The Grove Dictionary of
American Music

Volume Six

The Grove Dictionary of
American
Music

Second Edition

Volume Six
NAACC – Quotation

Edited by
Charles Hiroshi Garrett

OXFORD
UNIVERSITY PRESS

OXFORD
UNIVERSITY PRESS

Oxford University Press is a department of the
University of Oxford. It furthers the University's objective
of excellence in research, scholarship, and education
by publishing worldwide.

Oxford   New York
Auckland   Cape Town   Dar es Salaam   Hong Kong   Karachi
Kuala Lumpur   Madrid   Melbourne   Mexico City   Nairobi
New Delhi   Shanghai   Taipei   Toronto

With offices in
Argentina   Austria   Brazil   Chile   Czech   Republic   France   Greece
Guatemala   Hungary   Italy   Japan   Poland   Portugal   Singapore
South Korea   Switzerland   Thailand   Turkey   Ukraine   Vietnam

Oxford is a registered trade mark of Oxford University Press
in the UK and certain other countries.

Published in the United States of America by
Oxford University Press
198 Madison Avenue, New York, NY 10016

The first edition was published as *The New Grove Dictionary of American Music*
Edited by H. Wiley Hitchcock and Stanley Sadie (Macmillan, 1986)

The Library of Congress Cataloging-in-Publication Data

The New Grove Dictionary of American Music
The Grove dictionary of American music / edited by Charles Hiroshi Garrett. -Second edition.
volumes ; cm.
Revision of *The New Grove dictionary of American music*, originally published in 1986.
Includes bibliographical references.
ISBN 978-0-19-531428-1 (print set : alk. paper)—978-0-19-999059-7 (v.1 : alk. paper)—978-0-19-999060-3
(v.2 : alk. paper)—978-0-19-999061-0 (v.3 : alk. paper)—978-0-19-999062-7 (v.4 : alk. paper)—978-0-19-999063-4
(v.5 : alk. paper)—978-0-19-999064-1 (v.6 : alk. paper)—978-0-19-999065-8 (v.7 : alk. paper)—978-0-19-999066-5
(v.8 : alk. paper)—ISBN (invalid) 978-0-19-973925-7 (e-book)   1. Music—United States—Encyclopedias.
2. Music—United States—Bio-bibliography.   I. Garrett, Charles Hiroshi, 1966–   II. Title.
ML101.U6N48 2013
780.973'03—dc23   2012002055

1 3 5 7 9 8 6 4 2

Printed in the United States of America
on acid-free paper

Contents

General Abbreviations

A	alto, contralto [voice]
a	alto [instrument]
AA	Associate of the Arts
AAS	Associates in Arts and Sciences
AB	Alberta; Bachelor of Arts
ABC	American Broadcasting Company; Australian Broadcasting Commission
Abt.	Abteilung [section]
ACA	American Composers Alliance
acc.	accompaniment, accompanied by
accdn	accordion
addl	additional
addn(s)	addition(s)
ad lib	ad libitum
AFM	American Federation of Musicians
AFRS	Armed Forces Radio Service
AFR&TS	Armed Forces Radio & Television Service
aft(s)	afterpiece(s)
Ag	Agnus Dei
AGMA	American Guild of Musical Artists
AIDS	Acquired Immune Deficiency Syndrome
AK	Alaska
AL	Alabama
all(s)	alleluia(s)
AM	Master of Arts
a.m.	ante meridiem [before noon]
AMC	American Music Center
Amer.	American
amp	amplified
AMS	American Musicological Society
Anh.	Anhang [appendix]
anon.	anonymous(ly)
ant(s)	antiphon(s)
appx(s)	appendix(es)
AR	Arkansas
arr(s).	arrangement(s), arranged by/for
ARSC	Association for Recorded Sound Collections
a-s	all-sung
AS	American Samoa
ASCAP	American Society of Composers, Authors and Publishers

ASOL	American Symphony Orchestra League
Assn	Association
attrib(s).	attribution(s), attributed to; ascription(s), ascribed to
Aug	August
aut.	autumn
AZ	Arizona
aztl	*azione teatrale*
B	bass [voice], bassus
B	Brainard catalogue [Tartini], Benton catalogue [Pleyel]
b	bass [instrument]
b	born
BA	Bachelor of Arts
bal(s)	ballad opera(s)
bap.	baptized
Bar	baritone [voice]
bar	baritone [instrument]
B-Bar	bass-baritone
BBC	British Broadcasting Corporation
BC	British Columbia
bc	basso continuo
BCE	before Common Era [BC]
Bd.	Band [volume]
BEd	Bachelor of Education
Beds.	Bedfordshire
Berks.	Berkshire
Berwicks.	Berwickshire
BFA	Bachelor of Fine Arts
BFE	British Forum for Ethnomusicology
bk(s)	book(s)
BLitt	Bachelor of Letters/Literature
blq(s)	burlesque(s)
blt(s)	burletta(s)
BM	Bachelor of Music
BME, BMEd	Bachelor of Music Education
BMI	Broadcast Music Inc.
BMus	Bachelor of Music

bn	bassoon
BRD	Federal Republic of Germany (Bundesrepublik Deutschland [West Germany])
Bros.	Brothers
BRTN	Belgische Radio en Televisie Nederlands
Bs	Benedictus
BS, BSc	Bachelor of Science
BSM	Bachelor of Sacred Music
Bte	Benedicite
Bucks.	Buckinghamshire
Bulg.	Bulgarian
bur.	buried
BVM	Blessed Virgin Mary
BWV	Bach-Werke-Verzeichnis [Schmieder, catalogue of J.S. Bach's works]
C	contralto
c	circa [about]
c	cent(s)
CA	California
Cambs.	Cambridgeshire
Can.	Canadian
CanD	Cantate Domino
cant(s).	cantata(s)
cap.	capacity
carn.	Carnival
cb	contrabass [instrument]
CBC	Canadian Broadcasting Corporation
CBE	Commander of the Order of the British Empire
CBS	Columbia Broadcasting System
CBSO	City of Birmingham Symphony Orchestra
CCNY	City College of New York
CD(s)	compact disc(s)
CE	Common Era [AD]
CeBeDeM	Centre Belge de Documentation Musicale
cel	celesta
CEMA	Council for the Encouragement of Music and the Arts
cf	confer [compare]
c.f.	cantus firmus
CFE	Composers Facsimile Edition
CG	Covent Garden, London
CH	Companion of Honour
chap(s).	chapter(s)
chbr	chamber
Chin.	Chinese
chit	chitarrone
cho-reog(s).	choreography, choreographer(s), choreographed by
Cie	Compagnie
cimb	cimbalom
cl	clarinet
clvd	clavichord
cm	centimetre(s); *comédie en musique*
CM	Northern Mariana Islands (US Trust Territory of the Pacific)
cmda	*comédie mêlée d'ariettes*
CNRS	Centre National de la Recherche Scientifique
c/o	care of

CO	Colorado
Co.	Company; County
Cod.	Codex
coll.	collected by
collab.	in collaboration with
colln	collection
col(s).	column(s)
com	*componimento*
comm(s)	communion(s)
comp.	compiler, compiled by
comp(s).	composer(s), composed (by)
conc(s).	concerto(s)
cond(s).	conductor(s), conducted by
cont	continuo
contrib(s).	contribution(s)
Corp.	Corporation
c.p.s.	cycles per second
cptr(s)	computer(s)
Cr	Credo, Creed
CRI	Composers Recordings, Inc.
CSc	Candidate of Historical Sciences
CT	Connecticut
Ct	Contratenor, countertenor
CUNY	City University of New York
CVO	Commander of the Royal Victorian Order
Cz.	Czech
D	Deutsch catalogue [Schubert]; Dounias catalogue [Tartini]
d.	denarius, denarii [penny, pence]
d	died
DA	Doctor of Arts
Dan.	Danish
db	double bass
DBE	Dame Commander of the Order of the British Empire
dbn	double bassoon
DC	District of Columbia
Dc	Discantus
DD	Doctor of Divinity
DDR	German Democratic Republic (Deutsche Demokratische Republik [East Germany])
DE	Delaware
Dec	December
ded(s).	dedication(s), dedicated to
DeM	Deus misereatur
Den.	Denmark
Dept(s)	Department(s)
Derbys.	Derbyshire
DFA	Doctor of Fine Arts
dg	*dramma giocoso*
dir(s).	director(s), directed by
diss.	dissertation
dl	*drame lyrique*
DLitt	Doctor of Letters/Literature
DM	Doctor of Music
dm	*dramma per musica*
DMA	Doctor of Musical Arts
DME, DMEd	Doctor of Musical Education

DMus	Doctor of Music		GEMA	Gesellschaft für Musikalische Aufführungs- und Mechanische Vervielfaltingungsrechte
DMusEd	Doctor of Music Education			
DPhil	Doctor of Philosophy		Ger.	German
Dr	Doctor		Gk.	Greek
DSc	Doctor of Science/Historical Sciences		Gl	Gloria
DSM	Doctor of Sacred Music		Glam.	Glamorgan
Dut.	Dutch		glock	glockenspiel
			Glos.	Gloucestershire
			GmbH,	Gesellschaft mit Beschränkter Haftung [limited-liability company]
E.	East, Eastern			
EBU	European Broadcasting Union		grad(s)	gradual(s)
EdD	Doctor of Education		GSM	Guildhall School of Music, London (to 1934)
edn(s)	edition(s)		GSMD	Guildhall School of Music and Drama, London (1935–)
ed(s).	editor(s), edited (by)			
EdS	Education Specialist		GU	Guam
EEC	European Economic Community		gui	guitar
e.g.	exempli gratia [for example]			
el-ac	electro-acoustic			
elec	electric, electronic		H	Hoboken catalogue [Haydn]; Helm catalogue [C.P.E. Bach]
EMI	Electrical and Musical Industries			
Eng.	English		Hants.	Hampshire
eng hn	english horn		Heb.	Hebrew
ENO	English National Opera		Herts.	Hertfordshire
ens	ensemble		HI	Hawaii
ENSA	Entertainments National Service Association		hmn	harmonium
EP	extended-play (record)		HMS	His/Her Majesty's Ship
esp.	especially		HMV	His Master's Voice
etc.	et cetera		hn	horn
EU	European Union		Hon.	Honorary; Honourable
ex., exx.	example, examples		hp	harp
			hpd	harpsichord
			HRH	His/Her Royal Highness
f	forte		Hung.	Hungarian
facs.	facsimile(s)		Hunts.	Huntingdonshire
fa(s)	farsa(s)		Hz	Hertz [c.p.s.]
fasc(s).	fascicle(s)			
Feb	February			
ff	fortissimo		IA	Iowa
f, ff	following page, following pages		IAML	International Association of Music Libraries
f., ff.	folio, folios		IAWM	International Alliance for Women in Music
fff	fortississimo		ibid.	ibidem [in the same place]
fig(s).	figure(s) [illustration(s)]		ICTM	International Council for Traditional Music
FL	Florida		ID	Idaho
fl	flute		i.e.	id est [that is]
fl	floruit [he/she flourished]		IFMC	International Folk Music Council
Flem.	Flemish		IL	Illinois
fp	fortepiano [dynamic marking]		ILWC	International League of Women Composers
Fr.	French		IMC	International Music Council
frag(s).	fragment(s)		IMS	International Musicological Society
FRAM	Fellow of the Royal Academy of Music, London		IN	Indiana
FRCM	Fellow of the Royal College of Music, London		Inc.	Incorporated
FRCO	Fellow of the Royal College of Organists, London		inc.	incomplete
			incid	incidental
FRS	Fellow of the Royal Society, London		incl.	includes, including
fs	full score		inst(s)	instrument(s), instrumental
			intl	international
			int(s)	intermezzo(s), introit(s)
GA	Georgia		IPEM	Instituut voor Psychoakoestiek en Elektronische Muziek, Ghent
Gael.	Gaelic			
GEDOK	Gemeinschaft Deutscher Organisationen von Künstlerinnen und Kunstfreundinnen		IRCAM	Institut de Recherche et Coordination Acoustique/Musique

ISAM	Institute for Studies in American Music
ISCM	International Society for Contemporary Music
ISDN	Integrated Services Digital Network
ISM	Incorporated Society of Musicians
ISME	International Society for Music Education
It.	Italian
Jan	January
Jap.	Japanese
Jb	Jahrbuch [yearbook]
JD	Doctor of Jurisprudence
Jg.	Jahrgang [year of publication/volume]
Jr.	Junior
jr	junior
Jub	Jubilate
K	Kirkpatrick catalogue [D. Scarlatti]; Köchel catalogue [Mozart: no. after '/' is from 6th edn; also Fux]
kbd	keyboard
KBE	Knight Commander of the Order of the British Empire
KCVO	Knight Commander of the Royal Victorian Order
kg	kilogram(s)
Kgl	Königlich(e, er, es) [Royal]
kHz	kilohertz [1000 c.p.s.]
km	kilometre(s)
KS	Kansas
KY	Kentucky
Ky	Kyrie
L.	no. of song in R.W. Linker: *A Bibliography of Old French Lyrics* (University, MS, 1979)
L	Longo catalogue [A. Scarlatti]
LA	Louisiana
Lanarks.	Lanarkshire
Lancs.	Lancashire
Lat.	Latin
Leics.	Leicestershire
LH	left hand
lib(s)	libretto(s)
Lincs.	Lincolnshire
Lith.	Lithuanian
lit(s)	litany (litanies)
LittD	Doctor of Letters/Literature
LLB	Bachelor of Laws
LLD	Doctor of Laws
loc. cit.	loco citato [in the place cited]
LP	long-playing record
LPO	London Philharmonic Orchestra
LSO	London Symphony Orchestra
Ltd	Limited
Ltée	Limitée
m	metre(s)
MA	Massachusetts; Master of Arts

Mag	Magnificat
MALS	Master of Arts in Library Sciences
mand	mandolin
mar	marimba
MAT	Master of Arts and Teaching
MB	Bachelor of Music; Manitoba
MBE	Member of the Order of the British Empire
MD	Maryland
ME	Maine
MEd	Master of Education
mel	*melodramma, mélodrame*
mels	*melodramma serio*
melss	*melodramma semiserio*
Met	Metropolitan Opera House, New York
Mez	mezzo-soprano
mf	mezzo-forte
MFA	Master of Fine Arts
MGM	Metro-Goldwyn-Mayer
MHz	megahertz [megacycles]
MI	Michigan
mic	microphone
Middx	Middlesex
MIDI	Musical Instrument Digital Interface
MIT	Massachusetts Institute of Technology
MLA	Music Library Association
MLitt	Master of Letters/Literature
Mlle, Mlles	Mademoiselle, Mesdemoiselles
MM	Master of Music
M.M.	Metronome Maelzel
mm	millimetre(s)
MMA	Master of Musical Arts
MME, MMEd	Master of Music Education
Mme, Mmes	Madame, Mesdames
M, MM.	Monsieur, Messieurs
MMT	Master of Music in Teaching
MMus	Master of Music
MN	Minnesota
MO	Missouri
mod	modulator
Mon.	Monmouthshire
movt(s)	movement(s)
mp	mezzo-piano
MPhil	Master of Philosophy
MP(s)	Member(s) of Parliament
Mr	Mister
Mrs	Mistress; Messieurs
MS	Master of Science(s); Mississippi
MSc	Master of Science(s)
MSLS	Master of Science in Library and Information Science
MSM	Master of Sacred Music
MS(S)	manuscript(s)
MT	Montana
Mt	Mount
MTNA	Music Teachers National Association
mt(s)	music-theatre piece(s)
MusB, MusBac	Bachelor of Music

muscm(s)	musical comedy (comedies)	op(s)	opera(s)
MusD,		opt.	optional
MusDoc	Doctor of Music	OR	Oregon
musl(s)	musical(s)	orat(s)	oratorio(s)
MusM	Master of Music	orch	orchestra(tion), orchestral
		orchd	orchestrated (by)
		org	organ
N.	North, Northern	orig.	original(ly)
nar(s)	narrator(s)	ORTF	Office de Radiodiffusion-Télévision Française
NB	New Brunswick	os	*opera seria*
NBC	National Broadcasting Company	oss	*opera semiseria*
NC	North Carolina	OUP	Oxford University Press
ND	North Dakota	ov(s).	overture(s)
n.d.	no date of publication	Oxon.	Oxfordshire
NDR	Norddeutscher Rundfunk		
NE	Nebraska		
NEA	National Endowment for the Arts	P	Pincherle catalogue [Vivaldi]
NEH	National Endowment for the Humanities	p.	*pars*
NET	National Educational Television	*p*	piano [dynamic marking]
NF	Newfoundland and Labrador	PA	Pennsylvania
NH	New Hampshire	p.a.	per annum [annually]
NHK	Nippon Hōsō Kyōkai [Japanese broadcasting system]	pan(s)	pantomime(s)
		PBS	Public Broadcasting System
NJ	New Jersey	PC	no. of chanson in A. Pillet and H. Carstens: *Bibliographie der Troubadours* (Halle, 1933)
NM	New Mexico		
n(n).	footnote(s)		
Nor.	Norwegian	PE	Prince Edward Island
Northants.	Northamptonshire	perc	percussion
no(s).	number(s)	perf(s).	performance(s), performed (by)
Notts.	Nottinghamshire	pf	piano [instrument]
Nov	November	pfmr(s)	performer(s)
n.p.	no place of publication	PhB	Bachelor of Philosophy
NPR	National Public Radio	PhD	Doctor of Philosophy
n.pub.	no publisher	PhDEd	Doctor of Philosophy in Education
nr	near	pic	piccolo
NRK	Norsk Rikskringkasting [Norwegian broadcasting system]	pl(s).	plate(s); plural
		p.m.	post meridiem [after noon]
NS	Nova Scotia	PO	Philharmonic Orchestra
NSW	New South Wales	Pol.	Polish
NT	North West Territories	pop.	population
Nunc	Nunc dimittis	Port.	Portuguese
NV	Nevada	posth.	posthumous(ly)
NY	New York [State]	POW(s)	prisoner(s) of war
NZ	New Zealand	*pp*	pianissimo
		p., pp.	page, pages
		ppp	pianississimo
		PQ	Province of Quebec
ob	*opera buffa*; oboe	PR	Puerto Rico
obbl	obbligato	pr.	printed
OBE	Officer of the Order of the British Empire	prep pf	prepared piano
obl	*opéra-ballet*	PRO	Public Record Office, London
OC	Opéra-Comique, Paris [the company]	prol(s)	prologue(s)
oc	*opéra comique* [genre]	PRS	Performing Right Society
Oct	October	pseud(s).	pseudonym(s)
off(s)	offertory (offertories)	Ps(s)	Psalm(s)
OH	Ohio	ps(s)	psalm(s)
OK	Oklahoma	ptbk(s)	partbook(s)
OM	Order of Merit	pt(s)	part(s)
ON	Ontario	pubd	published
op. cit.	opere citato [in the work cited]	pubn(s)	publication(s)
op., opp.	opus, opera [plural of opus]	PWM	Polskie Wydawnictwo Muzyczne

QC	Queen's Counsel
qnt(s)	quintet(s)
qt(s)	quartet(s)
R	[in signature] editorial revision
R	photographic reprint [edn of score or early printed source]
R.	no. of chanson in G. Raynaud, *Bibliographie des chansonniers français des XIIIe et XIVe siècles* (Paris, 1884)
R	Ryom catalogue [Vivaldi]
r	recto
R	response
RAAF	Royal Australian Air Force
RAF	Royal Air Force
RAI	Radio Audizioni Italiane
RAM	Royal Academy of Music, London
RCA	Radio Corporation of America
RCM	Royal College of Music, London
rec	recorder
rec.	recorded [in discographic context]
recit(s)	recitative(s)
red(s).	reduction(s), reduced for
reorchd	reorchestrated (by)
repr.	reprinted
re(s)	response(s) [type of piece]
resp(s)	respond(s)
Rev.	Reverend
rev(s).	revision(s); revised (by/for)
RH	right hand
RI	Rhode Island
RIAS	Radio im Amerikanischen Sektor
RIdIM	Répertoire International d'Iconographie Musicale
RILM	Répertoire International de Littérature Musicale
RIPM	Répertoire International de la Presse Musicale
RISM	Répertoire International des Sources Musicales
RKO	Radio-Keith-Orpheum
RMCM	Royal Manchester College of Music
rms	root mean square
RNCM	Royal Northern College of Music, Manchester
RO	Radio Orchestra
Rom.	Romanian
r.p.m.	revolutions per minute
RPO	Royal Philharmonic Orchestra
RSFSR	Russian Soviet Federated Socialist Republic
RSO	Radio Symphony Orchestra
RTÉ	Radio Telefís Éireann
RTF	Radiodiffusion-Télévision Française
Rt Hon.	Right Honourable
RTVB	Radio-Télévision Belge de la Communauté Française
Russ.	Russian
RV	Ryom catalogue [Vivaldi]
S	San, Santa, Santo, São [Saint]; soprano [voice]
S	sound recording

S.	South, Southern
s	soprano [instrument]
s.	solidus, solidi [shilling, shillings]
SACEM	Société d'Auteurs, Compositeurs et Editeurs de Musique
San	Sanctus
sax	saxophone
SC	South Carolina
SD	South Dakota
sd	*scherzo drammatico*
SDR	Süddeutscher Rundfunk
SEM	Society for Ethnomusicology
Sept	September
seq(s)	sequence(s)
ser.	series
Serb.	Serbian
ser(s)	serenata(s)
sf, sfz	sforzando, sforzato
SFSR	Soviet Federated Socialist Republic
sing.	singular
SJ	Societas Jesu [Society of Jesus]
SK	Saskatchewan
SMT	Society for Music Theory
SO	Symphony Orchestra
SOCAN	Society of Composers, Authors and Music Publishers of Canada
Sp.	Spanish
spkr(s)	speaker(s)
Spl	Singspiel
SPNM	Society for the Promotion of New Music
spr.	spring
sq	square
Sr.	Senior
sr	senior
SS	Saints (It., Sp.); Santissima, Santissimo [Most Holy]
SS	steamship
SSR	Soviet Socialist Republic
Staffs.	Staffordshire
STB	Bachelor of Sacred Theology
Ste	Sainte
str	string(s)
St(s)	Saint(s)/Holy, Sankt, Sint, Szent
sum.	summer
SUNY	State University of New York
Sup	superius
suppl(s).	supplement(s), supplementary
Swed.	Swedish
SWF	Südwestfunk
sym(s).	symphony (symphonies), symphonic
synth	synthesizer, synthesized
T	tenor [voice]
t	tenor [instrument]
tc	*tragicommedia*
td(s)	*tonadilla(s)*
TeD	Te Deum
ThM	Master of Theology
timp	timpani
tm	*tragédie en musique*

TN	Tennessee		VHF	very high frequency
tpt	trumpet		VI	Virgin Islands
Tr	treble [voice]		vib	vibraphone
trad.	traditional		viz	videlicet [namely]
trans.	translation, translated by		vle	violone
transcr(s).	transcription(s), transcribed by/for		vn	violin
trbn	trombone		vol(s).	volume(s)
tr(s)	tract(s); treble [instrument]		vs	vocal score, piano-vocal score
TV	television		VT	Vermont
TWV	Menke catalogue [Telemann]		v, vv	voice, voices
TX	Texas		v., vv.	verse, verses
U.	University		W.	West, Western
UCLA	University of California at Los Angeles		WA	Washington [State]
UHF	ultra-high frequency		Warwicks.	Warwickshire
UK	United Kingdom of Great Britain and Northern Ireland		WDR	Westdeutscher Rundfunk
Ukr.	Ukrainian		WI	Wisconsin
unacc.	unaccompanied		Wilts.	Wiltshire
unattrib.	unattributed		wint.	winter
UNESCO	United Nations Educational, Scientific and Cultural Organization		WNO	Welsh National Opera
			WOO	Werke ohne Opuszahl
UNICEF	United Nations International Children's Emergency Fund		Worcs.	Worcestershire
			WPA	Works Progress Administration
unorchd	unorchestrated		WQ	Wotquenne catalogue [C.P.E. Bach]
unperf.	unperformed		WV	West Virginia
unpubd	unpublished		ww	woodwind
UP	University Press		WY	Wyoming
US	United States [adjective]			
USA	United States of America		xyl	xylophone
USO	United Service Organisations			
USSR	Union of Soviet Socialist Republics		YMCA	Young Men's Christian Association
UT	Utah		Yorks.	Yorkshire
			YT	Yukon Territory
v	verso		YWCA	Young Women's Christian Association
v.	versus		YYS	(Zhongguo yishu yanjiuyuan) Yinyue yanjiusuo and variants [Music Research Institute (of the Chinese Academy of Arts)]
V	versicle			
VA	Virginia			
va	viola			
vc	cello		Z	Zimmermann catalogue [Purcell]
vcle(s)	versicle(s)		zargc	*zarzuela género chico*
VEB	Volkseigener Betrieb [people's own industry]		zar(s)	zarzuela(s)
Ven	Venite			

Discographical Abbreviations

The abbreviations used in this dictionary for the names of record labels are listed below. In recording lists the label on which each recording was originally issued is cited, and no attempt is made here to indicate the affiliations of labels to companies. The names of a number of record labels consist of series of capital letters; although these may be abbreviated forms of company names they are not generally listed here as they constitute the full names of the labels concerned.

AAFS	Archive of American Folksong (Library of Congress)	Ev.	Everest	OK	Okeh
A&M Hor.	A&M Horizon	EW	East Wind	Omni.	Omnisound
ABC-Para.	ABC-Paramount	Ewd	Eastworld	PAct	Pathé Actuelle
AH	Artists House	Fan.	Fantasy	PAlt	Palo Alto
Ala.	Aladdin	FaD	Famous Door	Para.	Paramount
AM	American Music	FD	Flying Dutchman	Parl.	Parlophone
Amer.	America	FDisk	Flying Disk	Per.	Perfect
AN	Arista Novus	Fel.	Felsted	Phi.	Philips
Ant.	Antilles	Fon.	Fontana	Phon.	Phontastic
Ari.	Arista	Fre.	Freedom	PJ	Pacific Jazz
Asy.	Asylum	FW	Folkways	PL	Pablo Live
Atl.	Atlantic	Gal.	Galaxy	Pol.	Polydor
Aut.	Autograph	Gen.	Gennett	Prog.	Progressive
Bak.	Bakton	GrM	Groove Merchant	Prst.	Prestige
Ban.	Banner	Gram.	Gramavision	PT	Pablo Today
Bay.	Baystate	GTJ	Good Time Jazz	PW	Paddle Wheel
BB	Black and Blue	HA	Hat Art	Qual.	Qualiton
Bb	Bluebird	Hal.	Halcyon	Reg.	Regent
Beth.	Bethlehem	Har.	Harmony	Rep.	Reprise
BH	Bee Hive	Harl.	Harlequin	Rev.	Revelation
BL	Black Lion	HH	Hat Hut	Riv.	Riverside
BN	Blue Note	Hick.	Hickory	Roul.	Roulette
Bruns.	Brunswick	Hor.	Horizon	RR	Red Records
BS	Black Saint	IC	Inner City	RT	Real Time
BStar	Blue Star	IH	Indian House	Sack.	Sackville
Cad.	Cadence	ImA	Improvising Artists	Sat.	Saturn
Can.	Canyon	Imp.	Impulse!	SE	Strata-East
Cand.	Candid	Imper.	Imperial	Sig.	Signature
Cap.	Capitol	IndN	India Navigation	Slnd	Southland
Car.	Caroline	Isl.	Island	SN	Soul Note
Cas.	Casablanca	JAM	Jazz America Marketing	SolS	Solid State
Cat.	Catalyst	Jlgy	Jazzology	Son.	Sonora
Cen.	Century	Jlnd	Jazzland	Spot.	Spotlite
Chi.	Chiaroscurro	Jub.	Jubilee	Ste.	Steeplechase
Cir.	Circle	Jwl	Jewell	Sto.	Storyville
CJ	Classical Jazz	Jzt.	Jazztone	Sup.	Supraphon
Cob.	Cobblestone	Key.	Keynote	Tak.	Takoma
Col.	Columbia	Kt.	Keytone	Tei.	Teichiku
Com.	Commodore	Lib.	Liberty	Tel.	Telefunken
Conc.	Concord	Lml.	Limelight	The.	Theresa
Cont.	Contemporary	Lon.	London	Tim.	Timeless
Contl	Continental	Mdsv.	Moodsville	TL	Time-Life
Cot.	Cotillion	Mel.	Melodiya	Tran.	Transition
CP	Charlie Parker	Mer.	Mercury	20C	20th Century
CW	Creative World	Met.	Metronome	20CF	20th CenturyFox
Del.	Delmark	Metro.	Metrojazz	UA	United Artists
Dis.	Discovery	MJR	Master Jazz Recordings	Upt.	Uptown
Dra.	Dragon	Mlst.	Milestone	Van.	Vanguard
EB	Electric Bird	Mlt.	Melotone	Var.	Variety
Elec.	Electrola	Moers	Moers Music	Vars.	Varsity
Elek.	Elektra	MonE	Monmouth-Evergreen	Vic.	Victor
Elek. Mus.	Elektra Musician	Mstr.	Mainstream	VJ	Vee-Jay
EmA	EmArcy	Musi.	Musicraft	Voc.	Vocalion
ES	Elite Special	Nat.	National	WB	Warner Bros.
Eso.	Esoteric	NewJ	New Jazz	WP	World Pacific
		Norg.	Norgan	Xan.	Xanadu
		NW	New World		

Bibliographical Abbreviations

The bibliographical abbreviations used in this dictionary are listed below. Full bibliographical information is not normally supplied for nonmusical sources (national biographical dictionaries) or if it may be found elsewhere in this dictionary (in the lists following the articles ("Dictionaries and encyclopedias," "Histories," and "Periodicals") or in *Grove Music Online* (in the lists that form parts of the articles "Dictionaries & encyclopedias of music," "Editions, historical," and "Periodicals"). The typographical conventions used throughout the dictionary are followed here: broadly, italic type is used for periodicals and reference works, and roman type for anthologies, series, etc.

19CM	*19th Century Music*
20CM	*20th Century Music* [retitled in 2000; see 21CM]
21CM	*21th Century Music* [see also 20CM]
ACAB	*American Composers Alliance Bulletin*
AcM	*Acta musicological*
AM	*American Music*
AMw	*Archiv für Musikwissenschaft*
AMZ	*Allgemeine musikalische Zeitung*
Anderson 2	E.R. Anderson: *Contemporary American Composers: a Biographical Dictionary* (Boston, 2/1982)
AnM	*Anuario musical*
AnMc	*Analecta musicological*
AnnM	*Annales musicoloques*
ANB	*American National Biography Online*
ARJS	*Annual Review of Jazz Studies*
ARSCJ	*Association for Recorded Sound Collections Journal*
AsM	*Asian Music*
Baker 5[–9]	*Baker's Biographical Dictionary of Musicians, 1958–2001*
Baker 20thC.	*Baker's Biographical Dictionary of 20th-Century Musicians*
BAMS	*Bulletin of the American Musicological Society*
BMw	*Beiträge zur Musikwissenschaft*
BPiM	*The Black Perspective in Music*
BWQ	*Brass and Woodwind Quarterly*
Campbell GC	M. Campbell: *The Great Cellists*
Campbell GV	M. Campbell: *The Great Violinists*
CBY	*Current Biography Yearbook*
CC	B. Morton and P. Collins, eds.: *Contemporary Composers*
CMc	*Current Musicology*
CMR	*Contemporary Music Review*
CohenE	A.I. Cohen: *International Encyclopedia of Women Composers*
COJ	*Cambridge Opera Journal*
DAB	*Dictionary of American Biography* (New York, 1928–37, suppls., 1944–81)
DB	*Down Beat*
DBL	*Dansk biografisk leksikon* (Copenhagen, 1887–1905)
DBL2	*Dansk biografisk leksikon* (Copenhagen, 2/1933–45)
DBL3	*Dansk biografisk leksikon* (Copenhagen, 3/1979–84)
DCB	*Dictionary of Canadian Biography*
Dichter-ShapiroSM	H. Dichter and E. Shapiro: *Early American Sheet Music*
DBY	*Down Beat Yearbook*
DNB	*Dictionary of National Biography* (Oxford, 1885–1901, suppls., 1901–96)
EDM	*Das Erbe deutscher Musik* (Berlin and elsewhere)
EitnerQ	R. Eitner: *Biographisch-bibliographisches Quellen-Lexikon*
EMC1	*Encyclopedia of Music in Canada* (Toronto, 1981)
EMC2	*Encyclopedia of Music in Canada* (Toronto, 2/1992)
ES	F. D'Amico: *Enciclopedia dello spettacolo*
EthM	*Ethnomusicology*
EthM News letter	*Ethno[-]musicology Newsletter*
EwenD	D. Ewen: *American Composers: a Biographical Dictionary* (New York, 1982)
FAM	*Fontes artis musicae*
Feather-Gitler BEJ	L. Feather and I. Gitler: *The Biographical Encyclopedia of Jazz* (New York, and Oxford, England, 1999)
FétisB	F.-J. Fétis: *Biographie universelle des musiciens*
FisherMP	W.A. Fisher: *One Hundred and Fifty Years of Music Publishing in the United States* (Boston, 1933)
FriedwaldB	W. Friedwald: *A Biographical Guide to the Great Jazz and Pop Singers* (New York, 2010)
GEWM	*The Garland Encyclopedia of World Music*
GMO	*Grove Music Online*
Grove 1[–5]	G. Grove, ed.: *A Dictionary of Music and Musicians*
Grove6	*The New Grove Dictionary of Music and Musicians*
Grove7	S. Sadie and J. Tyrell, eds.: *The New Grove Dictionary of Music and Musicians* (2/London, 2001)
GroveA	*The New Grove Dictionary of American Music*
GroveAS	W.S. Pratt, ed.: *Grove's Dictionary of Music and Musicians: American Supplement* (New York, 1920, 2/1928, many reprs.)

GroveI	*The New Grove Dictionary of Musical Instruments*		*MSD*	*Musicological Studies and Documents* (Rome)
GroveJ	*The New Grove Dictionary of Jazz*		*MT*	*The Musical Times*
Grove J2	*The New Grove Dictionary of Jazz* (2/2002)		*MTNAP*	*Music Teachers National Association: Proceedings*
GroveO	*The New Grove Dictionary of Opera*		*MusAm*	*Musical America*
GroveW	*The New Grove Dictionary of Women Composers*		*NAW*	E.T. James, J.W. James, and P.S. Boyer, eds.: *Notable American Women* (Cambridge, MA, 1971; suppl., 1980)
GSJ	*The Galpin Society Journal*			
GV	R. Celletti: *Le grandi voci: dizionario critico-biografico dei cantanti*		*NOHM*	*The New Oxford History of Music*, ed. E. Wellesz, J.A. Westrup, and G. Abraham (London, 1954–)
HDM4	*Harvard Dictionary, 4th ed.*			
HiFi	*High Fidelity*		*NRMI*	*Nuova rivista musicale italiana*
HiFi/ MusAm	*High Fidelity/Musical America*		*NZM*	*Neue Zeitschrift für Musik* [retitled 1920, see ZfM]
HMYB	*Hinrichsen's Musical Year Book*		*ÖMz*	*Österreichische Musikzeitschrift*
IAJRCJ	*International Association of Jazz Record Collectors Journal*		*ON*	*Opera News*
IMSCR	*International Musicological Society Congress Report*		*OQ*	*Opera Quarterly*
			PAMS	*Papers of the American Musicological Society*
IRASM	*International Review of the Aesthetics and Sociology of Music*		*PASUC*	*Proceedings of the American Society of University Composers*
ISAMm	*Institute for Studies in American Music* (New York)		*PMA*	*Proceedings of the Musical Association* [retitled 1944, see PRMA]
ITO	*In Theory Only*		*PNM*	*Perspectives of New Music*
JAMIS	*Journal of the America Musical Instrument Society*		*PRMA*	*Proceedings of the Royal Music Association* [see *PMA*]
JAMS	*Journal of the American Musicological Society*		*RaM*	*La rassegna musicale*
JazzM	*Jazz Monthly*		*RBM*	*Revue belge de musicologie*
JbMP	*Jahrbuch der Musikbibliothek Peters*		*RdM*	*Revue de musicology*
JEFDSS	*The Journal of the English Folk Dance and Song Society*		*ReM*	*La revue musicale*
			RiemannL	*Riemann Musik Lexicon*, rev. W. Gurlitt (Mainz, Germany, 12/1959–75)
JEMF	*J[ohn] E[dwards] M[emorial] F[oundation] Quarterly*		*RISM*	*Répertoire international des sources musicales*
JFSS	*The Journal of the Folk-song Society*		*RN*	*Renaissance News*
JIFMC	*Journal of the International Folk Music Council*		*RRAM*	*Recent Researches in American Music* (Madison, WI)
JJI	*Jazz Journal International*		*RS*	*Rolling Stone*
Jm	*Jazz magazine* (Paris)		*Schuller-EJ*	G. Schuller: *Early Jazz* (New York, 1968/R)
JMT	*Journal of Music Theory*		*Schuller-SE*	G. Schuller: *The Swing Era* (New York, 1989)
JRBM	*Journal of Renaissance and Baroque Music*		*Schwarz GM*	B. Schwarz: *Great Masters of the Violin*
JRME	*Journal of Research in Music Education*			
JSAM	*Journal of the Society for American Music*		*SIMG*	*Sammelbände der Internationalen Musik-Gesellschaft*
JT	*Jazz Times*		*SMA*	*Studies in Music*
JVdGSA	*Journal of the Viola da Gamba Society of America*		*SMz*	*Schweizerische Musikzeitung/Revue musicale suisse*
KdG	*Komponisten der Gegenwart*, ed. H.-W. Heister and W.-W. Sparrer		*SouthernB*	E. Southern: *Biographical Dictionary of Afro-American and African Musicians*
LAMR	*Latin American Music Review*		*Thompson*	O. Thompson: *The International Cyclopedia of Music and Musicians*
LaMusicaD	G.M. Gatti and A. Basso: *La musica: dizionario*			
MB	*Musica britannica* (London)		*VintonD*	J. Vinton, ed.: *Dictionary of Contemporary Music* (New York, 1974)
MEJ	*Music Educators Journal*		*VMw*	*Vierteljahrsschrift für Musikwissenschaft*
MF	*Die Musickforschung*		*Waterhouse-LangwillI*	W. Waterhouse: *The New Langwill Index: a Dictionary of Musical Wind-Instrument Makers and Inventors*
MGG	F. Blume, ed.: *Die Musik in Geschichte und Gegenwart*			
MJ	*Music Journal*		*YIFMC*	*Yearbook of the International Folk Music Council*
ML	*Music and Letters*			
MM	*Modern Music*		*ZfM*	*Zeitschrift für Musik* [see *NZM*]
MMR	*The Monthly Musical Record*		*ZIMG*	*Zeitschrift der Internationalen Musik-Gesellschaft*
MO	*Musical Opinion*			
MQ	*The Musical Quarterly*			
MR	*The Music Review*			

Library Abbreviations

AAu	Ann Arbor, University of Michigan, Music Library	*Bc*	Boston, New England Conservatory of Music, Harriet M. Spaulding Library
AB	Albany (NY), New York State Library	*Bfa*	Boston, Museum of Fine Arts
AKu	Akron (OH), University of Akron, Bierce Library	*Bgm*	Boston, Isabella Stewart Gardner Museum, Library
AtaT	Talladega (AL) Talladega College	*Bh*	Boston, Harvard Musical Association, Library
ATS	Athens (GA), University of Georgia Libraries	*Bhs*	Boston, Massachusetts Historical Society Library
ATet	Atlanta (GA), Emory University, Pitts Theology Library	*Bp*	Boston, Public Library, Music Department
ATu	Atlanta (GA), Emory University Library	*Bu*	Boston, Boston University, Mugar Memorial Library, Department of Special Collections
AU	Aurora (NY), Wells College Library		
AUS	Austin, University of Texas at Austin, The Harry Ransom Humanities Research Center		
AUSm	Austin, University of Texas at Austin, Fine Arts Library	*CA*	Cambridge (MA), Harvard University, Harvard College Library
		CAe	Cambridge (MA), Harvard University, Eda Kuhn Loeb Music Library
BAR	Baraboo (WI), Circus World Museum Library	*CAh*	Cambridge (MA), Harvard University, Houghton Library
BAep	Baltimore, Enoch Pratt Free Library	*CAt*	Cambridge (MA), Harvard University Library, Theatre Collection
BAhs	Baltimore, Maryland Historical Society Library	*CAward*	Cambridge (MA), John Milton Ward, private collection [on loan to CA]
BApi	Baltimore, Arthur Friedheim Library, Johns Hopkins University	*CF*	Cedar Falls (IA), University of Northern Iowa, Library
BAu	Baltimore, Johns Hopkins University Libraries	*CHAhs*	Charleston (SC), The South Carolina Historical Society
BAue	Baltimore, Milton S. Eisenhower Library, Johns Hopkins University	*CHH*	Chapel Hill (NC), University of North Carolina at Chapel Hill
BAw	Baltimore, Walters Art Gallery Library	*CHua*	Charlottesville (VA), University of Virginia, Alderman Library
BER	Berea (OH), Riemenschneider Bach Institute Library	*CHum*	Charlottesville (VA), University of Virginia, Music Library
BETm	Bethlehem (PA), Moravian Archives	*CIhc*	Cincinnati, Hebrew Union College Library: Jewish Institute of Religion, Klau Library
BEm	Berkeley, University of California at Berkeley, Music Library	*CIp*	Cincinnati, Public Library
BL	Bloomington (IN), Indiana University Library	*CIu*	Cincinnati, University of Cincinnati College - Conservatory of Music, Music Library
BLl	Bloomington (IN), Indiana University, Lilly Library	*CLAc*	Claremont (CA), Claremont College Libraries
BLu	Bloomington (IN), Indiana University, Cook Music Library	*CLU*	USA, Los Angeles, CA, University of California, Los Angeles
BO	Boulder (CO), University of Colorado at Boulder, Music Library		
BU	Buffalo (NY), Buffalo and Erie County Public Library		
Ba	Boston, Athenaeum Library		

CLp	Cleveland, Public Library, Fine Arts Department
CLwr	Cleveland, Western Reserve University, Freiberger Library and Music House Library
COhs	Columbus (OH), Ohio Historical Society Library
COu	Columbus (OH), Ohio State University, Music Library
CP	College Park (MD), University of Maryland, McKeldin Library
CR	Cedar Rapids (IA), Iowa Masonic Library
Cn	Chicago, Newberry Library
Cp	Chicago, Chicago Public Library, Music Information Center
CtY	USA, New Haven, CT, Yale University
Cu	Chicago, University, Joseph Regenstein Library, Music Collection
Cum	Chicago, University of Chicago, Music Collection
DAVu	Davis (CA), University of California at Davis, Peter J. Shields Library
DAu	Dallas, Southern Methodist University, Music Library
DLC	USA, Washington, DC, Library of Congress
DMu	Durham (NC), Duke University Libraries
DN	Denton (TX), University of North Texas, Music Library
DO	Dover (NH), Public Library
DSI (JOHP)	USA, Washington, DC, Smithsonian Institution: Jazz Oral History Program
Dp	Detroit, Public Library, Main Library, Music and Performing Arts Department
E	Evanston (IL), Garrett Biblical Institute
EDu	Edwardsville (IL), Southern Illinois University
EU	Eugene (OR), University of Oregon
Eu	Evanston (IL), Northwestern University
FAy	Farmington (CT), Yale University, Lewis Walpole Library
FW	Fort Worth (TX), Southwestern Baptist Theological Seminary
G	Gainesville (FL), University of Florida Library, Music Library
GB	Gettysburg (PA), Lutheran Theological Seminary
GR	Granville (OH), Denison University Library
GRB	Greensboro (NC), University of North Carolina at Greensboro, Walter C. Jackson Library
HA	Hanover (NH), Dartmouth College, Baker Library
HG	Harrisburg (PA), Pennsylvania State Library
HO	Hopkinton (NH), New Hampshire Antiquarian Society

Hhc	Hartford (CT), Hartt College of Music Library, The University of Hartford
Hm	Hartford (CT), Case Memorial Library, Hartford Seminary Foundation [in ATet]
Hs	Hartford (CT), Connecticut State Library
Hw	Hartford (CT), Trinity College, Watkinson Library
I	Ithaca (NY), Cornell University
ICJic	USA, Chicago, IL, Jazz Institute of Chicago
ICU	USA, Chicago, IL, University of Chicago
IDt	Independence (MO), Harry S. Truman Library
IO	Iowa City (IA), University of Iowa, Rita Benton Music Library
InUAtm	USA, Bloomington, IN, Indiana University Archives of Traditional Music
K	Kent (OH), Kent State University, Music Library
KC	Kansas City (MO), University of Missouri: Kansas City, Miller Nichols Library
KCm	Kansas City (MO), Kansas City Museum, Library and Archives
KN	Knoxville (TN), University of Tennessee, Knoxville, Music Library
LAcs	Los Angeles, California State University, John F. Kennedy Memorial Library
LApiatigorsky	Los Angeles, Gregor Piatigorsky, private collection [in STEdrachman]
LAs	Los Angeles, The Arnold Schoenberg Institute Archives
LAuc	Los Angeles, University of California at Los Angeles, William Andrews Clark Memorial Library
LAum	Los Angeles, University of California at Los Angeles, Music Library
LAur	Los Angeles, University of California at Los Angeles, Special Collections Dept, University Research Library
LAusc	Los Angeles, University of Southern California, School of Music Library
LBH	Long Beach (CA), California State University
LEX	Lexington (KY), University of Kentucky, Margaret I. King Library
LNT	USA, New Orleans, LA, Tulane University [transcripts of interviews held at LNT were published on microfilm as New York Times Oral History Program: New Orleans Jazz Oral History Collection (1978–9)]
LOu	Louisville, University of Louisville, Dwight Anderson Music Library
LT	Latrobe (PA), St Vincent College Library
Lu	Lawrence (KS), University of Kansas Libraries
M	Milwaukee, Public Library, Art and Music Department
MAhs	Madison (WI), Wisconsin Historical Society

MAu	Madison (WI), University of Wisconsin
MB	Middlebury (VT), Middlebury College, Christian A. Johnson Memorial Music Library
MED	Medford (MA), Tufts University Library
MG	Montgomery (AL), Alabama State Department of Archives and History Library
MT	Morristown (NJ), National Historical Park Museum
Mc	Milwaukee, Wisconsin Conservatory of Music Library
MoKmb	Kansas City, MO, Kansas City Museum of History
MoUSt	USA, St. Louis, MO, University of Missouri
NA	Nashville (TN), Fisk University Library
NAu	Nashville (TN), Vanderbilt University Library
NBu	New Brunswick (NJ), Rutgers - The State University of New Jersey, Music Library, Mabel Smith Douglass Library
NCH (HCJA)	USA, Clinton, NY, Hamilton College: Hamilton College Jazz Archive
NEij	Newark (NJ), Rutgers - The State University of New Jersey, Rutgers Institute of Jazz Studies Library
NH	New Haven (CT), Yale University, Irving S. Gilmore Music Library
NHoh	New Haven (CT), Yale University, Oral History Archive
NHub	New Haven (CT), Yale University, Beinecke Rare Book and Manuscript Library
NNC	USA, New York, NY, Columbia University
NNSc	USA, New York, NY, Schomburg Collection, New York Public Library
NNSc (HBC)	USA, New York, NY, Schomburg Collection, New York Public Library, Hatch-Billops Collection
NNSc (LAJOHP)	USA, New York, NY, Schomburg Collection, New York Public Library, Louis Armstrong Jazz Oral History Project
NO	Normal (IL), Illinois State University, Milner Library, Humanities/Fine Arts Division
NORsm	New Orleans, Louisiana State Museum Library
NORtu	New Orleans, Tulane University, Howard Tilton Memorial Library
NYamc	New York, American Music Center Library
NYbroude	New York, Broude private collection
NYcc	New York, City College Library, Music Library
NYcu	New York, Columbia University, Gabe M. Wiener Music & Arts Library
NYcub	New York, Columbia University, Rare Book and Manuscript Library of Butler Memorial Library
NYgo	New York, University, Gould Memorial Library [in NYu]
NYgr	New York, The Grolier Club Library
NYgs	New York, G. Schirmer, Inc.
NYhs	New York, New York Historical Society Library
NYhsa	New York, Hispanic Society of America, Library

NYj	New York, The Juilliard School, Lila Acheson Wallace Library
NYkallir	New York, Rudolf F. Kallir, private collection
NYleh-man	New York, Robert O. Lehman, private collection [in NYpm]
NYlibin	New York, Laurence Libin, private collection
NYma	New York, Mannes College of Music, Clara Damrosch Mannes Memorial Library
NYp	New York, Public Library at Lincoln Center, Music Division
NYpl	New York, Public Library, Center for the Humanities
NYpm	New York, Pierpont Morgan Library
NYpsc	New York, New York Public Library, Schomburg Center for Research in Black Culture in Harlem
NYq	New York, Queens College of the City University, Paul Klapper Library, Music Library
NYu	New York, University Bobst Library
NYw	New York, Wildenstein Collection
NYyellin	New York, Victor Yellin, private collection
Nf	Northampton (MA), Forbes Library
NjR	USA, Newark, NJ, Rutgers, the State University of New Jersey
NjR (JOHP)	USA, Newark, NJ, Rutgers, the State University of New Jersey: Jazz Oral History Project
Nsc	Northampton (MA), Smith College, Werner Josten Library
OAm	Oakland (CA), Mills College, Margaret Prall Music Library
OB	Oberlin (OH), Oberlin College Conservatory of Music, Conservatory Library
OX	Oxford (OH), Miami University, Amos Music Library
PHci	Philadelphia, Curtis Institute of Music, Library
PHf	Philadelphia, Free Library of Philadelphia, Music Dept
PHff	Philadelphia, Free Library of Philadelphia, Edwin A. Fleisher Collection of Orchestral Music
PHgc	Philadelphia, Gratz College
PHhs	Philadelphia, Historical Society of Pennsylvania Library
PHlc	Philadelphia, Library Company of Philadelphia
PHmf	Philadelphia, Musical Fund Society [on loan to PHf]
PHphs	Philadelphia, The Presbyterian Historical Society Library [in PHlc]
PHps	Philadelphia, American Philosophical Society Library
PHu	Philadelphia, University of Pennsylvania, Van Pelt-Dietrich Library Center
PO	Poughkeepsie (NY), Vassar College, George Sherman Dickinson Music Library

PROhs	Providence (RI), Rhode Island Historical Society Library
PROu	Providence (RI), Brown University
PRV	Provo (UT), Brigham Young University
PRs	Princeton (NJ), Theological Seminary, Speer Library
PRu	Princeton (NJ), Princeton University, Firestone Memorial Library
PRw	Princeton (NJ), Westminster Choir College
Pc	Pittsburgh, Carnegie Library, Music and Art Dept
Ps	Pittsburgh, Theological Seminary, Clifford E. Barbour Library
Pu	Pittsburgh, University of Pittsburgh
Puf	Pittsburgh, University of Pittsburgh, Foster Hall Collection, Stephen Foster Memorial
R	Rochester (NY), Sibley Music Library, University of Rochester, Eastman School of Music
SA	Salem (MA), Peabody and Essex Museums, James Duncan Phillips Library
SBm	Santa Barbara (CA), Mission Santa Barbara
SFp	San Francisco, Public Library, Fine Arts Department, Music Division
SFs	San Francisco, Sutro Library
SFsc	San Francisco, San Francisco State University, Frank V. de Bellis Collection
SJb	San Jose (CA), Ira F. Brilliant Center for Beethoven Studies, San José State University
SL	St Louis, St Louis University, Pius XII Memorial Library
SLC	Salt Lake City, University of Utah Library
SLug	St Louis, Washington University, Gaylord Music Library
SM	San Marino (CA), Huntington Library
SPma	Spokane (WA), Moldenhauer Archives
SR	San Rafael (CA), American Music Research Center, Dominican College
STEdrach mann	Stevenson (MD), Mrs Jephta Drachman, private collection; Mrs P.C. Drachman, private collection
STO	Stony Brook (NY), State University of New York at Stony Brook, Frank Melville jr Memorial Library
STu	Palo Alto (CA), University, Memorial Library of Music, Department of Special Collections of the Cecil H. Green Library
SY	Syracuse (NY), University Music Library

SYkrasner	Syracuse (NY), Louis Krasner, private collection [in CAh and SY]
Su	Seattle, University of Washington, Music Library
TA	Tallahassee (FL), Florida State University, Robert Manning Strozier Library
TNF	Nashville (TN) Fisk University
TxU	Austin (TX) University of Texas
U	Urbana (IL), University of Illinois, Music Library
Uplame nac	Urbana (IL), Dragan Plamenac, private collection [in NH]
V	Villanova (PA), Villanova University, Falvey Memorial Library
WB	Wilkes-Barre (PA), Wilkes College Library
WC	Waco (TX), Baylor University, Music Library
WGc	Williamsburg (VA), College of William and Mary, Earl Gregg Swenn Library
WI	Williamstown (MA), Williams College Library
WOa	Worcester (MA), American Antiquarian Society Library
WS	Winston-Salem (NC), Moravian Music Foundation, Peter Memorial Library
Wc	Washington, DC, Library of Congress, Music Division
Wca	Washington, Cathedral Library
Wcf	Washington, Library of Congress, American Folklife Center and the Archive of Folk Culture
Wcg	Washington, General Collections, Library of Congress
Wcm	Washington, Library of Congress, Motion Picture, Broadcasting and Recorded Sound Division
Wcu	Washington, Catholic University of America, Music Library
Wdo	Washington, Dumbarton Oaks
Wgu	Washington, Georgetown University Libraries
Whu	Washington, Howard University, College of Fine Arts Library
Ws	Washington, Folger Shakespeare Library
Y	York (PA), Historical Society of York County, Library and Archives

Volume Six

NAACC – Quotation

A Note on the Use of the Dictionary

This note is intended as a short guide to the basic procedures and organization of the dictionary. A fuller account will be found in "About the Dictionary," pp. xxi–xxiv, vol. one.

Alphabetization of headings is based on the principle that words are read continuously, ignoring spaces, hyphens, accents, parenthesized and bracketed matter, etc., up to the first punctuation mark, then again thereafter if that mark is a comma. "Mc" and "Mac" are alphabetized as "Mac," "St." as "Saint."

Cross-references are shown in small capitals, with a large capital at the beginning of the first word of the entry referred to. Thus "The UNIVERSITY OF MICHIGAN was founded in Detroit in 1817" means that the entry referred is not "University of Michigan" but "Michigan, University of."

Abbreviations used in the dictionary are listed on pp. vii–xx, in the order General (beginning on p. vii), Discographical (p. xiv), Bibliographical (p. xv), and Library (p. xvii).

Work-lists are normally arranged chronologically (within section, where divided), in order of year of composition or first publication (in the latter case dates are given in parentheses). Italicized abbreviations (such as *DLC*) stand for libraries holding sources and are explained on p. xvii.

Recording-lists are arranged chronologically (within section, where divided), typically in order of date of issue. Abbreviations standing for record labels are explained on p. xiv.

Bibliographies are arranged chronologically (within section, where divided), in order of year of first publication, and alphabetically by author within years. Abbreviations standing for periodicals and reference works are explained on p. xv.

N

NAACC. National Association for American Composers and Conductors; *see* NATIONAL ASSOCIATION OF COMPOSERS, USA.

NABBA. *See* NORTH AMERICAN BRASS BAND ASSOCIATION.

Nabokov, Nicolas [Nikolay] (*b* Lyubcha, Novogrudok, nr Minsk, Belorussia, O.S. 4/17 April 1903; *d* New York, NY, 6 April 1978). Composer of Russian birth, cousin of the writer Vladimir Nabokov. He first studied composition privately with Vladimir Ivanovich Rebikov in Yalta and St. Petersburg (1913–20), then at the Stuttgart Conservatory (1920–22) and the Berlin Hochschule für Musik with Paul Juon and Ferruccio Busoni (1922–3). He studied at the Sorbonne in the years 1923–6 and was awarded the degree of Licence ès Lettres. He taught in Paris and Germany from 1926 to 1933, then immigrated to the United States, where he became a citizen in 1939.

Nabokov taught at Wells College, Aurora, New York (1936–41); St. John's College, Annapolis (1941–4); and the Peabody Conservatory (1947–52). During and after World War II he held several United States government cultural positions in Europe. From the 1950s he lived chiefly in Paris, although he was active as a composer and a promoter of music festivals all over the world. He became secretary-general of the Congress for Cultural Freedom in 1951 and organized the Paris festival Oeuvre du XXe Siecle (1952), the Music in Our Time Festival (Rome, 1954), and the East-West Music Encounter (Tokyo, 1961). He served as director of the Berlin Festival (1963–6) and was composer-in-residence at the Aspen Institute for Humanistic Studies (1970–73).

As a composer Nabokov is closely identified with music for dance. His first important work, the ballet-oratorio *Ode* (1927), was commissioned by Sergei Diaghilev, who produced it in London, Paris, and Berlin. A pronounced lyricism, occasionally infused with bitonality, informs both this work and his ballet *Union Pacific*, which was written to commemorate the completion of the transcontinental railroad and makes use of popular 19th-century American tunes. Whether or not conceived for the stage, Nabokov's music shows strong dramatic powers and unusual orchestral eloquence. He wrote an entertaining volume of essays, *Old Friends and New Music* (Boston, 1951), the books *Igor Stravinsky* (Berlin, 1964) and *Bagázh: Memoirs of a Russian Cosmopolitan* (New York, 1975), and articles—mainly on Russian music and musicians—for numerous periodicals including *Atlantic*, *Harper's*, *Musical America*, *New Republic*, and *Partisan Review*.

WORKS
(selective list)

STAGE
Ode: Méditation sur la majesté de Dieu (ballet-orat, R. Desormières, after M. Lomonosov, choreog. L. Massine), Paris, 6 June 1928; La vie de Polichinelle (ballet), Paris, 1934; Union Pacific (ballet, A. MacLeish, choreog. Massine), Philadelphia, 6 April 1934; Samson Agonistes (incid music, J. Milton), Aurora, NY, 14 May 1938; The Last Flower (ballet, after J. Thurber), 1941; The Holy Devil (op, 2, S. Spender), Louisville, KY, 16 April 1958, rev. as Der Tod des Grigorij Rasputin (3), Cologne, 27 Nov 1959; Don Quixote (ballet, 3, Nabokov and G. Balanchine), Aug 1965; The Wanderer (ballet), 1966; Love's Labour's Lost (op, W.H. Auden, C. Kallman, after W. Shakespeare), Brussels, 7 Feb 1973;

VOCAL
Choral: Collectionneur d'échos, S, B, unison vv, perc, 1932; Job (orat, J. Maritain), male vv, orch, 1933; America was Promises (cant., MacLeish), A, Bar, male vv, perf. 1940
Solo vocal: The Return of Pushkin (elegy, Nabokov, after A. Pushkin), S, T, orch, perf. 1948; Vita nuova (after Dante), S, T, orch, perf. 1951; Symboli chrestiani, Bar, orch, perf. 1956; 4 poèmes de Boris Pasternak, 1v, pf (1961); 6 Lyric Songs (A. Akhmatova: Requiem), 1966

INSTRUMENTAL
Orch: Symphonie lyrique, perf. 1930; Pf Conc., 1932; Le fiancé, ov. after Pushkin, 1934; Sinfonia biblica, perf. 1941; Fl Conc., 1948; Conc. corale, fl, str, pf, 1950; Les hommages, conc., vc, orch, perf. 1953; The Last Flower, sym. suite, 1957; [4] Studies in Solitude, perf. 1961; Sym. Variations, 1967; Sym. no.3 "A Prayer," perf. 1968; Variations on a Theme by Tchaikovsky, vc, orch, 1968
Other works: Pf Sonata (1926); 3 Dances, pf (1929); Serenata estiva, str qt, 1937; Pf Sonata (1940); Sonata, bn, pf, 1941; 3 Sym. Marches, band, 1945; Canzone, Introduzione e Allegro, vn, pf (1950)

Principal publishers: Editions Russes, Senart

BIBLIOGRAPHY

EwenD

A. Danielou: "Nicolas Nabokov is Dead," *The World of Music*, xx/1 (1978), 127–8

A. Hughes: "Nicolas Nabokov, 75," *New York Times* (7 April 1978)

I. Wellens: "Music on the Frontline: Nicholas Nabokov's Struggle against Communism and Middlebrow Culture," *Tempo*, lvii/July (2003), 63–72

BRUCE CARR/KATHERINE K. PRESTON/MICHAEL MECKNA

NACUSA. *See* NATIONAL ASSOCIATION OF COMPOSERS, USA.

Nagano, Kent (George) (*b* Morro Bay, CA, 22 Nov 1951). Conductor. The son of Japanese American parents, he studied both Asian and Western music. He began studying piano with his mother at the age of four and specialized in koto during his high school years. He was educated at Oxford University (1969) and the University of California, Santa Cruz (BA 1974); later he studied composition and analysis with Grosvenor Cooper and music history with Edward Houghton. He then studied conducting with Laszlo Varga and piano with Goodwin Sammel at San Francisco State University (MM 1976) before attending the University of Toronto (1977–9). During these years he worked as a *répétiteur* and assistant conductor for the Opera Company of Boston and conducted chamber opera in San Francisco and ballet in Oakland. He was invited to become music director of the Berkeley SO in 1978. Over two decades he turned the ensemble into a progressive force in Northern California music-making. His long association with Olivier Messiaen began with the Berkley SO, after he met Messiaen during the American premiere of *La transfiguration de notre seigneur Jésus-Christ* in Berkeley; Nagano was subsequently Seiji Ozawa's assistant for the premiere of *Saint François d'Assise* (Paris, December 1983). Ozawa arranged for Nagano to join the faculty at the Tanglewood Music Center and to have his debut with the Boston SO in 1984 as assistant conductor.

Nagano was music director of the Ojai Music Festival (1985–6) and principal guest conductor for the Ensemble Intercontemporain (1986–9). He was the first winner with Hugh Wolff of the Affiliate Artists' Seaver Conducting Award. During the 1990s he was music director of the Lyons Opera (1989–98), associate principal guest conductor of the LSO (1990–98), and music director of the Hallé Orchestra in Manchester (1992–2000). Although he revived the status of this last orchestra, his expensive programming of primarily contemporary works led to empty seats. Nagano was blamed for the near bankruptcy of the orchestra in 1998, and Mark Elder replaced him in 2000. Nagano then was principal conductor and artistic director of the Deutsches SO Berlin (2000–06) and principal conductor of the Los Angeles Opera (2001–06). In 2006 he became music director of the Montreal SO and general music director of the Bayerische Staatsoper.

Nagano has excelled at complex late 19th- and 20th-century scores and has been praised for his technique, if not always his warmth, especially in performances and recordings of Messiaen and Mahler. His exuberant and graceful movement on the podium is reminiscent of that of his mentor, Ozawa, and, like him, conducts without a baton. In Lyons he performed and recorded rare repertory, including Ferruccio Busoni's *Doktor Faust*, *Arlecchino*, and *Turandot*, Debussy's *Rodrigue et Chimène* (orchestrated by Edison Denisov), Peter Eötvös's *Trois soeurs*, Carlisle Floyd's *Susannah*, Bohuslav Martinů's *Les trois souhaits*, Francis Poulenc's *Dialogues des Carmélites*, Sergei Prokofiev's *The Love for Three Oranges* (*Gramophone* magazine's Record of the Year in 1990), and the first recording of Richard Strauss's *Salomé* with the original French text by Oscar Wilde. At the Salzburg Festival he conducted *St. François d'Assise* in 1998 and *Doktor Faust* in 1999.

Nagano has conducted the world premieres of John Adams's *The Death of Klinghoffer* (Brussels, Théâtre Royal de la Monnaie, March 1991), Schoenberg's *Pierrot Lunaire* (with Björk, Verbier Festival, August 1996), Kaija Saariaho's *L'amour de loin* (2000), and Adams' nativity oratorio *El niño* (Paris, Théâtre du Châtelet, December 2000). His extensive discography includes works by Adams, Bartók, Hector Berlioz (an excitingly theatrical *La damnation de Faust*), Leonard Bernstein, Benjamin Britten, Darius Milhaud, Prokofiev, Ravel, Schoenberg, and Stravinsky. Through Nagano's initiative the International Arnold-Schönberg-Prize was established in 2001, which has been awarded to such composers as George Benjamin, Unsuk Chin, and Aribert Reimann.

BIBLIOGRAPHY

H. Traber: *Kent Nagano: Musik für ein neues Jahrhundert* (Berlin, 2002)

JOSÉ A. BOWEN/RICHARD WIGMORE/
MICHAEL BAUMGARTNER

Nagel, Robert (*b* Freeland, PA, 29 Sept 1924). Trumpeter, composer, and educator. A graduate of the Juilliard School, he regularly performed in New York with orchestras, in recording studios, and for radio and television broadcasts. Among his most prominent recordings are the first of the Igor Stravinsky *L'histoire du soldat* and *Octet for Wind Instruments*. One of his singular achievements involved his founding and directing the NEW YORK BRASS QUINTET in which he performed as first trumpet from 1954 to 1984. Important commissions by the quintet include Malcolm Arnold's *Brass Quintet* and Gunther Schuller's *Music for Brass Quintet*. Nagel served on the music faculties of Yale, the Juilliard School, Manhattan School of Music, Hartt School of Music, Rutgers University, Hofstra University, and the University of South Carolina. His many original and arranged works for trumpet and brass quintet have become standard repertoire. Among his many honors are the Brass Congress Award, International Trumpet Guild Honorary Award, Cesare Bendinelli Award, and the Platinum Piston Award.

JASON S. BERGMAN

NAJE [National Association of Jazz Educators]. An organization dedicated to JAZZ EDUCATION founded in 1968 and disbanded in 2008.

Nakai, R(ay) Carlos [R.C.] (*b* Flagstaff, AZ, 16 April 1946). Flutist, composer, educator, and author of Navajo and Ute descent. He earned a master's degree in American Indian Studies from the University of Arizona and was awarded an honorary doctorate from Northern Arizona University (1994). By the early 2010s he had released more than 45 albums for various record labels, earned two gold records, and sold more than four million albums. He has received eight Grammy nominations spread across three categories, a Governor's Arts Award (1992, Arizona), two Indie Awards, and eight Native American Music Awards, and has been inducted into the Arizona Music & Entertainment Hall of Fame. In collaboration with composer James DeMars and ethnomusicologist David McAllester, Nakai wrote *The Art of the Native American Flute* (Phoenix, 1996). His music has been featured in such films as *The New World* (2005), *Geronimo: An American Legend* (1993), and *How the West was Lost* (1993). The Martha Graham Dance Company performed his *Cycles* in 1988 to accompany Graham's final choreographed work, *Night Chant*.

Formally trained as a trumpet player, Nakai began playing Native American flute in 1973 and released his first album, *Changes*, in 1983. His album *Canyon Trilogy* (1989) was the first-ever Native American gold record. By the early 2010s he had performed as a soloist internationally and with more than 25 orchestras. He has often been credited for the late 20th-century resurgence and evolution of the Native American flute and its popularity with non-Native and Native people. His work is characterized by a blend of Western European and Native American techniques, and he has collaborated with a wide range of performers of traditional, jazz, classical, new age, Japanese, Tibetan, Hawaiian, Jewish, and Arabic music, among other styles.

SELECTED RECORDINGS

Changes (Canyon, 1983); *Cycles* (Canyon, 1985); *Canyon Trilogy* (Canyon, 1989); *Island of Bows* (Canyon, 1994); *Kokopelli's Café* (Canyon, 1996); *Two World Concerto* (Canyon, 1997); *Big Medicine* (Canyon, 1999); *Ancient Future* (Canyon, 2000); *In Beauty, We Return* (Canyon, 2004); *Reconnections* (Canyon, 2006); *Dancing Into Silence* (Canyon, 2010)

BIBLIOGRAPHY

D.P. McAllester: "The Music of R. Carlos Nakai," *To the Four Corners*, ed. E.C. Leichtman (Warren, MI, 1994), 189–210

P. Conlon: "The Native American Flute: Convergence and Collaboration as Exemplified by R. Carlos Nakai," *The World of Music*, xliv/1 (2002), 61–74

"Icons of Echoes: R. Carlos Nakai" <http://www.echoes.org/onlinenakai.html> (2013)

KAY EDWARDS

Nakamura, Daniel M. *See* DAN THE AUTOMATOR.

Nakasone, Harry [Seisho] (*b* O'ahu, Territory of Hawai'i, 12 Feb 1912; *d* Honolulu, HI, 19 March 2011). *Sanshin* player. Born in Hawai'i to Japanese immigrant parents, he was taken by his mother to her native Okinawa to be raised by his grandparents. There at the age of nine he began playing the Okinawan *sanshin*. The *sanshin* is a three-stringed instrument with a skin-covered soundbox, which predates the similar Japanese shamisen. He was given a *sanshin* by his uncle—also an accomplished player of the instrument—when he returned to Hawai'i in 1925 and began formal instruction in 1933, taking lessons from a number of *sanshin* grand masters and visiting Okinawa whenever possible. For the next six decades Nakasone performed *sanshin* at gatherings for the Okinawan community in Hawai'i, playing for festivals and various celebrations. He also taught *sanshin* in college classes and gave private lessons, led the Okinawan classical music ensemble Seifu Kai, and became the first non-Japanese citizen to receive a teaching certificate from the nationally recognized Nomura Music Academy in Okinawa. Nakasone was on the ethnomusicology faculty at the University of Hawaii, Manoa, from 1966. He became the music director of the Okinawan American music and dance organization Kariyushi-Kai in 1990 and received an NEA National Heritage Fellowship in 1991. Beyond Japan and Hawai'i, Nakasone performed in Brazil, Los Angeles, the Pacific Northwest, and the San Francisco Bay area.

MEGAN E. HILL

Nakota [Yankton]. Native American group belonging to the SIOUX.

Nambe. Native Americans belonging to the TEWA subgroup of the EASTERN PUEBLO.

NAMT [National Association for Music Therapy].
See MUSIC THERAPY.

Nancarrow, (Samuel) Conlon (*b* Texarkana, AR, 27 Oct 1912; *d* Mexico City, Mexico, 10 Aug 1997). Composer. Having been sent by his father (the mayor of Texarkana) to the Western Military Academy in Illinois, he started playing trumpet there and later attended the national music camp at Interlochen, Michigan. His father pushed him toward an engineering career, for which purpose Nancarrow briefly attended Vanderbilt University. Enrollment in Cincinnati College (1929–32) did not result in graduation, but it did, in 1930, expose him to Stravinsky's *The Rite of Spring*, which sparked an interest in rhythmic complexity. In 1934 he moved to Boston and studied privately with ROGER SESSIONS, WALTER PISTON, and NICOLAS SLONIMSKY. A Communist Party member, he volunteered for the Abraham Lincoln Brigade and fought in the Spanish Civil War. After returning home, he reacted to growing anti-communist activity in America by moving to Mexico City in 1940, where he lived until his death.

Nancarrow's works from 1930 to 1945 were for piano (*Prelude* and *Blues*), small orchestra, string quartet, and small chamber ensembles. Best known, however, are his series of about 50 (the numbering is ambiguous) studies for player piano, which explore a fascinating range of techniques for achieving extreme rhythmic complexity. In 1947, living on inherited money and inspired by Henry Cowell's book *New Musical Resources* (in which Cowell recommended using a player piano to achieve complex polyrhythms), Nancarrow traveled to New York to buy a player piano and have a roll-punching machine built for him. His first pieces, later gathered together as Study no.3, were experiments in extremely fast jazz pianism, influenced by Nancarrow's favorite pianists Art Tatum and Earl Hines. The piece officially numbered Study no.1 spun fragments of a 30-note pitch row around marching major triads in two simultaneous tempos of four against seven.

Considering that three quarters of Nancarrow's output is for the same instrument, the variety of his musical strategies is astonishing. Nevertheless, his music can be summed up as deriving from four basic rhythmic ideas: ostinato, isorhythm, tempo canon, and acceleration. The early blues-influenced studies, nos. 1, 2, 3, 5, and 9, are generated by setting ostinatos against each other at different tempos. In studies 6, 7, 10, 11, and 20, he revived the medieval technique of isorhythm (although inspired by a strong interest in the tala structure of Indian music), employing multiple repetition of the same rhythm against different pitch sequences. The climax of the early studies is no.7, in which three isorhythms are set against each other in myriad combinations and at lightning-fast speed. Even here the feeling for jazz harmony remains strong, and the isorhythms simulate the freedoms of a wild jazz pianist.

With studies 13–19, Nancarrow discovered the technique with which he would be most identified: tempo canon. In the tempo canons, a melody (or, later, textual block) is superimposed upon itself at different levels of transposition and at varying tempo ratios, for example 4:5, 12:15:20, and so on. Formal variety is achieved by varying the placement of the convergence point, i.e., the moment at which the melodies reach the same point in their respective material. For instance, the simple Study no.14 has two voices at a 4:5 ratio, with the convergence point at the exact mid-point of the piece. Study no.31 ends just seconds before its three voices (at ratios 21:24:25) would have converged. Starting with Study no.24, Nancarrow worked with highly elaborate schemes in which the melodies begin at a convergence point, grow further and further apart, switch tempos, grow back together, reach a second convergence point, and repeat the process over and over again.

In his most elegant canons (studies 24, 32, 33, 36, 37, 43) this process achieves a classic interdependence between form and content. Near a convergence point, the motives tend to be brief and to echo from voice to voice quickly. In between such coincidences, the melodies tend to stretch out at greater length. As Nancarrow developed this technique, his rhythmic ratios grew to almost unimaginable complexity: the square root of 2 against 2 in no.33, *e* against π in no.40 (*e* being the base of natural logarithms), and in no.37 a scale of 12 tempos analogous to the pitch ratios of a justly-tuned chromatic scale (similar to a scale Karlheinz Stockhausen had used in Gruppen, and which both may have taken from Cowell's book).

The remaining rhythmic idea is acceleration (and deceleration), employed in studies 8, 21, 22, 23, and 27 to 30. Study no.27, for instance, is a canon in which the voices accelerate (and decelerate) at rates of 5%, 6%, 8%, and 11%. (In a 5% acceleration, each note is 5% shorter in duration than its predecessor.) While acceleration was arguably Nancarrow's most original device (though again suggested by Cowell), it was difficult to control structurally in the pre-computer era, and did not prove as fertile as tempo canon or isorhythm.

In Nancarrow's early works, these rhythmic ideas remain fairly distinct. In his late studies, though—nos. 25, 35, 41, 42, 45, 46, 47, and 48—he begins, as Beethoven did in his last sonatas and string quartets, to combine his structures into hybrid forms. For example, in nos. 45–7, a tempo canon based on an isorhythm creates an acceleration effect as it nears a convergence point. Also, beginning with the spectacular Study no.25, Nancarrow began to develop what was idiomatic about the player piano, indulging in superfast glissandos and arpeggios, figures that traverse the keyboard within a split second. At the thunderous climax of no.25, 1028 notes swirl by in 12 seconds. Perhaps his greatest works, though, are his chaotic-sounding late canons, studies 41 and 48, in which frenetic glissandos and jazz gestures are flung together according to well concealed accelerative structures.

Nancarrow composed in almost total isolation until the late 1970s, when Peter Garland began publishing his scores in *Soundings* and the studies started appearing on record. Starting in 1983 his increasing fame brought a series of commissions for live-performed works (Tango?, String Quartet no.3, Piece no.2 for small orchestra, Three Canons for Ursula) and invitations to major music festivals in America and especially Europe; in 1983 the MacArthur Foundation awarded him its prestigious "genius" award of $300,000. After his death some 68 unlabeled piano rolls, some containing seemingly complete works, plus a number of smaller scores, were found in his studio, adding some posthumous works to his output and creating some ambiguities in terms of titling. Nancarrow's player piano studies have had a tremendous impact on young composers for their almost unparalleled fusion of visceral excitement and structural elegance.

WORKS

CHAMBER AND ORCHESTRAL

Sarabande and Scherzo, ob, bn, pf, 1930; Toccata, vn, pf, 1935; Septet, 1940; Trio no.1, cl, bn, pf, 1942; Piece no.1, small orch, 1943; Str Qt no.1, 1945; Str Qt no.2, late 1940s, inc.; Piece no.2, small orch (1985); Str Qt no.3, 1987; Trio no.2, ob, bn, pf, 1991

PLAYER PIANO
(unless otherwise stated all extant as piano rolls and in MS score)
Studies nos.1–30, *c*1948–60, incl. no.2b [based on final movt of Piece no.1, small orch]; no.13, no score extant; no.30, prep player pf, no score extant; no.34, arr. str trio; Studies nos.31–7, 40–51, *c*1965–92; nos.38 and 39 renumbered as 43 and 48; For Yoko, 1990; Conc. for Player Pf and Orch (arr. of Study no.49), 1992; 3 Movts for Chbr Orch (partly orchd C. Sandoval), 1992; Contraption no.1, cptr-driven prep pf, 1993

PIANO
Blues, 1935; Prelude, 1935; Sonatina, 1941; 3 Two-Part Studies, early 1940s; Tango?, 1983; 3 Canons for Ursula, 1989

MSS in *CH-Bps*
Principal publishers: Boosey & Hawkes, Peters, Smith, Soundings

BIBLIOGRAPHY
E. Carter: "The Rhythmic Basis of American Music," *The Score and I.M.A. Magazine*, xii (1955), 27–32
G. Mumma: "Nancarrow Notes," *Desert Plants: Conversations with 23 American Musicians*, ed. W. Zimmermann (Vancouver, 1976), 247–51
P. Garland, ed.: *Conlon Nancarrow: Selected Studies for Player Piano* (Berkeley, 1977) [incl. interview with Nancarrow and articles by G. Mumma, R. Reynolds, J. Tenney, and others]
R. Commanday: "The Man who Writes for Player Piano," *San Francisco Chronicle* (30 June 1981)
J. Rockwell: "Conlon Nancarrow: Poet of the Player Piano," *New York Times* (28 June 1981)
C. Gagne and T. Caras: "Conlon Nancarrow," *Soundpieces: Interviews with American Composers* (Metuchen, NJ, 1982), 281–303
P. Garland: "Conlon Nancarrow: Chronicle of a Friendship," *Americas: Essays on American Music and Culture (1973–80)* (Santa Fe, 1982), 157–85
J. Jarvlepp: "Conlon Nancarrow's *Study ♮27 for Player Piano* Viewed Analytically," *PNM*, xxii (1983–4), 218–22
M. Fürst-Heidtmann: "Conlon Nancarrow's 'Studies for Player Piano'/ Time is the Last Frontier in Music," *Melos*, xlvi (1984), 104–22
J. LaBarbara: "The Remarkable Art of Conlon Nancarrow," *Musical America*, xxxiv (1984), 12–13
R. Reynolds: "Conlon Nancarrow: Interviews in Mexico City and San Francisco," *American Music*, ii/2 (1984), 1–24
M. Fürst-Heidtmann: "Ich bin beim Komponieren nur meinen Wunschen gefolgt," *MusikTexte*, no.21 (1987), 29–32
P. Carlsen: *The Player-Piano Music of Conlon Nancarrow: an Analysis of Selected Studies* (New York, 1988)
M. Furst-Heidtmann: "Conlon Nancarrow und die Emanzipation des Tempos," *NZM*, Jg.150, nos.7–8 (1989), 32–8
K. Gann: "Private Bells," *VV* (14 Nov 1989)
K. Gann: "Conlon Nancarrow's Tempo Tornados," *VV* (5 Oct 1993)
K. Gann: *The Music of Conlon Nancarrow* (Cambridge, 1995)
J.R. Greeson, and G.B. Gearhart: "Conlon Nancarrow: an Arkansas Original," *Arkansas Historical Quarterly*, lxiv/4 (1995) 457–69
Obituaries: *New York Times* (12 Aug 1997), *VV* (2 Sept 1997)
M.E. Thomas: "Nancarrow's Canons: Projections of Temporal and Formal Structures," *PNM*, xxxviii/2 (2000), 106–33
C. Callender: "Formalized Accelerando: an Extension of Rhythmic Techniques in Nancarrow's Acceleration Canons," *PNM*, xxxix/1 (2001), 188–210
J. Hocker: *Begegnungen mit Nancarrow* (Mainz, Germany, 2002)
E. Drott: "Conlon Nancarrow and the Technological Sublime," *American Music*, xxii/4 (2004), 533–63
D. Stojanovic-Novicic: "Sound in a Paper Roll: the Creative Network of Conlon Nancarrow," *Music & Networking: Belgrade 2005*, 111–18
D. Stojanovic-Novicic: "Misunderstandings about Conlon Nancarrow, with a Little Help from the Composer himself," *(Auto)Biography as a Musicological Discourse: Belgrade 2010*, 398–407
D. Stojanovic-Novicic: "The Carter-Nancarrow Correspondence," *American Music*, xxix/1 (2011)

KYLE GANN

NANM. *See* NATIONAL ASSOCIATION OF NEGRO MUSICIANS (NANM).

Nanton, Tricky Sam [Joe; Irish, Joseph N.] (*b* New York, NY, 1 Feb 1904; *d* San Francisco, CA, 20 July 1946). Jazz trombonist. His parents immigrated from the West Indies, and some musicians felt that his improvisations reflected the cadences of his parents' speech patterns; Duke Ellington observed: "When a guy comes here from the West Indies and is asked to play some jazz, he plays what he thinks it is, or what comes from his applying himself to the idiom." Nanton worked with Earl Frazier at Edmond's Cellar and with Cliff Jackson at the Nest Club, both in Harlem, in the mid-1920s and recorded with Sidney Bechet, Don Redman, Elmer Snowden's Westerners, and Clarence Williams's Stompers (alongside Bubber Miley). He joined Ellington in 1926, following the departure of Charlie Irvis, who had contributed to Ellington's "jungle style" with a unique muted trombone sound. Although Nanton also played open horn solos, he invented his own growling, muted approach and employed a rubber plunger, somewhat borrowed from and compatible with that of Ellington's trumpeter Miley. Nanton's muted wah-wah sound rang with a unique, primitive-sounding, almost vocal quality. "Blues with a Feeling" (OK, 1928) exemplifies the successful Miley–Nanton relationship. Nanton explained: "Trombonists try the plunger and discover it's way out of tune…they don't understand that it takes a helluva lot of experimentation and above all the ears have to be in tune. They have to violate all the principles of trombone playing to use the plunger properly…You have to play about a quarter tone flatter…when they see the kind of mute I use and get one, they find they're sharp…It's not all slide…you have to use your lip, too, and work it out until the desired effect is obtained." The precision of the technique, or musical tricks, that Nanton devised specifically for Ellington's music earned him the nickname "Tricky Sam." Additional outstanding examples of Nanton's work are his solos on "Blue Harlem" (Bruns., 1932), "Dear Old Southland' (Vic., 1933), and "Sidewalks of New York" (Vic., 1940). Nanton died of a stroke while touring with Ellington. Ellington, the cornetist Rex Stewart, and other band members described him as being impressively erudite with a highly developed yet limited melodic sense, enhanced by a pervasive and appealing sense of humor.

BIBLIOGRAPHY
D. Ellington: *Music is my Mistress* (New York, 1973)
R. Stewart and C. Gordon: *Boy Meets Horn* (Ann Arbor, 1991)
E. Lambert and E. Norsworthy: *Duke Ellington: a Listener's Guide* (London, 1999)
S. Lasker: disc notes, *The Complete 1932–1940 Brunswick, Columbia and Master Recordings of Duke Ellington and his Famous Orchestra*, Mosaic (2010)

PATRICIA WILLARD

Na'ope, George L(anakilakekiahiali'i) (*b* Honolulu, HI, 25 Feb 1928; *d* Hilo, HI, 26 Oct 2009). Hawaiian hula master, dancer, and musician. He was born into a poor family in the Kalihi district of Honolulu and began his studies in hula at the age of three with his grandmother. After studying under Mary Kanaele, he moved to Hilo, where at the age of 13 he began to teach the art of Hawaiian dance and music for 50 cents per lesson. He studied with Joseph Ilala'ole until he was 20 and later with Lokalia Montgomery and Tom Hiona. In 1936 he opened his first hula studio in Honolulu, where he taught traditional chant and dance to a wide range of students. He also performed regularly with several organizations, including Ray Kinney's dance troupe. Eventually, Na'ope gained an international reputation and traveled widely to Europe and Asia popularizing hula. In 1964 he founded the Merrie Monarch Festival, which subsequently became the top hula competition in the world. He received an NEA National Heritage Fellowship Award in 2006.

JONAS WESTOVER

Narcocorrido [Narco-corrido]. *Corridos* (Mexican heroic ballads) related to the drug traffic between Mexico and the United States. The term *narcocorrido* became common in the late 1980s or early 1990s; such songs, however, have existed since the 1920s, when Prohibition spawned a wave of *corridos* of *tequileros*, or bootleggers. In the 1930s and 1940s, *corridos* such as "Carga blanca," a hit for Los Alegres de Terán, dealt with smugglers of other drugs, but the modern trend began in the mid 1970s, when Los Tigres del Norte recorded "Contrabando y traición" and "La banda del carro rojo," huge hits which were made into popular movies and followed by multiple sequels and imitations. These hits helped to revive the *corrido* form. Some scholars have argued that because many *narcocorridos* are fictitious they should not be considered alongside the older, historically based *corridos* (*see* Corrido). *Narcocorridos* continue to be based on true stories, however, and their listeners regard them as continuing the tradition of celebrating brave men and women, albeit in an illegal business.

A new wave of *corrido*-focused artists appeared in the 1990s, inspired by the Sinaloan-born, Los Angeles-based singer-songwriter Chalino Sánchez. Sánchez wrote many of his songs on commission for their protagonists, and though some of his followers have had little personal connection to the world they chronicle, others have continued this trade.

In general, *narcocorridos* are about gun battles and personal bravery, and most do not even mention drugs. In the 1990s, though, Los Tucanes de Tijuana recorded "Mis tres animales," a song that used code words to talk about cocaine, marihuana, and heroin, and later singers such as Lupillo Rivera have taken inspiration from gangsta rap, writing about crack dealers and cocaine parties. *Narcocorridos* remain most popular in the Mexico–United States border region and Mexico's drug-growing states, but are now also performed and written in much of Latin America, and have been particularly successful in Colombia.

BIBLIOGRAPHY

E. Wald: *Narcocorrido: a Journey into the Music of Drugs, Guns, and Guerrillas* (New York, 2001)

J.M. Valenzuela Arce: *Jefe de jefes. Corridos y narcocultura en México* (Mexico City, 2002)

ELIJAH WALD

Narell, Andy [Andrew] (*b* New York, NY, 18 March 1954). Pannist, composer, and leader. He discovered jazz by listening to Billy Taylor on WLIB in New York. He was introduced to steel pan through his father's work at the Educational Alliance on the Lower East Side of Manhattan. From 1970 to 1973 he studied music at the University of California at Berkeley.

Narell's style combines jazz with such Latin and Caribbean musics as calypso, *biguine*, rumba, and *son*. He has recorded numerous studio albums as a leader for the Inner City, Hip Pocket, Windham Hill Jazz, and HeadsUp labels and as a co-leader with Paquito D'Rivera and Dave Samuels of the Caribbean Jazz Project and with Mario Canonge, Michel Alibo, and Jean Philippe Fanfant of Sakésho. As a studio musician Narell has appeared on albums with artists including Bela Fleck, Marcus Miller, Spyro Gyra, Vince Mendoza, Jesús "Chucho" Valdés, Angelique Kidjo, and Nancy Wilson. He has also worked with such film composers as James Horner, Elmer Bernstein, Hans Zimmer, and Thomas Newman.

Narell has pioneered steel pan as a solo jazz instrument and has composed innovative jazz-influenced music for large steel bands; such soloists as Michael Brecker, Hugh Masekela, Mike Stern, and David Sanchez have played on his orchestral recordings. In 1999 he was the first foreigner to arrange music for the Trinidad and Tobago annual Panorama steel band competition. Other projects include the University of Calypso, a collaborative effort with the Trinidad calypsonian Relator.

BIBLIOGRAPHY

A. Martin: "Words of Steel: Pete Seeger and the US Navy Steel Band," *Voices: the Journal of New York Folklore*, xxxiv/1 (2008), 20–27

A. Martin: *Pan-America: Calypso, Exotica and the Rise of the American Steel Band Movement* (diss., U. of Minnesota, 2011)

ANDREW R. MARTIN

Nas [Jones, Nasir bin Olu Dara] (*b* New York, NY, 14 Sept 1973). Rapper. He is the son of jazz musician OLU DARA. Nas was among the most influential rap artists to emerge in the 1990s. He gained recognition for his poetic, street-level lyrics and rhythmically intricate flow. He began playing trumpet and composing rhymes as a child in New York's Queensbridge project. As a youth he developed an interest in African culture and the Qu'ran, aligning himself with the Five Percent Nation. His unique rapping and poetic talents attracted MC Serch of hip-hop crew 3rd Bass; Serch became Nas's manager and helped the rapper secure a contract with Columbia Records in 1992. In 1994 the rapper's debut album, *Illmatic* (Col.), drew critical acclaim for its gritty, evocative portrayals of ghetto life enhanced by creative lyrics and skillful delivery. Awarded five Mics from *The Source* magazine, the album included tracks produced by Q-Tip, DJ Premier, and Large Professor, and a cameo by Nas's father. Journalist Henry Adaso hailed it as the "greatest hip-hop recording of all time." In 1996 Nas followed with *It Was Written* (Col.). This double-platinum album premiered at number 1 on both the pop and R&B charts and showcased collaborations with Mobb Deep's Havoc, Dr. Dre, and DJ Premier. It marked the premiere of the Firm, a hip-hop supergroup comprised of Nas, Cormega, Foxy Brown, and AZ. Nas then released *I am...* (Col., 1999, number 1 R&B and pop), which included the track, "Hate Me Now," a duet with Sean Combs featuring a sample from Carl Orff's *Carmina Burana*. The song's video elicited controversy when Combs allegedly became violent with Nas's manager over images that portrayed the rapper nailed to a cross. Beginning in 2001 Nas was involved in a public rivalry with rapper Jay-Z in which both men verbally attacked one another on their albums. The feud ended in 2005, and Nas signed with Def Jam Records, where Jay-Z was serving as CEO, the following year. Their first collaboration yielded the provocatively titled *Hip-hop is Dead* (Def Jam, 2006). The album's title track, which sampled Nas's single "Thief's Theme" (2004) and Iron Butterfly's "In-A-Gadda-Da-Vida," sparked debates about the relevance of hip hop and the impact of Southern crunk music on the genre in the new millennium. In 2007, citing Nas's criminal record, commentator Bill O'Reilly claimed it was inappropriate for the artist to perform at a concert for students at Virginia Technical University. Nas released the single "Sly Fox" (Def Jam, 2008) in response. In 2008 Columbia Records released a collection of Nas's greatest hits.

BIBLIOGRAPHY
A. Light: *The Vibe History of Hip Hop* (New York, 1999)
D. Ross: *The Nightmare and the Dream: Nas, Jay-Z and the History of Conflict in African-American Culture* (Jersey City, NJ, 2008)
M.E. Dyson: *Born to Use Mics: Reading Nas's Illmatic* (New York, 2010)

MARGARET JACKSON

Nascimento, Milton (*b* Rio de Janeiro, Brazil, 26 Oct 1942). Brazilian singer, instrumentalist, and songwriter. He was raised in the town of Três Pontas in the state of Minas Gerais by an adoptive couple. His adoptive mother, Lília Silva Campos, taught him piano when he was young. He also learned accordion, guitar, and bass. He recorded his first song, "Barulho de trem," in 1962. He also publicly performed with Wagner Tiso's vocal group W's Boys at dance parties. He moved to Belo Horizonte in 1963 where he established musical relationships with Fernando Brant, Márcio Hilton Borges, Ronaldo Bastos, and later Beto Guedes, Lô Borges, and Toninho Horta. The group Clube da Esquina formed the basis of many musical collaborations. They later released the double-album *Clube da esquina* (EMI-Odeon, 1972), which demonstrates the musical relationships between group members. The vocalist Elis Regina was also an early interpreter of Nascimento's music. Nascimento became famous through a series of nationally televised song festivals. In 1968 he accepted Eumir Deodato's invitation to record in the United States for A&M Records. The resulting album, *Courage*, featured Herbie Hancock and Airto Moreira. Nascimento's music has an international following and orientation. He collaborated with jazz saxophonist Wayne Shorter for his album *Native Dancer* (Col., 1974), and Shorter appeared on Nascimento's own recording the following year, *Minas* (EMI).

Nascimento's compositional style draws on religious imagery, folk styles, and such topics as poverty and social justice. He also cites influences from other countries around the world. He has maintained working relationships with many artists in the *nueva canción* movement, and the Beatles have been a major compositional influence. He has collaborated with such artists as Duran Duran, Cat Stevens, and Daniel Barenboim. Nascimento's fans have cited his vocal timbre, extraordinary range, and social consciousness as enduring reasons for his appeal.

BIBLIOGRAPHY
Grove7 (G. Béhague)
C.A. Perrone: *Masters of Contemporary Brazilian Song: MPB 1965–1985* (Austin, TX, 1989)
M. de U. Carvalho: "*Canção da América*: Style and Emotion in Brazilian Popular Song," *Popular Music*, ix (1990), 321–49
M. Borges: *Os sonhos não envelhecem: histórias do clube da esquina* (São Paulo, 1996)
C. McGowan and R. Pessanha: *The Brazilian Sound: Samba, Bossa Nova and the Popular Music of Brazil* (Philadelphia, 2/1998)
J.S. Roberts: *Latin Jazz: the First of the Fusions, 1880s to Today* (New York, 1999)

KARIANN GOLDSCHMITT

Nash, (Frederic) Ogden (*b* Rye, NY, 19 Aug 1902; *d* Baltimore, MD, 19 May 1971). Poet and lyricist. He studied at Harvard University and worked in New York before settling in Baltimore as a full-time writer. He produced several volumes of light and satiric verse, a few screenplays, and lyrics for Broadway and television shows. More than 65 of his published poems have been set to music, the majority from his many verses about animals. The earliest known setting, *Quartet for Prosperous Love Children* (1933) by Robert Armbruster, is included in Nash's *Happy Days* (also 1933). Most of the settings are found in a few choral and song cycles, the earliest of which was *Ogden Nash's Musical Zoo* (1947) by Vernon Duke. Other cycles include *Who's Who in the Zoo* by Jean Berger, *Ogden Nash Suite* by Jerry Bilik, *Essays on Women* by Arthur Frackenpohl, and *A Musical Menu* and *A Musical Menagerie* by Philip Hagemann. Recent settings that include texts by Nash are by Timothy Hoekman (*The Nash Menagerie*), Bob Chilcott (*Fragments from his Dish*), Jeffrey Rickard (*Four, Plus One*), Phillip Schroeder (*Ogden Nash Songs*), Stephen Paulus (*Bittersweet*), Marion Verhaalen (*Animal Verses of Ogden Nash*), and Roger Vogel, ("Have You Heard That I Love You?" a letter from Ogden Nash to Frances Rider, 25 August 1929, in *Love Letters*).

Nash was a skilled and prolific lyricist. He and S.J. Perelman collaborated with Kurt Weill on the popular Broadway musical *One Touch of Venus*. With Vernon Duke and others he wrote the musical comedy *Sweet Bye and Bye* and the musical revues *Two's Company* and *The Littlest Revue*. He also wrote verses to accompany Saint-Saëns's *Carnival of the Animals* and lyrics for two television programs, "Art Carney Meets 'Peter and the Wolf'" and "Art Carney Meets 'The Sorcerer's Apprentice,'" which featured the Baird Marionettes with music adapted from Prokofiev and Dukas and composed by Paul Weston.

BIBLIOGRAPHY

D. Ewen: *New Complete Book of the American Musical Theater* (New York, 1970)

R. Lewine and A. Simon: *Songs of the American Theater* (New York, 1973)

C.D. Kinsman, ed.: *Contemporary Authors*, i (Detroit, 1975), 475 only

G. Bordman: *American Musical Theatre: a Chronicle* (New York, 1978)

M.A. Hovland: *Musical Settings of American Poetry: a Bibliography* (Westport, CT, 1986) [incl. list of settings]

R. Gottlieb and R. Kimball, eds: *Reading Lyrics, More Than a Thousand of the Century's Finest Lyrics* (New York, 2000)

MICHAEL HOVLAND

Nash, Grace (Elinor) C(hapman) (*b* rural Garrettsville, OH, 19 Nov 1909). Music educator, author, and violinist. Educated at Hiram College and Ohio Wesleyan University (BA in French and music, 1930), she completed a Master's degree in performance and composition at Chicago Musical College in 1936. She married Ralph Nash in 1936 and soon accepted a position as assistant concertmaster with the Manila Symphony Orchestra in the Philippines. She and her family became prisoners of war in 1942 when the Japanese invaded Manila. They were released in 1945. Her book *That We Might Live* (Scottsdale, AZ, 1984) tells the story of their internment. Nash taught violin and music theory in the Chicago area until the 1960s, when she began to study with CARL ORFF, ZOLTÁN KODÁLY, and Rudolph Laban. She integrated their methodologies into her teaching as illustrated in her book *Creative Approaches to Child Development with Music, Language, and Movement* (Van Nuys, CA, 1974). The Orff Schulwerk is the approach into which the others are woven. Nash became prominent as a teacher trainer in the Orff style from 1979 to 1999, and she authored many publications used by music teachers. She was the first recipient of the American Orff-Schulwerk Association's Distinguished Service Award (1989).

BIBLIOGRAPHY

M.S. Orrell: *The Work of Grace Nash in Music Education in the United States, 1960–1990, and Her Influence upon Members of the American Orff-Schulwerk Association in the States of Arizona and Colorado* (diss., U. of Houston, 1995)

J. Cole: "Nine Decades of Graceful Teaching," *Teaching Music*, vii/6 (2000), 44–48

ALAN L. S. SPURGEON

Nash, Lewis (Douglas) (*b* Phoenix, AZ, 30 Dec 1958). Drummer. He developed an early interest in music and began playing drums at age ten. By his late teens he was performing locally with small jazz ensembles and had garnered invaluable experience as a sideman for Sonny Stitt, Art Pepper, Red Garland, Lee Konitz, and Slide Hampton. He moved to New York with hopes of procuring steady work and soon joined Betty Carter and her trio (1981); his four-year association with the singer included international tours and collaboration on her Grammy Award winning album, *Look What I Got!* (1988). His versatility attracted other top-flight musicians such as bass player Ron Carter, who featured him on several recordings and within the context of varied ensembles. Nash remained active throughout the 1980s, supporting the work of Branford Marsalis, J.J. Johnson, Willie Nelson, and Natalie Cole, among others. He has made a number of albums as a leader including his first, *Rhythm Is My Business* (1989). In the 1990s Nash formed his own ensembles, which ranged from a duo to a septet. In the 2000s he became a highly regarded clinician and consequently spurred the careers of younger drummers. His melodic sensibility, vast array of percussive effects, and tremendous sense of swing were put to use as he became a member of the Blue Note 7 (2008), which was formed to honor the 70th anniversary of Blue Note Records. They have continued to tour the United States performing the music of various Blue Note artists.

BIBLIOGRAPHY

Feather-Gitler BEJ

K. Micallef: "Lewis Nash: the Business of Rhythm," *Modern Drummer*, xvi/10 (1992), 32 [incl. discography]

K. Micallef: "Lewis Nash: Jazz's Most Valuable Player," *Modern Drummer* (2009)

MICHAEL CONKLIN

Nashville. Capital city of Tennessee (population 626,144; metropolitan area 1,550,733; 2010 US Census). Founded in 1779 and incorporated as a town in 1806. Although internationally known as the home of country music, a distinction given to the city due to the broadcasting and publishing industries of the 20th century, the city has a long history as a center for music performance, publication, and pedagogy in a variety of music genres.

1. Art music. 2. 19th-century vernacular music. 3. Country music. 4. Rhythm-and-blues. 5. Nashville in the early 21st century.

1. ART MUSIC. The development of Nashville's early concert life was directly linked to the importance placed on education by the region's earliest settlers and the increase in numbers of European immigrants during the 19th century who served as music instructors, established music schools, and organized concerts. Davidson Academy, Nashville's first school, was established in 1785. By 1816 the Nashville Female Academy opened and soon included music instruction in the curriculum. Following the success of these early institutions, a number of schools were chartered; many included musical training. Due to an emphasis on education and the arts, Nashville was dubbed the "Athens of the South."

By 1820 a musical society was established to promote musical instruction and organize music events in the city. Early concerts were held at the Nashville Inn,

The Nashville Symphony Orchestra at Schermerhorn Symphony Center. (Photo: Harry Butler)

City Hall, the Masonic Hall, area churches, and established educational institutions. The first formal concert held in Nashville was in 1819 at the Masonic Hall and included a mixture of popular songs and opera overtures. Throughout the early 19th century, Nashville hosted a series of concerts featuring both classical pieces and the most popular music of the era. By 1850 Nashville was gaining a national reputation as a city of the arts. The Adelphi Theater, built in 1850, became the center of Nashville's concert life, and the city witnessed an increase in music events performed by local musical organizations and national and international acts. Notable performers in Nashville's early concert life included Luigi Arditi's Italian Opera Company, Ole Bull, Jenny Lind, Camillo Sivori, Henri Herz, and Maurice Strakosch.

In 1861 Tennessee seceded from the union and was soon occupied by federal troops. Many area newspapers ceased publication, resulting in the scarce documentation of concert life. Following the Civil War, Nashville reclaimed its title as a center for education and the arts. Three institutions were established in Nashville to educate emancipated slaves: Nashville Normal and Theological Institute, later named Roger Williams University (1865); Central Tennessee College (1865); and Fisk University (1866). The JUBILEE SINGERS, a choral group from Fisk University, performed a concert tour in 1871 to raise funds for their struggling institution, introducing new audiences to the African American spiritual tradition. The success of their US tours led to international tours. Money raised by their performances secured the University, purchased the current Fisk campus, and provided funds for the construction of Jubilee Hall. Other Nashville educational institutions established in the late 19th century include Vanderbilt University (1873), Belmont Junior College (1890), and Nashville Bible School, later named Lipscomb University (1891).

Concert life also saw a rebirth in the years following the Civil War. In 1887 the Vendome Theater opened; it was Nashville's finest concert hall to date. The first production in the new hall was Giuseppe Verdi's *Il trovatore*. In 1889 Riverboat Captain Tom Ryman began construction on the Union Gospel Tabernacle, which he envisioned as a space for religious revivals. After Ryman's death in 1904, the hall was renamed the Ryman Auditorium. In addition to religious gatherings, the hall also served as an important venue for national and international musical and theatrical acts. Notable artists who appeared on the Ryman stage included the Chicago Orchestra with Theodore Thomas, the Ballets Russe with Vaslav Nijinsky, Ignance Jan Paderewaki, Giuseppe Campanari, John Phillip Sousa, Edward Strauss and the Vienna Orchestra, the Metropolitan Opera Company, and Enrico Caruso. In 1941 the Ryman became the home of Nashville's most famous musical institution, the Grand Ole Opry, and it has continued to serve as a live music venue for local, national, and international acts.

In 1904 J. Hough Guest organized Nashville's first symphonic orchestra. Comprised of 38 members, the orchestra held its premiere performance at the Vendome Theater. The second attempt at forming a symphonic orchestra occurred in 1920 under the direction of F. Arthur Henkel. The current Nashville Symphony, established in 1946, was largely due to the vision and financial support of Walter Sharp. Conductors for the symphony have included William Strickland (1946–51), Guy Taylor (1951–9), Willis Page (1959–67), Thor Johnson (1967–75), Michael Charry (1976–82), Kenneth Schermerhorn (1983–2005), Leonard Slatkin, artistic director (2006–09), and Giancario Guerrero (from 2009). Early performances were held at the War Memorial Auditorium. In 1980 the symphony relocated to the Tennessee Performing Arts Center and in 2003 broke ground on its $123.5 million Schermerhorn Symphony Center, which opened to the public with a concert conducted by Leonard Slatkin in 2006. After the historic May 2010 Nashville flood, the hall closed for repairs, and concerts were held at other area venues. The symphony hall reopened on New Year's Eve, 2010, with a concert featuring violinist Itzhak Perlman. In the 2000s

Statue of country music producer Owen Bradley by artist Gary Ernest Smith, Owen Bradley Park, Nashville. (AP Photo/Curtis Hilbun)

the Nashville Symphony recorded 18 albums with the Naxos label (now located in the Nashville Metropolitan area) and one with the Decca Label. For these recordings, the symphony received 13 Grammy nominations and six Grammy awards.

2. 19TH-CENTURY VERNACULAR MUSIC. Ballads such as "Barbara Allen," "The King's Daughter," and "The House Carpenter," collected by George Boswell in the middle Tennessee area, suggest the presence of European folk music in Nashville during the 19th century. African American vernacular and religious songs such as "The Good Old Way," "Sinner Won't Die No More," and "The Gold Band" were collected in Nashville by William Francis Allen, Charles Pickard Ware, and Lucy McKim Garrison, and documented in *Slave Songs of the United States* (New York, 1867). These early vernacular traditions led to the creation of new forms of vocal and instrumental music throughout the 19th and early 20th centuries and laid the foundation for popular musical forms that would later be broadcasted from Nashville.

Vernacular music could also be heard performed at religious gatherings and revival meetings, common events in Middle Tennessee during the 19th century. The popularity of religious gatherings and the importance they placed on music led to the 1818 publication of *Tennessee Harmony*. The success of this tunebook led to a series of religious tunebooks published in the Nashville area, including *The Western Harmony* (1824), *The United States Harmony* (1829), *The American Harmony* (1839), *The Cumberland Harmony* (1834), and *The New Harp of Columbia* (1867).

Nashville's vibrant concert life in the mid-19th century led to visits by traveling minstrel troupes, including the Northern Serenades, Old Joe Swensy's Virginia Minstrels, the Empire Minstrels, and Mat Peel's Campbell Minstrels, who played to sold-out crowds at local venues such as the Masonic Hall. Minstrel troupes as well as vaudeville troupes and popular artists remained popular in the local theaters and venues well into the 20th century.

3. COUNTRY MUSIC. The history of country music in Nashville is directly connected to the history of broadcasting. WSM 650 AM, established by the National Life and Accident Insurance Company, first broadcasted in 1925. Shortly after the station went on the air, George D. Hay was hired as the program manager. Of the many programs Hay championed, the most long lasting and influential on Nashville's and the nation's music identity was the WSM barn dance, renamed the GRAND OLE OPRY in 1927. Performances of the Opry were held in several venues throughout the city, including the National Life and Insurance Company building, the Belcourt Theater, the Dixieland Tabernacle, and the War Memorial Auditorium. In 1943 the Opry moved to the Ryman Auditorium, where it would reside for the next 31 years. The Opry gained national attention in 1932 when WSM increased its frequency to 50,000 watts. Combined with the station's clear channel status, this increase in frequency wattage allowed the Opry to be heard across much the country. Its national popularity led to a syndicated broadcast by NBC affiliates in 1939. Notable performers of the early Opry included Uncle Dave Macon, the Carter Family, Hank Williams, Patsy Cline, Deford Bailey, Roy Acuff, Minnie Pearl, and Bill Monroe's Bluegrass Boys. In 1974 the Grand Ole Opry relocated to the Grand Ole Opry House, located at the Opryland complex.

Although Opryland, the amusement park associated with the location, closed in 1997, the Opry continues to perform at this venue. The Grand Ole Opry House was damaged during the May 2010 flood. While closed for repairs, the Opry performed at venues across the city, including its former home, the Ryman Auditorium. The Grand Ole Opry House reopened in September 2010 with a special edition of the Opry, titled "Country Comes Home." In the 2010s the Opry was still being performed every Saturday night, making it the longest running live radio program.

While most of the country was introduced to the sounds of hillbilly and country music through the Opry's live broadcast, Nashville did not become a center for the country music recording industry until the late 1940s. Castle Studio, Nashville's first professional studio, was opened in 1945. A number of recording studios and independent labels followed. By 1948 national labels were frequenting the Nashville area to record the many musicians performing on the Opry stage. In 1955 Bradley Film and Recording Studio, later known as the Quonset Hut, was founded by Harold Bradley and his brother Owen Bradley, an arranger and songwriter for Decca Records. Following the Bradley studio's success, RCA Records built a studio in Nashville in 1957, with Chet Atkins as producer. The artists recorded at these two studios, such as Patsy Cline, Kitty Wells, Brenda Lee, Jim Reeves, George Jones, Eddy Arnold, Don Gibson, and Elvis Presley, represent the Nashville sound, a 1950s sub-genre of country music that incorporated pop characteristics and production such as string sections and background vocals. The popularity of this sound and these artists retuned country music to the mainstream and further established Nashville as the home of country music. Following the success of the Nashville Sound, a number of publishing houses, recording studios, and musicians were established on Nashville's Music Row.

4. Rhythm-and-blues. While Nashville is best known for its close ties to country music, the city was also a hotbed for rhythm-and-blues, jazz, and gospel music. In the early decades of the 20th century Jefferson Street and Fourth Avenue North served as entertainment districts for African American audiences and performers. One notable venue was the Bijou Theater, which was part of the Theater Owner Booking Association and hosted a number of artists on the vaudeville circuit and the earliest African American jazz and blues recording artists, including Bessie Smith and Doc Cheatham. In the mid-20th century Nashville also became known for its gospel music tradition, largely due to the broadcasts of the Fairfield Four from Nashville's Fairfield Baptist Church. Beginning in 1941 their music was featured on WLAC, which broadcasted to a large portion of the country. In the 1940s, 1950s, and 1960s Nashville became a regular stop on the national Chitlin' circuit. Venues included War Memorial Auditorium and the Ryman Auditorium as well as clubs in the already-established black entertainment districts. Notable local and national acts played these venues, including Cecil Gant,

Earl Gaines, the Prisonaires, Etta James, Sam Cooke, Ray Charles, Little Richard, and Jimi Hendrix. Like country musicians, rhythm-and-blues musicians were attracted to Nashville because of broadcasting opportunities. Beginning in 1946 WLAC programmed late night shows featuring the sounds of rhythm and blues. Like WSM, WLAC broadcasted with 50,000 watts and obtained clear channel status, allowing a large portion of the country to hear rhythm and blues over the airwaves for the first time. With the success of the radio broadcasts and the presence of a rich gospel and rhythm and blues scene, several labels were established in Nashville, including Bullet Records (1946), Tennessee Records (1949), Excello Records (1952), and Nashboro records (1952). In 1964 R&B performers were given the opportunity to appear on television through the local program *Night Train*, broadcasted on WLAC- TV.

5. Nashville in the early 21st century. Nashville's reputation as a city for music performance and production has continued into the 21st century with a number of major and independent labels, live venues, and publishing houses that promote artists in many genres, including country, bluegrass, Americana, gospel, Christian contemporary, rock and roll, and art music. Several organizations in Nashville have promoted and preserved musical forms and their history: the Country Music Hall of Fame and Museum, the Nashville Symphony, the Country Music Association, the Americana Music Association, the Barbershop Harmony Society, the Gospel Music Association, the International Bluegrass Association, the Nashville Songwriters Association, and the Nashville Jazz Workshop.

Nashville's continued emphasis on education and the arts has been apparent in the number of institutions of higher education that have offered degrees in musical performance, business, education, theory and composition, and church music, including Belmont University, Fisk University, Lipscomb University, Tennessee State University, Trevecca Nazarene University, and Vanderbilt University. Through professional, private, communal, and educational organizations, Nashville has continued to provide a number of opportunities in a wide variety of musical traditions, further laying claim to its moniker "Music City, USA."

BIBLIOGRAPHY

C.R. Crain: *Music Performance and Pedagogy in Nashville, Tennessee, 1818–1900* (diss., George Peabody College for Teachers, 1975)

J. Egerton: *Nashville: the Faces of Two Centuries 1780–1980* (Nashville, TN, 1979)

C.K. Wolfe, ed.: *Folk Songs of Middle Tennessee: The George Boswell Collection* (Knoxville, TN, 1997)

J. Jensen: *The Nashville Sound: Authenticity, Commercialization and Country Music* (Nashville, TN, 1998)

C.K. Wolfe: *A Good Natured Riot: the Birth of the Grand Ole Opry* (Nashville, TN, 1999)

Night Train to Nashville: Music City Rhythm & Blues 1945–1970 (Nashville, TN, 2004)

T. Sharp: *Nashville Music Before Country* (Charleston, SC, 2008)

ROBERT WEBB FRY II

Nashville Sound. A term that denotes a pop-leaning style of country music, an era (*c*1957–72) in which this style gained favor, and Nashville's informal approach to recording, regardless of musical genre. The term also carries a mystique that heightened its effectiveness as a marketing slogan.

Although Nashville had yielded country, pop, gospel, and rhythm-and-blues hits since 1947, the term first appeared in *Music Reporter* in 1958, when country music was coping with a sales slump attributed to the rise of rock and roll. Accordingly, country record producers including Chet Atkins, Owen Bradley, Ken Nelson, and Don Law targeted young listeners with rockabilly stars (Elvis Presley), held core audiences with new hard-country singers (Porter Wagoner), and sought a larger adult following with the Nashville Sound, a country-pop sound foreshadowed by Red Foley, among others, in the late 1940s and early 1950s.

Musically, Nashville Sound recordings de-emphasized steel guitar and traditional fiddle playing, stressing instead lush string, and sometimes horn, arrangements and choral backing, which enhanced the cross-market appeal of smooth singers such as Eddy Arnold, Jim Reeves, and Patsy Cline. Subsequent hits boosted country's appeal to broadcasters and advertisers and helped increase the number of full-time country radio stations from 81 in 1961 to more than 600 in 1972. In so doing the Nashville Sound strategy helped to establish a broadcasting infrastructure that supported a wide variety of country styles.

Nashville's country-pop recordings were not uniform, but their remarkable similarities reflected the fact that a small group of producers then supervised most country singers, who were in turn supported by a small cadre of studio professionals. Certain artists began to challenge this system in the early 1970s, insisting on selecting studios, musicians, and even producers, and the Nashville Sound's heyday subsequently faded. Nevertheless, classic Nashville Sound hits continued to set high standards into the 2010s, and the city's relaxed, cooperative approach to recording continued to attract artists and producers from around the world.

BIBLIOGRAPHY

B. Ivey: "The Bottom Line: Business Practices that Shaped Country Music," *Country: the Music and the Musicians*, ed. P. Kingsbury and A. Axelrod (New York, 1988), 406–51

J. Jensen: *The Nashville Sound: Authenticity, Commercialization, and Country Music* (Nashville, 1998)

D. Pecknold: *The Selling Sound: the Rise of the Country Music Industry* (Durham, NC, 2007)

JOHN W. RUMBLE

NASM. *See* National association of schools of music [nasm].

National Academy of Recording Arts and Sciences [NARAS]. Music industry organization based in Santa Monica, California, that was founded in 1957. The most notable and visible event sponsored and run by the organization is the annual Grammy awards, which has recognized outstanding achievement by musicians, producers, and other professionals in the field of recorded music. The Grammy Foundation, established in 1989, has been responsible for the planning and operation of the awards. In 1997 NARAS launched its first international venture, the Latin Academy of Recording Arts and Sciences, which has produced the Latin Grammy Awards. The organizational structure of NARAS has consisted of three levels, including a select group of individually elected trustees, the boards of each chapter, and the general membership from each of the 12 chapters across the United States. More specialized wings have also existed in the academy. For instance, the producers and engineers wing has encompassed engineers, remixers, producers, technologists, and manufacturers. This wing has promoted the development of recording technologies, new standards for industry practices, history and archiving, and music education.

Overall, the multi-layered organization has provided arts advocacy, outreach and education, and support services to professionals in the recording industry. Its most evident goal has been to recognize exceptional achievement in the field through the awards process. It has also sought to archive and preserve recorded works in partnership with the Smithsonian Institution. Additionally it has provided a network of support through the MusiCares Foundation, which has provided funds to help music industry people in crisis. Finally, the organization has served as an advocate for the entertainment community, more specifically the music industry, fighting for intellectual property rights, protection of music copyright, and performance opportunities for members.

TIMOTHY M. CRAIN

National Anthem, the. *See* Patriotic music.

National Association for American Composers and Conductors [NAACC]. The original name of the National association of composers, USA.

National Association for Music Education, the. *See* Music educators national conference: the national association for music education.

National Association for Music Therapy. Organization founded in 1950 by a group of practicing music therapists and college teachers; *see* Music therapy.

National Association of College Wind and Percussion Instructors [NACWPI]. Organization for teachers of wind and percussion instruments in American institutions of higher education, founded at the University of Michigan in 1951. The aims of the organization are to encourage and develop more effective ways of teaching wind and percussion instruments on the college level; to provide for an efficient interchange of information, ideas, and materials among members; to encourage the publication, recording, composition, and distribution of good music for wind and percussion instruments; to foster the development and manufacture of the best in wind and percussion instruments; to coordinate the activities of the membership with other groups having common interests; and to encourage the performance of solo and chamber music in which wind or percussion instruments have significant roles. The association publishes the quarterly *NACWPI Journal* (founded in 1952) and supports a composition project devoted to the commissioning and publishing of works for wind and percussion instruments. The association's archives are maintained at the University of Maryland's Michelle Smith Performing Arts Library.

RAOUL F. CAMUS

National Association of Collegiate and High School Gospel Choirs. Choral association. The mission of the National Association of Collegiate and High School Gospel Choirs (NACHSGC) is to support a greater vision of faith, fellowship, and education by preserving the musical heritage of college and high school gospel choirs, fostering gospel music excellence, promoting artistic expression, and developing leaders who will enrich the futures of gospel music and society. In 2007 the National Association of Collegiate Gospel Choirs and the National Association of High School Gospel Choirs merged to form the National Association of Collegiate and High School Gospel Choirs. NACHSGC represents college and high school choirs from campuses across the United States and Canada. Gospel artist Kim Burrell was elected the first chair of the board of directors. The organization supports program initiatives including Training & Enrichment, Performing Arts, Education & Outreach, and Health & Wellness. NACHSGC publishes a quarterly journal, *College Gospel Magazine*, containing articles and highlighting nationwide gospel events. Initially financed by interested board members, the NACHSGC now relies on membership dues, community and foundation support, and private funding sources to further its mission and initiatives.

GARY D. PACKWOOD

National Association of Composers, USA [NACUSA]. Organization devoted to the promotion and performance of American concert hall music. It was founded in 1933 as the National Association for American Composers and Conductors under the guidance of Henry Hadley "to arrange and encourage performances of works by American composers and to help develop understanding and friendly cooperation between composers and conductors." Over 5000 American works were presented during its first 40 years, including 2000 premieres and many performances of early-period works. In later years, under its president Leon Barzin, the final concert of each season was given by a full orchestra in Carnegie Hall as part of the American Music Festival. Other presidents over the years have included Lawrence Tibbett, Sigmund Spaeth, Robert Russell Bennett, and Daniel Kessner. The organization later established an archive of American music at the New York Public Library and held an annual concert and reception at which the Henry Hadley Medal was awarded to individuals or institutions for distinguished services to American music. It also cosponsored the Lado Composition Competition and, in the 1950s, arranged orchestral readings of works by member composers. At the height of its activities, the

association had 1200 members in 48 states. It became considerably less active after the death in 1971 of Inez Barbour Hadley, who had been the guiding spirit and benefactor since her husband's death in 1937. In 1975 the association was reorganized by John Vincent, professor of composition at UCLA, and changed its name to National Association of Composers, USA (NACUSA); it had about 750 members spread across ten chapters as of 2011. It sponsors annual competitions for young composers and performers, and has continued to produce concerts in New York, Los Angeles, San Francisco, and other sites across the country. The *Annual Bulletin* published between 1933 and 1970 was superseded by the quarterly journal *Composer USA* in 1976. Issues have been published tri-annually since 1994 and have concentrated on members' activities and opportunities for composers, along with feature articles and reviews of relevant concerts and recordings. The organization's website (<http://www.music-usa.org/nacusa/>) has featured streaming audio and has housed an extensive catalog of American music.

JOHN SHEPARD/MICHAEL MAUSKAPF

National Association of Jazz Educators [NAJE]. An organization dedicated to jazz education founded in 1968 and disbanded in 2008.

See JAZZ EDUCATION.

National Association of Negro Musicians [NANM]. Organization founded in 1919 in Chicago to promote interest in African American music. Earlier efforts to found such an organization had been made by Clarence Cameron White in 1916 and R. Nathaniel Dett in 1918, both of whom participated in the first convention of the association and served as president during the 1920s. Governed by a board of directors and elected officers, the organization has met annually in various cities during the summer for workshops, concerts, recitals, panel discussions, business meetings, and youth concerts. Its numerous regional branches have sponsored other activities throughout the year. Among the recipients of national awards and special tributes early in their careers have been Hazel Harrison, Marian Anderson, Julia Perry, Arthur LaBrew, Grace Bumbry, Leon Bates, and Awadagin Pratt.

BIBLIOGRAPHY

SouthernB

L.H. White: "The NANM," *American Musician*, ii/2 (1921), 18

J.A. Mills: "The National Association of Negro Musicians," *HiFi/MusAm*, xxix/8 (1979), 14–15

D.E. McGinty: *A Documentary History of the National Association of Negro Musicians* (Chicago, 2004)

DOMINIQUE-RENÉ DE LERMA

National Association of Schools of Music [NASM]. Accrediting body for music in postsecondary education in the United States. In the early 21st century its membership included more than 640 institutions and consisted of colleges, universities, conservatories, and non-degree-granting postsecondary schools; membership indicates accreditation and is voluntary. Community and precollegiate arts schools that offer programs in music may gain membership in NASM through accreditation with the Accrediting Commission for Community and Precollegiate Arts Schools (ACCPAS).

NASM was founded in 1924 by a group of representatives from conservatories and university schools of music to secure a better understanding among institutions; to establish a more uniform method of granting credit for music studies; and to set and evolve threshold standards for the granting of degrees and other credentials. Its accrediting activities began in 1928 with the establishment of standards for undergraduate degrees in music. In addition to its accrediting activities, NASM has provided a national forum for the discussion of issues related to music in American life, especially in higher education. It has provided professional development for music administrators, management-oriented data through the Higher Education Arts Data Services (HEADS) project, and policy analysis focused on education and the arts. The association has been governed by a board of directors and an executive committee, members of which have been elected by representatives of the accredited institutional members. Institutional membership functions have been conducted by an elected Commission on Accreditation and a Commission on Community/Junior College Accreditation. In the early 21st century the executive director and staff occupied offices in Reston, Virginia.

BIBLIOGRAPHY

C.M. Neumeyer: *A History of the National Association of Schools of Music* (diss., Indiana U., 1954)

B.C. Tuthill: *NASM: the First Forty Years* (Washington, DC, 1973)

R. Glidden: "An Introduction to NASM: Purpose and Philosophy," *Proceedings of the 59th Annual Meeting* (Reston, VA, 1984)

S. Barrows: *Historical Perspectives 1924–1999: National Association of Schools of Music Seventy-Fifth Anniversary* (Reston, VA, 1999)

ROBERT GLIDDEN/SAMUEL HOPE

National Association of Teachers of Singing [NATS]. Professional organization for voice teachers. It was founded in Cincinnati, Ohio, in 1944. In the 2010s it was headquartered in Jacksonville, Florida, and the organization's mission has been to "encourage the highest standards of the vocal art and of ethical principles in the teaching of singing; and to promote vocal education and research at all levels, both for the enrichment of the general public and for the professional advancement of the talented." Full membership has been limited to teachers and coaches of singing who have the requisite years of experience, training, and academic degrees. Associate and affiliate memberships have also been available. NATS has counted more than 6500 members in the United States, Canada, and over 25 other countries. It has offered a variety of educational opportunities such as workshops, intern programs, master classes, and conferences beginning at the chapter level and progressing to national events. Students of NATS members have been permitted to compete at local and national levels through the National Association of Teachers of Singing Artist Awards (NATSAA). The organization has also sponsored the Art Song Competition, established

to stimulate the creation of vocal literature through the cooperation of singer and composer. The *NATS Bulletin*, which first appeared in 1944 and was later renamed *The Journal of Singing*, has been a scholarly, peer-reviewed journal that has published articles on all aspects of singing, repertoire, and vocal health and pedagogy.

RICHARD R. BUNBURY

National Band Association (NBA). Professional organization founded in 1960 and affiliated with the Music Educators National Conference. Its general purposes as stated in its constitution are "to promote the excellence of band performance throughout the world; to encourage the composition and performance of quality band music at all levels; to assist directors at all levels of experience to identify areas of mutual concern; to promote pride and continued enthusiasm among band directors; to encourage quality students to pursue careers in music; and to promote a spirit of cooperation and continued dialogue among directors, performers, the music industry, and all other band support organizations at all levels." Membership includes a subscription to the monthly *The Instrumentalist* magazine and the biannual *NBA Journal*. The organization meets every year at the Midwest Clinic in Chicago, and offers various services and projects to members. The NBA sponsors the Academy of Wind and Percussion Arts Award (in recognition of those who have made outstanding contributions to bands and band music); the NBA Hall of Fame of Distinguished Conductors on the campus of Troy University, Troy, Alabama; the NBA/William D. Revelli Memorial Band Composition Contest for new band works; the biennial NBA/Merrill Jones Memorial Young Composers Band Composition Contest for composers under 40; the biennial Young Composer Mentor Project; the biennial Young Conductor Mentor Project; the International Conducting Symposium; annual Research Grants; and the NBA Citations of Excellence awarded to outstanding band directors.

RAOUL F. CAMUS

National Baptist Music Convention. The National Baptist Convention, USA (NBC) was organized in 1895 in an effort to unite, at the national level, the growing numbers of black Baptists in the United States. Its general objectives were domestic and foreign missions, education, and the publication and dissemination of religious literature. Structurally, the NBC operated through several Boards, each with specifically defined duties. A music department was introduced into the Convention in 1916 as part of the Baptist Young Peoples Union (BYPU) and Sunday School Board, under the direction of Lucie Eddie Campbell. The Convention published *Gospel Pearls* (1921), a songbook intended to accompany the music and worship services of black Baptists. While not wholly endorsed by the more conservative members of the Convention leadership, Thomas A. Dorsey introduced his gospel blues songs to the Convention in 1932. Under strict supervision of the Music Committee, which included Campbell, the Convention developed into the premiere performance venue for gospel singers. Gospel composers also capitalized on the outlet to demonstrate and sell compositions. The NBC established the National Baptist Music Convention (NBMC, 1948) to train musicians for the denomination. Theodore Frye, a prominent gospel singer and Music Committee member, was a key figure in the NBMC's creation.

BIBLIOGRAPHY

L. Fitts: *A History of Black Baptists* (Nashville, TN, 1985)

H.C. Boyer: *How Sweet the Sound: the Golden Age of Gospel* (Washington, DC, 1995)

ROXANNE R. REED

National Barn Dance. Between 1924 and 1960, the "National Barn Dance," owned by Sears-Roebuck Agricultural Foundation and later by Burridge D. Butler's *Prairie Farmer* magazine, was broadcast on Chicago's WLS each Saturday evening from 7:30 to 9:30pm and from 10:00pm to midnight. With its clear-channel signal and 50,000-watt transmitter, acquired in 1931, listeners throughout the Midwest could tune their radios to the barn dance program or attend a live performance in the Eighth Street Theatre, after it was built in 1932. Beginning in 1933, the NBC Blue network broadcasted a one-hour segment of the show, sponsored by Miles Laboratories and Alka-Seltzer, on radio stations throughout the United States.

The "National Barn Dance" catered to a diverse audience of rural midwesterners, displaced white southerners, Northern European immigrants, and Chicago urbanites with an eclectic mix of popular and "hillbilly" musics and comedic skits. Continuing the practices of minstrelsy and vaudeville, the programming appeared in a variety-show format that evoked the boisterous setting of the Saturday night barn dance. The broadcasts juxtaposed the Hoosier Hot Shots' jazz playing on homemade instruments to the Prairie Ramblers' western swing numbers and the Georgia Wildcats' southeastern string band music. Its comedic skits included a master of ceremonies, originally George D. Hay (who later established the "Grand Ole Opry"), bantering with characters such as "Spare-ribs," a blackface character played by Malcolm Clair, as well as Arkie the Arkansas Woodchopper and Ole Yonson the Swiss immigrant, both of whom appeared in rural garb. The program also reached into the domestic sphere by presenting intimate forms of vocal music, such as Grace Wilson's sentimental songs, the De-Zurik Sisters' yodeling imitations of bird calls, Mac and Bob's duet singing, the Three Little Maids' blended harmonies, and the Maple City Four's barbershop arrangements.

Furthermore, the "National Barn Dance" pulled the diverse strands of country music—ballads, fiddling contests, square dances, sentimental parlor songs, western tunes—together to market "hillbilly" or "old-time" music to audiences outside of the South. In the 1920s, Chubby Parker sang folksongs to his banjo accompaniment, and Bradley Kincaid established himself as a "singing mountaineer" of ballads from southern Appalachia. In the 1930s, John Lair, originally from Kentucky, formed the string band ensemble Cumberland Ridge Runners with performers who would lead significant careers in country music: Red Foley, Linda Parker, Doc Hopkins, Karl Davis, and Hartford Taylor. The 1930s also saw the rise of the "Queen of Radio," Lulu Belle, who with Scotty Wiseman formed a long-lasting duo.

In addition to music that gestured to the rural South, the "National Barn Dance" cultivated the western imagery of singing cowboys and cowgirls. Gene Autry's crooning cowboy persona over the airwaves of WLS led to his starring roles in Republic's western films. Singing cowgirls, the Girls of the Golden West, Louise Massey, and Patsy Montana joined the myriad women singers predominant on the program. With the growing prominence of the "Grand Ole Opry" and the rise of rock and roll, the "National Barn Dance" waned in popularity during the 1950s. When WLS was sold to ABC in 1960, the program moved to Chicago's WGN, where it broadcast until 1970.

BIBLIOGRAPHY

F. Evans: *Prairie Farmer and WLS* (Urbana and Chicago, 1969)

C. Berry, ed: *The Hayloft Gang: the Story of the National Barn Dance* (Urbana and Chicago, IL, 2008)

K. McCusker: *Lonesome Cowgirls and Honky-Tonk Angels: the Women of Barn Dance Radio* (Urbana and Chicago, IL, 2008)

S. Vander Wel: *I Am a Honky-Tonk Girl: Country Music, Gender, and Migration* (diss., U. of California Los Angeles, 2008)

STEPHANIE VANDER WEL

National Collegiate Choral Organization [NCCO]. Organization founded in 2004 by William Bausano (Miami University), William Dehning (University of Southern California), Buddy James (California State University, East Bay), and Lisa Graham (Wellesley College) to create national opportunities for university and collegiate choral conductors in the areas of choral performance, scholarship, and research. The inaugural conference was held in San Antonio in 2006. Beginning in 2009, the national conferences have been offered biennially in the fall, and are usually held on university campuses. Conference sessions include choral performance, lectures, literature sessions, and panel discussions that relate directly to the needs of the collegiate choral professional including areas such as promotion and tenure, recruiting, and the teaching of conducting. NCCO has awarded noted conductors Dale Warland, Robert Page, and Vance George life membership for their extraordinary contributions to choral music in the United States. In 2008, the NCCO created the online, peer-reviewed journal *The Choral Scholar*, which publishes relevant articles in English on topics relating to choral music as well as reviews of books, recordings, and musical scores. In 2010, NCCO published on its website *The Conductor as Scholar: National Guidelines for the Promotion and Tenure of Collegiate Choral Conductors*, which seeks to clarify expectations for promotion and tenure. National officers are elected biennially, and the national board is comprised of representation of collegiate choral conductors from nearly all 50 states.

BONNIE BORSHAY SNEED

National Conservatory of Music of America. Music conservatory established with private donations in New York in 1885 by Jeannette Meyer Thurber. Although intended as a national institution, the only federal contribution was $200,000 in 1891. ANTONÍN DVOŘÁK was director from 1891 to 1895. Influential in its prime, the conservatory quietly closed around 1930.

BIBLIOGRAPHY
E. Rubin: "Jeannette Meyer Thurber (1850–1946): Music for a Democracy," in R.P. Locke and C. Barr, eds., *Cultivating Music in America: Women Patrons and Activists Since 1860* (Berkeley, CA, 1997), 134–59

CAROLYN LIVINGSTON

National Convention of Gospel Choirs and Choruses. Convention founded in 1933 by Thomas A. Dorsey, Sallie Martin, Magnolia Butts, Theodore Frye, and Henry J. Caruthers. As a mass expansion of the first gospel choral union, founded by Dorsey in 1932, the National Convention of Gospel Choirs and Choruses (NCGCC) was dedicated to fostering and promoting musical and spiritual growth for Christian musicians. Dorsey was the first president of the convention and held that post for nearly five decades. Sallie Martin served initially as National Organizer. In this role she was instrumental in extending the convention's reach across regional lines and was also a key contributor in the distribution of gospel sheet music. The convention experienced significant growth in visibility and programs during the early years. By 1945 activities and initiatives included scholarship, artist development, and youth programs, as well as extensions of their mission that included the preservation of sacred music traditions. The convention operated as the largest national body devoted to gospel music, its preservation, and promotion through the 1960s. In the 2010 the convention boasted over 45 chapters/unions, and it has met annually at various locations throughout the United States. Notable affiliates of the convention include Mahalia Jackson, James Cleveland, and Hezekiah Walker.

BIBLIOGRAPHY
M.W. Harris: *The Rise of Gospel Blues: the Music of Thomas Andrew Dorsey in the Urban Church* (New York, 1992)
J.A. Jackson: *Singing in my Soul: Black Gospel Music in a Secular Age* (Chapel Hill, NC, 2004)

HORACE J. MAXILE, JR.

National Council for the Traditional Arts. Based in Silver Spring, Maryland, the National Council for the Traditional Arts (NCTA) derived from the National Folk Festival Association, established in 1933 by Sarah Gertrude Knott. Knott, born in Kentucky in 1895, was a proponent of community arts. In 1934, with a group of advisors that included folklorists Zora Neale Hurston and George Lyman Kittredge, she established the National Folk Festival in St. Louis. The annual event contrasted with folk festivals of the era in championing ethnic and regional diversity. Following Knott's retirement in the 1970s, the organization renamed itself the National Council for the Traditional Arts, in an attempt to revitalize a festival that, with many costumed presentations, had begun to seem dated. Long under the stewardship of JOE WILSON, a National Heritage Fellowship awardee and Living Legend (Library of Congress) designee, the NCTA broadened its portfolio. It has sponsored the National Folk Festival (which has changed locations every few years), "partner" festivals such as the Lowell Folk Festival, touring programs, and the Blue Ridge Music Center in Galax, Virginia. The extensive NCTA audio archives have been held by the American Folklife Center at the Library of Congress. In the early 2010s Julia Olin was the director, and the NCTA has continued to present a broad range of grassroots musical traditions from around the world.

BIBLIOGRAPHY
J. Wilson and L. Udall: *Folk Festivals: a Handbook for Organization and Management* (Knoxville, TN, 1982)
M.A. Williams: *Staging Tradition: John Lair and Sarah Gertrude Knott* (Urbana, IL and Chicago, 2006) <http://www.ncta.net>

BURT FEINTUCH

National-Dobro [National String Instrument Corporation; Valco]. Musical instrument manufacturer, primarily of fretted resonator and electric instruments. The company originally took shape through the pioneering work of John Dopyera (*b* Dolná Krupá, Slovakia, 1893; *d* Rouge River, OR, 3 Jan 1988), who belonged to a family of influential musical instrument makers. George Beauchamp, a vaudeville entertainer, came to Dopyera's Los Angeles violin repair shop in 1926 and inquired about producing a louder guitar to use on stage. Dopyera was skilled, creative, and experienced, holding several musical instrument patents and having recently made banjos. As an outsider to guitar making, he was also prepared to come up with something revolutionary, which would help the guitar to be heard over the din of drums and horns in ensembles of the time.

Beauchamp commissioned the guitar, and the arrangement soon yielded a whole new category of six-strings—"resophonic" or resonator guitars (*see* RESONATOR GUITAR). After a forgettable attempt with a Victrola-like amplifying horn, John Dopyera went to work on a metal-body instrument nicknamed the "tricone." Equipped with three pie-pan-like diaphragms (resonators) inside the body, the tricone produced a bold, cutting tone. Beauchamp rounded up investors and in 1927 the pair founded the National String Instrument Corporation.

National dominated Los Angeles instrument making until the Great Depression. The company made tricones followed by single-cone Hawaiian guitars, Spanish guitars, ukuleles, and mandolins. Workers assembled Nationals with the care of craftsmen, while the metal bodies were stamped out on a huge press originally designed to make automobile fenders. National made plain, economical instruments for the Sears catalog and expensive, highly engraved models for serious professionals.

Beauchamp and Dopyera had a major falling out in 1929, and John left to form the Dobro Manufacturing Corporation with his brothers Emil (Ed) (*c*1902–77) and Rudy (Rudolph) (1895–1978). Dobro guitars had a unique single-resonator design that used what John called a "spider bridge." The company set up a factory in Los Angeles and licensed the Regal company in Chicago to make instruments. Dobro instruments and those that mimic the originals have been extremely popular in both bluegrass and country music.

In an attempt to hogtie his new competition, Beauchamp told instrument dealers that Dobro guitars violated National's patent. It was a lie that backfired. At first the story paralyzed Dobro, but it eventually spawned a lawsuit that National lost. The settlement turned National stock over to Dobro, and that laid the groundwork in 1933 for a takeover and the creation of the National-Dobro Corporation.

National-Dobro is best remembered for the electric guitars it introduced in the 1930s. The resonator guitar business waned in the shadow of the new technology. Close behind Electro String (Rickenbacker) in the race to create successful electric guitars, National-Dobro moved to Chicago in 1936 where its electronic parts suppliers and distributors were headquartered. Facing economic hard times, it struggled through the end of the 1930s until World War II.

In 1942 National-Dobro became Valco, with partners Victor Smith, Al Frost, and Louis Dopyera (1896–1964). After the war, the government lifted restrictions on important materials, and Valco quickly became one of the leading manufacturers of lap steels and lower-end electrics. The company also sold acoustic guitars and arch top electrics. Valco was quite successful, especially selling amplifiers (under names including National, Supro, Oahu, Kay, Gretsch, and Airline) from the 1940s through the mid-1960s. In the 1960s Valco produced electrics made with Fiberglass bodies, called the Res-O-Glas models. A bit too radical even for the 1960s, they failed to catch on.

Al Frost retired in 1964 as Valco's success started to unravel. Its mounting financial difficulties, caused in part by an inability to make products fast enough, led to bankruptcy in 1968. The National brand name was used for a time by a Japanese company. In 1989 the National Reso-Phonic Company was founded to build National-style resonator guitars, but it had no connection to the original National company. For a time in the 1960s Mosrite, the California concern, used the Dobro trademark. Rudy and Emil Dopyera regained the title in 1970 and used it for guitars made by their company, Original Musical Instruments. In 1993 Gibson acquired the Dobro name and has made several designs with the trademark spider bridge.

BIBLIOGRAPHY

B. Brozman: *The History and Artistry of National Resonator Instruments* (Fullerton, CA, 1993)

T. Gray and J.P. Quarterman: *Dobro Guitars: a Pictorial History* (Anaheim, CA, 2009)

RICHARD R. SMITH

National Endowment for the Arts [NEA]. An independent grant-making agency established in 1965 by the United States Congress to advocate for and foster excellence, diversity, and vitality in the arts; the NATIONAL ENDOWMENT FOR THE HUMANITIES was established in the same year. The NEA has provided funding to organizations in a number of categories, including dance, design, education, folk and traditional arts, literature, media arts (radio, television, film), museums, music, musical theater, opera, (arts) presenting, theater, and the visual arts. Most grants for individual artists were discontinued following an incident in 1990, when the NEA chairman at the time, John Frohnmayer, withheld funding from four performance artists (thereafter known as the NEA Four) due to the controversial nature of their work. The artists fought for and eventually received their grants in 1993. The individual awards subsequently bestowed by the NEA have included the Jazz Masters Fellowship, Opera Honors, the National Heritage Fellowship, and the National Medal of Arts, the last of which is the highest award given to artists and art patrons by the US government. The agency's programs relating to music have included fellowships, support for professional training and career development for musicians, and funding for chamber, jazz, choral, and orchestral ensembles. Large-scale research studies on the impact of the arts and trends in arts participation have been contracted and published on a yearly basis and have included *The Arts and Civic Engagement: Involved in Arts, Involved in Life* (2006), *Artists in the Workforce: 1990–2005* (2008), and *2008 Survey of Public Participation in the Arts* (2009).

The endowment has been run by a chairman and the National Council for the Arts, which has comprised 26 distinguished citizens widely recognized in their respective disciplines. Both the chairman and the council have been appointed by the President and subject to Senate confirmation. Beginning in the 1980s federal support for the arts began to fall out of favor, and the agency's appropriation was greatly reduced. Although higher levels of funding were later reinstated, the NEA's budget has represented a small portion of the government's total expenses. By 2008 the agency had administered more than 130,000 grants totaling more than $4 billion. In 2011 Congress forwarded a bill that would have effectively discontinued the NEA and NEH altogether.

BIBLIOGRAPHY

M. Straight: *Twigs for an Eagle's Nest: Government and the Arts, 1965–1978* (New York, 1979)

F. Taylor and A.L. Barresi: *The Arts at a New Frontier: the National Endowment for the Arts* (New York, 1984)

R. Bolton, ed.: *Culture Wars: Documents from the Recent Controversies in the Arts* (New York, 1992)

J.W. Ziegler: *Arts in Crisis: the National Endowment for the Arts versus America* (Pennington, NJ, 1994)

D.M. Binkiewicz: *Painting, Politics, and Cold War Culture: United States Arts Policy and the Formation of the National Endowment for the Arts, 1960–1975* (diss., UCLA, 1997)

D.A. Smith: *Covered Wagons of Culture: the Roots and Early History of the National Endowment for the Arts* (diss., U. of Missouri-Columbia, 2000)

D.M. Binkiewicz: *Federalizing the Music: United States Arts Policy and the National Endowment for the Arts 1965–80* (Chapel Hill, NC, 2004)

M. Bauerlin, ed.: *National Endowment for the Arts: a History, 1965–2008* (Washington, DC, 2008)

MICHAEL MAUSKAPF

National Endowment for the Humanities [NEH]. An independent grant-making agency established in 1965 by the United States Congress (together with the NATIONAL ENDOWMENT FOR THE ARTS) to advance knowledge and understanding of the humanities in the United States. Areas funded by the NEH include the history, theory, and criticism of the arts; literature; history; jurisprudence; philosophy; archaeology; comparative religion; and ethics. Grants are awarded for individual and collaborative scholarly projects; editions and translations; summer research seminars; projects in libraries and museums; radio and television programming; educational resources, preservation of and access to humanities resources; digital projects; and others. The endowment has four main divisions (Education Programs, Public Programs, Research Programs, and Preservation and Access) and three offices (Digital Humanities, Federal-State Partnership, and Challenge Grants). The NEH is headed by a chairman and the 26-member National Council for the Humanities; both are appointed by the President of the United States and are subject to Senate confirmation. Awards are selected through evaluation by peer reviewers. Application guidelines and evaluation criteria, lists of funded projects, and information about current and past projects supported by NEH are available on the NEH website (<http://www.neh.gov>). The agency has published the magazine *Humanities* since 1969. Notable music projects that have received NEH support include a critical edition of the *Works of Giuseppe Verdi*; the *Retrospective Index of Music Periodicals* (*RIPM*), which provides access to three centuries of literature relating to music; *Jazz*, an eight-part, 12-hour documentary film series on the history of jazz; a book on Ethiopian music in the United States; biographical works on Aaron Copland, Antonín Dvořák, George Gershwin, Kurt Weill, Lou Harrison, Edgard Varèse, Béla Bartók, William Schuman, Georg Philipp Telemann, and Enrique Granados, among others; "Voices Across Time: Teaching American History through Song," an NEH summer institute for school teachers; and a challenge grant awarded to the American Musicological Society to endow publication subventions and an award program in musicology.

ELIZABETH A. ARNDT

National Federation of Music Clubs NFMC. One of the world's largest music organizations with 200,000 senior, student, and junior members in 6500 clubs and organizations in the United States. (*See* CLUBS, MUSIC.) Chartered in Illinois in 1898, the NFMC grew out of a gathering of music clubs at the 1893 World's Columbian Exposition in Chicago assembled by Rose Fay Thomas, president of the Amateur Musical Club of Chicago, and wife of the founder of the Chicago Symphony, Theodore Thomas. In its early years the NFMC focused on developing new clubs and organizing state federations, but soon it enlarged its mission to include managing artists' concerts through an Artist Bureau and promoting music by American composers. By 1907 the NFMC had established an American Music Department to encourage clubs to give preference to American music

and musicians in their programs and had inaugurated a biennial competition for American composers. Before long the organization was working to found local music libraries, donate money to a fund for needy musicians, encourage the founding of local bands and orchestras, and promote music in public education.

Over its more than 100 years of service, the NFMC has sought to stimulate American composition, promote American performers, foster cooperation among people and organizations in furthering musical education, and integrate music into civic, educational, and social life. In its efforts to support and develop American music and musicians, the NFMC has since 1924 marshaled its local organizations in nationwide community festivities during its National Music Week in May that celebrate the role of music in American life. During World War II, the NFMC War Service Committee distributed records, music, and equipment to American Armed Forces, and immediately after the war, the federation gave instruments and repair kits to European orchestras that had suffered losses or damage to their instruments. Since 1955 it has encouraged the performance of American works through a sponsorship program called the Parade of American Music. It has also promoted American music and composers through its American Music Month (November) and Crusade of Strings programs.

Intent on supporting young talent, the federation has offered more than three quarters of a million dollars in state and national competitions, including biennial Young Artists awards and the Ellis Award for Duo-Pianists, which have launched hundreds of performers in professional careers. Additional competitions in numerous categories have also been sponsored: voice, instrumental music, composition, dance, conducting, handicapped and visually impaired, and music therapy, as well as awards for students to attend summer music centers. The federation's interests have also included advocacy for music education legislation, sponsorship of music therapy programs, partnering with higher education, and campaigning for higher musical standards in the media. In 1948 the NFMC was accredited by the United Nations as a nongovernmental organization, and in 1982 it was chartered by the Congress of the United States.

BIBLIOGRAPHY

National Convention of Women's Amateur Musical Clubs (Chicago, 1893), repr. as *The Record of the Founding Meeting of the National Federation of Music Clubs* (Green Bay, WI, 1973)
<http://nfmc-music.org>

JOHN SHEPARD/LINDA WHITESITT

National Flute Association. Organization formed to encourage a higher standard of artistic excellence for the flute, its performers, and its literature. The group was founded in November 1972 at an organizational meeting in Elkhart, Indiana, convened by Mark Thomas, during which a slate of officers was proposed. The first annual convention was held in Anaheim, California, in August 1973, and was attended by about 170 people. The National Flute Association (NFA, <http://www.nfaonline.org>) has since grown to about 6000 members from the United States and some 70 other countries.

Originally, membership included a subscription to *Woodwind World* (published 1957–74); the group began its own newsletter in 1975, which became *The Flutist Quarterly* in Fall 1990. Additional special publications have included a republication of Leonardo De Lorenzo's *My Complete Story of the Flute* (1992), *The NFA 20th Anniversary Anthology of American Flute Music* (1993), and a second edition of John Krell's *Kincaidiana* (1997).

The annual meetings have featured competitions, concerts, lecture-demonstrations, master classes, and industry-related exhibits. Various performance competitions have been held; there have also been competitions for composition and for graduate research. Prizes have been awarded for performance at the high school and young artist levels, and for piccolo artist (since 1993) and baroque-flute artist (since 1995). The NFA has also awarded several scholarships and has sponsored commissions for new works for flute and piccolo.

The NFA Music Library Collection, a lending library of some 15,000 scores, including rare editions and out-of-print scores, has been located at the University of Arizona, in Tucson. Since 1990 an Oral History Committee has carried out interviews with significant flutists, flute makers, and composers. An NFA Archives was established at the Library of Congress in 1996.

CAROLYN BRYANT

National Guild of Piano Teachers. An organization founded in 1929 by Irl Allison as the Piano Guild, a division of the American College of Musicians. Its purpose is to provide incentives for piano students and to promote education in music through examinations, auditions, and competitions. With headquarters in Austin, Texas, the National Guild of Piano Teachers (NGPT) has grown to more than 118,000 participants who participate in annual auditions in 863 cities in the United States and 17 other countries. The NGPT has held non-competitive auditions for which students of all ages have striven to reach specific goals and have been rewarded for their achievements. Participants have performed for and received feedback from internationally recognized judges, and numerous $100 scholarships have been awarded annually. The organization has also provided training and certification programs for teachers, and it has added a highly successful composition contest. The NGPT has published the bimonthly journal *Piano Guild Notes* since 1945.

JOHN SHEPARD/KAREN M. BRYAN

Nationalism. Nationalism reflects and promotes the belief that, in fundamental terms, an individual belongs to a *people*, most often defined by race, ethnicity, language, or religion, who may collectively lay rightful and exclusive claim to a specific *homeland*. Not all manifestations of nationalism insist on an exclusive alignment between people and territory; "cultural nationalism," for example, makes no specific territorial claim. But the growing prevalence of nationalism across the 19th century and after has tended to blend more narrow applications into a broader conceptual category, so that cultural nationalism has often directly supported political nationalism, even if unintentionally.

Nationalism is almost always couched in idealistic terms and has indeed contributed in many instances to the amelioration of political repression. However, because it imposes alignments between peoples and territories, nationalism has also done tremendous harm. Thus, during the 20th century, nationalism sparked several wars, fomented terrorism, excused forced migrations and mass murder as modes of "ethnic cleansing," and, more specifically, laid the foundation for the Armenian genocide, two world wars, and the Holocaust.

The United States has to some extent escaped such extreme negative consequences, at least on the home front. To be sure, a developing sense of nation fueled western expansion in the 19th century, with extreme negative consequences for American Indian populations through war, appropriation of lands, and forced migrations. Moreover, the Civil War had a partly nationalist basis, not least because slavery itself depended on differentiating sharply among peoples regarding their capacities and entitlements, leaving a bitter legacy of racial tension. But the nation's founding principles of inclusivity and equality, combined with balances of power on the federal level, strong attachments to regional difference, legally structured independence at the state level, freedom of mobility, and a constitutional emphasis on individual rights, helped stave off more dire potential consequences of nationalism. Even so, many marginalized ethnic groups have had to contend mightily for the supposedly guaranteed rights of all peoples in the United States. Besides African Americans and Native Americans, other groups who have been marginalized and sometimes persecuted include the Irish, Asians, Jews, and Latinos/as, among others.

Because qualities and behaviors imputed to specific peoples have been more aspirational than real, nationalist projects have typically offered idealized versions of their heroes and citizenry, established standards for the latter, and mounted agendas for their collective betterment. Thus, growing alongside the prevalence of nationalism across the 19th century were associated concepts involving cultural hierarchies, tradition, and "respectability." The latter two have contributed to the disenfranchisement of some groups even apart from ethnicity, including, most importantly in historical terms, women and homosexuals. In other ways, notions of cultural hierarchy have significantly affected the development of musical nationalism in the United States.

1. Musical nationalism. 2. Musical nationalism in the United States. 3. Respectability. 4. Aspiration. 5. Vernacular song. 6. The modern *Volksgeist* option.

1. MUSICAL NATIONALISM. Although the roots of nationalist thought go far back, its modern forms rest, philosophically, on German Idealism, and, by dint of model, on the successes of the British, Italian, and German nationalist projects in the 18th and 19th centuries, with the first of these achieving milestone alliances in 1707 and 1800, and the latter two reaching fruition in 1870 and

1871, respectively. German Idealism, in projecting a deep connection between individual subjectivity and some larger construct (Absolute Consciousness, Infinity, the Will, etc.), proved a natural ally of nationalism. Moreover, German Idealism emerged at a key historical moment in the late 18th century, not only rechanneling the Enlightenment's focus on the individual towards something larger but also, by around 1800, designating *music* as the highest of the arts, prized especially for its capacity, through contemplation, to connect individual subjectivities to whatever larger construct might be imagined.

That nationalist feeling might be fostered through music had already by then been shown through the tradition of presenting large-scale performances in England of George Frideric Handel's oratorios. These works, in which the "Nation of Israel" could be understood as an allegory for the modern British nation, combined the ontological sanguinities of Handel's musical rhetoric with Biblical authority, imparting a strong sense of rightness to the established order, reinforced in performance through the grand effect of choral singing accompanied by an orchestra (R. Smith; R. Taruskin). All of these dimensions of public musical performance—narrative allegory, musical ontology, religious feeling, and a sense of collective aspiration—would continue to make music a strong component of European nationalism. To these dimensions were added music's capacities to evoke a sense of myth (most often the basis for nationalist claims), to suggest specific land- and seascapes, and to induce an impression of what Johann Gottfried Herder (a student of Immanuel Kant) termed the *Volksgeist* ("spirit of the people"; Taruskin). The latter might be conveyed not only by applying Herder's speculations about folk music—hence the heavy dependence on (often simulated) folk music in nationalist musical repertories—but also by presenting, through recognizable musical topics, specific positive qualities imputed to the *Volk* in question, such as a collective cherishing of a shared valuable heritage, heroism, striving, perseverance, aspiration, or the capacity both to enjoy life and to feel deeply.

Across the 19th century, opera and symphony became the principal genres for nationalist music in Europe, in part because of their suitability for large-scale public performance. Opera served particularly well, both because its (possibly allegorical) dramatic content could be more obviously grounded in a particular language and culture, and because its choruses could evoke large-scale political action (Taruskin). But the symphony, especially as repurposed by Ludwig van Beethoven, early on became the genre of choice for Germany, advanced as "serious" music whose contemplation would foster the depth of soul requisite to German *Kultur* through processes sanctioned by German Idealism. As orchestral works after Beethoven came increasingly to evoke specific peoples and places, the symphony, as the most serious orchestral genre, became by the late 19th century a central vehicle of musical nationalism even beyond Germany. In parallel to these developments, musicology developed as a

scholarly discipline with a clearly nationalist agenda, tasked to recover the valuable musical pasts of (initially and especially) Germany, France, and Italy; signal early achievements were the Johann Sebastian Bach and Giovanni Pierluigi da Palestrina editions, launched in 1850 and 1862, respectively.

2. MUSICAL NATIONALISM IN THE UNITED STATES. Because of the diverse ways nationalist thought has influenced the development and preservation of music in the United States, we may distinguish among four modes of nationalist musical practices. The "respectability" mode lies closest to European models, based in the traditions now commonly known as "classical" music. Aspirational nationalist music originates stylistically in a lower cultural stratum but seeks to move upward, sometimes overtly parallel to national aspirations. Vernacular musical nationalism ignores the upper cultural strata, addressing particular constituencies more directly. And, in the "modern *Volksgeist*" option, once-discounted musical genres are "reclaimed," providing a revisionist account of what the United States has been, and what from its past should be valued.

3. RESPECTABILITY. Especially after the Civil War, concerted efforts were made to elevate musical culture, so that the United States could take its place among the European nations that were seen to be its most appropriate cultural siblings. While this project was pursued most vigorously in the Northeast (Boston, New York, and Philadelphia), other cities were also involved in similar projects of cultural uplift, according to evolving, often regionally specific situations and needs. Many among the *nouveaux riches* pursued societal leadership through cultural philanthropy. Those in the South desired to reclaim genteel traditions associated with the antebellum era. And the rapidly expanding West sought to "catch up" with the cultural standards of eastern cities and Europe. The nationalist basis for these efforts became especially evident when ANTONÍN DVOŘÁK was brought to New York in 1892 by Jeannette Thurber and the National Conservatory of Music, specifically to help develop an "American" music. Among several works he contributed, the most successful was the Symphony "From the New World," in E Minor (1893), although for most listeners its character seemed more Bohemian than American (M. Beckerman).

"From the New World" drew on a wide variety of practices and idioms, some imported from Europe and others native to the United States. The symphony as a genre—including the institution of the public orchestra concert—was distinctly European and had by then become an established purveyor of nationalist sentiment. But there were more specific imported elements, as well, including the "Rimsky" scale (later called octatonic) that Dvořák uses to evoke a sense of mythic wonder in the introductions of the first two movements, and the substitution of ethnic dance for the traditional minuet or scherzo movement. These European conventions provided the context for an array of specifically American elements, most prominently a sense of primitive grandeur that comes across as almost scenic, actual and invented "Negro melodies" (i.e., spirituals, which blend Anglo-American hymnody with African traditions), and Indianist musical tropes. Within the finale, moreover, Dvořák interwove his disparate themes together in a quasi-Wagnerian, leitmotivic manner, as if to suggest the "commingling of races" he wrote about after his return to Bohemia, which he saw as distinctively American, and wherein he foresaw the future of American music.

Dvořák's projection of an American "melting-pot" musical aesthetic, though resulting in works of lasting popularity, was roundly rejected in its time as a potential model, due largely to the racialized political realities of the United States. Although other American composers had anticipated Dvořák's orchestral use of African American idioms, and would continue to indulge a nascent vogue for Indianist music (T. Browner; M.V. Pisani), they did not mean thereby to *represent* the United States directly, and many resented Dvořák's naïve presumption to do so on their behalf. Soon after the *New World*, AMY MARCY BEACH (*née* Cheney, a largely self-taught New England composer who also wrote some Indianist music) began work on her "Gaelic" Symphony in response to Dvořák's *New World*, employing the same key. Beach's symphony—the first by an American woman, and widely performed after its 1896 premiere—exemplifies the inherent conflict within the nationalist music aesthetic as transplanted to an American context, between courting respectability and relying on materials borrowed from a lower cultural stratum. Professionally, Beach was herself a partial victim of "respectability," largely forsaking her performance career at the request of her husband, and thereafter signing her works "Mrs. H.A.A. Beach." In the "Gaelic" Symphony, she ensures a kind of musical respectability by grounding its discourse directly in a series of other E minor symphonies, by Dvořák, Johannes Brahms, and Arthur Sullivan (the "Irish"), alluding as well to Felix Mendelssohn's "Scottish," in the related key of A Minor. Within this context, she develops a "folk" element more respectable for late-19th-century New England than Dvořák's interracial mix, using Irish-derived tunes and idioms that bespeak both her own Anglo-American heritage and the upward mobility that had by then lifted Irish Americans into the ranks of ethnic respectability (hence the authenticating term, "Gaelic"). Yet, perhaps inevitably, despite the work's sure-handed competence, it seems tame compared to Dvořák's bold treatment of less reputable material.

What eventually displaced Dvořák's musical image of the American landscape, some four decades later, in a form suitable for the concert stage and answering to mainstream national myths, was the "empty" soundscape introduced by Virgil Thomson and AARON COPLAND in the 1930s, as part of the then-current "populist" movement. Copland, for example, once freed of his infatuations with overt jazz idioms in the 1920s, developed his "open plains" idiom and proceeded to "people" it (often through ballet) with a variety of European-derived communities in the process of nation-building.

Among these and related works partaking of a sense of nationalism were Copland's *Billy the Kid* (1938), *Lincoln Portrait* and *Rodeo* (1942), *Appalachian Spring* (1943), and Symphony No.3 (1944, including the 1942 *Fanfare for the Common Man* as a culmination).

Alongside this development, film music in the first full decade of the "sound" era reclaimed a vital place for older "classical" traditions, with scores derived from Wagnerian practices and written by European-trained composers working in Hollywood, often supporting "American" content and in some instances employing the new "American" idiom to set landscapes, an approach pioneered by Thomson (*The Plow that Broke the Plains*, 1936; *The River*, 1937) and Copland (*Of Mice and Men*, 1939; *Our Town*, 1940; *The Red Pony*, 1948). In establishing "place," film music partook of a wide array of styles, often far removed from the world of classical music, such as jazz for cityscapes or nightclubs, or "cowboy" or "western" styles for exterior settings. Although distinctive as a type, the latter echoed Copland's "American" style in exploiting the capacity for directly simple styles to evoke spatial vistas, a line of development that would extend to Philip Glass's score for *Koyaanisqatsi* (1982) and beyond.

4. ASPIRATION. Dvořák's challenge to employ African American idioms as part of a spectrum of styles that might represent "America" was for a long time mostly ignored by American composers working primarily in the "classical" milieu. But the advent of blues and jazz in the early 20th century began to change these attitudes—if only gradually, since opposition to jazz on moral grounds for a long time kept pace with its growing popularity. As with other American-grown artistic products (most notably, film), the prestige of jazz and blues in the United States was given a significant boost by its enthusiastic acceptance abroad, especially in France, where respected composers were quick to incorporate these idioms into their compositions, including Darius Milhaud (*La création du monde*, 1923) and Maurice Ravel (Violin Sonata, 1923; Piano Concerto in G, 1931). But the first uses of concert jazz in an overtly nationalist context came not from established concert-hall composers, but from jazz musicians aspiring to bring this music to the concert hall, an aspiration that had several notable precedents.

Long before jazz caught on in Europe after the First World War, blackface minstrelsy enjoyed a similar kind of European success in the 19th century. Stephen Foster, who wrote many songs for the minstrel stage, also wrote a more "elevated" version of this type of song, helping to create a repertory of respectable American parlor songs. Later in the century and well into the 20th, spirituals became a concert staple. And, as ragtime emerged near the turn of the 20th century, African American composer Scott Joplin began to publish rags mounted in a fashion similar to European piano music, following a "classicizing" impulse similar to Foster's. Although Joplin's ambitions along these lines also led him to compose operas (*A Guest of Honor*, 1902, now lost; *Treemonisha*, 1910, unstaged during his lifetime), however, it wasn't until such figures as GEORGE GERSHWIN, DUKE ELLINGTON, and WILLIAM GRANT STILL began writing for the concert hall and opera stage that music in this vein achieved lasting success and became understood as part of a legitimate "nationalist" voice.

The phenomenal success of Gershwin's jazz-based *Rhapsody in Blue* (1924) provided the impetus for him to compose more concert music in this idiom. Particularly interesting from a nationalist context is *An American in Paris* (1928), which provides a direct parallel to Dvořák's "From the New World," since, in trying to capture impressions of a world different from his own, each composer also delineates his own character—generally taken to be a quintessentially *national* character—in such vivid terms that the ostensible subject ("the New World," "Paris") has seemed incidental to the overall effect and success of the piece.

Still's *Afro-American Symphony* (1930) is more directly nationalist in intent. Based on a blues tune, it attempts to suggest a blended heritage, as a reflection both of Still's own mixed race (African, Native American, and European) and of the "comingling of races" Dvořák claimed as a hallmark of the United States. The work's trajectory is intensely aspirational, using the poetry of Paul Laurence Dunbar, in African American dialect, to map its programmatic course from "Longing" and "Sorrow," through "Humor" (the widely performed "banjo" scherzo), to "Aspiration," the latter presented in a hymn-driven finale that builds to a culminating series of iterations of an Indianist motive from the scherzo of Dvořák's "New World." The dual basis of this narrative, in a projected American blend and in Still's own story, becomes most intensely personal when, during the scherzo, a sharply profiled quotation of Gershwin's "I Got Rhythm" (introduced earlier that year) lays claim to the song's melodic hook as Still's own figure, which, as he claimed in interviews, he had often used as the basis for improvisation.

The implicit claim Still makes, of a kind of musical theft, has been a common theme throughout the history of African American idioms emerging into mainstream American popular and concert musics, dating back at least to minstrelsy. For example, as the theme of the Largo from the "New World" became popular as the spiritual "Goin' Home," claims regarding which version was the original began to surface on both sides. Similarly, Irving Berlin was accused of basing "Alexander's Ragtime Band" on a tune from Joplin's *Treemonisha*. To some extent, flexibility regarding creative propriety is built into the shared improvisational milieu of jazz, providing the partial basis for claims that Billy Strayhorn should be given more credit for his collaborative contributions to Ellington's concert works, including several that may be understood as nationalist (i.e., *Black, Brown, and Beige*, 1943, intended as a kind of African American history). More generally, however, such claims give specific focus to a larger issue of collective creative propriety (a concept based in nationalist ideology), that in the United States it was white (often Jewish) artists who most often profited and received credit for idioms that originated in African American musicking—including

ragtime, blues, jazz, tap dance, R&B, and rock—even as some of these figures also worked hard to open doors that remained effectively closed to African Americans for most of the 20th century. This sharp differential regarding public access, venue, and markets has reinforced what may be described as parallel nationalisms within the United States, in which blacks and other racialized groups remained sharply segregated from the mainstream until the CIVIL RIGHTS MOVEMENT began to bring gradual political change on behalf of racial equality (R. Radano and P.V. Bohlman).

This context of perceived appropriation deeply affected the production and reception of Gershwin's *Porgy and Bess* (1935), the most important of many attempts to create a distinctively "American" opera based on American themes and musical idioms. Deriving, as a "folk opera," from a 1924 book by white writer DuBose Heyward, who also contributed lyrics (along with Ira Gershwin), *Porgy and Bess* mythologizes the experiences of poor blacks in the Southern city of Charleston, but from a perspective very different from that of Still or Ellington's musical engagements with race. Negative criticism of the show has tended to see it as a show by and for whites, as reinforcing rather than challenging the status of African Americans; these criticisms point to (among other things) its focus on a romanticized lower stratum of society and its use of dialect. From a nationalist perspective, the black community in *Porgy and Bess* represents a separate nation, which does not map easily onto either the actual experiences of African Americans or some larger vision of America's realities and possibilities. Yet, Gershwin himself mixed easily with African American musicians, and clearly meant the piece as a means to bring them into mainstream high culture—insisting against fierce resistance, for example, that its sung roles be performed only by black actors. As a work of American nationalism, it has shared the reception profile of the "New World" Symphony: while loved and respected as a dramatic musical work, it has also been resented for its presumption to speak for a population to which its creators did not belong, its sensibilities undermined at every turn by its outsider perspective.

The culturally aspirational dimension of *Porgy and Bess* is consistent with Gershwin's work not only for the concert stage but also for Broadway musicals; thus, his *Of Thee I Sing* (1931), a satire of national politics, was the first musical to win a Pulitzer Prize. Indeed, the musical as a genre has proven to be among the most effective and enduring musical venues for aspirational American nationalism, since among its core recurring themes has been the nature of national identity, with generally assimilationist plots celebrating the inclusivity of the United States (R. Knapp; A. Most, 2004). Already in 1904, less than a decade after Beach's "Gaelic" Symphony, GEORGE M. COHAN's *Little Johnny Jones* presented an Irish American jockey in London, proud of his nation ("Yankee Doodle Boy") and homesick for New York ("Give My Regards to Broadway"). In line with the show's larger strategies, "Yankee Doodle Boy" constructs a musical map of the United

States, interweaving strains of "Yankee Doodle," "Dixie," "Auld Lang Syne," and the "Star Spangled Banner," while referring verbally to Johnny's girl, "Goldie Gates" of San Francisco. As Cohan knew and exploited, the American musical stage had already been the principal site of Irish emergence into respectability, as it would be also for Jews, Italians, and eventually (if less decisively) African Americans.

A key element in this process of assimilation is the capacity of each group to maintain critical aspects of its identity even in the process of becoming "American." Johnny Jones (played by Cohan himself) remains the scrappy Irishman even as he claims his birthright as an American. Likewise, American Jews working on Broadway, creating and performing in assimilationist plots, with romantic pairings providing a means for outsiders to become insiders, projected an image of the American melting pot that gradually became, to a large extent, a Jewish American reality. Within this process, the Jewish character fused with the American character, creating what has been termed "theatrical liberalism," in which even the popular theater becomes a sacred place where people become who they are through performance, where performance underwrites freedom, and where communal obligations take precedence over rights (A. Most, 2010). In countless musicals, communities comprising disparate elements are built along these lines, open to anyone who may share these tenets. Samson Raphaelson's *The Jazz Singer* (Broadway, 1925; filmed in 1927) provides a classic example of this fusion, as the protagonist insists to his cantor father that becoming a jazz singer extends rather than denies his traditional Judaism.

Over several decades, many high-profile American musicals may be understood as American nationalist in positioning each such community as America *in nuce*. Rodgers and Hammerstein's *Oklahoma!* (1943), a pivotal work in this development, is most overtly nationalist in the title song, directly tying its people to a specific landscape, and finding the basis for that connection in intimate reflection, *à la* German Idealism:

> Ev'ry night my honey lamb and I,
> Sit alone and talk
> And watch a hawk
> Makin' lazy circles in the sky.
> We know we belong to the land,
> And the land we belong to is grand!

Similarly, communities in musicals reconcile apparent opposites (*Guys and Dolls*, 1950) and find enrichment through absorbing outsiders (*The Music Man*, 1957). Musicals also imagine the United States as a model for solving widespread problems and realizing potential (*The King and I*, 1951; *The Sound of Music*, 1959), or reimagine its possibilities within cycles of generational renewal (*Flower Drum Song*, 1958; *Hair*, 1967). Equally important to American nationalism have been the many musicals that have been critical of the United States, whether explicitly or implicitly, whether in satire or in earnest. Because the genre is basically affirmative, these criticisms seem generally to come from a place of deep personal investment in the United States even as they

criticize; particularly successful examples include *Show Boat* (1927), *Of Thee I Sing, The Cradle Will Rock* (1938), *South Pacific* (1949), *Candide* (1956), *West Side Story* (1957), *Gypsy* (1959), *How to Succeed in Business without Really Trying* (1961), *Cabaret* (1966), *Chicago* (1975), *Pacific Overtures* (1976), *Dreamgirls* (1981), *Assassins* (1991), *Rent* (1996), *Ragtime* (1998), and *Parade* (1998). Among the aspects of America these shows criticize, the most frequently recurring is its racial politics, even as many of them also indulge in Orientalist practices—a common element in nationalist discourses, since defining the Other is crucial to issues of self-identity. The focus on race in musicals bespeaks not only the inclusive nationalist agenda of many who have written and performed in musicals but also the intractability of the problem itself, particularly regarding the divide between black and white. Hopeful narratives regarding the latter have been extremely rare on Broadway.

5. VERNACULAR SONG. Many political songs have a nationalist basis. Couched in a style that allows them to be taken up by many voices, such songs are inherently invitational, promoting communal feeling and helping to persuade people to political action. Their plain-spoken manner allows them more aggressively to pursue agendas where culturally elevated genres have failed to make much headway. Although conducive to many nationalist agendas, they implicitly oppose the idea that nationalism must entail collective cultural betterment. Rather, these songs remain resolutely within their lower cultural stratum, often in order to validate a more broadly based heritage.

Folksongs, and songs written in that style, are traditionally one of the richest sources for nationalist musics. Among the most important contributors to this kind of song in the United States was WOODY GUTHRIE, whose "This Land Is Your Land" (1940, recorded 1944) achieved long-lived popularity, buoyed by the FOLK REVIVAL of the 1950s and 1960s. Like Irving Berlin's anthem "God Bless America" (1918, rev. 1938), which Guthrie disliked, "This Land" is in the style of a hymn; indeed, it borrows its melody from a Baptist hymn that had already been used by other folk singers. Originally, the song's claim of collective ownership—the very basis for nationalism—was extended even further in a verse long-suppressed for being too "Communist":

> There was a big high wall there that tried to stop me;
> Sign was painted, it said "private property;"
> But on the back side it didn't say nothing;
> That side was made for you and me.

A similar flirtation with Communist ideology energizes "The Hammer Song" ("If I Had a Hammer"; Pete Seeger and Lee Hays, 1949), which also achieved great success during the folk revival, including a 1962 cover by Peter, Paul, and Mary. The song's title hints at the "hammer and sickle" of Communism, but with crucial deniability. Thus, the "hammer of justice" has the "safe" explanation of a judge's gavel, but can quite easily suggest instead the "distributive justice" of Communism. The song maintains a balance between its call to action and its call to love, which fully makes sense only when its Communist dimension is rightly understood, and placed within a nationalist context, with "love" being what binds together "my brothers and my sisters/All over this land" in common cause.

The folk revival coincided productively with the Civil Rights Movement, reinforcing the spirituals-based soundtrack heard in news coverage of the day, as provided by arrested protesters joined in song. Among the most important of the hymns popular at the time is "We Shall Overcome," another song brought out by Pete Seeger in the 1940s, deriving from a 19th-century spiritual (sharing specific lineage with Bob Dylan's "Blowin' in the Wind"). Revived in the late 1950s, the song became associated with Reverend Martin Luther King, but was also widely sung and recorded by other activists in the movement, including Pete Seeger and Joan Baez. The song's "We" is usefully ambiguous, allowing the plight of one people (or nation) to be shared by another when both join in song; as suggested by the sentiment of later verses ("We shall live in peace"), the expansiveness of the song's "We" is its real point. Significant as well is its emphasis on a deeply shared feeling ("Deep in my heart/I do believe"), a vital part of effective nationalist music, deriving from German Idealism.

6. THE MODERN *VOLKSGEIST* OPTION. One of the foundational notions of nationalism is that the "spirit of the people" may be gleaned from vernacular music that has been protected from the corruptive influence of modernity, so that collecting folk music becomes part of a larger project of recovering a shared valuable past. In the United States, this has involved some fairly traditional folkloric research by, among others, Alan Lomax and Charles Seeger (Pete's father) and his wife, Ruth Crawford Seeger. Interest in America's musical past has extended to many other repertories, including shape-note hymnody, spirituals, minstrel and parlor songs, ragtime, blues, and early Tin Pan Alley, as well as regional folk traditions, work songs, prison songs, hobo songs, and the like—much of which is now categorized as "roots" music.

Despite a clear nationalist basis, the recovery of these musics has only indirectly served nationalist agendas in the United States, remaining instead largely an academic interest that occasionally emerges in popular culture (e.g., in movies such as *O Brother, Where Art Thou?* 2000). More directly relevant to American nationalism has been the reissue of its legacy of recorded music in the United States, greatly facilitated by several anthologies released by Smithsonian Folkways, which have led to the reclamation of previously discounted repertories and sometimes elevated them to the highest cultural status, most spectacularly in the case of early jazz (that is, pre-bop). This enshrinement of early jazz, leading up to a kind of "golden age" of swing, was codified as "America's classical music" in the ten-part documentary *Jazz* (2001, dir. Ken Burns, with Wynton Marsalis as artistic director). In line with many other nationalist accounts of musical traditions, the documentary mythologizes jazz as an art form brought to perfection within

the incubator of a nation, under the direction of a few enormously talented artists. Thus, *Jazz*'s claim that "Ellington is our Mozart" draws a direct parallel between America's veneration of its jazz legacy and early German nationalist claims concerning their pantheon of great composers.

Two other kinds of American music with a substantial recorded legacy have increasingly been regarded as a kind of "national treasure." The six-part documentary *Broadway: the American Musical* (2004) exemplifies the generally higher regard recently being accorded the musical, as a specifically *American* development, an elevation aided by the increased commercial viability of revivals, the formation of a canonic repertory, the ballyhooing of a supposed "golden age" (creating a mythology of the musical akin to Burns's veneration of the swing era), and an upsurge in academic work concerning the musical. As a separate development, movie scores have found their way into the concert hall, both because of their capacity to engage audiences directly, and as part of a general veneration for classic Hollywood film—again, as a specifically *American* art form.

BIBLIOGRAPHY

Grove7 (R. Taruskin)

C. Hamm: *Music in the New World* (New York and London, 1983)

L. Levine: *Highbrow/Lowbrow: the Emergence of Cultural Hierarchy in America* (Cambridge and London, 1988)

J. Horowitz: *Wagner Nights: an American History* (Berkeley, CA, 1994)

G. Bederman: *Manliness and Civilization: a Cultural History of Gender and Race in the United States, 1880–1917* (Chicago, 1995)

R. Smith: *Handel's Oratorios and Eighteenth-Century Thought* (Cambridge and New York, 1995)

T. Browner: "'Breathing the Indian Spirit': Thoughts on Musical Borrowing and the 'Indianist' Movement in American Music," *American Music*, xv/3 (1997), 265–84

E. Gellner: *Nationalism* (London, 1997)

R. Locke and C. Barr, eds.: *Cultivating Music in America: Women Patrons and Activists since 1860* (Berkeley, CA, 1997)

S. Scheckel: *The Insistence of the Indian: Race and Nationalism in Nineteenth-Century American Culture* (Princeton, NJ, 1998)

R.J. Scott-Childress, ed.: *Race and the Production of Modern American Nationalism* (New York and London, 1999)

R. Radano and P.V. Bohlman, eds.: *Music and the Racial Imagination* (Chicago and London, 2000)

R.A. Reuss and J.C. Reuss: *American Folk Music and Left-Wing Politics, 1927–1957* (Lanham, MD, 2000)

C.P. Smith: *William Grant Still: a Study in Contradictions* (Berkeley, CA and Los Angeles, 2000)

R. Crawford: *America's Musical Life: a History* (New York and London, 2001)

E.N. Glenn: *Unequal Freedom: How Race and Gender Shaped American Citizenship and Labor* (Cambridge and London, 2002)

M. Beckerman: *New Worlds of Dvorak: Searching in America for the Composer's Inner Life* (New York and London, 2003)

N. Hubbs: *The Queer Composition of America's Sound: Gay Modernists, American Music, and National Identity* (Berkeley, CA, Los Angeles, and London, 2004)

A. Most: *Making Americans: Jews and the Broadway Musical* (Cambridge, MA, 2004)

R. Knapp: *The American Musical and the Formation of National Identity* (Princeton, NJ, and Oxford, 2005)

M.V. Pisani: *Imagining Native America in Music* (New Haven, CT, and London, 2005)

E.J. Blum: *Reforging the White Republic: Race, Religion, and American Nationalism, 1865–1898* (Baton Rouge, LA, 2007)

C.H. Garrett: *Struggling to Define a Nation: American Music and the Twentieth Century* (Berkeley, CA, Los Angeles, and London, 2008)

R. Locke: *Musical Exoticism: Images and Reflections* (Cambridge and New York, 2009)

A. Most: "The Birth of Theatrical Liberalism," *After Pluralism: Reimagining Religious Engagement*, ed. C. Bender and P.E. Klassen (New York, 2010), 127–55

RAYMOND KNAPP

National League of Musicians. Musicians' union founded in 1886; *see* UNIONS, MUSICIANS'.

National Music Council of the United States. Organization whose members are national music organizations. Founded in 1940 by Julia Ober, Harold Spivacke, Franklin Dunham, and Edwin Hughes, the Council has provided a forum for the discussion of issues and problems concerning music in the United States and has acted as a liaison among member organizations. It has advised Congress on proposed legislation pertaining to music and in 1956 was granted a congressional charter. The Council has encouraged the formation of the American String Teachers Association, and both the National Association for Music Therapy and the National Opera Association were founded under its auspices. In 1959, with funds from the Ford Foundation, it established one of the first programs placing composers in public schools. It has cosponsored an annual Arts Advocacy Day and has worked closely with federal legislators "to promote and support music and music education as an integral part" of the public school curricula. It has also sponsored the concert series "Bicentennial Parade of American Music" (1976) and the National Black Music Colloquium and Competition at the Kennedy Center for the Performing Arts (1980). The activities of the Council and its members have been reported in the *National Music Council Bulletin* (1940–82) and the *National Music Council News* (renamed the *National Music Council Newsletter* in 2004). Each year the Council has presented the American Eagle Award for distinguished service to American music; past recipients include Dizzy Gillespie, Morton Gould, Dawn Upshaw, and Kenny Rogers.

BIBLIOGRAPHY

E. Hughes: "The National Music Council, 1940–1960," *National Music Council Bulletin*, xx/3 (1960), 1–4

J. Browning: "National Music Council—25 Years of Service," *MJ*, xxiv/1 (1966), 77 only

Contemporary Music for Schools: a Catalog...sponsored by the Ford Foundation and the National Music Council, ed. MENC (Washington, DC, 1966)

EMILY GOOD/MICHAEL MAUSKAPF

National Music Publishers' Association [NMPA]. Trade association. Founded in 1917 as the Music Publishers' Protective Association, the NMPA has communicated with agencies of the United States federal government on legislation that affects its members and has studied technological developments that have implications for the publishing industry. The association set up and has continued to operate the Harry Fox Agency (*see* PERFORMING RIGHTS SOCIETIES), which has acted as its members' agent in administering mechanical rights licenses and has represented their interests before the federal government. The NMPA was an influential organization in the development and enactment of the Copyright Act of 1976. Since 1980 the NMPA has given awards to its members for the best-selling songs in various categories, including popular, rhythm-and-blues, country, Latin, and gospel. Membership in the NMPA is open to firms that have published music for one year, including compositions that have been used commercially. In the early 21st century the association's headquarters were in Washington, DC. In conjunction with the Music Publishers' Association, the NMPA has issued the *Music Publishers Sales Agency List*. By 2010 the organization represented over 800 publishers. In the early 21st century the NMPA became a leading voice surrounding the protection of recorded music on the Internet.

JOHN SHEPARD/JONAS WESTOVER

National Negro Opera Company [NNOC]. It was founded in Pittsburgh by MARY CARDWELL DAWSON in 1941. The Company grew out of a performance of Giuseppe Verdi's *Aïda* at the annual meeting of the National Association of Negro Musicians (Pittsburgh, August 1941) during Dawson's presidency. The group's first independent production was a repeat performance of *Aïda* at Pittsburgh's Syria Mosque in October of the same year. Dawson moved the Company to Washington, DC, in 1942, producing performances in Pittsburgh, Washington, DC, Chicago, and New York in venues ranging from New York's YWCA and Madison Square Garden; Pittsburgh's Syria Mosque; and Washington's Watergate Park and Griffith Stadium. They were the first outside company to perform on the stage of the Metropolitan Opera House, where on 27 May 1956 they staged Clarence Cameron White's *Ouanga!* (1932). In addition to *Aïda* and *Ouanga!* the Company's repertoire included *La traviata*, *Faust*, and R. Nathaniel Dett's *The Ordering of Moses*, the latter performed in 1951 at Carnegie Hall. Artists who performed with the NNOC included Lillian Evanti, William Franklin, Robert McFerrin, Camilla Williams, Carol Brice, Edward Boatner, and McHenry Boatwright.

In later years the company was unable to perform regularly because of financial difficulties and continuing disputes with the American Guild of Musical Artists and the American Federation of Musicians. The company disbanded after Dawson's death in 1962; company records can be found within Dawson's archive in the Music Division of the Library of Congress.

KAREN M. BRYAN

National Opera Association [NOA]. Organization founded in 1955 under the auspices of the National Music Council to support all phases of opera production, composition, promotion, and appreciation in the United States and Canada. Members have hailed from North America, Europe, Asia, and Australia, and have been composers, conductors, directors, managers, producers, publishers, librettists, teachers, scholars, translators, and organizations (opera companies, colleges and universities, and schools). NOA awards have been given annually through its Professional Voice Auditions,

Chamber Opera Competition for composers, Scholarly Paper and Dissertation Competitions for scholars, and the Opera Production and Opera Scenes Competitions for institutions. Publications have included a monograph series (of which Boris Goldovsky's *Touring Opera*, 1975, is vol. iii), an annual directory of members by profession or vocal category, *The Opera Journal* (founded in 1968), and the cumulative *NOA Catalogue of Contemporary American Operas* (1976). NOA special initiatives have included an outreach program, Opera for Youth; the Sacred in Opera project, which has encouraged operatic representations of the religious quest; and the Legacy Project, which began in 1995 in an effort to honor and promote contributions to racial diversity in opera. Recipients of Legacy "Lift Every Voice" Awards have included singers Robert McFerrin, Leontyne Price, and Shirley Verrett, scholar Eileen Southern, and composer George Walker.

JOHN SHEPARD/STEPHANIE JENSEN-MOULTON

National Opera Company. Opera company founded in 1885 as the AMERICAN OPERA COMPANY.

National Orchestral Association. Organization founded in 1930 "to train American orchestra musicians in orchestral techniques and repertoire, providing them with the necessary experience and level of expertise to enter professional orchestra careers." Originally called the American Orchestral Society and later reorganized by Mary Flagler Cary, Franklin Robinson, and Léon Barzin, the Association gave its first concert at Carnegie Hall on 28 October 1930, making it the oldest training orchestra in the United States. Barzin, who later became founding music director of the New York City Ballet, led the Association until 1958 and again from 1970–76. He remained involved with the organization into his 90s, and an annual award has been given in his honor. The orchestra has not only explored the standard repertory but has also given more than 60 world premieres, 25 American premieres, and 60 New York premieres. It has rehearsed and performed under such guest conductors as Aaron Copland and Bernard Haitink, and has accompanied soloists such as Emanuel Feuermann, Myra Hess, Philippe Entremont, and Itzhak Perlman. During World War II, the orchestra played at army camps and hospitals and gave 25 warbond concerts over the New York radio station WQXR. It was the official orchestra of the Festival of Two Worlds in Spoleto in 1973, and it represented New York State at the Kennedy Center Bicentennial Celebration. In 1984 the association became affiliated with Columbia University through the Institute for Orchestral Studies, a one-year fellowship program for graduate students. It has cosponsored an annual workshop for conductors and promoted the careers of young composers by producing world premiere performances at Carnegie Hall each year. In the early 2010s its headquarters were in New York.

JOHN SHEPARD/MICHAEL MAUSKAPF

National Peace Jubilee. *See* PEACE JUBILEES.

National School Band Association. An organization founded in 1926 to administer contests for school wind bands; *see* BAND.

National String Instrument Corporation. *See* NATIONAL-DOBRO.

Native American flute [Courting flute; Indian courting flute; Indian love flute; various tribal names]. The primary wind instrument of Native American culture. Similar to the European recorder, it is a block flute in which air is forced across a fipple by a blockage in the wind chamber. It was traditionally made of wood or cane, with an external duct. The instrument may have from four to six finger holes and may be elaborately decorated by painting or carving of totemic designs. It was originally found among the Plains tribes; tribes known to have used the courting flute include the Iroquois, Winnebago, Sioux, Omaha, Crow, Nez Percé, Northern Ute, Apache, and Seminole. Traditional Native literature traces the origins of the flute to prehistoric times through stories crediting sacred animals or other forms of divine intervention with the creation of the instrument and directions for its use. References to the flute are found in writings and diaries of European explorers and settlers, including the Lewis and Clark journals.

Plains flutes were commonly made of red cedar, although other straight-grained woods were also used in the Plains–Plateau area; cane flutes were made in the Southwest. Flutes have also been made from metal gun barrels and nickel tubing, among other materials. The traditional method of construction was such that no two instruments were identical. Typically, a man would make his own instrument and create a personal courting song, which he would then play outside the lodging of a young woman of the tribe. If the woman was interested in the man, she would emerge from the lodging and courtship would ensue. Some courting songs passed through several generations of a family.

The first recordings of the Native American flute date to the early 20th century and include an example of Kiowa flute song with the performer telling his tribe's story of how the flute came to his people. Doc Tate Nevaquaya's recordings from the 1940s are credited with renewing interest in the flute tradition and leading to a renaissance of flute performance in the latter decades of the century. The instrument has become part of the musical practices of tribes throughout North and Central America across a broad range of styles and for many functions, including social and ceremonial practices. The instrument has also been used in popular music, jazz, film scores, symphonic and chamber works, and New Age recordings. R. Carlos Nakai's album *Canyon Trilogy* (1989) was the first gold record to feature Native American flute. Among other prominent flutists are Keith Secola (Anishinabe), Robert Tree Cody (Dakota-Maricopa), Tom Ware (Comanche), Robert Mirabal (Taos), and Kevin Locke (Lakota). Historically, only men played the flute, but contemporary women flutists, including Alice Gomez, Lillian Rainer, Mary

Youngblood, and Geraldine Barney, have gained widespread recognition.

DISCOGRAPHY

R.T. Cody: *Young Eagle's Flight* (Canyon CR-553, 1991); R.C. Nakai: *Spirit Horses* (Canyon CR-7014, 1991); R.T. Cody: *Dreams from the Grandfathers* (Canyon CR-554, 1993); K. Locke: *Dream Catcher* (Earthbeat 9 42538-2, 1993); K. Locke: *The Flash of the Mirror* (Makoche MC0104, 1996); J. Rainer, Jr.: *Songs of the Indian Flute, Volume 1* (self-published, 1996); J. Rainer, Jr.: *Songs of the Indian Flute, Volume 2* (self-published, 1996); R.C. Nakai: *In Beauty we Return* (Canyon CR-7064, 2004); D.T. Nevaquaya: *Comanche Flute Music* (Folkways SFW-50403, 2004)

BIBLIOGRAPHY

D.C. Miller: "Flutes of the American Indian," *The Flutist*, ii (1921), 509
M.F. Riemer: *Instrumental and Vocal Love Songs of the North American Indians* (thesis, Wesleyan U., 1978)
B. Burton: *Moving Within the Circle: Contemporary Native American Music and Dance* (Danbury, CT, 1993, 2/2008)
R.C. Nakai, K. Light, and D.P. McAllester: *The Art of the Native American Flute* (Phoenix, AZ, 1996)
B. Burton: *Voices of the Wind: Native American Flute Songs* (Danbury, CT, 1998)

BRYAN BURTON

Native American music. In this article the term "Native American" is used to refer to the native peoples who occupied the North American continent above Mexico before the advent of western European exploration and colonization in 1492 and their descendants. Similar populations in Mexico, Central America, and South America are not discussed here other than occasional references in connection with other groups or in general discussions of history.

Native Americans appear to have come into the Western Hemisphere from Asia in a series of migrations across the Bering Strait or a land bridge that existed during the late Ice Ages. Their common origin explains the physical characteristics that many Native Americans have in common, while the several waves of migration are supposed to account for the many native linguistic families. DNA and linguistic studies have confirmed their origins as lying in East Asia, with evidence of additional linguistic connections with Siberian peoples and a tribal history of the Lenape in Eastern North America has been interpreted as show origins near Lake Baikal in Siberia. In addition, rituals among some Athabaskan peoples, including Navajo and Apache, show striking similarities to animist and proto-Buddhist practices. There is evidence of the presence of Native Americans in the Americas for at least 15,000–20,000 years. In pre-Columbian times the population of the area north of Mexico is estimated to have been several million.

1. Music. (i) Terminology. (ii) Music and society. (iii). Geographical and cultural style areas. (iv) Regional styles. (a) The Plains. (b) The Eastern Woodlands. (c) The Southwest and California. (d) The Great Basin. (e) The Northwest Coast. (f) Arctic and Subarctic. (g) Intertribal. (v) Musical instruments. (a) Idiophones. (b) Membranophones. (c) Chordophones. (d) Aerophones. (vi) Composition, learning, and rehearsing. (vii) Developments after European contact. (a) Early influences. (b) Peyote music. (c) The Ghost Dance. (d) New Native American musics. (viii) Research. 2. Dance. (i) Introduction. (ii) Social contexts. (iii) Choreography and music. (iv) Regalia. (v) Theatrical productions.

1. MUSIC.

(i) Terminology. Native American is but one of many labels employed by scholars to identify the native peoples of North America. Indian, American Indian, Amerindian, and Indians of North America, used in academic and popular writings from the 19th through 21st centuries, derive from the belief prevalent at the time of Columbus that the Americas were the outer reaches of the East Indies. Matthiessen suggests that the use of *indios* by Columbus may have be a corruption of the phrase *una gente in dios* (a people in God), which Columbus and other early explorers used to describe the idyllic lifestyle of the first people encountered during their voyages of discovery. Increasingly, "Indian" and variations of the term have been seen by some as both inaccurate and racially insensitive; others continue to embrace these terms. The term "Amerind," although popular in scholarly writing in the early 20th century, is now used almost exclusively in reference to native peoples of Central and South America.

First Nations, First People, Native Peoples, and Original People are terms used increasingly in contemporary scholarship. Aboriginal People, although often used in Canada, is seen to carry a connotation of inferiority of culture by most Native Americans. "Tribe" is also viewed

Anonymous North American Indian courting flute, 19th century (Dayton C. Miller Flute Collection, Music Division, Library of Congress)

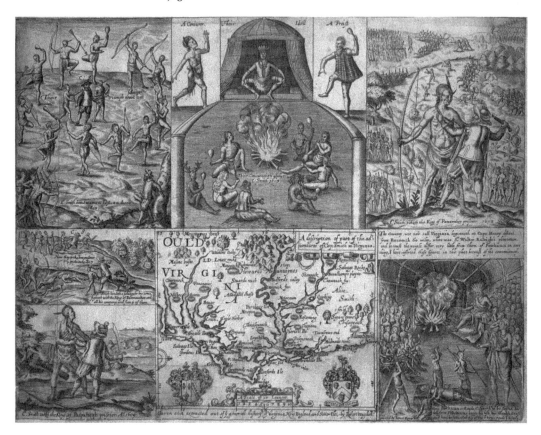

Captain John Smith engraving of Native American musicians with container rattles, 1624. (Wilson Special Collections Library, UNC Chapel Hill)

as deprecatory by many Native Americans because of its association in the popular mind with "primitive." "Nation" has gained acceptance for cultural identification, and it has gradually replaced "reservation" in recent years. In this and other entries, "tribe" and "nation" will be used interchangeably according to source usage.

Beginning in the late 20th century, Native Americans began returning to the use of original tribal names replacing designations assigned by explorers and settlers. Many of these latter names were misinterpretations of original names (Crow, for "Children of the Long Beaked Bird"), derogatory terms used by other groups (Apache, or "enemy of my people" in Zuni), or names referring to locale or type of dwelling (Pueblo). A few examples of this trend include: Inde' (Apache), Dineh (Navajo), Chattah (Choctaw), Tsalagi (Cherokee), and Tohono O'odham (Papago). The majority of the original tribal names translated as "the people," often qualified with a distinguishing term to identify a locale of practice: Tohono O'odham, for example, translates as "People of the Desert," while Haudenosaunee (Iroquois) translates as "People of the Longhouse." In this and other entries on Native American music, traditional names and original names will be used interchangeably according to source usage.

(ii) Music and society. Music is a central element in Native American culture from the time before contact with Europeans to the modern era. From birth to death,

music is part of each rite of passage, each celebration, each social event, and each moment of solemnity. Explorers and settlers from the 16th century to the 20th century wrote descriptions of Native American songs and dances, marking the frequency of musical activities, and noting that, often, a musical celebration would last an entire night. Journals also noted individuals respected within a specific tribe as outstanding singers or dancers, often expressing surprise that warriors and leaders such as Geronimo, Sitting Bull, and Quanah Parker were as famed within their own culture as musicians and creators of songs as much as they were for their leadership in war.

In most cultures, music was intimately connected with religion: it was the most important element in worship and in rituals such as the ceremonies of age-grade (peer group) societies and gambling games. Music was also used to accompany social dances, games, calendar rituals, and events in the life cycle. Music was also an essential part of healing rituals. Music evidently symbolized and personalized supernatural power: it was believed that spirits gave this power to human beings by teaching them songs, and individuals who were thought to have a supernatural association had a special relationship with music. As well as being an accompaniment to ceremonies, music was in many instances a form of prayer, and its presence was an important factor in religious experience. Music and performance were judged less by specifically musical crite-

Peyote meeting of Comanche Indians, c1923: Marcus Poco (center) and Chebahta (extreme right) hold gourd rattles; the body of the drum (left of center) is an iron pot and its skin is fastened by rawhide thongs wound around stones. (Roger Cunningham/Photo courtesy Research Division Oklahoma Historical Society)

ria than by how well they fulfilled religious and other functions and were effective in providing food, water, healing, and so on. Although most Native Americans had relatively simple material cultures and economic systems, each tribe had many varied ceremonies, public and private, which required songs, and native American song repertories often included thousands of items.

Music and dance are closely related in Native American cultures. Traditionally, most musical genres accompanied dances performed during communal ceremonies. These dances, many of which persist, are thought to unite members of the community with one another, with the spirits of their ancestors and with supernatural beings. Although each tribe has its distinctive style, Native American dances generally move in a circular pattern and feature a dignified style of frontal body movement. Often dance steps, hand gestures, and spatial designs have symbolic meaning linked to the ceremony. Depending on performance context and community practice, dance outfits range from everyday attire to intricately detailed costumes, head-dresses, and body paint. Often the dancers also sing and accompany themselves with hand-held rattles or sound-makers worn on their bodies or sewn on their outfits. The structure of the music usually reflects the structure of the dance. Dancers follow the beat of the rhythmic accompaniment, and the duration of a song is often determined by the time required for all the dancers to complete a full circuit of the dance ground.

Similarly, since most Native American poetry is sung, there is a close relationship between the structures of poems and songs. Song texts often use verbal structures that do not normally occur in the spoken language. One typical example is the Plains tribes' use of non-lexical syllables, which surround the meaningful text and are interpolated in it. In the Southwest, archaic words or words borrowed from neighboring tribes are often used in songs. Indeed a great many Native American songs have no lexical words, using instead vocables which may be defined as "meaningful syllables without direct translation"; in such songs, however, a fixed succession of syllables constitutes the poetic text. Peyote songs, for example, have a distinctive musical style and a repertory of fixed non-lexical syllables and syllable sequences that closely follow the rhythmic patterns of the melodies. The absence of lexical words, particularly in the songs of certain Plains tribes, may be connected with the relative lack of instrumental music; the songs fulfill both vocal and instrumental functions.

The relationship between music and language in Native American songs has not yet been fully investigated. There is some indication that syllabic and melodic elements coincide well, though not precisely, and that non-lexical syllables may be used to shift important words of the text to a rhythmically logical position. The Native Americans of the Southwest have elaborate poems set to music, in which the relationship between musical and textual lines is very close. In the Great Basin of Nevada, song forms such as *AABBCC* are accompanied by precisely the same textual forms. The content of these song texts varies from simple description of everyday events to symbolic and philosophical statements. However, in some Native American cultures, the words and music of a song are not inextricably bound; indeed, new words may be added to an existing melody and a new melody may be composed for an old text.

Formerly, Native Americans had few professional musical specialists or professional training of musicians in

Zuni musicians performing on wooden flute, pueblo cottonwood drum, and deer-toe rattles, Albuquerque. (Nativestock.com/Marilyn Angel Wynn)

the Western sense of these terms. Nevertheless, certain individuals in each group were regarded as superior performers or as the originators of music—composers in Western terms. Because of the close association of music with spirituality, the ritual specialist, shaman, or medicine man has usually been the person most involved with music. However, any member of the tribe may create new songs or dances, particularly social dances, or individual dances in which improvisation of music and dance is a central feature.

Historically, men have had a more public role in ceremonial life than women, leading earlier scholars to assume that music in Native American cultures is a largely male domain. Recent research has challenged that assumption, showing how the development of new performance contexts for traditional repertories has created new performance opportunities for women. Contemporary researchers have discovered that there have long been entire genres and styles of music and dance reserved for women, created by women, or created for women. Such music was often overlooked because Native Americans were reluctant to share women's music and dance with male researchers. Beginning in the 1960s, women have also played a central role in the development of syncretic popular music. Women have also begun to take roles in music formerly reserved for males. For example, there are now numerous drum groups that showcase women performers and compete in powwows and cultural fairs.

(iii) Geographical and cultural style areas. In certain respects, Native American culture appears homogeneous: its musical styles are broadly similar throughout the continent, as are its myths and religious practices, which show similarities to those of Central and South America. Recent examinations of traditional beliefs and literature have also shown links with Asian practices. In other respects, however, the Native American cultures as they were before the forced moves to reservations may be divided into distinct areas, coinciding with the physical divisions of the continent: the Eastern Woodlands (known as Eastern Sedentary in Canada and subdivided into northeast and southeast in the United States), the Plains, the Southwest and California, the Great Basin, the intermountain Plateau (largely in Nevada and Utah), the Northwest Coast, and the far North (subdivided into Western Subarctic and Arctic). These areas appear to have developed more or less independently for several centuries: each area had its own political and economic system, largely shaped by the exigencies of the natural environment.

Scholars have identified approximately 1000 tribal units, almost as many languages, and about 60 independent language families in North America. But the boundaries of the language groups did not at all coincide with the boundaries of the cultural areas, which shows that the cultural areas became defined fairly late in Native American history. There is substantial evidence that Native American cultures were influenced by cultures outside the North American borders. Traits from the cultures of Mexico and Central America, for instance, are found among the Indians of the Southwest, the Southeast, and the Northwest Coast; the Native Americans of the far North and the Inuit (Eskimo) share certain traditions with tribal groups of northeast Asia. Menzies theorizes additional contacts and influences from Asian cultures (including China) from the early 15th century.

(iv) Regional styles. A number of attempts have been made, by Roberts, Nettl, McAllester, and Burton, among others, to indicate the geographic distribution of musical styles in Native American culture. The main culture areas are the Plains, the Plateau, the East (subdivided into Northeast and Southeast), the Southwest (including California), the Great Basin, the Northwest Coast, and the North; the musical culture of the Plateau Indians—principally the Flathead and the Salish—shares traits with the cultures of the Plains and the Northwest Coast (respectively) and is not separately dealt with here. In general, stylistic boundaries tend to coincide with cultural boundaries though not necessarily with language groupings; the music of a culturally and geographically homogeneous group of tribes tends also to be homogeneous. Thus the greater cultural diversity in the western half of the country, resulting perhaps from its greater geographical diversity and the isolating effect of its mountain ranges, is reflected in its greater musical diversity.

The usefulness of these groupings is limited by the fact that although there are perhaps 1000 separate cultures or tribes, in the case of only about 100 is enough known to make reliable characterizations possible. Further difficulties arise because the music was collected at different times: one cannot productively compare a tribe whose music was recorded in the late 19th century with one whose repertory is known only from the 1950s, by which time intertribal contacts and Westernization may have effected substantial changes. Styles also have been affected by intermarriage between members of different cultures and the disruption of traditional cultural boundaries by the placement of Native Americans on reservations which were sometimes far from their original homeland and often shared with Native Americans from different tribes and culture groups. Further relocation efforts during the 1950s and 1960s may be seen as an attempt to dilute Native American identity and force a merger with mainstream American culture. Native Americans have also adopted musical styles and genres from Western popular music involving style, genre, and instrumentation. For example: Mohawk singer Murray Porter, who performs jazz and blues, uses a singing voice that closely remembers such African American singers as Louis Armstrong and Ray Charles. Given these influences, drawing an accurate map of cultural styles becomes an impossible task. The descriptions and discussions of regional styles below apply best to archival recordings and scholarly studies of ritual and ceremonial musics in which authenticity of style is of spiritual importance.

(a) The Plains. The best-known regional style is that of the Plains culture (including the Arapaho, Blackfoot, Kiowa, Pawnee, and Sioux tribes), whose territory extends from the Mississippi River to the Rocky Mountains; it is largely shared by some Plateau Indians, notably the Flathead. This style (ex.1) is characterized by descending (sometimes terraced) melodic lines, a predominance of pentatonic scales (using intervals

Map of North America showing the culture areas of Native Americans.

approximating major 2nds and minor 3rds), substantial use of hexatonic and tetratonic scales (with occasional use of other scales as well), and a harsh, pulsating vocal production. Among the differences between men's and women's singing is that men make use of dynamic pulsations, while women usually achieve a similar effect by slight changes in pitch. Forms are most frequently of the incomplete repetition type (e.g., *AABCDBCD*); and often material from the beginning of the song is repeated an octave lower at the end (*AABCBDC'B'CBDC'B'*). The words of the songs are often entirely or largely nonlexical, but if meaningful words are used they

Ex.1 Arapaho song, transcr. B. Nettl. Courtesy of Bruno Nettl

ö pulsated beats

appear at the beginning of the incomplete repetition (i.e., the second appearance of B in the first scheme given above). Drum and rattle accompaniment is usual, as elsewhere on the continent, but the Plains styles are distinguished by the use of slightly off-the-beat drumming, the drumstrokes sounding just before or after the beats of the melodic rhythm.

See ARAPAHO, BLACKFOOT (i), CROW, FLATHEAD, KIOWA, OMAHA (i), PAIUTE, PAWNEE, and SIOUX.

(b) The Eastern Woodlands. The music of tribes who live east of the Mississippi (e.g., the Cherokee, Choctaw, Creek, and Seminole of the Southeast; the Iroquois (Onondaga, Oneida, Cayuga, Mohawk, and Seneca) and Wabenaki (Penobscot and Passamaquoddy) of the Northeast; and the Ojibwe (or Chippewa) of the Great Lakes area) is in some ways similar to that of the Plains tribes. Descending melodic lines, a pulsating singing style, and the incomplete repetition form are common. The phraseology of their songs is more even and symmetrical; whereas Plains songs often consist of phrases of varying length and seem to have a blurred rhythmic structure, songs of the eastern tribes tend to have phrases of the same length and a readily distinguishable rhythm (ex.2). In addition, some tribes of the Southeast, as well as the Iroquois of the Northeast, may use antiphonal and responsorial singing, consisting of short, alternating phrases. A simple type of polyphony naturally arises from the overlapping of phrases that sometimes occurs in this technique. The singing style of the East is somewhat more relaxed, and singers do not use the high part of the register as regularly as do Plains singers. Percussion accompaniment coincides with the melodic rhythm. Scales are more frequently anhemitonic pentatonic, the tetratonic scales appearing less frequently than in Plains music.

Ex.2 Creek ballgame dance-song (Speck, 1911)

Generally speaking, the music of the Southeast appears to have been more complex than that of the Northeast, perhaps because the Southeast formerly had some relationship with the complex musical styles of native peoples from Mexico and Central America through extensive trade routes. The Northeastern tribes, largely Algonquian-speaking, are more closely related musically to the Native peoples of the Plains, perhaps because certain Plains tribes (e.g., Blackfoot, Cree, Arapaho) are also Algonquian-speaking. Some tribes in the Great Lakes region (e.g., the Winnebago and Menomini) have music very similar to that of the typical Plains tribes.

See CHEROKEE, CHOCTAW, CREEK, IROQUOIS, OJIBWE, SEMINOLE, and WABENAKI.

(c) The Southwest and California. The Indians of the Southwest exhibit great diversity in their cultures and languages. Notable among the area's inhabitants have been the Pueblo (including the Hopi, Zuni, Taos, and Tewa tribes), who created tiny city-states with the most complex societies to be found north of Mexico; the semi-nomadic Apache and Navajo, related to other Athapaskan-speaking tribes in western Canada, whence they probably migrated before 1500; and desert-dwelling tribes such as the Yuma, Pima, and Tohono O'odham (formerly Papago). These groups have had much cultural interchange, so that Yuman songs can be found in the Pima repertory and substantial Pueblo influences in Navajo music.

Pueblo music is the most complex and varied among Native Americans: lengthy melodies use a variety of pentatonic, hexatonic, and heptatonic scales, and many songs show the incomplete repetition principle. The large variety of Pueblo songs and styles is due to the complexity of the tribal religion, with its many-sided public and private ceremonial life. The singing style has vocal tension and pulsation, but, different from Plains music, the Pueblo sing in a low, growling voice. Melodic contours tend to be series of broad, sweeping, descending lines, though occasionally the terraced melodic descent prevalent in the Plains is used. The most complex music exists among the western groups, mainly in Arizona, including the Hopi and Zuni. The music of the eastern Pueblo, in New Mexico (e.g., the Taos), is somewhat simpler and more closely related to that of the Plains peoples (ex.3).

Ex.3 Laguna Pueblo corn-grinding song (Herzog, 1936)

◡ = note shortened by no more than 1/3 of value indicated
↑ = pitch slightly raised
↓ = pitch slightly lowered
small notes indicate dynamic weakness
parentheses indicate uncertainty as to pitch or duration

The music of the Navajo and Apache has several distinctive characteristics, in particular a singing style that is nasal, light, and relatively free of pulsations. The Navajo normally prefer the high vocal register, while the Apache sing in the middle of the vocal range. Both tend to use intervals approximating 3rds (more so than do other Indian cultures), which gives a triadic sound to their songs. The Navajo have some songs with a large range and others with a range of only a 5th. Apache songs generally have smaller ranges and less complex forms than those of the Navajo. It may be that Navajo music was once almost identical stylistically with that of the Apache, but that it became increasingly more complex (though using the same general principles), possibly through increased contact with the Pueblo Indians. Many forms in Navajo and Apache music consist of alternation between melodic elements at different pitch levels. Some Apache songs alternate two phrases, one slightly higher than the other but otherwise melodically related. At the other extreme, some Navajo songs consist of alternation between a low, repeated note and a flowing melody sung falsetto at a much higher pitch level. The rhythms in Navajo and Apache songs usually employ only two note values (notated in ex.4 as quarter- and eighth-notes).

Ex.4 *Gift-song from the Navajo Enemy Way ceremony (McAllester, 1954) Peabody Museum of Archaeology and Ethnology*

The third style found in the Southwest belongs to speakers of the Yuman language family, and is shared with at least some of the small tribal groups in southern and central California. It is characterized by a more relaxed singing style and in many cases a special melodic form, similar to that of the Navajo and Apache songs described earlier. A melodic unit (a phrase or a more complex tune built of several phrases) is repeated many times, occasionally interrupted by a slightly higher-pitched melody, resulting in such schemes as *AAAA-BAABABABAAABAAB*. Section B, the higher, is referred to among some Yuma as the "rise" (ex.5), and in dances it is accompanied by a raising of the hands.

Ex.5 *Yuma song, part of myth-telling (Herzog, 1928)*

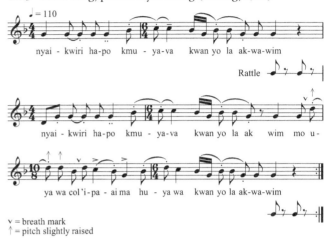

v = breath mark
↑ = pitch slightly raised

Throughout the Southwest, songs are set to intricate texts, often arranged strophically, whereas those of the Plains Indians frequently employ vocables, that is, meaningful syllables without direct translations. Flutes are among the most important melodic instruments in this area.

See APACHE *and* NAVAJO (Athapaskan groups); CAHUILLA, CHUMASH, DIEGUEÑO, HAVASUPAI, MAIDU, MOJAVE, PAIUTE, PIMA, POMO, SHASTA, TOHONO O'ODHAM, WINTUN, YAQUI, YOKUTS, *and* YUROK (California-Yuman); *and* HOPI, PICURIS, EASTERN PUEBLO, TAOS, TEWA, *and* ZUNI (Pueblo).

(d) The Great Basin. The desert plateau (Great Basin) region of Utah and Nevada, extending into Northern California, was inhabited by tribes who had simple hunting and gathering cultures (including the Paiute and the Shoshone). Their music was also relatively simple and consisted of short songs with small range sung in a vocal style substantially like that of the Plains but with less emphasis on the high register. Many of the songs were cast in a form that Herzog identified and called the "paired-phrase" pattern (ex.6): single, consecutive repetitions of each phrase occur in such combinations as *AABB* and *AABBCC*, or in the more complex (and perhaps Plains-related) *AABBCCBBCC*. Scales are typically tetratonic but sometimes pentatonic, using major 2nds and minor 3rds. The Great Basin style was the basis of the much more widespread Ghost

Ex.6 *Ute song (Herzog, 1935)*

Dance style, which was diffused throughout the Plains near the end of the 19th century.

See Paiute and Shoshone.

(e) The Northwest Coast. The music of the Native Americans of the Northwest Coast—in the United States the Nuu-chah-nulth (Nootka), or Makah, and Salish—is among the more complex styles in North America, as might be expected from their highly developed social and economic system and their achievements in wood sculpture and textile design. One possible reason for this flowering of the arts is the presumed contact with Mexican cultures, evidence for which is seen in some design motifs and musical instruments. Music of the Northwest Coast native peoples is characterized by the use of small intervals such as minor 2nds, a large variety of complex forms built from short phrases, and a frequently complex rhythmic accompaniment. Whereas the percussion rhythms in most Native American music rely on the repetition of a single note value (or sometimes the simple alternation of two, such as quarter- and eighth-notes, producing a 6/8 effect), some songs of the Northwest Coast have accompaniments with more complex structures (ex.7). These characteristics are also found to a lesser degree in the music of the Salish tribes, who live south of the main Northwest Coast culture area.

Ex.7 Drum rhythms found in Northwest Coast music

Ex.7a

Ex.7b

Ex.7c

See Nuu-chah-nulth and Coast salish.

(f) Arctic and Subarctic. The northernmost inhabitants of North America are the Inuit (Eskimo), living largely near the sea, and the northern Athapaskan- or Nadéné-speaking tribes who inhabit the inland area of Alaska and western Canada (e.g., the Dogrib, Kutchin, Slavey, and Tlingit). The music of the Athapaskan tribes is related to those of the Athapaskan-speaking Navajo and Apache but incorporates melodic contours and singing style akin to Plains practices.

Despite the substantial cultural and racial difference between Native Americans and the Inuit, Inuit music belongs stylistically with that of Native Americans. It is a music of considerable variety, including songs in a simple style consisting of short, repeated, and varied melodies of three or four notes. Other songs are more complex, using pentatonic scales with and without semitones; their melodic contours may have an undulating and arc-shaped form or a terraced descent reminiscent of Plains melodic types. The simplest Inuit

songs appear to have much in common with those of the Palaeo-Siberian groups in eastern Siberia, but in other respects Inuit music shows apparent Plains and Athapaskan relationships. The relatively complex rhythms sometimes found in Inuit drum accompaniments may stem in part from the practices of Northwest Coast tribes. In its use of pulsations on long notes, Inuit singing style has much in common with a large proportion of Native American culture.

See Inuit, Tlingit, and Canadian first peoples.

(g) Intertribal. During the 20th century, the intermingling of Native Americans from varied cultural groups at powwows, cultural fairs, and so on, as well as the impact of intermarriage, and Western influences led to an intertribal style (sometimes referred to as pan-Indian in earlier studies and publications). Characteristics of the Plains style form the core of intertribal music with elements of other styles integrated on a broad regional basis. Contemporary Powwow performances feature a mixture of traditional and intertribal styles.

(v) Musical instruments. Native Americans have a great variety of instruments, many of them used in a percussive role. The main melodic instruments are flutes; other melody-producing instruments, now known only from descriptions in the ethnographic literature, appear to have served mainly as drones. The Apache violin and other violin-like instruments are used primarily in the Southwest United States. In some cases, instruments are used purely for their tone-color; sometimes they imitate sounds of nature (e.g., animal cries and birdcalls) or suggest the voices of supernatural beings. Instruments of indeterminate pitch are often associated with ceremony and ritual, often as a background to singing. An example is the bullroarer, whose non-melodic sonorities serve both to accompany singing and to mesmerize when they help to induce the shaman's state of trance.

(a) Idiophones. The most widespread Native American instruments are those that vibrate when struck, shaken, rubbed, or plucked. Among the simplest are those that are rhythmically struck with sticks: boxes and poles have been used for this purpose on the Northwest Coast and by the Salish tribes; bark idiophones are found among the tribes of the north-east; baskets have been used similarly by the Yuma and Apache tribes of the Southwest and in Southern California; and turtle shells were once important rhythmic instruments in southern Mexico. Among the Plains Indians, a suspended piece of unmounted hide (technically a membranophone, not an idiophone) was beaten by several singers simultaneously; one might well regard this as an ancestor of the drum. (This instrument is more fully described under membranophones.) Finally, the "foot drum," a plank or log rhythmically stamped upon, was known in California, the extreme Southwest, and possibly also on the Northwest Coast.

Among the more complex idiophones, the log drum was evidently diffused from central Mexico to cultures on the West Coast of North America; in a simplified form (without a slit), it became an important instrument of the Northwest Coast tribes.

The most frequently used idiophone was the rattle, which still exists in innumerable forms; most prominent is the container rattle, essentially a handle and a closed container holding pebbles or seeds. Most, if not all, Native American cultures had some form of container rattle, but the materials used varied from area to area, and the different ceremonial uses in each tribe gave rise to a great regional variety of decoration. Many Native American rattles are art objects as well as sound-producing instruments.

The most widespread containers were gourds (found throughout the United States but particularly in the eastern half of the country) and leather spheres sewn from rawhide (used in the Plains). Basket rattles were used on the West Coast, coconuts in parts of the southeast, and cocoons in California. Turtle shells were used for container rattles in the Eastern Woodlands and the Southwest and horn in isolated spots throughout the country. After the coming of Europeans and the introduction of metal, bells (sleigh bells) came to be used as container rattles among some Apache groups and have since spread to other tribes, where they are sometimes worn on ceremonial costumes, enhancing the dance with rhythmic jingles.

The other important rattle, particularly in the West, is the suspension type, consisting of a series of perforated objects that are strung together and shaken. Among the objects used are deer-hooves (particularly in the Great Basin area of Nevada and Utah); rattles taken from rattlesnakes (in the Southeast and California); bird beaks, bones, and animal claws (on the Northwest Coast); animal shells (by the Pueblo of the Southwest); and, in more recent times, metal (in many different areas).

Finally, there are split-stick clappers, played in California and on the Northwest Coast, and the rasp, a notched stick placed on a basket or an inverted piece of pottery for resonance and scraped with another stick. The rasp is used in the Great Basin, the Plains, and in the area round the Gulf of Mexico. On the northeast coast of the United States and the Canadian maritime provinces, an instrument in which the wood is split in a fan-like pattern may be used to strike the palm of the hand or "strummed" to produce a rippling sound effect.

(b) Membranophones. Membranophones are, with idiophones, the only type of instrument widely used by Native Americans. Most widespread is the single-headed frame drum, held in one hand and struck with the other. Its one skin is attached to a frame typically about 12 to 24 inches in diameter, with four thongs (or sets of thongs) tied on the opposite side from the skin into a massive knot that is used as a handle for the instrument. This type of drum is found in the vast majority of Native cultures; the only important exception appears to be the California culture area. Contemporary Native Americans have begun to substitute artificial skins to create more durable and reliable instruments. Snare drum and bass drum heads such as used by US marching bands are employed by a number of performers, while the Orff Studio 49 hand drums, originally intended for educational use in music classrooms, have been observed in powwows and hand drumming competitions. A larger drum is used in social dances and powwow settings. This drum, often the size of a small bass drum, may be single- or double-headed and is typically suspended in a frame and played by multiple performers. The instrument, the players, and singers around it are referred to collectively as "The Drum" and strict protocols are observed in its playing. Modern drums may use artificial heads such as are used on Western bass drums.

Double-headed drums are found aboriginally in only a few places: isolated spots in the Great Lakes area, the Gulf Coast, the Great Basin, and New England. They may be of recent origin, influenced by European bass and snare drums. In any event, drums with two heads, particularly large drums capable of being beaten by several players, became widespread throughout the eastern two-thirds of the United States during the 20th century.

Water-drums held and beaten by one player are found in much of the United States, from the East Coast to the Plains. They are filled with water to permit tuning and to effect a distinct sonority. Among Apaches and Navajo, a coal is placed inside the drum to manipulate the tension through heating and cooling. Plains Native America employ the WATER-DRUM for the Peyote ritual. (*See* PEYOTE DRUM and PEYOTE RATTLE.)

Throughout the United States, drums are generally beaten with wooden sticks whose ends are sometimes padded with rawhide. The beating of drums with hands or fingers has been relatively uncommon and is restricted to a few tribes in the Great Basin and California.

(c) Chordophones. Chordophones were infrequently used among Native Americans. The only documented instruments are the TSII'EDO'A'TL (Apache violin or Navajo fiddle) and other violin-like instruments in the Southwest United States and northern Sonora, and the musical bow; scholars do not universally agree whether such instruments are truly indigenous or result from the influence of Western cultures.

Made of the century plant (agave) stalk, the Apache violin is used in social, ritual, and healing music of the Apache and related tribes in the Southwest. The instrument has one or two strings made of horsehair and played with a bow made from a thin branch of wood and horsehair. In most modern instruments, standard violin strings have been substituted for horsehair for the purpose of increasing sound projection. Because the Apache violin is made from a plant stalk, scholars have difficulty documenting the instrument prior to the 19th century. However, Apache musicians and instrument makers cite traditional beliefs that the instrument has been with them in perpetuity. Supporting this view are one-string box violins from Siberia that could be ancestors of the modern instrument. Best known among makers of the Apache violin include

Geronimo, Amos Gustina, and Chelsey Wilson. Instruments by these makers are found in museum collections throughout the Southwest as well as the Peabody and Smithsonian museums. Another single string violin is found among the Seri of northern Sonora.

The use of homemade violin-like instruments by the Yaqui, Tarahumara, Tohono O'odham, and related tribes is traced to the 16th century when Native Americans observed Spanish musicians playing in church services. Although these instruments are derived from Western models, the handmade nature of the instruments and their use in social and ceremonial functions is now a centuries-old Native American tradition. The instruments are irregularly shaped and strings are made from a variety of materials including animal gut, horsehair, baling wire, and discarded guitar strings. The violin is added to other instruments including Western-derived homemade harps and guitar-like instruments, rattles, rasps, and drum to form ensembles playing CHICKEN SCRATCH (waila) music. Contemporary musicians sometimes use commercially produced violins, guitars, and other chordophones, but often turn to handmade instruments, which feature a lower, flatter bridge, variable tunings, and against-the-chest playing position.

Other Western-derived fiddle traditions are found among the Metis and Micmac of Canada. The instruments are based on standard European violin and the repertoire combines Scottish fiddle tunes, French voyageur and folk songs, and Native American songs. Drums, rattles, and rasps are sometimes included as part of the fiddle band ensemble.

The musical bow was used by Native Americans prior to European contact, though this simple instrument is not substantially documented: its existence can be inferred only from reports, and hardly anything is known of its music. The musical bow appeared only in the Southwest, California, and (sporadically) the Great Basin. In most cases, it appears to have been a simple hunting bow, occasionally adapted to musical use. Among the Apache it was fitted with a resonator, and in California bows were sometimes built specifically for music. Information about the music produced on the musical bow is suggested by the music of certain Indian tribes in South America, where it has been used as a solo instrument or to accompany singing, normally with a range of two or three notes within an interval of a 4th.

(d) Aerophones. The most important melodic instrument is the flute, found in many different forms over much of the country, but especially in the West and South. Flutes are almost always solo instruments, though in some cultures, such as that of the Plains, the flute repertory appears to have consisted largely of music that could also be sung.

The most important materials used to make flutes have been wood, cane, or bark. Pottery flutes have been sporadically used in the Southwest, and bone flutes on the Northwest Coast, in California, and on the Plains. The number of finger-holes in flutes has varied from three to six. The majority of Native American flutes are end-blown, but there are also duct flutes, in which a hole is drilled into the side of the flute, a plug inserted, and the hole partly covered by a separate, often elaborately sculpted piece of wood that is tied to the instrument. Occasionally (in the Great Basin and among the Salish-speaking tribes of the plateau of Washington and Idaho), side-blown flutes have been used, and nose flutes appear to have been known in the Great Basin. Single-note bone and wood whistles were widely used, for musical and ritual purposes, in the West; in California, they were sometimes tied together in groups to form panpipes. Contemporary flute makers have produced instruments made from synthetic polymers, ceramics, crystal, and metal. Electronic adapters have been attached for performances in large venues.

Multi-tubed whistle flutes are also found in the Northwest Coast cultures. Bone flutes, either without finger-holes or having up to six, were used as a courting instrument in Plateau cultures and have also been located in archaeological sites in Newfoundland. Whistles made out of quills or goose feathers had ceremonial uses in the Inuit cultures of Baker Lake and the Mackenzie Delta. The willow flute, with one to six finger-holes, occurred in cultures as widely separated as the Mi'kmaq (Mi'kmaw; Micmac), Nlaka'pamux (Thompson), Caribou Inuit, and the Slavey. The most distinctive type is the vertical whistle flute with a sliding external block and gasket to cover the tone-hole. In Canada this instrument was used by Eastern woodlands groups, both nomadic and sedentary, in the Northern Plains, the Plateau, and some of the Northwest Coast cultures. It uses a whistle mechanism to produce the sound, with the "block" (also referred to as saddle, bird, or rider) forming the windway for the air located on the outside of the flute. It may vary in length (13 to 33 inches) and diameter (0.75 to 2 inches). Its mouth end may be blunt, tapered, or a small tube. Many examples are beautifully carved from wood and decorated with leather, beading, or feathers. Usually there are six open finger-holes but both the literature and examples found in museums indicate that these varied from four to seven holes. The ideal flute was one that produced a full, vibrating sound when all of the holes were closed. Its main traditional use was as a courting instrument by young men, but it could also be used for signaling in wars. (*See also* NATIVE AMERICAN FLUTE.)

Reeds have occasionally been used for producing sound, and there have been trumpets of various sorts—gourd, shell, wood, and bark. Little is known about these instruments, but they appear to have been used ceremonially and to have played only single notes. In the Maritime provinces of Canada and the Northeastern United States, a trumpet-like instrument made from birch bark was used primarily in hunting, perhaps as an animal call. This instrument resembled a small megaphone and was played by buzzing the lips using the small end of the "megaphone" as a trumpet mouthpiece.

The bullroarer consists of a flat piece of bone or wood with serrated edges, which is attached to a string or rawhide thong and whirled rapidly through the air. It has been used most widely in the West, extending eastwards into the Plains. Shamans used the bullroarer when seeking to control the weather (as in the Great Basin area of Nevada and Utah) or to invoke a trance; sometimes it was a signal for the assembly of the tribe, and in recent times it has been a toy. A similar instrument, the bone buzzer, consists of a rounded piece of bone with holes; two pieces of twined string are attached and as they are pulled apart the buzzer rotates rapidly, producing a low, whining sound. Similar to both the bullroarer and bone buzzer is the bird roarer, which may be made from wood or bone with notches and slits in the body of the instrument to produce a bird-like chirping sound when the instrument is whirled through the air.

Native Americans along the Gulf of Mexico, as well as in Mexico and the Caribbean, used shells as trumpet-like instruments. The end of a large shell, such as the conch shell, is cut open to produce a hole to be used as a mouthpiece. Occasionally, other holes would be drilled so several pitches could be produced. These instruments were used primarily for signaling and in ritual music. Cowhorn whistles and gourd ocarinas were used by Iroquois nations.

(vi) Composition, learning, and rehearsing. Native American attitudes to musical composition contrast with those found in other cultures. Generally speaking, human beings were not considered to be the active originators of music, but rather the recipients of music imparted to the tribe by spirit beings, either through dreams and visitations or, more directly, at the legendary time of the tribe's origin. Plains tribes, for example, believed that songs could come to a tribe either through its members' visions or as borrowings from other tribes, although a few songs are traditionally thought to have been with the tribe from its beginning. The Pima, according to George Herzog, seem to think of songs as having an independent existence, and a person to whom a song appears in a dream is said to have "unraveled" the song. Many Native Americans believe that music exists all around and melodies are "caught" by individuals. Thus, those who Western culture would label as composers are frequently called songcatchers. Zuni musician and dancer Fernando Cellicion refers to the composition process as "remembering" a song from its creation at the beginning of time. Other Native American cultures believe that a song is made from the elements provided by the Creator and nature. Contemporary Apache instrument maker and performer Chesley Wilson explains that he makes songs and credits earlier songmakers for traditional repertoire.

Song learning is accomplished by rote, and the accuracy with which it is done reflects the degree of the culture's interest in precise reproduction. On the Northwest Coast, for example, and among the Navajo of the Southwest, a single lapse in accuracy of performance may invalidate a ritual, so a fairly stable tradition can be assumed. The Plains tribes, by contrast, do not expect great precision, so that one might expect that their songs have changed substantially over a period of time. The idea of learning songs from human beings is related to that of learning songs from guardian spirits in dreams or visions; in the latter case, a visionary was thought to be able to learn a song in a single hearing, and Native Americans have maintained that they are able to learn a song very rapidly, perhaps after having heard it only once, even where visions are not involved. Rehearsing of songs is found in a few cultures, such as those of the Northwest Coast or Pueblos; generally, however, systematic musicianship is unusual. During the late 20th century, culture camps were developed by a number of southwestern and Plains tribes in which young children, particularly those living away from the reservation, gather to learn songs, dances, instrument making and performance, and other skills from master musicians.

Native Americans have developed several different modes of communicating about music, most of which involve gestural and cosmological systems rather than musical notation. However, some tribes have developed graphic notations as mnemonic aids, for example, song-counting sticks of Osage singers, roll-call canes of the Cayuga Condolence Council ritual, and Ojibwa birch-bark rolls or music boards. Among some Native Americans, markings on instruments provide aids to recalling a particular song or set of songs.

Native Americans believe that the best way to learn and appreciate music is through direct experience, and traditionally most singers do not verbalize about music theory. In fact, almost all theoretical writing and terminology about Native American music has been the product of Western ethnomusicologists. Nevertheless, clearly formed musical thought, values, aesthetics, and concepts of musicianship underlie all Native American performances, and compositional guidelines as well as details of form and design are articulated by experienced musicians. The ability to perceive melodic difference and to distinguish hundreds of songs within a stylistically homogenous and sometimes narrow repertory is highly developed. Typical of respected tribal musicians of all Nations, Wilson has a memorized repertoire of over 1000 songs and dances for use in specific ceremonies and social occasions. In repertories of recent origin, such as intertribal music, names for sections within a song form and for types of drumbeat are common.

(vii) Developments after European contact. Native American musics, like all other musical traditions, have continually changed, reflecting native concepts of history and underlying attitudes toward change itself. Many groups believe that history proceeds along a recursive spiraling path rather than a linear chronology. Therefore, Native Americans tend to adapt historic repertories to new social realities, blending older styles with fresh components and merging the genres of one community with those of another. Western influence has sometimes resulted in more abrupt musical change.

Entire tribes were obliterated through disease and war brought by contact with Europeans. Conversion to Christianity and the Westernization of native social and economic patterns prompted the adoption of new repertories and the creation of new performance contexts. In the 20th and 21st centuries, tourism has also played a significant role in the development of Native American music and dance. Through adaptation, blending, and merging, Native Americans have adapted European musical values, styles, and instruments to enrich and diversify their own traditions.

(a) Early influences. The first substantial contact that Native peoples had with European music occurred in Mexico and the southwestern United States as early as the late 15th and early 16th centuries with the arrival of missionaries (sacred) and explorers (secular). The first mass was sung in Mexico City (Tenochtitlán) in 1521 with musical training in performance, composition, and instrument making established in the Tiripitio monastery by 1533. Also in the 16th century, Taqui and Tarahumara Native Americans observed violins used in religious services in northern Sonora and began hand crafting violins, harps, and guitars that were used in a unique syncretic music. Similar patterns continued in the southwestern United States. One description tells of an early 17th-century incident in which friars taught the Pueblo Indians to sing and to play instruments; a Navajo chief came to visit the Santa Clara Pueblo, and the friars, who wished to convert him to Christianity, had bells rung and trumpets and shawms played, which evidently impressed him greatly.

Throughout the continent, the teaching of Western church music to Native Americans was a major missionary activity. Nevertheless, Native Americans usually maintained a separation between their knowledge of Western music and their traditional music. Until the late 20th century, they did not develop the kinds of mixed styles that arose in Africa, in black cultures of the New World, in India, and in the Middle East. This lengthy stylistic separatism is probably due to the great differences between the Native American styles and those of the European music known to them.

The greatest degree of integration occurred in the Southwest, where Spanish became a common language. The Pueblo have many rituals of Hispanic origin that exist side by side with their Amerindian traditions. An example is the Tewa Pueblo MATACHINES dance, which has acquired a respected place in Pueblo ceremonial repertories. Some of the tunes are European in origin, with guitar and rattle accompaniment, but some are probably of Native American origin. Pueblo music, with its variety of scales and melodic forms, evidently lent itself better to the creation of mixed styles than did other North American styles.

During the 19th century, Native American schools, both tribal and governmental, created curricula giving music a prominent role in the daily life of the school. During the 1840s and 1850s, both instrumental and vocal music instruction were offered through the Indian Territory (Oklahoma and parts of Kansas). Instrumental

and vocal ensembles primarily Western-style works, but programs included arrangements of Native American melodies (in a Western style). "Indian" bands were featured at performances throughout the Midwest including the St. Louis World's Fair.

(b) Peyote music. The peyote cactus, whose buttons are chewed for hallucinogenic effect, was the basis of a religious cult in central Mexico several centuries ago. By the early 18th century, the cult had penetrated to the southwestern United States, where it was practiced by the Apache. After that time, it spread to many tribes, particularly those of the Plains and the West, bringing with it a special religious cult and a peculiar musical style. By the middle of the 20th century the Peyote religion—officially the Native American Church, with headquarters in Washington, DC—was the most important religious movement among Native Americans, and Peyote music perhaps their most prominent musical style.

Peyote meetings consist largely of singing, and Peyote songs may be sung outside the religious context. The tenor of the religion is conciliation with non-Native Americans, and it has Christian overtones. The rapid spread of the religion has given many tribes a new musical style and repertory, which have accompanied or sometimes supplanted older traditions. This religious and musical phenomenon is primarily a result of modernization, arising from the greater need for mutual support and friendly contact among Native Americans facing the problems resulting from Westernization.

The style of Peyote music probably derives from Apache and Navajo styles. It has long tunes made up of short phrases, frequently using a single main rhythmic motif and closing with a standardized final formula (ex.8). The form is frequently the incomplete repetition form of the Plains. The melodic contour may be undulating or descending in the terraced fashion common in Plains music. The singing style is more relaxed and gentler in tone than Plains singing and, indeed, is different from all other known Native American singing styles. Contemporary Peyote music singers, such as Primeaux and Mike, often add a second melodic line, creating a sound reminiscent of Christian plainsong. The tempo is quick, and the accompaniment uses a gourd rattle and a small kettledrum partly filled with water. The texts are frequently non-lexical but use characteristic configurations of syllables such as 'he yo wi ci na yo' or 'he ne yo wi ci ne'. Such syllabic combinations are employed by all Amerindian tribes using the Peyote ceremony and are thought by each tribe to have originated in another. Occasionally words in the Amerindian vernacular are used and sometimes English words with Christian content as well.

See PEYOTE DRUM and PEYOTE RATTLE.

(c) The Ghost Dance. In contrast with the Peyote religion, which has a history of several centuries and finally became a movement of reconciliation with

Ex.8 Comanche Peyote song (McAllester, 1949)

⌣ = note shortened by no more than 1/3 of value indicated
↑ = pitch slightly raised
↓ = pitch slightly lowered

(d) New Native American musics. In addition to adapting Christian hymnody and developing pan-tribal styles such as the Ghost Dance and Peyote music, Native Americans have adopted styles and repertories from other American ethnic groups. Many tribes in the Northeastern United States and Maritime provinces of Canada have developed fiddle traditions based on those introduced by their European neighbors in the 18th and 19th centuries, while Southwestern Native Americans continue to transform the popular "chicken scratch" (waila) music. Native composers and performers participate in the full range of popular idioms, including rock and roll, folk rock, jazz, gospel, and country and western music.

Contemporary bands such as Xit and KEITH SECOLA's Wild Band of Indians write song lyrics that comment on current sociopolitical concerns and issues, or reflect the realities of contemporary Native American life. Individual performers, including singer BUFFY SAINTE-MARIE and saxophonist JIM PEPPER, achieved renown in mainstream circles. The vocal group ULALI has explored inter-ethnic musical and historical connections by combining southeastern Native song genres, English lyrics, and African American vocal harmonies. WALELA, formed by Rita Coolidge, a popular rock singer of the 1970s, has combined Cherokee music with gospel and blues. The Plains courting flute has become an icon of the New Age movement through the success of figures such as R. CARLOS NAKAI and ROBERT TREE CODY. The newest generation of Native American popular musicians includes Derek Miller, Susie Morningstar, Annie Humphrey, and Red Thunder. To recognize musical achievement among Native Americans across many musical genres, the Native American Musicians Association created the Native American Music Awards (NAMMYS) in 1998.

See also ALTERNATIVE MUSIC and NATIVE AMERICAN POPULAR MUSIC.

Since the 19th century, Native Americans have also composed in European genres using European notation. Thomas Commuck (1805–55), of the Narragansett tribe, wrote and published a collection of 120 hymns for the Methodist Episcopal Church in 1845. More recent Native American composers include Jack Kilpatrick (Cherokee), LOUIS BALLARD (Cherokee-Quapaw) and BRENT MICHAEL DAVIDS (Mohican). Davids, who has been commissioned by the Joffrey Ballet, the Kronos Quartet, and the National Symphony Orchestra, composes music that draws on images and concepts from contemporary Native American life and also incorporates musical instruments and instruments of his own design into the European symphony orchestra, string quartet, and other traditional ensembles. Nakai and Secola have composed television and motion pictures scores, and Nakai has teamed with non-Native American composer James Demars to compose a series of works for Native American flute and orchestra. Other contemporary Native American composers, including GEORGE QUINCY (Choctaw), JEROD IMPICHCHAACHAAHA' TATE (Chickasha), and Steven Alveraz (Apache), create works that combine traditional themes and instruments with Western orchestral traditions.

non-Native Americans, the GHOST DANCE was cultivated for only a short time, representing a final attempt by some Native Americans to rid themselves of the effects of Westernization. Like the Peyote religion, its practice became an intertribal movement and gave rise to a peculiar musical style that was adopted by various tribes and provided diversification. It began in 1870 among the Paiute of western Nevada and spread rapidly during the 1880s, particularly among the Sioux, culminating in the "Sioux Outbreak" of 1890, after which it was outlawed. The musical style that accompanied it was derived from that of the Great Basin of Nevada, whence the movement came, and consisted of relatively simple songs with a small melodic range and a characteristic form in which each phrase was repeated (e.g., *AABB, AABBCC,* or *AABBCCAABB*). The phrases are short and unequal, and the singing style relatively tense and pulsating. The Ghost Dance was revived during the 1970s as part of civil rights activism of such groups as the American Indian Movement. Contemporary Ghost dance practice has neither the influence nor significance of the 19th-century movement, and few new songs have been added to the repertoire.

(viii) Research. Native American music has been much studied by American scholars because many groups have been readily accessible and because most Native Americans have been able to speak English for several generations. Other causes have included the growth of American musical nationalism during the late 19th and early 20th centuries and the growing interest of Americans in the cultures of minority groups. More recently, Native American operated schools, museums, and tribal centers have actively promoted a renaissance of cultural traditions including music. Profits from tribally owned casinos have provided funding for not only these efforts but also to sponsor performances, offer grants for the study of Native American culture, and commission compositions (often film scores for Native American produced motion pictures).

Scholars have published transcriptions of Native American songs in Western notation, comparative studies covering the entire continent, monographs on individual tribal styles, and investigations of special historical and theoretical topics. Among the most enterprising and distinguished have been Frances Densmore, who recorded, transcribed, and published songs of many tribes for the Bureau of American Ethnology; Alice C. Fletcher, Theodore Baker, and Benjamin Ives Gilman, who were early pioneers in this field; Willard Rhodes, who made large numbers of recordings and published a number of studies; David P. McAllester, whose work focused mainly on music of the Southwest, especially the Navajo tribe; Gertrude P. Kurath, who made significant contributions in the area of Native American dance; Alan P. Merriam, who in his monograph on the music of the Flathead tribe gave equal attention to the anthropological and structural aspects of their music; and Bruno Nettl, whose work on Blackfoot music and ritual drew on ethnohistory and mythology as well as contemporary fieldwork. Nettl is also known for his contributions to mapping the musical areas of the Native Americans (1954). The ethnomusicologists Hornbostel, Stumpf, and Otto Abraham, and the anthropologist Franz Boas, though their main work lay elsewhere, also made important contributions to the study of Native American music.

Scholars of the next generation include Charlotte Frisbie, who has focused on the Navajo; Leanne Hinton, who has studied Havasupai music and language; William Powers, Orin Hatton, and Tara Browner, who have emphasized the Plains region; Thomas Vennum, whose work centers on the Ojibwa; Richard Keeling, who has focused on Northern California; Judith Vander, who has studied Shoshone music and the Ghost Dance; Charlotte Heth, Marcia Herndon, David Draper, and Victoria Lindsay Levine, who have focused on the Southeastern region; Richard Haefer and Brenda Romero, whose work emphasizes the Southwest; Virginia Giglio, who has worked with southern Cheyenne singers; Beverly Diamond, whose work focuses on Native Americans of Canada and eastern North American, and who has written arguably the most comprehensive text on Native American instruments; and Bryan Burton, who has researched Western Apache music traditions, the Native American flute, and Native American popular music.

While 20th-century Native American music is fairly well known, scholars have only recently begun to develop methods to research its earlier history. Some tribes used graphic notations, but these were not widespread, and tended to convey information about song texts, and their number and sequence in ceremonies, rather than melodies or rhythm. Archaeology has not contributed greatly to music research as most Native American musical instruments were made from natural materials subject to deterioration. Scholars interested in historical processes have often worked with ethnohistorical materials, sacred narratives, and oral history, combined with what is known of the movements of tribes and the geographic distribution of stylistic features. Therefore, most scholars have concentrated on the period since 1890, when sound recording began. Extensive collections of recordings have been deposited at various archives—notably the Library of Congress (Washington, DC) and the Archives of Traditional Music, Indiana University (Bloomington). Many historic and contemporary recordings are available commercially from the Library of Congress Archive of American Folk Culture, Smithsonian/Folkways Recordings, Indian House and Canyon Records.

2. DANCE.

(i) Introduction. Native American dances embody and dramatize core spiritual, social, and cultural values through organized, patterned movement accompanied by music. Regional ecologies, numerous distinctive tribal languages, and individual or collective creativity have produced marked differences in Native American dance styles; this diversity is reflected in dance terminology, which includes many tribe-specific terms in Native languages as well as English and, in the Southwest, Spanish. Little historical documentation exists for Native American dance prior to contact with Europeans, although archaeological evidence suggests that genres such as Pueblo *kachina* dances and Eastern Woodlands stomp dances have existed for at least 800 years. This deep history is corroborated through tribal origin narratives and oral histories. European explorers and missionaries left written descriptions of Native dance that reveal historical continuity in many genres as well as adaptations and innovations through time. Despite oppressive efforts by the US and Canadian governments to suppress Native dance through legal bans as well as assimilationist policies, particularly from the late 19th through the mid-20th century, Native people throughout North America continue to perform traditional dances, which have been fundamental to their cultural survival as well as the preservation and ongoing renewal of their unique identities.

(ii) Social contexts. Native Americans perform traditional dances in the context of collective, communal ceremonies that seek healing, mark the passage of seasons, or celebrate life cycle events. A strict division

Members of Comanche tribe perform War Dance, Inter-Tribal Indian Ceremony, Gallup, New Mexico. (Haga Library/Lebrecht Music & Arts)

between sacred and secular is not part of the traditional Native North American world view. Therefore, although most communities categorize dances as either sacred or social, both of these categories may be performed in ceremonial contexts at ritually prepared dance grounds. Sacred dances are often performed by separate groups of either men or women during the daytime, while social dances are mixed and take place at night. Following colonization, some Native peoples indigenized ceremonial dances of European origin, augmenting their traditional repertories through the creation of innovative hybrid genres. In addition, since the early 20th century, Native people have developed new social contexts for the performance of traditional dance, focused on general affirmation of tribal and intertribal Indian identities rather than on specific ceremonies. Native communities thus sustain a rich variety of social contexts for the performance of traditional dance, and Native dance events occur every week throughout the year in both rural and urban communities. Some dances are open to community members only, but outsiders are welcome at many events, as long as they conform to Native ceremonial etiquette.

Curing ceremonies focus on a particular patient but involve as many as several hundred participants from a given community. Spiritual healing is the main goal of these ceremonies; the patient derives a sense of wellbeing from all of the relatives and friends who attend the event to offer their prayers and support. Therefore, the social functions of the ceremony, including dance, play an integral role in the healing process. Examples include the Navajo Nightway and Enemyway ceremonies. On the ninth night of the Nightway, which may be performed during the winter months, teams of 14 dancers each impersonate *ye'i* or spirit beings. The dancers represent the presence of the *yeis* at the ceremony and

help to bring their healing power to the patient. They wear hide masks and dance in a double file, shaking gourd rattles while singing intricate *yeibichai* songs. At the conclusion of the dancing, the patient's family gives a special gift to the dance team that has presented the most impressive performance in terms of outfits, singing, and dance. On the second and third nights of the Enemyway, which may be performed during the summer months, participants perform social dances such as the Two-Step and Skip Dance. These are couples dances in which ladies choose their partners; the man and woman dance side by side, sometimes with a blanket draped over them. The Two-Step involves a trotting step with lifted feet, while the Skip Dance features a skipping step. At the conclusion of the dance, the man pays his partner a token coin to represent goods obtained through a raid; this is a symbolic reference to the sacred narrative dramatized by the Enemyway as a whole.

Ceremonies that mark the passage of seasons celebrate the first ripening of wild fruits, as in the Ute Bear Dance. In addition, seasonal ceremonies may invoke spiritual assistance or give thanks for the agricultural cycle, observe the winter and summer solstices, or honor game animals during hunting season. Pueblo peoples of New Mexico celebrate each phase of the agricultural cycle, from the preparation of irrigation ditches through the growth, maturity, and harvest of the crops. Ceremonies associated with agriculture are also widely practiced among Eastern Woodlands tribes. The Seminole, Creek, Cherokee, Yuchi, and some other Southeastern peoples perform the Green Corn ceremony during the summer growing season. Some daytime dances performed during the Green Corn ceremony include the Feather Dance, performed only by men, and the Ribbon Dance, performed only by women.

Hopi Indians performing Antelope Dance, c1920. (Library of Congress, Prints & Photographs Division, LC-USZ62-102175, J246061 U.S. Copyright Office, No. 86.)

Stomp Dances belong to the nighttime part of the event and include men and women dancing together. (*See* STOMP DANCE.) In the Northeast, Haudenosaunee women perform summer ceremonies to honor their staple foods: corn, beans, and squash. For example, the society of women planters welcomes the growing season with round dances, while they perform the Women's Shuffle Dance at harvest festivals.

Seasonal ceremonies often include ritual elements that affirm relationships between humans and other beings; therefore, these events may feature specialty dances designed to honor and give thanks to animals and plants that provide for the needs of human life. Some of these dances involve mimesis, such as the Ojibwe and Menomini Fish Dance in which men imitate fish by flapping their hands like fins, or the Eastern Cherokee Bear Dance, in which men and women imitate bears while dancing in a circle. Men and women tread heavily in the Cherokee and Haudenosaunee Buffalo Dance, whereas in the Yuchi Buffalo Dance, men lean on sticks to simulate walking on four legs. The Pueblo tribes perform many variants on the Buffalo Dance. In some versions, two men disguised with buffalo heads dance with one or two buffalo maidens, or there may be double files of buffalo men and women. In other versions, a large assembly of dancers dressed as game animals, including elk, mountain sheep, buffalo, and deer, all wear appropriate antlers and lean on sticks to enhance the realism of their movements. Native Americans perform many kinds of Deer Dances, including the version performed by the Yaqui of southern Arizona and northern Mexico. Other animal dances honor small game, such as rabbits, as well as several bird species. In the Pueblo Eagle Dance, a pair of dancers wearing feathered wings on their arms circle, swoop,

and hop, imitating the eagle's soaring flight. Women imitating swans or wild geese sway and flap their arms in performances by Great Lakes tribes who live on the migration routes of these birds. Among the Eastern Woodlands tribes, the Robin Dance, Duck Dance, and Passenger Pigeon Dance are entertaining social dances performed during the nighttime portion of seasonal ceremonies.

Life cycle ceremonies, also known as rites of passage, articulate transitions in a person's life from one social status to another through a symbolic enactment of transformation. Dance figures prominently in life cycle ceremonies; for example, the Mescalero Apache girl's puberty or Sunrise ceremony incorporates several genres of dance. The girl at the center of the ceremony dances for many hours over the four-day event, in a demonstration of her physical and spiritual preparedness to become a mother of her people. While much of the ritual dancing takes place in private, public genres include Mountain God dances and social dances. The Mountain God dancers perform at night, using a trotting step as they perform a series of dips while circling the central fire. Each dancer personifies a Mountain Spirit, who brings blessings and spiritual protection to the girl undergoing the ceremony. As the Mountain Gods dance, women from the community dance in support of them. Social dancing takes place late at night, after the Mountain Gods have completed their performance. In addition to Apache ceremonial dances, powwow dancing may take place in an adjacent area throughout the duration of the girl's puberty ceremony.

Some tribes have adapted European dances, creating hybrid genres that fuse Native and non-Native steps, forms, and symbolism. For example, in 1881 the Salish of Puget Sound introduced other northwestern tribes to the Shaker Church, a Christian sect that practiced an ecstatic round dance. Some two centuries earlier, Catholic missionaries introduced a dance-drama to the Yaqui and Pueblos that became the MATACHINES dance. *Matachines* dances differ from indigenous dances in that they are accompanied by guitars and fiddles, using tunes that resemble European dance music. The exception is Santa Clara Pueblo, where the accompaniment for *Matachines* dances is provided by singers and drum. The choreography includes Native stomping steps with European dances such as the polka and *pas de basque*. Although the *Matachines* dance represents a blending of Native American and European elements, it constitutes a genre of traditional dance among the peoples who perform it. Often it is a Christmas pageant in New Mexico and part of Catholic feast days among the Yaqui, where the *Matachines* represent soldiers of the Virgin Mary. Other examples of hybrid genres include Yaqui Easter fiestas, in which the *pascola* dance, accompanied by a flute and drum, symbolizes the blending of Native and Spanish spiritual and cultural elements.

Native Americans began to develop new social contexts for the performance of traditional dance in the early 20th century. These include performances at fairs, non-ceremonial community celebrations, folkloric demonstrations, and commercial shows. However, powwows are the best-known and most widespread example. Based on older ceremonial dances conducted by men's warrior societies among the Plains tribes, the powwow emerged during the late 19th century and became widely popular throughout Native North America by the 1950s. The focal point of powwows is the War Dance. For men, the War Dance demonstrates physical prowess, while for women, the dance demonstrates agility and grace. Older men tend to dance in the dignified Men's Traditional style, in which the dancer holds his back straight and flexes his arms close to his torso, subtly tilting his shoulders and turning his head as he progresses around the dance circle with a slow double step. Younger men and boys may perform the Men's Fancy or Grass Dance styles, in which the performer can twist and flex his torso, bob his head vigorously, cross or twist his feet, or twirl in place. Women's Traditional dancers circulate around the arena singly or in groups of twos, threes, or fours, moving with a graceful step-bend. Alternatively, Women's Traditional dancers may bend their knees rhythmically while standing in place. Younger women and girls in Fancy Shawl or Jingle Dress regalia employ a more energetic style of movement with spins, turns, and athletic footwork. Each dancer improvises combinations of his or her favorite steps, but all movements must be in time with the drumbeat and end exactly on the last beat and last note of the song.

In addition to War Dances, social dances and exhibition dances are usually performed during powwows. Social dances include the Two-Step (also called Rabbit Dance or Owl Dance), Round Dance, Snake Dance, and Buffalo Dance. The Two-Step is a partners dance in which the couple holds hands in the skater's position.

In the Round Dance, participants dance in a clockwise circle, stepping sideways and sometimes holding hands. The Snake Dance is a follow-the-leader dance with a running step. The leader guides the line of dancers in a counterclockwise direction, then meanders, winds into a spiral, unwinds, and continues to meander. Several variants can be performed on this basic pattern. To represent the snake sloughing its skin, the first two dancers in line may form an arch by holding up their arms for the other dancers to pass through; subsequent pairs join the arch after passing through it, creating a progressively longer tunnel for dancers who are farther back in the line. The Snake Dance may be followed by the Buffalo Dance, where dancers mime the movements of bison. The most popular exhibition dance is the Hoop Dance, in which a performer dances with several hoops, stepping through them and passing them over his or her body to create complex shapes. Another social dance, the Forty-Nine, takes place late at night after the powwow has ended. In this dance, which is mainly for young people, participants dance in concentric circles around the singers.

Humor plays an integral role in American Indian dance events, in public jokes told by a master of ceremonies, in more private interactions among family and friends, and in the performance of dancers known in English as clowns. Operating through symbolic reversals, ceremonial clowns reinforce social expectations by displaying incorrect behavior. Humor lifts the spirits of ceremonial participants who strive to maintain a

Johnson Jimerson of the Seneca Nation performs Smoke Dance, New York State Fair, 2010. (NICHOLAS LISI/The Post-Standard/Landov)

cheerful, cooperative attitude throughout physically and emotionally demanding events in order to preserve the social harmony necessary to achieve a positive outcome. Among the Onondaga of New York, clowns wearing masks made of corn husks parody their own sacred ceremonies, evoking awe as well as laughter. Among the Pueblo peoples of the Southwest, ritual clowns parody the behavior of outsiders including mainstream pop stars as well as certain ethnic groups as a whole, such as Anglo-Americans and other Native peoples.

(iii) Choreography and music. Dance and music are strongly interconnected for Native Americans. In Native languages, the same word may refer to both music and dance, and typically, many different songs in one category bear the same generic title of the dance they accompany. Each tribe has its own distinctive choreographies, but common features include a dignified, elastic style of frontal body movement, a slightly downward gaze, knee flexion, and agile footwork. Posture is usually erect or slightly bent forward from the waist. For the most part, dancers use a relatively narrow range of motion in the arms, hands, shoulders, and head. Torso movements may be more expressive than arm gestures in some dances. For example, male powwow dancers tilt their heads and twist, flex, and bend their torsos in time with the drum beat. Perhaps most importantly, Native American dancers remain close to the earth, avoiding large leaps and acrobatics, in part to express respect for and a profound spiritual connection to the earth, and in part to maintain the stamina required for dancing outdoors all day or throughout the night.

Directionality and repetition play an important role in Native American choreographies. In many cases, sets of movements must be repeated four times to express cultural concepts of balance and completion. For example, Pueblo peoples emphasize their sacred number four by repeating a dance four times, once in each of the cardinal directions, over the course of one day. This pattern also governs rain and animal dances, which are performed in the Pueblo's central plaza. Southeastern peoples dance counterclockwise, which is the metaphorical direction of spiritual growth in Eastern Woodland thought. The cardinal directions guide practices of the Plains and western Great lakes tribes, but the direction is clockwise—east, south, west, and north—the customary ritual direction for these peoples. Repetition and directionality in Native American dance embody traditional concepts of time and space through the physical, kinesthetic representation of cyclic recurrence and emplacement. In addition, since community members evaluate traditional dances primarily on the level of participation, repetition in choreography enables everyone present to join the performance, regardless of prior knowledge or experience.

Most traditional dances move in a circle, symbolizing cultural metaphors for continuity, wholeness, and unity. In many cases, the spatial arrangement of the dance ground itself is conceptualized as a series of concentric circles. For example, Native Southeastern peoples build a sacred fire at the center of the ceremonial ground; dancers spiral around the fire and men's ceremonial arbors mark the cardinal directions on three sides of the ground. Those who are not dancing sit on folding chairs on a berm that articulates the ground's periphery; a dirt road rings the ground, and family camps surround the road. Similarly, Lakota powwow spaces are organized as concentric circles, with dancers at the center, surrounded by drum groups. Audience members sit on folding chairs on the periphery of the dance area, and vendors set up stalls in the ring beyond. Some Native people feel the presence of spirit beings at traditional dances, who may make their presence known either at the center or the outermost circle of the dance ground.

A fundamental dance step throughout Native North America is known by the English term "stomp." It features a shuffling trot that may be varied in several ways. The step may involve a single or double stomp, and the stomp may be light or heavy. The step may involve a forward shuffle or a quick, graceful back-and-forth shake just before the foot is placed. For some ceremonials, a line of Eastern Pueblo dancers moves in place, using a foot-lifting step called *antege*. The *antege* steps coordinate with the characteristic duple pulse of most American Indian dance music, but some Pueblo ceremonial dance songs briefly shift from duple to triple meter at certain points. This produces a patterned pause in the dance step, called a *ta'a*, in which the dancer holds his right foot suspended on the third beat. In the Northwest Coast, the Nootka use the term *quoqaccupita* to refer to a similar change of meter; they refer to steady, even steps as *xaeskaanal*, and to short, fast steps as *tsaxailala*. Plains Indian social dance songs employ a triple beat, in which dancers step on the first and third beats. Some Native American dances employ mimetic movements to enact activities such as corn husking or grinding among the Cherokee and Haudenosaunee.

The relationship between the singers' melody and the drumbeat can be complex in Native American music, but dancers synchronize their movements with the drum. In powwow music, for example, the singers' beat and tempo may correlate loosely with the drum, but the dancers follow the drum beat. The dancers' relation to the music is most intimate when they accompany themselves either with a rattle or a sound-maker attached to the body or dance outfit. The dancers may provide the sole accompaniment, or they may fit their rhythms to the sounds made by a separate group of musicians. Suspension rattles made of deer hooves may be worn behind the knee or attached to a belt, apron, or robe. Yaqui dancers wrap strings of dried cocoons filled with gravel around their legs. Alaska Native dancers wear gauntlet gloves decorated with amulets made from bone, ivory, shells, and other materials that rattle gently during the performance.

Hand-held container rattles provide the most common form of self-accompaniment. Rattles are often made of gourds, which are readily available in various shapes and sizes. These containers, which are considered female, may be filled with their own dried seeds, corn kernels, chokecherry seeds, or even buckshot. Pueblo people believe that dancers enhance their rain-bringing power by thrusting flat gourd rattles toward the earth as they sing and dance. Male buffalo dancers also shake large, round gourd rattles. In the Haudenosaunee Eagle Dance, performers shake small egg-shaped gourds in time with their movements. The Haudenosaunee also use other natural materials for rattles, such as a section of cow horn with a wooden handle, used by special singers or for self-accompanied dances. For introductions and interludes the dance leaders shiver the rattle; during the dance they alternately strike it on the palm of the left hand and shake it in the air. False-face dancers pound large rattles made of snapping turtle shells, while women of the planter's society shake small tortoise-shell rattles. Rawhide formerly provided the material for the cylindrical rattle used by Ojibwe shamans and for various spherical and disc-shaped rattles of Plains peoples. Wooden rattles, often elaborately carved in animal or bird images, serve shamans in Northwest Coast communities.

One masterly combination of movement and music occurs in the Yaqui Deer Dance. The *maso* (deer impersonator) accompanies his sensitive, quivering mime of a hunted deer with passive and active instruments. As his feet strike the ground, the cocoon leg rattles whisper and the deer hooves clatter; he shakes two large gourds, the right one with a vertical impulse, the left one with a rotary swish. At the same time, an accompanist scrapes a notched stick on a gourd resonator and a singer strikes a special kind of water drum (actually a struck idiophone), consisting of a half-gourd floating in a tub of water. Three shaman-clowns, called *pascolas*, pursue the deer. Their grotesque, angular shoulder jerks and leaps fit the uncanny black, bearded mask of the *pahko'ola* (old man of the *fiesta*). Their cocoon anklets swish, but the bronze bells on their belts clang more harshly than the deer hooves, and their *sonazo* (sistrum) makes a sharply metallic sound. The *sonazo*, an ironwood frame to which brass discs are attached by nails, is struck against the palm of the left hand to produce syncopated rhythms. At the same time, musicians play a notched stick and a one-man flute and drum combination.

(iv) Regalia. Native American dancers refer to their clothing and personal adornment, including the paraphernalia and musical instruments they carry, as regalia or outfits rather than costumes. Most dancers make their own regalia by hand and may assemble an outfit over several years. Dancers also inherit or receive pieces of regalia as gifts from relatives or friends, and they sometimes purchase pieces from skilled artisans. In this way, each dancer's regalia becomes a unique expression of individual taste, style, identity, and personal history. Native American dance outfits extend movement patterns through the fringes, feathers, and other mobile parts that are incorporated into the clothing and head-

dresses; they also enhance the musical accompaniment through sound-makers worn on the dancer's outfit or body.

Dance regalia varies by tribe and performance context. For example, among the Pueblo peoples of New Mexico, women usually wear a knee-length dress, called a *manta*, woven from wool or heavy cotton, with a shawl pinned on the right shoulder, a woven sash around the waist, deerskin moccasins, and jewelry made of silver, turquoise, spiny oyster, coral, or stones. Depending upon the dance, women may wear painted wooden headdresses called *tablitas* and may carry evergreen sprigs or ears of corn in their hands. Men usually wear white woven kilts with their chests bare or painted, a woven sash and bells around the waist, and moccasins. They carry sprigs of evergreens and a gourd rattle, and may wear feathers in their hair (Sweet, 1985/R). By contrast, Choctaw dancers wear outfits derived from the clothing worn by Anglo-American southerners during the 19th century. Women wear a long, solid-colored cloth dress with a rectangular yoke, long sleeves, and one or two ruffles near the hem. The ruffles and yoke feature appliqué in a contrasting color, using designs such as diamonds, half-diamonds, the Saint Andrew's cross, or reversed spirals, which carry symbolic significance. They wear a white apron over the dress, a beaded collar at the neck, and moccasins or street shoes. Some women wear a silver comb on the crown of the head from which they suspend a bunch of long, colorful ribbons; others pin ribbons on the dress at the nape of the neck. Choctaw men wear a solid-color cotton shirt with a rectangular yoke and long sleeves, featuring appliqué trim in a contrasting color on the sleeves, yoke, and hem. They wear black slacks or jeans, street shoes, a beaded medallion or baldric, and a black felt hat, sometimes with a beaded or ribbon hatband and feather. Some men wear a bunch of long, colorful ribbons fastened at the waist on one or both sides (Howard and Levine, 1990).

Powwow dancers wear regalia derived from 19th-century Plains Indian ceremonial attire, but contemporary powwow outfits often incorporate fluorescent colors, iridescent synthetic fabrics, and references to popular and foreign cultures. For example, a teen-aged Fancy Dancer incorporates the comic book character Spider Man into his outfit with a red and blue color scheme and spider appliqué; an adult Grass Dancer wears a beadwork medallion replicating a professional football team logo; and a college student sews rows of Indonesian coins onto her Women's Traditional dress to commemorate a meaningful study abroad experience. A powwow dancer's regalia reflects the dance style he or she performs. The main categories include Men's and Women's Traditional Dance, Men's and Women's Fancy Dance, Men's Grass Dance, and Women's Jingle Dress Dance. Men's Traditional dancers usually carry a feather fan and wear a long shirt and leggings, a bone breastplate, and a feather bustle with cloth trailers on the lower back. Women's Traditional dancers wear a long dress or skirt and blouse with a belt and a neck scarf; they carry a fringed shawl and a feather fan. Men's Fancy dancers wear a large feather bustle on both the upper and lower back, as well as a small feather bustle on each arm. They carry spinners and wear beaded yokes and aprons. Women's Fancy or Fancy Shawl dancers wear a dress or skirt and blouse with a fringed shawl over their shoulders, moccasins, and leggings. Grass Dancers wear shirts and aprons with thick, long fringes made of yarn or chainette; they carry a feather fan in one hand and mirror or small shield in the other. Jingle Dress dancers sew rows of tin cones onto their dresses, which they wear with leggings, moccasins, and a neck scarf. Male dancers in all categories wear roach headdresses with feather spinners, while women dancers wear feathers and ermine wraps tied in their hair.

For some tribes, masks constitute an important part of the regalia worn for ceremonial dances. Navajo *yeibichai* dancers wear masks made of ritually harvested deerhide, painted and decorated to represent spirit beings who possess healing powers. Similarly, Apache Mountain God dancers perform during the girl's puberty ceremony; they wear a black head covering with holes for the eyes and mouth, topped with an elaborate wooden headdress. A Hopi *kachina* dancer becomes one with the spirit he represents when he dons his mask. In one Haudenosaunee curing ceremony, dancers wear carved and painted wooden masks with grotesque features, representing spirits of wind and disease. In a different ceremony, Haudenosaunee dancers wear masks made of braided corn husks. Among the Makah people of the Pacific Northwest, ceremonial dance masks are considered animate and they constitute an important part of a family's property. Makah dancers use sleight of hand to change masks in the midst of a performance, enhancing its dramatic impact (Goodman and Swan). Several Northwest Coast tribes use transformation masks in ceremonial dances. These transformation masks represent animals or other beings on the outside, but may be opened by the dancer during performance to reveal an inner mask.

Native American dancers honor their relationships with other people by wearing or carrying pieces of regalia they have inherited or received as gifts from relatives and friends. Similarly, they honor human relationships to plants, animals, and the earth itself by wearing materials such as feathers, sea shells, animal fur, buffalo horns, deer hooves, antlers, elk teeth, porcupine quills, turtle shells, cocoons, plant greenery, gourd rattles, beads (to represent seeds), paint made from clay or pulverized minerals, and metal bells or tin cones. Vanessa Brown, a Navajo powwow dancer, explains that "When I dance with all my regalia on—animal skins, feathers, shells, ermine furs…I feel like all the living beings of the world are with me. There are the wingeds, the four-leggeds, the ocean beings, and the fur-bearers; when you dance surrounded by them, it makes you feel majestic," (Toelken, 2003, 80).

(v) Theatrical productions. In the late 19th century, some Native American peoples began to perform staged dances based on traditional choreographies for theatrical productions. These included Wild West shows, traveling carnivals, fairs, expositions, Chautauqua presentations, and "Indian Detours," tours of Pueblo communities offered to travelers in New Mexico. Thousands of Native people supported themselves through these kinds of performances between 1880 and 1930. At a time when government policies banned American Indian dances in ceremonial contexts, participation in theatrical productions provided an outlet for both the preservation of tribal customs and the public expression of ethnic identity. Furthermore, performance in theatrical productions created opportunities for Native people to travel both domestically and internationally, and many relished this opportunity, although considerable debate about these shows took place at the time among Indian reformers as well as Native people.

Most early 20th-century theatrical productions were organized and sponsored by Anglo-American promoters, but within a few decades, some Native communities had begun to organize their own events. Among the best known was the Puye Cliffs Ceremonial sponsored by Santa Clara Pueblo in New Mexico from 1957 until 1981. A similar event, the Nambe Falls Ceremonial, has been held nearly every year since 1961. The Nambe Falls Ceremonial includes dancers from the Pueblos of Nambe, San Ildefonso, San Juan, and Santa Clara. Native American theatrical productions of traditional dance took a new direction in the 1980s, with the emergence of the AMERICAN INDIAN DANCE THEATRE, founded in 1987 by Barbara Schwei and Hanay Geiogamah (Kiowa). This company, described as "the high-water mark of Native American tribal dancing performed on stage" (Jones, 1992, 172), presented traditional and modern dance in highly choreographed, professionally produced concerts featuring some of the top Native performers in North America.

Native Americans also participate in European genres of dance, and by the early 20th century some began to achieve international acclaim, most notably the Osage ballerinas Marjorie and Maria Tallchief. By the late 20th century, Native American composers and performers working in diverse European musical genres incorporated elements of indigenous dance into their work. These elements include traditional dancers in full regalia, elaborate sets and lighting that reference ritual contexts, and dance pieces inspired by Native myths and legends. Examples include the *Powwow Symphony* (1998) by the Mohican composer Brent Michael Davids and the multimedia show *Music from a Painted Cave* (2001) by the Taos Pueblo rock singer, poet, and Native flute player Robert Mirabal. *BONES: an Aboriginal Dance Opera* also premiered in 2001, produced and directed by Sadie Buck (Seneca) with David DeLeary (Anishnabe). This project grew out of the Aboriginal Women's Voices and Chinook Winds Aboriginal Dance programs at the Banff Centre for the Arts in Canada. The choreography blends music, modern dance, and indigenous aesthetics to challenge operatic conventions while it transforms intercultural relationships (Diamond, 2011).

BIBLIOGRAPHY
GENERAL

F. Densmore: *The American Indians and their Music* (New York, 1926, 2/1937)

G. Herzog: *Research in Primitive and Folk Music in the United States* (Washington, DC, 1936)

H.H. Roberts: *Musical Areas in Aboriginal North America* (New Haven, CT, 1936)

F. Densmore: "Imitative Dances among the American Indians," *Journal of American Folklore*, no.235 (1947), 73–8

C. Haywood: *A Bibliography of North American Folklore and Folksong*, ii (New York, 1951, 2/1961)

W. Rhodes: "North American Indian Music: a Bibliographical Survey of Anthropological Theory," *Notes*, x (1952–3), 33–45

G.P. Kurath: "Native Choreographic Areas of North America," *American Anthropologist*, lv/1 (1953), 60–73

B. Nettl: *North American Indian Musical Styles* (Philadelphia, 1954)

J. Hickerson: *Annotated Bibliography of North American Indian Music North of Mexico* (diss., Indiana U., 1961)

A. Briegleb, ed.: *Directory of Ethnomusicological Sound Recording Collections in the U.S. and Canada* (Ann Arbor, MI, 1971)

R. Stevenson: "English Sources for Indian Music until 1882," *EM*, xvii (1973), 399–442

R. Stevenson: "Written Sources for Indian Music until 1882," *EM*, xvii (1973), 1–40

M. Herndon: *Native American Music* (Norwood, PA, 1980)

D.W. Krummel and others, eds: *Resources of American Music History* (Urbana, IL, 1981)

M. Maguire: *American Indian and Eskimo Music: a Selected Bibliography Through 1981* (Washington, DC, 1983)

R. De Cesare: *Myth, Music and Dance of the American Indian* (Van Nuys, CA, 1988)

R. Keeling, ed.: *Women in North American Indian Music: Six Essays* (Bloomington, IN, 1989)

G. McDow: *Instrumental Music Education in the Indian Schools of Oklahoma Before Statehood (1852–1907)* (diss., U. of Oklahoma, 1989)

P. Matthiessen: *In the Spirit of Crazy Horse* (New York, 1991)

C. Heth, ed.: *Native American Dance: Ceremonies and Social Traditions* (Washington, DC, 1992)

B. Diamond, S. Cronk, and F. Von Rosen: *Visions of Sound: Musical Instruments of First Nations Communities in Northeastern America* (Waterloo, IA, 1994)

D.B. Lee, ed.: *Remaining Ourselves: Music and Tribal Memory, Traditional Music in Contemporary Communities* (Oklahoma City, 1995)

I. Goddard, ed.: *Languages: Handbook of North American Indians*, xvii (Washington, DC, 1996)

R. Keeling: *North American Indian Music: a Guide to Published Sources and Selected Recordings* (New York, 1997)

E. Koskoff, ed.: "Music of the American Indians/First Nations in the United States and Canada," *The Garland Encyclopedia of World Music: The United States and Canada*, iii (New York, 2001), 363–570

V.L. Levine: *Writing American Indian Music: Historic Transcriptions, Notations, and Arrangements* (Middleton, WS, 2002)

G. Menzies: *1421: The Year China Discovered America* (London, 2002/R)

B. Toelken: *The Anguish of Snails: Native American Folklore in the West* (Logan, 2003)

B. Wright-McLeod: *The Encyclopedia of Native Music: More Than a Century of Recordings from Wax Cylinder to the Internet* (Tucson, AZ, 2005)

REGIONAL STUDIES

F. Densmore: *Chippewa Music* (Washington, DC, 1910–13)

F.G. Speck: *Ceremonial Songs of the Creek and Yuchi Indians* (Philadelphia, 1911)

H. Thuren and W. Thalbitzer: *The Eskimo Music* (Copenhagen, 1911)

F. Densmore: *Teton Sioux Music* (Washington, DC, 1918)

F. Densmore: *Papago Music* (Washington, DC, 1929)

F. Densmore: *Pawnee Music* (Washington, DC, 1929)

F. Densmore: *Nootka and Quileute Music* (Washington, DC, 1939)

M.W. Smith, ed.: *Indians of the Urban Northwest*, ed. M.W. Smith (New York, 1949)

F. Densmore: *Seminole Music* (Washington, DC, 1956)

G.P. Kurath: *Iroquois Music and Dance: Ceremonial Arts of Two Seneca Longhouses* (Washington, DC, 1964)

A.P. Merriam: *Ethnomusicology of the Flathead Indians* (Chicago, 1967)

G.P. Kurath and A. Garcia: *Music and Dance of the Tewa Pueblos* (Santa Fe, NM, 1970)

C.J. Frisbie: *Music and Dance Research of Southwestern United States Indians: Past Trends, Present Activities, and Suggestions for Future Research* (Detroit, 1977)

C.J. Frisbie, ed.: *Southwestern Indian Ritual Drama* (Albuquerque, NM, 1980)

L.D. Koranda: "Music of the Alaskan Eskimos," *Musics of Many Cultures: An Introduction*, ed. E. May (Berkeley and Los Angeles, 1980), 332–62

M. La Vigna: "Okushare, Music for a Winter Ceremony: the Turtle Dance Songs of San Juan Pueblo," *Selected Reports in Ethnomusicology*, iii/2 (1980), 77–100

N. Yeh: "The Pogonshare Ceremony of the Tewa of San Juan, NM," *Selected Reports in Ethnomusicology*, iii/2 (1980), 101–46

F.W. Champe: *The Matachines Dance of the Upper Rio Grande: History, Music, and Choreography* (Lincoln, 1983)

J.D. Sweet: *Dances of the Tewa Pueblo Indians: Expressions of New Life* (Santa Fe, NM, 1985/R)

L. Evers and F.S. Molina: *Yaqui Deer Songs/Maso Bwikam: A Native American Poetry* (Tucson, AZ, 1987)

J. Vander: *Songprints: the Musical Experience of Five Shoshone Women* (Urbana, IL, 1988)

B. Nettl: *Blackfoot Musical Thought: Comparative Perspectives* (Kent, MD, 1989)

J. Howard and V.L. Levine: *Choctaw Music and Dance* (Norman, OK, 1990)

W. Suttles, ed.: *Handbook of North American Indians: Northwest Coast*, vii (Washington, DC, 1990)

C.R. Farrer: *Living Life's Circle: Mescalero Apache Cosmovision* (Albuquerque, NM, 1991)

P. Conlon: *Drum-Dance Songs of the Iglulik Inuit in the Northern Baffin Island Area: a Study of their Structures* (diss., U. of Montreal, 1992)

R. Keeling: *Cry for Luck: Sacred Song and Speech among the Yurok, Hupa, and Karok Indians of Northwestern California* (Berkeley, 1992)

C. Mishler: *The Crooked Stovepipe: Athapaskan Fiddle Music and Square Dancing in Northeast Alaska and Northwest Canada* (Urbana, IL, 1993)

V. Giglio: *Southern Cheyenne Women's Songs* (Norman, OK, 1994)

L.P. Valentine: *Making it their Own: Severn Ojibwe Communicative Practices* (Toronto, 1995)

C.G. Wilson, R.L.H. Wilson, and B. Burton: *When the Earth Was Like New: Western Apache Songs and Stories* (Danbury, CT, 1995)

D.E. Walker, ed.: *Handbook of North American Indians: Plateau*, vii (Washington, DC, 1998)

R.J. DeMallie, ed.: *Handbook of North American Indians: Plains*, xiii (Washington, DC, 2001)

E. McCullough-Brabson and M. Help: *We'll Be in your Mountains, We'll Be In Your Songs: A Navajo Woman Sings* (Albuquerque, 2001)

L.J. Goodman and H. Swan: *Singing the Songs of my Ancestors: the Life and Music of Helma Swan, Makah Elder* (Norman, OK, 2003)

J.B. Jackson: *Yuchi Ceremonial Life: Performance, Meaning, and Tradition in a Contemporary American Indian Community* (Lincoln, NB, 2003)

R.D. Fogelson, ed.: *Handbook of North American Indians: Southeast*, xiv (Washington, DC, 2004)

B. Diamond: *Native American Musics in Eastern North America* (New York, 2008)

For further bibliography, see entries on individual regions and groups.

DEVELOPMENTS AFTER EUROPEAN CONTACT

J. Mooney: *The Ghost-dance Religion and the Sioux Outbreak of 1890* (Washington, DC, 1896, 2/1965)

L. Spier: "The Sun Dance of the Plains Indians: its Development and Diffusion," *Anthropological Papers of the American Museum of Natural History*, xvi (1921), 451

D.P. McAllester: *Peyote Music* (New York, 1949)

W.N. Fenton and G.P. Kurath: *The Iroquois Eagle Dance* (Washington, DC, 1953)

D.P. McAllester: *Enemy Way Music: a Study of Social and Esthetic Values as Seen in Navaho Music* (Cambridge, MA, 1954)

J.H. Howard: "Pan-Indian Culture of Oklahoma," *Scientific Monthly*, viii (1955), 215

J.G. Jorgensen: *The Sun Dance Religion: Power for the Powerless* (Chicago, 1972)

R. Witmer: "Recent Change in the Musical Culture of the Blood Indians of Alberta, Canada," *Yearbook for Inter-American Musical Research*, ix (1973), 64

T. Hatton: "Performance Practices of the Northern Plains Powwow Singing Groups," *Yearbook for Inter-American Musical Research*, x (1974), 123

B. Black Bear Sr. and R.D. Theisz: *Songs and Dances of the Lakota* (Aberdeen, SD, 1976)

C.J. Frisbie and D.P. McAllester, eds.: *Navajo Blessingway Singer: the Autobiography of Frank Mitchell, 1881–1967* (Tucson, AZ, 1978)

J.H. Howard: "Pan-Indianism in Native American Music and Dance," *EM*, xxvii (1983), 71

W.C. Wickwire and W. Cochrane: *Cultures in Contact: Music, the Plateau Indian and the Western Encounter* (diss., Wesleyan U., 1983)

C. Heth: "Update on Indian Music: Contemporary Trends," *Sharing a Heritage: American Indian Arts* (Los Angeles, 1984)

D. Whitehorse: *Pow-Wow: The Contemporary Pan-Indian Celebration* (San Diego, 1988)

W.K. Powers: *War Dance: Plains Indian Musical Performance* (Tucson, AZ, 1990)

D. Zotigh: *Moving History: Evolution of the Powwow* (Oklahoma City, 1991)

R. Jones: "Modern Native Dance: Beyond Tribe and Tradition," *Native American Dance: Ceremonies and Social Traditions*, ed. C. Heth (Washington, DC, 1992), 169–83

B. Burton: *Moving Within the Circle: Contemporary Native American Music and Dance* (Danbury, CT, 1993, 2/2008)

T. Browner: *Heartbeat of the People: Music and Dance of the Northern Pow-wow* (Champaign, IL, 2002)

C. Ellis: *A Dancing People: Powwow Culture on the Southern Plains* (Lawrence, KS, 2003)

C. Ellis, L.E. Lassiter, and G.H. Dunham, eds: *Powwow* (Lincoln, NB, 2005)

B. Diamond: "Decentering Opera: Early Twenty-First-Century Indigenous Production," *Opera Indigene: Re/presenting First Nations and Indigenous Cultures*, ed. P. Karantonis and D. Robinson (Surrey and Burlington, 2011), 31–56

BRUNO NETTL/VICTORIA LINDSAY LEVINE/
BRYAN BURTON (1), GERTRUDE PROKOSCH KURATH/
VICTORIA LINDSAY LEVINE (2)

Native American popular music. Native American popular music combines elements of Western popular music with traditional Native American musics and storytelling including use of Western and Native American instruments, Native languages, socio-political and cultural issues, and Native regalia. Lyrics may be in a Native language, vocables, English or a combination and often follow traditional uses of music to teach history, cultural values, and social/political issues. Music styles may draw from a single popular genre or combine elements of several Western popular and traditional Native genres. The terms AlterNATIVE and AlterNative music are used as synonyms by some musicians (*see* ALTERNATIVE MUSIC).

In the years following World War I, Native veterans brought western popular music styles home from military service, and by the 1930s there were Native American bands covering popular songs and performing in local venues drawing their repertoire from radio broadcasts and recordings. Lyrics were sometimes translated into a Native language or set to more traditional Native melodies. Such groups were primarily semi-professional and played only local venues. Native or Native descendant musicians such as Robbie Robertson (Jewish-Mohawk), Rita Coolidge (Cherokee), Cher (Cherokee), and Buffy Sainte-Marie (Cree) rose to national attention in the mainstream popular music world in the 1960s and 1970s. XIT, an all-Native rock band formed in 1970, released the first commercially successful Native American popular music album, *Plight of the Redman*, in 1972. Widespread industry discrimination in obtaining

Black Eagle at the 2005 Grammy Awards, Los Angeles. (REUTERS/Gary Hershorn /Landov)

studio time and distribution during this era limited the audience for most Native popular musicians to local venues and powwows. Sainte-Marie, Johnny Trudell (Santee), Peter LaFarge (Narragansett), and country singer/actor Floyd Red Crow Westerman (Wapheton-Sisseton) are among those to use music as a vehicle for political activism.

The 1980s and 1990s were decades of rapid growth both in availability and recognition of Native American popular music. The years 1982 and 1983 saw the rerelease and wider distribution of Westerman's 1969 album *Custer Died for your Sins* and Golden Globe and Academy Awards honors for Sainte-Marie's "Up Where We Belong." (Although the film version of Sainte-Marie's song was strictly pop in style, her other recordings of "Up Where We Belong" feature Native American flute and tribal singing.) Tom Bee (Lakota), founder of XIT, released and distributed XIT's initial recordings while working as a producer for Motown Records and founded Sounds of America Records (1989) and SOAR Distribution LTD (1995) to allow native Artists greater access to recording and distribution. In the mid-1980s, Keith Secola (Anishnabee) wrote "NDN Karz" often identified as "the Indian national anthem." R. Carlos Nakai's (Navajo-Ute) *Canyon Trilogy* (1989) became the first gold record released by a Native performer. Robbie Robertson's score for *The Native Americans* (1994) featured a compilation of works by numerous Native performers. Its soundtrack and Robertson's Red Road Ensemble performances increased awareness of Native American popular musicians and launched the careers of the groups Ulali and Walelea. In 1998 Native American Music Association established the Native American Music Awards to recognize musical achievement among Native Americans.

Entering the 21st century, Native American popular music has established a secure place within Native American musical culture due, in part, to greater production and distribution networks through Native-owned or Native-sympathetic studios and production companies, including Canyon Records Productions, Sound of America Records (Tom Bee), Akina records (Keith Secola), Indian House, and Silver Waver Records. Digital distribution through networks such as iTunes and Rhapsody has also contributed to the music's growth and popularity. In addition, the growth of the tribal casino industry provides innumerable new performance venues for Native artists. Composer-performers such as Keith Secola, R. Carlos Nakai, and Brent Michael Davids also have expanded into writing scores for popular television series and motion pictures.

BIBLIOGRAPHY

D. McAllester: "The Beginning of a New Genre," *The Art of the Native American Flute* (Phoenix, AZ, 1996), 79–108

B. Diamond: "Native American Contemporary Music: the Women," *Worlds of Music*, xliv/1 (2002), 9–35

B. Burton: *Moving Within the Circle: Contemporary Native American Music and Dance* (Danbury, CT, 2/2008), 117–29

B. Diamond: *Native American Music in Eastern North America* (New York, 2008), 117–52

BRYAN BURTON

Naughton, James (*b* Middleton, CT, 6 Dec 1945). Actor, singer, and director. A graduate of Brown University with a Master of Fine Arts degree from Yale University, he has compiled Broadway credits that equally reflect his gifts as a musical actor, non-singing actor, and director. Following critical recognition as Edmund in a revival of *A Long Day's Journey into Night* (1971), Naughton made his Broadway musical debut (alongside Joanna Gleason) playing Wally in Cy Coleman's *I Love My Wife* (1977). Naughton created the role of the fictional detective Stone in *City of Angels* (1989) and played Billy Flynn in the revival of *Chicago* (1996); he won Tony Awards for both portrayals. Naughton directed actor Paul Newman in the part of the Stage Manager in *Our Town* on Broadway (2002) and as a television (PBS) movie (2003). His solo cabaret show *James Naughton: Streets of Dreams* has played successfully in New York and on tour. He also has many nonmusical film and television credits.

Naughton's handsome stage presence exudes mellowness and masculinity. His superb comic timing is understated; even in a madcap moment, he seems centered and imperturbable. Naughton's singing style is often described as "crooning," an apt term to convey that his voice and phrasing are evocative of popular singers of the mid-20th century, but inaccurate if conveying a lack of vocal presence. Naughton uses his sizeable voice in a wide range of dynamics and vocal color, but in an unobtrusive manner that preserves the audience's sense of his coolness and control.

BIBLIOGRAPHY

M. Rothstein: "The Case of an Actor who Loves his Craft," *New York Times* (18 Dec 1989), C11

M. Gussow: "James Naughton: an Actor Singing for the Joy of It," *New York Times* (26 June 1998), E2

SHARON O'CONNELL CAMPBELL

Naumburg, Walter Wehle (*b* New York, NY, 25 Dec 1867; *d* New York, NY, 17 Oct 1959). Banker and music patron. Naumburg's father, Elkan, came to the United States in his late teens and established a successful clothing company. Reportedly the son of a cantor, the elder Naumburg was himself an amateur musician and hosted weekly chamber music performances attended by important figures such as Leopold Damrosch, Theodore Thomas, and Marcella Sembrich. The Damrosch Oratorio Society of New York was conceived in his home. Thus, Walter Naumburg grew up in a musical environment; he began studying the cello at eight years of age. While a student at Harvard, Naumburg regularly performed in the Pierian Sodality orchestra; he graduated *cum laude* in 1889. He briefly entered his father's business before its dissolution; thereafter he formed E. Naumburg & Co., a lucrative commercial lending firm. The family maintained a box at the newly constructed Carnegie Hall, and his father donated a bandstand to the city for Central Park, where he established a series of four concerts every summer. Walter and his brother, George, continued to fund the concerts after their father's passing.

In 1926 Walter created the Naumburg Fund to sponsor debuts for three promising musicians every year.

The enterprise launched the careers of pianist William Kapell, mezzo-soprano Regina Sarfaty, soprano Laurel Hurley, cellist Phyllis Kraeuter, and violinist Betty Jean Hagen. Naumburg retired from business in 1931 to pursue his musical interests full time. In 1935 he was appointed head of the Town Hall music committee. He headed Musicians Foundation, which cared for indigent musicians, served on the advisory committees to the music departments at Harvard and Princeton, and was appointed a trustee of the New England Conservatory of Music. He was an organizer of the Society of Amateur Players and continued playing cello until 1953. He hosted and performed in Wednesday night sessions devoted to chamber music. He expressed a particular fondness for Ludwig van Beethoven's string quartets. His memorial service featured music by the Kreutzer Quartet.

BIBLIOGRAPHY

Obituary, *New York Times* (18 Oct 1959)

The Walter W. Naumburg Foundation Fiftieth Anniversary, 1926–1976 (New York, 1976)

GARY GALVÁN

Navajo [*Diné*]. Native American tribe. Among the largest existing Native American tribes, known as *Diné* in their own language, the Navajo are descended from Athabascan-speaking hunter-gatherers who entered what is now the southwestern United States by about 1000 CE. The Navajo were strongly influenced by neighboring Pueblos (*see* PUEBLO, EASTERN and PUEBLO, WESTERN), from whom they adopted some technologies, such as weaving, and certain other cultural traits. Following their acquisition of sheep from Spanish settlers, Navajos developed a transhumant lifestyle, characterized by seasonal movement of sheep from lowland to highland pastures. As of 2011 the Navajo number some 300,000 people, many of whom were living on the Navajo reservation in northeastern Arizona, southeastern Utah, and northwestern New Mexico. The reservation covers 27,425 square miles and is the largest Indian reservation in the United States. The Navajo are culturally and linguistically related to the APACHE, who also live in the southwest.

Navajo traditional music centers on some 50 healing ceremonies, called chantways, each having a large repertory of songs. The chantways restore harmony between the universe and an individual who has become ill; chantways may be combined with Western medicine to restore the patient's health and well-being. Chantways are performed by ritual specialists, called Singers, who require years of focused training to learn all of the songs, prayers, dry paintings, and other components of a ceremony; accuracy of memorization is of the utmost importance. Ceremonies recount episodes from the Navajo creation narrative in thousands of lines of ritual poetry recited in prayers or sung in song cycles. They may take as many as nine days and nights to complete. Many family members, neighbors, and friends may attend a ceremony, and the family of the patient provides food and gifts for all participants; therefore ceremonies can be quite costly.

Ceremonial songs are performed in unblended unison by the Singer and a group of male helpers, who employ tense, nasal vocal production. Depending on the ceremony, instrumental accompaniment may include handheld container rattles, an inverted basket struck with a stick, or a water drum. Water drums are made from a small ceramic vessel with a skin head, partially filled with water and played with a stick that has a small hoop at the distal end. Ceremonial songs feature a kind of strophic form in which a chorus alternates with a verse; the chorus may be repeated one or more times before the reprise of the verse. The chorus features an animated, often triadic melody in contrast with the verse, which employs a more level melodic contour. Song texts combine vocables with lyrical poetry, alternating descriptions of male and female deities or attributes, reflecting the gender complementarity that shapes much of Navajo thought. Texts of dance songs are often romantic or humorous.

Some of the most common ceremonies include the Enemyway, Nightway, and Blessingway. The Blessingway involves a network of interrelated ceremonies that are central to traditional Navajo religion and philosophy. Its purpose is to create and maintain conditions of harmony, through reference to sacred narratives in which a principal figure is Changing Woman, a spirit being who is consistently benevolent toward humans. An important kind of Blessingway is the *Kinaaldá*, or girl's puberty rite, which initiates a girl into adulthood after the onset of menses. The marriage ritual and the House Blessing are other kinds of Blessingway. Each of these ceremonies reenacts the story of Changing Woman's birth, growth, and maturity. Parts of the Blessingway are often included in other ceremonies in order to protect the participants from dangerous powers invoked in the course of the ritual.

Recordings of Navajo sacred ceremonial songs are not available to the public, but songs of a more social nature appear on commercial recordings. These include genres associated with the nighttime portion of the Enemyway ceremony, including the Skip Dance, Two-Step Dance, Sway Songs, and Circle Dance. Similarly, Yeibichai songs, which belong to the nighttime portion of the Nightway ceremony, may be recorded and performed outside of the ceremonial context, during the appropriate season. Other traditional genres include Moccasin Game songs, Corn Grinding songs, songs associated with work, and social songs. This music is buoyantly melodic and encompasses a range of styles; new songs in these genres continue to be composed.

In addition to traditional repertories, the Navajo participate in mainstream musical life as composers, performers, and listeners. Abbreviated forms of some ceremonies have been developed for public events; for example, a shortened House Blessing can be incorporated into the dedication of a new school or chapter house. Thousands of Navajos participate in multi-tribal musical styles, such as those belonging to the Powwow or the Peyote religion. On the reservation there are many Christian sects who sing hymns with English or Navajo words. Country and western music is very popular; two well-known Navajo country and western bands are the Fenders and the Navajo Sundowners. Rock, hip hop, acoustic folk, and other styles of popular music are composed and performed by Navajo artists. Perhaps the best-known Navajo musician is R. Carlos Nakai, whose virtuoso technique and spirit of experimentation on the Plains courting flute have brought him international acclaim. New roles for Navajo women singers have emerged since the 1970s, with the advent of traditional groups such as the Southern Maiden Singers or the Sweethearts of Navajoland, and singer-songwriters including Arlene Nofchissey Williams, Sharon Burch, and Geraldine Barney. Thus, innovations in Navajo music reflect broader changes in Navajo culture.

DISCOGRAPHY

Night and Daylight Yeibichai (Indian House 1502, 1968); *Navajo Skip Dance and Two-step Songs* (Indian House 1503, 1969); *Music of New Mexico: Native American Traditions* (Smithsonian Folkways 40408, 1992); *Navajo Songs Recorded by Laura Boulton* (Smithsonian Folkways 40403, 1992); *Heartbeat: Voices of First Nations Women* (Smithsonian Folkways 40415, 1995)

BIBLIOGRAPHY

G.A. Reichard: *Navaho Religion* (New York, 1950)

D.P. McAllester: *Enemy Way Music* (Cambridge, 1954)

C.J. Frisbie: *Kinaaldá: a Study of the Navaho Girls' Puberty Ceremony* (Middletown, CT, 1967)

L.C. Wyman: *Blessingway* (Tucson, AZ, 1970)

G. Witherspoon: *Language and Art in the Navajo Universe* (Ann Arbor, MI, 1977)

F. Mitchell: *Navajo Blessingway Singer* (Tucson, AZ, 1978)

C.J. Frisbie: *Navajo Medicine Bundles or Jish* (Albuquerque, NM, 1987)

C.J. Frisbie: "Gender and Navajo Music," *Women in North American Indian Music*, ed. R. Keeling (Bloomington, IN, 1989), 22–38

E. McCullough-Brabson and M. Help: *We'll Be in your Mountains, We'll Be in your Songs: a Navajo Woman Sings* (Albuquerque, NM, 2001)

DAVID P. MCALLESTER/VICTORIA LINDSAY LEVINE

Navarro, Fats [Theodore; Fat Girl] (*b* Key West, FL, 24 Sept 1923; *d* New York, NY, 7 July 1950). Jazz trumpeter. He played piano and tenor saxophone while growing up before switching to trumpet at age 13. He developed quickly and when he was 17 joined the territory band of Snookum Russell. During the period 1943–4 he was a member of the Andy Kirk Orchestra, in which he sat next to Howard McGhee, who was one of his main influences, along with Charlie Shavers, Roy Eldridge, and Dizzy Gillespie. When Gillespie left the Billy Eckstine Orchestra in January 1945, he recommended that Navarro be his replacement. The 18 months that he spent with Eckstine solidified Navarro's bop style and large tone. He spent the remainder of his career mostly playing with small bop combos. Navarro recorded many significant record sessions between 1946 and 1949 including dates with the Bebop Boys, Coleman Hawkins, Eddie "Lockjaw" Davis, Dexter Gordon, Don Lanphere, Kenny Clarke, Illinois Jacquet, and Tadd Dameron. He also led his own recording dates for Savoy and Blue Note. Although he was not a major composer, his line on "Out of Nowhere" that was called "Nostalgia" became a bop standard.

The year 1948 was a particularly busy period for the trumpeter: he toured with the Lionel Hampton big band, was briefly a member of Benny Goodman's small group and big band (recording a boppish "Stealing Apples"), and worked regularly with Dameron. Several existing radio broadcasts show that his playing was perfect for both Dameron's band and his music. Navarro also excelled during a trumpet battle recording date with McGhee. In 1949 he toured with Jazz at the Philharmonic and was in excellent form on a quintet session with Bud Powell and the young Sonny Rollins. In the same year he recorded with the Metronome All Stars next to Gillespie and Miles Davis. Navarro's last existing recordings are surprisingly joyful and fiery and took place during a live date with Charlie Parker from 1950 that, if dated with accuracy, took place less than two months before his death. A heroin addict, Navarro was stricken by tuberculosis, and the once-overweight trumpeter wasted away and died when he was just 26.

During a period when few trumpeters could closely emulate Gillespie's complex virtuosity, Navarro became a major musical role model. His tone was beautiful and large, he had complete command of his horn, and the logic that he employed during his solos was advanced. He was considered by many of his contemporaries to be second only to Gillespie among the bop trumpeters.

SELECTED RECORDINGS

As leader: Fat Girl (Savoy, 1947); Ice Freezes Red (Savoy, 1947); Goin' to Minton's (Savoy, 1947); Nostalgia (Savoy, 1947); Barry's Bop (Savoy, 1947)

As sideman: B. Eckstine: "Air Mail Special" on *Together!* (Spot., 1945); K. Clarke: Epistrophy/Oop Bop Sh'bam (Swing, 1946); 52nd Street Theme/Royal Roost (Swing, 1946); E. Davis: Calling Dr. Jazz/Stealin' Trash (Savoy, 1946); Hollerin' and Screamin' (Savoy, 1946); T. Dameron: The Squirrel/Our Delight (BN, 1947); The Chase/Dameronia (BN, 1947); A Bop Carol (Savoy, 1947); B. Goodman: Stealin' Apples (Cap., 1948); H. McGhee: Boperation/The Skunk (BN, 1948); Double Talk (BN, 1948); B. Powell: Bouncing with Bud/Wail (BN, 1949); Dance of the Infidels/52nd Street Theme (BN, 1949); C. Parker: *One Night in Birdland* (Col., 1950)

BIBLIOGRAPHY

I. Gitler: *Jazz Masters of the Forties* (New York, 1966/R), 97

R. Russell: "Fat Girl: the Legacy of Fats Navarro," *DB*, xxxvii/4 (1970), 14

W. Balliett: "Jazz: Fat Girl," *New Yorker* (12 June 1978)

J.L. Collier: *The Making of Jazz: a Comprehensive History* (New York, 1978), 398

M. Ruppli: "Fats Navarro Discography," *DF*, no.42 (1979), 4; no.43 (1980), 7; no.44 (1981), 3; no.45 (1982), 11

S. Yanow: *Trumpet Kings* (San Francisco, CA, 2001), 276–7

SCOTT YANOW

Navy School of Music. Band personnel training school located on Naval Amphibious Base Little Creek, Norfolk, Virginia. It provides initial musical training and specialized courses for musicians in bands of the US Army, Navy, and Marine Corps. It was established on 26 June 1935 under the auspices of the US Navy Band, and was organized and led by James Morgan Thurmond. It was separated from the Navy Band and relocated to Anacostia Naval Receiving Station in 1943, and then to Little Creek in 1964. It has been called the US Navy

School of Music (1935–48), US Naval School of Music (1948–64), School of Music (1964–2004), and Navy School of Music (2004–). Its unofficial name is the Armed Forces School of Music.

BIBLIOGRAPHY

P.M. Jones: *A History of the Armed Forces School of Music* (diss., Pennsylvania State U., 2002)

PATRICK M. JONES

Naxos. Multinational record company and distributor. Established in Hong Kong by German-born entrepreneur Klaus Heymann in 1987, it began issuing classical music titles throughout Asia and Europe. Initially distributed in the United States under the banner of Enigma Classics in 1988, Naxos ended the joint venture in 1990 to issue recordings in North America under its own name. Early releases (the first 30 of which Naxos licensed, rather than owned) largely featured standard classical repertoire recorded in central European countries, though the label later branched out into rarities and works by modern composers including Gyorgi Ligeti, Arvo Pärt, and Krzystof Penderecki. The Naxos World label, featuring traditional and folk music, was launched in 2000. Other imprints include HK, Marco Polo, Naxos Educational, Naxos Historical, Naxos Jazz Legends, and Naxos Nostalgia. The label also produces audio and video DVDs and operates an audiobooks division, a subscription online radio service, an online streaming music library, and a book-publishing imprint.

BIBLIOGRAPHY

B.L. Scherer: "Mr. Heymann's Opus: The Naxos Catalog," *Wall Street Journal*, 15 Jan (2003)

K. Wangler: "Naxos – A Classic Example of Marketing Principles: A Case Study of the Four P's of Marketing Techniques as Used by a Classical Music Record Label," *Journal of the Music and Entertainment Industry Educators Association,* ix/1 (2009), 95–112

THANE TIERNEY

NBA. *See* NATIONAL BAND ASSOCIATION [NBA].

Ndegeocello, Meshell [Johnson, Michelle Lynn; Bashir-Shakur, Meshell Suhaila] (*b* Berlin, Germany, 1968). Electric bassist, singer, and songwriter. As a teenager she changed her name to Ndegeocello ("free as a bird" in Swahili), the spelling of which has shifted over the years. Since 1997 she has also called herself Meshell Suhaila Bashir-Shakur, a reference to her (professedly unconventional) affiliation with Islam. Raised in Washington, DC, she attended arts schools, debuted at 17 as a jazz bassist, and cut her teeth in the local go-go scene. A jazz history major at Howard University, she dropped out to have a son and was among the first musicians to sign with Maverick.

Ndegeocello has refused most identity categories, but has described herself as "a female Homo sapien...sexually functional with both sexes" and black. Traversing genre, her music draws from soul, R&B, funk, hip hop, jazz, go-go, dub, and rock. *Plantation Lullabies* (Maverick, 1993), a self-produced album featuring Ndegeocello on most instruments, garnered attention across the United States and Europe, contributing to the soul revival with a politically conscious musical examination of African American history and contemporary politics. Recorded with a full band, *Peace Beyond Passion* (Maverick, 1996) bravely critiqued homophobia in the black Christian community while developing her signature sensual, spiritual, funky musicality.

In 1999 she released *Bitter*, an intimate, jazz-influenced album that garnered critical acclaim but proved a commercial disappointment and signaled growing problems with Maverick, which considered her music "not black enough." As a response she released *Cookie: the Anthropological Mixtape* (Maverick, 2002), which intersperses clips of famous black activists (often Marxists) with "go-go" spoken word and song, set to black and Latino dance beats. *Comfort Woman* (Maverick, 2003) fulfilled her contract.

She subsequently formed the Spirit Music *Jamia* (an Arabic word for gathering or school), an instrumental jazz fusion sextet with a DJ with which she released *The Spirit Music Jamia: Dance of the Infidel* (Shanachie, 2005). Following albums, *The World Has Made Me the Man of My Dreams* (Decca, 2007) and *Devil's Halo* (Mercer Street, 2009), contend with decades of strife over musical and personal identity through philosophical, stylistically shifting music. *Weather* (Naïve, 2011) hearkens back to *Bitter*'s acoustic intimacy and zen-like sparseness. *Pour une âme souveraine: a dedication to Nina Simone* (Naïve, 2012) makes material Ndegeocello's connections to the late "High Priestess of Soul." As of 2011 Ndegeocello had been nominated for ten Grammy Awards.

BIBLIOGRAPHY

L. Burns and M. Lafrance: *Disruptive Divas: Feminism, Identity and Popular Music* (New York, 2001), 133–67

M. Mockus: "MeShell Ndegéocello: Musical Articulations of Black Feminism," *Unmaking Race, Remaking Soul: Transformative Aesthetics and the Practice of Freedom,* ed. C.D. Acampora and A.L. Cotton (Albany, NY, 2007), 81–102

S. Goldin-Perschbacher: *Sexuality, Listening, and Intimacy: Gender Transgression in Popular Music, 1993–2008* (diss., U. of Virginia, 2008), 60–102

SHANA GOLDIN-PERSCHBACHER

NEA. *See* NATIONAL ENDOWMENT FOR THE ARTS.

Neblett, Carol (*b* Modesto, CA, 1 Feb 1946). Soprano. Her father was an accomplished pianist and her grandmother a renowned violinist. After early training in both of these instruments, Neblett studied singing privately with WILLIAM VENNARD and at the University of Southern California with LOTTE LEHMANN and Pierre Bernac. She left without graduating in 1965 and became a soloist for a short time with the Roger Wagner Chorale. Encouraged by the impresario Sol Hurok, she embarked on a career in opera and made her debut with the New York City Opera in 1969 as Musetta. Her subsequent debuts included Chrysothemis in *Elektra* at the Chicago Lyric Opera (1975), Antonia in *Les contes d'Hoffmann* at the Dallas Civic Opera (1975), Minnie in *La fanciulla del West* at the Vienna Staatsoper (1976) and Covent Garden (1977), and Senta in *Der fliegende Holländer* (1979). Among her other roles are Margherita and Elena (in Arrigo Boito's *Mefistofele*), Claudio Monteverdi's Poppea, Marietta-Marie (in Erich Wolfgang Korngold's *Die tote Stadt*), Alfredo Catalani's Wally, and Yaroslavna (in Aleksandr Borodin's *Prince Igor*). She has appeared with many of the leading American orchestras, including the Los Angeles PO in Ludwig van Beethoven's Ninth Symphony under Carlo Maria Giulini, and performed the role of Vitellia in Jean-Pierre Ponnelle's film version of *La clemenza di Tito*. In 1973 the statuesque Neblett gained considerable notoriety in a production of Jules Massenet's *Thaïs* in New Orleans by removing her costume at the end of the first act.

She has recorded widely, including *La bohème* for Angel/EMI with James Levine conducting (1979); *La fanciulla del West*, under Zubin Mehta (Deutsche Grammophon, 1977); *Die tote Stadt*, with Erich Leinsdorf (RCA, 1975); Gustav Mahler's Symphony no.2 with Claudio Abbado and the Chicago SO (Deutsche Grammophon, 1996). Her marriage in 1975 to conductor Kenneth Schermerhorn ended in divorce. Neblett has served on the music faculty of Chapman University in Southern California and the International Lyric Academy in Rome.

BIBLIOGRAPHY

E. Myers: "Reunion: Carol Neblett," *ON*, lxviii/3 (2003), 14–6

JAMES WIERZBICKI/JAMES BASH

Nebraska, University of. State university with campuses in Lincoln, Omaha, and Kearney. The flagship campus in Lincoln (UNL) was founded in 1869. It opened a music school as an independent but credit-awarding conservatory in 1894. Enrollment grew rapidly from 57 students to 200 by the end of the first academic year. The School of Music was sold to the Standard Chautauqua System of Lincoln in the early 20th century, but reacquired by the university in 1930. The school was in the College of Arts and Sciences from the 1930s until 1993, when it became part of a new College of Fine and Performing Arts. In 2000 the college was renamed the Hixson-Lied College of Fine and Performing Arts following receipt of a naming gift from Christina Hixson and the Lied Foundation Trust. In the fall of 2008 the School of Music enrolled approximately 400 music majors (250 undergraduate and 150 graduate students) and 20 dance majors, employed 57 faculty and 13 staff, and offered the BA, BM, BME, MM, and DMA, as well as a collaborative PhD with the College of Education and Human Sciences. Targeted program areas include chamber music, composition, jazz studies, modern dance, music education, and opera. UNL is the first research university to offer a music education degree track in music composition and pedagogy.

Today, in addition to the main campus at Lincoln and a medical campus at Omaha, the University of Nebraska at Omaha general campus (added to the state university system in 1968) is home to a Department of Music that offers BM and MM degrees taught by a faculty of 39. The University of Nebraska at Kearney (added in 1991) Department of Music & Performing Arts offers the BA, BM, BA in Ed, and MA in Ed taught by a faculty of 20.

BIBLIOGRAPHY

R.E. Knoll: *Prairie University: a History of the University of Nebraska* (Lincoln, NE, 1995)

O.B. Pollak and L. Valentine: *University of Nebraska at Omaha* (Chicago, 2007)

JOHN W. RICHMOND

Negrete (Moreno), Jorge (Alberto) (*b* Guanajuato, Mexico, 30 Nov 1911; *d* Los Angeles, CA, 5 Dec 1953). Mexican film actor and singer. Jorge Negrete was the second of five children born into an upper-class military family. In 1931 he debuted on Radio XETR singing operatic arias and romantic ballads. During this time Negrete also studied voice with José Pierson, a respected vocal coach in Mexico City. In 1936, at the request of Emilio Azcárraga, owner of Radio XEW, Negrete moved to New York City to costar on an NBC radio show entitled *The Mexican Caballeros*. Although his movie career began in 1937, it was the 1941 film *¡Ay, Jalisco…no te rajes!* (Hey Jalisco…Don't Give Up) that made Negrete a star. The singing *charro* (cowboy) role as played by Negrete displayed the character qualities of what would become the model for the singing *charro* of the 1940s and 1950s—a brave, God-fearing, macho figure with "right" on his side.

Jorge Negrete emerged as the quintessential singing charro of the comedia ranchera film genre and reached iconic status within Mexican popular culture. Numerous songs from Negrete's films such as "¡Ay Jalisco…no te rajes!," "Cocula," and "Yo soy mexicano" became classics of the mariachi repertory and he was revered by audiences in Mexico, Spain, and throughout the Americas.

BIBLIOGRAPHY

D. Negrete: *Jorge Negrete* (México City, 1987)

E. Serna: *Jorge el bueno: la vida de Jorge Negrete, vols. I and II* (México City, 1993)

DONALD A. HENRIQUES

NEH. *See* NATIONAL ENDOWMENT FOR THE HUMANITIES.

Neidich, Charles (*b* New York, NY, 26 Aug 1953). Clarinetist, teacher, and conductor. He began studying clarinet with his father; his principal teacher was New York pedagogue Leon Russianoff. After graduating from Yale in anthropology, Neidich enrolled at the Moscow State Conservatory studying with clarinetist Boris Dikov (1975). He was the first American recipient of a Fulbright grant for study in the Soviet Union. Neidich has won numerous competitions, including the Munich competition (1982) and the Atlantic Richfield Foundation Competition (1985), a special addition to the Naumburg series of competitions. He has been a faculty member of the Juilliard, Manhattan, and Mannes schools of music as well as SUNY Stony Brook and the Aaron Copland School of Music at Queens College, New York. He has been a celebrated soloist, having performed with the Minnesota, BBC Symphony, Royal Philharmonic, Saint Louis Symphony, Tafelmusik Baroque, and Orpheus Chamber orchestras, and as a guest of the Juilliard, Guarneri, Brentano, Colorado, and Cavani string quartets. Neidich has recorded and performed on period instruments and produced a reconstructed version of Wolfgang Amadeus Mozart Clarinet Concerto. His premieres include works by Milton Babbitt, Elliott Carter, Edison Denisov, and Joan Tower. In 2004 he was the recipient of Juilliard's William Schuman Scholars Chair award. As a conductor he has appeared with the New World and San Diego symphony orchestras.

BIBLIOGRAPHY
K.K. Ho: *Interpretation, Pedagogy, and Technique in Clarinet Repertoire as Reflected in the Practice of Contemporary New York Clarinetists* (diss., CUNY, 1998)

JONATHAN HOLDEN

Neidlinger, William Harold (*b* Brooklyn, NY, 20 July 1863; *d* East Orange, NJ, 5 Dec 1924). Composer, voice teacher, conductor, and organist. In New York, Neidlinger took composition lessons with DUDLEY BUCK and C.C. Müller; he continued his training in London with Edward Dannreuther. Performing as an organist and choral conductor in Brooklyn and Philadelphia until 1896, Neidlinger then lived abroad, working as a voice teacher in London and Paris. In 1901 he moved to Chicago, where his voice students included Frank King Clark, the bass. He composed the cantata *Prayer, Promise and Praise* (1906); two comic operas, *Ulysses* (1901) and *Sweet Anne Page* (1903); and approximately 200 sacred and secular solo songs, including the popular "Serenade" (1889). An interest in child psychology prompted Neidlinger's many compositions for children, including *Small Songs for Small Singers* (New York, 1896), used widely in kindergarten classrooms around the country. Other volumes in this vein include *A Primer on Voice and Singing* (New York, 1903), and a collection of nature songs for children, *Earth, Sky, and Air in Song* (New York, 1900). In the preface to this latter volume, Neidlinger writes of his desire to capture children's sense of language and humor in his songs. After moving to East Orange, New Jersey, he became interested in working with mentally disabled children, founding the Neidlinger School for the Unusual Child.

BLAKE HOWE

Neikrug, Marc (Edward) (*b* New York, NY, 24 Sept 1946). Composer and pianist. From 1964 to 1968 he studied with the opera composer Giselher Klebe at the Hochschule für Musik in Detmold. Subsequently he attended SUNY, Stony Brook (MM, composition 1971). He has received two awards from the NEA and commissions from, among others, the Houston SO, the Saint Paul Chamber Orchestra, the Deutsche Oper Berlin, the Pittsburgh SO, the Aldeburgh Festival, and the New York Philharmonic. He has served as a contemporary music consultant for the Saint Paul Chamber Orchestra (1978–85) and as the founder and director of Melbourne Summer Music in Australia (1986–91) and Santa Fe Chamber Music Festival (from 1998).

Whether writing in an atonal or a chromatically tonal idiom, Neikrug has been above all a harmonist. His orchestral works, which move in long, carefully orchestrated chordal blocks punctuated by virtuoso, repetitive

fragments of melody, reveal the influence of the composer Per Nørgård. Attacks of acoustically based harmonies and chord clusters lend his duo sonatas their rhythmic drive. Among his best known works is the theater piece *Through Roses* (1979–80), which dramatizes the nightmares of a Jewish violinist who survived in a concentration camp by playing for members of the SS; the film version received prizes at both the Besançon Film Festival (1981) and the International Film and Television Festival, New York (1982). His opera, *Los Alamos* (1988), the first American work commissioned by the Deutsche Oper Berlin, states its anti-nuclear position by juxtaposing commentaries on the "Star Wars" program and rituals practiced by the Pueblo Indians. Pueblo culture also inspired Neikrug's *Pueblo Children's Songs* for soprano and piano (1995) and *Healing Ceremony* (2009) commissioned by the University of New Mexico Cancer Center.

As a pianist, Neikrug has appeared in a duo with the violinist Pinchas Zukerman—they gave the first performance of Neikrug's Duo no.1 and the *Sonata concertante*—and was the soloist in the first performance of his Piano Concerto. He has conducted a number of performances of his works by American and European orchestras and has been composer-in-residence at the Aspen Music Festival.

WORKS

Stage: Through Roses (Neikrug), actor, 8 insts, 1979–80; Los Alamos (Neikrug), 1988; Death Cell Memoirs of an Extraterrestrial (Neikrug), actor, cl, vn, pf, 2010

Orch: Pf Conc. no.1, 1966; Cl Conc. no.1 1967; Va Conc., 1974; Eternity's Sunrise, 1979–80; Mobile, 14 insts, 1981; Vn Conc. no. 1, 1984; Chettro Ketl, chbr orch, 1986; Conc., 2 vn, va, vc, orch, 1987; Fl Conc., 1989; Sym. no.1, 1990; Fanfare, 1994; Pf Conc. no.2, 1996; Vn Conc. no.2, 1999; Rosaceae, orch, 2004; Sym. no.2 ("Quintessence"), 2007; Cl Conc. no.2, 2008; Conc. for Orch, 2011

Solo vocal: Nachtlieder, S, orch 1988; Pueblo Children's Songs, S, pf, 1995; Healing Ceremony, M/B, orch, 2009

Chbr and solo inst: Sonata, vc, 1967; 2 str qts, 1969, 1972; Suite, vc, pf, 1974; Rituals, fl, hp, 1976; Concertino, fl, ob, cl, vn, va, vc, pf, 1977; Continuum, vc, pf, 1978; Kaleidoscope, cl, pf, 1979; Duo no.1, vn, pf, 1983; Voci, cl, vn, vc, pf, 1988; Stars the Mirror, str qt, 1988; "Take Me T"/Susan's Gift, perc, 1989; Duo concertante, vn, pf, 1995; Str Qnt, 1996; Petrus, vc, pf, 2001; Pf Qnt, 2 vn, va, vc, pf, 2003; Duo no.2, 2006; Three Wine Pieces, vn, pf, 2006; Ritual, vc, pf, perc, 2007; Passions Reflected, pf, 2008; Green Torso, vn, va, vc, pf, 2009; Cl Qnt, 2010

Some early works withdrawn

Principal publishers: Bärenreiter, Chester, Hansen, Presser, Salabert

SEVERINE NEFF

Neil A. Kjos Music Company. Music publisher. The company was founded in 1936 by Neil A. Kjos Sr. Originally headquartered in the suburbs of Chicago, it relocated in 1975 to San Diego, California. The firm is especially noted for its instructional books for beginners. Choral music and pedagogical literature have remained staples since the firm opened. Neil A. Kjos Jr. joined the business in the 1960s and took over operations in 1968. Under his leadership the company expanded into piano pedagogy, working with music educators to create a comprehensive and facile series. Frequent collaborators include Jim and Jane Bastien, who contributed a series of almost 400 books for beginning pianists, and Bruce

Pearson, who has written for beginning band and orchestra. The firm has also targeted international markets and was one of the first to introduce recordings alongside method books. Upon his retirement in 1998, Kjos Jr. passed the business on to his two sons, Mark and Tim.

JONAS WESTOVER

Neill, Ben (*b* Winston-Salem, NC, 14 Nov 1957). Composer and trumpet player. He studied at Youngstown State University (BM 1980, MM 1982), the Manhattan School of Music (DMA 1986), and with LA MONTE YOUNG, whose meditatively long-toned brass music was a primary influence. He also played guitar with Rhys Chatham, later following him as music curator of The Kitchen, New York (1992–8). Neill has done commercial work for television and films, and since 2008 has taught music industry and production at Ramapo College. His performing and composing careers have centered on the Mutantrumpet, a three-belled instrument of his own invention with pressure-sensing pads that connect it to MIDI controller. Using this instrument, Neill has triggered sound-transforming computer sequences during performance, a technique that shares characteristics with the music of David Behrman, with whom he has worked closely.

Neill's computer installations have developed from both pitch and rhythmic manifestations of the overtone series. *678 Streams*, for example, unleashes computerized beats in patterns of six against seven against eight. Works such as *Green Machine* exist not only as performances but also as ambient installations. The theater pieces *ITSOFOMO (In the Shadow of Forward Motion)* and *Downwind* express liberal political views. Heavily beat-oriented, his music has gained a considerable following of ambient rock fans; in *Night Science* (2009) he combined his mutantrumpet improvisation with the rhythms of dubstep, an electronic dance-music genre that originated in London. *Persephone*, a music theater piece presented at the Brooklyn Academy of Music in 2010, combined samples of 19th-century Romantic music with electronica and rock, while *Posthorn* (2008) used a solo from Gustav Mahler's Third Symphony as the basis for computer-enhanced video. The rhythmic complexity of his works made him a seminal figure in the Totalist movement of the 1990s in Manhattan, and his music continues to explore harmonic ratios and numerical structures.

WORKS

MULTIMEDIA

(mtpt—mutantrumpet; †—collab. D. Wojnarowicz)

Orbs, mtpt + elecs, perc, slide projections, 1984; Aggregation†, mtpt + elecs, perc, video, 1989; AIDS Ragtime†, mtpt + elecs, perc, video, 1989; The Industrial Section/High Tech Accelerando†, mtpt + elecs, perc, video, 1989; Intermezzo†, mtpt + elecs, perc, video, 1989; ITSOFOMO (In the Shadow of Forward Motion)†, mtpt + elecs, perc + elecs, video, 1989; Liberty†, mtpt + elecs, perc, video, 1989; Downwind, spkr, 2 trbn, elec gui, pedal steel gui, perc, slide projections, 1992; Green machine, mtpt + elecs, cptr, interactive projections, 1994 [also interactive installation]; *Palladio*, 3 vv, el-ac gui,

mtpt + elecs, interactive video samples (collab. B. Jones, based on novel by J. Dee), 2005; *Persephone*, S, 5 female vv, mtpt + elecs, vc, elec b gui, drums, samples (collab. Ridge Theater, M. Goese, and W. Leght), 2010

FOR MTPT AND ELECS

Schizetudes 1–3, 1988–92; Clandestinetude no.3, 1992; Blues' Yellow Shadow, 1993; Music for the King of Thule, 1993; 678 Streams, 1993; Auricle, 1994; Critical State, 1994; Ether, 1994; Night Vision, 1994; 689 Pleasures, 1994; Sistrum, 1994; Chemistry of 7, 1995; Pentagram (collab. P. Miller), 1995; Somnabula, 1995; Blue Maroon, 1996; Dream Phase, 1996; Flotation Device, 1996; Propeller, 1996; Triptycal, 1996; Twelfth Flight, 1996; Freezer Burn, 1997; Goldbug, 1997; Route Me Out, 1997; Syntonic, 1997; Tunnel Vision, 1997; Lookinglast, 1998; Posthorn, 1998; Turbonium, 1999; Bouquet, 2000; Turbonium X, 2001; First Kiss, 2004; Hummer Symphony, 2004; Mal's Theme, 2004; Laudanum, 2007; Novalis, 2007; Oberon, 2007; Lonesome Wood, 2008; Futura, 2009; Monochromatic, 2009; Afterimage, 2009; Seeker, 2009; Alpha Dub, 2009; Gaugear, 2009; Hudsonic, 2009; Booster, 2009; Hearthrob, 2009; Menace Ultimo, 2009; Outlands, 2009

With other insts: Bal, mtpt + elecs, 2 trbn, pedal steel gui, perc, 1985; 2 Dances, mtpt + elecs, 2 trbn, pedal steel gui, perc, 1985; Mainspring, mtpt + elecs, 2 trbn, pedal steel gui, perc, 1985; Sarabande, mtpt + elecs, 2 trbn, pedal steel gui, perc, 1985; Dis-Solution 2, mtpt + elecs, perc, 1986; Money Talk, mtpt + elecs, perc, tape, 1987; Torchtower, spkr, mtpt + elecs, perc, gui, 1992; Dark Gift, mtpt + elecs, vc, 1997; It's Only Money, mtpt + elecs, vc, gui, 1997; Shirt Waste, mtpt + elecs, gui, 1988; Pulstax, mtpt + elecs, drums, 1999; 6 of the Other, mtpt + elecs, drums, 1999; Salvia Mea, mtpt + elecs, drums, 1999; Ambulance Sym., v, mtpt + elecs, drums, text by A. Montgomery, 2000; West Nile Fever, v, mtpt + elecs, drums, cowritten with A. Montgomery, 2000; Subway Surfers, v, mtpt + elecs, drums, cowritten with A. Montgomery, 2000; Palladio Theme/Kicked, 2004, v, mtpt + elecs, drums, cowritten with L. Jensen, 2000; Molly's Theme, v, mtpt + elecs, cowritten with L. Jensen, 2004; Swimming with the Fishes, v, gui, mtpt + elecs, cowritten with L. Jensen, 2004; Last Kiss, v, gui, mtpt + elecs, cowritten with L. Jensen, 2004; Truth Transmitters, v, mtpt + elecs, cowritten with L. Jensen, 2004; Color Bar Remix, mtpt + elecs, gui, 2004; Cusp, v, mtpt + elecs, cowritten with M. Goese, 2007; Resonata, v, mtpt + elecs, cowritten with M. Goese, 2007; Elegy, v, mtpt + elecs, cowritten with M. Goese, 2007; World's End, v, mtpt + elecs, cowritten with M. Goese, 2007; New Green, v, mtpt + elecs, cowritten with M. Goese, 2007; Stargazer, v, mtpt + elecs, cowritten with M. Goese, 2007; Roma, v, mtpt + elecs, cowritten with M. Goese, 2007; Blackpool, v, mtpt + elecs, cowritten with M. Goese, 2010; If You Lie Awake, v, mtpt + elecs, cowritten with M. Goese, 2010; A Lovely Goodbye, v, mtpt + elecs, cowritten with M. Goese, 2010

OTHER WORKS

Magnetic Etudes, chbr orch, 1983; Dis-Solution 1, 2 melody insts, elec gui, elec kbd, drum machine, 1986; No More People, S, mtpt, str qnt, elec gui, drums, 1987, orchd 1995; Abblasen House, 2 mtpt, 2 trbn, elec gui, perc, drum cptr, 1988; Dromosolo, spkr, mtpt + cptr, interactive elecs, 1988; Aria di Battaglia, mtpt, 2 trbn, pedal steel gui, perc, 1990; Mojave, insts, tape, 1990; Nuerplay, 15 or more insts, 1990; After Haydn, mtpt + elecs, trbn-propelled elecs, collab. N. Collins, 1991; Antiphony, 4 tpt, 2 perc, live elecs, 1991; Clandestinetude no.1, elec gui, 1992; Clandestinetude no.2, 2 trbn, 1992; Kama rupa, elecs, 1994; Sargasso, elecs, 1994; Counting Laughter, 2 tpt, 2 perc, elecs, 1995; I am a girl who loves to shoot, S, orch, 1995; 3 Way 150 voice, elecs, 1999; Man's Best Friend, elecs, 1999; Dead Plants, slide whistle, elecs, 1999; Nite Nite, fl, elecs, 2000; Ice Cream, gui/elecs, 2000; Passing, gui/elecs, 2000; Whisper, elecs, 2000; Funk Stop, elecs, 2000; Spheramid, sax/elecs, 2000; Concessions, elecs, 2000; Red Calle, gui/elecs (co-composed with R. Poss), 2000; Bugfunk, gui, elecs, 2001; Iceman, gui, elecs, 2001

BIBLIOGRAPHY

B. Neill: "Pleasure Beats: Rhythm and the Aesthetics of Current Electronic Music," *Leonardo Music Journal, xii: Pleasure* (2002), 3–6

KYLE GANN

Nelhybel, Vaclav (*b* Polanka nad Odrou, Czechoslovakia, 24 Sept 1919; *d* Scranton, PA, 22 March 1996). Czech composer, naturalized American. He studied classics and musicology at Prague University and conducting and composition at the Prague Conservatory. In 1942 he continued his musicological studies at Fribourg University in Switzerland, where he taught music theory from 1947. He also held conducting positions with Radio Prague and the Stadttheater (1939–42), the Czech PO (1945–6), Swiss Radio (1946–50), and Radio Free Europe (1950–57). In 1957 he emigrated to the United States, becoming an American citizen in 1962. He taught at the University of Massachusetts, Lowell (1978–9), and the University of Scranton, Pennsylvania (1994–6), where he co-founded the World Premiere Composition Series.

Synthesizing several musical styles by incorporating various elements from existing systems, Nelhybel's music demonstrates a linear-modal orientation in which functional tonality does not apply. An interaction of autonomous melodic lines and complementary rhythmic patterns creates a vigorous drive that is the hallmark of his style. This whirlwind propulsion is the result of a generation of tension through the accumulation of dissonance, increases in textural density, and the use of a wide range of dynamics and timbres. Thematic material was often borrowed from his Czech heritage. *Music for Orchestra and Woodwind Quintet* (1987), for example, quotes his favorite Slovak folksong and a well known Bohemian chorale.

Nelhybel wrote three operas, *Legend* (1954), *Everyman* (1974), and *Station* (1978). Of these, *Everyman*, based on the medieval morality play, is the best known. Essentially tonal with modal coloring to evoke the feeling of the medieval original, the orchestration employs winds, brass, chimes, bells, organ, and percussion. The harmonic language is chromatic, especially in scenes where the character of Death is important.

WORKS

Stage: Morality e feux (ballet), 1942; Cock and the Hangman (ballet), 1946; In the Shadow of a Lime Tree (ballet), 1946; Legend (op), 1954; Everyman (op), 1974; Station (op), 1978

Vocal: Cantata pacis, 6 solo vv, chorus, wind, perc, org, 1965; Epitaph for a Soldier (W. Whitman), solo vv, chorus, 1966; Dies ultima, 3 solo vv, chorus, jazz band, orch, 1967; Sine nomine, 4 solo vv, chorus, orch, tape, 1968; America Sings, Bar, chorus, band, 1974; Estampie natalis, chorus, ens, 1975; Adoratio, chorus, 1979; Fables for all Time, nar, chorus, orch, 1980; Let there be Music, Bar, chorus, orch, 1982; songs; anthems

Sym. band/wind ens: Caucasian Passacaglia, 1963; Conc. antiphonale, brass, 1964; Sym. Requiem, with Bar, 1965; Festivo, 1969; Yamaha Conc., 1971; Concertino da camera, vc, wind, pf, 1972; Toccata, hpd, wind, perc, 1972; Cantus and Ludus, pf, wind, perc, 1973; Dialogues, with pf, 1976; Counterpoint no.2, trbn, perc, 1979; Ritual, 1979; Music, 12 tpt, wind, 1980; Sinfonia resurrectionis, 1980; Conc., grosso, 1981; Ps xii, wind, perc, 1981; Cl Conc., 1982; Concertante, 1982; Trittico, 1993; Conc., t trbn, b trbn, wind ens, 1995

Orch: Sym., 1942; Etude symphonique, 1949; Sinfonietta concertante, 1960; Va Conc., 1962; Houston Conc., 1967; Polyphonies, 1972; Polyphonic Variations, tpt, str, 1976; Slavonic Triptych, 1976; Music for Orch and Ww Qnt, 1987; Conc., b trbn, orch/band, 1992

Chbr: Wind Qnt [no.1], 1948; Str Qt [no.1], 1949; Wind Qnt [no.2], 1958; Wind Qnt [no.3], 1960; Brass Qnt [no.1], 1961; Str Qt [no.2], 1962; Brass Qnt [no.2], 1965; Quintetto concertante, vn, tpt, trbn, xyl, pf, 1965; Conc., perc, 1972; Conc. spirituoso nos.1–4, 1974–7; Ludus, 3 tubas, 1975; Music, 6 tpt, 1975; Praeambulum, org, timp, 1977; Variations, hp, 1977; Oratio no.2, ob, str trio, 1979; Sonate da chiesa; many other small chbr works; many pf and org pieces

Many pieces for children; arrs. of own works

Principal publishers: Barta, Belwin-Mills, Christopher, General, Kirby, Presser

WRITINGS
"A Creative Climate for Composers," *The Instrumentalist*, xxv/8 (1970), 18–9
"The Composer Conducts," *The Instrumentalist*, xxviii/11 (1974), 42–3
"An Approach to Analysis of a Score," *School Musician*, xlii/6 (1981), 8–10

BIBLIOGRAPHY
J. Blahnik: "Nelhybel's Concept of Conducting," *The Instrumentalist*, xxiii/12 (1968), 33–6
P. Michaelides: "Nelhybel—Composer for Concert Band," *Music Educators Journal*, liv/4 (1968), 51–3 [analysis of *Cantata pacis*]
P.L. Boonshaft: *Vaclav Nelhybel: a Biographical Study and Survey of his Compositions with an Analysis for Performance of "Caucasian Passacaglia"* (diss., U. of Hartford, Connecticut, 1991)
J.D. Knapp: *Vaclav Nelhybel: his Life, Influences on his Compositional Style and a Review of his Published Choral Compositions* (diss., U. of Missouri, Kansas City, 1991)
W.H. Rehrig: *The Heritage Encyclopedia of Band Music* (Westerville, OH, 1991/*R*); repr. on CD-ROM, 2005) [includes extensive works list]
J. Smolka: "Václav Nelhýbel: Český skladatel a dirigent v USA," *Hudební rozhledy*, xliv/2 (1991), 79–82
J. Knight: "Conducting Nelhybel's *Festivo*: Greatness in Grade 3 Music," *The Instrumentalist*, li/1 (1996), 18–22
P.L. Boonshaft: "Discovering a Treasure of 160 Nelhybel Works," *The Instrumentalist*, liii/1 (1998), 68–72
N.E. Smith: *Program Notes for Band* (Lake Charles, LA, 2000), 442–4
R.L. Tucker: *A Historical Examination of the Hymn Tune Ein feste Burg and its Treatment in Selected Twentieth-century Concert Band Literature* (diss., Texas Tech U., 2001) [incl. chapter on Nelhybel's *Festive Adorations*]
H.D. Bath. "Vaclav Nelhybel's *Trittico*: a Symphonic Painting in Sound," *The Instrumentalist*, lvi/5 (2002), 32–6

JAMES P. CASSARO

Nelson, Ken (*b* Caledonia, MN, 19 Jan 1911; *d* Somis, CA, 6 Jan 2008). Country music record producer. One of the most prolific, influential, and successful record producers in the country arena, Ken Nelson was raised in a Chicago orphanage and struck out on his own at the age of 14. He had a brief performing career as a member of the Campus Kids but soon thereafter achieved more success on Chicago radio. His promotion of country music received the attention of Los Angeles-based Capitol Records, which hired him as producer in 1947. Nelson was appointed head of the country division in 1951 and remained in the post until 1971. Over that period he produced thousands of sessions and achieved more than 100 number-one hits. The roster of artists with whom he was associated is astounding: Ferlin Husky, Red Simpson, Faron Young, Jean Shepard, Tommy Collins, Merle Travis, Wynn Stewart, Rose Maddox, the Farmer Boys, Hank Thompson, and Sonny James. Nelson also helped establish the commercial and aesthetic preeminence of the Bakersfield Sound by producing the career-establishing recordings of Merle Haggard and Buck Owens. He made his mark in other genres as well by signing humorist Stan Freberg to the label, recording rock and roll pioneers Wanda Jackson and Gene Vincent, promoting session musician Glen

Campbell into a pop star, and bringing the Beach Boys to the attention of the company. Nelson retired from Capitol in 1976. He was inducted into the Country Music Hall of Fame in 2001 and published an autobiography, *My First 90 Years Plus 3* (Pittsburgh, 2003).

DAVID SANJEK

Nelson, Oliver (Edward) (*b* St. Louis, MO, 4 June 1932; *d* Los Angeles, CA, 27 Oct 1975). Composer, arranger, and saxophonist. He studied piano and saxophone during his childhood and theory and composition at Washington University in St. Louis (BM 1957) and Lincoln University (MM 1958). He was also a private composition student of ELLIOTT CARTER. Nelson performed with various territory bands (late 1940s), Louis Jordan's orchestra (1950–51), and the US Marine Band (1951–3). He moved to New York in 1959 and made a series of highly regarded recordings, many of which included his own compositions. The most important of these was the album *The Blues and the Abstract Truth* (Imp., 1961), which also featured Freddie Hubbard, Eric Dolphy, and Bill Evans. Nelson toured with the Quincy Jones Orchestra (1960–61) and was briefly a substitute in Duke Ellington's group (1961). As a composer he is best known for his jazz works, such as "Stolen Moments" (which has become a standard), *Jazzhattan Suite* (1967), *Black, Brown and Beautiful* (1969), and *Berlin Dialogue for Orchestra* (1970). He also wrote in classical forms, but most of this music was not well received and remains unpublished. As an arranger Nelson was in high demand, and his arrangements appeared on the recordings of Wes Montgomery (including the Grammy-winning album *Goin' Out of My Head*, Verve, 1965), Count Basie, Lee Morgan, and Buddy Rich, among others. In 1967 he moved to Los Angeles to pursue a career scoring for film and television; his work in this field included music for the television show *The Six Million Dollar Man* and the film *Death of a Gunfighter*. Nelson's most important contribution as a jazz educator is the book *Patterns for Improvisation* (Hollywood, 1966).

RECORDINGS
(selective)

As leader: *Meet Oliver Nelson* (NewJ, 1959); *Screamin' the Blues* (NewJ, 1960); *Taking Care of Business* (NewJ, 1960); *The Blues and the Abstract Truth* (Imp., 1961); *Straight Ahead* (NewJ, 1961); *More Blues and the Abstract Truth* (Imp., 1964); *Live from Los Angeles* (Imp., 1967)

As sideman: L. Bellson: *The Brilliant Bellson Sound* (Verve, 1959); E. Davis: *Trane Whistle* (Prst., 1960); D. Ellington: *Paris Blues* (UA, 1961); J.J. Johnson: *The Dynamic Sound of J.J. with Big Band* (Vic., 1964)

BIBLIOGRAPHY

P. Garland: "The Many 'Bags' of Oliver Nelson," *Ebony*, xxiv/1 (1968), 108–20
D. Baker, L. Baker, and H. Hudson, eds.: *The Black Composer Speaks* (Metuchen, NJ, 1978)
A. Homzy: "Nelson, Oliver Edward," *International Dictionary of Black Composers*, ed. S. Floyd (Chicago, 1999) [incl. works list]
M.D. Moss: *Concert Band Music by African-American Composers: 1927–1998* (diss., U. of Michigan, 2000)

LARS HELGERT

Nelson, Ricky [Nelson, Eric Hilliard; Rick] (*b* Teaneck, NJ, 8 May 1940; *d* DeKalb, TX, 31 Dec 1985). Singer, actor, and songwriter. Born into a performing family, Nelson was given a boost towards stardom at a young age, and even his first forays into music were successful. The second son of bandmaster Ozzie and singer Harriet Nelson, he was already an actor on the radio series "The Adventures of Ozzie and Harriet" by 1949. The family's popularity inspired a film (*Here Come the Nelsons*, 1952), which led to the popular television series, also titled "The Adventures of Ozzie and Harriet" (1952–66), on which he premiered as a singer. His good looks and clean image helped turn Nelson into a teen idol. In 1957, when he was 16, his first release became a hit: "A Teenager's Romance" with "I'm Walkin'" on the flip side. Numerous hits followed, including "Stood Up" (1958), "Travelin' Man" (1961), "Young World" (1962), and "For You" (1963). He landed a five-year deal with Imperial Records, and his career further blossomed. His first album, *Ricky* (1957), sold over a million copies, fueled by the hit "Be Bop Baby." At first he worked mainly with studio jazz musicians, but as he became more interested in rock, Nelson insisted on a "younger" sound that was more akin to the music of Carl Perkins and Elvis Presley (whose backup vocalists worked uncredited for Nelson). He also performed musical numbers on the family's television program, one of the early cross-marketed TV superstars. His next and perhaps greatest hit was "Poor Little Fool" (1958), which reached number one. He managed to work his way out from under his family's shadow by appearing in a number of movies, including *Rio Bravo* (1959, which earned Nelson a Golden Globe), *The Wackiest Ship in the Army* (1960), and *Love and Kisses* (1965). Into the late 1960s, drug use slowed Nelson's productivity, and in the early 1970s, he struggled to regain his earlier musical footing. He continued to appear on television throughout the decade and into the next before his death in an accidental plane crash in 1985. Though Nelson's success as a musician owed much to the exposure he received on television, his songs were often first-rate; he chose good material; and his accounts of white, middle-class, teenage life were evocative and memorable.

BIBLIOGRAPHY

P. Bashe: *Teenage Idol, Travelin' Man: the Complete Biography of Rick Nelson* (New York, 1992)

JONAS WESTOVER

Nelson, Ron (*b* Joliet, IL, 14 Dec 1929). Composer and conductor. He studied with HOWARD HANSON, BERNARD ROGERS, LOUIS MENNINI, and WAYNE BARLOW at the Eastman School (1948–57), where he received the BMus, MMus, and DMA degrees, and with Tony Aubin in Paris at the Ecole Normale de Musique (1954–5). In 1956 he joined the faculty of Brown University, where he served as chairman of the music department (1963–73) and as professor from 1968 until his retirement in 1992. He has received many honors, among them a Fulbright award (1954–5), a Ford Foundation fellowship (1963), a Howard Foundation grant (1965–6), NEA grants (1973,

1976, 1979), and many commissions (including the National SO, the Rochester PO, the USAF Band and Chorus, the Rhode Island PO, the Aspen Music Festival, and many colleges and universities). In 1993 his Passacaglia (Homage on B-A-C-H) made history by winning all three major wind band competitions—the National Association Prize, the American Bandmasters Association Ostwald Prize, and the Sudler International Prize. He was awarded the Medal of Honor of the John Philip Sousa Foundation in Washington, DC, in 1994. He has appeared as guest composer and conductor at numerous colleges and universities.

From early on Nelson's music has revealed fine craftsmanship, particularly in its subtle control of rich and varied textures, and a keen sense of instrumental and vocal color. It explores a wide range of styles while remaining accessible in its tonal focus, melodic inventiveness, and formal clarity. Nelson's exposure in the mid-1960s to non-Western cultures, particularly those of East Asia, and his growing fascination with meditation and music that would induce states of meditative calm have strongly influenced his mature style. His skilled and sympathetic writing for the voice and his concern for rich and sonorous harmony give his choral works a consistency that transcends stylistic shifts. In a number of later works, gamelan-like percussion textures, often created through a controlled aleatorism that can also affect the length of the work, provide kaleidoscopic canvases upon which lyrical melodies are drawn. The textures of Psalm XCV grew out of experiments with meditation and biofeedback devices; in the Mass of St. La Salle, Nelson drew on the music of medieval and Renaissance composers, using specific traits such as the relentless modal rhythms of Perotinus to serve as a point of departure for his own musical imagination. His *Five Pieces after Paintings by Andrew Wyeth* explore a number of styles, from sophisticated chromatic counterpoint to rock and jazz rhythms to Ivesian collage and layering, resulting in a vivid programmatic tapestry characteristic of his instrumental palette.

WORKS

Ops: The Birthday of the Infanta (Nelson), 1955–6; Hamaguchi (M. Miller), 1981

Choral: The Christmas Story (Bible), cantata, Bar, nar, SATB, brass, perc, org, 1958, arr. SATB, orch; 5 Anthems for Young Choirs (Heb. Book of Prayer), SA, pf, 1961; 3 Ancient Prayers (Heb. Book of Prayer), SATB, org, 1962; Triumphal Te Deum, SSAATTBB, org, brass, perc, 1963; What Is Man? (S. Miller), oratorio, Bar, S, nar, SATB, orch/org, brass, perc, 1967; Prayer of Emperor of China on the Altar of Heaven, 21 Dec 1539 (Emperor of China), SATB, wind, perc, 1972; Psalm XCV, SATB, insts ad lib, 1971; 4 Pieces after the Seasons (T. Ahlburn), SATB, insts ad lib, 1977; 3 Autumnal Sketches (Ahlburn), S, SATB, insts, 1980; Mass of St. La Salle, inst ens, 1981; 3 Nocturnal Pieces (Ahlburn), SATB, insts, 1982; 3 Seasonal Reflections (Ahlburn), 1982; Three Settings of the Moon, SA, pf, mar, glock, 1983; Three Pieces after Tennyson, TTBB or SATB, pf, 1987; Three Mountain Ballads, SATB, pf, 1988; Invoking the Powers, SATB, pf, perc, 1990; And this shall be for music, SATB, brass, 1990; Songs of Praise and Reconciliation, SATB or TTBB, pf, perc, 1991; Proclaim this day for music, SATB, brass, perc, 2001; Let us find a meadow, SATB, pf, 2005; other pieces, incl. several on biblical texts

Large Ens: Conc. for Pf and Symph Band, 1948; Savannah River Holiday, 1955, arr. band 1973; Mayflower Ov., band, 1958, rev. 1997;

Ballet: Dance in Ruins, orch, 1964; Sarabande: for Katharine in April, orch, 1954; Jubilee, orch, 1960; This Is the Orchestra, nar, orch, 1960; Ov. for Latecomers, orch, 1961; Toccata for Orch, 1961; Rocky Point Holiday, orch/band, 1969; Trilogy: JFK-MLK-RFK, tape, orch, c1969–70; 5 Pieces after Paintings by Andrew Wyeth, orch 1976; Meditation and Dance, orch, 1977; Fanfare for a Celebration, band, 1982; Medieval Suite, band, 1983; Fanfare for a Celebration, orch, 1983; Pebble Beach Sojurn, org, brass, perc, 1983; Aspen Jubilee, band, 1984; Danza Capriccio, a sax, wind ens, 1988; Brevard Fanfare, brass, 1986; Te Deum Laudamus, SATB, wind ens, 1988; Elegy II for Strings, 1988; Morning Allelusia, wind orch, 1989, 1989; Fanfare for the Jour of Sunrise, wind ens, perc, 1989; Resonances I, winds, perc, 1990; Lauds (Prasie High Day), band, 1991; To the Airborne, band, 1992; Passacaglia (Homage on B-A-C-H), band, 1992; Epiphanies (Fanfares and Chorales), band, 1994; Chaconne (In Memoriam…), band, 1994; Sonoran Desert Holiday, band, 1994; Courtly Airs and Dances, band, 1995; Nightsong, euph, wind ens, 1995; Fanfare for the Kennedy Center, brass, perc, 1995; Panels (Epiphanies II), orch, 1996; Resonances II, orch, brass, 1997; Elegy I, str orch, 1998; Fanfare for the New Millennium, band, 2 ant brass choirs, 1999; Pastorale: Autumn Rune, band, 2006

Chbr: Kristen's Song, vn, fl, org, 1982; And the Moon Rose Garden, vc, pf, 1982; Nightsong, instr/acc., 1986

Film scores: many documentary and educational film scores

Principal publishers: Boosey & Hawkes, Carl Fischer, Ludwig Music, Theodore Presser

BIBLIOGRAPHY

Baker8

J. Vinton, ed.: *Dictionary of Contemporary Music* (New York, 1974)

LANCE W. BRUNNER/GREG A STEINKE

Nelson, Tracy (*b* Madison, WI, 27 Dec 1944). Singer. An underrated and insufficiently recognized artist, she is accomplished in country, blues, rhythm-and-blues, and rock. She began performing in college and released her first solo recording, *Deep Are the Roots*, in 1964. She joined the ensemble Mother Earth (named after a Memphis Slim song), who were signed to Mercury Records in 1968. Their first album, *Living with the Animals*, includes Nelson's signature self-penned song, "Down So Low," a grieving but never glum ballad. Mother Earth recorded three other albums on Mercury and one each for Reprise and Columbia, before breaking up in 1973. Nelson also released a splendid solo album of country songs in 1970. She has subsequently performed solo or as a member of star-studded ensembles. Her 1974 duet with Willie Nelson, "After the Fire Is Gone," received a Grammy nomination in 1974. Owing to discomfort with the state of the music business, Nelson dropped out for the better part of the 1980s, although she sang back-up for Neil Young and appeared with him at Live Aid in 1985. In the 1990s she released several albums on Rounder, including *Sing It*, a 1998 collaboration with Marcia Ball and Irma Thomas; it received a Grammy nomination. Nelson released her first live recording, *Live from Cell Block D*, in 2004 and a second country release, *You'll Never Be a Stranger at My Door*, in 2007.

DAVID SANJEK

Nelson, Willie (Hugh) (*b* Abbott, TX, 30 April 1933). Singer, songwriter, and actor. A member of the Country Music Hall of Fame (1993) and Songwriters Hall of Fame (2001), Nelson received his first guitar from his paternal grandparents at the age of six. Absorbing the sounds of western swing, gospel convention singing, and the Czech and German bands that played in the Texas Hill Country, he composed his first songs at the age of seven, debuted as a singer in a West, Texas bar at age nine, and worked as a rhythm guitarist in John Raycheck's polka band at age ten.

Following service in the US Air Force and a year of agricultural studies at Baylor University, Nelson set out to become a professional musician, playing clubs throughout Texas; working as a disc jockey on radio stations in Hillsboro (KHBR), Pleasanton (KBOP), and Fort Worth (KCNC, KCUL); and developing a portfolio of songs. In 1956, he moved to Vancouver, Washington, where he was a disc jockey on KVAN. There, he used the radio studio to record his first two sides, "No Place for Me" and "Lumberjack." Returning to Fort Worth in 1958, Nelson joined KCUL's "Cowtown Hoedown" as the house band's lead guitarist, which led to contracts with D Records and publisher Glad Music in 1959.

In 1960, Nelson traveled to Nashville, where he signed with publisher Pamper Music. The following year, his song "Crazy" became a major hit for country crooner Patsy Cline, and Faron Young's recording of his "Hello Walls" sold over a million copies. Widely recognized by his peers as one of the most evocative songwriters of his generation, Nelson did not enjoy similar initial success as a recording artist. He recorded briefly for Liberty Records before signing with RCA Victor in 1965, where, until 1972, producers Chet Atkins and Felton Jarvis struggled to develop a sound and image that suited his musical approach.

Despite becoming a member of the "Grand Ole Opry" in 1965, Nelson frequently returned to the Texas dancehalls to entertain his most supportive audiences. When his Nashville home burned in December 1969, Nelson returned to Texas permanently and began reading the work of poet Khalil Gibran and psychic Edgar Cayce, whose influence can be heard in his concept albums *Yesterday's Wine* (RCA Vic., 1971) and *Phases and Stages* (Atl., 1974). Nelson also became a leader of the progressive country music scene that flourished around the Armadillo World Headquarters in Austin, Texas between 1972 and 1978, performing regularly in the city; investing in the city's entertainment industry; and, beginning in 1973, staging an annual Fourth of July Picnic to showcase songwriters, country legends, and promising new acts. Following the release of his concept album *Red Headed Stranger* (Col., 1975), Nelson also became associated with the "Outlaw country" movement in Nashville, led by Waylon Jennings and Tompall Glaser and culminating in the platinum-selling release *Wanted! The Outlaws* (RCA Vic., 1976).

Always an eclectic musician, Nelson recorded prolifically in the late 1970s and 1980s, creating collections of pop standards, soundtracks to feature films, and duets with such artists as Ray Charles, Emmylou Harris, George Jones, and Julio Iglesias. In 1985, Nelson organized Farm Aid, a benefit concert and non-profit organization which, to 2010, has raised $37 million in support of family farmers in the United States. That year, Nelson joined Kris Kristofferson, Waylon Jennings, and Johnny Cash to form the country supergroup the

Highwaymen, which recorded three albums and toured for a decade. Throughout the 1990s and early 2000s, Nelson maintained a rigorous touring and recording schedule, releasing as many as three albums a year and performing as many as 200 nights annually.

RECORDINGS
(selective list)
Country Willie: His Own Songs (RCA Vic. LSP-3418, 1965); *Yesterday's Wine* (RCA Vic. LSP-4568, 1971); *Phases and Stages* (Atl. SD 7291, 1974); *Red Headed Stranger* (Col. KC-33482, 1975); with W. Jennings, J. Colter, and T. Glaser: *Wanted! The Outlaws* (RCA Vic. APL1-1321, 1976); *Stardust* (Col. KC-35305, 1978); with J. Cash, W. Jennings, and K. Kristofferson: *The Highwaymen* (Col. CK-40056, 1985); *Teatro* (Isl. 52454, 1998)

BIBLIOGRAPHY
M. Bane: *The Outlaws: Revolution in Country Music* (n.p., 1978)
W. Nelson and B. Shrake: *I Didn't Come Here and I Ain't Leavin'* (New York, 1988; repr. 1988 as *Willie: an Autobiography*)
W. Nelson: *The Facts of Life and Other Dirty Jokes* (New York, 2002)
J. Reid: *The Improbable Rise of Redneck Rock* (Austin, 1974, 2/2004)
J.N. Patoski: *Willie Nelson: An Epic Life* (New York, 2008)

TRAVIS D. STIMELING

Nelsova [Katznelson], **Zara** (*b* Winnipeg, MB, 24 Dec 1917; *d* New York, NY, 10 Oct 2002). Cellist of Canadian birth; naturalized American. She began lessons in early childhood with her father, later studied with Dezsö Mahalek, and then moved with her family to London, where she studied at the London School of Violoncello and privately with its principal, Herbert Walenn. She was heard by John Barbirolli and introduced by him to PABLO CASALS, from whom she received additional lessons. She also had brief periods of study with EMANUEL FEUERMANN and GREGOR PIATIGORSKY. In 1932 she gave a London debut recital and appeared as a soloist with Malcolm Sargent and the LSO, playing Edouard Lalo's Concerto. Later she joined her two older sisters, a violinist and a pianist, and as the Canadian Trio they toured extensively in Britain, Australia, northern Africa, and South Africa. During World War II she was principal cellist of the Toronto SO, and in 1942 she made her US solo debut, at Town Hall, New York. From 1949 she was based in London and introduced to Britain new works by Samuel Barber, Paul Hindemith, Dmitry Shostakovich, and Ernest Bloch, who dedicated to her his three suites for unaccompanied cello; later, she gave the premiere of the concerto by Hugh Wood at the 1969 Promenade Concerts. In 1955 she took American citizenship and in 1963 married pianist Grant Johannesen, with whom she gave numerous duo recitals. In 1966 she became the first American cellist to tour the USSR, where she played sonatas by Zoltán Kodály and Serge Rachmaninoff. Although noted as an interpreter of the contemporary cello repertory, Nelsova also excelled in Romantic works, compensating for some lack of force with a sensitive feeling for melodic phrase and formal development. Among her recordings are Edward Elgar's Concerto, Bloch's *Schelomo* (with the composer conducting), Barber's Cello Concerto, also under the composer's direction, and Ludwig van Beethoven's piano trios with Glenn Gould and Alexander Schneider. She also premiered Paul Hindemith's *A*

Frog He Went A-Courting in London in 1947, Alexander Brott's *Arabesque* in Montreal in 1958, Alexei Haieff's Cello Sonata in 1963, and gave the US premiere of Robert Casadesus's Sonata in 1972. She taught at the Juilliard School of Music from 1985 until the year of her death. In 1960 she was bequeathed a Stradivari cello, the "Marquis de Corberon," dated 1726.

NOËL GOODWIN/RICHARD WIGMORE/
MEGAN E. HILL

Neo-soul. Musical genre. Dating from the mid-1990s, neo-soul typically features heartfelt love songs that reflect the complexity of contemporary romantic relationships. In its emotional depth it recalls bluesy, gospel-based soul music of the 1960s but is rendered through a more nuanced set of musical conventions. The genre definition is contested because, although the term has been used by music writers, industry publicists, and musicologists, the musicians whom it purportedly identifies have tended to reject it. Nonetheless, there are a number of artists, songs, and aesthetic features that distinguish it as a unique style of contemporary black popular music.

Neo-soul often contains spoken-word poetry or a vocal delivery that is more restrained than traditional soul. It is also rendered in a relatively narrow pitch range that is much less melismatic than its predecessor. Tempos tend to favor slow to mid-tempo grooves and the style draws from jazz, gospel, blues, funk, hip-hop, and world music. It largely ignores digital synthesizers in favor of traditional horns, drums, percussion, and older instruments such as the Fender Rhodes electric piano and the Hammond B3 organ, as well as acoustic and electric guitars. Subtle use of drum machines and turntable sampling is employed on occasion but rarely foregrounded.

Bassist-vocalist MESHELL NDEGEOCELLO is considered a foundational neo-soul artist whose eclectic 1993 debut album *Plantation Lullabies* produced the popular crossover dance single "If That's Your Boyfriend (He Wasn't Last Night)". It was multi-instrumentalist crooner D'ANGELO, however, who became the most influential progenitor of the style based on the atmospheric albums *Brown Sugar* (1995) and *Voodoo* (2000), both critical and commercial successes. D'Angelo opened the door for artists such as Maxwell, Erykah Badu, India.Arie, Eric Benet, Macy Gray, Raphael Saadiq, Jill Scott, and others. Although many of these artists have achieved significant mainstream success, the music remains primarily confined to a small but loyal fan base and is supported by a cottage industry of small independent record labels devoted to the genre. Neo-soul has also influenced a number of UK soul artists including Joss Stone, Amy Winehouse, and Corinne Bailey Rae.

MILES WHITE

Neruda, Pablo [Reyes Basoalto, Neftalí Ricardo] (*b* Parral, Chile, 12 July 1904; *d* Santiago, Chile, 23 Sept 1973). Chilean poet and politician. Neruda was a highly prolific author whose main subjects were love and eroticism (*Veinte Poemas de Amor y una Canción Desesperada*, 1924), metaphysics (*Residencia en la tierra*, 1933), and

politics (*Canto General*, 1950). Between 1927 and 1943 he held consular posts in Burma, Java, Singapore, Argentina, Spain, and Mexico. Neruda's time in Spain coincided with the start of the Spanish Civil War, an event that marked him profoundly. He published a collection of poetry in support of the Republican movement (*España en el corazón*, 1937) and in 1939 oversaw the immigration of over 2000 Spanish refugees to Chile. From this point on, sociopolitical themes become central to Neruda's oeuvre. He was awarded the Nobel Prize for literature in 1971.

Neruda's works, particularly his political and love poems, have inspired musical settings by numerous composers. Major classical settings of his works include Sergio Ortega's *Fulgor y muerte de Joaquín Murieta* (1967), Samuel Barber's *The Lovers*, op. 48 (1971), Alberto Ginastera's *Serenata* (1973), Allan Pettersson's Symphony no. 12 (1973–4), Peter Schat's *Canto General* (1974), Luciano Berio's *Coro* (1975–6), Mikis Theodorakis's *Canto General* (1971–82), and Peter Lieberson's *Neruda Songs* (2005). His poetry has also been set to popular music songs, such as Vicente Bianchi's "Tonadas de Manuel Rodríguez" (1955) and Víctor Jara's "Poema 15" (1972), and concept albums, such as Aparcoa's *Canto General* (1970), Los Jaivas's *Alturas de Macchu Picchu* (1981), and Luciana Souza's *Neruda* (2004).

BIBLIOGRAPHY

R. de Costa: *The Poetry of Pablo Neruda* (Cambridge, MA, 1979)
M. Kadlec: *Selected Works for Solo Voice Set to Texts of Pablo Neruda* (diss., Indiana U., 1982) [incl. list of settings]
F. Aparicio: "Música y poesía en *La Barcarola* de Pablo Neruda," *Revista Iberoamericana*, 1987 liii, 767–86
H.C. Woodbridge and D.S. Zubatsky: *Pablo Neruda: an Annotated Bibliography of Biographical and Critical Studies* (New York, 1988)

DANIEL PARTY

Nestico, Sammy (Samuel Louis) (*b* Pittsburgh, PA, 6 Feb 1924). Arranger and composer. He taught himself to play trombone and was a member of his high school band. He earned a degree in music education from Duquesne. After being a high school band director for one year in Wilmerding, Pennsylvania, he joined the US Air Force Band and was a staff arranger for 15 years. He then served with the US Marine Band as chief arranger. In 1968 he moved to Los Angeles where he composed many television and movie scores, and arranged and/or conducted albums for many popular recording artists. From 1970 to 1984 he was composer and arranger for the Count Basie Orchestra. In 1998–9 Nestico served as a professor at the University of Georgia. He has received many awards, is a member of the American Bandmasters Association, and has published nearly 600 works for professional and school groups.

BIBLIOGRAPHY

N.E. Smith: *Program Notes for Band* (Lake Charles, LA, 2000), 445
W.H. Rehrig: *The Heritage Encyclopedia of Band Music* (Westerville, OH, 1991, 1/1996); CD-ROM (Oskaloosa, IA, 2005)
S. Nestico: *The Complete Arranger* (Delevan, NY, 1993; rev. ed. Carlsbad, CA, 2006)
S. Nestico: *The Gift of Music* (Carlsbad, CA, 2009)

WILLIAM BERZ

Netrebko, Anna (Yuryevna) (*b* Krasnodar, Russia, 18 Sept 1971). Soprano of dual Russian and Austrian citizenship. She studied at the St. Petersburg Conservatory, and after winning first prize in Moscow's 1993 Glinka Competition was invited by Irina Arkhipova to take part in a concert at the Bolshoi. This in effect launched her career, and the following year she made her stage debut with the Kirov Opera (of which she is a permanent member) as Susanna in *Le nozze di Figaro*. Netrebko's international breakthrough came in 1995 when she made a sensational United States debut as Lyudmila in *Ruslan and Lyudmila* at the San Francisco Opera, in which she was admired both for her magnificent, dark-toned singing and her alluring stage presence. She has subsequently appeared frequently at San Francisco and other American houses, especially in Russian roles (including Natasha in Prokofiev's *War and Peace*, Louisa in his *Betrothal in a Monastery*, and Marfa in Rimsky-Korsakov's *The Tsar's Bride*), in Italian roles such as Gilda, Musetta, Nannetta, and Giulietta (in *I Capuleti e i Montecchi*), and also in Mozart (Ilia and Susanna).

In 2002 she made her debut, as Natasha, at the Metropolitan Opera. Her Munich debut, as Violetta, in the 2002–3 season prompted one critic to write "there is none lovelier, none who sings more excitingly, none more charming—there were cheers, madness, and cries of 'the new Callas.'" Her first appearance at Los Angeles, as Lucia, in 2003 provoked similar praise. Netrebko is also in demand as a recitalist in the Russian and Italian bel canto repertory, and has appeared frequently on television and in film. Her beautiful, highly distinctive voice, wide ranging, powerful yet flexible, combining sensuous warmth with steely-edged purity, and her flair for vivid characterization can be heard in two discs of operatic arias and complete opera recordings, including *Betrothal in a Monastery*, *The Love for Three Oranges*, and *La traviata*, recorded at the 2005 Salzburg Festival.

BIBLIOGRAPHY

GMO

E. Myers: "Learning to Brake in the Fast Lane…," *ON*, lxx/10 (April 2006), 16–22

H. Canning: "Anna Netrebko," *Opera*, lviii/6 (June 2007), 644–51

RICHARD WIGMORE/R

Nettl, Bruno (*b* Prague, 14 March 1930). Ethnomusicologist of Czech birth. He was educated at Indiana University (AB 1950; MA 1951; PhD 1953) and the University of Michigan (MALS 1960). His distinguished teaching career has been anchored at the University of Illinois at Urbana-Champaign (appointed associate professor of music, 1964; professor of music and anthropology, 1967–92; emeritus professor, 1992), but has included numerous guest professorships, including Kiel (Fulbright professor, 1956–8), Washington (1985, 1988, 1990), Louisville (Bingham Professor, 1983), Colorado College (1992, 1998), Harvard (1990), and Chicago (1996). Among numerous honors are four honorary doctorates (Chicago 1993; Illinois 1996; Carleton College 2000; Kenyon College 2002), the Fumio Koizumi Prize (Tokyo 1993), and a Festschrift (1991).

Nettl's scholarship has been seminal for the growth of ethnomusicology during the second half of the 20th century. He has written or edited numerous works surveying and broadening theoretical and methodological principles, notably *Theory and Method in Ethnomusicology* (1964), *The Study of Ethnomusicology: 29 Issues and Concepts* (1983), and *Comparative Musicology and Anthropology of Music* (with P.V. Bohlman, 1991). He has also published extensively on a variety of topics, including Native American music, folk and traditional music, the Middle East (especially Iran), the intellectual history of ethnomusicology, urban ethnomusicology, local music ethnography, and improvisation. He has influenced musical scholarship through extensive editorial activities, from journal editorships (*Ethnomusicology*, 1961–5, 1998–2002) to advisory boards (AMS committee for publications of American music and *Garland Encyclopedia of World Music*) to monograph series (Detroit Monographs in Musicology and Chicago Studies in Ethnomusicology).

Nettl's influence on modern musical scholarship crosses disciplinary as well as international borders. He has encouraged rapprochement and cooperation among all domains of musical scholarship, and has strengthened the interdisciplinary potential of ethnomusicology by drawing from folklore studies, anthropology, and the social sciences. The influences of his approaches to world music are also evident in his activities as a teacher, which embrace all levels of music education, and appear in his articles and classroom textbooks, as well as the characteristically lucid quality of all his published work. Many leading ethnomusicologists have studied with Nettl and written dissertations advised by him. It has been the greatest measure of his intellectual breadth and diversity that his former students have not formed a single school, but have established new directions both for ethnomusicology and modern musical scholarship generally.

WRITINGS

American Indian Music North of Mexico: Its Styles and Areas (diss., Indiana U., 1953; Philadelphia, 1954 as *North American Indian Musical Styles*)

"Stylistic Variety in North American Indian Music," *JAMS*, vi/2 (1953), 160–8

"Musical Culture of the Arapaho," *MQ*, xli/3 (1955), 325–31

Music in Primitive Culture (Cambridge, MA, 1956)

"The Hymns of the Amish: an Example of Marginal Survival," *Journal of American Folklore*, lxx/278 (1957), 323–8

"Historical Aspects of Ethnomusicology," *American Anthropologist*, lx/3 (1958), 518–32

"Notes on Musical Areas," *AcM*, xxx/3 (1958), 170–7

An Introduction to Folk Music in the United States (Detroit, 1960, enlarged 3/1976 as *Folk Music in the United States*)

Cheremis Musical Styles (Bloomington, IN, 1960)

Reference Materials in Ethnomusicology (Detroit, 1961, 2/1967)

Theory and Method in Ethnomusicology (New York, 1964)

Folk and Traditional Music of the Western Continents (Englewood Cliffs, NJ, 1965, 3/1990)

"Studies in Blackfoot Indian Musical Culture," *EM*, xi (1967), 141–60, 293–309; xii (1968), 11–48 (with S. Blum), 192–207

with B. Foltin: *Daramad of Chahargah: a Study in the Performance Practice of Persian Music* (Detroit, 1972)

with R. Riddle: "Taqsim Nahawand: a Study of Sixteen Performances by Jihad Racy," *YIFMC*, v (1973), 11–50

"Thoughts on Improvisation: a Comparative Approach," *MQ*, lx/1 (1974), 1–19 with C.E. Hamm and R. Byrnside: *Contemporary Music and Music Cultures* (Englewood Cliffs, NJ, 1975)

"On the Question of Universals," *World of Music*, xix/1–2 (1977), 2–12

ed.: *Eight Urban Musical Cultures: Tradition and Change* (Urbana, IL, 1978)

"Some Aspects of the History of World Music in the Twentieth Century: Questions, Problems, and Concepts," *EM*, xxii/1 (1978), 123–36

The Study of Ethnomusicology: Twenty-Nine Issues and Concepts (Urbana, IL, 1983; rev. as *The Study of Ethnomusicology: Thirty-one Issues and Concepts*, Urbana, IL, 2005)

"In Honor of our Principal Teachers," *EM*, xxviii/2 (1984), 173–85

"Western Musical Values and the Character of Ethnomusicology," *World of Music*, xxiv (1984), 29–43

The Western Impact on World Music (New York, 1985)

"World Music in the Twentieth Century: A Survey of Research on Western Influence," *AcM*, lviii/2 (1986), 360–73

The Radif of Persian Music: Studies of Structure and Cultural Context (Champaign, IL, 1987, 2/1992)

"The IFMC/ICTM and the Development of Ethnomusicology in the United States," *Yearbook for Traditional Music*, xx (1988), 19–25

Blackfoot Musical Thought: Comparative Perspectives (Kent, OH, 1989)

ed., with P.V. Bohlman: *Comparative Musicology and Anthropology of Music: Essays on the History of Ethnomusicology* (Chicago, 1991) [incl. "The Dual Nature of Ethnomusicology in North America: the Contributions of Charles Seeger and George Herzog," 266–74]

with others: *Excursions in World Music* (Englewood Cliffs, NJ, 1992, 2/1997, 3/2001)

"Mozart and the Ethnomusicological Study of Western Culture," *Disciplining Music: Musicology and Its Canons*, ed. K. Bergeron and P.V. Bohlman (Chicago, 1992), 137–55

"La musica dell'antropologia e l'antropologia della musica: una prospettiva nord-americana," *Antropologia della musica e culture mediterranee: Venice 1992*, ed. T. Magrini (Bologna, 1993), 37–56

"Recent Directions in Ethnomusicology," *Ethnomusicology: an Introduction*, ed. H. Myers (London, 1992), 375–99

ed., with others: *Community of Music: an Ethnographic Seminar in Champaign-Urbana* (Champaign, IL, 1993) [incl. "A Place for All Musics? The Concentric Circles of the Music Building," 93–105]

Heartland Excursions: Ethnomusicological Reflections on Schools of Music (Urbana, IL, 1995)

ed., with M. Russell: *In the Course of Performance: Studies in the World of Musical Improvisation* (Chicago, 1998)

"The Institutionalization of Musicology: Perspectives of a North American Ethnomusicologist," *Rethinking Music*, eds. M. Everist and N. Cook (New York, 1999), 287–310

Encounters in Ethnomusicology: a Memoir (Warren, MI, 2002)

"We're on the Map: Reflections on SEM in 1955 and 2005," *EM*, l/2 (2006), 179–89

ed., with G. Solis: *Musical Improvisation: Art, Education, and Society* (Urbana, IL, 2009)

BIBLIOGRAPHY

S. Blum, P.V. Bohlman, and D.M. Neuman, eds.: *Ethnomusicology and Modern Music History: Festschrift Bruno Nettl* (Urbana, IL, 1991) [incl. list of writings, 278–305]

PHILIP V. BOHLMAN/R

Nettleton, Asahel (*b* North Killingworth, CT, 21 April 1783; *d* East Windsor, CT, 16 May 1844). Evangelist and hymnbook compiler. He was one of the earliest itinerant New England evangelists, and began preaching and conducting revival meetings throughout New England and New York in 1811. In response to the demand for a broader selection of hymns appropriate to evangelistic use, he compiled *Village Hymns for Social Worship* (Hartford, CT, 1824), a landmark in American hymnody in that it moved away from the dominance of Isaac Watts and his school. The collection of 600 hymns was drawn partly from earlier American compilations, including Nathan Strong's *Hartford Selection* (1799),

Samuel Worcester's *Select Hymns* (1819), and Leonard Bacon's missionary *Hymns and Sacred Songs* (1823), but also contained new hymns and some published for the first time in the United States. It was widely used as a source by later American and British compilers and went through numerous editions up to 1858. Nettleton approved the publication of a small tunebook, *Zion's Harp* (1824), to accompany his collection; of its 60 tunes, all but one, Jacob French's "Pilgrim's Farewell," were British.

BIBLIOGRAPHY

DAB (H.E. Starr)

B. Tyler: *Memoir of the Life and Character of Rev. A. Nettleton* (Hartford, CT, 1844, rev. 2/1854)

R.S. Smith: *Recollections of Nettleton and the Great Revival of 1820* (Albany, NY, 1848)

J.B. Waterbury: *Sketches of Eloquent Preachers* (New York, 1864), 42–51

F.J. Metcalf: *American Writers and Compilers of Sacred Music* (New York, 1925/R1967), 65, 142

P.G. Hammond: *Music in Urban Revivalism in the Northern United States, 1800–1835* (diss., Southern Baptist Theological Seminary, 1974)

J.F. Thornbury: *God Sent Revival: the Story of Asahel Nettleton and the Second Great Awakening* (Darlington, CO, 1977/R1988)

T. Nettles: *Asahel Nettleton: Sermons from the Second Great Awakening* (Ames, IA, 1995)

B. Tyler and A. Bonar: *Nettleton and his Labours* (Edinburgh, PA, 1996)

PAUL C. ECHOLS/R

Neubauer, Paul (*b* Los Angeles, CA, 17 Oct 1963). Violist and educator. He made his solo debut at age 13 with the Los Angeles Philharmonic. He studied with Alan de Veritch, PAUL DOKTOR, and WILLIAM PRIMROSE and attended the Juilliard School (BM 1982, MM 1983). He won the Lionel Tertis International Viola Competition (1980) and the Mae M. Whitaker and D'Angelo international competitions. In 1984, at age 21, he became the youngest principal string player in the history of the New York Philharmonic and remained its principal violist until 1990 when he pursued further opportunities as a soloist and chamber musician. Noted for his exceptional musicality and effortless playing, Neubauer became an artist member of the Chamber Music Society of Lincoln Center in 1989. He has frequently collaborated with the Emerson, Juilliard, Cleveland, Fine Arts, Orion, Borromeo, Miami, and Brentano quartets and other artists. He has also been the music director of the OK Mozart Festival. He has given many world premieres, including Béla Bartók's Viola Concerto (revised), Max Bruch's Double Concerto for Clarinet and Viola with clarinetist David Shifrin, Tobias Picker's Viola Concerto, Gordon Jacob's Viola Concerto no.2, Joan Tower's *Purple Rhapsody*, and David Ott's Viola Concerto. He gave the US premiere of Krzysztof Penderecki's Viola Concerto, with Penderecki conducting, and Richard Suter's Three Nocturnes for Viola and Orchestra. In 1989 Neubauer made his Carnegie Hall debut, playing the first performance of Joel Philip Friedman's Concerto for Viola and Orchestra with the National Orchestral Association. He has performed as a soloist with orchestras and festivals around the world, and his extensive discography ranges from Bright Sheng's "Three Chinese Love Songs" to Johann Sebastian Bach's "Brandenburg Concerti." He has taught at Mannes College, The New School for Music, the Juilliard School, and Rutgers University.

JAMES BASH

Neuendorff, Adolf [Adolph] (*b* Hamburg, Germany, 13 June 1843; *d* New York, NY, 4 Dec 1897). Conductor, composer, theatrical impresario, and violinist of German birth. He arrived in New York in June 1855 and soon began as timpanist at the German-language New York Stadttheater, eventually becoming concertmaster, assistant conductor under KARL ANSCHÜTZ, and music director in 1867. Neuendorff made his solo violin debut at Dodworth Hall on 21 March 1859, and after musical studies with Gustav Schilling (1801–83), violin lessons with GEORGE MATZKA, composition work with Anschütz, and singing lessons with Joseph Weinlich, he undertook a South American recital tour *c*1860–61. Returning to the United States by 1862, he was appointed music director at Milwaukee's German theater a year later. In the mid-1860s, along with Anschütz, he conducted Grover's German Grand Opera Company. G.C.D. Odell described this touring company as presenting "among the most famous German singers heard up to that time in America" (*Annals of the New York Stage*, vol. 7, 676). In 1867–8 Neuendorff also performed in the New York Philharmonic's violin section.

Between 1872 and 1881, in addition to conducting, he managed New York's Germania Theater, offering a constantly changing bill of German-language musical plays and farces, operettas, and occasionally operas. Neuendorff wrote the music for more than 20 German theatrical works, all with an abundance of songs. His most important operettas include *Der Rattenfänger von Hameln* (1880), still known today for its aria "Wandern, ach Wandern," sung by the Pied Piper; *Don Quixote* (1882); and *Prinz Waldmeister* (1887). He presented the US debut of Johann Strauss's *Die Fledermaus* on 21 November 1874 at the Stadttheater, and in fall 1875 his German company, starring tenor Theodore Wachtel and soprano Eugenie Pappenheim, appeared at the Academy of Music. Neuendorff opened his second and larger Germania Theater in the former Wallack's Theater in 1881, but because of greater expenses he was forced to close in 1883 and he left theatrical management permanently thereafter.

Neuendorff had an extensive and varied career conducting opera and orchestral music throughout the United States: American premieres in German of three of Richard Wagner's operas: *Lohengrin* (3 April 1871, Neues Stadttheater), *Der fliegende Holländer* (12 March 1877, Academy of Music), and *Die Walküre* (2 April 1877, Academy of Music); music director of the New York Philharmonic, 1878–9 (US premiere of Pyotr Tchaikovsky's Symphony no.3); first conductor of the forerunner of the Boston Pops Orchestra, 1885–9; Midwestern tour performances by the Metropolitan Opera, 1886; conductor for pianist Amy Marcy Beach's debut with the Boston SO, 28 March 1885, and the American debut of pianist Josef Hofmann at the Metropolitan Opera House, 29 November 1887. From 1889 to 1891 he was the music director of Emma Juch's English Opera Company, which toured the United States, Canada, and Mexico. His wife, soprano Georgine von Januschowsky (1850–1914), who earlier appeared at the Germania, was a member of this troupe.

Neuendorff was also an accomplished writer. He chronicled the history of New York's German theater in a series of articles that appeared in Germania Theater programs in the 1870s, and in September 1876 he reported on the Bayreuth premiere of Wagner's *Ring* cycle in a 3500-word essay in the *New Yorker Staats-Zeitung*. Although other conductors such as Leopold and Walter Damrosch, Theodore Thomas, and Anton Seidl overshadowed him, Neuendorff worked tirelessly to promote European artistic culture (especially Wagner's operas) and to develop the German American stage in New York.

WORKS
(selected list)

THEATRICAL WORKS
(all premiered in New York except where noted)
New Yorker Leben (Volksstück, F. Berg), Neues Stadttheater, 20 April 1869; Gefahrvolle Wege (musical farce, C. Sturenburg), Germania Theater, 29 April 1876; Die Reise durch New York in 80 Stunden (based on H. Salingré's Die Reise durch Berlin in 80 Stunden, a parody of J. Verne's Le Tour du monde en quatre-vingts jours), Germania Theater, 3 Nov 1876; Der Berliner in Philadelphia (musical farce), Cincinnati, Deutsches Theater, 23 March 1878; Onkel Knusperich, oder eine Nacht in New York (musical farce, H. Raberg and H. Italianer), Germania Theater, 14 April 1880; Die Rattenfänger von Hameln (operetta, H. Italianer [German], F. Williams [English]), Germania Theater, 13 Dec 1880; Don Quixote (operetta, H. Italianer), Neues Germania Theater, 9 Jan 1882; Der Pawnbroker von Harlem (Volksstück, E. Boremsky and M. Cohnheim), Neues Germania Theater, 16 Nov 1882; Prinz Waldmeister [Waldmeisters Brautfahrt] (operetta, H. Italiener), Thalia Theater, 2 May 1887; Der Minstrel [Der Schalk von Aberdeen] (operetta, H.F. Urban), Amberg Theater, 18 May 1892;

OTHER WORKS
Two syms., smaller orch works, qts for male vv, solo songs, and other compositions

BIBLIOGRAPHY
G. Kadelburg: *Das deutsche Theater in New York* (New York, 1878)
G.C.D. Odell: *Annals of the New York Stage*, 15 vols. (New York, 1927–49)
V.B. Lawrence: *Strong on Music: the New York Music Scene in the Days of George Templeton Strong, 1836–1875. Volume 3: Repercussions, 1857–1862* (Chicago, 1999)
J. Koegel: "The Development of the German-American Musical Theater in New York, 1840–1890," *European Music and Musicians in New York City, 1840–1900*, ed. J.M. Graziano (Rochester, NY, 2006), 149–81
J. Koegel: *Music in German Immigrant Theater: New York City, 1840–1940* (Rochester, NY, 2009)
J. Spitzer, ed.: *American Orchestras in the Nineteenth Century* (Chicago, 2012)

JOHN KOEGEL

Neuhaus, Max (*b* Beaumont, TX, 9 Aug 1939; *d* Maratea, Italy, 3 Feb 2009). Sound artist, visual artist, inventor, percussionist, and author. He enjoyed a distinguished career as a percussionist: he studied at the Manhattan School of Music, performed new works by avant-garde luminaries at major venues worldwide, and recorded for Columbia Masterworks. In 1968 he chose to stop performing and to devote himself to what he would later name "sound works." In these diverse pieces, which technically included sound sculptures, installations, performances, soundwalks, and electroacoustic music, Neuhaus related sound to space and site in unique ways that, he believed, exceeded terms such as "music," "sound art," and "sound installation." Instead, he grouped the works in his oeuvre according to their themes or "vectors": walking, place, passage, moment, sensation, network, performance, and invention. The vectors were Neuhaus's avenues of approach to sound: through them, he explored creative relationships with sonic realms. He coined the broad term "sound works" to encapsulate pieces that traveled all of these diverse vectors, without incurring the baggage attendant on the term "art."

1. Walks. 2. Place. 3. Passage. 4. Moment. 5. Sensation. 6. Networks, performances, inventions.

1. WALKS. Neuhaus's first sound works were 15 soundwalks entitled *LISTEN* (1966–76), executed throughout the United States and Canada. Having served as a percussionist in pieces by John Cage, Edgard Varèse, and others who had introduced "noise" into music, Neuhaus decided to take the next step: introducing music's audiences to the noisy streets beyond the concert hall. He invited audience members to an urban location, a Manhattan street corner, for instance, that was not typically part of the "artworld"; he rubber-stamped their hands with the word *LISTEN*, and led them through the city, saying nothing. The idea, as in most of Neuhaus's works, was to initiate an experience that each listener would undergo privately, in his or her own way. Although he led some soundwalks personally, he also encouraged listeners to develop them on their own, guiding them with written and illustrated publications, including his poster of the Brooklyn Bridge, emblazoned with the word *LISTEN*. By publicly encouraging urban dwellers to savor and appreciate city sounds, Neuhaus launched a political attack against the US Government's (1974) condemnation of "noise pollution," which he saw as a propaganda campaign meant to eclipse an actual problem: air pollution.

2. PLACE. Many of Neuhaus's works are site-specific, meant not only to highlight the sounds already present at the site but also to construct new sounds that invite listeners to reimagine the site. Each of Neuhaus's "place works" animated a sound by molding and positioning it according to the character of a particular site, and animated the site by filling it with new sound. For example, in *New Work (Underground)* (1978), Neuhaus placed a recorded, growling sound beneath a grate in the sculpture garden at New York's Museum of Modern Art. In *untitled* (1979–89), he set a 30-channel amplifier in a hollow stairway at the Chicago Museum of Modern Art. In all of Neuhaus's place works, the goal was to create a new, quasi-imaginary place from an existing site filled with original sounds. In his view, this new place was synonymous with his artwork: in discovering and "entering" this new place, listeners "entered" his artwork. They enter the work by realizing that the subtle sound they are hearing (the growl, the amplified footsteps) is in fact out of place relative to the site. They may then refocus their attention: from moving through the site in pursuit of some objective, to savoring the site and the sound itself. Neuhaus's aim is to incite this shift of attention. His best-known place works include *Walkthrough* (1973–7), soft sounds placed in a subway station, and *Times Square* (1977–92, reinstated 2002), a permanent installation of tones in a grate beneath a pedestrian median in Times Square, New York. Unlike music, in which listeners seem to "follow" sounds' apparent changes over time, the fixed sounds in Neuhaus's place works may be traversed and explored like rooms and sculptures. Also unlike music, *Times Square* is anonymous: there are no signs or framing devices to demarcate the artwork from the everyday bustle of the Square; the sounds are so subtle that they may pass unnoticed. The piece issues invitations, not commands, for passersby to relish the city and urban sounds instead of hurrying through them, oblivious.

3. PASSAGE. Contrasting place works, in which listeners pause to listen, passage works require movement through a sound-filled space. The sounds shape the spaces by partitioning them into segments, and by accentuating their dynamic qualities. Additionally, listeners' movements through the passageways play active roles in generating their experiences, thus in creating the works themselves. In *untitled* (1999) and *Suspended Sound Line* (1999), Neuhaus placed loudspeakers at various points along an office-building corridor and suspension bridge, respectively. In his first passage work, *Drive-In Music* (1967), listeners guided their cars along a boulevard; microphones and transmitters hidden in the trees broadcasted sounds to the passing car radios. Passengers' experiences varied as their cars passed under different trees. This piece was the first manifestation of Neuhaus's lifelong interest in creating art for public spaces: sounds accessible to everyone.

4. MOMENT. Where place and passage works inserted sounds into sites, Neuhaus's moment works created sudden absences of sound that seized listeners' attention. Only in the moment of the sounds' disappearances did listeners notice them, either perceiving "after-images" of the sounds, or realizing that the ensuing silence was shaped by the recently dissipated sounds. For *Time Piece Stommeln*, installed at a vacant German synagogue (2007), Neuhaus constructed a sound based on the noises of the traffic surrounding the site. Twelve times each day, this sound grows from near inaudibility until it emerges from the crowded atmosphere as a distinct event. But as soon as listeners realize that they are hearing something out of place, it disappears, fading back into the traffic. The sound is timed according to

Jewish law's division of the day into 12 ritual hours, and the sudden absences remember the extermination of Jewish people during the Third Reich. Other moment works include *Time Piece Graz* (2003) and *Time Piece Beacon* (2005).

5. SENSATION. Neuhaus's 17 *Water Whistle* pieces (1971–4) experimented with underwater sound and listening. As his first site-specific works, these pieces were realized in swimming pools throughout the United States and Canada. He used hydraulic sound sources as well as venues: for each pool, he designed a unique configuration of mobile water hoses fed through complex underwater whistles. Since the sounds were audible only underwater, listeners lay in the pools, submerged their ears, and experienced how different aural sensations are when water—instead of air—mediates sound.

6. NETWORKS, PERFORMANCES, INVENTIONS. A perennial interest of Neuhaus's was music-making in collaboration with a massive public. In *Public Supply* (1966), he created a collage composition, live and in real time, from sounds sent via telephone to a radio station. *Radio Net* (1977) was a live event during which sounds telephoned to Washington, DC, by listeners in five American cities, were collected, mixed, and broadcasted by a device of Neuhaus's invention. He created a similar arrangement for the Internet in *Auracle* (2004). Not a piece but a system, *Auracle* takes vocal sounds, transmitted online, as commands for the activation of other sounds stored within the system. Participants can experiment alone or collaborate with others in real time.

Musical performance and composition thus remained central components of Neuhaus's oeuvre. In fact, he did not sharply distinguish his activities as a percussionist from his other sound works; instead he considered performance one of his vectors. Similarly, his inventions—redesigned sirens for emergency vehicles, with more bearable and locatable sounds (patented 1991)—were distinct from his artworks but born from the same drives: the desire to engage the urban public in learning to enjoy and shape the sounds (and hence the places) amid which they lived.

BIBLIOGRAPHY
GMO (H. Davies and J. Rockwell)
J.C. Ammann, M. Neuhaus, C. Ratcliff: *Max Neuhaus—Sound Installation* (Basel, 1983)
C. Ratcliff: "Max Neuhaus: Aural Spaces," *Art in America*, lxxv/10 (1987), 154–63
M. Neuhaus: *Max Neuhaus: Elusive Sources and "Like" Spaces* (Turin, 1990)
M. Neuhaus: "Siren—Aural Design," *Kunst & Museumjournaal*, iv/6 (1993), 12–8
M. Neuhaus: *Max Neuhaus—Sound Works*, 3. vols. (Osfildern, Germany, 1994)
M. Tarantino: "Two Passages," (1998), <http://www.max-neuhaus.info/soundworks/vectors/passage/twopassages/>
Y. Safran: "Shaping Sound," *Domus*, 876 (2004), 72–7
B. LaBelle: *Background Noise: Perspectives on Sound Art* (London, 2006)
A. Licht: *Sound Art: Beyond Music, Between Categories* (New York, 2007)
L. Cooke and K. Kelly, eds.: *Max Neuhaus: Times Square, Time Piece Beacon* (New York, 2009)
C. Cox: "Enduring Work: On Max Neuhaus (1939–2009)," *Artforum*, xlvii/9 (2009), 49–52

MANDY-SUZANNE WONG

Neumeyer, David Paul (*b* Bay City, MI, 1 June 1950). Musicologist and music theorist. He received the BM from Michigan State University in 1972, and the PhD in music theory at Yale University in 1976. At Yale he studied with Allen Forte and Claude Palisca; the former supervised his dissertation, a pitch-class-set analysis of the early compositions of Paul Hindemith. After two years of teaching at Kansas State University (Manhattan), Neumeyer took a position at Indiana University (Bloomington), where he taught from 1978 to 2000. Since the fall semester of 2000 he has held the Leslie Waggener Professorship in the College of Fine Arts at the University of Texas at Austin.

Neumeyer's early research focused on the works of Paul Hindemith, including a monograph (*The Music of Paul Hindemith*) and numerous articles. Beginning in the early 1990s, most of Neumeyer's research has shifted to issues regarding film music, including a key review in the *Journal of the American Musicological Society*, coauthored with James Buhler, which offered a critical assessment of the state of film music studies in 1994, just before interest in the topic exploded later in the decade.

WRITINGS
The Music of Paul Hindemith (New Haven, CT, 1986)
with J. Buhler: "C. Flinn, *Strains of Utopia* and K. Kalinak, *Settling the Score*," *JAMS*, xlvii/2 (1994), 364–85 [review article]
coeditor with J. Buhler and C. Flinn: *Music and Cinema* (Middletown, CT, 2000)
"Film Theory and Music Theory: On the Intersection of Two Traditions," *Music in the Mirror: Reflections on the History of Music Theory and Literature for the 21st Century*, ed. T. Mathiesen and A. Giger (Lincoln, NE, 2002), 275–94
with J. Buhler: "Music-Sound-Narrative: Analyzing *Casablanca*," *Interdisciplinary Studies in Musicology*, v, ed. M. Jablonski and M. Klein (Poznan, Poland, 2005), 277–91
with L. Neumeyer: "On Motion and Stasis: Photography, 'Moving Pictures,' Music," *Music, Meaning and Media*, ed. R. Littlefield, E. Pekkilä, and D. Neumeyer (Imatra/Helsinki, 2007), 11–33
"Diegetic/Nondiegetic: a Theoretical Model," *Music and the Moving Image*, ii/1 (2009), 26–39
with J. Buhler and R. Deemer: *Hearing the Movies: Music and Sound in Film History* (New York, 2009)

DANIEL GOLDMARK

Nevada [née Wixom], **Emma** (*b* Alpha, nr Nevada City, CA, 7 Feb 1859; *d* Liverpool, England, 20 June 1940). Soprano. A pupil of Mathilde Marchesi, she made her opera debut in 1880 at Her Majesty's Theatre, London, in *La sonnambula*, an opera that brought some of her greatest successes (her medallion was later placed with those of Giuditta Pasta and Maria Malibran on Vincenzo Bellini's statue at Naples). She appeared to great acclaim in Italy and Paris, where her roles included Lucia and Mignon. Returning to the United States in 1884 she appeared at the New York Academy of Music, and, the following year, on alternate nights with Adelina Patti. She made several further tours of the United States and Europe, but sang at Covent Garden only in 1887 as Amina and Charles Gounod's Mireille, her intonation and flexibility being admired but not her free treatment of Gounod's score. In England she frequently sang in oratorio, including the first performance of Alexander Mackenzie's *Rose of Sharon* (1884), the soprano part of which had been written for her. Despite its lack of dramatic power, her light, clear, and controlled tone was highly admired. A noted feature of her concerts were her many changes of dress, culminating in the appearance of her wedding dress, in which she was said almost to "defy description." Among her pupils was her daughter Mignon Nevada.

BIBLIOGRAPHY

A.W. Thayer: "Emma of Nevada," *Dwight's Journal of Music*, xl/1034 (4 Dec 1880), 198–9

W. Armstrong, ed.: "Reminiscences of Emma Nevada," *New York Tribune Sunday Magazine* (28 Oct 1906), 7

P.G. Davis: *The American Opera Singer* (New York, 1997), 192–4

J.B. STEANE/KATIE BUEHNER

Nevaquaya, Joyce Lee Tate [Doc Tate]   (*b* Fletcher, OK, 3 July 1932; *d* Lawton, OK, 5 March 1996). Visual artist, flute player, and composer; member of the Comanche Nation. He graduated from high school at Fort Sill Indian School in Lawton, Oklahoma (1951) and attended Haskell Indian Institute in Lawrence, Kansas (1951–2). A natural leader, he was a self-taught artist, flutist, composer, dancer, lecturer, and lay minister. The Smithsonian Institution commissioned him to perform on the Native flute on a Goodwill Tour of England (1970), at the National Folk Festival (1973), and to record *Comanche Flute Music* for Folkways Records (1979). He performed flute at the Night of the First Americans, Kennedy Center for the Performing Arts (1982), United Nations Mission (1985), and Code Talkers Decoration Ceremony, Oklahoma City (1989). He was the first Native American musician to give a solo recital in Carnegie Hall, New York (1990), and was commissioned by the Oklahoma Arts Council to compose and perform the Native flute piece *Flight of the Spirit* (1991). His numerous awards include the National Heritage Fellowship from the NEA (1986) and a designation as Oklahoma Treasure from the Governor's Arts Awards (1995). His experimentation in the 1970s with cross-fingerings, development of ornamentation techniques, and extension of the lowest note's warbling sound to all of the available pitches resulted in a substantial expansion of the flute's repertoire. He played a key role in the rejuvenation of the NATIVE AMERICAN FLUTE, which has continued to flourish in the 21st century.

BIBLIOGRAPHY

P.D. Lester: "Nevaquaya, Doc Tate," *The Biographical Directory of Native American Painters* (Tulsa, OK, 1995), 390–1

E. Wapp: liner notes, *Comanche Flute Music Played by Doc Tate Nevaquaya*, Smithsonian Folkways (2004), 4–13

P. Conlon: "Nevaquaya, Joyce Lee 'Doc' Tate," *Encyclopedia of Oklahoma History and Culture*, ii, ed. D. Everett (Oklahoma City, 2009), 1014

PAULA J. CONLON

Neville Brothers, the. Rhythm-and-blues, funk, soul, and rock performers. The brothers include Art (Arthur Lanon Neville; *b* New Orleans, LA, 17 Dec 1937; keyboards and vocals), Charles (*b* New Orleans, LA, 28 Dec 1938; saxophone and flute), Aaron (*b* New Orleans, LA, 24 Jan 1941; keyboards and vocals), and Cyril (*b* New Orleans, LA, 10 Jan 1948; vocals). The collective experience of the Neville Brothers distills the musical and cultural heritage of New Orleans over the course of the last century. The quartet was born, raised, and saturated in the city's 13th Ward, a blue-collar neighborhood on the edge of the Garden District. While their parents were not themselves musicians, one of their father's closest friends was the vocalist Smiley Lewis, and their classmates included the celebrated keyboard players Allen Toussaint and James Booker. They began their individual professional lives early. Charles joined the Rabbit Foot Minstrel Show as the "Boy Wonder of Sax" in his teens; Art hung about Cosimo Matassa's studio at a similar age and sang backup on Little Richard's "The Girl Can't Help It"; and Aaron initiated his singing career as a protégé of vocalist Larry Williams. Aaron was the first to break commercially in 1966 with the chart-topping single "Tell It Like It Is." Art followed as a member of the influential instrumental ensemble THE METERS. The single "Sophisticated Cissy" and its follow-up "Cissy Strut" ascended the charts in 1969. The independent label Josie marketed the initial releases, though the Meters were later signed to Reprise Records. The fraternal ensemble first assembled as participants in the 1976 recording *The Wild Tchoupitoulas*; the ensemble was led by the Indian chief, vocalist, and family friend George "Big Chief" Jolly. The Neville Brothers released their first eponymous group recording in 1978 on Capitol Records, and subsequently would be affiliated with Black Top, Rhino, Spindletop, A&M, and Columbia. "Healing Chant" from the 1989 A&M release *Yellow Moon*, produced by Daniel Lanois, won a Grammy Award for Best Pop Instrumental. Subsequently, Aaron reexperienced a successful solo vocalist career, and received Grammys for "Don't Know Much" and "All My Life," both duets with Linda Ronstadt. After several of the brothers were displaced by Hurricane Katrina, the group returned to the city in 2008 to headline and close the New Orleans Jazz and Heritage Festival.

BIBLIOGRAPHY

D. Snowden: liner notes, *The Very Best of the Neville Brothers* (1997, Rhino R2 72626)

A. Neville et al.: *The Brothers* (New York, 2000)

DAVID SANJEK

Nevin [Dale], **Arthur (Finley)**   (*b* Edgeworth, PA, 27 April 1871; *d* Sewickley, PA, 10 July 1943). Composer, conductor, and ethnomusicologist, brother of ETHELBERT NEVIN. After early musical instruction from his father, an amateur composer and biographer of Stephen C. Foster, he studied at the New England Conservatory (1889–93). In 1893 he traveled to Europe, where his teachers included Karl Klindworth (piano), and OTIS BARDWELL BOISE and Engelbert Humperdinck (composition). Upon his return to the United States in 1897 he taught, composed (often using the pseudonym Arthur Dale), and conducted concerts of his own works.

During the summers of 1902 and 1903 Nevin lived among the Blackfoot Indians of Montana, documenting folklore and transcribing music. His study of Native American culture resulted in the composition of the opera *Poia*. In 1907, following an invitation from President Theodore Roosevelt, he presented an illustrated lecture on the work at the White House. Although an American production was not staged, *Poia* was performed at the Royal Opera, Berlin in 1910, the first American opera to be produced in a European court theater. After dividing his time between composing and conducting at the MacDowell Colony, Nevin joined the music department at the University of Kansas, Lawrence, in 1915. During World War I he directed choirs and bands at Camp Grant, Illinois. In 1920 he was appointed director of municipal music and drama in Memphis, where he also conducted the symphony orchestra. He moved to New York in 1922. The last 20 years of his life were spent in declining health.

Although Nevin's compositional style grows out of the salon music of the latter 19th century, his earliest works are characterized by an expansiveness that challenges the predictability of that tradition. His fusion of standard forms and freely tonal harmonies often projects an Impressionistic style. His instrumental works are almost exclusively programmatic.

WORKS
(selective list)

Stage: The Economites (comic op, 3, W.G. Mudie), Sewickley, PA, ?2 Feb 1899; A Night in Yaddo Land (masque, E. Stebbins and W. Chance) (1900); Poia (op, 3, E. von Huhn, after R. Hartley), Berlin, 23 April 1910; The Daughter of the Forest (op, 1, Hartley), Chicago, 5 Jan 1918; At the Tavern (op impressionistic, 3, Hartley), Peterborough, ?1920; 4 other stage works

Vocal: 3 Songs (1895); Chrysoar (H.W. Longfellow), SATB, pf (1907); The Djinns (cant., after V. Hugo), SATB, pf (1913); Mother Goose Fantasy, S, SA, pf (1921); Sleep Little Blossom (A. Tennyson) (1922); Eros (R.H. Davis) (1925); 60 other songs, additional partsongs, cantatas, choruses, fantasies, serenades

Inst: Lorna Doone, suite, orch (1897); Str Qt, d (1897); Suite miniature, orch (1903); At the Spring, str orch (1911); Midnight Forrest, humoresque, orch (1930); Arizona, orch (1932); Woodland Rhapsody, pf, orch (1941); other movts for str qt, orch suites, tone poems

Kbd (pf, unless otherwise stated): 2 Dances (1895); Ballet Waltz (1899) [from the Economites]; From Edgeworth Hills, suite (1903); 2 Impromptus to the Memory of Edward MacDowell (1914); Southern Sketches (1923); Chanson triste, org (1925); other descriptive pieces

BIBLIOGRAPHY

"Explains Berlin's Attack upon *Poia*," *Musical America*, xii/2 (1910), 25 only [interview]

A. Nevin: "Two Summers with the Blackfeet Indians of Montana," *MQ*, ii (1916), 257–70

N. Slonimsky: "Musical Oddities," *The Etude*, lxxiii (1955), 4 only

JOHN C. FRANCIS

Nevin, Ethelbert (Woodbridge) (*b* Edgeworth, nr Pittsburgh, PA, 25 Nov 1862; *d* New Haven, CT, 17 Feb 1901). Composer and pianist. His father, Robert Peebles Nevin, was an author, poet, and newspaper publisher; his mother, Elizabeth Duncan Oliphant, was a pianist for whom the first grand piano had been carried across the Allegheny Mountains to western Pennsylvania. Nevin was the fifth of eight children; his youngest sibling, ARTHUR NEVIN, also was a musician.

Nevin received his first musical training at home. He could sing and play his own accompaniments at the piano by age six, and subsequently studied with music teachers in Pittsburgh. At the age of 11 he wrote his first published work, *Lilian Polka*. During a family year abroad he studied the piano with Franz Böhme in Dresden. In 1881–3 at Boston he studied the piano with B.J. LANG and harmony with STEPHEN ALBERT EMERY, then returned to Pittsburgh to teach and perform recitals, often including his own songs, chamber works, and piano pieces.

In the years 1884–6 Nevin studied in Berlin with Karl Klindworth (piano) and Karl Bial (composition). He also took lessons in composition from Otto Tiersch and studied piano with HANS FREIHERR VON BÜLOW. He intended a career as a virtuoso pianist, establishing himself in Boston. Dividing his time between composing and performing, he found success with his published works, beginning with *Sketchbook* and then *Water Scenes*, including a piece Nevin himself tired of performing, *Narcissus*. He spent the years 1891–2 in Berlin and Paris, where he taught the piano, composed, and lectured on Wagner. Back in Boston he taught and performed—interrupted by a nervous breakdown and extended voyage to recover in 1894—increasingly including performances of his own compositions. Seeking serenity, he spent the years 1895–6 in Florence, Montepiano, and Venice, where he wrote impressionistic piano suites. He resumed his recitals in New York; he shared one program in 1898 with Isadora Duncan who "illustrated in classic dances" his piano pieces *Narcissus, Ophelia*, and *Water Nymph*. There in 1897 he wrote in one day his most popular song, *The Rosary*. In 1898 Nevin moved back to "Vineacre," the family's estate, which Willa Cather described in "An Evening at Vineacre" (quoted in Thompson). He wrote his last successful songs there and died during a winter sojourn in New Haven.

Nevin was a miniaturist who used short musical forms and emphasized seemingly simple and spontaneous melody, providing accompaniments that support without seeking the foreground. He wrote some 55 piano pieces, 85 songs, 20 choral works, and miscellaneous other pieces, all distinguished by their sentiment, grace, and charm. Liu provides stylistic analysis of individual works. A few—most prominently *Narcissus* and the piano etude op.18 no.2—have continued to find a place on vocal and piano recitals in the 21st century.

WORKS
(selective list)

op.

2   Sketchbook (Boston, 1888): 7 songs (H. Heine, C. Kingsley, R.L. Stevenson): Im wunderschönen Monat Mai, Du bist wie eine Blume, Lehn deine Wang' an meine Wang', Oh, that we two were maying, In winter I get up at night, Of speckled eggs the birdie sings, Dark brown is the river; 1 chorus, vn obbl: The night has a thousand eyes; 5 pf pieces: Gavotte, Love Song, Berceuse, Serenata, Valse rhapsodie

6   Three Duets, pf (Boston, 1890)

7   Four Compositions, pf (Boston, 1890): Valzer gentile, Slumber Song, Intermezzo, Song of the Brook

9   Wynken, Blynken and Nod (E. Field), chorus, pf 4 hands (Boston, 1890)

12   Five Songs (Boston, 1891): A Summer Day (Nesbit), Beat upon mine, little heart (A. Tennyson), In a Bower (L.C. Moulton), Little Boy Blue (Field), At Twilight (P. van Rensselaer)

13   Water Scenes, pf (Boston, 1891): Dragon Fly, Ophelia, Water Nymph, Narcissus, Barcarolle

16   In Arcady, pf (Boston, 1892): A Shepherd's Tale, Shepherds all and Maidens Fair, Lullabye, Tournament

18   Etude in the form of a Romance; Etude in the form of a Scherzo, pf (Boston, 1892)

20   A Book of [10] Songs (Boston, 1893): A Fair Good Morn, Sleep, little tulip (Field), Ev'ry Night (Stevenson), Airly Beacon (Kingsley), When the Land was White with Moonlight (A.R. Aldrich), A Song of Love (E.L. Tomlin), Nocturne (T.B. Aldrich), Dites-moi (O. Boise), Orsola's Song (J. Richepin), In der Nacht (G. Platen)

21   Maggio in Toscana, pf suite (Boston, 1896): Arlecchino, Notturno, Barchetta, Misericordia, Il rusignuolo, La pastorella

—   The Rosary (R.C. Rogers), 1v, pf (Boston, 1898)

25   A Day in Venice, pf suite (Cincinnati, 1898): Alba, Gondolieri, Canzone amoroso, Buona notte

28   Songs from Vineacre (pubd separately, Cincinnati, 1899–1900): A Necklace of Love (F.L. Stanton), Sleeping and Dreaming (R.P. Nevin), Mon désir (J. Ahrem), The Nightingale's Song (A.H. King), The Dream-maker Man (W.A. White), The Silver Moon (P. Verlaine), Ein Heldenlied (Heine), Ein Liedchen (Heine)

29   Captive Memories (J.T. White), song cycle, bar, 4vv, pf (Cincinnati, 1899)

30   En Passant, pf suite (pubd separately, Cincinnati, 1899): A Fontainebleau, In Dreamland, Napoli, At home

—   Mighty Lak' a Rose (F.L. Stanton), 1v, pf (Cincinnati, 1901)

—   The Quest (R. Hartley), cant., vs (Cincinnati, 1902), orchd H. Parker

MSS at *Pu*

Principal publishers: Boston Music Co. (G. Schirmer), Schott, John Church Co.

BIBLIOGRAPHY

DAB (R.G. Cole)

V. Thompson: *The Life of Ethelbert Nevin from his Letters and his Wife's Memories* (Boston, 1913)

F. Rogers: "Some Memories of Ethelbert Nevin," *MQ*, iii (1917), 358–63

J.T. Howard: *Ethelbert Nevin* (New York, 1935) [incl. list of works, chronology, bibliography]

Y. Wang: *Ethelbert Nevin Collection* (MS, U. of Pittsburgh, 1987) [incl. list of music, programs, clippings, correspondence, photographs, mementos]

H. Liu: *The Piano Music of Ethelbert Nevin* (thesis, U. of Florida, 1995)

R. Schempf: *The New England Character Piece: A Comparative Study of Four Representative Composers* (diss., Manhattan School, 1995)

DEANE L. ROOT

New Age. An ideology based on the belief in the ultimate cultural evolution of human societies through the transformation of individuals. New Age thought surfaced in alternative healing communities in the United States during the late 1970s; its manifestations are varied, including sound and music. A particular link is invoked connecting music, meditation, and mind. In many cultures, specific musical practices are used in religious ceremonies to induce altered states of consciousness. New Age offers explanations of such phenomena by merging North American shamanic traditions with the scientific approaches of psychology, neurophysiology, and particle physics, as well as Indian mystical theories of perception.

As a musical genre New Age has gained a lucrative niche within the international music industry, especially since the 1980s. An early example of what would later be described as a New Age album is Tony Scott's *Music for Zen Meditation* (1964), where, as in so many subsequent releases, Asian and Western musical instruments and styles are combined. The term itself was introduced in 1976 with Will Ackerman's first release of acoustic guitar solos, *In Search of the Turtle's Navel*. The stylistic range of New Age music is broad. Early New Age pioneers included progressive rock groups (Pink Floyd, Harmonium), jazz musicians (Paul Horn, Paul Winter Consort), and composers of electronic music (Wendy Carlos, Klaus Schulze). New Age often echoes the legacy of minimalism, whether in its repetition, instrumentation, or lengthy duration. Because of its ambient qualities, New Age music often accompanies yoga, meditation, and relaxation.

BIBLIOGRAPHY

GMO

R. Garneau: "Ritual and Symbolism in New Age Music," *Pacific Review of Ethnomusicology*, iv (1987), 57–74

R. Basil, ed.: *Not Necessarily the New Age: Critical Essays* (Buffalo, NY, 1988) [incl. L. Berman: "New Age Music?," 250–68]

A. Laurier: "Jazz? New Age? Classical?," *Canadian Composer*, ccxxv (1989), 24–7

H.C. Zrzavy: "Issues of Incoherence and Cohesion in New Age Music," *Journal of Popular Culture*, xxiv/2 (1990), 33–53

P.C. Blum: "Typification, Transcendence, and Critique: On the Social Construction of New Age Music," *All Music: Essays on the Hermeneutics of Music*, F. Dasilva and D. Brunsma, eds. (Brookfield, VT, 1996), 117–32

DIANE SCHREINER/R

New Albion. Record company. Founded in 1984 in San Francisco, California, by Foster Reed, it moved to Elizaville, New York, in 2005. Early recordings featured experimental electro-acoustic and minimalist music by California composers and ensembles, including Ingram Marshall (*Fog Tropes*), John Adams (*Shaker Loops*), Daniel Lentz ("O-Ke- Wa"), Stephen Scott's bowed piano ensemble, the Paul Dresher Electro-Acoustic Band, the California EAR Unit, and the Deep Listening Band. In addition, Reed has built a catalog of music by international composers, including Somei Satoh (Japan) and Ge Gan-ru (China), Karlheinz Stockhausen (Germany), Silvestre Revueltas (Mexico), and Arvo Pärt (Estonia), and expanded to include an earlier generation of American experimentalists, including Henry Cowell, Lou Harrison, Ruth Crawford, Johanna Beyer, John Cage, Leo Ornstein, Morton Feldman, and Terry Riley. During the 1990s the firm released on average 12 albums per year and diversified its catalog with a series of early music recordings with Ensemble Project Ars Nova and orchestral recordings by the New Century Chamber Orchestra, whose CD of music by Dmitry Shostakovich, *Written with the Heart's Blood* (1996), was nominated for a Grammy Award. Since the early 2000s, with the downturn in the recording industry, Reed has limited the number of recordings released per year and shifted its distribution to the Internet. In the early 2010s the catalog included over 136 recordings that reflected an eclectic range of performers, ensembles, and composers, including pianists Sarah Cahill and Margaret Leng Tan; singer Joan La Barbara; cellist Joan Jeanrenaud;

double-bassist Stefano Scodanibbio; composers Evan Ziporyn, Stephen Vitiello, Erdem Helvacioglu, Kyle Gann, and Roberto Sierra; and the Brooklyn-based new music ensemble Slow Six.

G. PAUL COX

New Amsterdam Singers. Choral ensemble. Founded in 1966 as "The Master Institute Chorus," the New Amsterdam Singers (NAS) have garnered substantial critical attention for an amateur chorus. Clara Longstreth, the group's head conductor since 1968, has assembled programs that have been acclaimed as colorful, complex, and textually rich. She has been with the group from its start, initially serving two years as assistant conductor to Allan Miller (1966–8). Since becoming a fully independent group in 1978, NAS included over 70 singers in the early 2010s. The group has been known for performing a wide assortment of music, ranging from 15th-century pieces to contemporary works, and for specializing in a cappella performance as well as double chorus repertoires. NAS has performed subscription concerts in New York and has sung in other venues around the metropolitan area annually. The group has also periodically toured abroad; international tour destinations have included Cuba, Argentina, Turkey, Russia, and Latvia. In December 2010 a subset of the group traveled to Washington, DC, to perform at the White House holiday open house festivities. The group has produced three CDs, which include selected live performances and highlight 20th-century choral music.

CATHERINE WOJTANOWSKI

Newark. City in New Jersey (pop. 277,140; metropolitan area 18,818,536; 2010 US Census). On the Passaic River, about 12 km west of Manhattan, it was founded by Puritan settlers from Connecticut in 1666 and incorporated in 1836.

1. Art music. 2. Popular music, jazz, and gospel music.

1. ART MUSIC. Early musical life centered around the church, which by 1720 was predominately Presbyterian. James Lyon (1735–94), the compiler of *Urania* (1761/*R*), an important early American tune book, was born and educated in Newark. By the late 18th century private teachers were offering musical instruction, and in 1797 the first musical band of Newark citizens participated in the Independence Day celebration. Trinity Church (subsequently Trinity & St. Philip Episcopal Church on Broad Street in downtown Newark) installed the first church organ in Newark in 1819. By 1830 Newark had three church organs, and the formation of three choral organizations, the Harmonic Society (1830), the Newark Handel and Haydn Society (1831), and the Mozart Sacred Society (1834), furthered the performance of sacred music. Henry Pilcher built his first organ in Newark in 1834. The composer William Batchelder Bradbury taught singing to children at the Presbyterian churches. The first oratorio held in Newark, George Frideric Handel's *Judas Maccabaeus*, was presented by the Newark Handel and Haydn Society in 1837. Between 1832 and 1841 there were 92 public concerts by well-known musicians, including violinists, pianists, opera singers, and the English singers Henry Russell and John Braham. The *New York Musical Review and Gazette* included reviews of concerts given by musicians resident in Newark.

The first secular music group, the Newark Amateur Glee Company, was organized in 1837, but concerts consisting principally of secular music were not tolerated by the churches and had to be held in hotels and the meeting halls of private clubs. Newark's Concert Hall, which was renamed many times after its inauguration in 1847, was the first public hall in the city to be lit by gas. Library Hall (capacity 600), which opened in 1848, and Oraton Hall (opened 1856) were also used for concerts.

By 1850 Newark had become the wealthiest and most populated city in New Jersey, and the wave of German immigrants who settled there in the middle of the century initiated a new era in the city's musical life. The first German singing-society, the Eintracht, was organized in 1846, followed by the Auyrora (1852), the Concordia (1857), the Arion Men's Chorus (1850), the Germania (1865), and the Harmonie (1883) societies. An auditorium to house these groups was built in 1884 by Gottfried Krueger, after whom it was named. Among the many other choral groups that formed around this time was the Newark Harmonic Society, which had its own orchestra and started sponsoring concerts in 1860.

The Orpheus Club, among the earliest glee clubs in the United States, was organized in 1889 by Samuel Augustus Ward, the organist and choirmaster at Newark's Grace Church who is remembered for his hymn tune "Materna" (1882, now sung as "America the Beautiful" with lyrics by Katherine Lee Bates). Newark's choral tradition continued with the formation in 1966 of the renowned Newark Boys Chorus (and School) and the legendary North Jersey Philharmonic Glee Club, inaugurated 1939. Originally founded as the New Jersey Symphony Boys Choir, the Newark Boys Chorus has performed at major venues around the United States and toured in Europe and Asia. The school is located in the Lincoln Park Arts District beside the historic landmark Newark Symphony Hall, formerly the Mosque Theatre. The all-male North Jersey Philharmonic Glee Club formed in 1939 under the directorship of Delores Collins Benjamin. It has performed European and African American classical songs for audiences at the Newark Museum, the White House, and many other key institutions.

The first opera performed in Newark was Carl Maria von Weber's *Der Freischutz*, presented in German on 2 June 1885 at the Concert Hall; in 1860 a season of Italian opera was given in English translation. Opera began to flourish in the city in the 1890s with performances at Miner's Newark Theater. Interest continued in the 1920s with the Newark Music Festivals and into the 1930s with performances sponsored by the Griffith Music Foundation, the Newark Opera House, and the Grand Opera Company of New Jersey, which gave its first performance in Newark in 1937. The Opera Theatre of New

Jersey moved to Newark and gave its first performance at Symphony Hall in November 1968; it was renamed the New Jersey State Opera in 1974. It moved to the New Jersey Performing Arts Center in 1998. The non-profit company Trilogy: An Opera Company has been led by opera bass Kevin Maynor, its founder and artistic director; it performs works by African American composers and operas that reflect the black experience at various community venues.

The city's first permanent orchestra, the Newark SO, was formed in 1914 as the Eintracht Orchestra. It was followed by the SO of Newark, the Newark Chamber Orchestra (1956), and the Little Symphony of Newark (1966). The New Jersey Symphony Orchestra, founded in 1928, has toured throughout the state and since 1964 has been based in Newark. It performed at Symphony Hall before moving to the New Jersey Performing Arts Center.

In 1938 Mrs. Parker O. Griffith established the Griffith Music Foundation, which for more than 20 years sponsored a variety of musical activities at the Mosque Theatre, including a piano master-class series, concerts by renowned conductors, instrumental virtuosos, and singers (e.g., Arturo Toscanini, Vladimir Horowitz, Rubinstein, Emanuel Feuermann, Marian Anderson—who came to Newark for seven seasons—and Ferruccio Tagliavini) and orchestras (e.g., the Boston SO, the Cleveland Orchestra, and the New York Pops Orchestra), as well as ballet, opera, and children's programs. The foundation was closed in 1959, but similar events were sponsored first by Garden State Concerts, Inc., and later by Moe Septee, who brought to Newark such organizations as the Moscow and Leningrad symphony orchestras and the Royal Ballet from London; Septee became manager of the Mosque Theatre after it was refurbished.

A number of significant festivals and outdoor musical events have taken place in Newark, the first of which were the concerts given by the Newark Philharmonic Concert Band and guest bands at Branch Brook Park for more than 50 years from 1904. In 1915 C. Mortimer Wiske organized the Newark Music Festival, which was held annually until 1930, usually in the First Regiment Armory. It boasted choruses of 500–3000 voices and audiences of up to 40,000. The second festival in 1916 was a historical pageant lasting four days, involving 4000 actors, 300 singers, and 90 instrumentalists in the celebration of the 250th anniversary of the foundation of Newark. In 1936 the Essex County Music Society, under the leadership of Mrs. Griffith, began to sponsor a music series called "Symphonies under the Stars." The concerts, attended by up to 25,000 people, were held at the Newark Schools Stadium until 1942, when war restrictions required them to be moved indoors. Among the soloists who participated in the series were Jascha Heifetz, Yehundi Menuhin, Fritz Kreisler, Ezio Pinza, Jussi Björling, and Paul Robeson.

The most significant contemporary arts institution in Newark is the New Jersey Performing Arts Center (NJPAC), which opened in 1997. It is located on Sarah Vaughn Way, near Park Place and Central Avenue in the Cultural Arts District of downtown Newark. Featuring the 2750-seat Prudential Hall, the 514-seat Victoria Theatre, and smaller venues, NJPAC is now home to the New Jersey SO and the New Jersey State Opera and host to international touring artists. The arts center offers wide-ranging programming to which the city has responded favorably, from hip-hop festivals and ballet performances to conversations with artists and educational programming. The world lives in Newark, a diverse and multicultural city, and the world's artists play NJPAC. Sweet Honey in the Rock has made annual appearances since the center opened, helping transform a formerly blighted area into a plaza of light for Newark, Greater Newark, in nearby New York.

2. POPULAR MUSIC, JAZZ, AND GOSPEL MUSIC. Vaudeville shows were produced in Newark during the 1870s, but it was not until 1902, when Proctor's Park Palace was built specifically as a music hall, that vaudeville could be considered to have been well established. The first burlesque shows were offered in Newark during the 1880s at Waldman's Opera House (the renamed Concert Hall), and performances of this kind took place until 1956, when an anti-burlesque amendment was added to the city's theatrical ordinance. In 1872 one theater and three music halls were in use; by 1922 there were 62 such venues, two of them for theater, two for burlesque, and five for vaudeville. Musical productions were in their heyday in Newark in the 1920s and early 1930s, and the Shubert Theater accommodated a great many of them.

Newark provided a congenial atmosphere for jazz, which by the 1930s had several small clubs, including the Piccadilly and the Alcazar, and such larger halls as the Adams, Orpheum, and Paramount theaters, where, among others, Louis Armstrong, Duke Ellington, and Jimmy Lunceford performed. The Kinney Club, Skateland, and the Savoy Ballroom offered big-band music. During the late 1930s two local bands were established, the Savoy Dictators and Gil Fuller's Barons of Rhythm, and Ellington, Art Tatum, Woody Herman, and Stan Kenton played at the Mosque and the Adams theaters in the 1940s, followed by Miles Davis, Art Blakey, and John Coltrane at various jazz clubs (Powell's Lounge, the Front Room, Sugar Hill, and the Key Club) in the 1950s. By the mid-1960s, however, when guitarist GEORGE BENSON was becoming known, only the Key Club remained. Jazz in Newark was revived in the 1970s, with jazz services at Memorial West Church, weekly jazz sessions at Pere's East, and activities at the Key Club and Sparky J's, located directly across the street from each other, right around the corner from Newark City Hall. Many Newark-born musicians have made major contributions to jazz, including composer and saxophonist WAYNE SHORTER and the Divine One, vocalist SARAH VAUGHAN.

In October 2000 Jazz Vespers was born at Bethany Baptist Church in Newark's Central Ward. It is held on the first Saturday of every month, highlighting luminaries such as vocalist Lizz Wright, bassist Mimi Jones, pianists Cedar Walton Trio and Randy Weston, and others.

The INSTITUTE OF JAZZ STUDIES, founded in 1952 by Marshall Stearts of Hunter College, CUNY, and housed on the Newark campus of Rutgers, the State University, since 1967, is a leading archival collection of jazz and jazz related material (*see* Libraries and collections). It publishes the *Journal of Jazz Studies* (formerly the *Annual Review of Jazz Studies*). The music department at Rutgers offers a BA in music, a sequence of courses in arts management, and a variety of student ensembles.

Gospel music became culturally more significant in Newark in the 1920s and 1930s with the growth in the black population and the number of black churches established at that time. Sarah Vaughan and Dionne Warwick both sang in Newark church choirs before they made their careers in jazz and popular music, as did Warwick's niece, Whitney Houston. Savoy Records, which was particularly successful in black gospel music, started as a Newark-based company, issuing its first recording, a bop session, in 1944. In 1978 the company moved to Elizabeth, New Jersey, where it was bought by Prelude Records five years later. An annual Gospel Fest is held at the Prudential Center in Newark, hosted by Cissy Houston (Whitney's mother and former member of the Sweet Inspirations). The Institute for Sacred Music was established in May 2011 at Bethany Baptist Church under the direction of Courtney Bryan, whose album *This Little Light of Mine* has attracted much attention.

Newark has been home to a myriad of internationally known popular artists, including composer Jerome Kern (born in New York but raised in Newark), singers Frankie Valli and Connie Francis, singer-songwriter Paul Simon, singer and actress Whitney Houston, and rapper/actors Ice-T and Queen Latifah. The city also nurtured local legends such as singer Viola Wells (1902–86), who adopted the stage name Miss Rhapsody. She shared the stage with top performers such as Nat "King" Cole, her exciting style reflected in billing as "Miss Rhapsody, the Ebony Stick of Dynamite." Late in her career, she won a local Citizen of the Year award, was honored for 60 years in show business by Essex County College in Newark and was presented with the key to the city by Mayor Kenneth Gibson.

BIBLIOGRAPHY

W.H. Shaw: *History of Essex and Hudson Counties, New Jersey* (Philadelphia, PA, 1884)

D.E. Hervey: "Music in Newark," *a History of the City of Newark, New Jersey…1666–1913*, ed. F.J. Urguhart (New York, 1913)

C.H. Kaufman: *Music in New Jersey, 1655–1860: a Study of Musical Activity and Musicians in New Jersey from its First Settlement to the Civil War* (East Brunswick, NJ, 1981)

G. Bishop: "Gems of New Jersey Music," *Sunday Star-Ledger* (2, 9, and 16 Oct 1983)

B.H. Kukla: *Swing City: Newark Nightlife, 1925–50* (Philadelphia, PA, 1991)

C. Kerlew: "The Institute of Jazz Studies and Rutgers University: From Academic Orphan to National Resource," *Public & Access Services Quarterly*, i/1 (1994), 43–65

D. Bischoff: "Shimmering glass lets Newark shine," *Star-Ledger* (20 Oct 1997)

R. Strauss: "New Jersey's Arts Center: 5 Years of Hybrid Success," *New York Times* (18 Nov 2002)

LYNNE M. SCHMELZ-KIEL/SANDRA L. WEST

Neway, Patricia (*b* Brooklyn, NY, 30 Sept 1919; *d* East Corinth, VT, 24 Jan 2012). Soprano. After graduating from Notre Dame College for Girls (BA 1939; the school subsequently became Saint John's University), she became seriously interested in music and developed her voice with Morris Gesell, whom she later married. In 1946 she made her solo debut as Fiordiligi in *Così fan tutte* at the Chautauqua Festival, and in 1948 she joined the New York City Opera and appeared as the Female Chorus in Benjamin Britten's *The Rape of Lucretia*. In 1950 she created the role of Magda Sorel in Gian Carlo Menotti's *The Consul*, which she sang in 269 performances on Broadway. In 1958 she created another Menotti role, the Mother in *Maria Golovin* at the Brussels World's Fair. She was the originator of the role of the Mother Abbess in Richard Rodgers and Oscar Hammerstein II's *The Sound of Music* (1959), for which she won the 1960 Tony Award for Best Featured Actress in a Musical. Her later career was devoted to concerts and guest opera appearances with numerous American companies, primarily in contemporary works by Britten, Alban Berg, Francis Poulenc, Lee Hoiby, and Hugo Weisgall.

PETER G. DAVIS/CHRISTOPHER E. MEHRENS

Newborn, Phineas Jr. (*b* Whiteville, TN, 14 Dec 1931; *d* Memphis, TN, 26 May 1989). Jazz pianist, composer, and bandleader. Born into a musical family that included his father, a drummer, and his brother Calvin, a guitarist, he grew up in Memphis where he heard major jazz artists. His influences included Nat "King" Cole, Fats Waller, Art Tatum, Bud Powell, and the little known Oscar Dennard. In his early career he worked with Booker Little, George Coleman, Sonny Criss, Jamil Nasser, and Charles Lloyd. He attended Tennessee State College before being drafted into the US Army in 1953. Following his discharge, in 1955 he moved to New York, where he remained until 1961. An Atlantic album and appearance at the Newport Jazz Festival (1956) were both enthusiastically received. Newborn subsequently recorded four albums for Victor and two for Roulette in the 1950s. During a period in Los Angeles (1961–71) he made five recordings for Contemporary Records before retreating from the public eye to Memphis. He recorded a second album for Atlantic in 1974 following a brutal beating that led to his hospitalization. In the late 1970s he made several more albums and returned to New York (1978) and toured Japan and Europe. Newborn made a last appearance in the mid-1980s before he succumbed to lung cancer. His work has been acknowledged by Memphis pianists of different generations, including Harold Mabern, James Williams, Mulgrew Miller, and Donald Brown.

BIBLIOGRAPHY

D.C. Hunt: "Phineas Newborn Jr.: Problems of a Virtuoso," *Jazz & Pop*, ix/6 (1970), 22–4

S. Booth: *Rythm Oil: a Journey through the Music of the American South* (New York, 1991)

C. Newborn: *As Quiet as it's Kept! The Genius of Phineas Newborn, Jr.* (Memphis, 1996)

C.J. Wagner: *Changing Contents for Jazz: American Cultural History, Art in the Market, and the Life of Phineas Newborn, Jr.* (diss., U. of Memphis, 1996)

MICHAEL FITZGERALD

Newbury, Mickey [Milton J.] (*b* Houston, TX, 19 May 1940; *d* Springfield, OR, 29 Sept 2002). Singer–songwriter. He occupies a singular place in American pop and country music. Although often grouped with the circle of Nashville revolutionaries that included Willie Nelson, Tom T. Hall, and Kris Kristofferson, Newbury wrote elegant, deceptively simple songs that seemed to arise from a mystical, distant plane known only to him. Paradoxically, his most familiar composition, "An American Trilogy," was original only in the way he blended the standards "Dixie," "Battle Hymn of the Republic," and "All My Trials." His recording of the song (Elektra, 1972) spotlighted his gorgeous, aching-heart tenor and was reprised in a hit version by Elvis Presley (RCA Victor, 1972).

Arriving in Nashville following overseas military service, he signed with the famed Acuff-Rose publishing company in the 1960s and, within the decade, had hit recordings of his songs by Don Gibson ("Funny familiar forgotten feelings" [RCA Victor, 1966]), Kenny Rogers and the First Edition ("Just dropped in [To see what condition my condition was in]" [Reprise, 1968]), Andy Williams ("Sweet Memories" [Columbia, 1968]), and Eddy Arnold ("Here Comes the Rain Baby" [RCA Victor, 1968]). Just a few of the additional artists to record Newbury's songs include Ray Charles, Johnny Cash, Brenda Lee, David Allan Coe, Glenn Campbell, and Solomon Burke. He also influenced countless performers with his matchless voice and folksy manner, along with distinctive compositions such as "Cortelia Clark," about a blind street singer, and the strikingly sad country ballad "She even woke me up to say goodbye."

During the 1970s Newbury, who had earlier recorded for RCA, released his own recordings in critically acclaimed albums such as *Looks Like Rain* (Mercury, 1969), *Frisco Mabel Joy* (Elektra, 1971), and *Heaven Help the Child* (Elektra, 1973). Failing to make a commercial impact with his own recordings, Newbury moved to Oregon and concentrated on his growing family. He continued recording throughout the 1990s, including wonderfully spare duets with violinist Marie Rhines, and some memorable live performances, but lung problems plagued him until his death in 2002.

THOMAS GOLDSMITH

New Dance Group. Performing arts organization. Established in 1932 by six young Jewish women on the Lower East Side of New York City, New Dance Group (NDG) has trained leaders of the American dance into the 21st century. Founded to combine the radical left with modern dance expression, NDG proclaimed in its first anniversary bulletin, "Dance Is a Weapon of the Class Struggle." The early NDG included concert dance soloists, a men's group, ensembles that performed in union halls, and a folk-dance unit. By the mid-1930s the school boasted an enrollment of 800 students.

Between 1932 and the 1970s the NDG retained its commitment to social justice through both protest works and dances that celebrated the United States. Members of NDG included the Jane Dudley–Sophie Maslow–William Bales Trio, Hadassah, Pearl Primus, Mary Anthony, Donald McKayle, and Jean-Léon Destiné. Woody Guthrie, Pete Seeger, Alex North, and Earl Robinson composed music for NDG choreographers. A myriad of dancers passed through the NDG studios for rehearsals, as teachers, or for meetings, including Anna Sokolow, Doris Humphrey, Charles Weidman, José Limón, Alvin Ailey, and Jerome Robbins. Styles taught at the school from the 1940s included Afro-Caribbean, modern, Middle Eastern, folk dance, and ballet.

In 1953 NDG produced its first Broadway season, and in 1955 the corporation purchased a building in Manhattan's theater district for school and company rehearsals. By the 1960s NDG's collective began to wane as leaders left for universities or formed independent studios, and financial problems plagued the Group. Yet in 1974 Joyce Trisler's NDG workshop production of Stravinsky's *Sacre du printemps* provided the seed for the Joyce Trisler Danscompany.

In 2000 the Dance Heritage Coalition named NDG's one of "America's Irreplaceable Dance Treasures." Celebrating the NDG seventieth anniversary in 2002, political luminaries from Vice President Dick Cheney to Senator Hillary Clinton wrote letters of congratulation. With deficits mounting, a new NDG Board elected to close operations in 2009. While the choreographic legacy remains with the estates of the individual artists, NDG's rich document-based and photographic archives have been deposited at the Library of Congress.

DISCOGRAPHY
New Dance Group Gala Historic Concert 1930's–1970's, American Dance Guild videotape (New York, 1993)

BIBLIOGRAPHY
S. Prickett: "From Workers' Dance to New Dance," *Dance Research*, vii/1 (1989), 47–64
S. Prickett: "Dance and the Workers' Struggle," *Dance Research*, viii/1 (1990), 47–61
M. Franko: *Dancing Modernism/Performing Politics* (Bloomington, IN, 1995)
E. Graff: *Stepping Left: Dance and Politics in New York City, 1928–1942* (Durham, NC, 1997)
B. Rosen, ed.: *The New Dance Group: Movement for a Change* (London, 2000)
V.P. Geduld: "Performing Communism in the American Dance: Culture, Politics, and the New Dance Group," *American Communist History*, vii/1 (2008), 39–65

VICTORIA PHILLIPS GEDULD

New England. This article broadly addresses music making since the early 17th century in the states comprising New England: Maine, New Hampshire, Vermont, Massachusetts, Connecticut, and Rhode Island. Although religious denomination, trade, and other factors connected New Englanders to Canadians to the north and fellow Americans in other regions, New England's colonial history and geography, and the importance of Boston as a cultural and trade center, fostered a regionally distinct musical identity. See individual city entries on BOSTON (i), HARTFORD, PORTLAND (i), PROVIDENCE, and SPRINGFIELD.

1. Music in the colonies. 2. The rise of singing schools. 3. 19th-century reform and immigration. 4. The Second New England School. 5. 20th-century plurality and dispersion. 6. New England as a region.

1. MUSIC IN THE COLONIES. Prior to the arrival of European colonists, the music of peoples who spoke Eastern Algonquian languages dominated New England. When the Puritans of the Plymouth (1620) and Massachusetts Bay (1628) Colonies arrived in the New World, they brought with them Psalters published in Europe. The latter colony's inhabitants, however, benefited from a geographical position between the Atlantic Ocean and the Charles and Merrimack Rivers, and by 1640 rapid growth fostered the publication of an American Psalter, the *Bay Psalm Book*. With its pedagogical "admonition to the reader," it demonstrates an interest in musical education that became a defining cultural characteristic of the region. Its publication also reflects New England's importance as a center of American music publishing, a position it held until New York became the publishing hub in the 1890s.

Religion did not preclude the Puritans' enjoyment of secular music. In addition, many of their fellow immigrants arrived as indentured servants, victims of poverty or famine, laborers, criminals, or political refugees. Secular songs thus played a major role in the working and social lives of all New Englanders, especially in rural settings such as the Connecticut River Valley, the White Mountains, and the rocky coast of Maine. Although New England was one of the most ethnically homogeneous regions of the United States until the mid-19th century, English ballads, folk songs, and sea chanteys vied with French Canadian, Scottish, and Irish traditional songs and performance styles to produce a variegated musical landscape.

The landscape itself likewise affected the nature of vernacular music in the region. Tunes such as "A Song on the Nantucket Ladies" and "The Lumberman's Alphabet" reflected geographically determined occupations such as farming, lumbering, fishing, whaling, and textile milling. Still other songs recalled historical events that impacted the lives of Northeasterners, ranging from the Boston Tea Party in 1773 to the sinking of the *Titanic* in 1912. In part because American musicians and musical influences played a far lesser role in the early growth of New England musical traditions, this music remained regionally distinct from similar ballads and folk songs in the South, with the fiddle taking on the prominent role that the banjo played in that region.

2. THE RISE OF SINGING SCHOOLS. During the mid-18th century, New Englanders in large towns and cities boasted access to an ever-widening variety of cultural activities. With the easing of religious strictures and an increase in discretionary income that accompanied advances in ship-building, urbanites could afford dancing lessons, instrumental concerts, and with the lifting of Blue Laws in the 1790s, theater. Most rural communities, on the other hand, relied upon singing schools, the result of an early 18th-century reform movement, for musical education. (*See* SINGING-SCHOOL.)

Prior to the 18th century, LINING OUT, a call-and-response style, was common practice among Northeastern congregations. A group of Harvard-educated clerics objected to its untutored sound and advocated a return to musically literate REGULAR SINGING. In 1721 the first singing school was founded in Boston, and with a rise in musical literacy arose America's first generation of native-born composers whose best-known representative was William Billings. Although singing schools eventually spread as far south as Virginia and Kentucky, they and their itinerant singing masters were most closely identified with small-town New England, as literature such as Washington Irving's *The Legend of Sleepy Hollow* (1820) demonstrates. Many composers of the First New England School were musical autodidacts, writing tunes that departed from European harmonic "correctness" in favor of personal expression. Their music thrived throughout the United States in the years following the American Revolution, but by the turn of the 19th century, it came under attack by fellow psalmodists, clergymen, and community leaders, and thereafter survived mainly in the South.

3. 19TH-CENTURY REFORM AND IMMIGRATION. As Richard Crawford (2001) has observed, musical reform was a regionally specific phenomenon centered in New England, and in the 19th century it went hand-in-hand with the rise of Transcendentalism, coupled with industrial and commercial prosperity. Following on the heels of the reformer Thomas Hastings, Massachusetts-born Lowell Mason used public interest in music's potential for intellectual, moral, and spiritual edification to raise funds for his Boston Academy of Music (1833–47) and to convince the Boston School Committee to include European-oriented music education in the nation's nascent public school curriculum. The growth of such organizations as the Boston Handel and Haydn Society (1815) similarly indicated a shift away from native composition, and the arrival of European musicians such as Ole Bull and Jenny Lind, as well as a steady influx of Germans from 1848 on, increased northeasterners' appreciation for and emulation of European music.

In the popular sphere, Tyrolean families of singers inspired the establishment of American troupes, most famously the Hutchinson Family Singers of New Hampshire. George Root, one of Mason's associates, became one of the most famous antebellum composers, known particularly for his Civil War songs, and in the postwar years, PEACE JUBILEES gave rise to music festivals throughout New England. Toward the end of the century, Henry Lee Higginson founded the Boston SO (1881), and as musical literacy yielded a First New England School, so the increase in such musical infrastructure as professional ensembles, conservatories, concert halls, and luthiers nurtured a second school of composers in New England.

4. THE SECOND NEW ENGLAND SCHOOL. By mid-century New York had overtaken Boston as the nation's leading city, but its competitive, commercial atmosphere contrasted with that of Boston, whose history of education, social reform, and philanthropy produced an environment more supportive of art music and its composers. During the 1890s New Englanders John Knowles Paine,

George W. Chadwick, Arthur Foote, Horatio Parker, and Amy Marcy (Mrs. H.H.A.) Beach, along with Boston transplants Charles Martin Loeffler and Edward Mac-Dowell, formed the first school of American composers since the Yankee tunesmiths and the Moravians. Although all of these composers wrote in an idiom whose roots lay in Germany, they approached European genres through a uniquely American sensibility, a process that produced such works as Chadwick's *Symphonic Sketches* and Beach's *Gaelic Symphony*.

At the intersection between these and early 20th-century modernist composers stood Charles Ives. On one hand, his Yankee upbringing in Danbury, Connecticut, belief in Transcendentalist ideals, and study with Horatio Parker at Yale connected him to the Second New England School. On the other, his radical musical experimentation, which his father George encouraged in order to "stretch the ears" of his son, informed a style quite different from that of his teacher, though he likewise integrated American and European traditions. Ives strongly identified with the region of his birth, evoking its places and people through the titles, subjects, and popular and sacred musical quotations in many of his works.

5. 20TH-CENTURY PLURALITY AND DISPERSION. While Ives mirrored the Northeast with the rough-hewn, individualistic Yankee character of his music, younger composers found it difficult to avoid the influence of European modernism during the first half of the 20th century. As French influence overshadowed that of Germany, and New York overtook Boston as America's cultural center, the regional connection between New England and the art music tradition loosened. Particularly after World War I, composers such as Walter Piston, Quincy Porter, Randall Thompson, and Carl Ruggles explored new modes of artistic expression, which frequently afforded them less public support than the more musically accessible Second New England School composers had received.

During the second half of the 20th century, New England's musical identity entered a period of transition. Many composers who were raised in New England left to pursue their educations and careers elsewhere (Alan Hovhaness, John Adams), while others came to New England for the same reasons (Leon Kirchner, John Harbison), and with this demographic fluidity came stylistic plurality. The above trends also touched rural New Englanders. While traditional song and dance continued in communities stretching from Rhode Island to the "north country," 20th-century technological advancement and sociocultural change opened gaps within traditionally tight-knit families and communities, altering the nature of rural social and religious music, as well as the number and background of practitioners.

Although New Englanders have had to adapt their sense of regional identity to such change, their performance and educational institutions and festivals have continued to play an integral role in American musical life. Boston has remained the region's cultural nerve center, with its leading ensembles, conservatories, and strong academic programs. The MACDOWELL COLONY,

in Peterborough, New Hampshire, has continued to support composers, artists, and writers during short periods of residence. In addition to well-established music festivals in Newport, Rhode Island, and Tanglewood, Massachusetts, other gatherings and festivals dedicated to a wide range of genres, some imported (bluegrass, blues, jazz) and others rooted in the region's musical history (folk, classical, sea music, traditional Irish music), have taken place annually in cities throughout the region.

6. NEW ENGLAND AS A REGION. While Americans have continued to perceive the six states that comprise New England as a distinct region, several factors have impacted New Englanders' sense of regional identity: the slow dissolution of their ethnic homogeneity, advances in transportation that have lifted geographical constraints on travel, the impact of two world wars on both cultivated and vernacular traditions, and the changes wrought by the birth of a mass culture. As the stylistic variety of 20th-century composition and the regular movement of Americans to and from the Northeast suggests, music of New England in the early 21st century was no longer as deeply rooted in the ethnic, religious, and cultural identity of its 17th-century western European practitioners and their descendants. Rather, their stamp is only one among many that has left its imprint on the region.

BIBLIOGRAPHY

G. Hood: *A History of Music in New England: with Biographical Sketches of Reformers and Psalmists* (Boston, 1846)

E.H. Linscott, ed.: *Folk Songs of Old New England*, 2nd edn, intro. by J.M. Carpenter (Hamden and London, 1939/R1962)

J.W. Worst: *New England Psalmody, 1760–1810: Analysis of an American Idiom* (diss., U. of Michigan, 1974)

B. Lambert, ed.: *Music in Colonial Massachusetts, 1630–1820* (Boston, 1980–5)

C. Hamm: *Music in the New World* (New York and London, 1983)

J.A.L. Lemay: 'New England's Annoyances': America's First Folk Song (London and Toronto, 1985)

G. Chase: *America's Music: From the Pilgrims to the Present* (Urbana and Chicago, 1987, 3/1992)

N.E. Tawa: *The Coming of Age of American Art Music: New England's Classical Romanticists* (Westport, CT, 1991)

N.E. Tawa: "Ives and the New England School," *Charles Ives and the Classical Tradition*, ed. G.H. Block and J.P. Burkholder (New Haven and London, 1996), 51–72

P. Benes, ed.: *New England Music: the Public Sphere, 1600–1900*, The Dublin Seminar for New England Folklife Annual Proceedings, 21 through 23 June 1996 (Boston, 1998)

P. Benes and J.M. Benes, eds.: *Bibliography of Studies of New England Music Before 1900* (Boston, 1998)

N.E. Tawa: "Why American Art Music First Arrived in New England," *Music and Culture in America, 1861–1918*, ed. M. Saffle (New York and London, 1998), 141–65

V.L. Levine: "Northeast," *GEWM Volume 3: the United States and Canada*, ed. E. Koskoff (New York, 2000), 461–5

R. Crawford: *America's Musical Life: a History* (New York and London, 2001)

N.E. Tawa: *From Psalm to Symphony: a History of Music in New England* (Boston, 2001)

A.C. Buechner: *Yankee Singing Schools and the Golden Age of Choral Music in New England, 1760–1800* (Boston, 2003)

J.C. Post: *Music in Rural New England Family and Community Life, 1870–1940* (Lebanon, NH, 2004)

N. Cohen: "Folk Music of the Northeast," *Folk Music: a Regional Exploration* (Westport, CT, and London, 2005), 83–107

LEAH G. WEINBERG

New England Composers, Schools of. Two groups of American composers. The members of each are considered by historians to be unified on account of the area of their activity (New England), their Anglo-Saxon ethnic background, and the similarity of their musical training, style, and career. Writers have used different terms to categorize them; the most neutral of these—First and Second New England schools—was introduced by Hitchcock (1969).

The First New England School, which has also been referred to as one of "native pioneers" (Chase) and "Yankee tunesmiths" (Hitchcock, 1966), includes the late 18th- and early 19th-century composers of music for singing schools. Most of them were singing-school teachers themselves and composed or compiled at least one tunebook; they worked in the New England states, especially Massachusetts and Connecticut. In some cases these composers worked at trades and taught singing schools or published music as a secondary vocation.

William Billings is typically reckoned as the chief composer in this group; other figures of note include Daniel Read, Timothy Swan, Stephen Jenks, Supply Belcher, and Justin Morgan. These composers wrote psalm or hymn tunes, anthems, and fuging tunes. While most of this repertoire fell out of favor in New England after the turn of the nineteenth century, many pieces from this tradition were preserved in the shape-note tunebooks that proliferated in the American West and South in mid-century.

The Second New England School, termed also the "Academics" (Hughes), the "Boston Group" (Howard), the "Boston classicists" (Chase), or New England "Classical Romanticists" (Tawa, 1991), includes a group of late nineteenth-century composers, among them John Knowles Paine, Arthur Foote, George Chadwick, Horatio Parker, and Amy Beach. Some sources also include lesser-known figures such as Arthur Whiting or Margaret Lang. A later generation of composers, including Frederick Converse, Edward Burlingame Hill, and Daniel Gregory Mason, received part of their musical education from the earlier composers (particularly Paine and Chadwick) and inherited some musical attitudes and attributes, even if they did not adhere to them throughout their careers.

The relationship of Edward MacDowell to this school is problematic. Nicholas Tawa includes MacDowell on the basis of his residency in Boston (1888–96) and his continuing relationship with that city's musical institutions and composers; most sources do not, based on clear stylistic and aesthetic musical differences between MacDowell and the other composers of the school.

Of the primary members, all but Foote and Beach completed their musical training in Germany; most pursued careers in the Boston area as organist or teacher (or both), and wrote songs, cantatas, oratorios, and instrumental works in the larger abstract forms of the Classic-Romantic European tradition. However, Chadwick, Parker, and Foote also ventured into more overtly Romantic genres such as the tone poem.

Aside from Beach, the Second New England School composers were important figures in musical higher education. Paine taught at Harvard; Chadwick was director of the New England Conservatory for thirty-three years; Foote taught privately most of his career. Parker and MacDowell left Boston for teaching positions at Yale and Columbia, respectively. While these teaching positions brought their holders a measure of prestige and influence, the time constraints of such work probably hindered their compositional efforts.

The composers of this school (MacDowell excluded) wrote in traditional Classic-Romantic instrumental genres such as the symphony, string quartet, and piano trio, and engaged with conventional formal structures such as sonata form and theme and variations. Nonetheless, each composer appropriated these traditions individually, and as a result the school is not characterized by any particular uniformity of musical voice. Rather, the group is unified by high aesthetic ideals and respect for musical traditions.

BIBLIOGRAPHY

R. Hughes: *Contemporary American Composers* (Boston, 1900)

J.T. Howard: *Our American Music* (New York, 1931, 4/1965)

H.C. MacDougall: *Early New England Psalmody: an Historical Introduction* (Brattleboro, 1940)

G. Chase: *America's Music* (New York, 1955, 2/1966/R)

H.W. Hitchcock: "William Billings and the Yankee Tunesmiths," *HiFi/Stereo Review*, xvi (1966), 55 only

H.W. Hitchcock: *Music in the United States: a Historical Introduction* (Englewood Cliffs, 1969, 4/1999)

N. Tawa: *The Coming of Age of American Art Music: New England's Classical Romanticists* (Westport, CT, 1991)

N. Tawa: *From Psalm to Symphony: a History of Music in New England* (Boston, MA, 2001)

CHARLES S. FREEMAN

New England Conservatory. School of music founded by EBEN TOURJÉE in 1867; *see* BOSTON (i), and LIBRARIES AND COLLECTIONS.

New Grass Revival. Bluegrass/newgrass group. The group was formed in 1971 when four members of BLUEGRASS ALLIANCE (Sam Bush, *b* Bowling Green, KY, 15 April 1952, mandolin, fiddle, vocals; Courtney Johnson, *b* 20 Dec 1939, *d* Glasgow, KY, 7 June 1996, banjo; Curtis Burch, *b* Montgomery, AL, 24 Jan 1945, guitar, dobro, vocals; Ebo Walker [Shelor, Harry], *b* Louisville, KY, 1941, bass) attempted to fire fiddler and bandleader Lonnie Peerce, but instead quit *en masse* when Peerce informed them that he owned the band name. Their self-titled debut album (Starday, 1972) exemplified the divide between traditional and "hippy" elements in bluegrass music and culture of the time by applying bluegrass instruments and techniques not only to bluegrass but also to rock, pop, jazz, reggae, soul, and other genres as well. The same year, bassist Butch Robbins replaced Shelor, and drummer Michael Clemm joined for approximately six months, the only drummer to be an official part of the group. John Cowan (*b* 24 Aug 1952, bass, lead vocals) soon replaced Robbins and established a lineup that recorded four LPs for Flying Fish (*Fly Through the Country* [1975]; *When the Storm Is Over* [1977]; *Barren County* [1979]; *Commonwealth* [1981]). From 1979 to 1981 the group toured with Leon

Russell as opening and backing band, after which Burch and Johnson quit, replaced by Pat Flynn (*b* CA, 17 May 1952, guitar, vocals) and Béla Fleck (*b* New York, NY, 10 July 1958, banjo). During the 1980s the group recorded prolifically, first for Sugar Hill Records and later for Capitol/EMI, for whom they placed six singles on *Billboard*'s "Hot Country Singles" chart between 1986 and 1989, reached the top 40 with "Callin' Baton Rouge" (1989), and earned three Grammy nominations. Their final concert performance was held at a Grateful Dead concert at the Oakland Coliseum on 31 December 1989; they reunited in 1997 to perform with Garth Brooks on *The Late Show with Conan O'Brien*, and for a spontaneous one-song reunion on stage with additional musicians at Merlefest in 2007.

BIBLIOGRAPHY

R.K. Oermann: *New Grass Revival: Grass Roots—The Best of New Grass Revival* (Capitol 72438-63425-2-2, 2005) [liner notes]

DAVID ROYKO

New Harmony [Harmonie]. Village situated on the Wabash River in southwestern Indiana, known primarily for its communalist, communitarian, and millennialist activities. Harmonie was the second of three settlements built by the Harmony Society under George Rapp (1757–1847). Vocal and instrumental music flourished among the Harmonists during their Indiana decade (1815–25). Instrumental ensembles comprised a community orchestra that performed public concerts and private chamber groups that entertained George Rapp and his adopted son Frederick Rapp (1775–1834). Vocal music was used primarily within the church and for various Harmonist festivals. The hymn repertory consisted mostly of chorale tunes and *contrafacta*; choral repertory drew from printed vocal collections, oratorio choruses, and topical odes composed for festival occasions, with original contributions to both performance arenas by resident composers Johann Christoph Müller (1777–1845) and Frederick Eckensperger (1779–1849). Occasionally, orchestral accompaniment supported choral and congregational singing.

When Robert Owen (1771–1858), the Welsh-born father of British socialism, and William Maclure (1763–1840) bought the village from the Harmony Society, Owen re-named the town New Harmony. During the short period of its communitarian existence (1825–7), instrumental music took prominence. Karl Bernhard, Duke of Saxe-Weimar-Eisenach, visiting in 1826, described a chamber ensemble performing formal concert and functional dance music for various social occasions. Owen, though a confirmed atheist, allowed religious observances with music in the village. Later in the century, the Golden Troupe, a repertory company, and its band, "The Superb Silver Band," was based in the Thrall Opera House; they also toured throughout the continental United States from 1875–90.

BIBLIOGRAPHY

H.D. Kring: *The Harmonists: a Folk-Cultural Approach* (Metuchen, NJ, 1973)

Indiana Historical Commission: New Harmony as Seen by Participants and Travelers (Philadelphia, 1975)

R.D. Wetzel: *Frontier Musicians on the Connoquenessing, Wabash, and Ohio: a History of the Music and Musicians of George Rapp's Harmony Society (1805–1906)* (Athens, OH, 1976)

K.J.R. Arndt: *A Documentary History of the Indiana Decade of the Harmony Society 1814–1824* (Indianapolis, 1978)

C.K. Sluder: *Music in New Harmony, Indiana, 1825–1865: a Study of the Music and Musical Activities of Robert Owen's Community of Equality (1825–1827) and Its Cultural Afterglow (1827–1865)* (diss., Indiana U, 1987)

NIKOS PAPPAS

New Haven. City in Connecticut on Long Island Sound (pop. 129,779; metropolitan area 571,310; 2010 US Census) founded by English Puritans in 1638, and site of Yale University from 1716.

New Haven first came to musical prominence in the late 18th century as the home of Daniel Read, a composer and compiler of tunebooks, and Amos Doolittle, an engraver and publisher. Read and Doolittle together produced the first American periodical music publication, the *American Musical Magazine* (1786–7), consisting of American and English musical scores. About half of the tunebooks published in Connecticut from 1778 to 1810 originated in New Haven, but the number quickly declined when printing from type became more popular than engraving.

Although a New Haven Musical Society met in 1832, public musical entertainment in the city did not become important until the mid-century. It blossomed then largely due to the efforts of GUSTAVE J. STOECKEL, who founded the Mendelssohn Society in 1858 and taught music at his conservatory and at Yale University, and through Morris Steinert, who organized a short-lived orchestra in 1867. In 1894 Steinert founded the New Haven SO, one of the oldest American professional orchestras in continuous existence; it gave its first performance in January 1895. Its conductors have included HORATIO PARKER, David Stanley Smith, Frank Brieff, Erich Kunzel, Murry Sidlin, and William Boughton, among others. Parker also founded a New Haven Oratorio Society (1903–14), and the Horatio Parker Choir was founded by Smith in 1920.

Yale University was founded in 1701 as a private institution in Saybrook and moved to New Haven in 1716. A musical society was established at the university by 1812, and in 1853 a book of Yale songs was published, supposedly the first college songbook in the United States. Stoeckel became the first music instructor and conductor at the school in 1855, and was appointed professor of music in 1890 when music was added to the formal curriculum. By 1894 a music school had been created and degrees in music were awarded. Parker served as the first dean of the school from 1904 to his death in 1919.

Yale University has two administrative units for the study of music, the School of Music and the Department of Music. The School of Music awarded its first MM in 1932. In 1958 it became exclusively a graduate professional school, and in 1968 it began a DMA program. The Institute of Sacred Music was established in 1973 in affiliation with both the School of Music and the School of Divinity. By 2011 the School of Music maintained a roster of nearly 50 faculty members. Concerts have been given in Woolsey Hall since 1902; a new building, Abby and Mitch Leigh Hall, was opened in 2001. Chamber music has been stressed at the Yale Summer School for Music and Art on the Battell Estate in Norfolk, Connecticut, first sponsored by Yale in 1941. Some of the ensembles supported by the school include Yale Opera, the Yale Percussion Group, and several bands and choirs. The Whiffenpoofs (founded 1909) were the first small, informal singing group on campus. The Glee Club was founded in 1861 and made its first European tour in 1928. The Philharmonia Orchestra of Yale has given concerts in the United States and abroad.

During the 1930s an MA program in music history was introduced in the Graduate School. This led to the creation in 1940 of the Department of Music, headed by Leo Schrade, serving both Yale College (undergraduates) and the Graduate School. This department enrolled about 40 graduate students and roughly 75 undergraduate music majors in the 2010–11 academic year; it had 33 faculty members, administering a BA program in music, and MPhil and PhD degrees in music history and theory. This branch of Yale's music program has supported a Baroque opera series; several world music groups, including an impressive gamelan ensemble and a klezmer band; and a New Music ensemble.

The Irving S. Gilmore Music Library, which opened in 1998, holds an extremely rich collection of music scores, books, recordings, and research materials. The core of its rare-book collection came with the donation of Lowell Mason's library in 1873. In 1955 the library acquired Charles Ives's manuscripts and papers (Ives graduated from Yale in 1898), and it has since become a center for archival materials of American composers, including Parker, Carl Ruggles, Virgil Thomson, Kurt Weill, and many others. The school also administers the American branch of the archives of Paul Hindemith, who taught at Yale from 1940 to 1953. Other musical resources of the university include the internationally known Yale Collection of Musical Instruments, a Historical Sound Recordings collection, an American Musical Theatre collection, and the archives of the Oral History of American Music project. (For further discussion of Yale's archival holdings, *see* LIBRARIES AND COLLECTIONS, §3, "CONNECTICUT.")

The Neighborhood Music School in New Haven was formed in 1915 as part of a settlement house, and it continued to provide music education for youth in the 21st century. The University of New Haven has also offered courses in music and performance.

Several venues devoted to traditional music, including the New Haven Gaelic Club, have existed in the New Haven area. Shape note singing has been practiced at several churches and on the Yale campus, while contra dancing remained active at the Branford Community House in the 2010s. Street fairs such as the International Festival of Arts and Ideas have brought significant numbers of folk artists to the community. Popular music also has found a home in New Haven.

Toad's Place (est. 1976) has offered an intimate setting for national and local groups. Café Nine and BAR has also featured live music. Miracle Legion and Hatebreed are two of the bands that got their start in New Haven. The city has also hosted various events featuring live performance, including the New Haven Jazz Festival (1982–2007) and the Concerts on the Green.

BIBLIOGRAPHY

E.E. Atwater, ed.: *History of the City of New Haven to the Present Time* (New York, 1887)

R.G. Osterweis: *Three Centuries of New Haven, 1638–1938* (New Haven, CT, 1953)

C.A. Grimes: *They who Speak in Music: the History of the Neighborhood Music School, New Haven, Conn.* (New Haven, CT, 1957)

H.H. Roberts and D. Cousins: *A History of the New Haven Symphony Orchestra Celebrating its Seventy-fifth Season 1894–1969* (New Haven, CT, 1969)

R. Crawford: "Connecticut Sacred Music Imprints, 1778–1810," *Notes*, xxvii/3 (1971), 445–52; xxvii/4 (1971), 671–79

B.M. Kelley: *Yale: a History* (New Haven, CT, 1974/R1999)

H.E. Samuel: "Yale's DMA: a Progress Report," *College Music Symposium*, xviii/1 (1978), 97–104

B. Cannon: *Music and the Performing Arts in Jonathan Edwards College, 1933–1983* (New Haven, CT, 1984)

L. Noss: *A History of the Yale School of Music, 1855–1970* (New Haven, CT, 1984)

L. Noss: "Music Comes to Yale," *American Music*, iii/3 (1985), 337–46

C. Williams: "Organ Splendour at Yale" *Organists' Review*, lxxxiii/1:325 (Feb 1997), 13–22

J.P. Burkholder: "Ives and Yale: the Enduring Influence of a College Experience," *College Music Symposium*, xxxix (1999), 27–42

W. Collins: "The Yale Song Books, 1853–1978," *Vistas of American Music: Essays and Compositions in Honor of William K. Kearns*, ed. S.L. Porter and J.M. Graziano (Warren, MI, 1999), 196–219

PEGGY DAUB (WITH VICTOR T. CARDELL)/
JONAS WESTOVER

New Horizons International Music Association. An organization of amateur bands, choirs, and orchestras for adults with and without music experience. The first New Horizons band was established by Roy Ernst in Rochester, New York, in 1991. It spawned a movement that exceeded 200 groups internationally by the 2010s.

New Horizons International Music Association, (<http://www.newhorizonsmusic.org>)

DON D. COFFMAN

New Jack Swing [Swingbeat]. A pop-oriented rhythm-and-blues style that fuses a soul-based vocal style, a funk- or go-go-based propulsive rhythmic swing, jazz glissandi, and rap, using sampled sounds (modified by turntable techniques), synthesized sounds (such as strings), and drum machines (that create insistent beats). New York artist and producer TEDDY RILEY is generally credited for creating New Jack Swing (a term coined by writer and director Barry Michael Cooper) in the late 1980s, influenced by his collaborations with artists such as Kool Moe Dee, Johnny Kemp, Heavy D, Al B. Sure! [Al Brown], Keith Sweat, and with members of Riley's band Guy. The no.1 rhythm-and-blues single "I Want Her" (1987) by Keith Sweat is considered to be the first New Jack Swing hit. Writer-producers such as Riley, L.A. REID, and Babyface set romantic lyrics to light, memorable melodies. New Jack Swing was instantly well received and found great commercial success. It also quickly demonstrated crossover ability with Bobby Brown's album *Don't Be Cruel* (1988), coproduced by Riley, which sold over seven million copies. At its peak during the early 1990s, several female groups emerged, such as TLC and SWV, whose music is referred to as New Jill Swing; major productions include the Grammy-winning album *CrazySexyCool* (1994) by TLC. Subsequent developments fused with, or emphasized, other music styles, such as soul, which led to the emergence of styles from hip hop soul to nouveau soul or alternative soul. New Jack Swing continued to propel productions by Brian McKnight, who worked with Boyz II Men, Vanessa Williams, and many others.

BIBLIOGRAPHY

B.M. Cooper: "Teddy Riley's New Jack Swing: Harlem Gangsters Raise a Genius," *Village Voice*, xxxiii/42 (18 Oct 1988), 9–10

E. Gardner: "Hip Hop Soul," *The Vibe History of Hip Hop*, ed. A. Light (New York, 1999), 307–17

B.M. Cooper: liner notes, "The New Jack Epoch," *New Jack Swing Gold* (Universal Music Enterprises B0010037-02, 2007) [liner notes]

NICO SCHÜLER

New Kids on the Block [NKOTB]. Boy band. The group originally comprised Joey McIntyre (*b* Joseph Mulrey McIntyre, 31 Dec 1972, Needham, MA), Jordan Knight (*b* 17 May 1970, Worcester, MA), Jonathan Knight (*b* 29 Nov 1968, Worcester, MA), Danny Wood (*b* Daniel William Wood Jr., 14 May 1969, Boston, MA), and Donnie Wahlberg (*b* Donald Edmond Wahlberg Jr., 17 Aug 1969, Dorchester, MA).

This popular boy band was created in 1985 by producer Maurice Starr to reproduce the success of African American teen groups such as New Edition (which he had mentored in the early 1980s) and the Jackson Five. New Kids drew on the musical styles of African American male R&B singing and rap, but was designed to reach a wider audience—adding mainstream pop influences and a conservative image that was styled after white groups such as the Osmonds. The strategy proved enormously successful. By the 2010s New Kids on the Block had sold almost 80 million records worldwide.

Starr held auditions in Boston, first hiring teen rapper and dancer Donnie Wahlberg who then helped to enlist the others—Jordan Knight, who contributed a trademark Motown falsetto, as well as McIntyre, Jonathan Knight, and Wood. The group was signed by Columbia and released its self-titled song and debut album in 1986. Success came with the second album, *Hangin' Tough* (1988), for which the members had creative input as associate producers. It included their first hit, "Please Don't Go, Girl," several top five songs, and reached eight-times platinum status.

The group suffered criticism for performing with prerecorded vocals. In 1993 an attempt was made to resuscitate its waning success with a name change to NKOTB but the group disbanded in 1994. Several members followed solo careers, and Donnie Wahlberg, like his brother Mark, made the transition from music to acting. In 2011 the group reunited, recorded a CD, and performed with the Backstreet Boys.

STEPHANIE CONN

New Lost City Ramblers, the. Old-time string band. The New Lost City Ramblers were pioneers in the old-time music revival that paralleled the great folk music boom of the 1960s. The city-born and suburban-bred Ramblers specialized in recreating the sounds of rural southern string band and early bluegrass music at a time when the folk music scene was dominated by commercial singers and political singer/songwriters.

Mike Seeger (1933–2009), John Cohen (*b* 1932), and Tom Paley (*b* 1928) formed the original trio in 1958, with Tracy Schwarz (*b* 1938) replacing Paley in 1962. Following a successful appearance at the 1959 Newport Folk Festival, the group spent the next two decades touring colleges, coffee houses, and folk festivals. They introduced their northern and West Coast audiences to the southern folk music they had learned from hillbilly records of the 1920s and 1930s, from Library of Congress field recordings, and from recordings of traditional musicians they had made themselves. Playing a variety of instruments including fiddle, banjo, guitar, mandolin, autoharp, and harmonica, they performed a diverse repertoire ranging from fiddle tunes and bluegrass breakdowns to ballads, blues, and gospel songs. Their approach to southern folk styles is well represented on their 1958 album, *The New Lost City Ramblers*, the first of some 20 recordings they released on Folkways Records between 1958 and 1975.

The Ramblers were tireless advocates for southern folk music, working simultaneously as performers, researchers, documentarians, and promoters. Thanks in large part to their efforts, Elizabeth Cotten, Doc Watson, Maybelle Carter, Roscoe Holcomb, Dock Boggs, the Stanley Brothers, and many other traditional southern artists assumed prominent roles in the urban folk revival. The Ramblers raised key questions over what constituted authentic folk music, encouraging musicians to concentrate on instrumental and vocal performance styles gleaned from recordings rather than depending on words and melodies learned from written collections. They served as models for scores of string bands that sprung up in cities and on college campuses during the 1960s, and for musicians who revitalized Cajun, Irish, klezmer, Balkan, and other ethnic American musics in the 1970s and 1980s.

BIBLIOGRAPHY

Always Been a Rambler, DVD, dir. Y. Aginsky, Arhoolie Foundation AFV-204 (El Cerrito, CA, 2009)

R. Allen: *Gone to the Country: the New Lost City Ramblers and the Folk Music Revival* (Urbana, IL and Chicago, 2010)

RAY ALLEN

Newman, Alfred (*b* New Haven, CT, 17 March 1901; *d* Los Angeles, CA, 17 Feb 1970). Composer and conductor. He was a piano prodigy, making his first public appearance at the age of eight. He studied in New York with RUBIN GOLDMARK and George Wedge. In 1914 he was offered a piano scholarship by Sigismond Stojowski for a place at the von Ende School of Music, New York. Family poverty compelled him to abandon a concert career while still young; instead, he played in Broadway theaters and on vaudeville circuits. He studied conducting with William Daly and was the youngest conductor to date to appear on Broadway. As well as serving as music director for the *George White Scandals* (1920) and for the *Greenwich Village Follies* (1922–5), he conducted shows by George and Ira Gershwin, Otto Harbach, and Rodgers and Hart. In 1930 Newman went to Hollywood, where he was soon appointed music director at United Artists. He worked primarily in film musicals but gradually became more interested in traditional Hollywood scoring, especially after the success of his score for *Street Scene* (1931). From 1940 to 1960 he was head of the 20th Century-Fox music department and divided his time between composing and supervising and conducting film scores. He also supported the careers of such composers as Bernard Herrmann and Alex North, whose music was often regarded as unconventional. Newman worked on more than 230 films, winning nine Academy awards and 45 nominations; his last score (for *Airport*) was completed just before his death. Other activities included recordings with the Hollywood Bowl orchestra and guest conducting appearances with various American orchestras. His brothers Emil and Lionel also composed and conducted film scores in Hollywood, as have his sons Thomas and David Newman, his daughter Maria Newman, and his nephew Randy Newman.

One of the key figures in the history of American film music, Newman was among the first screen composers to establish the romantic symphonic style of Hollywood film scores, prevalent from the early 1930s to the mid-1950s. In comparison to composers such as Erich Wolfgang Korngold and Max Steiner, he was essentially self-taught as a composer; the few private lessons he took with Arnold Schoenberg in Hollywood had no appreciable effect on his musical style. His musical talents and fine dramatic sensibility, however, enabled him to learn on the job. When he encountered his first truly challenging scores around 1935, he began to show a knack for developing motivic material and an appreciation for the sound track's potential to incorporate new and interesting musical effects. By 1939 his music had developed into the style with which his name is associated. Well wrought and full textured, his scores sometimes (especially in the string writing) attain a high degree of lyrical and dramatic expressiveness. The manner in which certain sequences follow overt or hidden implications of the dialogue resembles the leitmotivic procedures of Richard Wagner and Richard Strauss.

Newman's scores for *Wuthering Heights, The Prisoner of Zenda, The Hunchback of Notre Dame, Captain from Castile,* and *The Robe* represent Hollywood film music at its best. As a conductor he had a great flair for molding music to the texture and rhythm of a picture and for coordinating the elements involved in the preparation and recording of a film musical. In his capacity as studio music director he encouraged the improvement of recording technique; the so-called Newman System for music synchronization, created for him during his United Artists years by musician Charles Dunworth, was still in use in the early 21st century.

WORKS
(selective list of film scores)
Street Scene, 1931; We Live Again, 1934; The Dark Angel, 1935; Beloved Enemy, 1936; The Prisoner of Zenda, 1937; Beau Geste, 1939; Gunga Din, 1939; The Hunchback of Notre Dame, 1939; Wuthering Heights, 1939; Young Mr. Lincoln, 1939; Brigham Young, 1940; How Green Was My Valley, 1941; The Song of Bernadette, 1943; Wilson, 1944; Captain from Castile, 1947; The Snake Pit, 1948; Prince of Foxes, 1949; Twelve O'Clock High, 1949; The Robe, 1953; The Egyptian, 1954, collab. B. Herrmann; A Man Called Peter, 1955; Anastasia, 1956; The Counterfeit Traitor, 1962; How the West Was Won, 1962; The Greatest Story Ever Told, 1965; Nevada Smith, 1966; Camelot 1967; Airport, 1970

BIBLIOGRAPHY
DAB (F. Steiner)
H. Brown: "The Robe," *Film Music*, xiii/2 (1953), 3–17
K. Darby: "Alfred Newman Biography and Filmography," *Film Music Notebook: a Complete Collection of the Quarterly Journal* (Sherman Oaks, CA, 1974–8), 219–27
F. Steiner: *The Making of an American Film Composer: a Study of Alfred Newman's Music in the First Decade of the Sound Era* (diss., U. of Southern California, 1981) [incl. complete list of film scores]
C. Palmer: *The Composer in Hollywood* (London and New York, 1990)
T. Thomas: *Film Score* (Burbank, CA, 1991)
K. Darby: *Hollywood Holyland: the Filming and Scoring of 'The Greatest Story Ever Told'* (Metuchen, NJ, and London, 1992), 163ff
M. Cooke: *A History of Film Music* (New York, 2008)
CHRISTOPHER PALMER/FRED STEINER/
JESSICA GETMAN

Newman, Anthony (*b* Los Angeles, CA, 12 May 1941). Organist, harpsichordist, and composer. In 1959–60 he studied in Paris with Pierre Cochereau and NADIA BOULANGER at the Ecole Normale de Musique. He received the BS degree in organ from the Mannes College in 1962, an MA in composition from Harvard University in 1963 after study with LEON KIRCHNER and LUCIANO BERIO, and the DMA in organ at Boston University in 1966. He served on the faculties of the Juilliard School (1968–73), was director of the graduate music program at Purchase College-SUNY (1975–8), and was professor of music at Indiana University from 1978 to 1981. He serves as director of music for St Matthew's Church in Bedford, New York. In 1967 Newman made his debut at Carnegie Recital Hall, New York, playing works by J.S. Bach on the pedal harpsichord. He is active as a recitalist, recording artist, and composer. His keyboard virtuosity is demonstrated not only at the organ, but also at the harpsichord and the fortepiano. His compositions include works for organ, piano, guitar, flute, chamber combinations, and orchestra. Newman's scholarly interest is in the Baroque era, especially in the keyboard works of J.S. Bach about which he has written several articles. He is a compelling performer whose high tempos are balanced by brilliant and innovative insights.

BIBLIOGRAPHY
A. Satz: "Musician of the Month: Anthony Newman," *HiFi/Musical America*, xxii/4 (1972), 4
T. Donahue: "Anthony Newman: Music, Energy, Spirit, Healing," *American Organist*, xxxv/6 (2001), 64
VERNON GOTWALS/JUDI CALDWELL

Newman, David "Fathead" (*b* Corsicana, TX, 24 Feb 1933; *d* Kingston, NY, 20 Jan 2009). Saxophonist and flutist. At an early age he moved with his family moved to Dallas, where he attended Lincoln High School. After graduation he earned a scholarship to study music and theology at Jarvis Christian College. After two years of college, Newman decided to perform professionally with alto saxophonist Buster Smith. While touring with Smith, he played with rhythm-and-blues bands that featured such musicians as Lowell Fulson and Ray Charles, who was Fulson's pianist. From 1954 he played in Charles's band and in 1958 made his first recording as a leader, the album *Fathead: Ray Charles Presents David "Fathead" Newman* for Atlantic Records. Newman left Charles's band in 1964 and moved to New York. From the late 1960s through the 1970s, he parlayed the fame garnered while working with Charles to record albums for Atlantic Records, Warner Bros., and Prestige, some of which were heavily produced and pop-oriented. He returned to his hard bop roots in the 1980s and began a productive association with HighNote Records in the 1990s that lasted until his death from pancreatic cancer. Newman's final two recordings, *Diamondhead* and *The Blessing*, illustrate the wide array of timbral colors that he was capable of producing as multi-instrumentalist: the warmth and depth of his tenor saxophone is wonderfully captured in tunes like George Gershwin's "Someone to Watch over me," and the airiness of his flute playing is nicely illustrated in "New York State of Mind" and "The Blessing."

BIBLIOGRAPHY

Feather-Gitler BEJ

M. Cuscuna: "Fathead Newman: King of the Texas Panhandle," *DB*, xli/20 (1974), 16

A. Little: "Fat Chance," *Cincinnati Magazine* (Dec, 2005), 34

MICHAEL CONKLIN

Newman, David (Louis) (*b* Los Angeles, CA, 11 March 1954). Composer, son of ALFRED NEWMAN, brother of THOMAS NEWMAN, and cousin of RANDY NEWMAN. He studied violin and piano as a child and earned music degrees from the University of Southern California (bachelor's in violin, master's in conducting). He worked regularly as a violinist in the Hollywood studios from 1977 to 1982, playing for such film composers as John Williams and Jerry Goldsmith.

Newman wrote his first film score in 1986 and was immediately embraced by the Hollywood community. He subsequently produced an average of five or six scores per year for his first few years in the business. Although a fine composer for dramas (*Hoffa, Brokedown Palace*), he became more sought-after for big-budget comedies (*The War of the Roses, The Nutty Professor, Galaxy Quest*) and animated films (*The Brave Little Toaster, Anastasia, Ice Age*). He received an Oscar nomination for his *Anastasia* score, 41 years after his father's Oscar nomination for a live-action version of the same story.

Unlike most of his colleagues, Newman has demonstrated a passion for unearthing and preserving American film music, wherever possible making it available for concert performance. In 1987 he launched a film-music preservation program at Robert Redford's Sundance Institute, which resulted in several high-profile

classic film-music concerts that he conducted. He has continued to conduct such programs at the Hollywood Bowl and elsewhere. He championed the work of Goldsmith, commissioning several new concert suites, during a three-year American Youth Symphony program that ended in 2010.

Newman has also written several concert works, including an unusual Los Angeles Philharmonic video-and-music collaboration (*1001 Nights*, 1998) and a six-movement woodwind concerto in which each of the first five movements is devoted to a single soloist and the final movement to all (2007).

WORKS
(selective list of film scores)

Vendetta, 1986; Critters, 1986; The Kindred, 1987; Malone, 1987; The Brave Little Toaster, 1987; Throw Momma from the Train, 1987; Bill & Ted's Excellent Adventure, 1989; Heathers, 1989; The War of the Roses, 1989; The Freshman, 1990; DuckTales: the Movie, 1990; Bill & Ted's Bogus Journey, 1991; Honeymoon in Vegas, 1992; The Mighty Ducks, 1992; Hoffa, 1992; The Sandlot, 1993; The Flintstones, 1994; Boys on the Side, 1995; The Phantom, 1996; The Nutty Professor, 1996; Matilda, 1996; Jingle all the Way, 1996; Anastasia, 1997; Galaxy Quest, 1999; Brokedown Palace, 1999; Bowfinger, 1999; Never been Kissed, 1999; Nutty Professor II: the Klumps, 2000; 102 Dalmations, 2000; Dr. Dolittle 2, 2001; The Affair of the Necklace, 2001; Ice Age, 2002; Scooby-Doo, 2002; Daddy Day Care, 2003; How to Lose a Guy in 10 Days, 2003; The Cat in the Hat, 2003; Scooby-Doo 2: Monsters Unleashed, 2004; Monster-in-Law, 2005; Serenity, 2005; Norbit, 2007; The Spirit, 2008; Alvin and the Chipmunks: the Squeakquel, 2009

BIBLIOGRAPHY

J. Burlingame: "L.A. Music's First Family: Range, Verstility David's Hallmark," *Daily Variety* (15 July 1997)

R. Koppl: "David Newman: the Calm before the Storm," *Film Music* (1998), Oct, 11–14

T. Greiving: "Prince David," *Film Score Monthly Online*, xiv/6 (2009) and xiv/7 (2009)

JON BURLINGAME

Newman, Lionel (*b* New Haven, CT, 4 Jan 1916; *d* Los Angeles, CA, 3 Feb 1989). Composer and conductor. The youngest of ten born to immigrant Russian-Jewish parents, his oldest sibling was ALFRED NEWMAN, who would become one of the pioneers of American film music. The younger Newman studied composition with JOSEPH SCHILLINGER in New York and, later in Los Angeles, with JOSEPH ACHRON and MARIO CASTELNUOVO-TEDESCO.

Like his older brother, Lionel Newman left school early to pursue a career as a musician. At the age of 15 he conducted for theater producer Earl Carroll in Florida (eventually conducting Carroll's *Vanities* show on Broadway in 1940), and in the 1930s he conducted touring shows for Tom Mix and Mae West. He followed his older brother to Hollywood and achieved early success as a songwriter (including a 1938 Oscar nomination for his title song for *The Cowboy and the Lady*).

Newman began stints as songwriter and rehearsal pianist at 20th Century-Fox in late 1939, soon after his brother Alfred became music director for the studio. All ten of his subsequent Oscar nominations were for Fox films, either as songwriter or musical director. He won the 1969 adaptation-score Oscar for *Hello, Dolly!* (with Lennie Hayton). Among his film songs were "As if I didn't have enough on my mind" (with Harry James, from *Do You Love Me?*) and "Never" (from *Golden Girl*), but his biggest hit was "Again" (sung by Ida Lupino in *Road House*), which spent 19 weeks on radio's *Hit Parade* in 1949 and generated six top-ten hits for performers including Doris Day, Mel Tormé, and Vic Damone.

Marilyn Monroe insisted on Newman as her personal musical director on Fox films including *Gentlemen Prefer Blondes*, *River of No Return*, *There's No Business Like Show Business*, and *Let's Make Love*. He was promoted to director of television music at Fox in 1959 and wrote some of the studio's best-known TV themes, including "Adventures in Paradise," "The Many Loves of Dobie Gillis," "Hong Kong," and "Daniel Boone." He also wrote several dramatic scores including *The Proud Ones*, *Love Me Tender*, *Compulsion*, *North to Alaska*, and *The Boston Strangler*. But his first love was conducting, and he conducted many Fox scores by Jerry Goldsmith, Alex North, and other composers during the 1950s, 1960s, and 1970s.

He succeeded Alfred as general music director for the studio in 1963, overseeing all feature and television music; he became vice president in 1977 and senior vice president in 1982, retiring in 1985. He briefly returned to the business as head of music for MGM-UA in 1988.

WORKS

Film scores: The Kid from Left Field, 1953; The Gambler from Natchez, 1954; The Killer Is Loose, 1956; The Proud Ones, 1956; A Kiss Before Dying, 1956; The Last Wagon, 1956; Love Me Tender, 1956; The Way to the Gold, 1957; Bernardine, 1957; Sing Boy Sing, 1958; Compulsion, 1959; North to Alaska, 1960; Move Over, Darling, 1963; Do Not Disturb, 1965; The Boston Strangler, 1968

Musical direction: You Were Meant for Me, 1948; Road House, 1948; Golden Girl, 1951; Gentlemen Prefer Blondes, 1953; Niagara, 1953; River of No Return, 1954; There's No Business Like Show Business, 1954; The Girl Can't Help It, 1956; Mardi Gras, 1958; Say One for Me, 1959; Let's Make Love, 1960; The Pleasure Seekers, 1964; Doctor Dolittle, 1967; Hello, Dolly!, 1969; At Long Last Love, 1975

BIBLIOGRAPHY

J. Tynan: "Lionel Newman," *BMI News* (Oct 1963), 30–3
"Lionel Newman," *BMI: The Many Worlds of Music*, (1974)
Obituary: *Los Angeles Times* (7 Feb 1989)

JON BURLINGAME

Newman, Randy [Randall Stuart] (*b* Los Angeles, CA, 28 Nov 1943). Popular singer, songwriter, and pianist. He was born into a musical family: three of his uncles, Alfred, Lionel, and Emil, composed and conducted film scores in Hollywood (*see* ALFRED NEWMAN and LIONEL NEWMAN). His family lived in various Southern cities, then, when Newman was seven, they settled in Los Angeles where he began to take piano lessons. He had begun writing songs by the age of 15 and while still in high school he was hired by Metric Music in California as a staff songwriter for a salary of $50 a week. Newman attended UCLA, where he studied music composition but left before completing his degree.

While at Metric, Newman wrote songs that were performed by many artists including the Fleetwoods, Gene McDaniels, and the O'Jays. One of his first songs to be widely recognized is "I think it's going to rain today,"

recorded by Judy Collins in 1966. Other artists have continued to record and perform his material over the years: Three Dog Night sang a truncated version of "Mama told me not to come" (1970), and Bonnie Raitt (1997) and Neill Diamond (2010) have both covered "Feels Like Home" from his musical *Faust*.

Newman began to record his own songs in 1968. He wrote and arranged all of the material on *Randy Newman Creates Something New under the Sun*, often using a full orchestra. It was this setting that allowed Newman's vocal delivery—drawling, untrained—to stand out, thus heightening the irony of his lyrics and the stories present in his songs. His concise songs—many of the early ones are less than two minutes long—generally narrate stories and often incorporate a device Newman refers to as the untrustworthy narrator. In "Davy the Fat Boy," for instance, the narrator presents himself as Davy's best friend, promising to take care of him when Davy's parents' die, yet he turns Davy into a carnival attraction sideshow. Newman has returned frequently to this device in various guises throughout his songwriting career. He is a slow songwriter and established an early pattern of completing enough songs to fill an album every two to three years, recording the album, and then making a tour. The songs range from the standard pop structure of verse and chorus to through-composed pieces. His work varies from a traditional rock style to jazz, blues, show tunes, and classical sources. Early songs that attracted attention include "Short People" (1977) and "I Love L.A." (1983).

In 1970 Newman began his foray into the world of film scores with his work on *Cold Turkey* with Norman Lear; that year he also conducted the music for *Performance*, which starred Mick Jagger. However, Newman dismissed this effort later, crediting his orchestrator Arthur Morton, instead. Newman did not compose for film again until 1981, when he wrote for Miloš Forman's *Ragtime*, which earned him an Academy Award nomination for the song "One More Hour." In 1984 he earned his second Academy Award nomination and a Grammy Award for Best Instrumental for his work on *The Natural*. Newman has subsequently continued to write film scores and has been nominated for and won several Academy Awards. He has had frequent pairings with the Walt Disney animation division, on such films as the *Toy Story* trilogy (1995, 1999, 2010), *Cars* (2006), and *The Princess and the Frog* (2009).

Despite his work in film, Newman has continued to write and produce albums of his own songs for release. *Harps and Angels* (Nonesuch, 2008) displays the same characteristics as his earlier albums. Newman is widely respected in both the rock and film score communities and continues to tour venues around the world.

SELECTED RECORDINGS

Randy Newman Creates Something New under the Sun (Reprise, 1968); *12 Songs* (Reprise, 1970); *Sail Away* (Reprise, 1972); *Good Old Boys* (Warner Bros. and Rhino, 1974); *Little Criminals* (Warner Bros., 1977); *Born Again* (Warner Bros., 1979); *Trouble in Paradise* (Warner Bros., 1983); *Land of Dreams* (Reprise, 1988); *Faust* (Reprise, 1995); *Bad Love* (Dreamworks, 1999); *Harps and Angels* (Nonesuch, 2008)

WORKS
Film scores: Cold Turkey, 1971; Herbstkatzen, 1981; Ragtime, 1981; The Natural, 1984; Gotcha!, 1985; Huey Long, 1985; ¡Three Amigos!, 1986; Avalon, 1990; Awakenings, 1990; Maverick, 1994; The Paper, 1994; Toy Story, 1995; James and the Giant Peach, 1996; Michael, 1996; Cats Don't Dance, 1997; Bug's Life, 1998; Pleasantville, 1998; Toy Story 2, 1999; Meet the Parents, 2000; Monster's, Inc., 2000; Mike's New Car, 2001; Seabiscuit, 2003; The Making of "Seabiscuit," 2003; Meet the Fockers, 2003; Cars, 2006; The Road to Cars, 2006 [TV film]; Leatherheads, 2008; The Princess and the Frog, 2009; Toy Story 3, 2010

BIBLIOGRAPHY
K. Courrier: *Randy Newman's American Dreams* (Toronto, 2005)
J. Matthews: *Randy Newman's Songs (1968–2008)* (diss., U. of Kentucky, forthcoming)

JON PARELES/JENNIFER MATTHEWS

Newman, Thomas (*b* Los Angeles, CA, 20 Oct 1955). Film composer. The youngest son of ALFRED NEWMAN, one of the central figures of Hollywood film music within the studio system of the mid-20th century, Thomas Newman has been a prolific, innovative, and influential composer of film scores in the late 20th and early 21st century. Newman was taught piano and violin as a child, then studied composition privately with GEORGE TREMBLAY and with Frederick Lesemann and DAVID RAKSIN during Newman's two years at the University of Southern California. After transferring to Yale University (BA 1977), Newman continued his compositional studies with Robert Moore, Bruce MacCombie, and JACOB DRUCKMAN, completing a master's degree in composition in 1978. Newman formed an important early connection with Broadway composer Stephen Sondheim, who helped Newman hone his interest in combining music and drama during the time when Newman wrote a musical theater piece, *Three Mean Fairy Tales*, which received a workshop performance. An opportunity to orchestrate a cue from John William's score for *Star Wars VI: Return of the Jedi* fueled Newman's growing interest in writing for film, and after working as a musical assistant on the 1984 film *Reckless*, Newman began to receive his own solo composing assignments. Consciously claiming the influence of composers such as Charles Ives, Igor Stravinsky, and Bernard Herrmann, Newman possesses a similarly pioneering spirit, and his imaginative approach to timbre has given his music a rare distinctiveness in a Hollywood landscape that often demands stylistic conformity. By the mid-1990s, Newman was recognized as one of the most original and influential composers working in Hollywood, as evidenced in part by his dual nominations for a Best Score Oscar for two 1994 scores, *Little Women* and *The Shawshank Redemption*. His music frequently blends digitally processed sounds together with acoustic instruments, and his strategic use of pedal points and drones highlights timbral qualities over harmonic progression and thereby lends his music an occasionally non-teleological quality. Newman has also created stirring symphonic scores in the tradition of his father's generation. Several of his scores show a fondness for pitched percussion, and compositions like his Oscar-nominated score for *American Beauty* quickly became

a stock sound for television commercials and derivative film scores. In addition to his dramatic works, Newman has received several commissions for concert works, including *Reach Forth Our Hands* for the 1996 Cleveland Bicentennial; a concerto for double bass and orchestra titled *At Ward's Ferry, Length 180 Ft.*, commissioned in 2001 by the Pittsburgh Symphony; and *It Got Dark*, initially commissioned by the Kronos Quartet in 2009 with a subsequent commission from the Los Angeles Philharmonic for a version for solo string quartet and orchestra.

WORKS
Film scores: Grandview, U.S.A., 1984; Reckless, 1984; Revenge of the Nerds, 1984; Desperately Seeking Susan, 1985; The Man with One Red Shoe, 1985; Real Genius, 1985; Jumpin' Jack Flash, 1986; Light of Day, 1987; Less Than Zero, 1987; The Lost Boys, 1987; The Great Outdoors, 1988; Welcome Home, Roxy Carmichael, 1990; Career Opportunities, 1991; Fried Green Tomatoes, 1991; The Linguini Incident, 1991; The Rapture, 1991; Scent of a Woman, 1992; The Player, 1992; Flesh and Bone, 1993; Josh and S.A.M., 1993; Little Women, 1994; The Shawshank Redemption, 1994; The War, 1994; Threesome, 1994; How to Make an American Quilt, 1995; Unstrung Heroes, 1995; American Buffalo, 1996; Phenomenon, 1996; The People vs. Larry Flynt, 1996; Up Close & Personal, 1996; Mad City, 1997; Oscar and Lucinda, 1997; Red Corner, 1997; Meet Joe Black, 1998; The Horse Whisperer, 1998; American Beauty, 1999; The Green Mile, 1999; Boston Public, television, theme, 2000; Erin Brockovich, 2000; Pay It Forward, 2000; In the Bedroom, 2001; Six Feet Under, television miniseries, theme, 2001; The Salton Sea, 2002; Road to Perdition, 2002; White Oleander, 2002; Finding Nemo, 2003; Angels in America, television miniseries, 2003; Lemony Snicket's A Series of Unfortunate Events, 2004; Cinderella Man, 2005; Jarhead, 2005; Little Children, 2006; The Good German, 2006; Towelhead, 2007; WALL-E, 2008; Revolutionary Road, 2008; Brothers, 2009; The Debt, 2010; The Adjustment Bureau, 2011; The Help, 2011

BIBLIOGRAPHY
D. Schweiger: "Thomas Newman: Scoring *The Shawshank Redemption*," [interview] *Film Score Monthly*, li (Nov 1994), 8–9
D. Adams: "Unstrung Newman: Thomas Newman Continues to Be Interesting and Good," [interview] *Film Score Monthly*, lxv–lxvii (Jan/Feb/March 1996), 10–3
L. Danly: "An Interview with Thomas Newman," *The Cue Sheet*, xii/3 (1996), 8–16
M. Schelle: "Thomas Newman," *The Score: Interviews with Film Composers* (Los Angeles, 1999), 267–92
R. Care: "Thomas Newman," *International Dictionary of Film and Filmmakers*, eds. S. Pendergast and T. Pendergast (Detroit, MI, 2000), 635–7
D. Adams: "Finding Newman," *Film Score Monthly*, ix/1 (Jan 2004), 14–7
S. Link: "Nor the Eye Filled with Seeing: the Sound of Vision in Film," *American Music* xxii/1 (Spring 2004), 76–90

NEIL LERNER

New media. The technological and cultural forms emerging from advances in digital computing, multimedia applications, and networked communication. Encompassing developments ranging from social media to interactive websites, new media have irrevocably transformed musical production and consumption in the late 20th and early 21st centuries. Its musical correlates—digital music, networked musical sound, and musical multimedia—have their own longer histories, but the conjunction of the three, aided by the rise of the personal computer in the late 1970s and the growth of the Internet, can be said to have produced a qualitatively new period in music history.

At the level of production, the rise of the Digital audio workstation (DAW)—incorporating the capabilities of recording machines, mixing boards, sequencers, synthesizers, drum machines, and effects processors—and DAW software packages such as ProTools have made high-level music recording widely available. During the 1990s and especially the early 21st century, digital audio files became networked across long distances via the Internet, with geographically and temporally separated musicians able to collaborate and record in synchrony.

The digital audio file is most familiar to consumers in its compressed format—particularly Mp3. Its relatively small file size was crucial to spurring the growth of peer-to-peer File sharing, enabling networked individuals to exchange music through various websites and web-based mechanisms such as Napster, Kazaa, LimeWire, and BitTorrent. Despite repeated failures to implement workable security measures (known as digital rights management, or DRM), changes in recording industry practices and the success of the Apple iTunes Store during the early 21st century made compressed sound files somewhat profitable as for-pay (rather than free) commodities. Online digital radio formats and recommendation engines such as Pandora, Last.fm, and Spotify also grew to reach networked listeners.

If music production itself has become centralized around the DAW, a number of old and new media have fully adopted digital audio, including film and television. Chief among the newer media would be the products of the Video games industry, which have become increasingly cinematic over the course of decades of development. Many of these games, such as multi-user dungeons and massively multiple online role-playing games, are networked on a very large scale. (Indeed, video game sales surpassed global music and then film industry revenues in the first decade of the 21st century.) Audio files also found homes in other networked contexts: web audio engines produced by such companies as Beatnik, Inc., helped sonify the Internet in the 1990s. But perhaps the most extraordinary development has involved the rise of YouTube, a video-sharing website launched in 2005 that became one of the central ways listeners would find and listen to digital music by the end of the decade. Because of legal actions from music and film copyright holders such as Viacom—reminiscent of the infamous lawsuits against file-sharers during the decade—the site, bought by Google in late 2006, has increasingly partnered with advertisers and the media industries. Attracting billions of views daily and quickly growing as a repository of music (with and without videos) created, uploaded, and edited by large corporate producers, independent artists, dedicated enthusiasts, and casual users, YouTube comprises one of the most celebrated and profoundly musical examples of "participatory culture."

The repurposing and wider distribution of digital audio during the late 1990s and early 21st century took place at a much greater scale through the development of "mobile media," made possible by the further miniaturization and networking of microprocessor-based devices and the expansion of communications network bandwidth. Such media include handheld (and often networked) portable media devices such as Laptop and tablet computers, mobile telephones, Blackberrys, personal digital assistants, handheld video game players, portable MP3 players (such as the extremely popular Apple iPod), and smartphones (such as Apple's iPhone) and have resulted in new media forms said to have converged with older (new) ones. The Ringtone became one example of digital music (and eventually digital audio) that was lucratively repurposed by the recording industry. Mobile Internet access brought downloaded music directly to cellular phones and other portable devices. And mobile software applications, or "apps," which burgeoned after the iPhone's release in 2007, have presented music software at the intersection of the portable audio player, digital musical instrument and performance/production gear, video game, social networking system, and concept album to generate wholly new popular forms of musical expression (such as Brian Eno's *Bloom*, Björk's *Biophilia*, or Smule's "Glee" app)—and, according to the marketing rhetoric, blur the boundary between the roles of producer and consumer.

Of course, the distinction has not been fully elided. Experimental communities of producers, often with the support of wealthy research institutions and media corporations, continue to explore the outer limits of digital and networked multimedia forms and performances. Gallery-based artists, established electro-acoustic music societies and communities, and newer gatherings such as the New Interfaces for Musical Expression conferences and the Mobile Music Workshops number among many examples. Moreover, large numbers of professional and amateur performing musicians have presented their musical recordings (as well as live-streamed performances) on personal websites, YouTube, and social networking sites such as MySpace and Facebook, using the networking capacities of the World Wide Web to build audiences for their musical products. Indeed, even quasi-nostalgic phenomena that can be seen as reactions to the new technical regimes of production—such as chiptune or 8-bit music producers or even analog-only record labels such as Daptone—depend largely on extant systems of networked new media, suggesting the degree to which the latter have become a crucial, perhaps dominant means of music distribution.

See also Computers and music, Intermedia art, Mobile telephone, and Portable media device.

BIBLIOGRAPHY

L. Manovich: *The Language of New Media* (Cambridge, MA, 2001)

M. Lister et al.: *New Media: a Critical Introduction* (London, 2003)

J. Sterne: "The MP3 as Cultural Artifact," *New Media & Society* viii/5 (2006), 825–42

H. Jenkins: *Convergence Culture: Where Old and New Media Collide* (New York, 2008)

J. Burgess and J. Green: *YouTube: Online Video and Participatory Media* (Cambridge, MA, 2009)

S. Gopinath: *The Ringtone Dialectic: Economy and Cultural Form* (Cambridge, MA, 2013)

S. Gopinath and J. Stanyek, eds.: *The Oxford Handbook of Mobile Music Studies* (forthcoming)

SUMANTH GOPINATH

New Music [New Music Edition]. Publishing and recording venture, founded in California by HENRY COWELL. The quarterly publication New Music, issued first in 1927, was the only series of its day dedicated solely to the publication of new scores. These pieces, described by Cowell as "non-commercial works of artistic value," often embraced advanced and innovatory compositional techniques for which publishing houses had little sympathy. The main series was supplemented by an Orchestra Series (1932–9) and occasional Special Editions. Many of the published pieces were also heard in San Francisco at concerts of the New Music Society (1925–36; founded by Cowell). In 1934 Cowell established New Music Quarterly Recordings. The discs, all first recordings, were more widely distributed than the scores, which were available only by subscription.

Cowell served as the head of all New Music projects until 1936. The recordings continued to be issued until 1942 under the direction of Otto Luening, while the New Music publications (New Music Edition from 1947) were edited by Gerald Strang, again by Cowell (1941–5), and later by Lou Harrison, Frank Wigglesworth, and Vladimir Ussachevsky. Among the composers to be published in *New Music* (often for the first time) were Babbitt, John Becker, Paul Bowles, Brant, Cage, Carter, Chávez, Copland, Cowell, Crawford, Creston, Feldman, Harrison, Ives, Luening, McPhee, Nancarrow, Piston, Riegger, Rudhyar, Ruggles, Strang, Thomson, Varèse, and Wolff. Although Americans dominated, Schoenberg, Webern, and several Latin American and Russian composers were also included. In 1954 New Music Edition experienced financial difficulties after the death of Charles Ives, who had for many years been its patron, and in 1958 it was transferred to Presser.

BIBLIOGRAPHY

R.F. Goldman: "Henry Cowell (1897–1965): a Memoir and an Appreciation," *PNM*, iv/2 (1965–6), 23–8

S.E. Gilbert, "'The Ultra-Modern Idiom': a Survey of *New Music*," *PNM*, xii/1–2 (Autumn 1973–Summer 1974), 282–314

R.H. Mead: "Cowell, Ives, and *New Music*," *MQ*, lxvi (1980), 538–59

R.H. Mead: *Henry Cowell's New Music, 1925–1936: the Society, the Music Editions, and the Recordings* (Ann Arbor, 1981)

D. Hall: "New Music Quarterly Recordings: a Discography," *Association of Recorded Sound Collections Journal*, xvi/1–2 (1984), 10–27

D. Nicholls, ed.: *The Whole World of Music: a Henry Cowell Symposium* (Amsterdam, 1997)

C.J. Oja and R. Allen, eds.: *Henry Cowell's Musical Worlds* (Brooklyn, 1997) [Henry Cowell Centennial Festival; program book]

EMILY GOOD/DAVID NICHOLLS/R

New Music USA. Organization based in New York, serving contemporary American composers and listeners. New Music USA was founded in 2011 as a result of the merger of the AMERICAN MUSIC CENTER and MEET THE COMPOSER.

New Orleans. City in Louisiana (pop. 343,829; metropolitan area: 1,017,000; 2010 US Census). Founded in 1718, it was the capital of French colonial Louisiana until 1762 and then in Spanish possession until 1800. It reverted briefly to French rule before it became a US territory as part of the Louisiana Purchase in 1803. Few towns in the United States have developed and preserved as rich and individual a musical tradition. A primary reason for this is its position at the mouth of the Mississippi River; it was the principal harbor serving the vast country to the north, from which raw materials were exported and to which manufactured goods were imported. In the 18th century and much of the 19th, New Orleans was a northern point of the French and Spanish Caribbean trade routes, which had a profound effect on its musical culture. So too did the city's prosperous economy: there were rich and noble families among the first settlers, who had not only a taste for culture but also the financial means to enjoy it. In the late 19th century and the early 20th the city's musical importance shifted from opera to jazz, which had its roots in the popular music of the city's numerous brass and string bands.

1. Opera. 2. Concert music. 3. Brass bands. 4. Jazz. 5. Publishing and recording. 6. Educational institutions.

1. OPERA. In cultural terms New Orleans became the Paris of America, and the early opera repertory shows a marked preference for French and Italian works. The city was the first in North America to have a permanent opera company and from 1859 to 1919 owned one of the biggest and most expensive opera houses in the Americas. Opera in New Orleans was initiated in 1792 with the building of the Théâtre de la rue St Pierre (by Louis Alexandre Henry), where the city's first known performance of opera, Grétry's *Silvain*, was given in 1796. Although documentation is scant before 1800, there are written references to two later performances, Dezède's *Blaise et Babet* (1796) and Dalayrac's *Renaud d'Ast* (1799). The theater was restored and reopened by Jean Baptiste Fournier in 1804. The first documented opera production under Fournier was François Devienne's *Les visitandines* (June 1805). Despite a prolific season (23 operas), Fournier was replaced in 1806 by Louis Tabary, a recent émigré from France. The ousted Fournier set up a rival theater and opera company in a dance hall called the Salle Chinoise (later renamed the Théâtre de la rue St Philippe), and a brisk competition between these two theaters resulted in a number of performances remarkable for a provincial city of 12,000 inhabitants. The general dearth of opera houses in North America meant that many of these performances were American premieres, including Grétry's *Le jugement de Midas* (1806), Méhul's *Une folie* (1807), and Boieldieu's *Le calife de Bagdad* (1805) and *Ma tante Aurore* (1807). The Théâtre de la rue St Pierre closed permanently in 1810, whereas the Théâtre St Philippe remained active until it was sold in 1832.

The most important opera house in New Orleans in the first half of the 19th century was the Théâtre d'Orléans. The original edifice, begun in 1806 by Tabary, opened belatedly in October 1815, only to burn down the next summer. It was rebuilt in 1819 by a French émigré, John Davis, under whose management it thrived as an opera center. In his first five years Davis produced 140 operas, 52 of which were American premieres.

Band playing on Bourbon Street, French Quarter, New Orleans. (Carol M. Highsmith's America, Library of Congress, Prints and Photographs Division.)

Again, French composers were favored (e.g. Boieldieu, Isouard, and Dalayrac), and the performances steadily improved in quality, owing to Davis's policy of engaging French professional singers, dancers, and instrumentalists. The Théâtre d'Orléans achieved national prominence when, between 1827 and 1833, Davis led the company on six acclaimed tours of the northeastern United States. In each of the cities visited (Boston, New York, Philadelphia, and Baltimore), much of the repertory was new. John Davis was succeeded in 1837 by his son Pierre, and in 1853, by Charles Boudousquié, an American-born impresario who sustained the theater's reputation until his resignation in 1859. Among the American premieres given by these latter directors were those of *Lucia di Lammermoor* (1841), *La juive* (1844), and *Le prophète* (1850). The theater went into decline in the 1850s and closed in 1866.

During the heyday of the Théâtre d'Orléans (1825–40) a rival impresario, James Caldwell, had produced ballad operas and Italian and French operas in English translation with an American company he brought from Virginia. He built the first two theaters in the city's new American sector, the Camp Street Theater (1824) and St Charles Theater (1835). Between 1827 and 1833 he mounted over 100 productions at the former, including *The Beggar's Opera*, *The Barber of Seville*, and *Cinderella* (*La Cenerentola*), and Boieldieu's *Jean de Paris*. In 1836 Caldwell introduced Italian opera to New Orleans with the Montresor troupe from Havana. In two successive seasons at the St Charles Theater the company performed such staples as *Norma*, *Semiramide*, and *Il barbiere di Siviglia*.

The city's musical importance increased with the opening of the French Opera House in 1859. Built by Boudousquié, it was one of the largest and most expensive theaters in the West and one of the finest in the United States. The opera ensemble Boudousquié established there was by no means provincial: many fine singers appeared, including Julie Calvé and Adelina Patti; the tenors Lecourt, Mathieu, and Escarlate; the baritones Victor and Melchisadels; and the bass Genibrel. 17 operas had their American premieres there, among them Meyerbeer's *Dinorah* (1861, with Patti in the title role), Massenet's *Le Cid* (1890), and Saint-Saëns's *Samson et Dalila* (1893). The French Opera House closed in 1913 and was purchased in 1919 by William R. Irby, who presented it to Tulane University with funds for its restoration. Its planned reopening in December 1919 was thwarted by a fire on the night of 2 December. Most of its archives were destroyed, along with its valuable collection of operatic properties, costumes, scores, and parts, and innumerable books and documents relating to opera.

New Orleans remained without a permanent opera organization until 1943, when Walter Loubart founded the New Orleans Opera Association. He was succeeded as music director by Walter Herbert (1944–54), Renato Cellini (1954–64), and Knud Andersson (1964–83). Performances (with visiting artists supported by local singers and chorus) were given in the city's Municipal Auditorium until 1973, when the New Orleans Theater of the Performing Arts was opened. The seasons (October to May) consisted of six to eight operas from the standard Italian, French, and German repertory; contemporary operas were avoided, though visiting companies staged *Lulu* (Sarah Caldwell, 1967) and *Gloriana* (ENO, 1984). After 1984 declining attendance and a reduced budget resulted in shorter seasons (three to five works) and a year-to-year reliance on guest conductors. Operas are presently sung in English or in the original language with English surtitles.

The New Orleans Opera Association was reformed in 1992 in celebration of the 50th anniversary of its founding. Operating with a more limited budget, the Association cut back to four operas in its annual season, two in the fall and two in the spring. In 1998 Robert Lyall was named General and Artistic Director of the New Orleans Opera Association. During his tenure the company has expanded its programming of 20th-century operas, among them Douglas Moore's *The Ballad of Baby Doe*; Gershwin's *Porgy and Bess*; Andre Previn's *A Streetcar Named Desire*; and, in 2003, the world premiere of Thea Musgrave's *Pontalba*, set in 18th-century New Orleans. The 2011–12 season included the first New Orleans performance of Britten's *Peter Grimes*.

2. CONCERT MUSIC. In 18th-century New Orleans concerts were given regularly as preludes to the numerous balls for which the city was famous. The concerts followed the European plan of a long and varied program, including orchestral works, chamber music, piano recitals, songs, and choral works. A mixed group of amateur and professional instrumentalists known as the Philharmonic Society was founded in 1824 and gave frequent concerts until 1829, performing thereafter only sporadically until 1848. By the second quarter of the 19th century, a considerable number of freed black musicians trained in art music were resident in New Orleans, a few of them having studied in France. In the late 1830s a Negro Philharmonic Society of over 100 performing and nonperforming members was organized to provide opportunities to hear music for those who objected to sitting in segregated sections in the public theaters. The society gave concerts and arranged for performances by visiting artists. For scores requiring larger forces the orchestra was augmented by white musicians. A small string orchestra, the Philharmonic Society of the Friends of Art, was formed in 1853 but survived less than a year because of a yellow fever epidemic. It was replaced by the Classical Musical Society, founded in 1855. Throughout the 19th century orchestral concerts were also given by the various theater ensembles. Although, in contrast to the opera, the repertory was conservative and consisted mainly of well-established works, these concerts were of a high standard, judging by the critical reaction to them in New Orleans, New York, Boston, and Philadelphia. The custom of engaging an outstanding soloist for a whole series of concerts began in the 1830s. Such artists as Ole Bull, Henry Vieuxtemps, Julie Calvé, and Jenny Lind included New Orleans in their tours, and singers often remained there to join one of the theater ensembles. Several musicians from New Orleans attained international prominence in the 19th century. Among them were Louis Moreau Gottschalk and Ernest Guiraud (1837–92), the teacher of Debussy and Dukas.

Many attempts to found an independent professional symphony orchestra between 1917 and 1934 failed for lack of financial support. The New Orleans Philharmonic SO was founded in 1936; its conductors have been Arthur Zack (1936–40), Ole Windingstad (1940–4), Massimo Freccia (1944–52), Alexander Hilsberg (1952–60), James Yestadt (1960–63), Werner Torkanowsky (1963–77), Leonard Slatkin (1977–9), Philippe Entremont (1979–86), and Maxim Shostakovich (1986–91). During Slatkin's tenure the orchestra moved into its own hall, the restored Orpheum Theater. Entremont shortened its name to the New Orleans Symphony and, in 1982, took the orchestra to Europe. After several years of financial insecurity, the orchestra folded in 1990. In 1991, it was succeeded by the Louisiana PO, a cooperative ensemble founded by former members of the New Orleans Symphony; as of 2010, it is the only musician-owned and collaboratively managed professional symphony in the United States. Its first conductor, Klauspeter Seibel, served from 1995 to 2005 and was succeeded in 2007 by Carlos Miguel Prieto, who maintains a full 36-week season of subscription concerts. The orchestra also offers children's concerts and pop concerts, and serves both the Opera Association and local ballet companies.

The LPO has expanded its reach by performing concerts across Louisiana and the Gulf South region. The orchestra also forms the core of the New Orleans Opera orchestra as well as the pit orchestra of Tulane's Summer Lyric Theater. The New Orleans Friends of Music, which entered its 57th season in 2011–12, continues its tradition of bringing world class chamber groups to the city. Since Hurricane Katrina (2005) they have expanded their season to seven concerts.

3. BRASS BANDS. The brass or military band, frequently augmented by woodwind and percussion, has long been important to the musical life of New Orleans, a southern Catholic city with a penchant for open-air festivities. Parades and parade music became the focal point of social life in the 19th century. On Sundays parades began early, their number and fervor increasing as the day wore on. Marching to bury the dead was customary as early as 1819, when the architect Benjamin Henry Latrobe, visiting the city, described the burial parades as "peculiar to New Orleans alone among American cities." By the 1830s notices of such parades often appeared in the newspapers. Members of militia companies, war veterans, freemasons, fire companies, benevolent societies, mechanics' societies, and others all marched at any time of day to bury their dead. The death of a hero anywhere was sufficient reason in New Orleans to hold a parade, or even two, as when General Lafayette died. Only during epidemics did the city experience a surfeit of brass band funerals, their mournful music mitigated by "gay and lightsome airs" as they left the cemetery, a practice imitated later in such jazz numbers as Jelly Roll Morton's *Dead Man Blues*. Military music flourished in New Orleans during the Civil War; in 1864 the famous bandleader Patrick S. Gilmore gave a concert there with 500 musicians.

A black marching-band tradition, which was of seminal importance in the genesis of jazz around 1900, originated in New Orleans after the Civil War (*see* §4). The presence of numerous concert-trained teachers and a plethora of military wind instruments at this time spawned a new generation of freed black bandsmen. A decade after the war there were several black wind bands fully competitive with the best white marching bands. By 1878 Kelly's Band and the St Bernard Brass Band were recognized as "splendid corps of musicians, excelled by none," and in 1885 the Excelsior Brass Band, considered the finest black band in the city, played for the formal opening of the Colored People's Exhibit at the New Orleans Cotton States Exhibition. An important early impetus for the proliferation of black street bands was the dynamic social change of Reconstruction. The stimulus of emancipation, the prolonged presence of federal troops and military bands in the city, and the promise of social and political equality for African Americans contributed to the style and content of the music. A particular catalyst was the establishment of numerous benevolent societies at the instigation of the black Reconstruction governor P.B.S. Pinchback. These black sociopolitical groups sponsored marching clubs and drill teams to perform at political rallies and outdoor social events with parades, including funerals.

While the earliest black marching bands were musically trained and polished ensembles, a trend toward extempore performances with ad lib embellishments developed among the New Orleans bands of the 1890s, leading eventually to the fully improvisational smaller jazz bands. Documentation is extremely scant, but it appears that this approach to playing was influenced by the gradual infiltration into the black bands of self-taught instrumentalists, some of whom came from rough country bands in the surrounding region. The repertory was thus extended to include, in addition to military pieces, music based on song: religious spirituals and gospel songs, as well as secular ballads, reels, rags, and blues. By 1900 such spontaneous performances by black bands, notably the Excelsior, Onward, Tuxedo, Eureka, and Olympia, were in great demand for all kinds of social occasions, including picnics, commercial publicity, boat excursions, and dancing. Concurrently this style of band music was emulated by a number of white brass bands, notably that of "Papa" Jack Laine, a mentor to many early white jazz musicians.

African American parade-band music thrived and developed alongside its offspring, jazz, in the early decades of the 20th century. The earliest recordings of it, between 1929 and 1945, reveal still-strong ties to the march and the gospel song, with jazzlike syncopated rhythm and melodic embellishment. By 1960 the music as a thriving tradition had all but disappeared, save for occasional performances by the Olympia, re-formed by Harold Dejan

In the 1970s and 1980s the New Orleans brass band tradition experienced a renaissance, with bands breaking away from traditional styles and adding elements of rhythm-and-blues, funk, hip hop, and bop to their repertoire. Some notable exponents of this updated brass band style are the Dirty Dozen Brass Band, Rebirth Brass Band, the Soul Rebels Brass Band, Youngblood Brass Band, the Hot 8, and the Stooges. It should be noted that this brass band revival has moved beyond the genre's original function as religious and social music of the local African American community to the broader tourist industry. While some traditional brass bands still play for neighborhood funerals and other events, the majority of younger bands sustain a purely commercial and touring career.

4. JAZZ. Although elements of a jazz style developed in several urban centers of the United States, the earliest examples of the genre arose in New Orleans, and therefore the city is generally regarded as the birthplace of jazz. The appearance of this style derived from many sources (church music, syncopated coon songs, ballads, folksongs, military brass bands, work songs, blues, etc.) and from the many races that inhabited New Orleans (African, Spanish, and French creoles and whites of European origin, mainly Italian).

Many early black jazz musicians received their musical training in the various black brass bands that paraded for social and religious occasions, such as funerals, while others began in the "string bands": small ensembles with violins and double bass, which played for dancing. Thus, the first recognized "jazz" band, led by the legendary cornetist Buddy Bolden, was a combination of both these sources, playing a repertory of written marches and freely improvised blues and ragtime themes. Bolden's powerful playing, colorful personality, and popularity earned him the title of "king" and established a highly competitive spirit among New Orleans musicians, particularly cornet players. Early jazz bands often challenged each other to musical duels when touring the city on open wagons to advertise a function. Later cornet "kings" included Freddie Keppard, King Oliver, and Kid René, along with other notable cornetists such as Buddy Petit, Chris Kelly, Mutt Carey, Bunk Johnson, and, of course, Louis Armstrong. Their expressive, almost vocal tones, harmonies around a written lead, and use of mutes created a distinctive style that was identified with the city.

Another recognizable characteristic was the clarinet style. The fluid technique and sensual tone were the hallmarks of the city's French and Spanish creoles, and combined with black elements of intense passion and sweeping lines, this style is evident in the work of early clarinetists such as Jimmie Noone, Johnny Dodds, Sidney Bechet, and, later, Barney Bigard and Edmond Hall. The percussive swing of the city's drummers was the third unique characteristic. The beat was relaxed, and the rhythmic texture varied to balance or motivate other performers. While a New Orleans band could be of any instrumentation, usually a vamping trombone, double bass (plucked rather than bowed), and banjo or guitar were added to the cornet/trumpet, clarinet, and drums. The inclusion of a piano, often played by a woman, was largely a later, post-1920, development.

Jazz played by white musicians at that time remained largely independent of the black and creole development. The earliest known figure in this genre was the percussionist "Papa" Jack Laine, who led various brass and ragtime bands from 1888 onwards. DIXIELAND JAZZ (as it was later termed) probably reached its fullest expression in the Original Dixieland Jazz Band, a group of white New Orleans musicians formed in Chicago and led by Nick LaRocca, formerly a cornetist with Laine. The worldwide success of the group as a result of its recordings, beginning in 1917, established this brand of jazz, with its driving tempos and attenuated black instrumental effects, as a potent force in American popular music. The spread of "jazz" began in about 1904, when New Orleans musicians settled in Texas and California and later in Chicago and New York. Foremost among these were the pianist-composer Jelly Roll Morton and, in 1922, Louis Armstrong. During the 1920s both musicians used the distinctive New Orleans sound to create some of the best jazz ever recorded.

Changing public taste in favor of larger orchestras during the 1930s meant small band jazz was less popular, although most New Orleans musicians were able to continue to find work. In the early 1940s there was a revival of interest in the New Orleans style and its musicians. The public acclaim of Kid Ory, Bunk Johnson, George Lewis, and Oscar "Papa" Celestin created a new white middle-class audience for traditional jazz, yet the essentially backward-looking nature of "revival" jazz has prevented New Orleans from reclaiming its former significance in this music. In the 1950s an indigenous style of rhythm-and-blues developed in the work of such musicians as Professor Longhair and Fats Domino, and in the 1970s a new young generation of African American musicians formed small brass bands to perform a mixture of rhythm-and-blues, soul, and jazz. The energy and percussive swing of these later bands retain many of the characteristics of New Orleans music. The historical interest in jazz led to the founding of the William Ransom Hogan Jazz Archive at Tulane University in 1958, bringing visitors and researchers to the city. Since 1969 New Orleans has held an annual spring music festival called the New Orleans Jazz and Heritage Festival, which features, in addition to traditional New Orleans jazz, various styles of modern jazz and a whole spectrum of allied genres.

Jazz in New Orleans continues to thrive in the 21st century in both traditional and modern genres. Traditional jazz is sustained by tourism, which is a primary part of the city's current economy. Venues such as Preservation Hall feature nightly performances by African American bands that are increasingly augmented by young white musicians, many of them of foreign birth. The Dixieland style is also featured in such French Quarter clubs as The Palm Court and Fritzl's European Jazz Pub. Modern jazz, on the other hand, is still a vital and evolving part of the city's local musical culture. The generation of post-bop figures such as Ellis Marsalis and Harold Battiste has given way, in the 1980s and 1990s, to a new generation of "cutting edge" players such as Wynton and Branford Marsalis, Donald Harris, and the younger Nicholas Payton and such white groups as Tony Dagradi's Astral Project. But, for all its authenticity, modern jazz remains a specialized genre of New Orleans music, featured in such local non-tourist venues as Snug Harbor and Sweet Lorraine's.

"Revival" jazz, while good for tourism, has failed to sustain this music as part of the city's contemporary life. By the 1950s that function was assumed by rhythm-and-blues, of which New Orleans was an early center with its own highly distinctive style. Marked by a joyous, leisurely dance rhythm with an overlay of Caribbean patterns, New Orleans R&B is the sound of such familiar figures as Fats Domino, Professor Longhair, Ernie K-Doe, Dr. John, and The Neville Brothers. Today this is the authentic musical voice of New Orleans, the music of "The Big Easy" to which local residents turn for parties and Mardi Gras. And in recent years, through the worldwide fame of its practitioners, New Orleans R&B and R&B-laced-funk/hip-hop have finally begun to eclipse jazz as the city's primary tourist attraction. Visitors in increasing numbers are turning from Preservation Hall to such temples of R&B as Tipitina's, Rock'n'Bowl, and The House of Blues.

5. PUBLISHING AND RECORDING. The thriving musical life of New Orleans enabled several music publishers to become established there. Among the earliest was Paul Emile Johns, a Polish-born emigrant from Vienna who opened a retail shop in 1830. In 1846 Johns sold his firm to William T. Mayo, who continued to print sheet music until he in turn sold the company in 1854 to Philip P. Werlein, a Bavarian emigrant known chiefly as the first Southern publisher of Dan Emmett's *Dixie* (as *I Wish I was in Dixie*, a pirated version preceding the authorized version of 1860). Werlein issued two sheet music anthologies as serials, the *Song Journal* (1870s) and *Werlein's Journal of Music* (1880s).

The firm of Armand Blackmar was active primarily during the Civil War years and was responsible for publishing some of the best-known music of the Confederacy, including *The Bonnie Blue Flag, Maryland! My Maryland!*, and an 1861 edition of *Dixie*. Louis Grunewald, a German emigrant who started a business in 1858, was the most prolific and versatile of all the New Orleans music publishers, extending his output in the 1880s to include religious and French Creole songs and piano compositions in the then popular "Mexican" style. Both the Werlein and Grunewald firms continued into the early 20th century, but by the 1920s music publishing in New Orleans had declined.

The first recordings of New Orleans music were by the Louisiana Phonograph Company, which recorded white and black artists as early as 1891. The earliest jazz recorded in the city was done by northern companies between 1924 and 1928; the first significant locally produced recordings were made during the New Orleans jazz revival of the 1940s, chiefly on the Southland label (1949–69). Cosimo Recording (1945–69), one of the leading recording studios for the national rhythm-and-blues industry by the mid-1950s, cut records for such artists as Fats Domino, Bobby "Blue" Bland, Big Joe Turner, Lloyd Price, and Ray Charles. Among companies established since 1960 was the short-lived All-For-One (1961–4); two major studios, Seasaint and Ultrasonic, opened in 1970. The closing of Cosimo Matassa's J&M Studios in the mid-1980s spawned several new studios, including The Music Shed, Piety Street Recording, Fudge Recording Studio, and Audiophile Recording Studio, which specializes in traditional jazz.

6. EDUCATIONAL INSTITUTIONS. The music department in Newcomb College of Tulane University was founded in 1909 by Leon Maxwell, who served as chairman until 1952. The department offers BA and MA degrees in history, theory, and composition, and BFA and MFA degrees in piano and other instruments and in singing. A BFA in Jazz Performance was added in 2004 with classes in jazz improvisation, jazz harmony, and a jazz orchestra and combos that perform every year at the New Orleans Jazz and Heritage Festival. Distinguished teachers have included Giuseppe Ferrata, Gilbert Chase, Howard E. Smither, and Charles Hamm. Among the university's libraries, the William Ransom Hogan Jazz Archive is important as a repository of early American jazz (prints, recordings, photographs, and taped interviews), and the Louisiana Division of the Howard-Tilton Memorial Library includes American sheet music and documents pertaining to the southern states. The Latin American Library is the second largest archive of its kind in the United States and contains many musical items. The Amistad Research Center, located at Tulane, is one of the most inclusive archives of ethnic minorities in America, especially African American, and there are significant musical documents.

The Loyola University College of Music, founded in 1931 as a music conservatory, retains its emphasis on performance, which is reflected in its most distinguished alumni, the singers Norman Treigle, Marguerite Piazza, Harry Theyard, Charles Anthony, and Anthony Laciura. It offers BM, BME, MM, and MME degrees in performance and music therapy. The music department at Dillard University, one of three black collegiate institutions in New Orleans, was established in 1936 with Frederick Douglass Hall as its first chairman; Hall established the department's policy of emphasizing black music, especially spirituals, in its curriculum. Among its most distinguished alumni are the composer Roger Donald Dickerson and the jazz pianist Ellis Marsalis. The music department of the New Orleans Baptist Theological Seminary was founded in 1919, primarily for the training of church organists and choirmasters. Undergraduate programs are also offered at Xavier University (music department founded 1934), for black Catholics, and at the University of New Orleans (music department founded 1963), which has recently established a degree in jazz performance. The Delgado Trade School was reorganized in the 1980s as the Delgado Community College and offers an undergraduate degree in music. The New Orleans Centre for the Creative Arts (NOCCA) is one of America's leading high schools for training musicians; among its graduates are Wynton Marsalis and Harry Connick Jr. There are substantial musical holdings in the libraries of Tulane University, the Theological Seminary, and at Louisiana State University.

See also BUDDY BOLDEN; DIXIELAND JAZZ; JAZZ; NEW ORLEANS JAZZ; NEW ORLEANS MUSIC; NEW ORLEANS MARDI GRAS MUSIC; NEW ORLEANS RHYTHM KINGS; PRESERVATION HALL JAZZ BAND; TRADITIONAL JAZZ.

BIBLIOGRAPHY

MGG1 (G.S. McPeek)

L.M. Gottschalk: *Notes of a Pianist* (Philadelphia, 1881); ed. J. Behrend (New York, 1964)

G.W. Gable: "The Dance in Place Congo," *Century Magazine*, xxxi (1885–6), 512–32

G. King: *New Orleans: the Place and the People* (New York, 1895/R)

J.G. de Baroncelli: *La théâtre français à la Nouvelle Orléans* (New Orleans, 1906)

J.G. de Baroncelli: *L'opéra français de la Nouvelle Orléans* (New Orleans, 1914)

D.B. Fischer: "The Story of New Orleans's Rise as a Music Center," *MusAm*, xix/19 (1914), 3

O.G.T. Sonneck: *Early Opera in America* (New York, 1915/R)

J.S. Kendall: *History of New Orleans* (Chicago and New York, 1922)

L. Gafford: *A History of the St. Charles Theater in New Orleans, 1835–43* (diss., U. of Chicago, 1930; part pubd Chicago, 1932)

J.E. Winston: "The Free Negro in New Orleans, 1803–1860," *Louisiana Historical Quarterly*, xxi (1938), 1075

A.L.W. Stahl: "The Free Negro in Ante-bellum Louisiana," *Louisiana Historical Quarterly*, xxv (1942), 301–96

J.S. Kendall: "New Orleans' Negro Minstrels," *Louisiana Historical Quarterly*, xxx (1947), 128

J.S. Kendall: "New Orleans Musicians of Long Ago," *Louisiana Historical Quarterly*, xxxi (1948), 130

J.S. Kendall: *The Golden Age of the New Orleans Theater* (Baton Rouge, LA, 1952/R)

G.S. McPeek: "New Orleans as an Opera Center," *MusAm*, lxxiv/4 (1954), 25, 136, 226 only

O. Keepnews and B. Grauer: *A Pictorial History of Jazz: People and Places from New Orleans to Modern Jazz* (New York, 1955, 2/1966/R)

W. Russell and S.W. Smith: "New Orleans Music," *Jazzmen*, ed. F. Ramsey Jr and C.E. Smith (London, 1957)

G.H. Yerbury: "Concert Music in Early New Orleans," *Louisiana Historical Quarterly*, xl (1957), 95

S.B. Charters: *Jazz: New Orleans, 1885–1957* (Belleville, NJ, 1958, 2/1963/R)

R.J. La Gardeur Jr: *The First New Orleans Theatre, 1792–1803* (New Orleans, 1963)

H.A. Kmen: *Music in New Orleans: the Formative Years, 1791–1841* (Baton Rouge, LA, 1966)

A. Rose and E. Souchon: *New Orleans Jazz: a Family Album* (Baton Rouge, LA, 1967, enlarged 3/1984)

M.T. Williams: *Jazz Masters of New Orleans* (New York, 1967/R)

G. Schuller: *Early Jazz: Its Roots and Musical Development* (New York, 1968/R)

E. Borneman: "Jazz and the Creole Tradition," *Jazzforschung/Jazz Research*, i (1969), 99–112

R.J. Martinez: *Portraits of New Orleans Jazz: Its Peoples and Places* (New Orleans, 1971)

J. Baron: "Paul Emile Johns of New Orleans: Tycoon, Musician, and Friend of Chopin," *IMSCR XI: Copenhagen 1972*, 246–50

H.A. Kmen: "The Roots of Jazz and the Dance in Place Congo: a Reappraisal," *Anuario Interamericano de Investigacion Musical*, viii (1972), 5–16

L. Panzeri: *Louisiana Composers* (New Orleans, 1972)

J.V. Buerkle and D. Barker: *Bourbon Street Black: the New Orleans Black Jazzman* (New York, 1973)

T. Stagg and C. Crump, eds.: *New Orleans, the Revival: a Tape and Discography of Traditional Jazz Recorded in New Orleans by New Orleans Bands, 1937–72* (Dublin, 1973)

J. Broven: *Walking to New Orleans: the Story of New Orleans Rhythm & Blues* (Bexhill-on-Sea, UK, 1974, 2/1977)

J. Joyce: "New Orleans Jazz: a Matter of Tradition," *New Orleans Review*, iv/1 (1974), 27

A. Rose: *Storyville, New Orleans, Being an Authentic, Illustrated Account of the Notorious Red-Light District* (University, AL, 1974)

L.B. Levy: *The Formalization of New Orleans Jazz Musicians: a Case Study of Organizational Change* (diss., Virginia Polytechnic Institute and State U., 1976)

P.C. Boudreaux: *Music Publishing in New Orleans in the Nineteenth Century* (thesis, Louisiana State U., 1977)

W.J. Schafer: *Brass Bands and New Orleans Jazz* (Baton Rouge, LA, 1977)

D.M. Marquis: *In Search of Buddy Bolden, First Man of Jazz* (Baton Rouge, LA, 1978)

L. Ostransky: *Jazz City: the Impact of our Cities on the Development of Jazz* (Englewood Cliffs, NJ, 1978)

R. Palmer: *A Tale of Two Cities: Memphis Rock and New Orleans Roll* (Brooklyn, NY, 1979)

J. Baron: *Piano Music from New Orleans 1851–1898* (New York, 1980)

K. Demetz: "Minstrel Dancing in New Orleans' Nineteenth Century Theaters," *Southern Quarterly*, xx/2 (1982), 28–39

F. Turner: *Remembering Song: Encounters with the New Orleans Jazz Tradition* (New York, 1982)

J. Berry, J. Foose, and T. Jones: *Up from the Cradle of Jazz: New Orleans Music since World War II* (Athens, GA, 1986)

J. Baron: "Music in New Orleans, 1718–1792," *AM*, v/3 (1987), 282–90

J. Hassinger: "Close Harmony: Early Jazz Styles in the Music of the New Orleans Boswell Sisters," *Women and Music in Cross-Cultural Perspective*, ed. E. Koskoff (New York, 1987), 195–201

K. Rose: *I Remember Jazz: Six Decades among the Great Jazzmen* (Baton Rouge, LA, 1987)

H.C. Boyer: "Tracking the Tradition: New Orleans Sacred Music," *Black Music Research Journal*, viii (1988), 135–47

L. Gushee: "How the Creole Band Came to Be," ibid., 83–100

K. McKnight: "Researching New Orleans Rhythm and Blues," ibid., 113–34

M. Sullivan: "Composers of Color of Nineteenth-Century New Orleans: the History behind the Music," ibid., 51–82

R. Wang: "Researching the New Orleans-Chicago Jazz Connection: Tools and Methods," ibid., 101–12

H. Eskew: "German Contributions to the Musical Culture of New Orleans," *Southern Quarterly*, xxvii/2 (1989–90), 25–39

A. Lemmon: "New Orleans Popular Sheet Music Imprints: the Latin Tinge prior to 1900," ibid., 41–57

M.S. Morrow: "Singing and Drinking in New Orleans: the Social and Musical Functions of Nineteenth-Century Männerchöre," ibid., 5–24

W.C. Fields: "Theodore La Hache and Music in New Orleans, 1846–1869," *AM*, viii/3 (1990), 326–50

C. Jerde: "Black Music in New Orleans: a Historical Overview," *Black Music Research Journal*, x (1990), 18–26

W. Carter: *Preservation Hall: Music from the Heart* (New York, 1991)

J. Johnson: "New Orleans's Congo Square: an Urban Setting for Early Afro-American Culture Formation," *Louisiana History*, xxxii (1991), 117–57

C.E. Kinzer: "The Tio Family and its Role in the Creole-of-Color Music Traditions of New Orleans," *Second Line*, xliii/3 (1991), 18–27

R.M. Sands: "Carnival Celebration in Africa and the New World: Junkanoo and the Black Indians of Mardi Gras," *Black Music Research Journal*, xi (1991), 75–92

B.B. Bisonette: *The Jazz Crusade: the Inside Story of the Great New Orleans Jazz Revival of the 1960's* (Bridgeport, CT, 1992)

J. Belsom: *Opera in New Orleans* (New Orleans, 1993)

M. Lemmon: "Te Deum laudamus: Music in St. Louis Cathedral from 1725 to 1844," *Cross, Crozier, and Crucible: a Volume Celebrating the Bicentennial of a Catholic Diocese in Louisiana*, ed. G.R. Conrad (New Orleans, 1993), 489–504

G. Lichtenstein and L. Dankner: *Musical Gumbo: the Music of New Orleans* (New York, 1993)

S.F. Starr: *Bamboula: the Life and Times of Louis Moreau Gottschalk* (New York, 1995)

D.M. Guion: "Felippe-Cioffe: a Trombonist in Antebellum America," *AM*, xiv (1996), 1–41

J.H. Baron: "New Orleans Composers of the 1990s," *Perspectives on American Music since 1950*, ed. J.R. Heintze (New York, 1999), 429–58

T. Brothers: *Louis Armstrong's New Orleans* (New York, 2006)

M. Burns: *Keeping the Beat on the Street: the New Orleans Brass Band Renaissance* (Baton Rouge, LA, 2006)

C. Hersch: *Subversive Sounds: Race and the Birth of Jazz in New Orleans* (Chicago, 2007)

J. Berry, J. Foose, and T. Jones: *Up from the Cradle of Jazz: New Orleans Music since World War II* (Lafayette, LA, 2009)

B.B. Raeburn: *New Orleans Style and the Writing of American Jazz History* (Ann Arbor, 2009)

R.B. Turner: *Jazz Religion, the Second Line, and Black New Orleans* (Bloomington, IN, 2009)

JOHN JOYCE (WITH GWYNN SPENCER MCPEEK) (1, 2);
JOHN JOYCE (WITH HENRY A. KMEN) (3);
J. BRADFORD ROBINSON/MIKE HAZELDINE/JOHN JOYCE (4);
JOHN JOYCE (5); JOHN JOYCE (WITH JOHN H. BARON) (6)

New Orleans jazz. A continuum of developing, inter-related, and community-based small band performance styles tied to the festival traditions of New Orleans. New Orleans style or traditional New Orleans jazz achieved its first idiomatic coherence between 1895 and 1917, the year it was first documented on phonograph records. What the music sounded like before 1917 remains a mystery. However, Jelly Roll Morton's interviews for the Archive of American Folk Song in 1938 and the oral histories of early New Orleans players collected by Bill Russell and Dick Allen between 1956 and 1978 for Tulane University's Hogan Jazz Archive enable an understanding of the music's basic parameters as envisioned by its practitioners. As a style New Orleans jazz has developed but not evolved, meaning that innovations have diversified its performance practices and repertoire, while older styles and repertoires have persisted. As such it can best be described as a contested tradition in a process of perpetual reinvention.

New Orleans jazz includes dance band and marching band variants. The former ensembles generally consist of five to seven instruments—although any configuration is possible, including solo piano and duos—the latter eight to 12 pieces. These groups perform a relaxed but highly syncopated dance music involving varying degrees of improvisation. The defining characteristics of the style are ensemble polyphony and heterophony, couched in a theoretical model of continuous collective improvisation but often relying on head arrangements worked out in advance. The objective is to furnish a rhythmically intense, emotionally satisfying performance to stimulate audience engagement and participation, such as dancing, clapping, foot tapping, and shouting. By the 1920s a New Orleans front line usually consisted of a cornet or trumpet, clarinet, and trombone. The trumpeter carried the lead and sometimes inserted what Joe Oliver described as "freakish" timbral effects such as baby crying and wah-wah through the ingenious use of mutes; the clarinetist provided obbligato, usually arpeggiated eighth-note runs; and the trombonist, who would originally have played a valve-operated instrument but subsequently always one with a slide, engaged in harmonic variations and smears and covered bass parts when necessary, providing the counterpoint. Although violin was found in ragtime and proto-jazz bands, its role as a lead instrument was gradually appropriated by cornet or trumpet, rendering it expendable in most New Orleans jazz bands after 1917. The front-line instruments, which routinely included saxophones by the mid-1920s, also accentuated rhythm through use of stop-time breaks and unison section playing. From 1922 wind instruments regularly supplemented the collective approach by engaging in solo improvisation during choruses and breaks, as exemplified by the work of such pioneers as King Oliver, Louis Armstrong, Leon Roppolo, and Sidney Bechet.

A full New Orleans rhythm section was made up of guitar (or banjo, especially after 1919), bass, and drums, although in many instances piano became a substitute for bass or guitar, especially for such early touring bands as Tom Brown's Band from Dixieland and the Original Dixieland Jazz Band. Before 1920 most New Orleans jazz bands did not include piano, but in the following decade its inclusion became routine. The function of the bass and drums was to provide a pulse and a strong, syncopated beat for dancers—what Jelly Roll Morton referred to as "plenty rhythm"—while also instigating various dynamic effects, such as choked cymbals to reinforce stop-time breaks, or cymbal crashes on the upbeat during out-choruses, which could alternately entail a shift to clave-based syncopation, as in Morton's "Original Jelly Roll Blues" (Bb, 1926). Although New Orleans jazz bass players were known for the percussive slap style associated with Steve Brown, Wellman Braud, and Sidney Brown, many were also adept at bowed technique and employed it to diversify the rhythmic and emotional content of the music. The New Orleans style was to a large degree the first popular music to benefit from the coalescence of the trap drum set, and there have been claims that the New Orleans drummers Dee Dee Chandler and Jack Laine invented the bass-drum foot pedal, when in fact, they merely built their own versions. Drummers tended to work primarily with snare and bass drum, relying on press rolls that could be adapted to any meter, including waltz, as needed. Unlike the collectors of "hot" recordings who apotheosized the New Orleans style and repertoire, New Orleans musicians were not purists and tended to give audiences what they wanted to hear, while also remaining true to the signature chemistry of the band and the individual voices of its players, which is usually why they were hired in the first place.

Because of the importance of rhythmic components to the style, some scholars have emphasized the shift from 2/4 to 4/4 (from a ragtime to a jazz feel) as emblematic of the completion of the New Orleans style's initial idiomatic development. However, it is perhaps more useful to consider the plethora of meters—along with the *tresillo* and *cinquillo* "Spanish tinge" elements described by Jelly Roll Morton—that is part of the repertoire of New Orleans rhythm sections because of the recurring nature of their use over time. Iconic practitioners such as Bechet refused to make distinctions between New Orleans ragtime and jazz styles, although others, such as cornetist Johnny DeDroit, emphasized the difference. As late as the 1950s the clarinetist George Lewis used the term "ragtime" to describe his jazz band and its traditional repertoire. Moreover, when one considers the contemporary reliance on clave-based rhythms among non-traditional new-wave brass bands such as the Rebirth (established in 1983) and the Hot Eight (established in 1995), the eclectic and continuous commingling of tradition and innovation becomes apparent. Although the Rebirth and Hot Eight ensembles have undeniably been part of the local brass band jazz tradition, they have drawn freely from Mardi Gras Indian music, hip hop, modern jazz, and rhythm and blues, incorporating those elements into what can nevertheless still be considered a New Orleans jazz performance. In the early 2010s the young New Orleans brass bands represented one of the most vital and community-oriented segments of the city's jazz scene, and their eclecticism was comparable to the ethos of diversification and variegation that fueled the style's original idiomatic development at the dawn of the 20th century.

See also JAZZ, NEW ORLEANS, and NEW ORLEANS MUSIC

BIBLIOGRAPHY

S.B. Charters: *Jazz: New Orleans, 1885–1957* (Belleville, NJ, 1958, 2/1963)

L.A. Pike: *Jazz, 1920 to 1927: an Analytical Study* (diss., U. of Iowa, 1962)

M. Williams: *Jazz Masters of New Orleans* (New York, 1967)

G. Schuller: *Early Jazz: its Roots and Musical Development* (New York, 1968/R)

L. Gushee: "The Nineteenth Century Origins of Jazz," *Black Music Research Journal*, xiv/1 (1994), 1–24

B. Russell: *New Orleans Style*, ed. B. Martyn and M. Hazeldine (New Orleans, 1994)

R. Knowles: *Fallen Heroes: a History of New Orleans Brass Bands* (New Orleans, 1996)

M.G. White, "The New Orleans Brass Band: a Cultural Tradition," *The Triumph of the Soul: Cultural and Psychological Aspects of African American Music*, ed. F. Jones and A.C. Jones (Westport, CT, 2001), 69–96

J. Stewart: "The Original Dixieland Jazz Band's Place in the Development of Jazz," *The Jazz Archivist*, no.19 (2005–6), 16–25

B. Raeburn: *New Orleans Style and the Writing of American Jazz History* (Ann Arbor, MI, 2009)

T. Herbert: "Trombone Glissando: a Case Study in Continuity and Change in Brass Instrument Performance Idioms," *Journal of the Historic Brass Society*, no.22 (2010), 1–19

BRUCE BOYD RAEBURN

New Orleans Mardi Gras Indians. The Mardi Gras Indians of New Orleans are African Americans who form "tribes" that confront one another in the streets during Mardi Gras, displaying elaborate hand-sewn costumes, challenging each other in artful language known as "Indian talk," and singing ceremonial chants. The chants are drawn from a common stock of call-and-response verses and accompanied by tambourines and other percussion instruments that typically adhere to a rhythmic cell called the "Indian beat" (ex.1).

Ex.1 "Indian beat" rhythmic cell

During Indian processionals and at weekly "practices" in local bars, the chants often serve a ceremonial function. For example, "Let's go get 'em" is a signal to approach a rival tribe while "Tu way pocky way" is a directive to clear a path for an approaching Indian. However, the rhythmic consistency and harmonic stability of the chants allow for much leeway. This is evident in the transposition of "floating verses" from different chants (so that "Shoo fly don't bother me" might morph into "Indians, here they come"); the improvisation of calls making reference to recent events and the experiences of the singer; and the addition of newly composed chants.

Accounts of New Orleanians "masking" in Indian suits date back to the 19th century, but the tradition was relatively confined to residential neighborhoods until the 1950s, when professional New Orleans musicians began recording Indian chants and composing Indian-themed songs in the prevalent styles of R&B and jazz. In 1954, James "Sugarboy" Crawford created a regional hit by taking the call-and-response chant "Iko, Iko" and restructuring it as a verse-refrain pop song, setting the vocal on top of a two-chord progression and adding a saxophone riff. The New Orleans girl-group the Dixie Cups recorded "Iko, Iko" in 1965 with the production team of Leiber and Stoller as a follow-up to their number one hit "Chapel of Love." Songwriter Earl King also created a Mardi Gras Indian anthem with "Big Chief," popularized on a 1964 recording by pianist Professor Longhair. These and other popular recordings initiated a radical shift in public awareness of Mardi Gras Indian activities.

In the 1970s, Indians themselves began making recordings of chants in highly orchestrated and harmonized arrangements, creating a genre called "Indian funk." The Wild Magnolias tribe, led by "chief" Bo Dollis, released a 45rpm record of Dollis's chant "Handa Wanda" backed by a funk band in 1970. The recording was produced by Jazz and Heritage Festival director Quint Davis, who arranged for the Wild Magnolias and other tribes to perform onstage in front of uninitiated and enthusiastic audiences. In 1976, Chief Jolly (George Landry) of the Wild Tchoupitoulas tribe made an album with his nephews Art, Charles, Aaron, and Cyril Neville, and soon after the group was featured performing "Meet de Boys on the Battlefront" in the documentary film *Always for Pleasure*.

"Meet de Boys on the Battlefront" now resides alongside "Handa Wanda," "Big Chief," and "Iko, Iko" as the most prominent and durable musical signs of the Mardi Gras Indian tradition. Recordings and performances by and about Mardi Gras Indians created an extensive listening public for what had been a relatively secretive community practice.

DISCOGRAPHY
Wild Tchoupitoulas: *The Wild Tchoupitoulas* (Island 054, 1976); Golden Eagles Featuring Monk Boudreaux: *Lightning and Thunder* (Rounder 2073, 1988); D. Harrison Jr.: *Indian Blues* (Candid 69514, 1992); various artists: *Mardi Gras Indians Super Sunday Showdown* (Rounder 2133, 1992); Wild Magnolias: *30 Years and Still Wild!* (AIM 5012, 2002)

BIBLIOGRAPHY
J. Berry, T. Jones, and J. Foose: *Up from the Cradle of Jazz: New Orleans Music since World War II* (Athens, GA, 1986)
M. P. Smith: *Mardi Gras Indians* (Gretna, LA, 1994)
M. Sakakeeny: "Indian Rulers: Mardi Gras Indians and New Orleans Funk," *Jazz Archivist*, no.26 (2002), 9–24
R.W. Lewis and R. Breunlin: *The House of Dance and Feathers: a Museum by Ronald W. Lewis* (New Orleans, 2009)

MATT SAKAKEENY

New Orleans music. Musical genre. New Orleans has enjoyed a reputation as an exceptionally musical place since the antebellum period, when the city's musical identity was based on an abundance of music representing the racial and ethnic heterogeneity of its inhabitants. (*See also* NEW ORLEANS.) Over the course of the twentieth century, the city's musical associations narrowed in scope, encompassing jazz, blues, rhythm and blues, soul, funk, brass band, and related styles bound together through an association with race, place, and functionality more firmly than many other locations in the United States. The term "New Orleans music" now refers primarily to black social dance music connected to the region's distinctive cultural traditions.

Historically, New Orleans music has been an integral part of a vibrant local public sphere, serving a function of assembling people in public spaces. Slaves were permitted to make music and dance, most notably in Congo Square, and musical opportunities only increased in the decades following the Civil War, when approximately 40,000 freed slaves and their offspring migrated to New Orleans from rural plantations. Around the turn of the 20th century a cultural efflorescence led to the emergence of JAZZ, which collected together a dizzying array of performance practices drawn from marching bands, social dancing, African-derived music making, Latin American rhythmic cells, ragtime, blues, the church, and more. Although African Americans were the primary architects of this new music, the heterogeneity of jazz was reflected in the diversity of its performers, which also included Creoles, Italians, Jews, Irish, and others who formed what Bruce Raeburn has termed an "incipient jazz community."

Jazz became an international popular music phenomenon in the 1920s, after Louis Armstrong, Sidney Bechet, Jelly Roll Morton, and many other New Orleanians relocated to New York, Chicago, Los Angeles, Paris, and beyond. The formative place of New Orleans within the development of jazz, however, does not appear to have been a significant consideration in public reception until the late 1930s, when the writing of jazz history began in earnest, and it was not until a decade later that the city's identification as the "birthplace" became common sense. The claim made most resoundingly in the book *Jazzmen* that jazz began "just [in New Orleans], not somewhere else" (Ramsey and Smith 1939, 5) changed the characterization of New Orleans as a musical city, altering understandings not only of where jazz came from but what constitutes the entirety of New Orleans music. In successfully arguing that jazz's emergence was locatable in a particular place and time and mainly attributable to a specific race, a process was set in motion that came to redefine New Orleans music as broadly synonymous with African American music, diminishing the history of diversity and intermixture that characterized the experiences of New Orleanians.

The remaking of New Orleans music was expedited by an infrastructural shift in the city's economy, as civic leaders began investing in tourism strategies that promoted local culinary and musical traditions. These changes coincided with the rise of the Civil Rights Movement; the dismantling of Jim Crow laws; and the mass popularity of recordings made by Fats Domino,

A member of the Golden Eagle Mardi Gras Indian gang performing at the New Orleans Jazz and Heritage Festival, New Orleans, 2011. (UPI/A.J. Sisco /Landov)

Lloyd Price, Professor Longhair, and other rhythm-and-blues artists at J&M Studios in the French Quarter. Institutions such as the Hogan Archive of New Orleans Jazz, Preservation Hall, and the Jazz & Heritage Festival ("Jazz Fest") sought to exhibit and preserve New Orleans music as it evolved through the continuous incorporation of soul, funk, and other new styles, all of which added value to local black music as a form of economic and cultural capital. A cursory glance at the roster for Jazz Fest, which has featured funk groups such as the Neville Brothers along with local jazz, blues, brass band, and Mardi Gras Indian musicians, reveals the multitude of black musical styles that constituted New Orleans music in the early 21st century.

Many of the forces that have shaped the development of New Orleans music are detectable in the city's most iconic and distinctive tradition, the brass band parade. In the 19th century funerals with music were common to many ethnic groups, but by the start of the 20th century the New Orleans brass band had been reconfigured as a black music ensemble; burial processions concluded with a second line dance propelled by upbeat dance music that emphasized improvisation, syncopation, and other African-derived musical practices. When the formative role of the brass band parade in the emergence of jazz was first recognized by researchers in the late 1930s, the tradition was relatively obscure to the majority of New Orleanians, but over the next two decades it was gradually made public through a series of sound recordings, film and television broadcasts, and media reports. By the 1960s brass bands performed weekly in Preservation Hall, Jazz Fest launched with a parade through the French Quarter, and tourism agencies began organizing staged parades for the benefit of tourists.

The increased value placed on the brass band parade, which occurred far from the city streets where the tradition originated, only enhanced its status within the local black community, which has continued to nurture the tradition through funerals—renamed "jazz funerals" in the 1960s—and weekly parades called "second lines." Contemporary bands, such as the Dirty Dozen and Rebirth, have updated the tradition with funky, hip-hop inflected songs that resonate with new audiences. Whether these bands are playing a community parade, a tourist parade in a hotel lobby, or the stage of a European concert hall, they are reinforcing and extending a legacy of New Orleans music that has transformed significantly over the course of several centuries.

In New Orleans musical performance has consistently served as a site of identity formation and social interaction due to the plenitude of offerings and their freedom of accessibility.

BIBLIOGRAPHY

F. Ramsey and C.E. Smith: *Jazzmen* (New York, 1939)

H.A. Kmen: *Music in New Orleans: the Formative Years, 1791–1841* (Baton Rouge, LA, 1966)

L. Gushee: "The Nineteenth Century Origins of Jazz," *Black Music Research Journal*, xiv/1 (1994), 1–24

L. Gushee: *Pioneers of Jazz: the Story of the Creole Band* (Oxford, 2005)

T. Brothers: *Louis Armstrong's New Orleans* (New York, 2006)

B. Raeburn: *New Orleans Style and the Writing of American Jazz History* (Ann Arbor, MI, 2009)

B. Raeburn: "Stars of David and Sons of Sicily: Constellations Beyond the Canon in Early New Orleans Jazz," *Jazz Perspectives*, iii/2 (2009), 123–52

M. Sakakeeny: "New Orleans Music as a Circulatory System," *Black Music Research Journal*, xxxi/2 (2011), 291–325

MATT SAKAKEENY

New Orleans Rhythm Kings [NORK], **the**. Jazz ensemble. Its nucleus consisted of trumpeter Paul Mares (1900–49), clarinetist Leon Roppolo (1902–43), and trombonist George Brunies (1902–74). Mares and Brunies moved to Chicago from New Orleans at the instigation of drummer Ragbaby Stevens in 1919. Roppolo arrived in 1921 after tours with Bea Palmer (who coined the name New Orleans Rhythm Kings) and Carlisle Evans stranded him. Their collaboration led to work at the Friars Inn as the Friars Society Orchestra, with Jack Pettis (tenor saxophone), Elmer Schoebel (piano), Louis Black (banjo), Arnold Loyacano (double bass, another hometown chum), and Frank Snyder (drums), where they performed for dancers and nascent jazz musicians. Recordings made for Gennett in August 1922 signaled a new phase in the stylistic development of jazz: their music was smoother, better integrated, and more technically proficient than that of the Original Dixieland Jazz Band, whose material they reinterpreted. They were also aware of their black counterparts, with Mares following King Oliver and Brunies developing a tailgate style parallel to Kid Ory's. Roppolo's coherent and lyrical solos on "Tiger Rag" signaled a notable departure from the front-line polyphony and rough-and-tumble improvisation that characterized most New Orleans jazz bands.

In 1923 the band adopted the name the New Orleans Rhythm Kings and recruited Mel Stitzel to replace Schoebel; Ben Pollack took over on drums, and New Orleans bass players Steve Brown and Chink Martin succeeded each other. In March 1923 the group recorded as a quintet, yielding a jazz interpretation of "Maple Leaf Rag" and three seminal versions of "Tin Roof Blues" featuring spectacular, variant solos by Roppolo. The New Orleans Rhythm Kings' recordings with Jelly Roll Morton in July 1923 hold a special significance as they took place at one of the earliest mixed-race recording sessions in jazz history. "Milenburg Joys," a restructuring of Mares and Roppolo's "Golden Leaf Strut" with an introduction by Morton, was a spontaneous collaboration. By 1924 work in Chicago was scarce, and the musicians drifted back to New Orleans, where they recorded as the New Orleans Rhythm Kings in January 1925 (when Santo Pecora replaced Brunies) and in March (when Charlie Cordilla replaced Roppolo). After the recordings failed to sell and hometown bookings did not materialize, the group disbanded. Mares retired from music before making a brief comeback in the 1940s. Brunies joined Ted Lewis's group and worked with Muggsy Spanier and Eddie Condon's circle in the 1930s, and enjoyed celebrity status during and after the New Orleans Revival. Roppolo's mental health deteriorated, and he died in a sanitarium.

SELECTED RECORDINGS
Eccentric (Gen., 1922); Panama/Tiger Rag (Gen., 1922); Weary Blues/ Wolverine Blues (Gen., 1923); Maple Leaf Rag (Gen., 1923); Tin Roof Blues (Gen., 1923); Milenburg Joys (Gen., 1923); She's Crying for Me Blues (OK, 1925)

BIBLIOGRAPHY
M. Stearns: "The History of Swing Music, Chapter IV: the White Tradition in Chicago: Did Rhythm Kings Borrow Ideas from Negroes?," *DB*, iii/9 (1936), 6–7; iii/10 (1936), 8
M. Williams: "N.O.R.K.," *Jazz Masters of New Orleans* (New York, 1967/*R*), 121–35

R.M. Sudhalter: *Lost Chords: White Musicians and their Contributions to Jazz, 1915–1945* (New York, 1999), 28–47

BRUCE BOYD RAEBURN

New River Shasta. Native American group of California, belonging to the SHASTA.

New thing. A term applied to the avant-garde jazz of the 1960s more commonly known as FREE JAZZ.

Newton, James (Weldon) (*b* Los Angeles, CA, 1 May 1953). Flutist and composer. He is best known for his work as a jazz flutist. His most popular album, *African Flower* (1985, BN), covers the works of Duke Ellington and Billy Strayhorn and won Album of the Year in the *Downbeat* International Critics Poll in 1986. Newton has received many *Downbeat* Awards as Jazz Flutist of the Year (1982–2004) and multiple ASCAP Standards Awards for classical composition. As a high school student he studied with the well-known Los Angeles jazz musician BUDDY COLLETTE. While attending California State University at Los Angeles, where he studied classical flute and graduated in 1980, he was also an active jazz performer, playing with Stanley Crouch, David Murray, Lester Bowie, and Cecil Taylor. Newton's skill and musical openness have allowed him to grow seamlessly into multiple musical spheres. He has led a variety of jazz ensembles under his own name as well as the Luckman Jazz Orchestra, based in California, and has frequently performed in ensembles with such musicians as the pianist Jon Jang, the tenor saxophonist David Murray, and the pianist Anthony Davis. He has also collaborated with musicians as diverse as Chet Baker, Jack DeJohnette, Stanley Turrentine, and Stevie Wonder. As a composer his efforts are just as varied, with classical works including *The Songs of Freedom Chamber Opera* (a two-act opera), *Looking Above: the Faith of Joseph* (for solo piano), *Prayers and Tears for the Broken* (for brass octet), and *Suite for Frida Kahlo* (for flute, reed player, tenor saxophone, bassoon, two trombones, piano, bass, and drums). His jazz works include *Nelson Mandela* and *Suite for Elizabeth Catlett*. Newton has also worked extensively as a classical performer, with such groups as the San Francisco Contemporary Music Players, the New York Philharmonic, and the Ensemble für Neue Musik Zurik.

E. RON HORTON

Newton-John, Olivia (*b* Cambridge, England, 26 Sept 1948). English singer and actress. Raised in Australia, where she began singing as a teenager, she is best known for her hits of the 1970s and early 1980s. She made her way from local television and radio appearances to national television contests, including "Sing, Sing, Sing," which won her a trip to England and the opportunity to begin recording. Newton-John's first album, *If Not for You* (Festival, 1971), brought her some attention in the UK and Australia, but it was not until the single "Let me be there" (1973) that she became known in the United States. *If You Love Me, Let Me Know* (MCA, 1974) included the song that was to become Newton-John's signature number, "I honestly love you," and garnered two Grammy awards for the singer, including Record of the Year. A string of chart-topping singles followed, making Newton-John well known before she took the iconic role as Sandy in the movie adaptation of *Grease* (1978), which solidified her standing in the history of film musicals. Her duet with John Travolta, "You're the one that I want," stayed at number one on the charts for 12 weeks. She continued recording a wide range of songs in the pop, country, and adult contemporary genres. Revamping her image, Newton-John released the album *Physical* in 1981, and the title track and its video were popular worldwide. After 1985 Newton-John recorded a few unsuccessful albums, and spent more time touring and devoting herself to social advocacy.

BIBLIOGRAPHY
T. Ewbank: *Olivia: the Biography of Olivia Newton-John* (London, 2009)

JONAS WESTOVER

New violin family. *See* HUTCHINS, CARLEEN.

New wave. References to new waves of music have appeared with regularity since the 1960s, but the most lasting genre association remains the period of the late 1970s and early 1980s. Critics attached the new wave label to British punk rock groups such as the Sex Pistols and the Clash, and then to a much broader range of artists who represented a more modern alternative to the stagnant clichés of mainstream rock. While punk rock wielded a major influence on the popular music scene in the United Kingdom, in the United States the music's stigma of violence and sexual deviance made it virtually unmarketable. Seymour Stein of Sire records is often credited with choosing the more neutral label of new wave to promote New York-based groups like Talking Heads, which previously had been lumped together with punk. Beyond the simple name change, the artists who increasingly came to be drawn under the new wave umbrella exhibited a cleaner, more commercially viable sound than punk's noisy, distorted style, while still retaining punk's edgy, irreverent attitude and determinedly antiromantic lyrical stance.

Part of what attracted Stein and others to new wave was the music's stripped back style and upbeat tempos, which they viewed as a much needed return to the energetic rush of rock and roll and 1960s rock that had dwindled in the 1970s with the ascendance of overblown progressive rock and stadium spectacles. This resurrection of the past took many different forms. Groups like the B-52's drew on early 1960s surf rock, girl group music, and thrift store fashions with a playful sense of irony, while power pop bands like the Knack looked more reverentially to the British Invasion sounds of the Beatles and the Who. The Cars incorporated rockabilly guitar licks, hand claps, and vintage 1960s combo organs into their songs, while also featuring modern electronic drums and synthesizer solos. Given this diverse stylistic range, it is difficult to generalize about an overarching new wave aesthetic.

If there was one element, however, that seemed to unify much of the new wave, it was the return to rock dancing that the music inspired as witnessed by the dramatic rise in urban "rock discos" at the turn of the 1980s. This association with dance increased even more with the emergence of British synth-pop artists, such as the Human League and Duran Duran in 1982 and 1983, who were featured heavily not only in American dance clubs but more crucially on the fledgling cable television network, MTV. Often referred to as a second British Invasion, these synthesizer-based groups, who brought a distinct disco and funk influenced flavor to their music, traveled both under the labels of new wave and "new music." By the mid to late 1980s these bands were largely on the decline and as they fell out of popularity, so did use of the new wave label. There have been numerous new wave revivals since the mid-1990s, and in general they have taken their inspiration from this last MTV synth-pop new wave era.

See also POP; PUNK; ROCK; SYNTHPOP.

BIBLIOGRAPHY
B. Gendron: *Between Montmartre and the Mudd Club: Popular Music and the Avant-Garde* (Chicago, 2002)
J. Covach: "Pangs of History in Late 1970s New-Wave Rock," *Analyzing Popular Music*, ed. A.F. Moore (Cambridge, MA, 2003), 173–95
C. Kronengold: "Exchange Theories in Disco, New Wave, and Album-Oriented Rock," *Criticism*, l/1 (2008), 43–82
T. Cateforis: *Are We Not New Wave? Modern Pop at the Turn of the 1980s* (Ann Arbor, MI, 2011)

THEO CATEFORIS

New World. Record company. It was established in New York in 1975 with a grant from the Rockefeller Foundation. The development of the nonprofit Anthology of Recorded Music, Inc., which oversees the New World Records label, was originally guided by label President Herman E. Krawitz, who has also served as board chairman, and A&R director Andrew Rayburn, whose initial mandate was to produce a 100-disc anthology of American music covering the widest possible spectrum of musical styles. That task was completed in 1978, and the anthology was distributed free of charge to nearly 7000 educational and cultural institutions worldwide. In the years since, the label's eclectic catalog has swelled to more than 400 recordings representing over 700 composers, from classical figures such as Samuel Barber, Leonard Bernstein, Aaron Copland, and Ned Rorem, to jazz performers including Cecil Taylor, Earl Hines, Roy Eldridge, and Terry Adams. The label has also compiled numerous anthologies, covering genres ranging from musical theater to Native American folk music.

Notable releases include three Grammy award winners: Barber's *Antony and Cleopatra* (1984), Bernstein's *Candide* (1986), and Rorem's *String Symphony/Sunday Morning/Eagles* (1989). The label has maintained an active release schedule, issuing approximately a dozen albums per year, covering virtually all styles of American music, exclusive of rock, hip-hop, new age, and country.

THANE TIERNEY

New World Symphony. An American fellowship-based professional training orchestra founded in 1987 in Miami Beach, Florida. Under the artistic direction of MICHAEL TILSON THOMAS in the 2010s, the program has prepared recent graduates from top music schools for leadership roles in orchestras worldwide. Students have been exposed to traditional and modern repertoire, leading guest conductors, soloists, and coaches.

STEPHEN F. ZDZINSKI

New York. City in the state of New York (pop. 8,175,133; metropolitan area 18,897,109; 2010 US Census). It is the largest city in the United States and the cultural center of the country. The fine natural harbor and waterways and the opening of the Erie Canal in 1825 quickly made New York the nation's principal commercial center. As the country's most important port until after World War II, the city has been the gateway for both visitors and immigrants to the United States, bringing a density and variety of cultural influences that have created a dynamic and varied musical life. The heart of America's music industry is in New York, and the city is a showcase for individuals and organizations from other parts of the continent and from abroad.

1. Before 1800. 2. Concert life. 3. Concert halls and other performance venues. 4. Opera and musical theater. 5. Orchestras and bands. 6. Chamber music. 7. Choral societies. 8. Religious music. 9. Avant-garde music. 10. Ragtime and jazz. 11. Popular music since 1950. 12. Ethnic music. 13. Education. 14. Associations and organizations. 15. Publishing, instrument making, broadcasting, and recording. 16. Criticism and periodicals. 17. Libraries.

1. BEFORE 1800. The first documented concert in New York was given on 21 January 1736 by the German-born organist and harpsichordist C.T. Pachelbel, son of the renowned Johann, at the house of Robert Todd, a vintner, next to Fraunces Tavern; an announcement of the event refers to songs and instrumental music with harpsichord, flute, and violin. Apparently the first organ was installed in the Dutch Reformed Church in 1724, followed in 1741 by an organ built by J.G. Klemm for Trinity Church. Forty-six concerts were advertised in New York between 1736 and 1775, more than in any other American city; they included a charity concert at City Hall after the installation of an organ in 1756 and, about 1766, the performance of a mar from Handel's *Judas Maccabaeus* "accompanied with a side drum" at the City Tavern.

Visiting musicians, usually from London, rarely remained long in New York; W.C. Hulett, who taught the violin and dancing in 1759 and was still in the city directory in 1799, was an exception. The arrival of WILLIAM TUCKEY in 1752 to become clerk of Trinity Church from 1 January 1753 marked a turning point in New York's musical life. Tuckey promptly took over the Trinity choir and became a champion of Handel's works; he organized subscription concerts and balls in the 1760s, and on 16 January 1770 sponsored a benefit at "Mr. Burns' New Room" with the first New York performance of the overture and 16 numbers from *Messiah*. Works by Haydn appeared on programs after 27 April 1782.

Various groups of New York musicians sporadically announced series of subscription concerts. "City Concerts" begun in 1793 by Henri Capron, James Hewitt (*see* HEWITT (1), and G.E. Saliment lasted until 1797, and included music by I.G. Pleyel, Haydn, A.-E.-M. Grétry, Adalbert Gyrowetz, Hewitt, and Benjamin Carr (*see* CARR (2); outdoor summer concerts initiated in 1765 by James Jones in the Ranelagh Gardens continued to be popular. Vocal and instrumental music by Haydn, Thomas Arne, and Carl Stamitz, as well as popular ballads, could be heard at Ranelagh Gardens and at Joseph Delacroix's Vauxhall Gardens in the late 1790s.

New York music organizations in the 18th century combining social and choral activities included the Harmonic (1773–4), Musical (1788–94), St. Cecilia (1791–9), Harmonical (1796–9), Columbian Anacreontic (1795–?), Uranian (1793–8), and Philharmonic (1799–c1816) societies. The repertory usually consisted of hymns and, occasionally, anthems. Few societies survived their good intentions.

Theater flourished and ballad opera was popular. Opera could be heard at the Nassau Street Theater from 1750; *The Beggar's Opera* was one of the first performed there. In 1753–4 a troupe from London directed by Lewis Hallam performed operas and plays; David Douglass reorganized it under the name of the American Company (later Old American Company), and it performed at the John Street Theatre and in other coastal cities from 1767 to 1774. During the British military occupation (1776–83) plays or ballad operas were occasionally performed, but it was not until 1785 that Lewis Hallam Jr. and John Henry reopened the Old American Company, which they operated more or less regularly until the turn of the century. The musical repertory consisted largely of pasticcio arrangements of such popular works as *Thomas and Sally, Rosina, Love in a Village, Lionel and Clarissa, The Adopted Child, The Duenna, No Song, No Supper,* and *The Flitch of Bacon*. Operas by Grétry (*Zémire et Azor*) and Egidio Duni (*Les deux chasseurs*) also served as a basis for local adaptation. For a short time in the 1790s French immigrants performed such works as *Les deux chasseurs*, Audinot's *Le tonnelier*, and Rousseau's *Le devin du village* in French.

Native musical theater came into its own in the last quarter of the 18th century. Among the earliest examples was *May Day in Town* (18 May 1788) with "music compiled from the most eminent masters." Hewitt's *Tammany, or The Indian Chief* (from which only one song survives), the first opera on a Native American subject, was produced on 3 March 1794; the libretto, by Anna Hatton, succeeded in its intention to arouse Federalist opposition, and *Tammany* had only three performances. The pantomime *The Fourth of July, or Temple of American Independence*, with music by Victor Pelissier, had one performance (4 July 1799), as did his *Edwin and Angelina*, based on Goldsmith (19 December 1796). More successful was Carr's opera *The Archers* (1796), from which only the introductory rondo and a single song survive.

JOHN JACOB ASTOR opened New York's first music shop in 1786, before concentrating on the fur trading business.

Jenny Lind's American debut, Castle Garden Theater, New York, 1850. (Music Division, The New York Public Library for the Performing Arts, Astor, Lenox and Tilden Foundations)

Carr and Hewitt were both important figures in the growth of music trades in the city: Carr arrived from England in 1793 and set up a music shop in Philadelphia in 1794 and in New York in 1795; he sold the latter to Hewitt in 1797. English popular music and American patriotic songs were the mainstay of their sheet music sales.

2. CONCERT LIFE. In the early 19th century concert life in New York centered on outdoor summer gardens, patterned on their London counterparts, and later on their attendant theaters. Popular establishments such as Castle Garden (1839–55) in the Battery and Niblo's Garden (1849–95) at Broadway and Prince Street presented ballad singers and mixed programs of instrumental music.

Economic opportunities in America and political uncertainties in Europe spurred the arrival of talented young musicians. A number of European singers, composers, conductors, and impresarios arrived during the early and mid-19th century, as well as popular virtuosos such as the violinist Sivori (1846–50) and the pianists Leopold de Meyer (1845–6, 1867–8) and Henri Herz (1846–8). Jenny Lind was on the stage of Castle Garden before a cheering audience of 7000 on the evening of 11 September 1850 for the first of about 20 concerts in New York, the last of which was on 24 May 1852. The significance of her tour, at first under the aegis of P.T. Barnum, lay less in her superb singing than in her impact on the box office, and the demonstration that a European artist of the first rank could find responsive audiences in the United States.

Virtuoso pianists such as Gottschalk, who gave 90 concerts in New York in seven seasons beginning in February 1853, and Thalberg, who played 56 concerts from November 1856 to April 1858, presented well-received programs. Both artists, playing American Chick-

ering pianos, concentrated almost exclusively on their own compositions, although Beethoven and Chopin were occasionally represented. Four resident pianists were active in the second half of the 19th century: HENRY CHRISTIAN TIMM (1835–92), RICHARD HOFFMAN (1847–97), SEBASTIAN BACH MILLS (1859–98), and William Mason (1855–1908). Each maintained a high standard of technical and interpretative excellence, and introduced to the American repertory works of a higher standard than the usual operatic potpourris, fantasies, and variations.

The impresario and conductor LOUIS JULLIEN arrived in New York in August 1853 to give light concerts, including works by the Americans W.H. Fry and G.F. Bristow, in the Crystal Palace. Other popular performers included the violinists Ole Bull and Henry Vieuxtemps, both of whom visited for the first time in 1843, and the pianist Alfred Jaëll (1851–2). Typical programs were mixed, usually including several arias and duets, one or two piano solos, a violin solo, an ensemble work, and, if there was an orchestra, an overture. The solo recital was virtually unknown, even the most celebrated virtuosos appearing with other performers.

The quality of visiting artists steadily improved. The arrival of Anton Rubinstein and Wieniawski on 23 September 1872 brought a serious note to concert programs of the day; a bold solo recital brought in more money than a troupe. Bülow visited in 1875–6 and again in 1889–90. Most Europeans arrived with their reputations already established at home, but Americans made their own evaluations; for example, free tickets were given for Paderewski's debut on 17 November 1891, but it was four seasons before he became a popular success.

After 1900 New York concert life differed little from that of a large European city. With a population of about three and a half million, improved transport, and an assured audience, the city's musical life became more

Carnegie Music Hall and Lyceum, 1905. (Museum of the City of New York, Postcard Collection)

predictable. Solo recitals became distinct from chamber concerts and orchestral programs, and European artists made repeated visits to the city. After 1914 both American and European musicians frequently established a New York base. By the middle of the century programs had changed; there were fewer solo recitals and more group events, chamber music was more popular, choruses were numerous but smaller, and the concert repertory became both more varied and more specialized within individual programs. A revitalization of the solo recital and further growth in chamber music activities took place from the 1960s, led by the city's two largest performing arts centers, Carnegie Hall and Lincoln Center. Concert activities prospered during the summer months after the founding at Lincoln Center of the Mostly Mozart Festival (1966) and the more general Lincoln Center Festival (1996).

3. CONCERT HALLS AND OTHER PERFORMANCE VENUES. The center of New York's musical life has moved steadily uptown since it began in what is now the financial district. For many years the principal musical activities were in the midtown area bounded by the Metropolitan Opera House in West 39th Street and Carnegie Hall at 57th Street and 7th Avenue. Carnegie Hall has played host to virtually every significant American or visiting musician since its opening on 5 May 1891, at which Tchaikovsky was guest of honor. The main hall, named in 1997 the Isaac Stern Auditorium, seats 2804 and is celebrated for its superb acoustics. Until the opening of Lincoln Center it was the home of the New York PO. The adjacent Carnegie Recital Hall (cap. 268, renamed Weill Recital Hall in 1986) is used for many debut recitals. Threatened with demolition when plans for Lincoln Center were announced in the mid-1950s, Carnegie Hall was saved through the efforts of a citizens' committee organized by Isaac Stern in 1960. New York City purchased the

hall and leased it to the newly formed Carnegie Hall Corporation, which became responsible for programming. The regular season includes classical, jazz, and popular concerts, as well as educational programs. In support of contemporary music, the corporation commissioned 21 new works between 1986 and 1999. A permanent exhibition on the history of Carnegie Hall is on display in the hall's Rose Museum (opened 1991).

Town Hall (cap. 1498, built 1921) on West 43rd Street was particularly popular as a concert hall in the middle decades of the 20th century. The hall was acquired by New York University in 1958 and closed temporarily in 1978; it reopened in 1984 after restoration. Radio City Music Hall in Rockefeller Center opened in 1932. Until 1974 it had a resident ballet company, and it continues to maintain its own orchestra and the Rockettes, a troupe known since 1933 for its precision chorus-line dancing. The *art déco* music hall seats 5874 and houses a noted Wurlitzer theater organ.

In the 1960s the axis of concert life moved further north with the establishment of Lincoln Center for the Performing Arts, a complex of buildings and organizations including almost a dozen theaters and concert and lecture halls. Philharmonic Hall opened on 23 September 1962 to a capacity audience of 2646; it was subsequently modified to improve its acoustics. In 1973 it was renamed Avery Fisher Hall and in 1976 was completely gutted and rebuilt to a new, successful acoustical design (cap. 2742 after renovation). The openings of the New York State Theater (1964, renamed in 2008 the David H. Koch Theater) and the new Metropolitan Opera House (1966), which also flank the main plaza, were followed in 1969 by that of Alice Tully Hall (cap. 1096), an ideal setting for solo and chamber concerts. The Vivian Beaumont Theater, the Mitzi E. Newhouse Theater, and the Library and Museum of the Performing Arts of the New York Public Library occupy a corner position at 65th Street and Amsterdam Avenue, while the Juilliard School and Alice Tully Hall are across 65th Street on Broadway. The Frederick P. Rose Hall, built in 2004, hosts jazz concerts and educational events programmed by Jazz at Lincoln Center. Free outdoor concerts are given each summer in the plaza of Lincoln Center and in the Guggenheim Bandshell of Damrosch Park (adjacent to the opera house).

Elsewhere in the city many colleges, museums, and other institutions include halls used for public concerts. Prominent among them are Merkin Concert Hall at Abraham Goodman House (opened 1978), Sylvia and Danny Kaye Playhouse at Hunter College, the Metropolitan Museum of Art's Grace Rainey Rogers Auditorium, the Kaufmann Auditorium at the East 92nd Street Young Men's–Young Women's Hebrew Association, Kathryn Bache Miller Theater at Columbia University, Aaron Davis Hall at City College, City Center for Music and Drama, Cooper Union, the Asia Society, and the Alternative Museum. Symphony Space, at Broadway and 95th Street, offers a varied program ranging from gospel and ethnic music to marathon concerts devoted to Bach, Ives, Cage, and others. Besides P.S. 122, the Clocktower Gallery and Franklin Furnace, the Kitchen has since 1971 been the most important center for Downtown experimental music, dance, performance art, video, and film.

Outside Manhattan the most important concert center is the Brooklyn Academy of Music, which opened in 1861 at a site in Montague Street; the present building on Lafayette Avenue opened in 1908. From the 19th century it was a cultural community and civic center presenting opera, oratorios, and plays. Since 1967 the academy has played a prominent role in sponsoring modern dance and theater as well as music. Since its first season in 1955, the Brooklyn Philharmonia (now PO) has performed at the academy. The "Next Wave" activities inaugurated in 1981 have expanded to include an annual festival and touring program featuring both contemporary music and less familiar works from the past. Outdoor summer concerts were held at Lewisohn Stadium from 1918 to 1966. Concerts are now held in Central Park and in parks in the other boroughs. The New York PO first gave outdoor concerts in 1965, and the Metropolitan Opera has done so since 1967.

4. Opera and musical theater. Italian opera first reached New York on 29 November 1825 with a performance at the Park Theatre of Rossini's *Il barbiere di Siviglia* by an Italian company led by Manuel García, the famous Spanish singer and teacher, who took the part of Count Almaviva. The ensemble of eight singers, four of them Garcías (including the 17-year-old Maria-Felicia, later Malibran), had been recruited in London by a New York vintner, Dominick Lynch. Encouraged by Lorenzo Da Ponte, then a professor of Italian at Columbia College, Lynch took García's troupe to New York for a season of 79 performances, accompanied by a local orchestra of 24; the repertory included *Don Giovanni*; Rossini's *Tancredi, Otello, Il turco in Italia,* and *La cenerentola*; Zingarelli's *Giulietta e Romeo*; and García's own *La*

figlia dell'aria. Before García's appearance opera in New York had consisted of makeshift adaptations of comic pasticcios with spoken dialogue and popular airs inserted in place of difficult arias, performed by actors. No female stars performed in New York until the 1820s. After the García's departure for Mexico in November 1826, a French company from New Orleans took a two-month season of French opera to the Park Theatre, opening on 13 July 1827 with Isouard's *Cendrillon*. The French repertory included at least ten operas, among them Cherubini's *Les deux journées*, Auber's *La dame blanche,* and Boieldieu's *Le calife de Bagdad*. The next opera company to appear was led by the tenor Giovanni Montresor in 1832–3; it gave about 50 performances of such works as Bellini's *Il pirata* and Mercadante's *Elisa e Claudio*, in addition to works of Rossini. Another French troupe from New Orleans introduced Rossini's *Le comte Ory* (Park Theatre, 19 August 1833) and Herold's *Zampa*.

New York's first venue for opera, the Italian Opera House at Church and Leonard streets, opened on 18 November 1833 with Rossini's *La gazza ladra*; among its backers were Lynch and Da Ponte. The second season was financially disastrous and in December 1835 the building was sold. When it reopened as the

TRINITY CHURCH.
Broadway, N.Y. rebuilt 1788.

Lithograph of Trinity Church after its rebuilding in 1788. (Emmet Collection, Miriam and Ira D. Wallach Division of Arts, Prints and Photographs, The New York Public Library, Astor, Lenox and Tilden Foundations)

The Cotton Club, Harlem, New York, c1938. (RA/Lebrecht Music & Arts)

National Theater, it joined other New York theaters as the home to British stars performing in the English-language repertory. The English opera was popular until the mid-1840s. On 3 February 1844 Ferdinando Palmo, a restaurateur, opened Palmo's Opera House (cap. *c*800) with the New York premiere of Bellini's *I puritani*. In four seasons Palmo introduced Bellini's *Beatrice di Tenda*, Donizetti's *Lucrezia Borgia* and *Linda di Chamounix*, and Verdi's *I Lombardi*. At other theaters pasticcios of opera in English by Balfe, Rooke, and Benedict remained popular. While Palmo's held sway in Chambers Street, 150 wealthy men were raising money for another opera house further uptown, and the Astor Place Opera House (cap. 1500–1800) opened on 22 November 1847 with Verdi's *Ernani*. The guaranteed support lasted only five years, financial returns were slight, and the house closed in 1852.

The period between 1847 and the founding of the Metropolitan Opera in 1883 was a turbulent one in New York's operatic history, dominated by colorful impresarios, competitive prima donnas, and constantly changing personnel who appeared in operatic performances in many New York theaters. After the closure of the house at Astor Place, the only theater devoted specifically to concert and opera was the Academy of Music at 14th Street and Irving Place, which opened on 2 October 1854 with a performance of Bellini's *Norma* starring Giulia Grisi and Giuseppe Mario; it continued to present regular operatic seasons until 1886. When it was built (at a cost of $335,000), the house contained the largest stage in the world (21·5 × 30 meters) and

seated 4,600. During the first 24 years the management changed every season.

MAX MARETZEK, who left London in 1848 to conduct at the Astor Place Opera, was among the more prominent impresarios. A frequent lessee and conductor at the Academy of Music, he was associated with the first New York performances of many operas there. Academy audiences heard *Rigoletto* (19 February 1855), *Il trovatore* (2 May 1855), *La traviata* (3 December 1856), Meyerbeer's *L'Africaine* (1 December 1865), and Gounod's *Roméo et Juliette* (15 November 1867), the last two in Italian. The brothers Max and MAURICE STRAKOSCH were also among the operatic producers active in New York from 1857. Most important was JAMES HENRY MAPLESON, who went to the Academy of Music in 1878 and directed operatic activities there and abroad until 1886. Many great singers appeared in New York; audiences in 1853, for example, heard the nine-year-old Adelina Patti, Giovanni Mario, Lind, Henriette Sontag, Giulia Grisi, and Marietta Alboni. Later decades saw the appearance of such singers as Christine Nilsson, Lilli Lehmann, and Italo Campanini. Thirty-nine American singers, among them Lillian Nordica, Clara Kellogg, Minnie Hauk, and Annie Louise Cary, sang at the Academy of Music before 1884. Local composers were not so fortunate, although Bristow's *Rip Van Winkle* ran for four weeks in 1855 at Niblo's Garden, and Fry's *Leonora* was heard in March 1858, 13 years after its premiere in Philadelphia. The first German operas (albeit English adaptations) performed in New York were *Der Freischütz* (1825), *Die Zauberflöte,* and *Fidelio* (both in the 1830s). The first

Lincoln Center, New York. (AP Photo/Matt Moyer)

opera by Wagner heard in the city was *Tannhäuser*, given on 4 April 1859 at the Stadt Theater.

The Metropolitan Opera House at Broadway and 39th Street opened with Gounod's *Faust* on 22 October 1883. Originally conceived as a social gesture by a score of millionaires who could not obtain boxes at the Academy of Music, the Metropolitan quickly achieved international eminence. The Metropolitan Opera Association has the longest uninterrupted existence of any organization of its kind in the United States: apart from 1892–3, when the house was closed because of a fire, and 1897–8, when MAURICE GRAU reorganized his company, a resident company has presented opera continuously at the Metropolitan since 1883. Henry Abbey, a well-known theatrical producer with little operatic experience, directed the first season and incurred a loss of $500,000. The artistic importance of the house dates from the following season when the board of directors accepted LEOPOLD DAMROSCH MANNE's proposal that he should direct a season of German opera. In the seven years after Damrosch's death in 1885 all of Wagner's operas from *Rienzi* to *Götterdämmerung* were conducted—five for the first time in America—by his successor, ANTON SEIDL. As in Europe, this was the peak period for Wagnerism, and this was particularly evident in New York. Celebrated European singers like Lehmann, Marianne Brandt, Amalie Materna, and Albert Niemann were members of the company, and in effect the Metropolitan became a German opera house; even *Il trovatore* and *Aida* were given there in German. Out of 17 operas in the repertory in the 1890–91 season, eight were by Wagner.

The sobriety of the programs eventually exhausted the patience of the box holders, and in 1891 Abbey returned as lessee, placing the management in the hands of Grau, a shrewd student of public taste. He built his company around such admirable singers as Emma Eames, the De Reszkes, Emma Albani, and Jean Lassalle, at first presenting the repertory exclusively in French and Italian. It was Grau's conviction that audiences attended opera primarily to hear fine singing, a belief he substantiated with some of the most brilliant casts Americans had ever heard. Among them were Nordica, Eames, Zélie De Lussan, Victor Maurel, Edouard De Reszke, and Giuseppe Russitano in *Don Giovanni*; Melba, Nordica, Sofia Scalchi, the De Reszkes, Maurel, and Pol Plançon in Meyerbeer's *Les Huguenots*; and Nordica, Marie Brema, the De Reszkes, and Giuseppe Kaschmann in *Tristan und Isolde* when the performance of German opera in German was resumed in 1896. In many respects these paralleled performances at Covent Garden, where Grau was also the impresario during part of this period.

Grau retired in 1903 and a new producing group was organized, with Heinrich Conried as manager. His theatrical experience as a producer of plays in German improved that aspect of the Metropolitan's productions considerably. Highlights of Conried's tenure included Caruso's Metropolitan debut (23 November 1903), a sensational *Salome* with Fremstad (22 January 1907), Chaliapin as an almost nude Méphistophélès (20 November 1907), and Mahler conducting *Tristan und Isolde* (1 January 1908).

Giulio Gatti-Casazza, the director of La Scala, was engaged as director in 1908, becoming general manager in 1910; Toscanini came to the Metropolitan with him, making his conducting debut in a performance of *Aida* (16 November 1908). With the musical cooperation of Toscanini and the financial assistance of Otto Kahn, Gatti-Casazza established an operatic enterprise of imposing scope and efficiency. Under him the policy of presenting opera in the language of its composition became the rule of the house. Important conductors during his 27-year tenure included GUSTAV MAHLER (1908–10), ARTURO TOSCANINI (1908–15), ALFRED HERTZ (1902–15), ARTUR BODANZKY (1915–39), and TULLIO SERAFIN (1924–34). The repertory was expanded to include as many as 48 different works in a 24-week season. Puccini's *La fanciulla del West* and Humperdinck's *Königskinder* had their world premieres at the Metropolitan in 1910. Gatti-Casazza continued to keep abreast of operatic developments in Italy and elsewhere, at the same time initiating the production of American operas, including Converse's *The Pipe of Desire* (18 March 1910), Parker's *Mona* (14 March 1912), and Taylor's *Peter Ibbetson* (7 February 1931). Although the company prospered under Gatti-Casazza's astute management, the 1929 stock market collapse and ensuing Depression severely depleted its reserve fund, and the season was shortened to 16 and later to 14 weeks. In 1935 Gatti-Casazza retired and was succeeded briefly by the singer Herbert Witherspoon, who died while planning his first season. His successor was the Canadian tenor Edward Johnson, long a member of the company, who managed the Metropolitan until 1950.

An experiment with a low-priced spring season featuring young American singers sponsored by the Juilliard Foundation lasted only two years (1936–7), but American singers such as Lawrence Tibbett, Eleanor Steber, Rose Bampton, Richard Crooks, Dorothy Kirsten, Leonard Warren, and Risë Stevens played an increasingly important role during Johnson's regime. Helen Traubel, Lauritz Melchior, and Kirsten Flagstad led a strong Germanic wing with outstanding Wagner performances in the late 1930s and early 1940s. Italian opera continued to dominate the repertory, French works being in the minority. Few modern operas were produced during Johnson's tenure, although the Metropolitan did give Walter Damrosch's *The Man without a Country* in 1937, Bernard Rogers's *The Warrior* in 1947, and Britten's *Peter Grimes* in 1948. The Metropolitan Opera Guild, a supporting organization founded in 1935 by Mrs. August Belmont, has a national membership of over 100,000 and sponsors an educational program and special performances for schoolchildren.

In 1950 SIR RUDOLF BING, a Viennese impresario who had managed the Glyndebourne and Edinburgh festivals, became general manager of the Metropolitan. His tenure, which lasted until 1972, was marked by modernization of stage techniques, an increasingly international cast, and the move of the company to new quarters in Lincoln Center. Although the repertory remained basically conservative, Bing introduced several American operas including Barber's *Vanessa*

(15 January 1958), Menotti's *Le dernier sauvage* (23 January 1964), and Levy's *Mourning Becomes Electra* (17 March 1967); light operas such as Strauss's *Die Fledermaus,* and Offenbach's *La Périchole* were also added to the repertory.

The new Metropolitan Opera House at Lincoln Center opened on 16 September 1966 with the world premiere of Barber's *Antony and Cleopatra*, in which Justino Díaz and Leontyne Price sang the title roles. Although the work was a spectacular failure, the house was a success. The seating capacity of the new auditorium (3788) is not much larger than that of the West 39th Street building (3625), but the inadequate staging facilities of the old house were replaced by a much larger stage and generous backstage quarters. The $46 million required for construction was raised in contributions by Lincoln Center and the Metropolitan Opera Association. The opera orchestra has 140 members and the chorus 80 full-time members.

In addition to accommodating the regular Metropolitan season of 32 weeks, the house is used by visiting opera and dance companies from the United States and abroad. Bing resigned in 1972 and his successor, the Swedish director Göran Gentele, died before his first season. Since then the Metropolitan Opera management has undergone several reorganizations, resulting in a gradual separation of the artistic and managerial functions. Artistic control was increasingly given to the conductor JAMES LEVINE, appointed music director in 1975. His interests ranged from the early Mozart operas to the classics of the 20th-century repertory. Notable new productions under his tenure have included *Idomeneo, Rinaldo, Lulu, Wozzeck, Mahagonny,* and *Moses und Aron*. In 2011 Fabio Luisi was named the company's principal conductor. Management of the company has been assumed by a succession of administrators: Schuyler Chapin (1972–5), Anthony Bliss (1975–85), with Levine and John Dexter, 1975–80), Bruce Crawford (1986–9), Hugh Southern (1989–90), Joseph Volpe (1990–96), and Peter Gelb (from 1996). The Metropolitan has maintained its international status as a showcase for singers suited to the scale of the auditorium, a scale that also helped determine the house production style of spectacular naive realism, represented particularly by the work of Zeffirelli. In the 1990s the company began to use in addition more exploratory directors and designers, and to broaden its hitherto traditional repertory. Corigliano's *The Ghosts of Versailles*, given its premiere on 19 December 1991, was the first new opera performed by the company since *Antony and Cleopatra*, and was followed by Glass's *The Voyage* (1992) and Harbison's *The Great Gatsby* (1999). During this period, too, Levine began giving concerts at Carnegie Hall with the Metropolitan orchestra.

Only two companies have challenged the hegemony of the Metropolitan on a regular basis. The first, Oscar Hammerstein's Manhattan Opera Company, opened in December 1906 in the Manhattan Opera House on 34th Street; Cleofonte Campanini was artistic director and conductor. Before frustrated guarantors of the Metropolitan bought him out in 1910, Hammerstein had introduced many French works to American audiences, including *Thaïs* (25 November 1907), *Louise* (3 January 1908), and *Pelléas et Mélisande* (19 February 1908), all with Mary Garden. He also presented such celebrated singers as Melba, Calvé, Tetrazzini, Renaud, and Dalmorès, in a varied repertory including the American premiere of Strauss's *Elektra* (1 February 1910).

The New York City Opera was founded as the City Center Opera Company in 1943. Opening at the City Center Theater in West 55th Street on 21 February 1944 with Dusolina Giannini as Tosca, the company has consistently encouraged participation by younger singers, composers, and audiences. At first seasons were short, a few weeks before and after the Metropolitan, but the spring and autumn periods were later lengthened to 11 weeks each, with about 175 performances given annually. A succession of conductor-managers—Laszlo Halász (1944–51), Josef Rosenstock (1952–5), Erich Leinsdorf (1956–7), and Julius Rudel (1957–79)—produced an imaginative repertory ranging from Prokofiev's *The Love for Three Oranges* (1949), Berg's *Wozzeck* (1959), Handel's *Giulio Cesare* (1971), and Monteverdi's *L'incoronazione di Poppea* (1973), to Gilbert and Sullivan, without neglecting standard works. American opera fared particularly well at the City Opera; premieres included Still's *Troubled Island* (1949), Copland's *The Tender Land* (1954), Kurka's *The Good Soldier Schweik* (1958), Douglas Moore's *The Wings of the Dove* (1961), Ward's *The Crucible* (1961), Rorem's *Miss Julie* (1965), Weisgall's *Nine Rivers from Jordan* (1968), and Menotti's *La loca* (1979). On 22 February 1966 the New York City Opera opened its spring season at its new home, the New York State Theater in Lincoln Center, with a performance of Ginastera's *Don Rodrigo*. The house (cap. 2800) was originally designed for the New York City Ballet, and was criticized as acoustically unsuited to opera, but a renovation in 1981–2 (cap. 2737) resulted in improved acoustics for opera performances.

The City Opera has always stressed ensemble production in contrast to the international star system, and has produced some fine singers, among them June Anderson, Patricia Brooks, Ashley Putnam, Samuel Ramey, John Reardon, Gianna Rolandi, BEVERLY SILLS, Norman Treigle, and Carol Vaness. Sills became director of the company in 1979, and Christopher Keene acted as music director (1982–6). Sills encouraged American conductors and opera in English. In 1984 the company was the first in the United States to introduce surtitles. The City Opera has continued to produce new works by American composers, among them Floyd's *Of Mice and Men*, Glass's *Akhnaten*, Anthony Davis's *X,* and Argento's *Casanova's Homecoming*. Productions of Bernstein's *Candide* (1982) and Sondheim's *Sweeney Todd* (1984) demonstrated Sills's interest in forging links between opera and musical theater. In 1984 the company received a gift of $5 million to make possible a regular spring season of musical comedy. Latterly one or two musical comedies have been performed each season along with traditional operas, new works (including Wiesgall's *Esther* in the company's 50th anniversary

season), and rare 20th-century European works, such as *Die Soldaten, Doktor Faust,* and *Mathis der Maler*, that became a specialty during Keene's term as general director (1989–96). Keene's successor, Paul Kellogg (1996–2007), turned attention more to the recent American past. Although its longtime Lincoln Center home, the David H. Koch Theater, underwent a substantial renovation in 2008–9. City Opera, under the leadership of George Steel (2009–), announced plans in 2011 to leave Lincoln Center and perform in other venues in New York.

Notable among the city's smaller opera companies are the Bronx Opera Company (1967), which juxtaposes standard repertory with lesser-known works; the Opera Orchestra of New York (1966), which gives unusual works in concert form; the Village Light Opera Group (1968); the New York Grand Opera (1973), which presents popular staged performances of more familiar operas, and the Dicapo Opera (1981), which mixes the familiar with the unfamiliar. Conservatories and schools combine training and performance in contemporary and standard repertory; among the most important are the Juilliard School's American Opera Center and the Manhattan School of Music. Besides the ensembles mentioned, over 40 organizations produce operas regularly.

The New York stage has also played host to more popular musical entertainment throughout its history. Following the success of ballad opera in the 18th century, parody burlesques, minstrel shows, and extravaganzas dominated the scene in the mid-19th century. *The Black Crook* (music by Thomas Baker and others, 1866), *Evangeline* (1874) by E.E. Rice, and Charles Hoyt's *A Trip to Chinatown* (1890) were particularly successful productions in a developing vernacular form that eventually fused song, dance, and plot into the American musical comedy. The musical has become an essential New York genre for theaters throughout the area, and by the 21st century, it encompasses houses outside of the aegis of the "Great White Way," including those in Brooklyn and Queens.

Operettas by Offenbach were popular from the 1860s, but in the two decades after the New York premiere of *H.M.S. Pinafore* (January 1879) European light opera by Sullivan, Audran, Millöcker, and others competed with local operetta by Caryll, Kerker, De Koven, and Herbert. Gilbert and Sullivan, Lehár, and Strauss still draw enthusiastic audiences to both opera houses and off-Broadway theaters.

GEORGE M. COHAN's first success, *Little Johnny Jones* (1904), popularized the patriotic American musical; "Give my regards to Broadway" became a theme that summed up the importance of the New York stage in the vernacular musical theater for the rest of the century. A Broadway run is an exciting opportunity for a successful musical comedy, and Broadway theaters have fostered such composers as Kern, Berlin, Gershwin, Porter, and Rodgers. Blitzstein, Menotti, Bernstein, and Sondheim have attempted to bridge the gap between the Broadway musical and opera with such works as *Regina* (1949), *The Consul* (1950), *Candide*

(1956), and *Sweeney Todd* (1979). After the Metropolitan Opera opened its house on Broadway in 1883, lavish theaters were soon built in the district around 42nd Street, such as the Lyceum (1903), Lyric (1903), Liberty (1904), Republic (later Belasco and Victory, 1907), Eltinge (later Empire, 1912), Harris (1914), Apollo (1920), and Ritz (later Walter Kerr, 1921). The area became the center of entertainment after the brothers SHUBERT began to operate their theaters in 1900. By the late 1920s the Shubert Organization owned more than 100 theaters around the country; among those in the city were the Winter Garden Theater (1911), Shubert Theatre, Booth Theater (both built in 1913), the Broadhurst Theater (1917), and the Barrymore Theater (1928), which the organization retained until the 1990s. In the mid-1990s the Shuberts owned and operated 16 Broadway theaters. Since its arrival on Broadway, the organization has produced over 500 melodramas, comedies, operettas, musicals, and reviews. The New York opening of the Walt Disney Company's first Broadway show, *Beauty and the Beast* (1994), coincided with the beginning of Disney's renovation of several theaters on 42nd Street, including the historic New Amsterdam, the theater that hosted Ziegfeld's *Follies* from 1907. As of 2011, Broadway's offerings remained a central feature of the cultural life of the city, especially as tourist attractions.

Dance also plays a vital part in New York's musical-theatrical life. Among the most prominent of the almost 100 dance companies in the city are the New York City Ballet (founded 1948), the Ballet Theatre (1939; renamed the American Ballet Theatre, 1956), the Alvin Ailey American Dance Theater (1958), the Martha Graham Dance Company (1926), and the Paul Taylor Dance Company (1961).

5. ORCHESTRAS AND BANDS. Amateur instrumental ensembles can be documented in New York at least as early as the 1770s. The St. Cecilia and Harmonical Societies joined to create the city's first Philharmonic in 1799—in which year it participated in the funeral ceremonies for George Washington. A musicians' cooperative, the Society offered semi-public Monthly Concerts plus an Annual Concert for which tickets were sold to nonmembers. It disbanded in 1816. A second Philharmonic Society, organized not by musicians but by wealthy and prominent laymen, existed from 1824 to 1827. Its conductor was Denis G. Etienne, a leading figure in the city's musical life since 1816. During the 1830s, New York orchestras increased in skill and size (in 1835, Ureli Corelli Hill observed abroad that some of the players in Spohr's Kassel orchestra were not up to New York standards). On 16 June 1842, Anthony Philip Heinrich conducted a "Grand Musical Festival" mainly featuring his own works; though he may not have realized his plan to lead 100 players, the orchestra, with Hill as concertmaster, was undoubtedly very considerable in size. A third Philharmonic Society, organized on 2 April 1842, was, like the first, cooperatively run by the musicians. Its inaugural program, at the Apollo Rooms on 7 December 1842, featured some 50 or 60 players performing for some 600 to 650 listeners. Beethoven's Fifth Symphony was led by Hill (who had introduced the work in 1841). Etienne conducted Weber's *Oberon* overture. H.C. Timm led an overture in D by Johann Wenzel Kalliwoda. Hummel's Piano Quintet in D minor and vocal selections by Beethoven, Mozart, and Rossini comprised the balance of the program (whose eclecticism of genre was typical for its time). This third New York Philharmonic is the oldest American symphonic organization in continuous existence to the present day. Its early programs included such landmark American premieres as Beethoven's Third Symphony (1843) and his Ninth (1846) for an audience of 2000 at Castle Garden. Its first season, however, numbered only three concerts. With few exceptions, four programs were given seasonally through 1857–8, five through 1867–8, six through 1896–7, eight through 1902–3, eight or nine through 1908–9. (Beginning in 1892–3, Philharmonic programs were paired with "public rehearsals"—de facto matinee concerts. As of 15 December 1905, the term "rehearsal" was dropped; the subscription programs thereafter came in pairs until the orchestra's 1909 expansion and reorganization).

That the Philharmonic remained a part-time band years after the founding of the Boston Symphony (1881) and Chicago Orchestra (1891), both with more substantial seasons, illustrates a larger reality: New York City lacked a central institution of musical performance. At the same time, according to Anton Seidl, in the 1890s it boasted the largest collection of first-rate instrumentalists of any city in the world. Its numerous theater orchestras and freelance concert ensembles performed with greater frequency than the Philharmonic or New York Symphony. In fact, a history of New York orchestras prior to World War I is best treated as a history of conductors. As the symphonic repertoire expanded and changed, as orchestras grew commensurately in size and complexity, the conductor's role was transformed. By the mid-19th century, conductors commanded special skills and authority, shaping interpretation, taste, and repertoire. In this context, Louis Jullien's New York concerts of 1853 and 1854 are a more notable benchmark than the nascent Philharmonic. However much a showman with jeweled baton, Jullien was an exacting leader whose numerous "Monster Concerts for the Masses" featured a skilled ensemble of foreign and local player in widely varied fare. Jullien's own *Firemen's Quadrille*, with simulated fire and real firemen, was one of his most popular numbers. He was also observed rehearsing Beethoven's *Pastorale* Symphony (in which he used a box of dried peas to "delineate" hail stones during the Storm) a dozen times and more to secure perfect balances and polish. His successful sponsorship of such William Henry Fry compositions as the *Santa Claus* Symphony set him apart from Germanic musicians who disdained American fare.

Of the Germans, THEODOR EISFELD became the Philharmonic's first "conductor for the season" in 1852. While Eisfeld's association with the orchestra continued through 1865, CARL BERGMANN ultimately made a more formidable impression, and may in fact be

Art Garfunkel and Paul Simon perform in Central Park, New York, 1981, for an estimated 400,000 people. (AP Photo/Handschuh)

regarded as the progenitor of New York's important Germanic conductors to come. Bergmann arrived in the United States in 1849 as a cellist with the GERMANIA MUSICAL SOCIETY, which set new performance standards throughout the United States; at its first New York concert, auditors were "awed by a sublimity of sounds too sensitively expressed to admit of more rapture than those created by supernatural agency." When the Germanians disbanded in 1854, Bergmann settled in New York. He frequently led the Philharmonic beginning in 1855, and was its sole conductor from 1865 until his retirement 11 years later. His electrifying performance of Wagner's *Tannhäuser* Overture on 21 April 1855—his first concert leading the Philharmonic—instantly made his reputation and was an early catalyst toward American WAGNERISM. Among Bergmann's other New York ventures was an 1856 series of 11 concerts with his own orchestra, including first American performances of Schumann's Fourth Symphony and Berlioz's overture *Le carnival romain*. Though Bergmann was an erratic musician (and a heavy drinker), William Mason judged him "an excellent, though not a great conductor."

THEODORE THOMAS, who displaced Bergmann in New York, was widely regarded as "great," however, and his itinerant Theodore Thomas Orchestra was judged world-class by such eminent visitors as Anton Rubinstein. Thomas's New York activities—as orchestral violinist (including concerts under Jullien), chamber musician (including concerts with Bergmann), and conductor—were multifarious. At Castle Park Gardens, beginning in 1868 with programs of light music, 1127 outdoor Theodore Thomas concerts rapidly evolved into a showcase for symphonies by Beethoven, Schubert, Mendelssohn, and Schumann. Thomas was also

conductor of the Philharmonic from 1877 to 1879 and 1879 to 1891. He also conducted the Brooklyn Philharmonic. Though he rarely led opera, he treated the symphonic Wagner and Beethoven as twin repertoire "pillars." Thomas the man was fiercely competitive. When another German conductor of consequence, Leopold Damrosch, appeared on the scene in 1871, Thomas is said to have greeted him at Schuberth's music store by vowing to "crush whoever crosses my path"—an anecdote which, if apocryphal, deserves to be true. No less than Bergmann or Thomas, Damrosch was a dedicated explorer of the newest music, especially if Germanic. Though attendance plummeted during his single season leading the Philharmonic (in programs including the entire first act of *Die Walküre* and generous excerpts from *Götterdämmerung*), he fought back with an orchestra of his own, christened the New York Symphony in 1878, by which time it had already preempted Thomas's scheduled premiere of Brahms's First Symphony. Damrosch in 1881 created a May festival of seven concerts in five days at the Seventh Regiment Armory; he conducted the American premiere of Berlioz's Requiem with a chorus of 1200. Thomas responded with *his* May festival, also at the armory, fielding a chorus of 3000. When Damrosch died suddenly in 1885, 23-year-old Walter Damrosch maintained his father's grand ambitions. A new balance of power pitted against one another Walter's New York Symphony and Oratorio Society, Anton Seidl's orchestra at the Met, and the three Thomas orchestras. If Walter was widely regarded as a mediocrity, Seidl, a charismatic Wagner protégé, introduced to New York a new podium species. In 1891—the same year that Walter Damrosch inaugurated Andrew Carnegie's Music Hall—Seidl took over Thomas's New York Philharmonic. Having previously transformed the

Metropolitan Opera into a leading German house, Seidl presided over a period of increasing Philharmonic revenues, additional Philharmonic concerts, and a new Philharmonic home: Carnegie's hall. Mainly, however, he conducted orchestras (typically contracted by Samuel Bernstein) called the Seidl Orchestra, Seidl Society Orchestra, or Metropolitan Orchestra. At Coney Island's Brighton Beach resort, he conducted 14 times a week in the summer. Seidl's New York orchestra, by whatever name, was remarkable for the size and freshness of its active repertoire. Though Wagner, Liszt, and Berlioz were favored causes, Seidl influentially led works by Edward MacDowell (whom he esteemed over Brahms), by his assistant Victor Herbert, and by his friend Antonin Dvořák, whose Symphony "From the New World" he premiered to resounding acclaim. When Seidl died in 1898, at the age of 47, he was poised to command a full time Seidl Orchestra, with Eugene Ysaÿe as concertmaster; it was to have become the pit orchestra at the Met as well as New York's premiere symphonic ensemble. Instead, the Philharmonic was cast adrift. Damrosch's New York Symphony, though a valued purveyor of novelties, lacked strong podium leadership. The Boston Symphony, a frequent New York visitor, set standards no local orchestra could meet.

This hiatus set the stage for the reorganization of the New York Philharmonic by a group of wealthy "guarantors" energetically led by Mrs. Mary Sheldon. In 1909–10, the orchestra—no longer a musicians' cooperative—expanded its season to 46 concerts, all led by Gustav Mahler. Mahler conducted 48 concerts in 1910–11 before a terminal illness forced his departure. His brief tenure was transformative but controversial. He galvanized the musicians without attaining Boston's polish. His interpretations were radically unorthodox. He feuded with the guarantors. His successor, Josef Stransky, was a lesser musician. The fate of the Philharmonic was eventually shaped by Clarence MacKay, who became chairman of the board in 1921, and ARTHUR JUDSON, who became manager in 1922. In 1928, the Philharmonic merged with the New York Symphony to become the "New York Philharmonic-Symphony Society"—a consolidation effected with the Philharmonic on top. Rather than a music director, Mackay and Judson opted for a multiplicity of conductors, with ARTURO TOSCANINI by far the dominant podium force. Toscanini's Philharmonic triumphantly toured Europe in 1930. But with his resignation in 1936 the orchestra's identity became newly diffuse. In David Sarnoff's Toscanini-led NBC Symphony (1937–54) the Philharmonic acquired a formidable rival, superior in energy, finesse, and musical leadership. Amid a plethora of guest conductors, the Philharmonic was entrusted to JOHN BARBIROLLI (1936–43), then ARTUR RODZIŃSKI (1943–47), then DIMITRI MITROPOULOS (1949–57). Aesthetically grounded in German Expressionism, Mitropoulos memorably championed such works as Mahler's Sixth Symphony (American premiere, 1947) and Berg's *Wozzeck* (1951). But he was frustrated in such efforts; his critics carped both about his programs and his performances.

Only with the departure of Judson in 1956, however, did the orchestra acquire a music director of effective missionary force: LEONARD BERNSTEIN (1958–69). Though his detractors found him too much the showman, and compared the Philharmonic unfavorably to the highly disciplined orchestras of Chicago and Cleveland, Bernstein proved a supreme educator. His impassioned advocacy of Mahler and Ives, embedded in nationally broadcast subscription concerts and nationally televised Young People's Concerts, made a permanent impact on symphonic repertoire in the United States. His thematic programming embracing surveys of American music, the 20th century symphony, and the "avant-garde"—topics of acute interest to Bernstein the composer. Though the New York Symphony had established Young People's Symphonic Concerts under Frank Damrosch in 1898, and the Philharmonic Society had launched a similar series under Ernest Schelling in 1924, the 47 televised Young People's Concerts Bernstein conceived, wrote, and narrated were a watershed; with the exception of Stokowski in Philadelphia, no previous conductor of comparable stature had so prominently embraced audiences of children and young adults. Of Bernstein's successors with the Philharmonic, PIERRE BOULEZ (1971–78) embodied the boldest artistic aspirations, peppered with new music and new formats. ZUBIN MEHTA (1978–91), KURT MASUR (1991–2002), and LORIN MAAZEL (2002–2009) pursued more conventional means and ends. Alan Gilbert, who assumed the music directorship in 2009, introduced a new emphasis on contemporary composers and community engagement.

Throughout the 20th century, innumerable smaller New York orchestras have contributed something distinctive to the city's musical life. The Russian SO (1904–18) under Modest Altschuler introduced works by Liadov, Rachmaninoff, Rimsky-Korsakov, and Scriabin; the American debuts of Josef Lhevinne (1906), Mischa Elman (1908), Rachmaninoff (1909), and Prokofiev (1918) were also made with the orchestra. The New Symphony Orchestra (1919–20), later the National Symphony Orchestra (1920–21), was led by Edgard Varèse, Artur Bodanzky, and Willem Mengelberg before merging with the New York Philharmonic. Of the city's radio orchestras, Toscanini's stellar NBC Symphony made famous recordings of the standard repertoire and toured the United States in 1950; upon Toscanini's retirement, the orchestra briefly survived as the Symphony of the Air. At CBS, Bernard Herrmann and Howard Barlow led an orchestra (1927–50) notable for repertoire excursions; Herrmann's studio guests included Bartók, Hindemith, Milhaud, Stravinsky, and Villa-Lobos. Alfred Wallenstein's Mutual Network orchestra (1933–43) also made American music a cause. Otto Klemperer and Thomas Beecham were among the conductors of a government-supported New York City Orchestra (1940–43). In 1944 a new orchestra under Stokowski was formed with the same name; the final season was conducted by Bernstein in 1947. Two post–World War II orchestras with a continuous history to the present day are the American Symphony Orchestra and American Composers

Orchestra. The former was begun by Stokowski in 1962 as an ensemble for young professionals. Since 1992 it has been sustained by Leon Botstein not as a training orchestra, but as a purveyor of thematic programs and unfamiliar repertoire; it also serves as the resident orchestra for Botstein's intellectually ambitious Bard Music Festival. The American Composers Orchestra, dedicated exclusively to native repertoire, was begun under Dennis Russell Davies in 1976; its activities diminished with his departure in 2002. Outside Manhattan, the Brooklyn Philharmonic was long the most important New York City orchestra. During its first incarnation (1857–91) the conductors were Eisfeld, Bergmann, and Thomas. A second Brooklyn Philharmonic was founded by Siegfried Landau in 1955. Under Lukas Foss (1971–90), the orchestra combined standard fare with "marathon" programming and a "Meet the Moderns" series. During the tenure of Dennis Russell Davies as principal conductor (1990–96), the Philharmonic undertook seasons of thematic, interdisciplinary programming initiated by its executive director, Joseph Horowitz, in collaboration with Harvey Lichtenstein, executive director of the Brooklyn Academy of Music (BAM). The subsequent music directors were Robert Spano (1996–2004) and Michael Christie (2005–10). A troubled relationship with BAM was largely responsible for a drastic reduction in activity; as of 2011, there were no Brooklyn Philharmonic concerts at BAM.

In New York today, Orpheus, the Orchestra of St. Luke's, and the Mostly Mozart Orchestra are prominent part-time ensembles. The Boston and Chicago Symphonies, and Cleveland and Philadelphia Orchestras are regular visitors. Carnegie Hall and Fisher Hall annually host the major orchestras of the world. As in 1900, New York in the early 21st century boasts the nation's most vigorous community of freelance orchestral musicians, competing for employment amidst a variety of symphonic institutions and events.

Bands in New York were frequently affiliated with military regiments, but played public concerts in the parks and at Manhattan and Brighton beaches. Among the most famous bandmasters in New York were the DODWORTH family, CLAUDIO S. GRAFULLA, CARLO ALBERTO CAPPA, PATRICK S. GILMORE, and later, EDWIN FRANKO GOLDMAN and his son RICHARD FRANKO GOLDMAN. The tradition of military bands in the city inspired founding of professional brass bands in the early to mid-19th century, the first of them being Thomas Dilka's Independent Band of New York formed in 1825. In 1835 Allen Dodworth took some of its members and formed the National Brass Band, which became the most successful and influential band in the city. In 1860 the bandmasters lived in the city: Harvey Dodworth led the Dodworth Band and the 13th Regiment Band of the New York National Guard; Grafulla and David L. Downing led the 9th Regiment Band; and Gilmore assumed in 1873 leadership of the 22nd Regiment Band, known from then as Gilmore's Band. After Gilmore's death in 1892, 19 musicians from the band joined the ensemble of J.P. Sousa, which became nationally renowned. Edwin Franko Goldman formed his own band in 1911, and it performed

continuously from 1918 to 1979 (from 1956 it was directed by Richard Franko Goldman). After 1980, the group was under the direction of Ainslee Cox as the Goldman Memorial Band until shutting down in 2005.

6. CHAMBER MUSIC. Few concerts devoted to chamber music were given publicly in New York before 1850. In 1851 Theodor Eisfeld initiated a series of quartet concerts including works by Haydn, Beethoven, and Mendelssohn; these were succeeded in 1855 by the renowned Mason and Thomas Chamber Music Soirées, which continued until 1868. Their fine programs included music by Schubert, Schumann, and Bach. On 27 November 1855 William Mason, Theodore Thomas, and Carl Bergmann gave the first performance of Brahms's Trio op.8. The New York Trio, founded about 1867 by Bernardus Boekelman, was active until 1888. The Kneisel Quartet (1885–1917) and the Flonzaley Quartet (1903–29), founded by the New Yorker Edward J. De Coppet, played frequently in private homes and at public concerts. The People's Symphony Concerts, a series of public chamber music concerts, were inaugurated in 1902. In 1914 the pianist Carolyn Beebe founded the New York Chamber Music Society, a group of about 12 musicians who gave regular concerts at the Plaza Hotel and elsewhere for about 25 years. The Society of the Friends of Music (1913–31) was chiefly a sponsoring organization that introduced many unfamiliar works to New York, among them Schoenberg's Chamber Symphony op.9 and Mahler's Eighth Symphony (April 1916). The Barrère Ensemble, a wind group organized in 1910 by the flautist Georges Barrère, expanded in 1915 to become the Little Symphony.

In 1936 the New Friends of Music began an annual series of 16 concerts with a repertory ranging from solo sonatas to works for chamber orchestra, carefully selected to review certain eras or specific composers; the series lasted until 1953. While groups like the New Friends of Music concentrated on 18th- and 19th-century music, contemporary music was presented in regular concerts sponsored by the League of Composers and the American section of the International Society for Contemporary Music (both founded in 1923; they merged in 1954) and the National Association for American Composers and Conductors (1933). The music of young composers was heard in the Composers' Forum, active in New York until 1940 from its foundation in 1935 by Ashley Pettis; it was revived and sponsored jointly by the New York Public Library and Columbia University from 1947 to 1980, when it was reorganized independently. Early music became popular in performances by the NEW YORK PRO MUSICA (1952–74), founded by the conductor Noah Greenberg; the 13th-century *Play of Daniel* was performed in costume in 1958 and aroused an interest in period performance.

In 1925, 40 chamber groups were identified as resident or as annual visitors; 50 years later at least 70 were resident and the number of visitors had increased. The Chamber Music Society of Lincoln Center, founded in 1968 by Charles Wadsworth with the support of Alice

Tully, gives a series of programs emphasizing unfamiliar repertory performed by outstanding musicians. Other mixed professional ensembles have included the New York Chamber Soloists (1957), Tashi (1974), the New York Philharmonia Virtuosi, the Bronx Arts Ensemble, and the Orpheus Chamber Orchestra (1972). Chamber groups based in New York have included the Juilliard (1946), Galimir, Guarneri (1964), Composers, American (1974), Concord, Emerson (1976), and Orion (1987) string quartets; the American Brass Quintet; and the New York (1947) and Dorian woodwind quintets. Ensembles specializing in contemporary music have included the Contemporary Chamber Ensemble (founded in 1960 by Arthur Weisberg), the Group for Contemporary Music (founded in 1962 by Harvey Sollberger and Charles Wuorinen), Continuum (founded in 1967 by Cheryl Seltzer and Joel Sachs as the Performers' Committee for 20th-Century Music), Speculum Musicae (1971), Parnassus, the Da Capo Chamber Players, and the New York New Music Ensemble, as well as several professional associations. Symphony Space hosts the annual New York Chamber Music Festival. Professional ensembles specializing in early music have included the Waverly Consort, the Ensemble for Early Music, the Western Wind, Music for a While, Pomerium Musices, the New York Renaissance Band, Calliope, Concert Royal, Anonymous 4, and the New York Cornet and Sackbut Ensemble. The Bach Aria Group (1946), the New York Collegium (founded in 1998 under the direction of Gustav Leonhardt), and the Neue Bach Band are among the leading specialist Baroque ensembles.

7. CHORAL SOCIETIES. The earliest choral societies included a Handel and Haydn Society, which sang the first part of *The Creation* on 10 June 1818 at St. Paul's (in Trinity Parish), and the New York Choral Society, under James Swindells, which sang there before Lafayette during his visit in July 1824. The first established group on record is the Sacred Music Society (1823–49), which sang *Messiah* (using Mozart's accompaniments) under URELI CORELLI HILL in November 1831; the society had a chorus of 73 and an orchestra of 38 at that time, and the receipts of $900 imply a large audience. In 1838 the society performed Mendelssohn's *St. Paul* and Mozart's Requiem. The first serious rival to the Sacred Music Society was the Musical Institute, founded in 1844 and directed by H.C. Timm. In 1849 the two groups merged to form the New York Harmonic Society, their first concert being a performance of Mendelssohn's *Elijah* (June 1851) in Tripler Hall. The society lasted until 1868 and its conductors included Timm, Eisfeld, Bristow, Bergmann, F.L. Ritter, and James Peck. An ambitious splinter group, the Mendelssohn Society, formed in 1863, was short-lived. In 1869 Peck directed the socially orientated Church Music Association; in 1873 Thomas imported a Boston chorus for a festival concert, an action considered an insult to the vocal and choral forces of New York.

New York's German population had two prominent men's choruses: the Deutscher Liederkranz, which gave its first concert on 17 May 1847 in the Apollo Rooms,

and the Männergesangverein Arion, an offshoot formed in 1854. The Liederkranz numbered Thomas, Bergmann, van der Stucken, and Leopold Damrosch among its conductors before 1895, while the Arion rose to prominence after getting Damrosch from Breslau to be its director in 1871. The two societies united in 1918 and celebrated a centenary in 1947. In 1866 a professional men's chorus, the Mendelssohn Glee Club, was formed, which also survived for a century. Its first permanent conductor (from 1867) was the violinist Joseph Mosenthal, a pupil of Spohr and one of the city's leading church musicians; he died in 1896 while conducting a rehearsal of the group. MacDowell then led the club until 1898; his successors were Arthur Mees, Frank Damrosch, Clarence Dickinson, Nelson Coffin, Ralph Baldwin, Cesare Sodero, and Ladislas Helfenbein. During the 20th century the membership shifted from professional to amateur singers, mainly businessmen, who sang popular favorites at private entertainments. Other men's clubs cultivating light music included the Downtown and University glee clubs, both conducted for many years by Channing Lefebvre and George Mead.

The longest-lived serious choral organization is the Oratorio Society of New York, founded in 1873 by Leopold Damrosch. Its first concert (3 December 1873) included works by Bach, Mozart, Palestrina, and Handel sung by a choir of about 50. In May 1874 the society gave Handel's *Samson* with orchestra, inaugurating the tradition of oratorio and large choral works that has continued to characterize the society's repertory. An annual Christmas performance of *Messiah* was inherited from the late Harmonic Society in 1874 and has continued to be a feature of the group's program. Late in the 19th century choruses of 400 to 600 sang Brahms's *German Requiem* (1877), Berlioz's *Grande messe des morts* (1881), Liszt's *Christus* (1887), and Saint-Saëns's *Samson et Dalila* (1892) and introduced *Parsifal* to the United States in concert form (1886). After Leopold Damrosch's death in 1885 conductors of the Oratorio Society included his sons Walter (1885–98 and 1917–21) and Frank (1898–1912), Albert Stoessel (1921–43), William Strickland (1955–9), T. Charles Lee (1960–73), Lyndon Woodside (1974–2005), and Kent Tritle (2006–).

Two organizations encouraging popular participation in music were the People's Choral Union and Singing Classes, organized in the city's Lower East Side by Frank Damrosch in 1892 and continuing into the 1930s, and the People's Chorus of New York, founded in 1916 and until 1954 conducted by Lorenzo Camilieri. Both groups sometimes assembled choirs of 1000 voices.

Musical life was enriched by the Musical Art Society, a professional mixed chorus conducted by Frank Damrosch for 26 years from 1894, which performed Palestrina, Bach, and the a cappella repertory. Contemporary choral music including Pfitzner's *Von deutscher Seele* (1923) and Honegger's *Le roi David* (1925) was presented by the Society of the Friends of Music (1913–31).

The Schola Cantorum grew out of a women's chorus established by Kurt Schindler in 1909, which became a mixed ensemble in 1910 and adopted its later name in 1912. Schindler conducted the choir until 1926, when Hugh Ross began a long tenure ending only with the group's final concert in 1971. The Schola Cantorum's programs often included unfamiliar works; Schindler introduced traditional and religious music from the Basque region and Catalonia, and Ross conducted the New York premieres of such works as Bloch's *Sacred Service* (1934), Walton's *Belshazzar's Feast* (1935), Stravinsky's *Perséphone* (1936), and Delius's *Mass of Life* (1938).

Baroque music performed in period style characterized the programs of the Cantata Singers, founded in 1934 by Paul Boepple, remaining active until 1969; later conductors of the ensemble—Arthur Mendel (1936–53), Alfred Mann (1953–9), Thomas Dunn (1959–67), and Robert Hickok (1968–9)—were also noted for their scholarship. The Dessoff Choirs grew out of Margarete Dessoff's Adesdi Chorus of women's voices organized in 1924; a mixed choir was begun in 1928, and from 1930 the combined ensembles directed by Dessoff performed under the present name. Boepple conducted the groups (which merged in 1942) from 1937 to 1968; subsequent conductors have included Michael Hammond (1973–82), Amy Kaiser (1983–95), and Kent Tritle (1996–2004). The Dessoff Choirs perform mixed programs ranging from Baroque to contemporary music. The Collegiate Chorale was founded in 1941 by Robert Shaw and conducted by him until 1954 with assistance (1949–52) from Margaret Hillis and William Jonson. Later conductors were Mark Orton (1953–4), Ralph Hunter (1954–60), Abraham Kaplan (1961–73), Richard Westenburg (1973–9), Robert Bass (1979–2008), and James Bagwell (2009–); this amateur ensemble has performed both large standard works and contemporary pieces.

Musica Sacra, organized by Westenburg in 1970 at the 5th Avenue Presbyterian Church, has become the most prominent professional choral ensemble in New York. Organizations employing professional choral singers have included the National Chorale (founded 1959) led by Martin Josman, the Amor Artis Chorus and Orchestra (1961) led by Johannes Somary, the Gregg Smith Singers (1961), Musica Aeterna (1969), Musica Viva of New York (1977) led by Walter Klauss, Musicians of Melodious Accord (1984), and the New York Concert Singers (1988). The amateur St. Cecilia Chorus, formed in 1906 by Victor Harris as a women's chorus, was expanded to a mixed ensemble in 1964. Other choruses have included the Canterbury Choral Society (1952), Masterwork Chorus (1955), the New York Choral Society (1959), Canby Singers (1960), the Boys Choir of Harlem (1968), the New Amsterdam Singers (1968–72 as the Master Institute Chorus), the Canticum Novum Singers (1972), the Sine Nomine Singers (1973), the Cappella Nova (1975), the New Calliope Singers (1976), the New York City Gay Men's Chorus (1980), the Riverside Choral Society (1980), the Russian Chamber Chorus of New York (1985), and the New York City Master Chorale (2005).

8. Religious music. Trinity Church at the top of Wall Street became the first important center of music in New York through the activity of William Tuckey, and the church continued to exert a powerful influence over sacred music in the city for more than two centuries. The first organist, John Clemm (1741–4), was probably the son of Johann Gottlob Klemm, the builder of the organ. After a fallow period, during which George K. Jackson's Te Deum in F was sung weekly for more than two decades, the newly rebuilt Trinity Church was consecrated in 1846, with the English musician Edward Hodges as its music director and organist. He introduced a boys' choir and a new repertory close to that of an English cathedral. Eighteen thousand people attended a two-day inauguration of a new organ by Henry Erben, installed in the rebuilt church in 1846. Later organists there included H.S. Cutler, A.H. Messiter, Victor Baier, Channing Lefebvre, George Mead, and Larry King, the last four of whom maintained the popular tradition of midday concerts.

One of the first examples of psalmody published in New York was *Psalms of David for the Dutch Reformed Church* (1767); a later important collection of psalm settings was *A Selection of Psalm Tunes for Use of the Protestant Episcopal Church in New York* (1812), revised in 1828 to include the works of five American composers. Thomas Hastings held various positions in New York from 1832 to 1872 and was an influential force in the city's musical development.

During the 19th century many churches developed extensive musical programs. Large mixed choirs, led by quartets of highly paid professional singers, and organs with several manuals became standard. Many distinguished organists, who often shared the duties of choir director, composer and teacher, served in the city, among them Samuel P. Warren at Grace Episcopal (1867–94), George W. Warren at St. Thomas's (1870–1900), and Harry Rowe Shelley at the Church of the Pilgrims and Central Congregational in Brooklyn and at the Fifth Avenue Baptist Church (1878–1936). G.W. Warren's son Richard held positions in various city churches for 50 years from 1880. William Crane Carl was at the First Presbyterian from 1892 to 1936, and Walter Henry Hall was active in New York from 1896 to 1935 at several churches, among them the Cathedral of St. John the Divine. Ives served at Central Presbyterian (1900–02), and in Brooklyn R. Huntington Woodman was at the First Presbyterian (1880–1941), John Hyatt Brewer in several positions from 1871 to 1930, and Dudley Buck at Holy Trinity (1877–1901).

Pietro Alessandro Yon at St. Francis Xavier (1908–26) and St. Patrick (1927–43), Clarence Dickinson at Brick Presbyterian (1909–59), and T. Tertius Noble at St. Thomas's (1912–47) had long, distinguished careers. Like many of their colleagues they published anthems and larger choral works, the octavo editions of which sold millions of copies. Seth Daniels Bingham at Madison Avenue Presbyterian (1912–51), Samuel A. Baldwin (active 1895–1932), and W. Lynnwood Farnam at the Church of the Holy Communion (1920–30) were especially fine organists.

Although choirs have become smaller, many churches maintain the practice of performing large-scale sacred works, often on Sunday afternoons or evenings. Among these musically active churches are St. Bartholomew, the Church of the Ascension, Riverside, St. Thomas, the Cathedral of St. John the Divine, the Church of our Savior, Holy Trinity Lutheran, St. Patrick's Cathedral, St. Ignatius Loyola, First Presbyterian, the Fifth Avenue Presbyterian, St. Mary the Virgin, Corpus Christi, and St. Peter Lutheran (noted for its jazz and choral programs). In the tower of the Riverside Church is the Laura Spelman Rockefeller Memorial Carillon, which with its 74 bells is the largest in the world. Significant music ensembles are also supported by the Russian Orthodox Cathedral of St. Nicholas and the Armenian St. Vartan Cathedral. Synagogues notable for their music are the Temple Emanu-El, Central Synagogue, and the Ashkenazi synagogue B'nai Jeshurun.

9. AVANT-GARDE MUSIC. The conscious cultivation of experimental musical activity in New York dates from the 1920s, and was the result of the convergence of several trends. One was the nascent self-awareness of American composers. Another was the rise of New York as the capital of American culture and its music business. A third was the sudden internationalism forced on American artists and intellectuals by the country's involvement in World War I. The timing meant that avant-garde activities in New York had a distinctively French cast: most of the composers active in New York between the world wars had studied in Paris with Nadia Boulanger (above all Copland and Thomson) or were part of EDGARD VARÈSE's circle.

Organizations sponsoring new music included the LEAGUE OF COMPOSERS (founded 1923), with which Copland was deeply involved (its journal *Modern Music*, 1924–46, was particularly influential), the American section of the INTERNATIONAL SOCIETY FOR CONTEMPORARY MUSIC (ISCM), and two organizations founded by Varèse—the International Composers' Guild and the Pan American Association of Composers. Cowell's series of scores (*New Music*), begun in 1927, was also important. The Composers' Forum, founded in 1935, carried on the sponsorship of new-music concerts.

The arrival in New York of many important European composers, notably Bartók and Wolpe, reinforced internationalist tendencies and fostered a younger generation of American composers who came to dominate new music after World War II. Beginning in the 1950s New York avant-gardism became marked by a division of sensibilities that was subsequently labeled "uptown" and "downtown." More visible at first was the "uptown" serialist school (and its non-serialist but equally rationalist allies), linked with the academy. This group not only controlled the concerts of the combined League of Composers and ISCM, but later founded new performance groups that specialized in dense, highly dissonant, chromatic music: the Group for Contemporary Music, Speculum Musicae (1971), and the New York New Music Ensemble (1975).

The rationalist sensibility was also active in the first American experiments in electronic music, which centered on New York. Landmark events included the

creation by Cage of the tape work *Imaginary Landscape no.5* (1951–2) and the first American tape-music concert, which Luening and Ussachevsky produced on 28 October 1952 at the Museum of Modern Art. In 1959 the RCA Mark II synthesizer was installed at Columbia University and the COLUMBIA-PRINCETON ELECTRONIC MUSIC CENTER, directed by Babbitt, Luening, Ussachevsky, and Sessions, was founded.

Cage's work became the focus of "downtown" new-music activity in the 1950s. His closest disciples were Christian Wolff, David Tudor, Morton Feldman, and Earle Brown; their work was paralleled by the New York activities of Fluxus, which prefigured the varied forms of mixed-media experimentation of the 1960s and beyond. Allan Kaprow, the inventor of "happenings," was part of the Cage circle, as were Toshi Ichiyanagi, Jackson Mac Low, Nam June Paik, and La Monte Young.

Experimental concerts were held at nightclubs such as the Electric Circus and at the major New York art museums (the Whitney, the Guggenheim, the Museum of Modern Art) long before they were accepted by the more conservative midtown musical organizations. But the bulk of experimental activity since the 1970s has taken place under the auspices of organizations located in lower Manhattan. Chief among them are the Kitchen, the Experimental Intermedia Foundation, Roulette, and the Alternative Museum. Bang On a Can, founded in 1987, has been a particularly active group.

Some performers, notably Glass, Reich, Laura Dean, and Laurie Anderson, succeeded in expanding their audiences by appearing in rock clubs. By the early 1980s experimental music in New York had begun to overlap with avant-garde jazz and rock. Composers such as Glenn Branca, Rhys Chatham, Peter Gordon, and John Zorn, and bands including Sonic Youth, moved freely between experimental performance spaces and rock clubs; avant-garde rock musicians, among them Arto Lindsay and Elliot Sharp, have attracted some attention from new-music circles, and jazz composers such as Henry Threadgill and Joseph Jarman played both at jazz clubs and in Weill Recital Hall.

Experimental music has long been a limited offering at the city's major halls. By the 1980s, however, signs were pointing to the acceptance of experimental music in more traditional locations. The Brooklyn Academy of Music became an important sponsor of new-music activities with its "Next Wave" events and festivals. At Lincoln Center, Horizons festivals in 1983 and 1984, sponsored by the New York PO under the direction of composer-in-residence Jacob Druckman, offered a dramatic midtown showcase for a wide variety of new music. Other performing groups—the American Composers Orchestra, the Composers' Showcase and Continuum—have specialized in contemporary music while steering a course between the various new-music factions.

10. RAGTIME AND JAZZ. New York's role in jazz history has always been significant, and from the mid-1920s decisive: it has attracted the finest musicians; provided the

most favorable opportunities for performing, hearing, broadcasting, and recording the music; and has been the home of most important innovations. It was the seat of the ragtime craze early in the 20th century: elements of the pioneering "classic" Missouri school, including ragtime king Scott Joplin and his publisher John Stark, transferred to New York in the first decade, and New York's own school of ragtime became the country's most active, and certainly the most published. Much of the style informed the Harlem school of stride pianists, who performed and entertained at clubs and private social functions; they were frequently recorded, and their high technical standards and inventive improvisation influenced many later jazz pianists.

Small- and large-band jazz were slower to develop, but the point of departure was again ragtime, especially as performed (and as early as 1898 recorded) by Sousa's Band and those of his rivals Arthur Pryor and Charles Prince. Later bands played orchestral ragtime well into the 1920s on a scale indicated by the names of groups like the Fifty Merry Moguls, whose leader Fred Bryan was known as "the jazz Sousa." These and New York's dance bands, which proliferated in the many large dance halls founded during Prohibition, became the basis of the city's orchestral jazz in the 1920s. The success of the ORIGINAL DIXIELAND JAZZ BAND on their appearance in New York in 1917 is not surprising; other white groups playing a similar bowdlerization of New Orleans style had already appeared in New York, but without the combination of showmanship and shrewd publicity that allowed the ODJB to bring jazz in quick succession to the city's, the nation's and Europe's attention. In January 1917 the ODJB made the first jazz recording; their second, made in February and featuring "Livery Stable Blues" and "Dixie Jass Band One Step," had sold two million copies by the end of the year. Their success spawned hundreds of similarly named white jazz groups in the city, of which the much recorded Original Memphis Five was the most important.

Jazz elements were also adopted by many of the city's dance bands, particularly that of PAUL WHITEMAN, whose name became a byword for jazz in the 1920s. Although Whiteman's "symphonic jazz" was later critiqued as a vitiated form of the music, he hired significant jazz performers such as Bix Beiderbecke and Frankie Trumbauer, and his performances set standards of musicianship that were emulated by large jazz ensembles throughout the country.

Among the important African American bands in New York were those of FLETCHER HENDERSON and DUKE ELLINGTON. Each of these leaders hired first-rate jazz soloists as early as 1924, notably Louis Armstrong (with Henderson) and Sidney Bechet (with Ellington). Henderson's arranger Don Redman was among the first to transform Armstrong's "hot" style into an orchestral idiom, developing a repertory that influenced much of the swing-band music of the following decade. Less influential, though of high artistic merit, were the experiments of Ellington, who from the mid-1920s combined commercial dance music with ingenious idiomatic arrangements and later produced what are widely regarded as the most significant jazz compositions.

By the end of the 1920s New York had become the center of the American jazz scene. Armstrong, Jelly Roll Morton, King Oliver, and Red Allen, the leading musicians in the late New Orleans style, all lived there, as did most of the important musicians of the Chicago school following the suppression of that city's underground speakeasy culture. Big bands following the Henderson model proliferated: bandleaders such as Henderson, Ellington, Luis Russell, Jimmie Lunceford, Cab Calloway, Chick Webb, Benny Goodman, and Charlie Barnet all performed, broadcast, and recorded in New York in the 1930s, and Count Basie's group, the most important jazz orchestra of the competing Kansas City tradition, was based in New York from 1937. The recognition of jazz by the country's established musical institutions was marked in 1938 by Goodman's concert at Carnegie Hall, and the country's historical interest in the genre was demonstrated there the same year by John Hammond's retrospective "Spirituals to Swing" concerts.

Small-ensemble jazz was generally not popular in the 1930s, but the repeal of the Prohibition Amendment had led to the establishment of numerous small clubs in New York, at some of which small jazz ensembles played. A number of clubs in 52nd Street (Onyx, Famous Door, and Kelly's Stable) promoted advanced swing jazz in small combinations. Minton's Playhouse and Monroe's Uptown House, both in Harlem, were later indispensable to the bop school, which originated in New York in the early 1940s and was almost exclusively a small-group form. Café Society, Birdland, Half Note, Five Spot, Village Vanguard, and Village Gate were all clubs that presented the most creative modern jazz of the 1940s and 1950s. The Five Spot in particular fostered avant-garde jazz, most famously through the appearances of Cecil Taylor in 1957 and Ornette Coleman in 1959. Although developments in this genre also took place in Europe, New York shared with Chicago the leadership of the free-jazz scene and saw the origins in the 1960s of groups such as the New York Contemporary Five with John Tchicai and Don Cherry, the New York Art Quartet, the Jazz Composer's Orchestra, and the musicians associated with LeRoi Jones's Black Arts Repertory Theater-School. Two developments of the late 1960s and early 1970s had a lasting effect on New York's jazz culture: the ascendance of rock music, which made it difficult for jazz musicians to find employment or recording opportunities, and a deep economic crisis, which caused many clubs to close and many musicians to relocate to other cities (particularly New Orleans and Los Angeles). Emulating visual artists and experimental classical musicians, some jazz players organized and performed in lofts, abandoned upper-story warehouses available at relatively low rents. The jazz loft scenes in SoHo (South of Houston Street) and Tribeca (Triangle Below Canal Street) led to highly interesting developments in avant-garde jazz in the work of such musicians as Sam Rivers, David Murray, Henry Threadgill, and Julius Hemphill, and groups such as the World

Saxophone Quartet. Many of their stylistic innovations also found their way into the postmodern aesthetic and "world music" of the late 1980s.

With the city's economic recovery from the late 1970s New York regained much of its former influence as a jazz capital. The revival of bebop brought many older musicians back to the United States from self-imposed European exile, and several excellent repertoire orchestras were founded with the object of cultivating the historical styles of the jazz tradition. Among these ensembles were the American Jazz Orchestra, the Carnegie Hall Jazz Orchestra, and the Lincoln Center Jazz Orchestra. In 1996, Jazz at Lincoln Center (JALC) became an autonomous division of the Lincoln Center for the Performing Arts. With Wynton Marsalis at the helm, JALC has presented an enormous array of jazz events, including thousands of concerts, lectures, and educational programs. Equally important was the recognition of mainstream jazz in the curriculum of Juilliard and other music schools, ensuring a continuous influx of talented and highly trained young musicians into the jazz scene. Avant-garde jazz continued to flourish at the Knitting Factory (founded in 1987), where experimentation and crossovers with ethnic musics, notably klezmer, were cultivated. Today New York's jazz scene is no longer confined to Manhattan and longstanding clubs such as the Village Vanguard; jazz can also be found in the city's other boroughs, particularly Brooklyn, to which the Knitting Factory relocated in 2008. Although many of today's jazz musicians are financially dependent on overseas tours for their livelihood, New York's concentration of media and creative artists is sufficient to ensure that the city remains the nerve center of America's jazz culture.

11. Popular music since 1950. Although rock and roll originated largely in the South and Midwest during the 1950s, Manhattan became a central location by the end of the decade. Most of the largest record labels, music publishers, television networks, and radio stations with the widest audience base were situated in New York, which prompted broadcasters, performers, producers, and songwriters to move to the city; disc jockey Alan Freed moved from his Cleveland radio station to become a personality at New York station WINS, and Dick Clark commuted from Philadelphia to broadcast his weekly television show.

New York-based pop songwriters, many of whom worked for music publishers in the Brill building on Broadway, were especially active in the late 1950s and early 1960s. Jerry Leiber, Mike Stoller, Burt Bacharach, Hal David, and Carole King, among others, wrote songs for girl groups (the Shangri-Las, the Ronettes), and male singers (the Drifters, Neil Sedaka, the Righteous Brothers). Some drew on Latin music they heard at the Palladium Ballroom (opened 1947; closed 1966) and integrated Puerto Rican and Afro-Cuban musical styles and rhythms. Successful producers such as Atlantic Records' Jerry Wexler released the latest R&B, soul, and rock hits.

In the 1960s Greenwich Village, a haven for folk music since the 1940s, fostered a new generation of folk-singers, performers, and singer-songwriters, many of whom later gained mainstream popularity. New York transplants Bob Dylan and Jimi Hendrix, as well as city natives Simon and Garfunkel, and Peter, Paul and Mary, gave critical early performances at Village clubs Café Wha?, Folk City, and the Bitter End.

During the 1970s, New York saw the development of glam, punk, disco, and hip hop. In the early 1970s the Velvet Underground held a regular residency at Max's Kansas City, a club that proved important to the glam rock and punk scenes and later featured early performances by Madonna (as lead vocalist for the group Emmy), the New York Dolls, Iggy and the Stooges, Blondie, and Patti Smith. CBGB (1973–2006; see CBGB & OMFUG) became popular for the fast-paced, often sharp-tongued rock music that would come to be called punk and also hosted new wave bands. The Ramones, Talking Heads, and other New York natives, as well as the Misfits, the Police, and Bad Brains, performed important early gigs at the small Bowery club.

Disco also flourished in 1970s Manhattan. In 1970 David Mancuso opened the Loft, which hosted members-only parties and featured recent dance music. As disco emerged from underground clubs around the city, DJs spun records for patrons at splashy New York disco clubs including Paradise Garage, Xenon, and, most famously, STUDIO 54. Disco, Latin dance music, and funk also contributed to the development of hip hop music at street parties and community events in the Bronx. While hip-hop recordings were not released until 1979, the club Disco Fever in the Bronx had begun supporting the hip-hop scene by 1977; pioneering Bronx rap group Grandmaster Flash and the Furious Five was among the first rap groups to perform there. In the 1980s and 1990s, hip hop continued to be a major force in New York. Independent New York record labels Def Jam Records (founded 1984) and Profile Records (founded 1981) released hip hop, rhythm-and-blues, house, and Latin freestyle. Many young New York City audiences embraced hip hop, metal, and hardcore punk alike. The Beastie Boys, a group comprised of such Brooklyn and Manhattan teens, moved between hardcore punk and hip hop in their early years; Queens rappers Run-D.M.C. became the world's biggest rap stars and pioneered rap-rock. These and other New York rap groups propelled the international popularity of hip-hop, which continued with Brooklyn rappers Notorious B.I.G. and Jay-Z, Staten Island hip-hop group Wu-tang Clan, and many more. (See Hip hop; Rap.)

Hip hop and post-disco musics such as house and techno filled popular dance clubs such as Area, Danceteria, and Limelight during the 1980s. DJs like Funhouse resident "JELLYBEAN" BENITEZ popularized the dance-pop of Madonna (whom he also produced), and the Latin freestyle of Shannon and the Cover Girls. New rock-inflected genres also emerged in the 1980s, as Sonic Youth helped usher in "noise-rock," a subgenre of post-punk, and local singer-songwriter Suzanne Vega was part of a folk-rock revival.

The 1990s saw a resurgence of dance music at Manhattan clubs MARS, Red Zone, The Tunnel, and MK.

Deee-Lite and other groups gained pop success with a dance style that blended hip-hop and house. Techno clubs such as NASA were among the first to popularize British rave culture and drum 'n' bass music in the United States. New York natives Mariah Carey and Jennifer Lopez found mainstream pop success mixing dance-pop, hip hop, and Latin freestyle.

In the 2000s a new generation of New York natives and local performing arts school alumni emerged as mainstream performers: singer/pianist Alicia Keys (Professional Performing Arts School), singer Lady Gaga (NYU Tisch School for the Arts), and rapper Nicki Minaj (LaGuardia High School for the Performing Arts) found pop stardom. Williamsburg (Brooklyn) and lower Manhattan became hosts to a new scene of progressive indie-rock bands including T.V. on the Radio, LCD Soundsystem, the Strokes, and the Yeah Yeah Yeahs.

12. ETHNIC MUSIC. "Ethnic" is an ambiguous term of difference typically associated with immigrant minority communities, and defining "ethnic music" in New York is particularly complicated. At the beginning of the 21st century, approximately 55% of New York's population—already far and away the most populous city in the country—was comprised of immigrants and their children. The number of ethnic New Yorkers grows higher once it includes those further removed from immigration, "internal immigrants" from other parts of the United States, and satellite communities outside the city. Each of these hundreds of ethnic communities is internally diverse, with complex relationships to a continually shifting set of neighboring groups. Furthermore, New York is the foremost symbol of American immigration, long associated with the "melting pot" (as in Israel Zangwill's famous play), "salad bowl," or "glorious mosaic." Considering these factors, much—or even most—of New York's musical life can be considered "ethnic" in one way or another.

The central importance of ethnic musical life in New York has contributed to a landscape in which public presentations of clearly bounded ethnic groups exist in tension with the internal needs and desires of variously constituted, ever-changing communities. Immigrants in New York have clustered in neighborhoods with mutual aid societies, music clubs, theaters, restaurants, houses of worship, and dance halls catering to their communities. Sometimes enclaves with proper names such as Little Italy and Chinatown—and sometimes existing within, overlapping with, or spread across other neighborhoods—these are sites of internal negotiation as people from different origins, often speaking different languages or dialects, live newly side-by-side under a singular umbrella of ethnic identity. Through the 19th and early 20th centuries, of the many different groups in New York, the Chinese (primarily Cantonese-speaking), German, Jewish (primarily Yiddish-speaking), Irish, and Italian communities made some of the most influential contributions to the city's musical life. Public displays with ethnic music such as the St. Patrick's Day parade (started in 1762) and the Feast of San Gennaro in Little Italy (started in 1926) have long been staples of New York life, attended by celebrants from all walks of life.

The close proximity of diverse ethnic populations has made New York a wellspring for cross-cultural interaction. New York has been a leading site of globally influential interethnic exchanges based in African diasporic musics, the most prominent being the multiple collaborations between African Americans, Jewish Americans, and Latin Americans in the broader spheres of jazz, American popular song, salsa, and later, hip hop. Many musicians and the styles they performed straddled the spheres of "ethnic" and mainstream musical contexts.

Ethnic music in New York underwent major transformations during the 20th century, along with new understandings of the idea of ethnicity and changes to the city's demographics. The emergence of multiculturalism in the 1960s led to increased public awareness of ethnic groups and performance opportunities. The Balkan Arts Center (later the Ethnic Folk Arts Center, and later still the Center for Traditional Music and Dance), founded in 1968, presents music of New York's immigrant groups and establishes institutions dedicated to the transmission of transplanted practices. In the last decades of the 20th century many more institutions, concert series, media outlets, and academic programs devoted to ethnic groups were developed, resulting in an unprecedented network of musicians, scholars, and agents of cultural institutions, with some individuals participating in all three roles. The World Music Institute, originally started in 1976, presents ethnic music, as do Carnegie Hall, Lincoln Center, and other mainstream venues. Public celebrations have become ubiquitous, some of the most prominent being the Lunar New Year and Eid al-Fitr events held throughout the city, the West Indian parade in Brooklyn, and the Holi celebration in Richmond Hill, Queens.

Since 1970 the landscape of ethnic New York has changed dramatically, characterized by tremendous diversity; before, most of New York's immigrants hailed from Europe. Over 130 languages are spoken in the borough of Queens alone. The ethnic communities that have partnered with the Center for Traditional Music and Dance gives a sense of the city's demographics at the beginning of the 21st century: these include the Albanian, Arab, Asian-Indian, Chinese, Colombian, Dominican, Filipino, Greek, Indo-Caribbean, Irish, Italian, Macedonian, Mexican, Peruvian, Puerto Rican, Soviet Jewish, Ukrainian, and West African communities. Some other immigrant groups with significant populations in New York are Afro-Trinidadians, Bangladeshis, Cubans, Ecuadorians, Guyanese, Haitians, Hondurans, Jamaicans, Koreans, Pakistanis, Poles, Russians, and Vietnamese. Many new immigrants have significantly altered the fabric of New York's historic ethnic communities. Chinese immigrants from various regions and ethnic groups have transformed Chinatown, once dominated by Cantonese; Jews from North Africa, Asia, and the former Soviet Union have changed the composition of the city's Jewish population; and African immigrants from Mali, Guinea, Sierra Leone, Senegal, and other countries have similarly transformed the city's African American community.

Multiculturalism has exerted strong pressures for immigrants and minorities in New York to define themselves in relation to one clearly bounded ethnicity, with ramifications for musicians and their repertoires. Some repertoires have been subject to reethnicization, such as the remodeling of various Eastern European repertoires performed by turn-of-the-century Jewish immigrants as a singular genre, klezmer music. Some particular styles have become symbolic loci of ethnic expression, such as bhangra for South Asians, plena and bomba for Puerto Ricans, and merengue and bachata for Dominicans. In some cases, music often glossed as universal or "Western classical" might be considered "ethnic," such as Italian opera among Italian Americans. One productive strategy for many musicians in New York has been to organize ethnic ensembles that draw on a variety of classical, light-classical, folk, and popular repertoires to represent one ethnic identity, such as Music from China or the Bukharan Jewish Ensemble Shashmaqam.

Musicians from various ethnic groups have also increasingly participated in intercultural fusion groups, inspired by the world music phenomenon, which depend on explicit combinations of ethnically marked instruments, rhythms, or other stylistic aspects; one example is Min Xiao-Fen's Blue Pipa Trio. Others have continued their careers with interethnic ensembles based in one style, such as Mamady Kouyaté, a guitarist with Guinea's Bembeya Jazz whose Afropop group in New York, the Mandingo Ambassadors, contains Guinean, Euro-American, African American, Israeli, and French Canadian members. It should also be noted that while certain repertoires operate as signals of ethnic identity in mainstream public or "world music" contexts, internal community events often reflect a tremendous amount of stylistic diversity, with folkloric and explicitly ethnic repertoires represented alongside globally popular styles such as Indian film music, American rap music and rock, or Cantopop. African American music, especially jazz and hip hop, has continued to be a tremendously important resource for immigrants— including, but not limited to, those from Africa and throughout the African diaspora—developing ethnic American musics.

13. EDUCATION. Music schools offering professional training became important in New York in the second half of the 19th century. One of the longest-lived was the New York College of Music, founded in 1878. Having absorbed the German Conservatory in 1920 and the American Conservatory in 1923, it was itself incorporated into New York University in 1968. The National Conservatory of Music in America, founded by JEANETTE THURBER in 1885, was granted a national charter in 1891, and ANTONÍN DVOŘÁK was director from 1892 to 1895. Although by 1910 the conservatory's reputation rivaled that of the Peabody, Cincinnati, and New England conservatories, it fell far behind these private institutions in funding and ultimately succumbed to public apathy.

A Metropolitan Conservatory, begun as a school of singing in 1886, became the Metropolitan College of Music in 1891 and the American Institute of Applied Music in 1900. It survived some 40 years but eventually succumbed to financial troubles. Settlement schools founded to provide musical training for underprivileged children fared better. The Henry Street Settlement (1893), Third Street Music School Settlement (1894), Greenwich House Music School (1906), and Turtle Bay Music School (1925) are among those that survive. In 1899 William C. Carl, a former student of Guilmant, founded at the First Presbyterian Church the Guilmant Organ School, the first American school devoted exclusively to the training of organists and choirmasters.

The Juilliard School, a conservatory of international reputation, was begun by Frank Damrosch in 1905 as the Institute of Musical Art. In 1924 the Juilliard Musical Foundation bestowed an endowment of approximately $23 million on a graduate school, which subsequently with the institute became known as the Juilliard School of Music. Later presidents have been John Erskine (1928–37), Ernest Hutcheson (1937–45), William Schuman (1945–62), Peter Mennin (1962–83), and Joseph W. Polisi (1984–). Before moving to Lincoln Center in 1968 the school incorporated a drama division, raised the dance department to divisional status and changed the name to the Juilliard School. Two notable components of the school are the Pre-College Division, devoted to teaching younger students in the arts, and the Music Advancement Program, which offers music lessons to underprivileged children in the city.

The Mannes College of Music was founded in 1916 by DAVID MANNES and his wife Clara Damrosch. First known as the David Mannes School, the college became a degree-granting institution in 1953, changing its name to Mannes College: the New School for Music in 2005; it was the first school of music in the United States to offer a degree in the performance of early music. Leopold Mannes was director from 1940 until his death in 1964. The school has played a particularly important role in the development of music theory in the United States. The Manhattan School of Music, a conservatory founded by Janet Schenck in 1917, offers undergraduate and graduate degrees. Its program in orchestral performance, founded in 1991, was the first of its kind in the United States. John Brownlee, president from 1966 to 1969, expanded the school's opera department, and in 1969 George Schick became president and the school moved to the Claremont Avenue building vacated by the Juilliard School. He was succeeded by John Crosby (1976–91), Marta Istomin (1992–2005), and Robert Sirota (2005–). The New School for Social Research added music to its curriculum in the 1920s. After 1933 it became a sanctuary for Jewish and socialist scholars who greatly influenced academic music education in the United States.

Two private universities in the city have strong academic courses in music. Columbia received its first endowment for the study of music in 1896. The first professor of music was EDWARD MACDOWELL. Paul Henry Lang was appointed professor of musicology at Columbia in 1939, and in

1944 Otto Leuning, a co-founder of the Columbia-Princeton Electronic Music Studio, became professor of the music department at Barnard College, then Columbia's women's affiliate. The university's Teachers College, devoted to graduate study in education, also maintains an active music department. New York University offers advanced degrees in musicology and education. Two of its specialties include writing for musical theater and film music composition; NYU hosts an annual conference, Music and the Moving Image, that celebrates the latter field of study. Union Theological Seminary's School of Sacred Music (1923–73) was absorbed by Yale University in 1974.

The City University of New York consists of a graduate center and many four- and two-year colleges, most of which offer both academic and practical instruction in music. Hunter, Queens, Brooklyn, and City colleges have traditionally strong music departments. In 1981 the Brooklyn and Queens departments were renamed respectively the Conservatory of Music and the Aaron Copland School of Music; the former is the seat of the H. Wiley Hitchcock Institute for Studies in American Music (founded 1971). A doctoral program at the CUNY Graduate Center at 365 Fifth Avenue was established in 1968 by Barry S. Brook. Since 1987 it has also offered a program in performance. The institution is the home of two bibliographical projects, the Répertoire International de Littérature Musicale (RILM) and the Répertoire International d'Iconographie Musicale (RIdIM), as well as the "Music in Gotham" Project, founded by John Graziano and Adrienne Fried Block.

State schools offered sporadic music education from 1856, but no clear course until 1898. In 1976 nearly 1700 music teachers served in elementary and secondary schools. The High School of Music and Art, from 1984 combined with the High School of the Performing Arts as the Fiorello LaGuardia High School, provides an opportunity for students to specialize in music theory, history, and performance, along with regular academic subjects. In addition to the settlement schools, instruction is available at such schools as the Harlem School of the Arts, the Dalcroze and Diller-Quaile schools, and the Bloomingdale House of Music. Several foundations and music schools exist across the five boroughs for the education of those wishing to study music, with many of these especially dedicated to teaching the youth of the city.

14. Associations and organizations. One of the first associations organized to promote the works of local composers was the Manuscript Society, founded in 1889 and reorganized in 1899 as the Society of American Musicians and Composers. In 1914 a group of men concerned principally with popular music, including Victor Herbert and Irving Berlin, formed the American society of composers, authors, and publishers (ASCAP), later the foremost American association for the protection of copyright musical works. ASCAP is a non-profit-making organization, representing both serious and popular music, which collects and distributes licensing fees for public performance. Broadcast music, inc. (BMI),

established in 1940, performs a similar function. The American composers alliance (ACA), founded in 1937 by Copland and others, was later affiliated with BMI. National in scope, these organizations have their headquarters in New York. Organized labor is represented in New York by Local 802 of the American Federation of Musicians, which includes instrumental ensemble musicians in all spheres, and the American guild of musical artists (AGMA), which has represented opera and concert artists since its formation in 1936.

Other non-profit-making organizations in the city have been actively concerned with the promotion of music and the welfare of musicians. The Beethoven Association (1918–40) under its president Harold Bauer was an important force in sponsoring concerts, publications, and charitable works. The National federation of music clubs (founded 1898) encourages young musicians throughout the country. The American Music Center (1939) has served as a reference and information center in New York, encouraging the performance of contemporary American music. The League of Composers, Composers' Forum, ACA, and National Association for American Composers and Conductors (1933) all sponsored many concerts locally.

The principal musicians' club in New York is the Bohemians, a service and social organization founded in 1907 by rafael joseffy. More specialized societies have included the Composers Collective of New York (1932–6); the New York Music Critics' Circle (1941–65); the American Guild of Organists, the headquarters of which have been in New York since its formation in 1896; and the Charles Ives Society, active from 1973. The Rodgers and Hammerstein Foundation has been active since 1953, and in 1983 the Kurt Weill Foundation for Music (founded 1962) opened its research center.

15. Publishing, instrument making, broadcasting, and recording. Early music publishers were often also dealers. James Hewitt (active 1793–1819) and his son James Lang Hewitt (1830–47) (see Hewitt) had a music shop and published music, as did John Paff from 1798 to 1817 and j.f. Atwill from 1833 to 1850. William DuBois (1813–54) also dealt in pianos, and Edward Riley (1806–50) taught music. In 1815 Firth & Hall, joined in 1832 by sylvanus billings Pond, began an important association that lasted under various names until 1884 (see Firth, hall & pond). Sheet music in the form of patriotic songs, simple operatic selections, and piano pieces dominated the repertory. In the second part of the 19th century Harvey B. Dodworth (1845–87) and the Schuberths, Julius and Edward (from 1858), achieved prominence. Of 27 firms belonging to the Board of Music Trade, however, only six were from New York. The introduction of the octave anthem by Novello in 1870 infused new strength into serious music publishing, especially by the firms of G. Schirmer (set up as Beer & Schirmer in 1861 by Gustav Schirmer) and Carl Fischer (established in 1872). The 1880s saw the founding of two important popular publishers, Harms (in 1875) and M. Witmark (in 1885); both are now subsidiaries of larger organizations. From the 1890s a large part of the

popular songwriting and music-publishing industry was in New York; becoming known as TIN PAN ALLEY, its center moved gradually uptown on Broadway. Leading music publishers in New York after 1945 included G. Schirmer, Carl Fischer, Boosey & Hawkes, Belwin-Mills, Associated Music Publishers (a division of Schirmer), C.F. Peters, Peer-Southern, and Chappell. Since the 1980s, many independent houses have been acquired by conglomerates. This has particularly affected the popular music publishing field, although by the 1990s the only important publishers of classical music left in New York were Boosey & Hawkes and G. Schirmer. The sweeping technology changes that have affected the publishing industry since 2000 have put severe pressure on music publishers, made especially acute with the advent of internet publishing as well as music-software programs such as Finale and Sibelius.

The manufacture of lutes and violins was reported in New York as early as the 1690s. Twenty-one instrument makers were active in the city in the 1790s, among whom Christian Claus (1789–99), Thomas Dodds (1785–99), and Archibald Whaites (1793–1816) frequently advertised in papers their abilities to make a dozen kinds of instruments. By the 1820s instrument making was the city's fifth-largest industry. A census of 1855 listed 836 instrument makers, among them 553 immigrants, mostly from Germany. In the 1890 census, there were 131 instrument firms employing 5958 craftsmen.

John Geib, an organ builder from 1798, was joined by his brothers Adam and William in a firm that manufactured pianos until 1872. The firm Dubois & Stodart made pianos from 1819 to the 1850s. Among the many piano-making firms active in the latter part of the century were Weber (founded 1852), Steck (1857), Hardman (1842), Bacon (1841), Haines (1851), Mathusek (1857), Behning (1861), Doll (1871), Sohmer (1872), and Behr (1881). The first three were absorbed by the AEOLIAN Corporation, which maintained its headquarters in New York into the 1970s. Most important among the city's piano makers has been STEINWAY & SONS, founded by Heinrich E. Steinweg in 1853. Some later publishers also dealt in instruments. E. Riley made flutes, and Firth, Pond & Co. made woodwind instruments from 1848 to 1865. A.G. Badger was an important flute maker from 1845, the business being absorbed by the Penzel & Mueller Co. after the turn of the century. Among brass instrument makers the Schreiber Cornet Co. (from 1867) and John F. Stratton (from 1859) were significant, the latter turning to guitar manufacture in 1890. August and George Gemunder and family arrived in the city from Germany before 1850 and made prizewinning violins for over 75 years. Rembert Wurlitzer Inc. was noted for the restoration and sale of rare violins from 1949 to 1974. By the start of the 21st century Steinway remained the only piano maker in the city.

New York became the national center of radio broadcasting with the founding of the first American radio networks—NBC in 1926 and CBS in 1927. For a while, before the impact of populist aesthetics and, later, television was felt, the networks attempted to emulate state-supported European broadcasters by sponsoring their own studio orchestras. The best known of these was the NBC SO. The New York PO has presented regular radio broadcasts since 1930, and occasional telecasts and concerts for young people. The Saturday matinée performances of the Metropolitan Opera have been broadcast since 1931. Since the 1970s performances at the Metropolitan and other Lincoln Center venues have been telecast on the Public Broadcasting Service network more recently, arts institutions have turned to cable and satellite broadcasting. New York supports a variety of radio stations, which broadcast classical, jazz, country music, rock, rap, and other genres.

New York was a center for the recording industry from its earliest days. Recordings of all musical genres were dominated by RCA Victor and Columbia, located in New York. After the rise of rock and the penetration of country music into the commercial mainstream, however, New York was successfully challenged by Los Angeles (for pop) and Nashville (for country) as a national recording center. But with the corporate headquarters of CBS, RCA, BMG, Sony, Angel/EMI, Polygram Classics, and Warner Communications, as well as specialized labels such as CRI, New World, and Nonesuch (now part of Elektra/Warner), and with ample recording facilities and an active musical community, New York has retained its leading position in the recording industry, especially for classical music, contemporary music, and jazz. Even though several of these companies have merged and transformed, they remain an important force in the industry. The RECORDING INDUSTRIES ASSOCIATION OF AMERICA (RIAA), a trade organization formed in 1952, is also based in the city.

16. CRITICISM AND PERIODICALS. Early reviews of public performances were unsigned. In the mid-19th century two literary figures, Walt Whitman in the *Brooklyn Eagle* (1841–5) and Margaret Fuller in Horace Greeley's *Tribune* (1844–6), included music in their critical writing. The city's first prominent music critic was the composer WILLIAM HENRY FRY, who wrote for the *New York Tribune* from 1852 to 1863. In 1880 HENRY EDWARD KREHBIEL joined the paper, for which he wrote distinguished critical commentary until 1923. HENRY T. FINCK contributed to the *Evening Post* from 1881 to 1924, and J.G. Huneker's columns appeared in various publications from 1891 to 1921. W.J. Henderson in the *New York Times* (1887–1902), *New York Sun* (1902–20, 1924–37), and the *New York Herald* (1920–24), and Richard Aldrich in the *New York Times* (1902–37) were particularly influential. These men were all cultivated university graduates with extensive musical training, as well as editors, lecturers, teachers, and authors; their newspapers gave them free rein, and their judgments have in the main stood the test of time.

The tradition of fine critical writing was continued by LAWRENCE GILMAN (active from 1901, with the *New York Tribune* 1923–39), DEEMS TAYLOR in the *New York World* (1921–5), and OLIN DOWNES in the *New York Times* (1924–55). VIRGIL THOMSON added his strongly individual voice to the *Herald-Tribune* from 1940 to 1954, followed by

Paul Henry Lang from 1954 to 1963. Chief music critics at the *New York Times* were H. Howard Taubman (1955–60), HAROLD C. SCHONBERG (1960–80), Donal Henahan (1980–91), Edward Rothstein (1991–5), BERNARD HOLLAND (1995–2008), and ANTHONY TOMMASINI (2008–). The paper, the most influential reviewing medium in the United States, had in 1999 five critics for classical and four critics for popular music, supplemented by freelance writers. Weekly periodicals also provide a forum for music critics, notably the *Village Voice,* which focuses on contemporary and popular music; the *New Yorker* was elevated to become a significant venue for music criticism during the tenure of ANDREW PORTER (1972–92), who was succeeded by Paul Griffiths (1992–7) and ALEX ROSS (since 1996); *Rolling Stone* (1977) is a primary source for rock criticism; and *Billboard* (1894) for popular music in general. Although challenges to print journalism have forced several publications to shed their critics entirely, the city remains the leading center for music criticism in the United States.

New York has long been a center of publishing activity of many kinds; 82 music periodicals appeared in the city between 1850 and 1900. Notable among them were the *Choral Advocate and Singing-Class Journal* (1850–73), what was eventually called *Watson's Art Journal* (1864–1905), the *Music Trade Journal* (from 1879), and *Music Trades* (from 1890); *Musical America* was founded in 1898 and merged with *High Fidelity* in 1965. General periodicals such as *Scribner's Magazine* (1887–1900) and *Harpers* (from 1850) have also carried articles of musical interest. *The Musical Observer* (1907–31) and *Modern Music* (1924–46) were influential. *The Musical Quarterly,* established in 1915, is a leading scholarly journal. Its editors have included Oscar Sonneck (1915–28), Carl Engel (1929–44), Gustav Reese (1944–5), P.H. Lang (1945–73), Christopher Hatch (1973–6), Joan Peyser (1977–84), Eric Salzman (1984–91), Paul Wittke (1992), and Leon Botstein (from 1993). Three important journals for organists, *Church Music Review* (1901–35), *American Organist* (1918–70), and the journal of the American Guild of Organists, *Music AGO/RCCO Magazine* (founded in 1967 and in 1980 renamed *The American Organist*) were published in New York. *Metronome* (1885–1961) has been superseded by a variety of magazines on jazz, pop, rock, salsa, rap, hip hop, and other genres of popular music. A thorough listing of music and other events held in the city can be found in *Time Out New York.* *Opera News* has been published since 1936 by the Metropolitan Opera Guild.

17. LIBRARIES. The New York Public Library, formed in 1895 by the amalgamation of the Astor (1849) and Lenox (1870) libraries with the Tilden Foundation (1887), includes one of the world's outstanding research collections. The Music Division (with nearly 700,000 titles as well as programs, clippings, photographs, and letters) is in the Library and Museum of the Performing Arts at Lincoln Center, and the Rodgers & Hammerstein Archives of Recorded Sound there include over 450,000 recordings of all kinds; in the same building the library maintains a circulating collection of more than 150,000 scores, books, and recordings. Another division of the New York Public Library, the Schomburg Center for Research in Black Culture, collects materials on jazz and the music of black musicians. In other parts of the city the Queensborough and Brooklyn public libraries maintain large music collections, and there are additional centers for circulating recordings in Manhattan and the Bronx. Theater life on 42nd Street is documented at the archives of the Shubert Organization on 45th Street, and the history of the Metropolitan Opera at the opera's archives in Lincoln Center. The American Music Center (founded 1940) has a collection of scores and sound recordings of contemporary American music, and the library of the Archive of Contemporary Music specializes in collecting pop, jazz, and rock and roll.

Each of the educational institutions offering advanced degrees has a good working collection to support its courses. Columbia, whose first music librarian, Richard Angell, was appointed in 1934, is one of the oldest. The Juilliard library has a collection of more than 50,000 books and scores. The Pierpont Morgan Library houses many valuable music manuscripts. The Department of Musical Instruments of the Metropolitan Museum of Art, whose origins go back to 1889, has a renowned collection of approximately 4500 Western and non-Western instruments. The curators of the collection have included Emanuel Winternitz and Laurence Libin. Collections of historical pictures of musical life can be found at the Research Center for Music Iconography at the City University of New York, and news photos of 20th-century musical life at the Battmann Archive. The Dance Notation Bureau (founded 1940) is one of the world's most important centers for research in dance notation. The Shubert Archive holds an enormous collection of theatrical materials that include music from the late 19th century onwards. The collection of the Museum of Television & Radio on 52nd Street preserves recordings of about 75,000 radio and television programs, a large number of them featuring music events.

BIBLIOGRAPHY
A General. B Opera and vocal music. C Orchestras. D Sacred music. E Musical theater. F Jazz and popular music. G Ethnic music.

A: GENERAL
H.E. Krehbiel: *Review of the New York Musical Season* (New York, 1886–90)

W.S.B. Matthews, ed.: *A Hundred Years of Music in America* (Chicago, 1889/R)

O.G. Sonneck: *Early Concert-Life in America (1731–1800)* (Leipzig, 1907)

I. Zangwill: *The Melting-Pot* (New York, 1909)

H.C. Lahee: *Annals of Music in America* (Boston, 1922)

J.T. Howard: *Our American Music: Three Hundred Years of it* (New York, 1931, enlarged 4/1965 as *Our American Music: a Comprehensive History from 1620 to the Present*)

H. Cowell, ed.: *American Composers on American Music: a Symposium* (Stanford, CA, 1933/R)

F. Damrosch: *Institute of Musical Art, 1905–1926* (New York, 1936)

E.R. Peyser: *The House that Music Built: Carnegie Hall* (New York, 1936)

V.L. Redway: "A New York Concert in 1736," *MQ*, xxii (1936), 170–7

N. Slonimsky: *Music since 1900* (New York, 1937, 5/1994)

R. Aldrich: *Concert Life in New York, 1902–1923* (New York, 1941)

V.L. Redway: *Music Directory of Early New York City* (New York, 1941)

G. Chase: *America's Music, from the Pilgrims to the Present* (New York, 1955, 3/1987)

H.W. Schwartz: *Bands of America* (Garden City, NY, 1957)

R. Schickel: *The World of Carnegie Hall* (New York, 1960)

D.D. Rogers: *Nineteenth Century Music in New York City as Reflected in the Career of George Frederick Bristow* (diss., U. of Michigan, 1967)

V. Thomson: *Music Reviewed 1940–1954* (New York, 1967)

M. Goldin: *The Music Merchants* (New York, 1969)

C. Gillett: *The Sound of the City* (New York, 1970, 2/1983)

D.D. Rogers: "Public Music Performances in New York City from 1800 to 1850," *Yearbook for Inter-American Musical Research*, vi (1970), 5–50

M.M. Lowens: *The New York Years of Edward MacDowell* (diss., U. of Michigan, 1971)

R.G. Martin: *Lincoln Center for the Performing Arts* (Englewood Cliffs, NJ, 1971)

J. Ogasapian: *Organ Building in New York City: 1700–1900* (Braintree, MA, 1977)

A. Aaron: "William Tuckey, a Choirmaster in Colonial New York," *MQ*, lxiv (1978), 79–97

A. Porter: *Music of Three Seasons, 1974–1977* (New York, 1978) [Reviews originally pubd in *The New Yorker*; see also *Music of Three More Seasons, 1977–1980* (New York, 1981) and *Musical Events: a Chronicle, 1980–1983* (New York, 1987)]

C.J. Oja: "The Copland-Sessions Concerts and their Reception in the Contemporary Press," *MQ*, lxv (1979), 212–19

L.A. Erenberg: *Steppin' Out: New York Nightlife and the Transformation of American Culture, 1890–1930* (Westport, CT, 1981)

R.A. Moog: "The Columbia/Princeton Electronic Music Center: Thirty Years of Explorations in Sound," *Contemporary Keyboard*, vii/5 (1981), 22–4

R.A. Lott: "New Music for New Ears: the International Composers' Guild," *JAMS*, xxxvi (1983), 266–87

G.W. Martin: *The Damrosch Dynasty: America's First Family of Music* (Boston, 1983)

J. Rockwell: *All American Music: Composition in the Late Twentieth Century* (New York, 1983)

B. Kellner, ed.: *The Harlem Renaissance: a Historical Dictionary for the Era* (Westport, CT, 1984)

J.W. Wagner: "New York City Concert Life, 1801–5," *American Music*, ii/2 (1984), 53–70

R. Holz: *Heralds of Victory: a History Celebrating the 100th Anniversary of the New York Staff Band and Male Chorus, 1887–c1986* (New York, 1986)

G.B. Anderson: *Music in New York during the American Revolution: an Inventory of Musical References in Rivington's "New York Gazette"* (Boston, 1987)

A. Dümling: "Massenlieder, Kollektivismus und Gebrauchsmusik: zum Einfluss deutscher Exil-Komponisten auf die Arbeitermusikbewegung und das Musikleben in der Vereinigten Staaten von Amerika der dreissiger Jahre," *Verdrängte Musik: Berliner Komponisten im Exil*, ed. H. Traber and E. Weingarten (Berlin, 1987), 141–64

M. McKnight: "Wagner and the *New York Press*, 1855–1876," *American Music*, v/2 (1987), 145–55

V.B. Lawrence: *Strong on Music: the New York Music Scene in the Days of George Templeton Strong, 1836–1874*, i: *Resonances (1836–1850)* (New York, 1988); ii: *Reverberations (1850–1856)* (Chicago, 1995); iii: *Repercussions (1857–1862)* (Chicago, 1999)

O.F. Saloman: "Margaret Fuller on Musical Life in Boston and New York, 1841–1846," *American Music*, vi/4 (1988), 428–41

T. Johnson: *The Voice of New Music: New York City, 1972–1982: a Collection of Articles Originally Published in "The Village Voice"* (Eindhoven, 1989)

D.-R. de Lerma: "Bibliography of the Music: the Concert Music of the Harlem Renaissance Composers, 1919–1935," *Black Music in the Harlem Renaissance*, ed. S.A. Floyd (Westport, CT, 1990), 175–217

T.J. Dox: "George Frederick Bristow and the New York Public Schools," *American Music*, ix/4 (1991), 339–52

N. Groce: *Musical Instrument Makers of New York: a Directory of Eighteenth and Nineteenth Century Urban Craftsmen* (Stuyvesant, NY, 1991)

B. Parisi: *A History of Brooklyn's Three Major Performing Arts Institutions: the Brooklyn Academy of Music, Brooklyn Center for the Performing Arts at Brooklyn College and St. Ann's Center for Restoration and the Arts, Inc.* (diss., New York U., 1991)

J. Graziano: "Music in William Randolph Hearst's *New York Journal*," *Notes*, xlviii (1991–2), 383–424

J. Horowitz: "Anton Seidl and America's Wagner Cult," *Wagner in Performance*, ed. B. Millington and S. Spencer (New Haven, CT, 1992), 168–81

R. Lee: *The Composers Collective of New York City and the Attempt to Articulate the Nature of Proletarian Music in the Writings of Charles Seeger, Marc Blitzstein and Elie Siegmeister in the 1930s* (diss., U. of Keele, 1992)

D.A. Day: *The New York Musical World, 1852–1860* (Ann Arbor, 1993)

M. Epstein: *The New York Hippodrome: a Complete Chronology of Performances, from 1905 to 1939* (New York, 1993)

E.M. Graff: *Stepping Left: Dance and Politics in New York City, 1928–1942* (diss., New York U., 1993)

E. Lott: *Love and Theft: Blackface Minstrelsy and the American Working Class* (New York, 1993)

D. Metzer: *The Ascendancy of Musical Modernism in New York City, 1915–1929* (diss., Yale U., 1993)

R. Breuer: *New Yorker Musik-Kaleidoskop, 1962–1990* (Trier, 1995)

K.J. Jackson: *The Encyclopedia of New York City* (New Haven, CT and London, 1995)

O.F. Saloman: *Beethoven's Symphonies and J.S. Dwight: the Birth of American Music Criticism* (Boston, 1995)

M.J. Pagano: *The History of the Third Street Music School Settlement, 1891–1984: Music School and Social Settlement—the Dual Identity of the Original Music School Settlement* (diss., Manhattan School of Music, 1996)

M.N. Grant: *Maestros of the Pen: a History of Classical Music Criticism in America* (Boston, 1998)

J. Horowitz: "The Imp of the Perverse: Mahler, New York, and a Question of 'Moral Aesthetics,'" *Times Literary Supplement* (8 Jan 1999)

W. Scott and P. Rutkoff: *New York Modern: the Arts and the City* (Baltimore, 1999)

S. Johnson, ed.: *The New York Schools of Music and the Visual Arts* (New York, 2000)

C.J. Oja: *Making Music Modern: New York in the 1920s* (New York, 2000)

M. Evans: *Waking Up in New York City: a Musical Tour of the Big Apple* (London, 2003)

K. Gann: *Music Downtown* (Berkeley, 2006)

J. Graziano, ed.: *European Music and Musicians in New York City, 1840–1900* (Rochester, NY, 2006)

B. Piekut: *Experimentalism Otherwise: the New York Avant-Garde and its Limits* (Berkeley, 2011)

B: OPERA AND VOCAL MUSIC

E. Singleton: "History of the Opera in New York from 1750 to 1898," *Musical Courier*, xxxvii/23 (1898), 10–24

G. von Skal: *History of the New York Arion, 1854–1904* (New York, 1904)

H.E. Krehbiel: *Chapters of Opera* (New York, 1908, 3/1911)

An Historical Sketch of 37 Seasons of the Oratorio Society of New York, 1873/74–1908/09 (New York, 1909)

F. Rogers: "America's First Grand Opera Season," *MQ*, i (1915), 93–101

O.G. Sonneck: *Early Opera in America* (New York, 1915)

J. Mattfeld: *A Hundred Years of Grand Opera in New York, 1825–1925* (New York, 1927)

G.C.D. Odell: *Annals of the New York Stage* (New York, 1927–49, 2/1970)

I. Kolodin: *The Metropolitan Opera* (New York, 1936, enlarged 4/1966)

W.H. Seltsam: *Metropolitan Opera Annals* (New York, 1947, 2/1949; suppls., 1957, 1968, 1978)

J.F. Cone: *Oscar Hammerstein's Manhattan Opera Company* (Norman, OK, 1966)

M. Nelson: *The First Italian Opera Season in New York City: 1825–1826* (diss., U. of North Carolina, 1976)

M.L. Sokol: *The New York City Opera* (New York, 1981)

J.F. Cone: *First Rival of the Metropolitan Opera* (New York, 1983)

M. Mayer: *The Met: One Hundred Years of Grand Opera* (New York and London, 1983)

Q. Eaton: *The Miracle of the Met: an Informal History of the Metropolitan Opera, 1883–1967* (New York, 1984)

P. Eisler: *The Metropolitan Opera: the First Twenty-Five Years, 1883–1908* (Croton-on-Hudson, NY, 1984)

G.W. Martin: "New York's Smaller Opera Companies," *Opera*, xxxvi (1985), 1001–7

B. McConachie: "New York Operagoing, 1825–50: Creating an Elite Social Ritual," *American Music*, vi/2 (1988), 181–92

G. Fitzgerald, ed.: *Annals of the Metropolitan Opera* (Boston and New York, 1989)

H.-L. de La Grange: "Mahler and the Metropolitan Opera," *SMH*, xxxi (1989), 253–70

R. Allen: *Singing in the Spirit: African-American Sacred Quartets in New York City* (Philadelphia, 1991)

J. Dizikes: *Opera in America: a Cultural History* (New Haven, CT, 1993)

J. Horowitz: *Wagner Nights: an American History* (Berkeley, 1994)

J.C. Ottenberg: *Opera Odyssey: Toward a History of Opera in Nineteenth-Century America* (Westport, CT, 1994)

K. Ahlquist: *Democracy at the Opera: Music, Theater and Culture in New York City, 1815–60* (Urbana, IL, 1997)

M. Johnson: *"The Masses Are Singing": Insurgency and Song in New York City, 1929–1941* (diss., CUNY Graduate Center, 2003)

A. Saposnik: *Women in the Spotlight: Divas in Nineteenth-Century New York* (diss., CUNY Graduate Center, 2003)

C: ORCHESTRAS

H.E. Krehbiel: *The Philharmonic Society of New York* (New York, 1892)

J.G. Huneker: *The Philharmonic Society of New York and its Seventy-Fifth Anniversary: a Retrospect* (New York, ?1917)

J. Erskine: *The Philharmonic Symphony Society of New York* (New York, 1943)

H. Shanet: *Philharmonic: a History of New York's Orchestra* (New York, 1975)

J. Horowitz: *Understanding Toscanini: How He Became an American Culture God and Helped Create a New Audience for Old Music* (New York, 1987)

H. Sachs: *Toscanini* (New York, 1988)

E. Schabas: *Theodore Thomas: America's Conductor and Builder of Orchestras: 1835–1905* (Urbana, 1989)

B. Bial: *Focus on the Philharmonic: in Celebration of the 150th Anniversary of the New York Philharmonic* (New York, 1992)

D.C. Meyer: *The NBC Symphony Orchestra* (diss., U. of California, Davis, 1994)

J. Doering: *A Salesman of Fine Music: American Music Manager Arthur Judson, 1900 to 1940* (diss., Washington U, St. Louis, 1998)

M.H. Frank: *Arturo Toscanini: the NBC Years* (Portland, OR, 2002)

J. Horowitz: *Classical Music in America: a History* (New York, 2005)

M. Edwards: *How Music Grew in Brooklyn: a Biography of the Brooklyn Philharmonic Orchestra* (Oxford, 2006)

H.L. de La Grange: *Gustav Mahler, Vol. 4: A New Life Curt Short (1907–1911)* (Oxford, 2008)

J. Canarina: *The New York Philharmonic from Bernstein to Maazel* (Portland, 2010)

J. Spitzer, ed.: *American Orchestras in the Nineteenth Century* (Chicago, 2012)

D: SACRED MUSIC

A.H. Messiter: *A History of the Choir and Music of Trinity Church* (New York, 1906)

L. Ellinwood: *The History of American Church Music* (New York, 1953)

S. Cornelius: *The Convergence of Power: an Investigation into the Music Liturgy of Santería in New York City* (diss., U. of California, Los Angeles, 1989)

D.A. Weadon: *Clarence Dickinson (1873–1969) and the School of Sacred Music at Union Theological Seminary in the City of New York (1928–1973)* (diss., Drew U., 1993)

J. Ogasapian: *English Cathedral Music in New York: Edward Hodges of Trinity Church* (Richmond, VA, 1994)

S. Basile: *Fifth Avenue Famous* (New York, 2010)

E: MUSICAL THEATER

C. Smith: *Musical Comedy in America* (New York, 1950, 2/1981)

G.M. Bordman: *American Musical Theatre: a Chronicle* (New York, 1978)

K.A. Kanter: *The Jews on Tin Pan Alley* (New York, 1982)

I. Heskes: "Music as Social History: American Yiddish Theater Music, 1882–1920," *American Music*, ii/4 (1984), 73–87

J. Schiffman: *Harlem Heyday: a Pictorial History of Modern Black Show Business and the Apollo Theatre* (New York, 1984)

R.C. Lynch: *Broadway on Record: a Directory of New York Cast Recordings and Musical Shows, 1931–1986* (New York, 1987)

T.L. Riis: *Just before Jazz: Black Musical Theater in New York, 1890–1915* (Washington, DC, 1989)

B. McNamara: *The Shuberts of Broadway: a History Drawn from the Collections of the Shubert Archive* (New York, 1990)

H. Alpert: *Broadway! 125 Years of Musical Theater* (New York, 1991)

J. Gavin: *Intimate Nights: the Golden Age of New York Cabaret* (New York, 1991)

M. Gottfried: *More Broadway Musicals: Since 1980* (New York, 1991)

M.E. Dorf: *Knitting Music: a Five-Year History of the Knitting Factory* (New York, 1992)

M. Lasser: "The Glorifier: Florenz Ziegfeld and the Creation of the American Showgirl," *American Scholar*, lxiii (1994), 441–8

D. Sheward: *It's a Hit! The Black Stage Book of Longest-Running Broadway Shows, 1884 to the Present* (New York, 1994)

S. Nelson: "Broadway and the Beast: Disney Comes to Times Square," *Drama Review*, xxxix/2 (1995), 71–85

E. Aleandri: *The Italian-American Immigrant Theatre of New York City* (Charleston, SC, 1999)

J. Sternfeld: *The Megamusical* (Bloomington, 2006)

S. Haenni: *The Immigrant Scene: Ethnic Amusements in New York, 1880–1920* (Minneapolis, MN, 2008)

J. Koegel: *Music in German Immigrant Theater: New York City, 1840–1940* (Rochester, NY, 2009)

F: JAZZ AND POPULAR MUSIC

S.B. Charters and L. Kunstadt: *Jazz: a History of the New York Scene* (Garden City, NY, 1962)

M. Williams: "Jazz Clubs, Jazz Business, Jazz Styles in New York: a Brief History and a Cultural Lag," *Jazz Masters in Transition, 1957–69* (New York, 1970/R), 89–93

J. Schiffman: *Uptown: the Story of Harlem's Apollo Theatre* (New York, 1971)

A. Shaw: *The Street that Never Slept: New York's Fabled 52nd Street* (New York, 1971/R1983 as *52nd Street: the Street of Jazz*)

J. Haskins: *The Cotton Club* (New York, 1977)

L. Ostransky: *Jazz City* (Englewood Cliffs, NJ, 1979), 179–230

T. Fox: *Showtime at the Apollo* (New York, 1983)

S.B. Charters and L. Kunstadt: *Jazz: a History of the New York Scene* (New York, 1984)

D. Such: *Music, Metaphor and Values among Avant-Garde Jazz Musicians Living in New York City* (diss., U. of California, Los Angeles, 1985)

E. Berlin: *Reflections and Research on Ragtime* (Brooklyn, NY, 1987)

E. Koskoff: "The Sound of a Woman's Voice: Gender and Music in a New York Hasidic Community," *Women and Music in Cross-Cultural Perspective* (New York, 1987), 213–24

D. Jasen: *Tin Pan Alley: the Composers, the Songs, the Performers and their Times: the Golden Age of American Popular Music from 1886 to 1956* (New York, 1988)

E. Pessen: "The Kingdom of Swing: New York City in the Late 1930s," *New York History*, lxx (1989), 276–308

S. Harrison-Pepper: *Drawing a Circle in the Square: Street Performing in New York's Washington Square Park* (Jackson, MI, 1990)

L.C. Gay: *Commitment, Cohesion and Creative Process: a Study of New York City Rock Bands* (diss., Columbia U., 1991)

P. Chevigny: *Gigs: Jazz and the Cabaret Laws in New York City* (New York, 1992)

C.H. Roell: "The Development of Tin Pan Alley," *America's Musical Pulse: Popular Music in Twentieth-Century Society*, ed. K.J. Bindas (Westport, CT, 1992), 113–21

H.A. Spring: *Changes in Jazz Performance and Arranging in New York, 1929–1932* (diss., U. of Illinois, 1993)

R. Woliver: *Hoot! A Twenty-Five Year History of the Greenwich Village Music Scene* (New York, 1994)

R. Kostelanetz: *The Fillmore East: Recollections of Rock Theater* (New York and London, 1995)

S.J. Tanenbaum: *Underground Harmonies: Music and Politics in the Subways of New York* (Ithaca, NY, 1995)

N. Groce: *Songs of the City* (New York, 1999)

K. Fikentscher: *"You Better Work!" Underground Dance Music in New York City* (Hanover, NH, 2000)

K. Emerson: *Always Magic in the Air: the Bomp and Brilliance of the Brill Building Era* (New York, 2005)

P. Shapiro: *Turn the Beat Around: the Secret History of Disco* (New York, 2005)

A. Stewart: *Making the Scene: Contemporary New York City Big Band Jazz* (Berkeley, 2007)

T. Fletcher: *All Hopped Up and Ready to Go: Music from the Streets of New York, 1927–77* (New York, 2009)

B. Gendron: *After the October Revolution: the Jazz Avant-Garde in New York (1964–65)* (New York, 2009)

T. Lawrence: *Hold on to your Dreams: Arthur Russell and the Downtown Music Scene, 1973–1992* (Durham, NC, 2009)

J. Schloss: *Foundation: B-boys, B-girls, and Hip-hop Culture in New York* (New York, 2009)

D. Charnas: *The Big Payback: the History of the Business of Hip-Hop* (New York, 2010)

H. Weinstein and J. Weinstein: *Buskers: the On-the-Streets, In-the-Trains, Off-the-Grid Memoir of Two New York City Street Musicians* (Berkeley, 2011)

J. Wriggle: *Chappie Willet and Popular Music Arranging in Swing Era New York* (diss., CUNY Graduate Center, 2011)

G: ETHNIC MUSIC

M. Slobin: *Tenement Songs: the Popular Music of the Jewish Immigrants* (Urbana, 1982)

K.K. Shelemay: "A Study of Syrian-Jewish Music in Brooklyn," *Jewish Folklore and Ethnology Newsletter*, viii (1986), 24–5

A.R. Schramm: "From Refugee to Immigrant: the Music of Vietnamese in the New York–New Jersey Metropolitan Area," *New Perspectives on Vietnamese Music*, ed. P.T. Nguyen (New Haven, CT, 1991), 90–102

L.E. Wilcken: *Music Folklore among Haitians in New York: Stage Representations and the Negotiation of Identity* (diss., Columbia U., 1991)

V.W. Boggs, ed.: *Salsiology: Afro-Cuban Music and the Evolution of Salsa in New York City* (Westport, CT, 1992)

S. Zheng: *Immigrant Music and Transnational Discourse: Chinese American Music Culture in New York City* (diss., Wesleyan U., 1993)

F.M. Figueroa: *Encyclopedia of Latin American Music in New York* (St. Petersburg, FL, 1994)

D.R. Hill: "A History of West Indian Carnival in New York City to 1978," *New York Folklore*, xx (1994), 47–66

L. Waxer: "Of Mambo Kings and Songs of Love: Dance Music in Havana and New York from the 1930s to the 1950s," *Latin American Music Review*, xv (1994), 139–76

R. Glasser: *My Music is my Flag: Puerto Rican Musicians and their New York Communities, 1917–1940* (Berkeley, 1995)

M.M. Vega: "The Yoruba *Orisha* Tradition Comes to New York City," *African American Review*, xxix (1995), 201–6

R. Allen and W. Wilcken, eds.: *Island Sounds in the Global City* (Chicago, 2001)

New York City Global Beat of the Boroughs: Music from NYC's Ethnic & Immigrant Communities, Smithsonian Folkways (2001) [CD]

S. Maira: *Desis in the House: Indian American Youth Culture in New York City* (Philadelphia, 2002)

M. Salazar and A. Angeloro: *Mambo Kingdom: Latin Music in New York* (New York, 2002)

E. Morales: *The Latin Beat* (Cambridge, MA, 2003)

R.Z. Rivera: *New York Ricans from the Hip Hop Zone* (New York, 2003)

New York City Department of City Planning Population Division: *The Newest New Yorkers 2000: Immigrant Population in the New Millennium, Briefing Booklet* (New York, 2004)

C. Washburne: *Sounding Salsa: Performing Latin Music in New York City* (Philadelphia, 2008)

S. Zheng: *Claiming Diaspora: Music, Transnationalism, and Cultural Politics in Asian/Chinese America* (New York, 2010)

IRVING KOLODIN, FRANCIS D. PERKINS/SUSAN THIEMANN SOMMER/ZDRAVKO BLAŽEKOVIĆ/R (1); IRVING KOLODIN, FRANCIS D. PERKINS/SUSAN THIEMANN SOMMER/ZDRAVKO BLAŽEKOVIĆ (WITH JOHN SHEPARD, SARA VELEZ)/R (2); IRVING KOLODIN, FRANCIS D. PERKINS/SUSAN THIEMANN SOMMER/ZDRAVKO BLAŽEKOVIĆ (WITH JOHN SHEPARD, SARA VELEZ)/R (3); IRVING KOLODIN, FRANCIS D. PERKINS/SUSAN THIEMANN SOMMER/ZDRAVKO BLAŽEKOVIĆ (WITH JOHN SHEPARD, SARA VELEZ)/R (4); JOSEPH HOROWITZ (5); IRVING KOLODIN, FRANCIS D. PERKINS/SUSAN THIEMANN SOMMER/ZDRAVKO BLAŽEKOVIĆ/R (6); IRVING KOLODIN, FRANCIS D. PERKINS/SUSAN THIEMANN SOMMER/ZDRAVKO BLAŽEKOVIĆ/R (7); IRVING KOLODIN, FRANCIS D. PERKINS/SUSAN THIEMANN SOMMER/ZDRAVKO BLAŽEKOVIĆ/R (8); JOHN ROCKWELL/ZDRAVKO BLAŽEKOVIĆ/R (9); EDWARD A. BERLIN, J. BRADFORD ROBINSON, JOHN ROCKWELL/ZDRAVKO BLAŽEKOVIĆ/R (10); WILL FULTON (11); EVAN RAPPORT (12); IRVING KOLODIN, FRANCIS D. PERKINS/SUSAN THIEMANN SOMMER/ZDRAVKO BLAŽEKOVIĆ (WITH JOHN SHEPARD, NINA DAVIS-MILLIS)/JONAS WESTOVER (13); IRVING KOLODIN, FRANCIS D. PERKINS/SUSAN THIEMANN SOMMER/ZDRAVKO BLAŽEKOVIĆ/R (14); IRVING KOLODIN, FRANCIS D. PERKINS/SUSAN THIEMANN SOMMER/ZDRAVKO BLAŽEKOVIĆ (WITH JOHN ROCKWELL, PAUL GRIFFITHS)/JONAS WESTOVER (15); IRVING KOLODIN, FRANCIS D. PERKINS/SUSAN THIEMANN SOMMER/ZDRAVKO BLAŽEKOVIĆ/JONAS WESTOVER (16); IRVING KOLODIN, FRANCIS D. PERKINS/SUSAN THIEMANN SOMMER/ZDRAVKO BLAŽEKOVIĆ/R (17)

New York Brass Quintet. Brass quintet established in 1954. Its first performance was in October of that year at the Carnegie Recital Hall (later Weill Recital Hall). Its founding members were Robert Nagel (trumpet), John Glasel (trumpet), Fred Schmidt (horn), Erwin Price (trombone), and Harvey Phillips (tuba). Initially formed to play children's concerts in cooperation with Young Audiences, Inc., the ensemble soon became recognized as one of the finest brass quintets in the United States and would eventually enjoy residencies at the Hartt School, the Yale School of Music, and the Manhattan School of Music. Performing music from all style periods, the group premiered numerous works including Malcolm Arnold's Quintet for Brass op.73 and Gunther Schuller's Brass Quintet. Recordings of Eugene Bozza's Sonatine and Alvin Etler's Quintet for Brass Instruments became listener favorites and received critical acclaim. The group saw many personnel changes during the late 1950s and early 1960s. By 1967 membership had stabilized and would remain the same for the next 17 years, with Robert Nagel (trumpet), Allan Dean (trumpet), Paul Ingraham (horn), John Swallow (trombone), and Thompson Hanks (tuba). The quintet collectively retired in 1984.

ERIC LYNN HARRIS

New York City Ballet. The performing company of the School of American Ballet, opened in New York City in January 1934. Successor to three companies directed by george Balanchine and lincoln Kirstein – the American Ballet (1935), Ballet Caravan (1936), and Ballet Society (1946) – New York City Ballet received its present name in 1948.

See also BALLET.

CLAUDE CONYERS

New York Dolls. Rock group. Formed in 1971 in New York, band members on its first two albums were vocalist David Johansen (*b* Staten Island, NY, 9 Jan 1950), guitarist Johnny Thunders [John Anthony Genzale Jr.] (*b* Queens, NY, 15 July 1952; *d* New Orleans, LA, 23 April 1991), guitarist Sylvain Sylvain [Sylvain Mizrahi] (*b* Cairo, Egypt, 14 Feb 1951), bassist Arthur Kane (*b* Bronx, NY, 3 Feb 1949; *d* Los Angeles, CA, 13 July 2004), and drummer Jerry Nolan (*b* Brooklyn, NY, 7 May 1946; *d* New York, NY, 14 Jan 1992). The band was instrumental in the development of the underground New York rock community in the 1970s.

The Dolls caught the attention of the New York rock community during a short residency at the Mercer Arts Center. Their first big break, in the fall of 1972, was an opening spot for Rod Stewart in England, where they met Malcolm McLaren. During their short UK tour, their first drummer Billy Murcia died of an accidental overdose. In New York the band remained notorious for their drug- and alcohol-fueled live concerts. On their first, eponymous album, one can hear influences from rock and roll, girl groups, and glam rock. The opening track, "Personality Crisis," characteristically combines Thunders's Chuck-Berry-influenced guitar riffs with Johansen's earnest sarcasm. On the tracks "Trash" and "Looking for a kiss" Johanson quotes girl group songs, including the Shangri-Las' "Give him a great big kiss." For their second album, *Too Much Too Soon* (1974), they hired the Shangri-Las' producer, Shadow Morton.

After the Dolls broke up, Thunders and Nolan formed the New York supergroup the Heartbreakers along with Richard Hell, Walter Lure, and Billy Rath. Later, David Johansen reinvented himself as Buster Poindexter and achieved significant commercial success. In 2004 the surviving members reunited for a series of concerts, eventually recording three new albums, *One Day It Will Please Us to Remember Even This* (2006), *Cause I Sez So* (2009), and *Dancing Backward in High Heels* (2011).

BIBLIOGRAPHY

R. Christgau: "New York Dolls," *Stranded: Rock and Roll for a Desert Island*, ed. G. Marcus (New York, 1979, R/1996), 132–47

N. Antonia: *The New York Dolls: Too Much, Too Soon* (New York, 2003)

CAROLINE POLK O'MEARA

New York Philharmonic. Symphony orchestra in New York City; founded in 1842, it is the oldest continually operating orchestra in the United States.

The "Philharmonic Society" was formed as a cooperative organization of musicians, led by the American-born violinist and conductor URELI CORELLI HILL. Sixty musicians performed its first concert on 7 December 1842 in the Apollo Rooms on lower Broadway before an audience of 600. Three concerts took place that first season, and throughout the 19th century the Philharmonic generally played between four and eight different programs each season, including the US premieres of Ludwig van Beethoven's Symphonies nos. 2, 3, 4, 7, 8, and 9.

In 1909 the Philharmonic musicians gave up their self-management system and joined a group of wealthy New Yorkers who guaranteed weekly salaries, increased the number of concerts in the first year to 54, and hired GUSTAV MAHLER as conductor. These "Guarantors" were led by Mary Sheldon, who raised $300,000. In 1913 a million dollar bequest from Joseph Pulitzer provided the financial footing necessary for a dramatic increase in activities, and required the organization to become a "membership corporation." In 2011 the Philharmonic had more than 11,000 members who had paid a minimum of $75 to join.

By the 1920s the Philharmonic began absorbing or merging with its competition: the short-lived National/New Symphony Orchestra and the City Symphony Orchestra were incorporated by 1923, and in 1928 the New York Symphony (founded as the Symphony Society in 1878 by Leopold Damrosch) agreed to merge. The official legal name of the combined ensemble became the Philharmonic-Symphony Society of New York.

A 1930 tour of Europe, under ARTURO TOSCANINI, began a tradition that has taken the ensemble on groundbreaking cultural exchanges to the Soviet Union (1959) and Pyongyang, D.P.R.K. (2008). As of 2011 the Orchestra has performed in 430 cities in 63 countries and travels abroad at least once a year.

The Philharmonic made its first recording in 1917 and first radio broadcast in 1922. National weekly radio broadcasts began in 1930, becoming a Sunday afternoon favorite, and continued for three decades until it was forced to move to Saturday night due to the popularity of Sunday afternoon football games. Between 1958 and 1972 LEONARD BERNSTEIN led 53 Philharmonic Young People's Concerts televised on CBS. Since 1976 *Live from Lincoln Center* has televised Philharmonic concerts at least twice a year.

In 1962 the Philharmonic moved from its long-time home Carnegie Hall to open Lincoln Center for the Performing Arts with a nationally televised concert from "Philharmonic Hall" (renamed Avery Fisher Hall in 1973). The Orchestra commissioned works from nine composers for the opening, establishing a tradition that has led to the creation of almost 150 new compositions.

In 1964 the Philharmonic became the first American orchestra to offer its musicians a 52-week contract. The orchestra musicians are members of Local 802 of the American Federation of Musicians. In 1973 contract negotiations with the musicians broke down which resulted in a ten-week strike. The Orchestra has 106 members, 50% of them women, and performs approximately 190 concerts each season.

The orchestra's website (<http://www.nyphil.org>) has hosted a variety of archival materials and also has presented audio streams of its national weekly radio broadcasts. In 2008 the orchestra presented its first webcast of a complete concert (from Pyongyang, North Korea). In May 2010 the Orchestra performed its 15,000th concert, a milestone unmatched by any other symphony orchestra in the world.

BIBLIOGRAPHY

H.E. Krehbiel: *The Philharmonic Society of New York: 'A Memorial'* (New York, 1892)

J.G. Huneker: *The Philharmonic Society of New York and its 75th Anniversary: a Retrospect* (New York, 1917)

J. Erskine: *The Philharmonic Society of New York: its First Hundred Years* (New York, 1943)

H. Shanet: *Philharmonic: a History of New York's Orchestra* (New York, 1975)

V.B. Lawrence: *Strong on Music: the New York Music Scene in the Days of George Templeton Strong*, vols. 1–3 (Chicago, 1999)

J. North: *New York Philharmonic Discography* (Lanham, MD, 2006)

J. Canarina: *The New York Philharmonic: From Bernstein to Maazel* (New York, 2010)

BARBARA HAWS

New York Pro Musica Antiqua. Instrumental and vocal early music ensemble. NOAH GREENBERG founded New York Pro Musica Antiqua in 1952 for the purpose of resurrecting the then largely neglected music of the Middle Ages, Renaissance, and early Baroque. Greenberg endeavored to produce historically informed performances, and the group, later renamed New York Pro Musica, developed a large repertory and achieved high standards of virtuosity. By 1960 Pro Musica maintained several subgroups, including consort vocal ensembles, a chamber choir of men and boys, and a Renaissance wind band. The ensemble attracted performers who had worked with Paul Hindemith and Erich Katz. Notable artists included Bernard Krainis (recorders), LaNoue Davenport (recorders and viols), and Russell Oberlin (countertenor).

Pro Musica maintained an active recording and touring schedule during its existence. It established a regular performing presence at New York's 92nd Street YMHA and the Metropolitan Museum of Art. The ensemble first toured nationally in 1956, and in 1957 launched an educational outreach program. In 1958 it transferred its recording production from Esoteric Records to the Decca label with which it recorded 23 albums. Pro Musica received financial support from the Rockefeller and Ford Foundations, as well as from the State Department, which enabled it to tour Europe, the Soviet Union, Israel, and South America.

Pro Musica created a sensation in the 1957–8 season with its production of the medieval liturgical drama *The Play of Daniel* which opened at the Cloisters at the Metropolitan Museum of Art. Performances were given annually and were later filmed for the Canadian Broadcasting Company and the BBC. *Daniel* was followed by the *Play of Herod* (1963) and the Tours Easter Play (1970).

After Greenberg's death in 1966, Pro Musica continued until 1974 under directors John Reeves White (1966–70), Paul Maynard (1970–72), and George Houle (1972–4). Many members of subsequent American early music ensembles studied with Pro Musica musicians, performing for audiences created by Greenberg's pioneering efforts. New York Pro Musica sold its collection of instruments to New York University, its library to SUNY, Purchase, and donated its archives to the New York Public Library.

BIBLIOGRAPHY

M. Davenport: "The New York Pro Musica's *Play of Herod*: Research Issues Then and Now," *Early Music America*, i/2 (Winter 1995), 26–34

J. Gollin: *Pied Piper: the Many Lives of Noah Greenberg* (Hillsdale, NY, 2001)

E. Aoyama: *Noah Greenberg and the New York Pro Musica: the Career, Reception, and Impact* (diss., U. of Cincinnati, 2004)

K. Yri: "Noah Greenberg and the New York Pro Musica: Medievalism and the Cultural Front," *American Music*, xxiv/4 (Winter 2006), 421–44

JOHN SHEPARD/RICHARD FRENCH/ANNE LYMAN

New York School. A loose confederation of painters, sculptors, dancers, composers, poets, and critics based in New York from approximately 1947 to 1963. Art historians apply the term to a group of artists, including Jackson Pollock, Willem De Kooning, Franz Kline, Robert Motherwell, Mark Rothko, and others, who collectively established the style of American painting known as Abstract Expressionism. Musicologists apply the term to a group of composers, including John Cage, Morton Feldman, Earle Brown, Christian Wolff, and David Tudor, who shared many aesthetic values with these artists, and in some cases formed deep friendships and synergies with them.

The group of New York School composers, however, was larger than the "circle of Cage." Edgard Varèse and Stefan Wolpe also belonged to the group, serving as mentors and teachers; Lucia Dlugoszewski, a Varèse student, had her compositions first performed by New York School artists; and Ralph Shapey attended some of their gatherings. The group often met at the Cedar Tavern or at The Club (39 East 8th Street), where Cage delivered several lectures, including his celebrated "Lecture on Nothing" (1949), and Varèse presented his "Music, an Art-Science" (1950). Cage and Motherwell coedited the Abstract Expressionist journal *Possibilities*, and Cage wrote essays for another of the group's journals, *The Tiger's Eye*. Varèse contributed an interview to *Possibilities*, as well as a page of the score of his unfinished *Espace*. Feldman's seminal essay "Sound. Noise. Varèse. Boulez" appeared in The Club's official journal *It is* (no.2, 1958, 46). While Cage, Feldman, Brown, and Varèse all painted in an Abstract Expressionist style, as composers their ties to the New York School painters varied. Cage admired the improvisation methods and the nonhierarchical, "all-over" surface of their paintings, yet he disliked their heroic posturing and the autobiographical impulses behind their work. He preferred to link himself with Marcel Duchamp and the Dada movement, not to Pollock. Brown's open-form procedure in such works as *Twenty-Five Pages* (1953), *Available Forms I* (1961), and *Available Forms II* (1961–2) owes a great deal to the improvisation method in Pollock's "drip" paintings, yet owes just as much to the mobile sculptures of non-New York School artist Alexander Calder, or to the nonnarrative writings of James Joyce. Feldman's connection to the artists was perhaps the strongest. He wrote: "the new painting made me desirous of a sound world more direct, more immediate, more physical than anything that had existed heretofore" ("Autobiography," *Essays*). His reliance on psycho-automatic instinct and his concern with abstract physical essences derive directly from Philip Guston, Rothko, and his other painter friends. He composed soundtracks for Hans Namuth's documentary films *Jackson Pollock* (1951) and *De Kooning* (1963) and titled works in homage to painters and poets of the group, including *For Franz Kline* (1962), *Piano Piece (to Philip Guston)* (1963), *Rothko Chapel* (1971), and *For Frank O'Hara* (1973).

See also EARLE BROWN; JOHN CAGE; MORTON FELDMAN; DAVID TUDOR; EDGARD VARÈSE; CHRISTIAN WOLFF.

BIBLIOGRAPHY

D. Ashton: *The New York School: a Cultural Reckoning* (New York, 1973/*R*)

L. Alcopley: "The Club," *ISSUE: A Journal for Artists*, iv (1985), 45–7

M. Feldman: *Essays*, ed. W. Zimmermann (Kerpen, 1985) [incl. "Autobiography," 36–40; "Give My Regards to Eighth Street," 71–8]

S. Johnson, ed.: *The New York Schools of Music and the Visual Arts* (New York, 2000)

STEVEN JOHNSON, OLIVIA MATTIS

New York, State University of [SUNY]. Public university system of the state of New York, headquartered in Albany. The SUNY system enrolled 464,981 students on 64 campuses in 2009. Founded in 1948, SUNY is the youngest system of public higher education in the 48 contiguous states and includes various community and technical college units as well as campuses offering bachelor's and master's degrees. The SUNY system's late appearance on the American higher education scene was the result of the longstanding presence of many prestigious private institutions within the state. Four campuses—Albany, Binghamton, Buffalo, and Stony Brook—are designated as major university centers and confer doctorates. Several SUNY units originated independently as academies and normal schools, the oldest of which, at Potsdam, was founded in 1816.

While many SUNY campuses offer BA degrees in music, only the campuses at Potsdam, Fredonia, Purchase, and Stony Brook offer BM and MM degrees. Potsdam Normal School introduced music and music pedagogy courses in the 1880s through an arrangement with Julia Crane's Crane Institute of Music, which became a department of the normal school in 1926. In 2009 the Crane School of Music enrolled approximately 600 students studying for undergraduate or graduate degrees in music education, performance, composition, music theory and history, and music business. The Fredonia campus (established 1867) offers the same concentrations in addition to majors in musical theater, sound recording technology, and music therapy. The SUNY campus at Purchase (established in 1967 on a conservatory model) focuses on performance and composition and offers performer's certificates and artist diplomas as well as BM and MM degrees. Degree programs include tracks for both classical and commercial (studio) musicians.

The music programs at the SUNY centers at Binghamton, Buffalo, and Stony Brook are perhaps best known for their graduate programs, including concentrations in composition, conducting, ethnomusicology, music history, theory, and performance. The Stony Brook campus, established in 1957, is the nearest of these four university centers to New York City, and maintains strong PhD and DMA programs in ethnomusicology and performance.

Many SUNY campuses feature performing arts facilities that serve as cultural focal points for their geographic areas. Community outreach programs in the arts are common.

NINA DAVIS-MILLIS/DAVID G. TOVEY

New York Voices. Vocal ensemble. New York Voices is grounded in the American jazz tradition, but its repertoire includes music with Brazilian, R&B, classical, and pop influences. Originally formed in 1987 by a quartet of alumni of Ithaca College (Peter Eldridge, Caprice Fox, Darmon Meader, and Kim Nazarian), Sara Krieger completed the quintet. When Krieger retired from the ensemble in 1992, Lauren Kinhan took her place. The group has retained a quartet voicing since Fox left the group in 1994. The four current members also maintain careers as solo performers, composers, and arrangers.

New York Voices has recorded seven solo albums, beginning with a self-titled debut CD in 1989, and made featured appearances on many other recordings, winning a 1996 Grammy with the Count Basie Orchestra (*Live at Manchester Craftsmen's Guild*) and a 2002 Latin Grammy for *Brazilian Dreams* with Paquito D'Rivera. The ensemble has performed with a number of influential jazz musicians, including Ray Brown, Bobby McFerrin, Nancy Wilson, and George Benson. *New York Voices Sing the Songs of Paul Simon* (1997) showcased their pop side, and it regularly collaborates with orchestras, especially the Boston Pops, on arrangements of big band tunes. It has appeared at diverse venues, including Carnegie Hall, Lincoln Center, The Kennedy Center, The Blue Note (Tokyo, NYC), and opera houses in Austria and Switzerland. The ensemble has recently increased its educational initiatives, giving workshops and clinics to high school and college-aged music students.

PATRICK K. FREER

New York Woodwind Quintet. Woodwind quintet formed in 1947. The ensemble made its New York debut in January 1954 and shortly thereafter began touring in the United States; tours followed under the auspices of the US State Department to Latin America (1956), Europe (1958), East Asia and the Pacific (1962), Central and South America (1969), and Russia (1972). It has given world premieres of works by such composers as Quincy Porter and Elliott Carter, and has also led the way in reviving lesser-known works by Franz Danzi and Anton Reicha, among others. The group has also commissioned and premiered more than 20 compositions, including Samuel Barber's *Summer Music*, and quintets by William Bergsma, Alec Wilder, Gunther Schuller, Ezra Laderman, William Sydeman, Wallingford Riegger, Jon Deak, and Yehudi Wyner. Through many school concerts given 1953–5, it developed the format for the Young Audiences program. The quintet was in residence at the University of Wisconsin for 15 summers (1954–69) with the pianist Frank Glazer and the

Fine Arts String Quartet, with whom it made a number of recordings. It has also served a summer residency at the Norfolk Festival at Yale University and a full-time residency at The Juilliard School, where it was appointed in 1987. As of 2013 its members were Carol Wincenc (flute), Stephen Taylor (oboe), Charles Neidich (clarinet), Marc Goldberg (bassoon), and William Purvis (horn).

JOANNE SHEEHY HOOVER/MEGAN E. HILL

Nézet-Séguin [Séguin], **Yannick** (*b* Montreal, PQ, 6 March 1975). Canadian conductor. He began to study piano at age five and decided to become an orchestral conductor at age ten. After attending the Conservatoire de Musique du Québec, he studied conducting under JOSEPH FLUMMERFELT at the Westminister Choir College, and CARLO MARIA GIULINI, among others. He became the musical director of the Chœur polyphonique de Montréal in 1994 and the Choeur de Laval in 1995. In 1995 he founded his own professional orchestral and vocal ensemble, La Chapelle de Montréal. From 1998 to 2002 he was chorus master, assistant conductor, and music adviser of the Opéra de Montréal. Since 2000 he has been the artistic director and principal conductor of the Orchestre Métropolitain of Montréal.

In November 2004 he made his European debut with Orchestre National du Capitole de Toulouse, and followed it with successful appearances with several prominent orchestras. His debut in 2005 with the Rotterdam PO resulted in reengagements the following year and his appointment as its music director in 2008, succeeding Valery Gergiev. After his impressive debut with the London PO in 2007, he was hired as its principal guest conductor the following year. In 2008 he began serving as the music director designate of the Philadelphia Orchestra, and in 2012 he took over its music directorship, a move that many believed would help reinvigorate the orchestra.

In the field of opera, career highlights for Nézet-Séguin include *Roméo et Juliette* at the Salzburg Festival (2008 and 2010), *The Makropoulos Case* (2009) and *Turandot* (2010) at Netherlands Opera, and *Carmen* and *Don Carlo* (2010) at the Metropolitan Opera. Noted for his charismatic conducting style, Nézet-Séguin has made 24 recordings in works from a variety of composers ranging from Nino Rota to Ludwig van Beethoven.

JAMES BASH

Ngek, Chum (*b* Anlong Vil village, Sangker City district, Battambang Province, Cambodia; March 1953). Cambodian musician. A master musician of Cambodian traditional music, Chum began studying the music of the *pinn peat* (court ensemble for dances, plays, and ceremonies), *mohori* (court ensemble for entertainment), and *phleng kar* (wedding ensemble), and the instruments *sralai* (oboe), *kong* (gong circle), and *sampho* (two-headed drum played with the hands) with his grandfather, Hieng Um, at age ten. As a young man, he continued his studies with several master musicians, becoming proficient on many instruments, including the *skor thom* (two-headed drum played with wooden sticks), *roneat ek* (21-keyed wooden xylophone), *tror*

(bowed fiddle), and *khimm* (hammered dulcimer). By age 18, he was already considered a master teacher (*krou*) and worked as a professional musician—employed by his home province and performing in official ceremonies. In 1974, he was selected to represent his province at a national contest and residency at the University of Fine Arts in Phnom Penh. During the reign of the Khmer Rouge, he lived in Cambodia, feigning no musical ability for fear of death, and working first in rice fields and then as a hospital orderly. In 1979 he left Cambodia, eventually immigrating to the United States in 1982 with the help of sponsors of the Khmer Classical Dance Troupe. His efforts to preserve Cambodian music in the United States earned him the Bess Lomax Hawes Award and a National Heritage Fellowship, both awarded by the NEA in 2004. He lives in Gaithersburg, Maryland, performing frequently and teaching in the Washington, DC area, with the Cambodian Buddhist Society and with Cambodian-American Heritage, Inc.

ALEXANDER M. CANNON

Nguyen, Phong Thuyet [Nguyễn Thuyết Phong] (*b* Tam Ngãi Village, Cầu Kè District, Cần Thơ [now Trà Vinh] Province, Vietnam, 9 Aug 1946). Vietnamese performer of traditional music and ethnomusicologist; naturalized American. Raised in the Mekong Delta of southern Vietnam, he began studying Buddhist chant and *nhạc lễ* (ritual music) at age five, followed by formal instruction with master musician Trầm Văn Kiên (Mười Kiên) at age ten. As a young man, he performed vocal and instrumental music in *đờn ca tài tử* (music of talented amateurs) ensembles and in *hát bội* (classical opera) and *cải lương* (renovated theater) troupes. He undertook undergraduate study at the University of Saigon, earning a bachelor's degree in Vietnamese literature and philosophy. After teaching literature in Saigon, he worked as a high school principal from 1970 to 1974, adding traditional music to the curriculum, which was considered an innovation at the time. After spending 1974–5 in Japan, he emigrated to Paris, where he earned a doctorate in ethnomusicology at the University of Paris–Sorbonne in 1982, writing a dissertation on Vietnamese and East Asian Buddhist chant under the direction of Edith Weber. After an appointment to the Centre National de la Recherche Scientifique, he began working in the United States in 1984, eventually becoming a citizen. He has held positions at UCLA, the University of Washington, the University of Pittsburgh, the University of Michigan, and Kent State University. In 1990, along with Terry E. Miller, he established the Association for Research in Vietnamese Music, later renamed the International Association for Research in Vietnamese Music and later still known as the Institute for Vietnamese Music. In the same year, he began publishing *Nhac Viet*, a newsletter designed to raise awareness about Vietnamese music and musicians in the United States.

After 17 years living abroad, he returned to Vietnam in 1991 to continue his research and followed this trip with others, including a 1994 trip to the previously restricted Central Highlands. Field recordings made on these trips provided the material for a six-CD set released by White

Cliffs Media in 2003. In 1992 he established *Nhac Viet: the Journal of Vietnamese Music*, which, until 1997, published works of scholarship about Vietnamese folk, traditional, and popular music by scholars based in North America, Europe, Australia, and Vietnam. He has furthered his performance activities and research with grants from the Social Science Research Council, the Asian Cultural Council, Earthwatch, and the NEA. In addition to being named a National Heritage Fellow by President Clinton in 1997, he has received awards in the United States and Vietnam, including the Đào Tân National Award (1996) and both the Vietnam Heritage Award and the Ohio Heritage Fellowship (2004). He was a Fulbright Scholar at the National Conservatory of Music from 2004 to 2005 in Hanoi, where he established an ethnomusicology program, and a Rockefeller Humanities Fellow from 2006 to 2007. As a player of the *đàn tranh* (seventeen-stringed zither), the *đàn nguyệt* (or *đàn kìm*, moon-shaped lute), the *đàn bầu* (monochord), and percussion, he has performed with the Phong Nguyen Ensemble since the 1980s, an ensemble that released the album *Song of the Banyan* in 1998, and as a solo and ensemble performer in North America, Europe, Asia, and the Middle East. He has also performed on many instruments of minority groups in Central Vietnam, including the *k'long put* (bamboo tubes), the *goong* (bamboo-tube zither), the *hiho* (bundle flutes), and the *t'rung* (bamboo xylophone). He has been recognized especially for his *đàn tranh*, *đàn nguyệt*, and vocal performances of *đờn ca tài tử* in addition to his extensive scholarship on the *nhạc tài tử* modal system. These efforts, and his establishment of a collection at the American Folklife Center and a collection of field slides, photographs, videos, and audio recordings at the Hobart and William Smith Colleges, have significantly increased the presence of Vietnamese music in the United States, where he continued to perform in the early 21st century. As of 2013 he resided in Hồ Chí Minh City and lectured at the National Conservatory of Music.

WRITINGS
(selective list on Vietnamese-American music)
GMO [includes further bibliography]
with P.S. Campbell and A.R. Schramm: *Searching for a Niche: Vietnamese Music at Home in America* (Kent, OH, 1995)
"Vietnamese Music in America," *Transcending Boundaries: Asian Musics in North America*, ed. Y. Terada (Osaka, 2001), 113–22

ALEXANDER M. CANNON

Niblock, James (Franklin) (*b* Scappoose, OR, 1 Nov 1917). Composer, educator, conductor, and violinist. He began musical studies in Portland, Oregon, with violinist Franck Eichenlaub and later studied with JASCHA BRODSKY. He earned a BA and BEd from Washington State University, served in the US Air Force (1942–6), and then earned his MA from Colorado College, where he studied violin with JOSEF GINGOLD and composition with PAUL HINDEMITH and ROY HARRIS. After accepting a teaching position at Michigan State University, he obtained his PhD at University of Iowa in 1954.

From 1948 through 1985 Niblock taught theory and composition at Michigan State University and performed in the Beaumont String Quartet. From 1963 to 1978 he served as chair of the College of Music and also served as the concertmaster of the Lansing SO. The music school grew in size and prestige, as he helped add numerous faculty members, oversaw the growth of the student population, initiated a ten-year residency with the Juilliard String Quartet, and was instrumental in the construction of an additional music building. Upon retirement from administrative duties, he returned to teaching and soon established Michigan State's first electronic music studio.

Niblock was an early supporter and board member of Blue Lake Fine Arts Camp in Twin Lakes, Michigan. Founded by two of his former students in 1966, the summer camp has grown to over 5000 students. He has continued to teach, conduct, and perform each summer, and has participated in numerous overseas tours with the orchestra. Blue Lake has commissioned several works, including chamber operas, a ballet, and a work for chorus and orchestra; it has also hosted premieres of Niblock compositions for the Verdehr Trio, Gary Karr, and others.

Niblock has continued an active career in composition in all genres. He describes his work as "mostly neo-classical," placing emphasis on melodic beauty and classical forms. He was awarded a MacDowell Colony Fellowship, an NEH grant, and Michigan State's first Distinguished Emeritus Faculty Award (2006) for his service to fine arts education, particularly for his association of more than four decades with Blue Lake.

Niblock's publishers include Broton & Mercadal, Michigan State University Press, Boosey and Hawkes, G. Billaudot, Hickeys, Interlochen Press, Southern Music, Shawnee Press, Theodore Presser, and others. His work has been recorded by Crystal Records and Michigan State University Press. His collection of manuscripts is held by Michigan State University Libraries.

WORKS
(selective list)
Chbr: Soliloquy, vn, chbr orch, 1987
Orch: Three American Dances, 1958; three double concs for vn, cl, and orch, 1998, 2004, 2011
Ops: Ruth, 2001; The Last Leaf, 2006; Ruth and Naomi, 2009
Chorus: Entreat me Not to Leave thee, 1961; That Music Always Round Me, SATB, orch, 1991

MARY BLACK JUNTTONEN

Niblock, Phill (*b* Anderson, IN, 2 Oct 1933). Composer, sound artist, multimedia artist, filmmaker, and photographer. His entire musical oeuvre consists of drone works: pieces of up to 70 minutes in duration, made of continuous, long tones. An idiosyncratic feature of his music is its dense and complex texture. As in his album *Touch Three* (2006), listeners may hear up to 32 layers sounding simultaneously—typically, by the composer's request, at the loudest possible volume. The relationship between the sounds in each layer is usually microtonal; and close-ratio tones at extremely high volumes produce overtones and difference tones. Thus, although each layer changes minutely and very slowly during the course of the piece, Niblock's music is very much alive:

the total, thickly textured sound of a piece itself produces more sounds and a palpable effect on listeners' bodies. Since 1998 he has used digital sound-editing tools to create these compound textures, although his early work relied on multitrack tape recorders.

Niblock has emphasized that his pieces do not typically develop over the course of their durations as most music does: while the microtones and overtones are constantly shifting, the pieces themselves do not usually consist of formal sections heard in succession. Thus in *Valence* (2005), for example, small alterations to the tones produce an overall texture that is at once shimmering and steady. He has described his music as an immersive experience, conceiving each piece as an architectural or environmental structure rather than as a linear event. In other words, he has envisioned his massive sounds as fixtures that one may enter and touch as well as hear.

Niblock has used both acoustic and electronic timbres in live and recorded performances. A single piece might be performed live in concert, then moved to a gallery to become a permanent sound installation, then released as an album for private listening. In performance, he has encouraged musicians to wander through the concert space while playing drones: interacting with the acoustics of the space, physically varying the distance between one another to alter the relationships between tones. He has often chosen unusual instrumental combinations, as in *Kontradictionaries* (2004) for contrabass-flute, contrabass-saxophone, and contrabass-tuba; and *Three Orchids* (2003) for three orchestras. *Pan Fried 70* (2003) is for a single performer who pulls a nylon thread that is tied to a piano string. *Hurdy Hurry* (2000) consists of layered samples of hurdygurdy tones (recorded by fellow drone artist Jim O'Rourke); *AYU AKA "As Yet Untitled"* (2000) applies similar layering processes to sounds produced by a single baritone voice.

Like many sound artworks, Niblock's pieces draw on both musical and visual elements. He has cited John Cage, Morton Feldman, David Tudor, and La Monte Young as important influences, as well as the photographer Edward Weston. Niblock's artistic career in fact began with photography: he made several portraits of jazz artists during the 1950s. More recently, he combined sound and video in the installation *The Movement of People Working* (2003), which he exhibited in London, New York, and elsewhere. At the London exhibition, 12 large video screens displayed Niblock's films of laborers at work, weaving, fishing, harvesting, and building walls in Mexico, Hong Kong, Peru, and Hungary. A live flutist and guitarist joined recorded tones coming from loudspeakers at high volumes, to create a complementary sonic tableau.

In addition to touring worldwide, and recording for Touch, Mokai, and Extreme Records, Niblock has been the director of Experimental Intermedia, a nonprofit organization based in New York and Belgium. This organization has sponsored, presented, and promoted experimental music and sound art. It has also operated a recording label dedicated to experimental sounds.

BIBLIOGRAPHY

M. Alburger: "Phill Niblock," *21st-Century Music*, xii/5 (2005), 1–3
V. Straebel: "Technological Implications of Phil Niblock's Drone Music, Derived from Analytical Observations of Selected Works for Cello and String Quartet on Tape," *Organised Sound*, xiii/3 (2008), 225–35

MANDY-SUZANNE WONG

Nicholas, Albert [Nick] (*b* New Orleans, LA, 27 May 1900; *d* Paris, France, 3 Sept 1973). Jazz clarinetist. A Creole of color, he studied solfège with Lorenzo Tio jr., before taking up clarinet around 1910. By 1916, when he joined the US Navy, he had professional experience with the bands of Buddy Petit and Billy Marrero. After returning to New Orleans in 1920, he worked with the Maple Leaf Orchestra and Manuel Perez's band. In the period 1923–4 he became known as a fluent improviser while leading a band at Tom Anderson's saloon that included Luis Russell and Barney Bigard. This group traveled to Chicago to join Joe Oliver in 1924. Nicholas recorded with Oliver, and his work on "Jackass Blues" shows a penetrating upper register tone, quick vibrato, and ability to execute liquid slides between clarionregister notes. After a tour of the Far East (1927), he moved to New York and worked through the 1930s with such leaders as Luis Russell, Jelly Roll Morton, and Louis Armstrong. Following World War II he teamed up with Kid Ory and led various groups. After moving to Paris in 1953, he performed throughout Europe until his death. He recorded extensively, and although his later style featured progressive elements he maintained a solid foundation in the blues, frequently augmenting his resonant tone with a growling effect.

BIBLIOGRAPHY

J. Chilton: *Who's Who of Jazz: Storyville to Swing Street* (London, 1970, enlarged 4/1985)
B. Bigard: *With Louis and the Duke*, ed. B. Martyn (London, 1985)
D. Barker: *A Life in Jazz*, ed. A. Shipton (London, 1986)

CHARLES E. KINZER

Nicholas Brothers. Tap dance duo. The elder brother was Fayard Antonio Nicholas (*b* Mobile, AL, 20 Oct 1914; *d* New York, NY, 24 Jan 2006); the younger was Harold Lloyd Nicholas (*b* Winston-Salem, NC, 27 March 1921; *d* New York, NY, 3 July 2000). They grew up in Philadelphia, the sons of professional musicians who played in their own band at the Standard Theater. Fayard learned to dance by watching the great African American dancers who performed there, and he later taught his little brother what he knew. Neither of them ever had any formal dance training. Notwithstanding, by 1932 they had become featured performers at Harlem's famed Cotton Club in New York City and had appeared in *Pie, Pie Blackbird* (1932), a short film that was the first of their more than 50 movies. Fayard was 18 and Harold was 11 when they began their professional career. After several other Hollywood movies, including *The All-Colored Vaudeville Show* and *The Big Broadcast of 1936* (both 1935), they appeared on Broadway in *Ziegfeld Follies* (1936) and *Babes in Arms* (1937).

The Nicholas Brothers were the preeminent exponents of "flash dancing," an exhilarating hybrid of tap dance, balletic movements, and acrobatic stunts. One of their signature moves was to dance down a flight of broad steps, leaping over each other and landing in the splits on each step. This sequence can be seen in the finale of their most famous film performance, in *Stormy Weather* (1943). Notable among their other films are *Tin Pan Alley* (1940), *Down Argentine Way* (1940), *Sun Valley Serenade* (1941), and *The Pirate* (1948).

See also MUSICAL THEATER DANCE.

BIBLIOGRAPHY

R.E. Frank: *Tap! The Greatest Tap Dance Stars and Their Stories, 1900–1955* (New York, rev. 1994)

C.V. Hill: *Brotherhood in Rhythm: the Jazz Dancing of the Nicholas Brothers* (New York, 2000)

CLAUDE CONYERS

Nicholl, Horace (Wadham) (*b* Tipton, UK, 17 March 1848; *d* New York, NY 10 March 1922). Composer and organist of English birth. After serving as organist at Dudley (1867–70) and Stoke-on-Trent (1868–70), he emigrated to the United States and, at the urging of friends, went to Pittsburgh to take up a post as organist of St. Paul's Cathedral; later he served as organist of the Third Presbyterian Church. In 1878 he moved to New York, where he was organist at several important churches in Manhattan and Brooklyn, and also worked as an editor for the firms of Schuberth and G. Schirmer. As a regular contributor to the *Musical Courier* he wrote detailed analyses of new works by the major European composers of the day. He taught harmony and composition privately, and from 1888 to 1895 was on the faculty of Miss Porter's School in Farmington, Connecticut. In 1900 he announced that he was returning to England, but the next year he was in Leipzig, where most of his organ works were published. By 1904 he had returned to New York, where he remained until his death.

As a composer Nicholl united great contrapuntal skill with a contemporary taste; his organ pieces include 12 symphonic preludes and fugues, a symphonic poem called Life in six movements, and a Symphonische Fantasie über Psalm 130. Among his vocal works are the first four of a projected cycle of 12 oratorios, Adam, Abraham, Isaac, and Jacob (1880–90), all in manuscript; a setting of Henry Wadsworth Longfellow's The Golden Legend; a Cloister Scene for chorus and orchestra (op.6); and a Mass in E major, which were published. His orchestral works are reflective of the harmonic styles of Richard Wagner and Franz Liszt and anticipate Richard Strauss in their virtuoso orchestration. They include a Suite op.3; Symphonic Fantasies opp.5 and 7; a Symphony in G minor, The Nation's Mourning op.8; another in C major, op.12; symphonic poems, Tartarus op.11 and Hamlet (after Shakespeare) op.14; and a Scherzo-Fugue for small orchestra op.15. Besides these he wrote numerous piano pieces, songs, and anthems, and some chamber music and textbooks.

DAVID KELLEHER/J.A. FULLER MAITLAND/
CHRISTOPHER KENT/R

Nicholls, David Roy (*b* Birmingham, UK, 19 Nov 1955). British musicologist and composer. He studied music at St. John's College, Cambridge University (BA 1978, MA 1982, PhD 1986). He taught at Keele University (1987–2000), where he also served as Professor of Music (1995–2000) and Research Dean on the Faculty of Humanities (1999–2000). He was Visiting Professor at the College of William and Mary, Virginia (1998). He is currently Professor of Music at the University of Southampton (2000–; Head of Department, 2001–3).

A prolific writer and reviewer of American music of the 20th century, Nicholls's interests often focus on experimental composers, among them Charles Ives, Henry Cowell, and John Cage. Having received numerous grants toward research and teaching in addition to other honors, including a special commendation to Royal Over-Seas League PRS Composers' Award (1991) and election to Fellowship of the Royal Society of Arts (2002), he has been an external examiner and consultant for university music programs in musicology and composition throughout the United Kingdom. Nicholls's compositions, frequently chamber music and featuring solo voice, have been performed throughout the UK as well as in South Africa, Australia, and the United States.

A member of several professional music societies, Nicholls has served on the board of the Society for American Music (1998–2000) and as the editor (2001–5) and on the editorial advisory board (1995–) of its journal. He was a member of the advisory board of *Grove Dictionary of American Music*, second edition.

WRITINGS

American Experimental Music, 1890–1940 (Cambridge, 1990)

Cambridge History of American Music (Cambridge, 1998, 2/2004)

John Cage (Champaign, IL, 2007)

DEBORAH CAMPANA

Nichols [Daniell], **Caroline B.** (*b* Dedham, MA, 1864; *d* Boston, MA, 17 Aug 1939). Violinist, conductor, and founder of the FADETTE LADIES' ORCHESTRA OF BOSTON (also known as the Fadette Women's Orchestra of Boston). She was one of the first American women to support herself for most of her career as a conductor. The second of four children of a musical father, Nichols studied violin with Julius Eichberg, Leopold Lichtenberg, and Charles Loeffler; and music theory and orchestration with Percy Goetschius and J.B. Claus. She began her career as a violinist. She was a founding member of the Marion Osgood Ladies Orchestra, founded by Osgood in Boston in 1884, but she soon broke off from that group and, with ETHEL ATWOOD and four others, founded the Fadette Ladies' Orchestra in October 1888. Although the orchestra began as a sextet with Nichols as first violin, it quickly expanded into a full-fledged chamber orchestra. Nichols soon abandoned the concertmaster's chair and took up the conductor's baton. Nichols led the Fadettes for their entire lifespan of more than thirty years, performing thousands of concerts across the United States, Canada and Europe, most notably as headliners on B.F. Keith's vaudeville circuit.

BIBLIOGRAPHY

B. Naylor: *Anthology of the Fadettes* (?1937)

ANNA-LISE P. SANTELLA

Nichols, Red [Ernest Loring] (*b* Ogden, UT, 8 May 1905; *d* Las Vegas, NV, 28 June 1965). Cornetist, composer, and bandleader. Regarded as a prodigy on cornet at a young age and aided by his father, a college music teacher, he began his music career with a band called the Syncopating Seven while still in his teens. In 1923 he moved to New York, where his clean sound and strong reading ability quickly earned him work as a sideman. Soon after moving to New York Nichols met trombonist Miff Mole, with whom he subsequently had a productive collaborative relationship in the late 1920s and early 1930s. During this period, Nichols recorded prolifically with various groups under the name Red Nichols and the Five Pennies for the Brunswick label, although the same groups often recorded for different labels under different names. These groups played a progressive version of DIXIELAND JAZZ, experimenting with odd instrumentations and adventurous harmonies while remaining staggeringly popular.

By the early 1930s, however, the popularity of swing had overtaken Nichols's traditional jazz and he was obliged to perform with show bands and pit orchestras rather than his own groups. Ultimately, a stint leading Bob Hope's orchestra led him to California, where economic hard times and family illness forced him to work in wartime shipyards. By 1944 Nichols had returned to music, reforming the Five Pennies band to play small Los Angeles area club gigs. He led this group for the next 20 years, recording and rebuilding the fame he had experienced in the 1920s. In 1959 Nichols recorded the soundtrack to the film *The Five Pennies*, which was loosely based on his own life. In 1965 he died only hours before a concert in Las Vegas. As a result of his commercial success during the 1920s and the fact that he never had the fiery improvisatory abilities of his two main influences, Louis Armstrong and Bix Beiderbecke, Nichols has often been regarded with suspicion as a sellout or a hustler. However, he made some of the most ambitious recordings of the 1920s, and the role his band played as a springboard for the careers of countless younger musicians, including Jimmy Dorsey, Benny Goodman, Jack Teagarden, and Artie Shaw, cannot be denied.

BIBLIOGRAPHY

S.M. Stroff: *Red Head: a Chronological Survey of "Red" Nichols and his Five Pennies* (Newark, NJ, 1996)

P.R. Evans: *The Red Nichols Story: after Intermission, 1942–1965* (Lanham, MD, 1997)

A.J. Sammut: "Red Nichols: the Red Heads," <http://www.allaboutjazz.com/php/article.php?id=39412> (2011)

DAVID CHEVAN

Nicholson, Stuart (*b* Cardiff, UK, 8 Jan 1948). British jazz journalist and historian. He studied music theory and clarinet at the Welsh College of Music and Drama (1967–71), followed by ten years leading a jazz-rock band under the stage name Nick Stewart. In the early 1980s he began writing on jazz for various magazines and newspapers in the UK. Since then his pieces have appeared in a range of publications in Europe and the United States, including *The Western Mail, Gramophone, The Observer, Jazzwise, Jazz Times,* and *The Wire*. His writing expanded to book-length studies in the 1990s, including highly regarded biographies of Ella Fitzgerald, Billie Holiday, and Duke Ellington, as well as broader surveys of jazz in the 1980s and jazz-rock. Since the early 2000s Nicholson has been a key chronicler of the European scene, especially movements blending jazz with local folkloric forms, classical music, and electronica. His controversial 2005 collection of essays *Is Jazz Dead? (Or has it Moved to a New Address)* examines this movement through the paradigm of "glocalization"—the localized application and interpretation of global phenomena. A second book on the topic was forthcoming as of 2011. He has lectured widely on jazz subjects and has held teaching posts at Leeds College of Music, where he was a visiting professor as of 2011.

WRITINGS

Ella Fitzgerald: a Biography of the First Lady of Jazz (London, 1993, 2/2004)

Billie Holiday (London, 1995/R)

Jazz: the Modern Resurgence (London, 1990; repr. as *Jazz: the 1980s Resurgence,* New York, 1995)

Jazz Rock: a History (London, 1998)

Reminiscing in Tempo: a Portrait of Duke Ellington (London, 1999)

Is Jazz Dead? (Or has it Moved to a New Address) (London, 2005)

MICHAEL C. HELLER

Nickelback. Canadian rock group. It formed in Vancouver in 1995. Members include vocalist Chad Kroeger, his brother, bassist Mike Kroeger, guitarist Ryan Peake, and drummer Daniel Adair, who replaced Ryan Vikedal in 2005. Nickelback's second studio album, *Silver Side Up* (Roadrunner, 2001), garnered mainstream success as a result of the ubiquitous single "How you remind me," which was number one on both Canadian and US charts and was the most played song of 2002 on US radio according to *Billboard*.

Although rooted in a postgrunge aesthetic dominated by distorted guitars and Kroeger's coarse vocal timbre, the band's longevity has allowed it to move into other musical territory. Subsequent studio albums—*The Long Road* (Roadrunner, 2003), *All The Right Reasons* (Roadrunner, 2005), and *Dark Horse* (Roadrunner/Atlantic EMI, 2008)—feature riff-based hard rock songs alongside anthemic power ballads that have found success in both mainstream rock and pop radio formats. This broad appeal owes much to Kroeger's narrative texts, which adhere to a distinct polarity between macho tales of sex and alcohol ("Something in your mouth") and earnest love songs ("If everyone cared"). The sardonic and self-reflexive single "Rock Star" is a notable exception to Nickelback's overall preponderance for sincere expression.

Nickelback's reception has been particularly divisive. While fans have propelled the band's worldwide sales to over 30 million albums, critics have consistently lambasted the group for its perceived inauthenticity. Accusations of overt commercialism and lack of originality have been intensified by the circulation of an Internet meme that superimposes "How you remind me" and "Someday" to highlight the musical similarities shared by the group's most successful singles. Despite

Nickelback's critical reception, however, the group's ability to craft memorable riffs and sing-along choruses and to connect with listeners through high-energy live shows represents a significant hard rock presence in contemporary mainstream music.

LEANNE FETTERLEY

Nickelodeon. In the early 20th century, a small storefront motion picture theater where the admission fee was five cents. It also may refer to a coin-operated player piano, often with added percussion effects, used in bars, dance halls, and amusement arcades.

Nickerson, Camille (*b* New Orleans, LA, 30 March 1888; *d* Washington, DC, 27 April 1982). Pianist, composer, and teacher. Her father, William, was a violinist, conductor, composer, and music teacher in New Orleans who founded the music department at Straight University, organizing both an orchestra and the Nickerson School of Music. Camille taught at the school after her graduation and, while a student, founded the B-Sharp Music Club. She obtained her formal training at Oberlin University, earning both bachelor's (1916) and master's degrees (1932), and was a member of Pi Kappa Lambda. She began composing while still a student and continued through her concert performances in the 1920s. Many of her compositions reflect her interest in Creole folk music. Assuming the stage name of "the Louisiana Lady," she promoted the music of that region in all her public appearances.

Nickerson abandoned active touring in favor of a faculty appointment at Howard University, where she taught piano (1926–62). She was active in a number of organizations, most notably in the National Association of Negro Musicians, of which she was named president in 1935. She encouraged emerging artists and performing organizations; she served as rehearsal accompanist and coach for some performances of the National Negro Opera Company in Washington, DC, in the 1940s. After her retirement in 1962 she became friends with William Grant Still, with whom she shared some of her compositions.

Her music includes original works and arrangements of folk songs, and she also wrote a number of works for younger pianists.

BIBLIOGRAPHY

D.E. McGinty and C. Nickerson: "The Louisiana Lady," *BPM*, vii/1 (1979), 81–94

A. Simpson: "The Louisiana Lady," *Louisiana History: the Journal of the Louisiana Historical Association*, xxxvi/4 (1995), 431–51

KAREN M. BRYAN

Nicks, Stevie [Stephanie] **(Lynn)** (*b* Phoenix, AZ, 26 May 1948). Singer-songwriter and rock musician. Nicks began her career with the San Francisco Bay Area band Fritz in the late 1960s. Her early influences were Janis Joplin, Jimi Hendrix, and Joni Mitchell. In the early 1970s she moved to Los Angeles with bandmate Lindsey Buckingham and recorded the album *Buckingham/Nicks* (Polydor, 1973). In 1975 the pair joined FLEETWOOD MAC and became integral to the band's change from blues rock to pop. Nicks wrote several of the band's hits (e.g., "Rhiannon" and "Dreams"). She sings in the alto range with a raspy timbre recognizable even amid close harmonies of other singers. Her voice, songwriting, and association with Fleetwood Mac made her one of the most important female rock musicians of the 1970s and 1980s. In the early 1980s, Nicks embarked on a solo career while still a member of Fleetwood Mac. Her first album, *Bella Donna* (Atlantic, 1981), included the hit "Edge of Seventeen" and duets with Tom Petty and Don Henley. Produced by Jimmy Iovine and backed by members of Petty's band, the recordings maintained a pop rock sound without the complex and polished production style of late-1970s Fleetwood Mac. Nicks added synthesizers on *The Wild Heart* (Atlantic, 1983). The album's primary single was "Stand Back," a dance-oriented hit featuring Prince (uncredited) on synthesizer. Nicks continued in a synth-rock style on *Rock a Little* (Atlantic, 1985), with singles "I can't wait" and "Talk to me," one of Nicks's few hits not self-penned. In 1993, she left Fleetwood Mac just before recording *Street Angel* (Atlantic, 1994), which was received poorly by critics. Nicks has since released two studio albums: *Trouble in Shangri-La* (Reprise, 2001), which was coproduced by Sheryl Crow, and *In Your Dreams* (Reprise, 2011).

OLIVIA CARTER MATHER

Nico [Päffgen, Christa] (*b* Cologne, Germany, 16 Oct 1938; *d* Ibiza, Spain, 18 July 1988). Singer, composer, instrumentalist, model, and actress of German birth. In her teens, she embarked on a successful modeling career, which led to roles in several European films, most famously in Federico Fellini's *La Dolce Vita* (1960). In 1963 she played the lead role in Jacques Poitrenaud's *Strip-Tease* (also called *Sweet Skin*); she also sang the theme song, a collaboration with Serge Gainsbourg. Her first recorded release was a single, "I'm Not Sayin'" (b side "The Last Mile"), for Rolling Stones manager Andrew Loog Oldham's Immediate label in 1965. After relocating to New York, Nico became a close associate of Andy Warhol, appearing in several of his experimental films and spending a brief tenure as singer with THE VELVET UNDERGROUND, contributing vocals to three songs on their first album, released in 1967. That year Nico also released her first solo album, *Chelsea Girl* (Polydor), but it was her second album, *The Marble Index* (Elektra, 1969), that was the first emphatic expression of her singular artistic vision. Devastatingly bleak and entirely self-penned, Nico accompanied herself on harmonium with sparse, experimental arrangements by John Cale. *Desertshore* (Reprise, 1970) mined similar territory, and more collaborations with Cale and Brian Eno followed. She continued her involvement in film throughout the 1970s, acting in and contributing music to the films of French experimental director Philippe Garrel. Her recorded output and touring became increasingly sporadic and chaotic as the result of chronic heroin addiction, but she continued to perform around the world until her death from a brain hemorrhage after a bicycling accident in 1988. She has been cited as a significant influence by a wide variety of musicians including Patti Smith, Lisa Gerrard, Elliott Smith, and Bauhaus.

BIBLIOGRAPHY

J. Young: *Nico: Songs they Never Play on the Radio* (London, 1992)

R. Witts: *Nico: the Life and Lies of an Icon* (London, 1993)

R. Unterberger: *White Light White Heat: the Velvet Underground Day by Day* (London, 2009)

LISA MacKINNEY

Nielsen, Alice (*b* Nashville, TN, 7 June 1868 or 1876; *d* New York, NY, 8 March 1943). Soprano. Her year of birth is ordinarily given as 1876, but according to her death record, she died at the age of 74. She began as a singer in church choirs, and made her professional debut in 1893 with the Pike Opera Company in Oakland, California. She was then engaged to sing at the Tivoli Theatre in San Francisco, where she soon became a favorite. Henry Clay Barnabee heard her sing, and offered her a position with what was then America's leading light opera company, the Bostonians. She spent two years with the ensemble, singing such roles as Maid Marian in De Koven and H.B. Smith's *Robin Hood* and Yvonne in Victor Herbert's *The Serenade*. After she left the troupe (taking with her several of its leading players and precipitating its demise), she starred in two operettas which Herbert composed especially for her, *The Fortune Teller* (1898; also in London, 1901) and *The Singing Girl* (1899). In 1902 she abandoned the popular musical stage to study opera in Rome. The following year she made her European debut in Naples as Marguerite in Gounod's *Faust*. Success in London with *The Fortune Teller* had brought her to the notice of the impresario Henry Russell, who introduced her to Covent Garden audiences in 1904. She was a "fresh and charming" Zerlina at her debut there in *Don Giovanni*; she also sang Mimì to Caruso's Rodolfo and Gilda to Victor Maurel's Rigoletto, as well as Susanna and Micaëla. She sang at the San Carlo, Naples before returning in 1905 to New York, where her appearances in *Don Pasquale* at the Casino Theatre failed to impress. With Henry Russell's San Carlo Opera Company she sang in *Don Pasquale* in a tour of the United States. In 1909 she joined the newly formed Boston Opera Company, under the direction of Russell, and remained with them as principal lyric soprano until 1914. Recognized as a "gentle and appealing artist," she also enjoyed popularity at the Metropolitan during this time, retiring to teach after a further short spell in operetta in 1917. Her clear, youthful-sounding voice took well to recording, though she lacked the individuality of style and timbre to achieve lasting distinction.

GERALD BORDMAN AND J.B. STEANE/R

Nigro, Susan (*b* Chicago, IL, 1951). Contrabassoonist. She holds bachelor's and master's degrees from Northwestern University and an additional degree from Roosevelt University. Among her teachers are Burl Lane and Wilbur Simpson. She was a member of the Civic Orchestra of Chicago, has appeared with the Chicago SO and St. Paul Chamber Orchestra, and is a founding member of the Chicago Bassoon Quartet and the contrabassoon duo The Two Contras. Most notably, she is one of the few contrabassoon soloists in the United States. Her efforts to promote the instrument have led her to commission and premiere multiple solo works, some of which can be heard on her CDs *The Big Bassoon* (Crystal Records, 1995) and *Little Tunes for the Big Bassoon* (Crystal Records, 1996).

KIMBERLY WOOLLY

Nikisch, Arthur (*b* Lébényi Szent-Miklós [now in Hungary], 12 Oct 1855; *d* Leipzig, Germany, 23 Jan 1922). Austro-Hungarian conductor. In 1866 he became a student at the Vienna Conservatory. He played violin in the famous performance of Ludwig van Beethoven's Ninth Symphony conducted by Richard Wagner in Bayreuth in 1872. In 1874 he joined the Vienna Court Orchestra, playing under Johannes Brahms, Franz Liszt, Giuseppe Verdi, and Wagner. In 1878 he become second conductor at the opera in Leipzig and was named principal conductor the following year.

Nikisch accepted the directorship of the Boston SO in 1889. His significance was instantly appreciated by such New York critics as Henry Krehbiel and W.J. Henderson. Anton Seidl had already accustomed them to "liberties" of tempo and expression, as prescribed by Wagner. "The man is full of magnetism," was Henderson's first impression. "He has a sympathetic appreciation of the composer's feeling…that seems contemporaneous with the birth of the work in the composer's mind." In Boston, however, Nikisch split opinion. His passion and spontaneity were favorably contrasted with the restraint of his Boston SO predecessor, Wilhelm Gericke. But Gericke was the superior disciplinarian, and some writers found Nikisch's "rubato effects" inauthentic and "theatrical." Nikisch's rendition of Beethoven's Fifth Symphony, on 8 November 1889, ignited a firestorm of controversy in the press lasting 24 days. Also, though he maintained the orchestra's allegiance to such local composers as George Whitefield Chadwick, Arthur Foote, Charles Loeffler, and Edward MacDowell, Nikisch's fundamental repertoire predilections—for Liszt, Wagner, and Pyotr Il'ych Tchaikovsky—were not Boston predilections. Nikisch left Boston after four seasons with one year left on his contract, having conducted 388 of the Boston SO's 398 nonsummer concerts, including 196 on tour in 32 cities. The circumstances of his departure were complex. It may be summarized that Nikisch and Henry Higginson, the orchestra's founder, grew antipathetic. Though Higginson preferred more conservative conductors, he recognized the genius in Nikisch and offered him the Boston directorship again in 1906; Nikisch surprised Higginson by declining.

As leader of both the Berlin PO and the Leipzig Gewandhaus Orchestra beginning in 1895, Nikisch became Europe's most famous and influential symphonic conductor. In addition, he became conductor of the PO concerts in Hamburg in 1897. He toured the United States in April 1912 with the London SO. His 1913 Berlin recording of Beethoven's Fifth, a reading mercurial in temper and flexible in pulse, documents what Boston was reacting to a quarter century before.

BIBLIOGRAPHY

Grove7 (H-H. Schönzeler and J. Horowitz)

A.M. Abell: "Arthur Nikisch: the World's Premier Conductor," *Musical Courier*, lxiv (3 April 1912), 5

"The Advent of Arthur Nikisch," *Musical Courier*, lxiv (10 April 1912), 21

E.S. Kelley: "The Art of Conducting as Exemplified in the Achievements of Arthur Nikisch," *Musical Courier*, lxix (16 Sept 1914), 5

M.A.D. Howe: *The Boston Symphony Orchestra: an Historical Sketch* (Boston, 1914, rev. and enlarged 2/1931/R 1978), 153

A.C. Boult: "Arthur Nikisch," *ML*, iii (1922), 117

A.C. Boult: "Nikisch and Method in Rehearsal," *MR*, xi (1950), 122

J. Horowitz: *Classical Music in America: a History* (New York, 2005)

JOSEPH HOROWITZ

Niles, John Jacob (*b* Louisville, KY, 28 April 1892; *d* nr Lexington, KY, 1 March 1980). Folksinger, folk-music collector, and composer. He began collecting and transcribing songs at age 14 and composed his first song, "Go 'way from my window," in 1907. A skilled pianist upon his graduation from Louisville's Dupont Manual High School, he continued his studies at Cincinnati Conservatory and the Schola Cantorum in Paris. A pilot with the US Army Signal Corps during World War I, he published two collections of wartime songs, *Singing Soldiers* (1927) and *The songs my mother never taught me* (1929).

While based in New York, Niles toured internationally with contralto Marion Kerby from 1929 to 1933, arranging African American and Appalachian material for their repertoire. He also began publishing his arrangements

John Jacob Niles with dulcimer, Cordia, Kentucky, 1937. (CBS/Landov)

and compositions with Carl Fischer and G. Schirmer and recording for Victor's Red Seal label. From 1931 to 1934 Niles collected folk music while accompanying photographer Doris Ulmann (1882–1934) on expeditions through the Appalachian Mountains. These trips provided material for his performances and culminated in publication of his *Ballad Book* (1961). He also composed original folklike songs including "I wonder as I wander" and "Black is the color of my true love's hair."

While at the John C. Campbell Folk School, Niles married journalist Rena Lipetz in 1936 and two years later they settled at Boot Hill Farm near Lexington, Kentucky. Titled the "dean of American balladeers" by *Time* magazine, Niles enjoyed an extensive performance career spanning 70 years that included concerts at the White House, New York's Carnegie Hall and Town Hall, and the first Newport Folk Festival. Niles's recordings were released by RCA, Folkways, Disc, Tradition, and his own Boone Tolliver label. His songs were widely performed by Metropolitan Opera divas such as Gladys Swarthout, Eleanor Steber, and Patrice Munsel. Niles's dramatic performance style was characterized by his highly enunciated, countertenor voice, accompanied by strums of his handcrafted dulcimers.

The John Jacob Niles Collection of manuscripts, field notebooks, photographs, instruments, and recordings is located at the University of Kentucky, as is the John Jacob Niles Center for American Music.

RECORDINGS
(selective)

I Wonder as I Wander, Carols and Love Songs (Tradition 1957; reissue Empire 2006)

WRITINGS

The Ballad Book of John Jacob Niles (New York 1960; rev. Lexington, KY, 1998)

John Jacob Niles Songbook (New York 1982/R2001)

BIBLIOGRAPHY

R. Pen: *I Wonder As I Wander* (Lexington, KY, 2010)

RON PEN

Nilsson [Svennsson], **(Märta) Birgit** (*b* Västra Karup, Sweden, 17 May 1918; *d* Västra Karup, Sweden, 25 Dec 2005). Swedish soprano. She studied at the Swedish Royal Academy of Music, Stockholm, where her teachers included Joseph Hislop. In 1946 she debuted at the Swedish Royal Opera, Stockholm, as Agathe (*Der Freischütz*), later singing Leonore, Lady Macbeth, the Marschallin, Sieglinde, Donna Anna, Venus, Senta, Aida, Tosca, and Lisa (*The Queen of Spades*). In 1951 she sang Electra (*Idomeneo*) at Glyndebourne, creating a stir with her keen-edged, forthright singing. During the 1954–5 season she sang her first *Götterdämmerung*, as Brünnhilde, and *Salome* at Stockholm and made her Munich debut as Brünnhilde in the complete *Ring*. Also in 1954 she first appeared in Vienna and, as Elsa, began her long association with Bayreuth, returning (1957–70) as Isolde, Sieglinde, and Brünnhilde. Her interpretation of Isolde in Wieland Wagner's 1966 production was of searing vocal and dramatic power. She first sang at Covent Garden in the 1957 *Ring*, returning as Isolde,

Amelia (*Un ballo in maschera*, with the Swedish Royal Opera in 1960), Strauss's Electra, and Turandot and Leonore. She made her American debut in San Francisco in 1956, and she first sang at the Metropolitan Opera in 1959 as Isolde. Because of difficulties with the Internal Revenue Service, Nilsson's North American career was interrupted from 1975 to 1979, at the height of her fame. But the issues were eventually resolved and she still managed to appear 223 times at the Metropolitan Opera in 16 roles, including two complete *Ring* cycles (1961–62, 1974–75).

Nilsson was generally considered the finest Wagnerian soprano of her day. Her voice was even throughout its range, pure in sound and perfect in intonation with a free-ringing top; its size was phenomenal. Her dramatic abilities were considerable. Electra was possibly her finest achievement, although the sheer power and opulence of her voice, coupled with a certain coolness, made her an ideal Turandot. In both of these, as well as in Wagnerian roles, her phenomenal stamina was perfectly suited to the rigorous demands of the music. Her many recordings include Brünnhilde and Isolde as well as the title roles in *Turandot* and *Elektra*. Her second recording of Isolde (Bayreuth, 1966), and her Electra remain perhaps her most thrilling achievements. In 1988 the American-Scandinavian Foundation established the Birgit Nilsson Prize, awarded to promising young opera singers, to commemorate the 350th anniversary of New Sweden, the first Swedish settlement in the United States. In 2008, the Birgit Nilsson Foundation announced that it would begin awarding another Birgit Nilsson Prize, this a million dollar prize awarded every second or third year, for outstanding achievement, to a concert or opera singer, a classical or opera conductor, or a specific production by an opera company. Plácido Domingo was the first recipient of the prize in 2009.

BIBLIOGRAPHY

W. Jefferies: "Birgit Nilsson," *Opera*, xi (1960), 607–12
A. Natan: "Nilsson, Birgit," *Primadonna: Lob der Stimmen* (Basle, 1962)
W. Weaver: "The Prima Donna at Work: Die Nilsson and La Nilsson," *HiFi/MusAm*, xv/2 (1965), 48–51, 119
A. Blyth: "Birgit Nilsson," *Gramophone*, xlvii (1969–70), 1123
J. Young: "Skanska: Birgit Nilsson on Home Ground," *ON*, xxxix/15 (1974–5), 48–51
B. Nilsson: *Mina minnesbilder* (Stockholm, 1977; Eng. trans. Garden City, NJ., 1981, as *My Memoirs in Pictures*)
S. Wadsworth: "And Still Champ…Birgit Nilsson Revisited," *ON*, xliv/13 (1979–80), 8–12, 35
R. Christiansen: *The Prima Donna* (London, 1984), 167–70
B. Nilsson: *La Nilsson* (Stockholm, 1995; Eng. trans. Lebanon, NH., 2007, as *La Nilsson: My Life in Opera*)
J.B. Steane: *Singers of the Century* (London, 1996), 131–40
Peter G. Davis: "Farewell to the Valkyrie," *ON*, lxx/10 (2006)

HAROLD ROSENTHAL/ALAN BLYTH/
JOSEPH E. MORGAN

Nilsson (III), Harry (Edward) (*b* Brooklyn, NY, 15 June 1941; *d* Agoura Hills, CA, 15 Jan 1994). Pop singer-songwriter. Commercial success in the United States eluded Nilsson for most of the 1960s, even though his early songs were recorded by producer Phil Spector and by television's the Monkees, and even though his own 1967 album *Pandemonium Shadow Show* (RCA)

received public praise from the Beatles. Finally, in 1969, Three Dog Night reached the American Top-10 with a recording of Nilsson's "One"; in that same year, the Oscar-winning film *Midnight Cowboy* featured Nilsson's cover of Fred Neil's "Everybody's Talkin'," for which Nilsson would win his first Grammy. He became known for his quirky compositional style and multitracked vocal arrangements. Further chart success came with a wildly popular, mawkish (and Grammy-winning) rendering of Badfinger's "Without you," as well as with his own calypso-folk song "Coconut," both singles from *Nilsson Schmilsson* (RCA, 1971). As the 1970s progressed, his career cooled; the deaths of friends Mama Cass and Keith Moon in Nilsson's London apartment (in 1974 and 1978, respectively) contributed to his withdrawal from the limelight. Since Nilsson's own death from a heart attack in 1994, his music has continued to be heard in television and film, especially when New York is the setting: Nilsson's songs and recordings have been used in the soundtracks for "Seinfeld," *Forrest Gump*, and, most thoroughly, *You've Got Mail*, which included "I guess the Lord must be in New York City" (1969), "The Puppy Song" (1969), "Remember (Christmas)" (1972), and Nilsson's rendition of "Over the Rainbow" (1988).

CHRISTOPHER DOLL

Nin-Culmell, Joaquín (María) (*b* Berlin, Germany, 5 Sept 1908; *d* Berkeley, CA, 14 Jan 2004). Composer and pianist of Cuban descent. The son of Joaquín Nin and the singer Rosa Culmell, he began his musical studies in Barcelona with Granados student Conchita Badia and later studied at the Schola Cantorum and the Paris Conservatoire, where his teachers included Paul Dukas. Alfred Cortot and Ricardo Viñes were among his piano teachers. During the summers of 1930, 1932, and 1934 Nin-Culmell studied with Manuel de Falla and in 1936 gave the first performance of de Falla's *Pour le tombeau de Paul Dukas*. In 1939 he moved to the United States, where he continued to give premieres of works by Spanish composers. His teaching appointments included positions at Williams College (1940–50) and the University of California, Berkeley (1950–74). In 1962 he was named a corresponding member of the Real Academia de San Fernando.

Nin-Culmell strove in his works to capture the spirit, rather than the letter, of Spanish folk music, often changing the rhythm, mode, or melodic contour of traditional melodies. A number of his works, including the ballet *El burlador de Sevilla* and the opera *La Celestina*, draw upon Spanish literature.

WORKS

Stage: Yerma (incid music, F.G. Lorca), 1956; El burlador de Sevilla (ballet, T. de Molina), 1957–65; La Celestina (op, F. de Rojas), 1965–85; Le rêve de Cyrano (ballet), 1978
Vocal: 2 Poems (J. Manrique), 1v, str qt, 1934–6; 3 Poems (G. Vicente), 1950; 3 Traditional Cuban Songs, chorus, 1952; 2 Spanish Christmas Villancicos, chorus, 1956–7; 24 Popular Songs of Catalonia, 1v, pf, 1957–61; 4 Popular Songs of Andalusia, 1v, pf, 1959–61; 4 Popular Songs of Catalonia, 1v, pf, 1959–61; 4 Popular Songs of Salamanca, 1v, pf, 1959–61; Cantata (J. Pradas), 1v, str orch, hp, clvd, 1965; Dedication Mass for St Mary's Cathedral, San Francisco, chorus, org,

1965–6; 5 Traditional Spanish Songs, 1v, pf, 1971; 6 Popular Sephardic Songs, 1v, pf, 1982; Afro-Cuban Lullaby, 1v, pf, 1985–90; ¡10 de octubre!, chorus, brass (J. Martí), 1985–90; 2 Songs (Martí), 1v, pf, 1985–90; Ragpicker's Song (A. Nin), chorus, pf, 1988; Canciones de la Barraca, 1v, pf, 1997–8; Te Deum, chorus, org, cymbals, 1999

Inst: 3 Impressions, pf, 1929; Sonata breve, pf, 1932; Homenaje a Falla, orch, 1933; Pf Qnt, 1934–6; 3 Homenajes, pf, 1941–90; 6 Variations on a Theme of Luis Milán, gui, 1945; Pf Conc., 1946; 2 Cuban Dances of Ignacio Cervantes, gui, 1947; Tonadas, 4 vols., pf, 1956–61; Diferencias, orch, 1962; Vc Conc., 1962–3 [after A. Viola]; Alejandro y Luis, pf, 1983; 12 Cuban Dances, pf, 1985; 6 Variations on a Theme of Bach, org, 1987; Sym. of the Mysteries, org, 1994; La Matilde y El Emilio, gui

Principal publishers: Belwin-Mills, Boileau, Broude, Eschig, Sacred

BIBLIOGRAPHY

G. Chase: *The Music of Spain* (New York, 2/1959)

A. Woehl: "Nin-Culmell: 'España me persigui'," *Clavier*, xxvi/1 (1987), 20–27

CAROL A. HESS

9/11. Almost immediately after four hijacked planes crashed on 11 September 2011 conversations started about how the tragedy should be understood in the context of popular culture. Discussions about violence and popular culture also arose, seemingly fed not only by the basic truth that 11 September was a day of terrible carnage but also by the notion that the mode of attack was inextricable from visual codes developed by Hollywood. During the first weeks after 9/11, numerous commentators insisted that Americans would be shaken out of their consumer habits and refuse to pay to see violent movies: it quickly became clear that music would play a special role as a cultural first responder on this new landscape.

Along with widely-circulated photographs and the *New York Times* series of impressionistic biographical life stories ("Portraits of Grief") popular song became the most widely-accepted "authentic" vehicle for commemorating American loss and expressing the grief and confusion that ensued after the attacks. For months and years after 9/11 popular musicians in the United States attempted to provide efficient articulations of American attitudes in the wake of the attacks. Two key television programs in the months following 9/11 capture the general outlines of the cultural industries' responses to the tragedy. On 21 September 2001 a telethon called *A Tribute to Heroes* was broadcast on all of the major networks. The performers on this widely-seen program included Bruce Springsteen, Billy Joel, Tom Petty, Paul Simon, Neil Young, and Sting, and its musical palette, while large enough to include some vague nods to hard rock and hip hop, was organized around evocations of a national togetherness defined by interracial unity. The visual and musical emblem of the show was the white lead singer performing with a Black gospel choir: this shorthand helped efface any of the complexities of identity (especially those having to do with Arabs, South Asians, or Muslims) that would vex so many Americans in the coming years. The racial unity of *Tribute* was communicated not only through the presence of gospel sounds, but also through the integration of various bands that do not usually feature African American musicians.

At the Country Music Awards held on 7 November 2001 Alan Jackson debuted his 9/11 song "Where Were You (When the World Stopped Turning)." Radio programmers had it on the air by the next morning and it topped the country music charts for five weeks from late December. The song's title became Jackson's vehicle for carrying a series of after-the-fact prescriptions for what Americans should have been doing as the planes hit, and then just after. The imagined "you" of Jackson's song is a teacher of "innocent children," who calls Mom, turns off the violent movie on the television (in favor of *I Love Lucy*), and most important, dusts off

Diddy (Sean Combs) performs at "United We Stand What More Can I Give," Washington, DC, 21 October 2001. (Greg E. Mathieson/MAI /Landov)

the Bible, presumably to read the verse from *1 Corinthians* that Jackson paraphrases in the chorus. While other country musicians—most notably Toby Keith—would record more militaristic songs, it was Jackson who most fully captured the mood described by Clint Eastwood on the *A Tribute to Heroes* telethon as "wounded" but also "renewed in strength."

The musical responses to 9/11 captured in the telethon and the Alan Jackson performance were powerful contributors to a culture that was struggling to figure out what "September 12th art"—to use British journalist Mark Lawson's formulation—should attempt to accomplish and what it should avoid. A major player here was Clear Channel Communications, a powerful media conglomerate that exerts its strength through its ownership of radio stations, its concert promotions, and its control of advertising venues. Media industry magazines reported on 14 September that Clear Channel Communications had released a list of "banned songs" that should not be played on their more than one thousand radio stations in the United States, out of sensitivity to their distraught listeners. The banned list is a bizarre and at times hilarious compendium of songs by bands from AC/DC to the Zombies. While Clear Channel's official position is that this "rumor" about censorship was not true, many local program directors admitted that in the wake of the circulated instructions numerous songs were removed from rotation.

The consensus position that developed in the first months after 9/11 reached an apotheosis of sorts with the release of Bruce Springsteen's record *The Rising* in the summer of 2002, about six weeks before the first anniversary of the attacks. No other work of 9/11 popular art has been met with the full-on media embrace that surrounded this release, which was carefully positioned by Springsteen and his marketing team as a major memorial. In countless print and broadcast interviews Springsteen has spoken eloquently about how he felt called to produce this work of remembrance, inspired first by a fan who yelled to him ("Hey, Bruce, we need you") out of a car window at the New Jersey shore. On *The Rising* Springsteen turns the camera *away* from the realities of the descent of planes, towers, and bodies that defined the day, and constructs instead a poetics of spiritual rebirth that is apparently apolitical.

Music-world objections to the consensus position took some time to develop, but when they did come (mostly in the world of hip-hop performance) the anger was palpable. These moments of protest were organized first around global concerns. Even in the midst of significant public support for the war in Afghanistan, rap artists, both mainstream and underground, launched critiques of American imperialism and militarism. Nas was one of the first major artists to speak against the seeming unanimity with his song "What Goes Around," which implies that that the destruction of the towers was inevitable and traceable to American hubris on the world stage. Boston-based indie rapper Mr. Lif was more concrete in "Home of the Brave" (2002), which expresses the belief that oil was the real reason for the war. Talib Kweli, who has been a major force in

independent rap music since the late 1990s, urged African Americans not to fall for the easy seductions of post-9/11 patriotism. Perhaps most galling to this generation of rappers was the virtually compulsory nature of patriotic declarations, and more particularly the culture-wide sanctification of police officers, the most visible figures of racist oppression for many young African Americans.

Hip-hop artists were in the vanguard again when it came to explaining how misleading (and politically motivated) it was for American government officials and media powers to try to project all post-9/11 evil in the world onto one-dimensional targets such as Osama Bin Laden or "the terrorists." Another of the fascinating and culturally complex ways that African American artists responded to the "blank check" of militarism that Congress handed the President to use in South Asia and the Middle East (as well as repressive surveillance measures in the United States) was to incorporate the sights and sounds of Middle Eastern and South Asian culture into their own work, whether this involved integrating the sounds of India's Bollywood or the images of Middle Eastern belly dancing into hip hop and rhythm and blues songs and videos. For young African Americans in the years after 9/11 to announce that their music *needs* South Asia and the Middle East must be heard as a cultural declaration of interdependence. From Jay-Z to Busta Rhymes and Erick Sermon, many hip-hop artists working in the aftermath of 9/11 have insisted that their culture relies on cultural synergies created by reaching out (or into) the various cultures of South Asia and the Middle East.

BIBLIOGRAPHY

M. Lawson: "After the Fall," *Guardian* (16 Aug 2002), <http://www.guardian.co.uk/film/2002/aug/16/artsfeatures.september11>
E. Nuzum: "Crash Into Me, Baby!: America's Implicit Music Censorship Since 11 September," *Freemuse* (2004), <http://freemuse.synkron.com/graphics/Publications/PDF/18.pdf>
D. Heller, ed.: *Selling 9/11: How a National Tragedy Became a Commodity* (New York, 2005)
J. Ritter and J. Martin Daughtry, eds.: *Music in the Post-9/11 World* (New York, 2007)
M. Sturken: *Tourists of History: Memory, Kitsch, and Consumerism from Oklahoma City to Ground Zero* (Durham, 2007)
J. Melnick: *9/11 Culture: America under Construction* (Malden, MA, 2009)
N.T. Sharma: *Hip Hop Desis: South Asian Americans, Blackness, and a Global Race Consciousness* (Durham, 2010)

JEFFREY MELNICK

Nine Inch Nails. Nine Inch Nails is the name given to the ever-changing musical collective brought together by leader TRENT REZNOR (Michael Trent Reznor, *b* Mercer, PA, 17 May 1965) to interpret his music in the studio and live on tour. Between 1988 and 1999, when the band ceased touring, over 20 different band members assisted Reznor. The most involved of these musicians included Charlie Clouser, keyboards (*b* Hanover, NH, 28 June 1963), Alessandro Cortini, keyboards (*b* Bologna, Italy, 24 May 1976), Jerome Dillon, drums (*b* Columbus, OH, 16 July 1969), Robin Finck, guitar (*b* Park Ridge, NJ, 7 Nov 1971), Danny Lohner, bass (*b* Corpus Christi, TX, 13 Dec 1970), Richard Patrick, guitar (*b* Needham, MA,

10 May 1968), and Chris Vrenna, keyboards (*b* Erie, PA, 23 Feb 1967). Reznor began recording his initial demos at the Right Track Studios in Cleveland for free when the studio was empty; he eventually played everything on the sessions except drums. The resultant album, *Pretty Hate Machine*, was a slow grower, but after two years of relentless touring across North America and Europe its sales picked up. Based around more of the same mix of industrial rock and electronica, the follow-up, *The Downward Spiral*, reached no.2 in the charts and propelled Reznor to stardom. A 1995 stadium tour with David Bowie followed. A lengthy break during which Reznor constructed his own studio and recorded a new album was rewarded with the chart topping *The Fragile*. In 2009 Reznor posted on the band's website that it was over for the foreseeable future.

RECORDINGS
(selective list)
Pretty Hate Machine (TVT, 1989), *The Downward Spiral* (Nothing, 1994), *Closure* (Nothing, 1997), *The Fragile* (Nothing, 1999), *And All That Could Have Been* (Nothing, 2002), *With Teeth* (Interscope, 2005), *Beside You in Time* (Interscope, 2007), *Year Zero* (Interscope, 2007), *Ghosts I–IV* (Null, 2008), *The Slip* (Null, 2008)

BIBLIOGRAPHY
M. Huxley: *Nine Inch Nails* (New York, 1997)
D. Carr: *Pretty Hate Machine* (New York, 2011)

ROB JOVANOVIC

Nirvana. Grunge band. Formed in 1987, it consisted of Kurt (Donald) Cobain (*b* Aberdeen, WA, 20 Feb 1967; *d* Seattle, *c*5 April 1994; guitar and vocals), Krist [Chris] Novoselic (*b* Compton, CA, 16 May 1965; bass), and from 1990 Dave Grohl (*b* Warren, OH, 14 Jan 1969; drums). It was one of the most popular of the Seattle grunge bands until Cobain's suicide in 1994. Influenced by other regional bands like the Melvins and Mudhoney, Nirvana developed a sludgy and distorted sound with Cobain's voice alternating between furious screams and lethargic mumbles. Their debut album, *Bleach*, was recorded for just over $600 and released through Sub Pop, the Seattle-based independent label, in 1989. Following a number of other drummers, Grohl, a veteran of the Washington, DC punk scene, joined the group. After touring with Sonic Youth as a supporting act, Nirvana signed with DGC Records, a subsidiary of Geffen Records, and released their breakthrough album, *Nevermind*, in late 1991. DGC originally had only modest hopes for *Nevermind*, but the first single and music video for "Smells Like Teen Spirit" gained extraordinary momentum and pushed the album to the top of the *Billboard* sales charts by early 1992.

Nirvana's success put Cobain in the spotlight as a spokesperson for the disaffected youths who had been labeled "Generation X." Resentful of the corporate machinery that had turned them into mass-marketed commodities, Nirvana turned to the post-punk engineer Steve Albini to create a more confrontational sound for their next album, *In Utero*. Cobain maintained a hostile attitude to his fame, and meanwhile his health problems and drug addiction continued to escalate in the time leading up to his death. After Nirvana, Dave Grohl moved on to form the Foo Fighters, while Krist Novoselic has primarily focused on political activism. The demos, "lost" recordings, and live performances of Nirvana have continued to be repackaged and released long after Cobain's death.

RECORDINGS
(selective list)
Bleach (Sub Pop, 1989); *Nevermind* (DGC, 1991); *In Utero* (DGC, 1993); MTV *Unplugged in New York* (DGC, 1994); *From the Muddy Banks of the Wishkah* (DGC, 1996)

BIBLIOGRAPHY
G. Arnold: *Route 666: On the Road to Nirvana* (New York, 1993)
M. Azerrad: *Come As You Are: The Story of Nirvana* (New York, 1993)
G. Gaar: *Nirvana's In Utero* (New York, 2006)
E. True: *Nirvana: The Biography* (New York, 2007)

RYAN MOORE

Nisenan. Native American group belonging to the MAIDU.

Nisqually. Native American group of the northwest coast; *See* SALISH.

Nissly, MaryBelle Johns (*b* Lancaster, PA, 1 May 1918; *d* Polaski, AR, 30 July 1999). Conductor and educator. She was the first female drum major at Lititz High School, PA. After earning a music education degree from West Chester State Teachers College (BS 1937) she became music supervisor of Lancaster Township Schools. During World War II she played piccolo and flute in the 400th Women's Army Corps (WAC) Band at Fort Des Moines, Iowa, eventually conducting the group until sent to attend the Army Music School, Fort Meyer, Virginia, to become an Army Band Leader. After graduation, she was assigned to the 400th WAC Band and then the 401st WAC Band, Fort Hamilton, NY. In 1944 she became the first woman to receive the rank of warrant officer. After the war she attended the University of Pennsylvania (MS 1949) and was an instrumental music teacher in Manheim Township Schools until 1951 when she accepted a captain's commission in the Air Force to organize and conduct the Women in the Air Force Band. She conducted the band for its ten-year existence, and remained in the service until 1968, eventually earning the rank of major. Her last music position was at the University of Arkansas, Little Rock.

BIBLIOGRAPHY
D.L Johnson: *The U.S. WAF Band Story* (Springfield, VA, 2004)
J.M Sullivan: "Women's Military Bands in a Segregated Army: the 400th and 404th WAC Bands," *Journal of Band Research*, xli/2 (2006), 1–35

JILL SULLIVAN

Nitty Gritty Dirt Band. Country rock band. Active since the beginning of country rock in Southern California during the late 1960s, the band has recorded and performed into the 2000s, making it one of the genre's longest standing groups. Over 15 musicians—including Bernie Leadon of the Eagles and Jackson Browne—have at some point been members but the most enduring contributors are Bob Carpenter, Jimmie Fadden, Jeff Hanna, Jimmy Ibbotson, and John McEuen, a banjo player who helped popularize the instrument among rock listeners. In its early years the group played a mix of folk, jug band, blues, novelty, and vaudeville that developed into a consistent country rock sound with heavy bluegrass influence by 1970. Their first important hit was "Mr. Bojangles" (1971, written by Jerry Jeff Walker) from the breakthrough album *Uncle Charlie and His Dog Teddy*. The band is most famous for its ambitious triple album, *Will the Circle Be Unbroken* (1972), a set of traditional country songs the band recorded in Nashville with legendary country musicians including Roy Acuff, Mother Maybelle Carter, Earl Scruggs, Merle Travis, and Doc Watson. The project was well received both in Nashville and among rock listeners, bringing country music to a wider audience and earning respect for country rock within traditional circles. Similar projects were released in 1989 and 2002 respectively, as volumes two and three of the same title. In the 1980s the band changed its sound to conform with mainstream country with a string of top-ten country hits, including three number ones ("Modern Day Romance," "Fishin' in the Dark," "Long Hard Road [The Sharecropper's Dream]").

OLIVIA CARTER MATHER

Nixon, Marni (*b* Altadena, CA, 22 Feb 1930). Singer and actress. From 1938–49 Nixon appeared as a child actor in over 50 films. Later, Nixon's coloratura soprano voice was used to dub Deborah Kerr in *The King and I* (1956) and *An Affair to Remember* (1957), Natalie Wood in *West Side Story* (1961), and Audrey Hepburn in *My Fair Lady* (1964). Nixon sang the role of Sister Sophia in the film version of *The Sound of Music* (1965). Her Broadway performing credits include Aunt Kate in *James Joyce's the Dead* (2000), Heidi Schiller in the revival of Sondheim's *Follies* (2001), and Guido's Mother in the revival of *Nine* (2003). A successful crossover artist, she enjoyed a substantial classical singing career. Her perfect pitch and flexibility made her a favorite of contemporary classical composers, including Igor Stravinsky. Of his works, she recorded *Les Noces, Nightingale, Mavra*, and *Cantata* (1952). She also recorded the complete vocal chamber works of Anton Webern, the "Improvisations sur Mallarmé I" by Pierre Boulez, and a Paul Hindemith anthology, among other works. Nixon's television career has included the children's show *Boomerang* (including four Emmy wins), *The Mothers-in-Law, Law & Order: Special Victim's Unit*, and appearances on game shows. From 1969–71 Nixon taught at the California Institute of the Arts and was on faculty at the Music Academy of the West. She also served as the diction coach for a recording of Carlisle Floyd's opera *Susannah*.

BIBLIOGRAPHY
W. Braun: "The Two Lives of Marni Nixon," *ON*, lxix/4 (Oct 2004), 30–34
M. Nixon: *I Could Have Sung All Night* (New York, 2006)

SYLVIA STONER-HAWKINS

Nixon, Roger (*b* Tulare, CA, 8 Aug 1921; *d* Burlingame, CA, 13 Oct 2009). Composer. Nixon attended Modesto (California) Junior College and the University of California, Berkeley (BA 1942, MA 1949, PhD 1952) where his composition teachers were Arthur Bliss, ERNEST BLOCH, and ROGER SESSIONS. He also studied privately with ARNOLD SCHOENBERG in 1948. He taught at Modesto Junior College (1951–9) and at San Francisco State University (1960–1990). Nixon received many commissions including one from the J.C. Penney Company to write a work for band celebrating the American Bicentennial. He won a number of awards, including the Neil A. Kjos Memorial Award, the Composers Press/Haubiel Solo Work Composition Contest, and the American Bandmasters Association Ostwald Award.

Nixon's compositional style is eclectic, especially in his use of tonality, in which he employs a mixture of different scales, modes, and various organizational systems. Even in compositions that are highly chromatic, pitch centers are emphasized, creating harmonic progressions and cadences that enhance the specific musical structure. In much of his music, themes tend not to be simple restatements but are altered and developed while retaining a strong connection to the original. A number of works are inspired by his native California. While many of his best known works are for band, he has written for other ensembles, including orchestra and chorus.

WORKS
Orch: Mooney's Grove Suite, 1964–8; Viola Concerto, 1969
Band: Elegy and Fanfare, March, 1956–7; Fiesta del Pacifico, 1958–60; Reflections, 1962; Pacific Celebration Suite, 1976; Chamarita! 1981; Monterey Holidays, 1999
Vocal: Six Moods of Love, song cycle, S, pf, 1950; Wonders of Christmas, SATB, 1980 rev. 1993
Pf: 24 Piano Preludes, 1946–2002

BIBLIOGRAPHY
A. Mazzaferro: "Roger Nixon and his Works for Band," *Journal of Band Research*, xxiv/1 (1988), 29–32
W.H. Rehrig: *The Heritage Encyclopedia of Band Music* (Westerville, OH, 1991, suppl. 1996); CD-ROM (Oskaloosa, IA, 2005) [includes list of works]
W. Berz: "Roger Nixon," *A Composer's Insight*, ed. T. Salzman, iii (Galesville, MD, 2006), 129–45
R. Nixon: "Roger Nixon," *Composers on Composing for Band*, ed. Mark Camphouse, iii (Chicago, 2007), 187–214

WILLIAM BERZ

Noack, Fritz (*b* Wolgast, Germany, 25 Sept 1935). Organ builder of German birth. He served his apprenticeship 1954–8 with Rudolph von Beckerath in Hamburg, subsequently working as a journeyman with Klaus Becker and Ahrend & Brunzema. He immigrated to the United States in 1959, working briefly for Estey, and then Charles Fisk, before opening a workshop in 1960 in Lawrence, Massachusetts, and shortly after, in nearby Andover, before moving to a larger facility in Georgetown, Massachusetts in 1970 under the name of Noack Organ Co., Inc. Among Noack's larger organs in this period are those for Unity Church, St. Paul, Minnesota (1965) and Trinity Lutheran Church, Worcester, Massachusetts (1967). Several practice and continuo organs were also built in this period.

At first influenced by German neo-Baroque tonal concepts and Bauhaus-style architecture, by the 1970s

Noack's organs, all of which have mechanical key action, were beginning to become more eclectic tonally, and more classical visually. The organ for First Lutheran Church in Seattle (1976) has Gothic casework, and others, such as that in Grace Episcopal Church in Grand Rapids, Michigan (1981), have casework inspired by North European Baroque designs. Some of Noack's larger organs include those in St. John's Cathedral, Wilmington, Delaware (1982) and Christ the King Lutheran Church, Houston, Texas (1995), the latter being based tonally and visually on the work of the Central German builder Hildebrandt. Noack's first exported organ was built in 1996 for Kwassui University in Nagasaki, Japan, followed in 1999 by an organ for Langholtskirkja in Reykjavik, Iceland. A large organ was built in 2003 for Lakeside Presbyterian Church in Lakeside Park, Kentucky, and in 2010 Noack completed a four-manual organ for the Cathedral of St. Joseph the Workman in LaCrosse, Wisconsin.

BIBLIOGRAPHY

G. Bozeman: "The Noack Organ Co. of Georgetown, Mass," *Art of the Organ*, i/2 (1971)

U. Pape: *The Tracker Organ Revival in America* (Berlin, 1978)

C. Cramer: "An Interview with Fritz Noack," *The American Organist*, xxi/8 (Aug 1989), 40–5

B. Jones: "The Organs of Fritz Noack," *Choir and Organ* (April/May 1995)

BARBARA OWEN

Noble, Johnny [John Avery] (*b* Honolulu, HI, 17 Sept 1892; *d* Honolulu, HI, 13 Jan 1944). Composer, arranger, and percussionist. He began to play several instruments in high school and graduated in 1911. Although he worked outside music for many years, he also found ways to make money as a performer, taking a position in 1919 with director Ernest Ka'ai in hotels around the island. Eventually he met Sonny Cunha, and the two combined jazz and ragtime with traditional Hawaiian music to reach a wider audience. Noble broke away and created his own band from the Moana Hotel in 1920, and was invited to take his group to San Francisco for a convention four years later. This move to the mainland offered him the opportunity to take the Johnny Noble Band throughout the United States, playing widely on the radio and recording over 100 sides on the Brunswick label. As a composer Noble penned songs that have become standards of Hawaiian music, including "My Little Grass Shack," "Hula Blues," and the "Kaimuki Hula." Many of his recordings included singer Emma Bush, whose throaty voice and soaring high notes nicely complemented Noble's sprightly orchestrations. Noble was one of the most important figures in popularizing Hawaiian music in America. In 1935 Noble became the first Hawaiian to be inducted into ASCAP. He also published several collections of music, including *Johnny Noble's Collection of Ancient and Modern Hulas* (New York, 1935).

BIBLIOGRAPHY

G.P. Noble: *Hula Blues: The Story of Johnny Noble, Hawaii, Its Music, and Musicians* (Honolulu, 1948)

JONAS WESTOVER

Noble, Ray(mond Stanley) (*b* Brighton, England, 17 Dec 1903; *d* London, England, 2 April 1978). English bandleader, arranger, and composer. He studied classical piano but became interested in dance music, serving as house conductor for HMV records from 1929 and attracting attention with the recordings of his New Mayfair Dance Orchestra (1930–34), particularly those with the singer Al Bowlly. He moved to the United States to direct his own band at the Rainbow Room in New York (1935–7), then went to Los Angeles and worked as a bandleader and radio personality into the 1950s. In the jazz field Noble's significance was as a catalyst rather than as a performer. His own arrangements and performances were generally of "sweet" dance music, and his major compositions were highly successful romantic ballads such as "Goodnight, sweetheart" (1931), "Love is the sweetest thing" (1932), "The very thought of you" (1934), "The Touch of your Lips" (1936), and "I hadn't anyone till you" (1938). However, his New York band, assembled by Glenn Miller (who also provided its more jazz-oriented arrangements, and thereby discovered his own distinctive way of writing), included such musicians as Pee Wee Erwin, Charlie Spivak, Sterling Bose, Johnny Mince, Bud Freeman, Will Bradley, and Claude Thornhill. Noble's instrumental composition "Cherokee" became the theme tune of Charlie Barnet's band (1938); as a familiar test piece for jazz musicians in the early bop style, Charlie Parker, among others, used its structure as the basis for new compositions, including "Koko."

BIBLIOGRAPHY

G.T. Simon: *The Big Bands* (New York, 1967, enlarged 2/1971, 4/1981), 383–5

A. McCarthy: *The Dance Band Era: the Dancing Decades from Ragtime to Swing, 1910–1950* (London, 1971/R), 62–4, 77–82

J.H. Klee: "Noble American, 1935–37," *Mississippi Rag*, iv/1 (1976), 1–3

C. Garrod: *Ray Noble and his Orchestra* (Zephyrhills, FL, 1991) [discography]

ANDREW LAMB/ALYN SHIPTON

Noble, T[homas] Tertius (*b* Bath, England, 5 May 1867; *d* Rockport, MA, 4 May 1953). Organist and composer of English birth. He became organist of All Saints, Colchester at the age of 12 and then attended the Royal College of Music (1884–9), where he studied organ with Water Parratt, theory with Frederick Bridge, and composition with Charles V. Stanford. After another church post in London he became assistant organist to Stanford at Trinity College, Cambridge (1890–92), organist and choirmaster of Ely Cathedral (1892–8), and of York Minster (1898–1913). While at York he founded the York Symphony Orchestra, became conductor of a revived York Musical Society, and was made an honorary Fellow of the Royal College of Organists. In 1913 he was appointed organist and choirmaster of St. Thomas Church in New York City, where he founded a boychoir school and implanted a traditional English cathedral practice. He became influential as a church musician and teacher and received several academic honors. In 1943 Noble retired from St. Thomas to pursue a more active recital career. His varied compositions (including some incidental music for the stage) number at least 35 for the organ, three complete

Anglican services and other liturgical music, as well as many anthems and orchestral music, including *Morris-Dance*, a suite for violin and orchestra, and an Introduction and Passacaglia played by the New York PO under the baton of John Barbirolli. He was editor of the 1916 Hymnal of the Protestant Episcopal Church and published two volumes of free organ accompaniments to hymns. Of his several hymn tunes, the best known is *Ora labora*, sung to words beginning "Come, Labor on" (1918). He also issued a widely used edition of Handel's *Messiah* (1912) and *The Training of the Boy Chorister* (1943). A collection of his manuscripts and memorabilia can be found in the Organ Library maintained by the Boston Chapter of the American Guild of Organists at Boston University.

BIBLIOGRAPHY

GMO
F.G. Edwards: "York Minster," *MT*, xliv/723 (1903), 297–304
W.G. Alcock: "Mr T. Tertius Noble," *MT*, liv/840 (1913), 97–98
"Dr. T. Tertius Noble," *The American Organist*, xxvii (1944), 273 [incl. a list of works]
Obituaries: *The Times* (6 May 1953); *MT*, xciv/1324 (1953), 281

WILLIAM OSBORNE

Noble, Timothy (*b* Peru, IN, 22 Feb 1945). Baritone. Known as one of the great interpreters of Verdi's male opera roles including *Rigoletto* and *Falstaff*, Noble completed his collegiate vocal training at Indiana University where he earned his bachelor's (1977) and master's (1981) degrees. Noble made his Metropolitan Opera debut on 22 February 1988 as Shaklovity in Mussorgsky's *Khovanshchina*. His performances with the Met continued through 1997, including roles in *Hänsel und Gretel, Rigoletto, Il Trittico, La Bohème, Don Giovanni, Aida, Cavalleria Rusticana, Pagliacci*, and as Christopher Columbus in Glass's *The Voyage*, a premiere to commemorate the 500th anniversary of Columbus's arrival in the New World. He has also sung with San Francisco Opera, Chicago Lyric Opera, Canadian Opera Company, La Fenice, Netherlands Opera, Santa Fe Opera, and the Glyndebourne Opera Festival.

As comfortable in the world of popular music as he is on the opera stage, Noble toured with Fred Waring and the Pennsylvanians as a young man and has recorded a collection of Cole Porter songs, *Simple Cole*, and a Grammy-nominated recording of *The Music Man*. In 1999 Noble concluded his stage career with his portrayal of Tony in an Indiana University production of *The Most Happy Fella*.

Noble became a Distinguished Professor at Indiana University in 2004, where his students have won national and international vocal competitions, become apprentices with virtually every young artist program in North America and have gone on as professionals to the Metropolitan Opera, San Francisco Opera, New York City Opera, and Chicago Lyric Opera.

BIBLIOGRAPHY

S. Scovasso: "Timothy Noble: Warrior on the Good Road," *Classical Singer*, xviii (April 2005), 8–17

TRUDI ANN WRIGHT

Noble, Weston (Henry) (*b* Riceville, IA, 30 Nov 1922). Conductor and teacher. He attended Luther College (BA 1943), finishing early to begin military service in World War II. He taught high school in LuVerne, Iowa (1946–8) and then returned to Luther as a "temporary" faculty hire, where he remained until his retirement in 2005. He received a master's degree from the University of Michigan (1951). During his time at Luther, Noble conducted the Concert Band (1948–73) and the Nordic Choir. His work with the band culminated in two solo concerts at Philharmonic Hall, Lincoln Center (1966, 1970). He built the 72-voice Nordic choir into one of the nation's leading collegiate choral ensembles, known for its exceptionally warm and blended choral tone and superb intonation. He has received five honorary doctorates, the Robert Shaw Award from American Choral Directors Association (1999), and the first Outstanding Music Educator award from National Federation of State High School Associations (1989). He is one of the few individuals invited to conduct all-state festivals for choir, band, and orchestra. His approach to conducting marries a respect for the technical demands of the art form with an emphasis on the power of music to change people's lives.

BIBLIOGRAPHY

W. Bunge: *Warmly, Weston: A Luther College Life* (Decorah, IA, 1998)
P.D. White: *The Whole Conductor: Weston Noble's Philosophies on the Psychology of Conducting and Musicianship* (diss., U. of Oklahoma, 1998)

STEVEN M. DEMOREST

No Doubt. Rock band. It formed in Anaheim, California, in 1986. Principal members are GWEN STEFANI, vocals (*b* Fullerton, CA, 3 Oct 1969); Eric Stefani, keyboards (*b* Fullerton, CA 17 June 1967); Tom Dumont, guitar (*b* Los Angeles, CA, 11 Jan 1968); Tony Kanal, bass (*b* London, England, 27 Aug 1970); Adrian Young, drums (*b* Long Beach, CA, 26 Aug 1969). John Spence (1969–87) and Eric Stefani formed the band, with Stefani's sister Gwen singing backup vocals. Tony Kanal joined after attending an early performance. After shifts in personnel following Spence's death in 1987, Gwen Stefani took over lead vocals, and Kanal, Tom Dumont, Adrian Young, and Eric Stefani (who left in 1994) formed the core of the group. Interscope Records signed No Doubt in 1991, and they achieved commercial success with 1995's *Tragic Kingdom*, which featured an eclectic mix of ska, new wave, pop, punk, and rock. Featuring the single, "Don't Speak," this album earned several Grammy nominations. While none of No Doubt's subsequent albums has matched *Tragic Kingdom*'s success, the group remained in the mainstream, winning Grammys for the singles "Hey Baby" (2003) and "Underneath It All" (2004). Gwen Stefani's charismatic performance style and fashion sense threatened to overshadow the band and by 2003, she began work on solo projects. No Doubt was on hiatus from 2004 to 2008, but they toured again in 2009 and began releasing albums again in 2010 with *Icon*.

COLETTE SIMONOT

Noehren, Robert (*b* Buffalo, NY, 16 Dec 1910; *d* San Diego, CA, 4 Aug 2002). Organist, organ builder, and composer. He studied under GASTON M. DETHIER at the Institute of Musical Art, New York, and under LYNNWOOD W. FARNAM at the Curtis Institute of Music, Philadelphia (1930–31), and served as organist and choirmaster at churches in Buffalo and Grand Rapids, Michigan. He received the BMus degree from the University of Michigan in 1948. After wartime service he taught from 1946 to 1949 at Davidson College, North Carolina, and in 1949 he moved to the University of Michigan in Ann Arbor, where he served as university organist and professor of music until his retirement in 1976. Well known as a recitalist, recording artist, and organ builder, he played extensively at home and abroad, and studied many historic European instruments. He designed and built many organs including those in St. John's Roman Catholic Cathedral, Milwaukee, the First Unitarian Church, San Francisco, and the First Presbyterian Church, Buffalo. He holds an American patent for a combination action that controls all pistons by a punched data-processing card. Noehren wrote numerous articles for professional journals as well as *An Organist's Reader: Essays by Robert Noehren* (1999). Among his compositions are two sonatas for organ.

BIBLIOGRAPHY
B. Petty: "Review [Johann Sebastian Bach: Organ Works, An Organist's Reader]," *Journal of American Organbuilding*, xvi/4 (2002)
W. Osborne: "Robert Noehren: In Memoriam," *The Diapason*, xciii/10 (2002), 14–17

VERNON GOTWALS/JUDI CALDWELL

Noge, Yoko (*b* Osaka, Japan, 1957). Jazz and blues pianist, singer, and composer of Japanese birth. She took piano lessons briefly as a child and was exposed to the blues while growing up in Osaka in the 1960s and 1970s. As a high school student, she formed the Yoko Blues Band with classmates. The band earned some success, winning first prize and a recording contract in a television-sponsored contest. In 1984 she moved to the United States to pursue a jazz and blues career in Chicago. Initially a singer, she studied piano with boogie, blues, and jazz pianist Erwin Helfer. In the early 1990s Noge established the Jazz Me Blues Band, which has played regularly in Chicago since its formation. In addition to Noge on piano and vocals, the ensemble has included Noge's husband, Clark Dean, on soprano saxophone, saxophonist Jimmy Ellis, trombonist Bill McFarland, and bassist Tatsu Aoki. In addition to playing more conventional jazz and blues, Noge has made a name for herself through the unique compositions she has written for the group, which meld Japanese folk music styles with Chicago blues. Active in the broader Asian American community, she cofounded the Chicago Asian American Jazz Festival in 1995, along with Tatsu Aoki and Francis Wong. Celebrated in her native country and her adopted home, Noge was named "Chicagoan of the Year" in 2006 by the editors of the *Chicago Tribune*, and was distinguished as "one of the most respected Japanese people in the world" by *Newsweek Japan* in 2009.

MEGAN E. HILL

Noise. Traditionally, noise has been thought of as the outside of music and meaning. In systems theory, noise is disruption of the signal or message; in biological terms, it is associated with pain, in legal terms it is associated with disturbance. Noise is also that which has hitherto been excluded from being proper music, so can include radical new directions in musical form (Wagner, Coltrane) as well as noises deemed unmusical. The term noise implies a judgement about the type of sound, performance, or piece, not an inherent quality of it. This means that the idea of noise has always been historicized within music philosophy. Luigi Russolo proposed (in 1913) that noise was both an essential part of nature and a new reality of the industrialized metropolis. Purposeful use of noise, would, ironically, bring a new social harmony. John Cage expanded the definition of what could occur in the place of music, from silence (more accurately, the absence of silence) to machine sounds (turntables, radios, prepared pianos). In 1977 Jacques Attali developed a Nietzschean argument wherein the history of music could be seen as the progressive domestication of noise, through familiarity, secularization of music, or legal controls (copyright, noise abatement, travel restrictions). More recently, Attali is often questioned, but it was his book, *Bruits*, that cleared the way for a contextualised understanding of noise and its relation to social and musical order, and established the idea that noise could work as a near-synonym for being avant-garde. Not all avant-gardism is noise—Arnold Schoenberg's system is a rethinking of musical systems, not a challenge to it, for example, and very often noise does feature explicit use of noises, in the form of extra-musical materials.

Erik Satie, Charles Ives, and Edgard Varèse join Cage at the forefront of incorporating noise into composition. After World War II, a series of sound laboratories allowed electronic composers such as Pauline Oliveros, Pierre Schaeffer, Delia Derbyshire, and Stockhausen to stretch the boundaries not only of musical material but also musical production. The borders between instrument, player, composition, sound, and music all blurred, while also in the 1960s, amplification and effects pedals stretched the range of instruments beyond their normal tolerance, producing feedback and distortion. What had been unwanted now became a musical tool, even a way of defining an individual player's style. Overload could even be used to convey a message, such as in Hendrix's playing of "The Starspangled Banner" at Woodstock in 1969. Extraneous sounds could now be valued in their own right: the sound of machines operating was not contrary to the music but would replace the correct use of an instrument (in free music as much as in post-punk *musique concrète*). As with Futurism, Fluxus radically rethought musical production as the result of interaction between different media, creating an interstitial form that Dick Higgins labeled "intermedia." Fluxus had preempted even early United States punk in its disavowal of virtuosity, musicality, and musical narrative development, with Nam June Paik, George Brecht, and Yoko Ono the tip of a noisy art iceberg. Industrial music of the late 1970s used aggressive electronics, high volume, seemingly low levels of skill, and violent performance to take noise to where it would represent a transgressive attack on established norms. Rock continued using more feedback as a central part of the sound (The Jesus and Mary Chain, Mudhoney, Sonic Youth), but noise was becoming a genuine form (or formless form) in Japan, with the likes of Masami Akita (Merzbow) constructing tracks from layers of brutal noises, oscillations, feedback, distortions, processed instrumentation, and field recordings left to loop recursively and ever louder. Recent years have seen the DIY noise of the early 1980s and also Japanese style noise music become integrated into avant rock. At the same time, the "harsh noise wall" subgenre smooths the layers of complex noise into a mass. After a brief period where noise was the essence of "noise music," the early 21st century has seen a return to a paradigm (in performance and recording) of musicalization of noise.

BIBLIOGRAPHY

L. Russolo: *L'arte dei Rumori* (Milan, 1913) [*The Art of Noises* (New York, 1986)]

J. Attali: *Bruits: essai sur l'économie politique de la musique* (Paris, 1977) [*Noise: The Political Economy of Music* (Minneapolis, 1985)]

D. Kahn: *Noise Water Meat: A History of Sound in the Arts* (Cambridge, MA, 1999)

P. Hegarty: *Noise/Music: A History* (New York and London, 2007)

S. Kim-Cohen: *In The Blink of an Ear: Toward a Non-Cochlear Sonic Art* (New York and London, 2009)

S. Goodman: *Sonic Warfare: Sound, Affect, and the Ecology of Fear* (Cambridge, MA, and London, 2010)

S. Voegelin: *Listening to Noise and Silence: Towards a Philosophy of Sound Art* (New York and London, 2010)

PAUL HEGARTY

Nolan [Nobles], **Bob (Clarence Robert)** (*b* Winnipeg, MB, 13 April 1908; *d* Newport Beach, CA, 16 June 1980). Cowboy singer, songwriter, and actor. Renowned for his ability to evoke the desert and woodland landscapes of western North America in both lyrics and music, Nolan was arguably the most influential western songwriter of his generation. As a child he moved frequently, living in British Columbia, New Brunswick, Boston, and Tucson. As a high school student in Tucson, he read the poetry of Shelley, Byron, and Keats and began writing his own poetry about the Arizona desert. After graduating from high school, he moved to Santa Monica, California, in 1929, where he worked as a lifeguard and began setting his poetry to music. In 1931 he joined Leonard Slye (later Roy Rogers) in the Rocky Mountaineers, and in 1933 they joined tenor Tim Spencer to form the Pioneer Trio (later the SONS OF THE PIONEERS). The Sons of the Pioneers frequently recorded Nolan's compositions, including such hits as "Cool Water," "Tumbling Tumbleweeds," and "Chant of the Wanderer." Nolan retired from the group in 1949, although he sporadically recorded with them until 1957 and occasionally appeared on their *Lucky "U" Ranch* program in

1951 and 1952. After 1957 Nolan retired from the industry, writing poetry and songs for his own enjoyment and fishing at Big Bear Lake, California. He briefly came out of retirement in 1979 to record a solo album with producer Snuff Garrett.

BIBLIOGRAPHY

K. Griffis: "The Bob Nolan Story," *JEMF Quarterly*, xvi (Summer 1980), 63–65

D.B. Green: *Singing in the Saddle: the History of the Singing Cowboy* (Nashville, 2002), 73–83

TRAVIS D. STIMELING

Nolen, Laura Vlasak (*b* Dallas, TX, 13 Jan 1977). Mezzo-soprano. She earned a degree in vocal performance at Texas Tech and went on to graduate work at Indiana University with teacher Costanza Cuccaro. She made her professional debut singing Third Lady in *Die Zauberflöte* at Cleveland Opera. Hailed for her "large and lush mezzo-soprano," Nolen debuted at the Metropolitan Opera as Waltrute in *Die Walküre* on 7 January 2008 and was reengaged with the Met for performances in the following season as Inez in *Il trovatore*, Guilietta (cover) in *Les contes d'Hoffmann*, The Countess (cover) in *The Nose*, Second Maidservant (cover) in *Elektra*, and a return as Waltrute.

Along with her work at the Met, she has performed with other prominent American opera companies including New York City Opera, Madison Opera, Lyric Opera of Kansas City, Dallas Opera, and Glimmerglass Opera, where she played the title role of *Guilio Cesare* in 2008. She has also appeared abroad as part of Ireland's Wexford Festival Opera, and with a Metropolitan Opera touring company of *Die Walküre* in Japan.

Equally comfortable on the concert stage, Nolen performed Haydn's Mass in Time of War with the Washington Chorus at the Kennedy Center in 2007 and in the same year Beethoven's Mass in C with the Honolulu Symphony, where her voice was described as "quite simply stunning: large, rich, warm butterscotch, beautifully placed."

BIBLIOGRAPHY

B. Kellow: "Laura Vlasak Nolen," *ON*, lxxi/9 (2007), 10–11

TRUDI ANN WRIGHT

Noll, Joseph (*fl* 1850–70). German violinist, conductor, and bandleader. Active in New York, he made his first known appearances in the 1849–50 chamber music series arranged by Theodore Eisfeld and presented by *Saroni's Musical Times*. In 1851 he was invited to join Eisfeld's new series of quartet soirées (alongside Charles Reyer, L. Eichorn, and Otto Dresel on piano) and remained with the ensemble until it folded in 1859. After four appearances as violin soloist with the New York Philharmonic Society in the early 1850s, Noll became a member of the orchestra and held the concertmaster chair for nearly two decades (1855–71). He served on their board of directors from 1856 to 1860. Noll also served as concertmaster of the Brooklyn Philharmonic Orchestra and the Theodore Thomas Orchestra. He frequently appeared as assisting artist and occasionally conductor at concerts headlined by others, notably with Jenny Lind, Henriette Sontag, Camilla Urso, and Louis Moreau Gottschalk. In 1852, Noll was invited to newly organize and lead New York's Seventh Regiment Band. The 42-piece band was noted for using both brass and woodwind instruments. The ensemble grew to 60 members before Noll was replaced by Claudio Grafulla in 1858.

BIBLIOGRAPHY

V.B. Lawrence, ed.: *Strong on Music: the New York Music Scene in the Days of George Templeton Strong* (New York, 1988 and Chicago, 1995 and 1999)

R.F. Camus: "Graffula and Cappa: Bandmasters of New York's Famous Seventh Regiment," *European Music and Musicians in New York City, 1840–1900*, ed. J. Graziano (Rochester, NY, 2006), 198–217

BETHANY GOLDBERG

Nollman, Jim [James Maurice] (*b* Boston, MA, 31 Jan 1947). Composer, guitarist, and animal communications researcher. He attended Tufts University (BA in English and music theater, 1969), and in 1970 became music consultant to the Children's Museum in Boston. After performing in nightclubs in New York and London for several years, he settled in the San Francisco Bay area and became music director of the Gallery Theater (1974–5). During this time he began experiments in communication with ocean mammals by means of amplified acoustic and electronic music. He founded and directed Interspecies Communication (Bodinas, CA, 1978–82), and was the principal investigator for the Greenpeace Iki Island project involving the slaughtering of dolphins (Japan, 1978–80) and John Lilly's Human/Dolphin Foundation (Careyes, Mexico, 1982–3). Other organizations to have sponsored his research include the World Wildlife Fund, the California Arts Commission, and the Fund for Animals.

Nollman seeks to create improvised musical dialogues with the animals he investigates, which include dolphins, turkeys, and orcas. Among the instruments he employs are electric guitars, wooden drums, *shakuhachi* (traditional Japanese flute), and dolphin sticks; he also uses special animal communications equipment and an underwater simultaneous listening, recording, and playback system of his own design. His musical technique requires improvisation and the exact matching of frequency, timbre, sonic gesture, and phrasing. Several recordings of his work, including *Interspecies Music* (1976), *Playing Music with Animals: Interspecies Communication of Jim Nollman with 300 Turkeys, 12 Wolves, and 20 Orcas* (1982), and *A Fish That's a Song* (1990) have been released on the Smithsonian Folkways label. Nollman also owns a recording studio on San Juan Island, Washington. He has not released much of his own music on disc; instead he has chosen to make them freely available on his website, including songs such as "The Salish Sea," "The Sign of Love," and "Your Biggest Fan." He has also experimented with ambient music, mixing a vast spectrum of sounds with whale calls and other animal calls to produce a larger soundscape.

WORKS
(selective list)

Opera: Hoon I Kwak (1, Nollman), 1972, San Francisco, 1975

Performance works with animals: Turkey Song (Music to Eat Thanksgiving Dinner by), 300 turkeys, 3 fl, 1974; Interspecies Music, acoustic and elec insts, 300 turkeys, 12 wolves, 20 orcas, 1976; Orca Reggae, elec gui, 20 orcas, 1980; Smithsonian Monkeys, elec gui, shakuhachi, monkeys, 1983; Orca Shooting, elec gui, orcas, 1983; Human-Dolphin Reggae, elec gui, kbd, swimmers, dolphins, 1983–4

BIBLIOGRAPHY

T. Crail: *ApeTalk & Whalespeak* (Los Angeles, 1981)

W. Doak: *Dolphin, Dolphin* (New York, 1981)

J. Obrecht: "Pro's Reply: Jim Nollman," *Guitar Player*, xv/1 (1981), 6

STEPHEN RUPPENTHAL/JONAS WESTOVER

Nomlaki. Native American group of California. Their music bore a resemblance to that of the WINTUN.

Nonesuch. Record company. It was originally established in New York in 1964 by Elektra Records Chairman Jac Holzman. Spurred by the concept of providing "fine records at the same price as trade paperbacks," Holzman undertook a project code-named Nonesuch (so that if anyone asked about it, they could truthfully say "there was no such project"). Initially, releases came largely from albums licensed through European labels, most importantly Club Français du Disque. In 1965 Teresa (Tracey) Sterne was brought in to manage the imprint, and under her guidance the label expanded to include original recordings, and embraced American composers from Scott Joplin to Morton Subotnick, as well as launching the Explorer series of indigenous world music.

In 1970 Holzman sold Nonesuch (along with its parent label, Elektra) to what would become Warner Communications. In 1979 the label moved its headquarters to Los Angeles as part of a major corporate restructure, then subsequently moved back to New York in 1983. In 1984 Robert Hurwitz took over the management of the label and Nonesuch embarked on an aggressive relaunch with titles from Steve Reich, the Kronos Quartet, and John Zorn. The label also branched out with artists such as *tropicalismo* singer Caetano Veloso, tango master Astor Piazzola, the Gipsy Kings, and the critically acclaimed *Le Mystère des Voix Bulgares*. In 1994 responsibility for Nonesuch corporate oversight was delegated to Warner Music International, during which time the label partnered with the World Circuit imprint for its biggest-selling release ever, the Grammy-winning *Buena Vista Social Club*. Nonesuch subsequently moved to Atlantic Records for oversight in 2001, and to Warner Bros. Records in 2004, where it remains committed to both adult contemporary and modern classical music, winning more than 30 Grammy awards in the past decade alone. Key artists include John Adams, k.d. lang, Emmylou Harris, Bill Frisell, Wilco, Pat Metheny, the Black Keys, the Magnetic Fields, and the Low Anthem.

THANE TIERNEY

Nonprofit organization. An organizational form that does not distribute profits to owners or shareholders, but instead reinvests them in pursuit of a goal or mission. A nonprofit organization (NPO) must serve some kind of public benefit and be privately governed by a board of volunteers. Any type of organization (e.g., association, corporation, trust, shareholder entity, membership or board managed) that meets these criteria may apply to receive tax exemption under section 501(c)3 of the United States Internal Revenue Code. State entities may also excuse NPOs from sales and property taxes. Such tax breaks reduce the cost of operation in exchange for public good and effectively provide public support for service innovation. Although nonprofit organizations have existed in some form or another for over 300 years, the legal criteria used to define the modern nonprofit have evolved mostly since about 1960. Nonprofits (typically known as non-governmental organizations or NGOs in Europe) include churches, universities, hospitals, service providers, and many arts and culture organizations.

1. Early history, 1700–1900. 2. Development of the nonprofit sector, 1900–2000. 3. Nonprofits and the performing arts in the 21st century.

1. EARLY HISTORY, 1700–1900. The nonprofit's early history can be traced to pre-Revolutionary America, when colonists took it upon themselves to meet certain responsibilities that in Europe had historically been assigned to the state. In the nation's first century, all US corporations were chartered by individual state bills that carried both the imperative to public service and government control. When a new political party won local control, corporate boards might be exchanged. The origins of the American nonprofit corporation stem from a controversy concerning the jurisdiction over one of America's oldest institutions. Established in 1636, Harvard University had to fight municipal and state government interests to maintain control of its admission policies and educational practices. This issue was addressed in Dartmouth College v. Woodward (1819) by the United States Supreme Court, which ruled that private corporations were protected from state control. This distinction between private and state organizations was an early and important marker of not only universities but religious and cultural institutions as well as for profit structures. The Chicago Symphony's Orchestral Association became one of the first nonprofits to incorporate for the purpose of supporting an orchestra in 1890, a year before the ensemble gave its first concert, charging a board of non-musicians to maintain the orchestra's artistic mission and raise funds to pay for it. Although musical organizations were first seen as educational entities providing charitable services to the general public, a growing tension between orchestras, opera companies, and popular audiences would lead to ongoing disagreement regarding their nonprofit status.

2. DEVELOPMENT OF THE NONPROFIT SECTOR, 1900–2000. By the turn of the 20th century, the nonprofit sector had begun to distinguish itself more clearly from the public and for-profit sectors by addressing societal needs not met by government or big business. Nonprofit organizations of all types appeared in industries where the government failed to provide adequate services and for-profit firms could not turn a profit (orphanages, museums, libraries, etc.). With the advent of the 501(c)3 designation in the 1960s, which excused NPOs from paying federal income tax and allowed philanthropists to remove their donations from these taxes, nonprofit activity greatly expanded in number and size, professionalizing their organizational frameworks and often expanding their paid staff. By the middle of the century, arts organizations had formalized complex governance and funding structures that are still in place today. Unlike their for-profit counterparts, nonprofit performing arts organizations (including orchestras, opera companies, and chamber music societies) remain tied to a social mission that supersedes—and often conflicts with—a financial bottom line. An unpaid board of directors keeps watch over this mission and provides guidance to the paid staff. This structure becomes increasingly complex and hierarchical in the context of the performing arts, where, for example, committees of musicians and union representatives negotiate contractual agreements with a governing board represented by professional staffers.

The financial structure accompanying the modern nonprofit is just as complex as its administrative structure. Along with ticket sales and other means of earned income, nonprofits depend on contributions from individuals, corporations, foundations, and in some cases the government. Indeed, much of the growth experienced by the nonprofit sector in the second half of the 20th century can be linked to the rise of philanthropy, both through foundations and wealthy patrons. The development of major funding initiatives through megafoundations like Ford, Rockefeller, and Mellon allowed arts organizations to grow at unprecedented rates in the 1960s, a development that was accentuated by the Great Society Programs under Lyndon Johnson and the rise of American wealth in general. In the performing arts, this has meant increased professional and sometimes full-time salaries for musicians, greater numbers of performances, and a focus on endowments to pay for increasing costs and revenue shortfalls.

3. NONPROFITS AND THE PERFORMING ARTS IN THE 21ST CENTURY. In the 21st century, the US nonprofit sector continues to develop. Since 1960, the percentage of the national population employed by nonprofits has grown from 1% to more than 10%. Universities boast multi-billion-dollar endowments and the annual expenditures of some of the country's leading orchestras exceed 60 million dollars. With this growth has come unparalleled diversity within the nonprofit sector, fostering breakthroughs in medicine, education, and art, and proving that nonprofits can indeed make money. Yet some of these organizations, especially those in the arts and culture sector, struggle to balance their budgets, especially in times of economic recession. Since productivity gains characteristic of the for-profit sector are difficult to achieve in nonprofits, especially in the arts, revenues (mainly ticket sales) typically cover less than one third of expenses for performing arts organizations. The

resulting income gap, or the difference between overall expenses and ticket sales, has put increasing pressure on fundraising and development staff and has forced many arts nonprofits to reevaluate their role and the publics they serve.

Nevertheless, new developments may help nonprofits reconcile their social or artistic mission with financial challenges. The social enterprise movement, which blends the nonprofit service with a focus on revenue-generating activities that contribute to the organization's mission, aims to foster a culture of self-sufficiency by reducing dependence on charitable donations. The invention of the low-profit limited liability company (L3C) offers a hybrid organizational form that loosens some of the advocacy and profit-making restrictions associated with the nonprofit sector, allowing for a more flexible approach to fundraising that may improve both social and financial return. Many argue further that cultural organizations might be better organized as standard (for-profit) corporations, relieving them of board management and some public reporting requirements.

BIBLIOGRAPHY

P. DiMaggio: *Nonprofit Enterprise in the Arts: Studies in Mission and Constraint* (New York, 1986)

H. Hansmann: "Economic Theories of Nonprofit Organizations," *The Nonprofit Sector*, ed. W. Powell (New Haven, 1987), 27–43

R. Bremner: *American Philanthropy* (Chicago, 1988)

D.C. Hammack: "Introduction: Growth, Transformation, and Quiet Revolution in the Nonprofit Sector Over Two Centuries," *Nonprofit and Voluntary Sector Quarterly*, xxx/2 (2001), 157–73

L. Salamon: "What is the Nonprofit Sector and Why Do we Have it?" *The Nature of the Nonprofit Sector*, ed. J.S. Ott (Boulder, CO, 2001), 162–6

D.C. Hammack: "Nonprofit Organizations in American History," *The American Behavioral Scientist*, vl/11 (2002), 1638–74

MARK CLAGUE, MICHAEL MAUSKAPF

Nooksack. Native American group of the northwest coast; *see* COAST SALISH.

Noone, Jimmie [Jimmy] (*b* Cut Off, nr New Orleans, LA, 23 April 1895; *d* Los Angeles, CA, 19 April 1944). Jazz clarinetist and bandleader. Raised in Hammond, LA, where he learned guitar, he moved to New Orleans in 1910 and took up clarinet, under the tutelage first of LORENZO TIO, JR., and then a precocious SIDNEY BECHET, who was two years his junior. He quickly followed his mentors into the elite circle of young Creole of color dance-band musicians. In 1913 he replaced Bechet in Freddie Keppard's Olympia Orchestra, which was active in Storyville. After Keppard had departed, Noone and the cornetist Buddy Petit formed the Young Olympia Band. Noone soon rejoined Keppard and toured the Midwest with the latter's Creole Band until it broke up in 1918. After a brief return to New Orleans he left the city permanently and traveled to Chicago with King Oliver to perform at the Royal Gardens. In 1920 he began a six-year stint playing saxophone and clarinet in Doc Cook's Dreamland Orchestra. During this period he undertook further study of the clarinet, with the classical teacher Franz Schoepp, and made around 20 recordings, for Gennett, Okeh, and Columbia, including four with Oliver in 1923.

Noone established himself as a bandleader in 1926 with a long residency at the Apex Club in downtown Chicago. His Apex Club Orchestra eventually included Joe Poston (alto saxophone) and Earl Hines (piano), and the format of shared lead for clarinet and alto saxophone gave it a unique sound. Its recordings "I know that you know," "Four or Five Times," and "Apex Blues" (all Voc., 1928) broke new ground for the post–New Orleans style, and Noone's playing in particular shows multiple techniques for ensemble clarinet. Except for brief engagements in New York, Noone continued to lead small groups in Chicago throughout the 1930s. Boosted by the New Orleans revival movement of the early 1940s, he toured widely and joined Kid Ory and Jack Teagarden, among others, for club dates and recording sessions in California. After moving to Los Angeles in 1943, he rejoined Ory and Zutty Singleton in an all-star band for Orson Welles's radio show shortly before his death of a heart attack.

Noone's chief importance lies in his status as a transitional figure in jazz history. His playing has been identified by scholars as providing a clear stylistic link between the older generation of New Orleans jazz clarinetists and the younger soloists of the swing era, as best represented by Benny Goodman, who cited Noone as a direct influence. In contrast to Johnny Dodds and Bechet—the other leading reed players of the New Orleans style—Noone used vibrato selectively as an ornament and generally employed a bright, full tone with consistent abdominal support, evidence of his systematic training. His solos often featured arpeggiations reminiscent of technical exercises from classical method books, which he articulated with a rapid staccato. Nonetheless, he also made expressive use of blue notes, wide trills, and bending of the pitch, especially on such numbers as "Sweet Lorraine" (Bruns., 1928) his signature ballad.

SELECTED RECORDINGS

As leader: I Know that you Know (Voc., 1928); Four or Five Times (Voc., 1928); Apex Blues/Sweet Lorraine (Bruns., 1928); The blues jumped a rabbit (Parl., 1936)

As sideman with K. Oliver: Chattanooga Stomp/New Orleans Stomp (Col., 1923); Camp Meeting Blues (Col., 1923)

BIBLIOGRAPHY

W. Neff: "Jimmie Noone," *Jazz Information*, ii/6 (1940), 6–9

A. McCarthy: "Jimmie Noone," *JazzM*, x/4 (1964), 10–14

M. Williams: *Jazz Masters of New Orleans* (New York, 1967/R)

W.H. Kenney: "Jimmie Noone: Chicago's Classic Jazz Clarinetist," *American Music*, iv/2 (1986), 145–58

B.H. Behnke and K.-U. Dürr: *Jimmie Noone* (Hamburg, Germany, 1996 [discography])

CHARLES E. KINZER

Nootka. Native American group of Cape Flattery, Washington; *see* NUU-CHAH-NULTH.

Nordenstrom, Gladys (Mercedes) (*b* Pokegama Township, MN, 23 May 1924). Composer. She studied singing, the trumpet, and the piano before enrolling at Hamline University in St. Paul, where she studied composition with ERNST KRENEK (BA 1946, MA 1947). In the summer of 1946 she also studied philosophy and literature at the University of Minnesota. She married Krenek in 1950 and moved with him to Los Angeles; they settled in Palm Springs in 1966. She composed independently of him, though they discussed the texts of their vocal works in detail. Her compositions are all atonal and highly expressionistic. Her *El Greco phantasie* (1965) is a strict 12-note work in which the row is constantly rotated, while the spirit of Webern informs the tightly knit and intense *Swift Is Death to Strike a Man (In Memoriam for Robert F. Kennedy)* (1968) and *Work for Orchestra no.3* (1975). Electronic sounds are combined with organ in *Signals from Nowhere* (1973). She has received several commissions and her works have been performed in America and Europe. After Krenek's death in 1991, Nordenstrom worked to preserve her husband's memory and compositions by founding the Ernst Krenek Institute (1998) and the private foundation Krems die Ernst Krenek (2004), both in Austria. Nordenstrom serves as Honorary President of the Ernst Krenek Institute. As a result of her philanthropic efforts, Nordenstrom was awarded the Decoration of Honor for Services to the Republic of Austria in 2006.

WORKS
(selective list)

Inst: Rondo, fl, pf, 1948; El Greco phantasie, str, 1965, rev. 1969; Swift Is Death to Strike a Man (In Memoriam for Robert F. Kennedy), orch, 1968; Signals from Nowhere, org, tape, 1973; Work for Orch no.3, 1975; Wind Qnt, 1977; Trio, cl, vn, pf, 1978
Vocal: Zeit XXIV (R. Pandula), S, pf, 1975–6; Parabola of Light (Nordenstrom), womens' vv, pf, 1980

Principal publisher: Bärenreiter

BIBLIOGRAPHY

W. Szmolyan: "Die Komponistin Gladys Nordenstrom-Krenek," *ÖMz*, xxxv/9 (1980), 445 only
B. Grigsby: "Women Composers of Electronic Music in the United States," *The Musical Woman: an International Perspective*, i, ed. J.L. Zaimont and others (Westport, CT, 1984), 193 only

GARRETT BOWLES/ELIZABETH PERTEN

Nordheimer. Canadian firm of music publishers, dealers, and piano manufacturers. It was established by Abraham and Samuel Nordheimer, who, having emigrated from Germany to New York in 1839, opened a music shop in Kingston in 1842 and moved to Toronto in June 1844. By 1845 they had issued Joseph Labitzky's *The Dublin Waltzes*, the earliest engraved sheet music in Canada. Despite provision for copyright protection under Canadian law, many of the firm's early publications were engraved in New York and registered there by agents; Nordheimer did not choose to begin registering works in Canada until 1859. That year the firm became the only Canadian member of the Board of Music Trade of the United States, and nearly 300 of its publications were included in the Board's catalog (1870).

A. & S. Nordheimer, as the company was first known, issued the usual reprints of popular European songs and piano pieces, as well as new works by such Canadian residents as J.P. Clarke, Crozier, Hecht, Lazare, Schallehn, and Strathy. Publications registered between 1846 and 1851 include plate numbers, but there is evidence that they were added to the plates after the first issue. Numbering resumed in the 1880s and continued after the firm changed its name, to Nordheimer Piano & Music Co., in 1898. But the highest numbers of both sequences do not even approach the number of publications issued between 1845 and 1927, of which about a thousand have been located. Nordheimer was by far the largest music publishing firm in 19th-century Canada.

Nordheimer began its piano operations in about 1845 as agents for US piano manufacturers including Stodart & Dunham in New York and Chickering in Boston. It established its own factory in 1890 and produced upright and grand pianos of high quality—21,500 by 1927 when the business was taken over by Heintzmann & Co., which kept the Nordheimer name for some styles until 1960.

After Abraham's death in 1862, Samuel was president of the firm until 1912, succeeded by his nephew Albert who retired in 1927. Branches were established at various times in Hamilton, London, Ottawa, St Catharine's, Montreal, Quebec, and Winnipeg. The Nordheimers were active also as impresarios, opening concert halls in Montreal and Toronto.

BIBLIOGRAPHY

The House of Nordheimer Celebrates its 63rd Anniversary (Toronto, 1903)
Piano Teacher's Thematic Guide (Toronto, 1914–18) [pubd by Nordheimer Piano & Music Co. Ltd]
M. Calderisi: *Music Publishing in the Canadas 1800–1867* (Ottawa, 1981)
H. Kallmann: "A & S Nordheimer Co.," *Encyclopedia of Music in Canada* (Toronto, 1981, 2/1992)

MARIA CALDERISI

Nordica [Norton; Norton-Gower], **Lillian** [Lilian] (*b* Farmington, ME, 12 May 1857; *d* Batavia, Java [now Jakarta, Indonesia], 10 May 1914). American soprano. She studied with John O'Neill at the New England Conservatory, graduating in 1876. Engaged by Patrick Gilmore, she made her concert debut with his band (Sept 1876), then toured America—and, in 1878, Europe—with the ensemble; her London debut was at the Crystal Palace (21 May 1878). She left Gilmore to study with Sangiovanni in Milan; he coined her stage name and arranged for her operatic debuts—as Donna Elvira in *Don Giovanni* (Teatro Manzoni, Milan, March 1879) and as Violetta (Teatro Guillaume, Brescia, April 1879). She sang in St. Petersburg (1880–82) and continued summertime studies in Paris with Giovanni Sbriglia; she also studied Marguerite (*Faust*) and Ophelia (*Hamlet*) with Gounod and Thomas, making her Paris Opéra debut in the former role (22 July 1882). In 1882 she married Frederick Gower, who disappeared three years later in the midst of their divorce proceedings. Nordica's American operatic debut, as Lillian Norton-Gower, was at the New York Academy of Music as Marguerite (26 Nov 1883). It marked the beginning of a long association with JAMES HENRY MAPLESON, with whose company she also made her Covent Garden debut (12 March 1887).

Nordica subsequently sang at Drury Lane (1887), Covent Garden (1888–93), and the Metropolitan Opera, where she made her debut as Leonora in *Il trovatore* (27 March 1890). In the 1890s she turned her attention to Wagner. After extensive coaching by Cosima Wagner, she sang Elsa in the first production of *Lohengrin* at Bayreuth in 1894. At the height of her Metropolitan Opera career (1893–1907) she was known primarily as a Wagnerian. In 1896 she married a Hungarian tenor, Zoltan Dome, whom she divorced in 1904. Between 1897 and 1908 she sang at the Metropolitan and with the Damrosch-Ellis Company (1897–8), at Covent Garden (1898, 1899, 1902), and with Hammerstein's Manhattan Opera Company (1907–8). From 1908 Nordica devoted herself to concert performances; her final appearance with the Metropolitan was in December 1909. That year she married George Washington Young; they lived in Ardsley-on-the-Hudson, New York. Nordica's final operatic appearance was in Boston (March 1913); shortly afterwards she embarked on a world concert tour. In December the steamer on which she was travelling struck a reef off New Guinea; Nordica contracted pneumonia, from which she later died.

Although not a strong actress, Nordica had a rich voice and a remarkable coloratura range. She knew 40 operatic roles in English, Italian, German, French, and Russian. A resolute and shrewd—but also generally good-natured—individual, she owed her stature as a great Wagnerian soprano to hard work, constant study, and determination. Late in her career she became a strong proponent of opera in English; she was also an ardent suffragist and had an unfulfilled dream of establishing a Bayreuth-like American Institute for Music. The Nordica Homestead Museum in Farmington, Maine, holds the singer's personal library and considerable correspondence.

BIBLIOGRAPHY

DAB (F.H. Martens); *NAW* (W. Lichtenwanger)

L. Nordica: *Lillian Nordica's Hints to Singers* (New York, 1923)

G.T. Edwards: *Music and Musicians of Maine* (Portland, ME, 1928/*R*)

O. Thompson: *The American Singer* (New York, 1937)

I. Glackens: *Yankee Diva: Lillian Nordica* (New York, 1963)

J.F. Cone: *First Rival of the Metropolitan Opera* (New York, 1983)

KATHERINE K. PRESTON/R

Nordoff, Paul (*b* Philadelphia, PA, 4 June 1909; *d* Herdecke, Germany, 18 Jan 1977). Composer and music therapist. He studied piano with D. Hendrick Ezerman at the Philadelphia Conservatory (diplomas 1926, 1928, MM 1934) and piano with OLGA SAMAROFF and composition with RUBIN GOLDMARK at the Juilliard School (graduated with distinction 1933). He taught at Philadelphia Conservatory (head of composition, 1938–43), Michigan State College (1945–49), and Bard College (1948–59), and was awarded two Guggenheim Fellowships (1933, 1935) and a Pulitzer Music Scholarship (1940). He composed in a neo-romantic style. From 1959 Nordoff and music therapist Clive Robbins (1927–2011) pioneered the application of improvisation and clinical composi-

tion for children with disabilities. The Nordoff-Robbins approach, also called "Creative Music Therapy," has had worldwide impact. Nordoff and Robbins composed numerous children's music therapy songs and coauthored several books, including *Music Therapy in Special Education* (New York, 1971), *Therapy in Music for Handicapped Children* (London, 1971), and *Creative Music Therapy: Individualized Treatment for the Handicapped Child* (New York, 1977; Gilsum, NH, R/2007).

See also MUSIC THERAPY.

WORKS

Stage: Mr. Fortune (op), 1936–7, rev. 1956–7; Every Soul Is a Circus (ballet, for M. Graham), 1937; The Masterpiece (operetta, I.F. Brewer), 1940; Salem Shore (ballet), 1943; Tally Ho (ballet), 1943; The Sea Change (op, Warner), 1951

Orch: Prelude and 3 Fugues, chbr orch, 1932–6; Pf Conc., 1935; Suite, 1938; Conc., vn, pf, orch, 1948; Vn Conc., 1949; The Frog Prince (H. Pusch, Nordoff), nar, orch, 1954; Winter Sym., 1954; Gothic Conc., pf, orch, 1959

Vocal: Secular Mass (W. Prude), chorus, orch, 1934; 34 Songs (Cummings), 1942–57; Lost Summer (Warner), Mez, orch, 1949; Anthony's Song Book (Nordoff), 1950; other songs and song cycles, choral pieces

Inst. Pf Qnt, 1936; Qnt. Wind, pf, 1948; Sonata, vn, pf, 1950; Sonata, fl, pf, 1953; pf pieces

Many works for children with disabilities

MSS in private collection, Waterloo, Ontario, Canada

Principal publishers: Associated, C. Fischer, Presser, G. Schirmer

BIBLIOGRAPHY

K. Aigen: *Being in Music: Foundations of Nordoff-Robbins Music Therapy* (Gilsum, NH, 1996)

K. Aigen: *Paths of Development in Nordoff-Robbins Music Therapy* (Gilsum, NH, 1998)

C. Robbins and C. Robbins, eds.: *Healing Heritage: Paul Nordoff Exploring the Tonal Language of Music* (Gilsum, NH, 1998)

RUTH C. FRIEDBERG/BARBARA L. WHEELER

Norfolk. City in Virginia (pop. 242,803; metropolitan area: 1,671,078; 2010 US Census). It is situated in southeast Virginia, about 20 miles from the Atlantic coast and is part of a greater metropolitan region including Virginia Beach, Portsmouth, Chesapeake, Newport News, and Hampton. The city was founded in 1682 and incorporated in 1736.

Wandering musicians frequented Norfolk in the 18th century, and the first notable choral group was organized in 1818. A "Philharmonic Association" was also founded shortly thereafter. Music performances during the 19th century often took place in Mechanics Hall and the city's several theaters, including the Avon Theater and what was called the "Opera House," built in 1856. A lively vaudeville scene grew in the early decades of the 20th century, with many performances taking place in the Granby Theater (1901), the New Wells Theater (1913), and the Attucks Theatre (1919).

Today the city boasts a thriving musical life. The Virginia Symphony Orchestra, founded in 1920 as the Norfolk Symphony, and led by music director JoAnn Falletta since 1991, performs more than 130 concerts every year. The amateur orchestra Symphonicity, established in 1981, is led by David Kunkel. Virginia Opera, based in Norfolk, is among the nation's finest regional opera companies. Organized in 1974, it was directed from 1975–2010 by Peter Mark. The company presents four productions each year, the majority of which take place in the Edythe C. and Stanley L. Harrison Opera House.

Norfolk is home to several choral ensembles, most notably the professional Virginia Chorale led by Scott Williamson. Founded in 1984 by Donald McCullough as the Norfolk Pro Musica, it originally specialized in Baroque and Renaissance music but now performs a wide range of choral repertoire. The Norfolk Symphony Chorus was established in 1990 and has been directed by Robert Shoup since 1997. Other choral groups include the Virginia Beach Chorale, the Schola Cantorum, and the women's group Bellissima!

The Virginia Arts Festival, established in 1996, is held annually in Norfolk. It attracts world-class musicians and performing groups and presents approximately 60 performances in classical, jazz, popular, and world-music styles in a span of about two months. Pop artists and touring Broadway productions frequent the area's larger performing venues, which include the Norfolk Scope Arena, Chrysler Hall, the Ted Constant Convocation Center, the NorVa, and Virginia Beach's Sandler Center for the Performing Arts. Musicals are occasionally presented by the Virginia Stage Company in the Wells Theater, while jazz artists often perform in the Attucks Theatre. Smaller concert series are also sponsored by Old Dominion University's Diehn Concert Series, which attracts several international-caliber groups and soloists each year, the Feldman Chamber Music Society, the Norfolk Chamber Consort, and many local churches and synagogues.

Norfolk is home to three universities offering music degrees. Old Dominion University has the largest program and offers the BM degree in performance, composition, and education, as well as the BA degree in Music and the MME degree. Norfolk State University offers the BM degree in music media and education and the MM degree in theory/composition, education, and performance. Virginia Wesleyan, a small Methodist college, offers a liberal arts degree in music and is noted for its Center for Sacred Music. Virginia Beach is also home to the Armed Forces School of Music, the largest training institution in the world for military musicians.

The Governor's School for the Arts, a secondary school program, offers preprofessional training for approximately 350 musicians, dancers, actors, and artists at no charge. Also notable is the Norfolk Academy of Music, a nonprofit community music school offering high-quality music instruction to nearly 250 students at little to no cost.

BIBLIOGRAPHY

W. Forrest: *Historical and Descriptive Sketches of Norfolk and Vicinity* (Philadelphia, 1853)

T.J. Wertenbaker: *Norfolk: Historic Southern Port* (Durham, NC, 1931)

B. Fahlman, B. Rossheim, D. Steadman, and P. Stewart: *A Tricentennial Celebration: Norfolk 1682–1982* (Norfolk, 1982)

R. Rose: *Norfolk: a People's History* (Charleston, SC 2007)

JASON PETERSON

Norman, Christina (*b* New York, *c*1960). Producer and media executive. Earning a degree from Boston University in film production, Norman began her career as an agent for television advertising until 1991. She then moved to MTV, taking on a series of jobs and rising through the company; she has held the positions of production manager, senior vice president for marketing, executive vice president, and senior manager of the sister channel VH1. In January 2004 Norman became president of the station. She immediately began to change the channel, which had been struggling to retain its adult-contemporary-oriented audience. She took the opportunity to greenlight several new television shows, including "I Love the 80s," "Bands Reunited," "Best Week Ever," and "Rock Behind Bars," that appealed to the station's demographic and significantly increased ratings. Interest in presenting a diversity of viewpoints and possessing an ability to lead creative teams, she also served as the executive director of Oprah Winfrey's OWN network.

JONAS WESTOVER

Norman, Jessye (*b* Augusta, GA, 15 Sept 1945). Soprano. She studied at Howard University, the Peabody Conservatory, and the University of Michigan (with, among others, Pierre Bernac and Elizabeth Mannion). She won the Munich International Music Competition in 1968 and made her operatic debut in 1969 at the Deutsche Oper Berlin, as Elisabeth (*Tannhäuser*), later appearing there as Countess Almaviva. Further engagements in Europe included Aïda at La Scala and Cassandra at Covent Garden, both in 1972. The following year she returned to Covent Garden as Elisabeth. For her American stage debut she sang Jocasta in Stravinsky's

Jessye Norman. (Laurie Lewis/Lebrecht Music & Arts)

Oedipus Rex and Purcell's Dido with the Opera Company of Philadelphia (1982); she appeared first at the Metropolitan Opera in 1983, once again as Cassandra. Other roles she has sung include Gluck's Alcestis, Strauss's Ariadne, Madame Lidoine (*Dialogues des Carmélites*), the Woman (*Erwartung*), Emilia Marty (*The Makropulos Affair*), Bartók's Judith, and Wagner's Kundry and Sieglinde.

In the 1990s Norman sang in the Metropolitan Opera's production of Strauss's *Ariadne auf Naxos* (1993) and has taken part in numerous galas and benefit performances, including the "Tribute in Light" memorial concert in New York City to honor those who died on 9/11. She has continued her recital career, and has expanded her repertoire to include Duke Ellington (*Sacred Concerts* at the Cathedral Church of St. John the Divine, New York, 2009).

Norman has a commanding stage presence; her particular distinction lies in her ability to project drama through her voice. Her opulent and dark-hued soprano is richly vibrant in the lower and middle registers, if less free at the top; although her extraordinary vocal resources are not always perfectly controlled, her singing reveals uncommon refinement of nuance and dynamic variety. Her operatic recordings include Countess Almaviva; Haydn's Rosina (*La vera costanza*) and Armida, Leonore, Euryanthe; Verdi's Giulietta (*Un giorno di regno*) and Medora (*Il corsaro*), Carmen, Ariadne, Salome; and Offenbach's Giuletta and Helen. Norman also appeared in jazz concerts including, in 1982, her own show *A Great Day in the Morning*. As her many discs reveal, she is also a penetrating interpreter of lieder and *melodies*, at her finest in the broader canvases of Mahler, Richard Strauss (whose *Vier letzte Lieder* she has recorded with distinction), and Debussy.

Norman has received a number of honorary doctorates (including Howard University and University of the South), the Kennedy Center Honors (1997), and the title of Commandeur de l'Ordre des Arts et des Lettres from the French government (1984); she was made an Honorary Ambassador to the United Nations (1990). She is on the board of a number of organizations, including the New York Public Library and the Board of Trustees of Paine College in Augusta, Georgia.

BIBLIOGRAPHY

SouthernB

"Jessye Norman: la vérité du chant," *Harmonie*, cxxxii (1977), 46–51

"Jessye Norman Talks to John Greenhalgh," *Music and Musicians*, xxvii/12 (1979), 14–15

M. Mayer: "Double Header: Jessye Norman in Her Met Debut Season," *ON*, xlviii/11 (1983–4), 8–11

J.M. Fischer: *Grosse Stimmen von Enrico Caruso bis Jessye Norman* (Stuttgart, 1993)

MARTIN BERNHEIMER/ALAN BLYTH/
KAREN M. BRYAN

Norman, Jim Ed (*b* Fort Myers, FL, 16 Oct 1948). Producer, arranger, and record executive. Norman met Don Henley when both were students at North Texas State University and formed the group Shiloh, which recorded a self-titled album (Amos, 1970), produced by Kenny Rogers, before disbanding in 1971. Norman, a keyboard player, began arranging for Henley's new group, the Eagles, as well as Linda Ronstadt, Kim Carnes, Bob Seger, and America. Between 1977 and 1983 he achieved great success as a record producer, working with Crystal Gayle, Hank Williams, Jr., Johnny Lee, Mickey Gilley, and Anne Murray, with whom he produced nine albums, received four Grammy Awards, and earned the Country Music Association's Single and Album of the Year awards for "A Little Good News" (Capitol, 1983).

In 1983 Norman joined Warner/Reprise as Vice-President of Artists & Repertoire, was named as Executive Vice President in 1984, and became President in 1989, a position he held until 2004. During his time with Warner/Reprise, Norman formed a gospel label, Warner Alliance, and Warner Western for western-themed music. He signed and produced noncountry acts Take 6 and Beth Nielsen Chapman and brought Béla Fleck and the Flecktones to the label. A prominent member of the Nashville music business community, Norman was founding president of Leadership Music, received the Time/Warner's Andrew Heiskell Community Service Award, the Anti-Defamation League's Johnny Cash Americanism Award, and Leadership Music's Bridge Award.

DON CUSIC

Norman, Larry (David) (*b* Corpus Christi, TX, 8 April 1947; *d* Salem, OR, 24 Feb 2008). Christian rock singer-songwriter. Larry Norman was born in Texas and grew up in San Francisco. He was raised as a conservative, evangelical Christian, and his conversion came at an early age. Fascinated with the countercultural youth movements of the 1960s, Norman chose to adopt the cultural vernacular, hoping to share his belief with hippies. Along with his long blond hair, Norman's unique mix of Christianity and rock and roll made him the perfect icon for the burgeoning Jesus Movement of the late 1960s and early 1970s. In the midst of a gospel music culture that tended to emphasize strong vocal technique, Norman's approach bore greater similarities to that of Neil Young or Van Morrison than to gospel music mogul Bill Gaither.

Norman is widely regarded as the "father of Christian rock." At the age of 18 he moved to San Jose, California, where he formed the band People! Their debut album featured a remake of "I Love You," earlier recorded by The Zombies. Norman hoped to title the album *We Need a Whole Lot More Jesus and a Lot Less Rock and Roll*, but Capitol Records released the work as *I Love You* in 1968. In 1970 Norman and Capitol Records released *Upon This Rock*, often called the world's first Christian rock album. Considered too Christian for the secular market and too rock and roll for the church, Norman eventually found himself rejected by both industries. Despite health problems and isolation from the official Christian music industry, during the 1980s Norman launched his own record label, Solid Rock.

Norman's albums were richly layered, following the style of the Beatles, the Rolling Stones, and Crosby, Stills, and Nash, but with a dark, apocalyptic streak. Among

Norman's most notable recordings are "The Rock that Doesn't Roll," "Sweet, Sweet Song of Salvation," "I wish we'd all been ready," "Six Sixty Six," "Why don't you look into Jesus?," "UFO," "Why should the Devil have all the good music?," "I Am the Six O'Clock News," and "The Great American Novel," a song Norman performed for President Carter at the White House in 1979. With the grit, authenticity, and shocking lyrics of *Street Level* (One Way Records, 1970) and *Bootleg* (One Way Records, 1972), his public persona earned him respect among numerous general market rock stars. *Only Visiting This Planet* (which included arrangements by Beatles producer George Martin) was ranked as the best Christian album of all time in 1988. His music has influenced artists such as Frank Black, U2, and John Mellencamp.

BIBLIOGRAPHY

J.R. Howard and J.M. Streck: *Apostles of Rock: the Splintered World of Contemporary Christian Music* (Lexington, KY, 1999)

M.A. Powell: *The Encyclopedia of Contemporary Christian Music* (Peabody, MA, 2002)

S.A. Marini: *Sacred Song in America: Religion, Music, and Public Culture* (Chicago, 2003)

J.J. Thompson: "Larry Norman: a Tribute," *CCM Magazine* (April 2008), 42

D.W. Stowe: *No Sympathy for the Devil: Christian Pop Music and the Transformation of American Evangelicalism* (Chapel Hill, NC, 2011)

SHAWN YOUNG

Nortec Collective. The Nortec Collective is a small, informal group of musicians, video and installation artists, and graphic and fashion designers from Tijuana, Mexico, working primarily near the border between the United States and Mexico. Members of the collective, who work pseudonymously, include Ramón Amezcua (Bostich), Pedro Gabriel Beas (Hiperboreal), Sergio Brown (VJ Brown), Ignacio Chávez Uranga (Plankton Man), Fernando Corona (Terrestre), José Luis Martín (VJ Mashaka), Roberto Mendoza (Panóptica), Jorge Ruiz and José Trinidad Morales "Pepe Mogt" (Fussible), and Jorge Verdin and Fritz Torres (members of Clorofila and Cha3).

Emerging onto the global club scene at the end of the 20th century, the group's music shares a common aesthetic known as Nor-tec, a neologism that evokes the two major stylistic elements from which the collective draws, namely, northern Mexican musical genres such as *conjunto norteño* and *banda sinaloense* and the foregrounded technological sounds of electronic dance music. More than just a combination of separate musical styles, Nor-Tec typifies the seeming contradictions and transnational circulations of border culture, highlighting and problematizing such binaries as tradition and modernity, the local and the global, and authenticity and kitsch.

The ability of this hybrid music to resonate with audiences in disparate locations, along with an aggressive and innovative campaign of promotion through alternative distribution channels, brought the Nortec Collective worldwide popularity during the first decade of the 21st century, with dozens of recordings, three Grammy nominations, and placement within multiple major corporate advertising campaigns. After 2007 the members

produced music only individually, and only four members of the collective, Bostich, Clorofila, Fussible, and Hiperboreal, were still touring as of late 2010, while Terrestre, Plankton Man, and Panóptica, no longer affiliated with the collective, still tour under the Nortec rubric.

BIBLIOGRAPHY

S. Asensio Llamas: "Tijuana Grooves: El borde revisitado en la electronica de Nortec," *Arizona Journal of Hispanic Cultural Studies*, v (2001), 55–72

A.L. Madrid: "Navigating Ideologies in 'In-Between' Cultures: Signifying Practices in Nor-tec Music," *LAMR*, xxiv/3 (2003), 270–86

S. Asensio Llamas: "The Nortec Edge: Border Traditions and Electronica in Tijuana," *Rockin' Las Americas: the Global Politics of Rock Music in Latin America*, ed. D. Pacini-Hernandez, H. Fernandez-L'Hoeste, and E. Zolov (Pittsburgh, 2004)

J.M. Valenzuela Arce: *Paso del Nortec/This Is Tijuana* (Mexico City, 2004)

A.L. Madrid: *Nor-tec Rifa! Electronic Dance Music from Tijuana to the World* (New York, 2008)

BILL BAHNG BOYER

Norteña music. Musical genre. Norteña music (*música norteña*) uses similar instrumentation to Texas-Mexican *conjunto*, featuring the accordion, *bajo sexto* (bass-rhythm guitar hybrid), electric bass, drums, and sometimes saxophone. It originated in the Northeastern region of Mexico, bordering the United States, particularly in the states of Nuevo León and Tamaulipas during the mid-19th century. German and Czech immigrants brought dance styles like the *redowa*, *mazurka*, *waltz*, *schottische*, and polka to cities like Monterrey and Matamoros in the region. Instrumental folk ensembles, called *tamborileros* (*picotas* in Tamaulipas), featuring one or two clarinets and a hand-held *tambora* drum (likely introduced by Spanish Jesuits), played these rhythms alongside Mexican *huapangos* and *sones* at secular and religious celebrations in rural towns and villages. Though there is evidence of the accordion's existence in Monterrey in the late 19th century, migrant workers who crossed the border to work as farm laborers, primarily in Texas, brought back cheap diatonic button models in the early-20th century, which quickly replaced the clarinets. Continued migration spurred the popularity of accordion and tambora ensembles on both sides of the border. The bajo sexto was added, eventually replacing the tambora, and the ensemble was solidified with the dissemination of recordings in the 1930s by Texas-based accordionist Narciso Martínez. By the mid-1940s, groups on both sides of the border featured *dueto* (duo) vocals to update the ensemble. Traditional and popular song genres, such as narrative ballads (*corridos*), country songs (*rancheras*), romantic songs, *boleros*, and, later, *cumbias*, were played by norteña groups.

By the late 1950s many Texas groups took on elements of country, rhythm and blues, and rock as Mexican Americans were participating more in American popular culture, thus creating an identity and music style separate from recent migrating Mexicans. Texas Mexicans, or Tejanos, used the term conjunto to refer to these ensembles and songs were increasingly bilingual or utilized less-complicated Spanish text. The 1964 termination of the Bracero Program coincided with a surge in Mexican migration that continues today, fueling the demand for the more Mexican-identified norteña music style across the United States. By the early 1970s norteña recordings were being produced and sold on both sides of the border by companies in Monterrey; Corpus Christi and San Antonio, Texas; and San Jose, California, focusing almost exclusively on the corrido. Traditionally, corridos told stories of Revolutionary heroes, the exploits of border heroes and bandits, and border-crossing. Modern norteña groups, like Los Tigres del Norte, Ramon Ayala y los Bravos del Norte, Los Cadetes de Linares, Luis y Julian, Los Humildes del Norte, Los Terribles del Norte, Los Tucanes de Tijuana, and many others, sing corridos about topics affecting a larger, Mexican laborer population now traveling from regions farther south in Mexico and spanning across the United States. Popular norteña topics include drug trafficking (*narcocorridos*), immigration policy, racism, discrimination, and, recently, corruption in Mexican politics. Largely due to the phenomenal success of multiple Grammy award-winning, 40-year veterans Los Tigres del Norte, popular Mexican rock bands such a Café Tacuba, El Gran Silencio, and electronic/experimental Nor-tec groups have mined stylistic elements of norteña music to create radio hits enjoyed by young fans in the United States, Mexico, and other Spanish-speaking countries.

BIBLIOGRAPHY

C. Ragland: *Música Norteña: Mexican Migrants Creating a Nation between Nations* (Philadelphia, 2009)

CATHY RAGLAND

North, Alex (*b* Chester, PA, 4 Dec 1910; *d* Los Angeles, CA, 8 Sept 1991). Composer and conductor. After attending the Curtis Institute, where he studied the piano with GEORGE FREDERICK BOYLE, he won a scholarship (1929) to the Juilliard School. He also studied on scholarship at the Moscow Conservatory (from 1933) and went on to serve as music director of the German Theatre Group and the Latvian State Theatre. He was the only American member of the Union of Soviet Composers, from which he received commissions for two choruses and a set of piano variations. In 1935 he returned to the United States and taught music for dance at Finch, Briarcliff, Sarah Lawrence, and Bennington colleges. In New York he studied composition with AARON COPLAND and ERNST TOCH and composed ballet scores for Martha Graham, Hanya Holm, and Agnes De Mille. In 1939 he went to Mexico as music director for Anna Sokolow's dance troupe, and while there he studied with SILVESTRE REVUELTAS and conducted concerts at the Palace of Fine Arts in Mexico City.

During World War II North served as a captain in the US Army; he organized therapeutic programs for veterans and scored more than 80 documentaries for the Office of War Information. In 1946 his *Revue* for clarinet and orchestra was performed by Benny Goodman with the City Symphony of New York under Leonard Bernstein. He continued to compose for the theater, particularly ballet scores, and after the success of his music for Elia Kazan's production of Arthur Miller's *Death of a Salesman*, Kazan invited him to write for the film version of Tennessee Williams's *A Streetcar Named Desire*. This, the first jazz-based symphonic score to be written for a film, brought North wide acclaim, and in the 1950s he became a leading Hollywood composer.

North made no stylistic distinction between his film music and his works in other genres; his entire output is grounded in the traditions of symphonic and chamber music. Fundamentally dramatic in conception, although often not emotionally demonstrative, his works include moments of light and dark, violent dissonance, and gentle lyricism or resignation. Although he used large symphonic forces to excellent effect (notably in the film scores for *Spartacus* and *Cleopatra*), he often wrote for smaller ensembles (as in *The Bachelor Party* and *Who's Afraid of Virginia Woolf?*). He was adept at integrating jazz elements (as in *A Streetcar Named Desire*, *The Long, Hot Summer*, and *The Rose Tattoo*) and like Bernard Herrmann preferred to exploit timbre, affect, and understated stylistic references, rather than referential themes and leitmotivic networks.

WORKS

FILM SCORES
(*-documentaries*)
*China Strikes Back, 1936; *Heart of Spain, 1937; *People of the Cumberland, 1937; *Mount Vernon, 1940; *A Better Tomorrow, 1944; *Library of Congress, 1945; *Venezuela, 1945; *City Pastorale, 1946; *Recreation, 1946; *Rural Nurse, 1946; *Coney Island USA, 1950; A Streetcar Named Desire, 1951; Death of a Salesman, 1951; The 13th Letter, 1951; Les misérables, 1952; Pony Soldier, 1952; Viva Zapata!, 1952; *The American Road, 1953; *Decision for Chemistry, 1953; The Member of the Wedding, 1953

Desirée, 1954; Go, Man, Go!, 1954; Man with the Gun, 1955; The Racers, 1955; The Rose Tattoo, 1955; Unchained, 1955; The Bad Seed, 1956; I'll Cry Tomorrow, 1956; The King and Four Queens, 1956; The Rainmaker, 1956; The Bachelor Party, 1957; Hot Spell, 1958; The Long, Hot Summer, 1958; South Seas Adventure, 1958; Stage Struck, 1958; The Sound and the Fury, 1959; The Wonderful Country, 1959; Spartacus, 1960; The Children's Hour, 1961; The Misfits, 1961; Sanctuary, 1961

All Fall Down, 1962; Cleopatra, 1963; The Outrage, 1964; The Agony and the Ecstasy, 1965; Cheyenne Autumn, 1965; Who's Afraid of Virginia Woolf?, 1966; 2001: a Space Odyssey, 1967 [not used]; The Devil's Brigade, 1968; The Shoes of the Fisherman, 1968; A Dream of Kings, 1969; Hard Contract, 1969; Willard, 1971; Pocket Money, 1972; The Rebel Jesus, 1972; Once upon a Scoundrel, 1973; Lost in the Stars, 1974 [adaptation of work by Weill, 1949]; Shanks, 1974; Bite the Bullet, 1975; Journey into Fear, 1975; The Passover Plot, 1976; Somebody Killed her Husband, 1978; Carny, 1980; Wise Blood, 1980; Dragonslayer, 1981 [after 2001: a Space Odyssey]; Under the Volcano, 1984; Prizzi's Honor, 1985; The Dead, 1987; Good Morning, Vietnam, 1987; The Penitent, 1988; The Last Butterfly, 1991; other documentaries

OTHER WORKS
Dramatic: Hither and Thither of Danny Dither (children's op, J. Gury), 1941; ballets and dance scores, TV scores, incid music and musical revues, other children's works

Inst: Quest, chbr orch, 1938; Suite, fl, cl, bn, 1938; Rhapsody, pf, orch, 1939; Suite, str qt, 1939; Trio, ww, 1939; Wind Qnt, 1942; Window Cleaner, cl, 2 pf, 1945; Revue, cl, orch, 1946; Sym. no.1, 1947; Dance Preludes, pf, 1948; Holiday Set, orch, 1948; A Streetcar Named Desire, suite, orch, 1951 [based on film score]; Death of a Salesman, suite, orch, 1951 [based on film score]; Viva Zapata!, suite, orch,

1952 [based on film score]; Rhapsody, tpt, pf, orch, 1956 [for film Four Girls in Town]; Sym. no.2, 1968 [based on TV score Africa]
Vocal: Negro Mother (cant., L. Hughes), A, chorus, orch, 1940; Ballad of Valley Forge (A. Kreymborg), Bar, chorus, orch, 1941; Rhapsody, USA (A. Hayes), S, A, T, B, chorus, orch, 1942; Morning Star (cant., M. Lampell), chorus, orch, 1946; many songs

Recorded interviews in *NHohMSS* in *Laum*
Principal publishers: Marks, Mills, North, Northern

BIBLIOGRAPHY

GroveA (C. Palmer/C. McCarty) [incl. further bibliography]
D. Kraft: "A Conversation with Alex North," *Soundtrack!*, iv/13 (1985), 3–8
W. Darby and J. Du Bois: *American Film Music: Major Composers, Techniques, Trends, 1915–1990* (Jefferson, NC, 1990), 398–424
T. Thomas: *Film Score: the Art and Craft of Movie Music* (Burbank, CA, 1991), 182–94
G. Burt: *The Art of Film Music* (Boston, 1994), 59ff
S.S. Henderson: *Alex North, Film Composer: a Biography, with Musical Analyses of* A Streetcar Named Desire, Spartacus, The Misfits, Under the Volcano, *and* Prizzi's Honor (Jefferson, NC, 2003)
P.A. Merkley: "'Stanley Hates This but I Like It!': North vs. Kubrick on the Music for *2001: a Space Odyssey*," *Journal of Film Music*, ii/1 (2007), 1–33
A. Davison: *Alex North's* A Streetcar Named Desire: *a Film Score Guide* (Lanham, MD, 2009)

CLIFFORD McCARTY/DAVID NEUMEYER

North American Brass Band Association [NABBA]. Nonprofit organization incorporated in 1983, made up of individual members and member bands. Devoted to British-type brass bands—ensembles that utilize the instrumentation of historic British brass bands of the late twentieth century, employing cornets, flugelhorn, E-flat tenor horns, B-flat baritones, euphoniums, trombones, tubas and percussion—this corporation was organized to foster, promote, and encourage the establishment, growth, and development of such ensembles throughout the United States and Canada. Its mission is, in part, to support and help further the music education of its members, as well as to advance the public's appreciation of British-type brass bands. A resource for musical and organizational assistance to such bands throughout North America, it also helps to sponsor and hold local, state, regional, national, and international contests and festivals for the purpose of improving the performing standards and abilities of its members. *The Brass Band Bridge*, its online quarterly publication, is devoted to disseminating news of, and scholarly articles on, all aspects relating to North American brass bands, and also reviews recently published brass band materials.

BIBLIOGRAPHY

D. Herak: *25-years of NABBA History* (Columbus, OH, 2007)

JAMES P. CASSARO

North Carolina, University of [UNC]. A statewide university system comprised of 17 institutions, more than 221,000 students, and a faculty of more than 12,000 (as of 2010). In 1931, UNC Chapel Hill was joined by North Carolina State University and UNC Greensboro to form the Consolidated University of North Carolina. In 1969, UNC Charlotte, UNC Asheville, and UNC Wilmington joined the system, and in 1971 all 16 public institutions in the state which at that time conferred bachelor's degrees became part of the system. The North Carolina

School of Science and Mathematics became a full member of the university in 2007.

The Chapel Hill campus (founded in 1789, enrollment of 29,390 in 2010) offers a BA with a major in music and a BM, both degrees with emphases in performance, music history, composition, jazz studies, popular music studies, and music education; an MA in teaching (MAT) with emphasis in music education; and an MA and a PhD in musicology. Fayetteville State University (1867, enrollment 5,781) offers a BA in general music with concentrations in instrumental music, keyboard, and voice and a BS in music education. North Carolina State University, Raleigh (1887, enrollment 34,376) offers only a minor in music. The Pembroke campus (1887, enrollment 6,944) offers a BA in music and in music with elective studies in business; a BM in music education and in musical theater; and an MA in music education and in teaching with specialization in music. Western Carolina University in Cullowhee (1889, enrollment 9,407) offers a BA in music; a BM in commercial and electronic music and in performance; a BM/BSEd in music education; a BFA with a concentration in music theater; and an MM in performance.

Elizabeth City State University (1891, enrollment 3,307) offers a BA in music with concentrations in composition, music education licensure, performance, music business, and sound recording technology. North Carolina Agricultural and Technical State University in Greensboro (1891, enrollment 10,795) offers a BA in general music and in music performance and a BS in music education. The UNC campus in Greensboro (1891, enrollment 18,771) offers a BA with a major in music; a BM in music education and in performance; an MM in performance, music education, music theory, and composition; post-master's certificates in music theory pedagogy and in ethnomusicology; a DMA in performance; and a PhD in music education. Winston-Salem State University (1892, enrollment 6,333) offers a BS in music business and in music education. Appalachian State University in Boone (1899, enrollment 17,222) offers a BM in music education, performance, sacred music, music therapy, and composition-theory; a BS in music industry studies; and an MM in music education, music education with a composition emphasis, music performance, and music therapy.

East Carolina University in Greenville (1907, enrollment 27,783) offers a BM in music education, music therapy, theory-composition, and performance and an MM in music education, music education with a concentration in music therapy, theory-composition, and performance. North Carolina Central University in Durham (1910, enrollment 8,645) offers a BA in music with concentrations in sacred music, music industry, ethnomusicology; a BA in music education and in music and liberal arts; and a BM and MM in jazz studies. The Asheville campus (1927, enrollment 3,967) offers the BA in music and in music with a concentration in jazz studies as well as a BS in music technology. The University of North Carolina, Charlotte (1946, enrollment 25,063) offers a BA in music and a BM in music education and in music performance. The Wilmington campus (1947, enrollment 13,071) offers a BA in music and a BM in music education and in performance. The UNC School of the Arts in Winston-Salem (1963, enrollment 872) offers a BM degree. The North Carolina School of Science and Mathematics (1980, enrollment 680), a public residential high school in Durham, offers instruction in music.

The archives and special collections of the UNC libraries hold a number of unique music resources. Chapel Hill is home to the Southern Folklife Collection, a preeminent archive dedicated to American folk music and popular culture. The UNC Chapel Hill Southern Historical Collection holds the papers of Paul Green, Lamar Stringfield, and Robert S. Phifer. The UNC Greensboro Martha Blakeney Hodges Special Collections and University Archives house an internationally known collection of cello music including books and manuscripts belonging to Elizabeth Cowling, Maurice Eisenberg, Bernard Greenhouse, Fritz Magg, Rudolf Matz, Janos Scholz, Luigi Silva, and Laszlo Varga. The Appalachian State University Libraries hold the papers and original manuscripts of the composer Tui St. George and the conductor Hans Schweiger.

CHRISTOPHER E. MEHRENS

North Carolina School of the Arts, University of [UNCSA]. State-supported arts conservatory. The North Carolina School of the Arts opened in Winston-Salem in 1965, joined the University of North Carolina system in 1972, and was renamed UNCSA in 2008. Five professional schools with a total enrollment of 1,100 provide training for high school through graduate students: Dance, Design and Production (including Visual Arts), Drama, Filmmaking, and Music. The High School and Undergraduate Academic Programs provide a strong curriculum of academic courses. The School of Music, with an enrollment of 260, offers a high school diploma, BM, College Arts Diploma, MM, and Professional Artist Certificate. The Music Library, a department in the UNCSA Library, holds nearly 120,000 items. The UNCSA Archives include published scores of Vittorio Giannini, scores of Louis Cheslock, papers of Gladys Swarthout, and the Benjamin Swalin Collection.

MARIE KROEGER/LESLIE E. KAMTMAN

Northeast Woodlands Indians. Group of Native American tribes that share certain cultural traits, living in New England, New York, New Jersey, Pennsylvania, eastern Virginia and Kentucky, northern Ohio and Indiana, Illinois, Michigan, Wisconsin, and northern Minnesota, and adjacent areas of Canada.

See Iroquois and Wabenaki; *see also* Native American music.

Northern Blackfoot. Native American tribe of Montana and Alberta, Canada; *see* Blackfoot (i).

North Texas, University of. State university in Denton, Texas. The institution dates to the founding of North Texas Normal College in 1890. It later became North Texas State College (1949), then North Texas State University (1961), and took its present name in 1988. The College of Music was founded in 1890, and currently

enrolls nearly 1,600 students with a full-time faculty of 95. It offers BM, MM, DMA, and PhD degrees in performance, composition, music education, music history, music theory, and jazz studies, and a (non-degree) Graduate Artist Certificate. The College of Music is internationally recognized for its comprehensive program, examples of which include opera, early music, chamber music, the Center for Experimental Music and Intermedia, and the Center for Music and Medicine. In addition to several performing groups for band, orchestra, and choir, the college offers many world music ensembles and nine jazz bands. The acclaimed One O'Clock Lab Band has been nominated for several Grammy awards. The music library (established in 1941) has one of the largest music collections in the United States, with over 300,000 volumes of books, periodicals, and scores, and approximately 900,000 sound recordings in various formats.

WARREN HENRY

Northwest Coast Indians. Group of Native American tribes that share certain cultural traits, living in a narrow band extending along the Pacific coast of North America from Northern California, Oregon, and Washington, through Canada, and into Alaska.

See Nuu-chah-nulth and Tlingit; *see also* Native American music.

Northwestern University. Privately endowed university in Evanston, Illinois, whose school of music was established in 1895.

See Chicago (i); *see also* Evanston, Illinois, in Libraries and collections.

Norvo, Red [Norville, Kenneth] (*b* Beardstown, IL, 31 March 1908; *d* Santa Monica, CA, 6 April 1999). Jazz xylophonist and vibraphonist. After touring with a marimba band in the late 1920s he joined Paul Whiteman's orchestra. Mildred Bailey, the singer in the band, became his first wife, and from 1936 to 1939 they led a small orchestra in New York. Norvo joined Benny Goodman's sextet in 1944, at which time he shifted from marimba to vibraphone. He was a soloist with Woody Herman's First Herd (1946) and toured with Billie Holiday. During the 1950s he led trios with guitar and double bass, one of which was an outstanding cool-jazz ensemble with Tal Farlow and Charles Mingus (1950–51). In 1959 he toured in Europe with Goodman. He toured there again in 1968 and 1969, but during the 1960s and 1970s he worked mainly in Nevada and California. Several albums with famous swing musicians announced his return to the international arena, and in the 1980s he toured Europe regularly.

In the early 1930s, with Whiteman and later with his own ensembles, Norvo proved himself an exceptional improviser on xylophone, a previously neglected instrument in jazz. He usually played vibraphone without vibrato, almost like a xylophone. His improvising, strongly influenced by Teddy Wilson's piano style, suffered an occasional rhythmic stiffness at fast tempos, but was outstanding on such jazz ballads as "Ghost of a Chance" (Baronet, 1945), recorded during a concert at Town Hall in New York. As a bandleader Norvo preferred delicate sounds. In the 1930s he led a drummerless sextet (trumpet, tenor saxophone, clarinet, xylophone, guitar, and double bass) and an orchestra noted for its subtle approach to swing. In the period 1936–7 this orchestra specialized in the performance of highly praised arrangements by Eddie Sauter, in particular "Remember" (Bruns., 1937), which has an outstanding solo by Norvo. Norvo later brought his concern for clarity and restraint to the trio with Farlow and Mingus, as may be heard on "Move" (Dis., 1950). Among the leading musicians of the swing era, he was unusually successful in making a transition to the bop style.

BIBLIOGRAPHY

G.T. Simon: *The Big Bands* (New York, 1967, 4/1981)

W. Balliett: "The Music is More Important," *Ecstasy at the Onion* (New York, 1971), 194–211; repr. in *Improvising: Sixteen Jazz Musicians and their Art* (New York, 1977), 113–35

A. Shaw: *The Street that Never Slept: New York's Fabled 52nd Street* (New York, 1971/R1977 as *52nd Street: the Street of Jazz*)

R. Stewart: "Red Norvo: a Tale of a Pioneer," *Jazz Masters of the Thirties* (New York, 1972/R), 71–9

S. Woolley: "Red Norvo: Interview," *Cadence*, ii/1 (1976–7), 3–5

J. McDonough: "Red Norvo: a Man for All Eras," *DB*, xliv/18 (1977), 16

S. Klett: "Red Norvo: Interview," *Cadence*, v/7 (1979), 5–8, 10–11, 16

L. Tomkins: "Happy Again with the Trio: Red Norvo," *CI*, xx/4 (1981), 22–3

B. Lylloff: "An Interview with Red Norvo," *Percussive Notes*, xxxi/1 (1992), 42

S. Klett: "Celebrating Red Norvo: 1908–1999," *The IAJRC Journal*, xxxii/3 (1999), 8–17

Oral history material in *NEij*

BARRY KERNFELD/R

Norwegian American music. *See* EUROPEAN AMERICAN MUSIC.

Norwood, Dorothy (*b* Atlanta, GA, 27 Nov 1935). Gospel singer and songwriter. Hailed by many as gospel's "greatest storyteller," Norwood's performing and recording career spans five decades. Her professional career began in the mid-1950s when she became a member of the Caravans. She left the Caravans in the late-1950s, developed her skills in songwriting and storytelling, and ultimately founded her own group (the Dorothy Norwood Singers) in the early 1960s. She and the Singers began recording shortly thereafter. By the end of that decade Norwood had recorded over ten albums, stamping many of them with her classic stories such as "The Old Lady's House" and "The Denied Mother." Norwood and the Norwood Singers toured with the Rolling Stones in 1972. Such visibility confirmed her status as an emerging force in the gospel music industry and introduced her and gospel music to new arenas and markets. Since that tour Norwood has released over 30 more recordings for various labels and with notable gospel groups such as the Mississippi Mass Choir. In complement to her unique storytelling ability is a deep and flexible alto voice that is as comfortable in ballad settings as it is with the spirited cries and hollers that sometimes punctuate her original stories.

BIBLIOGRAPHY

H.C. Boyer: *How Sweet the Sound: The Golden Age of Gospel* (Washington, DC, 1995)

R. Darden: *People Get Ready: A New History of Gospel Music* (New York, 2004)

HORACE J. MAXILE, JR.

Norworth, Jack [Knauff, John] (*b* Philadelphia, PA, 5 Jan 1879; *d* Laguna Beach, CA, 1 Sept 1959). Vaudeville performer and composer. After leaving home to join a minstrel show, he also tried his hand at vaudeville and straight drama. A man of small stature, he quickly became popular as a song-and-dance man, but he enjoyed his greatest success between 1907 and 1913, when he was partnered by his second wife, NORA BAYES; their celebrated billing read "Nora Bayes, Assisted and Admired by Jack Norworth." They played together in vaudeville and on Broadway and introduced Norworth's best-known song, "Shine on, Harvest Moon," in Ziegfeld's *Follies of 1908*. Among the other songs for which Norworth is remembered are "Take Me Out to the Ball Game" and "Sister Susie's Sewing Shirts for Soldiers." He spent most of World War I performing in London, and during the early 1920s played important roles for companies in Chicago. Although he continued to be a favorite in vaudeville, his popularity gradually lessened, and one of his last appearances was in 1938 as the elderly stage doorman in *The Fabulous Invalid*.

BIBLIOGRAPHY

A.W. McGuiggan: *Take Me out to the Ball Game* (Lincoln, NE, 2009)

GERALD BORDMAN/R

Nostalgia. Nostalgia refers to an emotional longing for home or an idealized time past, particularly of one's childhood or youth. While the term's roots are in the late 17th century, when it first appeared as a medical diagnosis for homesick soldiers, its connection to American music dates to the 19th century. Nostalgia has been associated with various genres and styles, ranging from Tin Pan Alley songs and Hollywood film scores to country and southern rock, as well as the numerous revivals, such as sacred harp singing and neo-swing, that emerged throughout the 20th century. No matter what musical shape nostalgia has taken, scholars have sought to illuminate the historical, social, and cultural conditions responsible for its emergence.

Two general strands of nostalgic songwriting dominated the 19th century. The first of these consisted of parlor ballads that conjured idyllic memories of female subjects lost to the passage of time, or in many cases even death. These songs, which found their largest audience in middle-class domestic settings, echoed the larger vogue for sentimentality in American culture at that time. The second type encompassed the numerous blackface minstrel songs that painted a nostalgic portrait of home and family life on the southern plantation. These were first popularized in the 1840s by white Northern songwriters, who drew on the suggestive power of a mythologized Old South as a pastoral alternative to the industrialization that was transforming the northern landscape. In the postwar years, as African

American performers took to the minstrel stage, the nostalgic plantation song remained an important part of the repertory, perpetuating a southern racial fantasy that belied the Reconstruction's traumatic ruptures.

In the 20th century's opening decades, nostalgia continued to figure prominently not only in musical theater, with its many minstrel retentions, but in the restless search for an authentic American compositional voice. Nowhere is this more evident than in the case of Charles Ives, who stands as the most widely analyzed nostalgic figure in American music history. The patch-work collage of 19th-century American musical quotations that run throughout Ives's music evokes memories of childhood, nature, and the small town values of his New England upbringing. As various scholars have suggested, Ives's nostalgic gaze was resonant with a larger societal reaction to and resistance against the alienating forces of modernity. Ives in particular chafed at the crass commercialism and passive easy-chair listening of the modern urban dweller, a development that threatened the active rural masculinity he believed was necessary to forging real American music.

This clash between modernity and tradition is crucial to understanding nostalgia in the first half of the 20th century. It is central, for example, to the pioneering work of folklorist John Lomax, whose reminiscences of a vanishing Old South partially fueled his quest for genuine American folk music. Convinced that such music could only be located in areas untouched by the corrupting hand of modern life, he turned first to the frontier ballads of the cowboys, whose isolated lifestyle ostensibly ensured their authenticity. Later, believing he had found an untapped wellspring of primitive purity in the music performed by black prisoners cut off from the outside world, he and his son Alan scoured the penitentiaries in the 1930s for original African American folk music, eventually landing their prize possession, the folk-singing convict, Leadbelly.

This same depression era also spawned one of the first major musical revivals of the 20th century, the return of the barbershop quartet. As with the many revivals that would follow in the decades to come, the barbershop revival drew on the nostalgic collective public memory of an idealized past era that no longer seemed continuous with the present. In the case of barbershop quartets, the close harmony of male voices offered the promise of camaraderie, and the comforting memories of an older, small town musical practice in the face of the depression's harsh realities. One could view the prominent return of 1950s rock and roll in the early 1970s similarly, as a nostalgic release from both the painful societal upheavals of the 1960s and the political and economic instability that followed in its wake. At the same time, the nature of the rock and roll revival and others of the late 20th century was much different in scope. The importance of reissued recordings, oldies radio stations, record collector publications, and the high profile return to the stage of authenticated performers from the original era, meant that memories of the earlier era would circulate in a much more heavily mediated fashion.

As the sounds and images of the 1950s became a commonplace of 1970s film, television sitcoms, and musical theater, and drew increasing coverage in the popular press, concerns arose that nostalgia had become little more than an emotionally manipulative marketing ploy. This dim view of nostalgia grew even more in the 1980s as influential cultural critics such as Fredric Jameson lamented the pastiche of "nostalgia films" like *American Graffiti*, and their effacement of history in favor of a stereotyped and misremembered past. Depicted or attacked as a regressive, politically conservative malady, nostalgia enjoyed little currency with leftist and liberal critics of the 1980s and early 1990s.

The late 1990s witnessed nostalgia's rehabilitation, however, as it was increasingly acknowledged as an active and meaningful presence in both the making and consumption of music. Vintage 1970s analogue synthesizers enjoyed a resurgence, as various musicians turned to them as an alternative to the digital keyboards and programming that dominated popular music. One could also see this "technostalgia" in hip-hop and electronica, where DJs sampled or simulated the surface noise of older vinyl recordings to lend their music a warm, or in some cases elegiac, authenticity. As vinyl sales plummeted, the figure of the nostalgic record collector consequently grew in prominence, appearing in movies such as *Ghost World* and as the subject of numerous academic studies. Given the accelerated rate of consumption that drives American society, it is unlikely that this link between musical nostalgia and obsolescent or residual media will dissipate anytime soon.

BIBLIOGRAPHY

F. Jameson: "Postmodernism, Or, the Cultural Logic of Late Capitalism," *New Left Review*, cxlvi (1984), 59–92

J. Hirsch: "Modernity, Nostalgia, and Southern Folklore Studies: the Case of John Lomax," *The Journal of American Folklore*, cv/416 (1992), 183–207

S. Key: "Sound and Sentimentality: Nostalgia in the Songs of Stephen Foster," *AM*, xiii/2 (1995), 145–66

L. Botstein: "Innovation and Nostalgia: Ives, Mahler, and the Origins of Modernism," *Charles Ives and his World*, ed. J. Peter Burkholder (Princeton, 1996), 35–74

L. Glazer and S. Key: "Carry me Back: Nostalgia for the Old South in Nineteenth-Century Popular Culture," *Journal of American Studies*, xxx/1 (1996), 1–24

D. Metzer: "'We Boys': Childhood in the Music of Charles Ives," *19CM*, xxi/1 (1997), 77–95

D. Shumway: "Rock 'n' Roll Soundtracks and the Production of Nostalgia," *Cinema Journal*, xxxviii/2 (1999), 36–51

J. Auner: "Making Old Machines Speak: Images of Technology in Recent Music," *Echo: a Music-Centered Journal*, ii/2 (2000), <http://www.echo.ucla.edu/Volume2-Issue2/auner/auner.html>

R. Rubin: "Sing Me Back Home: Nostalgia, Bakersfield, and Modern Country Music," *American Popular Music: New Approaches to the Twentieth Century*, ed. R. Rubin and J. Melnick (Amherst, MA, 2001), 93–109

T. Taylor: *Strange Sounds: Music, Technology & Culture* (New York, 2001)

G. Averill: *Four Parts, No Waiting: a Social History of American Barbershop Harmony* (New York, 2003)

T. Anderson: "As if History was Merely a Record: the Pathology of Nostalgia and the Figure of the Recording in Contemporary Popular Cinema," *Music, Sound and the Moving Image*, ii/1 (2008), 51–76

L. Kramer: "Music and the Politics of Memory: Charles Ives's *A Symphony: New England Holidays*," *JSAM*, ii/4 (2008), 459–75

J.M. Runowicz: *Forever Doo-Wop: Race, Nostalgia and Vocal Harmony* (Amherst, MA, 2010)

THEO CATEFORIS

Notation. Any graphic means of representing musical sounds, either by symbolizing them, or by providing instructions for producing them physically. This article is concerned with notations unique to, or originating in, the United States; these systems have developed from attempts to facilitate music reading or have been innovations resulting from compositional impulses and applications of digital technology.

1. Notations for ease of reading and musical computing. 2. Notations for 20th-century innovations.

1. NOTATIONS FOR EASE OF READING AND MUSICAL COMPUTING. The first music printed in the English-speaking colonies of North America was a group of psalm tunes, with bass lines, added to the ninth edition of the Bay Psalm Book (1698). Their notation and the solmization system by which they were taught were the foundation of the first specifically American notational developments. Fig.1 shows the combination of staff notation and letters beneath the staves representing a four-syllable solmization system (*fa, sol, la, fa, sol, la, mi*); this was an adaptation of earlier English psalm notation (*see* FASOLA). In the early 18th century a movement to improve church music by encouraging congregations to sing in "regular" fashion (i.e., by note-reading) arose in New England; one of its first proponents, John Tufts, further adapted the earlier notation in *A Very Plain and Easy Introduction to the Singing of Psalm Tunes* (1721). He eliminated conventional note shapes but kept the staff, on which he placed letters representing the solmization syllables, adding dots to double their durations, and slurs between them to halve their durations (fig.2). This "plain and easy method" of literal notation had an explicit pedagogical aim: to enable the novice at reading music, "with a little practice, to sing all the tunes in this book in any of their parts, with ease and pleasure." Although the *Introduction* had appeared in 11 editions

2. *Literal notation on staves (John Tufts, "An Introduction to the Singing of Psalm-tunes," 10th edition; Boston, 1738); the dots double and the slurs halve the notes' duration*

by 1744 (the earliest extant edition is the third, 1723), Tufts method was not adopted by other New Englanders; they continued, as the singing-school movement grew during the 18th century, to use staff notation with conventional note shapes.

An important notational innovation was introduced by William Little and William Smith in their singing-school tunebook *The Easy Instructor* (1801), which used four differently shaped note heads to represent the four solmization syllables: ◺ (*fa*), ○ (*sol*), □ (*la*), and ◇ (*mi*) (fig.3). This "shape-note" system was used in many later tunebooks, especially in the South and West, among them the extremely popular and long-lived *Southern Harmony* (1835) of William Walker, and *The Sacred Harp* (1844) of B.F. White and E.J. King. The four-shape system was challenged, however, by the rising influence of European seven-syllable solmization: Jesse B. Aikin added three new shapes to the four of earlier shape-note tunebooks in *The Christian Minstrel* (1846; fig.4a);

1. *Early American notation: staff and literal notation based on a four-syllable solmization system (Bay Psalm Book, supplement to the 9th edition; Boston, 1698)*

3. *Four-shape notation, in which distinctive note heads represent the four solmization syllables (William Little and William Smith, "The Easy Instructor"; Albany, NY, 1808 edition); though the excerpt is in E minor, the shapes are determined by the solmization of G major*

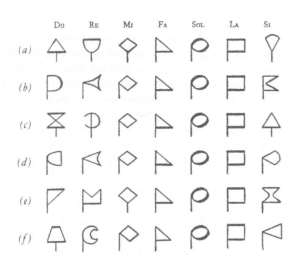

4. *Systems of seven-shape notation used by (a) Jesse B. Aikin in "The Christian Minstrel" (1846), (b) A. Auld in "The Ohio Harmonist" (1847), (c) W.H. Swan and Marcus Lafayette Swan in "The Harp of Columbia" (1848), (d) Joseph Funk in "Harmonia sacra, being a Compilation of Genuine Church Music" (5th edition, 1851), (e) A.W. Johnson in "The Western Psalmodist" (1853), and (f) William Walker in "Christian Harmony" (1867); each of the systems has conventional staff notation apart from the shape of the note heads (G.P. Jackson, "White Spirituals in the Southern Uplands," Chapel Hill, NC, 1933)*

other tunebook compilers, under the impression that Aikin's new shapes were patented, invented other systems (figs.4b–f). (*See also* SHAPE-NOTE HYMNODY.)

Various other notations, mostly numerical and aiming similarly to simplify the task of learning to read music by combining some kind of staff notation with cues for solmization, were developed. In Thomas J. Harrison's *Sacred Harmonicon* (1839) the seven scale steps are represented by the numbers 1 to 7, which replace conventional note shapes; the staff is reduced to two lines, the space between them representing a "middle" octave (within which

most vocal lines lie); and durations of notes and rests, as well as inflections of pitch, are represented by various signs and letters. Augustus D. Fillmore and his son James Henry Fillmore of Cincinnati both published tunebooks in which numbers (again, 1 to 7) either replaced note heads in an otherwise conventional staff notation, as in *The New Harp of Zion* (1866), or were placed in the note heads, as in *Songs of Gratitude* (1877; fig.5). Nineteenth-century American pedagogical ardor, expressed in novel attempts to make music reading easier, knew no bounds; the immense variety of short-lived notational self-help systems reached a climax when an "animalistic" shape-note method was proposed (probably facetiously) in the *Musical Million* (xxi, 1890; fig.6).

Related to these kinds of notation, although not so explicitly pedagogical in their aim, were various methods developed in communities of SHAKERS between about 1825 and 1870. Some Shaker manuscripts are written in adaptations of four-shape (fig.7a) and seven-shape systems; others display different kinds of literal notation (fig.7b) and numerical notation (fig.7c). Several Shaker scribes learned or invented shorthand systems (fig.7d), and one Shaker song—"learned by [the scribe] while sailin on de sea of de fate in de canoo. 6th November 1842"—is uniquely notated in symbols apparently derived from Native American pictographs.

In the first third of the 20th century certain practices arose in the notation of popular music and jazz which aimed at facilitating performance. In particular two ways of indicating the basic harmonies of a song were developed, either or both of which could supplement or supplant the standard score layout that notated a detailed accompaniment below the solo voice. The first of these is a capital letter placed above the staff to indicate the root of a major triad, with suffixes to indicate alteration of the chord quality to minor ("m" or "mi"), or to diminished and augmented triads, signified respectively by "dim" (or a superscript zero) and "aug" (or a plus sign). Numerals, with or without accidentals, are used for chords larger than triads ($\flat$7, 9, $\sharp$11, etc.) or to signify

5. *Numerical notation combined with conventional staff notation (James Henry Fillmore, "Songs of Gratitude"; Cincinnati, 1884 edition)*

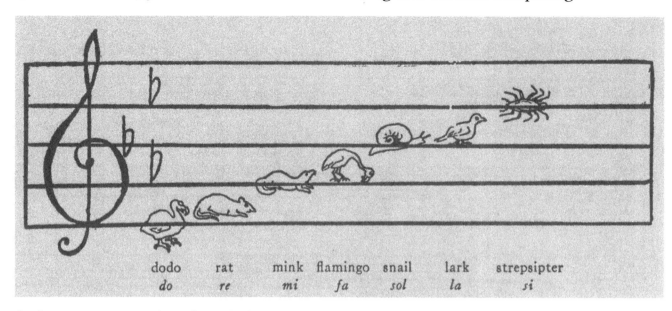

dodo	rat	mink	flamingo	snail	lark	strepsipter
do	*re*	*mi*	*fa*	*sol*	*la*	*si*

6. *Shape notation using outlines of animals, the names of which supply mnemomics for the seven solmization syllables (Aldine S. Kieffer, "Musical Million," xxi; Dayton, VA, 1890)*

7. *Shaker notation systems in 19th-century manuscripts: (a) adaptation of four-shape notation ("That Beautiful City," 1830s; OClWHi); (b) small literal notation ("Come up Hither," 1855–63; private collection); (c) numerical notation ("S.O. Watervliet," 1838–42; OClWHi); (d) shorthand notation ("The Humble Heart," c1845–67; DeWint-M)*

particular "tensions" that incorporate non-triadic tones, a special case of which is the suspension of a tone from the previous chord, more often marked simply "sus." Like Baroque figured bass, this shorthand notation adapts to differences of genre, personal taste, and opportunity for improvisation. It further allows condensation of the musical texture in simple song books for amateurs and essentials-only "fake books" for professionals. Another shorthand notation for harmony is a form of tablature, which became ubiquitous in popular guitar music. In the most common form a six-by-six grid or "tab" corresponds to the crossing of strings and frets on the instrument. Dots represent the positions of the fingers on the strings required to form the prescribed chord. As in the letter notation for chords, these guitar tabs do not specify the rhythms to be played but rather serve as a starting point for rhythmic elaboration within stylistic conventions. Often the literal transcription of finger positions is intended only to aid beginners, while advanced players will substitute different fingerings satisfying the same harmony. Often the letter and tab systems are combined, or supplied together with the fully notated accompaniment, allowing a song book to adapt to different accompanying instruments (fig.8). A more complete form of tablature, similar to that used in Renaissance compositions for lute and viola da gamba, was developed to notate performance of a composition by showing a "staff" that corresponded to the strings of the instrument. Rhythm is shown using standard note stems, flags, and beams, but note heads are replaced with numbers indicating where to stop the string against the fret (fig.9).

Representation of music in alphanumeric coding systems has interacted with graphical systems to enable pedagogy (letter names or solfège), comparative musical ethnology, analysis of structure and style, music printing, and performance with automated instruments. Like music notation, music encoding systems may construct synthetic representations, tempo-

rally encoding a performer's physical motion, qualities of sound, and formal organization. An encoding system may also specialize, as in two early systems developed for computer-based data processing, Stefan Bauer-Mengelberg's DARMS (from 1963, in several dialects) and Leland Smith's SCORE (1971), which encoded music symbols and their placement for visual displays and printing. SCORE, which was originally designed to drive an automated drawing machine (a pen plotter), retained some conceptual links to music calligraphy, yet provided a consistency of graphical quality that attracted the attention of music publishers as an alternative to typesetting, notably because corrections could be made relatively quickly, as editing of input codes. SCORE became a commercially available program and by the mid-1980s many music copyists converted their practice to use computers. Music notation software proliferated in the 1990s as the graphical displays for computers became commonplace, larger, and sharper in image, and as input devices became hand-held, bringing the process of notating music closer to that of working on paper. By the end of the century, music engraver's house rules were increasingly better integrated to software, which, along with the integration of sound playback capabilities through MIDI (an encoding of performance on electronic instruments) moved most composers not only to produce their own finished scores but to use such software as a tool for composing. Many composers and their advocates were quick to point out the detriments of this practice, in that it had the potential to constrain creativity to the design of software, which favored standard practices and concepts of sound modeled on keyboard instruments. Not all such composers avoided the use of software, but rather more freely notated their ideas using drawing software or drawing-oriented notation software. Others developed specialized self-designed computer programs for the stage of composition before transferring the

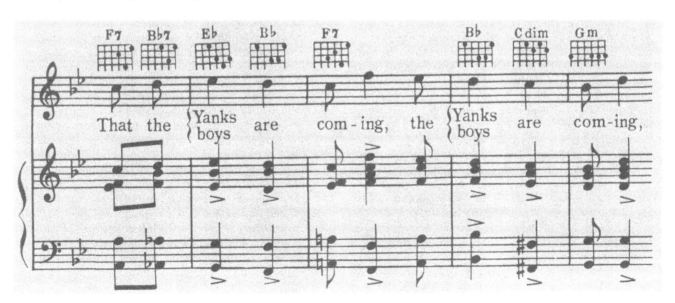

8. *Tablature for guitar, with chord indications, added above the staves (George M. Cohan, "Over there"; New York: Leo Feist, 1917)*

9. *Guitar tablature notating finger-picking figuration, with corresponding staff notation below: the six-lines represent the guitar strings, numerals on the lines indicate frets, and the other numerals and letters show fingering (H. Vinson, "A Folksinger's Guide to the Classical Guitar"; New York, 1971)*

musical information (via MIDI or generalized encodings such as MusicXML) to notation software. In the 2000s transfers of musical data are used in live interactive performance and integrate with real-time rendering of graphics, facilitating the extemporization of either prescriptive or representational notation as an integral part of the performance.

2. NOTATION FOR 20TH-CENTURY INNOVATIONS. The traditional staff notation of Western music, originally designed for modal and diatonic vocal music, became increasingly inadequate over the late 19th and early 20th centuries. The graphical complexity of the system already had increased over the 17th and 18th centuries as instrumental idioms became increasingly fixed into notation. Over the century and a half following, Romantic expressionism, incorporation of folkloric realism and non-Western musical concepts, and the general influence of modernism further pushed the boundaries of musical vocabularies to the point of requiring an astounding level of complexity in their graphical representation. From the 1920s radio broadcasting and sound recordings became more and more widely available and free from dissemination through print, which accelerated the proliferation and intermingling of musical styles, and increased the opportunity for repeated listening to a wider variety of music, including experimental avant-garde music. These trends, along with the extraordinary influence of electronic music, created from the 1950s onward demands to rethink notation in radically new terms.

The pioneers in 20th-century American notation were Charles Ives and Henry Cowell. Like his unconventional musical style, Ives's notations featured alterations of conventions. In the song *Charlie Rutlage*

(1920/21) he abandoned note heads briefly to encourage the singer into realistic unpitched declamation, but retained stems and flags to communicate the need for precise rhythmic delivery (fig.10). In *The Cage* (1906) he achieved a meterless freedom of rhythm by omitting time signature and most barlines. In other works without time signature he changed bar lengths frequently to coordinate meter with phrasing. In the "Hawthorne" movement of the Second ("Concord") Piano Sonata (1916–19) Ives notated high-pitched cluster chords to be played with a wooden board by enclosing the notes in boxes (fig.11).

Cowell's approach to notational extensions was both more radical and more systematic. He devised alternate notations for tone clusters which not only simplified their reading but more accurately illustrated their intended effect (fig.12). His notation of polyrhythm adapted shape-note notation in an original way to illustrate the layering of musical lines in rhythmic divisions beyond binary and ternary, as in *Fabric* (fig.13) where after initial brackets over triple, quintuple, and septupal rhythms, he allows the reader to continue by following different note shapes. For *The Banshee* (1925), his approach to notating its extraordinary and unprecedented methods of performing inside the piano was appropriately pragmatic, simply using letters as signs to indicate shifts in performance technique (fig.14). He used a similar notation in *Sinister Resonance* (1930) to indicate means of obtaining stopped pitches, muting, harmonics, and controlled resonances on the piano strings. Cowell's publication of modernist compositions in the periodical *New Music* (1927–36) and his *New Musical Resources* (1930) provided later composers with many examples of notational practices.

10. *Headless notes, indicating that the text should be recited rhythmically at no specific pitch (Charles Ives, "Charlie Rutlage," 1920/21, published in "114 Songs"; Redding, CT, 1922/R1975)*

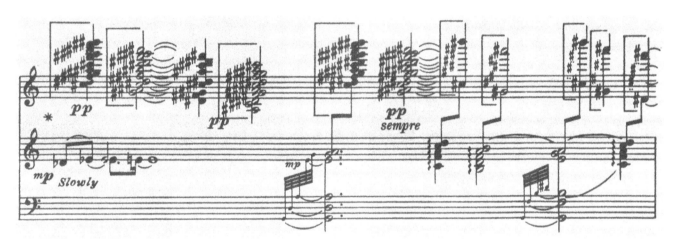

11. *Cluster chords enclosed in boxes (Charles Ives, "Hawthorne," Second Piano Sonata, first published 1920; revised edition, New York, 1947); the chords are played with a wooden board*

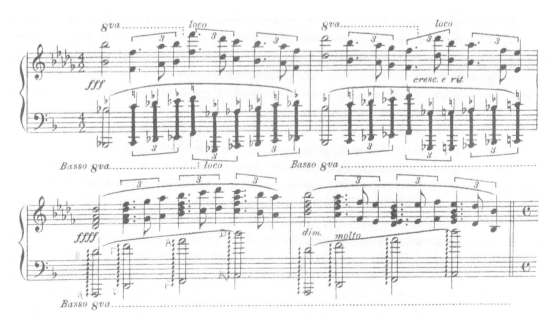

12. *Notation for tone clusters (lower staff), the superscript ♭ indicating black keys only and the ♮ white keys only (Henry Cowell, "The Tides of Manaunaun," ?1917; New York, 1922); the distinction between void and solid note heads is purely durational*

13. *Notation of polyrhythms (Henry Cowell, "Fabric," 1920; New York, 1922); the meaning of the note heads of different shapes (upper staff) for odd-numbered (non-duple) divisions of the beat is explained in the first two bars by the use of traditional numerals and braces*

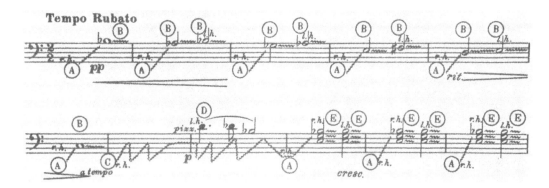

14. *Letters indicating methods of manipulating piano strings (Henry Cowell, "The Banshee," 1925; Los Angeles, 1930) (the work is played an octave lower than written pitch and the damper pedal is held down throughout): Ⓐ sweep with the flesh of the finger from the lowest string up to the note given; Ⓑ sweep with the flesh of the finger lengthwise along the string of the note given; Ⓒ sweep up and back from lowest A to the highest B♭ in the composition; Ⓓ pluck string with flesh of finger, where written, instead of octave lower; Ⓔ sweep along three notes together, in the same manner as Ⓑ*

Another innovator whose compositions and theoretical ideas called for new approaches to notation was Harry Partch, who constructed microtonal scales from principles of just intonation, composing from a large palette of available tones. To clarify the importance of exact tuning, as opposed to microtones being inflections of diatonic scales, notation in his early works dispenses with staff notation and simply inscribes interval ratios under the text, as in *Two Psalms* (1931, fig.15). Because tempo and rhythm were determined by the natural syllabic pulsations in the flow of speech, vertical alignment of ratios with the text was both an efficient and aesthetically appropriate notation. As Partch's compositions responded to the expanded orchestral resources brought about by his invention of unique in-

struments, his scores mixed the ratio notation with staff notation and tablatures relating to the unique physical layout of these instruments.

Composers also explored microtonality in terms of equal-tempered scales, the most common being those constructed of quarter-tones. In *Three Quarter-tone Pieces* (1924) Ives indicated pitches quarter- and three-quarter-tone sharp using arrows on conventional signs for natural and sharp. In *Music for Prague* (1968) Karel Husa appends both upward and downward arrows to conventional accidentals, thus adding or subtracting a quarter tone from either sharps or flats. Another method of adapting conventional signs is to remove, reiterate, or reverse graphical features of accidentals, such as removing from or adding to the lines forming the sharp

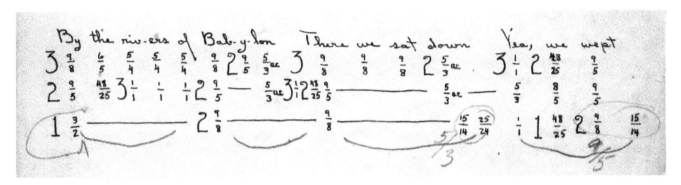

15. *Harry Partch's early interval-ratio notation: the top line is for intoning voice, the middle and bottom line are a two-part texture for Partch's adapted viola (a later version reorchestrated this part for his free-reed keyboard instrument, the chromolodeon with interval ratios marked on the instrument's keys); the larger numbers prior to the ratios indicate changing register (Two Psalms, 2. By the Rivers of Babylon, 1931)*

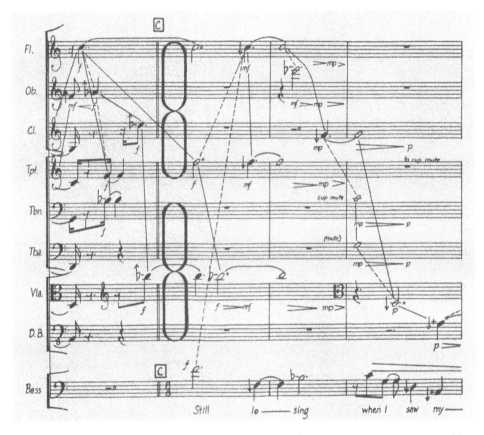

16. *Microtonal inflections, shown by arrows and plus and minus signs, sometimes in combination with accidentals (Ben Johnston, "Two Sonnets of Shakespeare," 1978; Baltimore, 1981)*

sign to indicate loss or gain of a quarter tone, as used by Brian Ferneyhough for his *Unity Capsule* (1976). Composers and theorists such as Easley Blackwood, who explored a large number of equal-tempered scales and evaluated them using electronic instruments, redefined the use of flats and sharps to indicate a progressive sequence of microtones rather than as alternate enharmonic spellings of the same tones. Ben Johnston, applying just intonation systems in works for standard instruments, elaborated conventional signs for accidentals to a high degree, adding both arrows and discrete

horizontal lines in the manner of flags. This system was further extended by appending plus and minus signs, as in his 1978 composition *Two Sonnets of Shakespeare* (fig.16). During the final two decades of the century, under the influence primarily of French and Romanian composers, microtonality was newly explored in terms of spectral composition, which constructs harmonies from analysis of the frequency spectrum of complex tones, or which more generally regards timbre to be the leading element in determining musical form. Especially in cases where written for acoustic rather than electronic instruments, notation of the finer gradations of pitch called for in this aesthetic will be resolved to the quarter-tone, or in some cases the eighth-tone.

Innovations in rhythm, influenced by the metrical complexity of Stravinsky, the increased formalization of note durations in post-Webern integral serialism, and by the more indigenous rhythmic inventiveness of ragtime and bebop, engendered alterations to the system of notation of both meters and note values. Meters became more irregular in both the number of beats and the durations of these beats, and changed more frequently within sections of a composition, even within a single phrase. Rhythmic flow incorporated higher-numbered bases of division, from quintuplets and septuplets eventually to very subtle gradations of rhythm built from 11- or 13-unit divisions. Perhaps more than the progress of chromaticism and experiments in microtonality, the advance of rhythmic complexity con-

tributed to the desire to reform notation. The first six bars of George Crumb's Five Pieces for Piano (1962; fig.17) provide examples of new notational practice with respect to both meter and rhythmic flow: a time signature showing the unit of time as a note shape rather than a number, a system which removed the need for mixtures of simple and compound time (two beats of dotted eighth value could be show directly, rather than surmising this from a 6/8 time signature), and rubato-like changes of speed within a subtle prime-number division, 13 notes within the time of a dotted quarter note. A manuscript reproduction from Elliott Carter's String Quartet no.2 (1959; fig.18) illustrates his attempt to realize in conventional notation the steady progress of the second violin part in 4/4 at ♩ = 140 while the other instruments proceed in 5/4 at ♩ = 175. Although in concept this is a simple bimetrical texture, because performers are very unlikely to maintain inde-

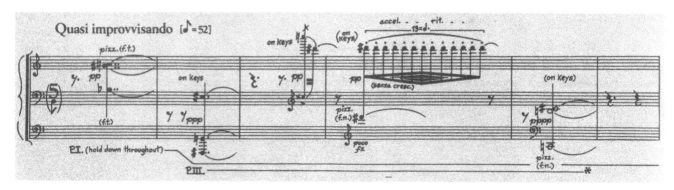

17. *Notational innovations for rhythm, including a note shape in the time signature and subtle rhythmic specification 13 = ♩., (George Crumb,* Five Pieces for Piano no. 1, *1962; New York, 1973)*

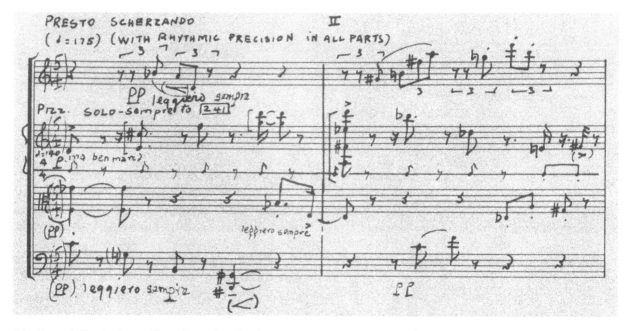

18. *One solution to the problem of notating simultaneous contrasting meters and tempi in conventional notation, with an additional interpretive guide line to indicate the true meter and rhythmic flow of the second violin part (Elliott Carter, String Quartet no.2, 1959, second movement; facs., New York, n.d.)*

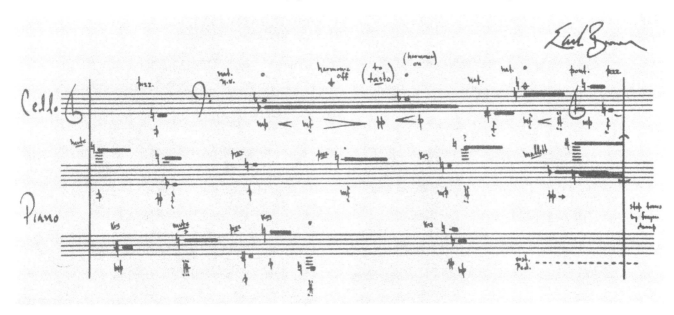

19. *Proportional (time) notation (Earle Brown,* Music for Cello and Piano, *1954–5; New York, 1961); the lengths of the note heads suggest the relative durations of the tones*

20. *Black note heads without stems, flags, or beams, allowing the pianist to determine durations (Morton Feldman, "Last Pieces" no.2, 1959; New York, 1963)*

pendent tempi when beyond simple binary or ternary proportions Carter selects one meter and tempo as a base, and notates the other against it taking advantage of the common rhythmic denominator. While ostensibly assisting the coordination of the ensemble, an unfortunate side effect is that the adjusted part (the second violin) must read a deceptively complex rhythm. Realizing this, Carter adds an extra cue line to clarify its true metrical and rhythmic intent. Stone (1963) and Charles Wourinen (1964) provided excellent analyses of complex rhythmic notation and problems of performance and interpretation, especially as existing in the music of Carter. Against the backdrop of rhythmic complexity the problems of a radical but wholly logical departure from conventional notation of duration was developed by Earle Brown. His "time notation" (later more commonly "proportional notation") showed durations of tones proportionally, independent of metric cadence and a regulating pulse. In *Music for Cello and Piano* (1954–5) the lengths of the note heads indicate the relative durations of tones within the time span repre-

sented by each system (fig.19). Morton Feldman, on the other hand, in compositions such as *Last Pieces* (1959), leaves the durations to the pianist, notating the pitches with conventional note heads, equally spaced apart, and without stems, flags, or beams (fig.20).

Brown was also one of the first to write in wholly "graphic notation," producing scores consisting of freely symbolic visual events that are to be translated, through the performers' imaginative interpretation of them, into sequences of musical sound. The best-known of these are from *Folio* (1952–3), notably the one-page *December 1952*. This score offers the performer not only a choice of sonic realizations for the durations suggested by the graphic, but also a choice in their sequence by means of reading the graphic in different directions. Brown cited inspiration for this concept to the mobiles of sculptor Alexander Calder and the working methods of painter Jackson Pollock. In the score for *Imaginary Landscape no.5* (1952), John Cage's practical use of graphical notation outlines a similar concept of "open form" which in this case leaves open the specific ordering

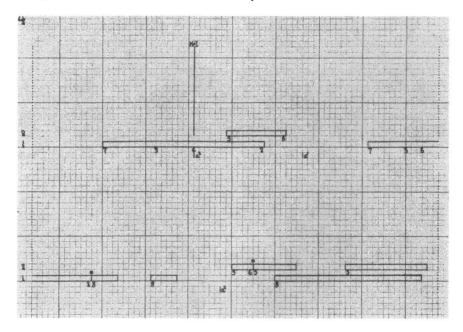

21. Graphic notation, conveying instructions for the creation of a recording on tape from phonograph records (John Cage, "Imaginary Landscape no.5," 1952; New York, 1961); each graph unit represents three inches of tape (only two of the eight tracks are active at this point), dots indicate changes of record, and the numerals 1–8 show amplitude

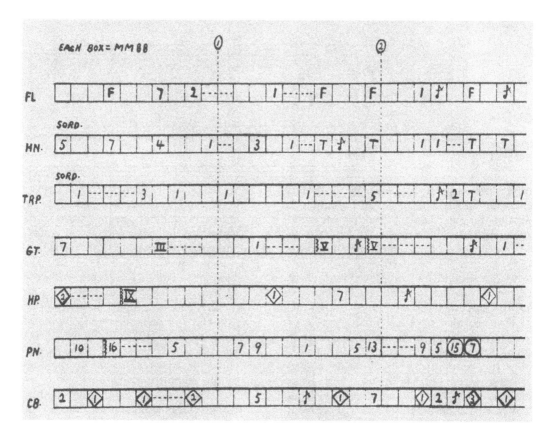

22. Graphic notation, using a line of boxes for each instrumental part (Morton Feldman, "The Straits of Magellan," 1961; New York, 1962); each box denotes one beat, with arabic numerals indicating the number of notes to be played consecutively within the beat, roman numerals the number of notes to be played simultaneously

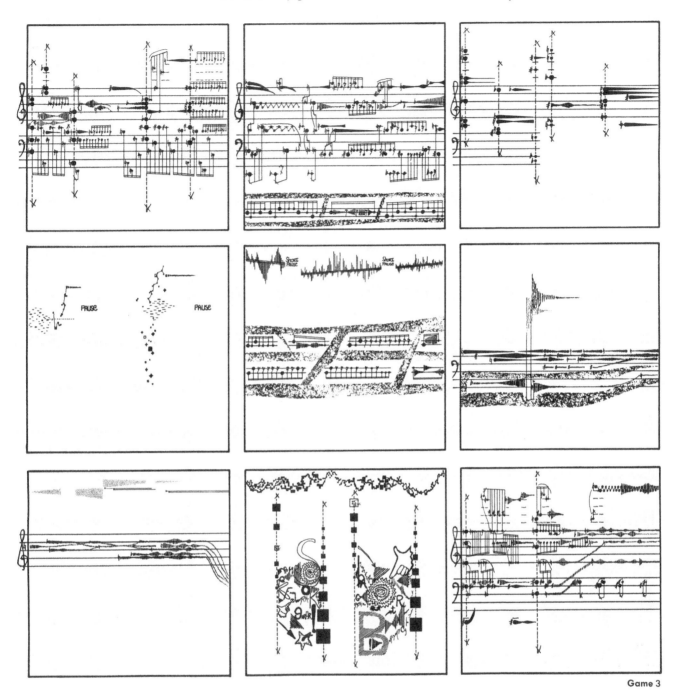

Game 3

23. *Robert Erickson's score for Scapes (1984) separates parts for performing groups into different areas of the score, which are to be performed as in a game of tic-tac-toe*

of material filling the specified rhythmic structure, here the recording on tape of excerpts from any 42 phonograph recordings (fig.21). Morton Feldman had used elements of graphic notation in his *Projection* series of 1950–51, in which for pitch is left unspecified except as to register (high, middle, and low), with dynamics and rhythm conventionally notated. For *The Straits of Magellan* (1961), however, the indeterminacy of musical elements is more pervasive, calling for a more completely graphic score. Each instrumental part

is notated within a series of boxes, each equaling one beat at metronome mark 88. Arabic numerals show the number of successive single notes to be played within that time, and roman numerals the number of simultaneous notes (fig.22). Robert Erickson's score for *Scapes* (1984) adapts a Medieval practice of laying out separate parts for performing groups into different areas of the score. He fills nine squares with graphic notation, which are ordered as the piece progresses as in a game of tic-tac-toe (fig.23). An especially provocative concept of

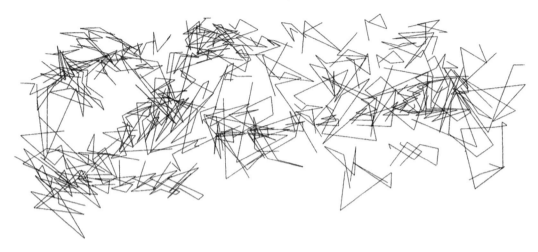

24. Herbert Brün's graphic for Mutatis Mutandis (1968) supplies an abstract representation of compositional processes for the performer to recreate not by improvisation but in the manner of constructing a new score

form and notational intent was explored by Herbert Brün, whose graphical scores supply direct abstract representations of compositional processes, provided with the intent that the performer analogically recreate this not by improvisation but in the manner of constructing a new score. In the instructions for *Mutatis Mutandis* (1968, fig.24) Brün clarifies that the graphic is not a musical score in the sense of providing instructions, even abstractly, for performance. Rather, the performer is asked to contemplate the graphics as "traces left by a process" and then to construct a version, even a new prescriptive score, that would share the same background process.

The development of electronic music opened an unprecedented level of opportunity for composers to specify details of sound characteristics and rhythmic subtlety, and to elevate the status of timbre from a matter of nuance and orchestration to one of an equal if not dominant contributor to formal design. Further, most early electronic composers served as their own technicians for synthesis of the sound used in their compositions, and this led to a more analytic and multilayered approach to compositional thought. Electronic music could not easily adapt existing notations without removing the very level of detail and uniqueness of construction that defined it as a genre. Confronting this problem, composers took two general approaches to notating a score for electronic music: the use of technical symbols, terms, and graphs to describe "how the sound at this point is made" in the manner of a schematic, or the use of drawings to create analogs of "how the sound here is perceived as a changing shape." A score notated using these approaches could serve as a study score for electronic music existing as recordings, a document for purposes of copyright, or as a prescriptive guide for the live creation of electronic sound.

Notation of electronic sounds to be combined with performance on traditional instruments presents a special case. In music where the electronic sounds interlock with the instrumental performance in a precisely measured contrapuntal texture, composers normally notate the electronic music in the manner of percussion instruments, mixing staff notation with shaped notes in mostly traditional rhythmic notation (fig.25). Where, however, the electronic sound is unpitched and of complex texture, composers represent these sounds using the analogical drawing technique, horizontally aligning the shape to the rhythmical spacing of performer's standard notation (fig.26). Representation of electronic sound in these scores often merges what is actually constructed from a mixture of several layers into a single note or drawn shape, in the manner of condensed orchestral score. In scores for compositions that are organized into pre-recorded electronic sequences, the starting positions for the playback of these sequences are indicated by numbered cues.

The analog-shape approach to electronic notation eventually entered the production of sound itself in the form of "graphical synthesis." In this technique, software is used to design sound synthesis using a drawing or sculpting metaphor. This technique had its roots in Max Mathews's GRIN program (1965), where one would draw controls for shaping sound using a light-sensing pen at the mainframe computer console. The UPIC program, created by Iannis Xenakis in 1977 but more widely available after 1992, allows the composer to draw controls for sound synthesis that span the duration of an entire composition, and thus constitutes a highly idiomatic form of notation of an electronic score (fig.27). The UPIC eventually became a real-time instrument and blurred the distinction between notation and musical performance. In the 2000s a new genre of electronic music emerged, "live encoding," a kind of improvisation in which the software that produces the musical sound is created and modified as part of the performance. In 2010 Roger Dannenberg created *Patterns*, a computer program that provided live encoding

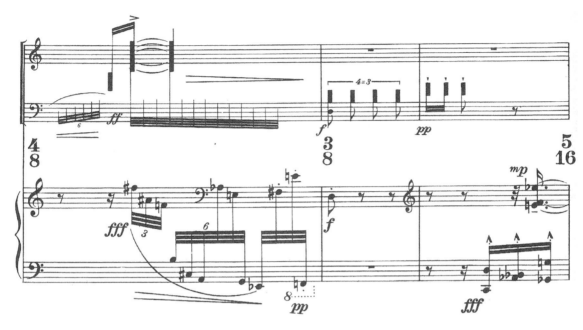

25. *Percussion-style notation used to represent electronic sounds in a highly contrapuntal composition for tape and traditional instrument (Mario Davidovsky, "Synchronisms No. 6," 1970)*

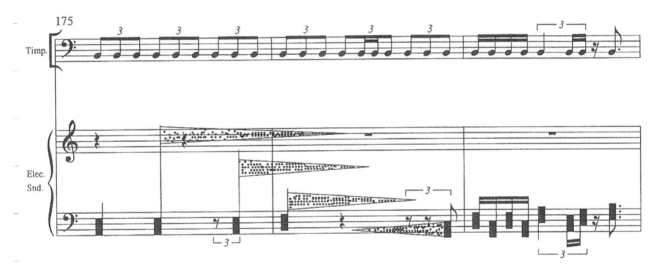

26. *Graphical analogies for shapes of electronic sound integrated with staff notation (Arthur Kreiger, "Occasional Demons" for timpani and electronic sounds, 2005)*

with an animated graphical notation to represent different processes and their transformations as they are created. The colorful symbolic animations provide a form of descriptive notation for the audience that itself develops during the performance.

Over the course of the 20th century, two opposing philosophies developed in relation to the intent of notation, pitting stability against innovation. Primarily addressing the practical problems for conventionally trained performers in navigating the proliferation of signs and symbols, analysts such as Gardner Read (1964/1971, 1978, 1987, 1990, 1998), Erhard Karkoschka (1966), Howard Risatti (1975), David Cope (1976), and Kurt Stone (1980) collected, codified, and evaluated new symbols and (especially by Karkoschka) issues of their arrangements in space and graphical alternatives. In 1974, Stone and others organized an international convention in Ghent to gather empirical data from delegates and publish recommendations for notational practice related to new music. Pursuing an opposite course, other authors sought to encourage and celebrate variety in notation, considering the notation of a composition to be an essential contributor to its artistic meaning. Cage in *Notations* (1969) assembled a compendium of facsimiles of manuscript scores by more than 250 composers with the purpose of documenting a great variety of graphical approaches. The 40th anniversary of this work was

27. An example of graphic sound synthesis as a hybrid of an instrument and a musical score; lines are drawn to determine frequency (pitch) on the vertical axis against time on the horizontal axis (Iannis Xenakis, "Mycenae-Alpha, 1980)

celebrated with the publication of *Notations 21* (2009) curated by Theresa Sauer, which demonstrated the continuing interest in experimental notations into the 21st century. The most radical expressions of what could constitute a musical score were published from 1967 through 1973 in Larry Austin's *Source: Music of the Avant Garde*. All 11 issues of this publication contain examples of innovative graphical expressions of musical ideas, including experiments with the use of color photography, mylar, and even fur. The second issue published the score for Cage's notorious *4'33"*, which notates three movements of silence on the part of the musical performer. In *Mind Models* (1975, 2005) Roger Reynolds provides a broad philosophical examination of notational issues at the end of the 20th century. He evaluates notation in relation to the stages of creative process, from idea through to performance, hearing, and interpretation, and considers these against not only good notational practice but deeper issues of intent, abstraction, and the effect of notation on the richness musical experience.

BIBLIOGRAPHY
STUDIES

Grove7 (Ian D. Bent and others)

H. Cowell: "Our Inadequate Notation," *MM*, iv/3 (1927), 29

H. Cowell: *New Musical Resources* (New York, 1930/R)

A. Copland: "On the Notation of Rhythm," *MM*, xxi/4 (1944), 217

H. Eimert, F. Enkel, and K. Stockhausen: *Problems of Electronic Music Notation* (Ottawa, 1956)

C. Seeger: "Prescriptive and Descriptive Music-Writing," *MQ*, xliv, 2 (1958), 184

B. Bartolozzi: "Proposals for Changes in Musical Notation," *JMT*, v (1961), 297

K. Stone: "Problems and Methods of Notation," *PNM*, i/2 (1963), 9 [repr. in *Perspectives on Notation and Performance*, 9]

W.T. Marrocco: "The Notation in American Sacred Music Collections," *AcM*, xxxvi (1964), 136

C. Wourinen: "Notes on the Performance of Contemporary Music," *PNM*, iii/1 (1964), 10

D. Behrman: "What Indeterminate Notation Determines," *PNM*, iii/2 (1965), 58 [repr. in *Perspectives on Notation and Performance* (1976), 74]

A. Kontarsky: "Notationen für Klavier," *Darmstädter Beiträge zur neuen Musik*, ix (1965) [Eng. trans. as "Notation for Piano" in *PNM*, x/2 (1972) and *Perspectives on Notation and Performance* (1976), 187]

E. Karkoschka: *Das Schriftbild der neuen Musik* (Celle, Germany, 1966; Eng. trans. as *Notation in New Music: a Critical Guide to Interpretation and Realization*, New York, 1972)

D. Martino: "Notation in General—Articulation in Particular," *PNM*, iv/2 (1966), 47 [repr. in *Perspectives on Notation and Performance* (1976), 102]

E. Brown: "Form in New Music," *Source: Music of the Avant Garde*, i (1967)

M.V. Mathews, and L. Rosler: "Graphical Language for the Scores of Computer-Generated Sounds," *PNM*, vi/2 (1968), 92 [repr. in *Perspectives on Notation and Performance* (1976), 153]

J. Cage: *Notations* (New York, 1969)

F. Pooler and B. Pierce: *New Choral Notation* (New York, 1971)

H. Cole: *Sounds and Signs: Aspects of Musical Notation* (London, 1974)

R. Reynolds: *Mind Models* (New York, 1975, 2/2005)

H. Risatti: *New Music Vocabulary: a Guide to Notational Signs for Contemporary Music* (Urbana, IL, 1975)

H. Sabbe, K. Stone, and G. Warfield, eds.: "International Conference on New Musical Notation: Proceedings," *Interface*, iv/1 (1975)

B. Boretz and E.T. Cone, eds.: *Perspectives on Notation and Performance* (New York, 1976)

D. Cope: *New Music Notation* (Dubuque, IA, 1976)

G. Warfield: *Writings on Contemporary Music Notation: an Annotated Bibliography* (Ann Arbor, MI, 1976) [452 titles cited and annotated]

P. Creston: *Rational Metric Notation* (Hicksville, NY, 1979)

S. Smith and S. Smith: "Visual Music," *PNM*, xx (1981–2), 75

W.Y. Elias: *Grapes: Practical Notation for Clusters and Special Effects for Piano and other Keyboards* (New York, 1984)

G. Read: *Source Book of Proposed Music Notation Reforms* (New York, 1987)

G. Read: *20th-century Microtonal Notation* (New York, 1990)

A. Brennink: *Equal Temperament Music Notation: the Ailler-Brennink Chromatic Notation: Results and Conclusion of the Music Notation Reform by the Chroma Foundation* (Victoria, BC, 1992)

T.S. Reed: *Directory of Music Notation Proposals* (Kirksville, MO, 1997)

E. Selfridge-Field: *Beyond MIDI: the Handbook of Musical Codes* (Cambridge, MA, 1997)

S. Smith, ed.: *The Sylvia Smith Archives of Smith Publications and Sonic Arts Editions,* (1997) <http://www3.uakron.edu/ssma/>

G. Read: *Pictographic Score Notation: a Compendium* (Westport, CT, 1998)

T. Wishart and S. Emmerson: *On Sonic Art* (London, 2002)

R. Rastall: *The Notation of Western Music: an Introduction* (London, 2008)

T. Sauer: *Notations 21* (New York, 2009; continued at <http://notations21.net/>)

J. Freeman and A. Clay: *Virtual Scores and Real-Time Playing* (Abingdon, 2010)

L. Austin and D. Kahn: *Source: Music of the Avant-garde, 1966–1973* (Berkeley, CA, 2011)

MANUALS

G. Read: *Music Notation: a Manual of Modern Practice* (Boston, 1964, 3/1971)

T. Ross: *The Art of Music Engraving and Processing* (New York, 1970)

K. Stone: *Music Notation in the Twentieth Century: a Practical Guide* (New York, 1980)

G. Schirmer, Inc.: *The G. Schirmer Manual of Style and Usage* (New York, 1990)

T. Gerou and L. Lusk: *Essentials of Music Notation* (Van Nuys, CA, 2009)

EXHIBITION BOOKS

Mappin Art Gallery, and Arts Council of Great Britain: *Eye Music: the Graphic Art of New Musical Notation* (London, 1986)

N.L. Perloff: *The Eye and the Ear: New Directions in Twentieth-Century Musical Notation,* Getty Center for the History of Art and the Humanities, 1 Feb – 28 April (Los Angeles, 1995)

A. Waterman, D. Singer, and M. Lyons: *Between Thought and Sound: Graphic Notation in Contemporary Music* (New York, 2007)

H. WILEY HITCHCOCK/CHRISTOPHER HOPKINS

Notorious B.I.G., the [Wallace, Christopher; Biggie Smalls; Biggie] (*b* New York, NY, 21 May 1972; *d* Los Angeles, CA, 9 March 1997). Rapper. Also known as Biggie Smalls or simply Biggie, The Notorious B.I.G. grew up in Brooklyn, spending much of his youth on the street as a small-time drug dealer and aspiring rapper who quickly became known for his smooth, swinging delivery and sharp wit. He was signed to a recording contract by SEAN COMBS, a former A&R man for Uptown Records who had recently started his own label, Bad Boy Records. His debut album, *Ready to Die*, was produced by Combs and released 13 September 1994. The album mixed B.I.G.'s streetwise lyrics with radio-friendly dance beats. Driven by hit singles including "Juicy," "One More Chance," and "Big Poppa," the album quickly sold over four million copies.

His success brought attention to Bad Boy Entertainment and its founder Combs. The focus and attention on an emerging East Coast label at a time when the West Coast had dominated the rap scene for two years (most notably the acts on Dr. Dre and Suge Knight's Death Row Records) was striking and led to a media-hyped rivalry between Death Row Records and Bad Boy Entertainment. Some maintain that the East Coast/ West Coast feud led directly to the unsolved killings of Tupac Shakur and Notorious B.I.G. who were gunned down within six months of one another. B.I.G.'s second album, *Life After Death*, was released only a few weeks after his death and has sold over ten million copies. A string of posthumous releases continue to be released and remixed (as is the case with Tupac Shakur), and Notorious B.I.G. continues to make the top of a variety of top-ten lists for his skills as MC.

BIBLIOGRAPHY

C. Scott: *The Murder of Biggie Smalls* (New York, 2000)

C.H. Coker: *Unbelievable: The Life, Death, and Afterlife of the Notorious B.I.G.* (New York, 2003)

J. Brown: *Ready to Die* (Phoenix, AZ, 2004)

JUSTIN A. WILLIAMS

Novacek, Stephanie (*b* Iowa City, IA, 31 Aug 1970). Mezzo-soprano. After studies at Cornell College (Iowa) and the University of Illinois, she became a member of the Houston Grand Opera Studio (1996–9). At Houston she created the role of Maria Callas in Michael Daugherty's *Jackie O* (1997) and the following year won acclaim as Jo in the world premiere of Mark Adamo's *Little Women*. Novacek had made her Houston Grand Opera debut as the Page in *Salome* in 1997, and has since sung additional roles for the company including Carmen, Maddalena (*Rigoletto*), Siebel (*Faust*), and Olga (*Yevgeny Onegin*). She is also a noted interpreter of Baroque opera. She sang Dido and the Sorceress in Mark Morris's production of *Dido and Aeneas* at the Brooklyn Academy of Music (1998) and has appeared in the title roles of Charpentier's *Médée* and Jean-Baptiste Lully's *Armide*, and as Monteverdi's Ottavia (*L'incoronazione di Poppea*) and Messaggiera (*Orfeo*), the last two with Canada's Opera Atelier. In 2004 she made her Geneva debut as Aljeja in Janáček's *From the House of the Dead*, and the following year her Covent Garden debut as Suzuki (*Madama Butterfly*). In 2006 she made her Chicago Lyric Opera debut as Annina in *Der Rosenkavalier*.

RICHARD WIGMORE/R

Novak, Yann (*b* Madison, WI, 1979). Sound artist, installation artist, electronic composer, laptop performer, and visual artist. Based in Los Angeles, he has collaborated with Will Long, Mise_En_Scene, and Marc Manning, among others, and exhibited and performed throughout the United States and Europe. He owns and operates Dragon's Eye Recordings, which promotes promising but under-recognized sound artists and composers.

Novak's installations, along with his electronic compositions and performances, typically consist of quiet, subtly shifting textures. These sounds are often field recordings of environmental sounds, digitally transformed into exquisite drones or slow-moving melodies, as in *+ROOM* (2009). Novak's work is often associated with AMBIENT MUSIC, demonstrating the fluid, and indeed questionable, nature of the boundary between music and field recording or, generally speaking, between music and sound art. However, unlike ambient music,

Novak's pieces are often programmatic. The goal, in many of his works, is to transform documentation into narrative by digitally altering prerecorded sounds and images. His alterations often consist not of fleshing out sounds and images by adding to their characteristics, but of digitally erasing their distinguishing features. He may obliterate the movement that we typically see in video, reducing it to a static expanse of color. Similarly, he alters environmental sounds beyond recognition into contemplative textures.

Novak's work narrates his own personal experiences; but he emphasizes the kind of experience that is familiar to many—the buzz of a bedside fan on a hot day, the emotional ordeal of moving to a new apartment. Each piece tends to draw its sounds, images, and narrative from a single source or location. In *The Breeze Blowing Over Us* (2008), the bedside fan generates source recordings that Novak turns into musical tones. The installations *Relocation. Vacant*, *Relocation.Mobile*, and *Relocation.Dislocation* (2009) recount the artist's move from Seattle to Los Angeles, using sounds recorded in his newly vacant apartment, on the freeway to California, and in his new apartment. *Relocation.Vacant* utilized an unadorned gallery space; but in the other two pieces, photographs offered partial views of where the sounds came from, even as the sounds themselves were altered beyond recognition. Though these pieces began as installations, Novak also released them on CD (by reducing their durations and excluding the images) and performed them live (in laptop extemporizations that drew upon the sounds exhibited in the installations). On his CD, *Two Segments* (2011), Novak and first-time collaborator Mise_En_Scene "narrated" their working relationship by making electronic sounds inspired by one another's previous work and placing them in a digital library, from which both artists drew in creating new compositions.

MANDY-SUZANNE WONG

Novarro, Ramón [Samaniego, José Ramón Gil] (*b* Durango, Mexico, 6 Feb 1899; *d* Los Angeles, CA, 30 Oct 1968). Film actor and singer of Mexican birth. He moved to Southern California with his family during the Mexican Revolution in the later 1910s, and worked in Hollywood as an extra in such silent films as Cecil B. De Mille's 1916 epic *Joan the Woman* (with Metropolitan Opera star Geraldine Farrar). By the early 1920s he was starring in high-budget films such as *The Prisoner of Zenda* (1922) and *Scaramouche* (1923). In the later 1920s, as one of MGM's biggest stars, he appeared as the romantic lead in a series of dramas and comedies, notably in *Ben Hur* (1925) and Ernst Lubitsch's silent version of *The Student Prince* (1927). He also performed as a singer and dancer in three early MGM film musicals by the composer-lyricist team of Herbert Stothart and Clifford Grey: *Devil May Care* (1929); *In Gay Madrid* (1930); and the English, Spanish, and French versions of *Call of the Flesh* (1930). His handsome physical appearance, dashing manner, fine acting ability, and pleasing operetta-style voice are seen and

heard to good advantage in the film version of the Jerome Kern operetta *The Cat and the Fiddle* (1934), costarring Jeanette MacDonald. He also appeared in the original film operetta *The Night is Young* (1935), with Evelyn Laye, for which Sigmund Romberg and Oscar Hammerstein II wrote their famous song "When I Grow Too Old to Dream." In the later 1930s, Novarro's career faltered, and he never again achieved star status. He died under tragic circumstances, murdered in an attempted robbery.

BIBLIOGRAPHY

D. Bodeen: "Ramon Novarro," *Films in Review*, xviii/9 (Nov 1967), 528–47

A.R. Ellenberger: *Ramon Novarro: A Biography of the Silent Film Idol, 1899–1968* (Jefferson, NC, 1999)

A. Soares: *Beyond Paradise: The Life of Ramón Novarro* (New York, 2002)

J. Koegel: "Mexican Musicians in California and the United States, 1910–1950," *California History*, lxxxiv/1 (2006), 6–29, 64–69

JOHN KOEGEL

Novelty piano. A term, used particularly in the 1920s, that was applied to a variety of piano music based on ragtime. Novelty piano music drew on sources as diverse as popular dance music, folk ragtime, and the music of the Impressionists (especially in its use of the whole-tone scale and the parallel 4th). Its most recognizable unifying feature was the "novelty break"—a stylized interruption of the melody and texture. This was often based on the motif of a tritone resolving onto a 3rd, although whole-tone passages and various figures used by dance orchestras and jazz bands of the 1920s were also employed. The novelty style was influenced by piano-roll arrangements, and many works demanded considerable pianistic skill; indeed, their composers were among the most adept pianists in the popular field.

The word "novelty" was used in association with various rags including Scott Joplin's *Euphonic Sounds: a Syncopated Novelty* (1909), but it was with the release on piano roll of Zez Confrey's *My Pet* in 1918 (published in 1921) that the identity of novelty piano was established. In such works as *Kitten on the Keys* (published in 1921, though released earlier on piano roll), *You Tell 'em Ivories* (1921), *Greenwich Witch* (1921), *Poor Buttermilk* (1921), *Coaxing the Piano* (1922), and *Nickel in the Slot* (1923), Confrey explored familiar territory with an inventiveness that places him among America's most imaginative composers. Another exponent was Roy Bargy, whose *Sunshine Caper, Jim Jams*, and *Pianoflage* all appeared in 1922. In New York Rube Bloom, Arthur Schutt, and Phil Ohman made contributions to the genre. Billy Mayerl adopted the style successfully and wrote novelties which are still played.

With the resurgence of ragtime in the 1950s the novelty style was revived to some degree. Although some ragtime enthusiasts dismissed novelty piano as frivolous and "inauthentic," the efforts of David Jasen and others fostered a more objective view of the style.

See also CONFREY, ZEZ.

BIBLIOGRAPHY

R. Blesh and H. Janis: *They All Played Ragtime* (New York, 1950, rev. 4/1971)

E.A. Berlin: *Ragtime: a Musical and Cultural History* (Berkeley, 1980/*R*)

D.A. Jasen: "Zez Confrey: Genius Supreme," *Zez Confrey Ragtime, Novelty and Jazz Piano Solos*, ed. R.S. Schiff (New York, 1982)

R. Riddle: "Novelty Piano Music," *Ragtime: Its History, Composers, and Music*, ed. J.E. Hasse (New York, 1985), 285–93

DAVID THOMAS ROBERTS/R

Novelty song. A comic popular song usually employing parody or a distinctive gimmick for humorous effect. The novelty song genre arose in the Tin Pan Alley era when artists and composers used the immediate appeal of musical puns, exaggerated voices, and silly lyrics to reach wider audiences through printed music, traveling shows, and radio. Strictly speaking, comic songs were not an innovation of the Tin Pan Alley era, but "novelty" songs represented a type of branding to set them apart from other types of popular music. These novelty songs often caricatured ethnic groups, poked fun at foreign cultures, and made light of other types of difference for the sake of humor (e.g., Irving Berlin's "Sweet Italian Love," 1910); their popularity speaks to norms, as in every age, that allowed for laughing at people considered atypical and reinforcing stereotypes of racial and cultural otherness through music.

Novelty songs transitioned well to recordings and, later, to videos. For example, Spike Jones and his City Slickers were catapulted to fame in 1942 with their novelty song rendition of "Der Fuehrer's Face" (recorded for radio broadcast and later released as a record single) which featured a raspberry at every iteration of "Heil" as well as an exaggerated German accent. In his traveling "Musical Depreciation Revue" and performances for film and television throughout the 1940s and 1950s, Jones took the novelty song to ridiculous levels through ruthless parody of popular songs and slapstick stage antics (e.g. "Cocktails for Two," 1944). In the 1950s artists such as Dickie Goodman created novelty records by sampling popular songs and combining these clips in humorous ways (e.g. "The Flying Saucer," 1956). Stan Freberg also produced records containing his comedic treatment of songs by popular musicians like Elvis Presley and Johnny Mathis.

A classic novelty song is "They're Coming to Take Me Away, Ha-Haaa!" (1966) by Jerry Samuels; in it, Napoleon XIV (Samuels) recounts his mental breakdown after losing his lover—who turns out to be his dog. As with many novelty songs of this era, "They're Coming" performed well on the charts. During the 1960s Tom Lehrer composed novelty songs of a distinctly political bent (e.g. "Who's Next?" in response to nuclear proliferation), and beginning with his 1965 album, *Freak Out!*, Frank Zappa devoted himself to the creation of humorous countercultural songs. In the 1970s and 1980s Zappa was eventually branded by his offbeat and patently satirical novelty music heard on radio or sold as self-produced albums (including *Joe's Garage*, 1979).

"The Dr. Demento Radio Show," started in 1970 by Barret Hansen (Dr. DEMENTO) and eventually syndicated across the United States, specialized in novelty songs. In his broadcasts Dr. Demento presented novelty music requested by fans as well as songs organized around a particular theme. His program is directly responsible for stimulating interest in novelty songs of earlier eras and for inspiring a new generation of musical parodists, including "WEIRD AL" YANKOVIC. Since the 1980s Yankovic has mocked not only popular musicians and popular culture but also music videos, including Michael Jackson's "Bad," which became Yankovic's "Fat." Novelty songs mocking musical conventions, politics, and popular musicians continued to emerge in the 2010s through the work of artists like Ray Stevens and in new forms, such as DJ mashups and the wealth of amateur videos produced for the Internet.

BIBLIOGRAPHY

C. Hamm: *Irving Berlin: Songs From the Melting Pot: The Formative Years, 1907–1914* (New York, 1997)

S. Otfinoski: *The Golden Age of Novelty Songs* (New York, 2000)

D. Goldmark: "Stuttering in American Popular Song, 1890–1930," *Sounding Off: Theorizing Disability in Music*, eds. N.W. Lerner and J.N. Straus (New York, 2006), 91–106

C.H. Garrett: "Chinatown, Whose Chinatown? Defining America's Borders with Musical Orientalism," *Struggling to Define a Nation: American Music and the Twentieth Century* (Berkeley, 2008), 122–64

JOHN MACINNIS

Novotná, Jarmila (*b* Prague, 23 Sept 1907; *d* New York, NY, 9 Feb 1994). Czech soprano. She studied in Prague with Emmy Destinn, and later in Milan. She made her debut in Prague as Mařenka in *The Bartered Bride* in June 1925. From 1933 to 1938 she sang at the Vienna Staatsoper, making regular appearances at Salzburg. In Vienna she created the title role in Lehár's *Giuditta* (1934) opposite Richard Tauber; the performance was broadcast by 120 radio stations. Her American debut was as Butterfly at San Francisco in 1939, and she was a valued member of the Metropolitan Opera from 1940 to 1956, where her repertory included Donna Elvira, Pamina, Octavian, Violetta, Freia, and Mélisande. She returned to Europe after World War II and was heard again at Salzburg, in Paris, and in Vienna. She appeared in *The Merry Widow* in San Francisco and on Broadway in the title role of Korngold's adaptation of *La belle Hélène*. Her recordings, which range from her early years in Prague to her postwar Salzburg *Rosenkavalier*, evince her charm and interpretative depth as well as occasional flaws in technique.

BIBLIOGRAPHY

P.G. Davis: "The Aristocrat," *ON*, lxxi/11 (2007), 46–9

HAROLD ROSENTHAL/ALAN BLYTH/R

Nowak, Lionel (*b* Cleveland, OH, 25 Sept 1911; *d* Bennington, VT, 4 Dec 1995). Pianist and composer. He made his debut as a pianist at the age of four and studied with BERYL RUBINSTEIN and Edwin Fischer; as a teenager he was an organist and choirmaster. At the Cleveland Institute he studied composition with HERBERT ELWELL, ROGER SESSIONS, and QUINCY PORTER (diploma 1936).

He taught at Fenn College (1932–8) and in 1938 became the composer and music director for the Humphrey-Weidman Company, a position which he held until 1942. From 1942 to 1946 he taught at Converse College and conducted the Spartanburg SO. He was professor of music at Syracuse University (1946–8) and then joined the faculty at Bennington College. He toured as a pianist and lecturer for the Association of American Colleges Arts Program (1945–63) and helped to plan the 1963 Yale Conference on Music Education; he was also chief consultant to the Manhattanville Music Curriculum Project (1965–72). The style of his dance scores is accessible; from the mid-1950s he made increasing use of serial techniques. The *Concert Piece* (1961) is among his recorded works. After suffering a stroke in 1980, Nowak paid special attention to composing piano pieces for the right hand alone and commissioned works from Otto Luening, Vivian Fine, and others.

WORKS

Dance scores: Square Dances (D. Humphrey), pf, 1938; Danzas mexicanas (J. Limón), pf, 1939; On my Mother's Side (C. Weidman), 1939; The Green Land (Humphrey), pf, 1941; Flickers (Weidman), 1942; House Divided (Weidman), 1944; Story of Mankind (Humphrey), orch, 1946

Inst: Concertino, pf, orch, 1944; Suite, 4 Pages from a Musical Diary, 1944; Suite, 4 wind, 1945; Sonata, ob, pf, 1949; Orrea Pernel, sonata, vn, 1950; Sonata no.1, vc, pf, 1950; Diptych, str qt, 1951; Fantasia, 3 insts, 1951; Sonata no.2, vc, pf, 1951; Qt, ob, str, 1952; Pf Trio, 1954; Duo, va, pf, 1960; Sonata no.3, vc, pf, 1960; Concert Piece, timp, str, 1961; Soundscape, pf, 1964; Soundscape, 3 ww; Soundscape, str qt; 4 Fancies for 5 Players, fl, cl, bn, va, vc, 1980; 4 Green Mountain Sketches, fl, vc, 1981; Suite, 2 vc, 1981; Games, suite, 4 fl, 1984; 4 Lemmas, vc, pf, ?1987

Vocal: Poems for Music (R. Hillyer), 5 songs, T, cl, 1951; Wisdom Exalteth her Children, double women's chorus, 1952; 4 Songs from Vermont, T, pf, 1953; 7 Songs from the Diary of Izumi Shikibu, 1v, pf, 1982

Edn: *Cowboys and the Songs they Sang*, collection of song settings, ed. S.J. Sackett (New York, 1967)

Principal publishers: ACA, New Music, Smith College Valley

BIBLIOGRAPHY

T. Strongin: "Composers on Main Street," *American Composers Alliance Bulletin*, xii/1 (1964), 1–8

B. Holland: "Cello-and-Piano Pieces by Bennington Teacher," *New York Times* (17 Nov 1987)

BARBARA L. TISCHLER

No Wave. A term used in the late 1970s to designate a subgenre of punk rock music. Critics writing for New York's alternative press, primarily between the years 1977 and 1979, dubbed a group of particularly discordant, dissonant, and often aggressive punk bands "no wave." The name was a play on the term new wave, at the time used interchangeably with punk. There is no evidence that the bands themselves used the term or considered themselves to be part of a unified scene prior to its appearance in publications like the *New York Rocker*. Nonetheless, no wave grouped together bands whose music was loosely affiliated around punk but abandoned much of its melodic and harmonic framework and instead pushed its abrasive timbres to the center of their sound. Some no wave bands, like D.N.A. and James Chance and the Contortions, embraced complex rhythmic structures. Others, including

Teenage Jesus and the Jerks, experimented with vocal and guitar dissonance over tom-heavy rock beats. An underground film movement in New York at this time was also dubbed no wave, with some performers and audience members traveling freely between the two mediums.

Brian Eno produced the primary document of no wave, the compilation album *No New York*, released in 1978 by Antilles records, which demonstrates the diversity of the no wave sound by the bands Teenage Jesus and the Jerks, Mars, the Contortions, and D.N.A. The Contortions, led by confrontational saxophonist James Chance, perform four songs, including "Dish It Out," that mix punk, funk, be-bop, and free jazz along with characteristic no wave dissonance. In the four songs by Teenage Jesus and the Jerks, all written and sung by 19-year-old Lydia Lunch, her assertive vocals stand against drummer Bradley Field's thudding drumbeats. A geographical divide separated the East Village bands archived by Eno and the groups based in SoHo, including Theoretical Girls, Static, and Gynecologists. These latter groups made up no wave's "art rock" contingent. Many no wave bands recorded a small number of singles, or nothing at all. In the mid-1990s, widely available reissues introduced no wave to a younger generation, and a decade later most no wave recordings could be easily found.

BIBLIOGRAPHY

B. Gendron: *Between Montmartre and the Mudd Club: Popular Music and the Avant-Garde* (Chicago, 2002)

S. Reynolds: *Rip It Up and Start Again: Post-punk 1978–84* (London, 2005)

M. Masters: *No Wave* (London, 2007)

T. Moore and B. Coley: *No Wave: Post-Punk. Underground. New York. 1976–1980* (New York, 2008)

CAROLINE POLK O'MEARA

NPR. NPR, formerly known as National Public Radio, is a privately and publicly funded nonprofit membership media group. Its primary focus involves the production, syndication, and distribution of news and cultural programming to US public radio stations. Individual NPR stations, however, may broadcast programming from various sources that have no formal affiliation with NPR. NPR also manages the Public Radio Satellite System, which distributes NPR programs and other programming from independent producers and networks.

In 1967 congressional passage of the Public Broadcasting Act established the Corporation for Public Broadcasting to provide federal financial support of local radio and television stations, nationally produced programming, and interrelated services. As a result, National Public Radio (NPR) was created in February 1970 to replace the National Educational Radio Network. NPR aired its first broadcast in April 1971 and soon launched national program services. Until 1977 NPR was primarily a production and distribution organization. When it merged with the Association of Public Radio Stations, however, it began to provide affiliated stations with training, promotion, and management, and to lobby Congress for funding. In 1983 the Corporation for Public

Broadcasting agreed to lend the network money in order to stave off bankruptcy. In exchange, NPR agreed to allow the Corporation for Public Broadcasting to distribute funding directly to the stations rather than to NPR. The result was a public radio environment driven by individual stations that would support NPR productions via subscription. NPR also agreed to turn its satellite service into a cooperative venture (the Public Radio Satellite System), making it possible for non-NPR shows to get national distribution.

Musical programming on NPR has been vital to its mission of cultural advancement from the beginning. Several programs produced by NPR include *All Songs Considered*, *Jazz Profiles*, *NPR World of Opera*, and *The Thistle & Shamrock*. Other productions distributed by NPR include *From the Top*, *Piano Jazz*, and *Sunday Baroque*. In November 2007 the website NPR Music was launched as a subsidiary of NPR to offer podcasts, live concert webcasts, reviews, and interviews from NPR and partner public radio stations across the country, as well as a list of stations on the internet offering live, streaming musical content.

See also Radio broadcasting and Radio, community.

TIMOTHY M. CRAIN

NRBQ [New Rhythm and Blues Quintet; New Rhythm and Blues Quartet]. Rock and roll band. NRBQ was fluent in numerous musical styles and known for their zany humor and high energy performances. It formed as a quintet in 1967 when pianist Terry Adams and guitarist/singer Steve Ferguson left their native Louisville, Kentucky, and met bassist Joey Spampinato, drummer Tom Staley, and singer Frank Gadler in Miami, Florida. The band relocated to New York City in late 1968. Their early years saw a number of personnel changes. Although Ferguson, a virtuoso rock and country picker, left in 1970, his song contributions and stylistic influence proved lasting. By 1974 the quartet of Adams, Spampinato, guitarist/singer Al Anderson, and drummer Tom Ardolino was in place, and would remain intact until 1994. Various horn players also contributed both on record and in performance, typically under the moniker of "The Whole Wheat Horns."

NRBQ's original songs, as well as its cover material, traversed a wide variety of musical styles, including pop, rockabilly, jazz, jump blues, country, and novelty songs. They often penned humorous lyrics, with subject matter embracing fossil fuel ("Get That Gasoline Blues"), food ("RC Cola and a Moon Pie," "Howard Johnson's Got His HoJo Working"), The Three Stooges ("Dr. Howard, Dr. Fine, Dr. Howard"), and marijuana ("Wacky Tobacky"). Other lyrics demonstrated a more traditional fondness for girls and cars. Several of NRBQ's more than 30 albums—studio releases, live recordings, reissues, and compilations—garnered critical acclaim, but only a few singles achieved moderate chart success. It was their live performances that led to cult status with fans and colleagues in the music business. Their sets were typically unplanned, with Adams often spontaneously calling out the next song. The band also was known to attempt to play songs chosen at random from a suggestion box.

The band's sound and texture were driven equally by its four core members. Adams possessed powerful honky-tonk piano skills and fluency with jazz harmony. He was an early pioneer on the Hohner Clavinet, utilizing it for rhythmic comping, harmonic washes, and melodic soloing. Anderson was a master picker with country and jazz leanings, and a worthy heir to Ferguson's legacy. Spampinato's washboard-style bass work and Ardolino's swinging drums created an infectious rhythmic foundation. Spampinato and Anderson were very capable singers, and the entire group pitched in with vocal harmonies and clever choral responses. Adams deployed his Kentucky drawl and sense of humor in his lead vocal parts.

In 1994 Anderson left the band to pursue a country music songwriting career, and was replaced by Spampinato's younger brother Johnny. The band continued to perform and record until 2004, at which point Adams and the Spaminato brothers parted ways. In 2011 Adams began using the moniker "NRBQ" in association with his own quartet.

JEFFREY T. ELDREDGE

*NSYNC. Boy band formed in Orlando, Florida in 1995. Its members are Lance Bass (*b* Laurel, MS, 4 May 1979), JC [Joshua Scott] Chasez (*b* Washington, DC, 8 Aug 1976), Joey Fatone (*b* New York, NY, 28 Jan 1977), Chris Kirkpatrick (*b* Clarion, PA, 17 Oct 1971), and Justin Timberlake (*b* Memphis, TN, 31 Jan 1981). The group's albums include **NSYNC* (1998), *Home for Christmas* (1998), *No Strings Attached* (2000), *Celebrity* (2001), *Greatest Hits* (2005), and *The Collection* (2010). Part of a hugely successful teen-pop influx during the late 1990s, they were widely known and celebrated in Europe before becoming popular in the United States, with a fan base consisting primarily of adolescent females. They have won awards from the Teen Choice Awards (1999, 2000, 2001), MTV Video Music Awards (2000, 2001), American Music Awards (2001), and received RIAA Diamond Awards for **NSYNC* and *No Strings Attached*. The group went on hiatus in 2002, citing Timberlake's busy solo career, and has released only two albums since: *Greatest Hits* and *The Collection*, both compilations of previously recorded material. Since their time with *NSYNC, Bass has received a Human Rights Campaign award for work in the gay community and has released an autobiography titled *Out of Sync*; Chasez released *Schizophrenic* (2004) and now writes for pop music acts including the Backstreet Boys; Fatone has become a television personality, hosting *The Singing Bee* and announcing on *Family Feud*; Kirkpatrick founded the Chris Kirkpatrick Foundation and performs with band Nigels11; Timberlake has released solo projects *Justified* (2002), *FutureSex/LoveSounds* (2006), and *The 20/20 Experience* (2013), produced albums, and acted in many films.

CRAIG JENNEX

Nueva canción [Nueva canción Latinoamericana]. Latin American song genre. Literally translated as "New Latin American Song," this term refers to interrelated musical movements that combined diverse folk music styles with socially engaged poetic content. These national expressions—including nueva canción in Chile, nuevo cancionero in Argentina, and nueva trova in Cuba—emerged in the 1960s, a decade marked by profound social transformations, political violence, and US military intervention in many parts of the Caribbean and Latin America. While their musical characters differed according to the local or popular sounds they absorbed, most manifestations of nueva canción shared a core membership of middle-class youth, a commitment to the causes of marginalized social and ethnic groups, and an anti-capitalist philosophy.

The origins of nueva canción movements are closely associated with musicians of the southern cone (Chile, Argentina, and Uruguay). Foundational figures include Violeta Parra (Chile) and Atahualpa Yupanqui (Argentina), folk artists who brought a new aesthetic, based in rural styles, to urban folk music performance in the 1950s. They influenced a younger generation of musicians who crafted their musical style as a homegrown, revolutionary alternative to both foreign commercial music and popular national genres of the early 20th century. By reaching across musical and cultural frontiers, artists sought to forge Pan–Latin American solidarity in the process of realizing social change. The aesthetics, politics, and ideologies of these movements were consolidated in both informal performance gatherings (peñas) as well as national and international festivals of song.

In Chile, Andean indigenous and mestizo genres were particularly influential in nueva canción, and instruments such as the quena, zampoña, and charango became core elements of ensembles including Quilapayún and Inti-Illimani. In Cuba, such musicians as Pablo Milanés drew from Afro-Cuban styles, while others such as Silvio Rodríguez created a cosmopolitan sound that was also influenced by North American rock and popular music. To many nueva canción musicians, the United States epitomized the capitalist imperialism against which they struggled. This ideological barrier did not inhibit the expression of political and aesthetic sympathies between specific artists, however. The identification of Latin American musicians with protest singers of North America is evident in Victor Jara's "El martillo" (an arrangement of "If I had a hammer" by Pete Seeger and Lee Hays) and the evocation of Bob Dylan's fingerpicking style in "Oleo de mujer con sombrero" by Silvio Rodríguez.

While military governments truncated many burgeoning nueva canción movements in the 1970s and 1980s, prominent musical groups in political exile established a powerful international arena for presenting Latin American song. Performances abroad generated great sympathy for nations under oppressive dictatorships. Chile's particular experience of violent political upheaval in 1973, especially the tragic death of Victor Jara, became a poignant basis for international artists to express solidarity and protest. Although for many listeners the original repertoire of nueva canción is symbolically linked to the specific social and political struggles of the mid-1960s and 1970s, many artists in Latin America and abroad maintain its aesthetic and activist discourses in performance today.

BIBLIOGRAPHY

GMO

E. Carrasco Pirard: "The nueva canción in Latin America," International Social Science Journal, xxxiv/4 (1982), 599–623

J. Fairley: "La Nueva Canción Latinoamericana," Bulletin of Latin American Research, iii/2 (1984), 107–5

O. Rodríguez Musso: La nueva canción chilena: continuidad y reflejo (Havana, 1988)

R. Moore: Music and Revolution: Cultural Change in Socialist Cuba (Berkeley, 2006)

F. Ríos: "La Flûte Indienne: the Early History of Andean Folkloric-Popular Music in France and its Impact on Nueva Canción," Latin American Music Review, xxix/2 (2008), 146–99

EMILY PINKERTON

Nugent [Jerome], **Maude** (*b* Brooklyn, NY, 12 Jan 1873 or 1874; *d* New York, NY, 3 June 1958). Singer and composer. She began her career in vaudeville, achieving tremendous success in 1896 with her song "Sweet Rosie O'Grady," which became the archetypal waltz ballad of the 1890s. Over the next few years Nugent's songs included "Mamie Reilly" (1897), "I can't forget you, Honey" (1899), and "Somebody Wants You" (1909), but none were more than minor successes. Nugent introduced many of her songs herself; for most she wrote both words and music, but the lyrics were occasionally supplied by her husband, William Jerome. At the age of 28 she retired from the stage to raise a family, although she made a brief return seven years later. After several decades in relative obscurity Nugent began appearing in "Gay Nineties" shows in the 1940s and, with her nostalgic appeal and lively presence, she enjoyed a brief vogue as a television personality in the 1950s.

BIBLIOGRAPHY

D. Gilbert: "Maude Nugent launched Sweet Rosie O'Grady, own song, at Tony Pastor's," *New York World Telegram* (14 April 1934)

E. Marks: *They All Sang: From Tony Pastor to Rudy Vallée* (New York, 1935)

Obituary, *New York Times* (4 June 1958)

J. Burton: *The Blue Book of Tin Pan Alley, A Human Interest Encyclopedia of American Popular Music* (Watkins Glen, NY, 1962)

WILLIAM BROOKS (WITH PAMELA FOX)/R

Numeral notation. A system using numbers instead of conventional round notes. The system, which was not written on a staff, used the numeral corresponding to the scale step of the desired pitch (1 for do, 2 for re, and so on). Various marks of punctuation denoted time value of notes. The Shakers used this experimental notation beginning as early as 1830, when David A. Buckingham introduced this notation at their community at Watervliet, New York. It was also used by a non-Shaker compiler, Thomas Harrison, in his book *Sacred Harmonicon* (1839). This system did not gain prominence in the United States, although Lowell Mason knew of it, and it is sometimes used by teachers of the Kodály Method.

See also NOTATION.

BIBLIOGRAPHY

G.P. Jackson: *White Spirituals in the Southern Uplands* (Chapel Hill, NC, 1933/*R*)

D.W. Patterson: *The Shaker Spiritual* (Princeton, NJ, 1979, 2/2000)

ROGER L. HALL

Nü Metal. Genre. This is an offshoot of HEAVY METAL which fuses the genre with the stylistic features of rap, funk, industrial, and alternative rock. Its antecedents comprised both rock and rap groups which aimed at stylistic crossover, including metal and alternative groups like Faith No More, Red Hot Chili Peppers, Jane's Addiction, and Rage Against the Machine, and rap groups like the Beastie Boys. The genre peaked in popularity between 1998 and 2002. Some of its most successful practitioners include Korn, Limp Bizkit, Slipknot, Linkin Park, Papa Roach, and the Deftones. Many, but not all, nü metal bands hail from California.

The genre's connection to heavy metal comes through its heavy riffing, screamed or growled vocals, down-tuned guitars, and aggressive attack. Unlike metal, the vocal stylings include rapping, and the bands sometimes include DJs. Riffs are commonly syncopated, and many bands emphasize rhythm and groove over melodic content. The lyrics tend to be introspective, reflecting on feelings of victimization, alienation, powerlessness, and abandonment. Korn's "Freak on a Leash" and Linkin Park's "In the End" typify the style during its most widely broadcast period of success. Nü metal's relationship to heavy metal at large is contested due to its rap content and the disempowerment expressed in the lyrics, a contrast with metal's more typically empowering, transcendent stance.

CHRIS MCDONALD

Nunn, Trevor (*b* Ipswich, England, 14 Jan 1940). British director. Nunn began his directing career with the Royal Shakespeare Company; he joined in 1964 and became its youngest director in 1968. He held the position until 1986, even as his sweeping, cinematic style also led him to the work for which he is best known: megamusicals and other high-profile musicals. His large-scale production of an adaptation of Dickens's *Nicholas Nickelby* (London, 1980) demonstrated his eye for the epic tale, and this aesthetic made him a good fit for the megamusical, starting with a long-term collaboration with composer ANDREW LLOYD WEBBER. *Cats*, their first show together, became the longest-running Broadway musical of all time (London, 1981; Broadway, 1982 with a run of 18 years). The most internationally successful musical, *Les Misérables* (by Schönberg and Boublil; London, 1985; Broadway, 1987), was a vehicle for the Royal Shakespeare Company, whom Nunn and co-director John Caird challenged to stretch their abilities for this epic megamusical. Other musicals directed by Nunn, many in association with the producer Cameron Mackintosh, include Lloyd Webber's *Starlight Express* (London, 1984; Broadway, 1987), *Aspects of Love* (London, 1989; Broadway, 1990), and *Sunset Boulevard* (London, 1993; Broadway, 1994), as well as the successful revival of *Oklahoma!* that reached Broadway in 2002 and the lauded revival of *A Little Night Music* that opened in 2009. He famously "saved" *Chess* (London, 1986; by Benny Andersson, Björn Ulvaeus, and Tim Rice) when director Michael Bennett was unable to complete the project, and then radically reworked it (to no avail) for its two-month run on Broadway in 1988.

Nunn also directs operas (including *Porgy and Bess* for Glyndebourne, 1988) and plays.

BIBLIOGRAPHY
J. Sternfeld: *The Megamusical* (Bloomington, IN, 2006)
M. Lundskaer-Nielsen: *Directors and the New Musical Drama: British and American Musical Theatre in the 1980s and 90s* (New York, 2008)

JESSICA STERNFELD

Nunns & Clark. Firm of piano manufacturers. As Nunns & Clark, it was active in New York from 1839 to 1860. The brothers Robert and William Nunns arrived in New York from London, England, around 1821 and first worked for Kearsing & Sons, piano makers. In 1823 they started their own firm, R. & W. Nunns. They are reputed to have introduced a French-style "rocker" action to American pianos and manufactured some instruments for sale under other makers' names (e.g. Dubois & Stodart). In 1833 the English immigrant John Clark joined the firm, which became known as Nunns, Clark & Co. William withdrew in 1839 and the business was thereafter known as (R.) Nunns & Clark; it continued until 1860, though Clark is not listed in city directories after 1858. William was in partnership with Augustus Brumley as Nunns & Brumley from 1836, then in 1843 he joined John and Charles Fischer under the name Nunns & Fischer, and in 1848 he withdrew from that firm to found William Nunns & Co. This went bankrupt in 1853 (at a time when William Steinway was an apprentice) and William retired. Ironically, in 1853 Nunns & Clark exhibited to general acclaim at the Crystal Palace, New York.

An extraordinarily ornate Nunns & Clark square piano, dated 1853 (held by the Metropolitan Museum of Art), shows the heavily carved rosewood casework for which the firm was renowned; though highly decorative, the piano is of standard design internally. In 1855 Nunns & Clark employed 83 men and boys and produced 300 pianos worth $150,000 at a factory at Setauket, Long Island. Robert continued to be listed in New York directories as late as 1868. William Nunns, Jr., Robert Nunns, Jr., and John Francis Nunns were also active in the trade into the 1860s.

BIBLIOGRAPHY
L. Libin: *American Musical Instruments in the Metropolitan Museum of Art* (New York, 1985)
N. Groce: *Musical Instrument Makers of New York: a Directory of Eighteenth- and Nineteenth-Century Urban Craftsmen* (Stuyvesant, NY, 1991)

LAURENCE LIBIN/R

Nunó, Jaime [Jaume Nunó i Roca] (*b* San Juan de las Abadesas, Catalonia, Spain, 8 Sept 1824; *d* Bayside, NY, 18 July 1908). Catalan composer, director, and organist. He acquired his musical skills primarily at the Barcelona cathedral and studied briefly in Italy, before becoming a military musician in 1845. He was sent to Havana, Cuba, to organize and direct regimental bands. In 1854 he left Cuba to work briefly for Mexican president Antonio López de Santa Anna, and soon after composed the Mexican National Anthem, for which he is best known. Later he became an opera director, managing troupes in New York City, Havana, and Mexico City. Tired of touring and relocating, he settled down in Buffalo, New York, in 1869, where he remarried and established himself as a choir director and music teacher in a city of commerce and theater life. In 1901 the Mexican musicians who played in the regimental band and the typical orchestra performing at the Pan American Exposition met with him and insisted that he return to Mexico for a triumphal tour. Unable to find steady employment as a director there, he returned to New York State, where he died in Bayside. His body was later returned to Mexico City and given a state funeral.

BIBLIOGRAPHY

GMO; Thompson

M. Talavera: *Miguel Lerdo de Tejada: su vida pintoresca y anecdótica* (Mexico City, 1940)

J.C. Romero: *La verdadera historia del Himno Nacional Mexicano* (Mexico City, 1961)

R. Stevenson: "Jaime Nunô after the Mexican National Anthem," *Inter-American Music Review*, ii/2 (1980), 103–16

JEAN DICKSON

Nurock, Kirk (*b* Camden, NJ, 28 Feb 1948). Composer, pianist, conductor, arranger, and teacher. He studied at the Eastman School's Arrangers' Lab with Rayburn Wright and at Juilliard (BM, MM) with LUCIANO BERIO and VINCENT PERSICHETTI. He also studied composition with Manny Albam and Johnny Richards. He taught at the Hanns Eisler Hochschule für Musik (1993–8) and at the New School for Jazz and Contemporary Music (1987–93, 1999–).

Nurock's compositional output crosses many stylistic boundaries. He has written chamber music, jazz tunes, and film scores, has orchestrated for pop and jazz productions (including work with Judi Collins, Bette Midler, James Taylor, and Nat and Cannonball Adderley), and has composed incidental music for numerous theatrical productions. He wrote the score for *Mowgli* (1985), based on Kipling's *The Jungle Book*, which was produced at the Judith Anderson Theater in New York, and has conducted orchestras, big bands, and for theater, including first productions by Bernstein, Sondheim, and others. In the 1970s he founded the Natural Sound Workshop, which explored the sonic possibilities of large groups of untrained voices. Similar techniques occupy numerous other works that involve audience participation. In the 1980s he began pursuing "cross-species communication," culminating in performances with sea lions, guinea pigs, canines, a screech owl, and more. Some of these works were captured in Burrill Crohn's video documentary *Animalsong* (1982). A cross-section of his work was also featured in a Bravo *Arts and Minds* documentary (2010).

Nurock's eclectic career includes collaborations with Art Baron, Leonard Bernstein, Theo Bleckmann, Jay Clayton, Marty Ehrlich, Dizzy Gillespie, the Israel Philharmonic, the Meridian Arts Ensemble, Meredith Monk, Bob Moses, the New World Symphony, Bobby Previte, and many more. His works have been performed at Carnegie Hall, Alice Tully Hall, Lukas Foss's "Meet the Moderns" at Brooklyn Academy of Music, the Metro-politan Museum of Art, Symphony Space, and more. He has also enjoyed great success as a solo pianist, playing original compositions and creative reinterpretations of jazz standards.

WORKS

(selective list)

Audience Oratorio, 1975; Mowgli, mus th, 1978–84; Bronx Zoo Events, 1980; Sonata for Piano and Dog, 1983; Haunted Messages, pf, barking audience, 1984; Expedition, jazz trio, Siberian Husky, 1984; The Incurable Dorothy Parker, S + pf, 1986; Gorilla, Gorilla, pf, 1988; 3 Screams, 2 amp. pf, 1990, 4 Imaginings, pf, 1999; (Unlikely) Aspirations, fl, "imaginary creatures," 2000; 6 Works for Children's Chorus, 2001–7; Trio for Piano, Trombone, and Terrier, 2003; Fables for Flügelhorn, tpt/flg, pf, 2005

CHRIS STOVER

Nuu-chah-nulth [Nootka]. A group of 19 Northwest Coast Indian tribes, formerly known as Nootka, who live in Canada and the United States and share common language and customs. Those inhabiting the west coast of Vancouver Island, British Columbia, now call themselves by the general term, Nuu-chah-nulth, while those on the northwest tip of the Olympic Peninsula in Washington State, call themselves Makah. Ocean and temperate rainforest produced a bounty of food for all these tribes and in addition provided materials for the creation of utilitarian items such as longhouses and clothing as well as ceremonial objects such as totem poles, masks, drums, rattles, and dance paraphernalia. The relative ease of food acquisition allowed time for the creation of complex political and social structures as well as elaborate musical and ceremonial activities.

Music has been an essential element in the proper functioning of these societies. Aside from supporting the power and status of chiefs, songs have played an important role in rites of passage (ceremonies connected with birth, puberty, marriage, and death); secret society activities; medicine and healing; whaling, hunting, and fishing; warfare; games; and other recreational activities. In addition, music served to renew myths, aid supernatural power, and foster enculturation. Most songs were privately owned pieces of personal property and could be performed only by the proper individuals in appropriate circumstances. An unwritten set of rules governed their correct use and inheritance.

1. Ceremonial practices. 2. Instruments. 3. Style. 4. Song texts and forms.

1. CEREMONIAL PRACTICES. In the past, ceremonial life and activities were largely governed by the sociopolitical organization. This hereditary, ranked system included three classes of people: chiefs and their immediate families; commoners, distant relatives of a chief; and slaves, individuals captured in warfare and their descendants born in captivity. Songs supported and reinforced this system: chiefs and their royal families owned the most important songs (as well as certain dances, costumes, and masks); commoners owned less important songs; and slaves generally were not allowed to own songs. Often a chief asked relatives to perform some of his songs and dances for him at ceremonials that he hosted.

The rainy winter months signaled the beginning of the ceremonial season, a time that included much feasting, singing, and dancing in the sturdy cedar longhouses. Former Makah and Nuu-chah-nulth ceremonies included the *Klukwali* (Wolf Ceremony), where children were initiated into a secret society of the same name. Abducted by members of the tribe who were dressed as wolves, the young initiates were carried into the woods where they spent four days learning tribal and familial history, and in addition, specific family songs and dances to be performed on their return. The *Tsayak*, a four-day secret society ceremony related to healing, involved singing and drumming by society members as well as activities of a medicine man who sang over and manipulated the patient's body. During the Makah *Tla'iihl* ceremony each participant entered a trance state and sang personal-guardian spirit songs in order to renew his or her individual power and strength. All three of these ceremonies have ceased to be observed over the past 75 to 100 years, and much of the music that accompanied them has been forgotten.

One lengthy ceremony that survives, however, is the potlatch. Given in the past principally to transfer chiefly status, names, and privileges (including songs) to successors, a potlatch often marked a rite of passage for one of the host chief's relatives while at the same time upholding the chief's own power and prestige. In addition to much feasting and speech-making, the chief displayed his wealth, songs, and dances before a large audience assembled from his own and other tribes. Because there was no system of writing, potlatch events had to be remembered and passed orally to the next generation. Therefore the chief gave special gifts to his invited guests as payment for witnessing and remembering.

Somewhat shorter in duration, the modern potlatch (now usually called a "party") was modified in part because the ceremony was outlawed by the US and Canadian governments in the 1880s (reinstated in the 1930s in the United States and 1950s in Canada). It remains a vehicle for emphasizing rites of passage, transfer of names and privileges, and display of wealth, songs, and dances by a host chief or his descendants. Transfers are occasionally made to a man being made a new chief, but more often to descendants of former chiefs. Feasts continue to be held and guests receive numerous gifts for witnessing potlatch events.

As the potlatch has changed over the years, so also has the three-tiered sociopolitical system, only vestiges of which remain. Among the Makah, for example, authority no longer rests with hereditary chiefs; rather, an elected tribal council has replaced them. Song ownership, however, remains important because chiefs' songs, when performed at potlatches, continue to symbolize status and prestige and thus are considered desirable property. Formerly, tribal members knew the ownership history of each others' songs, and thus conflicts were said to be infrequent. However, largely as a result of changes imposed by governments and missionaries, lines of ownership have become clouded. Conflicts have developed between those who can trace their traditional hereditary ownership rights and others who claim they have such rights. Currently, feuding over song ownership continues and is sometimes expressed during the course of contemporary potlatches.

2. INSTRUMENTS. Since vocal music has always been of primary importance among the Nuu-cha-nulth and Makah, most instruments have been used to support the voice and provide percussive accompaniment. The handheld frame drum, personally owned and often displaying a family crest or other Northwest Coast design on the drumhead, accompanies most songs. Two other powerful instruments used previously in longhouse ceremonies included a large cedar box drum (four feet high, six to eight feet long) that was pounded with the feet, and a hollowed log drum (about 30 inches long) played with wooden beaters. A plank drum (a long, wooden plank raised slightly above the ground), also played with wooden beaters, continues to be used at times by the Nuu-chah-nulth in Canada but not by the Makah.

Several types of rattles, formerly quite common, but used infrequently today, include a scallop-shell rattle (scallop shells strung on a hoop), a baleen rattle (a piece of baleen whale bone folded in half with pebbles inside), an elk horn rattle, and a bird-shaped rattle (carved of two pieces of wood, with pebbles inside). Newer carved wooden rattles in the shapes of wolf, grizzly bear, or thunderbird have been appearing at potlatches for about the past 30 years. Wooden whistles of several different lengths and sizes, rarely heard today, were not used to accompany songs; rather they announced the presence of supernatural beings. Bull roarers, also connected with supernatural creatures, are seldom used.

3. STYLE. Although most Nootka music is monophonic, two-part singing in 4ths is not uncommon. It is not known whether this polyphonic phenomenon, rare in American Indian music generally, came from missionary influence or was indigenous. The range of most songs is about an octave. Minor and major 2nds and minor and major 3rds are characteristic intervals; 4ths and 5ths occur less frequently. Three- and four-note scales are sometimes used, but five- and six-note scales are more common. Most melodies begin with a rising pattern, followed by undulation; there may be a descending phrase at the end. Prolongation of tones often occurs at the beginning or end of a phrase. Most songs are sung at the low end of the vocal register; when a song is begun too low, one or more half-step upward adjustments may be made in performance for the singer's comfort. Vocal ornaments, such as turns and grace notes, are fairly common. Rhythms are often complex, with a variety of drum patterns. The basic beat patterns, mostly in groups of two or three, may be used alternately within a song or may be played and sung simultaneously, creating cross-rhythms. It is proper for voices and drums to be out of synchronization in some songs.

4. SONG TEXTS AND FORMS. Many songs are composed entirely of vocables; others contain some lexical text,

but vocables often predominate. A story is connected with almost every song, and song and story are learned together; therefore most texts are brief, only a few key words being necessary to evoke the complete story. Non-Nuu-cha-nulth words, altered linguistic structures, and altered pronunciation may appear in these song texts.

Typically a Nuu-cha-nulth or Makah song opens with a section called the "Beginning," (no native term available), that has a variable number of phrases and may or may not include meaningful text. Normally this section is repeated one or more times during the song, and some songs consist solely of varied repeats of this section. The "Beginning" is frequently followed by a "Verse" (*Q'abaatchatl*) that usually has meaningful text; this also has a variable number of phrases, and may be repeated one or more times. Frequent repetition and variation of a small number of musical motifs or short phrases adds variety while maintaining the unity of a song. Formerly each song was sung four times through, but this practice has been largely abandoned. Despite a number of changes, this native song tradition remains strong.

Recordings of Nootka, Nuu-cha-nulth, and Makah music are held at the Archive of Folk Culture, Library of Congress, Washington, DC; the Archives of Ethnic Music and Dance, University of Washington School of Music, Seattle; and BC Archives, Royal British Columbia Museum, Victoria.

RECORDINGS

Northwest (Puget Sound), recorded 1950 by W. Rhodes (Library of Congress, AAFS L34, 1952) [reissued 1985 with descriptive notes]

Songs of the Nootka and Quileute, recorded 1923–6 by F. Densmore (Library of Congress AAFS L32, 1952)

Nootka Indian Music of the Pacific Northwest Coast, recorded by I. Halpern (FW FE 4524, 1974)

BIBLIOGRAPHY

J. Swan: *The Indians of Cape Flattery* (Washington, DC, 1870)

F. Boas: "The Nootka," *British Association for the Advancement of Science*, lx (1890), 582, 668

E. Sapir: "Some Aspects of Nootka Language and Culture," *American Anthropologist*, xiii/1 (1911), 15–28

E.S. Curtis: *The North American Indian*, xi (Cambridge, MA, 1916)

F. Densmore: *Nootka and Quileute Music*, Bureau of American Ethnology Bulletin, no.124 (Washington, DC, 1939)

E. Sapir and M. Swadesh: *Nootka Texts* (Philadelphia, 1939)

P. Drucker: *The Northern and Central Nootkan Tribes*, Bureau of American Ethnology Bulletin, no.144 (Washington, DC, 1951)

A. Ernst: *The Wolf Ritual of the Northwest Coast* (Eugene, OR, 1952)

P. Drucker: *Indians of the Northwest Coast* (New York, 1955)

H. Roberts and M. Swadesh: *Songs of the Nootka Indians of Western Vancouver Island*, Transactions of the American Philosophical Society, xlv/3 (1955), 199–327

L.J. Goodman: *Music and Dance in Northwest Coast Indian Life* (Tsaile, AZ, 1977)

L.J. Goodman: *This is my Song: the Role of Song as Symbol in Makah Life* (diss.,Wash. State U., 1978)

E. Arima and J. Dewhirst: "Nootkans of Vancouver Island," *Handbook of North American Indians, Vol 7: Northwest Coast*, ed. W. Suttles (Washington, DC, 1990), 391–411

L.J. Goodman: "Traditional Music in Makah Life," *A Time of Gathering: Native Heritage in Washington State*. ed. R.K. Wright (Seattle, 1991), 223–33

L.J. Goodman: "Aspects of Spiritual and Political Power in Chiefs' Songs of the Makah Indians," *The World of Music: Journal of the International Institute for Traditional Music*, xxxiv/2 (1992), 23–42

L.J. Goodman and H. Swan: "Makah Music: Preserving the Traditions," *Spirit of the First People: Native American Music Traditions in Washington State*, ed. W. Smyth and E. Ryan, (Seattle, 1999), 81–105

K. Robinson and C. Little: "Memorial Potlatch: *Laakt'uula*," *Nuu-chah-nulth Voices, Histories, Objects, and Journeys*, ed. A.L. Hoover (Victoria, BC, 2000), 131–2

L.J. Goodman and H. Swan: *Singing the Songs of My Ancestors: The Life and Music of Helma Swan, Makah Elder* (Norman, OK, 2003)

LINDA J. GOODMAN

N.W.A. [Niggaz with Attitude] Rap group. Its members included Eazy-E (Eric Wright; *b* Los Angeles, CA, 7 Sept 1963; *d* 26 March, 1995), DR. DRE (Andre Young; *b* Los Angeles, CA, 18 February 1965), Ice Cube (Oshea Jackson; *b* Los Angeles, CA, 15 June 1969), MC Ren (Lorenzo Patterson; *b* Los Angeles, CA, 14 June 1969), and DJ Yella (Antoine Carraby; *b* Los Angeles, CA, 11 Dec 1967).

Formed by rapper and entrepreneur Eazy-E, who founded Ruthless Records in 1987 with group manager Jerry Heller, N.W.A. was central to the development and spread of gangsta rap. Its first single "Panic Zone" (Ruthless, 1987) featured Arabian Prince (Mik Lezan; *b* Los Angeles, CA), an early member of the group. The group's debut album *N.W.A. and the Posse* (1987) was largely a compilation of Ruthless artists, and featured members Dr. Dre and DJ Yella (formerly of the group the World Class Wreckin' Cru), Ice Cube, and MC Ren.

N.W.A. gained nationwide prominence and notoriety with their second album *Straight Outta Compton* (1988), produced by band members Dr. Dre and DJ Yella, with raps by Eazy-E, MC Ren, Dre, and Ice Cube. The ultra-violent and misogynist lyrics on raw and confrontational tracks such as "Fuck the Police," "Straight Outta Compton," and "Gangsta Gangsta" precipitated an FBI investigation and media outcry. N.W.A. countered with the defense that they were simply journalists recording the reality of black life in deprived areas such as South Central Los Angeles. Yet by their own later admission, Eazy-E and Heller were aware of the commercial value of controversy and explicit lyrics, and in great part crafted the group's music and image to elicit a media reaction. Despite a lack of radio or television support, the album sold in large quantities and popularized West Coast rap to a national audience. Soon after their rise to fame, however, the group began to split apart.

In 1989, Ice Cube left to pursue a highly successful solo career. N.W.A.'s next releases, the EP *100 Miles and Runnin'* (1989) and the album *Efil4zaggiN* (1991) displayed the evolution of Dr. Dre's production, while the lyrical content was increasingly exploitative and misogynist, and lacked the social commentary evident on *Straight Outta Compton*. In the UK, copies of *Efil4zaggin* were seized under the Obscene Publications Act and only returned after a successful court action by Island Records, the distributing company.

In 1991, Dr. Dre left the group to become one of the most significant and sucessful rap producers and entrepreneurs of all time, working with Snoop Doggy Dogg, Tupac Shakur, Eminem, and others. After a career of acrimony and controversy, N.W.A. splintered into various solo projects, finally ending with the AIDS-related death of Eazy-E in 1995. Part of the group's legacy was a rise in hip hop's gangster posturing and an increased awareness among artists of the power of controversial and shocking lyrics to sell records.

BIBLIOGRAPHY
C. Keyes: *Rap Music and Street Consciousness* (Urbana, IL, 2002)
J. Heller: *Ruthless: a Memoir* (New York, 2006)
DAVID TOOP/WILL FULTON

Nyiregyházi, Ervin (*b* Budapest, Hungary, 19 Jan 1903; *d* Los Angeles, CA, 8 April 1987). Pianist and composer of Hungarian birth. His father and paternal grandfather were choristers in the Royal Hungarian Opera, his mother an amateur pianist. Raised in a Jewish family, he began at the age of three to play the piano and to compose; at the age of six he gave his first concert, in Fiume, and published three original works; at the age of eight he gave a command performance at Buckingham Palace. (As a child prodigy, he was the subject of a detailed study; *see* Révész.) At the National Hungarian Royal Academy of Music, he studied piano with Thomán (1907–8) and Székely (1908–14), and theory with Siklós and Weiner. He later took piano lessons with Dohnányi in Berlin (1914–15) and Budapest (1917–18), and with Lamond in Berlin (1916), and he made his orchestral debut, in Beethoven's Third Piano Concerto, with the Berlin Philharmonic under Fiedler (1915). Later public appearances in Europe, Scandinavia, and North America won much acclaim, though occasionally aroused controversy, too. His career was derailed, however, by a 1924–5 lawsuit against his manager and by his own plentiful neuroses. Although he performed occasionally through the 1950s, he never again had a major career. He lived mostly in Los Angeles from 1928, often in poverty and dissolution; between 1926 and 1978, he married ten times. He did some work for film studios (1928–30, 1944–7), and continued to compose, eventually completing well over 1000 works (a few were published 1950–51); he also wrote an unpublished book of essays (manuscript lost). In 1972–3, in San Francisco, he gave several public and private recitals, and he made recordings for the International Piano Archives in 1974 and 1978. In 1980 and 1982, he performed in Japan, and Toshiba-EMI released some concert recordings in 1981.

Liszt was at the heart of Nyiregyházi's aesthetic and repertory, and he played Liszt's music with particular authority. He played a little 18th-century music but much 19th and early-20th-century repertory (notably Beethoven, Brahms, Chopin, Debussy, Grieg, Rachmaninoff, Schubert, Schumann, Scriabin, and Tchaikovsky), and he played many operatic and other transcriptions (usually his own). His arch-romantic piano style was influenced by Liszt, Busoni, and Paderewski; his slow tempos, ardent singing tone, immense dynamic range, textual freedoms, and individuality of interpretation aroused particular comment. (Schoenberg was much impressed by his free, romantic style in 1935).

As of 2012 Nyiregyházi's papers are held at the University of Creation: Art, Music, and Social Work (Souzou Gakuen University) in Takasaki, Japan. An International Ervin Nyiregyházi Foundation, in Krommenie, The Netherlands, administers his posthumous affairs. Two CDs have been released: *Nyiregyházi at the Opera*, mostly studio recordings from 1978 (VAI Audio, 1992); and *Ervin Nyiregyházi in Performance: Live Recordings 1972–1982* (Music and Arts, 2007).

BIBLIOGRAPHY
G. Révész: *Erwin Nyiregyházi: psychologische Analyse eines musikalisch hervorragenden Kindes* (Leipzig, 1916; Eng. trans., London, 1925/*R* as *The Psychology of a Musical Prodigy*)
K. Bazzana: *Lost Genius: the Story of a Forgotten Musical Maverick* (Toronto and New York, 2007)
KEVIN BAZZANA

Nyro, Laura (*b* New York, NY, 18 Oct 1947; *d* Danbury, CT, 8 April 1997). Songwriter and singer. She became known initially as the composer of songs popularized by other artists (notably, Barbra Streisand and Peter, Paul and Mary); but a comparison of their performances with Nyro's own, earlier, recordings of this material reveal her to have exercised an important influence on the sound of popular music in the late 1960s and early 1970s. Unlike most prominent singer-songwriters of her generation, she wrote songs that derived largely from Tin Pan Alley forms and styles and the more popular idioms of jazz, rarely suggesting any folk influence, either urban or rural (she accompanied herself on piano rather than guitar). Her performance at the Monterey Pop Festival in 1967 helped her land a contract with Columbia Records, for whom she recorded her critically acclaimed albums *Eli & the 13th Confession* (1968) and *New York Tendaberry* (1969). Only on later albums does the sound and style of rock become a significant factor in her work; *Nested* (1978) reflects a mature synthesis of the varied aspects of her style. Though she took several breaks from the music business she recorded ten studio albums. On 8 April 1997 she died of ovarian cancer. A tribute concert was held in Manhattan's Beacon Theater on 27 October 1997, with performers including Patti LaBelle, Sandra Bernhard, and Phoebe Snow. A tribute album, *Time and Love: The Music of Laura Nyro*, was also released the same year. A posthumous album, *Angel in the Dark* (2001), contained material Nyro had recorded in 1994 and 1995. In 2011 *To Carry On*, an Off-Broadway play paying tribute to Nyro and her music, was performed by Mimi Cohen demonstrating the longevity of Nyro's cultural significance.

LAWRENCE STARR/CAROLYN BRUNELLE

Oakland. City in California, part of the SAN FRANCISCO Bay area.

Oak Publications. Firm of music publishers. It was founded in New York in the late 1950s by Irwin Silber, who was associated with Folkways Records and was editor of the folk music journal *Sing Out!*, to publish songbooks that would be of interest to his readers. Oak's catalog includes instruction manuals for guitar, dulcimer, banjo, pedal steel guitar, fiddle, and blues harp, and songbooks chiefly of blues, ragtime, bluegrass, folk, and country music. Its list includes such names as Alan Lomax, Woody Guthrie, Pete Seeger, Tom Paxton, Samuel Charters, and Jean Ritchie. The firm also published collections of folk music from other countries. In 1967 Oak was purchased by Music Sales Corporation.

BIBLIOGRAPHY

H. Traum: "The Story of Oak," *Sing Out!*, xxv/6 (1977), 26

FRANCES BARULICH

Oak Ridge Boys, the. Gospel and country music quartet. After 30 years together as a southern gospel group, it became widely successful by the early 1970s with its most popular lineup: Duane David Allen, lead (*b* Taylortown, TX, 29 April 1943); Joseph Sloan Bonsall, tenor (*b* Philadelphia, PA, 18 May 1948); William Lee Golden, baritone (*b* Brewton, AL, 12 Jan 1939); and Richard Anthony Sterban, bass (*b* Camden, NJ, 24 April 1943). Formed in 1943 in Knoxville, Tennessee, as part of Wally Fowler's Georgia Clodhoppers, the group took its name from the nearby town of Oak Ridge, first calling themselves The Oak Ridge Quartet. Under lead singer Fowler's management, they joined the *Grand Ole Opry* in 1945. In 1948 they helped establish all-night gospel singings at Nashville's Ryman Auditorium, a development important to the growth of the group's popularity as well as that of southern gospel generally. In 1956 E. Smith "Smitty" Gatlin assumed leadership and changed the name to The Oak Ridge Boys. Having topped the southern gospel market, they were initially unable to cross over to the country market. In 1975 "The Oaks" completed that difficult transition with the single "Y'all Come Back Saloon" (ABC/Dot, 1977), soon followed by "I'll Be True to You" (ABC/Dot, 1978). Their crossover extended to the pop market with "Elvira" (MCA, 1981). The Oak Ridge Boys have won numerous awards, including Grammys, Dove Awards, and Country Music Association Awards, some as recently as 2008. In 2000 they were inducted into the Gospel Music Association Hall of Fame. The group has had over 40 members since its inception, most of them before 1964. As of 2011 they remained active.

BIBLIOGRAPHY

E. Widner and W. Carter: *The Oak Ridge Boys* (Chicago and New York, 1987)

J.R. Goff, Jr.: *Close Harmony: a History of Southern Gospel* (Chapel Hill, NC, and London, 2002)

B.C. Malone: *Country Music, U.S.A.* (Austin, TX, 2/2002)

STEPHEN SHEARON

Oberheim, Thomas Elroy (*b* Manhattan, KS, 7 July 1936). Designer of electronic instruments. His name is primarily associated with the range of synthesizers designed by him and manufactured since 1974 by Oberheim Electronics in California. While working as an electronics engineer for a small computer company in the late 1960s, Oberheim was asked to construct a ring modulator, and the success of the original device (on the soundtrack of 1970s *Beneath the Planet of the Apes* and among jazz keyboardists) led to requests for others. In 1971 Maestro marketed both Oberheim's ring modulator and his phase shifter; Oberheim Electronics was set up in connection with their production.

In 1973, when he was an agent for ARP synthesizers, Oberheim devised a digital sequencer (DS-2), and the following year his company developed the Synthesizer Expander Module (SEM), a small monophonic synthesizer with two oscillators. The SEM had no keyboard control and was designed not as a standalone unit but, rather, as a tone generator that could work alongside the DS-2 or existing synthesizers like the ARP 2600 and Minimoog.

Oberheim is credited as one of the first to develop polyphonic synthesizers (the 2-Voice and the 4-Voice). These were marketed in 1974–5 and were based on the SEM (one Module for each voice) but featured a keyboard developed by the newly formed E-mu Systems. The 8-Voice and less popular 6-Voice followed soon after. The company then produced two programmable synthesizers, the monophonic OB-1 (1978) and the polyphonic OB-X (1979). Several variants of the latter followed (the OB-Xa being the most recognizable for its use on Van Halen's 1984 song "Jump"), as well as a further Expander Module, the Matrix 6 and 12 synthesizers, a digital sequencer, and a drum machine.

In 1985 Oberheim lost control of the company he had founded, which became part of ECC Development Corporation; he left the company in 1987. After producing the Matrix 1000 and a sample player, Oberheim/ECC went bankrupt in 1989. It was briefly owned by Suzuki, then relaunched in 1991 by Gibson Guitars. The trademark was then licensed to Viscount, an Italian electronic organ manufacturer that released products such as the OB*12 (2000), an analog-modeling digital synthesizer.

In 1987 Oberheim founded Marion Systems, specializing in sampler and synthesizer modules, and carrying out external design work (including nonmusical consulting). After the company closed its doors in the mid-1990s, he went on to found another short-lived enterprise, Seasound (1999–2001), known primarily for producing an audio interface for digital home-studio recording called the Solo. By 2010, partly in response to a resurgence of interest in analog synthesis among musicians, Oberheim reissued several of his 1970s designs under his own name, including the SEM.

BIBLIOGRAPHY

T.E. Oberheim: "A Programmer for Voltage Controlled Synthesizers," *Audio Engineering Society Preprint*, no.1172 (1976)

D. Heckman: "Tom Oberheim's Magical Music Machines," *HiFi/MusAm*, xxvii/4 (1977), 127–30

D. Milano: "Tom Oberheim: Designer of Synthesizers," *Contemporary Keyboard*, iii/5 (1977), 20–21, 32 only; repr. in *The Art of Electronic Music*, ed. T. Darter and G. Armbruster (New York, 1984), 92–97

P. Forrest: *The A–Z of Analogue Synthesisers*, i: *A–M* (Crediton, England, 1994, 2/1998), 259–60; ii: *N–Z* (Crediton, England, 1996), 7–24

G. Reid: "Tom Oberheim SEM," *Sound on Sound* (Sept 2010), 30–33

HUGH DAVIES/KYLE DEVINE

Oberhoffer, Emil (*b* Munich, Germany, 10 Aug 1867; *d* San Diego, CA, 22 May 1933). German conductor, organist, and teacher. Oberhoffer's first musical instruction was from his father, an organist. He later studied both piano and composition under Cyril Kistler and piano in Paris with Isidor Philipp. After immigrating to the United States around 1890, he settled in St. Paul, Minnesota in 1897 as conductor of the Apollo Club. When he became the conductor of the Philharmonic Club of Minneapolis in 1901, he started campaigning for the establishment of a permanent orchestra. In 1903 the Minneapolis Symphony Orchestra was established with Oberhoffer as conductor, a position he held until his resignation in 1923. He was also professor of music at the University of Minnesota and served as organist at the Church of the Redeemer in Minneapolis. Later he served as guest conductor of the St Louis Symphony, then retired and moved to California, where he died in 1933. His summer home in Lakeville, MN (built 1914–18) was designed by Paul Haugen, a leading proponent of Prairie School architecture, and is now on the National Register of Historic Places.

BIBLIOGRAPHY

Baker4; Grove3, Amer. suppl.

W.S. Pratt, ed.: *The New Encyclopedia of Music and Musicians* (New York, 1929)

JOSEPH A. BOMBERGER

Oberlin, Russell (Keys) (*b* Akron, OH, 11 Oct 1928). Countertenor and teacher. He was educated at the Juilliard School of Music (diploma 1951). Oberlin was a founding member in 1952 of the NEW YORK PRO MUSICA ANTIQUA with Noah Greenberg, and also appeared as a countertenor with numerous opera companies, orchestras, and ensembles, and in theatrical productions. He performed extensively in concert, recital, opera, and oratorio with many of America's foremost musical organizations. Oberlin is widely recognized by many critics as the leading countertenor of his time. He has been appreciated for his rare vocal quality, fluent technique, sensitive musicianship, and mastery of style. Admired also for his virile, sweet tone and subtle phrasing, he was a leading exponent of early music, and through his many recordings and appearances helped to popularize not only music at that time unknown but also the repertory of the countertenor voice. He has researched and offered commentary on the countertenor voice, distinguishing it from falsetto approaches. In 1961 he sang Oberon in the first Covent Garden production, and the US premiere in San Francisco, of Britten's *A Midsummer Night's Dream*. In the mid-1960s Oberlin retired from active singing and turned to teaching: he appeared as lecturer and lecture-recitalist at colleges and universities throughout the United States and abroad. In 1971 he was appointed professor of music at Hunter College, CUNY, and director of the Hunter College Vocal Collegium, serving there until his retirement in 1994.

BIBLIOGRAPHY

C. Yiannoudes: *Russell Oberlin: his Life and his Voice* (diss., CUNY, 2006)

PATRICK J. SMITH/NICOLA BADOLATO

Oberlin College Conservatory of Music. A conservatory attached to a private college in Oberlin, Ohio, near Cleveland. The college was founded by Congregationalists in 1833. In 1837 a student named George N. Allen was designated instructor of sacred music. He later became a professor (1841–64), and in 1865 two of his students, John P. Morgan and George W. Steele, established a conservatory that became affiliated with the college the following year. It is the oldest continuously operating conservatory in the United States. Under the directorship (1871–1901) of Fenelon B. Rice, the conservatory attained a position of national prominence it still holds. The conservatory enrolls about 600 students and has a faculty of 88. The college awards, on recommendation from the conservatory, BM degrees in performance, composition, music history, historical performance, electronic and computer music, music theory, jazz studies, a double major in piano and vocal accompanying, and also a performance diploma. Nearly one-third of students are enrolled in a double-degree (BM/BA) program offered jointly with the College of Arts and Sciences. The MM in historical performance, MMT in music education, and artist diploma are offered at the graduate level. Combined BM/MM programs in opera theater, conducting, and historical performance also are offered. An electronic music studio, an organ center, a jazz center, and a vocal arts laboratory are among the available facilities. The conservatory sponsors a collegium musicum and owns more than 1500 instruments for student use. Its library holdings total over 172,000 books and scores and over 70,000 sound recordings.

BIBLIOGRAPHY

R.D. Skyrm: *Oberlin Conservatory: a Century of Musical Growth and Influence* (diss., U. of Southern California, 1962)

BRUCE CARR/KAREN L. WOLFF

Oboe. Double-reed instrument. Into the early 20th century, many oboists in the United States were European visitors or immigrants, and most instruments were imported (the latter situation still prevailed in the early 21st century). As either skill in reed-making or a reliable source of reeds is necessary to play the instrument, the oboe was less common in America than the flute and clarinet. In early references, it is sometimes difficult to be certain when an oboe was being played, as in the 18th century the term "hautboy" (oboe) often served for all musicians of a wind band, and even into the mid-19th century many woodwind players were double-handed. In the 20th century, a distinctive "American school" of oboe playing developed and flourished.

Instruments called "hautboy" and other shawms were heard on plantations in New England, Maryland, and Virginia in the 17th century, and missionaries to New Mexico used *chirimias* and *bajóns* to accompany the singing in church. The earliest US players of the new oboe (also called "hautboy") that developed in the mid-17th century were German or British immigrants. The Hermits of Wissahickon, a pietist group that settled near Philadelphia in 1694, played hautboy, among other instruments. Edward Enstone, who arrived in Boston in 1714, was by 1716 offering for sale "Haut-Boys" and "Reads for Haut-Boys." By the mid-18th century, the oboe was being used by both British and American regiments, and in church and concerts. The Regiment and Artillery Company of Philadelphia, commanded by Benjamin Franklin, paraded in 1756 with "Hautboys [a wind band] and Fifes in the Ranks." In the same year, Franklin was "entertained with good music," by an ensemble including oboes at the Moravian church in Bethlehem. Instruments, reeds, and instruction books were advertised for sale and lessons offered in Philadelphia, New York, Boston, Baltimore, Charleston, and elsewhere.

Boston Concerts of the 1770s used military musicians, especially of the 64th Regiment; Josiah Flagg's concert of 17 May 1771, included "vocal and instrumental musick accompanied by French horns, hautboys, etc." In Charleston in 1773 a band of "six violins, two hautboys and bassoon, with a hand-taber played excellently well." Concerts were heard there in the early 1780s during the occupation by British and German Regiments; at one of these, an oboist of the 3rd Regiment named Smith, "a particularly powerful performer," played a concerto by Johann Christian Fischer.

A few Native Americans also took up the oboe. In Carolina or Florida Native Americans were reported to have learned to play "Flute, Hautboy and Flagelet," taught by a traveling French dancing master in 1700. The oboe also was probably among the European instruments brought by Jesuit missionaries to California in the 18th century and played by Native musicians in worship services. A request list from the San Francisco Mission in 1806 included a pair of oboes.

By the turn of the 19th century, the clarinet had overtaken the oboe in popularity. The best-known oboist was GOTTLIEB GRAUPNER (1767–1836), who arrived in the United States in 1795. He first played in the City Theatre Orchestra in Charleston, but by early 1797 he had moved to Boston, where (among other musical activities) he frequently appeared as an oboe soloist. Graupner also offered lessons and sold "Tipt Italian Hautboys with silver keys," as well as reeds and reed cases.

Oboists were among the many foreign musicians who visited or immigrated to the United States in the 19th century. Peter Gilles Sr. was active in Philadelphia and his son Henri-Noël (1778–1834) in Baltimore. Signor Paggi (1806–87), "Professor of the Oboe and English Horn," arrived in the orchestra of an Italian opera company in 1832, made a career as a soloist and teacher, and departed in 1843. In the 1840s and 50s, oboe soloists included Ferdinand Wiese, an early member of the Philharmonic Society of New York, and Antoine-Joseph Lavigne (1816–86), who toured with Louis Jullien's orchestra in 1853–4. The most frequently heard soloist was Antonio Lorenzo Ribas, who arrived in 1839. He appeared in New York, Philadelphia, and Boston, usually playing fantasias of his own composition based on operas or popular songs. Like Paggi, he also played english horn. Ribas was still active in 1867, when he performed Robert Schumann's *Drei Romanzen* at a Boston concert. But there were not enough competent players to staff the many theater and concert orchestras then active; the parts were assigned to other instruments or played by non-specialists, or sometimes simply omitted.

Many oboists (and musicians in general) in 19th-century America were Germans or of German origin, and one such was George Meinberg, "an artist of rare skill" brought from Berlin in 1871 by Carl Wolffson to perform in his orchestra in Philadelphia. Joseph Eller, active from *c*1865 until the end of the century, was a member of Theodore Thomas's orchestra and the New

York Philharmonic Society, soloist with Gilmore's ensemble, a frequent chamber music performer, and teacher at the New York College of Music. In 1885, Thomas dismissed Eller from his orchestra and replaced him with a Paris-trained Belgian, Felix Joseph Bour. The Musicians Mutual Protective Union sought to prevent the newly imported oboist from playing; legal action followed, and Thomas prevailed. The considerable newspaper commentary surrounding this case reveals that the oboe's sound was a matter of controversy, and suggests that American audiences in the East Coast cities had developed—some years before the advent of the "American school"—a preference for a full sound that blended well with the other woodwinds, as opposed to the thinner, more distinctive sound of the French-trained player.

The French sound gained favor, and by the end of the century many Belgian and French woodwind players had joined American orchestras. At least 15 students of the oboist Georges Gillet at the Paris Conservatory took positions in America, among them Georges Longy, who joined the Boston Symphony in 1898; Alfred Barthel (Chicago Symphony, 1903–29), Fernand Gillet (Boston Symphony, 1925–46); and Marcel Tabuteau (Philadelphia Orchestra, 1915–54). Henri de Busscher (1880–1975), a Belgian, was recruited for the New York Philharmonic by Walter Damrosch in 1915 and played there until joining the Los Angeles Philharmonic in 1920. He was solo oboe in the Columbia Pictures Studio Orchestra, 1948–56. There were also Italians such as Caesar Addimando and Bruno Labate, both active in New York in the early 20th century; Addimando moved to San Francisco in 1914.

Gillet's students played oboes by the firm of F. Lorée, Paris, and these became ubiquitous among American professional players. The most influential Gillet student in the United States was MARCEL TABUTEAU (1887–1966). His attention to detail, his focus on tone color and breath control, and his experiments with reeds and oboes (working both with Lorée and the respected technician Hans Moennig of Philadelphia) raised his playing to a high level and allowed him to produce a large, warm sound able to blend with the other wind players of the Philadelphia Orchestra—a style of playing known as the "American school." To meet his requirements, he developed a new style of reed, known as the "long scrape" or "American scrape": reeds are not evenly tapered from back to tip, but have a pronounced heart, a visible spine that runs the length of the reed, and an inverted V that defines the structure between the heart and the tip. Tabuteau trained several generations of students by rigorous methods, many during his tenure at the Curtis Institute, 1924–46.

Important performers of the 20th century have included Robert Bloom (1908–94); Harold Gomberg (1916–85), principal oboe of the New York PO 1943–77; his brother Ralph Gomberg (1921–2006), principal oboe of the Boston Symphony 1950–87; Ray Still (b 1920), principal oboe of the Chicago Symphony Orchestra 1954–93; John de Lancie (1921–2002), principal oboe of the Philadelphia Orchestra 1954–77 and teacher

at the Curtis Institute; John Mack (1927–2006), principal oboe of the Cleveland Orchestra 1965–2001 and a noted teacher; Ronald Roseman (1933–2000), also a composer; Thomas Stacy (b 1938), english hornist for the New York Philharmonic; and Richard Woodhams (b 1949), principal oboe of the Philadelphia Orchestra from 1977 and teacher at the Curtis Institute. By the early 21st century, oboe playing in the United States had become more varied and international, a trend exemplified by the appointment of Eugene Izotov as principal oboe of the Chicago Symphony in 2005 (trained in Russia and with Ralph Gomberg) and of Laing Wang as principal oboe of the New York PO in 2006 (trained in China and at the Curtis Institute).

Women first gained access to major professional orchestras in the United States in the late 1930s. Lois Wann was one of the first women to join an oboe section; after a stint in the New York Women's Symphony, she played in the San Diego and Pittsburgh Orchestras and went on to teach at the Juilliard School. Laila Storch, who persisted in pursuing lessons with Tabuteau after being initially rejected by the Curtis Institute due to her gender, was in 1945 the Institute's first female graduate. Other prominent women include Elaine Douvas, Principal of the Metropolitan Opera Orchestra since 1977, Kathryn Greenbank, Principal with the St. Paul Chamber Orchestra since 1982, and Katherine Needleman, Principal of the Baltimore Symphony since 2003.

The oboe has also been heard in jazz, fusion, and popular music, although never prominently; players have included Garvin Bushell (with John Coltrane), Mitch Miller, Yusef Lateef (with Cannonball Adderley), Bob Cooper (with Stan Kenton), Marshall Allen (with Sun Ra), Joe Farrell (born Joseph Carl Firrantello; with Chick Corea, and Hall and Oates), Dick Hafer (with Charlie Mingus), Paul McCandless (Oregon, the Paul Winter Consort). William Criss (1921–84) was heard in many film scores. Oboe players in North America became interested in period instruments after the mid-20th century: early players were Josef Marx, James Caldwell (whose Oberlin Baroque Performance Institute, founded in 1972, gave many players their first taste of the instrument), and Bruce Haynes. Other prominent players have included Stephen Hammer and Geoffrey Burgess.

From the 20th century, American composers wrote frequently for the oboe. Notable concertos have been written by Lukas Foss, John Corigliano, Elliott Carter, Ellen Taaffe Zwilich, Michael Daugherty, Ned Rorem (english horn concerto), and Eric Ewazen. Sonatas and chamber works have been composed by Walter Piston, Henry Cowell, William Grant Still, Ned Rorem, Samuel Barber, Ronald Roseman, Vincent Persichetti, Daniel Pinkham, Joan Tower, Katherine Hoover, and Daniel Asia, among others.

Oboe makers in the United States have been few, most instruments being imported. The earliest known maker was David (Gottlieb?) Wolhaupter (fl New York 1761–75). Other early makers were Jacob Anthony Sr. and Jr. of Philadelphia (active 1764–1811) and Isaac Greenwood of Boston and Salem (active 1773–81).

Makers active around Hartford, CT, in the early 19th century were Meacham (*fl* 1806–32) in Hartford and Albany, and Uzal Miner (*fl* Hartford 1807–15). George Catlin, active in Hartford and Philadelphia, 1799–1850, advertised that he made instruments of all kinds including hautboys, "30% cheaper than imported." Other 19th-century makers were William Callender (Boston, *fl* 1796–1825); Charles G. Christman (*fl* New York, 1823–58); Henry H. Prentiss (1801–*c*1860, *fl* Boston 1830–60); William Rönnberg (1803–*c*1889, *fl* New York 1834–89); Edward Baack (1809–93, *fl* New York 1837–72); Thomas J. Weygandt (1800–1874, *fl* Philadelphia, *c*1832–74); Theodore Berteling (1821/22–90, *fl* Boston and New York, 1848–89; the firm continued after his death); and Franz Lauter (*fl* New York 1845–85).

Professional instruments have been made in the 20th and 21st centuries by A. Läubin, founded by Alfred Laubin (1906–1976)—the firm's instruments have been favored by many American players; Fox, which began manufacturing oboes in 1974; Paul Covey, founded in 1970 by Paul Marshall Covey (1947–2008) and since carried on as Covey and Ramsay; and Thomas Hiniker (*b* 1963), who has made both oboes and bocals. Instruments for the student and amateur market have been made by firms including C.G. Conn, Linton, Selmer, MCW (Mark Chudnow Woodwinds), and Fox. Although never very popular, Boehm-system oboes were known in the United States. Lavigne had played one, and such instruments were later made by Berteling (advertised 1893–5) and Conn (*c*1900). They were also imported, and gained use in American military and jazz bands in the early 20th century. Period oboes have been made in the United States by Harry vas Dias, Bosworth & Hammer, and Sand Dalton, among others.

BIBLIOGRAPHY

Waterhouse-Langwill I; *Grove7* (J.K. Page)

F.L. Ritter: *Music in America* (1890; with new intro. by J. Riedel, New York, 1970)

H.E. Krehbiel: *The Philharmonic Society of New York: a Memorial* (New York, 1892; repr. in *Early Histories of the New York Philharmonic*, with intro. by H. Shanet, New York, 1979)

R.R. Drummond: *Early German Music in Philadelphia* (New York, 1910/*R*)

L. Ellinwood and K. Porter: *Bio-bibliographical Index of Musicians in the United States since Colonial Times* (Washington, DC, 1956/*R*)

H.E. Johnson: *Musical Interludes in Boston, 1695–1830* (New York, 1967)

R.F. Camus: *Military Music of the American Revolution* (Westerville, OH, 1975)

B. Lambert: "Social Music, Musicians, and Their Musical Instruments in and around Colonial Boston," *Music in Colonial Massachusetts, 1630–1820: a Conference held by the Colonial Society of Massachusetts, May 17 and 18, 1973* (Boston, MA, 1975), 409–514

R.E. Eliason: "Oboe, Bassoons, and Bass Clarinets, Made by Hartford, Connecticut, Makers before 1815," *GSJ*, xxx (1977), 43–51

D.A. Ledet: *Oboe Reed Styles: Theory and Practice* (Bloomington, IN, 1981)

R.L. Davis: *A History of Music in American Life* (Malabar, FL, 1982)

G.A. Conrey: "Story of a Great Oboist: Alfred Charles Barthel (1871–1957)," *Journal of the International Double Reed Society*, vi/4 (1983), 18–31

D.L. Hefner: *The Tradition of the Paris Conservatory School of Oboe Playing with Special Attention to the Influence of Marcel Tabuteau* (diss., Catholic U. of America, 1984)

R. Howe: "Historical Oboes," *The Double Reed*, xxiii/4 (2000), 21–8

G. Burgess and B. Haynes: *The Oboe* (New Haven, CT, 2004)

G. Burgess: *The Oboe on Record, 1903–1953*, Oboe Classics CC2012 (2005)

L. Storch: *Marcel Tabuteau: how Do You Expect to Play the Oboe If You Can't Peel a Mushroom?* (Bloomington, IN, 2008)

D. Lasocki: "New Light on the Recorder and Flageolet in Colonial North America and The United States, 1700–1840, from Newspaper Advertisements," *JAMIS*, xxxv (2009), 5–80

Annotated Checklist of Oboes and Related Instruments, National Music Museum, University of South Dakota, <http://orgs.usd.edu/nmm/Oboes.html> [online database]

JANET K. PAGE AND MICHELLE VIGNEAU

O'Brien, Eugene (*b* Paterson, NJ, 24 April 1945). Composer. He studied with Robert Beadell at the University of Nebraska (BM 1967, MM 1969), with Bernd Alois Zimmermann at the Staatliche Hochschule für Musik in Cologne on a Fulbright scholarship (1969), and with JOHN C. EATON and Iannis Xenakis at Indiana University (1970–71). In 1971 he won the Rome Prize for the *Elegy for Bernd Alois Zimmermann*. He joined the faculty of the Cleveland Institute in 1973, then moved on to Indiana University, where he is professor and associate dean. O'Brien's music is frequently pictorial and suggestive, with titles that often reflect the emotions prompting his work (e.g., *Embarking for Cythera*). His use of electronics is idiomatic rather than imitative, and a sparing use of aleatory procedures in such works as *Allures* lends an improvisatory dimension to his style.

WORKS
(selective list)

Orch: sym., 1969; 2 concs., vc, perc, 1967–71, 1983; Rites of Passage, 1978; conc., sax, orch, 1993; The Clouds of Magellan, 1996; 3 early works, withdrawn

Chamber: Ambages, pf 4 hands, 1972; Intessitura, vc, pf, 1975; Tristan's Lament, vc, 1977–9; Embarking for Cythera, chamber ens, 1978; Allures, perc, 1979; Fancies and Goodnights, chamber ens, 1981; Black Fugatos, chamber ens, 1983; Taking Measures, vn, 1984; Mysteries of the Horizon, chamb ens, 1987 [in memory of Paul Fromm]; Fancies and Goodnights, fl, cl, db, 1994; many early inst works, withdrawn

Instrumental: Close Harmony, 2 pfs, 4 hands, 1986; Rhyme and Reason, mar, 2002 (commissioned by Percussive Arts Society)

Vocal: Elegy for Bernd Alois Zimmermann (Pss.), S, chbr ens, 1970; Lingual, S, fl, vc, 1972; Dédales (Michelangelo, O. N. Yakamochi), S, orch, 1973; Dreams and Secrets of Origin (P. Neruda), S, chbr ens, 1982; *c*20 early vocal works, withdrawn

Principal publisher: Boosey & Hawkes

BIBLIOGRAPHY

"Eugene O'Brien: Winner of the Prix de Rome," *Your Musical Cue*, vii/7 (1971), 17

W. Salisbury: "Coup for Composer," *Cleveland Plain Dealer* (6 April 1980)

M. Evett: "Sounds of the City," *Live*, v/3 (1984), 63

MICHAEL MECKNA

O'Brien, Paddy (*b* Castlebarnagh, Daingean, Co. Offaly, Ireland, 13 Sept 1945). Accordion player of Irish birth. One of today's most celebrated and respected Irish American musicians, Paddy O'Brien is known for having an enormous personal repertoire, estimated to be close to 4000 tunes, learned strictly via oral tradition. He has recorded 1000 of these pieces on two volumes (500 tunes each) of *The Paddy O'Brien Tune Collection* (1995 and 2011), consisting of multiple CDs and extensive annotation.

Born in County Offaly, O'Brien spent much time in his youth learning from older musicians throughout Ireland. He played with several noted ensembles, including the Castle Céilí Band (1969–78) and Ceoltoiri Laighean (1971–8), and won many musical competitions. In 1978 he immigrated to the United States, where he toured and recorded with fiddler James Kelly and guitarist Dáithí Sproule. Since that time he has performed and recorded both as a solo artist and as leader of various ensembles, including Chulrua, The Doon Céilí Band, and O'Rourke's Feast. O'Brien has been the recipient of numerous grants and artist fellowships, and has taught at major Irish music summer schools in the United States and Ireland.

O'Brien is sometimes confused with another Paddy O'Brien (1922–91), from County Tipperary, who was highly influential as both an accordion player and composer. The older musician lived in New York City from 1954–62 but spent most of his life in Ireland.

RECORDINGS
(selective)
Traditional Music of Ireland (with J. Kelly and D. Sproule) (1995, Shanachie 34014) [CD reissue of two LPs recorded in 1978 and 1982]; Chulrua, *Down the Back Lane* (2003, Shanachie 22001); Chulrua, *The Singing Kettle* (2007, Shanachie 23002); *The Sailor's Cravat* (2011, New Folk Records WCM0001); *Mixing the Punch* (2011, New Folk Records WCM0003)

PAUL F. WELLS

Ochs, Michael (*b* Cologne, Germany, 1 Feb 1937). Music librarian, musicologist, and editor of German birth. Ochs immigrated to the United States in September 1939. He graduated from City College of New York (BA 1958), then earned degrees at Columbia University (MS in library service, 1963), New York University (MA in musicology, 1964), where he studied under Gustave Reese, and Simmons College (DA in library administration, 1975). After serving as creative arts librarian at Brandeis University (1965–74), he taught library science at Simmons (1974–8), where he introduced the college's first course in music librarianship. In 1978 he was appointed music librarian and lecturer on music at Harvard University, where he supervised the establishment of the US RISM office and directed the computerization of the music library's vast catalog. In 1988, Ochs became Richard F. French Librarian, the first endowed chair in music librarianship. He moved back to New York to become music editor at W.W. Norton publishers (1992–2002), where he edited two Pulitzer Prize finalists and other books that won major awards. Ochs chaired various committees of the Music Library Association between 1971 and 1987, edited the Association's journal, *Notes* (1987–92), and served as president (1993–5). In 2002 he established the Michael Ochs Endowment for *Notes*.

WRITINGS
(selected)
"A Taxonomy of Qualifications for Music Librarianship: the Cognitive Domain," *Notes* xxxiii/1 (1976), 27–44
"Qualifications for Music Librarianship in the U.S.A.," *FAM*, xxv (1978), 64–9
"Musical Americana in Harvard Libraries," *Harvard Library Bulletin*, xxxi (1984), 408–26
ed.: *Music Librarianship in America* (Cambridge, MA, 1991)
"In Eitner's Footsteps," *Notes*, xlviii (1992), 1216–24
"'L.m.i.A.': Mozart's Suppressed Canon Texts," *Mozart-Jahrbuch 1991* (Kassel, 1992), 254–61
"What Music Scholars Should Know about Publishers," *Notes*, lix (2002), 288–300
"You Say 'Sabachthani' and I Say 'Asabthani': a St. Matthew Passion Puzzle," *About Bach*, ed. G. Butler and others (Urbana, IL, 2008), 61–7

RUTHANN B. McTYRE

Ochs, Phil(ip David) (*b* El Paso, TX, 19 Dec 1940; *d* Far Rockaway, NY, 9 April 1976). Singer, songwriter, and political activist. Ochs grew up in a somewhat conservative middle-class home, but became active in radical leftist politics while at Ohio State University, where he studied journalism. After being introduced there to the protest songs of Woody Guthrie and Pete Seeger, Ochs took up acoustic guitar and folk singing, and performed in the folk duo The Sundowners (originally called The Singing Socialists) as an outlet for political commentary. He dropped out in 1962 and joined the folk scene in New York City's Greenwich Village, where he crossed paths with Bob Dylan, an important influence. Like Dylan at the time, Ochs specialized in the political topic song, and after Dylan left the genre, Ochs became its leading proponent. He was a sincere activist, and is most remembered for the songs of this time. They were alternately lamenting ("Too Many Martyrs," 1964), defiant ("I Ain't Marching Anymore" and "Draft Dodger Rag," 1965), narrative ("The Highwayman," 1965), satirical ("Love Me, I'm a Liberal," 1966), and often a mix of these qualities.

In his three albums for Elektra, Ochs used only acoustic guitar and voice, the expected instrumentation of a folk troubadour at the time. When he moved in 1967 to A&M Records and embraced more intricate studio production and arrangement, it was not only a musical break from the past, but also a reshaping of his identity into a folk-rock musician. While the political lampooning continued ("Outside of a Small Circle of Friends," 1967), he increasingly wrote personal songs as well, such as "Crucifixion." His last two studio albums were musically more intricate and adventurous than in the mid-60s heyday, but less commercially successful. Ochs continued performing in the last years of his life but also struggled increasingly with depression, alcohol, and drugs. In 1976 he took his own life.

BIBLIOGRAPHY
J.L. Rodnitzky: *Minstrels of the Dawn: the Folk-Protest Singer as a Cultural Hero* (Chicago, 1976)
M. Schumacher: *There but for Fortune: the Life of Phil Ochs* (New York, 1996)
D. Cohen: *Phil Ochs: a Bio-Bibliography* (Westport, CT, 1999)

MARK C. SAMPLES

O'Connor, Donald (*b* Chicago, 28 Aug 1925; *d* Calabasas, CA, 27 Sept 2003). Dancer, singer, and actor. Born into a theatrical family, he had a lengthy career in musical theater, spanning all forms from vaudeville to television, but was noted particularly for his performances in movie musicals. A talented tap dancer, singer, and comedian, he made his film debut at age 12 with his brothers in *Melody for Two* (1937), which led to a co-starring role in *Sing, You Sinners* (1938), and several youth-oriented pictures at Paramount. During the 1940s he made a number of low-budget musicals at Universal and, after wartime military service, the first of six memorable movies opposite Francis the talking mule. His best movie role was as Cosmo Brown in MGM's *Singin' in the Rain* (1952), dancing and singing in thrilling tap duets with Gene Kelly in "Fit as a Fiddle" and "Moses Supposes" and in the hilarious solo turn in "Make 'Em Laugh." His later movies include *I Love Melvin* (1953), *Call Me Madam* (1953), *There's No Business Like Show Business* (1954), *Anything Goes* (1956), and *The Buster Keaton Story* (1957). Hesitant to name a favorite film, he admitted that his favorite number was in *Call Me Madam*, in which he danced in a garden with Vera-Ellen to Irving Berlin's "It's a Lovely Day Today," a lyrical dance that shows the two fresh-faced performers at their elegant, lighthearted best.

BIBLIOGRAPHY

J. Kobal: *Gotta Sing, Gotta Dance: a Pictorial History of Film Musicals* (London, 1971)

T. Thomas: *That's Dancing!* (New York, 1984)

R.E. Frank: *Tap! The Greatest Tap Dance Stars and their Stories, 1900–1955* (New York, rev. 1994)

C.V. Hill: *Tap Dancing America: a Cultural History* (New York, 2010)

CLAUDE CONYERS

O'Connor, Mark   (*b* Seattle, WA, 5 Aug 1961). Multi-instrumentalist, composer, and educator. A teenaged multi-instrument prodigy in country and bluegrass styles, he won the National Junior Fiddle Championships (1974–7), the Grand Masters Fiddle Championship (1975), the National Flatpick Guitar Championship (1975), and the National Mandolin Championship (1979). His early mentor was noted Texas-style fiddler BENNY THOMASSON, and he later studied with jazz violinist Stephane Grappelli.

In 1980 O'Connor joined the David Grisman Quintet as guitarist, absorbing Grisman's progressive blend of bluegrass and swing-era "hot club" jazz. Two years later he became violinist in The Dregs (formerly The Dixie Dregs), a jazz-rock fusion band. O'Connor's early solo recordings, such as *On the Rampage* (Rounder, 1980) and *Meanings of* (Warner Bros., 1985), showcase his virtuosity on guitar and violin and demonstrate the influence of Grisman and the Dregs. Since 1982 O'Connor has worked extensively as a session musician, recording with numerous bluegrass, country, and pop artists.

In the 1990s O'Connor began to collaborate with broad-minded classical musicians and to compose concert pieces that incorporate many of his eclectic stylistic interests. Critical acclaim for O'Connor's *The Fiddle Concerto* (1992), his first orchestral score, led to other works, including *Appalachia Waltz* (1993; arranged and released on a CD of that title with Yo-Yo Ma and Edgar Meyer in 1996), a Double Violin Concerto (2008), three string quartets, and the *Americana Symphony* (2009). In these works O'Connor blends Coplandesque American pastoralism with his own deep knowledge of country, bluegrass, and jazz idioms. O'Connor's work as an educator began with the opening of his String Camp in the summer of 1994, and in 2009 he began publishing a series of method books for orchestral string instruments, combining classical techniques with traditional American musical repertoire.

BIBLIOGRAPHY

B. Smith: "Mark O'Connor: Winning it All by 14 (Grand Master's Fiddling Championship)," *Bluegrass Unlimited*, x (1976), 34–40

M.L. Small: "Dual Virtuoso: the Multi-Instrumental Mastery of Mark O'Connor, the Paganini of Nashville," *Acoustic Guitar*, iii (1993), 62–70

C. DeWitt: "Mark O'Connor: Blurring the Boundaries," *Sing Out*, xlix/2 (2005), 18–23

R. Maxham: "Mark O'Connor's Distinctively American Journey," *Fanfare*, xxxii/5 (2009), 34–42

GREGORY N. REISH

O'Day [Colton], **Anita (Belle)**   (*b* Chicago, IL, 18 Oct 1919; *d* Los Angeles, CA, 23 Nov 2006). Jazz singer. She began to appear in show business as a dancer on the endurance dance contest circuit, where she was occasionally invited to sing. At age 18 she became determined to become a professional singer. While working her way through numerous Chicago venues, she was seen at the Off Beat club by Gene Krupa, who hired her to sing with his band. The result for O'Day was almost instant success; not only did her recording of the song "Let me off Uptown" (1941, OK) become a huge hit, but she was also named New Star of the Year by *Downbeat*. Together with Krupa, O'Day recorded 34 songs plus two film shorts. She stayed with him until his group was disbanded in 1943 and returned to sing with him again in 1946. In the meantime she worked with Stan Kenton, recording a number of sides including "And her Tears Flowed like Wine" (1944). Although she struggled to match her success of the late 1940s, starting with *Anita O'Day Sings Jazz* (1952) her solo albums, for Norgran and Verve, were wildly popular, with her generally percussive vocal style matched with powerful support. She recorded an album almost every year until 1979 and continued performing regularly. Several live recordings were released in the 1990s, and her last studio album, *Indestructible!*, appeared in 2006. A documentary about her career, *Anita O'Day: Life of a Jazz Singer* (2007), received critical acclaim and a Grammy nomination.

WRITINGS

High Times, Hard Times (New York, 1981/*R*)

JONAS WESTOVER

O'Day, Molly [Williamson, LaVerne]   (*b* McVeigh, KY, 9 July 1923; *d* Huntington, WV, 5 Dec 1987). Country music singer, banjoist, and guitarist. She was considered by many to be the greatest female country music singer of her time. She began her radio career in 1939 while playing in a family string band with brothers

Skeets and Duke. She used the stage names Mountain Fern, Dixie Lee, and then (from 1942) Molly O'Day. In 1941 she married singer Lynn Davis, and for most of the 1940s the couple moved from one radio station to another. In 1945 publisher Fred Rose heard O'Day sing the gospel song "Tramp on the Street" in Knoxville and arranged a contract for her with Columbia Records. She recorded it along with a new song by Hank Williams, "Six More Miles to the Graveyard," at her first session (16 December 1946). Between 1946 and 1952 she made three dozen recordings, ranging from the traditional murder ballad "Poor Ellen Smith" (1949) to the apocalyptic gospel favorite "Matthew Twenty Four" (1948). By 1950, though, the Davises had abandoned secular music in favor of preaching and gospel music. They entered the ministry and settled in Huntington, West Virginia, where Lynn Davis pastored churches and established a long-term radio ministry over WEMM radio, broadcasting daily from a studio in their home. Molly O'Day was inducted posthumously into the West Virginia Music Hall of Fame in 2007. At a time when country music was becoming increasingly pop-oriented, Molly O'Day's short career in secular country music reasserted the vitality of the distinctive mountain singing style and helped to show that women could perform serious lyrical and emotional material with conviction.

CHARLES K. WOLFE/JOHN LILLY

Ode. By the late 19th century in America, the term ode became nearly synonymous with its counterpart, the CANTATA. As large multi-movement secular works for chorus, soloists, and orchestra, the texts to these odes were lengthy poems with many verses, accommodating both solos and choruses. Allusions to Greek and Roman classical poetic forms, salutations, and commendations were often imitated and included. These odes were often commissioned for important occasions, such as the Bicentennial in Philadelphia in 1876 (*The Centennial Meditation of Columbia* with text by Sidney Lanier and music by Dudley Buck), the Chicago World's Fair of 1893 (Amy Beach's *Festival Jubilate*, op.17, and George W. Chadwick's *Ode for the Opening of the Chicago World's Fair*—a partial setting of the 400-line poem by Harriet Moore for the occasion), and the bicentennial of the founding of Yale University in 1901 (Horatio Parker's *Hymnos Andron*) and Edward Burlingame Hill's *Ode* (for the Boston Symphony Orchestra's 50th Anniversary). Other odes include Parker's *Ode for the Commencement Day at Yale University* (1895) and *Spirit of Beauty* (1905) for the dedication of an art gallery, George Frederick Bristow's *The Great Republic: Ode to the American Union*, op.47 and *The Pioneer*, op.49 and John Knowles Paine's *Song of Promise* (1888). On a much smaller level the term "ode" was applied to the hymns and songs for groups such as the Freemasons, the Odd Fellows, and the Daughters of the American Revolution. In the political sphere, the ode was also used in conjunction with the ballad, glee, and song for 19th-century American political parties and presidential campaigns.

BIBLIOGRAPHY
R.L. Davis: *A History of Music in American Life*, ii (Huntington, NY, 1980)
B.A. Tischler: *An American Music: the Search for an American Musical Identity* (New York, 1986)
W. Miles: *Songs, Odes, Glees, and Ballads: a Bibliography of American Presidential Campaign Songsters* (New York, 1990)
D. Shrock: *Choral Repertoire* (New York, 2009)

CHARLES JURGENSMEIER

Odell. Organ building firm. It was founded in New York as J.H. & C.S. Odell in 1859 by brothers John Henry Odell (1830–99) and Caleb Sherwood Odell (1827–92), who had previously worked for Ferris & Stuart and William Robjohn. They succeeded the latter, who, along with his brother Thomas, subsequently worked for the Odells as voicers. Although not the largest organ building firm in New York, their factory on 42nd Street was turning out an average of 10 to 12 organs annually by the 1870s. Many of their organs were installed in New York and vicinity, including that in Fifth Avenue Presbyterian Church (1893), but a substantial organ was built in 1876 for the Fort Street Presbyterian Church of Detroit, and another went in 1881 to the Music Hall in Troy, New York. After the deaths of the founders, John Henry's son George Washington Odell became President of the firm, and significant organs built under his direction included those for Temple Emanu-El in New York (1901) and St. Joseph's Church, Albany (1912). He is also credited with some improvements in the firm's electro-pneumatic actions. He was eventually succeeded by Caleb's grandson, Caleb Herbert Odell (1879–1944), then his son, William H. Odell (1909–79); other members of the Odell family were also connected with the company at various times. In 1928 the firm relocated to a new factory in suburban Mount Vernon, but after the market crash of the following year, production was never restored to its previous amount and the firm henceforth survived largely by doing rebuilding and maintenance. It remained a family-owned business, and while its major assets were sold in 1983, family members retained rights to the company name and continued to do minor maintenance work. Edward Odell, a descendant of Caleb S. Odell, had worked for various relatives in his youth, and title to J.H. & C.S. Odell & Co. eventually fell to him, although he was then working for the Austin Organ Co. in Hartford. In 2002 he left Austin to reestablish the family firm with a modern workshop in East Hampton, Connecticut, engaged in rebuilding, restoration, and construction of new organs.

BIBLIOGRAPHY
"American Organ Builders of Today: J. H. & C. S. Odell & Co.," *The Diapason*, xvi/9 (1926), 36
J. Ogasapian: *Organ Building in New York City, 1700–1900* (Braintree, MA, 1977)
F.R. Webber: "A Century of Odell Organs." *The Tracker*, xxvi/4 (1981–82), 8–13

BARBARA OWEN

Odetta [Gordon, Odetta Felious Holmes; Holmes, Odetta] (*b* Birmingham, AL, 31 Dec 1930; *d* New York, NY, 2 Dec

2008). Singer, guitarist, and activist. Described by Dr. Martin Luther King, Jr., as the "Voice of the Civil Rights Movement," she initially came to fame while working the coffee houses and nightclubs of the West coast arm of the folk revival of the late 1950s and early 60s. Although she trained during her early years for a career in opera, she came to love the folk music and song traditions of America's various ethnic groups while living and working between Los Angeles and San Francisco. She borrowed a guitar and began developing a repertory of folk songs that extended from spirituals to ballads and the blues. While working at the Tin Angel in San Francisco, she developed such a following that the club's owner Peggy Tolk-Watkins suggested that she purchase her own guitar and shorten her name to Odetta. She eventually made her way to New York, where she became entrenched in the urban folk song movement of the early 1960s. Unlike many of her contemporaries Odetta did not write her own original songs, but chose to create her own interpretations of traditional material. These performances were chronicled in a number of landmark albums including *Odetta Sings Ballads and Blues* (1956), which Bob Dylan credited with influencing his decision to sing folk music, *At the Gate of Horn* (1957), and *Ballad for Americans and Other American Ballads* (1960), which was the first of several albums augmented with guitar, bass, and a number of different choral groups. Odetta's performances stretched the definition of folk music during the 1960s and her deep and resonant voice was accented by her rhythmic guitar playing. She lent her celebrity and voice to the Civil Rights Movement and was one of a few women musicians to perform at the historic March on Washington in 1963. Songs such as "I'm On My Way," "Oh Freedom," and "Sometimes I Feel Like a Motherless Child" served as part of her core repertory during this period. Her natural hairstyle foreshadowed the emerging consciousness that by the mid-1960s would coincide with the rise of Black Nationalism. Even as the popularity of folk music waned, Odetta continued to maintain her popularity. In her later years she lent her voice to domestic and global social causes and in 1999 was awarded the National Endowment of the Arts' National Medal of Arts by President Clinton. She was hoping to sing for the inauguration of Barack Obama, but died of heart disease before the date.

BIBLIOGRAPHY

J.S. Wilson: "Odetta: Folksinger Who Survived the Rock Years," *New York Times* (13 Jan 1981)

R. Lankford: *Folk Music USA: the Changing Voice of Protest* (New York, 2005)

L. Barnett: *I Got Thunder: Black Women Songwriters on their Craft* (New York, 2007)

M. Weil and A. Bernstein: "Odetta: Matriarch for Generation of Folk Singers," *Washington Post* (4 Dec 2008), B06

TAMMY L. KERNODLE

O'Dette, Paul (Raymond) (*b* Pittsburgh, PA, 2 Feb 1954). Lutenist, conductor, and musicologist. Initially a guitarist, O'Dette began playing the lute while in high school in Columbus, Ohio. He then studied with Thomas Binkley at the Schola Cantorum Basiliensis, an early music conservatory in Basel, Switzerland, from 1973–6. O'Dette has made more than 100 recordings as a soloist, accompanist, and conductor. The five-volume *Dowland: Complete Lute Works* (1995–7) is his best-known recording as a solo lutenist; other notable solo recordings are the Grammy-nominated *Daniel Bacheler: The Bachelar's Delight* (2006), *Johann Sebastian Bach: Lute Works, vol. 1* (2007), and *Marco dall'Aquila: Pieces for Lute* (2010). As an accompanist and ensemble member, O'Dette has performed on a variety of instruments. He plays the archlute on Sylvia McNair's Grammy-winning *The Echoing Air* with Christopher Hogwood and the Academy of Ancient Music (1995), the baroque guitar on *¡Jácaras!* (1998), and the theorbo on *Italian Baroque Trumpet Music* with Peter Holman and the Parley of Instruments (1988). In his capacity as artistic director of the Boston Early Music Festival, O'Dette has edited scores and conducted performances of several operas, including Mattheson's *Boris Goudenow*, Conradi's *Ariadne*, and Lully's *Thésée* and *Psyché* (recordings of the latter three operas were nominated for Grammys). He has written articles on Renaissance and 17th century music and coauthored the *New Grove* entry on John Dowland. O'Dette has taught at the Eastman School of Music since 1976.

BIBLIOGRAPHY

B. Duffie: "Lutenist Paul O'Dette: a Conversation with Bruce Duffie," <http://www.bruceduffie.com/odette2.html> (5 Oct 1993)

R. Couch: "Confronting an Original: a Conversation with Paul O'Dette," *Fanfare—The Magazine for Serious Record Collectors*, xxi/1 (1997), 30–40

J. Nelson: "Interview with Paul O'Dette, 6/25/08," *Lute Society of America Quarterly*, xliv/2 (2009), 24–29

LARS HELGERT

O'Farrill, Chico [Arturo] (*b* Havana, Cuba, 28 Oct 1921; *d* New York, NY, 27 June 2001). Cuban trumpeter, arranger, and composer, father of the pianist Arturo O'Farrill. He studied classical music with Felix Guerrero and STEFAN WOLPE, discovered jazz at the end of the 1930s, and played in Cuba with Isidro Perez and Armando Romeu. After moving to New York in 1948, he started working as an arranger for Benny Goodman (for whom he wrote the successful tune "Undercurrent Blues"), Stan Kenton, Count Basie, Art Farmer, and Machito. He also worked with Charlie Parker and Dizzy Gillespie on several key Afro-Cuban jazz classics recorded by Norman Granz. From 1957 to 1965 he lived in Mexico with his wife, the singer Lupe Valero, recording for Panart and Gema; he then returned to New York, where he worked for CBS television and wrote arrangements for pop tunes. In the 1970s he wrote scores for Kenton and Gato Barbieri as well as for an orchestra co-led by Machito and Gillespie. In his later years O'Farrill recorded for Verve and Milestone, led jazz big bands, and was commissioned by Wynton Marsalis to write a trumpet concerto. He remains well regarded as one of the most significant contributors to Cubop and Afro-Cuban jazz.

BIBLIOGRAPHY

B. Ratliff: Obituary, *New York Times* (29 June 2001)

L. Acosta: *Cubano be Cubano bop: One Hundred Years of Jazz in Cuba* (Washington, DC, 2003)

LUCA CERCHIARI

Offenbach, Jacques [Jacob] (*b* Cologne, Germany, 20 June 1819; *d* Paris, France, 5 Oct 1880). French composer of German origin. As one of the most successful composers of 19th-century comic opera, Offenbach was a primary influence on American musical comedy. He was also one of the most famous European musicians to visit the United States before 1900. Following bankruptcy in 1874, due to both poor business decisions and an extravagant lifestyle, Offenbach accepted an offer to perform in the United States during the Centennial year. He arrived in New York on 6 May 1876 and soon began a series of 30 concerts at the Hippodrome. Despite having a large and skilled orchestra, with John Philip Sousa as its concertmaster, Offenbach was initially not well received. Changes to the program—including the addition of Offenbach's *American Eagle Waltz*, newly composed for cornet virtuoso Jules Levy, and more appearances on the podium by Offenbach—improved the situation, as did productions of *La vie parisienne* and *La jolie parfumeuse*. Offenbach then went to Philadelphia to lead additional concerts and operettas before returning to France in July. His memoirs of this trip, published the following year, deal more with his impressions of life in the United States and less with music.

BIBLIOGRAPHY

GMO

J. Offenbach: *Orpheus in America: Offenbach's Diary of his Journey to the New World*, trans. L. MacClintock (Bloomington, IN, 1957)

SCOTT WARFIELD

Ogdon, Will [Wilbur Lee] (*b* Redlands, CA, 19 April 1921). Composer and arts administrator. After attending the University of Wisconsin, Madison (BM 1942), he studied with ERNST KRENEK at Hamline University, St. Paul (MA 1947), and with ROGER SESSIONS and Manfred Bukofzer at the University of California, Berkeley (1949–50). As a Fulbright scholar in 1952–3, he was a pupil of Honegger and René Leibowitz in Paris at the Ecole Normale de Musique. In 1955 he received a PhD in music theory from Indiana University, Bloomington, where he also studied musicology with Apel and Paul Nettl. He taught at the University of Texas, Austin (1947–50) and at Illinois Wesleyan University (1956–64). In 1965 he became Director of Music Programming at the University of Illinois, but left the next year when Krenek recommended him to administrator John Stewart at the University of California, San Diego. Ogdon became the founding Chair of the new music department at UCSD in 1966 and taught there until his retirement in 1991. He played a major role in bringing San Diego's program to national prominence, primarily due his belief in faculty-driven academic programming, and a focus on experimental new music. He led the recruitment of Pulitzer Prize–winning composer Roger Reynolds (1969) and was awarded an NEA grant in 1975. In addition to publishing more than two dozen works, he wrote (with Krenek and J. Stewart) a book on Krenek's music,

entitled *Horizons Circled* (1974), and has made important contributions to the study of early atonal music (published in the *Journal of the Arnold Schoenberg Institute*). Ogdon's music is known for its brevity; most of his works are less than ten minutes in length. He combines a liberal use of serial techniques with a refined sense of lyricism, drama, and comedy. His works are regularly performed by University of California, San Diego faculty members and by SONOR, the university's faculty and graduate student new music ensemble, which recorded a volume of his compositions in 1997.

WORKS

Dramatic: The Awakening of Sappho (chbr op, 4 episodes, Ogdon, after L. Durrell), 1976–80

Orch: Un tombeau de Jean Cocteau (I) (Cocteau), S, pf, 1964; By the Isar, S, afl, db, 1969; Un tombeau de Jean Cocteau (II) (Cocteau) S, pf, cl, chbr ens, 1972; Un tombeau de Jean Cocteau (III) (Cocteau), S, pf, ob, cl, nar, tape, slides, 1976; Five Comments and Capriccio, orch, 1979; Images, a Winter's Calendar, S, fl, cl, tpt, pf, 1980; Images of Spring and Summer, S, str qt, 1981

Vocal: Three Songs, Bar, pf, 1955; Two Kechwa Songs, S, pf, 1955; Three Sea Choruses, SATB, 1962; Four Tonal Songs, Bar, pf, 1988–90; Four Women's Choruses, 1990; Four D.H. Lawrence Songs, S, pf, 1991

Chbr: Three Trifles, vc, pf, 1957; Variations and Palindrome, str qt, 1962; Three Pieces, cl, pf, 1966; Five Pieces, vn, pf, 1982; Six Small Trios, xyl, mar, cimb, pf, tpt, 1982; Serenade no.1, ww qnt, 1986–7; Four Chbr Songs, S, fl, ob, cl, hp, va, vc, 1989; A Modern Fable, S, S, Bar, cl, bcl, perc, vn, vc, 1990; Serenade no.2, ww qnt, 1990–1; 13 Expressions, solo vn, fl, ob, cl, va, vc, pf, 1993; Nine Short Pieces and a Finale, str qt, 1995

Inst: Sonatina, pf, 1947; Three Pieces, pf, 1949; Five Preludes, vn, 1982; Two Capriccios, pf, 1992; Variations Suite, vn, va, 1996

Principal publisher: Association for the Promotion of New Music

BIBLIOGRAPHY

V. Scher: "UCSD Honors Will Ogdon, who set the stage, and the experimental tone, for its highly regarded music department," *San Diego Union-Tribune* (13 Nov 2005), <http://legacy.signonsandiego.com/news/features/20051113-9999-1a13ucsd.html>

"A Tribute to Will Ogdon," Videorecording, *UCSD TV* #11305, (2006), 86 minutes, <http://musicweb.ucsd.edu/media/mov/UCSDTV_Tribute_to_Will_Ogdon_256.mov>

DAVID COPE/JONATHAN KUUSKOSKI

Oglala. Native American group belonging to the Teton division of the SIOUX.

Ohio Players. Funk septet. The group formed in 1959 in Dayton, Ohio; key members included Leroy Bonner, guitar and voice; Clarence Satchell, saxophone; Ralph Middlebrooks, trumpet; Gregory Webster, drums; Billy Beck, keyboards; Marvin Pierce, trumpet; and Marshall Jones, bass guitar. The group had its first success in 1962 as the backup band on the Falcons' hit "I found a love." During the next 11 years they made many unsuccessful recordings, but in 1971 they signed a contract with Westbound and in 1973 their "Funky Worm" sold a million copies. After the group moved to Mercury in 1974 its next eight singles all reached the Top Ten on the soul chart; three of these ("Skin Tight," 1974; "Fire," 1974; and "Love Rollercoaster," 1975) were awarded gold records. The Ohio Players' style of "street" funk—based more on hypnotic rhythms than melody—was distinctive for its lusty, overpowering rhythm section, and the jazzy, rapid vocal delivery of Bonner and others.

Satchell described the group's sound as "progressive rock with a touch of jazz and blues"; the influence on its style of Sly and the Family Stone and of James Brown was very clear. The Ohio Players' stage show was elaborate and glittery, featuring bizarre costumes, intricate lighting, and bubble and smoke machines; the group also gained attention for the mildly pornographic photographs that were used for its album covers. The Ohio Players' popularity faded in the late 1970s, but they continued to record for Arista and Boardwalk before disbanding in the 1980s.

GARY THEROUX/R

Ohio State University. State-supported university in Columbus (founded 1870; opened 1873). Its school of music was established in 1945, though music instruction was introduced shortly after the opening of the university. The school resides in the Division of Arts and Humanities in the College of the Arts and Sciences. Its first director was Eugene J. Weigel (1894–1973), who was also the leader of the university's renowned marching band. David Meeker, appointed director in 1979, fostered the expansion of an analog and digital sound-synthesis laboratory and computer-based instruction in music theory. In 1971 the music library became one of the first research collections to be cataloged on computer. By the early 2000s, through the leadership of directors Don Gibson, Mellasenah Morris, and interim director Edward Adelson, a music business program and increased community outreach initiatives were established. The school has more than 600 students, a faculty of approximately 60, and houses three research laboratories. BM, BMEd, and BA degrees are offered, along with MA, MM, DMA, and PhD degrees in music history, theory, education, pedagogy, performance, conducting, and composition. Weigel Hall (completed 1980) features a recital hall with a movable ceiling and other acoustical refinements.

BIBLIOGRAPHY
E.W. Aho, ed.: *Script Ohio: the Ohio State University Marching Band* (Columbus, OH, 1979)

BRUCE CARR/ROBERT GILLESPIE

Ohlsson, Garrick (Olof) (*b* Bronxville, NY, 3 April 1948). Pianist. He attended the Westchester Conservatory of Music where he had lessons with Thomas Lishman, and then he went to Juilliard at age 13 where he studied with SASCHA GORODNITZKI and ROSINA LHÉVINNE. Other teachers include Olga Barabini, Irma Wolpe, and CLAUDIO ARRAU. Awards early in his career include first place in the Busoni Piano competition in 1966 and winner of the Montréal Piano Competition in 1968. Ohlsson firmly established his reputation as virtuoso when he won the gold medal at the 1970 Chopin International Piano Competition, the first American to do so. Other honors include the Avery Fisher Prize in 1994 and the University Musical Society Distinguished Artist Award at the University of Michigan in 1998.

Ohlsson travels extensively every year and has performed throughout the world in solo programs and with leading orchestras. In addition, Ohlsson is an avid chamber player and has performed with the Cleveland, Emerson, Takács, and Tokyo String Quartets, as well as with the FOG trio, of which he is a founding member with violinist Jorja Fleezanis and cellist Michael Grebanier. His recordings are numerous and celebrated and include a set of Chopin's complete works and the complete Beethoven Sonata Cycle, disk three of which won the Best Instrumental Soloist Performance Grammy Award in 2008.

A poet of the piano, Ohlsson's prodigious technique balances his richly expressive playing with a deeply intellectual interpretation of a vast repertory of music. He is known for his powerful yet intimate performances of Chopin's works. In 2010, the bicentennial of the composer's birth, he performed all-Chopin programs.

BIBLIOGRAPHY
A. Marcus: "Garrick Ohlsson," *Great Pianists Speak with Adele Marcus* (Neptune, NJ, 1979), 120–43
D. Dubal: "Garrick Ohlsson," *Reflections from the Keyboard: the World of the Concert Pianist* (New York, 1984), 248–55
E. Mach: "Garrick Ohlsson," *Great Pianists Speak for Themselves*, ii (New York, 1988), 173–97

MICHAEL STEINBERG/REBECCA SCHWARTZ-BISHIR

Ohman, Phil [Fillmore] **W(ellington)** (*b* New Britain, CT, 7 Oct 1896; *d* Santa Monica, CA, 8 Aug 1954). Pianist and composer. Although he composed over a dozen piano novelties and popular songs (including "Lost" in 1936 with Johnny Mercer), Ohman is better remembered as a notable pianist of the 1920s and 30s. Born to a Swedish immigrant Lutheran minister, Ohman began piano lessons as a child, later studying piano and organ with ALEXANDER RUSSELL, from whom he learned harmony and music theory. At 18 he ventured to New York City where he found work as a piano salesman, demonstrator, accompanist, and piano roll arranger and recording artist for QRS. In 1919, while at QRS, he was teamed with VICTOR ARDEN, and the two began a successful career as duo-pianists. They found regular work on radio, in clubs, and on Broadway, co-leading the pit orchestra for several Gershwin shows including *Lady Be Good* (1924), *Tip Toes* (1925), *Oh, Kay* (1926), and *Funny Face* (1927). From 1921 to 1932 the two were nominal leaders on a series of dance band recordings made for the Brunswick and Victor labels that featured their virtuosic arrangements of popular songs, with Ohman generally playing the piano's treble range and Arden playing in the bass range. Ohman and Arden dissolved their partnership amicably in 1934 and Ohman moved to Los Angeles, where he led a Hawaiian-flavored band and worked as pianist, arranger, and composer for several Hollywood films.

BRYAN S. WRIGHT

Ohrlin, Glenn (*b* Minneapolis, MN, 26 Oct 1926). Cowboy singer. Ohrlin left home at age 16 to travel throughout the West as a working cowboy and rodeo bronc rider, through which he acquired an extensive repertory of traditional cowboy songs (*see* COWBOY SONG). In 1973 he published *The Hell-bound Train: a Cowboy Songbook*, including

100 of his favorite cowboy songs; the book has become a classic. His performances are notable for the laconic and understated style of his singing and spare guitar accompaniment, as well as for his storytelling and humor. He has appeared on the folk revival circuit since the 1960s.

In 1983 and 1984, Ohrlin joined eight other cowboys from varying ranching traditions as they traveled with the National Council for the Traditional Arts' *The Cowboy Tour*, presenting storytelling, music, and cowboy poetry as they visited small cowtowns across the western United States.

In 1985 Ohrlin was awarded a National Heritage Fellowship by the NEA, and in that same year was involved in creating the first *Cowboy Poetry Gathering* in Elko, Nevada. In the succeeding years Ohrlin has come to be revered as the elder statesman of authentic cowboy performers and one of the last with connections to the earlier generations of cowboy performers.

CHARLIE SEEMANN

Oja, Carol J(ean) (*b* Hibbing, MN, 18 March 1953). Musicologist. Oja received her BA from St. Olaf College in 1974 and her MA from the University of Iowa in 1976, writing the masters' thesis "Musical Subjects in the Paintings of William Michael Harnett." She did her doctoral work with H. Wiley Hitchcock, Barry Brook, and Sherman Van Solkema at CUNY, completing her degree in 1985 with a dissertation on Colin McPhee. She taught at Brooklyn College and the Graduate Center at CUNY beginning in 1985. In 1993 she became Director of the Institute for Studies in American Music at Brooklyn College. In 1997 she and her husband, MARK TUCKER, accepted the David N. and Margaret C. Bottoms Professorship of Music and of American studies at the College of William and Mary, a position they held jointly until his death in 2000. In 2003 she became the William Powell Mason Professor of Music at Harvard University. Working from a wide array of primary sources, Oja focuses her work primarily on the classical and theatrical music of the 20th and 21st centuries. Her publications, often biographical in nature, reach across the lives and work of numerous major composers, treating the historical contexts and creative forces that supported, attracted the attention of, and drove the work of these men and women. Her first biography, *Colin McPhee: Composer in Two Worlds* (Washington, DC, 1990/R 2004), addresses the creative impetus of the exotic "other" in classical composition. *Making Music Modern* (New York, 2000), winner of the Lowens and ASCAP-Deems Taylor book awards, develops the contexts of classical music composition and performance in the city of New York during the 1920s. This work and others take up American relationships of classical and popular music and touch on issues of gender. During the 2000s her work turned toward musical theater and its relationship to political issues including race—a theme that runs through much of Oja's work—and immigration.

WRITINGS

"The Still-Life Paintings of William Michael Harnett: Their Reflections upon Nineteenth-Century American Musical Culture," *MQ*, lxiii/4 (1977), 505–23

"The Copland-Sessions Concerts and Their Reception in the Contemporary Press," *MQ*, lxv/2 (1979), 212–29

"Trollopiana: David Claypoole Johnston Counters Frances Trollope's Views on American Music," *College Music Symposium*, xxi/1 (1981), 94–102

ed.: *American Music Recordings: a Discography of 20th-Century US Composers* (Brooklyn, NY, 1982)

ed.: *Stravinsky in "Modern Music," 1924–1946* (New York, 1982)

Colin McPhee (1900–1964): a Composer in Two Worlds (diss., CUNY, 1985; Washington, DC, 1990)

"Composer with a Conscience: Elie Siegmeister in Profile," *AM*, vi/2 (1988), 158–80

"Cos Cob Press and the American Composer," *Notes*, xlv/2 (1988–89), 227–52

"Marc Blitzstein's *The Cradle Will Rock* and Mass-Song Style of the 1930s," *MQ*, lxxiii/4 (1989), 445–75

ed., with R.A. Crawford and R.A. Lott: *A Celebration of American Music: Words and Music in Honor of H. Wiley Hitchcock* (Ann Arbor, MI, 1990) [incl. "Virgil Thomson's Harvard Years," 323–45]

"'New Music' and the 'New Negro': the Background of William Grant Still's *Afro-American Symphony*," *Black Music Research Journal*, xii/2 (1992), 145–69

"The USA, 1918–1945," *Modern Times from World War I to the Present*, ed. R.P. Morgan (London, 1993), 206–30

"Gershwin and American Modernists of the 1920s," *MQ*, lxxviii/4 (1994), 646–68

ed., with R. Allen: *Henry Cowell's Musical Worlds* (Brooklyn, NY, 1997)

"Women Patrons and Activists for Modernist Music: New York in the 1920s," *Modernism/Modernity*, iv/1 (1997): 129–55

"Women Patrons and Crusaders for Modernist Music," *Cultivating Music in America: Women Patrons and Activists since 1860*, ed. R.P. Locke and C. Barr (Berkeley, 1997)

"Dane Rudhyar's Vision of American Dissonance," *AM*, xvii/2 (1999), 129–45

"George Antheil's *Ballet mécanique* and Transatlantic Modernism," *A Modern Mosaic: Art and Modernism in the United States*, ed. T. Ludington, T. Fahy, and S.P. Reuning (Chapel Hill, NC, 2000)

Making Music Modern: New York in the 1920s (New York, 2000)

ed., with J. Tick: *Aaron Copland and His World* (Princeton, NJ, 2005)

"*West Side Story* and *The Music Man*: Whiteness, Immigration and Race in the U.S. during the Late 1950s," *Studies in Musical Theatre*, iii/1 (2009), 13–30

ed., with S. Adams and K.K. Shelemay: *Leonard Bernstein in Boston*. Special issue of the *JSAM*, iii/1 (2009)

VIRGINIA DANIELSON

Ojai Music Festival. A spring series of weekend concerts initiated in 1947 at Ojai, California, a small community near Los Angeles by music aficionado John Bauer. The festivals began with a recital by the French baritone Martial Singher. Most of the performers are Los Angeles musicians, including members of the Los Angeles PO, the New Wave Chamber Players, and amateur and professional choruses. The artistic director of the festival through the late 1960s was Lawrence Morton; the position of music director has been held for short terms by Thor Johnson, Pierre Boulez, Michael Tilson Thomas, Esa-Pekka Salonen, and other leading conductors. Composers John Adams, Ingolf Dahl, Peter Maxwell Davies, Lukas Foss, John Harbison, Kent Nagano, and Oliver Knussen, as well as instrumentalists Emanuel Ax and Mitsuko Uchida have also served as music director. In 2011 the position was held by Dawn Upshaw. The festival's programs range from music of the 13th century to the avant garde, with an emphasis on rediscovered or rare works of the past and on new compositions; Copland's *Elegies for Orchestra* and Wuorinen's *A Reliquary for Igor Stravinsky* received their world premieres at the festival in 1973 and 1975 respectively. Although the repertory is broadly international, American composers, including many from Southern California, have been generously represented. Participants have included Aaron Copland, Lukas Foss, Igor Stravinsky, Milton Babbitt, Elliott Carter, Olivier Messiaen, György Ligeti, Steve Reich, Magnus Lindberg, Thomas Adès, Mark-Anthony Turnage, and Osvaldo Golijov.

RITA H. MEAD/MEGAN E. HILL

O'Jays, the. Soul vocal group. After singing together as a gospel duo, Walter Williams (*b* 25 Aug 1942) and Eddie Levert (*b* 16 June 1942) formed a doo-wop quintet, the Mascots, in Canton, Ohio, in 1958. The other original members were Bill Isles, Bobby Massey, and William Powell. They renamed their group after a Cleveland disc jockey, Eddie O'Jay, who had encouraged them. For ten years the O'Jays played concerts and recorded, with little success, for Wayco, Little Star, Apollo, King, Minit, Bell, and Imperial. Isles left the group in 1965. In 1968 the group signed a contract with the songwriting and production team of GAMBLE AND HUFF for their Neptune label, but that company shortly went out of business. The group stayed together, despite Massey's departure in 1971. Later that year Gamble and Huff formed a new label, Philadelphia International, and organized an efficient distribution system through CBS Records. As a result of that arrangement, as well as fine songs and inspired production marked by powerful orchestral arrangements and a driving beat, the O'Jays, now a trio, began to have major hits: "Back Stabbers" (1972), "Love Train" and "Put your hands together" (1973), "For the Love of Money" (1974), "I love music (part 1)" (1975), and "Livin' for the weekend" (1976). In 1976 the group lost its momentum when William Powell left (he died of cancer in 1977); his replacement, Sammy Strain (formerly of Little Anthony and the Imperials), participated in such later hits as "Use Ta Be My Girl" (1978) and "Forever Mine" (1979). The group recorded eight albums that earned gold records during the 1970s, their most successful decade. They crafted a sophisticated style of hard-edged soul music, skillfully orchestrated and joyfully performed. In 2005 the group was inducted into the Rock and Roll Hall of Fame.

GARY THEROUX/R

Ojibwe [Anishinaabe, Ojibway, Ojibwa, Chippewa]. A Native American tribe living principally in the western woodlands area of the United States and Canada, including portions of what is now Ontario, Manitoba, Minnesota, Wisconsin, and northern Michigan, having migrated from the eastern shores of Lake Superior beginning in the 17th century. Culturally they belong to the central Algonquian family and speak a language related to Odawa, Menominee, Potawatomi, and Cree.

The Ojibwe people were one of the first North American tribes whose music received serious attention from ethnographers; Frederick Burton's *American Primitive Music* (1909) and Frances Densmore's *Chippewa Music* (1910, 1913) include transcriptions of 513 songs based on wax-cylinder recordings made by Burton at Desba-

rets, Ontario, and Densmore on reservations in Minnesota and Wisconsin. Many of these recordings are in the process of being repatriated to the families of the original singers by the Smithsonian Institution.

Ojibwe performance traditionally spanned a wide variety of contexts, a number of which were nearly lost by the mid-20th century but have made a resurgence since the 1970s. In addition to the songs of the medicine lodge (*midewiwin*), the primary traditional religious society where membership is limited and obtained through formal initiation, there are songs for healing (dream songs), gambling (moccasin game songs), gift exchange (woman's dance songs), general entertainment (pipe dance songs), storytelling, courtship, warfare, and hunting. With the exception of *mide* and love songs, which had full texts, most songs contain only a brief text performed once during each strophe, with the remainder of the melody sung to vocables. The songs of the medicine lodge, accompanied by either water drum (constructed from a portion of a hollowed log) or birch bark rattle, are stylistically distinct from mainstream Ojibwe music and are characterized by deliberately unfocused intonation, unusually wide vibrato applied as an ornament to sustained tones, and the use of spoken exclamations between strophes. Texts, often archaic, have vocables inserted between syllables to disguise their meaning.

As the result of the ongoing consequences of colonization and culture loss, there was a gradual reduction throughout the 20th century in the number of song types in Ojibwe music. With settlement on reservations, increasing urbanization, and the incursion of nontraditional religions, many of the traditional occasions for music ceased to exist, and many song types have fallen into disuse. Whereas once a great variety of genres existed, the POWWOW or war dance song form constitutes the greatest portion of the repertory, borrowed from tribes to the north and west of the Ojibwe. The continuing influence of Dakota and Lakota structures—begun long ago through sporadic warfare, peace, cultural exchange, and intermarriage—on Ojibwe music is significant. Midewiwin lodge activity has been revitalized since the 1970s, with lodges scattered throughout Minnesota, Wisconsin, and Ontario, and as a result those songs are still being practiced.

Drums are prominent in Ojibwe communities. Double-headed frame drums, as well as single-headed hand drums in a range of sizes—covered most commonly in elk or cow hide—are used in a variety of public and ceremonial settings. The drum was used increasingly to accompany songs after its introduction around 1880 through contact with the Dakota. Occasionally commercially made bass drums are still used in Ojibwe powwow settings, but are becoming less common. Traditional drums have a drum keeper and are elevated on a wooden stand, with an eagle feather hanging from each of four slender poles representing the spirits of the four cardinal directions. In addition, such drums are often elaborately decorated with cloth, ribbon, beads, or fur, and their heads painted with symbolic designs. Colors and patterns are frequently dreamed, and are chosen for ritual connotation. All drums require special care, feasting, and purification, and are treated with the same respect given to people.

The two most common settings for singing with drums include Big Drum ceremonies—representing another central ceremonial society of the Ojibwe—which take place during the fall and winter, and powwows throughout the spring and summer. At powwows the most common genres sung are Grass Dance, Men's and Women's Traditional, Fancy, Crow-Hop, Sneak-Up, Intertribal, and Jingle Dress songs. While the Jingle Dress has made its way throughout the North American powwow circuit, it is widely recognized as having originated in Ojibwe culture around the time of World War I; its construction, songs, and dances have healing connotations.

After the drum, the other traditional instrument found most commonly in Ojibwe culture is the courting flute (*see* NATIVE AMERICAN FLUTE). A flute similar to those of other woodlands and Plains tribes is 15 to 20 inches long (somewhat shorter than those of neighboring cultures) usually with six holes, and constructed of cedar; its tone is regulated by a carved, movable block. Flute melodies are usually love-songs; there is historical evidence that in performance, a young man would alternate singing with the playing of slow, *rubato* melodies. Today a number of expert flute players are teaching younger generations, but the drum still remains most prominent.

Since the 1990s the revitalization of Ojibwe language and culture has driven a renewal of expertise in traditional forms on the one hand and fueled a creative surge in popular music genres on the other. While handdrum singers are helping recreational genres such as moccasin game songs to make a comeback, many contemporary Ojibwe artists write and perform folk, blues, rock, and heavy metal music. Hip hop has been increasingly popular among Ojibwe musicians since the 1990s, both in reservation communities and in cities such as Minneapolis and Winnipeg. A number of Ojibwe popular musicians draw upon traditional spiritual values and address contemporary cultural and political concerns.

Recordings of Ojibwe music are held at the Archive of Folk Culture, Library of Congress, Washington, DC; and the Archives of Traditional Music, Indiana University.

See also NATIVE AMERICAN MUSIC.

DISCOGRAPHY

Songs of the Chippewa, recorded 1907–10 by F. Densmore (1950, Library of Congress)

Chippewa: War Dance Songs for Powwow (1971, Canyon)

Chippewa Grass Dance Songs (1973, Canyon)

Ojibway Music from Minnesota: A Century of Song for Voice and Drum (1989/R, Minnesota Historical Society, St. Paul, MN)

Annie Humphrey: The Heron Smiled (2000, Makoche)

Keith Secola: Native Americana (Akina, 2005)

Eyabay Singers: No Limit (2007, Arbor)

Oshkii-Giizhik Singers: It Is a New Day (2008, Jaakola)

Wab Kinew: Live by the Drum (2009, Indie Ends)

Pipestone Singers: As the Rez Turns: Round Dance Songs (2010, Canyon)

BIBLIOGRAPHY

W.J. Hoffman: "The Midewiwin, or 'Grand Medicine Society' of the Ojibwa," *Bureau of American Ethnology, Seventh Annual Report, 1885–86* (Washington, DC, 1891), 143–300

F.R. Burton: *American Primitive Music, with Especial Attention to the Songs of the Ojibways* (New York, 1909)

F. Densmore: *Chippewa Music* (Washington, DC, 1910, 1913)

S.A. Barrett: "The Dream Dance of the Chippewa and Menominee Indians of Northern Wisconsin," *Bulletin of the Public Museum of the City of Milwaukee*, i (1911), 251–407

R. Landes: *Ojibwa Religion and the Midewiwin* (Madison, WI, 1968)

T. Vennum, Jr.: *Southwestern Ojibwa Music* (diss., Harvard U., 1975)

T. Vennum, Jr.: "Ojibwa Origin-Migration Songs of the *Mitewiwin*," *Journal of American Folklore*, xci/361 (1978), 753–91

T. Vennum, Jr.: *The Ojibwa Dance Drum: Its History and Construction* (Washington, DC, 1982, R/2009)

T. Vennum, Jr.: "The Ojibwa Begging Dance," *Music and Context: Essays for John M. Ward*, ed. A.D. Shapiro (Cambridge, MA, 1985), 54–78

T. Vennum, Jr.: "The Alice C. Fletcher Ojibwe Indian Recordings," *Discourse in Ethnomusicology. III: Essays in Honor of Frank J. Gillis*, ed. N.C. McEntire (Bloomington, IN, 1991), 73–103

M. McNally: *Ojibwe Singers: Hymns, Grief, and a Native Culture in Motion* (New York, 2000)

E. Carter Vosen: *Seventh-Fire Children: Gender, Embodiment, and Musical Performances of Decolonization* (diss., U. of Pennsylvania, 2001)

T. Browner: *Heartbeat of the People: Music and Dance of the Northern Pow-wow* (Urbana, IL, 2002/R)

A.S. Treuer: *Ojibwe in Minnesota* (St. Paul, MN, 2010)

THOMAS VENNUM, JR./ELYSE CARTER VOSEN

OKeh. Record company. It was established in 1918 by General Phonograph, an enterprise set up in New York in 1916 by Otto Heinemann to manage the American operations of Carl Lindström's German company. Jazz recordings began with items by the New Orleans Jazz Band. Recordings by Mamie Smith established OKeh's primacy in the field, which was reinforced in 1921 by the setting up of a race series (until 1923 called the Colored Catalog). It became an important jazz, blues, and gospel catalog and included material by Clarence Williams (from 1921), King Oliver (1923), Louis Armstrong's Hot Five and Hot Seven (1925–9), Lonnie Johnson, Mississippi John Hurt, J.M. Gates, and Bennie Moten's band (1923–5). Discs by Frankie Trumbauer, Bix Beiderbecke, and Eddie Lang were issued in a general popular series, and there were also separate series for country music, calypso, Jewish music, European popular music (for postwar immigrants), and Mexican music. The company's activities were little affected when it was taken over by Columbia in 1926; Heinemann ran OKeh as a new subsidiary specializing in jazz, blues, gospel, and popular music but also including violin solos by Eugene Ormandy and a huge novelty hit, the "Original Lauf-Aufnahme." Control passed to ARC–BRC in August 1934; later that year the race series was discontinued after almost 1000 issues. ARC–BRC dropped the name OKeh but CBS, which acquired the company in 1938, revived it and continued the numerical series of the Vocalion label, pressing early issues anew with OKeh labels. In the early 1950s the label became CBS's main outlet for rhythm-and-blues but was discontinued in 1970. The label was reactivated by Sony in the mid-1990s, then retired once more.

BIBLIOGRAPHY

OKeh Race Records (New York, c1924/R)

OKeh Race Records: the Blue Book of Blues (New York, c1927/R)

R.D. Kinkle: "OKeh Numerical List," "Vocalion-Okeh Numerical List," *The Complete Encyclopedia of Popular Music and Jazz, 1900–1950*, iv (New Rochelle, NY, 1974), 2123, 2255

R. Laird and B. Rust: *Discography of OKeh Records, 1918–1934* (Westport, CT, 2004)

HOWARD RYE/R

Oklahoma, University of. State-supported university founded in 1890, with campuses in Norman, Oklahoma City, and Tulsa. The music department was founded in 1893 and renamed the School of Music in 1899. Today, the school is part of the College of Fine Arts and is housed in the Catlett Music Center (completed in 1998), the Donald W. Reynolds Performing Arts Center (renovated in 2005), and Carpenter Hall. Graduate degrees have been granted from 1900 and PhDs from 1929. The School of Music has an enrollment of 400 students and a full-time faculty of about 50. In addition to the BMA and BFA, the School of Music awards the BME and MME in music education; the BM and MM in performance, composition, history, theory, piano pedagogy, and theory; the DMA in performance, composition, and piano pedagogy; and the PhD in music education. The school presents over 250 performances each year.

GRAYDON BEEKS/WARREN HENRY

Okwanachu. Native American group of California belonging to the SHASTA.

Olatunji, (Michael) Babatunde (*b* Ajido-Badacry, Nigeria, *c*1920; *d* Sabinas, CA, 6 April 2003). Nigerian drummer, composer, and music organizer and promoter. Educated at the Baptist Academy in Lagos, he moved to the United States in 1950 where he took the BA at Morehouse College in Atlanta, Georgia, in 1954. He settled in New York in 1954, enrolling in a graduate program at New York University, and later established the Center of African Culture in Harlem in the 1960s, a cultural performing arts school. He collaborated with artists such as John Coltrane, Max Roach, Yusef Lateef, Freddie Hubbard, Sonny Rollins, Jerry Garcia, and the Grateful Dead drummer Mickey Hart. His recordings and touring ensemble introduced countless audiences throughout North America and the world to West African performance traditions. In addition he wrote about African music and composed several film scores. His association with Hart led to several recording projects and further performing opportunities.

WRITINGS

with B.W. Dietz: *Musical Instruments of Africa: their Nature, Use and Place in the Life of a Deeply Musical People* (New York, 1965)

Yorùbá òde òní (Lagos, 1980)

Drums of Passion Songbook: the Songs of Babatunde Olatunji (New York, 1993)

with R. Atkinson and A. Akiwowo: *The Beat of My Drum: an Autobiography* (Philadelphia, 2005)

SELECTED RECORDINGS

Drums of Passion (Col., 1960); *Afro-Percussion Zungo!* (Col., 1961); *Flaming Drums!* (Col., 1962); *High Life!* (Col., 1963); *More Drums of Passion* (Col., 1966); *Soul Makossa* (Para., 1973); *Dance to the Beat of my Heart, Blue Heron* (1986); *Drums of Passion: the Invocation* (Rykodisc, 1988)

BIBLIOGRAPHY

G. Stewart: "The Beat Goes On: Olatunji," *Breakout: Profiles in African Rhythm* (Chicago, 1992), 87–96

J. Pareles: Obituary, *New York Times* (9 April 2003)

GREGORY F. BARZ/R

Olcott, Chauncey [Olcott, Chancellor John] (*b* Buffalo, NY, 21 July 1858; *d* Monte Carlo, 18 March 1932). Singer, composer, and lyricist. He toured with several minstrel and opera companies, then went to London for two years, where he studied singing and appeared in comic opera. He achieved fame after his return to the United States when he joined forces with Augustus Pitou in 1893 and succeeded William J. Scanlan as the leading singer in Pitou's productions of sentimental operettas on Irish themes. His success, founded on his sweet tenor voice and his ingratiating acting and appearance, led to his concentrating on Irish roles for the remainder of his career.

He contributed librettos, songs, and lyrics to many of the works in which he appeared, and wrote the complete scores of *Sweet Inniscarra* (1897), *A Romance of Athlone* (1899), *Garrett O'Magh* (1901), and *Old Limerick Town* (1902). His song "My Wild Irish Rose" (1899) and the lyrics "Mother Machree" (1911) and "When Irish Eyes Are Smiling" (1912), both with music by Ernest R. Ball, have attained lasting popularity. He made a few recordings of Irish American ballads between 1913 and 1920, but his popularity waned after World War I and he retired in 1925. Olcott was considered neither a great singer nor actor, but at the height of his popularity commanded a large and loyal audience among the Irish American community. His life was the subject of the Hollywood film *My Wild Irish Rose* (1947).

BIBLIOGRAPHY

DAB (W.P. Eaton)

"Olcott, Chancellor John (Chauncey Olcott)," *The National Cyclopaedia of American Biography*, xi (New York, 1901/R), 519

R.O. Olcott: *Song in his Heart* (New York, 1939)

J. Walsh: "Favorite Pioneer Recording Artists: Chauncey Olcott," *Hobbies*, lxxv (1970), no.6, p.37, no.7, p.37

D. Carroll: *The Matinee Idols* (New York, 1972)

M.K. Fiedler: "Chauncey Olcott: Irish-American Mother-Love, Romance and Nationalism," *Éire/Ireland: a Journal of Irish Studies*, xxii/2 (1987), 4–26

MICHAEL J. BUDDS/R

Oldberg, Arne (*b* Youngstown, OH, 12 July 1874; *d* Evanston, IL, 17 Feb 1962). Composer, pianist, and teacher. His father Oscar was a Swedish pharmaceutical chemist, who brought the family from Ohio to Washington, DC, and eventually to the Chicago area where Oscar founded the School of Pharmacy at Northwestern University in 1886 and where Arne would spend virtually his entire career. While not a prodigy, Arne Oldberg was an accomplished pianist at an early age. He studied with August Hyllested at the Chicago Musical College before traveling to Vienna in 1893 for two years of instruction with Leschetizky.

Oldberg began composing in the early 1890s, and his teachers included organist WILHELM MIDDELSCHULTE, Adolph Koelling, and FREDERICK G. GLEASON. His most important early scores were keyboard works, including organ fugues and piano suites, and chamber music. He returned to Europe in 1898, this time to study in Munich with JOSEPH RHEINBERGER. After a single year of concentrated work, he returned to Evanston and joined the faculty at the Northwestern University School of Music. He was elected to the National Institute of Arts and Letters in 1915 and won prizes from the National Federation of Music Clubs. Upon his retirement from Northwestern after more than 40 years of teaching, a city park near the University was named in his honor.

Oldberg composed mostly during the summer months, which he spent near Estes Park, Colorado, and occasionally in California. In addition to a substantial body of piano and chamber music, he produced more than 20 orchestral scores, usually employing conventional forms and colorful melodic material. These include at least six symphonies, six concertos, and a variety of single-movement pieces, most notably a dramatic overture called *Paolo and Francesca* (1899, rev. 1906) and *Symphonic Poem "The Sea"* (1936). His Symphonic Concerto (Piano Concerto no.1) (1907) was published by Arthur Farwell in the Wa-Wan Press. More than a dozen of Oldberg's pieces were programmed by Frederick Stock and the Chicago SO, including his Piano Concerto no.2, which had been premiered in Southern California after winning first prize in a contest sponsored by the Hollywood Bowl in 1931.

Oldberg continued composing through the 1950s and he retained strong ties to Chicago-area musical institutions that he himself had helped to establish, including the Cliff Dwellers (Chicago's artistic social club), the Chicago Manuscript Society, and the Chicago North Shore Music Festival. Many of his manuscript scores and papers are held at the Library of Congress.

BETH E. LEVY

Old-folks concert. A type of entertainment, popular in the second half of the 19th century, which revived the music and performance practices of the 18th-century New England singing-schools. Accounts of early amateur old-folks concerts in New Haven, and Fall River, Massachusetts, suggest their rural origins. They began in the 1850s and peaked in the 1860s, but endured through the century in various forms, taking on aspects of broad caricature and minstrelsy after the Civil War. Although FATHER KEMP is credited with originating the genre, it is more likely that he professionalized amateur songfests which featured the "good old tunes" that had been superseded by 19th-century styles of church hymnody. Even before Kemp's first concert in 1855, there had been organized efforts to sustain the singing-school repertory. The Billings and Holden Society was established in Boston in the mid-1830s, and it soon published a collection called *Ancient Psalmody* (1836) in order that the music "might not only be rescued from oblivion, but again be presented to the public in its original form." Other anthologies were issued in conjunction with the old-folks concerts between 1857 and 1875, including *Father Kemp's Old Folks' Concert Tunes* (1860) and *The Continental Concert Tunes for Ye Olde*

Folkes' Concerts, edited by John Church (1874). Among the most popular tunes were "Sherburne" by Daniel Read, "Northfield" by Jeremiah Ingalls, and "Anthem for Easter" and "Majesty" by William Billings. Kemp's Old Folks Concert Troupe added theatrical elements to the entertainment; performers impersonated Revolutionary War figures in costume and parodied old-time dialects.

BIBLIOGRAPHY

R.J. Kemp: *Father Kemp and his Old Folks* (Boston, 1868/R1982)

J.T. Steinberg: "Old Folks Concerts and the Revival of New England Psalmody," *MQ*, lix/4 (1973), 602–19

JUDITH TICK

Oldham, Kevin (William) (*b* Kansas City, MO, 30 Aug 1960; *d* Kansas City, MO, 11 March 1993). Composer and pianist. He studied at Northwestern University and at the Juilliard School, where his teachers included Herbert Stessin and SASCHA GORODNITZKI. He made his orchestral debut with the Detroit SO under Erich Kunzel in 1980, and throughout that decade presented highly regarded piano recitals in New York, Chicago, Washington, DC, and Los Angeles. In 1988, after learning that he was infected with HIV, he abandoned the concert stage and devoted the rest of his life to composition. He checked himself out of a New York hospital to rehearse and perform his Piano Concerto with the Kansas City SO under William McGlaughlin in January 1993. The following day he was readmitted to a local hospital, where he died six weeks later.

Oldham's neo-Romantic style combined the lush virtuosity of early 20th-century Russian music (by composers such as Rachmaninoff and Prokofiev) with a jaunty American manner that owed much to film scores and music theatre. The simple and haunting Andante tranquilo from his Piano Concerto has been especially admired. Several of his works have been recorded.

WORKS

Stage: Therese Raquin (op), unfinished; Titanic (musical theatre), unfinished

Vocal: 5 Songs, op.2: I am your friend; Do I know why; Intermezzo, pf; Prelude, pf; Song without Words in C; Gaspard de la nuit, 3 songs, op.3, S, pf: Ondine, Le gibet, Scarbo; 2 Waltzes, op.4, 3 S, pf, str qnt: Dingbat Waltz, Vocalise Waltz; 4 Songs, op.5: Will you ever dance to my songs again?, Pretending, All my Thoughts of you, Give me a Break; 4 Songs, op.11, S, unfinished; 5 Songs, op.12, Bar, unfinished; 3 Spirituals, op.13, unfinished; The Boulding Chorales, op.16, pubd: Can I Imprisoned; Small Flowers; Are there no armies; My Lord, Thou Art in Every Breath I Take; 3 Carols, op.20, pubd: Away in a Manger, Joy to the World, Silent Night; 3 Pss: cxxi, cxxx, cl

Inst: Toccata, op.1, pf; 2 Inst Pieces, op.6; Variations on a French Noel, op.7, pf, pubd; Fuge, op.8, s cl, a cl, cel, pf; Sym. no.1, op.9, org, pubd; Pf Conc., op.14, pubd; 2 Nocturnes, op.15, pf; Ballade, op.17, pf, pubd; Prelude, Saraband and Toccata, op.19 [Toccata completed by S. Cohen] [see also VOCAL: 5 Songs, op.2]

Transcrs. of works by Bach (Sinfonia, D, BWV29; Fugue, G; Prelude and Fugue, D, BWV532), M. Duruflé (Org Suite, op.5)

BIBLIOGRAPHY

T. Page, "The Ordeal of Kevin Oldham," *Tim Page on Music: Views and Reviews* (Portland, 2002), 169–80

TIM PAGE

Oldmixon [née Sidus], **Mrs. (Georgina)** [Miss George] (*b* Oxford, England, c1767; *d* Philadelphia, PA, 3 Feb

1835). Soprano of English birth. She made her debut with the stage name of Miss George at the Haymarket Theatre, London, on 2 June 1783, and distinguished herself as a soloist in Handel's oratorios. Later disputes with her associate Mrs. Billington probably contributed to her decision to move to the United States, where she joined Wignell's and Reinagle's company at the Chestnut Street Theatre in Philadelphia and made her debut on 14 May 1793 as Clorinda in *Robin Hood*. Decidedly a character actress, Oldmixon excelled in dramatic roles, such as Ophelia, Juliet's Nurse, and Mrs. Candour in *The School for Scandal*. She married Sir John Oldmixon of Bath, who became an ardent democrat and gardener. In 1805 she moved to New York, but returned to Philadelphia for a farewell benefit on 19 February 1814, where she remained to manage her Female Academy. Parker (1825) mentions her wide vocal range, dramatic talents, and fine sense of the Italian style. Oldmixon was a favorite with American audiences due to her vocal expertise and the distinction of her performances in comic opera.

BIBLIOGRAPHY

J.R. Parker: *Musical Biography* (Boston, 1825)

W.T. Parke: *Musical Memoirs* (London, 1830)

C. Durang: "The Philadelphia Stage," *Philadelphia Sunday Dispatch* (1854) [series of articles, continued in 1856, 1860; compiled by T. Westcott as *History of the Philadelphia Stage, between the Years 1749 and 1855*, 1868, *PHu*; similar compilations as *The Philadelphia Stage* in *PHlc*, *History of the Philadelphia Stage* in *PHbs*]

O.G.T. Sonneck: *Early Concert-life in America (1731–1800)* (Leipzig, 1907/*R*1978)

O.G.T. Sonneck: *Early Opera in America* (New York, 1915/*R*1963)

D.W. Krummel: "The Displaced Prima Donna: Mrs. Oldmixon in America," *MT*, cviii/1487 (1967), 25, 27–8

G. Smith: *Thomas Abthorpe Cooper: America's Premier Tragedian* (Madison, WI, 1996), 64, 75

D.W. KRUMMEL/R

Old-time music. A loosely defined term that is applied variously to older (i.e. pre–World War II) forms of country music, to a variety of traditional fiddling styles, and to modern performers who draw on or seek to perpetuate older styles. The history of the term has yet to be fully researched, but it was being used at least as early as the mid-1920s. In 1924 OKeh records used the term "Old Time Pieces" in ads to describe the music of two artists, Fiddlin' John Carson and Henry Whitter. Carson and Whitter were among the first southern rural artists to be recorded, at a time when the genre that later came to be called HILLBILLY MUSIC, and subsequently COUNTRY MUSIC, had yet to acquire an overarching rubric. The term was also used liberally during the nationwide, nostalgia-driven craze for "old-time" fiddling and dancing that was instigated by industrialist Henry Ford; this fad peaked in 1926.

The term gained renewed currency during the folk revival when northern, urban musicians and fans developed an interest in the older forms of rural music. One key use of the term is to distinguish the older STRING BAND style of music from the more modern form of BLUEGRASS MUSIC, but it is also used to describe forms of vocal music, especially close harmony singing in the manner of the Carter Family or the Blue Sky Boys.

BIBLIOGRAPHY

A. Green: "Commercial Music Graphics: Two," *JEMF Newsletter* (later *Quarterly*), iii/7 (1967), 15–16

M. Seeger: "What is Old-Time Music?," *Bluegrass Unlimited* (May 1997), 1–3 [reprinted online at <http://www.mikeseeger.info/music.html>]

PAUL F. WELLS

Old way of singing [common way; usual way]. A term used from the 18th century for a slow, heterophonic style of unaccompanied congregational singing found in rural Protestant churches in Britain and the United States, also variously called the common way and the usual way, to distinguish it from what was known as regular singing. In the early 21st century it was the oldest continuous tradition of English-language sacred song in the United States. Since the mid-17th century it has generally been associated with LINING OUT. The essence of the old way is the manner in which the tunes are sung by the congregation. The tunes are not written down; they are transmitted orally. The tempo is extremely slow, synchronized to the breath rather than to any common pulse beat: singers deliberately diverge on their way from one tune note to the next, some with more and some with less melodic elaboration.

The origins of the old way are uncertain. Similar practices have been noted among German-speaking groups tracing their descent from the 16th-century Anabaptists (*see* AMISH AND MENNONITE MUSIC) and in several parts of Scandinavia. This gives rise to the possibility that the old way preserves an ancient, pre-Reformation mode of popular singing that was once prevalent in Northern Europe. It may, on the other hand, have developed independently in various Protestant churches, where organs and choirs were outlawed for many generations.

Prevalent in English and Scottish churches by the early 17th century, the old way of singing was evidently brought to America by the colonists and flourished there in the absence of professional guidance for several generations. In Massachusetts lining out is mentioned with approval as early as 1647, by John Cotton. The heterophony that resulted was described by would-be musical reformers as "indecent," "like the braying of asses," and "tortured and twisted as every unskillful throat saw fit." Nonetheless, contemporary practitioners expressed a preference for the liberty given individuals to "curve" the tunes as they like and to communicate with the divine each in their own way, while experiencing the support of group participation. We can imagine that the colonists who resisted the musical reforms felt the same. Something of the difficulites that on occasion prevailed among precentors attempting to remember tunes and set the pitch in a comfortable range by ear may be gathered from entries in Judge Sewall's *Diary*, in which he describes services at the South Meeting House, Boston:

> 1705, Dec. 28. Mr. Willard...spoke to me to set the tune; I intended Windsor and fell into High-Dutch, and then essaying to set another tune went into a key much too high. So I pray'd Mr. White to set it; which he did well, Litchf[ield] Tune.
>
> 1718, Feb. 2. In the Morning I set York Tune, and in the 2d going over, the Gallery carried irresistibly to St. David's which discouraged me very much.

Regular singing in the American colonies began effectively in 1700 with the visit of Dr. Thomas Bray to the Anglican churches in Maryland, and thereafter leaders such as Cotton Mather, Thomas Symmes, and Nathaniel Chauncey spearheaded the reform movement in the Congregational churches of New England (*see* PSALMODY), where the old way was in gradual decline throughout the 18th century.

The influx of Scottish and Scots-Irish immigrants in the late 17th and early 18th centuries brought a distinctive brand of Presbyterianism, whose firmly held traditions included the Scottish psalter of 1650 sung in the old way with lining out. In urban centers there were schisms in the Presbyterian communities: "new side" synods welcomed the influence of the Evangelical movement, but "old side" synods staunchly resisted all reforms. In 1774 John Adams, accustomed to the New England choir singing, reported in his diary that the Old Presbyterian Society of New York was still "in the *old way*, as we call it."

The old way was never incorporated into the Methodist movement, being antithetical to John Wesley's ideas about singing. Baptists had been slow to accept congregational singing in worship at all, because it was a set form rather than a spontaneous act of praise; that issue was still alive in the 18th century, but by then many Baptists had already been singing in the old way. In the revival movement that swept the South and West in the early 19th century, Baptists were strong among those who adopted the lively camp-meeting, shape-note, and eventually gospel hymn singing. As the 19th century wore on, camp-meeting and gospel hymnody prevailed among most Baptist and Methodist denominations in the South, often with part-singing and hymn books. There the *Sacred Harp* and other Southern shape-note tunebooks inaugurated a literacy movement designed to drive out the old way, just as shaped notes and musical reform had done in New England a century earlier. But the most doctrinally conservative Baptist denominations in the South resisted these musical reforms as well as other reforms (such as Sunday school) and kept to the old way and lined-out hymnody, with melodies in oral tradition sung in heterophonic unison.

The old way of singing was still being practiced in the early 21st century in some white churches, principally among Old Regular Baptist congregations in the coal-mining regions of the southern Appalachian mountains. These communities have regarded their musical practice as an essential part of their home and church worship and have resisted any attempt to change it. Tallmadge (1975) reported the use of "lined hymns" in several hundred white Primitive and Old Regular Baptist churches in Kentucky, North Carolina, and Virginia. The lyrics were drawn chiefly from the 18th-century devotional composers such as Isaac Watts and circulated in favorite 19th-century compilations such as the *Sweet Songster* (1854) and the *Thomas Hymnal* (1877), as well as in newer compilations; the tunes, still entirely in oral tradition, included gospel and camp-meeting melodies, and even older ballad and fiddle tune airs (Cornett, Titon, and Wallhausser, 1997).

African American slaves, indentured servants, and freed slaves and their descendants learned the old way from Presbyterian and Baptist practice; the last have continued it with their own expressive alterations, slowing down the tempos further while engaging in greater melodic elaboration and improvisation. Dargan (2006) describes these "Dr. Watts hymns"—sometimes called meter hymns, surge songs, or deacons devotional—in some black Baptist churches, where in the early 2010s the traditional practice was geographically widespread rather than confined to the South and generally took place at the beginning of worship services.

BIBLIOGRAPHY

J. Cotton: *Singing of Psalms a Gospel Ordinance* (London, 1647)
G. Hood: *A History of Music in New England* (Boston, 1846/R)
M. van Doren, ed.: *Samuel Sewall's Diary* (New York, 1927)
G.P. Jackson: *Spiritual Folk-songs of Early America* (Locust Valley, NY, 1937, 3/1965)
G. Chase: *America's Music* (New York, 1955, 2/1966/R)
L.H. Butterfield, ed.: *Diary and Autobiography of John Adams*, ii (Cambridge, MA, 1961), 104 only
W.H. Tallmadge: "Baptist Monophonic and Heterophonic Hymnody in Southern Appalachia," *Yearbook for Inter-American Musical Research*, xi (1975), 106
N. Temperley: "The Old Way of Singing: its Origins and Development," *JAMS*, xxxiv (1981), 512
E. Cornett, J.T. Titon, and J. Wallhausser: liner notes, *Songs of the Old Regular Baptists* Smithsonian Folkways CD 40106 (Washington, DC, 1997)
W. Dargan: *Lining out the Word* (Berkeley, CA, 2006)

NICHOLAS TEMPERLEY/JEFF TODD TITON

Olefsky, Paul (*b* Chicago, IL, 4 Jan 1926; *d* Austin, TX, 1 June 2013). Cellist. He studied at the Curtis Institute with Daniel Saidenberg and GREGOR PIATIGORSKY; later he worked with PABLO CASALS and studied conducting with Herbert von Karajan and PIERRE MONTEUX. He received first prize in the Naumburg and Michael Memorial International Solo Competitions. He was a member of several American orchestras, including the Philadelphia Orchestra, becoming the youngest principal cellist in the ensemble's history, and the Detroit SO. He appeared as a recitalist in North America and Europe in repertory ranging from the Bach suites to Kodály's unaccompanied Cello Sonata. He gave the premieres of works by Kurt George Rogers, Virgil Thomson, Milhaud, Shapleigh, and Alexander Tcherepnin, among others. In 1974 he was appointed professor of cello and chamber music at the University of Texas, Austin, where he served as Emeritus Professor of Music. He gave master classes in the United States and internationally, including at Oxford and Cambridge. Olefsky's playing has been noted for its energy and sensitivity. His recordings include the complete sonatas of Beethoven and Brahms.

MARGARET DOUTT/MEGAN E. HILL

Oliva, Giacomo (Mario) (*b* New York, 14 Sept 1949). Pianist, percussionist, and music educator. He attended Chatham Square Music School in New York City (1956–67), Montclair State University (BA cum laude 1971, MA 1975), Seton Hall University (1976), and New

York University (EdD 1980). He taught and was a music administrator in the New Jersey public schools (1973–85), and at Mississippi State University (1985–92) and the University of Florida (1992–2001). He was percussionist with the New Jersey Opera (1972–4), musical director for the entertainer Connie Francis (1981–4), first assistant musical director for *Opera at Florham* (NJ) (1983–5), and a collaborative pianist for more than 30 years. Oliva has also presented papers and lecture recitals for professional organizations, and served as a reviewer for books and on journal editorial boards. He was president of the International Society for Music Education (2002–4), and has been an accreditation reviewer and music program consultant for over 20 institutions of higher education in the United States and abroad. Since 2001 he has served as the dean of the Hixson-Lied College of Fine and Performing Arts at the University of Nebraska–Lincoln. He has been named Nebraska Educational Administrator of the Year and National Administrator of the Year.

JERE T. HUMPHREYS

Oliveira, Elmar (*b* Waterbury, CT, 28 June 1950). Violinist. The son of Portuguese immigrants, Oliveira was nine when he began studying the violin with his brother John. At the age of 11 he received a scholarship to study at the Hartt School of Music with Ariana Bronne; he completed his studies with Raphael Bronstein at the Manhattan School, where he also received an honorary doctorate. While still a student he made his debut in 1964 as soloist with the Hartford SO. Two years later he was chosen by Bernstein to perform at a New York PO Youth Concert which was televised nationally. Oliveira made his New York recital debut at Town Hall on 18 March 1973. In 1975 he won the Naumburg Award, and in 1978 he became the first American violinist to win a gold medal at the Tchaikovsky Competition in Moscow. In December 1980 he gave the world premiere of Laderman's Second Violin Concerto, composed for him, with the Philadelphia Orchestra under the composer's direction. He won the Avery Fisher Prize in 1983. Since then his solo career expanded rapidly; he has played with the Chamber Music Society of Lincoln Center, as well as orchestras in Boston, Buffalo, Chicago, Cleveland, Colorado, Detroit, Helsinki, Leipzig Gewandhaus, London Philharmonic, Los Angeles, New York, Philadelphia, Rochester, Saint Louis, San Francisco, Seattle, and the Zurich Tonhalle, among others. He has also made extensive recital tours of North and South America, Australia, New Zealand, and Asia. He has taught at SUNY, Binghamton, where he received an honorary doctorate, and is currently a Distinguished Artist in Residence at the Lynn University Conservatory of Music in Boca Raton, Florida. He is a recipient of Portugal's highest civilian honor, the Order of Santiago.

Oliveira's playing is distinguished by smooth elegance, taste, and impeccable technique. His temperament is warm but controlled in a wide-ranging repertory. Among his recordings is Tchaikovsky's Piano Trio, performed with Mikhail Pletnyov and Nathaniel Rosen, fellow prizewinners of the Tchaikovsky Competition. Oliveira's discography on Artek, Angel, SONY Masterworks, Vox, Delos, IMP, Naxos, Ondine, and Melodiya covers a wide range of works from the Baroque period to the present. He has recorded the Brahms Concerto and Saint-Saëns Concerto no.3 with Gerard Schwarz and the Seattle Symphony, the violin sonatas of Respighi and Pizzetti, the complete Brahms sonatas with pianist Jorge Federico Osorio, the Joachim Concerto with the London Philharmonic, and the Tower Concerto (composed for him) with the Louisville Orchestra. Of note are two unique projects: a CD released by Bein & Fushi of Chicago, featuring Mr. Oliveira performing on some of the world's greatest violins (15 Stradivarius and 15 Guarneri del Gesus), and a CD of short pieces highlighting the Library of Congress's collection of rare violins. He is a well-known interpreter of modern works for violin, and has premiered works by Morton Gould, Aaron Kernis, Ezra Laderman, Benjamin Lees, Andrzej Panufnik, Krzysztof Penderecki, Joan Tower, and Charles Wuorinen. He performs on a 1729/30 Guarneri del Gesu called the "Stretton," and on several contemporary violins.

BIBLIOGRAPHY

J. Hiemenz: "Elmar Oliveira," *HiFi/MusAm*, xxx/12 (1980), 4

B. Schwarz: "The American School: the Younger Generation," *Great Masters of the Violin* (New York, 1983), 588–9

BORIS SCHWARZ/SARAH EYERLY

Oliveira, Jacques (Abraham) (*b* Amsterdam, The Netherlands, 1836; *d* New Orleans, LA, 18 June 1867). Violinist of Dutch birth. A student of Charles de Bériot, he frequently performed concertos and other works by de Bériot as well as numerous opera fantasies and Paganini's variations on "Carnival of Venice." In 1858 he was performing in Britain with a touring troupe headed by the American entertainer Tom Thumb. He arrived in New York late in 1859 and made his American début on 12 December as a soloist with the Drayton Parlor Opera Company. He continued to perform in New York and other cities of the northeast with the Draytons, with Tom Thumb, and with the Hooley and Campbell minstrel troupe. By 1862, he had settled in New Orleans, which was then occupied by federal troops. He quickly became a leading figure in that city's musical community, appearing regularly as a soloist at benefit concerts and other musical events. With Theodore La Hache, Gustave Smith, Marguerite Élie, and others, he organized chamber music concerts at the Opera House and other venues. In 1864 he appeared as a soloist at events staged in New Orleans by bandleader Patrick Gilmore. He died at the age of 31 during an outbreak of yellow fever, just as he was about to embark upon a concert tour.

BIBLIOGRAPHY

"Drayton's Parlor Operas," *New York Musical World* (24 Dec 1859)

"Musical," *New York Times* (13 Dec 1859)

BRIAN C. THOMPSON

Oliver, King [Joe] (*b* Abend, LA, 11 May or 19 Dec 1885; *d* Savannah, GA, 10 April 1938). Jazz cornetist and bandleader. He moved to New Orleans around 1900, after his father's death. He may have first studied music as a trombonist, but from 1907 he played cornet in street parades with brass bands such as Walter Kinchen's and the Onward and at parks, bars, dance halls, and cabarets with such bands as the Eagle, the Olympia, and Kid Ory's ensemble. After being arrested with Ory in June 1918, he relocated to Chicago at the dual invitations of Bill Johnson and Lawrence Duhé. According to Paul Barbarin, Oliver became known as "King" after playing "I'm not rough" (a "talking horn" specialty) with Johnson in February 1919 at the Royal Gardens. In October 1919 he took over Duhé's band. At Ory's behest he took his Creole Band to San Francisco and Oakland in 1921, but returned with the group to Chicago after being stranded in Los Angeles. In June 1922 he premiered his new ensemble, the Creole Jazz Band, at Lincoln Gardens, and the following August LOUIS ARMSTRONG arrived from New Orleans to become its second cornetist. With a stable lineup of New Orleans musicians—Johnny Dodds (clarinet), Honore Dutrey (trombone), Johnson (double bass and banjo), Baby Dodds (drums)—and Lil Hardin on piano, Oliver began recording in April 1923. Many jazz critics and "hot" record collectors have since come to prize these records as representing the first flowering of New Orleans jazz.

Success led to dissension—the band operated democratically until Oliver demanded more authority—with various defections occurring throughout 1923. By late 1924 the reorganized band included three reeds, with Barney Bigard and Albert Nicholas (clarinet/saxophone), Luis Russell (piano), and Paul Barbarin (drums) recruited from New Orleans, and this lineup performed as the Dixie Syncopators from February 1925 to March 1927. Oliver relocated to New York and enjoyed some success at the Savoy Ballroom in May 1927, after which he was offered an engagement at the Cotton Club, which he refused. When bookings became scarce, competitors picked off his musicians. Oliver remained in New York, sustained by recording sessions, until the bank crash of 1929 wiped out his savings. In 1931 the recording stopped, and he began relentless touring, mostly for white audiences, from the Midwest to Texas. Poor management, ramshackle transportation, and changing fashion thwarted all attempts to regain his former glory. Ill health curtailed his playing during the 1930s, yet he did his best to promote talented younger musicians including Clyde Bernhardt, Polo Barnes, and Lester Young.

Oliver is generally considered one of the most important musicians in New Orleans jazz. He played with a relatively foursquare rhythm and clipped melodic style and had a repertory of expressive deviations of rhythm and pitch, some verging on theatrical novelty effects and others derived from blues vocal style. He often used timbre modifiers and was especially renowned for his wah-wah effects, as in his three-chorus solo on "Dipper Mouth Blues" (1923, OK). As a soloist he can be best heard in a number of blues accompaniments, notably with Sippie Wallace. In contrast to Freddie Keppard and

Bunk Johnson, he integrated his playing superbly with his ensemble and was an excellent leader. Of the earlier New Orleans cornetists, only Oliver was extensively recorded in the 1920s with an outstanding ensemble, and the revival of New Orleans style owed much to the rediscovery of his Creole Jazz Band recordings. After 1924 the quality of his recordings declined, due partly to tooth and gum ailments and partly to his inability to assemble a rhythm section adequate to his stylistic requirements; yet he was capable of coherent and energetic playing as late as 1930. Oliver's influence is difficult to assess: his playing during his New Orleans period (his best years, according to Souchon) was not recorded, and by 1925 his style had largely been superseded by Armstrong's. He had a formative impact on BUBBER MILEY and perhaps on such white musicians as Muggsy Spanier. Johnny Dunn copied his mute tricks; and such trumpeters as Natty Dominique and Tommy Ladnier, who remained apart from Armstrong's influence, may have derived their styles from Oliver. In the early 2010s, the extent of Oliver's influence on Armstrong himself, although clearly audible and significant, had not yet been examined properly.

SELECTED RECORDINGS

As leader of the Creole Jazz Band: Canal Street Blues (1923, Gen.); Mandy Lee Blues/I'm going to wear you off my mind (1923, Gen.); Chimes Blues (1923, Gen.); Weather Bird Blues/Dipper Mouth Blues (1923, Gen.); Snake Rag/High Society Rag (1923, OK); Zulu's Ball/Working Man's Blues (1923, Gen.); Chattanooga Stomp/New Orleans Stomp (1923, Col.); London Cafe Blues/Camp Meeting Blues (1923, Col.)

As leader of other groups: Deep Henderson/Jackass Blues (1926, Voc.); Someday, Sweetheart/Dead Man Blues (1926, Voc.); Call of the Freaks/The Trumpet's Prayer (1929, Vic.); St. James' Infirmary/When you're Smiling (1930, Vic.)

As sideman: S. Wallace: Morning Dove Blues/Every Dog has his Day (1925, OK); Devil Dance Blues (1925, OK); V. Spivey: My Handy Man/Organ Grinder Blues (1928, OK); T. Alexander: 'Frisco Train Blues (1928, OK)

BIBLIOGRAPHY

F. Ramsey Jr.: "King Oliver," *Jazzmen*, ed. F. Ramsey Jr., and C.E. Smith (New York, 1939/R), 59–91

W. Allen and B. Rust: *King Joe Oliver* (London, 1957)

E. Souchon: "King Oliver: a Very Personal Memoir," *JR*, iii/4 (1960), 6–11; repr. in *Jazz Panorama*, ed. M. Williams (New York, 1962/R), 21–30

M. Williams: *King Oliver* (London, 1960); repr. in *Kings of Jazz*, ed. S. Green (South Brunswick, NJ 1978), 241–72

L. Gushee: "King Oliver," *Jazz Panorama*, ed. M. Williams (New York, 1962)

L.O. Koch: "Structural Aspects of King Oliver's 1923 Okeh Recordings," *JJS*, iii/2 (1976), 36–46

G. Anderson: "The Genesis of King Oliver's Creole Jazz Band," *American Music*, xii/3 (1994), 283–303

B.B. Raeburn: "King Oliver, Jelly Roll Morton, and Sidney Bechet: Ménage à Trois, New Orleans Style," *The Oxford Companion to Jazz*, ed. B. Kirchner (New York, 2000), 88–101

D. Vernhettes and B. Lindström: "Joe 'King' Oliver," *Jazz Puzzles* (Paris, 2012), 85–104

LAWRENCE GUSHEE/BRUCE BOYD RAEBURN

Oliver, Paul (Hereford) (*b* Nottingham, England, 25 May 1927). English writer on jazz and blues. He wrote articles and reviews for *Jazz Journal* (1952–c1960), *Music Mirror* (1954–9), and *Jazz Monthly* (1956–70), columns for *Jazz Beat* (in the 1960s) and *Hi-fi News and Record Review* (from the 1960s to 1980), and many disc notes. He became particularly well known for his writings on early jazz and the blues; he also gave broadcasts for the BBC from 1954. Oliver successfully brought the techniques of ethnomusicology to the study of blues; he made field visits to Africa and the American South, and challenged many of the assumptions of such earlier writers on jazz as Rudi Blesh by finding a stronger kinship with the blues and early jazz in the music of the savannas than in that of West Africa. He has also conducted important research into the influence of the songster and sermon traditions on race records. In addition to his work as a writer he has given lectures on jazz at the University of Cambridge, and his drawings of jazz and blues musicians have appeared in *Jazz Journal* and *Radio Times*. He is also well-known as an architectural historian and critic.

WRITINGS
Bessie Smith (London, 1959); repr. in *Kings of Jazz*, ed. S. Green (South Brunswick, NJ, 1978)
Blues Fell this Morning: the Meaning of the Blues (London, 1960, New York, 1961, repr. as *The Meaning of the Blues*, 1963, 2/1990)
Conversation with the Blues (London, 1965, 2/1997)
Screening the Blues (London, 1968/R; New York, 1970, as *Aspects of the Blues Tradition*)
The Story of the Blues (London, 1969/R, 2/1998)
Savannah Syncopators: African Retentions in the Blues (London and New York, 1970)
Blues off the Record: Thirty Years of Blues Commentary (New York and Tunbridge Wells, UK, 1984/R) [collection of previously pubd items]
Songsters and Saints: Vocal Traditions on Race Records (Cambridge and New York, 1984)
ed.: *The Blackwell Guide to Blues Records* (Oxford, 1989, 2/1991; as *The New Blackwell Guide to Recorded Blues*, 3/1996)
Broadcasting the Blues: Black Blues in the Segregation Era (New York, 2005)
Barrelhouse Blues: Location Recording and the Early Traditions of the Blues (New York, 2009)

BIBLIOGRAPHY
T. Mazzolini: "A Conversation with Paul Oliver," *Living Blues*, liv (1982), 24–30
J.M. Dougan: *Two Steps from the Blues: Creating Discourse and Constructing Canons in Blues Criticism* (diss., College of William and Mary, 2001)
D. Horn and A.F. Moore, eds.: *Popular Music*, xxvi/1 (2007) [whole issue]

ROBERT GANNON/R

Oliver, Sy [Melvin James] (*b* Battle Creek, MI, 17 Dec 1910; *d* New York, NY, 28 May 1988). Arranger, composer, producer, bandleader, trumpeter, and singer. Growing up as an African American musician in Zanesville, Ohio, Oliver was self taught as a trumpeter and arranger. After playing in territory bands in and around Zanesville and Columbus, he became a member of Jimmie Lunceford's orchestra in 1933. His charts for the Lunceford band were distinguished by contrasts, crescendos, and unexpected melodic variations, thereby setting new standards in big band swing and close-harmony singing. His use of two-beat rhythms also set his arrangements apart.

In 1939 Oliver was hired by the trombonist Tommy Dorsey and turned his band into one of the hardest swinging and most sophisticated ensembles of the early 1940s. In 1946 he started his own big band. During the late 1940s and 1950s he mainly did studio work, as a music director for the labels Decca, Bethlehem, and Jubilee. He continued to lead big bands and smaller ensembles, recycling his old Lunceford and Dorsey successes and performing new arrangements. Along with Duke Ellington and Fletcher Henderson, Oliver must be rated one of the top arrangers of the swing era and infused almost every chart with vigor and surprise.

SELECTED RECORDINGS
As leader: Siesta at the Fiesta (1950, Decca); Then I'll be Happy (1958, Dot); Intermezzo (Souvenir) (1960, Secan); Easy Walker (1962, Secan)
As sideman with J. Lunceford: Dream of You (1934, Decca); Swanee River (1935, Decca); Organ Grinder's Swing (1936, Decca); Annie Laurie (1937, Decca); 'Tain't what you do (1939, Voc.); Ain't she sweet? (1939, Voc.)

SELECTED ARRANGEMENTS
Recorded by T. Dorsey: The one I love belongs to somebody else (1940, Vic.); Well, git it! (1942, Vic.); On the Sunny Side of the Street (1944, 20CF)
Recorded by L. Armstrong: C'est si bon (1950, Decca); Skokiaan (1954, Decca)
Recorded by E. Fitzgerald: The Hot Canary (1951, Decca)

BIBLIOGRAPHY
S. Dance: *The World of Swing* (New York, 1974)
Z. Knauss: *Conversations with Jazz Musicians* (Detroit, 1977)
H. O'Neil: *The Ghosts of Harlem: l'Histoire du quartier mythique du jazz* (Paris, 1997; Eng. trans., enlarged, 2009, as *The Ghosts of Harlem: Sessions with Jazz Legends*)

EDDY DETERMEYER

Oliveros, Pauline (*b* Houston, TX, 30 May 1932). Composer, improviser, and accordionist. Born into a musical family, Oliveros played the piano, violin, accordion, and French horn in her childhood. She studied music at the University of Houston (1949–52) and at San Francisco State College (BA 1957). From 1954 to 1965 she studied composition with ROBERT ERICKSON at the San Francisco Conservatory of Music, where, together with Ramon Sender, she established the group Sonics to explore electroacoustic improvisation. During this period she also explored free improvisation with Terry Riley and Loren Rush. With Subotnick and Sender, in 1962 she co-founded and co-directed (until 1965) the SAN FRANCISCO TAPE MUSIC CENTER. In 1966 she studied electronic music with Hugh LeCaine and from 1966 to 1967 was the first director of the Mills College Tape Music Center. From 1967 to 1981 she taught at the University of California in San Diego, where she was the director of the Center for Music Experiment (1976–9) and founded the ♀ Ensemble. Thereafter she founded and directed the non-profit Pauline Oliveros Foundation in Kingston, New York, which in 2005 became the Deep Listening Institute. In 1988 with Stuart Dempster and Panaiotis (Peter Ward) she co-founded the Deep Listening Band to perform and record in exceptionally resonant spaces. She has also regularly offered Deep Listening workshops to advance creative listening and innovative music making. She has made worldwide appearances as a composer, improviser, and performer

Pauline Oliveros. (Photo by Pietr Kers)

on the accordion, earning international recognition. Oliveros has served as visiting professor and composer-in-residence at such institutions as Oberlin, Stanford, and Northwestern and has been a Distinguished Research Professor of Music at Rensselaer Polytechnic Institute and Milhaud Professor at Mills College. Her many awards include the Bonn Beethoven Prize; Columbia University's William Schuman Award; awards from ASCAP and the Foundation for Contemporary Performance; and Gaudeamus, Seamus, Fulbright, Guggenheim and NEA Fellowships; honorary doctorates from DeMontfort University, Mills College, and the University of Maryland; an honorary membership in the Society for American Music, as well as commissions from the Fromm Foundation, Lincoln Center, Meet the Composer, SEM Ensemble, and the West German Radio. Among her students are Sidney Corbett, PAUL DRESHER, and Alexina Louie.

Oliveros's wide-ranging creative activities are marked by a strong focus on improvisation, heightened sonic awareness, and innovative uses of music technology. Oliveros began her compositional career with works featuring sustained sounds, highly differentiated timbres, and traditional notation. Much of her early music, including *Variations for Sextet* (1960), was based on improvisatory and intuitive creative processes. Exploring improvisation and live-electronic and electroacoustic music intensely in the 1960s, she increasingly drew upon indeterminate graph and verbal scores and unconventional sounds. In *Sound Patterns* (1961), rhythm and vocal extended techniques are precisely indicated, but pitch is free. Electronic works such as *Bye Bye Butterfly* and *I of IV* (1966) are based on improvisation, having been created in real time without preconceived structures and scores. In the 1960s, Oliveros began to compose so-called *Theater Pieces*, which in addition to improvisation comprise lighting, costumes, actors, film

and electronics, often tailored to specific performers and improvisers such as Stuart Dempster and William O. Smith.

In the 1970s, having immersed herself in the study of Asian and Native American cultures, including different types of meditation, Karate and T'ai Chi, Oliveros aimed at greater body, environmental, and sonic awareness, which led to numerous, mostly verbally notated *Sonic Meditations* and to the practice of Deep Listening. In some of the musical meditations the performers concentrate on "unchanging tonal centers with emphasis on changing partials," but changes may also "occur involuntarily, or without conscious effort, while sustaining a sound voluntarily." Developed with her ♀ Ensemble, these meditations as well as such other works as *To Valerie Solanas and Marilyn Monroe in Recognition of their Desperation* (1970) and *Njinga the Queen King* (1993) reflect her preoccupation with feminism and queer identity.

From the 1980s, Oliveros has broadly explored the concept of Deep Listening as a performer with Dempster, David Gamper, Panaiotis, and other members of the Deep Listening Band, playing in caverns, cisterns, cathedrals, and other uniquely resonant spaces. Oliveros usually performs on her accordion tuned in two different just intonation systems and often uses the Expanded Instrument System, a sophisticated electronic sound-processing environment, which she designed and which provides feedback to her and her fellow musicians' sonic input in the form of iterated or modified spatialized sounds. She has taught the philosophy and practice of Deep Listening, which centers on a very attentive and ecologically motivated approach to listening and performing, whereby trained and untrained musicians and non-musicians achieve a high level of acoustic interconnection with each other and their environment. Oliveros has also composed specific Deep Listening exercises and pieces, drawing on improvisation, meditation, and electronics, and in 1990 she founded the Deep Listening Catalog, a publishing enterprise.

In recent years, Oliveros has developed new performance technology. Through her Telematic Circle, she has pursued composition in virtual worlds and cyber jamming and examined possibilities of telepresent music performed in real-time and simultaneously by musicians in different locations who use the Internet (or other broadband transmission systems) and her Adaptive Use Music Instruments software. She is currently exploring assistive software for the physically and cognitively challenged to include them in various types of music making.

WORKS
(selective list)

STAGE

Seven Passages for Elizabeth Harris, dancer, mobile, tape, 1963; Apple Box Conc., amp apple boxes, 1964; Pieces of Eight, wind octet, tape, 1964; Before the Music Ends, tape, dancer, 1965; George Washington Slept Here Too, amp vn, film, projections, tape, 1965; Seven Sets of Mnemonics (mixed media), 1965; Theater Piece for Trbn Player, garden hoses, tape, 1966; Double Basses at 20 Paces, 2 db, tape, slides, cond. and referee, 2 pfmrs, 1968; The Dying Alchemist Preview, mixed media, 1969; Please Don't Shoot the Piano Player, He's Doing the Best He Can, mixed media,1969; Sonic Mediations, vv, insts, pfmrs, 1971–2; Postcard Theater (multimedia event), 1972; What to Do, pfmrs, sonic and mixed media, 1972; Crow Two (ceremonial op), 1974; Theatre of Substitution, 1 pfmr, 1975; Bonn Feier, 1977; Theatre of Substitutions: Blind/Dumb/Director, 1977; Yellow River Map, 50 or more pfmrs, 1977; Travelling Companions, dancers, perc ens, 1980; Dream Horse Spiel, radio play, vv and sound effects, 1988; Njinga the Queen King, 1993; Tribute to Jerry Hunt, accdn, video, 1994; Ghost Dance, tape, ens, dancer, actors with choreographer Paula Josa Jones, 1998; Paulina!, film soundtrack for insts and elecs, 1998; Io and Her and the Trouble with Him, opera, 2001; Drifting Depths, film sound track, 2008; Urban Echo: Circle Told, large chorus, dance, 2008

INSTRUMENTAL

Orch: To Valerie Solanas and Marilyn Monroe in Recognition of their Desperation, orch/chbr ens, 1970; Tashi Gomang, 1981; Lion's Eye, gamelan orch/synclavier, 1985; Tasting the Blaze, perc, elecs, trbn, vc, cl, 4 accdn, gagaku orch, 1985; Arctic Air, 1992; Inside/Outside/Space/Is, 1992; Tropical Air, 1994; Four Meditations, 1997; Out of the Dark, str orch, 1998; One Hundred Meeting Places, 2006

Chbr: Trio, cl, hn, bn, 1955; Variations for Sextet, fl, cl, tpt, hn, vc, pf, 1960; 1000 Acres, str qt, 1961; Trio, fl, pf, page turner, 1961; Outline, fl, perc, db, 1963; Apple Box, amp apple box, small objects, 1964; Duo, accdn, bandoneon, opt. mynah bird, 1964; Circuitry, 5 perc, lights, 1967; Engineer's Delight, pic, 7 cond., 1967; Aeolian Partitions, fl, cl, vc, pf, 1969; Horse Sings from Cloud, hmn, accdn, bandoneon, concertina, 1975; Double X, pairs of like insts with overlapping compasses, 1979; Gone with the wind, mixed ens, 1980; Monkey, ens, 1981; Mother's Day, 2 concertinas, 1981; The Wanderer, accdns, perc, 1982; The Wheel of Time, str qt, 1983; Spiral Mandala, 4 cl, 8 crystal glasses, b drum, finger cymbals, 1984; Tree/Peace, pf trio, 1984; Wings of Dove, 2 pf, double wind qnt, 1984; Portrait of Qnt of the Americas, fl ob/eng hn, cl/bcl, 1988; Portraits for Brass qnt, 1989; Grand Improvisation, ob, db, synth, 1990; Epigraphs in the Time of AIDS, long str inst, accdn, trbn/didjeridu, kbd, elecs, 1994; From Unknown Silences, ens, 1996; Primordial Lift, ens, elecs, 1998; Saxual Orientation, sax qt, 1998; Sound Geometries, chbr orch, elecs, 2003; 70 Chords for Terry: A Meditation on String Theory, str qt, 2005; Inner/Outer Matrix, mixed ens, 2007; Heart of Tones—Mixed Realities, vv, trbn, Avatar Orch Metaverse, 2008; Magnetic Trails, pf, vn, 2008; Oracle Bones, nar, accdn, koto, elecs, light, 2009; Waking the Noise Intoners, 16 players, 2009; Olas, Sobre Las Olas, any ens, 2010

Solo: Rattlesnake Mountain, accdn, 1982; The Seventh Mansion: from the Interior Castle, amp accdn, effects, 1983; Waking the Heart, accdn, 1984; All Fours for the Drum Bum, perc, 1990; St. George and the Dragon, accdn, 1991; What If, accdn, 1991; Call to Listening: Space, accdn, 1992; Four for Forty, any inst, 1994; Cicada Song, accdn, 1996; From Unknown Spaces, accdn, elecs, 1998; Pigeon, accdn, elecs, 1998; Heart of Tones, trbn, elecs, 1999; Quintuplets Play Pen, pf, 2001; Scratching Back, perc, 2001; Sister Dreams, perc, 2001; Vigil, pf, 2002; Big Room, trbn, elecs, 2003; Quantum Flirts and Fits, accdn, 2003; Spirit Light, accdn, elecs, 2003; Sound Light Migrations, accdn, elecs, light, 2009

VOCAL

Choral: Sound Patterns, chorus, 1961; O HA AH, chorus, cond., 2 perc, 1968; AOK, chorus, accdn, vns, conds., 8 country fiddles, tape, 1969; Meditations on the Points of the Compass, 12 solo vv, chorus, perc, 1970; Angels and Demons, chorus, ens, 1980; Drama of the Five Families, nar, 1v, chorus, 1984; Legend, amp, accdn, chorus, perc, 1985; Midnight Operas, chorus, 1992; Sound Patterns and Tropes, chorus, perc, 2001; A New Indigo Peace, pf, chorus, 2008

Other vocal: 3 Songs (R. Duncan, C. Olson), S, pf, 1957; The C(s) for Once, vv, fls, tpts, tape delay, 1966; Music for Tai Chi, vv, accdn, str, wind, perc, 1970; Horse Sings from a Cloud (Rose Mountain), 1v, accdn, 1977; The Wheel of Life, vv, 1978; The Wandering, 1v, digital delay, 1984; Oh Sister Whose Name Is Goddess, 1v, digital delay, 1984; Song of the Ancestors, 1v, shell tpt, didjeridu, 1984; The Chicken Who Learned How to Fly, vv, nar, synth, 1985; The New Sound Meditation, vv, 1989; Deep Listening Pieces, 1v, ens, 1990; In Memory of the Future, 1v, 1991; Reflections on the Persian Gulf, 1v, accdn, 1991; Beyond the Mysterious Silence, 1v, cl, trbn, pf, accdn, 1996; A Song for Margrit, v, 1998; The Space of Spirit, vv, org, carillon, 1999; For the Memory of Christine, vv, perc, 2006

ELECTRONIC

Time Perspectives, tape, 1961; Bye Bye Butterfly, oscillators, amps, tape, 1965; Mnemonics I, II, and V, tape, elecs, 1965; Rock Sym., live elecs, tape, 1965; Big Mother Is Watching You, tape, 1966; The Day I Disconnected the Erase Head and Forgot to Reconnect It, tape elecs, 1966; 5000 Miles, tape, 1966; I, II of IV, tape, 1966; Participle Dangling in Honour of Gertrude Stein, tape, mobile, work crew, 1966; Music for Lysistrata, tape, elecs, 1968; Live Electronic Piece for Merce Cunningham's Dance, 1969; Bog Road with Bird Call Patch, tape 1967; Tara's Room, tape, 1988; Contenders, tape, 1990; Listening for Life, 1991; Sound Signum, tape, 1997; Ear Piece, radio/tape, 1998; Murphy Mixup, laptop orch, 2006; Sudophonia, sudophone orch, 2008; DroniPhonia, 6 iPhones, multi-instrumentalist(s), 2009

Principal publishers: Deep Listening, Smith

WRITINGS
(selective list)

"Karl Kohn: *Concerto Mutabile*," *PNM*, ii/2 (1963–4), 87–99
Pauline's Proverbs, ed. L. Montano (Berkeley, 1976)
Initiation Dream (Los Angeles, 1982)
Software for People: Collected Writings, 1963–80 (Baltimore, 1984)
"Cues," ed. P.P. Smith, *MQ*, lxxvii (1993), 373–83
The Roots of the Moment: Collected Writings, 1980–1996 (New York, 1998)
Deep Listening: a Composer's Sound Practice (Bloomington, IN, 2005)
"My American Music: Soundscape, Politics, Technology, Community," *American Music*, xxv/4 (2007), 389–404
Sounding Margins: Collected Writings, 1992–2009 (Kingston, NY, 2010)

BIBLIOGRAPHY

KdG (E. Rieger)
M. Subotnick: "Pauline Oliveros: Trio," *PNM*, ii/1 (1963), 77–82
W. Zimmermann: "Pauline Oliveros," *Desert Plants: Conversations with 23 American Musicians* (Vancouver, BC, 1976)
H. Von Gunden: *The Music of Pauline Oliveros* (Metuchen, NJ, 1983)
G. Gronemeyer: "Hast Du jemals den Klang eines schmelzenden Eisbergs gehört? Porträt von Pauline Oliveros," *Neuland*, no.4 (1983–4), 277–86
M.E. Young: *Tashi gomang. Pauline Oliveros: a Biography and Descriptive Catalog of Compositions* (diss, U. of Minnesota, 1991)

M.F. Schloss: *Out of the Twentieth Century: Three Composers, Three Musics, One Femininity* (diss., Wesleyan U., 1993)

T. Taylor: "The Gendered Construction of the Musical Self: the Music of Pauline Oliveros," *MQ*, lxxvii/3 (1993), 385–96

E. LeGuin: "Uneasy Listening," *repercussions*, iii/1 (1994), 5–21

S. Feisst: *Der Begriff "Improvisation" in der neuen Musik* (Sinzig, 1997)

K. Setar: *An Evolution in Listening: an Analytical and Critical Study of Structural, Acoustic, and Phenomenal Aspects of Selected Works by Pauline Oliveros* (diss. U. of Southern California, 1997)

M. Ahrens and P.N. Wilson: "Häutungen: Über Pauline Oliveros," *MusikTexte*, no.76–7 (1998), 75–82

K. Setar: "Watertank Software: Eine Interaktion zwischen Pauline Oliveros und einem halligen Raum," *MusikTexte*, 76–7 (1998), 96–101

B. Barnett et al.: "30 Years of Listening: Recollections of Sonic Meditations with Pauline Oliveros," *Musicworks*, lxxviii (2000), 36–40

T. Browner: "'They should have an Indian soul': Crow Two and the Processes of Cultural Appropriation," *Journal of Musicological Research*, xix/3 (2000), 243–63

C. Omlin: "Pauline Oliveros: Pionierin auf dem Gebiet der Elektronik, der Improvisation und des von ihr entwickelten Deep Listening," *clingKlong* , no.44 (2000), 14–15

D. Reason-Myers: *The Myth of Absence: Representation, Reception and the Music of Experimental Women Improvisers* (diss., U. of California, San Diego, 2002)

D. Bernstein and M. Payne: "Pauline Oliveros," *The San Francisco Tape Music Center: 1960s Counterculture and the Avant-Garde*, ed. D. Bernstein (Berkeley, 2008), 95–111

B.R. Lange: "The Politics of Collaborative Performance in the Music of Pauline Oliveros," *PNM*, xlvi/1 (2008), 39–60

M. Mockus: *Sounding Out: Pauline Oliveros and Lesbian Musicality* (New York, 2008)

M.E. Tote: *La Monte Young, Terry Riley, Pauline Oliveros and the Emergence of the American Postmodern Drone Aesthetic, 1957–1964* (diss., Tufts U., 2010)

SABINE FEISST

Olivia. An independent lesbian-feminist record collective. Named for the heroine of a lesbian pulp fiction novel, it was founded in 1973 by young lesbian-feminist activists in Washington, DC. Judy Dlugacz (president), Meg Christian, Ginny Berson, Jennifer Woodhul, and Kate Winter relocated the company to California in 1974.

Olivia not only promoted music by female singer-songwriter guitarists but also employed female studio musicians, engineers, and distributors. Members lived and worked together as a collective. Side-stepping mainstream music distribution channels, Olivia reached audiences through mail order, feminist bookstores, touring, and women's music festivals. Their first album (Christian's *I Know You Know*, 1974) sold ten thousand copies in its first year. Their second album, Cris Williamson's *The Changer and the Changed* (1975), became one of the top-selling albums on any independent label. In response to evangelical singer and orange juice spokeswoman Anita Bryant's antigay crusading, Olivia recorded *Lesbian Concentrate* (1977), promoting lesbian visibility (and humor) and contributing financially to the Lesbian Mothers National Defense Fund. It was not until the following year that Olivia released its first albums by African American artists (Linda Tillery and Mary Watkins).

Olivia's idealist, inexperienced business practices led to financial hardship and, in 1978, a demoralizing reorganization. Despite a celebratory sold-out tenth-anniversary show at Carnegie Hall, and support from Second Wave (Olivia's subsidiary, non-separatist label), Chris-

tian left in 1984, and by 1993 Olivia's operations had morphed into running a lesbian cruise line.

BIBLIOGRAPHY

Olivia Records: More than Music, 1979 [documentary, dir. A. Clearfield]

Radical Harmonies, 2002 [documentary, dir. D. Mosbacher]

J. Peraino: "Homomusical Communities," *Listening to the Sirens: Musical Technologies of Queer Identity from Homer to Hedwig* (Berkeley, 2006), 152–94

"Olivia Records," Queer Music Heritage, <http://www.queermusicheritage.us/olivia.html> [discography]

SHANA GOLDIN-PERSCHBACHER

Ollmann, Kurt (*b* Racine, WI, 19 Jan 1957). Baritone. His principal teachers were Yolanda Marculescu, Gérard Souzay, and Marlena Malas. As an operatic performer he has appeared with New York City Opera, Santa Fe Opera, Washington Opera, La Monaie (Brussels), and La Scala Milan. In 1987 he sang the title role in Peter Sellars's production of *Don Giovanni* at the Pepsico Summerfare in New York. A protégé of Bernstein, he appeared in the local premiere of *A Quiet Place* at the Vienna Staatsoper in 1986 and recorded *Candide* and *West Side Story* under him. In addition to his operatic career he has appeared with orchestras including the Boston Pops, Boston Symphony, New York Philharmonic, Orchestre de Paris, and Philadelphia Orchestra. Ollmann's clear, lyric voice and musical suavity have also distinguished him as a recitalist. Major recital appearances include performances at Town Hall (New York City), Wigmore Hall, and Tanglewood. A champion of new music he performed the premiere of the *AIDS Quilt Songbook* at Lincoln Center in 1992, and has premiered works by Torke, Lieberson, and Rorem.

BIBLIOGRAPHY

D. Kubiak: "Embracing the Unexpected: an Interview with Kurt Ollmann," *Classical Singer* (Nov 2004), 8–13, 32–34

CORI ELLISON/MICHAEL HIX

Olmstead, Andrea (*b* Dayton, OH, 5 Sept 1948). Musicologist. She studied violin with Burton Kaplan in New York and Lea Foli at the Aspen Music Festival and played in the New York Youth Symphony and the National Orchestral Association. She studied musicology with Gustave Reese, GEORGE PERLE, H. WILEY HITCHCOCK, BARRY S. BROOK, James Haar, BRIAN FENNELLY, and Jan LaRue. She taught music history at the Juilliard School (1972–80), the Aspen Music School (1973–6), the Boston Conservatory (1981–2004), the New England Conservatory (2006–), and the University of Massachusetts, Amherst (2009–10).

She is the author of five books as well as numerous articles, reviews, program notes, and CD liner notes; she has also produced CDs and given many preconcert lectures. Her published works concentrate on the composer Roger Sessions, the Juilliard School, and composers associated with the American Academy in Rome, where she was a Visiting Scholar at various periods since 1982. Critics have hailed her writings as "illuminating" and "fascinating." Not only has her work on Juilliard been considered groundbreaking, but her books on Sessions are lauded as the authoritative works on this important composer. From 2005 to 2007 she served as Christopher Hogwood Research Fellow at the Handel and Haydn Society Orchestra and Chorus. In 2009 she adapted Romulus Linney's play *Holy Ghosts* as an opera libretto (for Larry Thomas Bell) and produced the premiere performance in Boston.

WRITINGS
(selective)

Roger Sessions and his Music (Ann Arbor, 1985)

with L. Bell: "Musica reservata in Frederic Rzewski's North American Ballads," *MQ*, lxxii (1986), 449–58

Conversations with Roger Sessions (Boston, 1987)

"The Schoenberg–Sessions Correspondence," *Journal of the Arnold Schoenberg Institute,* xii/1 (1991), 47–62

ed.: *The Correspondence of Roger Sessions* (Boston, 1992)

"The Toll of Idealism: James Loeb—Musician, Classicist, Philanthropist," *JM*, xiv/2 (1996), 233–62

Juilliard: a History (Urbana, IL, 1999)

Roger Sessions: a Biography (New York, 2008)

"'Like one of the Trees': Roger Sessions and Hadley," *Cultivating a Past: Essays on the History of Hadley, Massachusetts,* ed. M.R. Miller (Amherst, 2009), 317–334

"The Rome Prize from Howard Hanson through David Diamond," *Music and Composition at the American Academy in Rome,* ed. M. Brody (forthcoming)

JONAS WESTOVER

Olmsted [Olmstead], **Timothy** (*b* Hartford, CT, 13 Nov 1759; *d* Phoenix, Oswego County, NY, 15 Aug 1848). Composer, tunebook compiler, singing master, and fifer. His known career as a musician began during the War of Independence, when he played fife in a Connecticut regimental corps (1775), becoming a fife major in 1776. He played in a regimental band from 1777 to 1780. After the war he apparently settled in Connecticut and worked as a singing master, though the only school of his that can now be documented was held at Wethersfield in 1804. He served in the War of 1812, and in his later years lived in Whitestown, New York.

Olmsted compiled *The Musical Olio* (Northampton, MA, 1805, 2/1811), which was devoted mostly to European pieces and favored the Methodist style, but also contained 25 of his own compositions. Drawing on his experience as a bandsman he also compiled *Martial Music* (Albany, NY, 1807), a collection of instrumental marches and dances, including nearly a dozen of his own. Olmsted's range as a musician was unusual for Americans of his generation. As a psalmodist, he composed in both the indigenous New England idiom and a more Europeanized style, and he also wrote with some skill for instruments.

BIBLIOGRAPHY

H.K. Olmsted and G.K. Ward: *Genealogy of the Olmsted Family in America* (New York, 1912), 40

F.J. Metcalf: *American Writers and Compilers of Sacred Music* (New York, 1925/R1967)

F.H. Johnson: *Musical Memories of Hartford* (Hartford, CT, 1931/R1970), 40

R.J. Wolfe: *Secular Music in America, 1801–1825: a Bibliography* (New York, 1964)

R. Crawford: *Andrew Law, American Psalmodist* (Evanston, IL, 1968/R1981), 65, 71, 178, 228

J. Downey: *The Music of American Revivalism* (diss., Tulane U., 1968), 43–5

R.F. Camus: *Military Music of the American Revolution* (Chapel Hill, NC, 1976)

R.M. Wilson: *Connecticut's Music in the Revolutionary Era* (Hartford, CT, 1979), 71, 76, 84

R.F. Camus: "A Source for Early American Band Music: John Beach's Selection of Airs, Marches, etc.," *Notes*, xxxviii/4 (1982), 792–809

A.P. Britton, I. Lowens and R. Crawford: *American Sacred Music Imprints 1698–1810: A Bibliography* (Worcester, MA, 1990)

M. Fawcett-Yeske and K. Kroeger: *The Collected Works of Eliakim Doolittle (1772–1850) and Timothy Olmsted (1759–1848),* Music of the New American Nation, xv (New York, 1999)

RICHARD CRAWFORD/DAVID W. MUSIC/R

Olsen, Edward (*b* Brooklyn, NY, 4 Feb 1925; *d* Old Saybrook, CT, 13 July 2009). Fifer and museum administrator. He joined his first drum corps at the age of nine, beginning a lifelong affiliation with fife and drum corps, including Brooklyn's Charles T. Kirk Fife, Drum & Bugle Corps (beginning in 1940) and the Sons of Liberty (1949), among others. In 1989 he founded the Sons of the Whiskey Rebellion.

Olsen recognized the historical importance of traditional "ancient" corps, whose music, dress, and drill retain vestiges of their 18th-century military heritage. In 1965 he and Bill Pace co-founded The Company of Fifers and Drummers "to perpetuate the tradition of early American martial music, to encourage greater knowledge of the historical significance of fife and drum music, and to foster the spirit of fellowship among fifers and drummers." In 1985 headquarters were established in Ivoryton, Connecticut, allowing the Company to open a Museum of Fife and Drum and the Drum Corps Archives, both comprised of Olsen's lifelong collection of drum corps materials. The Company, whose membership consists of ancient corps and friends, proved vital in guiding the community through rapid growth during and after the Bicentennial by hosting performances, publishing music, assisting newly formed corps, and uniting the heretofore loosely connected ancient community.

SUSAN CIFALDI

Olympia Brass Band. Brass band. The group was founded in New Orleans in 1962 by saxophonist Harold Dejan (1909–2002), a Creole of mixed African and European ancestry who played in numerous jazz, rhythm-and-blues, and brass bands. Typical of the brass band tradition, the Olympia featured trumpets, trombones, reeds, tuba, sousaphone, and snare drum, and marched in burial processions known as "jazz funerals" and community parades called "second lines." Their initial repertoire featured Baptist hymns, standard marches, and popular songs.

The Olympia was the first brass band to fully capitalize on the introduction of local brass band practices to wider audiences via sound recordings, film and television broadcasts, media reports, and international tours. For instance, at the 1970 Super Bowl halftime show, the Olympia staged a jazz funeral in the traditional uniform of white shirt, black pants and shoes, and a visored cap. Weekly concerts at Preservation Hall were frequently interrupted by tours throughout Europe, Japan, and America.

The global success of the Olympia only enhanced their credibility within the local black communities that had initially nurtured them. After the addition of trumpeter (and later, assistant bandleader) Milton Batiste in 1964, they earned a reputation as the most progressive local band. Batiste updated their sound by drawing on the popular music rhythm-and-blues style adding repertoire from singers such as Fats Domino, Professor Longhair, and Ray Charles. The band modernized their appearance at community parades by wearing matching T-shirts printed with their logo, reserving the formal uniforms for funerals and staged concerts. By recalibrating the tradition to resonate with diverse audiences in varied performance contexts, they laid the groundwork for a "brass band renaissance" that flourished with the emergence of the young Fairview Baptist Church Christian Marching Band and the Dirty Dozen Brass Band. The Olympia disbanded after the deaths of Batiste in 2001 and Dejan in 2002.

RECORDINGS
(selective)
Olympia Brass Band 1962, Eureka Brass Band 1966/1968 (2004, AMCD-95)
Here Come Da Great Olympia Band. (2009, Preservation Hall, VPS-4)

BIBLIOGRAPHY
H. Dejan: *Everything is Lovely!* (Pijnacker, Netherlands, 1989)
M. Burns: *The Great Olympia Band* (New Orleans, 2001)
M. Sakakeeny: "New Orleans Music as a Circulatory System," *Black Music Research Journal*, xxxi/2 (2011), 291–325

MATT SAKAKEENY

Omaha (i). Native American tribe of the north-central Plains, members of the Siouan language family. Before relocation to their present-day reservation in Nebraska, they ranged over the upper Missouri River Valley, leading a semisedentary life that combined horticulture and buffalo-hunting. Music was an integral part of traditional Omaha life, and the focus of religious rituals and secret societies. Songs had various sources; they could be composed by an individual, borrowed from a neighboring tribe, or, according to traditional belief, received from a supernatural being in a dream or vision. Since songs were considered property, they could also be purchased, though only personal songs were transferable in this manner. The right to sing songs that belonged to a society or tribal group came only through membership or hereditary privilege.

Like many other Plains tribes the Omaha lived in a state of continual conflict with their neighbors. War parties were organized to secure horses and property, and to avenge previous injuries. Before departure, a feast and dance were held in which members of the war party performed the Wolf Dance (the wolf was the patron of warriors), which, with trotting steps and sudden stops, was imitative of a wolf's movements. At this time a warrior also sang his personal medicine song, typically received from a guardian spirit in a vision. A successful return prompted a victory dance, performed by both men and women, around a central pole to which scalps of the enemy were tied. Men who had distinguished themselves in war usually belonged

to one of several warrior societies; by the mid-19th century the *Haethu'shka* was the largest. Meetings included dances that pantomimed battle movements, a feast, and honor songs. These were either new compositions or reworkings of existing songs, the texts of which were altered by the addition of another warrior's name and descriptions of his deeds. The use of one item of *Haethu'shka* regalia, a long bunch of grass (representing scalps), gave rise to the name "Grass Dance," as it was adopted by the Dakota Indians. On the northern Plains the war dance performed at contemporary pow-wows is still called the Grass or Omaha Dance. The Omaha also performed the *Wa'wan*, a ceremony in which calumets were presented to unrelated groups or distant tribes as a peace offering. Songs, which accompanied the "waving of the pipes" by two dancers who simulated the flight of eagles, were an important feature. As the *Wa'wan* was not the exclusive privilege of any group, its songs were widely known and sung by both men and women.

The most important religious ceremony of the Omaha, involving two elaborate song cycles, occurred annually in July following the summer buffalo hunt. The first song cycle thanked the Creator for the buffalo; the second recounted the events of the hunt. In their narrative function the songs had repetitive and recitative-like qualities, and their sacred nature required performance in a rigidly prescribed sequence. After these rites the annual tribal dance, *He'dewachi*, was held. Originally associated with the cultivation of corn, by the mid-19th century this showed many similarities with the Sun Dance of nonagricultural Plains tribes. In the dance, which lasted one day, two concentric circles, one formed of men and the other of women, moved in opposite directions around a pole. The Omaha had several secret medicine societies, each with sacred songs and dances to be performed during a healing ceremony. Membership was open to men and women who had a vision or dream in which a medicine song was received from the supernatural being that was the society's patron.

As music played a significant part in many Omaha ceremonies, singers who knew the repertory and had strong, reliable voices were sought after and paid to perform. Singing technique was typical of the Plains style, with a fair amount of tension in the voice, a high tessitura, high dynamic level, and pulsations on longer tones. Women often accompanied male singers, doubling the melody at the octave. Songs, which were fairly short, usually consisted of five to eight phrases that became longer towards the end of the piece. A common song form consisted of one long section of three to five phrases, all of which save the first were then repeated (e.g. *ABB'* or *ABCBC*). Others were through-composed, with no repetition of melodic material, but with repeated rhythmic motifs. The range of Omaha songs varied greatly; some, as was typical of the Plains style, had a range of an octave or more; others, especially older songs associated with the cultivation of corn, had a range of a 5th. Melodies were most often pentatonic with a descending contour. The most common intervals were major 2nds, minor 3rds, and to a lesser extent perfect 4ths. Drum accompaniment with a steady, regular pulse was the rule, the beats consistently falling either just ahead of or behind the pulse of the song. Most sacred songs had texts, but these consisted only of a few words that were liberally interspersed with vocables to suit the melodic phrase. Songs of the *Wa'wan* ceremony differed from other Omaha music, exhibiting characteristics of the eastern woodlands musical style: a more undulating melodic contour, stepwise descent, and a drumbeat synchronized with the voice.

The Omaha instrumentarium was fairly large. A waterdrum, made from a hollowed section of a tree partially filled with water and covered with buffalo hide, was used to accompany most songs, both sacred and secular. Before playing the drum was tuned by wetting the hide and stretching it tightly over the frame. Frame drums with single heads were used by members of medicine societies during healing ceremonies. A sheet of rawhide was beaten by women as they sang songs intended to give strength to warriors away from home. For the *Haethu'shka* meetings, a large drum, suspended on four stakes and struck with padded beaters, was played by two to four singers. Three types of rattle provided rhythmic accompaniment: gourd rattles, used in the *Wa'wan* and by the medicine societies; and hide-container and cluster rattles, made of deer hooves tied to the end of a stick, which were part of the regalia of the warrior societies. The eagle-bone whistle was used only in the *Wa'wan*, and the cedar flute, with an external duct and six fingerholes, was played by young men during courtship.

By 1900 traditional Omaha culture had nearly disappeared. Nevertheless the Omaha continue to participate in the pan-Indian songs and dances of the northern Plains, and hold an annual powwow in August at Macy, Nebraska. Recordings of Omaha music are held at the Bureau of American Ethnology, Smithsonian Institution, Washington, DC; the Archive of Folk Culture, Library of Congress, Washington, DC; and the Archives of Traditional Music, Indiana University, Bloomington, Indiana. Historic wax cylinder recordings made by Alice Fletcher and Francis LaFlesche are gathered on *Omaha Indian Music: Omaha Pow-Wow Songs* (A2ZCDS, 2006). The Omaha White Tail Singers are among the contemporary groups to record traditional songs.

BIBLIOGRAPHY
J.O. Dorsey: "Songs of the Hecucka Society," *Journal of American Folklore*, i/1 (1888), 65–8
A.C. Fletcher: "A Study of Omaha Indian Music," *Archaeological and Ethnological Papers of the Peabody Museum*, i/5 (Cambridge, MA, 1893)
A.C. Fletcher and F. LaFlesche: *The Omaha Tribe*, 27th Annual Report of the Bureau of American Ethnology, 1905–6 (Washington, DC, 1911)
R.F. Fortune: *Omaha Secret Societies* (New York, 1932/R1969)
J.H. Howard: "Notes on the Dakota Grass Dance," *Southwestern Journal of Anthropology*, vii/1 (1951), 82–5

MARY RIEMER-WELLER/R

Omaha (ii). City in Nebraska (pop. 408,958; metropolitan area: 865,350; 2010 US Census). It is situated at the confluence of the Platte and Missouri rivers on the Nebraska–Iowa border. In 1819 the regimental band at Fort Atkinson offered concerts and evenings of musical entertainment. 15 years later, a Baptist missionary, Moses Merrill, taught music to the Otoe Indians and transcribed a book of hymns into their language. Shortly after the Nebraska Territory was opened for settlement in 1854, Peter Sarpy, a fur trader with the American Fur Company, shipped the first piano up the Missouri River from St. Louis, and the territory's musically inclined European settlers established the Germania Männerchor, a philharmonic society, and a singing society.

When Nebraska became a state in 1867, Omaha opened a music school. During the next two decades the citizens formed many musical organizations, including the Omaha City and Union Pacific bands; the Swedish Brass Band; the Arion Singing Club; the Omaha and Norden glee clubs; the Apollo Club; the Omaha Harmonic Society; the Schumann, Beethoven, and Orpheus quartets; the Haydn Trio; and a number of church choirs. Several theaters and opera houses were built, including Redick's Opera House, the Grand Opera House, the Farnam Street Theatre, and Boyd's Opera House. The Orpheum Theater, a magnificent example of late 19th-century architecture that was completely restored in 1974, continues to be used for musical performances; it also serves as the home of Opera Omaha, a company that spotlights local talent. By the end of the 19th century the Musical Mutual Protection Union (later the Musicians' Union) had been formed, the Apollo Club had received national recognition at the World's Columbian Exposition (1893), and Dvořák had visited Omaha, where he was entertained by the Czech Band and the Seventh Regiment Band. Music also played an important role at the city's Trans-Mississippi and International Exposition (1898).

In the 1920s several jazz bands became prominent, including the Dan Desdunes Band, Maceo Pinkard's Jazz Band, and the Ted Adams Orchestra. Musical activity was encouraged during the Depression by the federal government, which sponsored the Omaha Civic Orchestra. By 1958 two semiprofessional companies, the Omaha Lyric Theatre and the Civic Opera Society, had been established. In 1965 the Omaha Regional Ballet Company was founded, and in 1976 the Omaha Sinfonia began a series of "Bagels and Bach" concerts on Sunday mornings at the Joslyn Art Museum. Hundreds of concerts are staged annually through such programs as Music in the Parks, the Summer Arts Festival, and the Septemberfest. The Jazz Society holds public jam sessions, and various rock, country music, and folk groups perform locally. The many African American artists who have made Omaha their home are celebrated at the Omaha Black Music Hall of Fame, founded in 2005. One the most successful contemporary Omaha groups is Mannheim Steamroller, whose recordings combine classical music and jazz, and make use of electronic materials. Saddle Creek Records was created in the city in 1993 and the indie bands they featured, including Bright Eyes, The Faint, and 311, comprise what has been dubbed the "Omaha sound," a type of country-infused rock; a documentary on the scene, *Spend an Evening with Saddle Creek*, was released in 2005. The city now features a venue for musical events that can seat 18,300 listeners, CenturyLink Center Omaha, constructed in 2003.

BIBLIOGRAPHY

A. Sorenson: *History of Omaha: From the Pioneer Days to the Present* (Omaha, 1889)

D.D. Dustin: *Omaha and Douglas Country: a Panoramic History* (Woodland Hills, CA, 1980)

KAREN M. DYER/JONAS WESTOVER

O'Meara, Eva Judd (*b* Seymour, CT, 10 March 1884; *d* New Haven, CT, 31 Oct 1979). Music librarian and bibliographer. She learned the profession through work experience, first in public libraries in Connecticut (1905–8), then at McGill University Library (1908–11), and as a cataloger for a private library (1911–13). In 1914 she became a cataloger (with responsibility for music) at the Yale University Library. In 1917, she merged three collections to form the Music Library in the new School of Music: the School's collection (2000 volumes), the university library's *Denkmäler* collection (600 volumes), and the Lowell Mason Library (10,300 volumes) from the department of theology. She worked in the music library part time until 1924, when she became the full-time librarian until her retirement in 1952. She also taught one of the nation's first two courses in music bibliography.

Miss O'Meara (as she was known) was a founding member of the Music Library Association (MLA) in 1931 and was elected as its first vice-president (1931–7). She also established, edited, and often wrote the first mimeographed series of MLA's *Notes*, nos. 1–15 (1934–42), as a mode of sharing practical information. In 1936 she was appointed chair of the music subcommittee for catalog code revision of the American Library Association. She worked in conjunction with MLA to establish a standard code for cataloging music, of which various chapters were jointly issued (1941–2). Her distinguished services to MLA were recognized by its Citation and Honorary Membership in 1965, and an award was named in her honor in 1988.

WRITINGS

"Notes on Stencilled Choir-Books," *Gutenberg-Jahrbuch*, viii (1933), 169–85

with K. Meyer: "The Printing of Music 1473–1934," *The Dolphin*, ii (1935), 171–207

"Music Library Association," *Library Journal*, lxi (1936), 571–3

"Cataloguing of Music: a Report of Progress for the Committee on a Code for Cataloguing Music," in "Papers Read at the Joint Meeting of the American Library Association and the Music Library Association, Columbia University, June 22, 1937," *Notes*, 1st ser., v (Nov 1937), 7–9

"Report of the Committee on the Code for Music Cataloguing," in "Proceedings of the Joint Meeting of the American Library Association and the Music Library Association, Kansas City, June 1938, Minutes of the Meeting and Papers," *Notes*, 1st ser., vi (Nov 1938), 12–14

"Lowell Mason Library of Music," *The Yale University Library Gazette*, xl (Oct 1965): 57–74

"The Lowell Mason Library," *Notes*, 2nd ser., xxviii (1971), 197–208

BIBLIOGRAPHY

Obituary, H.E. Samuel, *Notes*, xxxvi (1980), 637–8

C.J. Bradley: "Eva Judd O'Meara (1884–1979)," *American Music Librarianship: a Biographical and Historical Survey* (New York, 1990), 109–21

Eva Judd O'Meara Papers, Music Library Association Archives, Special Collections in the Performing Arts, Michelle Smith Performing Arts Library, University of Maryland Libraries

MARY WALLACE DAVIDSON

ONCE. A series of concerts and musical/theatrical events produced by a group of avant-garde composers in Ann Arbor, Michigan, during the 1960s. The founders were ROBERT ASHLEY, GORDON MUMMA, DONALD SCAVARDA, GEORGE CACIOPPO, and ROGER REYNOLDS. Although all had connections to the University of Michigan (UM), ONCE was an independent venture.

Ashley, who completed a bachelor's degree at UM in 1952, returned to Ann Arbor in 1956 and began working at the university's Speech Research Institute and writing music for light shows devised by Art Professor Milton Cohen. Also working with Cohen at this time was Mumma, who had studied at UM from 1952 to 1954. By 1958 Ashley and Mumma had formed the Cooperative Studio for Electronic Music, using homemade or modified equipment and providing electronic sounds to accompany Cohen's Space Theatre shows and other theatrical activities in the community. Cacioppo and Scavarda completed bachelor's and master's degrees at UM in 1951 and 1952. Reynolds held a degree in engineering physics, but returned to UM in 1957 to enter the music program.

A series of events in May–August 1960 stimulated the first ONCE festival: the residency of composer Roberto Gerhard in the spring semester; performances by John Cage and David Tudor (14/16 May) sponsored by the College of Architecture and Design and the town's Dramatic Arts Center (DAC); a lecture/demonstration by Luciano Berio at Uolevi Lahti's record store; and an international composers' conference in Stratford, Ontario.

On 16 October 1960, Ashley and Reynolds proposed a concert series to DAC, which sponsored about a half-dozen arts activities annually. DAC contributed to ONCE throughout its history, but the annual festivals were mostly self-supporting.

The first festival (four concerts, 24 February–4 March 1961) featured Berio's Domaine Musical Ensemble, pianist Paul Jacobs, and works by ONCE composers. Subsequent festivals (1962–5) included four to seven concerts each February–March. In September 1965 an additional festival took place on the roof of a parking garage, featuring Cage, Tudor, and the Judson Dance Company. As ONCE moved to increasingly larger venues, it hosted prominent guest ensembles such as the Dorian Wind Quintet, Alvin Lucier's Brandeis University Chamber Chorus, and the University of Illinois Chamber Players. Programs for the first five years included 170 works by 92 composers, most on the cutting edge of the new music scene. Late in 1962 Reynolds left for Europe, but others arrived in Ann Arbor, among them two from Texas: Philip Krumm and Robert Sheff ("Blue" Gene Tyranny).

Ancillary events, supplementing the annual festivals and taking place at other times during the year, mushroomed: ONCE Friends, ONCE Removed, ONCE a Month. Concerts by the founders and collaborators also took place in Detroit, Toronto, Richmond, St. Louis, Hartford, Boston, and New York. Teams of players (notably Ashley and Mumma's "Music for Pianos" series) performed nationally and internationally, including a production of Cohen's Space Theatre at the Venice Biennale in 1964. After 1965 ONCE events occurred sporadically for the next three years.

ONCE had an interdisciplinary character from the outset, including films by George Manupelli, unscheduled dramatic events in the city staged before unsuspecting public audiences (*Truck*, spearheaded by Mary Ashley), and the participation of architects Joseph Wehrer and Harold Borkin. The dramatic element became increasingly pronounced, however, eventually constituting a ONCE hallmark. The group's goal was to explore the intersections of the theater, music, art, and film—and to push the boundaries of performer-audience interaction.

The most significant legacy of ONCE is the new music created for the festivals. The works are highly diverse in style, but the founders were united by their exploration of sound, whether through the medium of extended techniques on traditional instruments, electronic (or electronically modified) timbres, or the intersection of musical sounds with those of the environment.

BIBLIOGRAPHY

G. Mumma: "The Once Festival and How it Happened," *Arts in Society*, iv/2 (1967), 380–98

Music from the ONCE Festival, 2003, New World Records 80567-2 (5 CDs and 136-page explanatory booklet with historical essay by Leta Miller and notes by the composers).

LETA E. MILLER

Onda Grupera [Música Grupera]. Mexican popular musical genre. The Spanish term *onda grupera* (literally "the group wave") refers to the "group phenomenon," one of Mexico's commercially most successful forms of popular music. *Grupos* (groups) are ensembles with electric guitar, synthesized instruments, and a lead vocalist which play easy-listening Mexican and international pop ballads, as well as *cumbias* (a typical Mexican style not to be confused with its Afro-Colombian source). *Grupos* are characterized by a common-denominator style or "bubblegum sound" rather than a distinctive Mexican regional style or flavor. Among the top bands are Los Bukis, Los Temerarios, Liberación, and Los Fugitivos.

Grupo is both a hybrid and a transnational genre. It has its origins in the 1960s Mexican pop ballad/rock groups that imitated English and American rock groups. The Mexican *rocanroleros* (rock 'n' rollers) Los Teen Tops and a number of rock groups signed on to the Peerless label. Despite a lack of access to the Mexican mainstream media, *rock en español* (rock in Spanish) soon surpassed English rock in popularity. *Grupo* also draws on the Colombian *cumbia* craze that swept Mexico in the late 1950s and early 1960s. During live performances, typically held at regional fairs and dance events in smaller towns and villages, Mexican groups would usually also interpret pop *baladas* (ballads) for romantic dancing. The first generation of *grupo* musicians in the 1970s developed a mixed repertoire that borrowed from the *balada pop* tradition (singers such as Julio Iglesias and José José), *cumbia tropical* (tropical cumbia), rock, and *ranchera* (Mexican country music). This hybrid music style appealed mainly to the working class. The pioneer groups hailed from anywhere between the southeastern peninsula of Yucatán to Acapulco on the Pacific coast, but eventually Mexico's northeast became the hub for the *grupo* movement.

During the 1980s, Monterrey's increasingly more professional recording and entertainment industries propelled the pop-influenced *grupera* music and *grupo/norteño* fusions (bands such as Los Mier, Bronco, and Grupo Límite) out of their regional confines. Although northern groups did not yet gain airplay in Mexico City, the music began to attract a larger audience, notably the growing immigrant population in the United States. After an earthquake devastated Mexico City in 1985, northern music made huge inroads into the capital. The *grupo* phenomenon peaked in the early 1990s when it became part of another expanding fashion in Mexico: massive, Woodstock-style dance concerts in major cities like Monterrey and Guadalajara.

BIBLIOGRAPHY

T. Carrizosa: *La Onda Grupera: Historia del Movimiento Grupero* (Mexico City, 1997)

R. Burr: *The Billboard Guide to Tejano and Regional Mexican Music* (New York, 1999)

HELENA SIMONETT

Oneida. Native American tribe of the Iroquois confederacy.

O'Neill, Francis [Captain Francis O'Neill] (*b* Tralibane, Co. Cork, Ireland, 28 Aug 1848; *d* Chicago, IL, 28 Jan 1936). Collector and publisher of Irish birth, naturalized American. O'Neill, who immigrated to the United States from Ireland and lived most of his adult life in Chicago, was the greatest collector and publisher of Irish traditional dance music. He left home at the age of 16 and served as a cabin boy on merchant vessels, sailing around the world and surviving shipwreck in the South Pacific. After settling briefly in Missouri, he moved to Chicago and joined the city's police force in 1873. He rose through the ranks to become Chicago's Chief of Police in 1901. He was renowned for his integrity, as well as for his supposed practice of finding employment on the police force for fellow Irish musicians. If police work was the public face of O'Neill, his private life revolved around his family and the traditional dance music that was his lifelong passion. He learned to play dance music on the simple-system flute from a neighbor in Bantry, and became an accomplished performer. As Irish dance music is an aurally transmitted form, O'Neill never learned to write or read music; his transcriptions were accomplished by collaborators, chief among them James O'Neill (from Co. Down). Francis O'Neill's great project of collection and transcription began in the 1880s as a memory aid for his own extensive repertoire, but was quickly expanded to include tunes contributed by many other musicians in the Chicago area. O'Neill's first musical publication was *The Music of Ireland* (Chicago, 1903). This huge volume contained 1850 melodies, including airs, songs, and harp compositions of Turlough Carolan, as well as the dance tunes for which his collections are better known. This collection was self-published and self-promoted, and was well received. After O'Neill's retirement from the Chicago Police Force in 1905, he revised his first collection to focus on dance music, as well as to add tunes and correct errors. The result of his revision was *The Dance Music of Ireland—1001 Gems* (Chicago, 1907). It became known as the definitive collection of Irish traditional dance music and was often referred to simply as "the book." O'Neill also wrote extensively on the Irish musicians and musical practices of his day in works such as *Irish Folk Music—A Fascinating Hobby* (Chicago, 1910) and *Irish Minstrels and Musicians* (Chicago, 1913). Along with his musical collections, these publications represent a definitive glimpse into Irish American musical life at the turn of the 20th century.

BIBLIOGRAPHY
B. Breathnach: *Folk Music and Dances of Ireland* (Dublin, 1971, R/1993)
N. Carolan: *A Harvest Saved: Francis O'Neill and Irish Music in Chicago* (Cork, 1997)
H. Bradshaw and L. Doherty: "O'Neill, (Captain) Francis," *The Companion to Irish Traditional Music*, ed. F. Vallely (Cork, 1999), 285–6
                    SALLY K. SOMMERS SMITH WELLS

One-step. A social dance for couples, consisting of a simple walking step for eight counts with a pivot on the first, danced to a fast march in 2/4 or 6/8 time, at about sixty bars per minute. It was popularized by the exhibition dancers Vernon and Irene Castle around 1910.

See RAGTIME DANCE.

Ono, Yoko (*b* Tokyo, Japan, 18 Feb 1933). Performance artist, composer, singer, and songwriter of Japanese birth. Ono was born into a wealthy banking family and raised in Tokyo. In 1953, she moved to New York to attend Sarah Lawrence College, where she studied music and philosophy. Ono married Ichiyanagi Toshi in 1956. In the early 1960s the couple's Manhattan apartment became the site of many performance events; several of the artists who performed there later became associated with Fluxus. Dubbed "the high priestess of the happening," Ono was a pioneer in the conceptual art movement. She once claimed that "the only sound that exists...is the sound of the mind." Her conceptual scores, described by George Maciunas as "Neo-Haiku Theater," often consist of only brief instructions. *Earth Piece* (1963), for example, instructs the performer to "listen to the sound of the earth turning." A specialist in extended vocal techniques, Ono performed self-composed pieces that featured her virtuosic vocal exploration of screams, sighs, moans, gasps, and multi-phonics.

After Ono's marriage to JOHN LENNON in 1969, the couple performed as a group throughout the late 1960s and 70s. A notable music project of this era was the Plastic Ono Band, a concept band consisting Ono, Lennon, and a rotating group of musicians. Ono conceived of the band first as an imaginary ensemble with tape recorders and microphones, as a supergroup with a flexible membership. Intersecting rock music and avant-garde styles, Lennon and Ono performed alongside Eric Clapton, Klaus Voorman, and Alan White at the *Toronto Rock 'n' Roll Revival*. The recording of this performance was released as a live album entitled *Live Peace in Toronto 1969* and was credited solely to the Plastic Ono Band. With a slightly different lineup featuring Ringo Starr and Voorman, Ono recorded *Yoko Ono/Plastic Ono Band* in 1970. This album contains "AOS," a live recording of a jam session directed by Ono, in collaboration with free jazz musician Ornette Coleman. The Plastic Ono Band went on a hiatus after 1975 and resumed in 2009 when Ono recorded *Between My Head and the Sky* with her son Sean Lennon, Yuka Honda (formerly of Cibo Matto), and Cornelius.

In addition, Yoko Ono has engaged in musical projects that foreground a pop music sensibility. On the *Double Fantasy* album (1980), the last of Ono and Lennon's musical projects, Ono contributed tracks that exemplified the then-emerging new-wave punk sound. In "Walking on Thin Ice," released a few months after the death of Lennon, Ono explored the intersection of avant-garde vocalization and dance-rock rhythm. Her music later influenced a number of dance music DJs including Danny Tenaglia and the Pet Shop Boys to remix her songs into top hits on the Billboard Magazine's Dance/Club Play Chart.

Yoko Ono's music centralizes themes of social change. Ono vocalized her commitment to the feminist movement in the albums *Feeling the Space* (1973) and *Blueprint for a Sunrise* (2001). To express her support for the gay rights movement, Ono re-recorded alternative versions of her track "Every Man Has A Woman Who Loves Him" (1980) and released them as "Every Man Has A Man Who Loves Him" and "Every Woman Has A Woman Who Loves Her" (2004). Continuing her and Lennon's anti-war efforts, Ono contributed to Amnesty International's production of the compilation album *Wake Up Everyone* (2004), a post-9/11, politically charged album containing her re-make of "Give Peace a Chance."

WRITINGS
Grapefruit (New York, 1964)
The Bronze Age (Detroit, 1989)
To See the Skies (Milan, 1990)

BIBLIOGRAPHY
J. Cott and C. Doudna, eds.: *The Ballad of John and Yoko* (New York, 1982)
M. Sumner, K. Burch, and M. Sumner, eds: *The Guests Go to Supper* (Oakland, CA 1986)
J. Hendriks, ed.: *Fluxus Codex* (Detroit 1988)
T. Johnson: *The Voice of New Music: New York City 1972–1982* (New York, 1989)
B. Haskell and J. Hanhardte: *Yoko Ono: Arias and Objects* (Salt Lake City, 1991)

G.G. Gaar: *She's a Rebel: the History of Women in Rock & Roll* (Seattle, 1992)

O.F. Smith: "Proto-Fluxus in the United States, 1959–1961: the Establishment of a Like-Minded Community of Artists," *Fluxus: a Conceptual Country*, ed. E. Milman (Providence, RI, 1992), 45–57

E. Gomez: "Music of the Mind from the Voice of the Raw Soul," *Yes Yoko Ono*, ed. D. Ross, M. Sayle, and J.S. Wenner (New York, 2000), 231–47

B. Jungr, A. Clayson, and R. Johnson: *Woman: the Incredible Life of Yoko Ono* (Surrey, UK, 2004)

T. Levitz: "Yoko Ono and the Unfinished Music of 'John and Yoko': Imagining Gender and Racial Equality in the Late 1960s," *Impossible to Hold: Women and Culture in the 1960s*, eds. A.H. Bloch and L. Umansky (New York, 2005), 217–40

DAVID W. BERNSTEIN/WENDY F. HSU

Onondaga. Native American tribe of the Iroquois confederacy.

Oohenonpa [Two-kettle]. Native American group belonging to the Teton division of the Sioux.

Opera. Generic term for a work combining music, drama, and spectacle, in which the onstage participants sing and act some or all of their roles. As a form of musical theater, in which music usually plays the dominant role, opera is perhaps the most elaborate of art forms; it may call on the united skills of composer, librettist, director, designer, choreographer, performers, and impresarios to attain realization. In its generally understood sense, opera originated in Italy about 1600 and originally catered to the élite of society. Since opera in America developed without the patronage system under which it flourished during its first two centuries in Europe, the genre took root in other ways, first as part of the varied repertoire of stock theaters, then under impresarios who established professional touring companies or designated opera houses, then among amateur organizations and schools giving local productions of mostly light opera and operetta, and finally in universities and colleges, where both professionals and students—and often composers—were brought together in a workshop environment that developed along uniquely American lines.

The first operatic works heard in the United States were examples of the English type known as ballad opera, which originated in London in the 1720s and was quickly transplanted to America; by the 1790s Americans were composing their own operas. Foreign-language operas were introduced at about that time: first French opera, in New Orleans, in the 1790s; then Italian opera, in New York, in the 1820s; then, slightly later in New York, German opera. Not until much later were operas in other languages performed in the United States. In the 20th century, the related but traditionally separated genres of opera and musical comedy enriched one another in new genres such as "Broadway Opera" or in the operatic dimensions of musical theater composers such as Loesser and Sondheim.

This article is concerned with both the native and imported (English-language and foreign-language) operatic traditions in the United States (they are sometimes differentiated as "American opera" and "opera in America") and with their synthesis in an American operatic culture of international outlook that has experienced remarkable growth since the mid-1960s. By the beginning of the 21st century, some new operas were being produced by several companies internationally, sometimes even with an international team of creators, making the designation of "American opera" somewhat imprecise.

Various aspects of American musical theater history are considered in detail elsewhere (*see* Ballad opera, Burlesque, Experimental music theater, Megamusical, Melodrama, Minstrelsy, Musical, Musical film, Musical theater, Musical theater dance, Operetta, Pantomime, Revue, Rock musical, Television musical, Variety, and Vaudeville). Information on opera houses and their resident companies will be found in entries on the cities in which they are situated. Individuals involved with opera—composers, librettists, directors, stage designers, singers, administrators, patrons, and critics—are discussed in their own entries.

1. English-language opera to 1815. 2. European opera to the mid-19th century. 3. English-language opera during the 19th century. 4. Operatic institutions, 1880–1930. 5. American opera, 1900–1970. 6. Opera in the academy. 7. Operatic institutions, 1930–. 8. American opera in the video and digital age.

1. English-language opera to 1815. The origins of American opera lie in early 18th-century England where the term "opera" was loosely applied to any stage work containing a substantial amount of music. As a result, early American opera, like its British counterpart, was alternately described by its creators as ballad opera, ballad farce, pasticcio, interlude, melodrama, pantomime, and comic opera, with little apparent concern for establishing clear-cut genre designations. Despite the confusion that may today result from this broad array of descriptive and seemingly contradictory titles, it is commonly agreed that the earliest operas to appear in America were, in fact, English ballad operas.

By nature, Ballad opera, a genre consisting of spoken dialogue interspersed with borrowed popular songs, was well suited to the unique cultural expression of colonial America. Its interpolation of pre-existing strophic tunes to set newly written lyrics provided its audiences with easy recognition, memorability, and adaptability. In addition, the genre's penchant for borrowing music whose prior use often had some relevance to the content of the newly written lyrics added to its satirical possibilities, and led to the appearance of works specially tailored to reflect America's changing tastes and values. In the 1730s, these tastes were not all that different from those in England; the first recorded opera to be performed in America dates from 1735, when Colley Cibber's ballad farce, *Flora, or Hob in the Well*, received its American premiere in Charleston, South Carolina. Over the next three decades, works such as John Gay's *The Beggar's Opera* (1728), Colley Cibber's *Damon and Phillida* (1729), and Thomas Coffey's *The Devil to Pay, or, The Wives Metamorphos'd* (1731) were regularly imported from England, quickly becoming audience favorites.

The late 1750s to 1760s marked a period of slow but steady operatic growth in America, with the opening of several new theaters in Williamsburg, New York, Charleston, and Philadelphia. Singers such as John Henry and Maria Storer (who may be regarded as America's first prima donna) began to be recognized for their talent and colorful performances both on and off stage. It was during this time also that the earliest manifestations of a uniquely American national identity began to appear onstage. In 1756, an adaptation of Thomas A. Arne's *Masque of Alfred* added new language and music to the British original in an attempt to make the work more relevant to its Philadelphia audiences. Soon after, American artists began to regularly modify the plots, language, and locales of English works in order to better reflect their own current socio-cultural and political climate. Perhaps most notably, in 1767, Andrew Barton's *The Disappointment, or The Force of Credulity*, a ballad opera in two acts, was published (though never performed) in Philadelphia. Often considered to be the first truly American opera, *The Disappointment* revealed its American origins by combining Pennsylvania-German dialect, satirical social commentary, and popular tunes, one of which would later become known as "Yankee Doodle."

The early 1770s saw a period of decline in theatrical and operatic activity that was partly due to puritanism and its aversion to theatrical morality and partly due to rapidly deteriorating political relations with England. In 1774, the Continental Congress resolved that they would "encourage frugality, economy and industry… [and] discountenance and discourage every species of extravagance and dissipation." Musical theater did, however, continue on a limited scale; in the northern cities, religious objections were avoided by the use of puppets or by billing theater productions as moral and entertaining lectures or as concerts. Meanwhile, southern cities like Charleston and Annapolis, free from puritan opposition, continued to produce lavish spectacles. The years of the Revolution itself (1775–81) saw the development of American opera come to a virtual standstill due to diminished financial resources and the association of the theater with Loyalist beliefs. During this period, amateur companies were sponsored by the three leading generals of the British expeditionary forces: William Howe, Henry Clinton, and John Burgoyne.

When the hostilities ceased, a new period of American opera began with theaters producing works celebrating the American victory and reflecting strong patriotic sentiments such as Francis Hopkinson's *America Independent, or The Temple of Minerva* (Philadelphia, 1781), and the anonymously written *The Blockheads, or Fortunate Contractor* (New York; published in England in 1782). Ironically, these distinctly American works appeared alongside the latest English imports in Philadelphia, New York, and Baltimore where the Old American Company (led by Lewis Hallam, Jr. and John Henry) and the Maryland Company of Comedians regularly performed British hits like Thomas Linley's *The Duenna* (1775), William Shield's *The Poor Soldier* (1783), and Stephen Storace's *No Song, No Supper* (1790) throughout the remainder of the decade.

The final decade of the 18th century saw an unprecedented increase in operatic activity that laid the foundation for opera until the mid-19th century. Theaters

Scene from the first performance of Shanewis or the Robin Woman, *1918. (The Metropolitan Opera Archives)*

with facilities for opera production were constructed by investors and leased to theatrical companies in commercially important seaport cities such as Boston, Newport (where the original Brick Market Theatre still stands), New York, Philadelphia, Charleston, and New Orleans. These theaters, in turn, attracted many talented and formally trained musicians, composers, and actors from England, Germany, and France, who became active as performers, teachers, music directors, and composers, supplying orchestral accompaniments and arrangements for English comic operas and writing original music. Among the most notable of these was Englishman ALEXANDER REINAGLE (1756–1809) who, together with actor THOMAS WIGNELL, co-founded the New Company (a theatrical company that performed in Philadelphia and Baltimore), built Philadelphia's Chestnut Street Theatre and Baltimore's Holliday Street Theatre, and served as orchestra director (directing from the piano), composer, and arranger for the company's productions. Other significant contributors to the developing genre were James Hewitt (1770–1827), whose *Tammany, or The Indian Chief* (New York, 1794) is the earliest American opera to set a libretto by a woman; Benjamin Carr (1768–1831), whose *The Archers, or The Mountaineers of Switzerland* (1796) was performed in Boston, New York, and Philadelphia; Victor Pelissier (c1740–c1820), who composed music for at least 84 theatrical works as well as the well-known opera *Edwin and Angelina* (New York, 1796); John Bray (1782–1825), whose *The Indian Princess, or La Belle Sauvage* was published in Philadelphia in 1808; and Raynor Taylor (1747–1825), a prolific composer of songs and operas including *Buxom Joan* (Philadelphia, 1801) and *The Aethiop* (Philadelphia, 1814).

2. EUROPEAN OPERA TO THE MID-19TH CENTURY. Foreign-language operatic activity in the United States began in 1791 in New Orleans, with the arrival of a French theatrical troupe headed by Louis Tabery. In 1792 he opened the city's first theater, later called the Spectacle de la rue St. Pierre. In the 1805–6 season alone the St. Pierre theater produced 16 different operas by nine composers including Pierre-Alexandre Monsigny, André Grétry, Nicolas Dalayrac, François-Adrien Boieldieu, Etienne-Nicolas Méhul, and Giovanni Paisiello. A permanent opera company was established at the Orleans Theater in 1810, and French opera continued to flourish in New Orleans in a succession of theaters and opera houses, the most important and elaborate of which, the French Opera House, opened in 1859.

French opera was introduced in the North during the same period, initially by a touring company from New Orleans led by John Davis, which appeared in Philadelphia and Baltimore as well as New York, Boston, and other eastern cities as far north as Quebec in the summers of 1827–33. Better received, however, than French operas were Italian works, at first in English adaptations. Henry R. Bishop's version of Mozart's *Don Giovanni* (as *The Libertine*) was presented at the Park Theatre in New York on 7 November 1817; his version of Rossini's *Il barbiere di Siviglia* (as *The Barber of Seville*) was produced there on 3 May 1819 and repeated during every season until 1824. Such adaptations of Italian operas were the most popular works on American musical-theater stages into the 1840s. The most successful of all was Rossini's *La Cenerentola* in a version by Rophino Lacy called *Cinderella, or The Fairy-Queen and the Glass Slipper*, which received its American premiere at the Park Theatre on 24 January 1831 and was performed in New York and many other American cities for three decades; it was the first opera to be produced in St. Louis (9 Oct 1837), and it became so widely known that it spawned burlesque and parody versions in the minstrel shows of the 1840s and 1850s.

Italian opera in the original language was introduced in 1825, when a Spanish company directed by the tenor Manuel García presented *Il barbiere di Siviglia* on 29 November at the Park Theatre, New York. During the next nine months it gave almost 80 performances, including Rossini's *La Cenerentola, Semiramide, Tancredi*, and *Il turco in Italia*, Mozart's *Don Giovanni*, and two of García's own operas. Exposure to such an expressive and powerful style of singing as offered that season by García, his daughter Maria Malibran, and his troupe in works of universal appeal was ultimately to divert one channel of American musical theater in a new direction. The older lyric-theater tradition—works in English with songs and choruses (written for singing actors) interspersed with spoken dialogue—continued; but the new European opera, with dialogue in recitative arias and ensembles written for virtuoso singers trained in the bel canto manner, and orchestral accompaniment in the Romantic style, soon began to take hold. Other troupes, both visiting and resident, rode the wave of enthusiasm, particularly evident in New York and Philadelphia, for Italian operas by Rossini, Bellini, Donizetti, and later composers. This vogue was reflected concretely in 1832, when LORENZO DA PONTE formed his own company and built the Italian Opera House in New York. It opened on 18 November 1833 with Rossini's *La gazza ladra*, but burned down two years later. The next opera house to be built in New York was the Astor Place Opera House (with 1500 seats the largest theater in the United States at that time); it opened on 22 November 1847 with Verdi's *Ernani*. The much larger Academy of Music (4600 seats) opened on 2 October 1854 with Bellini's *Norma*.

Although German opera, sung in German, did not gain a foothold in the United States until the 1850s, English-language paraphrases and pastiches—adaptations with deletions and insertions—of Weber's *Der Freischütz* had been heard in 1825, his *Oberon* in 1827, Mozart's *Die Zauberflöte* in 1832, and Beethoven's *Fidelio* in 1839. (*See* §3 below.) In 1855 a series of German operas in the original language was presented at Niblo's Garden in New York; important American premieres that followed were of the complete *Fidelio* (1856), Wagner's *Tannhäuser* (Stadt-Theater, New York, 4 April 1859), Mozart's *Die Entführung aus dem Serail* (Brooklyn Athenaeum, 16 Feb 1860), and Wagner's *Rienzi* (Academy of Music, 5 March 1878).

During the half century between 1825 and 1875 operatic activity increased and spread significantly, with regular visits by operatic divas such as JENNY LIND, MARIA MALIBRAN, ADELINA PATTI, and Christine Nilsson, all of whom sang a primarily Italian repertory. As operatic excerpts were published, local bands in towns large and small more frequently included them on their concerts. In addition, piano versions of much of this music became available to be played at home. New influences would emerge with the arrival of large numbers of immigrant musicians, many from Germany. Just as the influx of English musicians had influenced the style and direction of American music during the Federal period, so in the mid-19th century the Germans led Americans into an appreciation of the passionate and sensitive aspects of European Romanticism—though not without some opposition. (For example, the opera manager and conductor Max Maretzek was accused not only of allowing immoral activities in his theater—the Academy of Music in New York—but of depicting them on stage in his production of Verdi's *Rigoletto*.)

In the 1860s, a demand for French operetta grew in the United States, notably under the efforts of H.L. Bateman and JACOB GRAU. Grau established the Théâtre Français in New York, which performed Offenbach's *opéra-bouffes* in their original language, generally with imported singers and dancers. After the success of *La Grande Duchesse de Gerolstein* in 1867, others soon followed, among the most successful and influential to be *Geneviève de Brabant*, and *La Vie Parisienne*, Bateman took an *opéra-bouffe* company to Boston, Philadelphia, Chicago, and other cities, and found themselves in com-

petition with the New Orleans French Opera Troupe. As early as 1867, Oliver Ditson in Boston published ten selections from French *opéra-bouffe* in *Gems from New Operas*. Similarly, in Chicago, Root transcribed selections from *Orphée aux Enfers* for piano. This more popular style of opera, along with the extravaganza, had a direct influence on the American musical, which began to diverge from grand opera with *The Black Crook* in 1869 and which received further stimulus from the importation of British operetta, most notably GILBERT AND SULLIVAN's *HMS Pinafore* in 1879, the most performed English-language opera in the United States in the late 19th century.

As more theaters were built specifically for imported grand opera in the United States, opera became equated with elevated and progressive taste. Yet even though some populist writers such as Walt Whitman celebrated its expressive sensuality and reveled in its mellifluous foreign tongues, a combination of the unintelligibility of its texts, the complexity of its vocal style, and the unacceptability of its scenarios (which often dealt with illicit erotic love, diabolism, or mythology) conspired to isolate "grand opera" from mainstream American culture. As a result it came to be considered by many somewhat suspect as entertainment for the elite. The coexistence of popular musical plays in English and a more formal grand opera has continued to characterize American musical theater; the former ultimately developed into the Broadway and Hollywood musicals, the latter gave rise to such cosmopolitan institutions as the Metropolitan Opera.

3. ENGLISH-LANGUAGE OPERA DURING THE 19TH CENTURY. The performance of English-language opera in America during the first decades of the 19th century was a natural outgrowth of the normal theatrical repertory on the 18th-century stage. Long a part of theatricals in the New World, English-comic and ballad operas were performed by stock company members, who were expected to sing as well as act. The advent and spread of the star system during the first decades of the century resulted in significant change in both the repertory and the production method of operatic works. Duos and trios of trained singers (primarily from the UK) began to visit the United States in the 1810s and to tour as small vocal-star troupes. In addition to the older English-comic opera repertory, these singers performed the lead roles in translations of continental operatic repertory that was too demanding for stock-company singing actors (who were relegated to the subordinate roles). As a result, English translations/adaptations of works by composers such as Weber, Auber, Rossini, Donizetti, and Bellini entered the repertory of American stock companies. This both expanded the repertory and raised audience expectations about calibre of performances.

The important vocal stars who appeared during the 1820s and 30s included soprano ELIZABETH AUSTIN (c1800–after 1835), who visited from 1828–35, and the husband and wife team of JOSEPH WOOD (1801–90) and MARY ANNE WOOD (1802–64), who visited in 1833–6 and 1840–41. Austin introduced Americans to Rossini's *La*

Olive Stanton, who played Moll in Project 891's performance of Marc Blitzstein's The Cradle Will Rock, *New York, 1938. (Photofest)*

cenerentola (in a pastiche/adaptation by Rofino Lacy, 1831) and the Woods gave the American premieres (in English) of Bellini's *La sonnambula* (1835) and *Norma* (1841); all three operas became extraordinarily popular. Information on the nature of the translations or adaptations presented by these (and later) singers is scarce, but visiting British vocal stars probably brought with them to America the same adaptations they performed in the United Kingdom—by composers such as Henry Bishop and others. Only recently has any scholarly work been conducted on such operatic adaptations. Several other influential singers arrived in the late 1830s, including two teams: soprano Jane Shirreff (1811–83) and tenor John Wilson (1800–49), who visited during 1838–40, and the Seguins, soprano Anne (?1809–88) and bass Arthur (Edward; 1809–52), who arrived in 1839 and settled permanently in America. These singers and numerous others toured the American theatrical circuit, performing (with stock companies) a repertory that included English-comic operas (by Thomas Arne, Henry Bishop, Thomas Linley, John Davy, Charles Dibdin, Stephen Storace, and Michael Rooke), *The Beggar's Opera*, and English translations of continental works (by Auber, Boieldieu, Mozart, Rossini, Bellini, Donizetti, Weber, and others).

During the 1840s the Seguins became synonymous in the mind of the American public with the performance of English opera; many believed that the company's performances during the depression years of the early 1840s (following the Panic of 1837) kept American theaters from bankruptcy. By the middle of the decade the Seguins had begun touring as a small opera troupe rather than as vocal stars. Their repertory now expanded to include English translations of additional works by continental composers as well as newer operas written in English; among the latter were Balfe's *The Bohemian Girl* (1844) and Wallace's *Maritana* (1846), both of which were premiered by the Seguins and would remain popular in the United States for most of the century. The Seguin Opera Company, in various incarnations, continued to tour until Edward Seguin's death in 1852.

By the late 1840s English opera in America was performed by medium-sized itinerant companies, which usually included principal and secondary singers and the nucleus of a chorus. These troupes still appeared in stock-company theaters, with local orchestras performing the accompaniment and some of the more musically skilled local thespians filling out the chorus. The repertory of these troupes was similar to that of the earlier vocal stars, although in the later 1850s companies incorporated such newer works as Verdi's *La traviata* and *Il Trovatore*. Some of the more prominent English-language prima donnas of the late 1840s and early 1850s include Anna Bishop (1810–84), who arrived in 1847, and Sophie Anne (Anna) Thillon (1819–1903), who visited from 1851–4. Both sopranos formed English opera companies that bore their names, and toured widely, including visits to California. The most prominent English-language troupe of the 1850s was the Pyne and Harrison Company, which featured the soprano Louisa Pyne (1832–1904) and tenor William Harrison (1813–68), both from the UK. This company toured all over the eastern half of the United States (1854–7), covering a geographical area bounded by Boston, New Orleans, and St. Louis, and giving more than five hundred performances of opera in English. Their repertory consisted primarily of works that had long been familiar to English-opera audiences: translations of continental operas by Auber (*Crown Diamonds* and *Fra diavolo*), Donizetti (*Daughter of the Regiment* and *Love Spell*), Bellini (*La sonnambula*), Rossini (*Barber of Seville* and *Cinderella*), English-language operas by Wallace (*Maritana*) and Balfe (*Bohemian Girl*), and some hold-overs from the vocal-star period such as *The Beggar's Opera* and Bishop's *Guy Mannering*. This company also gave the premiere of George Frederick Bristow's *Rip van Winkle* (27 Sept 1855), which subsequently enjoyed a run of 18 performances at Niblo's Garden in New York.

When the Pyne and Harrison Company left in 1857, opera in English declined precipitously in popularity. English troupes (such as the Lyster and Durand, Caroline Richings, and Cooper opera companies) continued to perform during the late 1850s and early 1860s, but were more successful away from the major population centers of the East Coast, where large and well-appointed Italian opera companies had become popular. The small English companies were increasingly considered old fashioned, especially in comparison with some of the larger Italian troupes, many of which now featured European operatic celebrities and mounted superior performances.

During the second half of the 19th century, however, English opera once again became a staple of the American stage. Caroline Richings (1827–82) led the way in the English-opera renaissance as the prima donna of a company organized in 1866–7. Described regularly in the press as her company's "manageress" or "directress," Richings was one of the first in a cohort of American women who organized and retained artistic control of English opera companies during the period, possibly because they were marginalized by the visiting Italian companies (which relied on European operatic celebrities as drawing cards) or because they followed the example of a several prominent American women theater managers. Regardless of the reasons, these prima donnas simultaneously found a performance niche and provided Americans with a version of opera that regained popularity in the late 1860s and retained it for the remainder of the century.

Richings' repertory was similar to that of the Pyne and Harrison troupe of a decade earlier, with the addition of newer works by Vincent Wallace (*Desert Flower* and *Lily of Killarney*), Michael William Balfe (*The Rose of Castille*), Eichberg (*Doctor of Alcantara*), and continental composers such as Verdi and Gounod; the foreign-language works frequently were adapted by Richings herself. The company confounded East Coast critics, who predicted failure: the troupe enjoyed three successful seasons (1866–9), demonstrating that American audiences were still interested in opera in the vernacular. In

Alan Oke as M. K. Gandhi in Philip Glass's Satyagraha, *performed by the English National Opera, 2007. (Tristram Kenton/Lebrecht Music & Arts)*

1869, however, the Scottish soprano EUPHROSYNE PAREPA (1836–74), Edward Seguin's niece, arrived in the United States to form an English company. She had visited America several times since 1865, performing both Italian and English opera. She and the impresario C.D. Hess lured many of Richings' best singers to their company (perhaps because several were Seguins); they mounted two extraordinarily successful seasons (1869–70 and 1871–2); Richings managed a successful company with Hess in 1870–71. Parepa-Rosa returned to Europe for the 1870–71 and 1872–3 seasons, but died suddenly in early 1874, ending the career of a promising proponent of English opera. Richings was unable to regain her momentum (because of debts from the disastrous 1869–70 season), but continued to perform until 1878.

In 1873 the soprano CLARA LOUISE KELLOGG (1842–1916) took over as the most prominent American prima donna with the formation of the Kellogg Grand English Opera Company. Kellogg had made her American debut in 1861 (as Gilda at the Academy of Music), and had spent the intervening years in the United States and abroad performing in Italian opera and in concerts. She served as prima donna and artistic director of her English company; C.D. Hess and Maurice Grau were her business managers. Kellogg was a proponent of "opera for the people," and for four years—during the worst of the post-panic depression—her company enjoyed extraordinary success, in dramatic contrast with the fate of Italian and German companies. Kellogg was widely touted as the "first American prima donna"; her company performed many of the standard operatic chestnuts that English opera troupes had been mounting for decades, as well as translations of the standard Italian repertory (including some German and French works such as *The Flying Dutchman*, *Mignon*, and *Faust*),

many of which she translated herself. After the 1876 season she disbanded her English company in order to resume performances of opera in Italian. She continued to sing in the United States and Europe until her retirement in 1887. During the mid-1870s numerous other English opera companies competed with Kellogg; the most active were the Hess, Richings-Bernard, and Holman troupes. Zelda Harrison Seguin (1848–1914) and her husband Edward (1837–79, son of Arthur and Anne) also continued the family tradition of English opera. An increasing number of comic opera troupes also emerged to take advantage of an insatiable American interest in *opéras-bouffes*. Some of Kellogg's competitors in this area were companies formed around Emily Soldene, Alice Oates, Fay Templeton, and Emily Melville; their repertories relied heavily on translations of works by Lecocq, Hervé, and (overwhelmingly) Offenbach.

The 1880s were an extraordinarily successful decade for English-language opera in the United States. Companies that performed during this period include the Max Strakosch English Opera Company (1877–80), the Emma Juch Opera Company (1888–91), and two of the most popular companies of the century, the Emma Abbott Opera Company (1879–91) and the Boston Ideals (later the Bostonians) (1879–1904). Unfortunately, the (historically) best-known English opera company from this decade was a very public failure; this has created an erroneous impression about the place of English opera in late-century American musical culture. The American (later National) Opera Company (1886–8) was founded by philanthropist JEANETTE THURBER (musical director was Theodore Thomas) for the purpose of performing English translations (not adaptations) of the same repertory that was mounted by the Metropolitan Opera, with the lead roles played by Americans. Use of native singers was both a nationalist gesture and an attempt to control costs, but the size of the company and the lavish nature of its productions resulted in high ticket prices. Despite good intentions, Thurber seriously misunderstood American opera audiences, and alienated both the middle-class supporters of English opera (because of the high ticket prices) and the wealthy patrons of foreign-language opera (who preferred the celebrity of expensive European stars and considered foreign-language productions a mark of exclusivity). The company fell apart while touring in 1887 and was disbanded in 1888.

A more accurate picture of English opera reception in late-century America is provided by the long-term success and popularity of the Abbott and Boston Ideals troupes, and a brief examination of each is illustrative. The Abbott troupe was formed around the Chicago-born soprano EMMA ABBOTT (1849–91), who was thoroughly trained in the Italian tradition in Milan and Paris during the mid-1870s. Abbott returned to the United States in 1876 and decided to pursue opera in the vernacular, in part because (as she noted) "English opera is what the people want." (interview, *Lowell Daily Citizen*, 31 October 1879). She sang with the Hess Company in 1878–9, then became prima donna and artistic director of the Abbott Grand English Opera Company, which performed both English works and some operettas, but relied primarily on translated versions of the traditional Italian-company repertory (including German and French works); she made many of the translations herself. During the mid-1880s, for example, the troupe performed English versions of more than half of the repertory mounted in the United States by James Mapleson's Italian companies. Abbott's most popular operas were *Bohemian Girl*, *Chimes of Normandy*, *Maritana*, and *Martha*; a few operettas by Arthur Sullivan, Franz Suppé, and Otto Nicolai; and continental works such as *Faust, Romeo and Juliet, Mignon, La Sonnambula, Lucia di Lammermoor, Il Trovatore*, and *Paul and Virginia* (Massé). Her versions of the continental repertory frequently included changes (in the tradition of musical theater), and she regularly interpolated songs—a practice that was still commonplace but increasingly coming under attack. As a purveyor of reasonably priced operatic entertainment, Abbott challenged a late-century trend in the United States to transform opera into Culture. As a result, she earned the contempt of some powerful American critics (most of them Wagnerians), but won the patronage of tens of thousands of Americans, who preferred their opera without the trappings that were increasingly attached to foreign-language (especially Italian) opera. Abbott became known as "the people's prima donna," and both re-established English opera in the eastern half of the United States and created an audience for it in the rapidly expanding west. Her career was cut short by her sudden death (by pneumonia) while on tour in Utah in January 1891.

The second influential troupe of the 1880s, the Boston Ideals, was the longest-lived English company active in 19th-century America. (*See* BOSTON IDEAL OPERA COMPANY.) The original troupe disbanded in 1885 (when founding

manager Effie H. Ober retired), the singers regrouped under their own management in 1887, renamed the company the Bostonians, and performed all over the United States until 1904 (some of the original members were still singing). The company's repertory illustrates well both a continued American interest in the standard English-language repertory and the growing appeal of operetta and comic opera during the last third of the century. The Ideals were originally formed to perform Sullivan's *Pinafore* in the Boston Theatre at the height of the American craze for that work. The company was so successful that at the conclusion of the engagement Ober formed an English opera troupe. The Ideals quickly expanded their repertory to include some of the usual English fare—operas by Balfe, Robert Planquette, Gaetano Donizetti, Edmond Audran, D.-F.-E. Auber, Albert Lortzing, Mozart, and Friedrich von Flotow—in addition to a wide selection of operettas by Sullivan, Suppé, Louis Varney, Jacques Offenbach, and Charles Lecocq. To a certain extent the Bostonians both reflected and helped to form American light-opera taste in the final years of the century. The company was also influential in its support of American composers; operettas by Americans, including Julius Eichberg's *Doctor of Alcantara* (1862); Reginald de Koven's *Robin Hood* (1891), *Rob Roy* (1894), *Don Quixote* (1889), and *The Knickerbockers* (1892); and Victor Herbert's *Prince Ananias* (1894) and *The Serenade* (1897), were a regular part of their repertory.

During the 1890s the most prominent English troupes were the Philadelphia-based Hinrichs Grand English Opera Company (1888–96) and the Castle Square Opera Company, founded in Boston in 1895. The former troupe was established as a summer opera company by GUSTAV HINRICHS (1850–1942) as a continuation of Thurber's mission of popularizing opera by mounting performances in English at reasonable prices (Hinrichs had been associate conductor for the American Opera Company). The troupe eventually metamorphosed into a touring ensemble, in the 1890s performing operas in German, Italian, French, and English. The latter company was organized by Henry W. Savage (1859–1927) to perform opera in English at the Castle Square Theatre; it continued to be active well into the 20th century. The troupe, which also performed on tour, had a repertory of English, German, and Italian operas (the latter in translation) as well as light operas, operettas, and musical comedies by such composers as Gustav Luders, Franz Lehár, Emmerich Kálmán, Sullivan, Edward Jacobowski, and Offenbach. There were other companies in the 1890s that continued to perform the English-opera repertory that had been popular for most of the century; these included the William Carleton, Minnie Hauk, Emma Juch, and Marie Tavary opera companies. In general, however, there was a inexorable move in the direction of light or comic opera or operetta, and many of the companies active during the last decade of the century—such as the McCaull, Templeton, J.C. Duff, Pauline Hall, and William Carleton opera companies, and the New York Casino troupe, Augustin Daly Musical Comedy Company, and Camille d'Arville, Rudolph

Aronson, de Wolf Hopper, Alice Nielsen, and Alice Oates comic opera companies—performed such fare. The appetite of the American public was clearly moving in the direction of light musical theater or operettas, heralding a change in taste that eventually would culminate in the development of American musical comedy in the early 20th century.

See also Opera companies, itinerant.

4. Operatic institutions, 1880–1930. One of the most fascinating chapters in the history of American opera is that of the leading operatic institution since the late 19th century, the Metropolitan Opera. Built to rival the Academy of Music, the Metropolitan Opera House (3625 seats, at Broadway and 39th Street in New York) in its first season offered exclusively Italian-language productions designed for a socially elite audience, opening on 22 October 1883 with Gounod's *Faust* (in translation). The new company's lavish production values and celebrity casts resulted in a substantial deficit and the replacement of Ohio-born impresario Henry E. Abbey with Leopold Damrosch (*see* Damrosch family, (1)), who assembled a company of German singers. The arrival of distinguished conductor Anton Seidl upon Damrosch's death in 1885 continued the inauguration, on a large scale, of the music dramas of Wagner to the United States. A multilingual repertoire regime was established in 1891 with the return of Abbey in partnership with John B. Schoeffel and Maurice Grau (nephew of Jacob).

Iréne Theorin, Marco Berti, and Joseph Frank in Giacomo Puccini's Turandot, San Francisco Opera, 2011. (AP Photo/San Francisco Opera, Cory Weaver)

Until Giulio Gatti-Casazza became director of the Metropolitan in 1908 (with Arturo Toscanini as conductor), no American opera was given there. Under a repertoire modernization scheme initiated by Metropolitan Opera Company chairman Otto H. Kahn, 14 new operas and two ballets with scores by Americans were presented across the next quarter century. Beginning with Converse's *The Pipe of Desire* (18 March 1910), the initial phase included a competition for American composers, with the prize awarded to Parker's *Mona* (14 March 1912). Having rejected Chadwick's realist *The Padrone*, Gatti-Casazza ventured into American repertoire again with Walter Damrosch's *Cyrano de Bergerac* (27 February 1913), Herbert's *Madeleine* (24 January 1914), De Koven's *The Canterbury Pilgrims* (8 March 1917), and Cadman's *Shanewis*, presented with a pantomimed version of Henry F. Gilbert's symphonic poem *The Dance in Place Congo* (23 March 1918). In the years immediately following World War I, film composer Joseph Carl Breil's *The Legend*, together with John Adam Hugo's *The Temple Dancer* (12 March 1919) and Hadley's *Cleopatra's Night* (31 January 1920), were featured. Failing to establish an enduring native repertory, Gatti-Casazza (who remained with the company until 1935) turned to commissioning new works. After unsuccessfully approaching Charles Martin Loeffler and John Alden Carpenter for operas, he produced the most successful American works of his regime, Deems Taylor's *The King's Henchman*, set to a libretto by Edna St. Vincent Millay (17 February 1927), and *Peter Ibbetson* (7 February 1931), the first American opera to be honored with a performance on a Metropolitan Opera season's opening night (26 December 1933). The second phase of the program also experimented with more modernist fare–Carpenter's ballet *Skyscrapers* (19 February 1926) and Gruenberg's *The Emperor Jones* (7 January 1933)–before concluding with Hanson's *Merry Mount* (10 February 1934) and John Laurence Seymour's *In the Pasha's Garden* (24 January 1935).

Once the Metropolitan Opera was on a firm financial footing, no other American company could rival it, particularly in world premieres of European works such as Puccini's *La Fanciulla del West*, Humperdinck's *Königskinder* (both 1910), and Granados' *Goyescas*, the first opera sung in Spanish at the theater (1916). Theatrical entrepreneur Oscar Hammerstein I organized the Manhattan Opera Company in 1906, and for four seasons it vied with the Metropolitan for star performers. It achieved its greatest distinction in French repertoire, giving the American premieres of Massenet's *Thaïs* (25 November 1907), Gustave Charpentier's *Louise* (3 January 1908), and Debussy's *Pelléas et Mélisande* (19 February 1908), as well as Richard Strauss's *Elektra* (1 February 1910, in French). Lacking the financial support to sustain so expensive an operation, Hammerstein eventually entered into a $1.2 million buyout agreement with the Metropolitan in 1910.

Elsewhere in the United States resident companies were established, but were able to survive only for a limited time. The Boston Opera Company, founded in 1909 by Eben D. Jordan, Jr., and Henry Russell, was to be part of an ambitious initiative spearheaded by Kahn for a network to include companies in New York, Chicago, Philadelphia, and possibly San Francisco. The plan did not fully materialize owing to the disruptions of World War I, and the Boston company was forced to declare bankruptcy in 1915. Chicago's first complete opera production (Bellini's *La sonnambula*) was in 1850, but its first resident ensemble, the joint Chicago-Philadelphia Grand Opera Company, coalesced only with network support in 1910; headed by Hammerstein music director Cleofonte Campanini with former Metropolitan tenor Andreas Dippel, it opened with Verdi's *Aida* at the Auditorium. Significant patronage from Harold F. McCormick and his wife Edith Rockefeller allowed Chicagoans to gain local control (and abandon the Philadelphia branch) in 1913. In competition with the Metropolitan, the company maintained a national touring schedule, actively sought US premieres of European operas (Wolf-Ferrari's *Il segreto di Susanna* and *I Gioielli della Madonna*; Leoncavallo's *I Zingari*; Mascagni's *Isabeau*; Montemezzi's *La nave*; Ravel's *L'heure espagnol*) and offered a roster of new American works: Herbert's *Natoma* (28 February 1911), Henry Hadley's *Azora* (26 December 1917), Arthur Nevin's *A Daughter of the Forest* (5 January 1918), and Carpenter's ballet *The Birthday of the Infanta* (23 December 1919). The company also commissioned operas in advance of the Metropolitan, among them De Koven's *Rip Van Winkle* (2 January 1920) and Leoncavallo's *Edipo re* (13 December 1920). Perhaps its high point was reached on 30 December 1921 under the single season led by soprano Mary Garden, when Prokofiev conducted the premiere of his *The Love for Three Oranges*; originally commissioned by Campanini for the 1919–20 season, the production was delayed by the conductor's death in 1919.

Utilities magnate Samuel Insull reorganized the Chicago company on a populist basis during the 1920s, completing construction on the massive Civic Opera House in 1929. The organization barely survived the stock market crash that year, however, and was dissolved in 1932. The Ravinia Opera, a summer festival organized under Louis Eckstein in 1912, likewise ceased operations in 1931. One of the few ventures to prosper was the touring San Carlo Opera Company, founded in 1910 by Neapolitan FORTUNE GALLO, which offered the standard Italian repertory at popular prices. In only a few cities have companies established in the first half of the 20th century survived. Cincinnati's Summer Opera Association was set up in 1920, when summer seasons in an open-air pavilion at the municipal zoo were introduced. In 1972 the same company was renamed the Cincinnati Opera; it performs in the Music Hall. The San Francisco Opera Company was founded in 1923 by the Italian conductor Gaetano Merola, a former chorus director for Hammerstein. With a season of works drawn from the standard repertory and casts closely linked to the Metropolitan Opera's roster, the company garnered sufficient public support for the War Memorial Opera House (opened 1932), the first municipally owned lyric theater in the United States.

5. AMERICAN OPERA, 1900–1970. Developments in 20th-century American opera reflect shifts in social and political climate, both in subject matter and musical style. Jazz inflects many operas of the first half of the century, setting a precedent of stylistic mingling among modern American operas in general. As well, 20th-century opera composers made their work available to the public through unconventional means, including new technologies such as radio and television. Many promising American operas never received premieres (or *only* received premieres) and many composers experienced decades-long delays between the composition of works and their respective premieres. Towards the middle of the century, the very nature of the operatic genre was brought into question by American operas that walked the lines between musical theater, operetta and opera, foreshadowing postmodern deconstructions of the genre in the 1970s and beyond.

At the turn of the century many American composers wrote operettas in the Romantic style of European works that had been produced in the United States in the previous decades. Among the best-known new additions were *El capitán* (1896) by John Philip Sousa and *Naughty Marietta* (1910) by Victor Herbert. Notably, Walter Damrosch's opera *The Scarlet Letter* (1896) brought the Wagnerian aesthetic to Hawthorne's sparse New England morality tale. George Chadwick's murderous *Judith* (1901) relied on a French aesthetic of Romanticism. Deems Taylor's Wagnerian *The King's Henchmen* (1926), with libretto by Edna St. Vincent Millay, became a reliable hit at the Metropolitan. A late phase of the Romantic operetta tradition brought to America by European-born composers is typified by the success of Rudolf Friml's *The Vagabond King* (1925) and Sigmund Romberg's *The Student Prince in Heidelberg* (1924).

In the years immediately before and after World War I, operas with Native American settings provided an outlet for racial tensions. All tried to find the path to a distinctive American style by using authentic or pseudo-authentic Native American music in combination with existing styles of vocal and orchestral expression, with varying degrees of success. Herbert's *Natoma* (1911, Metropolitan Opera House, Philadelphia) portrays an Indian girl (sung in the premiere by Mary Garden) linked romantically with an American naval lieutenant who, in turn, is in love with her Mexican mistress. Arthur Nevin's *Poia* (1907, concert performance, Pittsburgh; first staging Berlin, 1910) was based on observation and collection of music of the Montana Blackfoot and strives more for anthropological accuracy than exotic romance. Though select arias from these are occasionally performed, the operas fell from notice for the most part because they failed to attract either the interest of the American opera companies, dominated by a repertory of foreign operas, or the support of American audiences.

In the years following World War I the very existence of opera in the United States was threatened. Its dramaturgical conventions and musical gestures seemed stale, and as the 1920s unfolded the developing Hollywood movie industry as well as two other new sources of entertainment—radio and recordings—undermined opera's audience base. Even more problematic was the fact that almost no composer had effectively met the challenge of creating opera based on a truly American-English prosody. Not until Virgil Thomson's *Four Saints in Three Acts* (1934), with a libretto by Gertrude Stein, were all the elements put together and extensively applied in a coherent manner. Thomson and Stein dismissed the obligatory love triangle from the plot, reestablishing poetry as the equal of music in opera. Significantly, *Four Saints* was first staged with an all-African American cast.

African American composers made important contributions to operatic repertory from the turn of the century onward. Scott Joplin's first opera *A Guest of Honor* (1903) was lost, but *Treemonisha* (1911) finally premiered in an orchestrated version in 1972, quickly receiving additional performances. Joplin's recovered opera features arias and recitative, but also African American call and response spirituals; *Treemonisha* hailed education as the "savior of the race," delineating characters according to whether or not they spoke in dialect. Harry Lawrence Freeman's best-known work, *Voodoo* (1913), received its premiere in 1928, but was called "unbeautiful discord" because of the jazz influences in its score. In 1933, Shirley Graham's *Tam-Tam* and Hall Johnson's *Run, Little Chillun'* both dealt with voodoo from the black perspective, as did the Haitian voodoo vehicles *Ouanga* (1932) and William Grant Still's *Troubled Island* (1937), the latter with a libretto by Langston Hughes and Verna Arvey.

Even as several African American composers wrote jazz-inflected operas, George Gershwin brought his own perspective on the African American experience to the operatic stage. Although Gershwin was not accepted as a member of the art-music community, either by its older Yankee constituents or by the younger modernists, his *Porgy and Bess* (1935) was hailed as an example of authentic American opera. Yet Gershwin himself composed the African American spirituals heard throughout the piece, and the melodic material in the opera is often reminiscent of Russian folk music. Ever the melodist, Gershwin's arias and choruses weave in and out of the operatic fabric creating themes as memorable as any of Gershwin's popular songs. Though it was many years before the work was performed by one of the major opera companies (Houston Grand Opera in 1976), *Porgy and Bess* is now part of the standard repertory.

After Gershwin's "American folk opera," composers continued to challenge and reshape operatic conventions both musically and theatrically. Marc Blitzstein, whose stage works reflect his political and social experiences during the Great Depression, wrote the libretto for his first well-known work, *The Cradle will Rock* (1937), as well as for *No for an Answer* (1941); both deal with the struggle for labor rights. *Regina* (1949), based on Lillian Hellman's *The Little Foxes*, transcends his earlier narrow ideological concerns to explore the nature of good and evil in advanced psychological

terms, drawing on such materials as black spirituals, jazz, Broadway and Yiddish musical theater, and even the music of Louis Moreau Gottschalk (mentioned by name in the score).

Gian Carlo Menotti's success began in 1937 with the Metropolitan Opera's production of his *Amelia al ballo*, and he went on to compose the first opera commissioned for radio, *The Old Maid and the Thief* (1939). Although Italian was his first language, he composed the majority of his own libretti, and American audiences and producers responded favorably to his "participant-observer's" perspective on American culture. Menotti's *The Medium* (1946) received a premiere at Columbia University, and was then produced on Broadway along with *The Telephone* (1946). Within only two years of its Broadway premiere, *The Medium* had already been performed over six hundred times by small companies across the United States; Menotti directed a film version of the opera with Marie Powers in 1951. *The Consul* (1950) also had extended runs on Broadway, and *Amahl and the Night Visitors*, the first opera written expressly for television, was written on commission from NBC (1951). It eventually achieved the reputation of being one of the most performed English-language operas in history. Menotti composed in a mildly dissonant style that retained much of the elegance of line associated with bel canto repertory; his operas form a cornerstone of the American operatic repertory, even as they call into question the differences between a Broadway musical and an opera.

Popular tunesmiths other than Gershwin have composed musicals that verge on operas. One example is Richard Rodgers's *Oklahoma!* (1943), in which choreography by Agnes de Mille approaches balletic sophistication and symphonic orchestral arrangements by Robert Russell Bennett help to integrate a racy Broadway style with operatic control and continuity. Another important work in this genre is Frank Loesser's *The Most Happy Fella* (1956). Weill's *Street Scene* (1947); Leonard Bernstein's *Trouble in Tahiti* (1952), *Candide* (1956), and *West Side Story* (1957); and William Bolcom's *Dynamite Tonite* (1963) are all examples of works by academically trained composers who have reached out to an audience that consists of both theater-goers and opera-lovers. These composers have used an orchestra smaller than is usual for opera, yet call upon singers to exhibit operatic virtuosity—*Candide*'s Cunegonde must sing repeated high Es in her aria—alongside actors and dancers, and in collaboration with directors who could create exciting stagings. This development of an American opera on Broadway overlaps with the musical, not only in its style, content, and presentation, but also in the custom of the composers' assignment to specialists of creative tasks such as orchestrating, making choral arrangements, and composing dance sequences.

Many American operas have drawn upon American literature for their libretti, as well as biographical explorations of major American historical figures. Julia Amanda Perry's *The Cask of Amontillado* (1953), based on Poe's short story, received performances in Italy and the United States, but its lyrical atonal style did not appeal to American audiences in the long term; likewise, Louise Talma's three-hour serial opera *The Alcestiad* (1960), with a libretto by Thornton Wilder, was performed only in German, but never received an American premiere. Similarly Martin David Levy's *Mourning Becomes Electra* (1867, Met), based on Eugene O'Neill's play, was problematic because its dense harmonic language seemed at odds with the American subject. Robert Ward's *The Crucible* (1961) and Carlisle Floyd's *Of Mice and Men* (1970), on the other hand, have received numerous performances, partly owing to the primarily tonal compositional style of these two composers. Biographical operas signaled a shift in operatic subject matter that continued with Philip Glass into the 1970s and 80s. Thomson's *The Mother of us All* (1947) explores the life of Susan B. Anthony; Douglas S. Moore treats pioneers as subject matter for his operas *The Devil and Daniel Webster* (1939) and *The Ballad of Baby Doe* (1958). Jack Beeson's *Lizzie Borden* (1965) showcases the composer's expert orchestration while unfolding a grizzly, true life crime: Borden's double axe murder of her parents.

Operas of merit have been written by a number of composers better known for their output in other genres, among them Antheil (*Transatlantic*, premiere 1930), Randall Thompson (*Solomon and Balkis*, 1942), Foss (*The Jumping Frog of Calaveras County*, 1950), Herrmann (*Wuthering Heights*, composed 1943–51), Schuman (*The Mighty Casey*, 1953), Copland (*The Tender Land*, 1954), Rorem (*The Robbers*, 1958, and *Miss Julie*, 1965), Samuel Barber (*Vanessa*, 1958, and *Antony and Cleopatra*, 1966), Sessions (*Montezuma*, 1964), and Siegmeister (*The Plough and the Stars*, 1969). Works that begin to turn toward late-20th-century aesthetic choices are theater pieces by John Corigliano, including his deconstructive work *The Naked Carmen* (1970); Lou Harrison's puppet opera *Young Caesar*, which calls for gamelan and other non-Western instruments; and Bernstein's semi-staged *Mass* (1971). These pieces further stretched the definition of opera and signaled coming upheavals in American opera composition.

6. OPERA IN THE ACADEMY. Some of the changes in repertoire in the middle part of the 20th century occurred not in the traditional operatic institutions, but in the growing number of music departments in colleges and universities. The directors of these programs were motivated by two goals. The first was to train young singers in the preparation of major operatic roles and techniques, preparing them to enter the audition market for professional and semi-professional companies. The second was to produce operas that were neither suitable nor commercially viable for the professional houses. In addition to the revival of Baroque and other little-performed repertory, the latter consisted of new operas by less established composers, operas in English, experimental opera, and—perhaps most unique to the academy—chamber operas, which featured small casts and often a small orchestra, sometimes even just a piano.

The college or university opera workshop—called an American phenomenon by Natalie Limonick in 1983—began as a union of "the uprooted Europeans of the World War II years and the open arms of American freedom and democracy." Many of these singers, directors, and choreographers who immigrated to the United States in the 1930s were trained in opera and sought opportunities in universities, colleges, and conservatories, where they established opera workshops modeled on Stanislavsky's famous Opera Studio of the 1920s.

One of the first of these in America was at Louisiana State University in 1929 under Pasquale Amato, who was succeeded by Peter Paul Fuchs. Other early workshop founders included Boris Goldovsky and Richard Rychtarik, who established an opera workshop at the Cleveland Institute of Music in 1936; Goldovsky then formed a workshop in 1942 at the New England Conservatory, where Sarah Caldwell joined him in 1949 as his assistant. In New York, opera workshops were organized at Columbia University in 1943 by Herbert Graf and Nicholas Goldschmidt and at the Juilliard School in 1947 by Frederic Cohen (with Frederic Waldman as associate director). Carl Ebert founded a workshop in 1948 at the University of Southern California, where he was joined in 1953 by Walter Ducloux and later replaced by Limonick. (Ducloux moved to a similar position at the University of Texas, Austin, in 1968.) The opera program at the Hartt School was begun by Elemer Nagy (1942); Hans Busch and Ernst Hoffman initiated an opera department at Indiana University (1948), as did Ludwig Zirner at the University of Illinois (1948), Jan Popper at UCLA (1950), and Josef Blatt at the University of Michigan (1952). Similar programs across the country quickly followed. One of the results of these partnerships between professional directors and student singers, designers, and orchestras was the decentralization of opera, away from the major metropolitan centers. The Hartt opera workshop presented the first complete opera on television in 1943 (*Hansel and Gretel*, WRGB, Schenectady).

The opera workshops also produced an abundance of gifted young native talent. For example, George London, whose exposure and early training in the workshop at Los Angeles City College, set him on a path to a successful professional career. Emerging professional companies presented only a few productions annually, and were not able to support all of these singers, but many found opportunities abroad, especially in Germany. In the years after World War II German opera houses began to reinstate their year-round seasons, and as the war had depleted the numbers of young, trained, native singers they welcomed Americans. During the 1950s an estimated 600–800 American singers performed on German opera stages; some of the most successful returned to the United States as stars.

Given its remarkable teaching faculty consisting of singers with international reputations, it is no surprise that the opera program at Indiana University became associated with performing major opera repertory including Verdi, Wagner, and Puccini. In its early years, the program more frequently commissioned and produced operas of American composers, among them Foss's *Jumping Frog of Calaveras County* (1950) and N. Dello Joio's *The Ruby* (1955). When John Eaton taught on the faculty, IU produced several of his gigantic microtonal operas, among them, *Danton and Robespierre* (1978).

Professional companies, dependent on box-office receipts and full houses, generally restricted their productions to the standard repertory, but the academic workshops, often with limited budgets but guaranteed support from their sponsoring institutions, could afford to be more adventurous. As director David DiChiera later noted, it was incumbent upon universities and conservatories "to lay a foundation for developing new works that will become tomorrow's traditions."

The program at Columbia University was instrumental in leading the way. Thanks to the foresight of Alice M. Ditson and her fund, the opera workshop gave regular premieres of several composers, some of whom remained closely associated with the academy. Among the world premieres by the students at Columbia were Benjamin Britten's *Paul Bunyan* (1941), Vittorio Giannini's *Blennerhasset* (1941), Bernard Wagenaar's *Pieces of Eight* (1944), Normand Lockwood's *The Scarecrow* (1945), Menotti's *The Medium* (1946), Thomson's *The Mother of Us All* (1947), Luening's *Evangeline* (1948), Ernst Bacon's *A Drumlin Legend* (1949), Jan Meyerwitz's *The Barrier* (1950), Douglas Moore's *Giants in the Earth* (1951) and *Gallantry* (1958), Beeson's *Hello Out There* (1954), and Chávez's *Panfilo and Lauretta* (1957).

Other college opera workshops—such as those at the University of Iowa and Kansas State—came to provide similar opportunities for composers, particularly in the area of works geared toward younger voices and smaller instrumental and production forces. Though some European music festivals had fostered chamber opera, the genre proliferated in college opera workshops. Composers such as Douglas Moore, Mark Bucci, Seymour Barab, and Martin Kalmanoff composed dozens of operas for school and amateur performances. Among noted premieres by American composers with chamber operas regularly in the repertory of college workshops were Carlisle Floyd's *Slow Dusk* (Syracuse University, 1949), Weisgall's *The Tenor* (Peabody Conservatory, 1952), Hamm's *The Secret Life of Walter Mitty* (Ohio U., 1953), Wilder's *Sunday Excursion* (Opera at 8:30, Chicago, 1953), Siegmeister's *Miranda and the Dark Young Man* (Hartt School, 1956), Argento's *The Boor* (Eastman, 1957), Barab's *A Game of Chance* (Augustana College, 1957), Hoiby's *The Scarf* (Curtis, 1958), Samuel Barbers' *A Hand of Bridge* (Mannes College, 1960), Jonathan Elkus's *The Outcasts of Poker Flat* (Lehigh University, 1960), Hovhaness's *Pilate* (Pepperdine, 1966), Rorem's *Three Sisters Who Are Not Sisters* (Temple U., 1971), Pasatieri's *Maria Elena* (U. of Arizona, 1983), and Paulus's *Heloise and Abelard* (Juilliard Opera Center, 2002).

The now-defunct Central Opera Service charted thousands of American opera premieres in colleges, universities, and other non-professional settings. Since the 1970s, these have diminished in number and have partly been replaced by opportunities for American composers in non-traditional venues—Victoria Bond's *Everyone is Good for Something*, Louisville Children's Theatre, 1986, for example—and by the workshopping of new operas in young artist programs, such as the opera studios of Houston, Santa Fe, Maryland, and other companies.

7. OPERATIC INSTITUTIONS, 1930–. In 1930 only two of today's major American opera companies, the Metropolitan Opera and the San Francisco Opera, existed. Other cities depended on touring companies or on tours either from those two or the soon-to-be-defunct Chicago Civic Opera. Today, the larger cities in every state have opera companies, and many have two or more, with the smaller companies often contributing original productions, talented young singers, and unusual repertory. In 2009–10 OPERA America counted 119 professional opera companies in the United States as members. Over half of these companies were established after 1970, and one quarter of the total were established since 1980 (see Table 1).

In the years preceding the stock market crash of 1929, the Metropolitan Opera, still a for-profit entity and often resorting to the aggressive methods of the business world, consolidated its position as the dominant American company and set the norm for others, that is, a roster of European star singers, European conductors and designers, and a repertory based on European composers of the 19th century, mainly Italian and German along with a few French: Verdi, Puccini, occasionally Mozart, Richard Strauss, Wagner, Bizet, and Gounod. The poor quality of the orchestra and the general absence of rehearsals were notorious.

There were regular American premieres of operas by leading European composers (Pizzetti, Respighi, Strauss, Krenek), but not many, and General Director GIULIO GATTI-CASAZZA attempted to continue the policy which he had established when he assumed his position in 1908 of producing at least one annual premiere of an English-language opera by an American composer. The Metropolitan gave weekly performances in Philadelphia—which continued, greatly reduced, until 1961—and a tour that followed the end of the main season and included Atlanta; Washington, DC; Baltimore; Boston; Rochester; and Cleveland. These continued until 1986. Earlier plans to expand the Metropolitan into a national company were never realized, but the tours as well as early radio broadcasts gave the Metropolitan the prestige of a national company.

The broadcasts developed during a financial reorganization brought on by the Great Depression. The 1929–30 season was the first to lose money in 20 years, and the situation worsened. Otto H. Kahn, longtime president and chairman, was replaced by his attorney Paul D. Cravath, who also represented Westinghouse and RCA. Cravath signed a contract with NBC for a fee of $5000 per radio broadcast, which exceeded box-office receipts. In 1932 the company was reorganized as the nonprofit Metropolitan Opera Association. In 1936 board member Eleanor Robson Belmont founded the Metropolitan Opera Guild and its magazine, *Opera News*, which, together with the broadcasts, became important fundraising tools. With Gatti-Casazza's retirement in 1935, his successor, Edward Johnson, a veteran tenor with the company, took the reins until 1950. Performances of Wagnerian operas by Flagstad and Melchior helped keep the company afloat. The onset of World War II required Johnson to hire primarily American singers, but several distinguished European conductors—Sir Thomas Beecham, George Szell, Fritz Reiner, and Bruno Walter—also became available. The company's financial struggles continued after the Depression, as expenses mounted and aging costumes and sets deteriorated. RUDOLF BING replaced Johnson in 1950, continuing until 1972, bringing the finest European singers to the Metropolitan and raising performance standards.

The original 1883 building was viewed as inadequate from the beginning because of its cramped quarters. The present house opened at Lincoln Center in 1966. During the eight decades in the old house, the company presented a total of 218 different operas in more than 11,000 performances (Kolodin, 1936, 4/1966). During this period only 20 American operas, including 16 premières, were presented. The operas that received more than 200 performances—all composed within the period 1816–1904 and more than half Italian, only two French, and none American—remain favorites today: Verdi's *Aida* (511 performances, in 74 seasons), Puccini's *La bohème* (444, 62), Bizet's *Carmen* (380, 59), Gounod's *Faust* (362, 63), Wagner's *Lohengrin* (341, 63), Verdi's *La traviata* (339, 65), Puccini's *Tosca* (326, 53) and *Madama Butterfly* (325, 52), Leoncavallo's *Pagliacci* (319, 59), Verdi's *Rigoletto* (312, 66), Wagner's *Tristan und Isolde* (299, 61) and *Die Walküre* (292, 63), Mascagni's *Cavalleria rusticana* (290, 59), Wagner's *Tannhäuser* (263, 54) and *Die Meistersinger* (243, 57), Verdi's *Il trovatore* (242, 59), Donizetti's *Lucia di Lammermoor* (234, 58), and Rossini's *Il barbiere di Siviglia* (200, 47). Since 1966 Mozart's operas have been staged more frequently, as *Don Giovanni* (514 performances) surpassed *Tannhäuser* (470) and *Le nozze di Figaro* (452) surpassed *Die Meistersinger* (408). After Gatti-Casazza's initiatives, the Met showed little interest in new American opera, aside from some sporadic Menotti productions of the early 1940s, until Samuel Barber's *Vanessa* (1957–8) proved a great success and was revived the following season and in 1964–5. The Met commissioned a second opera from Barber, his *Antony and Cleopatra* (1966–7) to inaugurate the new opera house at Lincoln Center in a lush production by Franco Zeffirelli.

After its move to Lincoln Center, the Metropolitan expanded its season from 150 performances annually to nearly 300—by far the most extensive in the United States. Since its move and the appointment of JAMES LEVINE as Principal Conductor in 1973, and Artistic Director from 1986 to 2004, the repertory expanded to include little-known works by canonical composers

(e.g., Rossini operas other than *Il barbiere di Siviglia*, Mozart's *Così fan tutte* and *Idomeneo*, bel canto repertory, early Verdi). Handel enjoyed three productions in the mid-1980s and returned in 2004. Gluck's *Iphigénie en Tauride* returned in 2007 after a 91-year absence. Tchaikovsky's major operas began to reappear in the 1950s through the 70s and finally found a regular place in the repertory in the 1990s. Janáček's operas took a firm hold, beginning the 1990s. Other 20th-century composers to have operas staged at the Met include Weill (*Mahagonny*, 1979), Busoni (*Doktor Faust* 2001), Schoenberg (*Moses und Aron* 1999, 2003), and Berg, whose *Wozzeck* has been a staple since the late 1950s and *Lulu* since 1977. Britten's operas have become quite popular at the Met and at other American companies. Before 1945 Wagner's *Ring* was performed yearly, sometimes with drastic cuts, sometimes more or less in full. Currently, only one or two Wagnerian operas are performed each season, and the *Ring* only every four years or so. Gershwin's *Porgy and Bess* was finally performed at the Met, beginning in 1985–6 and continuing in 1989–90 and 1990–91.

JOSEPH VOLPE was appointed the company's General Manager in 1990, remaining until 2006. In 1991–2 the Met began once again to commission new works from American composers. First came John Corigliano's *The Ghosts of Versailles* in 1991–2, then Philip Glass's *The Voyage* in 1995–6, then in 1999–2000 and 2001–2, John Harbison's *The Great Gatsby*. *A View from the Bridge* was commissioned from William Bolcom for performance in 2002–3, and *An American Tragedy* from Tobias Picker in 2005–6.

The most significant changes at the Met within the last 50 years have involved the more elaborate productions possible at Lincoln Center as well as the improvement in the orchestra, which was one of James Levine's mandates. Peter Gelb, who succeeded Volpe in 2006, initiated a policy of hiring prominent international stage directors to produce innovative productions. Financial support for the Metropolitan, as for other American companies, comes almost entirely from private sources, supplemented by ticket sales. In fiscal year 2009 government agencies, including the National Endowment for the Arts as well as state and municipal organizations, contributed a total of $3.2 million, or 1.2% of the company's operating expenses. The rise of regional opera companies in the last decades of the 20th century has compromised the Met's *de facto* position as a national company, making it more of a *prima inter pares*. The economic collapse of 2008 also had a serious effect on the Met's finances, but cutbacks in programming, new production strategies, income from its Live in HD broadcasts, rush tickets, and an underwritten lottery for prime seats at bargain prices have had limited success in shoring up attendance and the balance sheet. During the 2011–12 season, operating losses grew by 7% to $135 million, the third consecutive increase, although, after donor income, the Met claimed that it broke even. In December 2012, the company offered a $100 million bond issue to pay off loans.

The New York City Opera, "the people's opera," whose first season was in 1944, cultivated aims complementary to those of the primary company. The City Opera engaged younger singers, especially Americans, presented more rarely performed or new operas, as well as works from the standard repertory in English, and maintained lower ticket prices. For a time it appeared that American operas would be especially favored among the new productions—indeed, with support from the Ford Foundation in 1958, 1959, and 1960, the spring seasons were all-American. By the mid-1980s the City Opera had produced more than 50 new American operas, maintained its policy of keeping American works in the repertory, and tried to bridge the gap between opera and musical theater. It was also more adventurous than the Metropolitan in presenting 20th-century works, reviving forgotten 19th-century and little-known 20th-century works, as well as Baroque operas.

The achievement of the City Opera continued steadily upwards through the directorships of Julius Rudel (1957–79), BEVERLY SILLS (1979–88), Christopher Keene (1989–95), and Paul Kellogg (1996–2007). With the appointment for the 2009–10 season of the Belgian director Gérard Mortier, it seemed that the company was destined to enter into timely and challenging international trends. However, Mortier resigned abruptly, when the budget he had been promised was reduced, and George Steele replaced him. Since then attendance and the finances of the company have spiraled downward. As of May 2011 the season's projected deficit of around $5 million is the fourth consecutive shortfall, totaling about $31 million since 2007. The endowment, which amounted to $64.5 million a decade ago, has been reduced to around $10 million. On 20 May, the company announced that it intended to leave the New York State Theater at Lincoln Center to reduce costs. Its future is uncertain.

Of the two major companies outside New York, the San Francisco Opera survived the Depression, but the Chicago Civic Opera did not, brought down by the financial ruin of its General Manager and chief supporter, Samuel Insull, in 1932. Its three successors were short-lived. Then the Lyric Opera of Chicago was founded in 1954. In 2011 it celebrated its 23rd year of operating in the black, selling 91% of available seats. It opened with a performance of *Don Giovanni*, followed by *Norma* with Maria Callas in the title role, her American debut. The Lyric seasons were distinguished by the greatest international singers, including Gobbi, Simionato, Björling, Simoneau, and di Stefano, and important world premieres: Penderecki's *Paradise Lost* in a co-production with La Scala, as well as three operas by William Bolcom.

In San Francisco GAETANO MEROLA continued to build on the democratic foundations of the San Francisco Opera. Its permanent home, the War Memorial Opera House, opened in 1931, funded, not by a small group of plutocratic box holders, but by a group of private citizens who encouraged thousands of ordinary San Franciscans to subscribe. Although rooted in the Italian traditions of its founder and the local Italian community, the San Francisco Opera embraced German opera as well. A 1935 production of the *Ring* with Kirsten Flagstad, Melchior, Schorr, Rethberg, and Emanuel List proved an enormous artistic and financial success.

The most significant change in American opera over the past generation has involved the growth of regional opera companies. Some of these, notably the Seattle Opera (1962), the Houston Grand Opera (1955), the Dallas Opera (1957), and the Los Angeles Opera (1986), have achieved such a high standard that they are almost equal to the three leading companies. In fact the American opera world has developed a larger and more fluid network of sophisticated companies that share co-productions with the Metropolitan and European houses. Other prominent regional companies include the Pittsburgh Opera (1939), the Tulsa Opera (1953), Opera Memphis (1956), the Santa Fe Opera (1956), Washington National Opera (1957), the Opera Company of Boston (1958–1990), the Lyric Opera of Kansas City (1958), the Boston Lyric Opera (1976), and the now-defunct Opera Boston (1980–2011). Many of these companies have featured the same international stars who sing at the Metropolitan. Some follow the model of the City Opera, with young American artists shaped into resident ensembles and a varied fare of classical, contemporary and rarely performed works. A few organizations, such as the Opera Orchestra of New York, have made rarely heard works available in concert performances.

Touring companies continued to bring opera to cities that lacked local organizations through the 1930s and beyond. Fortune Gallo's San Carlo Opera carried on into the 1950s. Several companies specialized in German opera. In 1931 the German Grand Opera Company brought the *Ring* and other Wagnerian works to Denver, Los Angeles, and other cities. The San Francisco Opera performed regularly in Los Angeles. The Turnau Opera, based in Woodstock, New York, flourished from the 1950s into the 1970s and earned serious respect. The group also toured and for some years brought a winter season to Sarasota, Florida.

Most opera companies have initiated special educational programs and performances in venues such as schools and community centers, as well as regional tours by subsidiary ensembles: the first of these was begun by the San Francisco Opera in 1966. The surge in the construction of performing arts centers from the 1960s onwards enabled more operas to be produced in more flexible ways. In 2009 the Dallas Opera moved into a new house and adopted a semi-repertory schedule. The Seattle Opera first presented Wagner's *Ring* in the summer of 1975. The high quality of its productions and ancillary educational and scholarly events have made Seattle into an American Bayreuth. The San Francisco Opera offers a four-week summer season in June, including, in 2011, the *Ring*. Other notable summer-season opera companies include the Chautauqua Opera (1929), Opera Saratoga (founded as the Lake George Opera Festival in 1962), and the Glimmerglass Festival

(1975). Since 1997, the Caramoor Center has offered two bel canto operas in concert performances. Open-air facilities have been built or adapted for opera, as at the Santa Fe Opera. Opera is also regularly presented at the Aspen Music Festival, the Tanglewood Festival, and Wolf Trap (Vienna, Virginia). In 1977 Menotti and Christopher Keene founded the Spoleto Festival USA—which has featured several important opera premieres—in Charleston, South Carolina as a counterpart to their Italian festival.

Some of the major opera companies also have mounted programs for young singers, including those of the Santa Fe Opera (founded 1956), the San Francisco Opera's Merola Program (1962), the Cincinnati Opera's Young American Artists Program (1974), the Houston Grand Opera Studio (1977), and the Metropolitan's Young Artists Development Program (1980).

Operatic activity in the United States has grown dramatically since the mid-1960s, reaching a peak in the early 1990s, and then declining. In 2007–8, US opera companies presented 1990 performances of 414 fully staged main season and festival productions, a decrease from 2004, when there were 2159 performances of 427 productions. Likewise, according to the NEA, 4.8 million adults (2.1% of the adult population) attended at least one opera performance in 2008, a significant decline from 6.2 million (3.3%) in 1992 and 6.6 million (3.2%) in 2002. Attracting audiences, especially younger opera fans, continues to present a challenge.

At the same time, interest in composing and producing opera remains high. Since 1990 North American opera companies have produced over 200 new operatic works. Although it was not until 1978 that US professional organizations created programs for composers and librettists to try out new operas, by the mid-1980s some 40 companies had such programs, including composer-in-residencies. NEA grants have also proven valuable in stimulating the composition and production of new operas. According to Opera America, during the 2010–11 and 2011–12 seasons, 33 US opera companies performed works by American composers, including nine world premieres.

8. American opera in the video and digital age. Considering that staging a new opera is usually a time-consuming, expensive, and risky endeavor, and that opera has had to compete with many new forms of 20th-century entertainment, it has been challenging for American opera composers to have their works staged and reach wide audiences. Since the mid-20th century most opera programming has remained quite conservative, and tried-and-true European operas are still the most frequently produced by US opera companies each year. Few American works have entered the standard repertory, and, more often than not, a newly composed opera enjoys only its premiere production. An equally significant challenge for contemporary composers involves attempting to meet audience expectations for opera that have been shaped profoundly by musical theater, audio recordings, popular culture, and, especially, film, video, and television.

Despite these challenges American composers continue to be drawn to creating new operas, and they have been supported to some extent by the premiere companies—including the commissioning program in the 1990s by the Chicago Lyric Opera under Ardis Krainik—and to a greater extent by regional companies, including the Houston Grand Opera (under David Gockley from the 1970s to the 2000s) and the Minnesota Opera, many of which have co-commissioned and co-produced new American operas. A number of composers have made notable contributions to opera since the 1970s: Mark Adamo (*Little Women*, 1998; *Lysistrata*, 2005); John Adams (*Nixon in China*, 1987; *The Death of Klinghoffer*, 1991; *Doctor Atomic*, 2005; *A Flowering Tree*, 2006); Argento (*Postcard from Morocco*, 1971; *Miss Havisham's Fire*, 1979; *Casanova's Homecoming*, 1985; *The Dream of Valentino*, 1994); Robert Ashley (*That Morning Thing*, 1968; and the television operas *Atalanta*, 1982, and *Perfect Lives* [*Private Parts*], 1984; *Yellow Man with Heart of Wings*, 1990; *Balseros*, 1997); Leonard Bernstein (*A Quiet Place*, 1983); Bolcom (*McTeague*, 1992; *A View From the Bridge*, 1999; *A Wedding*, 2004); Corigliano (*The Ghosts of Versailles*, 1991); Danielpour (*Margaret Garner*, 2005); Daugherty (*Jackie O*, 1997); Anthony Davis (*X, or the Life and Times of Malcolm X*, 1986; *Under the Double Moon*, 1989; *Amistad*, 1997; *Wakonda's Dream*, 2007); Deborah Dratell (*Lilith*, 2001); Tan Dun (*The First Emperor*, 2006); Eaton (*Myshkin*, 1971; *The Cry of Clytaemnestra*, 1980; *The Tempest*, 1985); Floyd (numerous operas, including *Of Mice and Men*, 1970; *Bilby's Doll*, 1976; and *Cold Sassy Tree*, 2000); Glass (including *Einstein on the Beach*, 1976; *Satyagraha*, 1980; *Akhnaten*, 1984; *The Voyage*, 1992; *Orphée*, 1993; *The White Raven*, 1998; *Appomattox*, 2007); Goldenthal (*Grendel*, 2006); Ricky Ian Gordon (*The Grapes of Wrath*, 2007); Hailstork (*Rise for Freedom: The John P. Parker Story*, 2007); Harbison (*Winter's Tale*, 1979; *The Great Gatsby*, 1999); Heggie (*Dead Man Walking*, 2000; *The End of the Affair*, 2004; *Moby-Dick*, 2010); Paula M. Kimper (*Patience and Sarah*, 1998); Larsen (*Clair de lune*, 1984; *Every Man Jack*, 2006; *Picnic*, 2009); León (*Scourge of Hyacinths*, 1999); Mechem (*John Brown*, 2008); Pasatieri (*Calvary*, 1971; *The Trial of Mary Lincoln*, 1972, *Washington Square*, 1976; *Maria Elena*, 1983; *Three Sisters*, 1986; *The Hotel Casablanca*, 2007); Stephen Paulus (*The Village Singer*, 1979; *The Postman Always Rings Twice*, 1982; *The Woodlanders*, 1985; *The Woman at Otowi Crossing*, 1995; *Summer*, 1999); Picker (*The Fantastic Mr. Fox*, 1998; *An American Tragedy*, 2005); Previn (*A Streetcar Named Desire*, 1997; *Brief Encounter*, 2009); Rorem (*Our Town*, 2005); and Stewart Wallace (*Harvey Milk*, 1995; *The Bonesetter's Daughter*, 2008).

These composers have drawn on a wide range of musical resources—from Bolcom's mixture of Pucciniesque lyricism with American popular song to Danielpour's incorporation of spirituals, gospel, folk, and jazz to Tan Dun's fusion of Western and Eastern musical practices—yet the musical language of mainstream American opera has remained relatively conservative, in keeping with genre traditions and audience expectations. Glass's

TABLE 1: Opera companies in the United States: size and seasons

The table below is based on OPERA America's national survey of the 2009–10 season. Not listed are music festivals that include opera performances, light opera companies, or musical theater companies. The numbers of productions and performances within parentheses indicate educational and touring activities by a subsidiary ensemble, operating under the same management as the principal company and within its budget. A comma between months indicates a break within a season; otherwise the season is continuous.

Company	First Season	Productions/Performances	Season
BUDGETS OVER $10 MILLION			
Metropolitan Opera	1883	26/229	Sept–June
San Francisco Opera	1923	10/75 (13/306)	Sept–Nov, June–Aug
Florida Grand Opera	1941	5/42	Nov, Jan, Feb, April
New York City Opera	1944; founded 1943	6/37	March, Apr, May, Oct, Nov
Lyric Opera of Chicago	1954	9/82 (2/3)	Sept–Feb
Houston Grand Opera	1956; founded 1955	7/31 (8/30	Oct, Jan, April
Dallas Opera	1957; founded 1956	5/20 (2/52)	Oct, Feb, April, May
Santa Fe Opera	1957; founded 1956	5/38 (3/3)	July–Aug
Washington National Opera	1957; founded 1956	7/48 (2/25)	Sept–Nov, March–May
Seattle Opera	1962 (reorganized 1964)	5/44 (3/16)	Aug, Oct, Jan, Feb, April, May
San Diego Opera	1965	5/23 (12/44)	Jan–May
Los Angeles Opera	1979	9/64 (8/55)	Sept, Nov, April–June
Utah Symphony | Utah Opera	1978 (reorganized 2002)	4/20	Oct, Jan, March, May
BUDGETS $3–$10 MILLION			
Cincinnati Opera	1920	4/9	June, July
Central City Opera	1932	6/51	June, July
Florentine Opera Company	1933 (reorganized 1950)	3/9	Nov, March, May
Pittsburgh Opera	1940	5/20	Sept, Oct, Jan, March, April
New Orleans Opera	1943	4/8	Oct, Nov, March, April
Fort Worth Opera	1946	3/8	April, May
Portland Opera	1951; founded 1950	5/20	Sept, Nov, Feb, Mar, May
Lyric Opera of Kansas City	1958	4/20	Sept, Nov, Mar, April
Skylight Opera Theatre	1959	6/113	Jan, May, Sept, Nov
Sarasota Opera	1960	5/42	Oct, Feb, March
Hawaii Opera Theatre	1961 (founded 1960)	3/12 (1/4)	Jan, Feb
Palm Beach Opera	1962	4/16 (2/2)	Dec–Feb, April
Minnesota Opera	1964	5/28	Sept, Nov, Jan, March, April
Virginia Opera	1974	4/28 (1/5)	Oct, Nov, Feb, April
Opera Company of Philadelphia	1975	4/20	Oct, March, May, June
Boston Lyric Opera	1976	3/18	Nov, Feb, March
Opera Theatre of St. Louis	1976	4/28	May, June
Atlanta Opera	1979	4/16	Oct, Nov, Feb, April
Opera Carolina	1979	4/13	Jan, March, May
Opera Colorado	1981	3/12	Nov, Feb, April
Opera San José	1984	4/32 (10/14)	Sept, Nov, Feb, April
Austin Lyric Opera	1985	3/12	Nov, Jan, April
BUDGETS $1–$3 MILLION			
Chautauqua Opera	1929	4/8 (13/16)	July–Aug
Kentucky Opera	1952	5/10	Sept–Nov
Tulsa Opera	1953	3/9	Oct, Feb, April
Madison Opera	1953	4/7	Nov, Jan, April, July
Opera Columbus	1958 (reorganized 1981)	2/4	Oct, Feb
Opera Omaha	1958	3/8	Nov, Feb, April
Dayton Opera	1960	4/11	Oct, April, May
Syracuse Opera	1963	3/6 (4/4)	Oct, Feb, April
Chicago Opera Theater	1973	3/15	April–May
Indianapolis Opera	1975	4/8.	Oct, Nov, March
Knoxville Opera	1976	3/5	Feb–April
Piedmont Opera	1977	2/6 (1/3)	Oct, April
Opera Boston	1980	3/9 (2/2)	Oct, Feb, April
Nashville Opera	1981	4/8	Oct, Nov, April
Pensacola Opera	1983	2/7	Jan, March
Opera Santa Barbara	1994	2/4 (4/4)	Sept, May
Opera New Jersey	2002	4/13	July, Feb
BUDGETS UNDER $1 MILLION			
Mississippi Opera	1945	3/3	Nov, Jan, April
Mobile Opera	1946	4/6	Oct, Feb, April
Tri-Cities Opera	1949	3/8	Nov, Feb, March
Lake George Opera at Saratoga	1962	3/10	June–July
Aurora Opera	1967 (reorganized 2010)	2/8 (1/1)	Oct
Fargo-Moorhead Opera	1968	3/6	Oct, Dec, April
Opera Southwest	1972	3/16	Oct, March
Opera Roanoke	1977	5/7	Oct, Nov, Jan, March, May
Long Beach Opera	1979	3/7 (3/3)	Jan, March, May
Opera North	1981	2/13 (1/1)	Aug

Company	First Season	Productions/Performances	Season
Tacoma Opera	1984	3/7	Nov, Feb, March
Townsend Opera Players	1984	8/34	April, Jan
Amarillo Opera	1988	4/4 (17/20)	Feb, March, April, Aug
PORTopera	1995	1/1	June
Opera in the Heights	1996	5/28	Sept, Nov, Jan, March
Long Leaf Opera	1998	8/14	June
Asheville Lyric Opera	1999	3/5 (8/8)	Oct, Nov, Jan
Opera Vivente	1999	3/12	Sept, Feb, May

Einstein on the Beach may have shocked audiences at its 1976 premiere, perhaps as much for its non-narrative presentation as its intensely repetitive score, but the tonal comfort of minimalism has proven effective in many subsequent works by Glass, Adams, and other composers. Sensational US opera events instead often center on bold stagings of established European operas in the hands of imaginative directors such as Peter Sellars, who placed *Così fan tutte* in a neon-lit roadside diner and *Don Giovanni* in Spanish Harlem, and Julie Taymor, who brought puppetry and acrobatics to *Die Zauberflöte*. Classic literary works have continued to inspire many new American operas (including *A View From the Bridge*, *The Grapes of Wrath*, *Little Women*, *Our Town*, and many others) but recent composers have also drawn on children's literature (*The Fantastic Mr. Fox*), crime fiction (*The Postman Always Rings Twice*), and contemporary novels (*The Bonesetter's Daughter*). In recent decades, a sufficient number of operas that addressed topical and political subject matter—including *Harvey Milk*, *Nixon in China*, and *The Death of Klinghoffer*—prompted some critics to disparage what they saw as tawdry examples of "CNN opera" or "headline opera." American operas more often revolve around distant historical figures—including the runaway slave Margaret Garner and the radical abolitionist John Brown—rather than contemporary figures facing hot-button issues. It remains to be seen whether works such as Nico Muhly's opera *Two Boys*, a tale of violence set against the backdrop of online relationships and Internet chatrooms to be staged at the Met in 2013, will end up charting a new course for American opera.

Less conventional opera productions—including cross-disciplinary works that integrate elements of theater, performance art, emerging technologies, avant-garde dance, and other artistic practices—are more often developed in the realm of EXPERIMENTAL MUSIC THEATER. The one-act opera *Death and the Powers* (2010), created at the MIT Media Lab by faculty member Tod Machover, offers one such futuristic vision of the genre. Composed by Machover with a libretto by the poet Robert Pinsky, the opera's lead character Simon Powers seeks eternal life by "downloading" himself into the various pieces—books, furniture, walls—of his environment. The opera features not only a cast of human performers but also a chorus of robots, and Powers's "voice" finds expression first through his human form and later through a musical chandelier and a technologically animated stage. The commercial viability of this sort of technologically advanced project is questionable, however, as such development needs tremendous institutional support, which in this case included outside funding from the Monaco-based Futurum Association.

Recognizing their aging clientele, many US opera companies have attempted, with some success, to attract younger and more diverse audiences through special promotions, educational programming, and student discounts. On the local level, grass-roots opera organizations have played an important role in demystifying opera for new audiences through inventive programming and alternative productions (including small ensembles and workshops of new operas). On a larger scale, the Metropolitan Opera has attempted to attract wider audiences by hiring well-known film directors (including Anthony Minghella and Zhang Yimou) to direct splashy new opera productions. Other film directors such as Baz Luhrmann have mounted Broadway productions of perennial favorites including *La bohème*. In fact, some of the most popular contemporary US operas have been inspired directly by the experience of watching Hollywood film, including Heggie's *Dead Man Walking* (2000), an extremely successful work that has been performed internationally over 150 times. The impact of Broadway (including "rock operas" such as *Rent*) can be heard in the musical language of works such as Gordon's *The Grapes of Wrath* and felt in programming choices, as when the Chicago Lyric Opera took the controversial yet increasingly common approach of presenting a Broadway musical (*Show Boat*) as part of their standard opera season. Some concerned observers fret that "opera" appears as if it is being redefined to refer to any production staged in an opera house. But even that definition has been challenged by those who have taken opera out of the opera house: for instance, Gordon's *Orpheus and Euridice* was staged by the Long Beach Opera in an Olympic-size swimming pool, and Diana Paulus directed *Il Mondo Della Luna* at the Hayden Planetarium in New York City.

Opera companies have continued to attempt to make the experience of attending opera more enjoyable and accessible to a wider public, from the widespread introduction of air conditioning to the construction of summertime open-air facilities, including the spectacular venue that houses the Santa Fe Opera. Supertitles projected above the proscenium, developed by the Canadian Opera Company in 1982, were introduced by the New

York City Opera the following year and adopted quickly throughout the US opera world, including regional companies and school productions. In 1995 the Metropolitan Opera further tailored this technology by installing individual screens on each seat back (patented as "Met Titles"). Opera purists have not responded as favorably, however, to all new uses of technology: the amplification of singing voices in John Adams's *Doctor Atomic* stirred substantial controversy.

Opera programming has been a fixture on US television since the mid-20th century. NBC commissioned Menotti's *Amahl and the Night Visitors* and produced it in 1951; beginning in 1954 with Strauss's *Salome*, its Opera Theater staged some 30 opera productions. Since the late 1960s the Public Broadcasting System has relayed operas in the series "Live from the Met" and "Live from Lincoln Center" (with performances by the New York City Opera), and occasionally in the series "Great Performances." PBS has also aired recorded operas performed in London, Salzburg, Milan, Bayreuth, and other opera centers. Video and audio quality of televised opera was enhanced through digital broadcasting during the 1990s and to an even greater extent by the spread of high-definition (HD) video during the 2000s. According to a 2002 study by the NEA, the number of adults who experienced opera on television, video, radio, audio recordings, or the Internet was around 37.6 million—more than five times the number who attended a live opera performance that year. Opera companies have increased their efforts to reach audiences through various new media channels. In December 2006, the Metropolitan Opera initiated Live in HD, a program that broadcasts live opera performance in high-definition video via satellite to various venues, primarily movie theaters, across the world. The audience for Live in HD—typically numbering around 10–12 broadcasts each season, plus "encore" performances—far exceeds the total annual number of attendees of live opera performances at the Met. During the 2011–12 season these broadcasts brought audiences to more than 750 theaters in the United States and Canada alone, drawn by the affordable pricing, the convenience and informality of local venues, audio and picture quality, and close-up camera work, among other attractions. Live in HD performances are also available by subscription through Met Player, an online streaming service that makes available hundreds of full-length operas. Other top US opera houses have installed permanent high-definition video production facilities, and North American opera aficionados may also watch HD-productions delivered by several overseas opera companies. While such initiatives have garnered high praise for helping to spread the joy of opera to wider audiences, concerns also have been voiced about the promotion of video over live performance—often, as some critics have observed, to the detriment of the experience in the house—the impact of premiere opera broadcasts on regional opera companies with fewer resources, and the increased significance of telegenic features in the development of future opera stars.

There is no doubt, however, that today's opera world has fully embraced new media. Twenty-first century opera companies have assembled snazzy websites—featuring interviews, highlights, and interactive activities—and advanced Web technology allows for delivering opera broadcasts through live, delayed, or archived video streams as well as via HD-video downloads. Some presentations enable a viewer to jump between multiple channels, one featuring on-stage action and another offering streaming commentary and backstage footage. Performances by premiere opera companies are also available on broadcast radio, Internet radio, and satellite radio, and they are often packaged in the most recent digital formats along with extra features such as documentary footage and interviews of cast and crew. As a result, experiencing opera in the early 21st-century United States involves new, different, and varying levels of mediation. Spending "a night at the opera" in the digital age represents a far cry from the days when operatic stars came to town, local theaters were outfitted with stage machinery, and orchestras and hometown singers were readied to support them. Today, experiencing opera in America more often as not means traveling to the local cinema or simply staying at home and turning on a big screen television.

BIBLIOGRAPHY
REFERENCES AND ANTHOLOGIES

J. Mattfeld: *A Handbook of American Operatic Premieres, 1731–1962* (Detroit, 1963)

H.E. Johnson: *Operas on American Subjects* (New York, 1964)

H.C. Lahee: *Annals of Music in America: a Chronological Record of Significant Musical Events, from 1640 to the Present Day, with Comments on the Various Periods into which the Work is Divided* (New York, 1970)

E.I. Zimmerman: *American Opera Librettos, 1767–1825* (diss., U. of Tennessee, 1972)

A.H. Drummond: *American Opera Librettos* (Metuchen, NJ, 1973)

M.F. Schleifer, ed.: *American Opera and Music for the Stage: Early Twentieth Century* (Boston, 1990)

R.H. Kornick, *Recent American Opera: a Production Guide* (New York, 1991)

E. Borroff: *American Operas: a Checklist* (Warren, MI, 1992)

P.G. Davis: *The American Opera Singer: the Lives and Adventures of America's Great Singers in Opera and Concert, from 1825 to the Present* (New York, 1997)

D.B. Wilmeth and C. Bigsby, eds: *The Cambridge History of the American Theater*, i, *Beginnings to 1870* (Cambridge, 1998)

C.T. McCants: *American Opera Singers and Their Recordings: Critical Commentaries and Discographies* (Jefferson, NC, 2004)

K. Wlaschin: *Encyclopedia of American Opera* (Jefferson, NC, 2006)

GENERAL STUDIES
ON

W. Dunlap: *A History of the American Theatre* (New York, 1832/*R*)

G.O. Seilhamer: *History of the America Theatre* (Philadelphia, 1891/*R*)

H.C. Lahee: *Grand Opera in America* (Boston, 1902/*R*)

O.G.T. Sonneck: "Early American Operas," *SIMG*, vi (1904–5), 428–95

H.E. Krehbiel: *Chapters of Opera* (New York, 1908, 2/1909/*R*, 3/1911)

O.G. Sonneck: *Early Opera in America* (New York, 1915/*R*)

H.E. Krehbiel: *More Chapters of Opera* (New York, 1919/*R*)

H.C. Lahee: *Annals of Music in America* (Boston, 1922/*R*)

A.H. Quinn: *A History of the American Drama from the Beginning to the Civil War* (New York. 1923, 2/1943/*R*)

E.E. Hipsher: *American Opera and its Composers* (Philadelphia, 1927/*R*)

H. Graf: *The Opera and its Future in America* (New York, 1941)

C. Smith and G. Litton: *Musical Comedy in America* (New York, 1950/*R*)

Central Opera Service Bulletin (1959–)

J. Mates: *The American Musical Stage before 1800* (New Brunswick, NJ, 1962)

J. Mattfeld: *A Handbook of American Operatic Premieres, 1731–1962* (Detroit, 1963)

C. Hamm: "Opera and the American Composer," *The American Composer Speaks*, ed. G. Chase (Baton Rouge, LA, 1966), 284 only

C. Northouse: *Twentieth Century Opera in England and the United States* (Boston, 1976)

G.J. Weisenthal: *An Anatomy of Regional Opera: a Study of American Opera, its Development, Practice, and Place in the Community* (thesis, U. of Louisville, 1980)

D.L. Root: *American Popular Stage Music, 1860–1880* (Ann Arbor, MI, 1981)

P.H. Virga: *The American Opera to 1790* (Ann Arbor, MI, 1982)

J. Mates: "The First Hundred Years of the American Lyric Theater," *American Music*, i/2 (1983), 22 only

J. Mates: *America's Musical Stage: Two Hundred Years of Musical Theatre* (Westport, CT, 1985)

K. Silverman: *A Cultural History of the American Revolution* (New York, 1987)

M.F. Schleifer, ed.: *American Opera and Music for the Stage: Early Twentieth Century* (Boston, 1990)

S. Porter: *With an Air Debonair: Musical Theatre in America, 1785–1815* (Washington, DC, 1991)

G. Block: "The Broadway Canon from *Show Boat* to *West Side Story* and the European Operatic Ideal," *JM*, xi (1993), 525–44

J. Dizikes: *Opera in America A Cultural History* (New Haven and London, 1993)

K.K. Preston: *Opera on the Road: Traveling Opera Troupes in the United States, 1825–1860* (Urbana-Champaign, 1993/*R*)

J.L. DiGaetani and J.P. Sirefman: *Opera and the Golden West: the Past, Present, and Future of Opera in the U.S.A.* (Rutherford, NJ, 1994)

J.C. Ottenberg: *Opera Odyssey: Toward a History of Opera in Nineteenth-Century America* (Westport, CT, 1994)

E.K. Kirk: *American Opera* (Urbana and Chicago, 2001)

K.K. Preston: "Nineteenth-Century Musical Theatre," *Cambridge Companion to the Musical*, eds. P. Laird and W. Everett (Cambridge, 2002/*R*), 3–28

J. McPherson: "The Savage Innocents Part 2: On the Road with Parsifal, Butterfly, the Widow, and the Girl," *OQ*, xix/1 (2003), 28–63

K.K. Preston: "Between the Cracks: the Performance of English-Language Opera in Late 19th-Century America," *AM*, xxi/3 (2003), 349–74

R.M. Wilk: *"Vox Populi: Popularization and Americanization of Opera in America, 1931–1966* (diss., New York U., 2006)

D.A. Herwitz and L.K. Stein, eds.: "Opera in the Americas/American Opera," *OQ*, xxii/3–4 (2006); *OQ*, xxiii/1 (2007)

K.K. Preston: "Notes from (the Road to) Stage," *OQ*, xxiii/1 (2008), 103–19

K.K. Preston: "To the Opera House? the Trials and Tribulations of Operatic Production in Nineteenth Century America," *OQ*, xxiii/1 (2008), 39–65

M. Esse, ed.: "Mediating Opera," *OQ*, xxvi/1 (2010)

OPERA IN AMERICAN CITIES

C. Durang: "The Philadelphia Stage," *Philadelphia Sunday Despatch* (1854, 1856, 1860) [series of articles; compiled by T. Westcott as *History of the Philadelphia Stage, between the Years 1749 and 1855*, 1868, *US-PHu*; similar compilations as *The Philadelphia Stage* in *PPL*, and *History of the Philadelphia Stage* in *PHhs*]

J.N. Ireland: *Records of the New York Stage* (New York, 1866–7/*R*)

H.P. Phelps: *Players of a Century: A Record of the Albany Stage* (Albany, 1880/*R*)

W.G. Armstrong: *A Record of the Opera in Philadelphia* (Philadelphia, 1884/*R*)

J.C. Baroncelli: *L'opéra français de la Nouvelle Orléans* (New Orleans, 1914)

J. Curtis: *One Hundred Years of Grand Opera in Philadelphia* (MS, 1920, *PHf, PHhs*)

J. Mattfeld: *A Hundred Years of Grand Opera in New York, 1825–1925* (New York, 1927/*R*)

G.C.D. Odell: *Annals of the New York Stage* (New York, 1927–49/*R*)

E.C. Moore: *Forty Years of Opera in Chicago* (New York, 1930)

R.D. James: *Old Drury of Philadelphia: a History of the Philadelphia Stage, 1800–1835* (Philadelphia, 1932/*R*)

I. Kolodin: *The Metropolitan Opera* (New York, 1936, rev. and enlarged 4/1966/*R*)

Works Progress Administration: *The History of Opera in San Francisco*, San Francisco Theatre Research, vii–viii (San Francisco, 1938)

W.H. Seltsam: *Metropolitan Opera Annals* (New York, 1947; suppls., 1957, 1968, 1978)

E.M. Gagey: *The San Francisco Stage: a History* (New York, 1950/*R*)

Q. Eaton: *Opera Caravan: Adventures of the Metropolitan on Tour, 1883–1956* (New York, 1957/*R*)

A. Bloomfield: *The San Francisco Opera, 1923–1961* (New York, 1961)

R.L. Davis: *A History of Opera in the American West* (Englewood Cliffs, NJ, 1965)

Q. Eaton: *The Boston Opera Company* (New York, 1965/*R*1980)

R.L. Davis: *Opera in Chicago: a Social and Cultural History, 1850–1965* (New York, 1966)

H.A. Kmen: *Music in New Orleans: the Formative Years, 1791–1841* (Baton Rouge, LA, 1966)

A. Stoutamire: *Music of the Old South: Colony to Confederacy* (Rutherford, NJ, 1972)

M. Nelson: *The First Italian Opera Season in New York City, 1825–1826* (diss., U. of North Carolina, Chapel Hill, 1976)

E. Scott: *The First Twenty Years of the Santa Fe Opera* (Santa Fe, NM, 1976)

A. Bloomfield: *The San Francisco Opera, 1922–1978* (Sausalito, CA, 1978)

H.F. Jennings: *Grand Opera in Kansas in the 1880s* (diss., U. of Cincinnati, 1978)

O.E. Albrecht: "Opera in Philadelphia, 1800–1830," *JAMS*, xxxii (1979), 499

C. Cassidy: *Lyric Opera of Chicago* (Chicago, 1979)

Q. Eaton: *The Boston Opera Company* (New York, 1980)

M.L. Sokol: *The New York City Opera* (New York, 1981)

J.F. Cone: *First Rival of the Metropolitan Opera* (New York, 1983)

M. Mayer: *The Met: One Hundred Years of Grand Opera* (New York, 1983)

L.R. Wolz: *Opera in Cincinnati: the Years before the Zoo, 1801–1920* (diss., U. of Cincinnati, 1983)

P.E. Eisler: *The Metropolitan Opera: the First Twenty-five Years* (Croton-on-Hudson, NY, 1984)

F.P. Fells, ed.: *The Metropolitan Opera on Record: a Discography of the Commercial Recordings* (Westport, CT, 1984)

D. Lloyd: "The Juilliard American Opera Center and the State of Opera Training in America," *Musiktheater-Ausbildung: Opera, Musical, Tanz, Technik* (Kassel, Germany, 1987)

G. Fitzgerald, ed.: *Annals of the Metropolitan Opera* (New York and Boston, 1989; available online as *MetOpera Database*, <http://archives.metoperafamily.org/archives/frame.htm>)

P. Jackson: *Saturday Afternoons at the Old Met: The Metropolitan Opera Broadcasts, 1931–1950* (Portland, OR, 1992)

G.W. Martin: *Verdi at the Golden Gate: Opera and San Francisco in the Gold Rush Years* (Berkeley, 1993)

J. Horowitz: *Wagner Nights: An American History* (Berkeley, 1994)

E.A. Thierstein: *Cincinnati Opera: From the Zoo to Music Hall* (Hillsdale, MI, 1995)

K. Ahlquist: *Democracy at the Opera: Music Theater, and Culture in New York City, 1815–60* (Urbana, IL, 1997)

J. Chatfield-Taylor: *San Francisco Opera: the First Seventy-Five Years* (San Francisco, 1997)

R.C. Marsh: "The Ravinia Opera, 1912–1931," *Opera Quarterly* xiii/3 (1997), 97–106

E.H. Cropsey: *Crosby's Opera House: Symbol of Chicago's Cultural Awakening* (Madison, WI, 1999)

R.L. Davis: *La Scala West: the Dallas Opera under Kelly and Rescigno* (Dallas, TX, 2000)

C. Guzski: *American Opera at the Metropolitan, 1910–1935: A Contextual History and Critical Survey of Selected Works* (diss., CUNY Graduate Center, 2001)

T.P. Lentz: *The History of Michigan Opera Theatre: the Formative Years, 1963–1985* (diss., Wayne State U., 2001)

J. McPherson: "The Savage Innocents: Part I, King of the Castle: Henry W. Savage and the Castle Square Opera Company," *OQ*, xviii/4 (2002), 503–33

P. Huscher: *The Santa Fe Opera: an American Pioneer* (Santa Fe, NM, 2006)

R.C. Marsh and N. Pellegrini: *150 Years of Opera in Chicago* (DeKalb, IL, 2006)

C.J. Ratner: *Chicago Opera Theater: Standard Bearer for American Opera, 1976–2001* (diss., Northwestern U., 2006)

J. Koegel: *Music in German Immigrant Theater: New York City, 1840–1940* (Rochester, NY, 2009)

OPERA IN THE ACADEMY

R. RePass: "Opera Workshops in the United States," *Tempo*, no.27 (1953), 10–18

R.L. Holden: "The Opera Workshop: From 'Rags' to 'Riches': the Story of the University of Louisville Opera Theatre," *OQ*, i/4 (1983), 22–43

N. Limonick: "The Opera Workshop: the University of California Opera Workshop," *OQ*, i/1 (1983), 79–92

J. Moriarty: "The Opera Workshop: Opera Training in Boston; Looking Toward the Future," *OQ*, i/2 (1983), 54–68

B. Glass: "The Opera Workshop: the University of Iowa Opera Theater," *OQ*, ii/1 (1984), 85–94

T.C. Hernandez and J. Langenkamp: "The Opera Workshop: Opera at Kansas State University," *OQ*, ii/2 (1984), 96–110

P.G. Horan: *American Opera in Higher Education: a Description of its Status at Selected Conservatories, Colleges, Universities* (diss., New York U., 1996)

T.L. Snyders: *History of the University of Iowa Opera Theatre, 1938–1998* (diss., U. of Iowa, 1998)

J. Beeson: "Opera at Columbia University, 1941–1958," *CM*, no.70 (2000), 193–211

M.R. Griffel: "Opera at Columbia: a Shining Legacy," *CMc*, nos.79–80 (2005), 95–133

M.W. Tobias, ed.: *Opera for All Seasons: 60 Years of Indiana University Opera Theater* (Bloomington, IN, 2010)

IMPRESARIOS AND MANAGERS

M. Maretzek: *Crotchets and Quavers* (New York, 1855/R)

J.H. Mapleson: *The Mapleson Memoirs* (New York, 1888, rev. 2/1966 by H. Rosenthal)

M. Maretzek: *Sharps and Flats* (New York, 1890/R)

H. Russell: *The Passing Show* (Boston, 1926)

G. Gatti-Casazza: *Memories of the Opera* (New York, 1941/R)

M. Garden and L. Biancolli: *Mary Garden's Story* (New York, 1951)

V. Sheean: *Oscar Hammerstein I: the Life and Exploits of an Impresario* (New York, 1956)

J.F. Cone: *Oscar Hammerstein's Manhattan Opera Company* (Norman, OK, 1966)

F.T. Gallo: *Lucky Rooster: the Autobiography of an Impresario* (New York, 1967)

L.M. Lerner: *The Rise of the Impresario: Bernard Ullman and the Transformation of Musical Culture in Nineteenth Century America* (diss., U. of Wisconsin, 1970)

R. Bing: *5000 Nights at the Opera* (Garden City, NY, 1972)

C. Bishop: *The San Carlo Opera Company, 1913–1955: Grand Opera for Profit* (Santa Monica, CA, 1980)

R. Bing: *A Knight at the Opera* (New York, 1981)

G.W. Martin: *The Damrosch Dynasty: America's First Family of Music* (Boston, 1983)

D. McKay: "Opera in Colonial Boston," *AM*, iii (1985), 133 only

M. Turnbull: *Mary Garden* (Aldershot, 1996, 2/1997)

E. Rubin: "Jeannette Meyer Thurber (1850–1946): Music for a Democracy," *Cultivating Music in America: Women Patrons and Activists since 1860*, ed. R.P. Locke and C. Barr (Berkeley, 1997), 134–63

J.C. Ottenberg: "Gustav Hinrichs and Opera in Philadelphia 1888–1896," *OQ*, xv/2 (1999), 197–223

G.N. Vetro: *Cleofonte Campanini: L'altro direttore* (Parma, 2001)

T. Collins: *Otto Kahn: Art, Money, & Modern Time* (Chapel Hill, 2002)

J.C. Ottenberg: *Gustav Hinrichs (1850–1942) American Conductor and Composer* (Michigan, 2003)

P. Mazzagatti: *Tricks of the Trade: the Role of the Impresario in the Development of 19th-Century American Concert Life* (diss., Manhattan School of Music, 2005)

R. Henderson: "A Confluence of Moravian Impresarios: Max Maretzek, the Strakosches, and the Graus," *European Music and Musicians in New York City, 1840–1890*, ed. J. Graziano (Rochester, NY, 2006), 235–52

R. Henderson, ed.: *Further Revelations of an Opera Manager in 19th Century America: the Third Book of Memoirs by Max Maretzek* (Sterling Heights, MI, 2006)

K.K. Preston: "'Dear Miss Ober': Musical Management and the Web of Musical Life in the United States, 1876–1883," *European Music and Musicians in New York City, 1840–1890*, ed. J. Graziano (Rochester, NY, 2006), 273–98

J. Volpe and C. Michener: *The Toughest Show on Earth: My Rise and Reign at the Metropolitan Opera* (New York, 2006)

D.P. Kessler: *Sarah Caldwell: the First Woman of Opera* (Lanham, MD, 2008)

SELECTED WORKS

K.E. Gombert: *Leonora by William Henry Fry and Rip Van Winkle by George Frederick Bristow: Examples of Mid-nineteenth-century American Opera* (diss., Ball State U., 1977)

C.W. Patton: "Discovering *The Tender Land*: a New Look at Aaron Copland's Opera," *American Music*, xx/3 (2002), 317–40

R. Allen and G.P. Cunningham: "Cultural Uplift and Double Consciousness: African American Responses to the 1935 Opera *Porgy and Bess*," *MQ*, lxxxviii (2005), 342–69

B. Soll: *I Dream a World: the Operas of William Grant Still* (Little Rock, AR, 2005)

G.K. Brown: *Problems of Race and Genre in the Critical Reception of Porgy and Bess* (diss., U. of Washington, 2006)

R.A. Crawford: "Where Did *Porgy and Bess* Come from?" *Journal of Interdisciplinary History*, xxxvi/4 (2006), 697–734

C. Reynolds: "Porgy and Bess: an American *Wozzeck*," *JSAMusic*, i (2007), 1–28

R.P. Kolt: *Robert Ward's* The Crucible: *Creating an American Musical Nationalism* (Lanham, MD, 2009)

R.S. Longobardi: "Re-producing Klinghoffer: Opera and Arab Identity Before and After 9/11," *JSAM*, iii (2009), 273–310

W.A. Sheppard: "Blurring the Boundaries: Tan Dun's *Tinte* and *The First Emperor*," *JM*, xxvi (2009), 285–326

MARIA PURCIELLO (1); MARIA F. RICH, VICTOR FELL YELLIN/H. WILEY HITCHCOCK/JUNE C. OTTENBERG (2); KATHERINE K. PRESTON (3); MARIA F. RICH, VICTOR FELL YELLIN/H. WILEY HITCHCOCK/CAROLYN GUZSKI (4); STEPHANIE JENSEN-MOULTON (5); MARIA F. RICH, VICTOR FELL YELLIN/H. WILEY HITCHCOCK/MICHAEL V. PISANI (6); MICHAEL MILLER (7); CHARLES HIROSHI GARRETT (8); MELANIE FEILOTTER (TABLE); MICHAEL V. PISANI (BIBLIOGRAPHY)

OPERA America. National service organization. At the instigation of Seattle Opera's Glynn Ross, 20 regional opera leaders came together in 1970 to explore ways in which they could collaborate to improve the quality of opera in America. Important early initiatives included regional auditions, for which impresarios nominated singers to be heard by an assembly of their colleagues; and coproductions, in which costs for building a new production were shared among several companies. By 1980 the organization's membership of more than 70 companies included virtually every professional opera company in the United States, ranging from the Metropolitan Opera to Shreveport Opera. In 1983 OPERA America launched its first program to fund the creation of new American operas, which led to the establishment of a permanent endowment to assist opera companies in the commissioning, development, and promotion of new work. In 1990 it developed *Music! Words! Opera!*, a multidisciplinary curriculum introduced to schools across the country. The organization moved from Washington, DC, to New York City in 2005 to build the National Opera Center, which was completed in September 2012. In addition to providing space for its own programs, the Opera Center allows for the conduct of business (auditions, readings of new works, production meetings) by visiting opera professionals from across the country and around the world. OPERA America conducts and disseminates research on all aspects of the opera industry; its library houses unique collections related to American opera companies and repertory. The organization hosts an annual conference each year, as well as a number of smaller forums and workshops designed around the needs of administrators, artists, and trustees. In addition to providing direct services to members, the organization works in coalition with other national arts service organizations to advocate for opera and the arts before legislators and federal agencies.

KELLEY ROURKE

Opera companies, itinerant. Since the earliest days of opera it has been economically more practical, in many sets of circumstances, for opera to be presented by traveling troupes rather than by resident companies. Such troupes flourished in the United States, particularly during the second two-thirds of the 19th century, largely because of the huge distances and isolated communities hungry for cultural entertainment.

The history of opera performance in the United States during the 19th century is for the most part a history of itinerant opera companies. Except for works mounted by theatrical stock companies and by the resident companies in New Orleans (founded 1790) and New York (Metropolitan Opera, founded 1883), the vast majority of opera productions witnessed by North Americans at this period were given by touring troupes. As a consequence, performances were much more numerous and geographically widespread than the rather checkered history of resident companies would seem to indicate. The repertory of the various companies (English, French, Italian, and German) further reveals that American operatic tastes closely mirrored those on the Continent and in England.

1. English companies to 1860. 2. English companies, 1860–1900. 3. French companies. 4. Italian companies to 1860. 5. Italian companies, 1860–1900. 6. German companies.

1. ENGLISH COMPANIES TO 1860. English comic and ballad operas, performed first by itinerant players and later by the stock companies of theaters in larger cities, were an indispensable part of the American theatrical repertory in the 18th century. The general adoption of the star system as a style of theatrical management in the early 19th century, however, eventually changed both the repertory and the method of opera production in the United States, taking opera away from singing actors and actresses and putting it into the hands of trained singers. This system meant that British vocal stars could travel to North America not to join the resident company of a particular theater but to perform for short-term engagements in theaters around the country, commanding high wages; the first important itinerant singers

arrived in 1817. Since they tended to form themselves into small troupes of two, three, or four singers, they could cover the principal roles in most operatic productions mounted by local stock companies. The assignment of principal operatic roles to specialized singers significantly improved the quality of opera performance during the 1820s, 30s, and 40s, resulting in a gradual elevation in the musical expectations of American audiences; raised expectations, in turn, created a demand for the importation of even better singers.

During these three decades a number of British singers visited the United States and Canada. Some elected to settle in North America, while others returned to Great Britain; all of them, however, toured widely in the east and south, appearing in concerts, and in opera productions in cities as far removed geographically as Quebec City and New Orleans. Singers of particular importance during the 1820s and 30s include ELIZABETH AUSTIN (toured 1828–35), Joseph and MARY ANNE WOOD (1833–6, 1840–41), Jane Shirreff and John Wilson (1838–40), William F. Brough (arrived in 1833) and Anne and Edward (better known as Arthur in England) SEGUIN (arrived 1838). All these stars (especially Austin and the Woods) had a significant impact on the development of opera appreciation in the United States; in particular, they helped to foster Americans' love for Italian melody by introducing works by Giacomo Rossini (*La cenerentola*, in M.R. Lacy's pastiche, retitled *Cinderella, or The Fairy Queen and the Little Glass Slipper*) and Vincenzo Bellini (*Norma* and *La sonnambula*, in adaptations by J.R. Fry and H.R. Bishop, respectively), which became extraordinarily popular. Their repertory

"*The Louisa Pyne Polka,*" *by S. Markstein. (Music Division, The New York Public Library for the Performing Arts, Astor, Lenox and Tilden Foundations)*

Marcella Sembrich, Enrico Caruso, and members of the Metropolitan Opera Company stop in Chicago on their way home from San Francisco where the Great 1906 Earthquake destroyed their sets and instruments. (The Metropolitan Opera Archives)

also included adaptations (by various individuals) of other foreign-language operas (D.-F.-E. Auber's *Fra Diavolo*, Carl Maria von Weber's *Der Freischütz*, Giuseppe Donizetti's *L'elisir d'amore* and *La fille du régiment*) as well as operas originally written in English (William Michael Rooke's *Amilie*, Michael William Balfe's *The Bohemian Girl*, Vincent Wallace's *Maritana*).

During the 1840s the Seguins, who settled in the United States, helped pave the way for the proliferation of English opera companies by forming small touring troupes of six to eight singers; they toured widely with these expanded vocal-star companies (all known as the Seguin Opera Company) until Edward Seguin's death in 1852. During the financially depressed years of the 1840s, the Seguin Company was credited with providing enough business to keep many American theaters open. Despite the company's success, however, by the end of that decade the halcyon days of vocal-star troupes had ended, and small groups of itinerant singers were replaced by moderate-sized English troupes that were less dependent on stock companies. To a great extent this change was a response to the appearance of large, highly qualified, completely self-sufficient Italian companies in the late 1840s. English opera companies varied in size, but usually included principal and secondary singers and the nucleus of a chorus; for instrumental accompaniment they still relied on resident theater orchestras. The repertory of these companies was similar to that of the earlier vocal stars: *The Enchantress* and *The Bohemian Girl*, *Les diamants de la couronne* (as *Crown Diamonds*) and *Fra Diavolo*, *Cinderella* (Rossini, arr. Lacy), *La sonnambula* and *La fille du régiment* (as *The Daughter of the Regiment*). In the 1850s English translations of more-current Italian operas, in particular *Il trovatore* and *La*

traviata, also became standard fare; there has been very little scholarship, however, on the translations/adaptations performed by these English troupes. ANNA BISHOP (1810–84), who arrived in 1847, toured the East, South and far West of the country until 1855, sometimes as the star of the Anna Bishop Opera Company, sometimes as part of a smaller concert ensemble formed from the ashes of her various opera companies, which tended to disintegrate in mid-tour. In August 1855 she left for Australia, returning to the United States only in 1858. Sophie Anne (Anna) Thillon (1819–1903) toured as the star of her own opera company from 1851 to 1854. This troupe, although small, was popular and widely traveled; Thillon performed in cities on the East Coast, in the Midwest (St. Louis, Memphis, Cincinnati), and the far West (San Francisco). Another important mid-century company singer who performed in an itinerant company that bore her name was the Irish soprano Catherine Hayes (1818–61), who arrived in the United States in 1851, made a side trip to South America in late 1852, then left for Australia (from San Francisco) in 1854.

Among the many other English opera troupes that toured the country in the 1850s were the Manvers, Durand, Cooper, New Orleans, Richings, and Escott & Miranda companies. But by far the most popular and successful English troupe of the decade was the Pyne-Harrison Opera Company, an ensemble formed around Louisa Pyne (1832–1904) and William Harrison (1813–58), two strong proponents of English opera from Covent Garden. Between 1854 and 1857 they traveled throughout the eastern half of the continent, performing in cities from Montreal to New Orleans and St. Louis. After their departure English opera temporarily lost ground to Italian as the fashionable or "proper" style of operatic performance. Despite an increasing anti-English bias during the 1850s, however, opera in the vernacular continued to be extremely popular, particularly in areas away from the eastern seaboard.

2. ENGLISH COMPANIES, 1860–1900. Some of the English troupes active in the antebellum period continued to perform after the Civil War. During 1866–7, for example, CAROLINE RICHINGS (1827–82) formed a new company that included some of the best English-speaking opera singers in America, and confounded the critics (who deemed English opera "unfashionable") with three successful seasons. Richings's company precipitated a revival of English-language opera that would last for the rest of the century. The success of her company, however, ended with the 1869–70 season, when the Scottish soprano EUPHROSYNE PAREPA lured away the American soprano's best singers to her own English troupe, which performed successfully for two seasons (1869–70 and 1871–2). Parepa-Rosa died suddenly in 1874, cutting short a promising career; Richings, who was hampered by financial losses from the 1869–70 season, continued to perform until 1878.

The successor to Parepa Rosa was the American soprano CLARA LOUISE KELLOGG (1842–1916), whose Kellogg Grand English Opera Company enjoyed four extraordinarily successful seasons (1873–7) in the financially depressed years following the Panic of 1873. Kellogg's troupe mounted many of the works long considered components of the "standard" English-opera repertory (by Balfe, Wallace, Auber, Donizetti, and others) as well as her own translations of the normal Italian repertory (which included also French and German operas). Her company toured all over the eastern half of the country, attracting enthusiastic audiences in the same cities that failed to support itinerant foreign-language opera troupes by keeping ticket prices low, presenting opera "for the people" in the vernacular, and capitalizing on a growing middle-class backlash against the increasingly aristocratic (and expensive) image of the foreign-language troupes. Kellogg, who was known as "the first American prima donna," encouraged young American singers, including Emma Abbott. Other English troupes included the Max Strakosch English Opera Company (early 1880s), the Emma Juch Opera Company, which toured in the United States, Canada and Mexico (1889–91) (see EMMA JUCH); and the American Opera Company, founded by Jeannette Thurber and led by Theodore Thomas, which was established in 1886 in a highly publicized but ill-fated attempt to encourage the performance of opera in English by American singers. (The company disintegrated on the road in 1887 and disbanded during the 1887–8 season.) The most successful and influential itinerant English company of the 1880s was the troupe formed around the American soprano EMMA ABBOTT, which toured all over the country from 1879 until Abbott's untimely death by pneumonia in 1891. The company, which never had a losing season, performed a large repertory of old and new operas in English, translations of the continental repertory (excepting Wagner), and some operettas. Abbott, who was called "the people's

prima donna," fed an interest in English opera among American audiences in the East, and introduced the art form to the burgeoning population of the West.

Another extraordinarily influential and long-lived English company was the Boston Ideals (1879–1904; after 1885 the Bostonians), a troupe that performed a repertory of operettas and other light operas in addition to standards of the English-opera stage (see BOSTON IDEAL OPERA COMPANY). Originally founded on the crest of the *Pinafore* craze, the troupe helped to fashion late-century American taste in English opera by combining some of the older repertory with many lighter operettas, including works by Julius Eichberg, Victor Herbert, and Reginald de Koven. Other English opera companies that were active in the United States in the 1880s and 90s followed the lead of the Bostonians (and the extraordinarily popular *opéra-bouffe* companies) by exploiting the new American passion for operetta, especially the works of Jacques Offenbach, Arthur Sullivan, Charles Lecocq, Hervé, Robert Planquette, and Franz von Suppé. Little is known about the itineraries or histories of most of these troupes; a few of the many include the McCaull Opera Company, Ford's Opera Company, Alice Oates Opera Company, Emelie Melville Company, Norcross Fifth Avenue Opera Company, William Lyster's English Opera and Opera Bouffe Company, and the Templeton Opera Company. Among the most prominent late-century English troupes were the Hinrichs Opera Company (1888–96), managed by the Philadelphia conductor Gustav Hinrichs, and Henry Savage's Castle Square Opera Company, which was founded in 1894 and continued to perform well into the 20th century.

3. FRENCH COMPANIES. The New Orleans Opera Company, under the direction of the impresario JOHN DAVIS, was the first opera troupe to mount a tour of the United States. From their base at the French-language Théâtre d'Orléans, they made six tours to the East Coast, presenting operas by Adolphe Adam, Nicolò Isouard, Adrien Boieldieu, Auber, Rossini, and others in New York, Philadelphia, Boston, and Baltimore (1827–33). During the 1840s various versions of the French Opera Company of New Orleans toured the Northeast; although not as important as Davis's companies, these troupes kept French-language opera before the American public. In 1859 the French Opera House opened in New Orleans to compete with the Théâtre d'Orléans. This theater's resident company, which included such singers as Julie Calvé, St Urban, Lecourt, Mathieu, Victor, and Genibrel, appeared in other parts of the country; during the 1840s and 50s troupes featuring Calvé, in particular, mounted acclaimed performances on the East Coast.

The first American performance of Offenbach's *La Grande-Duchesse de Gérolstein* in 1867 marked the beginnings of an *opéra bouffe* craze in the United States that persisted throughout the 1870s. The important early troupes—which mounted the repertory in French—included companies managed by Henry L. Bateman and Jacob Grau, which toured regularly. By

the mid-1870s American audiences were already exhibiting an almost-insatiable appetite for operettas by such
composers as Lecocq, Edmond Audran, Planquette,
Hervé, von Suppé, Carl Millöcker, Johann Strauss II,
and Sullivan. One of the longest-lived and most successful troupes was the Aimée French Opera Company
(formed around the French soubrette Marie Aimée and
under the management of MAURICE GRAU). Aimée arrived
in the United States in 1870 and established her own
company in 1871–2 to perform (in French) a repertory
of works by Offenbach, with the occasional nod to
Hervé and Lecocq. The heyday of Aimée's troupe was
the mid-1870s, during these years (and later, into the
1880s) the company toured as far afield as San Francisco. Aimée began to sing in English in 1884. Other
important comic-opera companies active during the
1870s and 80s were the troupes of Sallie Holman (dates
unknown), Alice Oates (1849–87), and Emily Soldene
(1838–1912). The Holman and Oates companies companies emerged in the late 1860s, and continued to perform for many years, combining the opéra-bouffe repertory with many works normally performed by English
opera companies. The Holman troupe was active for 30
years and did not disband until the mid-1880s. The
Oates company traveled widely and very successfully
(as far west as San Francisco); the caliber of her troupe
declined in the mid-1880s as it turned increasingly to
burlesque. Soldene was an English soprano and manager who specialized in performing the opéra bouffe
repertory in English; her company (which was based in
the UK) visited the United States three times—in 1874–
5, 1876–7, and 1880–81—and toured all over the country, including visits to the West Coast.

4. ITALIAN COMPANIES TO 1860. From 1825 until 1847 the
history of Italian opera performance in the United
States is a chronicle of fits and starts. No company
active in this period lasted longer than a year or two
before going bankrupt; many remained intact for a
shorter length of time. There were also stretches of
years during which no Italian companies were active,
and opera was known to Americans only through presentations by English and French troupes. To the mid-
1840s the performance of opera in Italian was a novelty
because most Americans preferred to hear Italian opera
sung in English. Until 1847 both New York and New
Orleans acted as headquarters for visiting Italian opera
troupes; companies visited nearby towns and cities only
after exhausting the market in one or the other of these
two centers.

The first Italian troupe to perform in the United States
was a traveling company only in the broadest terms:
Manuel García's Italian Opera Company performed at
the Park Theatre in New York from November 1825
until September 1826, then left for Mexico. This brief
introduction to the Italian style, coupled with the growing American taste for Italian melody as performed by
such vocal stars as Austin and the Woods, resulted in
several attempts to establish Italian opera in New York
during the 1830s. The Montresor Opera Company, recruited from Italy by Lorenzo da Ponte, mounted two

seasons in New York and one in Philadelphia during
the winter–spring of 1832–3. When it disbanded, many
of the singers traveled to Havana, where they sang with
Francesco Brichta's Havana Opera Company for the
1833–4 season. Two other short-lived troupes were attempted on the East Coast: the Rivafinoli Company
(New York and Philadelphia, 1833–4) and the Porto-
Sacchi Company (New York and Albany, 1834–5). In
1836 the Montresor company resurfaced in New Orleans, where the De Rosa Company (1836–7) and Brichta's Havana Opera Company (1837) also appeared. Italian opera production then ceased in the country for
five years because of depressed economic conditions.
In 1842 a new version of the Havana company visited
New Orleans. This troupe, which numbered 57 (including
principal singers, chorus, and orchestra), had been assembled by the Cuban businessman Marti y Torrens.
After further performances in the city in spring 1843,
the troupe embarked on the first extended tour of the
United States undertaken by an Italian troupe, in nine
months visiting Cincinnati, Pittsburgh, Philadelphia,
New York, Baltimore, Washington, and (again) New Or-
leans. Their repertory included principally works by
Bellini and Donizetti, and their success was marked.

Italian opera performance entered a new phase
during the period 1847–60, when between three and
six Italian troupes were performing somewhere in the
United States in any single year. The activities of over
70 different troupes have been documented for this
period; itineraries of these companies expanded significantly—away from the East Coast and the towns and
cities on the Ohio and Mississippi Rivers, and ever
deeper into the interior of the country. This sudden es-
calation was the result of three factors: renewed economic prosperity, a realization by European performers
that an American tour would bring enormous riches,
and the appearance of the impresarios BERNARD ULLMAN,
MAX MARETZEK, and MAURICE STRAKOSCH.

It is almost impossible to ascertain clearly the names,
personnel, itineraries, and repertories of all the troupes
active during this time. Italian companies formed, broke
down, reformed, and merged with a dismaying frequency; furthermore, each company is typically referred
to in the contemporary press by a variety of names. A
broad summary of the activities of some of the most
important troupes should suffice to suggest the wealth
of activity. The Havana Opera Company of Marti y Torrens made extended tours of the eastern and southern
United States during 1847, 1848, and 1850 with troupes
that sometimes numbered more than a hundred musicians (including principal and secondary singers,
chorus, and orchestra). Companies from the Astor Place
Opera House in New York (from 1849 under the management of Maretzek) toured widely (principally on the
East Coast, but also including New Orleans and Mexico)
from 1847 until 1853. Maurice Strakosch managed a variety of troupes from 1848 until 1861, Bernard Ullman
was active as a manager from the early 1840s until
1862, and Maretzek continued to act as an impresario
after the ultimate failure of the Astor Place House; all
three managed troupes under their own names (e.g.,

the Strakosch Opera Company, the Maretzek Italian Opera Company) and occasionally embarked on joint endeavors (the Ullman-Strakosch Opera Company). These companies toured as far as the Midwest as well as in the south and north. In addition, companies named for visiting European celebrities were numerous and highly visible as they toured throughout the eastern half of the continent and as far west as California (via Panama); these troupes took the names of such artists as Henriette Sontag, Marietta Alboni, Balbina Steffanone, Grisi and Mario, Teresa Parodi, Adelaide Cortesi, Anna de LaGrange, and Luigi Arditi. The Academy of Music companies, nominally resident at the opera house of that name in Manhattan, also toured regularly, appearing principally in East Coast cities. The repertory of the 1850–51 Astor Place company is fairly representative of that performed by most of these Italian troupes; it included operas by Bellini (*Norma, La sonnambula,* and *I Capuleti e i Montecchi*), Donizetti (*Lucia di Lammermoor, Gemma di Vergy, Parisina, Lucrezia Borgia,* and *La favorite*), Rossini (*Semiramide* and *Il barbiere di Siviglia*), Verdi (*Ernani*), and Mozart (*Don Giovanni*).

5. ITALIAN COMPANIES, 1860–1900. The performance of Italian opera greatly accelerated in the years after the Civil War. The expansion of the American railroad system made longer and more distant tours an economic proposition, while continued growth of the American population and the unceasing expansion westward meant that there were more towns of a size large enough to support a two- or three-night visit by an itinerant company. Large cities along the rivers had been visited by itinerant troupes for years; now it was also economically feasible for companies to stop at many of the smaller towns in between. The completion of the transcontinental railroad in 1869 and the subsequent settling of the western interior opened a vast market for itinerant performers of all types; opera houses opened in such small towns as Ogden City, Utah; Central City, Colorado; and Grand Forks, North Dakota as well as larger urban areas such as Kansas City, Denver, and Omaha.

The period of economic expansion that followed the Civil War encouraged impresarios such as Maretzek and Strakosch to import some of the best European operatic stars for their companies; this practice resulted in escalating ticket prices. These companies continued to rely on middle-class Americans for support, but the wealthy—especially in large urban areas such as New York—were increasingly prominent in their patronage. The period of economic expansion came to a sudden halt with the Panic of 1873, and during the depression years of the mid-1870s, Italian opera company managers struggled to find audiences. Managers were unable to lower ticket prices because their wealthy patrons (including, increasingly, the nouveaux riches) demanded expensive European operatic celebrities; as a result, middle-class Americans began to regard foreign-language opera as an expensive luxury and turned instead to English opera and operetta. It was during this period

Marie Aimée. (Billy Rose Theatre Division, The New York Public Library for the Performing Arts, Astor, Lenox and Tilden Foundations)

that Italian opera (in particular) became "aristocratic" and elite in the eyes of many Americans.

The companies managed by Maretzek and Strakosch endured several disastrous years in the mid-1870s; by around 1877, however, the economic tide had begun to turn and Italian language troupes began once again to prosper. The most important Italian-language ensemble at the end of the 1870s was Her Majesty's Italian Opera Company of Drury Lane (London), which arrived in New York in 1878. The company manager, JAMES HENRY MAPLESON, had accepted a three-year contract to produce opera at the New York Academy of Music; his company performed there from mid-October to December, then toured for three months, appearing in Chicago, Boston, St. Louis, Cincinnati, Washington, Baltimore, and Philadelphia. The success of Mapleson's company (and the insufficient number of boxes at the Academy of Music) resulted in the establishment in 1883 of the Metropolitan Opera Company, intended to serve as competition to Mapleson's troupe.

Throughout the 1880s and 90s, although numerous Italian opera companies traveled throughout the United States, the two most important ones were Mapleson's Academy of Music company and the Metropolitan Opera (the latter also gave seasons of opera in German) The London-based company continued to perform successfully in New York and elsewhere (e.g., Detroit, Indianapolis, Syracuse, Albany, Buffalo, Pittsburgh, and

Cleveland) into the early 1880s, but strong competition from the Metropolitan Opera spelled the end for the London-based impresario. After two debilitating tours in the far West Mapleson abandoned the contest in 1886.

The Metropolitan Opera Company, although firmly based in New York, was an itinerant troupe from its first season (1883–4), when the manager, Henry Abbey, took the company on the road for four months. Seasons were then mounted almost every year in Boston, Philadelphia, Chicago, St. Louis, Cincinnati, Washington, and Baltimore, and during the next decade tours were extended to include San Francisco and Mexico as well as small towns in the eastern states.

6. GERMAN COMPANIES. The performance of opera by German companies in the United States was sporadic at best during the first half of the 19th century; the few troupes that were formed (usually in New York) were not sufficiently successful to mount tours. A company organized around Bertha Johannsen (from New York) gave a season at the Philadelphia Academy of Music in 1857. During the Civil War years, New Yorkers could attend performances by German opera companies organized by Karl Anschütz and Leonard Grover; the former, in particular, managed a successful (but overly ambitious) company in 1862–3 that mounted performances of such repertory as *Martha, Der Freischütz, Der Wildschütz, Die Zauberflöte,* and *Fidelio,* as well as translations of operas in Italian (*Le nozze de Figaro*) and French (*Fra Diavolo, Le postillon de Lonjumeau, Joseph,* and *Jean de Paris*). During 1864–5 Grover managed a German company that was fairly successful and that toured away from New York. During the 1870s, in the midst of the financial crisis that gripped the country following the Panic of 1873, several German troupes nevertheless enjoyed some success performing in cities with significant populations of German immigrants (Cincinnati, St. Louis, Louisville). The Louise Lichtmay German Opera Company (which did not fare well financially) mounted seasons in late 1874 and early 1875 in Cincinnati, and a troupe directed by Theodor Habelmann performed in St. Louis in 1875. The Wachtel Opera Company (directed by Adolph Neuendorff and featuring Theodor Wachtel and Eugenia Pappenheim) performed in New York, Philadelphia, and St. Louis in 1875–6.

German opera truly flourished in the United States during the 1880s, when the New York Metropolitan Opera adopted a completely German format in its second season (1884–5) under the direction of Leopold Damrosch, and went on to give several entirely German tours. When the company resumed Italian and French productions, opera in German was essentially banished, and to fill the void Leopold's son Walter Damrosch (*see* DAMROSCH family, (3)) organized the Damrosch Opera Company in 1894. In its first season the troupe performed exclusively Wagner, making a five-month tour that extended as far west as Kansas City. During the next season Damrosch added several non-Wagner operas and the troupe toured in the south. By the late 1890s it had become clear that Americans were interested in German as well as French and Italian opera and both the Met and the Damrosch company adopted the wing system of opera production, obviating the need for a separate German company; in 1896–7 and 1897–8 the German wing of the Damrosch troupe performed in Boston, Chicago, Cincinnati, Cleveland, Buffalo, and Detroit.

See also OPERA.

BIBLIOGRAPHY

M. Maretzek: *Crotchets and Quavers* (New York, 1855)

H.P. Phelps: *Players of a Century. A Record of the Albany Stage,* second edition (Albany, 1880/R)

R.G. White: "Opera in New York," *Century Magazine,* xxiii (1881–2), 686–703, 865–82; xxiv (1882–3), 31–43, 193–210

J.H. Mapleson: *The Mapleson Memoirs* (New York, 1888); ed. H. Rosenthal (London, 1966)

M. Maretzek: *Sharps and Flats* (New York, 1890)

S.E. Martin: *The Life and Professional Career of Emma Abbott* (Minneapolis, 1891)

H.E. Krehbiel: *Chapters of Opera* (New York, 1908, 3/1911)

H.C. Barnabee: *Reminiscences of Henry Clay Barnabee,* ed. G. L. Varney (1913/R)

K. Hackett: *The Beginnings of Grand Opera in Chicago (1850–1859)* (Chicago, 1913)

C.L. Kellogg: *Memoirs of an American Prima Donna* (New York, 1913)

G.C.D. Odell: *Annals of the New York Stage* (New York, 1927–49)

W.G. Carson: *The Theatre on the Frontier: the Early Years of the St. Louis Stage* (Chicago, 1932)

L. Gafford: *A History of the St. Charles Theatre in New Orleans, 1835–1843* (Chicago, 1932)

O. Thompson: *The American Singer: a Hundred Years of Success in Opera* (New York, 1937)

Works Progress Administration: *The History of Opera in San Francisco,* San Francisco Theatre Research, vii–viii (San Francisco, 1938)

R.A. Gerson: *Music in Philadelphia* (New York, 1940)

R.M. Gipson: *The Life of Emma Thursby, 1845–1931* (New York, 1940)

N. Smither: *A History of the English Theatre in New Orleans* (New York, 1944)

W.G. Carson: *St. Louis Goes to the Opera, 1837–1941* (St. Louis, 1946)

W.S. Hoole: *The Ante Bellum Charleston Theatre* (Montgomery, AL, 1946)

G.E. Schiavo: *Italian Music and Musicians in America* (New York, 1947)

E.M. Gagey: *The San Francisco Stage: a History* (New York, 1950)

S. Chevalley: "La première saison théâtrale française de New-York," *French Review,* xxiv (1951), 471–9

S. Chevalley: "Le Théâtre d'Orléans en tournée dans les villes du nord, 1827–1833," *Comptes rendus de l'Athénée louisianais* (New Orleans, 1955), 27–71

H.A. Kmen: *Music in New Orleans: the Formative Years, 1791–1841* (Baton Rouge, LA, 1966)

H. Pleasants: *The Great Singers: From the Dawn of Opera to Caruso, Callas and Pavarotti* (New York, 1966)

L. Lerner: *The Rise of the Impresario: Bernard Ullman and the Transformation of Musical Culture in Nineteenth Century America* (diss., U. of Wisconsin, 1970)

J.A. Belsom: *Reception of Major Operatic Premières in New Orleans during the Nineteenth Century* (diss., Louisiana State U., Baton Rouge, 1972)

A. Stoutamire: *Music of the Old South: Colony to Confederacy* (Rutherford, NJ, 1972)

M. Nelson: *The First Italian Opera Season in New York City: 1825–1826* (diss., U. of North Carolina, Chapel Hill, 1976)

Q. Eaton: *Opera Caravan: Adventures of the Metropolitan on Tour, 1883–1956* (New York, 1978)

H.F. Jennings: *Grand Opera in Kansas in the 1880s* (diss., U. of Cincinnati, 1978)

O. Albrecht: "Opera in Philadelphia, 1800–1830," *JAMS,* xxxii (1979), 499–515

C. Hamm: *Yesterdays: Popular Song in America* (New York, 1979)

J.F. Cone: *First Rival of the Metropolitan* (New York, 1983)

P.D. Wolz: *Opera in Cincinnati before 1920* (diss., U. of Cincinnati, 1983)

D. Cooper: *Opera in Montreal and Toronto: a Study of Performance Traditions and Repertoire* (diss., U. of Toronto, 1984)

T.G. Kaufman: "The Arditi Tour: the Midwest gets its First Real Taste of Italian Opera," *OQ*, iv/4 (1986), 39–52

V.B. Lawrence: *Strong on Music: the New York Music Scene in the Days of George Templeton Strong, 1836–1874*, i: *Resonances (1836–1850)* (New York, 1988); ii: *Reverberations (1850–1856)* (Chicago, 1995); iii: *Repercussions (1857–1862)* (Chicago, 1999)

J. Rosselli: "The Opera Business and the Italian Immigrant Community in Latin America, 1820–1930: the Example of Buenos Aires," *Past and Present*, no.127 (1990), 155–82

E. Rubin: "Jeannette Meyers Thurber and the National Conservatory of Music," *American Music*, viii/3 (1990), 294

K.K. Preston: *Opera on the Road: Traveling Opera Troupes in the United States, 1825–1860* (Urbana, IL, 1993)

K. Ahlquist: *Democracy at the Opera. Music Theater, and Culture in New York City, 1815–60* (Urbana, IL, 1997)

P.G. Davis: *The American Opera Singer* (New York, 1997)

E. Rubin: "Jeannette Meyer Thurber (1850–1946): Music for a Democracy," *Cultivating Music in America: Women Patrons and Activists since 1860*, ed. R.P. Locke and C. Barr (Berkeley, 1997), 134–63

B.F. Walsh: "Catherine Hayes An Early Donizetti Prima Donna," *OQ*, xiv/3 (1998), 45–54

E.H. Cropsey: *Crosby's Opera House: Symbol of Chicago's Cultural Awakening* (Madison, 1999)

J.C. Ottenberg: "Gustav Hinrichs and Opera in Philadelphia 1888–1896," *OQ*, xv/2 (1999), 197–223

B.F. Walsh: *Catherine Hayes (1818–1861): The Hibernian Prima Donna* (Dublin, 2000)

J. McPherson: "The Savage Innocents. Part I, King of the Castle: Henry W. Savage and the Castle Square Opera Company," *OQ*, xviii/4 (2002), 502–33

K.K. Preston: "Nineteenth-Century Musical Theatre," *Cambridge Companion to the Musical*, ed. P. Laird and W. Everett (Cambridge, 2002), 3–28

J. McPherson: "The Savage Innocents Part 2: On the Road with Parsifal, Butterfly, the Widow, and the Girl," *OQ*, xix/1 (2003), 28–63

J.C. Ottenberg: *Gustav Hinrichs (1850–1942): American Conductor and Composer* (Michigan, 2003)

K.K. Preston: "Between the Cracks: The Performance of English-Language Opera in Late 19th-Century America," *American Music*, xxiii/3 (2003), 349–79

J. Graziano: "An Opera for Every Taste: the New York Scene, 1862–1869," *European Music and Musicians in New York City, 1840–1890*, ed. J. Graziano (Rochester, 2006), 253–72

R. Henderson: "A Confluence of Moravian Impresarios: Max Maretzek, the Strakosches, and the Graus," *European Music and Musicians in New York City, 1840–1890*, ed. J. Graziano (Rochester, 2006), 235–52

R. Henderson, ed.: *Further Revelations of an Opera Manager in 19th Century America. The Third Book of Memoirs by Max Maretzek* (Sterling Heights, MI, 2006)

K.K. Preston: "'Dear Miss Ober': Musical Management and the Web of Musical Life in the United States, 1876–1883," *European Music and Musicians in New York City, 1840–1890* , ed. J. Graziano (Rochester, 2006), 273–98

K. Gänzl: *Emily Soldene: In Search of a Singer* (Wellington, New Zealand, 2007)

K.K. Preston: "To the Opera House? The Trials and Tribulations of Operatic Production in Nineteenth Century America," and "Notes from (the Road to the) Stage," *OQ*, xxiii/1 (2008), 39–65; 103–19

J. Koegel: *Music in German Immigrant Theater. New York City, 1840–1940* (Rochester, NY, 2009)

KATHERINE K. PRESTON

Opera Ebony. Opera Company. Benjamin Matthews, Wayne Sanders, Margaret Harris, and Sister Mary Elise (Sisters of the Blessed Sacrament) founded the company in 1973 "to ease the plight of black and minority artists finding it difficult to assimilate into a fundamentally European cultural tradition of opera." (*Crisis*, 1983). Under the leadership of Matthews as artistic director and Sanders as music director, the company has been home to numerous performers, directors, conductors, and technical crews and has provided a forum for new works by underrepresented composers. Opera Ebony (<http://www.operaebony.org/>) has performed in the major venues of New York City and has toured to Brazil, Russia, Estonia, Sweden, Finland, Iceland, Canada, Switzerland, and Martinique. In addition to works from the standard repertory, the company has produced premieres and commissions including *Frederick Douglass* (Moore, 1985); *Sojourner Truth* (Capers, 1986); *The Outcast* (Ain, 1990); *Oh Freedom* (McLin and Matthews, 1990); *Journin'* (Matthews, 1991); and *The Meetin'* (Watson, 1998).

BIBLIOGRAPHY

H. Williams: "National Opera Ebony is Alive and Doing Well," *The Crisis*, xc/4 (1983), 25

R. Gover: "Opera Ebony's Artistic Landmarks: Their Contribution to History," *OQ*, ii/2 (1984), 57–68

KAREN M. BRYAN

Opera/South. Opera company founded in 1970 as a collaborative effort between the music departments of Tougaloo College, Utica Junior College, and Jackson State University in Mississippi. Sister Mary Elise, SBS (1898–1982) initiated the program, prior to her involvement with Opera Ebony. Elise produced opera at Xavier University in New Orleans and after retiring moved upstate to develop operatic possibilities at these institutions. The group was chartered under the Mississippi Intercollegiate Opera Guild (1971) and adopted the name Opera/South at a time when there were very few opera companies in that region. Led by a Board of Directors the company produced operas annually from 1970 through the 1983–4 season, hiring professional singers for the leads but relying on student talent for the secondary roles, chorus, and production support. In addition to traditional works such as *Aida*, *Carmen*, and *Così fan tutte*, the group performed William Grant Still's *A Bayou Legend* (1974; filmed in 1979 for the Public Broadcasting System) and *Highway 1, U.S.A.* (1972), as well as the premiere of Ulysses Kay's *Jubilee* (1976).

BIBLIOGRAPHY

B. Bailey: "Opera/South: a Brief History," *The Black Perspective in Music*, xiii/1 (Spring 1985), 48–78

KAREN M. BRYAN

Operetta. Musical theater genre dominated by its score, which typically requires a variety of voice types, ranging from the operatic to the comic. Stories usually take place in a foreign land, often an imaginary Central European kingdom. While the genre is commonly associated with Central Europe, American operettas thrived on Broadway from the 1890s through the late 1920s and later in Hollywood.

See also MUSICAL THEATER.

Oppens, Ursula. (*b* New York, NY, 2 Feb 1944). Pianist and teacher. She began studying piano with her mother, Edith Oppens, but before settling on a career as a pianist, she attended Radcliffe College, where she earned a BA in English and Economics (1965). Oppens studied with LEONARD SHURE and Guido Agosti, and then with FELIX GALIMIR and ROSINA LHÉVINNE while earning a Master's degree from Juilliard (1966–9). In 1969 she won the Busoni International Piano competition and debuted at Carnegie Hall under the sponsorship of Young Concert Artists, Inc. She was awarded the *Diploma d'onore* from the *Accademia Chigiana* in 1970, and in 1976 she received an Avery Fisher Career Grant. Oppens has performed around the world with leading orchestras, as a solo artist, as a musician for the Mark Morris Dance Company, and at many prominent music festivals. She was the John Evans Distinguished Professor of Music at Northwestern University (1994–2008), and she currently is a Distinguished Professor at Brooklyn College Conservatory of Music and CUNY Graduate Center.

Oppens is a champion of contemporary piano music as well as the traditional repertoire. She co-founded the modern music group SPECULUM MUSICAE (1971), which won the Naumburg Chamber Music Award (1972). She has commissioned works from Anthony Braxton, Elliott Carter, Joan Tower, and other well-known composers. Three of her numerous recordings have been nominated for Grammy Awards. Oppens commands dynamic touches that evoke everything from tickling to supple sinking, to lightning strikes, to thunder claps. Crisp execution and clarity of tone and concept are hallmarks of her style.

BIBLIOGRAPHY

C. Field: Interview, *Clavier*, xxvi/4 (1987), 6–10
S. Kagan: Interview, *Fanfare*, xv/2 (1991–2), 156–61
D. McGown: "The Feast of 'Saint Ursula': a Conversation with Ursula Oppens," *The American Music Teacher*, xxxxix/4 (2000), 38–40

ELLEN HIGHSTEIN/REBECCA SCHWARTZ-BISHIR

Oquendo, Manny [José Manuel] (*b* Brooklyn, NY, 1 Jan 1931; *d* Bronx, NY, 25 March 2009). Percussionist and bandleader. Oquendo, whose heritage was Puerto Rican, grew up in Harlem. He took drum set lessons with Sam Ulano (alongside Max Roach). Ubaldo Nieto, timbale player for Machito and his Afro-Cubans, was an early influence. In the late 1940s, Oquendo began playing professionally with bandleaders Jose Budet, Pupi Campo, José Curbelo, Luis del Campo, Frank García (alongside "Chano" Pozo), Marcelino Guerra, Carlos Medina, Juanito Sanabria, Juan Torres, and Charlie Valero. In 1950, he joined Tito Puente's orchestra on bongo. In 1954 he was recruited by Puente's archrival, Tito Rodriguez, and a year later by Vicentico Valdés. Pianist Eddie Palmieri hired him in 1962 as timbale player for his seminal La Perfecta, a band credited for introducing a brass line-up of trombones and adapting the hard-driving style of Arsenio Rodriguez. In 1974 he formed Manny Oquendo y Libre (known as Conjunto Libre), leading the group for the rest of his professional career. In the early 1970s, he was also part of the groundbreaking Group Folklórico Experimental Nuevayorquino. His style and sound (low pitched drums, in the manner of Cuban players Ulpiano Díaz and Orestes Varona) reflected a strong aesthetic of restraint.

BIBLIOGRAPHY

F.M. Figueroa: "Manny Oquendo: Up Close and Personal (interview)," *Latin Beat Magazine*, vii (1997), 20–3
A.E. Velez: "Manny Oquendo, Latin Band Leader and Stylistic Innovator, Dies at 78," *New York Times* (12 April 2009)

JAIRO MORENO

Oral tradition. The term, broadly construed, refers to any music not transmitted in writing—that is music learned aurally, whether played or sung, including learning from recordings, though this extension of the term is more controversial. In common parlance the term is often used as a substitute for the problematic term FOLK MUSIC. Technically the term should be "aural/oral/visual/kinesthetic tradition," since the ear, the mouth, and/or the viewing and handling of an instrument are often used for this kind of music transmission. In the North American context, oral tradition looms large, since for a great part of history its inhabitants were either indigenous people with no means of or need for writing down tunes; new immigrants without any formal institutions to support their music-making; or people, including slaves, who because they were poor and itinerant were unable to own instruments or take formalized lessons. Yet even when settled, the bulk of the population continued—and continues—to engage oral transmission as the mainstay of their music-making. (McLucas, 2010). Here, besides the use of oral tradition in folk communities, we also consider its roles in art, popular, and children's music.

1. Oral traditions in music and text. 2. Oral repertories. 3. The oral process. 4. Recordings and oral tradition. 5. Oral tradition and art music. 6. Oral traditions in popular and children's music. 7. Ongoing controversies in the study of oral tradition.

1. ORAL TRADITIONS IN MUSIC AND TEXT. There are two streams of oral tradition within American musical culture—song texts and music, both vocal and instrumental—and they do not always coincide. While the majority of the North American population became literate by sometime in the 19th century, musical literacy was and continues to be a much rarer trait. Singers of ballads in the 18th and 19th centuries, for example, could learn texts aurally, but also often wrote out their texts or learned them from broadside ballad sheets or newspapers. Few of these sources contained notated melodies, which instead were passed on orally by street singers, professional singers in theatrical productions, and by non-professional performers simply singing to one another. The musical literacy of instrumentalists was more in evidence than for singers, as evidenced by manuscripts and prints with notation for tunes for fife, flute, violin, and other instruments that exist in the American context from as early as the 1720s (Keller). However, even among musically literate performers, the aurally-communicated content of both texts and tunes is of primary importance.

The oral tradition of songs and instrumental music forms the backbone of much of America's musical heritage, both in the repertoire of tunes that it has preserved and in the melodic and harmonic content, which has been absorbed into much of our popular and art music as well (McLucas).

2. ORAL REPERTORIES. The oldest and possibly largest repertoire of orally transmitted music is that of the thousands of Native American tribes who inhabited both North and South America for centuries before European contact. From the evidence gathered since contact, native religious ceremonies and secular activities were inextricably linked with song. These songs accompanied healing, gambling, the hunting and taming of animals, dancing of all kinds, and preparing for battle. For most Indian tribes pre-contact, vocal music with drums and rattles was the most prevalent, along with wooden and reed flutes, whistles, bullroarers, and rasps for some occasions. (The exceptional single-string Apache fiddle, *kízh kízh díhí*, may have originated pre-contact or it may be an imitation of the fiddle brought by Europeans.) Just as there are some 300 native languages still spoken in North America, and many more in South America, there are hundreds of different styles of Native American singing, ranging from the low-pitched, rehearsed unison of the Pueblo peoples to the falsetto range, nasal choruses in loose unison of the Apachean peoples—both Navajos and Apaches (Nettl). The pan-American powwow, an invention of native practitioners working in the 20th century, still relies on oral tradition for sharing songs and expanding the repertoire (Browner, 2002).

The immigrants from the British Isles and Ireland and their descendants have developed a repertoire numbering in the tens of thousands of tunes, and it is the one that has most often been collected, studied, and written about. Tunes dating from as far back as the early 17th century bear resemblance to songs that have been collected in the late 20th and 21st centuries (*see* TUNE FAMILIES). For example, the most ubiquitous ballad tune in North America, "Barbara Allen," has a tune recognizably similar to those used in Scotland since the 17th century (Seeger, 1966). At the same time, new texts have been put to old tunes and new texts and tunes have been composed to fit the old models, thus continually expanding the repertoire, while leaving its basic structures intact.

In addition, there are hundreds of repertoires perpetuated in the ethnic communities of other immigrant groups: the Hispanic, the Scandinavian, the Cajun, the many different Asian cultures, and, most significantly, the African Americans (Southern; Epstein) whose oral repertoire and processes have deeply influenced the course of American jazz (Gillespie); the blues (Evans); and popular music from the 19th century onwards.

3. THE ORAL PROCESS. The process of passing down a tune without written notation involves functions of memory that are only now becoming understood. Instead of considering aural memory as an anatomical recording apparatus that simply captures the minutiae of sounds in full and then either reproduces them accurately or not, neuroscience research suggests that sounds when first heard are separated into component parts, which are extracted and stored in different neuronal networks,

so that when "remembering" a tune one is really "reconstituting" it from the extracted elements, which include rhythm, timbre, pitch, as well as text and other associated memories of the context in which it was learned (Rubin; Snyder). Thus passing along a tune in oral tradition almost inevitably involves some forms of change, whether large or small (one could say this of performance in general). Among the most stable properties of a tune are its contour (Dowling), its overall form, and at least the memory of its timbre, whether that can be reproduced exactly or not (Levitin). Among the least stable of a remembered melody are its rhythm, often varying according to text and/or dance type, and its exact tonal content (including mode). In communities in which oral tradition is the predominant means of transmission, the idea of singing a tune exactly as learned is not necessarily a priority (though in certain American Indian ceremonial traditions, singing a song correctly is considered a necessity—the definition of "correctly," however is not clear). While novelty may not be sought, melodic variation often happens, even from one verse to another within the same song (see ex.1), and, as Spitzer has shown, even with the intervention of printed documents, the impact of orality can affect aspects of a tune's contour and rhythm.

Ex.1 Three variants of phrase 3 in the performance of "Tom Sheraman's Barroom" by Dick Devall (Timely Tunes C 1563 and Aurora 36–115), recorded 13 Oct 1929

4. RECORDINGS AND ORAL TRADITION. Just as the invention of printing brought forth much more fixity in texts than had previously existed, the invention of recording technologies introduces the idea of fixity into the tune repertoire, even among those who do not know notation. Because a recording can be played over and over, music can be committed to memory without notation and without direct human contact. Depending upon the listener and his or her background, the recording (or multiple recorded performances) may simply be substituted for hearing live performers and the same kinds of changes ordinarily made in memorizing tunes will ensue. But for communities in which oral traditions have largely waned, the idea of reproducing a tune more or less exactly is both more possible and more desirable. At times fidelity to a particular tradition can

stifle competing traditions, as seems to have been the case with the American recordings of Irish fiddler Michael Coleman, whose performances have held a place of honor for many decades among Irish musicians, who devote considerable time to imitating the musical style and repertoire evidenced on his commercial recordings (Grasso, 2011). In addition, as Alan Lomax emphasized, the commercial interests behind recordings often succeed in inundating smaller oral communities with ready-made music, which can drown out their oral traditions. Others counter that such communities often turn these new means of making music to their own ends.

5. ORAL TRADITION AND ART MUSIC. While it might seem that concert or art music does not rely much on oral tradition, depending as it does on written scores, a great deal of what is taught and played does not appear anywhere in the musical notation. Nuances of rhythm, timbre, ornamentation, vibrato—much of what makes a musical performance live—are handed down from musician to musician in lessons or in imitation of recordings. Even traditions of altered pitches are conveyed through generations of teachers, as taught by their teachers (Eigeldinger, 1970). In fact whole schools of thought about how an instrument should be played are also passed down orally through generations of teachers of a certain "school." See, for instance, Ethel Newcomb's comments about studying the Leschitzky method of playing piano.

6. ORAL TRADITIONS IN POPULAR AND CHILDREN'S MUSIC. While the term is most often used in connection with so-called folk music, oral tradition also forms the backbone of current-day popular music, even more so than in the past. Since many modern popular musicians work directly with electronic equipment, producing their own orchestrations in the studio, there is often no need for the intervention of notation. Likewise, the garage band movement (Hicks, 1999), and the advent of the bedroom beat-producer (Schloss, 2004) have depended upon learning and imitating by ear, and the Internet often plays the role of intermediary between the producer and his or her audience without the intervention of any form of notation.

Perhaps the purest form of musical oral tradition exists in the play of children. Opie and Opie and others have documented the tradition of childhood playground songs, and more recently Campbell and Marsh have studied the improvised singing and the important role of oral creativity in children's play (Campbell, 1998; Marsh, 1999).

7. ONGOING CONTROVERSIES IN THE STUDY OF ORAL TRADITION. The major themes still at issue in oral tradition are competing definitions of orality; the role of recordings in perpetuating—or corrupting—oral traditions; and the mechanisms by which the human memory preserves the traditions transmitted. How much does the process of oral tradition change what it receives; how much does it preserve accurately? Is oral tradition in danger of dying out in the face of new technologies? The answers

to these questions require further study and may vary from tradition to tradition and culture to culture.

BIBLIOGRAPHY

F.J. Child: *English and Scottish ballads* (Boston, 1880)
E. Newcomb: *Leschetizsky as I knew him* (New York, 1921)
C. Seeger: "Oral Tradition" *Funk and Wagnall's Standard Dictionary of Folklore and Mythology*, ii (New York, 1949–50)
T. Coffin: *The British Traditional Ballad in North America* (Philadelphia, 1950)
B. Nettl: *North American Indian Musical Styles* (Philadelphia, 1955)
G.M. Laws: *American Balladry from British Broadsides* (Philadelphia, 1957)
G.M. Laws: *Native American Balladry: a Descriptive Study and a Bibliographical Syllabus* (Philadelphia, 1964)
C. Seeger: "Versions and Variants of 'Barbara Allen' in the Archive of American Folk Song in the Library of Congress: with Comments on the Words by Ed Cray," *Selected Reports*, i/1 (1966), 120–67
A. Lomax: *Folk Song Style and Culture* (Washington, DC, 1968)
J.-J. Eigeldinger: *Chopin: vu par ses élèves* (Neuchâtel, 1970; Eng. trans., 1986, as *Chopin: Pianist and Teacher*)
E. Southern: *Music of Black Americans: a History* (New York, 1971), 27–9, 64–6
D. Buchan: *The Ballad and the Folk* (London, 1972)
D. Epstein: *Sinful Tunes and Sspirituals: Black Folk Music to the Civil War* (Urbana, IL, 1977)
W.J. Dowling: "Scale and Contour: Two Components of Memory for Melodies," *Psychological Review*, lxxxv/4 (1978), 341–54
K.V.W. Keller: *Popular Secular Music in America through 1800: a Preliminary Checklist of Manuscripts in North American Collections* (Philadelphia, 1981)
I. Opie and P. Opie: *The Singing Game* (New York, 1985)
L.O. Gillespie: "Literacy, Orality, and the Parry-Lord 'Formula: Improvisation and the Afro-American Jazz Tradition," xxii/2 (1991), 147–64
J. Spitzer: "'Oh! Susanna': Oral Transmission and Tune Transformation," *Journal of the American Musicological Society* xlvii (1994), 90–136
D.C. Rubin: *Memory in Oral Traditions: the Cognitive Psychology of Epic, Ballads, and Counting-out Rhymes*, (New York, 1995)
P.S. Campbell: *Songs in their heads: music and its meaning in children's lives* (New York, 1998)
M. Hicks: *Sixties Rock: Garage, Psychedelic, and Other Satisfactions* (Urbana, IL, 1999)
K. Marsh: "Mediated Orality: The Role of Popular Music in the Changing Tradition of Children's Musical Play," *Research Studies in Music Education*, xiii/1 (1999), 2–12
B. Snyder: *Music and Memory* (Cambridge, MA, 2000)
T. Browner: *Heartbeat of the People: Music and Dance of the Northern Pow-wow* (Urbana, IL, 2002)
J. Schloss: *Making Beats: The Art of Sample-Based Hip-Hop.* (Middletown, CT, 2004)
D.J. Levitin: *This is your Brain on Music: the Science of a Human Obsession* (New York, 2006)
D. Evans: "Formulaic Composition in the Blues: A View from the Field," *Journal of American Folklore*, no.120 (2007), 482–99
A. McLucas: *The Musical Ear: Oral Tradition in the USA* (Farnham and Burlington, VT, 2010)
E. Grasso: *Melodic Variation in the Instrumental Dance Music Tradition of Ireland* (diss. U. of Oregon, 2011)

ANNE DHU McLUCAS

Oratorio. A concert-length setting of a sacred subject for voices and instruments. An oratorio usually involves solo voices, chorus, and orchestra presented in concert with no costumes, scenery, or action. The musical styles and forms tend to reflect those of opera; the text—generally derived from the Bible—is dramatic in nature and includes narrative and reflective passages. Its nearest relative is the CANTATA; the only reliable distinctions between the two genres lie in length and subject. Cantatas generally run from ten to 60 minutes and are based on secular or sacred subjects, whereas oratorios last from one to three hours and involve sacred, dramatic texts.

The oratorio in the United States never achieved the popularity of the cantata, which held stronger appeal to Americans owing to its shorter length and less operatic style. American choral groups have generally preferred oratorios by European composers such as George Frederick Handel, Franz Joseph Haydn, and Felix Mendelssohn. Nevertheless, American composers produced a number of important oratorios, especially towards the end of the 19th century. Five oratorios had been written in this country by 1840 and 12 by the Civil War; by 1900 about 35 had been added. American oratorios were modeled in form and style on those by German and English composers and, like theirs, have several large sections and use librettos based on the Bible rather than newly penned verse. The librettos drew from the Old and the New Testaments in about equal proportions.

Oratorios were performed in the late 18th century in the larger cities of the Northeast. English immigrant William Selby's Musical Society of Boston performed the first complete oratorio, Samuel Felsted's *Jonah*, for George Washington during his visit to the city in December 1789. The earliest oratorios known to be composed in America were *Jersualem in Affliction* (1828) and *The Daughters of Zion* (1829) by Italian-born Filippo Trajetta in Philadelphia. Bohemian immigrant A.P. Heinrich, one of the first professional composers in this country, voiced his patriotism in *The Jubilee* (1841), an extended composition for chorus, soloists, and orchestra which probably never found performance.

Popular song composer John Hill Hewitt wrote the first known oratorio by an American, *Jephtha* (1845), intended for amateurs with its simple melodies, diatonic harmony, and uncomplicated accompaniments. He also penned three juvenile oratorios—popular shorter secular choral works intended for schools: *Flora's Festival* ("Pastoral Oratorio") for pupils of the Baltimore Musical Institute (1838), *The Revellers: a Juvenile Temperance Oratorio* (1848) set to a moralizing libretto denouncing the evils of alcohol, and *The Fairy Bridal: an Oratorio* (1845), which drew from the fairy wedding in Shakespeare's *Midsummer Night's Dream* for its libretto.

After mid-century, American composers continued to produce oratorios patterned after European models. George F. Bristow's *Daniel* premiered in 1867 in New York with a large chorus, noted soloists, and orchestra. In 1873 John Knowles Paine's *St. Peter* was premiered in its entirety in Portland, Maine, with a chorus of 150 and orchestra from Boston. The work was one of the finest American oratorios in the Handelian/Mendelssohnian tradition, with its lyrical solos, chorales, and active role for the chorus. A year later, Leopold Damrosch wrote *Ruth and Naomi* for his recently founded New York Oratorio Society. Dudley Buck's lengthy, three-part *The Light of Asia* (1886) is not only the sole work during the period celebrating the life of Gautama Buddha, but also the first American oratorio published abroad; Novello, in England, issued the vocal score in 1886.

American oratorios composed at the turn of the century reflected the modernizing influence of Wagner with continuous music, increased chromaticism, and the use of leitmotifs. Around 1890 Horace Wadham Nicholl finished his remarkable cycle of four oratorios: *Adam*, *Abraham*, *Isaac*, and *Jacob*, which appear not to have been performed. Horatio Parker established an international reputation with his *Hora novissima*, which premiered in England at the Three Choirs Festival and in London in 1899. With its elegant melodic lines, restrained chromaticism, colorful orchestration, and effective counterpoint, it remains the only 19th-century American oratorio still in the repertoire. Parker also wrote two striking dramatic oratorios: *The Legend of St. Christopher* (1897) and *Morven and the Grail* (1915). George Chadwick's stylistically modern *Judith: Lyric Drama* (1900) was conceived as an opera but has always been performed as an oratorio. Frederick Converse's *Job: Dramatic Poem* (1906), with its serene atmosphere, modal harmony, and plainchant-influenced melodies, looks to the past for its musical inspiration.

After World War I, composers and choral groups preferred the cantata to the oratorio for extended works. Nevertheless, 20th-century composers wrote a number of stylistically diverse oratorios, which continued to draw upon biblical subjects. Among these are Nathaniel Dett's *The Ordering of Moses* (1937), Bernard Rogers's *The Passion* (1942), Paul Creston's Christmas oratorio *Isaiah's Prophecy* (1962), Vincent Persichetti's *The Creation* (1969), and Dominick Argento's *Jonah and the Whale* (1973). Mona Lyn Reese's *Choose Life (Uvacharta Bachayim)*, which takes the Holocaust as its theme, was nominated for a Pulitzer Prize in 1995. In recent years the form has included other texts that are not biblical narratives, for example, Henry Brant's *Wind, Water, Clouds, and Fire* (2004) and Neely Bruce's *The Portals of St. Bartholomew* (2008).

BIBLIOGRAPHY
GMO
H.E. Krehbiel: *Notes on the Cultivation of Choral Music and the Oratorio Society of New York* (New York, 1884/R1970)
D.P. DeVenney: *Nineteenth-Century American Choral Music: an Annotated Guide* (Berkeley, 1987)
D.P. DeVenney: *American Choral Music since 1920: an Annotated Guide* (Berkeley, 1993)
D.P. DeVenney: *Varied Carols: a Survey of American Choral Literature* (Westport, CT, 1999)
N.L. Orr and W.D. Hardin: *Choral Music in Nineteenth-Century America: a Guide to the Sources* (Lanham, MD, 1999)
H. Smither: *A History of the Oratorio*, iv (Chapel Hill, NC, 2000)
N.L. Orr: "Choral Music and Music Making in the United States," *Nineteenth-Century Choral Music*, ed. D.M. Di Grazia (New York, 2013), 475–99

N. LEE ORR

Orbach, Jerry [Jerome Bernard] (*b* New York, NY, 20 Oct 1935; *d* New York, NY, 28 Dec 2004). Actor and singer. The son of Leon Orbach, a vaudeville performer, Jerry Orbach studied drama with Lee Strasberg at the Actors Studio in New York. Orbach performed on Broadway in *The Threepenny Opera* as a replacement for Smith, the Police Constable (1955). He was the original El Gallo, the narrator in the cast of the long-running off-Broadway musical *The Fantasticks* (1960). His character opens the show with the now famous song "Try to Remember." He returned to Broadway to play Paul Berthalet in *Carnival* (1961). Orbach received a Tony award nomination for his performance of Sky Masterson in a revival of *Guys and Dolls* (1965). He won the Tony Award for Best Actor in a Musical (1969) as Chuck Baxter in *Promises, Promises* (1968). Two of Baxter's songs, the title tune and "I'll Never Fall in Love Again," became popular hits. Orbach's pleasing lyric baritone presented text in a clear and lyrical manner. He received another Tony nomination for Best Actor (1976) as Billy Flynn in Kander and Ebb's *Chicago*, directed by Bob Fosse. Orbach played Julian Marsh in the original production of *42nd Street* (1980) by Warren and Dubin. He was the voice of Lumière in the Disney animated version of *Beauty and the Beast* (1991). In the 1980s Orbach pursued a full-time career in film and television, including playing Lennie Briscoe in the series *Law and Order*.

BIBLIOGRAPHY

G. Bordman: *American Musical Theater: a Chronicle* (New York, 2001)

Obituary, *Daily Variety*, cclxxxv/63 (30 Dec 2004)

SYLVIA STONER-HAWKINS

Orbison, Roy (Kelton) (*b* Vernon, TX, 23 April 1936; *d* Hendersonville, TN, 6 Dec 1988). Rock and roll singer, songwriter, and guitarist. Possessing one of the most distinctive and acclaimed voices in the history of rock music, Roy Orbison grew up singing country western and big band tunes. His early groups included the Wink Westerners and The Teen Kings. The Teen Kings were signed by Sam Phillips of Sun Records in 1956 and, increasingly influenced by rockabilly and rock and roll, Orbison recorded "Ooby Dooby" (1956), selling over 200,000 copies. In 1958 Orbison penned "Claudette," which he sold to The Everly Brothers and which appeared on the B-side to "All I Have to Do Is Dream." In 1960 his contract was bought by Nashville's Monument Records. Teaming up with Joe Melson, Orbison co-wrote and recorded "Only the Lonely" (1960) which became an instant hit in the United States and UK. Now in high demand Orbison wrote "Running Scared" (1961) loosely based on the rhythm of Ravel's *Bolero*. This was closely followed by "Crying" (1961) and "Dream Baby" (1962).

During the early 1960s Orbison adopted his trademark look of prescription sunglasses and black clothes. This combined with his naturally quiet, somewhat shy, personality and emotionally vulnerable songs and performances created a public aura of brooding man of mystery and introversion—characteristics not in keeping with Orbison's engaging sense of humor—but which helped market him to teenage audiences.

The hits continued in the early 1960s, including "In Dreams" (1963), "Mean Woman Blues" (1963), "Blue Bayou" (1963), and what later became a signature song, the ballad "It's Over" (1964). 1964 also produced Orbison's biggest hit, "Oh, Pretty Woman," characterized by

Orbison's guttural growl and a driving guitar line. Seemingly impervious to the success of the British invasion, *Billboard* magazine noted: "In a 68-week period that began on 8 August 1963, Roy Orbison was the *only* American artist to have a number one single in Britain." It was a feat which he accomplished twice with "It's Over" on 25 June 1964 and "Oh, Pretty Woman" on 8 October 1964.

Following the death of his wife and the onset of more psychedelically inspired music, Orbison's career went into a decline. While continuing to record in the 1970s he was mostly remembered for cover versions of his songs including Linda Rondstadt's "Blue Bayou" (1977) and Don McLean's "Crying" (1980). Bruce Springsteen regularly included Orbison's songs in his concerts and would later induct him into the Rock and Roll Hall of Fame in 1987.

The late 1980s saw a major revival in Orbison's career. In 1987 he won a Grammy award for "Crying," a duet with k.d. lang. In 1988 he joined The Traveling Wilburys with George Harrison, Jeff Lynne, Tom Petty, and Bob Dylan. 1988 also saw the release of *Mystery Girl*, featuring the hit "You Got It." Tragically, Orbison died of a heart attack later in the same year at the height of his resurgent popularity. While most men in rock and roll in the 1950s and 60s portrayed a defiant aggressive masculinity, many of Orbison's songs and vocal performances instead conveyed a quiet, if often impassioned, vulnerability. He remains one of the most universally admired writers and performers in the history of popular music.

RECORDINGS

(selective)

Roy Orbison and the Teen Kings, "Ooby Dooby" (1956, Sun Records); *Roy Orbison at the Rock House* (1961, Sun); *Lonely and Blue* (1961, Monument); *Crying* (1962, Monument); *In Dreams* (1963, Monument); *Orbisongs* (1965, Monument); *The Classic Roy Orbison* (1966, MGM); *Cry Softly, Lonely One* (1967, MGM); *Roy Orbison's Many Moods* (1969, MGM); *Mystery Girl* (1989, Virgin); *Roy Orbison and Friends: a Black and White Night Live* (1989, Virgin)

BIBLIOGRAPHY

K. Emerson: *Roy Orbison* (New York, 1976)

P. Lehman: *Roy Orbison: the Invention of an Alternative Rock Masculinity* (Philadelphia, 2003)

A.J. Zak: "Only the Lonely: Roy Orbison's Sweet West Texas Style," *Sounding Out Pop: Analytical Essays in Popular Music*, eds. M.S. Spicer and J. Covach (Ann Arbor, MI, 2010), 18–41

KEN McLEOD

Orbón (de Soto), Julián (*b* Avilés, 7 Aug 1925; *d* Miami Beach, 20 May 1991). Cuban composer of Spanish birth. He settled in Havana with his family in 1940. Considered a child prodigy of composition, he took lessons with JOSÉ ARDÉVOL and from 1942 to 1946 was a member of the Grupo de Renovación Musical, which had strong leanings towards neo-classicism. During the 1940s and 50s he was active as a pianist and music critic. He was associated with the literary group Orígenes (which included the writers José Lezama Lima and María Zambrano and the painter Wilfredo Lam), and published several essays in the group's journal that exhibit the refined, poetic use of language and imagery and the passionate phenomenological perspective, filtered through Catholicism, characteristic of the group's aesthetic. He directed the Orbón Conservatory (1946–60). In 1946 he studied composition with AARON COPLAND at Tanglewood, which strongly influenced his style of orchestration. In 1960 he moved to Mexico City where he assisted Carlos Chávez in the composition workshop at the Conservatorio Nacional. In 1963 he chose not to return to Cuba and moved to the United States without, however, fully integrating into the Cuban community in exile. He taught at Lenox College, Washington University, St. Louis; Barnard College; and the Hispanic Institute of Columbia University. He received two Guggenheim fellowships (1959, 1969), the Juan Landaeta Prize at the First Latin American Music Festival in Caracas (1954), and an award from the American Academy of Arts and Letters (1967). His work was commissioned by the Fromm and Koussevitzky Foundations and by the Dallas SO under Eduardo Mata. As an essayist, Orbón was particularly interested in the issue of style, and posited that the tradition of variation, as both structure and process, forms the backbone of Spanish and Spanish American musics, as opposed to the developmental procedures of the German musical world. Informed by his profound historical and literary interests, Orbón's music re-enacts the synthesis of the Spanish with the African that took place in Cuba and most of Latin America in the centuries after 1492. Particularly remarkable is the stylistic confluence of Spanish traditions of melodic ornamentation and structural variation, the modality of Spanish art- and traditional musics (which he saw as coming directly from Gregorian chant), Catholic liturgy, and African rhythms, some of them already transcultured into the Cuban guajiras and sones. The result is a highly personal style, vital and spiritually exalted, with a unique melos and strong rhythmic vitality.

WORKS
(selective list)
(most works written before 1947 are now lost)

Orch: Homenaje a la tonadilla, 1947; Tres versiones sinfónicas, 1953; Danzas sinfónicas, 1955; Conc. grosso, 1958; Partite no.3, 1965; Partite no.4, pf, orch, 1985
Choral: Crucifixus, 1953; Introito, vv, orch, 1968; Dos canciones folclóricas, vv, 1972; Liturgia de tres días, vv, orch, 1975
Solo vocal: Himnus ad galli cantum, S, fl, ob, cl, hp, str qt, 1955; Tres cantigas del rey, S, hpd, perc, str qt, 1960; Monte Gelboé, T, orch, 1962; Libro de cantares, 1v, pf, 1987
Chbr and solo inst: Tocata, pf, 1943; Preludio y danza, gui, 1951; Str Qt, 1951; Partitas no.1, hpd, 1963; Partita no.2, hpd, vib, cel, hmn, str qt, 1964; Preludio y fantasía tiento, org, 1974

Principal publishers: Boosey & Hawkes, Broude, Instituto Interamericano de Musicología, Presser, Southern

WRITINGS
En la esencia de los estilos y otros ensayos (Madrid, 2000)

BIBLIOGRAPHY
A. Carpentier: *La música en Cuba* (Mexico City, 1946/R)
A. Copland: "Festival of Contemporary Latin American Music," *Tempo*, no.35 (1955), 4–10
Pan American Union, ed.: *Compositores de América Composers of the Americas*, vi (Washington, DC, 1960), 83–7
V. Yedra: *Julián Orbón: a Biographical and Critical Essay* (Miami, 1990)

E. Mata: "Tres conferencias sobre Julián Orbón," *Eduardo Mata (1942–1995): fuentes documentales*, ed. G. Carmona (Mexico City, 2001/R), 266–98
A. West-Durán: "*En la esencia de los estilos y otros ensayos* by Julián Orbón," *LAMR*, xxiii (2002), 150–54

LEONORA SAAVEDRA

Orchestra. As used here an instrumental ensemble containing bowed strings with more than one player to a part, combined with wind, brass, and percussion instruments in varying proportions. The discussion focuses on orchestras in the United States and is arranged chronologically.

1. Before 1800. 2. 1800–65. 3. 1865–90. 4. 1890–1945. 5. 1945–present.

1. BEFORE 1800. Orchestras began to appear in England's North American colonies in the first half of the 18th century, some 70 or 80 years after the earliest European orchestras. The development of orchestras was slower in the new world due to sparse population, harsh material conditions, and the absence of aristocratic, court culture. Additionally there were religious restrictions on public theaters in many of the colonies and on instrumental music in church. In the 1730s newspapers in Boston, New York, and Charleston began to announce public performances by singers and "consorts" of instruments. The size of these ensembles cannot be ascertained, nor what instruments they comprised or what repertory they played. Many of them included amateur as well as professional musicians.

By the 1760s Philadelphia, New York, Boston, and Charleston had become important English provincial cities, whose musical life resembled that of cities such as Bristol, Birmingham, Edinburgh, and Dublin. Orchestras could be found in theaters, at the so-called pleasure gardens, and in various concert settings. (*See* PLEASURE GARDEN.) Philadelphia, with over 17,000 residents, offered subscription concerts from 1757, theaters from 1766, and pleasure gardens by the 1790s. A Philadelphia newspaper in 1771 advertised a benefit concert, "commencing and ending with favourite Overtures, performed by a full Band of Music, with Trumpets, Kettle Drums, and every Instrument that can be introduced with Propriety" (Sonneck, 1907, 75). Philadelphia's Chestnut Street Theater, when it opened in 1794, boasted an orchestra of 20 professional musicians. Charleston, the largest city in the southern colonies and unhindered by religious restrictions, had a vigorous public musical life. Concerts "of vocal and instrumental music" were given as early as 1733. The first theater was built in 1736, another in 1763. In the 1773–74 season this theater presented some 13 different English-language operas, suggesting that it had a resident orchestra. In 1762 the ST. CECILIA SOCIETY was organized and began to sponsor concerts, which in the 1770s included overtures and symphonies by Handel, Abel, Richter, and the Earl of Kelly. The Society recruited instrumentalists from other American cities and from England and by the 1780s had an orchestra of 20 instruments. Boston followed a similar pattern, with concerts "of vocal and instrumental music" from the 1730s on,

Park Theatre, New York, 1822. (© Collection of the New-York Historical Society, USA/ The Bridgeman Art Library)

and beginning in the 1760s there were concert societies in which professional and amateur performers combined to play orchestral music. Programs in the 1770s featured symphonies and overtures by Handel, J.C. Bach, and Stamitz—evidently an orchestral repertory. Because of religious restrictions there were almost no theatrical entertainments in Boston until after the American Revolution, and the first public theater was erected only in 1793.

In New York the John Street Theater in 1767 had a small orchestra; the Park Theater, which opened in 1798, had an orchestra of 14, led by James Hewitt. Subscription concerts began in New York in the 1760s, featuring overtures, songs, and instrumental solos, followed by dancing. Also beginning in the 1760s New York's pleasure gardens offered summer orchestral concerts. New York also had a number of musical societies in which professional musicians and amateurs banded together to offer concerts, some of them with orchestras. The Musick Club gave a concert as early as 1744, the Harmonic Society from 1773. By the 1790s the roster of societies included the Columbian Anacreontic Society, the Uranian Society, the Harmonical Society and the St. Cecilia Society. In 1799 these last two combined to form The Philharmonic Society of New York. Each member paid an initiation fee of $8 and yearly dues of $12, which went toward rent, refreshments, and the salary of the "leader" (principal violinist). The Society's weekly concerts were restricted to members and amounted to readings or rehearsals. Monthly concerts were semipublic: tickets were not sold to the general public, but each member received tickets which could be given to his

family and friends. The Society's programs were very much like those of comparable orchestras in London and on the continent, but the society itself differed from them in its governance, which was democratic, with a constitution, bylaws and elected officers.

Eighteenth-century American orchestras tended to be smaller than comparable European orchestras, and the performance standards were almost certainly lower. Instrumentalists were in short supply, most of them immigrants from England fleeing from London's overcrowded musical marketplace or occasionally from some personal scandal. The French Revolution brought an influx of French musicians in the 1790s, from France and also from Haiti. Absent court and church patronage, America's orchestra musicians pieced together a living by playing in the theaters, playing for dances and concerts, teaching, and dealing in instruments and printed music.

2. 1800–65. In the first half of the 19th century American musical life became more extensive geographically and also more cosmopolitan. Orchestras appeared in the interior of the country as well as on the Atlantic coast. New immigrants, especially from Germany, many of them well-trained and experienced, joined American orchestras. German immigrants also swelled audiences for instrumental performances and introduced America to a well-developed culture of orchestral concerts. Almost all 19th-century American orchestras were commercial ventures, selling tickets to performances in the theater, at concerts, and in other entertainment venues.

Theaters formed the core of orchestral employment in the United States. Almost every American city had at least one theater with a standing orchestra. Larger cities had several. In 1865 Boston had four theaters, Baltimore five, Cincinnati four, and Chicago three. New Orleans, which became an American city in 1803, had three theaters already in the 1830s, all of which offered opera, and all of which had standing orchestras. The Camp Street theater staged *Robert le Diable* in 1835 with an orchestra of 15; the St. Charles Theater for *The Marriage of Figaro* in the same year had an orchestra of 29. New York had by far the greatest number of theaters in the country—eight or ten theaters with standing orchestras. The orchestra at the Astor Place opera house (1847–53) was probably the largest: it numbered about 30 players, but could be expanded to 40 or more when the occasion demanded. Orchestras for theaters that presented spoken drama were considerably smaller. A *New York Tribune* article described the instrumental forces at four New York theaters in 1863: an orchestra of 19 at Wallack's Theatre; 16 players at Laura Keene's theatre; 16 at Niblo's and 13 at the Winter Garden. Violins, trumpets and clarinets were doubled; violas, cellos and basses and the rest of the winds played one-on-a-part. In the spoken theater orchestras played before and after the show and between the acts; they also accompanied songs and underscored dramatic moments. Their repertory mixed overtures, by Beethoven, Weber, Rossini, and others with popular songs and dances—everything arranged for the ensemble by that theater's violinist-leader. Theater orchestras in other American cities were similar to those in New York. They remained central to American music-making through the end of the century.

Orchestra concerts became more common in the first half of the 19th century, sometimes organized as a single benefit for an individual musician or a charity, sometimes as a subscription series. The organizational energy for concerts often came from the musicians themselves who wanted to play more ambitious repertory than they were able to perform in the theaters. At concerts the musicians could play symphonies by Beethoven and Spohr and concertos by Mendelssohn and Moscheles. However, in order to appeal to a broader audience, they took care to alternate such "classical" selections with arias from Italian operas, songs in English, and solo numbers for instrumental virtuosos. Concerts were scheduled in the afternoon or on Sundays when theater musicians were available.

Concert series could also be organized by a "philharmonic society" which aspired to give seasons of subscription concerts year after year. There was a Philharmonic Society in Boston from 1810 until 1815 or so and another from 1843 to 1855. Orchestras in Boston were also sponsored by the Academy of Music (1841–7) and the MUSICAL FUND SOCIETY (1847–55). The Academy of Music was originally organized to accompany the performance of sacred vocal music and was led by clergymen, whereas the Musical Fund Society was organized and run by the musicians themselves, who shared the profits (if any) at the end of the season. All these Boston orchestras were staffed by more or less the same musicians, most of whom also played in the theaters. In Cincinnati a Philharmonic Society was organized in 1857 in conjunction with a society of amateur singers. The Society announced that it proposed to form a "permanent, large and fine orchestra" with over 50 instruments; however the program for the second concert listed just 27 musicians. Cincinnati's Philharmonic Society lasted only until 1868, but many of the same musicians continued to perform in orchestras together for the next two decades. The musicians of St. Louis organized themselves in 1845 as a "Polyhymnia," then as a "Philharmonic" (1860–70). Chicago had a succession of "Philharmonics": one in 1850–51, a second from 1853 to 1856, a third from 1860 to 1866. Each began with a burst of optimism, flourished for a few years, then withered as subscriptions dwindled and audiences drifted away to other entertainments. This pattern was typical for 19th-century American concert societies; audiences, it seemed, were reluctant to pay for the music that the musicians wanted to play.

The exception was New York City, where the Philharmonic Society founded in 1842 managed to achieve institutional stability as a permanent orchestra. New York in 1840 had already replaced Philadelphia as the nation's largest city, and between 1840 and 1865 its population more than doubled to around 800,000 in Manhattan alone. There was an ample market for all types of music, including the "serious" repertory that orchestra musicians wanted to play. The Philharmonic

Society of New York (the third of that name) was organized as a musicians' cooperative, with members sharing the profits at the end of each season. In its first season the orchestra comprised 53 member-musicians, and it played just three concerts. By 1865 the orchestra had expanded to 80 players and the season to five concerts. Not only were the officers of the Society democratically elected, the conductors were elected too: at first they were chosen from among the society's members and shared duties at each concert; then one conductor was chosen for each concert. Beginning in 1866 the conductor was elected for the entire season and paid a salary rather than a share of the profits. The Philharmonic stated its purpose as "the advancement of instrumental music," and its programs emphasized "Symphonies, Overtures and the many pieces for smaller combinations of instruments, of Beethoven, Haydn, Mozart, Spohr, Weber, Mendelssohn, &c.," that offered "enjoyment of the highest intellectual character" (*Sixth Annual Report*, 1848). Evidently there was an audience in New York for this sort of music, because attendance and revenues increased steadily through the 1840s and 1850s. The panic of 1857 led to a momentary setback, but during the Civil War they resumed their upward course. As the nation's only "permanent" concert orchestra, the NEW YORK PHILHARMONIC served during much of the 19th century as a inspiration and a model for orchestras in other American cities.

Similarly inspiring were several European orchestras that performed in the United States during the 1840s and 1850s. The first was the Steyermarkische Musical Company, comprising 19 Austrian musicians who arrived in Boston in 1847, gave several weeks of concerts there, and then embarked on a tour that took them through Philadelphia, Baltimore, and Charleston all the way to New Orleans. The Steyermarkers seem to have been something of a novelty act, with military-style uniforms and small cymbals attached to their boots that jingled in time with the music. A more famous visitor was Joseph Gungl, well-known as a composer of dance music and leader of a successful orchestra in Berlin. Gungl and his orchestra arrived in November 1848 in New York, where they gave 14 concerts, then continued to Boston, Philadelphia, Baltimore, and Washington DC, where they played at President Zachary Taylor's inaugural ball. Gungl's orchestra, only half the size of his Berlin ensemble, drew modest audiences and did not get very favorable reviews. Moreover, several of his musicians left the ensemble and remained in the United States to join local theater orchestras. Returning to Berlin, Gungl published a letter in a newspaper criticizing the performance standards in New York and American musical taste in general.

Also arriving in 1848 was the GERMANIA MUSICAL SOCIETY, which exerted a lasting influence on American orchestras. The Society was an idealistic undertaking—24 young musicians from Berlin imbued with the ideas of utopian socialism, who organized themselves as an orchestra with the motto "equal rights, equal duties, and equal rewards" and resolved to realize their goals in the New World. Arriving in New York in April, 1848, they were immediately acknowledged as setting a higher standard of performance than American orchestras and previous visitors. The Germanians survived as an ensemble for six years (1848–54), giving over 900 performances in dozens of cities and towns along the eastern seaboard and as far west as St. Louis. They also served as the accompanying orchestra for sopranos Jenny Lind and Henriette Sontag and violinists Ole Bull and Miska Hauser. After the Germania disbanded in 1854 most of its members remained in the United States, organizing, conducting, and playing in orchestras from Boston to Philadelphia to Cincinnati to Chicago. Almost as influential was the American tour of LOUIS JULLIEN in 1853–4. Already famous in England for his promenade concerts, the charismatic Jullien came to the United States with a corps of soloists and section leaders and added New York's best musicians to make an orchestra of about 100 players, which played to ecstatic audiences for two months in New York and then embarked on a seven-month tour to some 20 American cities, large and small. Everywhere Jullien evoked the same enthusiastic response, not only for virtuoso showpieces and operatic potpourris, but for symphonies by Beethoven and Mendelssohn. In addition, the Jullien orchestra was the first in the United States to perform a significant number of works by American composers, including George Bristow, William Henry Fry, Vincent Wallace, and songs by Stephen Foster.

The visiting orchestras of the 1840s and 50s set a new standard of orchestral execution, and they demonstrated that orchestra concerts could draw large audiences and pay for themselves at the box office, not just in New York, but throughout the country. They introduced many works new to American audiences and helped turn American musical tastes toward "serious" music by classical composers. Finally, they also brought a cadre of young, well-trained orchestra musicians to the United States, many of whom remained to lead American orchestras during the second half of the century.

3. 1866–90. During the second half of the 19th century orchestras became ubiquitous in American urban life. Before the advent of amplification and recorded sound, an orchestra could fill a large indoor space with sound, provide continuity for a performance, and add aural and visual glamour to a public event. A visitor to an American city in the 1880s would have heard orchestras giving concerts; accompanying operas; playing for the spoken theater, as well as for vaudeville and burlesque; performing in parks, restaurants, hotels, and resorts; and contributing *éclat* to a variety of special events. Orchestras also expanded their geographical reach. Whereas in the first half of the century they were restricted to a few large cities, mainly on the east coast, by the 1880s orchestras could be found in most western cities, smaller manufacturing towns, and even mining camps. This increase in the number of orchestras was accompanied by an increase in the numbers of orchestra musicians, largely filled by immigration (first from Germany, then from Italy), but also by musicians trained

in America—in military bands, in private studios, and at newly founded conservatories.

An important new venue for orchestras were the "beer gardens," large establishments, mainly indoors, where concerts of orchestral and vocal music were presented in a casual atmosphere, with food and drink (mostly beer). Such "gardens" were already common in Europe in the 1830s and 40s, especially in German-speaking countries, and they sprang up in American cities where German immigrants settled. In smaller gardens the music was little more than songs, instrumental solos, and novelty acts, but the larger ones presented full-scale orchestral concerts, with a repertory similar to what would be heard in a concert hall or a theater. In the gardens, however, admission was free or cheap, since expenses were defrayed by the sale of food and drink. Many gardens hired the same orchestra for several years at a time, and this orchestra became a central component of the establishment's identity. Others engaged orchestras for single concerts or short seasons. In New York City there were scores of beer gardens. At the Broadway Garten the orchestra was directed in the 1860s by Carl Bergmann, conductor of the Philharmonic; THEODORE THOMAS (see below) led orchestras at a succession of gardens in the 1860s and 70s; at the Atlantic Garden patrons were entertained in the 1880s and 90s by the "Ladies Elite Orchestra," an all-woman ensemble. Similar gardens with similar orchestras could be found in Philadelphia, Baltimore, Cincinnati, Chicago, St. Louis, and Milwaukee, outdoors during the summer months.

After the Civil War New York increasingly became the center of a national entertainment industry, and likewise of American orchestral activity. The *New York Times* estimated in 1870 that there were 2218 orchestra musicians in the Manhattan, with 1800 more in the boroughs and suburbs. These instrumentalists (55% of them German, according to the *Times*) not only staffed the orchestras of the theaters, beer gardens, concert halls, and public festivals in the metropolis; they played in similar venues in other cities as well. Orchestras were assembled in New York for opera companies, minstrel shows, circuses, and other entertainments, and they accompanied these shows on regional or national tours. Other kinds of shows, for example, musicals and English-language opera, traveled with a skeleton crew of New York musicians, then filled out the orchestra with local musicians in the cities where they played.

An important example of the national reach of New York orchestras was the Theodore Thomas Orchestra. After playing violin in Jullien's 1853–4 orchestra and conducting the Brooklyn Philharmonic, Thomas assembled his own orchestra and in 1864 began giving concerts in New York concert halls and in the beer gardens. Thomas rapidly turned his ensemble into America's first full-time concert orchestra—modeled on European "enterprise orchestras" like those of Gungl, Jullien, and Johann Strauss, where an entrepreneur-conductor ran the orchestra as a full-time business operation. This form of organization had considerable advantages. Unlike concert-society orchestras such as the New York

Philharmonic, the Thomas orchestra rehearsed and played together almost every day and thus achieved a much higher standard of ensemble. And Thomas paid his men top dollar, so a musician in the Thomas orchestra did not have to work in the theaters or accept jobs he did not care for. The drawback was that a full-time orchestra had to work full time. To meet his payroll, Thomas had to schedule the orchestra to play as often as possible—in concert halls, in the beer gardens, for choral festivals, for private parties. Even in New York the market for concert music was not large enough to support an orchestra that played every day, so beginning in 1869, Thomas took his orchestra on the road to cities in New York and New England, then west through Pittsburgh, Cleveland, and Cincinnati to Chicago. The tour was a critical and financial success, the orchestra was hailed as the finest ensemble in America, and Thomas continued to tour almost every year until the 1890s. He also booked his orchestra to play at festivals throughout the country, like the May Festival in Cincinnati, the 1876 Centennial Exhibition in Philadelphia, and choral festivals (*Sängerfeste*) around the Midwest. From 1869 to 1890 Theodore Thomas and his orchestra exerted a massive effect on the development of American orchestras and on American music in general. They introduced millions of Americans to orchestral concerts and orchestral repertory, they set a new standard for orchestra performance, and they created wide support and patronage for orchestral music. At the same time they competed with local musicians and siphoned off support that otherwise might have gone to local orchestras.

When the Thomas orchestra was back in New York it continued to play in several concert halls, at Terrace Garden, and later at Central Park Garden. In concert halls Thomas emphasized symphonies, concertos and more "serious" repertory. In the garden concerts and on tour he refined the three-part format introduced to the United States by Gungl and Jullien: a first part consisting of crowd-pleasers and opera excerpts; a second part containing "serious" symphonic works (often just one or two movements), and a final section featuring soloists and dance music. This mixture of popular and classical, serious and light was designed to attract, amuse and educate a large and diverse audience. In addition to his activities with his own orchestra, Thomas was elected conductor of the New York Philharmonic and led that orchestra from 1877 on. The market for orchestral concerts in New York was growing stronger: in 1878 Leopold Damrosch organized the Symphony Society of New York, a third permanent orchestra, competing with the Thomas orchestra and the Philharmonic for audiences and patronage. Other American cities lagged behind New York but followed a similar pattern: expansion of the entertainment industry, growing numbers of musicians and orchestras, theaters as the basis of musical employment, concerts in diverse venues with mixed repertory, yearly visits by the Theodore Thomas orchestra, and ongoing efforts to form a "permanent" local concert orchestra.

Baltimore can serve as an example. By the 1870s the city had six or seven theaters with standing orchestras,

several German beer gardens that engaged orchestras for the summer, promenade concerts at the Maryland Institute and the Academy of Music, at least one local enterprise orchestra, and periodic public music festivals for which large orchestras were engaged. In addition the Theodore Thomas Orchestra played a short season in Baltimore at least once a year. Baltimore also had the Peabody Conservatory, which opened a music school in 1866. From 1873 to 1895 the conservatory operated the Peabody Orchestra, composed of faculty, students, and professionals, and offering a yearly subscription series, usually of eight concerts. In 1895, however, the Conservatory withdrew financial support, and the orchestra was dissolved.

Cincinnati had a large German community which provided the city both with musicians audiences for orchestral music. Beginning in 1873 and continuing every second or third year until the present, Cincinnati put on a MAY FESTIVAL of choral and orchestral music. The director of the May Festival was Theodore Thomas, who brought his orchestra to Cincinnati for the event. In 1878 Thomas was persuaded to come to Cincinnati as Director of the newly-founded College of Music, with the mission of making it a "school for orchestra." The college orchestra was dissolved in 1880, when Thomas resigned, then revived in 1886 with a local conductor, then disbanded again in 1888. In Cincinnati as in Baltimore, the expenses of a professional orchestra were too high for a conservatory to underwrite. An effort in 1884–6 to organize a Cincinnati Philharmonic as a musicians' cooperative on the model of the New York Philharmonic was no more successful. Meanwhile flutist Louis Ballenberg and cellist Michael Brand enjoyed greater success with a series of enterprise orchestras, beginning in 1872 and continuing into the 1890s. Their flexible ensemble, made up mainly of theater musicians, offered a subscription series, it played for public events, it gave promenade concerts at the hilltop resorts outside town. Despite the musicians' obligations in the theater, This "Cincinnati Grand Orchestra" toured a good deal—a summer season at New York's Brighton Beach in 1883, festivals in Cleveland, Nashville, Dayton, and Columbus (1885–7), an appearance at the Chicago World's Fair in 1893. Although it had little prestige and less financial backing, this ensemble, under changing names, amounted to a permanent concert orchestra in Cincinnati.

Chicago by the 1880s was rapidly approaching a population of a million and was home to every type of orchestra discussed so far. There were at least 11 theaters, each with its own resident orchestra. Several Chicago orchestras were organized as cooperatives with elected leaders and shared profits, a reflection of the socialist traditions of Chicago's many German immigrants. Co-op orchestras tended to be replaced in the 1880s by enterprise orchestras, where the leader paid the musicians a regular wage and kept any profits for himself. The Chicago Conservatory of Music, founded in 1865 by Florenz Ziegfield (father of the Broadway impresario) sponsored an orchestra from 1869 on, giving a yearly series of eight concerts. A philharmonic society—Chicago's fourth—was organized in 1881 but lasted for only one season. A "Chicago Orchestra" the following year was no more successful. Looming over orchestral music in Chicago was the long shadow of Theodore Thomas, who brought his orchestra to Chicago both in the course of his annual tours and again for the "Summer Nights" concerts at the lakeside Exhibition Building, and who enjoyed the support of the press and of wealthy patrons. Local orchestras in Chicago thrived in the theaters and beer gardens but found it hard to compete with Thomas as concert orchestras.

Boston in the second half of the 19th century had several theaters with resident orchestras, but its German population was relatively small, and a culture of orchestras in beer gardens and fraternal societies did not develop as in other American cities. However, there was a strong tradition of public concerts in theaters and auditoriums. Boston was home to several choral societies, it had a lively chamber music scene, and it welcomed a succession of visiting orchestras. After the Civil War the leading local orchestra was Harvard Musical Association Orchestra, founded in 1865 and managed not by a musician but by a music critic, JOHN SULLIVAN DWIGHT. The HMA engaged musicians from theater orchestras to play programs of classical music that were "pure" according to Dwight's exacting standards. Initially popular and financially successful, the orchestra found it increasingly difficult over the years to attract good musicians, pay for adequate rehearsal time, and achieve a satisfactory level of performance, particularly in comparison to the Thomas Orchestra, which visited Boston almost every year. Unable to sell enough tickets to meet its expenses, the HMA Orchestra ceased operations in 1882. It was replaced that same year by an orchestra on a new model—a concert orchestra supported by ongoing philanthropic subsidy. The Boston Symphony Orchestra was founded by HENRY LEE HIGGINSON, a Boston banker who had studied music in his youth. As he watched the HMA orchestra collapse, Higginson decided "to hire an orchestra of sixty men and a conductor, paying them all by the year, reserving to myself the right to all their time needed for rehearsals and for concerts..." (Howe, 1914, 27). True to his resolve, Higginson hired his orchestra, hired a conductor (George Henschel), managed the orchestra's activities and its finances, and made up its yearly deficits out of his own pocket. This system, which continued for 35 years, had many advantages: because the orchestra offered at least six months of full-time employment, it could recruit the best musicians, nationally and internationally; the conductor was responsible only for artistic leadership, not for management or fund-raising; the orchestra could increase its revenues by offering a summer season of popular concerts (this became the Boston Pops); and the orchestra did not have to abide by the rules of the musicians' union. The Boston Symphony quickly reached a high standard, and in 1887 it played a triumphal concert at Steinway Hall in New York, which the *Times* (15 February 1887) acknowledged was superior to the performance of any of the New York orchestras.

Musicians and critics in other cities began to ask who would be the "Higginson" for their community.

American orchestras in the second half of the 19th century were staffed for the most part by professionals, that is, musicians who made their living primarily from musical performance. To safeguard their livelihood, these musicians organized themselves into unions that encompassed almost all the professional musicians in their city. (*See* UNIONS, MUSICIANS'.) The first union, the Mutual Musical Protective Society of New York, founded in 1863, conducted a short, successful strike against theater owners that raised wages from $10 to $12 per week; the mere threat of a strike the next year brought weekly wages up to $14. Musicians in other cities followed their lead: Philadelphia in 1863, Chicago in 1864, and Washington in 1865. By 1892 there were something like 50 local unions, loosely affiliated in a National League of Musicians. Strikes were rare. The unions' aims were to reserve all orchestral work for union members and to regulate wages by setting a minimum price for every sort of musical job. By the end of the 19th century almost every American orchestra—theater orchestras, concert orchestras, dance orchestras, beer garden orchestras—was a union orchestra. The exception was the Boston Symphony, where a condition of employment was that the players not join the union.

4. 1891–1945. In the first half of the 20th century concert orchestras established themselves on a permanent basis in many of America's larger cities. Many orchestras that still exist were founded between 1891 and 1914, and a distinctive "American model" of organization emerged, in which the orchestra was a non-profit corporation, supported by civic philanthropy, with responsibility shared between a board of directors, a permanent conductor, and a professional manager.

The Chicago Symphony, America's first corporate orchestra, combined the musical vision of Theodore Thomas with the business acumen of Charles Norman Fay, a public utilities executive. Exhausted with touring and unable to support a full-time orchestra with New York engagements, Thomas had decided in 1889 to disband his orchestra. "Would you come to Chicago," Fay asked him, "if we could give you a permanent Orchestra?" "I would go to hell," Thomas famously answered, "if they gave me a permanent Orchestra" (Otis, 1924, 26). Initially Fay sought to raise a "guarantee fund" from a few wealthy donors, a variation on Higginson's Boston model. However, Fay quickly perceived the potential for broader support and solicited pledges of $1000 per year from over 50 donors to bring Thomas to Chicago and cover the first three years of the orchestra's operations. An "Orchestral Association" was formed and registered as a public corporation. In 1895 Fay's plan was further broadened by creating "Associate Memberships" for donations between $50 and $1,000. The campaign in 1902–3 to build Orchestra Hall expanded the base of support yet further. Thus, although the business of the orchestra was tightly controlled by Fay, thousands of Chicagoans came to have a stake in the organization. Thomas's Chicago Symphony Orchestra was staffed mainly with musicians from the Theodore Thomas Orchestra who moved with Thomas from New York, plus a few new players from Chicago and elsewhere. The 20-week subscription season, plus a summer popular series and limited touring provided the musicians with almost full-time employment. This configuration—a full-time orchestra, recruited nationally, organized as a corporation, with professional management, a charismatic conductor, broad community involvement, and a wide base of philanthropic support—became the model for a generation of new American orchestras.

The Cincinnati Symphony Orchestra, founded in 1895, followed with Chicago model but with local variations. Organizational leadership in Cincinnati came not from a businessman but from a group of wealthy women with extensive experience in artistic, charitable, and civic ventures, led by Mrs. William Howard Taft. They constituted themselves in 1894 as the Orchestra Association Company, a joint-stock corporation with an all-woman board of directors. In addition, the Cincinnati Symphony was not a full-time orchestra: it was composed mainly of musicians from the local theaters, released by agreement with the theater managers and paid by the concert. In its third season the orchestra began recruiting first chair players from out of town with a guaranteed salary and 20 weeks of work. This two-tier system continued well into the 20th century. The Cincinnati Symphony was led during its first season by three conductors, one of whom, Frank van der Stucken, was offered the job on a long-term basis and proved himself a dynamic leader and also an advocate of American music.

Other variants on the Chicago model emerged in Pittsburgh, Minneapolis, and St. Louis. The Pittsburgh symphony began in 1895 with a conductor (Frederick Archer), a Board of Directors led by a business executive (Charles Scovel), a three-year guarantee fund, and 50 local musicians, mainly from the theaters. After the first three years the number of guarantors was increased to 50, Archer was replaced with the more charismatic Victor Herbert, and first-chairmen were brought in from outside with guaranteed salaries. The orchestra was unable, however, to broaden its base of support sufficiently to cover this added expense, and operations were suspended in 1910, resuming only in1926. The Minneapolis variant was more successful. The orchestra was founded in 1903 by Emil Oberhoffer, conductor of a local choral society, who was joined in the enterprise by Elbert L. Carpenter, a civic-minded businessman. By1905 the orchestra had 60 players, a manager, and a guarantee fund. With inventive management, the Minneapolis Symphony Orchestra (today the Minnesota Orchestra) added to its regular subscription concerts such projects as Sunday popular concerts and children's concerts. It also toured extensively, mainly in the Midwest. By 1914 the Minneapolis Orchestra was playing 175 concerts per season. The St. Louis Symphony began similarly with a German choral society and a "Musical Union" orchestra that often accompanied them. In 1890 the two organizations were merged as the St. Louis Choral Symphony Society, led by conductor Joseph Otten and businessman Robert

S. Brookings, and incorporated in 1893. The society divided its performances between choral and orchestral concerts until 1907, when it discontinued the choral concerts, hired a new conductor (Max Zach), enlarged the orchestra, lengthened its season, added a series of popular concerts, and changed its name to the St. Louis Symphony Orchestra.

In Philadelphia the formation of a permanent orchestra was inhibited by the proximity of New York and the Thomas orchestra, later by the tours of the Damrosch orchestra and the Boston Symphony. The Philadelphia Orchestra originated almost serendipitously in a pair of benefit concerts in 1900 for the families of soldiers killed in the Spanish-American War. The concerts were organized by a Committee of Women, who engaged local theater musicians and Fritz Scheel, the conductor of the orchestra at a local amusement park. The benefit concerts were an artistic and financial success, and the Women's Committee added male members and set about raising a guarantee fund to make the orchestra permanent. Local players were gradually replaced with imported musicians, and the Philadelphia Orchestra rapidly achieved a high profile (Richard Strauss came to conduct in 1904) and correspondingly high expenses, to which the Women's Committee responded with more energetic fundraising. Finally, with Leopold Stokowski in place as conductor and Arthur Judson as manager, the Board of Directors undertook to raise an endowment large enough that the interest on it would make up the orchestra's deficits in perpetuity. "The Orchestra," said the Board in a 1916 circular, "is a civic asset. If it is to fulfill its destiny and place Philadelphia in the front rank among the musical cities of the world, it must be endowed." By the end of the year the endowment stood at $500,000, by 1919 at $1 million. Philadelphia represented a strikingly successful implementation of the Chicago model, which by then had become the "American Model" of orchestral organization.

Other members of this first generation of permanent American orchestras included Portland (1896), Seattle (1903), San Francisco (1911), and Detroit (1914). All of them were composed initially of theater musicians along with other local musicians, playing a relatively short season of symphony concerts and usually a summer pops season as well. Most of them were organized along the same lines as Chicago, as corporations with Boards of Directors, a salaried conductor, a professional manager, and a guarantee fund. Most of the first generation orchestras fell on hard times at one point or another; a couple suspended operations, then resumed. But all maintained their organizational identities and have endured into the 21st century. Similar orchestras founded between the first and second world wars included the Cleveland Orchestra (1918), the Los Angeles Philharmonic (1919), the Indianapolis Symphony (1930), the National Symphony (Washington DC, 1931), and orchestras in Rochester, Syracuse, Denver, Buffalo, New Orleans, and San Antonio. The Baltimore Symphony, founded in 1916, was a special case in that it was organized as a city orchestra, financed by a yearly appropriation and managed by a Municipal Department of

Music. The city insisted on low ticket prices in return for the subsidy, but it could not create a broad base of civic support, and the orchestra was reorganized in 1942 following the "American model," that is, a private corporation with a board of directors and a professional manager. Another example of government involvement in this generation of American orchestras was in San Francisco, where, after the 1935 Symphony season was cancelled due to lack of funds, city voters overwhelmingly approved a half-cent surcharge on their property tax to support the San Francisco Symphony.

One American orchestra that had not followed the "American model" was the New York Philharmonic, which, as the 20th century began, remained a musicians' cooperative, with shared profits and an elected conductor. The Philharmonic, however, was in dire straits. Its season was only five concerts long, and the musicians made most of their income playing in other orchestras. When other engagements conflicted with Philharmonic rehearsals or concerts, they sent substitutes. Many Philharmonic members resigned to take jobs in orchestras in other cities. By the 1908–9 season only 37 out of 100 players in the orchestra were actually members of the Society. To address the situation Mary R. Sheldon and several other prominent New Yorkers, most of them women, formed a committee that proposed to raise enough money to turn the Philharmonic into a full-time orchestra with a high-profile conductor. In return for full-time salaries, three years of guaranteed funding, and a future endowment, the musicians agreed to give up their democratic bylaws and the orchestra's co-op structure. Mrs. Sheldon and her associates in 1909 engaged Gustav Mahler as conductor, increased the number of concerts from 18 to 46, and raised more than $118,000 to cover the initial deficit. In 1912 an endowment was started with a large contribution bequest in the will of publisher Joseph Pulitzer, and the orchestra became a public corporation.

Although Mahler conducted only two seasons at the Philharmonic (1909–11), his appointment was characteristic of a new trend in American orchestras. In the 19th century most conductors had been "leaders": they played an orchestral instrument, composed and arranged music for their orchestra, managed its finances, and belonged to the same union as the men. As orchestras became corporations, the conductor's role was increasingly separated from both management and the players. The conductor became a star, whose performances and personality were marketed to the public, like those of a singer or a virtuoso instrumentalist. Boards of directors brought conductors directly from Europe and installed them in American orchestras with the mission of improving the quality of the orchestra (which usually involved wholesale changes in personnel) and raising its public profile. Henry Higginson initiated this pattern in at the Boston Symphony with a series of European conductors: George Henschel, Wilhelm Gericke, Artur Nikisch, Emil Paur, and Karl Muck. Cincinnati, after beginning with an American-born conductor (Frank van der Stucken), imported Leopold

Stokowski, Ernst Kunwald, Eugene Ysaÿe, Fritz Reiner, and Eugene Goossens. All but Stokowski were established stars before they arrived in America. After Mahler at the Philharmonic came Joseph Stransky and Willem Mengelberg; then in 1926 the Philharmonic appointed Arturo Toscanini, who led the orchestra for the next ten years and represented the quintessential 20th-century conductor: hyper-charismatic, autocratic, technically prodigious, devoted to his art, remote from both management and musicians.

The first two decades of the 20th century marked a high point for orchestras in America, in terms of the number of orchestras, the number of venues where orchestras played, and the general social and cultural reach of orchestras. Large cities now had permanent symphony orchestras with seasons of 20 weeks or more. Theaters continued to employ pit orchestras, playing six nights a week and usually a couple of matinees as well. Thousands of vaudeville theaters, from the Palace in New York to the Orpheum in Los Angeles, maintained house orchestras that accompanied touring acts. In addition movie theaters became an important venue for orchestras during the first quarter of the 20th century. Because most films were silent, music was even more necessary in movie theaters than for live theater. In 1920 it was estimated that out of 15,000 motion pictures theaters in the United States, 7000 had orchestras of some sort, ranging in size from eight or ten musicians in "main street" theaters to 70- and 80-piece orchestras in the New York movie palaces. Beer gardens, city parks, resorts, hotels, and cruise ships all employed orchestras. It seemed as though the American demand for entertainment could only grow larger, and with it the demand for orchestras.

The proliferation of orchestras was reversed abruptly in the 1920s. Many theaters had already switched from live theater or vaudeville to movies. In 1926 the first "talkies" were introduced. They were an immediate hit with the public, and by 1930 3500 theaters nationwide had been wired for sound. Orchestras were now superfluous: between 1927 and 1931 American theaters laid off some 20,000 musicians. There was little that the players or their union could do about it, particularly not after the onset of the Great Depression, which forced theater owners to lower ticket prices and lay off even more musicians.

The collapse of theater orchestras brought about a fundamental reorientation in the world of American orchestras. For something like 150 years the theater had provided the core of the orchestral musician's livelihood, a steady (though low-paying) job that allowed him the flexibility to take other work as it came his way. Now that livelihood was gone. Changes in popular music during the first quarter of the 20th century only made matters worse. During most of the 19th century orchestras had been the preferred accompaniment for social dancing. After a concert in a hall or a beer garden, the orchestra often played for dancing until the small hours of the morning. But with advent of ragtime and then jazz in the 20th century, dance music was taken

The Fadette Ladies' Orchestra of Boston, c1900. (Special Collections, University of Iowa Library)

over by bands and small ensembles composed mainly of wind and rhythm instruments. Dance orchestras declined and disappeared at just the same time as theater orchestras.

As theater and dance orchestras withered and died in the 1920s and 30s, "orchestra" came increasingly to mean "symphony orchestra": professional musicians, playing a repertory of classical music in a concert format. Symphony orchestra personnel overlapped with the orchestras that remained in the theaters—for opera, musicals, and ballets—but less than previously, because there was less work in the theater, and also because symphony orchestra positions were now full-time during the subscription season. In the 1930s Americans heard live orchestras in fewer venues and fewer public contexts than they had in the 1890s.

At the same time many new orchestras were created in the first half of the 20th century to play symphonic music. Community orchestras, school orchestras, women's orchestras, and others performed symphonic repertory in a concert setting. Community orchestras were sometimes founded by groups of musical amateurs seeking a musical outlet and sociable diversion, sometimes by music teachers seeking to expand opportunities for their students, sometimes by governmental bodies, such as school boards and recreation departments. (*See* COMMUNITY MUSIC ENSEMBLE.) They were encouraged by the introduction of instrumental music into public school curricula after the First World War. By the late 1920s there were community orchestras across the country, from Portland, Oregon to Portland, Maine. There was a doctors' orchestra in Akron, a businessman's orchestra in Chicago, women's orchestras in Cleveland, St. Louis, and Detroit. Many community orchestras combined amateurs with paid professional players. The Chicago Civic Orchestra functioned as a

training orchestra: over half of its members were professional musicians, mostly young, and it was conducted by Frederick Stock, who also led the Chicago Symphony. In the 1930s the US government undertook to sponsor community orchestras through the Federal Music Project, a branch of the Depression-era Works Progress Administration (WPA) (*see* WORKS PROGRESS ADMINISTRATION, FEDERAL MUSIC PROJECT OF THE). These were professional orchestras, ranging in size from 10 to over 100 musicians, whose aim was to provide employment to instrumentalists put out of work by the collapse of employment in the theaters. By 1938 there were some 127 Federal orchestras. The Federal Music Project wound down in 1941–2, as out-of-work musicians became soldiers or replaced men who had gone to war.

Another kind of community orchestra was associated with educational institutions—particularly colleges and universities. The orchestras of 19th-century music conservatories were composed mainly of theater musicians and faculty, with a smattering of students. Students at colleges and universities organized themselves into extracurricular, all-student orchestras which became institutionalized as music departments were created in the late 19th and 20th centuries. By 1940 there were over 100 college and university orchestras in the United States, about half of them sponsored and run by the school, the remainder extracurricular. They included undergraduates, graduate students, faculty from several departments, and amateur musicians from the surrounding community.

Community orchestras were also created to provide opportunities to instrumentalists excluded from other kinds of orchestras—in particular female and African American musicians. All-woman orchestras were formed already in the 1870s and 80s, some as ladies clubs, which gave occasional benefit concerts, and others as professional orchestras, playing in beer gardens and on

James Levine conducts the Boston Symphony Orchestra, 2007. (C. Christodoulou/Lebrecht Music & Arts)

the vaudeville circuit. Examples of club-model orchestras include the Los Angeles Women's Orchestra (1893–1945), the Ladies Philharmonic Orchestra of Boston (*c*1889–*c*1926), and the Women's Philharmonic Society of New York (1889–*c*1916). Some professional orchestras were the Lady Elite Orchestra at the Atlantic Garden in New York (1880–*c*1916) and THE FADETTE LADIES' ORCHESTRA (1888–1920), which began as a club but later played in vaudeville and movie theaters. In the 20th century, as women were trained at music conservatories, many more women's orchestras were founded, several with female conductors: the Women's Symphony of Chicago (1925–45), The Boston Women's Symphony (1926–30, conducted by Ethel Leginska), the Long Beach Women's Symphony (1925–48, conducted by Eva Anderson), the Orchestrette Classique (New York, 1932–43, conducted by Frederique Petrides), and the Women's Symphony of New York (1934–8, conducted by Antonia Brico). All-black orchestras were typically composed of professional instrumentalists who wanted an opportunity to play symphonic music. Two such orchestras were formed in New Orleans already in the 1890s; two also in Washington, DC; and one in Philadelphia in 1904. In New York James Reese Europe conducted concerts by the Clef Club Orchestra at Carnegie Hall from 1912 to 1915 that featured music by black composers. The "Baltimore Colored Orchestra," founded in 1929, was successful enough that the Municipal Department of Music appropriated money and ran it as a municipal orchestra like the Baltimore Symphony until the 1940s.

The development of electronic media—radio, movies, and recordings—offered opportunities and challenges for American orchestras in the first half of the 20th century. They brought orchestras to much larger audiences, but they also made it possible to replace many with fewer orchestras. Early recording processes were not kind to orchestras: strings had to be reinforced with wind instruments; operatic and symphonic excerpts were often recorded with bands. Electronic recording, introduced in 1925, was more successful, and American orchestras began to record the repertory of musical classics. The first American orchestra to make electronic recordings was the Philadelphia Orchestra under Leopold Stokowski. In 1925 he recorded Saint-Saëns *Danse Macabre* for RCA Victor, then Dvořák's *New World Symphony* on five 78 RPM disks. The Boston Symphony, New York Philharmonic, Minneapolis, Los Angeles, Cleveland, Chicago, and San Francisco orchestras all recorded in the 1930s, and income from recordings began to form a significant part of these orchestras' revenues. As recorded sound came into the movies, orchestral work moved from the theater to the studio: a few orchestras, most of them in Los Angeles, recorded sound tracks for almost all the movies that Americans saw. Some 300–500 instrumentalists—members of house orchestras at the major studios plus pick-up orchestras organized by contractors—supplied the music that 20,000 theater musicians had played during the previous decade. A cadre of instrumentalists coalesced in Los Angeles, excellent sight-readers, highly skilled and highly paid, but invisible to the public and outside the mainstream of American orchestras.

In the early days of radio many local stations engaged their own orchestras for live broadcasts. With the rise of the networks in the early 30s, however, these house orchestras were replaced by a much small number of network orchestras, and there was a shift toward regional and national broadcast of symphonic music. Already in 1922 the Detroit Symphony, the New York Philharmonic and the St. Louis Symphony transmitted concerts by means of "wireless telephone" to local radio stations, which broadcast them to regional audiences. The San Francisco Symphony began regular weekly broadcasts in 1926 sponsored by the Standard Oil Company of California. Symphonic music on the radio was often presented in the guise of education: Walter Damrosch in 1926 began a weekly show on NBC that combined lectures with orchestral selections performed by the New York Symphony, which he conducted. Incorporated into school curricula across the country, the NBC Music Appreciation Hour continued until 1942. Other orchestras, including the New York Philharmonic, the Boston Symphony, the Philadelphia Orchestra, and the San Francisco Symphony, broadcast their subscription concerts every week for adult audiences. The high point of orchestral broadcasting in America was the NBC Symphony Orchestra, created for and conducted by Arturo Toscanini, which broadcast 17 seasons of weekly concerts beginning in 1937 and continuing until 1954. The orchestra gave very few conventional concerts; most of its performances took place before an invited studio audience and were broadcast by NBC affiliates to a rapt national audience. The NBC Symphony also made hundreds of recordings, and between 1948 and 1952 a few of its concerts were televised. With Toscanini's retirement in 1954, the orchestra was disbanded. Because orchestra concerts have limited visual interest, television proved to be a less successful medium than radio. In the 1960s broadcast media were replaced by LP records as the main electronic medium by which orchestras reached the public.

5. 1945–PRESENT. The developments of the preceding period were consolidated in the second half of the 20th century. The role of orchestras in entertainment continued to decline; the symphony orchestra was confirmed as the paradigm American orchestra; the corporate, non-profit model of orchestra organization was retained and refined. As well as consolidation it was a period of tremendous expansion. The number of orchestras of all types playing classical repertory increased; there were

more full-time professional orchestras; orchestra seasons got longer; orchestra budgets got larger; more Americans attended orchestra concerts. Table 1 illustrates the large increases in total number of orchestras and in orchestra budgets between 1937 and 2009. The table shows a more than 500% increase in the number of orchestras in all categories between 1937 and 2009. The budgets of American orchestras increased still more, particularly in the "regional" category and even after adjusting for inflation.

The categories in Table 1 are derived from those used by the League of American Orchestras and the American Federation of Musicians and may be defined as of 2009 as follows. Most "major" orchestras have budgets of $10 million or more, seasons of 40 weeks or more, and are staffed with professional musicians most of whom have full-time positions. Most "regional" orchestras have budgets of $1 to $10 million, seasons of 15 weeks or more, and the musicians are professionals but not full time. "Community" orchestras have budgets under $1 million and are composed of a mixture of professionals and amateurs or entirely of amateur musicians.

As the 21st century begins, there are approximately 30 "major" American orchestras (including a few opera orchestras). They are formidable corporate entities. Their budgets range from about $15 million (Utah Symphony) to $99 million (Los Angeles Philharmonic). They have endowments ranging from $16 million (Buffalo Philharmonic) to $350–$400 million (Boston Symphony). They are incorporated as tax-deductible, charitable corporations with responsibility vested in a board of directors, which hires the music director (conductor) and an executive director. Besides 100 or so musicians, major orchestras employ large staffs of managers, administrative assistants, marketing and development personnel, custodial and maintenance workers, and more. They own a good deal of property, including real estate (usually a concert hall), equipment and furnishings, musical instruments, and a music library. Over half of the major orchestras have 52-week seasons—that is, the musicians are hired on a full-time basis with annual salaries—the remainder have seasons of 40 weeks or more. After their subscription season of eight or nine months, many orchestras have a summer season, usually of a more popular character, often in a festival setting. All major orchestras are unionized: wages, benefits, and the daily details of orchestra operations are governed

TABLE 1: Expansion of American orchestras, 1937–2009

	Major orchestras		Regional orchestras		Community orchestras (excluding college and university orchestras)
Date	Number of orchestras	Average budget in 2009 dollars	Number of orchestras	Average budget in 2009 dollars	Number of orchestras
1937	16	$4,910,000	34 (34)	$104,000	c250
1950	26 (21)	$4,118,000	54 (5)	$246,000	c400
1971	26	$13,200,000	100 (58)	$1,370,000	c600
2009	28	$31,395,000	350 (71)	$3,867,487	c1200

Compiled from Grant and Hettinger (1937), Hart (1971), American Federation of Musicians, *Wage Scales and Conditions* (2009), and data provided by the League of American Orchestras. Budgets have been adjusted for inflation; parentheses indicate how many orchestras furnished budget data.

by a contract negotiated between each orchestra's management, its musicians, and the American Federation of Musicians, usually on a multi-year basis. Musicians are recruited internationally through a elaborate audition process in which an audition committee evaluates hundreds of applicants in a series of increasingly selective rounds, first on recordings, then in person. Live auditions are often conducted behind a screen so that the committee does not know the identity of the candidate. Orchestra conductors are also recruited internationally; indeed many hold simultaneous appointments in different countries or make extensive guest appearances: they have been called "jet-set conductors." Consequently the music director of most major American orchestras conducts only a portion (sometimes less than half) of the orchestra's subscription season; the remaining concerts are taken by guests. Responsibility for programming is shared between the music director, the executive director, and the representatives of various soloists and guest conductors. The music director has a great deal of authority over hiring, firing, and seating of musicians, though here too the responsibility is shared with management and players' representatives.

"Regional" orchestras are more diverse, with budgets ranging from as little as $500,000 per year up to $10 million and more, and seasons from a few weeks at intervals during the year up to several months. Most are based in medium-sized cities or in metropolitan areas that also have a major orchestra. Few own their own concert halls, and some play at several locations within their region. Some regional orchestras try to create a special niche for themselves—as a chamber orchestra (e.g. St. Paul Chamber Orchestra), a period-instrument orchestra (Philharmonia Baroque), a new-music orchestra (American Composers Orchestra), or a training orchestra (New World Symphony). Many opera and ballet orchestras can also be considered "regional." The corporate structure of regional symphonic orchestras resembles that of the majors, with a board of directors, an executive director, a music director, and departments for development and marketing. Most regional orchestras are unionized: wages and working conditions are regulated by a contract. Musicians are selected by audition, but because the jobs are not full-time and the pay is considerably lower than in the major orchestras, the pool of applicants tends to be regional rather than national or international. Specialist orchestras tend to recruit more from a national pool of musicians and have more of a national profile than other regional orchestras. Musicians often play in several regional orchestras in the same metropolitan area, leading to a phenomenon known as the "freeway philharmonic," where the same instrumentalists staff several regional orchestras within driving distance of one another. Conductors, on the other hand, are recruited nationally, and some conduct two or more regional orchestras a considerable distance apart.

Community orchestras are an even more diverse group, ranging from orchestras devoted to particular repertories, to amateur orchestras in small towns, to gay and lesbian orchestras, to doctors' orchestras, to youth orchestras, to college and university orchestras. (See also YOUTH ENSEMBLES.) Their numbers, as Table 1 shows, are large, and estimates are speculative, as orchestras are formed, dissolved, revived, and combined. Budgets (not shown in the table) are even harder to estimate, since they are not reported systematically. Community orchestra musicians are overwhelmingly amateurs—they play for their own entertainment, edification, and education. Audition processes, if they exist at all, tend to be informal. Occasionally a few professionals are hired at the last moment to steady the ensemble in concert. Community orchestra budgets are much smaller than the budgets of major or regional orchestras. Since the players are unpaid, the principal expenses are the conductor's salary and rental of rehearsal and performance space. Fund raising and administrative support are typically provided by volunteers, themselves often players in the orchestra. Conductors of community orchestras tend to take on more managerial responsibility than conductors of major or regional orchestras. They are often among the orchestra's founders and often function as its manager as well. Community orchestras play tens of thousands of concerts for audiences across the United States who otherwise do not hear live orchestral music.

A few orchestras remain in theaters, movie, and television studios, and other venues in the 21st century. However, most of the "orchestral" music heard in movies and commercials is produced by computers. Musical theater still employs pit orchestras, but these are usually small and invariably amplified. In some cases they are "virtual" orchestras, that is, computer-produced sounds synchronized in real time with singers and sometimes a few live instrumentalists. Virtual orchestras have also been used for ballet and even operas. On the whole it seems clear that the day of the orchestra in American entertainment has passed.

The system of financing orchestras was consolidated in the second half of the 20th century. As orchestras became separated from entertainment, philanthropic funding became an increasingly important part of orchestras' budgets, first as short-term guarantee funds, then as endowments. Public funding, which began with the Baltimore Symphony and the Federal Music Project orchestras, increased decisively in the 1960s. (See FOUNDATIONS.) The Ford Foundation Symphony Program beginning in 1966 gave grants totaling $85 million to 56 major and regional orchestras on the condition that they raise matching funds. The aim of the Ford program was to strengthen American orchestras by extending their seasons, enlarging their audiences, and increasing the pay of orchestra musicians. The Ford program led to a large increase in the endowments of major and regional orchestras, also to longer seasons, higher musician salaries, and an expansion of orchestra management, especially "development" departments. Another public funding source was the National Endowment for the Arts, created in 1965 to distribute and administer grants to arts organizations on a project by project basis. Initially NEA support for orchestras was modest (about 2 percent of all NEA grants between 1966 and 1971), but it increased rapidly in the 1970s, as major and regional orchestras reconciled themselves to the idea of federal funding. In 1973 orchestras received grants of $4 million from the NEA; by 1980 the figure was over $15 million. NEA support for orchestras remained substantial through the 80s, then declined precipitously in the late 1990s, as complaints about NEA-funded art (mostly visual art) led to cuts in the agency's budget. Many states provide financial support to orchestras, as do regional and local governments. As of 2009, state and local funding exceeded federal by a considerable margin.

The patterns of income and expenses for American orchestras in the first decade of the 21st century are shown in Figs. 1 and 2, which average data across major and regional orchestras for the 2008–9 season. The two primary sources of orchestra income are ticket sales and private donations. "Other earned income" includes record royalties, broadcast income, rental income, and concession income. In general the major orchestras derive a larger proportion of their income from performance activities and from return on endowment than do regional orchestras, which rely more on private contributions and government grants. Community orchestras realize still less income from performance. On the expense side, "artistic personnel"—that is, player salaries, soloist fees, and payments to conductors—is the largest expense, followed by the costs involved in renting or operating a concert hall and touring. Total management expenses (fund raising, marketing, administrative, other) are almost as large as payments to musicians. Patterns of income and expenses changed considerably over the last half of the 20th century. Comparing the data in Fig. 1 to data from 1950 (not shown), performance revenue declined as a proportion of orchestra income, while the proportion from contributions and interest on endowment increased. Government grants increased only slightly as a proportion of income. Expenses (Fig. 2) changed over the same period: artist expenses, which in 1950 claimed almost 60 percent of orchestra budgets, declined, while administrative and

production expenses rose. Although musician salaries were significantly higher in 2009 than in 1950, musicians received a smaller percentage of the orchestra budgets.

American orchestras are chronically short of money: each year many orchestras report that they are operating at a deficit. An influential study by economist William Baumol, published in 1966, argued that these deficits were inherent in the nature of orchestras and were bound to increase over time, since the "productivity" of an orchestra cannot be increased, whereas player salaries rise to keep pace with productivity increases in other sectors of the economy. Baumol and others used the prospect of an ever-increasing revenue gap as an argument for government funding of orchestras. Curiously, though, despite the rise in musicians' salaries and a decline in concert attendance since the 1960s, orchestra deficits have not increased in real terms. Government funding has declined, but support from private sources has increased. Musicians wages have risen, but so have ticket prices. Economists, including Baumol himself, have acknowledged that the revenue gap grew no worse (also no better) over the last quarter of the 20th century. At most it may be said that since the beginning of the 20th century live orchestral music has become more and more of a luxury good; however the demand for this luxury is strong enough to keep a large number of American orchestras in business.

Labor relations in American orchestras changed significantly in the second half of the 20th century. Orchestra musicians had belonged to unions since the 1860s, but their principal concern was to regulate wages and conditions in the theater and on casual jobs. As orchestras separated themselves in the 20th century from other musical entertainment, orchestra musicians felt increasingly that they were not adequately represented by the American Federation of Musicians, which negotiated contracts with little input from the players. In 1961 orchestration musicians organized themselves within the American Federation of Musicians as ICSOM, the Inter-

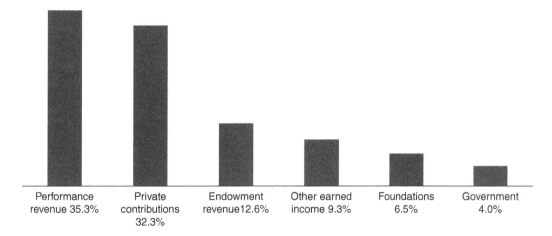

1. *Income of American orchestras, 2009. (Averaged across major and regional orchestras; data courtesy of the League of American Orchestras)*

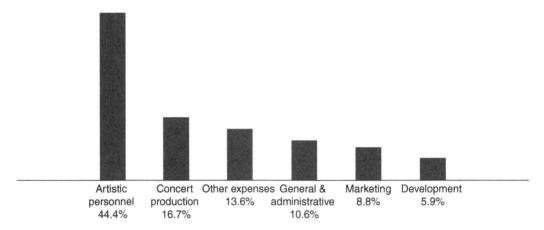

2. *Expenses of American orchestras, 2009. (Averaged across major and regional orchestras; data courtesy of the League of American Orchestras)*

national Conference of Symphony and Opera Musicians, and began to play a much larger role in contract negotiations with major orchestras. A series of bitter strikes ensued, resulting in much improved wages and benefits, 52-week seasons in many orchestras, musician participation in audition, dismissal, and seating processes, and three decades of bad feelings between musicians and orchestra management. The expansion of orchestra seasons, orchestra budgets, and orchestra fundraising that marked the second half of the 20th century may have resulted as much from ICSOM and its demands as from the Ford Foundation and NEA programs. A parallel organization, ROPA (Regional Orchestra Players Association) was formed in 1984 for smaller orchestras.

One of the most striking changes in American orchestras in the second half of the 20th century was the integration of women. Women had played in American orchestras since the 19th century. However, they had been largely excluded from professional concert orchestras. The Cleveland Orchestra hired four women in 1923 and the San Francisco Symphony five in 1925. Philadelphia, Pittsburgh, and the National Symphony hired a handful of women players in the 1930s. During World War II, however, as many male musicians went into military service, orchestras found themselves obliged to replace them with women. After the war the number of women declined somewhat as men returned, but the possibility of integration had established itself, and a few big orchestras (Baltimore, Los Angeles, Indianapolis, San Francisco) remained significantly integrated, with 10 to 15 percent women players. The big change came in the 1960s and 70s: all of the major orchestras hired significant numbers of women, and the representation of women in professional American orchestras rose to 40 percent in 1980. The change resulted from the general transformation of career expectations for women in the second half of the 20th century but also from the introduction of "blind" auditions, where the audition committee and conductor could not tell the sex of the candidate until the end of the audition process. In 2009 47 percent of

the players in major and regional orchestras were women. Women form a larger percentage of players in smaller orchestras than larger, and they are better represented among string players than brass and among section players than among first chair players. But gender equality has become a fact of life in all American orchestras.

Racial integration, also a goal during the last half of the 20th century, proved more elusive. Notwithstanding the long history of black musicians and of "colored" orchestras in the United States, and despite several affirmative action and outreach programs, only 1.4 percent of regular positions in American orchestras in 1990 were held by black musicians. In 2009 the figure stood at 1.8 percent. These figures are low in comparison to the proportion of African Americans in the US population and probably reflect the separation of orchestras from general entertainment in the 20th century. On the other hand the number of musicians of Asian ethnicity in American orchestras increased considerably during the last quarter of the 20th century, reflecting the increased interest and training in Western classical music in Asian countries and also among Asian Americans.

The repertory of American orchestras in the second half of the 20th century continued the focus on musical "classics" that had established itself in the late 19th century. A survey of the subscription concerts of 25 American orchestras between 1965 and 1989 showed that 20 composers accounted for more than 70 percent (by performance time) of the music played. The top five were Beethoven, Mozart, Brahms, Mahler, and Tchaikovsky. Over half of the composers in the group of 20 lived during the 20th century, although only one (Stravinsky) was still alive in 1965. The survey found a similar consistency among works: many of the works performed frequently at the beginning of the period were still performed frequently at the end. Thus the repertory of late 20th-century American orchestras was "classical" both in its coherence and its stability. Works by American composers constituted slightly over 10 percent of the total number of works programmed by slightly different group of orchestras. These data offered much less coherence: only one composer (Aaron Copland) was programmed often enough to be considered anything approaching "classic." At the same time, significantly more American works were performed in 1985–9 than had been performed in 1965–9. Contrary to what is sometimes stated, American orchestras at the beginning of the 21st century are not playing a repertory of 19th-century European music exclusively. But they are playing a "classical" repertory that changes very slowly and into which new composers and new works are only grudgingly accepted. The repertory is also "classical" in that it is distinguished categorically from "popular" music which is either not played at all or is cordoned off in separate "pops" concerts and summer seasons.

As the 20th century expired there was a great deal of angst over the condition of American orchestras. Complaints were voiced about limited repertory, aging audiences, chronic deficits, underrepresentation of minorities, musicians' strikes, and decreasing government support. Orchestras, it seemed, were rapidly making themselves irrelevant to the rest of American life. Yet looking back over more than 200 years of history, it is hard to point to a time when American orchestras were in better condition than they are at the beginning of the 21st century. Were things any better in the 1850s when instrumentalists labored in the theaters, played weekends in the beer gardens, and assembled a few times a year to give philharmonic concerts? Had conditions improved by the 1880s when the Thomas orchestra was the only full-time concert orchestra in the country and had to tour for months out of the year to make ends meet? In the 1920s when thousands of musicians lost their jobs in the theaters and movie palaces and were lucky to find part-time work in a federal orchestra? In the 1950s when women were excluded from the major orchestras and conductors hired and fired musicians at will? The problems of 21st-century American orchestras are real and urgent. But American orchestras have faced great challenges in the past, and they have always found ways to grow, prosper, and transform themselves.

BIBLIOGRAPHY

GENERAL

F.L. Ritter: *Music in America* (New York, 1883; 2/1890 with new intro. by J. Riedel, *R*1970)

W.S.B. Mathews: *A Hundred Years of Music in America* (Chicago, 1889, 2/1900, *R*1970)

M.A. De Wolfe Howe: *The Boston Symphony Orchestra: an Historical Sketch* (Boston, 1914, enlarged 2/1931 by J.N. Burk as *The Boston Symphony Orchestra, 1881–1931*)

M. Grant and H.S. Hettinger: *America's Symphony Orchestras, and How They Are Supported* (New York, 1940)

J.H. Mueller: *The American Symphony Orchestra: a Social History of Musical Taste* (Bloomington, IN, 1951)

J.K. Sherman: *Music and Maestros: the Story of the Minneapolis Symphony Orchestra* (Minneapolis, MN, 1952)

H. Kupferberg: *Those Fabulous Philadelphians: the Life and Times of a Great Orchestra* (New York, 1969)

P. Hart: *Orpheus in the New World: the Symphony Orchestra as an American Cultural Institution – Its Past, Present, and Future* (New York, 1973)

K.H. Mueller: *Twenty-Seven Major American Symphony Orchestras: a History and Analysis of Their Repertoires, Seasons 1842–43 through 1969–70* (Bloomington, IN, 1973)

G. Seltzer: *The Professional Symphony Orchestra in the United States* (Metuchen, NJ, 1975)

H.J. Shanet: *Philharmonic: a History of New York's Orchestra* (Garden City, NY, 1975)

J.A. Taylor: *The Emergence of the Black Performing Musician in the American Symphony Orchestra* (diss., Indiana U., 1976)

H.J. Shanet, ed.: *Early Histories of the New York Philharmonic* (New York, 1979) [annotated edition of Krehbiel, 1892; Huneker, ?1917; Erskine, 1943]

G. Martin: *The Damrosch Dynasty: America's First Family of Music* (Boston, 1983)

D. Schneider: *The San Francisco Symphony: Music, Maestros, and Musicians* (Novato, CA, 1983)

R.R. Craven, ed.: *Symphony Orchestras of the United States: Selected Profiles* (Westport, CT, 1986)

E. Schabas: *Theodore Thomas: America's Conductor and Builder of Orchestras, 1835–1905* (Urbana, IL, 1989)

G. Seltzer: *Music Matters: the Performer and the American Federation of Musicians* (Metuchen, NJ, 1989)

K.G. Wells and G.R. McIntosh: *Symphony and Song: the Saint Louis Symphony Orchestra* (Tucson, AZ, 1993)

J.P. Kraft: *Stage to Studio: Musicians and the Sound Revolution, 1890–1950* (Baltimore, MD, 1996)

E. Southern: *The Music of Black Americans* (New York, 3/1997)

D. Rosenberg: *The Cleveland Orchestra Story: "Second to None"* (Cleveland, c2000)

J. Spitzer and N. Zaslaw: *The Birth of the Orchestra: History of an Institution, 1650–1815* (New York, 2004)

J. Graziano, ed.: *European Music and Musicians in New York City, 1840–1900* (Rochester, NY, 2006)

C.P. Smith: *Making Music in Los Angeles: Transforming the Popular* (Berkeley, CA, 2007)

L.E. Miller: *Music and Politics in San Francisco: From the 1906 Quake to the Second World War* (Berkeley, CA, 2011)

J. Spitzer, ed.: *American Orchestras in the Nineteenth Century* (Chicago, 2012)

D. Hildebrand and E. Schaaf: *Musical Maryland: a History of Song and Performance from the Colonial Period to the Age of Radio* (Baltimore, MD, forthcoming)

BEFORE 1800

O. Sonneck: *Early Concert-Life in America (1731–1800)* (Leipzig, 1907/*R*1978)

O. Sonneck: *Early Opera in America* (New York, c1915)

C.J. Bagdon: *Musical Life in Charleston, South Carolina, from 1732 to 1776, As Recorded in Colonial Sources* (diss., U. of Miami, 1978)

V.B. Lawrence: "Mr. Hewitt Lays it on the Line," *19CM*, v/1 (1981), 3–15

J.W. Wagner: "New York City Concert Life, 1801–5," *American Music*, ii/2 (1984), 53–69

1800–65

H.E. Krehbiel: *The Philharmonic Society of New York: a Memorial* (New York, 1892)

H.E. Johnson: *Musical Interludes in Boston, 1795–1830* (New York, 1943)

A. Carse: *The Life of Jullien: Adventurer, Showman-Conductor and Establisher of the Promenade Concerts in England* (Cambridge, 1951)

H.A. Kmen: *Singing and Dancing in New Orleans: a Social History of the Birth and Growth of Balls and Operas, 1791–1841* (diss., Tulane U., 1961)

V.B. Lawrence: *Strong on Music: the New York Music Scene in the Days of George Templeton Strong, Volume 1, Resonances, 1836–1849* (New York, 1988/*R*)

J. Graziano: "Jullien and His *Music for the Millions*," *A Celebration of American Music: Words and Music in Honor of H. Wiley Hitchcock*, ed. R. Crawford, R.A. Lott, and C.J. Oja (Ann Arbor, MI, 1990), 192–216

M. Broyles: *"Music of the Highest Class": Elitism and Populism in Antebellum Boston* (New Haven, CT, 1992)

K.K. Preston: *Opera on the Road: Traveling Opera Troupes in the United States, 1825–60* (Urbana, IL, 1993)

R. Beck and R. Hansen: "Joseph Gungl and his Celebrated American Tour: November 1848 to May 1849," *SMH*, xxxvi (1995), 53–72

V.B. Lawrence: *Strong on Music: the New York Music Scene in the Days of George Templeton Strong*, ii, *Reverberations: 1850–1856* (Chicago, 1995)

V.B. Lawrence: *Strong on Music: the New York Music Scene in the Days of George Templeton Strong*, iii, *Repercussions: 1857–1862* (Chicago, 1999)

1865–90

T. Ryan: *Recollections of an Old Musician* (New York, 1899/R1979)

T. Thomas: *A Musical Autobiography*, ed. G. P. Upton (Chicago, 1905)

J.R. Commons: "Types of American Labor Unions: the Musicians of St. Louis and New York," *Quarterly Journal of Economics*, x/3 (1906), 419–42

R.F. Thomas: *Memoirs of Theodore Thomas* (New York, 1911)

J.E. Holliday: "The Cincinnati Philharmonic and Hopkins Hall Orchestras, 1856–1868," *Bulletin of the Cincinnati Historical Society*, xxvi (1968), 158–73

E.C. Krohn: *Missouri Music* (New York, 1971) [Originally published as *A Century of Missouri Music* (St. Louis, MO, 1924)]

S.R. Mazzola: *When Music Is Labor: Chicago Bands and Orchestras and the Origins of the Chicago Federation of Musicians, 1880–1902* (diss., Northern Illinois U., 1984)

S.R. Mazzola: "Bands and Orchestras at the World's Columbian Exposition," *American Music*, iv/4 (1986), 407–24

K.K. Preston: *Music for Hire: A Study of Professional Musicians in Washington (1877–1900)* (Stuyvesant, NY, 1992)

J. Horowitz: *Wagner Nights: an American History* (Berkeley, CA, 1994)

J.P. Kraft: "Artists as Workers: Musicians and Trade Unionism in America, 1880–1917," *MQ*, lxxix (1995), 512–43

A.F. Block: "Matinee Mania, or the Regendering of Nineteenth-Century Audiences in New York City," *19CM*, xxxi (2008), 193–216

J. Spitzer: "The Entrepreneur-Conductors and their Orchestras," *Nineteenth-Century Music Review*, v/1 (2008), 3–24

J. Koegel: *Music in German Immigrant Theater: New York City, 1840–1940* (Rochester, NY, 2009)

N. Newman: *Good Music for a Free People: The Germania Musical Society in Nineteenth-Century America* (Rochester, NY, 2010)

M. Reichert: *Carl Bergmann in New York: Conducting Activity, 1852–1876* (diss., Graduate Center of the City U. of New York, 2010)

1890–1945

P.A. Otis: *The Chicago Symphony Orchestra: its Organization, Growth, and Development, 1891–1924* (Chicago, 1924)

F.A. Wister: *Twenty-Five Years of the Philadelphia Orchestra, 1900–1925* (Philadelphia, PA, 1925)

K.S. Clarke: *Baltimore: "Cradle of Municipal Music"* (Baltimore, MD, 1932, 2/1941)

E.H. Pierce: "When Main Street Had an Orchestra," *MQ*, xx (1934), 426–34

R.J. Wolf: *A Short History of the Pittsburgh Orchestra, 1896 to 1910* (diss., Carnegie Institute of Technology, 1954)

S.S. Fain: *A Study of the Community Symphony Orchestra in the United States, 1750–1955* (diss., U. of Southern California, 1956)

C.B. Canon: *The Federal Music Project of the Works Progress Administration: Music in a Democracy* (diss., U. of Minnesota, 1963)

E. Arian: *Bach, Beethoven, and Bureaucracy: the Case of the Philadelphia Orchestra* (Tuscaloosa, AL, 1971)

L.R. Thomas: *A History of the Cincinnati Symphony Orchestra to 1931* (diss., U. of Cincinnati, 1972)

C. Neuls-Bates: "Women's Orchestras in the United States, 1925–45," *Women Making Music*, ed. J. Bowers and J. Tick (Urbana, IL, 1986), 349–69

J. Horowitz: *Understanding Toscanini* (New York, 1987)

J.B. Groh: *Evening the Score: Women in Music and the Legacy of Frédérique Petrides* (Fayetteville, AK, 1991)

E. Fones-Wolf: "Sound Comes to the Movies: the Philadelphia Musicians' Struggle against Recorded Music," *Pennsylvania Magazine of History and Biography*, cxviii/1–2 (1994), 3–31

J. Horowitz: *Wagner Nights: an American History* (Berkeley, CA, 1994)

J.P. Kraft: "The 'Pit' Musicians: Mechanization in the Movie Theaters, 1926–1934," *Labor History*, xxxv/1 (1994), 66–89

S.M. Jagow: "Women Orchestral Conductors in America: the Struggle for Acceptance – An Historical View from the Nineteenth Century to the Present," *College Music Symposium*, xxxviii (1998), 126–45

C. Ammer: *Unsung: a History of Women in American Music* (Portland, 2/2001)

S.W. Howe: "The NBC Music Appreciation Hour: Radio Broadcasts of Walter Damrosch, 1928–1942," *JRME*, li (2003), 64–77

R. Altman: *Silent Film Sound* (New York, 2004)

K.H. Marcus: *Musical Metropolis: Los Angeles and the Creation of a Music Culture, 1880–1940* (New York, 2004)

L. Dempf: "The Woman's Symphony Orchestra of Chicago," *Notes*, lxii (2006), 857–903

O.L. Krasner: "A Capital Idea: Reginald de Koven and the Washington Symphony Orchestra," *Music, American Made: Essays in Honor of John Graziano*, ed. J. Koegel (Sterling Heights, MI, 2011), 123–59

1945–PRESENT

American Federation of Musicians: *Wage Scales and Conditions in the Symphony Orchestra: ICSOM Orchestras* (1963–)

W.J. Baumol and W.G. Bowen: *Performing Arts: The Economic Dilemma* (New York, 1966)

National Endowment for the Arts: *Annual Report* (1967–)

R. Faulkner: *Hollywood Studio Musicians* (Chicago and New York, 1971)

W.J. Baumol and H. Baumol: "On Finances of the Performing Arts during Stagflation: Some Recent Data," *Journal of Cultural Economics*, iv/2 (1980), 1–14

P. Lehman: "Women in Orchestras: the Promise and the Problems," *Symphony* (December, 1982), 8–15, 56–60

American Federation of Musicians: *Wage Scales and Conditions in the Symphony Orchestra: ROPA Orchestra* (1985–)

American Symphony Orchestra League: *Participation of Blacks in Professional Orchestras: Survey and Study* (New York, 1990)

H. Price: "Orchestral Programming 1982–1987: an Indication of Musical Taste," *Bulletin of the Council for Research in Music Education*, no.106 (1990), 23–35

Wolf Organization and American Symphony Orchestra League: *The Financial Condition of Symphony Orchestras: Final Version, June 1992* (Cambridge, MA, 1992)

A.C. Gilbert: *Women in the Big Five Orchestras: an Exploratory Study of the Factors Affecting Career Development* (diss., U. of Akron, 1994)

J. Allmendinger, J.R. Hackman, and E.V. Lehman: "Life and Work in Symphony Orchestras," *MQ*, lxxx (1996), 194–219

T. Cowen and R. Grier: "Do Artists Suffer from a Cost-Disease?" *Rationality and Society*, viii/1 (1996), 5–24

E.C. Hall: *Survey and Analysis of the Repertory of Twenty-Six American Symphony Orchestras, 1982–83 through 1993–94* (diss., Peabody Institute, John Hopkins U., 1997)

D.A. Hardy: *Black Women in American Bands and Orchestras* (Lanham, MD, 2/1998)

H. Fogel: "Are Three Legs Appropriate? Or Even Sufficient," *Harmony*, no.10 (April 2000), 11–34

C. Goldin and C. Rouse: "Orchestrating Impartiality: the Impact of 'Blind' Auditions on Female Musicians," *American Economic Review*, xc/4 (2000), 715–41

D. Dempster: "The Wolf Report and Baumol's Curse: the Economic Health of American Symphony Orchestras in the 1990s and Beyond," *Harmony*, no.15 (October 2002), 1–23

T.J. Dowd, K. Liddle, K. Lupo, and A. Borden: "Organizing the Musical Canon: the Repertoires of Major U.S. Symphony Orchestras, 1842 to 1969," *Poetics*, no.30 (2002), 35–61

J. Ayer: *More Than Meets the Ear: How Symphony Musicians Made Labor History* (Minneapolis, MN, 2005)

HOWARD SHANET/JOHN SPITZER
(1, 2), JOHN SPITZER (3–5)

Orchestral music. The foundations of American orchestral music were laid in the 18th century by immigrant musicians who established and manned small orchestras, usually associated with theater and opera companies, and composed music for them. From the mid-19th century on, independent orchestras were established, and, influenced primarily by the Classical and Romantic music of central Europe, American composers increasingly produced music to be played by them. In the early 20th century, and especially after World War I, the Austro-German influence on American orchestral music yielded to a French one and the influence of jazz and popular music also began to be felt; these new currents led to a transformation of American orchestral music, which culminated, in the 1930s and 40s, in a "golden age." The far-reaching effects of World War II included the immigration of many important European composers to the United States whose own music as well as that of their American-born students had a huge impact on the subsequent development of American orchestral music. The postwar years saw a new diversity of ideals and expression (including serial and aleatory procedures and the development of electroacoustic music). Out of this diversity there emerged, by the 1970s, a "new romanticism," the proponents of which included conductors and instrumentalists as well as composers. While new romanticism remains popular, today's American orchestral repertoire encompasses a broad range of styles. Detailed discussion of individual items of American orchestral music may be found in articles on composers; for information on orchestral music written for films see FILM MUSIC. The history of American orchestras is discussed in ORCHESTRA, and to some extent in individual articles on conductors. The commissioning of orchestral compositions is addressed in AWARDS, FOUNDATIONS, and PATRONAGE, and in articles on individual music patrons and organizations.

1. Beginnings (to 1850). 2. An emerging identity (1850–1920). 3. Americana, ultramodernism, and the jazz age (1920–45). 4. The postwar years (1945–70). 5. Exploring new paths (1970–95). 6. The "end of history" and a new millenium (1995–2010).

1. BEGINNINGS (TO 1850). Lacking the powerful sources of patronage—church, state, and aristocracy—which in Europe had made possible the development of orchestras and the composition of music for them, musicians in colonial America produced no such music. Nevertheless, in the 18th century the cities of Boston, New York, Philadelphia, and Charleston attracted musicians in sufficient numbers to form small orchestras, and orchestral performances are reported from the 1770s on. A symphony by J.C. Bach was performed in Boston on 17 May 1771; one by Haydn was played in New York on 14 May 1774, and his Symphony no.85 ("La reine") was given in Philadelphia on 29 December 1792. The first American performance of a symphony by Beethoven seems to have been on 13 June 1813, in the Moravian community of Nazareth, Pennsylvania.

It is unclear exactly when orchestral music was first composed in the New World; 18th-century programs are ambiguous in their naming of composers and performers, and terminology is often confused. The earliest orchestral score published in the United States was *The Death Song of an Indian Chief*, by Hans Gram, a Danish composer who arrived in Massachusetts in 1785. The score, which calls for tenor voice and two clarinets, two horns, and strings, appeared in the *Massachusetts Magazine* in March 1791. German émigré John Christopher Moller published a sinfonia in the first issue of *Moller and Capron's Musical Numbers* (1793), but it is in short score with only a few instrumental indications.

James Hewitt, an exact contemporary of Beethoven who immigrated to New York from London shortly after his 22nd birthday, composed two potpourris, *New Medley Overture* (1799–1800) and *The New Medley Overture* (1801–2), which were published for piano but were possibly reductions of orchestral scores. Probably such piano scores, of which a large number appeared during the Federal era, served as the basis for ad hoc orchestrations depending on the instrumental resources at hand. But no other materials are extant.

Several scores from the first third of the 19th century survive in Pennsylvania, including a two-movement symphony in D (Andante and Rondo) composed in 1831 by another composer originally from England, William Cumming Peters, for George Rapp's Harmony Society (in the archives of the society in Old Economy Village at Ambridge; fig.1, p.426). There is also an overture in C and a four-movement symphony in E♭ by Philadelphia-born Charles Hommann, a score for which is in the archives of the Bethlehem Philharmonic Society. Hommann's Overture in D, housed in the library of the Musical Fund Society of Philadelphia, won a prize in 1835. These are all well-crafted, pleasant works, close in style to Haydn and Ignace Joseph Pleyel (both of whom figured prominently on American concert programs in this period). Anthony Philip Heinrich, who was born in Schönbuchel (now Krásný Buk in the Czech Republic) and arrived in Boston in 1810, left a much more impressive body of orchestral works and was sometimes described by his contemporaries as "the Beethoven of America." As a composer he was an autodidact and, though it is apparent that Haydn and Beethoven were his models, he brought to his music an individualistic penchant for wild fantasy and a fascination with American Indian lore (without, however, incorporating any Indian music in his works) and romantic natural phenomena. These are reflected in such orchestral extravaganzas as the fantasia *Pushmataha, a Venerable Chief of a Western Tribe of Indians* (1831), the concerto grosso *The Treaty of William Penn with the Indians* (1834, rev. 1847), and the symphony *The Ornithological Combat of Kings, or The Condor of the Andes and the Eagle of the Cordilleras* (1847, rev. 1856). Heinrich's works were performed in both the United States and Europe, and he was regarded with affection, though not universally with respect. John Sullivan Dwight took him to task (in *The Harbinger*, 4 July 1846) for his preoccupation with "mere outward scenes and histories [which] seem to have...disturbed the pure spontaneous inspiration of his melodies." Modern critics have noted that his music lacks development, but they find in it an interesting additive structure, if also a tendency to overembellish melodies.

2. AN EMERGING IDENTITY (1850–1920). The period 1850–1920 saw the rise of stable, "permanent" symphony orchestras in the United States, the first of which, the Philharmonic Society of New York, had been founded in 1842. In 1864 the Theodore Thomas Orchestra was founded (also in New York), and in 1878 the New York Symphony Society was formed by Leopold Damrosch,

the first of a family of conductors important in New York musical circles until the late 1920s. The Boston SO was founded in 1881. In 1891 a group of Chicago businessmen engaged Thomas to organize an orchestra there, which became the Chicago SO; and in 1900 a group of civic leaders organized the Philadelphia Orchestra. By 1920 most of the major American symphony orchestras were in operation.

Composers of American orchestral music continued to model their works on the European compositions that dominated concert programs. The first American-born composer whose works were performed by the New York Philharmonic Society was George F. Bristow, a violinist in the orchestra. His Overture in E♭ (1845) was played on 9 January 1847, and the next year his Sinfonia in E♭ received a performance in an open rehearsal. The Philharmonic also presented his Second Symphony (the "Jullien" Sinfonia) (1 March 1856) and Third Symphony in F♯ minor (26 March 1859). The latter's programmatic tendencies (its second movement is a nocturne and the scherzo is titled "Butterfly's Frolic") were confirmed in Bristow's Fourth Symphony ("The Pioneer," retitled "Arcadian"), first played by the Brooklyn PO on 8 February 1873, and in his grandiose Niagara Symphony for vocal soloists, chorus, and orchestra (1893), apparently modeled on Beethoven's Ninth Symphony and Mendelssohn's Second ("Lobgesang"). Bristow's music is more than a reflection of such models: it flows, the themes are apt, and the orchestration is colorful and effective. A solo trombone in the "Jullien" Sinfonia has elaborate passagework in the first movement, and is assigned the cantabile theme of the third, a usage Bristow must have learned from the brass bands of his time since it has no precedent in conventional European orchestral practice. Popular-music idioms often influenced the shape of Bristow's melodic material.

William Henry Fry also composed some ambitious orchestral works, including descriptive symphonies with such titles as *The Breaking Heart* (1852), *Santa Claus* (1853), *A Day in the Country* (c1853), *Childe Harold* (1854), *Niagara* (1854), and *Hagar in the Wilderness* (1854). All of these were performed in New York soon after their composition; half of them are lost. The style of Fry's orchestral music depends primarily on Italian models, especially Donizetti and Bellini; formally, it is programmatic, based on elaborate scenarios that are followed in minute detail.

New Orleans-born Créole Louis Moreau Gottschalk, arguably the most internationally prominent American musician of this period, has been known principally for the mostly short virtuosic piano pieces he composed for his own performance. But over the past decade conductor Richard Rosenberg has reconstructed and recorded Gottschalk's orchestral compositions which include two works he called symphonies—*A Night in the Tropics* and *À Montevideo*—but which are actually closer in construction to tone poems. Rosenberg subsequently revived orchestral scores by other Créole composers including Edmond Dédé, whose *Mon Pauvre Coeur* (1848) was the first music by a black composer to be published in the United States.

The orchestral music of John Knowles Paine (1839–1906) is the first by an American to demonstrate a complete grasp of the symphonic idiom. Paine wrote two symphonic poems (*The Tempest, c*1876, and *An Island Fantasy, c*1888), an overture to Shakespeare's *As You Like It* (1876), and a *Duo concertante* for violin, cello, and orchestra (c1877), as well as two symphonies. The Symphony no.1 (1875) is Beethovenian in its first and second movements (the latter a scherzo), but the slow movement, an outpouring of tranquil beauty, owes little to anyone; the finale, which stays close to convention, is Schumannesque. The Second Symphony ("In the Spring," 1879) is entirely different: in it Paine reveals a remarkable ability to build extensive formal structures and to integrate them with subtle cyclic procedures. The opening motif of the introduction to the first movement is interwoven, in many permutations, with the melodic material of every other movement save the Scherzo. Paine's use of such thematic procedures predates similar techniques in the symphonies of Brahms.

Paine was the mentor and patriarch of the Second New England School of American composers, which included Arthur Foote, George W. Chadwick, Horatio Parker, and Amy Marcy Cheney Beach. All composed orchestral music of distinction, though only Chadwick and Beach wrote symphonies. Beach's single symphony, the "Gaelic" in E minor (1894), has a fine sweep and sense of spontaneity; her Piano Concerto (1899) is notable for its brief but charming Scherzo. Chadwick produced a significantly larger body of orchestral works, from his early overture *Rip Van Winkle* (1879)—a success in Leipzig while he was still a conservatory student there—to the late "symphonic ballad" *Tam O'Shanter* (1914–15). The Celtic atmosphere of *Tam O'Shanter* appears in others of his works: the Symphony no.2 (1883–5) contains modal and rhythmic elements associated with Scottish folk music, and the Symphony no.3 (1893–4) is replete with them. Especially attractive are the four *Symphonic Sketches* (1895–1904). Foote favored writing for string orchestra; his works include: a Serenade (1891); two suites: D (1889) and E (1907, rev. 1908); and *A Night Piece* (1922), an arrangement for flute and strings of his *Nocturne* (1918). Parker, after some student efforts composed in Munich, left five major mature works for orchestra: the overture *Count Robert of Paris* (1890), the symphonic poem *A Northern Ballad* (1899), an organ concerto (1902), the symphonic poem *Vathek* (1903), and a suite arranged in 1915 from the opera *Fairyland*. The orchestral works may have influenced Parker's compositions in other genres: *A Northern Ballad* shares certain gestures and motifs with his oratorio *A Wanderer's Psalm* (1900), while *Vathek*, which shows some influence of Richard Strauss, is close to the idiom of the opera *Mona* (composed 1910).

Related aesthetically and stylistically to these Bostonians was Edward MacDowell, who completed eight orchestral works. The two piano concertos (1882 and 1884–6) are very different from each other: the first is quite conventional in shape and expression; the second is unusual in its design (it has a fleet scherzo as the second movement, flanked by a first movement marked "Larghetto calmato" and a fast finale with a slow introduction) and (in the view of some critics) its foreshadowing of Rachmaninoff's style. The three symphonic poems—*Hamlet and Ophelia* (1884–5), *Lancelot and Elaine* (1886), and *Lamia* (1887–8)—as well as the two completed movements ("Die Sarazenen," "Die schöne Alda") of an unfinished program symphony (1886–90) after *The Song of Roland* and the First Suite for orchestra (1888–93), are all characterized by a fertile melodic invention, chromatic harmony, and a rhythmic quality that often seems to suggest that the music was written to words. MacDowell's last and in some ways best orchestral work, the Suite no.2 ("Indian," 1891–5), is ironically the least characteristic, being based on American Indian melodies; of the five movements ("Legend," "Love Song," "In War Time," "Dirge," and "Village Festival"), "Dirge" is especially successful, and has been compared favorably with Wagner's funeral music for Siegfried.

A number of other composers wrote distinguished orchestral works during this period. Arthur Bird and George Templeton Strong both became expatriates and their music offers no hints of their American origins. Bird composed more than a dozen orchestral works beginning with his Symphony (1885). Strong was more prolific; a notable work is *Sintram* (Symphony no.2, 1887–8), based on the novel by the German writer Friedrich Heinrich Karl de la Motte Fouqué and Albrecht Dürer's print *Ritter, Tod und Teufel*. As an orchestral composer, Irish-born Victor Herbert is best known for his Cello concerto no.2 (1894), which inspired Dvořák to compose his Cello Concerto, but Herbert's greatest contribution is the sweep, skill, and imagination he brought to the orchestration of his operettas. Arthur Farwell and Henry F. Gilbert turned for inspiration respectively to the music of American Indians and black Americans. Farwell looked also to Russia and France for models that might liberate his work from Austro-German hegemony, but periodically returned to Indian themes, as in the fantasia *Dawn* (1904) and the Indian Suite (1944). Gilbert's best-known orchestral works are the *Comedy Overture on Negro Themes* (c1906) and the symphonic poem *The Dance in Place Congo* (c1908, rev. 1916); his last piece for large orchestra, Nocturne (1925–6), based on a passage from Whitman, is attractive and skillfully orchestrated, and shows no ethnic influences. A long-time member of the Boston SO, Charles Martin Loeffler developed a style heavily influenced by French music, but he also drew on other national styles (Russian, Spanish, and Irish) and on American popular music. Many of his orchestral works utilize chorus or solo singers; he also scored for unusual instruments, including viola d'amore and saxophone. (Loeffler, who emigrated to the United States at the age of 20, stated throughout his life that he was originally from Alsace, France, although there is now some speculation that he might have been born and raised in Germany.) Henry Hadley amalgamated elements of late German romanticism and early French impressionism in five symphonies, overtures, suites, and tone poems, bringing to them also, as a prominent

conductor, a profound knowledge of orchestration. His ambitious and once widely performed Fourth Symphony (1911) is an attempt to translate North, East, South, and West into music, and the final movement contains a Native American–inspired theme.

The work of Charles Griffes reflects the stylistic reorientation of American orchestral music in the years around World War I. His first piece for orchestra was the *Symphonische Phantasie* (1907), a very Germanic, Romantic, sprawling—and lovely—work; at about the same time he began sketching the *Notturno* (completed ?1918), which is reminiscent of Richard Strauss. During the next years Griffes concentrated on songs and piano works, and the style of his music veered towards French impressionism and even oriental music. *The Pleasure-Dome of Kubla Khan* (1917), a recasting of a piano work of 1912, was his first orchestral piece in the new idiom; his only other major original composition for orchestra (as distinct from arrangements of earlier works) was the *Poem* for flute and orchestra of 1919, skillfully constructed, sensitively orchestrated, and, though recalling Griffes's interest in oriental melody, lacking any hint of "chinoiserie."

Unquestionably the most original of American composer of this period, however, is Charles Ives (1874–1954) who created four numbered symphonies, two additional works incorporating the word symphony in their titles, two orchestral sets, and several smaller works for orchestra during the first two decades of the 20th century. Of his numbered symphonies the last, the Symphony no.4 (1909–16, but not heard in full until 1965), is full of multiple layers of simultaneous events, montages based on sacred and secular tunes, and harmonic aggregates sometimes involving microtones; the third movement is by contrast an almost academically conventional fugue (its principal subject is derived from a hymn tune by Lowell Mason); and these movements are framed by brooding outer movements in which the orchestra is joined by a chorus. Ives's other numbered symphonies are less challengingly complex, but parts of the four-movement quasi-symphony *Holidays* (c1917–19) come close. Some of the smaller orchestral works are unprecedented in their originality, notably *The Unanswered Question* (1908) and its companion piece *Central Park in the Dark* (c1909), as well as the three-part tone poem *Three Places in New England* (c1912–17) and the similarly conceived and shaped *Second Orchestral Set* (c1915–29). But the most experimental of all of Ives's works is the Universe Symphony, a work for multiple orchestras, which he first conceived in 1915 and worked on sporadically for many years, never completing it. In the 1990s, three different performing editions were assembled, and two have been commercially recorded.

American orchestras also performed popular material during this era. In 1910, African American composer, arranger, and band leader James Reese Europe organized the Clef Club Orchestra, the first all-black orchestra in the United States, which performed at Carnegie Hall as early as 1912 and boasted having as many as 150 musicians.

3. Americana, ultramodernism, and the jazz age (1920–50). The impulse of American composers to turn away from central European, postromantic models, already in evidence in the first two decades of the 20th century, increased after World War I. Piano virtuosos such as the Russian émigré Leo Ornstein, Henry Cowell, and George Antheil gained considerable notoriety for performances of their dissonant, "ultramodernist" original compositions and each eventually also began composing for the orchestra. Ornstein had written a piano concerto by 1921, at the height of his popularity, but after fading from the limelight created little else besides solo and chamber works. Antheil's initial forays into larger scale composition, created while in Berlin and Paris, were as radical as his solo piano pieces, the most extreme being his *Ballet Mécanique* (1923, later revised) for an all-percussion orchestra featuring propellers, siren, and 16 player pianos. While less confrontational, the first of his two piano concertos, completed a year earlier, and the first of his six numbered symphonies, all more conventionally-scored, are nevertheless very progressive. However, most of the music Antheil composed after his return to the United States, which includes many scores for motion pictures, is less extrovertedly avant-garde. Cowell's earliest orchestral music extends the experimentation of his piano music, which is arguably the most experimental of the three because of its use of such unusual techniques as playing across the keys with the forearms (tone-clusters) and inside on the strings. The 1928 Piano Concerto is filled with tone clusters both in the solo part and spread across the orchestra. The Sinfonietta, composed that same year but not performed until 1931, is filled with dissonant counterpoint; in 1932, Anton Webern conducted it in Vienna. Hans Barth, who immigrated to the United States from Germany in 1907 and was an associate of Ives, went even further, composing concertante works for orchestra featuring a portable quarter-tone piano of his own design. Leopold Stokowski premiered Barth's first quarter-tone Piano Concerto in 1930. Ruth Crawford Seeger composed very little for orchestra: *Music for Small Orchestra* (1926), which is the largest ensemble example of her use of dissonant counterpoint, and much later, a brief folk song arrangement, *Rissolty Rossolty* (1939). Johanna Magdalena Beyer also composed a few works for orchestra, but none have been yet been revived.

The earliest success of Aaron Copland, who would later be acknowledged as "the dean of American composers," was his 1924 Symphony for Organ and Orchestra, a hybrid symphony–concerto, premiered by conductor Walter Damrosch who famously remarked on stage following the performance, "If a young man in his twenties can compose a piece like that, by the time he is thirty he should be ready to commit murder." Carl Ruggles completed most of his uncompromisingly modernist orchestral output in the 1920s—*Men* (1921), *Men and Mountains* (1924) and *Sun-treader* (?1920; rev. 1926–31)—as did Paris-born composer Edgard Varèse, who immigrated to New York in 1917. *Amériques* for orchestra, the earliest work he acknowledged, was finished in 1921 but unperformed until 1926 when Stokowski pre-

miered it with the Philadelphia Orchestra. Stokowski also premiered Varèse's only other full orchestral work, *Arcana*, the following year. These works display Varèse's obsession with extreme dissonance and insistent rhythms, which was further developed in his later compositions for smaller forces. In 1927, Frederick Converse, whose Walt Whitman–derived tone poem *The Mystic Trumpeter* (1904) had already demonstrated an appreciation for American themes if not necessarily American sounds, composed another tone poem, *Flivver Ten Million*, inspired by the sale of the 10 millionth Ford automobile, which is filled with car horn allusions and other industrial sonorities.

On 12 February 1924, danceband leader Paul Whiteman, who had previously been a violist in the Denver and San Francisco symphonies, led an ensemble called the Palais Royal Orchestra in a concert of symphonic jazz featuring works by Victor Herbert as well as popular pianist Zez Confrey. But the most memorable work premiered that evening was *Rhapsody in Blue* for piano and jazz band by George Gershwin in an arrangement by Ferde Grofé. Grofé later reorchestrated the work for symphony orchestra and it quickly entered the repertory, as did Gershwin's subsequent tone poem *An American in Paris* (1928) and his Concerto in F for piano and orchestra (1925), both of which he orchestrated himself. Grofé, a composer in his own right, also explored the intersection of classical and popular idioms in more than a dozen works, of which his *Grand Canyon Suite* (1931) has been the most often performed. By the late 1920s, most popular jazz big bands, both white and black, were calling themselves orchestras. Glenn Miller and Benny Goodman led the most popular of the white swing ensembles, although Goodman was among the first to perform with a racially-integrated group. Among the most notable of the African American swing orchestras were those led by Fletcher Henderson, Bennie Moten, Jimmie Lunceford, Count Basie, and most importantly Duke Ellington, who as early as 1935 had already recorded an original extended multi-movement composition, *Reminiscing in Tempo*, and in later decades composed numerous large-scale works for his big band as well as several works, such as *Night Creature* (1955), which also involve symphony orchestra.

Another African American jazz composer/pianist James P. Johnson also wrote a great deal of music for symphony orchestra, much of which is presumably lost and most of which has remained neglected since his death except for a handful of works that were revived in the early 1990s by jazz historian James Dapogny and conductor Marin Alsop. William Grant Still, the first African American to compose a symphony performed by a major American orchestra as well as the first to conduct a major orchestra, was a prolific composer of orchestral music including five symphonies (1930–58), seven symphonic poems (1924–60), and a number of suites (1926–62). Still drew often on black popular styles, especially the blues, as in his Symphony no.1 (the "Afro-American") of 1930; Howard Swanson drew on similar sources for a number of orchestral works including the award-winning Short Symphony (1948), as did WILLIAM LEVI DAWSON and Florence Price, the first recognized female African American symphonic composer.

American popular and folk idioms were fundamental resources for many other composers as well. In 1925, Antheil composed *A Jazz Symphony*. Early ragtime and jazz also influenced John Alden Carpenter whose orchestral works include the "jazz pantomime" *Krazy Kat* (1921) and the ballet score *Skyscrapers* of 1923–4, built from alternating sections of "work" and "play," both of which are informed by varied elements of popular music. Copland ventured into jazz-inspired orchestral music with his suite *Music for the Theatre* (1925) and Piano Concerto (1926). In the 1930s, influenced by the populism and socialist realism of the Depression era, Copland began to investigate American folksong and folklore. The first result of this new orientation was *El salón México* (1933–6); this was followed by the ballets *Billy the Kid* (1938) and *Rodeo* (1942), *Lincoln Portrait* for speaker and orchestra and *Fanfare for the Common Man* for brass and percussion (both 1942), and the "ballet for Martha [Graham]" *Appalachian Spring* (1943–4), awarded the Pulitzer Prize in 1945. This phase of Copland's career as an orchestral composer culminated in the Third Symphony (1944–6); which, in the last movement, incorporates *Fanfare for the Common Man*. Folksong quotation makes no appearance in it, but so deeply had this influence permeated Copland's subconscious that a folkish atmosphere pervades the work.

The Chicago Symphony Orchestra's long-term conductor Frederick Stock, championed many local composers, collectively described at the time as a "Chicago School," many of whose works were, to varying degrees, rooted in the American vernacular. Among them were Edward Joseph Collins who, in addition to composing grandiose symphonic and concertante works in a romantic idiom, created orchestral miniatures such as *Cowboy Breakdown* (1935) and *Lil' David Play on Yo' Harp* (1940), a reworking of an African American gospel song. The output of David Van Vactor, a flutist in the CSO under Stock, is predominantly European in inspiration, but another romantic, Leo Sowerby, now principally known for his organ works, also composed tone poems such as *Prairie* (1929) and the early program overture *Come Autumn Time* (1919), which was the most widely performed American orchestral composition throughout the 1920s and much of the 1930s.

Virgil Thomson also incorporated such elements in his concert music, beginning with his *Symphony on a Hymn Tune* (1928), as well as in his film scores, which include *The Louisiana Story*, the only soundtrack thus far to be awarded the Pulitzer Prize in Music (1949). Howard Hanson, composer of seven symphonies and many other orchestral compositions, is rightly considered a neo-Romantic, but such a work as his Symphony no.2 (the "Romantic") of 1930 is in fact permeated with harmonic progressions typical of popular song; the second (1932) of three symphonies by Randall Thompson reveals the same influence, as does the Symphony

no.2 in A (1945) by Douglas S. Moore, a composer now remembered primarily for his operas. In 1946, California-based composer Vera N. Preobrajenska wrote *American Tone Poem* (also known as *Symphony in Blues*), an orchestration of three of the four movements of her 1945 Piano Sonata No. 1, each of whose movements is based on a different American popular music idiom.

Much American orchestral music in the three decades after 1920 was shaped under the combined influences of the teacher Nadia Boulanger and the conductor Serge Koussevitzky. Many promising American composers went to France for study with Boulanger (and through her were exposed to the works of Stravinsky and the younger French composers such as Les Six); once back in the United States, a number of them received commissions and performances from Koussevitzky, who had left Paris in 1924 to direct the Boston SO. Copland, who studied with Boulanger in the early 1920s, was the first to benefit from this support. Boulanger's very first American student, Marion Bauer, primarily remembered today for her advocatorial writings about contemporary music, composed several contrapuntal works for string orchestra as well as the populist American Youth Concerto (1945). Another pupil of Boulanger, who was also supported strongly by Koussevitzky, was Roy Harris, who began composing for orchestra early in his career (Andante, 1926; *American Portrait 1929*, 1929) and for whom orchestral music remained the main focus. He composed a total of 14 symphonies as well as many smaller works. The *Symphony 1933*, his first symphony, was a response to Koussevitzky's call for "a great symphony from the West." The Symphony no.3 (1937), in one movement, became Harris's most frequently performed work; abandoning most elements of conventional structure, he here permitted the musical materials to develop and shape their own forms. Thereafter, he tended to alternate between multi-movement design (e.g., the Fifth Symphony, 1942) and single-movement form (Seventh Symphony, 1952). In some of his later symphonies Harris added solo vocal and choral parts, and in his last, written on the occasion of the US Bicentennial, he included passages of choral declamation. Upon his return to the United States after studying with Boulanger, Elliott Carter composed several works which are imbued with the spirit of "Americana," including the Symphony no.1 (1942, rev. 1954) and Holiday Overture (1944, rev. 1961), celebrating the liberation of Paris during World War II.

Other major composers of orchestral music who were less influenced by the so-called "Boulangerie" included Walter Piston (though in fact he studied with Boulanger), Wallingford Riegger, and Roger Sessions. All three shared a lack of interest in "Americanism" as an aesthetic goal and wrote in a comparatively abstract, international style. Piston composed many orchestral works, including eight symphonies; his style is characterized by classic clarity of form, and a mixture of triadic and quartal harmony that emphasizes the linear integrity of the texture. Riegger developed his own brand of dodecaphony, which he employed with exemplary clarity of line and texture. He achieved significant recognition with his Third Symphony (1946–7), first performed in 1948. Sessions composed a total of nine symphonies, but most were composed after World War II after he adopted serial techniques. But even such early works as the First Symphony (1927), the Violin Concerto (1935), and Second Symphony (1946), which grow increasingly chromatic, exhibit the long lines that remained the hallmark of his mature style.

Another prolific contributor to the orchestral repertory from the 1930s on was William Schuman, who wrote ten symphonies and many other works, including ballet scores, symphonic poems, concertos, and suites. His Symphony no.3 (1941)—the earliest one he acknowledged—turns to neo-Baroque formal principles in its two double movements ("Passacaglia and Fugue," "Chorale and Toccata"). His fifth symphony, from two years later, is scored exclusively for strings. The Symphony no.6 (1948) is a departure from earlier symphonies in form (being in one movement) and harmonic vocabulary (it eschews polychords). Schuman's later works show an increasing density of harmonic material but no basic change in idiom. Some are in a somewhat more popular vein, however, like the New England Triptych (1956) and A Song of Orpheus (1961), a fantasia for cello and orchestra based on an earlier song. Samuel Barber, an American romantic of unabashedly European inclinations, created elegant and deeply expressive music. His ability to infuse elaborate contrapuntal technique with evocative expression is perhaps best displayed in the Adagio for Strings (1936), his best-known work, which is an expansion of a movement from his String Quartet. His popular Violin Concerto (1939) is a virtuoso tour-de-force. The first (1936) of his two symphonies combines dramatic gesture, prickly wit, and effusive lyricism in a single, compact, four-part movement. The three works titled Essay (1937, 1942, 1978) are in an original form in which two themes are set in opposition to each other rather than being developed.

4. THE POSTWAR YEARS (1945–70). By the 1940s a number of European composers had immigrated to the United States, among them Ernest Bloch, Sergei Rachmaninoff, Max Steiner, Dimitri Tiomkin, Franz Waxman, Darius Milhaud, Paul Hindemith, Arnold Schoenberg, Erich Wolfgang Korngold, Miklós Rózsa, Ernst Toch, Ersnt Krenek, Béla Bartók, and Igor Stravinsky. Even though, for the most part, the styles of their orchestral music did not change appreciably after their arrival in the United States, their presence, established reputations, occupancy of academic posts, and their ability to attract performances of their works meant that much contemporary music was heard during this period. Bloch's best-known works, such as Voice in the Wilderness (1936) and Suite hébraïque for violin or viola and orchestra (1951), are based on Jewish themes, though he also wrote in a neoclassical vein (in the two concerti grossi, 1924–5, 1952) and occasionally in a self-consciously American manner (as in America, 1926, an "epic rhapsody" for chorus and orchestra). Rachmaninoff, far more active as a pianist than a composer after

emigrating from Russia, composed only a handful of works in his later years, but his final score, the Symphonic Dances, was completed on Long Island in 1940 and premiered by the Philadelphia Orchestra. Scores by Steiner, Tiomkin, and Waxman, all of whom were classically trained composers, defined the sweeping orchestral sound of Hollywood motion pictures for decades. Milhaud's compositional style was well established before he settled in the United States in 1940, and after World War II he spent equal time in France and at Mills College. But he paid homage to his adopted home in such works as Kentuckiana (1948), Aspen Serenade (1957), A Frenchman in New York (1962), Meurtre d'un grand chef d'état (1963), Music for Boston (1965), Music for New Orleans (1966), and Music for San Francisco (1971). Schoenberg's 12-tone Violin Concerto (1935) and Piano Concerto (1942) date from his American years, but even more important was his influence as the symbolic embodiment in the United States of serial thought. In America, Krenek was an influential teacher and also a steadfast proponent of 12-tone music. Hindemith asserted his concept of a functional harmony in the best-known orchestral works of his American years, the jaunty Symphonic Metamorphosis on Themes of Carl Maria von Weber (1943) and the cantata When Lilacs Last in the Dooryard Bloom'd: a Requiem for those we Love (1946), composed in memory of FDR and the dead of World War II. During Bartók's four final years in the United States, he composed the Concerto for Orchestra (1943), to a commission from Koussevitzky, the mostly complete Third Piano Concerto (1945), and the unfinished Viola Concerto (1945). Stravinsky settled in the United States in 1940, though he had been a frequent visitor for the preceding 15 years and his Symphony of Psalms (1930), which gives chorus and orchestra equal weight, was written to a commission from the Boston SO. His early American works include the neoclassical Symphony in C (1939–40) and the lively Symphony in Three Movements (1942–5). Though both primarily composed concert works before arriving in the United States, Korngold and Rózsa were mostly known here for their orchestral film scores. Toch worked in Hollywood as a composer and conductor as well, but he also composed seven symphonies in America, the third of which won the Pulitzer Prize.

A number of younger American-born composers also came to prominence in the 1940s, making the period a "golden age." Robert Ward wrote the first of his five euphonious symphonies in 1941 (among his other orchestral pieces is one of 1954 titled Euphony). The Concertante for Piano and Orchestra (1944) by Vivian Fine, written during her studies with Sessions, remains one of her most effective works. The second and third symphonies (1944, 1946) of Peter Mennin brought him to public attention while he was still a student. In these, and the six others he wrote over the next 30 years, he forged an intense and energetic contrapuntal style. The single-movement Symphony no.1 (1945) of Halsey Stevens, who studied with Bloch at Berkeley and taught for decades at USC, shows the influence of Bartók, about whom Stevens later wrote a definitive analytical biography. The Symphony no.3 (1946) of Vincent Persichetti was championed by Ormandy and the Philadelphia Orchestra, but his works for band have remained better known than his nine symphonies; all are informed by a fluent craftsmanship covering a wide range of styles. The Symphony for Classical Orchestra (1947) by Harold Shapero was directly modeled the music of Beethoven. The rigorous pandiatonic style of David Diamond reached its climax in his Fourth Symphony (1945). By the time of his Symphony no.5 (1951), Diamond's idiom had developed into an extremely chromatic one. He wrote his next three symphonies while based in Europe, where he was untouched by avant-garde movements, and revised the Fifth Symphony in 1964 before returning to the United States the following year. It took him 20 years to complete his next symphony (no.9), a two-part work scored for bass-baritone and orchestra, with texts by Michelangelo Buonarroti. Leroy Anderson composed novelty miniatures, many for the Boston Pops Orchestra, with catchy rhythms, singable melodies, and creative use of instruments. Among these are *The Syncopated Clock* (1945), *Sleigh Ride* (1948), *A Trumpeter's Lullaby* (1949), and *The Typewriter* (1950). Larger-scale pops-oriented works also were written by Don Gillis and Morton Gould.

During the 1950s, under the influence of Schoenberg, Krenek, and other influential teachers, many American composers began employing the 12-tone method. Then only a few years after Schoenberg's death in 1951, his lifelong nemesis Stravinsky, in an extraordinary *volte-face*, began adopting serial techniques. Stravinsky's 12-tone orchestral works include the ballet score *Agon* (1953–7) and *Movements* (1958–9). This watershed conversion had a ripple effect on other composers, both those who were already established and others who were emerging at this time. Several prominent members of the "Boston School" of composers, which clustered around Copland at Tanglewood, gradually adopted serial procedures, among them Arthur Berger, Lukas Foss, and Irving Fine whose final work is an extremely effective 12-tone symphony (1962). Copland, too, in his late orchestral scores, *Connotations* (1962) and *Inscape* (1967), made use of serial methods, although in the former piece only as "building blocks" for a succession of variations based on the opening four-note chords and their implied melodic intervals. Leon Kirchner, a student of Schoenberg, modeled his first Piano Concerto (1953) on that of Schoenberg. The Symphony no.2 (1956) of George Rochberg is another powerful 12-tone work as is the radically atonal sole Symphony of émigré Stefan Wolpe, completed that same year but not performed in full until 1965. Ross Lee Finney also created vital dodecaphonic symphonies.

Sessions's densely contrapuntal, elegantly arched symphonies of the 1950s and 1960s range from the Third (1957), his first to incorporate the 12-tone method, to the exuberant Sixth (1966) and the fluid and expressive Eighth (1968). He was tied to no specific structure: the symphonies vary in number of movements; some contain prologues and epilogues;

several are played through without pause. He celebrated the virtuosity of the Boston SO (especially woodwind and brass players) in his last completed work, the epigrammatic Concerto for Orchestra (1981). Andrew Imbrie, a student of Sessions, adopted the long lines favored by his teacher and energized them, while keeping the overall texture clear; this is evident in his three symphonies (1965, 1970, 1970), concertos for violin (1954), piano (1973, 1974), and flute (1977), and *Prometheus Bound* for soloists, chorus, and orchestra (1980; fig.2). The earliest acknowledged orchestral work by George Perle, whose theoretical writings about 12-tone music are as significant as his own compositions, is Three Movements for Orchestra (1960). He later composed a concerto for cello and two for piano as well as an exciting compact Concertino for piano, winds and timpani (1979).

Other composers pursued a more rigorous and uncompromising approach to 12-tone music. Milton Babbitt, beginning in the late 1940s, extended serial concepts to all musical parameters including rhythm and timbre. But *Relata I* (1965) is his earliest orchestral composition using his advanced system. *Correspondences* (1967) for violin and strings has an additional timbral layer provided by an electronic tape. *Spectra* (1958) by composer/conductor Gunther Schuller, who conducted the premiere of *Relata I*, uses 12-tone principles to construct an orchestral palette of pure *klangfarbenmelodie*. But Schuller has also been heavily involved with jazz and the promulgation of THIRD STREAM music; among his own "third stream" works are the Concertino for jazz quartet and orchestra (1959), and *Journey into Jazz* for narrator and orchestra (1962). But even some of Schuller's non-jazz work like *Seven Studies on a Them by Paul Klee* (1959) demonstrates how malleable serialism can be. By the late 1950s, even David Van Vactor started using tone-rows and 12-tone orchestral music was featured in motion pictures including *The Cobweb* (music by Leonard Rosenman, 1955) and *The Planet of the Apes* (Jerry Goldsmith, 1968). But some prominent composers, including Barber, Hanson, Quincy Porter, Vittorio Giannini, Paul Creston, Norman Dello Joio, and Ned Rorem resisted this trend and steadfastly clung to a tonal language in their orchestral works during this time.

One of the most remarkable developments in American orchestral music in the 1950s was the LOUISVILLE ORCHESTRA COMMISSIONING PROJECT. From 1948 to 1960 over 100 works, mostly by American composers, were commissioned for an orchestra of 50 players. The range of compositions and composers was staggering: from works by established composers such as Copland (Orchestral Variations, 1957), Harris (Piano Concerto no.2, 1953), Riegger (Variations for piano and orchestra, 1952–3, and Variations for violin and orchestra, 1958), and Schuman—whose *Judith* (1949) was danced to by Martha Graham—to compositions by younger composers such as Foss (*A Parable of Death*, 1954), Rorem (*Design for Orchestra*, 1953), and Chou Wen-chung, who had immigrated to the United States from China in 1946 (*And the Fallen Petals*, 1953). Louisville also premiered experimental works such as the Rhapsodic Variations (1953-4), a collaborative piece for tape and orchestra by Otto Luening and Vladimir Ussachevsky. The project, with funding from the Rockefeller Foundation, established a record label, which ensured the widespread distribution of classical American music through the then relatively new medium of the LP.

Carter's Variations for Orchestra (1954–5), a Louisville commission, was the first of his orchestral works to embody the characteristics of form, texture, tempo, rhythm, and harmony found in his mature music. The Variations consist of a theme and two ritornellos, which have contrasting (and changing) tempos. Strings, winds, and brass have separate and distinct functions. The nine variations move with diminishing textural contrast from activity (variations 1–4) to stasis (5) and, with increasing contrast, back to activity (6–9); Carter's innovative "metric modulation" is found in variations 4 and 6. He explored similar terrain in his Double Concerto for harpsichord and piano (1961), which also moves to and from its midpoint in a symmetrical manner. The solo instruments are given contrasting rhythmic and melodic material and each is accompanied by an independent ensemble, which solves the problem of balancing instruments of such different volume and timbre; moreover the percussion and pitched instruments are assigned different functions, the keyboard instruments acting as intermediaries. Both the Piano Concerto (1964–5) and the Concerto for Orchestra (1969) utilize virtuoso concertino groups within the orchestra which have their own chordal harmonies; the latter piece is as glittering as the former is dark. A Symphony of Three Orchestras (1976) further extends Carter's handling of simultaneous events and spatial relationships. Each orchestra plays four movements, which intersect and lash the others to create a complex collage. The 12 movements have distinct and unique tempos, characters, harmonies, and timbres. Carter has continued to compose orchestral music past his centenary.

If Carter's mid-period music presents a stringent complexity, necessitating virtuoso performances in order to be properly realized, the music of John Cage is at the opposite extreme. Although a student of Schoenberg, Cage was subsequently influenced by Zen Buddhism and the I Ching which led him to explore chance music, in which sound in and of itself is more important than the composer's intentions. (*See* ALEATORY.) While his earliest orchestral work, *The Seasons* (1947), composed for a ballet by Merce Cunningham, is derived from numerical charts, the subsequent Concerto for prepared piano and chamber orchestra (1950–51) introduces elements of chance. Even the concept of "musical" sound is extended, for lengthy silences are a fundamental component of the third movement. Indeterminacy was a key factor in Cage's work by the time of the *Concert for Piano and Orchestra* (1957–8), in which the solo part and the 13 other instrumental parts can be played in any order with any portion omitted, for any length of time, and (for the "orchestral" parts) by any number of players; the piece may also be performed simultaneously with other compositions by Cage from the same period. *Atlas eclipticalis* (1961), written with the aid of I Ching operations, calls for optional live electronics and 86 parts that need not all be used in full; the notation for these is based on patterns derived from an astronomical atlas. Later orchestral works by Cage have utilized voices (*Renga*, 1976, and *Atlas borealis*, 1982), more than one orchestra (*30 Pieces for 5 Orchestras*, 1981), and no conductor (*A Collection of Rocks*, 1984). In the last six years of his life, Cage composed a series of works collectively called the Number Pieces using a time bracket technique; the number of players involved form the titles of these works. Six require an orchestra: *68, 74, 80, 101, 103,* and *108*.

Cage's associate, Morton Feldman, was principally interested in timbral relationships: his characteristic orchestral sound is soft and static, and consists of isolated events. Early in his career he adopted graphic notation, which functions as a blueprint for the production of sounds of indeterminate pitch and length. In *Marginal Intersection* (1951), Feldman determines relative pitches (high, middle, and low) for wind, brass, and strings, while allowing piano, guitar, and percussion to choose pitches from any register; within the confines of the graph structure, specific entrances and durations are chosen by the performer. By the 1960s he had moved back towards conventional notation, assigning pitches but not durations. *First Principles* for chamber orchestra (1966–7) contains notated changes from sound to sound, but the changes are so broadly spaced that they are difficult to discern. Feldman ultimately found that he wanted precise control over musical events—*The Viola in my Life IV* (1971) is a conventionally notated orchestral work; such procedures were, however, presaged in *Structures* (1960–62), where he did "'fix' (precisely note) what might occur if the work utilized indeterminate elements." In the 1970s, Feldman composed a series of works for soloists and orchestra, titled simply based on the combination, for example, *Flute and Orchestra* (1978). Feldman's final orchestral composition, *Coptic Light* (1985), was inspired by Coptic textiles. Feldman's scores are meant to be played very quietly throughout which makes his orchestral pieces, in particular, all the more surreal.

Composer–conductors such as Leonard Bernstein and Lukas Foss enjoyed a degree of success with their orchestral works, which derived in part from their ability to conduct them. Bernstein's first three symphonies ("Jeremiah," 1942, "Age of Anxiety," 1947, and "Kaddish," 1963), are intensely personal, post-Mahlerian cris-de-coeur about 20th-century crises of faith. In each, Bernstein goes beyond the boundaries of the standard symphony orchestra, using a mezzo-soprano soloist in the First Symphony, a pianist as "protagonist" in the Second, and speaker, mezzo-soprano, and chorus in the Third. The "Kaddish" Symphony represents Bernstein's attempt to come to grips with atonality and the ultimate confirmation of his faith in tonality. The most successful moments in these works come when Bernstein lets loose with breezy, jazzy music, as in the Masque in the "Age of Anxiety." He acknowledges the theatricality of his orchestral music, and in fact it has been the arrangements of his theater pieces, notably the overture to *Candide* and the Symphonic Dances from *West Side Story*, that have attained the most enduring place in the orchestral repertory. Foss's orchestral compositions are also eclectic, but more experimental than Bernstein's: he borrows chorale settings by Bach for his Symphony of Chorales (1956–8) and themes by Scarlatti, Handel, and Bach for his *Baroque Variations* (1967). Early works, such as the two piano concertos, Symphony in G, and *Recordare*, are neoclassical, while his suite from the cantata *The Prairie* (1944) contains hints of Americana. *Concert for Cello and Orchestra* (1966) pits a cellist against a prerecorded tape; here again a piece by Bach is used, and is gradually distorted by cellist and tape. *Time Cycle* for soprano and orchestra (1959–60), one of Foss's most important works, explores the nature of time; it originally included improvisatory sections. The wit and humor that mark many of these works are completely absent from *Exeunt* (1982), a serial composition concerned with the vision of human annihilation.

5. Exploring new paths (1970–95). Throughout the 1960s and into the 70s, scores of great complexity proliferated, especially by composers who studied with Sessions and Babbitt at Princeton University or at the Juilliard School (where Carter also taught). But the technical difficulties of such orchestral works have meant that they only receive occasional performances; as a result these composers' chamber works have been much more widely disseminated. Such is the case with Mario Davidovsky and Donald Martino, both of whom studied with Babbitt. Davidovsky in his earlier years mostly eschewed the orchestra in favor of combinations of solo instruments with electronic tape. In 1960, however, he composed *Contrastes* for string orchestra and electronic tape. In his later, non-electronic work, such as the 1984 Divertimento for cello and orchestra, his experiments with electronics inform his detailed exploration of orchestral timbre. Among Martino's orchestral output is a Piano Concerto (1965) and *Mosaic* (1967) as well as an intensely virtuosic Triple Concerto for Clarinet, Bass Clarinet, and Contrabass Clarinet with Chamber Orchestra (1977). Charles Wuorinen, who studied at Columbia University and has performed many of his own pieces as pianist or conductor, was drawn to the music of Babbitt, Schoenberg, Stravinsky, and Varèse, and early assimilated a wide variety of techniques into his own clear, uncompromising compositions. Before he was 25 he had written three symphonies and four concertante works, marked by rhythmic buoyancy and striking timbres. Serial techniques appear in *Orchestral and Electronic Exchanges* (1965), but Wuorinen found them less binding than many of his contemporaries. *A Reliquary for Igor Stravinsky* (1975) incorporates the late composer's last sketches, while the Two-part Symphony (1978) is a Stravinskian homage of another kind (to the Symphony in C) in its clear rhythms, concertante writing, and wit. Both the Violin Concerto no.2 (1972) and the Piano Concerto no.2 (1973) use amplified solo instruments,

while *Bamboula Squared* (1984) effectively combines orchestra and quadraphonic tape in a driving, suspenseful manner.

An unprecedented level of experimentation also pervaded popular music in America throughout the 1960s and 1970s, and many of these experiments involved the incorporation of orchestral sonorities into popular songs. Phil Spector described his orchestra-heavy productions of girl group singles as "little symphonies for the kiddies" and other producers such as Shadow Morton created equally orchestral arrangements. Later on, American rock bands such as the Beach Boys; Blood, Sweat and Tears; and Chicago created heavily orchestrated albums. All of this activity was foreshadowed in the orchestrations of such popular 1950s arrangers as Nelson Riddle, who worked most notably with Frank Sinatra, and film/TV composer Henry Mancini, whose theme from the soundtrack to *Peter Gunn* was widely emulated by rock musicians. Some jazz figures continued to pursue orchestral aspirations. Composer/arrangers such as Stan Kenton, Gil Evans, Melba Liston, and Gary McFarland eroded the boundaries between musical genres even further as did the big band of Don Ellis which explored complex meters and at one point incorporated a string section. The most experimental of all the jazz big band leaders was Sun Ra, who from the 1950s until his death fronted a peculiar large ensemble he called his Arkestra, which performed an amalgam of bebop, total free improvisation, and electronic music. In the 1960s, a number of progressive composer/musicians coming out of the jazz tradition formed the Association for the Advancement of Creative Musicians (AACM) to perform each other's music; among them were Muhal Richard Abrams, Anthony Braxton, Anthony Davis, Leroy Jenkins, George Lewis, Roscoe Mitchell, and Henry Threadgill, all of whom later would write works for symphony orchestra incorporating improvisation and other indeterminate elements.

On the West Coast a number of composers followed the lead of Luening and Ussachevsky and experimented with combining orchestra with tape or computer. Morton Subotnick, director of the San Francisco Tape Music Center in the 1960s, wrote for tape and orchestra in *Play! no.2* (1964), *Laminations* (1968), and *Before the Butterfly* (1975). After completing *Two Butterflies* (1975) for amplified orchestra, he began a series of "ghost pieces" in which a digital program (the ghost) modifies the pitch, timbre, attack, volume, and direction of instrumental sounds; among the "ghost" orchestral scores are *Axolotl* and *Liquid Strata* (both 1982). The music of Roger Reynolds often combines live performers, electronically altered tape of conventional instruments, and computer-generated sound; the results, as in *Transfigured Wind II* (1984), are complex but expressive. In his *Symphony [Vertigo]* (1987), dedicated to Wuorinen, a large orchestra is further enhanced by quadraphonic computer-processed sounds. Robert Erickson, a colleague of Reynolds at the University of California, San Diego, made use of tape in some works of the 1960s and 70s, but his later orchestral works derived unusual sonorities from the use of homemade instruments such as stroked rods (in *Aurora*, 1982).

Exposure to non-Western cultures has exerted a tremendous influence on a number of composers since the late 1950s onwards, as it had the Canadian composer Colin McPhee and others in the 1920s. Henry Cowell's travels were increasingly reflected in his later orchestral works, which unlike his earlier audacious music attemped a more universalist approach based on folk music traditions from around the world. Among Cowell's 21 symphonies, his 13th, "Madras" (1956–8), incorporates Indian ragas. Lou Harrison, like Cowell a champion of Ives and his radical experimentation, had long been interested in integrating East Asian elements as well as just intonation into his musical language (as in his Suite for violin, piano, and small orchestra, 1951; Four Strict Songs for eight baritones and orchestra, 1955; and Suite for Symphonic Strings, 1936–60); after traveling to the East Asian in 1961–2 he wrote *Pacifika Rondo* (1963) for 'a chamber orchestra of Eastern and Western instruments. In the 1970s, Harrison composed extensively for gamelan; his works include a concerto for piano and gamelan as well as a double concerto for violin and cello with Javanese gamelan. In his final years, Harrison continued to compose for symphony orchestra, but always permeated with an alternate sensibility as in his Piano Concerto (1985), in which the piano is retuned into a temperament proposed by J.S. Bach's disciple Kirnberger, Symphony no.4 (1990, rev. 1995) which includes a narration of Navajo Coyote tales, and a concerto for Japanese koto and strings (1997). *Meteor Farm* (1982) by Henry Brant is a large work involving traditional music of Java, India, and West Africa performed by two choruses, symphony orchestra, and jazz orchestras. Like many of his works since *Antiphony I* (1953, rev. 1968), it is "spatial music," in which separated groups of musicians are assigned contrasting music; the procedure owes much to Ives. Alan Hovhaness heard Indian music in Boston in the 1930s, but it was not until after extensive travels in the 1950s that he began to incorporate elements of Asian music—instruments, modes, rhythms—further affected by his intense involvement with meditation and mysticism, into his extensive output for orchestra, which includes 67 symphonies and many concertos. Asian music was also of significance for the early minimalist composers.

While minimalism has been one of the most important new styles in American music, it has evolved largely outside the orchestra. Terry Riley's pioneering *In C* (1964), in which all musicians play a series of repeating cells from the same part and a multi-part texture is created as a result of the musicians moving from cell to cell at their own pace, can be played by any ensemble including an orchestra and several orchestras have performed the work, albeit less effectively than more malleable ensembles. Riley has only composed a handful of works for standard orchestra, among them *June Buddhas* and *The Sands*, a concerto for string quartet and orchestra premiered by the Kronos Quartet (both 1991). Steve Reich has mostly eschewed the orchestra in favor of more clear articulations attained when there is only one player per part, with amplification. Several of his works, such as *Tehillim* (1981) and Triple Quartet (1998) have been adapted for orchestral performance, but his only compositions conceived specifically for a standard orchestra are *The Desert Music* for chorus and orchestra (1984), *Three Movements* (1986), and *The Four Sections* (1987), although his earlier *Music for a Large Ensemble* (1978), requiring 30 players, has clear orchestral aspirations. Beginning in the 1980s, another pioneering minimalist, Philip Glass, who had previously composed almost exclusively for his own ensemble, started writing for symphony orchestras. To date, he has now composed nine symphonies (two of which are based on rock albums by David Bowie—*Low* and *Heroes*) and numerous concertos, which have been performed internationally and most of which have been commercially recorded. Although most of the ritualistic compositions of Meredith Monk have been created for her own small ensemble and evolve during an intensive workshop process, she has also created an unusual work for orchestra, *Possible Sky* (2003).

But the most effective extension of the minimalist style of composition to encompass the forces of a large symphony orchestra has been in the music of John Adams. In three scores written for the San Francisco SO—*Harmonium* for chorus and orchestra (1980), *Grand Pianola Music* (1982), and *Harmonielehre* (1984–5)—he uses a rich, modulating, harmonic vocabulary to maintain the listener's involvement over the length of a composition. His similarly expansive, but brief *Short Ride in a Fast Machine* (1986) has become one of the most widely performed recent American compositions. Minimalism is only one of the elements that informs his later poly-stylistic orchestral scores, such as the quasi-expressionist Violin Concerto (1993), the epic *Naïve and Sentimental Music* (1998), *On the Transmigration of Souls* for chorus, orchestra and tape (2002), written to commemorate the events of September 11, 2001, the microtonally-infused *Dharma at Big Sur* (2003), and the frenetic *City Noir* (2009).

Far greater than the impact of minimalism on the composition of new orchestral music has been the so-called "new romanticism," a conscious return to tonality, sometimes in direct emulation of earlier music, other times imbued with a completely contemporary sensibility and occasionally informed by popular music which has, for the most part, remained tonal. The mid-career rejection of serial music by Rochberg, one of its most successful practitioners, was arguably as significant on composers as Stravinsky's adoption of serialism a generation earlier. Another composer whose initial works were 12-tone, but who subsequently created lush, expansive, tonal scores was David Del Tredici, whose obsession with Lewis Carroll's *Alice's Adventures in Wonderland* yielded a number of grandiose Straussian tone poems and symphonies (1968–84), culminating in *Final Alice* (1976) and *Child Alice* (1980–81). Later on, he celebrated his homosexual identity in the orchestral song cycle *Gay Life* (2000), and has taken inspiration from iconic early American themes in *Paul Revere's Ride* and *Rip Van Winkle*, both 2005. Another extremely effective neo-romantic work is the Piano Concerto (1988) by Robert Beaser.

Jacob Druckman eschewed serialism to write dramatic, colorful scores, quoting or alluding to earlier music (Debussy in *Windows*, which won the Pulitzer Prize in 1972, Bernstein's "Kaddish tune" in *Aureole* of 1979) without losing his own brilliant voice. Alive with color, also, are the scores of Joseph Schwantner; his use of the more ethereal-sounding percussion instruments—gongs, bowed cymbals, and particularly water goblets—permeates his works, but compositions such as *Magabunda* for soprano and orchestra (1983) have enormous dramatic impact because the colors are used so masterfully. The wondrous timbral explorations of George Crumb, most celebrated for his chamber works, have found their way into his occasional forays into orchestral compositions, such as *Star-child* (for soprano, children's chorus, and orchestra) of 1977 and *A Haunted Landscape* (1984).

The explosion of orchestral activity in recent decades—year-round orchestras, national and international tours, commissions, recordings—owes much to the creation of the NATIONAL ENDOWMENT FOR THE ARTS (NEA) in 1965. The existence of nationally supported funding for programs that hitherto had existed through the vision and generosity of individual patrons, private foundations, or local institutions (many of whom now teamed up with the NEA to create grander programs), provided new-found stability for composers, performers, and orchestras alike. One manifestation of this activity has been the proliferation of professional chamber orchestras, the most prominent of which are the St. Paul Chamber Orchestra (founded 1959), the Concerto Soloists of Philadelphia (1965), the Los Angeles Chamber Orchestra (1968), the 92nd Street "Y" Chamber Orchestra (1977), and the conductor-less Orpheus Chamber Orchestra. Each of these has presented new works, often their own commissions.

A combination of commissions from orchestras and relationships developed between individual composers and performers has accounted for the composition, in particular, of many important new concertos since 1970, including Michael Colgrass's *Déjà vu* (1977) for percussion quartet and orchestra (which won the Pulitzer Prize), John Corigliano's Clarinet Concerto (1977), and Druckman's Viola Concerto (1979). Schuller has also contributed extensively to the concerto repertory with works for instruments that are seldom used in a soloistic capacity—double bass (1968), contrabassoon (1978), and alto saxophone (1983)—as well as concertos for orchestra, piano, violin, and horn. Rochberg's five-movement Violin Concerto (1975), written for Isaac Stern, is perhaps his best-known orchestral score since his rejection of serialism and return to tonality in the 1960s. John Harbison wrote his three-movement, classically drawn Violin Concerto (1980) with the virtuosity of his wife, Rose Mary, in mind; Peter Serkin's suggestion that Peter Lieberson write him a piano concerto resulted in Lieberson's first orchestral work (1983), but his most striking work thus far has been

the Grawemeyer Award-winning *Neruda Songs* for mezzo soprano and orchestra (2005), composed for his wife Lorraine Hunt Lieberson, who premiered the work shortly before her untimely death in 2006.

For the US Bicentennial the NEA helped to document the state of American orchestral music by providing funds for a dozen orchestras to commission works: Leslie Bassett's *Echoes from an Invisible World*, Cage's *Renga* and *Apartment House, 1776*, Carter's *A Symphony of Three Orchestras*, Colgrass's *Theater of the Universe*, Del Tredici's *Final Alice*, Druckman's *Mirage*, Morton Gould's Symphony of Spirituals, Rochberg's Violin Concerto, Rorem's *Air Music*, Loren Rush's *Song and Dance*, Schuller's Concerto for Orchestra no.2, and Subotnick's *Before the Butterfly*. American orchestral music has at times suffered from a lack of repeated hearings. To address that problem, this program called for each orchestra to perform not only the composition it had commissioned but others of the Bicentennial pieces. The result was widespread dissemination and, perhaps more important, a number of interpretations of works containing an impressive range of styles. The performance of American orchestral music of many styles and periods has been a goal of the AMERICAN COMPOSERS ORCHESTRA (ACO), founded in 1977. In addition to maintaining an annual season of concerts devoted to American repertoire, the ACO has also embarked on festivals devoted to works for orchestra and electronics as well as orchestral music involving improvisation.

The NEA was also active, with the Rockefeller Foundation, Exxon, and MEET THE COMPOSER, in an important program of the early 1980s that appointed Adams, Druckman, Harbison, William Kraft, Robert X. Rodriguez, and Schwantner composers-in-residence with five leading American orchestras; subsequent participants included Libby Larsen, Stephen Paulus, Wuorinen, Stephen Albert, Tobias Picker, Christopher Rouse, Alvin Singleton, and Joan Tower. Composers, chosen by the orchestras' music directors, worked with orchestral musicians before composing their commissioned works, and also learned about administrative and economic structures of professional orchestras. Conductors have often repeated the commissioned pieces on their orchestra's tours as well as when they have conducted other orchestras. New-music festivals sponsored by the orchestras have exposed audiences to works by other composers than those in the residency program, and many of the commissioned pieces have been recorded. Many of these composers have striven to write practical, relatively brief works that can easily be learned by an orchestra in the short rehearsal periods available for professional ensembles.

6. THE "END OF HISTORY" AND A NEW MILLENIUM (1990–2010). While an immense amount of new orchestral music has continued to be commissioned, composed, and performed in the closing years of the 20th century and the beginning of the new millennium, the notion of what constitutes an orchestra has been challenged over the past generation. The rise of MIDI technology and

the proliferation of home computers and notation software have made it possible to create a kind of synthetically generated orchestral music: composers such as Jerry Gerber have worked almost exclusively in this medium. The earliest prominent work of this genre was *Digital Moonscapes* for the "LSI Philharmonic" (large scale integration) by Wendy Carlos, who is most widely known for her Switched-On Bach recordings. Composers who work in this medium contend that it offers a greater opportunity to explore such areas as metrical complexity, alternate tunings, and a wider array of timbre than is possible within standard symphony orchestras, with their institutional constraints, limited rehearsal schedules, and commitment to older, standard repertoire. Some composers instead opt to write for the symphonic wind bands (essentially an orchestra without strings) which proliferate throughout the United States in schools, universities and the military, and offer more opportunities for repeat performances of new works. In 2004, one of America's most high-profile orchestral composers, John Corigliano, created a major work for symphonic winds, Symphony No. 3 "Circus Maximus." Nowadays many composers create both orchestra and band versions of their pieces. There has also been a resurgence of music for big band, the orchestra of jazz. While contemporary motion picture soundtracks no longer always feature a lavish orchestral score—some use electronics and many are simply collections of pre-existing popular recordings—the orchestra is the timbral palette for Hollywood mainstays John Williams and Canadian-born Howard Shore. And in recent years, highly successful orchestra film scores have been composed by Corigliano, Philip Glass, Tan Dun, and other composers more frequently associated with the concert hall.

Other composers have created their own different kinds of large ensembles, some describing such configurations as "orchestras." Of the 15 symphonies of Glenn Branca, only his 7th and 9th are scored for a standard symphony orchestra; the others are for his own "orchestras" of heavily-amplified electric guitars. Another composer for "guitar orchestra," Rhys Chatham, created a work for 400 electric guitars. It has been argued that many of the ensembles formed by Frank Zappa, who first came to prominence for the unconventional rock music he created for his band the Mothers of Invention, are in fact orchestras. However, in later years Zappa also composed works expressly for conventional orchestras and these works have continued to be performed since his death. In 2003, Daniel Goode, a founding member of the Gamelan Son of Lion (a traditional Indonesian "orchestra" built by Barbara Benary to perform contemporary music), established the Flexible Orchestra, an ensemble with a rotating personnel with combines single instruments of various types with multiples of one instrument (one year cellos, another year trombones). Many composers have written music for malleable chamber orchestra configurations that have been formed all across the country specifically for the performance of new music, such as Philadelphia's Orchestra 2001, the Cleveland

Chamber Orchestra, the Seattle Creative Orchestra, and the Boston Modern Orchestra Project, which frequently expands to a full orchestra and has had the greatest ability to disseminate the music it has championed through its own recording label. Yet many active composers today eschew the creation of large ensemble music altogether.

Still, composers from a very wide range of backgrounds and stylistic inclinations continue to create music for the conventional symphony orchestra. A post-minimalist aesthetic informs a broad range of recent orchestral compositions such as the mysterious *Shadows* (1987) by Alvin Singleton, the propulsive *All In Good Time* (1993) by Barbara Kolb, the electronically enhanced *Kingdom Come* (1996) by Ingram Marshall, the vibrant color-named pieces of Michael Torke, including *Ecstatic Orange* (1985) and *Purple* (1987), and the expansive large scale sonic frescoes of Aaron Jay Kernis, such as *Symphony in Waves* (1989) and *Color Wheel* (2001). Michael Daugherty creates postmodern works in response to popular culture such as Superman-inspired *Metropolis Symphony* (1988–93) and the piano concerto *Le Tombeau de Liberace*, while the Alaska-based John Luther Adams and the expatriate Gloria Coates, an extremely prolific female symphonist, compose broad experimental orchestral canvasses. Others such as Corigliano, Harbison, Larsen, Rouse, Margaret Brouwer, Richard Danielpour, Lowell Liebermann, and Ellen Taaffe Zwilich, the first female composer to win the Pulitzer Prize in Music, continue to create a formidable body of more traditionally-oriented repertoire in recognizable orchestral forms such as symphonies and concertos. A relative newcomer to the role of concerto soloist has been the percussionist, but in recent years there have been a numerous works for such soloists, including works by Daugherty, Schwantner, Torke, Nancy Van de Vate, and Jennifer Higdon, which involve elaborate choreography involving numerous instruments. Many composers following in the tradition of Bartók have also written concertos "for orchestra" showcasing all of the musicians' virtuosity; among the more notable have been Tower, Rouse, Higdon, and Steven Stucky.

Orchestral works from a more modernist aesthetic orientation, albeit one that is seemingly less overtly at odds with standard practice, also continue to be composed by such established figures as Wuorinen and George Walker, the first African American composer to be awarded the Pulitzer Prize, as well as composers from later generations like Maurice Wright, Shulamit Ran, Melinda Wagner, David Rakowski, Augusta Read Thomas, and Michael Hersch. But the most prominent modernist remains Carter, who from his 80th year to beyond his 102nd, has been extremely prolific in his orchestral output. Starting with his Violin Concerto (1989), Carter began eschewing the complex simultaneities which were a hallmark of his earlier work, in favor of clearer, massed sonorities. Works such as his massive three-movement *Symphonia: Sum fluxae pretium spei* (1993–6), the Cello Concerto (2001), *Dialogues* for piano and chamber orchestra (2003), and the Horn Concerto (2007) at times almost suggest a *rapprochement* with the standard repertoire and as a result have been more widely performed.

One of the most exciting developments has been the proliferation of orchestral works by composers from cultures not previously associated with this tradition. In the 1980s, Chou Wen-chung was responsible for bringing many of China's most important young composers to the United States to study with him at Columbia University, among them Zhou Long, Chen Yi, Ge Gan-ru, Bright Sheng, and Tan Dun, and each has composed significant orchestral scores incorporating Chinese elements, among them Sheng's *H'un* (Lacerations) composed in memory of the Cultural Revolution (1988), Ge's *Chinese Rhapsody* (1992), Zhou's *Poems from Tang* (1995), and Chen's *Si Ji*, a Chinese Four Seasons (2005). Tan Dun's wildly theatrical orchestral works frequently evoke ancient Chinese shamanism and include concertos for his own devised water percussion (1998), paper instruments (2003), and stone and ceramic instruments (*Earth Concerto*, 2009). Korean-born composer Jin Hi Kim and Japanese American Ken Ueno have also created significant orchestral works inspired by ancient Asian traditions. Zhou and Chen, who are married, have become highly influential teachers and have now inspired generations of composers who create orchestral music infused with Asian sensibilities. There has been an equally significant outpouring of American orchestral works inspired by Latin American musical traditions. Cuban émigré Tania León, Puerto Rico-born Roberto Sierra, and Peruvian American Gabriela Lena Frank each create vibrant orchestral works incorporating the rhythms from their ethnic backgrounds, while some of the orchestral works of Argentina-born Osvaldo Golijov involve additional musicians from a wide array of world music backgrounds. Jerod Impichchaachaaha' Tate, a citizen of the Native American Chickasaw Nation, has composed a series of Native American themed orchestral works, such as the double bass concerto *Iyaaknasha'* (1993) and the flute concerto *Tracing Mississippi* (2002).

Others, mostly composer/performers, have introduced instruments and styles into orchestral music from other musical genres. In addition to writing many more conventional works for orchestra, Steven Mackey has composed two concertos featuring the electric guitar—*Deal* (1995) and *Tuck and Roll* (2000)—which celebrate his background as a rock musician and feature him as soloist. Composer/violinist Daniel Bernard Roumain has created a series of orchestral works incorporating funk and hip hop such as *Hip-Hop Essay* (1995) and *Voodoo Violin Concerto* (2002–6). *Liquid Interface* by Mason Bates incorporates trip-hop electronica into the orchestra via the composer's own performance on laptop. Such juxtapositions are becoming more and more common as younger generations who have been exposed to a broad range of musical genres, and freely move between them, have begun composing for the orchestra.

There have been orchestral initiatives specifically targeted to younger composers. The American Composers Orchestra (ACO) devotes two days to readings of works every year. There have been similar readings in Los Angeles and Tampa as well. The Minnesota Orchestra's Composer Institute offers a group of emerging composers a week-long immersion into the process of working with an orchestra, culminating in a concert of their works. Recently, the ACO initiated EarShot to encourage mid-sized orchestras across the country to also do reading seasons. Thus far, the Buffalo Philharmonic and the Colorado, Nashville, and Pioneer Valley (MA) symphonies have participated. Several of the works that have received their first performances as part of these various program have gone on to be performed by established orchestras during their regular concert seasons, such as <<*rewind*<< (2005) by Anna Clyne, *Earth and Green* (2006) by Clint Needham, and *These Worlds in Us* (2006) by Missy Mazzoli. For established composers the most ambitious recent initiative has been the Ford Made in America project, a collaboration between the Ford Motor Company Fund, the League of American Orchestras, and Meet The Composer. The project secures a commission by a prominent American composer that is then performed by orchestras in all 50 states. There have been two works created for the project thus far, Tower's *Made in America* and Schwantner's *Chasing Light*.

Overall, it continues to be an extremely fruitful time for new orchestral music in the United States. As of 2010, based on the information available to the League of American Orchestras, well over a thousand world premieres have already been performed in the 21st century by American orchestras.

BIBLIOGRAPHY

F.O. Jones, ed.: *A Handbook of American Music and Musicians* (Canaseraga, NY, 1886/R1971)

W.S.B. Mathews, ed.: *A Hundred Years of Music in America* (Chicago, 1889/R1970)

H.E. Krehbiel: *The Philharmonic Society of New York* (New York, 1892); ed. in Shanet (1979)

L.C. Madeira: *Annals of Music in Philadelphia and History of the Musical Fund Society from its Organization in 1820 to the Year 1858* (Philadelphia, 1896/R1973)

O.G.T. Sonneck: *Early Concert-life in America (1731–1800)* (Leipzig, 1907/R1978)

M.A.D. Howe: *The Boston Symphony Orchestra: an Historical Sketch* (Boston, 1914, enlarged 2/1931/R1978)

J.G. Huneker: *The Philharmonic Society of New York and its 75th Anniversary* (New York, ?1917; ed. in Shanet, 1979)

H.C. Lahee: *Annals of Music in America* (Boston, 1922/R1969)

P.A. Otis: *The Chicago Symphony Orchestra* (Chicago, 1925/R1972)

A.G. Rau and H.T. David: *A Catalogue of Music by American Moravians, 1742–1842* (Bethlehem, PA, 1938/R1970)

List of American Orchestral Works Recommended by WPA Music Project Conductors (Washington, DC, 1941)

J. Erskine: *The Philharmonic-Symphony Society of New York: its First Hundred Years* (New York, 1943; ed. in Shanet, 1979)

H. Leichtentritt: *Serge Koussevitzky, the Boston Symphony Orchestra and the New American Music* (Cambridge, MA, 1946/R1978)

M. Smith: *Koussevitzky* (New York, 1947)

W. Mellers: *Music in a New Found Land* (New York, 1964)

P.J. Korn: "The Symphony in America," *The Symphony*, ii, ed. R. Simpson (Harmondsworth, England, 1967), 243 only

R.C. Marsh: *The Cleveland Orchestra* (Cleveland, 1967)

R.S. Hines, ed.: *The Orchestral Composer's Point of View: Essays on Twentieth-century Music by those who Wrote it* (Norman, OK, 1970)

American Composers' Concerts, and Festivals of American Music, 1925–1971: Cumulative Repertoire (Rochester, 1972)

K. Krueger, ed.: The Musical Heritage of the United States: the Unknown Portion (New York, 1973)

H. Shanet: Philharmonic: a History of New York's Orchestra (Garden City, NY, 1975)

H.E. Johnson: First Performances in America to 1900: Works with Orchestra (Detroit, 1979)

H. Shanet, ed.: Early Histories of the New York Philharmonic (New York, 1979) [annotated edn of Krehbiel, 1892; Huneker, ?1917; and Erskine, 1943]

K.M. Famera: Catalog of the American Music Center Library, iii: Music for Orchestra, Band and Large Ensemble (New York, 1982)

C. Hamm: Music in the New World (New York and London, 1983)

J. Rockwell: All American Music: Composition in the Late Twentieth Century (New York, 1983)

J. Horowitz: Understanding Toscanini (Berkeley, 1987)

J.W. Struble: The History of American Classical Music (New York, 1995)

K. Gann: American Music in the Twentieth Century (New York, 1997)

J. Horowitz: Classical Music in America: a History of its Rise and Fall (New York and London, 2005)

R. Taruskin: The Oxford History of Western Music (New York, 2005)

K. Gann: Music Downtown: Writings from the Village Voice (Berkeley, 2006)

B.L. Scherer: A History of American Classical Music (Naperville, IL, 2007)

RODNEY H. MILL/FRANK J. OTERI (1, 2), RODNEY H. MILL AND SUSAN FEDER/FRANK J. OTERI (3), SUSAN FEDER/FRANK J. OTERI (4–5), FRANK J. OTERI (6)

Oregon. Jazz chamber ensemble. Its original members were Paul McCandless (oboe, english horn, bass clarinet), Glen Moore (double bass, violin, piano, flute), Ralph Towner (acoustic guitar, piano, french horn, trumpet, flugelhorn), and Collin Walcott (tablā, sitar, clarinet, percussion). They all played in the PAUL WINTER CONSORT before forming their own group in 1970; the percussionist Trilok Gurtu joined the group after Walcott's death in 1984 and the drummer Mark Walker replaced Gurtu in 1993. Oregon's style combines an eclectic mix of classical music, modern jazz, and non-Western musics and prefigured developments in what was subsequently marketed as world music; the timbre and sensitivity of their chamber style offered a sonic precedent for new age music. Their sensitive interaction in performance has allowed them to improvise collectively without assuming rigidly defined roles. Their recordings include pieces based upon complex harmonies, such as "Yellow Bell," and others based on a drone or free improvisation. While the soaring oboe in "Icarus" is typical, the fact that the musicians play 60 to 80 different instruments has given the group a wide palette of sounds. The group was still performing and touring in the early 2010s and has continued to push and blur musical boundaries, as evidenced by their acclaimed collaboration in 2000 with the Moscow Tchaikovsky Symphony Orchestra.

RECORDINGS
(selective list)

Our First Record (1970, Van.); Together (1976, Van.); Friends (1977, Van.); Violin (1978, Van.); Out of the Woods (1978, Elek.), incl. Yellow Bell; Oregon in Performance (1979, Elek.), incl. Icarus; Oregon (1983, ECM); Crossing (1984, ECM); 45th Parallel (1988, Portrait); Always, Never, and Forever (1990, VeraBra); In Moscow (2000, Intuition); 1000 Kilometers (2007, Cam Jazz)

BIBLIOGRAPHY

S. Larson: Some Aspects of the Album "Out of the Woods" by the Chamber Ensemble "Oregon" (thesis, U. of Oregon, 1981)

S. Larson: "Yellow Bell and a Jazz Paradigm," In Theory Only, vi/2 (1982), 31

J. Diliberto: "Oregon: Beauty, and the Beat," DB, lv/2 (1988), 24 [incl. discography and interviews]

STEVE LARSON/R

Oregon, University of. State university, founded in Eugene in 1876. It is the oldest of the state's seven institutions of higher education. Music became a professional school in 1886 and remained independent and self-supporting until 1915. Dance was founded in 1959 and merged into the School of Music and Dance in 1991. The school offers the BA and BS in music and dance, MFA, MA, and MS in dance, and BMus, MMus, DMA, and PhD in music, with strengths in music and dance performance, music education, historiography, and theory. In 2008–9, the school enrolled about 260 undergraduate and 140 graduate music students, and 55 undergraduate and 10 dance graduate students. There were 44 full-time and 22 part-time music faculty members, and 7 full-time and 6 part-time dance faculty. The present facilities were constructed in 1921, enlarged in 1950 and 1978, and renovated along with a major addition in 2009. The facilities include a 550-seat concert hall that houses one of the largest instruments of German organ builder Jürgen Ahrend. The main library of the university houses the substantial music collection (28,000 books and 51,000 manuscripts), musical Oregoniana, special collections, and 26,000 items of sheet music of the period 1896–1956.

DOUGLAS LEEDY/HARRY E. PRICE

Oregon Bach Festival. Founded in 1970, the Oregon Bach Festival takes place each year during June and July in Eugene, Oregon. Led by artistic director Helmuth Rilling, the Oregon Bach Festival emphasizes the music of Johann Sebastian Bach, but over the years it has expanded to include music from a wide array of composers. By 2010, it offered over 50 events encompassing a repertory extending from before Bach's time to contemporary music. Sponsored by the University of Oregon, the Oregon Bach Festival events take place primarily at Eugene's Hult Center for the Performing Arts and at Beall Hall at the University of Oregon's School of Music and Dance. A professional chorus and orchestra maintain the festival's focus on choral-orchestral repertoire. The Oregon Bach Festival also provides many educational activities. Its conducting masterclass draws participants from around the world, and the Stangeland Family Youth Choral Academy, directed by Anton Armstrong (St. Olaf College) attracts young singers from all across the nation.

The festival has commissioned, co-commissioned, and presented the first performances of numerous musical works, including the world premières of Felix Mendelssohn's The Uncle from Boston (from a rediscovered manuscript), Stephen Paulus's Symphony for Strings, Arvo Pärt's Litany, Osvaldo Golijov's Oceana, Krzyztof Penderecki's Credo, Sven-David Sandström's Messiah, and the US première of Tan Dun's Water

Passion. Since 1990, it has released or participated in 12 commercial recordings. Its recording of Penderecki's *Credo* won the 2001 Grammy Award for Best Choral Performance. Helmuth Rilling has created the Internationale Bachakademie Stuttgart and several other Bach Academies around the world, modeled on the Oregon Bach Festival and building on its success.

BIBLIOGRAPHY

M.C. Donnelly: *The Oregon Bach Festival, 1970-1994* (Eugene, OR, 1994)

S.M. Rilling, trans. G. Paine: *My Father Helmuth Rilling* (Eugene, OR, 2010)

JAMES BASH

Orff, Carl (*b* Munich, Germany, 10 July 1895; *d* Munich, Germany, 29 March 1982). German composer and music educator. Orff attended the Munich Academy of Music (graduating in 1914) and later studied composition with Heinrich Kaminsky. A successful composer in many genres, he is best known for the choral/orchestral ballet *Carmina Burana* (1937). It was in the field of music education, however, that he made his most important contributions. In 1924 Orff and dancer Dorothee Günther founded the Güntherschule of gymnastics, music, and dance in Munich, where he began to formulate his ideas about music education. Orff came to believe that musical performance should combine music, text, and movement, the kind of creative thinking encouraged by the artistic environment in Munich during the 1920s and 30s. In 1926 Gunild Keetman (1904–90) enrolled at the Güntherschule and began a lifetime of collaboration with Orff. Both believed that all children could take part in the joys of music making through speech, rhythmic activities, singing, and movement. Orff developed specially designed barred instruments for children based on the Indonesian gamelan and African percussion instruments, and Orff and Keetman published *Music for Children* (1950–54). The Orff approach became prominent in North America in the 1960s, when Keetman and Orff taught summer teacher training courses at the University of Toronto. The American Orff-Schulwerk Association was founded in 1968 to promote Orff education in the United States. The Orff Institute in Salzburg, Austria, is the international research and teaching center for the Orff approach.

BIBLIOGRAPHY

GMO

G. Keetman: *Elementaria: First Acquaintance with Orff-Schulwerk* (London, 1970)

J.R. Soderberg: *Developments of the Orff-Schulwerk in American Elementary Education* (thesis, San Francisco State College, 1970)

S.C. Munsen: *A Description and Analysis of an Orff-Schulwerk Program of Music Education* (diss., U. of Illinois, 1986)

ALAN L. SPURGEON

Organ (from Gk. *organon* via Lat. *organum*). A keyboard instrument having one or more manual keyboards and usually a pedal-board, the keys of which operate valves that admit air under pressure (supplied by a wind-raising device) to pipes arranged in one or more scale-like rows. The earliest, simplest organs consisted of one set of pipes, each pipe corresponding to one key of the keyboard. Beginning in the 15th century organs could include many sets of pipes of different pitches and tone-colors, and multiple keyboards. Modern organs are found in all sizes, from one-manual instruments with two or three sets of pipes, to ones with four or more manuals and several thousand pipes.

The first organs in the Americas were brought from Spain to Central America by Franciscan and Dominican missionaries in the mid-16th century. During the 17th century the use of organs—both imported and locally built—was widespread throughout Spanish colonial America; 17 small organs are reported as being in use in 1630 in what is now New Mexico, and one is later recorded in present-day Florida. By the early 18th century many Mexican cathedrals had organs equal to any on the Iberian Peninsula, among them the two instruments of 1688 and 1735 extant in Mexico City Cathedral, and indigenous schools of organ-building were established in Oaxaca, Puebla and elsewhere in Mexico. By the early 19th century small organs are recorded as having been used in distant Spanish mission outposts, including some in present-day California.

1. Up to 1800. 2. The 19th century. 3. The 20th century.

1. UP TO 1800. In the northern French Canadian colonies, there was a church organ at Quebec City as early as 1657, and between 1698 and 1705 a two-manual organ was imported for the Notre Dame Parish Church in Montreal. The first documented use of an organ in a church in the British or German colonies of the eastern seaboard dates from 1703. A small German religious colony had settled near Philadelphia in 1694, apparently bringing with it a small positive organ, and this was lent in 1703 for use at a Lutheran ordination ceremony in the "Old Swede's" Church, Philadelphia. In 1713 a four-stop English chamber organ, having characteristics of the "Father Smith" school, was placed in King's Chapel, Boston; it was mentioned as early as 1708 in connection with its original owner, Thomas Brattle, Treasurer of Harvard College, by the diarist Samuel Sewall, and it may have been imported before 1700. English organs, including some significant examples of the work of Bridge, Jordan, Green, England, and Snetzler, continued to be imported in increasing numbers to the eastern coastal colonies during the rest of the 18th century, almost entirely for Anglican churches.

The first person known to have built an organ in the colonies was Johann Gottlob Klemm, a Saxon who immigrated in 1733, and who built several organs, the largest of them a three-manual instrument installed in Trinity Church, New York, in 1739. His work was carried on by his apprentice, DAVID TANNENBERG, who built more than 40 organs between 1758 and his death in 1804, mostly for Moravian and other ethnic German churches in a small area of Pennsylvania. His largest instrument was built for Zion Lutheran Church in Philadelphia. Other German-born builders, notably Philip Feyring, were active around Philadelphia in the late 18th century.

Robert J. Barrow plays the newly-completed organ at the Washington Cathedral as the organ's builder, E.M. Skinner, looks on, 1938. (Library of Congress, Prints & Photographs Division, photograph by Harris & Ewing, LC-DIG-hec-24439)

Tannenberg's work reflected the influence of the Central German tradition, as transmitted by Klemm, but he also kept pace with newer European developments and was familiar with the writings of the theorist Georg Andreas Sorge. Following in his footsteps were Conrad Doll and several generations of the Krauss and Dieffenbach families, who, culturally removed from the English-influenced urban mainstream of East Coast organ building, continued to produce small organs in the "Pennsylvania Dutch" tradition for rural churches well past 1850.

Puritan (Calvinist) objections to the use of instruments in worship was strong throughout the northern colonies until the last decade of the 18th century, so that most of the early church organs were built for the Anglicans, Lutherans, and Moravians. There is also evidence for a number of domestic chamber organs, including claviorgans and barrel organs, in this period. Most organs (of all types) were still imported, but after the mid-18th century American builders began to appear in the colonies north of Pennsylvania.

The first true organ builder in Boston was THOMAS JOHNSTON, who, beginning about 1753, built a small number of church and chamber organs modeled after imported English instruments. Among his followers were Josiah Leavitt and HENRY PRATT, both of whom built several small church and chamber organs, primarily for rural churches west and north of Boston. The prejudice against instruments began to break down in churches of the Puritan tradition by the 1790s, creating a new demand for church organs that was increasingly met by American builders.

These early New England builders were essentially self-taught and at first supported themselves only partly through organ building. New York and Philadelphia,

however, attracted some English-trained builders during the final years of the 18th century. One of the earliest to arrive was CHARLES TAWS, who in 1786 advertised himself as a builder of "finger and barrel organs" in New York. He later moved to Philadelphia, where he was joined in 1795 by John Lowe, trained in the workshop of Gray of London. JOHN GEIB, trained in Germany and England, shortly after his arrival in New York around 1798 built several substantial church organs, most of them for that city.

2. THE 19TH CENTURY. None of the late 18th-century builders, whether foreign-trained or self-taught, seemed able to found a true "school" in their respective areas. None but Geib had familial successors (though Geib's sons soon abandoned organ building for the burgeoning piano trade). Yet in the first decades of the 19th century foundations were laid for two very important and influential centers of organ building in New York and Boston. The founder of the New York school was THOMAS S. HALL, who worked briefly for Lowe in Philadelphia before moving to New York in 1817. He soon secured substantial contracts in both New York and the coastal cities of the South; one of his largest instruments was built in 1820 for the Catholic cathedral of Baltimore. An early apprentice of Hall was his brother-in-law HENRY ERBEN, later briefly his partner, who in 1824 founded the firm that virtually dominated organ building in New York for 60 years, providing many organs there (notably the large 1847 one for Trinity Church) and in other cities.

The founder of the Boston school was WILLIAM MARCELLUS GOODRICH. Like other early New England builders, he was largely self-taught but had been briefly associated with Leavitt and Pratt as well as the piano maker

Organ, Fort Street Presbyterian Church, Detroit. (Library of Congress, Prints and Photographs Division, Detroit Publishing Company Collection, LC-D4-43831)

Crehore. He learned tuning from a French organist, metalworking from a pewterer, and virtually everything else from the study of English organs in Boston and a copy of Bédos de Celles' *L'art du facteur d'orgues* (1766–78). Goodrich began making chamber organs and claviorgans (known as "organized pianofortes") in 1804, and by his death in 1833 had built significant instruments for many churches in Boston and elsewhere as far south as Savannah, his largest being a three-manual organ completed in 1827 for St. Paul's Church, Boston. The entire next generation of Boston organ builders—Goodrich's brother Ebenezer, THOMAS APPLETON, George and William Stevens, Josiah H. Ware, and Elias and George Hook (*see* HOOK & HASTINGS)—were all trained in his workshop. Appleton, known for his handsome casework, eventually replaced Goodrich as the leading Boston organ builder, but was subsequently overtaken after 1850 by the Hook brothers and his own former apprentice, WILLIAM BENJAMIN DEARBORN SIMMONS.

For the first half of the 19th century, organ building in both New York and Boston was strongly influenced by late 18th- and early 19th-century English work. Specifications were conservative, manual compasses usually began at G below the C of the modern organ keyboard, pedals were of short compass or nonexistent, Swell divisions of short compass (from F or G below middle C), and until nearly 1850 variants of meantone tuning were in common use. Metal pipework was usually about 25% tin and 75% lead. Zinc for bass

pipes did not come into general use until after 1850; spotted metal (50% tin) did not begin to appear until after 1860. Around the mid-century New York once more saw an influx of immigrant builders. A few, notably GEORGE JARDINE and his sons, remained; others, such as Henry Pilcher and George Kilgen, worked there briefly before seeking their fortunes to the west.

Fewer immigrants settled in Boston, but several influential Boston organists returned from European study in the 1850s and 60s, bringing new ideas. Boston builders, particularly Simmons and the Hook brothers, studied European publications and experimented with new ideas from abroad. Pedal compasses increased, eventually to a standard 27 notes, and such stops as the Gamba and Harmonic Flute began to appear in specifications. Although the classic slider chest remained in use by most builders until the end of the 19th century, in 1859 Simmons experimented briefly with the use of cone-valve wind-chests. However, another recent European invention, the pneumatic-lever (Barker) action, was found very useful in larger organs, and both the Hook firm and Simmons had employed it by 1860. Developments in Boston soon spread to western Massachusetts, where they were adopted by such builders as WILLIAM ALLEN JOHNSON and JOHN WESLEY STEERE, whose trade was expanding into the northwestern states and included substantial contracts in Buffalo, Chicago, and elsewhere. Organ production increased steadily throughout the second half of the 19th century, spurred by urban growth and westward expansion. Beginning with an instrument by Hook for Tremont Temple, Boston (1853; four manuals, 70 stops), organs began to be installed in concert halls throughout the United States, and organ recitals (in both halls and churches) became popular. The importation of an organ from Walcker of Germany for Boston Music Hall in 1863 was in some ways anticlimactic, yet it introduced novelties such as free reeds, the Vox Humana stop, and the crescendo mechanism. It was followed by a Hook organ in Mechanics Hall, Worcester (1864), a Hook & Hastings in Cincinnati Music Hall (1878), a Roosevelt in Chicago Auditorium (1892), and others.

Organ building in Philadelphia had virtually stagnated by mid-century; John Standbridge and Henry Corrie, both British-born, were by then the only builders of any consequence there. In New York, however, Erben, Jardine, J.H. & C.S. ODELL, and Hall & Labagh were making important contributions, and in 1869 HILBORNE LEWIS ROOSEVELT, a 19-year-old former apprentice of Hall & Labagh, drew attention by exhibiting an organ with a primitive electrically operated action at an industrial fair. With his brother Frank he visited Europe to study the latest developments there, and founded his own company in 1872. Until his death in 1893 he was an uncontested pioneer among the New York builders.

German-born August Pomplitz and Henry Niemann of Baltimore were the only builders of consequence in the South, but during the second half of the 19th century organs were being built in the rapidly growing western cities as the frontier advanced. Nearly all the inland builders were also immigrants, including Matthias P. Möller, in Hagerstown, Maryland; John Gale

Marklove in Utica, New York; and Garrett House in Buffalo. German organ builders were active throughout the United States, beginning with Matthias Schwab and J.H. Koehnken, who were well established in Cincinnati before 1850. Later builders included A.B. Felgemaker in Buffalo; J.G. Pfeffer in St. Louis; WILLIAM SCHUELKE in Milwaukee; John HINNERS in Pekin, Illinois; G.F. Votteler, Carl Barckhoff, and Philip Wirsching in Ohio; and Joseph Mayer and Felix Schoenstein in California, the last an orchestrion maker who settled in San Francisco in 1877.

New tonal and technical resources continued to be developed in the large eastern factories, and their work reached all parts of the country. Simmons died in 1876 and was followed as one of the leaders of the Boston trade by George S. Hutchings, who had been trained at the firm of E. & G.G. Hook (known as HOOK & HASTINGS after 1871). Hutchings and Hook & Hastings, as well as Roosevelt in New York, were responsible for many of the developments that would shape the 20th-century organ. Farrand & Votey bought the Roosevelt firm in 1893 and merged with Aeolian of Garwood, New Jersey, in 1897; having patented many improvements in organ mechanism, Votey turned increasingly to automatic instruments. ERNEST M. SKINNER, who had worked in Hutchings's factory, invented the "pitman" type of electro-pneumatic wind-chest and was a strong proponent of orchestral tonal design. At the turn of the century this influential builder was joined by two innovative builders from England: JOHN TURNELL AUSTIN, who founded an organ company in Hartford, Connecticut on the strength of his unique "universal air chest" designs, and ROBERT HOPE-JONES, whose iconoclastic tonal and mechanical designs led to his later becoming known as "the father of the theater organ."

3. THE 20TH CENTURY. The early 20th century was a period of great change and much tonal and mechanical experimentation. Electrically controlled key and stop actions soon superseded all earlier forms, including mechanical and pneumatic-lever ones, and the intermediate types of tubular-pneumatic action initially developed by John W. Steere, ESTEY ORGAN CO., and KIMBALL. Transcriptions of orchestral works and compositions in the orchestral style assumed great prominence in the repertory, and for a few decades the organ was popularly regarded more as an imitator of the orchestra than an instrument with its own characteristic sound and literature. Secular use of the organ was widespread—in concert halls and ballrooms, at trade fairs and expositions, and perhaps most significantly in theaters and residences (see THEATER ORGAN). Hope-Jones devised means for making a few sets of pipes do service at several pitches on different manuals and named his creation the "unit orchestra"; his patents ultimately were assigned to the WURLITZER firm, which, along with Robert Morton and others, built thousands of organs of this type (usually with elaborate sound-effects) for movie theaters during the silent film era. The AEOLIAN CO. had become the leading maker of domestic player organs, often sizable and with elaborate consoles. Concert

Hall organs proliferated in the early 20th century, and Kimball, Skinner, Möller, Kilgen, and Austin built a number of these, some of which, for example, the 1911 Austin in the City Hall of Portland, Maine, are still in regular use. Size sometimes became an end in itself, resulting in huge organs such as those in the grand court of the department store of John Wanamaker & Co. in Philadelphia, and the Convention Hall in Atlantic City, New Jersey.

The theater organ era ended around 1930 with the introduction of the film soundtrack, and the reversal of fortunes caused by the Depression coupled with the technical progress of the phonograph and radio virtually eliminated the market for domestic player organs. In this same period a younger generation of organists—among them E. POWER BIGGS, CARL WEINRICH, MELVILLE SMITH, ERNEST WHITE, and Arthur Howes—began to be concerned with the loss of the organ's historical repertory, particularly the contrapuntal music of Bach, for which the orchestral organ was an inappropriate vehicle. Influenced by Albert Schweitzer's writings and the growing European "organ reform" movement, they actively advocated a return to a more eclectic organ design, incorporating a completely developed principal chorus along with reeds and flutes consciously based on historical concepts, while retaining some stops of a more Romantic-period nature.

Certain prominent organ builders and voicers, including Walter Holtkamp, Sr. (see HOLTKAMP ORGAN CO.), G. Donald Harrison of the AEOLIAN-SKINNER ORGAN CO., and Richard Whitelegg of the Möller firm, received encouragement for experimentation along "reformed" tonal lines in the 1930s. Holtkamp went even further, becoming an early and influential advocate of slider chests and the open, unencumbered placement of pipes. Between 1937 and 1940 Harrison built a few small unenclosed organs of severely classical tonal design, one of which, in the Germanic (now Busch-Reisinger) Museum at Harvard University, achieved widespread acceptance through its use for many years in E. Power Biggs's Sunday morning radio broadcasts. Biggs, an outspoken advocate of organ reform, also made recordings on this organ and encouraged contemporary composers to write for it.

Progress was suspended during World War II because of restrictions on necessary materials; organ factories had to restrict themselves to rebuilding, or convert to production of war material, and some firms closed. In the late 1940s and early 50s, however, the eclectic "American Classic" tonal design developed in the 1930s was becoming the standard for the older firms, and many important organs, such as the 1949 Aeolian-Skinner in Boston's Symphony Hall, were still built to this model. The reform movement, however, received new impetus from organists and builders who had visited the historic organs of Europe while on duty with the occupation forces, as well as from a younger generation of organists who studied abroad under Fulbright grants. Several of these organists, along with some of the younger organ builders, felt that tonal reform was not enough, and that classic principles of mechanical action, wind systems, and casework were also important musically. Significant imported organs by leading European "reform" builders such as Dirk Flentrop and Rudolf von Beckerath earned additional converts to the reform cause. Flentrop's first major organ in the United States was built for the Busch-Reisinger Museum at Harvard University in 1958, and other Flentrop instruments of the 1960s and 70s included organs for St. Mark's Cathedral, Seattle; Salem College, Winston-Salem, North Carolina; Warner Hall, Oberlin Conservatory, Oberlin, Ohio; and Duke University Chapel, Durham, North Carolina. Beckerath's work in that period included organs for Trinity Lutheran Church, Cleveland, Ohio; St. Paul's Cathedral, Pittsburgh; and Dwight Chapel, Yale University.

The challenge of the reform cause was first taken up in the United States by less-established and younger builders. Otto Hofmann's all-mechanical encased organ of 1956 in Matthews Memorial Church, Albany, Texas, and CHARLES BRENTON FISK's similar though larger instrument of 1961 in Mt. Calvary Church, Baltimore, Maryland, were early landmarks that attracted much attention. Such builders were shortly followed by FRITZ NOACK and JOHN BROMBAUGH, both of whom had European training. By the mid-1960s the larger companies, less flexible in their production methods, began to heed the trend, and certain of them—notably Schlicker (see HERMAN L. SCHLICKER), Casavant, and later Holtkamp— began to produce a few classically conceived mechanical-action organs in addition to electric-action ones. With few exceptions (notably Fisk's eclectic 1967 instrument for Memorial Church, Harvard University), these American "reform" instruments at first tended to emulate the rather strict "neo-Baroque" style of contemporary European examples. During the 1970s organists and organ builders alike became aware of a greater need to study the historic instruments of all countries and periods. Brombaugh and Fisk were among the first to do so, soon to be followed by younger builders such as TAYLOR & BOODY, GENE R. BEDIENT, MANUEL J. ROSALES, HELLMUTH WOLFF, GEORGE BOZEMAN JR., PAUL BYARD FRITTS, LYNN A. DOBSON, MARTIN PASI, Juget-Sinclair, and Richards & Fowkes, among others. This study resulted in both the conscious copying of historic examples (primarily for educational institutions) and a new kind of eclecticism, particularly evident in some of these builders' larger instruments, in which Renaissance, German Baroque, French classic, and 19th-century Romantic tonal elements are harmoniously combined.

A particular avenue opened to exploration in the late 1970s was that of temperament. Interest in the authentic performance of early keyboard music initiated a growing concern with various historical unequal temperaments. Tunings such as Werckmeister, Chaumont, and Kirnberger were gaining acceptance and being used by many builders of mechanical-action organs, along with their own "shop" temperaments; some of these builders now tune even sizable instruments in some form of "compromise" temperaments, as well as in the traditional equal-beating temperament. Although intended mainly for didactic purposes, instruments with subsemitone keys have been built by Brombaugh

(Oberlin College, Ohio, 1981), Fisk (Wellesley College, Massachusetts, 1981), and others.

Among the larger firms that have continued to work mostly with electro-pneumatic action—Schantz, Möller, Holtkamp, Austin, Reuter, Casavant, as well as newer ones such as BUZARD and QUIMBY—a similar eclecticism of tonal design is evident, but one more strongly rooted in the "American classic" style of the 1950s and 60s and more influenced by the "Romantic revival" of the early 1980s. A renewed interest in the early 20th century "symphonic" aesthetic emerged during the 1990s, its strongest proponent being the SCHOENSTEIN firm of San Francisco, which has built several substantial organs in this style, both for churches and concert halls.

The early decades of the 21st century have witnessed the side-by-side production in North America of high quality organs in almost every style, from the most severely authentic historical reproductions to modern eclectic instruments incorporating several tonal influences, with mechanical, electro-pneumatic, or solid-state actions (or combinations of these). The best of these contemporary organs represent a modern-day flowering of the ancient art of organ building, and have in common refined voicing tailored to specific acoustical environments, well-engineered and responsive mechanical design, and artistic visual design in both traditional and contemporary styles.

See also BAND ORGAN; CONCERT ORGAN; ORGAN MUSIC; PLAYER ORGAN; REED ORGAN; THEATER ORGAN.

BIBLIOGRAPHY

Grove7

The Great Organ in Boston Music Hall (Boston, 1865)

G.W. Nichols: *The Cincinnati Organ* (Cincinnati, 1878)

H. Lahee: *The Organ and its Masters* (Boston, 1902)

G.L. Miller: *The Recent Revolution in Organ Building* (New York, 1909/R)

R. Hope-Jones: *Recent Developments of Organ Building* (North Tonawanda, NY, 1910)

E.M. Skinner: *The Modern Organ* (New York, 1917)

G.A. Audsley: *The Organ of the Twentieth Century* (New York, 1919/R)

W.H. Barnes: *The Contemporary American Organ* (Glen Rock, NJ, 1930)

E.W. Flint: *The Newberry Memorial Organ at Yale University* (New Haven, CT, 1930/R)

C.G. Vardell: *Organs in the Wilderness* (Winston-Salem, NC, 1944)

F.R. Orr: *Twentieth Century Organ Design in America* (thesis, Northwestern U., 1954)

V.A. Bradley: *Music for the Millions: the Kimball Piano and Organ Story* (Chicago, 1957)

T.W. Dean: *The Organ in Eighteenth Century English Colonial America* (diss., U. of Southern California, 1960)

J.E. Blanton: *The Revival of the Organ Case* (Albany, TX, 1965)

B. Owen: *The Organs and Music of King's Chapel* (Boston, 1966)

W.H. Armstrong: *Organs for America: the Life and Work of David Tannenberg* (Philadelphia, 1967)

P.A. Getz: *Organ Mixtures in Contemporary American Practice* (diss., U. of Rochester, 1967)

J. Johnson: *Henry Erben, American Organ Builder: a Survey of his Life and Works* (thesis, Yale U., 1968)

W.H. Barnes and E.B. Gammons: *Two Centuries of American Organ Building* (Glen Rock, NJ, 1970)

J.R. Sharp: *Tonal Design of the American Organ, 1910–1969* (diss., Michigan State U., 1970)

W.J. Beasley: *The Organ in America, as Portrayed in Dwight's Journal of Music* (diss., U. of Southern California, 1971)

J.T. Fesperman: *Two Essays on Organ Design* (Raleigh, NC, 1975)

O. Ochse: *The History of the Organ in the United States* (Bloomington, IN, 1975)

B.W. Downward: *G. Donald Harrison and the American Classic Organ* (diss., Eastman School of Music, 1976)

A.F. Robinson, ed.: *The Bicentennial Tracker* (Wilmington, OH, 1976)

J. Ogasapian: *Organ Building in New York City, 1700–1900* (Braintree, MA, 1977)

L.J. Schoenstein: *Memoirs of a San Francisco Organ Builder* (San Francisco, 1977)

U. Pape: *The Tracker Organ Revival in America* (Berlin, 1978)

J.A. Ferguson: *Walter Holtkamp: American Organ Builder* (Kent, OH, 1979)

B. Owen: *The Organ in New England* (Raleigh, NC, 1979)

J.T. Fesperman: *Organs in Mexico* (Raleigh, NC, 1980)

J. Ogasapian: *Henry Erben: Portrait of a 19th Century American Organ Builder* (Braintree, MA, 1980)

U. Pape: *Organs in America*, i (Berlin, 1980)

J.T. Fesperman: *Flentrop in America* (Raleigh, NC, 1982)

M.D. Coffey: *Charles Fisk: Organ Builder* (diss., Eastman School of Music, 1984)

J.V.V. Elsworth: *The Johnson Organs* (Harrisville, NH, 1984)

U. Pape: *Organs in America*, ii (Berlin, 1984)

D.J. Holden: *The Life & Work of Ernest M. Skinner* (Richmond, VA, 1985)

S.L. Pinel: *Old Organs of Princeton* (Harrisville, NH, 1989)

R.J. Brunner: *"That Ingenious Business:" Pennsylvania German Organ Builders* (Birdsboro, PA, 1990)

C. Callahan, ed.: *The American Classic Organ: a History in Letters* (Richmond, VA, 1990)

B. Owen: *The Mormon Tabernacle Organ: an American Classic* (Salt Lake City, 1990)

D.H. Fox: *A Guide to North American Organbuilders* (Richmond, VA, 1991)

L. Edwards, ed.: *The Historical Organ in America* (Easthampton, MA, 1992).

K.J. Raudsepp: *Organs of Montreal* (Montreal, 1993)

J.O. Wilkes: *Pipe Organs of Ann Arbor* (Ann Arbor, MI, 1995)

R. Biswanger: *Music in the Marketplace* (Bryn Mawr, PA, 1999)

W.B. Clarke and J.A. Royal: *Organs of Savannah* (Savannah, GA, 2000)

A.M. Laufman: *Pipe Organs of Arlington, Massachusetts* (Harrisville, NH, 2000)

C.A. Traupman-Carr, ed.: *"Pleasing for Our Use." David Tannenberg and the Organs of the Moravians* (Bethlehem, PA, 2000)

O. Ochse: *Austin Organs* (Richmond, VA, 2001)

D.R. Traser: *The Organ in Richmond* (Richmond, VA, 2001)

C.R. Whitney: *All the Stops: the Glorious Pipe Organ and its American Masters* (New York, 2003)

J. Parkinson-Tucker: *Behind the Pipes: the Story of the Kotzschmar Organ* (South Portland, ME, 2005)

C.W. McManis: *Wanted: One Crate of Lions* (Richmond, VA, 2008)

J. Lewis: *Organs in the Land of Sunshine* (Richmond, VA, 2009)

J. Lewis: *The King of Instruments in the Crown City* (South Freeport, ME, 2009)

L. Luberoff: *The Organ Industry Takeover* (Richmond, VA, 2010)

B. Owen: *Music on the Green* (Richmond, VA, 2010)

S.L. Pinel: *Organbuilding along the Erie and Chenango Canals* (Richmond, VA, 2010)

J. Lewis: *Mr. Searles and the Organ* (Richmond, VA, 2011)

B. Owen: *The Great Organ at Methuen* (Richmond, VA, 2011)

D.H Fox: *Hilborne and Frank Roosevelt* (Richmond, VA, 2012)

J. Lewis: *Forgotten Organ Builders of Old California* (Exeter, NH, 2012)

BARBARA OWEN

Organ Historical Society [OHS]. American-based society with international membership promoting musical and historical interest in American organ building through collection, preservation, and publication of historical information and via recordings and public concerts. Founded 1956, incorporated 1961, and headquartered in Richmond, Virginia, the Society formed its American Organ Archives in 1961, storing them first at the Historical Society of York County, Pennsylvania; then in 1967 at the library of Ohio Wesleyan University in Delaware, Ohio; and in 1984 at Talbott Library, Westminster Choir College, Rider University, Princeton, New Jersey. The Archives, now employing an archivist and directed by its own board of governors, has become the largest repository of organ research materials in the world. *The Tracker* is the quarterly journal of the Society and is one of the publications of the OHS Press, overseen by a board of governors and director of publications. The Historic Organs Citations Program recognizes pipe organs deemed to be of historical value and worthy of preservation, while the Phoenix Project is the Society's initiative to help preserve unwanted or displaced organs. The Society's convention relocates annually to visit and hear performances on American organs of particular merit.

ALLISON A. ALCORN

Organization of American Kodály Educators [OAKE]. Professional organization for Kodály teachers. The organization's goal is to enrich the quality of life in the United States through music education following the principles set forth by Hungarian composer and educator ZOLTÁN KODÁLY (1882–1967). Kodály devoted a significant portion of his creative endeavors to the musical education of the Hungarian nation, and the approach bearing his name is based on his work and that of his students. He believed that the acquisition of basic musical skills is the right of every individual. In the Kodály approach comprehensive musicianship is nurtured through the teaching of musical literacy. The approach is vocally based, with folk songs of the culture as the repertoire and solfège as the basic teaching methodology. Only music of the highest quality is used in teaching and the approach is highly sequential in presenting musical concepts. Established in 1975, OAKE is affiliated with the International Kodály Society. The organization holds annual national conferences, has local chapters that sponsor workshops for teachers, reviews teaching standards for Kodály training programs, and supports the *Kodály Envoy,* a quarterly journal founded in 1974. Auditioned children's and youth choirs are features of the national conferences.

ALAN L. SPURGEON

Organ music. Before the end of the 18th century little organ music was written in America owing to a lack of viable instruments and Calvinist proscriptions of instrumental music in their churches. The continuous arrival of European immigrants began to change this situation as they began assuming positions in the more important churches of the eastern seaboard cities with increasingly imposing instruments. Notable musicians such as William Selby, Benjamin Carr, Raynor Taylor, Francis Linley, Henry C. Timm, Edward Hodges, Samuel P. Jackson, A.W. Haytor, Charles Zeuner, and John Zundel wrote modest voluntaries on the English model, variation sets, and pedagogical works, of which little was substantial.

During the final four decades of the 19th century the situation changed radically. John Knowles Paine, a seminal figure, was a practicing organist who received advanced training in Germany and then at home promoted the works of Bach, Mendelssohn, and Louis Thiele. Paine, the first American composer who successfully cultivated the classical German forms of symphony and sonata, wrote large-scale works for the organ, particularly variation sets, but also one-movement character pieces intended either for use in church or recital. Paine's teacher in Berlin, Karl-August Haupt and others, such as Joseph Rheinberger in Munich, served as mentors to several generations of American organist-composers; their more prominent pupils included Thayer, Buck, Whiting, Chadwick, and Parker (Foote remained at home but received similar training in Boston under Paine). These German-trained composers produced for the organ a considerable body of sonatas, suites, and variation sets, as well as preludes and postludes, canzonettas, impromptus, romanzas, and "concert pieces." Mendelssohn was at first their implicit model, but hints of Wagnerian chromaticism gradually intruded, and some eventually came to an awareness of what was referred to as "the modern French school." The more long-lived, however, never managed to reconcile themselves to 20th-century innovations, maintaining a retrospective stance to the end. This same pattern prevailed with lesser lights, such as James H. Rogers and others of his contemporaries.

After about 1890 the growing fascination with the French symphonic style of Franck and his followers supplanted the Germanic orientation. Prominent recitalists competed to play the first American performances of the new symphonies of Widor. Guilmant was invited by Clarence Eddy to headline the group of organists engaged to give a series of 62 recitals at the 1893 World's Columbian Exposition in Chicago; increasing numbers of Americans went to Paris to study with Widor, Guilmant, and Joseph Bonnet. In 1899 Guilmant's disciples even established an organ school in New York named after him intended for those unable to travel abroad. French influence was also mirrored in the organ symphonies, splashy toccatas, and evocative program works of composers such as Clarence Dickinson, Eric DeLamarter, Seth Bingham, and Garth Edmundson.

The fashion for explicitly programmatic music coincided with the development of instruments that incorporated simulated orchestral sounds. An especially popular example was Alexander Russell's suite-like *St. Lawrence Sketches* (1921). The trend perhaps reached its apex in the works of Ray Spalding Stoughton, whose Persian and Egyptian suites are almost outrageously vivid in their descriptiveness. The impulse to explore the organ's new coloristic possibilities resulted in many more transcriptions of instrumental works, a category that at least decorated or dominated recital (even church) programs into the 1930s. Long derided, this literature has in recent years found new favor. Some virtuosos specialized in rousing versions of the overture to Rossini's *William Tell*, or in storm pieces so suggestive that

listeners reputedly reached for their umbrellas. The work of Europeans such as William T. Best predominated at first, but soon Americans such as Samuel P. Warren, Samuel A. Baldwin, and English-born Edwin Lemare acquired a reputation for their skillful and often dazzling borrowings, particularly from Wagner. The evolution of the "orchestral" instrument reached its culmination in the theater organ, which enjoyed its heyday in America during the 1920s and 30s, when movie palaces across the country were fitted with "mighty Wurlitzers," or comparable instruments by other builders. With the great advantage over an orchestra of being able to extemporize, skilled theater organists could provide individualized accompaniments for silent films, often eliciting as much admiration as the films themselves.

Even while German and then French idioms dominated the field, British influence remained strong in the realm of church music. The larger Episcopal churches sometimes called on Englishmen such as T. Tertius Noble to introduce musical practices based on the British cathedral traditions. The hymn-tune preludes of Joseph Clokey, Everett Titcomb, and others satisfied a widespread need for such literature. Leo Sowerby was surely the most important composer to work within this tradition, evolving an entirely personal idiom in his diverse preludes and meditations on hymn melodies; he also made important contributions to the concert literature with one-movement display pieces, a suite and symphony, chamber music with organ, and several concerted pieces for organ and orchestra.

A number of prominent 20th-century composers, although not themselves organists, composed for the instrument. The important Contemporary Organ Series from the H.W. Gray Company included works by Copland, Piston, Sessions, Cowell, Quincy Porter, Ulysses Kay, and Douglas Moore, none of whom wrote more than a handful of organ pieces; to these names might be added Roy Harris, Luening, Barber, Menotti, Dello Joio, Finney, and Bassett. Despite his experience as a church organist, Ives wrote little organ music, and his quirky *Variations on America* (1891) is equally well known in its orchestral transcription by William Schuman.

However, others have created a more considerable repertory for the instrument. Virgil Thomson, a practicing organist early in his career and often mentioned only for his irreverent *Variations on Sunday-school Tunes* (1926–7), wrote more sober pieces in his lean, transparent idiom during that same decade and later. Daniel Pinkham, a successor of Thomson's at King's Chapel in Boston, left an immense number of organ works, ranging from utilitarian service music to substantial recital pieces in several movements, which often have a programmatic intent; they employ an austere neoclassical idiom, but later demonstrate the influence of serialism. During the 1970s Pinkham, Richard Feliciano, and others experimented in combining prerecorded sounds with those made live at the organ.

A substantial body of chamber music for conventional instruments with organ has been produced by

Pinkham, as well as Piston, Hovhaness, Rayner Brown, Samuel Adler, and others. Americans also seem to have developed a special predilection for works for solo organ with orchestral accompaniment: Parker, Dunham, DeLamarter, Dickinson, Bingham, Pinkham, Hanson, Harris, Copland, and Barber.

Other mainstream figures who have contributed to the organ repertory include Persichetti, Rorem, Libby Larsen, Stephen Paulus, and Conrad Susa. Experienced organists who in recent decades have added to the literature include William Albright, William Bolcom, Dan Locklair, Pamela Decker, Emma Lou Diemer, and Calvin Hampton. A cross-section of this literature can be found in *The AGO 90th-Anniversary Anthology of American Organ Music* (1988).

Although much of the recent repertoire for the instrument remains tradition-bound, some have written in advanced idioms employing spatial notation, tone clusters, aleatory techniques, and antimetrical rhythms, sometimes, particularly with Albright and Bolcom, combining their often witty musical language with an awareness of more traditional modes of expression. Others have attempted to exploit the organ as a sound source, achieving effects similar to those available on a synthesizer.

The American bicentennial provoked several anthologies of American organ music, including Beck and Woomer's *A Collection of 19th-century American Organ Music* (1975), Hart's *American Organ Music: a Glance at the Past 100 Years* (2 vols., 1975), and Owen's *A Century of American Organ Music (1776–1876)* (3 vols., 1975–83).

For works by Hailstork, Hancock, Hurd, Walker, and others, see M.T. Terry's six-volume *African-American Organ Music Anthology* (2000–6).

BIBLIOGRAPHY
GMO

B. Owen: "American Organ Music and Playing, from 1700," *Organ Institute Quarterly*, x/3 (1963), 7–13

W. Osborne: "Five New England Gentlemen," *Music: the AGO and RCCO Magazine*, iii/8 (1969), 27–9

M.S. Anderson: *"The Organ without a Master": a Survey of Nineteenth-century Organ Instruction Books in the United States* (diss., U. of Minnesota, 1977)

B. Owen: *The Organ in New England* (Raleigh, NC, 1979)

M. Kratzenstein: *A Survey of Organ Literature and Editions* (Ames, IA, 1980)

J.B. Clark: "American Organ Music Before 1830," *The Diapason*, lxxii/11 (1981), 1–3

P.B. Curtis: *American Organ Music North of Philadelphia before 1860: Selected Problems and an Annotated Bibliography* (diss., Manhattan School of Music, 1981)

C.R. Arnold: *Organ Literature: a Comprehensive Survey* (Metuchen, NJ, 2/1984)

M.C. Munday: *A Selected Bibliography of Solo Organ Works by Black Composers* (diss., Florida State U., 1992)

L.P. Spelman and J.R. Engquist: *Organ Plus: a Catalogue of Ensemble Music for Organ with other Instruments* (New York, 4/1992)

M.T. Terry: "African-American Organ Literature: a Selective Overview," *The Diapason*, lxxxvii/4 (1996), 14–17

S.L. Hettinger: *American Organ Music of the 20th Century* (Warren, MI, 1997)

WILLIAM OSBORNE

Orientalism. *See* EXOTICISM.

Original Dixieland Jazz (Jass) Band [ODJB]. Jazz ensemble. Organized in Chicago after the breakup of Stein's Dixieland Jass Band, a group of New Orleans musicians recruited by the drummer Johnny Stein (15 June 1891/5–30 Sept 1962) for a job at the Schiller Café in Chicago in March 1916, the Original Dixieland Jazz Band is generally credited as the first band to make a jazz record. Shortly after the band had arrived in Chicago, the cornetist Nick LaRocca (11 April 1889–22 Feb 1961), the trombonist Eddie Edwards (22 May 1891–9 April 1963), the pianist Henry Ragas (1891–18 Feb 1919), and the clarinetist Alcide "Yellow" Nunez (17 March 1884–2 Sept 1934) abandoned Stein and recruited another New Orleans drummer, Tony Sbarbaro (27 June 1897–30 Oct 1969), to replace him. In October 1916 Larry Shields (13 Sept 1893–21 Nov 1953), a refugee from Tom Brown's Band from Dixieland, replaced Nunez on clarinet, thus completing the lineup for the Original Dixieland Jass Band that would record in New York four months later.

Success performing at cabarets and theaters in Chicago brought them to the attention of the booking agent Max Hart, who arranged an engagement at Reisenweber's Restaurant in New York for January 1917, by which time LaRocca had become de facto leader. According to LaRocca, audience reaction was negative until he demonstrated how to dance to the music, after which the group attracted large and enthusiastic crowds, initiating a jazz craze. Given the band's burgeoning popularity, the Columbia Phonograph Company and the Victor Talking Machine Company became interested in recording the band. Columbia struck first, but the audition went badly when its engineers failed to achieve a satisfactory blending of instruments with the acoustical equipment available. On 26 February 1917 Victor's engineer Charles Sooy solved the problem by experimenting with the placement of musicians vis-à-vis the pick-up horns, leading to the commercial release of "Dixie Jass Band One-Step/Livery Stable Blues" within days of the recording. Estimates that the record sold more than 1.5 million copies are difficult to verify, but an advertisement in the New Orleans *Times–Picayune* in April 1917 provides insight into its immediate impact on the popular imagination: "Here is positively the greatest dance record ever issued. Made by New Orleans musicians for New Orleans people, it has all the 'swing' and 'pep' and 'spirit' that is so characteristic of the bands whose names are a by-word at New Orleans dances." This description of the music as being "characteristic" of New Orleans bands contradicts LaRocca's subsequent claims to have been the sole "originator" of jazz, a position that has diminished the Original Dixieland Jazz Band's credibility among critics and historians despite the enduring appeal of such compositions as "Skeleton Jangle," "Tiger Rag," "Bluin' the Blues," "Sensation Rag," "Fidgety Feet," and "Clarinet Marmalade Blues" (all 1918, Vic.), most of which became staples of the traditional jazz repertoire.

Following its initial success in disseminating New Orleans jazz, the Original Dixieland Jazz Band was afflicted by a series of personnel changes occasioned by

World War I (Edwards was drafted), the concomitant influenza pandemic (Ragas died and was replaced by J. Russel Robinson, 8 July 1892–30 Sept 1963), a tour of England (1919–20), record company machinations, and a moralistic backlash directed against jazz, culminating with LaRocca's retirement in 1925 after he suffered a nervous breakdown. An initially promising comeback intended to challenge Benny Goodman's status as the "King of Swing" with new recordings for RCA in 1936 ended prematurely with a letter from LaRocca dissolving the band because of "internal friction" in January 1938.

See also DIXIELAND JAZZ.

SELECTED RECORDINGS

Livery Stable Blues (1917, Vic.); Clarinet Marmalade Blues (1918, Vic.); Sensation Rag (1918, Vic.); Tiger Rag (1918, Vic.); Sphinx (1920, CoE); Margie (1920, Vic.); Jazz me Blues (1921, Vic.); Original Dixieland One-Step/Barnyard Blues (1936, Vic.)

BIBLIOGRAPHY

H.O. Brunn: *The Story of the Original Dixieland Jazz Band* (Baton Rouge, LA, 1960/R)
L. Abbott: "'Brown Skin, Who You For?' Another Look at Clarence Williams's Early Career," *The Jazz Archivist*, viii/1–2 (1993), 1–15
R.M. Sudhalter: *Lost Chords: White Musicians and their Contributions to Jazz, 1915–1945* (New York, 1999), 3–27
J. Stewart: "The Original Dixieland Jazz Band's Place in the Development of Jazz," *The Jazz Archivist*, no.19 (2005–06), 16–25

BRUCE BOYD RAEBURN

Original Gospel Harmonettes. Female gospel ensemble. It was formed in Birmingham, Alabama, in 1940 and became a leading African American gospel group in the 1950s. The original members were pianist Evelyn Starks, first soprano Vera Conner Kolb, second soprano Mildred Madison Miller, first alto Willie Mae Brooks Newberry, and second alto Odessa Glasgow Edwards. It began as the Gospel Harmoneers and later became the Gospel Harmonettes. To distinguish it from lesser-known groups performing under the name, it changed again to the Original Gospel Harmonettes. The group became known regionally from singing for a half-hour weekly radio program, an engagement that lasted a year. The first recording in 1949 with Miller as the main lead singer yielded little results. When the group recorded again in 1951, Birmingham native Dorothy McGriff Love—wife of Willie Love of the Fairfield Four—was recruited. Love proved to be a formidable singer and songwriter, which led to several successful recordings during the 1950s. Later, Love married Carl Coates of the Sensational Nightingales, changing her name to DOROTHY LOVE COATES. Known for her Pentecostal-style emotionalism and preacher-like delivery, her presence was so dominant that the group was often called Dorothy Love Coates and the Original Gospel Harmonettes. Following the group's retirement near the end of the 1950s, Coates organized the Dorothy Love Coates Singers and continued to perform throughout the 1960s.

BIBLIOGRAPHY

H.C. Boyer: *How Sweet the Sound: the Golden Age of Gospel* (Washington, DC, 1995)

B. Carpenter: *Uncloudy Days: the Gospel Music Encyclopedia* (San Francisco, 2005)

CEDRIC DENT

Orioles, the. The beginnings of the Orioles' career entwine a memorable personal narrative with the origins of doo-wop. An 18-year-old, Baltimore-based, white Jewish woman, Deborah Chessler, was passionate about songwriting, but devoid of any strategy as to how to achieve success. She had sold a song, "Tell Me So," to the African American vocalist Savannah Churchill, but the record came and went without a trace. In 1948 a friend interceded and alerted Chessler to a local vocal ensemble, the Vibranaires, which lead vocalist Sonny Til had formed around 1947. She contacted them and the group auditioned over the phone, convincing Chessler to become their agent. She subsequently contacted Jerry Blaine, the owner of Jubilee Records, who signed the group and changed their name to the Orioles, the state bird of Maryland. Chessler wrote songs for the group, including "It's too soon to know," composed expediently on a scroll of toilet paper. The record was released in November 1948, and reportedly sold 30,000 the first week. It quickly rose to no.1 on the national rhythm & blues charts and crossed over to no.13 on the pop charts; it also received cover recordings by the Ravens, Ella Fitzgerald, and Dinah Washington. Equally important was the fact that while the Orioles achieved crossover success, they were marketed explicitly to a black urban audience, many of whom idolized lead singer Til. However, a car accident in 1950 devastated the group, as guitarist Tommy Gaither was killed and other members severely injured. The Orioles rebounded and achieved another career plateau in 1953, when their cover version of Darrell Glenn's country song "Crying in the Chapel" went to no.1 on the rhythm & blues charts for five weeks and ascended to no.11 on the pop charts. Chessler left the group as manager in 1955, and the group disbanded a year later. Subsequent reunions failed to achieve success, yet their meteoric rise, establishment of a novel vocal genre, and unique relationship with Chessler guarantees the Orioles a place in music history. They were inducted into the Rock & Roll Hall of Fame in 1995.

BIBLIOGRAPHY

G. Marcus, ed.: "The Debra Chessler Story," *The Dustbin of History* (Cambridge, MA, 1995), 225–40

DAVID SANJEK

Orion String Quartet. String quartet. Formed in 1987, the Orion String Quartet consists of Todd and Daniel Phillips, brothers who alternate on first and second violin, violist Steven Tenenbom, and cellist Timothy Eddy. The ensemble is a member of The Chamber Music Society of Lincoln Center, quartet-in-residence at the Mannes College of Music, and resident quartet at Indiana University's Jacobs School of Music. The OSQ's members teach at the Mannes College of Music, Curtis Institute of Music, The Juilliard School, Queens College, Rutgers University, and the Bard College Conservatory of Music. In addition to holding invited residencies, they also participate as faculty at the Isaac Stern Chamber Music Workshop at Carnegie Hall and the Summer Institute for Advanced Quartet Studies in Aspen.

The OSQ, known for its diverse repertoire, performs over 50 concerts every year and has released 11 recordings. The ensemble's 1999 Sony Classical recording with Wynton Marsalis featured his first classical composition for strings, *At the Octoroon Balls* (String Quartet no.1). On the Arabesque label, the OSQ recorded Dvořák's "American" String Quartet and Piano Quintet with Peter Serkin and Mendelssohn's Octet with the Guarneri String Quartet. For Koch in 2006 the ensemble recorded Chick Corea's *The Adventures of Hippocrates*, John Harbison's Quartet no.4, and Marc Neikrug's Piano Quintet. In 2010 the OSQ released the premiere recording of Peter Lieberson's Piano Quintet with Peter Serkin on Bridge Records. The OSQ has recorded all of the Beethoven string quartets on Koch, and the complete string quartets of Leon Kirchner on Albany Records.

JAMES BASH

Orlando. City in Florida (pop. 238,300; metropolitan area: 2,134,411; 2010 US Census). Incorporated in 1876, it soon anchored a prosperous citrus-growing and resort area. Following World War II, aerospace industries emerged, initiating growth that exploded with the opening of Walt Disney World in 1971. Today, Orlando is one of the world's leading tourist destinations in a region of over two million inhabitants.

Orlando's 19th-century musical activities were limited. Built in 1875–6, the Court House was the first site of public performances, and the Opera House (erected 1884), the city's first amusement hall, hosted "home talent shows." In 1886 the Orlando Cornet Band organized with 15 members, and its appearances at statewide events garnered positive notices for the city. Following reorganization of the county in 1887, the school board ordered that music be included in the public schools' daily instruction. In about 1900 several private schools also included music in their curricula.

In the 20th century, art music began to thrive on the support of Orlando's leading citizens, notably citrus magnate Philip Phillips, who hosted performances by visiting opera stars and chamber music groups in his own home. In 1909, the Mendelssohn Club, which gave recitals and even Gilbert and Sullivan operettas with piano accompaniment, was organized, and the women's Wednesday Music Club (founded 1919) was active into the late 1950s. As early as 1910, Phillips supported concerts in the Lucerne Theatre, and in 1917 he built the Phillips Theatre. The Beacham Theatre opened in 1921 as a vaudeville house but also hosted operas in its early years. It later became a movie theater and occasional hall for popular concerts. Orlando's Municipal Auditorium was built in 1925–6 as a traditional concert hall, and the renovated structure, renamed for music-supporting mayor Bob Carr, continues as of 2011.

During the era of segregation, Orlando had separate facilities, including the Lincoln Theatre (opened 1937), for African Americans. South Street Casino (opened 1924) featured such "Chitlin Circuit" performers as Count Basie, Cab Calloway, Ray Charles, and Ella Fitzgerald and succeeded chiefly on the initiative of William Monroe Wells—one of Orlando's first African American physicians and civic leaders. In 1926 he erected the Wells'Built Hotel next to the casino for African American travelers. Similar venues, including the Sunshine Club, Elks Club, Club Eaton, Two Spot, and Club 436, also benefited from proximity to Wells's hotel.

From about 1937 to at least 1972, classical artists of international stature were brought to the area by the Central Florida Civic Music Association. The Orlando Community Concert Association (later the Festival of Orchestras) operated similarly from 1984 until 2011. Orchestral music was provided by volunteer ensembles until the Florida Symphony organized in 1950 under music director Yves Chardon; two years later it became Florida's first fully professional orchestra, lasting until 1993. Within two years, the defunct ensemble was reorganized as the Orlando Philharmonic, with musicians having greater control over operations.

The Orlando Opera began with a singers' gala performance sponsored by the Junior League in 1958; its first fully mounted production was Giacomo Puccini's *La bohème* in 1963. The group reached a high point in 1988 with the appearance of Luciano Pavarotti, but bankruptcy closed the company in 2009. Founded in 1935 at Rollins College, the 160-voice, volunteer Bach Festival Society of Winter Park offers the third-oldest Bach festival in the United States annually.

Post-secondary music education is found locally at the University of Central Florida (BA, BM, BME, and MA) and Rollins College (BA) and at Stetson University (BM and BME) in nearby DeLand.

Orlando's tourist industry provides regular work for a sizable corps of commercial musicians who perform at amusements such as Disney World, corporate events, and restaurants. A small, vibrant independent music scene revolves around a downtown club district featuring local bands. In the 1990s, Orlando was home base for teen-pop acts promoted by Lou Pearlman, notably the Backstreet Boys and *NSYNC.

BIBLIOGRAPHY

W.F. Blackman: *History of Orange County* (DeLand, FL, 1927)
E.H. Gore: *From Florida Sand to "The City Beautiful": a Historical Record of Orlando, Florida*, 2d ed (Orlando, 1951)
E. Bacon: *Orlando: a Centennial History*, 2 vols. (Chuluota, FL, 1975)
R.G. Smith: *The Florida Symphony Orchestra* (Orlando, 1975)
S. Rajtar: *A Guide to Historic Orlando* (Charleston, SC, 2006)
Orange County Regional History Center. Papers. (Orlando)

SCOTT WARFIELD

Ormandy, Eugene [Blau, Jenő] (*b* Budapest, Hungary, 18 Nov 1899; *d* Philadelphia, PA, 12 March 1985). Conductor of Hungarian birth. He was proficient enough as a violinist to enter the National Hungarian Royal Academy of Music at five, and by the age of seven he was giving concerts. He began studying with Jenő Hubay two years later and graduated with a master's degree at 14. After performing as leader of the Blüthner Orchestra in Germany and as a soloist on tours of central Europe, he was appointed professor of violin at 17. A concert agent persuaded him to immigrate to New York, but when he finally arrived in 1921 he found work hard to come by. He was forced to suffer the indignity of playing in the back of the orchestra at the Capitol Theatre in New York, but within a year he had graduated to leader. He made his debut there when the regular conductor fell ill in September 1924, and was appointed associate music director in 1926. In 1927 he became an American citizen and met Arthur Judson, who helped him find guest conducting work (mostly light music for radio broadcasts) to supplement his activities at the Capitol. Judson brought him to Philadelphia to substitute for an indisposed Toscanini in 1931; this led to his appointment as music director of the Minneapolis SO (1931–6), where he became nationally known through his recordings, including the first-ever recordings of Kodály's *Háry János* Suite and Schoenberg's *Verklärte Nacht*. He returned to Philadelphia in 1936 to share the podium with Stokowski for two years, before becoming sole music director for 42 years (1938–80), after which he became conductor laureate. He took the orchestra on numerous transcontinental and international tours, and also appeared as a guest conductor in Europe, Australia, South America, and East Asia.

Ormandy was quick to learn new works and usually conducted without baton or score. With a notably fine ear, he built on Stokowski's voluptuous "Philadelphia Sound" and soon added even greater polish and precision. Philadelphia paid the musicians well so he could afford the best; and, like Stokowski, he worked with them daily, often conducting over 100 concerts a year. Despite the glory he brought to his orchestra and his numerous awards (including an honorary KBE in 1976) and honorary doctorates, critics were always slightly circumspect in their praise. Whether the gloss of the orchestra offended a Puritan streak or the brilliance seemed too easy, his intepretations were often thought to be vulgar or shallow. Ormandy perhaps contributed to this image by playing so much of the late-Romantic and early 20th-century repertory which showed to advantage the lush sound he could command: Tchaikovsky, Dvořák, Strauss, Bruckner, Debussy, Ravel, and reorchestrated Bach were his staple fare. He was less successful with Beethoven and Brahms. But he conducted much new music and gave the premieres of Rachmaninoff's *Symphonic Dances*, Bartók's Piano Concerto no.3, and works by Britten, Hindemith, Martinů, Milhaud, Persichetti, and Webern. His large and enterprising discography includes the first recordings of Shostakovich's Cello Concerto no.1 and Symphony no.4, and of Mahler's Tenth Symphony in the performing version by Deryck Cooke. He also played much American music and gave premieres of works by Barber, Creston, Diamond, Ginastera, Hanson, Piston, Rorem, Schuman, Sessions, Thompson, and Villa-Lobos.

See also PHILADELPHIA.

BIBLIOGRAPHY

R. Gelatt: *Music Makers* (New York, 1953/R)

H.C. Schonberg: *The Great Conductors* (New York, 1967/R)

H. Kupferberg: *Those Fabulous Philadelphians: the Life and Times of a Great Orchestra* (New York, 1969) [with discography of Philadelphia records]

P. Hart: *Orpheus in the New World: the Symphony Orchestra as an American Cultural Institution* (New York, 1973), 139–68

J.L. Holmes: *Conductors: a Record Collector's Guide* (London, 1988), 214–17

J. Bewley: "Marking the Way: the Significance of Eugene Ormandy's Score Annotations," *Notes*, lix/4 (2003), 828–53

P.W. Rodríguez-Peralta: *Philadelphia Maestros: Ormandy, Muti, Sawallisch* (Philadelphia, 2006)

JOSÉ A. BOWEN

Ornstein, Leo (*b* Kremenchug, Ukraine, 2 Dec[?] 1893; *d* Green Bay, WI, 24 Feb 2002). Composer and pianist of Ukrainian birth. As a child, he studied at the Petrograd Conservatory. Immigrating to New York in 1906, he studied piano at the Institute of Musical Art with Bertha Fiering Tapper, who became his most important mentor. In 1911, after a brief European visit, where he performed for Theodore Leschetizky, he made his New York debut playing standard repertoire. Two years later, in 1913, he wrote his first modernist compositions, *Dwarf Suite* and *Wild Men's Dance (Danse sauvage)*. According to Ornstein they came to him unbidden in a single intuitive flash, although the exact date of their creation is impossible to ascertain. That same year he went back to Europe with Tapper, where he met Busoni and M.-D. Calvocoressi and became familiar with the newest European trends. He also made the acquaintance of a group of English composers that included Roger Quilter, Percy Grainger, and Cyril Scott. Quilter and Ornstein formed a particularly strong bond. Ornstein's first major appearance as a virtuoso specializing in modern music took place in London on 27 March 1914, where he performed his own music, together with that of Schoenberg and a group of Bach transcriptions by Busoni.

In January and February 1915 Ornstein gave a series of four recitals at the Bandbox Theatre in New York, which quickly established his reputation. He played all modern music, including Ravel, Schoenberg, and his own compositions. For audiences that still considered Richard Strauss and César Franck's Sonata in A for Violin and Piano modern music, these concerts were considered a revelation. Following these performances Ornstein concertized extensively. Critics called him "the most salient musical phenomenon of our time," and "the sum of Schoenberg and Stravinsky squared." Waldo Frank, also comparing him to Schoenberg and Stravinsky, wrote "Ornstein, the youngest of these, gives promise to be the greatest."

From 1915 to the early 1920s Ornstein had an extremely successful concert career, entirely in the Americas, while continuing to compose. He began to withdraw from concertizing in 1922, and by 1925, when he accepted the position as head of the piano department at the Philadelphia Academy of Music, he had virtually left the concert stage, except for a few occasional appearances. In 1935 he and his wife Pauline founded the Ornstein School of Music in Philadelphia. He retired from teaching in 1953. On the national stage Ornstein remained in obscurity from the 1930s to the 1970s, when he was rediscovered by Vivian Perlis and others. Recordings of his music began to appear at that time, and he received the Marjorie Peabody Waite Award from the National Institute of Arts and Letters in 1975. This renaissance reinvigorated his creativity, and he returned to composition, which he had all but abandoned by the late 1930s. Two of his finest works, the Piano Sonatas nos.7 and 8, were written when he was in his 90s.

Ornstein's compositions divide into three large groups: experimental works (almost all dating from the 1910s), more conservative pieces that hint of Eastern Europe (from the same period and after), which he called his "expressive" works, and later pieces that integrate the two extremes. His highly dissonant music, which gained him *infant terrible* notoriety, lasted only for a brief time, from 1913 to 1915. Dissonant and atonal, these early pieces often display an individual use of gapped, chromatic clusters, quite apart from the manner of Cowell, Ives, or Bartók. Most of his experimental works, such as the *Wild Men's Dance*, were for piano, though the Violin Sonata op.31 is his most uncompromisingly modernist. Thoroughly atonal, Ornstein years later commented, "I would say that Op. 31 had brought music just to the very edge....I just simply drew back and said, beyond that lies complete chaos." After op.31 Ornstein's music, although still modernist in character, is more tonal, less dissonant, and evokes his Eastern European origins. Much of it has a lyrical quality, one of Ornstein's greatest strengths. This style reached its apogee in 1927 with his *Quintette for Piano and Strings*, probably his best piece.

Most of his instrumental music is programmatic. Some works, such as *Impressions de Notre Dame* or *Three Moods*, evoke places or emotional states, many building on Debussy-like practices, from filigree semiquaver textures to extended triadic harmonies, pentatonicism, and parallelisms. This period is also distinguished by the use of structures that give the impression of a spontaneous composition process. Beneath the striking surface elements, however, often lie traditional ABA forms. In many ways his short instrumental works exemplify the creative spontaneity espoused at the time by the philosopher Henri Bergson, although Ornstein never acknowledged Bergson's influence. Ornstein claimed that he worked intuitively, with his compositions coming to him in a flash, although manuscripts for some of his larger works betray that claim. Because he depended upon his intuition and eschewed formal methods, Ornstein never mastered counterpoint, the absence of which is the most glaring weakness in his larger compositions. During his performing years Ornstein would often carry his compositions in his head, writing them down only when publishers insisted. As a result many of his earlier works are lost, including his first three piano sonatas.

Many of Ornstein's efforts on behalf of musical modernism have escaped the standard historical narrative. Not only did he introduce the latest pieces from Europe and his own radical style through performances beginning in January 1915, but he placed music into the elaborate network of modernist activity that existed in the other arts from the early 20th century. Hardly the lone wolf in the wilderness, Ornstein had around him a co-terie of friends, followers, and champions who included painters John Marin, William Zorack, Leon Kroll, and Georgia O'Keeffe, writers Paul Rosenfeld, Waldo Frank, and Edmund Wilson, the music activist Claire Reis, and the dancer Isadore Duncan. These connections place Ornstein squarely in the Stieglitz circle, the most important locus of US modernism. Even before his Bandbox appearances some members of this group plotted with him to find a place for musical modernism, not only with his own work, but in the creation of societies that would further the cause. This did not happen until the 1920s, with the founding of the International Composers Guild and the League of Composers, but it was in part because of Ornstein the idea was born. Historically his role in laying the groundwork for musical modernism in the United States may be his most important legacy.

WORKS
(selective list)
INSTRUMENTAL
Orch:
Evening Song of the Cossack, chbr orch, op.14 no.1, 1923; Pf Conc., 1923; Lysistrata Suite, 1930; Nocturne and Dance of the Fates, *c*1937

Chbr:
Sonata, op.31, vn, pf, *c*1915; 3 Russian Impressions, vn, pf, 1916; Sonata, op.26, vn, pf, *c*1918; 2 Sonatas, op.52, vc, pf, *c*1918; *c*1920; Pf Qnt, 1927; 3 str qts, op.28, op.99, *c*1929, no.3, 1976; 6 Preludes, vc, pf, 1931; Allegro (Intermezzo), fl, pf, 1959; Fantasy Pieces, va, pf, 1972; Hebraic Fantasy, vn, pf, 1975; Poem, fl, pf, 1979

Pf (solo unless otherwise stated):
6 Lyric Fancies, op.10, 1911; A Paris Street Scene at Night, op.4 no.3, 1912; Suicide in an Airplane, *c*1913; Pièce, pf 4 hands, op.19 no.1, 1913; Wild Men's Dance (Danse sauvage), op.13 no.2, *c*1913; 3 Preludes, op.20, *c*1914; Cossack Impressions, op.14, *c*1914; Impressions de la Tamise, op.13 no.1, 1914; Impressions de Notre Dame, op.16 nos.1–2, 1914; Suite russe, op.12, *c*1914; Three Moods, 1914; Dwarf Suite, op.11, *c*1915; A la Chinoise, op.39, *c*1918; Poems of 1917, op.41, 1918 [after W. Frank]; Serenade, op.5 nos.1–2, 1918; A la Mexicana, op.35, *c*1920; Arabesques, op.42, *c*1920; 2 Improvisations, pf 4 hands, op.95, 1921; 6 Watercolors, op.80, *c*1921; Nocturnes nos.1–2, *c*1922; 2 Lyric Pieces, *c*1924; Sonata no.4, *c*1924; 15 Waltzes and 42 numbered pieces, 1950–72; Tarantelle diabolique, 1960; 5 Intermezzi, 1965–8; 3 Landscapes, 1968; A Morning in the Woods, 1971; Some New York Scenes, 1971; Biography in Sonata Form, 1974; Burlesca, 1976; Impromptu no.1 (Epitaph), no.2 (A Bit of Nostalgia), 1976; A Dream almost Forgotten, 1978; An Autumn Fantasy, 1978; Barbaro, 1978; 5 pieces, 1978; Just a Fun Piece, 1978; The Recruit and the Bugler, 1978; A Small Carnival, 1978; Valse diabolique, 1978; A Reverie, 1979; Chromatic Dance, 1980; Sonata no.6, *c*1981; The Deserted Garden, 1981; 2 Legends, 1982, Sonata no.7, 1988; Sonata no.8, 1990; Works for children

VOCAL
Songs (1v, pf):
3 Songs, op.33, *c*1915; Mother o'mine (R. Kipling), *c*1916; There was a Jolly Miller Once, *c*1916; The Corpse, 1917; Two Oriental Songs (F. Martens), *c*1918; 5 songs (W. Frank), op.17, *c*1928, arr. 1v, orch, *c*1929 [untitled]; 4 songs without words, 1928 [untitled]; Lullaby

Choral:
3 Russian Choruses, SATB, op.61, 1918; America [various arrs.]

MSS in *US-NH*
Principal publishers: Joshua, Poon Hill Press

BIBLIOGRAPHY
EwenD
C. Van Vechten: "Leo Ornstein," *Music and Bad Manners* (New York, 1916), 229–43

C.L. Buchanan: "Ornstein and Modern Music," *MQ*, iv (1918), 174–83

F. Martens: *Leo Ornstein: the Man, his Ideas, his Work* (New York, 1918/*R*)

L. Ornstein: "The Trend of Ultra-Modern Composition," *Musical Observer*, xxi (1922), 54–5

V. Perlis: "The Futurist Music of Leo Ornstein," *Notes*, xxxi (1974–5), 735–50

T.E. Darter jr: *The Futurist Piano Music of Leo Ornstein* (diss., Cornell U., 1979)

C.J. Oja: "Leo Ornstein: "Wild Man" of the 1910s," *Making Music Modern: New York in the 1920s* (New York, 2000)

M. Broyles and D. Von Glahn: *Leo Ornstein, Modernist Dilemmas, Personal Choices* (Bloomington, IN, 2007)

CAROL J. OJA/MICHAEL BROYLES, DENISE VON GLAHN

Orpheus Chamber Orchestra. New York City-based ensemble. It was formed by the cellist Julian Fifer in 1972 and has since operated without a conductor, performing diverse orchestral repertoire using chamber music techniques. Although the group employs a professional staff, ensemble members (numbering 34 in 2011) hold administrative as well as artistic responsibilities, including programming, and they rotate seating and section leadership. Orpheus presents an annual series at Carnegie Hall, and tours regularly throughout the world. Since 2003 they have administered the Orpheus Institute, through which group members share their unique philosophy, methodology, and skills with college and conservatory students. They have released over 70 recordings, many of which feature Orpheus musicians as soloists; one, *Shadow Dances: Stravinsky Miniatures*, was honored with a 2001 Grammy Award. A documentary film titled *The Orpheus Chamber Orchestra Presents: Music Meets Business* was released in 2005. The group's unique operating model has generated interest from the business world as well as the music community; Orpheus has worked with New York University and the University of Chicago on projects related to issues of collaborative leadership and self-governance, and has been studied extensively by J. Richard Hackman (Harvard Business School), among others. In 1998 the group was awarded "Ensemble of the Year" by *Musical America*, and since 2007 has been named one of the Most Democratic Workplaces by WorldBlu, Inc.

BIBLIOGRAPHY

J. Traub: "Passing the Baton: Workplace Democracy in the Orpheus Chamber Orchestra," *New Yorker* (26 Aug 1996)

H. Seifter and P. Economy: *Leadership Ensemble: Lessons in Collaborative Management from the World's Only Conductorless Orchestra* (New York, 2001)

J.R. Hackman: *Leading Teams: Setting the Stage for Great Performances* (Cambridge, MA, 2002)

ELLEN HIGHSTEIN/MICHAEL MAUSKAPF

Orquesta típica. The orquesta típica is a Latin American ensemble that integrates "typical" or regional instruments with standard European orchestral instruments in performances of folk and popular music. Probably its first published use was in Cuba in the 1870s, to describe Miguel Faílde's *danzón* band, consisting of a cornet, a valve trombone, a *figle* (ophicleide), two C clarinets, two violins, a contrabass, timbales, and a güiro. In Argentina the term was used for tango bands. The famous Mexican Typical Orchestra was formed in August 1884 by musicians at the Conservatorio of Mexico City, directed by Carlos Curti. It combined bandolones, guitars, salterios, and sometimes marimbas and native percussion instruments, with violins, bass viol, and cellos, often with female dancers and singers. In March 1885 the Orquesta Típica Mexicana performed in New Orleans, joining an outstanding Mexican regimental band, at the World International Industrial and Cotton Exposition, where they were received with great acclaim, followed by a successful tour of the United States.

JEAN DICKSON

Orrego-Salas, Juan (Antonio) (*b* Santiago, Chile, 18 Jan 1919). Chilean composer and musicologist, active in the United States. Between 1936 and 1943 he studied composition under Pedro Humberto Allende and Domingo Santa Cruz in Chile. Grants from the Guggenheim and Rockefeller foundations allowed him to reside in the United States between 1944 and 1946, where he studied composition with AARON COPLAND and RANDALL THOMPSON, counterpoint with WILLIAM MITCHELL, and musicology with Paul Henry Lang and GEORGE HERZOG. After his return to Chile he was appointed professor of composition at the University of Chile, editor of the *Revista Musical Chilena* (1949–53), and music critic for newspaper *El Mercurio* (1950–61). Thanks to a second Guggenheim Fellowship he returned to the United States in 1954 to spend a year composing and lecturing. In Chile he next became director of the University of Chile's Instituto de Extensión Musical (1957–9), and later founded and became the first dean of the Music Department at the Catholic University in Santiago (1959–61).

In 1961 he relocated permanently to the United States to teach composition at the School of Music at Indiana University and to establish the Latin American Music Center at Indiana University, which he directed until 1987. Under his leadership, the Center became one of the most important repositories of 20th-century Latin American Art Music. Orrego-Salas has been honored with multiple awards, including the Chilean Music Festival four times (1948, 1950, 1952, 1998), the Olga Cohen Prize twice (1956 and 1958), the Organization of American States' Gabriela Mistral Prize in 1988, and the Chilean Government's National Arts Prize in 1992. He has received numerous commissions, most notably from the Koussevitzky, Coolidge, Kindler, Wechsler, and Riley foundations, and from the Louisville Orchestra and the National Symphony Orchestra.

Orrego-Salas' compositional output includes over 125 works, including a mass, an oratorio, three cantatas, two operas, an operetta, three ballets, seven concertos, and music for theater and film. His pieces of the 1940s and 50s embrace a neoclassical nationalism that emphasizes melodic lyricism and privileges instrumental over music with text. Starting in the early 1980s many of his works address sociopolitical issues. *Un canto a Bolívar*, op.78 (1981), for voices and traditional Andean instruments, is based on a poem by Pablo Neruda and advocates for Latin American integration. The opera *Viudas*, op.101 (1987–90), based on a novel by Ariel

Dorfman, through allegory expresses the composer's opposition of Augusto Pinochet's military dictatorship of Chile. His work as a musicologist encompasses books, edited collections, articles published in prestigious journals such as *Musical Quarterly* and *Ethnomusicology*, and dictionary and encyclopedia entries on the music of Latin America.

SELECTED WORKS

Op: El retablo del rey pobre, op.27, 1950–2; Viudas, op.101, 1990

Orch (with or without soloists): Escenas de cortes y pastores, op.19, 1946; Obertura festiva, op.21, 1948; Sym. no.1, op.26, 1949; Pf Conc. op.28, 1950; Sym. no.2 "To the Memory of a Wanderer," op.39, 1954; Serenata concertante, op.40, 1954; Jubilaeus musicus, op.45, 1956; Sym. no.3, op.50, 1961; Conc. a 3, op.52, 1962; Conc., w orch, op.53, 1964; Sym. no.4 "Of the Distant Answer," op.59, 1966; Ob Conc., op.77, 1980; Vn Conc., op.86, 1983; Pf Conc. no.2, op.93, 1985; Riley's Merriment (Scherzo), op.94, 1986; Fanfare, op.97, 1987; Vc Conc., op.104, 1992; Sym. no.5, op.109, 1995; Sym. no.6 "Semper reditus," op.112, 1997

Chbr Orch: Variaciones serenas, str orch, op.69, 1971; Introduction and Allegro Concertato, 4-hand pf, chbr ens, op.117, 1999; Fantasias, vc, small orch, op.119, 2000; Conc. Grosso, ob, vn, str orch, op.122, 2002

Choral: Alboradas, op.56, 1965; América, no en vano invocamos tu nombre, op.57, 1966; 3 Madrigals, op.62, 1967; Missa in tempore discordiae, op.64, 1969; The Days of God, op.73, 1976; Un canto a Bolívar, op.78, 1981; Bolívar, op.81, 1982; Yo digo lo que no digo, op.83, 1982; La ciudad celeste, op.105, 1992; The Goat that Couldn't Sneeze, op.106, 1992; 3 canticos sagrados, op.108, 1995; Ave Maria, op.111b, 1996; Canto a la Cordillera, op.113, 1997

Works published by MMB Music, Peer-Southern, Boosey & Hawkes, Albany Music

BIBLIOGRAPHY

L. Merino: "Visión del compositor Juan Orrego-Salas," *Revista Musical Chilena*, xxxii/142–4 (1978), 5–105

R. Lorenz: "El Concierto para violín y orquesta de Juan Orrego-Salas," *Revista Musical Chilena*, xxxviii/162 (1984), 147–53

G.R. Benjamin: "Dramme per musica en las obras de Juan Orrego-Salas, opera 76–106," *Revista Musical Chilena*, xlviii/182 (1994), 44–100

J. Orrego-Salas: *Encuentros, visiones y repasos: Capítulos en el camino de mi música y mi vida* (Santiago, Chile, 2005)

DANIEL PARTY

Orth, Robert (*b* Chicago, IL, 21 Jan 1947). Baritone. He studied music education at Wheaton College and taught elementary school music for nine years while performing musicals in summer stock. He made his opera debut in a 1974 production of *Così fan tutte* at Chicago Opera Theater, and his theatrical versatility, intelligence, and crisp English diction made him a natural fit for the growing American opera repertory. He created the title role in Stewart Wallace's *Harvey Milk* (Houston Grand Opera, San Francisco Opera, and New York City Opera) and has portrayed many other American icons on the opera stage, including Richard Nixon (in John Adams's *Nixon in China*), Frank Lloyd Wright (in Daron Hagen's *Shining Brow*), and Lyndon B. Johnson (in Steven Stucky's *August 4, 1964*). He has appeared in world premieres including Jake Heggie's *Dead Man Walking*, *The End of the Affair*, and *Moby-Dick*; André Previn's *Brief Encounter*; Ricky Ian Gordon's *The Grapes of Wrath*; John Musto's *The Inspector*; Hiram Titus's *Rosina*; and Garrison Keillor's *Mr. and Mrs. Olson*. A champion of contemporary music, he has sung works by John Adams, Dominick Argento, David Carlson, Lee Hoiby, Michael John LaChiusa, and Stanley Silverman. In addition to performances in opera houses across the country and concerts with major symphony orchestras, he continues to appear in musicals. His recordings include *Nixon in China*, *The Grapes of Wrath*, *Six Characters in Search of an Author* (Weisgall), *Harvey Milk*, *Dead Man Walking*, *Hansel and Gretel* (Humperdinck), *Shining Brow*, and *The Telephone* (Menotti).

BIBLIOGRAPHY

S. Kubian: "Clear Voice of Reason," *Chicago Tribune* (16 Aug 1992)

S.D. Eisenberg: "Coming Soon to a Theater Near You," *ON*, lxxv/3 (Sept 2010), 40–44

KELLEY ROURKE

Orthodox Church. When Orthodox worshippers gather together as the Church of God they truly believe that not only is Christ there in the midst of them, but so is the whole church as the Body of Christ (*1 Corinthians* xii.27), including the dead and especially the saints and the angels. Worship here on earth is joined with the heavenly worship. Singing brings the inhabitants of heaven and earth together in a common assembly where there is one thanksgiving and one joyful chorus.

Byzantine mystical thought stressed the belief in the angelic transmission of the chants of the church. The hymns that are sung by the angels around the throne of God (*Revelation* iv.8; *Isaiah* vi.1–4; *Ezekiel* iii.12) are passed on from one order or rank to the next until they are received by the hymnographer through a sense of spiritual hearing. By divine grace the hymnographer is able to compose melodies which are viewed as "echoes" or "models" of the heavenly songs and serve as the foundation for all musical creativity. To an Orthodox Christian the act of worship expresses the beauty and the joy of the Kingdom of Heaven. In a classic expression of this attitude, when the emissaries of Vladimir, Great Prince of Kiev, returned from Constantinople in 988, they reported that while at worship in the Church of Hagia Sophia, they did not know whether they were in heaven or on earth.

1. Forms of liturgical song. 2. Cathedral rite and monastic rite. 3. Orthodox Church singing in America. 4. Restoring the liturgical tradition.

1. FORMS OF LITURGICAL SONG. All liturgical services in the Orthodox Church use singing and chanting extensively; music and liturgy are interdependent. The liturgical forms of prayer that call for the use of song in the liturgical services of the Orthodox Church are *dialogue*, *psalmody*, and *hymnody*, all of which are unaccompanied except in some Greek Orthodox churches in the United States.

Dialogue, the most common form of liturgical prayer, has occupied a central place in worship from the earliest days of Christianity. The most common form of dialogue in Orthodox worship is the litany, from the Greek word *lite*, which means "entreaty or intercession." The celebrant calls upon the faithful to pray for various intentions, and to each petition the congregation, led by the choir, responds with *Lord, have mercy.* An *Amen-* completes a litany. The main types are the Great Litany, occurring at the beginning of Vespers, Matins, and the Divine Liturgy, the Little Litany, usually occurring between sections of psalmody or hymnody, the Litany of Fervent Supplication, and the Augmented Litany, with the response to its petitions being a threefold *Lord, have mercy.*

Scholars generally agree that by the year 375, according to the testimony of St Basil the Great (*c*330–79), the chanting of psalms was prevalent throughout all the churches of the Christian East.

Direct or alternating psalmody is commonly used for the chanting of a complete psalm or set of psalms. For liturgical use in Orthodox worship, the psalter (containing 150 psalms) is divided into 20 sections or *kathismata* with three sets of psalms in each section. Especially in monasteries, all 150 psalms are chanted in the course of a week, beginning at Vespers on Saturday evening and concluding at Matins on the following Saturday. In direct psalmody the set of psalms is chanted by a soloist while the people listen. In alternating psalmody the assembly (or choir) is divided into two groups who sing to each other, alternating psalm by psalm or verse by verse.

Responsorial psalmody has its roots in the original poetic form and structure of many of the psalms themselves. An example of such a form is Psalm 136 (135:Septuagint [LXX]), in which the second half of each verse is exactly the same: "for His mercy endures forever." In practice, a soloist chants the first half of each psalm verse and the congregation or choir concludes the verse with the refrain, "for his mercy endures forever."

The most common example of responsorial psalmody in contemporary Orthodox worship is the *Prokeimenon* ("that which comes before," i.e., an introduction, especially to readings from sacred scripture), sung at daily Vespers and Matins and at the Divine Liturgy. A selected verse from a particular psalm is first intoned by the solo chanter in order to cue the people and establish the pitch. This verse (or half-verse or simply a final element of a verse) is then repeated by the people (choir). The chanter then begins to chant selected verses of the psalm, and after each verse or half-verse the people, forming one choir, chant their refrain again. As a conclusion, the solo chanter sings the first half of the selected "response," and the people conclude with the second half. The Prokeimenon of Great Vespers celebrated on Saturday evenings, taken from Psalm 93 (92:LXX), is a good example of the responsorial form:

Soloist (deacon): The Lord is King; He is robed in majesty. (v.1a)

Choir (people): The Lord is King; He is robed in majesty.

Soloist (deacon): The Lord is robed, He is girded with strength. (v.1b)

Choir (people): The Lord is King; He is robed in majesty.

Soloist (deacon): For He has established the world so that it shall never be moved. (v.1c)

Choir (people): The Lord is King; He is robed in majesty.

Soloist (deacon): Holiness befits Thy house, O Lord, forever. (v.5b)

Choir (people): The Lord is King; He is robed in majesty.

Soloist (deacon): The Lord is King;

Choir (people): He is robed in majesty.

Antiphonal psalmody calls for the division of the people into two choirs, each of which responds alternately with a short, common refrain to psalm verses chanted by one (or two) solo chanters. The short refrain may be a selected psalm verse, an Alleluia, a short non-scriptural phrase (such as "Glory to You, O Lord!") or an independent sacred strophic hymn called a *troparion*.

Hymnody. In the New Testament, and especially in the Book of Revelation, fragments of hymns are found that the early Christians composed, knew by memory, and passed on orally to one another. The central Vesperal hymn, "Gladsome Light," which glorifies God as Father, Son, and Holy Spirit, already referred to as an ancient hymn by St. Basil the Great, is an example of a *troparion*, as is the hymn "Only-Begotten Son," ascribed to Justinian I (527–65), that is sung at the Divine Liturgy.

A *kontakion* consists of 18 to 30 metrical stanzas (each called an *oikos*), all structurally alike, which are preceded by a rhythmical and melodic independent stanza, the *prooemion*, whose last line serves as a common refrain for all stanzas. Kontakia were sung at Matins by a soloist, with the choir or congregation joining at the singing of the refrain. In today's liturgical services, the Kontakion consists of only the introductory *prooemion* and the first *oikos*.

The *kanon*, introduced into the morning service (Orthros) towards the end of the 7th century, is a complex poetical form made up of from two to nine *odes*, each of which consists of from six to nine stanzas (*troparia*). The first troparion of each ode (called an *heirmos*) serves as a model, establishing both the melody and rhythm for all subsequent troparia in that ode. Whereas the theme of the heirmos is taken from one of the biblical canticles, the troparia that follow develop themes related to the feast or saint for which the kanon is written. The introduction of the kanon is attributed to Andrew of Crete (*c*660–*c*720).

Of the more than 50,000 individual hymns found in the printed liturgical books (Horologion, Octoechos, Menaia, Triodion, and Pentecostarion) the most numerous are those that are referred to as *stichera* (from *sticheron*, "sing"). The earliest stichera were verses that were sung after a verse (*stichos*) of a psalm, but later they increased in length.

All the types of hymnography are organized for use in worship according to the church's division of liturgical time. This time is comprised of a daily cycle, between morning and evening; a weekly cycle, between Sunday and Sunday; and a yearly cycle, between Pascha and Pascha.

2. CATHEDRAL RITE AND MONASTIC RITE. The signing of the Edict of Milan in 313 ended the persecution of Christians and made it possible for them to express more freely their faith and belief in Jesus Christ. In the 4th

century both the monastic ordo and the so-called Cathedral rite began their paths of development.

The "chanted rite" (*asmatika akolouthia*), also referred to as the Cathedral Rite, originated in and evolved from the services of the great urban centers of the Roman Empire: Rome, Alexandria, Jerusalem, Antioch, and Constantinople. Characteristics of the cathedral ordo included extensive chanting, with refrains sung by the people to psalm verses chanted by a soloist, entrances, and processions. Parallel with this liturgical ordo was another pattern of worship that was being developed in the Egyptian, Palestinian, and Syrian monasteries. Monks who lived in the desert, especially those who settled in the Egyptian desert, emphasized the recitation of the psalter, called the "canon of psalmody," biblical readings, and penitential prayer. However, monks who resided in or near the cities, coming into frequent contact with the worship of the secular churches, added to their canon of psalmody certain cathedral usages, resulting in the development of a type of mixed monastic rite.

In the 6th century, especially under Justinian I, who was the Byzantine emperor from 527 to 565, Christianity became essentially the religion of the empire. This development gave rise to a flurry of activity in the building of churches and their artistic decoration, including the Great Church of Hagia Sophia in Constantinople. The cathedral rite reached its apex at this time, influencing the rites of all the cathedral churches of the Orthodox world. The fusion of elements of one rite to those of another was not unusual during this process of development and transference, and eventually it was the monastic ordo that prevailed over the "cathedral rite" for the services of the Divine Office. For the Eucharistic Liturgy, however, the usages of the Constantinopolitan cathedral rite predominated. Thus, the *Typikon* in use by Orthodox churches today represents a synthesis or "mixed rite," combining elements from the cathedral and the monastic traditions.

3. ORTHODOX CHURCH SINGING IN AMERICA. Orthodoxy was first brought to America via Alaska. In 1794 eight monastic missionaries from the Valaam Monastery near St Petersburg, Russia, arrived in Kodiak and began to establish Orthodox parishes throughout the mainland, the Aleutian Islands, and the Kenai Peninsula. In accordance with the Orthodox principle that the language of the prayer of the church is the language of the people, liturgical texts were translated into the various native languages. To this day the distinctive chants in the various native languages can be heard in Alaskan churches.

Soon after the sale of Alaska to the United States in 1867, the diocesan center of the Orthodox Church in Alaska was transferred from Sitka to San Francisco. During the next five decades, parishes that were canonically under the jurisdiction of the Russian Orthodox Church were established not only in port cities such as New Orleans, Philadelphia, New York, and Boston but also in industrial centers and mining and farming areas throughout the United States and Canada.

Mission schools were established, and a pastoral school for choir directors and readers was organized. Catechisms and liturgical texts in English were provided, and liturgical services were usually celebrated in several languages, among them Greek, Church Slavonic, Arabic, and English.

The Russian Revolution of 1917 resulted in the loss of support from the Russian Church and the establishment and strengthening of local ethnic jurisdictions in the United States. In addition, the great wave of emigration of the 1920s, 1930s, and 1940s from Slavic, Balkan, and Mediterranean countries greatly contributed to the increased use of Greek, Church Slavonic, Arabic, Romanian, Albanian, and other tongues in liturgical services of Orthodox churches belonging to the ethnic jurisdictions. Today in the United States there are 15 Orthodox jurisdictions, the three largest being the Autocephalous Orthodox Church in America (749 parishes and missions), Greek Orthodox Archdiocese (540 parishes), and the Antiochian Orthodox Christian Archdiocese (276 parishes); liturgical services, for the most part, are celebrated in English.

Both unison Byzantine chant with the *isokratima* (vocal drone) sung by cantors and polyphonic arrangements of liturgical texts sung by choirs were used for worship in the churches whose parishioners were mostly of Greek, Middle Eastern, or Balkan backgrounds. Although the medieval churches of Greece and the Balkan countries had used the unison Byzantine chant, already in the 19th century polyphonic works for church services were written by composers in Greece (John Sakellarides, c1853–1938), Serbia (Stevan Mokranjac, 1856–1914), Romania (Gavriil Musicescu, 1847–1903), and Bulgaria (Dobri Christov, 1875–1941). Congregational singing or plainchant (*prostopenie*) was employed by Galician and Carpathian parishes that entered the Orthodox diocese. Priests and choir directors who were trained in Russia, San Francisco, or Minneapolis organized choirs who sang the music customary to the Russian church in those churches whose parishioners were mostly of Slavic background.

Western-style polyphonic music was introduced to the Orthodox churches of southwestern Russia in the 17th century and quickly spread throughout all parts of the country. Choral works of such Russian church composers as Dmitry Bortniansky (1751–1825), Maxim Berezovsky (1745–77), Alexis L'vov (1798–1870), Nikolai Bakhmetev (1807–91), Aleksandr Arkhangel'sky (1846–1924), Stepan Smolensky (1848–1909), Aleksandr Kastal'sky (1856–1926), Pavel Chesnokov (1877–1944), Pyotr Tchaikovsky (1840–93), Aleksandr Grechaninov (1864–1956), and Sergei Rachmaninov (1873–1944), all can be heard today in Orthodox churches in America. Although traditionally all singing and chanting in the Orthodox Church is *a cappella* and the use of musical instruments is not permitted, many churches of the Greek Archdiocese in America use the organ to assist the choir at the Sunday services.

4. RESTORING THE LITURGICAL TRADITION. The very fact that Orthodox music is referred to as "liturgical" indicates

that there is a relationship between music and the liturgy. Types of melodies and their forms are closely connected with the liturgical action, for example, the musical form for the litany, being a people's response, is syllabic in form and rather simple in terms of melodic content. On the other hand, the Alleluia, whose function in the liturgy is to announce the reading of the Gospel, can be more melismatic, corresponding to the exultant character of this acclamation.

The question of "church singing with the participation of all the people" was raised by the bishops of the Russian Church in 1905. Participation in the common prayer of the church is an important sign of belonging to the one Body of Christ. The restoration of congregational singing was not simply a desire to comply with a canonical standard or a historical precedent; it was seen as a measure that would assist in giving to liturgy the life, the joy, and the power that is inherent in its purpose, content, form, and message. Congregational participation and the availability of suitable music are issues that are being raised in churches today in America and beyond.

Sacred scripture and Orthodox theology provide the content for most of the Greek liturgical hymnody, so the meaning of words is critical. Any translation must communicate correctly the Church's teaching. At the same time the poetic structure—rhythm, meter, rhyme, word-imagery, syntax—is an essential element of Byzantine hymnody and is important to the "transcendent beauty" of worship. The singing of hymns is seen by the Orthodox to be the expression of worship itself; therefore, the translation process must result in the production of texts that preserve the meaning without destroying the inherent beauty of the original.

Translated Orthodox hymnody must be able to be combined with a musical form so that the music is neither a detriment to the understanding of the content of the hymn nor to its poetic beauty. The music should not be in conflict with the text so as to cause words or syllables to be repeated in order for the text to fit the melody. All of the elements of the music—contour, phrasing, rhythm, form—should align with the poetic patterns inherent in the text. The authors of Orthodox hymns, Romanos the Melodos (6th century), Andrew of Crete (7th and 8th centuries), John of Damascus (8th century), Theodore of Studios (8th and 9th centuries), Joseph the Hymnographer (9th century), and others, were not only musicians but poets and theologians as well, and thus were able to keep an appropriate balance between music and text in their works. Composers of Orthodox music must always keep this in mind so that the integrity of the text is maintained and not destroyed because of particular musical demands.

Throughout most of the 20th century, the composing of music for the Orthodox churches in America was, for the most part, limited to adapting to English preexisting music written to Greek or Slavonic texts. This includes English "settings" based on traditional chant forms—Byzantine, Znamenny (Old Believers), Kievan, Serbian, Romanian—as well as adaptations of works identified with the numerous "national" Orthodox churches writ-

ten by composers such as Bortniansky, Chesnokov, Kastal'sky, Sakallarides, Musicescu, and Mokranjac. The results of these efforts vary widely, depending mostly on methodology. Where the main concern is the preservation of the original melody, as evident especially in the earliest settings of English translations, one generally finds repetition of words, poor phrasing, and improper or simply incorrect accentuation. For example, the first line of the translated Cherubic Hymn "Let us who mystically represent the Cherubim," set to or, rather, pasted under a Byzantine or Slavic melody, produces "Let us, let us, let us who mystically, mystically represent, represent the Cherubim."

Much of this has changed, especially since the 1970s, with the establishment of programs of music in the theological seminaries, the sponsorship of national and regional church music workshops, and the development of national departments of music in the various Orthodox jurisdictions, whose work is readily available on ecclesiastical websites. Translations into English of the complete corpus of liturgical texts now exist, and new compositions reflecting an understanding of both liturgical function and textual-musical cohesion are gradually entering the repertory. Special interest in Byzantine and Znamenny chant is on the rise, and music written with simple melodies, at times comprising only two parts, is being made available to small and mission parishes. All of this has contributed to a better and richer understanding of the relationship between music and worship in the Orthodox Church.

BIBLIOGRAPHY

E. Wellesz: *A History of Byzantine Music and Hymnography* (Oxford, 1961)

C. Tarasar, ed.: *Orthodox America 1794–1976* (Syosset, NY, 1975)

J. Quasten: *Music and Worship in Pagan and Christian Antiquity* (Washington, DC, 1983)

D. Conomos: *Byzantine Hymnography and Byzantine Chant* (Brookline, MA, 1984)

D. Conomos: *The Late Byzantine and Slavonic Communion Cycle: Liturgy and Music* (Washington, DC, 1985)

S. Glagolev: "The Sound of Sacred Music," *Orthodox Church Music* (Syosset, NY, No. 2, 1985)

V. Morosan: *Choral Performance in Pre-Revolutionary Russia* (Ann Arbor, MI, 1986)

J. Roccasalvo: *The Plainchant Tradition of Southwestern Rus'* (New York, 1986)

A. Schmemann: *Introduction to Liturgical Theology* (Crestwood, NY, 1986)

R. Taft: *The Liturgy of the Hours in East and West: the Origins of the Divine Office and Its Meaning for Today* (Collegeville, MN, 1986)

J. McKinnon: *Music in Early Christian Literature* (Cambridge, UK, 1989)

R. Taft: *The Byzantine Rite: a Short History* (Collegeville, MN, 1992)

M. Bailey: "Composing Orthodox Liturgical Music in the Contemporary World," *St Vladimir's Theological Quarterly*, xl/1–2 (1996), 65–75

D. Drillock: "Early Slavic Translations and Musical Adaptations of Byzantine Liturgical Hymnody," *St Vladimir's Theological Quarterly*, lxiv/3–4 (2000), 375–407

A. Rentel: "Byzantine and Slavic Orthodoxy," *The Oxford History of Christian Worship*, eds. G. Wainwright and K. Tucker (Oxford, 2006), 254–306

DAVID DRILLOCK

Ortiz, Luis [Perico] (*b* Santurce, Puerto Rico, 26 Dec 1949). Puerto Rican trumpet player, arranger, producer, and record company executive. Ortiz began his career as a trumpet player in San Juan playing for dance bands while also arranging for television shows. He moved to New York in 1972, where he was involved with the salsa scene as a producer, arranger, and studio musician. One of Ortiz's earliest arrangements for Fania Records was the bolero "Sálvame," recorded in 1973 on the album *Así se compone un son* by Ismael Miranda. Ortiz arranged for many other Fania artists throughout the 1970s, including Johnny Pacheco, Celia Cruz, and Héctor Lavoe. He was also a member of the Fania All-Stars, participating in the historic *Fania All-Stars Live at Yankee Stadium* (1973). In 1979 *Latin NY* magazine recognized Ortiz as the best arranger, best trumpet player, best orchestra leader, and musician of the year. He also arranged and recorded with many Puerto Rican salsa bands, including Tommy Olivencia's. Ortiz continues to perform, record, arrange, and teach. Most recently, he established his own record company. Besides his virtuosity and much-admired tone on the trumpet, he is hugely respected for his abilities to arrange in a wide variety of styles from traditional Afro-Caribbean to experimental and jazz.

DAVID F. GARCIA

Ortiz, Pablo (*b* Buenos Aires, 1 May 1956). Argentinean composer. He studied piano and accordion as a child and began his studies of composition under Gerardo Gandini at the Universidad Católica Argentina. In 1984 he moved to the United States where he received a doctoral degree from Columbia University, studying under MARIO DAVIDOVSKY. He has been the recipient of numerous prizes, among them a Guggenheim Fellowship (1993), the Charles Ives Fellowship (1996), and the Academy Award in Music (2008) by the Academy of Arts and Letters. He has received commissions by the Fromm Foundation, the Centro Experimental Teatro Colón, the Koussevitzky Foundation, the Gerbode Foundation, and the Fideicomiso para la Cultura Mexico–U.S., among others.

Ortiz's works include two chamber operas, electronic, orchestral, vocal, chamber, and solo music, as well as compositions for theatre and film. His choral music shows an influence of Renaissance counterpoint and often reflects his interest in Mexican poetry. In *Oscuro* (2004), for mixed voices and Pierrot ensemble, he sets texts by Francisco Alarcón and Amado Nervo in rich dissonant harmonies interspersed with rhythmically complex instrumental interludes. In *Fear of Tango* (1992), for two pianos, Ortiz inaugurated a series of tangos for different instrumental forces. He currently teaches composition at the University of California, Davis.

ANA R. ALONSO-MINUTTI

Ortiz Alvarado, William (*b* Salinas, PR, 30 March 1947). Puerto Rican composer. Raised in New York, Ortiz studied at the Conservatory of Music of Puerto Rico under composition teacher HÉCTOR CAMPOS PARSI. He received a master's degree (1976) from SUNY, Stony Brook, where he studied with BILLY JIM LAYTON and BÜLENT AREL, and a

PhD (1983) from SUNY, Buffalo, where he studied with LEJAREN HILLER and MORTON FELDMAN. Ortiz has been the assistant director of Black Mountain College II/SUNY Buffalo, music theory and composition professor, and organizer of student concerts in support of Hispanic students in the United States. He has served as chair of the department of humanities and as band conductor of the University of Puerto Rico, Bayamón, where he currently serves as music professor. He has also contributed as a music critic to the Puerto Rican newspaper *The San Juan Star*. Ortiz has received many commissions and awards, such as commissions for the Casals Festival (1995) and the Felipe Gutiérrez Espinosa Award (1980). His compositions include songs, chamber music, and symphonic works as well as electronic music. His music has been described as a Nuyorican artistic expression of cultural forms. Ortiz's inspiration comes from urban street subculture and embraces more universal forms of expression. He conceives of his music as "the 'violent beauty' of urban life, as the expression of the cries and shouts of the street—cries and shouts that reflect the thoughts of those who feel, of those who are oppressed." His works have been recorded and published by Ricordi, A.M. Percussion Publications, Smith Publications, Opus One Records, New World Records, and Centaur Records.

WORKS

Opera: Rican, 1986

Orch: Kantuta (ritual para orquesta), 1976; Suspensón de soledad en 3 tiempos, 1990; Música de ciudad, SATB, orch, 1996; Tropicalización, gui conc., 1999; Piano al tiempo de 3 voces, pf conc., orch, 1999; Esta es la tierra de los que aguantan callados por un nuevo despertar, gui conc., orch, 2001; Montage para un sueño en mi, 2001; Elogio a la plena, concert band or orch, 2002; Ciudad en tropical jubilation, pf, band, or orch, 2004; Música con calle, perc. conc., orch, 2006

Chbr: Rapsodia, gui, 1970; Pavana, gui or pf, 1977; 124 E. 107th St., perc, tape, narrator, 1979; Amor, cristal y piedra, gui, hp, hpd, 1980; Street Music, fl, trbn, perc, 1980; Piezas típicas puertorriqueñas, 2 gui, 1981; Composición para violín, violonchelo y piano, vln, vc, pf, 1982; Graffiti nuyorican, pf, perc, 1983; Abrazo, 4 gui, 1984; Urbanización, perc, 1985; Bolero and Hip-Hop en Myrtle Avenue, ob, pf, 1986; Carteto de arcos, No. 2, str qt, 1987; Cantinela, gui, 1996; Ricanstructions, fl, gui, 1999; Reminiscencias: Tapia 1882, str qt, pf, 2008

Voice: Madrigal, Ct, T, B, 1984; A Delicate Fire, C, gui, 1986; Dos gritos y una canción, T, pf, 1986; Ghetto, singer/narr, fl, amp. gui, perc, 1987; Romance, boy S or S, gui, 1988; Tríptico, Mez, fl, ob, cl, hrn, bn, 1990; Unknown Poets from the Full-Time Jungle, S, pf, 1992; Guakia Baba, Mez, fl, 1993; Songs from the Bilingual, Bar, gui, 2000; Cantos juveniles, children's choir, 2000; Canción del hijo no nacido, 3 child S, fl, pf, 2003; Cántico, chorus, band, or pf, 2004; Himno de la hermandad, v, pf, 2006

Pf: Sonatina, 1971; 4 piezas para piano, 1974; Transformaciones, 1975; Montuno, 1981; Del tingo al tango, 1984; De barrio obrero a la quince, 4 hand, 1986; Danza para Rhonda, 1986; Mulata fantasía, 1987; Bella Aleyda, 1989; Página en blanco y staccato, 1989

Principal publishers: American Composers Editions, A M Percussion, Instituto de Cultura Puertorriqueña, North/South, Quadrivium Music, Smith Publ.

BIBLIOGRAPHY

D. Thompson: "Contemporary String Music from Puerto Rico," *American String Teacher*, xxxiv/1 (1984), 37–41

D. Thompson: "La musica contemporanea en Puerto Rico," *Revista Musical Chilena*, xxxviii (1984), 110–17

C. Toro Vargas: *Diccionario biográfico de compositores puertorriqueños* (Ponce, PR, 2003)

R.A. de Souza: *The Percussion Music of Puerto Rican Composer William Ortiz* (diss., U. of Oklahoma, 2006)

MARYSOL QUEVEDO

Ortmann, Otto Rudolph (*b* Baltimore, MD, 25 Jan 1889; *d* Baltimore, MD, 22 Oct 1979). Music educator and administrator. He received his formal education at Baltimore City College and then at the Peabody Conservatory, where he gained a teacher's certificate in piano (1913) and an artist's diploma in composition (1917). From 1917 to 1941 he served on the faculty of Peabody (1928–41 as its director), and from 1942 to 1957 taught in the music department at Goucher College (1948–57 as its chairman). He also taught courses in the psychology of music at Johns Hopkins University (1921–4). He combined research on acoustics, anatomy, physics, and physiology with an investigation of musical talent and problems of music pedagogy, making a valuable contribution by synthesizing various conflicting historical principles and schools of technical thought; his articles and books in the area of piano pedagogy, in particular, gained for him national and international recognition.

BIBLIOGRAPHY
D.J. Gonzol: *Otto Rudolph Ortmann's Theories of Musical Experience and their Implications for Music Education* (diss., U. of Maryland, College Park, 1995)
A.E. Gustafson: *Tone Production on the Piano: the Research of Otto Rudolph Ortmann* (diss., U. of Texas at Austin, 2007)

WILLIAM McCLELLAN/R

Ory, Kid [Edouard, Edward] (*b* LaPlace, LA, 25 Dec 1886; *d* Honolulu, HI, 23 Jan 1973). Jazz trombonist, composer, and bandleader. He began playing banjo as a child, but by his teens had switched to trombone and begun leading successful bands in his hometown of LaPlace. At age 21 he moved to New Orleans, where his band quickly became one of the most sought after in the city. Ory's bands featured many of the finest musicians in early jazz, including the cornetists King Oliver and Louis Armstrong and the clarinetist Johnny Dodds. In 1919 he moved to Los Angeles, where he led and recorded with a new band that included the clarinetist Mutt Carey and the double bass player Ed Garland. In 1925 he moved to Chicago, where he was reunited with many of the musicians with whom he had played in New Orleans, including Armstrong, Jelly Roll Morton, Oliver, and Dodds. During Ory's Chicago period he appeared on landmark recordings with groups including Armstrong's Hot Five and Morton's Red Hot Peppers. After remaining virtually absent from jazz during the 1930s, he returned with a new band in 1943 and became a major force for the revival of traditional New Orleans jazz. Between 1944 and 1961, Ory toured with his band and performed on radio, including several notable appearances on the show *Orson Welles' Almanac*. He finally retired from music in 1966 and spent the last years of his life in Hawaii.

Ory was an essential figure in the development of jazz trombone and is credited with originating the tailgate style of trombone playing wherein glissandos and slurs are used to create a rhythmic backbone underneath the more ornamental playing of clarinet and cornet.

BIBLIOGRAPHY
Giltrap and Dixon: *Kid Ory* (London, 1958)
D. Dicaire: *Jazz Musicians of the Early Years, to 1945* (Jefferson, NC, 2003)

DAVID CHEVAN

Osborne, Conrad L(eon) (*b* Lincoln, NE, 22 July 1934). Music critic and singer. He attended Columbia University and also studied singing with Cornelius Reid and acting with FRANK CORSARO. He has acted in the theater and on television and has sung operatic baritone roles with various musical organizations in the New York area. As a writer he was chief vocal critic and contributing editor of *High Fidelity* (1959–69), and New York music critic of the London *Financial Times* (1962–9). In 1970 he was appointed advisory editor of the *Musical Newsletter* and in 1978 his critical guide *The Complete Operas of Mozart* (New York, 1978/R) was published. Osborne has contributed numerous articles to publications in the United States and England, including detailed critical discographies of the operas of Verdi (1963), Wagner (1966–7) and Russian composers (1974–5) for *High Fidelity*, and articles and reviews for *Opus* (from 1984). In the 1990s Osborne regularly contributed to *The New York Times*. His chief interest is opera, and his background as a performer has strongly influenced his critical writing on the subject. He has devoted much of his time to teaching singing privately. Osborne is widely regarded as one of the most discriminating vocal critics in the United States.

PATRICK J. SMITH/JONAS WESTOVER

Osborne [Osborn], **John** (*b* New England, *c*1792; *d* New York, 27 May 1835). Piano maker. He was one of several apprentices who learned their craft under BENJAMIN CREHORE of Milton, Massachusetts. He is said to have served this apprenticeship during the years (*c*1810–14) when Crehore was associated with the Boston shop of Lewis and Alpheus Babcock and Thomas Appleton. By 1815 Osborne had set up his own shop on Newbury Street, Boston, and by 1820 had moved to Orange Street. Among his Boston apprentices were Jonas Chickering, TIMOTHY AND LEMUEL GILBERT, and Ebenezer R. Currier. Osborne entered into a short-lived partnership with James Stewart in 1822, and in that year removed his shop to Boylston Square. From about 1830 until his death Osborne worked primarily in New York, although it appears that for much of that time he concurrently had business relationships in Albany, New York, first with Meacham and Pond, and then as a partner with Peter King. According to Spillane, in October 1834 Osborne moved into a large factory that he had built on Third Avenue at 14th Street.

Osborne described himself as a builder of upright, grand, square, and cabinet pianos. His pianos won several awards, including the first premium at the American Institute. Of the relatively few Osborne pianos that survive, most are squares, several of which incorporate a longitudinal metal bar that was patented on 29 July 1824 by a Boston medical doctor and inventor named John Dwight. Two extant upright pianos of Osborne's made between 1818 and 1821, with a range of six octaves (F' to f''''), are among the earliest such pianos built in America. Representative instruments are at the Smithsonian Institution, Washington, DC, and at Sturbridge, Massachusetts.

BIBLIOGRAPHY

R.G. Parker: *A Tribute to the Life and Character of Jonas Chickering by One Who Knew Him Well* (Boston, 1854)

H.K. Oliver: *Reports and Awards of the International Exhibition, 1876* (Philadelphia, 1878)

D. Spillane: *History of the American Pianoforte* (New York, 1890/R)

CYNTHIA ADAMS HOOVER, DARCY KURONEN

Osborne [Orsborn], **Mary (Estella)** (*b* Minot, ND, 17/18 July 1921; *d* Bakersfield, CA, 4 March 1992). Jazz guitarist and singer. One of 11 children born to Elvy and Estelle Orsborn, she was raised in Bismarck, North Dakota. Both parents played guitar and at an early age Osborne learned to play ukelele, violin, guitar, and bass. She played banjo in her father's string band at ten and by 15 was a featured instrumentalist, singer, and dancer in a local trio. After hearing Charlie Christian in Bismarck, she switched to electric guitar. One of its early pioneers, she developed a single-line playing style influenced by Christian and Django Reinhardt. She played in an all-female band that later joined Buddy Rogers' ensemble. In November 1942 she married the trumpeter Ralph Scaffidi. After Rogers' band broke up, its members were stranded in New York, and Osborne found work as a radio musician and session player. In the late 1940s she led her own trio and recorded with Mercer Ellington and Coleman Hawkins, among others. From 1945 to 1948 she recorded 11 sides with Mary Lou Williams' Girl Stars, providing vocals for two of them. "D.D.T" (1946, Cont.) is representative of her hard-swinging solo and comping style. Osborne's interpretation of a standard popularized by Billie Holiday, "(She's) He's Funny that Way" (1946, Cont.), features her sensitive alto voice. During the following decade Osborne returned to touring. Although she considered herself primarily a jazz guitarist, she backed the R&B singer Wynonie Harris and blues shouter Joe Turner, both of whom were prominent in rock and roll's early development. From 1952 to 1960 she played with the Elliot Lawrence Quintet, which was regularly featured on Jack Sterling's CBS radio show. She and Scaffidi moved to Bakersfield, CA, in 1968 and founded the Osborne Guitar Company and the Osborne Sound Laboratories, which manufactured guitars and amplifiers. She resumed performing in the early 1980s with festival and nightclub appearances in New York and Los Angeles. She died of liver failure in 1992.

BIBLIOGRAPHY

L. Dahl: *Stormy Weather: the Music and Lives of a Century of Jazz-women* (New York, 1984)

Obituary: *New York Times* (6 March 1992)

GAYLE MURCHISON

Osborne Brothers. Country music duo. As children, Bobby (Robert Jr.; *b* Hyden, KY, 7 Dec 1931) and Sonny Osborne (*b* Hyden, KY, 29 Oct 1937) were exposed to a variety of religious music and to that of Jimmie Rodgers and the Carter Family. Bobby made his professional debut in Dayton, OH, playing guitar with Junior Collett and Dick Potter. He later played with the Lonesome Pine Fiddlers and the Stanley Brothers, switching from guitar to mandolin in 1951. Sonny played banjo in Bill Monroe's Blue Grass Boys (1952–3). The Osborne Brothers were first billed as such in 1953 on Knoxville, TN radio station WROL, where their backup band, the Sunny Mountain Boys, consisted of Enos Johnson and L.E. White. In 1954, the Osbornes worked in Detroit with the singer and guitarist Jimmy Martin, who had just left Monroe, and recorded for RCA Victor. In 1955, they went to work for Charlie Bailey at Wheeling, WV station WWVA, but left by mid-1956 and signed with MGM Records. They made their first guest appearances on the *Grand Ole Opry* in 1959 and became regular cast members in 1964. In 1963, they began a long association with Decca (later MCA) Records. Their choice of songs was considerably more eclectic than the usual bluegrass repertory, encompassing both folk ("Take This Hammer," 1963) and mainstream country ("Making Plans," 1965) styles. Aiming their music at the basic country audience, the duo they attained modest chart placement in the mid-1960s with records featuring instruments atypical in bluegrass, such as electric guitar, steel guitar, drums, and piano. Their most memorable release was Boudleaux and Felice Bryant's "Rocky Top" (1968), which later became a Tennessee state song. The Osborne Brothers performed at several Newport Folk Festivals during the 1960s, and in the mid-1970s signed with the CMH label. The duo's return to a traditional bluegrass sound was followed by decades of festival and recording successes. Sonny retired in 2005, but Bobby continues to record and tour with his band, the Rocky Top X-Press. Noted for their high, intricate harmonies, for developing the now popular "high lead" vocal trio concept, as well as for their virtuoso mandolin and banjo picking, the Osborne Brothers have been a progressive force in bluegrass music.

BIBLIOGRAPHY

N. Rosenberg: "Osborne Brothers Discography," *Bluegrass Unlimited*, i (1967), no. 12, p.2; ii (1967), no.1, p.6; no.3, p.2

N. Rosenberg: "The Osborne Brothers," *Bluegrass Unlimited*, vi (1971), p.5; vi (1972), no.8, p.5

P. Kuykendall: "The Osborne Brothers – from Rocky Top to Muddy Bottom," *Bluegrass Unlimited*, xii/6 (1977), 10

RONNIE PUGH/LEE BIDGOOD

Osby, Greg(ory Thomas) (*b* St. Louis, MO, 3 Aug 1960). Alto and soprano saxophonist. After studying clarinet, flute, and alto saxophone privately, he graduated from Howard University with jazz studies as his major in 1980. He continued his education at the Berklee College of Music in Boston until 1983. After moving to New York in the same year, he played as a sideman with Herbie Hancock, Dizzy Gillespie, Andrew Hill, Muhal Richard Abrams, and Jaki Byard. In 1985 he joined Jack DeJohnette's group Special Edition. From the same year through the early 1990s he worked with the M-BASE collective, of which he was a founding member with Steve Coleman and Cassandra Wilson, among others. Having released three albums with the German label JMT, Osby signed a contract with Blue Note Records in 1990, for which he recorded 13 albums as a leader from 1991 to 2005. On several of these he featured Coleman, Jim Hall, and Hill. In 2008 he founded his own label, Inner Circle Music, and a sextet with the Portuguese vocalist Sara Serpa. Osby is a saxophonist with a warm, rich sound and virtuoso playing technique. He has a pragmatic, versatile approach to jazz and experiments with different styles from different periods.

BIBLIOGRAPHY

D. Helland: "Greg Osby: Open on All Sides," *DB*, lvi/10 (1989), 26–8
W. Jenkins: "Greg Osby: Taking It All in," *JT*, xxv/10 (1995), 54–7
G. Osby: "A Wizard's Approach," *DB*, lxviii/7 (2001), 2 only
G. Osby: "'If You Don't Create It, It Won't Exist'," *DB*, lxxiv/5 (2007), 34–6
M.D. Clayton: *M-Base: Envisioning Change for Jazz in the 1980s and Beyond* (diss., Harvard U., 2009)

MICHAEL BAUMGARTNER

Oscar Schmidt. Manufacturer and distributor of string instruments. Oscar Schmidt (*b* Dresden, Germany, 21 Sept 1857; *d* Karlsbad, Czechoslovakia, Oct 1929), originally a bookbinder, founded an eponymous business following his immigration to New York in 1871, though it was not formally incorporated until 31 March 1911 as Oscar Schmidt, Inc., in Jersey City, New Jersey. While the company began in music publishing, a partnership with Friedrich Menzenhauer began manufacturing fretless zithers in 1897. Schmidt was producing a variety of stringed instruments, including guitars, mandolins, banjos, ukuleles, and zithers in the early 20th century at his Ferry Street factory. Many of the products made by Schmidt bore other trade names. In 1909 Schmidt registered Sovereign and Stella as trademarks, though the company also made instruments for other vendors bearing house brands or no identification. Schmidt was a co-owner of the International Musical Corporation, founded on 26 April 1926, and he provided much of the autoharp manufacturing work for this successor to the Phonoharp Company. Following some legal disputes between the companies, and Schmidt's death in 1929, a new organization, the Oscar Schmidt-International Corporation, was founded in 1931 to manufacture zithers and autoharps, while Oscar Schmidt, Inc., continued to manufacture other types of stringed instruments. A series of restructurings occurred during the 1930s, and the fretted instrument construction was done by Fretted Instrument Manufacturers, Inc., owned by John Carner, though at the same factory facility as previously. In 1939 the Stella and Sovereign brand names were sold to Harmony of Chicago. Oscar Schmidt continued to produce autoharps and guitars until 1975. Now, guitars, ukuleles, and autoharps bearing the Oscar Schmidt name are sold by the US Music Corporation of Mundelein, Illinois.

The Schmidt organization and its related companies are notable for the production of inexpensive, accessible musical instruments, many of which were sold through catalogs or by door-to-door salesmen. Stella guitars dating from before World War II were used by many blues artists of modest means, and the distinctive sound of the company's birch or oak guitars had become a recognized part of the classic blues sound by the 1960s. The company's pre–World War II 12-string guitars have become particularly collectible and influential. Oscar Schmidt promoted the autoharp heavily after World War II as an instrument suitable for music education, prompting a revival of its use in schools and the folk music movement.

BIBLIOGRAPHY

B. Blackley: *The Autoharp Book* (Brisbane, CA, 1983)
N. Harpe: *The Stella Guitar Book* (Annapolis, MD, 2005)

ARIAN SHEETS

Osgood, (Emma) Aline (*b* Boston, MA, 1849; *d* Philadelphia, PA, 8 Nov 1911). Soprano. She was born in Boston and studied at the New England Conservatory. As a young woman, Osgood sang at the Old South Church, performing with well-known local singers and conductors such as Theodore Thomas and Carl Zerrahn. During 1873 she sang with the Mendelssohn Quintette Club and toured the United States and Canada with that group. From 1875, Osgood resided in England and concentrated her performing career on oratorio singing. She enjoyed wide success as an oratorio soloist throughout England, and her career included two performances before Queen Victoria. Beginning in 1878, Osgood made several trips to the United States, notably appearing in Thomas' May Festivals, first in Cincinnati and later in New York and Chicago. Osgood was also known for singing "ballads" such as "Home Sweet Home." Ultimately Osgood retired from the public stage and was married to E. Milton Dexter. She relocated to Philadelphia and continued to work as a voice teacher.

BIBLIOGRAPHY

Grove2, Amer. suppl
"Mrs. Aline Osgood," *Brainard's Musical World*, xix/222 (1882), repr. in *Brainard's Biographies of American Musicians*, ed. E.D. Bomberger (Westport, CT, 1999)
F.O. Jones, ed.: *Handbook of American Music and Musicians* (Canaseraga, NY, 1886/R)
W.S.B. Mathews: *A Hundred Years of Music in America: an Account of Musical Effort in America During the Past Century* (Chicago, 1889/R), 565

LAURIE BLUNSOM

Osgood, George Laurie (*b* Chelsea, MA, 3 April 1844; *d* Petersham, England, 12 Dec 1922). Tenor, conductor, and composer. He graduated with honors from Harvard in 1866, where he led the Glee Club and the orchestra, studying organ and composition with Paine. In Germany he studied for three years with Karl August Haupt, Ferdinand Sieber, and Robert Franz, and then another two years with Francesco Lamperti in Milan. After a performance tour in Germany, he returned to America, where he toured with the Theodore Thomas orchestra, then settled in Boston in 1872 as a voice teacher. In 1875 he became director of the Boylston Club choral society, which he transformed from a male choir to a mixed chorus of over 200 voices; it was reorganized in 1890 as the Boston Singers' Society. He became choir-master of the Emmanuel Church in 1882. For a number of years, Osgood presented a series of chamber music concerts, including much historical repertoire. He re-tired to England in 1904. His publications included *Guide in the Art of Singing* (1874), with at least eight editions, and *The Boylston Collection*. His compositions numbered over fifty songs, as well as church anthems, choruses, and part songs, including "In Picardie," "Wake not, but hear me, Love," "Thou'rt like a flower," and "Christmas Carol."

BIBLIOGRAPHY

Grove2, Amer. suppl.

"Osgood, George Laurie," *The National Cyclopaedia of American Biography*, vii (New York, 1892), 436 only

L.C. Elson: *The History of American Music* (New York, 1904), 251–2

Obituary, *Boston Daily Globe* (13 Dec 1922)

JOHN C. SCHMIDT

Osgood, Marion G. (*b* Chelsea, MA, Jan 1859; *d* Chelsea, MA, after 1940). Violinist, conductor, and composer. Osgood was born in the Boston suburb of Chelsea. She came from a musical family: her father was a teacher for Lowell Mason, her mother a composer, and her cousin, George L. Osgood, a well-known Boston musi-cian and composer. Osgood studied violin with JULIUS EICHBERG, a teacher known to encourage female partici-pation in music. She became one of Boston's best-known violin teachers and was known throughout the country as a leading solo violinist. She also composed and published works for violin and some songs. Os-good's most notable accomplishment was the formation of the Marion Osgood Ladies Orchestra in 1884, the first professional women's orchestra in the United States. In 1890 the orchestra consisted of 30 players, constituting a full complement of strings and wood-winds as well as brass and percussion, instruments that were traditionally considered unacceptable for women to play. Osgood directed the orchestra from the first violin. The orchestra continued to perform throughout the United States until at least 1911 and was the forerunner of the more famous Fadettes all-women or-chestra, which was led by a former player in Osgood's orchestra, Caroline Nichols.

BIBLIOGRAPHY

"Women Who Win their Way," *The Illustrated American* (23 August 1890)

F.E. Willard and M.A. Livermore, eds.: *Woman of the Century: Fourteen Hundred-Seventy Biographical Sketches Accompanied by Portraits of Leading Women in All Walks of Life* (Buffalo, 1893)

F.E. Willard and M.A. Livermore, eds.: *American Women: Fifteen Hun-dred Biographies with over 1,400 Portraits* (New York, 1897)

M.G. Osgood: "America's First 'Ladies Orchestra,'" *The Etude*, lviii (1940), 713

LAURIE BLUNSOM

Osmonds, the. Musical family and popular music group. Although many members of the Osmond family have

made careers as performers, the two most prominent are the brother and sister Donny [Donald] (*b* Ogden, UT, 9 Dec 1957) and Marie (*b* Ogden, 13 Oct 1959). Other brothers include Alan, Wayne, Merrill, Jay, and Jimmy. Based in Ogden, Utah, this large family has been well known for its association with the Jesus Christ Church of Latter Day Saints, and their religion has influ-enced their musical choices. The elder brothers of the family began by performing in barbershop quartets and by the early 1960s had landed a job at Disneyland. This led to regular appearances on *The Andy Williams Show* between 1962 and 1969; their younger siblings began to contribute to family shows during this time. After a European tour in 1969, the group released "One Bad Apple" (1971), which became their biggest hit. The light pop sound of the band incorporated bells and an or-chestrated background. The Osmonds released several more hits, including "Yo-Yo," "Down the Lazy River," and "Love Me for a Reason." As their musical success peaked, television opportunities appeared; for a season beginning in 1972 they were featured on an animated program, and for three seasons from 1976 the family produced *The Donny and Marie Show*, a variety show reflecting the rising success of the two younger sib-lings. Donny also had a strong run as a solo teen idol in the 1970s while Marie recorded some successful coun-try pop tunes in the 1970s and 80s. Both subsequently remained active in different facets of the entertainment business. Other family members continued recording and touring into the 21st century.

JONAS WESTOVER

Osorio, Jorge (Federico) (*b* Mexico City, Mexico, 22 March 1951). Mexican pianist. Widely regarded as one of the foremost pianists to emerge from Mexico, he attended the National Conservatory of Mexico before embarking on a strikingly cosmopolitan education, studying at the Paris Conservatoire (with Bernard Flavigny and Monique Haas), the Moscow Conservatory (Jacob Milstein), in Positano, Italy, with Wilhelm Kempff, and privately in New York with NADIA REISENBERG. He made his official debut in 1964 at the Palacio de Bellas Artes in Mexico City. His many awards include prizes at the Rhode Island International Master Piano Competition and the Dallas SO's Gina Bachauer award. Although widely known for championing Mexican piano music (particu-larly that of Manuel M. Ponce) and the great Spanish composers (Albéniz, Falla, Granados, and Soler), he made his name with warm but classically proportioned interpretations of Mozart, Beethoven, Schumann, Brahms, Rachmaninov, and such lesser-known compos-ers Carlos Chávez and Jacob Weinberg. He has also proved to be a sensitive interpreter of Debussy and Schubert. His playing has combined a beautiful, rounded tone with an impressive grasp of large-scale structure. Osorio's interpretations have shown a classical sense of proportion and an eloquence which always puts the composer first. A true virtuoso, his musical tempera-ment has precluded exhibitionism, even in such invita-tions to flamboyance as the Tchaikovsky concerto. His concert tours have taken him to five continents, with notable North American appearances at the Hollywood Bowl, Ravinia, and Grant Park festivals. Two works by the Mexican composer Carlos Jiménez Mabarak have been dedicated to him, and in 1969 he gave the first ever performances in Mexico and Guatemala of Mozart's Piano Concerto in C, K503. Formerly the artistic director of the Brahms Music Festival in Mexico, he has always excelled in chamber music, playing with the violinist Mayumi Fujikawa and the cellist Richard Markson, the Moscow and Tel Aviv quartets, and the violinist Henryk Szeryng. He joined the faculty at Roosevelt University's Music Conservatory in 2005.

JEREMY SIEPMANN

Ossman, Vess L. [Sylvester Louis] (b Hudson, NY, 21 Aug 1868; d Fairmont, MN, 8 Dec 1923). Banjoist and composer. Self-taught on the five-string banjo which he played finger-style, he benefited from the ability of 1890s acoustic recording technology to record the banjo (it was unable at that time to capture other instruments such as the piano well). He arranged piano music for banjo and had a prolific recording career (1893–1917) which including collaborations with the singer Len Spencer (1898, 1903, 1904). He was an early recording artist for Victor. His compositions include "The Darkey's Barbecue" (1894), "Rusty Rags Medley" (1901), and "Honolulu Cake Walk." In 1900 and 1903 he recorded in England with the pianist Landon Ronald. Hundreds of recordings that he made in New York and London remained in catalog, although after 1904 recording engineers were able to add small orchestras to support his banjo. Ossman also performed and recorded with the mandolinist Audley Dudley in the Ossman–Dudley Trio and as the Vess Ossman Banjo Orchestra. He worked in clubs and hotels in Indianapolis and Dayton. Rudi Blesh claimed that ragtime's origins were on the banjo and had been concertized for the piano, and that Ossman's recordings sought to reverse that process. For more information see U. Heier and R.E. Lotz: *The Banjo on Record: a Bio-discography* (Westport, CT, 1993), 305–31.

JEFFREY GREEN

Ostertag, Bob [Robert] (b Albuquerque, NM, 19 April 1957). Composer, performer, instrument builder, and journalist. In high school he learned to play guitar, flute, violin, and percussion. In 1976 he enrolled at the Oberlin Conservatory, where he built a Serge modular synthesizer. He also formed the Fall Mountain ensemble with the reed player Ned Rothenberg and the violinist Jim Katzin. After leaving Oberlin in 1979 without a degree, he toured with Anthony Braxton's Creative Music Orchestra then settled in New York. There he began playing with John Zorn, Eugene Chadbourne, Wayne Horvitz, and Fred Frith and embarked on an idiosyncratic and individualistic career.

Ostertag's work is holistic; he has developed his compositions inseparably from the instruments he has designed, the musicians with whom he has collaborated and improvised, and the explicit and passionate political opinions he has sought to express. In 1980 he released his first solo album, *Getting a Head* (Rift Records, 1980). The music features an instrument that he designed with Bryan Medwed that linked together three open-reel tape recorders via helium balloons. A technical and musical breakthrough, it could be played in live performance and was suitable for improvisation. In 1980 Ostertag began committing more time to politics: he traveled to Nicaragua under the new Sandinista regime and fundraised and spoke on behalf of the El Salvador guerillas. One work of this period, *General Hospital*, was based on a collage text combining a *TV Guide* article and news reports of atrocities committed by the National Guard in Nicaragua. His album *Voice of America* (Rift, 1981) made use of telephone answering machine cassettes, each of varying length, played back on deliberately malfunctioning equipment. The audio content consists of recordings from television broadcasts made during the week of the presidential inauguration of Ronald Reagan, the return of the American hostages held in Iran, and the Super Bowl. He used this method to record Frith and the singer Phil Minton in performance, and used the recordings for live playback, anticipating the concept and use of the digital sampler.

After a technical mishap destroyed his analog sampling equipment and he had no means to replace it, Ostertag abandoned music and dedicated himself for several years to the cause of the Salvadorian revolution, working in Central America, giving speeches, and publishing in such periodicals as *Mother Jones* and *The Guardian* (London). In 1988 an invitation from Frith to tour with his new band, Keep the Dog, drew Ostertag back into music, and in this context he began to use both MIDI and digital samplers. With these instruments, he also appeared in duos with Frith and Zorn at the Knitting Factory and recorded *Attention Span* (Rift, 1990) and *Sooner or Later* (Rift, 1991). The latter work is the most famous and notorious of his career, and perhaps the most emotionally and politically expressive; it is made from a sample of Frith's guitar and a recording of a Salvadorian boy burying his father. In 1992 Ostertag was commissioned by the Kronos Quartet to compose *All the Rage*, which is built around the transcription of a riot for gay rights in San Francisco. The work became the title piece of a Kronos album recorded in 1993. Ostertag followed this with *Burns like Fire*, a solo piece made from the same audio recording, dedicated to the artist, writer, and AIDS activist David Wojnarowicz. He went on to lead the Say No More Quartet (1993–8), his first ensemble in decades, with Mark Dresser, Gerry Hemingway, and Phil Minton. Ostertag recorded the group's improvisations, used that material as a source for musique concrète, then transformed the result into scores for the instrumentalists.

In 1998 Ostertag received a commission to commemorate the 50th annniversary of the Universal Declaration of Human Rights for UNESCO and German radio. The following year he moved from the sampler to a laptop computer, for which he wrote his own audio performance software. At STEIM he created *Yugoslavia Suite* in response to the NATO bombing of Serbia and performed the work in the Balkans with his collaborator, the lighting designer Richard Board; the two were briefly arrested in Serbia. In the first decade of the 21st century he produced radiophonic works, including *Post Paradise* (2003) and *Creative Life* (2010). Ostertag's recordings have been released on several labels that have since become defunct; in 2006 he began making all recordings for which he owned the rights available for free download under a Creative Commons License. In 2007 he was appointed associate professor of technocultural studies at the University of California, Davis.

GEORGE J. GRELLA, JR.

Ostin, Mo (*b* New York, NY, 27 March 1927). Record executive. Trained as an accountant, he started his career in the record business at Verve Records, where he worked with Ella Fitzgerald and Sammy Davis Jr. He was subsequently hired as the president of Reprise, partially due to the influence of Frank Sinatra. He eventually became head of Reprise's parent company, Warner Bros., for which he signed and fostered the careers of such notable musicians as the Beach Boys, Frank Zappa, Paul Simon, and Prince. He worked at Warner Bros. from 1963 to 1994, where he was known particularly for his openness towards musical experimentation and the rights of artists. Ostin believed that the financial bottom line was not always the most significant factor in choosing the right music or musicians. In 1996 he and his fellow executive Larry Waronker moved to Dream Works Records, again taking risks with especially creative talent. Ostin was inducted into the Rock and Roll Hall of Fame in 2003 and retired from the business in the following year. For more information, see R. Sanjek and D. Sanjek, *American Popular Music Business in the 20th Century* (New York, 1991).

JONAS WESTOVER

Ostling, Acton Eric, Sr. (*b* Chester, CT, 13 April 1906; *d* Sarasota, FL, 1 Sept 1993). Educator and composer. While attending the Conway Band School at Ithaca College, Ostling was invited to perform with Patrick Conway's professional band. In 1927 he went to Endicott, New York, where he began the instrumental music program. He remained there for 36 years, serving as director of the Union-Endicott High School Band, and Supervisor of Music. A trombone and baritone horn player, his Connecticut heritage spawned an interest in New England fife and drum corps, and he became the first to conduct legitimate research into the history of that music. He also organized his high school students into an ancient fife and drum corps in 1938, one of the earliest corps formed outside Connecticut. He became an expert rudimental drummer, and published solos, ensembles, and method books, most notably *The Three Rs of Drumming*. He became well known for other educational materials based on his teaching. He was a co-author of the *First Division Band Method*, organizing solo and ensemble compositions and arrangements for that series. He originated the "Bandette" scoring procedure for marching bands, reducing the separate parts for maximum sound outdoors while retaining the music's essence. As a pioneer in the development of school

bands his performing groups were among the finest in New York State.

BIBLIOGRAPHY
W.H. Rehrig: *The Heritage Encyclopedia of Band Music* (Westerville, OH, 1991, suppl. 1996); CD-ROM (Oskaloosa, IA, 2005) [includes selective list of works]

ACTON OSTLING JR.

Oswald, Genevieve (Mary) (*b* Buffalo, NY, 24 Aug 1923). Archivist, writer, and teacher. Educated in music, with a Bachelor's degree from the University of North Carolina and postgraduate work at the Juilliard School and New York University Graduate School of Music, she acquired performing experience as a modern dancer and a lyric soprano. Following study at the Columbia University School of Library Service, she was entrusted in 1947 with the seed of New York Public Library's Dance Collection (now the Jerome Robbins Dance Division), then comprising a modest two shelves of material in the Music Division. As curator, she embarked on the task of enlarging the collection by soliciting donations from the dance community and raising funds for purchases of materials. Her vision was panoramic and global in scope: she included folk, ethnic, and popular dance forms as well as theatrical dance, and with projects such as the Asia Dance Archive soon expanded the collection's range beyond the western world. She did not limit the collection to print materials: the Film Archive, begun in 1961, soon grew into an invaluable trove of moving images on various film and video formats. Under her leadership, the Collection's very catalog advanced pioneering technology in the form of a groundbreaking fully-automated book catalog in 1974. In 1964 the Dance Collection became an independent division of the library, and moved in 1965 to its present-day quarters at Lincoln Center. Recognized as one of the world's leading collections of dance materials, it is utilized by creative artists as well as scholars and students. Oswald retired as curator in 1987 but continues to be active in the dance world. Her activities past and present include teaching dance history at New York University, serving as coordinator of the Americas Center of the World Dance Alliance, and assisting other dance archives with her experience and expertise.

WRITINGS
"Where are the Organized Sources for Scholarly Research?" *Research in Dance* (1968), 51–4
"Creating Tangible Records for an Intangible Art," *Special Libraries* (1968), 146–151
"Some Random Observations on the Teaching of Dance History," *CORD News*, ii (1970), 17–21
"Myth and legend in Martha Graham's Night Journey," *CORD Dance Research Annual*, xiv (1983), 42–9
"One Approach to the Development of a Dance Archive: the Dance Collection in the Library and Museum of the Performing Arts (The New York Public Library at Lincoln Center)," in *Libraries, History, Diplomacy, and the Performing Arts*, ed. I. J. Katz (New York, 1991), 77–84

BIBLIOGRAPHY
International Encyclopedia of Dance (New York, 1998)

SUSAN AU

Oswald, John (Anthony) (*b* Kitchener, ON, 30 May 1953). Composer, media artist, record producer, saxophonist, dancer, and writer. His composition teachers included R. MURRAY SCHAFER and Barry Truax at Simon Fraser University, Vancouver, and DAVID ROSENBOOM, Casey Sokol, RICHARD TEITELBAUM, and JAMES TENNEY at York University, Toronto (BFA 1977).

As a saxophonist specializing in improvisatory music, Oswald has performed widely in North America and Europe and recorded with the guitarist Henry Kaiser (*Improvised*, Music Gallery Editions, 1978), the trumpeter Toshinori Kondo (*Moose and Salmon*, Music Gallery Editions, 1982), among others; he has also released a solo album (*Alto Sax*, Metalanguage, 1981). He has been associated with the Music Gallery in Toronto since the 1970s and has performed with ensembles including Pitch, the Glass Orchestra, the New Music Co-op, and the trio CCMC (with Michael Snow and Paul Dutton).

Long involved with dance, Oswald has created electroacoustic music for such dance companies as Dancemakers, Tangente, Toronto Independent Dance Enterprise, and Bill Coleman and his North American Experience (*Shane* and *Baryshnikov*, both 1987, *Zorro*, 1989), as well as for choreographers including William Douglas (*Anima*, 1990), Denise Fujiwara (*Loud Colors*, 1990), Paula Ravitz (*Skindling Shades*, 1987), James Kudelka (*Case of Death*, 1991), Jennifer Mascall (*Parade*, 1986, *Elle*, 1989), and Holly Small (*Wounded*, 1988, *Small Attack*, 1990). His *A Disembodied Voice* (1999), created for the National Ballet of Canada, is scored for orchestra, "robot piano" (disklavier), and the sampled singing voice of Glenn Gould. He has also danced with Fujiwara, Danceworks, North American Experience, and Small, among others, and founded Art Wrestling, a weekly improvisatory dance enterprise in Toronto.

Oswald has received commissions from numerous organizations, including Arraymusic (*Acupuncture*, 1991), the Kronos Quartet (*Spectre*, 1990, *preLieu*, 1991, *Mach*, 1993), and RectoVerso Theatre in Quebec (*Parcours scénographique*, 1997). He created the soundtracks for *Stress*, an avant-garde multi-screen film by Bruce Mau premiered at the Vienna Festival (2000), and an outdoor sound and image installation, *Eislaufen*, created for the Tonspur festival in Vienna (2010).

Founder of the FONY label, Oswald is best known for coining the term "plunderphonics" to describe exploiting the familiarity of recognizable audio samples, the component parts of which are re-purposed to create new musical works. After establishing the Mystery Laboratory project in Toronto in 1980, he began distributing audio cassettes of sound collages he created. In 1987 he released *Plunderphonics* (Mystery Tape Laboratory), an EP that used samples of recordings by Count Basie, Dolly Parton, Elvis Presley, and Stravinsky's *The Rite of Spring* which had been manipulated in the studio (speeds and pitches altered and contents segmented, re-ordered, and reversed). An album version of *Plunderphonics*, which contained additional samples of the Beatles, Beethoven, Gould, Michael Jackson, Liszt, Verdi, and Webern, was released in 1989 (FONY); despite distributing it free of charge and acknowledg-ing all source materials used, Oswald was accused by the Canadian Recording Industry Association (CRIA) of flouting copyright restrictions. He subsequently surrendered his master recordings and the remaining stock of copies to be destroyed by CRIA. The notoriety of that case, however, led to a series of lucrative projects for Oswald: *Rubáiyát* (Elektra, 1991), a plunderphonic album commissioned by Elektra Records to mark its 40th anniversary; *Plexure* (Avant, 1993), with transmogrified samples of music by more than a thousand pop artists; and *GrayFolded* (Swell/Artifact, 1994–5), a two-disc plunderphonic audio tour through 25 years of live performances of the Grateful Dead's signature improvisation, "Dark Star." *GrayFolded* was selected as one of the best recordings of the year by *Rolling Stone* and the *New York Times*, among other publications.

In 2004 the New Millennium Players performed a retrospective of Oswald's music at Walt Disney Hall (Los Angeles) that included *Oswald's 1st Piano Concerto by Tchaikovsky (as suggested by Michael Snow) in B minor* (2000) and his Concerto for Wired Conductor and Orchestra (2001), as well as chamber and solo works. Described variously as a "God-like being" (*Eye Weekly*) and "the maddest man on the planet" (*The Observer*), he also won a Governor General's Award in Media Arts (2004), the jury for which wrote: "John Oswald has created an art—and vocabulary—of his own in his exceptional and innovative work as a sound artist, image alchemist, composer, and media artist…His influence on an entire generation of artists and his international reputation attest to his free-ranging spirit of innovation and exploration."

BIBLIOGRAPHY

C. Cutler: "Plunderphonia," *Musicworks*, lx/Fall (1994), 6–19

K. Holm-Hudson: "John Oswald's 'Rubaiyat (Elektrax)' and the Politics of Recombinant Do-Re-Mi," *Popular Music and Society*, xx/3 (1996), 19–36

K. Holm-Hudson: "Quotation and Context: Sampling and John Oswald's Plunderphonics," *Leonardo Music Journal*, vii/1 (1997), 17–25

N. Igma: "Plunderstanding Ecophonomics: Strategies for the Transformation of Existing Music," *Arcana: Musicians on Music*, ed. J. Zorn (New York, 2000), 9–17 [interview]

D. Keenan: "Undoing time: Interview with Samplist John Oswald," *The Wire*, no.219 (2002), 42–9 [interview]

S. TIMOTHY MALONEY

Oteri, Frank J. (*b* Miami, FL, 12 May 1964). Composer, musician, impresario, editor, and journalist. He graduated from Columbia University with a double concentration in Music and Literature (BA 1985), and served at WKCR, the campus radio station, as classical music and world music director (1984–5). He returned to Columbia as a graduate student in ethnomusicology (MA 1990). Oteri is an active and decorated composer, with a style that Peter Frank has described as "supple and self-effacing yet still distinctive," and "spiced with tangy sonorities." His pieces have been performed by Sarah Cahill, Dominic Frasca, the Sylvan Winds, and the Magellan String Quartet, and include the stage work *MACHUNAS* (1998–2002), an oratorio inspired by Fluxus founder George Maciunas, which he created in collaboration with Lucio Pozzi; vocal works that include *if by yes* (1994) to poems of E.E. Cummings; *as long as forever* (2003) from the poetry of Dylan Thomas; and *The Other Side of the Window* (1995), from texts by Margaret Atwood. He has explored microtonality in *Just Salsa* (1991) for 11-limit just intonation salsa band; *circles in wood* (2002), a quarter-tone wind quintet; *Fair and Balanced?* (2004) for quarter-tone saxophone quartet, recorded by the PRISM Quartet for release in 2011; and *Imagined Overtures* (2005) for a rock band playing in 1/6th tones.

Oteri is also an accomplished and important advocate for contemporary music, as reflected by his professional work, extensive writings, and public and media appearances. He joined the staff at the American Music Center in 1998 and founded the Center's online magazine, *NewMusicBox* (<http://www.newmusicbox.org/>), the following year. As Editor, he has conducted and published interviews with over 100 leading American composers and musicians, including Milton Babbitt, Wendy Carlos, Elliott Carter, Ornette Coleman, Mario Davidovsky, Philip Glass, Jennifer Higdon, Meredith Monk, Pauline Oliveros, Terry Riley, Ned Rorem, Tan Dun, Henry Threadgill, Joan Tower, Charles Wourinen, and LaMonte Young. He is a frequent contributor to *Chamber Music* magazine, *Symphony* magazine, and *Playbill*, and his book on the *Rautavaara Orchestral Works* was published in 1999.

He has appeared as either guest or moderator for pre-concert and post-concert panels at Lincoln Center, Carnegie Hall, Walt Disney Hall, and Meet the Composer's "The Works" in Minneapolis, Minnesota. He also participates in music conference panels in both the United States and abroad, including those for Chamber Music America, Opera America, League of American Orchestras, Music Critics Association of North America (for which he also served two two-year terms on its Board of Directors), and the International Association of Music Information Centres. He has been a guest in conversations about new music on radio programs in North America, Asia, Europe, and Australia. Since 2003, he has hosted the 21st Century Schizoid Music concert series at Cornelia Street Cafe in New York City. He is the recipient of the National League of American Pen Women Prize for Musical Composition (1981), the George W. Woodbury Poetry Prize from Columbia (1985), the Deems Taylor Award (1999), and the ASCAP Victor Herbert Award (2007), which cited his "distinguished service to American Music" and "vision as a composer, journalist, editor, broadcaster and impresario."

GEORGE J. GRELLA JR.

Otis, Johnny [Veliotes, John Alexander] (*b* Vallejo, CA, 28 Dec 1921; *d* Los Angeles, CA, 17 Jan 2012). Producer, label owner, scout, broadcaster, author, visual artist, preacher, farmer, and political activist. Although born a Greek American, he chose to live as if he were an African American, marrying a black woman and committing himself to the values and culture of that community. He began his career as a drummer, formed his own band, and recorded his first hit, "Harlem Nocturne," in 1945. He subsequently produced major hits for other artists, including Big Mama Thornton's "Hound Dog" in 1953. Otis possessed a particular eye for talent and discovered a number of successful performers, including Esther Phillips, Etta James, Big Jay McNeely, Jackie Wilson, and Little Willie John. He also hit the charts with "Willie and the Hand Jive" in 1958. He burst back upon the scene with a spectacular revue featured at the Monterey Jazz Festival in 1970, which also encouraged public interest in his guitar-playing son Shuggie, who subsequently recorded several solo albums. Otis published two memoirs, released a lavish collection of his paintings, and was the subject of a full length biography. A sign of the breadth of his musical skills and range of his musical influence, Otis was inducted into the Rock and Roll, Rhythm and Blues, and Blues halls of fame.

BIBLIOGRAPHY
J. Otis: *Listen to the Lambs* (Minneapolis, 1968/*R*)
J. Otis: *Upside your Head: Rhythm & Blues on Central Avenue* (Middletown, CT, 1993)
G. Lipsitz: *Midnight at the Barrelhouse: the Johnny Otis Story* (Minneapolis, 2010)

DAVID SANJEK

Oudin, Eugène (Espérance) (*b* New York, 24 Feb 1858; *d* London, 4 Nov 1894). Baritone of French descent. He studied with Moderati in New York, where he made his debut in 1886 at Wallack's Theatre with the M'Caul Opéra-Comique Company as Montosol in an English version of Roger's *Joséphine vendue par ses soeurs*. He was engaged by Sullivan to create the part of the Templar in *Ivanhoe* at the Royal English Opera House, London, in 1891. He sang the title role in the English premiere of *Yevgeny Onegin* (1892) at the Olympic Theatre, and in 1893 he sang the High Priest in the first performance in England (a concert version) of *Samson et Dalila*, in his own translation. Oudin sang with notable success in 1893 and 1894 at St. Petersburg as Wolfram, Telramund, and Albert (*Werther*).

HAROLD ROSENTHAL/R

Oundjian, Peter (*b* Toronto, ON, 21 Dec 1955). Canadian conductor, violinist, and teacher. Of Armenian-British heritage, he was educated in England where he studied piano, took violin lessons, and sang in the choir of Westminster Abbey as a boy soprano. During this time he met Benjamin Britten, who included him in three of his recordings. He studied violin with Manoug Parikian before entering the Royal College of Music in London. He transferred to the Juilliard School where he studied violin with IVAN GALAMIAN, ITZHAK PERLMAN, and DOROTHY DELAY. After winning first prize at the 1980 International Violin Competition in Viña del Mar, Chile, Oundjian played first violin with the Tokyo String Quartet (1981–95). The ensemble's intense schedule of more than 130 concerts and five recordings per year prompted his retirement because of focal dystonia, a muscle condition that affected his left hand. Since 1981 Oundjian has also taught at the Yale School of Music.

His conducting debut took place in 1995 at the Caramoor International Music Festival with the Orchestra of St. Luke's. From 1997 to 2003 he served as the festival's artistic director. Other conducting posts include music director of Amsterdam's Nieuw Sinfonietta (1998–2003) and principal guest conductor of the Colorado Symphony in Denver (2003–6) and the Detroit SO (2006–9). Oundjian became music director of the Toronto SO in 2004 and has been associated with reinvigorating this orchestra, which had been on the brink of collapse. With this orchestra, he established the New Creations Festival to showcase contemporary orchestral music. He has released four recordings on the self-produced record label, tsoLIVE. He was named music director of the Royal Scottish National Orchestra for the 2012–13 season.

BIBLIOGRAPHY
V. Cruice: "From First Violin to Artistic Director," *New York Times* (22 June 1997)
C. Eatock: "Oundjian on Board" *Opus*, (Fall 2004), 12–15; repr. <http://www.colineatock.com/peter-oundjian.html> (2013)

JAMES BASH

OutKast [Outkast]. Rap duo. It comprises Andre 3000 (André Lauren Benjamin; *b* Atlanta, GA, 27 May 1975) and Big Boi (Antwan André Patton; *b* Atlanta, 1 Feb 1975). One of their defining features has been constant reinvention, and their music has evolved significantly since their debut in 1994. At a time when East and West Coast artists dominated the charts, the duo brought increased attention to southern hip hop, effectively putting their hometown of Atlanta on the hip-hop map.

Andre 3000 and Big Boi met and formed Outkast at Tri-Cities High School, an arts-based institution in Atlanta. In 1992 they signed with LaFace Records. Their recording debut came with an appearance on a remix of TLC's hit "What about Your Friends" (1993). In 1994 the group released their debut album *Southernplayalisticadillacmuzic*, which attained platinum certification. Produced by Organized Noize, who had originally recruited them to LaFace, the album was noted for its use of live instrumentation and laid-back, soul-heavy sound, which can be heard on the hit single "Git up, Git out."

In 1996 Outkast released the double platinum *ATLiens*, which debuted at number two on the Billboard album charts. The album once again featured production from Organized Noize but leaned more towards atmospheric sounds than their debut. Their next recording *Aquemini* (1998) solidified the group's reputation as one of the most dynamic and consistent in popular music. It was also certified double platinum. In 2000 the duo released their critically acclaimed fourth album, *Stankonia*, which surpassed their previous successes, selling more than four million copies. Outkast's creative and commercial peak came in 2003 with the release of the double album *Speakerboxxx/The Love Below*. This was actually two solo projects: Big Boi's *Speakerboxxx* and Andre 3000's *The Love Below*. Big Boi's album was heavily rooted in bounce and traditional southern hip hop; Andre 3000's disc experimented with electronic pop, funk, and even drum and bass. The album was

certified platinum 11 times and produced two number-one songs: Big Boi's "The Way You Move" and Andre 3000's "Hey Ya!" In addition the album won the Grammy award for Album of the Year in 2004.

The pair then began working in the film industry. In 2006 they starred in Bryan Barber's musical *Idlewild* for which they also co-wrote the soundtrack. Big Boi released his first official solo album, *Sir Lucious Leftfoot: the Song of Chico Dusty*, in 2010. Andre 3000 has made several appearances on singles by UGK, Jay-Z, and John Legend.

BIBLIOGRAPHY
C. Norris: "Funk Soul Brothers," *Spin*, xvi/12 (2000), 142–8
R. Sarig: *Third Coast: OutKast, Timbaland, and how Hip-hop Became a Southern Thing* (Cambridge, MA, 2007)

JARED PAULEY

Outsider music. A term coined by the radio DJ and author Irwin Chusid in 1996 to describe a loosely related set of recordings that do not fit well within any pre-existing generic framework. The art critic Roger Cardinal first used the term "outsider" in 1972 in relation to visual art. His usage translated into English the French artist Jean Dubuffet's term *art brut*, which arose from Dubuffet's interest in the artwork of criminals and the mentally ill. The term "outsider art" was in wide circulation during the 1970s and 80s, when many examples of what became now known, after Chusid, as "outsider music" were first being analyzed by collectors of outré records; Lester Bangs mentioned two key outsider musicians, Wild Man Fischer and Jad Fair, in his essay "A Reasonable Guide to Horrible Noise" (1981). V. Vale explored similar terrain in the early 1990s. Outsider music does not involve any definite stylistic qualities; criteria for inclusion are generally either negational or relational. Much outsider music exhibits idiomatic characteristics of established genres, ranging from opera (Florence Foster Jenkins) to country music (the Legendary Stardust Cowboy), although in an idiosyncratic fashion. Other examples defy precedent, leaving the critical listener understanding initially only what the music is not (as with Fischer's a cappella compositions). The term "outsider" is, almost by definition, controversial. From Dubuffet to Chusid, it has concurrently carried connotations of both psychological pathologies and an assumption of a purity of expression at the boundaries of culture.

The relationship between outsider music and mental illness is apparent from the biographies of the artists Chusid profiles in *Songs in the Key of Z: the Curious Universe of Outsider Music*; five of the 20 examples in his book concern musicians whose psychological problems are documented: Joe Meek (paranoid/depressive; murdered his landlady before committing suicide), Daniel Johnston (bipolar disorder), Wesley Willis (schizophrenic), Syd Barrett (erratic behavior compounded by the use of LSD), and Fischer (both bipolar and schizophrenic). At the least, nearly all outsider musicians display eccentric personal habits. There are serious questions regarding the exploitation of such individuals within the commercial music industry.

However, it is also worth noting that many artists within the loose "canon" of outsider music were avid self-promoters. Furthermore, many of them were not bereft of some type of musical training. The composer Harry Partch, noted for his homemade instruments, held residencies at several universities. Tiny Tim, who wrote "Tiptoe through the Tulips," had an almost encyclopedic knowledge of Tin Pan Alley. Willis, Fischer, and Daniel Johnston all worked to ingratiate themselves within the rock scenes of their times and locales. Meek, Barrett, and Captain Beefheart each enjoyed some level of popular success and not necessarily in the context of novelty, a category that sometimes overlaps with outsider music.

Rather than simply existing outside of society, as the term might imply, many outsider artists aspired to mainstream success. That neither Foster Jenkins nor the Shaggs could competently adhere to the conventions of their chosen genre did not lessen their ambition. Nevertheless, the combination of unusual personalities and unconventional music ensured that even if these were not pure expressions beyond the social, they still called into question the perimeter that contains what is and is not culture.

BIBLIOGRAPHY
L. Bangs: "A Reasonable Guide to Horrible Noise," *Psychotic Reactions and Carburetor Dung*, ed. G. Marcus (New York, 1988), 301–4
V. Vale: *Incredibly Strange Music*, i (San Francisco, 1993)
V. Vale: *Incredibly Strange Music*, ii (San Francisco, 1994)
I. Chusid: *Songs in the Key of Z: the Curious Universe of Outsider Music* (Chicago, 2000)
MungBeing <http://www.mungbeing.com/issue_2.html> [outsider art and stuckism issue]

JOHN CLINE

Ovation. Firm of guitar manufacturers. It was founded in Bloomfield, Connecticut, in the 1960s by Charles Huron Kaman (1919–2011) as a subsidiary of the aerospace products manufacturer Kaman Corporation. Kaman became interested in guitars and guitar production and began to test for this purpose materials that the company had developed in experiments on the vibrational and acoustical properties of helicopter rotor blades. The result was the first series of Ovation acoustic guitars, introduced in 1966 and 1967, which included the Balladeer six-string and the Pacemaker 12-string models. Both had Ovation's distinctive rounded back, made from a synthetic material resembling fiberglass (patented by Ovation as Lyrachord), which enhances reflection, and thereby projection, of the sound.

Three years later Kaman unveiled another innovation in the form of a pickup built into the bridge saddles of the instrument; this sensed vibrations in both the strings and the top of the guitar and was connected to a small preamplifier inside the body, which was controlled by a volume potentiometer mounted on the heel of the instrument. This device effectively created a hybrid "electricacoustic" guitar, which has become the first choice of many pop guitarists interested in achieving the sound quality of a good acoustic instrument at relatively high amplification levels on stage. Ovation has also produced some less successful solid-body

electric guitars, including the Breadwinner (1972) and the UK II (1979), the body of which was made of another plastic developed by Ovation ("Urelite") over an aluminum frame. The most expensive and distinguished of Ovation's guitars have been the Adamas models, launched in the mid-1970s. The top was made from a sandwich of rigid graphite fiber and wood and had multiple sound holes, positioned at the upper end, for extra projection.

In 2007 the Kaman Music Corporation was purchased by FENDER and has subsequently operated as KMC Music, Inc.

BIBLIOGRAPHY
T. Bacon, ed.: *Rock Hardware: the Instruments, Equipment and Technology of Rock* (Poole, England, 1981)
T. Wheeler: *American Guitars: an Illustrated History* (New York, 1982)
W. Carter: *The History of the Ovation Guitar* (Milwaukee, 1996)
"Charles Huron Kaman," *Music Trades* (1 March 2011), 186–89

TONY BACON/ARIAN SHEETS

Overton, Hall (*b* Bangor, MI, 23 Feb 1920; *d* New York, NY, 24 Nov 1972). Composer. He began his music studies in Grand Rapids, Michigan, and composed an overture and a polytonal orchestral piece while still in high school. He pursued studies in counterpoint with Gustav Dunkelberger (1940–42) and in composition with VINCENT PERSICHETTI at the Juilliard School (1947–51); later he took private lessons with WALLINGFORD RIEGGER and DARIUS MILHAUD. Serving overseas in the US Army (1942–5), he developed remarkable skill in jazz improvisation and later appeared with such jazz musicians as Stan Getz, Oscar Pettiford, Teddy Charles, and Jimmy Rainey; he also made arrangements for the Thelonious Monk Orchestra and contributed to *Down Beat* and *Jazz Today*. His own music was deeply influenced by jazz but without his trying to make jazz "respectable" through the unnatural imposition of classical forms or materials. He taught at the Juilliard School (1960–71); the New School, New York (1962–6); and the Yale School (1970–71). Among his many honors were two Guggenheim Fellowships (1955, 1957), a BMI award (1962), and the combined award of the American Academy of Arts and Letters and the National Institute of Arts and Letters (1964).

WORKS
(selective list)

Dramatic: The Enchanted Pear Tree (op buffa, 4 scenes, J. Thompson, after Boccaccio: *Decameron*), 1950; Nonage (ballet), 1951; The New Look is the Anxious Look (film score), 1960; Pietro's Petard (chbr op, 1, R. DeMaria), 1963; Huckleberry Finn (op, 2, Overton, J. Stampfer, after M. Twain), New York, May 1971

Orch: Sym. Movt, 1950; Sym. no.1, str, 1955; Concertino, vn, str, 1958; Sym. no.2, 1962; Dialogues, chbr orch, 1963; Interplay, 1964; Sonorities, 1964; Rhythms, vn, orch, 1965; Pulsations, chbr orch, 1972

Chbr and solo inst: Str Qt no.1, 1950; Sonatina, vn, hpd, 1956; Fantasy, brass qnt, pf, perc, 1957; Str Trio, 1957; Polarities no.1, pf, 1959; Sonata, va, pf, 1960; Sonata, vc, pf, 1960; Pf Sonata, 1963; Processional, brass qt, perc, 1965; Str Qt no.2, 1967; Str Qt no.3, 1967; Polarities no.2, pf, 1971; other pf and chbr pieces

Vocal: Captivity (G. Chaucer), male vv; 3 Elizabethan Songs (B. Jonson), S, pf, 1953; other songs

Principal publishers: ACA, Peters

BIBLIOGRAPHY

J.T. Howard: *Our American Music: Three Hundred Years of it* (New York, 1929, enlarged 4/1965 as *Our American Music: a Comprehensive History from 1620 to the Present*), 613–4, 808, 913–4

D. Cohen: "The Music of Hall Overton," *ACAB*, x/4 (1962), 8–12

W. Mellers: *Music in a New Found Land* (London, 1964/R), 229–30, 540

G. Green: "Current Chronicle," *MQ*, lvii (1971), 659–64 [analysis of Va Sonata]

OLIVER DANIEL

Owen, [Esther] **Anita** (*b* Brazil, IN, Nov 1874; *d* New Haven, CT, 25 Oct 1932). Songwriter and publisher. She was among the most successful female songwriters of her generation. The daughter of John Dale Owen, a composer born in Wales, she was raised in Indiana and went to school near Terre Haute at St. Mary's in the Woods. While there she sold her first song, evidently a setting of "Ave Maria." Her obituary in the *New York Times* describes Owen as the composer of 200 works, yet it is unlikely that more than about half of those were ever published. In 1894 she composed and published her first and most enduring hit, the sentimental waltz song "Sweet Bunch of Daisies," which sold a million copies. This song, the first of several about daisies, became a standard with country string bands and Appalachian fiddlers, and was also recorded by the blues harmonica player El Watson in 1928.

As Carrie Jacobs-Bond did a few years later, Owen founded a music publishing company, the Wabash Music Co., in Chicago and designed the covers of her songs. From the beginning she wrote her own texts, but after 1898 she only set her own poems to music. After moving to New York in 1904, she published with Jerome H. Remick & Co. from 1908 until she married Arthur J. Jones in 1917. He then founded the Jones Music Co. and issued her last songs in 1919 and 1920. She also composed a comic opera, *The Great Mogul* (1903).

CHRISTOPHER A. REYNOLDS

Owen, Barbara (*b* Utica, NY, 25 Jan 1933). Organist and organ scholar. Owen studied organ at Westminster Choir College and received a MusB in 1955 before earning a MusM from Boston University in 1962. Her organ teachers included Edward Broadhead, ALEXANDER McCURDY, and George Faxon. She later attended summer courses at the North German Organ Academy (1975, 1977) and the Academy of Italian Organ Music (1985), and she earned the American Guild of Organists Choir Master certificate in 1982. After graduating from Westminster Choir College, Owen served as organist in various Connecticut and Massachusetts churches before accepting a position as Music Director at First Religious Society Unitarian Church in Newburyport, Massachusetts (1963–2002). After her retirement there, she became organist at St. Anne's Episcopal Church, Lowell, Massachusetts (2002–7). She has been the librarian of the American Guild of Organists' Organ Library at Boston University since 1985. Owen has been dean and councilor for several AGO regions as well as councilor and president of the Organ Historical Society, an advisory board member for the Instituto de Organos Historicos de Oaxaca since 2005, and a trustee of Methuen Memorial Music Hall since 1990. A leading organ scholar, she has won numerous awards including an NEH Fellowship (1974–5); the Westminster Choir College Alumni Citation of Merit (1988); the Organ Historical Society Distinguished Service Award (1988); the American Musical Instrument Society Curt Sachs Award (1994), and the AGO Organ Library Max Miller Book Award (2009). In 2005 Owen was honored by the Organ Historical Society with a festschrift, *Litterae Organi: Essays in Honor of Barbara Owen* (Richmond, VA).

SELECTED WRITINGS

The Organs and Music of King's Chapel (Boston, 1965, 2/1993)

The Organ in New England: an account of its use and manufacture to the end of the nineteenth century (Raleigh, 1979)

E. Power Biggs: Concert Organist (Bloomington, 1987)

ALLISON A. ALCORN

Owen, Charlotte Louise Plummer (*b* Minneapolis, MN, 31 Jan 1918; *d* Ann Arbor, MI, 18 Dec 2004). Conductor. She studied piano, saxophone and clarinet as a child, playing weekly jobs with the family's dance band, and was an award-winning clarinetist at Eugene High School in Eugene, Oregon. She studied music education at the University of Oregon and during this time she was hired to direct the University High School band. After graduation in 1939, she was an assistant band director in La Grande, Oregon, then moved to Commerce High School in Portland to teach instrumental and vocal ensembles. In 1943, during World War II, she enlisted in the Marine Corps Women's Reserve (MCWR) to play clarinet in the band and was appointed director at the rank of Master Technical Sergeant. In this capacity, she was the first woman band director in the Marine Corps and was the first woman to guest conduct the US Marine Corps Band. In 1945, after the war ended, she married, played principal clarinet in orchestras, raised a family, and taught private instrumental lessons for over 60 years. From 1986–2001, she directed the Ann Arbor Civic Band. In 1997 she was invited to direct a band of women veterans at the dedication of the Women in Military Service of America Memorial in Washington, DC.

BIBLIOGRAPHY

"Marine Corps Women's Reserve Band," *Music Educators Journal*, xxx/1 (1943), 26, 51

P. Meid: *Marine Corps Women's Reserve in World War II* (Washington, DC, 1968)

E. Stone and B.S. Medin: "*Music Women Marines:* the Marine Corps Women's Reserve Band in World War II" (unpublished manuscript, 1981).

M.V. Stremlow: "Marine Corps Women's Reserve," *In Defense of a Nation: Servicewomen in World War II*, ed., J.M. Holm and J. Bellafaire (Washington, DC, 1998).

J.M. Sullivan: Interview with Charlotte Owen, 2 August 2001, Ann Arbor, MI. Transcripts and videotape recordings [See <http://www.public.asu.edu/~jmsulli/Webpages/marine.html>]

M. Chavez: "Women Marine Band," *Leatherneck—Magazine of the Marines*, lxxxvi/2 (2003), 44–8

J.M. Sullivan: "A History of the Marine Corps Women's Reserve Band," *Journal of Band Research*, xlii/1 (2006), 1–41

JILL SULLIVAN

Owens, Buck [Alvis Edgar] (*b* Sherman, TX, 12 Aug 1929; *d* Bakersfield, CA, 25 March 2006). Country musician and businessman. He is widely considered the central figure of the Bakersfield sound, and his dominance of the country charts in the 1960s challenged Nashville's hegemony and bolstered the West Coast country scene in Bakersfield and Los Angeles. During the 1950s he worked as a guitarist and session player for several Bakersfield artists before signing with Capitol Records in 1957. In 1963 he began a streak of 14 consecutive number-one country hits with "Act Naturally," which was later covered by the Beatles. Other hits included "Together Again" (1964), "I've got a tiger by the tail" (1965), and a cover of "Johnny B. Goode" (1969).

Owens's songs eschewed themes of hard living and rambling for a portrayal of the male subject as a lonely victim of romance. With his backing band, the Buckaroos, he developed a bright, driving sound which he described as a freight train feel: heavy bass and drums accompanying two Fender Telecaster electric guitars played by Owens and the guitarist Don Rich. The twangy Telecaster sound and high, close harmony of Owens and Rich characterized many of his recordings. The Buckaroos both toured and recorded with Owens, a contrast to country norms. Owens thus established an alternative to the popular "countrypolitan" sound produced in Nashville (he also never joined the "Grand Ole Opry"); in doing so he inspired such country-rock musicians as Gram Parsons and the Flying Burrito Brothers. He also marketed himself as a hard-country artist free of pop influence; in 1965 he published his famous "Pledge to Country Music" in which he committed to sing and produce only country music.

Owens's recording career declined in the 1970s following the death of Rich, but he won new fame as cohost of the television show *Hee Haw*. He also managed business ventures that he had begun developing early in his career, eventually building an empire that included ownership of country radio stations, publishing and management companies, a television show, and Bakerfield's Crystal Palace dancehall. Collaborating with Dwight Yoakam brought him attention in the 1980s and produced Owens's final number-one hit, "Streets of Bakersfield" (1988).

BIBLIOGRAPHY

M. Fenster: "Under his Spell: how Buck Owens Took Care of Business," *Journal of Country Music*, xii (1989), 18–27

M. Fenster: "Buck Owens, Country Music, and the Struggle for Discursive Control," *Popular Music*, ix (1990), 275–90

B. Ching: "Drawing Hard Lines: Buck Owens, Dwight Yoakam, and the Bakersfield Sound," *Wrong's What I Do Best: Hard Country Music and Contemporary Culture* (New York, 2001), 89–118

E. Sisk: *Buck Owens: the Biography* (Chicago, 2010)

OLIVIA CARTER MATHER

Owens, Harry Robert (*b* O'Neil, NE, 18 April 1902; *d* Eugene, OR, 12 Dec 1986). Bandleader, composer, and songwriter. He studied cornet and by 1916 had joined the vaudeville circuit. He started his first band in 1926 in Los Angeles, where he auditioned and befriended the young singer Bing Crosby at the Lafayette Hotel. Owens' transformation into a prominent figure in Hawaiian music began when he was hired in 1934 to be the director of the band at the Royal Hawaiian Hotel in Waikiki. Actively studying the area's traditions, native music, songs, and lyrics, Owens became one of the first to write down many of these tunes, often orchestrating them for use by his band the Royal Hawaiians. During his first year in residence, he composed the famous song "Sweet Leilani," which became the band's signature piece. The number was heard during a visit to the islands by Crosby, who requested its inclusion in his upcoming film, *Waikiki Wedding* (1937). It went on to win the Oscar for Best Original Song and became an enormous hit for Crosby and was sung in other movies during the 1940s. Owens appeared regularly on television, where he continued to popularize his own and native Hawaiian music. A composer of more than 300 hapa haole songs, which mixed modern styles and traditional Hawaiian music, Owens also recorded many records for Decca in the 1940s and 50s. For further information see G.S. Kanahele, ed., *Hawaiian Music and Musicians: an Illustrated History* (Honolulu, 1979).

JONAS WESTOVER

Ozarks, the. Predominantly rural region including much of southern and central Missouri, northern Arkansas, and arguably parts of Oklahoma, Kansas, and Illinois. Musically, the Ozarks is known for contributing to folk and popular genres associated with the Upland South. Its musical history bespeaks diversity, however, and, in many respects, parallels that of the nation.

Native Americans residing in the Ozarks before white settlement included the OSAGE, who performed ceremonial dances and songs. Though most Native people left the region in the early 1800s, their musical influences remained. CHEROKEE and other Native people migrated to the region in anticipation or because of forced removal from homelands in the Southeast in the 1830s; many residents today claim Native ancestry. Intertribal powwows featuring music occur annually.

An 1807 report suggests that bands in Ste. Genevieve, Missouri, the first organized settlement established by French colonists, played cotillions and other popular dances of the time. French folk traditions persist in parts of southeast Missouri. Traditional fiddling from the Old Mines area appears on *I'm Old but I'm Awfully Tough: Traditional Music of the Ozark Region* (Missouri Friends of the Folk Arts, c1977) and recordings by Dennis Stroughmatt. Residents of some communities sing centuries-old song *La Guignolée* (or *La Guiannée*) each New Year's Eve.

Culture introduced by Anglo- and Celtic-American settlers, predominantly from southeastern states, largely eclipsed that of the French in the Ozarks within the early 1800s. Vernacular dance music was integral to that culture. Explorers witnessed informal dances in rural Arkansas in the 1810s; a square dance accompanied by fiddling was documented in central Missouri in 1818. The Anglo- and Celtic-American fiddling and string band traditions initiated in the Ozarks in the early 1800s are related to those established in Appalachia and other regions of the Upland South. Stylistic traits and repertoire from various other sources have been integrated into those traditions. These influences include ragtime and other African American music; German American and parlor styles from points north, and, since the early 1900s, media-transmitted old-time, country, bluegrass, and Western swing idioms.

Commercial use of Ozarks vernacular instrumental music beyond the region has occurred at least since the mid-1800s, when a humorous sketch called "The Arkansas Traveler," featuring fiddling, became popular nationally. Ozarks string music was recorded in conjunction with the popularization of square dancing in the 1920s and 30s. Fiddle contests, which tend to emphasize Texan and pan-regional styles, and country and bluegrass performances have superseded square dances as the principal public contexts for fiddling. Nonetheless, jam sessions, festivals, and institutions such as the Ozark Folk Center in Arkansas feature traditional fiddling exhibiting distinctly regional characteristics and aurally transmitted repertoire. Gordon McCann and others have documented traditional fiddling extensively in recent decades; recordings on several labels provide examples. Ozarks old-time fiddlers who have received national recognition since the mid-20th century include Violet Hensley, Lyman Enloe, Art Galbraith, Gene Goforth, Bob Holt, and Lonnie Robertson. Increasingly, younger women conserve and perform Ozarks traditional fiddle music.

Anglo- and Celtic-Americans also introduced ballads and songs of both Old and New World origin. The older ballads (narrative songs of both oral and broadside origin) constituted approximately the same repertoire as that of the Appalachian tradition (e.g., "Barbara Allen," "The House Carpenter"). The Ozarks also shared with Appalachia lyric, blues, and play-party songs. Singing was largely unaccompanied; more recently, traditional singers have used instruments (guitar and sometimes banjo or dulcimer) to accompany themselves.

The 1800s witnessed commercial production of numerous songs disseminated via sheet music, notably "parlor ballads," which proved popular in aural tradition nationwide. (See PARLOR MUSIC.) Other 19th- and early-20th-century songs transmitted both in print and aurally included those associated with minstrelsy, the Civil War, cowboy life, and the music hall. Singing games or "play-parties" occurred in many rural communities. Since the advent of recordings and radio, Ozarks traditional singers have also learned repertoire from those sources, first- or second-hand; many songs recorded by musicians from elsewhere entered the Ozarks vernacular repertoire. Beginning in the early 1900s, folksong collectors, notably Henry Belden, Vance Randolph, John Quincy Wolf, Alan Lomax, Max Hunter, and W.K. McNeil, notated, recorded, and published songs from the region. Their fieldwork brought several singers to prominence, including Almeda Riddle, Ollie Gilbert, May Kennedy McCord (also a folk music collector and radio personality), and Jimmy Driftwood (also a songwriter and cultural conservator), many of whom

later made recordings and performed nationwide during the folk revival.

Nineteenth-century German immigrants, settling largely near the Missouri and Mississippi rivers, established musical organizations and introduced cultivated and vernacular repertoire. Founders of the Lutheran Church-Missouri Synod contributed to the reintroduction of pre-Bach versions of chorales. Community events feature German-American instrumental music and dancing.

Vocal and instrumental parlor music, brass bands, and barbershop quartets were common among townspeople in the late 1800s-early 1900s. Blackface minstrelsy persisted into the mid-1900s in some communities.

The region contributed significantly to ragtime. The House of Lords saloon, operating from 1899 to 1922 in Joplin, Missouri, hosted performances by such important pianist-composers as Scott Joplin, Jelly Roll Morton, and Joplin native Percy Wenrich (1887–1952). Notable ragtime musicians from the Missouri Ozarks include Theron Bennett (1879–1937), JAMES SCOTT (1886–1938), considered one of the "big three" classic ragtime composers, and Clarence Woods (1888–1956); pianist-historian Bob Darch (1920–2002) was based in the region for much of his career.

Music representing predominantly white Evangelical and Independent Protestant traditions has long been central to Ozarks culture. Use of *Missouri Harmony* (1820), a four-shape-note tunebook, was once widespread. No uninterrupted tradition of four-shape singing remains, but singers including composer-scholar P. Dan Brittain engage in it as a revived practice. Singing from *Christian Harmony* (1866), an early seven-shape tunebook, occurred in the Arkansas and Missouri Ozarks through much of the 1900s. Field recordings made in the 1940s to 60s indicate that some folk hymnody associated with the 19th-century tunebook tradition remained in oral circulation; religious folksongs reflecting influences including camp-meeting spirituals, early gospel music, Holiness and Pentecostal religiosity, and secular popular song were also documented. Primitive Baptist congregations sing repertoire associated with the tunebook tradition; some occasionally sing by lining out. The Ozark Folk Center annually hosts a National Shape-Note Gathering encompassing multiple traditions.

Gospel music is more prevalent than older traditions of white spirituals and folk hymnody. Gospel songwriter E.M. Bartlett (1885–1941) co-founded Hartford Music Company in Arkansas in 1918. Hartford songwriter ALBERT E. BRUMLEY (1905–77) achieved preeminence in Southern gospel, composing such standards as "I'll Fly Away." His own Missouri-based company, Albert E. Brumley and Sons, still publishes music and hosts an annual "sing" featuring famous performers. The Stamps-Baxter Music Company maintained an Ozarks office in the mid-1900s. Singing schools—brief courses in music theory, seven-shape notation, and ensemble singing—occurred in many rural communities in the 20th century, often using materials published by Hartford or Stamps-Baxter. The Brockwell Gospel Music School in

Arkansas, a 1948 outgrowth of such courses, remains influential. Several renowned Southern gospel ensembles, including the Jordanaires and Foggy River Boys, originated in the Missouri Ozarks. BRANSON, Missouri, is a center of southern gospel, contemporary Christian, and Evangelical-themed music theater performances. Gospel music provides the core repertoire for congregational singing in many churches. Church-hosted gospel "sings" and county singing conventions occur frequently. Local musicians spanning the gospel stylistic spectrum participate in community events. Old-time, bluegrass, and country musicians often perform gospel songs. African American gospel, though not as prominent as white gospel, is also represented in the Ozarks.

As elsewhere, country music emerged in the Ozarks as interrelated traditions of folk music (incorporating popular music in aural circulation) became the bases of radio programming and recordings in the early to mid-1900s. Recordings by Ozarks musicians in the earliest years of the country recording industry (the mid-1920s to early 30s), though few compared with those by musicians from Appalachia and the Deep South, are considered noteworthy; examples by various Arkansas and Missouri string bands appear on *Echoes of the Ozarks* (County Records, 1969). George D. Hay attended a hoedown near Mammoth Spring, Arkansas, while on a journalistic assignment in 1919; it piqued his interest in rural string music, leading to his involvement in early country radio programming and eventually his founding of the *Grand Ole Opry* in Nashville.

Country music soon developed a symbiosis with its antecedent traditions as media-transmitted repertoire was integrated into participatory music-making. Radio stations broadcast live-in-the-studio performances by local musicians beginning in the late 1930s. Stylistically, this programming was largely typical of "hillbilly" radio throughout the Upland South but incorporated more western swing-influenced music, reflecting the Ozarks' proximity to the southwest. In the 1940s and 50s, KWTO in Springfield, Missouri, syndicated country programming to stations nationwide. Such influential musicians as Chet Atkins and the Carter Family spent time in residence at KWTO. ABC began national telecasts of the weekly *Ozark Jubilee* from Springfield in 1955. Featuring regional and nationally known performers, it continued (under various titles) until 1961. Historian Bill Malone calls it "the king of the televised barn dances."

Ozark Jubilee alumnus and Missouri native PORTER WAGONER (1927–2007) made numerous popular recordings and appeared regularly on the *Grand Ole Opry* and his own television program in the mid- and late 1900s. Singers Ferlin Husky (1925–2011) and Wynn Stewart (1934–85), both Missourians, influenced the development of the Nashville Sound and the Bakersfield, California, country scene, respectively. The Wilburn Brothers (Doyle, 1930–82, and Teddy, 1931–2003) from Arkansas contributed to the Nashville milieu as a vocal duo, executives, and television hosts. Jan Howard (*b* 1930) and Leona Williams (*b* 1942), Missouri natives, have achieved acclaim as singers. Many other Ozarkers have attained prominence in various facets of mainstream country music and western swing. Branson, Missouri, has been a major hub of country performance and base of operations for many musicians since the 1980s. Alternative country and neo-traditional music also contribute to the Ozarks' musical milieu and vice versa, as evidenced by the career of Missouri band Big Smith and the soundtrack of the 2010 film *Winter's Bone*.

Bluegrass music seems almost ubiquitous in the Ozarks. Symbioses between bluegrass and local traditions of music-making in antecedent genres developed by the mid-1900s. The Dillards are the most influential bluegrass band to have originated in the region. Other accomplished Ozarks bluegrass musicians include Lonnie Hoppers, Guy Stevenson, and Dale Sledd. Nationally significant annual bluegrass festivals occur in Arkansas and Missouri. Amateur and semi-professional bluegrass musicians, often stylistically conservative but occasionally more progressive, appear at jam sessions, social events, and "opries" throughout the region.

Ozarks natives Ronnie Hawkins (*b* 1935), Ronnie Self (1938–1981), and Steve Cropper (*b* 1941), have contributed significantly to rock and roll and rhythm-and-blues. The Back-to-the-Land movement of the 1970s contributed to the popularity of rock in the region. Several Ozarks-based rock bands whose identities reflect their regional origins (e.g., Ozark Mountain Daredevils, Ha Ha Tonka) have achieved prominence.

Blues has contributed to musical life in Springfield for many decades; substantial annual blues festivals occur there and in Eureka Springs, Arkansas. Jazz has been performed in the region since the early 1900s. Several Ozarks-based ensembles representing various idioms, including Alphonso Trent's Orchestra, Joe Haymes' Springfield Band, and the Hardin Brothers, an African American vocal quartet, achieved national prominence in the 1920s to 30s. Bassist-composer Dallas Bartley performed with such notable mid-20th-century jazz musicians as Earl Hines and Louis Jordan's Tympany Five. Perhaps the most renowned jazz musician from the Ozarks is bassist-composer CHARLIE HADEN (*b* 1937), known for his work with Ornette Coleman and his own Liberation Music Orchestra. Other jazz musicians who have achieved prominence within and beyond the region since the 1960s include John "Bebop" Brown, Dave Bedell, Bob Betts, Claudia Burson, and Dave Scott. Several clinics, societies, and academic programs have provided jazz education in the Ozarks in recent decades, including the Stan Kenton Clinic, North Arkansas Jazz Society, and Missouri State University jazz studies program.

Cultivated ("classical") music, introduced by European colonists and immigrants, expanded with the founding of conservatories and music programs at area colleges (e.g., the University of Arkansas, 1873; Drury College, 1875; Missouri State University, 1908). In the first half of the 1900s, collegiate vocal and instrumental ensembles developed, concert venues were established in larger towns, and several nationally respected soloists performed in Springfield. The Springfield Symphony Orchestra, founded in 1934, has collaborated with eminent musicians, including Percy Grainger, who made Springfield his base throughout World War II. Other instrumental and choral ensembles include the Chamber Orchestra of the Ozarks, Southern Symphony Orchestra, Mid-America Singers, and Symphony of Northwest Arkansas. Opera workshops and festivals began developing in the 1950s. The Springfield Regional Opera (now SRO Lyric Theatre) has produced a wide variety of operas since its 1979 founding by Dawin Emanuel. Tenor James Billings (*b* 1932) has sung with ensembles in Boston, New York, and Chicago, and directed the SRO. Other prominent operatic musicians from the Ozarks include soprano Willa Stewart (1917–2002) and conductor-impresario Sarah Caldwell (1924–2006).

Contributors to the ongoing evolution of music in the Ozarks range from families maintaining 200-year-old traditions to recent immigrant communities.

BIBLIOGRAPHY

H.M. Belden, ed.: *Ballads and Songs Collected by the Missouri Folk-Lore Society* (Columbia, MO, 1940, 2/1955)

V. Randolph: *Ozark Folksongs* (Columbia, MO, 1946–1950/*R*)

W.J. Geil: *Christian Harmony Singing in the Ozarks* (thesis, U. of Illinois, 1967)

V. Randolph and G. McCann: *Ozark Folklore: an Annotated Bibliography* (Columbia, MO, 1972/*R*)

D.S. McIntosh: *Folk Songs and Singing Games of the Illinois Ozarks*, ed. D. Whiteside (Carbondale, IL, 1974)

J. Olin, J. Olin, and B. Bergey: liner notes, *I'm Old, but I'm Awfully Tough*, Missouri Friends of Folk Arts LP 1001 (1977)

W.K. McNeil: "A Discography of Folk Music from the Ozark States," *Mid-America Folklore*, viii (1980), no.3; ix (1981), no.2; x (1982), no.1

R. Gilmore: *Ozark Baptizings, Hangings, and Other Diversions: Theatrical Folkways of Rural Missouri, 1885–1910* (Norman, OK, 1984)

L.A. Wolz: "Folk Music in Missouri: an Annotated Bibliography," *Missouri Folklore Society Journal*, viii–ix (1986–1987), 193–213

E.D. McKinney: *Images, Realities, and Cultural Transformation in the Missouri Ozarks, 1920–1960* (diss., U. of Missouri, 1990)

R. Spears-Stewart: *Remembering the Ozark Jubilee* (Springfield, MO, 1993)

W.K. McNeil: *Ozark Country* (Jackson, MS, 1995)

C.K. Wolfe: liner notes, *Echoes of the Ozarks*, County CD-3506, CD-3507 (1995)

W.K. McNeil: liner notes, *Somewhere in Arkansas: Early Commercial Country Music Recordings from Arkansas, 1928–1932*, Center for Arkansas and Regional Studies (1997)

R. Cochran: *Singing in Zion: Music and Song in the Life of One Arkansas Family* (Fayetteville, AR, 1999)

M. Wilson: liner notes, *Traditional Fiddle Music of the Ozarks*, Rounder CD 0435, CD 82161-0436-2, CD 82161-04376-2 (1999–2000)

D. Deller: "The Songbook Gospel Movement in Arkansas: E.M. Bartlett and the Hartford Music Company," *The Arkansas Historical Quarterly* lx/3 (2001), 284–300

B. Blevins: *Hill Folks: A History of Arkansas Ozarkers and Their Image* (Chapel Hill, NC, 2002)

W. Glenn: *The Ozarks' Greatest Hits: a Photo History of Music in the Ozarks* (Nixa, MO, 2005)

C. Langley: "Opera in the Ozarks Celebrates 55 Years," *Music Clubs Magazine*, lxxxv/2 (2005–6)

D. Beisswenger and G. McCann: *Ozarks Fiddle Music: 308 Tunes Featuring 30 Legendary Fiddlers with Selections from 50 Other Great Ozarks Fiddlers* (Pacific, MO, 2008)

J.J. Castro: *Music Heard Deeply: Song and Ethnic Interaction in the Cherokee Ozarks* (diss., U. of Central Oklahoma, 2008)

Dallas Bartley: Small Town Boy, Special Collections and Archives Department, Missouri State University, <http://library.missouristate.edu/archives/exhibits/bartley/index.htm>

John Quincy Wolf Folklore Collection, Lyon College, <http://web.lyon.edu/wolfcollection/>

Max Hunter Folk Song Collection, Missouri Sate University, <http://maxhunter.missouristate.edu/>

DREW BEISSWENGER, JULIE HENIGAN, AND MATT MEACHAM

Ozawa, Seiji (*b* Fenytien [now Shenyang], China, 1 Sept 1935). Conductor of Japanese descent. Born to Japanese parents, he learned piano from an early age, studying Bach with Noboru Toyomasu from the age of 12. He entered the Tōhō School of Music in Tokyo at 16 as a pianist, but after breaking two of his fingers playing rugby, he switched to conducting and composition and studied with Hideo Saito. In 1954 he first conducted the NHK SO and the Japan PO, and in 1958 he won first prizes in both conducting and composition at the Tōhō School. He moved to Paris and took first prize in the International Competition for Young Conductors at Besançon and befriended two of the judges—Eugène Bigot, who gave him conducting lessons, and Charles Münch, who invited him to the Berkshire Music Center at Tanglewood, where he studied with Münch and Claude Monteux and won the Koussevitzky Prize. He then traveled to Berlin where he won a scholarship to study with Herbert von Karajan; Leonard Bernstein noticed him there and offered him a job as an assistant conductor with the New York PO, a post he held from 1961 to 1965.

In 1962 Ozawa made his debut with the San Francisco SO and soon began to work as a guest conductor with the Chicago SO during the Ravinia Festival, where he subsequently became artistic director (1965–9). He was also music director of the Toronto SO (1965–9) and began appearing with the Boston SO, the Philadelphia Orchestra, the Japan PO, and the San Francisco SO, of which he was music director (1970–76). In 1970, along with Gunther Schuller, he became artistic director of the Berkshire Music Festival (later the Tanglewood Music Center); he served until 2002, and a concert hall built in 1994 was named in his honor. Ozawa served as music director of the Boston SO from 1973 to 2002 and was named music director laureate following his retirement. In addition to his activities with the Boston SO and Tanglewood, he has led an active musical life in Japan and Europe. He was made honorary artistic director of the Japan PO (later the New Japan PO) in 1980 and founded the Saito Kinen Orchestra in 1984. Ozawa has been increasingly interested in opera following his opera debut at Salzburg with *Così fan tutte* in 1969. In addition to concert performances of opera in Boston, he has appeared at Covent Garden (debut 1974), La Scala, the Vienna Staatsoper, and the Paris Opéra. He made his Metropolitan Opera debut in 1992 and served as principal conductor of the Vienna Staatsoper from 2002 to 2010.

Ozawa has attributed his graceful podium style to his first conducting teacher, Saito, and to the language barrier which he has said he has continued to face. Although audiences have responded to his dance-like conducting, he has been well respected by musicians for his skilled baton and rehearsal technique, his even temperament, and his detailed, intensive preparation.

He has routinely conducted even the most difficult scores from memory. His repertory has favored large-scale works by Berlioz, Brahms, and Mahler as well as much modern music. While in San Francisco, he performed nearly all of Schoenberg's orchestral music and a wide range of Stravinsky's works. Some of his best early recordings are of Witold Lutosławski, Arthur Honegger, and Messiaen's Turangalîla. Strauss, Bartók, Debussy, Ravel, Messiaen, and Tōru Takemitsu have all remained in his repertory, and he has given the premieres of new works by Peter Maxwell Davies and Lukas Foss, among others. In Boston he improved technical precision and developed a darker, weightier sound for the Romantic German repertory; but he has been criticized for a lack of expressive depth on the relatively infrequent occasions when he has conducted Mozart, Haydn, and Schubert. Similarly, his opera performances, both on stage and in the recording studio, have received a mixed reception, a brilliant recording of *Elektra* being followed by a lush but lethargic *Carmen*. But his bold 1990s Boston Mahler cycle, recorded by Philips, has been widely admired, and his world premiere of Messiaen's *St. François d'Assise* (1983, Paris) received worldwide acclaim.

BIBLIOGRAPHY

P. Hart: *Conductors: a New Generation* (New York, 1979), 165–94, 287–90

H. Matheopoulos: *Maestro: Encounters with Conductors of Today* (London, 1982), 384–404

B.L. Scherer: "Ozawa at the Met," *ON*, lvii/7 (1992–3), 9–10, 54

T. Page: "Keeping Time at Tanglewood," *ON*, lxviii/12 (2004), 26–9

JOSÉ A. BOWEN/R

Ozomatli. Popular music group, emergent from the multiethnic communities of Los Angeles, California, that successfully blends Chicano, African American, and Latin American styles. The elements of the band are guitar, bass, drums, percussion (Afro-Caribbean and world-beat), horns, various folk guitars (Cuban *tres*, Mexican *jarana* and *guitarra de son*), and predominantly Spanish vocals, coupled with a rapper. Rooted in East Los Angeles's Chicano cultural scene of the mid-1990s, the band's multiethnic membership complicates ethnic identification. Originally a Latin-based jam band that performed at protest rallies, the players first united under the name Todos Somos Marcos (We are all Marcos), a reference to the Zapatista revolutionary spokesperson Subcomandante Marcos in solidarity with domestic ethnic and marginalized groups. Ozomatli (monkey in Nahuatl) is an Aztec symbol of movement. Appropriately the group's music is significantly based on Latin and African American dance rhythms, which their first album—*Ozomatli* (Almo Sounds, 1998)—aptly documents. The album demonstrates not only a mastery of various Latin dance rhythms (*cumbia*, salsa, *danzón*) but also a keen sense of blending these rhythms with American popular styles of rock and hip-hop. Here and in subsequent recorded and live performances the band achieved a transnational urban musical aesthetic that spoke to both the creative possibilities of multiethnic Los Angeles and the global popularity the band would soon achieve.

BIBLIOGRAPHY

V. Viesca: "Straight Out the Barrio: Ozomatli and the Importance of Place in the Formation of Chicano/a Popular Culture in Los Angeles," *Cultural Values*, iv (2000), 445–73

G. Johnson: "A Sifting of Centuries: Afro-Chicano Interaction and Popular Musical Culture in California, 1960–2000," *Decolonial Voices: Chicana and Chicano Cultural Studies in the 21st Century*, ed. A. Aldama and N. Quiñones (Bloomington, IN, 2002)

ESTEVAN CÉSAR AZCONA

P

Pablo. Record company. It was formally established in Los Angeles in August 1974 by the jazz impresario NORMAN GRANZ (who had sold his previous label, Verve, to MGM in 1960), although issues had begun in Europe and Japan in 1973. The initial roster included Ella Fitzgerald, Oscar Peterson, Joe Pass, Duke Ellington, Joe Turner, and Count Basie. The label was originally distributed by RCA Records (subsequently part of Sony/ BMG).

In January 1977 the company launched a sister label, Pablo Live, which featured live recordings both of contemporary jazz artists and reissues of concerts recorded in the 1950s and 60s culled from Granz's vaults. Artists who appeared on the Live label included John Coltrane, Lester Young, Stephane Grappelli, and Mongo Santamaria; the label also released a recording of a legendary jam session that took place in Hartford, Connecticut, in 1953 (*Norman Granz' Jazz at the Philharmonic/Hartford, 1953*).

Throughout the 1970s and 80s, Pablo maintained an aggressive release schedule and compiled a catalog of more than 350 albums. Granz sold the label in 1987 to Fantasy, which continued to issue albums under the imprint. In the early 2010s Pablo was a subsidiary of Concord, which acquired the assets of Fantasy in 2004, and was largely dormant.

THANE TIERNEY

Pace, Charles Henry (*b* Atlanta, GA, 4 Aug 1886; *d* Pittsburgh, PA, 16 Dec 1963). Gospel composer and publisher. When he was 13 he settled with his family in Chicago, where he continued to study piano and began to write gospel songs and arrange spirituals for the Beth Eden and Liberty Baptist churches. In 1925 he formed the Pace Jubilee Singers, an early conservative gospel group which recorded songs by Pace, Tindley, and others for Victor and Brunswick (1926–9). For a short time the group was accompanied by Thomas A. Dorsey, for whom Pace published several songs through his Pace Music House (established in Chicago in 1910). Pace moved to Pittsburgh in 1936 and shortly afterwards organized the Pace Gospel Choral Union, a 25-member ensemble that was enlarged to as many as 300 singers for special celebrations; its repertory consisted of gospel songs and spirituals. Pace also founded two highly successful music publishing houses in Pittsburgh—the Old Ship of Zion Music Company (1936–51) and Charles H. Pace Music Publishers (1952–63)—from which he published most of his 104 sacred compositions and arrangements and 26 secular songs. Pace's gospel songs, the best known of which are "Bread of Heaven," "Hide my soul," and "Nobody but you, Lord," are in the style of Tindley's songs, with a verse–chorus structure, memorable melodies, and simple, effective harmonies.

BIBLIOGRAPHY
M.A.L. Tyler: *The Music of Charles Henry Pace and its Relationship to the Afro-American Church Experience* (diss., U. of Pittsburgh, 1980)

HORACE CLARENCE BOYER

Pace, (Tarrian) LaShun [Pace-Rhodes, Shun] (*b* Atlanta, GA, 6 Sept 1963). Gospel singer and songwriter. After honing her skills with her family's group, the Anointed Pace Sisters, she emerged as a lead singer as a teenager in the mid-1980s. Her first solo recording, *He Lives* (1991), was released under the name Shun Pace-Rhodes and contains one of her best-known pieces, "I know I've been changed." Her signature on this black folk church song is one that evokes utterances of traditional gospel performance emblems and exhibits the melismatic styles of contemporary gospel singers. Some of her traditional pieces contain brief sermons that feature compelling episodes of pitched speech. Pace followed *He Lives* with three more solo projects in the 1980s; each contained songs that demonstrated her distinctive skill in singing traditional gospel music. On these recordings renditions of folk flavored classics, such as "I promised the Lord" and "Another Day's Journey," are mixed with songs that are representative of contemporary trends. In the early 21st century Pace has remained true to traditional gospel while exploring intriguing connections to its more modern developments. Her brazen and dexterous soprano adds flair to *God is faithful*

(2001), on which hymns, original works, and cover tunes are treated with tinges of jazz and R&B.

HORACE J. MAXILE, JR.

Pace, Robert (*b* Newton, KS, 22 June 1924; *d* Chatham, NY, 5 Sept 2010). Pianist and piano pedagogue. After serving as an infantryman in Europe during World War II (1943–5), he resumed his studies at the Juilliard School with JOSEF LHÉVINNE and ROSINA LHÉVINNE (BS 1948). He then concertized under Columbia Artists Management (1948–51), taught piano classes at Juilliard, and started a private studio. He studied with Raymond Burrows and obtained degrees at Teachers College, Columbia University (MM 1949, EdD 1951), after which he taught and served in various administrative roles at that institution (1953–95). His pedagogy focused on musical literacy, creativity, and independent learning, and he was known for his innovative incorporation of peer-teaching psychology into group music (piano) teaching; his comprehensive musicianship curriculum that interrelated repertoire, technique, composing, improvising, analysis, theory, and musicality; his "multi-key" curriculum, in which transposition and multiple tonalities were basic; and his adaptation of ideas by Jerome Bruner and other learning theorists. He also supervised numerous dissertations. Pace wrote a large number of books and articles, including the *Robert Pace Piano Series* (Bryn Mawr, PA, 1954), *Piano for Classroom Music* (Englewood Cliffs, NJ, 1956), and *Music for Piano* (New York, 1961), as well as his own compositions and arrangements. He held leadership positions in many national and international organizations and was appointed by President John F. Kennedy to a four-member panel to evaluate the status of music in the United States (1962–3). Pace received the Music Teachers National Association Music Achievement Award (2003), an honorary doctor of music degree from Westminster Choir College (2003), and the Music Educators National Conference Lifetime Achievement Award (2008).

BIBLIOGRAPHY

J.J. Forester: *Robert Pace: his Life and Contributions to Piano Pedagogy and Music Education* (diss., U. of Miami, 1997)

D.A. Gallaway: *A History of the National Piano Foundation 1962–2007* (diss., U. of Oklahoma, 2008), 63–108

JERE T. HUMPHREYS

Pacheco, Johnny (*b* Santiago de los Caballeros, Dominican Republic, 25 March 1935). Flutist, bandleader, and producer of Dominican birth. Pacheco's early exposure to Cuban radio fostered a lifelong passion for Cuban dance music. The family moved to New York in 1946, where he began to play Cuban music professionally with Gilberto Valdés's *charanga* (dance ensemble). With Valdés's encouragement, Pacheco learned the traditional five-keyed Cuban wooden flute. In 1959 he joined Charlie Palmieri's charanga La Orquesta Duboney and then formed his own charanga the following year. Their first LP, *Pacheco y su charanga* (1960), sold over 100,000 copies, an unprecedented amount for a Latin band. In 1965 he abandoned the charanga format for

the trumpet-based *conjunto* ensemble, reinterpreting the music of La Sonora Matancera, Arsenio Rodríguez, Félix Chappottín, and Cheo Marquetti. That same year he and Italian American lawyer Jerry Masucci started Fania Records, which would become the most successful salsa record company in the 1970s. As Fania's musical director, Pacheco played a formative role in the international popularization of Willie Colón, Pete "El Conde" Rodríguez, Celia Cruz, and others. In his heyday Pacheco was a charismatic bandleader and musician in tune with the roots of Cuban popular music. But it was his acumen for the commercial music industry that accounts for his importance in the history of Latin popular music.

DAVID F. GARCIA

Pachelbel [Patchelbel, Patchable], **Charles Theodore** [Carl Theodor] (*b* Stuttgart, Germany, bap. 24 Nov 1690; *d* Charleston, SC, bur. 15 Sept 1750). German organist, harpsichordist, music teacher, and composer; naturalized American, son of Johann Pachelbel. He immigrated to the New World around 1730. His brother Johann Michael appeared as a violinist in Jamaica as early as 1728. Pachelbel was in Boston by 1732, before serving as organist of Trinity Church in Newport, Rhode Island, in the years 1734–5. He played harpsichord at concerts in New York in 1736. He had settled in Charleston, South Carolina, by the summer of 1737, where that year he advertised the performance of an unspecified cantata on St. Cecilia's Day (22 November) at the theater in Queen Street (also called the Dock Street Theatre). In Charleston he established himself as a music teacher; his pupils included Peter Pelham and Eliza Lucas. In February 1737 or 1738 he married Hannah Atkins Poitevin, although he may have brought to America a daughter from a previous marriage: a woman called Elizabeth Pachelbel married in Charleston in June 1750.

On 25 February 1739 or 1740 Pachelbel was elected organist of St. Philip's Church, the principal Anglican church of the colony. Although he did not advertise his services over the next several years, he probably enjoyed the patronage of numerous wealthy pupils, both urban and rural, during the last decade of his life. In March 1749 he advertised his intention to open a singing school in Charleston, although this new venture may have been motivated by an increasing debility. In September 1749 he complained to the vestry of St. Philip's Church of "a lameness in his hands" and in November that year publicly thanked the benefactors who had contributed "towards his necessary Voyage for restoring his Health." His will, written in October 1749, was witnessed by two fellow musicians, the New England psalmodist Jonathan Badger and the Scotsman James McAlpine. Pachelbel was buried at St. Philip's on 15 September 1750. The inventory of his estate included "Sundry books English and German, Sundry books on Musick," a spinet, a clavichord, and two slaves. In the early 2010s his sole extant composition was a *Magnificat* for eight voices and continuo, composed before he moved to America.

BIBLIOGRAPHY

V.L. Redway: "A New York Concert in 1736," *MQ*, xx (1936), 170–77

V.L. Redway: "Charles Theodore Pachelbell: Musical Emigrant," *JAMS*, v (1952), 32–6

R. Stevenson, ed.: "Caribbean Music History: a Selected Annotated Bibliography," *Inter-American Music Review*, iv/1 (1981–2), 1–112, esp. 82

K.J. Welter: *Johann Pachelbel, Organist, Teacher, Composer: a Critical Reexamination of his Life, Works, and Historical Significance* (diss., Harvard U., 1998)

ROBERT STEVENSON/NICHOLAS MICHAEL BUTLER

Pacifica Quartet. String quartet. Based in Illinois, it was formed in 1994 by Simin Ganatra and Sibbi Bernhardsson (violins), Masumi Per Rostad (viola) and Brandon Vamos (cello). It quickly established itself as one of the most polished and musically perceptive of North American quartets and won the Coleman Chamber Ensemble Competition (1996), the Concert Artists Guild Victor Elmaleh Competition (1997) and the Naumburg Chamber Music Award (1998). Further honors include Chamber Music America's prestigious Cleveland Quartet Award (2002), *Musical America*'s Ensemble of the Year (2009), and a Grammy Award for Best Chamber Music Performance for their recording of Elliott Carter's first and fifth string quartets (2009). The Pacifica also received the Avery Fisher Career Grant (2006), becoming the second chamber music ensemble to be recognized in the grant's history. The group's repertory has been unusually wide, ranging from the Viennese classics to contemporary music, with the quartets of György Ligeti and Carter something of a specialty. They have also regularly commissioned new works and have given as many as eight world premieres a year.

The Pacifica has toured widely in Europe, Australia, and the United States. Their discography includes the first recordings of quartets by Easley Blackwood, quartets by Antonín Dvořák, and complete cycles of the Felix Mendelssohn and Carter quartets. In 2005 the group attracted widespread praise for their performance at Wigmore Hall of Beethoven's A minor string quartet, op.132, prefaced by readings of T.S. Eliot's *Four Quartets*. The performance was characteristic of the players' desire to explore new ways of presenting the core quartet repertory. The Pacifica was appointed resident quartet of Lincoln Center Chamber Music Society Two in 2002 and acted as quartet-in-residence of the Metropolitan Museum of Art for the 2009–10 season. In the early 2010s it was faculty quartet-in-residence at the University of Illinois, Urbana-Champaign, and its members were resident performing artists at the University of Chicago and the Longy School.

RICHARD WIGMORE/ELIZABETH PERTEN

Packard. Reed organ and piano firm. It was founded in 1850 by Isaac T. Packard (*b* North Bridgewater, MA, 29 June 1817; *d* Ft. Wayne, IN, 11 Sept 1873) as Packard, Foss & Co., but it was renamed Packard Brothers after his brother Edmund joined in 1854. After Edmund left to found his own workshop in 1857, the firm continued as I.T. Packard & Co. In 1865 Packard moved to Chicago as superintendent of the Estey Organ Company's branch office, and between 1867 and 1870 he was superintendent for the Riley Burdett & Co. factory, during which time he was granted four patents. Following the Chicago fire of 1871, Packard, with the backing of banker S.B. Bond (1833–1907), established a new company in Fort Wayne, Indiana, under the name of the Fort Wayne Organ Co. After Packard's death, it continued under Bond's direction, making reed organs, such as the "Grand" model (1891), that were notable for their cabinetry. His son Albert S. Bond became manager in 1886 and expanded operations in 1893 to include piano making, followed by a change of the firm's name to the Packard Company. Pianos became the predominant activity after 1900 and included the successful Packard player piano. Reed organ manufacture had ceased by 1914, after which the company went by the name of the Packard Piano Co. It was forced into receivership in 1930 by the depression, when the Packard trademark was sold to Story & Clark Pianos.

BIBLIOGRAPHY

A. Dodge: *Pianos and their Makers* (Covina, CA, 1911/*R*)

R.F. Gellerman: *The American Reed Organ* (New York, 1973)

W.J.G. Ord-Hume: *Harmonium: the History of the Reed Organ and its Makers* (London, 1986)

BARBARA OWEN

Paderewski, Ignacy Jan (*b* Kuryłówka, Podolia, 6/18 Nov 1860; *d* New York, NY, 29 June 1941). Polish pianist and composer. In 1891 the Steinway Co. sponsored Paderewski's first American tour: 107 concerts in 117 days beginning in New York with three orchestral concerts at Carnegie Hall. Impressed by his musicianship and stamina, critics and scholars including William James Henderson, Philip Hale, Richard Aldrich, William Foster Apthorp, Reginald De Koven, William Hubbard, Henry T. Finck, James Gibbons Huneker, Daniel Gregory Mason, and Olin Downes became friends. Ultimately he made 20 tours of the United States, the last of which took place in 1939. He traveled in his own rail car and eventually visited all 48 states.

The piano for his second tour—Steinway Grand no.71227, held at the National Museum of American History—bears the inscription: "This piano has been played by me during the 1892–1893 season in seventy-five concerts. I.J. Paderewski." Starting at Carnegie Hall, as usual, his 1895 tour included more than 30 cities from coast to coast. Paderewski was present for the American premiere of his opera, *Manru*, at the Metropolitan Opera House (14 February 1902). The premiere of his Symphony in B minor op.24 (12 February 1909) by the Boston SO under Max Fiedler was followed by performances by the orchestra on a tour to Brooklyn, Philadelphia, Baltimore, and Washington, DC.

Between 1914 and 1916 Paderewski acquired more than 5000 acres in Paso Robles and Santa Maria Valley, California. From 1906 until his death he made recordings, first for Welte-Mignon and later for Victor. His recitals were never recorded, but sometimes started half an hour late and concluded with an hour or more of encores with modulations from one to the next. Sometimes pieces—e.g., nocturnes, waltzes, and rhapsodies—would be promised but not specified, the choice being made at the moment. He played from memory, usually on American Steinways, and did not use the middle pedal.

Paderewski also owned the villa Riond-Bosson, near Morges, Switzerland, which he purchased in 1900. Following the outbreak of World War I, Paderewski returned from his villa to the United States in April 1915 hoping to involve the United States in Polish affairs. A recital and speech at the White House in Woodrow Wilson's presence (22 February 1916) led to a conference with Wilson (6 November). On 8 January 1918 the 13th of Wilson's Fourteen Points called for the restoration of Poland; the 14th point resulted in the formation of the League of Nations. Paderewski, a signatory of the Versailles Peace Treaty which determined Poland's borders, became Poland's prime minister, secretary of foreign affairs, and delegate to the league in 1918. Around this time Charles E. Chambers created three of the five portraits of Paderewski commissioned by Steinway.

Paderewski's political career was brief, and he returned to the stage in 1922. His 13th tour of the United States began that November. His 20th was cut short by a heart attack in May 1939. World War II compelled Paderewski again to leave his residence in Switzerland and return to the United States. He earned approximately $5 million from US tours and gave almost $3 million to Poland during World War I. His coffin was escorted with military honors to St. Patrick's Cathedral, New York, on 2 July 1941, where Archbishop Francis J. Spellman celebrated the Mass with music by Pietro Alessandro Yon and Lorenzo Perosi. President Franklin Roosevelt instructed that the remains be laid to rest at Arlington National Cemetery. In 1963 President John F. Kennedy installed a plaque at the site. In 1992, at the request of the Polish president Lech Wałęsa, President George Bush ordered the return of Paderewski's remains to his native land. Paderewski's heart remains in the United States in a bas-relief by the sculptor Andrzej Pitynski for the National Shrine of Our Lady of Czestochowa in Doylestown, Pennsylvania.

BIBLIOGRAPHY

Grove7

H.T. Finck: "Mr. Paderewski in America," *Forum*, xv (1893), 416–27

"Paderewski Here Again," *New York Times* (24 Oct 1895)

L. Gilman: "Not Really a Good Pianist, Only a Great One," *Musician*, xxxi/Jan (1926), 14, 32

I.J. Paderewski and M. Lawton: *Paderewski Memoirs* (New York, 1938)

Obituary, *Time* (7 July 1941)

"Paderewski Mass at St. Patrick's," *Musician*, xlvi/July–Aug (1941), 119

H.L. Anderson: "Ignace Jan Paderewski Discography," *British Institute of Recorded Sound*, x (1958), 2–7

M. Perkowska, ed.: "List of Works by Ignacy Jan Paderewski," *Polish Music Journal*, iv/Winter (2001)

B. McGinty: *Paderewski at Paso Robles* (Scottsdale, AZ, 2004)

MARK A. RADICE

Padilla, Juan de (*b* Andalusia, Spain, *c*1500; *d* nr Quivira, Kansas plains [now Lyons, KS], Dec 1542). Missionary and music educator. He was probably the first European to teach music in territory that is now part of the United States. He was trained and ordained by the Franciscans in Spain and in 1528 or 1529 traveled to New Spain (now Mexico), where he served in various missions. On 17 November 1532 he and nine other Franciscans wrote from the convent at Guatitlán to the King of Spain describing their missionary work, which included teaching Indian children to sing plainchant and part-singing. In 1540 he went with the expedition led by Francisco Vásquez de Coronado, with the intent to evangelize native peoples in New Mexico, working for a time there among the Moqui Pueblo and Zuni Indians. He traveled north as far as Kansas with Coronado the following year, then returned to New Mexico, and set out again with three companions in 1542. The four missionaries reached a large settlement of Pawnee near present-day Junction City, Kansas, where they spent four months successfully teaching. Padilla's expedition at the end of the year to preach to a nearby camp of Kansa Indians led to hostilities between the two tribes, however, and he was killed by the Pawnee.

BIBLIOGRAPHY

A.F. Bandelier: "Fray Juan de Padilla: the First Catholic Missionary and Martyr in Eastern Kansas, 1542," *American Catholic Quarterly Review*, xv (1890), 551–65

L.M. Spell: *Musical Education in North America during the Sixteenth and Seventeenth Centuries* (diss., U. of Texas, 1923)

G.N. Heller: "Fray Juan de Padilla: the First Euro-American Music Educator," *Kansas Music Review*, xliv/4 (1982)

J. Koegel: "Spanish and French Mission Music in Colonial North America," *JRMA*, cxxvi/1 (2001), 1–53

GEORGE N. HELLER/JOHN KOEGEL

Page, Hot Lips [Oran Thaddeus] (*b* Dallas, TX, 27 Jan 1908; *d* New York, NY, 5 Nov 1954). Jazz trumpeter and singer. He worked as a professional musician in his home state of Texas during the 1920s and later maintained that he learned to play authentic blues by listening to the local performers there. He played with Walter Page's Blue Devils (1928–30) then with Bennie Moten's band (1931–3 and 1934). In 1936 he worked briefly with Count Basie's band as a principal soloist, but left to become a solo artist at the behest of Louis Armstrong's manager Joe Glaser, a move generally regarded as having crippled a potentially illustrious career. Page gained much publicity during a brief stay with Artie Shaw's band (1941–2). He also made many fine recordings under his own name (1938–54), often leading bands with some of the finest swing musicians, including Earl Bostic, Don Byas, J.C. Higginbotham, and Ben Webster, among his sidemen. His purposeful, exciting trumpet playing and deeply felt blues singing were probably too rugged to gain widespread favor. Throughout his career he thrived on the atmosphere of impromptu jam sessions, in which his searing tone, dramatic phrasing, and improvised blues lyrics were a source of considerable inspiration to fellow musicians.

BIBLIOGRAPHY

SouthernB

J.G. Jepsen and K. Mohr: *Hot Lips Page* (Basel, Switzerland, 1961) [discography]

N.W. Pearson Jr.: *Goin' to Kansas City* (Urbana, IL, 1988)

T.B. Weeks: *Luck's in my Corner: the Life and Music of Hot Lips Page* (New York, 2008)

JOHN CHILTON

Page, Patti [Fowler, Clara Ann] (*b* Claremore, OK, 8 Nov 1927; *d* Encinitas, CA, 1 Jan 2013). Singer and actress. At the age of 18 she landed a job as a singer on KTUL, a local radio station in Oklahoma. Her work on the Page Milk Company's brief segment led to her stage name. In the period 1946–7 she traveled widely with the Jimmy Joy Band; while in Chicago she played a show with Benny Goodman that led to her first recording contract, with Mercury Records. In 1947 she began to release hits, starting with "Confess"; produced by Mitch Miller, it used overdubbing technology with Page's own voice. Her version of Cole Porter's "So in Love" (from *Kiss me, Kate*) was a chart-topping triumph in 1949, with "Money, Marbles and Chalk" performing well the same year. In 1950 she recorded what became her signature song, "The Tennessee Waltz." On her way to becoming the top-selling female artist of the 1950s, she also succeeded with "I went to your wedding" (1952) and "(How much is that) Doggie in the Window" (1953). Her smooth voice and light fare proved appealing just before the rock and roll explosion, but she managed to remain in the spotlight despite changing tastes. Page began working with producer Vic Schoen in 1956, and this collaboration changed her sound by increasing the tempos and jazzing up the arrangements. With Schoen, Page released what became her best-selling album, *Manhattan Tower* (Mercury, 1956), a dramatic tone poem that included narration and sung material. She appeared often on television during the 1950s and briefly hosted her own program in 1955; some minor acting roles followed into the 1960s. Although her last major pop hit was "Hush…hush, sweet Charlotte" (1965), Page managed to extend her longevity as a singer by turning towards country and western sounds. Among her singles to climb the *Billboard* country charts were "We're lonely" (1973) and "I may not be lovin' you" (1974). Page continued to record into the 1990s and remained active as a performer in the early 21st century. For more information see P. Page and S. Press: *This is my Song: a Memoir* (New York, 2009).

JONAS WESTOVER

Page, Robert (*b* Abilene, TX, 17 April 1927). Conductor and educator. After early musical training from his parents, he studied at Abilene Christian College (BA, 1948), where he met his wife, soprano Glynn Castleberry, and Indiana University (MM, 1951), with doctoral studies at New York University (1955–9). He was Music Director of the Mendelssohn Club of Philadelphia (1964–76), Cleveland Orchestra Chorus (1971–89), Mendelssohn Choir of Pittsburgh (1979–2006), and Robert Page Singers (1982–98), and has held conducting appointments with the Cleveland Orchestra (1979–89), Cleveland Opera (1980–88) and Pittsburgh SO (1989–2006). He has premiered many significant works and served as guest conductor with orchestras, choruses and opera companies in the United States and Europe. His extensive discography includes a number of prize-winning recordings. Page has taught at Eastern New Mexico (1951–5), Temple (1956–75), and Carnegie-Mellon Universities (1975–80 and again 1988–2013), and has served on numerous arts councils, including panels for the National Endowment for the Arts. He was president of Chorus America (1990–93).

Page has had notable success in both academic and professional arenas. At Temple University his choruses sang and recorded frequently with the Philadelphia Orchestra, where he enjoyed a close association with Eugene Ormandy. With the orchestras in Cleveland and Pittsburgh he worked closely with Lorin Maazel.

Drama, clarity, and dynamic singing characterize Page's performances and recordings. He is a sought-after guest conductor and teacher, and many of his students hold prominent professional and academic positions. Page is a strong advocate for the establishment and support of professional choral singing in America.

BIBLIOGRAPHY
M. Munson: "An Interview with Robert Page," *Choral Journal*, (2009), 34–41

WILLIAM WEINERT

Page, Ruth (*b* Indianapolis, IN, 22 March 1899; *d* Chicago, IL, 7 April 1991). Ballet dancer, choreographer, and company director. Trained in classical ballet by Adolph Bolm, Enrico Cechetti, and Edna McRae and in modern dance by Harald Kreutzberg, she enjoyed a thirty-year career as soloist and ballerina with various companies, but it was as a company director and choreographer that she had greatest effect. In 1935 she formed a partnership with Bentley Stone, which led to the creation of the Page-Stone Ballet in 1938. Thereafter she served as director and choreographer of numerous companies, including several based in Chicago. She is revered as a pioneer in creating ballets on American themes and/or set to American music. In 1933 she choreographed *La Guiablesse* (The Devil Woman) to a libretto by Lafcadio Hearn and music by William Grant Still. The title role was danced by Katherine Dunham; Page herself was the only white dancer in a cast of fifty. Notable among her later works are *Hear Ye! Hear Ye!* (1934; music by Aaron Copland), *An American in Paris* (1936; music by George Gershwin), and *An American Pattern* (1937; music by Jerome Moross). Her best works of Americana are *Frankie and Johnny* (1938; music by Jerome Moross) and *Billy Sunday* (1946; text by J. Ray Hunt, music by Remi Gassman; later restaged to music by Carmon DeLeone), both of which fuse the vocabulary of classical ballet with movements from vernacular dance, sports, and everyday actions. Page spent much of the latter part of her career creating ballet versions of popular operas and operettas.

WRITINGS
A.M. Wentick, ed.: *Page by Page* (Brooklyn, 1978)

BIBLIOGRAPHY
J. Martin: *Ruth Page: an Intimate Biography* (New York, 1977)
A. Barzel: "Page, Ruth," *International Dictionary of Ballet*, ed. M. Bremser (Detroit, 1993)

CLAUDE CONYERS

Page, Tim (*b* San Diego, CA, 11 Oct 1954). Writer. He studied with Leonard Altman at the Tanglewood Music Center and CHARLES JONES at Mannes College before attending Columbia University (BA 1979). Page wrote on culture and music for the *New York Times* (1982–7). He then served as chief classical music critic for *Newsday* (1987–95) and the *Washington Post* (1995–9, 2000–8), where he won a Pulitzer Prize (1997). He has subsequently taught music and journalism at the University of Southern California.

Page has shown a particular interest in 20th-century music and a special attraction to minimalism. But his music writing—some of which appears in the collections *Music from the Road* (New York, 1992) and *Tim Page on Music* (Portland, OR, 2002)—displays an expansive knowledge of classical and popular repertories, and he has blurred perceived boundaries between these categories. Page also hosted the radio program *New, Old, and Unexpected*, which aired on WNYC-FM from 1981 to 1992. Among his music-related book projects are his biography of American pianist William Kapell (College Park, MD, 1992) and the edited volume *The Glenn Gould Reader* (New York, 1984). In addition Page led the BMG Catalyst record label (early 1990s) and served as an administrator with the St. Louis Symphony (1999–2001).

Page's writings extend beyond music to include his biography of American novelist Dawn Powell (New York, 1998), as well as a memoir, *Parallel Play* (New York, 2009), in which a major theme is the author's life with Asperger's syndrome. His abiding interest in film dates back to his childhood; he was featured as a young amateur filmmaker in David and Iris Hoffman's documentary *A Day with Timmy Page* (1967).

MATTHEW MUGMON

Page, Walter (Sylvester) (*b* Gallatin, MO, 9 Feb 1900; *d* New York, NY, 20 Dec 1957). Jazz double bass player and bandleader. He played occasionally with Bennie Moten's band in the early 1920s and in 1925 founded his own band, the Blue Devils, in Oklahoma City. At various times this group included in Hot Lips Page, Buster Smith, Count Basie, Jimmy Rushing, Lester Young, and other leading figures in the Southwest style, making the Blue Devils, along with Moten's group, the most influential jazz band in the area. However, they made only one record, "Blue Devil Blues/Squabblin'" (Voc., 1929). In 1931 Page was forced, for financial reasons, to give up the leadership of the Blue Devils, and he played with Moten until 1933. After playing briefly with Basie and then with the Jeter-Pillars band in St. Louis, he began a fruitful association with the Count Basie Orchestra (1935–43, 1946–9). He was a mainstay of Basie's celebrated rhythm section, where the solidity and swing of his playing enabled Basie to dispense with left-hand stride patterns and Jo Jones to transfer the pulse to the hi-hats. "Pagin' the Devil" (Com., 1938), recorded with the Kansas City Six, a unit from the Basie band, includes one of the earliest jazz solos on double bass. These and other performances established Page as the leading jazz bass player of the late 1930s and a creator of the walking-bass style. After his tenure with Basie's group ended in 1949, he played mainly on a freelance basis with various swing and dixieland groups in New York. He participated in the seminal

mainstream-jazz recordings of Vic Dickenson (1953–4) and Buck Clayton (1953–6).

BIBLIOGRAPHY

W. Page and F. Driggs: "About my Life in Music," *JR*, i/1 (1958), 12–15

G. Schuller: *Early Jazz: its Roots and Musical Development* (New York, 1968/*R*)

R. Russell: *Jazz Style in Kansas City and the Southwest* (Berkeley, CA, 1971, 2/1973/*R*)

G. Schuller: *The Swing Era: the Development of Jazz, 1930–1945* (New York, 1989)

D.H. Daniels: *One o'Clock Jump: the Unforgettable History of the Oklahoma City Blue Devils* (Boston, 2005)

J. BRADFORD ROBINSON/R

Pageant. Although the term "pageant" has a substantial history in reference to European liturgical drama and postwar beauty contests, the dramatic form known as the pageant held special significance for American composers between the 1910s and the 1930s. Combining spoken dialogue, dance or pantomime, and musical numbers, pageants were most often staged outdoors and were usually characterized by some type of civic or social aim and by amateur or community involvement, sometimes on a massive scale.

The most widely propagated type of pageant was the community or historical pageant. Bringing the ideals of the new pageantry movement in Great Britain across the Atlantic, William Chauncy Langdon and the American Pageant Association (founded in 1913) advocated an episodic, locally generated drama in which "the place is the hero and its history is the plot." For such productions the music was often a pragmatic pastiche of old favorites, *contrafacta*, and newly composed scores. Ernest Richard Kroeger and Frederick Shepherd Converse wrote music for the gargantuan *Pageant and Masque of St. Louis* (1914), which featured a cast of thousands. Arthur Farwell, Walter Damrosch, and Chalmers Clifton wrote music for community pageants in New England in the 1910s; Farwell also created a number of pageants on the West Coast (1918–26). Of particular interest is *The Pilgrim Spirit* (1921), for which the pageant master George Pierce Baker commissioned music from George Whitefield Chadwick, Converse, Arthur Foote, John Powell, Leo Sowerby, Clifton, Edgar Stillman Kelley, Edward Burlingame Hill, and Henry Gilbert.

In addition to retelling local history, many pageants combined their underlying progressive message of education through participation with an overt message about social justice. Among these may be counted numerous pageants devoted to women's suffrage, to the labor movement, and to black history, including *The Star of Ethiopia*, with text by W.E.B. Du Bois. Other productions had allegorical plots and were often called masques or pageant-masques. These include *Caliban by the Yellow Sands* written for the Shakespeare tercentenary with music by Farwell; the *Rosaria* pageant in Portland (1925) with music by Charles Wakefield Cadman; and the religious dramas created by Christine Wetherill Stevenson out of the same ecumenical civic spirit that led to the creation of the Hollywood Bowl. Many pageants have been devoted to holiday or patriotic celebrations (Christmas, Fourth of July) or historical anniversaries, especially those relating to the Civil War and World War I. Others were staged specifically for world's fairs or similar events. The best known among these occasional works may be the pageant *Railroads on Parade* (1939–40), produced for the New York World's Fair with music by Kurt Weill.

While most pageants were ephemeral, achieving only a scant handful of performances, others became significant, annual tourist attractions for their communities. These include a variety of Hiawatha-based pageants (initially at Kensington Point on Lake Huron, later as a standing attraction in Pipestone, MN); the *Ramona* pageant, adapted by Garnet Holme from Helen Hunt Jackson's 1884 novel and staged annually in southern California since 1923; and *The Lost Colony*, created by Paul Green and produced under the auspices of the Federal Theater Project of the WPA with musical contributions by Lamar Stringfield. With the significant exception of Green and a circle of North Carolina pageant performers, who continued to produce and encourage historical pageantry into the mid-20th century, historical pageantry seems to have declined after World War II. In the early 2010s much research remained to be carried out on the musical components of these multimedia works and the opportunities they provided for composers, performers, and audiences.

BIBLIOGRAPHY

D. Glassberg: *American Historical Pageantry: the Uses of Tradition in the Early Twentieth Century* (Chapel Hill, NC, 1990)

N. Prevots: *American Pageantry: a Movement for Art & Democracy* (Ann Arbor, MI, 1990)

J. Graziano: "Community Theater, *Caliban by the Yellow Sands*, and Arthur Farwell," *Vistas of American Music*, ed. J. Graziano and S. Porter (Warren, MI, 1999), 293–308

BETH E. LEVY

Pahinui. A family of Hawaiian *ki hoʻalu* (slack-key) guitarists. The patriarch, Charles Phillip "Gabby" Pahinui (1921–80), has been celebrated as the father of modern slack-key guitar playing. His style and repertoire initiated a slack-key revival that has continued into the early 21st century. Three of his sons have enjoyed high profile careers, and members of the third and fourth generations were coming of age in the early 21st century to maintain the legacy even as it was spreading beyond Hawaii.

Gabby was known affectionately as Pops, much as jazz musicians referred to Louis Armstrong. Like Armstrong, Gabby was a charismatic free spirit who played at high levels of skill and feeling and broke new ground, especially by emphasizing improvisation. He began his professional career at age 12 playing bass in small clubs around Honolulu. At that time he preferred jazz to Hawaiian music. His playing shows strong jazz influences, especially in the use of augmented chords, rhythmic variation, and improvisation. Of course by the 1920s many Hawaiian artists, especially steel guitarists, were integrating jazz into their work.

Adding steel guitar, ʻukulele, and slack-key guitar to his arsenal, Gabby performed with many leading artists, including Andy Cummings and his Hawaiian Serenaders. He acquired a wide repertoire, which included pop hits of the day, Hawaiian standards, marches, and old parlor songs. He sang in a smooth tenor with a solid low range and sweet falsetto. By all accounts he had a marvelous ear and was strict about playing in tune.

As a slack-key guitarist Gabby favored four tunings: *taro patch* (D–G–d–g–b–d'), C *wahine* (C–G–e–g–b–e'), C Mauna Loa (C–G–e–g–a–e'), and F *wahine* (F–c–e–g–c'–e'). He tended to pick with thumb and index finger or with two fingers for rolls.

Beginning in 1946 Gabby recorded five tracks with slack-key guitar as the main focus. "Hiʻilawe" proved especially popular and became his signature tune. These releases brought what had previously been a private, closely guarded music into the commercial mainstream. They also inspired a host of other players to take their music public, such as Leonard Kwan, Sonny Chillingworth, and Raymond Kane. In 1957 Gabby relocated to Waimanalo on Oahu's windward coast, where jam sessions in his yard lasted for days and attracted musicians like EDDIE KAMAE. With Kamae he formed the popular revivalist group Sons of Hawaii in 1959. Gabby also recorded side projects for a variety of labels. In live performances he dazzled audiences and band mates with his musicality, charisma and *kolohe* ("rascal") persona. All the while he maintained a day job with the City and County of Honolulu road crew, switching later to the Parks and Recreation Department.

In the early 1960s two of Gabby's ten children, Bla (*b* 1942) and Cyril (*b* 1950), began their music careers, in the rock band the Characters. With Peter Moon, Palani Vaughan, and Baby Kalima, they also recorded the first album by the group the Sunday Manoa (1966), demonstrating that younger musicians were getting interested in Hawaiian music.

In 1972 Gabby released his first solo album, *Gabby*. By this stage his primary instrument was the 12-string guitar. His voice had taken on a gruffer edge, which enhanced his down-to-earth image. His core group included his friends Atta Isaacs and Chillingworth along with four of his sons including Bla, Cyril, and Martin (*b* 1951). Some traditionalists criticized Gabby's free-wheeling approach to Hawaiian lyrics (he sang phonetically), but he became a huge star. The album *Gabby Pahinui Hawaiian Band* (1975) included Ry Cooder and was an enormous hit, outselling most pop records in Hawaii. In 1976 Gabby and Isaacs performed on several tracks for Cooder's album *Chicken Skin Music*, which was named after the Hawaiian term for goose bumps. Although he received offers to tour off island, Gabby chose to stay in Hawaii, which limited his exposure to international audiences. His death in 1980 made front-page news in Hawaii and led to a precedent-setting wake at Honolulu Hale (the city hall) attended by hundreds of fans and leading musicians.

In the 1980s Cyril and Martin worked with the Peter Moon Band. Both also released solo albums, as did Bla. All three reunited with Cooder for *The Pahinui Brothers* in 1992. Since then Martin has performed in a number of groups, primarily a trio with Aaron Mahi (bass) and George Kuo (guitar). Bla has released solo material and added vocals to Cooder's album *Chavez Ravine* (2005). Cyril has toured widely and recorded with groups and as a soloist, playing mainly in a C major tuning (*C–G–e–g–b–e'*). He has also held regular sessions in the old family house for young musicians who want to learn slack key. Gabby's grandaughter, Anita Nakamura, and her son Mika have lived in the house and have also learned slack-key guitar. Several other descendants have worked as singers, such as Gabby's grandson Kunia Galdeira, who has performed with Sonny Lim, among others.

JAY W. JUNKER

Paine, John Knowles (*b* Portland, ME, 9 Jan 1839; *d* Cambridge, MA, 25 April 1906). Composer and teacher. He was the first native-born American to win acceptance as a composer of large-scale concert music, and one of the first to be named professor of music in an American university (Harvard).

1. Life. 2. Works.

1. LIFE. Paine came from a musical family. His father ran a music store, published sheet music, and conducted the town band; two uncles were professional musicians; his grandfather built one of the first pipe organs in Maine and conducted a band. As a youth, Paine studied organ, piano, harmony, and counterpoint with HERMANN KOTZSCHMAR, a conservatory-trained musician who had emigrated from Germany in 1848 and settled in Maine. After a thorough musical grounding, Paine sailed for Europe in September 1858, accompanied by Ludwig van Beethoven biographer Alexander Thayer. In Berlin he studied organ with Karl-August Haupt (who was apparently his principal mentor) and orchestration and composition with Wilhelm Friedrich Wieprecht, among others. He remained abroad for three years, traveling during vacations, playing the organ, and giving recitals in Germany and England. He met and played for Clara Schumann, and he was affected by the rediscovery of the music of Johann Sebastian Bach, then current in Berlin. In his recitals he included his own works, as well as those of Bach, Felix Mendelssohn, and Ludwig Thiele. During this visit and also during a second, lengthy one to Germany in 1866–7, Paine absorbed the style, manner and taste of the German musical world, and put them to immediate use upon his return to the United States.

When he settled in Boston in 1861, Paine started a series of organ recitals and public lectures on musical style, forms, and history; these ultimately won him an appointment to the faculty of Harvard (Assistant Professor in 1873, Professor in 1875), which he retained until retirement in 1905. The department of music that he organized was to be a model for many others in American universities. Paine became the idol of the arbiter of the Boston genteel tradition in the arts, John Sullivan Dwight, whose Boston-based *Journal of Music* was always flattering when reporting Paine's concerts and lectures and, more importantly, when lobbying for more attention to music at Harvard.

Paine was a charter member of the American Guild of Organists and played first at Boston's West Church, then at Harvard's Appleton Chapel for several decades before his energies were directed towards composition and teaching. His early organ recitals were models of catholicity and included major works of Bach, not often heard in the United States at that time. Paine also lectured at the New England Conservatory, on whose board he sat as a friendly adviser; he taught at Boston University; and he appears to have had a large circle of musical friends, notably conductor Theodore Thomas, pianist Amy Fay, and singer Emma Eames. Paine's composition students at Harvard included JOHN ALDEN CARPENTER, FREDERICK SHEPHERD CONVERSE, MABEL WHEELER DANIELS, ARTHUR FOOTE, EDWARD BURLINGAME HILL, CLAYTON JOHNS, Daniel Gregory Mason, CARL RUGGLES, and Walter Spalding; his students in music history and style included RICHARD ALDRICH, A.T. DAVISON, M.A. DeWolf Howe, OLIN DOWNES, HENRY T. FINCK, HENRY LEE HIGGINSON, Hugo Leichtentritt, and Owen Wister. Paine advised Higginson in the founding and early development of the Boston SO. In 1898 he became a member of the National Institute of Arts and Letters. Paine married Mary Elizabeth Greeley (1836–1920), a native of Portland, Maine, in 1869; following his death, she arranged for several of his larger works to be published by Breitkopf & Härtel. She also established the John Knowles Paine Traveling Fellowship, awarded to Harvard students who show "distinguished talent and originality" in musical composition and scholarship.

Paine served the Harvard community for 43 years. By his presence and by his serious concern with music in a liberal arts college, he awakened a regard for music among many generations of Harvard men. His writings testify to his insistence upon the place of music within the liberal arts. Performances of his compositions were treated as major cultural events in Boston and Cambridge, and attracted frequent interest in New York, Brooklyn, Chicago, and Philadelphia, to judge from reviews in the principal literary journals. He was commissioned to write a major commemorative composition for each of America's expositions during his lifetime. His compositions formed a prominent part of the musical activities in Cambridge, most notably his music for the performance in Greek of Sophocles' *Oedipus tyrannus* (at Harvard's Sanders Theatre in 1881). Paine nourished the Harvard community with over 100 original musical compositions for use in campus plays, concerts, and other diversions; with numerous lectures and prose articles; and by his presence as college organist, teacher, and companion. He made Cambridge a center of musical America and attracted such members of the Cambridge and Boston intelligentsia as H.W. Longfellow, R.W. Emerson, O.W. Holmes, J.R. Lowell, J.G. Whittier, C.W. Eliot, J. Fiske, W.D. Howells, the James brothers, F.J. Turner, C.E. Norton, and G. Santayana. He was a pioneer not only in setting up a collegiate department of music, but in being a "composer-in-residence," in contrast to the nature of appointments in contemporary European universities.

2. WORKS. Paine modeled his early works upon the style of the masters he had studied, especially Bach and the Viennese classicists. The early keyboard music, the Mass in D, the First Symphony, the oratorio *St. Peter*, and the early cantatas are all in the accepted academic style prevalent before 1860 in German and German American circles. Some of them, notably the Mass in D, go beyond mere competence to genuine inspiration and grandeur. Then, in a desire to align himself with musical progress (even after having written scathingly against the corruption of chromaticism), Paine altered his musical style by infusing it with greater chromatic activity, although never losing the strength and vigor of his individual style. A decline in health brought on by diabetes, bitterness at the lack of acceptance of his opera *Azara* (never staged; it was initially scheduled for the 1905–6 season at the Metropolitan Opera, but the company resisted preparing an opera in English), and the wear upon him of the academic ennui of such a long teaching career contributed to a slackening of compositional activity in the last two decades of his life.

The change in style may be seen by comparing his two symphonies. The first, while not of uniformly superior quality, states its classical case with force and eloquence. A masterly handling of the sonata idea is notable in the opening movement and a lovely, mid-19th-century melodic slow movement. In the second symphony Paine incorporates elements of program music and organizes a much larger work in an almost Wagnerian manner through transformation and thematic recurrence. Another work from this period, perhaps his finest from his later years, is the Prelude to *Oedipus tyrannus*, which shows clear examples of thematic transformation, cyclic construction, and chromatic key relationships. A more pronounced stylistic change may be seen in the two versions of the violin sonata, extensively rewritten in the last year of his life. Traditional key relationships and diatonic voice leadings in the original are replaced by chromatic mediant and semitone key relationships and non-functional chord resolutions in the later version. For the most part, these changes greatly strengthen the musical statements. Throughout his career, Paine's music in general was characterized by a strong sense of tonality, by regular metric organization and distinctive rhythmic figuration, by sensitive orchestration and textural devices, and by controlled harmony marked by an increasing chromaticism.

Paine was rewarded in his lifetime by great attention to his large works: the Mass in D, the oratorio *St. Peter*, the two symphonies, some of the cantatas, and music for plays. His music was performed frequently by the Boston SO and the Theodore Thomas orchestra. In 1883 George Henschel, then the conductor of the Boston SO, was sent the following Valentine greeting:

> Oh, Henschel, cease thy higher flight!
> And give the public something light;
> Let no more Wagner themes thy bill enhance
> And give the native workers just one chance.
> Don't give the Dvořák symphony again;
> If you would give us joy, oh give us Paine!

WORKS

EDITIONS

The Complete Organ Works of J.K. Paine, ed. W. Leupold (Dayton, OH, 1975) [L]

J.K. Paine: Complete Piano Music, ed. J.C. Schmidt (New York, 1984) [S1]

Democratic Souvenirs: an Historical Anthology of 19th-century American Music, ed. R. Jackson (New York, 1988) [J]

Three Centuries of American Music: a Collection of American Sacred and Secular Music (Boston, 1989–92) [T]

John Knowles Paine: Three Chamber Works for Piano and Strings, ed. J.C. Schmidt, RRAM, xvii (1991) [S2]

John Knowles Paine: the Complete Organ Works, ed. W. Leupold and M.F. Somerville (Boston, 1996) [LS]

John Knowles Paine: Vocal Chamber Music, ed. J.C. Schmidt, RRAM, xxxv (1999) [S3]

John Knowles Paine: The Nativity, Opus 39, ed. J.C. Schmidt, RRAM, xlvi (2004) [S4]

John Knowles Paine: Symphony No. 2 in A Major (Spring) *Op. 34*, ed. J.C. Schmidt, RRAM, lxx (2010) [S5]

STAGE

op.

— Il pesceballo (comic op, F.J. Child, Eng. trans. J.R. Lowell, based on G.M. Lane: *The Lone Fishball*), 1862, lib. (Cambridge, MA, 1862); ms. includes recitatives for soloist(s) and continuo and chorus parts; arias adapted from ops by Donizetti, Rossini, Mozart, and Bellini are lacking; ed. Mary Ellen Brown, (Bloomington, IN, 2008)

35 Oedipus tyrannus (incidental music, Sophocles), T, male chorus, orch, 1880–1, Cambridge, 17 May 1881 (Boston, 1881); rev. 1895 (Boston, 1895/*R*); version for large orch (Boston, 1908); Prelude pubd separately (Leipzig, 1903/*R*)

— Azara (grand op, 3, Paine), 1883–98, concert perf., Boston, 7 May 1903 (Leipzig, 1901 vs, 1908 fs and parts); J (Act II/v)

— The Birds (incidental music, Aristophanes), T, male chorus, orch, 1900, Cambridge, 10 May 1901 (Boston, 1902)

CHORAL

— Agnus Dei, 1861, lost

— Benedictus, 1861, lost

— Hymn for Harvard Commencement (J.B. Greenough), 1862, rev. 1883 (Boston, 1883)

8 Domine salvum fac, inauguration hymn for Harvard president, male chorus, orch, 1863, Cambridge, 4 March 1863 (Cambridge, 1915)

10 Mass, D, S, A, T, B, chorus, org, orch, 1865, Berlin, 16 Feb 1867 (New York, 1866)

14/1 Funeral Hymn for a Soldier, male chorus, c1863; S3

14/2 The Summer Webs, male chorus, c1863; S3

14/3 Minstrel's Song (T. Chatterton), male chorus, c1863; S3

— Peace, peace to him that's gone (T. Moore), male chorus, c1863; S3

— Radway's Ready Relief (advertisement text), male chorus, c1863 (Boston, 1883); S3

— Soldier's Oath (C.T. Brooks), male chorus, 1865, Cambridge, 21 July 1865 (Cambridge, 1865); S3

— O bless the Lord, my soul (I. Watts), male chorus, org (Boston, 1911); S3

20 St. Peter (orat), S, A, T, B, chorus, org, orch, 1870–2, Portland, ME, 3 June 1873 (Boston, 1872/*R*); T, vii; J, nos.34–5

27 Centennial Hymn (J.G. Whittier), chorus, org, orch, 1876, Philadelphia, 10 May 1876 (Boston, 1876), for Centennial Exposition, Philadelphia, 1876

36 The Realm of Fancy (after J. Keats), cant., S, A, T, B, chorus, orch, 1882, Boston, 2 March 1882 (Boston, 1882)

37 Phoebus, Arise! (W. Drummond), cant., T, male chorus, orch, 1882, Boston 26 April 1882 (Boston, 1882/*R*)

38 The Nativity (after J. Milton), cant., S, A, T, B, chorus, orch, 1883, Boston, 2 May 1883 (Boston, 1883), for Handel and Haydn Society, Boston; rev. 1903 as op.39, Boston, 22 March 1903 (Boston, 1903); S4

— Divine Love (C. Wesley), 1886, Portland, 4 July 1886, lost

43 Song of Promise (after G.E. Woodberry), cant., S, chorus, org, orch, 1888, Cincinnati, 22 May 1888 (Cincinnati, 1888/*R*), for Cincinnati May Festival

—   Columbus March and Hymn (Paine), chorus, org, orch, 1892, Chicago, 21 Oct 1892 (Boston, 1892), for World's Columbian Exposition, Chicago, 1893

—   Freedom, our Queen (O.W. Holmes), children's chorus, 1893, for World's Columbian Exposition, Chicago, 1893 (London, 1893); arr. SATB (New York, 1902)

—   Hymn of the West (E.C. Stedman), chorus, orch, 1903, St. Louis, 30 April 1904 (St. Louis, 1904/R), for Louisiana Purchase Exposition, St. Louis, 1904

Other occasional works, chorus, kbd

SONGS
(all for 1v, pf)

29   Four Songs, c1866–c1878 (Boston, 1879): Matin Song (B. Taylor), ed. R. Hughes, Songs by Thirty Americans (Boston, 1904/R) [T, ii]; I wore your roses yesterday (C. Thaxter); Early Springtime (T. Hill); Moonlight (J. von Eichendorff); S3

—   Spring, 1869; S3

—   The Fountain (G.P. Lathrop), c1878; S3

—   The clover blossoms kiss her feet (O. Laighton), 1882; S3

40/1   A Bird upon a Rosy Bough (C. Thaxter) (Boston, 1884); S3

40/2   A Farewell (C. Kingsley) (Boston, 1885); S3

40/3   Beneath the Starry Arch (H. Martineau) (Boston, 1885); S3

40/4   Music When Soft Voices Die (P.B. Shelley), lost

Other songs

ORCHESTRAL

23   Symphony no.1, c, 1875, Boston, 26 Jan 1876 (Leipzig, 1908); repr. in H.W. Hitchcock, ed., Earlier American Music, i (New York, 1972)

28   As you Like it, ov., c1876, pubd as Was ihr wollt, Cambridge, 21 Nov 1876 (Leipzig, 1907/R)

31   The Tempest, sym. poem after Shakespeare, c1876, New York, 2 Nov 1877 (Leipzig, 1907/R)

33   Duo concertante, vn, vc, orch, c1877, Cambridge, 23 April 1878

34   Symphony no.2 "In the Spring," A, 1879, Cambridge, 10 March 1880 (Boston, 1880); S5

44   An Island Fantasy, sym. poem, c1888, pubd as Poseidon and Amphitrite: an Ocean Fantasy, Boston, 19 April 1889 (Leipzig, 1907/R); T, x

—   Lincoln: a Tragic Tone Poem, c1904–6, inc.

CHAMBER

5   String Quartet, D, c1855 (New York, 1940)

22   Piano Trio, d, c1874, Cambridge, 18 Dec 1874

24   Violin Sonata, b, 1875, Boston, 11 May 1876; rev. c1905, Cambridge, 22 March 1906; S2

30   Romanza and Humoreske, vc, pf, c1875, Boston, 3 Nov 1876; S2

32   Larghetto and Humoreske, vn, vc, pf, c1877, Boston, 9 Feb 1877; S2

ORGAN

—   Prelude and Fugue, g, 1859; LS

—   Prelude, c; LS

2/1   Fantasia and Fugue, e, 1860; LS

2/2   Double Fugue on God Save the Queen or Heil dir im Siegerkranz, D, 1860; LS

3/1   Concert Variations on the Austrian Hymn, F, 1860 (Boston, 1876); L, LS

3/2   Concert Variations on The Star-Spangled Banner, c1861 (Boston, 1865); L [as op.4], LS

—   Concert Variations upon Old Hundred, c1861 (Cambridge, 1916); L, LS

6   Fantasia, F, 1865, lost

—   Reverie, after Longfellow's Song of the Silent Land, c1862, lost

17   Andante can variazioni, from lost Fantasia Sonata, c1863; LS

—   Caprice, c1863, lost

19   Two Preludes, Db, b, c1864 (Boston, 1892); L, LS

—   Fantasia on the Portuguese Hymn, c1864, lost

—   Pastorale, c1865, lost

13   Fantasie on Ein' feste Burg, c1869 (Cambridge, 1916); L, LS

Other pieces

PIANO

1   Sonata no. 1, a, 1859

4   Sonata no. 2, f#, before 1861, lost

7   Christmas Gift, 1862 (Boston, 1864); Piano Music in 19th-century America, ed. M. Hinson, ii (Chapel Hill, 1975); S

9   Funeral March in Memory of President Lincoln, 1865 (New York, 1865); S

—   Valse Caprice

11   Four Character Pieces, c1868: Frisch (Vivace); Feierlich (Largo); Etwas Bewegt (Con moto); Willkomen (Giojoso) (Leipzig and Boston, 1872), incl. Welcome Home to my Darling Lizzie! From John

12   Romance, c, c1868 (Boston, 1869); S

15/1   Prelude and Fugue, b, before 1865

15/2   Prelude, f#, before 1865

15/3   Fugue, A, before 1865

25   Four Characteristic Pieces, 1876: Dance; Romance; Impromptu; Rondo Giocoso (Boston, 1876); S

26   Ten Sketches: In the Country, c1873: Woodnotes; Wayside Flowers; Under the Lindens; The Shepherd's Lament; Village Dance; Rainy Day; The Mill; Gipsies; Farewell; Welcome Home (Boston, 1876); S

39   Romance, Db, c1882 (Boston, 1883); S

41   Three Piano Pieces, c1882–4: A Spring Idyl; Birthday Impromptu; Fuga Giocosa (Boston, 1884); S; no.2 previously pubd (Boston, 1882); nos.2–3, Nineteenth Century American Piano Music, ed. J. Gillespie (New York, 1978)

45   Nocturne, Bb, c1889 (Boston, 1889); S

MSS of most unpubd works in MH

Principal publishers: Ditson, Schmidt, Breitkopf & Härtel

WRITINGS

"The New German School of Music," North American Review, cxvi (1873), 217–45

with T. Thomas and K. Klauser: Famous Composers and their Works (Boston, 1891, 2/1894, 3/1901) [incl. "Beethoven as Composer" and "Music in Germany" by Paine]

"Shall we have endowed opera?" Forum, xiii (1892), 507–18

The History of Music to the Death of Schubert (Boston, 1907/R)

BIBLIOGRAPHY

ANB (B. Owen); DAB (R. Aldrich); EwenD

G.L. Osgood: "St. Peter, an Oratorio," North American Review, cxvii (1873), 247

W.F. Apthorp: Reviews of Paine's music, Atlantic Monthly, xxxi (1873), 506; xxxvii (1876), 633; xxxviii (1876), 124

J. Fiske: Reviews of Paine's music, Atlantic Monthly, xxxii (1873), 248; xxxvii (1876), 763; repr. as "Paine's 'St. Peter,'" The Unseen World, and other essays (Boston, 1876), 266–79

L.C. Elson: "Native Music and Musicians," Musical Herald, iii (1882)

W.S.B. Mathews, ed.: A Hundred Years of Music in America (Chicago, 1889/R), 675

A. Fields and R. Lamb, eds.: Letters of Celia Thaxter (Cambridge, MA, 1895)

J.L. Mathews: "Music in American Universities—in Harvard University—an Interview with J. K. Paine," Music [Chicago], ix (1896), 644–9

G.P. Upton, ed.: Theodore Thomas: a Musical Autobiography (Chicago, 1905/R)

L.C. Elson: "John Knowles Paine," The Etude, xxiv (1906), 104

W.S.B. Mathews: "German Influence upon American Music as Noted in the Work of Dudley Buck, J.K. Paine,…," The Musician, xv (1910), 160

R.F. Thomas: Memoirs of Theodore Thomas (New York, 1911/R)

E. Eames: Some Memories and Reflections (New York, 1927)

G.T. Edwards: Music and Musicians of Maine (Portland, ME, 1928)

W.R. Spalding: Music at Harvard: a Historical Review of Men and Events (New York, 1935/R)

A. Foote: "A Bostonian Remembers," MQ, xxiii (1937), 37–44

M.A.D. Howe: "John Knowles Paine," MQ, xxv (1939), 257–67

E. Fisk, ed.: The Letters of John Fiske (New York, 1940)

K.C. Roberts: John Knowles Paine (thesis, U. of Michigan, 1962)

R. Stevenson: Protestant Church Music in America (New York, 1966)

J.C. Huxford: John Knowles Paine: Life and Works (diss., Florida State U., 1968)

J.W. Barker: "A Report on the Society for the Preservation of the American Musical Heritage," *American Record Guide*, xxxiv (1968–9), 766–74

J.A. Mussulman: *Music in the Cultured Generation: a Social History of Music in America, 1870–1900* (Evanston, IL, 1971)

R. Smith: "American Organ Composers: John Knowles Paine," *Music: the AGO and RCCO Magazine*, x/2 (1976), 31

P.E. Stone: Liner notes, *John Knowles Paine Mass in D*, NW 262–3 (1978)

B. Owen: *The Organ in New England* (New York, 1979)

J.C. Schmidt: *The Life and Works of John Knowles Paine* (Ann Arbor, MI, 1980)

D.P. DeVenney: *A Conductor's Study of the 'Mass in D' by John Knowles Paine* (diss., U. of Cincinnati, 1989)

E.A. Sears: *The Art Song in Boston, 1880–1914* (diss., Catholic U. of America, 1993)

R.I. Van Hooser: *John Knowles Paine's 'St. Peter': a Stylistic and Dramatic Analysis* (diss., U. of Cincinnati, 1994)

N.E. Tawa: *From Psalm to Symphony: a History of Music in New England* (Boston, 2001)

G.W. Cook III: "Dwight's 'Diarist' and '"John," a Portland boy,'" *The Beethoven Journal*, xxiii/1 (2008), 4–14

Letters, scrapbooks, programs, etc. in *MB, MH*

KENNETH C. ROBERTS, JR./JOHN C. SCHMIDT

Paine, Thomas D(udley) (*b* Foster, RI, 1813; *d* Woonsocket, RI, 1 June 1895). Instrument maker and inventor. In 1848 he patented a rotary valve with three passages through the rotor instead of the usual two. His instruments are also the earliest known to use string linkage to turn rotary valves. A set of Paine brass instruments won a first prize at the 1852 exhibit of the Franklin Institute in Philadelphia.

Paine's early work was in the Woonsocket woolen mills, followed by an apprenticeship and work in watch- and clock-making from 1832 to 1837. He also played the violin for dancing. Paine first appears as a musical instrument maker in the Boston City Directory of 1841. It is thought that he may have worked with E.G. Wright while in Boston, as both he and Wright exhibited keyed trumpets at the Massachusetts Charitable Mechanic Association fair in that year. From 1842 to about 1857 he worked in Woonsocket, supplying valve brasses of all sizes to many amateur bands. He was evidently assisted in the business by a younger brother, Emery A. Paine, and by his father, John O. Paine. Several examples of Paine's instruments are found at the Rhode Island Historical Society in Providence. After 1857 he seems to have worked mostly as a watchmaker and repairer, but after 1885 he listed himself as a violin maker. He is known to have made more than 130 violins.

BIBLIOGRAPHY
Waterhouse-Langwill1

R.E. Eliason: "Early American Valves for Brass Instruments," *GSJ*, xxiii (1970), 86–96

R.E. Eliason: *Early American Brass Makers* (Nashville, TN, 1979/*R*), 5–14

ROBERT E. ELIASON

Paiute. Native Americans of the Great Basin area of Nevada, southern Idaho, Oregon, Utah, and eastern California. They comprise many small bands or groups, each of which has political autonomy and its own informal social organization, and all of which share a common language, culture, and territory. Many groups, such as the BANNOCK, SNAKE, PIAVOSOTO, and KAIBAB, are known by their band names, although all are Paiute.

The most important Paiute instrument is the split-stick clapper, used to accompany most social and ceremonial songs; the most unusual instrument is the shaman's rattle, made from a cocoon filled with rattling pieces and suspended from a forked stick. The flute, bone whistle, small double-headed drum, and bull-roarer are also used. The musical bow, once prominent among many Paiute bands, was made from a piece of elderberry or maple wood 1.2 to 1.5 meters long; it was plucked with the finger, using the mouth as a resonating chamber.

The unique Paiute song form has influenced the music of Plains tribes and other cultures, chiefly through the GHOST DANCE songs of the late 19th century as sung by Wovoka after 1889 and to a lesser extent by his father around 1870. This form, called the paired-phrase pattern, is typical of the Great Basin area and is nearly always present in Paiute song. It is characterized by symmetrical sections with each phrase repeated *(AA BB CC*, etc.); phrases may be established by textural or accentual qualities or by melodic or rhythmic movement, and are frequently of unequal length. A second Paiute musical genre is song recitative, in which narrative portions of Paiute myths are recited in a musical style unique to the animal character who is believed to be speaking. For example, Badger-chief recitations sound the same in any myth, and Badger recitations sound different from Wolf recitations. The recitation of Badger chief consists of a single measure of five beats with an anticipation of the second beat and a staccato final note (ex.1). Textural phrases with fewer than eight syllables are lengthened by adding non-lexical vowels, while longer phrases of text are split between musical repetitions. This type of recitative occurs in a less developed state in other American Indian cultures.

Ex.1 Paiute Badger-chief recitation (from Sapir, 1910, p.461)

An interesting type of borrowing, the use of the Yuman rise, may be observed in a few Paiute songs. This may have entered the Paiute repertory through the so-called southern Paiute (Chemehuevi or Kawai-isu), who live along the Colorado River and have borrowed complete song cycles from the Yuma, including funeral songs, and Salt, Deer, and Mountain-sheep cycles. Most songs have a comparatively narrow range, and their phrase endings tend to cluster around the final pitch (usually the lowest of the song). They employ three to five tones and intervals of major 2nds and minor 3rds. Paiute music is representative of simpler Indian musical style but it has profoundly influenced other North American Indian cultures from the 19th-century Ghost Dance to the pan-Indian songs of the modern era.

Collections of Paiute music are held at Indiana University's Archives of Traditional Music.

See also NATIVE AMERICAN MUSIC.

SELECTED RECORDINGS

Great Basin: Paiute, Washo, Ute, Bannock, Shoshone (AAFS, 1954); *Chants of the Native American Church of North America*, iii (Can., 1971); *Songs of the Warm Springs Indian Reservation* (Can., 1974); J. Treje: *Stick Games Songs of the Paiute* (Can., 1999); Chemawai Singers: *Chemawa Indian School Singers* (Can.)

BIBLIOGRAPHY

E. Sapir: "Song Recitative in Paiute Mythology," *Journal of American Folklore*, xxiii (1910), 455–72

F. Densmore: *Northern Ute Music*, Bureau of American Ethnology Bulletin, no.75 (Washington, DC, 1922)

E. Sapir: "Texts of the Kaibab Paiutes and Unitah Utes," *Proceedings of the American Academy of Sciences*, lxv (1930), 297–535

I. Kelly: "Ethnography of the Surprise Valley Paiutes," *University of California Publications in American Archaeology and Ethnology*, xxxi (1932), 67–210

J.H. Steward: "Ethnology of the Owens Valley Paiute," *University of California Publications in American Archaeology and Ethnology*, xxxiii (1933), 233–350

G. Herzog: "Plains Ghost Dance and Great Basin Music," *American Anthropologist*, xxxvii (1935), 403–19

A. Merriam: "Washo Peyote Songs," *American Anthropologist*, lix (1957), 615–41

A. Pietroforce: *Songs of the Yokuts and Paiutes* (Healdsburg, CA, 1965)

J. RICHARD HAEFER

Pakistani American music. *See* ASIAN AMERICAN MUSIC.

Palange, Louis S(alvador) (*b* Oakland, CA, 17 Dec 1917; *d* Burbank, CA, 8 June 1979). Conductor, composer, and arranger. His early musical training included clarinet and bassoon lessons as well as composition studies with his father and with Domenico Brescia at Mills College, Oakland. He settled in Los Angeles in 1936 and became assistant conductor, composer, and arranger for the Los Angeles County Band and arranger for the United Artists Studio and the Werner Janssen SO of Los Angeles. He also studied composition privately with WESLEY LA VIOLETTE. During World War II Palange served in the US Navy, conducting and composing much music for the Naval Training Center orchestra in San Diego (1942–3) and documentary film scores for the Photographic Science Laboratory in Washington, DC (1943–6). From 1946 until 1962 he worked as an arranger, composer, and instrumentalist for various television studios in the Los Angeles area; during these years he was one of Hollywood's busiest professionals. One of his most regularly performed compositions has been a work for flute and orchestra entitled *Pictures* (1948). Palange conducted numerous amateur and semi-professional orchestras, including the Los Angeles Philharmonic Band (1953–79), for which he served as music director; the West Coast Opera Company, which he founded (1962–79); the Downey SO (1967–79); and the Los Angeles County Concert Orchestra (1972–9). His vast collection of scores was donated to the Guthrie Music Rental Library.

WORKS

Stage: Handsome Harpy (operetta, F. Smithee), 1965

Orch: Evangeline, tone poem, 1943; The Plagues of Egypt, tone poem, 1945; Sym. no.1 "Invasion," 1946; Pictures, fl, orch, 1948; Poker Deck Ballet Suite, 1949; Romantic Conc., pf, orch, 1949; Sym. no.2, 1950; 2 vn concs., 1950, n.d.; *c*30 shorter works; arrs. of opera excerpts, popular songs, and inst works

Sym. band: Sym. in Steel, 1940; Hollywood Panorama, tone poem, 1950; Campus Bells, ov.; Jazz Rhumba; Brass Woodwind Clique; Navy Forever March; Intrigue; Driftwood; Beginning of Time, suite; more than 20 short works; arrs. of popular songs, orch works, opera excerpts, and other inst works

Chbr: Classical Trio, fl, vn, va, 1942; 4 Generations, str qt, 1950

Film scores: Dark Venture (1956); The Delinquents (1957); 6 US Navy documentaries; more than 50 scores for short clips

Principal publishers: Boosey & Hawkes, Highland, Presser

GENE BIRINGER/JONAS WESTOVER

Palestine, Charlemagne [Charles Martin] (*b* Brooklyn, NY, 15 Aug 1947). Composer, pianist, organist, carillonneur, vocalist, and visual artist. He studied composition first at Mannes College, then with MORTON SUBOTNICK at New York University. He later studied voice with PANDIT PRAN NATH. He cites Indonesian music, African music, and Jewish and Russian Christian-Orthodox chanting as his primary influences. In fact, he is reluctant to call himself an American composer, since his music and thought derive from multicultural sources. Although he is acknowledged to have influenced the development of 20th-century Western music, Palestine sees in his own work a reaction against the American and European avant-gardes, which seem to him callous and lacking in true spirituality. In an effort to convey a sense of the sacred without subscribing to any particular religion, he has conceived idiosyncratic approaches to composition and performance. He finds kindred spirits in electronic, noise, and rock musicians of the 21st century, who hear his echo in their own techniques.

Palestine's experiences as a carillonneur in New York, from 1962 to 1970, inaugurated his belief in the physicality of music and performance. The pounding gestures required by the carillon and the immense resonances of the bell tower remained central to his techniques throughout his career. Intent on summoning similar colossal sounds from other instruments by activating all their overtones, Palestine experimented with full-bodied drones throughout the 1970s. His *Spectral Continuum Drones*, for organ, calls for up to four hours of sustained sound. He composed similar pieces for piano, also titled *Spectral Continuum*, and for electronic oscillators, for instance *Four Manifestations on Six Elements*.

In 1970 Palestine met the dancer Simone Forti, and they collaborated on *Illuminations*, a performance-artwork they performed throughout Europe. Two years later Palestine embarked on his own video- and performance-artwork, *Body Music*. The performing body and the ritualistic essence of live performance have remained integral to his work. In 1974 he composed his best-known piece, the 45-minute *Strumming Music*, for piano. Inspired by flamenco guitar playing, "strumming" on the keyboard—a technique invented by Palestine—involves repeating a small number of notes quickly and loudly for an extended period of time, while keeping the sustain pedal depressed. In *Strumming Music* a quickly alternating pair of notes expands gradually into clusters, so that constant application of the pedal activates all available overtones. Palestine believes that this technique unlocks, from within the piano, potential normally obscured by traditional playing, unleashing thick sounds reminiscent not only of the bell tower, but also of a jet engine.

Palestine's music often explores trance-like states and destructive gestures, in reaction to what he saw as contrived spirituality embraced by American minimalists like La Monte Young. For instance, in certain of his vocal pieces, Palestine recreates the self-sacrificial, trance-inducing gestures of shamans, hurling his body at the walls. He believes that listeners may choose to hear very little in his music or to be overwhelmed by it. He therefore does not conceive his music as "minimal," despite the extended durations that it shares with minimalism.

A performance by Palestine is a ritual for all the senses. Attended by a retinue of stuffed animals, he typically wears a carefully chosen uniform, decorates the piano with candles and other accoutrements, and releases incense. While he plays, he consumes cognac and Kretek Indonesian cigarettes. For Palestine, the animals are meant to convey power and security, enlarging and strengthening the presence of sound.

Between 1980 and 1996 Palestine's musical performances were rare. Instead he focused on creating sculptural objects and musical scores that did not call for sound, such as *Books of Continuity*. In 1995 he renewed his relationship with music by working with electronic and rock musicians who drew inspiration from the intensity of his early work. In addition to recording alongside Pan Sonic, Scanner, and others, and creating new solo works for piano and organ, Palestine has begun to revisit his early pieces for release on CD.

WORKS
(selective list)

Performance art: Illuminations, 1970, collab. S. Forti; Body Music, video and performance artwork, 1972

Pf: Spectral Continnuum, 1970; Strumming Music, 1974, arr. pf, hpd, str ens, 2010; Lower Depths, 1974–5; Wallenda, 1979; Timbral Assault, 1980; Musashi, 1981

Other: Etudes, carillon, 1964–82; L'avventura, elec series, 1966–70; Birth of a Sonority, elec, 1966–81, arr. str ens as Evolution of a Sonority, 1975–80; Spectral Continuum, org, 1970–81; Four Manifestations on Six Elements, 1974; Duo Strumming for Two Harpsichords, 1978; Diverse Schlingen Blaengen, org, 1988; Schlongo!!! DaLUVDrone, organ, 1998; Mort Aux Vaches, elec, 1999, collab. Pan Sonic

BIBLIOGRAPHY

T. Johnson: "Charlemagne Palestine Ascends," *Village Voice* (18 April 1977); repr. in *The Voice of New Music* (Eindhoven, 1989), 159–60

E. Strickland: *Minimalism: Origins* (Bloomington, 2000)

B. Deguid: "Charlemagne Palestine Interview" <http://media.hyperreal.org/zines/est/intervs/palestin.html> (2013)

D. Varela: "Sensual, Physical, and Visceral Music Trance: Interview by Daniel Varela," <http://www.furious.com/perfect/charlemagnepalestine.html> (2013)

S. Williams: "Charlemagne Palestine" <http://www.frieze.com/comment/article/charlemagne_palestine/> (2013)

MANDY-SUZANNE WONG

Palladium Ballroom. This second-floor dance hall on the corner of Broadway and West 53rd Street in New York City became famous as a center of Latin music and dancing from 1948 until 1966. Owned by Maxwell Hyman, the Palladium had been successful during the big band era, but by 1947 its popularity with its largely white clientele had waned. Its manager approached Caribbean music promoter Federico Pagani about booking a Latin band, hoping to attract New York's burgeoning Hispanic community. Their first Latin dance concert, to music by Machito and His Afro-Cubans, was held on a Sunday afternoon. It was a huge success. Soon, Latin music was played on Wednesday evenings as well as Sunday afternoons, with Tito Puente's Piccadilly Boys alternating with Machito's band. Within a year, the Palladium was devoted exclusively to Latin music, and dancers clamored for space on its large dance floor.

By 1950, singer-bandleader Tito Rodríguez had joined Machito and Tito Puente as a headliner at the Palladium, and the Mambo craze was in full swing. The "big three" of Latin bands produced hit after hit, including Puente's "Picadillo," Rodríguez's "Mambo Mona," and Machito's "Babarabatiri." Among many other Latin musicians and singers who starred at the Palladium were Arsenio Rodríguez, Celia Cruz, Beny Moré, and Miguelito Valdés.

Besides the best of Latin music, the Palladium was known for the innovation and spectacular technique of its dancers, displayed in weekly dance competitions. Pedro Aguilar ("Cuban Pete") and his partner Millie Donay were frequent contest winners, but the indisputable star dancers were Augie and Margo Rodríguez, who developed the mambo to dazzling heights.

BIBLIOGRAPHY

M. Salazar: *Mambo Kingdom: Latin Music in New York* (New York, 2002)

J. Behrens: *Big Bands and Great Ballrooms: America Is Dancing…Again* (Bloomington, 2006)

C. Hamer-Hodges: *The Opening Act: the Love Story of Augie and Margo Rodriquez* (Seattle, 2006)

CLAUDE CONYERS

Palmer, Earl (Cyril) (*b* New Orleans, LA, 25 Oct 1924; *d* Banning, CA, 19 Sept 2008). Drummer. He began his career as a tap-dancer, performing in vaudeville houses soon after his fifth birthday. He and his mother, a singer, were part of Ida Cox's blues and jazz revue, which traveled the country widely. Palmer only began to play drums after completing military service during World War II. He attended the Grunewald School in New Orleans, where he studied piano and percussion and first learned how to read and write music. Soon afterwards he became sought after as a drummer, known for his impeccable sense of rhythm and timing. One of his first jobs in the 1940s came with the Dave Bartholomew Band, and he also played in the house band for J&M Studios. After moving to Los Angeles in 1957, Palmer worked as a session drummer, as well as a regular, for Aladdin Records. It was his session work that brought him lasting fame, in which setting he worked with artists ranging from such early rock and roll stars as Fats Domino and Little Richard to the popular singers Doris Day and Frank Sinatra and the jazz vocalist Sarah Vaughan. His versatility brought constant studio work, and he was also recruited to play on such television theme songs as "Green Acres" and "Mission: Impossible." After the 1970s he spent more time performing live jazz. He was inducted into the Rock and Roll Hall of Fame in 2000.

BIBLIOGRAPHY

T. Scherman: *Backbeat: Earl Palmer's Story* (New York, 2000)
Obituary, *Los Angeles Times* (21 Sept 2008)

JONAS WESTOVER

Palmer, Horatio R(ichmond) (*b* Sherburne, NY, 26 April 1834; *d* Yonkers, NY, 15 Nov 1907). Music educator and composer. He was educated by his father and at Rushford Academy, New York, where he taught from 1855 to 1865 as well as giving singing classes in the surrounding area. After the Civil War he moved to Chicago, where he directed the music in the Second Baptist Church, published the monthly magazine *Concordia*, and taught at assemblies throughout the Midwest and Canada. The success of his compilation *The Song Queen* (1867) encouraged Palmer to issue other collections, including *The Song Monarch* (1874) and *The Choral Union* (1884), and pedagogical works, such as *Palmer's Theory of Music* (1876) and *The Common Sense Music Reader* (1883). In the 1870s and 1880s his publications were among the most popular of their type in the United States. In 1874 Palmer returned to New York, where he organized the Church Choral Union in 1881. Since this proved successful, he was called upon to organize similar groups in other eastern cities. He was active at the Chautauqua assemblies as early as 1879 and was director of music there from 1888 to 1901; under his guidance performances of secular music at Chautauqua were expanded significantly. Although Palmer composed much music, only the hymn tunes "Yield not to temptation" (1868) and "Vincent" (1887) achieved wide popularity. As a pedagogue, however, his impact was substantial; widely traveled and widely read, he was an engaging lecturer and a forceful conductor and teacher.

BIBLIOGRAPHY

DAB (F.J. Metcalf)
W.S.B. Mathews, ed.: *A Hundred Years of Music in America* (Chicago, 1889/*R*1970)
G.H. Jones: "Dr. Palmer," *The Musician*, iv (1899), 427–8

WILLIAM BROOKS

Palmer, Job (*b* Falmouth, MA, 1747; *d* Charleston, SC, 30 Jan 1845). Psalmodist. Shortly after settling in Charleston, South Carolina, as a carpenter, he first advertised in May 1772 the opening of a school to teach "Psalmody and all branches of Vocal Music." Palmer's seasonal singing courses soon became affiliated with the city's Independent Congregational Church, which was composed primarily of New Englanders. He served as the church's clerk and choirmaster for 39 years, and then as deacon for a further 30 years. During that time he cultivated a repertoire of sacred hymnody and psalmody that historians usually associate with the New England states. Palmer was exiled to Philadelphia after the British Army captured Charleston in 1780. Shortly after his return in 1783, Palmer's choir of the Independent Congregational Church garnered much local praise, especially during

the reception of President George Washington in Charleston in May 1791. Palmer's sacred vocal music courses were a regular feature of Charleston's Independent Congregational Church into the early 19th century and may have established the groundwork for the formation of the city's Union Harmonic Society in 1816. His sons and grandsons, who became prominent theologians in the Congregational and Presbyterian denominations, continued his legacy.

NICHOLAS MICHAEL BUTLER

Palmer, Larry (*b* Warren, OH, 13 Nov 1938). Harpsichordist and organist. He received undergraduate training at the Oberlin College Conservatory and completed his DMA at the Eastman School in 1963. His organ teachers included Fenner Douglass and DAVID CRAIGHEAD; he studied harpsichord with Isolde Ahlgrimm and Gustav Leonhardt. From 1969 he has been harpsichord editor of *The Diapason*. Palmer has published English-language editions of Distler's choral works and written *Hugo Distler and His Church Music* (St. Louis, 1967); his recordings include organ works of Distler, as well as harpsichord and organ music of the 17th, 18th, and 20th centuries. Palmer's monograph *Harpsichord in America: a Twentieth-Century Revival* (Bloomington, IN, 1989/*R*1993) offers a unique look at the American harpsichord world until the 1960s. *Letters from Salzburg: a Music Student in Europe, 1958–1959* (Eau Claire, WI, 2006) chronicles Oberlin's bold experiment in international education—sending its entire junior music class to study at the Mozarteum. He has performed as a recitalist throughout the United States and Europe and has commissioned and premiered numerous works for harpsichord by such composers as Neely Bruce, Rudy Shackelford, Ross Lee Finney, and Persichetti. In 1970 he was appointed professor of harpsichord and organ at Southern Methodist University in Dallas, where he is now head of organ and harpsichord, director of graduate studies in music, and university organist.

CHARLES M. JOSEPH, ALLISON A. ALCORN

Palmer, Robert (Moffat) (i) (*b* Syracuse, NY, 2 June 1915; *d* Ithaca, NY, 3 July 2010). Composer and teacher. He won a scholarship to the Eastman School of Music as a pianist, but gradually shifted his emphasis to composition, studying with BERNARD ROGERS and HOWARD HANSON (BM 1938, MM 1940). He went on to study composition with ROY HARRIS, AARON COPLAND and, most important, QUINCY PORTER. He taught at the University of Kansas (1940–43) and Cornell University (1943–80). His honors include an American Academy of Arts and Letters award (1946), Guggenheim Fellowships (1952–3, 1960–61), and a Fulbright Senior Fellowship (1960–61). He received commissions from the Koussevitzky Foundation (1943, for the String Quartet no.2), the Elizabeth Sprague Coolidge Foundation (1950, for the Piano Quintet), the National Association of Educational Broadcasters (1960, for the *Memorial Music*), the Lincoln Center (1965, for the *Centennial Overture*), and Cornell University.

Palmer's distinctive style can be seen as an outgrowth of the styles of his teachers, though it is also connected with the work of Milhaud, Hindemith, Michael Tippett, Petrassi, and Bartók. His best-known piece, the *Toccata ostinato* for piano (1945), is an exciting treatment in 13/8 time of a boogie-woogie inspiration, familiar to Palmer from his experience playing jazz duets. The Piano Concerto (1971) is noteworthy for its culmination in a swinging long-breathed tune that incorporates motifs from the first movement, which have been developed fugally and combined with contrasting motifs.

WORKS

Orch: Poem, vn, chbr orch, 1938; Conc., small orch, 1940; K 19, sym. elegy, 1945; Variations, Chorale and Fugue, 1947, rev. 1954; Chbr Conc., vn, ob, str, 1949; Sym. no.1, 1953; Memorial Music, 1960; Centennial Ov., 1965; Sym. no.2, 1966; Choric Song and Toccata, band, 1968; Pf Conc., 1971; Symphonia concertante, 9 insts, 1972; Ov. on a Southern Hymn, sym. band, 1979; Conc., 2 pf, 2 perc, str, brass, 1984; incid music

Vocal: 2 Songs (W. Whitman), 1v, pf, 1940; Abraham Lincoln walks at midnight (V. Lindsay), chorus, orch, 1948; Carmina amoris (Sappho, others), S, cl, vn, pf, 1951, arr. with chbr orch; Slow, slow, fresh fount (B. Jonson), SATB, 1953, rev. 1959; Of Night and the Sea (chbr cant., Whitman, E. Dickinson, others), S, B, orch, 1956; And in that day (Bible: *Isaiah*), anthem, chorus, 1963; Nabuchodonosor (Bible: *Daniel*), T, B, TTBB, wind, perc, 2 pf, 1964; Portents of Aquarius, nar, SATB, org, 1975

Chbr and solo inst: Str Qt no.1, 1939; Conc., 5 insts, 1943; Str Qt no.2, 1943, rev. 1947; Pf Qt no.1, 1947; Pf Qnt, 1950; Sonata, va, pf, 1951; Qnt, cl, str trio, pf, 1952, rev. 1953; Str Qt no.3, 1954; Sonata, vn, pf, 1956; Pf Trio, 1958; Str Qt no.4, 1960; Organon I, fl, cl, 1962; Epithalamium, org, 1968; Sonata, tpt, pf, 1972; Pf Qnt no.2, 1974; Organon II, vn, va, 1975; Sonata no.1, vc, pf, 1978; Sonata no.2, vc, pf, 1983

Pf: Sonata no.1, 1938, rev. 1946; 3 Preludes, 1941; Sonata no.2, 1942, rev. 1948; Sonata, 2 pf, 1944; Toccata ostinato, 1945; Sonata, pf 4 hands, 1952; Evening Music, 1956; 7 Epigrams, 1957; Morning Music, 1973; Sonata no.3, 1979

MSS and scores in *I*

Principal publishers: Elkan-Vogel, Peer, Peters, G. Schirmer, Valley

BIBLIOGRAPHY

GroveA (W.W. Austin) [incl. further bibliography]; *EwenD*

W.W. Austin: "The Music of Robert Palmer," *MQ*, xlii (1956), 35–50

R. Salvatore: "The Piano Music of Robert Palmer," *Clavier*, xxviii/4 (1989), 22–30

S. Stucky: "Remembering Robert Moffatt Palmer (1915–2010)," *NewMusicBox*, <http://www.newmusicbox.org/article.nmbx?id=6481>

WILLIAM W. AUSTIN/R

Palmer, Robert (ii) (*b* Little Rock, AR, 19 June 1945; *d* New Orleans, LA, 20 Nov 1997). Rock and jazz critic. As a youth he played reed instruments with rock, country, and soul bands and later with an eclectic, psychedelically tinged group called the Insect Trust, with which he recorded two albums. He was a co-founder of the Memphis Blues Festival (1966) and reviewed books and music for the *Arkansas Gazette* before graduating from the University of Arkansas (BA 1967). In New York thereafter he became a widely published freelance writer; from 1975 he was a regular reviewer for the *New York Times* and in 1981 he was appointed to its staff of jazz and pop critics. He wrote several books, the most important being his study of the Delta blues (*Deep Blues*, New York, 1981), and held teaching positions at Bowdoin College, Memphis State University, Brooklyn College, CUNY, and Yale University. He also collaborated musically on informal projects with Ornette Coleman, Sid Selvidge, and CeDell Davis, among others.

Palmer's writing reflects his interest in all forms of pop, jazz, and avant-garde music and an encyclopedic knowledge of the blues and early rock; his prose style is direct and unmannered. More a celebrator than a critic, he brought a musician's understanding and sympathy to his subjects.

WRITINGS

Baby, that was Rock and Roll: the Legendary Leiber and Stoller (New York, 1980)

Deep Blues (New York, 1981)

Jerry Lee Lewis Rocks! (New York, 1981)

The Rolling Stones (New York, 1983)

Rock and Roll: an Unruly History (New York, 1995)

A. DeCurtis, ed.: *Blues and Chaos: the Music Writing of Robert Palmer* (New York, 2009)

JOHN ROCKWELL/R

Palmieri, Charlie (*b* Bronx, NY, 21 Nov 1927; *d* New York, NY, 12 Sept 1988). Pianist, arranger, and bandleader. Initially self-taught, Palmieri started piano lessons at seven. He began performing professionally in 1943 with the Osario Selasie Orchestra, eventually making his first recording, "Se va la rumba," with the Rafael Muñoz Band in 1946. He pursued training in harmony, composition, and arranging with Otto Chesna while continuing piano studies with Margaret Bonds. After performing with Tito Puente's band from 1951 to 1953 he joined Pupi Campo's band performing on Jack Paar's *Today* show on CBS Television. In 1959 he debuted his popular *charanga*, La Orquesta Duboney, featuring Johnny Pacheco on flute. La Duboney recorded Cuban *charanga* music and American pop-inspired music for United Artists Records, while also popularizing the *pachanga* with Alegre Records in the early 1960s. Palmieri supplemented his performance career with teaching assignments in the public schools and at City College of New York in the early 1970s. For the next two decades he recorded and performed mostly as a featured artist with New York–based Latin bands, including that of his younger brother, Eddie Palmieri. Beloved and respected by musicians for his musical talent, knowledge, and professionalism, Palmieri was one of the most important Puerto Rican musicians to popularize and develop Latin music in New York.

DAVID F. GARCIA

Palmieri, Eddie [Eduardo] (*b* New York, NY, 15 Dec 1936). Pianist, bandleader, composer, and arranger. Palmieri is considered to be a forerunner of key SALSA music developments. La Perfecta, his small charanga ensemble, founded in 1961, featured an independent section of wailing trombones that became the standard format for most salsa orchestras after 1968. His album *Azúcar pa' ti* (Fania, 1965) is seminal for his extended *montuno* sections and the use of atonal melodies, keyboard clusters, and polytonal riffs. Patterned on formal paradigms by Cuban musician Arsenio Rodríguez, and in line with the jazz styles of Thelonious Monk and McCoy Tyner, Palmieri's daring piano style often weaved within experimental arrangements and alongside fellow musicians who were granted considerable freedom. At the risk of financial instability during salsa's most prosperous years

(1971–5), he turned down proposals from the music industry that could have compromised his creative independence; he was seen by salsa moguls, and even by conservative followers, as an "anarchist." His mechanical adoption of rock and funk music in "Azúcar," from his *Recorded Live at Sing Sing* (Fania, 1972), portrays a sense of alienation, exploitation, and poverty, as felt among marginalized Latino groups in New York, but his *montunos* often evoke idyllic worlds of freedom, as expressed in the lyrics of "Vámonos pa'l monte" and "Libertad, lógico" (1971). In these and other respects, his album *The Sun of Latin Music* (Musical Prod, 1974) is regarded as Palmieri's masterpiece. Since 1975, his relevance and value grew with a catalog reaching dozens of recordings and numerous awards. He continues to demonstrate a commitment to Latin jazz styles without abandoning his role as a salsa bandleader.

BIBLIOGRAPHY
C.M. Rondón: *El Libro de la Salsa* (Caracas, 1980)
EDGARDO DIAZ DIAZ

Palombo, Paul (Martin) (*b* Pittsburgh, PA, 10 Sept 1937; *d* Stevens Point, WI, 2 July 1987). Composer. He attended Indiana University of Pennsylvania (BME 1962), where he studied composition with Charles Hoag; his other teachers were ROBERT HALL LEWIS at the Peabody Conservatory (1963–6) and WAYNE BARLOW and BERNARD ROGERS at the Eastman School (PhD 1969). While at Eastman he was awarded the Howard Hanson Prize for composition. In 1981 he was named composer of the year for the state of Washington. From 1969 to 1978 he taught at the College-Conservatory at the University of Cincinnati; there he developed and then directed the conservatory's electronic music studio, where he produced most of his music dating from this period. In 1978 he was appointed director of the music school at the University of Washington, Seattle; he became composer-in-residence there in 1981. He was then appointed dean of the College of Fine Arts at the University of Wisconsin, Stevens Point, where he served until his death in 1987. Palombo's early works exemplify a strongly motivic and pointillistic approach, but from 1981 he employed a lyrical, even popular idiom in works that rely more on intuitive energy than on methodical structures. With Lucas Drew he edited Barry Green's *Advanced Techniques of Double Bass Playing* (Cincinnati, 1976), an important two-volume compendium of bass techniques. Over the years he also presented many invited papers on a variety of topics in music and the arts.

WORKS
(all works composed 1978–9 were withdrawn)
Large ens: Serenade, str orch, 1964; Sinfonietta, chbr orch, 1965; Movt for Orch, 1967; Variations, orch, 1968; The Dance, dance band, 1980
Chbr and solo inst: Pf Sonata, 1965; Miniature, fl, 1966; Vc Sonata, 1966; Composition for 3 Insts, fl, cl, bn, 1967; Str Qt, 1967; 3 Manners of Chance, ob, cl, bn, 1967; Metatheses, fl, ob, hpd, db, 1970; Montage, vn, pf, 1971; Ritratti anticamente, va, pf, 1972; Variants, hpd, 1975; Music for Triceratops Americus, elec, 1977; Variatione de camera, fl, cl, va, vc, pf, 2 perc, 1980

Tape: Proteus (C. Geerling), orch, tape, 1969; Miniature, org, tape, 1970; Morphosis, ballet, 1970; Crystals, 1971; Sonos I–III, 1 inst, tape, 1972–3; Et cetera, ballet, 1973–4; Sonos IV, str trio, tape, 1974; Music for Stego-wagenvolkssaurus, 1974; Theme: Horizons of the Air, 1974; Theme: We the Women, 1974; Laser Images, film score, 1975; Laser Music, 1975; Sound of Seattle: New Faces '82, stage music, 1982
Vocal: It's Over, 1v, pf, 1981; Moody, Moody Blues, vv, dance band, 1981; Morning Memories (C. Henry), 1v, pf, 1981

BIBLIOGRAPHY
Baker8
E.R. Anderson: *Contemporary American Composers* (Boston, 1976)
DAVID COPE/GREG A STEINKE

Pamela Z [Brooks, Pamela] (*b* Buffalo, NY, 13 July 1956). Composer, performer, vocalist, and media artist. Her creative output has focused on the combination of two primary elements: her vocal performance (capable of operatic lyricism as well as extended techniques) and her use of computer technology. Z began experimenting with recording devices in her youth and made pieces that layered her voice with homemade instruments and concrete sounds. She went on to study classical vocal performance at the University of Colorado at Boulder and performed as a singer-songwriter. She relocated to San Francisco in 1984 where she began performing her own inter-media theatrical works and concerts. Her performance pieces have situated her in a field of processed and live sound accompanied by video or projected images.

A prominent feature of Z's compositional practice is her use of various delay and sound processing technology. Her early works used digital delays, effects units, and samplers that manipulated her voice, MIDI-generated sounds, and samples. In 2000 she began working with Max/MSP software to produce loops and delays, as well as other effects and textures. She has also made use of gesture-based MIDI controllers such as the BodySynth—a set of electrode sensors worn on her body with which she has triggered and manipulated sounds via muscle movements and physical gestures—as well as Donald Swearingen's Ultrasound controller.

Z's musical aesthetic is one of sonic accretion. With her electronics she has created sound beds built up from her voice as well as sampled sounds. She has also been interested in language as a compositional resource and explored the musicality of spoken words by subjecting them to looping and delay. With her use of gesture as well as her physical presence in her performances, Z has offered a humanistic musical technology. By manipulating her own voice as well as exploring the physicality of computerized performance through the BodySynth, she has allegorized technology not as an alienating force but as an extended network of human agency and emotion. In her performance pieces she has explored a number of recurring themes: the materiality of voices and language (*Voci*, *Parts of Speech*), dislocation and alienation (*Gaijin*, *Baggage Allowance*), and the production of knowledge (*The Pendulum*, *Wunderkabinet*).

Z's oeuvre includes sound installations, concert pieces, and chamber works written for ensembles including

ETHEL, the California E.A.R. Unit, and the Bang on a Can All-Stars. She has received numerous awards including a Guggenheim Fellowship and the CalArts Alpert Award in the Arts.

WORKS
(selective list)
Stage: Parts of Speech, 1v, elecs, video, projections, 1998; Gaijin, 1v, elecs, dancers, video, 2001; Voci, 1v, elecs, video, 2003; Metal/Vox/Water, 1v, elecs, video, amp metal, 2005; Wunderkabinet, 1v, vc, elecs, video, 2005, collab. M. Brubeck; The Pendulum, 1v, elecs, video, 2008; Baggage Allowance, 1v, elecs, video, 2010

Chbr: The Schmetterling, 1v, chbr ens, elecs, 1998; Shifting Conditions in the Southland, 1v, chbr ens, elecs, 1998; Persistence, 1v, chbr ens, elecs, 2001; Ethel Dreams of Temporal Disturbances, str qt, tape, 2005; Twenty Answers, chbr ens, 2008

Vocal: Badagada, 1v, elecs, 1988; Bone Music, 1v, elecs, perc, 1992; Pianobend, 1v, elecs, 1994; Broom, 1v, elecs, 2009; Flare Stains, 1v, elecs, 2010

BIBLIOGRAPHY
T. Sellar: "Parts of Speech: Interview with Pamela Z," *Theater Magazine*, xxx/2 (2000), 59–64
P.Z.: "A Tool is a Tool," *Women, Art, and Technology*, ed. J. Malloy (Cambridge, MA, 2003), 348–61
H. Gray: *Cultural Moves: African Americans and the Politics of Representation* (Berkeley, 2005)
F. Uitti: "Pamela Z," *CMR*, xxv (2006), 587–9
G. Lewis: "The Virtual Discourses of Pamela Z," *JSAM*, i/1 (2007), 57–77
K. Kennedy: "A Few Facets of Pamela Z," *Musicworks*, no.76 (2000); repr. at <http://www.pamelaz.com/musicworks.html> (2013)

RYAN DOHONEY

Pan, Hermes [Hermes Panagiotopoulos] (*b* Memphis, TN, 10 June 1905; *d* Beverly Hills, CA, 19 Sept 1990). Dance director of Hollywood films. His mother moved him and his sister to New York City when they were children. He learned tap dancing on the city sidewalks and began his career dancing in amateur theatricals and speakeasies before finding work on Broadway in the late 1920s. While assisting Le Roy Prinz in staging musical numbers for *Top Speed* (1929; music by Bert Kalmar and Harry Ruby), he met Ginger Rogers, a featured player in the show, and may have helped with her first-act song-and-dance number, "Keep your undershirt on." In 1930 he went to Hollywood, where his connection with Prinz led to one job after another and eventually to working with Fred Astaire and Ginger Rogers on their first film, *Flying Down to Rio* (1933). Their relationship turned into a lifelong friendship and an enduring professional association. Pan collaborated with Astaire and Rogers on all nine of their RKO films (1933–9) and on their tenth, *The Barkleys of Broadway* (1949), at MGM. When his RKO contract ended in 1939, he worked at other studios and created dances for some of the greatest musical films of the next forty years. A good-looking man with a courtly manner, he often appeared on screen as the dancing partner of the stars of his films, including Betty Grable, Rita Hayworth, and Carmen Miranda. His agreeable personality, remarkable dance vocabulary, innovative stagecraft, and expertise in choreographing for the camera made him a leading exponent of the golden age of movie musicals in Hollywood. He was honored by the National Film Society Achievement in Cinema Award in 1980.

BIBLIOGRAPHY
J. Kobal: *Gotta Sing, Gotta Dance: a History of Movie Musicals* (New York, rev. 1983)
J. Mueller: *Astaire Dancing: the Musical Films* (New York, 1985)
R.E. Frank: *Tap! The Greatest Tap Dance Stars and Their Stories, 1900–1955* (New York, rev. 1990)
L. Billman: *Film Choreographers and Dance Directors* (Jefferson, NC, 1997)
F.W.D. Ries: "Pan, Hermes," *American National Biography Online* (New York, 2000), <http://www.anb.org>

CLAUDE CONYERS

Pan American Association of Composers. Composers' organization dedicated to the performance of contemporary music from the United States and Latin America. It was founded by Edgard Varèse, Carlos Chávez, and Henry Cowell in New York (1928) to replace the INTERNATIONAL COMPOSERS' GUILD (1921–7). As part of the political spirit of Pan-Americanism between the world wars, this association was the first to foster musical cooperation among composers throughout the Americas. It was also one of the first organizations dedicated to the performance of American music in Europe. Between 1929 and 1934 it presented at least 35 concerts, in New York, Havana, Paris, Berlin, Madrid, Dessau, Vienna, Budapest, and Hamburg. It also sponsored a series of radio broadcasts in 1933. Charles Ives provided financial support, and Nicolas Slonimsky conducted most of the concerts. Members Adolph Weiss, Pedro Sanjuán, Amadeo Roldán, and Alejandro García Caturla also conducted association concerts. Anton Webern, Fritz Reiner, and Albert Stoessel were guest conductors. After Varèse had moved to France in fall 1928, Cowell was acting president until December 1933. Following Varèse's return, he assumed the role of president and presented two final concerts in 1934. The association's notable premieres included Ives's *Three Places in New England* and *The Fourth of July*; Varèse's *Ionisation* and *Ecuatorial*; and Carl Ruggles' *Sun-treader*.

BIBLIOGRAPHY
D. Root: "The Pan-American Association of Composers (1928–1934)," *Anuario Interamericano de investigation musical*, viii (1972), 49–70
C. Oja: *Making Music Modern* (New York, 2003)
S. Stallings: *Collective Difference: the Pan-American Association of Composers and Pan-American Ideology, 1925–1945* (diss., Florida State U., 2009)

STEPHANIE STALLINGS

Panassié, Hugues (*b* Paris, France, 27 Feb 1912; *d* Montauban, France, 8 Dec 1974). French writer on jazz. He was one of the founders (1932) and later president of the Hot Club de France. After taking saxophone lessons as a child, he turned to writing about jazz as an adult; he published *Le jazz hot* (1934) and edited the journal *Jazz-hot* (1935–46), to which he contributed many articles. He regarded Louis Armstrong as "the greatest of all hot soloists" and in 1947 published Armstrong's first biography. In 1938 Count Basie recorded a composition called "Panassié Stomp," dedicating it to the writer; later that year, Panassié organized several small-group recording sessions with Mezz Mezzrow which included sessions with Tommy Ladnier and Sidney Bechet, which helped bolster the New Orleans revival movement. He also recorded a swing septet under the leadership of Frankie Newton.

In his voluminous writings Panassié sought to put jazz on an equal footing with art music by denouncing an "artistic conscience" that required developed musical theories which "muzzle inspiration…restrain and cripple the creative effort" (*The Real Jazz*, 1942). From the mid-1940s he controversially distinguished "real jazz" ("the music of the Negro orchestras of the South of the United States") from "commercial counterfeits" which he identified with Jack Hylton, Paul Whiteman, and bebop, thus delimiting the genre to the 1920s and 30s.

WRITINGS
(selective list)
Le jazz hot (Paris, 1934; Eng. trans., rev. 1936/*R*)
The Real Jazz (New York, 1942, enlarged 2/1960/*R*; Fr. orig. pubd as *La véritable musique de jazz*, Paris, 1945, enlarged 2/1952)
Louis Armstrong (Paris, 1947/*R*)
Jazz panorama (Paris, 1950)
with M. Gautier: *Dictionnaire du jazz* (Paris, 1954/*R*, enlarged 4/1987; Eng. trans., 1956, 2/1956 as *Guide to Jazz*, ed. A.A. Gurwitch)
Louis Armstrong (Paris, 1969; Eng. trans., New York, 1971)

DAVID TRIPPETT

Pandit Pran Nath (*b* Lahore, India [now Pakistan], 3 Nov 1918; *d* Berkeley, CA, 13 June 1996). Indian vocalist and composer, naturalized American. From the age of 13 he studied for 20 years as a disciple of Abdul Waheed Khan. He established his reputation as a leading interpreter of Kirana style with an exceptional knowledge of traditional compositions and the delineation of raga. From 1960 to 1970 he taught at Delhi University. His first appearances in the West in 1970 brought the vocal tradition of Hindustani classical music to the United States; subsequently he performed extensively in Europe, the United States, and elsewhere. He became a permanent resident of the United States and in 1971 established a school in New York, the Kirana Center for Indian Classical Music; in 1973 he was artist-in-residence at the University of California, San Diego, and from 1973 to 1984 was on the faculty of Mills College in Oakland, California. His awards in composition include a Guggenheim Fellowship (1975) and an NEA award (1978). He continued to teach and perform through his final years.

Pran Nath's majestic expositions of the slow *ālāp* sections of ragas, together with his emphasis on perfect intonation and the clear evocation of mood, profoundly influenced Western composers and performers; LA MONTE YOUNG, TERRY RILEY, and the artist-performer Marian Zazeela became his disciples, and JON HASSELL, RHYS CHATHAM, DON CHERRY, JON GIBSON, LEE KONITZ, CHARLEMAGNE PALESTINE, and DOUGLAS LEEDY all studied with him. Also known as a designer of instruments, Pran Nath after coming to the United States contributed innovations to the design of the tamboura, and his unvarnished Pandit Pran Nath–style instrument achieved worldwide recognition. Another of his instruments, the *prānda nāda*, which produces a continuous drone, is based on the tuning fork. Pra Nath is the subject of the documentary film *In Between the Notes: a Portrait of Pandit Pran Nath, Master Indian Musician* (1986).

BIBLIOGRAPHY
L. Young: "Singing of Pran Nath: the Sound is God," *Village Voice* (30 April 1970)
R. Palmer: "India's Master of Breath," *Rolling Stone* (30 Sept 1971)
J. Pareles: Obituary, *New York Times* (17 June 1996)

LA MONTE YOUNG/R

Pan-Indianism. An inter-tribal movement of Native Americans; *see* NATIVE AMERICAN MUSIC.

Pans. The individual instruments of a steel band, made from oil drums whose ends are hammered into a concave shape and tuned; *see* AFRO-CARIBBEAN MUSIC and UNITED STATES NAVY STEEL BAND.

Pantomime. (from Gk. *pantomimos*: "one who does everything by imitation") A theatrical genre in which mimed action is accompanied by music, sometimes combined with dialogue and sung text. In colonial America pantomime was an offshoot of the English tradition and in the 1790s French pantomime and *ballet d'action* were influential. After 1810 indigenous pantomime declined in popularity, but was incorporated into circus acts, where vestiges still remain in the mimed antics of the clowns and some of the equestrian routines. The influence of the mimed action, stage machinery, and action music of pantomime are also found in 19th-century genres such as melodrama and vaudeville. By the 20th century, it had become a much more idiosyncratic genre, depending upon the composer, but it resurfaces in the films of Chaplin and other comedians and in animated cartoons.

1. The colonial period. 2. The post-Revolutionary period. 3. The 19th century. 4. The 20th century.

1. THE COLONIAL PERIOD. The first documented performance of musical theater in America was *The Adventures of Harlequin and Scaramouch*, a pantomime performed as an afterpiece to Thomas Otway's play *The Orphan* as seen in Charleston on 4 February 1735, two weeks before the production there of the first ballad opera to be heard in America, *Flora*, by the English dramatist Colley Cibber. Like the dozen other pantomimes known to have been presented in the 1750s and 60s, it was based on an English model, probably the comic portion of *Perseus and Andromeda* (1730) by Lewis Theobald with music by John Ernest Galliard. However, just as its title differs from that of the English version, so too must the music, stage design, and choreography have been reworked for the more modest theatrical capabilities of the colonies. In English pantomimes, besides an overture, there were often songs similar to those of BALLAD OPERA and "comic tunes"— short binary instrumental pieces to accompany the grotesque and stylized dances that formed an important part of the entertainment. Pantomimes in this period were most often presented as "afterpieces" to full-length plays or ballad operas.

Besides *The Adventures of Harlequin*, at least a dozen more pantomimes (most of them also based on the characters of the traditional harlequinade) were presented in the colonies (in New York, Philadelphia, and Annapolis) between 1750 and the Revolution. A few of these are known to have been English works, and it is probable that most were. The American composers of music for these productions remain unidentified and no music or librettos for pantomimes of the colonial period are extant; some indication of performance practices may be obtained, however, from playbills and from descriptions of differences between American and English productions.

2. THE POST-REVOLUTIONARY PERIOD. There are a few extant pieces of pantomime music (dances, songs, and overtures) written by American composers between the years 1784 and 1812, including five by Pelissier and four by Reinagle. There is evidence from reviews, playbills, and librettos that a great many more were composed; Pelissier, for example, is known from advertisements to have composed or arranged music for 14 pantomimes, Reinagle for more than half a dozen, Rayner Taylor for five, and Benjamin Carr for two. Overtures were frequently advertised as having been composed by local musicians; extant examples by Reinagle (*Harlequin's Invasion*, 1795) and James Hewitt (two overtures for unknown works) are of the medley type, characterized by the combination of fragments of popular tunes. Most of the surviving pieces, however, are single songs or dances that were published in anthologies of piano and vocal music; Reinagle's "Hunting Song" (published *c*1804) from *Harlequin's Almanac* (*c*1800) is a typical example. Most pantomimes were still re-makes of English productions, although some titles indicate American situations (e.g., "Harlequin Panattaha or The Genii of the Algonquins" of 1810).

Certain performers became particularly well known for their pantomime roles: John Durang and Lewis Hallam, director of the Old American Company, were famous as Harlequin, and Alexander Placide, a theater manager in Charleston, as a clown. French actors such as M. Francisquy, M. Quesnet, and Mme. Gardie, unable to perform English-language roles, appeared almost exclusively in pantomime, and they brought with them from France a new style of ballet-pantomime influenced by the *ballet d'action* of J.G. Noverre. This was grander, more spectacular, and more serious than the works based on the antics of the *commedia dell'arte* characters; the short, comic tunes depicting specific actions were mostly replaced by more extended but nonetheless expressive music characteristic of late 18th-century English and French ballet.

3. THE 19TH CENTURY. While pantomime did not flourish in the United States in the 19th century, as it had in the 18th, English pantomime continued to be imported; among the most popular works were *Cinderella* (1804), *Mother Goose* (1805), and *Dick Whittington* (1814). Several imports were devised by James Byrne, the Harlequin and ballet-master at Drury Lane and Covent Garden, London, who was born in Philadelphia and had worked at the Chestnut Street Theatre before going back to England. According to Charles Durang, pantomime ceased to be attractive to audiences after about 1810 and, except in Philadelphia, where an English-style pantomime was

presented during the Christmas season well into the 1850s, pantomime performances were rare. The shift in performance style was also recorded by Durang; writing in 1856 of Lewis Hallam as a Ground Harlequin in the 1780s he states, "The modes of then executing that agile parti-colored cavalier's movements are now entirely obsolete and unpracticed by the modern representatives of his antics."

At Niblo's Garden in New York, however, the French ballet-pantomime (with the addition of acrobatics and rope-dancing), as choreographed by Mazurier and perfected by the Ravel family in the 1830s and 40s, was more successful, and they carried their ballet-pantomimes to many eastern cities. In the 1860s, a return to slapstick antics within a fairytale plot, characteristic of earlier pantomime, was offered by Thomas Baker at Niblo's and Wallack's and by George Fox at the Bowery Theatre. Starting in 1865, Fox moved to the Olympic, and his *Humpty Dumpty*, a highly successful send-up of New York politics, using elements of the old English harlequinade, outdid even *The Black Crook* in number of performances. The music, arranged by Anthony Reiff, was a pastiche of existing songs and dances, as was normal for this genre in both Britain and America.

Although pantomime as a separate type of theater was dying out in the 19th century (with the exception of the occasional imported English production), elements survived in other genres, such as burlesque and melodrama. By the end of Fox's career in the late 1870s his pantomime had become mixed with other specialty acts to form the VAUDEVILLE show. Patriotic and spectacular pantomime had meanwhile found a permanent home in the circus: John Durang and others performed such works as *The Independence of America, or The Ever Memorable 4th of July, 1776*, with music by Reinagle, for Ricketts' Circus already in the 1790s. The true legacy of American pantomime music, however, is probably to be found in the machinery and scenic effects of 19th-century MELODRAMA, where music, often cued using the same titles as those used for 18th-century pantomime—for example, "hurry," "fright," "battle"—is used to underline the most dramatic scenes.

4. THE 20TH CENTURY. Although the British style of pantomime had ceased to exist in the United States, composers and choreographers turned to new models of musical pantomime to create new works in the 20th century. For example, the French-influenced John Alden Carpenter's jazz-pantomime "Krazy Kat" (1921) based on the comic strip by George Herriman was danced at Town Hall in 1922, with Adolf Bolm, the choreographer, in the title role. Blair Fairchild's 1921 ballet-pantomime *Dame Libellule*, was the first work by an American to be produced at the Paris Opéra. Harry Partch's revised version of *Oedipus* (1952–4) has a dance-pantomime section, and Herb Haufrechts' 1953 work, *Bone Quillen* is termed an "opera-pantomime." More recently, Pauline Oliveros's *Rose Moon* (1984) is a pantomime to be performed by "more than 24 people, including vocalists, percussionists, mimes, and 'lunatics.'" Seymour Barab's six-part "Tales of Rhyme and

Reason" is scored for narrator, dance-pantomime, and orchestra. Many other works are on the boundary between pantomime and dance.

Old-style pantomime music and antics, however, are most easily found in animated cartoons, which still have "hurry music" for their chase scenes, and in the comedy films of such actors as Charlie Chaplin, W.C. Fields, Red Skelton, Danny Kaye and Carol Burnett. Chaplin's classic silent film *City Lights* of 1931, made three years after the advent of sound films, is subtitled "a comedy romance in pantomime" and has a score by Chaplin himself.

BIBLIOGRAPHY
W. Dunlap: *A History of the American Theatre* (New York, 1832)
C. Durang: "The Philadelphia Stage," *Philadelphia Sunday Dispatch* (1854, 1856, 1860) [series of articles; compiled by T. Westcott as *History of the Philadelphia Stage, between the Years 1749 and 1855*, 1868; *PHu*; similar compilations as *The Philadelphia Stage* in *PPL, History of the Philadelphia Stage* in *PHbs*]
E. Willis: *The Charleston Stage in the 18th Century* (Columbia, SC, 1924)
G.C.D. Odell: *Annals of the New York Stage* (New York, 1927–49/R)
L. Moore: "John Durang: the First American Dancer," *Dance Index*, i (1942), 120–39
D. Mayer: "The Pantomime Olio and Other Pantomime Variants," *Theatre Notebook*, xix (1965), 22–28
A.S. Downer, ed.: *The Memoirs of John Durang, American Actor, 1785–1816* (Pittsburgh, 1966)
D. Mayer: *Harlequin in his Element, 1806–1836* (Cambridge, MA, 1969)
P. Tyler: *Chaplin: Last of the Clowns* (New York, 1947, 2/1972)
J. Moy: *John B. Ricketts' Circus, 1793–1800* (diss., U. of Illinois, 1977)
A.D. Shapiro [McLucas]: "Action Music in American Pantomime and Melodrama 1730–1913," *American Music*, ii/4 (1984), 49–72
L. Senelick: *The Age and Stage of George L. Fox, 1825–1877* (Hanover and London, 1988)
D.L. Root: "Music Research in Nineteenth-Century Theater: or, The Case of a Burlesquer, a Baker, and a Pantomime Maker," *Vistas of American Music: Essays and Compositions in Honor of William K. Kearns*, ed. S.L. Porter and J. Graziano (Warren, MI, 1999)
D. Goldmark: *Tunes for 'toons: music and the Hollywood cartoon* (Berkeley, 2005)
D. Kamin: *The Comedy of Charlie Chaplin: Artistry in Motion* (Lanham, MD, 2008)

ANNE DHU McLUCAS

Paoli, Antonio [Marcano, Antonio Emilio Paoli] (*b* Ponce, PR, 14 April 1871; *d* San Juan, PR, 24 Aug 1946). Puerto Rican tenor. Encouraged by his elder sister Amalia, a singer active in Spain, he studied in Madrid and Milan. During his early career (and while studying singing in Milan), he adopted the name Ermogene Imleghi Bascarán. He made his debut in Paris as Arnold in *Guillaume Tell* (1899) and developed a career as a dramatic tenor in the tradition of Francesco Tamagno. Paoli toured with a company headed by Pietro Mascagni in 1902, singing in Chicago and New York. Following his debut as Otello in Madrid (1905), he sang that role some 570 times; he had also given, by the end of his career, 425 performances of Manrico. Other important appearances were at the new Teatro Colón, Buenos Aires, in 1908, and at La Scala as Samson in 1909–10. His many recordings include excerpts from *Pagliacci*, under the direction of Ruggero Leoncavallo (1907). He occasionally performed in Puerto Rico during his tours of North and South America and retired there in the early 1920s; his last public appearances were in San

Juan in 1928 as Manrico and Otello with a visiting New York company. In such roles as Samson, Canio, and Otello he contributed to the development of a true dramatic tenor style of characterization as distinct from that of the "elevated baritone."

BIBLIOGRAPHY
GV (R. Celletti; R. Vegeto)
J. López, E. Arnosi, and L. Alvarado: "Antonio Paoli" *Record Collector*, xxii (1974–5), 5 [with discography by J. Dennis]
J. López: *Antonio Paoli, "el león de Ponce": la vida del célebre tenor* (Waterbury, CT, 1997)
J. Martínez Solá: *Antonio Paoli: el tenor puertorriqueño* (San Juan, 2003)

DONALD THOMPSON/R

Papago. *See* TOHONO O'ODHAM.

Papakhian, A[rsen] Ralph (*b* Detroit, MI, 28 Dec 1948). Music librarian. He graduated from Western Michigan University (BA 1971; MMus 1973; MLS 1973), began working in the Music Library's Technical Services Division of Indiana University in 1975, and became head of the division in 1985. Papakhian has been an advocate for cooperative cataloging of music from its inception in 1976. He was co-founder of the Music OCLC Users Group, the first effort to implement a MARC format prior to its introduction by the Library of Congress, and served as its chair (1993–7). He managed Indiana's participation in the Associated Music Libraries Group Title II-C grant (1984–90) for retrospective conversion, the computerization of cataloging data. The NACO-Music Project, the first such cooperative project, grew out of this grant and sought to create authoritative headings for music in the Library of Congress files; he has coordinated it since 1988. He has contributed to the education of music catalogers through the summer Workshop in Music Cataloging since 1996. He has served the Music Library Association, most notably as a founder of the MLA listserv and the MLA Clearinghouse, an on-line document repository. These have revolutionized information sharing among music librarians. In 1992 he received the first MLA Special Achievement Award.

WRITINGS
with R. Smiraglia: "Music in the OCLC On-Line Union Catalog," *Notes*, xxxviii (1981), 257–74
"The Frequency of Personal Name Headings in the Indiana University Music Library Card Catalogs," *Library Resources & Technical Services*, xxix (1985), 273–85
"Music Librarianship at the Turn of the Century: Cataloging," *Notes*, lvi (2000), 581–90

J. BRADFORD YOUNG

Papapostolou, Harilaos (*b* Agrinion, Greece, 22 April 1932; *d* Baltimore, MD, 30 Nov 1998). Greek chanter and choir director, naturalized American. He came from a long line of Orthodox priests and continued in the footsteps of his father as a *psalti*, or chanter. Beginning at five years old he studied with professional church singers, learning the liturgical elements of the Greek Orthodox tradition. He attended Athens Conservatory, earning degrees in both Western classical and Byzantine traditional musical styles, and Athens University, where he studied theology. He returned to Agrinion after graduating and became the *protopsaltis* (head chanter) of his church. In the 1950s and early 60s he founded and maintained a music conservatory and promoted traditional Greek music on radio and television. In the mid-1960s he moved to Washington, DC, and in 1967 became head chanter and choir director at St. Sophia Greek Orthodox Cathedral. Through public forums and an educational system of his own design, Papapostolou helped keep Byzantine sounds alive in the Western world. He was particularly known for blending a strong faith with his own powerful musical expression. In 1998 he received a National Heritage Fellowship from the NEA.

JONAS WESTOVER

Papas [Papadopoulos], **Sophocles** (*b* Sopiki, Greece, 18 Dec 1893; *d* Alexandria, VA, 26 Feb 1986). Guitar teacher and publisher, born in Greece. At the age of 14 he moved from Greece to Cairo, Egypt, where he learned to play the mandolin. He returned to Greece in 1912, but in 1914 immigrated to the United States. After serving in the US Army, he settled in Washington, DC, in 1920, where he taught fretted instruments, played mandolin and banjo on the radio, and studied the guitar seriously with William Foden and George Krick. By the late 1920s he was one of the few Americans (other than Bickford, Krick, and Foden) promoting European guitar music. Papas befriended the guitarist Andrés Segovia soon after the latter's 1928 New York debut and effectively promoted Segovia's American career thereafter. As a publisher, he established the Columbia Music Company in Washington (1928) and eventually published his *Segovia Scales* (1953), a notable, often reprinted book on technique for aspiring classical guitarists. Papas himself was the author of a popular *Method for the Classic Guitar* (enlarged ed. 1963). He was also the proprietor of a succession of music schools in Washington, DC: Papas Studios (1938–47), the Columbia School of Music (1947–56), the Guitar Shop (1956–68), and a private studio in the Dupont Circle Building (1968–82). Notable among his students were Aaron Shearer, John Marlow, Clare Callahan, Sharon Isbin, Charlie Byrd, Dorothy DeGoede, Alvino Rey, and Joe Breznikar.

BIBLIOGRAPHY

E.P. Smith: *Sophocles Papas: the Guitar, His Life* (Chapel Hill, 1998)
P. Danner, ed.: "Papas on Papas with Reflections on Segovia," *Soundboard*, xxv/1 (1998), 29–32

THOMAS F. HECK/PETER DANNER

Pape, René (*b* Dresden, Germany, 4 Sept 1964). German bass. He was a member of the Dresden Kreuzchor as a child (1974–81) and made his stage debut in 1988 at the Berlin Staatsoper, where he has since been a member of the regular ensemble, singing Sarastro, Rocco, Ramfis, Fasolt, Hunding, King Mark, and Pogner, among other roles. His first appearance at the Salzburg Festival was as Don Fernando (*Fidelio*) and in Johann Sebastian Bach's *St. Matthew Passion* in 1990. He sang Fasolt at Bayreuth each year from 1994 to 1998; Wagner roles have become a specialty for him. Pape's debut at La

Scala was in 1991 as Sarastro, and he first appeared at the Vienna Staatsoper as Hunding (1996), at Covent Garden as Heinrich der Vogler (1997), and at the Metropolitan as Fasolt (1997). In 2000 he returned to the Metropolitan as an athletic Escamillo, and he has subsequently performed there regularly, appearing as Boris Godunov in the 2010–11 season. His other roles include a saturnine, beautifully sung Leporello, heard at the 1999 Salzburg Festival. He is also a concert artist, delivering notable performances in Giuseppe Verdi's Requiem and making his solo recital debut at Carnegie Hall in 2009. His well formed, compact bass and refined, shapely phrasing can be heard in recording as Pogner and in *The Creation, The Seasons*, and Mozart's Requiem, all with Sir Georg Solti. In 2008 Pape released a new recording of solo arias entitled *Gods, Kings, and Demons*, with the Staatskapelle Dresden. He can also be seen on a number of DVDs, including *Die Zauberflöte* and his signature role, King Mark in *Tristan und Isolde*. Pape has received several awards for his work, including being named Singer of the Year by *Musical America* in 2001.

ALAN BLYTH/JONAS WESTOVER

Papo Lucca [Quiñonez, Enrique Arsenio Lucca] (*b* Ponce, PR, 10 April 1946). Puerto Rican salsa pianist, instrumentalist, producer, and arranger. The son of a prominent Puerto Rican bandleader, he studied at Ponce's Free School of Music. He also took lessons from pianist Ramon Fernandez and had begun his performing career by the age of 11. He subsequently worked with his father's group, La Sonora Ponceña, and eventually inherited the band as his own. During the 1950s he played alongside such musical luminaries as Machito and Obdulio Morales Ríos and appeared regularly on television, especially on Ruth Fernández's variety show. After graduating from the University of Puerto Rico, Lucca gained greater prominence through his affiliation with La Sonora Ponceña and his work with other artists. In 1976 he served as performer and producer of La Sonora Ponceña's *Conquista Musical* (Fania). He also became the pianist for the Fania All-Stars. One of his notable achievements came with the album *La Ceiba* (Fania, 1979), in which he and La Sonora Ponceña collaborated with vocalist Celia Cruz. Although he has recorded solo piano works, Lucca has tended to work more often as part of salsa ensembles. He has been included in many films about salsa and is recognized as one of the most important contributors to the genre.

JONAS WESTOVER

Paramount. Record label. Established in 1916, it was the main label of the New York Recording Laboratories of Port Washington, Wisconsin. A race series began in August 1922 and proved extremely successful; by the time it was discontinued in 1932 more than 1100 releases had been made. The work of jazz and blues singers predominated, including that of Ma Rainey, Ida Cox, Alberta Hunter, Charley Patton, and Blind Lemon Jefferson. Many discs in the race catalog are now acknowledged to be classics, including recordings by King

Oliver, Lovie Austin's Blues Serenaders, and Jimmy O'Bryant's Original Washboard Band. Paramount's General Series contained a smaller proportion of jazz, but included some discs by Fletcher Henderson and the Original Memphis Five and a considerable amount of hot dance music.

During the early 1920s Paramount was closely associated with the Bridgeport Die & Machine Co. and also exchanged many masters with Plaza (later part of ARC). In 1929 it moved to Grafton, Wisconsin; operations ceased in 1932. Thereafter, however, a small number of race issues appeared in a Paramount series produced by ARC. The collector John Steiner revived the label in the late 1940s, putting out both reissues and new material; LPs of the latter were released until the early 1950s.

BIBLIOGRAPHY

M. Wyler: *A Glimpse of the Past: an Illustrated History of some Early Record Companies that Made Jazz History* (West Moors, England, 1957)

R.M.W. Dixon and J. Godrich: *Recording the Blues* (London, 1970)

M.E. Vreede: *Paramount 12/13000 Series* (London, 1971) [discography]

C. Hillman: "Paramount Serenaders 1923–1926," *Storyville*, no.67 (1976), 8–13; no.68 (1976), 52–4; no.69 (1977), 91–4; no.70 (1977), 149–50; no.72 (1977), 226–7; no.73 (1977), 29–30; no.74 (1977), 67–8; no.75 (1978), 84–5 [incl. discography]

B. Rust: *The American Record Label Book* (New Rochelle, NY, 1978), 226

HOWARD RYE/BARRY KERNFELD

Paray, Paul (M.A. Charles) (*b* Le Tréport, France, 24 May 1886; *d* Monte Carlo, France, 10 Oct 1979). French conductor and composer, active in the United States. He studied with his father, an organist, and in Rouen, France, where he became an organist at 17. A year later he entered the Paris Conservatoire, won a *premier prix* in harmony and, in 1911, the Prix de Rome. After being conscripted into the French army in 1914, he was taken prisoner until 1918. He made his debut at a test concert with the Lamoureux Orchestra in 1920 and as a result was appointed assistant conductor of the Concerts Lamoureux, succeeding Camille Chevillard as principal in 1923. Five years later Paray became conductor of the Monte Carlo PO, and from 1933 he was principal conductor of the Concerts Colonne in Paris.

During World War II Paray conducted in Marseilles and Monte Carlo, and returned to Paris in 1944 to reorganize the Colonne Orchestra after the liberation. He remained with the Concerts Colonne until his appointment as principal conductor of the Detroit SO (1952–63). At Detroit he inaugurated the Henry and Edsel Ford Auditorium in 1956 with his *Mass of Joan of Arc*, originally composed in 1931 for the quincentenary commemoration at Rouen and first performed there. He also recorded the mass and made several discs of French works, notably by Hector Berlioz, Georges Bizet, Emmanuel Chabrier, Maurice Ravel, and Albert Roussel. Paray acquired a reputation as a reliable conductor in a wide range of the classical repertory. As a composer he tended towards academic propriety. His works include the symphonic poem *Adonis troublé* (1921, staged at

the Paris Opera in 1922 as the ballet *Artémis troublée*), two symphonies, a *Fantaisie* for piano and orchestra, and various chamber and piano works.

BIBLIOGRAPHY

L'art musical (7 Jan 1938) [Paray issue]

W.L. Landowski: *Paul Paray: musicien de France et du monde* (Lyons, France, 1956)

H. Stoddard: *Symphony Conductors of the U.S.A.* (New York, 1957), 160–70

J.-P. Mousnier: *Paul Paray* (Paris, 1998)

J. Hunt: *A Gallic Trio: Charles Munch, Paul Paray, Pierre Monteux, Discographies* (London, 2003)

NOËL GOODWIN/R

Paredes, Américo (*b* Brownsville, TX, 3 Sept 1915; *d* Austin, TX, 5 May 1999). Scholar. Born to a family of Mexican American ranchers on the border of Texas and Mexico, he grew up in Brownsville and dedicated his life to promoting the culture of Mexican Americans and combating racism. Paredes worked as a journalist while attending junior college. In 1937 his first book of poetry, *Cantos de adolescencia*, was published. In 1944 he enlisted in the US Army, and after his active tour ended he worked as a journalist for the army journal *Stars and Stripes*, first as correspondent, then as political editor of the Pacific edition. By 1956 he had completed his bachelor's, master's, and doctoral degrees in English and folklore studies at the University of Texas at Austin. Two years later his dissertation on Gregorio Cortez and the *corrido* song form was published as *"With his Pistol in his Hand": a Border Ballad and its Hero*; it eventually became a cornerstone of folklore and anthropological research. Paredes taught folklore and creative writing at his alma mater, training an entire generation of scholars, and founded centers for folklore and Mexican American studies. The Mexican government bestowed upon him the Order of the Aztec Eagle, its highest award for non-citizens, in 1990. After his retirement in 1984, he continued to publish poetry, fiction, and scholarly research.

BIBLIOGRAPHY

M.F. Medrano: *Américo Paredes: in His Own Words, an Authorized Biography* (Denton, TX, 2010)

M. Meier: "Américo Paredes, 1915–99: Mexican American Folklorist, Writer, Poet, Musician," <http://www.lib.utexas.edu/benson/paredes/biography.html> (2013)

MARK LOMANNO

Pareles, Jon(athan) (*b* Connecticut, 1953). Music critic. Raised in Connecticut, he played piano from an early age and took up jazz flute in high school. He attended Yale University, where he majored in music and was music director of the university radio station, WNHC. After graduating in 1974 he moved to Boston, where he launched his professional career as a freelance music critic. He wrote reviews for the "PopTop" section in *Fusion*, a free Boston newspaper, and at the same time contributed to the alternative weekly publication *Real Paper*. In 1975 his first submission to the pioneer rock-and-roll magazine *Crawdaddy* was accepted by writer John Swenson, catapulting Pareles into the national world of popular music criticism. After two years of freelancing, he became music editor at *Crawdaddy*, and he moved to New York in 1977. He left the magazine shortly before it folded in 1979 and became assistant editor at *Rolling Stone*. Pareles stayed at the magazine only briefly, however, and accepted a position at the *Village Voice* in 1980. There he temporarily replaced Robert Christgau and worked as music editor until 1981. In 1982 he began making regular freelance contributions to the *New York Times*, where he covered both popular music and jazz. The *Village Voice* offered Pareles a full-time position in 1985, but instead he became a staff writer at the *New York Times*. He has been chief popular music critic from 1988 into the early 2010s, and his byline has continued to appear frequently in the "Arts & Leisure" section.

Pareles's career is distinguished by his coverage of a wide variety of music genres, including rock, pop, hip hop, jazz, avant-garde, punk, metal, and musics from around the world. Although his primarily contributions have been as a music critic, he has also engaged in traditional journalistic reporting. Until he became a staff writer at the *New York Times* in 1985, he divided his time between writing and working as an editor. He co-edited *The Rolling Stone Encyclopedia of Rock & Roll* (New York, 1983, 3/2001) with Patricia Romanowski. He has continued to live and work in New York.

GLENDA GOODMAN

Parent Music Resource Center (PMRC). Organization formed in May 1985 to address sexual and violent content in American popular music. The tax-exempt PMRC comprised only a board of directors headed by a group of so-called Washington Wives—women such as Tipper Gore and Pamela Howar who were married to prominent public and political figures. The PMRC quickly gained national attention, launching a media blitz that attributed social ills to depravity in music. Formed with the expressed intent of providing information, the group soon used their clout to meet with the Recording Industry Association of America (RIAA) and demand labeling of records for content along with self-censorship from the industry. They identified 15 contemporary popular songs to exemplify their charges of pornography and violence:

The PMRC Filthy Fifteen		
1.	Prince	"Darling Nikki"
2.	Sheena Easton	"Sugar Walls"
3.	Judas Priest	"Eat Me Alive"
4.	Vanity	"Strap on Robbie Baby"
5.	Mötley Crüe	"Bastard"
6.	AC/DC	"Let Me Put My Love into You"
7.	Twisted Sister	"We're Not Gonna Take It"
8.	Madonna	"Dress You Up"
9.	W.A.S.P.	"Animal (Fuck Like a Beast)"
10.	Def Leppard	"High 'n Dry"
11.	Mercyful Fate	"Into the Coven"
12.	Black Sabbath	"Trashed"
13.	Mary Jane Girls	"In My House"
14.	Venom	"Possessed"
15.	Cyndi Lauper	"She Bop"

On 19 September 1985 the US Senate Committee on Commerce, Science, & Transportation commenced a series of hearings to investigate pornographic content in popular music. Notably the committee chairman, John Danforth, and two of its members, Al Gore and Ernest Hollings, were married to leaders of the PMRC. Testimony included statements from Frank Zappa, Dee Snider (lead singer of Twisted Sister), and John Denver, all of whom objected to the threat of government censorship and legislative action based on subjective interpretations. Before the series of meetings had ended, the RIAA, which was looking for support from four senators on the committee for the Home Audio Recording tax bill, agreed to a labeling system. In 1990 the system was standardized with the generic but distinctive wording "Parental Advisory Explicit Content," which was colloquially dubbed the Tipper Sticker. After her husband's election to the vice-presidency in 1992, Tipper Gore resigned from the PMRC, and the group soon dissolved.

See also CENSORSHIP.

BIBLIOGRAPHY

United States Senate: *Record Labeling: Hearing before the Committee on Commerce, Science, and Transportation* (Washington, DC, 1985)

R. Cutietta: "Rock Music Gets a Label," *Music Educators Journal*, lxxii/April (1986), 36–8

C. Chastanger: "The Parents' Music Resource Center: from Information to Censorship," *Popular Music*, xvii (1999), 179–92

GARY GALVÁN

Parepa(-Rosa), Euphrosyne [De Boyescu, Parepa] (*b* Edinburgh, Scotland, 7 May 1836; *d* London, England, 21 Jan 1874). Scottish soprano. Her father was Baron Georgiades de Boyescu, a Walachian magnate, and her mother the soprano Elizabeth Seguin, with whom she studied. After making her debut in Malta as Amina in *La sonnambula* in 1855, she appeared in many European cities for the next decade. Possessing a two-and-a-half octave range and a voice that combined power and sweetness, she was one of the best and most popular singers of her era in opera, concert, and oratorio. She went to the United States in 1865 to take part in a concert tour with Theodore Thomas's orchestra. In February 1867, she married her second husband, Carl Rosa, a violinist on the tour. She appeared in Patrick S. Gilmore's Peace Jubilee in Boston in 1869 and gave concerts with her husband, with whom she formed the Parepa-Rosa English Opera Company (1867–71). It toured the United States extensively, presenting operas in English translation, and was successful both artistically and financially. Parepa-Rosa suspended the activities of her troupe in 1871, and with her husband formed a new group that featured the German tenor Theodor Wachtel and the English baritone Charles Santley. She returned to Europe in 1872. Her husband endowed the Parepa-Rosa Scholarship in her memory at the Royal Academy of Music.

BIBLIOGRAPHY

Grove7; DNB (R.H. Legge)

Obituary, *New York Times* (23 Jan 1874)

G.P. Upton: *Musical Memories* (Chicago, 1908)

E.B. Marks: *They all had Glamour* (New York, 1944)

HAROLD ROSENTHAL/ELIZABETH FORBES/DEE BAILY/R

Paris (Wright), Twila (*b* Fort Worth, TX, 28 Dec 1958). Contemporary Christian music singer, songwriter, author, and pianist. Her musical gifts were apparent when she was young, and her family encouraged her to both sing and learn piano, which she began at age six. Her father was the founder and chancellor of an evangelical school, Ecclesia College, as well as a musician. Her first album of evangelical songs was *Little Twila Paris* (1965). She began to write and record her own music, eventually releasing the album *Knowin' You're Around* (Milk and Honey, 1980). Once she found her niche, she gained popularity on Christian adult contemporary radio and produced a tremendous amount of music in a short period of time. Successful albums quickly followed, including *Keepin' my Eyes on You* (1982) and *Kingdom Seekers* (1985). Her style is contemporary Christian, featuring rock instruments and piano complementing hymn-like melodies. In the 1980s she had 13 singles that landed in the top ten on the contemporary Christian music chart; six of those, including "Runner" (1984) and "True Friend" (1989), hit number one. Her efforts have garnered a host of Dove Awards, including Female Vocalist of the Year in three consecutive years (1993–5). Throughout the 1990s and into the 2000s she continued to record regularly, including *Small Sacrifice* (2007), to tour widely, and to preach through song. Paris has also written books on Christian themes.

JONAS WESTOVER

Parisot, Aldo (Simoes) (*b* Natal, Brazil, 30 Sept 1920). Cellist of Brazilian birth. He made his debut at the age of 12 and studied first with his stepfather Thomazzo Babini and then for five years with Iberê Gomes Grosso in Rio de Janeiro. He also studied architectural engineering. He moved to the United States in 1946 to study at Yale University (MA), and the next year made his debut as a soloist with the Boston SO at the Berkshire Music Center; he served as principal cellist of the Pittsburgh SO in the years 1949–50. Since 1948 tours have taken him throughout the United States and to Europe, Asia, Africa, and South America. Although he favors suites by Bach and sonatas by Beethoven and Brahms, he has also championed contemporary music and his recordings cover a wide repertoire. He has given premieres of works composed for him by Quincy Porter (*Fantasia and Dance*, 1950), Heitor Villa-Lobos (Cello Concerto no.2, 1955), Camargo Guarnieri (*Choro*, 1962), Cláudio Santoro (Cello Concerto, 1963, Sonata no.3, 1964), Alvin Etler (Cello Concerto, 1971), Yehudi Wyner (*De novo*, 1971), and Donald Martino (*Parisonatina al'dodecafonia*, 1976), among others. Parisot taught at the Peabody Conservatory (1956–8) before joining the faculty at Yale in 1958, where he was still teaching in the early 2010s; he also held positions at the Mannes College (1962–6) and the New England Conservatory (1966–70) and was artist-in-residence at the Banff Center, Canada (1981–3). He has received many awards, among them numerous honorary degrees as well as the United Nations Peace Medal (1982).

BIBLIOGRAPHY

M. Fellowes: "Mastering the Cello: from an Interview with Aldo Parisot," *Etude*, lxxi (1953), 17, 61
A. Parisot: "Parisot on Parisot," *MusAm*, lxxxii/12 (1962), 64
S. Fleming: "The Aldo Parisot International Cello Competition," *HiFi/MusAm*, xxxii/6 (1982), 34

MINA F. MILLER

Park, Sue-Yeon (*b* Ganghwa Island, South Korea, 1954). South Korean dancer, naturalized American. She was exposed to traditional Korean dance from a young age through the shamanistic Buddhist rituals that her family hosted when she was a child. At the age of four she moved with her family to the capital city of Seoul. From age six she was encouraged by her parents to study dance, and at age 13 she entered an art and performance school (*kwonbon*). She immigrated to the United States after she finished a tour there in 1981.

Park became involved with the Korean immigrant community in New York, including the Association for Korean Performing Arts. She later established a branch of the Korean Traditional Music Association in New York (1993) under the appellation Korean Traditional Performing Arts Association and founded Sounds of Korea, a performance group dedicated to preserving Korea's traditional performing arts.

She has studied *salpuri-chum*, a Buddhist shamanic dance, in South Korea with the renowned female dancers You Lim Jin and Yi Mae-bang, and the *seungmu* Buddhist drum dance with Chang-bae Yi, a master in that discipline. In 2003 she became the only American to be designated a *yisuja* by the South Korean government, a title denoting the highest level of mastery in traditional arts, which she earned for *salpuri-chum*. She has also achieved the highest designation of *jeonsuja* for her mastery of *seungmu*. She has received many awards recognizing her dedication to her art, including the New York Governor's Award of Excellence (2004). She has also been the recipient of the Best Artist of the Year Award from the Foundation for Korean Arts and Culture in Korea, and in 2008 was awarded the prestigious NEA National Heritage Fellowship, the US government's highest recognition for excellence in folk and traditional arts.

MEGAN E. HILL

Parkening, Christopher (William) (*b* Los Angeles, CA, 14 Dec 1947). Classical guitarist. Inspired by the guitar playing of his cousin Jack Marshall, he took up the instrument at the age of 11. After several years' study with Celedonio Romero and Pepe Romero, he participated in the master classes of Andrés Segovia at the University of California, Berkeley, and subsequently studied privately with him. He spent a year at UCLA (1964–5) but then transferred to the University of Southern California as a cello student of Gabor Rejto (the guitar was not yet taught at the university). Asked to found the guitar department there, he eventually became its head (1971–5). Meanwhile, his first recordings were released in 1968 (*In the Classic Style* and *In the Spanish Style*, Angel Records), and his first concert tour began the same year. For the next decade he enjoyed a successful career as a performer, and his recordings from this period, including *Parkening and the Guitar* (Angel, 1976, nominated for a Grammy Award), are notable for their energy and bravura. By 1977, however, he had become disenchanted with his increasingly stressful career. After abandoning the concert stage, he moved to a ranch in Montana, where he taught guitar and appeared only rarely as a recitalist (for example, in Washington, DC, 1979). About 1981, after becoming a committed Christian, he resumed his performing career, with the stated intention of playing "only for God's glory" (quoting Johann Sebastian Bach); since that time his recordings (various reissues apart) have often included overtly religious works. In performance he gradually recaptured the successful formula of his earlier recitals, which centered on colorful shorter pieces, and critics have drawn particular attention to his greater subtlety of expression. Since the mid-1980s he has often been joined in concerts by guitarist David Brandon. He has collaborated with singers Kathleen Battle (their recording *Pleasures of Their Company*, EMI, 1986, earned Parkening his second Grammy nomination) and Jubilant Sykes (*Jubilation*, EMI, 2007). He has performed with many top orchestras, including the London SO, with which he made the first recording of Elmer Bernstein's Guitar Concerto (EMI, 2000). Parkening's aesthetics and repertoire choices have leaned heavily toward traditional classical works; he has sometimes been criticized for neglecting modern music. He has published *The Christopher Parkening Guitar Method* (Chicago, 1972/R), several volumes of transcriptions, including one of works by Bach (Chicago, 1973/R), and *Joaquin Rodrigo: Music for Guitar*, an edition of 19 Rodrigo pieces for solo guitar (Mainz, 1995). He has taught at Pepperdine University since 2002, which is the site of the Parkening International Guitar Competition.

BIBLIOGRAPHY

C. Cooper: "Christopher Parkening," *Classical Guitar*, v/6 (1987), 12–5

J. Gore: "Christopher Parkening," *Guitar Player*, xxvii/5 (1993), 31–4

L. Sharken: "Seeking Beauty," *Guitar Player*, xxxv/4 (2001), 78–82

C. Parkening and K. Tyers: *Grace like a River: an Autobiography* (Carol Stream, IL, 2006)

<http://www.parkening.com> (2013)

THOMAS F. HECK/LARS HELGERT

Parker, Alice (*b* Boston, MA, 16 Dec 1925). Composer, conductor, and teacher. She studied at Smith College (BA 1947) and the Juilliard School (MS 1949), where her teachers included ROBERT SHAW, JULIUS HERFORD, and VINCENT PERSICHETTI. She worked as an arranger for the Robert Shaw Chorale (1949–67) and taught at Westminster Choir College; she founded and directs Melodious Accord, Inc. Her more than 400 compositions include operas, cantatas, choral pieces, and song cycles on Amerindian texts and poems by Emily Dickinson, Edna St. Vincent Millay, and Archibald MacLeish, among others. Her association with Shaw produced numerous choral settings of American folksongs, hymns, and spirituals. Her many honors include a MacDowell Colony Fellowship; the Smith College Medal; ASCAP awards; honorary

doctorates; grants from the NEA, NYSCA, and AMC; and commissions from Chanticleer, the Vancouver Chamber Singers, and the Atlanta SO. She is the author of *Musical Reference Crammer* (New York, 1964), *Creative Hymn Singing* (Chapel Hill, NC, 1976), *Folk Song Transformations* (New York, 1985), *Melodious Accord* (Chicago, 1991), and *The Anatomy of Melody* (Chicago, 2006). Often writing for small groups of voices and instruments, Parker's focus on choral chamber music stems from her belief that music is first and foremost composed of sound, with the human voice as its most natural and essential realization.

WORKS
(selective list)

Ops: The Martyrs' Mirror (2), Lansdale, PA, 1971; The Family Reunion (1), Norman, OK, 1975; Singers Glen (prol, 2), Lancaster, PA, 1978; The Ponder Heart (2), Jackson MS, 1982

Choral-orch: Journeys: Pilgrims and Strangers, 1975; Gaudete: 6 Latin Christmas Hymns, 1976; Commentaries (E. Dickinson; trad. folksongs), SSA, SSAA, orch, 1978; Songs from the Dragon Quilt (S. Nickerson), nar, SATB, orch, 1984; Earth, Sky, Spirit, children's vv, orch, 1986; The World's One Song, 1990; That Sturdy Vine (J. Janzen, trad. hymns), SATB, children's vv, S, orch, 1991; Singing in the Dark, male vv, orch, 1995

Cants.: A Sermon from the Mountain (M.L. King), nar, SATB, str, ad lib jazz inst, 1969; The Feast of Ingathering, SATB, org, 1972; Melodious Accord, SSATB, brass qt, hp, 1974; In Praise of Singing, SATB, str qnt, 1981; Sacred Syms., SATB, fl, vn, vc, org, 1983; Elinor Wylie: Incantations, SSA, cl, pf, 1984; Kentucky Psalms, SATB, str qnt, 1984; The Babe of Bethlehem, SSAA, handbells/pf, 1986; Angels and Challengers (M. Sarton), SATB, ob, 2 cl, bn, pf, 1990; Listen, Lord (J.W. Johnson, spirituals), SATB, A, db, perc, pf, 1991; Clearings (W. Berry), SATB, S, B, chbr ens, 1992; Harmonious Herbst (trad. Moravian), SATB, S fl, ob, bn, str insts, 1992

Other choral: Psalms of Praise, TB, perc, 1964; Street Corner Spirituals, SATB, tpt, drum, gui, 1964; 5 American Folk Songs, SATB, 1968; Away, Melancholy, SSA/SSAA, tambourine, 1971; Carols to Play and Sing, SATB, perc, org, 1971; 6 Hymns to Dr Watts, (SATB)/(Bar, ww qt), 1975; There and Back Again, SATB, ww qt, 1977; Play-Party, Songs, SATB, pf, 1982; 3 Folksongs, SAB, pf, 1983; SongStream, SATB, pf 4 hands, 1983; Millay Madrigals, SATB, 1985; Stars and Stones, SATB, ob, vn, pf, 1987; Dem Bells, chorus, handbells, 1988; Women on the Plains, SSA, pf, 1988; American Dances, SA, pf, 1989; Anniversary hymns, SATB, 1989; Roll Round with the Year, TTBB, gui/pf, 1989; Sacred Madrigals, SSATB, 1989; Three Seas, SSAA, fl, bn, hp, 1989; Water Songs, unison/SA, pf, 1989; Wren Songs (Brian Wren), SATB, 1991; Great Trees (Berry), SATB, kbd, 1991; Hollering Sun (N. Wood, Amerindian), SATB, 1992; Zimre Chayim (trad. Hebrew), SATB, Mez, 1994; Sweet Manna, SATB, 1998; Sing Now of Peace (Bible, W. Shakespeare, Amerindian), SATB, vibraphones, perc, 1999

Song cycles: Astrometaphysical: 4 Songs to Robert Frost, S, pf, 1968; A Gnasherie (O. Nash), Mez, pf, 1971; Songs for Eve (A. MacLeish), 4vv, str qt, 1975; Echoes from the Hills (E. Dickinson), S, fl, cl, hn, str, 1979; Of Irlaunde, Bar, fl, pf, 1979; 3 Mountain Hymns, S, pf, 1982; Songs of the Turtle (Amerindian), S, str qt, 1994

Chbr and solo inst: Four Hymn Preludes, org, 1970; Partita in A, hpd, 1978; Double Concerto, ob, va, str orch, 1980; Cello Sonata, vc, pf, 1982; Dances, str qt, 1988; A Windmere Suite, pf, 1992

Principal publishers: ECS, Hinshaw, GIA, Lawson-Gould, G. Schirmer
Principal recording companies: Musical Heritage Society, GIA

BIBLIOGRAPHY

A. Meier: "Alice Parker: Working toward a Musical Society," *Music Educators Journal*, lxxiii/5 (1986–7), 36–41

J.S. King: *Three Choral Compositions by Alice Parker: a Conductor's Analysis of Songstream, Angels and Challengers, and Songs from the Dragon Quilt* (diss., Louisiana State U., 2005)

SHARON PRADO HOWARD (text, bib),
CHRISTINE AMMER (works)/ELIZABETH PERTEN

Parker, Charlie [Charles Christopher Jr; Bird; Yardbird; Charlie Chan] (*b* Kansas City, KS, 29 Aug 1920; *d* New York, NY, 12 March 1955). Jazz alto saxophonist. Parker was one of the most innovative and influential instrumentalists of jazz. He and John Birks "Dizzy" Gillespie were most influential in developing the modern jazz style called bebop (or Bop).

1. Life. 2. Music.

1. Life. Parker's parents were Charles and Addie Parker. His mother stated that her son had no middle name, but at least one document has been found on which he signed his name Charles Christopher Parker Jr., and perhaps that was how Parker thought of himself. He and his mother moved to Kansas City, Missouri, most likely during the summer of 1927, and that is where Parker grew up. Around 1933, Parker asked for and received from his mother an alto saxophone, but he soon lost interest in the horn and loaned it out. A few years later, Parker got the instrument back and tried to teach himself to improvise.

Two often-cited Kansas City jam sessions found a naive Parker unable to keep up with professionals and being asked to leave the bandstand. Around 1935, Parker, who only knew the song "Honeysuckle Rose" (in the key of F) all the way through, tried to sit in with some musicians. When they played "Body and Soul" (in the key of D♭), Parker found that his "Honeysuckle Rose" didn't fit and he was "laughed right off the bandstand." He joined the semi-professional Deans of Swing, although bassist and friend Gene Ramey judged him "the saddest thing in the band." By September 1935, Parker and the Deans of Swing had been mentioned in the *Kansas City Call* newspaper. Perhaps in connection with joining the group, later in 1935 Parker began the process of joining Kansas City's Local 627 of the American Federation of Musicians, finally joining the union in 1936. Ramey and Parker attended a circa-1936 jam session with pianist Count Basie and drummer Jo Jones, as Ramey recalled: "I remember one night in particular when we were to jam with Basie…Jo Jones waited until Bird started to play and, suddenly, in order to show how he felt about Bird, he threw a cymbal across the dance floor. It fell with a deafening sound, and Bird, in humiliation, packed up his instrument and left." Parker realized there was more to jazz than he had thought and redoubled his practicing efforts. In a 1953 interview, he recalled "I used to put in at least eleven, eleven to fifteen hours a day.…I did that for over a period of three or four years." Also around this time, aged 16, Parker began using heroin and formed an addiction that would plague him for the rest of his life. In 1936, he married Rebecca Ruffin, and in 1938 his first child, Leon, was born.

By 1936, tenor saxophonist Lester Young had become a major influence upon Parker's melodic concept and sense of swing. Around 1937, Kansas City alto saxophonist Henry "Buster" Smith took Parker under his wing and became an influence upon

Parker's timbre and his melodic line. Parker's first major breakthrough came in that summer while he was playing an extended engagement in the Ozark mountains. He memorized and studied recordings of Lester Young with Count Basie that he had taken with him, and learned much from Young's solos. Upon his return to Kansas City, a much-improved Parker began an association with pianist Jay McShann. This association was interrupted by Parker's 1939 trip to New York City, where he reportedly heard pianist Art Tatum for the first time in person. Parker later told of a second artistic breakthrough of December 1939 in which while improvising on the chord progression to Ray Noble's "Cherokee," Parker could finally play the advanced ideas that he had been hearing in his mind. Soon after, Parker left New York and returned to Kansas City, and was soon recorded non-commercially on at least three occasions. These 1940 recordings document that by the age of 20, Parker was the technical, melodic, rhythmic and harmonic equal of most or all well-known national-class altoists. After joining Jay McShann's big band, Parker began touring the United States and made his first commercial recordings that were available to the public.

While with McShann, Parker met another major influence, trumpeter Dizzy Gillespie. Gillespie was conversant with music theory, an area that Parker never studied. Gillespie was also a virtuoso improviser, and at the time was one of the few of their generation who could keep step with Parker in performance. The McShann band soon got a recording contract with Decca, and Parker recorded his first solos that were available to the public. The band soon went on the road, and arrived in New York in early 1942. At the time, Parker participated in New York jam sessions, many at Monroe's Uptown House in Harlem where he was informally recorded playing a lengthy "Cherokee." Finally issued in the 1970s, this recording documented his continued development as an improviser much better than the Decca recordings had done. In 1942–3, Parker and Gillespie went on to play in the big bands of Earl Hines (in which Parker played tenor sax) and then Billy Eckstine. The latter is often called the first bebop big band. In 1943, while with Hines, Parker married Geraldine Scott, although the marriage may not have been legal. They had no children together.

Parker and Gillespie's professional partnership produced many important studio recordings in 1945, most led by Gillespie, who sought career opportunities more concertedly than did Parker. In November 1945, Parker made his first recordings as a leader, with an 18-year old Miles Davis featured on many of the selections. In late 1945 Gillespie brought to Los Angeles a modern jazz group that included Parker, and in early 1946, Parker and Gillespie first performed under the aegis of concert promoter Norman Granz. Soon after, when Gillespie returned to New York, the Parker-Gillespie partnership effectively ended as a regular collaboration. Parker's life spun out of control in Los

Angeles; he was not able to obtain heroin regularly, and was close to being homeless. In late July, suffering from drug withdrawal, Parker was nearly unable to play at a recording session. This episode is usually called Parker's "breakdown," although Parker was no stranger to drug-caused crises. That evening, Parker was arrested at his hotel reportedly after an accidental fire in his room and perhaps appearing undressed in the hotel lobby. As an alternative to Parker being sent to prison, it was arranged for him to be committed as a mental patient to California's Camarillo State Hospital, in effect an intervention that temporarily stopped his decline in health. Upon his release in 1947, Parker returned to New York and formed his "classic quintet" with Miles Davis (trumpet), Duke Jordan (piano), Tommy Potter (bass) and Max Roach (drums). This basic group (with occasional personnel changes) would make a long series of recordings that are now considered classic. Initially, Parker's health was better, but heroin and alcohol use increasingly took their toll. Parker married Doris Sydnor in 1948, but again the marriage may not have been legal, and they also had no children together.

In 1949, Parker took his first trip to Europe for the *Festival International de Jazz* in Paris, where he met classical saxophone virtuoso and teacher Marcel Mule (who heard Parker in concert and later said that he did not care for Parker's music). Parker was reportedly touched by the reception of jazz fans and critics who viewed him as an artist (not just an entertainer) and a genius. A live recording of "Salt Peanuts" from one of his sets at the festival documents Parker quoting the opening bassoon part of Igor Stravinsky's *Le Sacre du Printemps*, which had infamously premiered in Paris in 1913.

After his return, Parker made his first recordings with a group that included violins, viola, cello, harp, and oboe/English horn in addition to the usual piano, bass, and drums. These and subsequent recordings with orchestral instruments reflected Parker's interest in Western classical music, although not the classical music repertoire that Parker had in mind. In 1950, Parker and Chan Richardson (born Beverly Dolores Berg) began a common-law marriage. Together they gave birth to a daughter, Pree, and a son, Baird. Late in 1950, Parker undertook a trip to Sweden and Denmark as a "single" (picking up accompanists while on tour), with a quick stop-over in Paris.

Gillespie and Parker reunited in the recording studio in 1950, and their live recordings of 1951 and 1953 find Parker very much inspired. Increasingly in the 1950s, for financial and legal reasons (Parker's New York City "cabaret card" was revoked after he was convicted for drug possession), Parker toured as a single, going to various cities and working with local musicians. Occasional tours organized by Norman Granz provided some of the few bright spots in Parker's later employment history. His daughter, Pree, who had a heart defect and perhaps cystic fibrosis, died in 1954. Parker's life became more chaotic under the stress of his heroin and alcohol use, and he was at times estranged from his wife and children. He attempted suicide in 1954, and was admitted to Manhattan's Bellevue hospital for recovery. His last engagement was March 4–5, 1955, at the night club Birdland (named for Parker) in New York City. Parker died a week later from multiple health problems brought on by drug and alcohol abuse.

2. MUSIC. Parker was one of the most brilliant and influential instrumentalists of jazz. As an improviser, he was highly creative melodically, rhythmically, and harmonically. Unusual among jazz musicians, he was equally creative in playing blues, up-tempo, and ballad material. Before Parker, the dominant models for alto saxophone tone quality were the lush and vibrato-laden sounds of Johnny Hodges and Benny Carter. Parker's bluesy and edgy timbre, with only selective use of vibrato, created a leaner sound that was effective for rapid melodic lines. He created a large musical vocabulary that was adopted by many musicians who followed.

Before 1945, only a handful of recordings featuring brief Parker solos had been issued to the public, so his early process of artistic development was little-known. Starting a few decades after his death, many non-commercial, pre-1945 recordings were discovered and gradually released to the public. Quite possibly the earliest of these is a disc labeled "Honey & Body," a solo alto saxophone performance in medley form, using the chord progressions of "Honeysuckle Rose" and then "Body and Soul." These of course were the same two songs involved in his disastrous circa-1935 jam session experience mentioned above. On "Body," Parker outlines the chord changes with an authority that was surpassed by few swing era wind players (Coleman Hawkins being an exception). On "Honey," Parker exhibits the influence of Art Tatum in his presentation of melodic motives at different pitch/harmonic levels (ex.1).

Ex.1

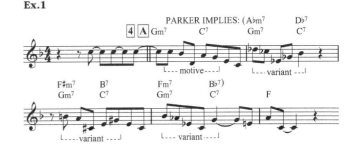

Throughout, Parker shows that his sense of time is already strong as he swings convincingly without any accompaniment. Tatum's practice of inserting brief melodic quotations from various sources may have influenced Parker to do the same. Especially in live performances, Parker was known to quote from a wide variety of sources ranging from other jazz artists' solos (such as Louis Armstrong's "West End Blues") to current popular songs to Western classical music compositions.

Ex.2

As discussed above, Parker had experienced an artistic breakthrough in 1939 while improvising upon the chord progression of the popular song "Cherokee," a song whose "B" section was considered particularly difficult to improvise upon. In two sessions from approximately 1942 and 1943, Parker was non-commercially recorded playing the song, and he shows his mastery of the piece by fluently playing—using in part prepared phrases—on the "B" sections.

In 1943, Parker (playing tenor sax) and Gillespie were members of the Earl Hines big band. Amateur recordings of the two jamming together illustrate Parker's mastery of creating complex melodic lines, even on the larger horn. Ben Webster heard Parker play the tenor and told him, "That horn ain't supposed to sound that fast." Parker was later commercially recorded playing tenor sax with Miles Davis in 1947 (for Savoy) and 1953 (Prestige).

In 1945, Parker, back on alto sax, began to be commercially recorded more frequently, sometimes under the leadership of Dizzy Gillespie. These recordings' improvisations by Gillespie, Parker, and pianist Al Haig—along with Gillespie's compositions—announced that a new, complex, modern jazz style had been developed. Live amateur 1945–6 recordings of the Gillespie group with Parker have since surfaced and feature longer solos and show how strongly the two were musically inspired by one another.

In November 1945, Parker recorded his first session as a leader, a session that produced three classic performances (Savoy label). In "Billie's Bounce" and "Now's the time," Parker's solos showed how the blues tradition was ever-relevant and malleable. Also recorded that day was "Ko Ko," a virtuoso, up-tempo improvisation on the "Cherokee" chord progression that had fascinated Parker since his late-1939 breakthrough. Even the fluent Parker tended to use prepared phrases on the difficult keys that begin the B section. When he was still with Jay McShann, Parker had advised his fellow musicians to play a simple figure based on the opening of the song "Tea for Two" while soloing on Cherokee's "B" section. In an amateur recording from around 1943, Parker uses that principle and plays four-note arpeggiated figures that pass through the melody notes of "Tea for Two" (circled in ex.2). Note the regular accents on beats one and three of each measure. During his 1947 recording of "Ko Ko," he returns to the idea, but begins the figure on beat two and rearranges the pattern to produce a more varied and more syncopated passage (ex.2).

One of the first live Parker recordings to be issued to the public was the January 1946 Los Angeles Jazz at the Philharmonic all-star concert performance of "Oh, Lady Be Good." The opening measures of Parker's solo illustrate how he could take a popular song and imbue it with a blues sensibility. In the next chorus Parker takes a more abstract tack by unleashing a double-time ii^7–V^7–I passage that includes the chromatic passing tones and altered dominant harmony that are associated with modern jazz.

By the 1945–7 period, most of Parker's melodic vocabulary was in place. He had at the ready an unusually large repertoire of melodic building blocks (some derived from earlier players, many his own) that would help him navigate chord progressions. Thomas Owens (1974) transcribed and labeled about 100 of Parker's short figures and organized them according to the context (key and chord progression) in which they were used by him. At his most inventive, Parker used these building blocks selectively and with great creativity while spinning forth melody.

Although Parker is justly famous for his rapid improvisations, his series of slower-tempo studio recordings from 1947–8 reveals just as much about his rhythmic, melodic, and harmonic art. These recordings were based on six American popular songs and a slow blues. Parker's second solo of take five (the master take) of the blues "Parker's Mood" begins with two short, earthy phrases (mm. 1–2) before proceeding in a more abstract direction. A few of the many other notable aspects include Parker's playful rhythms in measure five and the beginning of six, an implied chromatic passing chord to join measures eight and nine, and his alterations on selected dominant chords. Throughout, Parker's "time" on the 16th-note level is stunning (ex.3).

When improvising, Parker often forged ahead with new ideas rather than developing the ideas that he had just stated. Unusually, on his 1947 recording of "Embraceable You" (take A), he develops the beginning of his solo using a six-note motive. Because he was recording more frequently beginning in 1947, Parker had reasons to compose more often than he had in the past. His compositions of the period tended to be "contrafacts," new melodies that were superimposed over existing chord progressions. If Parker was using an AABA pop song form, he would often only set eight

Ex.3

measures to be played on the A sections; the B section would generally be improvised. In the case of a blues form, he would set 12 measures. Unlike Dizzy Gillespie, Parker did not compose melodic introductions, interludes, and codas, although his rhythm section was sometimes charged with improvising introductions. Parker went to greater compositional lengths in two contrapuntal pieces, "Ah-Leu-Cha" and "Chasing the Bird" in which the saxophone and trumpet play independent lines.

In his live appearances, Parker tended to perform the same group of compositions (and thereby chord progressions) over and over. For that reason, and because of his continuing addictions and other factors, Parker relied more on his stock building blocks and some longer set phrases for improvisation than he had just a few years earlier. Ironically, in 1949 he had criticized Dizzy Gillespie for "repeating patterns" in his solos, something that Parker was increasingly doing. In that same year, Parker told pianist Lennie Tristano that "he had said as much as he could in this particular idiom.... He was tired of playing the same ideas." Around the same time, Parker told the trumpeter Red Rodney, "Jazz has to go on from here, we just can't stop with this." One way that Parker hoped to expand his musical universe was through his occasionally expressed intention to study, compose and perform notated Western classical music. Parker was especially interested in 20th-century composers such as Béla Bartók, Igor Stravinsky, Paul Hindemith, and Jacques Ibert. After Parker's 1949 trip to Paris, he reportedly wanted to study composition with French composer Nadia Boulanger. Later the same year, Parker recorded

with an ensemble that featured many instruments associated with classical music (a string quartet, harp, oboe or English horn) plus a jazz rhythm section. For this session and one in 1953, Parker wanted to record an undefined classical repertoire, but he did not have the musical knowledge or stable lifestyle required to organize such a session, and his record producer, Norman Granz, was unwilling to commission newly composed pieces. Instead, Granz commissioned arrangements of American popular songs to be played by these ensembles.

In his later career, Parker was often stimulated to produce fresher improvisations when presented with chord progressions not from popular songs or blues, such as the introductions, transitions, and codas found in arrangements commissioned by Granz. A good example is Parker's outpouring of melody over the introduction to "Just Friends," from his 1949 studio recording with a string section. Parker's recordings of the 1950s are problematic. Granz actively tried to present Parker in a wide variety of settings, not all of which were stimulating to him, and none of which involved the Western classical music repertoire that Parker at times wanted to try. Granz also had strong ideas about having Parker record standard compositions from American popular song, so Parker had less motivation to compose new pieces. Parker's live recordings of the period are more revealing of the state of his improvisational art. Although he occasionally expressed a desire to further develop his art, Parker's soloistic vocabulary of the time was largely but not entirely stagnant. A few of Parker's live recordings of the 1950s show him sequencing short intervallic patterns as a way of creating chromaticism. The pattern shown in ex.4, from a 1952 live recording of "Rocker," descends by whole steps (the circled notes), and cuts across the piece's tonality as created by the chord progression.

Ex.4

Of course, saxophonist John Coltrane would a few years later be highly associated with playing such sequential chromatic patterns across the prevailing tonality. Conceivably Parker wanted to expand on this technique (he had occasionally used such patterns in live recordings at least as early as 1946), but as was the case for many of his stated desires for new musical horizons, he did not or could not develop it. Despite Parker's unrealized goals, in his last years he could still spin forth creative melody with gifted harmonic awareness and with great rhythmic quality, as heard in many live recordings that have been issued since his death.

3. INFLUENCE. Parker influenced not only saxophonists, but also players on all instruments, along with many composers, arrangers, and certain singers. On a general level, Parker (along with Art Tatum, Coleman Hawkins, Dizzy Gillespie and others) set new standards for instrumental virtuosity and musical complexity, and younger musicians responded by setting their technical sights higher. More specifically, to a greater degree than any musician of Parker's generation, young musicians transcribed his improvised solos and studied his vocabulary. Many of his short phrases were adopted by instrumentalists and used as raw material for navigating chord progressions.

Among the prominent alto saxophonists of the 1940s and 50s highly influenced by Parker were Sonny Stitt, Jackie McLean, Phil Woods, Lou Donaldson, and Cannonball Adderley. When saxophonist Ornette Coleman first emerged in the late 1950s, he was characterized by pianist John Lewis as "an extension of Charlie Parker."

A number of musicians recorded Parker in his live appearances and studied the results for inspiration. The most famous of these was saxophonist Dean Benedetti, most of whose recordings were first issued to the public in 1990.

Trumpeter Shorty Rogers transcribed part of one of Parker's solos on "Dark Shadows" (Dial, 1947; take 3) and arranged it for Woody Herman's saxophone section, as heard on his 1947 recording of "I've got news for you." This concept was later developed in the 1970s and 80s by the band Supersax, which featured Parker solos arranged (most often by Med Flory) for a five-person saxophone section.

Beginning in the late 1950s, Parker's influence waned gradually with the ascendency of modal and non-tonal concepts, plus chromaticism derived from pentatonic- and fourth-derived patterns. The publication of the *Charlie Parker Omnibook* (Parker solo transcriptions) in 1978, the rise of jazz college-based education programs, and a post-1980 trend toward re-examining jazz's past led to a resurgence in interest in Parker's music.

RECORDINGS
(selective list)

ISSUED UNDER PARKER'S NAME
Bird: The Complete Charlie Parker on Verve, Verve 837 142-152 (1988) (10 discs); *The Complete Dean Benedetti Recordings of Charlie Parker*, Mosaic 129 (1990) (7 discs); *Young Bird 1940–44*, Masters of Jazz MJCD 78/79 (1995) (2 discs); *The Complete Live Performances on Savoy*, Savoy Jazz SVY 17021 (1998); *The Complete Savoy and Dial Recordings 1944–1948*, Savoy SVY-17079 (2000) (8 discs); *Complete Jazz at Massey Hall*, Jazz Factory JFCD-22856 (2003); *Bird in Time 1940–1947*, ESP-Disc ESP 4050 (c2008) (4 discs); *Complete Live at the Rockland Palace*, Rare Live Recordings RLR 649641 (2008); *Complete Live at Birdland May 17, 1950*, Rare Live Recordings RLR 88647 (2009) (2 discs); *Bird's Eyes, vol. 7*, Philology W 57 (n.d.) [1950 Parker interview with Marshal Stearns and John Maher]; *Bird's Eyes, vol. 8*, Philology W 80 (n.d.) [1954 interview with John McLellan and Paul Desmond]; *Bird's Eyes, vol. 18*, Philology W 848 (n.d.) [1953 interview with John McLellan]

ISSUED UNDER OTHERS' NAMES OR WITH PARKER AS CO-LEADER
Jay McShann: *Blues from Kansas City*, Decca GRD-614 (1992); with Dizzy Gillespie: *Diz 'n' Bird at Carnegie Hall*, Roost CDP 7243 8

57061 2 7 (1997); with Dizzy Gillespie: *Town Hall, New York City, June 22, 1945*, Uptown UPCD 27.51 (2005)

BIBLIOGRAPHY AND OTHER RESOURCES
TRANSCRIPTIONS AND COMPOSITIONS
[M. Feldman, ed.]: *Charles Parker's Bebop for Alto Sax: 4 Solos* (New York, 1948)

P. Pinkerton, ed.: *Charlie Parker: Nine Solos Transcribed from Historic Recordings* (New York, 1961)

W.D. Stuart: *Famous Transcribed Recorded Jazz Solos: Charlie 'Bird' Parker* (New York, 1961)

Charlie Parker: Sketch Orks, Designed for Small Groups (New York, 1967)

T. Owens: *Charlie Parker: Techniques of Improvisation*, ii (diss., UCLA, 1974) [190 pieces]

S. Watanabe, ed.: *Jazz Improvisation: Transcriptions of Charlie Parker's Great Alto Solos* (Tokyo, c1975) [25 pieces]

J. Aebersbold and K. Slone: *Charlie Parker Omnibook* (New York, 1978) [59 pieces]

A. White, ed.: *The Charlie Parker Collection: 308 Transcribed Alto Saxophone and Tenor Saxophone Solos* (Washington DC, 1978–9)

DOCUMENTS AND SOURCES
L. Feather: "Yardbird Flies Home," *Metronome*, lxiii/8 (1947), 14, 43–4; repr. in Woideck 1998

L. Feather: "A Bird's-ear View of Music," *Metronome*, lxiv/8 (1948), 14, 21–2; repr. in Woideck 1998

M. Levin and J.S. Wilson: "'No Bop Roots in Jazz': Parker," *Down Beat*, xvi/17 (1949), 1, 12–13; rev. as "The Chili Parlor Interview," *Down Beat*, xxxii/6 (1965), 13–15; repr. in Woideck 1998

C. Parker and F. Paudras: *To Bird with Love* (Antigny, 1981) [photographs and documents]

Pop, Including Bird—The Chan Parker Collection, Christie's, 8 Sept 1994 (London, 1994) [auction catalog]

E. Bubley and H. O'Neal: *Charlie Parker* (Levallois, 1995) [photographs and essay]

K. Vale: *Bird's Diary: The Life of Charlie Parker 1945–1955* (London, 1996) [chronology and reprints of collected source material]

C. Woideck, ed.: *The Charlie Parker Companion: Six Decades of Commentary* (New York, 1998)

N. Saks and K. Vail: *Charlie Parker & Jazz Club Memorabilia* (New York, 2007)

Oral history material in *AUSm*

DISCOGRAPHIES
R. Bregman, L. Bukowski, and N. Saks: *The Charlie Parker Discography* (Redwood, NY, 1993)

E.M. Komara: *The Dial Recordings of Charlie Parker: a Discography* (Westport, CT, 1998)

P. Losin: *Charlie Parker Sessions: 1940–1955* <http://www.plosin.com/milesAhead/BirdSessions.aspx>

BIOGRAPHIES AND BOOKS WITH BIOGRAPHICAL MATERIAL
L. Feather: "Chapter II," *Inside Be-bop* (New York, 1949/R1977 as *Inside Jazz*/R2010 as *Inside Be-bop*), 11–18

R. Reisner: *Bird: the Legend of Charlie Parker* (New York, 1961)

I. Gitler: "Charlie Parker and the Alto and Baritone Saxophonists," *Jazz Masters of the Forties* (New York, 1966), 15–57

R. Russell: *Bird Lives: the High Life and Hard Times of Charlie "Yardbird" Parker* (New York, 1973)

I. Gitler: *Swing to Bop: an Oral History of the Transition in Jazz in the 1940s* (New York, 1985)

G. Giddins: *Celebrating Bird: the Triumph of Charlie Parker* (New York, 1987)

M. Miller: *Cool Blues: Charlie Parker in Canada 1953* (London, Ontario, 1989)

C. Parker: *My Life in E-Flat* (Columbia, SC, 1999)

F. Driggs and C. Haddix: *Kansas City Jazz: From Ragtime to Bebop: a History* (New York, 2005)

B. Priestley: *Chasin' the Bird: the Life and Legacy of Charlie Parker* (New York, 2005) [incl. discography]

ANALYTICAL AND DESCRIPTIVE MATERIAL
D. Heckman: "Bird in Flight: Parker the Improviser," *Down Beat*, xxxii/6 (1965), 22–4

J. Patrick: "Charlie Parker and Harmonic Sources of Bebop Composition: Thoughts on the Repertory of New Jazz in the 1940s," *Journal of Jazz Studies*, ii/2 (1975), 3–23

L. Bash: "The Historical and Pedagogical Implications of Motivic Formulas as Supplied by the Charlie Parker Recordings of 'Cherokee'," *Jazz Research Papers*, i (1981), 1–9

P. Schaap: "The Sessions," *Bird: The Complete Charlie Parker on Verve*, Verve 837 142–152 (1988) [liner notes]

S. Sandvik: "Polyharmony, Polyrhythm and Motivic Development in Charlie Parker's *Klact-Oveeseds-Tene* (Take 1) Solo," *Jazzforschung*, xxiv (1992), 83–97

K. Engelhardt: "Young Charlie Parker and Side-Slipping: the Efferge Ware Connection," *Jazz Research Papers*, xvi (1996), 177–88

C. Woideck: *Charlie Parker: His Music and Life* (Ann Arbor, MI, 1996/1998)

H. Martin: *Charlie Parker and Thematic Improvisation* (Lanham, MD, 1996)

S. Larson: "The Art of Charlie Parker's Rhetoric," *Annual Review of Jazz Studies*, viii (1997), 141–66

K. Jones-Quartey: "'Parker's Mood' Revisited," *Annual Review of Jazz Studies*, x (1999), 221–35

L.O. Koch: *Yardbird Suite: a Compendium of the Music and Life of Charlie Parker* (Boston, MA, 1999)

T. Owens: "Bird's Children and Grandchildren: The Spread of Charlie Parker's Musical Language," *Jazzforschung/Jazz Research*, xxxi (1999), 75–88

B. Kirchner: "The Dial, Guild, Bel-Tone and Comet Recordings," *The Complete Savoy and Dial Recordings 1944–1948*, Savoy SVY-17079 (2000) [liner notes]

J. Patrick: "The Savoy Recordings," *The Complete Savoy and Dial Recordings 1944–1948*, Savoy SVY-17079 (2000) [liner notes]

P. Baudoin: "Le vol de l'oiseau" (or "La valse des vilains copieurs"), *Les cahiers du jazz*, no.3 (2006)

VIDEO

Bird, dir. C. Eastwood, Warner Brothers (1988)

Celebrating Bird: the Triumph of Charlie Parker, dir. G. Giddins and K. Simmons, Pioneer Entertainment (1991)

Norman Granz Presents Improvisation, dir. N. Granz, Eagle Rock Entertainment (2007)

CARL WOIDECK

Parker, Horatio (William) (*b* Auburndale, MA, 15 Sept 1863; *d* Cedarhurst, NY, 18 Dec 1919). Composer and church musician. At 14 he took piano and organ lessons with his mother; he later studied composition with GEORGE WHITEFIELD CHADWICK, piano with John Orth, and theory with STEPHEN ALBERT EMERY in Boston. He was church organist in Dedham, Massachusetts, 1880–82. His first compositions were 50 songs on poems by Kate Greenaway, written shortly after his first year of musical study; within the next few years he composed keyboard, chamber, and some short orchestral pieces. From 1882 to 1885 he studied at the Königliche Musikschule in Munich, including composition under Josef Rheinberger. During this time he wrote his first extensive compositions, including the *Ballad of a Knight and his Daughter*, the cantata *King Trojan*, and the Symphony in C.

On returning to America, Parker spent several years in New York, where he taught at the cathedral schools of St. Paul and St. Mary (1886–90), at the General Theological Seminary (1892), and at the National Conservatory of Music (1892–3). He was organist and choirmaster at St. Luke's in Brooklyn (1885–7), St. Andrew's in Harlem (1887–8), and at Holy Trinity in Manhattan (1888–93).

Parker's reputation as a composer was established during the early 1890s with performances of his student works, the publication of a considerable amount of church music, and major works including the overture *Count Robert of Paris*, heard at the first public concert of the New York Manuscript Society in 1890; the cantata *Dream-King and his Love*, which won the National Conservatory prize in 1893; and the oratorio *Hora novissima*, written for the Church Choral Society of New York in 1893. There followed a series of major vocal and choral compositions, including *Cáhal Mór of the Wine-Red Hand*, a rhapsody for baritone and orchestra first performed by the Boston SO (1895); the dramatic oratorio *The Legend of St. Christopher*, a commission from the Oratorio Society of New York (1897); and the motet *Adstant angelorum chori*, which received a prize and performance by the Musical Art Society of New York (1899).

Frequent performances of *Hora novissima* during the 1890s brought Parker to national prominence. In autumn 1893 he left New York to become organist and choirmaster at the fashionable Trinity Church in Boston. The following year he received an honorary MMus from Yale University and accepted the Battell Professorship of the Theory of Music there, a position he retained until his death. In 1904 he was made dean of the School of Music, and under his guidance Yale gained a national reputation for training composers. Parker's reputation as a teacher was later clouded by the negative recollections of his most famous student, CHARLES IVES, whose damaging comments were published years after Parker's death. Recent research has demonstrated that Ives's characterization of Parker as an inflexible conservative was developed only after he came into contact with Henry Cowell and other ultra-modernists in the 1920s; before that time he held his former teacher in high regard.

Parker also became an important musical figure in the New Haven community by organizing and conducting the New Haven SO (1895–1918) and the Choral Society (1903–14). He conducted various choral societies and glee clubs both in the vicinity of New Haven and as far away as Philadelphia. He continued in his post at Trinity Church in Boston until 1902, when he left to take up a similar post at the collegiate church of St. Nicholas in New York; he served this Dutch Reformed church until 1910.

A performance of *Hora novissima* at the Three Choirs Festival in Worcester in 1899 was the first of a series of activities in England which included the commission of *A Wanderer's Psalm* for the Hereford Festival and the performance of *Hora novissima* in Chester (both in 1900) and of Part 3 of *St. Christopher* at Worcester and *A Star Song* at Norwich (both in 1902). He received an honorary MusD from Cambridge University in 1902.

Significant vocal and choral compositions from his later years include *Crépuscule*, a prizewinning concert aria performed by the Philadelphia Orchestra in 1912; the cantata *King Gorm the Grim* (1908) and the morality *The Dream of Mary* (1918), both for the Norfolk (Connecticut) Festival; and the oratorio *Morven and the Grail* (1915), commissioned for the centennial celebration of the founding of the Handel and Haydn Society of Boston.

Parker's second area of composition was theater music. After writing incidental music for two plays, *The*

Eternal Feminine (1904) and *The Prince of India* (1906), he composed music for two grand operas: *Mona*, which won a prize offered by the Metropolitan Opera Company and received four performances in that house (1912); and *Fairyland*, which won a prize offered by the National Federation of Music Clubs and six performances in Los Angeles (1915).

Parker composed numerous songs, anthems, and hymns. Apart from some character-pieces for organ and piano, his instrumental composition was infrequent after the early years; however, the symphonic poem *A Northern Ballad* (1899) and the Concerto for Organ and Orchestra were performed by major American orchestras. Parker performed his Concerto with the Boston SO (1902) and the Chicago SO (1903).

Parker's health, which had been uncertain since his youth, deteriorated rapidly during World War I, and he died of pneumonia contracted while on a recuperative trip to the West Indies in 1919. His last compositions, *The Red Cross Spirit Speaks* (1918) and *AD 1919*, are marked more by emotional fervor than by his creativity.

Parker composed steadily throughout his life, although his church, educational, and conducting duties were extensive. He was capable of intense concentration and frequently used the time while commuting from New Haven to Boston or New York for composing. After 1907, many of his largest works were written during summers at his family's vacation home in Blue Hill, Maine.

His career as a composer can be divided into three periods. The first was strongly eclectic and included the student and New York cantatas as well as the oratorio *Hora novissima*. The latter contains flowing, balanced melodic lines, moderately chromatic harmony, colorful orchestration, and stirring polyphonic effects.

The second period was marked by an increasing concern for dramatic expression in several of the larger choral works, and the fulfillment, with *Mona*, of a desire to write an opera. The contrasting, sectional structures of the first period gave way to an increasingly unified, highly expressive style. The key works are *Cáhal Mór of the Wine-Red Hand*, with its integration of solo voice and orchestra; *The Legend of St. Christopher*, with its well-developed leading motif technique; *A Star Song*, with its long-phrased melodies, tonally evasive harmony and unified structure; and finally *Crépuscule* and *Mona*, with their pervading chromaticism, vacillating tonalities, and sometimes angular, disjunctive melodies.

During this same period Parker wrote a number of cantatas and ceremonial pieces, which had a more conservative cast and sustained his reputation as a traditionalist. They include *Adstant angelorum chori*, with its allusions to Renaissance polyphony; *A Wanderer's Psalm*, with its contrasting sections and unifying *tonus peregrinus*; *Hymnos Andron*, with its application of the rhythm and structure of Greek poetry; and the occasional pieces *Union and Liberty* and *Spirit of Beauty*, with their balanced sections.

The third period, following *Mona*, was stylistically regressive: for example, *An Allegory of War and Peace*, *The Dream of Mary*, *The Red Cross Spirit Speaks*, and *AD 1919* are marked by a return to diatonic harmony, more traditional key relationships, balanced structures and clearly defined melody. Parts of *Morven and the Grail* and *Fairyland* also show these tendencies. These works reflect Parker's concern, during his last few years, to communicate more directly with the American public.

During his lifetime Parker was considered a craftsman without equal and was one of America's most highly respected composers, but since his death, the number of performances of his major works has declined steadily. Even his more imaginative works, in which he attempted to follow such composers as Richard Wagner, Vincent d'Indy, Richard Strauss, Claude Debussy, and Edward Elgar, are received no better than the more conservative pieces, which show the influence of Johannes Brahms, Antonín Dvořák, and Charles Gounod. Parker's inability to achieve a strongly individualistic style and his reliance on chromatic formulas that are now considered too sentimental have undoubtedly contributed to the neglect of his music. *Hora novissima*, *A Northern Ballad*, and a few anthems are still occasionally heard, and several of his songs have a beauty that should rescue them from obscurity.

WORKS
(printed works published in New York unless otherwise stated)

CHORAL

op.

25   Part Songs, 1882; listed in Strunk

—   2 Gesänge für gemischten Chor, 1882; listed in *9. Jahresbericht der Königlichen Musikschule in München* (1882–3), 37

1   Mountain Shepherd's Song (Uhland), TTBB, pf, 1883 (Boston, 1884)

3   Psalm 23, S, women's chorus, org, hp, 1884; Munich, Königliche Musikschule, 23 Dec 1884 (pubd as The Lord is my Shepherd, 1904)

6   Ballade (F.L. Stolberg), f, chorus, orch, 1884; Munich, Königliche Musikschule, 7 July 1884 (pubd as The Ballad of a Knight and his Daughter, 1891)

8   König Trojan (A. Muth), ballad, T, Bar, SATB, orch, 1885; Munich, Königliche Musikschule, 15 July 1885 (pubd as King Trojan, Boston, 1886)

15   Idylle (cant., J.W. von Goethe), T, B, SATB, orch, 1886 (1891)

14   Blow, Blow, thou Winter Wind (W. Shakespeare), TTBB, pf, 1888 (1892)

16   Normannenzug (cant., H. Lingg), TTBB, orch, 1888 (pubd as The Norsemen's Raid, Cincinnati, 1911)

—   Ecclesia, SATB, SSA boys' chorus, org, 1889, *NH*

21   The Kobolds (cant., A. Bates), SATB, orch, 1890; Springfield, MA, Choral Festival, 7 May 1891 (London, 1891)

26   Harold Harfager, partsong, SATB, orch, 1891 (1891)

31   Dream-King and his Love (cant., Geibel, trans. E. Whitney), T, SATB, orch, 1891; New York, 30 March 1893 (1893)

27   2 Choruses for Women: The Fisher (Goethe), The Water Fay (H. Heine), SSAA, pf (1892)

30   Hora novissima (orat, B. de Morlaix), S,A,T,B, SATB, orch, 1893; New York, Church Choral Society, 3 May 1893 (London, 1893)

33   3 Choruses, male vv: My Love (L.E. Mitchell), Three Words (W.B. Dunham), Valentine (C.G. Blanden) (1893)

37   The Holy Child (Christmas cant., I. Parker), S, T, B, SATB, pf/org, 1893 (1893)

39   4 Choruses, male vv: Behold, how good and joyful; Blest are the departed; Lord dismiss us with thy blessing; Softly now the light of day, 1893 (1894)

42   Ode for Commencement Day at Yale University (E.C. Stedman), 1895 (1895)

—   In May, partsong, female chorus, hp, orch, 1897 (1897)

—   Laus artium (cant.), solo v, SATB, orch, 1898, *NH*

43   The Legend of St Christopher (dramatic orat, I. Parker), solo vv, chorus, orch, 1897; New York, Oratorio Society, 15 April 1898 (London and New York, 1898)

45	Adstant angelorum chori (Thomas à Kempis), motet, 8vv, 1899; New York, Musical Art Society, 16 March 1899 (1899)
50	A Wanderer's Psalm (cant., after Ps cvii), solo vv, chorus, orch, 1900; Hereford, Three Choirs Festival, 13 Sept 1900 (London, 1900)
48	3 Part Songs, TTBB: Awake, my Lady Sweetlips (E. Higginson), The Lamp in the West (Higginson), The Night has a Thousand Eyes (F.W. Bourdillon) (Cincinnati, 1901)
53	Hymnos Andron (T.D. Goodell), solo vv, TTBB, orch, 1901; Yale U., 23 Oct 1901 (pubd as Greek Festival Hymn, 1901)
54	A Star Song (H.B. Carpenter), lyric rhapsody, solo vv, chorus, orch, 1901; Norwich (England) Festival, 23 Oct 1902 (Cincinnati, 1902)
54b	Come Away! (J. Dowland), SATB (London, 1901)
—	The Robbers (J. Baillie), SATB, pf; in W.L. Tomlin: *The Laurel Song Book* (Boston, 1901)
—	An Even Song (C. Thaxter), SA, pf (London, 1901)
60	Union and Liberty (O.W. Holmes), chorus, band/orch, 1905; commissioned for and perf. at inauguration of President T. Roosevelt (1905)
61	Spirit of Beauty (ode, A. Detmers), male chorus, band/orch, 1905; Buffalo, NY, ded. of Albright Art Gallery, 31 May 1905 (1905)
63	The Shepherds' Vision (Christmas cant., F. Van der Stucken, trans. A. Jennings), solo vv, chorus, org, (ob, str, hp ad lib), 1900 (1906)
64	King Gorm the Grim (T. Fontane, trans. M.P. Whitney), ballad, chorus, orch, 1907; Norfolk Festival, 4 June 1908 (1908)
	Piscatrix, TTBB (1908)
—	Songs for Parker daughters, trios, female vv, 1911: I Remember the black wharfs and ships (H.W. Longfellow), September Gale (C.H. Crandall), Rollicking Robin (L. Larcom), no.1 (Boston and New York, 1923)
66	School Songs, SATB, pf: no.1 unidentified, Springtime Revelries (N. Waterman), The Storm (Waterman), Freedom Our Queen (O.W. Holmes); nos.2–4 (Boston, 1912, 1919, 1911)
—	The Song of the Swords (from op, Mona), SATB, pf (New York and Boston, 1911)
73	A Song of Times (cant., J.L. Long), S, SATB, bugle corps, band/orch, org, 1911; Philadelphia, Wanamaker Dept Store, 1 Dec 1911 (1911)
—	A Song of a Pilgrim Soul (H. Van Dyke), partsong, vv, pf (1912)
74	7 Greek Pastoral Scenes (Meleager, Argentarius), SA, female chorus, ob, hp, str, 1912 (1913)
75	The Leap of Roushan Beg (Longfellow), ballad, T, TTBB, orch; Philadelphia, Orpheus Club, 1913–14 season (1913)
76	Alice Brand (cant., Scott), solo vv, SSA, pf (1913)
—	Gloriosa patria, patriotic hymn (1915)
79	Morven and the Grail (orat, B. Hooker), solo vv, chorus, orch, 1915; Boston, 13 April 1915 (Boston, 1915)
—	Ave virgo gloriosa (from op, Fairyland), female chorus, pf, 1915 (1915)
82	The Dream of Mary (J.J. Chapman), morality, solo vv, children's chorus, chorus, congregation, org, orch, 1918; Norfolk Festival, 4 June 1918 (1918)
—	Triumphal March (D.K. Stevens), SATB, pf; in G. Parsons: *High School Song Book* (Boston, 1919)
84	AD 1919 (cant., B. Hooker), S, chorus, orch, 1919; Yale U., June 1919 (New Haven, CT, 1919)
—	I Remember (Longfellow), female vv, pf; in *A Book of Choruses for High Schools and Choral Societies* (Boston, 1923)

STAGE

—	The Eternal Feminine (incid music, F. Nathan), chorus, orch, 1903–4; New Haven, CT, 7 Nov 1904; lost
—	The Prince of India (incid music, J.I.C. Clarke, after L.E. Wallace), 1v, chorus, orch, 1905; New York, Broadway Theatre, 24 Sept 1906, *NH*
71	Mona (op, 3, Hooker), 1910; New York, Metropolitan, 12 March 1912 (1911)
77	Fairyland (op, 3, Hooker), 1914; Los Angeles, 1 July 1915 (1915)
80	Cupid and Psyche (masque, 3, J.J. Chapman), 1916; New Haven, 16 June 1916, *NH*
81	An Allegory of War and Peace (F.H. Markoe), chorus, band, 1916; New Haven, CT, 21 Oct 1916, *NH*

SONGS
(1v and pf unless otherwise stated)

—	Kate Greenaway Songs, 50 settings, 1878; see Kearns (1990) for individual listing, *NH*
—	La coquette, 1879, *NH*
—	3 Songs: Goldilocks, Slumber Song, Wedding Song, 1881 (Boston, 1882)
10	3 Love Songs: Love's Chase (T.L. Beddoes), Night Piece to Julia (R. Heink [Herrick]), Orsame's Song (Suckling), 1886 (Boston, 1886)
—	2 Sacred Songs: Rest, There is a Land of Pure Delight, 1890 (Boston, 1890)
22	3 Sacred Songs: Evening, Heaven's Hope, Morning (1891)
23	3 Songs: My Love, O Waving Trees, Violet, 1891 (1891)
24	6 Songs: Cavalry Song (E.C. Stedman), Egyptian Serenade (G.W. Curtis), O ask me not (H. Hopfen), Pack, clouds, away! (T. Heywood), Spring Song (Curtis), The light is fading (E.A. Allen) (1891)
—	Come see the place (1893), also arr. as anthem
34	3 Songs: I know a little rose, My Lady Love, On the Lake (1893)
—	In Glad Weather (C.B. Going) (1893)
—	A Rose Song, unison chorus, pf (London, 1893)
—	2 Songs: Fickle Love (L.C. Moulton), Uncertainty (C. Swain) (Boston, 1893)
—	2 Songs: A Song of Three Little Birds, Love is a Rover (S.M. Peck), 1893 (Cincinnati, 1893)
—	Divine Love (A. Jennings) (Boston, 1894)
—	2 Shakespeare Songs: A poor soul sat sighing, It was a lover and his lass (Boston, 1894)
40	Cáhal Mór of the Wine-Red Hand (J.C. Mangan), rhapsody, Bar, orch, 1893; Boston, 29 March 1895 (1910)
—	Salve regina (1895)
—	Spanish Cavalier's Song (I. Parker) (Boston, 1896)
47	6 Old English Songs: Come, O come, my life's delight (T. Campion), Love is a sickness (S. Daniel), He that loves a rosy cheek (T. Carew), Once I loved a maiden fair (Old English), The Complacent Lover (C. Selby), The Lark (W. Davenant), 1897–9 (Cincinnati, 1899)
—	The Green is on the grass again, 1900, *NH*
51	4 Songs: A Spinning Song (I. Parker), At Twilight (E.A. Baker), June Night (E. Higginson), Love in May (Higginson), 1901 (Cincinnati, 1901)
—	The Toedt Songs, S, vn, pf, 14 songs as Christmas gifts for children of close friends, 1903–16, microfilm of MS, *NH* (for individual listing see Kearns (1990)), no.5 (1939)
59	4 Songs: Good-Bye (C. Rossetti), Serenade (N.H. Dole), Songs (R.L. Stevenson), The Blackbird (W.E. Henley) (1904)
—	2 Songs from Tennyson's Queen Mary: Lute Song, Milkmaid's Song (1904)
58	3 Sacred Songs, org acc.: Come, Holy Ghost (St. Ambrose), Declining Now, the Sun's Bright Wheel (C. Coffin), Lo, Now the Shades of Night (St. Gregory) (London, 1905)
—	Springtime of Love (F.D. Sherman), 1905 (1905)
—	Last Night the Nightingale (T. Marzials); The Garden Pirate (G. Rogers); The Reason Why (G. Cooper); 1906, *NH*
62	Crépuscule (J. de Beaufort, trans. E. Whitney), concert aria, Mez, orch, 1907; Philadelphia, 27 March 1911 (1912)
—	The First Christmas, 4 S, pf, 1907, *NH*
—	The Wandering Knight's Song (Cincinnati, 1908)
—	O, I will walk with you; On the Hillside; The Presence Dwells among the Starlit Places; Lamentation (trans. G. Morris), 1909, *NH*
70	7 Songs (B. Hooker): A Man's Song, A Robin's Egg, A Woman's Song, I shall come back, Offerings, Only a Little While, Together, 1910 (Cincinnati, 1910)
—	A Christmas Song (J.G. Holland), 1911; in *Century Illustrated Monthly Magazine* (Dec 1911)
—	Rollicking Robin (L. Larcom), 1911, *NH*
—	2 Songs: A Perfect Love (A.H. Hyatt), 1913, Her cheek is like a tinted rose (F.E. Coates), 1912 (Boston, 1914)
—	3 Songs: Across the Fields (W. Crane), 1906, Morning Song (M. Schütze), 1908, Nightfall (Schütze), 1908 (Boston, 1914)
78	The Progressive Music Series for Basal Use in Primary, Intermediate and Grammar Grades, 61 songs, 1914–9 (Boston and New York, 1914–9); for individual listings see Kearns (1990)

— It was a Lover and his Lass (W. Shakespeare), 2 S, vn, pf, 1916, *NH*
— Tomorrow (F.E. Coates), 1915; The Pearl (A. Hyatt), 1916; *NH*
83 The Red Cross Spirit Speaks (J. Finley), 1v, orch, 1918 (1918)
— Hymn for the Victorious Dead (H. Hagedorn); in *The Outlook* (18 Dec 1918)

ANTHEMS, SERVICES
(for SATB, org; solo vv as indicated)

— Christ our Passover (1890)
— Bow down thine ear; Deus misereatur, E, 1890; Magnificat, E, with solo v; Nunc dimittis, E; The Lord is my light; There is a land of pure delight, with solo v (all pubd in 1890)
— Give unto the Lord, 1890; I will set his dominion in the sea (1891)
— The Riven Tomb, in *New York Herald* (29 March 1891); Te Deum, A (1891); Who shall Roll us away the Stone?, with S solo (1891)
— 12 Christmas Carols for Children, unison chorus, pf (1891)
— The Morning and Evening Service, E, together with the Office for The Holy Communion, 1890 (London, 1892)
— Let us rise up and build, 1892, *NH*
— Before the Heavens were Spread Abroad, with T solo (London, 1893)
— Come see the place, arr. as anthem, 1v, chorus/qt, org (1893)
34b Magnificat and Nunc dimittis, E, 1893 (London, 1893)
— Te Deum, B (1893)
— Rejoice in the Lord; Look ye Saints, the Sight is Glorious, 1894 (1976)
— Light's Glittering Morn, with B solo, 1894 (1894)
— Far from the World, with S/T solo (1896)
— O Lord, I will exalt thee, 1897 (1897)
— Calm on the Listening Ear of Night, with S/T solo, 1898; in *The Churchman* (10 Dec 1898)
— Grant, we beseech thee, merciful Lord, 1899 (Boston, 1898)
— Behold, ye Despisers, with B solo (London, 1899)
— Now sinks the sun (from The Legend of St. Christopher), a cappella, 1897 (London, 1900)
— In Heavenly Love Abiding, with S solo; While we have Time; 1900 (both pubd London, 1900)
— Thou shalt remember, with Bar solo, 1901 (London, 1901)
— Come, gentles, rise (D. Evans), unison chorus, org, 1903 (1905)
— God, that Makest Earth and Heaven (1903/*R*)
— Brightest and Best, with S solo, 1904 (1904)
57 The Office for the Holy Communion, B, 1904 (New York and London, 1904)
— It came upon the Midnight Clear, solo vv, chorus, org, (vn, hp ad lib), 1904 (Boston, 1904)
— I shall not die but live, with Bar solo, 1905 (Boston, 1905)
— To whom then will ye liken God, with T solo, 1909 (1909)
— The Voice that Breathed o'er Eden, unison chorus, kbd, 1916, *NH*
— He faileth not, with S/T solo, 1919 (1919)
— He who hath led will lead, *NH*

The following hymnals contain the majority of Parker's hymn settings (for individual listings see Kearns, 1990):

H. Parker, ed.: *The Hymnal, Revised and Enlarged...of the Protestant Episcopal Church in the USA* (1903)
H. Parker and H.B. Jepson, eds.: *University Hymns for Use in the Battell Chapel at Yale with Tunes Arranged for Male Voices* (1907)
The Hymnal...of the Protestant Episcopal Church in the USA (1918)
The Hymnal of the Protestant Episcopal Church in the USA (1943)

KEYBOARD
(individual listings in Kearns (1990))

— Geschwindmarsch für zwei Orgelspielern, 1881 (Carol Stream, IL, 1975)
9 5 morceaux caractéristiques, pf (Boston, 1886)
19 4 Sketches, pf (Boston, 1890)
17 4 Compositions, org (1890)
23 6 Lyrics, pf (1891)
20 4 Compositions, org (1891)
28 4 Compositions, org (1891)
32 5 Sketches, org (1893)

36 4 Compositions, org (1893)
— 2 Compositions, pf; in *Famous Composers and their Works*, xiii (Boston, 1895), 1097–106
— 3 Compositions, org; in D. Buck: *Vox organi* (Boston, 1896)
49 3 morceaux caractéristiques, pf (Cincinnati, 1899)
— Praesentir Marsch, pf 4 hands, 1906, *NH*
65 Organ Sonata, E (1908)
67 4 Compositions, org (pubd as op.66, 1910)
68 5 Short Pieces, org (1908)
— Introduction and Fugue, e, org, 1916, *NH*

ORCH AND CHBR

4 Concert Overture, E, orch, 1884; Munich, Königliche Musikschule, 7 July 1884, *NH*
5 Regulus, ov. héroïque, orch, 1884, *NH*
12 Venetian Overture, B, orch, 1884, *NH*
13 Scherzo, g, orch, 1884, *NH*
7 Symphony, C, orch, 1885; Munich, Königliche Musikschule, 11 May 1885, *NH*
11 String Quartet, F, 1885; Detroit, MI, 29 Nov 1887; in J. Graziano, ed.: *Three Centuries of American Music*, viii (1991), 245–313
24b Count Robert of Paris, ov., orch, 1890; New York, 10 Dec 1890, *NH*
35 Suite, pf, vn, vc, New York, 3 March 1893 (1904)
38 String Quintet, d, 1894; Boston, 21 Jan 1895, *NH*
41 Suite, e, pf, vn, 1894; Boston, 15 Jan 1895, *NH*
46 A Northern Ballad, sym. poem, 1899; Boston SO, 29 Dec 1899, *NH*
55 Organ Concerto, 1902; Boston SO, 26 Dec 1902 (London, 1903)
56 Vathek, sym. poem, 1903, *NH*
72 Collegiate Overture, with male chorus, 1911; Norfolk Festival, 7 June 1911, *NH*
77d Fairyland Suite (prelude, int, ballet from op, Fairyland), 1915, *NH*

WRITINGS

"Concerning Contemporary Music," *Proceedings of the American Academy of Arts and Letters*, i (1909–10), 36–43; repr. in *North American Review*, cxci (1910), 517–26
"Some Orchestral Conditions," *Atlantic Monthly*, cxix (1917), 485–90
"Our Taste in Music," *Yale Review*, 2nd ser., vii (1917–8), 777–88; repr. in *Yale Review*, xcix/3 (July 2011), 31-41

BIBLIOGRAPHY

R. Hughes: *Contemporary American Composers* (Boston, 1900, rev. 2/1914/*R* by A. Elson as *American Composers*)
J. van Broekhaven: "*Mona*: a Thematic Analysis," *Musical Observer*, vi/4 (1912), 22–8
G.W. Chadwick: *Horatio Parker* (New Haven, 1921/*R*)
E.E. Hipsher: *American Opera and its Composers* (Philadelphia, 1927, 2/1934/*R*)
D.S. Smith: "A Study of Horatio Parker," *MQ*, xvi (1930), 153–69
O.W. Strunk: "Works of Horatio W. Parker," *MQ*, xvi (1930), 164–9
J.T. Howard: *Our American Music: Three Hundred Years of it* (New York, 1931, enlarged 4/1965 as *Our American Music: a Comprehensive History from 1620 to the Present*)
I.P. Semler and P. Underwood: *Horatio Parker: a Memoir for his Grandchildren* (New York, 1942/*R*)
V.F. Yellin: Review of Charles Ives' *The Celestial Country*, *MQ*, lx (1974), 500–8
W.C. Rorick: "The Horatio Parker Archives in the Yale University Music Library," *FAM*, xxvi (1979), 298–304
W.K. Kearns: "Horatio Parker's *Mona*: its Place in the Composer's Career and in American Opera," *Sonneck Society Newsletter*, vi/3 (1980), 11–2
J.J. Butera: *Form and Style in Two American Organ Sonatas: the Grand Sonata in E-Flat, Op. 22, of Dudley Buck; and the Sonata in E-Flat, Op. 65, of Horatio Parker* (diss., American Conservatory of Music, 1982)
W.K. Kearns: "Horatio Parker and the English Choral Societies," *American Music*, iv/1 (1986), 20–33
W.K. Kearns: *Horatio Parker, 1863–1919: his Life, Music, and Ideas* (Metuchen, NJ, and London, 1990)
W.K. Kearns: "Horatio Parker's Oratorios: a Measure of the Changing Genre at the Turn of the Twentieth Century," *Inter-American Music Review*, xi/2 (1990–1), 65–73

N.E. Tawa: *The Coming of Age of American Art Music: New England's Classical Romanticists* (New York, Westport, CT, and London, 1991)

A.B. Scott: "Medieval and Renaissance Techniques in the Music of Charles Ives: Horatio at the Bridge?" *MQ*, lxxviii (1994), 448–78

S.E. Scroggins: *The Songs of Horatio Parker* (diss., U. of Maryland, 1995)

N.E. Tawa: "Charles Ives and the New England School," *Charles Ives and the Classical Tradition*, ed. G.H. Block and J.P. Burkholder (New Haven, CT, 1996), 51–74

W.K. Kearns: "Horatio Parker, Edward Elgar, and Choral Music at the Turn of the Twentieth Century," *Elgar Society Journal*, x/i (1997), 4–24

H.L. Yang: *A study of the overtures and symphonic poems by American composers of the Second New England School* (diss., Washington U, 1998)

H.E. Smither: *A History of the Oratorio, v.4 The Oratorio in the Nineteenth and Twentieth Centuries* (Chapel Hill, NC, 2000), 493–506

R.A. Clark: *American Choral Music in Late Nineteenth-Century New Haven: the Gounod and New Haven Oratorio Societies* (thesis, U. of North Texas, 2001)

E.D. Bomberger: "Layers of Influence: Echoes of Rheinberger in the Choral Works of Horatio Parker," *Josef Rheinberger: Werk und Wirkung*, ed. S. Hörner and H. Schick (Tutzing, 2004), 225–41

C.J. Song: *Pianism in Selected Partsong Accompaniments and Chamber Music of the Second New England School (Amy Beach, Arthur Foote, George Whitefield Chadwick, and Horatio Parker), 1880–1930* (diss., Ball State U, 2005)

G.S. Magee: *Charles Ives Reconsidered* (Urbana, IL, 2008)

WILLIAM KEARNS/E. DOUGLAS BOMBERGER

Parker, J(ames) C(utler) D(unn) (*b* Boston, MA, 2 June 1828; *d* Brookline, MA, 27 Nov 1916). Composer, organist, and teacher. A graduate of both the Boston Latin School and Harvard College (1848), he decided to abandon law (after reading it 1848–51) in favor of music. From 1851 to 1854 he studied with Moritz Hauptmann, Ignaz Moscheles, Louis Plaidy, E.F. Richter, and Julius Rietz in Leipzig. When he returned to Boston he began teaching the piano, organ, and harmony, serving on the faculty of the New England Conservatory from 1871 to 1897. He founded an amateur vocal ensemble called the Parker Club in 1862 and served as organist for more than a quarter century at the fashionable Trinity Church (1864–91). His major compositions were written for the Handel and Haydn Society, of which he was organist: *Redemption Hymn*, for alto solo and chorus, was written for its fourth triennial Festival of 1877; the cantata *St. John* was written for the 75th anniversary of the society; an Easter oratorio, *The Life of Man*, was sung by the society in 1895. He published a *Manual of Harmony* (Boston, 1855), edited a large anthology called *Sacred Choruses: Selected, Translated, and Arranged from the Works of Celebrated Composers* (Boston, 1861), and translated theoretical works by Plaidy (*Technical Studies for the Piano Forte*, 1855), Nicola Vaccai (*Practical Method of Italian Singing*, 1865), and Richter (*Manual of Harmony*, 1873, with many later editions), as well as the texts of some of Mendelssohn's partsongs (1856) and Niels Gade's *Comala* (1875). He was among the most respected American composers of sacred choral music in the late 19th century.

WORKS
(selective list)
(all published in Boston)

7 Part Songs (1875)
Redemption Hymn, A, 4vv, vs (1877)

The Blind King (after L. Uhland), ballad, Bar, male vv, orch, vs (1883)
St. John, cantata, solo vv, 4 vv, orch, vs (1890)
The Life of Man, oratorio, solo vv, 4vv, orch, vs (1894)

BIBLIOGRAPHY
DAB (F.W. Coburn)

C.C. Perkins and others: *History of the Handel and Haydn Society of Boston, Massachusetts* (Boston and Cambridge, MA, 1883–1934/*R*), i, 511, 515; ii, 50

W.S.B. Mathews, ed.: *A Hundred Years of Music in America* (Chicago, 1889/*R*), 700

L.C. Elson and others: "Passing of J.C.D. Parker," *New England Conservatory Magazine-Review*, vii (1916–17), 45

J.T. Howard: *Our American Music* (New York, 1931, 4/1965), 296

ROBERT STEVENSON/E. DOUGLAS BOMBERGER

Parker, John Rowe (*b* Boston, MA, 24 Oct 1777; *d* Boston, MA, 29 Dec 1844). Music dealer and publisher. After a brief career as a merchant and importer he opened a music store, the Franklin Music Warehouse, at 6 Milk Street, Boston, in 1817. According to an announcement made in 1819 he sold pianofortes and church and chamber organs, all built on the premises; in 1820 he published a 55-page catalog, one of the earliest extant music trade catalogs in the United States. The same year he began publication of a weekly music periodical, *The Euterpeiad: or Musical Intelligencer, Devoted to the Diffusion of Musical Information and Belles Lettres* (1820–23/*R*). Each issue contained some historical narrative and a musical biography or "scientific" report, drawn mostly from English sources; short musical anecdotes alternated with serious commentary on music publications and performances, mainly in the Boston area. A musical supplement, in the form of a sheet of piano or vocal music, was included; the works were often by contemporary European masters, but such Americans as Lowell Mason and Anthony Philip Heinrich were also represented. The bias toward European music, criticized by one subscriber, Benjamin Carr, was typical of the period.

The Euterpeiad ceased publication in March 1823; a year later Parker brought out a compilation of reprints from it under the title *A Musical Biography*. He left the Franklin Warehouse in 1824 to become an import agent. His last contribution to the musical life of Boston was his participation with Mason, George James Webb, and John Sullivan Dwight on the editorial board of the *Boston Musical Gazette*, founded in 1838. Although he was not active as a musician, Parker played an important role in the dissemination of American and European music and musical opinion in the early 19th century. Some of his correspondence, dating from 1802 to 1840, is at the University of Pennsylvania, and a manuscript daybook is in the Reynolds Collection at Brown University.

BIBLIOGRAPHY
H.E. Johnson: "Early New England Periodicals Devoted to Music," *MQ*, xxvi (1940), 153

H.E. Johnson: *Musical Interludes in Boston, 1795–1830* (New York, 1943)

J.C. Haskins: "John Rowe Parker and *The Euterpeiad*," *Notes*, viii (1950–51), 447

C.E. Wunderlich: *A History and Bibliography of Early American Music Periodicals, 1782–1852* (diss., U. of Michigan, 1962)

H.E. Johnson: "The John Rowe Parker Letters," *MQ*, lxii (1976), 72–86

R.J. Wolfe: *Early American Music Engraving and Printing* (Urbana, IL, 1980)

J.A. Cuthbert: "John Rowe Parker and *A Musical Biography*," *American Music*, i/2 (1983), 39–52

ANNE DHU MCLUCAS

Parker, William (*b* Bronx, NY, 10 Jan 1952). Jazz bass player, bandleader, and composer. He grew up listening to such swing artists as Duke Ellington and played trumpet, trombone, and cello. Inspired by Ornette Coleman, John Coltrane, Archie Shepp, Cecil Taylor, and Albert Ayler, he took up bass in his teens and had formal studies, first with Paul West, then with RICHARD DAVIS, Art Davis, and MILT HINTON at Jazzmobile. Later he studied privately with JIMMY GARRISON and Wilbur Ware and developed a unique style featuring a propulsive alternation between rapid-fire upper-register playing and low punctuating open-string strums, along with vamps, walking "freebop" lines, and lyrical arco work. In 1973 Parker launched his professional career in the downtown New York loft-jazz scene, performing with Muntu and the Music Ensemble, and making his recorded debut on Frank Lowe's album *Black Beings* (1973, ESP). Soon he was playing in bands led by Cecil Taylor and Don Cherry at Carnegie Hall and the Five Spot Café, jointly organizing loft concerts and festivals, and leading his own Centering Orchestras. By the early 1980s he had become Taylor's main bass player and he eventually filled the chair from 1980 until 1992. He also co-founded the collective quartet Other Dimensions and began an association with German bass player Peter Kowald, with whom he organized the seminal Sound Unity Festivals in 1984 and 1988. Parker continued leading bands and organizing festivals throughout the 1980s, as well as performing solo and with bands led by Bill Dixon, Peter Brötzmann, and David S. Ware and working with Cecil Taylor's Unit and Orchestra. In the 1990s Parker founded his quartet In Order to Survive and the Little Huey Creative Music Orchestra and performed with some of the leading figures in the European and American jazz avant-garde at the Vision Festival in New York. He also toured and recorded with such groups as the David S. Ware Quartet, Peter Brötzmann's Die Like a Dog, and Other Dimensions in Music. He has subsequently focused on projects including the William Parker Quartet and the Inside Songs of Curtis Mayfield.

SELECTED RECORDINGS

As leader: *Through Acceptance of the Mystery Peace* (1974, Centering); *In Order to Survive* (1993, Black Saint); *Sunrise in the Tone World* (1997, AUM Fidelity); *Lifting the Sanctions* (1998, No More); *O'Neal's Porch* (2001, Centering); *Inside Songs of Curtis Mayfield: Live in Rome* (2007, RAI Trade)

A. SCOTT CURRIE

Parkhurst, Susan McFarland [Parkhurst, Mrs E.A.] (*b* Leicester, MA, 5 June 1836; *d* Brooklyn, NY, 4 May 1918). Composer. She composed popular songs and parlor piano solos during the 1860s. A skillful writer, she gained most recognition for songs on such topical themes as temperance and abolition. "Father's a drunkard and mother is dead" (1866)—which she and her daughter ("Little Effie") performed at concerts and temperance meetings in New York—became a standard of the period. Other successful songs include "New Emancipation Song," "There are voices," "Spirit Voices," and "Weep no more for Lilly" (all 1864).

Horace Waters, the New York publisher associated mainly with Stephen C. Foster, promoted Parkhurst's work, printing a *Select Catalogue of Mrs. E.A. Parkhurst's Compositions* in 1864. She contributed tunes to Waters' collections of Sunday school hymns, *The Athenaeum* (1863), *The Golden Harp* (1863), and *Zion's Refreshing Showers* (1867). In the early 1860s Parkhurst worked at Waters' music store, where she encountered Foster. She published "Personal Recollections of the Last Days of Stephen Foster" in the September 1916 issue of the magazine *The Etude*, describing herself as a "lady who in her youth was known as a successful composer, and who, when a young girl, took a friendly interest in Stephen Foster."

Writing in the standard song-and-chorus format of the period, Parkhurst infused popular song formulae with a more ambitious musical language. Her harmonic vocabulary was more expansive and richer than that found in most average songs of the period, and the piano postludes she often used to round off her songs were more imaginative. Original prints of about 60 songs are held in the Music Division of the New York Public Library; instrumental works are at the American Antiquarian Society, Worcester, Massachusetts.

BIBLIOGRAPHY

E.M. Smith, ed.: *Women in Sacred Song: a Library of Hymns, Religious Poems and Sacred Music by Women* (Boston, 1885)

M.R. Turner: *The Parlour Song Book* (London, 1972)

R. Crawford, ed.: *Civil War Songs* (New York, 1977)

J. Tick: *American Women Composers before 1870* (Ann Arbor, MI, 1983, 2/1995)

K. Pendle, ed.: *Women and Music: a History* (Bloomington, IN, 1991)

J. Finson: *The Voices that are Gone: Themes in 19th-century American Popular Song* (New York, 1994)

JUDITH TICK

Parks, Van Dyke (*b* Hattiesburg, MS, 3 Jan 1943). Composer, lyricist, producer, arranger, actor, and singer. He is best known for collaborating with other artists and for writing the lyrics to the Beach Boys' album *Smile* with Brian Wilson. Although he began his career as a child actor throughout the 1950s, he turned to music in his teens, learning guitar and performing with his brother, Carson. He landed a record contract in 1964 with MGM, then moved to Warner Bros. two years later, mostly working as an arranger and a session musician. In 1966 he recorded on the Byrds album *Fifth Dimension* (Columbia) and began his work on *Smile*. His songs such as "Surf's Up" and "Wind Chimes" impressed Wilson, who championed Parks's work. However, due to strife within the band—caused partly by objections to such songs as "Cabinessence"—*Smile* went unreleased at the time. Parks went on to work on solo projects, and in 1968 he released his first album, *Song Cycle* (Warner Bros.). A critical success but a commercial disappointment, the recording fused a variety of musical styles within a rock context, placing such dissimilar elements as ragtime, jazz, and orchestral music within a psychedelic framework. Parks subsequently worked more on producing, collaborating with top artists including Bonnie Raitt, U2, Rufus Wainwright, Ringo Starr, and Fiona Apple. After a visit to the West Indies in the early 1970s, he released a calypso-based record, *Discover America*, in 1972 and then a follow-up in 1975. Parks has subsequently composed film scores such as those for Robert Altman's fascinating musical *Popeye* (1980), *Follow that Bird* (1985), and *The Two Jakes* (1990). His hugely varied projects have included further albums, songs recorded by other artists, music for television, and more collaborative work. Wilson and Parks have reunited several times, finally releasing *Smile* and performing it on tour in 2004.

BIBLIOGRAPHY

J. Fitzgerald: "Musical Transport: Van Dyke Parks, Americana, and the Applied Orientalism of *Tokyo Rose*," *Perfect Beat*, iv/2 (1999), 145–67

D. Carter: "'What's still Left of my Memory': Recovery and Reorientation in the Songs of Van Dyke Parks," *Popular Music and Society*, xxvii (2004), 387–405

D. Carter: "Beyond the Stars and Stripes: Charting Van Dyke Parks' New World Musical Voyage," *Popular Music*, xxviii (2009), 197–216

R. Henderson: *Van Dyke Parks' Song Cycle* (New York, 2010)

JONAS WESTOVER

Parlan, Horace (Lumont) (*b* Pittsburgh, PA, 19 Jan 1931). Pianist. He began piano study at the age of eight as a therapeutic device to counteract the effects of polio, which he had contracted at age five. He developed his own technique that accommodated the permanent partial paralysis of his right hand. Briefly a law student at the University of Pittsburgh, Parlan established himself on that city's jazz scene in the early 1950s. In 1957 he moved to New York, where he recorded with Charles Mingus (appearing on albums such as *Mingus Ah Um*, 1959, Col.), Lou Donaldson, and Tommy Turrentine before making a series of recordings as a leader between 1960 and 1963 for the Blue Note label. The first of these albums was *Movin' & Groovin'* (1960, BN). He also recorded as a sideman with Stanley Turrentine, Dexter Gordon, Grant Green, Tubby Hayes, Eddie "Lockjaw" Davis, and Slide Hampton during the 1960s. Parlan left the United States for Denmark in the early 1970s; he has cited crime, stress, and the decreasing popularity of jazz as the reasons for his relocation, and since then nearly all of his recordings have been made in Europe. These include albums with Archie Shepp (*Goin' Home*, 1977, Ste. and *Trouble in Mind*, 1980, Ste.), his own trio (*No Blues*, 1975, Ste.), his quintet (*Glad I Found You*, 1984, Ste.), and Christina von Bülow (*My Little Brown Book*, 2007, Stunt). He has also toured extensively, appearing with Sonny Rollins, Dizzy Gillespie, and various European jazz musicians. A documentary film about his life, *Horace Parlan by Horace Parlan*, was released in 2002.

BIBLIOGRAPHY

S. Nicholson: "Horace Parlan: Return Engagement," *JT*, xxxi/1 (2001), 58–62

A. Lubet: *Music, Disability, and Society* (Philadelphia, 2011)

H. Parlan and H. Barfod: *My Little Brown Book: Seventy Years of Jazz Life* (Copenhagen, 2011)

LARS HELGERT

Parliament/Funkadelic. The name by which the loose agglomeration of musicians led by GEORGE CLINTON in the 1970s is commonly known; they formed the constantly changing membership of groups known as Parliament and Funkadelic.

Parlor music. Parlor music generally refers to music composed for domestic use from *c*1820 to World War I, consisting primarily of songs for voice and piano but also including compositions for solo piano as well as transcriptions and arrangements adaptable for a variety of instruments. Both vocal and instrumental music were aimed at an amateur market and intended for performance in the home, primarily but not exclusively by females. Instrumental music for the parlor was most commonly for piano or melodeon but demonstrated flexibility according to circumstances, with interchangeable parts for a variety of popular domestic instruments such as flute, guitar, or violin. The music was published in individual SHEET MUSIC editions, often with elaborate engraved covers. All aspects of the genre—music, texts, and the material cultural of sheet music and instruments—both reflected and affected the technology, social mores, and cultural values of this period.

1. History and significance. 2. Musical characteristics.

1. HISTORY AND SIGNIFICANCE. The emergence of parlor music in the 19th century was a result of three interrelated phenomena: technological developments, the growth of the middle class, and changes in domestic architecture. Technical advances in the manufacture and dissemination of sheet music and musical instruments fostered music-making in American homes. In the 18th century, only a few hundred musical titles were published in the United States; the first quarter of the 19th century saw the publication of 10,000 titles, and the industry continued to expand until World War I. The growth of a middle class with more leisure time led to greater opportunities for music lessons and domestic entertainment. The 19th century saw sharp increases in the number and frequency of native-born music teachers who offered music training in school, home, and church settings. Finally, changes in domestic architecture created a room removed from the daily functions of cooking, eating, and sleeping, which served as a marker of social stature for Americans. Derived from the French word *parler* ("to talk"), the American parlor became an important site to display the family's best furnishing, to engage in the short, ritualized visits known as "calling," and for various entertainments, including panoramas, *tableaux vivants*, and musical performance.

The initial wave of parlor songs that circulated in the United States was written by British composers. Prominent among these were Thomas Haynes Bayly ("Long Long Ago"), Henry Bishop ("Home, Sweet Home" on lyrics by John Howard Payne), THOMAS MOORE (*Irish Melodies*), and HENRY RUSSELL (1812–1900; "Woodman, Spare that Tree" on lyrics by George Pope Morris). The songs were popularized in concerts by touring singers, such as the Hutchinson Family Singers, and then published for the home market in sheet music form. In 1837, Austrian emigré Francis J. Grund described "the parlor amusement in the United States, which consists principally in vocal and instrumental music. The performers, on such occasions, are usually ladies; the gentlemen's accomplishments in the arts being commonly confined to the flute."

The genre reached maturity in the songs of Stephen Foster, the United States's first professional musician, and his contemporaries George Frederick Root, Henry Clay Work, Septimus Winner, and William Shakespeare Hays. Charles K. Harris and Harry von Tilzer, among many others, gained popularity at the turn of the 20th century. In addition to original music composed specifically for the parlor, these composers wrote arrangements and transcriptions of religious and classical pieces. Often young women made personalized albums that gathered together a heterogeneous mixture of music.

Integral to the rise of the parlor music industry was the increasing availability of musical instruments for the amateur market. In 1843 Chickering (which began making pianos in 1823) patented a one-piece metal frame that facilitated mass production. An 1849 article in *Ladies Repository* noted: "Within the memory of a generation, the entire country, as well as our village, has been flooded with pianos." Music publishers were quick to take advantage of the new market. In 1867, the catalog of publisher Oliver Ditson offered 33,000 pieces of music for piano. By the turn of the 20th century a piano could be ordered from Sears Roebuck for less than $100, a melodeon for less than $50.

While parlor music was intended for mass consumption, it was identified with a genteel tradition somewhere between the noisy, lowbrow genre of blackface minstrelsy and the aristocratic pretensions of symphonic and operatic music. It represented the aspirations of economic status (the ability to afford lessons, sheet music, and a piano) along with the perceived superior values that accompanied gentility. Yet because it also represented the virtues of democracy, uniting idealism with broad popular appeal, it stood apart from the European-identified genres of symphonic and operatic music. Magazines such as *Godey's Lady's Book* promoted the uplifting qualities of music through articles, fiction, and poetry. The rise of commercial engraving by popular artists such as Currier and Ives produced a new artistic form whose increasingly elaborate covers underscored the social significance of the music.

The popularity of parlor music began to decline in the last decade of the 19th century, as social, economic, and technological developments eroded the function of the parlor. Americans increasingly lived in homes with a living room and a phonograph for entertainment. Additionally, increasing professional opportunities for women within the music field drew attention away from the amateur nature of home music. The composers and publishers that settled in New York's Tin Pan Alley continued to take advantage of the appeal of sentimental themes, but no longer was popular song identified with genteel aspirations. With the parlor went the musical genre that bore its name.

2. MUSICAL CHARACTERISTICS. The most common characteristic of parlor music is its simplicity, a result of its orientation toward the amateur market. In song, the simplicity of vocal line, often based on stepwise motion and/or a pentatonic scale, made it easier for amateurs to sing. Similarly, the piano accompaniments reveal simple repeated chords designed to keep the singer on pitch and to fill in gaps between the verse and chorus; these could also be readily transferred to guitar or other chordal instrument. Transcriptions and arrangements were similarly simplified. This simplicity was not merely a practical choice for the composer but an ideal of performance practice, as *Harper's* expressed in 1851, in a column on "Mems for Musical Misses": "Study simplicity: it is better to give no expression than false expression." In 1869, the *Atlantic Monthly* advised that "the music of the parlor…ought always to be of a simple but tasteful character."

Parlor music drew from a wide range of historical, topical, and scenic themes. The predominance of topics concerning love, home, and children reflected the genre's identification with women and the 19th-century "cult of domesticity." For piano, short lyric pieces predominated, but there were also longer and more challenging descriptive scenes and depictions of historical events (e.g., the *Battle of Prague*) and dance music—such as quadrilles, polkas, waltzes, and schottisches.

Whatever the theme, its treatment was nearly universally sentimental and nostalgic; the portrayal of bittersweet emotions stimulated by the contemplation of a person or object lost to the narrator was the songwriter's favorite device. Even in songs on current social and political topics, in which sentimentality was fused to the perception of music's inherent ennobling effect, reformers used the sentimental ballad as an effective vehicle to sway listeners on behalf of causes such as temperance and abolition. Similarly, during the Civil War, in addition to direct propaganda, many songs reflected the pervasive sentimentality of the day, e.g. Root's "Just Before the Battle, Mother."

Reinforcing the primacy of emotion was form. The parlor ballad was not a true narrative ballad but rather employed a verse-chorus form, with the chorus conveying the central emotional message. A chorus sometimes featured four-part harmony similar to the minstrel song, particularly by mid-century, when the parlor and minstrel genres became more similar musically.

Some parlor music reflected sacred themes, as songwriters often adapted religious words to parlor tunes or wrote parlor music on sacred texts. In addition to his minstrel and parlor music, Stephen Foster published the collections *Waters' Golden Harp for Sunday Schools* and *The Athenaeum Collection of Hymns and Tunes for Church and Sunday School*. Such religious sentiments, expressed through religious or semi-religious imagery and rhetoric, were compatible with the genre's connection with values. The four-part, note-against-note texture of the chorus linked the ballad stylistically to the hymn, reinforced by textual nuances such as the use of *thou* and *thee*.

In 1909, the Chapple Publishing Company published a collection of *Heart Songs*—400 songs drawn from entries sent in from over 20,000 Americans over a four-year period. Along with selections from "the great masters" (including Giuseppe Verdi, Gaetano Donizetti, Richard Wagner, Wolfgang Amadeus Mozart, and Franz Schubert), songs by the British and Irish composers, Bayly, Russell, and Moore remain popular. "Negro Melodies and Minstrel Songs" and "sacred songs and revival hymns" each appear in a separate section. The majority of the songs in the collection were composed before 1880, and about a quarter are from the Civil War era. There are a few newer songs, which tend to follow the sentimental style of the older ones: for example, Victor Herbert's "Because You're You" (1906). The editors noted that "few 'rag time' songs were sent in; operatic selections were not largely in favor. Love ballads, patriotic, sacred and concert melodies were the most popular."

The editors of *Heart Songs* looked forward to the demand for a subsequent volume, but the "rag time" and other new popular styles were fast supplanting the mood and practice of parlor music. Although the era of parlor music was over, many of the songs lived on in home, school, or religious settings, and the legacy of sentimentality continues to be a hallmark of American vernacular styles.

BIBLIOGRAPHY

F.J. Grund: *The Americans in their Moral, Social, and Political Relations* (Boston, 1837/*R*)

E. Douglas Branch: *The Sentimental Years: 1836–1860. A Social History* (New York, 1934/*R*)

R. Lynes: *The Domesticated Americans* (New York, 1957)

W. Austin: *Susanna, Jeanie, and The Old Time Folks at Home: the Songs of Stephen C. Foster from his Time to Ours* (New York, 1975, 2/1987)

C. Hamm: *Yesterdays: Popular Song in America* (New York and London, 1979, 2/1983)

N.E. Tawa: *Sweet Songs for Gentle Americans: The Parlor Song in America* (Bowling Green, OH, 1980)

L.L. Stevenson: *The Victorian Homefront: American Thought and Culture, 1860–1880* (New York, 1991, repr with new preface, 2001)

J.H. Foy and K.A. Marling, eds.: *The Arts and the American Home: 1890–1930* (Knoxville, TN, 1994)

S. Key: "Sound and Sentimentality: Nostalgia in the songs of Stephen Foster," *American Music*, xiii/2 (1995), 145–66

K. Emerson: *Doo-Dah! Stephen Foster and the Rise of American Popular Culture* (New York, 1997)

J. Tick: "Passed Away Is the Piano Girl: Changes in American Musical Life, 1870–1900," *Women Making Music: the Western Art Tradition, 1150–1950*, ed. J. Bowers and J. Tick (Urbana, IL, 1986), 325–48

R. Crawford: *The American Musical Landscape: the Business of Musicianship from Billings to Gershwin* (Berkeley and Los Angeles, 2000)

N.E. Tawa: *High-Minded and Low-Down: Music in the Lives of Americans, 1800–1861* (Boston, 2000)

SUSAN KEY

Parly, Ticho [Christiansen, Frederick] (*b* Copenhagen, Denmark, 16 July 1928; *d* Seattle, WA, 21 June 1993). Tenor of Danish birth. He studied in Paris, Bloomington, Indiana (where he took part in the premiere of Dello Joio's *The Ruby*, 1955), and New York. In 1958 he made his debut in New Orleans as Pong (*Turandot*) and the following year sang Radames in Aachen, Germany. In San Francisco (1960) he sang the Emperor (*Die Frau ohne Schatten*), the Drum Major, and Rinuccio. In Wuppertal, Germany (1961), his roles included Ferruccio Busoni's Mephistopheles and Peter Grimes. In 1963 he sang Leandro (Hans Werner Henze's *Il re cervo*, the revised version of *König Hirsch*) in Kassel and made his Bayreuth debut as Vogelgesang (*Die Meistersinger*); he returned to the latter as Siegmund (1966) and Siegfried (1968). In 1966 he made his debuts at Covent Garden (Siegfried), the Paris Opéra (Tannhäuser), the Metropolitan (Tristan), and the Colón (Tristan). He sang Herod at La Scala (1967) and returned as the Drum Major. For Scottish Opera he sang Siegfried (1971) and Peter Grimes (1973), before performing Loge in San Diego (1974) and Seattle (1975–7). He appeared frequently in Copenhagen in Wagner roles and also as Florestan, Shuysky, and Otello, the last of which he sang in 1988 as a last-minute replacement. He created a sense of youthful exuberance on stage to second a strong, rather baritonal voice.

ALAN BLYTH

Parmentier, Edward (*b* 1946). Harpsichordist and organist. As the Arthur F. Thurnau Professor of Harpsichord and director of the Early Music Ensemble at the University of Michigan, he has been a recognized specialist in the music of J.S. Bach, the English virginalists, and the French *clavecinistes*. He is known for his compelling and passionate musical interpretations, commitment to the use of mean-tone tunings, performances on unique period instruments, and recordings of rare 17th-century keyboard works. He studied harpsichord with ALBERT FULLER while earning degrees in classical languages and literatures, humanities, and musicology at Harvard and Princeton. He also studied with Dutch organist, harpsichordist, conductor, and pedagogue Gustav Leonhardt at the Amsterdam Conservatory. Parmentier has performed widely throughout the United States, Russia, Europe, and Asia. His solo appearances include recitals on harpsichord and on historic organs. He has also appeared as a continuo player and concerto soloist, and conducts chamber orchestras. A distinguished performer of Baroque music on period instruments, Parmentier has released numerous recordings that have garnered critical and popular acclaim, notably *Bach: Well-Tempered Clavier, Book I* (2004), *Early Italian Harpsichord Music* (2003), *Bach: English Suites* (2000), and the anthology *Splendor of the Harpsichord* (1997). He also has recorded Iberian music performed on an 18-century Portuguese fortepiano, Arcangelo Corelli's ensemble works, Scarlatti sonatas, and the complete Bach partitas.

ELDONNA L. MAY

Parnas, Leslie (*b* St. Louis, MO, 11 Nov 1931). Cellist. He studied under GREGOR PIATIGORSKY at the Curtis Institute (1948–53) and then served as principal cellist of the St. Louis SO (1954–62). Parnas has won several coveted awards and competitions: he came second in the Geneva International Music Competition (1957), won the Prix Pablo Casals at the International Cello Competition in Paris (1957), gained top honors at the Trofeo Primavera

(1959), and was awarded joint second prize in the Tchaikovsky International Competition in 1962 (no first prize was awarded that year). Since then Parnas has appeared nationally as a soloist with the New York Philharmonic, the Boston PO, the Philadelphia Orchestra, the National SO, and the St. Louis SO, with which he performed the premiere of Dmitry Borisovich Kabalevsky's Cello Concerto no.2 op.77 in 1964, and internationally with the Hamburg and Moscow symphonies and the Leningrad PO, among others. Parnas has also given recitals, performing regularly with the CHAMBER MUSIC SOCIETY OF LINCOLN CENTER. He has also toured widely with the Buswell-Parnas-Luvisi Trio and has participated in the Marlboro, Berkshire, Casals, Mostly Mozart, and Spoleto (USA) music festivals. In addition to serving as artistic director of the Kneisel Hall Summer Music School in Blue Hill, Maine, for 12 years (1973–85), Parnas has also twice acted as juror for the Tchaikovsky International Composition (1990, 1995). He has taught at Boston University since 1962. His playing is characterized by a sure technique and an aggressive approach to phrasing. He has played the "Rosette" cello made by Matteo Goffriller in 1698 since acquiring it in 1955.

JAMES WIERZBICKI/ELIZABETH PERTEN

Parra (Sandoval), Violeta (del Carmen) (*b* San Carlos, Ñuble, Chile, 4 Oct 1917; *d* La Reina, Chile, 5 Feb 1967). Chilean folk music performer, composer, and researcher. She began playing music at an early age, learning guitar and performing with her brothers and sisters in rural areas of the southern Central Valley in Chile. In her teens she moved to Santiago where she studied at the Escuela Normal. After leaving school she made her living performing at urban nightclubs and bars, singing popular music of the time, including corridos, rancheras, and boleros.

Encouraged by her older brother, the poet Nicanor Parra, she began to comb the Chilean countryside in 1953 to make field recordings of rural musicians. This investigative work, along with her own rural background, shaped the musical form, humanist poetry, and social critique of her original songs. In 1954 she hosted a music program on Radio Chilena, becoming a well known public figure and also winning the Premio Caupolicán for best folklorist of the year. She realized several extended stays in Europe where she performed actively and exhibited her embroidered tapestries at the Louvre in Paris. She recorded her most recognized songs, "Gracias a la vida," "Volver a los diecisiete," and "Run run se fue pa'l norte," on her last album, *Las Últimas Composiciones de Violeta Parra* (RCA Victor, 1966). Parra is considered a seminal figure of the nueva canción movement, and her tradition-infused original compositions influenced artists such as Víctor Jara, Patricio Manns, Rolando Alarcón, and her children Ángel and Isabel Parra.

BIBLIOGRAPHY

Grove7
I. Parra: El libro mayor de Violeta Parra (Madrid, 1985)
F. Sáez: La vida intranquila: Violeta Parra, biografía esencial (Santiago de Chile, 2007)

EMILY PINKERTON

Parris, Robert (*b* Philadelphia, PA, 21 May 1924; *d* Washington, DC, 5 Dec 1999). Composer and music critic. After graduating from the University of Pennsylvania (BS 1945, MS 1946), he studied composition at the Juilliard School of Music (BS 1948) with PETER MENNIN and WILLIAM BERGSMA, and at Tanglewood (1950–51) with Jacques Ibert and AARON COPLAND. A Fulbright Fellowship (1952–3) enabled him to continue his studies with Arthur Honegger at the Ecole Normale, Paris. From 1961 to 1975 he served as music critic for the *Washington Post* and *Washington Star*. He also wrote articles for *The Juilliard Review* and *The Kenyon Review*. After teaching at Washington State College and the University of Maryland, he served as professor of composition and music theory at George Washington University from 1963 to 1999. He received commissions from the Detroit SO (*The Phoenix*, 1969), the Albany SO (*The Messengers*, 1974), the Contemporary Music Forum (*The Book of Imaginary Beings II*, 1983) and the National SO (*Symphonic Variations*, 1987).

Parris's music balances a keen sense of order with an imaginative exploration of extreme registers, wide-ranging textures, intricate rhythmic/metric schemes and virtuosic performance techniques. Together with a penchant for counterpoint, his music demonstrates a striking economy of means, an emboldened sense of contrast, and a passionate lyricism. His works are often darkly introspective, even macabre, a feature enhanced by intense chromaticism and expressionistic orchestration. The mystical visions evoked in his preferred texts are often transmuted into musical imagery.

WORKS
(selective list)

INSTRUMENTAL

Orch: Harlequin's Carnival, 1949; Sym. no.1, 1952; Pf Conc., 1954; Conc., 5 timp, orch, 1955; Va Conc., 1956; Vn Conc., 1958; Conc., trbn, chbr orch, 1964; Fl Conc., 1964; Timp Conc. (The Phoenix), 1969; The Messengers (Angels), 1974; The Unquiet Heart, vn, orch, 1981; Three Chorale-Preludes, 1983; Chbr Music, 1984; Metamorphic Variations, 1986; Sym. Variations, 1987; 13 Pieces, 1986; Nocturnes, 1992
Chbr: Str Qt no.1, 1951; Str Trio no.2, 1951; Str Qt no.2, 1952; Sinfonia, brass, 1963; Book of Imaginary Beings I, fl, vn, vc, pf, 2 perc, 1967; Conc., vn, vc, pf, perc, 1967, rev. 1977; Book of Imaginary Beings II, cl, vn, va, vc, 2 perc, 1983; Metamorphic Variations, fl, cl, vn, vc, perc, 1986; Sonata, vc, pf, before 1949; Variations, pf, 1952; Fantasy and Fugue, vc, 1955; Cadenza, Caprice and Ricercar, vc, pf, 1961; 3 Duets, elec gui, amp hpd, 1985; 22 other chbr works

VOCAL

Choral: The Hollow Men, T, male chorus, chbr ens, 1949; Hymn for the Nativity (Peter the Venerable), SATB, 8 brass, 3 timp, perc, 1962; Reflections on Immortality, brass, chorus, 1966; 6 other choral works
Solo: The Leaden Echo and the Golden Echo (G.M. Hopkins), Bar, orch, 1960; Cynthia's Revells (B. Jonson), Bar, pf, opt. gui, 1979; 10 other solo vocal works

Principal publishers: ACA, Peters

BIBLIOGRAPHY

Baker8; EwenD

CECELIA H. PORTER

Parsons, Albert Ross (*b* Sandusky, OH, 16 Sept 1847; *d* Mount Kisco, NY, 14 June 1933). Pianist, teacher, composer, and writer. He studied with Frédéric Ritter in

New York (1863–6), with Ignaz Moscheles, Carl Reinecke, Benjamin Papperitz, E.F. Wenzel, and E.F. Richter at the Leipzig Conservatory (1867–9) and with Carl Tausig, Theodor Kullak, and Carl Friedrich Weitzmann in Berlin (1870–72). Having settled permanently in New York, he was organist at Holy Trinity Church (1872–6) and at the Fifth Avenue Presbyterian Church (1876–85), but he attained greater prominence as a piano teacher. He maintained a private teaching studio in the city for more than 50 years and also taught from 1886 at the Metropolitan Conservatory of Music (from 1891 the Metropolitan College of Music, and reorganized in 1900 as the American Institute of Applied Music). Parsons composed mostly songs and piano arrangements (transcriptions and paraphrases). A man of many interests, he wrote a book on Egyptology, studied philosophy and genealogy, and published poetry. He was an early promoter of Wagner in America, and made an English translation of Wagner's *Beethoven* (1872); he also wrote *Parsifal, or The Finding of Christ through Art* (1893). His pedagogical works include *The Science of Pianoforte Practice* (1886) and *The Virtuoso Handling of the Pianoforte* (1917). He translated O. Lessmann's *Franz Liszt*, and revised Kullak's edition of Chopin and Alexis Holländer's edition of Schumann, translating the commentaries into English.

BIBLIOGRAPHY

DAB (J.T. Howard)
Obituary, *New York Times* (15 June 1933)

JOHN GILLESPIE

Parsons, Gram [Connor, Ingram Cecil] (*b* Winter Haven, FL, 5 Nov 1946; *d* Joshua Tree, CA, 19 Sept 1973). Singer-songwriter. His output as a solo artist and as a member of the Byrds and of the Flying Burrito Brothers laid the foundation for COUNTRY ROCK. He grew up in a wealthy but troubled household: his father committed suicide and his mother died of cirrhosis due to heavy drinking. Parsons played in a number of rock and roll cover bands in his teens, but moved on to folk and then country while attending Harvard University for a semester. He then formed the International Submarine Band in 1966 with musicians from the Boston folk scene, although the band had broken up by the time its debut album, *Safe at Home*, was released.

Parsons was friends with Chris Hillman of THE BYRDS and was recruited to the band following the departures of David Crosby and Michael Clarke in 1967. While technically only a sideman in legal terms, he played a crucial role in shaping *Sweetheart of the Rodeo* (1968), a country-influenced album recorded in Nashville. Legal issues led to three of Parsons' vocals being re-recorded by Roger McGuinn, but he contributed several of the record's key tracks, including "You're still on my mind" and "Hickory Wind." He left the band soon thereafter due to concerns over a planned concert in apartheid-era South Africa.

After spending time with the Rolling Stones—Parsons was particularly close with Keith Richards—he formed the Flying Burrito Brothers with Hillman. The band released two albums and was the opening act for the Stones' concert in 1969 at the Altamont Speedway, but Parsons' increasing drug use made for erratic live performances. He left following the release of *Burrito Deluxe* (1970), and his subsequent attempts to record a solo album were stalled by drug use.

A friendship with the singer-songwriter Emmylou Harris got Parsons back into the studio, resulting in his first solo album, *G.P.* (1973). Its follow-up, *Grievous Angel*, was also recorded with Harris and has since become recognized as a landmark album in country-rock. Parsons did not live to see its release: he died of an overdose of morphine and alcohol in September 1973 while on an excursion to Joshua Tree. Famously, his friend Phil Kaufman stole his body from the airport and drove it back to Joshua Tree to be burned.

Drawing on the melancholy of classic honky tonk and the energy of amplified 1960s rock, Parsons' music grew in popularity after his death, proving a key influence on contemporaries like Harris and the Eagles and later artists like Elvis Costello and Uncle Tupelo.

BIBLIOGRAPHY

S. Griffin: *Gram Parsons: a Music Biography* (Pasadena, 1985)
B. Fong-Torres: *Hickory Wind: the Life and Times of Gram Parsons* (New York, 1991)
P. Doggett: *Are You Ready for the Country: Elvis, Dylan, Parsons and the Roots of Country Rock* (New York, 2001)
J. Hundley and P. Parsons: *Grievous Angel: an Intimate Biography of Gram Parsons* (New York, 2005)
O.C. Mather: "'Regressive Country': the Voice of Gram Parsons," *Old Roots, New Routes: the Cultural Politics of Alt.Country Music*, ed. P. Fox and B. Ching (Ann Arbor, MI, 2008), 154–74
D. Meyer: *Twenty Thousand Roads: the Ballad of Gram Parsons and his Cosmic American Music* (Villard, 2008)

RYAN R. McNUTT

Pärt, Arvo (*b* Paide, Estonia, 11 Sept 1935). Estonian composer. Arvo Pärt's works since the late 1970s have gained a popularity that is almost unique in the world of classical music. Pärt studied composition at the Tallinn Conservatory (1957–63) with Heino Eller, and became a recording engineer with Estonian Radio. During his early career he wrote stage and film music and was one of the first composers in the Soviet Union to explore serialism (*Nekrolog*, 1960). In the late 1960s Pärt introduced the use of musical quotations and references to older music in his works, such as "Credo" for chorus, piano, and orchestra (1968). Because "Credo" drew from religious texts, it was banned in the Soviet Union. Pärt later emigrated in 1980, settling in Berlin.

Following "Credo," Pärt engaged in extended periods of contemplative silence during which he studied early polyphony. He composed the Third Symphony (1971) during this interim period, and in 1976 he reemerged with a new style that he called "tintinnabulation," based on a slow modulation of sounds, such as those produced by bells and pure voice tones. The technique is reminiscent of both the medieval Notre-Dame school of composition and the Eastern Orthodox tradition of sacred music. In 1977 Pärt used tintinnabulation in three works that remain among his most well loved: *Fratres, Cantus in Memoriam Benjamin Britten*, and

Tabula Rasa. Most of his later works set sacred texts, often in Latin, and many are large in scale, such as *Passio* (1982), *Te Deum* (1984–6, rev. 1993), and *Litany* (1994). His shorter works, such as the *Magnificat* (1989) and *The Beatitudes* (1990) have become standard repertoire for choirs all over the world.

Pärt has received numerous honors and awards, including election to the American Academy of Arts and Letters. In 2007 the Best Choral Performance Grammy was awarded to Paul Hillier and the Estonian Philharmonic Chamber Choir for Pärt's *Da Pacem.* In 2009 he was awarded the Léonie Sonning Music Prize. Over 40 recordings have been produced of his music, and his work has been heard in dozens of movies, from *There Will Be Blood* to *Fahrenheit 9/11.* Several conferences, such as "Arvo Pärt and Contemporary Spirituality" at Boston University (March 2010), have explored the effect of Pärt's music on humanity and culture.

BIBLIOGRAPHY

Grove7 (P. Hillier)

D. Clarke: "Parting Glances: David Clarke Reappraises the Music and Aesthetics of Arvo Pärt," *MT*, cxxxiv (1993), 680–4

P. Hillier: *Arvo Pärt* (London, 1997)

G. Smith: "An Interview with Arvo Pärt: Sources of Invention," *MT*, cxl (1999), 19–25

P. Quinn: "Out with the Old and in with the New: Arvo Pärt's 'Credo'," *Tempo*, no.211 (2000), 16–20

A. Ross: *The Rest Is Noise* (New York, 2007)

JAMES BASH

Partch, Harry (*b* Oakland, CA, 24 June 1901; *d* San Diego, CA, 3 Sept 1974). Composer, theorist, instrument maker, and performer. He dedicated most of his life to implementing an alternative to equal temperament—which he found incapable of the true consonance his ear and essentially tonal aesthetic demanded—and to fermenting a more holistic manner of composition and performance influenced by ancient and non-Western traditions. He invented an approach to just intonation he called monophony as it grew from a single tone, from one voice. Realizing that traditional instruments and performers would be inimical to his system, he designed and constructed new and adapted instruments, developed notational systems, and trained performing groups wherever he was living and working. By the 1940s he had transformed his profound antipathy to the European concert tradition into the idea of "corporeality," the performative aspect of monophony, which emphasized the physical and communal qualities in music.

Born in California to Presbyterian missionaries who had served in China, Partch grew up in the American Southwest where he imbibed a diverse array of musical experiences: "Christian hymns, Chinese lullabyes, Yaqui Indian ritual, Congo puberty ritual, Cantonese music hall, and Okies in California vineyards" (see the preface to the second edition of his *Genesis of a Music*). His own musical training began on piano, organ, mandolin, and cornet, and Partch played piano well enough to accompany silent films in Albuquerque. By 1920 he had returned to California, where he spent the next 13 years as a proofreader, piano teacher, and violist. Frustrated that his formal music education at the University of

Southern California papered over music's acoustical bases, Partch began to research intonation independently. In 1923 he discovered a new foundation for his musical thought in Hermann von Helmholtz's *On the Sensations of Tone*: he was particularly influenced by Helmholtz's preference for just intonation and by the translator A.J. Ellis's discussions of 19th-century experimental keyboard instruments, most of them English. He experimented with just intonation on string instruments and eventually developed the "adapted viola" by attaching a cello fingerboard to a viola and indicating appropriate finger positions through brads and lines; he finished the instrument in 1930 during a one-year sojourn in New Orleans. By 1928 he had completed the first draft of a theoretical treatise, *Exposition of Monophony*, which extended triadic consonance to include the 7th, 9th, and 11th partials. He also posited a symmetrical 29-note-per-octave scale, or gamut, for the adapted viola. Acknowledging the text-setting principles of early opera, Gluck, Mussorgsky, Debussy, Mahler, and the Schoenberg of *Pierrot lunaire*, his first "monophonic" works set texts by Li Po and Shakespeare and from the Biblical Psalms; they featured an "intoning" voice that used Sprechgesang in a non-expressionist manner and were accompanied (in the period 1930–33) by the adapted viola. From the outset he used pitches outside his chosen gamut, never restricting himself dogmatically.

Partch presented his first recitals in the years 1932–3. By 1933 his gamut had evolved to 37 tones (after flirtations with 39, 41, and even 55 tones), and the last draft of *Exposition of Monophony* was finished (although subsequently lost until the early 1980s). Partch went to New York and won a grant from the Carnegie Foundation to do research in England (1934–5), where he studied the work and instruments he had read about in *On the Sensations of Tone*; he also met William Butler Yeats, Arnold Dolmetsch, Edmund Dulac, George Russell (also known as the poet A.E.) and (in Rapallo) Ezra Pound. In addition to the new adapted guitar, he had a first keyboard instrument, the Ptolemy, built in London—although he abandoned it after shipping it to California—and met with Kathleen Schlesinger to discuss her recreation of a Greek kithara from a vase in the British Museum. He returned to the United States in the spring of 1935; by June he had begun a nine-month transient existence in the Western states, the subject of his socio-musical diary, *Bitter Music*. This narrative of life on the road and in Depression-era federal work camps mixes irony, nostalgia, and homoeroticism with keen observations of the effect New Deal-era policies had on transients and Dust Bowl migrants. Partch interpolated drawings of his surroundings and voice-and-piano renderings of transcribed speech-music along with more complex settings of conversations and Protestant hymnody to round out this remarkable document. He nearly published it in 1940, but later tried to destroy all copies; it resurfaced in the 1980s.

By 1941 Partch was in Chicago. He subsequently lived in New York and its environs, where he expanded his instrumentarium: he notably added two chordophones (a kithara and harmonic canon) and an adapted harmonium (the chromelodeon). He also set a final

Harry Partch with his instruments on the set for the film The Dreamer that Remains, *1972. (Betty Free-man/Lebrecht Music & Arts)*

43-tone gamut and began to compose for larger ensembles. During the early 1940s he concentrated on works with Americana texts, including hitchhikers' inscriptions (*Barstow*), newsboys' cries (*San Francisco*), transient missives (*The Letter*), and a hobo's train journey (*US Highball*). In the same period he received a measure of acclaim, including two Guggenheim grants, the support of composers ranging from Otto Luening to Quincy Porter to Howard Hanson, and a concert of his music sponsored by the League of Composers at Carnegie Hall (April 1944). He had his first semi-official university association at the University of Wisconsin in Madison from 1944 to 1947; his anti-academic views were reinforced by the music faculty's generally hostile attitude towards his music (Wiecki).

Partch returned to California and composed smaller pieces suffused with the melancholy of his first "monophonic" music. The University of Wisconsin Press finally published his treatise *Genesis of a Music* in 1949; in it the "expanded tonality diamond," based on the consonant hexad and revealing an interlocking series of common tones, reached fruition. Partch worked with Ben Johnston (1950–51) and presented the original version of *King Oedipus* at Mills College, Oakland (1952). His Gate 5 Ensemble (1953–5) performed and recorded *Plectra and Percussion Dances* and the revised *Oedipus* for his private record label (later also called Gate 5). These large-ensemble works have a mixture of tragic solemnity and vigorous rhythm, the latter due to his newly created percussion instruments: the diamond marimba, bass marimba, marimba eroica, cloud-chamber bowls, and spoils of war.

In 1956 Partch moved to Urbana, where Johnston taught at the University of Illinois, to produce *The Bewitched*, a dance drama featuring a coloratura witch leading a group of "lost musicians" through a dramatic haze; the premiere (1957) barely survived the friction between composer and choreographer Alwin Nikolais (Gilmore, 1995). In 1958 he embarked on one of his only long-term collaborations, with the director Madeline Tourtelot; this association produced six films: *Windsong* (1958), *Harry Partch: Music Studio* (1958), *US Highball* (1958, completed 1968), *Rotate the Body in all its Planes* (1961), *The Renascent* (1963), and *Delusion of the Fury* (1969). He returned to Urbana in January 1959 to compose and produce *Revelation in the Courthouse Park* and *Water! Water!* Another major event at Urbana was his meeting Danlee Mitchell, a percussionist who became his foremost performer, conductor, assistant, amanuensis, and friend for the rest of his life.

Partch returned to California for good in 1962. With the exception of a few smaller pieces, his music since the early 1950s had been truly "corporeal": dramaturgically intense, musically eclectic, and with the instruments (by this point more than 20) and their performers in full view of the audience. These works were influenced by East Asian theatrical traditions, in which Partch found an artistic integration that he believed the West had abandoned. This adoption of non-Western musical traditions mirrors his aesthetic evolution from monophony to corporeality, from the one voice to many voices working as one. The culmination of his theatrical and musical theories was *Delusion of the Fury*, a two-act work in which he used two non-European myths: a Japanese Noh tale of a pilgrim doing penance for a killing and an African story of a quarrel judged by a deaf and near-sighted judge. The work has some of Partch's most beautiful as well as most invigorating music; the variety of textures allows the subtleties of his harmonies and instrumental timbres to come forward.

Partch was never in good health, a problem exacerbated by his time as a hobo and migrant worker in the 1930s and early 40s, and his physical and mental stability began to give way in the last decade of his life. In 1973 he managed to compose the score for *The Dreamer that Remains*, a documentary filmed by Stephen Pouliot and produced by Betty Freeman which, although episodic, is a touching mesh of reminiscences and music in an earlier style that aptly summarizes his multitudinous achievements. He died of a heart attack a year after the film's completion.

For many, Partch's idiosyncratic menagerie of instruments remains the most striking feature of his life's work. Indeed Partch himself remarked in his manual on the instruments' repair and maintenance that the instruments give his music its character. His move from instruments focused on discrete pitches—the adapted viola, the chromelodeon—to those focused on sound and movement—the spoils of war, the quadrangularis reversum—matches his move from the one voice to corporeal theatrical works and traces the evolution of his aesthetic. By his life's end his instrumentarium, excluding small hand instruments, comprised the following:

chordophones (plucked or struck with mallets unless otherwise stated): adapted guitars I and II, adapted viola (bowed), kithara I and II, surrogate kithara, harmonic canons I, II (Castor and Pollux) and III (blue rainbow), crychord, koto (a gift from Lou Harrison and not altered)

idiophones (all tuned unless otherwise stated): diamond marimba, quadrangularis reversum, bass marimba, marimba eroica, mbira bass dyad (all wood); boos I and II, eucal blossom (bamboo); gourd tree, cone gongs (metal); cloud-chamber bowls, mazda marimba (glass); zymo-xyl (glass and wood), spoils of war (metal and wood, includes whang gun)

aerophones: chromelodeons I and II (modified reed organs), bloboy (pipes and bellows)

As Johnston noted soon after Partch's death, the problems in preserving a music so intimately tied to its creator and a fragile and unique instrumentarium are immense. In the early 1990s Danlee Mitchell, Partch's executor, gave the instruments to Dean Drummond, a Partch performer in the 1960s and founder of the New York group Newband. They have subsequently been held at Montclair State University, New Jersey, as part of the Harry Partch Institute and have been used regularly in Partch performances and new works by Drummond and others. Although copies have been made of some, most remain singular originals. Reproductions of the composer's tablature scores, transcriptions into expanded conventional notation, and recordings and films proliferated beginning in the late 1990s, particularly through Philip Blackburn's work at Innova recordings. These documents remain the primary means by which to study and hear the music—a somewhat ironic situation given Partch's lifelong ambivalence about recording.

Nevertheless interest in Partch has increased greatly since his death and overtaken the view held of him in life as quixotic or worse. His eclecticism, especially his unfettered use of non-Western musical traditions, anticipated many late 20th-century trends, and he has served as a model for developments in intonation, acoustic instruments, and timbre. He influenced the percussive motor-rhythm music of the minimalists of the 1960s and 70s, and his theater works are precursors of numerous experiments since the mid-1950s. His life provides an example of curmudgeonly but humane courage.

See also INSTRUMENTS; SOUND SCULPTURE; and TUNING SYSTEMS.

WORKS
(all in just intonation unless otherwise stated)

Works in equal temperament, incl. pf conc., sym. poem, *c*50 songs, 1910s–20s, destroyed 1930

Str Qt, vn, 2 va, vc, *c*1925–7, lost

My Heart Keeps Beating Time, equal temperament (L. Yoell), 1v, pf, 1929, rev. 1935 (in *Bitter Music*)

17 Lyrics of Li Po (trans. S. Obata), 1v, adapted va, 1930–33; San Francisco, 9 Feb 1932

By the Rivers of Babylon (Ps cxxxvii), 1v, adapted va, 1931; San Francisco, 9 Feb 1932; final rev., 1v, vc, kithara II, chromelodeon, 1955

Potion Scene from *Romeo and Juliet* (W. Shakespeare), 1v, adapted va, 1931; San Francisco, 9 Feb 1932; rev., 1v, 2 S, vc, orig. insts, 1955

The Lord is my Shepherd (Ps xxiii), 1v, adapted va, 1932; San Francisco, 9 Feb 1932; rev., 1v, chromelodeon, kithara, 1943

Barstow: Eight Hitchhiker Inscriptions from a Highway Railing at Barstow, California, 1v, adapted gui, 1941; New York, 22 April 1944; final rev., 2 vv, orig. insts, 1968, facs. and transcr. ed. R. Kassel (Madison, 2000) [1st of 4 works in The Wayward cycle]

December, 1942: 3 Settings, 1v, adapted gui: Come Away, Death (Shakespeare: *Twelfth Night*), The Heron (Tsuryuki, trans. A. Waley), The Rose (E. Young); nos.2–3 rev., 1v, orig. insts, in Intrusions

Dark Brother (T. Wolfe: *God's Lonely Man*), Bar, adapted va, chromelodeon, kithara, Indian drum, 1942–3; Madison, WI, 3 May 1945; rev., addl bass mar, after 1951

Mad Scene from *King Lear* (Shakespeare), 1v, chromelodeon, kithara, *c*1942–3, lost

US Highball: a Musical Account of a Transcontinental Hobo Trip (Partch), vv, gui I, kithara, chromelodeon, 1943; New York, 22 April 1944; rev., 2 vv, large ens of orig. insts, 1955 [2nd of 4 works in The Wayward cycle]

San Francisco: a Setting of the Cries of Two Newsboys on a Foggy Night in the Twenties, 1v, adapted va, chromelodeon, kithara, 1943; 22 April 1944; rev., 1v, vc, kithara II, chromelodeon, 1955 [3rd of 4 works in The Wayward cycle]

The Letter: a Depression Message from a Hobo Friend, 1v, adapted gui, kithara, 1943; final rev., 1v, large ens of orig. insts, 1972 [4th of 4 works in The Wayward cycle]

2 Settings from *Finnegans Wake* (J. Joyce): Isobel, Annah the Allmaziful, S, double flageolet/2 fl, kithara, 1944; Madison, 7 March 1945

Y[ankee] D[oodle] Fantasy (Partch), S, tin fls, tin ob, flexatone, chromelodeon, 1944; New York, 22 April 1944

"I'm very happy to be able to tell you about this …" (W. Ward, BBC transcr.), S, Bar, kithara, Indian drum, 1945; Madison, 3 May 1945; lost

Polyphonic Recidivism on a Japanese Theme (The Crane), equal temperament, SATB, 1945

Intrusions, incl. Study on Olympos' Pentatonic, Study on Archytas' Enharmonic, The Waterfall (Young), The Street (W. Motley: *Knock on any Door*), Lover (G. Leite), Soldiers–War–Another War (G. Ungaretti, trans. W.F. Weaver), Vanity (Ungaretti, trans. Weaver), Cloud Chamber Music, 1v, orig. insts, last work with chorus, Indian deer-hoof rattle, 1946–50

Sonata Dementia (Partch), 1v, insts, 1949–50; rev. as Ring around the Moon

The Wooden Bird (incid. music, W. Leach), 1v, insts, 1950, collab. B. Johnston; Charlottesville, VA, 10 Jan 1951

Plectra and Percussion Dances: Castor and Pollux, a Dance for the Twin Rhythms of Gemini, 1952, rev. 1968; Ring around the Moon, a Dance Fantasm for Here and Now (Partch), 1952–3; Even Wild Horses, Dance Music for an Absent Drama (A. Rimbaud: *A Season in Hell*), vv, large ens of orig. insts, 1949–52; Berkeley, CA, 19 Nov 1953

King Oedipus (1, after W.B. Yeats, after Sophocles), 10 solo vv, chorus, large ens of orig. insts, 1951 (begun 1933); Oakland, CA, 14 March 1952; rev. as Oedipus (Partch and J. Churchill, after Sophocles), 1952–4; Oakland, 2 June 1954; final rev., 1967; New York, 24 April 1997

2 Settings from Lewis Carroll: O Frabjous Day!, The Mock Turtle Song, 1v, orig. insts, 1954; no.1, Mill Valley, CA, 13 Feb 1954

Ulysses at the Edge, vv, tpt, db, model skindrums, boo, 1955; final rev., vv, a sax, bar sax, orig. insts, 1961–2; added to The Wayward cycle

The Bewitched (dance satire, 1, Partch), S, chorus, dancers, large ens of orig. and trad. insts, 1955–6; Urbana, IL, 26 March 1957

Windsong (film score, dir. M. Tourtelot), large ens of orig. insts, 1958; rev. as Daphne of the Dunes (dance), 1967

Revelation in the Courthouse Park (1, after Euripides: *Bacchae*), 16 solo vv, 4 speakers, chorus, dancers, large ens of orig. and trad. insts, 1959–60; Urbana, 11 April 1961

Bless this Home (V. Prockelo), 1v, ob, orig. insts, 1961

Rotate the Body in all its Planes (ballad for gymnasts, based on Revelation in the Courthouse Park, Chorus 3), S, chorus, large ens of orig. and trad. insts, 1961; Urbana, 8 April 1962

Water! Water! (satirical "intermission," 2, Partch), solo vv, choruses, large ens of orig. and trad. insts, 1961; Urbana, 9 March 1962

Jine the Calvary (trad.), 1v, orig. insts, 1963

Study, harmonic canon I and kithara I, 1963–4

And on the Seventh Day Petals Fell in Petaluma, large ens of orig. insts, 1963–6; Los Angeles, 8 May 1966

Delusion of the Fury: a Ritual of Dream and Delusion (2, Partch, after Jap. and African trad.), actors, chorus, dancers, large ens of orig. and small hand insts, 1965–6; Los Angeles, 9 Jan 1969

The Dreamer that Remains: a Study in Loving (film score, dir. S. Pouliot), vv, chorus, large ens of orig. insts, 1972; La Jolla, CA, 25 March 1973

WRITINGS

T. McGeary, ed.: Harry Partch: "Bitter Music": Collected Journals, Essays, Introductions and Librettos (Urbana, IL, 1991) [hereafter BM]

Exposition of Monophony (c1927–1933), excerpts in Interval, iv/2 (1983), 6 only; iv/3 (1984), 8–9

"Ratio Keyboard Design, 8 Sept 1932," Interval, v/3 (1986–7), 14–17

Analysis and Transcription of California Indian Melodies from the Lummis Cylinder Collection at the Southwest Museum, Los Angeles (1933), excerpts in Kassel (1991)

"A New Instrument," MO, lviii (1934–5), 764–72

Bitter Music (1935–6, rev. 1940)

Preface to Patterns of Music (1940) [in BM]

Review of J. Yasser: Theory of Evolving Tonality (c1942–4), Interval, iv/4 (1985), 5–6

"Show Horses in the Concert Ring," Circle, no.10 (1948), 43–50; repr. in Soundings [Los Angeles], no.1 (1972), 66–76 [in BM]

Genesis of a Music: an Account of a Creative Work, its Roots and its Fulfillments (Madison, WI, 1949, enlarged 2/1974)

"The Rhythmic Motivations of Castor and Pollux and even Wild Horses" (1952) [in BM]

"Life in the Houses of Technitution" (c1953), Allos, ed. K. Gaburo (La Jolla, CA, 1980), 291–301

"Some New and Old Thoughts after and before The Bewitched" (1955) [in BM]

"Selected Correspondence to Lou Harrison 1955–1970," A Lou Harrison Reader (Santa Fe, 1987), 54–62

"The Ancient Magic," Music Journal, xvii/5 (1959), 16 only [in BM]

Manual on the Maintenance and Repair of, and the Musical and Attitudinal Techniques for, Some Putative Musical Instruments (1963), Interval, i/2 (1978), 8–12; i/3 (1979), 7–14; i/4–5 (1979), 15–18, 31–4

"The University and the Creative Arts: Comment," Arts in Society, ii/3 (1963), 22 only [in BM]

Lecture, Source, i/1 (1967), 103 only [in BM]

A Quarter-saw Section of Motivations and Intonations (1967) [lecture] [excerpt in BM]

P. Blackburn, ed.: Enclosures, iii (St. Paul, 1997) ["scrapbook" of Partch materials]

BIBLIOGRAPHY

GroveA (P. Earls)

S.N. Mayfield: "Student Devises 29-Degree Octave Theory of Music," *Times-Picayune* [New Orleans] (16 Nov 1930)

J.M. Barbour: Review of Genesis of a Music, MQ, xxxvi (1950), 131–5

W. Leach: "Music for Words Perhaps," Theatre Arts, xxxvii/1 (1953), 65–8

P.M. Schafer: "New Records," Canadian Music Journal, iii/2 (1959), 55–8 [on US Highball]

M.J. Mandelbaum: Multiple Division of the Octave and the Tonal Resources of 19-tone Temperament (diss., U. of Indiana, 1961)

W. Mellers: "An American Aboriginal," Tempo, no.64 (1963), 2–6

"Harry Isn't Kidding," Time (5 July 1963)

P. Earls: "Harry Partch: Verses in Preparation for Delusion of the Fury," Yearbook: Inter-American Institute for Musical Research, iii (1967), 1–32

A. Woodbury: "Harry Partch: Corporeality and Monophony," Source, i/2 (1967), 91–3

E. Friedman: "Tonality in the Music of Harry Partch," Composer [Hamilton], ii/1 (1970), 17–24

A. Hiss: "Hobo Concerto," New Yorker (7 Feb 1970)

S.L. Pouliot: "Filming the Work of Harry Partch, or Get to Know Your Genius," American Cinematographer, lv (1974), 322–5, 333, 344–5

J. Cott: "The Forgotten Visionary," Rolling Stone, no.158 (1974), 32–4, 36, 38

G. Kvistad and A. Otte: "Harry Partch (1901–74): Genesis of a Music," Numus West, i/6 (1974), 29 only

B. Johnston: "The Corporealism of Harry Partch," PNM, xiii/2 (1974–5), 85–97

W. Zimmerman: "Ben Johnston on Harry Partch," Desert Plants: Conversations with 23 American Musicians (Vancouver, 1976), 347–71 [incl. score of The Letter]

R. Wernick: Review of Genesis of a Music, JMT, xx (1976), 133–7

J. Fritsch: "Die Tonalität des Harry Partch," Feedback Papers, no.14 (Cologne, 1977), 17–26; repr. in R. Brinkmann, ed.: Avantgarde Jazz Pop (Mainz, 1978), 31–41

G.A. Hackbarth: An Analysis of Harry Partch's "Daphne of the Dunes" (diss., U. of Illinois, 1979)

J. Smith: "The Partch Reverberations: Notes on a Musical Rebel," San Diego Weekly Reader (25 Sept 1980); repr. in Interval, iii (1981), no.1, pp.7–12; no.2, pp.6–9, 12; repr. in Soundings, xii (1982), 46–59

M. Stahnke: "Gedanken zu Harry Partch," Neuland: Ansätze zur Musik der Gegenwart, ii (1981–2), 242–51

W. Burt: The Music of Harry Partch (Melbourne, 1982)

P. Garland: Americas: Essays on American Musicians and Culture, 1973–80 (Santa Fe, 1982), 56–63, 267–90

W. Salmon: "The Influence of Noh on Harry Partch's Delusion of the Fury," PNM, xxii/1–2 (1984), 233–45

K. Gaburo: "In Search of The Bewitched: Concerning Physicality," The Percussionist, xxiii/3 (1985), 54–84

T. Kakinuma: The Musical Instruments of Harry Partch as an Apparatus of Production in Musical Theatre (diss., U. of California, 1989)

T. McGeary: The Music of Harry Partch (Brooklyn, 1991) [catalog incl. bibliography (to 1974) and discography]

R. Kassel: "Harry Partch in the Field," Musicworks, no.51 (1991), 6–15

W. Mellers: "An Authentic American Composer," Times Literary Supplement (31 May 1991), 16 [on Bitter Music]

R.V. Wiecki: "Relieving '12-Tone Paralysis': Harry Partch in Madison, Wisconsin, 1944–1947," American Music, ix/1 (1991), 43–66

R. Maltz: "Microtonal Techniques in the Music of Harry Partch and Ben Johnston," Music Research Forum, vii (1992), 14–37

B. Gilmore: "On Harry Partch's Seventeen Lyrics of Li Po," PNM, xxx/2 (1992), 22–58; erratum, PNM, xxxi/1 (1993), 332–3

J. Schneider: "Bringing Back Barstow," Guitar Review, no.95 (1993), 1–13

"Remembering Harry Partch," 1/1: The Journal of the Just Intonation Network, viii/4 (1994) [Partch issue]

B. Gilmore: "'A Soul Tormented': Alwin Nikolais and Harry Partch's The Bewitched," MQ, lxxxi (1995), 80–107

R. Kassel: The Evolution of Harry Partch's Monophony (diss., CUNY, 1996)

D. Dunn, ed.: Harry Partch: an Anthology of Critical Perspectives (Amsterdam, 1998/R)

B. Gilmore: *Harry Partch: a Biography* (New Haven, 1998)

R. Kassel, ed.: *Barstow, Eight Hitchhiker Inscriptions from a Highway Railing at Barstow, California [1968 Version]* (Madison, WI, 2000)

B. Gilmore: "The Climate since Harry Partch," *CMR*, 22/1–2 (2003), 15–33

S.A. Granade: *I was a Bum once Myself: Harry Partch, U.S. Highball, and the Dust Bowl in the American Imagination* (diss., U. of Illinois, 2005)

B.A. Blackburn: *Tonal Modulation with Just Intonation: Corporeality and Musical Gesture in the Music of Harry Partch* (diss., U. of Illinois, 2006)

E. Green: "Just how Radical was Harry Partch? A Consideration of 'The Long-Departed Lover' in the Light of Traditional Techniques of Songwriting," *1/1: The Journal of the Just Intonation Network*, xii/2 (2006), 16–24

B.T. Harlan: *One Voice: a Reconciliation of Harry Partch's Disparate Theories* (diss., U. of Southern California, 2007)

S.A. Granade: "Rekindling Ancient Values: the Influence of Chinese Music and Aesthetics on Harry Partch," *JSAM*, iv/1 (2010), 1–32

S.A. Granade: "When Worlds Collide: Harry Partch's Encounters with Film Music," *Music and the Moving Image*, iv/1 (2011), 9–33

Recorded interviews in *NHoh and U*

RICHARD KASSEL/S. ANDREW GRANADE

Parton, Dolly (Rebecca) (*b* Pigeon Forge, TN, 9 Jan 1946). Country singer-songwriter, multi-instrumentalist, and actress. Known for her soprano voice, fluttering vibrato, instrumental ability, humor, outrageous appearance, philanthropy, and business empire, Dolly Parton sprang from the depths of poverty in Appalachia. One of 12 children born to a sharecropper, Parton grew up in a one-room cabin near Sevierville, Tennessee. Music was central to her family life; her mother taught her old-time Appalachian songs and she sang in her grandfather's church. Parton began writing her own songs and playing guitar at a young age and landed a role on Cas Walker's television show in Knoxville, Tennessee, when she was 10 years old. In 1960, Parton recorded several songs in the Brenda Lee rockabilly style with Goldband Records in Lake Charles, Louisiana. Her first song, "Puppy Love" landed her an appearance on the *Grand Ole Opry*. The day after her high school graduation, Parton boarded a bus for Nashville. She secured a songwriting contract in 1966 and a year later cut her first single with Mercury Records ("Dumb Blonde"). In 1967, Parton replaced Norma Jean on *The Porter Wagoner Show*, marking the beginning of a successful professional relationship with Wagoner that resulted in 13 duet albums on RCA Victor. In 1971, she had her first number-one hit with "Joshua," and she scored three more in 1974 with "Jolene," "Love is like a butterfly," and "I will always love you." Parton left the *Porter Wagoner Show* in 1974, but retained Wagoner as her producer for two more years. Throughout the 1970s, she won numerous awards and obtained a syndicated television show (*Dolly*). In the 1980s, Parton began to appear as an actress, starring alongside Jane Fonda in the film *9 to 5* (1980), *The Best Little Whorehouse in Texas* (1982), and *Steel Magnolias* (1989). She has collaborated with numerous musicians, including Emmylou Harris and Linda Ronstadt on the Grammy Award–winning albums *Trio* (Warner Bros., 1986) and *Trio II* (Elektra, 1999), and with Loretta Lynn and Tammy Wynette on *Honky Tonk Angels* (Columbia 53414, 1993).

Parton successfully crossed over with her 1977 hit "Here you come again," which featured purposefully glossier production as a crossover strategy. Her music and business acumen have helped change women's roles within the country industry, and she has been a fierce advocate for gender equality. In the title track of her first album, *Just Because I'm a Woman* (RCA, 1968), Parton reprimands her boyfriend for questioning her previous sexual partners. Other songs have addressed prostitution, emotional and societal inequalities, and her mother's experience of remaining with a cheating husband ("To Daddy," 1975). Following the path of Loretta Lynn, Parton also wrote songs about her poor upbringing. "Coat of Many Colors" (1971) related Parton's embarrassment of being picked on by other children for her patchwork coat, while *My Mountain Tennessee Home* (RCA, 1973) reveals nostalgia for her rural upbringing. Parton has since built an East Tennessee empire to strengthen the economy of her hometown, largely through Dollywood, a theme park that attracts more than three million visitors each year. In 1999, she was inducted into the Country Music Hall of Fame.

BIBLIOGRAPHY

D. Parton: *Dolly: My life and other unfinished business* (New York, 1994)

W. Parton: *Smoky Mountain memories: Stories from the Parton family* (Nashville, TN, 1996)

P. Wilson: "Mountains of Contradictions: Gender, Class, and Region in the Star Image of Dolly Parton," *Reading Country Music: Steel Guitars, Opry Stars, and Honky-tonk Bars*, ed. C. Tichi (Durham, NC, 1998), 98–120

S. Miller: *Smart blonde: Dolly Parton* (London, 2008)

N. Cardwell: *The Words and Music of Dolly Parton: Getting to Know Country's "Iron Butterfly"* (Westport, CT, 2011)

JADA WATSON

Partsong [part song; part-song]. A term referring to works of modest dimensions built on secular texts, which are normally unaccompanied and less often supported by the piano. "Part" refers to multiple voice parts—distinguished from works for solo voice and piano—rather than to sectional structures, and suggests works for mixed voices, as well as all-female or all-male ensembles. Most are designated for choral performance, with multiple singers in each section, although some suggest the possibility of presentation by groups of solo voices.

The genre has ample European antecedents with composers ranging from Mozart and Haydn through Franz Schubert and Robert Schumann to Johannes Brahms and beyond. In the United States, as in Europe, hundreds of such works were generated by the needs of a host of private singing societies spread across the country. These were independent organizations that concentrated on the performance of this literature. The first of these English-language ensembles was the Mendelssohn Glee Club, organized in New York during the fall of 1866; its second music director was composer Edward MacDowell, although he served in that capacity for only two years, due to his declining health.

Even though pieces written before and later might well fit the label, the heyday of what composers, performers, and listeners referred to as "partsongs" in the United States ran roughly from the 1860s through the 1930s, after which the term lost its currency. Usually they appear as single movements, although one finds that multi-movement sets and others were issued in anthologies of such works. Initially partsongs were usually published in folio form, but soon publishers including Arthur P. Schmidt in Boston and G. Schirmer in New York turned to the more economical and handy octavo format. The principal composers of the genre were Dudley Buck, George Whitefield Chadwick, Arthur Foote, Horatio Parker, MacDowell, Amy Marcy Beach, Margaret Ruthven Lang, and Henry Hadley. Some of the composers sporadically became their own lyricists. The words of some of the most prominent poets of the period, such as Henry Wadsworth Longfellow, Robert Lowell, Walt Whitman, and Sidney Lanier, appear only sparingly and are surpassed by those of lesser lights like Cale Young Rice, Clinton Scollard, and David Stevens. The composers were aware of their constituency, writing in a conservative homophonic, homo-rhythmic idiom, with only modest amounts of contrapuntal imitation. Reflecting larger trends, earlier works in the tradition reflect an obvious awareness of Felix Mendelssohn, their harmonic language quite straightforward; later works became increasingly chromatic and complex.

BIBLIOGRAPHY
D. DeVenney: *Nineteenth-Century American Choral Music: an Annotated Guide* (Berkeley, CA, 1987)

W. Osborne: *American Singing Societies and their Partsongs* (Lawton, OK, 1994)

WILLIAM OSBORNE

Pasatieri, Thomas (*b* Brooklyn, NY, 20 Oct 1945). Composer. Though his family was not musically sophisticated, he started piano lessons at age nine and began writing music soon thereafter. A prolific composer by the age of 14, he worked briefly with NADIA BOULANGER before entering the Juilliard School, where he studied composition with VITTORIO GIANNINI and VINCENT PERSICHETTI. He cited as his most influential teacher Giannini, who encouraged him to follow his own artistic inclinations and validated his commitment to a neo-romantic style. He credits Persichetti with helping him to refine his craftsmanship. At 23 he received the first doctorate awarded by the Juilliard School.

Vocal music has always been Pasatieri's chief interest. Strongly drawn to opera, he wrote his first at age 19; by the time he was 35 he had completed 15, most of which have been performed numerous times. He came to national prominence in 1972 with *The Trial of Mary Lincoln*, commissioned and premiered by National Educational Television. Set to a libretto by television writer Anne Howard Bailey, the work is a moving portrait of the first lady in her later years, during the court trial that judged her insane. Tailored to the intimacy of television, the opera uses flashbacks, dissolves, and voice-overs. Pasatieri's operas tend to focus on highly emotional characters in the throes of extreme situations, with subjects drawn from well-known literary works by writers such as Anton Chekhov, Eugene O'Neill, and Henry James. These qualities, combined with his post-Puccinian neo-romantic style rooted in the *bel canto* tradition, found favor with singers and audiences during the 1970s. Evelyn Lear, Frederica Von Stade, Richard Stilwell, John Reardon, Lili Chookasian, Lauren Flanigan, and Jennie Tourel are just some of the well-known singers who have championed his works. However, the ease with which he turned out opera after opera, his defiance of then-fashionable atonal styles, and the success he achieved at a relatively young age resulted in a vicious critical backlash.

In 1984 with 17 operas to his credit but discouraged by the antipathy of critics and the financial uncertainty of a composer's life, Pasatieri ceased writing operas and moved to Hollywood. There he found lucrative work in the film industry as an orchestrator, scoring the music for many highly acclaimed films. He also continued to compose a number of choral and instrumental works. In 2003 having achieved financial stability, he moved back to New York and returned to the world of musical theater, revising several of his earlier operas and completing five new ones by 2010. Revivals of some of his earlier operas as well as multiple performances and recordings of some of his later works have been received favorably by critics, as more conservative musical styles have become acceptable. Pasatieri's finest efforts, such as *Black Widow*, *Washington Square*, and *Frau Margot*, are among the most powerful and moving works of the American operatic repertoire.

Pasatieri has taught at Juilliard, the Manhattan School of Music, and the Cincinnati Conservatory; he was director of the Atlanta Opera from 1980 until 1984.

WORKS
OPERAS
The Trysting Place (1, Pasatieri, after B. Tarkington), 1964, unperf; *Flowers of Ice* (2, R. Rogers), 1964, unperf; *The Women* (chbr op, 1, Pasatieri), Aspen, CO, 20 Aug 1965; *La Divina* (op buffa, 1, Pasatieri), New York, Juilliard School, 16 March 1966; *Padrevia* (1, Pasatieri, after G. Boccaccio), New York, Brooklyn College, 18 Nov 1967; *The Penitentes* (3, A.H. Bailey), 1967, Aspen, CO, 3 Aug 1974; *Calvary* (church op, 1, Pasatieri, after W.B. Yeats), Bellevue, WA, 7 April 1971; *Black Widow* (3, Pasatieri, after M. Unamuno), Seattle, WA, 2 March 1972; *The Trial of Mary Lincoln* (TV op, 17 scenes, A.H. Bailey), WNET, 14 Feb 1972; *The Seagull* (3, K. Elmslie, after A. Chekhov), Houston, 5 March 1974; *Signor Deluso* (op buffa, 1, Pasatieri, after Molière), Wolf Trap, VA, 27 July 1974; *Ines de Castro* (3, B. Stambler), Baltimore, 30 March 1976; *Washington Square* (2, K. Elmslie, after H. James), Detroit, 1 Oct 1976; *Three Sisters* (1, K. Elmslie, after A. Chekhov), 1979, Columbus, OH, 13 March 1986; *Before Breakfast* (1, F. Corsaro, after E. O'Neill), New York, 9 Oct 1980; *The Goose Girl* (children's op, 1, Pasatieri, after Bros. Grimm), Fort Worth, TX, 15 Feb 1981; *Maria Elena* (1, Pasatieri), Tucson, AZ, 6 April 1983; *Frau Margot* (3, F. Corsaro), Fort Worth, TX, 2 June 2007; *The Hotel Casablanca* (op buffa, 2, Pasatieri, after G. Feydeau), San Francisco, 3 Aug 2007; *The Heir Apparent* (F. Corsaro, after H. James) 2008; *The Family Room* (D. Malfitano), 2009, Princeton, NJ, 23 July 2011; *God Bless Us, Everyone!* (1, M. Capasso, B. Van Horn), New York, 16 Dec 2010; *The Martyrs* (D. Malfitano), 2012, New York, 8 Nov 2012

VOCAL
Songs (1v, pf, unless otherwise stated): 3 American Songs (L. Phillips), 1971; 3 Coloratura Songs (L. Phillips, J. Fletcher), 1971; 2 Shakespeare Songs, 1971; Heloïse and Abelard (L. Phillips), S, Bar, pf, 1973; 3 Poems (J. Agee), 1974; Rites de passage (L. Phillips), 1v, chbr orch/str qt, 1974; Far from Love (E. Dickinson), S, cl, vn, vc, pf, 1976;

Day of Love (K. van Cleave), song cycle (1983); 3 Sonnets from the Portuguese (E.B. Browning), 1984; 7 Lehmannlieder (L. Lehmann), song cycle, 1v, pf/orch, 1988; Windsongs (R. Ramsay, R.H. Deutsch, R. Nixon), S, pf (1989); Alleluia (Latin, trans. Pasatieri) (1991), arr. SATB, pf; Canciones del barrio, 1v, str qt, 1993; A Rustling of Angels (various, 12 songs), 2000; Three Poems of Oscar Wilde, 2001; Letter to Warsaw (P. Braun), S, chbr ens, 2003; The Daughter of Capulet (monodrama, W. Shakespeare), S, pf, 2007; Lady Macbeth (monodrama, W. Shakespeare), S, pf, 2007; Bel Canto Songs (W. Blake), 2009; The Bride of the Moor (W. Shakespeare), S, pf, 2010; Due Sonnete del Petrarca, 2010; Trois Chansons de la Lune, 2011; numerous additional songs

CHORAL
Permit Me Voyage (J. Agee), S, SATB, orch, 1976; Mass, S, Mez, T, B, SATB, orch, 1983; A Joyful Noise, SATB, brass sextet, org, perc, 1985; 3 Mysteries (W. Whitman, G. Meredith, P. Sidney), SATB, 1991; The Harvest Frost (C. Sandburg), SATB, chbr ens, 1993; Bang the Drum Loudly, children's chorus, 1994; Canticle of Praise, SATB, org, 1995; Mornings Innocent (gay and lesbian poets), male vv, ob, vc, hp, pf, 1995; A Charm of Moonlight, 2010; In the Light of Angels, S, Mez, children's chorus, baroque orch, 2012

INSTRUMENTAL
Orch: Invocations, 1968; Symphony no.1, 2009; Symphony no.2, 2011
Solo instrument with orch: Conc., pf, orch, 1993; Conc., 2pf, str, 1994; Conc., hpd, str, 2007; Conc., va, orch, 2012
Chbr: Theatrepieces, cl, vn, pf, 1987; Sonata, vn, pf, 1994; Qt, fl, va, vc, pf, 1995; Serenade, vn, chbr orch/pf, 1995; Sonata, va, pf, 1995; Sonata, fl, pf, 1997; Rhapsody, trbn, pf, 2006; Rhapsody, b, pf, 2008; The Dimming of the Day, va, hpd, 2009; Manifesto, va, 2012; 3 pf Sonatas (1966, 1969, 1999); Cameos, pf, 1969

FILMSCORE ORCHESTRATIONS
(selective list)
Little Shop of Horrors (1986); La Bamba (1987); Dirty Rotten Scoundrels (1988); The Little Mermaid (1989); Fried Green Tomatoes (1991); Scent of a Woman (1992); The Shawshank Redemption (1994); Primary Colors (1998); The Green Mile (1999); Erin Brockovich (2000); Road to Perdition (2002)

Principal publishers: Presser, G. Schirmer, Belwin-Mills

BIBLIOGRAPHY
S. Fleming: "Pasatieri's *The Seagull,*" *High Fidelity/Musical America,* xxiv/6 (1974), 32–3
R. Jacobson: "Thomas Pasatieri: Opera is the Plural of Opus," *After Dark,* vi/11 (1974), 45–9
H.C. Schonberg: "*Ines de Castro* in Baltimore," *New York Times* (1 April 1976)
P.G. Davis: "They Love Him in Seattle," *New York Times Magazine* (21 March 1976)
A. Hughes: "Pasatieri's *Washington Square* Opera States its Case," *New York Times* (15 Oct 1977)
J. Rockwell: "Baltimore Opera's Three Portraits of Women," *New York Times* (3 Feb 1985)
W. Simmons: "Pasatieri's *The Three Sisters,*" *Fanfare,* xi/2 (1987), 193–4
R.H. Kornick: *Recent American Opera: a Production Guide* (New York, 1991), 222–32
W. Simmons: "Pasatieri: *Frau Margot* [premiere]," *American Record Guide,* lxx/5 (2007), 47–8
R. Dyer: "Reunion—Thomas Pasatieri," *Opera News,* lxxi/10 (2007)

WALTER SIMMONS

Pasi, Martin (*b* Bregenz, Austria, 21 Dec 1953). Organ builder of Austrian birth. After serving a four-year apprenticeship with the Rieger firm in Austria, he moved to the United States in 1981 and worked for several organ builders, including Paul Byard Fritts, before opening his own workshop in Roy, Washington, in 1990 under the name of Pasi Organ Builders. Pasi's organs are influenced by historical models, and all components are custom made in-house. The casework of the instruments ranges in design from traditional to contemporary. Among his most significant organs are those in Trinity Lutheran Church, Lynnwood, Washington (1995), which was designed and voiced in the Italian manner, and in St. Cecilia's Cathedral, Omaha, Nebraska (2003), a distinctive 55-stop instrument in which the *Hauptwerk, Positiv,* and Pedal have dual temperament and can be played in both meantone and well-tempered tuning systems. One of Pasi's largest organs, completed in 2010, is a four-manual instrument of 76 stops located in the Co-Cathedral of the Sacred Heart in Houston, Texas, but his workshop has also produced small continuo and house organs.

BIBLIOGRAPHY
J. Ambrosino: "Mean and Keen," *Choir and Organ,* xiv/6 (2006), 54
K.C. Vogt: "A Dual Temperament Organ in America's Heartland," *ISO Journal,* no.32 (2009), 8

BARBARA OWEN

Pasito Duranguense [Chicago sound]. Mexican American musical style. The *pasito duranguense* (little Durango step) or "Chicago sound" emerged in the early 21st century in the Mexican communities of greater Chicago. A number of groups, made up of mostly young Mexican immigrants, recreated traditional Mexican brass-band sound with synthesizers and drums to interpret Mexican *rancheras* and *baladas* (rustic and refined love songs) as well as more upbeat tunes that became known as "El pasito duranguense," a couple-dance style mixing *merengue* and *ranchera*. Invested emotionally in the Mexican homeland by insisting in regional sound aesthetics, the music appealed to a new transnational audience but also gained considerable popularity in northern Mexico. Promotion of the bands in the United States included national TV campaigns, street marketing, and strong radio airplay on Spanish-language stations across the country. The "Chicago sound" made inroads into the 2003 Billboard Latin charts and topped the 2003 Billboard charts of "Regional Mexican" music. The *pasito duranguense* has been compared to the *technobanda* movement that swept Southern California a decade earlier. The Duranguense movement included bands such as Grupo Montéz de Durango, Alacranes Musical, K-Paz de la Sierra, Patrulla 81, Los Horóscopos de Durango, Braceros Musical, and Conjunto Atardecer (from Durango).

BIBLIOGRAPHY
S. Hutchinson: *From Quebradita to Duranguense: Dance in Mexican American Youth Culture* (Tucson, AZ, 2007)
H. Simonett: "Quest for the Local: Building Musical Ties between Mexico and the United States," *Postnational Musical Identities: Cultural Production, Distribution and Consumption in a Globalized Scenario,* ed. I. Corona and A.L. Madrid (Lanham, MD, 2008), 119–35

HELENA SIMONETT

Paso doble [pasodoble]. A fast duple-meter march-like music and its corresponding two-step couple dance. Originating in France, the dance became associated with Spanish dance culture; theatrical presentations have used music and movements to evoke elements of a bullfight (for example, the lead dancer as matador, the follower as the matador's cape). Gaining popularity with French competition dancers in the early 20th century, it has developed primarily into a competitive BALLROOM DANCE, rather than a social or theatrical dance. Although it has not been one of the primary competitive ballroom dances in the United States, it has been a fixture on the international scene as one of the dances in the International Latin program. The brisk, agile couple dance is characterized by quick, march-like steps, with emphasis on every second step. The structure of each dance includes an introduction and three main sections, including climactic moments that typically prompt dramatic poses. The dance has often been choreographed to "España cañí" or appropriate pieces composed in *paso doble* style.

Pass, Joe [Passalaqua, Joseph Anthony Jacobi] (*b* New Brunswick, NJ, 13 Jan 1929; *d* Los Angeles, CA, 23 May 1994). Jazz guitarist and bandleader. Soon after beginning his career he began to take drugs and spent many years in prisons, hospitals, and halfway houses. In 1961, together with other jazz musicians in Synanon, a self-help organization for drug addicts, he issued a collective album which attracted some critical attention to his easygoing manner and astounding technical prowess. He then worked for several years in Los Angeles studios, recording with Johnny Griffin, Gerald Wilson, and Les McCann, among others, but remained more or less in obscurity until 1973, when he was retained for the Pablo label and recorded his first solo album, *Virtuoso*. The success of this recording catapulted him to fame and Pass immediately began to dominate jazz popularity polls for his instrument. For the rest of the decade and through the 1980s he was in high demand for concerts, festivals, and recording sessions, notably as an accompanist to Ella Fitzgerald and Sarah Vaughan, and as a member of Oscar Peterson's groups.

Pass was one of the few jazz guitarists to master the technique of fingerpicking, which allowed him to produce satisfying performances as an unaccompanied soloist. Like Art Tatum, with whom he was often compared because of his remarkable technique, he excelled when elaborating solo paraphrases of popular songs, revealing a refined sense of harmony and an uncommonly wide array of accompaniment textures.

BIBLIOGRAPHY
J. Tynan: "Joe Pass: Building a New Life," *DB*, xxx/17 (1963), 18
"Joe Pass Discography," *SJ*, xxix/6 (1975), 238
B. James: "Joe Pass Interview," *JJ*, xxix (1976), no. 5, p.12; no. 5, p.24
L. Underwood: "Joe Pass: Virtuoso Revisited," *DB*, xlv/7 (1978), 16
J. Ferguson: "Joe Pass: Reflections of a Jazz Virtuoso," *GP*, xviii/9 (1984), 51
W. Enstice and P. Rubin: *Jazz Spoken Here: Conversations with Twenty-two Musicians* (Baton Rouge, LA, 1992), 226

J. BRADFORD ROBINSON/R

Passamaquoddy. Native American tribe of the WABENAKI confederacy.

Pasticcio. A dramatic vocal work, the music for which is wholly or partly borrowed from existing works by various composers. The Italian for "mess" or "hodge-podge" and related to the French word *pastiche*, the term originated in Italian operatic practices of the 18th century. For a discussion of the pasticcio in the United States *see* BALLAD OPERA.

Pastor, Tony [Antonio] **(i)** (*b* New York, NY, 26 April 1833; *d* Elmhurst, NY, 26 Aug 1908). Circus performer and variety manager. He was the third of six children of a Spanish immigrant barber, Antonio Pastor, and his American wife Cornelia Pastor (née Buckley). He was apprenticed to John Jay Nathans, a circus equestrian, in 1847, but gravitated towards a career as a clown. In the latter role he was expected to sing and dance as well as take part in comic minstrel and pantomime skits, which were a standard part of 19th-century circus entertainments.

By the end of the 1850s Pastor had moved into variety entertainment. It was not uncommon for variety theaters to hire circus acts, and Pastor found his first steady employment with Frank Rivers, a Philadelphia manager, and then with Robert Butler, the manager of the American Music Hall in Manhattan. Pastor worked with Butler for several seasons and established himself as a hugely popular performer with a diverse range of skills. A new theater licensing law in 1862 fundamentally changed the economic model for variety and temporarily shut theaters as police raided them; the memory of these events almost certainly prompted Pastor to

Tony Pastor. (Courtesy of Gillian Rodger)

reform the most rowdy elements of variety when he himself became a manager.

In 1865 Pastor opened the Opera House at 201 Bowery and by 1870 he was one of the leading variety managers in the country. He continued in this position until the late 1880s, when a younger generation of entrepreneurial managers began to cut into his profits.

Pastor was one of the earliest managers to pioneer the matinee performance in variety in order to attract women and children to his theater, and his evening show was deemed suitable for women. He was one of the earliest variety managers to lead touring troupes across the country; by the late 1870s he traveled from coast to coast in the summer months, and during the extended depression of the mid-1870s he maintained a troupe on the road year round. As his reforms became standard practice in "refined" variety, Pastor relocated his New York hall closer to the established dramatic houses. In 1875 he moved into the Metropolitan Theater at 585 Broadway, christening the establishment Tony Pastor's New Theater. He stayed there until 1881, when he moved further north into the heart of Union Square's fashionable theater district and leased a theater space in Tammany Hall, where he remained until 1908.

Pastor was associated with all of the leading variety performers of his time, many of whom, including Ella Wesner, Gus Williams, Lillian Russell, and John and Harry Kernell, began their careers on his stage. He was one of the first variety managers to book English acts, such as the male impersonators Bessie Bonehill and Vesta Tilley, both of whom drew huge audiences. When variety performers began to unionize in response to the business tactics of Keith and Albee and other entrepreneurial managers, Pastor not only supported the performers' cause but also helped to underwrite their union, the White Rats. Known throughout his career as a generous and benevolent manager, he always gave old-time performers facing hard times a spot on his bill. Despite his success he left only a small estate, for he returned most of his wealth to the profession through charity.

BIBLIOGRAPHY

P. Zellers: *Tony Pastor: Dean of the Vaudeville Stage* (Ypsilanti, MI, 1971)

S. Kattwinkel: *Tony Pastor Presents Afterpieces from the Vaudeville Stage* (Westport, CT, 1998)

A. Fields: *Tony Pastor: Father of Vaudeville* (Jefferson, NC, 2007)

GILLIAN M. RODGER

Pastor, Tony [Pestritto, Antonio] **(ii)** (*b* Middletown, CT, 26 Oct 1907; *d* Old Lyme, CT, 31 Oct 1969). Bandleader, singer, and saxophonist. He began playing as a sideman in the orchestras of John Cavallaro, Irving Aaronson, and Vincent Lopez, before joining Artie Shaw's band (1936), in which he was a tenor saxophone soloist and singer; "Indian Love Call" (1938, B♭) offers a good example of his throaty, somewhat gruff vocal style. After Shaw dissolved the band Pastor formed his own in 1940, taking some of Shaw's players with him. Many of the group's arrangements were written by the guitarist

Al Avola, although Budd Johnson, Walter Fuller, and Ralph Flanagan also made contributions. Pastor's singing was greatly influenced, he acknowledged, by Louis Armstrong and was always an important part of his shows. In the late 1940s Pastor also performed with Betty and Rosemary Clooney. He broke up his big band in 1959 and led a smaller group with his two sons, appearing with them in nightclubs until his retirement in 1968.

BIBLIOGRAPHY

GroveJ2

G. Simon: *The Big Bands* (New York, 1967, 4/1981), 391

C. Garrod: *Tony Pastor and his Orchestra* (Zephyrhills, FL, 1973, 3/1997) [discography]

L. Walker: *The Big Band Almanac* (Pasadena, CA, 1978, 2/1989)

MARK TUCKER/R

Pastorela. A pageant-like Christmas drama combining music, dance, and theater cultivated in Mexico and in Mexican American communities in the United States. At the core of the *pastorela* tradition is the Biblical narrative of the annunciation of the birth and adoration of the Christ child, retold in the folk play *Los pastores* (the Shepherds), which itself is based on a medieval script credited to St. Francis of Assisi in 1223. The *pastorela* focuses on the experiences of a group of shepherds who fend off devils and other evils as they persevere on their journey to Bethlehem, the site of the nativity.

When the 16th-century colonizers and missionaries first brought the shepherd plays to New Spain, indigenous peoples accustomed to their own musical-religious dramas adopted and adapted them, using the dramas as frames for the preservation of select indigenous customs. As variant practices emerged, significant differences between indigenous and mestizo choreographic customs, musical assignments, and costumes developed. A wide array of special and distinctive masks exist for each of the stock characters, which typically include the Archangel Michael, Joseph, Mary, the infant Jesus, a hermit, a group of shepherds who include Bato and his wife Gila, and Lucifer (Luzbel) and other devils.

Mexican and American versions of the *pastorelas* often preserve archaic customs of Hispanic speech and song. Colonial-era *pastorelas* included *villancicos* and *tonadas* set to Golden Age verse that have been handed down by word of mouth over the centuries. Copies of written scripts and music for historic versions are scarce, but Gaspar Fernandes's *La adoración de los Santos Reyes a Jesu Christo* (1833) records a popular version of the nativity story performed in Latin America and Spain dating from the 18th century.

Although the *pastorela* became a treasured tradition throughout Mexico and in Mexican American communities in the United States, its performance, particularly in urban areas, began to decline in the mid-20th century. A resurgence of enthusiasm in folkloric traditions in the wake of the new folk movement, along with new attention from theaters, helped spur renewed interest in the *pastorela* in the 1970s. In San Juan Bautista, California, Luis Valdez, the founding director of El Teatro

Campesino, began offering a modern staged version of the *pastorela* in 1971. His version, told through the eyes of a young daughter of farm laborers, was re-created for a PBS film production in 1991 starring Linda Ronstadt, Paul Rodriguez, and Cheech Marin. Theaters in other US cities with sizeable Hispanic populations, particularly in the American Southwest, followed with their own adaptations. In 2007 the *pastorela* of the Borderlands Theater in Tucson, Arizona, opened with a skit ridiculing thinly veiled immigration battles in the debate over whether the Mexican flag should fly alongside the US flag at the Arizona-Sonora Desert Museum. The show also incorporated songs by the Beatles as well as Lalo Guerrero, and featured an accordion-based dance band led by Native American *waila* musicians.

Beyond its religious purpose, the *pastorela* carries special meaning in the Americas. It offers participants a frame for defining and reinforcing community, as well as a means to renew and reinterpret Hispanic inheritance.

BIBLIOGRAPHY

J. Romero Salinas: *La pastorela mexicana: origen y evolución* (Mexico City, 1984)

C. Shelton: *Los Pastores* (San Antonio, 1990)

R. Flores: *Los Pastores: History and Performance in the Mexican Shepherd's Play of South Texas* (Washington, DC, 1995)

N. Kanellos: *Noche Buena: Hispanic American Christmas Stories* (New York, 2000)

T. Knighton and A. Torrente: *Devotional Music in the Iberian World, 1450–1800* (New York, 2007)

M. Herrera-Sobek: "Luiz Valdez's La Pastorela, the Shepherd's Play: Tradition, Hybridity and Transformation," *Mexican American Religions*, ed. G. Espinoza and M.T. Garcia (Durham, NC, 2008), 325–37

"Celebrating Los Pastores in San Antonio, Texas: Photographs from the Mary Ann Smothers Bruni Collection," <http://www.lib.utexas.edu/benson/lospastores/index.html> (2013)

"La Pastorela," <http://hidvl.nyu.edu/video/000539578.html> (2013)

JANET L. STURMAN

Pastorius, Jaco [John Francis] (*b* Norristown, PA, 1 Dec 1951; *d* Fort Lauderdale, FL, 12 Sept 1987). Bass guitarist. He grew up in Fort Lauderdale and as a teenager accompanied rhythm-and-blues and pop artists, including the Temptations and the Supremes. In 1975 he worked with Pat Metheny in Boston, and the following year he attracted widespread notice with his performances on the album *Heavy Weather* (Col.) by Weather Report, with whom he had a long association. From that time he was much in demand as a bass player and producer in a wide variety of settings, which included performances on a number of albums by Joni Mitchell in the late 1970s. From 1980 to about 1983 he toured with his own group, Word of Mouth. He died as a result of injuries sustained during a brawl at the Midnight Club in Fort Lauderdale.

Unlike many jazz and rock bass guitarists, Pastorius used a fretless instrument, and he played with immaculate intonation and melodic clarity, as heard on "Donna Lee" (from his album *Jaco Pastorius*, Epic, *c*1975). Although sometimes faulted for his flamboyant stage personality and eclecticism, he won the admiration of jazz and rock bass players for his fleet technique, which incorporated among other features an unprecedented facility for producing artificial harmonics on the instrument ("Portrait of Tracy," from *Jaco Pastorius*) and the imaginative fusion of styles in his solos. In his own groups, he often preferred to omit chordal instruments from the line-up, thereby leaving space for his own chords and those he implied in his imaginative lines (for example, the title track from *Invitation*, WB, 1982). Stanley Clarke should be credited with pioneering a new melodic role for the electric bass guitar in jazz fusion, but Pastorius soon proved to be the greater player, pursuing creative new paths as Clarke settled into a lightweight fusion style. Pastorius's performances set the standard for this style of bass playing.

BIBLIOGRAPHY

N. Tesser: "Jaco Pastorius: the Florida Flash," *DB*, xliv/2 (1977), 12–13, 44 [incl. discography]

D. Roerich: "Jaco Pastorius: the Musician Interviewed," *Musician*, no.26 (1980), 38–42

C. Silvert: "Jaco Pastorius: the Word is Out," *DB*, xlviii/12 (1981), 17–19, 71

J. Mitchell: "Jaco," *The Jazz Musician*, ed. M. Rowland and T. Scherman (New York, 1994), 191–200

B. Milkowski: *Jaco: the Extraordinary and Tragic Life of Jaco Pastorius, "the World's Greatest Bass Player"* (San Francisco, 1995/R)

L.A. Wayte: *Bitches Brood: the Progeny of Miles Davis's* Bitches Brew *and the Sound of Jazz-rock* (diss., UCLA, 2007)

J. BRADFORD ROBINSON/BARRY KERNFELD/R

Patchwork. A melody composed of multiple short segments borrowed from two or more existing melodies, sometimes elided through paraphrase or linked by new material. The term also refers to the technique of creating such a melody or to a piece that uses such a melody. It is borrowed from quilting and evokes an image of stitching together numerous fragments to form a new pattern. Patchwork differs from medley in using melodic fragments or phrases rather than whole tunes, resulting in a new melody that has its own integrity but contains more than one QUOTATION; its focus on creating a linear melody differs from the often polyphonic juxtapositions of COLLAGE.

Like patchwork quilts, patchwork melodies are a typically American form. Tin Pan Alley songwriters such as Charles K. Harris, Paul Dresser, Harry Von Tilzer, George M. Cohan, and Irving Berlin used the technique: the verse of Cohan's "The Yankee Doodle Boy" (1904), for example, interweaves quotations from "Yankee Doodle," "Dixie," "The Girl I Left Behind Me," and "The Star-Spangled Banner" with some original material in ragtime style. Many patchwork songs, including "The Yankee Doodle Boy," are on patriotic subjects, while others, such as Harris's "Songs of Yesterday" (1916) and Berlin's "Alexander's Bag-pipe Band" (1912), are about making music; the references to a single genre of songs, whether patriotic or popular, reinforce the meaning of the text through association in an effect similar to stylistic ALLUSION. Charles Ives used patchwork in several of his art songs, including "The Last Reader" and "Hymn" (based on hymn tunes), "The Things Our Fathers Loved" and "Old Home Day" (popular songs), and "In Flanders Fields" and "He Is There!" (patriotic songs). He also composed a few instrumental patchworks, such as the first movement of *Three Places in New England*.

Rare in the mid-20th century, patchwork became current again with the introduction of SAMPLING AND SEQUENCING, as producers of HIP HOP and other genres linked elements of two or more existing songs to create a new verse or chorus. John Oswald's album *Plexure* (Avant, 1993) is an extreme case, with several thousand samples used in only 22 minutes. A master of patchwork is DJ Earworm (Jordan Roseman), who has created songs that consist entirely of snippets of vocal lines from existing recordings over a sampled accompaniment, a process also called quilt-pop. Prime examples include the MASH-UP tracks he creates annually; titled United State of Pop, each of these contains a patchwork of segments drawn from the top 25 pop songs of the year according to *Billboard* magazine, accompanied by a music video that is also a patchwork of music videos for these songs.

BIBLIOGRAPHY

J.P. Burkholder: *All Made of Tunes: Charles Ives and the Uses of Musical Borrowing* (New Haven, 1995)

A. Houtchens and J.P. Stout: "'Scarce Heard amidst the Guns Below': Intertextuality and Meaning in Charles Ives's War Songs," *JM*, xv/ Winter (1997), 66–97

<www.djearworm.com> (2013)

For further bibliography *see* BORROWING.

J. PETER BURKHOLDER

Patent notes. Notes used in shape-note notation; *see* SHAPE-NOTE HYMNODY.

Patinkin, Mandy [Mandel Bruce] (*b* Chicago, IL, 30 Nov 1952). Actor and singer. He attended the University of Kansas and later graduated from the Drama Division of the Juilliard School. In 1975 Joseph Papp of the New York Shakespeare Festival gave him his first break, a Broadway role in *Trelawny of the "Wells"* at Lincoln Center. Patinkin created the roles of Che Guevara in Andrew Lloyd Webber's *Evita* (1979) and George in Stephen Sondheim's *Sunday in the Park with George* (1984). For the former, he won a Tony Award and for the latter a nomination. He returned to Broadway to perform the hunchbacked uncle, Archibald Craven, in *The Secret Garden* (1991) and Burrs in Michael LaChiusa's *The Wild Party* (2000), for which he earned a Tony Award nomination. As a singer, Patinkin is best known for his expressive performances and distinctive sound as a falsetto tenor. He has released seven solo albums and has appeared in several other recordings. Touring the United States, Australia, and New Zealand since 1989, Patinkin has expanded his concert repertoire to include three different solo shows, *Dress Casual, Celebrating Sondheim*, and *Mamaloshen*, and one with Patti LuPone, *An Evening with Patti LuPone and Mandy Patinkin*. He has also performed extensively on the small and silver screens. For his portrayal of Dr. Jeffrey Geiger in the 1994–5 season of the CBS series *Chicago Hope*, Patinkin received an Emmy Award and a Golden Globe nomination. He starred as Jason Gideon in the CBS series *Criminal Minds* (2005–7) and as Saul Berenson

in the Showtime series *Homeland* (2011–). His film roles include Inigo Montoya in *The Princess Bride* (1987), Avigdor in *Yentl* (1983), and Detective Francisco in *Alien Nation* (1988).

BIBLIOGRAPHY

R. Tichler and B.J. Kaplan: *Actors at Work* (New York, 2007), 104–26

LARA E. HOUSEZ

Patitucci, John (James) (*b* Brooklyn, NY, 22 Dec 1959). Electric and acoustic bass player. He learned electric bass as a child and studied classical bass at both San Francisco State and Long Beach State universities. He is well known for his technical prowess and command of both instruments. He gained recognition as a top Los Angeles studio musician and moved to high profile stints with Chick Corea's Elektric and Akoustic bands in the 1980s and 90s. He has recorded numerous albums as leader (first with GRP and then with Concord), won Grammy awards for playing and composing, and explored classically themed composition and performance opportunities. Patitucci's studio credits include work with Herbie Hancock, Bon Jovi, Dizzy Gillespie, Queen Latifah, George Benson, and Sting. A NARAS Most Valuable Player award winner in 1986, he garnered multiple Best Electric Bassist awards from both *Guitar Player* and *Bass Player* readers' polls in the 1990s. His albums range from his self-titled debut (1988), which topped the *Billboard* Jazz chart, to the acclaimed releases *Communion* (2001) and *Songs, Stories & Spirituals* (2003). Patitucci has also recorded and performed as a sideman, with such jazz musicians as Wayne Shorter, Wynton Marsalis, and Joshua Redman; pop and Brazilian musicians including Aaron Neville, Natalie Cole, Airto Moreira, and João Bosco; and the film composers Jerry Goldsmith, John Williams, and Mark Isham. He also boasts teaching credits with the Thelonious Monk Institute of Jazz, the Betty Carter Jazz Ahead program in Washington, DC, and the City College of New York. Patitucci has also composed chamber music.

SELECTED RECORDINGS

As leader: *John Patitucci* (1988, GRP); *Communion* (2001, Conc.); *Songs, Stories & Spirituals* (2003. Conc.); *Remembrance* (2009, Conc.)

As sideman with C. Corea: *The Chick Corea Akoustic Band* (1990, GRP); *The Chick Corea Elektric Band* (1990, GRP)

JEFFREY HOLMES

Patrick, Julian (*b* Mississippi, 1927; *d* Santa Fe, NM, 8 May 2009). Baritone. He was known for his work in opera and on the Broadway stage. Encouraged by his musical family, he performed regularly with the Apollo Boys Choir in Birmingham, Alabama. He continued his music studies at the College-Conservatory of Music in Cincinnati, but was interrupted when he was drafted to serve in the Korean War. In the early 1950s he worked with the impresario Boris Goldovsky and received his first opportunities to perform in opera. He made his Broadway debut as Achilles in *The Golden Apple* (1954) and later appeared in *Bells are Ringing, Juno*, and *Once upon a Mattress*, among other shows. As an operatic baritone, Patrick was best known for his tenure with the Seattle Opera. He also appeared at the Metropolitan Opera, Volksoper Vienna, Welsh National Opera, New York City Opera, San Francisco Opera, Chicago Lyric Opera, Houston Grand Opera, and Dallas Opera, among others. Among the roles he created was George in Carlisle Floyd's *Of Mice and Men* (1969).

BIBLIOGRAPHY

Obituaries: *Seattle Times* (16 May 2009); *New York Times* (31 May 2009)

JONAS WESTOVER

Patriotic music. Music that expresses devotion to the nation. In the United States, love of country has inspired a wide range of musical works, including concert music, hymns, marches, and, most especially, songs, celebrating their authors' vision of the nation and inviting citizens to participate. Such visions may tap generally accepted ideological themes or attempt to reshape American identity, negotiating symbolic meaning or giving voice to new ideas or peoples. Although often inspired by times of national crisis, especially war, patriotic songs are less born of the moment than made and remade over decades by historical circumstance and national trends that draw the national imagination. Competitions to solicit patriotic songs rarely succeed; rather, inspiration and circumstance cohere to create famous or influential patriotic tunes (e.g., "The Star-Spangled Banner," see below). Once established, patriotic music can become a site for rehearsal, reinterpretation, and even protest by individual performers or as mass singing. Patriotic songs often figure in social rituals—military pageantry, funerals, concerts, legislative sessions, graduations, and so on— and their performance traditions and even musical details may shift over time in both new arrangements and the oral tradition.

1. Up to the Civil War. 2. After 1865.

1. UP TO THE CIVIL WAR. The resistance of the American colonists to the British Stamp Act (1765) inspired songs expressing solidarity with fellow colonists. Among the most widely circulated was the "Liberty Song" (published 1768), which declared that "In freedom we're born, and in freedom we'll live." John Dickinson, an ardent colonial statesman, wrote the words to an English tune (a tradition known as broadside ballad), and this song, together with similar ones published in newspapers, magazines, almanacs, and sheet music, stimulated the revolutionary spirit.

William Billings, a Boston composer and patriot, first published the anthem "Chester" in 1770; its text (likely by Billings himself) asserts the fearlessness of the American colonists and New England's divine protection. Additional stanzas from 1778, celebrate the prowess of the colonial militia, further strengthening the tune's function as an anthem of the Revolution. It was second in popularity only to "Yankee Doodle," a song that survives in the popular imagination. Its origins are not precisely known, but its earliest written reference appears in the libretto (published in New York in 1767) of *The Disappointment*, an American comic opera; in

1768 a newspaper reported that when the British warships arrived in Boston "the Yankee Doodle song was the Capital Piece in their Band of Music." The British used the tune derisively, but the young Americans made it their patriotic song and are believed to have played it at Cornwallis's surrender at Yorktown in 1781. The word "Yankee" refers to a New Englander; "doodle" originally referred to a "fool" or "simpleton" most likely, but became a point of resistance and pride. Lyrics varied, but were often humorous and jaunty (the verse containing the rhyme "pony" and "macaroni" did not appear until 1842). (*See* REVOLUTIONARY WAR, THE.)

The words of "The Star-Spangled Banner" were written in September 1814 by Georgetown lawyer Francis Scott Key, who wrote lyrics to a popular melody (to which he had previously composed separate lyrics nine years earlier). The melody was composed in England *c*1770 by organist and composer John Stafford Smith to set lyrics beginning "To Anacreon in Heaven" and known as "The Anacreontic Song." It was sung by the club president of a gentlemen's amateur musical club in London known as the Anacreontic Society. The tune inspired newly written lyrics from many American composers, including Robert Treat Paine, whose "Adams and Liberty, or The Boston Patriotic Song" (1798) helped spread further awareness of the melody. Other American lyrics fall into traditional pub drinking song, by which reputation the Anacreontic Society's anthem is less appropriately known. Key's 1814 lyrics were originally circulated via broadside and entitled "The Defence of Ft. M'Henry." The words "the star-spangled banner" occur near the end of each stanza, and the present title may have been suggested by a sheet music publisher. The song accompanied flag-raising ceremonies during the Civil War, and was at times claimed by both sides in the conflict, and gradually became the sonic accompaniment for the Union flag, particularly because of its lyric. The song became the official flag-raising anthem of the US Navy in 1898, and of the entire military in 1916 by order of President Woodrow Wilson. In 1918 the National Society of the United States Daughters of 1812 embraced the cause of making it the US national anthem. And with the support of Maryland Congressman J. Charles Linthicum a bill making "The Star-Spangled Banner" the US national anthem made its way slowly through Congress, before being signed into law by President Herbert Hoover in 1931.

Since its creation, the anthem has undergone musical transformation, both gentle and provocative. As national anthem a typical performance is slower than the original tune, which celebrated military victory, using dotted rhythms to restrain the tempo. Jimi Hendrix's 1969 Woodstock rendition, however, adds psychedelic pictorialisms that depict "rocket's red glare" and "bombs bursting in air" and further interpolates the bugle call "Taps," apparently offering a critique of America's war in Vietnam and race riots at home, while affirming the nation. Similarly personal renditions have been made famous by Jose Feliciano, Marvin Gaye, Whitney Houston, and others. No single official version of the anthem has been named, allowing the song to give voice to

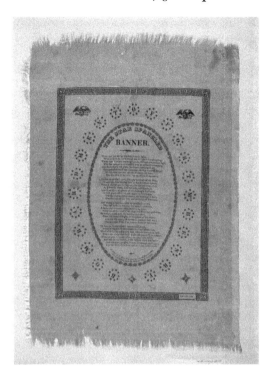

"The Star Spangled Banner," by Francis Scott Key, printed on silk to commemorate the bombardment of Fort McHenry, 1814. (Library of Congress, Rare Book and Special Collections Division)

American citizenship in all its diversity. (*See also* WAR OF 1812, THE.)

During the undeclared naval war with France in 1798 "Hail Columbia!" was written by Joseph Hopkinson to the melody of Philip Phile's *The President's March,* originally written for George Washington's inauguration. It was used frequently as a US national anthem until 1931. The words of "America" or "My Country, 'Tis of Thee" were written in 1831 by a young clergyman, Samuel Francis Smith (1808–95), who had been asked to write English texts to certain German music. He chose one German hymn, not recognizing that its melody was that of the British anthem "God Save the King," and promptly wrote the words of "America" at one sitting. Smith's words were sung on 4 July 1831 under the title "Celebration of American Independence" in Boston. The poem originally had five stanzas; the third—calling the British "tyrants"—is not typically sung today. "America" is now also considered a hymn, partly because of the final stanza that begins "Our fathers' God! to Thee" and ends "Great God, our King!"

"Hail to the Chief" has been played for many years to announce the arrival, or to acknowledge the presence, of the President of the United States; the first presidential inauguration at which the march was played was President Martin Van Buren's on 4 March 1837. The words are by Sir Walter Scott and first appeared in his poem *The Lady of the Lake* (1810), written in honor of a favorite chief of the highlanders of Scotland. The music is usually ascribed to "Mr. Sanderson," apparently

the English songwriter James Sanderson; however, the earliest printings (about 1812) are American.

There has been controversy as to whether "Columbia, the Gem of the Ocean" is an American song or an adaptation of the British "Britannia, the Pride of the Ocean." However, the American song was copyrighted in the United States in 1843 under the title "Columbia the Land of the Brave," "Columbia" being a frequently used name for the United States during its early history, as a reference to Christopher Columbus's discovery. The song was another alternative national anthem. No British printing is known until 1852, and this bears the legend "Melody collected...abroad." The song is also known in both the United States and England as "The Red, White, and Blue," after the colors of the flags of both countries. David T. Shaw, a singer, and Thomas à Beckett, a musician and actor, separately claimed authorship of the American version.

Many strongly patriotic songs were composed and sung during the American CIVIL WAR. After Fort Sumter had been fired on in April 1861, "Glory Hallelujah" was played publicly in May at a flag-raising ceremony for the training of Northern recruits near Boston, and contemporary newspapers reported that troops sang the song as they marched in Boston in July. One magazine that month claimed it was a "people's tune" and that "one can hardly walk on the streets for five minutes without hearing it whistled or hummed." Carrying the lyrics "Canaan's Happy Shore" or "Brothers, will you meet me?" the tune was written around 1856 by William Steffe. Julia Ward Howe's poem "Battle Hymn of the Republic" was written to this music in or near Washington in November 1861. Howe had heard soldiers singing the song and was asked to provide a worthier text. A pioneer for women's rights, she said "My poem did some service in the Civil War. I wish very much that it may do good service in the peace."

"Dixie" is attributed to Dan Emmett in 1859 as a blackface minstrel number, but it was performed only intermittently and without much success until it was sung without authorization in New Orleans in April 1860; it created such excitement that it was repeated 13 times that month, and unauthorized sheet music editions were published in New Orleans. The song would become the unofficial national anthem of the Confederacy, but Northern publishers also printed it before, during, and after the Civil War. Only a few days before his assassination President Abraham Lincoln proclaimed "Dixie" a national song and asked a serenading band at the White House to play it. A contemporary explanation of the word "Dixie" is given in a program of Bryant's Minstrels dated February 1861: "As many inquiries have been made in regard to the meaning of 'Dixie Land,' and as to its location, it may be well to remark that, with the Southern Negroes, Dixie Land is but another name for home." (*See* CONFEDERATE MUSIC.)

Two other patriotic songs of the Civil War are George F. Root's "The Battle Cry of Freedom" and "Tramp! Tramp! Tramp!" President Lincoln wrote to Root: "You have done more than a hundred generals and a thousand orators." Another Civil War song is the rousing

"When Johnny Comes Marching Home," usually credited to Patrick Gilmore, though its melody is apparently of Irish origin. Stephen Foster also wrote several patriotic songs during the Civil War, including "We Are Coming, Father Abraam, 300,000 More."

2. AFTER 1865. The lofty words of "America the Beautiful," or "O beautiful for spacious skies," were inspired by Katherine Lee Bates's view from Pike's Peak in Colorado in summer 1893 and describe the splendors of the possessions given to the American people. The poem by Bates, an English professor at Wellesley College, was published on 4 July 1895, but it is not known who set it to the music of "Materna" by Samuel Augustus Ward; "Materna" had been composed in 1882 and was published a few years later. The first known printing of poem and music together was in 1910, after Ward's death.

John Philip Sousa composed his stirring march *The Stars and Stripes Forever!* on a ship from England to the United States in 1896; "I paced the deck with a mental brass band playing the march fully a hundred times during the week I was on the steamer." Sousa said "A march should make a man with a wooden leg step out," and *The Stars and Stripes Forever!* epitomized the enthusiastic optimism of a country then beginning to come into its own. In December 1987, Congress made *The Stars and Stripes Forever!* the national march of the United States.

The most famous patriotic song from WORLD WAR I, George M. Cohan's "Over There," was written in 1917, after the United States had entered the war, and was introduced by Nora Bayes at a Red Cross benefit performance. Largely for this song Cohan was awarded the Congressional Medal; as one observer commented, "there is the whole arrogance of the strength of the New World in its lines."

Irving Berlin wrote "God Bless America" in 1918 as a finale for the soldier show *Yip, Yip, Yaphank*, but he did not consider it appropriate, and the song was not performed until Kate Smith asked him for a patriotic song to introduce on the radio on Armistice Day (the earlier name for Veterans Day) 1938. Berlin altered the words slightly to change it into a peace song, and as an expression of gratitude to the country he assigned all his royalties from it to the Boy Scouts of America and Girl Scouts of America. Largely in recognition of "God Bless America," Berlin received a gold medal from President Eisenhower by act of Congress. The composer stated that he never expected it to be a great national song, as it is a prayer and lacks the nobility of an anthem; and yet some have argued that this sincere, simple, and effective song should replace "The Star-Spangled Banner" as the national anthem.

The words "Praise the Lord and pass the ammunition!" were spoken by Chaplain William Maguire on board a US Navy warship during the Japanese attack on Pearl Harbor in December 1941; they inspired the best-known American patriotic song of WORLD WAR II, written shortly afterwards by Frank Loesser.

America's involvement in the VIETNAM WAR inspired many popular songs, the majority of which expressed antiwar sentiment and disapproval of government policy, such as "Feel Like I'm Fixin' to Die Rag" (1967) by Country Joe and the Fish and "War" (1969) performed by Edwin Starr. Musical responses expressing patriotism in many different forms emerged after 9/11, including Alan Jackson's country tribute, "Where were you (when the world stopped turning)" (2001), Ani DiFranco's critique of US governmental policy, "Self Evident" (2001), and Toby Keith's militaristic "Courtesy of the Red, White and Blue (The Angry American)" (2002). The era also saw a renewed interest in earlier patriotic songs including "God Bless America" as well as Lee Greenwood's "God Bless the USA," which was originally released in 1984, but climbed the country charts again upon its re-release in 2001.

A number of patriotic songs have strong associations with the military services. The army's "The caissons go rolling along" was written in 1907 by Edmund L. Gruber, an officer in the Philippine Islands; it was occasioned by the reunion of two portions of his regiment which had been separated. The US Navy's "Anchors Aweigh" was written for the Army–Navy football game in 1906 by Alfred H. Miles and Charles A. Zimmerman, the former an undergraduate at the Naval Academy and the latter the academy bandmaster. The music of *The Marines' Hymn* is by the French composer Jacques Offenbach; it was written for the 1867 revision of his *Geneviève de Brabant*. The author of the words is unknown, and no printing of them is known until 1918. The Air Force's *The Army Air Corps Song* was written in 1939 by Robert

Original manuscript of Irving Berlin's "God Bless America," c1918. (Library of Congress, Music Division)

Crawford, a member of the music faculty at Princeton University.

Some of the most gifted American composers have contributed in various ways to the repertory of patriotic music. Charles Ives composed orchestral works with patriotic titles: *Washington's Birthday* (1909) and *The Fourth of July* (1911–13). In 1931 George and Ira Gershwin wrote a patriotic lovesong, "Of thee I sing" ("Thee" referring to the United States), and a satirical patriotic piece, "Wintergreen for President," for the musical comedy *Of Thee I Sing*, the title of which was derived from the first stanza of "America."

See also Battle music and Campaign music.

BIBLIOGRAPHY

O.G.T. Sonneck: *Report on "The Star-Spangled Banner," "Hail Columbia," "America," "Yankee Doodle"* (Washington, DC, 1909/R1972, enlarged 2/1914/R)

American War Songs (Philadelphia, 1925/R)

J. Muller: *The Star Spangled Banner: Words and Music Issued between 1814–1864* (New York, 1935, 2/1973)

H. Dichter and E. Shapiro: *Early American Sheet Music: its Lure and its Lore, 1768–1889* (New York, 1941/R)

S. Spaeth: *A History of Popular Music in America* (New York, 1948)

R.S. Hill: "The Melody of 'The Star Spangled Banner' in the United States before 1820," *Essays Honoring Lawrence C. Wroth* (Portland, ME, 1951), 151–93

E.D. Snyder: "The Biblical Background of the 'Battle Hymn of the Republic'," *New England Quarterly*, xxiv/2 (1951), 231–38

I. Silber: *Songs of the Civil War* (New York, 1960)

G. Svejda: *History of the Star Spangled Banner from 1814 to the Present* (Springfield, VA, 1969)

H. Nathan: *Dan Emmett and the Rise of Early Negro Minstrelsy* (Norman, OK, 1962/R)

J.J. Fuld: *The Book of World-Famous Music: Classical, Popular and Folk* (New York, 1966, 2/1971)

P.W. Filby and E.G. Howard: *Star-Spangled Books: Books, Sheet Music, Newspapers, Manuscripts, and Persons Associated with "The Star-Spangled Banner"* (Baltimore, MD, 1972)

V.B. Lawrence: *Music for Patriots, Politicians and Presidents* (New York, 1975)

J.A. Leo Lemay: "The American Origins of 'Yankee Doodle'," *William and Mary Quarterly*, xxxiii (1976), 435–64

R. Crawford: *The Civil War Songbook* (New York, 1977)

W. Lichtenwanger: *The Music of The Star-Spangled Banner from Ludgate Hill to Capitol Hill* (Washington, DC, 1977)

W. Lichtenwanger: "The Music of 'The Star-Spangled Banner'," *College Music Symposium*, xviii (1978), 34–81

J.A. Summit: "'I'm a Yankee Doodle Dandy?': Identity and Melody at an American Simh at Torah Celebration," *EthM*, xxxvii (1993), 41–62

A. Collins: *Songs Sung Red, White, and Blue: The Stories behind America's Best-Loved Patriotic Songs* (New York, 2003)

K. Smith: *God Bless America: Tin Pan Alley Goes to War* (Lexington, KY, 2003)

J.B. Jones: *The Songs that Fought the War: Popular Music and the Home Front, 1939–1945* (Lebanon, NH, 2006)

W. Gibbons: "'Yankee Doodle' and Nationalism, 1780–1920," *American Music*, xxvi (2008), 246–74

S.R. Kaskowitz: *As We Raise Our Voices: a Social History and Ethnography of "God Bless America"* (diss., Harvard U., 2011)

Star Spangled Banner Sheet Music Collection in *BAhs*

JAMES J. FULD/R

Patronage. Cultural life in America came of age in the 19th century just as the system of aristocratic, royal, and ecclesiastical patronage in Europe was in decline and being replaced with state support, often with a strong central authority. American musicians, in contrast, never benefited from the support of kings, nobles, or a central church. As a society, Americans have preferred a pluralistic approach to supporting creative artists that emphasizes diversity and places responsibility for constructing a living directly on the artist. Composers and musicians have had to rely on a complex web of support that includes private patrons, philanthropic foundations, and federal, state, and local governments. In addition, there remains an emphasis on sustaining oneself through the marketplace with the sales of sheet music, scores, recordings, concert tickets, and similar products.

During the Colonial period in America, the infrastructure to nurture and support composers and musicians barely existed. Helped in large part by private patrons, it evolved in the 19th century with the creation of educational opportunities, the formation of performance organizations and venues, and the development of appreciative audiences. As the new country stabilized and grew wealthy, some Americans began to engage in philanthropic activities, though they initially concentrated on social issues such as poverty and illness. By the middle of the 19th century, however, some philanthropists turned their attention towards the arts and culture. The wealthiest patrons, such as Andrew Carnegie, were able to build concert halls or finance an orchestra as Henry Lee Higginson did. Other patrons provided assistance to individual musicians and composers. For instance, many composers sought training in European conservatories because of the lack of available institutions in the United States. Some composers secured financing for their travels from wealthy patrons: Arthur Farwell received support from Thomas Mott Osborne, a wealthy industrialist from Auburn, New York, who financed his first year and a half of study in Europe.

Some patrons supported composers with the basic living necessities, such as lodging and living expenses. For example, Judge John Speed provided Anthony Heinrich with a small cabin on his estate outside of Louisville, and Mrs. Ole Bull provided Farwell a place to live in 1897. Gertrude Vanderbilt Whitney supplied Edgard Varèse with an allowance in 1921 so that he might focus on composition, and Alma Morgenthal Wertheim gave stipends to composers such as Aaron Copland and Israel Citkowitz. Betty Freeman paid annual grants to John Cage for living expenses from 1965 until his death, and financially aided Harry Partch and Paul Dresher in a similar fashion. A few patrons were able to extend this concept by forming artist retreats. Two notable ones include the Macdowell colony in Peterborough, New Hampshire, founded in 1907 by Edward and Marion MacDowell, and Yaddo in Saratoga Springs, New York, founded in 1900 by Spencer and Katrina Trask.

Other patrons created opportunities for new works to be heard, an essential component to the success of any composer. Throughout the late 19th and early 20th century, patrons hosted "at homes," in imitation of the famous French parlors and salons. Isabella Stewart Gardner held many such concerts in her home in Boston around the turn of the 20th century. The patrons of the modernist composers in the 1920s often hosted recitals in their homes in New York City, inviting an impressive list of guests who could assist composers in furthering their work. In addition to these smaller gatherings, some patrons arranged larger performance opportunities such as concerts and festivals and often commissioned works or awarded prizes in conjunction with them. For example, Carl and Ellen Stoeckel began the Norfolk Music Festival in 1900 in Litchfield, Connecticut, and commissioned works by numerous composers, including George Chadwick and Horatio Parker. In 1918 ELIZABETH SPRAGUE COOLIDGE built an auditorium near her home Pittsfield, Massachusetts, to host chamber music festivals.

Commissioning works was one of the most significant ways that individual patrons could support composers. Commissioners have ranged from those with modest means to the very wealthiest and from those who are simply interested in music to fully trained professional musicians. This last category includes patrons such as Elise Boyer Hall, who commissioned many works for the saxophone in the early 20th century, and SERGE KOUSSEVITZKY, who personally commissioned many symphonic works. Jack and Linda Hoeschler, who commissioned their first piece from Stephen Paulus in the 1980s, have since arranged for and financed the creation of around 70 works and formed the Minnesota Commissioning Club with four other couples. Other commissioning clubs formed around the country in the late 20th century, including Sound Investment, run by the Los Angeles Chamber Orchestra, and Bang on a Can's People's Commissioning Fund.

By the early 20th century, the wealthiest philanthropists found themselves inundated with requests for financial aid from individuals and organizations. The use of an organized and administered corporate structure in the form of a charitable foundation provided a buffer between supplicants and the fortunes of these men and women. Changes in tax laws in the 20th century also contributed to the formation of foundations. The Sixteenth Amendment to the US Constitution, ratified in 1913, instituted a federal income tax levied on individuals and corporations. The War Revenue Act of 1917 included a provision to allow for the deduction of charitable donations, and the Revenue Act of 1935 substantially increased the tax rate for wealthy Americans and corporations. These measures influenced some to give away portions of their wealth through philanthropy to avoid taxation. Tax-exempt foundations became the preferred method of distribution, a consequence of which has been fewer private patrons in the later 20th century and onward.

FOUNDATIONS, as defined by the Internal Revenue Code of the United States, are nonprofit corporations or charitable trusts whose primary aim is to issue grants to individuals or organizations for scientific, educational, cultural, religious, or other charitable purposes. One of the earliest foundations was the Carnegie Foundation, founded by Andrew Carnegie in 1910. Other millionaires such as the Rockefellers soon followed. Foundation support for performing arts organizations and composers was initially low but grew significantly in the 1950s and 60s.

Large foundations, such as the Carnegie, Rockefeller, and Ford Foundations, have tended to award grants to institutions rather than individuals, and music has represented a small portion of the total monies distributed. Their efforts on behalf of music have typically been directed towards larger projects such as purchasing instruments and equipment, funding commissioning programs through specific orchestras, and supporting educational and performance institutions. Numerous smaller foundations have formed over the years, however, that focus more specifically on music and on composers. These include the Elizabeth Sprague Coolidge Foundation, the Serge Koussevitzky Music Foundation, the FROMM MUSIC FOUNDATION, the John Simon Guggenheim Foundation, and the Martha Baird Rockefeller Fund for Music. (*See* KOUSSEVITZY FOUNDATIONS and MARTHA BAIRD ROCKEFELLER.) These smaller organizations concentrate on the commissioning and performance of new works, funding residencies, subsidizing the recording of new works, and sponsoring seminars, educational opportunities, and journals. Some organizations award grants to very specific populations, such as the New York Foundations for the Arts, which supports residents of New York. Others support specific genres of music such as rhythm and blues, Jewish music, and musical theater. The John Simon Guggenheim Memorial Foundation, founded in 1925, awards fellowships to scholars, scientists, and artists, allowing them to further their studies. Numerous composers have been among the recipients. Similarly, the American Academy in Rome awards the Rome Prize, which allows artists and scholars to reside at the Academy and pursue their independent projects. Since 1943, the Pulitzer Prize for Music has recognized composers for an existing musical composition; the prize serves to both acknowledge and sustain the winners. (*See* AWARDS.)

Several foundations act as agents for other foundations, private donors, and federal, state, and local governments by accepting large grants and redistributing them to individuals and organizations in the form of grants, fellowships, scholarships, commissions, awards, or prizes. The most active organizations in this respect are the American Composers Forum, the AMERICAN MUSIC CENTER, and MEET THE COMPOSER. All three organizations assist composers through programs for commissioning, performing, and recording new American music. All together, foundations have become the main source of commissioning funds for composers in America.

While patronage through individuals and, later, foundations grew along with cultural life in the United States, government support took longer. Unlike in Europe and elsewhere, the government of the United States was reluctant to enter the business of directly supporting the arts. In the 19th century, any efforts on behalf of culture were typically concerned with the visual arts, particularly the acquisition of works to adorn federal buildings. The exception for music during this period was the granting of a national charter for the establishment of a National Conservatory of Music. The first government-sponsored program came as a result of the severe economic conditions of the Depression of the 1930s. The FEDERAL MUSIC PROJECT OF THE WORKS PROGRESS ADMINISTRATION established three temporary work relief programs for artists: the Federal Art Program, the Federal Theater Program, and the Federal Music Program. Musicians were typically employed by the federal government in orchestras that performed throughout the country, especially in rural areas with limited access to performances. After World War II, serious debate over government support of the arts began. Arguments in favor of support often cited the advantage of cultural exchange programs in cementing relationships with allies, as well as the notion that federal support for the arts would enhance the perception of American cultural life in comparison to its European counterparts. Finally, some argued that art should be available to all Americans and that federal support was critical to achieving that access. Those against federal funding argued that the cost of such a program would be too high, that the arts should not be subjected to the possibility of government control and censorship, and that more pressing issues should occupy the federal government. Musicians and composers themselves were divided, largely over the issue of artistic control. After 15 years of proposals and debate, legislation was passed in 1964, creating the National Council on the Arts. The following year, the National Foundation on the Arts and Humanities was created. The Foundation includes two endowments, one for art and one for humanities, funded through Congressional appropriations.

From 1966 until 1972, the NATIONAL ENDOWMENT FOR THE ARTS awarded grants to composers through the Composer Assistance Program. These grants assisted composers with copying costs for a completed work. In 1973 the Endowment created the Composer-Librettist Fellowship. Until direct grants to individuals were discontinued in 1995, the Endowment awarded over 1000 grants to composers, including composers of large orchestral works, small ensemble pieces, and works in less conventional genres such as electronic music and sound installations. Composers in all stages of their careers have received grants and nearly every state has been represented. In addition to direct assistance to composers, the Endowment has supported performing arts organizations, some of which perform new music by American composers. Since the elimination of direct grants to individuals, funds now pass through qualified re-granting authorities such as state arts councils and organizations such as Meet the Composer and the American Music Center.

Throughout the history of the arts in the United States, commerce has played a vital role in the support of music. Sheet music publishers, record companies, radio and television broadcasters, and other commercial entities have supported the work of composers, songwriters, and musicians while also benefiting from their creative efforts. The support offered has typically been in the form of royalties to the creator, but companies have participated in the process by providing studios, instruments, marketing and sales support, or even financial support. This tinge of commerce has led some to view music as entertainment rather than art, making the role of a patron ambiguous: should an artist be able to profit from her work while receiving financial aid from a patron, foundation, or the government? On the other hand, the publishers, record companies, and others with a financial interest in the creative work become, in effect, patrons.

BIBLIOGRAPHY

R. Ericson: "Foundations—Patrons of Music," *Musical America*, 76 (1956), 14ff
L. Trompeter: "Patronage Then and Now," *Musical Courier*, 159 (1959), 3
G. Larson: *The Reluctant Patron: the United States Government and the Arts, 1953–1965* (Philadelphia, 1983)
R. Bremner: *American Philanthropy* (Chicago, 1988)
M. Cummings: *Public Money and the Muse: Essays on Government Funding for the Arts* (New York, 1991)
R. Locke and C. Barr: *Cultivating Music in America: Women Patrons and Activists since 1860* (Berkeley, CA, 1997)
T. Adam: *Philanthropy, Patronage, and Civil Society: Experiences from Germany, Great Britain, and North America* (Bloomington, IN, 2004)
L. Botstein: "Music in Times of Economic Distress," *MQ*, xc (2007), 167–75

PAULA J. BISHOP

Patsy Montana [Blevins, Ruby] (*b* Beaudry, AR, 30 Oct 1908; *d* San Jacinto, CA, 3 May 1996). Singing cowgirl and songwriter. One of the most prominent singing cowgirls of the 1930s, she performed music that demonstrated an independent model of womanhood in musical settings that romanticized the West. Her music reached a broad audience through radio, recordings, and film, and her signature tune, "I want to be a cowboy's sweetheart" (1935), featured her virtuosic yodeling and became the first song written and recorded by a female country artist to sell one million copies.

In the late 1920s Montana started her radio career as a member of the Montana Cowgirls with Lorraine McIntire and Ruth DeMondrum. Under Stuart Hamblen's tutelage, the trio performed on his program on KMIC, a radio station based in Inglewood, California. They played at other radio stations throughout California and Oregon and starred in the movie short *Lightning Express* (1932). After the ensemble disbanded, Montana sought to establish herself on a prominent radio station by securing the position as the lead singer of the Prairie Ramblers, a string band on Chicago's WLS. Montana and the Prairie Ramblers performed on various WLS programs, including *Smile-a-While* and *National Barn Dance*.

Montana and the Prairie Ramblers also recorded throughout the 1930s for the American Record Company, where A&R man Art Satherley oversaw the recording sessions and encouraged Montana to write songs that resembled her first successful single. Montana performed "I want to be a cowboy's sweetheart" in Gene Autry's film *Colorado Sunset* (1939). In the 1940s Montana left WLS and the Prairie Ramblers for a solo career on the West Coast, where she established and hosted her own radio show, *Wake Up and Smile*, on ABC. She was inducted into the Country Music Hall of Fame in 1996.

BIBLIOGRAPHY

P. Montana: "Portraits from the Most Popular Country Show on the Air, 1924–1939," *Journal of Country Music*, x/3 (1985), 33–48

P. Montana with J. Frost: *Patsy Montana: the Cowboy's Sweetheart* (Jefferson, NC, 2002)

S. Vander Wel: *I am a Honky-Tonk Girl: Country Music, Gender, and Migration* (diss., UCLA, 2008)

S. Vander Wel: "The Lavender Cowboy and 'The She Buckaroo': Gene Autry, Patsy Montana, and Depression-Era Gender Roles," *Musical Quarterly*, xcv/2-3 (Summer–Fall 2012), 207–251

STEPHANIE VANDER WEL

Patti, Adelina [Adela] **(Juana Maria)** (*b* Madrid, Spain, 19 Feb 1843; *d* Craig-y-Nos Castle, nr Brecon, Wales, 27 Sept 1919). Soprano. She was the youngest daughter of the tenor Salvatore Patti (*b* Catania, Italy, *c*1800; *d* Paris, France, 21 Aug 1869) and the soprano Caterina Chiesa Barili-Patti (*b* Rome, Italy; *d* Rome, 6 Sept 1870). She had two older sisters, both sopranos: Amalia (*b* Paris, 1831; *d* Paris, 1915), who appeared in opera and concerts in the United States from 1850 until her marriage with the pianist and impresario MAURICE STRAKOSCH; and Carlotta (*b* Florence, Italy, 30 Oct 1835; *d* Paris, 27 June 1889), who, after making her debut in 1861 at a concert in New York, sang for one season in opera at the Academy of Music and then devoted the rest of her career to concert performances in Europe and the United States.

In 1846 the Patti family left Europe for New York, where Caterina sang for a few years before retiring. Salvatore managed Italian opera at Palmo's Opera House and later at the Astor Place Opera House for several seasons, but neither venture was successful and he eventually returned to Europe. Adelina first sang in public on 22 November 1851 in a charity concert at Tripler Hall, New York. Accompanied by Strakosch and violinist Ole Bull, she toured the United States for three years as a child prodigy, and from the start it was on her earnings that the family lived. In 1857 she embarked on another tour, this time through the southern states and to the West Indies with the pianist and composer Louis Moreau Gottschalk. She made her stage debut on 24 November 1859 at the Academy of Music, New York, as Gaetano Donizetti's Lucia, having studied the role with Emanuele Muzio. The following winter, after a tour of eastern cities, she returned to the Academy for a second season.

On 14 May 1861 Patti made a spectacular European debut at Covent Garden as Amina in Vincenzo Bellini's *La sonnambula*, and for the next two decades sang exclusively in Europe with great success. During the winter of 1881–2 she returned to the United States for the first time in 20 years. Beginning this tour in New York City at the Academy of Music, she performed in concert and was accompanied by her second husband, French tenor Ernesto Nicolini, as well as by several other artists. By the end of the tour, she capitulated to demands by American audiences to hear her in fully staged opera and appeared in *La traviata*, *Il barbiere di Siviglia*, and *Faust* (sung in Italian), among other works.

For the next three winters she was engaged by J.H. Mapleson for his opera tours of the United States, appearing in New York at the Academy (where as Lady Harriet in Friedrich von Flotow's *Martha* she celebrated the 25th anniversary of her operatic debut), as well as in Philadelphia, Chicago, Cincinnati, Washington, Boston, and other cities. During these tours she received exorbitant fees; she also endorsed many commercial products. Another tour, this time managed by H.E. Abbey and announced as her farewell to the American stage, began in November 1886 and included six performances at the Metropolitan Opera in April 1887. She was back with Abbey's company in 1889–90 and again in January through May of 1892. Among many highlights of the later tour were three concerts that she gave at greatly reduced prices in Madison Square Garden in May 1892, attracting audiences numbering as high as 12,000. In 1893–4 she embarked on a tour throughout the United States—managed by Marcus Mayer—that consisted primarily of concerts. Her final American sojourn (also a concert tour) began in New York at Carnegie Hall on 2 November 1903 and ended unexpectedly early in Hot Springs, Arkansas, on 8 March 1904. The abrupt cancellation was publically attributed to fatigue on Patti's part, but was more likely because ticket sales had been disappointing for many of the concerts, some of which even had to be canceled due to low box-office receipts.

Patti also performed frequently in Latin America. Her 1886–7 tour of the United States, for instance, brought her on a side trip to Mexico City. She also toured South America exclusively in the spring and summer of 1888 and 1889, appearing at the Politeama Argentino in

Adelina Patti. (Lebrecht Music & Arts)

Buenos Aires, Argentina, and at the Teatro Solis in Montevideo, Uruguay.

In the early years of her long career, the roles that formed the staples of her repertory included Lucia, Amina, Rosina, Elvira (*I puritani*), Norina, Adina, Lady Harriet, Zerlina, Violetta, and Gilda. She later added a number of heavier parts, including Valentine (*Les Huguenots*), Charles Gounod's Marguerite and Juliet, Aida, and even Carmen (one of the very few mistakes that she made). She was a competent actress, particularly in comedy, while the purity of tone and flexibility of voice that she retained for well over half a century were proof of the exemplary way in which she used and nurtured her extraordinary gifts.

BIBLIOGRAPHY

NAW

T. de Grave: *Le biographie d'Adelina Patti* (Paris, 1865)

M. Strakosch: *Souvenirs d'un impresario* (Paris, 1866, 2/1887)

L. Lauw: *Fourteen Years with Adelina Patti* (New York, 1884/*R*1977)

J.H. Mapleson: *The Mapleson Memoirs* (London, 1888; ed. H. Rosenthal, 1966)

M. Maretzek: *Sharps and Flats* (New York, 1890/*R*1968)

L. Arditi: *My Reminiscences* (New York, 1896/*R*1977)

H. Klein: *The Reign of Patti* (New York, 1920/*R*1978)

H. Pleasants: *The Great Singers* (New York, 1966), 204

J.F. Cone: *Adelina Patti: Queen of Hearts* (Portland, OR, 1993)

H. Poriss: "She Came, She Sang…She Conquered? Adelina Patti in New York," *European Music and Musicians in New York City, 1840–1900*, ed. J. Graziano (Rochester, NY, 2006), 218–34

ELIZABETH FORBES/HILARY PORISS

Pattison, John Nelson (*b* Niagara Falls, NY, 22 Oct 1845; *d* New York, NY, 27 July 1905). Pianist and composer. He showed musical talent at an early age, and by age 15 had attracted attention as a performer. He studied in Germany with prominent teachers, including Sigismond Thalberg, Adolph von Henselt, Hans von Bülow, Karl August Haupt, Moritz Hauptmann, Carl Reinecke, Julius Stern, and Adolf Bernhard Marx, and also had lessons with Liszt. After returning to the United States briefly, he went back to Germany for a concert tour, performing as well in Paris and cities in Italy. In 1862 he settled in New York into a teaching career, and in the following years performed in more than 800 concerts. He toured with the Parepa-Rosa Opera Company, Clara Louise Kellogg, Emma Albani and Pauline Lucca, performed with the New York and Brooklyn Philharmonic Societies, and gave a striking series of recitals at the Centennial Exposition in 1876. Pattison initiated a music therapy project in 1878, involving 40 members of D.L. Downing's Ninth Regiment Band and several singers in a study at Blackwell's Island lunatic asylum in New York City. An 1869 marriage to Adelaide Mangam failed, amid claims of "ill treatment," drunkenness, and bigamy. His works include *Niagara*, a symphony for orchestra and military band, a concert overture, a piano concerto, songs, and many piano pieces.

BIBLIOGRAPHY

Grove2, Amer. suppl.

"Pattison, John Nelson," *Cyclopedia of Music and Musicians*, ed. John Denison Champlin, Jr. (New York, 1899), III, 96

"Pattison, John Nelson," *The American History and Encyclopedia of Music: Musical Biographies*, ed. W. L. Hubbard (Toledo, 1908), II, 139

W.B. Davis: "Music Therapy in 19th Century America," *Journal of Music Therapy*, xxiv/2 (1987), 76–87

JOHN C. SCHMIDT

Pattison, Lee (*b* Centralia [now Wisconsin Rapids], WI, 22 July 1890; *d* Claremont, CA, 22 Dec 1966). Pianist. He studied piano with CARL BAERMANN and composition with GEORGE WHITEFIELD CHADWICK at the New England Conservatory, graduating in 1910, and then studied with ARTUR SCHNABEL in Berlin. In 1916 he formed a two-piano team with GUY MAIER, and the two performed together regularly from 1919 to 1931. A number of composers, including John Alden Carpenter, Edward Burlingame Hill, and Leo Sowerby, dedicated works to them. From 1932 until 1937 he was head of the piano department at Sarah Lawrence College; he was also on the summer school faculty of the Juilliard School and the New England Conservatory. He composed several pieces for piano, including *Florentine Sketches* and *Told in the Hills*.

R. ALLEN LOTT

Patton, Charley (*b* nr Bolton, MS, *c*1891; *d* Indianola, MS, 28 April 1934). Blues singer and guitarist. In 1912 he moved to the Dockery plantation near Drew, Mississippi, where he performed with Tommy Johnson, Willie Brown, and other Mississippi blues singers who exchanged songs and techniques. He claimed to have been a lay preacher and recorded a few gospel items, including "Prayer of Death" (1929). A professional musician and songster, Patton was noted for his clowning and entertaining, but the majority of his recordings, made from 1929 until his death, present a more serious artist. Generally regarded as the archetypal Mississippi African American blues singer, he traveled as far as Milwaukee to play, and his fame extended far beyond the Mississippi area. He had a rasping voice of the "heavy" kind admired by many other singers. "Pony Blues" (1929, Para.), included in his first recording session, was his most celebrated blues item, although "Down the Dirt Road" (1929, Para.) and "Moon Going Down" (1930, Para.), the latter with Willie Brown playing the flat-pick guitar in accompaniment, are perhaps his best recorded blues. The themes of his blues were often autobiographical, although sometimes the stanzas were confused; "High Sheriff Blues" (1934, Voc.) is among the more consistent narratives. Patton's recordings are somber, often with percussive accompaniment on a guitar in open G tuning. He also performed ballads, including "Elder Greene Blues" and "Frankie and Albert" (both 1929, Para.), ragtime or dance-songs such as the spirited "A Spoonful Blues" (1929, Para.), and spirituals from the songster repertory. His blues influenced Bukka White, Howlin' Wolf, and many later singers.

BIBLIOGRAPHY

SouthernB

P. Oliver: *The Story of the Blues* (London, 1969/*R*)

J. Fahey: *Charley Patton* (London, 1970)

G. Oakley: *The Devil's Music: a History of the Blues* (London, 1976)

J.T. Titon: *Early Downhome Blues: a Musical and Cultural Analysis* (Urbana, IL, 1977)

R. Sacre, ed.: *The Voice of the Delta: Charley Patton and the Mississippi Blues Tradition* (Liège, 1987)

S. Calt and G. Wardlow: *King of the Delta Blues: the Life and Music of Charlie Patton* (Newton, NJ, 1988)

E. Wald: "Charley Patton, King of the Delta Blues: a Look under the Mask," *Sing Out!*, xlvi/2 (2002), 46–52

PAUL OLIVER/R

Patton, Willard (*b* Milford, ME, 26 May 1853; *d* Minneapolis, MN, 12 Dec 1924). Singer, teacher, conductor, and composer. Patton studied voice under F.S. Davenport, J. Whitney, and W.W. Davis. He later received instruction from ACHILLE ERRANI and DUDLEY BUCK in New York. From 1877 to 1882 he gave concerts and sang tenor in oratorios, as well as being a chorus trainer in Maine from 1875. He organized the Handel Association in Bangor, Maine (1877). After touring the Midwest in 1883, he moved to Minneapolis to be a concert singer and teacher. From 1886 to 1889 he served as vocal instructor at Hamline University. In 1890 he founded the Philharmonic Club, which he conducted until 1894. One of the organizers of the Minnesota State Music Teachers Association, he twice served as president. His compositions include the operettas *The Gallant Garroter* (1882) and *La Fianza* (1889); the oratorio *Isaiah* (1897); two musical epics, *The Star of Empire* (1900) and *Foot-Stones of a Nation* (1906); the opera *Pocahontas* (1911); and a symphonic fantasy, *The Spirit of '61* (1915), as well as the cantatas *The Call of Spring* and *Summer* (both for female ensemble) and *The Atonement*, a Te Deum in D-flat, and several choruses and songs.

BIBLIOGRAPHY

Baker4Grove3, Amer. suppl.

E. E. Hipsher: *American Opera and its Composers* (Philadelphia, 1927/R)

W.S. Pratt, ed: *The New Encyclopedia of Music and Musicians* (New York, 1929)

JOSEPH A. BOMBERGER

Patty, Sandi [Sandra Faye] [Patti, Sandi] (*b* Oklahoma City, OK, 12 July 1956). Singer-songwriter. Born into a family of church musicians belonging to a restorationist Church of God congregation, she began singing and taking piano lessons as a young child and soon joined her family's group, the Ron Patty Family. She finished her undergraduate degree in music education at Anderson College in Anderson, Indiana, which was also home to the gospel group the Gaither Vocal Band. In the 1970s Patty recorded vocals for commercial jingles at Bill Gaither's studio and in the early 1980s sang backup with his band. In 1978 her self-produced album *For my Friends* caught the attention of the Christian media company Zondervan and brought Patty her first major recording contract. In 1986 her rendition of the US national anthem accompanied a video montage of the Liberty Weekend celebration on ABC television, leading to national recognition. Patty has since sung at several presidential inaugurations. Her divorce in 1990 scandalized the Christian music fan community and years later continued to evoke criticism, demonstrating the complicated moral code enforced by the Christian music industry and its fans.

Patty is known for her four-octave range, which has earned her the nickname the Voice, and for songs that feature dramatic symphonic accompaniment. Throughout her career she has drawn on Southern gospel and praise and worship traditions, sometimes described by the industry as inspirational music. While other Christian pop stars have sought to cross over into the secular marketplace, Patty has continued to sing only unambiguously Christian music, asserting her commitment to her music as ministry. By the early 2010s she had released more than 30 albums, and her songs had appeared on many Christian compilations. She had won numerous awards including five Grammys, a number of Dove Awards, and four Billboard Music Awards. She was inducted into the Gospel Music Hall of Fame in 2004. For more information see D. Cusic: *Sandi Patti: the Voice of Gospel* (New York 1988).

SELECTED RECORDINGS

Sandi's Song (Singspiration, 1979); *Love Overflowing* (Impact, 1981); *Hymns Just for You* (Benson, 1985); *Morning like this* (Word, 1986); *Another Time, Another Place* (Word, 1990); *Le voyage* (Word, 1993); *O Holy Night* (Word, 1995); *Artist of my Soul* (Word, 1997); *Libertad de mas* (Word, 1999); *All the Best…Live!* (Epic, 2001); *The Edge of the Divine* (Stylos, 2010)

ANNA NEKOLA

Patwin. Native American group in California whose music resembles that of the WINTUN.

Paukert, Karel (*b* Skuteč, Czechoslovakia [Czech Republic], 1 Jan 1935). Organist of Czechoslovakian birth; naturalized American. He studied oboe and organ at the Prague Conservatory and at the Royal Conservatory of Ghent, Belgium. His organ teachers included Jan Bedřich Krajs and Gabriel Verschraegen. He obtained permission to leave Czechoslovakia to become principal oboist with the Iceland National SO (1961) and later deputy organist of St. Bavon Cathedral in Ghent. After gaining notice at an international improvisation competition in Haarlem, the Netherlands, Paukert came to the United States (where he became a citizen in 1972) and taught at Washington University, St. Louis; Northwestern University, Evanston, Illinois; the Cleveland Institute of Music; and the Oberlin Conservatory of Music. In addition to his teaching, he directed the music program at St. Luke's Episcopal Church in Evanston. In 1974 he became curator of musical arts at the Cleveland Museum of Art, where he played more than 800 recitals, commissioned music from local and international composers, mounted the Aki Festival of New Music, enlarged the museum's keyboard collection, and made recordings on the McMyler Memorial Organ before retiring in 2005. Since 1979, he has directed the music program at St. Paul's Episcopal Church in Cleveland Heights. Paukert has made several recordings on the Azica label.

ALLISON A. ALCORN

Paul, Les [Polfuss, Lester William] (*b* Waukesha, WI, 9 June 1915; *d* White Plains, NY, 12 Aug 2009). Guitarist and guitar maker. He was largely self-taught on guitar and played with country-music groups before performing on his own radio show in Chicago during the 1930s. A growing interest in jazz led to the formation of the Les Paul Trio with the singer Jimmy Atkins and the bass player Ernie Newton; after moving to New York in the late 1930s, the group appeared with Fred Waring and his Pennsylvanians for five years and later performed with Bing Crosby and the Andrews Sisters. Paul's childhood fascination with radio technology led to his early adoption of electric amplification and the propensity for technical experimentation throughout his career. He was actively involved in testing and adapting hollow- and solid-body electric guitars with electromagnetic pickups in the 1930s and 40s, sometimes in conjunction with guitar makers. In 1941 he created a prototype instrument, known as the Log, which he fashioned from a four-foot wooden board. With Paul's input Gibson introduced the Les Paul model in 1952 with a gold-finish top; later versions of this guitar have been the favored instrument for many guitarists, especially rock musicians. In addition to exploring various techniques of multitrack recording, he invented "sound-on-sound" recording (overdubbing), the floating bridge pickup, the electrodynamic pickup, and various types of electronic transducers, innovations that made a great impact on the recording industry in general and guitarists in particular. He also created the Les Paulveriser, a machine used in performance to record sounds, play them back, and electronically modify them. He applied his inventions with some success in recordings, such as "How High the Moon" and "Vaya con Dios," made during the 1950s with his wife, the singer Mary Ford (Colleen Summers; *b* Pasadena, CA, 7 July 1924; *d* Los Angeles, CA, 30 Sept 1977). Paul's technical wizardry gave the music novelty value and also pointed the way for future recording processes. In subsequent decades Paul collaborated on recordings with the country-music guitar virtuoso Chet Atkins and the jazz guitarist Al Di Meola. He released his final album, *American Made, World Played* (Cap.) in 1995. In recognition of his contributions as a musician and inventor, he was inducted into the Rock and Roll Hall of Fame (1988) and the National Inventors Hall of Fame (2005) and awarded the National Medal of Arts (2007).

BIBLIOGRAPHY

P. Day and T. Bacon: *The Gibson Les Paul Book: a Complete History of Les Paul Guitars* (San Francisco, CA, 1993)

M.A. Shaugnessy: *Les Paul: an American Original* (New York, 1993)

Obituaries: *New York Times* (13 Aug 2009); S. Waksman, *Popular Music and Society*, xxxiii/2 (2010), 269–73

MARK TUCKER/R

Paul, Thomas (Warburton) (*b* Chicago, IL, 22 Feb 1934). Bass. He studied violin and viola as a child. After graduating from Occidental College, Los Angeles (BA 1956), he immediately began studies in violin, viola, and conducting at the Juilliard School. During military service (1957–60) he joined the US Army Chorus in Washington, DC, and this encouraged him to embark on a career as a singer. In 1961 he made his debut at Carnegie Hall in Handel's *Belshazzar*, won first prize in the Liederkranz Foundation vocal competition, and was awarded a Ford Foundation grant. From 1962 to 1971 he worked with the New York City Opera, with which he made his debut as Sparafucile in *Rigoletto*. He then joined the faculty of the Eastman School as visiting professor and became professor there in 1974 and artist-in-residence in 1993.

Paul's diverse roles with American opera companies include Pimen (*Boris Godunov*), Tiresias (*Oedipus Rex*), Ramfis (*Aida*), Seneca (*L'incoronazione di Poppea*), Sarastro (*Die Zauberflöte*), and Mephistopheles (Arrigo Boito's *Mefistofele*). His oratorio roles have also been numerous. He made his European debut with the Gächinger Kantorei Stuttgart in J.S. Bach's *St. Matthew Passion* in 1976. In 1978 he performed with Jan DeGaetani and Speculum Musicae in the world premiere of Elliott Carter's *Syringa*, a work he recorded in 1983. His recital debut took place in 1980 at Alice Tully Hall. Paul has also appeared with orchestras throughout North America and was principal bass of the Aspen Music Festival from 1971 to 1990. During the 1980s he frequently toured with the Bach Aria Group.

In 1990 Paul sang with the Boston SO in the 50th anniversary celebrations of the Tanglewood Music Center. He has recorded for such labels as Columbia, Deutsche Grammophon, Marlboro Recording Society, Nonesuch, RCA Victor, Vox, and CRI.

BIBLIOGRAPHY

R. Ericson: "About Two Basses," *New York Times* (7 Dec 1980)

P.G. Davis: "Bass: Thomas Paul, Solo," *New York Times* (10 Dec 1980)

MARY A. WISCHUSEN

Paulus, Stephen (Harrison) (*b* Summit, NJ, 24 Aug 1949). Composer. He studied piano from age ten and began composing in his early teens. At the University of Minnesota (BA 1971, MA 1974, PhD 1978) he studied composition with Paul Fetler and DOMINICK ARGENTO. He was awarded an NEA Composer Grant (1978) and a Guggenheim Fellowship (1982). He won third prize in the Kennedy Center Friedheim Award (1988, for his Concerto for Violin and Orchestra) and won the Distinguished Composer Award from the American Guild of Organists (2007–8). He has also received an honorary doctorate from Macalester College in St. Paul, Minnesota. Since 1990 Paulus has served as concert music representative of the ASCAP board of directors. In the early 2010s he was also board vice president of the American Composers Forum, formerly the Minnesota Composers Forum, which he co-founded with Libby Larsen in 1973. He has been composer-in-residence for the orchestras of Atlanta (1988–92), Minnesota (1983–7), Tucson, and Annapolis and for the Dale Warland Singers (1991–2). He has been guest composer at the Santa Fe Chamber Music Festival, the Tanglewood Festival, the Aspen Music Festival, the Oregon Bach Festival, and in the UK the Aldeburgh Festival and the Edinburgh Festival.

His prolific output—by the early 2010s he had composed more than 400 works—represents many genres, including music for orchestra, opera, chorus, chamber ensembles, solo voice, concert band, organ, and piano. His works have been commissioned by private patrons, musicians, and organizations including William Preucil, Thomas Hampson, Robert McDuffie, Håkon Hagegård, Robert Shaw, Doc Severinsen, Leo Kottke, the Cleveland Orchestra, the New York Philharmonic, Friends of Music at the Supreme Court, the Chamber Music Society of Lincoln Center, Berkshire Music Center, and the National Society of Arts and Letters.

Paulus's works have generally been tonal, melodic, and rhythmically active, and his style has been compared to that of Benjamin Britten and William Schuman. He has described his music as "colorful, anchored in tonality but not without dissonance, used sometimes in obvious, sometimes in more subtly prepared ways." Some works, such as his string quartet *Quartessence* (1990) and *Explosions* for solo piano (2007), feature angular and sometimes dissonant melodies. Paulus is also known for melodic lyricism, found particularly in his choral anthems such as "The Old Church" (2001) and "The day is done" (2006). He has explained that he has prioritized rhythm as the foundational core of his pieces. Whether fast and busy, as in his song-cycle *A Heartland Portrait* (2006), or slow and calm, as in *Hallelu! (Sing Hallelu!)* (1975), his compositions convey a compelling rhythmic energy. In his setting of poet Richard Cranshaw's *Welcome all Wonders* (2005), Paulus combines many of his typical musical characteristics by setting a rhythmically and melodically adventurous oboe part over a more declamatory, homophonic, and tonal SATB choir. He has stated his aim to write music that is paradoxically both "surprising and inevitable."

Paulus first came to national fame through his operas, four of which were commissioned and first performed by the Opera Theatre of St. Louis, Missouri. His music provides clear characterizations, as well as dramatic and lyrical expressivity, which can be heard in *The Postman Always Rings Twice* (1982), his most successful opera and the first American opera produced at the Edinburgh Festival. Colored by a lush, symphonic score, the work combines a well-structured libretto with relentless cinematic flow.

In the early 2010s Paulus was considered by some to be one of the greatest living choral composers. His choral composing career began in the late 1960s, when he worked as a church choir director, and by the early 2010s he had composed more than 250 choral works. In 1996 he became the first American composer to be commissioned to write a new carol, "Pilgrim Jesus" (1996), for the Festival of Nine Lessons and Carols at King's College, Cambridge, UK. His popular choral work "Pilgrim's Tune," adapted from the finale of his one-act opera *The Three Hermits* (1997), was performed at the funerals of the American presidents Ronald Reagan and Gerald Ford.

Many of Paulus's works reflect a deeply spiritual ideology; in particular, many of his choral anthems display a Christian perspective, and his works celebrating Christmas are among his most popular and most recorded. Yet, he has often gone beyond specific religious beliefs and engaged with broader spiritual themes. For example, the Concerto for Violin, Cello, and Orchestra, *The Veil of Illusion* (1994), inspired by Shakti Gawain's *Living in the Light*, draws the listener through a veil of materialism into a world of spiritual truth.

WORKS
(selective list)
Op: Summer, 1999; Heloise and Abelard, 2002; Hester Prynne at Death, 2004; The Star Gatherer, 2006
Orch: Spectra, 1980; Conc. for Orch, 1983; Sinfonietta, 1991; Tpt Conc., 1991; Org. Conc., 1992; Conc. in the American Style, orch, 1998; The Five Senses, narr, orch, 2003; Conc. for Org, Chorus, Orch, 2002; Erotic Spirits, S, orch, 2004; Vc Conc., 2009
Band: Over One Hundred Years, 2002; Bounce Back for Ellis, 2008
Choral: North Shore (M.D. Browne), S, Mez, Bar, SATB, orch, 1977; Jesu Carols, SATB, hp, 1985; Meditations of Li Po, SATB, 1994; Mass, SATB, str, harp, perc, org, 1999; To Be Certain of the Dawn, S, Mez, T, B, SATB, orch, 2005; God be with us, SATB, perc, pf, 2006; Stabat Mater, 2 SATB, 2009
Chbr and solo inst: Colors, brass qnt, 1974; Partita, vn, pf, 1986; American Vignettes, vc, pf, 1988; Fantasy in 3 Parts, fl, gui, 1989; Air on Seurat, vc, pf, 1992; Exotic Etudes, vn, 2 va, vc, pf, 2000
Solo vocal: 3 Elizabethan Songs, S, pf, 1973; Artsongs, T, pf, 1983; Letters from Colette, S, pf, str qt, perc, 1986; Songs of Love and Longing, S, pf, 1992; Dylan Thomas Songs, S, orch, 2009

BIBLIOGRAPHY
A. Porter: "Musical Events," *New Yorker* (25 June 1979)
M.A. Feldman: "Triple Header," *ON*, xlix/17 (1984–5), 24–6
B. Cartland: "Stephen Paulus and his 'Postman,'" *Opera Monthly*, i/10 (1989), 24–32
R.H. Kornich: *Recent American Opera: a Production Guide* (New York, 1991)
R. Markow: "Paulus: Music of the Night," *Classical Music*, xviii/3 (1995), 25 only
M. Gresham: *Choral Conversations: Selected Interviews from Chorus! Magazine* (San Carlo, CA, 1997), 73–84
B. Taylor: "An Interview with Stephen Paulus," *Choral Journal*, xxxvii/8 (1997), 17–22
B. Johnson: "New York: Stephen Paulus's 'Voices of Light,'" *Tempo*, no.218 (2001), 41–2
S.L. Kruger: *The Three Hermits: Study of an Opera by Stephen H. Paulus* (diss, U. of Oklahoma, 2003)
S. Jackson: *Stephen Paulus's First Organ Concerto (1992): an Organist's Study Guide and Rehearsal Score* (diss., Juilliard, 2004)

ELISE KIRK/ANNA NEKOLA

Paul Winter Consort. Musical ensemble. Founded in 1967 by saxophonist and composer Paul Winter (*b* Altoona, PA, 31 Aug 1939), the ensemble is one of the earliest exponents of world music. Blending African, Asian, and South American elements with jazz, the self-described "contemporary consort" uses woodwinds, strings, and percussion and also draws on the recorded voices of humpback whales, wolves, and birds. Winter's professional career began while he was a student at Northwestern University, after his jazz sextet won an international jazz festival and was signed to Columbia Records. He recorded several albums in Brazil in the mid-1960s and formed Living Music Records in 1980 as a platform for his symbiotic music and ecology-driven "Earth Music." David Darling, Eugene Friesen, Ralph Towner, Paul Halley, Oscar Castro-Neves, Glen Velez, Paul McCandless, and Paul Sullivan are among the musicians to perform with (and compose for) the consort. "Icarus" (1972, written by Towner) is perhaps its best-known individual piece. The group has won multiple Grammy Awards and additional Grammy nominations in the New Age category. In performance settings ranging from cathedrals to the Grand Canyon to impromptu environmental stages, the sound of Winter's soaring and lyrical soprano sax leads the consort through classical and folk-driven themes, both old and new. Cathedral organs, voices, strings, and world percussion produce an eclectic and inclusive musical palette.

JEFFREY HOLMES

Paur, Emil (*b* Czernowitz, Austria [now Chernivtsi, Ukraine], 29 Aug 1855; *d* Frýdek-Místek, Czechoslovakia, 7 June 1932). Austrian conductor, violinist, and composer. After early studies with his father, the director of the Vienna Musikverein, he entered the Vienna Conservatory in 1886, studying composition with Dessoff and violin with Hellmesberger. He became a member of the court orchestra in 1870, and from 1876 held conducting posts in Kassel, Königsberg, the Mannheim Hofoper (1880), and the Leipzig Stadttheater (1891). In 1893 he went to the United States, succeeding Nikisch as conductor of the Boston SO.

In 1898 Paur succeeded Seidl as music director of the New York Philharmonic Society, and in 1899 he filled Dvořák's position as director of the National Conservatory of Music in New York. He left both posts in 1902, returning first to Austria and then touring as guest conductor with many leading European orchestras. He conducted German opera at Covent Garden (1900) and in Madrid (1903) as well as in Berlin. His period as conductor of the Pittsburgh Orchestra (1904–10, succeeding the popular Victor Herbert) raised it to international standards and introduced much new European and American music, including works by Smetana, Goldmark, Rubinstein, MacDowell, and Amy Beach. Paur's own symphony, *In der Natur*, was performed in 1909. Unfortunately, his classically oriented programming (emphasizing the German Romantic repertoire) and insistence on importing European musicians led to the orchestra's demise in 1910. Upon returning to Europe, Paur succeeded Carl Muck as director of the Berlin Opera (1912) but resigned after a few months, remaining in Berlin as a concert conductor. His other compositions include the Piano Concerto in A (1909), a violin concerto, and chamber music.

BIBLIOGRAPHY

E. Kenny: "Some Letters to Emil Paur," *Notes*, viii (1950–51), 631–49

F. Dorian and J. Meibach: *A History of the Pittsburgh Symphony Orchestra* (Pittsburgh, 1987)

R.F. Schwartz: "Paur and the Pittsburgh: Requiem for an Orchestra," *American Music*, xii/2 (1994), 125–47

J.A. FULLER MAITLAND/MALCOLM MILLER/
JAMES DEAVILLE

Pavarotti, Luciano (*b* Modena, Italy, 12 Oct 1935; *d* Modena, 6 Sept 2007). Italian tenor. He sang, along with his father Fernando, in Modena's city chorus. He studied in Modena with Arrigo Pola and in Mantua with Ettore Campogalliani. In 1961, after winning the Concorso Internazionale, he made his debut at Reggio nell'Emilia as Rodolfo (*La bohème*) and quickly made an impression for his eloquent lyrical singing. In 1963 he sang Edgardo (*Lucia*) in Amsterdam and made his Covent Garden debut as Rodolfo, returning as Alfredo,

Elvino, Tonio (*La fille du régiment*), Gustavus III, Cavaradossi, Rodolfo (*Luisa Miller*), Radames, and Nemorino (1990). In 1964 he sang Idamantes at Glyndebourne; in 1965 he made his American debut at Miami, toured Australia with the Sutherland-Williams company, as Edgardo, and made his La Scala debut as Rodolfo, returning for the Duke, Vincenzo Bellini's Tebaldo, and Jules Massenet's Des Grieux. At La Scala he also sang in a remarkable performance of Giuseppe Verdi's Requiem to mark the centenary of Arturo Toscanini's birth. He first sang at San Francisco in 1967 as Rodolfo and the following year made his Metropolitan debut, again as Rodolfo, later singing Manrico, Fernand (*La favorite*), Ernani, Cavaradossi, Idomeneus, Arturo (*I puritani*), Radames, Rodolfo (*Luisa Miller*, 1991), and the Italian Singer (*Der Rosenkavalier*).

Pavarotti had a bright, incisive tenor with a typically free, open, Italianate production and penetrating high notes. He made it a practice never to sing beyond his own means; even when he tackled more dramatic roles such as Otello late in his career he never forced his fundamentally lyric tenor. Above all he had a directness of manner that went straight to his listeners' hearts. His voice and style were ideally suited to Gaetano Donizetti, the early and middle-period works of Verdi (he was particularly admired as Alfredo and Gustavus III), and to Giacomo Puccini's Rodolfo and Cavaradossi. His impassioned singing of Calaf's "Nessun dorma" (*Turandot*) turned the aria into a bestseller, though in this role and some of the other heavier parts he essayed he arguably lacked the true *spinto* power. He performed alongside all of the brightest stars of opera and also made appearances at concert halls, arenas, and stadiums throughout the United States, Asia, Australia, Europe, the Middle East, and South Africa.

Pavarotti's art is liberally preserved on disc and video, which give a true reflection of his voice and personality: no opera singer understood better than he the new power of the media. He recorded most of his major roles, some of them twice, and was one of the "Three Tenors" combination (with Plácido Domingo and José Carreras: their first concert was held in Rome in July 1990) that brought opera to an unprecedentedly wide public. His genial looks and generous, outgoing personality were ideally suited to that kind of phenomenon; indeed, it might well have not existed without his enthusiastic participation. Despite his enormous popular acclaim, Pavarotti was anxious to preserve his reputation as a serious artist, and his voice retained much of its color and vibrancy into his 60s. In 1999 he sang Cavaradossi at the Metropolitan, followed in 2001 by Radames, although by then the tone production had become noticeably more effortful. His last opera performance was Cavarodossi at the Metropolitan in 2004, and he retired, following a farewell tour, in 2005.

Pavarotti devoted himself to the development of young singers and initiated an international vocal competition in Philadelphia. In his last years he continued to audition new voices and to give singing lessons in his home. He was also known as an expert equestrian and organized a show jumping competition on the international circuit, the Pavarotti International. Coinciding with this annual event held in Modena, he staged a charity concert that brought together the top names in rock, pop, and jazz. Pavarotti was honored with countless international accolades and awards, including an appointment in 1998 as the United Nations Messenger of Peace. In 2007 his hometown of Modena renamed its opera house in his name.

BIBLIOGRAPHY

G. Gualerzi: "Luciano Pavarotti," *Opera*, xxxii (1981), 118–24

L. Pavarotti: *My Own Story* (London, 1981)

M. Mayer: *Grandissimo Pavarotti* (Garden City, NY, 1986)

L. Magiera: *Luciano Pavarotti: metodo e mito* (Milan, 1990)

J. Kesting: *Luciano Pavarotti: ein Essay über den Mythos der Tenorstimme* (Düsseldorf, 1991; eng. trans., 1996)

L. Pavarotti and W. Wright: *Pavarotti, my World* (New York, 1995)

A. Midgette: "In Search of Luciano Pavarotti," *ON*, lxiii/5 (1998), 22–30

H.H. Breslin and A. Midgette: *The King and I* (New York, 2004)

P.G. Davis: Obituary, *ON*, lxxii/5 (2007), 16–9

J. Allison, ed.: "Pavarotti in Opera," *Opera*, lix/3 (March supplement 2008), 1–49

G. Guandalini: *Luciano Pavarotti. Il trionfo della voce* (Rome, 2008)

L. Magiera: *Pavarotti visto da vicino* (Milan, 2008; eng. trans. *Pavarotti up Close*, 2008)

M. Balestrazzi: *Pavarotti dossier* (Palermo, 2009)

ALAN BLYTH, STANLEY SADIE/NICOLA BADOLATO/R

Pavement. Rock band. Formed as a studio noise experiment by two school friends, the singer and guitarist Stephen Malkmus (*b* Santa Monica, CA, 30 May 1966) and the guitarist Spiral Stairs (Christopher Scott Kannberg; *b* Stockton, CA, 30 Aug 1966), the group added the drummer Gary Young (*b* Mamaroneck, NY, 3 May 1953) and started playing often shambolic shows around northern California in 1989. Young frequently could be seen performing handstands rather than playing the drums or handing out toast to the audience before a show. The trio recorded their seminal debut album, *Slanted & Enchanted* (Matador, 1992), at Young's studio. With the addition of the bass player Mark Ibold (*b* 17 Oct 1962) and the percussionist Bob [Robert] Nastanovich (*b* Rochester, NY, 27 Aug 1967), a friend of Malkmus from the University of Virginia, the band set out as a more coherent but still sometimes sloppy live outfit. *Crooked Rain* (1994) threatened to push them into the mainstream with a string of catchy singles. By now Young's eccentricities had seen him depart, and he was replaced by Steve West (*b* Charlottesville, VA, 8 Dec 1966). The band took a step back towards their alternative roots with the rambling but brilliant *Wowee Zowee* (Matador, 1995). *Brighten the Corners* (Matador, 1997) and the long tour that followed sowed the seeds of doubt that saw the finale of *Terror Twilight* (Matador, 1999) become almost a Malkmus solo project. The group disbanded at the end of that tour in late 1999 before reforming for a series of summer dates in 2010. For more information see R. Jovanovic: *Perfect Sound Forever* (Boston, 2004).

SELECTED RECORDINGS

Slay Tracks (1933–1969) (Treble Kicker, 1989); *Demolition Plot J-7* (Drag City, 1990); *Perfect Sound Forever* (Drag City, 1991); *Slanted & Enchanted* (Matador, 1992); *Watery Domestic* (Matador, 1992); *West-ing by Musket and Sextent* (Drag City, 1993); *Crooked Rain, Crooked Rain* (Matador, 1994); *Wowee Zowee* (Matador, 1995); *Brighten the Corners* (Matador, 1997); *Terror Twilight* (Matador, 1999)

ROB JOVANOVIC

Pawnee. Native American tribe of the south-central Plains, formerly a confederacy of the Skiri, Chawi, Pithawirata, and Kitkahahki Indians. Before the mid-19th century the Pawnee lived in permanent earth-lodge villages along the rivers of Nebraska and northern Kansas. They subsisted by cultivating corn, beans, and squash, and by taking part in buffalo hunts twice a year. During the 19th century the traditional life of the Pawnee was threatened by a severe population decline and by their relocation to Oklahoma, directed by the US government, during the period 1875–6. This article is principally a description of Pawnee culture before its disruption.

1. Music and ceremonial life. 2. Instruments. 3. Composition. 4. Style.

1. MUSIC AND CEREMONIAL LIFE. The Pawnee are noted for their elaborate religious system and mythology based on cosmological powers, and for the beauty of the songs and rituals related to their ceremonial life. Almost all important ceremonies were associated with sacred bundles believed to have derived from supernatural powers. Bundles attributed to celestial powers were owned by each village and used by priests to perform ceremonies necessary for the welfare of the community; those attributed to animal supernatural powers belonged to doctors' and warriors' societies and were used for the benefit of the individual.

The ceremonial season, which lasted from early spring through the autumn harvest, was prescribed by stellar observation, the occurrence of natural phenomena, and the yearly agricultural cycle. A ceremony might consist of several ritual acts such as a smoke offering, food offerings of corn and meat, and gift giving, but sacred songs were its essential feature. The season began with the Thunder, or Creation, Ceremony, in which the priests sang for the revitalization of the earth. The songs, the meanings of which were generally obscure to the listeners, were long and formulaic. They were based, as were many of the priests' ritual songs, on a series of word substitutions called steps; there were 26 steps for women and 30 for men. Women's steps used words associated with the fields and home life, men's with animal powers and warfare. The first song of the Thunder Ceremony used the complete series of women's and men's steps. Its basic form (a four-line stanza sung twice) was extended in performance to 448 lines as each of the steps was substituted during 56 repetitions of the eight lines. Subsequent songs were rendered in abbreviated form, using only four women's and six men's steps. The descending melodic line of the songs and the priests' manner of singing were intended to imitate the descent from heaven to earth of rolls of thunder.

The agricultural cycle continued with rituals to ensure the growth and abundant harvest of corn. At planting time the women danced with hoes and baskets, in imitation of the motions of ground-breaking and planting.

Students from the Pawnee Indian School perform on the weekly radio program, Indians for Indians, *University of Oklahoma at Norman, 1943. (AP Photo)*

After the corn sprouted the priests led a procession to the fields while singing songs to Mother Corn. A final ceremony after the harvest replenished the sacred bundles with new corn. Beyond the agricultural ceremonies the priests were responsible for rituals to purify the sacred bundles, rituals associated with the buffalo hunt, and others not part of the yearly cycle. The Calumet Ceremony (also called Hako, from the Wichita word for "pipe") could be initiated in any season except winter to maintain peace and trade between the Pawnee and neighboring tribes. During this elaborate, four-day ceremony the priests sang for the welfare of the people.

Traditional Pawnee society was hierarchical and had, beyond its hereditary classes of chiefs and priests, a group of doctors organized into several secret medicine societies. Each society centered around an animal guardian (such as bear, buffalo, otter, beaver, or owl) that was its source of power. Membership, although sometimes obtained by means of a vision (common among other Plains tribes), was more often achieved through long apprenticeship. Among the Skiri, the societies met in combination after the harvest for the grand Thirty Day, or Medicine Lodge, Ceremony. Here each doctor was required to demonstrate his powers to his fellows and the public. Performances were elaborate and dramatic, involving sleight-of-hand, hypnotism, and trance-induction. Each doctor dressed as his animal

benefactor to reaffirm kinship with it, and sang and danced the story of the original vision experience. Although these songs were the individual creations of each doctor, they generally followed a standard pattern, consisting of four to eight stanzas (usually six), each with two lines (*AB*) alternating with a refrain and a longer, repetitive chorus. Dances were mimetic, and their rhythmic accompaniment suggested a particular animal's movements. Buffalo Society songs, for example, had a steady, unchanging accompaniment that imitated the sound of a running herd. For "bear" singing the beat was slow and heavy. Each class of songs also had a particular formulaic ending (such as *o ho o* or *ha wa wa*) that further distinguished the type of song.

In pre-reservation days most young men could belong to a number of warrior societies, each of which had its own songs, dances, and costume. Although most were disbanded after the Pawnee were relocated to Oklahoma, a few societies were revived around 1900 under the impetus of the GHOST DANCE movement. After the demise of the movement the Pawnee continued the dance in a syncretic form called the Ghost Dance Hand Game, in which the songs of the Ghost Dance were combined with the old Hand Game (a guessing game widely distributed among Indian tribes) and elements of Pawnee ritualism. In intervals between games the Pawnee danced slowly in a large circle, moving clockwise, to Ghost Dance songs. Songs of the old warrior societies were also part of the ceremony.

2. INSTRUMENTS. Pawnee instrumentation was extensive and varied, with many instruments having particular ritual significance. Gourd rattles were shaken during priests' rituals and ceremonies of the medicine societies. Rawhide rattles, either spherical or ring-shaped, were part of the regalia of several warriors' societies. Buffalo dancers carried cluster rattles made of small pieces of buffalo hoof that were strung on leather thongs attached to the end of a stick covered with buckskin; similar rattles were also made of deer hoof. Several types of drum were known. A WATER-DRUM, used in doctors' ceremonies, was made of a hollowed cottonwood log half-filled with water; it was covered with a water-soaked hide and struck with an unpadded beater. During preparation of the drum doctors breathed into its cavity; thus they intended both to give the instrument life and inhale its healing power. The drum's "voice" was believed capable of driving away disease. Doctors' apprentices, who sang at certain medicine society meetings, accompanied themselves by beating on a large, dry cowhide without a resonating chamber; a single-headed frame drum was used by some warrior societies. With the development of the Ghost Dance Hand Game a large double-headed drum, suspended from forked sticks, came into use. Wind instruments included small reed and eagle-bone whistles used by the doctors' and warriors' societies, and a flute used for courting.

3. COMPOSITION. Songs were actively sought by all young men and were essential to members of warriors' and doctors' societies; the sounds of nature often provided inspiration. Commonly a song would come to an individual while he wandered over the prairie; a person who received a song in this way was said to have been in an uncommon state of heightened awareness. Songs received during the day were dance songs, or songs that could only be sung in the daytime; those dreamed were sung only at night. An individual's songs were his personal property and were usually passed on through inheritance. Songs of the sacred bundle ceremonies and of the medicine societies were said to have been received in visions; these were passed on to new priests and doctors during their apprenticeship. Occasionally entire ceremonies and their songs were borrowed from neighboring tribes, for example, the Deer Dance from the Wichita.

4. STYLE. Pawnee singing style was characterized by a moderately high degree of vocal tension, with pulsation on long notes and downward glides at phrase endings. Songs related to the sacred bundles and those of the medicine societies usually had meaningful texts, set syllabically, while songs of the warrior societies more often contained vocables. The average range was an octave to a 10th; larger ranges of up to two octaves occurred occasionally in warrior songs. Pentatonic scales without half-steps predominated. A song generally began on its highest note, descended in terrace fashion, and ended on its lowest note, which usually was also the tonic. Intervals of the melodic line were mostly major 2nds and minor 3rds, with 4ths common in songs of the warrior societies. Often several phrases of a song shared the same rhythmic pattern. Rhythmic accompaniment varied according to song type, but a regular steady beat that coincided with the melodic pulse was most common. Drum beats occurring regularly just before or after the pulse were usually found in warriors' songs. Pawnee songs exhibited a wide variety of forms. Commonly a song consisted of repetitions of several short phrases in various orders; their reiterations were often a 5th or octave lower than their initial statement. Incomplete repetition (i.e., *AA' BC A' BC*) was found principally in warriors' songs. Ghost Dance song form was typically *AABB* or *AABBCC*.

Both traditional and modern elements are present in contemporary Pawnee music and dance. At hand games, Ghost Dance songs are still occasionally performed, as are two dances from old warriors' societies, the Young Dog Dance and the Iruska. The Pawnee also perform the popular powwow dances of the southern Plains, such as the War, Round, Forty-niner, Two-step, Buffalo, and Gourd dances.

Recordings of Pawnee music are held at the Archive of Folk Culture, Library of Congress, Washington, DC (including recordings by James R. Murie); the Indiana University Archives of Traditional Music, Bloomington (recordings by Murie, George Dorsey, Alexander Lesser, and Gene Weltfish); the Bureau of American Ethnology, Smithsonian Institution, Washington, DC (recordings by Alice C. Fletcher); the Nebraska State Historical Society, Lincoln; and the Columbia University Department of Anthropology, New York (recordings by Weltfish).

SELECTED RECORDINGS
Songs of the Pawnee and Northern Ute (AAFS, 1951); *Plains: Comanche, Cheyenne, Kiowa, Caddo, Wichita, Pawnee* (AAFS, 1954); *Music of the Pawnee: Sung by Mark Evarts* (FW, 1965)

BIBLIOGRAPHY
G.B. Grinnell: "The Young Dog's Dance," *Journal of American Folklore*, iv (1891), 307–13
A.C. Fletcher: *The Hako: a Pawnee Ceremony* (Washington, DC, 1904/R)
N. Curtis: *The Indians' Book* (New York, 1907, 2/1923/R)
J.R. Murie: "Pawnee Indian Societies," *American Museum of Natural History Anthropological Papers*, xi (1914), 543–644
H.H. Roberts: *Ceremonial Songs of the Pawnee: Transcriptions of Music and Musical Analysis* (MS, 1922)
R. Linton: "Annual Ceremony of the Pawnee Medicine Men," *Field Museum of Natural History, Department of Anthropology, Leaflet*, no.8 (1923), 1–10
F. Densmore: *Pawnee Music* (Washington, DC, 1929/R)
A. Lesser: *The Pawnee Ghost Dance Hand Game: a Study of Cultural Change* (New York, 1933)
J.R. Murie: *Ceremonies of the Pawnee* (Washington, DC, 1981/R)
G.E. Hyde: *The Pawnee Indians* (Norman, OK, 1988)
A. Lesser: *The Pawnee Ghost Dance Hand Game: Ghost Dance Revival and Ethnic Identity* (Lincoln, NE, 1996)
T.E. Leahy: "The Pawnee Ghost Dance and Cultural Renaissance," *Chronicles of Oklahoma*, lxxxv/3 (2007), 324–41
A. Lesser: *The Pawnee Ghost Dance Hand Game: a Study of Cultural Change* (Whitefish, MT, 2008)

MARY RIEMER-WELLER/R

Paxton, Tom [Thomas Richard] (*b* Chicago, IL, 31 Oct 1937). Singer, author, and songwriter. Paxton grew interested in folk music at the University of Oklahoma. In 1960 the army brought him near New York, where he met other young folk musicians such as Bob Dylan and Phil Ochs. Following his discharge, Paxton sang in coffeehouses in Greenwich Village, and his songs began to attract the attention of other folk musicians, notably the Chad Mitchell Trio ("The Marvelous Toy") and Pete Seeger, who performed his "Ramblin' Boy" at the Weavers' Carnegie Hall reunion (1963). Paxton's first Elektra album, recorded in 1964, contained a number of still-popular songs such as "I can't help but wonder where I'm bound" and "The Last Thing on My Mind." Five more albums appeared in the 1960s, containing numerous topical protest songs. From 1965 on, Paxton performed frequently in the United States, England, and Europe, even settling in the UK for four years. He returned to the United States in 1977 and released the much-heralded *New Songs from the Briar Patch*. Paxton estimates that he has written 500 songs ranging from gentle, nostalgic love songs to political commentary that can be passionate or keenly ironic; his work is often seen as an extension of the tradition of socially conscious folk music. His compositions have been recorded by Judy Collins, Doc Watson, Dave Van Ronk, Porter Wagoner, Arlo Guthrie, Peter, Paul, and Mary, Holly Near, Dolly Parton, Delroy Wilson, and Willie Nelson.

While continuing his primary career, Paxton also recorded and performed children's music extensively from 1987 through 2002, earning Grammy nominations in that field. During this time he also published many books for children. Several feature Paxton retelling Aesop's fables in verse; later titles feature his original verse stories. By 2009 he had reduced his schedule to about forty appearances per year. He has continued to record, and since 2000 he has released songs such as "Sarah Palin" that he describes as having a "short shelf life" (<http://www.tompaxtom.com>) as free Internet downloads. Paxton has received Lifetime Achievement Awards from ASCAP, the BBC, the Folk Alliance, and the Recording Academy.

BIBLIOGRAPHY
G. Friesen: "Something New has Been Added," *Sing Out!*, xiii/4 (1963), 12–23
A. Means: "The Politics of Paxton," *Melody Maker* (20 Feb 1971)
A. Edelstein: "The Last Thing on Tom Paxton's Mind is Writing Safe Songs," *Songwriter*, v/5 (Feb 1980)
T. Paxton: *The Honor of Your Company* (New York, 2000)
J. Freedom du Lac: "Alexandria Resident & Folk Icon Tom Paxton Gets Lifetime Achievement Grammy Today," *Washington Post* (7 Feb 2009)

TERENCE O'GRADY/ART MENIUS

Payne, John Howard (*b* New York, NY, 9 June 1791; *d* Tunis, Tunisia, 9 April 1852). Actor, playwright, translator, and lyricist. He first appeared on stage in Boston at age 12 in school productions. Two years later he founded the *Thespian Mirror*, New York's first periodical devoted to the theater. He attended Union College for two years before leaving in 1809 to make his professional acting debut. His success in New York led to a well received American tour (1809–12), which included appearances as the first Hamlet in the United States. In 1813 he moved to England, where he became the first American actor to appear on the European stage. For 20 years he lived in London and Paris, where he was best known as a translator and adaptor of French works for London theaters. In 1822 he reworked a Parisian ballet into the operetta *Clari, the Maid of Milan* for Covent Garden. Its second-act aria "Home, Sweet Home," set to music by Henry R. Bishop, became one of the most popular songs of the 19th century, although neither Payne nor Bishop received any royalties. Payne returned to the United States in 1833 and became active in politics. He served twice as the American consul to Tunis (1842–5 and 1851–2). His enduring fame as the author of "Home, Sweet Home" was such that 30 years after his death, American philanthropist W.W. Corcoran paid to have Payne's body brought back to the United States. In 1970 Payne was inducted into the Songwriters Hall of Fame.

BIBLIOGRAPHY
R.P. Chiles: *John Howard Payne: American Poet, Actor, Playwright, Consul and Author of "Home, Sweet Home"* (Washington, DC, 1930)
G. Overmeyer: *America's First Hamlet* (New York, 1957)

SCOTT WARFIELD

Payne, Maggi (*b* Temple, TX, 23 Dec 1945). Composer, flutist, recording engineer, and video artist. She began playing flute at age ten. Soon after she received a tape recorder and began experimenting with distortion and layering. She studied flute with Walfrid Kujala and composition with ALAN B. STOUT, M. WILLIAM KARLINS, and Theodore Ashford at Northwestern University (BMus 1968). While in college she performed much contemporary music, including Mario Davidovsky's *Synchronisms no.2* and Roman Haubenstock-Ramati's *Interpolation, mobile pour flute*. After a brief period at Yale University (1969), she continued her studies in flute performance at the University of Illinois (MM 1970) and took lessons with GORDON MUMMA, BEN JOHNSTON, SALVATORE MARTIRANO, and James Beauchamp. Further postgraduate study in electronic music and recording media at Mills College (MFA 1972) led to posts there as recording engineer, assistant professor, and (from 1992) co-director of the college's Center for Contemporary Music. Her honors include multiple grants from the NEA and the Mellon Foundation.

Payne has composed primarily for electronic tape, and her early works feature the Moog III synthesizer. In some of her early pieces, such as *Spirals* (1977), *Spheres* (1977), and *Circular Motions* (1981), Payne experimented with spatial concepts, such as how to manipulate sound vertically, as well as with Doppler effects. Spatialization has continued to be an important concern in her compositions. She was drawn to Edgard Varèse's ideas about crystallization, as evidenced in *Crystal* (1982), which, like many of her compositions, features a video element, a microscopic observation of crystal growth. She has frequently combined tape music with visual elements, such as dance and electronically manipulated video images of nature, including moving water (*Liquid Metal*, 1994) or a plethora of isolated landscapes (*Apparent Horizon*, 1996). Payne is interested in film herself and has collaborated with the video artist Ed Tannenbaum since the 1990s. In 1999 Mumma commissioned her to add visuals to his work *Pontpoint*. Additionally Payne has often drawn on urban sound sources recorded in the San Francisco area, as in *Airwaves (realities)* (1987) and *Resonant Places* (1992). She transforms these intrusive human sounds, such as those of motorcycles and airplanes, into seemingly natural phenomena.

Although the majority of Payne's compositions have been electro-acoustic, she has written several works for the acoustic medium. In 2003 the flutist Nina Assimakopoulos commissioned the solo flute work *Of all*. Payne's composition *fff*, for solo flute (2006), explores timbre and extended techniques without any electronic modifications. She has also written for women's choir and for voice and piano.

Payne has remastered performances of Béla Bartók's string quartets by groups such as the Fine Arts Quartet, the Hungarian String Quartet, and the Végh Quartet. Her piece *break/motors* (2001) comes from her restoration work. She fashioned the composition from removed fragments, undesirable hisses, squeaks, and noise found on historic recordings.

WORKS

STAGE

Dance scores (all for tape): House Party (choreog. C. Brown), 1974; Synergy II (choreog. Brown), 1974; Inventory (choreog. M. Sakamoto), 1980; Rondo (choreog. B. Kagan), 1984; The Living Room (choreog. N. Bryan), 1987
Other: The Winter's Tale (incid music, W. Shakespeare), 1975

TRADITIONAL MEDIA

Inflections, fl, 1968; Songs of Flight (G. Snyder), S, pf, 1988; Desertscapes (M. Payne), 2 choruses, 1991; Minutia 0–13, 1–3 pf, 1996; Suspended Time, orch, 2000; Reflections, fl, 2003; Of all, fl, 2003; Ringtones, carillon, 2004; fff, fl, 2006

ELECTRO-ACOUSTIC AND MULTIMEDIA

Video scores (all for tape, dir. E. Tannenbaum): 3 Movts with 2 Movts, 1982; Maytricks, 1983; Dance, 1984; Hikari, 1984; Contest, 1985; Gamelan, 1985; Hands, 1985; Shimmer, 1985; Back to Forth, 1986; Flights of Fancy (Viscous Meanderings), 1987; Ahh-Ahh (Queue the Lizards), 1987; Heavy Water, 1991
Video scores (all for tape, dir. M. Payne): Circular Motions, 1981; Crystal, 1982; Io, 1982; Solar wind, tape, video/slide projections, 1983; Airwaves (realities), 1987; Liquid Metal, 1994; Apparent Horizon, 1996
Tape and slide projections: Farewell, 1975; Transparencies, 1976; Spheres, 1977; Spirals, 1977; Lunar Earthrise, 1978; Lunar Dusk, 1979; Blue Metallics, tape, slide projections/film, 1980; Rising, tape, slide projections, opt. dancers, 1980; Ling, 1981
Installations (audio/video): Effervescence, 2008; Cloud Fields, 2008
Other (tape unless otherwise stated): Ametropia, 1970; HUM, fl, tape, 1973; Orion (film score), 1973; VDO (film score), 1973; Allusions, dancers, tape, 16mm film, lighting, 1974; Scirocco, fl, tape, 1983; White Night, 1984; Subterranean Network, 1986; Phase Transitions, 1989; Resonant Places, 1992; Aeolian Confluence, 1993; Moiré, 1995; Raw data, 1998; Close-ups, 1999; Sweet Dreams, 1999; breaks/motors, 2001; FIZZ, 2004; Arctic Winds, 2007; Electric Ice, 2007; Glassy Metals, 2009; Surface Tension, 2010

BIBLIOGRAPHY

B. Demetz: "New Faces," *Ear*, xii/6 (1987), 23
K. Gann: "Medium Rare," *Village Voice* (27 Oct 1987)
G. Borchert: "American Women in Electronic Music, 1984–94," *CMR*, xvi/1–2 (1997), 89–97
A.E. Hinkle-Turner: *Women Composers and Music Technology in the United States: Crossing the Line* (Burlington, VT, 2006)
T. Rodgers: *Pink Noises: Women on Electronic Music and Sound* (Durham, NC, 2010)

GAVIN BORCHERT/ALYSON PAYNE

Paynter, John Philip (*b* Mineral Point, WI, 29 May 1928; *d* Glenview, IL, 4 Feb 1996). Conductor, composer, arranger, and educator. Named for John Philip Sousa, Paynter studied piano, organ, and clarinet in his public school years. He earned degrees at Northwestern University (BM 1950, MM 1951). He was appointed director of the marching band, assistant director of bands, and instructor of theory in 1951. He worked closely with, and was influenced by, Glenn Cliffe Bainum, Northwestern's director of bands, and succeeded him upon his retirement. A prolific composer and arranger with over 400 works, Paynter taught band repertoire, conducting, and arranging. A strong advocate of community bands, he helped found and conducted the Northshore Concert Band, Chicago, in addition to traveling throughout the United States and four continents providing leadership and support for high level amateur band performances. Paynter also served as president of the Mid-West International Band and Orchestra Clinic, the American Bandmasters Association, the World Association for Symphonic Bands and Ensembles (WASBE), and the National Band Association (co-founder and Honorary Life President.) He was awarded an Honorary Doctorate of Humane Letters by DePaul University (1992) and received the Northwestern Alumni Association Excellence in Teaching Award (1987). He also received many honors from fraternal and educational organizations. The archives of the Northshore Concert Band are held at *Eu*.

BIBLIOGRAPHY

W. Saxon: Obituary, *New York Times* (11 Feb 1996)

DONALD HUNSBERGER

Payola. A practice involving record companies or promoters paying or inducing radio DJs or stations to play certain records. Such arrangements were common until the 1950s, but created a national scandal in the United States when made widely public during the rise of rock and roll in the middle of that decade. Although the practice was subsequently made illegal, government crackdowns against payola have continued into the 21st century. Third-party promoters often have been used to sidestep legal restrictions. The term derives from a combination of the words "pay" and "Victrola" and was used to describe the process by which a recording could be financially engineered to become a hit. For more information see F. Dannen: *Hit Men: Power Brokers & Fast Money inside the Music Business* (New York, 1991).

JONAS WESTOVER

Payton, Nicholas (Anthony) (*b* New Orleans, LA, 26 Sept 1973). Jazz trumpeter and bandleader. He began playing trumpet at the age of four and was playing with the Young Tuxedo Brass Band by the age of nine and performing and touring professionally in the All Star Brass Band at 12. During his high school years he studied with Clyde Kerr Jr. at the New Orleans Center for Creative Arts and subsequently with Ellis Marsalis at the University of New Orleans. He made his Carnegie Hall debut in 1991 with Marcus Roberts and from 1992 to 1994 performed with Elvin Jones's Jazz Machine. He has also performed with the Lincoln Center Jazz Orchestra and Carnegie Hall Jazz Band, among other ensembles.

Payton plays piano, bass, drums, tuba, trombone, clarinet, and saxophone but is best known for his work on trumpet. His solo style is extremely agile, including fast and nimble navigation through the registers and expert glissandi through the whole tonal range of the trumpet. He has released numerous albums as a leader for Verve, Milestone, and Warner Bros. and won a Grammy Award with the trumpeter Doc Cheatham for *Doc Cheatham & Nicholas Payton* (1996, Verve). He has also performed on the soundtracks for films and documentaries about the jazz scenes of Kansas City and New Orleans.

DANIEL JOHN CARROLL

Pazmor, Radiana [Pasmore, Harriet Horn] (*b* San Francisco, CA, 12 May 1892; *d* Sonoma, CA, 25 Jan 1986). Contralto, teacher, and music therapist. After attending the University of California, Berkeley (BA, French, 1914), she taught piano and then voice at Pomona College in Claremont, California (1914–20). After study and concert performances in Europe (1920–25) she returned to the United States and performed and taught privately in New York (1925–35) and Hollywood, California (1936–40). During the 1930s Pazmor was noted for her performances of contemporary American art songs. Her programs regularly included works by Charles Ives, Henry Cowell, Carl Ruggles, John Cage, Ernst Bacon, Ruth Crawford, Roger Sessions, Lou Harrison, Aaron Copland, and William Grant Still. She gave recitals for organizations such as the League of Composers and the Pan American Association of Composers, and at academic institutions including the New School for Social Research, Columbia University, Princeton University, and Harvard University. She studied music therapy at Boston University (MM 1955) while teaching music at Converse College in Spartanburg, South Carolina (1940–60). From 1960 to 1969 she helped rehabilitate patients with vocal disorders and from 1963 to 1969 served as a visiting music professor at St. Andrew's Presbyterian College in Laurinburg, North Carolina. She retired in 1969, and after sustaining injuries in an automobile accident in 1970 she moved to Sonoma, California. Throughout her concert career Pazmor was lauded for her exceptional dramatic sense, articulation, diction, and tone quality, her ability to sing difficult music with apparent ease, and her gift of ironic humor. Tall and striking in appearance, she was known for her magnetic personality and her poise on stage.

Some of Pazmor's correspondence, programs, music, and memorabilia are held in the Mickel Library at Converse College; other correspondence is held in the Irving S. Gilmore Music Library at Yale University and the music divisions of the Library of Congress and the New York Public Library at Lincoln Center.

BIBLIOGRAPHY

C. Lengyel, ed.: *Early Master Teachers* (San Francisco, 1940), 65–66

J. Rodriguez, ed.: *Music and Dance in California* (Hollywood, CA, 1940), 411–12

L. Kibler: *The History of Converse College* (Spartanburg, SC, 1973), 376, 381–82

R. Mead: *Henry Cowell's New Music, 1925–1936* (Ann Arbor, MI, 1981), 127, 242–46, 255, 280, 319–320, 357, 363, 430

N. Lindley: *Singer Radiana Pazmor and American Music: the Performer as Advocate* (diss., U. of Maryland, College Park, 1993)

JOHN A. EMERSON/CHRISTOPHER E. MEHRENS

P. D. Q. Bach. *See* SCHICKELE, PETER.

Peabody. Ballroom dance that evolved from the fast Foxtrot of the ragtime era. Soon after the introduction of the foxtrot in 1914, two variations developed: a slow version done at about 40 measures per minute and a fast version done at over 50 measures per minute. In England, the fast foxtrot was called the Quickstep; in America it was called the Peabody, named after a New York policeman, Lieutenant William Frank Peabody (1873–1939). Charged with questionable activities, Peabody had twice been dismissed from the police force but had been exonerated and reinstated; he was eventually promoted to captain and put in charge of a Brooklyn precinct. He was a large, good-natured bachelor who, despite his considerable weight, was light on his feet and who loved to dance. A popular member of New York ragtime dancing circles, he especially enjoyed dancing the fast foxtrot, which was gaining popularity in 1915. Because of his huge girth, however, Officer Peabody was unable hold his partner directly in front of him, so he held her on his right side, in a sort of promenade hold known as the English or the right-outside position. The dance that came to be called the Peabody was thus based on an unusual dance position for the partners, which led to some unique steps and floor patterns. Today, the Peabody and the quickstep bear little resemblance to each other, although some of the steps are the same.

The Peabody is a brisk dance that covers a lot of space on the dance floor. Danced to almost any 2/4 or 4/4 ragtime tune of appropriate tempo, it is essentially a fast one-step, with long, gliding strides and a few syncopations. Other basic steps, developed in the 1920s, are the cross-step and the lock step. The leader changes sides as he travels around the floor and adds promenades and simple turns as the dance progresses. The partners may also add slight dipping motions with their upper bodies once they master the rhythm and flow of movement. In competitions and exhibitions, Peabody dancers sometimes wear appropriate ragtime dress: suits and bowler hats for the gentlemen and long, full dresses for the ladies. Music suitable for dancing the Peabody includes "When the Saints Go Marching In," "Ain't She Sweet,"

"Yes, we have no bananas," "Tiger Rag," "Bourbon Street Parade," and other ragtime tunes of New Orleans jazz men of the late 1910s and early 1920s.

BIBLIOGRAPHY

T.E. Parsons: *Popular Ballroom Dances, Including Westchester, Tango, Waltz, Riviera, Peabody, [and] Collegiate Swing* (New York, 1936)

A. and J. Butler: *The Encyclopedia of Social Dance* (New York, 1967)

R.M. Stephenson and J. Iaccarino: *The Complete Book of Ballroom Dancing* (New York, 1980)

CLAUDE CONYERS

Peabody, George (*b* South Danvers [now in Peabody], MA, 18 Feb 1795; *d* London, UK, 4 Nov 1869). Philanthropist, active in England. From 1807 he worked in retail stores and dry-goods businesses in New England, Baltimore (with branches in New York and Philadelphia), and Great Britain. After living in Baltimore for twenty-two years (1815–37), he settled in London, establishing the firm of George Peabody & Co. (1843–64), which specialized in foreign exchange and American securities. His business prospered, and he spent most of his fortune in philanthropy; his gifts enabled several institutes, libraries, lyceums, and museums to be established in the United States during the 1850s and 1860s, and he was also a major benefactor of the poor by financing housing in London. On visits to the United States he promoted public education in the southern states, made substantial gifts to museums at Harvard and Yale universities, and founded the Peabody Institute (Peabody, Massachussetts) and the Peabody Academy of Science (Salem, Massachussetts). In Baltimore, he gave $1,400,000 to establish the Peabody Institute in 1857; it included a free library, an endowment for lectures, an art gallery, and an academy of music—the first music conservatory in the United States, later renamed the Peabody Conservatory (*see* BALTIMORE). In Great Britain he came to be regarded as an unofficial Anglo-American ambassador; his honors included a doctorate from Oxford University (1867).

BIBLIOGRAPHY

DAB (S.H. Paradise); *DNB* (J.R. MacDonald)

F. Parker: *George Peabody: a Biography* (Nashville, 1971/*R*)

WILLIAM McCLELLAN/BLAKE HOWE

Peabody Conservatory. Music conservatory, part of the Peabody Institute of the John Hopkins University, founded by George Peabody in BALTIMORE in 1857; *see also* LIBRARIES AND COLLECTIONS.

Peace Jubilees. Massive music festivals held in Boston after the Civil War. Known as Peace Jubilees, they were organized by bandleader PATRICK S. GILMORE, and each was intended to commemorate a specific occasion, with thousands of instrumentalists and singers performing before a huge audience in a specially built Coliseum. It has been reported that there were two Peace Jubilees in Boston (1869, 1872). There was also a third one (1889). The music consisted mainly of operatic arias and choruses (Wolfgang Amadeus Mozart, Gioachino Rossini), oratorio choruses (George Frideric Handel, Joseph Haydn, Felix Mendelssohn), and a few overtures and symphonies (Ludwig van Beethoven, Franz Schubert).

The National Peace Jubilee was held for one week in June 1869 to commemorate the end of the Civil War and carried the motto, "Let Us Have Peace." On opening day, US President Ulysses S. Grant and other officials heard a new *Hymn of Peace*, a setting of a poem by Oliver Wendell Holmes, with music by Matthias Keller. With 103 different choruses from as far away as Ohio and Illinois, totaling 10,404 singers, and a band and orchestra totaling 1011, this was the first great "monster" festival held in 19th-century America. Among the featured guest musicians were violinist Ole Bull and

Rehearsal for the National Peace Jubilee, Boston, 1869. (Library of Congress)

soprano Euphrosyne Parepa-Rosa. This Jubilee was very successful and made a profit. A portion of the money was given to Gilmore for organizing and planning the event.

Due to the success of the first one, a second even larger event, the World's Peace Jubilee and International Music Festival, was held for 18 days in Boston (1872) to celebrate the end of the Franco-Prussian War. Featuring twice as many musicians as the first one, there were days set aside for bands from England, Germany, France, and Austria. Invited guests included composers Franz Abt and Johann Strauss, who conducted several of his famous waltzes and premiered a new "Jubilee Waltz," dedicated to P.S. Gilmore. Other premieres were a *Festival Hymn* with words and music by Dudley Buck; a psalm setting by Alberto Randegger; and several sections from a new oratorio, *St. Peter*, by John Knowles Paine. Yet, this Jubilee was not financially successful, the audience was smaller, and some were critical of its enormous size and scope.

Gilmore organized a third Peace Jubilee for one week in Boston in June 1889 to celebrate the 20th anniversary of the first Jubilee, a smaller event featuring Gilmore's Band with a chorus of 1000, and 1000 children from the Boston public schools.

BIBLIOGRAPHY

Music to be performed in the Grand National Peace Jubilee (Boston, 1869)
"The Boston Peace Jubilee," *New York Times* (20 June 1869)
P.S. Gilmore: *History of the National Peace Jubilee and Great Music Festival held in the City of Boston, June 1869* (Boston, 1871)
Music to be performed at the World's Peace Jubilee and International Musical Festival (Boston, 1872)
"The Jubilee: Opening of the International Musical Festival in Boston," *New York Times* (18 June 1872)
H.C. Schonberg: "Jubilee Maker: Patrick Gilmore and His Gigantic Music Festivals," *Musical Digest* xxix/10 (June 1947), 8, 34–5
R. Jarman: "Big Boom in Boston," *American Heritage Magazine*, xx/6 (1969)
F.J. Cipolla: "Patrick S. Gilmore: The Boston Years," *American Music*, vi/3 (1988), 281–92
R.L. Hall: *'Angel of Peace': the Boston Peace Jubilees* (Stoughton, MA, 2010)

ROGER L. HALL

Peacock, Gary (*b* Burley, ID, 12 May 1935). Bass player. He grew up in the Pacific Northwest and had begun taking piano and drum lessons by the age of 13. He moved to Los Angeles at 17 to study at the Westlake School of Music before enlisting in the army in 1954. He played piano and drums in military bands for two years while stationed in Germany before switching to bass. After his discharge he performed with Hans Koller, Albert Mangelsdorff, Bud Shank, and Attila Zoller and then moved back to Los Angeles (1958). Peacock toured with Terry Gibbs, played with Art Pepper, Dexter Gordon, Harold Land, and Paul Bley, and recorded with Barney Kessel, Don Ellis, and Clare Fischer. He moved to New York in 1962 where he was a member of Bley's quartet with Don Cherry. He also worked with George Russell, Bill Evans, Miles Davis, and in gradually freer contexts with Jimmy Giuffre, Roland Kirk, Roswell Rudd, Steve Lacy, and Archie Shepp. He con-

tinued in this direction, recording and touring as a member of Albert Ayler's groups with Cherry and Sonny Murray (1964).

Health concerns led to a brief departure from music towards studies of Eastern philosophy and medicine. He moved to Japan in 1969 where he played with Sadao Watanabe and Masabumi Kikuchi; he returned to the United States in 1972 and studied biology at the University of Washington and later taught music at the Cornish College of the Arts in Seattle. He toured Japan with Bley and Barry Altschul in 1976 and recorded *Tales of Another* (1977, ECM) as a leader with Keith Jarrett and Jack DeJohnette. Peacock, Jarrett, and DeJohnette reformed in 1983 as Jarrett's trio Standards and maintained an active international touring and recording schedule as one of jazz's most influential modern ensembles. In the 1980s and 90s Peacock also worked with Jan Garbarek, Tomasz Stańko, Ralph Towner, Bill Frisell, and Paul Motian.

BIBLIOGRAPHY

M. Williams: "Gary Peacock: the Beauties of Intuition," *DB*, xxx/13 (1963), 16–7
M. Solomon: "Bassist Peacock into Zen, Est and ECM," *DB*, xlvi/10 (1979), 9 only
J. Rosenbaum: "Gary Peacock: the Experience of Music," *Bass Player*, iv/4 (1993), 54–6
J. Ephland: "Why Play Standards?" *DB*, lxiii/2 (1996), 16 only [incl. discography]
D. Adler: "Standard Bearers: Keith Jarrett, Gary Peacock, and Jack DeJohnette," *JT* (2010), Jan

BARRY LONG

Pearce, S(tephen) Austen (*b* Brompton, Kent, England, 7 Nov 1836; *d* Jersey City, NJ, 9 April 1900). Organist of English birth. As a child he was a cathedral chorister in Rochester and Chatham before studying at Oxford University (BM, 1859, DM, 1864). He played at various London churches and gave recitals at the Hanover Square Rooms and elsewhere before immigrating to New York in 1872. He played successively at St. Andrew's, St. George's, St. Stephen's, Zion Church, Church of the Ascension, and the Fifth Avenue Collegiate Church (1879–85). He ended his career at the Jersey Heights Presbyterian Church in Jersey City. Pearce was also active as a teacher and writer. He taught and lectured at Columbia College, New York College of Music and General Theological Seminary, and in Baltimore at the Peabody Conservatory and Johns Hopkins University. Pearce was appointed music editor of the *Evening Post* in 1874 and contributed to the *Musical Courier, Harper's*, and *Encyclopedia Americana*. His major literary effort was a *Pocket Dictionary of Musical Terms* in twenty languages (1889). In 1877 he published a collection of *Columbia College Chapel Music* and a *Method for the Pianoforte* in 1888. His compositions, mostly unpublished, include a three-act children's opera, *La Belle Américaine*, an oratorio *Celestial Visions*, a cantata *Psalm of Praise*, orchestral music, songs, and works for piano and organ.

BIBLIOGRAPHY

DAB (F.C.G. Cole)

WILLIAM OSBORNE

Pearl, Minnie [Cannon, Sarah Ophelia; née Colley, Sarah Ophelia] (*b* Centerville, TN, 25 Oct 1912; *d* Nashville, TN, 4 March 1996). Country music singer and comedienne. Raised in a wealthy family and educated at the private Ward-Belmont College in Nashville, she was one of the most successful vaudeville-styled country music humorists, performing her rural spinster character on radio, stage, and national television for more than 50 years. After joining the Wayne P. Sewall Production Company shortly after graduation, she worked in minstrel and musical shows in small southern towns, where in 1936 she met the prototype for the character that eventually became Minnie Pearl. She began to portray this character using rural anecdotes and jokes she had collected in her travels, adding to the act burlesque versions of country songs sung in a cracked, out-of-tune voice. By 1939 she was making appearances in the guise of Minnie Pearl, recounting family happenings at Grinder's Switch, a fictional hamlet based on a settlement near Centerville, TN. In 1940 she joined the cast of the *Grand Ole Opry*, where she continued to refine the character of Minnie Pearl under the tutelage of George Dewey Hay, the show's announcer. In 1946 she began a 12-year association with comedian Rod Brasfield. Unlike most earlier country humor, which had depended heavily on visual jokes, slapstick, and exaggerated accents, the Pearl–Brasfield routines on the *Grand Ole Opry* were tailored to radio and were based on verbal humor and quick repartee. In later years Pearl was better able to exploit her visual image, including her famous hat with a $1.98 price tag, on a series of national television shows, notably *Hee Haw*, the most popular country-music show of the 1970s and 80s. She was elected to the Country Music Hall of Fame in 1975 and awarded the National Medal of Arts in 1992. Her performing career ended in 1991 after an acute stroke. Pearl rarely recorded songs and had only one hit single, in 1966; her significance was in perfecting the country vaudevillian type, which was an important component to the country music industry for most of the 20th century.

BIBLIOGRAPHY

M. Pearl and J. Dew: *Minnie Pearl: an Autobiography* (New York, 1980)

R. Peterson: *Creating Country Music: Fabricating Authenticity* (Chicago, 1997)

C. Havighurst: *Air Castle of the South: WSM and the Making of Music City* (Urbana, 2007)

CHARLES K. WOLFE/CLAY MOTLEY

Pearl Jam. Rock band. It was formed in 1990 in Seattle, Washington. Key members have included Jeff(rey Allen) Ament (*b* Havre, MT, 10 March 1963; bass), Stone (Carpenter) Gossard (*b* Seattle, WA, 20 July 1966; guitar), Mike [Michael David] McCready (*b* Pensacola, FL, 5 April 1966; guitar), Eddie Vedder (Edward Louis Severson; *b* Evanston, IL, 23 Dec 1964; vocals and guitar), and Dave Krusen (*b* Tacoma, WA, 10 March 1966; drums). Pearl Jam formed from the remnants of the Seattle-based band Mother Love Bone after that band's vocalist Andrew Wood died from a heroin overdose in March 1990. Vedder moved north to Seattle from San Diego to join the new band and they set about recording their debut album, *Ten*. Boosted by the singles "Alive" and "Jeremy," the album had sold more than 13 million copies worldwide by the early 2010s. Although they had a heavy rock influence in their music the band struggled to emerge from being labeled as just another grunge band, especially after their appearance in the prototypical grunge movie *Singles* (1992). As the decade moved on they proved to be more versatile and hooked up with likes of Neil Young and R.E.M. to show their more melodic and acoustic sides. The band has also exhibited a longevity that their early 1990s Seattle counterparts have failed to match, and apart from a series of different drummers the other members of the band remained in the early 2010s. Matt(hew David) Cameron (*b* San Diego, CA, 28 Nov 1962; drums) joined in 1998 and was the band's fifth drummer. As well as issuing nine studio albums the band have been prolific with their release of live material. Around the turn of the millennium they put out 72 live shows on CD from one tour alone. As these shows were issued by the band themselves they have been referred to as official bootlegs. There have been further official bootlegs issued from many subsequent tours, and in the early 2010s these numbered almost 700.

SELECTED RECORDINGS

Ten (Epic, 1991); *Vs* (Epic, 1993); *Vitalogy* (Epic, 1994); *No Code* (Epic, 1996); *Yield* (Epic, 1998); *Binaural* (Epic, 2000); *Riot Act* (Epic, 2002); *Pearl Jam* (J, 2006); *Backspacer* (Monkeywrench, 2009)

BIBLIOGRAPHY

M. Clarke: *Pearl Jam and Eddie Vedder: None too Fragile* (London, 2009)

Pearl Jam and C. Crowe: *Pearl Jam Twenty* (London, 2011)

ROB JOVANOVIC

Pearson, Stephen Funk (*b* Poughkeepsie, NY, 22 Jan 1950). Composer, guitarist, author, and television host. He gained undergraduate degrees from Vassar College in philosophy and music, and a master's degree (MM) in composition and performance from Hunter College. He studied guitar with Alexander Bellow, Frederic Hand, ALICE ARTZT, David Russell, John Mills, José Tomás, and Oscar Ghiglia. His composition teachers include Lennox Berkeley, Robert Middleton, RICHARD WILSON, and ANNEA LOCKWOOD. He also has gained extensive experience with folk, rock, and jazz. His compositional style is notable for a fusion of diverse genres and his experimentation with prepared guitars. Representative works for prepared guitar include *Pongue*, which involves the use of carefully prepared ping-pong balls, and *South China Sea Peace*, which employs unusual *scordatura* and an additional bridge placed under the 12th fret. The recording *Artists around the World Perform Stephen Funk Pearson* (CDBY, 2009) showcases Pearson's compositions for traditional folk instruments (mandolin, flute, guitar, and marimba) often performed in unorthodox manners. His music has premiered at major venues including the Kennedy Center, Alice Tully Hall at Lincoln Center, Queen Elizabeth Hall, and Carnegie Recital Hall. An accomplished guitarist, he won top prize at the International Guitar Competition of Puerto Rico. His album *Live in Concert: London* (Kyra-Clio) showcases traditional repertoire for the classical guitar among some of his own compositions. He also is the creator and host of the syndicated television series *Funk-TV*, and the author of "Cacophony Corner," a cartoon series that has appeared in *Soundboard* magazine.

M. RUSTY JONES

Pease, Alfred H(umphreys) (*b* Cleveland, OH, 6 May 1838; *d* St. Louis, MO, 12 July 1882). Composer and pianist. According to family genealogies, his mother was a descendant of the English composer Pelham Humfrey. From 1855 to 1857 he studied classics at Kenyon College, Gambier, Ohio; he then went to Berlin, where he studied piano and composition until about 1860. After a brief return to the United States he spent another three years in Germany as a pupil of Bülow. He made his debut as a pianist on 8 February 1864 at Dodworth's Hall, New York, and continued to perform both as a soloist and as an assisting artist until his death. In his last months he drank excessively, staying in St. Louis under an assumed name, and he dropped dead in the street, unnoticed and at first unidentified.

Pease wrote about 100 songs noteworthy for their sensitive text settings and for harmonies that are more striking than those of his contemporaries; among them were Break, break, break; Blow, bugle blow; Ay!; Bedouin Song; Forever More; Good Night; I love my love; O love come back; O Morning Star; Stars of the Summer Night; The Miller's Daughter; and Tender and True. He also wrote many piano compositions, as well as a piano concerto in E-flat, performed at Philadelphia on 19 July 1876 in an all-American concert conducted by Theodore Thomas. His other orchestral works, *Reverie and Andante, Andante and Scherzo*, and *Romanze*, were also performed by Thomas's orchestra.

BIBLIOGRAPHY

DAB (F.L.G. Cole)
"Pease, Alfred H.," *Brainard's Musical World* (August 1879), repr. in *Brainard's Biographies of American Musicians*, ed. E.D. Bomberger (Westport, CT, 1999)
Obituary, *New York Times* (16 July 1882)
W.T. Upton: *Art-song in America* (Boston, 1930/R1969 with suppl. 1938)

CARL S. ROGERS/JOHN C. SCHMIDT

Pease, James (*b* Indianapolis, IN, 9 Jan 1916; *d* New York, NY, 26 April 1967). Bass-baritone. He studied at the Curtis Institute and made his debut with the Philadelphia Opera Company as Méphistophélès in Gounod's *Faust* (1941). He sang with the New York City Opera (1946–53), where his repertory included Escamillo, Wozzeck, Ochs, Hans Sachs, and Mozart's Figaro. At the Berkshire Music Festival (1946–9) he sang in the American premieres of *Peter Grimes* (Captain Balstrode) and *Albert Herring* (Mr. Gedge). He worked with the Hamburg Staatsoper (1953–8), making his debut there as Orestes and later singing Falstaff, Mandryka, Count Almaviva, Briano (*Aroldo*), and Wotan; he also appeared as Socrates in the premiere of Krenek's *Pallas Athene weint* (1955). He sang Don Giovanni at Glyndebourne in 1954 and the following year made his debut at Covent Garden (Wotan), where he continued to sing until 1961.

His roles included Boris, which he sang at Graz in 1966. Pease's performances, if not profound, were pleasing and well conceived. Although his voice was light by Wagnerian standards, it was well focused, and he made good interpretations of Wotan and Hans Sachs; perhaps his finest role was Captain Balstrode.

CHARLES A. JAHANT/ELIZABETH FORBES

Peaslee, Richard Cutts (*b* New York, NY, 13 June 1930). Composer. He graduated from Yale University and the Juilliard School and also studied privately with NADIA BOULANGER and WILLIAM RUSSO. His compositional style is eclectic, encompassing jazz influences, folk-like idioms, extended instrumental techniques, and electronic sound resources. His early works for jazz ensemble culminated in *Stonehenge* (1963) for the London Jazz Orchestra. Many of his compositions exploit the virtuosity of particular performers. *Chicago Concerto* (1967) was written for Gerry Mulligan (baritone saxophone), *Nightsongs* (1973) for Harold Lieberman (trumpet and flugelhorn), *The Devil's Herald* (1975) for Harvey Phillips (tuba), and *Arrows of Time* (1994–6) for Joseph Arlessi (trombone).

In the mid-1960s Peaslee began composing extensively for the stage. An early success was *Marat/Sade* (1964), a score that juxtaposed diverse elements drawn from 18th-century classicism and 20th-century compositional techniques as well as folk music and popular idioms. Other musicals include *Animal Farm* (1984), *Miracolo d'amore* (1988), and *The Snow Queen* (1990). He has collaborated with the choreographers Twyla Tharp (*Happily Ever After*, 1976), David Parsons (*Ring around the Rosie*, 1994; *Touch*, 1996), and Elisa Monte (*Feu follet*, 1996) and has composed music for the Joffrey and the New York City ballet companies. He also has written for film and television, including the Joseph Campbell/Bill Moyers series *The Power of Myth*, for which his music was nominated for an Emmy Award.

Peaslee is the recipient of several grants and awards such as the American Academy of Arts and Letters Marc Blitzstein Award and Obie, Drama Desk, and Villager awards, in addition to NEA and NFA fellowships. A former board member of the American Composers Orchestra and a board member of American Opera Projects, Peaslee has also taught at the Lincoln Center Institute and as part of New York University's Music Theatre Program.

WORKS
(selective list)

DRAMATIC

Musical theater: Marat/Sade (P. Brook), 1964; The Serpent (J. van Itallie), 1970; The Fable (J. van Itallie), 1975; The Children's Crusade (K. Cavander), 1981; Animal Farm (P. Hall, A. Mitchell), 1984; Garden of Earthly Delights, 1984; Vienna: Lusthaus (C.L. Mee), 1986; Miracolo d'amore (M. Clarke), 1988; The Snow Queen (A. Mitchell), 1990; Moby-Dick (Peaslee and A. Mitchell, after H. Melville), 2005, rev 2008
Opera: Sir Gawain and the Green Knight, 2001
Dance music: Happily Ever After (T. Tharp), 1976; Ring around the Rosie (D. Parsons), 1994; Feu follet: a Cajun Tale (E. Monte), 1995; Touch (Parsons), 1996; The Four Humours (Pilobolus), 2002
Film and television: Marat/Sade, 1966; Wild Wild World of Animals, 1977; The Power of Myth (J. Campbell, B. Moyers), 1988; Blown Sideways through Life, 1995
Incid music for more than 40 productions in London, New York, and Paris

OTHER
Orch: Stonehenge, jazz ens, 1963; Chicago Conc., jazz ens, 1967; October Piece, 1970; Afterlight, 1985; Tarentella, 1988
Choral: Missa brevis for St. John the Divine, SATB, org, 1994
Chbr: Nightsongs, tpt, hp, str, 1973; The Devil's Herald, 4 hn, tuba, perc, 1975; Distant Dancing, brass qnt, 1992; Arrows of Time, trbn, pf, 1994, orchd 1996
Principal publishers: Boosey & Hawkes, E.C. Schirmer, Margun, European American, Galaxy, Boonin
JOSEPH BRUMBELOE/ELIZABETH PERTEN

Pedal steel guitar [pedal steel, steel guitar, steel]. A musical instrument that is a technological expansion of the lap steel guitar. The pedal steel rests on four legs with the string plane parallel to the ground and is played from a seated position. The strings are stopped with a smooth steel bar held in the left hand and plucked with metal or plastic plectra worn on the thumb, index, and middle fingers of the right hand. The use of the bar produces a characteristic tone and allows for expressive vibrato and portamento effects. The bar is laid across the string plane, restricting players to the intervals of the open strings. In the 1910s through 1930s mechanisms were introduced to lap steel guitars to allow players to change between popular tunings without manually retuning individual strings. In the 1950s players began to use devices activated by foot pedals and knee levers to produce melodic and harmonic effects as they played. The popularity of this style drove the refinement of the technology and the establishment of the pedal steel as a distinct instrument.

A typical modern pedal steel comprises two ten-string necks that are affected by eight foot pedals and four or five knee levers. Each of these devices can be configured to alter any string or combination of strings, and each string can be raised or lowered by one to three semitones. Most players utilize two standard tunings: an E9 tuning that is strongly associated with country music, and a C6 tuning that is most often used in western swing and jazz. Each tuning has a typical series of pitch changes, referred to as a "copedant," which is initially set up by the manufacturer. Players often analyze those of musicians they seek to emulate. Popular models aside from the double-neck E9/C6 pedal steel include a single-neck with an E9 tuning and a single-neck with a 12-string "universal" tuning that combines aspects of the E9 and C6.

The earliest pedal mechanisms were similar in principle to the pedal harp and were intended to alter the instrument's tuning to match the key of a particular piece. Among the instruments of this type are the Electraharp, manufactured by Gibson from 1939 to 1941, and the Multi-Kord, manufactured by Harlin Brothers from the 1940s to the 1960s.

A second wave of development began in the late 1940s with the innovative instruments of the California-based luthier Paul Bigsby. A major landmark came in 1954 with the release of "Slowly," a number one single by the singer Webb Pierce. On this track the steel guitarist Bud Isaacs used the pedals of his Bigsby steel to combine the tone of the steel with a harmonic gesture that was impossible to execute on a standard steel guitar. This new sound captivated audiences, significantly steel guitar players, many of whom claim to have subsequently taken their non-pedal instruments to their garage workshops to reverse-engineer Isaacs' mechanisms.

Throughout the 1950s and 60s professional steel guitarists in tandem with instrument makers developed the technology and techniques of the modern pedal steel. Players credited with major innovations include Buddy Emmons, Jimmy Day, Ralph Mooney, Maurice Anderson, and Lloyd Green; key manufacturers include Sho-Bud, Fender, Emmons, and MSA.

The pedal steel has often been used to signify country music in other genres. This is particularly true of hybrid genres such as country rock of the late 1960s and early 1970s and alternative country of the 1990s and 2000s. Divergent pedal steel styles can be heard in jazz, Nigerian juju, and the sacred steel tradition of the House of God Pentecostal church.

See also COUNTRY ROCK; HAWAIIAN GUITAR; and SACRED STEEL.

BIBLIOGRAPHY
W. Winston and B. Keith: *Pedal Steel Guitar* (New York, 1975)
W. Winston, ed.: *Pedal Steel Guitar: a Manual of Style* (Henderson, TN, 1980)
W. Carter: *Gibson Guitars: 100 Years of an American Icon* (Los Angeles, 1994)
G. Gruhn and W. Carter: *Electric Guitars and Basses: a Photographic History* (San Francisco, 1994)
G. Gruhn and W. Carter: *Gruhn's Guide to Vintage Guitars: an Identification Guide for American Fretted Instruments* (San Francisco, 1999)
T. Miller: "The Origins and Development of the Pedal Steel Guitar" (thesis, U. of South Dakota, 2007)
A. Babluk: *The Story of Paul Bigsby: Father of the Modern Solidbody Electric Guitar* (Savannah, GA, 2008)
TIMOTHY D. MILLER

Pedreira, José Enrique (*b* San Juan, PR, 2 Feb 1904; *d* San Juan, PR, 6 Jan 1959). Puerto Rican music educator, composer, and performer. He took piano lessons in San Juan with Ana and Rosa Sicardó before studying piano and composition in New York for five years with ZYGMUNT STOJOWSKI. In 1928 he returned to Puerto Rico and embarked on a performing tour of the island. He and his wife, Alicia Hutchinson, then founded the Academia de Piano Pedreira in San Juan. Among his pupils were Alba Rosa Castro and Irma Isern. In 1953 he formed a piano-organ duo with former student José Raul Ramírez. The Pedreira-Ramírez Duo performed for weekly radio and television broadcasts and in various other venues in Puerto Rico and New York. Pedreira is acknowledged as the most significant Puerto Rican composer of his generation. His stylistic evolution was gradual, from Romanticism through an identifiably Puerto Rican Impressionism to a more personal idiom that is particularly evident in his eloquent danzas. He represents the transition between Quintón (1881–1925) and nationalist composers of the 1950s. He received awards from the Ateneo of Puerto Rico, University of Puerto Rico, and Juilliard School of Music. He was inducted into the *Danza* Composers Hall of Fame in 1985.

WORKS
Inst: Pf Conc., d, 1936; vn, pf duos, incl. Elegía India; numerous pf works, incl. mazurkas, waltzes, danzas, op fantasias, nocturnes, études, caprices, and 1 sonata

Vocal: 3 diálogos con el silencio, song cycle, 1956; many songs, 1934–54
El jardín de piedra (ballet), 1957

Principal publisher: Asociación Pro Divulgación de Música, Inc.

BIBLIOGRAPHY
R. Sacarello: "José Enrique Pedreira y la Escuela de Stojowsky," *Puerto Rico Ilustrado*, xxviii/1578 (1940), 9
H. Campos-Parsi: "El Fin del Modernismo: Pedreira," *Le Gran Enciclopedia de Puerto Rico*, ed. V. Báez, vii (Madrid, 1976), 266–8
D. Thompson and F. Schwartz: *Concert Life in Puerto Rico, 1957–1992: Views and Reviews* (Puerto Rico, 1998)
J.R. Ramírez: Liner notes, *José Raúl Ramírez Interpreta a José Enrique Pedreira, Vol. 1*, Asociación Pro Divulgación de Música Inc., 92-1 (n.d.)

GUSTAVO BATISTA/JEFFREY P. THUERAUF

Peer, Ralph S(ylvester) (*b* Independence, MO, 22 May 1892; *d* Los Angeles, CA, 19 Jan 1960). Talent scout, producer, and music publisher. He began his career in the Kansas City offices of the Columbia Phonograph Co. He eventually worked for the company full time and transferred to its Chicago headquarters. Following World War I, he moved to a rival label, the General Phonograph Co.'s OKeh, which focused on blues and jazz recordings. In 1920 Peer and his supervisor Fred Hager oversaw the recording of Mamie Smith's "Crazy Blues," a record that sold more than a million copies and illustrated the commercial potential of African American music. By the following summer Peer was appointed recording director of OKeh's new 8000 "race" series; he has been regularly credited for coining the term "race records."

As a talent scout Peer's approach involved field trips to find local talent in various cities across the country. On one such trip to Atlanta in search of black performers, a furniture storeowner, Polk Brockman, insisted that Peer record the popular musician Fiddlin' John Carson playing "The Little Old Cabin in the Lane." Initially Peer doubted that there was any sort of market for such a recording; however, its success changed his mind. He created the record label number 4890 for a second shipping of Carson's song, and with recordings of Virginia Millhand and the harmonic player Henry Whittier, OKeh began its hillbilly series.

Peer left OKeh in 1925 and agreed to work for the Victor Talking Machine Co. for one dollar a year on the condition that Victor would allow him to copyright the music that was recorded. By securing these copyrights, Peer became the de facto publisher and recipient of royalties earned by these compositions. A common record industry practice, Peer's innovation was the idea of actively encouraging early country and black artists to generate original material to record, avoiding already copyrighted selections. In 1927 Peer recorded dozens of performers in Bristol, Tennessee, an event referred to as the Big Bang of country music owing to the recordings of the Carter Family and Jimmie Rodgers. Rodgers, the so-called Father of Country Music, became a star and the Carter Family sold more records for RCA-Victor than any other artist except for Rodgers.

Peer founded Southern Music Publishing in 1928. In addition to country and blues, Peer also recorded popular music and Western art music and expanded operations into Latin America and Europe. In 1940 he established the Peer International Corporation, which together with Southern, became the Peer-Southern Organization. In the early 2010s it was known as peermusic.

BIBLIOGRAPHY
R.A. Peterson: *Creating Country Music: Fabricating Authenticity* (Chicago, 1997)
B.C. Malone: *Country Music, U.S.A.* (Austin, TX, 2002/R)
C.K. Wolfe and T. Olson, eds.: *The Bristol Sessions: Writings About the Big Bang of Country Music* (Jefferson, NC, 2005)
<http://www.peermusic.com> (2013)

NANCY P. RILEY

Peerce, Jan [Perelmuth, Jacob Pincus] (*b* New York, NY, 3 June 1904; *d* New York, NY, 15 Dec 1984). Tenor. He studied with Giuseppe Borgatti and from the mid-1940s was chosen by Arturo Toscanini to sing in his broadcasts and recordings of *La bohème*, *La traviata*, *Fidelio*, *Un ballo in maschera*, and the last act of *Rigoletto*. He made his stage debut in Philadelphia in 1938 as the Duke of Mantua and joined the Metropolitan in 1941, making his first appearance as Alfredo; he stayed with that company until 1968. He toured abroad with many ensembles, specializing in the Italian and French spinto repertories, and in 1956 he became the first American to sing with the Bol'shoy since the war. In 1971 he made his Broadway debut as Tevye in *Fiddler on the Roof*. He also appeared in films, and recorded popular songs in addition to Jewish liturgical music. In his prime Peerce was most admired for a remarkably even scale, a strong technique, and a voice with a dark vibrancy in the middle register and a metallic ring at the top, points confirmed by his recordings under Toscanini. Although his diminutive size precluded an ideal romantic illusion, he was an actor of restraint and dignity.

BIBLIOGRAPHY
GV (G. Gualerzi; S. Smolian)
A. Levy: *The Bluebird of Happiness: the Memoirs of Jan Peerce* (New York, 1976)
J. Hines: "Jan Peerce," *Great Singers on Great Singing* (Garden City, NY, 1982), 224–30
Obituary, *New York Times* (17 Dec 1984)

MARTIN BERNHEIMER/R

Peerless Quartet. Close-harmony vocal group active between 1906 and 1928. It was among the most prominent and best-selling close-harmony vocal groups of the acoustic era, recording hundreds of songs for many record labels including Columbia, Victor, and Edison. Formed from members of the Columbia and Invincible quartets, the original group consisted of Frank Stanley (leader), Henry Burr, Albert Campbell, and Steve Porter. The name "Peerless" was adopted so that they could record for other record labels, although they continued to appear as the Columbia Quartet on the Columbia label until 1912. Early hits included "By the Light of the Silvery Moon" and "Let me call you sweetheart." Sometimes using other names, they also recorded comic sketches and minstrel songs.

In 1910 Stanley died and Burr took over as leader and manager for the remainder of the group's existence. In the years before and during World War I they recorded "I didn't raise my son to be a soldier" (1915) and George

M. Cohan's patriotic "Over There" (1917), reflecting popular sentiment of the moment. There were numerous membership changes, with nearly a dozen singers over the quartet's lifespan. After the war the group's popularity declined, and by the mid-1920s its sound was considered outdated. Burr reorganized the group but disbanded it in 1928. For more information see G. Averill: *Four Parts, No Waiting: a Social History of American Barbershop Harmony* (New York, 2003).

JEFFERY WANSER

Peermusic. *See* PEER-SOUTHERN.

Peer-Southern [peermusic]. Firm of music publishers founded by talent scout and entrepreneur RALPH S. PEER in 1928. It has subsequently had a major impact on the development of many musical genres. Peer worked for the record companies OKeh and Victor in the 1920s, recording Mamie Smith, Louis Armstrong's Hot Five, and Fiddlin' John Carson. He discovered the Carter Family and Jimmie Rodgers and recorded both in the Bristol sessions (1927), which are considered the first recordings of commercial country music. With the help of Victor, Peer founded Southern Records, which originally focused on country and jazz artists. Southern's early jazz roster included Jelly Roll Morton, Louis Armstrong, and Count Basie. Many of the songs it recorded in its early days, such as "Georgia on my Mind," "Will the Circle be Unbroken," and "You are my sunshine," became standard repertoire. Peer has been criticized for taking advantage of many of his early recording artists, as he encouraged many to write their own songs but subsequently retained the publishing rights and accompanying royalties.

In the late 1920s through the 30s Southern expanded into Latin America through joint ventures with international publishers. From 1931 it acquired large holdings in South and Central America, including the music of Raphael Hernández, Pedro Flores, Paquito Lopez, Benny Moré, and Tito Puente, and helped introduce these artists to audiences in the United States. Over the next 15 years the company expanded into Europe, Australia, South Africa, and East Asia under the name Peer International. Associated European artists include Edith Piaf, Maurice Chevalier, and Henri Salvador. Southern and Peer International then became known as the Peer-Southern Organization and acquired the American Performing Rights Society, Melody Lane Publications, La Salle Music Publishing Company, and the Charles K. Harris Music Publishing Company. From 1948 Peer-Southern worked with art music and music education, signing such composers as Charles Ives, Manuel Ponce, and David Diamond. In the 1950s it branched out into early rock and roll and signed Buddy Holly, Little Richard, and the Platters, among others. The Rolling Stones and Donovan recorded their early albums at Peer-Southern's London studios.

Ralph Peer died in 1960. His widow, Monique, ran the company until their son Ralph Peer II took control. The company continued global expansion into Asia-Pacific and became the first international music company to pursue online recording sales. In the early 2010s it was called peermusic and operated 32 offices in 28 countries. Its artist roster included a wide range of styles including hip hop, new age, Celtic, and electronic music.

BENJAMIN J. HARBERT

Pelham, Dick [Pell, Richard Ward] (*b* New York, NY, 13 Feb 1815; *d* Liverpool, England, 8 Oct 1876). Minstrel. A talented singer, dancer, and actor, he made his debut on the New York stage in 1835 in Thomas D. Rice's blackface farce *O, Hush! or, the Virginny Cupids!* He subsequently toured with Turner's Circus doing song and dance, and teamed with his younger brother Gilbert W. Pell (*b* New York, NY, *c*1825; *d* Lancashire, England, 21 Dec 1872). Together they presented "negro extravaganzas" featuring comic songs, dialogue, and lively dancing to banjo accompaniment, with Gilbert billed as Pelham's "pupil, the little ace of spades." Pelham wrote many of their songs, notably "Massa is a stingy man" (1841) and "Ginger Blue" (1841). In 1840 Pelham lost a $500 challenge dance to John Diamond.

With DAN EMMETT, BILLY WHITLOCK, and FRANK BROWER he founded the VIRGINIA MINSTRELS, the first blackface minstrel troupe, in early 1843. Playing tambourine on the left end, Pelham's boisterous stage antics—like those of Brower on the opposite end—created the convention of the end man. His virtuosic breakdowns became legendary: like Brower, he was a top-ranked dancer whose moves were imitated by William Henry Lane, among others. The Virginia Minstrels dissolved in July 1843 but reunited briefly in spring 1844 at Pelham's instigation, with Joel Sweeney replacing Whitlock. Pelham married an actress and remained in England for the rest of his life. When Gilbert brought his Pell's Ethiopian Serenaders, featuring Lane, to England in 1848, Pelham managed them for a time. He continued to perform with various minstrel troupes; his last engagement was in Birmingham, England, on 19 August 1856.

BIBLIOGRAPHY

E.L. Rice: *Monarchs of Minstrelsy: from 'Daddy' Rice to Date* (New York, 1911) , 11–12, 13, 48

T.A. Brown: "Early History of Negro Minstrelsy," *Burnt Cork and Tambourines: a Source Book for Negro Minstrelsy*, ed. W.L. Slout (San Bernardino, CA, 2007), 9, 10, 11, 12, 14, 124, 194, 195, 200, 260; repr. at <http://www.circushistory.org/Cork/BurntCork4.htm>

SANDRA JEAN GRAHAM

Pelham, Peter (*b* London, England, 9 Dec 1721; *d* Richmond, VA, 28 April 1805). Organist, harpsichordist, teacher, and composer of English birth. He was the son of Peter Pelham, a mezzotint portrait engraver who settled in Boston in 1726. The family hosted one of the earliest known public concerts of secular music in the New World at their house on 30 December 1731. Pelham studied with CHARLES THEODORE PACHELBEL, the son of Johann Pachelbel, for nine years from the age of 12, first in Newport, Rhode Island, and later in Charleston, South Carolina. In the latter he subsequently taught spinet and harpsichord, and his students described him as "a Genteel Clever young man" and "verey chomical and entertaining." He was the first organist at Trinity

Church, Boston (1744–9) and the organist of Bruton Parish Church in Williamsburg, Virginia (1755–1802); his evening performances at Bruton Church in 1769 included works by George Frideric Handel, Antonio Vivaldi, and William Felton. He conducted the Virginia Company of Comedians' production of *The Beggar's Opera* in 1768 and performed a dirge (now lost) at a Masonic funeral at Bruton Church in 1773. Pelham also held non-musical posts in Williamsburg: he was supervisor for the printing of money (1758–75), governor's clerk (1769–70), and jail keeper (1770–?80). He became blind in 1802, after which his daughter Elizabeth briefly succeeded him as organist at Bruton Church.

Few works by Pelham survive. The melody of a minuet has been found in Williamsburg (published in J.S. Darling, ed.: *A Little Keyboard Book*, Williamsburg, VA, 1972). His 1744 manuscript copybook of harpsichord lessons (held at the Colonial Williamsburg Foundation's John D. Rockefeller Jr. Library) contains two complete minuets that may also be by Pelham. These simple, didactic works are well crafted and appealing. The book also includes works by Handel, Thomas Arne, J.C. Pepusch, Maurice Greene, Davidson Russel, Marchant, Robert Valentine, Jean Baptiste Loeillet [John Loeillet of London], and Charles Theodore Pachelbel. Pelham's keyboard arrangements of orchestral and operatic works display solid musicianship; accuracy and clarity are exemplary throughout the volume.

BIBLIOGRAPHY

N.A. Benson: *The Itinerant Dancing and Music Masters of Eighteenth Century America* (diss., U. of Minnesota, 1963)

R. Stevenson: "The Music that George Washington Knew: Neglected Phrases," *Inter-American Music Review*, v (1982–3), 19–77

H.J. Butler, ed.: *The Peter Pelham Manuscript of 1744: an Early American Keyboard Tutor* (Colfax, NC, 2005)

H. JOSEPH BUTLER

Pelissier [Pelesier, Pelliser, Pellisier], **Victor** (*b* ?Paris, France, *c*1740–50; *d* ?New Jersey, *c*1820). French composer, arranger, and horn virtuoso. After fleeing the native and black uprisings in St. Domingue (now Haiti), he was first mentioned in an advertisement for a concert in Philadelphia (1792) as "first French horn of the theatre in Cape François." In 1793 he joined the orchestra of the Old American Company in New York, living in lower Manhattan from 1797–1806, and became one of its principal composers and arrangers. From 1811 to 1814 he was back in Philadelphia, where he published *Pelissier's Columbian Melodies* (1811–2), in 12 volumes containing 46 songs, dances, and instrumental pieces arranged for piano, many of them originally written for New York and Philadelphia theaters, including some bravura arias for leading singers. He may also have composed the Symphony in G in the 1780s before his emigration from France, but probably not the *Amusements variés* mentioned by Eitner, or *L'Amour de l'Age d'Or*, mentioned by Saloman, both of which are stylistically distinct.

Pelissier's American career extended through a change in theatrical music from an emphasis on historical spectacle, pantomime, and comic opera to an age of sentimental melodrama. His *Ariadne Abandoned by Theseus in the Isle of Naxos* (1797) was one of the earliest and most influential melodramas composed in America, though a more complete idea of his style is shown in the incidental music to William Dunlap's play *The Voice of Nature* (1803) and in the *Ode on the Passions...every stanza expressing a different passion*, included in the *Columbian Melodies*. Pelissier was a prolific composer who, in his scores for over 80 theatrical works, displayed "variety of thought and readiness of invention, with the full knowledge of all the powers of an orchestra" (Parker). A victim of failing eyesight, he was honored in 1814 and 1817 with benefit concerts given by New York musicians.

WORKS

Collection: *Pelissier's Columbian Melodies*, i–xii (Philadelphia, 1811–2) [PCM]; ed. K. Kroeger, RRAM, xiii–xiv (1984)

STAGE

Operas: *Edwin and Angelina, or The Banditti* (3, E.H. Smith, after O. Goldsmith), New York, 19 Dec 1796, 2 songs in PCM, i, vi; *Sterne's Maria, or The Vintage* (2, W. Dunlap), New York, 14 Jan 1799, 3 songs in PCM, xi

Pantomimes: *The Death of Captain Cook*, New York, 1793, lost; *Sophia of Brabant*, Philadelphia, 1 Nov 1794, lost; *Harlequin Pastry Cook*, Philadelphia, 21 Nov 1794, lost; *La forêt noire*, New York, 30 March 1795, lost; *Danaides, or Vice Punished*, Philadelphia, 1795, lost; *Robinson Crusoe*, New York, 15 June 1796, lost; *The Fourth of July, or Temple of American Independence*, New York, 4 July 1799, lost; *Obi, or Three-fingered Jack*, Boston, 1801, dances in PCM, vii, ix; *Gil Blas*, New York, 1802, fandango in PCM, xi; *La fille hussar*, New York, 1803, lost; *Raymond and Agnes, or The Bleeding Nun*, New York, 1804, lost; *Mother Goose*, Philadelphia, 1810, lost; *The Milleners*, allemande in PCM, xi; *The Archers*, Philadelphia, air in PCM, xi

Melodramas: *Ariadne Abandoned by Theseus in the Isle of Naxos*, New York, 1797, lost; *A Tale of Mystery* (3, T. Holcroft), New York, 16 March 1803, collab. J. Hewitt, 2 dances in PCM, i; *The Bridal Ring*, Philadelphia, ov., dances, 2 marches in PCM, iii–vii; *Valentine and Orson*, New York, 1805, song in PCM, xii; *The Lady of the Lake*, Philadelphia, songs in PCM, iii, iv; "Ode on the Passions," speaker, pf, PCM

Incidental music: *The Mysterious Monk* (tragedy, Dunlap), New York, 31 Oct 1796, ode and choruses, lost; *Virgin of the Sun* (5, A. von Kotzebue, trans. Dunlap), 12 March 1800, Chorus of Priests, lost; *The Voice of Nature* (3, Dunlap), New York, 1803, 2 choruses, processional music, score and parts *NYp*; modern ed. Karl Kroeger in *Early Melodrama in America* (New York, 1994)

Arrs. of orch accs. to stage works by other composers, perf. New York, Philadelphia, most lost

OTHER

Vocal: 24 songs, some in PCM, others also pubd; "Return, O Love" in *Pioneer American Composers, a Collection of Early American Songs*, ed. H.V. Milligan (Boston, 1921), pf v

Inst: Sym., G, *c*1780, Berne, Stadt- und Universitätsbibliothek, repr. *The Symphony in France, 1730–1790*, ed. J.A. Rice (New York, 1984); 3 ovs., arr. pf, PCM, i–iii, v, ix; Conc. for Cl (perf. Philadelphia 1810), lost; *Funeral Dirge* (perf. New York, 1801), lost; *Masonic March* (Philadelphia, *c*1807–14); Qt (perf. Philadelphia, 1792), lost; dances, marches, variations, arr. pf, PCM; *March to Canada*, pf (Philadelphia, 1813); 22 other pieces, arr. pf, PCM; Waltz, pf, in *A Program of Early American Piano Music*, arr. J.T. Howard (New York, 1931)

BIBLIOGRAPHY

EitnerQ

J.R. Parker: "Musical Reminiscences: Pelliser," *The Euterpeiad*, iii/3 (1822), 18

W. Dunlap: *History of the American Theatre* (New York, 1832)

C. Durang: "The Philadelphia Stage," *Philadelphia Sunday Dispatch* (1854, 1856, 1860) [series of articles; compiled by T. Westcott as

History of the Philadelphia Stage, between the Years 1749 and 1855, 1868, *PHu*; similar compilations as *The Philadelphia Stage* in *PHlc*, and *History of the Philadelphia Stage* in *PHbs*]

O.G.T. Sonneck: *A Bibliography of Early Secular American Music* (Washington, DC, 1905; rev. and enlarged by W.T. Upton, 2/1945/*R*1964)

O.G.T. Sonneck: *Early Concert-life in America (1731–1800)* (Leipzig, 1907/*R*1978)

O.G.T. Sonneck: *Early Opera in America* (New York, 1915/*R*1963)

W.T. Upton: *Art-song in America* (Boston, 1930/*R*1969 with suppl. 1938)

J.T. Howard: *Our American Music* (New York, 1931, 4/1965) [incl. list of works]

J. Mates: *The American Musical Stage before 1800* (New Brunswick, NJ, 1962)

R.J. Wolfe: *Secular Music in America, 1801–1825: a Bibliography* (New York, 1964)

O.F. Saloman: "Victor Pelissier, Composer in Federal New York and Philadelphia," *The Pennsylvania Magazine of History and Biography*, cii/1 (1978), 93–102

E. Zimmerman: *An American Opera Composer: Victor Pelissier, Practitioner of an Elusive Art Form* (Lawrence, KS, 1978)

K. Kroeger, ed.: *Pelissier's Columbian Melodies*, i–xii (Philadelphia, 1811–12) RRAM, xiii–xiv (1984)

J.L. Snedeker: "The Horn in Early America," *Perspectives in Brass Scholarship: Proceedings of the International Historic Brass Symposium, Amherst, 1995*, ed. S. Carter (Stuyvesant, NY, 1997), 151–69

ANNE DHU McLUCAS

Pellegrino, Ron(ald Anthony) (*b* Kenosha, WI, 11 May 1940). Composer and performer. After early training as a clarinetist, he studied theory, composition, and philosophy at Lawrence University (BM 1962) and later studied with RUDOLF KOLISCH, René Leibowitz, and Robert Crane at the University of Wisconsin (MM 1965, PhD 1968). He began working in electronic music in 1967 at the University of Wisconsin and in 1969 published *An Electronic Music Studio Manual* (Columbus, Ohio), which became the standard text on the Moog synthesizer. He directed the electronic music studios at Ohio State University (1968–70) and the Oberlin Conservatory (1970–73) and was associate professor at Texas Tech University, Lubbock (1978–81). Since that time he has served on the faculties of Miami University, Sonoma State University, and Western Carolina University. In the early 2010s he was conducting research in the studios of Electronic Arts Productions and presenting at seminars, workshops, presentations, expositions, and events covering emerging technology in the arts, communications, and education throughout the world. He has received two Ford Foundation awards (1967, 1969) and grants from the NEA and NEH for establishing the Leading Edge music series (a forum for contemporary music performance and scholarship) and for research on his book *The Electronic Arts of Sound and Light* (New York, 1983). Pellegrino's works reflect his interest in psychoacoustics and psycho-optics. His main concerns have been the composition of sound and light structures derived from common electronic sources, the process of improvisation, and the creation, using electronic instruments, of works whose sonic and visual aspects are fully integrated. He has further explored these areas by founding two electronic music performance ensembles, the Real Electric Symphony (R*ES) and the Sonoma Electro-acoustic Music Society (SEAMS), and has developed a theory of music based on the structure and behavior of waves and vibrations, which he calls cymatic music. He has written articles on topics including synthesizers and laser composition. His other publications from Electronic Arts Productions are *Emergent Music and Visual Music: Inside Studies* (2009) and *Realizing Electronic Dreams: a Composer's Notes and Themes* (2010).

WORKS

Elec and mixed media: S&H Explorations, cl, elec, 1972; Metabiosis IV, mixed media, 1972; Figured, film, perc, tape, 1972; Cries, film, perc, tape, 1973; Kaleidoscopic Electric Rags, 1974; Video Slices, film, perc, tape, 1975; Ephemeral Forms, mixed media, 1976; Metabiosis VI, mixed media, 1977; Setting Suns and Spinning Daughters, mixed media, 1978; Words and Phrases, 1v, perc, elec, 1980; Siberian News Release, perc, elec, 1981; Spring Suite, elec, 1982; Laser Seraphim and Cymatic Music, mixed media, 1982; Soft Candy, elec, 1986; Winter Reflections, elec, 1999; The Dev Fox Heterophonic Alchemical Tours, mixed media, 2001; other works

Tape and inst: The End of an Affair, perc, tape, 1967; Dance Drama, S, timp, 1967; Passage, tape, 1968; Markings, S, timp, tape, 1969; ETT/Y, 4-track tape, 1970; Leda and the Swan, S, synth, 1970; Phil's Float, cl, tape, 1974; Wavesong, pf, tape, 1975; Issue of the Silver Hatch, perc, 1979

Principal publishers: American Society of University Composers, Electronic Arts Productions, Society of Composers

STEPHEN RUPPENTHAL/GREG A STEINKE

Pelletier, (Louis) Wilfrid (*b* Montreal, ON, 20 June 1896; *d* New York, NY, 9 April 1982). Canadian conductor and music educator. After studying with François Héraly (1904–14) and subsequently working with Alexis Contant and Alfred Laliberté, in 1915 Pelletier won the Prix d'Europe and moved to Paris with his first wife, Berthe Jeannotte. There he studied with ISIDORE PHILIPP (piano), Marcel Samuel-Rousseau (harmony), Charles Bellaigue (opera repertory), and Charles-Marie Widor (composition). After moving to New York in 1917 he was engaged on the recommendation of Pierre Monteux as a *répétiteur* at the Metropolitan Opera. In 1921 he was made assistant conductor. In 1928 he became director of the company's French repertory and in 1932 conductor of the Sunday Night Opera Concerts. He served as house conductor until 1950, during which time he initiated the Metropolitan Auditions of the Air (1936), regularly conducted the New York Philharmonic's children's concerts and was guest conductor under Arturo Toscanini of the NBC SO.

In April 1935 he gave his first concert as founding conductor of the reorganized Montreal SO and in November instigated a series of children's concerts. In June 1936 he led the inaugural programme of the Montreal Festival. In 1940 he left the Montreal SO and in 1942, together with Claude Champagne, persuaded the provincial government to establish the Conservatoire de Musique de Québec à Montréal. Pelletier was director until 1961 and made it the pre-eminent musical institution in French Canada. From 1951 to 1966 he was artistic director of the Quebec SO and from 1961 to 1970 music director in the Ministry of Cultural Affairs of the Quebec government. His honours included CMG (1946), Chevalier of the Légion d'Honneur (1947), and Companion of the Order of Canada (1968). In 1966 the largest concert hall at the new Place des Arts in Montreal was named Salle Wilfrid-Pelletier. Pelletier married the American singer Queena Mario in 1925 and the soprano Rose Bampton in 1937.

BIBLIOGRAPHY

W. Pelletier: *Une symphonie inachevée* (Montreal, 1972) [autobiography]

C. Huot: *Evolution de la vie musicale au Québec sous l'influence de Wilfrid Pelletier* (diss., U. de Toulouse, Le Mirail, 1973)

M. Kendergi: "La musique des années cinquante au Québec," *Studies in Music from the University of Western Ontario*, ix (1984), 27–36

C. Huot: *Wilfrid Pelletier: un grand homme, une grande oeuvre* (Montreal, 1996)

CHARLES BARBER, JOSÉ A. BOWEN

Peloubet. Family of instrument makers.

1. Joseph-Alexandre de Chabrier de Peloubet. 2. (Louis Michel François) Chabrier (de) Peloubet.

1. JOSEPH-ALEXANDRE DE CHABRIER DE PELOUBET. (*b* nr Lauzun, France, 4 March 1764; *d* Bloomfield, NJ, 8 March 1844). Maker of woodwind instruments. He worked as a French merchant seaman before serving in the royal army at the start of the French Revolution. He was arrested and sentenced to death, but escaped and made his way to Germany, where he learned the trade of making woodwind musical instruments. In October 1803 he moved to New York, where he married in 1805. He was active as an instrument maker in different New York locations. He advertised in the New York *Morning Chronicle* (6 November 1804) as Monniot, Peloubet & Co. for making and repairing "all sorts of instruments, viz., Violins, Piano Fortes, Harpsichords, Organs, Clarinets, Flute, Octaves, Flageolets, &c." In 1810 and 1811 he advertised in the *Albany Argus* as a "musical instrument maker."

The only instrument which can be attributed to him is a five-key boxwood clarinet with ivory trim and five flat brass keys, pitched quite low and stamped "Peloubet." This appears to be the earliest extant clarinet made in the United States.

2. (LOUIS MICHEL FRANÇOIS) CHABRIER (DE) PELOUBET. (*b* Philadelphia, PA, 22 Feb 1806; *d* Bloomfield, NJ, 30 Oct 1885). Maker of woodwind instruments and reed organs, son of (1) Joseph-Alexandre de Chabrier de Peloubet. He used "Chabrier" as his given name (the family name); "Peloubet" is the name of an estate near Lauzon in southwestern France. He probably learned woodwind making from his father, and at age 17 he apprenticed with Firth & Hall in New York. In 1830 he went into business for himself at Heather Street, making flutes, clarinets, piccolos, and flageolets. In 1836 he moved his family to Bloomfield, New Jersey, where he established a factory in Pierson's Mill, and in 1842 to 86 Orange Street. After these premises were destroyed by fire in 1869, he built two new factory buildings on Orange Street. Peloubet maintained connections in New York: a number of his woodwind instruments carry the stamp "Atwill's Music Saloon, N-York." Other Peloubet instruments are stamped "Factory at Bloom-field," or "Factory at Bloomfield, N.J."

About 1842 the firm began producing melodeons and in 1849 cabinet reed organs; at that time they evidently stopped production of woodwind instruments. Peloubet advertised melodeons and reed organs in newspapers in Newark, New Jersey, during the 1850s

and 60s, during which time the company grew, with Peloubet's son Jarvis (1833–1902) joining him in the family business. In 1860 they produced 90 melodeons at a value of $8000, most of them small home instruments. The company also operated as C. Peloubet & Son, Peloubet & Pelton Standard Organ Co. (in partnership with J.M. Pelton, 1873–*c*1882), and Peloubet Standard Organ Co.

LYON & HEALY of Chicago purchased the Peloubet company in 1890 and continued their line of organs. A large number of flutes by C. Peloubet has survived and ranges in complexity from simple, one-key instruments to eight-key flutes, one made of ivory, with silver keywork and trim (Dayton Miller Collection no.73), also stamped "P.H. Taylor's Approved, (No.) 315." In addition to flutes, there exist numerous clarinets, piccolos, and flageolets. For further information see C.H. Kaufman: *Music in New Jersey, 1655–1860: a Study of Musical Activity and Musicians in New Jersey from its First Settlement to the Civil War* (Rutherford, NJ, 1981).

DOUGLAS KOEPPE

Peña (Plaza), Lito [Ángel] (*b* Humacao, PR, 17 July 1921; *d* San Juan, PR, 18 June 2002). Saxophonist, bandleader, composer, and arranger. A member of one of Puerto Rico's most respected musical families, he was trained in the practices of old Spanish military-band traditions by his father, Juan Peña Reyes (1879–1948). After playing in a band led by his cousin Rafael González Peña and another by Armando Castro, he was hired in 1947 as saxophone soloist for the César Concepción Orchestra. Divisions within this orchestra in 1954 led him and fellow members to create the 15-piece Orquesta Panamericana, which performed various Latin American genres. The ensemble also offered an early showcase for Ismael Rivera, who was later known as el Sonero Mayor. Popularly known as La Panamericana, the group conspicuously presented fresh Afro-Puerto Rican sounds on radio and television, helping *bomba* and *plena*—genres associated with marginal barrios—to become the most visible musical products of Puerto Rico. Peña's training in music theory with Amaury Veray and Julián Bautista led to a strong catalog of nationalist compositions, including his *Fantasía Caribe* for orchestra (1962), which introduced the sounds of *bomba* to the concert hall. From 1984 until his death, he conducted the Puerto Rico State Band.

BIBLIOGRAPHY

A. Peña: *Juan Peña Reyes: su música y su tiempo*, ed. T. Peña Plaza (San Juan, PR, 1994)

J. Santiago: *Nueva ola portoricensis* (San Juan, PR, 1994)

M. Peña Plaza: "Lito Peña: retrato," *El Centro Cultural Informa* (Humacao, PR, 2003)

EDGARDO DIAZ DIAZ

Pendergrass, Teddy [Theodore DeReese] (*b* Kingstree, SC, 26 March 1950; *d* Bryn Mawr, PA, 13 Jan 2010). Soul singer and songwriter. He was ordained a minister at an early age and was introduced to secular music by his mother. He taught himself to play drums and several other instruments and sang with a local group in Philadelphia while in his teens. When he was 19 he became the drummer for the Cadillacs. A year later he joined HAROLD MELVIN AND THE BLUE NOTES and soon replaced John Atkins as the group's lead singer, in which role he sang on a number of Philly soul classics. Melvin remained its nominal leader, however, and Pendergrass's dissatisfaction with this arrangement led him to leave the ensemble in 1976 and begin a career as a soloist. In the late 1970s and early 1980s he had several hit recordings, including "I don't love you anymore" (no.41, 1977), "Close the Door" (no.25, 1978), and "Love TKO" (no.44, 1980); these were lavishly produced soul ballads notable for their rich vocal textures, elaborate instrumental arrangements, and overt sensuality. Pendergrass's career was interrupted in 1982 by an automobile accident that left him partially paralyzed; it resumed in 1984 when he recorded an album of new material, *Love Language*, that strongly recalled his earlier style. "Joy" (1988, from the album of the same name) was a number one hit on the R&B charts and allowed him to continue his career in high standing. As he recorded throughout the 1990s, he was featured in both live performances and videos that received significant attention on BET (Black Entertainment Television). His final major hit was "Believe in Love" (1994). He also released live concerts on DVD, including *From Teddy, with Love* (2002). Although he retired from making music commercially in 2006, he continued to work as a singer with charities. For more information see T. Pendergrass: *Truly Blessed* (New York, 1992).

JONAS WESTOVER

Penn, William (Albert) (*b* Long Branch, NJ, 11 Jan 1943). Composer. He attended SUNY, Buffalo, where he studied trumpet (BFA 1964) then composition (MA 1967, with Henri Pousseur and Mauricio Kagel). He received a PhD from Michigan State University (1971). At the Eastman School he pursued further studies in composition with WAYNE BARLOW and served as a faculty member in composition and theory (1971–8). From 1974 to 1976 he was staff composer for the New York Shakespeare Festival and from 1975 he was associated with the Folger Shakespeare Theatre and Sounds Reasonable Records in Washington, DC. He later taught at the University of Connecticut, served as director of the electronic studio at the University of Arizona, and was both a visiting faculty member and composer-in-residence at the University of South Carolina. He has received a number of awards; by 2012 these included one from Meet the Composer, more than 30 from ASCAP, and three NEA fellowships (1974–6). His output covers a wide range of genres including jazz and mixed media works. He has also contributed music for Broadway and off-Broadway productions, as well as for both feature films and television. In the early 2010s he was running an independent recording company and occasionally composing music for theatrical productions. For more information see E. Smedley: *William Penn's "Garland Songs": an Orchestration and Examination of Music and Text Association* (diss., U. of Washington, 2010).

WORKS

Str Qt, 1968; At Last Olympus!, musical, 1969; Spectrums, Confusions, and Sometime: Moments beyond the Order of Destiny, orch, 1969; The Pied Piper of Hamlin, musical, 1969; Chbr Music no.1, vn, pf, 1971, no.2, vc, pf, 1972; Sym., 1971; The Boy who Cried "Wolf" is Dead, musical, 1971; Ultra mensuram, 3 brass qnts, 1971; And among the Leaves we were Passing, synth, 1972; Designs, wind, jazz qnt, perc, 1972; The Canticle, musical, 1972; Inner Loop, band, 1973; Niagara 1678, band, 1973; Night Music, fl choir, 1973; Miroirs sur le Rubaiyat, pf, nar, 1974; Confessions of a Serial Killer, film score, 1987; A Cornfield in July and the River, voice, band, 1991; Mr. Toad's Wild Adventure, orch, 1993; Sax Conc., 1994; The Revelations of St. John the Divine, wind ens, 1995; Capriccio, tuba, mar, 1998; incid music, mixed media works, songs, other inst pieces

Publishers: C.F. Peters, Ludwig, Marimba, Seesaw

DAVID COPE/ALAN SHOCKLEY

Pennario, Leonard (*b* Buffalo, NY, 9 July 1924; *d* La Jolla, CA, 27 June 2008). Pianist. His earliest teachers included the pianists ISABELLE VENGEROVA and Olga Steeb, and the composer ERNST TOCH. At the age of 12 he made his debut playing Edvard Grieg's concerto with the Dallas SO. His New York debut came seven years later in Liszt's E♭ concerto with the New York Philharmonic under Artur Rodziński in Carnegie Hall. In 1952 he gave his first European performances, including his London debut, and then toured extensively, winning praise for the power and brilliance of his playing. As a chamber musician he worked and recorded with Jascha Heifetz and Gregor Piatigorsky, among others. He gave the first performance of Miklós Rózsa's Piano Concerto (1966), composed for him, with the Los Angeles PO under Zubin Mehta. In the 1970s he expanded his repertory to include popular works, notably music by Louis Gottschalk and George Gershwin.

BIBLIOGRAPHY

"It Is the Ultimate Reward," *Piano Quarterly*, no.82 (1973), 3–7 [interview]
J. Barron: Obituary, *New York Times* (28 June 2008)

GEORGE GELLES/BETH E. LEVY

Pennington, Eddie (*b* Madisonville, KY, 22 March 1956). Guitarist. A native of Hopkins County, Kentucky, he is known as a master of the intricate fingerpicked guitar style known as Kentucky thumb-picking or Travis-style picking (for Merle Travis, its best known practitioner). Originally a regional style emerging from the coal fields of Western Kentucky, the music is characterized by the use of a thumb-pick to create a bluesy bass line, while fingers pluck lively, percussive rhythm, melody, and harmony.

Pennington was born to a family especially rich in fiddlers; the fiddle was his first instrument. In 1974, however, he met the legendary thumb-picker Mose Rager of Drakesboro, Kentucky, whose performance style shaped a generation of guitarists, including Travis and Chet Atkins. Smitten with Rager's sound, Pennington divided his time between pre-med studies at Western Kentucky University and less formal instruction by example from Rager. He left college and completed work at the Kentucky College of Mortuary Science in 1977; he subsequently worked as a funeral director and as Hopkins County coroner from 1986 to 2010. He continued music as a serious avocation and eventually dropped his other occupational commitments.

Inspired by Travis's musicianship, Pennington has also developed a winning stage presence reflecting his hero's jaunty charm. He has served as an informal ambassador of Muhlenberg County guitar style throughout the United States and Europe. In 2003 he received an honorary doctorate from Western Kentucky University, triumphantly completing the effort begun in the 1970s. In 2002 he received a National Heritage Fellowship from the NEA, the highest honor offered to traditional artists by the federal government.

SELECTED RECORDINGS

As leader: with C. Black: *Just my Style* (Bee/Nephi, 2000); *Eddie Pennington Walks the Strings…and Even Sings* (Folkways, 2004); *Atonathum'* (That Muhlenberg Sound, n.d.)

ERIKA BRADY

Pennsylvania, University of. Privately endowed university founded in Philadelphia in 1740 and offering music courses from 1875; *see also* Libraries and collections.

Pennsylvanians, the [Fred Waring and His Pennsylvanians]. Instrumental ensemble, vocal band, and choral ensemble. Formed in 1918 at Pennsylvania State University, The Pennsylvanians were originally known as the "Waring-McClintock Snap Orchestra" (for co-founding brothers Fred and Tom Waring, and friends Freddy Buck and Poley McClintock). They were later billed as "Waring's Banjo Orchestra," and then "Waring's Pennsylvanians" by the time of their first hit record, *Sleep* (1923). The initially became popular by performing at college campuses, vaudeville houses, and movie theaters. Over six decades, the ensemble recorded more than 1500 songs on over 100 albums, producing hit recordings and radio/television programs until Waring's death in 1984.

Over the years, the group changed its emphasis substantially, shifting from an instrumental ensemble to a vocal jazz ensemble, and eventually to a choral ensemble. The Pennsylvanians' repertoire was eclectic, encompassing popular, folk, romantic, holiday, patriotic, and Broadway idioms. The group became one of the most popular choral ensembles in America despite not focusing on classical choral repertoire. Waring's influence on the teaching of choral music paralleled the focus of the ensemble and included a series of choral workshops that introduced his method of employing unique syllables to provide textual emphasis. Fred Waring did not rehearse the ensemble, though he did oversee issues of interpretation and textual phrasing, developing what became known as the "Waring Sound." Rather, The Pennsylvanians, and its companion studio ensemble called Glee Club, employed some of the most notable choral conductors of the twentieth century, including Robert Shaw (1939–44), Don Craig (1944–8), Lara Hoggard (1948–55), and Jack Best (1955–84).

PATRICK K. FREER

Penobscot. Native American tribe of the Wabenaki confederacy.

Pentecostal and Renewal music. The music and worship of (1) that group of Christian sects whose defining characteristic is the belief that the occurrence on the day of Pentecost recounted in the second chapter of the *Acts of the Apostles* not only signaled the birth of the Church but described an experience available to believers in all ages, namely, baptism in the Holy Spirit; and (2) those churches, either belonging to or outside the mainstream denominations, that were touched by the Charismatic Renewal movement of the latter half of the 20th century. Associated with these traditions is a distinctive repertory of songs and choruses expressing, often in a vivid and personal manner, individual and collective experience of the Christian faith.

1. The Pentecostal tradition. 2. The Charismatic tradition.

1. The Pentecostal tradition. The Pentecostal Movement in America, strongly influenced by Methodism and the Holiness Movement (out of which it grew), is considered to have emerged at the turn of the 19th and 20th centuries, with outpourings of the Holy Spirit manifested in North Carolina (1896), Kansas (1901), and California (1906). At the beginning all leaders preached the Wesleyan doctrine of sanctification as a "second work of grace," and the "third blessing" as baptism in the Holy Spirit, with speaking in tongues as evidence. So strong was the teaching on baptism in the Holy Spirit that at a very early stage at least six hymnals with the title *Pentecostal Hymns* were used within the movement. From its meager beginnings Pentecostalism has grown into a global force within Christendom, crossing denominational barriers in a way that few other movements have managed. Missionary activity on the part of several of the long-established Pentecostal Churches, international crusades by leading evangelists such as Oral Roberts, religious broadcasting and the proliferation of Christian television networks have all contributed to its worldwide spread. Today, there are three broad groups of Pentecostal believers: (1) classical Pentecostals, belonging to churches whose origins date back to the beginning of the 20th century, for example, the Assemblies of God, the Church of God (Cleveland, Tennessee), the Pentecostal Holiness Church, and the International Church of the Foursquare Gospel (*see* Aimee Semple McPherson); (2) neo-Pentecostals, who accept baptism in the Holy Spirit but choose to stay within the mainstream denominations; and (3) charismatics, whose affiliation and doctrinal beliefs lie outside the classical Pentecostal or main denominational frameworks, but whose faith is centered on the distinctively Pentecostal blessings and phenomena, namely, baptism in the Holy Spirit with the spiritual gifts, such as divine healing, of *1 Corinthians* xii.8–10. In 2008 it was estimated that about a quarter of all Christians belonged to Pentecostal or charismatic denominations.

Music, often highly spiritual and improvisatory, has always been a significant feature of Pentecostal worship. The Movement's immediate musical roots lay in the traditional congregational songs common to many other denominations, particularly the hymns of Isaac Watts and Charles Wesley. But even more widespread and characteristic were the Holiness Movement songs, which focused on purity of heart, eradication of sin and a deeper walk with God (e.g. "The Cleansing Wave"), camp-meeting songs, concerned with man's earthly trials, conversion to the Christian life, and the experience of joy on the path to heaven (e.g. "Our Lord's Return to Earth"), and gospel songs, which were songs of personal testimony and heartfelt belief in Jesus Christ, especially during times of trial (e.g. "Blessed Assurance"). The more distant origins of Pentecostal music, however, may be found in biblical traditions of music and worship. In the Old Testament music clearly had both a "functional" and a "spiritual" aspect: in everyday life it was used, for example, in social contexts, as a martial accompaniment to physical work, for didactic purposes, and as an element in liturgy; but sacred song could also be a vehicle for expressing the deeper dimensions of human thought and experience. The functional aspect is of primary importance to Pentecostals, for whom music must be easily accessible, capable of reflecting the "everyday life" of the believer and allowing the worshiping community to convey its needs to God (as, for example, in Reuben Morgan's "Your Unfailing Love": "When my burden keeps me doubting, when my memories take the place of you, Jesus come"). But it is also necessary for sacred music to reinforce theological belief and impart spiritual truths, thus helping people to grow closer to their Creator (as in songs concerned with healing, the second coming of Christ, spiritual baptism and the workings of the Holy Spirit). The use of various musical instruments, the importance of singing psalms and scriptural songs, and the rebirth, within the Charismatic Movement, of dance in worship, may be directly attributed to Old Testament example (see Alford, 688).

2. THE CHARISMATIC TRADITION. During the early decades of the 20th century, as the Pentecostal Movement developed, a freer, more demonstrative kind of worship evolved whose influence would eventually leave no branch of the Western Church untouched. In the 1950s and 60s a "neo-Pentecostal" style of worship began to appear, particularly in the United States and Great Britain, among small groups of Christians belonging to the mainstream denominations. At first these "charismatic fellowships" would mainly gather in homes or in smaller rooms of churches for prayer-meeting type services. But as the Charismatic Renewal movement gathered worldwide momentum, it was only a matter of time before its characteristic style of worship, known as "Praise and Worship," whose hallmark was an intensely personal form of group singing called "praise singing," began to be incorporated into the normal services of individual churches. Many Christians of hitherto traditional persuasion—Methodists, Presbyterians, Baptists, Mennonites, Anglicans/Episcopalians, Lutherans, Roman Catholics—came to realize that their worship, though outwardly proper and beautiful, seemed inwardly void and unimaginative, lacking freshness and life-giving spirituality. By contrast, Charismatic Renewal brought a fresh "wind of the Spirit," imparting a new vitality and meaning by restoring an emphasis on dynamic worship,

in both a personal and corporate way. Worship could be an experience of joy and celebration, often manifested in enthusiastic, winsome singing, the raising of hands, exclamations of verbal praise, and, at times, spontaneous spiritual dance. The study of scripture (aided by new versions of the Bible) also plays a vital part in this type of worship, and in many churches there has been a renewed interest in the Eucharist, but praise and praise singing remain central.

Although a casual observer might easily interpret congregational praise singing as primarily emotional, its authenticity is supported by biblical practice. Some theologians see the 20th-century Charismatic Renewal movement as the spiritual restoration of Davidic worship around the Ark of the Covenant, especially through praise singing. A number of elements in Praise and Worship are based on Old Testament models and represent a liberating trend by allowing expression of the whole body and person. The joyous intensity and robust, exuberant style of praise singing is a response to Psalm lxvi.1–2, "Make a joyful noise unto God all ye lands: sing forth the honour of his name: make his praise glorious," as well as other exhortations such as "cry aloud" (Psalm lv.17) and "shout for joy" (Psalm v.11); even "laughter" is not excluded (Psalm cxxvi.2) from worship. Such singing is often accompanied by bowing and kneeling (Psalm xcv.6: "Come, let us worship and bow down; let us kneel before the Lord our maker"), clapping of hands and shouting (Psalm xlvii.1: "O clap your hands all peoples; shout to God with a voice of triumph"), lifting up of hands (Psalm cxxxiv.2: "Lift up your hands in the sanctuary, and bless the Lord") and—perhaps the most surprising of all—dancing (Psalm cl.4: "Praise him with the timbrel and dance"; and 2 Samuel vi.14: "David danced before the Lord with all his might").

The charismatic service allows for a type of freedom and spontaneity whereby pastor and "worship leader," who form a dual team, do not feel the need to be in complete control of the progress of the meeting. It is assumed that unexpected changes of direction will occur, as motivated by the Holy Spirit, although this does not mean that an eclectic, free-for-all pattern emerges but rather that a type of "guided spontaneity" prevails in which events in the service are anticipated but not prescribed or predicted. The worship leader—a kind of master of ceremonies responsible for guiding the direction of the service—chooses and leads the songs, leads prayer, quotes scripture and provides commentary. The ability of the congregation to "flow with the Spirit" as directed through the worship leader is essential. A common freedom and excitement of praise is often shared by worship leader and congregation alike, resulting in improvised and creative worship that emanates from the very hearts of the participants, who may express themselves in prayer, testimonies, word of knowledge, prophecy, and expressions of praise in singing, shouting, and dancing.

The key to praise singing lies in the participation of the congregation, for praise music is not primarily to be listened to but rather to be sung (choir items and organ playing, therefore, are usually of lesser importance). The music generally consists of short, often repetitive choruses and other scripture songs, whose antecedents may be found in the Pentecostal camp-meeting and gospel songs. The voice of the worship leader, amplified by an efficient sound system, is of primary importance in leading the singing, although gestures (not necessarily the conventional directing patterns) are often used to indicate the beginning and ending of phrases. The singing is usually reinforced by a back-up group of "praise singers" (or an individual co-singer) and instrumentalists, but rather than functioning as a choir the singers encourage participation through their visual exuberance and their leadership in physical movements.

The musical characteristics of praise singing are very much bound up with popular music styles and performing practice, for example, the use of pop-derived harmonies, rhythms and instrumentation (drums, piano, synthesizers, guitars and, in large churches, wind instruments). Some of the most prominent charismatic churches engage arrangers and copyists to provide new instrumental charts for praise singing. The result is a type of "sacra-pop" that has become the dominant musical style in such worship. The development of electronic technology has been an important factor in the growth of the genre, for sound reinforcement systems and electronic and amplified instruments permit an enormous array of sounds and dynamic levels not previously available. Nevertheless, a wide range of practice exists, and in many churches the style of singing remains simple, with minimal use of instruments and electronic support.

The kind of praise singing described above has somewhat displaced traditional congregational song and the use of the hymnal, not least because holding a hymnbook inhibits the worshippers from raising or clapping their hands. The most widespread practice is to sing from memory; some congregations use projectors to display the words. "Liturgical" churches of charismatic persuasion tend to blend their use of memorized choruses and scripture songs with use of the hymnal and the service book. In the early stages, Praise and Worship music was mostly passed on by oral tradition, for example, the chorus "Seek ye first" (1972) and the simple repetitive "Alleluia" (1972). Other typical and universally known charismatic songs, many of them in a direct, folklike idiom, include "This is the day" (1967), "I exalt Thee" (1976), "I will enter his gates with thanksgiving" (1976), "Praise the name of Jesus" (1976), "Give thanks" (1978), "I love you Lord" (1978) and "We bring the sacrifice of praise" (1984). What is considered to be the first published collection of Praise and Worship music, *Scripture in Song* by David and Dale Garratt, appeared in New Zealand in 1968. Today most collections are published in the United States, by companies such as Maranatha Music, Vineyard Music, and Integrity Music, including, respectively, *Maranatha! Music, Praise, Hymns and Choruses* (1987, 4/1997), *Songs of the Vineyard* (1980s–) and *Hosanna Music Songbooks* (1987–). Another significant source, devoted primarily to Praise and Worship music, is the Word Music series initiated by *Songs and Praise for Worship* (1992). Praise and Worship choruses also appear side by side with more traditional hymns in various denominational hymnals, for example, *The United Methodist Hymnal* (1989), *The Baptist Hymnal* (2008) and the Church of the Nazarene's *Sing to the Lord* (1993), and also in such nondenominational books as *The Hymnal* (1986) and *Celebration Hymnal* (1997). New resources supply downloadable sheet music and instrumental tracks to accompany selected Praise and Worship songs.

The Praise and Worship phenomenon, with its central activity of praise singing, is regarded by some commentators as a peripheral movement. But this is to fail to recognize its extraordinary growth and impact during the 20th and 21st centuries. Praise singing is not bound by denominational barriers but rather fosters a natural ecumenicity: persons of all ages, from varying theological, ethnic and cultural traditions, can share in it together, bringing with them the distinctiveness of their backgrounds. It would not be unreasonable to predict that the new spirit of praise singing will exert an increasing influence on Christian worship as the 21st century moves forward.

BIBLIOGRAPHY

GENERAL

P. Fleisch: *Zur Geschichte der Heiligungsbewegung* (Leipzig, 1910)

D. Gee: *The Pentecostal Movement* (London, 1949)

C. Conn: *Like a Mighty Army* (Cleveland, 1955)

K. Kendrick: *The Promise Fulfilled: a History of the Modern Pentecostal Movement* (Springfield, MO, 1961)

E. Bucke: *The History of American Methodism* (Nashville, TN, 1964)

F. Bruner: *A Theology of the Holy Spirit: the Pentecostal Experience and the New Testament Witness* (Grand Rapids, MI, 1970)

W. Menzies: *Anointed to Serve: the Story of the Assemblies of God* (Springfield, MO, 1971)

V. Synan: *The Holiness-Pentecostal Movement in the United States* (Grand Rapids, MI, 1971)

D. Dayton: *Theological Roots of Pentecostalism* (Grand Rapids, MI, 1987)

J.M. Spencer: "The Heavenly Anthem: Holy Ghost Singing in the Primal Pentecostal Revival (1906–1909)," *Journal of Black Sacred Music*, i/1 (1987), 1–33

D. Alford: 'Pentecostal and Charismatic Music,' *Dictionary of Pentecostal and Charismatic Movements*, ed. S.M. Burgess, G.B. McGee and P.H. Alexander (Grand Rapids, MI, 1988), 688–95

R. Webber: *Signs of Wonder: the Phenomenon of Convergence in Modern Liturgical and Charismatic Churches* (Nashville, TN, 1992)

D. Hustad: *Jubilate II: Church Music in Worship and Renewal* (Carol Stream, IL, 1993)

B. Liesch: *The New Worship* (Grand Rapids, MI, 1996)

R. Webber: *Ancient–Future Worship: a Model for the 21st Century* (Wheaton, IL, 1999)

M.L. Butler: "Musical Style and Experience in a Brooklyn Pentecostal Church: an "Insider's" Perspective," *Current Musicology*, lxx (2000), 33–60

J.W. Jones, Jr.: *Modern American Pentecostalism: the Significance of Race, Class, and Culture in Charismatic Growth* (Ph.D. diss., University of Arkansas, 2002)

J. Becker: *Deep Listeners: Music, Emotion, and Trancing* (Bloomington, 2004)

A. Yong and E.Y. Alexander: *Afro-Pentecostalism: Black Pentecostal and Charismatic Christianity in History and Culture* (New York, 2011)

PRAISE AND WORSHIP

G. Truscott: *The Power of his Presence* (San Diego, CA, 1969)

B. Mumford: *Entering and Enjoying Worship* (Greensburg, PA, 1975)

C. Baker: *On Eagles' Wings* (Seattle, 1979)

R. Allen: *Praise: a Matter of Life and Breath* (Nashville, TN, 1980)

R. Allen and G. Borror: *Worship: Rediscovering the Missing Jewel* (Portland, OR, 1982)

A. Ortlund: *Up with Worship: how to Quit Playing Church* (Ventura, CA, 1982)

J. Cornwall: *Let us Praise* (South Plainfield, NJ, 1983)

J. Cornwall: *Let us Worship* (South Plainfield, NJ, 1983)

C. Johansson: *Music and Ministry* (Peabody, MA, 1984)

P. Baker: *Contemporary Christian Music: Where it Came from, What it Is, Where it's Going* (Westchester, IL, 1985)

J. Cornwall: *Elements of Worship* (South Plainfield, NJ, 1985)

T. Law: *The Power of Praise and Worship* (Tulsa, 1985)

R. Webber: *Worship is a Verb* (Waco, TX, 1985)

L. Boschman: *The Prophetic Song* (Shippensburg, PA, 1986)

J. Hayford: *Worship his Majesty* (Waco, TX, 1987)

K. Osbeck: *The Endless Song: 13 Lessons in Music and Worship of the Church* (Grand Rapids, MI, 1987)

B. Sorge: *Exploring Worship: a Practical Guide to Praise and Worship* (Buffalo, NY, 1987)

D. Bloomgren, D. Smith and D. Christoffel: *Restoring Praise and Worship to the Church* (Shippensburg, PA, 1989)

L. Boschman: *The Rebirth of Music* (Shippensburg, PA, 1990)

J. Cornwall: *Worship as David Lived it* (Shippensburg, PA, 1990)

M. Evans: *Open up the Doors: Music in the Modern Church* (London, 2006)

G. Scheer: *The Art of Worship: a Musician's Guide to Leading Modern Worship* (Grand Rapids, MI, 2006)

R. Woods and B. Walrath: *The Message in the Music: Studying Contemporary Praise and Worship* (Nashville, TN, 2007)

D.S. Pollard: *When the Church Becomes Your Party: Contemporary Gospel Music* (Detroit, 2008)

G.A. Adnams: *The Experience of Congregational Singing: an Ethnophenomenological Approach* (Ph.D. diss., U. of Alberta, 2008)

B.J. Johnson: *"Oh, for a thousand tongues to sing": Music and Worship in African America Megachurches of Los Angeles, California* (Ph.D. diss., UCLA, 2008)

J. RANDALL GUTHRIE/R

Pentecostalism. *See* PENTECOSTAL AND RENEWAL MUSIC.

Pepper, Art(hur Edward) (*b* Gardena, CA, 1 Sept 1925; *d* Panorama City, CA, 15 June 1982). Jazz alto and tenor saxophonist. In 1943 he played in the big bands of Benny Carter and Stan Kenton. After serving in the US Army he toured with Kenton as the band's outstanding soloist (1946–51) and also performed freelance in Los Angeles. Thereafter his career was hampered by a series of prison terms for drug abuse, although he attempted several times to resume playing and issued several acclaimed recordings for the Contemporary label between 1957 and 1960, including *Intensity* (1960). In 1964 he adopted the tenor saxophone and began to play free jazz, then in 1968 returned to mainstream jazz by joining Buddy Rich's band; serious ailments forced his departure in the following year, however. From 1977 until his sudden death he gave a series of sensational bop performances in Japan and New York. He was the subject of a documentary, *Art Pepper: Notes from a Jazz Survivor* (1982).

Pepper was a leading figure in West Coast jazz, a movement with which he was associated not only because of his choice of location and musical colleagues but also because of his light, clear, precise sound on the alto saxophone. However, he was a stronger, more fiery improviser than his fellow West Coast musicians, as is amply demonstrated by his recordings in 1957 and 1960 with Miles Davis's rhythm section. In the mid-1960s, under the overwhelming influence of John Coltrane, he

took up the tenor saxophone, on which his playing stressed intense and expressive noise elements. Eventually, having returned to the alto instrument, he combined the two approaches in performances such as "Cherokee" (on the album *Saturday Night at the Village Vanguard*, Cont., 1977), in which traditional bop lines erupt at explosive moments into squeals, growls, and flurries of notes.

BIBLIOGRAPHY

GroveJ2

J. Tynan: "The Return of Art Pepper," *DB*, xxvii/8 (1960), 17–18

J. Tynan: "Art Pepper's Not the Same," *DB*, xxxi/22 (1964), 18–19, 40

C. Marra: "Art Pepper: 'I'm Here to Stay!'," *DB*, xl/4 (1973), 16–17

L. Underwood: "Pepper's Painful Road to Pure Art," *DB*, xlii/11 (1975), 16–17, 34

A. Pepper and L. Pepper: *Straight Life: the Story of Art Pepper* (New York, 1979, 2/1994) [incl. discography by T. Selbert]

P. Welding: "Art Pepper: Rewards of the Straight Life," *DB*, xlvi/18 (1979), 16–19 [incl. discography]

T. Selbert, ed.: *The Art Pepper Companion: Writings on a Jazz Original* (New York, 2000)

Oral history material in *NEij*

BARRY KERNFELD/R

Pepper, J(ames) W(elsh) (*b* Philadelphia, PA, 1853; *d* Philadelphia, PA, 28 July 1919). Music publisher and band instrument maker. He worked as an engraver in his father's printing business, gave music lessons, and in 1876 founded a publishing house at 9th and Filbert streets in Philadelphia. From copper plates and a manually operated press he issued instrumental tutors, quicksteps, and from 1877 to 1912 a monthly periodical entitled *J.W. Pepper's Musical Times and Band Journal* (later the *Musical Times*). Around 1887 he acquired a structure at 8th and Locust streets which came to be known as the J.W. Pepper Building, accommodating a large salesroom, an instrument factory, and a printing plant, equipped with steam-powered presses to produce sheet music on a large scale. During the next four decades the firm published nearly 200 new titles a year; except for a small group of sacred songs issued by Pepper Publishing Co. in 1901–4, these were all orchestral and band works intended for civic, commercial, and school ensembles. Many compositions and arrangements appeared in journals—*Quickstep, Brass and Reed Band, Ballroom, Theatre and Dance*, and *Opera House*. The *J.W. Pepper Piano Music Magazine* was begun in 1900 and a separate 20th-century series was also established. Among the composers whose works were published by Pepper were John Philip Sousa, Arthur Pryor, Claudio S. Grafulla, George Southwell, William Paris Chambers, Nick Brown, Thomas H. Rollinson, William Henry Dana, and Fred Luscomb. Publication of new works ceased in 1924.

Pepper sold more than 70,000 brass instruments and a similar number of drums, woodwind, and string instruments. His instruments were moderately priced and, like his sheet music, intended for a mass audience. Controversy concerning the invention of the SOUSAPHONE culminated in a claim by C.G. Conn to have invented it in 1898, although Pepper had introduced a prototype as early as 1893. The manufacture of Pepper instruments continued until J.W. Pepper & Son was formed in 1910, after which most instruments sold by the firm were imported. On Pepper's death the direction of J.W. Pepper & Son was assumed by Howard E. Pepper (1882–1930), in turn succeeded by his widow, Maude E. Pepper. The firm was sold in 1942 and moved to Valley Forge, Pennsylvania, in 1973. Guided by Harold K. Burtch and his son Dean C. Burtch, who became president on his father's death in 1963, the firm eventually became the world's largest retailer of sheet music, with 14 branch locations and a strong Internet presence serving consumers in the 2010s.

BIBLIOGRAPHY

J.W. Pepper's Musical Times and Band Journal (Philadelphia, 1877–1912)

W.H. Dana: *J.W. Pepper's Guide…Arranging Band Music* (Philadelphia, 1878)

W.H. Dana: *J.W. Pepper's Guide…Orchestra Music* (Philadelphia, 1879)

LLOYD P. FARRAR/R

Pepper, Jim [James Gilbert] (*b* Salem, OR, 18 June 1941; *d* Portland, OR, 10 Feb 1992). Tenor and soprano saxophonist, singer, bandleader, and composer. Of Native American (Creek and Kaw) heritage, he was raised in Oregon and Oklahoma. Early musical influences included tap dance, big band jazz, Southern Plains powwow music and dance, and peyote music. Pepper moved to New York in 1964 and joined the Free Spirits (1966), an early fusion jazz ensemble featuring Larry Coryell and Bob Moses. After forming the group Everything is Everything (1967) with former members of Free Spirits Chris Hills and Columbus Baker, Pepper recorded "Witchi Tai To," a composition fusing a peyote song with jazz, rock, and country influences. Released on *Everything is Everything featuring Chris Hills* (Vanguard Apostolic, 1969), "Witchi Tai To" peaked at number 69 on the Billboard pop charts. By 2011 it had been covered by at least 90 artists ranging from Brewer & Shipley, Jan Garbarek, and Oregon to the Paul Winter Consort and Joy Harjo. Pepper released four albums as a leader: *Pepper's Pow Wow* (Embryo, 1971), *Comin' and Goin'* (1987, Antilles), *Dakota Song* (1987, Enja), and *The Path* (1988, Enja), and performed throughout the United States and in Europe and Africa. His credits as a sideman include work with Archie James Cavanaugh, Don Cherry, Charlie Haden, Paul Motian, Nana Simopoulos, and Mal Waldron. He is the subject of the documentary film *Pepper's Pow Wow* (dir. S. Osawa, 1996).

BIBLIOGRAPHY

J. Berry: "Comin' and Goin': Memories of Jazzman Jim Pepper," *Oregon Historical Quarterly*, cvii/1 (2006), 122–9

J-C. Perea: "The Unexpectedness of Jim Pepper," *MUSICultures*, xxxix/1 (2012), 70–82

JOHN-CARLOS PEREA

Perabo, Johann Ernst (*b* Weisbaden, Germany, 14 Nov 1845; *d* Boston, MA, 29 Oct 1920). Pianist, teacher, and composer of German birth. He was the youngest of ten children, all of whom became musicians. His music lessons began at age five. Three years later he could play J.S. Bach's *Das wohltemperierte Clavier* from memory.

His family came to New York in 1852, relocated to Dover, New Hampshire, and then to Boston and Chicago. The father, whose finances were strained, asked for assistance from the federal government towards the boy's musical education, but President Buchanan explained that neither the administration nor Congress had any interest in the development of the fine arts. Fortunately, private patrons financed a voyage in 1858 to Hamburg, where Perabo furthered his education. He entered the Leipzig Conservatory in 1862 and received instruction on the piano from Ignaz Moscheles and Ernst Wenzel and in composition from Carl Reinecke. In 1865 he returned to the United States and made a triumphant concert tour through the Midwest. By March 1866 he had settled in Boston, where he remained until his death.

Perabo gave solo recitals, played in chamber ensembles, and performed as a soloist with symphony orchestras. His interpretations of the Beethoven and Schubert piano sonatas were admired. Lilian Whiting wrote: "To hear Mr. Perabo interpret Beethoven, Schubert, and Bach is a joy for a lifetime. His marvelous technique, his refinement of expression, the depth of significance whose inner meaning his rendering translates…is all beyond the power of words to describe." As a piano teacher he was surpassed by few. Among his students was the noted composer and pianist Amy Beach.

His compositions, largely for the piano, were published in America and Germany. Among them are *Moment Musical*, op.1; Scherzo, op.2; Prelude, op.3; Waltz, op.4; 3 Studies, op.9; *Pensées*, op.11; *Circumstance, or Fate in a Human Life*, op.13; Prelude, Romance, and Toccatina, op.19; and songs.

BIBLIOGRAPHY

F.O. Jones, ed.: *A Handbook of American Music and Musicians* (Canaseraga, NY, 1886)

A. Ehrlich: *Celebrated Pianists of the Past and Present* (Philadelphia, 1894), 258–60

The National Cyclopaedia of American Biography (New York, 1898), 446

L. Whiting: *Boston Days: the City of Beautiful Ideals* (Boston, 1902), 307–9

NICHOLAS TAWA

Perahia, Murray (*b* New York, NY, 19 April 1947). Pianist and conductor. He began piano lessons at an early age with Jeanette Haien and later graduated from Mannes College, where he majored in conducting and composition, while continuing his piano studies with ARTUR BALSAM. Before embarking on a solo career, he also spent summers at Marlboro, Vermont, where he was encouraged by RUDOLF SERKIN and collaborated in chamber music with such outstanding musicians as Pablo Casals and members of the Budapest Quartet; he also studied at this time with the veteran pianist MIECZYSŁAW HORSZOWSKI. In March 1972 he made his debut with the New York PO and later that year won first prize at the Leeds International Piano Competition. That led in the following year to his first London recital, at Queen Elizabeth Hall, and his first concert at the Aldeburgh Festival, where he became a regular visitor, often accompanying Peter Pears; from 1981 to 1989 he was one of the artistic directors of the festival. In the 21st century he became the principal guest conductor of the Academy of St. Martin in the Fields and has toured with that ensemble extensively throughout the world. His activities after 2000 include recording and touring, as well as editing the Henle Urtext Edition of Ludwig van Beethoven's complete piano sonatas. He has also produced, edited, and released discs of the pianist Alfred Cortot's recorded master classes. Perahia has been awarded two Grammy awards for his own recordings and has been nominated for six others. He was made a Knight of the British Empire in 2004 by Queen Elizabeth II. For his numerous services to music, he has been awarded honorary fellowships at Jesus College, Cambridge, and at the Royal College of Music.

Perahia's sensibility and the naturalness and lyrical impulse of his phrasing, together with the polish of his playing, were always recognized as exceptional. After he placed first at the Leeds competition it was predictable that he would become a distinguished pianist, but the direction and extent of his development as a solo player might not have been foreseen. He acknowledges that he owes much to the advice, inspiration, and friendship of Vladimir Horowitz. During the 1980s and 90s his playing acquired a more sharply defined declamation and the command of a larger scale than it had before; whereas early in his career he was not thought of as a virtuoso player or one with a "big" production, after 2000 listeners could sense in his playing a bolder rhetoric and more space for the music to breathe.

Perahia is a consummate player of J.S. Bach's music and has recorded the six English suites, and he has also made a successful case for re-establishing the suites of Handel and many of the sonatas of Domenico Scarlatti as rewarding repertory for pianists. In the late 1970s he began to record all the concertos of Wolfgang Amadeus Mozart with the English Chamber Orchestra, directing them from the piano, and achieved a set of consistent excellence. His discography also includes recordings of Felix Mendelssohn (a composer he has consistently championed), together with Beethoven's sonatas and all his piano concertos (with the Concertgebouw Orchestra conducted by Bernard Haitink). His recordings of Robert Schumann's *Kreisleriana* and Piano Concerto and Frederic Chopin's Ballades and two concertos have been acclaimed; his Chopin discography is substantial and has been particularly admired. His repertory in the 20th century hardly extended beyond Béla Bartók, although it included Michael Tippett's First Sonata. In all his work, whether as concerto soloist, solo recitalist, chamber musician, accompanist, or conductor, he has brought distinction and a musical ease that has seemed effortless.

BIBLIOGRAPHY
A. Blyth: "Branching Out," *Gramophone*, lxix/Oct (1991), 60–1

STEPHEN PLAISTOW/JONAS WESTOVER

Perantoni, Daniel (*b* Ridgway, PA, 5 May 1941). Tuba player and teacher. He studied at the Eastman School of Music (BM 1964) and Catholic University of America (MM 1968). Perantoni has made an international impact on musical life for over four decades. He has been a leading performer in a variety of genres as a solo recitalist and chamber musician and has made legendary recordings of such works for the tuba as Anthony Plog's *Three Miniatures*, Krzysztof Penderecki's *Capriccio*, Scott Wyatt's *Three for One*, Robert Jager's Concerto, and Francis McBeth's *Daniel in the Lion's Den*. He has championed the use and design of new instruments and equipment, and is largely responsible for the popularity of the F tuba. His work in the Matteson-Phillips Tuba-jazz Consort paved the way for the tuba-euphonium jazz explosion. He has performed with the Summit Brass (as a founding member), Symphonia, and the St. Louis Brass Quintet. In addition to maintaining an extremely active performing career, Perantoni has held professorships at the University of Illinois (1968–82), Arizona State University (1982–94), and Indiana University (1994–). His former students hold prestigious positions in major performing ensembles throughout the world. He received the Lifetime Achievement Award from TUBA (Tubists Universal Brotherhood Association) (2000).

PATRICE MADURA WARD-STEINMAN

Peraza, Armando (*b* Havana, Cuba, 30 May 1924). Cuban percussionist. Orphaned at a young age he began supporting himself while still a child. In 1941, when he heard a local group needed a conga player, he offered to the fill the position, despite having no prior musical experience. He subsequently earned an engagement as *bongocero* with Conjunto Kubavana alongside Carlos "Patato" Valdés. In 1947 Mongo Santamaria, who was ill, called Peraza to fill in for him in Mexico. The two later moved to New York together. Peraza was soon sitting in with the Machito Orchestra at the Palladium Ballroom, where Charlie Parker (with whom he later recorded) was in the audience. An autodidact, Peraza has been renowned for his unorthodox but inventive performance style. After several years with Slim Gaillard, Peraza worked with the pianist George Shearing in a decade-long collaboration which produced many albums, including *Latin Affair* (Cap., 1958). Peraza also joined the groups of Cal Tjader (*Soul Sauce*, Verve, 1964), Santamaria (*Mongo*, Fan., 1959), and Carlos Santana (*Lotus*, Col., 1973) for extended periods. Peraza has lived in the San Francisco area since the early 1950s, emerging as an influential advocate of Afro-Cuban culture and music.

BIBLIOGRAPHY
C. Gerard: *Music from Cuba: Mongo Santamaría, Chocolate Armenteros, and Cuban Musicians in the United States* (Westport, CT, 2001)

MARK LOMANNO

Percussion music. Music written for, or performed on, any one or more of those instruments acoustically or scientifically classified as producing sounds by striking, rubbing, or scraping. Acoustically, the instruments are generally divided into the categories of either pitched or non-pitched instruments, and therefore often have music composed with this distinction in mind. Specifically, these instruments include any type of drum, shaken or struck idiophone (cymbals, gongs, maracas, and so on), or constructed melodic instruments such as xylophone, marimba, vibraphone, glockenspiel, and chimes. In addition, several electronic or MIDI instruments, which are activated by striking, have been developed. This article focuses primarily on music by American composers and performers of the music.

1. Historical overview. 2. Percussion music categories. (i) Percussion ensemble music. (ii) Percussion concertos. (iii) Percussion solos. (iv) Keyboard percussion concertos. (v) Marimba solos. (vi) Vibraphone solos. (vii) Timpani concertos. (viii) Timpani solos. 3. Music publishing.

1. HISTORICAL OVERVIEW. Percussion music has existed on the American continent from earliest known times. 16th century watercolors by John White and engravings by Thoedore De Bry show Native Americans with rattles and shakers while dancing, and subsequent depictions include drums of both wood and skin. The arrival of Europeans to America brought military drumming traditions, most of which were un-notated until the publication of method books in the United States began with Herman Mann's *The Drummer's Assistant* (1808). This established a long-standing and continuing tradition of military-styled drumming, first in military bands, and later in public school institutions or community corps of bugles (or fifes) and drums.

Although incorporated as part of traditional bands and orchestras, percussion instruments sometimes assumed a solo role early in the history of these ensembles. Beginning in the 1870s, solos for xylophone or bells appear in the publications of Harry Braham's music to accompany the musical productions of Harrigan and Hart, and a featured solo for drums (snare, bass, and cymbals), timpani, xylophone, bells, and bird whistle (all performed by one player) appears as early as 1908 in *The Drummer's Escapade* by George D. Barnard.

The growth of university and public school music ensembles provided the impetus to establish marching and concert types of ensembles, both of which gradually evolved from utilization of percussion in a traditional section of 3 or 4 players on timpani, snare drum, bass drum, and xylophone or glockenspiel, to sections of 10, 20 or 30 players for modern marching bands or drum corps and expanded numbers in concert bands and orchestras. (*See* BAND.) The performance of percussion music in the military tradition, known as rudimental drumming, as well as marching ensembles, can be traced through the history of DRUM CORPS organized by the VFW, DCI, MBA, and WGI, as well as through the National Association of Rudimental Drummers (NARD), and the Percussive Arts Society (PAS) competitions and publications. Recent technical evolution of solo rudimental drumming in America can be traced through the music of John Pratt (1950s to 60s), Mitch Markovich (1960s to 70s), and Jeff Queen (1990s to 2000s). Solos for snare drum in a non-rudimental style are best illustrated by Colgrass (*Six Unaccompanied Solos for Snare Drum*, 1957), Benson (*Three Dances for Solo Snare Drum*, 1962), and the *Noble Snare Drum*, volumes I–IV (1988–90).

A natural outgrowth in the marching arena was the need to expand the concert percussion section in both types of instruments and numbers of participants during non-marching months, resulting in a wide-spread popularity of the concert percussion ensemble utilizing graded literature for didactic purposes, removed from the original band and orchestral ensembles.

Throughout the 20th century, developments in concert, symphonic, and orchestral music continued its expansion of percussion instruments and increase in numbers of personnel. This process drew on the artistic creations of major composers from the 1930s, such as George Antheil, Edgard Varèse, Charles Ives, and Henry Cowell, utilizing the expanded sonorities of percussion instruments in the second half of the 20th century.

The development of silent motion pictures and sound recordings brought increased attention to music for percussion and contributed to the notion that sound effects or "traps" were to be performed by the drummer, on the "trap set" or "drum set," which was also employed in popular genres such as ragtime, jazz, swing, and later styles. Though largely improvised, the concept of one player performing on multiple drums and percussion instruments laid the foundation for the modern "multiple-percussion" compositional style, utilized by Stravinsky in *L'Histoire du Soldat*, which continues to receive specialized treatment in solo or ensemble compositions. Percussion remains important to scoring films and television. Hollywood percussionists Emil Richards, Shelly Manne, and Joe Porcaro have made extensive contributions in this medium.

2. PERCUSSION MUSIC CATEGORIES. Percussion music is often categorized into that for percussion ensembles, often grouped by number of players or type of instruments, such as mallet/keyboard ensembles; percussion concertos and solos, specified by instrument; and chamber music for percussion with other, non-percussion instruments or voices.

(i) *Percussion ensemble music.* Following World War I, American composers began to experiment with percussion instruments as an exploratory medium to organize sounds in ways which resulted in compositions based on concepts other than melody, harmony and standard rhythms. Early American composers were influenced by the Italian futurists prior to World War I and by George Antheil (*Ballet Mécanique,* 1923–5). Cowell, a major American innovator and composer for percussion, treated the piano as a percussion instrument as early as 1914; wrote for exotic percussion instruments, such as American Indian bullroarers, in his *Ensemble* (1924); and was especially attracted to non-Western tunings and timbres. Many composers, such as William Russell, were influenced by jazz or Latin American dances. Early percussion music often made use of instruments from Latin America and Asia or "found" instruments, such as rice bowls, brake drums, or anvils. As a result of these influences, percussion music has frequently incorporated a world-music approach to timbre, rhythm, and instrument choices.

Varèse's *Ionisation* (1929–31), scored for 13 percussionists on 40 instruments, was the earliest piece for percussion written in the United States and was premiered in New York in 1933. Also appearing on the concert was William Russell's *Fugue for 8 Percussion Instruments* (1931–2). The Pan American Association of Composers, founded by Varèse, included Cowell, Russell, Amadeo Roldán, and Carlos Chávez, and provided exposure and impetus to the Pan-American "experimentalists," many of whom contributed to the earliest literature for percussion ensemble, or influenced those who heard their music. Formative compositions in this genre include music by Roldán (*Ritmicas* no.5 and no.6, 1930), Russell (*Three Dance Movements*, 1933; *Ogun Badagri*, 1933), José Ardévol (*Study in the Form of a Prelude and Fugue*, 1933), John J. Becker (*The Abongo*, 1933), Johanna Beyer (*IV*, 1935), Harold G. Davidson (*Auto Accident*, 1935), Gerald Strang (*Percussion Music for Three Players*, 1935), Ray Green (*Three Inventories for Casey Jones*, 1936), Cowell (*Ostinato pianissimo*, 1934; *Pulse*, 1939) and Chávez (*Toccata*, 1942).

Lou Harrison and John Cage, both pupils of Cowell, followed his lead and continued to experiment with both the timbres and use of exotic instruments. Harrison expanded the use of exotic instruments in his *Symphony in Free Style* (1939), *Canticle No. 3* (1941), and *Labyrinth* (1941), with the use of gongs, cowbells, elephant bells, brake drums, iron pipes, sistrums (metal rattles), maracas, and woodblocks. His output reflects a substantial contribution to the genre with such compositions as his *Fifth Simfony* (1939), *Canticle no.1* (1940), *Song of Quetzalcoatl* (1940), *Canticle no.3* (1941), *Fugue* (1941), Concerto for violin and percussion orchestra (1942, rev.1959), and Suite (1942).

Cage developed the prepared piano (*Bacchanale*, 1940) and continued to include additional "found" or experimental instruments and concepts in his music with such pieces as *First Construction (in metal)* (1939), which calls for graduated thunder sheets, scraped piano strings, sleigh bells, and Japanese temple gongs; his *Imaginary Landscape no.1* (1939), composed for two variable-speed turntables, muted piano, and cymbals; and his *Amores* (1943), which includes prepared piano and bean pod rattles. Harrison and Cage collaboratively composed *Double Music* (1941), a quartet which includes water gongs, brake drums, water buffalo cowbells, and sistrum. Conventional percussion instruments were also used at times as exemplified by *October Mountain* (1942) by Alan Hovhaness.

Harry Partch, using instruments of his own construction that featured microtonal tunings, created experimental music including percussion (*Oedipus*, 1951; *The Bewitched*, 1955). Other experimental pieces of the period include Henry Brant's *Origins, a percussion symphony* (1950) and James Wood's *Village Burial with Fire* (1989), which includes a part for the microxyl (a 36-pitched dowel instrument tuned at three-quarter tone intervals), as well as several other quarter-tone instruments.

The establishment by Paul Price of the first US percussion ensemble program at the University of Illinois in 1950 ushered in a new era in both education and composition for percussion ensemble music, laying the foundation for contemporary percussion ensembles housed by most American universities and high schools. After two decades of formative growth, percussion ensemble music achieved full recognition of its potential by the 1970s with significant amounts of music written for didactic purposes as well as for emerging professional ensembles. Significant ensembles that have contributed to the medium include Dick Schory's Percussion Pops Orchestra (1950s to 60s); the short-lived New Percussion Quartet of Buffalo (1965–8), comprised of members of the Buffalo Philharmonic and the faculty at the University of Buffalo; Repercussion Unit (established 1970) by John Bergamo; the Blackearth Percussion Group (1972–9), which was the first ensemble-in-residence at a major university (Northern Illinois University and then the College-Conservatory of Music, University of Cincinnati); the Percussion Group, established in 1979 by Allen Otte, James Culley, and William Youhass as a continuation of Blackearth, with replacements for Youhass including Jack Brennan, 1985–7, Benjamin Toth, 1987–92, and since 1992, Russell Burge; and NEXUS, established in 1971 by Bob Becker, William L. Cahn, Michael Craden, Robin Engelman, Russell Hartenberger, and John Wyre (replaced in 2002 by Garry Kvistad). These ensembles collaborated closely with and commissioned leading composers such as George Crumb, John Cage, Steve Reich, Herbert Brün, Toru Takemitsu, Ellen Taaffe Zwilich, Peter Schickele, James Tenney, William Albright, John Luther Adams, Russell Peck, Qu Xiao-Song, Mark Saya, and Larry Austin.

Significant diversification in compositional processes, such as serialism, aleatory techniques, graphic notation, and the use of tape or electronic accompaniments, shaped percussion music during the 1950s and 1960s. Notable for the use of one or more of these approaches are Earle Brown's *Synergy* (1952), Krenek's *Marginal Sounds* (1957), Donald Erb's *Four* (1963), and Mario Davidovsky's *Synchronism no.5* for tape and percussion (1969). Other notable or influential compositions from these decades, primarily composed in more traditional structures or using standard instruments, include *Three Brothers* (1951) and *Percussion Music* (1954) by Michael Colgrass, *Orchestral Prelude for Percussion* (1956) by Malloy Miller, *Evolution* (1954) and *Variations on a Familiar Theme* (1956) by Harold Farberman, and *Streams* (1961) by Warren Benson, noted for its use of voices. *Encore in Jazz* (1964) by Vic Firth and *Jazz Variants* (1969) by John Beck incorporated jazz and rock concepts into the percussion ensemble, a stylistic trend greatly explored and continued to the present day.

The music of two European composers, Karlheinz Stockhausen (*Schlagquartett*, 1952, rev. 1974 as *Schlagtrio*) and Iannis Xenakis (*Persephassa*, 1969), and Argentinean-born Mauricio Kagel (*Transicion II*, 1958–9) influenced American composers and performers of percussion ensemble and chamber music. Works such as Chávez's *Tambuco* (1967), which uses rasping stick, water gourd, clay rattle, tap-a-tap, sistrum, and Swiss brass bells, continued the use of non-traditional or ethnic instruments combined with more traditional instruments. Representative works for percussion ensemble of all sizes dating from this period and since include music by Gordon Peters (*Swords of Moda Ling*, 1957), William Kraft (*Suite for Percussion*, 1958), Ben Johnston (*Knocking Piece*, 1962), Russell Peck (*Lift Off!*, 1966), Charles Wuorinen (*Ringing Changes*, 1969), Steve Reich (*Marimba Phase*, 1967, *Drumming*, 1971, *Clapping Music*, 1972, *Music for Pieces of Wood*, 1973, *Nagoya Marimbas*, 1994, *Mallet Quartet*, 2009), William Albright (*Take That*, 1972), Michael Udow (*African Welcome Piece*, 1973, *Four Movements*, 1974, *Bog Music*, 1978), Herbert Brün (*At Loose Ends*, 1974), Walter Mays (*Six Invocations of the Svara Mandala*, 1974), Kagel (*Dressur*, 1977), Christopher Rouse (*Ogoun Badagris*, 1976, and *Ku-Ka-Ilimoku*, 1978), Cage (*but what about the noise of crumpling paper...*, 1985), Michael Hennagin (*Duo Chopinesque*, 1986), David Gillingham (*Stained Glass*, 1991), David Maslanka (*Crown of Thorns*, 1991), Eric Ewazen (*The Palace of Nine Perfections*, 1999), and David Lang (*The So-Called Laws of Nature*, 2002).

The above compositions lead to general observations regarding major compositional procedures or influences, as well as methods of selecting and organizing instruments for percussion ensembles. First, performers are assigned either one or many instruments per part (similar to a multiple percussion setup); sometimes multiple performers are assigned to a single instrument (as in two performers striking the inside of a piano). Second, no standard instrumentation and no typical number of performers exists in this genre. Third, compositions frequently have only battery instruments, or make primary use of melodic instruments supported by battery instruments. Fourth, the repertoire consistently incorporates rhythmic and stylistic elements from all parts of the world. Fifth, new sounds and timbres are produced not only by the extensive use of "found" instruments (brake drums, gourd rattles, pots, bowls, buckets, and so on), but through the invention, extensive development, or modification of numerous new instruments for percussion. Sixth, the use of innumerable specialized mallets, beaters, sticks and other striking implements made of various woods, plastics, rubbers, metals, organic materials (such as rattan, seeds or beans) and various methods of actuating an instrument by striking, buzzing, plucking, bowing and scraping, as well as the use of the fingers and hands, have created an unlimited palette of musical color available to a composer or performer. Seventh, the many combinations of instruments and approaches has led to great advances in notation of percussion music. Eighth, much percussion music is composed whereby overlapping ostinato patterns are established as an underlying support mechanism in most parts as individual parts or performers are featured in turn. Ninth, a significant number of "novelty" compositions which feature striking one's body, stomping, clapping, popping bags, or other entertaining methods of creating a sound are found in the repertoire and have crossed-over into popular culture. Tenth, didactic percussion music occupies a prominent position for percussion music in the United States, in stark contrast to teaching methods employed in European or other countries throughout the world.

A significant number of arrangements and original compositions have been developed for ensembles or orchestras of marimbas or other combinations of keyboard percussion instruments that range in size from three to 100 players. Pioneered by Clair Omar Musser in the 1930s, these types of ensembles include the music of the Marimba Masters (1954–9) led by Gordon Peters, the novelty arrangements of solo xylophone music performed by Nexus, and Reich's *Six Marimbas* (1973, rev. 1986) and *Mallet Quartet* (2009).

(ii) Percussion concertos. Percussion soloists, due to both the aural and visual appeal of the instruments, have appeared more frequently in concertos with American orchestras since the latter part of the 20th century. Representative compositions include those by Darius Milhaud (Concerto for percussion and small orchestra, 1931); Ben Johnston (Concerto for percussion, 1952); Robert Suderberg (Concerto for solo percussion and orchestra, 1979), commissioned by Michael Bookspan and the Philadelphia Orchestra; Russell Peck (*The Glory and the Grandeur*, 1988) for percussion trio, written for the Percussion Group–Cincinnati; Richard Rodney Bennett (Concerto for percussion, 1990), James MacMillan, a Scottish composer (*Veni Veni Emmanuel*, 1992), and Joan Tower (*Strike Zones*, 2001), all commissioned by Scottish percussionist Evelyn Glennie; Joseph Schwantner (*Concerto for Percussion and Orchestra*, 1995), commissioned for the 150th Anniversary of the New York Philharmonic; and Ellen Taaffe Zwilich (*Rituals for Five Percussionists and Orchestra*, 2005), written for NEXUS.

(iii) Percussion solos. The tradition of composed solos for multiple percussion instruments performed by one person, though having roots in such pieces as Stravinsky's *L'Histoire du Soldat*, or Milhaud's *La creation du monde*, begins in 1956 with John Cage's *27' 10.554" for a percussionist*, which divides freely-chosen instruments into four categories (metal, wood, skin, and all others), all performed by a single performer. The influence of Stockhausen, with *Zyklus* (1959) and *Mikrophonie* (1964) strongly influenced American composer/performers such as Max Neuhaus. Music in this genre is typically composed specifically for a single performer and often commissioned or collaboratively developed. Performers such as Steven Schick, William Winant, and Glennie champion this genre. Major works in this genre include: William Kraft's *French Suite* (1962) and *English Suite* (1974); Morton Feldman's *King of Denmark* (1964); Rickey Tagawa's *Inspirations Diabolique* (1965); Charles Wourinen's *Janissary Music* (1966); Herbert Brün's *Plot* (1967), *Touch and Go* (1967), and *Stalks and Trees and Drops and Clouds* (1967); William Hibbard's *Parson's Piece* (1968); Paul Zonn's *Andrea's Dancing Music* (1974); Stuart Saunders Smith's *Songs I–IX for Actor-Percussionist* (1980–82); Iannis Xenakis's *Psappha* (1976) and *Rebonds* (1989); Frederic Rzewski's *To the Earth* (1985); Brian Ferneyhough's *Bone Alphabet*

(1992); David Lang's *Anvil Chorus* (1991); Roger Reynolds's *Watershed* (1995); and John Luther Adams's *The Mathematics of Resonant Bodies* (2003).

(iv) Keyboard percussion concertos. A substantial number of solos for xylophone with band or orchestral accompaniment were published in the United States beginning in the 1870s and featured by such prominent musical organizations as the Sousa Band. Many were arrangements, or sets of variations on popular folk songs, but significant numbers of original solos, often in popular dance forms, were also composed. The marimba largely superseded the xylophone in the 1930s, but concertos for each or both have since been written by Creston (Concertino for marimba, 1942), Milhaud (Concerto for marimba and vibraphone, 1947), Kurka (Concerto for marimba, 1959), Jorge Sarmientos (*Concertino para Marimba y Orquestra*, 1957), and Hovhaness (*Fantasy on Japanese Woodprints*, 1967). In recent decades, Ney Rosauro's Concerto for marimba and orchestra (1992) has received the most performances in this genre in recent decades. Vida Chenoweth pioneered the earliest concerto performances and Glennie is most often heard as a soloist in recent decades.

(v) Marimba solos. Beginning with the etudes and preludes of Clair Omar Musser (1940s), original compositions for the marimba have appeared for both didactic and concert recital purposes. Representative literature includes Peter Tanner's *Sonata* (1974), Gordon Stout's *Two Mexican Dances* (1975), David Maslanka's *Variations on Lost Love* (1977), Raymond Helble's *Toccata Fantasy* (1980), Andrew Thomas's *Merlin* (1985), Jacob Druckman's *Reflections on the Nature of Water* (1986), and Joseph Schwantner's *Velocities* (1990). The solo marimba recital was pioneered by Vida Chenoweth and is well-illustrated by the touring careers of Linda Maxey and Keiko Abe.

(vi) Vibraphone solos. Invented in the United States in 1922, the vibraphone has been predominantly found in jazz, played by such notable performers as Lionel Hampton, Red Norvo, Milt Jackson, and Gary Burton. Some works have been written for the concert stage, including Mark Saya's *The Murphy Sonata* (1978, rev. 1994) and Stuart Saunders Smith's *Links*, nos.1–11, (1974–94).

(vii) Timpani concertos. Concertos for timpani, though written as early as the 18th century, have only recently come to the fore in the United States. Representative compositions are those by William Kraft (Concerto for timpani and orchestra, 1984); James Oliverio (Timpani Concerto no.1 "The Olympian," 1990; Timpani Concerto no.2, 2007; Double Timpani Concerto, 2011; Philip Glass (*Concerto Fantasy* for two timpanists and orchestra, 2000), commissioned by Jonathan Haas; and Russell Peck (Concerto for timpani and orchestra "Harmonic Rhythm," 2000), commissioned by a consortium of 39 orchestras.

(viii) Timpani solos. Solo literature for timpani is generally unaccompanied. Most composers have concentrated on the rhythmic interaction of the drums (often exploring polymeter or metric modulation) or the timbral possibilities of the drums and bowls when struck with various types of beaters or implements, such as brushes, hands, fingers, or tuning forks, or the placement of another instrument, such as an inverted cymbal, on the head. Among the most significant works are Elliott Carter's *Eight Pieces* for four timpani (1950–66), Jan Williams's *Variations for Solo Kettledrums* (1964), William Cahn's *Raga no.1* (1968), John Beck's Sonata for timpani (1969), Paul Zonn's *Xoe* for four timpani and snare drum (1971), Chávez's *Partita* for solo timpani (1973), John M. Floyd's *Theme and Variations* for four timpani (1974), Murray Houllif's *Four Verses* for timpani (1976), William Kraft's *Variations on King George* (1980), John Beck's *Three Episodes for Timpani* (1980), and Bruce Hamilton's *Rituals* (1998).

3. MUSIC PUBLISHING. In addition to major music publishing companies, such as Carl Fischer and C.F. Peters, numerous smaller companies specialize in percussion music. Among these are Music for Percussion, Media Press, Smith Publications, Permus, Kendor, Studio 4, Keyboard Percussion Publications, C-Alan Publications, Honeyrock, Row-Loff, Drop 6, and Oklahoma University Percussion Press. Significant numbers of pieces are the result of commissions or collaborations by such artists as Evelyn Glennie (156+ commissions), NEXUS (75+), Blackearth (35+), Percussion Group–Cincinnati (75+), Leigh Howard Stevens (30+), Robert van Sice (100+), and Steven Schick (150+).

BIBLIOGRAPHY

BeckEP; *BladesPI*

M. Ward: "Percussion's 'Top 75 Compositions'," *Percussive Notes*, x/3 (1972), 16–18

D. Eyler: "The Top 50 Percussion Solo and Ensemble Compositions of Today," *Percussive Notes*, xviii/1 (1979), 38–9

K.L. Reiss: *The History of the Blackearth Percussion Group and Their Influence on Percussion Ensemble Literature, Performance, and Pedagogy* (diss., U. of Houston, 1987)

K.L. Reiss: "An Overview of the Origins and Development of the Percussion Ensemble," *NACWPI Journal*, xxxvii/4 (Summer 1989), 10–17

S. Smith: *The Development of the Marimba as a Solo Instrument and the Evolution of the Solo Literature for the Marimba* (diss., Ohio State U., 1995)

S. Gerber: *Karlheinz Stockhausen's Solo Percussion Music, a Comprehensive Study* (diss., U. of Cincinnati, 2003)

L. Rogers: "Choices: Researching Percussion Ensemble Literature," *Percussive Notes*, xlii/6 (2004), 64–8

N.V. Gagné: "The Beaten Path: a History of American Percussion Music," *NewMusicBox* (1 April 2004), <http://www.newmusicbox.org/articles/The-Beaten-Path-A-History-Of-American-Percussion-Music/>

A. Smith: *An Examination of Notation in Selected Repertoire for Multiple Percussion* (diss., Ohio State U., 2005)

S. Schick: *The Percussionist's Art* (Rochester, NY, 2006)

J. Hall: *Development of the Percussion Ensemble Through the Contributions of the Latin American Composers Amadeo Roldán, José Ardévol, Carlos Chávez, and Alberto Ginastera* (diss., Ohio State U., 2008)

T. Kernan: *The Percussion Group: Cincinnati: A History of Collaboration between Ensemble and Composer* (diss., U. of Cincinnati, 2010)

JOHN H. BECK/JAMES A. STRAIN

Percussive Arts Society [PAS]. International organization established in 1961 to promote percussion education, research, performance, and appreciation. In 2011 it had more than 8500 members, with 49 chapters in the United States and around 30 in other countries. Since 1976 it has held the annual Percussive Arts Society International Convention (PASIC) with performances, workshops, exhibits, lectures, and panel discussions, and competitions in composition and in solo and ensemble playing. As part of its educational function, the society sponsored a revision and standardization of drum rudiments, resulting in the PAS International Drum Rudiments, adopted in 1984 and subsequently used by many percussion educators.

PAS has issued two alternating bi-monthly publications, *Percussive Notes* (begun in 1967 as a newsletter, later expanded to a journal) and *Percussion News* (a newsletter begun in the mid-1980s). Earlier publications were *Percussionist* (1963–80), renamed *Percussive Notes Research Edition* (1981–6).

In 2009 PAS consolidated its operations in Indianapolis, Indiana, allowing it to have its offices, annual convention, museum, and library in the same city. The museum, which houses instruments donated over a period of years, opened in 1992 in Lawton, Oklahoma. Renamed the Rhythm! Discovery Center when it reopened in Indianapolis in 2009, it displays rare and historical percussion instruments from around the world. The library's collections include archival and reference material, scores, and recorded music. PAS also maintains an extensive website (<www.pas.org>) that includes publication archives, research databases, and online tours of its library and museum collections.

BIBLIOGRAPHY

J. Wanamaker: "PAS International Drum Rudiments," *Percussive Notes*, xxvi/4 (1988), 6–9
R. Mattingly: "50 Years of PAS," *Percussive Notes*, xlix/1 (2011), 6–12; xlix/2 (2011), 8–15; xlix/3 (2011), 8–11; xlix/4 (2011), 12–17; xlix/5 (2011), 8–15
G. Cook: "PAS Museum: History and Metamorphosis," *Percussive Notes*, xlix/2 (2011), 18–23

CAROLYN BRYANT

Perera, Ronald (Christopher) (*b* Boston, MA, 25 Dec 1941). Composer. He studied with LEON KIRCHNER at Harvard University (BA 1963, MA 1967), then with Gottfried Michael Koenig at the University of Utrecht's electronic music studio (1968). An extended study of electronic and computer music culminated in his editing with Jon H. Appleton *The Development and Practice of Electronic Music* (Englewood Cliffs, NJ, 1975), a major text. He has received fellowships from the MacDowell Colony three times (1974, 1978, 1981) and the National Institute for the Arts (1976). Both the Paderewski Fund (1972) and the Goethe Institute (1974) have commissioned works from him. He taught at Syracuse University from 1968 to 1970 and at Dartmouth College in 1970. The following year he joined the faculty of Smith College, Massachusetts, where he was the Elsie Irwin Sweeney Chair in Music. He retired from teaching in 2002.

In *Alternate Routes* (1971), a score for the Dartmouth Dance Company, Perera conceived of all sounds as having kinetic properties: either wild runs and spins or delicate, subtle departures from complete stillness. In contrast to this physical orientation, his settings of three poems by Günter Grass (1974) use quotations of jazz, march music, and a waltz by Johann Strauss to evoke the nostalgic or even bizarre inner experiences of the personae. His treatment of text is often remarked upon as being particularly impressive among American composers. His two-act chamber opera *The Yellow Wallpaper* (1989, with libretto by Constance Congdon adapted from the Charlotte Perkins Gilman novella) premiered in Northampton and received its New York premiere at the Manhattan School (1992). His cantata *The Golden Door* (1998, based on Ellis Island archives) evokes the sounds of bustle, heartbreak, and ultimately triumph that characterize so much of the American immigrant experience. Perera wrote a children's opera for the Manhattan School of Music Opera Studio, Educational Outreach division (*The Araboolies of Liberty Street*), which has received numerous performances in New York schools. Perera's music has been performed by the Cleveland Chamber Symphony, the Springfield SO, Boston Musica Viva, the ensemble Lontano, Sanford Sylvan, Karen Smith Emerson, Jane Bryden, and Jon Humphrey, among others. It has been recorded principally on the Albany, CRI, and Opus One labels.

WORKS

Stage: Alternate Routes, dance score, elec, 1971; The Yellow Wallpaper (op, C. Congdon, after C.P. Gilman), 1989; S. (op, C. Congdon, after J. Updike), 1995; The Araboolies of Liberty Street (op, C. Congdon, after S. Swope), 2001
Orch: Chanteys, 1976; The White Whale, 1981; Music, fl, orch, 1990; other works
Other inst: Suite, pf, 1966; Improvisation for Loudspeakers, tape, 1969; Reverberations, org, tape, 1970; Reflex, va, tape, 1973; Fantasy Variations, pf, elec, 1976; Bright Angels, org, perc, tape, 1977; Tolling, 2 pf, tape, 1979; Sonatina, va, pf, 1986; Fanfare, va, pf, 1987; Sun's Rising, org, 1986; Out of Shadow, org, 1987; Triptych, org, 1997; other works
Choral: Mass, solo vv, chorus, orch, 1967; Did you hear the angels sing? (S. Miller), S, SATB, org, 1968; 3 Night Pieces, S, A, SSAA, vc, perc, pf, 1974; Everything that has Breath (Pss. cxlviii, cl), male/female/mixed 2vv, tape, 1976; The Canticle of the Sun, SATB, narr, 1984; The Golden Door, SATB, narr, 1998; other works
Solo vocal: Dove sta amore (L. Ferlinghetti), S, tape, 1969; 5 Summer Songs (E. Dickinson), S, pf, 1972; Apollo Circling (J. Dickey), S, pf, 1972; 3 Poems of Günter Grass, Mez, chbr ens, tape, 1974; Children of the Sun (R.L. Stevenson), S, hn, pf, 1979; The White Whale (H. Melville), Bar, orch, 1981; other works
Principal publishers: Boosey & Hawkes, E.C. Schirmer, Music Associates of New York, Pear Tree Press

DAVID COPE/ANDERS TOBIASON

Peresson, Sergio (*b* Udine, Italy, 29 March 1913; *d* Haddonfield, NJ, 16 April 1991). Italian violin maker, naturalized American. He initially learned to make violins as a hobby in Udine. After World War II he moved to Venezuela, where he took up violin making professionally. In 1963 he became associated with Moennig & Son, Philadelphia, and about the same time established his own workshop in New Jersey. His instruments were modeled on an amalgamation of the Stradivari and Guarneri "del Gesù" patterns. Their tone quality was strong and even, although the resonance of some was inconsistent. He made violins for Isaac Stern and Ivan Galamian, among others, and a cello for Jacqueline du Pré. His violins were highly sought after, and he was also successful with his violas. In his later years, he was considered to be the leading North American luthier.

JAAK LIIVOJA-LORIUS/R

Pere Ubu. Rock group. Pere Ubu was formed in 1975 in Cleveland, Ohio, by David Thomas (*b* 14 June 1953; vocals), Peter Laughner (*b* 22 August 1952; *d* 22 June 1977; guitar), Tom Herman (*b* 19 April 1949; guitar), Tim Wright (*b* 1952; bass), Allen Ravenstine (*b* 9 May 1950; synthesizer), and Scott Kraus (*b* 19 November 1950; drums). Fronted by Thomas, the initial line-up recorded two singles in 1975 and 1976 before disbanding. Laughner died due to alcohol and drug problems in 1977 and the band reformed with Tony Maimone (*b* 27 September 1952; bass) replacing Wright.

Pere Ubu was named after surrealist Alfred Jarry's protagonist in the French play *Ubu Roi*, and helped usher in New Wave with their first single "30 Seconds Over Tokyo." The band utilized various non-musical sounds and unconventional instrumentation behind Thomas's "careening vocals" to create a unique experimental garage rock sound. The first two albums released by the band, *The Modern Dance* (1978) and *Dub Housing* (1979), became underground successes, influencing musicians of the postpunk and art rock genres, in particular R.E.M. and the Pixies. A tour of England in 1978 garnered the band new heights of popularity, but internal problems caused the band to break up in 1982. Thomas embarked on a solo career and moved to England before reforming Pere Ubu with *The Tenement Year* (1988). The retrospective *Datapanik in the Year Zero* (1996) emphasized Pere Ubu's impact on popular music and the band entered a new phase of productivity, including expansion into film score and theatrical stage productions.

BIBLIOGRAPHY

H. George-Warren and P. Romanowski, eds.: *The Rolling Stone Encyclopedia of Rock & Roll* (New York, 1983, 3/2001), 749–50

Ubu Projex, <http://ubuprojex.net/>

RICHARD D. DRIVER

Pérez, Danilo (*b* Monte Oscuro, Panama, 29 Dec 1966). Panamanian pianist, bandleader, and composer. Born in Panama to a musical family, he began playing piano at the age of three. He studied classical piano at the National Conservatory before moving to the United States, where he studied jazz piano and composition at Indiana University of Pennsylvania and Berklee College of Music in Boston. In his early career Pérez performed with Paquito D'Rivera and Dizzy Gillespie, both of innovators of Afro-Cuban jazz. He was the youngest member in Dizzy Gillespie's United Nations Orchestra (1989–92). In addition to his own critically acclaimed work as a bandleader, Perez has performed with Wynton Marsalis, Wayne Shorter, Steve Lacy, Arturo Sandoval, and Roy Haynes. He also served as a cultural ambassador of Panama.

Pérez's compositions blend diverse musical idioms, drawing from folk and popular music of Latin America, the African diaspora, and jazz. His album *The Journey* (1994, Novus) reflects the experiences of Africans during the slave trade and was performed in an orchestral arrangement by the National SO of Panama in 1995. The album *PanaMonk* (1996, GRP) paid tribute to the composer Thelonious Monk and included both Pérez's own compositions inspired by Monk's characteristic musical language and reinterpretations of Monk's work. Pérez's Grammy-nominated album *Central Ave* (1998, GRP) featured the Panamanian singer Raúl Vital and the traditional Panamanian style of *mejorana* singing. The Pan-American scope of Pérez's output is evident in *'Til Then* (2003, Verve), which includes his arrangements of North American pop songs by Joni Mitchell and Stevie Wonder alongside compositions by the Panamanian composer Rubén Blades and the Chilean composer Violeta Parra.

RUTH E. ROSENBERG

Pérez, Irvan (*b* Delacroix Island, LA, 29 Dec 1923; *d* New Orleans, LA, 8 Jan 2008). Isleño *décima* singer and composer. Perez was born into and was an advocate of the Isleño culture, descendents of Canary Islanders who settled in St. Bernard Parish in southern Louisiana in the late 1700s. He was a proponent of the traditional *décima*, a narrative song using ten-line stanzas, with origins in medieval Spain and the Canary Islands. His father, Erafin Pérez, taught him the art. Irvan also composed his own décimas in his native Isleño dialect, a combination of Old Spanish and Cajun French. His compositions dealt with a wide variety of subjects, from love to weather to the hardships experienced by the Isleños. Pérez was featured in the 1999 PBS series *River of Song: A Musical Journey*, and he made numerous recordings. He also performed at prominent music festivals and venues, including Wolf Trap and Carnegie Hall. In 1991 he received a National Heritage Fellowship from the National Endowment for the Arts, and in 2001 he performed for the Spanish king and queen during their trip to Mississippi; he also performed many times in the Canary Islands.

BIBLIOGRAPHY

S. Armistead and I. Katz: *The Spanish Tradition in Louisiana* (Newark, DE, 1992)

S. Armistead, M. Wood Wood, and I. Katz: *La tradición hispano-canaria en Luisiana: la literatura tradicional de los isleños* (Las Palmas de Gran Canaria, 2007)

WALTER AARON CLARK

Pérez Prado, (Dámaso) (*b* Matanzas, Cuba, 11 Dec 1917 or 1918; *d* Mexico City, Mexico, 14 Sept 1980). Cuban bandleader, composer, pianist, and arranger. He studied classical piano in Matanzas before moving to Havana, where he worked and recorded with such ensembles as the Orquesta Casino de la Playa. These recordings feature a modern piano style with syncopated riffs that characterize *guaracha* and *danzón de nuevo ritmo*, which in the 1950s also characterized mambo.

Between 1947 and 1949 Pérez Prado composed instrumental works such as "Trompetiana" (1946) and

"Rumbambó" (1946) that were already generically labeled as mambo. His recordings "Hembra mala," "Mi cazuelita," "Mambo 5" (different from his well known 1950s theme), and "Habana" were also called mambos although they exhibit little relation to the later mambo style. In 1948 Pérez Prado started working as a composer and arranger for Mexican films and soon thereafter moved to Mexico. In April and June 1949 he recorded "El manisero," "Tacuba," "Pachuca," "Macomé," and "José," stylistically complex mambos that RCA asked him to simplify. This change in accessibility led to the most popular 1950s mambo genre better exemplified in "Al compás del mambo," "Mambo no.5," and "Qué rico el mambo." During this time Pérez also collaborated with the singer Benny Moré.

In 1951 he toured the United States for the first time; two years later he moved to the country after being expelled from Mexico (he was not allowed to return there until 1964). His recordings of "Cerezo rosa" (1953) and "Patricia" (1955) sold millions of copies, and the latter was used by Federico Fellini in *La dolce vita* (1960). In the 1960s he tried to introduce new styles, like the *dengue*, which never achieved his earlier level of success. In the 1970s he re-recorded his earlier mambos with electric bass and a modern drum kit.

BIBLIOGRAPHY

R. Giró, ed.: *El mambo* (Havana, 1993)
C.J. Sierra: *Pérez Prado y el mambo* (Mexico City, 1995)
M. Salazar: *Mambo Kingdom: Latin Music in New York* (New York, 2002)
R. López Cano: 'Apuntes para una prehistoria del mambo,' *Latin American Music Review*, xxx (2009), 213–42

RUBÉN LÓPEZ CANO

Performance art. An umbrella term that encompasses a wide array of performance traditions. As the name implies, performance art tends to be driven by a solo performer or a small group of performers; indeed, the presence of a performer or performers is one of the few things that characterizes most performance art. Performance art frequently engages with mixed media and multiple performance traditions; it tends to involve elements of theater, both narrative and non-narrative, and often borrows from experimental music, video art, dance, and visual art. It shares much with conceptual art, an artistic genre in which the concept supplants the object as the essence of the artwork. Depending on the performer's goals, performance art may contain various levels of scriptedness, from fully texted scenarios to primarily improvisatory works: however, it is usually characterized by a certain amount of textual flexibility, which allows room for performer–spectator interaction.

The framework of performance art encompasses several international mid-20th century movements, including the situationists, the Viennese actionists, practitioners of happenings (*see* HAPPENING), the loose international group FLUXUS, the Living Theater, and the Black Power-driven BLACK ARTS MOVEMENT (BAM). These movements can trace their origins to the solo and small-group theatrics staged by the Dada, futurist, and constructivist movements in Europe during the first decades of the 20th century, along with the experimental dramaturgy

of Antonin Artaud. Like their forebears, these mid-century movements embraced a political aesthetic that was strongly critical of commercialization in concert culture and the art world, and their works often treated artistic institutions in critical or ironic ways. These critiques ranged from the controversial decision in 1964 by members of Fluxus to picket the New York premiere of Karlheinz Stockhausen's *Originale* to *Malcolm '71: or, Publishing Blackness*, a dramatic piece by the BAM-affiliated writer and performer Ed Bullins, which critiques the perceived inequities of university black studies programs.

The late 1960s and 70s saw a rise in individualistic solo performance and the emergence of New York as a center for performance art. In 1964 former Fluxus artist Nam June Paik and cellist Charlotte Moorman began a collaboration, and together they created a series of pieces that fused Moorman's cello with text, action, and live electronics; among these was Paik's *Opéra sextronique* (1967), in which a topless Moorman was briefly arrested for indecency. The 1970s and 80s also blurred the line between performance art and rock and roll, a distinction that continued to weaken with the advent of the commercial rock video in the early 80s. Such artists as Patti Smith and Laurie Anderson, who combined speech, song, instrumental virtuosity, and charismatic stage personae, were able to move fluidly between the parallel cultures of downtown New York rock and performance art.

Although most performance art has been staged before small audiences, some of its proponents have

Meredith Monk in "Turtle Dreams," 1986. (Dee Conway/Lebrecht Music & Arts)

worked on a larger scale: from the late 1960s Robert Wilson devised elaborate spectacles such as *The Life and Times of Joseph Stalin* (1973), a 12-hour piece that eschewed narrative, focusing instead on the slow movement of performers and objects. The composer Philip Glass, who had collaborated with Wilson on *Einstein on the Beach* (1976), staged a number of operas in the 1970s and 80s, including *Satyagraha* (1980) and *Akhnaten* (1983), that drew equally from conventional opera and performance art. The composer Robert Ashley's operatic trilogy, *Perfect Lives* (1977–83), *Atalanta* (1982), and *Now Eleanor's Idea* (1993), fuses the symbolic abstraction and performer-centricity of performance art with experimental sound collage and video projection. Similarly, Meredith Monk's works (among them, *Quarry*, 1976) draw from the worlds of opera, solo performance, feminist theater, and video art.

Since the early 1980s many artists' interest in live electronics has expanded to include engagements with computers and computer-generated sound (*see* INTERMEDIA ART and NEW MEDIA). These experiments run the gamut from simple sound-generating programs to works that incorporate computers and the Internet as primary texts; Cory Arcangel's work, for example, has appropriated and reworked a variety of preexisting electronic media, from analog video games to YouTube videos. The increasing cultural prominence of performance art has also led to a number of high-profile collaborations between performance artists and popular musicians; one notable example is *Drawing Restraint 9* (2005), a film collaboration between the singer and composer Björk and her partner, the performance artist and sculptor Matthew Barney. Performance art has increasingly become an international phenomenon; in particular, the collapse and weakening of a number of state-centered regimes, including the Soviet Union, in the 1980s prompted a surge of interest in performance art outside the United States. At a performance art retrospective, *100 Years*, held at the New York Museum of Modern Art in 2010, many of the artists chosen to represent the most modern face of performance art hailed from post-Soviet bloc nations, as well as from Cuba, Thailand, and China.

BIBLIOGRAPHY

R. Goldberg: *Performance Art: from Futurism to the Present* (New York, 1988)

S. Banes: *Subversive Expectations: Performance Art and Paratheater in New York, 1976–85* (Ann Arbor, MI, 1998)

A. Kaprow: *Essays on the Blurring of Art and Life* (Berkeley, CA, 2003)

M. Sell: *Avant-Garde Performance and the Limits of Criticism* (Ann Arbor, MI, 2005)

K. Gann: *Music Downtown: Writings from the Village Voice* (Berkeley, CA, 2006)

J. Harding and C. Rosenthal, eds.: *Restaging the Sixties: Radical Theaters and their Legacies* (Ann Arbor, MI, 2006)

JOHN ROCKWELL/KELSEY COWGER

Performing rights [copyright collecting] **societies**. Organizations that protect musical works registered by their members and collect fees payable in respect of the performance of such works.

1. Definition. 2. American societies: (i) American Society of Composers, Authors and Publishers (ASCAP) (ii) Broadcast Music, Inc. (BMI) (iii) SESAC Inc. (iv) Harry Fox Agency, Inc.

1. DEFINITION. The legal provisions described in the article COPYRIGHT give rise to certain economic rights, which are enjoyed by the owner of the copyright. In music, the most important is the right of public performance, known as the "performing right." Others include the right to reproduce musical works in sound recordings (such as phonograph records, audio tapes, CDs, and digital formats), known as the "mechanical right," and the right to reproduce musical works in the soundtracks of audio-visual recordings (such as films, videotapes and DVDs), known as the "synchronization right." In some countries a right exists in the public use or transmission of sound recordings, so that performers in particular recordings receive royalties for the use of their music. The civil right in the recorded performance as such (not to be confused with the performing and broadcasting right in the works performed) is not widely established internationally, and does not exist in the United States.

Once these rights are established, the problem of collecting license fees arises. It is almost always impossible for an individual copyright holder to recover royalties on more than a very small number of the performances on which they are due. Even one could locate a few of the performances, that individual would not always have the means or the expertise to negotiate appropriate royalties and issue licenses. Collection for performances nationwide or overseas would be out of the question for the individual or small publishing company. Societies have therefore been set up in most countries to collect royalties for the use of copyrighted music and to distribute the revenue among the parties entitled to it. It is, equally, an immense advantage to the music user to have a central body that can be approached for licenses and will clear the rights automatically with each copyright owner, not only in his own country, but also in virtually every other country in the world. Performing rights societies offer a blanket license to the music user who would otherwise be put to considerable administrative expense in acquiring these rights and would also have to pay the individual copyright owners in respect of each use.

Performing rights societies typically license only the right of nondramatic public performance (the "small right"). They do not license the "grand right," i.e., the right of dramatic public performance, which attaches to all forms of musical theater, such as operas, ballets, and musicals. Works such as these can be staged only in a limited number of places and can therefore be traced comparatively simply. It is much more difficult to collect in respect of the small right, and it is in the administering of this right that the collecting societies have performed a needed function for creators and copyright owners of music. Collection of mechanical-right fees is usually the province of the copyright owner; in the United States many publishers use the services of the Harry Fox Agency, Inc., for this purpose.

The members of the two international organizations of copyright collecting societies, the Confédération Internationale de Sociétés d'Auteurs et Compositeurs (CISAC), founded in 1928, and the Bureau International de l'Edition Mécanique (BIEM), are linked by international contracts of affiliation, whereby each society collects on its own territory for the works of its own members and the members of the other societies with which it is affiliated. By the same contract, each national society is empowered to grant licenses on its own territory in respect of the repertoires of each society with which it is affiliated, so that the society is able to offer its licensees access to a virtually worldwide range of copyright music. Thus, a licensee in Chicago, for example, has available almost the whole catalog of music that is likely to be needed.

2. AMERICAN SOCIETIES. Copyright owners may not concurrently be members of more than one American performing rights organization. However, it is possible to resign from one organization and join another after contracts have been fulfilled. Publishers, following carefully established procedures and regulations of the various societies, may set up different companies in each. In this way they can handle the works of writers they wish to represent without restrictions incurred from societal affiliation.

(i) American Society of Composers, Authors and Publishers (ASCAP). Until 1897 Congress had not included in the copyright law a performing right in musical works, and it was not until 1914 that the first performing rights society, ASCAP, was founded. A performing right offered a collecting society in the United States enormous scope, for although the territory was large, communications were good and the population was spread much more evenly than in other large countries, such as Canada, making it practical to collect in cities and large towns. As various types of popular music spread across the country, there were countless performances in dance halls, nightclubs, restaurants, and cafés, which had previously been beyond the control of an individual copyright owner but which a central agency such as ASCAP could effectively monitor. A further enormous increase in the performance of popular music came with the introduction of radio broadcasting in the 1920s and the establishment in a single year of more than 500 radio stations. Naturally, not all music users immediately accepted the claims of the new society, and ASCAP was obliged to establish its position by court actions against users of music, such as restaurants, dance halls, background-music operators, concert promoters, and broadcasters.

ASCAP is an unincorporated membership association managed by a board of 24 directors (12 writers and 12 publishers); ASCAP's writer members elect the writer-directors, and its publisher members elect the publisher-directors; as such, ASCAP is the only performing rights society in the United States that is owned, controlled, and run by the creators and copyright owners of music. The directors hold office for two years.

Any writer or publisher meeting minimal requirements may become an ASCAP member; the estates of deceased writers may also become members. Members (who pay annual dues to the society) are elected by a majority of the board, and upon election, must sign an agreement by which they assign to the society the non-exclusive right to license the non-dramatic public performance of their works for the period of the agreement. ASCAP itself is not a "copyright owner." However, because earlier American copyright law did not acknowledge divisibility of ownership, and lawsuits had to be brought in the name of the copyright owner, the society sought and acquired the right to sue in the member's name. Under the 1976 law, the ownership of copyright may be transferred in part or subdivided. Members assign rights in all compositions then or thereafter written, composed, published, acquired, or owned by the member, whether alone, jointly, or in collaboration with others.

ASCAP distributes all the revenues it collects after deducting its expenses and payments to foreign societies, operating in this sense on a nonprofit basis. Half of all royalties are distributed to writer-members and half to publisher-members. Distribution is accomplished by means of a sampling survey that represents all licensed performances. Performances are given values relative to each other through a complex weighting formula; by way of illustration, television performances are weighted in such a way that feature performances are worth more than background performances, which in turn are worth more than theme-music performances, which in turn receive higher credits than advertising jingles. Domestic royalties are distributed quarterly and foreign royalties semi-annually; a writer member may not irrevocably assign his royalties to another.

ASCAP typically negotiates license agreements with trade associations or groups representing user industries. The licenses granted are termed "blanket" licenses because, in return for payment of a specified (usually an annual) fee, the music user is entitled to perform any works in the ASCAP repertory. The rate for each license is structured for the particular user industry involved. For example, hotels pay fees dependent on their annual expenditures on live entertainment and their use of recorded music; colleges and universities pay a fee dependent on the number of full-time students. Radio and television broadcasting organizations choose one of two kinds of license, either of which gives them the right to perform any work in the ASCAP repertory: under one type, also called a "blanket" license, an organization pays a percentage of its total advertising revenue, and a fixed sum for music used on unsponsored programs; under the "per program" license, a relatively higher percentage of advertising receipts is paid, but only on income from programs making use of ASCAP music. Virtually all broadcasters choose the "blanket" license.

The federal government has attempted through antitrust litigation to promote competition in the area of musical performing rights. In 1941, after the Department of Justice took action against ASCAP under the

Sherman Act, the society agreed to a consent decree (i.e., it was deemed not to have broken any law, nor was evidence taken or judgment given). The decree, which has been amended from time to time and regulates virtually all aspects of ASCAP's operations, established membership requirements, the principles of the distribution system, and licensing procedures (the "per program" license for broadcasters was one result of the decree). The decree made two provisions of particular significance for music users. First, if ASCAP and a potential licensee fail to agree on a royalty, the user may apply for a determination of a reasonable license fee by the US District Court for the Southern District of New York, which supervises the decree; pending judgment, the licensee may have access to works in the society's repertory, and ASCAP may ask the court to fix an interim license fee. Second, ASCAP may not discriminate in the license fees, terms, or conditions between "similarly situated users."

After a case in 1948 that deemed ASCAP to be in violation of the antitrust laws (and eventually made it impossible for the society to license the public performance of music in the theatrical exhibition of motion pictures), the consent decree of 1941 was completely altered: in the words of one court, the resulting amended decree (1950) "disinfected" ASCAP of any antitrust taint. In subsequent court decisions, the blanket license ASCAP offered was repeatedly, but unsuccessfully, attacked on antitrust grounds, on behalf of users such as local radio broadcasters, television networks, "general" establishments (such as taverns, restaurants, and nightclubs), and local television stations. The legality of the blanket license is now well established.

In terms of the number of works in its repertory and amount of revenue it collects, ASCAP is the largest performing rights society in the United States. It is a member of CISAC. For the society's activities outside the area of performing rights see AMERICAN SOCIETY OF COMPOSERS, AUTHORS AND PUBLISHERS.

(ii) Broadcast Music, Inc. (BMI). A number of broadcasting organizations opposed ASCAP's attempts to license them in the early days of radio, but ASCAP succeeded in setting up a procedure for licensing them for a fixed lump sum, which persisted until 1932, when the concept of a percentage of the broadcaster's revenue was introduced. Such a fee was unwelcome to the National Association of Broadcasters, but the association had to accept the society's terms. In 1940 ASCAP again sought to introduce new license terms, but this time the members of the National Association of Broadcasters decided to boycott ASCAP music by using material in the public domain (some of it in versions updated to suit the popular styles of the time) and to arrange for new music to be composed that would not pass into ASCAP's net.

ASCAP's repertory was very extensive, and up to 1940 the society had an effective monopoly. It was at this time that some 600 enterprises, most of them engaged in broadcasting, formed Broadcast Music, Inc. (BMI), for the sole purpose of creating a competitive

source of music licensing in the USA. At the time, ASCAP was also involved in antitrust proceedings and was obliged to settle its dispute with the broadcasters. Few at ASCAP expected BMI to survive, but by the mid-1960s its share of the market (the amount of music played by American broadcasting organizations) had become greater than ASCAP's, although its repertory was smaller. BMI is the world's largest performing rights organization in terms of the number of affiliated songwriters and publishers (more than 500,000 members in 2011). BMI's initial success was largely attributable to its open-door policy. For the first time, writers of country music, jazz, gospel, rhythm-and-blues, and other types of music that had not previously been eligible to earn performing money could share in performing rights income.

The prospectus under which stock in BMI was originally offered stated that no dividends were to be expected from the company, and no dividends have been paid. Stock in the company continues to be held by members of the broadcasting industry, and the board of directors is drawn from this area. Except for operating expenses all the collected revenue from the works that it has logged in broadcast and live performances is redistributed to its writer and publisher affiliates. Like ASCAP, BMI is subject to a consent decree under antitrust legislation, and disputes between BMI and licensees are settled according to the rules of the American Arbitration Association. For the company's activities outside the area of performing rights, *see* BROADCAST MUSIC, INC.

(iii) SESAC Inc. Founded in 1931 as the Society of European Stage Authors and Composers, SESAC Inc. (now the official name of this organization) is a private licensing company owned by the Heinicke family. Unlike ASCAP and BMI, SESAC collects in respect of mechanical and synchronization rights (covering commercial recordings for private use, and films) as well as in respect of the performing right. Royalty distributions (made quarterly) are based on such external factors as the number of recordings released, placement and movement on popularity charts, and local surveys. Both ASCAP and BMI levy their royalties as a percentage of the licensee's revenue, but SESAC's charges are based on fixed, lump-sum payments according to a broadcasting user's advertising rates and the population of the market it serves. (Assessment according to the number of hours of broadcasting was dropped in favor of charges based on advertising rates.) A SESAC license is taken out by virtually all broadcasting organizations in the country. At one time SESAC maintained what was known as the "transcribed library," a program service it made available to broadcasters. For the society's activities outside the area of performing rights, *see* SESAC INC.

The scale of the activities of the three American organizations can be compared by looking at their receipts from performing rights licenses in particular years. In 1952 ASCAP received over $17 million, BMI over $5 million, and SESAC about $1 million. By 1957 ASCAP's receipts were about $27 million and BMI's about

$9.5 million, while SESAC's remained at $1 million. In 1963 ASCAP's income had risen to $38 million and BMI's to about $15 million, while SESAC's income was still $1 million. In 1982 ASCAP's total receipts came to about $187 million, BMI's to nearly $120 million, and SESAC's to approximately $5 million. In 2010, ASCAP's distributed $846.3 million in royalties, BMI distributed $789 million in royalties, and SESAC remained a distant third.

(iv) Harry Fox Agency, Inc. In 1927 the Music Publishers' Protective Association (later the National Music Publishers' Association) set up the Harry Fox Agency to license musical copyrights other than the performing right on behalf of its members and other, non-member publishing firms. The rights in respect of which it collects are the mechanical and synchronization rights, the right in broadcast commercials (for which the royalties for each use, as in the case of films, are negotiated by the agency), and the right to transmission of recorded music by radio and in public places such as restaurants, stores, and airplanes. The agency grants licenses to recording companies and others availing themselves of the mechanical right and collects the royalties from them. The revision of the copyright act that came into effect on 1 January 1978 stipulated the royalty in respect of each work on a phonograph recording or tape to be 2¾¢ per composition or ½¢ per minute of playing time, whichever is the greater; a commission of 4½% for discs and tapes is charged by the agency on the royalties it collects. The current mechanical royalty rate is 9.1¢ each for a recording of a composition of five minutes or less in duration and 1.75¢ per minute or fraction thereof for recordings of a composition of over five minutes in length. The Fox agency has an effective collection system in Japan through the Japanese Society for Rights of Authors, Composers and Publishers, and works through various other foreign societies as well.

See also COPYRIGHT; INTELLECTUAL PROPERTY; and LICENSING.

BIBLIOGRAPHY

T. Solberg: *Copyright Enactments 1783–1900* (Washington, DC, 1900, rev. 5/1973 as *Copyright Enactments: Laws Passed in the United States since 1783 Relating to Copyright*)
R. Hubbell: *The Story of ASCAP by a Founder* (MS, c1937, *NN*)
The ABC of BMI (New York, 1940)
D. MacDougald Jr.: "The Popular Music Industry," *Radio Research, 1941*, ed. P.F. Lazarsfeld and F. Stanton (New York, 1941), 65–109
A. Green and J. Laurie Jr.: *Show Biz, from Vaude to Video* (New York, 1951)
H. Finkelstein: "The Composer and the Public Interest—Regulation of Performing Right Societies," *Law and Contemporary Problems*, xix (1954), 275
E.N. Waters: "ASCAP," *Victor Herbert: a Life in Music* (New York, 1955/R), 431
A.D. Neale: *The Antitrust Laws of the United States of America: a Study of Competition Enforced by Law* (Cambridge, England, 1960)
S. Shemel and M.W. Krasilovsky: *This Business of Music* (New York, 1964, rev. and enlarged 5/1985)
S. Shemel and M.W. Krasilovsky: *More about this Business of Music* (New York, 1967, rev. and enlarged 3/1982)
D.D. Braun: *The Sociology and History of American Music and Dance* (Ann Arbor, MI, 1969)
M. Goldin: *The Music Merchants* (New York, 1969)
I. Tarr: "Tape Systems—Cartridge and Cassette: Current Impact in the United States—and Prospects," *The Complete Report of the First International Music Industry Conference, April 1969* (New York, 1969)
B. Ringer: *Two Hundred Years of Copyright in America* (Washington, DC, 1976)
B.L. DeWhitt: *The American Society of Composers, Authors, and Publishers 1914–1938* (diss., Emory U., 1977)
L.S. Schultz: "Performing-Rights Societies in the United States," *Notes*, xxxv (1978–9), 511
L. Feist: *An Introduction to Popular Music Publishing in America* (New York, 1980)
G.W.M. McFarlane: *Copyright: the Development and Exercise of the Performing Right* (London, 1980)
G.W.M. McFarlane: *A Practical Introduction to Copyright* (London, 1982)
G.W.M. McFarlane: *Copyright through the Cases* (London, 1985)
J. Ryan: *The Production Of Culture in the Music Industry: the ASCAP-BMI Controversy* (Lanham, MD, 1985)
R. Sanjek: *American Popular Music and Its Business: the First Four Hundred Years* (New York, 1988)
R. Sanjek and D. Sanjek: *Pennies From Heaven: American Popular Music and Its Business* (New York, 1996)
C. Wildpaner: *The U.S. Digital Millennium Copyright Act: a Challenge for Fair Use in the Digital Age* (Vienna, 2004)
R.S. Rosen: *Music and Copyright* (Oxford, New York, 2008)

GAVIN MCFARLANE/DAVID SANJEK

Perich, Tristan (*b* New York, NY, 24 May 1982). Composer and visual artist. After attending Phillips Academy in Andover, Massachusetts, he studied math, music, and computer science at Columbia University (BA 2004). He subsequently received a masters in art, music, and electronics at the interactive telecommunications program at Tisch School of the Arts (2007). He also attended the first Bang on a Can Summer Institute (2002).

Perich has been inspired by the aesthetics of math and physics and has worked with simple forms and complex systems. His compositions, which offer an austere meeting of electronic and organic sounds, have been performed internationally by ensembles including Bang on a Can, the Calder Quartet, Sonic Generator, and Ensemble Pamplemousse. In 2010 Rhizome commissioned him to create an audio installation with 1500 speakers.

In 2004 he began work on *1-Bit Music* to experiment with the foundations of electronic sound. The result was a physical "album," released by Cantaloupe Music in 2006, that contained an electronic circuit assembled inside a CD case with a headphone jack on the side. The device played back 40 minutes of lo-fi one-bit electronic music, the lowest possible digital representation of audio. *Surface* magazine called the *1-Bit Music* boxes "profound throwbacks to the traditional album, a response to the intangibility of iTunes and mp3s in the form hand-held artwork." Working with one-bit music conceptually influenced his music for acoustic ensembles, resulting in dual compositions for musicians with one-bit music accompaniment, pairing the performers with on-stage speakers. His subsequent circuit album, *1-Bit Symphony* (Cantaloupe, 2010), is a long-form electronic composition in five movements. Its music explores the intricate, polyphonic potential of one-bit music, uniting simple with complex and celebrating the virtuosity of electricity.

As a visual artist Perich has staged many solo exhibitions and participated in a variety of group shows in New York and Europe. His *Machine Drawings*, pen-on-paper drawings executed by machine, were featured in the book *Makers* (Cambridge, MA, 2005). Expressing digital processes in traditional media, these drawings explore order and randomness within compositional frameworks, delicately executed by the minimal drawing machine.

Perich's experimental group, the Loud Objects (with Kunal Gupta and Katie Shima), has performed electronic music by soldering their own noise-making circuits from scratch in front of the audience, often displayed from the top of old overhead projectors to render transparent the meaning of their physical gestures. They have performed and exhibited in Asia, Europe, Scandinavia, and North America. In 2009 they received a commission from Turbulence.org to create a networked noise toy development tool for open experimentation in hardware audio programming, and in 2010 they were artists-in-residence at Art on Air.

Perich was a featured artist at the Sonár festival in Barcelona (2010) and was presented with the Award of Distinction for his composition *Active Field* by the Prix Ars Electronica in Austria (2009). He was artist-in-residence at Issue Project Room in 2008, at Mikrogalleriet in Copenhagen in 2010, and at the Addison Gallery in Andover, Massachusetts, and Harvestworks in New York in fall 2010. His work has received support from the New York State Council on the Arts, the American Music Center, and Meet the Composer, among others. He has spoken about his work and taught workshops around the world.

WORKS
(selective list)
Active Field, 10 vn, elec, 2007; Telescope, 2 b cl, 2 bar sax, elec, 2007; All Possible Paths, cl, vc, db, gui, pf, mar, elec, 2008; Observations, crotales, 2 perc, elec, 2008; Dual Synthesis, hpd, elec, 2009; Half-tone, 3 pic, elec, 2010; Elevation Maps, 5 accdn, elec, 2010; Woven, cl, vn, vc, pf, amp. perc with effects, 2010

ELIOT GATTEGNO

Periodicals. Periodicals are publications issued at recurring intervals (e.g., annually, quarterly) featuring essays, reports, critiques, or news. Whether published regularly or occasionally, they differ from continuations or those works appearing in fascicles, insofar as their periodicity (represented by issue or volume numbers) implies continuing and contemporary relevance as determined by a publisher, editor, or sponsoring organization. In music, examples of periodicals include yearbooks, annual reports, journals, or newsletters.

This article provides a general account and history of music periodicals in the United States. A comprehensive list of music periodicals and alphabetical index follows the bibliography.

1. History. (i) To 1915. (ii) 1915–65. (iii) 1965–90. (iv) 1990–2010. 2. List. 3. Index.

1. HISTORY.

(i) To 1915. The forerunners of true American music periodicals were influenced by earlier English publications. *American Musical Magazine* (1786–7), edited by Amos Doolittle and Daniel Read, consisted of compositions by American and English composers, and its successor, *Musical Magazine* (1792–1801), edited by Andrew Law, featured psalm and hymn tunes as well as essays. Primarily a literary journal, *Ladies' Literary Museum, or Weekly Repository* (1817–20) also included musical supplements with an occasional article on a musical topic.

Considered the first American music periodical, *Euterpeiad, or Musical Intelligencer* (1820–23), edited by J.R. Parker, featured news of Boston's musical culture together with a serial conspectus of music history. The scope of a later, New York–based counterpart, *Euterpeiad* (1830–31), expanded to include essays on music and style, biography and anecdotes about well-known musicians as well as reviews of printed music and concert performances. Perhaps the most ambitious early American music periodical, *Dwight's Journal of Music* (1852–81), was published in Boston and contained essays on composers and music history, theory, education, and style along with critical reports on the musical culture and announcements of new compositions. Its editor, JOHN SULLIVAN DWIGHT, indicated in an early circular his hope for its tone to be "impartial, independent, catholic, conciliatory, aloof from musical clique and controversy, cordial to all good things, but not eager to chime in with any powerful private interest of publisher, professor, concert-giver, manager, society, or party."

Toward the late 19th century, changing cultural trends could be witnessed in the rise of new periodical content. For example, the revival of church music and sung services (already the focus of the German publication *Caecilia*) could be found in the New York–based journal of the American Cecilia Society, and in *Church Music Review* of the American Guild of Organists. Evidence of a growing interest in a nascent music industry could be seen in *Music Trades* (1890–), the sale of musical instruments in *Music Industry* (1906–), and musical entertainment in *Billboard Advertising* (1894–). At the same time, music education reform inspired publications such as *The Etude* (1883–1957), *The Musician* (1896–1948), and the *Tonic Sol-fa Advocate* (1881–6). By the turn of the century, music periodicals with content focused on a variety of musical activities within their locales were published in cities across the nation; for example, in New York, *Musical America* (1898–1964); in Chicago, *The Musical Leader and Concert-goer* (1895–1967); and in Los Angeles, *Pacific Coast Musician* (1911–48), recognized as the oldest significant Californian music periodical.

(ii) 1915–65. In 1915 OSCAR G.T. SONNECK founded the first comprehensive musicological periodical, *The Musical Quarterly*. In addition to articles on musicological topics, *MQ* included book, music, and record reviews together with "Current Chronicle" (reports on performances of new music), as well as quarterly book and recording lists. The American Musicological Society began publishing its journal in 1948, whereas the Music Library Association, having begun its occasional *Notes for the Members of the Music Library Association* in 1934, initiated a more comprehensive quarterly second series in 1943, entitled *Notes*, which featured articles in

addition to lists and reviews of new music, books, and recordings. Recognizing the need to discover articles written about music, Florence Kretzschmar, with help from the Music Library Association and assistance from Dorothy Tilly and Kurtz Myers, started *The Music Index* in 1949, a monthly author and article title index, which was cumulated annually. Soon thereafter, in 1953, the Society for Ethnomusicology founded its *Ethno-Musicology Newsletter* (later journal, *Ethnomusicology*).

The growing number of music periodicals reflected new needs for professionals in the field of music to share information with one another. Instrumental music teachers saw the first publication of *School Band and Orchestra Musician* (later *School Musician* then *Musician/Director & Teacher*) in 1929, and the *Instrumentalist* in 1946. The American Guild of Organists began *American Organist* in 1918, whereas piano teachers began *Piano Guild Notes* in 1945; and the Symphony Orchestra League (later League of American Orchestras) began its newsletter (later entitled *Symphony*) in 1948.

Another trend in the development of American music periodicals during these years focused on the sound recording industry. *The Phonograph, a musical news weekly*, perhaps the first publication of its kind in the United States, began in 1916, and in later years also featured articles on the talking machine, radio, and even television. From 1926–32 the *Phonograph Monthly Review*, also known as *Music Lovers' Phonograph Monthly review, an independent American magazine for amateurs interested in recorded music and its development*, served the public's need to learn more about recordings currently available. Perhaps the dominant publication of this realm was first established in 1949 (concurrent with *Music Index*): the Schwann catalogs and discographic periodicals, extremely popular, comprehensive guides to currently issued recordings. The Schwann titles followed the sound recording format evolution from the periodical's first incarnation, *Long Playing Record Catalog*, to *Schwann Compact Disc Catalog* (which ended publication in 1990). Schwann's last publications, *Opus* and *Spectrum*, featured information on classical and popular music recordings respectively and ceased publication in 2001.

(iii) 1965–90. Music periodical offerings after the mid-1960s grew steadily in number and theme. In addition to the comprehensive approach to the study of music discussed above, more specialized examination of the aural art form defined by specific time periods, for example, could be found. Among such titles were *19th Century Music* (1977–) and *20th Century Music* (later *21st Century Music*) that incorporated descriptive and analytical treatment of music and genres in articles. *Divisions* (1978–) featured discussion of Baroque improvisational techniques, guidelines for performance and English translations of theoretical works. At the same time, titles centered on specific musical genres were also flourishing such as *Chamber Music Magazine* (1984–; later *Chamber Music*), *Opera Journal* (1968–), and *Opera Quarterly* (1983–).

American music became the focus of the publications from the Sonneck Society (later the Society for American Music), initially the *Sonneck Society Newsletter* (1975–) and subsequently the quarterly *American Music* (1983–; the *Journal of the Society for American Music* since 2007). African American music was explored in the publication of the Institute for Research in Black American Music of Fisk University, *The Black Perspective in Music* (1973–90), and the Society for Asian Music began publishing its periodical, *Asian Music*, in 1968. The H. Wiley Hitchcock Institute for Studies in American Music examines art music as well as folk and urban music of North America in its newsletter (1971–), whereas *Revista de música Latino Americana/Latin American Music Review* (1980–) contains articles on musical traditions of people from Latin America, Mexico, Puerto Rico, and Cuba.

In 1979 soon after the Society for Music Theory's inception, the Society began publishing *Music Theory Spectrum* featuring articles on theory and analysis as well as aesthetics. Interest in examining new musical forms and thought continued to grow over time as demonstrated in other journals such as the *Computer Music Journal* (1977–), and those publications highlighting examples of newly composed scores together with discussion of compositional technique such as *Source* (1967–72), *Soundings* (1972–90), and *Ear* (1973–88). Continuing in the analytical vein but involving the psychological, perception-based or therapeutic applications of music include titles such as *Psychology of Music* (1973–), *Psychomusicology* (1981–), *Music Therapy Perspectives* (1982–), and *Music Perception* (1983–).

One of the longer lived titles devoted to the music of a single composer, *Bach*, the organ of the Riemenschneider Bach Institute (1970–), offers analyses and essays on the forms, styles and performances of Johann Sebastian Bach and other Baroque composers. Other such publications based on the music of individual composers include the *Beethoven Journal* (1986–) published by the Ira F. Brilliant Center for Beethoven Studies and the American Beethoven Society, *Fritz Reiner Society Newsletter* (later *Podium*, 1975–88), and *Journal of the Arnold Schoenberg Institute* (1975–). Of similar note are journals devoted to individual musical instruments, such as *Clarinet* (1973–), *Modern Drummer* (1977–), *Double Reed* (1978–), *Flute Talk* (1981–), and *Bass Player* (1990–). In 1975 the American Musical Instrument Society began publishing its journal.

The development of jazz and popular music continued to be documented in the magazine and journal literature from the mid-1960s forward. The National Association of Jazz Educators published a newsletter (1968–) that later grew into the *NAJE Educator* then *Jazz Educators Journal*, which ceased publication in 2007. More popular treatment of jazz could be found in *Living Blues* (1970–) from Chicago and *Jazz Times* (1980–) from Washington, DC. The world of rock music has also grown extensively during this period. *Rolling Stone* (1967–) focused initially on music of the 1960s to 70s, but later grew to include a more expansive view of popular music as well as contemporary film reviews and political, economic, and popular culture commentary. Other long-standing magazines include *Crawdaddy* (1966–78) and *Creem* (1969–), both devoted to rock and roll music in a popular treatment. A more scholarly approach to the topic can be found in *Popular Music and Society* (1971–) based in Bowling Green University, which features historical, theoretical, critical, sociological, and cultural examination of the topic.

(iv) 1990–2010. As in earlier times, periodical literature of the late 20th century reflected musical as well as contemporary societal awareness. Perhaps the most important thread weaving through all music-related subjects by this point, however, was technological progress as it impacted the world of music. The results can be seen in pervasive Internet accessibility, widespread availability of sound recording sharing, and, therefore, the opportunity for American music developments to be easily observed and globally influential.

A second thread, the interdisciplinary relationship of music with another subject, can also be observed. With regard to music and culture, for example, a major movement, women and music, can be easily observed in titles such as *Women of Note* (1993–), and *ROCKRGRL* (1994–2005), as well as *IAWM Journal* (1995–). By 1997 *Women & Music: a Journal of Gender and Culture* began publication, expanding serious deliberations on gender theory into the realm of music. Publications focusing on film music arose including *Film Music* (1999–), *Journal of Film Music* (2002–), and *Music and the Moving Image* (2008–). Music blended with science and technology may be observed in the journal *Leonardo: Arts, Science and Technology* (particularly in an annual issue devoted to music), and technology becoming part of the music curriculum is at the heart of *Journal of Technology in Music Learning* (2001–) and *Music Education Technology* (2003–).

With advances in computing and networking technology in the last decades of the 20th century, access to periodicals changed, eventually causing the use and nature of this literature to evolve as well. By the mid-1990s, for example, libraries were able to provide online public access to their catalogs, the contents of which were once only available in their card catalogs. Libraries also began associations with one another that encouraged cooperation in developing their collections and sharing digitally offered services. As a result, library consortia such as OhioLINK or the California Digital Library, for example, could share and archive resources digitally. At the same time, journal publishers began providing digital editions of titles once only available in paper-based subscriptions. Periodical vendors would then aggregate collections of these titles and dispense online subscriptions.

To collect and preserve digital periodical and journal titles, new cooperatives emerged, opening the door to full-text electronic availability of music journal titles. Project MUSE (started at Johns Hopkins University in 1993) and JSTOR (started at the University of Michigan in 1995) are two examples of not-for-profit organizations working with publishers to preserve journal literature while delivering full-text digital content to users via subscription-based services. In 2003 JSTOR announced the beginning of the Music Collection; having worked with *RILM* and other societies such as the Music Library Association to target specific publishers and titles, the complete runs of 32 new titles were added to JSTOR's holdings (over 40 titles in 2010). Project MUSE currently provides full-text access to 12 music journals.

In 2002 another perspective on digital journals began with an idea emanating from discussion at the Open Society Institute (OSI). As a result, Open Access Journals, or peer-reviewed publications available only in digital form, allow any user to read, download, copy, distribute, print, or search such publications without direct cost. *The Directory of Open Access Journals* (DOAJ) provides the means for accessing such titles including *Journal of Seventeenth-Century Music* (1995–) and *Music & Politics* (2007–).

In addition to continual online access to journal literature, digital functionality enables music periodical users to benefit from the enhanced effectiveness afforded by electronic indexing and abstracting resources. Once only available in paper format, for example, *Music Index*, *RILM Abstracts of Music Literature*, and *RIPM* not only provide online access to citations or abstracts but can also lead directly to articles in full-text format. One disadvantage to digital access, the loss of all access to past issues of a title if the title stopped publication, for example, was alleviated by the emergence of programs providing long-term protection for libraries' holdings. LOCKSS (based at Stanford University), Portico, and CLOCKSS, all preservation programs designed to protect libraries' digital content against journal cancellation or other lapses in content provision, ensure access to subscribed content if digital access somehow disappears.

BIBLIOGRAPHY

GENERAL

Grove5 (A.H. King); *Grove7* (I. Fellinger and others); *MGG* ("Zeitschriften," I. Fellinger)

E. von Lannoy: "Was ist die Aufgabe einer musikalischen Zeitung?" *Neue Wiener Musik-Zeitung*, i (1852), 1–2

G.W. Cooke: *John Sullivan Dwight: Brook-farmer, Editor, and Critic of Music* (Boston, 1898/R)

O.G.T. Sonneck: "Die musikalische Zeitschriften-Literatur," *ZIMG*, i (1899–1900), 388–90

L.N. Richardson: *A History of Early American Magazines, 1741–1789* (New York, 1931)

E.N. Waters: "John Sullivan Dwight, First American Critic of Music," *MQ*, xxi (1935), 69–88

F.L. Mott: *A History of American Magazines* (Cambridge, MA, 1938–68)

H.E. Johnson: "Early New England Periodicals devoted to Music," *MQ*, xxvi (1940), 153–61

J.C. Haskins: "John Rowe Parker and *The Euterpeiad*," *Notes*, viii (1950–51), 447–56

C.E. Wunderlich: *A History and Bibliography of Early American Musical Periodicals, 1782–1852* (diss., U. of Michigan, 1962)

D.W. Krummel: "Twenty Years of 'Notes'—a Retrospect," *Notes* xxi (1963–4), 56–82

P.L. Miller: "Twenty Years After," *Notes*, xxi (1963–4), 55–6

E. Salzman: "Modern Music in Retrospect," *PNM*, ii (1964), 14–20

J.R. Holmes: '*The Musical Quarterly*': *its History and Influence on the Development of American Musicology* (thesis, U. of North Carolina, 1967)

J.F. Schoof: *A Study of Didactic Attitudes on the Fine Arts in America as expressed in Popular Magazines during the Period 1786–1800* (diss., Ohio U., 1967)

I. Fellinger: *Verzeichnis der Musikzeitschriften des 19. Jahrhunderts* (Regensburg, Germany, 1968)

N. Zaslaw: "Free Music Periodicals," *CMc*, no.10 (1970), 140–43

R. Ceely: "Communications," *PNM*, xi (1972), 258–61

M.V. Davison: *American Music Periodicals, 1853–1899* (diss. U. of Minnesota, 1973)

H.E. Karjala: *A Critical Analysis of 'School Music' Magazine 1900–1936* (diss., U. of Minnesota, 1973)

C.B. Grimes: *American Musical Periodicals, 1819–1852: Music Theory and Musical Thought in the United States* (diss., U. of Iowa, 1974)

J.H. Alexander: "Brainard's (Western) Musical World," *Notes*, xxxvi (1979–80), 601–14

M. Lederman: *The Life and Death of a Small Magazine (Modern Music 1924–1946)* (Brooklyn, NY, 1983)

G.B. Anderson: "Unpublished Periodical Indexes at the Library of Congress and Elsewhere in the United States of America," *FAM*, xxxi (1984), 54–60

C. Lindahl: "Past Efforts regarding Union Catalogues of Periodicals in the United States of America," *FAM*, xxxi (1984), 50–51

I. Fellinger: *Periodica musicalia 1789–1830* (Regensburg, Germany, 1985)

G.B. Anderson: *Music in New York during the American Revolution: an Inventory of Musical References in 'Rivington's New York Gazette'* (Boston, MA, 1987)

I. Fellinger: "Periodica," *Modern Music Librarianship: Essays in Honor of Ruth Watanabe*, ed. A. Mann (Stuyvesant, NY, 1989), 193–214

C. Clark: "POMPI: Popular Music Periodicals Index," *FAM*, xxxviii (1991), 32–7

R. Kitson: "English and American Periodicals Treated by *RIPM*: a Report," *Periodica musica*, ix (1991), 23–7

B.H. Miller: "Household Periodicals: an Unstudied Source of American Music," *FAM*, xlii (1995), 311–9

M. Colby: "Music Periodical Indexing in General Databases," *Notes*, liv (1997–8), 27–37

M.W. Davidson: "Mid-Nineteenth-Century American Periodicals: a Case Study," *Notes*, liv (1997–8), 371–87

K. Kroeger: "*The Musical Quarterly* and *American Music*," *Vistas of American Music: Essays and Compositions in Honor of William K. Kearns*, ed. S.L. Porter and J. Graziano (Warren, MI, 1999), 309–20

LISTS OF PERIODICALS

HDM4 (H.E. Samuel and L. Coral); *RiemannL12*

"Periodische Schriften," *Jahrbuch der Musikbibliothek Peters* (Leipzig, Germany, 1894–1938)

Union List of Serials in the Libraries of the United States and Canada, ed. W. Gregory (New York, 1927, 2/1943, rev. 3/1965 by E.B. Titus; suppls., Washington, DC, 1973– as *New Serial Titles*, from 1982 in 3-month cumulations)

Bibliographie des Musikschrifttums (1936–88)

D.H. Daugherty, L. Ellinwood, and R.S. Hill: *Bibliography of Periodical Literature in Musicology and Allied Fields and a Record of Graduate Theses* (Washington, DC, 1940–43/R)

L. Fairley: "A Check-list of Recent Latin-American Music Periodicals," *Notes*, ii (1944–5), 5, 120

F. Campbell, G. Eppink, and J. Fredericks: "Music Magazines of Great Britain and the United States," *Notes*, vi (1948–9), 239–62, 547; vii (1949–50), 372–6

I. Lowens: "Writings about Music in the Periodicals of American Transcendentalism (1835–1850)," *JAMS*, x (1957), 71–85

C.E. Wunderlich: *A History and Bibliography of Early American Musical Periodicals, 1782–1852* (diss., U. of Michigan, 1962)

Early American Periodicals Index to 1850 (New York, 1964)

F. Blum: "Music Serials in Microfilm and Reprint Editions," *Notes*, xxiv (1967–8), 670–9

I. Fellinger: *Verzeichnis der Musikzeitschriften des 19. Jahrhunderts* (Regensburg, Germany, 1968); suppls. in *FAM*, xvii (1970), 7–8; xviii (1971), 59–62; xix (1972), 41–4; xx (1973), 108–11; xxi (1974), 36–8; xxiii (1976), 62–6

W.J. Weichlein: *A Checklist of American Music Periodicals, 1850–1900* (Detroit, 1970)

T.G. Everett: "An Annotated List of English-Language Jazz Periodicals," *Journal of Jazz Studies*, iii/2 (1975–6), 47–57; v/2 (1978–9), 99–103; cont. in *Annual Review of Jazz Studies*, iv (1988), 214–6

C.E. Lindahl: "Music Periodicals: New Music and the Composer," *Notes*, xxxii (1975–6), 784–93

Ulrich's International Periodicals Directory (New York, 1975–80)

C.E. Lindahl: "Music Periodicals: Early (and Later) Musical Instrument Journals," *Notes*, xxxiii (1976–7), 86–102

C.E. Lindahl: "Music Periodicals," *Notes*, xxxiii (1976–7), 308–16, 851–64; further lists in xxxiv (1977–8), 883–93; xxxv (1978–9), 323–35, 895–902; xxxvi (1979–80), 662–72; xxxix (1982–3), 106–16

C. Lawrence Mekkawi: "Music Periodicals: Popular and Classical Reviews and Indexes," *Notes*, xxxiv (1977–8), 92–107

J.M. Meggett: *Music Periodical Literature: an Annotated Bibliography of Indexes and Bibliographies* (Metuchen, NJ, 1978)

J. Hoornstra and T. Heath, eds.: *American Periodicals, 1741–1900: an index to the microfilm collections* (Ann Arbor, MI, 1979)

Northern California Chapter of the MLA: *A Union List of Music Periodicals in the Libraries of Northern California* (Berkeley, CA, 6/1979)

C.E. Lindahl: "Music Periodicals in U.S. Research Libraries in 1931: a Retrospective Survey, Part iii: The United States," *Notes*, xxxviii (1981–2), 320–6

L.I. Solow: "Index to Music Periodicals Reviewed in *Notes* (1976–1982)," *Notes*, xxxix (1982–3), 585–90

H.R. Cohen: "An Introduction to the Fourth 'R': Le répertoire international de la presse musicale du dix-neuvième siècle (RIPMxix)," *Periodica musica*, i (1983), 1–2

"New Periodicals" or "New Music Periodicals," *Notes* (1983–4) [recurring column]

K.P. Glennan: "Music periodicals published in Los Angeles County, 1900–1985: a Bibliography," *California's Musical Wealth* (Glendale, CA, 1985), 107–22

T.E. Warner: *Periodical Literature on American Music, 1620–1920: a Classified Bibliography with Annotations* (Warren, MI, 1988)

L.M. Fidler and R.S. James, eds.: *International Music Journals* (New York, 1990)

INDEXES AND ABSTRACTING RESOURCES

The Music Index. Information Service Coordinators; Harmonie Park Press, Detroit, 1949–2009; later *Music Index Online*. EBSCO Publishing, Ipswich, MA, 2010–

Music Article Guide. Philadelphia, 1965–96

RILM Abstracts of Music Literature. New York, 1967–99; later, RILM [Online]. New York, 1997–

Répertoire international de la presse musicale. Ann Arbor, MI, 1987–97; later, *RIPM Retrospective Index to Music Periodicals, 1800–1950*. Baltimore, MD, 1997–

ONLINE RESOURCES

CLOCKSS, <http://www.clockss.org/clockss/Home>

DOAJ, <http://www.doaj.org/>

JSTOR: Announces Music Collection. JSTORNEWS 7, 2 (June 2003), <http://news.jstor.org/news/2003.06/music.html>. Accessed 4 Nov 2010

LOCKSS, <http://lockss.stanford.edu/lockss/Home>

Portico, <http://www.portico.org/digital-preservation/>

Project MUSE. What is Project MUSE?, <http://muse.jhu.edu/about/muse/index.html>

RILM, <http://www.rilm.org/index.php>

RIPM, <http://www.ripm.org/>

2. LIST. Much of the information related to titles that began publication prior to 1950 has been retained from the first edition and, when necessary or possible, updated. Titles dating from 1950 forward have likewise been retained and when necessary updated, but many additional titles have also been added. Because much more extensive data is readily available for publications in the latter class, only title and publication information has been provided.

1 *Euterpeiad*, or *Musical Intelligencer* (Boston, 1820–23; new ser. 1823) 3 vols., new ser. 2 nos., W; from 1821, F; from 1822–3, no. 14, M

2 *Lyre*, or *New York Musical Journal* (New York, 1824–5) 1 vol., M

3 *Theatrical Censor and Musical Review* (Philadelphia, 1828) 28 nos., D, from no.4; 3 nos. W

4 *Euterpeiad: an Album of Music, Poetry, and Prose* (New York, 1830–1) 2 vols., S

5 *American Musical Journal* (New York, 1834–5) 1 vol., B; from Feb 1835, M

6 *Boston Musical Gazette* (Boston, 1838–9) 2 vols., F

7 *Musical Review and Record of Music Science, Literature, and Intelligence* (New York, 1838–9) 2 vols.

8 *Parlour Review and Journal of Music, Literature, and the Fine Arts* (Philadelphia, 1838) 10 nos., W [also Fr. edn]

9 *Proceedings of the Musical Convention* (Boston, etc., 1838–) later, *American Musical Convention*, Y

10 *Musical Magazine, or Repository of Musical Science, Literature, and Intelligence* (Boston, 1839–42, except 4–18 Sept 1841 and 4 Dec 1841 to 10 April 1842) 78 nos. in 3 vols., F; from 1841/2, no.71, O

11 *Boston Eoliad: devoted Exclusively to the Science of Music* (Boston, 1840–1) 2 nos., H

12 *Musical Visitor* (Boston, 1840–6); later, *Boston Musical Visitor* (1842–4); then later, *American Journal of Music and Musical Visitor* (1844–6) 5 vols., S

13 *Musical Cabinet: a Monthly Collection of Vocal and Instrumental Music and Musical Literature* (Boston, 1841–2) 1 vol., M

14 *Musical Reporter* (Boston, 1841) 9 nos. in 1 vol., M

15 *World of Music* (Bellows Falls, VT, 1843–8) 5 vols., S. Continued as *Philharmonic Journal* (Claremont, NH, 1848–9) 24 nos. in 1 vol., F

16 *Boston Musical Review* (Boston, 1845) 4 nos., S

17 *Musical Gazette* (Boston, MA, and Bellows Falls, VT, 1846–50), later, *Boston Musical Gazette* (1847–50) 5 vols., F; from 1848–9, S. Continued as *Message Bird*.

18 *American Musical Times* (New York, 1847–9) 3 vols., W. Continued from *New York Musical Chronicle and Advertiser*.

19 *Message Bird: a Literary and Musical Journal* (New York, 1849–60) later, *Journal of the Fine Arts* (1 May 1851), then *Arts and Musical World* (from 16 June 1851), then *Musical World and Journal of the Fine Arts* (from 2 Feb 1852). Incorp. *Saroni's Musical Times* (15 July 1852) to form *Musical World and New York Musical Times*, and later, *Musical World* (from 9 Sept 1854), and *New York Musical* (from 2 Jan 1856), and then later, *Musical* (from 5 Jan 1858); 25 vols., S, from 4 Sept 1852, W. Continued from *Musical Gazette*; incorp. into *Choral Advocate*.

20 *Saroni's Musical Times* (New York, 1849–52) 5 vols., W. Incorp. into *Message Bird*.

21 *American Musical* (Huntington, NY, 1850–51, Huntington & Savage, from 1851), later, *Monthly Musical Review and Choir Singers' Companion* (from 1850, no.3) pubd 2 vols., Q; from 1850, no.2, M. Incorp. into *Choral Advocate*.

22 *American Musical Fund Society: Annual Report* (New York, 1850–60) 10 vols., Y

23 *Baltimore Olio and American Musical Gazette* (Baltimore, 1850) 1 vol., M

24 *Choral Advocate and Singing-class Journal* (Mason [& Law], New York, 1850–73). Incorp. *American Musical* (Jan 1852) to form *Musical Review and Choral Advocate* (wrapper title *American Musical Review and Choral Advocate*), later, *New-York Musical Review and Choral Advocate* (1854). Incorp. *Musical Gazette* (1855, no. 11) to form *New-York Musical Review and Gazette*, incorp. *Message Bird* (1860, no. 16) to form *Musical Review and Musical World*, later, *New York Weekly Review of Music, Literature, Fine Arts, and Society* (from 1865), then *New York Weekly Review* (from 1867), pubd 766 nos. in 24 vols., M; from 1854, S; from 1865 W

25 *Lorgnette, or Studies of the Town, by an Opera Goer* (New York, 1850) 24 nos.

26 *North-western Musical Herald* (Detroit, 1851) 2 nos., M

27 *Dwight's Journal of Music* (Boston, 1852–81) 1051 nos. in 41 vols., W; from April 1863, F

28 *Boston Musical Journal* (Boston, 1853–4) 19 nos., S

29 *Monthly Musical Gazette* (New York, 1853) 10 nos. in 1 vol., M

30 *Musical Gazette* (Mason, New York, 1854–5) 26 nos. in 1 vol., W. Incorp. into *Choral Advocate*.

31 *Massachusetts Musical Journal* (Boston, 1855–7) later, *Boston Journal and Literary Gazette* (1856) 2 vols., S

32 *New York Musical Pioneer and Choristers' Budget* (Huntington, NY, 1855–71 except Oct–Dec 1868) later, *New York Musical Pioneer* (from Oct 1859), then later, *Musical Pioneer* (Jan 1865) 16 vols., M

33 *Deutsche Musikzeitung für die Vereinigten Staaten (Staaten von Nordamerika)* (Philadelphia, 1856–61) 5 vols., S, later M, W, F; suppl.: *Die Wespe* (1859–61), O [in Ger.]

34 *Philadelphia Musical Journal and Review* (Philadelphia, 1856–7) 26 nos. in 1 vol., F

35 *Western Journal of Music* (Chicago, 1856–) 1 no., F

36 *Educational Herald and Musical Monthly* (New York, 1857–64) 8 vols., M

37 *Kleine Musik-Zeitung: Musical Gazette* (New York, 1858–70) later, *Little Musical Gazette: kleine Musik-Zeitung* (Oct/Dec 1867 to Dec 1868) 13 vols., Q; from 1868, 4; in 1870, 2 nos. M [in Eng., Ger.]

38 *Chorister* (New York, 1859–65 except Oct 1861 to May 1862, July–Sept 1862, and Jan–April 1864) later, *Chorister and Musical Advisor* (from 1861) 5 vols., M

39 *Southern Musical Advocate and Singers' Friend* (Mountain Valley, VA, and Singer's Glen, VA, 1859; Singer's Glen, 1860, 1867–9) later, *Musical Advocate and Singers' Friend* (1866–9) 5 vols., M. Continued as *Musical Million*.

40 *Boston Musical Times* (Boston and New York, 1860–71) later, *Musical Times* (from Feb 1869) 13 vols., F

41 *Bühnen-Almanach des St. Louis-Opern Hauses* (St. Louis, 1861) 1 vol., Y [in Ger.]

42 *Monthly Choir and Organ Journal* (New York, 1862–3) 1 vol., M

43 *Song Messenger of the Northwest* (Root & Cady, Chicago, 1863–75 except Dec 1872 to Feb 1873) later, *Song Messenger* (from 1870); then later, *Messenger Monthly* (from 1874) 13 vols., M. Incorp. into *Church's Musical Visitor*.

44 *Orpheonist and Philharmonic Journal* (New York, 1864–80) later, *Philharmonic Journal and Orpheonist* (from Nov 1873), and then *Advertiser*. 108 nos. in 16 vols., M; from 1875–6, S; from 1876–7, M

45 *Watson's Weekly Art Journal* (New York, 1864–1905) later, *American Art Journal* (from 1866), and then *Watson's Art Journal* (1867–75, no. 10) 87 vols., W. Incorp. into *American Musician*.

46 *Western Musical World* (Cleveland, later Chicago, 1864–95) later, *Brainard's Musical World* (from Jan 1869) 32 vols., M. Incorp. into *Etude*.

47 *Music-class Journal and Organist's Companion* (Dubuque, IA, 1865–6) 2 vols., M

48 *Musical Visitor* (Indianapolis, IN, 1865–7) later, *Butterfield's Musical Visitor* (from March 1867) 3 vols., M. Continued as *Williard's Musical Visitor*.

49 *New-Yorker Musik-Zeitung* (New York, 1865–79) later, *New-Yorker Musik- und Unterhaltungs-blätter* (from 1877), then later *New-York Musik-Zeitung* (from 1878) 22 vols., F; from 1866, W [in Ger.]

50 *Orpheus: a Repository of Music, Art, and Literature* (New York and Boston, 1865–80) 16 vols., M

51 *Seven Sounds: a Musical Magazine devoted to the Youth* (Chicago, 1865–) 3 nos. in 1 vol., Q

52 *Chicago Musical Review* (Chicago, 1866–7) later, *Higgins' Musical Review* (from no.3) 9 nos. in 1 vol., M

53 *Concordia* (Chicago, 1866–7) 2 vols., M

54 *Neue New-Yorker Musik-Zeitung*, also *New Yorker Musik-Zeitung* (New York, 1866–71) 5 vols., W [in Ger.]

55 *New York Musical Gazette* (Mason, NY, 1866–74; Biglow & Main, 1869–74) 8 vols., M

56 *Vermont Musical Journal* (Burlington, VT, 1866–8) later, *American Musical Journal* (from Jan 1868) 2 vols., M

57 *Western Musical Review* (Indianapolis, IN, and Cincinnati, OH, 1866–83) later, *Benham's Musical Review* (from Jan 1870), then later, *Baldwin's Musical Review* (from July 1879) M

58   *Albany Musical Bulletin* (Albany, NY, 1867–8) 2 vols., M
59   *Compton's St. Louis Musical Journal* (St. Louis, 1867–) 5 nos., M
60   *Loomis Musical Journal* (New Haven, 1867–1900) later, *Musical and Masonic* (from 1870) 34 vols., M
61   *Moore's Musical Record* (Manchester, NH, 1867–70) 5 vols., M
62   *Musical Bulletin-Extra* (Troy, NY, later also New York, 1867–73) later, *Musical Bulletin* (from no.2) 7 vols., M
63   *Musical Journal* (Philadelphia, 1867) 1 vol., M
64   *Pacific Musical Gazette* (San Francisco, 1867–) M
65   *Southern Journal of Music* (Louisville, KY, 1867–) 14 nos. in 1 vol., S, later M
66   *United States Musical Review* (New York, 1867–74) later, *Peters' Musical Monthly* (from 1869) 14 vols., M
67   *Walter S. Pierce's Musical Circular* (San Francisco, 1867–) F
68   *Whitney's Musical Guest* (Toledo, OH, 1867–81) later, *Guest and Literary Journal* (from Jan 1873) 14 vols., M
69   *Figaro: devoted to Music and Drama* (New York, 1868–72) M
70   *Green Mountain Musical Journal* (Fair Haven, VT, 1868–) M
71   *Mellor's Musical Mirror* (Pittsburgh, 1868–9) 1 vol., M
72   *Musical Independent* (Chicago, 1868–73 except Nov 1871 to Nov 1872) 4 vols., M. Continued as *Goldbeck's Monthly Journal of Music.*
73   *New York Journal of Music* (New York, 1868–) 7 nos., M
74   *Folio: a Journal of Music, Art, and Literature* (Boston, 1869–95) 42 vols., M
75   *Hitchcock's New Monthly Magazine: Choice Music, Art Notes, and Select Reading for the Family Circle* (New York, 1869–70) 2 vols., M
76   *Rochester Musical Times* (Rochester, NY, 1869–72) later, *Musical Times* (1871–2) 4 vols., M
77   *National Peace Jubilee and Music Festival Reporter* (Boston, 1869) Q, later W
78   *Silver Tongue and Organists' Repertory* (New York, 1869–71) 3 vols., M
79   *Singing People: an Advocate for Congregational Singing* (New York, 1869–71) 2 vols., Q; from Jan 1871, M
80   *Amateur: a Repository of Music, Literature, and Art* (Philadelphia, 1870–74; new ser. 1875) 5 vols., new ser. 11 nos., M
81   *Chicago Magazine of Fashion, Music, and Home Reading* (Chicago, 1870–76) 7 vols.
82   *Musical Million* (Dayton, VA, and Singer's Glen, VA, 1870–1913) 44 vols., M. Continued from *Southern Musical Advocate.*
83   *Musical Monthly* (Chicago, 1870–77) M
84   *Willard's Musical Visitor* (Indianapolis, 1870–71) 1 vol., M.
85   *Zundel's Organ and Choir Monthly* (Zundel and Zundel & Brand, Brooklyn, NY, and Toledo, OH, 1870–) 1 no., M
86   *Church's Musical Visitor* (Cincinnati, 1871–97) 26 vols., M
87   *Metronome: a Monthly Review of Music* (Boston, 1871–4) 3 vols., M
88   *Newburgh Musical Bulletin* (Newburgh, NY, 1871–2) 2 vols., M
89   *Southern Musical Journal* (Savannah, GA, 1871–82) 11 vols., M. Combined with *Georgia Music Eclectic* to form *Southern Musical Journal and Educational Eclectic.*
90   *Song Journal* (Detroit and New York, 1871–97) 18 vols., M. Continued as *Concert-goer.*
91   *Winner's Musical Trumpet* (Philadelphia, 1871–) 2 nos., Q
92   *American Musical Gazette* (New York, 1872–3) 2 vols., M
93   *Dexter Smith's Musical, Literary, Dramatic, and Art Paper* (Boston, 1872–8), later, *Dexter Smith's Musical, Dramatic, Literary, Humorous, Art, Household, and Fashion Magazine* (from July 1873) then later, *Smith's Pictorial* (from March 1876) 14 vols., M. Incorp. into *Ditson and Co.'s Musical Record.*
94   *Musical Visitor and Lesson Manual for the Sunday-school and Home Circle* (Lebanon, PA, 1872–6) 5 vols., M
95   *New Hampshire Journal of Music* (Manchester, NH, 1872–82) later, *Whitney's New Hampshire Journal of Music* (from 1874) 11 vols., M
96   *Vox humana: a Journal of Music and Musical Information* (Cambridgeport [Cambridge], MA, and Chicago, 1872–9) 8 vols., M
97   *Zundel and Brand's Quarterly* (Zundel & Brand, Toledo, OH, 1872–) 1 no., Q
98   *Echo: devoted to Music, Literature, Art, and Drama* (Providence, RI, 1873–4) 2 vols., M

99   *Georgia Music Eclectic* (Atlanta, 1873–4) 2 vols. Combined with *Southern Musical Journal* to form *Southern Musical Journal and Educational Eclectic.*
100   *Goldbeck's Monthly Journal of Music* (Chicago, 1873) 2 nos., M. Continued from *Musical Independent.*
101   *Globe: Music, Drama, Literature, and Art* (New York, 1873–6), later, *Musical Globe and Ladies Fashion Bazaar* (from 1876) 5 vols., M
102   *Kansas Folio: a Monthly Journal of Music, Art, and Literature* (Leavenworth, KS, 1873–) 2 nos., M
103   *Musical Bouquet* (New York, 1873–) 1 no., M
104   *Musical Echo* (Milwaukee, 1873–5) 6 vols., M
105   *Amphion* (Detroit, 1874–85, except Oct–Nov 1877) 11 vols., M
106   *Caecilia: Vereinsorgan des Amerikanischen Caecilien-Vereins* (Regensburg, Germany, 1874–6; New York, 1877–) Incorp. *Catholic Choirmaster* to form *Sacred Music* (Pustet, Church Music Assn of America) M, later Q
107   *Organist's Quarterly Journal and Review* (Boston, 1874–7) 3 vols., Q
108   *Sherman and Hyde's Musical Review* (San Francisco, 1874–9) 6 vols., M
109   *Leader: devoted to Music and General Literature* (Boston, 1875–1904) 30 vols., M
110   *Music Trade Review* (New York, 1875–80) later, *Review* (from Nov 1878), then later, *Music Trade Review* (from Dec 1878), then later, *Musical Times* (from Sept 1879), and then *Musical and Dramatic Times and Music Trade Review* (from 1879) 11 vols., S; from Nov 1878, W
111   *Musical Casket* (Singer's Glen, VA, 1875–6) M
112   *Musical Gazette* (Chicago, 1875–) 1 no., M
113   *Trumpet Notes: a Monthly Paper devoted to the Interests of Amateur Bands* (Elkhart, IN, 1875–81) 10 vols., M
114   *Daniel F. Beatty's Illustrated Piano and Organ Advertiser* (Washington, DC, and Warren County, NJ, 1876–7) 7 nos., M
115   *Footlight: devoted to Art Industries of California—Music and the Drama* (San Francisco, 1876–80) D
116   *Knake's Monthly Journal of Music and General Miscellany* (Pittsburgh, 1876–83) 5 vols., M
117   *Lauter's Monthly Journal of Music and General Miscellany* (Newark, NJ, 1876–8) 3 vols., M
118   *Music Teachers National Association: Proceedings of the Annual Meeting* ([Delaware, OH] 1876–8, 1880–90, 1892–1905) 27 vols., Y. Continued as *Studies in Musical Education, History, and Aesthetics.*
119   *Musician and Artist* (Boston, 1876) 5 nos., M
120   *New England Monthly Journal of Music and General Miscellany* (Boston, 1876–) 1 no., M
121   *Utah Musical Times* (Salt Lake City, 1876–8) 2 vols., M
122   *J. W. Pepper's Musical Times and Band Journal* (Philadelphia and Chicago, 1877–1912) later, *Musical Times,* M
123   *Musical Advocate* (Altoona, PA, 1877–82) 5 vols., M
124   *Musical Review* (Chicago, 1877) 1 no., M. Probably continued from *Musical Monthly.*
125   *Score* (Boston, 1877–82) 10 vols., M
126   *Seltzer and Ammel's Monthly Journal of Music and General Miscellany* (Columbus, OH, 1877–) 1 no., M
127   *Baton* (Richmond Mozart Assn, Richmond, VA, 1878–88) 11 vols., W; from 1886, S
128   *Brainard's Sunday-school Singer* (Cleveland, 1878–) 1 no., M
129   *Ditson and Co.'s Musical Record* (Ditson, Boston, 1878–1903), later, *Musical Record* (from 1879, no. 17), then *Record and Review* (from 1900, no.468), 504 nos., M; Sept 1878, 2 nos. in 1 vol.; from Oct 1878, F; from Oct 1878, W; from Oct 1883, M. Incorp. *Dexter Smith's Musical, Literary, Dramatic, and Art Paper*; incorp. into *Musician.*
130   *Indicator* (Chicago, 1878–1930) later, *Music Trade* (from 2 Oct 1915) 52 vols., W. Incorp. into *Music Industry.*
131   *Kunkel's Musical Review* (St. Louis, 1878–1909) 32 vols., M
132   *Musician's Journal* (Somerset, PA, 1878–) 1 no., M
133   *Thomas Brothers' Musical Journal* (Catskill, NY, 1878–85) 6 vols.
134   *Art Critic: devoted to Music, Art, and Literature* (Jersey City, NJ, and New York, 1879–80) 3 vols., M

135 *Figaro: Wochenschrift für Theater, Kunst, und Literatur* (New York, 1879–81) later, *New York Figaro: belletristische Wochenschrift für Theater, Musik, Kunst, Literatur, und Unterhaltung* (from 1879, no. 12) 3 vols., W.

136 *Foster's Musical Journal* (Geneva, OH, 1879–84) 5 vols., M

137 *J.W. Smith, Jr., & Bro's Musical Journal,* sometimes *Smith's Monthly Journal of Music and General Miscellany* (Brooklyn, NY, 1879–) M

138 *Music Trade Journal* (New York, 1879–) later, *Musical Critic and Trade Review* (from 20 Aug 1885), then, *Music Trade Review* (from March 1956) and then, *Piano and Organ Review*. Incorp. *Musical Merchandise* (Jan 1958) to form *Musical Merchandise Review* (S, from 20 Aug 1892; W, from July 1929; M). Incorp. *Keynote* (1898); incorp. as a section into *Talking Machine World* (March–May 1933), into *Radio-journal* (April 1942–Jan 1943), and then into *Musical Merchandise* (Feb 1943–Jan 1945).

139 *Musical Bulletin* (Hershey School of Musical Art, Chicago, 1879–83) 4 vols., M

140 *Musical Bulletin* (Washington, DC, 1879–80) 2 vols., M

141 *Musical Review* (New York, 1879–81) 3 vols., W. Continued as *Studio and Musical Review*.

142 *Musician* (Philadelphia, 1879–80) 2 vols., M

143 *Princeton Musical Journal* (Princeton, NJ, 1879–) 10 nos., M

144 *Song Friend* (Chicago, 1879–94) M

145 *Voice: an International Review of the Speaking and Singing Voice* (New York, 1879–1902) later, *Werner's Voice Magazine* (from 1889), then later, *Werner's Magazine* (from 1893) 30 vols., M. Incorp. into *Philharmonic*.

146 *Young Folks' Musical Monthly* (Strongsville, OH, 1879–80) 2 vols., M

147 *Zitherplayer* (Washington, DC, 1879–81) O

148 *Molineux' Organists' and Conductors' Monthly* (Brooklyn, NY, 1880–) 1 no., M

149 *Monthly Musical Review* (Indianapolis, IN, and Warren, OH, 1880–82) 11 nos., M

150 *Musical and Sewing Machine Gazette* (Philadelphia, 1880–84; New York, 1884–1961; Evanston, IL, 1961–2) later, *Musical and Sewing Machine Courier* (from 1880, no.4), then later, *Musical Courier* (from 1880, no.9), and then *Musical and Dramatic Courier* (from no. 41), then, *Musical Courier* (from 1884, no.24), then, *Courier and Review of Recorded Music* (from Feb 1961). Incorp. *Music Magazine* to form *Music Magazine and Musical Courier* (Oct 1961) 164 vols., W; from 15 June 1937, S; from June 1941, S; Oct–May, M; June–Sept, from Oct 1954, S; Nov–Feb and M March–Oct from March 1958, M; directory issue, 1957–61, Y. Incorp. *Musical Observer* (Dec 1931), and later, *Review of Permanent Recorded Music* (June 1958).

151 *Musical Banner* (Mondamin, IA, 1880–) 1 no., M

152 *Musical Harp* (Berea, OH, 1880–97)

153 *Musical Herald* (Boston and Chicago, 1880–93), later, *Boston Musical Herald* (from 1889), and then *Musical Herald of the United States* (from Nov 1892) 14 vols., M

154 *Musical People* (Cincinnati, 1880–4) 8 vols., M except 1882 to April 1883, W

155 *Musical News* (New York, 1880–1) 26 nos. in 1 vol.

156 *Orchestra* (Boston, 1880) 5 nos., M

157 *Chicago Musical Times* (Chicago, 1881–1926) 51 vols., M, from Nov 1887, S; from April 1891, W. Incorp. into *Presto*.

158 *Hovey's Musical Review* (Three Rivers, MI, 1881–) 1 no., M

159 *Musical Messenger* (Battle Creek, MI, 1881–2) 2 vols., M

160 *New York Figaro: belletristische Wochenschrift für Theater, Musik, Kunst, Literatur, und Unterhaltung,* new ser. (New York, 1881–1900) 20 vols., W; suppl.: New York Phonograph. In Ger. Continued from *Figaro*.

161 *Studio and Musical Review* (New York, 1881) 13 nos., W. In 2 pts: Art Department and Musical Department. Continued from *Musical Review*.

162 *Tonic Sol-fa Advocate* (Tonic Sol-fa Movement in the US and Canada, New York, 1881–6) 5 vols., M, from Jan 1886 Q. Continued as *Musical Reform*.

163 *América musical* (New York, 1882–4) 36 nos., M [in Sp.]

164 *American Musical Journal* (Chicago, 1882–) 4 nos. in 1 vol., M

165 *Apollo: a Journal of Music, Literature, and Art* (Boston, 1882–3) 5 nos., M

166 *Courier: a Monthly Review devoted to Music and Literature* (Cincinnati, 1882–6) 5 vols., M. Continued as *Courier*.

167 *Echo* (Amer. St. Cecilia Soc, Pustet, New York and Cincinnati, 1882–5) 3 vols., M

168 *Freund's Daily Music and Drama* (New York, 1882–3) 78 nos., D

169 *Goldbeck's Musical Instructor* (St. Louis, 1882–5) later, *Goldbeck's Musical Art, or Practical Exposition of the Art of the Music* (April 1883), then *Goldbeck's Art Critic or Musical and General Observer* (from Oct 1884) 3 vols., M; F

170 *Music: a Review* (New York, 1882–3) later, *Music & Drama* (from 29 April 1882), and then *Weekly Music and Drama* (from 13 Jan 1883), and then *Music and Drama* (from 2 June) 7 vols., W. Suppl.: *Music Trade*. Continued as *Freund's Weekly*.

171 *Music and Drama* (San Francisco, 1882–1901) later, *San Francisco Music and Drama*

172 *Songster and Fireside Friend* (Springfield, OH, 1882–) 6 nos., M

173 *S.S. Stewart's Banjo and Guitar Journal* (Philadelphia, 1882–1902) later, *Stewart's Banjo, Guitar, and Mandolin Journal*. 19 vols., B; from Dec 1900, M; bibl.

174 *Boston Musical Year-book* (Boston, later Chicago, 1883–93), later, *Year-book and Musical Year of the United States* (from 1885–6), then *Musical Yearbook of the United States* (from 1886–7) 10 vols., Y

175 *Concert Quarterly* (Buffalo, NY, 1883–4) 2 vols., Q

176 *Echo: a Music Journal* (Lafayette, IN, in 1894 also Chicago, 1883–1901) 17 vols., M

177 *Etude* (Lynchburg, VA, 1883–4; Philadelphia, 1884–1957) later, *Etude and Musical World* (1896 to Dec 1897), then *Etude Music Magazine* (from Feb 1922), and then *Etude: the Music Magazine* (from Dec 1948) 75 vols., M, from May 1956, B; later M, B. Incorp. *Western Musical World* (Nov 1895).

178 *Freund's Weekly* (New York, 1883–92) later, *Music and Drama* (from 1884–5, no.8) 17 vols., W; suppl.: *Music Trade Review* (from 15 Aug 1885), *Music Trade* (1885–92) W. Continued from *Music, a review*.

179 *Keynote: a Weekly Review devoted to Music and the Drama* (New York, 1883–97) 19 vols., W; from Oct 1886, M. Incorp. into *Music Trade Journal*.

180 *Keynote: Topics of Musical and Literary Interest* (Harrisburg, PA, 1883–) 1 no., M

181 *Musical Items* (New York, 1883–7) 4 vols., M

182 *Musical Observer* (Boston, 1883–4) 2 vols., mainly W

183 *New England Conservatory of Music: Alumni Annual* (Boston, 1883–93) 11 vols., Y. Continued as *New England Conservatory Quarterly*.

184 *Southern Musical Journal and Educational Eclectic* (Macon, GA, 1883–) 10 nos., M. Continued from *Southern Musical Journal and Georgia Music Eclectic*.

185 *American Music Journal* (Natl League of Musicians, New York, 1884–1915), later, *American Musician and American Music Journal* (from 1886, no. 16), then, *American Musician* (from 1888). Incorp. *Art Journal* (1906) to form *American Musician and Art Journal* (from 1914, no.8), *American Musician* (1915, no.4), *Music Publisher and Dealer* (1884–8), and *Musical Mutual Protective Union* (1886–7) 31 vols., M, from 1885, S, later W, S, M.

186 *Galop: devoted to Dancing, Music, Etiquette, and Dress* (Boston, 1884–1900) 17 vols., M

187 *Music and Drama* (Chicago, 1884–) W

188 *Musical and Home Journal* (Brooklyn, NY, 1884–91) M

189 *Musical Visitor* (Dalton, GA, later Dallas, 1884–1915), later, *Music Teacher* (from 1885) M

190 *Parmelee's Musical Monthly* (New London, CT, 1884–5) M.

191 *Presto* (Chicago, 1884–1941) Incorp. *Chicago Musical Times* (April 1926) to form *Presto-Times*, later, *Presto Music Times* (from 1938) M; from Nov 1887, S; from 9 April 1891, W; from 1 March 1929, S; later M, B; from Feb 1939, mainly M; yb, 1887–9

192 *Propaganda musical* (New York, 1884–5), later, *Musical Propaganda* (from Nov 1884) 2 vols., M

193 *Schleicher and Sons' Musical Monthly* (Mount Vernon, NY, and Stamford, CT, 1884–96) 113 nos., M

194 *Shoninger Musical Monthly* (Chicago; South Norwalk, CT, 1884–94) 115 nos., M

195 *American Tonic Sol-fa Normal* (Rocky Hill, OH, 1885–) 3 nos., M

196 *Chicago Music and Drama* (Chicago, 1885–) 1 no., W

197 *Metronome* (New York, 1885–1961) later, *Music U.S.A.* (Jan 1959 to April 1960) 78 vols., mainly M; music suppl., 1914, M. In 2 edns: *Metronome Orchestra Monthly* and *Metronome Band Monthly* (Oct 1914 to Dec 1924); either Orchestra Edition or Band Edition (Jan 1925 to Jan 1932). Incorp. *Dominant* (Jan 1925)

198 *School Music Journal* (Boston, 1885–7) 3 vols., M in school year

199 *Tway's Musical Guest* (New York, 1885–92) 10 vols., M, later Q

200 *Brooklyn Musical Monthly* (Brooklyn, NY, 1886–98) M.

201 *Gleaner* (Pittsburgh, 1886–1900) M

202 *Musical Advocate* (Cleveland, 1886–90), 5 vols., M

203 *Musical Reform* (New York, 1886–8) 2 vols., M. Continued from *Tonic Sol-Fa Advocate.*

204 *North's Philadelphia Musical Journal* (Pennsylvania State MTA, Philadelphia, 1886–90) later, *Philadelphia Musical Journal* (from April 1889) 5 vols., M, also W edn

205 *Opera Glass* (New York, 1886–) 8 nos. in 1 vol., W

206 *People's Educational Quarterly* (Dayton, VA, 1886–) 1 vol., Q

207 *Reading Musical Monthly* (Reading, PA, 1886–) 1 no., M

208 *Worch's Musical Monthly* (Washington, DC, 1886–97) 131 nos., M

209 *Ziarno: wydawnictwo poświecone miłośnikom muzyki i śpiewu narodowego oraz życiu społeczno-towarzyskiemu Polaków w Ameryce/The seed: pubn dedicated to lovers of music, folksong, and the community life of Poles in America* (Chicago, 1886–1903), later, *Soc. of Pol. Singers* (from 1890) M, in Pol. Incorp. into *Harmonia.*

210 *Clef: published in the Interests of Organists, Choir Leaders, Vocal Societies, and the Music Public Generally* (New York, 1887–9) 3 vols., M

211 *Courier* (Cincinnati, 1887–93), later also *Cincinnati College of Music Courier,* new ser. 11 vols., M. Continued from *Courier.*

212 *Gatcomb's Banjo and Guitar Gazette* (Boston, 1887–99), later, *Gatcomb's Musical Gazette* (from 1892) 12 vols., M, later B

213 *Illinois Music Teachers Association: Proceedings* (Lincoln, IL, 1887–1920) 32 vols.

214 *Preacher and Chorister* (Tipton, MO, 1887–9) 3 vols., M

215 *Concert-goer* (Denver, 1888–97) 218 nos.

216 *Lights of Music and the Stage* (New York, 1888) 1 no., M

217 *Muse: Music, Drama, Literature, Social Science* (Minneapolis, 1888–90) 2 vols., M

218 *Musical Enterprise* (Camden, NJ, and Atlantic City, NJ, 1888–1931) 43 vols., M

219 *Musical Messenger* (Washington, DC, 1888–9) 2 vols., M

220 *Tam-tam: Almanach* (Chicago, 1888–97) 10 vols., Y

221 *Voice Quarterly* (New York, 1888–97) later, *Vocalist* (from Jan 1892) 13 vols., Q; from Jan 1892, M

222 *Musical Advance* (Minneapolis, 1889) 6 nos., M

223 *Universal Song* (Amer. Tonic Sol-fa Assn and Coll. of Music, New York, 1889–92) 2 vols., mainly Q

224 *Violin* (Boston, 1889–90) 2 vols., M

225 *J. E. Henning's Elite Banjoist and Guitar and Mandolin News* (Chicago, 1890–91) 2 nos., Q

226 *Music Trades* (New York, 1890–1971; Englewood, NJ, 1972–), later, *Music Trades* (Feb–July 1929), W, from Feb 1929 M. Incorp. *Music Trade News* (1933).

227 *Musical Gazette* (Brooklyn, NY, 1890–92) later, *Musical Magazine* (from May 1891) 2 vols., M, later Q

228 *New York Musical Era* (New York, 1890–91) 2 vols.

229 *Organ* (New York, 1890–1914) 150 nos. in 25 vols., B

230 *Organist's Journal* (Arlington, NJ, and New York, 1890–1903) 14 vols., M

231 *Philadelphia Music and Drama* (Philadelphia, 1890–92) 3 vols., W

232 *American Musical Times* (Youngstown, OH, 1891–5) 5 vols., M

233 *At Home and Abroad: a Monthly Review devoted to Music and the Kindred Arts* (New York, 1891–5) 8 vols., M

234 *Denver Music and Drama* (Denver, 1891–) 36 nos., W

235 *Deutsch-amerikanische Chor-Zeitung* (Chicago, 1891–4) 3 vols., M [in Ger.]

236 *Home Music Journal* (Logansport, IN, 1891–1900), later, *Choir Music Journal* (from Aug 1898) 9 vols., M

237 *Music: a Monthly Magazine* (Chicago, 1891–1902 except May–Aug 1902) 22 vols., M. Incorp. into *Muse.*

238 *Music Review* (Chicago, 1891–4) 4 vols., M. Continued as *Music Review,* new series (1900)

239 *Musical Advocate* (Oxford, GA, 1891–2) 9 nos. in 1 vol.

240 *Musical Age: a Monthly Magazine devoted to Music and Kindred Arts* (Jersey City, NJ, 1891–) 1 no., M

241 *Musical Messenger: a Monthly Magazine* (New York and Cincinnati, 1891–1917) 13 vols., M

242 *Salmisten: kirkelig sång og musiktidende för kirker, skoler, hjem, og foreninger* (Chicago, 1891–) 5 nos., M [in Nor.]

243 *Utah Musical Journal* (Salt Lake City, 1891–) 1 no., M

244 *American Musical Journal: a Literary Monthly devoted to the Mutual Advancement of the Interests of the Musical Producer and Consumer* (Chicago, 1892–) 4 nos., M

245 *Cabinet: a Journal of Music, Education, Art* (Michigan MTA, Detroit, 1892–3) 10 nos.

246 *Gittit: manadtlig sangtidning för hemmet, söndagsskolan, och församlingen* (Minneapolis, 1892–1903) 17 vols., M [in Swed.]

247 *M.T.N.A. Messenger* (Music Teachers Natl Assn, Wellesley Hills, MA, 1892–1905), later, *Messenger* (from March 1898) 6 vols., Q, later B; from April 1903, W

248 *Organ* (Boston, 1892–4) 2 vols.

249 *School Record* (Michigan MTA, Detroit, 1892–9) 7 vols., M

250 *Violin World* (New York, 1892–1928) 35 vols.

251 *Amusement Globe: devoted to the Dramatic, Theatrical, Musical, Vaudeville, and Circus Professions* (New York, 1893–) 23 nos. in 1 vol., W

252 *Choir Herald* (Chicago, 1893–7) 5 vols., M. Continued as *Choir Herald* [new series].

253 *Dominant* (Philadelphia and New York, 1893–1925, except Dec 1914) 32 vols., M. Incorp. into *Metronome.*

254 *Freund's Weekly* (New York, 1893–1914) later, *Musical Weekly* (from 2 Dec 1893), then *Musical Age* (from 15 Jan 1896) 85 vols., W

255 *Musical Notes: a Monthly Journal for the Studio and Home* (New York, 1893–) 2 nos., M

256 *Musical Recorder* (Brooklyn, NY, 1893–) 1 no., M

257 *National Home and Music Journal* (Chicago, 1893–5) 3 vols., M

258 *Opera* (New York, 1893–5) 68 nos. in 2 vols., B

259 *Wing's Musical Journal* (Lynn, MA, 1893–) 2 nos., M

260 *Ashmall's Monthly Vocalist* (Arlington, NJ, 1894) 2 nos., M

261 *Billboard Advertising* (Cincinnati, later New York, 1894–1971; Los Angeles, 1971–), later, *Billboard* (from 1 Nov 1896), then *Billboard Music Week* (from 9 Jan 1961), then *Billboard: the International Music-record* (from 5 Jan 1963), then *Newsweekly Music-record-tape* (from 7 June 1969) W, c.i. 1972–3; suppls.: *Billboard: Index of the New York Legitimate Stage* (1931–9), Y; *Band Yearbook* (1939–42), Y; *Talent and Tunes on Music Machines* (1939–41), Y, which later became a separate pubn: *Who's Who in the World of Music* (1961–), Y

262 *Cadenza* (Amer. Guild of Banjoists, Mandolinists, and Guitarists, Kansas City, 1894–1900; New York, 1900–08; Boston, 1908–24) 31 vols., B, from Sept 1900, M. Incorp. *Concerto* (1901); incorp. into *Jacob's Orchestra Monthly.*

263 *Choir Leader* (Dayton, OH, 1894–) M

264 *Harmony, People's Choral Union and Singing Classes* (New York, 1894–1900, 1903) 5 vols., M. Continued as *Harmony.*

265 *Musical News* (New York, 1894–5) 4 nos. in 1 vol., M

266 *New England Conservatory Quarterly* (Boston, 1894–1904) 10 vols., Q; from 1898–9, 5 nos. Y in school term. Continued from *New England Conservatory Alumni Annual*; continued as *New England Conservatory Review.*

267 *Opera* (Chicago, 1894–5) 2 vols., W; 1895, F

268 *Opera Glass: a Musical and Dramatic Magazine* (Boston, 1894–8) 5 vols., M

269 *Pacific Coast Musical Journal* (San Francisco, 1894–6) later, *California Musical Journal* (from May 1895) 3 vols., M

270 *Two-step* (Buffalo, NY, and Chicago, 1894–1935) later, *Dancing Master* (after 1900) 44 vols., M except July–Aug

271 *American Federation of Musicians: Official Proceedings* (St. Louis, 1895–)

272 *Baton: a Monthly Journal devoted to Western Music Matters* (Kansas City, 1895–7) 4 vols., M, later B

273 *Ev'ry Month: an Illustrated Magazine of Literature and Popular Music* (New York, 1895–1903). Incorp. *J.W. Pepper Piano Music Magazine* (Oct 1902) to form *Ev'ry Month and Piano Music Magazine.* 15 vols., M

274 *Levassor's Musical Review* (Cincinnati, 1895–) M

275 *Looker-on: Musical, Dramatic, Literary* (New York, 1895–7) 4 vols., M

276 *Musical Clipper* (Philadelphia, 1895) 6 nos. in 1 vol., M

277 *Musical Leader and Concert-goer* (Chicago, 1895–1967) later, *Musical Leader: with which is incorporated the Concert-goer of New York* (1907, no. 14) then, *Musical Leader: a Weekly Record of Musical Events, Dramatic, and Society Topics* (1910, no. 14), and then *Musical Leader* (1933, no.24) 99 vols., W, from 1934, F, later M, S; from Oct 1942, M. Incorp. *Concert-goer* (1903).

278 *Phonograph Record* (Chicago, 1895–6) 2 vols., M

279 *Pianist* (Amer. Guild of Organists, New York, 1895–8) later, *Pianist and Organist* (from July 1896), 5 vols., M

280 *Song Writer* (New York, 1895–6) 16 nos., M

281 *Allegretto* (Natl League of Musicians of the US, Minneapolis, 1896–8) 2 vols., M or B

282 *American Choir* (New York, 1896–9) 78 nos.

283 *Jennings Musical Tidings* (Cincinnati, 1896–) M

284 *Missouri Music Teachers Association: Official Report of the Annual Convention* (Kansas City, 1896–1918) Y

285 *Musical Trio* (Waco, TX, 1896–1917) 21 vols., M

286 *Musical Worker: a Journal of Music, Musical Literature, and Social Ethics* (Atlanta, 1896–) 2 nos., M

287 *Musician* (Philadelphia, 1896–1903; Boston, 1903–18; New York, 1919–48) 53 vols., M. Incorp. *Ditson and Co.'s Musical Record* (Dec 1903), incorp. *Musical World* (1904)

288 *Aeolian Quarterly* (New York, 1897–9) 3 vols., Q

289 *American Home Journal* (Amer. Musical Assn, Chicago, 1897–1903) later, *Conkey's* (from April 1898) 11 vols., M

290 *American Musician* (AFM, Cincinnati, 1897–1903) 7 vols., M

291 *Chicago Trio: a Banjo, Guitar, and Mandolin Journal devoted to the Interests of Teachers, Players, and Makers* (Chicago, 1897–) 4 nos., B

292 *Choir Herald,* new ser. (Dayton, OH, 1897–) 19 vols., M. Continued from *Choir Herald.*

293 *Concert-goer* (NY State MTA, New York, 1897–1903) 220 nos., M, from May 1899, W; suppl.: Report of the Annual Meeting (1899–1902), Y. Continued from *Song Journal*; incorp. into *Musical Leader.*

294 *Herald of Music* (St. Louis, 1897–) 3 nos., M

295 *Kirchenchor* (Dayton, OH, 1897–1930) 33 vols., M [in Eng., Ger.]

296 *Musical Critic* (Chicago, 1897–1900) 3 vols., M

297 *Musical Herald* (W. W. Kimball Company, Chicago, 1897–1916) mainly M

298 *Musical News* (St. Louis, 1897–) 11 nos. in 1 vol., M

299 *Musical Temple: a Monthly devoted to the Interests of Mandolin, Guitar, and Banjo Players* (Philadelphia, 1897) 1 no.

300 *School Music: a Journal devoted to Music Education* (New York, 1897) 2 nos., M

301 *American Musician* (St. Louis, 1898–1922; Newark, NJ, 1922–75; New York, 1975–) later, *International Musician* (from 1901), then subtitle added, *Official Journal of the American Federation of Musicians of the United States & Canada* (from 1919–20) M

302 *Music and Literature* (Frederick, MD, 1898–9) 2 vols., M

303 *Music Review* (Ditson, Boston, 1898–1900) 3 vols., M

304 *Music, Song, and Story* (New York, 1898, except April 1898 to March 1899) 4 nos. in 1 vol., M

305 *Musical America* (New York, 1898–9, 1905–64) 84 vols., W; from 1929, varies between S and M; from Feb 1960, M; directory issue, 1930–, Y. Incorp. into *High Fidelity.*

306 *Musical Gem* (San Francisco, 1898–) 1 no., M

307 *Musical Mirror* (Indiana MTA, Lafayette, IN, 1898–1901) 4 vols., M except Aug

308 *Symphony: a Magazine devoted Entirely to Music in Every Form* (Cleveland, 1898–) 1 no., M

309 *American Phonographic and Literary Journal* (Allentown, PA, 1899–1900) 2 vols.

310 *Brainard's Musical* (New York and Chicago, 1899–1909) Q

311 *Choir: a Monthly Journal of Church Music* (Cincinnati, 1899–1922) 23 vols., M

312 *Choral Society Bulletin* (Washington, DC, 1899–)

313 *Edgewood Music and Home Journal* (Cincinnati, 1899–1903) later, *Columbia Music and Home Journal* (from 1900) 4 vols., M

314 *Gleanings from the World of Music* (Cleveland, 1899–) 1 vol., B

315 *Harmonia* (Buffalo, NY, from 1903 Bay City, MI, 1899–1905) 6 vols., M, in Pol.; Incorp. *Ziarno*; continued as *Harmonia.*

316 *Music and Childhood* (chicago, 1899–1900) 11 nos. in 1 vol., M

317 *Music Life* (New York, 1899–1905) 6 vols., M except July–Aug

318 *Music Lover* (Worcester, MA, 1899–) 6 nos. in 1 vol., M

319 *Piano, Organ, and Musical Instrument Workers' Official Journal* (Piano, Organ, and Musical Instrument Workers of America, Chicago, 1899–1911) 13 vols., M

320 *Choir Journal* (Boston, 1899–1908) 240 nos., S

321 *American Music Journal* (Natl Qualified Music Teachers League, Cleveland, 1900–07) 7 vols.

322 *Chicago Music Journal* (Chicago, 1900–01) 2 vols., M

323 *F.O.G. Mandolin, Banjo, and Guitar Journal* (Qualified Teachers League, Cleveland, 1900–04) 4 vols.

324 *J.W. Pepper Piano Music Magazine* (Philadelphia, 1900–02) 24 nos. in 4 vols. Incorp. into *Ev'ry Month.*

325 *Key Note: a Magazine of Music, Society, and the Stage* (Elmira, NY, 1900–04) 4 vols.

326 *Lyra: populäre Monatsschrift für Musik, Kunst, Wissenschaft, und Leben, Verband Deutscher Chordirigenten Amerikas* (New York, 1900) 1 vol., M [in Ger., sometimes in Eng.]

327 *Music Review, devoted to the theory, analysis, review and practice of music.* New ser. (Chicago, 1900–02) 1 vol., M except July–Aug. Continued from *Music Review.*

328 *School Music* (Quincy, IL, 1900; Keokuk, IA, 1901–33; Mount Morris, IL, 1934; Chicago, 1935–6) 3 vols. Incorp. into *School Music Monthly.* Later returned to *School Music.* 36 vols., M; c.i. 1927–31, 1932–4, 1935–6; Jan 1905

329 *Violinist* (Chicago, 1900–37, except Jan–Sept 1930 and 1932 to Sept 1935) 50 vols., M, from 1929, 3–5 nos. Y; from 1935, Y; 1937, 2 nos. Y. Incorp. into *Musical Standard* (Sept 1905–Sept 1908)

330 *Western Music Trades Journal* (Los Angeles, 1900–10). Continued as *Western Music.*

331 *Western Musician* (Dixon, IL, 1900–07) 7 vols., M

332 *Bohémienne* (San Francisco, 1901–33 except Oct 1928 to July 1930) later, *Musical Review* (from 1903) then Pacific Musical (from 1907), then *Pacific Coast Music Review* (from 1931–3, no.3) 57 vols.

333 *Church Music Review* (Amer. Guild of Organists, New York, 1901–35), later, *New Music Review and Church Music Review* (from Nov 1904) 404 nos., M

334 *Music and Stage: New York, London, Paris* (New York, 1901–2) 2 nos.

335 *Music of the Future and of the Present* (Chicago, 1901–7; Berlin and Chicago, 1907–1912) *Das Musizieren der Zukunft* (from 1907, no.4) 2 vols. [in Eng., from 1901–7; later in Ger.]

336 *Musical Century* (Springdale, PA, 1901–) 2 nos., M

337 *Musical Life* (New York, 1901–4) 3 vols., M

338 *Musical World* (Boston, 1901–4) 4 vols., M. Incorp. into *Musician.*

339 *National Federation of Music Clubs: Biennial Proceedings* (Chicago, 1901–34) 18 vols., biennially. Continued as *National Federation of Music Clubs: Book of Proceedings.*

340 *Philharmonic: a Magazine devoted to Music, Art, Drama* (Chicago, 1901–3) later, *Muse* (from April 1903) 3 vols., Q, in 1902; 6, in 1903, 5 nos. Y. Incorp. *Voice* (Jan 1903); incorp. *Music, a monthly magazine* (Feb 1903)

341 *School Music Success* (Paterson, NJ, 1901–2) 3 vols.

342 *Negro Music Journal* (Washington Conservatory of Music, Washington, DC, 1902–3) 2 vols., M

343 *Philharmonic Review: a Monthly Magazine devoted to Musical Subjects and the Official Program of the Great Philhar-*

monic Course (Los Angeles, 1902–), later, *Magazine of Celebrities* (from 1939) M

344 *Profession* (New York, 1902–4), later, *Musical Profession: a Magazine for Teachers and Students of Music* (from 1904) 3 vols.

345 *Calendar of the University School of Music* (U. of Michigan, Ann Arbor, MI, 1903–5) 2 vols., Y

346 *Exchange Journal of Music* (New York, 1903–5), later, *Journal of Music* (from May 1904) 2 vols.

347 *Focus: a Weekly devoted to the Musical and Theatrical World* (New York, 1903–4) 3 vols., W

348 *Harmony: a Bulletin of the P.S.M.* [People's Singing Movement] (New York, 1903–5), later, *Harmony: devoted to the Interests of the People's Choral Union and People's Singing Classes* (from March 1904), new ser. 2 vols., M, later O. Continued from *Harmony, People's Choral Union and Singing Classes.*

349 *Masters in Music: a Monthly Magazine* (Boston, 1903–5) 36 pts in 6 vols., M

350 *Mirth and Music* (New York, 1903–)

351 *University School of Music Record* (U. of Michigan, Ann Arbor, MI, 1903–) M

352 *Conservatory: a Journal devoted to Music and the Kindred Arts* (New York, 1904–9) 6 vols.

353 *Knocker: a Humorous Musical Monthly* (New York, 1904–) 1 no., M

354 *Musical Messenger* (Chicago and Cincinnati, 1904–24) 20 vols., M. Incorp. into *Jacobs' Orchestra Monthly* and also *Jacobs' Band Monthly.*

355 *Music and Story* (Florence, CO, 1904–) 1 no., M

356 *Music Land Messenger* (Chicago, 1904–) 2 nos., B

357 *Music Student* (Springfield, MO, 1904–) 7 nos. in 1 vol., O

358 *Southern Music Teachers Association: Quarterly Bulletin* (Washington, DC, 1904–) Q

359 *Church Music* (Philadelphia, 1905–9) 4 vols., Q; from 1906, B.

360 *Harmonia* (Choral Soc. of Milwaukee, Milwaukee, 1905–10) [in Pol.]. Continued from *Harmonia.*

361 *Institute: a Periodical devoted to Singers and the Voice* (Chicago, 1905–7) 2 vols.

362 *Monthly Music Folio* (Memphis, 1905–) M

363 *Musical Standard: incorporating The Violinist* (Chicago, 1905–8) 9 vols., M. Incorp. *Violinist* (Sept 1905 to Sept 1908). Continued as *Music News.*

364 *Neume* (New England Conservatory of Music, Boston, 1905–13) 9 vols.

365 *Talking Machine World* (New York, 1905–34), later, *Radio Music Merchant* (from Aug 1930), then *Radio-merchant* (from May 1932) 30 vols. Incorp. *Radio-merchant* as a section (March–May 1933).

366 *Triangle of Mu Phi Epsilon* (1905–) Q

367 *Aus der musikalischen Welt* (New York, 1906–9) 3 vols., Q [in Ger., sometimes Eng.]

368 *Green-room-book, or Who's Who on the Stage* (New York and London, 1906–7; London, 1907–9) 4 vols., Y

369 *Music Industry* (New York, 1906–) later, *Piano Magazine and Music* (from 1910, no.4). Incorp. *Piano Trade* (Oct 1915) to form *Piano Trade Magazine*, later, *Piano Trade and Radio Magazine* (from 1929, no.5), then *Piano Trade Magazine* (from 1932, no.8), and then *PTM: Piano Trade Magazine* (from 1953, no.4), *PTM Magazine* (from 1965), and then *World of Music* (from 1971) M; from 1967, F; from May 1968; M. Incorp. *Music Trade Indicator* (in March 1930).

370 *Studies in Musical Education, History, and Aesthetics: Papers and Proceedings of the Music Teachers National Association* (Hartford, CT, 1906–28; Oberlin, OH, 1929–38; Pittsburgh, 1939–50). Titled *Papers and Proceedings of the Music Teachers National Association* (1927) then *Volume of Proceedings of the Music Teachers National Association* (from 1928) 44 vols., Y; c.i. 1906–15, 1918–29, 1930–36, 1937–46. Continued from *Music Teachers National Association: Proceedings of the Annual Meeting.*

371 *Symphony* (Southern MTA and Georgia MTA, Atlanta, 1906–) 1 no., M

372 *Western Musical Herald* (Des Moines and Chicago, 1906–16) 9 vols.

373 *Edward MacDowell Memorial Association Report* (New York, 1907–) later, *Annual Report.* Y

374 *Fortnightly: a Journal of Music, Letters, Painting, and General Civic Interest* (Philadelphia, 1907–8) 7 nos., F

375 *Music Supervisors' National Conference: Journal of Proceedings* (Madison, WI, 1907–26; Chapel Hill, NC, 1927–8; Ithaca, NY, 1929–30; Chicago, 1931–40) later, *Yearbook of the Music Supervisors National Conference* (from 1931), then *Yearbook of the Music Supervisors Educators National Conference* (from 1934) 31 vols. to 1938, 1939–40 pubd as vol.xxx, Y; c.i. 1925–38.

376 *Music World* (Philadelphia, 1907–8) 3 vols.

377 *Musical Medium* (New York, 1907–8) 17 nos. in 2 vols., M

378 *Musical Observer* (New York, 1907–31) 30 vols., M. Incorp. into *Musical and Sewing Machine Gazette.*

379 *Musician's Chronicle* (New York, 1907–) 4 nos. in 1 vol., O

380 *Musician's Monthly Magazine* (Cleveland, 1907–9) 3 vols., M

381 *Steinway Bulletin* (New York, 1907) 8 nos. except no.6, M

382 *Allegro: a Magazine of Music and Literature* (Aurora, NY, and Washington, DC, 1908) 4 nos. in 1 vol., M

383 *American Bandsman* (New York, 1908–) 5 nos. in 1 vol.

384 *American Music Society: Bulletin* (New York, 1908) 2 nos.

385 *Barde: devoted to Art, Music, Literature* (New York, 1908–9) 2 vols. [in Ger.]

386 *Crescendo* (Amer. Guild of Banjoists, Mandolinists, and Guitarists, Boston, 1908–28; Hartford, CT, 1929–33) 25 vols., M

387 *Journal of School Music* (Chicago, 1908–9) 9 nos. in 1 vol., M

388 *Music News* (Chicago, 1908–52) 44 vols., W; from 1933, no.25, M; later W, B; from 1935, B; Oct–June and M, July–Sept, from 1945, M. Continued from *Musical Standard.*

389 *Musical Light* (Fort Worth, TX, 1908–15) 8 vols.

390 *Saugerties Musical Review* (Saugerties, NY, 1908–9) 1 vol., M

391 *Tone: the Only Musical Magazine* (New York, 1908–) 1 no., M

392 *C. G. Conn. Ltd. Musical Truth* (Elkhart, IN, 1909–41), later, *Musical Truth* (from 1928, no.45) 30 vols., O

393 *Diapason* (Chicago, 1909–), official journal of Organ Builders Assn of America (1918–27), Natl Assn of Organists (1919–34), Canadian Coll. of Organists (1934–), Amer. Guild of Organists (1934–), Hymn Soc. of America (1936–), M.

394 *Musical Messenger* (New York, 1909) 2 nos. in 1 vol., M

395 *Musical Register: America's Leading Musical Journal* (Chicago, 1909–10) 2 vols., M

396 *Musical Squibs* (New York, 1909–) 2 nos., W

397 *Opera News* (Philadelphia and New York, 1909–20) 11 vols., W aut.–spr. Continued as *Music Record and Opera News.*

398 *Pan Pipes of Sigma Alpha Iota* (Sigma Alpha Iota Intl Music Fraternity for Women, Menosha, WI, later Sarasota, FL, 1909–) 4 nos. Y

399 *Jacobs' Orchestra Monthly* (Boston, 1910–41). Incorp. Musical Messenger (March 1924), then incorp. *Cadenza* (April 1924) to form *Jacobs' Orchestra Monthly and The Cadenza*, then back to *Jacobs' Orchestra Monthly* (Nov 1927) 32 vols., M

400 *Music Era* (Boston, 1910–16) 7 vols., M

401 *Psycho-vowel Herald and Voice Building* (New York, 1910–) 1 no.

402 *Studio: a Monthly Magazine devoted to the Interests of Music Teachers, Music Students, and all Music Lovers* (Michigan MTA, Detroit, 1910–14) 5 vols., M

403 *Music* (Boston, 1911–12) 18 nos. in 1 vol.

404 *Music Teachers Association of California: Official Bulletin* (San Francisco, 1911–35) 25 vols.

405 *Musical Advocate: a Journal of Music, Poetry, and Chaste Literature* (Little Rock, AR, 1911–14) 4 vols.

406 *New England Conservatory Review* (Alumni Assn, Boston, 1911–18) later, *Magazine and Alumni Review* (from Sept 1913), then *Magazine–Review* (from Dec 1914), 8 vols., Y, from 1913 2 nos. Y, from Sept 1913 Q. Continued from *New England Conservatory Quarterly*; continued as *New England Conservatory News and Alumni Bulletin.*

407 *Pacific Coast Musician* (Los Angeles, 1911–48) 37 vols., M; from Sept 1923, W; from Feb 1935, S.

408 *Player Piano* (New York, 1911–19), later, *Player Piano Journal* (from March 1913), then *Piano Journal* (from 1917) 8 vols., M. Incorp. into *Mist.*

409   *Scherzo: a Quarterly Bulletin of New Music* (New York, Boston, and Chicago, 1911–) 1 vol., Q

410   *Thoth-Apollo Magazine: devoted to Speech, Art, and Music* (Columbus, OH, 1911–) 1 no., M

411   *True Tone Musical Journal* (Elkhart, IN, 1911–41), later, *Buescher: True Tone Musical Journal* (1940, no.4) 30 vols., Q

412   *Western Music* (Los Angeles, 1911–33), later, *Music and Radio Trades Journal* (from 1927), then *Radio and Refrigeration Journal* (from Nov 1931) 14 vols. Continued from *Western Music Trades Journal*.

413   *Art and Music* (Cleveland, 1912–17) 17 nos. in 1 vol.

414   *Harvard Musical Review* (Cambridge, MA, 1912–16) 4 vols., M except Aug–Sept.

415   *Institute of Music Pedagogy: Monthly News Letter* (Northampton, MA, 1912–15; Yonkers, NY, 1916–18; Flint, MI, 1919; Hartford, CT, 1920–28) 17 vols., M, from 1921 Q

416   *Manager and Musician* (Chicago, 1912–13) 6 nos. in 1 vol., O

417   *Musical Progress* (Washington, DC, 1912–14) 3 vols.

418   *Musical World* (Chicago, 1912–17; New York, 1917–24), later, *Monitor* (1912, nos. 7–8), then *World* (from 1912, no.9), and then *Monitor and World* (from 1913, no.7), back to *Monitor* (from 1915, no.5). Published by Natl Assn of Organists, 1912 to June 1913; Natl Assn of Teachers of Singing, 1913–14; Natl Fed. of Music Clubs, Sept 1913–24. 14 vols., O; from 1913, M.

419   *Wisconsin Music Teacher* (Wisconsin MTA, Madison, WI, 1912–19) 7 vols.

420   *Century Opera Weekly* (New York, 1913), later, *Opera* (from no.8) 13 nos. in 1 vol., W

421   *Foyer: Music and Drama* (Philadelphia, 1913–16) 3 vols.

422   *Music and Health* (Croton-on-Hudson, NY, 1913) 3 nos., Q

423   *Music Magazine and Musical Stage Review* (Boston, 1913) 4 nos. in 1 vol., W

424   *Musical Advance* (New York, 1913–48, except June–Sept 1913) 36 vols., mainly M

425   *Musicians' Journal* (MTA of California, San Francisco, 1913–15; new ser. 1929–30) 3 vols., new ser. 4 nos., W

426   *Tuner's Magazine* (Cincinnati, 1913–16) 4 vols., M

427   *United States Service Musician* (Elkhart, IN, 1913) 3 nos. in 1 vol., M

428   *Volunteer Choir* (Dayton, OH, 1913–39) 27 vols., M

429   *Christiansen's Ragtime Review* (Chicago, 1914–18) later, *Ragtime Review* (from 1916, no.6) 4 vols.

430   *Console* (Natl Assn of Organists, New York, 1914–19) 5 vols.

431   *International Music and Drama* (Bertrand De Berny's Opera and Oratorio Soc., New York, 1914–16) 4 vols., W

432   *Minnesota Music* (St. Paul, 1914–19) 6 vols.

433   *Music Bulletin* (New York, 1914–32) 17 vols., M; from 1916–17, Q

434   *Music Supervisors' Journal* (Music Supervisors' Natl Conference, later MENC, Madison, WI, 1914–) later, *Music Educators Journal* (from 1934–) Q; from 1919–20, 5 nos. Y; from 1934–5, 6 nos. Y; from 1966–7, M. Incorp. *Eastern School Music Herald* (1926)

435   *Opera Magazine* (New York, 1914–16) 3 vols., M

436   *Catholic Choirmaster* (Soc. of St. Gregory of America, Baltimore, 1915–17; Philadelphia, 1917–38; Arlington, VA, …Buffalo, 1938–64) 50 vols., 3 nos. Y, from 1916 Q. Incorp. into *Caecilia*.

437   *Gospel Choir* (Philadelphia, 1915–) M

438   *Illinois Music Teachers Association: Bulletin* (Lincoln, IL, 1915; new ser. 1916–18) 1 vol., new ser. 4 vols.

439   *Music and Musicians* (Brooklyn, NY, 1915–22, except July–Oct 1920, and early 1921) 8 vols., S, from (1916, no.5) M; from 1918, W; later S, M.

440   *Music and Musicians* (Seattle, 1915–37) 23 vols., M

441   *Music Lover* (Philadelphia, 1915–) 4 nos. in 1 vol., M

442   *Music Merchant* (New York, 1915–) 1 no.

443   *Music Student* (Los Angeles, later Chicago, 1915–17) 4 vols., M

444   *Music Survey* (Jacksonville, IL, 1915–17) 2 vols.

445   *Musical Art* (Inst. of Musical Art, Detroit, 1915–17) 2 vols.

446   *Musical Messenger* (Pittsburgh, 1915–16) 6 nos. in 1 vol.

447   *Musical Quarterly* (New York, 1915–) Q

448   *Musicale* (Texas MTA, Dallas, TX, and Arlington, VA, 1915–33), later, *Southwestern Musicale* (from 1930, no.10) 19 vols., M. Continued as *Southwestern Musician*.

449   *Sharps and Flats* (Chicago, 1915–)

450   *Southern Musician* (Maryland Musical Assn, Baltimore, 1915–)

451   *United Musician* (New York, 1915–) M

452   *Wheel of Delta Omicron* (Delta Omicron Intl Music Fraternity, Columbus, OH, 1915–) Q

453   *Art and Artists* (Detroit Orchestral Assn, Detroit, 1916–22) later, *All the Arts* (from 1920–21) then *Arts, Commerce, and Government* (from 1921–2) 4 vols., Q

454   *Jacobs' Band Monthly: a Music Magazine* (Boston, 1916–41) 26 vols., M. Incorp. *Musical Messenger* (1924).

455   *Mist* (New York, 1916–22), later, *MIST: Musical Instrument Sales Tips* (April 1920) 13 vols., M. Incorp. *Player Piano* (Feb 1919)

456   *Selmer's Modern Musician* (New York, 1916–)

457   *Standard Player Monthly* (New York, 1916–29) 15 vols., M

458   *Phonograph* (New York, 1916–), later, *Phonograph and Talking Machine Weekly* (from July 1919), then *Talking Machine and Radio Weekly* (from Sept 1928), then *Radio* (from Dec 1933), then *Radio and Television Weekly* (from May 1939), and then *Electronic Industry Weekly* (from Jan 1978) W

459   *Washington Musician* (Musicians' Protective Union, Washington, DC, 1916; new ser. 1929–32) 9 nos., new ser. 3 vols.

460   *Eastern School Music Herald* (Eastern Music Supervisors' Conference, Yonkers, NY, and Ithaca, NY, 1917–26) 9 vols., 9 nos. Y. Incorp. into *Music Supervisors' Journal*.

461   *Teachers' Music Sentinel* (Hudson, NC, 1917–19) 2 vols.

462   *Tuneful Yankee* (Boston, 1917–30) later, *Melody* (from 1918) 14 vols., M

463   *American Organist* (Amer. Guild of Organists, New York, 1918–70) 53 vols., M; bibl.

464   *Community Music Service Weekly* (Community Music League, New York, 1919–20) later, *Community Music Service* (from Sept 1919) then, *Music Service* (from Nov 1920) 2 vols., W

465   *Marley Musical Review* (Dallas, 1919–28) later, *Southern Musical Review* (from May 1920), then *Whittle Musical Review* (from Nov 1920) 7 vols., M

466   *Master Musician* (Philadelphia, 1919–22) later, *American Musician and Sportsman Magazine* (from Sept 1920) 2 vols.

467   *Music Lover: devoted to the Interests of Earnest Music Students* (Denver, 1919–) 3 nos., B

468   *Musical Field* (New York, 1919–23) 5 vols.

469   *New England Conservatory News and Alumni Bulletin* (Boston, 1919–37) 18 vols., M. Continued from *New England Conservatory Review*; continued as *New England Conservatory, Boston: Alumni Quarterly*.

470   *American Organ Monthly* (Boston, 1920–34) later, *American Organ Quarterly* (from 1922) 15 vols., M; except July–Aug, from April 1922, Q.

471   *Flutist* (Asheville, NC, 1920–9) 10 vols., M

472   *Musical Digest* (New York, 1920–48) 30 vols., W, from 1927, no.8, M; from 1941, B; later Q, B, M. Incorp. *Top Notes*.

473   *Educational Music Magazine* (Chicago, 1921–57) B. Incorp. into *Music Publishers Journal*.

474   *Eolian Review* (Natl Assn of Harpists, New York, 1921–32) later, *Eolus* (from 1925) 11 vols., 3 nos. Y, from 1925, H; from 1927, Y.

475   *Music and Poetry* (Chicago, 1921–) 10 nos.

476   *Music Record and Opera News* (New York, 1921–). Continued from *Opera News*.

477   *Musical Forecast* (Musicians' Club of Pittsburgh, Pittsburgh, 1921–48) 45 vols., M

478   *Overture* (Musicians' Mutual Protective Assn, later Local 47 of the AFM, Los Angeles, 1921–) M

479   *Baton* (Inst. of Musical Art, New York, 1922–32) 11 vols., M except sum.

480   *Baton: a Monthly Journal published in the Interests of Professional and Amateur Musicians* (Los Angeles, 1922–3) 2 vols., M

481   *Music Box* (New York, 1922–34) 13 vols.

482   *Music Education* (Washington, DC, 1922–5) 4 vols.

483   *Music Lover's Magazine* (Portland, OR, 1922–3) 2 vols.

484   *National Federation of Music Clubs: Official Bulletin* (Peoria, IL, 1922–) later, *Music Club Magazine* (from 1928–9), then *Music Clubs Magazine* (from 1931–2) then *Showcase: Music*

(1960–63) Incorp. *Church Music Bulletin and National Federation of Music Clubs* (in 1931) and *Showcase: American Music Clubs Magazine* (in 1962)

485   *Sheet Music Trade News* (New York, 1922–33) later, *Music Trade News* (from April 1924) 11 vols. Incorp. into *Music Trades.*

486   *Northwest Musician* (San Francisco, 1923–37) later, *Musical West and Northwest* (from 1925), then *Musical West: Music and the Dance* (from 1927) 14 vols., M

487   *Echo muzyczne* (Chicago, 1924–37) 14 vols., M [in Pol.]

488   *League of Composers' Review* (New York, 1924–46) later, *Modern Music* (from Nov 1925) 23 vols.; suppls., 1930, 1931

489   *Music* (New York, 1924) 1 no., M

490   *Music Hour* (Chicago, 1924) 3 nos., M

491   *Music Journal for Music Lovers* (Sharon, PA, 1924–6) later, *Youth's Musical Companion* (from Feb 1926) 3 vols.

492   *Musical Booster* (Kansas City, 1924–6) 2 vols.

493   *Music and Youth* (Boston, 1925–30) M

494   *Musical Merchandise* (New York, 1925–57) later, *Merchandise Magazine* (from Feb 1953) 65 vols., M. Incorp. into *Music Trade Journal.*

495   *Pierre Key's Music Year Book* (New York, 1925–38) later, *Pierre Key's International Music Year Book* (1928–30) 6 vols., O

496   *Sänger-Zeitung* (Fed. of Workers' Singing Socs. of the USA, New York, 1925–48) M

497   *Musical Washington* (Washington, DC, 1926) 3 nos.

498   *Musicians' Service Magazine* (Chicago, 1926–9) later, *Musicians' Magazine* (from 18 June 1926) then *Music Magazine* (from Aug 1927) 4 vols., W. Continued as *School Band and Orchestra Musician.*

499   *Northwest Musical Herald* (St. Paul, 1926–34) 9 vols., 5 nos. Y

500   *Pianist Pedagogue* (Chicago, 1926–7) later, *American Musician* (from 1926, no.5) 2 vols.

501   *Phonograph Monthly Review* (Boston, 1926–32) later, *Music Lovers' New England Conservatory Review* (from July 1927) 6 vols., M. Continued as *Music Lovers' Guide.*

502   *Woodwind News* (New York, 1926–7) later, *Woodwind Ensemble* (1927) 2 vols., Q

503   *Church Music Bulletin* (Natl Fed. of Music Clubs, Los Angeles, 1927–31) later, *Music in Religious Education* (from 1929). Incorp. into *National Federation of Music Clubs.*

504   *Keynote* (Associated Glee Clubs of America, New York, 1927–65)

505   *Matthay News* (Amer. Matthay Assn, Springfield, OH, later Gettysburg, PA, 1927–)

506   *Musical Philadelphia* (Philadelphia, 1927–8) 2 vols.

507   *Musical Record* (Natl Acad. of Music, New York, 1927–) 2 nos.,

508   *National Federation of Music Clubs: Junior Bulletin* (Merchantville, NJ, 1927–31) 5 vols., 9 nos. Y. Incorp. into *National Federation of Music Clubs: Official Bulletin.*

509   *Fortnightly Musical Review* (New York, 1928) F

510   *Harmony: a Liberal Education in Music* (Chicago, 1928–) 4 nos.

511   *Musical Re-education* (Soc. for Musical Re-education, New York, 1928) 1 no.

512   *Triad* (Ohio MEA, Fairfield, OH, later Elyria, OH, 1928–) 6 nos. Y

513   *Western Musical Times* (San Francisco, 1928–9) 9 nos., S

514   *Baton: Magazine for School Music Supervisors* (Elkhart, IN, 1929–) O

515   *Blues: Magazine of the New Rhythms* (Columbus, MS, 1929–30) 9 nos.

516   *School Band and Orchestra Musician* (Natl School Band and Orchestral Assn, later Amer. School Band Directors' Assn, Chicago, 1929–54; Joliet, IL, 1954–) later, *School Musician* (from Sept 1930) then *Musician/Director & Teacher* (from 1963), M except July–Aug. Continued from *Musicians' Service.*

517   *Top Notes* (East Stroudsburg, PA, 1929–30) Incorp. into *Musical Digest.*

518   *Bulletin of the Folk-song Society of the Northeast* (Cambridge, MA, 1930–37) 12 nos., O; c.i.

519   *Disques* (Philadelphia, 1930–33) 3 vols., M

520   *Music World* (Los Angeles, 1930–32) M

521   *Musical Instrument Merchandiser* (Elkhart, IN, 1930–32) 2 vols.

522   *Musical Review for the Blind* (New York, 1930–33) 42 nos. in 4 vols.

523   *Wisconsin School Musician* (Wisconsin School Music Assn, Madison, WI, 1930–) 4 nos. Y

524   *Collaborator* (New York, 1931) 2 nos., M

525   *Lilly-Foster Bulletin* (Indianapolis, IN, 1931–5, 1940) later, *Foster Hall Bulletin* (from 1931, no.3) 12 nos., O

526   *New York Musicological Society Bulletin* (New York, 1931–4)

527   *Brooklyn and Long Island Musical Review* (New York, 1932–48 except Feb–Sept 1932 and June 1942–Nov 1943) later, *Musical Review* (from Feb 1934) then *Music Teachers' Review* (from Sept 1936) and then *Music Teachers' Review Quarterly* (from 1942) 14 vols.

528   *Chord and Discord* (Bruckner Soc. of America, New York, 1932–63, 1969, 1979–) O

529   *Music Lovers' Guide* (New York, 1932–5) 3 vols., M. Continued as *American Music Lover.*

530   *Sacred Musician* (South Pasadena, CA, 1932–)

531   *Hawaiian Guitarist* (Cleveland, 1933–) later, *Guitarist* (from Feb 1935), then *Music Today* (from Nov/Dec 1942), and then *Music* (from 1945) M

532   *Musical Record* (Baltimore and Philadelphia, 1933–4) 1 vol., M

533   *National Association for American Composers and Conductors: Annual Bulletin* (New York, 1933–70) 37 vols., Y

534   *Tempo* (United Hot Clubs of America, Los Angeles, 1933–40) 8 vols.

535   *Down Beat* (Chicago, 1934–) M

536   *Jewish Music Journal* (New York, 1934–5) 1 vol., B

537   *Musical Mercury* (New York, 1934–49) 17 vols.

538   *National Association of Schools of Music: Bulletin* (Cincinnati, 1934–) 38 nos.

539   *Notes for the Members of the Music Library Association* (Rochester and Buffalo, NY, 1934–8, 1940–42) later, *Notes for the Music Library Association* (from 1940, no.7) 15 nos. Continued as *Notes.*

540   *Opera, Concert, and Symphony* (San Francisco, 1934–53), later, *Counterpoint.* 18 vols.

541   *Southwestern Musician* (Lubbock, TX, 1934–) incorp. *Texas Music Educator* (Sept 1954) to form *Southwestern Musician/Texas Music Educator* (Texas MEA, Texas MTA, etc.). Continued from *Southwestern Musicale.*

542   *Tempo* (Music Educ. League, New York, 1934–5) 2 vols.

543   *Texas Music Educator* (Texas MEA, Borger, TX, 1934–54) Incorp. into *Southwestern Musician.*

544   *American Music Lover* (New York, 1935–41; Pelham, NY, 1941–57; New York, 1957–72; Melville, NY, 1976–) later, *Listener's Record Guide* (Sept 1944) and then *American Record Guide* (from Oct 1944) M. Continued from *Music Lovers' Guide.*

545   *Music Front* (Pierre Degeyter Music Club of New York City, New York, 1935–6) 2 vols.

546   *Music Vanguard: a Critical Review* (New York, 1935) 2 nos.

547   *National Federation of Music Clubs: Book of Proceedings* (Chicago, 1935–). Continued from *National Federation of Music Clubs: Biennial Proceedings.*

548   *Women in Music* (Orchestrette Classique, New York, 1935–40) M

549   *Accordion World* (Mount Kisco, NY, 1936–71) later, *Accordion and Guitar World* (also *Magazine*) (from 1958) M; later B

550   *Bulletin of the American Musicological Society* (New York, 1936–48) 13 nos., Y. Continued as *Journal of the American Musicological Society.*

551   *Music Teachers National Association: Advisory Council Bulletin* (Lincoln, NE, 1936–50) later, *Music Teachers National Association Bulletin* (from 1938) 15 vols., O. Continued as *American Music Teacher.*

552   *Opera News* (Metropolitan Opera Guild, New York, 1936–)

553   *Papers read at the Annual Meeting* (Oberlin, NY, 1936–8, 1940–41) later, *Papers read by Members of the American Musicological Society* (from 1937), *Papers of the American Musicological Society* (from 1940) 5 vols., Y. Continued as *Abstracts of Papers read at the Annual Meeting of the American Musicological Society.*

554 *School Music News* (New York State School Music Assn, Little Falls, later Schenectady, NY, 1936–) M.

555 *Fretted Instrument News* (Amer. Guild of Banjoists, Mandolinists, and Guitarists, Providence, RI, 1937–57) B

556 *New England Conservatory of Music, Boston: Alumni Quarterly* (Boston, 1937–) Q. Continued from *New England Conservatory News and Alumni Bulletin.*

557 *ACA Bulletin* (New York, 1938, 1952–65) later, *Bulletin of the American Composers Alliance* (from 1952) then *American Composers Alliance Bulletin* (from 1961) 13 vols., mainly Q.

558 *Gramophone Shop, Inc., Record Supplement* (New York, 1938–54) 17 vols., M

559 *Violins* (Evanston, IL, and Chicago, 1938–60) later, *Violins and Violinists* (from 1938) then *Violins' and Violinists' Magazine* (from Feb 1942) 168 nos. in 21 vols., O; from 1953, B.

560 *Jazz Information* (New York, 1939–41) 2 vols.

561 *Journal of Musicology* (Greenfield, OH, 1939–47) 5 vols., Q

562 *Keyboard* (New Haven, 1939–42) 4 vols., M

563 *Steinway Review of Permanent Music* (New York, 1939–58 except June–July 1941 and Nov 1943) later, *Steinway Review of Permanent Recorded Music* (from 1950) 21 vols. Incorp. into *Musical Courier.*

564 *Composers and Authors of America* (Composers' and Authors' Assn of America, Cleveland and San Antonio, 1940–) Q

565 *Guild of Carillonneurs in North America: Bulletin* (Darien, CT, 1940–) O

566 *Jewish Music Forum: Bulletin* (Soc. for the Advancement of Jewish Musical Culture, New York, 1940–59) O

567 *Listen: the Guide to Good Music* (New York, 1940–51) 12 vols., M

568 *Music and Rhythm* (Chicago, 1940–) O

569 *Music Makers of Stage, Screen, Radio* (Dunellen, NJ, 1940) 3 nos.

570 *Musical Facts* (Chicago, 1940–41) 2 vols.

571 *Musical Record* (New York, 1940–41) 2 vols., M

572 *National Music Council Bulletin* (New York, 1940–) 3 nos. Y; from 1975, H

573 *Nebraska Music Educator* (Nebraska MEA, Lincoln, NE, 1940–) 4 nos. Y

574 *Film Music Notes* (Natl Film Music Council, New York, 1941–) later, *Film Music* (from 1951) then *Film and TV Music* (from 1956), B

575 *Journal of Aesthetics and Art Criticism* (Amer. Soc. for Aesthetics, Baltimore, later Cleveland, 1941–) Q

576 *Musician* (Chicago, 1941–) M

577 *Recorder Review* (Amer. Recorder Soc., New York, 1941–3)

578 *Cadenza* (Montana MEA, Bozeman, MT, 1942–) 4 nos. Y

579 *Cash Box: the International Music-record Weekly* (New York, 1942–) W

580 *Illinois Music Educator* (Illinois MEA, Mendota, IL, later Urbana, IL, 1942–72) 5 nos. Y, later Q

581 *International Records Agency: Bulletin* (Richmond Hill, NY, 1942–) O

582 *Leschetizky Association of America: News Bulletin* (New York, 1942–) O

583 *Piano Technician* (Amer. Soc. of Piano Technicians, Delavan, WI, 1942–57) 16 vols. Continued as *Piano Technicians Journal.*

584 *Record Changer* (Fairfax, VA, 1942–57) 15 vols., M

585 *SESAC Music* (SESAC Inc., New York, 1942–) M, later O

586 *Song Hits* (Derby, CT, 1942–) M

587 *Army and Navy Musician* (Bandsmen's Assn, New Haven, 1943–) later, *Musicana, US Army, Navy, and Air Force* (from March 1951)

588 *Braille Musician* (Library of Congress, Division for the Blind and Physically Handicapped, Washington, DC, 1943–69) 27 vols., B. In Braille; continued as *New Braille Musician.*

589 *Classical Recordaid* (Philadelphia, 1943–71) M

590 *Keyboard, Jr.: the Magazine for Young Musicians* (New Haven, 1943)

591 *Mississippi Notes* (Mississippi MEA, Hattiesburg, MS, 1943–74) later, *Mississippi Music Educator.*

592 *Music Dial: a Musician's Magazine* (New York, 1943–)

593 *Music Publishers' Journal* (New York, etc., 1943–) later, *Music Journal* (from 1946); suppl.: *MPJ New Music List*, from 1947 *Index to New Music*, 1946–9, 4 vols.; incl. *Music Journal;*

Journal Annual (from 1958), *Journal Anthology* (from 1962), *Journal Annual Anthology* (1970–71) Incorp. *Educational Music Magazine* (April 1957); incorp. *Music and Artists* (Feb 1973).

594 *Northwest Music Review* (Washington State MTA and Washington MEA, Seattle, 1943–9) 5 vols.

595 *Notes* (Music Library Assn, Washington, DC, 1943–) 2nd ser., Q; suppl.: *Notes for Members*, 1947–64, 36 nos. Continued from *Notes for the Members of the Music Library Association.*

596 *Notes from Purdue University Musical Organizations* (Lafayette, IN, 1943–) later, *P.M.O. Notes*; M

597 *Washington Music Review* (Seattle, 1943–4) 10 nos., M

598 *American Musicological Society News Letter* (New York, 1944–)

599 *Bulletin: the official magazine of the National Association of Teachers of Singing* (Natl Assn of Teachers of Singing, New York, 1944–66) later, *NATS Bulletin* (from 1962) 22 vols., 5 nos. Y, from 1953/4 Q. Continued as *NATS Journal.*

600 *Gopher Music Notes* (Minnesota MEA, Alexandria, MN, 1944–) Q

601 *Music* (New York, 1944) 1 no.

602 *Score* (Amer. Soc. of Music Arrangers, Beverly Hills, CA, 1944–53 except Nov 1946 to Dec 1949 and April 1950 to 1952) 5 vols., B

603 *Tune-dex Digest* (Amer. Soc. of Disc Jockeys, New York, 1944–65) later, *Music Business* (from 1946), M. Incorp. into *Music Vendor.*

604 *Music of the West* (Music Trades Assn of Southern California, Pasadena, CA, 1945–50)

605 *Musicology* (Middlebury, VT; New York, 1945–9) 2 vols., O.

606 *Piano Guild Notes* (Natl Guild of Piano Teachers, Austin, 1945–)

607 *A.T.G. Bulletin* (Accordion Teachers Guild, Minnetonka, MN, later Rochester, NY, 1946–) 10 nos. Y, later B

608 *Guitar Review* (Soc. of the Classic Guitar, New York, 1946–) O

609 *Indiana Musicator* (Indiana MEA, Indianapolis, later Muncie, IN, 1946–) Q

610 *Instrumentalist* (Assn for the Advancement of Instrumental Music, Glen Ellyn, IL, and Evanston, IL, 1946–)

611 *International Lyric Courier* (New York, 1946–) B

612 *Jewish Music News* (Jewish Music Council of Philadelphia, Philadelphia, 1946–)

613 *Jewish Music Notes* (Natl Jewish Music Council and Natl Jewish Welfare Board, New York, 1946–9) 4 vols., O. Continued as section 3 of *Circle* (from March 1950)

614 *Journal of Renaissance and Baroque Music* (Inst. of Renaissance and Baroque Music, Cambridge, MA, 1946–7) later, *Musica disciplina* (American Inst. of Musicology, Rome, 1948–)

615 *Music Studio News* (Oakland, CA, 1946–) M

616 *Music Vendor* (New York, 1946–) later, *Record World* (from 1964) Incorp. *Music Business* (1965)

617 *Songwriter's Review* (New York, 1946–) B

618 *Year in American Music* (New York, 1946–8) 2 vols., Y

619 *Western Music, Drama, and Art* (Phoenix, 1946–8)

620 *Choir Guide* (Intl Choir Directors' League, New York, 1947–64) later joined *Organ Guide* (Feb 1952) to form *Choral and Organ Guide*; M

621 *Composer's News Record* (League of Composers, New York, 1947–9) 9 nos., O

622 *Hymn Writers' Magazine* (Los Angeles, 1947–) later, *Hymn Lovers' Magazine* (from Nov/Dec 1948) then *Christian Etude, Hymn Writers' (Lovers') Fellowship* (from July 1952) B

623 *Music Dealer* (New York, 1947–55) 9 vols., M

624 *Pianist* (Intl Piano Teachers Assn, Erie, PA, 1947–)

625 *School Director* (Florida MEA, Tampa, FL, 1947–) later, *School Music Director* (from 1959) then *Florida Music Director* (from 1969)

626 *Woodwinds* (New York, 1947–8) 2 vols. Continued as *Woodwind Magazine.*

627 *Allegro* (Associated Musicians of Greater New York, New York, 1948–) M

628 *Arpeggio Music Magazine* (Philadelphia, 1948–9) 7 nos., M

629 *ASSW News* (Amer. Soc. of Songwriters, Boston, 1948) 1 vol., O
630 *Bulletin for Northern California Music Libraries* (Music Library Assn, San Francisco, later San Jose, 1948–53; new ser. 1953) later, *Notes for the Northern California Music Libraries* (April–Dec 1948) 6 vols., new ser. 1 no.
631 *CMEA News* (California MEA, San Diego, CA, later Bakersfield, CA, 1948–67)
632 *Cantors Voice* (Cantors Assembly of America, New York, 1948–66)
633 *Catholic Music Educators Bulletin* (Natl Catholic MEA, Hyattsville, MD, later Washington, DC, 1948–76) later, *Musart.* 28 vols. Y. Continued as *Pastoral Music.*
634 *Harmonizer* (Soc. for the Preservation and Encouragement of Barber Shop Quartet Singing in America, Detroit, MI, later Kenosha, WI, 1948–) Q, later 6 nos. Y
635 *Hospital Music Newsletter* (Committee on Music in Hospitals, Natl Music Council, New York, 1948–51) 3 vols., O. Continued as *National Association for Music Therapy Bulletin.*
636 *Independent Songwriter* (Independent Song-writers Assn, Somerville, NJ, 1948–) B
637 *Iowa Music Educator* (Iowa MEA, Des Moines, 1948–) Q
638 *Journal of the American Musicological Society* (Boston, 1948; Richmond, VA, 1949–) 3 nos. Continued from *Bulletin of the American Musicological Society.*
639 *Just Records* (New York, 1948–50) 34 nos., M
640 *Life with Music* (Bureau of Musical Research, Hollywood, CA, 1948–) M
641 *MTA California Keynotes* (MTA of California, Burbank, CA, 1948–) O
642 *Music and Art* (Fresno, CA, 1948–)
643 *Music Magazine of Los Angeles* (Los Angeles, 1948–)
644 *Music-Q* (Washington, DC, 1948–) M
645 *Music Reporter* (New York, 1948–9) M
646 *Musical News* (AFM, San Francisco, 1948–) M
647 *News Letter of the American Symphony Orchestra League, Inc.* (Charleston, VA, 1948–61; Vienna, VA, 1962–82; Washington, DC, 1982–) later, *Newsletter* (from 1952), then *Symphony News* (from 1971) and then *Symphony Magazine* (from 1980) B; directory issue, 1980–, Y
648 *News Sheet* (Pennsylvania Fed. of Music Clubs, Pittsburgh, 1948–) 4 nos. Y
649 *Phonolog Reporter* (San Diego, CA, 1948–) W
650 *Plein jeu: the Quarterly Magazine devoted to the Electronic Organ* (Olympia, WA, 1948–) Q
651 *Symphony* (New York, 1948–) M except Aug
652 *Tennessee Musician* (Tampa, FL, 1948–) Q
653 *Woodwind Magazine* (New York, 1948–55) 7 vols. Continued from *Woodwinds.*
654 *AGMAzine* (Amer. Guild of Musical Artists, New York, 1949–) Q
655 *CMC Journal* (Student Assn of the Chicago Musical Coll., Chicago, 1949–) O
656 *Country Song Roundup* (Derby, CT, 1949–54) 33 nos., M; suppl.: *Country Song Roundup Annual*
657 *Georgia Music News* (Georgia MEA, Collegeboro, later Athens, GA, 1949) Q
658 *Hymn* (Hymn Soc. of America, New York, 1949–76; Springfield, OH, 1976–) 3 nos. Y; from 1952, Q
659 *Kansas Music Review* (Kansas MEA, Emporia, later Wichita, KS, 1949–) 6, later 5 nos. Y
660 *Long Playing Record Catalog* (Cambridge, MA, 1949–53; Boston, 1953–) title varies, from *Schwann-1 Record & Tape Guide* (Jan 1972), *New Schwann* (from Dec 1983) M; artist index, 1953–, O; incorp. *Schwann Catalog of Imported Records* (1983)
661 *MPA Bulletin* (Music Publishers' Assn of the US, New York, 1949–) O
662 *M.S.V.A. Journal* (Michigan School Vocal Assn, Port Huron, MI, 1949–) 4 nos. Y
663 *Music Forum* (New York, 1949–50) later, *Music Forum and Digest* (from 1949, no.3) 2 vols., M
664 *Music Index* (Detroit, 1949–) M, cumulations Y
665 *Music News Directory* (Washington MTA, Washington, DC, 1949–) H

666 *Oregon Music Educators News* (Salem, later Roseburg, OR, 1949–) later, *Oregon Music Educator* (from 1954) 3 nos. Y
667 *Pittsburgh Musician* (Local 60 AFM of the Pittsburgh Musical Soc., Pittsburgh, 1949–) M, later B
668 *Soundings: a Monthly Sounding of the New Records* (New York, 1949–) M
669 *String News* (Division of U. Extension, U. of Illinois Music Section, Urbana, IL, 1949–) O
670 *Texas String News* (Amer. String Teachers Assn, Dept of Music, U. of Texas, Austin, 1949–) Q
671 *V.M.E.A. Notes* (Virginia MEA, Richmond, VA, 1949–) 6 nos. Y
672 *Young Keyboard, Jr.: the Magazine for Music Appreciation* (New Haven, 1949–)
673 *American Recorder Society: Newsletter* (New York, and Stony Point, NY, 1950–59) 38 nos., O. from 1963, Q. Continued as *American Recorder*
674 *Boletín de música y artes visuals* (Unión Panamericana, Departamento de Asuntos Culturales, Washington, DC, 1950–56) 76 nos., M in Sp. Continued as *Boletín interamericano de música* (Unión Panamericana, Departamento de Asuntos Culturales, Washington, DC, 1957–73) from 1970, Organización de los Estados Americanos 87 nos., B; from 1970, 3 nos. Y [in Sp., parallel Eng. edn]
675 *Church Musician* (Sunday School Board, Southern Baptist Convention, Nashville, 1950–) M
676 *Clarinet* (New York, 1950–57) 26 nos. Continued as *Woodwind World.*
677 *Harp News of the West* (Northern California Harpists' Assn, Oakland, CA, 1950–66) later, *Harp News* (from 1950, no.2) 4 vols., H. Continued as *American Harp Journal.*
678 *Notes a tempo* (West Virginia MEA, West Liberty, WV, 1950–) M Sept–June
679 *Second Line, New Orleans Jazz Club* (New Orleans, 1950–) O
680 *Sing Out! The Folk Song Magazine* (New York, 1950–) B
681 *American Music Teacher* (Music Teachers Natl Assn, Pittsburgh, 1951–63; Cincinnati, 1963–). Continued from *Music Teachers National Association Bulletin.*
682 *American String Teacher* (Amer. String Teachers Assn., Urbana, IL, 1951–60; Mankato, MN, 1960–71; Trenton, NJ, 1972–) Q
683 *High Fidelity* (Great Barrington, MA, 1951–) later, *High Fidelity and Audiocraft* (1958–9) Incorp. *Musical America* (Feb 1965) to form *High Fidelity/Musical America*; *High Fidelity/Musical America: Special Directory Issue* (1968–); *Musical America: Annual Directory Issue* (1965–), Y. Incorp. *Hi-Fi Music at Home.*
684 *Organ Institute Bulletin* (Andover, MA, 1951–64) later, *Organ Institute Quarterly*
685 *NACWPI Bulletin* (Natl Assn of Coll. Wind and Percussion Instructors, Washington, 1952–) later, *NACWPI Journal*
686 *Piano Quarterly Newsletter* (Piano Teachers Information Service, Wilmington, VA, 1952–92) later, *Piano Quarterly*
687 *PMEA News* (Pennsylvania MEA, West Chester, PA, 1952–)
688 *Ethno-Musicology* (Soc. for Ethno-Musicology, Middletown, CT, 1953–76) later, *Ethnomusicology Newsletter*
689 *Journal of Research in Music Education* (MENC Chicago, 1953–)
690 *New Mexico Musician* (New Mexico MEA, Albuquerque, 1953–)
691 *Selmer Bandwagon* (Elkhart, IN, 1953–79)
692 *Berlioz Society Newsletter* (New York, 1954–60)
693 *Gregorian Review* (Toledo, OH, 1954–8)
694 *Juilliard Review* (Juilliard School of Music, New York, 1954–62). Continued as *Juilliard News Bulletin.*
695 *Michigan Music Educator* (Michigan MEA, Ypsilanti, MI, 1954–88)
696 *Musical Box Society Bulletin* (Musical Box Society, St. Paul, MN, 1954–85; 1988–) later, *Mechanical Music*
697 *Washington Music Educator* (Washington MEA, Ellensburg, WA, 1955–) later, *Voice of Washington Music Educators*
698 *American Guild of Organists Quarterly* (New York, 1956–67)
699 *Musical Americana Newsletter* (Philadelphia, 1956–)
700 *Tracker* (Organ Historical Society, Richmond, VA, 1956–)
701 *Brass Quarterly* (Durham, NH, 1957–65). Continued as *Brass and Woodwind Quarterly*

702   *Journal of Music Theory* (Yale U. School of Music, New Haven, 1957–)

703   *Nevada Notes* (Nevada MEA, Reno, NV, 1957–71); new series (1979–84)

704   *News and Notes* (Los Angeles, 1957–75) later, *Composer and Conductor*. Continued as *Composer/USA*

705   *News Bulletin of the Moravian Music Foundation* (Winston-Salem, NC, 1957–) later, *Bulletin*, and then *Moravian Music Foundation Bulletin*, then *Moravian Music Journal*

706   *American Choral Review* (Assn of Choral Conductors, Amer. Choral Fdn, [New York], 1958–)

707   *Cornell University Music Review* (Dept of Music, Cornell U., Ithaca, NY, 1958–68)

708   *Folklore and Folk Music Archivist* (Indiana U., Bloomington, IN, 1958–68) Q (1963–)

709   *Hi Fi and Music Review* (New York, 1958–) later titles, *Hi Fi Review*, *Hi Fi Stereo Review*, and *Stereo Review*. Merged with *Video Magazine* to form *Stereo Review's Sound and Vision* (2001–)

710   *Jazz Review* (New York, 1958–61)

711   *Musica liturgica* (Cincinnati, 1958–60)

712   *Musik aus Amerika* (US Information Service, Vienna, Austria, 1958–62) 5 vols.

713   *NSOA Bulletin* (Natl School Orchestra Assn, Terre Haute, IN, 1958–98)

714   *Piano Technicians Journal* (Piano Technicians Guild, Seattle, 1958–)

715   *Reihe: a Periodical devoted to Developments in Contemporary Music* (Bryn Mawr, PA, 1958–68) [Amer. edn of Austrian ser., Vienna, 1955–62]

716   *Central Opera Service Bulletin* (Metropolitan Opera Natl Council, Central Opera Service, New York, 1959–90)

717   *Choral Journal* (Amer. Choral Directors Assn, Tampa, FL, 1959–)

718   *Close-up* (Country Music Assn, Nashville, 1959–67) later, *CMA Close-up*

719   *Journal of Church Music* (Lutheran Church in America, Philadelphia, 1959–88)

720   *Music Ministry* ([United] Methodist Church, Nashville, 1959–78)

721   *Quarterly Check-list of Musicology* (Darien, CT, 1959–77)

722   *Research Memorandum, American Choral Foundation* (Assn of Choral Conductors, New York, 1959–82)

723   *Response in Worship, Music, the Arts* (Lutheran Soc. for Worship, Music, and the Arts, St. Paul, 1959–78)

724   *Theatre Organ* (Amer. Assn of Theatre Organ Enthusiasts, Middleburg, VA, 1959–66) later, *Theatre Organ/Bombarde*

725   *American Recorder* (Amer. Recorder Soc., New York, 1960–)

726   *Critics Criteria* (Rockville, MD, 1960–93) later, *Newsletter of Music Critics Association*

727   *FIGA News* (Chicago, 1960–78) later, *Fretted Instrument Guild of America*

728   *Jazz Report* (Ventura, CA, 1960–82) Incorp. into *Music Memories and Jazz Report*

729   *BMI: News About Music & Writers* (Broadcast Music, Inc., New York, 1961–4) later, *BMI: the Many Worlds of Music*

730   *College Music Symposium* (Coll. Music Soc., [Binghamton, NY], 1961–)

731   *Music Memories* (Birmingham, AL, 1961–) Incorp. into *Music Memories and Jazz Report*

732   *Clavier* (Evanston, IL, 1962–2008)

733   *Jazz* (New York, 1962–71) later, *Jazz and Pop*

734   *Juilliard News Bulletin* (Juilliard School of Music, New York, 1962–84)

735   *Missouri Journal of Research in Music Education* (Missouri MEA, St. Louis, 1962–)

736   *Percussive Notes* (Percussive Arts Soc., Urbana, IL, 1962–) Incorp. *Percussionist* (1983)

737   *Perspectives of New Music* (Fromm Music Fdn, Annandale-on-Hudson, NY, 1962–)

738   *Stereophile* (Philadelphia, 1962–)

739   *AMICA Bulletin* (Automatic Musical Instrument Collectors' Assn, Campbell, CA, 1963–72)

740   *Council for Research in Music Education Bulletin* (School of Music, Coll. of Educ., U. of Illinois, and Office of the Superintendent of Public Instruction, Champaign, IL, 1963–)

741   *Juilliard Review Annual* (Juilliard School of Music, New York, 1963–8)

742   *Junior Musician* (Sunday School Board, Southern Baptist Convention, Nashville, 1963–70) later, *Young Musicians*

743   *Musician's Voice* (New York, 1963–70)

744   *Musigram* (Natl Sheet Music Soc., Covina, CA, 1963–6)

745   *Percussionist* (Urbana, IL, 1963–82) later, *Percussive Notes/Percussionist Research Edition* (Percussive Arts Soc., 1981–2) Incorp. into *Percussive Notes*

746   *American Old Time Fiddlers' News* (Amer. Old Time Fiddlers' Assn, Lincoln, NE, 1964–)

747   *Catgut Acoustical Society Newsletter* (Montclair, NJ, 1964–84)

748   *Colorado Journal of Research in Music Education* (Boulder, CO, 1964–73)

749   *Disc Collector Newsletter* (Cheswold, DE, 1964–80) later, *Disc Collector*

750   *Grand Baton: Journal of the Sir Thomas Beecham Society* (Cleveland, 1964–)

751   *Journal of Band Research* (Amer. Bandmasters Assn, Coll. Band Directors Natl Assn, Natl Band Assn, and Amer. School Band Directors' Assn, College Park, MD, 1964–)

752   *Journal of Music Therapy* (Natl Assn for Music Therapy, Lawrence, KS, 1964–)

753   *Journal of the Viola da Gamba Society of America* (Memphis, 1964–)

754   *Music City News* (Nashville, 1964–2000) later, *Country Music City News*

755   *Notes of N.A.O.T.* (Natl Assn of Organ Teachers, Hammond, IN, 1964–84) later, *Organ Teacher*

756   *Viola da Gamba Society of America: News* (Edgewater, MD, 1964–) later, *VDGSA News*

757   *Boosey and Hawkes Newsletter* (New York, 1965–)

758   *Brass World* (Des Moines, 1965–74)

759   *Current Musicology* (Dept of Music, Columbia, New York, 1965–)

760   *JEMF Newsletter* (John Edwards Memorial Fdn, Los Angeles, 1965–88)

761   *Bluegrass Unlimited* (Broad Run, VA, 1966–) M

762   *Brass and Woodwind Quarterly* (Durham, NH, 1966–9)

763   *Church Music* (Concordia Teachers' Coll., River Forest, IL, 1966–80)

764   *Crawdaddy: Magazine of Rock* (New York, 1966–78)

765   *Lute Society of America, Inc.: Newsletter* (San Francisco, 1966–88)

766   *Notes from Eastman* (Eastman School of Music, Rochester, NY, 1966–78) later, *Eastman Notes*

767   *American Harp Journal* (Amer. Harp Soc., Los Angeles, 1967–)

768   *ASCAP Today* (Amer. Soc. of Composers, Authors and Publishers, New York, 1967–78). Continued as *ASCAP in Action*

769   *Contemporary Music Newsletter* (Columbia U., New York, 1967–77)

770   *Electronic Music Review* (Independent Electronic Music Center, Trumansburg, NY, 1967–8)

771   *Ernest Bloch Society Bulletin* (Portland, OR, 1967–91)

772   *Guitar Player: the Magazine for Professional and Amateur Guitarists* (Saratoga, CA, 1967–71)

773   *Journal of Synagogue Music* (Cantors Assembly of America, New York, 1967–)

774   *Music in Higher Education* (Natl Assn of Schools of Music, Washington, DC, 1967–82)

775   *Music: the A.G.O. Magazine* (American Guild of Organists and Royal Canadian Coll. of Organists, New York, 1967–) later, *Music: the A.G.O. and R.C.C.O. Magazine*, then *American Organist*

776   *Rag Times* (Maple Leaf Club, Los Angeles, 1967–)

777   *RILM Abstracts of Music Literature: répertoire international de la littérature musicale/International Repertory of Music Literature* (Intl Musicological Soc., Intl Assn of Music Libraries, and Amer. Council of Learned Socs., at the Graduate School, CUNY, New York, 1967–)

778   *Rolling Stone* (San Francisco, 1967–)

779   *S.E.M. Newsletter* (Soc. for Ethnomusicology, Milwaukee, etc., 1967–)

780   *Source: Music of the Avant Garde* (Davis, CA, 1967–72)

781   *American Society of University Composers: Newsletter* (New York, 1968–87)

782   *Asian Music* (Soc. for Asian Music, New York, 1968–)
783   *Association for Recorded Sound Collections: Journal* (Silver Spring, MD, 1968–84)
784   *Country Dance and Song Society News* (New York, 1968–96)
785   *Early Music Laboratory Bulletin* (Los Angeles, 1968–80)
786   *Harpsichord* (Intl Soc. of Harpsichord Builders/Intl Harpsichord Soc., Denver, 1968–76)
787   *IAJRC Record* (Intl Assn of Jazz Record Collectors, Naperville, IL, 1968–) later, *IAJRC Journal*
788   *International Alban Berg Society Newsletter* (Durham, NH, 1968–93)
789   *Lute Society of America, Inc. Journal* (Lexington, VA, 1968–)
790   *Music and Artists* (New York, 1968–72)
791   *National Association of Jazz Educators Newsletter* (Manhattan, KS, 1968–) later, *NAJE Educator*, then *Jazz Educators Journal*
792   *Opera Journal* (Natl Opera Assn, Columbia, MO, 1968–)
793   *Composer* (Redondo Beach, CA, 1969–81) later, *Composer Magazine*
794   *Creem* (Pelham Manor, NY 1969–)
795   *Music Library Association Newsletter* (Ann Arbor, MI, 1969–)
796   *New Braille Musician* (Library of Congress, Division for the Blind and Physically Handicapped, Washington, DC, 1969–77). Continued as *Musical Mainstream*
797   *Orff Echo* (Amer. Orff Schulwerk Assn, Cleveland, 1969–)
798   *Singing News: the Printed Voice of Gospel Music* (Pensacola, FL, 1969–83)
799   *To the World's Bassoonists* (Intl Double Reed Soc., Fort Worth, TX, 1969–77) Incorp. into *Double Reed*
800   *Yearbook of the International Folk Music Council* (Urbana, IL, 1969–80; New York, 1981–) later, *Yearbook for Traditional Music*
801   *Bach* (Riemenschneider Bach Inst., Baldwin-Wallace Coll., Berea, OH, 1970–)
802   *Living Blues* (Chicago, 1970–)
803   *Music Cataloging Bulletin* (Music Library Assn, Ann Arbor, MI, 1970–)
804   *World Saxophone Congress Newsletter* (Evanston, IL, 1970–74). Continued as *Saxophone Symposium: a Newsletter* (N. Amer. Saxophone Alliance of the World Saxophone Congress, Northwestern U., School of Music, Evanston, IL, 1975–)
805   *AMS Newsletter* (Amer. Musicological Soc., New Haven, 1971–)
806   *Horn Call* (Intl Horn Soc., Elmhurst, IL, 1971–)
807   *Institute for Studies in American Music: Newsletter* (Brooklyn, NY, 1971–2008)
808   *Music at Yale* (New Haven, 1971–)
809   *Musical Newsletter* (New York, 1971–7)
810   *Newsletter of the Historical Musical Society* (Massapequa Park, NY, 1971–) later, *Newsletter of the American Musical Instrument Society*
811   *Popular Music and Society* (Center for the Study of Popular Culture, Bowling Green State U., Bowling Green, OH, 1971–)
812   *Country Music* (New York, 1972–2003)
813   *Dead Relix* (New York, 1972–) later, *Relix*
814   *Electronotes: Newsletter* (Ithaca, NY, 1972–83) later, *Electronotes, Musical Engineering Group*
815   *Keyboard Arts* (Princeton, NJ, 1972–7)
816   *Musical Analysis* (Denton, TX, 1972–4)
817   *NUMUS-West: North America's New Music Journal* (Mercer Island, WA, 1972–5)
818   *Soundings* (Santa Fe, NM, 1972–90)
819   *To the World's Oboists* (Intl Double Reed Soc., Fort Worth, TX, 1972–7) Incorp. into *Double Reed*
820   *Absolute Sound* (Seacliff, NY, 1973–)
821   *American Suzuki Journal* (Suzuki Assn of the Americas, Boulder, CO, 1973–)
822   *Ancient Times* (Company of Fifers and Drummers, Deep River, CT, 1973–)
823   *Antique Phonograph Monthly* (New York, 1973–92)
824   *Banjo Newsletter* (Greensboro, MD, 1973–)
825   *Bells, a newsletter of opinions, news & reviews of improvised music* (Berkeley, CA, 1973–9)
826   *Black Perspective in Music* (Fdn for Research in the Afro-Amer. Creative Arts, New York, 1973–90)

827   *Boombah Herald: a Band History Newsletter* (Lancaster, NY, 1973–98)
828   *Clarinet* (Intl Clarinet Soc., Pocatello/Dept. of Music, Idaho State U., 1973–)
829   *Computational Musicology Newsletter* (San Francisco, 1973–)
830   *Different Drummer: the Magazine for Jazz Listeners* (Rochester, NY, 1973–5)
831   *Ear* (San Francisco, 1973–92) later, *Ear Magazine West*
832   *Folk Harp Journal* (Mount Laguna, CA, 1973–)
833   *Folk Mass and Modern Liturgy Magazine* (San Jose, CA, 1973–) later, *Modern Liturgy*
834   *Guild of American Luthiers Newsletter* (Tacoma, WA, 1973–84) later, *Guild of American Luthiers Quarterly*
835   *International Trombone Association Journal* (Youngstown, OH, 1973–) later, *ITA Journal*
836   *Journal of Jazz Studies* (Inst. of Jazz Studies, Rutgers U., New Brunswick, NJ, 1973–9; 1982–) later, *Annual Review of Jazz Studies*
837   *Journal of the International Double Reed Society* (School of Fine Arts, Texas Christian U., Fort Worth, TX, 1973–98)
838   *Mississippi Rag* (Minneapolis, 1973–2006)
839   *Mountain Newsreal* (Tucson, AZ, 1973–85) later, *Newsreal*
840   *Psychology of Music* (Thousand Oaks, CA, 1973–)
841   *Senza sordino* (Intl Conference of Symphony & Opera Musicians, Chicago, 1973–)
842   *T.U.B.A. Newsletter* (North Amer. Region of Tubists Universal Brotherhood Assn, Denton, TX, 1973–2001) later, *T.U.B.A. Journal*
843   *Violone* (Ohio State U., School of Music, Columbus, OH, 1973–9)
844   *American Society for the Advancement of Violin Making News Bulletin* (New York, 1974–) later, *Violin Society of American News Bulletin*, and then *Journal of the Violin Society of America*
845   *Analog Sounds* (New York, 1974–9)
846   **Asterisk: a Journal of New Music* (Ann Arbor, MI, 1974–6)
847   *Guitar and Lute* (Honolulu, 1974–83)
848   *International Society of Bassists: Newsletter* (Coll.-Conservatory of Music, U. of Cincinnati, Cincinnati, 1974–) later, *Bass World: Annual Journal*, and then *Journal*. Incorp. *Bass Sound Post*
849   *International Trumpet Guild Newsletter* (Bloomington, IN, 1974–82) later, *ITG Newsletter* Incorp. into *ITG Journal*
850   *Pickin': the Magazine of Bluegrass & Old-time Country Music* (Philadelphia, 1974–9) Incorp. into *Frets*
851   *Soundboard* (Guitar Fdn of America, Los Angeles, 1974–)
852   *Xenharmonikôn: an Informal Journal of Experimental Music* (Highland Park, NJ, 1974–98)
853   *American Musical Instrument Society Journal* (Shreveport, LA, 1975–) later, *Journal of the American Musical Instrument Society*
854   *Arnold Schoenberg Institute Bulletin* (U. of Southern California, Los Angeles, 1975–96) later, *Journal of the Arnold Schoenberg Institute*
855   *Contemporary Keyboard* (Cupertino, CA, 1975–) later, *Keyboard*
856   *Dulcimer Players News* (Front Royal, VA, 1975–)
857   *Fritz Reiner Society Newsletter* (Novelty, OH, 1975–88) later, *Podium*
858   *Ha'ilono mele* (Hawaiian Music Fdn, Honolulu, 1975–82)
859   *In Theory Only* (Michigan Music Theory Soc., School of Music, U. of Michigan, Ann Arbor, MI, 1975–)
860   *ILWC Newsletter* (Intl League of Women Composers, Framingham, MA, 1975–95) later, *International League of Women Composers newsletter*, then *ILWC Journal*
861   *International Society of Bassists* (Ann Arbor, MI, 1975–96)
862   *International Trumpet Guild Newsletter* (School of Music, Indiana U., Bloomington, IN, 1975–82)
863   *Polyphony: Electronic Music and Home Recording* (Oklahoma City, OK, 1975–) later, *Electronic Musician*
864   *RIdIM/RCMI Newsletter: répertoire international d'iconographie musicale/International Repertory of Musical Iconography* (Research Center for Musical Iconography, Graduate School, CUNY, New York, 1975–97)
865   *Sonneck Society Newsletter* (Sonneck Soc., Brighton, MA, later Lima, OH, 1975–99) later, *Bulletin of the Society for American Music*

866   *AIVS Newsletter* (Amer. Inst. for Verdi Studies, Dept of Music, New York U., New York, 1976–98) later, *Verdi Newsletter*

867   *Cadence, the American Review of Jazz & Blues* (Redwood, NY, 1976–)

868   *Composer/USA* (Natl Assn of Composers, USA, Los Angeles, 1976–)

869   *Cum notis variorum: Newsletter, U. of California Music Library* (Berkeley, CA, 1976–89)

870   *ITG Journal* (Intl Trumpet Guild, Nashville, 1976–)

871   *Musica judaica: Journal of the American Society for Jewish Music* (New York, 1976–2006)

872   *National Flute Association Newsletter* (Royal Oak, MI, 1976–87) later, *Flutist Quarterly*

873   *Pastoral Music* (Natl Assn of Pastoral Musicians, Washington, DC, 1976–)

874   *Pro musica* (El Cerrito, CA, 1976–7)

875   *19th Century Music* (Berkeley, CA, 1977–)

876   *ARSC Newsletter* (Assn for Recorded Sound Collections, Albuquerque, 1977–)

877   *Black Music Research Newsletter* (Inst. for Research in Black Amer. Music, Fisk U., and Center for Black Music Research, Columbia Coll., Chicago, 1977–87)

878   *Computer Music Journal* (People's Computer Co., Menlo Park, CA, 1977–)

879   *Dialogue in Instrumental Music Education* (Madison, WI, 1977–98)

880   *Fanfare: the Magazine for Serious Record Collectors* (Tenafly, NJ, 1977–)

881   *Indiana Theory Review* (Graduate Theory Assn, School of Music, Indiana U., Bloomington, IN, 1977–)

882   *Journal of the American Liszt Society* (Louisville, KY, 1977–) later, *American Liszt Society Journal*

883   *Modern Drummer* (Clifton, NJ, 1977–)

884   *Musical Mainstream* (Library of Congress, Natl Library Service for the Blind and Physically Handicapped, Washington, DC, 1977–)

885   *NARAS Institute Journal* (Natl Academy of Recording Arts and Sciences, Atlanta, 1977–80)

886   *Rockingchair: the Review Newsletter for Libraries who Buy Records* (Philadelphia, 1977–82)

887   *American Ensemble* (Chamber Music America, New York, 1978–) later, *Chamber Music Magazine*, then *Chamber Music*

888   *Chinese Music General Newsletter* (Chin. Music Soc. of North America, Woodridge, IL, 1978–) later, *Chinese Music*

889   *Double Reed* (Intl Double Reed Soc., East Lansing, MI, 1978–)

890   *Inter-American Music Review* (Los Angeles, 1978–)

891   *Interval: a Microtonal Newsletter* (San Diego, 1978–87)

892   *World of Opera* (New York, 1978–)

893   *Frets Magazine: the Magazine of Acoustic Stringed Instruments* (Cupertino, CA, 1979–89)

894   *Journal of Musicological Research* (New York, 1979–)

895   *Music Theory Spectrum* (Soc. for Music Theory, School of Music, Indiana U., Bloomington, IN, 1979–)

896   *Recordings of Experimental Music* (Audubon, NJ, 1979–85)

897   *Black Music Research Journal* (Inst. for Research in Black Amer. Music, Fisk U., and Center for Black Music Research, Columbia Coll., Chicago and Nashville, 1980–)

898   *Circular* (Library of Congress, Natl Library Service for the Blind and Physically Handicapped, Washington, DC, 1980–) later, *Music Circular*

899   *International Banjo* (Kissimmee, FL, 1980–84)

900   *Jazz Times* (Washington, D.C., 1980–)

901   *Journal of Guitar Acoustics* (Michigan Center, MI, 1980–83)

902   *Journal of the Conductors' Guild* (Washington, DC, 1980–)

903   *MadAminA! a Chronicle of Musical Catalogues* (Music Associates of America, Englewood, NJ, 1980–99)

904   *Ovation: the Magazine for Classical Music Listeners* (New York, 1980–89)

905   *Revista de música Latino Americana/Latin American Music Review* (U. of Texas, Austin, 1980–)

906   *SONUS: a Journal of Investigations into Global Musical Possibilities* (Cambridge, MA, 1980–)

907   *Winds Quarterly* (Needham, MA, 1980–81)

908   *Ars lyrica: Newsletter of the Society for Word-music Relationships* (New Haven, 1981; 1983–) later, *Lyrica Society*

909   *Ex tempore* (Dept of Music, U. of California at San Diego, La Jolla, CA, 1981–)

910   *High Performance Review: the Magazine for Perceptive Listeners* (Stanford, CA, 1981–96)

911   *Psychomusicology: a Journal of Research in Music Cognition* (Nacogdoches, TX, 1981–)

912   *Black Sheep Review* (Cambridge, MA, 1982–5)

913   *Chamber Music Quarterly* (St. Cloud, MN, 1982–4)

914   *ClariNetwork* (Hilliard, OH, 1982–8)

915   *Impromptu* (Library of Congress, Music Division, Washington, DC, 1982–5)

916   *Music Therapy Perspectives* (Natl Assn for Music Therapy, Washington, DC, 1982–)

917   *Resound: a Quarterly of the Archives of Traditional Music* (Indiana U., Bloomington, IN, 1982–2007)

918   *Sheet Music Exchange* (Winchester, VA, 1982–9)

919   *Suzuki World* (Ability Development Associates, Athens, OH, 1982–7)

920   *Update: the Applications of Research in Music Education* (Dept of Music, U. of South Carolina, Columbia, SC, 1982–)

921   *American Brahms Society Newsletter* (Seattle, 1983–)

922   *American Music* (Sonneck Society/Society for American Music, Champaign, IL, 1983–2007; University of IL Press, 2008–) See *Journal for the Society of American Music* (1085).

923   *Ethnomusicology at UCLA* (U. of California at Los Angeles, Los Angeles, 1983–9)

924   *International Congress on Women in Music Newsletter* (Los Angeles, 1983–90)

925   *Kurt Weill Newsletter* (Kurt Weill Fdn for Music, New York, 1983–)

926   *Living Music* (Desert Hot Springs, CA, 1983–)

927   *Music Explorer* (Evanston, IL, 1983–)

928   *Music Perception: an Interdisciplinary Journal* (Berkeley, CA, 1983–)

929   *Musical Woman: an International Perspective* (Westport, CT, 1983–90)

930   *Opera Quarterly* (Chapel Hill, 1983–)

931   *Review of Popular Music: RPM* (Intl Assn for the Study of Popular Music, 1983–)

932   *American Liszt Society, Inc., Newsletter* (Washington DC, later Rochester, NY, 1984–)

933   *Archer* (St. Louis, 1984–) later, *Schütz Society Reports*, then *Newsletter of American Schütz Society*, and then *17th Century Music*

934   *Balungan* (Amer. Gamelan Inst. for Music and Educ., Oakland, CA, 1984–)

935   *College Band Directors National Association Journal* (Buffalo, NY, 1984–94) later, *CBDNA Journal*

936   *Cue Sheet* (Soc. for the Preservation of Film Music, Los Angeles, 1984–)

937   *Forte* (Milwaukee, 1984–7)

938   *GAMUT* (Georgia Assn of Music Theorists, Atlanta, 1984–)

939   *Jazz Newsletter* (Kerrville, TX, 1984–6) M. Continued from *Jazzologist*

940   *Jazziz* (Gainesville, FL, 1984–)

941   *Modern Percussionist* (Cedar Grove, NJ, 1984–7). Incorp. into *Modern Drummer*

942   *National Music Council News* (New York, 1984–)

943   *Opus: the Magazine of Recorded Classics* (Harrisburg, PA, 1984–8). Incorp. into *Musical America*

944   *Pacific Review of Ethnomusicology* (UCLA Ethnomusicology Students Assn, Los Angeles, 1984–2002)

945   *Percussion News* (Percussive Arts Soc., Lawton, OK, 1984–)

946   *Sound Post, dedicated to Scandinavian Folk Music and Dance* (Hardanger Fiddle Assn of America, Richfield, MN, 1984–)

947   *1/1: The Journal of the Just Intonation Network* (San Francisco, 1985–2007)

948   *American Lutherie* (Guild of Amer. Luthiers, Tacoma, WA, 1985–). Continued from *Newsletter of Guild of American Luthiers*

949   *Bandworld* (Ashland, OR, 1985–)

950   *Darius Milhaud Society Newsletter* (Cleveland, 1985–)

951   *Electronic Musician* (Nashville, TN, 1985–). Continued from *Polyphony*

952   *Experimental Musical Instruments* (Point Reyes Station, CA, 1985–99)

953   *Full Score* (UCLA Music Library, Los Angeles, 1985–90)

954   *Journal of the American Viola Society* (Section of the Intl Viola Soc. and Assn for the Promotion of Viola Performance and Research, Provo, UT, 1985–2003)

955   *Spin* (New York, 1985–)

956   *Allegro* (Assn of Friends of Plácido Domingo, New York, 1986–)

957   *Beethoven Newsletter* (Brilliant Center for Beethoven Studies and Amer. Beethoven Soc., San Jose, CA, 1986–) later, *Beethoven Journal*

958   *College Musician* (Burbank, CA, 1986-8)

959   *EMA News* (Early Music America, New York, 1986–88). Continued as *EMA Bulletin.*

960   *Encore* (Grove's Dictionaries, New York, 1986–9)

961   *Hazard's Pavilion* (Soc. for the Preservation of Southern California Musical Heritage, Lomita, CA, 1986–9)

962   *Inside CBMR* (Center for Black Music Research at Columbia Coll., Chicago, 1986–7). Continued as *CBMR Digest*

963   *Journal of American Organbuilding* (Amer. Inst. of Organbuilders, Houston, 1986–) Q

964   *Journal SEAMUS* (Soc. for Electro-Acoustic Music in the United States, Los Angeles, 1986–)

965   *Los Angeles Songwriters Showcase* (Hollywood, CA, 1986–99) later, *SongWriters*, then *National Academy of Songwriters Musepaper*

966   *Music Notation News* (Music Notation Modernization Assn, Kirksville, MO, 1986–2004)

967   *Music Research Forum* (Coll.-Conservatory of Music at the U. of Cincinnati, OH, 1986–)

968   *Newsletter of the American Handel Society* (College Park, MD, 1986–)

969   *Opera Fanatic* (Bel Canto Soc., New York, 1986–)

970   *Pitch* (Amer. Festival of Microtonal Music, New York, 1986–90)

971   *Score* (Soc. of Composers & Lyricists, Beverly Hills, 1986–)

972   *Songtalk* (Natl Acad. of Songwriters, Los Angeles, 1986–96)

973   *Strings: the Magazine for Players and Makers of Bowed Instruments* (San Anselmo, CA, 1986–)

974   *Vintage Guitar Magazine* (Bismarck, ND, 1986–)

975   *Violexchange: Quarterly Review of String Literature and Repertoire* (Ann Arbor, MI, 1986–92)

976   *General Music Today* (Soc. for General Music and Natl Assn for Music Educ., Reston, VA, 1987–2002). Continued from *Soundings*

977   *Integral: the Journal of Applied Musical Thought* (Eastman Theory Assn, Rochester, NY, 1987–)

978   *IPAM Newsletter* (Intl Piano Archives at Maryland, College Park, MD, 1987–)

979   *Journal of Black Sacred Music* (Durham, NC, 1987–95)

980   *Journal of Music Theory Pedagogy* (Gail Boyd de Stowlinski Center for Music Theory Pedagogy at the U. of Oklahoma, Norman, OK, 1987–)

981   *Leitmotive* (Wagner Soc. of Northern California, San Francisco, 1987–)

982   *Musletter* (IBM Los Angeles Scientific Center and U. of Southern California School of Music, Los Angeles, 1987–)

983   *New York Opera Newsletter* (Maplewood, NJ, 1987–) later, *Classical Singer*

984   *Old Time Herald: a Magazine dedicated to Old-Time Music* (Durham, NC, 1987–)

985   *Schirmer/News* (New York, 1987–)

986   *Serial, Newsletter of the Friends of the Arnold Schoenberg Inst. at the USC School of Music* (Los Angeles, 1987–9)

987   *Ars musica Denver* (Lamont School of Music at the U. of Denver, 1988–95)

988   *CBMR Digest* (Center for Black Music Research at Columbia Coll., Chicago, 1988–). Continued from *Inside CBMR*

989   *Dirty Linen: the Magazine of Folk, Electric Folk, Traditional and World Music* (Baltimore, 1988–)

990   *Historical Performance* (Cleveland, 1988–94). Continued as *Early Music America*

991   *Modern Keyboard* (New York, 1988–)

992   *Newsletter, American Bach Society* (Rochester, NY, 1988–90)

993   *Opera Monthly* (New York, 1988–94)

994   *Performance Practice Review* (Fallbrook, CA, 1988–97)

995   *SEAMUS Newsletter* (Soc. for Electo-Acoustique Music in the US, Denton, TX, 1988–)

996   *Berklee Today: a Forum for Contemporary Music and Musicians* (Berklee Coll. of Music, Boston, 1989–)

997   *Computers in Music Research* (Wisconsin Center for Music Technology at the U. of Wisconsin School of Music, Madison, WI, 1989–99)

998   *Country America* (Des Moines, IA, 1989–98)

999   *Drums & Drumming* (San Francisco, 1989–91)

1000   *EMA Bulletin* (Early Music America, Cleveland, 1989–2007). Continued from *EMA News*

1001   *Historic Brass Society Journal* (New York, 1989–)

1002   *JazzSouth* (Southern Arts Fed., Atlanta, 1989–)

1003   *Open Ear: a publication dedicated to sound and music in health and education* (Bainbridge Island, WA 1989–) later, *Open Ear Journal*

1004   *Request* (Minneapolis, 1989–)

1005   *Southeastern Journal of Music Education* (U. of Georgia School of Music, Athens, GA, 1989–)

1006   *Traverso: Baroque Flute Newsletter* (Hudson, NY, 1989–)

1007   *Acoustic Guitar* (San Anselmo, CA, 1990–)

1008   *Bass Player* (San Mateo, CA, 1990–)

1009   *Blues Access* (Boulder, CO, 1990–2002)

1010   *Film Score Monthly* (Vineyard Haven, MA, 1990–) later, *Film Score Magazine*, and then *Soundtrack Club*

1011   *Quarterly Journal of Music Teaching and Learning* (Center for Research in Music Learning and Teaching at the U. of Northern Colorado, Greeley, CO, 1990–97)

1012   *Score* (Nashville, TN, 1990–) later, *Gospel Today*

1013   *Bellows* (Friends of the Accordion, Van Nuys, CA, 1991-7)

1014   *California Jazz Now* (Oakland, CA, 1991–) later, *Jazz Now*

1015   *Creem: America's Only Rock and Roll Magazine* (New York, 1991–4). Continued from *Creem Magazine*

1016   *Erzähler* (Symphonic Organ Soc., Dorchester, MA, 1991–6)

1017   *GLSG Newsletter for the Gay and Lesbian Study Group of the American Musicological Society* (Los Angeles, 1991–2005)

1018   *Hymnology Annual* (Hymn Soc. in the US and Canada, Hymn Soc. of GB and Ireland and Internationale Arbeitsgemeinschaft für Hymnologie, Berrien Springs, MI, 1991–)

1019   *International Journal of Arts Medicine* (Intl Arts Medicine Assn and Intl Soc. for Music in Medicine, St Louis, 1991–2000)

1020   *Journal of Music Teacher Education* (Soc. for Music Teacher Educ. of the Music Educators Natl Conference, Reston, VA, 1991–2002)

1021   *Latin Beat Magazine* (Gardena, CA, 1991–)

1022   *Leonardo Music Journal: LMJ; Journal of the International Society for the Arts, Sciences and Technology* (Cambridge, MA, 1991–)

1023   *Mobile Beat: the DJ Magazine* (East Rochester, NY, 1991–)

1024   *New England Organist* (Lawrence, MA, 1991–7) later, *Northeast Organist*

1025   *Banda élastica: rockanrol y otros rollos* (Long Beach, CA, 1992–)

1026   *Beethoven Forum* (Lincoln, NE, 1992–2000; Champaign, IL, 2002–)

1027   *Catholic Music Educator* (Natl Assn of Pastoral Musicians Music Educator Division, Washington DC, 1992–2008)

1028   *Music Reference Services Quarterly* (Binghamton, NY, 1992–)

1029   *Repercussions: Critical & Alternative Viewpoints on Music and Scholarship* (Berkeley, 1992–2007)

1030   *Rhythm Music Magazine* (Cambridge, MA, 1992–) later, *Rhythm*

1031   Sacred Music News & Review (Franklin, TN, 1992–2001)

1032   *Society for the Preservation of Film Music News* (Hollywood, CA, 1992–7) later, *SPFM Newsletter*, then *Film Music Society Newsletter*

1033   *Songwriter's Monthly* (Feasterville, PA, 1992–2001)

1034   *Stentor* (Friends of the Wanamaker Organ, Bryn Mawr, PA, 1992–)

1035   *International Jazz Archives Journal* (Intl Acad. of Jazz Hall of Fame at the U. of Pittsburgh, Pittsburgh, PA, 1993–)

1036   *Jazz Player* (Medfield, MA, 1993–2002)

1037   *Parterre Box: the Queer Opera Zine* (New York, 1993–2001)

1038   *Performing Songwriter* (Nashville, TN, 1993–)

1039   *Philosophy of Music Education Review* (Music Educ. Dept at Indiana U., Bloomington, IN, 1993–)

1040   *Teaching Music* (Music Educators Natl Conference, Reston, VA, 1993–)

1041   *Women of Note Quarterly* (Pullman, WA, 1993–)

1042   *Woodwind Quarterly* (Maple Valley, WA, 1993–2001; 2003–) later, *Journal of Musical Instrument Technology*

1043   *Vibe* (Boulder, CO, 1993–)

1044   *20th Century Music* (San Anselmo, CA, 1994–) later, *21st Century Music*

1045   *ASCAP Playback* (Amer. Soc. of Composers, Authors and Publishers, New York, 1994–) later, *Playback*

1046   *Blues revue* (West Union, WV, 1994–)

1047   *Fiddler Magazine* (Los Altos, CA, 1994–)

1048   *ROCKRGRL: No Beauty Tips or Guilt Trips* (San Mateo, CA, 1994–2005)

1049   *Sondheim Review* (Chicago, 1994–)

1050   *TuTTi* (Coconut Grove, FL, 1994–)

1051   *5-String Quarterly* (Austin, 1995–6)

1052   *Bach Perspectives* (Amer. Bach Soc., Lincoln, NE: U. of Nebraska Press, 1995–)

1053   *Early Music America* (Cleveland, OH, 1995–)

1054   *Harmony* (Symphony Orchestra Inst., Evanston, IL, 1995–2003)

1055   *IAWM Journal* (Intl Alliance for Women in Music, Indiana, PA, 1995–)

1056   *Journal of Seventeenth-Century Music* (Cambridge, MA, 1995–)

1057   *Lenox Avenue* (Center for Black Music Research at Columbia Coll., Chicago, 1995–9)

1058   *Music Theory Online* (Santa Barbara, 1995–)

1059   *Antiphon, Journal for Catholic Liturgy* (Salt Lake City, 1996–)

1060   *Cross Accent* (Assn of Lutheran Church Musicians, Worcester, MA, 1996–)

1061   *Gig Magazine* (NY, 1997–2003)

1062   *Jazz improv* (Jenkintown, PA, 1997–)

1063   *Organized Sound: An International Journal of Music and Technology* (New York, 1997–)

1064   *Women & Music, Journal of Gender and Culture* (Intl Alliance for Women in Music, Washington DC, 1997–2008; Lincoln, NE, 2008–)

1065   *Studies in Penderecki* (Princeton, 1998–2003)

1066   *Echo, a music-centered journal* (Los Angeles, 1999–)

1067   *Film Music: The Professional Voice of Music for Film and Television* (Glendale, CA, 1999–)

1068   *Free-Reed Journal* (Center for the Study of Free-Reed Instruments, the Graduate Center, CUNY, Hillsdale, NY, 1999–2002)

1069   *Journal of Music in China* (Los Angeles, 1999–2002)

1070   *Country Music Annual* (Lexington, KY, 2000–02)

1071   *MEIEA/Music & Entertainment Industry Educators Association* (New Orleans, 2000–)

1072   *Journal of Technology in Music Learning* (Tallahassee, FL, 2001–)

1073   *Journal of Texas Music History* (San Marcos, TX, 2001–)

1074   *Naturlaut: the Quarterly Journal of the Chicago Mahlerites* (Chicago, 2001–)

1075   *Pendragon Review* (Hillsdale, NY, 2001–3)

1076   *Remix* (Emeryville, CA, 2001–)

1077   *Journal of Film Music* (Claremont, CA, 2002–)

1078   *Music Education Technology* (Overland Park, KS, 2003–)

1079   *Colloquium, Music, Worship, Arts* (Yale Institute of Sacred Music, New Haven, CT, 2004–)

1080   *Journal of Schenkerian Studies* (Center for Schenkerian Studies, Denton, TX, 2005–)

1081   *VSA Papers* (Violin Society of America, Poughkeepsie, NY, 2005–)

1082   *Activate!* (Dayton, OH, 2006–)

1083   *Empirical Musicology Review* (Columbus, OH, 2006–)

1084   *Jazzed: the Jazz Educator's Magazine* (Needham, MA, 2006–)

1085   *Journal for the Society of American Music* (Society for American Music/Cambridge UP, NY, 2007–). See also *American Music* (922).

1086   *Music & Politics* (Santa Barbara, CA, 2007–)

1087   *Music and the Moving Image* (Champaign, IL, 2008–)

3. Index.

1/1, 947

5-String Quarterly, 1051

17th Century Music, 933

19th Century Music, 875

20th Century Music, 1044

21st Century Music, 1044

ACA Bulletin, 557

AIVS Newsletter, 866

AMICA Bulletin, 739

AMS Newsletter, 805

ARSC Newsletter, 876

ASCAP in Action, 768

ASCAP Playback, 1045

ASCAP Today, 768

ASSW News, 629

A.T.G. Bulletin, 607

Absolute Sound, 820

Abstracts of Papers read at the Annual Meeting of the American Musicological Society, 553

Accordion World, 549

Accordion and Guitar World, 549

Acoustic Guitar, 1007

Activate, 1082

Advertiser, 44

Aeolian Quarterly, 288

AGMAzine, 654

Albany Musical Bulletin, 58

All the Arts, 453

Allegretto, 281

Allegro, 627, 956

Allegro: a Magazine of Music and Literature, 382

Amateur: a Repository of Music, Literature, and Art, 80

América musical, 163

American Art Journal, 45

American Bandsman, 383

American Brahms Society Newsletter, 921

American Choir, 282

American Choral Review, 706

American Composers Alliance Bulletin, 557

American Ensemble, 887

American Federation of Musicians: Official Proceedings, 271

American Guild of Organists Quarterly, 698

American Harp Journal, 677, 767

American Home Journal, 289

American Journal of Music and Musical Visitor, 12

American Liszt Society Journal, 882

American Liszt Society, Inc., Newsletter, 932

DEBORAH CAMPANA

Perkins, Carl (Lee) (*b* Tiptonville, TN, 9 April 1932; *d* Jackson, TN, 19 Jan 1998). Rockabilly guitarist, songwriter, and singer. He was born to the only white sharecropping family in Tiptonville, Tennessee. As a child he was influenced tremendously by the radio broadcasts of the *Grand Ole Opry* and the blues and gospel songs that African Americans sang while working. A black neighbor taught him to play guitar, and Perkins formed a band with his two brothers as a teenager. In 1954 he heard Elvis Presley's rendition of the bluegrass classic "Blue Moon of Kentucky." Because it sounded much like his own music, Perkins drove to Memphis to audition for Presley's producer, Sam Phillips, at Sun Records. Impressed with his originality and energy, Phillips agreed to record him. In 1955 Perkins recorded the song "Blue Suede Shoes," which became an anthem of the growing rockabilly genre and Sun's first million selling record. It was the first single to simultaneously top the Billboard pop, R&B, and country charts.

In March 1956, while en route to New York for his first national television appearance, Perkins was involved in a near-fatal automobile accident. While he recovered, Presley signed with RCA Records and released his own version of "Blue Suede Shoes." Although Perkins recorded again for Sun, none of his songs achieved the same widespread success. He instead flourished as a songwriter, penning hits for Patsy Cline, Johnny Cash, and Bob Dylan, among others. In 1987 he was inducted into the Rock and Roll Hall of Fame and received the Academy of Country Music's Lifetime Achievement Award.

SELECTED RECORDINGS
Carl Perkins: the Essential Sun Collection (Recall, 1999); *Carl Perkins & Friends: Blue Suede Shoes, a Rockabilly Session* (Snapper Classics, 2006)

BIBLIOGRAPHY
C. Escott with M. Hawkins: *Good Rockin' Tonight: Sun Records and the Birth of Rock n' Roll* (New York, 1991)
C. Morrison: *Go, Cat, Go! Rockabilly Music and its Makers* (Champaign, IL, 1996)
C. Perkins with D. McGee: *Go, Cat, Go! The Life and Times of Carl Perkins, the King of Rockabilly* (New York, 1996)

J. MICHAEL BUTLER

Perkins, Charles C(allahan) (*b* Boston, MA, 1 March 1823; *d* Windsor, VT, 25 Aug 1886). Art and music historian and arts advocate. Born into a wealthy family, he graduated from Harvard University in 1843 and went to Rome and Paris to study drawing and painting. After returning to Boston in 1849 he turned to music and studied composition in Leipzig during the years 1851–4. A third trip to Europe, to Florence in 1855, convinced him to focus on historical writing. He soon published two important volumes, *The Tuscan Sculptors* (London, 1864) and *The Italian Sculptors* (London, 1868), each illustrated with his own drawings. Because of these volumes he became the first American selected to the French Académie des Beaux-Arts. After returning to Boston he assumed a leading role in the founding of the Museum of Fine Arts.

Perkins was active in the Harvard Musical Association and the HANDEL AND HAYDN SOCIETY. He participated in concerts given by both groups and conducted some of the Handel and Haydn Society concerts. He served as its president from 1876 to 1886. He had completed the first chapters of a history of the Handel and Haydn Society when he was thrown from a carriage and died instantly. The history was completed by John S. Dwight.

BIBLIOGRAPHY
C.C. Perkins and J.S. Dwight: *History of the Handel and Haydn Society of Boston*, i (Boston, 1883–93)
Obituary, *Proceedings of the American Academy of Arts and Sciences*, xxii/May–Dec (1886), 534–39

MICHAEL BROYLES

Perkins, Henry S(outhwick) (*b* Stockbridge, VT, 20 March 1833; *d* Chicago, IL, 20 Jan 1914). Educator and composer. He studied at the Boston Music School (1857–c1861), observed teaching methods in Europe, and studied singing with Pierre Wartel in Paris and Luigi Vannuccini in Florence (1875–6). He was principal of the Iowa State Normal Academy of Music (1867–72) and professor of music at the state university (1867), both in Iowa City, and director of the Kansas Normal Academy of Music in Leavenworth (1870–74). These academies consisted of multiple sessions of six to eight weeks per year. He also conducted over 200 musical workshops known as conventions, and taught in normal schools in eight states during this period. Perkins was a founder and the first life member of the Music Teachers National Association (1876), and an organizer and first president of the Illinois Music Teachers Association (1886–96). He founded and became director of the Chicago National College of Music in 1891, with which he was associated for the remainder of his life. He composed a considerable amount of music, mostly songs and hymns, published as sheet music and in approximately 40 collections. His father, Orson Perkins (1802–82), was a singing school teacher in Vermont.

BIBLIOGRAPHY
R.D. Comstock: *Contributions of the Orson Perkins Family to Nineteenth Century American Music Education* (diss., U. of Iowa, 1970)

RAYMOND D. COMSTOCK/PATRICK M. JONES

Perkins, John MacIvor (*b* St. Louis, MO, 2 Aug 1935; *d* St. Louis, MO, 12 Nov 2010). Composer and teacher. He was educated at Harvard University (BA 1958) and the New England Conservatory (BMus 1958); he also studied with NADIA BOULANGER in Paris, Roberto Gerhard and Edmund Rubbra in London (1958–9), and ARTHUR BERGER, HAROLD SHAPERO, and IRVING FINE at Brandeis University (MFA 1962). He taught at the University of Chicago (1962–5), Harvard (1965–70), and Washington University, St. Louis (1970–2001); at the last he served as chairman of the music department. After his retirement he continued as professor emeritus at Washington University, teaching master classes and composing and directing his own works. His honors include a Woodrow Wilson National Fellowship (1959–61), commissions from the Fromm Music Foundation, the St. Louis Bicentennial, and the Smithsonian Bicentennial, and an award from the National Institute of Arts and Letters (1966).

Perkins composed about 35 major works. He frequently used serial procedures to generate pitch and interval successions. In the course of a work, musical events, such as thematic structures or sections of textural density, often occur at different rates of speed, and textures are subjected to modifications of density (as in *Music for 13 Players*). Perkins's compositions are notable for virtuoso instrumental writing and for their sonorous integrity. His work with interwoven or contrasting tempo characteristics resulted in in his authorship of theoretical studies such as "Note Values" (*PNM*, iii/1, 1965, p.47–57) and in articles on the music of Luigi Dallapiccola and Berger. Some of his compositions were recorded by CRI and re-released on CD.

SELECTED WORKS LIST

Stage: Divertimento, chbr op, 1958; Andrea del Sarto, 1980
Inst: Canons, 9 insts, 1958; Fantasy, Intermezzo, Variations, pf, 1959–62, orch, 1961; 5 Miniatures, str qt, 1962; Qnt Variations, 1962; Caprice, pf, 1963; Music for Carillon, 1963; Music for Orch, 1964; Music for 13 Players, 1964–6; Music for Brass, 1965; Cadenza, 1978; Lyric Variations, vn, pf, 1989; After and Before, orch, 2004
Vocal: Strike, Churl, high v, pf, 1959; 8 songs, 1956–62; 3 Studies, chorus, 1958; Alleluia, 1971; After a Silence: Alpha, 1976

BIBLIOGRAPHY

C. Spies: "John M. Perkins: Quintet Variations," *PNM*, ii/1 (1963), 67-76
B. Boretz and E. Cone, eds.: *Perspectives on Notation and Performance* (New York, 1976)
H. Pollack: *Harvard Composers: Walter Piston and his Students, from Elliott Carter to Frederic Rzewski* (Metuchen, NJ, 1992)

RICHARD SWIFT/JOANNA R. SMOLKO

Perkins, Pinetop [Joseph William; Joe Willie] (*b* Belzoni, MS, 7 July 1913; *d* Austin, TX, 21 March 2011). Blues pianist and singer. Professionally active by the late 1920s, he was a fixture in his hometown early in the next decade, which gave him the chance to appear on the radio with the slide guitarist Robert Nighthawk. Although his first instrument was the guitar, Perkins switched to piano after an injury in the 1940s. He played alongside Sonny Boy Williamson on the King Biscuit Time radio show in Arkansas for three years and also accompanied B.B. King in Memphis. In the early 1950s he began a long association with Earl Hooker; the two recorded "Pinetop Boogie Woogie" (Sun, 1953), which brought them increased renown. After a brief retirement from music in the 1960s, Perkins was convinced to return to performing in 1968. He took the coveted position of pianist with Muddy Waters' band the following year and remained with the ensemble until 1980. The band morphed into the Legendary Blues Band that year and began recording regularly on the label Rounder; it achieved significant success, including several Grammy nominations. Perkins' first major solo release was *After Hours* (Blind Pig, 1988), on which his flamboyant piano style, deeply anchored in Delta Blues traditions, won him critical acclaim. He continued to release albums throughout the 1990s and into the next century. At the age of 91 he recorded *Last of the Great Mississippi Delta Bluesmen: Live in Dallas* with other blues legends Henry Townsend, Robert Lockwood Jr., and David Edwards; released by Blue Shoe Project in 2007, it earned Perkins his first Grammy Award.

JONAS WESTOVER

Perkins, (David) Walton (*b* Rome, NY, 16 Nov 1847; *d* Chicago, IL, 8 Feb 1929). Pianist and educator. He studied with S.B. MILLS and ALFRED H. PEASE, then with Theodor Kullak and Anton Rubinstein in Berlin. His debut as a pianist was in New York in 1869; he remained active as a pianist until 1887, when he became a teacher. Having settled in Chicago, he helped William H. Sherwood found the Sherwood School of Music in 1897 and served as its associate director until 1901. From 1907 until his death he was president of the Chicago Conservatory of Music. He also composed piano pieces, songs, and choral works, and contributed to the journal *Music Magazine*.

R. ALLEN LOTT

Perkinson, Coleridge-Taylor (*b* Winston-Salem, NC, 14 June 1932; *d* Chicago, IL, 9 March 2004). Composer and conductor. Perkinson was named after the African-British composer Samuel Coleridge-Taylor. He studied composition with VITTORIO GIANNINI and CHARLES MILLS at the Manhattan School (BM 1953, MM 1954), and with EARL KIM at Princeton University, and conducting at the Berkshire Music Center (1954). He studied at the Salzburg Mozarteum in the summer of 1960 and at the Netherlands Radio Union in Hilversum, where he worked with conductor DEAN DIXON in the summers of 1960, 1962, and 1963. Perkinson held conducting positions with the Dessoff Choirs (1956–7), the Brooklyn Community SO (1959–62) and the Symphony of the New World, of which he was co-founder (1965–75). He also appeared as guest conductor of the Dallas SO, the Bogotá PO, the Albany SO), and the North Carolina SO. Perkinson also served as music director of the American Theater Lab (1966–7, with Jerome Robbins) and the Alvin Ailey American Dance Theater (1968, 1978). His music draws on elements of Baroque counterpoint, American Romanticism, blues, spirituals, and rhythmic ingenuity.

WORKS

Ballets: Ode to Otis, 1971; Carmen (after Bizet) 1972–3; Forces of Rhythm, 1972–3; Beber, 1982; To Bird with Love, 1984
Inst: Variations and Fugue on The Ash Grove, 1950s; Str Qt no.1 "Calvary," 1952; Scherzo, 1953; Toccata, 1953; Grass, pf, str, percussion, 1956; Sinfonietta no.1, 1956; Commentary, orch, 1964; Sonatina, perc, 1965; Pf Sonata, 1965; Blues Forms, vn, 1972; Lamentations: a Black Folk Song Suite, 1973; Pf Sonata no.2 "Statements," 1975
Many vocal works, incl.: Elizabethan Love Lyrics, 1952; Song to Spring, late 1960s; 13 Love Songs in Jazz Settings, late 1960s; Fredome-Freedom, 1970; The Legacy, 1982
Incid. music: To Damascus, 1960; Songs of the Lusitanian Bogey, 1967; God is a Guess What?, 1968; Malcachon, 1969; Man Better Man, 1969; The Great MacDaddy, 1974; The Emperor Jones, 1984
Film scores: Crossroads Africa, 1962; Montgomery to Memphis, 1969; The McMasters, 1969; Happy Birthday Mrs. Craig, 1971; A Warm December, 1972; Together for Days, 1972; Amazing Grace, 1974; The Education of Sonny Carson, 1974; Thomasine & Bushrod, 1974; Freedom Road, 1979; Boardwalk, late 1970s; Bearden on Bearden, 1980; 10 television series, incl. A Woman Called Moses, 1978

CARMAN MOORE/ANYA LAURENCE

Perle, George (*b* Bayonne, NJ, 6 May 1915; *d* New York, NY, 23 Jan 2009). Composer and theorist. He studied composition with WESLEY LA VIOLETTE (1934–8) and ERNST KRENEK (early 1940s) and was awarded a BA at DePaul University (1938) and a PhD at New York University (1956). A member of the faculty at the University of Louisville (1949–57), the University of California, Davis (1957–61), and Queens College, CUNY (1961–84), he also held visiting professorships at Yale University (1965–6), the University of Southern California (summer 1965), SUNY, Buffalo (1971–2), the University of Pennsylvania (1976, 1980), Columbia University (1979, 1983), the University of California, Berkeley (Ernest Bloch Professor, 1989), and New York University (1994). He was elected to the American Academy of Arts and Letters (1978) and the National Academy of Arts and Sciences (1985), and his awards included the Pulitzer Prize in music (1986, for Wind Quintet no.4), the MacArthur Fellowship (1986), and two Guggenheim Fellowships (1966, 1974). His book *The Operas of Alban Berg* (Berkeley, 1980) won the AMS Otto Kinkeldey Award and the ASCAP Deems Taylor Award (1981). His articles on Webern and Berg also won Deems Taylor awards in, respectively, 1975 and 1978. He was composer-in-residence at Tanglewood Music Center (1967, 1980, 1987), at the Marlboro Music Festival (1993), and with the San Francisco SO (1989–91). He was elected to the Institute of the American Academy and Institute of Arts and Letters in 1978.

In the 1930s Perle was among the first American composers to be attracted by the music and thought of Schoenberg, Berg, and Webern. His interest, however, was not so much in the 12-note system itself as in the idea of a generalized systematic approach to dodecaphonic composition. Using some of the fundamental concepts of the 12-note system, such as set and inversion, he developed an approach to composition that attempts to incorporate such 12-note ideas with some of the basic kinds of hierarchical distinction found in tonal practice, such as the concept of a key as a primary point of reference. Originally referred to as "the 12-tone modal system," his system of "12-note tonality" developed continuously from 1939 (and in collaboration with Paul Lansky, 1969–73). In simple terms it is an attempt to create useful distinctions and differentiations in a 12-tone context by defining functional characteristics of pitch-class collections, in terms of the intervals formed by component pairs of notes, on the one hand, and the properties of these same pairs with respect to axes of symmetry, points about which they are symmetrically disposed, on the other. In an abstract sense these two concepts are roughly analogous to notions of mode and key in tonal music.

The harmonic vocabulary of 12-note tonality is exclusively derived from "cycle sets," ordered 12-note statements of complete collections of symmetrically related dyads. The cyclic set differs from the general 12-note series not only in its structure but also in its use: akin to a scale in diatonic tonality, its function is referential, not literally determining note-to-note motion on the compositional surface. Paired forms of the cyclic sets generate arrays of chords that are related to one another by different types of symmetry. This approach was anticipated in some works by Berg (the first movement of the *Lyric Suite* and Act 2 scene i of *Lulu*) and Béla Bartók (the fourth and fifth quartets) in their use of symmetrical relations as a basis for their harmonic language. Perle's approach does not define explicit procedures for composition but rather outlines a large and highly structured network of pitch-class and formal relations which can then serve as points of reference for compositional development. In this sense, too, it is like tonal composition in that the composer's "system" is a general guide to a musical language and a given composition constructs a unique interpretation of that language.

Although most of Perle's compositions to 1967 and all since then were based on this approach, Perle also wrote works that he described as

"freely" or "intuitively" conceived, combining various serial procedures with melodically generated tone centers, intervallic cells, symmetrical formations, etc. A rhythmic concept, or rather ideal, toward which I progressed in these and other works was that of a beat, variable in duration but at the same time as tangible and coherent as the beat in classical music, and of an integration between the larger rhythmic dimensions and the minimal metric units.

These works include the Quintet for Strings (1958), three wind quintets (1959, 1960, 1967), and a series of monophonic works for solo instruments (1942–65). A consistent thread that runs through these pieces, as well as later works, is the construction of rhythmic relations through inter-tempo equivalences: e.g. triplet eighth notes in one tempo might equal quarter notes in another. Although this was a widely used technique, Perle used it in a highly personal way, which has the effect of creating a general feeling of continuous rubato, adding a subtle flexibility to the underlying rhythmic sense. Interrelations of meter, rhythm, tempo, phrase structure, and formal design are basic to his compositional thinking.

In comparison with much music of the time, the sound of Perle's music and the manner in which his musical ideas unfold are usually straightforward and relatively uncomplicated. His music eschews the veneer of the avant-garde and what he considered the wrongheaded association of musical complexity with perceptual difficulty. The complexities that concerned him were those arising from the many levels on which his pitch, pitch-class, and motivic relations interacted and interrelated, and for him difficulties were only in making these relations as interesting and understandable as possible. In many of his compositions a few relatively simple musical ideas appear in different ways and contexts so that the character and quality of these ideas become richer in the process.

Perle's writings on 20th-century music, particularly that of Schoenberg, Berg, Webern, Bartók, and Skryabin, have contributed much to a wider and deeper understanding of it. His work on Skryabin has made an important contribution in showing how analytical insights may be derived from idiosyncratic features of a composer's notation, and his book *Serial Composition and Atonality* has become a standard text. His most extensive work was on the music of Berg and revealed in great depth and detail the richness and subtlety of Berg's work, dispelling popular notions that Berg's music, in contrast with that of Schoenberg and Webern, is arbitrary in its use of 12-note and serial procedures. After studying the materials for the incomplete third act of *Lulu*, in 1963, he published a series of articles which conclusively demonstrated that the opera could be accurately completed and prepared the way for the publication of the complete opera in 1985. In January 1977 Perle discovered a score of Berg's *Lyric Suite* which had been annotated by the composer. The annotations unfolded a secret program inspired by Berg's love for Hanna Fuchs-Robettin, the wife of a Prague industrialist and sister of Franz Werfel. Her initials combine with Berg's to give the basic cell of the work, B–F–A–B♭ (in German, H–F–A–B). This discovery, together with Berg's letters to Hanna Fuchs-Robettin, uncovered by Perle at the same time and spanning the period from 1925 to Berg's death in 1935, refuted the description of Berg's life and character that had been authorized by his widow and accepted by every biographer of the composer.

Perle's work is deeply conservative in that his main effort was to build a musical world whose logic and power is as consistent as that of traditional tonal practice. While this was also Schoenberg's aim in constructing the 12-note system, for Perle there was an intolerable contradiction in Schoenberg's concept of the 12-note series as "invented to substitute for some of the unifying and formative advantages of scale and tonality" at the same time as it "functions in the manner of a motive." Perle's cyclic sets act solely as the basis of the harmonic and contrapuntal syntax of his music: they do not function as motifs. Although initially inspired by the Vienna school, his later writings (*The Listening Composer*) reveal a close connection with Skryabin, Bartók, and Stravinsky as well. Perle argues that the seemingly disparate aspects of post-tonal music share structural elements that derive from a common source—inversional and cyclic symmetry inherent in the 12-note scale—and that this implies a system of relations as coherent as that of diatonic tonality.

WORKS
(selective list)

ORCHESTRAL
Solemn Procession, band, 1947; 3 Movts for Orch, 1960; Serenade no.1, va, chbr orch, 1962; 6 Bagatelles, 1965; Vc Conc., 1966; Serenade no.2, 11 insts, 1968; Concertino, pf, wind, timp, 1979; A Short Sym., 1980; Serenade no.3, pf, chbr orch, 1983; Dance Fantasy, 1986; New Fanfares, brass ens, 1987; Lyric Intermezzo, 15 players, 1987; Sinfonietta I, 1987; Pf Conc., no.1, 1990; Sinfonietta II, 1990; Adagio, 1992; Pf Conc. no.2, 1992; Transcendental Modulations, 1993

CHAMBER
For 6 insts: For Pf and Wind, fl, eng hn, cl, hn, bn, pf, 1988; Critical Moments, fl + pic, B♭ cl + E♭ cl + b cl, vn, vc, pf, perc, 1996; Critical Moments 2, fl + picc, B♭ cl + E♭ cl + b cl, vn, vc, pf, perc, 1998
5 insts: Str Qnt, 1958; 4 Wind Qnts no.1, 1959; no.2, 1960; no.3, 1967; no.4, 1984; Sonata a cinque, b trbn, A cl + E♭ cl + b cl, vn, vc, pf, 1986; Nightsong, fl, cl, vn, vc, pf, 1988; Duos, hn, str qt, 1995
4 insts: Str Qt no.2, 1942, unpubd; Str Qt no.5, 1960, rev. 1967; Str Qt no.7, 1973; Sonata a quattro, fl, cl, vn, vc, 1982; Windows of Order (Str Qt no.8), 1988; Brief Encounters (Str Qt no.9), 1998
2 insts: Lyric Piece, vc, pf, 1946; Sonata quasi una fantasia, cl, pf, 1972; Sonata, vc, pf, 1985; Sonata for Vc and Pf, 1985; Tryptich, vn, pf, 2003

SOLO INSTRUMENT
Str: Sonata, va, 1942; Hebrew Melodies, vc, 1945; Sonata, vc, 1947; Sonata no.1, vn, 1959; Monody II, db, 1962; Sonata no.2, vn, 1963; Solo Partita, vn, va, 1965

Winds: 3 Sonatas, cl, 1943; Monody I, fl, 1960; 3 Inventions, bn, 1962; A Flourish for Barry Brook, tpt/cl, 1989; Bassoon Music, 2004
Pf: Pantomime, Interlude, and Fugue, 1937; Little Suite, 1939, unpubd; Modal Suite, 1940; 6 Preludes, 1946; Sonata, 1950; Short Sonata, 1964; Toccata, 1969; Suite in C, 1970; Fantasy-Variations, 1971; 6 Etudes, 1976; Ballade, 1981; 6 New Etudes, 1984; Sonatina, 1986; Lyric Intermezzo, 1987; Phantasyplay, 1995; 6 Celebratory Inventions, 1995; Chansons cachées, 1997; Musical Offerings, left hand, 1998; 9 Bagatelles, 1999

VOCAL
2 Rilke Songs, Mez, pf, 1941; "And so the Swans …," a cappella chorus, 1961; Sonnets to Orpheus, a cappella chorus, 1974; Songs of Praise and Lamentation, chorus, orch, 1974; 13 Dickinson Songs, S, pf, 1977–8

INCIDENTAL MUSIC
The Birds (Aristophanes, trans. W. Arrowsmith), solo vv, chorus, fl + pic, E♭ cl + bar sax, tpt, trbn, va, cel + hpd + hmn + pf, perc, 1961

Principal publishers: Presser, Boelke-Bomart, Gunmar, ECS Publishing

WRITINGS
"Evolution of the Tone-row: the Twelve-tone Modal System," *MR*, ii (1941), 273–87; It. trans. in Boletín latíno-americano de música, v (1941), 421–34
"Twelve-tone Tonality," *MMR*, lxxiii (1943), 175–9
"The Harmonic Problem in Twelve-tone Music," *MR*, xv (1954), 257–67
"The Possible Chords in Twelve-tone Music," *The Score*, no.9 (1954), 54–63
"The Music of Miriam Gideon," *Bulletin of American Composers Alliance*, vii/4 (1958), 2–6
"Theory and Practice in Twelve-tone Music (Stadlen Reconsidered)," *The Score*, no.25 (1959), 58–64
"Atonality and the Twelve-note System in the United States," *The Score*, no.27 (1960), 51–9; Sp. trans. in *Buenos Aires musical*, xiv (1959), 40–51
Serial Composition and Atonality: an Introduction to the Music of Schoenberg, Berg, Webern (Berkeley, 1962, 6/1991)
Twelve-tone Tonality (Berkeley, 1977, enlarged 2/1996)
"Berg, Alban," *Grove6*
with P. Lansky: "Atonality," "Twelve-Note Composition," *Grove6*
The Listening Composer (Berkeley, 1990)
"Symmetry, the Twelve-tone Scale, and Tonality," *CMR*, vi/2 (1992), 81–96
The Right Notes: Twenty-three Selected Essays by George Perle on Twentieth-century Music (Stuyvesant, NY, 1995)

BIBLIOGRAPHY
Grove7 ("Perle, George") [includes list of writings]
H. Weinberg: "The Music of George Perle," *American Composers Alliance Bulletin*, x/3 (1962), 6–11
L. Kraft: "The Music of George Perle," *MQ*, lvii (1971), 444–65
P. Lansky: *Affine Music* (diss., Princeton U., 1973)
B. Saylor: "A New Work by George Perle," *MQ*, lxi (1975), 471–5
O. Knussen: "George Perle, Composer," *Tempo*, no.137 (1981), 38–40
R. Swift: "A Tonal Analog: the Tone-centered Music of George Perle," *PNM*, xxi (1982–3), 257–84
M. Boriskin: "Six New Etudes: a Strand of Perle's," *Clavier*, xxvi/4 (1987), 11–15
D. Miller: "Perle on Perle," *George Perle* (Englewood, NJ, 1987), 5–22 [interview]
J. Carson: "A Talk with George Perle on Music History, Tonality, and Composing," *Strings*, iv (1989), 40–43
P. Lansky: "The Listening Composer," *George Perle: a Catalog of Works* (Boston, 1991), 6–7
E. Antokoletz: "Twelve-tone Tonality," *Twentieth-century Music* (Englewood Cliffs, NJ, 1992), 426–7
P. Carrabré: *Twelve-tone Tonality and the Music of George Perle* (diss., CUNY, 1993)
International Journal of Musicology, iv (1995) [Perle 80th birthday Festschrift issue; incl. E. Antokoletz: "George Perle's *The Listening Composer*," 13–23; J. Smith: "George and the Dragon: Reflections from a Chopin Etude," 25–43; J. Carr: "George Perle and the Computer: an Uneasy Alliance," 207–15; C. Porter: "Five to Four Complexities in George Perle's *Nocturne*," 217–29; P. Carrabré: "Music as Linguistic

Analog," 231–9; P. Lansky: "Being and Going," 241–52; J. Leleu: "La notion de 'Background Structure' chez George Perle: de l'étude du langage musical au déchiffrement des oeuvres," 253–90, Eng. trans. in *International Journal of Musicology*, v (1996), 287–322; D. Pitt: "What is Tonality?," 291–300; D. Headlam: "Tonality and Twelve-tone Tonality: the Recent Music of George Perle," 301–33]

S. Rosenhaus: *Harmonic Motion in George Perle's Wind Quintet no.4* (diss., New York U., 1995)

M. Graubart: "The Writings of George Perle," *Tempo*, no.196 (1996), 37–41

A. Whittall: "Double Dealer," *MT*, cxxxvii (1996), 25–7

M. Steinberg: *The Concerto* (New York, 1998), 337–42

G.C. Foley: "Arrays and K-nets: Transformational Relationships within Perle's Twelve Tone Tonality," *Indiana Theory Review*, xxiii (2002), 69–97

D. Headlam: "Perle's Cyclic Sets and Klumpenhouwer Networks: a Response," *Music Theory Spectrum*, xxiv/2 (2002), 246–56

P. Lambert: "Isographies and Some Klumpenhouwer Networks they Involve," *Music Theory Spectrum*, xxiv/2 (2002), 165–95

D. Lewin: "Thoughts on Klumpenhouwer Networks and Perle-Lansky Cycles," *Music Theory Spectrum*, xxiv/2 (2002), 196–230

P. Stoecker: "Klumpenhouwer Networks, Trichords, and Axial Isography," *Music Theory Spectrum* xxiv/2 (2002), 231–45

D. Schober: *George Perle's Six New Etudes: Symmetry, Audibility, and the Rhetoric of Reconciliation* (diss., U. of Michigan, 2004)

C. Nam: *George Perle's Bagatelle no.1: a Study of Design, Pitch Relations, and Metric Pattern* (diss., U. of Houston, 2006)

E. Antokoletz: "From Bartók and Berg to Perle: a New Concept of Tonality and Means of Progression as Shown in no.5 of George Perle's *Thirteen Dickinson Songs*," *Theory and Practice*, xxxiii (2008), 121

D. Headlam: "George Perle: an Appreciation," *PNM*, lxvii/2 (2009), 159–95

PAUL LANSKY/R

Perlis, Vivian (*b* Brooklyn, NY, 26 April 1928). Musicologist and librarian. She was educated at the University of Michigan (BM 1949, MM 1952), where she studied the history of music and also piano and harp. A graduate student in musicology at Columbia University (1962–4), she taught the history of music at several colleges in New England before becoming a reference librarian at Yale University in 1967. There she founded the Oral History of American Music project and has continued as its director. The project is an extensive repository on tape and videotape of source material on composers and other major figures in American music. Perlis's other activities have included lecturing and teaching for the American studies program and the Yale music department. She has collaborated on several recordings and television documentaries, the latter including "Memories of Eubie" (1980) on the jazz pianist Eubie Blake. Her work represents an imaginative and timely contribution to the investigation of the history of American music.

WRITINGS
"Ives and Oral History," *Notes*, xxviii (1971–2), 629–42

Charles Ives Remembered: an Oral History (New Haven, CT, 1974)

ed., with H.W. Hitchcock: *An Ives Celebration: Brooklyn, NY and New Haven, CT, 1974*

"The Futurist Music of Leo Ornstein," *Notes*, xxxi (1974–5), 735–50

Two Men for Modern Music: E. Robert Schmitz and Herman Langinger (Brooklyn, NY, 1978)

"Charles Ives: Victorian Gentleman or American Folk Hero?," *Folk Music and Modern Sound*, ed. W. Ferris and M.L. Hart (Jackson, MS, 1982), 141–50

ed.: *Charles Ives Papers* (New Haven, CT, 1983)

with A. Copland: *Copland* (New York, 1984–9) [Copland's autobiography]

"Monumenta Americana Revisited," *A Celebration of American Music: Words and Music in Honor of H. Wiley Hitchcock*, ed. R.A. Crawford, R.A. Lott, and C.J. Oja (Ann Arbor, MI, 1990), 439–48

"Dear Aaron, Dear Lenny: a Friendship in Letters," *Aaron Copland and his World*, eds. C.J. Oja and J. Tick (Princeton, NJ, 2005), 151–78

"Aaron Copland and John Kirkpatrick: 'Dear John, can you help me out?'," *Copland Connotations: Studies and Interviews*, ed. P. Dickinson (Woodbridge, UK, 2002)

with L. Van Cleve: *Composers' Voices from Ives to Ellington: an Oral History of American Music* (2005)

PAULA MORGAN/R

Perlman, Itzhak (*b* Tel-Aviv, Palestine [now Israel], 31 Aug 1945). Israeli violinist. He initially taught himself to play, first on a toy fiddle and then on a child's violin. At four he was stricken with poliomyelitis which left him permanently disabled. During a year's convalescence he continued to practice and he then entered the Tel-Aviv Academy of Music to study with Rivka Goldgart. By the time he gave his first solo recital, at ten, he had already made a number of appearances with the Ramat-Gan and Broadcasting Orchestras. In 1958 he played twice on television for *The Ed Sullivan Show* in New York and decided to remain there, making a nationwide US tour and entering the Juilliard School of Music to study with DOROTHY DELAY and IVAN GALAMIAN. He made his Carnegie Hall debut in 1963 and the following year won the Leventritt Memorial Award. In 1965 he toured his native country and in the 1965–6 and 1966–7 seasons he visited most of the major North American cities. In the 1967–8 season he made major debuts in Europe, including in London and Paris, and since then he has been recognized not just as the finest violinist of his generation but as one of the greatest musical talents to emerge since World War II.

Although he has to play sitting down, Perlman is an immensely strong violinist with no discernible flaws in his technique; he produces a big tone of great beauty and phrasing with immense breadth when the music demands it. His numerous recordings include the Bach solo sonatas and partitas, the Paganini caprices and much of the virtuoso repertory, as well as profound interpretations of Bach's Double Concerto and Mozart's Sinfonia concertante with Pinchas Zukerman; the Mozart sonatas with Daniel Barenboim; the Beethoven and Brahms concertos with Barenboim conducting; the Beethoven sonatas with Vladimir Ashkenazy; and the Berg and Stravinsky concertos with Seiji Ozawa. In chamber music he has often been heard, in the concert hall or on recordings, with such colleagues as Barenboim, Zukerman, Ashkenazy, Martha Argerich, Bruno Canino, Lynn Harrell, and Rohan De Silva. Perlman also conducts professionally; he has directed a number of leading chamber and orchestral ensembles throughout the United States and around the world. Beyond classical music, he has also played jazz and has garnered acclaim for his 1995 PBS television special on Klezmer music *In the Fiddler's House*, in which he performed in Poland with four of the world's most respected Klezmer bands. He has won four Emmy awards for his television work, most notably performing arts features and documentaries for PBS. He has been featured on the soundtracks of several films, including the Academy Award winning *Schindler's List* (music by John Williams).

For many years Perlman has been associated with the Aspen Music Festival in Colorado, and he teaches at Brooklyn College, New York. A dedicated educator, Perlman is a co-founder, along with his wife, Toby Perlman, of the Perlman Music Program for which he has worked as a teacher and conductor each summer since its inception in 1993. He also holds the Dorothy Richard Starling Foundation Chair at the Juilliard School. In 1996 he was awarded the Royal Philharmonic Society's gold medal and in 2003 the Kennedy Center Honor. He has won 15 Grammy Awards over the course of his 50-year career, including a Grammy Lifetime Achievement Award in 2008. Although he has generally made light of his disability, he has on occasion been a trenchant spokesman for the disabled and has given performances to raise awareness and funding to fight polio. Works have been written for him by Robert Mann, Earl Kim, and Robert Starer. He performed along with the cellist Yo-Yo Ma, the pianist Gabriela Montero, and the clarinetist Anthony McGill at President Barack Obama's inauguration in 2009 premiering a piece written for that event by John Williams. He has also performed for President George W. Bush and Queen Elizabeth II. He plays the 1714 "Soil" Stradivari.

BIBLIOGRAPHY

B. Schwarz: Great Masters of the Violin (London, 1983), 601–6
D. Rooney: "Courage and Ability," The Strad, c (1989), 300–03
R.D. Lawrence: "Pearls of Wisdom," The Strad, c (1989), 304–8
B.L. Sand: "Introducing Professor Perlman," The Strad, cvi (1995), 1146–51
H. Roth: Violin Virtuosos from Paganini to the 21st Century (Los Angeles, 1997), 220–27

TULLY POTTER/MEGAN E. HILL

Perry, Douglas (b Buffalo, NY, 19 Jan 1945). Tenor. Although his repertoire includes more than 90 operatic roles, he is best known as an interpreter of the operas of Philip Glass and Benjamin Britten. He performed the role of Mahatma Gandhi in Glass's opera Satyagraha with the Netherlands Opera, Lyric Opera of Chicago, San Francisco Opera, and Seattle Opera and was featured in the CBS recording of this work. Other notable recordings include Glass's Songs from Liquid Days and Virgil Thomson's The Mother of us all. Perry made his Metropolitan Opera debut in the world premiere of Glass's The Voyage and appeared in the world premiere of Glass' White Raven in Lisbon; he also performed in the latter work at the Teatro Real in Madrid and in his debut with the Lincoln Center Festival. He was a featured soloist in Leonard Bernstein's A Quiet Place (Deutsche Grammophon). As a specialist in the works of Britten, Perry has sung the roles of the Mayor in Albert Herring, Quint in The Turn of the Screw (with Glimmerglass Opera, Montreal Opera, Kentucky Opera), Flute in A Midsummer Night's Dream, and Nebuchadnezzar in The Burning Fiery Furnace (Utah Opera, Opera Colorado). In addition to numerous performances in works from the standard repertoire, he created the role of Marquis de Lisle in the premiere of Dominick Argento's Casanova's Homecoming at Minnesota Opera and participated in the American premiere

of Judith Weir's A Night at the Chinese Opera produced by Santa Fe Opera.

MATTHEW ALAN THOMAS

Perry, Edward Baxter (b Haverhill, MA, 14 Feb 1855; d Camden, ME, 13 June 1924). Pianist and author. He lost his sight in an accident at the age of two. After studying the piano with Junius W. Hill in Boston, he went in 1875 to Germany, where he studied with Theodor Kullak, Dionys Pruckner, Clara Schumann, and in 1878 with Liszt. He taught at Oberlin College (1881–3) and then in 1885 devoted himself to a performing career. In his recitals he presented explanatory comments on the works performed, thus originating the lecture-recital. The concept was well received, and he gave more than 3300 such programs throughout the United States, appearing multiple times over the years in the same cities and reaching a new level of smaller towns, such as Brownwood, Texas; Emporia, Kansas; Lawton, Oklahoma; and Waterloo, Iowa. He toured Europe in 1897–8. Louis C. Elson claimed in 1904 that Perry had given more recitals than any other American. He also contributed several hundred articles to music magazines, principally The Etude, and wrote two books, Descriptive Analyses of Piano Works (Philadelphia, 1902) and Stories of Standard Teaching Pieces (Philadelphia, 1910). In his lectures and writings he offered fanciful literary programs, what he called an "aesthetic analysis," rather than technical descriptions of the music in an attempt to make art music more accessible to general audiences. He focused on the music of Schubert, Chopin, Schumann, Liszt, and Rubinstein, which lent itself to such narratives, and wrote his own programmatic compositions, including Last Island, inspired by the destruction of a resort island in Louisiana by a hurricane in 1856, and Die Lorelei, based on the Heine poem. He later taught at Woman's College, Montgomery, Alabama (1917–20), Hood College, Frederick, Maryland (1921–2), and Lebanon Valley College, Annville, Pennsylvania (1922–4).

BIBLIOGRAPHY

DAB (F.L.G. Cole).
W.F. Gates: "Edward Baxter Perry," Musical Courier, xxxiv/22 (1897), 10
L.C. Elson: The History of American Music (New York, 1904)
J.A. Bowen: "Liszt the Teacher," Journal of the American Liszt Society, lii–liii (2002–3), 1–63 [includes "Annotated Bibliography of Students and Observers of Liszt's Teaching" in collaboration with E.D. Bomberger]

R. ALLEN LOTT

Perry, Julia (Amanda) (b Lexington, KY, 25 March 1924; d Akron, OH, 24 April 1979). Composer. Perry was born in 1924, confirmed by her birth certificate and passport, not 1927, which is found on her gravestone and may have been used sometimes by Perry. Raised in an upper middle class African American household, she studied violin, voice, and piano from age six. After completing studies at Akron University for one year and then Westminster Choir College (BM 1947, MM 1948) with support from a Knight Memorial Education Fund scholarship, she taught at Hampton Institute in Virginia (1948–9) and later at Florida A&M (1967–8). Perry preferred to focus on composition and conducting. She spent two summers at the Berkshire Music Center, studying choral singing under HUGH ROSS (1949) and composition with Luigi Dallapiccola (1951), and took a conducting course at the Juilliard School of Music (1950–51). She went on to study with Dallapiccola in Florence, briefly with NADIA BOULANGER in France (1952), winning the Prix Fontainebleau for her Viola Sonata, and conducting at Accademia Chigiana in Siena with Emanuel Balaban, Alceo Galliera, and Adone Zecchi (summers 1956–8). Other honors included Guggenheim Fellowships (1954, 1956), a National Institute of Arts and Letters Award (1964), and a posthumous Alumni Merit Award Citation from Westminster Choir College (1984). Perry was at the MacDowell Colony on several occasions (1954, 1959, 1962, 1967) and was hired by the US Information Service to lecture and conduct in Europe (1955, 1957). *Stabat mater* (1951), which launched her career, was also her most performed work; her *Study for Orchestra*, a reorchestration of *A Short Piece*, was performed by the New York PO led by William Steinberg in 1965. Recognized as an individual of great promise during her twenties, Perry had many opportunities, published her work, and received favorable notices. The 1960s, perhaps her most productive decade in terms of the quantity of large-scale compositions, brought Perry distribution by established publishers and the release of three works on separate recordings by Composers Recordings, Inc. Her career was curtailed because of health problems, especially a paralytic stroke affecting her right side in 1971. Her letters reveal her effort to walk, talk, and conduct again. She did learn to write with her left hand and resumed composing; however, she endured tragic emotional and financial difficulties, and compositions from her last decade are generally not her best work.

Perry's early works, mostly songs and choral music, may have roots in her experience as a gifted singer whom Italian music critics praised in the early 1950s (she inexplicably abandoned this artistic avenue by 1953). Some early works show a strong influence of spirituals while *Prelude for Piano* draws on the blues, using an extended harmonic vocabulary of major 7ths, 9ths and 11ths, blue notes, chord substitutions, and the common blues poetic form *AAB*. Perry's study with Dallapiccola came after he began using twelve-tone technique to achieve motivic unity, to create melodies, and to transform small melodic cells. These stylistic elements significantly influenced her *Short Piece, Homage to Vivaldi, Symphony in One Movement*, and *Miniature* for piano. While living in Europe, primarily Florence and Siena, her music became increasingly instrumental and abstract, focusing on the concise treatment of small motivic cells. Overt references to black culture are absent in these restrained, neo-classical works. Pitch centers are established through reiteration, the melodic-harmonic language is often dissonant, and rhythmic complexity emerges in shifting subdivisions and syncopation. *Homunculus C.F.*, written shortly after her return to the United States in 1959, is among her most innovative works, gradually unfolding pitches in a

chord of the 15th. With the civil rights struggles of the 1960s, she renewed her use of African American musical idioms but shifted her references to contemporary, urban genres. *A Suite Symphony* draws on rock and roll and rhythm and blues. *Bicentennial Reflections* offers a cautionary tale of American race relations, developing a racial dynamic with the aid of visual and textual elements.

WORKS
(of her known works, over one hundred, about half are currently lost)

OPERAS
3 Warnings (op or dramatic cant. for Columbia Opera Workshop), 1950; The Cask of Amontillado (The Bottle) (Perry and V. Card, after E.A. Poe), 1953; The Selfish Giant (Perry, after O. Wilde), 1964; The Symplegades (Mary Easty, also: Gallows Hill), c1960–74, unfinished

VOCAL
Choral: Carillon Heigh-ho (Perry), SATB (New York, 1947); Is There Anybody Here?, women's vv (1st perf. 1947); The Lord is Risen, men's vv (1st perf. 1947); Chicago (C. Sandburg, secular cant.), Bar, nar, chorus, orch, 1948; Missa brevis, SATB, org, by 1950; Ruth (sacred cant.), SATB, org, (1st perf. 1950), lost; Our Thanks to Thee (Perry), A, SATB, org (New York, 1951); Ye Who Seek the Truth (Perry), T, SATB, org (New York, 1952); Be Merciful Unto Me, O God (Ps lvii.1–2), S, B, SATB, org (New York, 1953); Song of Our Savior (Perry), S, SATB (New York, 1953); Frammenti dalle lettere di Santa Caterina, S, SATB, chbr orch, 1953, rev. 1957; Hymn to Pan (J. Fletcher), SATB, org/pf, 1963; Sym. no.7 "USA", SATB, chbr orch, 1967 or ?1969

Other vocal: Deep Sworn Vow, 1v, pf (1st perf. 1947); King Jesus Lives, 1v, pf (1st perf. 1947); To Elektra, 1v, pf (1st perf. 1947); Lord, What Shall I Do?, spiritual, high v, pf (Boston, 1949); By the Sea (Perry), high v, pf (New York, 1950); Free at Last, spiritual, high v, pf (New York, 1951); Stabat mater (Latin plus Eng. singing trans. by Perry), A/[Mez], str qt/str orch, 1951; I'm a Poor Li'l Orphan in This Worl' (?I'm a Poor Little Orphan Girl), spiritual, medium v, pf (New York, 1952); Alleluja (Matthew xxviii.1, 2, 5, 6), medium v, org, 1950s?; A Short Service from "The Mystic Trumpeter" (W. Whitman), T/[S], tpt, 1954; How Beautiful are the Feet (Isaiah lii.7), medium v, pf/org (New York, 1954); Parody (P. Sides), Bar, pf, 1954; Resurrection (P. Sides), v, pf, 1959; Quinary Quixotic Songs (Triptych) (Perry), B-Bar, fl, cl, va, bar hn, pf, 1976; Bicentennial Reflections (Perry), T, 2 cl, 3 perc, elec b gui, 1977; 5 Songs (?5 Songs for S and Pf, 1963), Mez, str qt, by 1977; 7 Contrasts (7 Songs, also: Contrasts), Bar, 7 insts, by 1977; Prayer, S, pf, n.d.

INSTRUMENTAL
Orch: A Short Piece, 1952 [reorchd 1955 as A Short Piece for Large Orch; reorchd 1965 as Study for Orch]; 3 Negro Spirituals, S, orch, 1956; Homage to Vivaldi (Requiem for Orch, also: Vivaldiana), 1959, rev. 1964; Sym. in 1 Movt (?Sym. no.1), vas, bs, 1961; 7 Sutures, 1961; Dance (Ballet), chbr orch (2 fl, 2 fl + pic, a sax, t sax, 4 hn, vas, bs), 1962; Sym. no.2, 1962; Sym. no.3, 1962, ?rev. 1970; Contretemps, 1963; Solstice, str, 1963; Vn Conc., 1963–5 (Peer-Southern), rev. 1968 (C. Fischer); 5 Negro Spirituals (2 movts added to 3 Negro Spirituals), Mez, orch, 1956–64; Sym. no.4, 1964–8?, incomplete?; 4 Spirituals (?expansion of 3 Spirituals for Orch), ?1965–7; Sym. no.5 "Integration," ob, a sax, 6 brass, mar, pf, hp, timp, perc, str, 1966–7; Sym. no.8, 1968–9; A Suite Sym. (?Sym. no.9), late 1960s?; Module (variations on Negro folktune), 1967–75; Pf Conc. no.2 (1 movt), 1964 and becomes 2nd movt of Pf Conc. "In 2 Uninterrupted Speeds," 1964–9, 1st movt lost; Sym. no.10 "Soul Sym." [some manuscript mislabeled as Sym. no.12], Bar, orch, 1972; Sym. no.12 "Simple Sym." (Children's Sym.), 1973

Band: Symphony Band Sym. (?Sym. no.6), ?1966; Marching Band Sym. (4 movts: Marching Band Salute, Venus Moon, Fireworks on Mars, Theme, Variations and Finale; ?also: Space Adventure Sym., also: Space Sym., maybe also: Sym. no.11), 1972; Football Game Salute, 1972; Panorama, by 1972; Theme Song "Gimme that Ol' Time Religion," mini-marching band, 1973; Suite, brass, perc, 1978

Chbr and solo inst: Trio, fl, cl, bn (1st perf. 1951 at Tanglewood); Sonata, va, pf, Prix Fontainebleau 1952, lost [sometimes listed for vn, which probably does not exist]; StrQ, 1954; Pastoral (Septet), fl, 2 vn, 2 va, 2 vc, 1959; Homunculus C.F., hp, cel + pf, 8 perc, 1960; The Beacon, 2 eng hn, 2 t sax, 2 bn, 2 tpt, 1963; Sym. no.13 (minor rev. of Quartette), fl, ob, cl, a sax, bn, 1963; Composition, opt. pf, 1960s, arr. as Serenity, cl, 1972; Soundouts, 3 tpt, 2 trbn, 1970–1; Tom Thumb Series, perc ens, 1972; Divertimento, fl, ob, a sax, t sax, bn, 1974–6

Pf: Prelude (Lament), 1946, rev. 1962; Pearls on Silk (1st perf. 1947); Suite of Shoes, (1st perf. of "Soldier's Boots" 1947); 2 Easy Pieces (Popping Popcorn; Spreading Peanut Butter), 1972; Miniature (in The New Scribner Music Library, vol. 11 [New York, 1973]); 3 Pf Pieces for Children

MSS and papers in NA; Jackson State U., Jackson MS; Center for Black Music Research, Columbia College, Chicago; American Music Research Center, U. of Colorado, Boulder; NYamc; peermusic; Carl Fischer; Composers Recordings Inc; Library of Congress; Westminster Choir College Archives

Principal publishers: Carl Fischer, Galaxy, peermusic (formerly Peer-Southern and Southern)

Principal recording companies: CRI, Koch, Leonarda, Senrab

BIBLIOGRAPHY

O. Smith: "Julia Perry Acclaimed in Europe for Music," Akron [OH] Beacon Journal (6 July 1952), 16A

W. Brinkey: "They All Say: 'Look at the American Signora!,'" Life (23 Dec 1957)

Obituary, BPM, vii (1979), 282; viii (1980), 264 [correction]

M.D. Green: Black Women Composers: a Genesis (Boston, 1983)

D. Thieme: "Julia Perry," Notable Black American Women, ed. J.C. Smith (Detroit, 1992), 841–2

J.M. Edwards: "Julia Amanda Perry," International Dictionary of Black Composers, ii, ed. S. Floyd (Chicago, 1999), 914–22

R.T. Payne: A Study of Julia Perry's Opera The Cask of Amontillado from a Director's Perspective (diss., U. of Illinois, 2001)

H. Walker-Hill: From Spirituals to Symphonies: African-American Women Composers and their Music (Westport, CT, 2002/R), 93–139

J. MICHELE EDWARDS

Perry, Linda (b Springfield, MA, 15 April 1965). Singer, songwriter, and producer. She was raised in a musical household, which exposed her to a wide variety of music. In 1989, while performing in a variety of small venues in San Francisco's Bay Area, she was recruited into the band 4 Non Blondes as lead singer. The band released their debut album, Bigger, Better, Faster, More! (Interscope, 1992); it contained the group's biggest hit, "What's going on?," which was written by Perry and brought the band's pop-rock sound and Perry's powerful voice to mainstream audiences. Perry has identified herself as a lesbian, and during the Billboard Music Awards in 1994 she attracted attention by performing with the word "dyke" on her guitar. Before 4 Non Blondes could complete a second album, Perry left the band to pursue a solo career. In 1996 she released In Flight to critical praise but poor commercial sales. In 1997 she started her own record label, Rockstar Records, to help local bands secure support. In 2001 she returned to performing and touring in the hope of releasing another album, but found greater success in writing songs for other female artists. She wrote Christina Aguilera's Grammy-winning single "Beautiful" (2004) and has both produced and co-written albums for numerous artists including P!nk (Missundaztood). Perry has since continued to release her own music independently through the Internet.

BIBLIOGRAPHY

G. Gaar: She's a Rebel: the History of Women in Rock & Roll (Seattle, 1992, 2/2002)

A. Stockwell: "Her Party's Started," The Advocate (10 Dec 2002)

JESSICA L. BROWN

Persichetti, Vincent (b Philadelphia, PA, 6 June 1915; d Philadelphia, PA, 14 Aug 1987). Composer, educator, and pianist. At the age of five he enrolled in the Combs Conservatory (Philadelphia), where he studied the piano, organ, and double bass; he also studied theory and composition with Russell King Miller, his most influential teacher. While in high school, he acquired professional experience performing on the radio, in churches, and in recital. After graduating from Combs (BMus 1935), he served as head of its theory and composition departments while studying the piano with OLGA SAMAROFF and composition with PAUL NORDOFF at the Philadelphia Conservatory (MMus 1941, DMus 1945), and conducting with FRITZ REINER at the Curtis Institute. In 1941 he was appointed head of the theory and composition departments at the Philadelphia Conservatory. He joined the faculty of the Juilliard School in 1947, where he became chairman of the composition department (1963) and of the literature and materials department (1970). From 1952 he also served as director of publications for Elkan-Vogel.

Persichetti's prodigious musical output exemplifies a principle that was also fundamental to his teaching and theoretical writing: the integration into a fluent working vocabulary of the wealth of materials placed at a composer's disposal by the expansion of musical language over the course of the 20th century. Drawing on a wide range of musical materials, from simple diatonicism to complex atonal polyphony, Persichetti produced an array of works whose breadth of expression and varied moods, styles, and levels of difficulty bewildered those who sought an easily identifiable musical personality or a conventional chronological pattern of development.

Despite Persichetti's precocious attainment of compositional fluency, his early works show the influence of Stravinsky, Bartók, Hindemith, and Copland; not until the 1950s did he truly achieve his own distinctive voice. Within that decade alone, however, he produced nearly 50 compositions, among them some of his finest and most frequently performed works. During this period he also developed a formal design particularly well suited to his creative temperament. This concept, in which a series of short sections, usually based on a single theme, is integrated into a large formal structure, underlies the Concerto for Piano—Four Hands, the Symphony no.5, the Piano Quintet, the Piano Sonata no.10, and the String Quartet no.3, all of which are among Persichetti's most fully realized compositions.

Persichetti himself identified two main currents within his creative disposition: one "graceful" and the other "gritty." Beyond this, his music is characterized by lucid textures, sparse gestures, epigrammatic forms, a fondness for pandiatonic and polytonal harmony, a playful rhythmic vitality, and a pervasive geniality of spirit. Like that of Mozart and Ravel, Persichetti's music often suggests the innocence and childlike joy of pure musical creativity. Hence many works for beginners stand, with neither condescension nor apology, alongside more difficult compositions. The importance with which he regarded his pieces for children is indicated by the fact that one of his most ambitious works, the opera *The Sibyl*, a harsh allegory based on the folktale *Chicken Little*, draws most of its thematic material from the *Little Piano Book*. *The Sibyl* was the 20th work in a series Persichetti called "Parables," which he defined as "non-programmatic musical essays about a single germinal idea." He began the series in 1965, completing the 25th addition in 1986. Many of the "Parables" are written for monophonic instruments and are based on motifs from other compositions.

Persichetti often "cross-referenced" his own works explicitly, regarding his output as a sort of bibliography from which he could draw at any time. Perhaps the most important of his "bibliographical" works are the two volumes of *Hymns and Responses for the Church Year*, contemporary hymnals with texts drawn from a variety of poetic sources, both traditional and modern. He returned to these collections frequently to borrow thematic material for compositions of many types and dimensions. Another quasi-religious work, which Persichetti often described as his most significant opus, is *The Creation*, a large oratorio on his own text, drawn from 53 mythological, scientific, poetic, and biblical sources.

Persichetti was a prodigious pianist, and although he made substantial contributions to many musical genres, his works for piano—including 12 sonatas—are worthy of particular mention. Comprising a large portion of his output, these provide a microcosmic representation of his work as a whole, while offering a comprehensive survey of 20th-century piano techniques. Toward the end of his life he became fascinated with the harpsichord, composing 10 sonatas and other pieces that constitute what is perhaps the most intensive modern contribution to the literature of that instrument. His most widely performed works, however, are those he composed for wind band, which reveal a natural affinity for the medium. Many of these pieces—most notably the Symphony no.6—have become classics of the band repertoire.

Persichetti's many works of intermediate difficulty, his ecumenical attitude regarding contemporary compositional techniques, and his warm, engaging, and witty personal manner made him a favorite on American college campuses, to which he was frequently invited as a guest lecturer. Among his many honors and awards are three Guggenheim Fellowships, two grants from the National Foundation on the Arts and Humanities, and a grant from the National Institute of Arts and Letters, of which he was a member from 1965. Many of his works were commissioned by the country's leading orchestras and institutions. His writings include the monograph *William Schuman* (with F.R. Schreiber, New York, 1954) and *Twentieth Century Harmony* (New York, 1961).

WORKS
(all published unless otherwise stated)

OPERA
The Sibyl (Parable XX) (1, Persichetti, after fable: *Chicken Little*), op.135, 1976; Philadelphia, Pennsylvania Op Theatre, 13 April 1985

LARGE INSTRUMENTAL ENSEMBLE
Orch: Concertino, op.16, pf, orch, 1941; Sym. no.1, op.18, 1942, unpubd; Sym. no.2, op.19, 1942, unpubd; Dance Ov., op.20, 1942; Fables, op.23, nar, orch, 1943; The Hollow Men, op.25, tpt, str, 1944; Sym. no.3, op.30, 1946; Serenade no.5, op.43, 1950; Fairy Tale, op.48, 1950; Sym. no.4, op.51, 1951; Sym. for Str (Sym. no.5), op.61, 1953; Sym. no.7 "Liturgical," op.80, 1958; Pf Conc., op.90, 1962; Introit, op.96, str, 1964; Sym. no.8, op.106, 1967; Sym. no.9 "Sinfonica janiculum," op.113, 1970; Night Dances, op.114, 1970; A Lincoln Address, op.124, nar, orch, 1972; Conc., op.137, eng hn, str, 1977

Band: Divertimento, op.42, 1950; Psalm, op.53, 1952; Pageant, op.59, 1953; Sym. for Band (Sym. no.6), op.69, 1956; Serenade no.11, op.85, 1960; Bagatelles, op.87, 1961; So Pure the Star, chorale prelude, op.91, 1962; Masquerade, op.102, 1965; Turn not thy Face, chorale prelude, op.105, 1966; O Cool is the Valley (Poem for Band), op.118, 1971; Parable IX, op.121, 1972; A Lincoln Address, op.124a, nar, band, 1973; O God Unseen, chorale prelude, op.160, 1984

VOCAL
Choral: Mag and Nunc, op.8, SATB, pf, 1940; Canons, op.31, SSAA/TTBB/SATB, 1947; 2 Cummings Choruses (E.E. Cummings), op.33, 2vv, pf, 1948; Proverb, op.34, SATB, 1948; 2 Cummings Choruses, op.46, SSAA, 1950; Hymns and Responses for the Church Year (W.H. Auden and others), op.68, 1955; Seek the Highest (F. Adler), op.78, SAB, pf, 1957; Song of Peace (anon.), op.82, TTBB/SATB, pf, 1959; Mass, op.84, SATB, 1960; Stabat mater, op.92, SATB, orch, 1963; Te Deum, op.93, SATB, orch, 1963; Spring Cantata (Cummings), op.94, SSAA, pf, 1963; Winter Cantata (11 Haiku), op.97, SSAA, fl, mar, 1964; 4 Cummings Choruses, op.98, 2vv, pf, 1964; Celebrations (cant., W. Whitman), op.103, SATB, wind ens, 1966; The Pleiades (cant., Whitman), op.107, SATB, tpt, str, 1967; The Creation (Persichetti), op.111, S, A, T, Bar, SATB, orch, 1969; Love (Bible: *Corinthians*), op.116, SSAA, 1971; Glad and Very (Cummings), op.129, 2vv, 1974; Flower Songs (Cant. no.6) (Cummings), op.157, SATB, str, 1983; Hymns and Responses for the Church Year, vol. 2, op.166, 1987

Solo: E.E. Cummings Songs, op.26, 1945, unpubd; 2 Chinese Songs, op.29, 1945; 3 English Songs (17th century), op.49, 1951, unpubd; Harmonium (W. Stevens), song cycle, op.50, S, pf, 1951; Sara Teasdale Songs, op.72, 1957, unpubd; Carl Sandburg Songs, op.73, 1957, unpubd; James Joyce Songs, op.74, 1957; Hilaire Belloc Songs, op.75, 1957; Robert Frost Songs, op.76, 1957, unpubd; Emily Dickinson Songs, op.77, 1957; A Net of Fireflies (Jap., trans. H. Steward), song cycle, op.115, 1970

CHAMBER AND SOLO INSTRUMENTAL
3 or more insts: Serenade no.1, op.1, 10 wind, 1929; Str Qt no.1, op.7, 1939; Concertato, op.12, pf qnt, 1940; Serenade no.3, op.17, vn, vc, pf, 1941; Pastoral, op.21, ww qnt, 1943; Str Qt no.2, op.24, 1944; King Lear, op.35, ww qnt, timp, pf, 1948; Serenade no.6, op.44, trbn, va, vc, 1950; Pf Qnt, op.66, 1954; Str Qt no.3, op.81, 1959; Parable II, op.108, brass qnt, 1968; Str Qt no.4 (Parable X), op.122, 1972; Parable XXIII, op.150, vn, vc, pf, 1981

1–2 insts: Suite, op.9, vn, vc, 1940, unpubd; Sonata, op.10, vn, 1940; Fantasy, op.15, vn, pf, 1941, unpubd; Vocalise, op.27, vc, pf, 1945; Serenade no.4, op.28, vn, pf, 1945; Sonata, op.54, vc, 1952; Little Rec Book, op.70, 1956; Serenade no.9, op.71, 2 rec, 1956; Serenade no.10, op.79, fl, hp, 1957; Infanta marina, op.83, va, pf, 1960; Serenade no.12, op.88, tuba, 1961; Serenade no.13, op.95, 2 cl, 1963; Masques, op.99, vn, pf, 1965; Parable [I], op.100, fl, 1965; Parable III, op.109, ob, 1968; Parable IV, op.110, bn, 1969; Parable VII, op.119, hp, 1971; Parable VIII, op.120, hn, 1972; Parable XI, op.123, a sax, 1972; Parable XII, op.125, pic, 1973; Parable XIII, op.126, cl, 1973; Parable XIV, op.127, tpt, 1973; Parable XV, op.128, eng hn, 1973; Parable XVI, op.130, va, 1974; Parable XVII, op.131, db, 1974;

Parable XVIII, op.133, trbn, 1975; Parable XXI, op.140, gui, 1978; Parable XXII, op.147, tuba, 1981; Serenade no.14, op.159, ob, 1984; Parable XXV, op.164, 2 tpt, 1986

KEYBOARD

Pf: Serenade no.2, op.2, 1929; Sonata no.1, op.3, 1939; Poems, vols.1–2, opp.4–5, 1939; Sonata no.2, op.6, 1939; Sonata, op.13, 2 pf, 1940; Poems, vol. 3, op.14, 1941; Sonata no.3, op.22, 1943; Variations for an Album, op.32, 1947; Sonata no.4, op.36, 1949; Sonata no.5, op.37, 1949; Sonatina no.1, op.38, 1950; Sonata no.6, op.39, 1950; Sonata no.7, op.40, 1950; Sonata no.8, op.41, 1950; Sonatina no.2, op.45, 1950; Sonatina no.3, op.47, 1950; Conc., op.56, 4 hands, 1952; Parades, op.57, 1952; Serenade no.7, op.55, 1952; Sonata no.9, op.58, 1952; Little Pf Book, op.60, 1953; Serenade no.8, op.62, 4 hands, 1954; Sonatina no.4, op.63, 1954; Sonatina no.5, op.64, 1954; Sonatina no.6, op.65, 1954; Sonata no.10, op.67, 1955; Sonata no.11, op.101, 1965; Parable XIX, op.134, 1975; Reflective Keyboard Studies, op.138, 1978; Little Mirror Book, op.139, 1978; 4 Arabesques, op.141, 1978; 3 Toccatinas, op.142, 1979; Mirror Etudes, op.143, 1979; Sonata no.12, op.145, 1980; Winter Solstice, op.165, 1986

Other: Sonatine, op.11, org pedals, 1940; Hpd Sonata no.1, op.52, 1951; Org Sonata, op.86, 1960; Shimah b'koli, op.89, org, 1962; Drop, Drop Slow Tears, chorale prelude, op.104, org, 1966; Parable V, op.112, carillon, 1969; Parable VI, op.117, org, 1971; Do Not Go Gentle, op.132, org pedals, 1974; Auden Variations, op.136, org, 1977; Dryden Liturgical Suite, op.144, org, 1980; Hpd Sonata no.2, op.146, 1981; Song of David, op.148, org, 1981; Hpd Sonata no.3, op.149, 1981; Hpd Sonata no.4, op.151, 1982; Hpd Sonata no.5, op.152, 1982; Parable XXIV, op.153, hpd, 1982; Hpd Sonata no.6, op.154, 1982; Little Hpd Book, op.155, 1983; Hpd Sonata no.7, op.156, 1983; Hpd Sonata no.8, op.158, 1984; Serenade no.15, op.161, hpd, 1984; Give Peace, O God, chorale prelude, op.162, org, 1985; Hpd Sonata no.9, op.163, 1985; Hpd Sonata no. 10, op.167, 1987

Principal publisher: Elkan-Vogel (Theodore Presser)

BIBLIOGRAPHY

EwenD

R. Evett: "The Music of Vincent Persichetti," *Juilliard Review*, ii/2 (1955), 15–30

D. Persichetti: *Vincent Persichetti's Music* (MSS, 1960), Persichetti Archive at New York Public Library, JPB 90-77, Box 103, Folders 17–18

W. Schuman: "The Compleat Musician," *MQ*, xlvii (1961), 379–85

D.M. Rubin: "Vincent Persichetti," *ASCAP in Action* (1980, spr.), 8

R. Shackelford: "Conversation with Vincent Persichetti," *PNM*, xx/1–2 (1981–2), 104–34

J. Hilfiger: *Comparison of Some Aspects of Style in the Band and Orchestral Music of Vincent Persichetti* (diss., U. of Iowa, 1985)

J.B. Smith: *Golden Proportion in the Published Solo Piano Music of Vincent Persichetti* (diss., U. of Missouri, Kansas City, 1987)

D.L. and J.L. Patterson: *Vincent Persichetti: a Bio-Bibliography* (Westport, CT, 1988, aut.)

D.A. Morris: *Life of Vincent Persichetti, with Emphasis on Works for Band* (diss., Florida State U., 1991)

D.A. Morris: "Persichetti Rediscovered: The Manuscripts of Vincent Persichetti's Band Works, Part One," *Journal of Band Research*, xxviii (1992, aut.), 21–30

F. Fennell: A Conductor's Interpretive Analysis of Masterworks for Band (Galesville, MD, 2008), 6–27

J.S. Smith: Vincent Persichetti's Choral Settings of E. E. Cummings' Poetry, with Special Emphasis on the "Flower Songs", Op. 157 (diss., U. of Houston, 2009)

M.A. Minut: *Style and Compositional Techniques in Vincent Persichetti's Ten Sonatas for Harpsichord* (diss., Ball State U., 2009)

W. Simmons: *Voices of Stone and Steel: The Music of William Schuman, Vincent Persichetti, and Peter Mennin* (Lanham, MD, 2011)

WALTER SIMMONS

Persinger, Louis (*b* Rochester, IL, 11 Feb 1887; *d* New York, NY, 31 Dec 1966). Violinist, pianist, and teacher. He had early lessons in Colorado and appeared in public at the age of 12. His main studies were at the Leipzig Conservatory (1900–4) under Hans Becker (violin), Carl Beving (piano), and Arthur Nikisch (conducting), who described him as "one of the most talented pupils the Leipzig Conservatory ever had." He then settled in Brussels for three years, combining studies under EUGÈNE YSAŸE with concerts in Belgium and Germany and two summers' coaching from Jacques Thibaud. After returning to the United States, he made his debut on 1 November 1912 with the Philadelphia Orchestra under Leopold Stokowski, followed by many engagements with orchestras. In 1914 Nikisch invited him to become leader of the Berlin PO, and in 1915 he became leader of the San Francisco SO. Two years later he resigned to form his own string quartet and to direct the Chamber Music Society of San Francisco (1916–28), where he began his teaching career. One of his earliest pupils was YEHUDI MENUHIN, whose family followed Persinger to New York in 1925. An accomplished pianist, he was the accompanist for Menuhin's first New York recital in 1926 and on his American tour in 1928–9. On his 75th birthday Persinger gave a recital at the Juilliard School, playing half the program on the piano and half on the violin.

Persinger taught at the Cleveland Institute of Music (1929–30), and in 1930 succeeded Leopold Auer at the Juilliard School, where he taught the violin and chamber music until his death. Among his pupils were ISAAC STERN, RUGGIERO RICCI, Guila Bustabo, and Camilla Wicks. He said that his unorthodox teaching method was "based on keeping a child's interest, in sensing what might be amusing or arresting to him, and in using as few pedantic words as possible. I teach through the sound of the instrument." Menuhin wrote that Persinger "has done perhaps more than anyone else to establish a genuine American school of violin playing." Persinger served as a member of the jury in the Queen Elisabeth and Wieniawski competitions, and published transcriptions and editions of violin music.

BIBLIOGRAPHY

CampbellGV; SchwarzGM

R. Magidoff: *Yehudi Menuhin: the Story of the Man and the Musician* (Garden City, NY, 1955/*R*, 2/1973)

M.C. Hart: "Louis Persinger: a Tribute on his 75th," *Juilliard Review*, ix/1 (1961–2), 4

Y. Menuhin: "Louis Persinger," *Juilliard Review Annual*, v (1966–7), 15

Obituary, *Juilliard News Bulletin*, v/3 (1966–7), 1

Obituary, *New York Times* (1 Jan 1967)

J. Creighton: *Discopaedia of the Violin, 1889–1971* (Toronto, 1974), 579

Y. Menuhin: *Unfinished Journey* (London, 1977, 2/1996)

M.M. Myers: *Louis Persinger: an American Violinist and his Treatise* (DMA thesis, U. of Houston, 2003)

BORIS SCHWARZ

Person, Houston (*b* Florence, SC, 10 Nov 1934). Tenor saxophonist. He studied music informally as a child and took piano lessons with his mother; he later turned to the tenor saxophone. He studied at South Carolina State College and then served in the armed forces during the Korean War. He joined the service band while stationed in West Germany and performed with pianist Cedar Walton and trumpeter Don Ellis. After his military service, Person continued his studies at the Hartt College of

Music. His warm, full, soulful sound attracted musicians like organist Johnny Hammond and Etta Jones; he procured valuable experience while working with Hammond from 1963 to 1966. He then made a series of albums, as a leader, for Prestige Records in the 1960s, including his initial release, *Underground Soul* in 1966 and later recorded for Mercury, Savoy, Muse, and High-Note. He has been active as a sideman for musicians Charles Earland, Ran Blake, Johnny Hammond, and perhaps most notably, pianist and composer Horace Silver. In 1984, he performed at the Grande Parade du Jazz in Nice, France. Throughout the 1990s and 2000s, he remained an active force in the jazz scene—continuing to be a soulfully potent interpreter of the standards and contemporary repertory.

BIBLIOGRAPHY

Feather-Gitler *BEJ*

E. Cook: "I Just Like People Who Swing: Houston Person," *JJI*, xxxviii/1 (1985), 13

MICHAEL CONKLIN

Persuasions, the. A cappella vocal group. Formed in 1961 by bass singer Jimmy "Bro" Hayes with Jerry Lawson (*b* Ft. Lauderdale, FL, 23 Jan 1944; lead), Jayotis Washington (first/second tenor), "Sweet" Joe Russell (second tenor), and Herbert "Toubo" Rhoad (baritone). Although they have never had a hit single, they have survived more than five decades as one of the most popular and influential black a cappella groups with 18 albums to their credit, interpreting music ranging from works by the Grateful Dead to Roy Hamilton and Elvis Presley. After singing together for eight years, they recorded their first commercial album for Frank Zappa's Straight Records in 1969, although it remained unreleased for a decade. They signed with Capitol Records in the early 1970s and recorded three albums for the label, including their biggest seller, *Street Corner Symphony* (1971). After a brief flirtation with instrumentally backed music, the Persuasions returned to a cappella music with *Chirpin'* (1977) on Elektra, which *Rolling Stone* named one of the 100 best albums of the 1970s. The group gained greater fame after performing in filmmaker Spike Lee's 1990 television special "Do It A Cappella" and singing on the subsequent recording. Over the years, the Persuasions have sung with such musical artists as Liza Minnelli, Stevie Wonder, Joni Mitchell, Paul Simon, and Patti LaBelle. Lawson left the group in 2003 and joined another a cappella group, the Talk of the Town, the following year. He has continued to perform and record with them. The Persuasions are the subject of the film documentary *Spread the Word: the Persuasions*.

RECORDINGS

(selective)

Street Corner Symphony, Collectables (1993)

BIBLIOGRAPHY

M. Rosalsky: *Encyclopedia of Rhythm and Blues and Doo-Wop Vocal Groups* (Lanham, MD, 2002)

J.M. Runowicz: *Forever Doo-Wop* (Amherst, 2010)

STEVE OTFINOSKI

Peter, Johann Friedrich (*b* 19 May 1746, Heerendijk, Holland; *d* 13 July 1813, Bethlehem, PA). German Moravian composer, musician, and minister active in Pennsylvania and North Carolina. He was educated at Moravian schools in Haarlem, Holland, and Niesky, Germany, where he may have received his first musical training from Moravian composer Johann Daniel Grimm. At the age of 19, he entered the Moravian seminary in Barby, Germany, and began making copies of musical works by other composers. He was called to service in America in 1770.

In Pennsylvania, his first work was as an instructor at the Moravian boys' school in Nazareth, and it was then that he composed his first-known music for the church. In 1773, he was called to work in Bethlehem, as a teacher and a bookkeeper, and he began copying anthems by Moravian composer Christian Gregor. In 1779, he was called to Lititz, Pennsylvania, as record keeper and secretary. He was called to Salem, North Carolina, in 1780, and was ordained a Moravian minister, serving a two-year interim pastorate; he was also supervisor of the boys' school. With the signing of the Peace of Paris in 1783, North Carolina governor Alexander Martin proclaimed 4 July a "Day of solemn thanksgiving." To the best of our knowledge, the Moravians were the only ones who celebrated the occasion. Peter assembled the music for the afternoon service, using selections from the music already on hand, some of which had been used at Moravian peace celebrations at the end of the Seven Years' War in 1763.

Peter married soprano Catherina Leinbach in 1786. He served pastorates in Graceham, Maryland (1790), Hope, New Jersey (1791–93), and Mount Joy, Pennsylvania (1802–04), and spent the last seven years of his life in Bethlehem. In 1811, he took part in what may have been the US premiere of Haydn's *Creation*.

Beginning in 1764, and continuing throughout his life, he copied hundreds of instrumental and vocal pieces. Among these are several that are the only known surviving copies, including four symphonies by J.C.F. Bach, and the earliest known copy of Haydn's Symphony no.17. Throughout most of his life, Peter served as teacher or supervisor at Moravian schools, and was also responsible for giving organ lessons to promising students. He found a great deal of satisfaction in this work, and his widespread influence is only beginning to be fully recognized.

Peter's efforts raised the level of the church's musical life, by means of his compositions, teaching, music direction, and preparation of service odes or "psalms." Using his own compositions, along with anthems by other composers, and interspersing them with appropriate hymns, he demonstrated the ability to manage larger-scale musical form and harmonic flow within the boundaries of a well-established liturgy. This grasp of large-scale musical flow is also seen in his six string quintets, which he completed in Salem in 1789; these are the earliest-known chamber music works written in the United States. Peter's vocal works, which date from 1770 to 1813, include some 80 choral anthems with orchestral accompaniment, and five vocal solos and five vocal duets with orchestra. His compositions feature graceful vocal writing and a considerable depth of musical expression. The orchestral accompaniments for strings and organ with occasional woodwind and brass, is always well worked out and often elaborate. His sacred vocal music is among the finest body of concerted church music written in North America at the time and compares well with that of European Moravian composers of his era. Manuscript copies of his music are in the holdings of the Moravian Music Foundation in Bethlehem, Pennsylvania, and Winston-Salem, North Carolina.

BIBLIOGRAPHY

M.P. Gombosi, ed.: *Catalog of the Johannes Herbst Collection* (Chapel Hill, NC, 1970)

W.E. Schnell: *The Choral Music of Johann Friedrich Peter* (diss., U. of Illinois, 1973)

M.P. Gombosi: *A Day of Solemn Thanksgiving* (Chapel Hill, NC, 1977)

J.S. Ingram: "A Musical Pot-pourri: the Commonplace Book of Johann Friedrich Peter," *Moravian Music Foundation Bulletin*, xxiv/1 (1979), 2–7

F. Cumnock: *Catalog of the Salem Congregation Music* (Chapel Hill, NC, 1980)

C.D. Crews: *Johann Friedrich Peter and His Times* (Winston-Salem, NC, 1990)

N.R. Knouse: *The Music of the Moravian Church in America* (Rochester, NY, 2008)

KARL KROEGER/NOLA REED KNOUSE

Peter, Paul and Mary. Folk group. It was formed in 1961 in New York by Albert Grossman, and it included Peter Yarrow (*b* New York, NY, 31 May 1938; guitar, vocals), (Noel) Paul Stookey (*b* Baltimore, MD, 30 Dec 1937; guitar, vocals), and Mary (Allin) Travers (*b* Louisville, KY, 9 Nov 1936; *d* Danbury, CT, 16 Sept 2009; vocals). The trio became one of the biggest acts in the 1960s and the most popular group to emerge out of THE FOLK REVIVAL.

Grossman encouraged the three to perform together in Greenwich Village; he hired Milt Okun to arrange their material, and he crafted their image as an offbeat group to counter the clean-cut Kingston Trio, with Yarrow as leader, Stookey as a comic, and Travers a silent and mysterious beauty. After seven months of rehearsals, the group was signed to Warner Bros. Records. Their self-titled debut album reached number one in August 1962 and included a cover of Pete Seeger and Lee Hays's "If I Had a Hammer," which charted at number ten. The group's second album included the number two hit "Puff the Magic Dragon" (May 1963); some claimed the song was about drugs and not a children's song as performed. The group's cover of Bob Dylan's "Blowin' in the Wind" hit number two in July 1963 and brought commercial success to the singer-songwriter.

The trio supported various political causes, notably the civil rights and antiwar movements of the 1960s. Their cover of the Weavers' "If I Had a Hammer" brought folk protest songs to the mainstream, and the group performed it at the March on Washington in 1963. The group hit number one with a cover of John Denver's "Leaving on a Jet Plane" in 1969 but decided to break up in 1970 after ten charting albums to pursue solo careers that proved to be less successful. The trio reunited in 1978 and went on a national tour continuing to record and tour until Travers died in 2009.

BIBLIOGRAPHY

H. George-Warren and P. Romanowski, eds.: *The Rolling Stone Encyclopedia of Rock & Roll* (New York, 1983, rev. 3/2001), 754–55

R. Cohen: *Rainbow Quest: the Folk Music Revival and American Society, 1940–1970* (Amherst, MA, 2002), 189–291

RICHARD D. DRIVER

Peter, Simon (*b* Heerendijk, Holland, 2 April 1743; *d* Salem [now Winston-Salem], NC, 29 May 1819). German Moravian composer and pastor active in Pennsylvania and North Carolina. The son of Moravian missionary parents, he was educated in the Moravian schools in Germany and taught at the Moravian boarding school in Neuwied, Germany. He came to America in 1770 with his brother, composer Johann Friedrich Peter, and taught at the Moravian schools in Nazareth and Lititz, Pennsylvania. After moving to North Carolina in 1784, he served several pastorates there for more than 20 years and was a member of the governing board of the Moravian Church in North Carolina. Simon Peter's musical compositions, though few in number, demonstrate a high degree of musical talent and skill. Most notable are his festive anthem, *Siehe, meine Knechte sollen essen*, written in 1803 for the 50th anniversary of the arrival of the Moravians in North Carolina and utilizing soprano solo, double choir, strings, and organ. His poignantly expressive *O Anblick, der mirs Herze bricht*, for Holy Week, is found in versions for soprano solo and for SSAB choir, both with accompaniment by strings and organ.

BIBLIOGRAPHY

C.D. Crews: "Memoir of Simon Peter (1743–1819)," *The Distinctiveness of Moravian Culture*, ed. C.D. Atwood and P. Vogt (Bethlehem, 2003), 35–46

N.R. Knouse: *The Music of the Moravian Church in America* (Rochester, 2008)

NOLA REED KNOUSE

Pete Rock and CL Smooth. Rap duo. It comprised Pete Rock (*b* Peter Phillips; Mt. Vernon, NY, 21 June 1970) and CL Smooth (*b* Corey Penn; New Rochelle, NY, 8 Oct 1968). Widely influential and popular for their soul-infused beats and introspective lyricism, Pete Rock and CL Smooth released three albums between 1991 and 1994. Their highly acclaimed *Mecca and the Soul Brother* (Elektra, 1992) included the tribute "They reminisce over you (T.R.O.Y.)," written for their late friend and fellow Mount Vernon native Troy "Trouble T-Roy" Dixon, a dancer and member of the group Heavy D and the Boyz. The song's memorable saxophone riff was sampled from Tom Scott's cover of the Jefferson Airplane song "Today." Other songs of note include "Straighten it out" and "Lots of Lovin'."

In 1993 the duo produced and performed with Run-D.M.C. on the song "Down with the King," a track that delivered the hip-hop legends from obscurity. They also contributed songs to the soundtracks for *Who's the Man* (1993) and *Menace II Society* (1993). Despite their success, Pete Rock and CL Smooth disbanded after 1994's *The Main Ingredient* (Elektra). Pete Rock went on to become one of the most in-demand producers in hip hop, while CL Smooth went largely unheard for the rest of the 1990s aside from a few guest appearances. The duo has occasionally worked together, CL Smooth appearing on Pete Rock's album *Soul Survivor* (Loud, 1998) and *Soul Survivor II* (BBE, 2004). Pete Rock also produced several songs for CL Smooth's solo releases in 2006 and 2007, respectively. In late 2010, the pair officially reunited, announcing plans to record a new album.

JARED PAULEY

Peters [Lazzara], **Bernadette** (*b* Queens, NY, 28 Feb 1948). Actor and singer. She began performing at the age of three and joined Actors Equity at nine. A year later Peters made her stage debut playing Tessie in the 1959 revival of *The Most Happy Fella* at the New York City Center. In 1968 she performed the role of George M. Cohan's sister, Josie, in *George M!* and scored her first major success as Ruby in the off-Broadway production of *Dames at Sea*. Over the course of a career that has already spanned more than half a century, Peters has demonstrated her tremendous talent and has emerged as one of Broadway's most versatile stars. Notable roles highlight her broad range of experience as an actor and singer: Mabel in *Mack and Mabel* (1974), Dot in *Sunday in the Park with George* (1984), Emma in *Song and Dance* (1985), the Witch in *Into the Woods* (1987), Marsha in *The Goodbye Girl* (1993), Annie Oakley in a revival of *Annie Get Your Gun* (1999), Rose in a revival of *Gypsy* (2003), and Desiree in a revival of *A Little Night Music* (2010). Widely acclaimed as the finest singing actress since Barbra Streisand, Peters has received nominations for seven Tony Awards, winning two (the first for *Song and Dance* and the second for *Annie Get Your Gun*), and nine Drama Desk Awards, winning three. Four of the Broadway cast albums on which she has been featured have won Grammy Awards. She has recorded six solo albums and several singles and has performed internationally in her own solo concert act. Her musical film credits include *Pennies from Heaven* (1981), for which she won a Golden Globe Award, and *Annie* (1982). Over the years, Peters has appeared in other films and television series and has authored two children's books.

BIBLIOGRAPHY
R. Viagas: *I'm the Greatest Star: Broadway's Top Musical Legends from 1900 to Today* (New York, 2009)

LARA E. HOUSEZ

Peters, C.F. Firm of music publishers. It was founded in New York in 1948 by WALTER HINRICHSEN, who had worked for his father, Henri Hinrichsen (head of the Peters firm in Leipzig), for five years before coming to the United States in 1936. Although a separate business from Peters in Leipzig (later Frankfurt am Main) and Peters in London (founded by Walter's older brother Max in 1938 as Hinrichsen Edition), it shares the same ideals. One of its first priorities was to reissue the "Edition Peters"

publications, a series known since its inception in 1867 for its superior quality of production and high editorial standards and for covering the standard repertory as well as including Urtext and scholarly editions. The Collection Litolff, the American Music Awards sponsored by Sigma Alpha Iota, the American Wind Symphony Editions, and the New York Public Library Music Publications have also been published by the firm. Another major commitment is to the publication of contemporary music. The Peters catalog lists among its composers Milton Babbitt, John Cage, Henry Cowell, George Crumb, Morton Feldman, Charles Ives, Krzysztof Penderecki, Arnold Schoenberg, Christian Wolff, and Charles Wuorinen. The firm has also become the American agent for a number of European publishers. After Hinrichsen's death, his widow Evelyn continued to maintain the high standards of the firm and expanded the catalog. His son Henry Hans Hinrichsen became president of the firm in 1978 and was succeeded in 1983. On 19 December 1983 Evelyn Hinrichsen and C.F. Peters were awarded the American Music Center's Letter of Distinction for their continued commitment to the advancement of new music. This goal has remained vital into the 21st century even as the company maintains its older catalog. The expansion of its different branches, in addition to the 1974 acquisition of Schwann and the 1989 acquisition of C.F. Kahnt, has allowed Peters to become one of the largest music publishers of the early 21st century.

BIBLIOGRAPHY
GMO ("Peters," H.-M. Plesske and F. Barulich)
"The C. F. Peters Company," *Music Journal Annual* (1973), 56, 96
H.W. Hitchcock: "C.F. Peters Corporation and Twentieth-century American Music," *An Introduction to Music Publishing*, ed. C. Sachs (New York, 1981), 15
I. Lawford-Hinrichsen: *Music Publishing and Patronage: C.F. Peters, 1800 to the Holocaust* (New York, 2000)

FRANCES BARULICH/JONAS WESTOVER

Peters, Roberta (*b* New York, NY, 4 May 1930). Soprano. She studied with William Hermann and was engaged by the Metropolitan at 19, without previous stage experience. She made her debut in 1950 as Zerlina, a last-minute replacement for Nadine Conner; her official debut was to have been as the Queen of Night, two months later. She appeared with the company for 35 years, giving hundreds of performances, closing with Gilda in *Rigoletta* in 1985. Her early roles included Despina (*Così fan tutte*), Rosina, Giuseppe Donizetti's Norina (*Don Pasquale*) and Lucia di Lammermoor, and Giuseppe Verdi's Oscar (*Un ballo in maschera*); in 1964 she sang the role of Kitty in the American premiere of Gian Carlo Menotti's *Le dernier sauvage*. Later she attempted to broaden her repertory in lyric soprano roles, playing Violetta, Mimì, and Jules Massenet's Manon outside New York and performing in musical comedy. She performed at Covent Garden (*The Bohemian Girl* under Sir Thomas Beecham, 1951), in Salzburg (*Die Zauberflöte*, 1963), Vienna (1963), Munich (1964), and Berlin (1971), and with the Kirov and Bol'shoy companies (1972). She also made numerous television appearances, most notably in her many dozens of performances on *The Ed Sullivan Show*. A singer of considerable charm and flute-like accuracy, Peters maintained the Lily Pons and Amelita Galli-Curci tradition of coloratura singing at a time when the more dramatic attitudes of Maria Callas and, later, Joan Sutherland were in vogue. She recorded several of her most successful roles, including Zerbinetta and Rosina with Erich Leinsdorf and the Queen of Night with Karl Böhm.

BIBLIOGRAPHY
R. Peters and L. Biancolli: *A Debut at the Met* (New York, 1967)
J. Hines: "Roberta Peters," *Great Singers on Great Singing* (Garden City, NY, 1982), 231–9

MARTIN BERNHEIMER/R

Peters, W(illiam) C(umming) (*b* Woodbury, Devon, 10 March 1805; *d* Cincinnati, OH, 20 April 1866). Music publisher, musician, and conductor. He immigrated to the United States from England in about 1820. In 1827 he was active in Pittsburgh as a clarinetist, music teacher, and proprietor of one of the city's first music shops. Early in his career Peters worked for George Rapp's HARMONY SOCIETY; between 1828 and 1831 he composed a Symphony in D in two movements, a Mass in D, numerous marches and dances, and arranged opera overtures for the Harmonist orchestra. He was also organist at Trinity Episcopal Church in Pittsburgh. In 1830 Peters's Musical Repository was located at 19 Market Street; in 1831 he was in partnership with W.C. Smith and J.H. Mellor at 9 Fifth Avenue. He sold his business interests to his partners in 1832 and moved to Louisville, establishing himself as a teacher and dealer in pianos and operating a school and circulating music library.

In the three decades before the Civil War about 200 of Peters's arrangements and compositions were published. Between 1838 and 1866 W.C. Peters owned or had an interest in no fewer than ten publishing companies in Louisville, Baltimore, Cincinnati, New York, and St. Louis. His earliest publications were his own songs and keyboard pieces that were first published by Hewitt & Jaques. Among his works are the "Citizens Guards' March" (1841), "Sweet Memories of Thee" (1839), and "Kind, kind, and gentle is she" (1840).

Peters, Browning & Co., Louisville, was formed in about 1840 by W.C. Peters, his brother-in-law Samuel Browning (*d* TX, 1844) and probably his brother Henry J. Peters (*d* TX, 1877). This was followed around 1841 by Peters & Co., Louisville, and Peters & Co., Cincinnati (W.C. Peters and Henry J. Peters). Peters & Webster, Louisville, was formed in 1845 at about the same time as Peters & Field, Cincinnati, and Peters & Field, St. Louis, with Joel Field. Popular composers in their catalog were Stephen Collins Foster, Henry Russell, E.W. Gunter, and William Striby. The inventory was increased with sheets acquired from John F. Nunns and Kretschmar & Nunns, Philadelphia.

In 1849 W.C. Peters established the firm W.C. Peters, Baltimore. Some sheets have the imprint W.C. Peters & Co., Baltimore, but no source has been found to identify a partner or partners. While in Baltimore W.C. Peters stated that he "still had an interest" in the Louisville and Cincinnati companies and for a time tried to unite them with interlocking plate numbers.

W.C. Peters's sons, William M. Peters, Alfred C. Peters, and John L. Peters, became active in the companies in the late 1840s and early 50s. In 1848 William M. Peters joined Peters & Field, which then became Peters, Field & Co. and began a new plate number series. One or more of the sons may have been part of W.C. Peters & Co., Baltimore, which published the *Baltimore Olio and Musical Gazette* (12 Numbers). This contained music, excerpts from pedagogical works, biographical sketches, reviews and notices of concerts, and other topics of current musical interest, some of the latter written by pianist-composer Charles Grobe.

In 1851 W.C. Peters moved to Cincinnati and with his sons William and Alfred formed W.C. Peters & Sons, "successors to Peters, Field & Co." W.C. Peters & Sons issued piano methods and exercises by Franz Hünten, Johann Friedrich Burgmüller, Carl Czerny, and Henri Herz, and teaching manuals for other instruments. They also published masses, motets, antiphons, hymns, and responses for the Roman Catholic Church, most of which were adapted and arranged or composed by W.C. Peters. Among the European composers represented are Giuseppe Baini, Anton Diabelli, Pietro Terziani, Gaspare Spontini, Louis Lambillotte, Michael Haydn, J.N. Hummel, and Vincent Novello. The Americans include Raynor Taylor, Benjamin Carr, Benjamin Carr Cross, H.D. Sofge, Henry Bollmann, and W.C. Peters.

In 1857 William M. Peters was replaced by his brother John L. Peters, and William appears to have established his own business. John L. Peters also opened stores in New York and St. Louis. Under the names W.C. Peters & Sons, A.C. Peters & Brother, and J.L. Peters & Brother they continued to publish popular songs, many with texts about the Civil War, and by 1862 the plate numbers on new sheets issued were above the number 4000. Popular composers in their inventory were Henri Herz, Vincent Wallace, William Iucho, Stephen Glover, and Charles Grobe.

In March 1866 the company premises were destroyed by fire and the Peters company lost its entire stock of music and all the plates acquired by W.C. Peters over a period of more than 40 years. On 20 April 1866, one month after the fire, W.C. Peters died of heart failure. John L. Peters then began to expand his New York and St. Louis businesses, buying the stock of H.M. Higgins, Chicago (1867), A.E. Blackmar, New York, J.J. Dobmeyer & Co., St. Louis, and DeMotte Brothers, Chicago (all 1869). J.L. Peters sold the Cincinnati firm to J.J. Dobmeyer & Co. in 1868 and the New York firm to C.H. Ditson & Co. in 1877. J.L. Peters, St. Louis, published until 1885 and was an active music store until 1892. Meanwhile, in Louisville Henry Peters and his partners had bought back the business from D.P. Faulds in 1855 (sold to them in 1851) and resumed business as Peters, Webb & Co. until 1861, when the company was named Webb, Peters & Co. Henry J. Peters dissolved his Louisville partnership in 1877 and moved to Texas where he died soon afterwards.

BIBLIOGRAPHY

H. Dichter and E. Shapiro: *Early American Sheet Music: its Lure and its Lore, 1768–1889* (New York, 1941, repr. with corrections as *Handbook of Early American Sheet Music, 1768–1889*)

E.G. Baynham: *The Early Development of Music in Pittsburgh* (diss., U. of Pittsburgh, 1944)

S.V. Connor: *The Peters Colony of Texas* (Austin, 1959)

E.C. Krohn: *Music Publishing in the Middle Western States before the Civil War* (Detroit, 1972)

R.D. Wetzel: *Frontier Musicians on the Connoquenessing, Wabash, and Ohio* (Athens, OH, 1976)

G.R. Keck: *Pre-1875 American Imprint Sheet Music in the Ernst C. Krohn Special Collections, Gaylord Music Library, Washington University, St. Louis, Missouri: a Catalog and Descriptive Study* (diss., U. of Iowa, 1982)

R.D. Wetzel: "The Search for William Cumming Peters," *American Music*, i/4 (1983), 27–41

E.C. Krohn: *Music Publishing in St. Louis* (Warren, MI, 1988), 51

R.C. Vitz: *The Queen City and the Arts: Cultural Life in Nineteenth-Century Cincinnati* (Kent, OH, 1989)

S. Saunders and D.L. Root, eds.: *The Music of Stephen C. Foster* (Washington, DC, 1990)

M. Korda: *Louisville Music Publications of the 19th Century* (Louisville, KY, 1991)

R.D. Wetzel: "Catholic Church Music in the Midwest before the Civil War: the Firm of W.C. Peters & Sons," *American Music Life in Context and Practice to 1865*, ed. J.R. Heintze (New York, 1994), 203–30

R.D. Wetzel: *Oh! Sing No More That Gentle Song: the Musical Life and Times of William Cumming Peters, 1805–66* (Sterling Heights, MI, 2000)

RICHARD D. WETZEL/R

Petersilea, Carlyle (*b* Boston, MA, 18 Jan 1844; *d* Tropico, CA, 11 June 1903). Pianist and teacher. Petersilea studied with his father Franz, a pupil of Hummel. He later attended the Leipzig Conservatory from 1862 to 1865, where he studied with Moscheles. He was selected on three occasions to play piano concertos in public performances in the Gewandhaus and earned the prestigious Helbig Prize at the conclusion of his studies. Upon his return to the United States he was active as a pianist, introducing unfamiliar works by Schumann and Beethoven to the Boston public. He founded and taught at the Petersilea Academy of Music in Boston from 1871 to 1886, then at the New England Conservatory from 1886 to 1892 before moving to California. In 1884 he took a group of students on an extended trip to Germany, where they visited Liszt in Weimar. His solo recital in Berlin on 10 April of that year earned accolades from the Berlin critics. In addition to a revision of his father's five-volume piano method, Petersilea authored a number of books on spiritualism and the afterlife, including *Letters from the Spirit World: Written through the mediumship of Carlyle Petersilea, by his Father, Franz Petersilea, and Other Spirit Celebrities.*

BIBLIOGRAPHY

F. Petersilea: *The Petersilea System for the Piano-forte* (Boston, 1872, enlarged 2/1888 by C. Petersilea)

"Carlyle Petersilea," *Brainard's Musical World* (1879); repr. in *Brainard's Biographies of American Musicians*, ed. E.D. Bomberger (Westport, 1999)

M.E. Benedict: *Musical People in Retrospect* (Boston, 1931)

E. DOUGLAS BOMBERGER

Peterson, Curt (*b* Colorado, 1967). Tenor. He studied at the Juilliard School's Opera Center after taking a degree in vocal performance at the University of Colorado at Boulder, and made his professional debut, as David in *Die Meistersinger*, with Opera Colorado in 1992. Since then he has made his name in North America as a fluent lyric tenor, equally adept in the bel canto repertory (with Gioachino Rossini's Count Almaviva a favorite role) and in contemporary opera. He is also a noted interpreter of the Classical oratorio repertory and of later works such as *Carmina burana*. His other operatic roles include Nadir (*Les pêcheurs de perles*), Tonio in *La fille du régiment* (which he sang for his Opera Lyra Ottawa debut in 2001), Ajax I in *La belle Hélène*, Lindoro (*L'Italiana in Algeri*), Ramiro (*La Cenerentola*), and Ernesto (*Don Pasquale*). In 1996 Peterson created the role of Matthew Gurney in Santa Fe Opera's 1996 world premiere production of Picker's *Emmeline*; he repeated the part for his New York City Opera debut the following season and also for the recording. In 2001 he made his French debut, at the Nantes Opera, in a production of Manfred Gurlitt's *Soldaten*. He joined the University of Colorado voice faculty in 2001.

RICHARD WIGMORE/R

Peterson, Hannibal (Marvin) [Marvin (Charles); Lokumbe, Hannibal; Hannibal] (*b* Smithville, TX, 11 Nov 1948). Trumpeter, composer, and poet. As a child, he was inspired by the music favored by his grandparents, including African American spirituals. He was given a trumpet at the age of 13 and quickly formed a band, the Soul Masters. They found success almost immediately as the backup group for a variety of performers traveling through the Texas area including Otis Redding, Jackie Wilson, Etta James, and T-Bone Walker. Peterson went to school at North Texas University (1967–9), and then moved to New York in 1970 to pursue a career as a jazz trumpeter. He resided there for 25 years, finding substantial success as both a sideman and as lead trumpet, and working with musicians such as Frank Foster, Roland Kirk, Pharaoh Sanders, Roy Haynes, Elvin Jones, McCoy Tyner, Don Pullen, and Gil Evans. He joined Evans on a number of albums, including *Svengali* (Atlantic, 1973) and *Priestess* (Polygram, 1977), and even after releasing his own significant solo work, continued to record with Evans into the 1980s. His trumpet playing draws from elements of hard bop and free jazz, alternating between clear, rapid lines and highly expressive swoops and piercing blasts. In 1974 he founded the Sunrise Orchestra, which performed frequently at international music festivals, including those in Japan, China, and Turkey. Since the mid-1970s he has recorded a wide range of music with a variety of artists. Some of his most prominent early releases include *Children of Fire* (Sunrise, 1974), *Hannibal* (MPS, 1975), *Tribute* (Baystate, 1979), and *The Angels of Atlanta* (Enja, 1981). He also reached out to different audiences by performing in schools, churches, and prisons. Adopting the name Hannibal Lokumbe, he continued to perform regularly as a trumpet player into the 2000s and has also branched out into composition, lecturing, and writing poetry. Peterson's compositions fuse elements of jazz, blues, gospel, African and African American rhythms, and Western classical components. He served as composer-in-residence (1999–2002) for the Pathways to Connections concert series in New Orleans. He often writes on a large scale for full orchestra and choir. He has published two volumes of poetry and has continued to write into the 21st century. Among the awards he has received include a grant from the NEA, a lifetime achievement award from the Detroit SO, and a Fellow Award in Music from United States Artists (2009).

BIBLIOGRAPHY
G. Endress: "Hannibal Marvin Peterson," *JP*, xxiv/5 (1975), 14
B.J. Primack: "Hannibal," *DB*, xliv/15 (1977), 24
L. Van Trikt: "Marvin 'Hannibal' Peterson," *Cadence*, xxii/3 (1996), 5

JONAS WESTOVER

Peterson, John Willard (*b* Lindsborg, KS, 1 Nov 1921; *d* Scottscale, AZ, 20 Sept 2006). Composer and publisher. He studied at the Moody Bible Institute and the American Conservatory of Music in Chicago. In 1954 he joined Singspiration, Alfred B. Smith's gospel music publishing firm, in Montrose, Pennsylvania; with P.J. and B.D. Zondervan he purchased the company in 1963 and moved to Grand Rapids, Michigan. In 1971 he moved to Arizona, but continued to serve as executive editor for Singspiration. Peterson received the International Gospel Songwriting Award of the Society of European Stage Authors and Composers in 1975. He established another firm to publish contemporary gospel music in 1977; Good Life Publications, of Scottsdale, Arizona, became a division of Belwin-Mills in 1982. He also founded the John W. Peterson Music Co. Peterson's cantatas for church use have sold nearly ten million copies. His most popular gospel songs include "It took a miracle," "Heaven came down," and "Surely Goodness and Mercy." He wrote an autobiography, *The Miracle Goes On* (1976), and a film of the same title was made about his life. He was inducted into the Gospel Music Hall of Fame in 1986.

BIBLIOGRAPHY
W.J. Reynolds: *Companion to Baptist Hymnal* (Nashville, 1976)

HARRY ESKEW/R

Peterson, Oscar (Emmanuel) (*b* Montreal, QC, 15 Aug 1925; *d* Mississauga, ON, 23 Dec 2007). Canadian jazz composer, pianist, and singer. Born into a musical Montreal family, he began to play trumpet before a bout of childhood tuberculosis moved him to piano. Peterson began studying with the Hungarian-Canadian pianist Paul de Marky, who taught the pedagogical method of Franz Liszt, perhaps explaining Peterson's lifelong foregrounding of technical virtuosity. Influenced by Teddy Wilson, Erroll Garner, Nat "King" Cole, and Art Tatum, Peterson gravitated towards boogie-woogie and jazz. Turning professional at age 14, Peterson established himself in Canada through his work with the CBC ("Light Up and Listen"), his soundtrack to Norman McLaren's animated *Begone Dull Care* (1949), his stay with the Johnny Holmes Orchestra, his 16 78 recordings for RCA Victor, and his engagement at Montreal's Alberta Lounge (1947–9). It was here

that Peterson was "discovered" by the impresario Norman Granz.

After hearing Peterson at the Alberta, Granz, who would become Peterson's manager, record producer, and lifelong friend, invited him to make his unannounced American debut at Carnegie Hall on 18 September 1949. Peterson joined Granz's traveling Jazz at the Philharmonic in 1950, playing in the drummer-less trio format (piano, guitar, bass) popularized by Tatum and Cole. Working with bassist Ray Brown and guitarists Barney Kessel and (more prominently) Herb Ellis, the trio became a favorite of Granz (who used Peterson and the others as accompanists for recordings by Ella Fitzgerald, Lester Young, Ben Webster, Roy Eldridge, and Stan Getz) and with audiences who found their swinging style accessible. Ellis's 1958 departure led to a change of instrumentation with the entry of drummer Ed Thigpen. This trio incarnation became among the busiest jazz ensembles of the 1950s and 60s, performing over one hundred concerts around the globe each year, while recording numerous albums for Granz's label, Verve. Still, Peterson found the time, along with Phil Nimmons, to open Toronto's Advanced School of Contemporary Music (ASCM) on 11 January 1960.

Throughout the 1970s and 80s Peterson continued to record and perform in various capacities—solo, duo with Joe Pass or Niels-Henning Ørsted Pedersen, in occasional small group format, and with symphony orchestras—until being waylaid by a stroke in 1993. Peterson's post-stroke playing emphasized a right-hand linear approach, and performances increasingly featured his own compositions, including *Canadiana Suite* and "Hymn to Freedom." Highly feted, Peterson, who became York University's Chancellor in 1991, remains, in death as in life, an iconic jazz figure.

RECORDINGS
(selective list)
As unaccompanied soloist: *My Favorite Instrument* (1968, MPS)
As leader: *The Oscar Peterson Trio at the Stratford Shakespearean Festival* (1956, Verve); *The Way I Really Play* (1968)
As sideman: S. Stitt: *Sonny Stitt Sits in with the Oscar Peterson Trio* (1959, Verve)

BIBLIOGRAPHY
B. James: "Oscar Peterson," *Essays on Jazz* (London, 1961), 134
L. Feather: "Piano Giants of Jazz: Oscar Peterson," *Contemporary Keyboard*, iv/7 (1978), 53
G. Lees: *Oscar Peterson: the Will to Swing* (London, 1989)
R. Palmer and O. Peterson: *A Jazz Odyssey: the Life of Oscar Peterson* (London and New York, 2002)

ANDREW SCOTT

Peterson, Wayne T. (*b* Albert Lea, MN, 8 March 1927). Composer. He studied at the University of Minnesota (BA 1951, MA 1953, PhD 1960) where his teachers included Paul Fetler, EARL GEORGE, and James Aliferis. A Fulbright Scholarship (1953–4) enabled him to spend a year at the RAM where he studied with Lennox Berkeley and Howard Ferguson. He has held teaching appointments at San Francisco State University (1960–1992), Indiana University (1992) and Stanford University (1992–4), and fulfilled commissions for the San Francisco

SO, Louisville Orchestra, Freiberg SO, and the American Composer's Orchestra and the Guggenheim, Fromm, Koussevitzky, Meet the Composer, Gerbode, and Djerassi foundations. He has received awards from the Minnesota Centennial Composition Contest (1958), the American Society of Harpists (1985), and the American Academy and Institute of Arts and Letters (1986). In 1990 he was a visiting artist at the American Academy in Rome and in 1992 won a Pulitzer Prize for *The Face of the Night, The Heart of the Dark*. He was guest composer at the Composer's Conference in Wellesley, Massachusetts, and the Festival of New Music, Sacramento State University. He has served on the Nomination Committee for the Pulitzer Prize in Music, 1999–2001, and was a jury member for the First Seoul International Competition for Composers, 2001. In addition, Peterson, in joint sponsorship with San Francisco State University, established and currently administers the Wayne Peterson Prize in Music Composition (since 1998).

Peterson is an open-minded enthusiastic listener and a self-confessed eclectic. He is a composer of great independence and boldness of spirit. His compositions, formed in the 12-tone idiom but without systematic application, are generated by intensely compacted ideas in combustive rhythmic play. His music is characterized by strikingly intricate and intensely active rhythms, profuse and inventive melodic and contrapuntal lines, and secure, if at times elusive, formal structures. His works range in mood from driving and devilishly playful to sensuous. The jazz that emerges here and there in certain of his chamber works is nothing contrived in the manner of so-called "fusion." It happens occasionally out of the recesses of Peterson's early life and the openness or breadth of his musical experience. Always in Peterson's music the driving force remains rhythmic, with an intricacy of the interaction of parts and an irregularity that develops fierce energy. In its larger design, the rhythm draws on advanced techniques such as metric modulation, maintaining an undiverted flow.

Peterson works with the colors and characters of the individual instruments like a master painter, matching and contrasting them, exploring their possibilities and the challenges of the particular medium, creating a changing field of textures. Thus, his music with its flux of tempos is imbued with an extraordinary fluidity of sonority. His craft incorporates a high specificity of performance directions, particularizing advanced playing techniques and tempo and expression indications. He provides the performers with a vocabulary of the symbols that have evolved in new music performance, many of his own invention. His music engages the listener in the challenge that animated it, embodying a creative process that anticipated the digital age.

Later compositions employ an increasingly tonal idiom. Originally a jazz pianist, he began composing under the influence of Copland and Stravinsky before becoming absorbed by the music of Schoenberg and Sessions. He has also acknowledged Boulez, Carter, and Wuorinen as important influences.

WORKS

INSTRUMENTAL

Orch: Free Variations, 1958; Introduction and Allegro, 1959; Exaltation, Dithyramb and Caprice, 1961; Clusters and Fragments, str, 1968; Transformations, chbr orch, 1986; Triology, chbr orch, 1988; The Widening Gyre, 1990; The Face of the Night, The Heart of the Dark, 1991; And the Winds Shall Blow, sax qt, orch, 1994; Theseus Ov, 1995

Chbr: Metamorphosis, wind qnt, 1967; Phantasmagoria, pic + fl + a fl, E♭ cl + cl + b cl, cb, 1969; Capriccio, fl, pf, 1973; Diatribe, vn, pf, 1975; Encounters, pic + fl, cl + b cl, hn, tpt, vn, vc, perc, pf, 1976; Rhapsody, vc, pf, 1976; An Interrupted Serenade, fl, vc, hp, 1978; Doubles, 2 fl, cl, b cl, 1982; Sextet, pic + fl + a fl, cl + b cl, vn, vc, perc, hp, 1982; Str Qt no.1, 1983; Ariadne's Thread, pic + fl + a fl, ob, cl + b cl, hn, vn, perc, hp, 1985; Duodecaphony, va, vc, 1987; Labyrinth, fl, cl, vn, pf, 1987; Mallets Aforethought, perc qt, 1990; Str Qt no.2 Apparitions, Jazz Play, 1991; Diptych: Aubade, Odyssey, pic + fl + a fl, cl + b cl, vn, vc, perc, pf, 1992; Duo, vn, pf, 1993; Janus, fl, ob, cl, hn, tpt, vn, va, vc, perc, pf, 1993; Vicissitudes, pic + fl + a fl, cl + b cl, vn, vc, perc, pf, 1995; Windup, sax qt, 1997; Peregrinations, solo cl, 1997; Monarch of the Vine, perc qt, 1998, unpubd; Str Qt no.3 "Pop Sweet," 1998; Colloquy, fl, hp, 1999, unpubd; Antiphonies, solo perc (mar, vib), 1999, unpubd; Inscape, fl/a fl, cl/b cl, perc, 2000, unpubd; Four Preludes for Piano, 2000, unpubd; Nonet, fl/pic/a fl, ob, cl/b cl, hn, perc, pf, vn, va, vc, 2001, unpubd; Quest, fl/a fl, pf, 2002, unpubd; A Three Piece Suite, fl/pic/a fl, cl/b cl, vn, vc, perc, pn, 2003, unpubd; Pas de Deux, fl/a fl, mar/vib, 2006, unpubd; Str Trio, 2007, unpubd; Scherzo, fl, cl, vn, vc, 2008, unpubd; Trap Drum Fantasy, trap drum set, 2009, unpubd; Full Circle, brass qnt, perc, 2009, unpubd; Excursion, vn, pf, 2010, unpubd; arrs. incl. works by Ravel (Sonatine), De Falla (4 Spanish Songs)

VOCAL

Choral: Can Death Be Sleep (J. Keats), 1955; Earth, Sweet Earth (G.M. Hopkins), 1956; Ps lvi, 1959; An E.E. Cummings Triptych, 1962; An E.E. Cummings Cant., SATB, pf/octet, 1964; Spring (T. Nash), 1970; A Robert Herrick Motley, 1997; Carol (W. Austin), 2000, unpubd; She Lives with the Furies of Hope and Despair; I Am Cherry Alive (D. Schwartz), 2006, unpubd

Solo: 3 Songs (L. Tennyson, T.S. Eliot, Hopkins), S, pf, 1957; Ceremony After a Fire Raid (D. Thomas), S, pf, 1969; Dark Reflections (J. Joyce, E. St. Vincent Millay, T. Campbell), S, vn, pf, 1980; Freedom and Love (T. Campbell), sop, 1 perc. 2004; arr. Debussy (Song Cycle) Debussy String Quartet, 1st movt, 8 cl, 1989; Ravel Sonatine, ww qnt, 1989; Four Spanish Songs (De Falla), ww qnt, 1991; Seven Debussy Songs for S or Mez, chbr orch, 1999; A Brahms Suite, Capriccio in B minor, op.76, no.2, Intermezzi, op.119, nos. 2 and 3, ww qnt, 2001; A Debussy Suite, from Suite Bergamasque and Preludes, ww qnt, 2002; Transcriptions of Piano Music, Chopin Valse Brillante, Bartók Rondo on a Folk Tune, Ravel Pavanne, ww qnt, 2002

Principal publishers: Peters, Trillenium, Seesaw, Lawson-Gould, Boosey & Hawkes

BIBLIOGRAPHY

R. Commanday: "Composer Wayne Peterson," *San Francisco Chronicle* (13 Oct 1991)

ROBERT COMMANDAY

Petit, Buddy [Crawford, Joseph] (*b*, New Orleans, LA, *c*1897; *d* New Orleans, LA, 4 July 1931). Jazz cornetist and bandleader. Buddy Petit began his professional career as a founding member of the Young Olympia Band, formed when Olympia Band cornetist Freddie Keppard left New Orleans to join the Original Creole Band in Los Angeles in 1914. Other members of the Young Olympia were clarinetist Jimmie Noone, trombonist Zue Robertson, banjoist Simon Marrero, bassist John Marrero, and drummer Arnold DePass, and shortly afterward Noone and Petit co-led a band of their own at places such as the Pythian Temple until the clarinetist left to join Keppard in Chicago for the Creole Band's final vaudeville season in 1917–8. Petit made a short trip to Los Angeles in 1917 to work with Jelly Roll Morton before returning to New Orleans and situating himself as one of the top bandleaders on the regional (Texas–Florida) scene. A photograph taken in Mandeville, Louisiana, c1920, shows Petit with a seven-piece band: Leon René (vocals), Edmond Hall (clarinet), George Washington (trombone), Buddy Manaday (banjo), Chester Zardis (bass), and Eddie Woods (drums). In an era when nascent New Orleans jazz trumpet and cornet players sought to define themselves and gain work by developing a unique signature "voice" on their instrument, Petit was renowned as a player who eschewed the high-note theatrics often relished by trumpeters in favor of a mid-range, blues-inflected expressive style relying on rich tone to elicit audience response. Petit never recorded commercially.

BIBLIOGRAPHY

J. De Donder: "My Buddy," *Footnote*, xiv/3 (1983), 24; xiv/4 (1983), 4
K. Koenig: *'Under the Influence': the Four Hornsmen of New Orleans Early Jazz* (New Orleans, LA, 1994)

BRUCE BOYD RAEBURN

Petri, Egon (*b* Hanover, Prussia [now in Germany], 23 March 1881; *d* Berkeley, CA, 27 May 1962). German pianist and teacher of Dutch descent, later active in the United States. At the age of five he had violin lessons with his father, Henri Petri, then leader of the Leipzig Gewandhaus Orchestra. Following the family's move to Berlin in 1889 he became a pupil of the pianist Teresa Carreño. He also learned the organ and the horn, and as a teenager studied composition and theory with Kretschmar and Draeseke. From 1901, when he joined FERRUCCIO BUSONI's master class at Weimar, the piano became his chosen instrument. Busoni took a deep interest in his development and later described him as being his "most genuine pupil." Petri corrected the manuscripts of Busoni's operas and piano works, and also collaborated with him in editing Bach's keyboard works.

He made his debut in Holland in 1902, although initially failed to establish a successful career. In 1905 he became a professor at the Royal Manchester College of Music, and he remained there until 1911, after which he returned to Berlin as Busoni's assistant. From 1921 to 1925 Petri taught at the Hochschule für Musik and pursued a busy concert schedule, with an intensive tour of Russia in 1923. He lived at Zakopane in Poland from 1925, and this remained his base until the outbreak of the Second World War. The 1930s was the busiest decade in his career. A notable American debut in January 1932 opened a new chapter in both his concert and teaching activity, and he subsequently became a naturalized American. From 1940 to 1946 he was visiting professor at Cornell University, but following a serious illness he decided to move to the West Coast and settled in California as a teacher and lecturer at Mills College, Oakland, where he remained for a further decade. He also taught at the San Francisco Conservatory. His pupils included Carl Szreter, Franz Joseph Hirt, Gunnar

Johansen, Vitya Vronsky, Earl Wild, Grant Johannsen, and Ernst Lévy, as well as John Ogdon, who attended his master classes in Basle.

Although Petri was a large-scale player in the Busoni mold, his playing differed in many respects to that of his teacher. He was considerably more dutiful in regard to both correct style and adherence to the printed text. In contrast to the tonal richness of Busoni's playing, Petri's piano sound frequently had a rough edge to it. His playing was noted for a massiveness of conception and for its dedicated interpretative insight. Particularly admired in Bach, Beethoven, and Liszt, Petri was also a staunch advocate of his mentor's compositions, a number of which he recorded.

BIBLIOGRAPHY

M. Benedict: "The Legacy of Egon Petri," *Clavier*, xxxvi/9 (1997), 19–23
F. Busoni and M. Weindel, ed.: *Briefe an Henri, Katharina und Egon Petri* (Wilhelmshaven, Germany, 1999)
D. Manildi, ed.: "Petri in Retrospect," *Pianists, on and off the Record: the Collected Essays of Jan Holcman* (College Park, MD, 2000), 47–51

JAMES METHUEN-CAMPBELL/R

Petrides, Frédérique Joanne [née Mayer, Frédérica Jeanne Elisabeth Petronille] (*b* Antwerp, Belgium, 1903; *d* New York, NY, 12 Jan 1983). Conductor. She studied violin with Mathieu Crickboom, Gösta Andreasson, and Paul Stassevitch. In 1923 she came to the United States and worked in New York as a freelance violinist and teacher. She married Peter Petrides in 1931. In 1932–3 she attended JOHN LAWRENCE ERB's summer conducting classes at New York University, but it was Mitropoulos, whose rehearsals with the New York PO she attended regularly from 1950 to 1956, who most strongly influenced her conducting. In 1933 she founded the Orchestrette of New York (known first as the Orchestrette Classique) for female instrumentalists; it gave concerts in Aeolian Hall and Carnegie Recital Hall from 1934 to 1943. The orchestra's newsletter, *Women in Music* (1935–40), edited by Petrides, was very effective in promoting the activities of women in professional music. In addition to the Orchestrette, Petrides conducted the Hudson Valley SO, the West Side Community Concerts, the Student Symphony Society of New York, and summer concerts in Washington Square and Carl Schurz parks. A pioneering woman conductor, she was one of the first to demonstrate that women could work successfully in the field of professional concert music.

BIBLIOGRAPHY

J.G. Pool: "America's Women Composers: Up from the Footnotes," *MEJ*, lxv/5 (1979), 28–41
C. Neuls-Bates: *Women in Music* (New York, 1982, 2/1996), 253, 259–64
J.B. Groh: *Evening the Score: Women in Music and the Legacy of Frédérique Petrides* (Fayetteville, AR, 1991)

JEAN BOWEN/R

Petrillo, James C(aesar) (*b* Chicago, IL, 16 March 1892; *d* Chicago, IL, 23 Oct 1984). Labor leader. He played trumpet and at the age of 14 organized a dance band. He was soon attracted to union activity, and in 1914 he was elected president of the American Musicians Union

(AMU) in Chicago. After being defeated for reelection three years later, he resigned from the AMU and joined the AMERICAN FEDERATION OF MUSICIANS (AFM). He became president of the Chicago local in 1922, was named to the parent union's executive board in 1932, and in 1940 was elected national president, a post he held until he retired in 1958 (although he retained the presidency of the Chicago local for another four years).

Petrillo was an aggressive, shrewd, and powerful fighter for the musicians in the AFM. He built the Chicago local into a disciplined force in municipal politics and worked to expand the membership at the national level (by 1951 the 20 largest AFM locals had a total of nearly 98,000 members). He was particularly active in the matter of the threat to musicians' income and employment posed by recorded music and in August 1942 called a strike banning AFM members from making recordings until the record manufacturers would agree to pay the union a fee for every disc produced. Decca Records signed such an agreement about a year later; RCA Victor and Columbia, the other major companies, held out until autumn 1944, when they too signed and agreed to pay between .25¢ and 5¢ per disc. The gain to AFM was reported to be $4 million per year. Through his political influence, he advocated for racial integration; for example, he canceled an AFM conference outing in St. Petersburg, Florida, in 1946 because local venues would not permit African American attendees. He became the head of the Civil Rights Division of the AFM in 1964. In 2009 he was posthumously inducted into the Illinois Labor History Society Union Hall of Honor.

See also UNIONS, MUSICIANS'.

BIBLIOGRAPHY

P.S. Carpenter: *Music: an Art and a Business* (Norman, OK, 1950), 137ff
R.D. Leiter: *The Musicians and Petrillo* (New York, 1953)
P. Hart: "James Caesar Petrillo and the Militant Musician," *Orpheus in the New World* (New York, 1973), 96
Obituary, *New York Times* (25 Oct 1984)
G. Seltzer: *Music Matters: the Performer and the American Federation of Musicians* (Lanham, MD, 1989)
C. Sengstock: *That Toddlin' Town: Chicago's White Dance Bands and Orchestras, 1900–1950* (Urbana, IL, 2004)
W.H. Young and N.K. Young: *Music of the World War II Era* (Westport, CT, 2008)

H. WILEY HITCHCOCK/JOANNA R. SMOLKO

Pettiford, Oscar (*b* Okmulgee, OK, 30 Sept 1922; *d* Copenhagen, Denmark, 8 Sept 1960). Jazz double bass player, cellist, and bandleader. Of mixed African American and Native American heritage, he was born into a large, musical family and learned many instruments in the family's touring band, which was based in Minneapolis. In 1943 he was engaged as a bass player for Charlie Barnet's band, with which he traveled to New York in the same year. After working with a quintet led by Roy Eldridge (1943), he found a place in the emerging bop scene; he worked as coleader, with Dizzy Gillespie, of a combo at the Onyx (1943–4). Personal differences caused this pioneering group to disband, but one year later he and Gillespie recorded together.

From 1944 Pettiford played in numerous small bop combos and in various big bands, notably Duke Ellington's (1945–8) and Woody Herman's (1949). In the mid-1950s he led his own big band that, though highly regarded for its inventive arrangements and instrumentation, suffered from instability of personnel, owing in part to Pettiford's difficult temperament. He immigrated to Europe in 1958, and in his final years was based in Copenhagen.

Pettiford was the first jazz bass player to adapt and elaborate the innovations of Jimmy Blanton within a bop context, and his ideas and discoveries had a lasting influence on the bop style as a whole. His earliest recorded solos, such as "The Man I Love" (Signature, 1943), were learned by rote by many aspiring bop bass players, though few could approach his penetrating tone and clear projection of ideas. Later, from about 1950, he transferred his solo style to amplified cello, which he played in a bouncy, dexterous style, reminiscent of Charlie Christian. Together with Ray Brown and Charles Mingus, who owed much to his influence, Pettiford was influential in establishing the double bass as a jazz solo instrument equal in importance to the winds.

BIBLIOGRAPHY

P. Harris: "Oscar Pettiford Now on Cello Kick," *DB*, xvii/26 (1950), 20
G. Hoefer: "Oscar Pettiford," *DB*, xxxiii/11 (1966), 25
I. Gitler: *Jazz Masters of the Forties* (New York, 1966/R1983 with discography), 150
J.-E. Berendt: "Thank You, Oscar Pettiford," *Ein Fenster aus Jazz* (Frankfurt am Main, Germany, 1977), 141
C. Gazdar: *First Bass: the Oscar Pettiford Discography* (Bangalore, India, 1991)

J. BRADFORD ROBINSON/R

Petty, Tom [Thomas] **(Earl)** (*b* Gainesville, FL, 20 Oct 1952). Rock singer, songwriter, and guitarist. In the early 1970s he moved to Los Angeles with his band Mudcrutch, which soon dissolved. Petty formed the Heartbreakers with former Mudcrutch members Mike Campbell (guitar) and Benmont Tench (keyboards), adding Ron Blair (bass) and Stan Lynch (drums). Other Heartbreakers have included Howie Epstein (bass), Steve Ferrone (drums), and Scott Thurston (guitar and vocals). Petty's early songs were short and riff-based in contrast to the "jam band" aesthetic prevalent in the South during the 1970s, earning him comparisons with New Wave. Influenced by Bob Dylan and Roger McGuinn, his rough, varied vocal delivery is one of the most recognizable in rock. After his first hit, "Breakdown" (1976), and the release of two studio albums, Petty challenged his record company (MCA) and was able to renegotiate a new contract, a rare feat for an artist at the time. He began working with producer Jimmy Iovine for his third album, *Damn the Torpedoes* (1979); the album's hits ("Refugee," "Don't do me like that") firmly established Petty's career.

In the early 1980s Petty struggled to generate hits, but a collaboration with Dave Stewart of the Eurythmics temporarily revived him with "Don't Come Around Here No More." The song's video starred Petty as the Mad Hatter from *Alice in Wonderland* and was played in heavy rotation on MTV, winning younger fans. In 1989 Petty had his second breakthrough with a solo album, *Full Moon Fever*. (In his solo work Petty employs members of the Heartbreakers, making solo and group projects difficult to distinguish.) On *Full Moon Fever* (1989) and *Into the Great Wide Open* (1991), Petty and producer Jeff Lynne added multiple acoustic guitar tracks to Petty's basic rock band line-up. The arrangements nodded back to one of Petty's influences, folk rock, but showcased the lush and polished sound for which Lynne was known. With Lynne, Dylan, Roy Orbison, and George Harrison, Petty founded the Traveling Wilburys in the late 1980s. *Wildflowers* (Warner Bros., 1994) marked a return to a simpler recording aesthetic with producer Rick Rubin. His later work *Mojo* (2010) is based in electric blues. Petty has participated in Live Aid, Farm Aid, and MUSE (Musicians United for Safe Energy, a.k.a. "No Nukes") concerts, and he performed in the halftime show for Super Bowl XLII in 2008.

BIBLIOGRAPHY
P. Zollo and T. Petty: *Conversations with Tom Petty* (London, 2005)
Tom Petty and the Heartbreakers: Runnin' Down a Dream, dir. P. Bogdanovich, Reprise, 2007 [video documentary]

OLIVIA CARTER MATHER

Petzold, Robert G(eorge) (*b* Milwaukee, WI, 25 Sept 1917; *d* Madison, WI, 9 July 1999). Music educator and scholar. He attended Milwaukee State Teachers College (BS 1938) and taught music in the Wisconsin public schools (1938–42, 1946–51), serving in World War II in the interim (1942–6). He completed two degrees at the University of Wisconsin–Madison (MM 1947, PhD 1950) and taught there for the remainder of his career (1951–86), also serving as chair of the Curriculum and Instruction Department (1965–7) and associate dean of the School of Education (1967–70). Petzold secured the first US Department of Education grant of its kind in music education, and five subsequent grants for his foundational studies on auditory perception and for research training projects. His landmark longitudinal study, *Auditory Perception of Musical Sounds by Children in the First Six Grades* (University of Wisconsin–Madison, 1966), and related studies have influenced subsequent research. He also held leadership positions in the International Society for Music Education Research Commission and the Music Educators National Conference Music Education Research Council, and sat on the editorial committees of the *Music Educators Journal* (1962–6) and *Journal of Research in Music Education* (1966–72), of which he was editor (1972–8). Petzold received the Wisconsin Music Educators Association's Distinguished Service Award (1990).

BIBLIOGRAPHY
R.G. Petzold and J.C. Dunbar: *Oral History Program Interview with Robert G. Petzold, 1994, University of Wisconsin–Madison Archives* (Madison, WI, 1994)
A.L. Barresi, G.B. Olson, and A. Lockwood: *Memorial Resolution of the Faculty of the University of Wisconsin–Madison: On the Death of Professor Emeritus Robert George Petzold, Faculty Document 1484, 6 March 2000* (Madison, WI, 2000)

DAVID L. PERRY

Peyote drum. A water drum used in meetings of the Native American (or Peyote) Church. The standard drum consists of a well-soaked buckskin head stretched over an iron kettle about 25 cm deep. The best skins are said to be "brain tanned." The head symbolizes the former war shield, now a spiritual shield. It is attached by an intricate tying method that has symbolic import. Symbolism and rules may vary from fireplace to fireplace with some ideas common throughout the religion. Seven stones or marbles indicating the seven days, the seven sisters (constellations), the seven senses (orifices) of the face, or, for the Sioux, the seven council fires, are tied to the head. The rope tying the head represents the rope used to tie enemies, the reins of war horses, or blood veins. The kettle is half-filled with water, which represents rain or the water of the earth; the sound of the drum represents thunder. Live coals (four to 12 depending on the fireplace) symbolizing lightning are put in the water before the head is attached. The skin is kept moist during meetings by vigorously shaking the kettle between songs or a quick shake during a song when the sound begins to change. At some fireplaces the drummer will suck or blow on the edge of the drum to force water onto the head, while at others this is prohibited.

The drum may be marked on the outside with ash, pollen, or red paint depending upon rules of the local fireplace. Though small, the peyote drum is considered more powerful than the large powwow drum because it contains all the elements of life. History indicates that a hand drum was used in the early years of the peyote cult and that use of the water drum was borrowed from the Apache.

The beater is an unpadded stick about 30 cm long, which may be carved and decorated; it strikes forcefully, producing a loud, resonant sound. Heads of canvas or rubber have been used when buckskin was not available. Earthenware crocks and tin cans have substituted for iron kettles, and in recent years aluminum copies of the standard kettle have been made especially for use as peyote drums; they are light and easy to handle. The drum rests on the ground, tilted towards the drumming hand of the kneeling player. The thumb of the hand holding the drum presses against its head to govern tone and pitch, though some fireplaces prohibit this action.

The songs are performed in sets of four; a fast, even drumbeat continues throughout each song but the tempo slows and the pitch drops between songs. Women attend meetings but ordinarily do not drum or sing. The drum is played at the same time as the PEYOTE RATTLE.

BIBLIOGRAPHY
D.P. McAllester: *Peyote Music* (New York, 1949)
M.E. Opler: *An Apache Life-Way* (New York, 1965)
W. La Barre: *The Peyote Cult* (New York, 1970)

DAVID P. MCALLESTER/J. RICHARD HAEFER

Peyote music. The music of the Native American Church, the beliefs and practices of which fuse Native religious practices with Christian elements; *see* Peyote drum; Peyote rattle; Native american music.

Peyote rattle. Small vessel rattle used by singers during ceremonies of the Native American (or Peyote) Church. It is a gourd about eight to nine cm in diameter containing pebbles, pierced by a straight wooden handle about 25 to 30 cm long that passes through the gourd and projects slightly. A circular stopper on the handle prevents the stones from falling out. A tuft of dyed horsehair, representing the peyote cactus blossom, is tied to the projecting end. The handle, which may be carved or beaded at the base, symbolizes the arrow or the riding crop used in war but now used in peace. The beadwork may show various symbolic designs: rainbow for beauty of life, red-white-blue for war veterans, fire, or water. 12 tassels cut from a bowstring (so it can never be used on a bow again) decorate the end of the handle to symbolize the months or yearly cycle. The user shakes the rattle with one hand and holds the peyote staff (symbolic of the broken bow) in his other hand. The stopper can be of wood or even a coin; it does not touch the edge of the gourd. Friction of the end of the handle projecting at the top (symbolic of the arrow head) holds the handle to the gourd. The rattle pebbles may have individual significance such as turquoise for an Apache, salt, ant, or ocean pebbles, etc. The outer surface of the rattle may be decorated in patterns related to the peyote ceremony or patterns important to the owner such as stars, moon, fire, or eagle; older rattles often had patterns scratched into the surface.

During a peyote ceremony the rattle, followed by the Peyote drum, is passed clockwise around the circle of participants starting from the west behind the altar. Each person is expected to sing (usually four songs) before passing it on. Often a song is introduced with a tremolo on the two instruments, which then maintain the same rather quick tempo of the song.

BIBLIOGRAPHY

D.P. McAllester: *Peyote Music* (New York, 1949)
M.E. Opler: *An Apache Life-Way* (New York, 1965)
W. La Barre: *The Peyote Cult* (New York, 1970)

MARY RIEMER-WELLER/J. RICHARD HAEFER

Peyser, Ethel R(ose) (*b* New York, NY, 6 March 1887; *d* New York, NY, 12 Sept 1961). Writer. She was educated at Vassar College, Barnard College, and Columbia University Teachers College (BS 1908). From 1912 to 1914 she worked in the editorial department of the *New York Herald Tribune* and in 1914 for the *New York Evening Mail*. She was music critic for the *Musical Leader* from 1926 until 1934 and contributed to other music journals; she also worked on the staff of general magazines and wrote articles and books on hobbies and domestic topics. In conjunction with Marion Bauer she wrote two successful popular histories of music: *How Music Grew* (1925, rev. 2/1939) and *Music through the Ages* (1932, rev. 3/1967). Her other books include *How to Enjoy Music* (1933), *The Book of Culture: the Basis of a Liberal Education* (1934/R1941), *The House that Music Built: Carnegie Hall* (1936), and *How Opera Grew* (1956).

BIBLIOGRAPHY

J.T. Howard: *Our American Music* (New York, 1931, rev. 4/1965), 566
E.N.C. Barnes: *American Women in Creative Music* (Washington, DC, 1937), 19
Obituary, *New York Times* (14 Sept 1961), 31

MARY A. WISCHUSEN/R

Peyser [née Gilbert], **Joan** (*b* New York, NY, 12 June 1931; *d* New York, NY, 24 April 2011). Editor and writer on music. Peyser began her musical career as a pianist, performing publicly at New York's Town Hall in 1944 at the age of 13. She studied at Smith College (1947–9), Barnard College (BA 1951), and with Paul Henry Lang at Columbia University (MA 1956, further study until 1958). She wrote numerous articles for such periodicals as *Commentary*, *Vogue*, *Hi-Fi/Stereo Review*, and *Opera News*, and authored many pieces for the Sunday *New York Times* which were based on interviews with European and American musicians. Peyser first won the ASCAP Deems Taylor Award for a 1966 article on Marc Blitzstein and went on to win four more times (1969, 1982, 1984, and 2001). From 1977 to 1984 she was editor of the *Musical Quarterly*. Her work on Leonard Bernstein, *Bernstein: a Biography* (1987, 2/1998), is considered by some critics to be one of the most important critical studies of the composer and his works. Peyser's books, *The New Music* (1971) and *Boulez* (1976), are intended as a history of music from 1880 to the present; the first discusses Arnold Schoenberg, Igor Stravinsky, Anton Webern, and Edgard Varèse, and the second, Karlheinz Stockhausen, John Cage, and Milton Babbitt, in addition to Pierre Boulez. The two books were revised and adapted as the single volume *To Boulez and Beyond* in 1999.

WRITINGS

ed.: *The Orchestra: Origins and Transformations* (New York, 1986)
The Memory of all That: the Life of George Gershwin (New York, 1993)
The Music of my Time (White Plains, NY, 1995)
To Boulez and Beyond: Music in Europe Since the Rite of Spring (New York, 1999)

PAULA MORGAN/JONAS WESTOVER

Pfatteicher, Carl F(riedrichs) (*b* Easton, PA, 22 Sept 1882; *d* Philadelphia, PA, 29 Sept 1957). Organist and teacher. He was trained in music and theology at Harvard (1912) and Freiburg University. From 1912 to 1947 he was professor of music at Phillips Academy in Andover, Massachusetts, where he established a tradition of playing the complete organ works of Bach each academic year in the college chapel. He then taught at Franklin and Marshall College, the University of Pennsylvania, and Trinity University in San Antonio. He edited a number of volumes of organ and choral music, including the organ works of John Redford, *The Christian Year in Part Songs* (1915), *The Christian Year in Chorals* (1917), *Thesaurus musicae sacrae* (1920), and *The Oxford American Hymnal* (1930). He was co-editor of *The Church Organist's Golden Treasury* (c1949) and *The Office Hymns of the Church in their Plainsong Settings* (1951).

MICHAEL FLEMING

Phạm Duy (Cẩn) (*b* Hà Nội, Việt Nam, 5 Oct 1921; *d* Hồ Chí Minh City, 27 Jan 2013). Vietnamese musician, composer, and educator. Born in Hà Nội's Old Quarter, he joined the Việt Minh resistance to French occupation in the 1940s as a performer and composer of resistance songs. He used his experiences touring with a small ensemble as material for songs—including "Về Miền Trung" ("Return to the Central Region") and "Bà Mẹ Gio Linh" ("The Mother of Gio Linh")—to depict the hardship of the soldiers and residents he encountered. He broke with Việt Minh leadership in the early 1950s when they attempted to regiment artistic production. He declined an invitation to join the Communist Party and study composition in Moscow, and he eventually moved to Sài Gòn, where he composed some of his best-known works, including the song cycle *Con đường cái quan* (*The Mandarin Road*) that depicts a north-to-south journey through Việt Nam, "Tình Hoài Hương" ("Feeling for One's Homeland"), and "Ngậm Ngùi" ("Melancholy"), in which he set a poem by poet and Democratic Republic of Vietnam statesman Huy Cận to music. In April 1975 he left Sài Gòn, settling in Ft. Walton Beach, Florida. He soon started Pham Duy Enterprises, selling copies of his cassettes via mail order, and began performing in refugee centers in the United States with his wife and daughter. The troupe later toured US universities as the Pham Duy Family Singers. In 1977 he moved to Midway City, California. He composed prolifically, published instructional and song books, and developed a reputation as a lecturer and educator. He also embraced technology, being the first Vietnamese in the United States to self-produce a CD in the late 1980s, and in 1995 released a visually and aurally rich CD-ROM titled *Trường Ca Con Đường Cái Quan* (*Voyage Through the Motherland*). As a corpus, his music depicts personal and refugee journeys, including the journeys of boat people in "Hát Cho Người Vượt Biển" ("Sing for the Boat People"); the experience of Vietnamese building lives in the United States; and places to which many Vietnamese cannot return, including the Vietnamese countryside and Sài Gòn. He is also known among non-Vietnamese audiences through *Musics of Vietnam* (Carbondale, IL, 1975), the first book in English on Vietnamese music. In 2005 he resettled in Hồ Chí Minh City where he lived until his death in 2013. His published memoirs, *Hồi ký I, II, III, IV,* and other writings are available online (<http://www.phamduy2010.com/e-books>).

RECORDINGS
(selective)
with B. Crofut and S. Addiss: *Music of Vietnam* (Folkways Records, 1965); *Folk Songs of Vietnam* (Folkways Records, 1968)
ALEXANDER M. CANNON

Phase music. A term applied to one of the compositional practices generally referred to as MINIMALISM; it is associated particularly with the work of STEVE REICH.

Phelps, Lawrence Irving (*b* Somerville, MA, 10 May 1923; *d* Boston, MA, 22 Feb 1999). Organ builder. Phelps's early education was directed toward a musical career, and he studied conducting, organ, and several orchestral instruments at the New England Conservatory, as well as electronics at Northeastern University. He sought to design an organ which would restore the fundamental principles of the so-called "classical" organ, typified by the German 17th-century school of the Schnitger family, yet which in its approach to technical problems and its greater versatility would be a genuinely modern instrument. In 1944 he was apprenticed to G. Donald Harrison at the Aeolian-Skinner Organ Co., Boston, and in 1949 spent a year as voicer and tonal finisher for Walter Holtkamp. He then became an independent consultant, his most important project being the large instrument he designed and tonally finished for the First Church of Christ, Scientist, Boston. This was the largest church organ in the United States, and in it he incorporated several technical and tonal innovations, among them dissonant mutations and modifications to the electrical and winding systems, exploring theories then considered radical but now generally accepted.

In 1958 he was appointed tonal director (becoming president in 1971) of the firm of Casavant Frères, Quebec, then one of the world's largest organ building companies, and in 1961 began making modern mechanical-action (tracker) organs, then largely unknown in North America. Not only were these instruments of a sophisticated tonal design, successfully reconciling the two main fundamental schools of organ building and composition (German Baroque and French Classical), but they also introduced advanced technical improvements in the action as well as special low pressure reeds and modern electronic control systems to aid the player. During his 14 years at Casavant, Phelps produced some 650 organs, of which in the United States a typical example in classical north German style is that at Colorado State University, Fort Collins; in contrast is the technically challenging four-manual circular organ (echoing the architecture) suspended from the roof of Lewis and Clark College in Portland, Oregon, the sound of which works entirely by reflection. From 1972 to 1981 he operated his own company in Erie, Pennsylvania, building in 1974 a much acclaimed mechanical-action instrument for the 1300th anniversary of Hexham Abbey, the first major pipe organ built in the United States for a European venue. In 1981 Phelps took up the challenge of applying his principles of design to furthering the development of the electronic organ, and for 14 years he directed the Custom Organ department of the Allen Organ Co., Pennsylvania, before returning to Boston in 1995 to oversee the major restoration of his instrument in the First Church of Christ, Scientist, where he remained as organ curator until his death.

Phelps's organs are noted for their musically functional qualities; their tonal design is based firmly on the requirements of the organ repertoire of all periods while eschewing antiquarianism, and their exceptionally subtle key action further assists the musician. With an original and constantly enquiring mind he rethought each principle of organ design, seeking to realize in the organ the same standards of blend, clarity, musical expressiveness, and above all balance that distinguish all fine musical instruments and ensembles; he wished to make his instruments the perfect vehicle for the expression of the organ's repertoire old and new and for sensitive players to convey their understanding of it.

Phelps was a board member of the International Society of Organ Builders and American editor of its journal until 1980, and a visiting lecturer at Westminster Choir College, Princeton, from 1969 to 1971. He was awarded an honorary doctorate of letters by Colorado State University in 1994. Exceptionally articulate and objective, he published frequently on the organ's history, design, and acoustical problems in such journals as *Diapason*, *Organ Institute Quarterly*, and the *International Society of Organbuilders Journal*. His influence as pioneer, reformer, and educator has been widespread.

BIBLIOGRAPHY

O. Ochse: *The History of the Organ in the United States* (Bloomington, IN, 1975)

J. Norman: *The Organs of Britain: an Appreciation and Gazetteer* (Newton Abbot, England, 1984)

M. Forsyth-Grant: *Twenty-one Years of Organ-Building* (Oxford, 1987)

J. D'Aigle: *L'histoire de Casavant Frères, facteurs d'orgues, 1880–1980* (Sainte Hyacinthe, 1988)

DAVID TITTERINGTON/GILLIAN WEIR

Phi Beta. A professional society for men and women in the creative and performing arts, founded in 1912; *see* FRATERNITIES AND SORORITIES.

Phi Beta Mu. Society for bandmasters, founded in 1937; *see* FRATERNITIES AND SORORITIES.

Philadelphia. City in Pennsylvania (pop. 1,526,006, ranked fifth largest in the United States; metropolitan area pop. 5,965,343; 2010 US Census). Recognized as one of the country's principal musical and cultural centers, it is home to world-renowned institutions such as the Philadelphia Orchestra and the Curtis Institute of Music. The city also hosts two unique music-lending collections at the Free Library of Philadelphia: the Fleisher Collection of Orchestral Music, the largest and most comprehensive collection of orchestral performance sets in the world, and the Drinker Choral Music Library, the largest source of choral works in the United States.

Originally inhabited by Lenape (Delaware) Indians, the area was occupied by Dutch and Swedish settlers in the early 17th century. In 1681 King Charles II of England granted the land now known as Pennsylvania to William Penn, a Quaker who sought refuge for victims of religious persecution. Penn established the city of Philadelphia (Greek for "brotherly love") the following year. Despite Quakers' open admonishments against musical practices, evidence survives of thriving musical activity. For example, German Protestant communities had instrument builders as early as 1700 and produced more than 20 editions of German hymns such as *Urania, or a Choice Collection of Psalm-Tunes, Anthems, and Hymns*, compiled by James Lyon (Philadelphia, 1761).

By 1750 Philadelphia had become the busiest port and largest city in the Colonies as well as a meeting place for the founders of the United States. It served intermittently as the new country's capital from 1776 until 1800 and dominated trade and culture until New York's ascent to prominence around 1820.

1. Concerts. 2. Opera. 3. Choral singing. 4. The Musical Fund Society. 5. Popular music and jazz. 6. Educational institutions. 7. Music publishing. 8. Instrument makers.

1. CONCERTS. Subscription concerts were given from 1757 by a chamber orchestra, largely through the efforts of FRANCIS HOPKINSON, one of the first American-born composers, and the city's governor, John Penn. The programs included music by the best English, Italian, German, and Bohemian composers of the time. A few months before his graduation in 1757 from the College of Philadelphia (later the University of Pennsylvania), Hopkinson mounted an elaborate performance of Thomas Augustine Arne's masque *Alfred*. The British occupation of the city by Lord Howe's army in 1777 was marked by the splendid musical pageant *Mischianza*.

After the Revolutionary War English emigrants Rayner Taylor, Alexander Reinagle, and Benjamin Carr led the city's musical life through the turn of the century and were active as performers, composers, conductors, teachers, and concert managers. Philadelphia had garden concerts in the summer imitating those at Ranelagh, Vauxhall, and other London pleasure gardens. However, it was not until the second half of the 19th century that the city had a resident orchestra of any importance. Taking its name from an earlier group that had come from Germany in 1848, the Germania Orchestra under the leadership of Carl Lenschow gave annual concert series from 1856 to 1895. During the celebration of the centenary of American independence in 1876, THEODORE THOMAS conducted a long series of concerts by his orchestra. The opening program included works by the American composers John Knowles Paine and Dudley Buck, as well as Richard Wagner's *Grosser Festmarsch*. But Thomas's programs were too weighty and difficult for the visitors and were given in a hall too far from the center of the city to draw a large audience; consequently they could not compete with the lighter program offered by Jacques Offenbach at the exhibition grounds. It was 12 years before Thomas was able to pay off the heavy debts resulting from this undertaking (*see also* CENTENNIAL EXHIBITION). Thomas settled permanently in Chicago in 1891. The loss of the annual concert series his orchestra had given in Philadelphia was only partly compensated for by concerts given by the Boston SO, the New York PO, and the New York SO from the 1890s to about 1926. In the late 1890s opera conductor Gustav Hinrichs, choral director Henry Gordon Thunder, and composer William Wallace Gilchrist tried to form a local orchestra on a permanent basis.

German conductor Fritz Scheel set the foundations for the Philadelphia Orchestra when he performed two benefit concerts for the families of soldiers killed in the

Philippines during the Spanish–American War. With a guarantee fund Scheel officially launched the Philadelphia Orchestra with 85 musicians on 16 November 1900 in a concert featuring works by Karl Goldmark, Ludwig van Beethoven, Pyotr Tchaikovsky, Carl Maria von Weber, and Wagner. At first Scheel employed predominately German musicians and conducted rehearsals in German; he later relied exclusively on European-trained players and premiered the works of major European composers. After Scheel's death in 1907, Austrian conductor Karl Pohlig took his place. Pohlig introduced Serge Rachmaninoff to the American stage before returning to Germany tainted by a personal scandal that shortened his tenure with Philadelphia.

After taking the helm as conductor in 1912, LEOPOLD STOKOWSKI steered the orchestra to international prominence. He experimented with orchestral seating to manipulate the sound, encouraged free bowing, and introduced works by Alban Berg, Ferruccio Busoni, Aleksandr Scryabin, Igor Stravinsky, Arnold Schoenberg, and Edgard Varèse. Stokowski's US premiere of Gustav Mahler's Eighth Symphony garnered national attention with 1068 musicians featured in each of nine performances. A staunch disciplinarian focused on accessibility, acculturation, and education, Stokowski also continued the tradition of children's concerts established under Scheel. With a lighter touch, he coordinated the appearance of live animals—including a baby elephant—from the Philadelphia Zoo for a presentation of Camille Saint-Saëns' *Le carnaval des animaux* at the Academy of Music. Stokowski proved himself a boisterous promoter, increased the orchestra to more than 100 members, produced the first recordings by an orchestra (1917), broadcast performances on radio (from 1929), pioneered stereophonic recording (1933), and guided the orchestra's first transcontinental tour, of 27 cities. Between 1937 and his retirement in 1941, he directed the orchestra in three films including the animated Disney epic, *Fantasia* (1940).

Appointed music director in 1938, EUGENE ORMANDY conducted the Romantically proportioned orchestra for 42 years before retiring, as conductor laureate, in 1980. A violinist by training, Ormandy built upon the Philadelphia Orchestra's unique sound by often doubling viola parts in the second violins or vice versa. Its dense strings became a defining characteristic of what became known as the Philadelphia sound. Ormandy conducted the first performances by an orchestra on national television (1948) and later toured with the orchestra through South America, Europe, and Asia. In 1973 the ensemble became the first American orchestra to perform in mainland China. Ormandy's chosen successor, RICCARDO MUTI, stripped down the orchestra between 1980 and 1992 to provide a leaner sound and deliver precise, historically informed performances of older works. He also became known for concert performances of complete operas as well as for programming an array of contemporary works. Wolfgang Sawallisch (1993–2003) brought more traditional, if less adventurous, Eurocentric fare. Subsequent directors Christoph Eschenbach (2003–2008) and Charles Dutoit

(2008–2012) kept the orchestra steeped in a more conservative repertory.

The failure of the orchestra's board of directors to balance the budget in the face of dwindling attendance and their declaration of Chapter 11 bankruptcy protection in the spring of 2011—despite a $120 million endowment—sparked controversy with the negation of contracts and prompted the exodus of several highly respected players on the eve of Yannick Nézet-Séguin's ascent to the role of music director in the 2012–13 season.

Originally housed in the Academy of Music—an operatic hall with inadequate acoustics for the performance of a symphony—the orchestra relocated to the newly constructed Kimmel Center for the Performing Arts in December 2001 where they have performed their regular season in the cello-shaped 2500-seat Verizon Hall.

Outdoor concerts have long been popular with Philadelphia audiences; between 1896 and 1920, for example, a concert series given at the suburban Willow Grove amusement park attracted thousands of listeners. During a three-month season, Frederick Stock with the Theodore Thomas Orchestra, Walter Damrosch with the New York SO, and Victor Herbert with his own group gave two concerts a day over two to five weeks. Band concerts were also given under the direction of John Philip Sousa, Arthur Pryor, and Giuseppe Creatore. A summer festival with indoor concerts was held at the suburban Ambler Campus of Temple University between 1967 and 1980. From 1930 the Philadelphia Orchestra has given outdoor summer concerts in Fairmount Park (the Robin Hood Dell Concerts, subsequently held in the Mann Music Center, an outdoor auditorium built in 1976). Following the establishment in 1966 of the SARATOGA FESTIVAL in New York State, the orchestra has played there each summer. Summer activities have also included international festivals around the world. Nearly all the world's great conductors and performing artists have appeared with the Philadelphia Orchestra, beginning with Ossip Gabrilovich, who was a soloist at the opening concert, and including Richard Strauss in 1904 and Felix Weingartner in 1905. Rachmaninoff, who lived for a period in Philadelphia, performed and recorded there, and dedicated several of his works to the orchestra (*see also* ORCHESTRA).

Chamber orchestras and small ensembles were established in Philadelphia as early as the 1750s, and countless amateur and professional organizations have subsequently been formed. Of particular note is the Symphony Club, founded in 1909 by EDWIN A. FLEISHER as the first training orchestra in the United States. It met weekly at 1235 Pine Street where members devoted half their rehearsal time to sight-reading symphonic pieces. Open to both sexes and all races, the Symphony Club had expanded to include three performing ensembles as well as theory and piano classes by 1915. Fleisher purchased more than 3000 orchestral sets to fill club needs and donated them in 1929 to the Free Library of Philadelphia as the basis of the Fleisher Collection. Akin in spirit to the Symphony Club, the

Orchestra Society of Philadelphia has served as a reading orchestra since its foundation by Morris Goldman and Sidney Rothstein in 1964. The Chamber Orchestra of Philadelphia (established in 1964 by Marc Mostovoy) and the Philadelphia Chamber Music Society (founded by Anthony Checchia in 1986) are among eight groups that have been resident in the Perelman Theater at the Kimmel Center for the Performing Arts and have provided access to thousands of concerts to the community.

Among the most prominent of the professional groups was the CURTIS STRING QUARTET (1932–81). The members were graduates of the Curtis Institute, and the quartet traveled widely and made many recordings. The Philadelphia String Quartet, made up of members of the Philadelphia Orchestra, was formed in 1959 and became the quartet-in-residence at the University of Washington in 1967.

In 1925 Fabien Sevitzky, a bass player in the Philadelphia Orchestra, established the Philadelphia Chamber String Sinfonietta, which consisted of 18 string players from the orchestra; the organization disbanded after its leader became conductor of the Indianapolis SO in 1937. The Society for Contemporary Music, founded in 1927, introduced a large number of important new scores in the few years of its existence.

The Bach Festival, the Amerita (American-Italian) Chamber Players, and 1807 and Friends are among dozens of non-profit musical organizations which have been active in the region during the late 20th and early 21st centuries. Several ensembles have specialized in the performance of early music on period instruments: the American Society of Ancient Instruments (founded by Ben Stad, 1925), Piffaro (1985, formerly the Philadelphia Renaissance Wind Band), and the Philadelphia Classical Symphony (founded by Karl Middleman, 1994). Groups specializing in contemporary music include Relâche (1977) and Orchestra 2001 (1988). The Network for New Music (1984) and the Composer's Forum sponsor performances of music by living composers. The Hildegard Institute, founded by Sylvia Glickman (1991), specializes in the music of women composers. The Sylvia Glickman Memorial Fund presents prizes annually for new chamber music compositions by women of 40 years or more and for outstanding students in the chamber music program at Haverford College.

In 1986 Andrea Clearfield established a music salon in her vaulted Center City apartment that has featured an eclectic array of high-level performances. Monthly concerts have included not only classical, chamber, and operatic works but also jazz, contemporary compositions, electronic music, improvisation, folk, experimental, and world music.

2. OPERA. The earliest known performance of a musical drama in Philadelphia was *Flora, or Hob in the Well*, a ballad opera given by an English company in 1754. Both the Society Hall Theatre, built by David Douglass in 1759, and the Southwark Theatre, which opened in 1766 with Arne's *Thomas and Sally*, staged productions

of plays and operas given by the American Company. Comic operas by leading British composers were frequently performed, often soon after their premieres in London. In 1767 the first performance of an American ballad opera, *The Disappointment* (attributed to Andrew Barton), was announced, but it was subsequently canceled at the last moment "as it contained personal reflections…unfit for the stage"; it was not performed until 1976, although two editions of the libretto were published in the 18th century. During the Revolutionary period expensive theatrical entertainments were prohibited, except during the time of the British occupation, and the ban remained in effect until 1789.

After the ban was lifted, Philadelphia became one of the nation's main theatrical centers. The New Company, founded in 1792 by ALEXANDER REINAGLE and Thomas Wignell, recruited a large number of singers and composers from England. Although the principal repertory was from London, several composers who lived in Philadelphia wrote original operas; among the most successful were *The Archers* (1796) by Carr, *The Volunteers* (1795) by Reinagle, and *The Aethiop* (1814) by Taylor. Of prime importance to the success of opera was the construction in 1793 of the New Theatre (later known as the Chestnut or Chestnut Street Theatre), one of the finest theaters in the United States; it seated nearly 2000 people, and its design was based on the Theatre Royal at Bath in England. The Chestnut Theatre burned to the ground in 1820.

Exceptions to the English character of the repertory were the performances by a troupe of French refugees from Santo Domingo (1796–7) and by John Davis's French Opera Company of New Orleans (1827); the latter troupe enjoyed such success that it returned eight times over a 16-year period. A familiar figure in Philadelphia during his later years, LORENZO DA PONTE was instrumental in bringing the first Italian companies to the city and in igniting an enthusiasm for Italian opera that has been maintained subsequently. Gioachino Rossini and Vincenzo Bellini were the most frequently performed composers by both the Montressor (1832–3) and the Rivafinoli (1834) opera companies. The immense popularity of Bellini's *La sonnambula* (1836, with 61 performances over the next three years) almost dealt a death-blow to English opera. One of the few exceptions was *The Enchantress* by Michael Balfe, which was given 32 times within a ten-week period in 1846. Philadelphia staged the premiere in 1845 of the first American grand opera, *Leonora* by William Henry Fry, which was written in the Italian style and admired so much that it was performed 16 times that season. The Havana Opera Company introduced the operas of Giuseppe Verdi to the city in 1847.

With the erection of the Academy of Music in 1857, the city acquired the finest opera house in the country. Built by the Philadelphia firm of Napoleon Le Brun and modeled after La Scala, the house had three balconies, an impressive interior, and nearly 3000 seats. In the early 2010s it was the oldest existing opera house in the United States and in 1963 was declared a National Historic Landmark; it has remained the principal opera and concert hall in the city. Many first American performances were given there, including *Faust* (in German, 1863), *Der fliegende Holländer* (in Italian, 1876), and Arrigo Boito's *Mefistofele* (1880). In the second half of the 19th century, two additional opera houses were opened: the Chestnut Street Opera House (1885) and the Grand Opera House (1888). With three houses available, the city was able to attract touring companies that featured the finest European stars. A number of American premieres were directed by Gustav Hinrichs at the Grand: *Cavalleria rusticana* (1891), *L'amico Fritz* (1892), *Les pêcheurs de perles* (1893), *Manon Lescaut* (1894), and Hinrich's own opera, *Onti-Ora* (1890).

The Metropolitan Opera of New York first appeared in Philadelphia in 1885 and gave the first complete performance in the city of the *Ring* cycle, under Anton Seidl in 1889. From that time until 1968, when production costs became prohibitive, the company presented an annual season in Philadelphia, ranging from six to 25 performances a year. Oscar Hammerstein I, challenging the supremacy of the Metropolitan, built an opulent 4000-seat theater called the Philadelphia Opera House (1908). It was sold to the Metropolitan in 1910 and was renamed the Metropolitan Opera House. After 1931 it was seldom used, and in 1948 it was destroyed by fire.

Since the end of World War I many local opera companies have been formed; the Philadelphia Civic Opera Company (1924–30) gave the American premieres of Strauss's *Ariadne auf Naxos* and *Feuersnot*, and the Philadelphia Grand Opera Company (1926–43) that of Berg's *Wozzeck* (1931) with the Philadelphia Orchestra conducted by Stokowski. The Pennsylvania Grand Opera Company (1927) was later re-formed as the Philadelphia–La Scala Company. After several mergers and name changes, the Civic Grand and the Lyric Grand emerged as the major opera companies in the city, performing primarily the popular Italian repertory. In 1976 they merged to form the Opera Company of Philadelphia. In addition to traditional works by Georges Bizet, Wolfgang Amadeus Mozart, and Giacomo Puccini, the company has occasionally programmed newer works such as Tan Dun's *Tea: a Mirror of Soul* and Nico Muhly's *Dark Sisters*. Other groups have included the Center City Opera Theater, founded by Andrew Kurtz in 1999, and Concert Opera Philadelphia, formed in 1995 to provide operatic works in concert settings.

3. CHORAL SINGING. Choral singing has flourished in Philadelphia since the end of the 18th century. In 1784 Andrew Adgate organized the Institution for the Encouragement of Church Music, later the Uranian Academy (1787–1800). The city's large German population supported several singing societies. The Männerchor (1835–1962), the Junger Männerchor (from 1850), and Arion (1854–1969) disbanded, but Harmonie (1855) and eight other German choral groups have remained active. Other important early choruses were the Abt Male Chorus, led successively by Michael Cross and Hugh Archibald Clarke; the Philadelphia Choral Society,

conducted by Henry Gordon Thunder (1897–1946); the Treble Clef Club (1884–1934) and the Eurydice Chorus (1886–1918), both for women; the Fortnightly Club (1893); the Palestrina Choir (1915–48); and the Accademia dei Dilettanti di Musica (1928–60). Still flourishing in the early 2010s were the male-voice Orpheus Club (from 1872), the Mendelssohn Club (from 1874), Singing City (from 1947), the Philadelphia Singers (from 1971, the city's principal professional choir), and the Choral Arts Society (from 1982).

4. THE MUSICAL FUND SOCIETY. In the early 2010s the MUSICAL FUND SOCIETY was the oldest continuing musical organization in the United States; it was founded in February 1820 by a group of professional and amateur musicians who had been playing quartets for their own enjoyment for several years. Among the founders were the musicians Benjamin Carr, Rayner Taylor, J. George Schetky, and Benjamin Cross and the painter Thomas Sully, who made portraits of his fellow members. Inspired by the Royal Society of Musicians of Great Britain, the society was dedicated to "the relief of decayed musicians and the cultivation of skill and diffusion of taste in music." Its initial public concert was presented on 22 April 1821 and featured Beethoven's Symphony no.2; in 1822 Joseph Haydn's *Creation* was given by more than 100 performers to an audience of nearly 2000. The society maintained its own orchestra and around 1900 was actively involved in the establishment of the Philadelphia Orchestra.

William Strickland, a distinguished architect and member of the society, designed the Musical Fund Hall (1824), which was used for the society's many concerts and for other musical and non-musical events. Noted for its fine acoustics, the hall attracted renowned artists such as Maria Malibran, Jenny Lind, Henriette Sontag, Adelina Patti, Henri Vieuxtemps, and Louis Moreau Gottschalk; *Die Zauberflöte* had its first American performance there (1841, in English). The building fell into disrepair in the 20th century and was demolished in 1982 after repeated efforts to preserve it had failed; the façade was left but the hall itself was replaced by a residential development. The society's large music and document collection, which includes early editions and manuscripts of European music as well as music by Pennsylvania composers, went to the library of the University of Pennsylvania.

In the late 20th century the society focused its attention on fostering the careers of emerging young artists and ensembles through the awarding of grants, scholarships, and the Musical Fund Society Career Advancement Award. It has also supported musicians and music education in the Philadelphia area, offered free public concerts, and sponsored occasional competitions for new music. Most notable is the international competition in 1928, whose first prize was shared by Béla Bartók, for his String Quartet no.3, and Alfredo Casella, for the original version of his *Serenata*. The competition has subsequently been sponsored by the society's Edward Garett McCollin Fund; in 1994 the prize was awarded to Judith Lang Zaimont for her Symphony no.1, which was performed by the Philadelphia Orchestra in January 1996.

5. POPULAR MUSIC AND JAZZ. Although some scholars cite the lack of documentation for early popular music practices in Philadelphia as evidence of Quaker suppression, published protests to musical practices from the Society of Friends more likely suggest the presence of a rote tradition shared between various communities. English influence was documented with the presence of strolling players and comedian acts in the early 1700s. By the end of the 18th century, evidence of songs and dances began appearing in Colonial presses. In 1759, for instance, Francis Hopkinson published "My days have been so wondrous free," a song in English style for voice and harpsichord that is regarded as the first secular song by an American-born composer. His deficiently titled *Seven Songs for the Harpsichord or Forte Piano* (it contains eight songs) published in 1788 bore a dedication to George Washington.

Throughout the 1800s Philadelphia served as an important stop for the Underground Railroad and grew as a major urban music center for African Americans. Frank Johnson's band frequently performed for dances during the 1820s and 30s, garnered national attention, and after appearing before Queen Victoria in England, introduced a series of well-received promenade concerts in 1838 that included a racially integrated concert on 29 December 1843. The leading artist in a small school of black composers that included Aaron J.R. Connors, James Hemmenway, Isaac Hazzard, and William Appo, Johnson had become the first African American to publish sheet music in 1818, with *Six Setts of Cotillions*; he had also produced piano arrangements of band music and penned such works as *Recognition March of the Independence of Hayti* (1825).

Sam Sanford built the first dedicated minstrel theater in 1853 and two years later added a second, more popular venue, the 11th Street Opera House. Prominent resident acts included the long-lived Carncross and Dixey's Minstrels and Frank Dumont's Minstrels. In 1863 the Ida Aldridge Troupe, one of the few troupes to feature black performers, appeared at Franklin Hall, a dance hall on east Spruce Street. Between 1890 and 1910 Benjamin F. Keith and Marcus Loew established theaters in northeast cities that included Philadelphia locations and featured vaudeville acts.

Philadelphia mummery represents a blend of British, German, Greek, Italian, and Swedish winter traditions that grew from neighborhood festivities into a citywide celebration by 1890. On 1 January 1901 the city sanctioned the first official Philadelphia Mummers Parade with fancy dress and comic club members participating. The following year string bands marched into the foray with their defining characteristic timbres derived from strings, reeds, and percussion. Instrumentation has typically included banjos, saxophones, accordions, glockenspiel, and drums. Early celebrations often incorporated elements of minstrelsy, including blackface (officially banned in 1964), and relied on arrangements of minstrel-like tunes such as James Bland's "O, dem Golden Slippers" (1879), the unofficial theme song of the Mummers. More than a century later, the annual Philadelphia Mummers Parade continued to provide the foundation for the region's New Year's Day celebration with some 15,000 participants, including 18 string bands, marching up South Broad Street in elaborate costumes to compete in nationally televised performances at the foot of City Hall.

From the 1920s the Earle Theatre on Market Street and "black and tan" clubs (racially integrated venues), such as entrepreneur John T. Gibson's Standard and Dunbar theaters, attracted the biggest touring acts, from Duke Ellington to Josephine Baker to Frank Sinatra. Philadelphia also has been home to such outstanding jazz performers as violinist Joe Venuti, guitarist Eddie Lang, singer Ethel Waters, trumpeter Lee Morgan, saxophonist Grover Washington Jr., and pianist McCoy Tyner. The Philadelphia Clef Club, a social club established in 1966 by local music union members, hosted scattered events into the late 20th century. The annual River Blues Festival on Penn's Landing on the Delaware River in the 1980s and 90s featured performances by a wide range of artists, including B.B. King, Taj Mahal, and Michael Hedges.

In October 1952 WFIL-TV in Philadelphia introduced *American Bandstand*, a televised dance program that kept thousands of Philadelphia area high school teens flocking to the studio or glued to their television sets. When the show went national in 1957 with its host DICK CLARK on the ABC network, *American Bandstand* grabbed the attention of more than 60% of afternoon television viewers and set popular music trends across the country.

In the early 1970s songwriter-producers Kenneth Gamble and Leon Huff (*see* GAMBLE AND HUFF) as well as THOM BELL spearheaded the Philly soul movement, a musical style tinged with gospel-influenced vocals, colored by lush string and horn arrangements, and driven by the signature smooth sounds of MFSB (Mother, Father, Sister, Brother), the studio band for Philadelphia International Records. The label produced chart-toppers such as the Spinners' "Could it be I'm falling in love" (1972), the Stylistics' "Betcha by Golly, Wow" (1970), Harold Melvin and the Blue Notes' "If you don't know me by now" (1972), and the O'Jays' "Love Train" (1972). An especially enduring example of the Philadelphia sound is the aptly named "TSOP (The Sound of Philadelphia)," which Don Cornelius commissioned as the theme for his own groundbreaking television dance program, *Soul Train*.

In addition to large stadiums that include the Philadelphia Sports Complex, respectable stages scattered across the city—like those at the Electric Factory, the Tower Theater, the Trocadero Theatre, and World Café Live—have made the city an attractive national tour stop for major performing acts. Before it was demolished in 1992, the city's John F. Kennedy Stadium was paired with Wembley Stadium in London to provide a stage for the dual-venue satellite-linked Live Aid benefit concert coordinated by Bob Geldof and Midge Ure and broadcast to nearly two million viewers in some 150 countries on 13 July 1985. From the late 1960s until the turn of the century, Veterans Stadium (affectionately dubbed the Vet by locals) and the Spectrum regularly hosted concerts by such artists as the Rolling Stones, Pink Floyd, David Bowie, Eric Clapton, and Aerosmith. Philadelphia performances by the Doors, the Grateful Dead, the Who, KISS, and Genesis, among others, exist on commercially released recordings. By 2011 Citizens Bank Park, Lincoln Financial Field, and the Wells Fargo Center had replaced the Spectrum and the Vet in the South Philadelphia Sports Complex. Other noteworthy annual traditions include the Philadelphia Folk Festival (from 1962) held in nearby Schwenksville and the Philly Caribbean Festival (from 1987) held on Penn's landing.

6. EDUCATIONAL INSTITUTIONS. The first institution for general musical instruction was the American Conservatorio (1822–54), founded by Filippo Trajetta. The Musical Fund Society established an academy of music (1825–32), but it was financially unprofitable. The two most significant music conservatories at the end of the 19th century were the Philadelphia Musical Academy and the Philadelphia Conservatory of Music (both 1870); they merged in 1963, and the institution, with an expanded curriculum, was renamed the Philadelphia College of the Performing Arts (1976). After its merger with the Philadelphia College of Art in 1985, the school was renamed the University of the Arts; in the early 2010s it was awarding both undergraduate and graduate degrees. The Settlement Music School opened in 1908; from a student body of 40 in its first year it grew to approximately 7000 students at its five branches. In the early 21st century it was the largest community arts school in the country and was providing high quality music instruction for its students regardless of age, background, or the ability to pay.

The Curtis Institute of Music has achieved a reputation as one of the foremost conservatories in the United States. Founded in 1924 by Mary Louise Curtis Bok, who was the president of the school until her death in 1970, it has offered scholarships in performance and composition and attracted internationally renowned musicians as teachers. Well-known alumni include Samuel Barber, Leonard Bernstein, Lukas Foss, Alan Gilbert, Hilary Hahn, Jennifer Higdon, Lang Lang, Gian Carlo Menotti, Anna Moffo, Vincent Persichetti, and Ned Rorem. It has offered both BM and MM degrees and a professional diploma. Another highly regarded institution, the Academy of Vocal Arts (1935), has awarded scholarships to most of its students.

Two large universities have offered undergraduate and graduate degrees in music. After being founded in 1740, the University of Pennsylvania appointed Hugh Archibald Clarke professor of the science of music in 1875; this, one of the earliest chairs of music in an American university, was held by Clarke for 50 years. He concerned himself only with theory and composition; music history was later added to the curriculum but not performance, although the university has maintained both choral and instrumental performing groups. In the 1960s the music department gained an international

reputation in composition, musicology, and music theory under the chairmanship of GEORGE ROCHBERG. The department has maintained a distinguished faculty and awarded BA, MA, and PhD degrees in these fields as well as a PhD in ethnomusicology. The university's music library, named after the musicologist OTTO E. ALBRECHT, is recognized as one of the finest on the East Coast.

The Temple University school of music dates from 1913, although honorary degrees in music were granted as early as 1897. A department of music education was initiated in 1923 and a separate college of music was established in 1962. In 1986 the New School of Music, founded in 1943 by the members of the Curtis String Quartet, merged with Temple to form the New School Institute, and in the same year the college was renamed the Esther Boyer College of Music in recognition of its benefactor. Temple University has awarded BM, MM, and MMT degrees, DMAs in composition and performance, and PhDs in music education and music therapy. It has offered performing experience in some three dozen ensembles and sponsored the Music Preparatory Division, the Community Music Program, and the Center for Gifted Young Musicians.

In the nearby suburbs, undergraduate and graduate music degrees have been awarded at Immaculata College and West Chester University. Other colleges, such as Haverford and Swarthmore, have offered music courses and supported choral and orchestral ensembles.

7. MUSIC PUBLISHING. Philadelphia was the pre-eminent music publishing center in the United States until about 1850, when it was superseded by New York. The earliest music published was in a hymnbook printed by Christopher Sauer in 1752, and the first publication to contain full pages of music using movable type was *The Youth's Entertaining Amusement*, compiled in 1754 by William Dawson. Early music publishers were John Aitken (1787–1811), Thomas Dobson (1787–98), John Christopher Moller and Henri Capron (1793–4), and Filippo Trisobio (1796–8). Benjamin Carr, with his family and his associate J. George Schetky, published great quantities of music intermittently from 1793 until 1830. The firm of George Willig, established in 1794, was the leading publishing house in the first half of the 19th century; it was sold to Lee & Walker in 1856 and to Oliver Ditson in 1875. Other significant firms include George E. Blake (1803–c1850), Allyn Bacon, under various firm names (1816–80), John G. Klemm (1823–83), Fiot, Meignen & Co. (1835–63), G. André & Co. (1850–79), and W.H. Boner (1865–1900). J.W. Pepper (1876) moved to the suburb of Valley Forge in 1973 and within a few years became the largest retailer of instrumental ensemble sheet music in the United States. Theodore Presser's firm moved to Philadelphia in 1884 and to the suburb of Bryn Mawr in 1949, acquired Oliver Ditson (1931) and Elkan-Vogel (1970), and became one of the foremost music publishing firms in the country. Presser is also known for its publication of the monthly music magazine *Etude* (1883–1957) and for its charitable work. In 1906 the firm established the Presser Home

for Retired Music Teachers, operated by the Presser Foundation. The foundation has also provided music scholarships and grants to colleges for the construction of music buildings. The Presser firm was acquired in 2004 by Carl Fischer.

8. INSTRUMENT MAKERS. From its earliest history, the city has had capable instrument makers. The Swedish organ builder Gustavus Hesselius constructed spinets and virginals as early as 1742, and John Behrent produced the first piano made in the colonies in 1775. James Juhan advertised himself in 1783 as the manufacturer of a "great North American fortepiano." In 1789 CHARLES ALBRECHT began making pianos and, shortly thereafter, CHARLES TAWS; his sons continued the business until the 1830s. John Isaac Hawkins took out the first patent for an upright piano (a "portable grand") in 1800. Thomas Loud Jr. began to manufacture pianos in 1816, and the business was continued by members of his family until 1854. From 1828 until 1878 Conrad Meyer was one of the country's leading piano makers. The Prussian piano maker Johann Heinrich Schomacker settled in Philadelphia in 1837; his firm continued under later generations until about 1935.

Violin makers also have a long history in Philadelphia. John Albert, like many other Germans, came to the United States in 1848; his shop was continued by family members until about 1921. Other important violin makers have included the formidable firm William Moennig & Son, which operated from 1909 to 2009 (*see* MOENNIG).

BIBLIOGRAPHY

C. Durang: "The Philadelphia Stage," *Philadelphia Sunday Despatch* (1854, 1856, 1860) [series of articles; compiled by T. Westcott as *History of the Philadelphia Stage, between the Years 1749 and 1855*, 1868, *PHu*; similar compilations as *The Philadelphia Stage* in *PHlc*, and *History of the Philadelphia Stage* in *PHbs*]

W.G. Armstrong: *A Record of the Opera in Philadelphia* (Philadelphia, 1884/*R*)

L.C. Madeira: *Annals of Music in Philadelphia and History of the Musical Fund Society from its Organization in 1820 to the Year 1858* (Philadelphia, 1896/*R*)

O.G.T. Sonneck: *Early Concert-Life in America (1731–1800)* (Leipzig, 1907/*R*), 65–157

R.R. Drummond: *Early German Music in Philadelphia* (New York, 1910/*R*)

H.M. Lippincott: *Early Philadelphia: its People, Life and Progress* (Philadelphia, 1917)

J. Curtis: *One Hundred Years of Grand Opera in Philadelphia* (MS 1920, *PHf*, *PHbs*)

Pennsylvania Composers and their Compositions, ed. Pennsylvania Federation of Music Clubs (Philadelphia, 1923)

F.A. Wister: *25 Years of the Philadelphia Orchestra, 1900–1925* (Philadelphia, 1925/*R*)

A. Aston and J. Kelpius: *Church Music and Musical Life in Pennsylvania in the Eighteenth Century*, ed. Pennsylvania Society of the Colonial Dames of America (Philadelphia, 1926–47)

A.A. Parker: *Music and Musical Life in Pennsylvania in the Eighteenth Century* (Philadelphia, 1926–7)

R.D. James: *Old Drury of Philadelphia: a History of the Philadelphia Stage, 1800–1835* (Philadelphia, 1932)

T.C. Pollock: *The Philadelphia Theater in the Eighteenth Century* (Philadelphia, 1933/*R*)

A.H. Wilson: *A History of the Philadelphia Theatre 1835 to 1855* (Philadelphia, 1935/*R*)

R.A. Gerson: *Music in Philadelphia: a History of Philadelphia Music, a Summary of its Current State and a Comprehensive Index Dictionary* (Philadelphia, 1940/*R*)

G.M. Rohrer: *Music and Musicians of Pennsylvania* (Philadelphia, 1940/*R*)

W.J. Perlman and S. Spaeth: *Music and Dance in Pennsylvania, New Jersey, and Delaware* (New York, 1954)

D.W. Krummel: *Philadelphia Music Engraving and Publishing, 1800–1820: a Study in Bibliographical and Cultural History* (diss., U. of Michigan, 1958)

H. Kupferberg: *Those Fabulous Philadelphians: the Life and Times of a Great Orchestra* (New York, 1969)

The Musical Fund Society of Philadelphia (Philadelphia, 1970)

E.C. Wolf: "Music in Old Zion, Philadelphia, 1750–1850," *MQ*, lviii (1972), 622–52

P. Hart: *Orpheus in the New World: the Symphony Orchestra as an American Cultural Institution* (New York, 1973), 139–68

J.J. Kelley: *Life and Times in Colonial Philadelphia* (Harrisburg, PA, 1973)

T. Cummings: *The Sound of Philadelphia* (London, 1975)

E. Southern: "The Philadelphia Afro-American School'," *BPM*, iv (1976), 238–56

E.J. Southern: "Musical Practices in Black Churches of Philadelphia and New York, ca.1800–1844," *JAMS*, xxx (1977), 296–312

O.E. Albrecht: "Opera in Philadelphia, 1800–1830," *JAMS*, xxxii (1979), 499–515

J.A. Taricani: "Music in Colonial Philadelphia: Some New Documents," *MQ*, lxv (1979), 185–99

D. Webster: "The Curtis Institute: a Decade of Change," *High Fidelity/Musical America*, xxx/3 (1980), MA20–22, 39

J.F. Marion: *Within these Walls: a History of the Academy of Music in Philadelphia* (Philadelphia, 1984)

S.L. Porter: *With an Air Debonair: Musical Theatre in America 1785–1815* (Washington, DC, 1991)

J.K. Kurnick: *Riccardo Muti: Twenty Years in Philadelphia* (Philadelphia, 1992)

K. Smith: *Catalog of the Music of Pennsylvania Composers* (Wynnewood, PA, 1992)

K.K. Preston: *Opera on the Road: Traveling Opera Troupes in the United States, 1825–60* (Urbana, IL, 1993)

S.E. Murray: "Music and Dance in Philadelphia's City Tavern 1773–1790," *American Musical Life in Context and Practice to 1865*, ed. J.R. Heintze (New York, 1994), 3–47

J. Shalom: "The Ira Aldridge Troupe: Early Black Minstrelsy in Philadelphia," *African American Review*, xxiii/4 (1994), 653–58

J. Ardoin, ed.: *The Philadelphia Orchestra: a Century of Music* (Philadelphia, 1999)

D. Burgwyn: *The Kimmel Center for the Performing Arts: Home of the Philadelphia Orchestra* (Philadelphia, 2001)

J.A. Jackson: *A House on Fire: the Rise and Fall of Philadelphia Soul* (New York, 2004)

P.W. Rodríguez-Peralta: *Philadelphia Maestros: Ormandy, Muti, Sawallisch* (Philadelphia, 2006)

H. Sheldon: *Philadelphia's History of Music* (Charleston, SC, 2011)

OTTO E. ALBRECHT/GARY GALVÁN (1–2),
OTTO E. ALBRECHT/R (3–4, 7–8), GARY GALVÁN (5),
OTTO E. ALBRECHT (with NINA DAVIS-MILLIS)/R (6)

Philadelphia Ballet. Company founded by catherine Littlefield and her mother, Caroline Littlefield, in 1935. Disbanded in 1942, it was the first ballet company made up almost exclusively of American dancers. The only non-American was Alexis Dolinoff, the principal male dancer and ballet master.

Philadelphia Woodwind Quintet. Woodwind quintet founded in 1950. All of the ensemble's members held positions in the Philadelphia Orchestra under Eugene Ormandy. Its original members were Burnett Atkinson (flute), Anthony Gigliotti (clarinet), John de Lancie (oboe), Sol Schoenbach (bassoon), and Mason Jones (horn). Later members included William Kincaid (flute), Robert F. Cole (flute), Murray Panitz (flute), and Bernard

Garfield (bassoon). In addition to many recording projects (now available as a complete four-CD set through Boston Records), the ensemble filmed a series of 30-minute kinescopes in cooperation with public television that were broadcast nationwide. In the early 1950s the quintet was invited to perform at the Spoleto Festival in Italy. The trip also included performances, staged in cooperation with the US Army, for American troops stationed in Iceland. In addition to their membership in the orchestra, all quintet members held university faculty positions. The ensemble disbanded following the conclusion of their last recordings in the 1960s.

ERIC LYNN HARRIS

Philately, musical. The study of postage stamps and related items containing musical allusions in the pictorial design or text.

1. Introduction. 2. List.

1. INTRODUCTION. The most popular philatelic items produced by the United States Postal Service (USPS) are regular-issue and special-issue stamps, pre-stamped postcards and envelopes, cancellation marks, first-day covers, and souvenir sheets. The stamps may be issued individually or in series, and may include commemoratives, which honor individuals, organizations, activities, and historical events. They can be printed in sets, booklets, sheets, or coils (continuous rolls), and be issued with descriptive booklets, art prints, CDs and other collectibles. Christmas and Easter seals and similar materials not issued by the USPS and vanity stamps (custom photo stamps issued under USPS licensing) are also popular collectibles but do not fall within the scope of this article.

First-day covers (envelopes bearing new stamps, which are canceled on the first day of issue) are important to music philatelists as much for the musical cachet on the envelope as for the stamp itself, which may not contain a musical allusion. Souvenir sheets (commemorative sheets containing one or more stamps that often bear a description) may also include music incipits, instruments, or other musicalia.

The US Postal Service has commemorated individual musicians on stamps only since 1940. However, from the 1970s the greatest and best known American composers and performers, representing jazz and blues, Broadway and films, folk and dance music, opera and classical music, have been honored with colorful and detailed stamps. Descriptions and documentation relating to the postal issues are vital aspects of philately, and the USPS provides extensive research information about its products and subjects.

In recent years USPS has issued compact disc recordings of performers on commemorative stamps, including American Indian Dances (1996), Folk Heroes (1996), the Gospel Singers Series (1998), the Hollywood Composers Series (1999), Frank Sinatra (2008), and Albert Von Tilzer's popular baseball song "Take me out to the ball game" (2008). In honor of the Billie Holiday stamp (1994), Verve Records issued a CD selected from the label's Holiday recordings from 1952–59 in their Verve Postage Stamp Series. Picture puzzles were issued with the Elvis Presley (1993), Marilyn Monroe (1995), and Lucille Ball (2001) stamps.

The largest organization devoted to music topical collecting has been the Philatelic Music Circle, founded in 1969 in Harrow, England, with members in many countries, including the United States. Until its termination in 2005, the group published *The Baton*, a journal devoted solely to musical stamp collecting. The journal was assimilated by *Der Musikus, Mitteilungsblatt der Motivgruppe Musik,* which publishes articles in German or French but includes English summaries.

The American Topical Association, based in Milwaukee, serves several groups of music topical collectors, and in addition to its journal, *Topical Times,* publishes a number of booklets with articles on music topicals. The *Fine Arts Philatelist* is published by the Fine Arts Unit of the ATA.

The first great American music topical collector was the piano manufacturer Theodore G. Steinway (1883–1957). His philatelic library now resides in the Collectors Club of New York. Frederic C. Schang (1884–1990), President of Columbia Artists Management, published six books illustrating his collection of autographed visiting cards and musical stamps. His papers are housed in the New York Public Library's Music Division. Conductor Leonard Slatkin (1944–) was the honorary Patron of the Philatelic Music Circle, succeeding American-born British violinist Lord Yehudi Menuhin (1916–1999). The large collection of the late violinist Jascha Heifetz (1901–1987) resides in the Cardinal Spellman Museum of Stamps and Postal History, Regis College, Weston, Massachusetts.

2. LIST. This list of regular and special issue stamps, airmail stamps, and stamped envelopes and postcards is arranged chronologically by issue date. Names, titles, series, issue series (if any), types (where necessary), postage values, and dates of issue are indicated. Other than names, distinctive titles printed on stamps appear in quotes. Stamp names are from *The Postal Service Guide to U. S. Stamps* and *USA Philatelic.* The list comprises stamps celebrating persons and entities that have contributed significantly to music or depicting musical instruments or other musical allusions. Not included are stamps commemorating amateur musicians (e.g., Albert Einstein, Benjamin Franklin) and those that have only a peripheral connection with music (e.g., Walt Disney, Joseph Pulitzer). All are regular issues unless otherwise stated.

"Troops Guarding Train" [soldier with bugle], Trans-Mississippi Exposition Issue, 8¢ (17 June 1898)

"Sesquicentennial Exposition" [Liberty Bell], 2¢ (10 May 1926), stamped envelope (27 July 1926)

"George Rogers Clark Commemorative" [soldier with drum], 2¢ (25 Feb 1929)

Stephen Collins Foster, Famous Americans Issue: Composers, 1¢ (3 May 1940)

John Philip Sousa, Famous Americans Issue: Composers, 2¢ (3 May 1940)

Victor Herbert, Famous Americans Issue: Composers, 3¢ (13 May 1940)

Edward MacDowell, Famous Americans Issue: Composers, 5¢ (13 May 1940)

Ethelbert Nevin, Famous Americans Issue: Composers, 10¢ (June 10 1940)

Thomas A. Edison [inventor of phonograph and recordings], 3¢ (11 Feb 1947)

Francis Scott Key [author of "Star Spangled Banner"], 3¢ (9 Aug 1948)

Paul Revere [music engraver, church bell caster, silversmith], Liberty Issue, 25¢ (18 April 1958) (coil issued 25 Feb 1965)

"The American Woman" [violin in inset], 4¢ (2 June 1960)

"And This Be Our Motto, In God Is Our Trust" [quotation from 4th verse of Francis Scott Key's "Star Spangled Banner"], American Credo Issue, 4¢ (14 Sept 1960)

"Mexican Independence: 1810–1960" [bell], 4¢ (16 Sept 1960) [issued with an identical Mexican stamp with Spanish text]

"Champion of Liberty: Ignacy Jan Paderewski," Champion of Liberty Issue, 4¢, 8¢ (8 Oct 1960)

"Let Freedom Ring," [Liberty Bell], airmail, 10¢ (10 June 1960), 13¢ (28 June 1961)

"American Music" [lute, horn and music score], issue commemorating the 50th anniversary of founding of ASCAP, 5¢ (15 Oct 1964)

Liberty Bell, stamped envelope, 1.25¢ (6 Jan 1965), 1.4¢ (26 March 1968)

"Christmas" [angel with trumpet], Christmas Issue, 5¢ (2 Nov 1965)

"First Stars and Stripes 1777" [designed by Francis Hopkinson, earliest American songwriter, musician, signer of Declaration of Independence], 6¢ (4 July 1968)

"W.C. Handy, Father of the Blues," 6¢ (17 May 1969)

"California,1769–1969"[Carmel Mission belfry with 6 bells], California Settlement, 200th Anniversary Issue, 6¢ (16 July 1969)

"American Painting: William M. Harnett" [painting with bugle, violin and bow], 6¢ (3 Dec 1969)

"On the First Day of Christmas My True Love Sent To Me" [quote from Christmas song "Partridge in a Pear Tree"], Christmas Issue, 8¢ (10 Nov 1971)

"Sidney Lanier, American Poet" [flutist and composer], 8¢ (3 Feb 1972)

"Wolf Trap Farm, Virginia; National Parks Centennial" [national park for the performing arts], 6¢ (26 June 1972)

"Masters of St. Lucy Legend, National Gallery of Art" [detail of angels playing vielle and shawm, from the anonymous painting "Mary, Queen of Heaven"], Christmas Issue, 8¢ (9 Nov 1972)

"'Twas the Night Before Christmas" [Santa Claus holding toy trumpet], 8¢ (9 Nov 1972)

"Rise of the Spirit of Independence" [drummer], American Bicentennial Issue: Communications in Colonial Times, 8¢ (28 Sept 1973)

"Rise of the Spirit of Independence" [post rider blowing bugle], American Bicentennial Issue: Communications in Colonial Times, 8¢ (28 Sept 1973)

George Gershwin, American Arts Issue, 8¢ (28 Feb 1973)

"Progress in Electronics" [microphone, speaker, vacuum tube, TV camera], Electronics Progress Issue, 15¢ (10 July 1973)

"Christmas" [Christmas tree in needlepoint with toy trumpet ornament], Christmas Issue, 8¢ (7 Nov 1973)

Bells, coil, 6.3¢ (1 Oct 1974)

"Early Card by Louis Prang" [cherubim ringing bell], Christmas Issue, 10¢ (14 Oct 1975)

"Proclaim Liberty Throughout All the Land" [Liberty Bell], Americana Issue, and coil, 13¢ (31 Oct 1975)

"Beat the Drum for Liberty and the Spirit of '76" [tenor drum], Music of America Issue, coil, bulk rate, 7.9¢ (23 April 1976)

"Marching in Step to the Music of the Union" [Saxhorns], Music of America Issue, coil, 7.7¢ (20 Nov 1976)

"Spirit of 76" [set of 3 stamps with drummer boy, old drummer, and fifer], American Bicentennial Issue, 13¢ (1 Jan 1976)

"Centennial of Sound Recording" [Edison's tin foil phonograph], Sound Recording Issue, 13¢ (23 March 1977)

"Cincinnati Music Hall," Historical Preservation Issue, postcard, 10¢ (12 May 1978)

"Jimmie Rodgers: Singing Brakeman" [with guitar], Performing Arts Series, 13¢ (24 May 1978)

"George M. Cohan: Yankee Doodle Dandy," Performing Arts Series, 13¢ (3 July 1978)

"Peace Unites a Nation Like Harmony in Music" [Steinway grand piano], Music of America issue, coil, bulk rate, 8.4¢ (13 July 1978)

"Listen With Love To the Music Of the Land" [guitar] Music of America Issue, coil, bulk rate, 3.1¢ (25 Oct 1979)

"The Music of America is Freedom's Symphony" [two Weaver violins], Music of America Series, coil, 3.5¢ non-profit; also stamped envelope (23 June 1980)

"Season's Greetings" [antique toy trumpet and drum], 15¢ (16 Oct 1980)

"For Amber Waves of Grain" [flag with quote from "America, the Beautiful"], Flag and Anthem Issue, 18¢ (24 April 1981)

"From Sea to Shining Sea" [flag with quote from "America, the Beautiful"], Flag and Anthem Issue, 18¢ (24 April 1981)

"For Purple Mountains Majesties" [flag with quote from "America, the Beautiful"], Flag and Anthem Issue, 18¢ (24 April 1981)

"Bernard Maybeck, 1862–1957: Palace of Arts, San Francisco" [popular venue for music, dance and theater events], American Architecture Series, 18¢ (28 Aug 1981)

"Philadelphia Academy of Music," postcard, 13¢ (13 June 1982)

"Wolf Trap Farm Park for the Performing Arts," 20¢ (1 Sept 1982)

Igor Stravinsky, Great Americans Issue, 2¢ (18 Nov 1982)

Scott Joplin, Black Heritage Issue, 20¢ (9 June 1983)

"Metropolitan Opera, 1883–1983," 20¢ (14 Sept 1983)

John McCormack, Performing Arts Issue, 20¢ (6 June 1984)

Jerome Kern, Performing Arts Issue, 22¢ (23 January 1985)

Duke Ellington, Performing Arts Issue, 22¢ (29 April 1986)

Julia Ward Howe [wrote poem "Battle Hymn of the Republic," important Civil War song], Great Americans Issue,14¢ (12 Feb 1987)

Enrico Caruso, Performing Arts Issue, 22¢ (27 Feb 1987)

James Weldon Johnson [with incipit of music and lyrics for "Lift Every Voice and Sing"], Black Heritage Series, 22¢ (2 Feb 1988)

Toscanini [Arturo Toscanini], Performing Arts Issue, 25¢ (25 March 1989)

"The Wizard of Oz" [Judy Garland with Toto], Classic Films Issue, 25¢ (23 March 1990)

Cole Porter [with music fragment], Performing Arts Issue, 29¢ (8 June 1991)

Jack Benny [with violin in Al Hirschfeld cartoon] Comedians Issue, 29¢ (29 Aug 1991)

Fanny Brice [singer, comedian, in Al Hirschfeld cartoon], Comedians Issue, 29¢ (29 Aug 1991)

Elvis Presley, American Music Series, 29¢ (8 Jan 1993, reissued 16 June 1993) [most popular US stamp ever issued]

Oklahoma!, American Music Series, 29¢ (30 March 1993)

Hank Williams [with guitar], American Music Series, 29¢ (9 June 1993)

Bill Haley [with guitar], American Music Series, 29¢ (16 June 1993)

Clyde McPhatter, American Music Series, 29¢ (16 June 1993)

Ritchie Valens, American Music Series, 29¢ (16 June 1993)

Otis Redding, American Music Series, 29¢ (16 June 1993)

Buddy Holly, American Music Series, 29¢ (16 June 1993)

Dinah Washington, American Music Series, 29¢ (16 June 1993)

Pony Express Rider, Civil War Soldier, Stage Coach [tenor drum], National Postal Museum issue, 29¢ (30 July 1993)

Patsy Cline [with microphone], American Music Series, 29¢ (25 Sept 1993)

The Carter Family [with guitar neck], American Music Series, 29¢ (25 Sept 1993)

Bob Wills [with violin], American Music Series, 29¢ (25 Sept 1993)

"Greetings" [toy soldier blowing horn], Christmas Issue, 29¢ (21 Oct 1993)

Charlie Chaplin [music hall performer, film composer, actor, film maker], Silent Screen Stars Issue, 29¢ (27 April 1994)

Al Jolson, American Music Series: Popular Singers, 29¢ (1 Sept 1994)

Bing Crosby, American Music Series: Popular Singers, 29¢ (1 Sept 1994)

Ethel Waters, American Music Series: Popular Singers, 29¢ (1 Sept 1994)

Nat King Cole, American Music Series: Popular Singers, 29¢ (1 Sept 1994)

Ethel Merman, American Music Series: Popular Singers, 29¢ (1 Sept 1994)

Bessie Smith, American Music Series: Popular Singers, 29¢ (17 Sept 1994)

Muddy Waters, American Music Series: Popular Singers, 29¢ (17 Sept 1994)

Billie Holiday, American Music Series: Popular Singers, 29¢ (17 Sept 1994)

Robert Johnson, American Music Series: Popular Singers, 29¢ (17 Sept 1994)

Jimmy Rushing, American Music Series: Popular Singers, 29¢ (17 Sept 1994)

"Ma" Rainey, American Music Series: Popular Singers, 29¢ (17 Sept 1994)

Mildred Bailey, American Music Series: Popular Singers, 29¢ (17 Sept 1994)

Howlin' Wolf, American Music Series: Popular Singers, 29¢ (17 Sept 1994)

Liberty Bell, stamped envelope, 32¢ (13 Jan, 1995), issued as security envelope (16 May 1995)

Marilyn Monroe [singer, actress], Legends of Hollywood Issue, 32¢ (1 June 1995)

Louis Armstrong, American Music Series: Jazz Musicians Series, 32¢ (1 Sept 1995)

Coleman Hawkins, American Music Series: Jazz Musicians Series, 32¢ (16 Sept 1995)

James P. Johnson, American Music Series: Jazz Musicians Series, 32¢ (16 Sept 1995)

Jelly Roll Morton, American Music Series: Jazz Musicians Series, 32¢ (16 Sept 1995)

Charlie Parker, American Music Series: Jazz Musicians Series, 32¢ (16 Sept 1995)

Eubie Blake, American Music Series: Jazz Musicians Series, 32¢ (16 Sept 1995)

Charles Mingus, American Music Series: Jazz Musicians Series, 32¢ (16 Sept 1995)

John Coltrane, American Music Series: Jazz Musicians Series, 32¢ (16 Sept 1995)

Thelonious Monk, American Music Series: Jazz Musicians Series, 32¢ (16 Sept 1995)

Santa Entering Chimney [toy drum in sack], Christmas Issue, 32¢ (30 Sept 1995)

Child Holding Jumping Jack [with toy bugle], Christmas Issue, 32¢ (30 Sept 1995)

Child Holding Tree [with toy bugle], Christmas Issue, 32¢ (30 Sept 1995)

Midnight angel [bells on garland], 32¢ (19 Oct 1995; reissued Oct 1996)

American Indian Dances [5 dancers, small bells on legs, drummer on souvenir sheet], 32¢ (7 June, 1996) Issued with CD.

Harold Arlen, Legends of American Music Series: Songwriters Issues, 32¢ (11 Sept 1996)

Johnny Mercer, Legends of American Music Series: Songwriters Issues, 32¢ (11 Sept 1996)

Dorothy Fields, Legends of American Music Series: Songwriters Issues, 32¢ (11 Sept 1996)

Hoagy Carmichael, Legends of American Music Series: Songwriters Issues, 32¢ (11 Sept 1996)

Count Basie, Legends of American Music Series: Big Band Leaders Issue, 32¢ (11 Sept 1996)

Tommy and Jimmy Dorsey, Legends of American Music Series: Big Band Leaders Issue, 32¢ (11 Sept 1996)

Glenn Miller, Legends of American Music Series: Big Band Leaders Issue, 32¢ (11 Sept 1996)

Benny Goodman, Legends of American Music Series: Big Band Leaders Issue, 32¢ (11 Sept 1996)

Harold Arlen, Legends of American Music Series: Songwriters Issues, 32¢ (11 Sept 1996)

Johnny Mercer, Legends of American Music Series: Songwriters Issues, 32¢ (11 Sept 1996)

Dorothy Fields, Legends of American Music Series: Songwriters Issues, 32¢ (11 Sept 1996)

Hoagy Carmichael, Legends of American Music Series: Songwriters Issues, 32¢ (11 Sept 1996)

Jukebox, coil, 25c (27, Jan, 1997; reissued as first-class presort 14 March 1997)

"The Stars and Stripes Forever" [uniformed musician with trumpet], 32¢ (21 July 1997)

Lily Pons, American Music Series, Opera Singers Issue, 32¢ (10 Sept 1997)

Richard Tucker, American Music Series, Opera Singers Issue, 32¢ (10 Sept 1997)

Lawrence Tibbett, American Music Series, Opera Singers Issue, 32¢ (10 Sept 1997)

Rosa Ponselle, American Music Series, Opera Singers Issue, 32¢ (10 Sept 1997)

Leopold Stokowski, Classical Composers and Conductors Issue, 32¢ (12 Sept 1997)

Arthur Fiedler, Classical Composers and Conductors Issue, 32¢ (12 Sept 1997)

George Szell, Classical Composers and Conductors Issue, 32¢ (12 Sept 1997)

Eugene Ormandy, Classical Composers and Conductors Issue, 32¢ (12 Sept 1997)

Samuel Barber, Classical Composers and Conductors Issue, 32¢ (12 Sept 1997)

Ferde Grofé, Classical Composers and Conductors Issue, 32¢ (12 Sept 1997)

Charles Ives, Classical Composers and Conductors Issue, 32¢ (12 Sept 1997)

Louis Moreau Gottschalk, Classical Composers and Conductors Issue, 32¢ (12 Sept 1997)

Charlie Chaplin [music hall performer, film composer, actor, film maker], Celebrate the Century Series: 1910s, 32¢ (3 Feb 1998)

"Flappers Do the Charleston" [with caricature trombone and sax players], Celebrate the Century Series: 1920s, 32¢ (28 May 1998)

Leadbelly [Huddie Ledbetter], Folk Musicians Issue, Legends of American Music Series, 32¢ (26 June 1998)

Woody Guthrie, Folk Musicians Issue, Legends of American Music Series, 32¢ (26 June 1998)

Sonny Terry, Folk Musicians Issue, Legends of American Music Series, 32¢ (26 June 1998)

Josh White, Folk Musicians Issue, Legends of American Music Series, 32¢ (26 June 1998)

Mahalia Jackson, Gospel Singers Issue, Legends of American Music Series, 32¢ (15 July 1998), CD issued

Roberta Martin, Gospel Singers Issue, Legends of American Music Series, 32¢ (15 July 1998), CD issued

Clara Ward, Gospel Singers Issue, Legends of American Music Series, 32¢ (15 July 1998), CD issued

Sister Rosetta, Gospel Singers Issue, Legends of American Music Series, 32¢ (15 July 1998), CD issued

"Radio Entertains America," Celebrate the Century Series: 1920s, 32¢ (28 May 1998)

"Jazz Flourishes" [with trombone and trumpet players and "Jazz Club" sign]. Celebrate the Century Series: 1920s, 32¢ (28 May 1998)

"Troops Guarding Train" [soldier with bugle], Reissue of the 17 June 1898 Trans-Mississippi Exposition Issue, 8¢ (18 June 1998)

"Jitterbug Sweeps Nation" [with bobby sox dancers and juke box], Celebrate the Century Series: 1940s, 33¢ (18 Feb 1999)

"The Big Band Sound" [with singer and instrumentalists], Celebrate the Century Series: 1940s, 33¢ (18 Feb 1999)

"I Love Lucy" [featuring movie singer Lucille Ball and Latin band leader Desi Arnaz], Celebrate the Century Series: 1950s, 33¢ (26 May 1999)

"Rock 'n' Roll" [with guitarist, drums, bass and dancers], Celebrate the Century Series: 1950s, 33¢ (26 May 1999)

Max Steiner, Legends of American Music Series: Hollywood Composers Issue, 33¢ (16 Sept 1999), issued with CD

Dimitri Tiomkin, Legends of American Music Series: Hollywood Composers Issue, 33¢ (16 Sept 1999), issued with CD

Bernard Herrmann, Legends of American Music Series: Hollywood Composers Issue, 33¢ (16 Sept 1999), issued with CD

Franz Waxman, Legends of American Music Series: Hollywood Composers Issue, 33¢ (16 Sept 1999), issued with CD

Alfred Newman, Legends of American Music Series: Hollywood Composers Issue, 33¢ (16 Sept 1999), issued with CD

Erich Korngold, Legends of American Music Series: Hollywood Composers Issue, 33¢ (16 Sept 1999), issued with CD

"Woodstock" [hand on guitar fingerboard], Celebrate the Century Series: 1960s, 33¢ (17 Sept 1999)

"The Beatles" [with cartoon yellow submarine], Celebrate the Century Series: 1960s, 33¢ (17 Sept 1999)

Ira & George Gershwin, Legends of American Music Series: Broadway Songwriters Issues, 33¢ (21 Sept 1999)

Lerner & Lowe, Legends of American Music Series: Broadway Songwriters Issues, 33¢ (21 Sept 1999)

Lorenz Hart, Legends of American Music Series: Broadway Songwriters Issues, 33¢ (21 Sept 1999)

Rodgers & Hammerstein, Legends of American Music Series: Broadway Songwriters Issues, 33¢ (21 Sept 1999)

Meredith Willson, Legends of American Music Series: Broadway Songwriters Issues, 33¢ (21 Sept 1999)

Frank Loesser, Legends of American Music Series: Broadway Songwriters Issues, 33¢ (21 Sept 1999)

"Disco Music" [with dancers], Celebrate the Century Series: 1970s, 33¢ (18 Nov 1999)

"Year 2000" [with cherub blowing noise maker and holding bell], 33¢ (27 Dec 1999)

"Musical Smash" [with character from "Cats"], Celebrate the Century Series: 1980s, 33¢ (13 Jan 2000)

"Compact Discs" [with CD and treble clef], Celebrate the Century Series: 1980s, 33¢ (13 Jan 2000)

"Hip Hop Culture" [with dancer and boom box], Celebrate the Century Series: 1980s, 33¢ (13 Jan 2000)

"Ryman Auditorium, Nashville, Tennessee" [home of "Grand Ole Opry" and other country music shows], postcard, 20¢ (18 March 2000)

Louise Nevelson [abstract sculptures titled "Silent Music I" and "Black Chord"], 33¢ (6 April 2000)

"Francis Hopkinson Flag 1777" [earliest American songwriter and musician, signer of Declaration of Independence], The Stars and Stripes Issue, 33¢ (14 June 2000)

Maxfield Parrish ["The Lute Players" picture with lutes], American Illustrators Issue, 34¢ (1 Feb 2001)

John Held, Jr. ["The Girl He Left Behind" illustration with guitar], American Illustrators Issue, 34¢ (1 Feb 2001)

"Northwestern University, Sesquicentennial, 1851–2001" [University Hall bell and clock tower], postcard, 20¢ (28 April 2001)

Leonard Bernstein, 34¢ (10 July 2001)

Lucille Ball [movie singer], Legends of Hollywood Series, 34¢ (6 Aug 2001)

19th Century Santa [with toys including trumpet], Christmas Issue, 34¢ (10 Oct 2001)

19th Century Santa [with toy drum and sticks], Christmas Issue, 34¢ (10 Oct 2001)

"Greetings from Pennsylvania" [Liberty Bell], Greetings from America Issue, 34¢ (4 April 2002)

"Greetings from Tennessee" [guitar], Greetings from America Issue, 34¢ (4 April 2002)

"Paul Strand, 1890–1976" [photograph "The Steeple," a church bell tower] Masters of American Photography Series (13 June 2002)

"God Bless America, Irving Berlin" [with musical incipit], 37¢ (15 Sept 2002)

"Music" [with arm of Max Steiner notating a film music score], American Film Making: Behind the Scenes Issue, 37¢ (25 Feb 2003)

Roy Acuff [with fiddle], 37¢ (13 Sept 2003)

"Cutler Hall, Ohio University" [former bell tower, now with chimes], postcard, 23¢ (10 Oct 2003)

Reindeer with Pan Pipes, Holiday Music Makers, Christmas Issue, also postcards, 37¢ (23 Oct 2003)

Santa Claus with Drum, Holiday Music Makers: Christmas Issue, also postcards, 37¢ (23 Oct 2003)

Reindeer with Horn, Holiday Music Makers: Christmas Issue, also postcards, 37¢ (23 Oct 2003)

Santa Claus Playing Trumpet, Holiday Music Makers: Christmas Issue, also postcards, 37¢ (23 Oct 2003)

Paul Robeson, Black Heritage Series, 37¢ (20 Jan 2004)

Henry Mancini [with Pink Panther and list of his films], 37¢ (13 April 2004)

Bambi and Thumper [animated musical motion picture], The Art of Disney: Friendship Issue, 37¢ (23 June 2004), also prints, stamped stationery, postcards.

Pinocchio [animated musical motion picture], The Art of Disney: Friendship Issue, 37¢ (23 June 2004), also prints, stamped stationery, postcards.

The Lion King [animated musical motion picture], The Art of Disney: Friendship Issue, 37¢ (23 June 2004), also prints, stamped stationery, postcards.

Moss Hart [musical theater director, playwright], Literary Arts Issue, 37¢ (25 Oct 2004)

Marian Anderson, Black Heritage Series, 37¢ (27 Jan 2005)

Edgar Y. "Yip" Harburg [with opening lyrics to "Over the Rainbow"], Literary Arts Issue, 37¢ (28 April 2005)

Walt Disney Concert Hall [architect Frank Gehry, 2003], Masterworks of Modern American Architecture Issue, 37¢ (19 May 2005)

Snow White and Dopey ["Snow White and the Seven Dwarfs," animated musical motion picture], The Art of Disney: Celebration Issue, 37¢ (30 June 2005), includes prints and postcards.

Alice and Mad Hatter ["Alice in Wonderland," animated musical motion picture], The Art of Disney: Celebration Issue, 37¢ (30 June 2005), includes prints and postcards.

Ariel [holding a harp] and Flounder ["The Little Mermaid," animated musical motion picture], The Art of Disney: Celebration Issue, 37¢ (30 June 2005)

Mambo [with cartoon orchestra in background], Let's Dance Issue, 37¢ (17 Sept 2005)

Lyra [Greek goddess holding lyre], Constellations Issue, 37¢ (3 Oct 2005)

Hattie McDaniel [actress, singer], Black Heritage Series, 39¢ (25 Jan 2006)

Cinderella and Prince Charming ["Cinderella," animated musical motion picture], The Art of Disney: Romance Issue, 39¢ (21 April 2006), includes prints and postcards.

Beauty and the Beast ["Beauty and the Beast," animated musical motion picture], The Art of Disney: Romance Issue, 39¢ (21 April 2006), includes prints and postcards.

Lady and the Tramp ["Lady and the Tramp," animated musical motion picture], The Art of Disney: Romance Issue, 39¢ (21 April 2006), includes prints and postcards.

Judy Garland, Legends of Hollywood Issue, 39¢ (10 June 2006)

Oklahoma Statehood [with quote "Oh, What a Beautiful Mornin'" from the musical "Oklahoma!"], 39¢ (11 Jan 2007)

Ella Fitzgerald, Black Heritage Series, 39¢ (10 Jan 2007)

"Forever" stamp [Liberty Bell], "first-class" (12 April 2007)

Mickey Mouse [as "The Sorcerer's Apprentice," a segment from Disney's animated musical motion picture "Fantasia"], The Art of Disney: Magic Issue, 41¢ (16 Aug 2007), includes prints and postcards.

Peter Pan and Tinker Bell ("Peter Pan," animated musical motion picture], The Art of Disney: Magic Issue, 41¢ (16 Aug 2007), includes prints and postcards.

Dumbo and Timothy Mouse ["Dumbo," animated musical motion picture], The Art of Disney: Magic Issue, 41¢ (16 Aug 2007), includes prints and postcards.

Aladdin and Genie ["Aladdin," animated musical motion picture], The Art of Disney: Magic Issue, 41¢ (16 Aug 2007), includes prints and postcards.

Frank Sinatra, 42¢ (13 May 2008), CD issued

Poster for "Black and Tan" [a motion picture featuring Duke Ellington and the Cotton Club Orchestra, with Ellington's silhouette, stylized orchestra and piano keyboard], Vintage Black Cinema Issue, 42¢ (16 July 2008)

Poster for "Prinsesse Tam Tam" [motion picture featuring Josephine Baker], Vintage Black Cinema Issue, 42¢ (16 July 2008)

Poster for "Caldonia" [movie short featuring Louis Jordan performing his hit song, with Jordan holding saxophone], Vintage Black Cinema Issue, 42¢ (16 July 2008)

Poster for "Hallelujah" [King Vidor's production of the MGM musical, with music by Irving Berlin; includes cartoon instruments and players on poster], Vintage Black Cinema Issue, 42¢ (16 July 2008)

"Take Me Out to the Ball Game, 1908-2008" [with brief incipit] (16 July 2008), CD issued

Pongo and Pup ["101 Dalmations," animated musical motion picture], The Art of Disney: Imagination Issue, 42¢ (7 Aug 2008)

Princess Aurora ["Sleeping Beauty," animated musical motion picture], The Art of Disney: Imagination Issue, 42¢ (7 Aug 2008)

Mowgli and Baloo ["The Jungle Book," animated musical motion picture], The Art of Disney: Imagination Issue, 42¢ (7 Aug 2008)

Latin Jazz [with stylized congas, bass, and piano players], 42¢ (8 Sept 2008)

Nutcracker drummer, Holiday Nutcrackers Series, 42¢ (23 Oct 2008)

Bob Hope [comedian, actor, singer], 44¢ (29 May 2009)

"The Dinah Shore Show" [Dinah Shore: singer, music variety show host], Early TV Memories Series, 44¢ (11 Aug 2009)

"The Ed Sullivan Show" [Ed Sullivan: music variety show host], Early TV Memories Series, 44¢ (11 Aug 2009)

"The Tonight Show" [Steve Allen: music variety show host, pianist, composer], Early TV Memories Series, 44¢ (11 Aug 2009)

"Ozzie and Harriet" [TV sitcom featuring orchestra leader and producer Ozzie Nelson, big band singer Harriet Nelson, and teen idol musician Ricky Nelson], Early TV Memories Series, 44¢ (11 Aug 2009)

"Thanksgiving Day Parade" [trombones, cornets, sousaphone and drum major in parade], 44¢ (9 Sept 2009)

Roy Rogers [singing cowboy actor], Cowboys of the Silver Screen Issue, 44¢ (7 April 2010)

Gene Autry [singing cowboy actor], Cowboys of the Silver Screen Issue, 44¢ (7 April 2010)

Kate Smith [singer], 44¢ (10 May 2010)

Angel with Lute [detail from 15th C. fresco by Melozzo da Forli], Christmas issue, 44¢ (21 Oct 2010)

Tito Puente [Puerto Rican American timbalist, and Latin music composer and band leader], "forever" issue, current first class denomination (16 March 2011)

Carmen Miranda [Brazilian singer and dancer who starred in American motion pictures], "forever" issue, current first class denomination (16 March 2011)

Selena [Selena Quintanilla-Pérez, Mexican American singer and songwriter], "forever" issue, current first class denomination (16 March 2011)

Carlos Gardel [Argentine singer, songwriter, and actor], "forever" issue, current first class denomination (16 March 2011)

Celia Cruz [Cuban Salsa music singer], "forever" issue, current first class denomination (16 March 2011)

Jazz [abstract tribute to jazz by artist Paul Rogers], "forever" issue, current first class denomination (26 March 2011)

Danny Thomas [popular singer, actor, producer, and humanitarian], "forever" issue, current first class denomination (16 Feb 2012)

José Ferrer [Puerto Rican actor, director, singer, and pianist], Distinguished American Series, "forever" issue, current first class denomination (26 April 2012)

Miles Davis [jazz trumpet player], joint issue with La Poste (French postal administration), "forever" issue, current first class denomination (12 June 2012)

Edith Piaf [French chanteuse], joint issue with La Poste (French postal administration), "forever" issue, current first class denomination (12 June 2012)

BIBLIOGRAPHY

Topical Time (Carterville, IL, 1949–)
A. Ragucci: *Musicos en el Sello Postal* (Buenos Aires, 1955)
H.O. Henneman: *Music on Stamps* (Milwaukee, 2/1956)
J. Watson: *Stamps and Music* (London, 1962)
N.A. Miller: *Encyclopedia of Music Philately* (Milwaukee, 1963)
The Baton (1969–2005) [journal of the Philatelic Music Circle]
S. Peat: *Music On Stamps* (Chippenham, 1972–5)
M.J. Whitehead: *Music World of Stamps* (Milwaukee, 1975)
G.K. Senior: *Music and Musicians on Postage Stamps* (Orrell, UK, 1979)
G.K. Megla: *Musik im Spiegel der Philatelie* (Tübingen, 1984)
Der Musikus, Mitteilungsblatt der Motivgruppe Musik (Berlin, 1985–)
A.H.R. Grimsey: *Check List of Postage Stamps About Music* (London, 2/1988)
USA Philatelic (Washington, DC, 1996–)
J.A. Norstedt: *A Checklist of Postage Stamps About Music* (Blacksburg, VA, 1997)
The Postal Service Guide to U. S. Stamps (Washington, DC, 37/2010)
Scott Specialized Catalogue of United States Stamps and Covers (New York, 167/2011)

STEPHEN M. FRY

Phile [Fyles, Pfeil, Phyles, etc.], **Philip** (*d* ?Philadelphia, PA, 1793). Violinist and composer. He was active in Philadelphia from 1784, becoming about that time leader of the orchestra of the Old American Company. He wrote a violin concerto that was performed in Philadelphia on 12 April 1787. His only extant composition is *The President's March*, said to have been written for the inauguration of George Washington in 1789, though the earliest printed editions date from 1793–4 (ed. V.B. Lawrence in *Music for Patriots, Politicians, and Presidents*, 1975). The tune was subsequently set to the text "Hail Columbia" by Joseph Hopkinson, and the song received its first performance on 25 April 1798.

BIBLIOGRAPHY

O.G.T. Sonneck: *A Bibliography of Early Secular American Music* (Washington, DC, 1905; rev. and enlarged by W.T. Upton, 2/1945/R1964)
R.R. Drummond: *Early German Music in Philadelphia* (New York, 1910/R1970)
R.J. Wolfe: *Secular Music in America, 1801–1825: a Bibliography* (New York, 1964)

J. BUNKER CLARK

Philharmonic Society (of Charleston, SC). The Philharmonic Society of Charleston, South Carolina, was a subscription concert organization that flourished between 1809 and 1814. Incorporated on 20 December 1810 as "The Philharmonic Society of South Carolina," its officers were professional musicians simultaneously engaged to perform at the city's theaters and at the St. Cecilia Society's concert series: Robert Léaumont, Louis DeVillers, Charles Gilfert, Philip Muck, Daniel Remoussin, Eugene Guilbert, Isadore Labatut, Augustus Remoussin, and Arnold Remoussin. Unlike the St. Cecilia Society, however, the Philharmonic Society was a purely commercial venture, with the musicians themselves serving as both its managers and performers. By presenting its fortnightly subscription concerts at an alternative venue (the long room of dancing master and violinist Peter Fayolle) on a different night of the week, the Philharmonic Society offered the public a musical alternative to the more exclusive St. Cecilia Society events. It concerts were still private subscription events, however, and the Philharmonic Society's advertisements repeatedly noted that tickets were not sold at the door.

The paucity of extant sources of information about the Philharmonic Society precludes a full description of its orchestra, repertoire, and audience. Since most of its members appear to have been French-speaking refugees of the revolutions in Europe and the West Indies, it is likely that the society sought to attract culturally astute but socially marginalized patrons excluded from the St. Cecilia Society's Anglophilic concerts. Since the Philharmonic Society's officers also formed a large portion of the professional contingent of the St. Cecilia Society's orchestra, they probably presented a similar repertoire of contemporary British musical fashions, including orchestral, chamber, and vocal works, mixed with elements of French concert repertoire of the 1790s and early 1800s.

The Philharmonic Society presented a seasonal series of fortnightly concerts between March 1809 and May 1812, but its activities declined sharply during the depressed years of the War of 1812. Following the conclusion of its regular concert season in May 1812, and the US declaration of war against Britain the following month, the society advertised only anniversary concerts in the spring of 1813 and 1814. No further advertisements of this organization appear after the death of its president, Robert Léaumont, in August 1814. The last known appearance of Charleston's Philharmonic Society dates from February 1820, when the organization joined forces with the city's Union Harmonic Society (founded in 1816) for a charity oratorio concert. The performing membership of these two organizations may have overlapped to some degree, but their respective activities represented differing musical styles and purposes.

The relatively brief existence of the Philharmonic Society occurred near the end of a long era of vigorous concert activity in Charleston that began in the 1760s. The society arose from a bounty of professional performers wishing to capitalize on the city's auspicious musical climate, but its demise a few years later proved to be among the first signs of a significant and lasting contraction in Charleston's musical vitality.

BIBLIOGRAPHY

N.M. Butler: *Votaries of Apollo: the St. Cecilia Society and the Patronage of Concert Music in Charleston, South Carolina, 1766–1820* (Columbia, SC, 2007)

NICHOLAS MICHAEL BUTLER

Philipp, Adolf (*b* Lübeck, Germany, 29 Jan 1864; *d* New York, NY, 30 July 1936). Composer, librettist, playwright, singer, actor, and theatrical impresario of German birth. In the early 1880s, Philipp began a career as a tenor in German operetta companies, and also wrote several operetta librettos. Gustav Amberg brought him to New York in 1890 to perform at his Amberg Theater. In 1893, Philipp opened the Germania Theater on 8th Street, where, up to 1902, he wrote and composed, directed, produced, and starred in an extensive series of German American Volksstücke ("folk plays" with music, or musical comedies). These works represent a new American hybrid mix of disparate theatrical and musical elements: German operetta and Volkstück, the American musical comedy, and aspects taken from Ned Harrigan's and David Braham's musical plays. Philipp's musicals such as *Der Corner Grocer aus der Avenue A* (1893) and *Der Pawnbroker von der East Side* (1894) presented portrayals of German American immigrant life in New York and captured the humorous and serious aspects of ordinary life for both the newly arrived Greenhorn and long-established immigrant population.

He wrote the libretti for his Germania Theater musicals and composed the music for most of them with Carl von Wegern (*b* Neiße, Germany, 30 May 1852; *d* Avalon, CA, 1 Nov 1916). Philipp's works usually ran for all or much of the theatrical season and he took some of them on tour. *Der Corner Grocer aus der Avenue A* was reportedly performed more than 1000 times into the 1920s.

In 1903, Philipp moved to Berlin and presented his musicals at the Deutsch-Amerikanischer Theater, including the very successful *Über'n grossen Teich*. He returned to New York by 1907, and presented his Parisian-styled musical farce *Alma, wo wohnst du?* (1909), translated as *Alma, Where do you Live?* (1910), which became his most popular work on Broadway and on tour; however, the racy German plot was tamer for the English version. His English-language operetta *Adele* had one of the longest runs of the 1913–14 Broadway season and also toured. Philipp adopted the pseudonyms Jean Briquet and Paul Hervé to add a continental French flair to his Broadway musicals. Anti-German prejudice after the United States entered World War I in 1917 reduced his activity, though he wrote and appeared in an English-language pro-American play, *Tell That to the Marines* (1918). After the war, he continued writing German American musical comedies on local New York themes, but for smaller and often bilingual audiences. Philipp was the most successful German American playwright and theatrical composer, and he wrote or adapted more than 100 stage works. His musicals exhibit an assimilation of many styles: the Viennese waltz operetta, German regional folk song, French comic opera, ragtime, march music, and the turn-of-the-century American musical theater.

WORKS
(selective list)
(except where indicated, all works with libretti and music were by Philipp, and all were performed in New York)
(AP = Adolf Philipp; CW = Carl von Wegern; RS = Rudolf Sinnhold)
Die Royalisten (operetta, music by Josef Mañas), 1888 (Braunschweig); Der Corner Grocer aus der Avenue A (music CW), 1893; Der Pawnbroker von der East Side (music AP, CW), 1894; Der New Yorker Brauer und seine Familie (music AP, CW), 1894; Der Butcher aus der Ersten Avenue (music AP, CW), 1895; New York in Wort und Bild (music AP, CW), 1895; New York bei Nacht (music AP, CW), 1896; Klein Deutschland (music AP, CW), 1897; Der glucklichste Mensch in New York (music AP, RS), 1897; Die Reise nach Amerika (music AP, RS), 1898; Die Geheimnisse von New York (music AP, RS), 1900; Im Lande der Freiheit, 1901; Über'n grossen Teich (Berlin), 1903; New York (Berlin), 1904; Aber, Herr Herzog (Berlin), 1905; Er und ich (Berlin), 1905; Im wilden Westen (Berlin), 1906; Alma, wo wohnst du?, 1909, trans. as Alma, Where do you Live? (lib. G. Hobart), 1910; Auction Pinochle, 1912, trans. as Auction Pinochle (lib. E. Paulton), 1914; Adele (lib. Paulton), 1913; Das Mitternachtsmaedel, 1913, trans. as The Midnight Girl (lib. Paulton), 1914; Zwei Lots in der Bronx, 1913, trans. as Two Lots in the Bronx (lib. Paulton), 1913; The Girl Who Smiles (lib. Paulton), 1915; Two Is Company, 1915; Sadie from Riverside Drive (in German), 1916; Mimi (lib. Paulton), 1920; Home Brew (in German), 1922; Also das ist New York, 1922; Ohne Louis geht es nicht, 1923; Die deutsche Marie, 1924; Wilhelminche, 1925; Die Trockenen und die Nassen, 1926; Der Tanz um den Dollar, 1928; Bertha von Ridgewood, 1928; Sie hat so etwas, 1928; Kultur (play), 1933; Hotel Alimony (play), 1934

Principal publisher: Remick

BIBLIOGRAPHY
K. Gänzl: "Philipp, Adolf," *The Encyclopedia of the Musical Theater* (New York, 2001)
J. Koegel: "Adolf Philipp and Ethnic Musical Comedy in New York's Little Germany," *American Music*, xxiv/3 (2006), 267–319
J. Koegel: "The Development of the German-American Musical Theater in New York, 1840–1890," *European Music and Musicians in New York City, 1840–1900*, ed. J. Graziano (Rochester, NY, 2006), 149–81
J. Koegel: "Non-English-Language Musical Theater in the United States," *The Cambridge Companion to the Musical*, ed. W.A. Everett and P.R. Laird (Cambridge, 2008), 29–53
J. Koegel: *Music in German Immigrant Theater: New York City, 1840–1940* (Rochester, NY, 2009)

JOHN KOEGEL

Philipp, Isidore (*b* Budapest, Hungary, 2 Sept 1863; *d* Paris, France, 20 Feb 1958). French pianist, teacher, and composer of Hungarian origin, active in the United States. He studied with Stephen Heller and Camille Saint-Saëns. He was professor of piano at the Paris Conservatoire from 1893 to 1934 and was extraordinarily successful as a teacher. With the outbreak of World War II he came to the United States where, despite his age, he continued to teach; he also arranged works for two pianos and edited many well-known piano pieces. He gave his last public performance in New York in 1955. Philipp's ability to solve pianistic problems has remained legendary. No fewer than 13 of his collections of piano exercises and studies were published in the United States between 1898 and 1953, and they are still highly regarded. In 1977 the American Liszt Society established the Isidore Philipp Archive and Memorial Library at the University of Louisville School of Music.

BIBLIOGRAPHY
H. Bellamann: "Isidor Philipp," *MQ*, xxix (1943), 417–25
D.M. Le Blanc: *The Life and Work of Isidor Philipp* (DMA thesis, U. of Cincinnati, 1989)
C. Timbrel: "Isidor Philipp, His Life and Legacy," *Journal of the American Liszt Society*, xl (1996), 48–83

MAURICE HINSON/R

Philips. Dutch recording company. Philips Gloeilampen-fabrieken entered the record industry in 1929, when it started producing hardware for shellac (78 r.p.m.) discs. In 1946 Philips took over the Dutch arm of Decca and in 1950, Philips entered the record business in its own right. The technical superiority of its pressings attracted a world-wide clientele, and the label established a reputation for the high technical quality of its recordings of Western classical music. Philips distributed recordings for various companies in Europe and the United States, including CBS (1951–60); from 1955 to 1968 Columbia Records distributed Philips material in the United Sates on the Epic label. Philips later found a new US partner in Mercury. Throughout the late 1950s and the 60s Philips built an impressive classical music catalog; they also found success with film soundtracks and, to a lesser degree, popular music. In 1964 Philips consolidated its technical leadership by introducing the Musicassette, which replaced the open-reel tape for domestic use. The convenience and low price of the new format contributed to massive growth in the recording industry which lasted until the recession of the late 1970s.

After a series of corporate maneuvers and mergers in the 1960s and 1970s, Polygram (a holding company formed by Philips) stood as the most powerful music group in the world upon its acquisition of Decca in 1979. Polygram's three classical-music labels, Decca, Deutsche Grammophon, and Philips, retained their independence with regard to artists and repertory. Philips turned their attention to opera, early music, 20th-century music, and classical crossover artists (fusing classical with jazz, pop, or light music). They also gained distinction for producing ambitious, multi-volume boxed sets. The invention by Philips Gloeilampenfabrieken of the CD, developed in collaboration with Sony and launched in 1982–3, further fueled the company's fortunes. Along with other CD companies, Philips benefited commercially from reissues of earlier analog recordings in digital form. With CD sales declining in the mid-1990s, Philips sold its majority share in Polygram to Seagram in 1998, breaking the link with Philips Gloeilampenfabrieken. A new company, Universal Classics, was formed from Philips, Decca, and Deutsche Grammophon; its parent company is the UNIVERSAL MUSIC GROUP. In 1999 Philips and Decca merged their operations, bringing Philips's location in the Netherlands to an end.

JAMES CHATER (with DAVE LAING and
JANET TOPP FARGION)/R

Phillipps, Adelaide (*b* Stratford-on-Avon, England, 26 Oct 1833; *d* Karlsbad [now Karlovy Vary, Czechoslovakia], 3 Oct 1882). Singer of English birth. Her family moved to Canada and then to Boston, where from 1842 she appeared as an actress, singer, and dancer, principally at the Boston Museum. In 1851 she studied singing with MANUEL GARCÍA in London and in 1853 made her operatic debut in Brescia, Italy. After two years of sporadic engagements in Italy as Signorina Fillippi, she returned to the United States and performed operatic roles under Max Maretzek in New York and Havana; her first important appearance in New York was as

Azucena in Verdi's *Il trovatore* on 17 March 1856. In 1861–2 she made a European tour, then appeared regularly throughout the United States in operas, concerts, and oratorios. After an unsuccessful season with her own Adelaide Phillipps Opera Company, she sang with the Boston Ideal Opera Company (1879–81).

BIBLIOGRAPHY

NAW

Mrs. R.C. Waterston: *Adelaide Phillipps: a Record* (Boston, 1883)

O. Thompson: *The American Singer* (New York, 1937/R1969), 42

C. McGlinchee: *The First Decade of the Boston Museum* (Boston, 1940)

Phillips, Burrill (*b* Omaha, NE, 9 Nov 1907; *d* Berkeley, CA, 22 June 1988). Composer and pianist. His theory and composition teachers were Edwin Stringham at the Denver College of Music (1928–31) and HOWARD HANSON and BERNARD ROGERS at the Eastman School (BM 1932, MM 1933). He was a faculty member at Eastman (1933–49, 1965–6), the University of Illinois (professor, 1949–64), the Juilliard School (1968–9), and Cornell University (1972–3), as well as a visiting composer at the universities of Texas, Kansas, Southern California, and Hawaii. Among his awards are two Guggenheim Fellowships (1942–3, 1961–2) and an award from the American Academy of Arts and Letters (1944). He was a Fulbright Lecturer at the University of Barcelona (1960–61). He received commissions from the League of Composers (Scherzo for orchestra, 1944), the Koussevitzky Foundation (*Tom Paine*, overture for orchestra, 1946), the Fromm Foundation (*The Return of Odysseus*, 1956), and the Elizabeth Sprague Coolidge Foundation (String Quartet no.2, 1958).

Phillips's first important orchestral work, *Selections from McGuffey's Reader* (1933), was an immediate success and established his reputation as a composer with a consciously American style—a reputation that has tended to overshadow the subsequent development of his musical language. The elements of his early style—an emphasis on melodic line, a rich harmonic texture, and rhythmic associations with jazz—had evolved by the late 1930s and early 1940s into a drier, more acerbic idiom, with asymmetrical rhythms and broadened expressiveness. Many of the works written in the 1940s and 50s reveal a new intensity and compression; imitative counterpoint is characteristic of the piano writing. In the early 1960s Phillips began to work with free serial techniques, less sharply accented rhythms, and an increasing sense of fantasy. Although he can in no sense be considered an imitator of earlier models, his works show a clarity of line and texture that reflects his great admiration for the music of Domenico Scarlatti and Purcell.

WORKS

STAGE

Katmanusha (ballet), 1932–3; Play Ball (ballet), 1937; Step into my Parlor (ballet), 1942; Don't We All (op buffa, 1, A. Phillips), 1947; Dr. Faustus (incid music, C. Marlowe), org, brass qt, timp, 1957; Nine from Little Rock (film score), 1964; La piñata (ballet, choreog. J. Limón), chbr orch, 1969; The Unforgiven (op, 3, A. Phillips), 1981; other incid music

ORCHESTRAL

Selections from McGuffey's Reader, 1933; Sym. concertante, chbr orch, 1935; Courthouse Square, 1935; Concert Piece, bn, str, 1942, arr. bn, sym. band/pf, 1953; Pf Conc., 1942; Scherzo, 1944; Tom Paine, ov., 1946; Scena, chbr orch, 1946; Conc. grosso, str qt, chbr orch, 1949; Triple Conc., cl, va, pf, orch, 1952; Perspectives in a Labyrinth, 3 str orchs, 1962; Soleriana concertante, 1965; Theater Dances, 1967; Fantasia, sym. band, 1968; Yellowstone, Yates, and Yosemite, t sax, sym. band, 1972

VOCAL

Declaratives (T. Boggs, E.E. Cummings, B. Phillips), SSAA, chbr orch, 1943; What will Love do and The Hag (R. Herrick), SSAA, 1949; A Bucket of Water (A. Phillips), SATB, pf, 1952; The Age of Song (W. Raleigh, T. Campion, J. Donne, W. Shakespeare), SATB, 1954; The Return of Odysseus (A. Phillips), Bar, nar, chorus, orch, 1956; The First Day of the World (A. Phillips), TTBB, pf, 1958; 4 Latin Motets, SATB, 1959; Canzona III (A. Phillips), S, fl, pf, perc, 1964; Canzona IV (A. Phillips), S, fl, perc, 1967

That Time may Cease (Marlowe), TTBB, pf, 1967; Canzona V (A. Phillips), SATB, pf, 1971; Eve Learns a Little (A. Phillips), S, 4 ww, pf, 1974; The Recesses of my House (A. Phillips), S, cl, pf, perc, 1977; Hernán y Marina (A. Hurtado), S, pf, 1981; Song in a Winter Night (B. Noll), S, pf, 1981; Letters from Italy Hill (A. Phillips), S, fl, cl, str qt, pf, 1984

CHAMBER AND SOLO INSTRUMENTAL

Pf works incl. 4 sonatas, 1942–60; Toccata, 1944; Music, 1949–50; Serenade, pf duet, 1956; Commentaries, 1983

Qts incl. 2 str qts, 1939–40, 1958; Partita, pf qt, 1947; Conversations and Colloquies, 2 vn, 2 va, 1950; Ob Qt, 1967

Sonatas: vn, pf, 1941; vc, pf, 1948; org, 1964; vn, hpd, 1965

Other: Trio, 3 tpt, 1937; Piece, 6 trbn, 1940; 4 Figures in Time, fl, pf, 1952; A Rondo of Rondeaux, va, pf, 1954; Music for this Time of Year, wind qnt, 1954; Sinfonia brevis, org, 1959; 3 Nostalgic Songs, fl, pf, 1962; Intrada, wind ens, perc, pf, vn, vc, 1975; Huntingdon Twos and Threes, fl, ob, vc, 1975; Scena da camera, vn, vc, 1978; Canzona VI, wind qnt, 1985

MSS in *R, Wc*

Principal publishers: Elkan-Vogel, Fallen Leaf, C. Fischer, Hargail, Presser, Southern

BIBLIOGRAPHY

J.T. Howard: *Our American Music* (New York, 1931, enlarged 4/1965)

C.R. Reis: *Composers in America* (New York, 1938, 2/1947/R)

J.T. Howard and A. Mendel: *Our Contemporary Composers* (New York, 1941/R)

B. Phillips: "Saluting the American Composer: Burrill Phillips," *Music Clubs Magazine*, 1 (1970–71), 6, 8–9, 19 [incl. autobiographical statement]

ANN P. BASART

Phillips, Esther [Jones, Esther Mae] (*b* Galveston, TX, 23 Dec 1935; *d* Carson, CA, 7 Aug 1984). Blues singer. She began singing in church as a child. In 1948 she won first prize in an amateur talent show in Los Angeles, and the following year joined the band of Johnny Otis, performing under the name Little Esther. With Otis she recorded "Double Crossing Blues" (1950), which reached number 1 on the rhythm-and-blues chart, and toured with his group until it disbanded in the early 1950s. She then moved to Houston and, on account of illness, retired from public life until 1962, when her version of the country-music standard "Release Me" became her only solo recording to reach the Top Ten. In the mid-1960s she had some success with jazz and pop audiences, and in 1972 she recorded what is probably her finest album, *From a Whisper to a Scream*. An intense, passionate singer whose performances recalled those of Dinah Washington, Phillips was acknowledged by the Beatles as an important influence on their work. In 1975 she issued "What a Difference a Day Makes," a disco single that reached number 20 on the pop chart; this exhibited her strong voice and versatility.

BIBLIOGRAPHY

SouthernB

S.A. Williams: "Returning to the Blues: Esther Phillips and Contemporary Blues Culture," *Callaloo*, xiv (1991), 816–28

JIM MILLER/R

Phillips, Harvey (Gene) (*b* Aurora, MO, 2 Dec 1929; *d* Bloomington, IN, 20 Oct 2010). Tuba player and teacher. He studied at the Juilliard School (1950–54) and performed with the New York City Opera and Ballet orchestras, NBC Opera Orchestra, and Sauter-Finegan Orchestra. He was a founding member of the New York Brass Quintet and Matteson-Phillips Tuba-Jazz Consort, was a free-lance tuba player in New York recording studios, and played on the Voice of Firestone, Bell Telephone Hour, and Band of America. He taught at Indiana University (1971–94), where he sponsored the First International Tuba Symposium and "OctubaFest" of student recitals (1973), and was named distinguished professor (1979) and professor emeritus (1994). He founded TubaChristmas in 1974 at Rockefeller Plaza in New York. He commissioned more than 200 works for tuba and served as executive editor of *The Instrumentalist* magazine (1986–96). He also co-founded several organizations, including T.U.B.A. (Tubists Universal Brotherhood Association, 1972) and the International Brass Society (1975). Regarded as the finest tuba player of his day, Phillips received many awards, including honorary doctorates from New England Conservatory (1971) and the University of Missouri (1987), Indiana University President's Medal for Excellence (2008), and induction into the American Classical Music Hall of Fame (2008).

DENNIS K. McINTIRE/PATRICE MADURA WARD-STEINMAN

Phillips, John (*b* Los Angeles, CA, 7 June 1948). Harpsichord maker. He graduated from the University of California, Santa Cruz (BA in German literature and music, 1973) and the University of California, Berkeley (MA in music history, 1975). In 1969, while still an undergraduate, he began building harpsichords from kits by S.R. Williams, completing four; his fifth instrument, in 1973, was a copy of the 1646 Andreas Ruckers double manual harpsichord enlarged in 1756 by Blanchet and again, in 1780, by Taskin (Paris, Musée de la Musique). He opened his shop in Berkeley in 1975. By 2011 he had completed more than 100 instruments, about half modeled on French harpsichords, the rest on Italian, Flemish, and German instruments. He usually works with one or two assistants, including decorator Janine Johnson.

Since 2000 he has performed major restorations on instruments acquired by a private collector, including a 1635 Ioannes Ruckers (2005), an anonymous Spanish instrument (2007), a 1627 Ioannes Ruckers (2008), and a 1707 Nicholas Dumont (2011). He has exhaustively studied the work of the Gräbner family of Dresden; copies of their instruments are among his specialties.

Phillips is known for the high quality and exacting decor of his work; his instruments are in the hands of institutions and musicians in the United States and Europe.

WRITINGS

"The 1739 Johann Heinrich Gräbner Harpsichord: an Oddity or a Bach-Fügel?" *Das deutsche Cembalo: Symposium im Rahmen der 24. Tage Alter Musik in Herne 1999*, ed. C. Ahrens, G. Klinke (Munich, 2000), 123–39

"The Surviving Harpsichords of the Gräbner Family: a Builder's Perspective," *Michaelsteiner Forschungsberichte 22: Das Mitteldeutsche Cembalo*, ed. M. Lustig, H. Weiner (Michaelstein, 2003), 53–84

BIBLIOGRAPHY

J.R. Lee: "John Phillips: Bringing Harpsichords Back to Life," *San Francisco Classical Voice* (8 Aug 2011)

EDWARD L. KOTTICK

Phillips, Liz [Elizabeth] (*b* Jersey City, NJ, 13 June 1951). Composer and artist. Phillips studied at Bennington College (BA 1973). Her work has focused on creating interactive multimedia installations, combining audio and visual art forms with new technologies to produce fascinating interactive experiences. In her early career as an artist she created sculptures using light. Later she incorporated sound as a logical extension of her work, explaining "What I wanted to do…was to change three-dimensional space over time, and sound was the best way to do this" (Close). She has earned considerable recognition for her sound sculptures, indoor and outdoor, that incorporate and react to wind, water, fish, light, sound, dance, and people. Her works often contain electronic circuitry that responds to elements of the environment in which it is positioned—in some cases responding to human movement (as in *Sunspots*) and in others a changing landscape (as in *Windspun* and *Come About*). From a visual standpoint, *Windspun* is typical of many of Phillips's sculptures in that the "sensor" (in this case a windmill) serves both an artistic and a practical purpose. Information about the speed and direction of the wind and the presence of nearby people is gathered by the sensor and transformed into sound by means of a synthesizer, using the hollow shaft of the windmill as a resonator. The changing environment may activate sound events, shifting their pitch, timbre, duration, and amplitude. Duration and physical dimensions are weighed and proportioned into intervals that make a vibrant density visible in her compositions. In 1981, she cofounded Parabola Arts Foundation, a not-for-profit organization created by five media artists from varied disciplines (music, sculpture, film, and video), which provides funding for art-related projects. She has made and exhibited interactive sound and multimedia installations at numerous art museums, alternative spaces, festivals, and public spaces throughout Europe and the United States. Selected venues include the Whitney Museum of American Art, the San Francisco Museum of Modern Art, the Spoleto Festival USA, the Walker Art Museum, Ars Electronica, Jacob's Pillow, the Kitchen, and Creative Time, among others. Phillips has also collaborated with the Merce Cunningham Dance Company, and her work was presented by the Cleveland Orchestra, IBM Japan, and the World Financial Center.

WORKS
(selective list)

Sound sculptures: T.V. Dinner, 1971; Electric Spaghetti, 1972; Sound Structure, 1972; Sumtime, 1973, collab. Y. Wada and A. Knowles; Broken/Unbroken Terracotta, 1975; Cityflow, 1977; Metrosonic Province, 1978; Sunspots, 1979; Windspun for Minneapolis, 1980; Come About, 1981; Windspun, 1981; Multiple Perspectives, 1982; Sound Syzygy, 1982; Sonar Eclipse, 1983, collab. M. Cunningham; Echo Evolution, 2002, Echo Location 2004.

BIBLIOGRAPHY

R. Cohen: "Sound Articulates Space," *Synapse* (Jan–Feb 1977), 14–15
J. La Barbara: "New Music," *HiFi/MusAm*, xxix/5 (1979), 12–13, 40
C. Drewes: "A Sculptor with Sound," *San Francisco Examiner* (21 June 1981)
D. Ahlstrom: "Liz Phillips: Sunspots," *Computer Music Journal*, vi/3 (1982), 5–6
R. Close: "Composer's Works Lend New Meaning to Movement," *St. Paul Pioneer Press* (13 Dec 1982)
P. Rabinowitz: "The Sound of Reformed Space: Liz Phillips's Response Installations," *PAJ: A Journal of Performance and Art*, xxiv/3 (2002), 35–43

CHARLES PASSY/BONNIE E. FLEMING

Phillips, Philip (*b* Chautauqua Co., NY, 13 Aug 1834; *d* Delaware, OH, 25 June 1895). Evangelistic singer, composer of Sunday school songs, and compiler of hymnbooks. He was largely self-taught in music and began teaching singing schools at the age of 19. In about 1863 he established Philip Phillips & Co. in Cincinnati to sell pianos and melodeons and to publish Sunday school songbooks. He later moved to New York where he became the music editor for the Methodist Book Concern. Phillips came to be known primarily as a singer of sacred and sentimental songs, and his appearance before President Abraham Lincoln in 1865 brought him widespread fame. He gave solo concerts in which he accompanied himself at the reed organ and was also associated with Dwight Moody and other evangelists. Moody invited Phillips to accompany him on his planned tour of England, but as Phillips had prior engagements, Moody took Ira D. Sankey instead, forming the famous partnership.

Phillips was known as the "Singing Pilgrim" and entitled one of his collections *The Singing Pilgrim, or Pilgrim's Progress Illustrated in Song* (New York, 1866). His *Hallowed Songs* (co-edited with Theodore E. Perkins and Sylvester Main; Cincinnati, 1865) was used in meetings by Moody and Sankey before the publication of Sankey and Bliss's gospel hymn collections. Phillips's *American Sacred Songster* (1868) sold very well in England. Two of Phillip's tunes, to the texts "Home of the Soul" and "One Sweetly Solemn Thought," were included in the *Broadman Hymnal* (1940). Phillips made singing tours to England and around the world. In 1875 he began a tour of Australia, India, Japan, Palestine, Egypt, Italy, Germany, and Austria, described in his autobiographical *Song Pilgrimage* (1882). His concerts and services in Great Britain paved the way for Sankey's singing a few years later by introducing English congregations to the practice of solo singing in religious services.

BIBLIOGRAPHY

DAB (F.H. Martens)

P. Phillips: *Song Pilgrimage around and throughout the World* (New York, 1882)

A. Clark: *Philip Phillips: his Songs and Tours* (New York, n.d. [c1887])

J.H. Hall: *Biography of Gospel Song and Hymn Writers* (New York, 1914/R1971)

HARRY ESKEW/MEL R. WILHOIT

Phillips, Sam(uel Cornelius) (*b* Florence, AL, 25 Jan 1923; *d* Memphis, TN, 20 July 2003). Record producer and label owner. In 1945 Phillips moved to Memphis to work as an announcer and engineer at radio station WREC. Four years later he opened the Memphis Recording Service at 706 Union Avenue. In addition to recording weddings, bar mitzvahs, speeches, and anything else that could generate cash flow, Phillips recorded local rhythm and blues artists such as Howlin' Wolf, Roscoe Gordon, and Ike Turner, licensing the finished masters to Chess Records in Chicago and the Bihari Brothers consortium of labels (Modern, Meteor, and RPM) on the West Coast. A number of these recordings were significant R&B chart hits including Howlin' Wolf's primal "How Many More Years" and "Moanin' at Midnight" (both 1951), Turner's seminal "Rocket 88" (issued by Chess as by Jackie Brenston and his Delta Cats—1951), and Roscoe Gordon's "Booted" and "No More Doggin'" (both 1952). "Rocket 88" sported distorted guitar, a screaming tenor sax solo, and lyrics built from a series of automotive and sexual metaphors; it is often referred to as the first rock and roll record.

In 1952 Phillips started his own label, SUN Records, achieving his first hit in the spring of 1953 with "Bear Cat" by Rufus Thomas, an answer song to Big Mama Thornton's hit recording of "Hound Dog." In August of that year, an unknown truck driver named Elvis Presley stopped by Sun to make a vanity recording as a birthday present for his mother. Presley paid to record another acetate in January 1954. Intrigued by Presley's eccentric style, in July 1954 Phillips produced the first of five 78s and 45s that Presley would release on Sun over the next two years, all of which featured a novel production technique that Phillips termed "slapback echo." These recordings were the first examples of rockabilly music and are among the most important recordings in history. At this point, Phillips, for all intents and purposes, stopped recording rhythm and blues artists, focusing his efforts on rockabilly and country.

When Presley became a national success in 1955, Phillips sold his contract to RCA for $35,000. Phillips used a portion of that money to launch radio station WHER-AM, the first ever all-women radio station. That same year he recorded Johnny Cash's first record. A year later Phillips produced Carl Perkins' "Blue Suede Shoes," which became Sun's first million-seller. Sun would go on to release and Phillips would produce the first recordings by such important American musicians as Jerry Lee Lewis, Roy Orbison, and Charlie Rich as well as extraordinary records by lesser-known musicians such as Billy Lee Riley and Sonny Burgess.

Phillips sold Sun Records in 1969 to Shelby Singleton. In 1986 he was inducted into the Rock and Roll Hall of Fame.

BIBLIOGRAPHY

P. Guralnick: *Feel Like Going Home: Portraits in Blues and Rock 'n' Roll* (New York, 1971)

C. Escott and M. Hawkins: *Good Rockin' Tonight: Sun Records and the Birth of Rock 'n' Roll* (New York, 1992)

K. Crouch and T. Crouch: *Sun King: the Life and Times of Sam Phillips, the Man Behind Sun Records* (London, 2010)

ROB BOWMAN

Philosophy of music. Philosophers of music aim to clarify fundamental aspects of music that typically go unexamined. The questions we will brush up against in this entry illustrate this: "What is musical experience?" "What is a musical work?" "How is music related to emotion?" This entry does not consist of short summaries of numerous philosophers' views; that sort of treatment can be found elsewhere (Kania, 2010; Kivy, 2006; Levinson; and on popular music, Gracyk, 2008); nor does this entry consider the history of the philosophy of music (see *Grove7*). This entry consists of relatively detailed considerations of fewer thinkers, with the goal of illuminating the issues above and of demonstrating central similarities and differences in the views emerging from the two principal Western philosophical traditions, analytic and continental philosophy. A reader might ask—given the title of this volume, why not simply survey the work of American philosophers of music? This would be misleading and artificially narrow due to the pervasive dialogue between American philosophers and those in other parts of the English-speaking world. A reader might continue—but in that case, why not focus only on the dominant philosophical tradition of these Anglo-American philosophers, namely, analytic philosophy? In addition to the fact that the Kania, Kivy, and Levinson entries mentioned above are almost entirely focused on analytic philosophy (as is Davies's section IV, "Anglo-American philosophy of music, 1960–2000," in *Grove7*; and Davies, 2011), an unavoidable portion of the interesting work in current Anglo-American philosophy of music grows out of the cross-pollination of the analytic and continental traditions. There are an increasing number of Anglo-American philosophers of music who either take themselves *to be* continental philosophers or who are influenced by the continental tradition. The intermingling of traditions takes place not only between Anglo-American analytic philosophers and *European* continental philosophers, but also between Anglo-American analytic philosophers and *Anglo-American* philosophers who are influenced by the continental tradition. One cannot ignore continental philosophy of music in this climate.

What is analytic and what is continental philosophy? Since the second half of the twentieth century, Anglo-American philosophers have referred to the kind of philosophy practiced in continental Europe as "continental philosophy," and they have dubbed their own "analytic." Analytic philosophy can be characterized as having "commitments to objective, clear argument and to an interpersonal, empirically oriented approach…[endeavoring to treat] specific philosophical issues and problems in a piecemeal or cumulative fashion" (Davies, 2011). While analytic philosophy is defined in terms of methodology, it seems that continental philosophy is defined simply as the philosophy practiced in a certain place, continental Europe. The categorization also suggests that continental philosophy is methodologically homogeneous (see Critchley); to the contrary, continental philosophy is a tradition of disparate movements: 19th-century German philosophy, phenomenology, existentialism, Marxism and critical theory, post-structuralism, postmodernism, and so on. Notwithstanding this diversity, there are attempts to define continental philosophy, but there are significant disagreements about how to do so (see, for example, Cooper, 1994; Critchley; and Levy). There is some doubt as to whether a definition is possible—or even desirable, given that the movements of continental philosophy were grouped together by analytic philosophers.

The manner of characterizing continental philosophy adopted here is contained within the *working principle* for differentiating between the traditions that structures this entry; the principle centers on two kinds of *detachment*. Continental philosophers of music tend to believe that it is ineffectual to examine music or some aspect of music as detached from its context; depending upon the philosopher, the context emphasized will be historical, social, political, and/or a context of lived-experience. Analytic philosophers of music, on the other hand, typically aim for such detachment, maintaining that it fosters clarity. Second, continental philosophers believe that a philosopher must take her own context into consideration in framing and carrying out her investigations (again, where the context is historical, social, political, and/or context of lived-experience). Analytic philosophers typically maintain that detaching themselves from their contexts fosters objectivity, and so aim for it.

1. Musical experience. 2. Musical work. 3. Emotion. 4. Conclusion.

1. MUSICAL EXPERIENCE. Musical experience does not consist of merely sound but of organized sound. Yet not just any organizing elements will do; the organizing elements commonly taken to be essential are pitch, rhythm, melody, and harmony. Some philosophers claim that we do not automatically hear music when presented with sound organized in this way; such organization is not a sufficient condition for hearing music. What is required for hearing music? What constitutes musical experience?

Consider Roger Scruton's view, which is situated (mostly) in the analytic tradition. Scruton (1997) distinguishes between hearing sounds and hearing tones; tones are the core of Scruton's account of musical experience (and musical understanding); tones are the constituents of music. In ordinary, non-musical cases, we hear a sound as conveying information about its cause; for example, when we hear the sound of screeching tires, we hear the sound as informing us about an abruptly stopping vehicle. Hearing tones is different. Sounds become tones when we experientially detach them from their sources, listening to them as ends in themselves, and they are organized in terms of pitch, rhythm, melody, and harmony. Sounds become tones, in other words, when we hear them in a musical context rather than in a worldly context.

Experientially detaching sounds in this way paves the way for hearing the sounds of music as "governed by a virtual causality that resides in the musical line" (Scruton, 2009, p.5); in these cases, one note can be experienced as the effect of another note, even when each note is the material effect of different musical instruments. "No longer does it seem as though the middle C that sounds is caused by someone blowing on the clarinet. Instead we hear it as a response to the B that preceded it, and as though calling in turn for the E that follows" (Scruton, 1997, p.19). This is what Scruton calls "the acousmatic experience of sound" (Scruton, 1997, drawing upon Pierre Schaeffer's use of the term).

Scruton claims that tones are intentional objects. This use of "intentional," in philosophy, does not refer to a purpose; the intentionality of a mental state is its *directedness*; an intentional object is that which an experience or thought is directed toward, or is *about*. In this case, intentional objects are the non-material objects of musical experience. Invoking these ideas connects Scruton, at least in this way, to phenomenology, and in this regard, Scruton has been criticized by other analytic philosophers for muddying the distinction between musical experience and music itself.

An additional, important aspect of Scruton's view is his claim that musical experience and understanding are essentially metaphorical. The melodic movement, harmonic closure, and so on, that we hear in music are not literally present in the sounds; rather, we imaginatively apply these spatial concepts to our experience; these concepts do accurately characterize our musical experiences, but these descriptions are irreducibly metaphorical. "The metaphor cannot be eliminated from the description of music, because it defines the intentional object of the musical experience. Take the metaphor away, and you cease to describe the experience of music" (Scruton, 1997, p.92). (For an interesting criticism of Scruton's appeal to metaphor in his account of musical understanding see Budd, chapter 6).

Scruton's distinction between sound and tone is related to—if not ultimately reducible to—one way of marking the distinction between ordinary experience and aesthetic experience, the thesis of aesthetic disinterest. Philosophers of art have often claimed that we must make an effort to experience the elements of an artwork in a non-instrumental way; we should not experience the features of a painting, for instance, as conveying practical information. Features of artworks are properly experienced as ends in themselves rather than as means. When I perceive a painting of a bowl of oranges, if I want to experience it aesthetically, I should not experience it as appetizing. (Aesthetic disinterest has been a central issue for a number of influential philosophers, such as Immanuel Kant and Monroe Beardsley.)

The work of the French sociologist Pierre Bourdieu has recently had a marked influence on philosophy of art, as has the work of other continental philosophers who also emphasize the relevance of historical, social, and political factors (such as Theodor W. Adorno). Bourdieu's criticism of aesthetic disinterest (1984; 1987) predates Scruton's work but serves as a thought-provoking criticism of it. The predominant view of art, according to Bourdieu, is that artworks are autonomous objects, understandable only through disinterested perception, which emphasizes artistic form over function and content (Bourdieu arrives at this claim about the predominant view of art through his interpretation of Kant). Bourdieu calls the aptitude for understanding and perceiving art in these terms "the aesthetic disposition" (this is his aesthetic *habitus;* a person with such competency has "taste"). Philosophers who make universal claims about the nature of art are unaware, according to Bourdieu, that the data for their claims consist of their own experiences, not a pure experience: "Kant's analysis of the judgment of taste finds its real basis in a set of aesthetic principles which are the universalization of the dispositions associated with a particular social and economic condition" (Bourdieu, 1984, p.493).

Regarding these socioeconomic conditions, in a series of surveys conducted in France in the 1960s and 70s, Bourdieu found that the aesthetic disposition is much more prevalent among the bourgeoisie, much less prevalent among the working-class. Although the aesthetic disposition is a historical invention, the bourgeoisie regard it as a natural gift that is possessed by superior individuals. The aesthetic disposition is a kind of cultural code, a product of formal education and social origin, cultivated through a bourgeois home life, frequenting of museums, a privileged education, and so on. This artistic milieu (roughly what Bourdieu calls the artistic "field") fosters the aesthetic disposition in individuals who occupy its various roles (artist, critic, art historian, art dealer, and so on). On Bourdieu's account, artworks are cultural objects, constituted within the artistic field by individuals possessing the aesthetic disposition; the field, in turn, is sustained by that very disposition.

Taste is a mark of distinction; it is possible to determine a person's class by determining which kinds of art she prefers. Bourdieu found that working-class individuals tend to be interested in art for its subject-matter, content, rather than form, and they prefer artworks on the basis of the real-world values depicted. Due to the absence of representational content, instrumental music stands out as an art that *distinguishes* more clearly than other arts; in the case of instrumental music, a person lacking the code (the aesthetic disposition) for understanding art will have no leverage for attaining a partial understanding: "nothing more clearly affirms one's 'class', nothing more infallibly classifies, than tastes in music" (Bourdieu, 1984, p.18). Taste not only *marks* those with certain preferences as lower in social status, it also *legitimizes* that status; a person's taste *justifies* her class status. Possessing taste is required for appreciating the trappings of a bourgeois lifestyle (fine furniture, haute couture, gourmet meals, and so on); a person who prefers popular music demonstrates that she does not have taste, and this lack of the aesthetic disposition

justifies her not having *access* to fine art as well as the finer things in general. It is in this sense that taste can function as a tool of domination.

If Bourdieu is right, his view pulls the carpet out from under some analytic philosophers. Scruton's acousmatic thesis seems a paradigmatic case of disinterested perception, and if Bourdieu is correct, this way of experiencing and explaining music is a mere creation of culture, a product of social and historical forces. In other words, Scruton has methodologically detached himself from his socio-economic context and has not acknowledged its role in shaping his view. Scruton has explicitly worried about this kind of criticism, and has dug in his heels: "Taste is as natural to humanity as law or mathematics, and just as free from the 'ideology of domination'" (Scruton, 1997, p.478). (For an additional criticism of Scruton's acousmatic thesis, see Hamilton.)

An aspect of Bourdieu's view that has sparked controversy is his claim that the popular aesthetic is not a true aesthetic but is defined negatively in contrast to the bourgeois aesthetic. For Bourdieu, a person possesses the bourgeois aesthetic disposition or she lacks taste. This leaves popular music out in the cold; it is not a legitimate artform. Some Anglo-American philosophers have defended popular music in the face of such criticisms. Consider Richard Shusterman's defense of rap/hip hop. Shusterman rejects the aesthetic of autonomy, in part by drawing upon John Dewey: aesthetic experiences result from a kind of refinement of ordinary experiences; art, at its very origin, is intrinsically connected to the practical world. Shusterman emphasizes that rap music rejects the disinterested attitude: rap is not only often concerned with political activism and social issues, but it is an artform that requires bodily engagement; "Hip-hop began explicitly as dance music to be appreciated through movement, not mere listening" (Shusterman, p.63; see also Gracyk, 2007).

2. MUSICAL WORK. Ontology is the subfield of philosophy concerned with the nature of existence, being. One task ontologists set themselves is to determine what kinds of things exist, and to determine the nature of those things. Until recently, philosophers of music have concerned themselves primarily with Western art music; having drawn a distinction between musical works and performances, musical ontology has focused primarily on the former—what is the musical work of art? (See Davies, 2001 and Kania, 2008 for useful surveys.) A musical work does not seem to be identical to a score, not even an original copy of the score; a work does not seem to be identical to a performance, not even a set of performances. An influential view of musical works maintains that works are types, sound-structures. The pure version of this view maintains that works are timeless, eternal sound-structures; this results in the counter-intuitive claim that musical works are not created but discovered (Kivy, 1983). Another version of this kind of view holds that works are, indeed, created. Consider Jerrold Levinson's influential account (Levinson, 1980). Although Levinson holds that musical works are abstract objects, he rejects the view that works are merely sound structures; works

are created abstract objects, contextualized types. For Levinson, it is a non-negotiable pre-ontological intuition that works are created. "There is probably no idea more central to thought about art than that it is an activity in which participants create things—these things being art-works" (Levinson, 1980, p.8). Works are not merely sound structures, but they also involve relational properties concerning the composer and the work's musico-historical context (these properties are what make claims of originality possible), and instrumentation specifica-tions ("performing-means structures"). "The type that is a musical work must be capable of being created, must be individuated by context of composition, and must be in-clusive of means of performance" (Levinson, 1980, p.19).

Lydia Goehr's *Imaginary Museum of Musical Works* (1992) can serve as an example of a continental approach to the topic. Goehr claims that the analytic approach cannot yield an adequate account of the mu-sical work because it prioritizes pure ontological con-cerns over musical practice: "While the analytic method has given theorists a way to account for the logic of phenomena, this has not been true for their empirical, historical, and, where relevant, their aesthetic charac-ter" (p.86). Goehr shifts the project of musical ontology away from the analytic approach of finding "the best description of the kind of object a work is" (p.4) toward giving an account of the emergence and function of the concept of the musical work in musical practice. This is her key methodological maneuver.

Goehr claims that the work-concept fully crystallized around the year 1800. She cites changes in the actions and attitudes of composers, audiences, and conductors, as well as changes in the ideals of notation and perfor-mance, changes in the function of scores, the shifting currents of aesthetics, and so on. For example, around 1800, composers began to view their compositions as ends in themselves rather than as music created to serve a religious or social function, notation became more precise, and audiences were increasingly rever-ent. "The ideal of *Werktreue* emerged to capture the new relation between work and performance as well as that between performer and composer. Performances and their performers were respectively subservient to works and their composers" (p.231). Instrumental music became "emancipated from the extra-musical" (p.155).

Goehr's view shows that some of the analytic assumptions—for example, that music is autonomous and ought to be examined in a detached manner—are only contingently true for a particular kind of music at a particular time. It's not difficult to see how Goehr's view attains critical traction vis-à-vis the view that works are eternal and uncreated (it seems reasonable to maintain that the view doesn't capture how the work-concept functions in musical practice). But at first glance, her critical traction is less obvious in the case where analytic philosophers, such as Levinson, *do* attempt to accommodate features of musical practice in their ontologies. Goehr's criticism of views like Levinson's is that an analytic philosopher's methods—"the theoretical limits provided by current strategies of analysis" (Goehr, 1992, p.55)—cannot adequately

determine which pre-ontological and aesthetic issues are relevant to ontology; a historical analysis is required for deciding which observations ought to be brought to bear on an ontology of musical works.

Regarding this line of criticism it will be illuminating to consider the connection between Goehr's historical method and Friedrich Nietzsche's genealogical method. Nietzsche holds that certain concepts are essentially historical; such concepts involve elements that can be multi-layered, through time, and more or less hidden. Disambiguating such a concept requires an examina-tion of its historical development. As Maudemarie Clark writes,

> Nietzsche suggests that concepts influenced by history are like ropes held together by the intertwining of strands, rather than by a single strand running through the whole thing. To analyze such concepts is not to find necessary and sufficient conditions for their use but to disentangle the various strands that may have become so tightly woven together by the process of historical development that they seem inseparable (Clark, p.22).

In a portion of his *On the Genealogy of Morality*, Nietz-sche discusses the genealogy of the concept of punish-ment; he emphasizes that the meaning of punishment is not singular and static: "Today it is impossible to say for sure why we actually punish....In an earlier stage, by contrast, the synthesis of 'meanings' still appears more soluble" (Nietzsche, II, §13; see also Goehr, 1992, p.90, note 105). Genealogy is required for elucidating those earlier meanings, their connection to the current meaning, and the current meaning itself. According to Goehr, the work-concept is an emergent, open-textured, cultural concept. The continuity of open concepts "prompts us to trace the genealogy of the concept or the history of its meaning as it has functioned within the relevant practice as a way to understand both the concept and the associated practice" (Goehr, 1992, p.93). Goehr's historical account is not merely an at-tempt to understand the history of the work-concept, it is a way of uncovering what it means and how it func-tions now.

Turning to more recent musical ontology, we find a number of analytic philosophers taking musical prac-tice very seriously; for example, Amie Thomasson writes, "We cannot discover the ontological status of paintings, symphonies, or novels first by referring to *this kind of thing* [ostending a sample] and then inves-tigating its true ontological nature...we must follow the method of analyzing the conception embodied in the practices of those competent speakers who ground and reground reference of the term" (Thomasson, p.226). (See also Kania, 2008 and the expansive Davies, 2001.)

The dominant analytic view of musical works—tak-ing works to be abstract structures—seems especially inadequate in regard to genres such as jazz and rock (regarding jazz in general, see Alperson, 1991; Brown, 2000; Hagberg, 2006; regarding jazz ontology, see Davies, 2001). Following Theodore Gracyk's *Rhythm and Noise: An Aesthetics of Rock* (1996), rock is a kind of popular music emerging around 1965, with origins in, but superseding, rock and roll. According to Gracyk, although rock music has stylistic roots in African

American music, rock is not defined in terms of musical style but in terms of its being centered on recording technology. In the case of rock, the primary target of evaluation and criticism does not seem to be a structure or a performance; rather, the musical work is the recording.

3. EMOTION. It has long been suggested that there is a special connection between music and the emotions, a connection more salient than between other arts and the emotions. One context in which this connection emerges is in considering the nature of musical understanding. At one level, understanding music is a matter of hearing the relations between pitches, rhythms, harmonies, and melodies as a composer intends. But a number of philosophers have argued that understanding a piece of music requires understanding the emotions it expresses (see Davies, 2003, chapter 8). Now, it is straightforward to grasp what we mean when we say that a *person* expresses an emotion (a person expresses an emotion when she behaves so as to communicate it), but how is it that *music* can express emotion? This question is even more challenging in light of philosophers' traditional assumption that we should only be considering instrumental music (the idea being that we ought to focus on music itself, not music and libretto, for example, where the libretto may do the lion's share of the expressive work).

What could we mean when we say that a piece of music is melancholy or exuberant? The most straightforward way of trying to make sense of the relationship between music and the emotions seems to be to maintain that a given piece of music expresses exuberance (say) in the sense that it *arouses* exuberance in listeners. Here are two challenges that an arousal theory, as it is called, must address. Some cases of arousal are merely idiosyncratic; for example, perhaps a particular piece of music makes me feel elated due to my associating the piece with the first weeks of my daughter's life. In such cases, the elation aroused by that music may have little to do with the characteristics of the piece itself; we wouldn't want to say that this aroused emotion is relevant to understanding that piece of music. Another worry for arousal theory is that it seems counterintuitive to maintain that in order to be able to judge a piece of music correctly as being remorseful a person must actually feel remorse. (For an illuminating discussion of arousal theories, see Matravers, 2011.)

Another approach, "expression theory," holds that music is sad (say) due to the composer's expressing her sadness through the music. On this view, if a piece of music is sad, the composer must have been sad during the act of composition. Among other shortcomings, this theory is commonly thought to involve an untenable picture of the creative process, given that there are certainly instances in which a composer writes a sad piece while not experiencing that emotion during the creative process. (For a subtler version of the theory, see Collingwood, 1938.) A related view maintains that the emotions expressed in a work of music are those of a character or persona whom we imaginatively hear in

the music (for a critical discussion, see Davies, 2003, chapter 10). (For an interesting hybrid view, maintaining that arousal plays an epistemological role in aiding a listener to grasp the expressive qualities of the music, see Ridley, 1995, and Robinson.)

The views above may be categorized as analytic views, as can Peter Kivy's influential theory of musical expressiveness. Kivy maintains that a piece of music can be rightly characterized as sad without expressing an agent's sadness. Rather than sad music being an expression of someone's sadness, sad music is *expressive of* sadness. Kivy invokes an analogy with a St. Bernard: "The St. Bernard's face is not expressing sadness. The face of the St. Bernard is sad even when the creature is happy, it being at the other end that she expresses her emotions" (Kivy, 2002, p.37). This sadness is a property of the music itself; it is an emergent, perceptual property of the music, in the same way that cheerfulness is a property of the color yellow. The music is sad in virtue of its formal properties; this is important, because it allows Kivy to maintain that music is expressive of emotion even though it is an autonomous sound-structure without extra-musical content (see Kivy, 1990). Kivy's "contour theory," as this is called, maintains that music can be expressive of the "garden variety" emotions in this way (sorrow, joy, fear, hope, etc.). The St. Benard's face has particular, droopy features that make it look sad; similarly, sad music has particular contours— features of the music's form, such as a slow tempo and halting rhythm—in virtue of which it sounds sad or melancholy. "The anguished melody, like the anguished speaking voice, shrieks and cries, leaps in dissonant intervals, and proceeds in 'jerks,' with irregular pauses" (Kivy, 2002, p.39). These features are expressive of emotions in that they resemble the way people possessing the same emotions move and talk. (Other, simple qualities of music, such as minor chords, are expressive of emotions but have no contour; another explanation is needed. Kivy suggests that they may be expressive by convention, customary association.)

Let us consider some comments from a continental perspective that are critical of Kivy's view; the intention here is to show just how different the problem of the relationship between music and the emotions looks from the continental side. Andrew Bowie claims that Kivy's move of locating the emotions in the music itself, combined with Kivy's assumption that the musical work is an autonomous object, ignores a context that is necessary for experiencing a given piece as melancholy (or whatever) to begin with. Bowie explains,

> The point Kivy should be making is made by Merleau-Ponty (1945), who rejects the objectifying language of perceived properties in favor of the idea that the perceived world, including music, is already full of meanings. These are of a kind which cannot be reduced to being 'perceived properties' because what they are depends both on the context in which they are encountered and on those encountering them (p.24).

If the initial detachment maneuver were not made, it would be easier to understand how we experience music as involving emotions: "If one tries to isolate music as an object in the world in the same way as one isolates the object of an explanatory theory, the first step causes the problem, because music and the world relate in ways which affect what both are understood to be" (p.32). (A more thorough analysis would show that invoking Merleau-Ponty does, indeed, set up a fruitful contrast in approaches to emotions in music, but Bowie's criticism of Kivy is remiss in that he doesn't consider Kivy's discussion of culture in *Sound Sentiment*.) In a methodological criticism related to Bowie's, Aaron Ridley has pointed out that if a philosopher takes music to be autonomous in this way, she will naturally tend to believe that the best way to examine it is to isolate it from its external contexts—the method will reinforce the theory (Ridley, 2004, chapter 1).

4. CONCLUSION. Regarding the analytic approach, as Ridley notes (2004), it is obviously reasonable for an investigator to aim to detach her target of investigation from irrelevant contextual elements. The crucial thing is to determine correctly just which contextual elements are irrelevant and which are connected to music in a way that cannot be ignored without resulting in a misdescription of the explanandum. Philosophers slip into a criticizable scientism when they unreflectively assume that the relevant and irrelevant elements are exactly those that are relevant and irrelevant in the investigation of *other* phenomena (that is, philosophers should not adopt, unreflectively, the sciences' way of settling these issues). Different continental philosophers explore different arguments in favor of not detaching music from one or another "extra-musical" context: history, politics, lived-experience, and so on. Analytic philosophers often criticize continental philosophers for being unclear, steeped in jargon, subjective, and for embedding their claims in grand theories (see Davies, 2011). One theme that emerges from these criticisms is that analytic philosophers believe that continental philosophers would be better off if they methodologically detached their explananda from various contexts more than they do. If philosophy of music has entered an especially fruitful period, this may be because each tradition is—explicitly and implicitly—pressing the other to reassess where to draw the methodological boundaries, to reassess which connections to the "extra-musical" are relevant and which are not. The dialogue between these traditions cannot but be fruitful for the future of Anglo-American philosophy of music.

BIBLIOGRAPHY

Grove 7 (L. Goehr and others: "Philosophy of Music")
R.G. Collingwood: *The Principles of Art* (Oxford, 1938/R)
M. Merleau-Ponty: *Phénoménologie de la Perception* (Paris, 1945)
P. Bourdieu: *Distinction: a Social Critique of the Judgement of Taste*, trans. R. Nice (Cambridge, MA, 1979, 2/1984)
J. Levinson: "What a Musical Work Is," *Journal of Philosophy*, lxxvii/1 (1980), 5–28
P. Bourdieu: "The Historical Genesis of a Pure Aesthetic," *The Journal of Aesthetics and Art Criticism*, Analytic Aesthetics, xlvi, (1987), 201–10
P. Kivy: *Sound Sentiment: An Essay on Musical Emotions* (Philadelphia, 1989)
P. Kivy: *Music Alone* (Ithaca, GA, and London, 1990)
P. Alperson: "When Composers Have To Be Performers," *Journal of Aesthetics and Art Criticism*, xlix (1991), 369–73

L. Goehr: *The Imaginary Museum of Musical Works: an Essay in the Philosophy of Music* (Oxford and New York, 1992)
M. Clark: "Nietzsche's Immoralism and the Concept of Morality," *Nietzsche, Genealogy, Morality*, ed., R. Schacht (Berkeley, Los Angeles, and London, 1994)
D.E. Cooper: "The Presidential Address: Analytical and Continental Philosophy," *Proceedings of the Aristotelian Society*, lciv (1994), 1–18
S. Davies: *Musical Meaning and Expression* (Ithaca, GA, and London, 1994)
A. Ridley: *Music, Value and the Passions* (Ithaca, GA, 1995)
T. Gracyk: *Rhythm and Noise: An Aesthetics of Rock* (London and New York, 1996)
S. Critchley: "What Is Continental Philosophy?" *International Journal of Philosophical Studies*, v/3 (1997), 347–65
R. Scruton: *The Aesthetics of Music* (Oxford, 1997)
J. Levinson: "Music, Aesthetics of," *Routledge Encyclopedia of Philosophy*, ed. E. Craig (London and New York, 1998)
F. Nietzsche: *On the Genealogy of Morality*, trans. M. Clark and A.J. Swensen (Indianapolis, IN, and Cambridge, 1998 [orig. published 1887])
L.B. Brown: "'Feeling My Way': Jazz Improvisation and Its Vicissitude—A Plea for Imperfection," *Journal of Aesthetics and Art Criticism*, lviii/2 (2000), 112–23
R. Shusterman: *Performing Live* (Ithaca, GA, and London, 2000)
S. Davies: *Musical Works and Performances* (Oxford and New York, 2001)
P. Kivy: *Introduction to a Philosophy of Music* (Oxford and New York, 2002)
N. Levy: "Analytic and Continental Philosophy: Explaining the Differences," *Metaphilosophy*, xxxiv (2003), 284–304
S. Davies: *Themes in the Philosophy of Music* (Oxford and New York, 2003)
A. Ridley: *The Philosophy of Music: Theme and Variations* (Edinburgh, 2004)
J. Robinson: *Deeper than Reason* (Oxford and New York, 2005)
A. Thomasson: "The Ontology of Art and Knowledge in Aesthetics," *The Journal of Aesthetics and Art Criticism*, lxiii (2005), 221–9
G. Hagberg: "Jazz Improvisation: a Mimetic Art?" *Revue Internationale de Philosophie*, lx (2006), 469–85
P. Kivy: "Music, Philosophy of," *Encyclopedia of Philosophy*, Second Edition, ed. D.M. Borchert (Macmillan, 2006), 436–40
A. Bowie: *Music, Philosophy, and Modernity* (Cambridge, 2007)
T. Gracyk: *Listening to Popular Music* (Ann Arbor, 2007)
A. Hamilton: *Aesthetics and Music* (London and New York, 2007)
M. Budd: *Aesthetic Essays* (Oxford and New York, 2008)
T. Gracyk: "The Aesthetics of Popular Music," *Internet Encyclopedia of Philosophy*, ed. J. Fieser and B. Dowden (2008) <http://www.iep.utm.edu/music-po/>
A. Kania: "The Methodology of Musical Ontology: Descriptivism and its Implications," *British Journal of Aesthetics*, xlviii/4 (2008), 426–44
A. Kania: "New Waves in Musical Ontology," *New Waves in Aesthetics*, ed. K. Stock and K. Thomson-Jones (London and New York, 2008)
R. Scruton: *Understanding Music* (London and New York, 2009)
A. Kania: "The Philosophy of Music," *The Stanford Encyclopedia of Philosophy*, ed. E.N. Zalta (2010) <http://plato.stanford.edu/archives/fall2010/entries/music/>
S. Davies: "Analytic Philosophy of Music," *The Routledge Companion to Philosophy and Music*, ed. T. Gracyk and A. Kania (London and New York, 2011)
D. Matravers: "Arousal Theories," *The Routledge Companion to Philosophy and Music*, ed. T. Gracyk and A. Kania (London and New York, 2011)

TIGER C. ROHOLT

Phi Mu Alpha Sinfonia Fraternity. Music society, founded in 1898; *see* FRATERNITIES AND SORORITIES.

Phi Mu Gamma. National professional fine arts sorority. *See* FRATERNITIES AND SORORITIES.

CLAUDE CONYERS

Phish. Rock group. It was formed in 1983 in Burlington, Vermont. Original members included Trey Anastasio (*b* Ernest Joseph Anastasio III, Fort Worth, TX, 30 Sept

1964; lead guitar), Mike Gordon (*b* Michael Eliot Gordon, Sudbury, MA, 3 June 1965; bass guitar), and Jon Fishman [Fish] (*b* Philadelphia, PA, 19 Feb 1965; drums). Page McConnell (*b* Philadelphia, PA, 17 May 1963; keyboards) joined in 1985. The group disbanded in 2004 then reunited in 2009.

Phish's music is eclectic and diverse; their extensive catalog of original songs touches on genres as varied as bluegrass, calypso, funk, and jazz. Some compositions feature dissonant melodies and harmonies, contrapuntal textures (including fugues), metric and rhythmic irregularities, and through-composed form, displaying the progressive rock influence of Genesis and Frank Zappa. Phish is often labeled a jam band, and most songs feature some element of improvisation. Some jams involve soloing over the song's chord changes. In other songs, such as Anastasio's iconic "You enjoy myself" or "David Bowie," a structured full-band improvisation over a simple chord progression is the last section of a through-composed form, building towards a climactic riff or lyric. Anastasio's virtuosic guitar soloing anchored many early jams. Beginning around 1993 Phish experimented more with free-form, full-band improvisation, leaving song structures behind entirely as exemplified by "Tweezer" from their live release, *A Live One* (1995). In 1997 the band incorporated a funkier, groove-based style, heard on *Story of the Ghost* (1998). Phish's live concert recordings better showcase their improvisational approach than their studio albums do.

Phish created a devout following (known as "Phishheads" or "phans") through extensive touring. Phish has never released a hit single, instead relying on word of mouth for promotion and allowing fans to make and trade recordings of live concerts. In this and other respects, Phish's devout fans, many of whom attend multiple shows within a tour, resemble those of the Grateful Dead, to whom Phish is often compared.

BIBLIOGRAPHY

R. Gehr and Phish: *The Phish Book* (New York, 1998)
The Phish Companion: a Guide to the Band and Their Music, 2nd ed., compiled by the Mockingbird Foundation (San Francisco, 2004)
P. Puterbaugh: *Phish: the Biography* (Philadelphia, 2009)

JACOB A. COHEN

Phoenix. City in Arizona (pop. 1,445,632; metropolitan area 4,192,887; 2010 US Census). First occupied by the Hohokam culture between 700 CE and 1400 CE, modern development began in 1867 and was followed by a formal incorporation in 1881. Phoenix is now the 6th largest city in the United States and the 14th largest metropolitan area, which includes the cities of Tempe, Mesa, Glendale, Scottsdale, and Sun City. It supports a broad range of cultures, musical traditions, and performing venues that set it apart from other cities of its size.

Since 1972 classical music in the city has been centered at the multi-purpose Symphony Hall, where both the Phoenix Symphony and Phoenix Youth Symphony have performed. Although both orchestras were formally founded in 1947, the Phoenix Symphony was active in various forms as early as the 1920s. The Phoenix Symphony, led by Michael Christie, is the state's only full-time performing orchestra, offering some 275 performances annually throughout central Arizona. Its music directors have included John Barnett, Robert Lawrence, Leslie Hodge, Guy Taylor, Philip Spurgeon, Eduardo Mata, Theo Alcantara, James Sedares, and Hermann Michael. Orchestral performance extends throughout the greater Phoenix valley with a number of professional-level groups. The Symphony of the Southwest (founded 1956) serves the city of Mesa and MusicaNova (founded 2003) serves Scottsdale. The West Valley Symphony (founded 1968) performs in Sun City.

Many of the players in Phoenix's professional orchestras are also busy in the city's thriving—and sometimes eclectic—mix of chamber music. The Phoenix Chamber Music Society, which was founded in 1961, focuses on the presentation of internationally renowned artists. An emphasis on cultural and international diversity is the mission of another group, the Pangean Orchestra (founded 2009), which features instruments from around the world such as the Iraqi kanun, African djembe, and the French horn. Other groups such as Duozona (founded 1997), Mill Ave Chamber Players (founded 2009), and the Phoenix Chamber Brass (founded 2007) present standard classical repertoire and modern music.

Vocal music is another source of music tradition in Phoenix with an array of popular and longstanding groups. Established in 1958, the Phoenix Chorale (formerly known as the Phoenix Bach Choir), has multiple Grammy awards and nominations. The Orpheus Male Chorus, established in 1929, is the oldest continuously performing choral ensemble in the state. Providing training for young boys is the internationally recognized Phoenix Boys Choir (founded 1947), which is one of the largest boy choirs in the country.

Opera and ballet are also well-represented in Phoenix. The Arizona Opera Company, founded in 1971 as the Tucson Opera Company, is headquartered in Phoenix and also serves Tucson and Flagstaff. Founded in 2007, the Phoenix Opera presents large-scale productions in the city's historic Orpheum Theatre (opened 1929). The premier ballet organization in central Arizona is Ballet Arizona, which was founded in 1986 out of a merger of three existing groups (Phoenix Ballet, Arizona Dance Theater, and Ballet West Arizona).

Throughout the valley a range of jazz styles can be found from 1920s swing groups like the Hot Club of Phoenix (founded 2007) to big bands such as the Extreme Decibel Big Band (founded 1987). Phoenix's jazz community is supported by several notable organizations and ensembles. Jazz in AZ (founded 1977) and the Arizona Classic Jazz Society (founded 1984) are the city's leading and most established organizations in promoting jazz traditions through concert sponsorship and community outreach. The country's oldest jazz youth ensemble, Young Sounds of Arizona (founded 1971), is also headquartered in the city and develops talent through students in middle school and high school.

Neighboring Tempe provides the metropolitan area with the Mill Avenue District and Arizona State University. The university campus is the largest by enrollment in the United States and was originally founded in 1885 as the Tempe Normal School. The university's school of music has over 850 students, 65 faculty, and several performing venues. Of considerable note is the university's iconic Gammage concert hall, which was designed by the architect Frank Lloyd Wright and opened in 1964. Adjacent to the campus, the Mill Avenue District has given birth to a number of popular groups in the rock genre including the Meat Puppets and the Gin Blossoms.

Much of Phoenix's appreciation for music can be seen in its community outreach programs and youth education. In 1995 the Arizona School for the Arts opened as one of Arizona's first charter schools. The school's emphasis in the performing arts prepares students for advancement into college. Another community organization is Rosie's House, which specializes strictly as a music academy and was established a year later in 1996. Rosie's House devotes its mission to helping underserved youth from diverse backgrounds through the teaching of community service and music education. The city is also home to the Musical Instrument Museum (opened 2010), which houses one of the largest and most comprehensive selection of instruments from around the world.

See also SOUTHWEST.

BIBLIOGRAPHY
Arizona: its People and its Resources (Tucson, 1960, rev. 2/1972)
D. Scoular: *The First Decade: a History of Events at Grady Gammage Memorial Auditorium, 1964–1974* (Tempe, 1976)
B.C. Stoneburner: *The Phoenix Symphony Orchestra, 1947–1978: Leadership, Criticism and Selective Commentary* (thesis, Arizona State U., 1981)

KEITH PAWLAK

Phonograph. *See* RECORDED SOUND; TURNTABLE; TURNTABLISM.

Piaf [Gassion], Edith (Giovanna) (*b* Paris, France, 19 Dec 1915; *d* Plascassier, nr Grasse, France, 10 Oct 1963). French singer and actress. Her mother was a singer and her father was a fairground acrobat. Her early childhood was fraught with illness, she became temporarily blind through infection, and she was passed from one lodging to another, eventually staying with her grandmother who worked in a bordello. At the age of nine she joined her father on tour and began to sing while he performed his routine. It was as a street singer that she was discovered in Paris by the proprietor of the nightclub Le Gerny's, Louis Leplée, who launched her as "La môme Piaf" ("the little sparrow") in October 1935. She was an immediate success and was engaged to record and to sing on radio. At first her repertory drew on popular songs of the day, but very soon songwriters began to write material especially for her.

A film career began almost as soon as she had achieved her early fame, and during World War II she remained in France and continued to record and make films. In 1945 she recorded the first of her worldwide successes, "Les trois cloches," with the group Les Compagnons de la Chanson, and the following year recorded "La vie en rose," her most famous song. She found huge success in New York in 1947 and for the next few years became a transatlantic star. Illness, drug addiction, and alcoholism dogged her later years, and her reputation was increased with several well-publicized affairs and marriages. Her love affair with the champion boxer Marcel Cerdan, who was killed in an air crash, caught the public's imagination and seemed to be the subject of some of her love songs such as "L'orgue des amoureux" (1949), "Hymne à l'amour" (1950), and "La belle histoire d'amour" (1960).

Piaf was the inheritor of a great tradition of Parisian chanson, the logical successor to *chanteuses réalistes* of the 1920s. At the same time she was one of the singers who began to create a new, more international style of Parisian song. Her early songs belong unmistakably to the old music-hall tradition. Although her voice was strong she soon developed a microphone technique and her later performances seem to belong to the world of international pop music rather than the Paris *café-concert*. Her later recordings, using larger orchestras, choirs, and echo-chambers, have none of the charm of her earlier performances and melodramatic effects detract from the simplicity of her singing. Her ability to invest the lyrics with pathos and, too seldom, humor, continued to be impressive. Despite, or perhaps because of, the sad personal life which she seemed to bring to her songs, Piaf's fame and popularity have remained in the decades since her death. All her recordings remain in print, and several plays and films about her have introduced her songs to later generations.

BIBLIOGRAPHY
GMO
E. Piaf: *Au bal de la chance* (Paris, 1958; Eng. trans. as *The Wheel of Fortune*, 1965)
E. Piaf: *Ma vie* (Paris, 1964; Eng. trans., 1990)
S. Berteaut: *Piaf* (Paris, 1969; Eng. trans., 1970)
J. Montserrat: *Edith Piaf et la chanson* (Paris, 1983)
P. Ribert: *Témoignages sur Edith et Chansons de Piaf* (Paris, 1984)
M. Crosland: *Piaf* (London, 1985)
B. Marchois: *Piaf: Emportée par la foule* (Paris, 1995)
K. Reader: "Flaubert's Sparrow, or the Bovary of Belleville: Édith Piaf as Cultural Icon," *Popular Music in France from Chanson to Techno: Cultural, Identity and Society*, ed. H. Dauncey and S. Cannon (Aldershot, UK, 2003), 205–223

PATRICK O'CONNOR/R

Piano [pianoforte; fortepiano]. A keyboard instrument, the strings of which are struck by rebounding hammers. It was originally called pianoforte (It.: "soft-loud") or fortepiano, because the loudness of its sound could be varied by the player's touch. The piano has played an important role in American life since the late 18th century, when learning the instrument was considered a genteel occupation for young ladies; by the late 19th century it had become an essential item in many homes. American piano builders, seeking to satisfy the taste of American musicians and to meet the challenges of the American climate, developed manufacturing and sales techniques and new features, such as the one-piece metal frame, which by the 1870s enabled them to dominate the world piano trade.

Pianos were used and made in North America by the 1770s. The earliest known reference to a piano there is

Square piano with a one-piece metal frame by Alpheus Babcock, c1835.
(Boston Museum of Fine Arts)

a notice in the *New-York Gazette* and *Weekly Mercury* of 17 September 1770 listing a "fortepiano" for sale by the Englishman David Propert; in Boston, Propert advertised that he taught the piano and in 1771 performed "some select pieces on the forte piano," at the Concert Hall. In the same year in Virginia Thomas Jefferson and Robert Carter bought pianos from London. In 1772 John Scheiuble [Sheybli] announced in New York that he made and repaired pianos, and in 1774 he advertised for sale "one hammer spinnet," which he may have made himself. Another German craftsman, John [Johann] Behrent, usually credited with making the first piano manufactured in North America, advertised in Philadelphia in 1775 that he had made an instrument "by the name of Piano Forte, of Mahogany, in the manner of an harpsichord, with hammers and several changes." Although both manufacture and emigration diminished during the Revolutionary War, from the mid-1780s many builders emigrated from Europe to the United States, among them Thomas Dodds (active in New York from 1785), CHARLES ALBRECHT (Philadelphia, c1785), CHARLES TAWS (New York, then Philadelphia, 1786), and John Geib (New York, 1797), who claimed by 1800 to have built 4910 pianofortes. In Milton, Massachusetts, the American-born BENJAMIN CREHORE was building pianos by the 1790s. The type most often played and owned by Americans was the square piano, which remained in favor until the 1880s. The typical early square had wooden framing, a range of five to five and a half octaves ($F'-c''''$), English action (although Albrecht made some with German action), and changes in registration activated by hand stops.

As early as 1792 DODDS & CLAUS noted the need to prepare their wood "to stand the effect of our climate," a prime concern of American builders throughout most of the 19th century. JOHN ISAAC HAWKINS, an English civil

engineer working in Philadelphia, included an iron frame and iron bracing rods in his ingenious 1800 patent for a small upright piano. Although his invention did not succeed musically, it represents one of the earliest attempts to use iron to withstand climatic changes. In 1825 ALPHEUS BABCOCK, a Boston maker who had worked with Crehore, was the first to be issued a patent (17 December 1825) for a one-piece metal frame, which he claimed would be "stronger and more durable than a wooden frame or case" and, because the strings and metal frame would expand or contract equally, would prevent the instrument being "put out of tune by any alteration in the temperature of the air." He fitted this frame in a piano typical of the late 1820s, a mahogany square with decorative stenciling, two pedals and a compass of six octaves ($F'-f''''$); only two Babcock squares with an iron frame are extant. Many builders, especially in New York and Baltimore, opposed the iron frame, claiming that it resulted in a thin and nasal tone quality. Instead, many used the heavy wooden bracing and a solid five-inch (12–7 cm) wooden bottom for stability in tuning. But by the 1840s wooden framing alone was not strong enough to withstand the enormous tension required by the piano's expanded compass (seven octaves, $A''-a''''$) and the rigors of American climatic extremes.

By the 1830s American makers of square pianos were using the Erard repetition action. In 1840 the Boston piano maker JONAS CHICKERING, with whom Babcock worked from 1837 to 1842, patented a metal frame with a cast-iron bridge for a square piano, and in 1843 he patented a one-piece metal frame for grands. He was the first to devise a successful method of manufacturing and selling pianos with metal frames and was the first major American builder to make grand pianos, for which he won special notice at the Great Exhibition in

London (1851). Metal frames and felt-covered hammers made American squares characteristically heavy and sonorous instruments. The Chickering factory, with about 300 workers, made over 10% of the 9000 pianos produced in the United States in 1851. After a fire destroyed the factory in late 1852 the firm built a vast new factory, and by the 1860s it employed over 500 workers. The Chickering firm set the standard for the American piano industry: production of high-quality pianos with metal frames, an extensive steam-powered factory operation whose workers developed highly specialized skills, an energetic sales program, and support for musical events and performers characterized its approach.

In 1853, the year of Jonas Chickering's death, the firm of Steinway & Sons was established in New York (see STEINWAY). Within a decade Henry Steinway and his sons, who had immigrated from Germany in 1850, had equaled the Chickering firm in production and prestige. Like Chickering, the firm designed pianos with metal frames. In 1859 Steinway patented a new arrangement for the grand piano, overstringing (US patent no.26,532): the bass strings were strung above the middle and upper register strings, permitting the use of longer strings for an extended lower range and provided a richer sound and locating the bridges closer to the middle of the soundboard for more efficient amplification. Soon after the 1867 Paris Exhibition, at which both Steinway and Chickering won gold medals, Steinway pianos had come to dominate the world trade. At the 1873 Vienna Exhibition, more than two-thirds of the pianos were overstrung. Between 1857 and 1885 the Steinways were granted 54 patents, 41 of them to C.F. Theodore Steinway (1825–89), whose designs aimed at greater strength and stability, more responsive action, and bigger, purer sound. By 1875 he claimed a metal plate that would sustain string pressure up to 35 short tons. Coming to New York in 1865 from Germany, where the square had lost favor in the 1840s, he improved and promoted the upright, which the firm had begun making in 1862. American makers continued to love the square, but Steinway made its last square in 1888. The combination of technical excellence, aggressive promotion through concerts and advertisements, especially by WILLIAM STEINWAY, efficient production, and a shrewd business sense made possible the company's rise to world prominence.

The Steinways, Chickerings, and numerous other piano builders, such as the English immigrants Thomas Loud and Robert and William Nunns (see NUNNS & CLARK), and the German-born William Knabe, Albert Weber, and HUGO SOHMER, supplied pianos primarily for the amateur musician. But they achieved world prominence by obtaining endorsements from performing artists, whose concerts were often organized and financed by the manufacturers. The earliest virtuosos to come to the United States, such as Leopold de Meyer (1845) and Henri Herz (1846), brought their own European pianos (Erard and Herz respectively). The American-born, Paris-trained Louis Moreau Gottschalk started his American tour in 1853 with a Pleyel piano, but he became an advocate of Chickering pianos, the tone quality of

which was compatible with his compositions and his playing style. After the 1866 opening of Steinway Hall in New York and the favorable notice at the 1867 Paris Exhibition, Steinway sponsored tours by Anton Rubinstein (1872), Ignace Paderewski (1891), and many others; Chickering arranged for Hans von Bülow to open Chickering Hall in New York in 1875. American pianists went to Europe to study, among them William Mason with Franz Liszt and Ignaz Moscheles, and Amy Fay with Liszt and Rubinstein. The excitement created by touring artists led thousands of Americans, mostly young women, to study piano and play and teach it in homes, schools, and churches, if not in concert halls. The piano became a staple of public entertainment, helped the development toward the end of the 19th century of new musical styles (ragtime and jazz), and promoted the burgeoning popular song business.

Though the Steinways and Chickerings dominated the American piano industry in the 19th century, many smaller firms flourished in New England and Philadelphia, in Charleston, South Carolina, and later in Cincinnati (e.g., BALDWIN) and Chicago (Kimball). Most obtained their parts from suppliers such as ALFRED DOLGE (felts for hammers, soundboards), Pratt, Read & Co. (keys and actions), and Wessell, Nickels & Gross (actions). Some, notably JOSEPH P. HALE, used the stencil system, providing piano sellers with finished instruments marked with whatever names they wished. A number of stencillers used names like Bradwood or Stinway & Sons, intended to make customers think of famous piano names. In financial depressions (late 1870s, 1884, 1893, 1907, 1921,

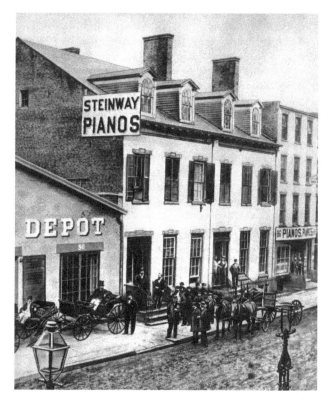

First permanent Steinway factory in New York, 1854–60. (Lebrecht Music & Arts)

1930s) many firms went out of business; others consolidated into larger piano groups such as the American Piano Company (1908) and the Aeolian Company (1895), which combined in 1932 to form the Aeolian-American Corporation (*see* Aeolian-skinner organ co.).

The demand for pianos was great. According to statistics gathered by Loesser, Ehrlich, and Dolge, one of every 4800 Americans bought a new piano in 1829, in 1851 one of 2,777, in 1870 one of 1540, in 1890 one of 874, and in 1910, a peak year when 350,000 pianos were produced, one person in 252. By 1919 the more than 333,000 pianos that were made included 177,000 regular pianos and 156,000 player pianos, a trend that had begun with the introduction of mechanically operated pianos at the end of the 19th century (*see* Player piano). The peak year for player pianos, more popular in the United States than in Europe, was 1923. The principal American names were Aeolian's Pianola and the later Duo-Art, Bush & Lane's Cecilian, and Ampico from the American Piano Company, but many smaller companies produced examples.

Increasing competition from radio and recordings, as well as the automobile, which had begun to replace the piano as a status symbol, is reflected in the 1929 statistics: only 130,000 were produced—a decrease of 180,000 in ten years. In 1932, three years into the Depression, only 25,000 pianos were made. Since then, the piano has never regained its former prominence, especially on the amateur level, where high fidelity systems, films, television, and instruments such as the electric guitar became more popular.

Piano sales did not cease in the 1930s. New piano models such as the "baby" grand and the small "spinet" upright were introduced then in an attempt to encourage sales. Beginning in the late 1960s, American piano manufacturers ranked second to the Japanese in world output and sales. Only one of every 1354 Americans bought a piano in 1983; 155,000 of those sold were produced in the United States (6500 grands) and 37,000 were imported (15,000 grands).

As the 20th century approached its end, the American piano industry underwent constant thinning. As Asian companies improved quality and production and lowered prices, American firms failed: Chickering had been absorbed by the America Piano Company in 1903, the Depression took more toll, but companies like Knabe, Sohmer, and other, smaller ones disappeared as the century wore on. Kimball in Chicago bought the Viennese Bösendorfer in 1966, but Kimball went out of business in 1996 and an Austrian company bought Bösendorfer back in 2002. Likewise, Baldwin bought Bechstein of Berlin in 1963, but a group of Bechstein employees bought it back. And Baldwin in its turn fell into bankruptcy in 2001, when the Gibson Guitar Company purchased it. But Baldwin ceased production in 2008, and the last major piano maker in the United States stopped production. That has left Steinway & Sons alone, along with several small producers, Astin-weight pianos, Walter piano co., Spreeman piano innovations (maker of the Ravenscroft piano), and Fandrich. But Fandrich, the inventor of a new upright action, does not manufacture pianos but instead retrofits instruments purchased from Europe and China. The highest numbers (by a very large margin) of pianos now being sold in the United States are produced by Asian manufacturers. At least one of those companies, Samick of Korea, does some preparation of their instruments in the United States; several others have stopped US manufacturing altogether. As the largest piano manufacturer in the world, Yamaha of Japan is the source of the greatest number of pianos sold in the United States. Sales figures are not available, but it is possible that electronic keyboards outpaced pianos in the early 21st century; many of them are also made in Asia.

Meanwhile, piano concerti played by splendid pianists remain staple offerings by symphony orchestras, jazz pianists continue to prosper, and composers provide new music for the instrument. Figures for the number of active piano teachers are not available, but there seems to be no shortage.

See also Electric piano; Novelty piano; Piano music; Player piano; and Prepared piano.

BIBLIOGRAPHY

Grove7 ("Pianoforte"; E.M. Ripin and others)

ClinkscaleMP and *Clinkscale Database of Early Pianos, 1700–1860* <http://www.EarlyPianos.org/>

"Felix": "Piano Fortes," *The Euterpeiad*, iii (1823), 179 only

The New York Book of Prices for Manufacturing Piano-fortes by the Society of Journeymen Piano-forte Makers (New York, 1835;, repr. with foreword by H.Z. Steinway and intro. by L. Libin, Malden, MA, 2009)

J.L. Bishop: *A History of American Manufactures from 1608 to 1860* (Philadelphia, 1861–6, enlarged 3/1868/R)

J. Parton: "The Piano in the United States," *Atlantic Monthly*, xx (1867), 82–98

H.K. Oliver: "Musical Instruments," *International Exhibition 1876: Reports and Awards, Group XXV* (Philadelphia, 1878)

T. Appleton and others: "The American Pianoforte Manufacture," *Musical and Sewing Machine Gazette* (21 Feb 1880)

D. Spillane: *History of the American Pianoforte* (New York, 1890/R)

W. Steinway: "American Musical Instruments," *One Hundred Years of American Commerce 1795–1895*, ed. C.M. Depew (New York, 1895), 509–15

A. Dolge: *Pianos and their Makers* (Covina, CA, 1911–3/R)

C.M. Ayars: *Contributions to the Art of Music in America by the Music Industries of Boston, 1640–1936* (New York, 1937/R)

T.E. Steinway: *People and Pianos: a Century of Service to Music* (New York, 1953, 2/1961)

A. Loesser: *Men, Women and Pianos: a Social History* (New York, 1954/R)

C. Ehrlich: *The Piano: a History* (London, 1976, 2/1990)

C.A. Hoover: "The Steinways and their Pianos in the Nineteenth Century," *JAMIS*, vii (1981), 47–89

E.M. Good: *Giraffes, Black Dragons, and other Pianos: a Technological History from Cristofori to the Modern Concert Grand* (Stanford, CA, 1982, 2/2000)

C.H. Roell: *The Piano in America, 1890–1940* (Chapel Hill, NC, 1989)

R. Palmieri: *Piano Information Guide: an Aid to Research* (New York and London, 1989)

N. Groce: *Musical Instrument Makers of New York: A Directory of Eighteenth- and Nineteenth-Century Urban Craftsmen* (Stuyvesant, NY, 1991)

R. Palmieri, ed.: *Encyclopedia of Keyboard Instruments*, i: *The Piano* (New York, 1994)

J. Parakilas, ed.: *Piano Roles: Three Hundred Years of the Piano* (New Haven, CT and London, 2000)

D.D. Fandrich, ed.: *Piano Tone Building 2006: Proceedings of the Piano Technicians' Conferences, Chicago, 1916, 1917, 1918, New York, 1919, Acoustic Department, American Steel & Wire Co.* (Centralia, WA, 2006)

CYNTHIA ADAMS HOOVER, EDWIN M. GOOD

Pianola. A piano-playing device invented and named by E.S. Votey in 1895 and subsequently made by AEOLIAN §1. The trademark "Pianola" was also used for Aeolian player pianos, and became widely adopted as a generic term for all piano-players and player pianos. The name also initiated the practice of including the suffix "-ola" in the names of many musical devices.

Piano music. The United States was established as an independent nation at about the time that the piano superseded the harpsichord in general use, and piano music and its composition have flourished in the United States since the colonial period. In the 19th century the piano was a standard item of drawing-room furniture in many homes; the manufacture and sale of pianos flourished, and American piano builders such as ALPHEUS BABCOCK, JONAS CHICKERING, and Henry STEINWAY were among the best in the world. Even in the 20th and 21st centuries, when radio, recordings, television, personal computers, and an increased popularity of other instruments for domestic use have threatened its dominance, the piano has remained in wide use in all kinds of music-making, amateur and professional. Accordingly, American music publishing has always tended to center on piano music: almost from the beginning of the printing of music in the United States, music for piano was rivaled in quantity of publication only by songs (most of which, of course, included a piano accompaniment), and an immense amount of piano music, by American as well as foreign composers, was issued. This article surveys the main lines of development of American piano music and the most important contributions of its chief composers.

1. To 1865. 2. 1865 to 1920. 3. After 1920. (i) The mainstream concert tradition. (ii) Music of popular inspiration. (iii) The avant garde and contemporary developments.

1. To 1865. The transition from harpsichord to piano as the principal keyboard instrument in use is reflected in the title of the first keyboard work to be published in the United States, William Brown's *Three Rondos for the Piano Forte or Harpsichord* (1787), and in that of Benjamin Carr's collection, including a set of six tiny sonatas, *A New Assistant for the Pianoforte or Harpsichord* (1796). Similarly titled is the group of eight songs for voice and keyboard that Francis Hopkinson had printed as *Seven Songs for the Harpsichord or Forte Piano* (1788). Such titles avoided designating a single instrument, undoubtedly to maximize sales. Another feature of the transitional period until about 1820 was the laying out of music in manuscripts and imprints in "keyboard score" (i.e., on treble and bass clefs) but without any instrumental designation; these may be simply skeletal cue sheets, to have been fleshed out by improvisation on whatever instruments were at hand, and this is almost certainly the case with the numerous anthologies of dance music, such as the anonymous *A Collection of the Most Favorite Cotillions* (n.d. [?1804]) and James Hewitt's compilation *A Collection of the Most Favorite Country Dances* (n.d. [? 1802]). Hewitt similarly

published in keyboard score *The Battle of Trenton* (1797), as did Carr his patriotic potpourri *The Federal Overture* (1794), though there is evidence that both were performed by ensembles. More clearly conceived for keyboard instrument (probably the piano) are some sets of variations by Carr and Hewitt, divertimentos and rondos by Rayner Taylor, and sonatas and rondos by J.C. Moller.

All these works are in the early Classical style: thin-textured, short-breathed, foursquare in phrase structure, and formally and harmonically simple. Much more sophisticated and with a broader stylistic and expressive range, approaching that of C.P.E. Bach's keyboard sonatas and rondos, are the four three-movement "Philadelphia sonatas" (1786–94), left in manuscript, by Alexander Reinagle; they are certainly the finest American keyboard music before 1820.

Between 1820 and the Civil War, American piano music, especially that intended for amateur performers and domestic use, developed rapidly. Publishers could hardly satisfy the demand, and a legion of minor figures, many of them amateurs themselves, appeared as composers of the airy trifles that were the principal products of the burgeoning sheet-music industry. The repertory consisted mainly of three kinds of pieces: sets of variations, usually based on popular songs, hymn tunes, or (from the 1830s on) opera arias; dances (waltzes, polkas, schottisches, galops, cotillions and quadrilles, and marches and quicksteps); and—distinctly in the minority—abstract genres (rondos are the most numerous). In time Romantic ideals of fantasy, irregularity, and individuality began to be reflected in American piano music—partly under the influence, from the 1840s, of touring European virtuosos (Leopold de Meyer, Henri Herz, and Sigismond Thalberg, among others); sets of variations took on the character of rhapsodic fantasies, simple dances became stylized—a tendency expressed in the appending of the phrase "de concert" to the dance title—and most piano works became programmatic or pictorial.

The first, and possibly the most extravagant, composer of piano music reflecting the new ideals was ANTHONY PHILIP HEINRICH: as John Sullivan Dwight put it (in *The Harbinger*, 4 July 1846), "Mr. Heinrich belongs to the romantic class, who wish to attach a story to everything they do." In about 100 compositions for piano, beginning with those in his op.1, *The Dawning of Music in Kentucky* (1820), Heinrich ranged from the naive to the prophetic, from the primitively simple to the elaborately grandiloquent. An ardent lover of the American wilderness, he celebrated it in such amazing works as *A Sylvan Scene in Kentucky, or the Barbecue Divertimento*, in which nearly 30 musical ideas appear without any repetitions, and *A Chromatic Ramble, of the Peregrine Harmonist*, a tour de force of harmonic and enharmonic complexity. He could take well-known tunes like "Hail! Columbia" and "Yankee Doodle" and place them alongside an endless, often bizarre volley of notes; the composer himself described the outcome as "full of strange ideal somersets and capriccios."

Only slightly less extravagant is much of the piano music by LOUIS MOREAU GOTTSCHALK, who triumphed in Paris in the 1840s as a young pianist and composer, then returned to the United States in 1853 to take up a nomadic life as a touring virtuoso, succeeding so dramatically that he has been called "our first matinee idol." His early pieces were the first to borrow from Afro-Caribbean and Creole sources; his later ones often draw on other folk, popular, and patriotic materials, as in *The Union* (1852–62), a grand "paraphrase de concert" on national airs (*Yankee Doodle, The Star-Spangled Banner, Hail Columbia!*, and some trumpet calls), or *Columbia, caprice américain* (1859), based on Stephen Foster's *My Old Kentucky Home*. Gottschalk seems also to have been the first American to write piano duets, for both one instrument (an arrangement of Gioachino Rossini's overture to *Guillaume Tell*, 1850–54) and two, and concerto-like works (*Grande tarantelle*, 1858–64, for piano and orchestra); he also organized grand concert extravaganzas at which such works as his arrangements of Charles Gounod (*Grande marche de Faust*) and Richard Wagner (*Grande marche de Tannhäuser*), both for 16 pianos (31 pianists) and orchestra, were performed.

Another folk-oriented composer of the time was Blind Tom (THOMAS BETHUNE), a black, blind savant with autism who was celebrated for his ability to duplicate at the keyboard anything he heard. Tom was born into slavery and sold to a promoter as a carnival attraction. His compositions included *The Battle of Mannasas*, in which the Union and Confederate armies are heard to draw closer to each other, patriotic themes and bombastic explosions flying. Gottschalk was aware of Blind Tom and dismissed reports of his gifts as mere hyperbole.

A much more restrained Romantic pianism is found in the music of Richard Hoffman (almost 100 pieces) and William Mason (like Hoffman a pupil of Franz Liszt in Weimar).

2. 1865 TO 1920. Piano music from the end of the Civil War to the early 20th century was dominated, as was other music of the increasingly assured "cultivated tradition" of American concert music, by central European models. Most members of the preeminent Second New England School studied in Germany and returned to the United States committed to the tradition of "the three Bs" (J.S. Bach, Ludwig van Beethoven, Johannes Brahms). Among the works of such composers as John Knowles Paine, George W. Chadwick, Arthur Battelle Whiting, Horatio Parker, Amy Marcy Beach, D.G. Mason, and Arthur Foote (all of them keyboard players), there is a liberal sprinkling of abstract piano music in the form of suites and sonatas, fugues, and sets of small pieces. Related to these Boston academics in his German training but more strongly influenced by the New German School of Liszt and Wagner, was EDWARD MAC-DOWELL, himself a virtuoso pianist. MacDowell's large body of piano music—four sonatas, two concertos, some suites, and 16 collections of character pieces—is stylistically the most individual of any American's after

Gottschalk. Moreover, his occasional allusions in titles to American subject matter, as in "From an Indian Lodge" and "From Uncle Remus" in *Woodland Sketches* and several compositions among the *Sea Pieces* and *New England Idyls*, are echoed musically (if only faintly) with evocations of American Indian and African American idioms.

More purposeful and consistent attempts to find a national identity in ethnic sources were made by others. An important influence was Antonín Dvořák, who during his years at the National Conservatory in New York (1892–5) urged the development of a national school based on the songs of African Americans and Indian Americans; among those who responded were Harvey Worthington Loomis (*Lyrics of the Red Man*, 1903–4) and Harry T. Burleigh (*From the Southland*, 1907). ARTHUR FARWELL, having founded the Wa-Wan Press in 1901 partly in "definite acceptance of Dvořák's challenge to go after our folk music," published several hundred works, many of them for piano, by 37 composers. Farwell himself left an important body of piano music, from his tiny, ingenious *What's in an Octave?* (1930) to the craggy Sonata (1949), as well as some overtly Indian works such as *From Mesa and Plain* (1905). HENRY F. GILBERT turned not only to Indian sources (*Indian Scenes*, 1912) but also to African American ones (*Negro Dances*, 1914), as did John Powell, a concert pianist (*Rhapsodie nègre*, for piano and orchestra, 1918; individual movements in several suites for piano).

Of the various attempts made by American composers of the early 20th century to break away from the musical domination of an Austro-Germanic vocabulary and aesthetic, CHARLES T. GRIFFES's was notably successful—in piano music as in songs and orchestral pieces. Having assimilated the idioms of French impressionism (as is shown by the original version, for piano, of *The Pleasuredome of Kubla Khan*, 1912, and "The White Peacock" and others of the *Roman Sketches*, 1915–6) and some aspects of Asian music (though these are not evident in solo piano works), Griffes completed before his early death a single sonata (1917–8), which, while owing something to Aleksandr Scryabin's sonatas, is his most original and powerful composition. Even more remarkably individual was the achievement of CHARLES IVES: although his music remained virtually unknown until many years later, by 1920 he had virtually completed his oeuvre, which includes two piano sonatas (Ives had the second, "Concord, Mass., 1840–1860," c1915–9, printed privately in 1920), an eight-minute *Three-page Sonata* (c1910–11), *Varied Air and Variations* (c1920–22; it has been suggested that the title is a pun on "Very Darin' Variations"), and a large number of briefer pieces and studies, many with provocative titles such as *The Anti-abolitionist Riots in Boston in the 1850s* (c1912–3) and *Some South-paw Pitching* (c1918–9). Ives's use of polytonality, collage, free-floating dissonance, unexpected juxtapositions, and trite-sounding quotations (with references ranging from Beethoven to folk ditties) conveys both sarcasm and sentimentality. He also experimented with microtonal tuning, notably in his *Three Quarter-Tone Pieces for Two Pianos* (1923–4).

3. AFTER 1920. To summarize the piano music written by Americans in the middle decades of the 20th century is a formidable task: it is not only extremely diverse in style but also vast in quantity and a remarkable amount is of high quality.

(i) The mainstream concert tradition. Most of the piano works written between the wars, and many written since World War II, may be seen as products of the serious, highly crafted tradition of abstract music established first in the United States by the composers of the Second New England School. Like them, the 20th-century composers in this tradition have been thoroughly grounded in European music, many having studied either in Europe (with teachers such as Nadia Boulanger and Luigi Dallapiccola) or at home with immigrant or resident European masters (Arnold Schoenberg, Paul Hindemith, Darius Milhaud, Luciano Berio, and others). As with their 19th-century forebears, "Americanism" in a stylistic sense has been of no particular concern to these composers; theirs has been, predominantly, a competent, well-crafted, but neutral music of individual expression, cast in traditional forms.

Although the works that have been written in the mainstream tradition are numerous, only a few have entered the permanent repertory. Perhaps at the head of the list are Aaron Copland's Piano Variations (1930), Piano Sonata (1939–41), Piano Fantasy (1952), and *Night Thoughts* (1972). Roger Sessions is known for his three sonatas (1928–65) and the serial set of Five Pieces (1974–5) but more especially for the four intense character pieces originally entitled *From my Diary* (1937–9), retitled *Pages from a Diary*. Ross Lee Finney's five sonatas (1933–61), smaller sets of pieces (including the attractive serial teaching pieces *Inventions*, 1956), and *Variations on a Theme by Alban Berg* (1952; Finney studied with Berg) are notable contributions, as are the many compositions for piano by the prolific Vincent Persichetti. Samuel Barber, with his single sonata (1949), added music of quality to the repertory but wrote little else for solo piano.

William Grant Still, dubbed the "Dean of African-American composers," collaborated with W.C. Handy and other jazz luminaries, yet retained European sensibilities in most of his writing. George Walker, the first African American to win a Pulitzer Prize, composed five piano sonatas but also avoided direct ethnic references or vernacular Americanisms, sticking closely to the conservatory-trained art music tradition.

More contemporary composers writing in a mainstream idiom include the Pulitzer Prize–winning Francophile Ned Rorem, perhaps best known for his profoundly lyrical songs; his piano works include three Sonatas (1948, 1949, 1954), Eight Etudes (1975), and numerous smaller pieces. John Harbison's piano works include the Piano Sonata no.1—*In Memoriam Roger Sessions* (1987), commissioned by the NEA, *Gatsby Etudes* (1999), based on his opera, *The Great Gatsby*, and *Ten Micro-Waltzes* (2004). Joan Tower's piano contributions include *Holding a Daisy* (1996), *Vast Antique Cubes/Throbbing Still* (2000), and *Ivory and Ebony*

(2009); Ellen Taaffe Zwilich, the first female composer to win a Pulitzer Prize, has written *Millennium Fantasy*, for piano and orchestra (2000); Lowell Liebermann, whose work is especially popular among students and at piano competitions, is represented by numerous keyboard works, from Piano Sonata no.1 (1977) to Nocturne no.11 (2010); and Pulitzer Prize–winner David Del Tredici combines his formidable pianism and compositional skill in piano works ranging from the thorny *Fantasy Pieces* (1959–60) to the sweepingly Romantic *Virtuoso Alice* (1984).

ELLIOTT CARTER's compositional approach was based on the idea of emotional counterpoint, with instruments or themes acting like individual characters in (an often raucous) conversation—often working at different speeds and inhabiting different behaviors. He produced an early piano sonata (1946) and much later wrote the dark, rhapsodic *Night Fantasies* (1980). He continued composing long past his one-hundredth birthday and created new repertoire for piano with increasing frequency. Among these, his *90+* (1994), written in honor of composer Goffredo Petrassi's 90th birthday, contains 90 staccato notes plus a coda; *Two Diversions*, written for a *Carnegie Hall Millennium Piano Book* (2000), are intended for students; *Intermittences* (2005), suggested by a chapter in Marcel Proust's work, was commissioned by the Carnegie Hall Corporation and the Gilmore International Keyboard Festival for Peter Serkin; and *Caténaires* (2006), for pianist Pierre-Laurent Aimard, is, explained the composer, "a fast one line piece with no chords…a continuous chain of notes using different spacings, accents and colorings, to provide a wide variety of expression." Carter's monumental *Double Concerto* for piano, harpsichord and two chamber orchestras (1959–61) and his Piano Concerto (1964–5) were declared by Igor Stravinsky to be masterpieces.

Among composers of 12-tone music must be cited Milton Babbitt, whose *Three Compositions for Piano* (1947) were among the first examples of total serialism, an approach he continued throughout his lifetime, and who completed his celebrated *Allegro Penseroso* in 1999. Babbitt also worked in electronic music, composing *Reflections* for piano and synthesized tape in 1972, following Mario Davidovsky's highly successful *Synchronisms no.6* for piano and electronic tape in 1971, which won a Pulitzer Prize. This combination of keyboard and electronics continues in the work of TOD MACHOVER, who spent time at Pierre Boulez's Institut de Recherche et Coordination Acoustique/Musique (IRCAM) in Paris; he created what he calls a "hyperpiano"—a Yamaha Disklavier whose sound is manipulated by means of computer programming. Machover's solo piano piece *Chansons d'Amour* (1982) is also considered an important contribution to the literature.

Other American composers influenced by the Second Viennese School included George Rochberg, whose first 12-tone work was the 12 Bagatelles (1952), and Charles Wuorinen, whose Piano Variations (1963), *The Blue Bamboula* (1980), and other pieces reflect his virtuosity as a pianist. Rochberg's 12-tone phase culminated (at least among his piano works) in the Sonata-fantasia

(1956); he later moved in other directions, making important neotonal statements (*Partita-variations*, 1976).

Some of the most unusual piano music in this tradition—on the edge of the avant-garde in its explorations of piano sonorities—is that by GEORGE CRUMB. *Makrokosmos I* (1972) and *Makrokosmos II* (1973) for amplified piano comprise 24 fantasies inspired partly by Claude Debussy's 24 *Préludes* and Béla Bartók's *Mikrokosmos*. Diverse in style, they call not only for traditional keyboard and pedal techniques but also for operations within the body of the instrument and a variety of sounds from the pianist (such as singing, speaking, and groaning). Collage also plays a part: in "Nightfall I" the pianist is to whistle phrases of the revival hymn "Will there be any stars in my crown?" and in "Dream Images" there are fragments of Fryderyk Chopin's *Fantaisie-impromptu*.

(ii) Music of popular inspiration. The syncopated music of ragtime and early jazz spread in modified form to mainstream white culture early in the 20th century, transforming the nature of American social dancing and popular music. Important ragtime composers included Scott Joplin, whose *Maple Leaf Rag*, *The Entertainer*, and the Mexican-tinged *Solace* stand as classics of the style; Tom Turpin; Louis Chauvin; Arthur Marshall; James Scott; Charles H. Hunter; and Eubie Blake, whose *Charleston Rag* of 1899 served as a transition to the Harlem Stride style.

From the 1920s there were attempts to adapt the new idioms to concert music, including music for piano. The best-known examples are those of GEORGE GERSHWIN, especially *Rhapsody in Blue* (1924), for piano and dance band, and the Concerto in F (1925); among his solo piano music are the lapidary Three Preludes (1926) and the 18 too-brief song transcriptions in *The Gershwin Song Book* (1932). Gershwin's pianism was an amalgam of styles: the "NOVELTY PIANO" tradition spearheaded by Zez Confrey, whose million-selling *Kitten on the Keys* and other piano works displayed bouncy rhythms and jazz-age filigree, often in quickly executed sequences and figures requiring alternations of the hands; the soaring melodies of Liszt; the impressionist harmonies of Debussy and Maurice Ravel; swing piano patterns he picked up from his mentors, Harlem Stride greats Willie "The Lion" Smith, James P. Johnson, and Thomas "Fats" Waller; and Jewish-inflected dance music from Eastern Europe. Gershwin remained adventurous, pursuing microtonal interests as well as developments in the work of Alban Berg before his life was cut short by a misdiagnosed brain tumor.

Many minor composers, especially during the Depression years when populist feeling was strong and in the war years when the prevailing sentiment was nationalistic, dabbled briefly in popular-music idioms, as did some major ones, among them Copland (*Four Piano Blues*, 1926–47), Virgil Thomson ("Ragtime Bass" in the Ten Etudes, 1943), Barber (*Excursions*, 1944), Roy Harris (*American Ballads*, 1942–5), and William Schuman (*Three-score Set*, 1943). Such borrowings were infrequent after World War II; however, with the revival in the 1970s of ragtime, some composers saw its pianistic possibilities and enlarged the repertory of piano rags (William Bolcom, with *Ghost Rags*, 1970–71, and other compositions), or composed larger works influenced by ragtime (William Albright, with *Grand Sonata in Rag*, 1968). Jazz too had some influence, both direct (as in Lalo Shifrin's *Jazz Sonata*, c1963) and indirect, as in FREDERIC RZEWSKI's *Four North American Ballads*, 1978–9 (and, in their underlying idea if not their idiom, aleatory works by various composers). Rzewski's leftist political bent shows up in his masterful variations on *The People United Will Never Be Defeated* (1975) and in *De profundis* (1992), which uses a letter written by a jailed Oscar Wilde; it requires the pianist to recite as well as play. Rzewski's music requires high virtuosity and a subtle command of the piano's pedals and dynamic range, producing dramatic and sometimes ethereal effects that the composer credits to the early avant-garde pianist David Tudor.

Jazz pianists themselves produced some of the most brilliant, inventive, and artful piano music of the era (although until transcriptions from recordings were made the music was not available for performance by other pianists unless they learned it by ear). Some were noteworthy for their originality (Duke Ellington, Keith Jarrett, Lennie Tristano, Thelonious Monk, Cecil Taylor); others offered music full of surprises and shifts of style and idea (Jelly Roll Morton, Dave Brubeck, Bill Evans, John Lewis, Dave McKenna, Jason Moran, Mary Lou Williams); still others produced pieces of coruscating virtuosity (Earl Hines, Erroll Garner, Bud Powell, and especially Art Tatum).

(iii) The avant garde and contemporary developments. A strong current in American music of the 20th and 21st centuries has been the continuing presence of avant-garde composers with private visions and unique voices; among them are a few who have expressed their ideas significantly, even predominantly, in piano music. Key voices were Charles Ives and HENRY COWELL. Ives not only wrote music for two pianos tuned a quarter-tone apart but also called for the performer of the "Concord" Sonata to depress the keyboard with a board (of a specific length) to produce massive cluster chords; in the accompaniment to the song "Charlie Rutlage" (1920/21) he requires the pianist to play with his fists (noting that the pitches are not important). Cowell arrived independently at the idea of tone clusters, produced by fists or forearms, first in *The Tides of Manaunaun* (?1917); he also, in *Fabric* (1920), wrote music of unprecedented poly-rhythmic complexity. Then in the following decade he wrote a whole series of pieces (including *Aeolian Harp*, c1923, *Sinister Resonance*, 1925, and *The Banshee*, 1930) that explored a previously untapped reservoir of sonorities produced by playing directly on the strings—plucking, stroking, or striking them, muting or stopping them, and producing harmonics on them.

Cowell's freethinking was passed on to his disciple JOHN CAGE. Cage had studied with Schoenberg, who informed him that he had no sense of musical harmony and would therefore run into a wall as a composer; a subsequent foray into Zen Buddhism convinced Cage that he should give up harmony and learn to embrace sounds of every kind. Cage's main contribution to avant-garde pianism was to turn the instrument into a kind of delicate-sounding one-man percussion band by "preparing" it—placing on and between the strings various objects and bits of material to transform the sound quality (see PREPARED PIANO). His works for prepared piano culminated in the 70-minute *Sonatas and Interludes* (1946–8), which became his most frequently performed piece. His efforts in the 1950s to reduce his role as composer—to let the music simply "happen"—were realized in the lengthy *Music of Changes* (1951), *4'33"* (1952; the notorious "silent" composition, most often performed as a piano solo), and *Music for Piano 4–19* (1953). Cage also wrote (and surely was the first to do so) for a child's miniature piano (Suite for Toy Piano, 1948). Many contemporary composers, including Erik Griswold, Toby Twining, and George Crumb, have begun to enlarge this repertoire, writing works especially for pianist Margaret Leng Tan, a toy piano advocate.

Cage inspired numbers of younger composers, some of whom produced remarkable piano music. Morton Feldman's *Last Pieces* (1959) consist of nothing but soft, complicated chords, their duration and that of the silences between them being left to the performer; Christian Wolff's *For Piano I* (1952) is even more spare and silence-dominated. The instructions for Robert Moran's *Composition for Piano with Pianist* (*c*1965) read: "A pianist comes onto the stage and goes directly to the concert grand piano. He climbs into the piano and sits on the strings. The piano plays him." Larry Austin calls for the performer of his *Accidents* (1967) to make not sounds but very rapid gestures; the player must repeat any gesture within which an unintended, accidental sound occurs, until it is free of "error."

Perhaps influenced by Cowell, CONLON NANCARROW pushed back even further the frontiers of rhythmic complexity, and also velocity, in his music, almost all of which is exclusively for player piano. Envisioning a literally superhuman music, Nancarrow learned how to punch his works onto player-piano rolls and, beginning with *Study for Player Piano I* (late 1940s), produced a long series of fantastic etudes, rich in canons and almost unfathomable polyrhythms, for one and two player pianos. Rhythmic complexity of a different nature has preoccupied STEVE REICH, one of whose first "live" instrumental works (most of his early works are for tape) of pulse music (or phase music) was *Piano Phase* (1967) for two pianists or marimba players, in which the same material is played by the two performers at slightly different speeds, creating constantly changing relationships (see MINIMALISM). The title of Reich's *Six Pianos* (1933) is self-explanatory.

Many other composers have produce music in the "minimalist" mode—so-called because of its minimal use of materials and highly repetitive patterns—including PHILIP GLASS, whose solo piano music includes *How Now* (1968) and *A Musical Portrait of Chuck*

Close (2005); his works for two pianos, such as *Four Movements for Two Pianos* (2009), have been performed by the composer with pianist/conductor Dennis Russell Davies. JOHN ADAMS, who, like Glass, has written several operas, produced the intricately structured solo piano works *Phrygian Gates* (1977–8)—in which constantly shifting modules move between the Lydian mode and Phrygian mode—and *China Gates* (1977), as well as *Hallelujah Junction* (1996) for two pianos, and a jazz-influenced piece, *American Berserk* (2001).

Yet another area in which music for piano has pursued new ground is that of the musical scale itself. In addition to Charles Ives, others have delved into the world of quarter-tones. German American composer HANS BARTH, influenced by the ideas of Ferruccio Busoni, developed a quarter-tone piano in 1928 and even interested George Gershwin in the possibilities of rendering his preludes in this tuning. More recently, JOHN CORIGLIANO, whose traditional compositions for piano include *Etude Fantasy* (1976), *Fantasia on an Ostinato* (1985), and *Winging It: Improvisations for Solo Piano* (2008), composed *Chiaroscuro* (1997) for two pianos tuned a quarter-tone apart.

Others have investigated an even wider world of microtonal shadings. Inspired in part by the work of Harry Partch (who wrote not for piano or other conventional instruments but for inventions of his own), composers such as BEN JOHNSTON (Sonata for Microtonal Piano, 1965) have sought, in music based on just intonation (giving untempered intervals), to "reopen doors closed by the acceptance of the 12-tone equal-tempered scale as the norm of pitch usage" (Hamm, 1976, quoting Johnston). Other composers have turned to the East for inspiration along these lines. Lou Harrison made use of Indonesian scales and gamelan-like sounds. His Piano Concerto (1983–5) made use of a well-tempered tuning, Kirnberger #2. LA MONTE YOUNG, a student of Indian raga master Pandit Pran Nath, developed an aesthetic based that employed just intonation and tones of exceedingly long duration. His most famous work is *The Well Tuned Piano* (1964—present in numerous realizations)—performances of which have taken over six hours. Young and his partner Marian Zazeela have created a permanent sound and light installation known as the "Dream House." Composer Michael Harrison, who tuned La Monte Young's piano and became his student (as well as Pandit Pran Nath's), has carried on the just intonation tradition, creating works like *Revelation*, a 75-minute extended exploration of his own tuning based on prime numbers. Harrison has stated that, just as Schoenberg emancipated the dissonance, he seeks to emancipate the "comma"—the harmonic collision that occurs in pure tunings because natural octaves, fifths, and thirds, as they are multiplied across the keyboard, arrive at different versions of the same scale tones. Thus, the grating sound that musicians once called "wolves"—and that equal temperament was created to avoid—has become a feature of Harrison's musical texture.

See also ART SONG; CHAMBER MUSIC; EXPERIMENTAL MUSIC; JAZZ; and RAGTIME.

BIBLIOGRAPHY
A. Loesser: *Men, Women and Pianos* (New York, 1954)
M.L. McKeon: *Stylistic Tendencies in Mid-twentieth-century American Piano Music* (diss., Eastman School of Music, 1957)
B.A. Wolverton: *Keyboard Music and Musicians in the Colonies and United States of America before 1830* (diss., Indiana U., 1966)
M. Williams: *The Jazz Tradition* (New York, 1970, 2/1983)
M. Hinson: *Guide to the Pianist's Repertoire* (Bloomington, IN, 1973; suppl., 1979)
J.B. Clark: "The Renaissance of Early American Keyboard Music: a Bibliographic Review," *CMc*, xviii (1974), 127–32
C. Hamm: Liner notes, *Sound Forms for Piano*, NW 203 (1976)
R. Offergeld: "Gottschalk and Company: the Music of Democratic Sociability," *The Wind Demon*, NW 257 (1976) [liner notes]
J.B. Clark: Preface, *Anthology of Early American Keyboard Music, 1787–1830*, RRAM, i–ii (1977)
R. Hopkins: Preface to *Alexander Reinagle: the Philadelphia Sonatas*, RRAM, v (1978)
K.R. Gartner: *The Expansion of Pianism since 1945* (diss., New York U., 1979)
E.A. Berlin: *Ragtime: a Musical and Cultural History* (Berkeley, CA, 1980/R1984 with additions)
W. Brooks: "The American Piano," *The Book of the Piano*, ed. D. Gill (Ithaca, NY, 1981), 172
B. Taylor: *Jazz Piano: A Piano History* (Dubuque, IA, 1983)
J. Gillespie and A. Gillespie, eds.: *A Bibliography of Nineteenth-century American Piano Music* (Westport, CT, 1984)
J. Bunker Clark: *The Dawning of American Keyboard Music* (New York, 1988)
S. Isacoff: *Temperament: How Music Became a Battleground for the Great Minds of Western Civilization* (New York, 2003)
K.C. Ward: *For the parlor and the concert stage: a guide to recent collections of American piano music from the classic and romantic eras* (Hillsdale, NY, 2010)
MAURICE HINSON, H. WILEY HITCHCOCK/
STUART ISACOFF

Piano Technicians Guild. An international nonprofit organization of piano tuners and technicians that monitors and maintains standards in the craft, in the absence of government licensing. Formed in 1958 by the merger of the National Association of Piano Tuners (founded 1908) and the American Society of Piano Technicians (founded 1940), the PTG is organized into regions throughout the United States and worldwide, offering to its members opportunities for accreditation, continuing education and professional development. Members may progress through an apprentice-like program of classes and examinations to improve their skills to the level of Registered Piano Technician (RPT). Additionally, the Guild serves as a public resource for piano technology and actively supports music education. In 2010, the Guild was headquartered in Kansas City and had over 4000 members worldwide. The organization publishes the monthly *Piano Technicians Journal* and a wide variety of technical manuals and bulletins, and offers a technician referral service on its website (<http://www.ptg.org>).

JOHN T. SHEPARD/ANITA SULLIVAN

Piantadosi, Al (*b* New York, NY, 18 July 1884; *d* Encino, CA, 8 April 1955). Songwriter, publisher, and composer. He initially studied medicine in college but changed fields and became a song plugger. He worked as a pianist in Callahan's saloon and other nightclubs in the Chinatown district of New York. His first song, "My Mariuccia Take a Steamboat" (1906), became especially popular for its "toot toot" sounds. He published several commercially successful songs before 1920, including the ethnic songs "I'm a Yiddish cowboy" (1908), "I'm awfully glad I'm Irish" (words by E. Leslie, 1910), and "That Italian Rag" (Leslie, 1910), and two sentimental ballads that sold over a million copies each: "That's how I need you" (J. McCarthy, J. Goodwin, 1912) and "The Curse of an Aching Heart" (H. Fink, 1913). He also wrote "I didn't raise my boy to be a soldier" (A. Bryan, 1915), which raised some controversy because of its isolationist stance toward World War I. As an accompanist for vaudeville performers such as Anna Chandler, Piantadosi toured widely in the United States and also traveled to Europe and Australia, where he often performed ragtime. On his return he worked in music publishing in New York and retired in 1930 to California, where he managed a variety of musicians. Piantadosi's music was widely recorded and resulted in several high-selling sides, including "If You Had All the World and its Gold" (1916).

BIBLIOGRAPHY
J. Burton: "The Honor Roll of Popular Songwriters: Al Piantadosi," *Billboard Magazine* (11 June 1949), 38 only
RONALD RIDDLE/JONAS WESTOVER

Piastro, Mishel [Michel] (*b* Kerch, Crimea, Russia, 19 June 1891; *d* New York, NY, 10 April 1970). Violinist. He attended the St. Petersburg Conservatory from 1903 to 1910, where he was a violin pupil of LEOPOLD AUER. He was active as a concert violinist before immigrating to the United States in 1920; that same year he made his debut in New York and then toured the country. In 1925 he was appointed concertmaster and assistant conductor of the San Francisco SO; from 1931 to 1943 he was concertmaster of the New York PO, under Toscanini and then Barbirolli, and while with the orchestra appeared frequently as a soloist. He was also first violinist of the New York Philharmonic-Symphony String Quartet, and in the 1930s and 1940s often appeared as a recitalist and chamber music performer in New York. For over 25 years beginning in 1941 he conducted radio station WOR's "Longines Symphonette." Piastro was also active as a teacher for most of his professional life.

Piatigorsky, Gregor (*b* Yekaterinoslav, Russia [now Dnepropetrovsk, Ukraine], 17 April 1903; *d* Los Angeles, CA, 6 Aug 1976). Cellist and composer of Ukrainian birth. He began to play the cello when he was seven and two years later was admitted to the Moscow Conservatory as a scholarship student of Alfred von Glehn; later he had some private lessons with Anatoly Andreyevich Brandukov. In 1919 he was invited to join Moscow's foremost string quartet, the Lenin Quartet, led by Lev Tseytlin, and the same year he was appointed principal cellist of the Bol'shoy Theater orchestra. He left the revolution-torn region surreptitiously in 1921, going first to Warsaw, then to Leipzig where he studied with Julius Klengel. In 1924 Wilhelm Furtwängler engaged him as principal cellist of the Berlin PO, a post he left in 1928 to devote himself to a solo career. In Berlin he formed a distinguished sonata partnership with Artur Schnabel and a trio with Schnabel and Carl Flesch. His American debut with the New York PO in December 1929 was the triumphant beginning of an international career. In 1930 he was heard in trios with Vladimir Horowitz and Nathan Milstein, and he formed another trio in 1949 with Jascha Heifetz and Artur Rubinstein. Having settled in California, in 1961 Piatigorsky joined Heifetz in establishing a chamber music series in Los Angeles known as the Heifetz-Piatigorsky Concerts; some of their programs were heard in New York in 1964 and 1966 and were also recorded. For a number of years he was director of chamber music at the Berkshire Music Center, Tanglewood, and from 1962 until his death he was a professor at the University of Southern California, Los Angeles, where his cello classes were renowned; in 1975 a Piatigorsky chair of music was established there. Piatigorsky performed until late in his life, playing at several concerts given for his 70th birthday in 1973 and in London in 1974.

At the height of his career Piatigorsky was acclaimed as a leading cellist of his generation, combining an innate flair for virtuosity with an exquisite taste in style and phrasing; technical perfection was never a goal in itself. His vibrant tone had infinite shadings and his sweeping eloquence and aristocratic grandeur created an instant rapport with his audience. He was at his best in emotional Romantic music, and Strauss commented after hearing him play *Don Quixote*: "I have heard the 'Don' as I thought him to be." He gave the premieres of concertos by Mario Castelnuovo-Tedesco (1935, with Arturo Toscanini), Paul Hindemith (1941) and William Walton (1957), and the first American performance of Prokofiev's concerto op.58 (1940). Besides original works for cello (including *Pliaska*, Scherzo, Variations on a Theme of Paganini for cello and piano or orchestra), he published some skillful transcriptions and collaborated with Igor Stravinsky on the cello version of the "Suite italienne" from *Pulcinella*. There is a rich legacy of Piatigorsky recordings in the solo and chamber music repertory. His autobiography *Cellist* (New York, 1965) has been translated into several languages. Among his numerous awards were several honorary doctorates and membership of the Légion d'Honneur. Piatigorsky owned two magnificent Stradivari cellos, the "Batta" (1714) and the "Baudiot" (1725).

BIBLIOGRAPHY

CampbellGC

M. Campbell: "Professor and Populariser," *The Strad*, civ (1993), 354–7

J.-M. Molkhou: "Discography," ibid., 881–4

M. Bartley: *Grisha: the Dramatic Story of Cellist Gregor Piatigorsky* (New Russia, NY, 2004)

T. King: *Gregor Piatigorsky: the Life and Career of the Virtuoso Cellist* (Jefferson, NC, 2010)

BORIS SCHWARZ/R

Piavosoto. Native American group of the Great Basin area, belonging to the Paiute.

Piazzolla, Astor [Ástor] **(Pantaleón)** (*b* Mar del Plata, Argentina, 11 March 1921; *d* Buenos Aires, Argentina, 5 July 1992). Argentine composer, arranger, bandleader, and *bandoneón* player. With just a few lessons on *bandoneón* and general music notions acquired from pianist Bela Wilda, he learned Tango (i) by listening to and emulating its key performers. After living most of his childhood and adolescence in New York, he moved to Buenos Aires and joined Anibal Troilo's influential *orquesta típica* in 1939. In addition to playing *bandoneón*, Piazzolla earned a living by writing arrangements for Troilo's and other important tango orchestras, including those led by Francini, Pontier, Basso, and Fresedo. In 1944 he left Troilo to form his own group. He began to study with composer Alberto Ginastera and in 1953 won the Fabien Sevitzky prize for his *Buenos Aires Symphony*, which earned him a scholarship to study in Paris with Nadia Boulanger. After his return in 1955, Piazzolla founded the Buenos Aires Octet, the first musical manifestation of his revolutionary style that came to be known as *nuevo tango*. Of his various instrumental ensembles that followed—quintet, nonet, electronic octet, and sextet, all of which experimented beyond the traditional lineup of the tango orchestra—his two quintets (1960–70, 1978–89) became the most emblematic.

Piazzolla's approach transforms some of the essential characteristics of traditional tango (phrasing, syncopation, rubato, swing), while incorporating classical (atonal passages, contrapuntal textures, ostinati) and jazz elements (walking bass, improvisation, drum set). Although progressive bandleaders, including Osvaldo Pugliese and Horacio Salgán, recognized his revolutionary talent, Piazzolla's *nuevo tango* was fiercely resisted by traditionalists and remained controversial until the 1980s. His compositions range from symphonic works to film music. However, it was through his own live performances with his ensembles that he achieved international fame.

During the 1970s Piazzolla's music found its European niche in jazz festival circles, where his nonet and electronic octet were appreciated as well-balanced combos. Unable to classify Piazzolla's music, the US market proved more resistant. Despite some performances in New York, at Philharmonic Hall and at Carnegie Hall, and work as a nightclub and studio musician (1965–8), it was not until the growth of the world-beat phenomenon in the 1980s—and the increasing demand for world music-influenced chamber music—that Piazzolla found his place in the American market. His pieces appeared in the successful Broadway show *Tango Argentino* and in his own concerts at the Public Theater (1986), Central Park's Naumburg Bandshell (1987), and Alice Tully Hall (1989). Two recordings released in the United States, *Tango Zero Hour* (1986) and *La camorra* (1989), positioned Piazzolla as a world-music composer in high demand. Concerts during the period 1988–90 with the Orchestra of St. Luke's and the Kronos Quartet led to an increased interest in Piazzolla's music at symphonic and chamber venues. After his death, his music found a place in the standard repertoire. His Concerto for *bandoneón* and orchestra and *Cuatro estaciones porteñas* have been frequently programmed by American orchestras.

WORKS

(selective list)

Stage: El hombre de la esquina rosada, v, nar, ob, 2 vn, va, vc, db, gtr, 2 bandoneón, pf, hp, perc, 1960; María de Buenos Aires, 2 vv, chorus, nar, fl, 2 vn, va, vc, db, gtr, bandoneón, pf, vib, perc, 1968

Film: La fiaca, 1968; Lumière, 1975; Voyage de noces, 1975; Henry IV, 1984; El exilio de Gardel, 1985; Sur, 1988

Orch: Tangazo, 1969; Conc. for bandoneón, 1979; Conc. for bandoneón and guitar, 1985

Chbr: Le grand tango, vc, pf, 1982; Woe/Five Tango Sensations, bandoneón, str qt, 1983–5; Four for Tango, str qt, 1988

Tangos: Triunfal; Tanguango; Prepárense; Contrabajeando; Adiós Nonino; Decarísimo; Calambre; Buenos Aires hora cero; Cuatro estaciones porteñas; Milonga del ángel; Balada para un loco; Tristezas de un Doble A; Libertango, Suite Troileana; Mumuki; Contrabajísimo; Vardarito

SELECTED RECORDINGS

As leader: Octeto Buenos Aires (1957, Disk Jockey); Piazzolla bailable y apiazzollado (1961, RCA Victor); Tango para una ciudad (1963, CBS); El tango: Jorge Luis Borges–Astor Piazzolla (1965, Polydor); María de Buenos Aires (1968, Trova); Adiós Nonino (1969, Trova); Pulsación (1970, Trova); Libertango (1974, Trova); Suite Troileana-Lumière (1975, Trova); Biyuya (1979, Interdisc); Piazzolla-Goyeneche (1982, RCA Victor); El exilio de Gardel (1986, RCA Victor); Cero Hour (1986, American Clavè); Tristezas de un doble A (1987, Messidor); La camorra (1989, American Clavè); The Central Park Concert (1994, Chesky); 57 Minutos con la realidad (1996, Intuition); Tres minutos con la realidad (1997, Milan Sur)

BIBLIOGRAPHY

GMO

C. Kuri: Piazzolla: la música sin límite (Buenos Aires, 1992)

M.S. Azzi and S. Collier: Le Grand Tango: the Life and Music of Astor Piazzolla (New York, 2000)

N. Gorín: Astor Piazzolla: a Memoir (Portland, OR, 2001)

G. Mauriño: "Raíces tangueras de la obra de Astor Piazzolla," LAMR, xxii (2001), 240–54

D. Butler Cannata: "Making it there: Piazzolla's New York Concerts," LAMR, xxvi (2005), 57–87

LORENA GUILLÉN

Picker, Tobias (*b* New York, NY, 18 July 1954). Composer and pianist. He studied with CHARLES WUORINEN (Manhattan School, 1972–6), ELLIOTT CARTER (Juilliard, 1976–8) and MILTON BABBITT (Princeton, 1978–80). He quickly attracted critical attention, being characterized at age 24 by Andrew Porter as "a genuine creator with a fertile, unforced vein of invention" (A. Porter: "Musical Events," *New Yorker*, 20 Nov 1978). At the age of 18, Picker was an improvising pianist for the Martha Graham School of Contemporary Dance, an experience that encouraged his intuitive, pulse-based musicality. His professed affinity for two composers, one romantic and one modern, also catalyzed his compositional style. He has met the challenge to reconcile the warm, earnest, arching continuity of Brahms and the cool, playful, fractured energy of Stravinsky with music distinctive for its emotional immediacy and impulsive, visceral rhythm.

Picker's early compositions, through to the age of 25, are exclusively chamber works that usually involve searching astringent harmonies, exclamatory gestures, and motoric drive; his serialized pitches are often used in a manner that implies a transient tonality within a succession of striking moments. In succeeding works involving full orchestra, these moments are protracted, often into textures of even more sharply defined character.

Breadth and grandeur are achieved through the slow, pulsed interlocking of theme and pedal point. Melodically elaborated and colorfully scored ostinato passages continually propel the music forward. Picker imbues romantic conventions with a modern spirit which rejects nostalgia but retains considerable expressive freedom.

One work tends to engender the next, usually with a shift in focus. The unremitting bravura and textural invention of the Violin Concerto (1981) is followed by the weighty, more integrated Symphony no.1 (1982). Piano Concerto no.2, "Keys to the City," commissioned for the centennial of New York's Brooklyn Bridge, effectively absorbs American vernacular elements, most conspicuously in a driving boogie-woogie passage. Picker's imagination responds particularly well to extramusical subjects. Based on a text by Hermann Melville, *The Encantadas* (1983), a concerto for narrator and orchestra distinctive for its wide variety of musical tableaux, has enjoyed successful productions internationally in seven languages. Another work which quickly gained popularity, especially in its orchestrated form, is *Old and Lost Rivers* (1986), a short, serene Texan pastorale for piano which Picker wrote while composer-in-residence for the Houston SO (1985–90). Its homogeneous polyphonic texture anticipates more extended works in which faster movements are balanced by those of slow, cursive chromatic lines stretched across sustained harmonies. Also representative is the string quartet, *New Memories* (1987), commissioned by the Santa Fe Chamber Music Festival to commemorate the 100th birthday of the local artist Georgia O'Keeffe, who died during the writing of the work. Her painting reinforced Picker's awareness of an American Southwest geologic time frame that informed his slowly unfolding works of this period. In the hybrid *Romances and Interludes* (1989), Picker confronts the 19th century directly by composing a prelude and two interludes around his orchestration of Schumann's *Drei Romanzen* op.94 for oboe and piano. Thematic allusion and mediating orchestration convincingly bind the otherwise disparate musics in a complementary relationship. *Two Fantasies* (1989) for orchestra revisits favored textures: a slow, expansive, though somewhat restive movement followed by a kaleidoscopic etude in motoric frenzy.

Between 1978 and 1992, Picker wrote eight songs for soprano and piano, one of which, *Aussohnung*, he orchestrated to become the culminating moment in his Symphony no.2 (1986–7). *The Rain in the Trees* (1993), for soprano, flute, and orchestra, based on a text by W.S. Merwin, represented his most expanded use of the voice to this time. Here purely instrumental blocks of stratified polyphony alternate between Ivesian vigor and Javanese serenity. It is, however, the rapturous vocal movements which make the lasting effect and anticipate the composer's first stage work, *Emmeline* (1994–6), commissioned by the Santa Fe Opera. Its story of a 19th-century New England woman's unwitting marriage to a son she bore at 14 and then abandoned entails a pathos appropriately met by primarily tonal music which is emotionally charged and theatrically effective. The opera's initial success was exceeded in a second production two years later by the New York City Opera, prompting international commitments and further opera commissions. Written for the Los Angeles Opera, *Fantastic Mr. Fox* (1998) is based on a children's story well served by pulsing, playfully angular counterpoint and tunes which drift in and out of tonality. Picker's third opera, *Thérèse Raquin,* (1999–2000) based on the novel by Émile Zola, was commissioned by a consortium of companies, including the Dallas Opera, San Diego Opera, and Opéra de Montréal. The work spins an engrossing tale of dangerous passion and desire. Picker's score uses a particularly sinister tonality for a libretto whose core represents an adulterous wife, her rapacious lover, and an unsuspecting husband. The success of these first productions brought Picker a new commission from Opera Theatre Europe for a chamber orchestra version of *Thérèse Raquin,* which premiered in March 2006 at the Linbury Studio of the Royal Opera House, Covent Garden, and received its US premiere at Dicapo Opera Theatre in New York one year later. Based on the success of the chamber orchestra version of *Thérèse Raquin,* Picker was commissioned to arrange *Emmeline* for chamber orchestra as well and the piece saw its premiere at Dicapo Opera Theatre in 2009 with its European premiere at Szeged, Hungary, at Hungary's National Theatre soon after. In 2004 The Metropolitan Opera commissioned Picker's fourth opera *An American Tragedy*, based on the novel by Theodore Dreiser. A progressive drama of temptation, responsibility, and faith, *An American Tragedy* centers on the love triangle spun by a mid-western missionary's son upon his arrival in New York. The opera, which features a lyrical score with passages of striking chromatic harmonies, saw its world premiere at the Met in December 2005.

The Rambert Dance Company premiered Picker's new ballet, *Awakenings,* in the fall of 2010 at the Lowry, Salford, UK. The ballet, inspired by true life stories, stems from Oliver Sacks's book of the same name. Picker's fifth opera, *Dolores Claiborne,* based on the book by Stephen King, was commissioned by the San Francisco Opera in 2011. Picker was named artistic director of The Opera San Antonio in 2010 and elected to the American Academy of Arts and Letters in 2012.

WORKS
(selective list)

Ops: Emmeline (2, J.D. McClatchy, after J. Rossner), 1994–6, Santa Fe Op, 27 July 1996; Fantastic Mr. Fox (3, D. Sturrock, after R. Dahl), 1998, Los Angeles Op, 9 Dec 1998; Thérèse Raquin (G. Scheer, after É. Zola), 1999–2000, Dallas Op, 30 Nov 2001; An American Tragedy (G. Scheer, after T. Dreiser) 2005, The Metropolitan Op, 2 Dec 2005; Dolores Claiborne (J.D. McClatchy, after S. King), 2011-13, San Francisco Op, 18 Sept 2013

Ballet: Awakenings, 2010, Rambert Dance Company, 22 Sept 2010

Orch: Pf Conc. no.1, 1980; Vn Conc., 1981; Sym. no.1, 1982; The Encantadas (H. Melville), nar, orch, 1983, arr. nar, chbr orch, 1986; Pf Conc. no.2, "Keys to the City," 1983; Pf Conc. no.3, "Kilauea," 1986; Old and Lost Rivers, 1986 [arr. of pf work]; Sym. no.2 "Aussöhnung," S, orch, 1986–7; Sym. no.3, str, 1988 [based on Str Qt with Bass]; Romances and Interludes, ob, orch, 1989 [from Schumann: Three Romances, op.94]; 2 Fantasies, 1989; Séance "Homage à Sibelius," 1991; Bang!, 1992 [2nd movt of 2 Fantasies]; Va Conc., 1990, rev. 1993; And Suddenly It's Evening, 1994; Tres Sonetos de Amor, 1v, orch, 2000

Chbr: Trio, ob, vc, pf, 1974, unpubd; Flute Farm, 4 fl, 1975; Septet, fl, bn, tpt, trbn, vn, pf, vib/glock, 1976; Sextet no.2, ob, cl, pf, vn, vc, vib/glock, 1976; Sextet no.3, fl, vn, vc, db, perc, 1976; Rhapsody, vn, pf, 1978; Octet, ob, b cl, hn, vn, vc, db, hp, vib/mar, 1978; Romance, vn, pf, 1979; Nova, vn, va, vc, db, pf, 1979; The Blue Hula (Sextet no.4), fl, cl, vn, vc, pf, vib/glock, 1981; Serenade, pf, ww qnt, 1983 [based on Nova]; Keys to the City, pf, 8 insts, 1986 [arr. of Pf Conc. no.2]; Str Qt, "New Memories," 1987; Str Qt with Bass, 1988, orchd; Invisible Lilacs, vn, pf, 1991; Suite, vc, pf, 1998; Str Qt no.2, 2008; Pf Qnt, Live Oaks, 2011

Pf: Duo, pf 4 hands, 1972, unpubd; When Soft Voices Die, 1977; Old and Lost Rivers, 1986; Pianorama, 2 pf, 1984; 3 Pieces, 1988; 4 Etudes for Ursula, 1995–6; 3 Nocturnes for Ursula, 2009

Songs (S, pf unless otherwise stated): Dayton (Picker), 1978; Alicante (Picker), 1978; Aussöhnung (J. Goethe), 1984, arr. as last movt of Sym. no.2; When We Meet Again (E. St Vincent Millay), 1985; Half a Year Together (R. Howard), 1987; Remembering (E. St. Vincent Millay), 1987; The Rain in the Trees (Merwin), S, fl, orch, 1993; S, orch, 2001; S, pf, 2006; Cuatro sonnets de amor (Neruda), v, pf, 1999-2003

BIBLIOGRAPHY
K.R. Schwarz: "Tobias Picker," *Music and Musicians*, ix (1985), 10–11

JOHN VAN DER SLICE

Pickett, Wilson (*b* Prattville, AL, 18 March 1941; *d* Reston, VA, 19 Jan 2006). Soul singer and songwriter. He moved to Detroit with his family at the age of 14. He first recorded in 1957 as part of the gospel quartet the Violinaires. Having decided to sing secular music, Pickett replaced Joe Stubbs in 1959 as lead singer of another Detroit-based vocal group, the Falcons, whose members included future soul stars Eddie Floyd and Mack Rice. In 1962 Pickett composed and sang lead on the Falcons' second hit, "I found a love," following which he began a solo career.

After brief stints with the Correctone and Double L labels, in 1964 he signed with Atlantic Records. After an undistinguished session in New York, Atlantic co-owner Jerry Wexler suggested that Pickett should record in Memphis at Stax Records. Wexler believed that the Southern musicians and their "live-in-the-studio" approach to recording would be better suited to Pickett's gospel-based style. In 1965 Pickett recorded three sessions at Stax where he was backed by the house band Booker T. and the MGs (without Booker T. Jones, who was away at college) and the Memphis Horns. Four hits resulted: "In the Midnight Hour," "Don't fight it," "634-5789 (Soulsville U.S.A.)," and "Ninety-nine and a Half (won't do)." After Stax closed its doors to outside sessions, Wexler took Pickett to record in Muscle Shoals, Alabama, where he cut such hits as "Land of 1,000 Dances," "Mustang Sally," and "Funky Broadway." Possessing perhaps the harshest voice in soul music, Pickett had landed more than 40 records in the rhythm-and-blues and pop charts by the mid-1970s. In 1991 he was inducted into the Rock and Roll Hall of Fame. Two years later he received a Pioneer Award from the Rhythm and Blues Foundation. In 1999 after a 12-year hiatus, Pickett cut his final album, the critically acclaimed *It's Harder Now*, with producer Jon Tiven.

BIBLIOGRAPHY
G. Hirshey: *Nowhere to Run: the Story of Soul Music* (New York, 1984)

P. Guralnick: *Sweet Soul Music* (New York, 1986)

J. Wexler and D. Ritz: *Rhythm and the Blues: a Life in American Music* (New York, 1993)

R. Bowman: *Soulsville U.S.A.: the Story of Stax Records* (New York, 1997)

ROB BOWMAN

Picon, Molly (*b* New York, NY, 1 June 1898; *d* Lancaster, PA, 6 April 1992). Yiddish singer, lyricist, actress, and comedienne. Raised in Philadelphia, where her mother worked as a seamstress in the Yiddish theater, Molly Picon made her debut in that city's Arch Street Theater as a child, exhibiting the irrepressible zest and high-octane antics for which she would become famous. During a trip to Europe, where her husband/manager Jacob Kalish brought her to improve her Yiddish, Picon made her first film *Ost und West* (re-released as "Good Luck") in Vienna in 1923. Returning home, she teamed as lyricist with composer Joseph Rumshinsky (1881–1956) for dozens of hit shows—including three in 1925.

Breaking her partnership with Rumshinsky in 1933, Picon next teamed with American-born composer Abe Ellstein, with whom she recorded many of the songs for which she would be remembered: "Abi Gezint" ("As Long As You're Healthy") and "Tif Vi Di Nakht" ("Deep As the Night.") Picon's popularity grew on the Yiddish screen with *Yidl Mitn Fidl* (Jew and His Violin, 1934) and *Mamele* (Little Mother, 1938), and on radio with appearances on *Der Tog Program* ("The Day Program," WABC, 1927–33), *I Give You My Life* (WMGM, 1939), and *Nancy from Delancey* (WHN, 1941).

One of the few Yiddish theater stars to cross over to an English-speaking audience, Picon enjoyed popularity on Broadway in *Morning Star* (1940) and *Milk and Honey* (1961–63), in Hollywood films such as *The Naked City* (1948) and *Fiddler on the Roof* (1971), and on television in *Car 54, Where Are You?* (1961–63) and *Gomer Pyle, USMC* (1968). Picon performed actively until shortly before her death.

HENRY SAPOZNIK

Picou, Alphonse (Floristan) (*b* New Orleans, LA, 19 Oct 1878; *d* New Orleans, LA, 4 Feb 1961). Jazz clarinetist. A Creole of color, he learned guitar and clarinet as a youth, and began playing clarinet professionally by the age of 16. He was adept at both reading and embellishment-oriented improvising, and moved easily among the brass bands, orchestras, and smaller dance bands of the downtown Creole community, remaining active into the 1930s. His light skin enabled him to work occasionally with white bands. He played B♭ and E♭ clarinets with brass bands, including the Excelsior and Tuxedo bands, and while with the latter is said to have developed an obbligato solo on "High Society" (a swinging paraphrase of the piccolo part from the standard march arrangement) that has since become a celebrated set-piece in the repertory of traditional jazz. During the Depression Picou left music to work as a tinsmith, but with the revival of interest in traditional jazz he returned, recording with Kid Rena in 1940. Prominent in the music scene of postwar New Orleans, he enjoyed stints with Papa Celestin (1940s), as a leader (1950s), and with Paul Barbarin towards the end of his life. His recordings reveal a clear tone with spare vibrato, fluency across registers, semi-staccato articulation, and a light swing.

BIBLIOGRAPHY

W.J. Schafer: "Breaking into 'High Society': Musical Metamorphoses in Early Jazz," *JJS* ii/2 (1975), 53

R.H. Knowles: *Fallen Heroes: a History of New Orleans Brass Bands* (New Orleans, 1996)

CHARLES E. KINZER

Picuris. Native American tribe of New Mexico; one of the eastern Pueblo groups. (*See* PUEBLO, EASTERN.) The Picuris language is a dialect of Tiwa; in their own language, they call themselves *P'iwwel*. They are descendants of the Ancestral Puebloans who have inhabited the southwestern United States for thousands of years. There are some 1800 enrolled members of the Picuris tribe, fewer than 90 of whom live in the pueblo.

Traditional Picuris music includes songs to accompany ceremonial dances, Catholic feast day dances, corn grinding, gambling games, social dances, ditch-cleaning, and ceremonial picnics. Other genres include songs in stories and lullabies. Picuris music is similar to that of the other eastern Pueblos, except the singers use a stronger degree of vocal tension. Men perform ceremonial songs in unblended unison. Instrumental accompaniment varies by genre; for example, ceremonial dance songs are accompanied by a drum and a hand-held container rattle, while picnic songs, performed as part of a five-day spring ceremony, are accompanied by striking arrows together. Men preparing to clean the irrigation ditches in March accompany their songs by tapping a stone or stick on their shovels. Sunset Dances, performed the night before ceremonial races take place, are accompanied by metal bells, perhaps worn on the dancers' outfits. Notched-stick rasps accompany Basket Dances. Bundle drums, made of rolled hides struck with sticks, have also been reported. The violin and guitar, played by Spanish New Mexican musicians, accompany MATACHINES dances.

Songs for ceremonies such as the Corn Dance or the Basket Dance employ a complex sectional form similar to the *AABBA* form heard in kachina and maskless kachina songs among other Pueblos. Songs for game animal dances, such as the Deer Dance, Buffalo Dance, or Mountain Sheep Dance, feature the form heard in other Pueblo animal dances. These songs begin with an unmetered introduction followed by a slow song and then a fast song. Both songs employ paired phrase structure, with patterned pauses created by shifts from duple to triple meter, as well as extended cadential phrases. Ditch-cleaning and picnic songs also use this form. Social dance songs use a simpler paired-phrase structure, while a Captive Dance song features the kind of strophic form with asymmetrical repetition heard in Plains Indian powwow songs.

The music of Picuris awaits thorough documentation; few recordings or scholarly studies exist, although annual dance events continue to take place at the pueblo.

DISCOGRAPHY

Picuris Indian Songs (Taos Recordings and Publications TRP-5, 1964)

"… So These Won't Be Forgotten" (Taos Recordings and Publications TRP-121, 1968)

Ditch-Cleaning and Picnic Songs of Picuris Pueblo (Indian House IH-1051, 1971)

Music of New Mexico: Native American Traditions (Smithsonian Folkways, SF CD 40408, 1992)

Proud Heritage: A Celebration of Traditional American Indian Music (Indian House IH-9601, 1996)

BIBLIOGRAPHY

J.P. Harrington and H.H. Roberts: *Picuris Children's Stories, with Texts and Songs* (Washington, DC, 1928)

D.N. Brown: "Picuris Pueblo," *Handbook of North American Indians, Vol. 9: Southwest*, ed. A. Ortiz (Washington, DC, 1979), 268–77

D.N. Brown: "Dance as Experience: the Deer Dance of Picuris Pueblo," *Southwest Indian Ritual Drama*, ed. C. J. Frisbie (Albuquerque, NM, 1980), 71–92

J.P. Harrington: *Indian Tales from Picuris Pueblo* (Santa Fe, NM, 1989)

DONALD N. BROWN/VICTORIA LINDSAY LEVINE

Pieczonka, Albert [Pięçonka, Albert Emil Theodor] (*b* Königsberg, East Prussia [now Kaliningrad, Russia], 10 Feb 1828; *d* New York, 12 April 1912). Prussian composer, pianist, and teacher. Pieczonka's paternal ancestors originated from Lissa, Prussia (now Leszno, Poland). He studied piano with Moscheles and composition at the Leipzig Conservatory. He moved to London in 1858 and became a successful performer, composer, and teacher. As a performer, he specialized in Beethoven. In 1879 he published the set of ten *Danses de Salon* for piano, the first of which is the *Tarantella* in A minor. In 1880, Pieczonka moved to New York where he formed the *Kempa Ladies' Orchestra* with his wife and six daughters. From 1882–7, the orchestra toured the United States and Canadian Maritimes.

Pieczonka was well-known during his lifetime for writing concert-pieces and parlor music for the piano. His compositional style is characterized by accessible melody and impressive pianistic effects that are technically not demanding. His *Tarantella* in A minor quickly brought him recognition in the United States and continues to be a popular pedagogical recital piece. He was also well-known for his works *Polish Chivalry*, *Dancing Waves*, and *Grande Polonaise Héroïque*. There are striking similarities between Pieczonka's *Grande Marche Triomphale* (1880) and the college fight song "On, Wisconsin!" (1909).

BIBLIOGRAPHY

S.P. Erickson: "Music in America: A New Nineteenth Century Composer," *Keyboard Companion*, xix/2 (2008), 6–15

STEPHEN P. ERICKSON

Piegan. Native American tribe of Montana, and Alberta, Canada; *see* BLACKFOOT (I).

Pierce, Webb (*b* nr West Monroe, LA, 8 Aug 1921; *d* Nashville, TN, 24 Feb 1991). Country-music singer, guitarist, songwriter, and publisher. He performed as a guitarist on radio station KMLB (Monroe, LA) before 1950, when he joined the "LOUISIANA HAYRIDE" on KWKH (Shreveport, LA). Recording contracts with the local Pacemaker label (*c*1950), Four-Star, and Decca (1951) allowed him to resign his part-time job as a clerk at Sears, Roebuck and concentrate on music. After his initial hit, "Wondering" (1952), he gained national attention with "Back Street Affair" (1952), one of the first country songs to deal forthrightly with adultery. An equally important landmark was "There stands the glass" (1953), a classic drinking song and the first country hit to use the pedal steel guitar, played by Bud Isaacs. It became the favorite backup instrument in country music for the next two decades, and Pierce was the first of many country singers whose slurs, octave jumps, and use of dynamics complemented its sound. During his peak years (1951–71), Pierce had eight no.1 hits, and 81 sides on the country chart; among the most influential were "Slowly" (1954); "In the Jailhouse Now" (1955), a remake of the old Jimmie Rodgers tune; and "Why, Baby, Why" (1955), a duet with Red Sovine. In 1952 he joined the cast of the *Grand Ole Opry*, where he inherited Hank Williams's mantle as the show's leading honky-tonk singer. With Opry manager Jim Denny he founded Cedarwood Music in 1953; it was a leading Nashville publishing firm whose writers included Danny Dill, John D. Loudermilk, Carl Perkins, and Mel Tillis. One of the most commercially successful of modern country singers, Pierce had a nasal tenor voice that was influential in defining the honky-tonk vocal style in the 1950s.

RECORDINGS
(selective list)
(all recorded for Decca)

As soloist: "Back Street Affair" (1952, 28369); "Wondering" (1952, 46364); "There stands the glass" (1953, 28834); "Slowly" (1954, 28991); "In the Jailhouse Now" (1955, 29391); "Holiday for Love" (1957, 30419); "A Thousand Miles Ago" (1959, 30858); "Sweet Lips" (1961, 31249); "Memory #1" (1964, 31617); "Fool, Fool, Fool" (1967, 32167)

With R. Sovine: "Why, Baby, Why?" (1955, 29755)

BIBLIOGRAPHY

T.E.W. Laird: *Louisiana Hayride: Radio and Roots Music along the Red River* (New York and Oxford, 2005)

CHARLES K. WOLFE/R

Pi Kappa Lambda. Music honor society, founded in 1918; *see* FRATERNITIES AND SOCIETIES.

Pikuni. Native American tribe of Montana and Alberta, Canada; *see* BLACKFOOT (I).

Pilafian, (J.) Sam(uel) (*b* Miami, FL, 25 Oct 1949). Tubist and educator. Pilafian studied with Rex Conner at the Interlochen National Music Camp, where he became the second tubist in 50 years to win the camp's concerto competition (1967). He attended the University of Miami where he studied with Constance Weldon. He may be best known for being a founding member of the Empire Brass Quintet, with which he performed from 1972 until 1993. During this same period he served on the faculties of the Tanglewood Institute and Boston University. Pilafian is also an active jazz tubist who taught at the Berklee College of Music (1971–4). His group Travelin' Light, with guitarist Frank Vignola, released several recordings in the 1990s. From 1994 to 2012 Pilafian served as Professor of Music on the faculty of Arizona State University, and he currently teaches at the University of Miami. In addition to his work as a recitalist, he has gained prominence as a composer and an author of pedagogical texts. With tubist Patrick Sheridan, he coauthored *The Breathing Gym* and *The Brass Gym*. He is the composer of *Relentless Grooves*, a series of compositions featuring electronic accompaniments that reflect various ethnic music sources.

BIBLIOGRAPHY

R.W. Morris and E.R. Goldstein, eds.: *The Tuba Source Book* (Bloomington, IN, 1996)
P. Sheridan and S. Pilafian: *The Brass Gym: A Comprehensive Daily Workout for Brass Players* (Mesa, AZ, 2008)

RICHARD PERRY

Pilcher & Sons. Firm of organ builders. It was founded by Henry Pilcher (1798–1880), a native of Dover, England, who had trained with his elder brother in London. He immigrated to the United States in 1832, first setting up a workshop in Newark, New Jersey, but moved to New Haven, Connecticut, in 1839, where he built at least two organs and was also organist of Trinity Church. In 1844 he returned to Newark, but moved in 1852 to St. Louis, Missouri, where his sons Henry Jr. (1828–90) and William (*b* 1830) joined him under the name of Henry Pilcher & Sons. There a substantial organ was built in 1850 for St. Paul's Church, St. Louis. In 1863 the company moved to Chicago; Henry Pilcher Sr. retired in 1872, and in 1874 under the direction of Henry Jr. and his four sons, the company made a final move to a new factory in Louisville, Kentucky, where it prospered in the early 20th century. In 1904 Pilcher built the organ for the Louisiana Purchase Exposition in St. Louis, and its largest instrument was built in 1929 for the Memorial Auditorium in Louisville. The firm carried on the English tonal tradition into the 20th century and was noted for its complex but reliable wind-chest design, patented by William E. Pilcher. His sons Gerard W. and William E. Jr. continued to run the company until shortly after Gerard's death in 1941, but the business never fully recovered from the depression years and was unable to survive the World War II era. It closed in 1944, and its assets were sold to the M.P. Möller firm of Hagerstown, MD.

BIBLIOGRAPHY

"American Organ Builders of Today: Henry Pilcher's Sons," *The Diapason*, xvi/6 (1925)
M. Lippincott: "Henry Pilcher: Organ Builder," *Quarterly Bulletin* [New York Historical Society], xxv/4 (1943), 87
S.E. Koehler: "Memoirs of an Organ Builder," *The Tracker*, ixx/2 (1975) 12–17
E.T. Schmitt: "The English Background of the Pilchers," *The Tracker*, xxxvii/1 (1993) 4–12

BARBARA OWEN

Pilsbury, Amos (*b* Newbury, MA, 15 Oct 1772; *d* Charleston, SC, 19 Oct 1812). Composer and tunebook compiler. Pilsbury and his family settled in Charleston, South Carolina, sometime before May 1798, when he first advertised there as a music copyist. In Charleston he worked primarily as a schoolmaster at the city's Orphan House and then at the private academy of the St. Andrew's Society. During his tenure in Charleston, however, Pilsbury never advertised to teach music. In late 1799 he published a compilation of 240 tunes called *The United States' Sacred Harmony* (Boston, 1799). Of the 30 previously unknown tunes in this compilation, Pilsbury claimed authorship of 25. In subsequent years, a few of Pilsbury's tunes appear in other published compilations, including the *Choral-book* (Boston, 1816) of Charleston Episcopal organist Jacob Eckhard. While in Charleston, Pilsbury also published a text-only anthology, *Sacred Songster* (Charleston, 1809). A later edition of Pilsbury's songster was advertised in Charleston as late as 1826. Although isolated from the mainstream of New England sacred music currents, Pilsbury's compilations and original works exerted a perceptible influence on the development of American folk hymnody, especially in subsequent tune compilations published in the southern states.

BIBLIOGRAPHY

K.D. Kroeger: "A Yankee Tunebook from the Old South: Amos Pilsbury's *The United States' Sacred Harmony*," *Hymn*, xxxii/3 (July 1981), 154–62
D.W. Music: "Seven 'New' Tunes in Amos Pilsbury's *United States' Sacred Harmony* (1799) and Their Use in Four-Shape Shape-Note Tunebooks of the Southern United States before 1860," *AM*, xiii/4 (1995), 403–47

NICHOLAS MICHAEL BUTLER

Pima. Native Americans of central Arizona. They inhabit a stark desert along the dry riverbeds of the Salt and Gila rivers; as recently as the early 20th century these rivers flowed year round, and the Pima practiced irrigation agriculture and ate fish. Owing to their central location on two important waterways, the Pima had regular contact with many other cultures. The Apache, to the northeast, and the Yuma, to the west, were dreaded enemies. The Maricopa, fleeing from the Yuma, eventually settled in central Arizona near the Pima, who learned from them much about Yuman lifestyle, including songs. The Pima (called Akimel O'odham by the Tohono o'odham) maintained friendly relations with their Tohono relatives (formerly called Papago), who lived to their south (they speak mutually intelligible dialects of the Piman language). In the last half of the 19th century, the Pima provided food and assistance to many English-speaking travelers (including missionaries) in Arizona; as a result of these friendly contacts many settled in the area. A majority of the Pima was Christianized by the early 20th century; Protestant missionaries (as opposed to the Catholics who came to the area before them) forbade the celebration of traditional ceremonies, dancing, and singing, resulting in a loss of many traditional song genres. Frank Russell, who visited the Pima in 1901–2, reported that no traditional songs were heard in the Pima villages, although he elicited over 200 song texts with the help of Jose Lewis, his Tohono interpreter.

Pima musical style is nearly identical to that of the Tohono O'odham, though more individual singing styles may be noted now, possibly because a strong performance continuum was lacking from the 1890s to the 1960s. The main accompanying instrument is the gourd rattle, used by some singers as a drumstick with which they strike an inverted cardboard box. The rasp (for healing songs), the inverted basket drum, and a three-hole cane flute were played but today are rarely encountered. According to Russell, eight categories of song existed: myth, game, Round Dance, hunting, medicine, girl's puberty, rain, and war, though song naming conventions indicate that many more genres existed previously. Only social and Round Dance songs remain widely known; these are often named for birds or other animals (such as the swallow, bluebird, oriole, or butterfly). Specific songs open and close the singing and dancing that take place during a night's ceremonies; the bulk of the songs are chosen, from a corpus of about 200, at the discretion of the lead singer. Each song cycle is said to have been dreamed by a Pima and is normally named for the being who taught the songs. The cycles often tell of a journey in which the singer and teacher are transported to important landmarks in Pima land. The songs describe various creatures and nocturnal objects made by Earth Medicine Man and are intended to help the Pima better understand their relation to the universe. The opening songs of a cycle usually speak of the sun setting in the west and the sound of songs in the distance, while the closing songs tell of the sky in the east becoming light and the animals waking.

In the 1960s and 70s several traditional song and dance genres were reintroduced to teach Pima traditions to younger members. At the Salt River Community Basket Dance songs were relearned, and young girls were taught how to make traditional dance dresses and yucca baskets and how to dance with the baskets. One of the Gila River communities now performs the *Matachina*, a dance of Spanish origin found throughout the Southwest, with both young men and girls participating (the latter a Piman invention). Another modern genre, developed in the 20th century, is the Heaven song. Heaven songs describe Jesus and Mary and tell of the salvation offered the Pima through Christian beliefs. They are not translations of Christian hymns but rather indigenous expressions of Christian doctrine in traditional Pima musical style. These songs also are dreamed, often in association with a ritual event such as baptism or first communion.

Nontraditional musical groups of the Pima include the Salt River Indian Band (an amateur community ensemble) and various rock and acculturated popular groups with varying organization and membership (for example, *see* CHICKEN SCRATCH). In the mid-1970s a pan-Indian style drum was developed in the town of Sacaton, Arizona. Powwow music can be heard at community events, such as annual rodeos. Due to the proximity of Piman lands to metropolitan Phoenix, many non-Piman Native American Church members began to hold meetings on Piman land and now some Pimas also practice the peyote way.

See also NATIVE AMERICAN MUSIC.

DISCOGRAPHY
Songs from the Pima (Can. ARP 6066, 1970)
Traditional Pima Dance Songs (Can. 8011, 1978)
Pima Express: *Time Waits for No One* (Can. CR8118, 2006)
Earl Ray: *Traditional Songs of the Salt River Pima* (Can. CR6324, 2005)

BIBLIOGRAPHY
F. Russell: "The Pima Indian," *Bureau of American Ethnology, 26th Annual Report* (Washington, DC, 1904–5/R1975)
G. Herzog: "A Comparison of Pueblo and Pima Musical Styles," *Journal of American Folklore*, xlix/194 (1936), 283–417
N. Ware: "Survival and Change in Pima Indian Music," *EthM*, xiv/1 (1970), 100–13
D. Bahr and J.R. Haefer: "Song in Piman Curing," *EthM*, xxii/1 (1978), 89–122
D. Bahr, J. Giff, and M. Havier: "Piman Songs on Hunting," *EthM*, xxiii/1 (1979), 245–96
J. Giff: "Pima Blue Swallow Songs of Gratitude," *Speaking, Singing and Teaching*, eds. F. Barkin and E. Brandt (Tempe, AZ, 1980)
D. Bahr: "Pima Swallow Songs," *Cultural Anthropology*, i/2 (1986), 171–87
D. Bahr: "Papago Ocean Songs and the Wi:gita," *Journal of the Southwest*, xxxiii/5 (1991), 539–56
D. Kozak: "Swallow Dizziness, the Laughter of Carnival, and Kateri," *Wicazo Sa Review*, viii/2 (1992), 1–10
D. Bahr, V. Joseph with L. Paul: *Ants and Orioles: Showing the Art of Pima Poetry* (Salt Lake City, UT, 1997)
R. Valenzuela: "The Pima and Maricopa Villages: Oases at a Cultural Crossroads," *Journal of Arizona History*, xxxix (1998), 345–78
                                                                  J. RICHARD HAEFER

Pimsleur, Solomon (*b* Paris, France, 19 Sept 1900; *d* New York, NY, 22 April 1962). Composer. His family immigrated to New York in 1903. He received an MA in literature at Columbia University (1923), where he studied composition with Daniel Gregory Mason. After receiving a fellowship in 1926, he studied with RUBIN GOLDMARK at the Juilliard School, and then at the Mozarteum in Salzburg. With his sister, Susan Pimsleur Puma, he ran an artists' agency and production company; he was also known as a pianist and lecturer. Pimsleur wrote over 120 works for a range of ensembles. He frequently combined musical with literary interests, setting to music poetry of William Shakespeare, the English Romantics, and 20th-century authors (including Kathleen Raine, Wilfred Owen, and himself). His romantic neoclassicism was often the vehicle for emotional indulgence (*Symphony to Terror and Despair* op.55, *Melancholy Sonata* op.56, *Heart Rending Sonata for String-Sextet* op.77), though he achieved a greater universality of expression in, for example, the *Symphonic Ballade* op.18, no.5. At the time of his death he had finished two acts of an opera based on the *Diary of Anne Frank*. His music manuscripts are at Columbia University and the Moldenhauer Archives at Washington State University.

BIBLIOGRAPHY
Compositores de América/Composers of the Americas, ed. Pan American Union, xiii (Washington, DC, 1967), 94 [incl. list of works]
                                                                  DAVID HUNTER/R

Pine, Rachel Barton (*b* Chicago, IL, 11 Oct 1974). Violinist. She began violin studies at the age of three. Her earliest teachers were Roland and Almita Vamos; she has also studied with Ruben Gonzalez, Werner Scholz, Elmira Darvarova, and several early music performance specialists. At the age of seven, Pine made her professional debut with the Chicago String Ensemble. Three years later she appeared with the Chicago SO performing Camille Saint-Saëns' *Introduction et Rondo Capriccioso* with Erich Leinsdorf conducting. Pine has won numerous international violin competition awards, including Montreal (1991), Kreisler (Vienna, 1992), Szigeti (Budapest, 1992), and the Queen Elisabeth (Brussels, 1993). In 1992 she became the first American and youngest performer to win a gold medal from the J.S. Bach International Violin Competition in Leipzig, Germany. She has worked with prestigious conductors including Charles Dutoit, Zubin Mehta, Neeme Järvi, and Plácido Domingo. Festival appearances include the Mozartwoche (2000), Salzburg Festival (2001), and the Montreal Chamber Music Festival (2006–11), where she premiered (2010) the last movement of Samuel Barber's long-lost 1928 Violin Sonata. Pine composes her own cadenzas to concertos by composers including Ludwig van Beethoven, Johannes Brahms, Franz Clement, Wolfgang Amadeus Mozart, and Niccolò Paganini. She also participates in historically informed interpretations of baroque, renaissance, and medieval music, performing with the period instrument ensemble Trio Settecento. To date Pine has released 16 recordings, including *Homage to Sarasate* (1992) with the pianist Samuel Sanders; *Brahms, Joachim: Violin Concertos* (2003) with the Chicago SO, which earned a Grammy Award nomination; and *Beethoven, Clement: Violin Concertos* (2008) featuring a newly published Concerto by Clement.

BIBLIOGRAPHY

"Rachel Barton Pine," *Strad*, cxix/1423 (Nov 2008), 30–4

R.B. Pine, ed.: *The Rachel Barton Collection: Original Compositions, Arrangements, Cadenzas and Editions for Violin* (New York, 2009)

ANNA E. KIJAS

P!nk [Moore, Alecia Beth] (*b* Doylestown, PA, 8 Sept 1979). Singer-songwriter. At the age of 16 Moore formed an R&B group called Choice with two other teenage girls, and they worked with industry producers for two years without releasing any studio albums before Moore chose to embark on a solo career. In 2000 she released her pop and R&B-influenced debut album *Can't Take Me Home* under the stage name P!nk. It went on to sell over 5 million copies in the United States, and she toured to support the album as the opening act for pop band *NSYNC's American tour. In 2001 she collaborated with Christina Aguilera, Mya, and Lil' Kim for their Grammy-winning interpretation of "Lady Marmalade" for the film *Moulin Rouge*, and later that year released her second album, *Missundaztood*. P!nk used the album to distance herself from her earlier pop-persona with a more intimate rock-influenced sound that won her two Grammy nominations. During this time she became actively involved with PETA, strongly advocating animal rights. In 2003 she released *Try This*, winning her another Grammy award, and followed it with 2005's *I'm Not Dead* and 2008's *Funhouse*. In 2010 P!nk released a compilation titled *Greatest Hits…So Far!!!*

JESSICA L. BROWN

Pinkard, Maceo (*b* Bluefield, WV, 27 June 1897; *d* New York, NY, 19 July 1962). Orchestrator and composer. An African American songwriter, he initially worked as a theatrical agent in Omaha, Nebraska, in 1914, publishing his first song in 1915. He moved to New York by 1920 where his "Don't cry little girl" was published in 1918 and the Original Dixieland Jazz Band recorded his "Sweet Mammy o' Mine" (1919). His writing for musicals included the book for *Liza* (1922) which moved from Daly's 63rd Street Theatre to 44th Street in 1923, the first black show on Broadway during the season, with 172 performances. Veteran Thaddeus Drayton recalled in 1963: "it was a great show with great tunes." Ethel Waters recorded several Pinkard songs including "Sugar" in 1925 (published 1927) and "Sweet Georgia Brown" (1925) which became one of the most frequently recorded tunes in jazz. In 1930 his "Them There Eyes" was published. His orchestrations were played by Paul Whiteman and Jean Goldkette, and recorded by Wilbur Sweatman (*Those Draftin' Blues*, 1918, Col. A-2645) and Fletcher Henderson (*Potomac River Blues*, 1923, Voc. B14740; *Come on, Baby*, 1928, Col. 14392-D). Bessie Smith recorded *Kitchen Man* (Col. 14435-D, words by Andy Razaf, composer identified as "Belledna," being Edna Bell Alexander or Mrs. Pinkard, but copyrighted by Razaf and Pinkard) in 1929 as did Sara Martin in 1928 (QRS R-7043-B). His music publishing house Pinkard Publications was still active in 1944.

BIBLIOGRAPHY

M. Stearns and J. Stearns: *Jazz Dance* (New York, 1968), 143

T. Lord: *Clarence Williams* (Chigwell, England, 1976), 286, 494

E. Southern: *Biographical Dictionary of Afro-American and African Musicians* (Westport, CT, 1982), 308

W.H. Kenney: "The Influence of Black Vaudeville on Early Jazz," *Black Perspective in Music*, xiv/3 (1986), 233–48

JEFFREY GREEN

Pinkham, Daniel (Rogers) (*b* Lynn, MA, 5 June 1923; *d* Natick, MA, 18 Dec 2006). Composer. He started playing the piano and composing at the age of five, and received organ and harmony lessons from CARL F. PFATTEICHER at Phillips Academy, Andover, Massachusetts (1937–40). Subsequently he studied composition with A.T. Merritt, A.T. DAVISON, WALTER PISTON and AARON COPLAND at Harvard University (1940–44) and with PAUL HINDEMITH, Arthur Honegger and SAMUEL BARBER at the Berkshire Music Center at Tanglewood. He took private lessons with NADIA BOULANGER in composition (1941–7), with Jean Chiasson, P.C. Aldrich, and WANDA LANDOWSKA on the harpsichord and with E. POWER BIGGS on the organ. He held teaching positions at the Boston Conservatory of Music, Simmons College in Boston, Boston University, Dartington Hall, and Harvard (1946–58); he became music director of King's Chapel, Boston (1958). In 1959 he joined the faculty of the New England Conservatory as a lecturer in music history, theory, composition, and the harpsichord, later establishing and chairing there the department of early music performance. He performed extensively on the harpsichord in a duo with the violinist Robert Brink, with the Boston SO and in solo recitals. Among his numerous awards are a Fulbright scholarship (1950), a Ford Foundation grant (1962), an American Academy of Arts and Sciences Prize, and five honorary doctorates. His works were commissioned by major institutions and have been widely performed.

Pinkham was a versatile composer whose prolific output covers a great variety of genres. His early involvement with church music as a student organist at Christ Church, Boston, and his attraction to biblical stories and liturgy led to a large body of work for organ, short choral pieces, songs, and extended sacred compositions for choir and instruments. Attracted to bell-like sonorities since his time as a school carillonneur at Andover, he incorporated the evocation of bells into many of his instrumental compositions. Reflecting the influence of Stravinsky and Hindemith and his commitment to the early music revival, Pinkham's music of the 1930s and 40s embraces church modes, 16th-century contrapuntal techniques and 17th-century forms and instruments. Though in the 1950s and 60s he employed chromaticism and dodecaphony and investigated new tonal and intervallic relationships, he never used serial techniques dogmatically, instead combining 12-note rows with tonal elements. In 1970 he began to explore electronic music, creating tapes in his own studio. In many of his numerous works for tape and live musicians, especially organ and voices, he allows the performer rhythmic flexibility and free choice in the order of events to avoid rigid synchronization. With his strong interest in theater and drama, Pinkham provided theatrical instructions for some of his cantatas, while other works, such as *The Passion of Judas* (1976), can be performed either in concert or as a theater piece. He wrote articles for journals on music.

WORKS
(selective list)

Stage: Passion of Judas (cant./op), 1976; Garden Party (op, Pinkham, N. Farber), S, Bar, 2 actors, chorus, 5 insts, tape, 1976; The Dreadful Dining Car (comic melodrama, Pinkham, after M. Twain, N. Farber), Mez, actors, solo vv, 7 insts, 1982; The Left-Behind Beasts (music play for children, Pinkham), actors, chorus, chbr ens, perc, 1985; The Cask of Amontillado (op, Pinkham, after E.A. Poe), T, Bar, chorus, 6 insts, 2002

Choral: Wedding Cant., opt. solo vv, chorus, insts, 1956; Christmas Cant., chorus, insts, 1957; Easter Cant., chorus, insts, 1961; Requiem, solo vv, chorus, insts, 1963; Stabat mater, S, chorus, orch, 1964; St. Mark Passion, solo vv, chorus, orch, 1965; Jonah, spkr, solo vv, chorus, orch, 1967; Ascension Cant., chorus, orch, 1970; To Troubled Friends (J. Wright), chorus, str, tape, 1972; Daniel in the Lions' Den, nar, solo vv, chorus, insts, tape, 1972; Fanfares (Bible), T, chorus, insts, tape, 1975; Descent into Hell (Pinkham), solo vv, chorus, insts, tape, 1979; Hezekiah, solo vv, chorus, tpt, org, 1979; When God Arose, solo vv, chorus, insts, 1979; Before the Dust Returns, chorus, insts, 1981; Lauds, 2vv, insts, 1983; Dallas Anthem Book, chorus, org, 1984; Advent Cant., chorus, insts, 1991; Christmas Syms., solo vv, chorus, insts, 1992; The Dryden Te Deum (J. Dryden), chorus, insts, 1992; The Creation of the World, nar, chorus, insts, 1994; The Covenant Motets, chorus, org, 2001; Three Spiritual Madrigals (G.M. Hopkins), chorus, 2002; Advent Canticles, chorus, 2004; A Symphony of Hallelujahs, chorus, 2 tpts, db, org, 2006; many Psalm motets and works for choir with acc.

Solo vocal: The Song of Jephtha's Daughter (R. Hillyer), S, pf, 1963; 8 Poems of Gerard Manley Hopkins, Bar, va, 1964; Letters from St. Paul, S/T, org, 1965; Safe in their Alabaster Chambers (E. Dickinson), Mez, tape, 1972; Charm me asleep, Bar/Mez, gui, 1977; Transitions, Mez, bn/pf, 1979; Manger Scenes (N. Farber), S, pf, 1980; The Death of the Witch of Endor, A, hpd, perc, 1981; Music in the Manger (Farber), S, hpd/pf, 1981; The Wellesley Hills Psalm Book, medium v, org, 1983; Called Home (Dickinson), Mez, pf, 1996; Songs of Innocence (Blake), high v, fl, pf, 2001; Tuba Mirum, Bar, trbn, 2002; The word was made flesh, 1v, hp, 2005

Orch: Vn Conc., 1956; Sym. no.1, 1961; Catacoustical Measures, 1962; Sym. no.2, 1962; Signs of the Zodiac, opt. nar, orch, 1964; Org. Conc. no.1, 1970; Serenades, tpt, wind orch, 1979; Sym. no.3, 1985–6; Sym. no.4, 1990; Ov. Concertante, org solo, orch, 1992; Org. Conc. no.2, 1995; Org. Conc. no.3, 1996; Make Way for the Ducklings, nar, orch, 2002; works for band, music for TV and film

Chbr and solo inst: Sonata no.1, org, str, 1943; Conc., cel, hpd, 1955; Concertante no.3, org, cel, perc, 1962; Partita, hpd, 1962; Sonata no.3, org, str, 1968; Lessons, hpd, 1971; Toccatas for the Vault of Heaven, org, tape, 1971; Blessings, org, 1977; Epiphanies, org, 1978; Masks, hpd, chbr ens, 1978; Miracles, fl, org, 1978; Vigils, hp, 1982; Brass Qnt, 1983; Psalms, tpt, org, 1983; Str Qt, 1990; Organbook nos.1 and 2, 1991; Nocturnes, fl, gui, 1992; Preludes, pf, 1995–6; Divertimento, tpt, hp, 1997; Str Trio, 1998; Aurora, cl, org, 2000; Lections, org, 2004; The Saint Luke Organ Book, 2005; works for carillon

Arrs., many vocal, of works by Handel, Purcell, Schubert, Selby

Principal publishers: Peters, E.C. Schirmer

BIBLIOGRAPHY
M.W. Johnson: *The Choral Works of Daniel Pinkham* (diss., U. of Iowa, 1968)

J. McCray: "Pinkham: On Composing: an Interview with Daniel Pinkham," *Choral Journal*, xvii/2 (1976), 15–17

D.K. Cox: *Aspects of Compositional Styles of Three Selected Twentieth-Century American Composers of Choral Music: Alan Hovhaness, Ron Nelson, and Daniel Pinkham* (diss., U. of Missouri, Kansas City, 1978)

M.L. Corzine: *The Organ Works of Daniel Pinkham* (diss., U. of Rochester, Eastman School, 1979)

L. Raver: "The Solo Organ Music of Daniel Pinkham," *American Organist*, xvii/6 (1983), 35–7

M.E. Stallings: *Representative Works for Mixed Chorus by Daniel Pinkham: 1968–1983* (diss., U. of Miami, 1984)

K. DeBoer and J.B. Ahouse: *Daniel Pinkham: a Bio-Bibliography* (Westport, CT, 1988)

H. Pollack: "A Heritage Upheld: Daniel Pinkham," *Harvard Composers: Walter Piston and his Students, from Elliott Carter to Frederic Rzewski* (Metuchen, NJ, 1992), 189–207

M.A. Radice: "An Interview with Daniel Pinkham," *American Organist*, xxxi/8 (1997), 56–61

D. Spirro-Allen: *The Choral Music of Daniel Pinkham: A Pedagogical Analysis* (diss., Boston U., 1999)

T.R. Brown: *Stylistic Influences and Application of "Gebrauchsmusik" in the late choral cantatas of Daniel Pinkham* (diss., U. of Arizona, 2009)

SABINE FEISST

Pinza, Ezio (Fortunato) (*b* Rome, Italy, 18 May 1892; *d* Stamford, CT, 9 May 1957). Italian bass. Having studied at the Bologna Conservatory, he made his debut in 1914 in Soncino, near Crema, as Oroveso in *Norma*. After World War I he sang in the principal Italian houses. His appearance at the Metropolitan Opera as the Pontifex Maximus in Spontini's *La vestale* in 1926 began a period of 22 consecutive years as a leading bass in New York, where he sang 50 roles and became a great favorite of the public, as much for his handsome presence, engaging personality, and spirited acting as for his beautiful and cultivated *basso cantante*. Besides all the main Italian bass roles (among which his Padre Guardiano in *La forza del destino* and Fiesco in *Simon Boccanegra* deserve special mention), he was outstandingly successful as Don Giovanni and as Figaro; he sang also in many French operas, occasionally essayed Wagner in German, and undertook the title role of Boris Godunov in Italian. After leaving the Metropolitan, at the age of 56, he began a second career in musical comedy, operetta, and musical films, scoring an enormous success on Broadway in *South Pacific* (1949, Rodgers and Hammerstein). Pinza was unquestionably the most richly gifted and most accomplished Italian bass of his day, as is demonstrated by his numerous recordings, especially those made for Victor (1927–30), when his voice was in its prime.

BIBLIOGRAPHY

GMO; *GV* (J.B. Richards; J.P. Kenyon)

E. Pinza and R. Magidoff: *Ezio Pinza: an Autobiography* (New York, 1958/*R*)

J.B. Richards, J.P. Kenyon, and J. McPherson: "Ezio Pinza," *Record Collector*, xxvi (1980–81), 51–95, 101–37 [incl. discography]

J.B. Steane: *Singers of the Century* (London, 1996), 56–60

DESMOND SHAWE-TAYLOR/R

Pipe Corps. *See* DRUM CORPS.

Pipedreams. Nationally syndicated weekly radio broadcast by American Public Media with host and senior executive producer Michael Barone (*b* Kingston, PA, 1946). The initial broadcast on 3 January 1982 was carried by 64 stations. The first 14 broadcasts consisted of performances taped during the 1980 American Guild of Organists National Convention in Minnesota. After a brief hiatus, *Pipedreams* resumed broadcasting in October 1983 and settled into a regular 90-minute format. As of fall 2008, *Pipedreams* was carried by 145 stations, broadcasting to a weekly audience of 226,500. *Pipedreams* is the only nationally distributed weekly radio program showcasing the art of the pipe organ. Barone has been recognized with numerous awards for his work with *Pipedreams*, including the American Guild of Organists President's Award (1996), the Distinguished Service Award of the Organ Historical Society (1997), and the ASCAP Deems Taylor Award (2001). In November 2002 he was selected for induction into the Minnesota Music Hall of Fame. For about a decade before *Pipedreams* debuted, Barone had produced *The Organ Program* on Minnesota stations KSJR and KSJN on behalf of St. John's Abbey and the University in Collegeville.

ALLISON A. ALCORN

Pips. *See* GLADYS KNIGHT AND THE PIPS.

Piquete típico. Also known as *Orquesta típica*. A phrase used in Cuba to denote wind ensemble groups associated primarily with the nineteenth century that played dance repertoire of the period, most often *contradanzas*, *danzas*, and *danzones*. The instrumentation of such groups typically included two or more violins, two clarinets, acoustic bass, bassoon, trombone, cornet or trumpet, a güiro scraper, and timbales. The *piquete típico* format remained popular from the early nineteenth century through the turn of the twentieth century. At that time its popularity began to decline and other ensembles began to take its place in public life, most notably the smaller Charanga francesa bands of flute and violin, and large jazz bands.

A group known as the Piquete Típico Cubano continues to exist in Havana. The revolutionary government formalized its status in 1963 under the direction of musicologist Odilio Urfé. The mission of the group is to maintain older repertoire that might otherwise not be heard. In the 1970s and 1980s, the Piquete recorded LP records of historical dance repertoire for the EGREM record label. Under the guidance of its current director, Jorge Vistel Columbié, the ensemble often performs together with dancers in Old Havana, and has created video shorts for educational purposes.

ROBIN MOORE

Piracy. Music piracy is commonly understood as the unauthorized duplication, dissemination, or broadcast of recorded or printed musical texts. There is some debate over whether music piracy necessarily involves seeking profit from the activity. At the national and international levels, combinations of discursive and punitive juridical and technological strategies have been employed to combat the practice.

1. Printed music. 2. Radio. 3. Recorded music. 4. The Internet.

1. PRINTED MUSIC. Before the emergence of recording, piracy centered on sheet music production and distribution, primarily in the industrialized nations. In the UK, music pirates contradicted first the Royal Charter of the Stationer's Company (1557) and later the Statute of Anne (1709) either as individuals, loose syndicates, or highly organized groups using up-to-date methods for managing production and distribution. Piracy of theatrical productions was also common, especially in the case of unlicensed British productions performed in the United States whose intellectual property laws did not initially apply to foreign works.

2. RADIO. Pirate radio emerged in earnest in the UK in the 1960s as an alternative to the BBC. Commercial and non-commercial stations broadcast contemporary popular music from ships or decommissioned military fortifications in international waters. A resurgence of Pirate Radio in UK in the 1980s renewed resistance to licensing authorities who were seen to restrict freedom of musical expression. In the United States, pirate radio is less developed, much smaller in scale, and oriented toward protesting government regulation and promoting freedom of speech.

3. RECORDED MUSIC. As personal recording devices became more accessible in the 1970s, unauthorized audience recordings of live concert performances, known as "bootlegs," circulated among fans, often for free, sometimes sold by street vendors or at record stores. Performers such as the Grateful Dead (and many artists since) encouraged fan taping and swapping. The practice has become more efficient and widespread since the rise of the Internet. Certain artists see the practice as impeding their ability to profit from their work and actively discourage concert recording, often through security searches at concerts.

"Home taping" describes the transfer of pre-recorded music onto cassettes by music consumers themselves. Reacting to a general downturn in the US music economy in the early 1980s, and despite home taping's primary use in sharing music for free among small groups, the recording industry saw home taping as a significant threat: it was assumed that consumers were purchasing fewer recordings since they were able to make their own duplicates. Similar concerns have resurfaced after the emergence of successive technologies that enable consumers to record and distribute music.

Highly organized mass duplication and sale of CDs constitutes a significant for-profit market. In China it is estimated that unauthorized CDs of major international artists dominate the music market and account for hundreds of millions of dollars in lost profit for the major record labels. Despite purported detrimental effects for major record labels, black markets allow for the widespread proliferation of a variety of music in regions where authorized copies are expensive or otherwise inaccessible.

4. THE INTERNET. The unauthorized distribution of music online has spurred one of the liveliest debates about the relationship between music and the Internet. National and international industry lobbying groups are at the forefront of efforts to curtail the activity, and international trade agreements are increasingly concerned with issues involving intellectual property. Artists are divided as to whether FILE SHARING benefits or hinders their ability to profit from their music careers, while music fans appear to favor the practice. Largely without concern for profit, digital music files are freely shared among Internet users through websites, "MP3 blogs," Internet Relay Chat, email, file hosting sites, and peer-to-peer (P2P) technologies. Napster (2000–02) was one of the earliest P2P file-sharing applications, with many more emerging following its court-mandated shutdown in 2002. As of 2010 the BitTorrent file-sharing protocol was the favored P2P technology because it was well suited to the efficient transfer large amount of data among many users. Internet practices have renewed focus on music piracy and its rich history. As a result, it is difficult to conceive of a musical world that does not include such heated debates over musical property.

BIBLIOGRAPHY
(and other resources)
C. Heylin: *Bootleg: the Secret History of the Other Recording Industry* (New York, 1995)
W. Wang: *Steal this File Sharing Book: What they Won't Tell you about File Sharing* (San Francisco, 2004)
Steal This Film (2006) [documentary]
Steal This Film (Part 2) (2007) [documentary]
Good Copy Bad Copy: A documentary about the current state of copyright and culture, dir. A. Johnsen, R. Christensen, and H. Moltke (2007)
On Piracy and the Future of Media, dir. J. McArdle (2007)
M. Mason: *The Pirate's Dilemma: How Youth Culture Reinvented Capitalism* (New York, 2008)
A. Johns: *Piracy: the Intellectual Property Wars from Gutenberg to Gates* (Chicago, 2009)
A. Langlois, R. Sakolosky, and M. van der Zon: *Islands of Resistance 2: Pirate Radio in Canada* (Point Roberts, WA, 2010)
PAUL A. AITKEN

Pisaro, Michael (*b* Buffalo, NY, 4 Nov 1961). Composer, educator, and guitarist. He studied composition at DePaul University (BM 1983) and at Northwestern University (MA 1985, DMA 1988). His primary teachers were GEORGE FLYNN, BEN JOHNSTON, and ALAN B. STOUT. From 1986 to 2000 he taught composition and theory at Northwestern University, then moved in 2000 to California

Institute of the Arts, where he has also co-chaired the composition department. His music has been performed frequently in the United States, Europe, and Japan. His pieces have been selected twice by the ISCM jury for performance at World Music Days festivals (Copenhagen, 1996; Manchester, 1998), and his music has been heard at festivals in Vienna (Wien Modern, 1997), London (Cutting Edge, 2007), Huddersfield (2009), Glasgow (INSTAL 2009), Berlin (Maerzmusik, 2010), New York (Amplify: stones, 2011), and elsewhere.

Pisaro's overarching compositional interests include the exploration of minute sonic and timbral details, silence, and the way in which these elements relate over time. In his formative years, the distorted organ and guitars of progressive rock proved catalytic, as did the innovative musical structures, timbres, and orchestrations of Eric Dolphy, Booker Little, John Cage, and Alvin Lucier. These diverse influences led Pisaro to an interest in the relationships between timbre and harmony that would become a determining factor in his compositional aesthetic. Beginning in the early 1990s exposure to works emanating from the Berlin-based Wandelweiser collective cemented his compositional and philosophical trajectory. The composers associated with Wandelweiser—including Antoine Beuger, Jürg Frey, and Radu Malfatti—frequently draw on works by American experimental composers, beginning with Charles Ives, as points of departure for their unconventionally scored compositions, often containing verbal instructions. In 1995 Pisaro joined the collective, with which he now publishes, and since has created over 120 works for a wide-ranging variety of instrumental, orchestral, and electroacoustic forces. Several adopt post-Cageian schemas for opening up performance situations, such as the two *Space* pieces for audience (1994 and 1997). Many other compositions highlight the timbral intricacies and decays associated with a single instrument, such as *Breath* for solo alto saxophone (1994), *Mind is Moving (I)* for solo guitar (1995), and *Fade* for solo piano (2000). *Hearing Metal 1* for recorded tam-tam and sine tones (2007) was composed in close collaboration with percussionist Greg Stuart, whose role in Pisaro's compositional process may be likened to David Tudor's association with Cage. Works for larger ensemble include *Ricefall* for 16 performers (2004) and *A Wave and Waves* for 100 percussionists (2007).

The recording process has become increasingly vital to Pisaro's compositional aesthetic. *The Transparent City* (2004–6) is a series of field recordings imbued with sine tones that emphasize and destabilize "harmonic" relationships in the recorded soundscapes. Subsequent pieces, such as *Asleep, Street, Pipes, Tones* (2009) and *July Mountain* (2009), juxtapose electronics and field recordings with conventional instruments.

BIBLIOGRAPHY
D. Warburton: "The Sound of Silence," *Signal to Noise*, xxiv (2002), 34–7
J. Gottschalk: *Perception and Actuality: an Application of William James's Experiential Approach to the Music of Alvin Lucier and Michael Pisaro* (diss., Northwestern U., 2008)
G. Stuart: *A Percussionist's Practice* (diss., U. of California, San Diego, 2009)
MARC MEDWIN

Pisk, Paul A(madeus) (*b* Vienna, Austria, 16 May 1893; *d* Los Angeles, CA, 12 Jan 1990). Composer and musicologist of Austrian birth. His teachers included Schreker (counterpoint) and ARNOLD SCHOENBERG (composition). After receiving the doctorate in musicology from the University of Vienna (1916) and a diploma in conducting from the Vienna Conservatory (1919), he helped to found the Austrian section of ISCM, worked as a periodicals editor and theory teacher (1920–34), and directed the music department of the Volkshochschule (1922–34). Pisk's connections with ISCM led to acquaintances with American composers such as Cowell and Sessions. Through Frederick Jacobi, he was invited to New York to play Austrian music on CBS and hear performances, sponsored by the League of Composers, of his own works. He immigrated to the United States in 1936, where he renewed contact with Schoenberg, Milhaud, and Hindemith. In 1937 he joined the faculty of the University of Redlands, California, becoming head of the music department in 1948. He was later appointed professor at the University of Texas, Austin (1951–63), and Washington University in St Louis (1963–72). He eventually settled in Los Angeles, where he continued to teach, compose, lecture, and write, his chief topics being Schoenberg and the Second Viennese School. Pisk's compositions tend towards atonality, but do not employ 12-note techniques. His thematic and motivic construction reveals a concern for linear relationships that develop contrapuntally within traditional forms and procedures. Harmonies are based on intervallic structures derived from the melodic contour. Many of his works, while chromatic, employ folk melodies. The American Musicological Society awards a prize in his name to the best scholarly paper presented by a graduate student at their annual conference.

BIBLIOGRAPHY

GMO

J. Glowacki, ed.: *Paul A. Pisk: Essays in His Honor* (Austin, TX, 1966)

T.W. Collins: *The Instrumental Music of Paul A. Pisk* (diss., U. of Missouri, Kansas City, 1972)

E. Antokoletz: "A Survivor of the Vienna Schoenberg Circle: An Interview with Paul A. Pisk," *Tempo*, cliv (1985), 15–21

H.-B. Dietz: "Paul A. Pisk: Eulogy," *Newsletter: The American Musicological Society*, xx/11 (1990), 8

ELLIOTT ANTOKOLETZ/R

Piston, Walter (Hamor) (*b* Rockland, ME, 20 Jan 1894; *d* Belmont, MA, 12 Nov 1976). Composer and teacher. His family was largely of English origin, though his paternal grandfather, Antonio Pistone, an Italian seaman, arrived in Maine from Genoa. In 1905 the family moved from Rockland, Maine, to Boston, where Piston, after concentrating on engineering in high school, studied art at the Massachusetts Normal Art School (1912–6). It was there that he met his future wife, painter Kathryn Nason. Largely self-taught as a musician, he earned money playing the piano and violin in dance bands. From 1917 to 1921 he also played the violin in orchestras and chamber ensembles under the direction of Georges Longy. When the United States entered World War I, he quickly learned to play the saxophone so that he could join the Navy Band. During his service in the Navy, he took up other band instruments as well.

Piston entered Harvard in 1919 as a special music student; he enrolled formally in 1920 and graduated with honors in 1924. His teachers included A.T. DAVISON and EDWARD BURLINGAME HILL, among others. From 1921 to 1924 he conducted the Pierian Sodality, Harvard's student orchestra. He pursued further studies with Paul Dukas, NADIA BOULANGER, and George Enescu at the Ecole Normale de Musique (1924–6), where he played the viola in the school orchestra. His two earliest extant works, Three Pieces for the flute, clarinet, and bassoon (1925) and the Piano Sonata (1926), reflect the influences of Boulanger and Dukas, respectively. The lean counterpoint of the former reveals a neoclassical elegance related to the styles of Igor Stravinsky and Paul Hindemith, while the romantic grandeur of the latter suggests an affinity with Johannes Brahms and César Franck. In subsequent scores, such as the Flute Sonata (1930), Piston merged these two aesthetics, forging a conservative modernist style of his own.

Upon his return to Boston in 1926 Piston joined the music department at Harvard, a position he held until his retirement in 1960. He did most of his composing during the summer months, which he spent on a dairy farm in Woodstock, Vermont. His occasional attempts at descriptive music, such as *Tunbridge Fair* for symphonic band (1950) and *Three New England Sketches* for orchestra (1959), took rural New England as their subject. Even in his more abstract works, his syncopated rhythms, austere textures, and clipped forms bespoke a special attachment to that part of the country. "Is the Dust Bowl more American than, say, a corner in the Boston Athenaeum?" he asked. "Would not a Vermont village furnish as American a background for a composition as the Great Plains?"

He found an early advocate in Serge Koussevitzky, the conductor of the Boston SO, for whom Piston wrote his first works for orchestra (although Koussevitzky handed over the baton to the composer for their premieres). Piston eventually wrote 11 works for that ensemble, as well as fulfilling commissions from the major orchestras of New York, Philadelphia, Cleveland, Dallas, Louisville, Minneapolis, and Cincinnati, among others. Aaron Copland also helped to bring him to national attention by featuring his music at Yaddo and the New School for Social Research, and by declaring him in 1936 to be "one of the most expert craftsmen American music can boast." He also earned the admiration of numerous other composers, including Stravinsky, Ernst Krenek, Roger Sessions, Howard Hanson, Virgil Thomson, and Elliott Carter, for whom in 1946 Piston offered "hope that the qualities of integrity and reason are still with us."

Piston's mastery took many forms, including a meticulous hand that allowed his publisher, AMP, to publish his scores in facsimile. (He penned all but one of the illustrations to his *Orchestration* text as well.) Intimately familiar with instruments and possessing a refined ear, he worked primarily at a desk, scoring his music as he composed it, rather than beginning with a piano reduction. His masterful orchestrations emphasize clarity and brilliance as opposed to novelty and effect. Along with a compelling sense of form, he also displayed a dazzling handling of canon, invertible counterpoint, melodic retrograde and inversion, and other contrapuntal techniques. The traditional forms of sonata, rondo, variation, fugue, and passacaglia acquired a distinctive lucidity and compression in his hands. One can readily discern in his music an engineer's concern for formal precision, a painter's care for coloristic detail, and a violist's attention to inner voices. "Melody and tonality are extended to allow for all sorts of new sounds and new rhythms," observed William Austin of the Fourth Symphony, "but melody and tonality organize the whole in essentially the same way they do in Mozart's world, as they rarely do in ours." While some thought the reserved quality of his music a limitation, his admirers extolled not only his impressive technical skills but also the "longing tenderness" of his slow movements and the "sparkling gaiety" of his scherzos.

Piston initially established a reputation as a composer's composer, although some of his more accessible efforts in the late 1930s and early 40s, notably *Carnival Song* for chorus (1938), the ballet suite from *The Incredible Flutist* (1938), and the Second Symphony (1943), were well received by the larger concert-going public. Symphony no.4 (1950) and Symphony no.6 (1955) also became particular favorites. Having absorbed Arnold Schoenberg's 12-tone method as early as the Flute Sonata (1930) and having composed a strict (albeit tonal) 12-tone work as early as the *Chromatic Study on the Name of Bach* for organ (1940), he made more extensive use of the 12-tone method in the 1950s and especially the 60s. His music accordingly became more chromatic and dense. These late works were also adventurous formally, featuring complex one-movement designs, rather than the more traditional three- and four-movement forms he generally had employed in the past.

A relatively slow worker, Piston joked that it took him an hour to decide upon a note and another hour to decide to erase it. He produced about one work a year, the eight symphonies and five string quartets representing the heart of his achievement. During his last two decades he produced a series of concertos (not necessarily titled as such) for viola (1957), two pianos (1959), violin (1960), harp (1963), cello (1966), clarinet (1967), flute (1971), and string quartet (1976). He often composed with the capabilities and traits of particular players, ensembles, and even halls in mind, and these concertos proved no exception. Some of them were written for such celebrated virtuosi as Salvatore Accardo, Nicanor Zabaleta, and Mstislav Rostropovich; others were undertaken for distinguished members of the Boston SO, such as the flautist Doriot Anthony Dwyer, and other friends. All attest to his great knowledge of instrumental technique.

As a teacher, Piston was the acclaimed author of a series of texts: *Principles of Harmonic Analysis* (Boston, 1933), *Harmony* (New York, 1941), *Counterpoint* (New York, 1947), and *Orchestration* (New York, 1955). Translated

into numerous languages, the latter three were among the most esteemed and widely used books of their kind. The harmony texts in particular helped to initiate a new era of music theory, in which theoretical principles were derived "from the observation of musical practice," as David Thompson has noted. These texts also shed new light on the relationship between harmonic root movement and rhythmic structure, and between orchestration and form. In his occasional critical essays, Piston wrote thoughtfully on subjects such as the music of Roy Harris and the limitations of the 12-tone method. Elliott Carter, Leroy Anderson, Arthur Berger, Gail Kubik, Irving Fine, Gordon Binkerd, Ellis Kohs, Leonard Bernstein, Robert Middleton, Robert Moevs, Harold Shapero, Allen Sapp, Daniel Pinkham, Noël Lee, Billy Jim Layton, Claudio Spies, Samuel Adler, Frederic Rzewski, and John Harbison, who numbered among his students at Harvard, benefited not only from, in Bernstein's words, his "non-pedantic approach to such academic subjects as fugue" but also from close familiarity with his finely crafted music. Although he encouraged them to find their own way, many of these composers show his stylistic influence, especially in matters of contrapuntal finesse and textural clarity.

Piston's achievements were recognized by Pulitzer prizes for the Symphonies nos.3 and 7, a Naumburg Award for the Symphony no.4 and New York Music Critics' Circle awards for the Symphony no.2, the Viola Concerto, and the Fifth String Quartet. He was elected to the National Institute of Arts and Letters in 1938, the American Academy of Arts and Sciences in 1940, and the American Academy of Arts and Letters in 1955. He also received a Guggenheim Fellowship, the Coolidge Medal, and numerous honorary doctorates. In addition, the French government bestowed upon him the decoration Officer of the Ordre des Arts et des Lettres.

WORKS

ORCHESTRAL

Orch Piece, 1925, unpubd; Sym. Piece, 1927, unpubd; Suite no.1, 1929; Conc. for Orch, 1933; Prelude and Fugue, 1934; Concertino, pf, chbr orch, 1937; Sym. no.1, 1937; The Incredible Flutist (ballet), 1938; Vn Conc. no.1, 1939; Sinfonietta, chbr orch, 1941; Fanfare for the Fighting French, brass, perc, 1942; Prelude and Allegro, org, str, 1943; Sym. no.2, 1943; Fugue on a Victory Tune, 1944, unpubd; Variation on a Theme by Eugene Goossens, 1944 [1 of 10 Jubilee Variations]; Suite no.2, 1947; Sym. no.3, 1947; Toccata, 1948; Sym. no.4, 1950; Tunbridge Fair (Intermezzo), sym. band, 1950; Fantasy, eng hn, hp, str, 1953; Sym. no.5, 1954; Sym. no.6, 1955; Serenata, 1956; Va Conc., 1957; Conc., 2 pf, orch, 1959; 3 New England Sketches, 1959; Sym. no.7, 1960; Vn Conc. no.2, 1960; Sym. Prelude, 1961; Lincoln Center Festival Ov., 1962; Capriccio, hp, str, 1963; Variations on a Theme by Edward Burlingame Hill, 1963; Pine Tree Fantasy, 1965; Sym. no.8, 1965; Variations, vc, orch, 1966; Cl Conc., 1967; Ricercare, 1967; Ceremonial Fanfare, brass, perc, 1969; Fantasia, vn, orch, 1970; Fl Conc., 1971; Bicentennial Fanfare, 1975; Conc., str qt, wind, perc, 1976

Arrs. (all unpubd): Debussy: Clair de lune, 1936; Fauré: Prométhée, Act II, scene i, 1945; Beethoven: Pf Sonata "Moonlight," op.14/2, 1st movt

CHORAL

Carnival Song (L. de Medici), TBB, brass, 1938; March, 1940; Psalm and Prayer of David, SATB, fl, cl, bn, vn, va, vc, db, 1958: O Sing unto the Lord a New Song (Ps xcvi), Bow Down Thine Ear, O Lord (Ps xxcvi)

CHAMBER

3 Pieces, fl, cl, bn, 1925; Minuetto in stile vecchio, str qt, 1927, unpubd, withdrawn; Sonata, fl, pf, 1930; Suite, ob, pf, 1931; Str Qt no.1, 1933; Pf Trio no.1, 1935; Str Qt no.2, 1935; Sonata, vn, pf, 1939; Interlude, va, pf, 1942; Qnt, fl, str qt, 1942; Partita, vn, va, org, 1944; Sonatina, vn, hpd, 1945; Divertimento, fl, ob, cl, bn, str qt, db, 1946; Str Qt no.3, 1947; Duo, va, vc, 1949; Pf Qnt, 1949; Str Qt no.4, 1951; Wind Qnt, 1956; Str Qt no.5, 1962; Pf Qt, 1964; Str Sextet, 1964; Pf Trio no.2, 1966; Souvenir, fl, vn, hp, 1967; Duo, vc, pf, 1972; 3 Counterpoints, vn, va, vc, 1973; Fugue…sur un sujet de Fenaroli, str qt, n.d., unpubd

KEYBOARD

Sonata, pf, 1926, unpubd, withdrawn; Chromatic Study on the Name of Bach, org, 1940; Passacaglia, pf, 1943; Improvisation, pf, 1945; Variation on Happy Birthday, pf, 1970, unpubd

MSS in *Bp*

Principal publishers: Associated, Boosey & Hawkes, E.C. Schirmer, G. Schirmer

WRITINGS

(for list of articles see Pollack (1981))

Principles of Harmonic Analysis (Boston, 1933)

Harmony (New York, 1941, 5/1987 with M. DeVoto)

Counterpoint (New York, 1947)

Orchestration (New York, 1955)

BIBLIOGRAPHY

T. Chanler: "New York, 1934," *MM*, xi/3 (1934), 142–7

A. Berger: "Walter Piston," *Trend* (1935), 210–22

I. Citkowitz: "Walter Piston: Classicist," *MM*, xiii/2 (1936), 3–11

R.L. Finney: "Piston's Violin Sonata," *MM*, xvii/4 (1940), 210–13

A. Copland: "Sessions and Piston," *Our New Music* (New York, 1941, 2/1968), 176–86

E. Carter: "Walter Piston," *MQ*, xxxii/3 (1946), 354–75

W.W. Austin: "Piston's Fourth Symphony: an Analysis," *MR*, xvi (1955), 120–37

O. Daniel and others: *Walter Piston* (New York, 1964)

C. Taylor: "Walter Piston: for his Seventieth Birthday," *PNM*, iii/1 (1964), 102–14

P. Westergaard: "Conversation with Walter Piston," *PNM*, vii/1 (1968), 3–17

H. Lindenfeld: *Three Symphonies of Walter Piston: an Analysis* (diss., Cornell U., 1975)

D.M. Thompson: *A History of Harmonic Theory in the United States* (Kent, OH, 1980)

W.D. Curtis: "Walter Piston (1894–1976): a Discography," *ARSCJ*, xiii/2 (1981), 76–95

H. Pollack: *Walter Piston* (Ann Arbor, MI, 1981) [incl. work-list, further bibliography, discography]

H. Pollack: *Harvard Composers: Walter Piston and His Students, from Elliott Carter to Frederic Rzewski* (Metuchen, NJ, 1992) [incl. list of writings]

R.C. Murrow: *Music Theory Textbooks in the United States, 1941–1992: Philosophical Trends in Written Skills* (diss., U. of Oklahoma, 1995)

C.J. Harris: *The French Connection: The Neoclassical Influence of Stravinsky, through Boulanger, on the Music of Copland, Talma, and Piston* (diss., SUNY Buffalo, 2002)

H. Eisenlohr, "Walter Piston," *Komponisten der Gegenwart*, v, ed. H. Heister and W. Sparrer (Munich, 2003)

R.M. Davis: *Walter Piston's Concerto no.1 for Violin and Orchestra; Thematic and Motivic Transformation, Style, and Violinistic Issues* (diss., U. of Texas-Austin, 2004)

M. DeVoto: "Two Composers on American Music at Mid-Century: Walter Piston in Conversation with Wilfrid Mellers, 1962," *American Music*, xxviii/1 (2010), 119–28

HOWARD POLLACK

Pitahawirata. Native American tribe of the PAWNEE confederacy.

Pitney, Gene (Francis Allen) (*b* Hartford, CT, 17 Feb 1941; *d* Cardiff, Wales, April 2006). Singer and song-writer. His career as a singer began while in high school where he was known as the "Rockville Rocket" and sang with his own group called Gene & the Genials. His first recordings came with the duo known as Jamie and Jane (Pitney and Ginny Arnell) and as a solo artist under the name of Billy Bryan, but the first recordings that would chart were "(I Wanna) Love My Life Away" and "Town Without Pity" which he cut under his own name for Musicor in 1961. Turning to songwriting, Pitney composed classic hits in the 1960s for the likes of Roy Orbison ("Today's Teardrops"), Bobby Vee ("Rubber Ball"), Ricky Nelson ("Hello Mary Lou"), and the Crystals ("He's a Rebel"). However, his darkly handsome and brooding looks along with his innate and emotionally, angst-ridden singing style kept him popular as a singer and caught the attention of other songwriters looking for a hit maker. In the early 1960s he would chart with the Goffen-King song "Every Breath I Take," the Bacharach-David songs "(The Man Who Shot) Liberty Valance" and "24 Hours from Tulsa," and the Jagger-Richards song "That girl belongs to yesterday."

In the mid-1960s, Pitney crossed over to country, making albums with George Jones and Jones' singing partner, Melba Montgomery. By the late 1960s Pitney found his popularity to be greater in Europe than in America, and he scored dozens of hits in England, including Randy Newman's "Nobody needs your love," "Something's gotten hold of my heart," a 1989 duet with Marc Almond that gave Pitney the only no.1 song of his career, and "Nessuno mi puo' giudicare," which placed second in Italy's San Remo Song Festival.

RECORDINGS

(selective list)

George Jones & Gene Pitney (1994, Bear Family); *Complete Duets 1965* (2007, EMI); *The Best of Gene Pitney* (2008, Collectables Records); *Recorded Live on Stage* (2009, Past Programs)

RANDOLPH LOVE

Pitot, Geneviève (Geneviève Sullivan; Mrs. Joseph Sullivan) (*b* New Orleans, LA, 20 May 1901; *d* New Orleans LA, 4 Oct 1980). Pianist, dance arranger, and composer. Born to a French Creole family, she was a child prodigy whose skills were recognized by pianist Alfred Cortot, who invited her to Paris for study (1919–22). She moved to New York in the mid-1920s, working as an accompanist, playing weekly programs on WOR Radio, and making piano rolls for the Aeolian Duo-Art Company. Her modern dance accompanying began in the late 1920s, including a 1927 program with Michio Ito. By 1929 Pitot had begun work with choreographer Helen Tamiris, a partnership that continued until Tamiris's death in 1966. From 1935 to 1939 Pitot composed for the WPA Federal Dance Project, creating works for Tamiris, Charles Weidman, and Nadia Chilkovsky, including *Salut du Monde* (1936), *Candide* (1937; in collaboration with Wallingford Riegger), *Adelante* (1939), and *How Long, Brethren?* (1937).

Characterized by one commentator as a "tiny, amusing fireball," Pitot worked with many important choreographers throughout her career, including Doris Humphrey, Hanya Holm, Daniel Nagrin, Agnes de Mille,

Jerome Robbins, Michael Kidd, and Donald Saddler. Until the late 1940s she presented solo recitals of French and modern American piano music. Pitot began her Broadway work in the 1940s, with credits including all or part of the dance music for *High Button Shoes* (1947), *Inside U.S.A.* (1948), *Kiss me, Kate* (1948), *Miss Liberty* (1949), *Call Me Madam* (1950), *Out of this World* (1950), *Two on the Aisle* (1951), *Two's Company* (1952), *Can-Can* (1953), *L'il Abner* (1956), *Destry Rides Again* (1959), *Saratoga* (1959), and *Milk and Honey* (1961), among others.

BIBLIOGRAPHY

W. Spratling and W. Faulkner: *Sherwood Anderson and Other Famous Creoles* (New Orleans, 1927)
J. Martin: *America Dancing: the Background and Personalities of the Modern Dance* (New York, 1936)
Obituary, *New York Times*, 9 Oct 1980
P. Tisch: "Remembering Helen Tamiris," *Dance Chronicle*, xvii/3 (1994), 327–60

JANE RIEGEL FERENCZ

Pittel, Harvey (*b* Great Falls, MT, 22 June 1943). Saxophonist. He studied clarinet with KALMAN BLOCH and Franklyn Stokes, and saxophone with Stokes from 1961 to 1965 while attending the University of Southern California, where he obtained his doctorate in music education. Further studies were with FREDERICK HEMKE at Northwestern University (1965–6) and with Joseph Allard (1966–9) while he was in the West Point Military Academy Band; he continued lessons with Allard sporadically for the next decade. In 1970 he won a silver medal at the Concours International in Geneva. He has since received two Martha Baird Rockefeller Fund grants and a National Endowment for the Arts Solo Recitalist Grant, and has won the Concert Artists Guild competition. He made his solo debut with the Boston SO in Ingolf Dahl's Saxophone Concerto (1971); his recital debut was in 1973 at Carnegie Recital Hall. He has performed throughout the United States, Europe, Mexico, and East Asia. In 1972 he formed a saxophone quartet; he has also performed in a trio consisting of saxophone, piano, and cello. Among the premieres he has presented are those of Berio's Chemins II b/c, Babbitt's Images and Chihara's Saxophone Concerto. Pittel has taught at the University of Southern California, California State University (Fullerton and Long Beach campuses), Boston University, the Mannes College, and from 1980, the University of Texas, Austin. He has also held workshops at the Aspen Music School and the Berkshire Music Center.

SORAB MODI/MEGAN HILL

Pitts, Lilla Belle (*b* Aberdeen, MS, 26 Sept 1884; *d* Nashville, TN, 24 Jan 1970). Music educator and author. Pitts studied piano, voice, and violin at Ward Seminary in Nashville (1900–05), and piano at North Texas Female College (1906) and the Chicago Conservatory of Music (1907–9), among other places. She was encouraged to become a public school supervisor by Birdie Alexander, a leading Texas music supervisor. Pitts taught studio piano briefly in Louisiana (1906), supervised vocal music in the schools of Amarillo (1910–14) and Dallas (1915–21), Texas, and worked for the Columbia Phonograph Company (1921–3). She subsequently taught at Elizabeth, New Jersey (1924–38), studying part-time with Charles H. Farnsworth and Peter W. Dykema at nearby Teachers College, Columbia University (BA 1935). She was on the faculty at Teachers College (1938–54) and later held several visiting professorships. Pitts wrote four books and many articles, mostly about music appreciation. She was best known for her *Music Integration in the Junior High School* (Boston 1938) and her editorial work for *Our Singing World* (Boston 1949). Pitts served as president of the Music Educators National Conference (1942–4) and was influential in developing the concept of "general music" among music teachers in the 1950s and 1960s. She was inducted into the Music Educators Hall of Fame in 1986.

BIBLIOGRAPHY

H.A. Goodman: *Music Education: Perspectives and Perceptions (37 Outstanding Music Educators)* (Dubuque, IA, 1982), 122–4
G.L. Blanchard: *Lilla Belle Pitts, Her Life and Contributions in Music Education* (diss., Brigham Young U., 1966) [includes list of writings]
Obituary, *Music Educators Journal*, lvi/7 (1970), 105 only

GEORGE N. HELLER/WILLIAM R. LEE

Pittsburgh. City in southwestern Pennsylvania (pop. 305,704; metropolitan area: 2,447,393; 2010 US Census). The city was founded in 1758 as a military settlement. With its location at the convergence of three major rivers and the abundance of coal in its hills, Pittsburgh was a busy commercial center with, until the turn of the century, little of the cultivated environment found in towns along the East Coast. The Scots-Irish, of whom many were conservative Presbyterians, influenced the development of the city both commercially and culturally well into the 20th century. The first piano by CHARLES TAWS (Philadelphia, 1791) arrived by pack mule team around 1796; it can be seen at the Heinz History Center along with the one surviving piano by Charles Rosenbaum, the city's earliest (1814) piano maker. Three early shape-note tune books were locally published: *Patterson's Church Music* (1813), *The Beauties of Harmony* (1814), and *The Pittsburgh Selection of Psalm Tunes* (1816). In the 1820s and beyond the Harmonists, whose third settlement was close by, attracted Pittsburgh musicians and composers to participate in their music programs. By the 1830s the Welsh were active with their singing festivals known as *gymanfa ganu*. By midcentury the Germans had established a Teutonia Männerchor and Pittsburgh's best-known native composer, STEPHEN C. FOSTER, was launching his career as a professional composer.

During the latter part of the 19th century and early 20th century, the city's population expanded to accommodate the burgeoning glass, iron, and steel industries and immigrants from Europe arrived eager for jobs. The result was a panoply of cultural traditions that defined the city's distinctive neighborhoods and some remain to this day. During this time, local choral and orchestra groups developed and traveling orchestras (including the Theodore Thomas Orchestra) as well as opera troupes and soloists performed as demands from immigrants and the industrial elite expanded the music activity of the city.

In addition to the city's professional music organizations, amateur and semi-professional organizations among them, the Tuesday Musical Club (1889), Bach Choir (1934), Pittsburgh Savoyards (1938), the Pittsburgh Civic Orchestra (1958), and Pittsburgh Banjo Club (1988) were established and many have remained an integral part of Pittsburgh's flourishing 21st-century arts community. The city's infamous industrial past belies what is now a geographically attractive, most livable city with a vibrant 14-square block Cultural District downtown overseen by the Pittsburgh Cultural Trust (1984) which serves as both an arts agency and economic development catalyst. The city's foundation community and the Allegheny Regional Asset District (1993), which distributes a percentage of a 1% sales and use tax, support music and other arts organizations in the region.

1. Orchestras and chamber music. 2. Opera. 3. Organs and the choral tradition. 4. Music education and libraries. 5. Business and broadcasting. 6. Traditional, folk, and popular music. 7. Jazz.

1. ORCHESTRAS AND CHAMBER MUSIC. Artist Samuel H. Dearborn founded Pittsburgh's first music organization, the Apollonian Society, in 1806. The society performed popular songs and marches of the day as well as the music of J.C. Bach, Wolfgang Amadeus Mozart, and Ignace Joseph Pleyel. The first ensemble in Pittsburgh that endured for more than a couple of concerts was the Pittsburgh Orchestral Society (1854–6). Many orchestras were subsequently organized to perform in the city's various choral festivals including the May Music Festival (1879–89). Most of the effort that went into organizing the financially unsuccessful festivals was transferred to the establishment of the city's first permanent professional orchestra, the Pittsburgh Orchestra, in 1895.

Backed by such prominent Pittsburgh residents as Andrew Carnegie, Henry Clay Frick, and George Westinghouse Jr., the Pittsburgh Orchestra had a brief but distinguished career under music directors Frederick Archer (1896–8), Victor Herbert (1898–1904), and Emil Paur (1904–10). It performed in Carnegie Music Hall (capacity 1972), part of the library/museum complex built in Oakland in 1895 and funded by Carnegie. The orchestra performed annually at Carnegie Hall in New York. Although it made extensive tours (performing in as many as 23 states in a single season) and was reported to rank third of the nation's orchestras in artistic importance, it disbanded in 1910 because of financial difficulties. The void was filled by visiting orchestras from Philadelphia, Cleveland, New York, and elsewhere.

The Pittsburgh SO was founded in 1926 and had its first season the following year amid a storm of controversy: the necessity of scheduling concerts on Sundays (because most of the players held weekday jobs) put the orchestra in conflict with Pennsylvania's Sunday Blue Laws of 1794, which forbade selling anything (including tickets) on the Sabbath. After the first concert (24 April 1927), nine of the board members were brought before a magistrate. The orchestra's ultimate victory in this case made it possible for other Pennsylvania orchestras to perform on Sundays.

The orchestra's permanent conductors include Antonio Modarelli (1927–37), FRITZ REINER (1938–48 following reorganization in 1937 by Otto Klemperer), William Steinberg (1952–76), SIR ANDRÉ PREVIN (1976–84), LORIN MAAZEL (1984–96), Mariss Jansons (1996–2004), Andrew Davis (artistic advisor 2005–8), and Manfred Honeck (2008–). MARVIN HAMLISCH served as principal Pops conductor from 1995 until his death in 2012. The orchestra gave its first performances at the 3750-seat Syria Mosque; since 1971 its concerts are in the 2847-seat Heinz Hall for the Performing Arts (formerly the Penn Theater) located in the downtown Cultural District.

Its affiliate, the Pittsburgh Youth Symphony (1945) for students age 13–20, is conducted by associate and assistant conductors of the Pittsburgh SO. The Three Rivers Young Peoples Orchestras (1974) provides training for 9–18 year olds. The American Wind Symphony (1957), conducted by founder Robert Boudreau, presented summer concerts on a custom-designed concert barge moored on the Allegheny River in downtown Pittsburgh and commissioned close to 400 new works. Determined to revive the American brass band tradition, the River City Brass Band played its first concert in 1981 and has maintained an active performance schedule in the city and away. Composer David Stock founded the Pittsburgh New Music Ensemble in 1976, and following Stock's retirement in 1999, it has presented contemporary music concerts under its conductor Kevin Noe (2001).

The Pittsburgh Chamber Music Society (1961) and the Renaissance and Baroque Society of Pittsburgh (1968) have each presented a full season of concerts featuring the best ensembles from the United States and abroad. Chatham Baroque (1990), an early music ensemble, has performed music of the 17th and 18th centuries on instruments of the period and is based in the city. The Pittsburgh Jewish Music Festival (2004) has been an annual event devoted to Jewish-themed classical music by Jewish composers.

2. OPERA. The first opera given in Pittsburgh was an English version of Gioachino Rossini's *Il Barbiere di Siviglia* in 1838 at the Old Drury Theatre (1833), but opera did not flourish in Pittsburgh until 1873, when the Frohsinn Society presented Friedrich Freiherr von Flotow's *Alessandro Stradella* (in German) to much acclaim. In 1874 the Gounod Club performed Flotow's opera *Martha* in its first operatic series. While opera companies (including New York's Metropolitan Opera) visited the city regularly on their tours in the early 20th century, the first permanent professional organization, the Pittsburgh Opera, was not established until 1939. Richard Karp, a violist in the Pittsburgh SO, directed the opera company 1942–75. His daughter Barbara followed until 1979 when James DeBlasis became artistic director. TITO CAPOBIANCO, general director 1983–2000, increased the budget and production values and moved the company into the state-of-the-art

Benedum Center (another renovated cinema seating 3800 in the Cultural District) in 1987. Mark Weinstein's rigorous financial management and strategic planning marked his successful tenure as director from the late 1990s until 2008 when Christopher Hahn took over. While focusing on the familiar repertory, the company has added contemporary opera to its offerings and supports the Pittsburgh Opera Resident Artist Program (early 1990s). In 1941 MARY CARDWELL DAWSON established the National Negro Opera Company in Pittsburgh where she had had a music teaching studio since 1927. The company performed works by Giuseppe Verdi, Georges Bizet, R. Nathaniel Dett, and others in Pittsburgh, Washington, DC, New York, and Chicago until Dawson's death in 1962 when the company ceased to exist. The Civic Light Opera (1945) has lit up the summer months with its professional musical theater performances. Their Gene Kelly Awards for Excellence in High School Musical Theater (1991) and their educational arm, the CLO Academy, have encouraged quality musical theater productions at the high school level in the city. Former Metropolitan Opera mezzo-soprano Mildred Miller Posvar founded the Opera Theater of Pittsburgh in 1978, and since then the company has promoted young professional singers in standard and modern repertory. Jonathan Eaton succeeded Posvar as director in 1999.

3. ORGANS AND THE CHORAL TRADITION. Organs first appeared in the city's churches in 1812 when the first Catholic church, St. Patrick's, installed one. Other churches followed soon after. While conservative Presbyterians kept both choirs and instruments out of their services before 1820, organs crept in to some of their more liberal churches as the century progressed.

In 1890 ANDREW CARNEGIE, who saw the organ as an economical means of bringing music to the general public, built for the city of Allegheny (annexed to Pittsburgh in 1906) a library and an attached music hall with a large organ. Leonard Wales, appointed city organist and supported by public funds, began the first known series of free organ recitals in the United States in this hall. The arrangement continued until 1974. Carnegie also installed an organ in 1895 in the Oakland Carnegie Music Hall, where a similar series of recitals was given (1895–1981). At both venues the public heard over 7000 recitals.

The formation of the Teutonia Männerchor brought the German choral tradition to Pittsburgh in 1854; other singing societies followed. After the Civil War, Pierre L.C. Tetedoux, a singing teacher and former pupil of Rossini, organized the Cantata Society (1870s) which gave elaborate performances of sacred music. The Mozart Club (1879–1919) presented oratorios and other large-scale works. The Mendelssohn Choir of Pittsburgh (1909), in the early 21st century a chorus of 120 with a 20-voice professional core, has sung oratorio, opera, and Broadway; has served as the choir of the Pittsburgh SO; and has supported the Junior Mendelssohn for qualified 8th–12th grade students. The Children's Festival Chorus of Pittsburgh (1983) has offered three choirs

for children ages 8–15. The Pittsburgh Camerata (1975) has been the city's professional chamber choir.

4. MUSIC EDUCATION AND LIBRARIES. Evidence of music teaching in Pittsburgh dates back to 1799 when Peter Declary arrived to teach violin and other instruments. Others followed, including in 1811 William Evens, who set up singing schools and amassed Pittsburgh's first music archive some of which came to the Carnegie Library of Pittsburgh Music Collection at the end of the 19th century. Pittsburgh was one of the first American cities to introduce music into the public schools (1844). Will Earhart, who became Director of Music for the city's public schools in 1912, wrote a widely read report, "Music in the Public Schools" (1914), which marked the beginning of a new era in music education. In 1979 the Pittsburgh School for the Creative and Performing Arts (CAPA), part of the Pittsburgh Public School system, was established and has served grades 6–12. Gateway to the Arts (1957, as Gateway to Music) has supported teacher training and artist residencies in the schools.

Three of the city's universities have had vigorous music degree programs. The University of Pittsburgh's Music Department has offered degrees through the Ph.D. in musicology, ethnomusicology, jazz studies, and music theory and composition. Students at Duquesne University's Mary Pappert School of Music have earned degrees at the bachelor's and master's levels in performance, music education, music technology, music therapy, and sacred music. The School of Music at Carnegie Mellon University has offered bachelor's and master's degrees in performance, composition, conducting, and music and technology. Students, faculty, and guests have presented public concerts and recitals on a regular basis. Each institution has had a music library focusing primarily on support for its curriculum. Pittsburgh's largest music library collection has resided at the Carnegie Library of Pittsburgh (the city's public library) with strong holdings in performing editions, opera, audio and video materials, and local historical resources. The Center for American Music (University of Pittsburgh) has had a research collection and museum with a focus on Stephen Foster.

Chatham Music and Arts Summer Day Camp (1956), City Music Center of Duquesne University (1989), the Afro-American Music Institute (1982), and Calliope School of Folk Music (1990) have been among those who provide learning opportunities for children and adults in the local community.

5. BUSINESS AND BROADCASTING. Music stores and instrument makers of primarily pianos and organs were in evidence by the early 1800s. By 1841 the city had four music stores. John H. Mellor, who came to the city in 1831 as an organist, was a partner in a musical instrument store that supplied the Chickering piano for Jenny Lind's concert in Masonic Hall in 1851; his firm also published the city's first known music magazine, *Mellor's Musical Mirror* (1868–9), and in the hands of his son and grandson remained a force in Pittsburgh's musical life into the next century. In 1846 composer and

businessman HENRY KLEBER (1816–1897), who had worked in the Mellor store as a younger man, opened a music store. He and Stephen Foster were friends and fellow composers. From 1921 to 1948 the monthly *Musical Forecast* reported the musical activity of the city and abroad.

Pittsburgh was an early center in the development of radio and the home of KDKA (1920), one of the first commercial radio stations in the United States. KDKA was the first to broadcast religious services (Calvary Episcopal, 1921) and the first to establish its own orchestra, Victor Saudek, conductor (1922). WQED-FM (1973) has been an all-classical station. WQED-TV (1954), the first community sponsored television station, produced the *Previn and the Pittsburgh* (1977–80) series of orchestra programs and *Mr. Rogers' Neighborhood* (1968–2001) in which music played an important part. WYEP-FM (1974) has played adult alternative, and WDVE-FM (1960s) has covered rock while also devoting time to local sports and to caricatures of local figures and of Pittsburghese, the local dialect. WDUQ-FM (1949–2011), a station for jazz and NPR news, was sold in 2011 and reemerged as WESA-FM, which has limited its jazz coverage in favor of news programming.

6. TRADITIONAL, FOLK, AND POPULAR MUSIC. In the 19th century, while upper-class residents were pursuing written, "cultivated" music, Pittsburgh's popular and folk music sprang from such disparate sources as the brass bands of volunteer fire companies, blackface minstrelsy, ethnic fraternal societies and weddings, and ensembles associated with local companies. Subsequent immigrant groups have established traditions; those from India, for example, enjoy a long-running radio show, improvisatory classical concerts, and Bhangra dance competitions.

Composer and lyricist STEPHEN C. FOSTER (1826–64) wrote both parlor songs in the European tradition that were accessible with simple accompaniment and minstrel songs that were immediately promoted on stage and spread nationwide. In the early 21st century, his works continued to be performed by classical as well as popular and folk artists. Pittsburgh's Allegheny Cemetery, Foster's burial place, has been the site of *Doo Dah Days!*, an annual festival celebrating his music and legacy.

In 1959, around the same time as the nationwide folk revival, Pittsburgh singers Robert Schmertz and Vivien Richman released albums on the Folkways label. Schmertz's *Sing Oh, the City Oh! Songs About Early Pittsburgh* contained his own compositions. *Vivien Richman Sings Folk Songs of West Pennsylvania* drew its songs from the collections of Jacob A. Evanson, the Director of Vocal Music for the Pittsburgh Board of Education. The NewLanders have continued this tradition of researching regional historical songs, although they have performed in a more contemporary rock and pop style.

Even if the city itself has moved beyond its smoky past, its musical culture often continued to reflect an industrial tradition. The Slovakian steelworker's song "Aja Lejber Man" ["I'm a Labor Man"], popular in the early 20th century, is about working every day, trying to save money to send back to the old country, but still buying everyone at the bar a drink on payday. These subjects still echoed in the 1970s and 80s rock music of bar bands such as Joe Grushecky and The Iron City Houserockers. Instrumental indie-rock group Don Caballero's 1995 album featured photographs of local smokestacks. *When We Shine: 15 Songs About Pittsburgh*, a 2008 project album of Calliope Folk Music School, includes songs titled "Workshop of America" and "Rust Belt Blues." Singer Anne Feeney has been prominent in the labor movement, but working-class protest music has also manifested in the punk rock of groups such as Aus-Rotten and Anti-Flag. Pittsburgh's image as a sports-crazed industrial town with a rich ethnic heritage is further demonstrated by Jimmy Pol's popular 1970s "Steelers Fight Song," based on the "Pennsylvania Polka." Every year, especially when the Steelers reach the postseason, more football fight songs have been created and played on local radio stations. The first rapper from Pittsburgh to achieve national success, Wiz Khalifa, did it with a song ("Black & Yellow," 2010) that cites local sports teams' colors.

Pittsburgh's music is not all hard-hats and helmets as some of the smoothest vocal music of the pop era has emerged from the region. PERRY COMO, a barber from the nearby town of Canonsburg, was one of the most popular singers of the 20th century, with stunningly frequent chart success from 1943 until 1974. Also from Canonsburg was Bobby Vinton, who had four number one hits in the 1960s but whose hit "My Melody of Love" (1974), sung partially in Polish, showed why he was nicknamed the "Polish prince." Lou Christie struck the top of the charts in 1965 with "Lightnin' Strikes." Still regionally active in the 2010s were white soul artist Billy Price and rocker Donnie Iris, whose hits in the 1980s impressively display his multitracked vocals.

Pop harmony groups also sprouted from Pittsburgh. Some also achieved racial harmony and many benefited from the color-blind "platter pushin'" of local radio DJ Porky Chedwick. The Del Vikings were formed at the Pittsburgh airport by African American Air Force members, but after incorporating a white member, they became in 1957 the first mixed-race pop group to chart a top-10 hit. The Marcels, who scored a no.1 hit in 1961 with their version of "Blue Moon," were another racially integrated group. The first single by a white group to hit no.1 on the Cashbox R&B charts was "Since I Don't Have You" by The Skyliners in 1959. Tommy James moved to Pittsburgh in 1965 after his single "Hanky Panky" became a local sensation and recruited a Pittsburgh backing group. The Vogues also had a number of hits in the 1960s and the Jaggerz (fronted by Donnie Iris) scored a hit with "The Rapper" in 1970. Even as national tastes have changed, vocal harmony groups, doo-wop, and other styles of oldies, including barbershop harmony, have remained popular in Pittsburgh, especially among the aging population.

Some successful music acts have come from genres one might not expect from a rust belt city. Rusted Root's neo-hippie fusion of rock and world music brought them national success in the 1990s. Songwriters and performers Bob Corbin and David Hanner found moderate success on the country charts from 1979 to 1993. The latest sensation is Girl Talk (Gregg Michael Gillis), a DJ and electronic artist whose albums consist solely of hundreds of samples of other musicians' songs.

7. JAZZ. Pittsburgh's jazz musicians have had a tremendous effect on the history and development of the genre. To pursue performing careers elsewhere, though, many of the most influential musicians left the city at a young age. Examples include pianists Earl [Fatha] Hines, Mary Lou Williams, Erroll Garner, Sonny Clark and Ahmad Jamal, trumpeter Roy Eldridge, drummers Kenny Clarke and Art Blakey, guitarist George Benson, bassist Ray Brown, arranger Billy Strayhorn, and vocalists Maxine Sullivan, Billy Eckstine, and Eddie Jefferson. Composers and arrangers Billy May, Henry Mancini, Sammy Nestico, and Peter Matz also left for the theaters, radio, and film studios of New York or Hollywood.

Occasionally, musicians returned to Pittsburgh after making a name for themselves elsewhere. The best example is drummer Roger Humphries, who first went on the road with Pittsburgh saxophonist Stanley Turrentine in 1962 and then played with Horace Silver in the mid-1960s before returning home to raise his family. Humphries might be considered a localized version of Blakey and his Jazz Messengers in that so many musicians have passed through his bands, jam sessions, or classes he taught at the local performing arts high school (CAPA) from 1980 to 2009. Other jazz artists who returned include guitarist Jimmy Ponder, trombonist Harold Betters, pianist Walt Harper, who opened venues such as Harper's Attic and performed at Steelers home games from the mid-1970s to 2002, and drummer Joe Harris, who played with Dizzy Gillespie and Charlie Parker in the 1940s and returned to teach at the University of Pittsburgh from 1972 to 1986. Saxophonist Nathan Davis also came to teach at the university in 1969 and started the jazz studies program, annual seminar, and concert there.

Locals have made great efforts to preserve the legacy of Pittsburgh jazz. Trombonist and composer Dr. Nelson Harrison created an online social networking site, the Pittsburgh Jazz Network. Trumpeter Chuck Austin spearheaded the African American Jazz Preservation Society of Pittsburgh, which specifically worked to research the African American Musicians Union Local 471 (in existence 1908–66). Saxophonist Hosea Taylor wrote a memoir about Pittsburgh jazz in the 1940s. Vibraphonist and radio host Tony Mowod founded the Pittsburgh Jazz Society in 1987.

In the Hill District, the former heart of Pittsburgh's African American cultural life and documented in the work of photographer Charles "Teenie" Harris, the Crawford Grill hosted many of the biggest names in jazz from the 1940s to the 70s. It and many other music venues such as the Hurricane, Midway Lounge, Balcony, Attic, and Dowe's on Ninth, closed especially as the city lost population and neighborhoods declined. Fortunately, Manchester Craftsmen's Guild (founded by Bill

Strickland in 1968) opened a 350-seat venue in 1986 and, in 1987, started the MCG Jazz concert series.

BIBLIOGRAPHY

G.M. Rohrer: *Music and Musicians of Pennsylvania* (Philadelphia, 1940)

J. Evanson: "Folk Music in an Industrial City," *Pennsylvania Songs and Legends*, ed. G.G. Korson (Philadelphia, 1949)

R.J. Wolfe: *A Short History of the Pittsburgh Orchestra 1896 to 1910* (thesis, Carnegie Institute of Technology, 1954)

J. Evanson, G. Swetnam, and R. Lahmer: *Early Western Pennsylvania Hymns & Hymn-Tunes, 1816–1846* (Pittsburgh, 1958)

E.G Baynham: *A History of Pittsburgh Music 1758–1958* (MS, 1970)

Carnegie Magazine, xlix/3 (1975) [whole issue]

C. Miner: *Pittsburgh Rhythms: The Music of a Changing City, 1840–1930* (Pittsburgh, 1991)

M. Brignano: *Pittsburgh Civic Light Opera: How Dreams Came True* (Pittsburgh, 1996)

H. McCullough: *The Illustrated History of Opera in Pittsburgh: the Pittsburgh Opera Story* (Pittsburgh, 2005)

K.S. Guffey: *Music as an Art: Pittsburgh's Music Societies 1860–1900* (thesis, Indiana U. of Pennsylvania, 2006)

C. Pena: *Pittsburgh Jazz Records and Beyond, 1950–1985* (thesis, U. of Pittsburgh, 2007)

C.P. Orr, A. Mendelson, and T. Clarke: *Pittsburgh Born, Pittsburgh Bred: 500 of the More Famous People Who Have Called Pittsburgh Home* (Pittsburgh, 2008)

Organ Historical Society: *Organ Atlas 2010: the City of Pittsburgh and Western Pennsylvania*, ed. R. Smith (Richmond, VA, 2010)

H. McCullough and M. Brignano: *Play On: an Illustrated History of the Pittsburgh Symphony Orchestra* (Pittsburgh, 2011)

IDA REED/KATHRYN LOGAN (1–5);
TIMOTHY R. WILLIAMS (7)

Pixies, the. Rock band. The Pixies were formed in Massachusetts by guitarist/vocalist Black Francis ("Frank Black"; Charles Michael Kittridge Thompson IV; *b* Boston, MA, 6 April 1965), guitarist Joey Santiago (*b* Manila, Philippines, 10 June 1965), bassist/vocalist Kim Deal (*b* Dayton, OH, 10 June 1961), and drummer David Lovering (*b* Burlington, MA, 6 Dec 1961). After signing with the British independent label 4AD in 1987, the Pixies released the EP *Come on Pilgrim* and two full-length albums often considered masterpieces of late 1980s alternative rock, *Surfer Rosa* and *Doolittle*. The Pixies' music, which proved influential in alternative rock circles, is distinguished by the harrowing screams of Black Francis, and his interplay with the cool, detached vocals of Kim Deal. The group broke up in 1993 after releasing *Bossanova* and *Trompe Le Monde*, leading Francis to rename himself Frank Black and begin a solo career, while Deal moved on to make music with her sister Kelly in the Breeders. The Pixies eventually reunited in 2004 for a world tour that included headlining performances at prominent festivals in Europe and North America.

BIBLIOGRAPHY

J. Frank and C. Ganz: *Fool the World: the Oral History of a Band Called Pixies* New York, 2006)

B. Sisario: *The Pixies' Doolittle* (New York, 2006)

RYAN MOORE

Pizarro, Artur (*b* Lisbon, Portugal, 17 Aug 1968). Pianist of Portuguese birth. A piano prodigy, he made his debut at the Lisbon Conservatory of Music at age three. He performed in 1981 at the São Luíz Theatre in Lisbon and in the same year appeared with the Gulbenkian Orchestra. He studied with Sequeira Costa in both Lisbon and in the United States after Costa was hired by the University of Kansas at Lawrence. He later studied with Aldo Ciccolini at the Conservatoire de Paris. Pizarro triumphed in the International Vianna da Motta Competition (Lisbon, 1987), the Greater Palm Beach International Competition (Florida, 1988), and in the Leeds International Piano Competition (1990), where his fine tone and effortless command were revealed notably in Fryderyk Chopin's op.25 Etudes. Since making his London debut at the Wigmore Hall in 1988, he has given recitals in Japan, Australia, and the United States and has appeared with many of the world's leading orchestras and conductors, including Charles Dutoit, Sir Charles Mackerras, Essa-Pekka Salonen, and Yuri Temirkanov. Pizarro has also performed a wide variety of chamber music; with violinist Raphaël Oleg and cellist Josephine Knight, he formed the Pizarro Trio in 2005, and he also regularly performs piano duets with Vita Panomariovaite. His repertory ranges from music by Franz Liszt and Serge Rachmaninoff to Aleksandr Skryabin, Dmitry Kabalevsky, Dmitry Shostakovich, Darius Milhaud, Rodrigo, and Jan Voříšek.

BRYCE MORRISON/JONAS WESTOVER

Pizer, Elizabeth [Faw] **Hayden** (*b* Watertown, NY, 1 Sept 1954). Composer and pianist. After completing her formal education at the Boston Conservatory of Music, she moved to the West Coast, working as an opera répétiteur at San Jose State University. She began her work in radio broadcast production in Berkeley and then worked in San Mateo. She has received several awards for her vocal and choral music, including first prize in the Delius Composition Contest (1982) for *Madrigals Anon* for unaccompanied chorus. Pizer has received several first prizes in the National League of Pen Women composition contests for works including *Five Haiku II*, her String Quartet, and *Nightsongs* for mezzo-soprano and piano with texts by Milton Blake. Her *Strains and Restraints* (1984) for solo piano received a first prize in the 1994 biennial composition contest of the National League of Pen Women. The three movement work features an additive theme, which begins as a small cell and expands upon each restatement. Additionally, Pizer served as an adjudicator for the National League of American Pen Women Competition for American Women Composers in 2000.

Pizer's style can be described as tonal, with impressionistic harmonies. Lyrical melodies are also a prominent feature of her style. Overall, Pizer's range of compositions exhibits her eclectic influences from jazz, opera, and Chinese music. In her electro-acoustic works, Pizer draws upon the influence of water. Often wanting to emulate the depth and motion of water, compositions such as *Sunken Flutes*, *The Infinite Sea*, and *Aquaspheres* are concerned with textures, creating dense layers that give way to silence.

Pizer dedicated her *Expressions Intimes* (1975) to Catalan composer and pianist Federico Mompou, about whom she later authored an article. Her piece, *Elegy in*

Amber: In Memoriam Leonard Bernstein (1993) for string orchestra, weaves in brief quotations from Bernstein's Mass, *West Side Story,* and *Trouble in Tahiti.* The work was given its Asian premiere by the Hong Kong Bach Choir in 2000. Pizer has written a large number of jazz-inspired instrumental works, such as *Zephyr, Leprechauns*, and *Eucalyptus*. Additionally, Pizer has written pieces for tape, such as *Sunken Flutes* (1979), *Arlington* (1989), *Embryonic Climactus* (1989), *The Infinite Sea* (1990), and *Aquasphere* (1990).

In 1974, she married composer Charles R. Pizer, and together they formed an archival library for music not commercially available. As an offshoot, in 1988 Pizer developed the International Women's Music Sound Archive, a collection of classical music by women composers. Pizer has always had an abiding interest in promoting the performance of female composers, working closely with the International League of Women Composers (ILWC), which she chaired from 1982 to 1983. She has also written for the *ILWC Journal*. She maintains the score and sound archives at her home in Three Mile Bay, New York.

WORKS
(selective list)
Orch: Under and Overture, op.37, orch without str, 1979; Elegy in Amber: In Memoriam Leonard Bernstein, str orch, 1993 Band: Fanfare Ov., 1977–9
Vocal: Alleluia, op.25, 2S, chorus, 1976; Kyrie, op.39, chorus, 1976; Look down, fair moon (W. Whitman), 1v, pf, 1976; Slow, slow, fresh fount (B. Jonson), fl, chorus, 1977; Holy Eucharist Rite II, op.46, 1v, chorus, pf/org, 1978; When to the sessions of sweet silent thought (W. Shakespeare), op.47, 1978; 5 Haiku, op.48, S, chamber ens, 1978; 5 Haiku II, op.50, Mez, pf, 1979; Madrigals Anon, op.51, chorus, 1979; Kyrie eleison, chorus, 1983
Chbr: Nocturne, op.28, ob, va, vc, cel, harp, 1976; Quilisoly, op.38, fl/vn, pf, 1976; Elegy, op.43, str orch/str qt/(fl, eng hn, hn, bn) 1977 [formerly known as Interfuguelude]; Piece of Eight, op.42, 2 ob, 2 cl, 2 hn, 2 bn, 1977; Str Qt, 1981; Nightsongs (M. Drake), vc, pf, 1986
Pf: Sonata no.2, op.10, 1974; 2 Brief Pieces, op.12–13, 1975; Expressions intimes, op.14–18, 1975; Jimnobody no.1, op.22, 1976; Jimnobody no.2, op.24, 1976; A mon père, pour mon père, op.40, 1977; Lyric Fancies, 1983; Strains and Restraints, 1984; Charms, 1987
Elec: In the Land of Nod, synth, tape, 1979; Sunken Flutes, synth, tape, 1979; Arlington, tape, 1989; Embryonic Climactus, tape, 1989; Aquasphere, tape, 1990; The Infinite Sea, tape/(nar, tape), 1990; Momentum: a Glimpse of the Sea, tape, 1990

BIBLIOGRAPHY
G. Straughn: "Composer Profile: Elizabeth Faw Hayden Pizer," *ILWC Journal* (1994), 33

ALYSON PAYNE

Pizzarelli, Bucky [John] **(Paul, Sr.)** (*b* Paterson, NJ, 9 Jan 1926). Guitarist. He was inspired to take guitar lessons when he heard his uncle Bobby Domenick play in a quartet led by a blind accordion player named Joe Mooney. He began playing professionally at the age of 17, when he got a job with Vaughn Monroe's dance band. He was drafted into the US Army in 1944 and played with Stéphane Grappelli in recently liberated France. Their long-lasting relationship produced several duo recordings including *Stéphane Grappelli/Bucky Pizzarelli Duet* (Ahead, 1979) and *Stéphane Grappelli Live at the Blue Note* (Telarc Jazz, 1995). He worked as a staff guitarist for NBC from 1952 to 1964 and played with Doc Severinsen in the Tonight Show Band. He began playing with Benny Goodman's combo in 1966 and continued to tour with Goodman into the 1970s.

In the early 1970s he organized duos with George Barnes and Les Paul. He toured Japan with Lionel Hampton, Dexter Gordon, and Hank Jones in 1977. He is the father of renowned jazz guitarist John Pizzarelli. Their recordings together include *Complete Guitar Duos* (Stash, 1984) and *Contrasts* (Arbors Records, 1999). Bucky has also recorded with his bassist son Martin *Triple Play* (Victoria Records, 2004) and guitarist daughter Mary *Green Guitar Blues* (Monmouth Evergreen, 1972). As a versatile studio musician, he recorded with rhythm-and-blues diva Roberta Flack, *Roberta Flack/First Take* (Atlantic, 1969) and played on the soundtrack for at least 20 film scores. He is known as a standard bearer of swing and is acclaimed for his unique chord voicing, succinct phrasing, and seven-string guitar technique. He is also the author of several books on guitar techniques including *Power Guitar* and *A Pro's Approach to Melody and Chord Playing*.

BIBLIOGRAPHY
T.M. Ripmaster: *Bucky Pizzarelli: a Life in Music* (Pacific, MO, 1998)
MATTHEW ALAN THOMAS

Place. Themes involving place, location, space, and geography have profoundly shaped American music and, consequently, led scholars to examine their relationship to music production, performance, and musical meaning. While American musicians have consistently incorporated, interpreted, and interrogated musical ideas surrounding place, it is only since the 1990s that an increasing number of scholars have begun to address such themes across a wide and diverse range of musical genres.

American composers have long drawn inspiration from American places, which gained momentum in the 19th century as art music composers sought to set American composition apart from its European counterparts. Even European visitors, such as Antonín Dvořák, attempted to convey of a sense of American vistas in works such as his New World Symphony (1893). Many 19th- and early 20th-century works sought to portray American landmarks and the natural landscape while largely depending on a musical language imported from European music (Fry, *Niagara Symphony* [1854]; Grofé, *Grand Canyon Suite* [1931]). The approach of Charles Ives represents an important break from the European tradition because of the way he situated much of his music in the sonic landscape of America in pieces such as *Central Park in the Dark* (c1909) and *Three Places in New England* (c1912–21). Later in the century, Aaron Copland composed the ballet scores *Rodeo* (1942) and *Appalachian Spring* (1944), which combine American vernacular music with orchestrations featuring wide spacing between instruments—a device used for a "landscape" theme in *Appalachian Spring* that has come to be regarded as a distinctively "American" sound. Other postwar American composers, including Walter Piston, Vincent Persichetti, and William

Bolcom, have explored the sounds of place in the United States, especially in their vocal works.

American musicians also have titled compositions after places in the United States, whether cultural landmarks, local neighborhoods, or special destinations. Duke Ellington named many works after locations that were significant to him personally or to the African American community generally, such as "Harlem Air Shaft" and "East St. Louis Toodle-oo." Similar practices have continued to occupy popular genres, including hip hop (Jay-Z's "Empire State of Mind"), punk rock (X's "Los Angeles"), and country (Merle Haggard's "Okie from Muskogee"). These songs variously celebrate or critique; some reference American geography as a means of promoting "American" values.

Many compositions address American places, and the experiences of American places, without direct reference in the title, or even the lyrics. Prime examples are the songs of Bruce Springsteen, such as "Born to Run," "Glory Days," and "The Rising," which conjure the landscape of his native state, New Jersey, interpretations backed by his public statements and album titles. His audience has subsequently found ways to map the experiences depicted in his songs onto their own experiences. In their Grammy-winning album *Suburbs* (2010), the Canadian band Arcade Fire addressed life in North American suburbs with a musical language based in 21st-century indie rock. In contrast, post-minimalist composer John Luther Adams finds inspiration in his adopted state, Alaska. The title of his installation "The Place Where You Go to Listen" (2006) refers to a spot on the Arctic Coast called Naalagiagvik but also evokes less localized experiences of vast American landscapes. His installation transforms real-time information about the Alaskan environment into colors and sounds. Some artists comment on more abstract places associated with the United States, such as highways, the dance floor, and the open plains, while other works have come to be associated with a place or space through acts of reception rather than as a product of the compositional process. Two examples would be psychedelic music in 1960s San Francisco and grunge in 1990s Seattle. In both cases, the local music community collaborated in the creation of a new subgenre of rock music, which became widely popular but was commonly associated with the place and time of its creation, even when some of the genre's innovators were not located in these cities.

When scholars encounter works and music cultures with strong ties to specific places, their analyses often begin by exploring social, economic, and political contexts. Scholarship on American music has examined the function within a given community of various American organizations and institutions, such as the Boston Philharmonic, the Juilliard School, and the Hollywood Bowl. Contemporary studies of sheet music, the recording industry, or live music promotion also consider how the specifics of place in cultural expression often become more significant as technologies of transportation and communication have made the world seem smaller. The experience of listening to (and dancing to) music at a specific location (for example, house music in Chicago) may promote connections between music, place, and time. Studying the communities created by these experiences thus can reveal how musical practices have roots in the places they are created and consumed. Alternative sites for musical production create and reproduce a location-specific sound for the marketplace. In the 1960s and 70s country music artists in Los Angeles, Austin, and Nashville developed distinct styles of country music (country rock, progressive country, and country pop) that enacted the values of these communities.

Many of today's scholars of American music and place take interdisciplinary approaches. Fieldwork-based studies of music communities present opportunities to theorize how local roots impact community music practices. (Fox, 2004). Music scholars also use the study of space and place to critique traditional historiography and conventions of other music-historical discourses, suggesting that if we limit our study to the progress and development of genres and other musical practices over time, we inevitably overlook other modalities of human experience and musical meaning. Theorizing the spatial insists on the multivalent connections between musicians, audiences, and their communities, widely defined, across space and time. Music can offer the listener a virtual environment, an arena for experiencing spatial relationships and exploring attitudes about place (Watkins, 2011).

The study of place is also crucial to our understanding of power dynamics expressed by American music. For example, Ellington's representation of places opens a musical window into the impact of segregation on African Americans' lives and artistic practices. Work on how hierarchies of place in the American landscape create and change music communities and their compositions remains central. Additionally, the study of sounding places intersects with other research areas, including ecocritical and urban musicology. An ecomusicologist might consider the affect of sprawl on the American SOUNDSCAPE (Schafer, 1977), while a scholar writing about music rooted in the postindustrial urban landscape might turn to the work of urban planners and cultural geographers (Forman, 2002; Krims, 2007). In the growing field of SOUND STUDIES, scholars often consider the everyday, localized sensory experience of sound and noise (Bijsterveld, 2008; Thompson, 2002), while asking what role sound has played in the formation of American culture (Keeling and Kun, 2011).

The transnational circulation of musical practices—originating in the flow of people and capital across national boundaries—does not necessarily divorce music from place. Thanks to recordings and the movement of people, musicians have access to sounds from cultures around the world, sometimes integrating this music without regard to its cultural origins or conventional practices. Appadurai's neologisms—ethnoscapes, technoscapes, finanscapes, and mediascapes—often populate contemporary scholarship as conceptual markers. Scholars also study communities that are located in a more abstract, mediated, and imagined space rather than a single geo-graphically situated location or a group of locations (Lipsitz, 1994).

Musicology is not the first discipline to take a spatial turn since the 1990s, however its object of study, music, has long been understood as the consummate art of time. Music scholarship informed by the critical analysis of place, space, and geography necessitates rethinking and grappling with not only historical narratives, but also approaches to sound, musical analysis, and understandings of the "music itself."

See also ECOMUSICOLOGY; GEOGRAPHY.

BIBLIOGRAPHY

S. Feld: *Sound and Sentiment: Birds, Weeping, Poetics, and Song in Kaluli Expression* (Philadelphia, 2/1990)
R.M. Schafer: *The Tuning of the World* (New York, 1977)
G. Lipsitz: *Dangerous Crossroads: Popular Music, Postmodernism, and the Poetics of Place* (New York, 1994)
A. Appadurai: *Modernity at Large: Cultural Dimensions of Globalization* (Minneapolis, MN, 1996)
A. Leyshon, D. Matless, and G. Revill: *The Place of Music* (New York, 1998)
A. Bennett: *Popular Music and Youth Culture: Music, Identity, and Place* (New York, 2000)
M. Forman: *The 'Hood Comes First: Race, Space, and Place in Rap and Hip-Hop* (Middletown, CT, 2002)
E.A. Thompson: *The Soundscape of Modernity* (Cambridge, MA, 2002)
D. Von Glahn: *The Sounds of Place: Music and the American Cultural Landscape* (Boston, 2003)
A. Fox: *Real Country: Music and Language in Working-Class Culture* (Durham, NC, 2004)
B. Toliver: "Eco-ing in the Canyon: Ferde Grofé's *Grand Canyon Suite* and the Transformation of Wilderness," *JAMS*, lvii/2 (2004), 325–67
I. Biddle and V. Knight: *Music, National Identity and the Politics of Location* (Burlington, VT, 2007)
A. Krims: *Music and Urban Geography* (New York, 2007)
K. Bijsterveld: *Mechanical Sound: Technology, Culture, and Public Problems of Noise in the Twentieth Century* (Cambridge, MA, 2008)
K. Keeling and J. Kun, eds.: *Sound Clash: Listening to American Studies*, Special Issue of *American Quarterly* (2011), 445–862
H. Watkins: "Musical Ecologies of Place and Placelessness," *JAMS*, lxiv/2 (2011), 404–8

CAROLINE POLK O'MEARA

Placide, Alexandre (*b* Paris, France, 1750; *d* New York, NY, 26 July 1812). French ballet dancer, choreographer, and theatrical entrepreneur. He was the head of a family of actors, singers, and theatrical managers in London, New York, and New Orleans. A renowned performer in France and England in the 1770s and 80s and dubbed "danseur au roi" by Louis XV, Placide immigrated to Saint-Domingue (Haiti) in 1788 and to Annapolis, Maryland, in 1791. He brought a talented ballet troupe whose repertory included harlequinades and ballets of his own composition, later adding melodramatic ballet pantomimes and French operas. Critics praised Placide for his graceful, noble bearing and stylishly executed ballets and pantomimes, as well as his inventive theatrical special effects and pageantry, fabulous costumes, massed processions, and special lighting and mechanical tricks. He specialized in rope dancing and developed it into a true art form.

The company appeared in Baltimore, Philadelphia, Boston, Newport, and finally Charleston, South Carolina, in 1794, joining another company of French dancers led by Jean-Baptiste Francisqui. The expanded company flourished, presenting ballets, pantomimes, acrobatics, operas, and French plays. In 1796 the company suddenly disbanded when Placide discovered that his leading dancer and common-law wife, Suzanne Taillandet, had eloped with someone else. Soon thereafter, Placide married teenage actress Charlotte Wrighten, daughter of the brilliant actress-singer-composer Mrs. Mary Ann Pownall, and trained her to take Suzanne's place. Placide joined West and Bignall's touring company briefly and then rebuilt his own French Theatre Company around his new wife's increasing abilities. As their children grew, they were apprenticed to the stage and by 1803 began to take small roles in Placide's productions. Keeping their home base in Charleston, the troupe toured East Coast cities. Placide's death while on tour in New York in 1812 came shortly after a devastating theater fire during his benefit performance in Richmond, Virginia.

BIBLIOGRAPHY

ANB (M. Needham)

E. Willis: *The Charleston Stage in the XVIII Century, with Social Settings of the Time* (New York, 1968)

S.L. Porter: *With an Air Debonair: Musical Theatre in America 1785–1815* (Washington, DC, 1991)

M. Needham: "Placide, Alexandre," *International Encyclopedia of Dance*, v (1998), 197–9

KATE VAN WINKLE KELLER

Plains Indians. Group of Native American tribes that share certain cultural traits. They live between the Mississippi River and the Rocky Mountains, including parts of Montana, North Dakota, South Dakota, Minnesota, Wyoming, Nebraska, Iowa, Colorado, Kansas, Missouri, Oklahoma, Arkansas, and Texas, as well as eastern Alberta, southern Saskatchewan, and southwestern Manitoba.

See ARAPAHO; BLACKFOOT (I); CROW; KIOWA; OMAHA (I); PAWNEE; and SIOUX; see also NATIVE AMERICAN MUSIC.

Plançon, Pol [Paul-Henri] (*b* Fumay, Ardennes, France, 12 June 1851; *d* Paris, 11 Aug 1914). French bass. A pupil of Gilbert Duprez and Giovanni Sbriglia, he made his debut at Lyons in 1877. He first sang at the Paris Opéra in 1883 as Gounod's Méphistophélès, and remained there for ten seasons, taking part in the premieres of Massenet's *Le Cid* (Count of Gormas) and Saint-Saëns's *Ascanio* (François I), among other operas in the French repertory. On 29 November 1893 he appeared for the first time at the Metropolitan Opera as Jupiter in Gounod's *Philémon et Baucis*. His first Mephistopheles for the Metropolitan was a month later, while the company was on tour. For the next 15 years he was a leading bass at the Metropolitan, where he participated in a number of American premieres, notably of Berlioz's *La damnation de Faust* (1906). Among the parts with which he was most closely associated were Capulet and Friar Laurence (Gounod's *Roméo et Juliette*), Hermann (*Tannhäuser*), Ramfis (*Aida*), and St. Bris (Meyerbeer's *Les Huguenots*), as well as Mephistopheles. He was also well known in the United States as a recitalist.

Judging by the recordings that survive, Plançon was the most polished singer of his time. His beautiful *basse*

chantante had been admirably schooled, and his style was extremely elegant; his many recordings (1902–8) embody standards otherwise outside the experience of a present-day listener. Not only his flawless trills and rapid scales but his cantabile and pure legato, as in "Voici des roses" (*La damnation de Faust*) and "Vi ravviso" (*La sonnambula*), are exemplary.

BIBLIOGRAPHY

L. Hervingham-Root and J.F.E. Dennis: "Pol Plançon," *Record Collector*, viii/7–8 (1953), 148–91 [incl. discography and commentary by L. Hevingham-Root]

DESMOND SHAWE-TAYLOR/R

Plantation song. A type of 19th-century popular song originating in the minstrel show and current from the 1840s, generally with a text in pseudo-black dialect. Plantation songs, especially those of STEPHEN C. FOSTER, had musical and poetic ties to sentimental balladry. Such songs became extremely popular as domestic music. *See also* MINSTRELSY.

PAUL R. LAIRD

Plateau Indians. Group of Native American tribes that share certain cultural traits, living in northern Oregon and Idaho, western Montana, eastern Washington, and British Columbia. *See* FLATHEAD and COAST SALISH.

Platters, the. Popular vocal group. Its principal members were Tony Williams (*b* New Rochelle, NY, 15 April 1928; *d* New York, NY, 14 Aug 1992; lead tenor), David Lynch (*b* St. Louis, MO, 1929; *d* 2 Jan 1981; second tenor), Zola Taylor (*b* Los Angeles, CA, 17 March 1938; *d* Los Angeles, 30 April 2007; soprano), Herb Reed, and Paul Robi (*b* New Orleans, LA, 1931; *d* 2 Jan 1989; baritone). During the second half of the 1950s they applied vocal harmonies derived from African American doo-wop to mainstream popular ballads with considerable commercial success. The purity and precision of Williams's singing were the principal features of the Platters' recordings of "Only You" (1955) and "The Great Pretender" (1956), both composed by the group's manager Buck Ram. Other hit records in the United States and abroad included versions of Jimmy Kennedy's "My Prayer" (1956), Jerome Kern and Otto Harbach's "Smoke gets in your eyes" (1959), and Ram's "Twilight Time" (1958). Williams left the group in 1960 and later formed his own Platters group. His replacement was Sonny Turner, but by 1970 a series of personnel changes had led to a proliferation of units calling themselves the Platters; Ram, a trained lawyer, expended much money and energy on suing these groups for trademark infringement.

DAVE LAING/R

Player organ. An organ, other than a mechanically operated barrel organ, which may be played either by hand or by automatic means. Invariably the term is applied to an instrument functioning pneumatically by perforated paper rolls and thus similar to a player piano. The earliest player organs were reed instruments and were developed from the organette or portable automatic reed organ. The first was the Wilcox & White Symphony, made in Meriden, Connecticut, and introduced in 1888. This was little more than an American organ with a roll-playing mechanism. Vocalion, the forerunner of the Aeolian Company, was producing a small 46-note roll-played organette called the Syreno. Several versions were made including one with a keyboard called the Tonsyreno. This sired the first Aeolian player organ built into a piano-type case and working on suction. The compass was extended to 58 notes and the instrument was named the Aeolian Grand. The improved sound, achieved through individual reed cells operated by a pressure air system, gave rise to the Aeolian Orchestrelle. A wide range of Orchestrelles was made between 1890 and 1918, all featuring Vocalion-patented "tone-ranks" of "orchestrally-voiced" reeds. Although generally retaining a single keyboard, "two-manual" Orchestrelles were made which used 112-note music rolls arranged to control two separate divisions of stops: these were particularly fine instruments. Manufacture was mostly in America but many were assembled for the British market by Aeolian's piano factory at Hayes, England. Despite their relatively high cost, Orchestrelles enjoyed a popularity only terminated by the aftermath of World War I. Other makers also built player reed organs but these were much less successful and proved marketing failures, two being Bell Organ Company's Bellollian and Malcolm & Company's Phoneon. The highest quality player reed organs, however, were far superior instruments, the finest being those made by Schiedmayer in Stuttgart (the Scheola), and Mustel in Paris (the Concertal). In America, reed-organ maker Estey produced a small number of very fine and expensive pneumatically played instruments which were superior in both quality and tonality to those of Aeolian. Player-organ technology was soon applied to the pipe organ and Aeolian built a number of costly domestic instruments including some which used the Duo-Art or "reproducing" system as developed for the reproducing piano. These pipe organs controlled their own stop registration and swell shutters from the music roll. Some of the finest player pipe organs were built by Estey and Skinner (which took over Aeolian's pipe-organ division) in America and by Welte in Germany. Just as in the 1800s barrel-organ builders offered automatic organs to churches that did not have competent organists, in the opening decades of the 20th century a number of church-organ builders offered pneumatic player actions to their instruments for use when the regular organist was not available. These generally were 88-note actions which would play piano rolls, but alternatively 58-note actions could be fitted to play the rich library of Aeolian music rolls.

BIBLIOGRAPHY

J. Fox: "The Aeolian Orchestrelle," *Music & Automata*, i (London, 1984), 253–62

A.W.J.G. Ord-Hume: *Harmonium* (Newton Abbot, England, 1986)

A.W.J.G. Ord-Hume: "Who Invented the Aeolian Orchestrelle? the Story of the Vocalion," *Music & Automata*, iv (Guildford, England, 1989), 240–57

A.W.J.G. Ord-Hume: *Automatic Organs* (Atglen, PA, 2007)

ARTHUR W.J.G. ORD-HUME

Player piano. A piano fitted with a self-playing mechanism. Its different forms vary considerably in their musical capabilities and the underlying mechanisms, as well as in the amount of human intervention required for their operation.

The earliest form, the barrel piano, first appeared around 1800 as a portable street instrument. Often very limited in range and typically lacking a keyboard, it was either carried by hand or wheeled on a cart by an operator who powered it by continuously turning a crank. During the 19th century these street pianos, sometimes referred to as "hurdy-gurdies," were a regular presence on streets of large cities in both Europe and America. Due to their generally poor intonation and coarse timbre, and the limited repertoire of melodies they were capable of playing, street pianos were often considered a nuisance by those who live and worked nearby. Most barrel pianos in American cities were made in Italy or England. However, George Hicks, a British maker, moved to the United States and opened a shop in Brooklyn; one of his large barrel pianos (c1860) is in the collection of the Metropolitan Museum of Art.

At the Centennial International Exposition, held in Philadelphia in 1876, French inventor Jean-Louis-Napoléon Fourneaux showed his Pianista (invented in 1863) a piano-playing device that operated from perforated cards and was the earliest player mechanism to use a pneumatic action. Late 19th-century developments transformed the domestic self-playing piano from a rare mechanical curiosity into a mass-produced musical instrument. The most significant of these was the adoption of the perforated paper roll (already widely in use on self-playing organs) as the dominant storage medium. Paper rolls were reproducible, relatively inexpensive to manufacture, and easily interchangeable by the instrument's operator. Early manufacturers in the United States included Needham & Sons (New York City) and Wilcox & White (Meriden, CT), while the Hupfeld firm of Leipzig, Germany, led the European market. In 1895, Edwin S. Votey, an organ builder in Detroit, developed a piano-playing device which, after being acquired by the Aeolian firm the following year, became known as the Pianola. The name, chosen by Votey as a blend of the words "piano" and "Aeolian," became widely adopted as a generic term for all piano-players and player pianos. The original Pianola was separate from the instrument that it played. Described variously as "piano-players," "cabinet players," or "push-up players," these mechanisms were designed to be placed in front of a piano so that a series of mechanical "fingers" were situated directly above the keys. Cabinet players generally operated on a limited subset of the piano's range—often as few as 58 notes—and remained the most common type of self-playing device until about 1905, when they were surpassed in popularity by integrated players, in which the playing mechanism was inside the piano cabinet, usually above the keyboard.

While player pianos are often thought of as autonomous music makers, early models required a significant amount of involvement from a human operator in order to produce convincingly musical performances. Most player pianos were motivated by foot pedals, requiring a player to be seated in front of the instrument during a musical performance. Standard piano rolls included only the pitch and duration of the each note, requiring the expressive variation of tempo and dynamics to be provided by the operator (sometimes called a "piano-list") through manipulation of levers mounted either on the front of the external player's cabinet or directly below the keyboard on a player piano. This need for an operator's creative intervention was often marketed as a feature of early player instruments—an opportunity to express oneself musically without having to spend years acquiring technique—and a number of player piano method books were published in the first decades of the 20th century, including Gustav Kobbé's *The Pianolist: a Guide for Pianola Players* (New York, 1907) and Sydney Grew's *The Art of the Player-Piano: a Text-Book for Student and Teacher* (London and New York, 1922).

In addition to a growing roster of companies offering all varieties of player instruments, an entire industry was developed to provide owners with a constant supply of new music to play. While early devices typically required proprietary media designed specifically for their use, the Buffalo Convention, held on 10 December 1908, in Buffalo, New York, established industry-wide specifications for two different sizes of piano rolls (65 and 88 notes). This standardization allowed owners to access a vast assortment of music offered for sale by different manufacturers. As an alternative to purchasing rolls, the Aeolian firm offered a lending library that allowed subscribers to pick a dozen new selections every two weeks from a catalog of 17,000. The most enduring manufacturer of the piano rolls is the QRS firm, founded in Chicago in 1900 as a subsidiary of the Melville Clark Piano Company. While most roll producers ceased production in the 1930s, QRS has continued to cut new piano rolls into the 21st century.

While the musicality of early player pianos was largely dependent on their operator's skill, technological developments in the first decade of the 20th century made it possible for manufacturers to encode an increasing amount of expressive data onto their piano rolls. The Aeolian Company's "Themodist" system, introduced in 1900, allowed specific notes on a roll to be emphasized to bring out a theme. Another innovation involved printing lines on the paper roll which, when tracked by an alert operator using a special pointer, would provide subtle variations in tempo. The increasing desire to be able to encode the piano roll with more nuanced performances culminated with the introduc-

tion of reproducing pianos. The first of these were built in 1904 by the Welte-Mignon of Freiburg, Germany. By 1913 American firms began offering their own reproducing instruments, starting with the Aeolian "Duo-Art" and the American Piano Company's "Ampico" piano. Where the basic player piano had offered the amateur the possibility of playing like a virtuoso, makers of reproducing pianos lured buyers with the promise of hearing works performed exactly as they had been performed by leading pianists of the day. The rolls for reproducing pianos used propriety technologies unique to each manufacturer, and the different companies competed to acquire prestigious artists for their catalogs.

By the 1910s the player piano had became a major cultural force in the United States. In 1919, self-playing instruments (including reproducing pianos) accounted for 61% of all pianos produced in the United States (see Table 1). The player piano's market dominance was short-lived, however, because of competition from the ever-improving phonograph and the newly introduced radio. Its popularity peaked in 1923, when over 200,000 player-pianos were manufactured, then declined through the end of the 1920s, and essentially ended during the economic depression of the 1930s. (Piano roll sales peaked slightly later, in 1927, a year in which QRS sold over 10 million rolls.) While impressive in its musical capabilities, the success of the reproducing piano was limited by its extremely high cost. (In 1914, when an Aeolian Pianola upright could be purchased for about $400—and a low-end Ford Model-T for $450—an upright Steinway Duo-Art reproducing piano cost $1500.) Even at the height of their popularity in the early 1920s, production of reproducing pianos never amounted to more than 10% of the total player piano market.

The popularity of player pianos had an impact on composers of both popular and art music. Tin Pan Alley songwriters and jazz musicians, including George Gershwin, Fats Waller, Jelly Roll Morton, and Zez Confrey, were employed by music publishers to arrange and record piano rolls. Confrey capitalized on the player piano's facile execution of flashy and virtuosic music figures in his novelty piano pieces, many of which achieved popularity first as piano rolls before being sold as sheet music. The idea of composing music specifically for the player piano was taken up by 20th-century composers such as Igor Stravinsky, George Antheil, Paul Hindemith, and, most notably, Conlon Nancarrow, whose rhythmically and melodically complex compositions far exceed the abilities of a human pianist. Additionally, the large number of reproducing piano rolls made by concert pianists of the early 20th century have become an important historical resource, since they

TABLE 1: Production of Player Pianos in the United States

	1909	1914	1919	1921	1923	1925	1927	1929	1931	1935
All pianos	364,545	326,274	341,652	221,210	347,589	306,584	218,140	130,973	51,370	61,198
Player pianos*	45,414	95,402	208,541	122,439	205,556	169,193	95,454	36,504	2171	418
Percentage	12.5	29.2	61.0	55.3	59.1	55.2	43.8	27.9	4.2	0.7

*Including reproducing pianos

often preserve performance details which could not be captured by the phonographic recording process of the time. In the 1980s the Yamaha Corporation introduced the Disklavier, a digitally controlled player piano capable of both recording and reproducing performances with a high degree of precision. The success of these instruments, as well as the availability of kits to automate existing pianos, has resulted in a new class of digitally-controlled player pianos.

BIBLIOGRAPHY

G. Kobbé: *The Pianolist: a Guide for Pianola Players* (New York, 1907)
J. McTammany: *The Technical History of the Player* (New York, 1915/*R*)
W.B. White: *Piano Playing Mechanisms* (New York, 1925/*R*)
L. Givens: *Re-Enacting the Artist: a Story of the Ampico Reproducing Piano* (Vestal, NY, 1970)
H. Roehl: *Player Piano Treasury* (Vestal, NY, 1961, 2/1973)
A.W.J.G. Ord-Hume: *Automatic Pianos: a Collector's Guide to the Pianola, Barrel Piano, and Aeolian Orchestrelle* (Atglen, PA, 2004)
B. Dolan: *Inventing Entertainment: the Player Piano and the Origins of an American Musical Industry* (Lanham, MD, 2009)

EDMOND T. JOHNSON

Playlist. A selection of popular songs guaranteed air time on a given radio station. It first originated in the 1940s and 50s in American radio broadcasting. The Top 40 playlist included those songs currently in the higher reaches of the chart, a selection of those records climbing the chart but still outside the Top 40, a number of new releases, mostly from major records labels and which were predicted to become hits, and a few older songs considered classics. Some of these records, for example the current number one, were played several times a day ("heavy rotation"), while other playlisted items were guaranteed to be heard only a few times each week. The format was open to corruption as record labels attempted to buy their records airtime ("payola"). Over the years concerns have also been raised about the inability of popular artists from contested genres, such as punk, metal, and hip hop, to gain access to spots on mainstream radio playlists. In the 1980s the term was adapted (as video playlist) to the videos played by channels such as MTV. Today *playlist* also refers to the customized list of songs that any individual can organize and play using software on a personal computer or by accessing various Internet-radio websites.

DAVID BUCKLEY/R

Pleasants, Henry (*b* Wayne, PA, 12 May 1910; *d* London, 4 Jan 2000). Author and critic. He trained as a singer and pianist at the Philadelphia Musical Academy and Curtis Institute of Music, with subsequent private studies in singing, piano, and composition. In 1930 he became music critic for the *Philadelphia Evening Bulletin*, and music editor from 1934. After army service (1942–50), mostly in North Africa and Europe, he joined the US Foreign Service and was based successively in Munich, Berne, and Bonn (1950–64). During this time (1945–55) he was also central European music correspondent for the *New York Times*. He settled in London and was London music critic for the *International Herald Tribune* (1967–97) and an editor for *Stereo*

Review, as well as a frequent contributor to the musical press in Britain and the United States. The Curtis Institute awarded him an honorary doctorate in 1977. He was married to the harpsichordist and fortepianist Virginia Pleasants.

Pleasants's writings extend and elaborate a critical principle which accords serious attention to the popular musical vernacular of the 20th century (jazz, musical theater, rock, and pop), in the belief that these styles have gained a dominant position in world music not only as commercial entertainment, but also as art. His study of great singers is related to this in suggesting that the art of singing reached its zenith in the Baroque period; since then it has been in conflict with the demands of emotional expression and compositional techniques and cannot survive if lyrical grace is not the chief element of its style.

WRITINGS
(*selective list*)

The Agony of Modern Music (New York, 1955)
Death of a Music? the Decline of the European Tradition and the Rise of Jazz (London, 1961)
ed. and trans.: *The Musical Journeys of Louis Spohr* (Norman, OK, 1961)
The Great Singers: From the Dawn of Opera to Our Own Time (New York, 1966)
Serious Music—and All That Jazz! (New York and London, 1969)
The Great American Popular Singers (New York, 1974)
ed. and trans.: *The Music Criticism of Hugo Wolf* (New York, 1978)
Opera in Crisis (London, 1989)

NOËL GOODWIN/R

Pleasure garden. An open-air venue featuring entertainment, music, and food. With the establishment of a stable middle-class in 18th-century England, gardens were created, such as London's Vauxhall Gardens, as an entertainment venue primarily for tradespeople. These featured flowering plants, musical performances (orchestral and vocal), fountains, light refreshments (especially tea), and various entertainments. Emulating the British concept, American pleasure gardens were created in colonial America, in cities such as Williamsburg and Jamestown. By the 19th century, gardens such as the Palace Garden in New York City became public gathering places for many recreational activities, including music and other stage performances, sports, games, and circuses.

BIBLIOGRAPHY

A. Scott-James and O. Lancaster: *The Pleasure Garden: an Illustrated History of British Gardening* (London, 1977)
P. Martin: *The Pleasure Gardens of Virginia: From Jamestown to Jefferson* (Princeton, 1991)
J.W. Frick: "Fireworks, Bonfires, Ballrooms and More: New York's Palace Garden," n.d., <http://www.circusinamerica.org/docs/frick_garden.pdf>

JOANNA R. SMOLKO

Plena. Puerto Rican music genre. Plena is a street genre of Puerto Rico that was born of the poor and largely black urban experience at the end of the industrial revolution. The most widely accepted history situates Plena's origins in the neighborhood of La Joya del Castillo in the southern town of Ponce during the turn of the 19th century. Plena is characterized by handheld drums. These *panderetas* (also called *panderos*) are pan drums that are held in one hand and played with the other; early pleneros (or plena practitioners) used two similarly sized drums. A lead drum identified as requinto was (and continues to be) used to improvise a variety of slaps; the seguidor (or second drum) provided the steady rhythm. The accordion, marimbula, and the güicharo are among the earliest accompanying instruments. Contemporary practice utilizes three drums: the largest is the *seguidor grande*; the midsize is the *seguidor pequeño* (also known as the *punteador* or *banao*); and the smallest is the *requinto*. Other instruments used in modern interpretations include the cuatro (a ten-string guitar-like implement) and various forms of percussion. The earliest pleneros included Carolina "Carola" Clark George, Bumbún [Joselino Oppenheimer], Gumersindo "Sindo" Mangual Oppenheimer, and Eustacio Flores Llano among others.

BIBLIOGRAPHY

J. Flores: "'Bumbún' and the Beginnings of Plena Music," *Divided Borders: Essays on Puerto Rican Identity* (Houston, 1993), 85–91

F. Echevarria Alvarado: *La plena, origen, sentido y desarrollo en el folklore puertorriqueño* (Santurce, 1984)

M. Miller: "Plena and the Negotiation of 'National' Identity in Puerto Rico," *Centro Journal*, xvi/1 (2004), 36–59

R. López: *Los Bembeteos de La Plena Puertorriqueña* (San Juan, 2007)

MELANIE MALDONADO

Pleskow, Raoul (*b* Vienna, Austria, 12 Oct 1931). Composer of Austrian birth. He immigrated to the United States in 1939 and was naturalized in 1945. From 1950 to 1952 he attended the Juilliard School; at Queens College, New York (BM 1956), he studied composition with KAROL RATHAUS, and at Columbia University (MM 1958) he was a pupil of OTTO LUENING. In 1959 he joined the faculty of C.W. Post College, Long Island University (from 1970 he was a full professor), where he was a colleague of Wolpe. He has received awards from, among others, the Ford Foundation (1972), the Martha Baird Rockefeller Fund for Music (1972), the NEA (1974, 1975, 1978), the National Institute of Arts and Letters (1974), and the Guggenheim Foundation (1977).

Pleskow has acknowledged the importance of his "apprenticeship" with Wolpe in learning a "manner of covering musical space" and speaks of his "admiration for the coolness and serenity of 'classicism.'" Earlier pieces such as Music for 7 Players, *Movement for Nine Players* (1965), and Three Bagatelles for solo piano (1969) are in an atonal, or loose 12-tone idiom; their motifs and melodies, disjunct in register and rhythmically asymmetrical, are punctuated by chordal attacks or silences. Since the 1980s, his pieces have combined tonal and atonal elements. The Four Bagatelles for Orchestra (1981), the best known of his early works in this style, are distinguished by their long Romantic melodies in tempo rubato, treated contrapuntally. Recent works written for saxophonist Marshall Taylor and pianist Samuel Hsu are highly sensitive to the implications of register and timbre in shaping both hybrid and nontonal forms. Pleskow claims to have composed these works by remembering dreams in which the new piece sounds in concert.

WORKS
(selective list)
(from a list compiled by Ephraim Schäfli)

ORCH

2 Movts, 1968; 3 Pieces, chbr orch, 1974; Fantasia Sopra Ave Regina Coelorum, solo inst, chbr orch, 1977; Suite, 1978; Music for Orch, 1980; 4 Bagatelles, 1981; 6 Epigrams, orch, 1984; 2 Preludes, 1987; Consort, str, 1987–8; Dezembermusik, chbr orch,1992; 5 Brief Episodes, pf, orch, 1996

INSTS

Form I, vn, pf, 1959; Qt, fl, cl, vn, vc, 1960; Crossplay, fl, cl, vib, pf, vn, vc, 1963; Music For 7 Players, fl, cl, hp, perc, pf, vn, vc, 1965; Movt for 9 Players, fl, tpt, cl, pf, cel, perc, vn, vc, db, 1965; 3 Movts for Qnt, fl, cl, pf, vn, vc, 1971; 2 Canzoni, ob + eng hn, vn, pf, 1973; Str Qt no.1, 1980; Str Qt no.2, 1981; Epigrams, str qt, 1985; 2 Arabesques, fl, 2 cl, vn, va, vc, db, pf, 1988; 6 Fancies on Pictures of Paul Klee, pf, vn, va, vc, 1992; Perc Duo, mar, pf, 1994; Soliloquy and Dialogue, s sax, pf, 1998, rev. 2000; Sextet "Wintergesänge," fl, cl, bn, vn, va, vc, 1999; 4 Bagatelles, str qt, 2005; 7 Canzoni, a sax, pf, 2006; Chbr Conc., tpt/a sax solo, fl, cl, bn, pf, vn, va, vc, 2007; Dialogue, pf solo, fl, cl/a sax, vc, 2009

SOLO INST

Piece, pf, 1967; Bagatelles, vn, 1968; 3 Pieces, pf, 1968; 3 Bagatelles, pf, 1969; Prelude and Bagatelle, pf, 1976; Prelude, Bagatelle, and Fantasiestück, pf, 1980; Caprice, pf, 1983; 4 Images/Pf Sonata no.1, 1989; 3 Laudi, org, 1989; Pf Sonata no.2, 1993; Pf Sonata no.3, 1997; Pf Sonata no.4, 1999; Albumblatt I and II (10/12/08, von meinen Winter bewußt), a sax, 2008; Maestro Hsu, His Fantasy, pf, 2010

VOCAL

3 Early Songs (Bible, hymn texts, R. Greene) v, pf, 1961; 2 Songs on Latin Fragments (Liber Usualis), (arr.), S, pf, 1972; Cant. no.1 (Bible), S, T, SATB, red. orch, 1975; On 2 Ancient Texts (trouvère song, Ave Regina Coelorum), S, fl, cl, pf, vc, 1975; On 3 Old English Rhymes (anon., 15th & 16th cen.), S, fl, cl, pf, vc, 1976; Cant. no.2 (Bible), T, Mez, SATB, fl, 2 cl, pf, vn, va, vc, 1979; 6 Brief Verses (Liber usualis), female vv, str orch, pf, 1983; Paumanok: a Long Island Cant. (W. Whitman), S, SATB, fl, cl, pf, timp, 2 vn, va, vc, 1985; 3 Songs on Texts of Oscar Wilde, v, pf, 1987; Te Deum (Catholic hymn), 2 S, T, chorus, chbr orch, 1994; Sextet with Voice (Hölderlin), S, ob/s sax, cl, str qt, 2010

Principal publishers: ACA, McGinnis & Marx

SEVERINE NEFF

Plimpton, Job (*b* Medway, MA, 27 Feb 1784; *d* Brookline, MA, 1864). Composer, compiler, teacher, and organ builder. He worked from 1806 to 1820 as a music teacher in New York City, though he spent some time in Albany in 1819. In September 1820 he performed at Boston's Columbian Museum on the Apollino, a panharmonicon that he claimed to have invented (announced in *The Euterpeiad*, i/23 (1820), 91). He later built reed organs and in 1836 exhibited an eight-stop instrument of his own design at Boston's Mechanic's Fair. He compiled *The Washington Choir* (Boston, 1843), a collection of temperance music that identifies him on its title-page as "pupil of Dr. G.K. Jackson," who was active in New York between 1802 and 1812. Plimpton's few surviving compositions include eight marches, an air, a waltz, and a minuet in *The Universal Repository of Music* (a collection now in the New York Public Library, which he copyrighted on 10 December 1808 but apparently never published), *Behold the Lovely Vernal Rose*, a song for voice and keyboard (New York, 1816), and a few songs in *The Washington Choir*.

BIBLIOGRAPHY
R.J. Wolfe: *Secular Music in America, 1801–1825: a Bibliography* (New York, 1964)
B. Owen: *The Organ in New England* (Raleigh, 1979), 410
RICHARD CRAWFORD

Plishka, Paul (*b* Old Forge, PA, 28 Aug 1941). Bass. He studied with Armen Boyajian at Montclair State College, making his debut with Paterson Lyric Opera, an opera workshop founded by Bisio and Boyajian, in 1961. At age 23 Plishka launched his career by winning the Baltimore Opera auditions and the Met Opera Regional Auditions. His Met career began in earnest in 1965, singing Mozart's Bartolo and Puccini's Colline. After the touring company ceased operations, he was selected to join the Metropolitan Opera at Lincoln Center in 1967 under the aegis of Risë Stevens, where he made his house debut as Monk in *La Gioconda* and his company debut as Bonze in *Madama Butterfly*. Since then he has appeared in more than 1600 Met performances in approximately 50 roles, both in the serious and *buffo* categories, including Leporello and the Commendatore, Oroveso (*Norma*), Silva (*Ernani*), Fiesco (*Boccanegra*), Philippe II (*Don Carlos*), Frere Laurent (*Romeo et Juliette*), and King Mark. During his long professional career he has sung virtually all of the major operatic roles for bass at principal opera houses in the United States and Europe, impressing audiences with his rich, clear, elegant, and powerful voice, as well as his stylistic flexibility and dramatic skill.

BIBLIOGRAPHY
B. Kellow: "Man About the House," *ON*, lv/14 (1991), 14–17
MARTIN BERNHEIMER/ELDONNA L. MAY

Plog, Anthony (*b* Glendale, CA, 13 Nov 1947). Composer, trumpet player, and educator. Plog began studying music at age ten; at age 19 he was performing as an extra musician with the Los Angeles Philharmonic. His orchestral experience includes serving as principal trumpet of the San Antonio Symphony and associate principal of the Utah Symphony. In 1990 he moved to Europe to play solo trumpet with the Malmö Symphony in Sweden, and since 1993 he has been a professor at the Staatliche Hochschule für Musik in Freiburg, Germany. He has also taught trumpet at California State University, Northridge, University of Southern California, Music Academy of the West, Schola Cantorum, Malmö Music Academy, and Accademia di Santa Cecilia in Rome. Since 2001 he has focused on composition, initially writing exclusively for brass instruments and then broadening his scope. In 2004 the Utah Symphony premiered his children's opera, *How the Trumpet Got Its Toot*. He has received grants and commissions from the National Endowment for the Arts, the Malmö Symphony, the Utah Symphony, the Summit Brass, and the Chicago Chamber Musicians.

JASON S. BERGMAN

Poe, Edgar Allan (*b* Boston, MA, 19 Jan 1809; *d* Baltimore, MD, 7 Oct 1849). Writer. Beyond its bizarre and otherworldly surface, his work reveals a rare psychological acuity, a willingness to plunge into the darkest areas of the human mind. This and his technique of symbol and suggestion recommended his writings to many composers at the turn of the century. Claude Debussy and Maurice Ravel claimed that they were more influenced by Poe than by any music or composer. Debussy, who was fascinated by the tales in Baudelaire's translation, planned a work based on *The Fall of the House of Usher* at least as early as 1890; eighteen years later he was projecting this (with *The Devil in the Belfry*) as a double bill for the New York Metropolitan. Poe's influence involves not just vocal settings of texts but a literary philosophy shaping a musical one, something far more intricate and mysterious. His advocacy of technical refinement and unity of atmosphere, as well as uncompromising anti-didacticism, attracted a variety of composers, including Serge Rachmaninoff, Florent Schmitt, Joseph Holbrooke, Darius Milhaud, and Olivier Messiaen. Poe's view of music as "suggestive and indefinite"—"sensations which bewilder while they enthrall"—bears comparison with that of the symbolists. The sympathy he found between musical sounds and mental states is most fully expounded in *The Bells*, which inspired Rachmaninoff's choral symphony of the same name; a similar parallel is found in the linking of the sensitive and troubled Roderick Usher with the vibrating strings of a guitar. The most European of American writers, Poe magnetized first European composers, but in the later 20th and early 21st centuries he inspired settings by numerous Americans, including Leonard Bernstein, Charles Sanford Skilton, George Crumb, Leonard Slatkin, Philip Glass, Damon Ferrante, Augusta Read Thomas, and Deborah Drattell. Among notable recent works are Han-Peter Kyburtz's apocalyptic *Maelstrom* and Einojuhani Rautavaara's ambitious *On the Last Frontier* which uses tight parallel harmonies to evoke the claustrophobic vastness of Poe's sea tales.

BIBLIOGRAPHY
GroveO (B.R. Pollin)
M.G. Evans: *Music and Edgar Allan Poe* (Baltimore, MD, 1939/*R*)
E. Lockspeiser: *Debussy et Edgar Poe: manuscrits et documents inédits* (Monaco, 1962) [incl. lib, scenario, and sketches by Debussy for Poe operas]
B.R. Pollin: "More Music to Poe," *ML*, liv (1973), 391–404
R. Orledge: *Debussy and the Theater* (Cambridge, MA, 1982)
B.R. Pollin: "Music and Poe: a Second Annotated Check List," *Poe Studies*, xv/2 (1982), 7–13, 42
J. Sullivan: "New Worlds of Terror: the Legacy of Poe," *New World Symphonies* (New Haven, CT, 1999), 61–94
J. Sullivan: "Poe and Music: a Continuing Legacy," *The Edgar Allan Poe Review*, iv/2 (2003), 72–76
PAUL GRIFFITHS/JACK SULLIVAN

Pointer Sisters, the. R&B group. Its key members have been sisters June, Bonnie, Anita, and Ruth, although Bonnie left the group prior to its greatest success. The sisters grew up with gospel music, performing in their church choir in Oakland, California. They formed a singing group in the early 1970s, and though an initial deal with Atlantic Records proved unsuccessful, they found opportunities providing backing vocals for other artists, including Grace Slick and Boz Scaggs. Signing with Blue Thumb Records, their 1973 self-titled debut featured a pop hit "Yes we can can" (no.11), written by Allen Touissant. Through the 70s their fame grew slowly with a sound and image that recalled the 1940s, complete with feather boas and floral dresses. This incarnation of the group found its greatest success with 1975's *Steppin'*, featuring the Grammy-nominated single "How Long (Betcha' Got a Chick on the Side)."

Following a brief breakup when Bonnie left the group for a modestly successful solo career, the remaining sisters reunited and began cultivating an upbeat modern pop sound. After signing with Planet Records, a series of successful hits followed, beginning with the Bruce Springsteen–composed "Fire" in 1979 and peaking with the 1983 album *Break Out* on RCA. That record garnered two Grammy Awards and featured the top-10 hits "Jump (For My Love)" and "I'm so excited." The group released three more albums in the 80s, though their success dwindled. The sisters continued to tour through the 2000s as a nostalgia act with Ruth's daughter Issa replacing June, who passed away in 2006.

BIBLIOGRAPHY
J. Slater: "They Update the Past," *Ebony*, xxix/2 (Dec 1973), 103–13
A. Collier: "Pointer Sisters Shed Old Look, Old Clothes to Reach New Heights," *Jet*, lxviii/5 (15 April 1985), 58–60

RYAN R. McNUTT

Poister, Arthur William (*b* Galion, OH, 13 June 1898; *d* Durham, NC, 25 Feb 1980). Organist, teacher, and clinician. Arthur Poister studied at the American Conservatory, Chicago (BM 1925, MM 1931). After teaching at Central High School in Sioux City, Iowa (1925), Poister studied abroad with Marcel Dupré (Paris, 1925–6, 1927–8) and with Karl Straube (Leipzig, 1933–4). He taught organ and theory at the University of Redlands, California (1928–37), and was professor of organ at the University of Minnesota (1937–8), Oberlin Conservatory (1938–48), and Syracuse University (1948–67), where he was also University Organist and Director of Music for Hendricks Chapel. He was recognized for excellence in teaching by a DMus degree from Morningside College in Sioux City and a Chancellor's medal from Syracuse University. After his retirement from Syracuse, he taught at Hollins College, Oberlin Conservatory, University of Colorado, Longwood College, and Meredith College. In his younger years Poister was a successful touring recitalist, but he is better known as a teacher. Among his many students were Will Headlee, Wayne Leupold, Leonard Raver, Roger Nuquist, Donald Sutherland, and Marianne Webb. In addition are the hundreds of other organists who came under his influence through workshops and master classes across the country. Poister also had a close working relationship with the Cleveland organ builder Walter Holtkamp Sr.

VERNON GOTWALS/SARAH L. MARTIN

Pojoaque. Native Americans of the Tewa subgroup of the Eastern Pueblo.

Polacco, Giorgio (*b* Venice, Italy, 12 April 1873; *d* New York, NY, 30 April 1960). Italian conductor. After studies in Venice, Milan, and St. Petersburg, he was engaged as an assistant at Covent Garden in 1890 and made his debut the next year at the Shaftesbury Theatre, conducting Christoph Willibald Ritter von Gluck's *Orfeo ed Euridice*. He quickly became a successful opera conductor in many European cities, in Russia, and in South America and conducted for Luisa Tetrazzini's American debuts in Mexico in 1905 and at San Francisco in 1906. In 1911 he directed the first English production in the United States of Giacomo Puccini's *La fanciulla del West* by the Savage company and took the production on tour. He made his Metropolitan debut the next year with *Manon Lescaut* and remained there until 1917, succeeding Arturo Toscanini as director of the Italian repertory in 1915. He conducted in Chicago (1918–19) and returned there in 1921 from Europe at the invitation of Mary Garden; the Chicago Civic Opera was formed in 1922, and Polacco was principal conductor until ill-health forced him to retire in 1930. His performances were noted for precision and vigor, and in addition to Wagner and Italian operas he became a leading conductor of French opera under Mary Garden's influence at Chicago. He appeared at Covent Garden in 1912–13 and made his last appearances there in 1930 conducting *Pelléas et Mélisande* with Maggie Teyte, who in her autobiography (London, 1958) described him as that opera's "ideal interpreter."

RICHARD D. FLETCHER

Polansky, Larry (*b* New York, NY, 16 Oct 1954). Composer, performer, and theorist. He began his career playing jazz and rock guitar before composition studies with James Tenney and Gordon Mumma at the University of California, Santa Cruz (BA mathematics and music 1976) and Ben Johnston at the University of Illinois, Urbana-Champaign (MA composition 1978). He taught at Mills (1981–90) and Dartmouth (1990–) and is coauthor (with David Rosenboom and Phil Burke) of the computer music language HMSL (Hierarchical Music Specification Language). Polansky has distributed American experimental music through Frog Peak Music, a composers' collective he founded in 1983, and his writings on American composers. A skilled performer on the guitar, mandolin, and *gendér*, he employs conventional Western instruments, Javanese instruments, interactive computer, instruments and computer, and tape. Following Tenney, Polansky's music focuses on the gradual transformation (or mutation, as he calls it) of elements through complex gradual processes. His compositions, which often require computer control of those processes, explore pure tunings, morphological metrics (the measurement of musical shapes), mutation functions (the transformation of one shape into another), societies of mind (complex systems made of simple parts), and world musics.

WORKS
(selective list)

Movt for Lou Harrison, 4 db, 1975, rev. 1988; Sh'ma (Fuging Tune in G), fl, a fl, vn, va, vc, db, perc, 1978; Psaltery, tape, 1979; Another You, hp, 1980; V'leem'Shol […and to rule…], 5 fl, 1984; Hensley Variations, fl, va, gui, 1985; Al Het, S, gender, gambang, 1986; Distance Music, cptr, 1986; Gottlieb Variations, vc, gui, hp, 1986; Simple Actions, cptr, 1986; Lonesome Road, pf, 1989; Bedhaya Sadra/Bedhaya

Guthrie, vv, insts, gamelan, 1990; 51 Melodies, 2 elec gui, rock band, 1991; The World's Longest Melody, cptr, 1992; The Casten Variation, pf, 1994; 51 Harmonies, perc, elec gui, cptr, 1994; for jim, ben and lou, gui, hp, perc, 1995; 17 Behaviors, cptr, 1996; II-V-I, 1/2 elec gui, 1997; Piker, pic, 1998; 3 Vc Tunes, 1998; 3 Shaker Songs, elec gui, v, 1999; 3 Fiddle Tune Transcriptions by R.C. Seeger, 2 gui, 2000; Astraphony, chorus, tape, 2001; to foster and encourage (Anna Study no.4), tape, 2005; Ladies Auxiliary, mix ens, 2006; 4 Voice Canons no.2–23b, various insts, 1975–2008; Pedagogy, 6 vv, 6 gui, 2009; Simple song (agnosia), pf, v, 2010

MSS in Paddock Music Library, Dartmouth College, Hanover
Publisher: Frog Peak Music

WRITINGS

The Early Works of James Tenney (Santa Fe, NM, 1983)
"Paratactical Tuning: An Agenda for the Use of Computers in Experimental Intonation," *Computer Music Journal*, xi/1 (1987), 61–8
"Morphological Metrics," *Journal of Contemporary Music Research*, xxv (1996), 289–368
with J. Kennedy: "'Total Eclipse': the Music of Johanna Magdalena Beyer," *MQ*, lxxx/4 (Winter 1996), 719–78
ed.: *The Music of American Folk Song* (Rochester, 2001)
with D. Rockmore, D. Repetto, M.K. Johnson, and W. Pan: "A Mathematical Model for Optimal Tuning Systems," *PNM*, xlvii/1 (Winter 2009), 69–110

CARTER SCHOLZ/S. ANDREW GRANADE

Polaski, Deborah (*b* Richmond Center, WI, 26 Sept 1949). Soprano. She studied at Marion College, Indiana, and with Irmgard Hartmann in Berlin and made her debut in 1976 at Gelsenkirchen. After appearing at Munich, Hamburg, Karlsruhe, and Ulm, she sang Death/Judas in Gottfried Einem's *Jesu Hochzeit* at Hanover (1980); Marie (*Wozzeck*), Isolde, and Kundry at Freiburg (1983–5); Katerina Izmaylova at Mannheim (1985–6); Amelia (*Un ballo in maschera*) at Essen and Chrysothemis at Geneva (1986); Senta at La Scala and in Prague (1988); Richard Strauss's Electra at Zurich (1991) and Salzburg (1994); and Kundry for her Metropolitan debut (1992) and at Bayreuth (1993). With a powerful, vibrant voice of true dramatic proportions, she is well equipped to tackle the heavier Strauss and Wagner repertory. She has sung Brünnhilde at Bayreuth in several seasons since 1988; she has also sung the part at Cologne (1990), the Berlin Staatsoper (1993–4), and Covent Garden (1994–5). Her other roles include the Marschallin, the Dyer's Wife, and Dido and Cassandra in *Les Troyens*, for which she was acclaimed at the 2000 Salzburg Festival. Polaski has recorded Electra, Brünnhilde, Isolde, Ortrud in *Lohengrin* (with Daniel Barenboim), and Ermanno Wolf-Ferrari's *Sly*. In 2010 she was awarded an honorary doctorate from the University of Cincinnati.

ELIZABETH FORBES/PETER MONDELLI

Poleri, David S(amuel) (*b* Chestnut Hill, PA, 10 Jan 1921; *d* Hanalei, HI, 13 Dec 1967). Tenor. He studied in Philadelphia and New York. In 1949 he made his operatic debut in the title role of *Faust* in Chicago with Fortune Gallo's touring San Carlo Opera. He sang with the New York City Opera (Alfredo and Massenet's *Des Grieux*, both 1951) and with other leading opera companies in the United States. He sang Don Alvaro (*La forza del destino*) with Glyndebourne Opera at Edinburgh in 1951, returning in 1955. At Florence (1953–4) he sang Hermann in *The Queen of Spades* and Andrey in *Mazepa*, and later he appeared at Perugia and Genoa. In 1954 he

created the role of Michele in Menotti's *The Saint of Bleecker Street* in New York, and then sang the role in the Italian premiere at La Scala; he appeared as Prince Troilus in the Italian premiere of *Troilus and Cressida* in 1956, the year of his Covent Garden debut as Riccardo. With the Chicago Lyric Opera (1961–2) he sang Don Alvaro and Vladimir Igorevich (*Prince Igor*). A pioneer in televised opera, in 1955 he sang Cavaradossi (*Tosca*) for NBC television. Poleri had a strong, ringing voice and a fine stage presence. He died in a helicopter crash.

CHARLES A. JAHANT, ELIZABETH FORBES

Police, the. Rock group. It was formed in London in 1977 by progressive rock drummer Stewart Copeland (*b* Alexandria, VA, 16 July 1952), who was inspired by new opportunities facilitated by the emergence of punk. He recruited jazz-fusion vocalist-bassist STING [Gordon Sumner] (*b* Wallsend, UK, 2 Oct 1951) and later that year the veteran guitarist Andy [Andrew] Summers (*b* Poulton-le-Fylde, UK, 31 Dec 1942). At first a vehicle for Copeland's punk-like songs, Sting soon came to the fore as the dominant songwriter. Performances on stage and record consciously channeled the energy of punk while avoiding its polemic, and the band began to experiment with dub reggae rhythmic and bass techniques in short, sharp, pop-punk compositions.

The bands breakthrough came in the United States with "Roxanne" and the album *Outlandos d'Amour* (1978), with the follow-up *Reggatta de Blanc* (1979) and songs "Message in a Bottle" and "Walking on the Moon" achieving international success. The band was at the vanguard of the new wave rock sound that became popular in the United States in the early 1980s.

Zenyatta Mondatta (1980), *Ghost in the Machine* (1981), and *Synchronicity* (1983) exposed the previously veiled jazz, world music, and progressive musical interests of the band, with the inclusion of synthesizer, saxophone, piano, and layered guitars and vocals that gradually eschewed the reggae references and musical minimalism of their early music, but retained a pop appeal. *Synchronicity*, including "Every Breath You Take," reached no.1 on the Billboard 200 but proved the band's musical swan song, although they reformed for a lucrative world tour in 2007–8.

RECORDINGS
(selective list)
Message in a Box: The Complete Recordings (1993, A&M Records)

BIBLIOGRAPHY
S. Dalton: "The Police (retrospective and interview)," *Uncut* (April 2002)
C. Campion: *Walking on the Moon: the Untold Story of The Police and the Rise of New Wave Rock* (London, 2010)

SEAN ALBIEZ

Polin, Claire (*b* Philadelphia, PA, 1 Jan 1926; *d* Merion, PA, 6 Dec 1995). Composer, flutist, and musicologist. She studied at the Philadelphia Conservatory (BMus 1948, MMus 1950, DMus 1955), where her teachers included VINCENT PERSICHETTI, and later with Mennin at the Juilliard School of Music, and with ROGER SESSIONS and

LUKAS FOSS at Tanglewood. A flute student of WILLIAM KIN-
CAID (with whom she wrote two books on flute playing),
she was active both as a solo performer and as a
member of the Panorphic Duo. She held teaching appointments at the Philadelphia Conservatory (1949–64)
and Rutgers University (1958–91). Among her honors
were a MacDowell Colony Fellowship (1968), the Delta
Omicron International Composers Award (1953, 1958),
and numerous ASCAP awards.

Polin's scholarly interests included early Welsh music;
she published several articles on the harp music found
in the Ap Huw Manuscript. Additionally, she had an
abiding interest of Russian folk and contemporary
music, particularly that composed by women. While in
Russia during the 1980s, she conducted interviews with
Sofia Gubaidulina, Elena Firsova, and Ivana Loudova.
Polin's compositions, generally scored for solo instruments or chamber groups, often reflected her research,
incorporating folk material into an otherwise freely
atonal idiom. Polin incorporated much natural imagery
as well. Her *Cader Idris* (1971) for brass quintet takes
its inspiration from birdsong heard on the Welsh mountain of the same name. The piece contains various fragments that the performers assemble, sounding much
like a chorus of birds randomly singing at dawn. *O
Aderyn Pur* (1973) for flute and alto saxophone also
incorporates tape featuring manipulation of birdsongs
into the final movement. *Windsongs* (1978) for soprano
and guitar offers two poems, one in Russian and one in
Old Welsh about the wind. Her *Mythos* (1982) harp concerto incorporates scales from the Near East. Overall,
her writing is quite difficult; sparse, delicate textures
and an emphasis on contemporary instrumental techniques are also characteristic of her works.

WORKS
(selective list)

Orch: Sym. in 2 Movts, 1960; Sym. no.2, 1963; Scenes from Gilgamesh,
fl, str, 1972; Journey of Owain Madoc, brass qnt, perc, orch, 1973;
Golden Fleece, 1979; Mythos, conc., hp, str, 1982

Chbr: Str Qt no.1, 1953; Sonata no.1, fl, hp, 1959; Str Qt no.2, 1959;
Sonata no.2, fl, hp, 1961; Str Qt no.3, 1961; Consecutivo, fl, cl, pf trio,
1966; Makimono, fl, cl, pf trio, 1968; Cader Idris, brass qnt, 1971; O,
Aderyn Pur, fl, sax, tape, 1973; Death of Procris, fl, tuba, 1973; Res
naturae, ww qnt, 1980; Felina, Felina, vn, hp, 1981; Ma'alot, va, perc
qt, 1981; Kuequenaku-Cambriola, pf, perc, 1982; Walum olum, cl, va,
pf, 1984; Freltic Sonata, vn, pf, 1985; Garden of Earthly Delights,
wind qnt, 1987; Phantasmagoria, pf 4 hands, 1990

Solo inst: Serpentine, va, 1965; Structures, fl, 1965; Summer Settings,
hp, 1967; Margoa, fl, 1972; Eligmos archaioi, hp, 1972; Pièce
d'encore, va/vn, 1976; Georgics, fl, 1981; Hortus nardiensis, hp,
1986; Shirildang, pf, 1991

Vocal: No-rai, S, fl, db, 1963–4; Infinito, nar, S, SATB, a sax, dancer,
1972; Isaiah Syndrome, SATB, opt. insts, 1980; Paraselen, song cycle,
S, fl, pf, 1982; Mystic rondo, song cycle, T, vn, pf, 1987–8

Principal publishers: Seesaw, Dorn

MARGARET E. THOMAS/ALYSON PAYNE

Polish American music. *See* EUROPEAN AMERICAN MUSIC.

Political music. While much American political music has
roots in traditional song and balladry, the category includes many other kinds of music. From electoral songs
of the 1730s to punk rock protests of the 1980s, political music belongs to no one form nor does it fall entirely
into any one of the categories of popular, traditional, or
art music. Music may be deemed political when its
lyrics or melody reflect a political stance or evoke a
political judgment in the listener. Thus in some cases,
depending on the period, performer, and audience, a
single piece may or may not qualify as political music.
Any comprehensive definition of political music must
also take into account the context in which it is performed. "Who killed Cock Robin?," for example, and
many other pieces now regarded as nursery rhymes,
began as political allegories and have themselves since
been parodied. Yet among the most common types of
political music are campaign songs and music of political protest, including labor, populist, suffragist, and
abolitionist songs.

1. To the Civil War. 2. From 1861 to World War I. 3. Since 1919.

1. TO THE CIVIL WAR. The history of political music in the
United States predates the founding of the Union. From
Europe, Britain, West Africa, the Caribbean, and elsewhere, settlers brought with them distinct musical traditions; and with these traditions settlers furnished new
socio-political contexts. The first colonial broadsides
were probably those sold on the streets of Boston complaining of injustices by colonial governors. (*See* BROAD-
SIDE.) In early 18th-century New York, during a period
when the laboring classes were disenfranchised, election
day inspired many class-conscious songs and verses. In
the 1760s, campaign songs dealing with the struggles
between American Whigs and Tories appeared in penny
broadsides and columns of colonial papers. Songs circulated against the Stamp and Game Acts and against the
British presence in North America. In the 1780s, songs
such as "God save George Washington" (sung to the tune
of "God save the King") helped to elect the first president. Other songs aided the campaign in ratifying the
constitution. According to Silber (1971), American campaign songs had their most sweeping effect in the election of 1840, when supporters of W.H. Harrison assembled collections such as *The Tippecanoe Songbook*. The
result was not only electoral victory but, during the next
75 years, also a stream of odes, songs, waltzes, marches,
and polkas for presidential candidates. (*See also* GLEE.)

Campaign music circulated initially in political journals. But there is little evidence that shows how widely
such songs were actually sung in the 18th century. By
the mid-19th century, the campaign songster (a collection of lyrics without printed music) had become stan-
dardly used in electoral campaigns. Use of songsters
flourished due to the many sheet music publishers who
looked for commercial success in a song about a popular candidate. The melodies were mostly popular or patriotic tunes, such as "The Star-Spangled Banner."

From its birth, the labor movement was rich with musical activity. With the formation of the first unions in
the early 19th century came the first union songs, which
opposed the outlawing of organized labor and protested against economic and social injustice. Foner
(1975) summarizes the themes of 19th-century labor
song as "the organizations and struggles of working

people, their hatred for the oppressors, their affirmation of the dignity and worth of labor, their determination to endure hardships together and to fight together for a better life." These early songs rarely appeared in songsters or hymnals such as the *Pocket Hymn Book* (a model for later political chapbooks). But they circulated in print as broadsides and orally at processions and parades. Their tunes were derived from popular songs and hymns, and reflected the exhortative tradition of Puritan and Methodist religious music.

Songs of class protest regularly appeared in the first labor newspapers, such as Philadelphia's *Mechanics' Free Press* and New York's *Working Man's Advocate*. Editors seldom published melodies, but they frequently printed columns of songs and doggerel contributed by readers and union members. When hardship struck industrial and self-employed craftsmen, as in the depression of 1819–22, songs were a convenient means of voicing discontent, and the labor press became a principal forum for sentiments that had previously been expressed only orally.

In the period of Jacksonian democracy in the 1820–30s, labor songs flourished alongside workers' political parties. The following lines, published in 1829 (in the Dec 5 issue of *Mechanics' Free Press*), predate the *Communist Manifesto* by almost 20 years:

> The poor could live without the rich
> As every man may know
> But none that labour for their bread
> Could by the rich be spared…
> A truth it is both clear and plain
> Which every one may know
> That always in the richest earth
> The rankest weeds do grow.

Political songs of the Jacksonian era were not, however, limited to labor issues; among other topics included imprisonment for debt, indentured servitude, public health, landlords, and term limits for public officials (elected and otherwise),

With the widespread industrialization of New England in the early 19th century came child labor and some of the most famous factory protest ballads. A well-known example is "The Factory Girl," which was a title given to half a dozen widely circulated songs. Each wave of industrial and social change was reflected in song, including the depression of 1837 and the utopian movements of the 1840s and 1850s. Songs were composed for political meetings and rallies. In particular, the growth of the abolitionist movement in the North produced a large repertory of song. The Hutchinsons, a family of singers and entertainers, performed traditional and topical songs for the abolitionist cause, using tunes such as "Old Dan Tucker" for their new text, "Get off the track!"

Abolitionist songs represented the culmination of a tradition of anti-slavery songs that dated back for two centuries. Living in isolation and denied literacy by their masters, black slaves preserved many elements of their distinctive oral culture, at least through the 19th century. For African Americans, more than for most other groups, political sentiments surfaced in folklore and folksongs, particularly in the music of black protest.

Examples include the FIELD HOLLER (a means of communication beyond the hearing of the field boss), the SPIRITUAL (with its veiled references to a "great getting-up morning"), WORK SONGS (allowing a degree of control over the pace of labor), and folksongs encoded with directions to the Underground Railroad (such as "Follow the drinking gourd," through which slaves were encouraged to follow the Big Dipper northwards to freedom). Slaves also made up ballads about outlaws, tricksters, and "bad" slaves such as High John the Conqueror. This music fueled political protests and more defiant acts of sabotage, escape, and revolt. For disenfranchised and illiterate African Americans, music was a principal means of expressing sentiments which could otherwise be uttered only on pain of death. Throughout the 19th century, spirituals expressed hopes of release from bondage on earth. The symbolic content of this music ranged from the fairly explicit "We shall be free" to more coded interpretations of biblical narratives, such as "Didn't my Lord deliver Daniel (and why not you or I)."

2. FROM 1861 TO WORLD WAR I. At about the time of the Civil War, the American trade union movement began to solidify its base in urban centers. A specialized labor culture emerged, which brought with it occupational songs that protested wages, working conditions, and industrial accidents. This trend combined with music of European immigrants to revitalize political song in the United States. The depression songs of 1873, like those of 1819, 1837, and 1857, highlighted the contrast between the actual conditions of labor and the supposed American dream offered to new immigrants and workers. The Knights of Labor, a national labor organization founded in Philadelphia in 1869, produced popular political songbooks. Believing that songs and ballads educated workers on political issues, the organization opened local assemblies with songs of labor unity.

Two other movements generated political music in the 19th century: the suffragists and the farmer-labor alliances. Agitation for female suffrage emerged soon after the Civil War with a referendum in Kansas. Wyoming became the first state with women's suffrage. Upon its admittance to the Union in 1890, a body of songs developed which advocated suffrage as a means of increasing democracy and keeping society "pure" by introducing a body of voters that could outnumber immigrants and African Americans. Suffrage songs continued to be sung (and parodied) until the passing of the 19th Amendment in 1920. Along with the suffragists should be mentioned the temperance movement, whose fiery songs helped to legislate Prohibition, also in 1920.

Another movement contemporary with the suffragists after the Civil War was that known as populism. As the army cleared the frontier of American Indian settlements earlier in the century, farming had spread through the Midwestern and Western states. Unfortunately for the farmers, working conditions were determined by large trusts comprising landholders, banks, and railroads. In the 1830s and 1840s, agrarian reform movements, such as Dorr's Rebellion in Rhode Island and the Anti-Rent Wars in upstate New York, gave birth to humorous and biting songs about landholders. After the Civil War, with rising costs for rail transportation and mortgage foreclosures, farm tenancy increased considerably. These developments led to the founding of the Farmers' Alliance in 1877. Members of this populist political movement parodied many popular tunes, such as "When Johnny Comes Marching Home" and "John Brown's Body." In the 1890s, the Farmer's Alliance merged with the Knights of Labor and published two popular political songsters, *The Alliance and Labor Songster* and *The Labor Reform Songster*. The simple, familiar tunes and direct, exhortative lyrics were sung in many farmhouses and at grange meetings. In 1892, the Alliance and Knights of Labor coalition formed the Populist (or People's) Party, which used traditional tunes such as "Rosin the bow" for campaign songs.

Toward the end of the 19th century, several bitter strikes and labor battles in part instigated the production of memorable political songs. The Coal Creek rebellion of 1892 is remembered in "Payday at Coal Creek." In addition, both the Homestead steel strike of 1892 and the Pullman strike of 1894 (watersheds in the development of American unionism) gave rise to a wealth of protest songs. Some of these were written to popular tunes such as "After the Ball" ("After the Strike") and "Old Black Joe" ("The Poor White Slave"). Mines and mills were well represented in this upsurge of political music. The feudal conditions under which many miners labored inspired the production of numerous protest songs, one of which, "Miner's Lifeguard," was written during the first national strike of the United Mineworkers in 1897. Songs of the New England textile industry, like others, expressed feelings about occupational safety, wages, and working hours. For example, a classic political song, "Bread and Roses," originated at a mill strike in Lowell, Massachusetts, in 1912.

Among the most vigorous political songs of the 20th century were those of the Industrial Workers of the World (IWW), which was formed in 1905 from the remains of the Socialist Labor Party, the Western Federation of Miners, and other socialist groups. The IWW's practice of combining singing and rousing speeches may have originated early in the century in Spokane, Washington, whereby the IWW parodied the hymns of Salvation Army street bands with verses that pleaded the IWW cause. The IWW opened its meetings with songs. Its songbook (*Songs of the Workers*, 1934, 34/1974) included the first printing of "Solidarity Forever," "The Preacher and the Slave" (or "Pie in the Sky"), "Hallelujah, I'm a bum," and "The Red Flag." The tunes were taken largely from popular songs of the period, 1909–15, or from familiar gospel revival songs.

3. SINCE 1919. Although most 20th century political musical campaigns came from the left-wing of the political spectrum, groups such as the Ku Klux Klan sponsored barbershop quartets to articulate their views about racial supremacy. Following the example of the IWW (which lost much of its membership after adopting an anti-war stance during World War I), a number of socialist and communist movements fashioned politically charged

music for their causes in the 1930s and 1940s. As part of the COMPOSERS' COLLECTIVE OF NEW YORK (1933–8), classically trained musicians collaborated to produce music that would serve on picket lines while simultaneously improving the supposedly poor taste of the proletariat. They believed that music itself, and not merely the lyrics, could stir a revolutionary impulse. But the 12-tone political music that some of them composed under the influence of Schoenberg, Webern, and Berg was wholly unsuited to the New York ethnic laborers who were expected to sing it. Some members of the group went on to use musical theater for their political aims in works such as Marc Blitzstein's *The Cradle will Rock*.

The ALMANAC SINGERS were a group of about 12 young musicians who provided support for political and labor campaigns sponsored by the Congress of Industrial Organizations. They adapted the texts of Appalachian folksongs in order to address topical issues and sang them mainly to Eastern European immigrants in New York unions. People's Songs (1945–9) was a national organization of radical songwriters and performers who set out to disseminate labor and political protest songs. The association, whose magazine, at its most successful, attracted as many as two thousand subscribers, employed various types of music (cabaret, jazz, ethnic, and folk music) to articulate its political message.

Following the dissolution of these groups, songs urging political change were adopted by various mass movements. Radio and television aided such developments. From 1954, civil rights campaigns in the South made effective use of spirituals and gospel songs such as "We are soldiers in the army." In a second phase, this movement adapted traditional songs and melodies, similar to what union organizers had done in radical labor schools in the 1930s. Perhaps the most famous example was the traditional hymn, "I'll overcome." Over a period of 15 years, the song's words, tempo, and meter were revised for mass singing before it ultimately became "We shall overcome." The musical and religious roots of such songs were so deeply embedded in the Southern black culture that they succeeded where previous political song campaigns did not. By 1965, however, songs began to disappear from civil rights marches as their novelty, along with the non-violent tactics associated with them, began to fade.

Songs composed specifically for presidential campaigns have generally declined in importance since World War I. Two candidates who used song effectively were Franklin Roosevelt, whose "Happy days are here again" and "We've got Franklin D. Roosevelt back again" came to symbolize his era, and Henry Wallace, for whose ill-fated 1948 campaign Woody Guthrie and Pete Seeger contributed music. Eubie Blake's "I'm just wild about Harry" was revived for Harry Truman's campaign that year, but songs such as "We're madly for Adlai" and "Go with Goldwater" were soon forgotten.

In the 1960s, songs of the nuclear disarmament movement, sung by a few artists in the late 1950s, found new life in the rising dissatisfaction with American involvement in Vietnam. Although rarely broadcasted, anti-war songs such as "I feel like I'm fixin' to die rag" by

Country Joe McDonald achieved wide popularity. During the same period, several of Bob Dylan's songs, including "Blowin' in the Wind" (1963), were adopted as anthems for protest and civil rights movements. Dylan had been greatly influenced by Woody Guthrie and Pete Seeger, both formerly members of the Almanac Singers. Joan Baez was another performer whose songs expressed a strong social and political concern. Since then, many political groups—including feminists, environmentalists, and gay rights activists—have increasingly turned to music for political expression, drawing frequently from contemporary styles including folk, rock, country, hip hop, and punk rock. To what extent music making directly leads to political action remains a source of inquiry and debate.

See also ABOLITION; CAMPAIGN MUSIC; CONFEDERATE MUSIC; CIVIL RIGHTS MOVEMENT; THE CIVIL WAR; THE FOLK REVIVAL; Folk Song; PATRIOTIC MUSIC; PROTEST SONG; RESISTANCE.

BIBLIOGRAPHY
M. Larkin: "Revolutionary Music," *New Masses*, viii/7 (1933), 27

E. Siegmeister: *Music and Society* (New York, 1938)

W. Alderson: "On the Wobbly 'Casey Jones' and Other Songs," *California Folklore Quarterly*, i (1942), 373

J. Greenway: *American Folksongs of Protest* (Philadelphia, 1953)

T.P. Coffin: "Folksongs of Social Protest: a Musical Mirage," *New York Folklore Quarterly*, xiv/1 (1958), 3

A. Green: "A Discography of American Coal Miners' Songs," *Labor History*, ii (1961), 101

A. Green: "A Discography of American Labor Union Songs," *New York Folklore Quarterly*, xi/3 (1961), 1

C. Keil: *Urban Blues* (Chicago, 1966)

M. Orth: "The Crack in the Consensus: Political Propaganda in American Popular Music," *New Mexico Quarterly*, xxxvi (1966), 62

J. A. Scott: "Ballads and Broadsides of the American Revolution," *Sing Out!*, xvi/2 (1966), 18

D.A. DeTurk and A. Poulin, Jr., eds.: *The American Folk Scene* (New York, 1967)

R. Brazier: "The Story of IWW's Little Red Songbook," *Labor History*, ix (1968), 91

R.S. Denisoff: "Protest Movements: Class Consciousness and the Propaganda Song," *Sociological Quarterly*, ix (1968), 228

L. Miller and J.K. Skipper, Jr.: "Sounds of Protest: Jazz and the Militant Avant-garde," *Approaches to Deviance: Theories, Concepts and Research Findings*, ed. M. Letton, J.K. Skipper, Jr., and C. McCaghy (New York, 1968), 129

J. Boskin and R.A. Rosenstone, eds.: "Protest in the Sixties," *Annals of the American Academy of Political and Social Science*, ccclxxxii (1969)

J.L. Rodnitzky: "The Evolution of the American Protest Song," *Journal of Popular Culture*, iii/1 (1969), 35

M. Truzzi: "The 100% American Songbag: Conservative Folksongs in America," *Western Folklore*, xxviii (1969), 27

R.S. Denisoff: "'Take It Easy, But Take It: the Almanac Singers,'" *Journal of American Folklore*, lxxxiii (1970), 21

F. Kofsky: *Black Nationalism and the Revolution in Music* (New York, 1970)

B.D. Collins: "Music in the Labor Movement," *Industrial and Labor Relations Forum*, vii/4 (1971), 41

R.A. Reuss: *American Folklore and Left-wing Politics, 1927–1957* (diss., Indiana U., 1971)

I. Silber: *Songs Americans Voted by: the Words and Music that Won and Lost Elections and Influenced the Democratic Process* (Harrisburg, PA, 1971)

J. Sinclair and R. Levin: *Music and Politics* (New York, 1971)

R.S. Denisoff: *Sing a Song of Social Significance* (Bowling Green, OH, 1972)

P. Seeger: "Some Folk Roots and Protest Traditions," *The Incomplete Folksinger* (New York, 1972), 62–151

G.H. Lewis: "Social Protest and Self Awareness in Black Popular Music," *Popular Music and Society*, ii (1973), 327

P. Foner: *American Labor Songs of the Nineteenth Century* (Urbana, IL, 1975)

B. Reagon: *Songs of the Civil Rights Movement 1955–1965: A Study in Cultural History* (diss., Howard U., 1975)

R.A. Reuss: "American Folksongs and Left-Wing Politics, 1935–1956," *Journal of the Folklore Institute*, xii (1975), 89

A. Paredes: "Songs of Border Conflict," *A Texas-Mexican Cancionero* (Urbana, IL, 1976), 59–109

D.K. Dunaway: "A Selected Bibliography: Protest Song in the United States," *Folklore Forum*, x/2 (1977), 8

L.W. Levine: *Black Culture and Black Consciousness* (New York, 1977)

R. Lieberman: *"My Song Is My Weapon": People's Songs, American communism, and the Politics of Culture, 1930–1950* (Urbana, IL, 1989)

R. Garofalo: *Rockin' the Boat: Mass Music and Mass Movements* (Boston, 1992)

G.H. Lewis: "La Pistola y El Corazón: Protest and Passion in Mexican-American Popular Music," *Journal of Popular Culture*, xxvi/1 (1992), 51–67

R. Pratt: *Rhythm and Resistance: The Political Uses of American Popular Music* (Washington, DC, 1994)

K.L. Sanger: *When the Spirit Says Sing!: the Role of Freedom Songs in the Civil Rights Movement* (New York, 1995)

M. Mattern: *Acting in Concert: Music, Community, and Political Action* (New Brunswick, NJ, 1998)

B. Ward: *Just My Soul Responding: Rhythm and Blues, Black Consciousness, and Race Relations* (Berkeley, CA, 1998)

R.A. Reuss with J.C. Reuss: *American Folk Music and Left-Wing Politics, 1927–1957* (Lanham, MD, 2000)

R.D. Lankford: *Folk Music USA: The Changing Voice of Protest* (New York, 2005)

I. Peddie, ed.: *The Resisting Music: Popular Music and Social Protest* (Burlington, VT, 2006)

R.M. Moore: *Sells Like Teen Spirit: Music, Youth Culture, and Social Crisis* (New York, 2010)

D. Lynskey: *33 Revolutions per Minute: a History of Protest Songs, from Billie Holiday to Green Day* (London, 2011)

DAVID K. DUNAWAY/R

Polka (i). A term used to describe both a style of dance and a complex of related styles of music. Originally it referred to a couple's dance in 2/4 time that originated in central Europe in the 1830s. A widespread legend, circulating nowadays on the Internet, attributes its origin to a Czech servant girl. The popularity of polka dancing coincided with the invention and development of free reed squeezeboxes, concertinas and accordions, and the booming popularity of brass bands, thus a style of music closely associated with squeezeboxes and brass band instruments has come to be known as "polka."

The ascendancy of polka dancing and its associated music and instruments also coincided with a key period of mass migration from Europe to the United States. (*See* POLKA (II).) As a result, polka dancing, usually to squeezeboxes and band instruments, became associated with the ethnic heritages of several European American ethnic groups, especially Germans, Poles, Czechs, Slovenes, Finns, and Swiss. Polka is also known among Swedes, Norwegians, Italians, Croatians, Ukrainians, Slovaks, Lithuanians, and others. Czech, German and Polish immigrants to Texas and Mexico established polka, complete with accordions and brass bands, among Mexicans on both sides of the Rio Grande.

The invention of the phonograph launched the first great wave of ethnic music recordings from 1910 to 1929, including much polka. By the later 1920s and 30s, polka bands, which had originally been anchored in the ethnic styles of particular US immigrant groups, began to be accepted by a wider public. Radio broadcasts also exposed polka to a wider audience. The popularity of ballroom

*Dancers at the Beachland Ballroom's first Polka Brunch, Cleveland, 2010. (LYNN ISCHAY/
The Plain Dealer/Landov)*

dancing to jazz bands surged from the 1920s through the 1940s. Running parallel to this trend, polka bands likewise filled ballrooms with avid dancers who preferred it to jazz. Many of the bands mediated between the polka and jazz idioms, including both "old time" (polka) and "modern" (jazz) numbers in their repertoires.

Five major ethnic-named polka styles coalesced in the 1930s and 1940s: Polish, German (or "Dutchman"), Slovenian, Bohemian (or Czech), and Mexican (or "Conjunto"). Although the core of the musicians and audiences has been from each style's designated ethnic group, most have become multiethnic to some degree. In some US areas, a particular ethnic style became the regional polka style. Thus, Dutchman is also known as "Minnesota style," and is popular throughout the rural Upper Midwest, Slovenian is known as "Cleveland style" and is predominant in Great Lakes industrial cities as well as in western Pennsylvania, and Bohemian is the dominant style in eastern Wisconsin and Nebraska where Czech-descended musicians have been very influential. The Mexican polka scene, however, is largely mono-ethnic. The patterns of US socio-cultural segregation has kept Mexican polka separate.

The bands led by key influential musicians such as JOHN WILFAHRT, WALTER JAGIELLO, FRANKIE YANKOVIC, ROMY GOSZ, and NARCISO MARTÍNEZ effectively codified each polka style. Their music was spread through touring and the media, and they were imitated by dozens of other bands, some of which developed their own versions of the style.

Polka achieved its greatest penetration into American commercial music in the decade following World War II. After the advent of rock 'n' roll in the later 1950s, polka declined in the commercial music realm, but remains popular in the ethnic and regional communities where it originated.

BIBLIOGRAPHY

C. and A. V. Keil: *Polka Happiness* (Philadelphia, 1992)

V. Greene: *A Passon for Polka: old-time ethnic music in America* (Berkeley, CA, 1992)

P. Savaglio: "Polka Bands and Choral Groups: The Musical Self-representation of Polish-Americans in Detroit," *EthM*, xl (1996), 35–47

J.P. Leary: "Czech American polka music in Wisconsin," *Musics of multicultural America: a Study of Twelve Musical Communities*, ed. A.K. Rasmussen and C. Lornell (New York, 1997), 25–47

R. March: "Polka and tamburitza: Ethnic music and dance traditions in the Upper Midwest," *Ethnic and Border Music: a Regional Exploration,* ed. N. Cohen (Westport, CT, 2007), 139–70

RICHARD MARCH

Polka (ii). A lively couple dance from Bohemia which spread throughout Europe and the United States in a widespread 1844 "Polkamania."

It is believed that the polka was developed in Prague around 1830 as an expression of native Bohemian culture during the Czech National Revival movement. In 1840 the Prague ballet master Raab traveled to Paris to exhibit Bohemian national dances, including the polka, on stage at the Odéon Theatre. During the previous year, the polka had enjoyed successful debuts in Vienna, Berlin, and St. Petersburg, and the reception was especially favorable in Paris. French audiences grew fonder of the dance, and by 1842 it began to spread from stages to the public dance gardens, where off-duty ballerinas went to dance with their patrons. The following year a few couples began to exhibit the polka at private salons and soirées, then in the famous Winter Season of 1843–4, the growing interest in the polka suddenly accelerated into a significant dance craze.

The WALTZ had preceded the polka as the prototypical turning couple dance, but during the first three decades of the 19th century Western European and American social arbiters widely considered the waltz to be too intimate for public display. However the new polka was so ebullient and good-natured that it couldn't be considered lascivious. Paris quickly became fascinated with the new step, now as a social dance for the ballroom. News of the Parisian polkamania (French: *polkamanie*) quickly spread to England and the United States, resulting in a similar wave of popularity in the same year. As in Europe, talk of the polka overshadowed politics for many Americans. Some believed that the unknown Tennessee governor James Polk won the race for the presidency in 1844 primarily because his name was fashionable that year. An English humorist doubted that Polk was even his real name, implying that it was an adopted pseudonym to capitalize on the American polkamania.

The polka revived the ballroom after the relatively quiet 1830s, and dancing was once again thrust to the forefront of social activities. The newfound passion for social dancing led to an appetite for more steps to enjoy. The rousing GALOP from the late 1820s was revived, often becoming the last dance of a ball, and the Mazurka, which had not gained a large following during the Regency era, was also revived, and now became the ultimate saltatorial experience for advanced dancers. Mazurka waltzes were created by Parisian dancing masters who combined the old waltz with various Polish and Bohemian steps, providing further challenges that the more adept dancers could master. As enthusiasm mounted, variety was added by the SCHOTTISCHE and Redowa. More significantly, the 1844 polkamania led to a wider acceptance of the waltz, once society acclimated to the closed embrace of turning couple dances.

Over the last one and half centuries, the polka has spread around the world, evolving into many regional and folk forms, often danced to music significantly faster than the original 104 beats per minute.

RICHARD POWERS

Pollack, Ben (*b* Chicago, IL, 22 June 1903; *d* Palm Springs, CA, 7 June 1971). Jazz drummer and bandleader. Born into a wealthy family, he began playing drums and was hired by the New Orleans Rhythm Kings, with whom he played and recorded in 1923. While with this band he became known as perhaps the best white drummer in the style and influenced the next generation of players, including Dave Tough and Gene Krupa.

After a year on the West Coast with the Harry Bastin band, he took over Bastin's group in 1925. For the next 15 years Pollack led big bands, primarily in Chicago and New York, before settling in Los Angeles in the late 1930s. His first band included such later jazz worthies as Benny Goodman, Bud Freeman, and Glenn Miller.

By the early 1930s Pollack had replaced his early stars with younger musicians. His affair with singer Doris Robbins caused friction in the new band and most of the musicians left to form a cooperative group later fronted by Bob Crosby. Pollack again reformed, using other young musicians including Harry James and Irving Fazola.

Pollack's career after the 1940s included numerous business ventures, including a record company and several restaurants in California. He continued leading bands in the Dixieland style through the 1960s. By then business reversals and bitterness over his musical career led to a depression that ended in his suicide.

BIBLIOGRAPHY

S.B. Charters and L. Kunstadt: *Jazz: a History of the New York Scene* (Garden City, NY, 1962/*R*1981), chap.13
A. McCarthy: *Big Band Jazz* (London, 1974), 182ff
T.D. Brown: *A History and Analysis of Jazz Drumming to 1942* (diss., U. of Michigan, 1976), 282ff, 560f

JOHN L. CLARK JR.

Pollack, Howard Joel (*b* Brooklyn, NY, 17 March 1952). Musicologist. He received his PhD from Cornell University in 1981 with a dissertation titled *Walter Piston and his Music*. He is the John and Rebecca Moores Professor of Music at the University of Houston, where he has taught since 1987. Pollack's work focuses on American musicians and musical cultures, particularly connections between 20th-century popular American idioms, including jazz and Broadway, and classical music composition. He has published five books on American composers and their compositions, including Walter Piston, John Alden Carpenter, Aaron Copland, and George Gershwin. Written for a broad audience, Pollack's books have been praised as both accessible and erudite; his book on Copland was awarded the Irving Lowens Award from the Society for American Music and a Deems Taylor Award from ASCAP. His book on George Gershwin also received awards, for Excellence in Historical Recorded Sound Research from the Association for Recorded Sound Collections and another Deems Taylor Award from ASCAP. Pollack is also the recipient of grants from the Society for American Music and the American Musicological Society, a Fellowship from the National Endowment for the Humanities, and a Newberry Library Fellowship.

WRITINGS

Walter Piston and his Music (diss., Cornell U., 1981; Ann Arbor, 1981)
Harvard Composers: Walter Piston and his Students, from Elliott Carter to Frederic Rzewski (Metuchen, NJ, 1992)
Skyscraper Lullaby: The Life and Music of John Alden Carpenter (Washington, DC, 1995; rev. as *John Alden Carpenter: A Chicago Composer*, Urbana, IL, 2001)
Aaron Copland: The Life and Work of an Uncommon Man (New York, 1999)
"The Dean of Gay American Composers," *American Music*, xviii (2000), 39–49
"Samuel Barber, Jean Sibelius, and the Making of an American Romantic," *MQ*, cxxxiv (2000), 175–205
George Gershwin: His Life and Work (Berkeley, 2006)
with A. Davis: "Rotational Form in the Opening Scene of Porgy and Bess," *JAMS*, lx (2007), 373–414

BIBLIOGRAPHY

J. Rockwell: "Sounds of America," *The New York Times Book Review* (14 March 1999)

KENDRA PRESTON LEONARD

Pollikoff, Max (*b* Newark, NJ, 30 March 1904; *d* New York, NY, 13 May 1984). Violinist and promoter of contemporary music. After showing early promise as a violinist he was awarded a scholarship in 1917 by the

MacDowell Club of New York to study violin (with LEO-POLD AUER), composition, and piano, and another scholarship the following year to continue his work with Auer. Pollikoff made his New York debut on 30 October 1923 at Aeolian Hall in a program which included his own *Légende* for violin, and pursued a successful career as a concert artist, often introducing works by relatively unknown composers. In 1950 he gave the first public performance of Ives's Violin Sonata no.1 (*c*1908–13). From 1953 to 1973 he was associated with the Bennington Composers and Chamber Music conferences, and in 1956 he instituted a series at Columbia University devoted to reading new compositions. His most important achievement, however, was the establishment in 1954 of "Music in Our Time," a series of chamber music concerts presented at the 92nd Street Y and later at Town Hall, New York. At first the series presented mainly works by well-known composers such as Gershwin, Copland, Hindemith, and Rorem; later several younger composers including Chou Wen-chung, Da Costa, Kupferman, and Wuorinen received commissions from the series. Altogether it presented more than 250 contemporary works by such composers as Babbitt, Brant, Luigi Dallapiccola, Davidovsky, Luening, Rochberg, Saburo Takata, Trimble, and Wolpe. Often several pieces would be performed concurrently in different rooms and repeated, while the audience would wander about at will. The series ended in 1974, although a few individual concerts were given in later years under its title. After 1974 Pollikoff performed as soloist, made recordings, assisted in television commercials, and continued to promote contemporary music.

BIBLIOGRAPHY

R. Parmenter: "Violinist Offers First of Eight Concerts," *New York Times* (6 Feb 1956), 27

R. Parmenter: "World of Music: Under the Door," *New York Times* (6 Dec 1959), X13

D. Henahan: "5 Musical Works Echo New Theory," *New York Times* (2 March 1970), 45

C. Moore: "New Concert Procedures, 'the Walk-Around'," *Vogue*, clvi/3 (1970), 38

J. Rockwell: "Music: 20th for Pollikoff," *New York Times* (19 April 1974), 26

J. Rockwell: "Max Pollikoff Plays New Compositions for Violin," *New York Times* (22 April 1978), 10

C.G. Fraser: "Max Pollikoff, Violinist, Dies; Created 'Music in Our Time'," *New York Times* (14 May 1984), D18

O. Luening: [letter] "An Invaluable Champion," *Keynote*, viii/5 (1984), 4

MARY A. WISCHUSEN

Polo, Danny (*b* Clinton, IN, 22 Dec 1901; *d* Chicago, IL, 11 July 1949). Jazz clarinetist. He worked in Chicago, New Orleans, and Florida before leaving for Europe in 1927. He settled in London as the featured soloist in Bert Ambrose's high society dance band in 1930. He recorded anonymously for Woolworth store's Crown label in the United States in 1935. When he returned to England in 1937, he rejoined Ambrose and made records with his Swing Stars. He then moved to Paris to join Ray Ventura, where he made six fine recordings for Decca, directed by Leonard Feather. His "Montmartre Moan" of this period is a fine Bigard-like blues. He returned to New York in late 1939 and recorded for the

movie *Birth of the Blues* before rejoining old friend Claude Thornhill until the latter joined the navy. He again worked with Thornhill from 1947 to 1949, working alongside Gerry Mulligan and Lee Konitz, and influencing the postwar "cool" jazz sound.

BIBLIOGRAPHY

Chilton W

J. Godbolt: *A History of Jazz in Britain 1919–50* (London, 1986), 191, 225

JEFFREY GREEN

Polynesian entertainment. The dances and music of the Polynesian peoples have had varying impact on the United States over the last one and half centuries. Of greatest importance are Hawaiian music and dance, including musical instruments such as the PEDAL STEEL GUITAR and UKULELE, and practices such as the HULA (*see* HAWAII). Owing to US colonial involvement in the region, exchange and influences transcend just the Hawaiian connection. For the 1909 production *Inside the Earth* at the New York Hippodrome 50 Maori performers were imported from New Zealand for the season. To promote her 1926 silent film, *Aloma of the South Seas*, the dancer Gilda Gray toured with a Polynesian band, The Royal Samoans, and performed her "Polynesian dance" before showings. The Royal Samoans capitalized on the craze for Hawaiian and Tahitian music and dancing. They performed throughout the United States in the interwar period, even obtaining a live cameo in the 1932 Betty Boop cartoon, *Bamboo Isle*, where they provided not only the music but also the movements for Betty's rotoscoped hip-shaking hula. Their use of ukuleles, guitars, and prolific borrowing from different islands demonstrated the emergence of a generic Polynesian sound in popular music, which also borrowed freely from American styles such as jazz and ragtime.

The 1950s saw the growth of faux-Polynesian nightlife known as tiki culture comprising bars, restaurants, and whole franchises exploiting an exoticized image of Polynesia. After 1945 Las Vegas proved a draw-card for many Polynesian performers. Of the Polynesian groups the most famous was perhaps the Maori showband "Mary and the Maori Hi Five" active there from 1965 to 1971. The group's impact was documented by the 2009 award of the 40th star on the Strip by the Las Vegas Walk of Stars Committee.

The most comprehensive Polynesian entertainment complex in the United States is the Polynesian Cultural Centre (PCC) located on Oahu, Hawaii. Managed by the Church of the Latter-day Saints, the PCC is a theme park encompassing eight different Polynesian villages presented in a putative precontact state. They represent themselves, sometimes in an ironic-parodistic mode, through the music and dance of their respective islands. In the famous evening shows, the emphasis is on traditional rather than popular Polynesian music and dance but often the borders between the two are fluid as popular tourist genres such as Samoan knife dances, Fijian fire-walking, Maori haka, and Hawaiian hula are integrated into loosely knitted dramatic narratives and spectacular acrobatic feats supported by high-tech lighting effects and pyrotechnics.

BIBLIOGRAPHY

M. Werry: "'The Greatest Show on Earth': Political Spectacle, Spectacular Politics, and the American Pacific," *Theatre Journal*, lvii/3 (2005), 355–82

C. Balme: *Pacific Performances* (New York, 2007)

C.H. Garrett: *Struggling to Define a Nation* (Berkeley, CA, 2008)

CHRISTOPHER BALME

Pomeroy, Jim [James Calwell, Jr.] (*b* Reading, PA, 21 March 1945; *d* Philadelphia, PA, 6 April 1992). Performance artist, composer, writer, and arts administrator. He studied sculpture at the University of Texas, Austin (BFA 1968), and at the University of California, Berkeley (MFA 1972). As an administrator he cofounded and was vice president and curator of the performance space, 80 Langton Street (San Francisco, 1975–6, later renamed New Langton Arts), and was a trustee of the San Francisco Art Institute (1975–8). As artist-in-residence at the Exploratorium in San Francisco (1976–7) he created the visual installation *Light Weight Phantoms*; and in 1977 he joined the sculpture department of San Francisco State University. He acted as consultant to museums and galleries and to the NEA, and his performances and sound sculptures have been presented in the San Francisco Museum of Modern Art (1979), the Los Angeles Institute of Contemporary Art (1979), and the CEPA Gallery, Buffalo (1981), and elsewhere. He served as a professor of art at the University of Texas, Arlington, from 1987 until his death.

Though Pomeroy was primarily a multimedia performance artist, his work also encompassed sound sculptures, handmade instruments, experimental music, and comic, ironic, and political vocal music. He performed under various names such as Blind Nake, Blind Snake, and Rod Staph 'n' th' Cumforts. Musicians and performers with whom he collaborated include Paul DeMarinis, Jock Reynolds, Tom Marioni, Suzanne Hellmuth, and Jim Melchert. *A Byte at the Opera* (1977), one of his best-known works, employs sound generated by a computer which is suspended from the ceiling on a panel (measuring about 120 × 180 cm), 150 cm above a powder-covered plane (485 × 485 cm) whose underside is displayed on a large video screen. The patterns of movement of small objects described on the plane are reflected on the screen and, with the aid of the accompanying sounds, the image eventually revealed is of a mechanic using a magnet to manipulate ball bearings. This image alters in the course of the work. A recording of his work, *Sound*, was produced by the Los Angeles Institute of Contemporary Art in 1979. *Double Read for Dubbled Reeds* (1980), commissioned by the oboist Joseph Celli, is the only work of Pomeroy's which he created for another performer. In 1999 the New Langton Arts collective created a retrospective of his work, including a memorial website. Many of his pieces have been collected within the Jim Pomeroy Archive in the Center for Photography at the University of Arizona.

WORKS

(all texts by Pomeroy)

Sound sculptures: 3 Music Boxes, watches, clocks, metronomes, 1974–5; Fear Elites, music boxes, 1975; Mozart's Moog, 49 amp music boxes, 1978; Hat Dance, amp hard hat, slides, 1979; Mechanical Music, combination wrenches, 1979; Back on the Ladder…, vacuum cleaners, pipes, 1979–83; Whillikers in G, 5-gallon cans, 1980

Others: A Byte at the Opera (collab. P. DeMarinis), cptr, visual effects, 1977; Light Weight Phantoms, 1976–7; Fluteloops, with North Beach Memoranda, fl, tape, 1979; Double Read for Dubbled Reeds, sloboe [mechanical inst], 5 tape recorders, 1980; Fl Trio, solo fl, 1981; Magnetic Music, amp fl, toys, 1981; Muzak of the Spheres, battery gramophone, 1982; Token Dreams, text, 1985; ZOOM BI-SPEEL, audio tape, 1985; Listen to the Rhythm of the Reign, videotape, 1985; Tiananmen Tango, videotape, 1989; Eine Kleine NachtVid, videotape, 1990; performance and improvisational works for insts, tape, mechanical insts, hardware

BIBLIOGRAPHY

S. Foley: *Space, Time, Sound: Conceptual Art in the San Francisco Bay Area, the 1970s* (Seattle, 1981)

K. Norklun: "View from Within," *Artweek* (San Francisco, 7 Nov 1981)

Soundings, xii (Santa Fe, NM, 1982)

T. Druckrey and N. Lemmon, eds.: *For a Burning World Is Come to Dance Inane: Essays by and about Jim Pomeroy* (Brooklyn, 1993)

STEPHEN RUPPENTHAL/JOANNA R. SMOLKO

Pomo. Native American tribe of northern California. They inhabited an area along the Pacific Coast extending from the mouth of the Russian River to what is now Fort Bragg, and inland slightly farther east than Clear Lake.

Like other tribes of the area (such as the Maidu and Wintun), the Pomo embraced the Kuksu cult, a religious complex centering on impersonation of supernatural beings in rituals that aimed to ensure communal welfare. The GHOST DANCE movement had a great impact among the Pomo and led to the origin of the Bole Maru (Dream Dance) cult. Music was a central feature of all Pomo ritual; it was principally vocal and bound to religion in purpose and conception. Lole Kilak dances and songs were performed to ensure the availability of food and other natural resources. These were performed at ceremonies that were mainly the province of women, who also presided over celebrations for each year's first issue of acorns, clover, manzanita, and wild strawberries. The Pomo also had songs for institutions that were virtually universal among California Indians: shamanistic songs, war dance songs, girls' puberty dance songs, gambling songs, and songs for ritual mourning. The Pomo instrumentarium included the clapstick, footdrum, cocoon rattle, deer-hoof rattle, whistle, flute, and musical bow (for descriptions *see* YOKUTS and MAIDU). Only the flute and musical bow were used independently of singing; these were played only as solo instruments.

White settlers in Pomo territory during the late 19th century brought disease and environmental destruction, both of which threatened the survival of Pomo culture. Nevertheless some traditional ceremonies are still observed at the Kashia Rancheria, Cloverdale Rancheria, and elsewhere, and Pomo musical practices have been comparatively well documented in early and recent recordings of Pomo songs.

The structure of Pomo song is similar to that of the songs of other northern and central California tribes in many respects: melodic form is generally based on rather steady repetition of short, litany-like phrases of a descending or undulating nature, and the ambitus of most songs is restricted to an octave or less; tonal material is based on pentatonic scales or fragments; and vocables are more common than lexically meaningful texts. Pomo songs show a number of distinctive performance characteristics, however. Besides solo and choral unison singing, some examples exhibit alternation between soloists, responsorial singing between soloist and chorus, or accompaniment of a soloist by another singer who sustains what may be called an ostinato or drone. This practice recalls the multipart styles of northwestern California groups (such as the Yurok).

The Pomo Dance Song was repeated as often as wanted in performance, with variation and alternating soloists. Since all parts save that of the soloist were of fixed or indistinct pitch, there was no intervallic coordination, and the main organizing principle was rhythmic. Asymmetric meter, such as 7/8, is another feature that distinguishes Pomo music from that of the Maidu, Yokuts, or Wintun, but it is not an element of all Pomo singing. Pomo singing is distinguished from that of other Native Americans of northern and central California in its vocal quality. It does not have the extreme raspiness, nasality, pulsation, and glottalization that gives northwestern California (e.g., Yurok) singing its dramatic character, nor is the voice so smooth and relaxed as among the central California tribes (e.g., Yokuts). Rather, the preferred vocal quality falls somewhere between these extremes, and songs are generally sung in the lower register of the singer's range.

Early recorded Pomo music (usually that of solo performers rather than ensembles) was on wax cylinders. Recordings of Pomo music are held at the Lowie Museum of Anthropology, University of California, Berkeley.

See also Native american music.

BIBLIOGRAPHY

E. Loeb: "Pomo Folkways," *University of California Publications in American Archeology and Ethnography*, xix/2 (1926), 149–405

J. de Angulo and B. d'Harcourt: "La musique des Indiens de la Californie du Nord," *Journal de la Société des Américanistes de Paris*, xxiii/1 (1931), 189–228

W.J. Wallace: "Music and Musical Instruments," *Handbook of North American Indians*, viii, ed. R.F. Heizer (Washington, DC, 1978), 642–8

RICHARD KEELING/R

Pomus, Doc [Felder, Jerome Solon] (*b* New York, NY, 27 June 1925; *d* New York, NY, 14 March 1991). Rock and roll songwriter. Using the stage name Doc Pomus, he started his career as an R&B singer, performing in and around New York City and cutting unsuccessful records for various independent labels. Notable for being a Jewish performer in a predominantly black musical scene, and for being dependent on crutches to stand during concerts (a consequence of childhood polio), he eventually left the stage in the mid-1950s to concentrate on the less conspicuous profession of songwriting. He scored his first R&B hit with Ray Charles's recording of "Lonely Avenue" in 1956; a year later the Coasters had a pop hit with "Young Blood" (a song started by Pomus and finished by his friends Jerry Leiber and Mike Stoller). In 1958 Pomus and pianist Mort Shuman formed a songwriting partnership at publishing company Hill & Range in New York's Brill Building; with Pomus as the official lyricist and Shuman as the official composer, the pair

would go on to become darlings of the pop-music industry. Teen idol Fabian achieved fame with their "Turn me loose" and "Hound Dog Man" (both 1959); Dion and the Belmonts succeeded with "A Teenager in Love" (1959); the Drifters maintained success with "This Magic Moment" (1960), "Save the last dance for me" (1960), and "Sweets for My Sweet" (1961). Elvis Presley made many recordings of the duo's songs, including the easy-listening hit "(Marie's the Name) His Latest Flame" (1961) and the cult favorite "Viva Las Vegas" (1964). In 1965 Pomus and Shuman went their separate ways, and in that same year Pomus suffered a severe fall that left him permanently confined to a wheelchair. He continued to write sporadically and involve himself in various musical projects until he succumbed to lung cancer in 1991.

BIBLIOGRAPHY

K. Emerson: *Always Magic in the Air* (New York, 2005), 31–50

A. Halberstadt: *Lonely Avenue* (Cambridge, MA, 2007)

J.A. Friedman: *Tell the Truth Until They Bleed* (New York, 2008), 78–93

CHRISTOPHER DOLL

Pond, (Harry) Donald (*b* Leyton, UK, 14 Oct 1906; *d* Santa Barbara, CA, 21 Aug 1983). English music educator and composer. He trained as a chorister, studied with Gustav Holst, and worked at Dartington Hall School before immigrating to New York City in 1934, where he co-founded the Children's Theater Arts Workshop and served as music director to the Federal Dance Theatre. Through experience at New York's progressive Dalton School, he met Leopold Stokowski, who was advising the Pillsbury Foundation on a large arts endowment in California. Stokowski suggested establishing a nursery school to study the musicality of young children and recommended Pond, together with Gladys Moorhead (1893–1976), as directors. The Pillsbury Foundation School opened in Santa Barbara, California in 1937. In copious notes, Pond recorded his observations of innate musical ability expressed spontaneously by young children in free play. The work of Pond and Moorhead was among the first major studies of formal early childhood music education in the United States and was published by the Pillsbury Foundation. Pond's papers and music are held by Special Collections of Music, University of Maryland, College Park.

WRITINGS

G.E. Moorhead and D. Pond: *Music of Young Children* (Santa Barbara, CA, 1941, 3/1944/R)

BIBLIOGRAPHY

J.K. Kierstead: *The Pillsbury Foundation School and Beyond* (thesis, U. of Maryland, 1991)

J.K. Kierstead: *Listening to the Spontaneous Music-Making of Preschool Children in Play: a Pedagogy of Wonder* (diss., U. of Maryland, 2006)

PETER DANNER

Pond, Sylvanus Billings (*b* 1792; *d* 1871). Music seller, publisher, and composer. He was a partner in the firm of Firth, hall & pond.

Pone [Poné], **Gundaris** (*b* Saldus, Latvia, 17 Oct 1932; *d* New York, NY, 15 March 1994). Composer of Latvian birth. He fled Latvia as a war refugee in 1944 and studied violin and composition at the University of Minnesota (BA 1954, MA 1956, and PhD 1962). From 1963 he taught music theory and composition at SUNY, New Paltz, where he founded and directed the Contemporary Chamber Orchestra, host of the annual Music in the Mountains Festival since 1982. From 1972 Pone visited Latvia as a conductor of his own works.

Pone's style changed from the Romanticism of his early works to radical serial and aleatory techniques, particularly after six months of study in Venice with Luigi Nono in 1967. After 1980 he turned to a synthetic post-serial style and a more multifaceted approach. A ballet of the history of Riga remained unfinished. Pone received first prize in the Kennedy Center Friedheim contest and the "Città di Trieste" award (both 1982).

WORKS
(selective list)

Orch: Vn Conc., 1959; Vivos voco, mortuos plango, 1972; Avanti, 1975; La Serenissima, 1979–81; Titzarin, 1984–6; Monumentum pro Galileo, 1990

Chbr and solo inst: Vc Sonata, 1966; Allintervallreihe (Klavierwerk I), pf, 1963; Montage-Demontage (Klavierwerk II), pf, 1967; San Michele della Lagune, cl, vn, pf, 1967; "-o-ssia …," pf, 1968; De mundo Magistri Ioanni, 2 vn, 2 cl, pf, perc, 1972; Diletti dialettici, fl, cl, hn, pf, vn, va, vc, perc, 1973; Gran duo funebre, va, vc, 1987; Pezzi del tramonto, vn, pf, 1989; Cartoline dalla Curlandia, pf, 1992

WRITINGS

"Action-Reaction," *MR*, xxvii (1966), 218–27

"Jaunās mūzikas forma un doma" [Form and idea of new music], *Jaunā Gaita*, no.62 (1967), 6–19; repr. in *Literatūra un Māksla* (14 Feb 1992); (6 March 1992)

BIBLIOGRAPHY

S. Vēriņa: "Vivos voco," *Māksla*, (1973) no.1, 29–30

K. Larsson: *Gundaris Pone: Composer and Conductor* (New York, 1984) [catalog]

ARNOLDS KLOTIŅŠ

Pons, Lily (Alice Joséphine) (*b* Draguignan, nr Cannes, France, 12 April 1898; *d* Dallas, TX, 13 Feb 1976). Soprano of French birth. A piano student at the Paris Conservatoire, she received her first vocal instruction from Alberti de Gorostiaga and then studied with Giovanni Zenatello in New York. She made her operatic debut in 1928 at Mulhouse as Lakmé, with Reynaldo Hahn conducting. She then sang in French provincial houses as Gretel, Cherubino, Blonde, the Queen of Night and Mimì. On the recommendation of Zenatello, she went to the Metropolitan, where she made her debut in 1931 as Lucia. She caused a sensation and thereafter remained with the company for 28 seasons. She had success as Gilda, Amina, Marie (*La fille du régiment*), Philine (*Mignon*), Olympia and, above all, Lakmé. In 1935 she sang Rosina at Covent Garden and Gilda and Lucia at the Paris Opera. She sang in South America, San Francisco (where her roles included the Queen of Shemakha and Violetta), Monte Carlo, and Chicago and made several films. Married to André Kostelanetz from 1938 to 1958, she made her stage farewell at the Metropolitan in 1958 as Lucia. Pons possessed a pure, agile, high coloratura voice, as can be heard on her many recordings.

BIBLIOGRAPHY

B. Park: "Lily Pons," *Record Collector*, xiii (1960–61), 245–71 [with discography]

L. Rasponi: *The Last Prima Donnas* (New York, 1982), 405–30

P. Jackson: *Saturday Afternoons at the Old Met* (New York, 1992)

N.M. Zirato and J.A. Drake: "Remembering Lily Pons," *OQ*, xv/2 (1999), 224–37

J.A. Drake and K.B. Ludecke, eds.: *Lily Pons: a Centennial Portrait* (Portland, OR, 1999)

DENNIS K. McINTIRE/ALAN BLYTH/R

Ponselle [Ponzillo], **Rosa (Melba)** (*b* Meriden, CT, 22 Jan 1897; *d* Green Spring Valley, MD, 25 May 1981). Soprano. She studied singing with her mother and then with Anna Ryan. She began to appear in film theaters and vaudeville, often with her elder sister Carmela (a mezzo-soprano who was to sing at the Metropolitan from 1925 to 1935). In 1918 her coach William Thorner brought her to the attention of Enrico Caruso and Giulio Gatti-Casazza. In the first Metropolitan *La forza del destino* she made an unprecedented debut—the first operatic performance of her life—as Leonora (1918), opposite Caruso and Giuseppe De Luca. She had prepared the role with Romano Romani, who remained her principal operatic and vocal tutor. She sang at the Metropolitan for 19 seasons, undertaking 22 roles. Perhaps most celebrated as Norma, she also enjoyed extraordinary successes in *Oberon, Ernani, Don Carlos, La Gioconda, Andrea Chénier, Guillaume Tell, L'amore dei tre re, Don Giovanni* (Donna Anna), *Cavalleria rusticana, La traviata, La vestale*, and *L'Africaine*. She also participated in Joseph Carl Breil's *The Legend*, Italo Montemezzi's *La notte di Zoraïma*, and Romani's *Fedra*. In 1935 she attempted Carmen and experienced her only notable failure. Two years later she retired from opera, reportedly

Rosa Ponselle as the title character in Amilcare Ponchielli's La Gioconda. *(Richard Bebb Collection/Lebrecht Music & Arts)*

after her request for a revival of *Adriana Lecouvreur* was rejected, and vowed never again to set foot in the Metropolitan after her final performance (*Carmen*, 1937). She made her Covent Garden debut as Norma in 1929 and returned there as Violetta, Leonora (*Forza*), and the heroine of Romani's *Fedra*; at the Florence Maggio Musicale in 1933 she sang Julia (*La vestale*). Although her repertory was broad, she never sang Puccini or Wagner, about which she later confessed regret.

Ponselle's voice is generally regarded as one of the most beautiful of the century. She was universally lauded for opulence of tone, evenness of scale, breadth of range, perfection of technique, and communicative warmth. Many of these attributes are convincingly documented on recordings, among them a nervously vital portrayal of Violetta from a complete Metropolitan recording of *La traviata* (1935). In 1939 and 1954 she made a few private song recordings, later released commercially, the later set revealing a still opulent voice of darkened timbre and more limited range.

BIBLIOGRAPHY

GV (L. Riemens and R. Celletti; S. Smolian and R. Vegeto)

O. Thompson: *The American Singer* (New York, 1937), 335–46

I. Cook: "Rosa Ponselle," *Opera*, iii (1952), 75–81

T. Villella and B. Park: "Rosa Ponselle Discography," *Grand Baton*, vii/1–2 (1970), 5–14

J.B. Steane: *The Grand Tradition* (London, 1974), 289–94

J. Ardoin: "A Footnote to Ponselle's Norma," *Opera*, xxvii (1976), 225–8

"Ponselle at 80," *Opera*, xxviii (1977), 13–25

J. Hines: "Rosa Ponselle," *Great Singers on Great Singing* (Garden City, NY, 1982), 250–57

N. Douglas: *Legendary Voices* (London, 1992), 197–212

J.A. Drake: "Rosa Ponselle Recalls Roles and Colleagues, 1918–1924," *OQ*, x/1 (1993–4), 85–108

M. Bernheimer: "The Golden Soprano," *Opera*, xlviii (1997), 138–45

J.B. Steane: *Singers of the Century* (London, 1997), 171–5

M.J. Phillips-Matz: *Rosa Ponselle: American Diva* (Boston, 1997)

J.A. Drake: *Rosa Ponselle: a Centenary Biography* (Portland, OR, 1997) [includes discography]

MARTIN BERNHEIMER/R

Ponti, Michael (*b* Freiburg, Germany, 29 Oct 1937). American pianist of German birth. Ponti studied in Washington, DC, with Gilmour McDonald (a former pupil of Leopold Godowsky) until 1955, when his parents returned to Germany. There he trained at the Hochschule für Musik in Frankfurt with Erich Flinsch, who had been an assistant to Emil von Sauer at the Vienna Conservatory. Ponti undertook his first concert tour in 1954 and two years later entered the Busoni Competition in Bolzano. He placed fourth and reentered the contest several more times before finally earning top prize in 1964. Shortly afterwards, he debuted in Vienna with five performances of Bartók's Second Piano Concerto under Wolfgang Sawallisch and the Vienna SO. Ponti built his reputation on numerous albums of neglected composers he recorded for Vox in the 1970s, including piano concertos by such 19th-century figures as Bronsart von Schellendorf, Goetz, Stavenhagen, Scharwenka, and Moszkowski, as well as long-awaited sets of complete piano music by Rachmaninoff, Skryabin, and Tchaikovsky. Ponti's impressive command of the intricacies of virtuoso pianism made him a prominent champion of this repertory,

although his technical wizardry occasionally overshadowed his expressive capacity. Aside from his solo career, Ponti has toured extensively with a piano trio, formed in 1977 with violinist Robert Zimansky and cellist Jan Polasek. He also recorded a disc of Ives songs with baritone Dietrich Fischer-Dieskau for Deutsche Grammophon.

BIBLIOGRAPHY

H. Klein: "Michael Ponti—'Brash, Dash and Bravado,'" *New York Times* (30 Jan 1972)

D. Dubal: *The Art of the Piano: Its Performers, Literature, and Recordings* (Pompton Plains, NJ, 1989, 3/2004)

JAMES METHUEN-CAMPBELL/LINCOLN BALLARD

Ponty, Jean-Luc (*b* Avranches, France, 29 Sept 1942). French jazz-rock violinist. He electrified the violin and extended its capabilities with electronic devices such as phase shifters and synthesizers, melding early classical training and virtuosity with an ever-expanding jazz vocabulary to explore the capabilities of the violin. The son of classically trained parents (his father was a violin teacher and his mother a piano teacher), Ponty was performing in one of France's premiere symphony orchestras, Concerts Lamoureux, by his late teens. He also performed on clarinet and then tenor saxophone, influenced by the music of Miles Davis and John Coltrane. Ultimately he chose to perform jazz on the violin. His horn-like approach brought critical acclaim and led to early recording collaborations with the veteran jazz violinists Stephane Grappelli and Stuff Smith. He soon worked with the Gerald Wilson Big Band and the George Duke Trio, which led to projects with the Mahavishnu Orchestra, Frank Zappa, and Elton John (*Honky Chateau*). After signing as a solo artist with Atlantic Records in 1975, Ponty landed 12 consecutive albums in the top five of the *Billboard* jazz chart, with *Enigmatic Ocean* (1977) and *Cosmic Messenger* (1978) also performing well on the pop chart. During the 1990s he worked on acoustic projects infused by West African music, and recorded an acoustic album with Al Di Meola and Stanley Clarke. He has continued to tour and record into the 2010s in various projects, including with the group Return to Forever IV.

JEFFREY HOLMES

Poole, Charlie [Charles] **(Cleveland)** (*b* Randolph Co., NC, 22 March 1892; *d* Spray [now Eden], NC, 21 May 1931). Hillbilly singer, banjoist, and string band leader. He grew up in the textile towns of the North Carolina Piedmont, where he began playing the five-string banjo around the age of nine and learned many old songs and tunes while working in the mills. Although he recorded traditional Southern fiddle tunes and ballads, the bulk of his recorded output consisted of arrangements of popular songs of the 1890s and 1900s. Around 1924 Poole began to tour and then, in 1925, record with his string band, the North Carolina Ramblers, comprising fiddler Posey Rorer and guitarist Norman Woodlieff. Later members of the band included guitarist Roy Harvey and fiddlers Lonnie Austin and Odell Smith. Poole and the North Carolina Ramblers' first release,

"Can I sleep in your barn tonight mister"/"Don't let your deal go down blues" (Columbia, 1925), sold more than 102,000 copies at a time when most hillbilly records averaged sales of about 10,000 copies. In an era when most traditional Southern banjoists played in an older, percussive "frailing" or "clawhammer" style, Poole used a three-finger picking technique (employing the thumb and two fingers), possibly learned from another Randolph County, North Carolina, banjoist, Daner Johnson, who had adapted traditional Southern tunes to the classic banjo styles of the 1890s. Poole's precise, melodic playing was matched by that of the band, which cultivated a highly disciplined and tightly interwoven sound. Between 1925 and 1930 Poole and his band recorded a total of 80 sides for the Columbia, Paramount, and Brunswick labels, many of which became bluegrass, folk, and country standards.

Beginning in 1927 Poole tried to broaden his style by experimenting with a larger, five-piece band and also recording several showcase banjo medleys and instrumentals (with piano accompaniment) that had originally been recorded by classic banjo virtuoso Fred Van Eps, Poole's idol and perhaps his most important musical influence. But Poole was frustrated by his producer, Columbia A&R man Frank B. Walker, who insisted that he conform to his older, proven formula. The Great Depression's devastating effect on the recording industry, combined with growing health problems, prompted Poole to abandon his professional music career and soon led to his increased drinking and ultimately his premature death.

Poole was one of the first commercially successful hillbilly singers to perform in a folk-derived style to string-band accompaniment. He and the North Carolina Ramblers created an enormously influential musical sound that other North Carolina and Virginia string bands sought to emulate, and Poole's banjo style is often considered one of the precursors of modern bluegrass banjo. Unlike those of most of his contemporaries, Poole's commercial recordings have enjoyed considerable popularity with modern listeners; as late as 2011 six boxed sets or single CDs, constituting about 95% of his output, were available.

BIBLIOGRAPHY

N. Cohen and E. Kahn: "Tapescripts: Interview with Charlie Poole, Jr.," *JEMF Newsletter*, i (1966), 31–35

N. Cohen: "Early Pioneers," *Stars of Country Music*, ed. B.C. Malone and J. McCulloh (Urbana, IL, 1975), 3–39

K. Rorrer: *Rambling Blues: the Life and Songs of Charlie Poole* (London, 1982, 2/1992)

H. Sapoznik: Liner notes to *"You Ain't Talkin' to Me": Charlie Poole and the Roots of Country Music*, three-CD boxed set (2005, Columbia/Legacy, C3K-92781-92783)

P. Huber: *Linthead Stomp: the Creation of Country Music in the Piedmont South* (Chapel Hill, NC, 2008)

CHARLES K. WOLFE/PATRICK HUBER

Pop. Often used as a term interchangeable with "popular music," pop refers more precisely to a genre of popular music or an attitude toward making popular music that is typically seen as distinct from other genres such as rock, soul, or country. Indeed, pop is often defined in negative terms; Simon Frith argues that pop is "what's left when all the other forms of popular music are stripped away.... From this perspective pop is defined as much by what it isn't as by what it is." While a genre like Rock has identifiable sonic markers and characteristics—such as an emphasis on electric guitar, extensive use of blues-influenced structures, an ideology of authenticity and sincerity—pop as a genre cannot be said to have a coherent style. Pop's voracious borrowing and adaptation leads not only to new stylistic combinations but also to "pop" versions of country, rock, hip hop, heavy metal, and other styles. Rather than a specific set of sounds, pop is a sensibility.

Pop performers frequently pick and choose repertoire and mimic effects from other genres in crafting new material. The magpie-like nature of pop leads Eric Weisbard to call it "a hybrid, a category fouler" and Ann Powers to identify Prometheus the thief, rather than Orpheus the rebel, as pop's favorite god. In the face of charges of being derivative and banal, pop remains cheerfully indifferent to the value of originality. At the same time, the creators and producers of pop are often pioneers of new technologies, sounds, and styles, so that pop is frequently at the vanguard of experimentation. This paradox is one of many that make definitions of pop slippery and elusive.

While "pop" derives from "popular," the designation is often applied in the absence of market success or other indicators of actual popularity. Thus, a song or other piece of music can achieve tremendous popularity without being thought of as pop, and a song with a certain sensibility is considered pop even if it does not catch on with a wide audience. Consider the massive popularity of Nirvana's 1991 "Smells Like Teen Spirit" in contrast to Debbie Gibson's release of that year, "Anything is possible," ineluctably pop even though its sales were modest. For such reasons pop is a classification that may be assigned on the basis of sonic qualities, expressive themes, expected fan base, or assumptions about artistic integrity, rather than empirical evidence of popularity.

Note also that this comparison points to gendered associations of rock with masculinity and pop with femininity. Pop of the type produced by Gibson is generally considered the province of female performers and listeners, if only because of its safe, predictable language and thematic content. While rock culture encourages rebellion, models a quest for independence, and fits well with the expectations and standards of manhood, pop is family-friendly and connected to women and girls above all, reaffirming the ideology of romance and the safe, domestic space. Thus, while a young female performer of rock like Joan Jett had to work hard to prove herself along the lines of an honorary male, a young male performer of pop like Justin Bieber finds that his masculinity is called into question.

Age also has a bearing on the "pop" associations of individual performers. Pop is often associated with youth (and childhood) and produced by young (and sometimes child) performers; a connection to young, female audiences and performers can be sufficient to conjure the designation pop. Thus, when 19-year-old former television star Miley Cyrus included "Smells Like Teen Spirit" in her 2011 "Gypsy Heart Tour" (dedicating it to her little brother at home, because they had grown up singing it together), she was seen to have brought the song into the realm of family-friendly pop rather than having the performance transform her into a rock artist, even though her raspy vocals evoked Nirvana's Kurt Cobain more than Debbie Gibson.

At the same time, pop is also linked to middle-aged listeners, particularly middle-class suburbanites and most particularly women. Comforting older artists such as Barry Manilow are overwhelmingly understood to offer tame material oozing with false sentimentality and clichés, and their fan bases are largely assumed to be housewives, seeking the illusion of intimacy. The anodyne character of music associated with middle-aged housewives also connects it more strongly with bland fare suitable for family consumption, reinforcing associations with domesticity, conventional femininity, and children. A young listener's turn away from family-sanctioned pop to music genres associated with nonconformity can be perceived as a step toward adulthood, so that adult listeners preferring pop can be seen as immature.

Pop music is inextricably associated with commercial concerns, mass production, and charges of pandering to the least sophisticated tastes. The songwriter Stephen Foster, arguably the first purveyor of pop in the United States, wrote unfailingly pleasing tunes that relied exclusively on diatonic melodies, major keys, and basic harmonic movement, although he had received formal training in music and presumably was capable of greater complexity. Foster sought simplicity and transparency, crafting a language that could be grasped quickly by the majority of listeners after only one or two hearings. Such direct and pleasing pop music is often criticized on the grounds that it is simple to the point of inanity, and its fans unsophisticated and passive. This line of analysis, expressed most forcefully in the work of Theodor Adorno, assumes the existence of cynical businessmen, with no genuine interest in making good music, assembling shoddy product and force-feeding it to the mindless masses. Whether or not one subscribes to Adorno's position, there is no doubt that pop's appealing hooks and grooves worm their way into our consciousness, often without our consent or awareness, as in the famous Noël Coward line "Extraordinary how potent cheap music is."

Much of pop music's simplicity is deceptive, however. The creations of Burt Bacharach and Hal David in the 1960s, for example, frequently employ shifting meters and surprising melodic and harmonic language, but this did not prevent songs like "I say a little prayer for you" (originally recorded by Dionne Warwick, 1967) from being "catchy" and popular. Bacharach, a formally trained composer, drew on his familiarity with the European art music repertoire, and many of his peers associated with the Brill Building similarly employed a harmonic palette wider than the I–IV–V language of the blues. Likewise, earlier Tin Pan Alley songwriters

reworked familiar classical works into songs such as "I'm always chasing rainbows" (1918, based on Chopin's Fantasy-Impromptu, op.66) or "Our Love" (1939, based on Tchaikovsky's *Romeo and Juliet*); this strategy is also used in the 1975 hit "Midnight Blue" (based on the second movement of Beethoven's "Pathétique" sonata, op.13). The association of this sort of pop music with learned music practices also connects it with privileged middle- and upper-class listeners.

Pop music is overcoded, rooted in its cultural moment without pretensions of transcendence or lasting value. Pop's appetites range widely, often irreverently combining sounds of the moment and fashioning new hybrids, as when heavy metal guitarist Eddie Van Halen soloed in support of Michael Jackson (the anointed "King of Pop") on "Beat It" (1984). Even before the studio wizardry of Phil Spector and Brian Wilson in the 1960s, pop has historically stood at the forefront of exploration with new technologies of music and recording. We hear these qualities in "This Diamond Ring," a 1965 multitracked and overdubbed studio recording attributed to Gary Lewis & the Playboys (though its vocals were not even provided by the ostensible singer, Gary Lewis) and "Believe," the 1998 single by Cher that became a worldwide sensation in large part for its intriguingly distorted vocals. The production used Auto-Tune, a studio tool, to create what would come to be called "the Cher effect." Although Auto-Tune was originally designed to unobtrusively correct imprecise intonation, her producers used it to exaggerate the artificiality of abrupt pitch correction, a technique that became widespread in pop recordings and live performance throughout the first decade of the 21st century.

Yet pop may also lean toward the old-fashioned and nostalgic, recycling sounds and styles that were once associated with other genres. Pop relies on cultural amnesia, presenting "new" music uncannily resembling old music and seeming tame, even quaint, in its new setting. Sounds that shocked audiences when played by punk bands in the 1970s had become mainstream pop 25 years later in the hands of pop-punk groups. Often, pop artists specifically revive long forgotten songs to appeal to new listeners; the careers of teen idols such as Connie Francis and Leif Garrett (among many others) involved the strategic use of decades-old hits such as "Who's Sorry Now" and "Put your head on my shoulder." Old songs presented by young performers—thus combining fresh, youthful energy with reassuringly old-fashioned sounds—offer reactionary alternatives to new, subversive musics. Pop thus presents its listeners a distraction from contemporary musics and subcultures that threaten the *status quo*. In times of widespread duress, pop music also can offer soothing relief, as Rudy Vallee demonstrated with "Life is just a bowl of cherries" (1931), recorded during the Great Depression.

Pop's preference for personal themes, involving relationships and feelings, rather than explicitly political ones, helps it to exist simultaneously on the margins and at the center of social experience. Pop's essence is, perhaps, its ephemerality; pop songs can seize the public ear for a brief time and then evaporate, often ceding the ground to other musical styles when histories of music come to be written. Thus, the accepted narrative of significant music in 1969 attaches importance to Jimi Hendrix's accomplishments, but not to those of the Fifth Dimension or Tommy James and the Shondells, both of which groups far outpaced Hendrix that year in terms of chart success. The pleasures of James and the Shondells' "Crimson and Clover," though widely enjoyed, were easily discarded, leaving no lasting trace on the historical record.

At the same time, some pop songs pass into the vernacular and endure for decades or more—like the song "Oh! Susanna" (1848), originally composed by Stephen Foster for performance on the minstrel stage—in some cases coming to be understood as folk songs that seemingly exist apart from the commercial music publishing industry. Pop's later inclination for the single format characteristically has made its recorded products quicker and cheaper to make and distribute than the album format long preferred in rock culture (particularly rock with pretensions of grandeur and timeless artistic merit). Even confections such as the Archies' "Sugar Sugar" (1969)—a studio concoction credited to the band from a children's cartoon—have proven relevant and recognizable 40 years on. Created in a single recording session as a novelty song, "Sugar Sugar" has proven surprisingly durable, gaining "oldies" radio play in the 2010s comparable to that of art rock album tracks months in the making (for example, "Money" from Pink Floyd's 1973 *Dark Side of the Moon*).

Arguably, the freshness and unambiguousness of a pop confection like "Sugar Sugar" is the key to its lasting appeal, still audible decades after its creation. The banality of clichés used to convey commonplace emotions and experiences are in this way crucial to pop, leading to songs that express the familiar and acutely personal to the widest possible range of listeners. Unburdened with any claim to serious artistic worth, a pop song can articulate profound personal sentiment with breathtaking immediacy. Urging its listeners to dance or sing along, pop music offers transparency, directness, and access to innermost feeling.

See also ADULT CONTEMPORARY; BOY BANDS; BUBBLEGUM; GIRL GROUPS; NOVELTY SONG; POPULAR MUSIC; SYNTHPOP; and TEEN IDOL.

BIBLIOGRAPHY

C. Hamm: *Yesterdays: Popular Song in America* (New York, 1979)

T. Scheurer: "The Beatles, the Brill Building, and the Persistence of Tin Pan Alley in the Age of Rock," *Popular Music and Society*, xx/4 (1996), 89–102

D. Brackett: *Interpreting Popular Music* (Berkeley, CA, 2000)

S. Frith: "Pop Music," *The Cambridge Companion to Pop and Rock*, ed. S. Frith and W. Straw (Cambridge, England, 2001), 93–108

G. Wald: "I Want it That Way: Teenybopper Music and the Girling of Boy Bands" *Genders*, no.35 (2002), <http://www.genders.org/g35/g35_wald.html>

I. Inglis: "'Some Kind of Wonderful': the Creative Legacy of the Brill Building" *American Music*, xxi/2 (2003), 213–35

E. Weisbard, ed.: *This is Pop: In Search of the Elusive at Experience Music Project* (Cambridge, MA, 2004) [incl. E. Weisbard: "Who'll Write the Book of Love? Pop Music and Pop Prose," 1–14; A. Powers, "Bread and Butter Songs: Unoriginality in Pop," 235–44; J. Clover, "Good Pop, Bad Pop: Massiveness, Materiality, and the Top 40," 245–56]

K. Dickinson: "'Believe': Vocoders, Digital Identity, and Female Camp," *Music, Space and Place*, ed. S. Whiteley and others (Salford, 2004), 163–79

R. Dyer: "Housewives' Choice: Female Fans and Unmanly Men," *The Popular Music Studies Reader*, ed. A. Bennett and others (New York, 2006), 377–81

K. Emerson: *Always Magic in the Air: the Bomp and Brilliance of the Brill Building Era* (New York, 2006)

J. Neal: "Analysis and Performance Across the Canon: 'When Recollection is all We've Got': Analytical Exploration of 'Catchy' Songs," *College Music Symposium*, xlvii (2007), 12–22

D. Scott, ed.: *The Ashgate Research Companion to Popular Musicology* (Salford, England, 2009)

E. Wald: *How the Beatles Destroyed Rock'n'Roll: an Alternative History of American Popular Music* (New York, 2009)

T. Cateforis: *Are We Not New Wave? Modern Pop at the Turn of the 1980s* (Ann Arbor, MI, 2011)

JACQUELINE WARWICK

Pop, Iggy [Osterberg, James Newell, Jr.] (*b* Ypsilanti, MI, 21 April 1947). Rock singer and songwriter. He got his start as drummer in a high school band the Iguanas, from which he derived his nickname "Iggy." In late 1965 he was invited to join the more "progressive" Ann Arbor band the Prime Movers, through which he developed a dedication to urban electric blues and formed an association with Chicago drummer, Sam Lay, who played with the Paul Butterfield Blues Band. After leaving the Prime Movers, he became the singer with the Psychedelic Stooges, which he formed in 1967 with brothers Ron Asheton, guitarist, and Scott Asheton, drummer, along with Dave Alexander, bass guitarist. The group, soon renamed the Stooges, played loud, droning, repetitive music, supplanting the virtuosic tendencies of so much psychedelic rock with a more rough and ragged form of noise. For a time Iggy was known as Iggy Stooge,

Iggy Pop, 2005. (Tony Bartolo/Lebrecht Music & Arts)

carrying his new band's name as part of his persona; the name "Iggy Pop" took hold gradually, started as a joke among his band mates. Pop's lyrics for the Stooges distilled an attitude of youthful nihilism in which hedonism and boredom coexisted, and his violent theatrical antics, involving physical contortions, leaping from the stage into the audience, and cutting himself with broken glass, prefigured the aggressive impulses that would find wider circulation with the mid-1970s rise of punk.

The Stooges released three principal albums in their short career. Their eponymous debut, issued in 1969, was produced by John Cale and included songs notable for their anti-hippie sentiments, such as "No Fun" and "I wanna be your dog." *Funhouse* (1970) added saxophone solos in a free-jazz style to the band's hard psychedelic sound and features some of Pop's most lacerating vocal performances. In 1973 David Bowie produced *Raw Power*, on which James Williamson played guitar while Ron Asheton moved to bass. Although Bowie's production has long been a source of controversy, with its uneven balance that makes the rhythm section into a faint presence beneath Pop's vocals and Williamson's guitar, *Raw Power* is considered a landmark of 1970s hard rock and often hailed as a founding document of punk.

After the breakup of the Stooges in 1974 and a hiatus of some time, Iggy Pop continued his collaboration with David Bowie. With Bowie producing, Pop issued two albums that ushered in the post-punk era: *The Idiot* and *Lust for Life*, both released in 1977, which incorporated keyboards and dance rhythms alongside stark guitar-oriented rock and featured Pop's deep monotone giving voice to sentiments of a modern alienated self. Throughout the 1980s and 90s Pop continued releasing albums under his own name with moderate success and inconsistent artistic results. In 2003, after close to 30 years of separation, he re-formed the Stooges with original band mates Ron and Scott Asheton, with Mike Watt taking the place of the deceased Dave Alexander on bass guitar. The band has issued one new record, *The Weirdness*, since their reformation, and, despite Ron Asheton's untimely 2009 death, has continued performing with James Williamson on guitar.

RECORDINGS

WITH THE STOOGES

The Stooges (1969, Elek. 74051); *Funhouse* (1970, Elek. 74071); *Raw Power* (1973, Col. KC32111); *Metallic K.O.* (1976, Skydog 1015); *The Weirdness* (2007, Virgin 64648)

AS IGGY POP

Lust for Life (1977, RCA AFL12488); *The Idiot* (1977, RCA APL12275); *TV Eye* (1978, RCA APL12796); *New Values* (1979, Ari. 4237); *Party* (1981, Ari. 9572); *Zombie Birdhouse* (1982, Animal FV-41399); *Brick by Brick* (1990, Virgin 91381–2); *American Caesar* (1993, Virgin 39002); *Skull Ring* (2003, Virgin 80774)

BIBLIOGRAPHY

D. Marsh: "The Incredible Story of Iggy and the Stooges," *Creem*, ii/13 (1970), 1, 29–33

I. Pop and A. Wehrer: *I Need More: the Stooges and Other Stories* (New York, 1982)

L. Bangs: "Of Pop and Pies and Fun: a Program for Mass Liberation in the Form of a Stooges Review, or, Who's the Fool?," *Psychotic Reactions and Carburetor Dung*, ed. G. Marcus (New York, 1987), 31–52

N. Kent: "The Four Ages of a Man Named Pop: Pictures of Iggy," *The Dark Stuff* (New York, 1995), 244–66

P. Trynka: *Iggy Pop: Open up and Bleed* (New York, 2007)

STEVE WAKSMAN

Pope, W(ilfred) Stuart (George) (*b* Folkestone, England, 9 Aug 1921; *d* New York, NY, 31 Jan 2005). English music publisher. Educated at the Royal College of Organists, he joined the publishing firm of Boosey and Hawkes in 1937, and after wartime service eventually became managing director of the company's affiliate in South Africa (1958). He was also active as an organist, serving at the Crown Court Church, London (1946–58), and St Mary's Cathedral, Johannesburg (1960–64). He came to the United States in 1964 as managing director of Boosey and Hawkes and was appointed president in 1974. In 1984 he retired from Boosey and Hawkes and became president of BTG Management, a division of Birch Tree Group, Ltd, of which he was vice-president. He served on the boards of directors of ASCAP, the American Music Center, and the Music Publishers Association.

ELLEN HIGHSTEIN/N. LEE ORR

Popovich, Adam (*b* Denver, CO, 24 Dec 1909; *d* Chicago, IL, 16 June 2001). Instrumentalist, singer, and composer. As a child he began studying music with his father, who was originally from Serbia. The music of his family's heritage became a central part of Popovich's life. In 1924 he took up the tambura, a Serbian long-necked lute, and soon became an accomplished performer on the celo (a type of tambura) and the violin; Popovich had to take lessons from a teacher in a nearby mining village. In 1925 he formed the Popovich Brothers Yugoslav Tamburitza Orchestra with his brothers Eli, Ted, and Marko; they toured extensively in the West, and in 1928 settled in the large Serbian community of South Chicago, where they became well-known. They performed at the Smithsonian Institution's 1973 Festival of American Folklife; in 1978 they were portrayed in a film, *The Popovich Brothers of South Chicago*. The brothers also opened a venue, Club Selo, where they served Serbian food and where the brothers regularly performed. Many of their recordings can be found on the Balkan Records label. Popovich became an accomplished singer starting in the 1920s, and has been very active with his local congregation; he studied piano, harmony, and composition with the church's choirmaster, Joseph Kindl. When Kindl retired, Popovich directed the Sloboda choir of the Serbian Orthodox Church (from 1936) and for it he made many arrangements of traditional folk melodies. He also composed several original works for chorus and for tamburitza ensemble. He received a National Heritage Fellowship from the NEA in 1982.

DANIEL SHEEHY/JONAS WESTOVER

Popping. *See* HIP-HOP DANCE.

Pops [Pop, Promenade] **concert.** Orchestral programs modeled after European promenade concerts of the

19th century, in which light classical music was played while the audience was served refreshments. The development of pops concerts in America reflected an emerging emphasis on the audience and an explicitly articulated division between so-called serious and light classical music propagated by conductor Theodore Thomas and others. Such concerts were traditionally structured in three parts, in which lively pieces—overtures, marches, and galops—were played in the outer sections while the middle section typically included waltzes and occasionally more serious works; encores were a regular feature. These concerts often took place in outdoor venues during the summer season, and featured audience promenades during the intermissions. Initially, works by European composers such as Rossini, Grieg, Liszt, and J. Strauss dominated the programs of pops concerts, but excerpts from musicals and operettas by De Koven and Herbert, among others, soon became a significant component. In general these concerts were understood as a vehicle to reach new audiences and broaden the appeal of orchestras and orchestral music.

Since at least 1885 there have been several types of ensembles that produce pops concerts: independent pops orchestras (such as the New York Pops), pops orchestras associated with "serious" symphony orchestras (such as the Boston and Cincinnati Pops), and orchestras that perform the occasional pops concert or arrangement. The Boston SO was the first institution to establish regular pops concerts in the United States, and thus has served as a model for others. The Boston Pops Orchestra consists of musicians from the symphony orchestra and is administered by the same staff, but it is branded as a separate entity. A number of works have been written especially for the Boston Pops, including those by Leroy Anderson and John Williams. Selections of patriotic music, especially *The Star-Spangled Banner* and Sousa's *The Stars and Stripes Forever!* (as well as others of his many marches), are regularly included on pops programs, particularly on Independence Day, when outdoor concerts often conclude with a display of fireworks. The conductor ARTHUR FIEDLER became inextricably identified with pops concerts through his leadership of the Boston Pops Orchestra (1930–79) and the San Francisco Pops Orchestra (1951–78), as well as his many recordings, television broadcasts, tours, and guest appearances. Other conductors associated with pops include JOHN WILLIAMS, who succeeded Fiedler in Boston, ERICH KUNZEL, who founded the Cincinnati Pops Orchestra in 1977, RICHARD HAYMAN (who held the title "principal pops conductor" for concerts presented by the Detroit SO and the St. Louis SO), SKITCH HENDERSON (whose New York Pops Orchestra made its debut in 1983), and KEITH LOCKHART, who has served as music director of the Boston Pops since 1995. The first all-student pops orchestra was created on the University of Michigan's campus in 1995. In recent years pops concerts have begun to incorporate film and video-game music, as well as special presentations in which orchestra musicians share the stage with well-known popular artists.

BIBLIOGRAPHY

S. Ledbetter: *100 Years of the Boston Pops*, ed. J.C. Marksbury (Boston, 1985)

L.C. Manning: *A Guide to Orchestral "Pops" Programming: a Repertoire Handbook* (diss., U. of South Carolina, 2005)

A. Adler: *"Classical Music for People Who Hate Classical Music": Arthur Fielder and the Boston Pops, 1930–1950* (diss., U. of Rochester, Eastman School of Music, 2007)

W. Weber: *The Great Transformation of Musical Taste: Concert Programming from Haydn to Brahms* (New York, 2008)

SUSAN FEDER/MICHAEL MAUSKAPF

Popular music. Although the term is used widely to refer to music that is readily accessible to large numbers of listeners rather than to an elite few, "popular music" is difficult to define precisely because its meaning has shifted historically and because its boundaries are unclear and contested. It has been conventional to conceive of three broad categories of music: popular, art (or classical), and folk. Just as "art music" may refer to Gregorian chant, grand opera, string quartets, and minimalist percussion music, "popular music" is an umbrella term that encompasses a wide set of variously distinct though often related genres. All of these designations are imperfect, and more nuanced understanding of popular music necessitates recognizing the fluidity of musical boundaries, and the constant transformation, adaptation, and impermanence of musical practices. Definitions of popular music seeking to distinguish it from art or folk music usually emphasize its wide appeal, means of dissemination (in particular, mass distribution), and social structure (music of the people; music for a non-elite audience; music for a mass audience).

1. European origins. (i) English traditions. (ii) Scottish and Irish melodies. (iii) Bel canto. (iv) Continuing European influences. 2. Early American song and piano music. (i) The expanding market. (ii) The first American songwriters. (iii) Songs of the minstrel stage. (iv) Singing families. (v) Stephen Foster. (vi) Popular piano music. (vii) The Civil War period. (viii) The postwar years. 3. The Tin Pan Alley era. (i) The early years. (ii) Mainstream developments between the world wars. (iii) Traditional and ethnic music. (iv) Synthesis with jazz. (v) The end of the era. 4. The rock era. (i) Introduction. (ii) Rock and roll. (iii) The 1960s. (iv) The 1970s. (v) The 1980s. (vi) The 1990s. (vii) The 2000s.

1. EUROPEAN ORIGINS.

(i) English traditions. The first secular music printed in North America was associated with the BROADSIDE ballad. Some broadsides were printed in England and brought to the colonies; others were printed in such American cities as Boston, Philadelphia, and New York. They usually consisted only of a text, which was intended to be sung to a tune already familiar to the purchaser through oral tradition; even when a melody was printed on a broadside, it served only as a reminder. Many of these tunes have been preserved in oral tradition, in notated instrumental music as airs for variation, or in tutors and such contemporary sources as *The English Dancing Master* (1651), published by John Playford. Popular ballads can be reconstructed by matching their lyrics, as printed in broadsides, with tunes from these and other sources. The printing of secular music in North America began in earnest only

after the Revolution. Early printers and publishers included Benjamin Carr (Philadelphia and New York), James Hewitt (New York), P.A. von Hagen (Boston), and George Willig (Philadelphia); most of their issues were songs, for voice and keyboard, that had been popularized on the stages of the theaters and pleasure gardens of the day.

Musical life in the new nation was closely linked with that of England. Ballad operas had been performed in America since 1735, when *Flora, or Hob in the Well* was staged in Charleston, South Carolina. (*See* BALLAD OPERA.) In 1752, an English troupe landed in Virginia at Yorktown, and gave its first performances in Williamsburg. It soon began calling itself the American Company, and traveled throughout the colonies, performing ballad and comic operas. Songs from the operas they performed were issued by early American music publishers.

Solo songs with instrumental accompaniment, either taken from stage works or written for concert performances, were sung at benefit and subscription concerts in various cities, as part of the programs of musical societies in Charleston, New York, Boston, and Philadelphia, and at the outdoor performances at many pleasure gardens. (*See* PLEASURE GARDEN.) Almost all of these were written by English composers in the "London" style fashionable at the time, which combined elements of English airs with stylistic traits from the works of Handel, J.C. Bach, and other European composers. They are strophic songs, the melodies of which are mostly diatonic, with scale passages and melodic skips outlining basic triads, and accompaniments that are confined to simple figuration and repeated chords; their texts are mostly pastoral, comic, or moralizing. James Hook's annual collections of songs written for Vauxhall Gardens in London (1774–c1820) furnished American publishers with several hundred items.

Many musicians who had been active in London immigrated to the United States soon after the Revolution, and helped shape the musical life of the new country by playing, singing, conducting, and organizing musical events. Most also composed songs in the London style. Benjamin Carr, who had been associated with the London Ancient Concerts, went to Philadelphia in 1793 and was active there and in New York as a pianist, singer, composer, and music publisher. Reinagle arrived in the United States in 1786 and worked as a conductor, performer, and impresario in several cities; most of his published songs, which number more than 50, are arrangements of pieces by Arnold, Kelly, Dibdin, and Shield. James Hewitt came to the United States in 1792; he composed and conducted ballad and comic operas. The songs written by these composers enjoyed considerable success and were an important part of the first body of popular song printed in the United States.

Among the most popular songs in the first decades of the 19th century were those of John Braham, including the duet "All's well" from his opera *The English Fleet in 1342*, and the ballad "Is there a heart that never lov'd?" The songs of Henry R. Bishop were even more popular in the United States at this time: "Home, Sweet Home" (1823) was almost immediately successful and became the most universally known song of the 19th century; others of his songs, such as "Love has eyes" from the comic opera *The Farmer's Wife* enjoyed almost equal, though less enduring, popularity. Bishop's songs, like the best work of other English songwriters of the era, have an easy melodic charm, express emotions directly, and use simple accompaniments that do not draw attention from the singer and the text. The style of American popular music to the mid-19th century was decidedly English, though it often drew on other national styles heard in the British Isles at the time; this reflected the close cultural ties that still existed between the United States and Britain.

(ii) Scottish and Irish melodies. James Hook and his contemporaries sometimes wrote songs derived from, or imitative of, Scottish and Irish tunes. Hook's "Within a Mile of Edinboro' Town" and several arrangements of the anonymous "The Blue Bells of Scotland" were among the most popular sheet-music publications in the United States at the turn of the 19th century, as were a number of songs by Robert Burns ("John Anderson my Jo," "Auld Lang Syne," and "Comin thro the Rye"), which were set to traditional Scottish tunes; first published in *The Scots Musical Museum* beginning in 1787, these songs were distributed in the United States in the form of separate sheet-music issues. Burns's songs and cultural legacy have been particularly important in Canada, with its significant Scottish presence.

By far the most successful of the many collections of Irish songs that appeared in the late 18th and early 19th centuries was the ten-volume *A Selection of Irish Melodies*, with texts by Thomas Moore and accompaniments by John Stevenson (i–vii, 1808–18) and Bishop (viii–x, 1821–34). Like Burns, Moore added his own poetry to tunes taken from traditional music; though arrangements in the original editions of the collection were for one to four voices, the pieces were most popular as solo songs with keyboard accompaniment. They were enthusiastically received in North America, as they had been in England; the first volume was printed, from new plates, by G.E. Blake in Philadelphia as early as 1808, and succeeding volumes were published in the United States soon after their first appearance in London and Dublin. Individual songs were published separately, and many of these ("Believe me if all those endearing young charms," "The Last Rose of Summer," "The Minstrel Boy," "The harp that once thro Tara's halls") became enduring parts of the North American musical heritage, remaining in print throughout the 19th century and in some cases passing into oral tradition (whence their melodies had come in the first place). His 1804 "Canadian Boat Song" was frequently republished in Canada and the United States into the 1840s, indicating widespread appeal. The immense popularity of Moore's songs, cutting across social and economic divisions, was due both to their texts, which were more concerned with the direct expression of universal human sentiments than had been those of the earlier song repertory, and to their melodies, which were drawn from a musical style already familiar to the American public.

(iii) Bel canto. The music of Italian opera of the early 19th century had a profound impact on popular song in the United States. Simplified arrangements, for voice and keyboard, of excerpts from operas by Mozart and Rossini enjoyed some currency in the first decades of the century. Productions of Italian operas in English at the Park Theatre in New York and in other cities became popular; an "Englished" version, by Bishop, of *Il barbiere di Siviglia* was first staged at the Park in 1819, and frequently repeated in the next years. Many other reworkings of Italian operas, by Bishop and Rophino Lacey, followed. Lacey's *Cinderella, or The Fairy-queen and the Glass Slipper*, based loosely on Rossini's *La Cenerentola*, was first performed at the Park in 1831 and was given some 50 times in its first season alone; it remained in the repertory for decades. Vincenzo Bellini's *La sonnambula* was first performed in the United States in an English version in 1835, and his *Norma* came to the United States in 1840; the latter became the most popular opera of the decade. At the same time European companies led by figures such as Manuel García were touring the United States and performing Italian opera in the original language. In 1832 the Montresor Company, brought to the United States through the efforts of Lorenzo da Ponte (then a professor of Italian literature at Columbia College), gave 30 performances in New York. Local residents subsequently raised $150,000 to construct the Italian Opera House and assemble a company of professional European musicians; the grand opening of the opera house took place on 18 November 1833 with a performance of Rossini's *La gazza ladra*, and 80 performances of various operas were given in its first season. The first fully staged opera in Canada was Bellini's *Norma*, in Toronto, 1853.

The influence of Italian melody on North American culture was felt outside the opera house as well. For several decades after 1820 the melodies of arias, ensembles, and choruses by Rossini, Bellini, Donizetti, and their contemporaries were arranged as simple, strophic songs for voice and keyboard, given English texts, and published as SHEET MUSIC; their sales approached, and sometimes surpassed, those of English and Irish songs. With the increasing popularity of the Italian style, English composers began emulating its most obvious characteristics; this is evident in the songs of Henry Russell, who enjoyed enormous success as a singer and songwriter after arriving in the United States in 1835. Schooled in Italian opera, he wrote and performed songs that had an easy, Italianate, melodic charm, and texts expressing nostalgia for lost youth (the principal theme of Moore's *Irish Melodies*) or addressing issues relevant to American life, such as the treatment of Native Americans and of slaves. Most of his songs were unadorned, strophic ballads, but some ("The Maniac" and "The Ship on Fire") were more extended, complex pieces resembling the scena of contemporary Italian opera. Russell's appealing, dramatic voice, and the intensity of his delivery, inspired by the oratorical style of Henry Clay, made him the most popular singer in the United States to that date; the widespread appeal of his songs, some of which remained in the repertory for more than half a century, brought further currency to the Italian style. For more than 50 years North American songwriters absorbed elements of Italian melody into their music. This influence remained strong even though Italian immigrants constituted only a tiny fraction of the population.

(iv) Continuing European influences. Even after American songwriters began to write in a distinctive, indigenous style, the flow of music from Europe continued. Charlotte Alington Barnard, who published songs and poetry under the pen name "Claribel," was popular in the United States just after the mid-century for several dozen exquisite miniatures, including "I cannot sing the old songs," "Come back to Erin," and "Take back the heart." Many German songs in English translation were widely disseminated and were sung in the concert hall and the parlor: Schubert's *Serenade* and *Ave Maria*, and Beethoven's *Adelaide* were particular favorites, especially among the classical-music audience. American songwriters paid such music little heed, and indigenous popular song had by this time developed such a lively, distinctive character that most Americans preferred it to its European counterpart.

See also PARLOR MUSIC.

2. EARLY AMERICAN SONG AND PIANO MUSIC.

(i) The expanding market. During the Revolutionary period few in the United States were musically literate, and the sale of sheet music was consequently a small business confined mostly to larger cities, and to the most affluent, best-educated members of society, who were also those most likely to have some acquaintance with classical music. The style of popular vocal and keyboard music offered for sale was not markedly different from that of the classical music of the era, merely simpler in structure and less technically demanding. The rise of music education soon contributed to a sharp increase in the market for sheet music for home use, and eventually to a much clearer distinction between the styles of art and popular music.

The early 19th century saw a sharp increase in the quality and quantity of pianos constructed in the United States and Canada; at the same time changes in the economic life of the country made it possible for more people to own such instruments. By 1830 2500 pianos were being manufactured in the United States alone every year; a significant proportion of the population owned or had access to a piano, and sheet music sold in ever larger quantities for use in the home.

(ii) The first American songwriters. Francis Hopkinson wrote songs as early as 1759, and his *Seven Songs for the Harpsichord* (1788) was one of the first publications of secular music in the new republic. In the last decade of the 18th century about 50 secular songs by musicians living in New England were published in *The*

American Musical Miscellany (1798) and in such periodicals as the *Massachusetts Magazine*. Oliver Shaw of Providence composed dozens of songs in the first decades of the 19th century, several of which (for example, "Mary's Tears" and "There's nothing true but heav'n," both settings of sacred poems by Thomas Moore) were published, sold, and sung throughout the country. These were solidly in the mold of the English songs of the day, as were the early songs of John Hill Hewitt, including his remarkably successful "The Minstrel's return'd from the war" (1825), strongly reminiscent of *The Wounded Hussar* by James Hewitt, his father.

(iii) Songs of the minstrel stage. In ballad and comic operas black slaves sometimes appeared as minor characters, singing songs considered appropriate in their music and texts; two examples are Stephen Storace's "Poor Black Boy" (from *The Prize*, 1793) and Charles Dibdin's "Yanko Dear," which have deliberately simplistic music (though they have nothing to do with African or African American styles) and lyrics in heavy dialect. Charles Mathews, an English stage comedian who came to the United States in 1822, was fascinated by the speech patterns and physical characteristics of African Americans; his subsequent incorporation into his popular stage acts of skits, mock lectures, and songs drawing on black material was largely responsible for the increasing trend towards stage impersonation of black characters. By the late 1820s several American entertainers—George Nichols, Bob Farrell, and George Washington Dixon—were making use of comic "negro" songs, many of them published as sheet music. "The Coal Black Rose" and "Long Tail Blue" were popularized by Dixon; others were "De Boatman's Dance," "Clare de Kitchen," and "Zip Coon," which later became popular as "Turkey in the Straw."

In 1828 Thomas Dartmouth ("Daddy") Rice introduced the song "Jim Crow" to audiences in the Midwest as part of his impersonation of a black man performing a comic dance; this piece enjoyed immediate success on the stage and, from 1829, as sheet music. Rice was acclaimed in Cincinnati, Pittsburgh, Baltimore, Washington, New York, and, eventually, London. Other white entertainers impersonated African Americans in the popular theater and, beginning with the Virginia Minstrels in 1843, entire troupes did so as well, the performers appearing with blackened faces. Christy's Minstrels, the Kentucky Minstrels, the Ethiopian Serenaders, and the Sable Harmonists were a few of the groups offering blackface minstrel shows made up of comic dialogues and skits interspersed with dance and song. By mid-century these shows had become the most popular and distinctive product of the American stage; they reached a new peak of popularity after the Civil War, were widely admired and imitated abroad, and persisted well into the 20th century (*see* MINSTRELSY).

The English, when introduced to the minstrelsy of Rice (1836) and the Virginia Minstrels (1843), viewed these entertainments as a purely American form of musical theater, and regarded minstrel songs as the first characteristically American music of any sort. In fact many minstrel songs were derived to some extent from music brought to the United States from the British Isles. "Jim Crow," which Chase called the "first great international song hit of American music," has melodic similarities to English folksong, as do many other early minstrel songs. A handful of them (including "Old Dan Tucker" and "De Boatman's Dance") are based on repetitive melodic figures possibly taken from slave songs of African origin. The process of preparing minstrel songs for mass distribution in the form of sheet music, which required their transcription into musical notation and a degree of adaptation to the musical tastes of the intended consumers, necessarily obscured much of their distinctive character. Minstrel songs as performed on the stage therefore differed somewhat in style from those sung to piano accompaniment in the American parlor—an early instance of the market shaping the product.

(iv) Singing families. In 1839–43 the Rainers, an Austrian singing family, performed with great success in the United States; they wore Tyrolean costumes, were influential in popularizing the yodel, and introduced a new song literature to American audiences. Other Tyrolean and Swiss family groups toured the United States in the same period. They were a model for similar American family groups, the most successful of which, the Hutchinson family, had a great impact on North American popular music. There were 13 Hutchinson children, most of whom sang in church and social gatherings in Milford, New Hampshire. Four of them began performing in villages in New Hampshire and Vermont, then moved on to more important communities such as Saratoga Springs and Albany in New York. In September 1842 they sang in Boston, then gave concerts in Canada and the United States, before performing for President John Tyler in 1844. By then they were the most successful popular entertainers in the country, with dozens of songs in print, and when they went to England in 1845 they were accepted as further evidence of the United States's growing indigenous popular culture.

At the core of the Hutchinsons' early repertory were sentimental and melodramatic ballads popular in the 1840s, such as "The Snow Storm," a tale of a young couple freezing to death in a blizzard, and Russell's "The Old Sexton." They were also concerned with social and political issues, and performed such temperance songs as "King Alcohol" and abolitionist songs like "The Bereaved Slave Mother" and "Get off the track" (set to the music of "Old Dan Tucker"). In 1851 they sang for the first Women's Rights Convention, in Akron, Ohio. They later popularized *The Indian's Lament*, which denounced the persecution of Native Americans. They campaigned for Lincoln, and performed and published songs on his behalf. Perhaps their chief contribution to the emerging character of American popular music was their demonstration that song could be as potent a force for arousing public sentiment on controversial issues as political oratory or crusading journalism.

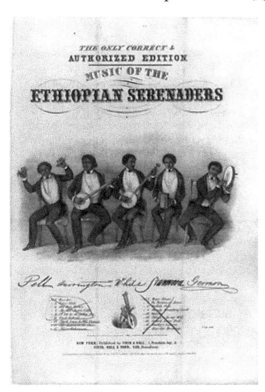

Sheet music cover, "Music of the Ethiopian Serenaders": Gilbert W. Pell, bones; George A. Harrington and William White, banjos; Moody Stanwood, accordion; and Francis Germon, tambourine. (Library of Congress, Prints & Photographs Division, LC-USZ62-66762)

(v) *Stephen Foster.* Born into an educated and well-to-do family in Pittsburgh in 1826, Foster wrote some of the best-loved songs of the 19th century, and more than any other songwriter, was responsible for forging a uniquely American style. His first song to be printed was "Open thy lattice, love" (1844); by the time of his death 20 years later he had written about 200 songs. He had an intimate knowledge of the various sorts of popular music of the day, including minstrel songs; his own first songs in this genre, written in 1847 and 1848 ("Lou'siana Belle," "Away down South," "Old Uncle Ned," and "Oh! Susanna"), have melodic similarities to the standard repertory. Other early songs, such as "Molly! Do you love me?" and "Stay, summer breath," reveal his familiarity with the English style of Henry Bishop and his peers. He knew the songs of Henry Russell, whom he heard in Pittsburgh, and is known to have been fond of attending the opera. His familiarity with melodies in the Italian style prompted him to imitate them in "The voice of bygone days," the duet "Wilt thou be gone love?," and a number of other songs. He was of Irish ancestry, and knew and admired Moore's *A Selection of Irish Melodies*; unmistakable traces of these tunes may be found in a number of his own songs, among them "Sweetly she sleeps, my Alice fair," "Gentle Annie," and "Jeanie with the light brown hair."

Foster's songs are astonishingly simple. The melodies are wholly diatonic, built on conjunct motion, and their phrase structure and larger forms are completely symmetrical. They are always in a major key. Harmonies are diatonic, relieved only occasionally by a secondary dominant; many songs, including some of the most familiar ones ("Oh! Susanna" and "Old Folks at Home"), use only tonic, dominant, and subdominant chords. This simplicity does not result from ignorance or poverty of invention: Foster had some knowledge of classical music, and in his early songs, such as "Wilt thou be gone love?," he sometimes devised more complex melodies and harmonies than he used later. He simply understood, as had no American songwriter before him, that to be universally popular music must be grasped and remembered after only a few hearings, and must be easily performed by those with only rudimentary musical skills. His texts, most of which he wrote himself, are rarely topical, and usually nostalgic. They reflect the events of his own, unhappy life, as well as the longing for a return to a simpler era that was the dominant mood of the period before the Civil War.

Around 1850 Foster began writing a new type of song, the "plantation melody," which synthesized several earlier styles into one that served several generations of American songwriters and came to be widely imitated in Europe. Examples of this new style are "Old Folks at Home," "My old Kentucky home, good night," and "Old Dog Tray." The melodic lines integrate elements of the Irish, Italian, and English styles so successfully that they have a character of their own; the harmonic and melodic language is still completely diatonic, and the accompaniment is further simplified; the verses, for a single voice, are followed by a refrain arranged in three- or four-part harmony. The texts are mostly nostalgic and lamenting, rarely refer specifically to black subjects, and do not attempt to imitate black dialect.

Foster's extreme simplicity of means reflected his decision to write songs that would appeal to the widest possible audience. By the early 1850s several of his songs had sold more than 100,000 copies, and though his share of the profit was small, he decided to give up other employment to devote himself completely to writing music; he was the first American composer to do so.

(vi) *Popular piano music.* Some of the sheet music published during the early 19th century consisted of pieces for keyboard; publication of marches and dances (mostly waltzes) had begun in the last decade of the 18th century. Some of this repertory was originally composed for keyboard, some was arranged from classical compositions or from pieces written for band or small dance orchestra. Many early waltzes were anonymous, identified only by such labels as "German Waltz" or "Hungarian Waltz." Others were simple arrangements of pieces by European composers such as Beethoven, Mozart, Muzio Clementi, and Johann Nepomuk Hummel; not all of these were waltzes in their original form. Still others were new pieces written in the United States by such composers as Charles Gilfert, who was active in Charleston and New York after his arrival from Europe, Peter K.

Moran, who came to New York from Dublin in 1813, and Peter Weldon, the most prolific composer of waltzes in the United States in the first quarter of the century. Whatever their origin, all these waltzes resemble one another in that they are simple pieces with several strains, capable of being played by amateur musicians of modest technique.

Other social dances also appeared in sheet-music form: first minuets, then reels and country dances used for the widely popular cotillion, and, in the early 1840s, polkas, brought to North America from central Europe. (*See* SOCIAL DANCE.) The schottische, mazurka, and polka redowa soon followed. The keyboard repertory also included descriptive BATTLE MUSIC (František Kočžwara's *The Battle of Prague* was a favorite, and was imitated by James Hewitt in *The Battle of Trenton*), variations on favorite airs, and various types of program piece and character-piece. As with vocal music in the decades following the Revolution, there was not always a clear distinction between classical and popular piano music; the latter, in fact, often consisted of simplified arrangements of the former. Selections from the classical repertory continued to be performed in the parlor well into the 19th century, just as some singers of popular songs had sufficient technique to sing operatic arias and lieder in their homes. Later in the 19th century there came to be a growing market for short piano works requiring modest technique and little musical sophistication on the part of performers and listeners. Eventually this repertory shifted from European pieces, and native works written in imitation of them, to compositions with a distinctively American character.

(vii) The Civil War period. The Civil War occurred just as popular music began to reach large numbers of Americans, and as popular songs began to deal with contemporary events and issues. As a result popular music just before and during the war not only concerned itself with political and military events, it also contributed to and affected them. There were great patriotic rallying songs that reflected the political sympathies of millions of people and sought to influence others; these included the "Battle Hymn of the Republic," "Dixie," "The Battle Cry of Freedom," and "The Bonnie Blue Flag." Other songs narrated military events and individual acts of heroism ("The Drummer Boy of Shiloh," "Stonewall's Requiem," "Marching through Georgia"), or treated serious and humorous aspects of life in the army ("Tenting on the Old Camp Ground," "Goober Peas"). Among the best songs were those that expressed the loneliness, fear, and sorrow of soldiers, their families, and their friends ("When this cruel war is over," "The Vacant Chair," and "When Johnny comes marching home").

Musically, most Civil War songs were cast in the verse–chorus patterns that had been popularized by Foster and widely imitated by his peers and successors, with their choruses set in four-part harmony. Foster's many war songs, however, are not among his best efforts. The most successful songwriters in the North were George Frederick Root, who wrote such popular songs as "The Battle Cry of Freedom" and "Just before the Battle, Mother," and Henry Clay Work, who wrote "Wake Nicodemus" and "Marching through Georgia." John Hill Hewitt was the leading Southern songwriter; his "All Quiet along the Potomac Tonight" is a poignant antiwar song, and like many pieces of the time was equally popular in the South and the North.

In many respects popular music and the traditional oral repertory were closely linked during the war years. A large proportion of Civil War songs consisted of arrangements of traditional Irish, Scottish, and English tunes with new, topical lyrics: "The Bonnie Blue Flag," the anthem of the Confederacy, uses the tune of "The Irish Jaunting Car"; Gilmore's "When Johnny comes marching home" is a clever reworking of "John Anderson my Jo," itself an arrangement by Robert Burns of an older traditional tune.

Many songs originated in popular minstrel shows, and a significant number of newly composed songs resembled traditional music in their melodic style; moreover, a number of songs composed during the war years passed quickly into the oral tradition. The Civil War was a "people's war," and it gave rise to a body of popular music that cut across class and ethnic divisions to an unprecedented extent.

See also THE CIVIL WAR; CONFEDERATE MUSIC; PATRIOTIC MUSIC; and POLITICAL MUSIC.

(viii) The postwar years. Many songwriters who first became successful during the war continued to write in the same style in the following years. Work's temperance song "Come home, Father" and his "Grandfather's Clock" (1875) are examples of this tendency, as are "Write me a letter from home" and "We parted by the river side" by Will Hays, whose first successful song had been "The Drummer Boy of Shiloh" (1862). With the exception of a number of songs concerned with temperance and women's rights, the texts of postwar songs were once again devoted to personal rather than public subjects, and musically the period saw little stylistic innovation. Among the most popular songs were H.P. Danks's "Silver threads among the gold" (1872), Thomas Westendorf's "I'll take you home again, Kathleen" (1875), Henry Tucker's "Sweet Genevieve" (1869), Charles A. White's "Put me in my little bed" (1869), Frank Howard's "When the robins nest again" (1883), Banks Winter's "White Wings" (1884), James A. Bland's "Carry me back to old Virginny" (1878), and David Braham's "Over the Hills to the Poor House" (1874).

The minstrel show continued to be the most popular form of American stage entertainment, and for the first time African American performers took part, not as members of a racially mixed cast but, beginning with the Georgia Minstrels in 1865, in separate black troupes. Kersands, Lucas, Bland, and Charles B. Hicks were among the successful black minstrel performers. Bland's "Oh, dem Golden Slippers" and "In the Evening by the Moonlight" were among the first pieces by a black composer to become widely known in the form of commercial sheet music; stylistically they were virtually indistinguishable from the work of white songwriters. A new type of piece for the minstrel stage, the "minstrel spiritual," developed when vocal groups from black schools, among them the Fisk Jubilee Singers, became popular for their performances of arrangements of prewar spirituals; "Angels, meet me at the cross road" (1875) by Hays and "Oh, dem Golden Slippers" are examples of this genre (*see* SPIRITUAL). At the same time the popular piano repertory began to reflect certain rhythmic aspects of black music (or, more accurately, white perceptions of them) in a number of character-pieces and "patrols," with their characteristic crescendo and decrescendo plan of dynamics.

The opening of Tony Pastor's Opera House in 1865, in the Bowery area of New York, was the first important step in the development of VAUDEVILLE, a stage genre that eventually eclipsed the minstrel show. The two forms were similar in that both consisted of songs, dances, comic acts, ensemble numbers, and other entertainments unencumbered by a plot. But while the minstrel show ostensibly referred constantly to the culture of the American South, and its music pretended to derive from African American culture, vaudeville was an urban, northern product that reflected the new ethnic mix of American cities. Vaudeville was also popular in the Canadian West in the 1890s and early 1900s, particularly in the Yukon and cities developing because of the Gold Rush. Initially most songs of the vaudeville stage were interchangeable with those of the minstrel show, and the minstrel song remained a staple of vaudeville well into the 20th century. Nevertheless vaudeville began developing characteristic song styles almost from its beginnings. David Braham, an English-born composer, was the most successful early vaudeville songwriter; he wrote hundreds of pieces for individual vaudeville entertainers, and for a succession of shows performed by the team of Ned Harrigan and Tony Hart during the 1870s and 80s.

American popular song of the late 19th century had a wide, varied audience. Songwriters lived and worked in the East, the Midwest, and the South; important music publishers were situated in various regions of the United States; minstrel and variety shows carried the latest repertory to almost every part of the country; musical style was similar to that of a cherished body of song familiar to most of the population; and song texts continued to mine the popular sentiments of nostalgia, faded love, lost youth, and the simple pleasures of pastoral life. The level of musical literacy continued to rise, and revenue from the sale of sheet music accounted for a growing share of the income of music publishers and songwriters.

3. THE TIN PAN ALLEY ERA.

(i) The early years. New York became the focus of the popular music industry in the last decade of the 19th century. The city began to play a more important role in musical and theatrical life in general, and a new generation of music publishers brought great energy, ambition, and foresight to their business in the 1880s and 90s. The most successful publishers were Thomas B. Harms, who brought out his first songs in 1881, Willis Woodward, who formed a business in 1883, and Isidore Witmark, who established M. Witmark & Sons in 1885. They specialized in popular songs, unlike such earlier publishers as Ditson of Boston, which had published a wide range of music, including classical, popular, and religious works, and instructional material. The key to their remarkable commercial success was their sophistication in identifying and appealing to their market; they conducted simple but effective surveys to determine the types of song that sold well, and tested new songs on prospective performers and listeners. "House" songwriters, who worked under contract, adapted their styles to the dictates of the publishers. By the turn of the century most of the successful publishers had offices on West 28th Street; this became known as TIN PAN ALLEY, supposedly from the sound of the inexpensive upright pianos on which song-pluggers accompanied themselves as they sang their compositions to potential buyers. The term "Tin Pan Alley" was eventually used to refer to the period of North American popular music history from the late 19th century to the 1920s, and the style then prevailing.

The first great songwriter of the era was Paul Dresser; his songs are mostly sentimental ballads in the style of the years after the Civil War. "The Pardon that Came too Late" (1891), "Just tell them that you saw me" (1895), "On the Banks of the Wabash" (1899), and "My Gal Sal" (1905) have simple melodies and nostalgic texts like the best songs of Foster, though they employ slightly more complex harmonies, with characteristic chromatic passages (often including a string of secondary dominants) at the approach to cadences.

More typical of the newer style is Charles K. Harris's "After the Ball," which sold more than 5 million copies following its publication in 1892. In its first decades Tin Pan Alley produced dozens of such songs, remarkable for their commercial success and their enduring quality: "Daisy Bell" (Harry Dacre, 1892), "The Sidewalks of New York" (Charles Lawlor and James Blake, 1894), "The Band Played On" (Charles Ward, 1895), "Sweet Rosie O'Grady" (Maude Nugent, 1896), "My Wild Irish Rose" (Chauncey Olcott, 1899), "A Bird in a Gilded Cage" (Harry Von Tilzer, 1900), "In the Good Old Summertime" (George Evans, 1902), "Sweet Adeline" (Harry Armstrong, 1903), "Give my regards to Broadway" (George M. Cohan, 1904), "Shine on, harvest moon" (Nora Bayes and Jack Norworth, 1908), "Let me call you sweetheart" (Beth Slater Whitson and Leo Friedman, 1910), and "When Irish Eyes are Smiling" (Ernest R. Ball, 1912). The texts refer mostly to urban life, picture the city as a lively, happy environment, and suggest that the United States was making an easy transition from rural to urban life. The popular image of the "gay nineties" as a carefree, untroubled time was formed in part by this music; Tin Pan Alley's publishers and songwriters were interested in selling songs rather than solving social problems, and found that this could best be accomplished by entertaining people with a product divorced from the unpleasant realities of day-to-day life.

Stylistically most early Tin Pan Alley songs are waltz songs. A few, based on march rhythms, also bear a relationship to dance music in that the popular two-step dance used music indistinguishable from the march.

The songs are strophic, with a succession of verses each followed by a chorus usually of 16 or 32 bars. Throughout the 19th century strophic forms had typically been used for popular songs with both narrative and contemplative texts; some had a brief refrain or chorus at the end of each verse (which often repeated or extended the musical material of the verse), but it was for its verses, not its chorus, that a song was usually known and remembered. In the Tin Pan Alley style, however, the principal melodic material was reserved for the chorus, and as the era progressed this gradually grew longer. The verse began to assume the role of an introduction, and its function became more narrative, establishing a dramatic situation that was treated lyrically in the chorus.

During its early history, the melodic and harmonic vocabulary of popular music was closely linked with that of classical music. Hook, Shield, and Braham had written music in the same style, albeit simplified, as that of contemporary classical composers. The melodies, harmonic progressions, and accompaniments of Bishop, Russell, and John Hill Hewitt are similar to those of Rossini, Bellini, and Mendelssohn. But by the middle of the 19th century the situation had changed: the songs of Foster, Root, and Work in no way approach the harmonic richness or the melodic complexity of Verdi, Chopin, or early Wagner. By the early 20th century the contrast between classical and popular styles was even greater; the songs mentioned above have no affinity with the music of Debussy, the early works of Stravinsky and Schoenberg, or the "Concord" Sonata and Second String Quartet of Ives.

It was precisely the simplicity and accessibility of Tin Pan Alley songs that accounted for their extraordinary popularity. While art music became increasingly complex in its harmony, melody, form, and instrumentation, popular composers continued to work in a common-practice style that was also the vernacular of church, dance, and band music. This style was closer to European music of an earlier time than to any body of folk music; but although it did not derive from traditional music, Tin Pan Alley song became folk music in that, owing to its great popularity, it passed into the oral tradition, absorbed by inhabitants of the rural South and other regions. The same process occurred among African American musicians, as can be seen from the role played by popular song in the early stages of jazz.

The early Tin Pan Alley era was also the age of RAGTIME. This was largely an improvised form of music, but some ragtime pieces did become popular as sheet music. Scott Joplin's "Maple Leaf Rag," the first ragtime piece to enjoy wide commercial success, was published in 1899. For more than a decade the sales of some published piano rags by Joplin, Tom Turpin, and others approached those of Tin Pan Alley songs. Ragtime's rhythms had a strong influence on American popular song. Its characteristic syncopations were quickly adopted, in simplified form, by songwriters to give their work spice and topical appeal. Coon songs, which derived from minstrel practices, used black dialect in their texts, and evoked syncopated dances in the ac-

companiments (see COON SONG), were published in large numbers in the 1880s and 90s, but later gave way to ragtime songs in the Tin Pan Alley style. These included Ben R. Harney's "You've been a good old wagon" (1895), Joe Howard's "Hello! Ma baby" (1899), Hugh Cannon's "Bill Bailey" (1902), "Under the Bamboo Tree" (1902) by Bob Cole, J. Rosamond Johnson, and James Weldon Johnson, and the early songs of Irving Berlin, including "Alexander's Ragtime Band" (1911), the most commercially successful example of the genre. By this time the ragtime song was the most popular type of vaudeville music, and sales of sheet music reflected its appeal.

Ragtime played a role in the early days of mechanical sound reproduction. Thomas A. Edison invented the phonograph in 1877, and by 1888 the "talking machine" was sophisticated enough for a recording of music to be attempted. Commercial phonographs and recordings were manufactured in Germany the following year, and in the 1890s, as the Tin Pan Alley era was beginning, the "nickel-in-the-slot" machine, the forerunner of the jukebox of the 20th century, became popular. As recording and playback equipment was not yet sophisticated enough to permit accurate reproduction of the human voice, the first mechanically reproduced popular pieces were instrumental; rags and other syncopated dance tunes, often played by woodwind or brass instruments, were most common. At the same time the player piano was enjoying its first vogue; ragtime pianists made numerous piano rolls, and these became the second medium, after sheet music, through which popular pieces became known.

The first decades of Tin Pan Alley also saw the development of a relatively sophisticated type of popular song, with melodies and harmonies reminiscent of European art music. A leading exponent of the genre was Victor Herbert, whose songs, such as "Ah! Sweet mystery of life," were often as successful as those of commercial songwriters. The songs of Reginald De Koven ("Oh Promise Me" from the opera *Robin Hood*, 1890), Ethelbert Nevin ("The Rosary," 1898), Carrie Jacobs-Bond ("I love you truly," 1901), and Ernest R. Ball ("Love me and the world is mine," 1906) are notable for their structural complexity, chromaticism, and elaborate accompaniments; they foreshadow the advanced style of a second generation of Tin Pan Alley songwriters.

A number of important works for the musical stage were written during the Tin Pan Alley era. Unlike earlier shows, which were sequences of unrelated musical numbers, these were based on coherent plots; as such they prefigured the American musical. Among the most important were Cohan's "musical plays," including *Little Johnny Jones* (1904) and *Forty-five Minutes from Broadway* (1906), and a number of stage works with music by Jerome Kern, including *The Red Petticoat* (1912) and *Very Good, Eddie* (1915), one of several shows written for the Princess Theatre. (*See* MUSICAL THEATER.)

(ii) Mainstream developments between the world wars. The period after World War I was marked by in-

novations that deeply affected the dissemination of popular music. At the turn of the century songs were introduced and popularized principally in musical stage productions (vaudeville, revue, operetta, and musical comedy), and the sale of sheet music was the music industry's main source of revenue. More than 100 American companies manufactured pianos, and most families with some degree of education owned a piano and played popular songs and piano pieces in their homes. As RECORDED SOUND became more sophisticated, however, the phonograph disc began challenging the primacy of printed sheet music. In 1919 the song "Mary" by George Stoddard, issued by the Victor firm, sold 300,000 copies without having been performed on the vaudeville stage. Later that year Selvin's Novelty Orchestra recorded for Victor "Dardanella," with words by Fred Fisher and music by Felix Barnard and Johnny S. Black; more than a million copies of the recording were sold. Whiteman's recording of "Whispering" (1920) more than doubled that figure. By 1920 there were almost 200 record companies in the United States, and it was common by the middle of the decade for sales of a recording of a song to surpass those of the sheet music. The introduction of electrical recording in 1925 increased audio fidelity and attracted even more consumers. The implications of this trend were not fully grasped by the music industry for some time, in part because the recording business was devastated for a number of years at the start of the Great Depression. (*See* MUSIC INDUSTRY.)

Experiments in the radio transmission of recorded music made by Frank Conrad of the Westinghouse Electric Company led to the establishment of one of the first commercial radio stations, KDKA, in Pittsburgh, in 1920. Within a decade more than 600 commercial stations were in operation, and the number of radio sets in American homes soon reached the millions. From the inception of broadcasting, radio programming emphasized popular music. Many performers whose reputations had been made on the stage moved successfully to the new medium; a new generation of singers adapted their vocal techniques to the new technology, and achieved a more intimate delivery through the use of the microphone (*see* CROONING). "Whispering" Jack Smith, Frank Parker, and Kate Smith were among the most successful radio performers. In 1935 *Your Hit Parade* began offering the most popular songs of the week to a nationwide radio audience of several million, and became a potent force in the popular music industry. (*See also* RADIO BROADCASTING.)

Popular music was closely linked with the film industry from 1927, when Al Jolson appeared in *The Jazz Singer*, the first commercial motion picture with continuous sound. *Broadway Melody* (1929) was the first successful MUSICAL FILM; early examples of the genre were little more than filmed versions of Broadway shows, but in the early 1930s Busby Berkeley's *Footlight Parade*, *42nd Street*, and *Gold Diggers of 1933*, with their extravagant production numbers, gave the musical film new dimensions and a distinct character. Songs were also interpolated into many other films. By the mid-1930s motion pictures had become the chief form of North American entertainment; some 60 million tickets were sold each week. Film companies engaged hundreds of songwriters, arrangers, and other musicians, for the most part recruited from Broadway and Tin Pan Alley.

The sale of sheet music continued to be the economic mainstay of the popular music industry in the 1920s and 30s, but phonograph recordings, radio, and film brought popular songs to millions who could not read music. Star performers were active across various media, and the market for American popular music, broadly defined, reached a mass audience across lines of gender, race, ethnicity, class, generation, and region. Increasingly the enjoyment of music took the passive form of listening rather than the active one of performing; a new type of consumer, one with no training in music, emerged and eventually predominated.

The style of popular song remained relatively constant during this period of technological revolution; while composers continually modified the musical means established in the first decades of Tin Pan Alley, they never broke away from them. Songs were cast in common structures and used a common harmonic and melodic vocabulary, which grew progressively closer to the style of such early 20th-century composers as Debussy, Grieg, Fauré, Puccini, and Rachmaninoff. The narrative character of many songs of the 1890s and early 1900s gave way to a lyric or reflective quality. Most songwriters of the second generation of Tin Pan Alley were schooled in European music, or were at least well acquainted with it. Almost all songs consisted of one or two verses, followed by a 32-bar "chorus" cast in

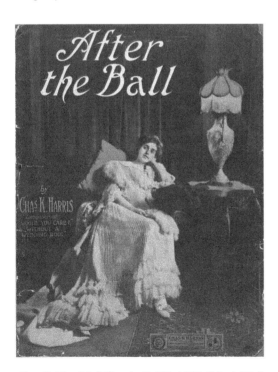

Chas K. Harris's "After the Ball," c1892. (Music Division, The New York Public Library for the Performing Arts, Astor, Lenox and Tilden Foundations)

four phrases and set in such patterns as *AABA*, *ABAB*, *ABCA*, or *AABC*. The verse was increasingly often omitted in performance and on recordings, and by the 1930s songwriters often did not write verses at all. Harmonically the music was basically triadic, diatonic, and tonal, but individual chords were often more complex, and included seventh and ninth chords, triads with added sixths and seconds, and a wide range of chromatically altered chords. Modulations to remote keys could occur in the second or third section of a song, or even within a phrase. The principal rhythmic characteristic continued to be the syncopations borrowed from American dances; the instrumental backings evoked the scoring of contemporary dance-band music, from the mixed wind and strings of the early 1920s, and the instrumentation of smaller jazz ensembles, to the big bands of the 1930s and 1940s.

In the early 1900s, for the first time in almost a century, many stylistic features of North American popular song resembled those of art music—not that of Stravinsky, Schoenberg, or Bartók, but that written by composers of the previous generation. Indeed, melodies from the classical repertory were, with some alteration of length, shape, and lyrics, made into successful popular songs, much as melodies by Mozart and Bellini had been adapted a century earlier. As early as 1918 Joseph McCarthy and Harry Carroll transformed a theme from Chopin's Fantasy-Impromptu op.66 into "I'm always chasing rainbows"; in 1920 Puccini's publisher successfully brought a suit against the American publisher of the song "Avalon" by Al Jolson and Vincent Rose, on the grounds that its tune was taken from *Tosca*. In 1939 "The lamp is low" was adapted from Ravel's *Pavane pour une infante défunte*, and many songs were reworkings of music by Tchaikovsky, including "Our Love" (1939, taken from *Romeo and Juliet*), and "Tonight we love" (1941, taken from his First Piano Concerto). As Tin Pan Alley strengthened its stylistic ties with European music in general, and the classical repertory in particular, its songs became more closely identified with middle- and upper-class American life, and few of them passed into oral tradition.

Tin Pan Alley's tendency to offer the public a familiar product led to a long period of stylistic equilibrium in American song. The AMERICAN SOCIETY OF COMPOSERS, AUTHORS AND PUBLISHERS (ASCAP), organized in 1914 to protect songwriters and publishers from unauthorized public performance of their music, contributed to the climate of stability and orthodoxy. After a number of court actions, a ruling by the US Supreme Court in 1917 allowed ASCAP to collect fees from restaurants, theaters, and other establishments offering live music to their customers. These fees, supplemented by those demanded of recording companies and broadcasters, came to represent a considerable sum. In 1921 $80,000 accrued to the society from performing rights; by the mid-1920s the figure exceeded $10 million. At that time membership of ASCAP was limited to 1000 composers and lyricists and 150 music publishers; new members were selected by the society itself, which insured a certain conformity of attitudes and musical styles.

Of the individual songwriters of the period, Irving Berlin must be considered first. His songs span almost the entire age of Tin Pan Alley, from 1907 to the 1950s; stylistically they range from rags and waltzes early in his career to more sophisticated ballads in his mature period. He is regarded by many as the most talented songwriter and lyricist of his age. Among his most famous songs, most of which were written for inclusion in stage revues and films, are, besides "Alexander's Ragtime Band," "God bless America" (1918), and "White Christmas" (1942), which is perhaps the most commercially successful American popular song of all time. His stage musicals, which include the *Ziegfeld Follies of 1919, 1920,* and *1927,* the *Music Box Revues* (1921–4), *Face the Music* (1932), *Louisiana Purchase* (1940), and *Annie Get your Gun* (1946), contain many more, such as "Oh! How I hate to get up in the morning" (*Yip, Yip, Yaphank,* 1918) and "Easter Parade" (*As Thousands Cheer,* 1933). These and many other songs by Berlin were performed on the stage, on the radio, and in films, by such leading entertainers as Eddie Cantor, Fanny Brice, Ethel Waters, Ethel Merman, Al Jolson, Ginger Rogers and Fred Astaire, Rudy Vallee, Bing Crosby, Bob Hope, and Judy Garland.

Jerome Kern wrote many songs, mostly for musicals and films, that achieved great critical and popular success. They include "Look for the silver lining" (from *Sally*, 1920), "Ol' Man River" (*Show Boat*, 1927), "Smoke gets in your eyes" (*Roberta*, 1933) and "The Last Time I saw Paris" (*Lady be Good*, 1941). George Gershwin was one of the most talented, successful composers of the era; most of his songs, also, were written for revues, musicals, or films, among them "Somebody loves me" (1924), "Embraceable You" (1930), and "The Man I Love" (1924). Cole Porter's best songs, written for stage musicals and films from the late 1920s, include "What is this thing called love?" (*Wake Up and Dream*, 1929), "Night and Day" (*Gay Divorce*, 1932), "Begin the Beguine" (*Jubilee*, 1935), and "So in Love am I" (*Kiss me, Kate*, 1948). Richard Rodgers collaborated with the lyricist Lorenz Hart on a number of musicals, which included many successful songs; after Hart's death, he wrote three of the most popular musicals of the century with Oscar Hammerstein II: *Oklahoma!* (1943), *Carousel* (1945), and *South Pacific* (1949). Each contained songs that became standards, including "O What a Beautiful Mornin'," "If I Loved You," and "Some Enchanted Evening." Among the other successful songs of the era were Harold Arlen's "Over the Rainbow" (1939) and "That Old Black Magic" (1942), Vincent Youmans's "Tea for Two" (1924), Jimmy McHugh's "I can't give you anything but love" (1928), Hoagy Carmichael's "Stardust" (1929), and Harry Warren's "Lullaby of Broadway" (1935).

In the first two decades of the 20th century the majority of Tin Pan Alley's successful songwriters were Jewish, and many of them were immigrants or first-generation Americans. A significant number of African American songwriters also figured prominently in Tin Pan Alley. Gussie Lord Davis (1863–99) wrote a number of successful songs, notably "In the Baggage Coach

Bessie Smith, c1925. (JazzSign/Lebrecht Music & Arts)

Ahead" (1896), of which more than a million copies were sold. A succession of musical comedies written and performed by black artists yielded many songs that enjoyed commercial success, including "Who dat Say Chicken" (1898) by Paul Laurence Dunbar and Will Marion Cook, "My Castle on the Nile" (1901) by James Weldon Johnson and Bob Cole, "Under the Bamboo Tree" (1902) by Cole, Johnson, and J. Rosamond Johnson, and "In Honeysuckle Time" and "I'm just wild about Harry" from the revue *Shuffle Along* (1921) by Noble Sissle and Eubie Blake. Later successes include "Honeysuckle Rose" (1929) by Fats Waller and a number of songs by Duke Ellington such as "Mood Indigo" (1931) and "Solitude" (1934).

Tin Pan Alley exemplified the conviction, developed as far back as the 1890s, that popular music was intended to entertain and therefore to steer away from painful and controversial subjects. WORLD WAR I produced a scattering of war songs—patriotic (Cohan's "Over There!," 1917), humorous (Berlin's "Oh! How I hate to get up in the morning," 1918), or sentimental (Richard A. Whiting's "Till we meet again," 1918)—but in general popular songs were concerned with personal, not public, matters. The cataclysmic events of the 1920s and 30s—THE GREAT DEPRESSION, the rise of totalitarian governments in Europe, the outbreak of WORLD WAR II—were largely ignored by North American songwriters, who continued to write love-songs, the tone of which was governed by the customs and mores of the mainstream of white American society. Even the US entry into the war inspired few topical songs, such as "Praise the Lord and pass the ammunition" (1942) by Frank Loesser, "I left my heart at the Stage Door Can-

teen" (1942) by Berlin, and "They're either too young or too old" (1943) by Loesser and Schwartz.

The years between the two world wars were a transitional period, during which the established music industry, still dominated by large publishers of sheet music, defined "popular music" in terms not only of sales but also of musical style; a Tin Pan Alley song was "popular" because of its musical idiom, whether or not it was financially successful. Technology brought popular music to a wider audience than ever before, but the style and content of the music remained essentially unchanged from before 1920. The most successful songwriters of the period were white, urban, and oriented towards the European style. At the same time a number of ethnic musical styles, derived from the oral tradition, reached new audiences through recordings and broadcasts.

(iii) Traditional and ethnic music. Wide areas of the rural southern and western United States, particularly the mountainous regions, and the fishing and mining communities of Atlantic Canada, were populated largely by descendants of English, Irish, and Scottish immigrants, who remained relatively isolated from the mainstream of North American life until well into the 20th century, and retained a close connection with their native traditions. The narrative ballad, an important type of secular music among these people, was often concerned with historical or mythical characters and events. Many ballads were variants of those brought over from the British Isles; others were written in the United States in the same general style. They were strophic pieces, often modal or pentatonic, and were originally sung by a single unaccompanied voice; by the 20th century they were often accompanied by banjo, fiddle, or guitar. Dance music, such as reels and hornpipes, was at first played by fiddle or pipe alone, but later banjo and guitar were used as well; many of these tunes, too, had been brought over from the British Isles. A number of composed songs of the 19th century had also passed into the oral tradition, including minstrel songs, many pieces by Foster, and some of the sentimental verse–chorus songs of the decades following the Civil War.

In the early 1920s the music of the rural United States, previously transmitted only through oral tradition, began to be disseminated by the mass media (*see* COUNTRY MUSIC). Victor, OKeh, and other recording companies issued phonograph discs of OLD-TIME MUSIC that were distributed regionally, and radio stations in the South, Midwest, and Southwest offered live programs devoted to the music. Individual performers and groups began to command wide audiences and sell significant numbers of recordings; among the most important were Fiddlin' John Carson, Charlie Poole, Uncle Dave Macon, Riley Puckett, and Ernest V. Stoneman. The Carter Family became the most successful early performers of HILLBILLY MUSIC. This consisted of solo singing, alternating with two- or three-part vocal harmony, accompanied by guitar, autoharp, and sometimes steel or Hawaiian guitar. Their repertory drew on traditional songs and ballads, composed songs of the 19th century, and new pieces in traditional styles. Jimmie Rodgers developed a more urban style; he sang mostly newly composed songs that combined traditional elements with traces of mainstream popular music and blues. The next generation of performers, which included Roy Acuff, Gene Autry, Bob Wills, Ernest Tubb, and Hank Williams, followed Rodgers's lead in forging a distinctive country-music style that retained some of the vocal timbre and instrumental sound of older music but made use of modern resources; among these were chord-playing instruments, which soon included the electric guitar; a rhythm section, which was unusual in traditional Anglo-American music; and a firm, sometimes sophisticated harmonic language. The distinctive sound of the music of the rural South was, for the most part, unacceptable to listeners accustomed to Tin Pan Alley songs. It can be understood as popular music, however, because of its wide currency and because most of its performers sought a national style that transcended regional differences.

The recording and broadcasting industries discovered another market in the early 1920s, that comprising African Americans. In 1920 the blues singer Mamie Smith made a series of recordings including "That Thing Called Love," "You can't keep a good man down," and "Crazy Blues"; their success set off a recorded BLUES craze that was followed by a number of jazz and religious recordings, released by both large and small companies. The music was extremely varied: it encompassed blues recordings; BOOGIE-WOOGIE piano; JAZZ played by small and large ensembles; recorded sermons; and religious pieces, inspired by 19th-century spirituals, sung either by male quartets and quintets, or—in the form that became known as GOSPEL MUSIC—by solo singers backed by a chorus and instruments. The recording industry classified all of these types as RACE RECORDS, and distinguished it from the popular music of Tin Pan Alley by listing it in separate catalogs. Yet its wide distribution and large audience soon integrated it into common conceptions of American popular music. (*See* AFRICAN AMERICAN MUSIC.)

Evidence of the Latin influence on mainstream American popular music, a number of fashionable dances, including TANGO, RUMBA, and MAMBO, had an impact on songwriting, musical, and dance practices across the nation. (*See* LATINO MUSIC.) Other types of regional and ethnic music disseminated by recording companies and radio stations included the distinctive music of the French-speaking Cajuns of Louisiana, and the songs and instrumental music of Slavic, Mediterranean, and Scandinavian immigrants in American cities (*see* EUROPEAN AMERICAN MUSIC).

(iv) Synthesis with jazz. Many Tin Pan Alley composers (particularly Gershwin, Arlen, and Berlin) listened with interest to syncopated dance music and early jazz, and incorporated rhythmic and melodic elements of these repertories into their own pieces. Conversely, many African American composers (including Waller and Ellington) and performers (including Billie Holiday, Nat "King" Cole, and Ella Fitzgerald) drew on the musical style and repertory of Tin Pan Alley.

Throughout the second quarter of the 20th century jazz and Tin Pan Alley were linked by a common repertory. The syncopated dance music of the 1910–20 period and the earliest styles of jazz used sectional two- or three-strain dance forms and the 12-bar blues. By the mid-1920s, as jazz ensembles increased in size, with many (including those of Ellington and Fletcher Henderson) depending on written arrangements, the repertory began to draw heavily on 32-bar, four-phrase songs. Some were newly written; others derived from the Tin Pan Alley song repertory. By the 1930s jazz musicians were expected to know the harmonic design (the "changes") of a core repertory of Tin Pan Alley songs by Gershwin, Green, Waller, Mercer, and others, and virtually every black jazz band (the best-known being those of Count Basie, Jimmie Lunceford, Cab Calloway, Louis Armstrong, Benny Carter, and Lionel Hampton) played versions of them.

White jazz bands with instrumentation and repertory similar to those of black bands were active in the 1920s and into the 30s. Paul Whiteman, who employed a number of the best white jazz performers of the 1920s, sold more recordings than any other group of the decade. Benny Goodman used arrangements by Benny Carter and Fletcher Henderson, and became a key figure of the SWING era. The bands of Jimmy and Tommy Dorsey, Artie Shaw, Woody Herman, Harry James, Glenn Miller, and many others soon contributed to the growing popularity of "big-band" music; for almost a decade, beginning in 1935, most best-selling recordings were of this sort of music, including such classics as Shaw's "Begin the Beguine" and Miller's "In the Mood."

Stylistically, swing stood between Tin Pan Alley and jazz. Bands often employed one or more singers; among the more notable were Frank Sinatra, Jo Stafford, Doris Day, Perry Como, Billie Holiday, Helen Forrest, and Bing Crosby. Instrumental pieces were usually fast, with the rhythm section maintaining a steady beat, the brass and reeds playing syncopated patterns, and various soloists improvising full or half choruses. The music was of the same sort as that played by the bands of Ellington, Basie, Lunceford, and Carter, sometimes even using the same arrangements, and the popularity of big-band music brought at least some recognition among white audiences of black jazz bands. Of all the genres of popular music in the prewar era, big-band swing came closest to representing a successful blend of white and black musical styles. But, with rare exceptions, bands remained segregated, either white or black, as were their audiences.

(v) The end of the era. By 1945 the Tin Pan Alley song had dominated North American popular music for more than half a century without undergoing significant changes in style; and although the demand for music had increased owing to the growth of the recording, broadcasting, and motion-picture industries, marketing techniques had essentially changed little since the turn of the century. During World War II, however, a number of forces were set in motion that threatened the prevailing equilibrium.

In 1940 ASCAP attempted to negotiate a new contract with radio networks in the United States, to ensure that its control over broadcast music would continue. Radio executives objected to the proposed fee structure, which would have doubled the amount paid to the society. During the stalemate no music protected by ASCAP could be broadcast, and a new organization of songwriters, lyricists, music publishers, and radio stations—BROADCAST MUSIC, INC. (BMI)—was formed. ASCAP settled its differences with its licensees within a year, but by this time it had a competitor in BMI. While some of BMI's songwriters remained faithful to the Tin Pan Alley style, many, some of whom were younger than most ASCAP members, and some of whom had a background in country music, sensed that the country was in a mood for change and explored new idioms. Large numbers of songs were produced that, although not written in an authentic country-music style, evoked the West; among them were "Deep in the Heart of Texas" (1941) by Don Swander and June Hershey, "Pistol Packin' Mama" (1942) by Al Dexter, and such adaptations of Latin pieces as "Tico-Tico" (1943), a reworking of a song by the Brazilian songwriter Zequinha Abreu. Half a century of stylistic consistency in mainstream popular song soon gave way to variety; the popular repertory became a miscellany of comic songs (Charles Grean's "The Thing," popularized in 1950 by Phil Harris; and Bob Merrill's "That Doggie in the Window," 1953), cover versions of country songs (Tony Bennett's recording of Hank Williams's "Cold, Cold Heart," 1951), songs in a cowboy vein (Frankie Laine's "Mule Train," 1949), instrumental pieces (Anton Karas's theme from the film *The Third Man*, 1949), and arrangements of traditional Anglo-American songs (the Weavers' "On Top of Old Smokey," 1951).

4. THE ROCK ERA.

(i) Introduction. Midway through the 20th century, commercially mediated, Southern-based music by black and white working-class musicians displaced Tin Pan Alley popular song to dominate national culture and lay the foundations of a new global lingua franca. "Untrained" performers replaced the previously dominant, professional network of composers, orchestrators, singers and studio orchestras; through the 1950s the major record labels lost nearly half their share of the popular music market to independent record labels. New cultural fusions were particularly encouraged by migrations from south to north and from country to city, as well as by new communications technologies that accelerated musical interactions and pushed music and musicians across geographical and cultural boundaries. Mass culture brought the views of marginalized groups to the mainstream, and previously separated groups discovered new identities and affinities through popular music. Such changes forced realignments of the genre categories that were in general use. The ways in which record companies separated artists and audiences by race, region, and class ("race records," "hillbilly," and

"popular," for example) hid the fact that such music had not developed from mutually exclusive sources, as genre labels have tended to reflect prevalent social, especially racial, categories as much as differences of musical style. In addition, commercial success and monetary rewards have not always matched up with musical traditions and creativity: although rock and roll was primarily created by African Americans, its financial rewards have gone disproportionately to white singers and businessmen.

"Rock and roll" had been used in blues lyrics to celebrate sexuality and dancing decades before its appearance (*Billboard*, 1946) to describe the RHYTHM-AND-BLUES of Joe Liggins and his Honeydrippers. The phrase has been used ever since: sometimes narrowly, to describe the music made by black and white popular musicians of the late 1950s; sometimes as a means of disguising black origins or of distinguishing white-identified music from soul, funk, disco, and hip hop; sometimes more broadly to label the whole range of popular styles that developed in the wake of the paradigm shift of the 1950s. Certain shared characteristics differentiated rock and roll, country music and rhythm-and-blues from Tin Pan Alley. Most notable were the blues influences, including forms derived from the 12-bar blues, amplified electric instruments and a rhythmic drive led by drums and bass. Yet the 32-bar verse–chorus forms of Tin Pan Alley persisted, as did a wide range of singing styles, and the new music's characteristic rocking rhythms can be heard as far back as the late 1920s in blues recordings, especially during the piano boogie-woogie craze of the 1930s, which supplied the left-hand ostinato pattern that became one of the foundations of rock and roll guitar style. Moreover, driving straight-eighth note grooves appeared in recordings by white country musicians of the same period. Although it was called hillbilly music until the mid-1940s, country music did not develop exclusively from Anglo-American folk traditions, but rather incorporated the multicultural influences of Spain, Hawaii, Africa, Italy, Switzerland, Tin Pan Alley popular song, black and white gospel music, and the blues.

Growing reliance upon the electric guitar is in some ways an index of the shift to rock and roll, yet such central figures of the 1950s as Jerry Lee Lewis and Little Richard continued to base their ensembles around the piano, and the guitar was not a prominent feature of the "girl group" performances of the early 1960s. New ways of drumming did most to unite the newer styles, but rock and roll still incorporated the crooning and song formats of previous popular song along with gospel, hillbilly, blues, and boogie-woogie characteristics. The adoption of the pedal steel guitar in the early 1950s helped make country music sound different from other popular postwar genres, but the growing use of drums from the late 40s brought it closer to other popular styles. However important these genres were as marketing categories, they grew from shared origins in blues, jazz, gospel, and country music, and they reflected their technological moment in their use of electric amplification, mass mediation, magnetic tape technology that spread from Germany after World War II, and commercial distribution.

The jazz, jump blues, and rhythm-and-blues of the 1930s and 40s established crucial conventions for later popular styles: the rhythmic energy and riff style of Count Basie's band; the honking saxophone solos and sexual energy of Wynonie Harris; the small jazz-influenced combos of Los Angeles's Central Avenue scene; the fusion of black and white styles that were heard in Louis Jordan's music; the gospel ecstasy that singers such as Sister Rosetta Tharpe, Little Richard, and Ray Charles brought to secular music; and T-Bone Walker's creation of an electric blues guitar style that Chuck Berry would later develop into the foundation of rock guitar playing.

There are not enough musical differences between songs such as Wynonie Harris's "Good Rockin' Tonight" (1948) and Big Joe Turner's "Shake, Rattle, and Roll" (1954) to justify the perception that a whole new style of music had emerged in the mid-1950s. Postwar cultural mixtures, migrations and technology brought Southern white and black working-class music to the attention of audiences that had previously not been exposed to its techniques and sensibilities. But earlier mixings have been too little acknowledged as well, such as the African American musicians who taught Hank Williams to play guitar and influenced his song-writing or the impact of country star Jimmie Rodgers's yodeling on the blues howl of Howlin' Wolf. Although record companies and radio stations marketed music according to the race of the performers (presumed to match that of their audiences), white listeners increasingly sought out black music in the late 1940s. Mass culture established a common frame of reference among previously separate communities, making regional, class-based, and ethnically specific cultural forms increasingly attractive and relevant to new audiences. Country and rhythm-and-blues artists often recorded versions of each other's songs, and the white team of Leiber and Stoller wrote many songs for black and Chicano artists that became hits on both the pop and rhythm-and-blues charts. Another important interaction was that of self-taught country and blues musicians with jazz-trained studio session players. As country music incorporated jump blues influences it became ROCKABILLY just as blues had evolved into rhythm-and-blues by embracing influences from jazz, Tin Pan Alley, and gospel; as the story is usually told, these two streams eventually united to produce rock and roll.

(ii) Rock and roll. Some historians date the beginning of this era to June 1955, when Bill Haley's "Rock around the Clock" became the no.1 record on *Billboard*'s "best sellers" chart and an icon of teenage rebellion. The early 1950s provide an alternative date, when white teenagers started to listen and dance to the rhythm-and-blues of black musicians, and the Cleveland disc jockey Alan Freed gained more and more white listeners for his rhythm-and-blues radio shows. By 1954, he was calling the music ROCK AND ROLL, a name that distracted attention from the cultural miscegenation that

was taking place. Records, jukeboxes and especially radio were particularly important for breaking down racial barriers still maintained in public spaces, and rock and roll concerts were the first integrated public events in many communities. (*See* JUKEBOX.) Despite the emphasis on youth culture in rock and roll—which established young audiences as a key arbiter of taste for popular music—the musics out of which it developed had been adult. Over-emphasis of teenage rebellion disguises the role of the music in breaking down racial boundaries, proposing new ideals of gender and sexuality, and promoting working-class perspectives through lyrics that criticized hierarchy and celebrated freedom, leisure, and community.

Most white rock and roll performers were Southern country musicians who adapted some of the features of rhythm-and-blues, and many of the best (such as Jerry Lee Lewis, Elvis Presley, and Carl Perkins) had grown up learning from black musicians. Bill Haley, Buddy Holly, and others kept their country instrumentation but developed rhythmic swing and blues inflections under the influence of jump blues artists such as Louis Jordan. Many of the most successful black rock and roll musicians (Fats Domino and Ruth Brown, for example) were established within rhythm-and-blues before they were redefined as part of a new cultural and commercial movement. The whole idea of rock and roll was "that Fats Domino had more in common with Bill Haley than he did with Wynonie Harris, that Elvis Presley had more in common with Ray Charles than he did with Ernest Tubb" (Ward, Stokes, and Tucker, A1986, p.97). Chuck Berry drew upon blues, country, and the jump blues of Louis Jordan to produce some of the founding conventions of rock and roll, including lyrics that celebrated mobility, play, and youth, as well as the double-string riffs that made him one of the most influential guitarists of the 20th century. His first record was a version of a country song, and he might have been categorized as a country singer if he had been white. Although tenor saxophone solos and rolling piano triplets continued to be used in rock and roll, the dominant trend was to move from horns, piano and swing rhythms to guitars and straight eighth-note grooves. Berry's "Rock and Roll Music" (1957) records a transitional moment, as some of the musicians swing the beat while others evenly subdivide it.

African American vocal groups, mostly male (the Coasters and the Drifters, for example), were among the most popular musicians of the decade, and sang romantic ballads with smooth harmonies (often based on I–VI–IV–V progressions) that extended the legacy of the gospel quartets and of popular 1940s vocal groups such as the Mills Brothers and the Ink Spots, while their up-tempo numbers displayed more overtly the rhythmic drive of rock and roll. Such groups typically placed less emphasis on instrumental backing, but singers often imitated instrumental sounds and sang non-verbal syllables that caused their music to be known as DOO-WOP. White groups such as Danny and the Juniors and the Crew Cuts contributed to the style but succeeded on the pop charts without first having to prove them-

Bill Haley and His Comets, from the film Rock Around the Clock, *1956. (AP Photo)*

selves through rhythm-and-blues chart success, as was normally required of black artists.

The most successful performer of this period was Elvis Presley, a white singer who learned to sing in the Pentecostal Church and by imitating the blues and country music he heard on the radio. Presley's musical talents, charisma, and sexiness soon made him the most successful figure in North American music, cemented through his successful appearances on the emerging medium of television and, later, film. His first commercial studio session yielded a cover of "That's all right, mama," which had been recorded by rhythm-and-blues artist Arthur "Big Boy" Crudup, paired with a version of Bill Monroe's "Blue Moon of Kentucky"—a white interpretation of a black song and a black-influenced performance of a white song. His commercial appeal, however, was still related to racial dynamics, as white audiences bought Presley's versions of rhythm-and-blues songs instead of those by the original African American performers. Still, he took as much from country as he did from rhythm-and-blues, and sales of country music suffered more from the popularity of rock and roll than did the rhythm-and-blues market.

The success of Presley and other rockabilly-styled artists helped undermine the music industry's assumptions about race-based genres and separate audiences. At this moment "one strain of popular music cut across racial, social, and geographic lines in a way not seen in the United States since the days of Stephen Foster" (Hamm, *c*1983, pp.62–3). By spreading elements of Southern working-class black and white culture to national and international audiences, Presley had a profound impact on music history.

Country music was divided by Presley's success, however, with the rockabilly singers such as Carl Perkins, Jerry Lee Lewis, Gene Vincent, the Everly Brothers,

Eddie Cochran, and Buddy Holly developing a style that reflected their absorption of black culture and that was distinct from the straight country singers who followed the example of Hank Williams. Country music expanded rapidly in the years after World War II and Nashville emerged as the center of its recording business. In the 1950s, the dominant country style was HONKY TONK, but Chet Atkins developed a new, Tin Pan Alley–influenced NASHVILLE SOUND, a country-pop fusion that was designed to attract larger audiences.

As white teenagers were increasingly moved by and moving like black entertainers, critics attempted to discredit rock and roll by linking it to racial conflicts, promiscuity and juvenile delinquency. With hindsight, such attacks are frequently dismissed as bigotry, misunderstanding and over-reaction, but censorship and other techniques for weakening rock and roll's impact reflect accurate perceptions of its power to challenge and disrupt accepted behaviors. At the end of the decade, the US Congress conducted hearings into the practice of payola, whereby disc jockeys were bribed to play particular records (*see* DJ (I)). This practice had been common since the rise of the music industry in the 1890s, and was not in fact illegal, but persecution of Alan Freed and other prominent figures was partly driven by the feeling that the music threatened social order. Meanwhile, the large record companies were regaining their control of the industry and promoting white singers, such as Pat Boone, who could outsell black performers with cover versions of the same songs (*see* COVER SONG); such adaptations served large white audiences who were attracted to rock and roll but resisted some of its cultural challenges. These events, along with the death of Buddy Holly and the disrupted careers of Presley, Chuck Berry, Little Richard, and Jerry Lee Lewis (by the draft, jail, religion, and scandal, respectively), have been regarded by many as marking the end of the original era of rock and roll, although its musical and social precedents resonated throughout the rest of the century.

(iii) The 1960s. The rock and pop of the 1960s differed from rock and roll of the 50s in several respects. Musicians embraced solid-body electric guitars, powerful amplification with deliberate distortion effects, new recording techniques and greater use of keyboard instruments. The longer playing time of the 33⅓ rpm album accommodated longer song forms that often included lengthy improvisations. Many song lyrics continued to be concerned with romance, but some now also participated overtly in political protest and the search for new identities and communities. Perceptions of a generation gap sharpened as 17-year-olds became the largest age cohort in 1964, and ROCK music dominated the output of the record industry. The diversity of the decade, however, can be lost to a collective memory that emphasizes Woodstock, psychedelia, sexual freedom, and transgression: the most popular musicians of the decade included not only the Beatles, Elvis Presley and Ray Charles, but also Connie Francis, Brenda Lee, and Percy Faith. It was because 1960s rock resounded in an environment that resisted many of its challenges that it proved so explosive and transformative.

Historians often characterize the early part of the decade as a lull between the interrupted careers of the first rock and roll generation and the arrival of the BRITISH INVASION. Neil Sedaka, Carole King, and other songwriters at the Brill Building in New York were moving popular music back towards the sentiments and production methods of Tin Pan Alley, while white "teen idols," such as Dion, Ricky Nelson, and Frankie Avalon, defused the dangerous sexuality of Presley, Little Richard, and Chuck Berry (*see* TEEN IDOL). Yet the same period (1959–63) saw the rise of SOUL music in Chicago and Memphis, the development of the MOTOWN sound, and a doo-wop revival that included tremendous popularity for GIRL GROUPS. The Shirelles, the Crystals, the Ronettes, and the Shangri-Las were among the most successful groups, and the most influential producer of such music was Phil Spector, who merged features of Tin Pan Alley song with the energy of rhythm-and-blues, and used innovative studio techniques to create his "wall of sound" (*see* RECORD PRODUCER). This golden age for female and African American artists was unjustly maligned by rock critics, who, until the 1990s, were almost all white men whose writings marginalized these groups. The most critically respected American group of the early 1960s was probably the Beach Boys, who used virtuosic vocal lines in the style of doo-wop, a rock and roll rhythm section, and adventurous recording practices to produce successful vignettes of surfing and other romanticized features of middle-class Californian culture.

Throughout the decade, country music remained marked by the influence of rock and roll, as electric instruments and drums became routinely used. The Country Music Association (founded in 1957) helped promote both the music and the industry, and the music

continued to grow in popularity, with three shows devoted to it appearing on network television by the end of the decade. Some of this increased popularity came from female stars who presented a new assertive image, such as Loretta Lynn and Tammy Wynette, and from singer-songwriters who crossed over to broader audiences, such as Willie Nelson and Kris Kristofferson.

The African American artists on Berry Gordy's Motown record label developed gospel-influenced, sexy but polished, elegant music that successfully crossed over to large white audiences. Its writers and producers (such as Holland, Dozier, and Holland) supplied songs and arrangements to a virtuosic house band (the Funk Brothers) and singers that included Stevie Wonder, the Temptations, the Four Tops, Diana Ross and the Supremes, Smokey Robinson and the Miracles, and Marvin Gaye. The "southern soul" of Stax Records in Memphis produced a more gritty and blues-derived style for mostly black audiences later in the decade, using an integrated house band to back singers that included Wilson Pickett, Aretha Franklin, and Otis Redding. James Brown invented FUNK and set the stage for subsequent dance music and rap by placing his rough, soulful vocals over instrumental grooves that suspended harmonic motion in favor of unprecedentedly percussive and polyrhythmic interlocking lines, including complicated, virtuosic bass lines.

Folk singers, many of whom were political activists, may have initially avoided the instrumentation and attitudes of rock and roll because of its location within commercial culture, but rock's rhythmic and timbral energy made it well suited to protest, and it became increasingly associated with protest movements, alternative lifestyles and perspectives and the breakdown of social and attitudinal barriers (*see* THE FOLK REVIVAL). Bob Dylan became arguably the most influential American musician of the 1960s by creating lyrics that pushed folk music towards a more critical, personal and self-consciously poetic tone, and his rough voice and loose intonation established an influential model for performance. He blurred the line between rock and folk with his controversial decision to "go electric" (1965), and brought rock and country closer together in 1968, just as the Byrds and the Band were also developing the COUNTRY ROCK fusions that would be followed by Buffalo Springfield, the Flying Burrito Brothers, the Grateful Dead, Neil Young and the Eagles. Rock criticism grew up around Dylan and the Beatles as the lyrics of both and the music of the latter provided material for complicated and serious analysis. Joan Baez, Tom Paxton and Phil Ochs were other protest singers who developed the poetic and political vocabulary of popular music and helped prepare for the boom, during the latter part of the decade, of personal, often confessional singer-songwriters such as Judy Collins, Joni Mitchell, Carole King, and Paul Simon (*see* SINGER-SONGWRITER). For the most part, African American audiences displayed little interest in FOLK ROCK or rock, despite the strong blues influences on the latter.

British bands were formed after the models set by US rock and roll musicians on recordings and tours. The extraordinary songwriting abilities of John Lennon and Paul McCartney helped earn the Beatles an extreme level of popular and critical success, and they produced catchy and memorable songs in a great range of styles, even as they explored unusual musical forms, harmonies, studio techniques, and instrumentation, as exemplified on their influential album, *Sgt Pepper's Lonely Hearts Club Band* (1967). Their success also helped establish an expectation that bands would write their own material, and their androgynous haircuts continued the rock and roll challenge to gender norms. Their string of number one singles in North America in 1964 paved the way for the other bands of the British Invasion: the Rolling Stones, Herman's Hermits, the Yardbirds, the Kinks, the Animals, and others. For many, these bands revived the interrupted energy of 1950s rock and roll, and they quickly displaced girl groups (except the Supremes) and soul singers on the pop charts.

BLUES ROCK and HARD ROCK developed as American and British musicians adapted and extended the blues, following such models as Robert Johnson and Muddy Waters, and the guitar became rock's main solo instrument. Jimi Hendrix's virtuosic technique reinvented the electric guitar, and Eric Clapton's blues-style playing also inspired many followers. The Doors' brooding music and the Who's forceful "power chords" (the interval of a 4th or 5th timbrally distorted by an amplifier to produce resultant tones) helped set crucial precedents for subsequent decades. Like the Beatles, the Rolling Stones made no secret of their debts to the African American musicians they had studied, although other bands, such as Led Zeppelin, took songwriting credit and royalties for music they had plainly copied.

Popular culture continued to be an important forum for challenges to dominant representations of identity and values in the late 1960s, reflecting the influences of civil rights struggles, global decolonization, the postwar diversity of higher education that made campuses an important site of activism, the working-class perspectives of many musicians, and a variety of disruptions of what had been taken to be "natural" gendered and sexual behavior. San Francisco became the main locus of the "counter-culture" of young people who explored alternatives that were meant to increase individual freedom and collective harmony. Psychedelic light shows, artwork, and drugs such as marijuana and LSD joined extended improvisatory jams and experiments with drones (inspired by the sitar playing of Ravi Shankar and the jazz of John Coltrane and Miles Davis) as means to the transformation of consciousness. Social harmony and equality remained paramount ideals of the counter-culture, emblematized by rock festivals such as the Monterey Pop Festival during the 1967 "Summer of Love."

The ideals of the ART ROCK and PROGRESSIVE ROCK of the late 1960s and 70s were often more elitist; taking their cue from *Sgt Pepper's Lonely Hearts Club Band*, groups such as the Moody Blues, Deep Purple, Yes, Pink Floyd, and Emerson, Lake, and Palmer incorporated musical techniques and references from classical music and various non-Western traditions in pursuit of what they saw as greater seriousness, complexity, and virtuosity. An-

other aesthetic development took place in the pages of such new magazines as *Hit Parader*, *Rolling Stone*, and *Crawdaddy*, as writers such as Lester Bangs, Dave Marsh, and Greil Marcus developed ways of arguing about the meanings and artistic significance of rock music, establishing the profession of the rock critic and furnishing influential models for subsequent criticism.

(iv) The 1970s. The music industry doubled in size between 1973 and 1978, and increased the efficiency of its marketing by hardening genre categories and by relying upon more narrowly defined radio formats. These changes helped fragment the rock community and largely resegregated broadcasting, despite the continued appeal to a broad audience of such artists as Elton John, Fleetwood Mac, and Stevie Wonder. FM-radio's new "album-oriented rock" format narrowed the popular definition of "rock," excluding music made by women and African Americans in favor of ARENA ROCK bands such as Led Zeppelin, REO Speedwagon, Rush, and Journey. Technological developments enabled some musicians, notably Stevie Wonder, Prince, and John Fogerty, to perform most or all of the instrumental and vocal parts on their albums. In live performance, amplification of all instruments, with their balance and timbre controlled by a sound mixing specialist, became standard practice.

Protests against social injustice and violence remained a theme for rock groups such as Crosby, Stills, Nash, and Young, as well as the Motown artists Marvin Gaye and Stevie Wonder. Gaye's *What's Going On* (1971) not only became Motown's best-selling album but also established the idea of unifying a concept album through social criticism. The singer-songwriter style of personal confession and introspection was a stronger trend, however, led by albums such as James Taylor's *Sweet Baby James* (1970), Carole King's *Tapestry* (1970), and Joni Mitchell's *Court and Spark* (1974), and work by Paul Simon, Neil Young, Jackson Browne, and Billy Joel. The folk-based singers of WOMEN'S MUSIC, such as Cris Williamson and Meg Christian, created a gentle, acoustic alternative to mainstream rock and pop, even as all-women bands like the Runaways and Fanny claimed rock's power for women. Bruce Springsteen began to make his prominent mark by combining the personal approach of the singer-songwriters, the grandeur of Spector's "wall of sound," lyrics that spoke to working-class concerns and experiences, a hard-edged rock sound and soul-inspired passionate, gritty vocals.

The continuing influence of Tin Pan Alley–styled pop, present in the 1960s music of the Lovin' Spoonful and the Mamas and the Papas, expanded in the 1970s with the success of Elton John, Olivia Newton-John, and ABBA. Miles Davis brought jazz to the pop charts with his fusion of rock, funk and modal jazz in *Bitches Brew* (1969), and JAZZ-ROCK bands such as Chicago and Blood, Sweat, and Tears flourished. Jazz could also be heard in the complex harmonies of Steely Dan, and in the continuing impact of 1960s guitarists who had been influenced by saxophonist John Coltrane. Carlos Santana's mixture of blues-based guitar virtuosity with Latin rhythms spoke from and to complex cultural identities. Blues and country influences were brought together by a number of Southern rock bands that emphasized their regional identity, most notably Lynyrd Skynyrd, the Allman Brothers Band, and ZZ Top.

Country rock grew as a genre with the Byrds, the Eagles, and the Nitty Gritty Dirt Band, all following in the wake of Dylan's success, while the most prominent musicians of mainstream country included Dolly Parton, Conway Twitty, Merle Haggard, Loretta Lynn, and the only African American major country star, Charlie Pride. A group of musicians in Austin, Texas, brought country music to larger youth audiences through the outlaw or Hard country style that was exemplified by Willie Nelson and Waylon Jennings. The perspectives of marginalized peoples also entered pop music through Bob Marley, the only Jamaican reggae musician to achieve great success in the United States. Reggae influences, especially off-beat guitar chords and fragmented, melodic bass lines, eventually showed up all across American popular music.

The tendencies of many 1960s bands to explore greater volume, distortion, and transgressive lyrics came to fruition in Heavy metal, established in 1970 by albums by Led Zeppelin, Black Sabbath, and Deep Purple. Drawing upon the world views and musical techniques of much earlier blues musicians like Robert Johnson and Howlin' Wolf, these bands explored occult topics, mysticism, and paranoia in their lyrics while developing heavier sounding drums, bass, distorted guitar, and wailing vocals. Guitar and drum solos became increasingly virtuosic, culminating in Van Halen's eponymous first album (1978), which revealed Eddie Van Halen as the most innovative and influential guitarist since Hendrix, and established the level of technique to which most metal guitarists of the 1980s would aspire. The spectacular costumes and stage sets of heavy metal contributed to its aura of power, and the experience of live concerts became particularly important for this genre, both because of the communal experiences it offered and because it was rarely played on the radio. In 1973 Led Zeppelin broke the concert attendance record held by the Beatles, and KISS became the most successful band of the decade, with 13 platinum albums. Grand Funk Railroad, Judas Priest, AC/DC, and Aerosmith confirmed these heavy metal conventions; some bands followed the lead of Deep Purple in adapting riffs, harmonies, and improvisatory styles from the music of Bach and Vivaldi, although this would become much more pronounced in the 1980s. Within heavy metal, KISS, Alice Cooper, and others appeared in gender-bending "glam" clothes and make-up, just as David Bowie and other transgressive androgynes were doing in other musical styles. (*See* Glam metal and Glam rock.)

Another spectacular genre, Disco dominated the latter part of the decade; the success of this often quite erotic style was in part due to advances in birth control methods, changes in the legal status and social position of women and sexual minorities, the laxity of US drug-enforcement policy, and other demographic shifts. Al-though it eventually crossed over into mainstream pop and achieved international success, disco began as the music of marginalized peoples, especially gay and black urban audiences. A dance-floor music, initially developed outside of the music industry, disco arose from the practices of New York and San Francisco DJs who cut and mixed records on two separate turntables, managing an uninterrupted flow of music and dancing all night. Using many of the soft soul techniques of the O'Jays and other groups on the Philadelphia International label, disco added an invariably fast (100–130 beats per minute) and heavy rhythmic pulse. It also drew upon salsa and funk, which was built on James Brown's rhythmic innovations but was expanded technologically and psychedelically by Earth, Wind, and Fire, George Clinton, and Sly and the Family Stone; the last group presented in every performance a microcosm of a society free of racism and sexism. Disco used few polyrhythms, however, and it even moved away from the dialectical bass drum-snare drum alternation of most rock and pop in favor of a rhythmic framework of regular, eighth-note thumping. It was a singer's music, often overtly incorporating the ecstatic techniques of gospel music, and "disco divas" such as Donna Summer were among its biggest stars. It was also a producer's music, with backing tracks often created in the studio by solo figures like Georgio Moroder. Sometimes using open grooves and accretionary structures rather than verse–chorus form, disco songs celebrated sustained pleasure in various forms: dance, sex, and communal identity.

These features helped make disco perhaps the most maligned genre of North American popular music. Racism, homophobia, and misogyny helped fuel a "disco sucks" backlash at the end of the decade, alongside criticism of its studio creation and trademark beat, the characterization of dancing as mindless, comparisons with art rock's complexity and live performance, and with the introspection of singer-songwriters. Disco's biggest stars were more representative of an international mainstream—the straight, white male Australian group the Bee Gees broke all previous sales records with *Saturday Night Fever* (1977)—and the genre brought together the most diverse fan base of any popular style since the rock and roll of the 1950s. From its peak in 1979, when 200 all-disco radio stations broadcast in the United States, it declined suddenly as a named genre, but its musical features remained a strong presence through subsequent decades, particularly in various forms of Electronic dance music.

Punk rock contrasted in nearly every way with disco: deliberately crude rather than polished in its musical techniques and performance styles; a guitar-driven instrumentation in place of lavish soundscapes filled with strings, horns and synthesizers; stripped-down harmonies insistently strummed, instead of lush chords and counterpoint; short, simple songs rather than extended dance grooves; ripped clothes and other signifiers of alienation from dominant conventions, all in strong contrast to disco's celebration of fantasy, attractiveness, and opulence. Influenced by the 1960s cynicism of Lou

Reed and the Velvet Underground, punk musicians explored calculatedly offensive topics and noisiness, downplaying virtuosity because it seemed artificial and elitist. It extended the rebellious aspects of the rock and roll tradition, only differing in its inclusion of mainstream rock among its targets. After the first American punk rockers, including the Ramones and Iggy Pop, Britain followed with younger and more working-class bands, of whom the Sex Pistols and the Clash were among the most influential. Black Flag, the Dead Kennedys, the Plasmatics, and others continued in a harder style of punk, HARDCORE, while others such as the Cars, Devo, and Talking Heads developed NEW WAVE by subtracting some of punk's anger and adding synthesizers and irony.

(v) The 1980s. Drum machines, samplers, synthesizers, personal computers, and sequencers became widely available in the 1980s, enabling musicians to create any imaginable sound, to use pre-existing music as compositional material, and to manipulate and store sounds as digital information. The worldwide spread of cassettes promoted more diversity in worldwide music production and distribution, reducing the dominance of North American music from two-thirds in the 1970s to one-third in the 80s. The introduction of the compact disc (1983) raised the quality of audio playback and increased industry profits, since they cost no more to produce but were sold at much higher prices. Global marketing plans became essential to the growth of the music industry, and although five huge corporations gained control of two-thirds of the world music markets, only one was US-owned, complicating debates over cultural imperialism.

Full-time cable television broadcasts of music videos began on MTV in 1981 and MuchMusic in 1984, increasing the popularity of bands and stars who had particular visual appeal and those whose audiences transcended narrow genre boundaries, including Madonna, Michael Jackson, Prince, and Bruce Springsteen (*see* VIDEO). Especially innovative videos helped build the careers of Jackson and Madonna, and other artists such as Peter Gabriel. Despite MTV's national scope and the expense of producing videos, it played a broader range of music than most radio stations and gave some artists easier access to audiences. Jackson's worldwide success with *Thriller* (1982), which sold an unprecedented 40 million copies worldwide, helped break down MTV's initially racist programming policies and revive a slumping music industry. Prince's fusions of rock and funk, particularly "Little Red Corvette" (1982) and "Purple Rain" (1984), helped break down some of radio's racially-defined boundaries at the same time that he challenged conventional gender norms. Music television's emphasis on spectacle had the effect of encouraging sexism and objectification in many videos, but several female performers, including Madonna, Tina Turner, Pat Benatar, and Cyndi Lauper, effectively used the new medium to project images that were both sexy and powerful.

Despite an increasingly centralized music industry, musical sounds and experiences were diverse. CHARITY ROCK concerts such as "Live Aid" and "USA for Africa" publicized campaigns against injustice and raised money on their behalf. Whitney Houston, Janet Jackson, Lionel Richie, and George Michael dominated the pop charts with songs about love and dance, along with the male vocal groups who developed NEW JACK SWING by combining smooth vocals with HIP HOP rhythms. U2's passionate vocals and polyrhythmic accompaniments, and R.E.M.'s fusion of country and punk influences, made them two of the most influential bands of the decade. Billy Joel and Paul Simon continued to extend the singer-songwriter tradition. Differing interpretations often add to the popularity of mass-mediated texts, as when Bruce Springsteen found that many listeners, including both major presidential candidates in 1984, heard only the celebratory music of his "Born in the USA," missing the lyrics' bitter indictment of US involvement in the Vietnam War and treatment of that war's veterans.

A revival of "traditional" elements was prominent in country music in the 1980s, with Randy Travis, Reba McEntire, Dwight Yoakam, George Strait, and Ricky Skaggs drawing upon earlier honky tonk, rockabilly, western swing, and bluegrass styles; many of the country stars of the 1970s continued their success in the 80s. Alabama, the Statler Brothers and others revived gospel influences and vocal harmonies within country music, and the film *Urban Cowboy* (1980) made "Western" dancing and clothing more broadly fashionable for a time.

Heavy metal grew to become the dominant genre of pop at the end of the 1980s. Recordings by Iron Maiden, Def Leppard, Motörhead, and others at the beginning of the decade became known as the "New Wave of British Heavy Metal," and the catchy songs and high production values of Def Leppard in particular set important precedents. Several factors contributed to the growth of the genre: the androgynous glam metal of Mötley Crüe, Ratt, and Poison; the success of Black Sabbath's singer, Ozzy Osbourne, as a solo artist; Bon Jovi's balance of pop romance and rock rebellion. It began to receive significant radio exposure, and MTV's *Headbangers' Ball*, first aired at the end of 1986, quickly became that station's most popular show. Throughout the decade, guitarists such as Randy Rhoads, Yngwie Malmsteen, and Steve Vai followed Van Halen in developing ever more virtuosic techniques. The influence of classical models (especially Bach, Vivaldi, and Paganini) on harmony, virtuosity, pedagogy, and analysis became paramount. The "underground" styles of THRASH METAL, death metal, and speed metal, with their faster tempos, heavier distortion, ensemble virtuosity, and more complicated song forms, arose primarily in the San Francisco Bay area and quickly spread, led by Slayer, Testament, Megadeth, and especially Metallica.

RAP, the aural component of a HIP HOP culture that included break dancing and graffiti writing, was perhaps the most innovative and influential musical development of the 1980s. During the previous decade, DJs at block parties and dances extended disco mixing techniques so that bits of one piece of music were

Tina Turner and Mick Jagger, Live Aid concert, Philadelphia, 1985. (AP Photo/Rusty Kennedy)

superimposed on another, and this recontextualizing of musical fragments (*see* SAMPLING AND SEQUENCING, HIP HOP) became basic to the style; manipulation of turntables as percussion instruments also provided rhythmically complicated patterns (*see* SCRATCHING and TURNTABLISM). MCs (from "master of ceremonies") who exhorted the crowd and advertised the group of musicians became rappers, whose intricately rhymed and phrased lyrics were rhythmically declaimed against the background of the DJs' music. Rap musicians drew upon long traditions of African American signifying and Jamaican toasting even as they utilized the latest technology, often (as in scratching) in unintended ways. Recordings of these practices began to be issued in 1979 and, in the early 1980s, Kool Moe Dee, L.L. Cool J and others demonstrated the virtuosic potential of the new style. Grandmaster Flash, with songs like "The Message" (1982), established a tradition of social critique through rap lyrics, which was extended later in the decade by the innovative music of Public Enemy. Female rappers such as Queen Latifah and Salt-N-Pepa positioned black women's concerns and perspectives prominently within popular culture and used rap as a forum for debate about gender. Later in the decade, Run DMC brought rap and heavy metal together by covering "Walk this way," a song by Aerosmith; fusions of these two styles were explored by many musicians in the following decade. Ice Cube, NWA, and Ice-T led GANGSTA RAP, and provoked great controversy by addressing racism and ghetto life in violent terms. Complex generational and class connections made African American rappers popular with large white audiences even as they became more Afro-centric. Particularly skilled and imaginative production teams, such as the Bomb Squad, combined dozens of sampled bits of previous music into noisy urban collages, often polyrhythmic and sometimes

polytonal. Extraordinarily virtuosic rappers, such as Rakim and Public Enemy's Chuck D, combined the rhetorical techniques of African American preaching with bebop's rhythmic flair as they delivered vivid and often critical lyrics.

Like heavy metal, rap was often deliberately noisy when compared to other styles, which often caused its particular forms of creativity and virtuosity to go unnoticed. Both genres were musically and lyrically diverse and differed greatly, but rap and metal fans and musicians often found themselves grouped together and demonized by politicians and the mainstream press. The PARENTS MUSIC RESOURCE CENTER, launched in 1985 by a group of Washington politicians' wives, instigated congressional hearings about "offensive" music, mostly metal and rap, promoted censorship campaigns against particular artists and brokered a "voluntary" program whereby record companies put warning stickers on certain albums, so making them unavailable in some parts of the United States. As had happened in the early days of rock and roll, such controversies betrayed fears about the reproduction of values, miscegenation, and the power of popular music to challenge and critique dominant assumptions and to present and naturalize alternatives.

(vi) The 1990s. During this period sampling and sequencing remained important compositional techniques, although increased corporate control of popular music and related changes in copyright law made it more difficult to sample pre-existing recordings freely. CD sales surpassed those of cassettes, and THE INTERNET emerged as an important and contested site for the distribution and exchange of music. The popular MP3 compression format preserved much of the high fidelity of a CD source but reduced sound files to a tenth of

their former size, making feasible the widespread transfer of music via personal computers. The music industry fought to regulate musical uploads and downloads, which they saw as a new frontier of piracy; in contrast, many fans and artists celebrated the new medium's potential to subvert corporate control of musical life.

Media conglomerates pursued mergers that enabled greater profits through synergy, as when soundtrack albums and films promote each other. The major record labels prioritized the music of a few consistent megastars, such as Michael Jackson, Janet Jackson, the Rolling Stones, Madonna, Prince, Aerosmith, and pop balladeers Mariah Carey and Whitney Houston, yet their dominance of the domestic market declined somewhat as smaller labels nearly tripled their share to one-fifth. Despite the emergence of new styles linked to youth culture, audiences for popular music remained generationally diverse; in 1992, only 24% of records were bought by people in their teens and younger.

A number of factors combined to end the unusual prominence of heavy metal at the turn of the decade. The rise of ALTERNATIVE MUSIC, especially as represented by the GRUNGE of Seattle-based Nirvana and other bands, blurred genre lines by retaining heavy metal's energy and distorted guitars but eschewing its overt instrumental virtuosity and spectacular stage style. The introduction of electronic point-of-sale reporting in 1991 showed that rap and country were much more popular than had been indicated by previous *Billboard* charts and other measures of sales, which had overstated the dominance of heavy metal. Besides the decline of heavy metal, the biggest musical trends of the 1990s were the movement of "alternative" to the mainstream, the growth of WORLD MUSIC as a marketing category, another period of crossover success for country music, the popularity of film soundtrack albums and the sudden expansion at the end of the decade of Latin pop, propelled by stars such as Marc Anthony, Ricky Martin, Enrique Iglesias, and Shakira, and supported by demographic changes that were making the United States ever more culturally diverse.

Growing out of the college radio and post-punk scenes of the 1980s, and building on the increasing popularity of R.E.M. during that decade, "alternative" emerged as a successful marketing category in 1991 when Nirvana's *Nevermind* unexpectedly sold over ten million copies, and led to international prominence a wave of grunge bands, including Soundgarden and Pearl Jam. The label "alternative rock" was also applied to the cryptic, moody, and rough-edged music of bands like Green Day, the Tragically Hip, the Breeders, and Hole, as well as female solo artists such as Tori Amos, Liz Phair, and Ani DiFranco. All-female RIOT GRRRL bands such as Bikini Kill and Sleater-Kinney were also part of this movement and influenced some of the most commercially successful artists of this period such as Alanis Morissette. The appeal of "alternative" music increasingly called its designation into question by outselling new releases by Michael Jackson and other "mainstream" stars. What united alternative musicians and fans was a generational identity characterized by disaffection and

Michael Jackson, 1989. (Vandell Cobb/Ebony Collection via AP Images)

malaise: with an ongoing decline in real wages, "Generation X" was the first cohort of Americans who could not expect to be better off than their parents. Thus, themes of downward mobility, loss of faith and an ironic, distrustful attitude towards modern life abound in alternative music. The more detached commentary of R.E.M. and Beck contrasted with the intense desire and frustration articulated by Nine Inch Nails, P J Harvey, and Nirvana.

Few people anticipated the tremendous breakthrough of country music to mainstream popularity in the 1990s, with new artists such as Brooks and Dunn, Allan Jackson, and sexy, often overtly feminist female singers like Martina McBride and Shania Twain, all led by the agile voice and sincere stage presence of Garth Brooks. Along with successful performers of the previous decade like Reba McEntire, Alabama and George Strait, these country stars accounted for as many as 40% of the top-selling albums. Early in the decade, the popularity of country music seemed to owe something to the fact that it offered a less aggressive alternative to the noisy sounds of rap, heavy metal, and grunge.

Gangsta rap was the decade's most controversial musical genre, with widespread debate as to whether rappers such as Ice Cube, Ice-T, Dr. Dre, and Tupac Shakur accurately depicted lives marked by racism and violence; critics alleged that they glorified criminality and misogyny. Such music responded to factors including the greater incidence of child poverty, infant mortality, and youth unemployment among black Americans, as well as disproportionate felony convictions and prison time for blacks and whites who committed the same crimes. The large white male audiences for gangsta rap were sometimes deliberately cultivated by rappers to interrupt the familial reproduction of white racism. Hip hop also flourished in other communities, leading to the wide spread of Latin hip hop and the virtuosic group of Filipino American turntablists who populated the San Francisco Bay Area. (*See* Asian american music.) Rapping also quickly spread around the world, as it served various cultural needs for working through local issues of identity and making connections with a global hip hop culture.

1980s styles of rap and pop ballads continued to be popular in the 90s, especially with hip hop touches introduced by such neo-doo-wop groups as Boyz II Men, En Vogue, a number of artists who worked with influential producer Kenneth "Babyface" Edmonds, and the best-selling female group TLC. Dance music achieved great popularity with new styles, such as "jungle" (soon renamed Drum 'n' bass), featuring virtuosic snare drum samples as a prominent part of the mix, Electro, Garage, House, and Detroit techno.

(vii) The 2000s. At the end of the millennium, the music of the 50-year rock and roll era was still widely perceived as comprising a reasonably coherent and living paradigm, despite accreted innovations in technology and musical style. The institutionalization of the music in college curricula, dissertations across fields, and museums such as the Experience Music Project (Seattle) and the Rock and Roll Hall of Fame (Cleveland), treated this period inclusively and with growing seriousness. Scholarly organizations devoted to popular music and culture such as the International Association for the Study of Popular Music (formed in 1981) became increasingly robust, sponsoring conferences and scholarly journals. Furthermore, established scholarly societies of music, such as the American Musicological Society and the Society for Ethnomusicology, began to make room for popular music scholars in their conference programs and journals; a serious interest in popular music was also seen in many other fields such as History, Cultural Studies, Gender Studies, Sociology, and Psychology. A proliferation of textbooks from major presses, designed for History of Rock and Roll classes, made it easier for universities to include popular music classes in their curriculum. Even within broad Music History classes, popular music genres became more and more likely to be treated with serious attention, reflecting the ecumenical listening and performing practices of professors and students alike.

As the generation that grew up with rock and roll moved grew older in the 2000s, and Generation X in turn became middle-aged, it became common for three generations to be familiar with the same repertoires and artists, harkening back to the broad appeal of popular music in the pre-rock and roll era. The term "dad rock" began to refer to the music enjoyed and imposed by parents, and radio stations specializing in Classic rock explicitly addressed themselves to middle-aged

suburbanites rather than youth. Combined with the development of the "box set" cataloguing a musician's entire oeuvre, and the rise of the Tribute band specializing in note-perfect reproductions of well-known artists' work, popular music increasingly took on a curatorial approach to documenting and packaging artifacts of presumed historic significance and cultural value.

The future of new music in the industry, however, seemed uncertain at best, in part because of sharp challenges presented by other forces in the entertainment industry: video game sales, for example, far surpassed global music revenues by the end of the decade. Traditional practices were thrown into further upheaval by the continuing growth of the Internet as a medium of musical exchange, the widespread ability for consumers to make or duplicate CDs, the sustained popularity of MP3 and other compression formats, the growth of digital radio formats and recommendation engines such as Pandora and Spotify, the success of Apple products such as the iPod (digital media player) and iTunes (an extremely successful online store, established in 2003, offering digital audio and video sales), and a decline in the need for authoritative taste-making institutions such as professional criticism, Top 40 charts, and record stores. The digital age therefore came to be characterized by a flattening of genre hierarchies and a diminished sense of a dominant mainstream. It became increasingly possible for artists to make high-quality recordings and connect with audiences outside the channels of the professional recording industry, and outside their geographical area, in a distant echo of the direct distribution methods of regional musicians selling 45s out of their car trunks in the mid-20th century. New stars of the 2000s were as likely to emerge from music scenes in Montreal (Arcade Fire), New Orleans (Lil Wayne) and Toronto (Justin Bieber and Drake) as from traditional hubs such as Nashville, New York, and Los Angeles. This renaissance of independent, self-managing musicians with home studios (*see* Digital audio workstation) that reached global fan bases, the renewed importance of the single as a commodity (as compared to the album), together with the rise of multiple small music scenes (virtual and otherwise), led to a dramatic drop in sales of individual records; the Recording Industry Association of America documents no "diamond" certified sales (more than 10 million) of a single album between 2005 and 2010. Sales of digital singles, which were not even monitored at the decade's start by Nielsen SoundScan, had outstripped the sales of physical CDs by 2006.

In the face of such challenges, the music industry consolidated further. Only four major record labels remained active into the 2010s—EMI, Universal Music Group, Sony Music Corporation, and Warner Music Group—each a subsidiary of a much larger company with broader goals in entertainment, media, and other industries. Much music industry activity turned toward cross-marketing musical artists through film, television, video games, the Internet, and other new media. Most prominent among such ventures was the immensely popular television show franchise *Pop Idol*, a singing talent show combined with elements of reality television whose US version premiered as *American Idol* in 2002, produced several stars including pop-rock singer-songwriter Kelly Clarkson and country artist Carrie Underwood, and dominated television ratings for the entire decade. The combined efforts of Disney Studios and Radio Disney also introduced a new parade of teen idols. Extending their earlier involvement with TV-Mouseketeers Britney Spears, Cristina Aguilera, and Justin Timberlake, Disney produced a stream of television stars and recording artists such as Miley Cyrus, the Jonas Brothers, and Selena Gomez to appeal to "tween" audiences.

Most of the commercially successful styles of the 1990s—including hip hop, pop, rock, country, and R&B—retained wide appeal into the new century, even as fans often gravitated toward more particularized subgenres or hybrids (such as alternative country, underground hip hop, and country-rap). Although other new styles hit the mainstream during the 2000s—ranging from the confessional approach of emo to the dance tracks of reggaeton—the decade as a whole may be best characterized as featuring a multiplicity of styles, scenes, and genres. Yet, just as technology reshaped music's production, distribution, and consumption, so too did its impact shape the sound of much popular music throughout the 2000s, supplying a continuous digital sheen. The impact of electronica was felt in the proliferation of electronica-influenced hybrids (such as electro hop, hip house, and nortec), the synthesized, beat-heavy, repeated loops that propelled dozens of chart-topping hits—by artists such as Britney Spears, Jennifer Lopez, Black Eyed Peas, Madonna, Justin Timberlake, Lady Gaga, and Kanye West—and the experimental electronic approaches that influenced the work of musicians as diverse as Radiohead, TV on the Radio, and Wilco. The impact of contemporary technology was also heard in the slick, glossy, pitch-perfect vocals that dominated mainstream popular music, often with the help of pitch-correction software such as Auto-Tune. The same technology, which is often used as a safety net in performance by contemporary vocalists in popular music and many other genres, was turned on its head during the 2000s by a steady stream of artists (led with enthusiasm by T-Pain) who wished to produce an artificial voice—a mechanical, futuristic, athletic, and highly processed vocal instrument that could leap suddenly and impossibly from pitch to pitch. Some musicians critical of widespread technological manipulation of music gravitated to Lo-fi recording methods while nostalgic interest in analog sound led to a mini-boom for older analog instruments as well as the vinyl LP.

Despite the growth of local, independent scenes, corporate influence on the popular world remained powerful throughout the decade. In 2000, Clear Channel Communications became the largest radio station owner in the United States; at its peak, it managed or owned more than 1200 radio stations and provided syndicated, branded, top-down programming for more than 5000 stations. Live Nation, a company that split off in 2005 from Clear Channel, not only became a multi-billion-dollar concert promoter but also began competing with the major labels by signing major artists such as Jay-Z, Nickelback, and Madonna to "360 deals" that encompassed recording, distribution, touring, management, and merchandizing. In 2010, the Live Nation operation grew through a merger with Ticketmaster, the nation's largest ticket sales agency.

In response to the sharp dip in album sales, touring and licensing became increasingly important revenue streams for popular artists. The renewed emphasis on live performance, combined with the nostalgia and buying power of older audiences, enabled long-established acts such as the Eagles, Madonna, U2, and Bruce Springsteen to stage especially lucrative tours. Many artists, young and old, turned to licensing their music, whether singles or entire albums, to commercial advertisers, often before the music itself had been officially released. Some corporations took even bolder steps to build ties with popular musicians. Converse, the sneaker manufacturer, opened Rubber Tracks, a recording studio in Brooklyn, that gave free studio time to recording artists in return for potential licensing deals and greater commercial exposure.

The accessibility of digital technology also enabled new strategies of listening and making music. The iPod transformed the nature and the portability of music libraries, and also permitted the crafting of playlists (whether deliberately constructed or generated at random) in a matter of seconds. In addition to releasing digital albums and singles, some artists created tracks designed to be used for mobile phone ringtones and other New media. The introduction in 2005 of YouTube, a video-sharing website, also played an important role in re-popularizing music videos and serving as a shared digital music warehouse. Digitized audio and user-friendly computer software also facilitated the combining of musical texts into new creations; although this practice had been used by creators of *musique concrète* such as Pierre Schaeffer beginning in the 1940s, and was termed "plunderphonics" by practitioner John Oswald in 1985, by the 2000s these techniques had been taken up by amateurs and professionals alike. A proliferation of amateur audio and video mash-ups have appeared on Internet sites such as YouTube, and commercial artists such as 2 Many DJs, Danger Mouse, and Girl Talk created popular Mash-up albums of collage-like songs crafted from pre-existing recordings. Some of these songs involved placing an entire vocal track from one recording over the instrumental material from one other, as in 2001's "A Stroke of Genie-us," which combined pop singer Christina Aguilera's hit "Genie in a Bottle" with indie rockers the Strokes's "Hard to Explain," while others combined shorter excerpts of music taken from a wider range of sources, as in Girl Talk's 2010 "All Day," which famously included 373 samples. Mash-up strategies soon became sufficiently established to drive episodes of the mainstream hit television series *Glee* and to charge performances on talent shows such as *The X-Factor*.

Curiously, the spread of collage techniques was complemented by a rise of old-fashioned pop singers in the 2000s and 2010s, though often these singers proved

Lady Gaga. (Imageclick/Lebrecht Music & Arts)

adept and creative in post-modern strategies and techniques. Singers such as Beyoncé, Rihanna, and Lady Gaga pleased intellectuals and ironists with their provocative, thoughtful challenges to convention, but they also attracted legions of fans with their skillful singing, appealing melodies, hook-laden choruses, and splashy performances across all media. The successful combining of avant-garde strategies with pop stylings suggested that opposition between art and commerce was becoming less rigid, a notion confirmed at the 2011 Grammy Awards, when cerebral indie rockers Arcade Fire won Album of the Year.

Mass mediated popular music has always depended upon commercial practices that can be exploitative, and it has often presented listeners with sanitized, anodyne versions of subversive, avant-garde musical expression. Tensions between mainstream and countercultural musics have often mirrored broader social values, and popular music has played central roles in social struggles and moments of cultural change.

Popular music's immediacy has allowed it always to register the desires and inequities of a conflicted world, and to facilitate the exchange of experiences and insights among people who have been separated by geography, power, and time.

BIBLIOGRAPHY

GENERAL
J.T. Howard: *Our American Music* (New York, 1931, 4/1965)
S. Spaeth: *A History of Popular Music in America* (New York, 1948)
G. Chase: *America's Music* (New York, 1955, 2/1966/R)
D. Ewen: *Popular American Composers, from Revolutionary Times to the Present* (New York, 1962; suppl. 1972)

W. Mellers: *Music in a New Found Land* (New York, 1964/R)
H.W. Hitchcock: *Music in the United States* (Englewood Cliffs, NJ, 1969, 2/1974)
D. Ewen: *All the Years of American Popular Music* (Englewood Cliffs, 1977)
C. Hamm: *Yesterdays: Popular Song in America* (New York, 1979)
D. Horn and P. Tagg, eds: *Popular Music Perspectives* (Göteborg, Sweden, and Exeter, England, 1982)
C. Hamm: *Music in the New World* (New York, 1983)
C. Small: *Music of the Common Tongue: Survival and Celebration in Afro-American Music* (London, 1987)
R. Middleton: *Studying Popular Music* (Buckingham, 1990)
D. Brackett: *Interpreting Popular Music* (Cambridge, 1995/R)
C. Hamm: *Putting Popular Music in its Place* (Cambridge, 1995)
D. Hesmondhalgh and K. Negus, eds: *Popular Music Studies* (London, 2002)
M. Spicer and J. Covach: *Sounding Out Pop: Analytical Essays in Popular Music* (Ann Arbor, 2010)

EARLY AMERICAN SONG AND PIANO MUSIC
T. Williams: *A Discourse on the Life and Death of Oliver Shaw* (Boston, 1851)
W. Chappell: *Popular Music of the Olden Time* (London, 1855–9/R as *The Ballad Literature and Popular Music of the Olden Time*)
J.H. Hewitt: *Shadows on the Wall* (Baltimore, 1877)
G. F. Root: *The Story of a Musical Life* (Cincinnati, 1891)
H. Russell: *Cheer Boys, Cheer! Memories of Men and Music* (London, 1895)
J.W. Hutchinson: *Story of the Hutchinsons (Tribe of Jesse)* (Boston, 1896/R)
O. G. T. Sonneck: *A Bibliography of Early Secular American Music* (Washington, DC, 1905, rev. and enlarged W.T. Upton 2/1945/R)
J.M. Chapple: *Heart Songs* (Boston, 1909/R)
H.V. Milligan: *Stephens Collins Foster* (New York, 1920)
G.C.D. Odell: *Annals of the New York Stage* (New York, 1927–49/R)
C. Wittke: *Tambo and Bones: a History of the American Minstrel Stage* (Durham, 1930)
S.F. Damon: *Series of Old American Songs, Reproduced in Facsimile* (Providence, RI, 1936)
D. Gilbert: *American Vaudeville: its Life and Times* (New York, 1940)
H. Dichter and E. Shapiro: *Early American Sheet Music: its Lure and its Lore, 1768–1889* (New York, 1941/R)
E.J. Kahn, Jr.: *The Merry Partners: the Age and Stage of Harrigan and Hart* (New York, 1955)
W.A. Heaps and W. Porter: *The Singing Sixties: the Spirit of Civil War Days Drawn from the Music of the Times* (Norman, OK, 1960)
H. Nathan: *Dan Emmett and the Rise of Early Negro Minstrelsy* (Norman, 1962/R)
P. Glass and L.C. Singer: *Singing Soldiers: a History of the Civil War in Song* (New York, 1964)
R.J. Wolfe: *Secular Music in America, 1801–1825: a Bibliography* (New York, 1964)
R.C. Toll: *Blacking Up: the Minstrel Show in Nineteenth-century America* (New York, 1974)
W.W. Austin: *"Susanna," "Jeanie," and "The Old Folks at Home": the Songs of Stephen C. Foster from his Time to Ours* (New York, 1975)
J.A. Stephens: *Henry Russell in America: Chutzpah and Huzzah* (diss., U. of Illinois, 1975)
R. Jackson: *Popular Songs of Nineteenth-century America* (New York, 1976)
H.T. Sampson: *Blacks in Blackface: a Source Book on Early Black Musical Shows* (Metuchen, NJ, 1980)
N.E. Tawa: *Sweet Songs for Gentle Americans: the Parlor Song in America, 1790–1860* (Bowling Green, OH, 1980)
D.L. Root: *American Popular Stage Music, 1860–1880* (Ann Arbor, MI, 1981)
S. Dennison: *Scandalize my Name: Black Imagery in American Popular Music* (New York, 1982)
R. Sanjek: *American Popular Music and its Business: the First Four Hundred Years, iii, From 1900 to 1984* (New York, 1988, rev. 2/1996 by D. Sanjek as *Pennies from Heaven: the American Popular Music Business in the Twentieth Century*)
E. Lott: *Love and Theft: Blackface Minstrelsy and the American Working Class* (New York, 1993)

J.W. Finson: *The Voices that are Gone: Themes in Nineteenth-century American Popular Song* (New York, 1994)

D. Cockrell: *Demons of Disorder: Early Blackface Minstrels and Their World* (New York, 1997)

K. Emerson: *Doo-dah! Stephen Foster and the Rise of American Popular Culture* (New York, 1997)

W.J. Mahar: *Behind the Burnt Cork Mask: Early Blackface Minstrelsy and Antebellum American Popular Culture* (Urbana, IL, 1999)

THE TIN PAN ALLEY ERA

G.M. Cohan: *Twenty Years on Broadway* (New York, 1924)

C.K. Harris: *After the Ball: Forty Years of Melody* (New York, 1926)

P. Dresser: *The Songs of Paul Dresser: With an Introduction by his Brother Theodore Dreiser* (New York, 1927)

J.W. Johnson: *Black Manhattan* (New York, 1930)

E.B. Marks: *They All Sang: from Tony Pastor to Rudy Vallée* (New York, 1934)

I. Witmark: *The Story of the House of Witmark: from Ragtime to Swingtime* (New York, 1939/R)

E.B. Marks: *They All Had Glamor: from the Swedish Nightingale to the Naked Lady* (New York, 1944/R)

R. Blesh and H. Janis: *They All Played Ragtime* (New York, 1950, 4/1971)

H. Meyer: *The Gold in Tin Pan Alley* (Philadelphia and New York, 1958)

D. Ewen: *The Life and Death of Tin Pan Alley* (New York, 1964)

A. Schoener, ed.: *Harlem on my Mind: Cultural Capital of Black America, 1900–1968* (New York, 1968)

N.I. Huggins: *Harlem Renaissance* (New York, 1971)

I. Whitcomb: *After the Ball* (London, 1972)

A. Wilder: *American Popular Song: the Great Innovators, 1900–1950* (New York, 1972)

J.R. Williams: *This Was "Your Hit Parade"* (Rockland, ME, 1973)

H. Pleasants: *The Great American Popular Singers* (New York, 1974, 2/1985)

B. Rust: *The American Dance Band Discography, 1917–1942* (New Rochelle, NY, 1975)

I. Whitcomb: *Tin Pan Alley: a Pictorial History (1919–1939)* (New York, 1975)

I. Howe: *World of our Fathers* (New York, 1976)

R. Pearsall: *Popular Music of the Twenties* (London, 1976)

E.A. Berlin: *Ragtime: a Musical and Cultural History* (Berkeley, CA, 1980, enlarged 2/1984)

L.A. Erenberg: *Steppin' Out: New York Nightlife and the Transformation of American Culture, 1890–1930* (Westport, CT, 1981)

J. Shepherd: *Tin Pan Alley* (London, 1982)

N.E. Tawa: *The Way to Tin Pan Alley: American Popular Song, 1866–1910* (New York, 1990)

A. Forte: *The American Popular Ballad of the Golden Era, 1924–1950* (Princeton, NJ, 1995)

W.H.A. Williams: *"Twas Only an Irishman's Dream": the Image of Ireland and the Irish in American Popular Song Lyrics, 1800–1920* (Urbana, 1996)

L. Abbott and D. Seroff: *Out of Sight: the Rise of African American Popular Music, 1889–1895* (Jackson, MI, 2002)

T. Brooks: *Lost Sounds: Blacks and the Birth of the Recording Industry, 1890–1919* (Urbana, 2004)

C.H. Garrett: *Struggling to Define a Nation: American Music and the Twentieth Century* (Berkeley, CA, 2008)

L. Hamberlin: *Tin Pan Opera: Operatic Novelty Songs in the Ragtime Era* (New York, 2010)

K.H. Miller: *Segregating Sound: Inventing Folk and Pop Music in the Age of Jim Crow* (Durham, NC, 2010)

THE ROCK ERA

B. Rosenberg and D.M. White, eds: *Mass Culture: the Popular Arts in America* (New York, 1957)

D.A. De Turk and A. Poulin, eds: *The American Folk Scene: Dimensions of the Folksong Revival* (New York, 1967)

C. Belz: *The Story of Rock* (New York, 1969, 2/1972)

D.D. Braun: *Toward a Theory of Popular Culture: the Sociology and History of American Music and Dance* (Ann Arbor, MI, 1969)

R.J. Gleason: *The Jefferson Airplane and the San Francisco Sound* (New York, 1969)

H. Pleasants: *Serious Music and all that Jazz* (London, 1969)

C. Gillett: *The Sound of the City: the Rise of Rock and Roll* (New York, 1970, 2/1972)

R. Middleton: *Pop Music and the Blues* (London, 1972)

I. Stambler: *Encyclopedia of Popular Music and Rock* (New York, 1973)

G. Marcus: *Mystery Train: Images of America in Rock 'n' Roll Music* (New York, 1975, rev. and enlarged 2/1982)

I. Stambler: *Encyclopedia of Pop, Rock & Soul* (New York, 1975)

T.W. Adorno: *Introduction to the Sociology of Music* (New York, 1976)

P. Hardy and D. Laing: *The Encyclopedia of Rock* (London, 1976)

J. Miller, ed.: *The Rolling Stone Illustrated History of Rock & Roll* (New York, 1976, 2/1980)

S. Chapple and R. Garofalo: *Rock 'n' Roll is Here to Pay: the History and Politics of the Music Industry* (Chicago, 1977)

J.S. Roberts: *The Latin Tinge: the Impact of Latin American Music on the United States* (New York, 1979, 2/1999)

D. Harker: *One for the Money: Politics and Popular Song* (London, 1980)

N. Tosches: *Unsung Heroes of Rock 'n' Roll* (New York, 1984)

E. Ward, G. Stokes, and K. Tucker: *Rock of Ages: the Rolling Stone History of Rock & Roll* (New York, 1986)

P. Van der Merwe: *Origins of the Popular Style: the Antecedents of Twentieth-Century Popular Music* (Oxford, 1989)

L.A. Lewis: *Gender Politics and MTV: Voicing the Difference* (Philadelphia, 1990)

G.G. Garr: *She's a Rebel: the History of Women in Rock and Roll* (Seattle, 1992)

R. Garofalo, ed.: *Rockin' the Boat: Mass Music and Mass Movements* (Boston, 1992)

R. Walser: *Running with the Devil: Power, Gender and Madness in Heavy Metal Music* (Hanover, NH, 1993)

T. Rose: *Black Noise: Rap Music and Black Culture in Contemporary America* (Hanover, NH, 1994)

S.A. Floyd: *The Power of Black Music: Interpreting its History from Africa to the United States* (New York, 1995)

S. Reynolds and J. Press: *The Sex Revolts: Gender, Rebellion and Rock'n' Roll* (Cambridge, MA, 1995)

S. Whiteley, ed.: *Sexing the Groove: Popular Music and Gender* (New York, 1997)

W.T. Lhamon: *Raising Cain: Blackface Performance from Jim Crow to Hip Hop* (Cambridge, MA, 1998)

S. Waksman: *Instruments of Desire: the Electric Guitar and the Shaping of Musical Experience* (Cambridge, MA, 1999)

C. Werner: *A Change is Gonna Come: Music, Race, and the Soul of America* (New York, 1999, 2/2006)

M.A. Neal: *What the Music Said: Black Popular Music and Black Public Culture* (New York, 1999)

A.J. Zak, III: *The Poetics of Rock: Cutting Tracks, Making Records* (Berkeley, 2001)

L. O'Brien: *She Bop II: the Definitive History of Women in Rock, Pop, and Soul* (London, 2002)

L. Burns and M. Lafrance: *Disruptive Divas: Feminism, Identity & Popular Music* (New York, 2002)

M. Cloonan and R. Garofalo, eds: *Policing Pop* (Philadelphia, 2003)

G.P. Ramsey, Jr.: *Race Music: Black Cultures from Bebop to Hip-hop* (Berkeley, 2003)

T. Lawrence: *Love Saves the Day: a History of American Dance Music Culture, 1970–1979* (Durham, NC, 2003)

J. Kun: *Audiotopia: Music, Race, and America* (Berkeley, CA, 2005)

K.R. Moon: *Yellowface: Creating the Chinese in American Popular Music and Performance, 1850s–1920s* (New Brunswick, NJ, 2005)

J. Chang: *Can't Stop Won't Stop: a History of the Hip-hop Generation* (New York, 2005)

S. Whiteley and J. Rycenga, eds: *Queering the Popular Pitch* (New York, 2006)

J. Warwick: *Girl Groups, Girl Culture: Popular Music and Identity in the 1960s* (New York, 2007)

F. Jarman-Ivens, ed.: *Oh Boy! Masculinities and Popular Music* (New York, 2007)

D. Brackett, ed.: *The Pop, Rock, and Soul Reader: Histories and Debates* (New York, 2/2009)

E. Wald: *How the Beatles Destroyed Rock 'n' Roll: an Alternative History of American Popular Music* (New York, 2009)

S. Waksman: *This Ain't the Summer of Love: Conflict and Crossover in Heavy Metal and Punk* (Berkeley, CA, 2009)

M.E. Cepeda: *Musical imagiNation: U.S.-Colombian Identity and the Latin Music Boom* (New York, 2010)

R. Avant-Mier: *Rock the Nation: Latin/o Identities and the Latin Rock Diaspora* (London, 2010)

D. Pacini Hernandez: *Oye como va! Hybridity and Identity in Latino Popular Music* (Philadelphia, 2010)

A. Sinnreich: *Mashed Up: Music, Technology, and the Rise of Configurable Culture* (Amherst, 2010)

T. Cateforis: *Are We Not New Wave? Modern Pop at the Turn of the 1980s* (Ann Arbor, 2011)

K. Meizel: *Idolized: Music, Media, and Identity in American Idol* (Bloomington, 2011)

For further bibliography, *see also*: ADULT CONTEMPORARY; ALTERNATIVE ROCK; ARENA ROCK; ART ROCK; BALTIMORE CLUB; BLUE-EYED SOUL; BLUES; BLUES ROCK; BOY BANDS; BUBBLEGUM; CHARITY ROCK; CONTEMPORARY CHRISTIAN MUSIC; CLASSIC ROCK; COON SONG; COUNTRY MUSIC; COUNTRY ROCK; CROONING; DETROIT TECHNO; DISCO; DOO-WOP; DRUM 'N' BASS; EASY LISTENING; ELECTRONIC DANCE MUSIC; FUNK; GARAGE; GARAGE ROCK; GHETTOTECH AND GHETTO HOUSE; GIRL GROUPS; GLAM METAL; GLAM ROCK; GO-GO; HIP HOP; GOTH ROCK; GRUNGE; HARD ROCK; HEAVY METAL; HOUSE; INDIE ROCK; JAM BAND; LO-FI; MIAMI BASS; MINSTRELSY; NEO-SOUL; NO WAVE; NOVELTY SONG; POP; PUNK; RAGTIME; RAP; REGGAE; RHYTHM-AND-BLUES; RIOT GRRRL; ROCK; ROCK AND ROLL; ROCKABILLY; SINGER-SONGWRITER; SOFT ROCK; SOUL MUSIC; SOUTHERN ROCK; STRAIGHT EDGE; SURF MUSIC; SYNTHPOP; TEEN IDOL; THRASH METAL; TRANCE; TRIBUTE BAND; WIZARD ROCK; and WOMEN'S MUSIC.

CHARLES HAMM/R (1, 2, 3), ROBERT WALSER/R (4, a–f),
JACQUELINE WARWICK,
CHARLES HIROSHI GARRETT (4, g)

Portable media device [portable media player]. An easily transported, often handheld machine that plays pre-recorded and/or broadcast media, sometimes possessing recording capability; the term is most often associated with portable digital audio and multimedia players. The history of the portable media device can be linked decisively, if not exclusively, to the invention of audio recording (portable magic lanterns and other cinematic precursors were common in the 19th century). Mechanical audio devices such as the suitcase gramophone, popular among sailors and soldiers, emerged during the first two decades of the 20th century, and early radio kits were portable, preceding the often-discussed "domestication" of the record player and the radio into household furniture. Radio sets became fitted components in automobiles around 1930, and so-called portable player pianos—portable player piano mechanisms applied to regular pianos—were even invented around the same time. But despite the commonplace description of such devices as "portable," the term has meant different things at different times and for different devices: one could articulate a scale-of-portability continuum dependent in part on object size, ranging from media playback and transmission machines that were transportable (which by definition would include all consumer models), to those moved about with relative ease while usually requiring stationary setup and usage (including the examples above), to handheld and pocket-sized devices that could allow for media consumption while on the move. Another consideration in portability was the power sources for such devices, which during the first half of the century shifted from the mechanical to the electrical but which were still hampered by the limitations of batteries, notably their cost, size, and storage capacity.

A conjunction of socioeconomic and technological advances after World War II transformed the portable media player irrevocably, making media consumption far more mobile. Global economic prosperity within a US-centered geopolitical system provided the backdrop for these advances, and technological developments from US corporations and research labs refined the transistor in the 1950s and the common alkaline battery towards the end of the decade. But another crucial economic force was developing at the same time: Japan. The Sony Corporation's entry in 1955 into the nascent portable transistor radio market in the United States and its breakthrough transformation of transistor production, which greatly decreased costs, led to an influx of radios from Japanese electronics goods firms into the US at the end of the decade. The subsequent decade witnessed a period of dominance of portable transistor radios from Japan and then Hong Kong: witness Van Morrison's song "Brown-eyed Girl" (1967), which highlighted the link between the transistor radio and rock music, as well as Allan Sherman's novelty parody "The Twelve Gifts of Christmas" (1963) which famously mentioned a "Japanese transistor radio." The growing prominence of the stereo cassette and cassette players as well as stereo headphones during the 1970s led to other exemplars of market dominance for Japanese electronics companies: the boombox, a portable stereo with cassette player and radio which emerged in the late 1970s and became associated with the rise of hip-hop music and culture; and, in 1979, Sony's famous Walkman, which became the subject of several well known studies (including those by Hosokawa and du Gay and others). With Japanese electronics production prominent in the US market through the next two decades, including the first portable compact disc player by Sony in 1984, one might describe this period of the broader American history of portable music devices as the "Sony conjuncture"—roughly coterminous with the postwar Japanese economic miracle and then its stalling-out in the 1990s.

All of this changed, and rather quickly, as a result of the Apple Corporation's release of a portable MP3 player, the iPod, in 2001. Precedents certainly existed before: prototype digital audio players apparently go back to 1979, and the first commercial MP3 players date from the mid-1990s. However, none had achieved the popularity of the iPod, whose latecomer status allowed it to bypass some legal battles surrounding MP3s and downloading, notably that of the Recording Industry Association of America against Diamond Multimedia in 1998. The iPod's prolonged success lay in Apple's strategy of pairing a well designed and cleverly marketed MP3 player with its own iTunes software (2001) and an easy-to-use and inexpensive online digital audio store, the iTunes Store (2003), which offered a legal and economically viable alternative to file sharing. Burgeoning iPod sales also drew attention to the fact that compressed sound files were constructed so as to be best heard in distracted contexts (Sterne, 2006 and 2012) and that the on-the-move usage seemed to transform listeners' experiences into quasi-cinematic mechanisms for mood management in ways similar to, but more supple than, those of previous portable audio players like the Walkman (Bull, 2007). Numerous book-length paeans to the new device were published during the decade, comprising one facet of a cultural phenomenon that also included parodies of the once-ubiquitous iPod silhouette advertisements and *Wired* magazine's iPod My Photo, an online engine imitating the ads with user-uploaded photos (Kahney, 2005). Various novel social uses of the iPod developed, from "silent raves" (flash mobs or more official gatherings in which listeners would dance to music heard on their headphones) to iPod DJing (in which iPod owners use their devices for mostly amateur DJing in a variety of public and private contexts). One study even examined the value chain of the iPod, demonstrating that the majority of its profits went to the United States despite being manufactured in China (Linden and others). Subsequent versions of the iPod revealed additional features (including camera, video player, and video camera), expanded memory capacity, and smaller size (iPod Mini and Nano), resulting in its transformation into a multimedia device capable of playing films and video games (although the original iPod included a game called Brick). Other companies like Microsoft, with its Zune player, sought to compete effectively with the iPod but were never able to do so in the US market.

As sales of the iPod soared during the 2000s, peaking globally in 2008, MOBILE TELEPHONE consumption was expanding at one order of magnitude greater—at the rate of billions, instead of hundreds of millions. By the early 2000s, however, mobile phones were not simply communication devices: they also included mechanisms for playing music, first as synthesizer files and later as sound files that served to customize the phone's RINGTONE, generating a multibillion dollar industry in the process. Not long afterwards, mobile phones became equipped with MP3 players, demonstrating a process of convergence with other devices and inspiring the "mobile music" market, in which music was downloaded directly to and listened to on mobile phones. Although this wasn't the case in the United States, by the mid-2000s in many countries the dominant MP3 player was the mobile phone. This fact prompted Apple to get into the phone business in 2007 by launching the iPhone, a smartphone (or combined phone and portable wireless computer) with numerous features including an MP3 player linked to the iTunes store; a phone-less but Internet-connected variant called the iPod Touch was released at the same time. The iPhone propelled smartphone sales more generally and helped to incubate a market for phone software called apps (applications), many of which were music-related. By the early 2010s phones had not, however, obviated other forms of portable media devices, such as portable DVD players, portable video game players, digital book readers, or even laptop and tablet computers (such as Apple's iPad), although the mobile phone remained the most common portable media device on the planet.

See also NEW MEDIA.

BIBLIOGRAPHY

S. Hosokawa: "The Walkman Effect," *Popular Music*, iv (1984), 165–80
M. Schiffer: *The Portable Radio in American Life* (Tucson, AZ, 1991)
P. du Gay and others: *Doing Cultural Studies: the Story of the Sony Walkman* (London, 1997)
M. Hilmes: *Radio Voices: American Broadcasting, 1922–1952* (Minneapolis, 1997)
S. Partner: *Assembled in Japan: Electrical Goods and the Making of the Japanese Consumer* (Berkeley, CA, 1999)
M. Bull: *Sounding Out the City: Personal Stereos and the Management of Everyday Life* (Oxford, 2000)
T. Day: *A Century of Recorded Music: Listening to Musical History* (New Haven, CT, 2002)
L. Kahney: *The Cult of iPod* (San Francisco, 2005)
J. Sterne: "The MP3 as Cultural Artifact," *New Media & Society*, viii (2006), 825–42
M. Bull: *Sound Moves: iPod Culture and Urban Experience* (London, 2007)
K. Bijsterveld and J. van Dijck, eds.: *Sound Souvenirs: Audio Technologies, Memory, and Cultural Practices* (Amsterdam, 2009)
G. Goggin: *Global Mobile Media* (London, 2011)
J. Sterne: *MP3: The Meaning of a Format* (Durham, NC, 2012)
S. Gopinath: *The Ringtone Dialectic: Economy and Cultural Form* (Cambridge, MA, 2013)
S. Gopinath and J. Stanyek, eds.: *The Oxford Handbook of Mobile Music Studies* (New York, 2013)
G. Linden and others: "Who Captures Value in a Global Innovation System? The Case of Apple's iPod," <http://pcic.merage.uci.edu/papers/2007/AppleiPod.pdf> (2013)

SUMANTH GOPINATH

Porter, Andrew (*b* Cape Town, South Africa, 26 Aug 1928). British writer on music. After playing continuo for Albert Coates in his teens, Porter studied English at University College, Oxford, where he was an organ scholar. While at the university he began reviewing concerts for *The New Statesman* and *The Times Literary Supplement*, accepting a position at the (London) *Times* upon graduation in 1951, and becoming music critic for the *Financial Times* in 1953. He later served as editor of *The Musical Times* (1960–7) and for two decades as music critic for the *New Yorker* (1972–92) before becoming music critic for *The Observer* (1992–7) and finally moving back to *The Times Literary Supplement* (1997–). During the 1950s and 60s he also wrote for a number of journals and magazines, including *Gramophone*, *High Fidelity*, and *Opera*.

As a Verdi scholar, he was appointed a Visiting Fellow at All Souls College, Oxford (1973–4), Regents Professor at the University of California, Irvine (1980), and Ernest Bloch Professor at the University of California, Berkeley (1980–1). He was an editorial board member of *19th-Century Music*, and for a time also edited the newsletter for the American Institute for Verdi Studies. His research in the archives of the Paris Ópera led to a rediscovery of excised material from the original version of Verdi's *Don Carlos* ("The Making of *Don Carlos*," 1972).

As a critic, Porter's clear, elegant literary style and keen, protean intellect won plaudits, with Virgil Thomson remarking in 1974: "Nobody reviewing in America has anything like Porter's command of [opera]. Nor has *The New Yorker* ever before had access through music to so distinguished a mind." He has also written about ballet, and given a number of radio broadcasts. In addition to criticism, Porter translated a number of libretti for performance at English National Opera, including Wagner's *Ring*, *Tristan*, and *Parsifal*; Verdi's *Otello*, *Falstaff*, *Don Carlos*, *Forza del destino*, and *Rigoletto*; Mozart's *Zauberflöte*; and Strauss's *Intermezzo*. More recently, however, Porter has lamented that "serious, scholarly music criticism [has] disappeared" from the daily press (Prince of Hesse Memorial Lecture, Aldeburgh, 2000).

Five volumes of his writing in the *New Yorker* have been published (*A Musical Season*, New York, 1974; *Music of Three Seasons*, New York, 1978; *Music of Three More Seasons*, New York, 1981; *Musical Events 1980–83*, New York, 1987; *Musical Events 1983–86*, New York, 1989). A Festschrift with 23 contributions, *Words on Music* (Hillsdale, NY), appeared in 2003.

Also see *Grove Music Online* for list of writings.

DAVID TRIPPETT

Porter, Cole (Albert) (*b* Peru, IN, 9 June 1891; *d* Santa Monica, CA, 15 Oct 1964). Composer, songwriter, and lyricist. One of the most celebrated Broadway and film composers of his era, Porter also penned his own lyrics, which were famous for their wit and sophistication.

1. Life. 2. Music. 3. Lyrics.

1. LIFE. The son of Kate Cole, an amateur pianist, and Sam Porter, an amateur guitarist, pianist, and singer, Cole Porter began his musical training at an early age. In addition to singing at the local Lutheran church, Cole studied the violin and the piano, attending the Marion Conservatory in Indiana at age six. He wrote his first song in 1901, "The Song of the Birds," and his first publication was a short piano work, *The Bobolink Waltz* (1902). As a youth, he played violin in the conservatory orchestra, provided piano accompaniment for silent movies, and even starred in a school production of *Snow White*. At age 14 he was sent to the Worcester (Massachusetts) Academy (1905–9), where the headmaster helped him transform an interest in poetry, which had been instilled by his father, into a gift for writing lyrics. The songwriting experience he gained in Worcester was put to good use during his undergraduate years at Yale University (1909–13), where he wrote the lyrics and music for at least 300 songs. This body of work included drama productions, Glee Club arrangements, and popular football songs such as "Bingo Eli Yale" and "Bulldog." Although his wealthy grandfather, James Omar Cole, pressured him into studying law at Harvard in 1913, he quickly transferred to the School of Music, where he pursued formal music study until opportunities on Broadway took him to New York.

Porter's initial Broadway ventures were unsuccessful. In 1915, his song "Esmerelda" was included in the musical *Hands Up* and "Two Big Eyes" made it into *Miss Information*. In 1916, his Gilbert and Sullivan–inspired show, *See America First*, opened on Broadway but closed after only 15 performances. Dejected, Porter returned to his studies, this time with PIETRO ALESSANDRO YON (the organist at St. Patrick's Cathedral in New York). When the United States declared war on Germany in 1917, Porter moved to Paris with an apparent desire to join the military efforts. His actions during this time are the subject of much debate, fed by Porter's own unsubstantiated claims that he was active in the French Foreign Legion. Some evidence suggests that he distributed relief supplies and then transferred from one regiment to the next until he was discharged in 1919. He remained in Paris and married a rich socialite, Linda Lee Thomas. Although Porter had a number of male lovers, he and Linda remained close, but likely platonic, partners until her death in 1954. The couple led a lavish lifestyle in Paris, the Riviera, and Venice throughout the 1920s. Their many parties were legendary, as was a passionate affair Cole had with Boris Kochno, a Russian dancer and librettist who collaborated with Sergei Diaghilev. During this period, and perhaps spurred by Thomas's desires that he should reflect his connections with high society by becoming a composer in the classical style, Porter returned to study with Vincent d'Indy at the Schola Cantorum. His only mature composition in this style, however, was the 1923 jazz ballet, *Within the Quota*, which premiered in Paris along with Milhaud's more enduring work, *La Création du Monde*. Porter's ballet features a nod to polytonality and limited whole-tone excursions, but generally evokes the harmonic and melodic language of his songs.

Meanwhile, Porter's continued attempts to garner success on Broadway achieved mixed results. His next three shows, *Hitchy-Koo of 1919* (56 performances), *Greenwich Village Follies of 1924* (127 performances), and *Paris* (1928, 195 performances) generated several hit songs, including "Let's do it." High volume sheet music sales of his love ballads "Old-Fashioned Garden" and "I'm in love again," however, reveal that American taste was not yet primed for Porter's sophisticated word play and droll humor. Indeed, Porter's *Wake Up and Dream* (1929) received 263 performances in London but floundered amid the economic tragedies of New York when it opened there in December (136 performances). Porter's first success in New York came when Irving Berlin, having turned down a commission to write the music for a show with a Parisian setting, recommended that producer E. Ray Goetz engage Porter for the job. The result was *Fifty Million Frenchmen* (1929), which ran for 254 performances.

The 1930s saw Porter moving into the American spotlight with eight Broadway openings, including *Gay Divorce* (1932) with Fred Astaire singing "Night and Day," *Red Hot and Blue* (1936), and *Du Berry was a Lady* (1939). The biggest hit of the decade, *Anything Goes* (1934), starred Ethel Merman and ran for 420 performances. Porter also made inroads into Hollywood, contributing to five Hollywood films during this period. His unique ability to balance catchy melodies with biting cynicism, clever rhymes, macaronic verse, and passionate feelings is evident in the many hit songs of this period, including "I get a kick out of you," "Begin the Beguine," "In the Still of the Night," "Just One of Those Things," and "You're the top."

A horseback riding accident on Long Island in 1937 crushed Porter's legs. Although the pain was constant, he continued for some time to lead a life of success and glamour, never allowing pity or pain to get in his way. He even claimed to have written the verse to his hit song "At Long Last Love" while waiting for the ambulance to remove him from the scene of the accident. Porter maintained a part-time residence at the Waldorf-Astoria in New York, but three years after the accident, Linda and Cole moved to a manor in Williamstown, Massachusetts, where Linda claimed that the fresh air bolstered her own poor health.

Porter had a number of successes in the 1940s, including scores for five movies and four hit shows that each ran for over 400 performances (*Panama Hattie*, *Let's Face It*, *Something for the Boys*, and *Mexican Hayride*). A 1946 film, *Night and Day*, starring Cary Grant as Cole Porter, romanticized Cole Porter's biography, conveniently disregarding his homosexuality and glorifying his limited military service. *Seven Lively Arts* (1944) and *Around the World in Eighty Days* (1946) opened and closed amid poor critiques and light audiences. Porter's 1948 Shakespearean masterpiece, *Kiss me, Kate*, however, saw unprecedented acclaim, running for 1077 performances. Based on *The Taming of the Shrew*, the show included several of the composer's most popular songs, including "So in Love," "Wunderbar," and "Too Darn Hot." Of his three later musicals, *Can-Can* (1953) was the most successful, with 892 performances. Porter's film credits of this period include a version of the 1955 show *Silk Stockings* and the very successful *High Society* (1956), which starred Bing Crosby, Grace Kelly, and Frank Sinatra.

Porter was greatly affected by the death of his mother in 1952 and his wife in 1954, and, after one leg was amputated in 1958, he stopped composing and lived as a recluse until his death from kidney failure on 15 October 1964. Many of Porter's shows were revived on Broadway in the decades after his death, including *Kiss me, Kate* (1999, 881 performances), and *Anything Goes* (1987, 784 performances; 2011, 553 performances). Porter songs have appeared in numerous films and Broadway shows, including a 2004 film biography, *De-Lovely*, starring Kevin Kline as Cole Porter.

2. MUSIC. Porter's songs were prepared for sheet music publication by Albert Sirmay (né Szirmai), music editor and arranger for Chappell Music. Porter's practice of notating much of the piano part is in direct contrast to the common tendency among contemporary songwriters and, although Sirmay often completed the arrangements for other composers, much of his job with Porter consisted of elaborating the piano parts for the amateur sheet-music market. Porter's unusual involvement in the creation of sheet music may have stemmed from his impressive music education, including formal studies in harmony and counterpoint, evidence of which is currently housed in Yale University's Beinecke Library.

Just as Porter's lyrics are characterized by their sophistication, so too is Porter's music, which includes some of the most extensive experimentation within the so-called Great American Songbook. Syncopated dance rhythms, modal mixture, intense chromaticism, motivic structuring, expressive text painting, and extended forms are common in his work. The well-known song, "Begin the Beguine," for instance, is extended to a surprising 108 measures and captures Latin rhythms in its alliterative titular phrase; see ex.1.

Ex.1 "Begin the Beguine" (1935), Titular phrase

Porter often began his songs in a key other than the "home" tonic, avoiding the fixed harmonic grounding in favor of the many potential continuations offered by a non-tonic beginning. Although he was not the only composer of the era to use this technique, his predilection for harmonic ambiguity is distinctive. Porter's F-major song, "Just One of Those Things," opens in a sultry D minor and its titular phrase is typical of his spontaneous and well-known response to common expressions; see ex.2.

Ex.2 "Just One of Those Things" (1935), Titular phrase

Porter explored several unusual and unexpected harmonic continuations of the ambiguous opening in the song's bridge (middle section). The section begins in the key of E♭ major, a radical departure from the poignant opening music in D minor, and moves through a series of chromatic melodic twists to the dominant of C major (G7). This change to the major mode and use of internal rhyme ("bit/it," then echoed on "aware/affair") is perhaps symbolic of the cheerful past reflected in the highly syncopated lyric: "when we started painting the town." The final section, however, contradicts this mood by resuming D minor. A touching return of the music from the titular phrase, now with the lyric "good-bye, dear," creates a cynical reminder of the song's underlying poignancy, despite its restoration of the F-major tonic in the final cadence; see ex.3.

"Night and Day" (1934), premiered by Fred Astaire, is perhaps the most innovative and best known of Porter's songs. The verse's 34 repeated Gs reflect Porter's tendency to juxtapose monotonous obsession with passionate chromaticism. Here, the repeated Gs mark the fixated longing of a beating heart: "keeps repeating you, you, you." The striking A♭ chord on the opening of the refrain arises from within a descending chromatic G–G octave in the bass, the goal tone of which is reserved for the critical lyrics "you are the one"; see ex.4. The bass motion foreshadows a similar chromatic line in the final line of the melody: "and this torment won't be through 'til you let me spend my life making love to you." Text-painting and motivic reference of this sort is often evident in Porter's songs, since he composed the lyrics and music in tandem.

Ex.3 "Just One of Those Things" (1935), Bridge

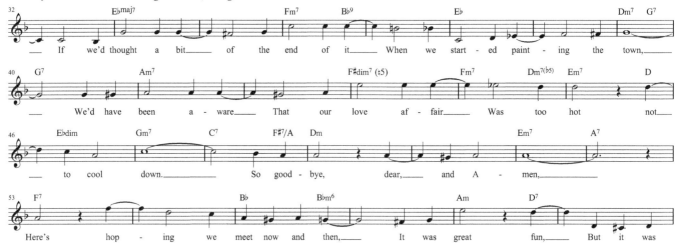

Ex.4 "Night and Day" (1934), Transition from verse to refrain

3. LYRICS. With their wit, art, and careful construction, Porter's self-scribed lyrics are timeless, speaking to contemporary audiences as they have to so many since his first Broadway production in 1916. They are characterized by clever rhymes, alliteration, *doubles-entendres*, and a penchant for the bawdy. Due to their explicit references to sex and drugs, a number of his songs were "Banned in Boston" by officials working in conjunction with the New England Watch and Ward Society. One song that tested these boundaries was "Love for Sale" (1930): "Love for sale/Appetizing young love for sale/Love that's fresh and still unspoiled/Love that's only slightly soiled/Love for sale."

The racy subject, clever rhymes ("unspoiled/soiled"), and excessive alliteration ("sale/still/unspoiled/slightly/soiled") identify it is the quintessential Porter lyric. The Boston censors spared this song despite an initially scandalous reception, partly because the song was transferred from the white singer Kathryn Crawford to the African American singer Elisabeth Welch, who sang it in a scene set in front of Harlem's Cotton Club. The racial politics at play were an unfortunate sign of the times, but, like so many of Porter's songs, this one has remained a hit among diverse audiences since its first performance due to its characteristic musical sophistication and remarkable use of text.

WORKS
(selective list)
EDITIONS
The Cole Porter Song Book (New York, 1959)
The Complete Lyrics of Cole Porter, ed. R. Kimball (New York, 1984)

Music & Lyrics by Cole Porter: A Treasury of Cole Porter (New York, 1972)
Music and Lyrics by Cole Porter: The Sassy, Sophisticated Sentimental Porter in Song (New York, 1975)
Unpublished Cole Porter (New York, 1975, 2/2003)
The Cole Porter Song Collection (Van Nuys, 2009)

STAGE
(professional works for which Porter wrote all or much of the score; lyrics are by Porter; names of librettists are given in parentheses; dates are those of first New York performance, unless otherwise indicated. Vocal selections were published for most works; complete lists of works are given in Eells, and Kimball and Gill; comprehensive list of films that include Porter songs can be found on The Internet Movie Database, <http://www.imdb.com>)

See America First (T.L. Riggs and Porter), 28 March 1916 [incl. I've a shooting box in Scotland]

Hitchy-koo of 1919 (revue, G.V. Hobart), 6 Oct 1919 [incl. Old-Fashioned Garden]

Within the Quota (ballet), Paris, 25 Oct 1923

Greenwich Village Follies of 1924 (revue), 16 Sept 1924 [incl. I'm in love again]

La revue des ambassadeurs, Paris, 10 May 1928 [incl. An Old-Fashioned Girl]

Paris (M. Brown), 8 Oct 1928 [incl. Let's do it]

Wake up and Dream (revue, J.H. Turner), London, 27 March 1929; New York 30 Dec 1929 [incl. What is this thing called love?]

Fifty Million Frenchmen (H. Fields), 27 Nov 1929 [incl. You do something to me; You've got that thing]

The New Yorkers (Fields, after E.R. Goetz and P. Arno), orchd H. Spialek, 8 Dec 1930 [incl. Love for Sale]

Gay Divorce (D. Taylor), orchd Spialek and R.R. Bennett, 29 Nov 1932 [incl. Night and Day; After You Who?]; contributed to the music for the film version, The Gay Divorcee (1934)

Nymph Errant (R. Brent, after J. Laver), orchd Bennett, London, 6 Oct 1933

Anything Goes (G. Bolton, P. Wodehouse, H. Lindsay and R. Crouse), orchd Bennett and Spialek, 21 Nov 1934 [incl. All Through the Night;

Anything goes; Blow, Gabriel, blow; I get a kick out of you; You're the top]; film, 1936

Jubilee (M. Hart), orchd Bennett, 12 Oct 1935 [incl. Begin the Beguine; Just One of those Things]

Red, Hot and Blue (Lindsay and Crouse), orchd Bennett, 29 Oct 1936 [incl. Down in the Depths, It's De-Lovely, Ridin' High]; film, 1949

You Never Know (R. Leigh), orchd Spialek, 21 Sept 1938 [incl. At Long Last Love]

Leave it to Me (B. and S. Spewack), orchd D. Walker, 9 Nov 1938 [incl. My heart belongs to daddy]

Du Barry was a Lady (Fields and B. DeSylva), orchd Spialek, Bennett and T. Royal, 6 Dec 1939 [incl. Do I love you?; Friendship]; film, 1943

Panama Hattie (Fields and DeSylva), orchd Bennett, Spialek and Walker, 30 Oct 1940 [incl. Let's be buddies]; film, 1942

Let's Face it (H. and D. Fields), orchd Spialek, Walker and Royal, 29 Oct 1941; film, 1944 [incl. Ace in the Hole]

Something for the Boys (H. and D. Fields), orchd Spialek, Walker, Bennett and Royal, 7 Jan 1943; film, 1944

Mexican Hayride (H. and D. Fields), orchd Bennett and Royal, 28 Jan 1944 [incl. I love you]; film, 1948

Seven Lively Arts (revue), orchd Bennett, Royal and Spialek, 7 Dec 1944 [incl. Ev'ry Time we say Goodbye]

Around the World in Eighty Days (O. Welles, after J. Verne), orchd Bennett and Royal, 31 May 1946

Kiss Me, Kate (B. and S. Spewack, after W. Shakespeare: *The Taming of the Shrew*), orchd Bennett, 30 Dec 1948 [incl. Another Op'nin', Another Show; So in Love; Wunderbar; Too Darn Hot]; films, 1953, 2003

Out of this World (Taylor, R. Lawrence), orchd Bennett, 21 Dec 1950 [incl. Use your imagination]

Can-Can (A. Burrows), orchd P.J. Lang and R. Noeltner, 7 May 1953 [incl. Allez-vous-en; Can-Can; C'est magnifique; I love Paris; It's all right with me]; film, 1960

Silk Stockings (G.S. Kaufman, L. McGrath and Burrows), orchd Walker, 24 Feb 1955 [incl. All of You]; film, 1957

Contributions to: Hands Up, 1915; Miss Information, 1915; Telling the Tale, London, 1915; Very Good Eddie, London, 1918; Buddies, 1919; The Eclipse, London, 1919; As You Were, 1920; A Night Out, London, 1920; Mayfair and Montmartre, London, 1922; Phi-Phi, London, 1922; The Sun never Sets, London, 1938

FILMS
(in addition to those cited above; not all scores wholly by Porter)

The Battle of Paris, 1929

Born to Dance, 1936 [incl. I've got you under my skin; Easy to Love]

Rosalie, 1937 [incl. In the Still of the Night]

Break the News, 1938

Broadway Melody of 1940, 1940 [incl. I concentrate on you; Between You and Me]

You'll Never Get Rich, 1941 [incl. Dream Dancing]

Something to Shout About, 1942 [incl. You'd be so nice to come home to]

Hollywood Canteen, 1944 [incl. Don't fence me in]

Night and Day, 1946

The Pirate, 1948 [incl. Be a clown]

Adam's Rib, 1949

High Society, 1956 [incl. True Love]

Les Girls, 1957

Aladdin (for television), 1958

At Long Last Love, 1975

You're the Top: Cole Porter Story (for television), 1990

De-Lovely, 2004

OTHER SONGS
(selective list)

Antoinette Birby, c1910; Bingo Eli Yale, 1910; Bridget, 1910; Bulldog, 1911; Esmerelda, 1915; Two Big Eyes, 1915; Let's misbehave, c1925; The Laziest Gal in Town, 1927; Miss Otis Regrets, 1934; Thank you so much, Mrs. Lowsborough-Goodby, c1935; From this moment on, 1950

Principal publishers: Chappell, Harms

BIBLIOGRAPHY
R. Kimball and B. Gill: *Cole* (New York, 1967) [incl. list of works]

A. Wilder: *American Popular Song: The Great Innovators, 1900–1950* (New York, 1972)

L.L. Siebert: *Cole Porter: an Analysis of Five Musical Comedies and a Thematic Catalogue of the Complete Works* (diss., CUNY, 1975)

C. Schwartz: *Cole Porter* (New York, 1977)

J. Johnson: "Cole Porter, 1944–1948: 'Don't fence me in'," *Musical Theatre in America: Papers and Proceedings of the Conference on the Musical Theatre in America*, ed. G. Loney (Westport, CT, 1984), 257–66

G. Mast: *Can't Help Singin': the American Musical on Stage and Screen* (Woodstock, NY, 1987) [incl. bibliography]

J.P. Swain: *The Broadway Musical: a Critical and Musical Survey* (New York, 1990), 129–52

S. Citron: *Noël and Cole: the Sophisticates* (London, 1992)

A. Forte: "Secrets of Melody: Line and Design in the Songs of Cole Porter," *MQ*, lxxvii (1993), 607–47

W.E. Studwell: "From Hammerstein to Hammerstein: the American Musical, 1927–1943," *Music Reference Services Quarterly*, iii (1994), 17–28 [incl. bibliography]

A. Forte: *The American Popular Ballad of the Golden Era, 1924–1950* (Princeton, NJ, 1995), 117–46

W. Rimler: *A Cole Porter Discography* (San Francisco, 1995)

J. Morella and G. Mazzei: *Genius and Lust: The Creative and Sexual Lives of Cole Porter and Noël Coward* (New York, 1996)

G. Block: "Anything Goes," "Kiss Me, Kate," *Enchanted Evenings: The Broadway Musical from "Show Boat" to Sondheim* (New York, 1997, 2/2009), 40–57, 215–32

W. McBrien: *Cole Porter: A Biography* (New York, 1998)

R. Kimball and R. Sudhalter: *You're Sensational: Cole Porter in the '20s, '40s, & '50s* (Indianapolis, 1999)

M. Shaftel: "From Inspiration to Archive: Cole Porter's 'Night and Day'," *JMT*, xliii (1999), 315–47

A. Forte: *Listening to Classic American Popular Songs* (New Haven, CT, 2001), 54–58, 95–102, 155–160

M. Buchler: "Every Love but True Love: Unstable Relationships in Cole Porter's 'Love for Sale'," *PopMusicology*, ed. C. Bielefeldt and R. Grossmann (Lüneberg, 2008), 184–200

MATTHEW R. SHAFTEL

Porter, Hugh (*b* Heron Lake, MN, 18 Sept 1897; *d* New York, NY, 22 Sept 1960). Organist and educator. The son of a Methodist minister, he received the BM degree from the American Conservatory in Chicago in 1920 and the BA from Northwestern University in 1924. He also studied with WILHELM MIDDELSCHULTE, W. LYNNWOOD FARNAM, T. TERTIUS NOBLE, and NADIA BOULANGER, and at Union Theological Seminary (MSM 1930, DSM 1944). He taught at Northwestern, the Juilliard School, New York University, the Mannes College, and, from 1931, the School of Sacred Music of Union Theological Seminary. In 1945 he became director there, following Clarence Dickinson, and was Clarence and Helen Dickinson Professor from 1947 until his death. Porter toured as a recitalist, served in many churches (including the Collegiate Church of St. Nicholas in New York), and was organist for several years at the Chautauqua Institution. He and his wife, Ethel K. Porter, were the music editors of the *Pilgrim Hymnal* (1958) of the United Church of Christ. Writing of his special talents, Bingham noted "a keen artistic sense, technical proficiency and mastery of style," and a "thorough knowledge of hymnody and liturgy." Porter died from a heart attack while he was inside the chamber of the new organ at James Memorial Chapel, repairing a cipher.

BIBLIOGRAPHY
S. Bingham: "An Appreciation of Hugh Porter", *Diapason*, li/12 (1960), 5

VERNON GOTWALS

Porter, (William) Quincy (*b* New Haven, CT, 7 Feb 1897; *d* Bethany, CT, 12 Nov 1966). Composer, viola player, and educator. He studied the violin as a child and began to compose at an early age. At Yale University (BA 1919, BMus 1921) he studied composition with HORATIO PARKER and DAVID STANLEY SMITH. In 1920 he took lessons in composition with d'Indy and in violin with Lucien Capet in Paris. On returning to the United States in 1921, he studied with ERNEST BLOCH in New York and later in Cleveland, where he joined the De Ribaupierre Quartet as viola player in 1922 and the staff of the Cleveland Institute of Music as a teacher of theory in 1923. With the aid of a fellowship from the Guggenheim Foundation, Porter returned to Paris in 1928 for a three-year stay, this time not to study but to compose.

During these years in Paris, Porter developed his personal style and produced the works which first established his reputation—in particular, the Violin Sonata no.2 and the String Quartet no.3, both of which won awards from the Society for the Publication of American Music. In 1932 Porter was appointed professor of music at Vassar College, where he remained until called in 1938 to become dean of the faculty of the New England Conservatory, assuming the position of director in 1942. In 1943 Porter was awarded the Elizabeth Sprague Coolidge Medal, and the following year he was elected to the National Institute of Arts and Letters.

In 1946 he returned to Yale as professor of music, a post he held until his retirement in 1965. Soon after he took up this position, Porter wrote a theoretical text entitled *Study of Sixteenth-Century Counterpoint, Based on the Works of Orlando di Lasso* (Boston, 1948). In 1939 he cofounded the AMERICAN MUSIC CENTER, eventually joining the Board of Directors in 1956 and remaining on it until his death. His papers, including many unpublished documents and his musical manuscripts, are held at the Irving S. Gilmore Music Library at Yale University. While Porter was at Yale, his major works included the *Concerto concertante*, which was awarded a Pulitzer Prize in 1954, and the Viola Concerto, which was first performed and recorded by Paul Doktor and taken up by other soloists, including Harry Danks and William Primrose. The latter described the work as "one of the most engaging of all viola concertos" (*Violin and Viola*, London, 1976/R, 186).

Porter's string quartets exhibit the key features of his style: smooth scalar melodic lines in a sometimes chromatic context, always rhythmically lively and characteristically idiomatic for the string player. Together, Porter's nine quartets form one of the most substantial contributions to the literature by any American composer. By their fluency and sensitivity, they reflect the composer's intimate involvement with the genre, and several were at one time in in the repertory of major ensembles.

WORKS
(juvenilia, composition exercises, incomplete works and sketches not listed)

ORCH

Ukrainian Suite, str, 1925; Suite, c, 1926, arr. pf/pf 4 hands/2 pf; Poem and Dance, 1932, arr. 2 pf; Sym. no.1, 1934, arr. 2 pf; Dance in 3-Time, chbr orch, 1937, arr. 2 pf; 2 Dances for Radio, in 4- and 5-Time, 1938; Music for Str, 1941; Fantasy on a Pastoral Theme, org,

str, 1943; The Moving Tide, 1944; Va Conc., 1948, arr. va, pf; The Desolate City (Arabian, trans. W.S. Blunt), Bar, orch, 1950; Fantasy, vc, orch, 1950; Conc. concertante, 2 pf, orch, 1953; New England Episodes, 1956 [based on Music for a Film on Yale Library]; Conc. for Wind Orch (Concertino), 1959; Hpd Conc., 1959; Sym. no.2, 1962; Ohio, ov., 1963; incid music, arrs.

CHBR AND SOLO INST

9 str qts: 1922–3, 1925, 1930, 1931, 1935, 1937, 1943, 1950, 1958
Boutade, pf, 1923; The Cloisters, pf, 1923; Nocturne, pf, 1923; Our Lady of Potchaiv, Ukrainian folksong, str qt, 1923; 2 preludes, str qt, 1923; Scherzo, str qt, 1923; Ukrainian Folk Songs, vn, pf, 1923; Sonata no.1, vn, pf, 1925–6; In monasterio, str qt, 1927, arr. small orch; Pf Qnt, 1927; Blues lointains, fl, pf, 1928; Counterpoint, str qt, 1928; Little Trio (Suite in E), fl, vn, va, 1928; Berceuse for Little Helen, vn/fl, pf; Cl Qnt, 1929; Sonata no.2, vn, pf, 1929; Toccata, Andante & Finale, org, 1929–32; Pf Sonata, 1930; Suite, va, 1930; Fl Qnt on a Childhood Theme, 1937; Lonesome, pf, 1940; Canon and Fugue, org, 1941; Fugue, str qt/ob qt, 1941; Pony Ride, 2 pf, ?1941; 8 Pieces for Bill, 1941–2, nos.2 and 8 lost; 4 Pieces, vn, pf, 1944–7; Sonata, hn, pf, 1946; Str Sextet on Slavic Folk Songs, 1947; Juilliard Pieces for Str, 1948–9; Divertimento, (2 vn, va)/(ob, vn, va), 1949; Fugue in d, pf/org, 1949; Promenade, pf, 1953, rev. 1956; Duo, vn, va, 1954; Nocturne, pf, 1956; Day Dreams, pf, 1957 [based on 8 Pieces for Bill]; Duo, va, hp, 1957; Divertimento, ww qnt, 1960; Hpd Qnt, 1961; Chorale, org, 1963; Variations, vn, pf, 1963; Ob Qnt, 1966
8 other vn, pf and org pieces; occasional pieces

VOCAL
(1 voice, piano, unless otherwise stated)

To the Moon (P.B. Shelley), 1922; And, Like a Dying Lady (Shelley), 1923, orchd; Go to sleep (Negro song), 1923, arr. Bar, str orch; Music, When Soft Voices Die (Shelley), 1924; The Silent Voices (A. Tennyson), 1924; 12 Songs for Helen on Nursery Rhymes, 1931, arr. 1v, 4 ww, str orch, 1955; This is the house that Jack built, 1937/8, orchd 1955; Cant. for the Composers' Guild, ?chorus, 1949; Introspections on The Banks o' Doon, 1v, fl, pf, 1955; 2 Songs (A. Porter), 1956; 7 Songs of Love (R. Graves), 1961; Jubilate Deo, men's chorus, org, 1965; [6] Songs for Rose Jackson (P. Colum, W. Shakespeare), 1966; incid music

MSS (incl. juvenilia and composition exercises), tape recordings, and memorabilia in *NH*
Principal publishers: ACA, Music Press, Peters, G. Schirmer, Valley Music

BIBLIOGRAPHY
EwenD
H. Elwell: "Quincy Porter," *MM*, xxiii (1946), 20–6
H. Boatwright: "'Quincy Porter (1897–1966)," *PNM*, v/2 (1967), 162–5
R.E. Frank: *Quincy Porter: A Survey of the Mature Style and a Study of the Second Sonata for Violin and Piano* (diss., Cornell U., 1973)
HOWARD BOATWRIGHT/JONAS WESTOVER

Portland (i). City in Maine (pop. 66,194; metropolitan area: 487,568; 2010 US Census). Formal interest in music is first evidenced in 1756, when the First Parish Church voted to raise £25 to purchase an edition of Tate and Brady's psalm book (with tunes annexed); the Second Parish Church installed the city's first church organ in 1798. A short-lived Handel Society of Maine, founded in Portland in 1814, was the first of several musical organizations formed in the first half of the 19th century: the Beethoven Musical Society of Portland, Maine (1819–26), the Handel and Haydn Society (1828–31), the Mozart Musical Society (1832–4), and the Portland Sacred Music Society (1836–54). The last had among its members the music retailer Jacob S. Paine and his brother David, an organist and teacher who compiled the *Portland Sacred Music Society's Collection of Church Music* (1839).

Jacob Paine's son, JOHN KNOWLES PAINE, born in Portland in 1839, was one of the first American composers to write large-scale musical works and the first full professor of music at Harvard University. A magnificent organ was presented to the city in 1912 by Cyrus H.K. Curtis, installed at the City Hall and named in honor of conductor, composer, and organist Hermann Kotzschmar (1829–1908). The Kotzschmar Club (formed in 1900) and the Marston Club for women (1887), named after the Portland composer and teacher George Marston, merged in 1965 to form the Marston–Kotzschmar Club. Among other early musical organizations that have remained active are the Portland Rossini Club (founded 1869 as a women's music society), and the MacDowell Club for women (1908).

The Maine Music Festival, promoted by William R. Chapman, was held annually in Portland and Bangor from 1897 to 1926. The Portland Choral Art Society (formed in 1972) and the Community Chorus (1979) of about 90 members continue the city's strong choral tradition. The Portland Band, organized in 1827 by Jacob Paine, was led from 1843 to 1860 by Daniel Hiram Chandler, who formed his own band in 1876; Chandler's Band continues to give concerts in the 21st century.

The Portland SO was organized in 1923–4 and incorporated in 1932; it became fully professional in 1953 and engaged its first resident conductor, Arthur Bennett Lipkin, in 1962. The orchestra presents annual series of classical, popular, and children's concerts in the Merrill Auditorium (capacity 1900), which was renovated in 1997. The Portland Symphony String Quartet (formed in 1969), originally affiliated with the orchestra and in residence at the University of Southern Maine from 1978, was renamed the Portland String Quartet in 1980. Further concert life is provided by the Portland Chamber Music Festival, which formed in 1994, and the Portland Ovations (founded 1931 as the Portland Concert Association), which sponsors an annual series of concerts by musicians of international reputation at Merrill Auditorium.

Popular music in Portland has focused on rock and folk music, with genres such as bluegrass, blues, and jazz also present. The primary local venue for popular music is One Longfellow Square, which opened in 2006. It hosts local and traveling musicians in an intimate setting. For larger, arena-style concerts and events, the Cumberland County Civic Center (capacity 8800–9500), which opened in 1977, is used. Local clubs such as Asylum and Styxx offer live and recorded dance music.

Although amateur productions of operetta have been given in Portland since the Revolutionary period, it was not until 1974, when Sarah Caldwell's Opera New England of Maine (one of eight regional branches that sponsor productions from the Opera Company of Boston) began presenting fully staged operas in the city, that a professional company could be heard on a regular basis. It continued staging operas in Portland into the mid-1980s. PORTopera began presenting a summer season of opera at the Portland State Theater in 1995. Founded in 1952, Portland Lyric Theater, a community theater organization, presents musicals.

The University of Southern Maine, with campuses in Portland and nearby Gorham, has an active undergraduate music program; a variety of student and faculty ensembles and guest performers bring additional concerts to the area. The university also sponsors a number of local youth music ensembles. Westbrook College also sponsors musical programs, as does the Portland Museum of Art. Early local musical groups are documented in the library of the Maine Historical Society and in the Portland Public Library, which has a special collection of sheet music by Maine composers, as well as a substantial lending collection of sheet and choral music, general music literature, and recordings.

BIBLIOGRAPHY

S. Freeman, ed.: *Extracts from the Journals Kept by the Rev. Thomas Smith* [1720–88] (Portland, ME, 1821, rev. and enlarged by W. Willis as *Journals of the Rev. Thomas Smith, and the Rev. Samuel Deane*, 2/1849)

W. Willis: *The History of Portland, from its First Settlement* (Portland, ME, 1831–3, rev. and enlarged 2/1865/R1972)

I. Berry: *Sketch of the History of the Beethoven Musical Society of Portland, Maine, 1819–1825* (Portland, ME, 1888)

G.T. Edwards: *Music and Musicians of Maine* (Portland, ME, 1928/R1970)

C.P. Small: *Handbook of First Parish Church of Portland* (Portland, ME, 1942)

F.T. Wiggin: *Maine Composers and Their Music: a Biographical Dictionary*, i (Rockland, ME, 1959), ii (Portland, ME, 1976)

D.A. Sears: "Music in Early Portland," *Maine Historical Society Quarterly*, xvi/3 (1977), 131–60

PRISCILLA HUBON McCARTY/JONAS WESTOVER

Portland (ii). City in Oregon (pop. 582,130; metropolitan area: 2,226,009; 2010 US Census). It was chartered in 1851.

1. Classical music. 2. Jazz. 3. Rock. 4. Traditional music.

1. CLASSICAL MUSIC. Music instruction was provided to settlers in the Oregon Territory by missionaries, among them Narcissa Whitman, a singer who settled across the Columbia River from present-day Portland in 1836. Music was also taught at the city's first school, St. Mary's Academy, founded in 1859. The Pillow and Drew Music Store, Portland's first music retail shop, opened in 1850 and specialized in "pianos of the most celebrated makers," accordions, and sheet music. Many of the city's early musical performances were provided by visiting groups, such as the Oregon City Chorus, which gave a concert in Portland in 1856, and the Bianca Opera Company, which presented Verdi's *Il trovatore* in 1867. The Fort Vancouver Post Band supplied music for weddings and ceremonial occasions until 1898. The band of the Aurora Colony, a nearby commune of German immigrants, performed frequently in Portland in the 1860s and 70s.

The Portland Mechanics Band was founded in 1864, and on 15 June 1866 the Philharmonic Music Society gave its first concert in Oro Fino Hall, the site of musical performances until 1878. An Apollo Club, which existed as early as 1883, continued to give choral concerts until it disbanded around 1960. The Portland SO, the sixth major orchestra to be established in the United

States and the first in the western United States, was formed in 1896 and renamed the Oregon SO in 1967. Carl Denton was resident conductor from 1918 to 1925, followed by Willem van Hoogstraten (1925–38), Werner Janssen (1947–9), James Sample (1949–53), Theodore Bloomfield (1955–9), Piero Bellugi (1959–61), Jacques Singer (1962–72), Lawrence Leighton Smith (1973–80), James DePreist (1980–2003), and Carlos Kalmar (from 2003). In 1924 an informal group of young musicians was organized under the guidance of Mary Dodge as the Portland Junior SO (renamed the Portland Youth PO in 1979), the first youth orchestra in the United States. It was conducted by the Russian immigrant Jacques Gershkovitch until his death in 1953, directed by Jacob Avshalomov from 1954 to 1995, and has been led by David Hattner from 2008. Metropolitan Youth Symphony was directed since its 1974 inception by Portland music professor and former Oregon Symphony violinist Lajos Balogh, who also founded and still conducts the summer Portland Festival Symphony, in 1980. Upon his retirement in 2012, Balogh was succeeded by Andres Lopera.

The city has supported numerous other concert music institutions. The Portland Baroque Orchestra, founded by local early music enthusiasts David Kerr, Douglas Leedy, Laura Migliori Cunningham, and others in 1983, ascended to national recognition under the directorship of famed Dutch conductor Ton Koopman and later English violinist Monica Huggett (from 1995). The Portland Columbia Symphony Orchestra, founded in 1982 by Jerry Luedders at Lewis and Clark College and taken off campus and brought to community-wide prominence by John Trudeau, offers performances in metro area churches and colleges. Portland Chamber Orchestra, founded 1947 and led for 20 years by Finnish composer and conductor Boris Sirpo, initially comprised music students at Lewis and Clark College; it is now led by Yaacov Bergman (from 2002) and offers some of the most innovative programming in the region.

Portland had a local opera company from 1917 to 1923. The Opera Association was founded in 1950. Directed by Christopher Mattaliano since 2003, Portland Opera holds performances in Keller Auditorium, Newmark Theatre, and its own Studio Theater. The city also embraces a wide variety of amateur, church, college, and professional choirs, including Cappella Romana (founded 1991 by Alexander Lingas), Portland Symphonic Choir (founded 1946), Oregon Repertory Singers (1974), Resonance Ensemble (2009), Portland Vocal Consort, Cantores in Ecclesia, Choral Arts Ensemble, Portland Symphonic Girlchoir, Pacific Youth Choir, In Mulieribus, Portland Gay Men's Chorus, and many others. Longtime conductors and college faculty members Bruce Browne, Gil Seeley, and Roger Doyle presided over the rise of Portland choral music.

The city's chamber music scene is also very active. The Friends of Chamber Music, which began an annual concert series in 1948, now presents leading touring chamber musicians. The Chamber Music Northwest summer festival (est. 1971 by Sergiu Luca and directed by David Shifrin since 1980) features top performers from around the nation, while the Portland Piano International attracts internationally acclaimed pianists to its summer festival and year-round recital series. In 1998 the William Byrd Festival began an annual summer program in which Cantores in Ecclesia and guests perform the English Renaissance composer's works. Beginning in 2009 the Oregon Bach Festival, founded in 1970 by Helmuth Rilling and based at the University of Oregon in Eugene, extended its reach to Portland, with several performances each summer.

The splendid Marquam Grand Theater, opened in 1890, gave impetus to Portland's musical life. It was succeed by a civic auditorium inaugurated in 1917, modernized to seat 3000 in 1968, and renamed Keller Auditorium, which hosts touring Broadway musicals, operas, and other national productions. Popular music concerts were long held at the Memorial Coliseum (capacity 11,500; opened 1960) and at the Paramount Theater (capacity 2800), rebuilt and renamed (after its principal private benefactor) the Arlene Schnitzer Concert Hall. It became the home of the Oregon SO in 1984 at the Portland Center for the Performing Arts, which includes three other performance halls and governs the nearby Keller. Many classical music concerts take place at Reed College's Kaul Auditorium, Portland State University's Lincoln Performance and Recital Halls, and other local venues. Area churches offer classical and world music events by local and touring artists every week, particularly the nonsectarian Old Church (capacity 350; built in 1883 and renovated in 1968), which has a restored organ of 1883 by Hook & Hastings. In 1949 the Portland Park Bureau began sponsoring free summer concerts ranging from opera to folk music in the Washington Park Amphitheater.

The most famous Portland composer, the maverick LOU HARRISON, was born in the city's Irvington neighborhood; he later returned for the summers of 1949–50 and worked with local ensembles on visits in the 1980s and 90s. Choral composer MORTEN LAURIDSEN grew up in Portland and has returned often for performances and recordings. Many local composers working in the classical tradition belong to NACUSA's Northwest chapter, Cascadia Composers. PSU professor Tomas Svoboda, Reed College professor David Schiff, and University of Oregon music professor Robert Kyr all work with area ensembles.

2. JAZZ. Portland's formidable jazz history began in the 1930s and accelerated after thousands of African Americans moved to the city to work in World War II shipyards. North Williams Avenue featured local and touring performers in jam sessions at clubs such as Lil' Sandy's, the Frat Hall, the Chicken Coop, Jackie's, and the Uptown Ballroom. The most celebrated, the Dude Ranch supper club and the Rhythm Room, hosted the most famous touring jazz stars. Early local jazz stars included Roy Jackson, Carl Thomas, Leo Amadee, Bobby Bradford, and many others. After urban renewal devastated the scene along with the rest of Portland's main African American neighborhood, jazz revived in the 1960s and 70s with performers such as Glen Moore

(who cofounded the influential world music jazz group Oregon with fellow Oregonian Ralph Towner). Famed composer and pianist Andrew Hill led the PSU jazz program for some years, and other well-known jazz musicians such as Jim Pepper, Nancy King, Dave Frishberg, Rebecca Kilgore, Esperanza Spalding, David Friesen, Darrell Grant, and Chris Botti either trained or established careers in the city. The city has several regular jazz venues, including Jimmy Mak's, a supper club that programs touring artists; its house band is led by the city's preeminent jazz figure, drummer Mel Brown. Each winter the city has staged Portland Jazz Festival, founded in 2004, directed by Bill Royston until 2011 and since then directed by Don Lucoff. In the summer, Mt. Hood Jazz Festival provides similar opportunities for local jazzers. The Creative Music Guild has since 1991 presented avant-garde improvised music, and the city has a small but vibrant experimental music scene.

3. ROCK. Rock and rockabilly emerged in the 1950s and 60s, often in informal venues such as high school auditoriums. Important early garage rock bands included the Kingsmen and Paul Revere and the Raiders; both recorded hit versions of the iconic rock song "Louie Louie" at the same studio in downtown Portland. A few R&B bands such as the Monterays earned regional reputations. By the 1980s, once restrictive cabaret liquor laws were eliminated, the live rock and pop scene steadily expanded, with heavy metal, punk/grunge/hardcore, hip hop and other genres finding local support. Important local bands from the 1980s and 90s included Dead Moon, Quarterflash, The Wipers, and Nu Shooz. A nascent funk/hip-hop scene spawned bands such as U-Krew and Pleasure. By the turn of the millennium, the Northwest's attraction to young musicians and other artists had spawned a burgeoning indie rock scene. National press attention focused on bands such as The Decemberists, Everclear, Dandy Warhols, Blitzen Trapper, Pink Martini, singers Elliott Smith and M. Ward, and many others. Instead of Portlanders leaving to find their fortunes in Los Angeles, Seattle, or other larger markets, the city attracted indie rock stars such as Sleater-Kinney, members of Death Cab for Cutie, The Shins, Spoon, and Modest Mouse, Stephen Malkmus of Pavement, and many others. Their music and those of other local bands are showcased at festivals such as MusicFest NW (founded 2000) and PDX Pop Now (founded 2004).

4. TRADITIONAL MUSIC. Folk music thrives in Portland, especially traditional Irish bands and fiddlers. English expatriate Kevin Burke, one of the world's leading Irish fiddlers, arrived in the early 1990s and performs often with Trail Band guitarist and songwriter Cal Scott, a fixture on the city music scene since the 1960s. An old time scene featuring ensembles such as Foghorn Stringband and Jackstraw has proved durable, and Portland has attracted important "newgrass" players like fiddler Darol Anger and banjo master Tony Furtado. That music finds a home at nearby outdoor festivals such as the annual summer Pickathon and Northwest String Summit.

The city's blues scene, which has featured current or former Portlanders such as Robert Cray and Curtis Salgado, convenes at each summer's Waterfront Blues Festival (founded 1987).

Portland world music ensembles include the Japanese dance-percussion Portland Taiko, Middle Eastern ensemble Al-Andalus, Venerable Showers of Beauty Javanese gamelan, Afrobeat bands such as Jujuba, traditional marimba groups, and more. Ghanaian drum master and music professor Obo Addy, who arrived in 1978, performed and taught in Portland until his death in 2012. Eastern European influences pervade popular fusion bands such as 3 Leg Torso (co-led by Lajos Balogh's son Bela) and Krebsic Orkestar. The Rasika and Kalakendra presenting organizations bring top Indian music performers to the city.

The public-school system once offered an excellent program in music performance, especially from 1947 to 1954 under the direction of Karl Ernst. A subsequent reduction of public-school music instruction has been partly offset by the activities of the Community Music Center (founded 1955), operated by the Portland Park Bureau. Private music schools included the Oregon Conservatory (1898–1932, 1945–54) and the Ellison-White Conservatory (later the Portland School of Music; 1918–59), but the city no longer has an independent music conservatory. Portland houses many institutions of higher education that offer undergraduate curricula in music, music education, composition, theory, and performance: Lewis and Clark College (founded in 1867, moved to Portland in 1942), the University of Portland (founded 1901), Reed College (1908), Concordia University (1905), Marylhurst College (1930), Portland State University (1946), and Mount Hood Community College (1966), which has a nationally recognized jazz curriculum. These schools also provide a home for some of the city's top musicians, and sponsor some of its most important concerts and student, faculty, and community performing groups.

BIBLIOGRAPHY
J. MacQueen: Pioneer Music of the Oregon Country (MS, 1935)
J. MacQueen: "Music in Portland," Oregon, End of the Trail, ed. Federal Writers Project (Portland, OR, 1940), 123–27
S.A. Smith: "Portland: The Musical Capital of the Northwest," University of Portland Bookman, vii/1 (1955) [extract]
D.M. Olsen and C.M. Will: "Musical Heritage of the Aurora Colony," Oregon Historical Quarterly, lxxix/3 (1978), 233–67
M.J. Harold: Music in the Oregon Province, 1859 to 1981 (Marylhurst, OR, 1982)
R. Dietsche: Jumptown: The Golden Years of Portland Jazz, 1942–1957 (Portland, OR, 2005)
M. Moscato, ed.: Northwest Passage: 50 Years of Independent Music from the Rose City (Portland, OR, 2010)
DOUGLAS LEEDY/BRETT CAMPBELL

Portman, Rachel (Mary Berkeley) (*b* Haslemere, England, 11 Dec 1960). English composer. She studied music at Worcester College, Oxford, and composition with Roger Steptoe; she also composed for productions at the Oxford Playhouse and scored a student film, *Privileged*, which was sold to the BBC. Her first professional film scoring commission came from David Puttnam in 1982 with *Experience Preferred…But Not Essential*. Her early television scores included *The Storyteller* (1986–8 and 1990), a series by Jim Henson, for which she was awarded the British Film Institute's Young Composer of the Year Award in 1988. In 1991 she composed for Mike Leigh's *Life is Sweet* (1990), her first feature film score. Since 1992 she has been in demand for Hollywood productions, and remains one of the few female composers to have achieved significant success at this level. With *Emma* (1996) she became the first female composer to receive an Academy Award.

Her film scores embrace a variety of styles, although she is best known for composing clear, string-dominated textures, often shaded with lyrical woodwind lines. She orchestrates much of her own music, but also works closely with orchestrator Jeff Atmajian. Although Portman gained renown as a composer for romantic comedies, her versatility is reflected in the many genres she has explored since the late 1990s, which range from serious drama to psychological thriller. In particular, she has collaborated with Lasse Hallström on *Cider House Rules* (1999) and *Chocolat* (2000), the scores of which were nominated for Academy Awards. Her scores for director Jonathan Demme's *Beloved* (1998) and *Manchurian Candidate* (2004) are especially striking; both scores depart from her more familiar orchestral sound. In particular, *Beloved* features solo voice, chorus, and African instruments instead of full orchestra. In 2003 her opera *The Little Prince* premiered at the Houston Grand Opera and has since been performed throughout the United States and recorded under the auspices of the BBC. Based on Antoine de Saint-Exupéry's novel of the same name, Portman's *The Little Prince* is one of relatively few operas intended for both children and adults. Characterized by cleanly etched vocal lines for boy soprano and lively children's choruses, the opera represents the composer's most ambitious work.

WORKS

FILM AND TELEVISION SCORES

Privileged, 1982; Experience Preferred...But Not Essential, 1982; The Storyteller, 1986–8, 1990; Oranges Are Not the Only Fruit, 1990; Life is Sweet, 1990; Antonia and Jane, 1991; Where Angels Fear to Tread, 1991; Used People, 1992; The Joy Luck Club, 1993; Benny and Joon, 1993; Friends, 1993; Ethan Frome, 1993; Sirens, 1994; Only You, 1994; War of the Buttons, 1994; A Pyromaniac's Love Story, 1995; Smoke, 1995; To Wong Foo, Thanks for Everything! Julie Newmar, 1995; The Adventures of Pinocchio, 1996; Marvin's Room, 1996; Emma, 1996; Addicted to Love, 1997; Beloved, 1998; The Other Sister, 1999; Ratcatcher, 1999; The Cider House Rules, 1999; The Legend of Bagger Vance, 2000; Chocolat, 2000; The Emperor's New Clothes, 2001; Hart's War, 2002; The Truth about Charlie, 2002; The Human Stain, 2003; Mona Lisa Smile, 2003; Lard, 2004; The Manchurian Candidate, 2004; Because of Winn-Dixie, 2005; Oliver Twist, 2005; The Lake House, 2006; Infamous, 2006; The Duchess, 2008; Grey Gardens, 2009; Never Let Me Go, 2010; Snow Flower and the Secret Fan, 2011

OPERA

The Little Prince (N. Wright), Houston, Houston Grand Opera, 31 May 2003

BIBLIOGRAPHY

H. Lumme: *Great Women of Film* (New York, 2002), 100–103
S. Kennedy: "A Night at the Opera: Rachel Portman Takes on Her First Concert Work, Saint-Exupéry's *The Little Prince*," *Film Score Monthly*, viii/6 (2003), 14–16

L.M. Timm: *The Soul of Cinema: An Appreciation of Film Music* (Upper Saddle River, NJ, 2003)
F. Karlin and R. Wright: *On the Track: A Guide to Contemporary Film Scoring* (New York, 1990, 2/2004)
C. DesJardins: *Inside Film Music: Composers Speak* (Los Angeles, 2006), 196–204

DAVID KERSHAW/NATHAN PLATTE

Portuguese American music. *See* EUROPEAN AMERICAN MUSIC.

Posselt, Ruth (*b* Medford, MA, 6 Sept 1911; *d* Gulfport, FL, 19 Feb 2007). Violinist. She studied with Emanuel Ondricek (1919–29) and made her debut appearances at Carnegie Hall and Boston's Symphony Hall at the age of 11. She continued to play frequently in Boston and made an appearance with Walter Damrosch and the New York PO when she was 17. After winning the Schubert Memorial Prize in 1929, she toured the United States and then went to France, where she studied with Jacques Thibauld. In 1932 she made her European debut in Paris; two years later she became the first American female violinist to tour the USSR. She first appeared with the Boston SO in 1935, performing the Tchaikovsky concerto under conductor Serge Koussevitsky. For the next 25 years Posselt was a regular soloist with the orchestra, premiering concertos by Walter Piston, Samuel Barber, Vladimir Dukelsky (Vernon Duke), and Edward Burlingame Hill. She also gave first performances of works by Henriette Bosmans, Paul Hindemith, Ernest Bloch, Aram Khachaturian, and Luigi Dallapiccola as well as world premieres of Aaron Copland's Violin Sonata, Bohuslav Martinů's Duo, and David Stanley Smith's Requiem. Posselt continued to tour nationally and internationally as a soloist and chamber music player, founding the Bell'Arte Trio (with the violist Joseph di Pasquale and the cellist Samuel Mayes) and participating in the revival of early music that began in Boston in the early 1950s. From 1963 to 1979 she taught at Florida State University, where she became professor of violin (1972) as well as a member of the Florestan Quartet. Nearly 30 recordings document her powerful tone, solid technique, authoritative style, and ability to realize demanding new works.

RICHARD DYER/ANYA LAURENCE

Post, Mike [Postil, Leland M.] (*b* Los Angeles, CA, 29 Sept 1944). Composer. Post grew up in the San Fernando Valley and, after high school, became a session musician for popular artists (he played guitar on Sonny and Cher's 1965 hit "I got you Babe"). In his early 20s he became an arranger and producer of pop material, including the First Edition (which catapulted Kenny Rogers to fame) and Mason Williams's "Classical Gas" (which earned Post a 1968 Grammy award).

In 1969 Post became musical director on *The Andy Williams Show*, the youngest person to hold such a post in the history of television variety shows. The year before he had befriended trombonist and arranger Pete Carpenter, then in his mid-50s, who possessed years of experience composing and orchestrating for television. The two launched a partnership writing dramatic underscores; their first series was *Toma* in 1973, one of several collaborations with producer Stephen J. Cannell over the next two decades.

"Music by Mike Post and Pete Carpenter" became a familiar television credit in the 1970s and 80s. They brought more contemporary sounds, including electric guitar, synthesizers, and backbeat, to the otherwise staid, traditional orchestral approach for most TV series. Their themes were also radio-friendly, generating pop hits for shows including *The Rockford Files*, *The Greatest American Hero*, and *Magnum, P.I.* Carpenter—with whom Post also scored *The White Shadow*, *The A-Team*, and *Hunter*—died in 1987, after scoring an estimated 1800 hours of television with Post.

On his own, Post enjoyed continued success with several Steven Bochco–produced series from the 1980s and 90s including *Hill Street Blues*, *Doogie Howser M.D.*, *L.A. Law*, *NYPD Blue*, and *Murder One* (the last of which won Post an Emmy). He also scored all of the *Law & Order* series beginning in 1990, creating a familiar transitional device often referred to as the "chung-chung," a musical sound effect similar to a jail cell slamming shut.

WORKS
(selective list)

Television series scores (with Pete Carpenter): *Toma*, 1973; *The Rockford Files*, 1974; *Baa Baa Black Sheep* (later *Black Sheep Squadron*), 1976; *Richie Brockelman, Private Eye*, 1978; *The White Shadow*, 1978; *The Duke*, 1979; *Tenspeed and Brown Shoe*, 1980; *Magnum, P.I.*, 1980; *The Greatest American Hero*, 1981; *Tales of the Gold Monkey*, 1982; *The A-Team*, 1983; *Hardcastle & McCormick*, 1983; *Riptide*, 1984; *Hunter*, 1984; *Stingray*, 1986. (Post co-wrote the themes for *Richie Brockelman*, *The Greatest American Hero*, *Hardcastle & McCormick*, *Blossom* and others with lyricist Stephen Geyer.)

Television movie scores (with Carpenter): *Two on a Bench*, 1971; *Gidget Gets Married*, 1972; *The Morning After*, 1974; *The Invasion of Johnson County*, 1976; *Coach of the Year*, 1980; *Will, G. Gordon Liddy*, 1982; *Hard Knox*, 1984

Television series scores (Post alone): *Hill Street Blues*, 1981; *Bay City Blues*, 1983; *L.A. Law*, 1986; *Hooperman*, 1987; *Wiseguy*, 1987; *Unsub*, 1989; *Quantum Leap*, 1989; *B.L. Stryker*, 1989; *Doogie Howser, M.D.*, 1989; *Law & Order*, 1990; *Silk Stalkings*, 1991; *The Commish*, 1991; *NYPD Blue*, 1993; *Murder One*, 1995; *Brooklyn South*, 1997; *Law & Order: Special Victims Unit*, 1999; *Law & Order: Criminal Intent*, 2001; *L.A. Dragnet*, 2003; *Law & Order: Trial by Jury*, 2005

Television movie scores (Post alone): *Adam*, 1983; *Heart of a Champion: The Ray Mancini Story*, 1985; *The Ryan White Story*, 1989; *Nashville Beat*, 1989; *Unspeakable Acts*, 1990; *Without Her Consent*, 1990; *The Gin Game*, 2003

Film scores: *Rabbit Test* (with Carpenter), 1978; *Deep in the Heart*, 1984; *The River Rat*, 1984; *Hadley's Rebellion*, 1987

BIBLIOGRAPHY

J. Burlingame: "Mike Post: He Makes TV Sound the Way It Sounds," *Washington Post* (TV Week, 24 July 1994), BD6–7, 41, 44

J. Burlingame: *TV's Biggest Hits: the Story of Television Themes from "Dragnet" to "Friends"* (New York, 1996)

E. Fink: "Episodic's Music Man: Mike Post," *Journal of Popular Film and Television*, xxv/4 (1998), 155–60

JON BURLINGAME

Postbop. Term that loosely refers to a body of music that emerged in the late 1950s and 60s that combined principles of bop, hard bop, modal jazz, and free jazz. Much of this music maintained standard bop and hard bop elements, including a "head—solos—head" format and accompanimental textures such as walking bass. But the music also departed from earlier traditions in the following ways: a slower harmonic rhythm characteristic of modal jazz, techniques for playing "inside" and "outside" the underlying harmonic structure, an interactive (or conversational) approach to rhythm section accompaniment, unusual harmonic progressions, use of harmonic or metric superimposition, unusual underlying formal designs for head statements and chorus structure improvisation, or the abandonment entirely of underlying chorus structure beneath improvisation. The recordings of the Ornette Coleman Quartet (*The Shape of Jazz to Come*, 1959), Miles Davis Sextet (*Kind of Blue*, 1959), Bill Evans Trio (*Portrait in Jazz*, 1959), the John Coltrane Quartet (*Live at the Village Vanguard*, 1961), and Eric Dolphy (*Far Cry*, 1961) are significant in that they maintain some inherited conventions of small group improvisation while enriching those conventions by establishing a degree of contact with the emerging free jazz movement. For many of these artists the notion of openness became a significant aesthetic principle.

The recordings of Miles Davis's "second classic quintet" of 1963–8 may be regarded as particularly important postbop documents. Their live performances of jazz standards developed a high degree of sophistication in harmonic and metric superimposition (even while frequently maintaining the underlying chorus structure). Improvisations on their studio recordings ("Orbits," *Miles Smiles*, 1966) often exhibit a technique known as "time, no changes," in which the rhythm section maintains walking bass and swing 4/4 accompanimental textures while abandoning the underlying chorus structure, harmonic progression, and form stated during the head. Further, on the trumpet solo to "Dolores" (*Miles Smiles*, 1966), bassist Ron Carter provides walking bass accompaniment that maintains the underlying 8 + 6 + 8 measure formal organization heard during the head, while Miles Davis organizes his solo in an 8 + 8 + 8 bar underlying form.

All of this suggests that distinctions between free and more traditional jazz idioms are frequently not particularly crisp, and that both approaches influenced compositional and improvisational solutions. Many of the innovations forged by these players remain fundamental to small group improvisation today.

BIBLIOGRAPHY

E. Jost: *Free Jazz* (Graz, Austria, 1974, repr. New York, 1994)

L. Porter: *John Coltrane: His Life and Music* (Ann Arbor, MI, 1997)

A. Kahn: *Kind of Blue: the Making of the Miles Davis Masterpiece* (New York, 2000)

J. Yudkin: *Miles Davis, Miles Smiles, and the Invention of Postbop* (Bloomington, IN, 2007)

K. Waters: *The Studio Recordings of the Miles Davis Quintet, 1965–68* (New York and Oxford, 2011)

KEITH WATERS

Postmodern dance. A short-lived dance movement of the 1960s and 1970s, growing out of modern dance and yielding to various forms of contemporary dance. Associated primarily with New York's Judson dance theater, postmodern dance focused more on the intellectual process of creating dance than the end result.

CLAUDE CONYERS

Postmodernism. A term carrying diverse and sometimes contradictory meanings, used to describe aesthetic tendencies as well as critical approaches beginning in the 1970s. There is considerable debate over whether its parameters are chronological or philosophical, and concerning the nature of its relationship with modernism.

Many have posited postmodernism as chronologically defined, resulting from disintegration of cultural paradigms established during a "modernist" era or socioeconomic condition variously defined as beginning sometime between the 15th and 17th centuries and ending at some point in the mid-20th century (Jameson, 1991). These paradigms include imperial expansion and centralization, meta-narratives of progress and enlightenment within European (and implicitly masculine) authority, and concerns with authorial originality within what has been characterized as an "anxiety of influence." In this sense postmodernity is marked by a breakdown of authority and orthodoxy, and a realization that multiplicity of voices and perspectives provides a more legitimate reflection of cultural realities (Jencks, 1986).

In stylistic terms, some have characterized postmodernism as prioritizing discontinuity and rupture over ideals of logic and completeness (Harvey, 1990); in this sense elements of the aesthetic can be seen to preexist a mid-20th-century chronological split, observed not only in the early 20th-century work of Duchamp and others in the Dada/Surrealist movements and the Italian futurists but also in the long tradition of quotation and "pasticcio" in various musical repertories. Indeed, some scholars (e.g., Kramer, 2002) have suggested that postmodernism is best understood as an aesthetic principle that is present in conjunction and opposition with modernism through several centuries of the Western musical tradition. In this sense, postmodernism is characterized by rejection of formal unity, positing other strategies of expressive coherence.

Some scholars (e.g., Hamm, 1997) have pointed to John Cage's experiments with aleatoric processes and audience-determined sound production in the early 1950s as an important milestone in the rejection of modernist unity and compositional control. Certainly subsequent experimentation in the third quarter of the 20th century by process-focused groups such as Fluxus, as well as Pauline Oliveros's "sonic meditations" and her ideas about "deep listening," were designed to posit creative overlap among composer, performer, and community. These approaches resonate with literary definitions of postmodernism that emphasize the importance of the reader in shaping the meaning of the creative work.

Another stylistic element that has also been called postmodern is a rejection of intellectual complexity in favor of increased accessibility. The variety of ways the notion of "accessible" has been framed can lead to the inclusion of vastly different approaches, and has encouraged critics to attempt to distinguish between various strands of postmodernism. Composers' "return" to tonality (whether explicit and rhetorical, as in the case of David Del Tredici, or more nuanced within a redefinition of parameters of consonance, as in the work of

John Corigliano or Ellen Taaffe Zwilich) has been characterized as a "postmodernism of reaction," a neoconservative turn in response to the sonic challenge of modernist dissonance (Foster, 1983). A second strand, called by some "radical postmodernism" (Kramer, 2002) or a "postmodernism of resistance" (Foster, 1983) has been characterized as providing a critique rather than an embrace of tonal and formal convention through the use of irony or defamiliarization. The repetitive patterns and pointedly nonteleological nature of process-based music by composers such as Terry Riley, Steve Reich, and Philip Glass, for instance, might be seen to bring into question the "master narratives" of functional harmony without rejecting its triadic sonorities. Along these lines, some of John Adams's work (e.g., his *Chamber Symphony*) juxtaposes elements of "high" and "low" culture with the effect of destabilizing the hierarchical opposition.

In order to transcend this binary opposition, Jann Pasler has suggested a third stylistic strand of postmodernism, "connection or interpenetration" (Pasler, 2008), which reflects neither an embrace nor a rejection of traditional narratives, but rather an awareness of their contingency and a "playfulness" with the collisions that can result through the juxtaposition of contrasting expressive resources. Pasler specifically cites the work of Cage and Oliveros as representative of this approach; an additional example of a contemporary American composer who can be seen as working within this model of postmodernism is Gabriela Ortiz, whose string quartet *Altar de Muertos* draws from both modernist and folk-Mexican elements in order to evoke what she has described as "chaos and the richness of multiple symbols."

Since postmodernism is also grounded in critical discourse, many have also seen it as an outcome of increased awareness of difference: in this sense, a postmodern critique of culture questions the power of Euro/North American institutional hegemonies (rightly or wrongly associated with modernism) to gloss over important diversities of experience and value grounded in gender, race, class, and/or geography. Postmodern scholarship on music thus seeks to avoid universalizing approaches, attempting to validate subaltern voices that speak to specificity of place or personal expression (Slobin, 1993; Lipsitz, 1994; Hisama, 2004). Some scholars have thus seen the potential for postmodernism as a resource for migrants and other displaced populations: for example, Coulombe (2002) has discussed the uneasy overlaps between postmodern and postcolonial issues in diasporic musical traditions. Beyond aesthetic considerations, Taylor (2002) has argued that postmodernism can be a marketing strategy rather than a true cultural shift, seeing this approach in the self-identification of composers such as Rouse and Jarvinen, who still subscribe to modernist notions of redemption of "popular" cultural elements through high-art processes. And while some have seen the juxtaposition of "serious" and "popular" styles as a feature of postmodernism that blurs or erodes boundaries between high and low cultures, Brackett (2002) has observed that systems of musical sponsorship, production, and marketing have maintained stable divisions established by an essentially modernist cultural frame despite occasional experimentation with "crossover."

While the chronological aspect of postmodernism may be less relevant to an application of the concept to diasporic traditions, since migrants have always built their musics though cross-cultural juxtaposition, the mobility and heterogeneity of North American populations has proven fertile ground for combination of vernacular musical styles. The media saturation of selected aspects of "high culture" has also facilitated appropriation by vernacular traditions. Brackett (2002) has placed the work of such artists as Beck and Björk, which builds on discontinuity and irony, as a postmodernist rhetorical opposition to the more modernist "authenticity" of pre-1970s rock. Stewart has sought to define a musical "Afro-postmodernism" that is deployed by hip-hop artists such as DJ Spooky as "an aesthetic strategy within polyculturalism that acknowledges the continuities between hip hop and earlier Afrological forms…while at the same time emphasizing the central role that hip hop cultures play in the contemporary postmodern, polycultural landscape" (2010, 340). While Stewart embraces the notion of postmodernity as inherently suitable to the cultural diversity of hip-hop, Madrid considers the label "postmodern" problematic in the context of Latino border musics such as Nor-Tec, characterizing it as reflecting an Euro-American condition, preferring to see such postcolonial repertories as expressing a "radical phase of modernity" that reappropriates modernist notions of technology towards utopian ideals, desiring "a modern condition that modernity itself fails to provide" (2008, 22).

The creative role of the performer, emphasized by various aspects of process-based postmodernism, has also been important through the rise of ensembles that reflect "postmodernisms of connection/interpenetration" through their programming choices. The Kronos Quartet is probably the most prominent and storied: since its establishment in 1973, it has gained both cultural prestige and significant market share through its pointed eclecticism, which has included substantial commissions of new works as well as recordings of canonic standards, and arrangements of vernacular repertories and various international traditions (Bennett, 2005), though some argue that the ensemble's approach is a continuation of modernist ideals about the role of the string quartet (Headlam, 2000). The Kronos Quartet and its activities represent an interesting study of the possible intersection of several of the different strands of postmodernism discussed above—including issues of marketing and self-presentation, engagement with audience response, and parallel presence of rejection and embracing of elements of the modernist preoccupation with "high culture."

BIBLIOGRAPHY

GMO (Pasler) [including further bibliography]

J. Cage: *Silence* (Middletown, CT, 1961)

H. Foster, ed.: *The Anti-Aesthetic: Essays on Postmodern Culture* (Port Townsend, WA, 1983)

A. Huyssen: *After the Great Divide: Modernism, Mass Culture, Postmodernism* (Bloomington, IN, 1986)

C. Jencks: *What is Post-Modernism?* (London, 1986)

R. Carl: "Six Case Studies in New American Music: a Postmodern Portrait Gallery," *College Music Symposium*, xxx/1 (1990), 45–63

D. Harvey: *The Condition of Postmodernity* (Oxford and Cambridge, MA, 1990)

F. Jameson: *Postmodernism, or the Cultural Logic of Late Capitalism* (London, 1991)

M. Slobin: *Subcultural Sounds: Micromusics of the West* (Middletown, CT, 1993)

G. Lipsitz: *Dangerous Crossroads: Popular Music, Postmodernism, and the Poetics of Place* (London, 1994)

K. McNeilly: "Ugly Beauty: John Zorn and the Politics of Postmodern Music," *Postmodern Culture*, v/2 (1994–5)

C. Hamm: "Privileging the Moment: Cage, Jung, Synchronicity, Postmodernism," *Journal of Musicology*, xv/2 (1997), 278–89

D. Headlam: "Re-Drawing Boundaries: the Kronos Quartet," *CMR*, xix/1 (2000), 113–40

J. Kramer: "The Nature and Origins of Musical Postmodernism," *Postmodern Music/Postmodern Thought*, ed. J. Lochhead and J. Auner (New York, 2002), 13–26

T. Taylor: "Music and Musical Practices in Postmodernity," *Postmodern Music/Postmodern Thought*, ed. J. Lochhead and J. Auner (New York, 2002), 93–118

R. Coulombe: "Postmodern Polyamory or Postcolonial Challenge? Cornershop's Dialogues from West, to East, to West," *Postmodern Music/Postmodern Thought*, ed. J. Lochhead and J. Auner (New York, 2002), 177–93

D. Brackett: "'Where's It At': Postmodern Theory and the Contemporary Musical Field," *Postmodern Music/Postmodern Thought*, ed. J. Lochhead and J. Auner (New York, 2002), 207–31

E. Hisama: "John Zorn and the Postmodern Condition," *Locating East Asia in Western Art Music*, ed. Y.U. Everett and F. Lau (Middletown, CT, 2004), 72–84

A. Dell'Antonio, ed.: *Beyond Structural Listening? Postmodern Modes of Hearing* (Berkeley, 2004)

D. Bennett: "Postmodern Eclecticism and the World Music Debate: the Politics of the Kronos Quartet," *Context*, xxix–xxx (2005), 5–15

A. Madrid: *Nor-Tec Rifa! Electronic Dance Music from Tijuana to the World* (New York, 2008)

J. Pasler: "Postmodernism, Narrativity, and the Art of Memory," *Writing Through Music: Essays on Music, Culture, and Politics* (New York, 2008), 49–81

J. Stewart: "DJ Spooky and the Politics of Afro-Postmodernism," *Black Music Research Journal*, xxx/2 (2010), 337–62

ANDREW DELL'ANTONIO

Poulton, George (*b* Cricklade, England, 1828; *d* Lansingburgh, NY, 17 Oct 1867). Composer, performer, and music teacher of English birth. Best known for penning the song "Aura Lea." Poulton emigrated at the age of seven from England to the United States with his parents. As an adult, he moved to Rochester, where he taught at a series of music schools. In 1859, however, he was fired from the Fort Edward Academy for imprudent behavior. Local newspapers reported that Poulton, already married, eloped with a student at the school, with her brother and friends in hot pursuit. Poulton was tarred and feathered at the hands of vigilante justice. "Aura Lea" was published in 1861, and remained popular through the Civil War. The song has also survived in various adaptations, including West Point's "Army Blue" (1865) and Elvis Presley's "Love me tender" (1956). Other publications include a number of songs, like "Johnny Darling," an answer to the popular "Katy Darling," and piano music, the most well-known of which was his piano setting of the hymn tune "Old Hundred" with variations. Poulton died at his parents' Lansingburgh home. The cause of death was listed as influenza.

SARAH GERK

Pound, Ezra (Loomis) (*b* Hailey, ID, 30 Oct 1885; *d* Venice, Italy, 1 Nov 1972). Poet and amateur composer. His musical achievements include an unorthodox *Treatise on Harmony*, a body of criticism, a role in the revival of older music, and, most notably, music for two "operas," *The Testament of François Villon* (1923) and *Cavalcanti* (1932). As a student Pound formed his taste on the Provençal troubadours, with their ideal union of composer and poet. Acquaintance with Arnold Dolmetsch deepened his love for early music, while other friendships broadened his experience. In 1913 the pianist Walter Rummel and Pound published arrangements of nine troubadour songs. From this unorthodox base, Pound, as "William Atheling," reviewed London concerts from 1917 to 1920 in the *New Age*, attacking current repertory and performance practice. In the 1930s local concerts sponsored by Pound in Rapallo formed a model for the 1939 Settimana Vivaldiana at Siena, which helped to establish Vivaldi's modern reputation.

Le Testament de François Villon, composed with help from George Antheil, illustrates Pound's theories of song, combining troubadour monody with rhythmic notation intended to reproduce asymmetrical word rhythms with scientific precision. Such complex meters as 7/16 or 19/32 are frequent. Harmony is minimal, instrumentation pointillist, dialogue perfunctory, staging stylized, the performer's personality effaced—all operatic resources are subordinated to the rhythmic-melodic verse line. Richard Taruskin has called *Villon* "a modernist triumph," Pound's "claim to musical immortality" (*New York Times*, 27 July 2003). Pound also produced a second version of *Villon* with simplified notation. First performed in 1926, the work has been produced twice by the BBC, staged by Robert Hughes at the Western Opera Theatre (1971), recorded by Fantasy Records of Berkeley, California (1972), and performed a number of times since. *Cavalcanti*, a similar work, was first performed by Hughes in 1983. A third opera on texts of Catullus and Sappho was left unfinished. A CD with excerpts from all three operas was produced by Other Minds, San Francisco, in 2003.

Pound's *Treatise on Harmony*, in his *Antheil and the Treatise on Harmony* (Paris, 1924, 2/1927/*R*), is a somewhat obscure attempt to substitute rhythmic organization for textbook harmony or the vertical sonorities of impressionism. Best understood against the background of Antheil's *Ballet mécanique*, Stravinsky's music of the 1920s, and the general revolt against tonality, it is one of the earliest attempts to theorize about music purely as an arrangement of *objets sonores*. Pound's complete music criticism was edited in 1977 by R. Murray Schafer.

Since 2002, Pound's music has entered a new era with the first publication of the scores, edited by Robert Hughes and Margaret Fisher. *Cavalcanti* was first to appear in 2002, followed by the violin compositions (2004) and the extant portions of an unfinished third opera (2005), and finally Pound's simplified version of *Le Testament* in 2008, which the editors believe to represent the composer's authorized version. When Antheil's original notation of *Le Testament* is released in

the near future, it will finally make all of Pound's music available for examination and performance.

Settings of Pound's poetry are not numerous. Among the early works are some songs by Rummel and male choruses by Granville Bantock. Jacob Avshalomov, Gordon Binkerd, and Copland have also composed choral settings. More recent compositions include those by Luciano Berio (*Laborintus II*), Elisabeth Lutyens, and David Wooldridge.

BIBLIOGRAPHY
GroveA; *Grove7* (S.J. Adams)

R. Merritt: *Early Music and the Aesthetics of Ezra Pound: Hush of Older Song.* (Lewiston, NY, 1993)

S.J. Adams: "Pound in the Theater: the Background of Pound's Operas," *Literary Modernism and Occult Tradition*, ed. L Surette and D. Tryphonopoulos (Orono, ME, 1996)

C. Mundye: *Ezra Pound's Operas: an Analytical and Contextual Study* (diss., U. of York, 1999)

Michael Ingham: "Pound and Music," *Cambridge Companion to Ezra Pound*, ed. Ira Nadel (Cambridge, 1999)

D. Albright: *Untwisting the Serpent: Modernism in Music, Literature, and Other Arts* (Chicago, 2000)

A. Conover: *Olga Rudge & Ezra Pound: "What Thou Lovest Well..."* (New Haven, CT, 2001)

B. Bucknell: *Literary Modernism and Musical Aesthetics* (Cambridge, 2001)

M Fisher: *Ezra Pound's Radio Operas: The BBC Experiments, 1931–1933.* (Cambridge, 2002)

R. Hughes and M. Fisher: *Cavalcanti: A Perspective on the Music of Ezra Pound* (Emeryville, CA, 2003)

M. Fisher: "Great Bass: Undertones of Continuous Influence," *Performance Research*, viii/i (2003), 23

R. Hughes and M. Fisher: *Complete Violin Works of Ezra Pound*, (Emeryville, CA, 2004)

M. Fisher: *The Recovery of Ezra Pound's 3rd Opera "Collis O Heliconii."* (Emeryville, CA, 2005)

C. Timbrell: *Prince of Virtuosos: a Life of Walter Rummel, American Pianist* (Lanham, MD, 2005)

M. Fisher: "The Music of Ezra Pound: a Facsimile Edition of Ezra Pound's Modernist Opera Le Testament in the Beinecke Library," *Yale University Library Gazette*, no.80 (2006), 139

M. Fisher and R. Hughes: *Le Testament: Paroles de Villon* (Emeryville, CA, 2008)

STEPHEN J. ADAMS

Powell, Ardal (*b* 22 April 1958, Bournemouth, England). Flute maker, musicologist, and publisher, of British birth; co-founder of FOLKERS & POWELL.

Powell, Bud [Earl] (*b* New York, NY, 27 Sept 1924; *d* New York, NY, 31 July 1966). Jazz pianist. Earl "Bud" Powell was born into a musical family in Harlem, New York, and rose to become one of the most important pianists in the modern jazz idiom, Bebop, a style that coalesced in the early 1940s. He began studying classical piano at the age of six, and was also tutored by his father, William Powell Sr., a stride pianist who worked as a building superintendent in Harlem. According to his father, the younger Powell could by the age of ten reproduce jazz recordings with ease, including the work of pianists Art Tatum and Fats Waller. His childhood musical experiences also included singing in the St. Charles Roman Catholic Church as well as playing the organ at its services and playing for teenage dances. Together with his boyhood friend, pianist Elmo Hope, Powell would listen to both classical and jazz recordings with equal enthusiasm. By the late 1930s Powell came under the influence of pianist Billy Kyle whose work with the John Kirby Sextet inspired the young pianist to mix his classical and jazz interests, as did Kirby. Although he continued to aspire to become a concert pianist as a teenager, the world of popular music became the realm in which his reputation would prosper. He dropped out of high school at age 15 to become a working musician, taking a variety of jobs throughout the New York City metropolitan area.

Sometime in the early 1940s Powell began to secure professional connections that would circulate news of his talents and ultimately provide opportunities to record. Among the most important would be pianist Thelonious Monk, whom he met in an uptown bar. Monk's influence would soon be felt profoundly on Powell and throughout an inner circle of musicians who were collectively and individually developing bebop, a demanding idiom of jazz in which each would be considered central figures on the piano. Powell's first major job in which he recorded and toured was with the well-known trumpeter Cootie Williams. Powell's recordings with Williams reveal a pianist comfortable in the language of swing but also pushing at edges of it with gestures of chromaticism, florid eighth- and 16th-note runs, harmonic expansion, and rhythmic complexity. It was during his tenure with Williams that Powell sustained a brutal head injury from police in Philadelphia who charged him with disorderly conduct. Shortly thereafter Powell endured the first of many institutionalizations in mental hospitals to treat his series of breakdowns that may have been a form of schizophrenia, which was exacerbated by alcohol and drug abuse. When Powell recorded his first album as a leader in January 1947, he had securely in place the mature bebop style to which generations of subsequent pianists would aspire: rapid right-hand virtuoso passages constructed of ingenious uses of dissonance, left-hand punctuations of 3rds, 5ths, and 7ths, and a rich and varied rhythmic schemata. Between institutionalizations during the 1950s he performed and recorded with checkered results as some of his work failed to live up to the artistic brilliance of his earlier music. In 1959 Powell moved to Paris where he toured, held residences in clubs, and recorded until his much heralded return in 1964.

Throughout his career Powell recorded with small groups that included horn players but he seemed most at home in the trio setting wherein his singular voice shined. In addition to his numerous recordings of the music of others, throughout his career Powell contributed highly original compositions to jazz literature, including "Hallucinations," "Tempus Fugue-it," "Webb City," "Glass Enclosure," "Celia," and his most well-known piece, "Un Poco Loco."

RECORDINGS
(selective list)

The Complete Bud Powell on Verve, PolyGram Records (1994); *Bud Powell: The Complete Blue Note and Roost Recordings*, Blue Note (1994)

BIBLIOGRAPHY

"Requiescat in Pace: Bud Powell—1924–66," *DB* (8 Sept 1966), 13

F. Paudras: liner notes, *Earl Bud Powell: Early Years of a Genius, 1944–1948*, Mythic Sound, 1989

A. Groves and A. Shipton: *The Glass Enclosure: the Life of Bud Powell* (Oxford and New York, 1993)

G. Giddins: liner notes, *The Genius of Bud Powell*, Verve, 1950 (reissued with Giddins' notes in 1993)

C. Smith: *Bouncing with Bud: All the Recordings of Bud Powell* (Brunswick, ME, 1997)

F. Paudras: *Dance of the Infidels: a Portrait of Bud Powell* (New York, [1986] 1998)

G. Ramsey: *The Amazing Bud Powell: Black Genius, Jazz History and the Challenge of Bebop* (Berkeley, CA, 2013)

GUTHRIE P. RAMSEY JR.

Powell, Dick [Richard Ewing] (*b* Mountain View, AR, 14 Nov 1904; *d* Los Angeles, CA, 2 Jan 1963). Actor and singer. A popular singer and bandleader, he became known as the perennial boyish and energetic star of numerous backstage musical films for Warner Bros. during the 1930s. He made his film debut playing a bandleading singer in *Blessed Event* (1932). He established himself playing the juvenile lead opposite the dancer Ruby Keeler in a string of films which included *42nd Street, Footlight Parade*, and *Gold Diggers of 1933* (all 1933). Other films included *Dames* (1934), *Gold Diggers of 1935* (1935), *Thanks a Million* (1935), *Gold Diggers of 1937* (1936), *On the Avenue* (1937), *Varsity Show* (1937), *Hollywood Hotel* (1938), and *Star Spangled Rhythm* (1942). He married his fellow singing actor JUNE ALLYSON in 1945. Powell later eschewed his clean-cut image and began to aspire to non-singing dramatic roles such as those he played in *Murder, my Sweet* (1944) and *The Bad and the Beautiful* (1952). He directed several films as well, but it is as the energetic wide-eyed dancer of the 1930s that Powell is best remembered. He had a fine clear tenor voice; with an instrument of moderate volume, Powell nonetheless possessed a technique which enabled him to be heard in a variety of musical venues with a solid sound and impeccable intonation.

WILLIAM A. EVERETT, LEE SNOOK

Powell, Edward (B.) (*b* Savanna, IL, 5 Dec 1909; *d* Los Angeles, CA, 29 Feb 1984). Orchestrator, arranger, composer, and conductor. As a teenager, he played alto saxophone in a St. Louis high school orchestra. His dissatisfaction with published dance band arrangements led him to write his own and eventually brought him to the attention of Fletcher Henderson in New York. Once there, Powell worked as a staff arranger at music publisher Harms from 1930 to 1934, orchestrating Broadway musical comedies, notably George and Ira Gershwin's *Let 'em Eat Cake*. Largely self-taught, he studied harmony and counterpoint with MORTIMER WILSON and JOSEPH SCHILLINGER, later taking up musical analysis with ARNOLD SCHOENBERG in Los Angeles. His petition for bankruptcy in 1933 may have prompted his relocation to Hollywood the following year. His long association with Alfred Newman began at Samuel Goldwyn Productions, where Powell was under contract from 1934 to 1939. At Goldwyn, drawing on his Broadway experience,

Powell excelled at arranging for musical pictures. He followed Newman to 20th Century–Fox, working as a staff arranger and orchestrator from 1940 to 1960. Powell also regularly orchestrated for Hugo Friedhofer, Cyril Mockridge, Alex North, and Franz Waxman. Freelancing in the 1960s, he worked on a handful of Alex North scores before retiring in the late 1960s. He did not always receive credit on the hundreds of films he orchestrated; contributions of original music to films scored by others also often went uncredited. Highly regarded and admired by his peers, he is widely considered to be one of the finest orchestrators ever to work in film.

WORKS
(selective list)
FILM SCORES
(as orchestrator and/or arranger)
The Goldwyn Follies, 1938 [score by A. Newman]; The Song of Bernadette, 1943 [score by Newman]; My Darling Clementine, 1946 [score by D. Buttolph]; Captain from Castile, 1947 [score by Newman]; All About Eve, 1950 [score by F. Waxman]; Broken Arrow, 1950 [score by H. Friedhofer]; The Robe, 1953 [score by Newman]; Prince Valiant, 1954 [score by Waxman]; There's No Business Like Show Business, 1954 [score by Newman]; The King and I, 1956 [score by Newman]; Peyton Place, 1957 [score by Waxman]; South Pacific, 1958 [score by Newman]; The Sound and the Fury, 1959 [score by A. North]; From the Terrace, 1960 [score by E. Bernstein]; Hang 'em High, 1968 [score by D. Frontiere]

FILM SCORES
(as composer)
Topper Takes a Trip, 1939 [with H. Friedhofer]; State Fair, 1945 [with A. Newman and others]

STAGE
(as orchestrator, all New York)
Garrick Gaieties, 1930; Earl Carroll's Vanities, 1932; Murder at the Vanities, 1933
MSS in *LAum*

BIBLIOGRAPHY
J. Rodriguez, ed.: *Music and Dance in California* (Hollywood, CA, 1940)
L. Maury: "Edward Powell," *The Score* iv/2 (1950), 5
WARREN M. SHERK

Powell, Eleanor (*b* Springfield, MA, 21 Nov 1912; *d* Los Angeles, CA, 11 Feb 1982). Tap dancer and actress. As a teenager she began performing her ballet and acrobatic act in supper clubs in Atlantic City, New Jersey, where she lived with her mother. Upon moving to New York City, she trained in tap dancing and soon found work on the Broadway stage, specializing in a style of rhythmic tap with balletic and acrobatic elements. Her appearance in *Fine and Dandy* (1930) led to further work as a soloist and featured performer on Broadway and in Hollywood. In MGM's *Broadway Melody of 1936* (1935) her dancing in top hat and tails to "Broadway Rhythm" was a sensational success, and her dance numbers in *Born to Dance* (1936) solidified her position as the new "Queen of Tap." Next came *Rosalie* (1937), *Broadway Melody of 1938, Honolulu* (1939), and *Broadway Melody of 1940*, which contains a duet with Fred Astaire to Cole Porter's "Begin the Beguine" that is considered her finest work. Among her later films are *Lady Be Good*

(1941), in which she dances to "Fascinatin' Rhythm"; *Thousands Cheer* (1943), including a boogie-boogie tap number; and *Sensations of 1945* (1944), in which she taps in a giant pinball machine. She was inducted into the International Tap Dance Hall of Fame in 2002.

BIBLIOGRAPHY
A.B. Levin: *Eleanor Powell: First Lady of Dance* (New York, 1997)
B.J. Evensen: "Powell, Eleanor," *American National Biography Online* (New York, 2000), <http://www.anb.org>
CLAUDE CONYERS

Powell, John (*b* Richmond, VA, 6 Sept 1882; *d* Richmond, VA, 15 Aug 1963). Pianist and composer. He attended the University of Virginia (BA 1901) and went on to study in Vienna, where his teachers included Theodor Leschetizky and Karel Navrátil. His early works, among them the *Sonata Virginianesque* (1906) for violin and piano, and the piano works *In the South* (1906), *At the Fair* (1907, a six-movement suite whose first and last movements are titled, respectively, "Hoochie-Coochie Dance" and "Banjo-picker"), and *Sonate noble* (1908) blend American folk material with traditional contrapuntal techniques, elements that remained important to his compositional style. He made his recital debut in Berlin in 1907 and subsequently performed in Paris, London, and Vienna to great critical acclaim. An interest in and admiration for German culture are manifest in *Sonate psychologique* (its title was originally in German) completed in 1905, while the epic *Sonata Teutonica*, also in a Lisztian post-Romantic German style was introduced in London by Benno Moisewitsch; paradoxically, its principal theme is derived from the folksong "Shenandoah."

After living in London for several years, Powell returned to Richmond, where he developed an interest in African American folksong. His reputation as an important American composer was established with the premiere of *Rhapsodie négre* for piano and orchestra (1918). Inspired by Joseph Conrad's *Heart of Darkness*, the work quotes African American melodies and uses syncopated ragtime rhythms. Powell, however, did not believe that African American melodies could serve as a basis for a national school of composition. In a lecture given in Houston on 6 April 1923 he expressed concern about the "melting pot" conception of America and about the possibility that the country might be peopled by an octoroon race. He was sympathetic to the eugenics movement and served as a leader in the formation of the Anglo-Saxon Club of America.

During the 1930s and 40s, Anglo-American folk influences took on increasingly important roles in his compositions, representative examples of which are the orchestral *Natchez on the Hill* and *In the South*. On a larger scale is the Symphony in A (1945, rev. 1951), which replaces the traditional third movement scherzo with a long slow movement, but is otherwise cast in traditional symphonic form. It is, however, written in a modal style and quotes many folk melodies. Powell also completed numerous arrangements of traditional folksongs, dances, and hymn tunes. He was a co-founder of the White Top Mountain Folk Festival (1931–41), taught at the University of Virginia, and gave recitals and lectures. Despite his championing of segregation, 5 November 1951 was declared "John Powell Day" by the Governor of Virginia. The building housing the music and art departments at Radford University in southwestern Virginia was designated Powell Hall in 1968. On 17 September 2010, the Board of Visitors at that institution abolished the building's name based upon Powell's racist past.

WORKS
(selective list)

Orch: Vn Conc., 1910 [2nd movt arr. as From a Love Past, vn, pf]; Rhapsodie nègre, pf, orch, 1918 [arr. 2 pf, 1922]; In Old Virginia, 1921; 2 Interludes, 1921; Natchez-on-the-Hill (3 Virginian Country Dances), 1932 [arr. vn, pf; 2 pf]; A Set of Three, 1935; Sym. in A [modal], 1945

Vocal: 5 Choral Works, 1902–7: Phantoms (J.B. Tabb), To a Butterfly (Tabb), Enigma (N. Lenau), Moonbalm (H. Heine), Nein (K. Burger); Lenztraum (Burger), 1v, pf, 1902–7; The Babe of Bethlehem, SATB, 1934; The Deaf Woman's Courtship, Mez, T, SATB, 1934, arr. Mez, T, male vv (1950); Soldier, Soldier, S, Bar, SATB, 1934; 5 Virginian Folk Songs, Bar, pf, 1938; other songs, choral works, hymns

Chbr: Sonata Virginianesque, vn, pf, 1906; Str Qt no.1, E, 1907; Sonata, A♭, vn, pf, 1918; Str Qt no.2, e, 1922, unfinished

Kbd (pf, unless otherwise stated): Sonate psychologique, 1905; In the South, suite, 1906; Variations and Double Fugue on a Theme by F.C. Hahr, 1906; At the Fair, suite, 1907; Sonate noble, 1908; Sonata Teutonica, 1913; In the Hammock, 2 pf, 8 hands, 1915; Dirge, 2 pf, 12 hands, 1928; Larry O'Garr, carillon, 1941; other unpublished works

MSS in *CHua*

Principal publishers: J. Fischer, G. Schirmer, Mathot-Paris, OUP

BIBLIOGRAPHY

M.L. Chapman: *The Piano Works of John Powell* (thesis, Indiana U., 1968)

P.L. Williams: *Music by John Powell in the Music Collection at the University of Virginia: a Descriptive Bibliography* (thesis, U. of Virginia, 1968)

L.M. Simms, Jr.: "Folk Music in America: John Powell and the 'National Music Idiom'," *Journal of Popular Culture*, vii (1973–4), 510 only

R.D. Ward: *The Life and Works of John Powell (1882–1963)* (diss., Catholic U. of America, 1973)

D.Z. Kushner: "John Powell: His Racial and Cultural Ideologies," *Min-Ad*, v/1 (2006), 1–14

DAVID Z. KUSHNER

Powell, Maud (*b* Peru, IL, 22 Aug 1867; *d* Uniontown, PA, 8 Jan 1920). Violinist. She began violin and piano lessons in Aurora, Illinois, then studied violin for four years with WILLIAM LEWIS in Chicago. She was a pupil at the Leipzig Conservatory under HENRY SCHRADIECK (1881–2) and at the Paris Conservatoire under Charles Dancla (1882–3), then in 1883 made a tour of England. The following year she studied with Joseph Joachim at the Berlin Hochschule für Musik. She made her European debut with the Berlin PO under Joachim in 1885, and her American debut with the New York PO under Theodore Thomas in the same year. She toured Europe with the New York Arion Society in 1892 and performed twice under Thomas at the World's Columbian Exposition, Chicago (1893), at which she delivered a paper, "Women and the Violin," to the Woman's Musical Congress.

Powell's mission was to advance America's cultural growth by bringing the best in classical music to Americans in remote areas as well as in the large cultural centers. She pioneered the violin recital in America. She was one of the first to champion works by American composers and introduced to the American public concertos by Pyotr Il'yich Tchaikovsky, Antonín Dvořák, Camille Saint-Saëns, Édouard Lalo, Jean Sibelius, Samuel Coleridge-Taylor, and Anton Stepanovich Arensky. She also toured widely in Europe and was particularly popular with audiences in England. Powell became one of the first women in Europe or America to form and lead a mixed gender string quartet (1894). The Maud Powell Concert Company, a group of six musicians, visited South Africa in 1905; she also formed the Maud Powell Trio with the company's cellist May Mukle and pianist Anne Mukle Ford and toured the United States in 1908–9. In 1904 she became the first solo instrumentalist to record for the Victor Talking Machine Company's celebrity artist series (Red Seal label), and her recordings became worldwide bestsellers. All were reissued on CD on the Naxos label in 2001–4. She made transcriptions for violin and piano, and composed an original cadenza for Brahms's Violin Concerto; many composers dedicated music to her. A collection of these works was published as *Maud Powell Favorites* in 2009 by the Maud Powell Society for Music and Education. She also contributed articles to music journals and wrote her own program notes. The brilliance, power, and finish of her playing, combined with an unusual interpretative gift, led her to be recognized as one of America's greatest violinists; contemporary reviewers ranked her alongside Fritz Kreisler and Eugène Ysaÿe.

BIBLIOGRAPHY

DAB (F.H. Martens); *NAW* (A.R. Coolidge)

F.H. Martens: "Maud Powell," *Violin Mastery* (New York, 1919), 183–97

E.L. Winn: "Maud Powell as I Knew her: a Tribute," *Musical Observer*, xix/3 (1920), 58–9

B. Schwarz: *Great Masters of the Violin* (New York, 1983), 494–7

K.A. Shaffer: "A Pioneer's Legacy," *The Maud Powell Signature: Women in Music*, i/1 (1985), 6–8

K.A. Shaffer: "Maud Powell: America's Legendary Musical Pioneer," *Journal of the Violin Society of America*, iii/2 (1987), 89–112

K.A. Shaffer: "Perpetual Pioneer," *The Strad*, xcviii (1987), 824–9

K.A. Shaffer and N.G. Greenwood: *Maud Powell: Pioneer American Violinist* (Ames, IA, 1988)

K.A. Shaffer: *Maud Powell Favorites*, (Brevard, NC, 2009), i

Maud Powell Society for Music and Education website, <http://www.maudpowell.org/>

KAREN A. SHAFFER

Powell, Mel(vin Epstein) (*b* New York, NY, 12 Feb 1923; *d* Sherman Oaks, CA, 24 April 1998). Composer and teacher. He studied piano with NADIA REISENBERG and was for some years noted as a jazz pianist, composer, and arranger (for Benny Goodman and Glenn Miller). After service in the US Army Air Forces, he attended Yale University where he studied composition with PAUL HINDEMITH (BM 1952). He taught at the Mannes College of Music and at Queens College, CUNY, before returning to Yale (1957–69), where he became chairman of the composition faculty and director of the electronic music studio, one of the first in the United States. In 1969 he went to the California Institute of the Arts as founding dean of the school of music; he was provost there from

1972 to 1976 and was appointed in 1978 to the school's first endowed professorship, the Roy E. Disney Chair, a position he held until his death. Among his many awards and commissions are those from Sigma Alpha Iota (1956), the Guggenheim Foundation (1960), the American Academy of Arts and Letters (1963), the NEA (1982), and Brandeis College (1989). He served as president of the American Music Center (1961–3) and on the editorial boards of *Perspectives of New Music* and *Journal of Music Theory*. In 1972 he was guest composer at the University of Wisconsin, River Falls, and at the Holland Festival, by invitation of the Dutch government. Powell won the Pulitzer Prize in Music in 1990 for the two-piano concerto *Duplicates*, a work commissioned by Betty Freeman for the LA Philharmonic. It was originally conceived to be performed with the composer and André Previn, then conductor of the orchestra, as soloists. Pianists Alan Feinberg and Robert Taub instead premiered it with the orchestra conducted by David Alan Miller.

Powell's use of 12-tone techniques makes possible the density of interval relationships and of durations, registers, and phrases that characterizes his music. In some works, such as *Filigree Setting* (1959), he uses quasi-improvisational techniques to extend durations and to permit the performer some choice of pitch succession or contour within an otherwise rigorously controlled context. In other compositions interval relations derived from pitch sets take precedence over ordered pitch succession, as in *Haiku Setting* (1961), to frame ordered elements. There is a similar use of pitch sets in his electronically synthesized music, which also takes into account the nontempered nature of the electronic medium. He also modified live sounds electronically in some of his works.

Later works, such as *Duplicates* and the chamber orchestra work *Modules*, deal with smaller segments of material. Powell varies the surface of the music and its instrumentation with increased eclecticism. While American serialism remains an important feature of his compositional language, one can also hear references to the coloristic writing and birdsong of Messiaen, Boulez's use of mobile forms, and the brash percussion writing of Varèse. *Duplicates* features the two piano soloists in the outer movements, accompanied by a large orchestra with an extensive and emphatically deployed percussion section. But its central movement, subdivided into three sections, "Madrigal," "Immobile," and "Mobile" (a cadenza for pianos), makes prominent use of other instrumental solos, often in pairs: winds, strings, pitched percussion, and even a few muted brass gestures reminiscent of Powell's jazz roots.

WORKS

Orch: Cantilena Conc., eng hn, orch, 1948; Stanzas, 1957; Settings, vc, orch, 1961; Immobiles 1–4, tape and/or orch, 1967; Modules, chbr orch, 1985; Duplicates, 2 pf, orch, 1987; Settings for Small Orch (in two parts), chbr orch, 1992

Inst: Beethoven Analogs, str qt, 1948; Capriccio, sym. band, 1950; Pf Sonatina, 1951; Recitative and Toccata Percossa, hpd, 1952; Pf Trio, 1954; Divertimento, vn, harp, 1954; Divertimento, wind qnt, 1955; Pf Qnt, 1956; Etude, pf, 1957; Miniatures, fl, ob, vn, va, vc, hpd, 1958; Filigree Setting, str qt, 1959; Improvisation, cl, va, pf, 1962; Str Qt,

1982; Intermezzo, pf, 1984; Madrigal, 2 pf, 1985; Nocturne, vn, 1985, rev. of Cantilena, 1970 [see "Tape"]; Wind Qnt, 1985; Setting, gui, 1986; Setting, 2 pf, 1988; Prelude, pf, 1988; Amy-Abilities, perc, 1988; Invocation, vc, 1988; Three Madrigals, fl, 1988; Piano Trio, pf, vn, vc, 1994; Sonatina, fl, 1995; Sexet, fl, cl, pf, perc, vn, vc, 1996

Vocal: 6 Love Songs, chorus, 1950; Sweet lovers love the spring (Shakespeare), female chorus, pf, 1953; Haiku Setting, S, pf, 1961; 2 Prayer Settings (Goodman, Gregory), T, ob, vn, va, vc, 1963; Settings (Joyce, Milton, Euripides, trad.), S, chbr ens, 1979; Little Companion Pieces (Baudelaire, W.C. Williams, Joyce, Asian and African trad.), S, str qt, 1980; Strand Settings: "Darker" (M. Strand), song cycle, Mez, elec, 1983; Die Violine (anon.), S, vn, pf, 1987; Letter to a Young Composer (Powell), S, perc, 1988; Levertov Breviary (Levertov), S, pf, 1996; Seven Miniatures, Women Poets of China, Mez, hp, 1998

Tape: Elec Setting, 1960; Elec Setting no.2, 1962; Events (H. Crane), 1963; Analogs 1–4, 1966; Immobile 5, tape, chbr ens, 1967; Cantilena (anon. Heb., Chin., Sanskrit), S, vn, tape, 1970, rev. as Nocturne, vn, 1985; Setting, wind insts, vn, tape, 1972; 3 Synth Settings, 1981; Cantilena, trbn, tape, 1982; Computer Prelude, tape, 1988

Principal publishers: MKS Music, G. Schirmer

BIBLIOGRAPHY

VintonD

J. Machlis: *Introduction to Contemporary Music* (New York, 1961)

H. Sollberger: "Mel Powell: *Haiku Settings*," *PNM*, iii/1 (1964), 147–55

L. Thimmig: "The Music of Mel Powell," *MQ*, lv/1 (1969), 31–44 [with list of works]

R. Robins: "An Interview with Mel Powell," *MQ*, lxxii/4 (1986), 476–93

"Points of Arrival: Mel Powell at 65'," *Aperiodical*, ii/1 (1988) [incl. work-list, discography]

RICHARD SWIFT/CHRISTIAN CAREY

Powell, Verne Q. (*b* Danville, IN, 7 April 1878; *d* Needham, MA, 3 Feb 1968). Maker of Boehm flutes and piccolos. As a boy he learned to play the flute and the piccolo and at seven made a fife. He worked at first as a jeweler and engraver in Fort Scott, Kansas. In 1910 Powell went to a concert in Chicago in which Georges Barrère played a Louis Lot silver flute; this inspired him to make a silver flute from melted-down teaspoons, watch cases, and coins. In 1913 WILLIAM S. HAYNES, who had been making wooden flutes, invited Powell to join his firm in Boston as foreman. In 1926 he started his own business, Verne Q. Powell Flutes, Inc., at 295 Huntington Avenue. Powell's first catalog (1927) advertised silver and gold flutes; among the first ten customers were John Wummer, Arthur Lora, and William Kincaid.

While working for Haynes, Powell was responsible for introducing French-model silver flute making to the United States. As an independent maker, he changed the design of his flutes, which were formerly on the Lot model, and made the first high C facilitator key. Besides silver flutes, Powell made wood and silver piccolos, silver alto flutes, and gold and platinum concert flutes. One platinum flute was made for the New York World's Fair in 1939 and was later purchased by Kincaid.

In 1961 Powell sold his business to four former employees, under whose management the firm expanded and moved to Arlington, Massachusetts. For most of the following 25 years it produced piccolos only sporadically; some of its employees made piccolos independently. In 1974 the firm introduced its Cooper scale for flutes, in collaboration with the English flute maker Albert Cooper. The firm holds a US patent (1990) for aurumite, a method of laminating 14-carat gold onto the outside and inside of the flute body. In 1997, working with the flutists András Adorján, Felix Skowronek, and Fenwick Smith, it resumed the manufacture of wooden Boehm system flutes. The firm changed hands several times; it moved in 1989 to Waltham, Massachusetts, and in 1999 to their current location in nearby Maynard. In 2002 the company created Sonaré Winds, a division that partners with other winds and brass makers. Many former Powell employees later founded their own firms, including Brannen Bros., Burkhart-Phelan, Edward Almeida, Dana Sheridan, Jack Goosman, Jonathon Landell, and Ostroff Sagerman.

BIBLIOGRAPHY

L.R. Gallese: "Two Companies are Most Noteworthy," *Wall Street Journal* (1 Feb 1977)

N. Toff: *The Development of the Modern Flute* (New York, 1979/*R*)

E.T. Livesey: "Makers of the Magic Flute," *Christian Science Monitor* (2 Jan 1980)

M. Goodman: *The Economics of Flute Production: an In-Depth Survey of the William S. Haynes and Verne Q. Powell Flute Companies* (diss., U. of Southern California, 1983)

S. Berdahl: *The First Hundred Years of the Boehm Flute in the United States, 1845–1945: a Biographical Dictionary of American Boehm Flutemakers* (diss., U. of Minnesota, 1986)

E. Machon: *High F'lutin* (Boston, 1986)

FRIEDRICH VON HUENE/NANCY TOFF/R

Powers, Ann (*b* Seattle, WA, 4 Feb 1964). Rock critic. After contributing to alternative publications in the Seattle and San Francisco Bay areas for a decade, she became a pop critic for the *New York Times* (1992–3, 1997–2001), an editor at *The Village Voice* (1993–6), a senior curator for the Experience Music Project (2001–5), and a senior critic at *Blender* magazine (2005–). For articles written during her tenure as chief pop-music critic of the *Los Angeles Times* (2006–11), Powers received the ASCAP Deems Taylor Award in 2010. She was the Distinguished Artist in Residence at the Norman Lear Center's Popular Music Project at the University of Southern California (2008–9), and guest-edited the 2010 edition of Da Capo Press's *Best Music Writing* series. In March 2011 she joined the staff of NPR Music.

Strongly dedicated to feminist cultural criticism, Powers and Evelyn McDonnell coedited *Rock She Wrote: Women Write about Rock, Pop, and Rap* (1995). She also explores new ways of writing biography in her memoirs, *Weird Like Us: My Bohemian America* (2001), which emphasizes how important it is for those with unconventional ideas to interact with mainstream society, and in the authorized and cowritten biography, *Tori Amos: Piece by Piece* (2005). Her book on Kate Bush's 1982 album *The Dreaming* is scheduled to be published in 2012.

What comes through most eloquently in Powers's writings is her personal investment in both the music she discusses and the sociocultural issues that this music raises. Her awareness of alternative viewpoints leads her to use a nondidactic tone, and this allows her readers to generate further debate and understanding.

ERIC HUNG

Powers, Marie (*b* Mount Carmel, PA, 1902; *d* New York, NY, 28 Dec 1973). Contralto. She studied music and languages at Cornell University before coming to New

York in the 1930s. Not finding immediate success, Powers traveled to Florence to study at the Royal Conservatory, where Toscanini heard and selected her to sing a series of Wagner operas at La Scala. Returning to New York, she sang standard contralto roles with the San Carlo Opera until Menotti asked her to sing Madame Flora in premieres of *The Medium* in New York (1947) and London (1948). She made her New York City Opera debut in 1948 in Menotti's *The Old Maid and the Thief*, and the following year created Azelia in Still's *Troubled Island*. After premiering the Mother in Menotti's *The Consul* in Philadelphia (1950), she sang Fricka (1951) and Mistress Quickly (1952) at the Paris Opéra. Her powerful acting led her to perform straight plays in later years, including a Broadway run of Anouilh's *Becket* with Laurence Olivier and Anthony Quinn (1960). She appeared in a televised performance of Britten's "Noye's Fludde" as Mrs. Noye on CBS in 1964.

ELIZABETH FORBES/STEPHANIE JENSEN-MOULTON

Pownall, Mary Ann [Mrs. James Wrighton] (*b* London, England, Feb 1751; *d* Charleston, SC, 12 Aug 1796). Actress, singer, and composer. She made her performing debut at Drury Lane in 1770 under the name Mrs. James Wrighton, and was praised by the English critics for her role as Lucy in John Gay's *The Beggar's Opera*. In 1792 she came to the United States with Mr. Pownall, her second husband, and became a member of the Old American Company. Before her death in 1796 she appeared in concerts in Charleston, Philadelphia, New York, and Boston. Her repertoire ranged from popular songs to opera, oratorio, and dramatic readings. One of her most successful appearances was at a "Grand Concert Spirituel" given in Charleston on 24 March 1796, consisting of songs, duets, and instrumental music from oratorios by Handel; such was the public interest that she gave an additional concert of sacred music two days later. Pownall's songs "Jenny of the Glen," "Lavinia," and "The Straw Bonnet" (all included in the volume *Six Songs for the Harpsichord*, 1794, written in collaboration with James Hewitt, director of the orchestra and house composer at the John Street Theatre), and "Kisses Sued For" (1795) were among the first by a woman to be published in the United States. Her vocal writing is characterized by strong leaps in the melody and a variety of rhythmic patterns; her harmonic language, however, is straightforward.

BIBLIOGRAPHY

E. Willis: *The Charleston Stage in the XVIII Century* (New York, 1933/*R*1968), 287–316, 331–7

O.G.T. Sonneck: *A Bibliography of Early Secular American Music* (Washington, DC, 1905, rev. and enlarged by W.T. Upton, 2/1945/*R*1964)

O.G.T. Sonneck: *Early Concert-life in America (1731–1800)* (Leipzig, 1907/*R*1978)

J. Tick: *American Women Composers before 1870* (Ann Arbor, MI, 1979/*R*2010)

P. Pohl: *The Artistic Contributions of Mary Ann Pownall to the American Theatre, 1792–1796* (thesis, San Jose State U., 1979)

S.L. Porter: *With an Air Debonair: Musical Theatre in America, 1785–1815* (Washington, DC, 1991)

C. Ammer: *Unsung: a History of Women in American Music* (Westport, CT, 1980/*R*2001), 18, 95

LORETTA GOLDBERG/R

Powwow. An intertribal Native American performance event derived from Plains Indian musical and cultural practices; the most public genre of Native performance in the United States and Canada. Powwows range from intimate, local gatherings of a few hundred people, to large arena shows with several thousand people from distant places. Locations include rural, outdoor dance grounds on private property, school gymnasiums, community centers, college campuses, and urban exposition arenas. As celebrations of contemporary Native life, powwows maintain family and community social networks while expressing modern Indian identities.

Powwow history is complex; it represents a creative adaptation to the forces of colonization. The musical form and style of modern powwow songs developed among the Plains tribes by the 1840s. By 1890 this style had diffused throughout the Plains. Government officials attempted to suppress Plains dances from the 1890s through the 1920s, while simultaneously, new contexts for Native dancing appeared, including Wild West shows. Thus the War Dance emerged in the 1920s through the blending of historic Plains genres with innovations from professionalized entertainments. The War Dance is a collective performance in which each participant dances independently while moving around a circle in coordination with the other dancers. It is the focal point of contemporary powwows.

Program details vary from one powwow to the next, depending in part on whether it is a traditional or contest powwow. Powwows open with a Grand Entry, when dancers process into the arena, led by flag bearers, a color guard, honored elders, head dancers, and the powwow princess. Flag Songs are sung, a prayer is offered in a Native language, the colors are posted, and a dance honoring veterans occurs; the emphasis on honoring veterans connects powwows to earlier traditions of Plains warrior societies. The remainder of the program features intertribal War Dances, alternating with social dances, exhibition dances, specials, and competition dances. The colors are retired at the conclusion of the powwow. Anyone may dance during intertribals and social dances, but only dancers wearing the appropriate regalia may perform during exhibition and contest dances. Styles of regalia correspond to different dance styles, including Men's Traditional, Men's Grass Dance, Men's Fancy Dance, Women's Traditional (Buckskin Dress or Cloth Dress), Women's Jingle Dress, and Women's Fancy Shawl. Specials include memorials, honorings, and demonstrations of Native dances from beyond the Plains area. Social dances, performed by couples, include Round Dances and Two-Steps.

War Dance songs are performed by a group of men, seated in a circle around a large drum; the men beat the drum in unison, each using a padded drumstick. The drum beat represents the heartbeat. The drum group may include women who stand behind the men, doubling their vocal line at the octave. In some groups, women also sit at the drum. The vocal phrasing is separate from the duple or triple drum meter, reflecting "the spiritual belief that the drum is a living being with a voice separate from that of the singers" (Browner, 2009, 224). Singers employ tense and nasal vocal production, pulsating on sustained tones. Songs emphasize five-tone gapped scales; melodies start high and descend in a terraced or undulating contour. War Dance songs use a two-part strophic form. The first part has one phrase, introduced by the head singer and then sung by the whole group. The second part has two phrases, which are repeated. The strophe may be diagrammed as: *A1 A/BC BC*. The strophe repeats many times, with subtle variations

Teri Hansen, Sheila and Jim Rich, Cougar Buschmann, and Sky Real performing at the Gathering of Oregon's First Nation Powwow, Salem, 2011. (MATT BUXTON/The Oregonian/Landov)

on each rendition. Singers call the strophe a "round," emphasizing the circular nature of the form. Some songs conclude with a coda or "tail." Powwow style has been incorporated into Native American popular music and orchestral works, by artists such as Buffy Sainte-Marie and Brent Michael Davids.

RECORDINGS
Honor the Earth Powwow: Songs of the Great Lakes Indians, 1991, Ryko, RACS 0199
Gathering of Nations Pow Wow 1999, 2000, SOAR, SOAR 200 CD
High Noon–Live at Taos 2000, 2000, IH, IH 4452
Thunder Hill: Relentless, 2009, Can., CR-6465

BIBLIOGRAPHY
G.A. Young: *Powwow Power: Perspectives on Historic and Contemporary Intertribalism* (diss., Indiana U., 1981)
O.T. Hatton: "In the Tradition: Grass Dance Musical Style and Female Pow-wow Singers," *EM*, xxx/2 (1986), 197–222
W.K. Powers: *War Dance: Plains Indian Musical Performance* (Tucson, AZ, 1990)
C. Heth, ed.: *Native American Dance: Ceremonies and Social Traditions* (Washington, DC, 1992)
T. Browner: *Heartbeat of the People: Music and Dance of the Northern Pow-wow* (Urbana and Chicago, 2002)
C.A. Ellis: *A Dancing People: Powwow Culture on the Southern Plains* (Lawrence, KS, 2003)
C.A. Ellis, L.E. Lassiter, and G.H. Dunham, eds.: *Powwow* (Lincoln, NE, and London, 2005)
T. Browner, ed.: *Songs From "A New Circle of Voices": the Sixteenth Annual Pow-wow at UCLA* (Middleton, WI, 2009)

VICTORIA LINDSAY LEVINE

Pozo, Chano [Pozo Gonzales, Luciano] (*b* Havana, Cuba, 7 Jan 1915; *d* New York, NY, 2 Dec 1948). Cuban drummer, singer, and dancer. His drumming and singing were rooted in Santeria, the *lucumí* faith derived from West African rituals. On 29 September 1947 he and the bongo player Chiquitico performed in a concert at Carnegie Hall with trumpeter Dizzy Gillespie—a landmark event in the history of fusing elements of jazz and Latin music. Pozo was murdered before he could fully develop his ideas with Gillespie, but during his brief career in the United States he provided the starting point for much popular music of the late 1940s and the 50s. The collaboration between the two men, which produced the infectious "Manteca" (1947), supplied the initiative for American musicians, and some of the listening public, to appreciate fully the tradition of Latin music.

BIBLIOGRAPHY
D. Gillespie and A. Fraser: *To Be, or Not…to Bop: Memoirs* (Garden City, NY, 1979; London, 1980, as *Dizzy: the Autobiography of Dizzy Gillespie*)
J.S. Roberts: *The Latin Tinge: the Impact of Latin American Music on the United States* (New York, 1979, 2/1999)
S. Yanow: *Afro-Cuban Jazz* (San Francisco, 2000)

JOHN STORM ROBERTS/R

Pratt, Awadagin (*b* Pittsburgh, PA, 6 March 1966). Pianist, conductor, and educator. He began his piano studies at the age of six and added the violin when he turned nine. At the age of 16 he entered the University of Illinois. He transferred to the Peabody Conservatory of Music and became its first student to graduate with performance diplomas in piano, violin, and conducting. In 1992 he became the first African American to win the Naumburg

International Piano Competition. In 1994 he made his debut at Lincoln Center with the New York Philharmonic Orchestra and received an Avery Fisher Career Grant. He has played with all of the major US orchestras and his summer festival appearances have included Ravinia, Blossom, Wolftrap, Caramoor, and Aspen, the Hollywood Bowl, and the Mostly Mozart Festival in Tokyo. He is the artistic director of the Next Generation Festival, based in Lancaster, Pennsylvania. He is famous for his flashy, untraditional concert attire and his dreadlocks.

As a conductor he has worked with Leonard Slatkin and led the National Symphony and the orchestras of Toledo, New Mexico, Winston-Salem, Santa Fe, and Prince George County, the Concertante di Chicago, and two orchestras in Japan. Since 2004 he has served as Associate Professor of Piano and Artist in Residence at the College Conservatory of Music at the University of Cincinnati and participates in numerous residency and educational outreach activities. He is the founder of the Pratt Music Foundation, which supports the musical development of children in the Bloomington-Normal area, Illinois. He has recorded several albums for Angel/EMI and in 2011 released a recording of Brahms sonatas for cello and piano with cellist Zuill Bailey on the Telarc label.

BIBLIOGRAPHY
T. Teachout: "You Can't Hear the Hair: Classical Pianist Awadagin Pratt Dresses Down—and Plays Up," *Mirabella* (Jan 1995)
J.V. Serinus: "Interview with Pianist Awadagin Pratt," *Secrets of Home Theater and High Fidelity*, x/2 (May 2003)

JAMES BASH

Pratt, Carroll C(ornelius) (*b* North Brookfield, MA, 27 April 1894; *d* Princeton, NJ, 8 Oct 1979). Psychologist and musicologist. He studied at Clark College (BA 1915), Clark University (PhD 1921), the University of Cambridge (1919), and the University of Berlin (1931). After serving as instructor and assistant professor of psychology at Harvard University (1923–38), he moved to Rutgers University, where he was professor and chair of the department (1937–45). He directed the Institute of Psychology and Philosophy at Ankara University (1945–7) before being appointed chairman and professor of psychology at Princeton University (1948–62) and then at Rider College (1962–71). He served as editor of the *Psychological Review* (1948–53) and as president of the American Society for Aesthetics (1950–2).

Pratt studied and wrote about various aspects of aesthetics and the psychology of music. Examining objective and subjective musical experience, he concluded that the hearer responds primarily to the inherent tonal design of the music rather than to its symbolic references, and therefore that some important aspects of musical response are not culturally determined. His writings include *The Meaning of Music* (New York, 1931, R/1968), *Music as the Language of Emotion* (Washington, DC, 1952), and *The Logic of Modern Psychology* (New York, 1939).

BIBLIOGRAPHY
"Carroll Cornelius Pratt (1894–1979)," *American Psychologist*, xxxv/11 (1980), 1044–6 [obituary]

RAMONA H. MATTHEWS/KAREN M. BRYAN

Pratt, Henry (*b* Wrentham, MA, 14 May 1771; *d* Winchester, NH, 28 Aug 1841). Organ builder. Son of Noah Pratt, a cabinetmaker who moved to Winchester, New Hampshire, in 1792. In addition to assisting his father, Henry was interested in music and mechanical pursuits such as clock making. In a church where his father was doing some work, Pratt encountered a small chamber organ, which he studied, and in 1799 essayed to construct one like it. This small organ of five stops was successful, and was placed in the town's Congregational church, launching him on his career, as other orders for organs followed. By 1834 he is recorded as having built 23 church organs and 19 chamber organs, largely for locations in New Hampshire and central Massachusetts, and at the time of his death is said to have built around 50 organs. Pratt's first organ still exists in the Conant Public Library of Winchester, and four other small Pratt organs survive, now all in museums, including those in Deerfield and Sturbridge, Massachusetts. They are notable for their careful craftsmanship, pleasing design and gentle sounds.

BIBLIOGRAPHY

"Organ-Building in New England," *New-England Magazine*, vi (March 1834), 205–15

W.J. Bruce: "A Chapter on Church Organs," *American Historical Record*, iii/28 (1874), 161–70

B. Owen: *The Organ in New England* (Raleigh, NC, 1979)

E.W. Atkins: "Henry Pratt Organ," *Winchester Star* (Nov 1990), 10

BARBARA OWEN

Pratt, Paul (Charles) (*b* New Salem, IN, 1 Nov 1890; *d* Indianapolis, IN, 7 July 1948). Ragtime composer and pianist. In 1909 he became the manager for the recently established popular-music publisher J.H. Aufderheide & Co. in Indianapolis. That same year Aufderheide issued Pratt's first piano rag, "Vanity," and in 1911 Pratt moved to Chicago to open a short-lived branch office for the firm, and began collaborating on popular songs with the lyricist J. Will Callahan (1874–1946). In 1914 John Stark issued Pratt's "Hot House Rag," a virtuoso showpiece and his finest work. From 1917, as a piano-roll artist for the United States Music Company, he recorded several of his own rags which were never published in sheet-music form. He wrote a few novelty songs, such as "Gasoline," which comments upon the increasing impact of automobiles on American culture. With the demise of ragtime Pratt began traveling as a piano accompanist in vaudeville, playing under the stage name of Paul Parnell. In 1924 he conducted Paul Whiteman's band The James Boys on a tour of the United States, and later conducted the orchestras in several Broadway musicals, including Rodgers and Hart's *Peggy-Ann* (1926) and *A Connecticut Yankee* (1927). The Depression ended his musical career, and from 1934 he lived in relative obscurity in Indianapolis and worked as a photographer. Pratt was a gifted pianist and composed several enduring rags noteworthy for their relative difficulty and their use of unconventional harmonic progressions. Though he was not prolific, his works stand alongside other noteworthy ragtime composers and his arrangements of other composers' works have given them an extended life and significance.

WORKS
(*selective list*)

Pf rags: Vanity Rag (Indianapolis, 1909); Colonial Glide (Indianapolis, 1910); Walhalla Rag (Indianapolis, 1910); Teasing Rag (Chicago, 1912); Hot House Rag (St. Louis, 1914); Spring-Time Rag (St. Louis, 1916); On the Rural Route (St. Louis, 1917)

Songs: Gee, but I'm Crazy for Rag (A. Warren) (Chicago, 1912); That Gosh Ding Hiram Tune (J.W. Callahan) (St. Louis, 1912); Gasoline (Callahan) (New York, 1914); Beneath Your Window (Callahan) (New York, 1925)

Orch: Siren of the Nile (Chicago, 1921)

Principal publishers: Aufderheide, Stark

BIBLIOGRAPHY

Obituary, *Indianapolis Star* (8 July 1948)

D.A. Jasen and T.J. Tichenor: *Rags and Ragtime: A Musical History* (New York, 1978), 180ff

J.E. Hasse: *The Creation and Dissemination of Indianapolis Ragtime, 1897–1930* (diss., Indiana U., 1981), 152ff

J.E. Hasse and F.J. Gillis: Liner notes, *Indiana Ragtime: a Documentary Album* (Indiana Historical Society, 1981)

T. Parrish: "The Paul Pratt Story," *Rag Times*, xvii/5 (1984), 2–5; xvii/6, 3–6

D.A. Jasen and G. Jones: *That American Rag: the Story of Ragtime from Coast to Coast* (New York, 2000)

H.L. White: *Ragging It: Getting Ragtime into History (and Some History into Ragtime)* (Lincoln, NE, 2005)

JOHN EDWARD HASSE/TIM SMOLKO

Pratt, Silas (Gamaliel) (*b* Addison, VT, 4 Aug 1846; *d* Pittsburgh, PA, 30 Oct 1916). Composer, pianist, and author. While working as a clerk for several Chicago music stores, including the firms of Root & Cady and Lyon & Healy, he saved enough money to spend the years 1869–71 in Germany studying piano and composition with Theodor Kullak, Franz Bendel, and others. A strenuous practice regimen caused a wrist injury that precluded him from pursuing an exclusive career as a virtuoso pianist. Along with George P. Upton, Pratt founded the Apollo Club of Chicago, a men's chorus, in 1872. On a short trip to Europe (1875–7), he took lessons with Liszt and conducted his own *Centennial Overture* in Berlin (4 July 1876) and later in London. After returning to Chicago, his reputation as a noteworthy composer solidified. In 1879 he led a series of orchestral concerts at Chicago's Central Music Hall that placed his second symphony, "The Prodigal Son," alongside symphonies by Beethoven, Schubert, and Mendelssohn. His opera *Zenobia, Queen of Palmyra* premiered in Chicago in 1882 and in New York the following year. In 1885 Pratt returned to London, where he directed performances of "The Prodigal Son" symphony and selections from *Zenobia*. His first opera, entitled *Antonio* when begun in 1870 but retitled *Lucille*, had a three-week run at the Columbia Theater in Chicago during March 1887. His third opera *Ollanta*, on an Inca subject, was never produced.

Pratt moved to New York in 1889 and began to diversify his musical activities considerably. He joined the faculty of the Metropolitan Conservatory of Music shortly after his arrival and later became principal of the West End School of Music. Between 1891 and 1892, he created an eclectic musical genre called "musical allegory," which included standard popular songs, newly composed symphonic interludes and operatic selections.

He also experimented with the use of visual media in musical performances, especially the stereopticon, a precursor to the motion picture. His musical allegory *America* (1894) combined all the elements of his previous compositional experiments. During his summers in the 1890s, he served as music director of the Surf Hotel on Fire Island, New York, where he directed elaborate water pageants. In 1906 he moved to Pittsburgh and founded the Pratt Institute of Art, which he directed until his death. An avid fan of Abraham Lincoln, he collected anecdotes about the former president in a tribute called *Lincoln in Story* (1901).

WORKS

OPERA

Antonio, 1870–71, selections perf. Chicago, Farwell Hall, 1874; rev. as Lucille, Chicago, Columbia, 14 March 1887
Zenobia, Queen of Palmyra, concert perf., Chicago, Central Music Hall, 15 June 1882; stage, Chicago, McVicker's, 26 March 1883; New York, 23rd Street Theatre, 21 Aug 1883; vocal score (Boston, 1881)
Ollanta, 1892, unperf.

OTHER WORKS

Centennial Ov.; perf. Berlin, 4 July 1876
3 sym. poems: Magdalena's Lament, *c*1870; Sandalphon; A Tragedy of the Deep [on the sinking of the *Titanic*], *c*1912
3 Syms, incl: no.1, perf. Chicago, 1871; no.2 in A Major, "Prodigal Son," 1875; Lincoln Sym.
The Musical Metempsychosis (musical entertainment), 1888
The Inca's Farewell (cant.), Bar, chorus, vocal score (Boston, 1891)
Serenade for Str Orch (1891)
The Civil War in Song: a Military and Musical Allegory (New York, 1891)
A Columbian Festival Allegory: the Triumph of Columbus; New York, Carnegie Hall, 10 Oct 1892, vocal score (New York, 1892)
America: a Musical Allegory; New York, Chickering Hall, 24 Nov 1894. This work includes "The Civil War in Song" and "A Columbian Festival Allegory," as well as newly composed music for the occasion.
*c*50 piano pieces

BIBLIOGRAPHY

A. Fay: "Musical Hours in Weimar with the Pianists of the Future," *Boston Daily Advertiser* (20 July 1876); repr. in *Inter-American Music Review*, vii/2 (1986), 79–83
W.S.B. Matthews, ed.: *A Hundred Years of Music in America* (Chicago, 1889)
K. Barne: *Listening to the Orchestra* (London, 1941)
R. Stevenson: "Musical Remembrances of Columbus's Voyages," *Inter-American Music Review*, xv/2 (1996), 32–47
E.D. Bomberger, ed.: *Brainard's Biographies of American Musicians* (Westport, CT, 1999)
E.D. Bomberger: *"A Tidal Wave of Encouragement": American Composers' Concerts in the Gilded Age* (Westport, CT, 2002)

ROBERT STEVENSON/DOUGLAS W. SHADLE

Pratt, Waldo Selden (*b* Philadelphia, PA, 10 Nov 1857; *d* Hartford, CT, 29 July 1939). Music scholar. He was educated at Williams College (BA 1878, MA 1881), and at Johns Hopkins University, where he studied Greek, archaeology, and aesthetics. He was largely self-taught in music. After two years with the Metropolitan Museum of Art in New York, he went to the Hartford Theological Seminary in 1882 as professor of ecclesiastical music and hymnology, a position he retained until his retirement in 1925. He taught concurrently at several other colleges, including the Institute of Musical Art in New York, and served as a church organist and a choral conductor. He was president of the Music Teachers National Association (1906–8), an editor of its *Proceedings*, and president of the American section of the International Musical Association (1911–16). He wrote a standard history of music and several books on the use of music in the church, and edited the American supplement to the second edition of *Grove's Dictionary*, a book of children's songs and a Sunday school hymnbook. He was awarded honorary degrees by Syracuse University (MusD 1898) and Williams College (LHD 1929).

WRITINGS

Musical Ministries in the Church (New York, 1901, enlarged 6/1923/*R*)
The History of Music (New York, 1907, repr. 1919 with supplementary death dates, enlarged 3/1935, with chap. on early 20th century by A. Mendel)
ed.: *Grove's Dictionary of Music and Musicians: American Supplement* (New York, 1920, rev. 2/1928/*R*)
The Music of the Pilgrims (New York, 1921/*R*) [on the Ainsworth Psalter]
The Problem of Music in the Church (Chicago, 1930)

BIBLIOGRAPHY

GMO
F.H. Johnson: *Musical Memories of Hartford* (Hartford, CT, 1931/*R*), 71ff
O. Kinkeldey: "Waldo Selden Pratt," *MQ*, xxvi (1940), 162–74

RAMONA H. MATTHEWS/R

Prausnitz, Frederik [Frederick] **(William)** (*b* Cologne, Germany, 26 Aug 1920; *d* Lewes, DE, 12 Nov 2004). Conductor of German birth. After immigration to the United States as a youth, he was trained at the Juilliard School, where he stayed on as a member of the conducting staff and faculty. He conducted the New England Conservatory SO (1961–9), was a staff conductor briefly at the BBC, and then was music director of the Syracuse (New York) SO (1971–4). The education of young professionals was one of his particular interests, and he joined the faculty of the Peabody Conservatory as music director of its symphony orchestra and opera in 1976; he became music director emeritus in 1980, continuing as director of the conducting studies program and the Contemporary Music Ensemble until 1998. He has been a visiting lecturer or consultant at Harvard, the University of Michigan, and Sussex University (England).

Prausnitz, a champion of contemporary music, has appeared widely as a guest conductor in the United States, Central America, and Europe. He gave the first American performances of works by, among others, Dallapiccola, Gerhard, Goehr, Lutyens, Petrassi, Schoenberg, Stockhausen, Varèse, and Webern; conversely, he introduced American composers such as Carter, Schuman, Sessions, and Wolpe to European audiences. He made a number of recordings of 20th-century music, ranging from the first complete recording of Walton's *Façade*, with Edith Sitwell, to Sessions's Symphony no.8; Sessions dedicated his Ninth Symphony to Prausnitz. He conducted the music of late 19th- and early 20th-century composers—including Mahler, early Schoenberg, and, notably, Elgar—with a special sense of identification and communicative power. By virtue both of technique and temperament, Prausnitz was most effective in music whose expressive gestures are sweeping and grand, but all his work was marked by the imprint of a probing and original mind. In 1974 he was awarded the Gustav Mahler Medal of Honor of the Bruckner Society of America. He wrote *Score and Podium: A Complete Guide to Conducting* (1983) and *Roger Sessions: How a "Difficult" Composer Got That Way* (2002). For the unusual spelling of his first name, he was indebted to an Italian poster printer, who omitted the penultimate "c" on the occasion of his Rome debut.

BIBLIOGRAPHY

N. Slonimsky: *Baker's Biographical Dictionary of Twentieth-Century Classical Musicians* (New York, 1997, ed. L.D. Kuhn, assoc ed. D. McIntire)

Obituary, *New York Times* (22 Nov 2004)

MICHAEL STEINBERG/GREG A STEINKE

Prepared piano. A piano in which the pitches, timbres, and dynamic responses of individual notes have been altered by means of bolts, screws, mutes, rubber erasers, and/or other objects inserted at particular points between or placed on the strings. JOHN CAGE devised the prepared piano for his *Bacchanale* (1940) and used it in a number of his subsequent compositions. Various attempts to alter piano strings, such as Maurice Ravel's inclusion of paper on the strings for *L'enfant et les sortilèges* (1920–5) and Henry Cowell's strumming, plucking, and muting of the instrument's interior in *Aeolian Harp* (c1923) and *The Banshee* (1925), predate Cage's invention.

Since the tonal alteration desired varies from one piece to another and depends on the nature and placement of the objects used to affect it, these must be indicated in the score, as shown in the table of preparations for Cage's *Sonatas and Interludes* (1946–8). However, with piano string layouts vary according to the maker, even careful preparation cannot guarantee the same effect when applied to different instruments; the prepared piano abounds with timbral possibilities. The sheer diversity of alterations employed by 20th-century composers has invited comparisons between the resulting sound of the prepared piano and that of the chamber orchestra, percussion ensemble, and gamelan.

Since around 1950 the prepared piano has grown in international popularity. Richard Bunger, the most frequent performer of the instrument during the latter half of the 20th century, identified more than 200 composers who contributed to the prepared piano repertoire, including the Americans Lou Harrison, Pauline Oliveros, James Tenney, and Christian Wolff.

Cage had already paired the prepared piano with other instruments, famously a percussion ensemble in *Amores* (1943); but the German composer Hans-Karsten Raecke went a step further in the 1970s by composing for ensembles comprising multiple prepared pianos. Other ensemble applications include compositions from vernacular traditions, as in John Cale's preparations for the Velvet Underground's song "All Tomorrow's Parties" (1967) and Ben Folds's preparation for "Free Coffee" (2008).

Other iterations of Cage's idea came with the preparation of player pianos by Conlon Nancarrow and of Harold Rhodes's electric pianos, most successfully by the experimentalist composer Eric Glick Rieman. Jazz musicians, including the American pianist Cecil Taylor, altered the hammers of their instruments with metal tacks. This represents a departure from the more ephemeral preparations championed by Cage and his immediate successors.

BIBLIOGRAPHY

R. Bunger: *The Well-prepared Piano* (Colorado Springs, 1973, 2/1981)

M. Fürst-Heidtmann: *Das präparierte Klavier des John Cage* (Regensburg, 1979)

D. Charles: "About John Cage's Prepared Piano," *Writings about John Cage*, ed. R. Kostelanetz (Ann Arbor, MI, 1993), 46–54

E. Salzman: "Cage's Well-tampered Clavier," *Writings about John Cage*, ed. R. Kostelanetz (Ann Arbor, MI, 1993), 55–7

L. Miller: "Cultural Intersections: John Cage in Seattle, 1938–1940," *John Cage: Music, Philosophy, and Intention, 1933–1950*, ed. D.W. Patterson (New York, 2002), 47–82

T. DeLio: *The Amores of John Cage* (Hillsdale, NY, 2009)

EDWIN M. RIPIN/HUGH DAVIES/THOMAS J. KERNAN

Presbyterian Church. Presbyterianism in North America consists of a cluster of Protestant denominations based on the ideas of the church reformers John Calvin and John Knox concerning theology and church government. The earliest congregations of Presbyterians in the American colonies were established in the 17th century by New England Puritans. In the same period, settlers from England, Scotland, Ireland, Wales, and elsewhere founded Presbyterian churches in Pennsylvania, Maryland, and Delaware; others established Presbyterian congregations in Canada in the 18th century.

Today, the largest of these denominations—the Presbyterian Church (USA)—offers guidance for church music through its Office of Worship, established in 1970, the same year the Presbyterian Association of Musicians was founded. These agencies publish a quarterly called *Reformed Liturgy and Music*. The association also sponsors music workshops and conferences, the largest of which is held each summer at the Presbyterian conference center in Montreat, NC.

1. Congregational singing in the United States. 2. Choral and instrumental music. 3. Congregational singing in Canada.

1. CONGREGATIONAL SINGING IN THE UNITED STATES. The Presbyterian Church in the American colonies followed the custom of metrical psalm singing favored by their Puritan and Presbyterian ancestors in Europe, notably of Calvin in Switzerland and Knox in Scotland. Calvin insisted on unison metrical psalm singing without accompaniment. The Scots and Irish colonists brought with them the Scottish Psalter (*Psalms of David in Meeter*, 1650), which drew on Francis Rous's psalter (1641) and the revision of Rous' version published by the Westminster Assembly of Divines (1643–7) as the *Psalms of David in English Meeter* (1646). Some of them also began to use the New England Puritans' Bay Psalm Book (1640), the first psalter published in North America.

The scarcity of psalters and a decline in musical literacy among these American pioneers led to the retention of only about a dozen psalm tunes, which in worship were "lined out" and sung with melodic and rhythmic liberties and at very slow tempos. The establishment of singing schools after 1720 by leaders such as John Tufts and Thomas Walter contributed notably to the improvement of psalm singing. Presbyterians came to enjoy "regular singing"—that is, reading by note and according to musical rules. Eventually the first American Presbyterian General Assembly recommended in 1788 that the custom of lining out be laid aside. The reformation of congregational singing continued into the 19th century; prominent in this effort was the Presbyterian composer and compiler Thomas Hastings.

During the Great Awakening (1726–44), the church split into two camps, the "Old Side" and the "New Side," in part because of differences over psalmody. The Old Side fought fiercely to retain their familiar Scottish Psalter, whereas the New Side favored the British New Version of Nahum Tate and Nicholas Brady (1696) and the *Psalms of David Imitated in the Language of the New Testament* by Isaac Watts (1719). This "psalm controversy" continued in some Presbyterian churches for decades; in many others it was soon eclipsed by the "great hymn controversy."

In addition to recasting the psalms, Watts also wrote a number of hymns, although hymns were controversial because of their "human composure." Benjamin Franklin reprinted Watts's psalms in Philadelphia (1729), and the Watts hymn texts became widely known to Presbyterians during the Great Awakening through the preaching of George Whitefield. *Urania, or a Choice Collection of Psalm-Tunes, Anthems, and Hymns* (1761), published by the Presbyterian James Lyon, psalm and hymn tunebooks such as *The New England Psalm Singer* (1770) by William Billings, and the evangelical hymns of Charles Wesley quickly gained popularity after the Awakening. Soon a large group of Presbyterians began to shift from psalmody alone to hymn singing. By 1788 the General Assembly could declare that the public praise of God was fulfilled "by singing psalms and hymns." In 1802 a revision of Watts's psalms with a collection of hymns was compiled by Timothy Dwight, the Presbyterian president of Yale College. In 1831 the Presbyterian Assembly authorized its first hymnal, a volume combining the two streams, suitably titled *Psalms and Hymns Adapted to Public Worship*. It included items by Watts and 70 other authors; it was revised and its hymnic content expanded in 1843.

The Civil War led American Presbyterians to divide into southern and northern denominations, which remained separated until their reunion in 1983. Before then, each denomination issued hymnals. The northern group, the Presbyterian Church in the USA, issued *The Hymnal of the Presbyterian Church* (1866), *The Presbyterian Hymnal* (1874), which was influenced by the British *Hymns Ancient and Modern* (1861), *The Hymnal* (1895, rev. 1911), edited by the distinguished hymnologist Louis Fitzgerald Benson, and *The Hymnal* (1933), edited by Clarence Dickinson, which took the Scottish *Revised Church Hymnary* (1927) as its model. Each of these contained few psalms. W. Covert and C. Laufer provided the Handbook (1935) to the 1933 volume.

In the latter half of the 19th century, some conservative southern Presbyterians embraced the hymnals of the minister Charles S. Robinson, including *Laudes Domini* (1884) and *In excelsis* (1897), though they were never officially adopted. In the early 20th century the predominantly southern Presbyterian Church in the United States published *New Psalms and Hymns* (1901) and *The Presbyterian Hymnal* (1927). The battle between psalms and hymns in much of American Presbyterianism was clearly won by hymnody by the turn of the 20th century.

In 1955 the two main Presbyterian branches joined three other Presbyterian and Reformed bodies in publishing *The Hymnbook,* edited by David Hugh Jones. Its 600 selections included more psalmody, New England content, and some gospel hymns. Before the 1983 reunion, both bodies also copublished *The Worshipbook* (1972), which included liturgical material and a collection of 373 hymns in alphabetical order of first line, for which Erik Routley provided an extensive commentary. The hymnal of the reunited Presbyterian Church (USA), *The Presbyterian Hymnal: Hymns, Psalms, and Spiritual Songs* (1990), edited by LindaJo McKim, contains 605 hymns in a range of musical styles, employs inclusive language, and incorporates psalmody and some African American, Hispanic, and Asian hymns. A separate publication, *Psalter* (1993), is available for speaking or singing the psalms. A new Presbyterian hymnal titled *Glory to God: the Presbyterian Hymnal,* edited by David Eicher, is expected to be published late in 2013.

Some Presbyterians have continued the tradition of singing only metrical psalms. The United Presbyterian psalters of 1871 and 1912 (prepared with assistance from eight other Presbyterian and Reformed denominations), *The Book of Psalms for Singing* (1973) of the Reformed Presbyterian Church, the *Trinity Psalter* (1994), and the *ARP Psalter* (2011) reflect this tendency. Some smaller Presbyterian bodies have issued their own hymnals, for example, the Orthodox Presbyterian Church's *Trinity Hymnal* (1961, 1990).

2. CHORAL AND INSTRUMENTAL MUSIC. Presbyterian choirs and singing societies originated in the early 18th century as a result of the movement toward "regular singing." During the second half of the 19th century, urban Presbyterian churches came to depend on quartets of paid singers, professionals who were frequently augmented by a volunteer choir of mixed voices. In most town and country congregations the choral leadership was provided entirely by volunteer singers.

The 20th century witnessed a flowering of choral music in Presbyterian churches under the leadership of two Presbyterian music educators. Clarence Dickinson established the School of Sacred Music at Union Theological Seminary in New York City in the late 1920s; at the same time John Finley Williamson founded the Westminster Choir College (now part of Rider University) in Princeton, NJ. Organist-choirmaster graduates of these and other schools began developing choirs in local congregations; in contemporary Presbyterian worship, such groups not only furnish leadership in hymn singing but also sing a wide repertory of anthems.

In 1763 James Lyon, compiler of *Urania,* argued for the lawfulness, excellency and advantage of instrumental music in the public worship of God. It was a plea for the pipe organ, and it was designed to improve singing in Philadelphia churches. Pipe organs were installed in the First Presbyterian Church of Alexandria, Virginia (1817), the Independent Presbyterian Church of Savannah, Georgia (by the 1820s), and the First Presbyterian Church of Rochester, New York (by 1830). Local congregations gradually came to employ a wide variety of instruments, but the organ predominated. On special occasions such as Christmas and Easter other instruments are frequently included, and, for oratorios and music dramas, a full orchestra may be employed. Handbell choirs are becoming popular, and sometimes Orff instruments are played for children's choir performances. Some more contemporary-style Presbyterian congregations use "praise teams" with vocal soloists or a small choral ensemble accompanied by keyboard, guitar, drums, and sometimes other instruments.

3. CONGREGATIONAL SINGING IN CANADA. Presbyterianism in Canada developed initially in Nova Scotia in the mid-18th century and gained momentum through continuing immigration from the British Isles (especially by members of the Church of Scotland) and the United States. A formal union of various Presbyterian congregations in 1875 led to the establishment of the Presbyterian Church in Canada. Their traditional use of the Scottish Psalter and the Scottish Paraphrases (1781) had already been complemented by psalms and hymns of Isaac Watts and hymnody of Charles Wesley. The Presbyterian *Book of Praise* (1897) was their first significant hymnal. Edited by Alexander MacMillan, its 621 selections included both metrical psalmody and a strongly British-oriented group of hymns; it was revised in 1918 to include more hymns from the United States. Two-thirds of Canadian Presbyterians joined with Methodists and Congregationalists to form the United Church of Canada in 1925. The nonuniting or "continuing" Presbyterians, called the Presbyterian Church in Canada, kept singing from their 1918 *Book of Praise.* The eventual dissatisfaction with the 1918 volume led the church authorities to authorize a supplement, *Praise Ways* (1975), which was further supplemented by the unofficial *Celebrate* (1983). A new psalter, *The Book of Psalms*, was issued in 1995, and was followed by a major revision of their old *Book of Praise.* Its 1997 edition consists of about 500 texts including modern hymns, scripture choruses, global hymns, and more works by Canadians, as well as 100 metrical psalms.

BIBLIOGRAPHY

L.F. Benson: *The English Hymn* (New York, 1915/R1962)

H.W. Foote: *Three Centuries of American Hymnody* (Hamden, CT, 1961)

J. Melton: *Presbyterian Worship in America: Changing Patterns since 1787* (Richmond, VA, 1967)

J.S. Moir: *Enduring Witness: a History of the Presbyterian Church in Canada* (Hamilton, ON, 1974)

N. Temperley: "The Old Way of Singing: its Origins and Development," *JAMS,* xxxiv (1981), 511–44

H.D. McKellar: "Hymnody of Canada: Presbyterian, Methodist, United Church" [unpublished typescript for the Hymn Society's Dictionary of American Hymnology, 1986]

M.F. Simmons: "Hymnody: Its Place in Twentieth Century Presbyterianism," *The Confessional Mosaic: Presbyterianism and Twentieth-Century Theology,* ed. M.J. Coalter, et al (Louisville, KY, 1990), 162–86

D.G. Hart and J.R. Muether: *Seeking a Better Country: 300 Years of American Presbyterianism* (Phillipsburg, NJ, 2007)

D.G. Hart: "Psalters, Hymnals, Worship Wars, and American Presbyterian Piety," *Sing a New Song: Recovering Psalm Singing for the Twenty-First Century,* eds. J.R. Beeke and A.T. Selvaggio (Grand Rapids, MI, 2010), 61–77

BERT F. POLMAN (1, 3) JAMES R. SYDNOR/
BERT F. POLMAN (2)

Prescott, Abraham (*b* Deerfield, NH, 5 July 1789; *d* Concord, NH, 6 May 1858). Maker of bowed string and keyboard instruments. He learned cabinet making from his uncle and made his first instrument, a "bass viol" or "church bass" (in fact, a large cello; *see* BASS VIOL), in 1809 in Deerfield. The instrument, bought by a local musician for use in church services, was the first of several hundred made and sold by Prescott by the 1840s. He played the "bass viol" (again, probably the cello) while attending Atkinson Academy, served as fife major in the 1812 war and later gave occasional singing lessons. He used his commercial acumen and his musical and religious associations (he was a deacon of the Baptist Church) to build a thriving music business. His apprentices included DAVID M. DEARBORN and Andrew Dearborn.

In 1831 Prescott opened a music store in Concord, New Hampshire; by 1833 he had moved the whole of his business there for better trade and shipping connections with Boston. In 1836 he pioneered the manufacture of small reed organs (known as "lap organs" or "rocking melodeons"; *see* REED ORGAN). In 1845 the Prescott firm, now Abraham Prescott & Son (his son was Abraham J. Prescott) turned its attention to seraphines, melodeons, and reed organs for church, school, and home use. The Dearborn brothers took over from Prescott's the manufacture of string instruments in about 1848, and after Prescott retired in 1850, the firm's constitution underwent several changes. From 1850 to 1852 it was known as Prescott & Brothers (in the hands of Prescott's sons, Abraham J., Joseph W., and Josiah B.); from 1852 to 1870 Prescott Brothers (after 1858 under Abraham J. & George D.B. Prescott); from 1871 to 1886 the Prescott Organ Co.; from 1887 to 1891 the Prescott Piano & Organ Co.; and from 1891 to 1912 the Prescott Piano Co. (which continued as piano dealers until 1917).

Prescott's instruments were well made. What he described as "bass viols" in his Deerfield business ledgers were no doubt the large cellos (typical dimensions: length 32¼ inches, lower bout 20 inches, upper bout 15¾ inches, neck 9⅞ inches) used in churches and now found in private collections and those of the Smithsonian Institution and at Yale University. Most Prescott basses are fitted with machine-head tuning devices in place of pegs. His double basses are still used today by leading orchestral and jazz players. Examples of his lap organs and larger reed organs can be found at the Smithsonian Institution and the New Hampshire Historical Society, where his business ledgers are also held.

BIBLIOGRAPHY

W. Prescott: *The Prescott Memorial* (Boston, 1870)
Over 100 Years of Musical Progress 1809–1910 (Concord, NH, 1910) [Prescott Piano Company pubn]
W. Henley: *Universal Dictionary of Violin and Bow Makers*, iv (Brighton, 1960)
S.R. Ogden: *Abraham Prescott and his Bass Viols* (MS, 1966, *CObs*)
B.D. Turcott: "Concord Instrument Makers," *Historical New Hampshire*, xxii/1 (1967), 18–27

CYNTHIA ADAMS HOOVER/R

Prescott, Gerald Roscoe (*b* Plymouth, IA, 19 July 1902; *d* Tampa, FL, 20 Nov 2005). Conductor and writer. His early musical instruction was on the reed organ, then piano. He joined a boys' band playing cornet. He majored in science at Upper Iowa University (BA 1924) and received his Master's degree from the University of Iowa in 1938. He taught science and developed a band and orchestra in Ida Grove, Iowa. Early in his career, Prescott spent summers in Chicago studying privately with FREDERICK NEIL INNES, Victor Grabel, and HALE A. VANDERCOOK. He led the Mason City (Iowa) High School Band from 1927–31. The band won many contests and Prescott's reputation grew; he was eventually recommended to become Director of Bands at the University of Minnesota (1932–57); he continued to teach music education courses there until 1967. From 1967 to 1972 he taught at the University of South Florida.

He developed the *Prescott Technic System*, a band curriculum based on methods developed in his early years of teaching high school bands and rooted in conservatory methods such as Arban and Klosé. His *Getting Results with High School Bands* (New York, 1938), co-authored with L.W. Chidester, was widely used. He was the second president of the College Band Directors National Association (1946).

BIBLIOGRAPHY

G.R. Prescott and L.W. Chidester: *Getting Results with School Bands* (New York, 1938)
A.M. Mast: *A History of the Mason City (Iowa) High School and Community Bands, 1920–1999* (diss., U. of Iowa, 2000)
C.L. Vermillion: *An Overview of Gerald R. Prescott's 1935 "The Prescott Technic System" With Recommendations for a Contemporary Edition* (diss., U. of Southern Mississippi, 2006)

WILLIAM BERZ

Prescott, Thomas M(ayhew) (*b* Beckley, WV, 11 May 1951). Maker of historical recorders. Prescott graduated from Lake Forest College, Illinois (BA in musicology, 1973). While in college, he attended the National Music Camp in Interlochen, Michigan, and developed an interest in the recorder and historical performance practice through the playing of Tom Butts, who was then studying with early music pioneer Robert Donington. In October 1973 Prescott was hired by the prestigious instrument maker FRIEDRICH VON HUENE, from whom he learned his craft. The first instruments he sold under his own name while working for Huene were Grenser baroque flute reproductions.

The two years Prescott spent in Huene's workshop provided the knowledge, experience, and income he needed to establish his own business, Prescott Workshop, in Cambridge, Massachusetts, in 1975; after several moves,

the workshop settled in Hanover, New Hampshire, in 1989. Following an initial offering of a single recorder, Prescott's catalog has since expanded to include ten different baroque-style recorders, four transitional instruments, six renaissance recorders, a J.C. Denner baroque bass in F, and a renaissance basset in G. His designs are informed by the instruments of Peter Bressan (1663–1731) and the calculations and construction principles of modern instrument builder Robert Marvin.

ELLEN EXNER

Preservation. The term *preservation* encompasses the broad variety of actions taken to prolong the useful life of an object. In American music libraries, approaches to preservation have evolved in response to three factors: the types of materials held in collections, technological innovations that altered our means of preservation, and the patterns of use that determine the best course of action.

1. TYPE OF MATERIALS. During the early history of American libraries, roughly through 1850, musical holdings mostly consisted of scores printed on rag paper made from cotton with long fibers. Because of the stable medium, preservation of collections primarily involved preventing and repairing damage and loss from external forces. Physical treatment of individual objects is also called conservation and remains an important preservation approach. New papermaking and printing techniques introduced after 1850 included higher wood pulp content with shorter fibers and acidic sizing, resulting in paper that was subject to rapid embrittlement. (*Sizing* is a substance employed in paper making to control ink absorption.) Though the problem began to be recognized early in the 20th century, the lack of a cost-effective means of deacidification or of reproducing acid-free printed volumes stymied systematic efforts to develop a solution for several decades, even as the amount of material published on acidic paper ballooned. The introduction of acid-free paper and a variety of deacidification processes at the end of the 20th century has ameliorated the situation for paper materials. During the same period, libraries began to collect recorded music in many formats, including cylinders, discs, magnetic tape, and digital formats. These have introduced new challenges, both of fragility and of obsolescence, but also new conceptual approaches.

2. TECHNOLOGICAL INNOVATIONS. Copying content from a brittle or obsolete older format to a more durable new format was first introduced as a marketing ploy in the 1920s when recording companies remastered cylinder recordings to the more popular disc format. Reformatting has been used for sound preservation since then. The development of microfilm in the 1960s permitted the reformatting of paper materials as well. Because polyester microfilm offered durability and inexpensive mass duplication, it unleashed a nationwide effort to preserve the printed content through reproduction on microfilms. One of the most important offshoots of this effort was the development of cost-effective coordinated

preservation administration within and among libraries. Between the 1970s and the 1990s, most major libraries built preservation departments and developed coordinated networks to avoid duplicate effort.

The digital technology that has arisen since the 1990s has introduced another new paradigm: repetitive digital duplication as a means of preserving a copy of an image or sound independent of physical format. In analog reproduction, both audio and visual, there is an incremental loss in quality with repeated copying, so the standard procedure is to make a very durable copy to last indefinitely. However, a digital file can, in principle, be duplicated repeatedly without loss of quality. The most recent phase of preservation history combines the administrative structure developed for microfilm projects with digital reproduction technology. Rather than depending on durable formats, institutions develop an organizational structure to support ongoing administration of multiple, easily duplicated (though individually fragile and quickly obsolescent) electronic copies. The capacity for high fidelity of digital duplication, the potential expanded accessibility of the copies, and the fact that for sound recordings no durable medium exists for large collections all promote the transition in content preservation from a dependence on a durable medium to long-term administration of multiple digital copies.

The rapid pace of technological development, however, threatens the complete loss of cultural content when a carrier format becomes obsolete before the content is copied to the next new format. In addition, the digitization of the original may introduce alterations, whether through intentional editing, poor duplication technique, or digital *aliasing* (the misreading of data due to sampling error). Different storage formats, whether analog or digital, offer various compromises between fidelity, economy, and ease of use. Prolonging the life of cultural content includes developing and following best practices to balance institutional resources with the need to maintain a level of reproduction fidelity that will satisfy both present needs and the unknowable requirements of future users. This includes the perpetual updating of records and developing metadata and other publication structures to make the content widely accessible.

3. PATTERNS OF USE. The final important consideration in preservation approach is the end use of the object being preserved. For unique cultural artifacts such as manuscripts, preservation of the physical object is paramount. This may include noninvasive protection, such as enclosing the individual pages of a manuscript in Mylar to allow close examination without contact. It may also include repair of damage or preventive treatment such as deacidification. A major challenge in conservation is to avoid treatments that obscure historical information, such as manuscript performance annotations that may have been mistaken for decay or damage. Objects in active use provide the greatest challenge for preservation, both because of the possibility of accidental damage and because of the potential for "restorative" care to cause unintended changes.

For mass-produced scores, reformatted copies that preserve the cultural content are the preferred substitutes for the user. Decisions to preserve performance markings are often complicated by lack of knowledge of their provenance. Another consideration is the preservation of advertising within publications, which may seem ephemeral but may also provide useful information for researchers.

Preservation of music collections now comprises three facets: conservation, including repair; security from disaster, theft, and abuse; and environmental controls. Preservation reformatting of cultural information involves deciding what information is salient and what level of fidelity is necessary, ranging from the simple iconic information of printed text to the extreme demands of recorded sound and images. Administration of the program includes setting priorities, finding and allocating resources, building durable organizations especially for digital preservation, and monitoring rights management for content not in the public domain. A full preservation program requires a significant investment but is an indispensable cost to preserve our history.

BIBLIOGRAPHY

W. Blades: *Enemies of Books* (London, 1880, 2/1888), <http://www. netLibrary.com/urlapi.asp?action=summary&v=1&bookid=2011401>

W.J. Barrow: *Manuscripts and Documents, Their Deterioration and Restoration* (Charlottesville, VA, 1955)

G.D. Cunha and D.G. Cunha: *Conservation of Library Materials* (Metuchen, NJ, 2/1971)

M.T. Roberts and D. Etherington: *Bookbinding and the Conservation of Books: a Dictionary of Descriptive Terminology* (Washington, DC, 1982). <http://palimpsest.stanford.edu/don/don.html>

S.G. Swartzburg: *Preserving Library Materials: a Manual* (Metuchen, NJ, 2/1995)

S. Honea: "Preservation at the Sibley Music Library of the Eastman School of Music," *Notes*, liii/2 (Dec 1996), 381–402

A. Carli: *Binding and Care of Printed Music* (Lanham, MD, 2003)

M. Casey and B. Gordon: *Sound Directions: Best Practices for Audio Preservation*, <http://www.dlib.indiana.edu/projects/sounddirections/bestpractices2007/>

The American Library Association and the Music Library Association both maintain web pages with information on library conservation and preservation issues, <http://www.ala.org/ala/mgrps/divs/alcts/mgrps/pars/index.cfm>, <http://www.musiclibraryassoc.org/committees/Preservation/>

ALICE CARLI

Preservation Hall Jazz Band. Jazz ensembles. Emerging from impromptu sessions at Larry Borenstein's Associated Artists Gallery on St. Peter Street in the 1950s, Preservation Hall was established in 1961 under the administration of Allan and Sandra Jaffe to ensure a place for New Orleans jazz bands to play free from commercial imperatives. The key to success was recording and touring, which created an international awareness of the Hall and its musicians. A succession of more than 25 bands, often working simultaneously, have operated under the Preservation Hall brand: Kid Thomas Valentine and George Lewis (first US tour 1963), George Lewis with Punch Miller (Japan tours 1963–5), De De Pierce (European tour 1967; Newport Festival 1970), Kid Thomas with Louis Nelson, Albert Burbank, and Emanuel Paul (tours of Australia, Japan, Canada, and Europe 1971; USSR 1972). By the mid-1970s trumpeter

Percy Humphrey led the principal touring band, featuring his brother Willie on clarinet. The band continued an active schedule of national and international touring for 20 years, complemented by three LPs for CBS (1977–83). Following the deaths of the Humphrey Brothers, John Brunious (or sometimes his brother Wendell) served as leader of the band. Since John's untimely death in 2008, Dr. Michael White and Gregg Stafford have fronted bands at the Hall. Under Benjamin Jaffe's (Allan and Sandra's son; bassist) guidance, significant experimentation and re-branding has occurred since Hurricane Katrina in 2005, including performances by the Preservation Hall Jazz Band at rock events, such as the Voodoo Festival in New Orleans.

BIBLIOGRAPHY
W. Carter: *Preservation Hall: Music from the Heart* (New York, 1991)
E. Abrams: *Preservation Hall: Interviews with Preservation Hall Band Members*, with photographs by S. Brinkman (Baton Rouge, LA, 2011)
BRUCE BOYD RAEBURN

Presley, Elvis (Aaron) [Aron] (*b* East Tupelo, MS, 8 Jan 1935; *d* Memphis, TN, 16 Aug 1977). Rock and roll singer, guitarist, and actor. As the most successful artist of the mid-1950s rock and roll explosion, Presley had a profound impact on popular music. His sense of style, musical and personal, was both the focal point of the media reaction to early rock and roll and the inspiration for many of the most important rock musicians to follow. The narrative of his meteoric rise and subsequent decline amid mysterious and tawdry circumstances fueled many myths both during his life and after his death at 42.

Presley was raised in extreme poverty in the deep South, and his earliest musical experiences came in the Pentecostal services of the First Assembly of God Church. Other formative influences included popular tunes of the day, country music, blues, and rhythm-and-blues. Although he had little experience as a performer, in 1954, at the age of 19, he came to the attention of Sam Phillips, owner of the Memphis recording company Sun Records. Phillips teamed Presley, who sang and played guitar, with local country and western musicians Scotty Moore (guitar) and Bill Black (bass). During their first recording session in June 1954, the trio recorded a single with the two sides "That's all right, mama," originally recorded in 1946 by the blues singer Arthur "Big Boy" Crudup, and "Blue Moon of Kentucky," originally recorded in 1946 by the bluegrass pioneer Bill Monroe. The group's style blended elements of country and rhythm-and-blues without being identifiable as either; the distinctive sound included Moore's rhythmically oriented lead guitar, Black's slapped bass, and Presley's forceful, if crude, rhythm guitar, with the recording swathed in a distinctive electronic echo effect. Presley's voice, however, attracted the most attention: swooping almost two octaves at times, changing timbre from a croon to a growl instantaneously, he seemed not so much to be synthesizing pre-existing styles as to be juxtaposing them, sometimes within the course of a single phrase. While the trio's initial record provoked enthusiastic responses immediately upon being broad-

cast on Memphis radio, it confused audiences, who wondered if the singer was white or black. Although white hillbilly musicians' music had incorporated African American instrumental and vocal approaches since the earliest recordings in the 1920s, no previous white singer had so successfully forged an individual style so clearly rooted in a contemporary African American idiom. Presley, Moore, and Black released four more singles with Sun Records (1954–5); each one featured a blues or rhythm-and-blues song backed with a country-style number; each one displayed increasing confidence on the part of Presley, and each recording was more commercially successful than the preceding one, with the last two, "Baby, let's play house" and "Mystery Train," reaching the top ten in the Billboard national country and western chart. Presley's uninhibited, sexually charged performances throughout the Southeast provoked frenzied responses and influenced other musicians: by the end of 1955 performers such as Carl Perkins and Johnny Cash had emerged with a style known as ROCKABILLY which bore a strong resemblance to Presley's.

Presley's growing popularity attracted the attention of promoter "Colonel" Tom Parker, who negotiated the sale of Presley's contract to RCA records for the unheard-of-sum of $35,000. His first recording for RCA, "Heartbreak Hotel," which was released in March 1956, achieved the unprecedented feat of reaching the top five on the pop, rhythm-and-blues, and country charts simultaneously. This recording and the songs that followed in 1956 all combined aspects of his spare Sun recordings with an increasingly heavy instrumentation that included piano, drums, and background singers, and so moved the sound closer to that of mainstream pop. Both sides of his third RCA single "Hound Dog" and "Don't be cruel" hit no.1 on all three charts. "Hound

Elvis Presley on The Ed Sullivan Show, *New York, 1956. (CBS/Landov)*

Dog" radically transformed Big Mama Thornton's 1952 rhythm-and-blues hit, while "Don't be cruel" was a more pop-oriented recording written specifically for him. Presley's vocal style already showed signs of mannerism, trading the unpredictable exchanges of different voices of the early recordings for a single effect throughout each song. At the same time he continued to explore new musical territory with the recording of "Love me tender" (1956), from his first movie, of the same title, an updated version of the Civil War song "Aura Lea."

Over the next two years, Presley released numerous successful recordings of fast or medium tempo rock and roll songs, and ballads derived from country music, Tin Pan Alley, or gospel music. He acted in three more films, *Loving You*, *Jailhouse Rock*, and *Kid Creole*, all of which were successful. His suggestive performing style as presented in recordings, films, and personal appearances generated a firestorm of critical disapproval, which did nothing to dim his popularity. Presley's induction into the US Army in early 1958 removed him from the public eye for two years, during which time recordings made previously continued to be released. After his return to civilian life in 1960, he recorded and released "Stuck on You," a song in the rock and roll style of his pre-army recordings. However, his next two hits represented a considerable change of direction: "Are you lonesome tonight?" and "It's now or never" (based on the Italian traditional "O sole mio" in the style of one of Presley's idols, Mario Lanza) were both ballads that showed Presley moving toward a middle-of-the-road blend of country and pop music. This move away from his raucous mid-1950s rock and roll style, and a simultaneous retreat from performing into a string of formulaic films, contributed to his waning popularity as a recording artist. Despite this, he continued to have numerous top ten songs up to 1963. The change in popular music tastes around 1964 with the sudden dominance of British bands such as the Beatles and the Rolling Stones and of artists recording for the Motown record label, such as the Supremes and the Four Tops, effectively ended his consistent success in the top 40.

In the late 1960s Presley attempted to re-establish himself as a creative artist. In 1968 he taped a television special clad in black leather in which he performed many of his older songs with a small, informal ensemble in front of a live audience. In 1969 he released the album *From Elvis in Memphis*, featuring his strongest material since his return to civilian life, and the two hit singles "In the Ghetto" and "Suspicious Minds." He returned to live performing that year as well; however, after an initial burst of energy, these performances soon degenerated into formula and self-parody. Although he had a few sporadic hits over the succeeding years, most notably with "Burning Love" (1972), he failed to achieve artistic or commercial consistency with his recordings. From 1972 to the time of his death Presley's performances became increasingly erratic as his health deteriorated and his behavior grew more eccentric and reclusive. His rise and fall have been exhaustively documented,

and perhaps no other celebrity has led such an active postmortem existence in the public imagination.

BIBLIOGRAPHY

J. Hopkins: *Elvis* (New York, 1971)
G. Marcus: *Mystery Train: Images of America in Rock 'n' Roll Music* (New York, 1975)
M. Farren and P. Marchbank: *Elvis in his own Words* (London, 1977)
D. Marsh: *Elvis* (New York, 1982)
K. Quain: *The Elvis Reader: Texts and Sources on the King of Rock 'n Roll* (New York, 1992) [incl. R. Middleton: "All Shook Up," 3–12; C. Wolfe: "Presley and the Gospel Tradition," 13–27]
P. Guralnick: *Last Train to Memphis: the Rise of Elvis Presley* (Boston, 1994) [incl. bibliography and discography]
G. Rodman: *Elvis after Elvis: the Posthumous Career of a Living Legend* (London, 1996)
P. Guralnick: *Careless Love: the Unmaking of Elvis Presley* (Boston, 1999)

DAVID BRACKETT

Presser. Firm of music publishers. It was founded in Philadelphia in 1883 by THEODORE PRESSER (*b* Pittsburgh, PA, 3 July 1848; *d* Philadelphia, PA, 28 Oct 1925), a musical philanthropist who had studied at the New England Conservatory in Boston. Earlier that year he had begun publication of a monthly magazine, *The Etude*, devoted to the interests of music teachers and students. In 1906 he opened in Philadelphia the Presser Home for Retired Music Teachers, the only such institution in the United States. In 1916 the Presser Foundation was established with funds of more than $1,000,000 for the support of the home, a department of scholarships (given directly to institutions and not to individuals), and a department for the relief of deserving musicians. After his death the firm was expanded by the acquisition of Church (1930), Ditson (1931), and the Mercury Music Corporation (1969), which included the catalogs of Beekman Music and Merrymount Music. In 1970 Elkan-Vogel became a subsidiary, and in 1981 the firm purchased the bulk of the copyrights of American Music Edition. Through Ditson, the company traces its history to 1783, making it the nation's oldest continuous music publisher. In 1949 Presser's main office was moved from Philadelphia to Bryn Mawr, Pennsylvania. The firm was acquired in 2004 by Carl Fischer.

Presser is the sole agent in the United States for a number of American publishers, including Columbia Music, Coronet, and Peermusic Classical, as well as for foreign firms. The company serves the needs of dealers, teachers, and musicians, drawing from a huge stock of classical, educational, and light music. It also maintains a large library of works for hire, including opera, ballet, and orchestral music. Among the many American composers represented by Presser are Donald Erb, Charles Ives, Vincent Persichetti, George Rochberg, Carl Ruggles, Peter Schickele, William Schuman, Roger Sessions, Ralph Shapey, Steven Stucky, Hugo Weisgall, Richard Wernick, and Ellen Taaffe Zwilich.

BIBLIOGRAPHY

A.A. Hauser: "American Music Publishing in 1958," *Notes*, xv (1957–8), 377–83
C. Yoder: *Theodore Presser, Educator, Publisher, Philanthropist: Selected Contributions to the Music Teaching Profession in America* (diss., U. of Illinois, 1978)

W.C. Rorick: "Theodore Presser Company: a Bicentennial Retrospect," *FAM*, xxxi (1984), 118–25

W. THOMAS MARROCCO, MARK JACOBS,
WARREN STOREY SMITH/LEAH BRANSTETTER

Presser, Theodore (*b* Pittsburgh, PA, 3 July 1848; *d* Philadelphia, PA, 28 Oct 1925). Teacher, editor, and publisher. Presser studied at the New England Conservatory in Boston and the Leipzig Conservatory. He established the music department at Ohio Wesleyan University, directed music at Hollins College, and worked at Randolph Macon College for Women in Lynchburg, Virginia. In 1883 in Virginia, with $250, he founded *The Etude*, a monthly music magazine containing compositions, informative articles, and advice for music teachers and students. Seeking larger quarters for the successful venture he moved to Philadelphia in 1884, then established the Theodore Presser Company, which continued to publish the magazine until 1957. The company, the oldest continuing music publisher in the United States, acquired other companies and today, as part of Carl Fischer, represents more than 70 US and foreign publishers. He opened the Presser Home for Retired Music Teachers in 1906, and established the Presser Foundation in 1916 with over $1 million to support the Home and to provide scholarships and a relief fund for musicians. In the philanthropic spirit of its founder the Foundation, dedicated to the support of music and music education, continues to award scholarships and grants.

BIBLIOGRAPHY
C. Yoder: *Theodore Presser, Educator, Publisher, Philanthropist: Selected Contributions to the Music Teaching Profession in America* (diss., U. of Illinois, 1978)
E.D. Bomberger, ed: *An Index to Music Published in "The Etude" Magazine, 1883–1957* (Lanham, MD, Toronto, and Oxford, 2004)

WARREN STOREY SMITH/MARTHA FURMAN SCHLEIFER

Pressing, Jeff (*b* San Diego, CA, 30 Nov 1946; *d* Melbourne, Australia, 28 April 2002). Australian American composer and writer. Born and educated in the United States, he moved to Melbourne in 1975 to teach jazz, electronic and computer music, and composition at La Trobe University (1975–93). In parallel, he pursued a career as a research scientist in cognitive psychology: from 1994 he was senior lecturer in psychology at the University of Melbourne. His compositions span a wide range of styles and influences, including fusion jazz, African drumming, chamber music in the tradition of Western art music, computer music, sound poetry, multi-cultural music, and multimedia presentations. As a performer he founded and performed with ensembles such as the World Rhythm Band, which specializes in jazz improvisation, the African drumming ensemble Adzohu, and the live-electronics ensemble OZDIMO. His compositions have been performed in Australia, the United States, Japan, Sweden, and elsewhere. Pressing's work was always marked by freshness and curiosity. His exploratory urge was strong, and his best work is marked by rhythmic liveliness, elaborate textures, and a sense of timbral fantasy, as illustrated by such electronic works as *The Butterfly's Dream* and *Zalankara*.

His sound poetry and verbal performances also contain humor and satire, an example being *The isms infecting musical thought*.

WORKS
Orch: Zalankara, multicultural sym., Western orch, transcultural orch, elec orch, 1991; Symphonia, 1992; Transliteration, str, 1993
Jazz ens: History, studio orch, 1973; Glyopsis, jazz qnt, 1974; Arrow, fl, kbd, bass, perc, 1975; Events, big band, 1976; Gait, 1v, jazz ens, 1976, rev. 2000; Mythical Creatures II, child nar, big band, 1976; Prime Funk, big band, 1976; Islands, big band, 1977; Torus, str qt, pf, synth, bass, drums, 1978; Stumbling Along, s sax, pf, synth, bass, 2 perc, 1980; Home and Mind, jazz qt, 1980; The Sun as a Golden Apple, vn, gui, tpt, elec pf, synth, bass, drums, perc, 1980; Lesser Trocanter, s sax, pf, synth, bass, 2 perc, 1981; Sex Life of the Snail, jazz qnt, 1982; The Earth is All that Lasts, 1v, acc., 1985
Chbr and solo inst: Tooth, fl, 1977; Request, trbn, vc, 1978; Tidbits, trbn, 1978; The Miracle of Skin, music theater, cl, pf, trbn, 1978; For Eight, 8 db, 1978; Familiar Artillery Implement, t sax ens, 2 kbd, 1979; Equator, trbn, pf, 1980; Songs for a Dying World, trbn, perc, pf, 1981; If Nineteen were Twelve, fl, trbn, vc, pf, elec pf/synth, perc, 1982; Gondwanaland, 5 West African perc (West African drums, bells, rattles), 1984; Cadenza, tpt, vc, pf, perc, elec pf/synth, 1985; Descent of the Avatar, a sax, trbn, perc, synths, 1987; Lizard Dance, pf, 1987; The Ticking Clock, pf, 1987; Sonata, vn, pf, 1991; Squeak, pf, 1991; Grace, ob, kbd, perc, 1992; Constructed Dreaming I, 4 perc, 1994; Simple Music I, gui, 1998; Vector, pf, 2001
Elec: Life on the Planet Earth, 1973; Tippety Tappety Torp, nar, 5 tape machines, 1977; Study no.1, 4 DX7 synths, 1985; 2 Fantasies for Harp, DX7 synth, 1987; The Sea, synths, sampler, 1987; Daru Dance, DX7 synth, perc, 1987; His Master's Voice, vv, sampler, synths, elecs, 1988–90; Jump Start, pf, synths, perc, 1988; Butterfly's Dream, DX7-II synth, 1989; 2 Generic Folksongs, sax, DX7-II, 1989; Ambient Complexities I and II, tape, 1992
Vocal: Allegory, music theater, 3 nar, cl, trbn, vc, pf, 1978; The Immortal's Story, orat., T, Bar, chorus, tpt, trbn, 3 perc, slides, 1983–4; Truth in Other Times and Places, female/boys' chorus, 2001
Other: On the Power of Women, 1v, perf, tape, pf, perc, 1982; Interactions with Kandinsky, pf, elec pf, synths, samplers, slides, 1984–8; The isms infecting musical thought: scientism, minimalism, maximalism, structuralism, reductionism, et al.: is there a doctor in the house?, perf. lecture, perf. as radio play, ABC radio, 1991; For and with MAX, ob, pf, synth, perc, projections, 1991

Principal publisher: La Trobe University Press
Principal recording company: Discovery

WRITINGS
"Pitch Class Set Structures in Contemporary Jazz," *Jazzforschung/Jazz Research*, xiv (1982), 133–72
"Cognitive Processes in Improvisation," *Cognitive Processes in the Perception of Art*, ed. R. Crozier and A. Chapman (Amsterdam, 1984), 345–63
"Improvisation: Methods and Models," *Generative Processes in Music*, ed. J. Sloboda (Oxford, 1988), 129–78
"Non-Linear Maps as Generators of Musical Design," *Computer Music Journal*, xii/2 (1988), 35–47
"Cybernetic Issues in Interactive Performance Systems," *Computer Music Journal*, xiv/1 (1990), 37–52
Synthesizer Performance and Real-Time Techniques (Madison, WI, and London, 1992)
"The Physicality and Corporeality of Improvisation," *Sounds Australia*, no.59 (2002), 22–4

BIBLIOGRAPHY
B. Williams: "Encomium for Jeff Pressing," *Music Perception*, xx/3 (2003) 315–21

WARREN BURT/R

Prestige. Record company. It was originally established in New York City in 1949 by record producer Bob Weinstock. At the age of 20 Weinstock made his first recordings, featuring pianist Lennie Tristano's quintet, and released them on the New Jazz label. Later that same year he started Prestige, which became the flagship of a family of imprints including Bluesville, Swingville, Moodsville, Par, Tru-Sound, and New Jazz. Because he had recorded so many saxophonists (including Sonny Stitt, Gene Ammons, Zoot Sims, Stan Getz, Wardell Gray, and others), an image of the instrument itself was integrated into the company's original logo. Weinstock's musical taste was not limited to the saxophone, though; singer Annie Ross, pianist Thelonious Monk, and trumpeter Miles Davis all called the label home during the 1950s. In 1971 Weinstock sold the label to a British firm, Regency Record Co., Ltd., which licensed the catalog to Fantasy Records for North America; Fantasy subsequently purchased the label's assets.

In 2004 Prestige was acquired by the Concord Music Group when it merged with Fantasy Records. Prestige remains an active imprint, primarily as a vehicle for reissues by artists including John Coltrane, Eric Dolphy, Art Farmer, and others.

BIBLIOGRAPHY

B. Ratliff: "Bob Weinstock, 77, Founder of the Jazz Label Prestige," *New York Times* (16 Jan 2006), A22 [obituary]

THANE TIERNEY

Preston, Billy [William] **(E.)** (*b* Houston, TX, 2 Sept 1946; *d* Scottsdale, AZ, 6 June 2006). Keyboard player, singer, and songwriter. Preston was a piano prodigy, who began learning when he was three and was playing live gigs with bands by the age of ten. Preston played with gospel stars Mahalia Jackson and James Cleveland, and landed a small acting role as a young W.C. Handy in the film *St. Louis Blues* (1958). In the 1960s he began to accompany various high profile artists, including Ray Charles, Sam Cooke, and Little Richard. In 1965 he released his solo album *The Most Exciting Organ Ever*. He released several additional albums, showcasing his remarkable keyboard skills and lively personality, but his connection with the Beatles brought him even greater prominence. Invited to the band's recording sessions by George Harrison, Preston played electric piano and organ on three of their late albums, contributing especially to *Abbey Road* (1969) and *Let It Be* (1970). He also landed a contract with Apple Records, for which he produced multiple albums. He went on to play with the Rolling Stones, Aretha Franklin, and Eric Clapton, among other stars. He also co-composed various successful songs, including "You are so beautiful" (1974), made popular by Joe Cocker. He continued to tour and record into the 21st century.

JONAS WESTOVER

Preston, Frances (*b* Nashville, TN, 27 Aug 1928; *d* Nashville, 13 June 2012). Music executive and philanthropist. Preston began her career as a messenger for the National Life and Accident Insurance Company. She soon became a receptionist at the company's radio station, WSM, and was largely responsible for organizing the early WSM Disc Jockey Convention, an event that would become the most important annual gathering for country music professionals. In 1958 she was hired to open a Nashville office for BROADCAST MUSIC, INC. Under her direction, BMI became the dominant performing rights organization in the region and, by offering advances to new publishers and songwriters, the central economic engine of the country music industry. By 1964 BMI Nashville had expanded from two people working in Preston's garage to 400 employees, and she reportedly became the first female executive in Tennessee when she was promoted to vice president. In 1985 she moved to BMI's New York office as senior vice president for performing rights, and a year later was named president and CEO, a position she held until her retirement in 2004. There she oversaw a major reconfiguration of the organization's financial structure, as international and new media licensing became increasingly important revenue streams. Preston served on numerous boards, including those of the National Music Council, the Rhythm & Blues Foundation, and the Rock and Roll Hall of Fame, and was appointed lifetime board member by both the Country Music Association and the Gospel Music Association. Widely known for her philanthropic work for cancer and AIDS research, she is the namesake for the Frances Williams Preston Laboratory at the Vanderbilt-Ingram Cancer Center.

BIBLIOGRAPHY

M.A. Bufwack and R.K. Oermann: *Finding Her Voice: the Saga of Women in County Music* (New York, 1993), 385–7

B. Holland: "Biz Bids Farewell to BMI's Preston," *Billboard*, cxvi/18 (2004), 6–7

DIANE PECKNOLD

Preston [née Imfeld], **Katherine K(eenan)** (*b* Hamilton, OH, 7 Dec 1950). Musicologist and educator. She studied music at Evergreen State College (BA 1974) and the University of Maryland (MM 1981) where she was recruited to study musicology by Eugene Helm. She interned at the Smithsonian Institution (1979–81) with CYNTHIA ADAMS HOOVER and WILLIAM BROOKS and studied with H. WILEY HITCHCOCK at the City University of New York (PhD 1989). She joined the department of music at the College of William and Mary in 1989, served as its chair (2000–07), and is currently the David N. and Margaret C. Bottoms Professor of Music. She has held visiting appointments at Keele University (England, 1998) and the University of Leiden (The Netherlands, 2009). She has won many prestigious fellowships such as a Fulbright award and has been active in both the Society for American Music (for which she was secretary 1997–2002) and the American Musicological Society.

Preston has been among the most prominent scholars of performance and the careers of performers in early America, seeking a broader understanding of music in American culture and advocating for 19th-century studies. *Opera on the Road*, her revised dissertation, portrays for the first time the work conditions and contributions of major traveling opera troupes in responding to and shaping the nation's taste for European opera, particularly performed in English. *Music for Hire*, her Smithsonian project and master's thesis study of "journeyman musicians" in the nation's capital, has influenced other scholars to explore the livelihoods of musicians and music as skilled labor.

WRITINGS
(selective)

Music for Hire: the Work of Journeymen Musicians in Washington, DC, 1875–1900 (New York, 1992)

Opera on the Road: Traveling Opera Companies in the United States 1825–1860 (Urbana, IL, 1993; 2001)

ed.: *David Braham: The Mulligan Guard Ball, and Reilly and the 400*, vol. 10 in series *Nineteenth-Century American Musical Theater* (New York, 1994)

ed.: *George Frederick Bristow: Symphony No. 2 ("Jullien")*, vol. 22 in the series *Music of the United States of America* (Madison, WI, 2010)

DEANE L. ROOT

Preston, Robert [Meservey, Robert Preston] (*b* Newton Highlands, MA, 8 June 1918; *d* Montecito, CA, 21 March 1987). Actor and singer. He grew up in Los Angeles and was a trained instrumental musician before joining the Pasadena Community Players. He was discovered by a talent scout from Paramount Pictures, and after signing a contract with the studio he appeared in numerous minor roles. He eventually moved to New York and made his Broadway debut succeeding José Ferrer as Oscar Jaffe in *Twentieth Century* (1950). In 1957 he created the character of Harold Hill in *The Music Man*, his most famous role, for which he won a Tony award and which he subsequently reprised in the 1962 film. Further Broadway roles included Michael in *I Do! I Do!* (1966)—a two-person show which co-starred Mary Martin and for which Preston won his second Tony award—and Mack in *Mack and Mabel* (1974). His film credits included *Mame* (1974) and *Victor/Victoria* (1982). A dramatic bass-baritone, Preston could make a very smooth transition from speech to song. His voice was very flexible and articulate and exuded power, strength, and masculinity. His distinctive sound was always immediately recognizable for its clarity, expression, and depth.

WILLIAM A. EVERETT, LEE SNOOK

Pretenders, the. English rock band. The Pretenders were formed in England in 1978 by American musician CHRISSIE HYNDE (vocals and guitar) and included guitarist and keyboardist James Honeyman-Scott, bassist Pete Farndon, and drummer Gerry McIlduff. Hynde formed the band after moving from Ohio to London, where she worked for both *NME* and at Malcolm McLaren's SEX boutique. She worked with a number of local musicians before attracting the attention of Dave Hill, a former A&R man who was starting his own record label. She gathered the other band members and in 1979 they released a cover of The Kinks' "Stop your sobbing." The single was a successful start, and they continued to release singles from Hill's Real Records label. McIlduff was replaced with drummer Martin Chambers before their self-titled debut album was released in 1980 to critical acclaim and international success. With all 12 songs written fully or in part by Hynde, their sound varied from accessible pop-influenced songs to harder rock, influenced by the aggressive and raw attitude of London punk music. Though Hynde was the only woman in the band, she was viewed as the one in control, and

was the only member who consistently stayed in the band throughout lineup changes and deaths of some members. She defined the image of the tough woman in rock for mainstream audiences, and did not flaunt her sexuality as a tool though she also hesitated to align herself with any feminist titles. *Pretenders* was followed by *Pretenders II* in 1981, but by July 1982, Hynde had fired Farndon from the band (he passed away a year later), and Honeyman-Scott had died from complications of his drug use. Guitarist Billy Bremner and bassist Tony Butler joined Hynde and Chambers to record and release the single "Back on the Chain Gang," which became one of their more successful singles and was featured on their 1983 album *Learning to Crawl*. By the time The Pretenders released their album *Get Close* in 1986, only Hynde remained from the original lineup. The Pretenders released four more albums between 1990 and 2002, with the lineup of Hynde, Adam Seymour, and Andy Hobson, with Chambers returning to perform with them again. Hobson was replaced with Nick Wilkinson before their 2008 release, *Break Up the Concrete*. In 2005 the group was inducted into the Rock and Roll Hall of Fame.

JESSICA L. BROWN

Previn, Sir André (George) [Priwin, Andreas Ludwig] (*b* Berlin, 6 April 1929). Composer, conductor, and pianist of German birth; naturalized American. The main characteristics of Previn's musicianship were developed early, including formidable virtuosity at the piano and a phenomenal sight-reading ability. While Previn studied piano with Rudolf Breithaupt at the Stern'sches Konservatorium in Berlin (renamed "Konservatorium der Reichshauptstadt Berlin" in 1936), the Jewish Priwins fled Germany in 1938. Via Paris, where Previn studied briefly with Marcel Dupré at the Conservatoire, the family went to Los Angeles, where friends like Jascha Heifetz and relatives like Charles Previn, at that time head of the music department at Universal Studios, lived. Previn became an American citizen in 1943. He started recording jazz in 1945 and received his first contract from MGM in 1946. At the same time, Previn continued his training, studying composition with JOSEPH ACHRON, ERNST TOCH, and MARIO CASTELNUOVO-TEDESCO, chamber music repertoire with violinist JOSEPH SZIGETI, orchestration and conducting from his colleagues at MGM, and, finally, around 1950, conducting from PIERRE MONTEUX, then music director of the San Francisco SO.

Most of Previn's musical likes and dislikes were established early. He has worked constantly throughout his life in several musical domains, including the composition of art music and playing chamber music and jazz in small groups. Writing film music for two and a half decades was important to him in many ways, too, as described in his comprehensive and entertaining autobiography *No Minor Chords: My Early Days in Hollywood*. But despite several elements of continuity, Previn's career after 1945 can be clearly divided into three stages in public perception: 1945–67, film music and jazz composer, arranger and pianist; 1967–91, conductor and pianist of classical music, casually composing contemporary art music; 1991–present, composer of contemporary art music, plus, in equal shares, conductor and pianist of classical music, jazz, and his own works.

In the first period of his career, Previn was primarily an instrumentalist and improviser within the West Coast jazz scene. He also wrote elegant scores for Hollywood films (e.g., *It's Always Fair Weather*, 1955; *Inside Daisy Clover*, 1965) and stage (*Coco*, 1969 in New York; *The Good Companions*, 1974 in London). In particular, he was a sophisticated arranger of material written by others, like George Gershwin, Frederick Loewe, or Cole Porter, adapting their work with great skill, creativity, and style to both film and jazz performance. For this work, Previn received four Academy awards (*Gigi*, 1958; *Porgy and Bess*, 1959; *Irma la Douce*, 1963; *My Fair Lady*, 1964) and several of his early Grammy awards (including a jazz version of songs from *West Side Story*, 1959).

Compared many times, unjustly and cursorily, and seldom to Previn's favor, to Leonard Bernstein, Previn's varied career as a versatile musician, primarily in art music, jazz, and film music (with short excursions to pop and musical theater), followed a unique path. In retrospect, both artists had some notable things in common, at least during the period when Previn was a full-time conductor of classical music in the mid-1960s through the 1980s. Unlike Bernstein, Previn, as a musician who established his career in film music and jazz (although from 1945 on he also regularly worked as a classical pianist, especially on the West Coast, and later increasingly as a conductor, too, making his official conducting debut with the St. Louis SO in 1962), had to work hard during the 1960s to make his way into conducting classical music. This was why he stopped performing and recording jazz for most of the time during the second stage of his career, although he was quite respected and successful as a jazz musician in the 1950s and early 60s (for example, his 1956 adaptation in West Coast style of *My Fair Lady* with Shelly Manne and Leroy Vinnegar was the first jazz record to sell more than a million copies). While Bernstein worked continuously as a distinguished conductor of classical music from the mid-1940s on and explored other areas of Western music and forms of musicianship, especially composing, from time to time, Previn radically redirected his career in the 1960s, moving from an established place in film and jazz to one focusing exclusively on performing classical art music as pianist and, especially, as conductor. Taking this astonishing risk led Previn to an illustrious second stage of his career, which included appointments with the Houston SO (1967–70), London SO (1968–79), Pittsburgh SO (1976–84), Los Angeles PO (1985–9), Royal PO London (1985–91), and Oslo PO (2002–6), supplemented by strong partnerships with the Boston SO, the NHK SO Tokyo, and the Vienna Philharmonic. Previn is widely respected for his outstanding performances and recordings of works by Haydn, Mozart, Russian 19th- and 20th-century works, and British 20th-century art music. He recorded extensively.

In the third stage of his career, Previn again refocused himself, this time on composing art music, on which he began concentrating during the 1970s. Previn has written works for, among others, John Williams, Itzhak Perlman, Janet Baker, Kathleen Battle, Vladimir Ashkenazy, Anne-Sophie Mutter, Yuri Bashmet, Renée Fleming, Yo-Yo Ma, the Emerson String Quartet, the San Francisco Opera, the Houston Grand Opera, and the Boston, Philadelphia, Pittsburgh, London, Leipzig, and Vienna orchestras. His most striking compositions (including a witty Trio for Piano, Oboe and Bassoon [1994]; two dramatically intense operas, *A Streetcar Named Desire* [1997] and *Brief Encounter* [2009]; the orchestral tour de force, *Diversions* [1999]; a violin concerto, written for Anne-Sophie Mutter [2001]; and a blues- and gospel-flavored song cycle, *Honey and Rue* [1992], a collaboration with poet Toni Morrison) combine expressionistic harmony with a strong tendency towards tonality. They are rhythmic and metrically complex, marvelously orchestrated, and include flashes of idioms associated with jazz and symphonic film music. Despite the crossover appeal that Previn's art music provokes in the ears of many commentators, Previn does not see himself as a postmodern musician, trying to mix musical styles and elements to create new kinds of aesthetic experiences. Rather, he defines himself as a "'compleat musician,' in the 18th-century sense" (Greenfield, *GMO*, 310), one working in different areas of Western music at the same time: "I adore just about every kind of music making there is.… Everything else, if it's well written or well performed, excites and enlightens me and makes me want to attempt it myself" (Previn, 1991, 131–2). Previn achieved extraordinary success in most of the musical areas he touched, giving him a rare status in contemporary Western music, due to his work as conductor, pianist, arranger, and composer in art, jazz, and film music, and as a charismatic media personality. He has received many awards in recent years for his lifetime achievements.

Previn has married five times, including to actress Mia Farrow and violinist Anne-Sophie Mutter, and is father of nine children.

WORKS
(selective list)

Stage: Coco (Musl, book and lib by A.J. Lerner), New York, 18 Dec 1969; The Good Companions (Musical, book by R. Harwood, lib by J. Mercer), London, 11 July 1974; Every Good Boy Deserves Favour (Operetta, book and lib by T. Stoppard), London, 1 July 1977; A Streetcar Named Desire (Op, lib by P. Littell, based on T. Williams' play, 1947, and E. Kazan's movie adaptation, 1951), San Francisco, 19 Sept 1998; Brief Encounter (Op, lib by J. Caird, based on N. Coward's play *Still Life*, 1936, and his own movie version called Brief Encounter, 1945), Houston, 1 May 2009

Orch: Overture to a Comedy, orch, 1962; Cello Conc., vc, orch, 1967; GuiConc., gui, jazz trio, orch, 1971; Principals, orch, 1980; Reflections, eng hn, orch, Philadelphia, 31 Aug 1981; Pf Conc., 1985; Honey and Rue: I. First I'll Try Love, II. Whose House Is This? III. The Town Is Lit, IV. Do You Know Him? V. I Am Not Seaworthy, VI. Take My Mother Home (T. Morrison), S, orch, New York, 5 Jan 1992; Vocalise, S, vc, orch, Boston, March 1996; Sallie Chisum Remembers Billy the Kid (M. Ondaatje), S, orch, Boston, March 1996; The Magic Number (D. Previn), S, orch, New York, 17 April 1997; Diversions, orch, Salzburg, 28 Jan 2000; Vn Conc. "Anne-Sophie," vn, orch, Boston, 14 March 2002; Night Thoughts, orch, Sacramento, 14 Oct 2006; Double Conc., vn, db, orch, Boston, 19 April 2007; Hp Conc., Pittsburgh, 7 March 2008; Owls, orch, Boston, 2 Oct 2008; Double Conc., vn, va, orch, New York, 26 April 2009; Vc Conc., Leipzig, 9 June 2011; Triple Conc., tpt, hn, tuba, orch, Pittsburgh, 9 March 2012

Chbr music: Two Little Serenades, vn, pf, 1970; 4 Outings for Brass, hn, 2 tpt, trbn, tuba, 1974; Peaches, fl, pf, 1978; Triolet for Brass, hn, 4 tpt, 4 trbn, tuba, 1985; A Wedding Waltz, 2 ob, pf, 1986; Sonata, vc, pf, 1993; Vocalise, S, vc, pf, 1995; Trio, pf, ob, bn, New York, 31 Jan 1996; Vn Sonata "Vineyard," vn, pf, New York, 14 July 1994; Bn Sonata, bn, pf, New York, 25 April 1999; Tango Song and Dance, vn, pf, Lucerne, 26 Aug 2001; Str Qt with S (C. Rossetti), New York, 4 May 2003; Piano Trio, New York, 22 April 2009; Cl Sonata, cl, pf, Prague, 28 May 2010; Octet for 11, fl, ob, cl, bn, hn, tpt, 2 vn, va, vc, db, Boston, 17 Oct 2010

Pf: Paraphrase on a Theme of William Walton, 1973; Invisible Drummer: 5 Preludes, 1974; 5 Pages from My Calendar, 1978; Matthew's Piano Book, 1979; Variations on a Theme by Haydn, 1990

Songs: 5 Songs: I. Morning has spread again, II. Home is so sad, III. Friday Night in the Royal Station Hotel, IV. Talking in Bed, V. The Trees (P. Larkin), Mez, pf, 1977; Sallie Chisum remembers Billy the Kid (M. Ondaatje), S, pf, Tanglewood, 24 Aug 1994; 4 Songs: I. Mercy, II. Stones, III. Shelter, IV. The Lacemaker (T. Morrison), S, vc, pf, New York, 27 Nov 1994; 2 Remembrances: I. A Love Song, II. Lyric (E. Lasker-Schüler, F. Ava), S, a fl, pf, Tanglewood, 1996; 3 Dickinson Songs: I. As Imperceptibly as Grief, II. Will there really be a morning?, III. Good morning midnight (E. Dickinson), S, pf, Quebec, 18 Dec 1999; The giraffes go to Hamburg (I. Dinesen), S, fl, pf, Newark, 3 May 2000; 4 Songs: I. Ad Infinitum, II. Is it for now, III. The Revelation, IV. To Write One Song (P. Larkin, W.C. Williams), T, pf, New York, 23 Oct 2004; 7 Lieder: I. Lied des Harfenmädchens, II. Abends, III. Mondlicht, IV. Wer je gelebt in Liebesarmen, V. Trost, VI. Letztes Blatt, VII. Oktoberlied (T. Storm), S, pf, San Francisco, 25 Feb 2009 (US premiere)

Film Scores: The Sun Comes Up, 1949; Bad Day at Black Rock, 1955; It's Always Fair Weather, 1955; Gigi, 1958; Porgy and Bess, 1959; Elmer Gantry, 1960; The Subterraneans, 1960; The Four Horsemen of the Apocalypse, 1962; Two for the Seesaw, 1962; Irma La Douce, 1963; My Fair Lady, 1964; Inside Daisy Clover, 1965; Valley of the Dolls, 1967; Paint Your Wagon, 1969; The Music Lovers, 1970

WRITINGS

with A. Hopkins: *Music Face to Face* (London, 1971)
ed.: *Orchestra* (Garden City, NY, 1979)
ed.: *André Previn's Guide to Music* (London, 1983)
ed.: *André Previn's Guide to the Orchestra* (East Rutherford, NJ, 1986)
No Minor Chords: My Early Days in Hollywood (New York, 1991)

BIBLIOGRAPHY

GMO (E. Greenfield)
E. Greenfield: *André Previn* (London, 1973)
M. Bookspan and R. Yockey: *André Previn: A Biography* (Garden City, NY, 1981)
H. Ruttencutter: *Previn* (London, 1985)
M. Freedland: *André Previn* (London, 1991)
L. Kramer: "The Great American Opera: *Klinghoffer, Streetcar*, and the Exception," *OQ*, xxiii/1 (2007), 66–80
F. Döhl: *André Previn* (Stuttgart, 2012) [incl. full works list and discography]

FRÉDÉRIC DÖHL

Prévost, Eugène-Prosper (*b* Paris, France, 23 April 1809; *d* New Orleans, LA, 19 Aug 1872). Conductor and composer of French birth. He studied with Jean François Le Sueur at the Paris Conservatoire where he won the *Prix de Rome* (1831) with his cantata *Bianca Capello*. He immigrated to New Orleans in 1838, where he was the principal conductor of the Théâtre d'Orléans until 1859, and the subsequent new French Opera House. Prévost conducted many European operas debuts not only in New Orleans, but also when the New Orleans French Opera Company toured the major northeast cities in the 1840s. With the onset of the Civil War, he returned to Paris in 1862 where he was the conductor for Offenbach's

theater "Les Bouffes Parisiens" and grand concerts of the "Champs Elysées." The luminaries of the Paris music scene praised Prévost for performing French opera in the New World. Prévost returned to New Orleans in 1868 as a teacher of music and was to have become the conductor for the opera company, but died suddenly in 1872.

As a composer, he wrote a variety of secular and sacred dramatic works: operas, cantatas, an oratorio, and a requiem for his son. He also wrote many pieces on regional and national themes, such as a patriotic overture, *L'Orléanaise*, and a march dedicated to President Zachary Taylor (1846). His songs demonstrate his dual national loyalties: some are topical American songs and others typical French ballads (ten of the latter were published in *Album musical*, n.d.) His captivating melodies reflect the influence of Cherubini, Le Sueur, and Plantade.

WORKS

Operas: L'hôtel des princes (1831); Le grenadier de Wagram (1831); Cosimo (1835); Les pontons de Cadix (1836); Le bon garçon (1837); Esmeralda (1842); La chaste Suzanne (1845); Adolphe et Clari (1846); L'illustre Gaspard (1863); Blanche et Renée (1871)

Other: Cantatas: La mort de Cléopâtre (1829); Bianca Capello (1831); Requiem (1857); Oratorio; Mass, chorus, orch; Several pieces, orch, Pn; Songs

BIBLIOGRAPHY

Grove6 (J. Mongrédien/H. Lacombe)
Obituary, *Bee* (New Orleans, 20 Aug 1872)
E.L. Jewell: *Jewell's Crescent City Illustrated* (New Orleans, 1873)
L. Panzeri: *Louisiana Composers* (New Orleans, 1972)
V.B. Lawrence: *Strong on Music, vol 1, Resonances, 1836–1850* (New York, 1988)

JOHN H. BARON/JENNIFER C.H.J. WILSON

Price [née Smith], **Florence Bea(trice)** (*b* Little Rock, AR, 9 April 1887; *d* Chicago, IL, 3 June 1953). Composer. She was the first African American woman to win widespread recognition as a symphonic composer, rising to prominence (with William Grant Still and William Dawson) in the 1930s. After early training with her mother she studied composition at the New England Conservatory in Boston with WALLACE GOODRICH and FREDERICK SHEPHERD CONVERSE (1903–6) and privately with GEORGE WHITEFIELD CHADWICK. She gained an Artist's Diploma (organ) and a piano teacher's diploma. She returned to the South to teach at the Cotton Plant–Arkadelphia Academy (1906–7) and Shorter College (1907–10) in Little Rock, then headed the music department of Clark College in Atlanta until 1912, when she returned to Little Rock to marry. In 1927, presumably to escape the increasing racial oppression in the South, the Price family moved to Chicago. There she began a period of compositional creativity and study at the American Conservatory and with CARL BUSCH, WESLEY LA VIOLETTE and Arthur Olaf Anderson at the Chicago Musical College. In the 1920s she began to win awards for her compositions, and in 1932 she achieved national recognition when she won first prize in the Wanamaker competition for her Symphony in E minor. With the symphony's premiere in 1933 by the Chicago SO under Stock, Price became the first African American woman to have an orchestral work performed by a major American orchestra. Her music was taken up by other orchestras, and she won further recognition after Marian Anderson's performance of her arrangement of the spiritual "My soul's been anchored in de Lord" and "Songs to the Dark Virgin." The latter, a setting of a text by Langston Hughes, is one of her most powerful art songs and was hailed by the *Chicago Daily News* as "one of the greatest immediate successes ever won by an American song." She remained active as a composer and teacher until her death.

Price played the theater organ for silent films, wrote popular music for commercial purposes and orchestrated arrangements for soloists and choirs who performed with the WGN Radio orchestra in Chicago. She is best known for her songs: her art songs and arrangements of spirituals were sung by many of the most renowned singers of the day including Marian Anderson, Blanche Thebom, Etta Moten, and Leontyne Price. Although her music was widely performed, her output, comprising over 300 compositions, remains unpublished, apart from a handful of songs and piano pieces. In her large-scale works Price's musical language is often conservative, in keeping with the Romantic nationalist style of the 1920s–40s, but it also reflects the influence of her cultural heritage and the ideals of the "Harlem renaissance" of the 1920s–30s. She incorporated spirituals and characteristic dance music within classical forms, and at times deviated from traditional structures in deference to influences which are implicitly African American, for example call-and-response techniques and Juba dance rhythms. To her art songs and piano music she brought a thorough knowledge of instrumental and vocal writing, colorful harmonies and exotic modulations.

WORKS
(selective list)

Orch: Sym. no.1, e, 1931–2; Ethiopia's Shadow in America, 1932; Mississippi River, sym., 1934; Pf Conc., d, perf. 1934; Sym. no.2, g; Sym. no.3, c, 1940, *NH*; Sym. no.4, d; Vn Conc. no.2, D, 1952; Chicago Suite; Colonial Dance, sym.; Dances in the Canebrakes [arr. of pf piece]; 2 concert ovs. [based on spirituals]; Ov. "Sinner please don't let this harvest pass"; Rhapsody, pf, orch; Songs of the Oak, tone poem; Suite of Negro Dances

Choral: The Moon Bridge (M.R. Gamble), SSA, 1930; The New Moon, SSAA, 2 pf, 1930; The Wind and the Sea (P.L. Dunbar), SSAATTBB, pf, str qt, 1934; Witch of the Meadow (Gamble), SSA (1947); Sea Gulls, female chorus, fl, cl, vn, va, vc, pf, by 1951; Nature's Magic (Gamble), SSA (1953); Song for Snow (E. Coatsworth), SATB (1957); Abraham Lincoln walks at midnight (V. Lindsay), mixed vv, orch, org; After the 1st and 6th Commandments, SATB; Communion Service, F, SATB, org; Nod (W. de la Mare), TTBB; Resignation (Price), SATB; Song of Hope (Price); Spring Journey, SSA, str qt

Solo vocal (all with pf): Dreamin' Town (Dunbar), 1934; 4 Songs, B-Bar, 1935; My Dream (Hughes), 1935; Dawn's Awakening (J.J. Burke), 1936; Songs to the Dark Virgin (L. Hughes), (1941); Hold fast to dreams (Hughes), 1945; Night (L.C. Wallace), (1946); Out of the South blew a Wind (F.C. Woods), (1946); An April Day (J.F. Cotter), (1949); The Envious Wren (A. and P. Carey); Fantasy in Purple (Hughes); Feet o' Jesus (Hughes); Forever (Dunbar); The glory of the day was in her face (J.W. Johnson); The Heart of a Woman (G.D. Johnson); Love-in-a-Mist (Gamble); Nightfall (Dunbar); Resignation (Price), also arr. chorus; Song of the Open Road; Sympathy (Dunbar); To my Little Son (J.J. Davis); Travel's End (M.F. Hoisington); c90 other works

Chbr: Suite for Brasses, c1949; Moods, fl, cl, pf, 1953; Negro Folksongs in Counterpoint, str qt; Spring Journey, 2 vn, 2 va, 2 vc, db, pf; pieces for vn, pf; 2 pf qnts; other works for str qt

Pf: At the Cotton Gin (1928); Sonata, e (1932); 3 Little Negro Dances, 1933, arr. sym. band, 1939, arr. 2 pf (1949); Bayou Dance, 1938;

Dance of the Cotton Blossoms, 1938; Dances in the Canebrakes (1953); c10 other works, c70 teaching pieces

Org: Impromptu, 1941; Adoration (1951); Evening Song, 1951; In Quiet Mood, 1951; Passacaglia and Fugue; Retrospection (An Elf on a Moonbeam); Retrospection (1995); Sonata no.1, 1927; Suite no.1 (1993); Festal March (1995); Offertory (1995); other works

Arrs. of spirituals: Fantasie nègre, e, 1929 (Sinner, please don't let this harvest pass); My soul's been anchored in de Lord, 1v, pf (1937), arr. 1v, orch, arr. chorus, pf; Nobody knows the trouble I see, pf (1938); Were you there when they crucified my Lord?, pf (1942); I am bound for the kingdom, 1v, pf (1948); I'm workin' on my building, 1v, pf (1948); Heav'n Bound Soldier, male chorus, 1949 [2 arrs.]; Variations on a Folksong (Peter, go ring dem bells), org (1996); I couldn't hear nobody pray, SSAATTBB; Save me, Lord, save me, 1v, pf; Trouble done come my way, 1v, pf; 12 other works, 1v, pf

MSS of 40 songs in *PHu*; other MSS in private collections; papers and duplicate MSS in U. of Arkansas, Fayetteville

Principal publishers: Fischer, Gamble-Hinged, Handy, McKinley, Presser

BIBLIOGRAPHY

GroveW (R.L. Brown, M.S. Nachman, B.G. Jackson) [incl. further bibliography]; *SouthernB*

E. Southern: *The Music of Black Americans: a History* (New York, 1971, 2/1983)

B.G. Jackson: "Florence Price, Composer," *BPM*, v (1977), 30–43

R.L. Brown: "William Grant Still, Florence Price, and William Dawson: Echoes of the Harlem Renaissance," *Black Music in the Harlem Renaissance*, ed. S.A. Floyd (Westport, CT, 1990), 71–86

R.L. Brown: "The Woman's Symphony Orchestra of Chicago and Florence Price's Piano Concerto in One Movement," *American Music*, xi/2 (1993), 185–205

P.M. Peters: "Deep Rivers: Selected songs of Florence Price and Margaret Bonds," *Canadian University Music Review*, xvi/1 (1995), 74–95

R.L. Brown: *The Heart of a Woman: the Life and Music of Florence B. Price* (Urbana, IL, 2002)

RAE LINDA BROWN/R

Price, Harry E(dward) (*b* Havana, Cuba, 11 Jan 1953). Music educator and scholar of Cuban birth. He received degrees from Florida State University (BME 1974, MME 1975) and Syracuse University (EdD 1981), where he was a University Fellow. He taught music in the Georgia public schools and at universities, including University of Alabama, Tuscaloosa (1986–2004) and the University of Oregon (2004–9), where he received the Excellence in Scholarship and Teaching Award (2009). Since 2009 he has been director of the School of Music at Kennesaw State University in Georgia. He was editor of the *Journal of Research in Music Education* (1994–2000) and is currently on the Executive Committee of the Society for Research in Music Education of the Music Educators National Conference. He has served on the editorial committees of the *Bulletin of the Council for Research in Music Education*, *Contributions to Music Education*, *International Journal of Music Education*, *Journal of Band Research*, *Journal of Research in Music Education*, *Psychology of Music*, *Research Studies in Music Education*, and *Update: Applications of Research in Music Education*. Price has made presentations in Asia, Australia, Eastern and Western Europe, and North and South America, and has published more than 70 articles in national and international journals.

JERE T. HUMPHREYS

Price, John Elwood (*b* Tulsa, OK, 21 June 1935; *d* Tuskegee, AL, 9 May 1995). Composer. He studied composition with DAVID BAKER at Lincoln University, Bela Rozsa at the University of Tulsa, and PAUL A. PISK and Robert Wykes at Washington University in St. Louis. He taught at Karamu Theater, Cleveland, Florida Memorial College, Eastern Illinois University, and Tuskegee University.

Price was committed to realizing an African-centered philosophy in his compositions, expressed through conventional Western musical notation. His works are characterized by polyrhythmic and polycentric structures, in which conflicting rhythmic and tonal patterns share equal prominence, a resistance to sharp formal definitions, and repetition (particularly of two- or three-note patterns) designed to achieve altered consciousness. His work also acknowledges a collective memory shared by successive generations of African Americans and stresses the importance of the communal over the individualistic. The majority of his *c*200 works have not been published.

WORKS
(selective list)

Orch: Scherzo I, cl, orch, 1952, rev. 1955;…And so Faustus Gained the World and Lost his Soul (Whatever Happened to Humanity?), 1963, rev. 1989

Chbr and solo inst: Meditation and Change of Thought, 4 brass, 1954; Hymn and Deviation, 4 brass, 1956; Blues and Dance I, cl, pf, 1957; Impulse and Deviation, vc, 1958; Impulse and Deviation I, db, 1976; 5 Folk Songs, pf, 1977; A Ptah Hymn, vc, 1978; On the Third Day…Osiris Rose, db, pf, 1988; Isis and Osiris, db, kbd, perc, dancers, 1992

Vocal: Mists, 1962; Ps cxvii, 1968; Prayer: April 15, 1968, 1972

BIBLIOGRAPHY

A. Tischler: *Fifteen Black American Composers* (Detroit, 1986), 213–57
J. Pickett: *John Elwood Price* (diss., U. of Wisconsin–Madison, 1996)

JACQUELINE L. PICKETT

Price, Lloyd [Mr. Personality] (*b* New Orleans, LA, 9 March 1933). Rhythm-and-blues and rock-and-roll singer. In the late 1940s he formed a rhythm-and-blues quintet in New Orleans, and composed and recorded for a local radio station. His first recording, "Lawdy, Miss Clawdy" (with the pianist Fats Domino), reached no.1 on the rhythm-and-blues charts in 1952. He had three more top ten hits before being drafted into the armed forces in 1954. After entertaining troops in the Far East until 1956, he moved to Washington, DC. There he formed his own company, KRC, to record his composition "Just Because," which was the first in a succession of his songs in the late 1950s to reach the top five on the rhythm-and-blues charts and to appear as well on the rock-and-roll charts; foremost among them were "Stagger Lee" (based on the traditional blues song "Stack-o-lee"), "Personality," and "I'm gonna get married," which were all composed by Price and his manager Harold Logan, and which display Price's round, deep, booming voice. In the 1960s Price founded the record labels Double L (for which Wilson Pickett first recorded) and Turntable, and continued to compose, record, and perform; he also established his own nightclub, the Turntable, in New York. He has since appeared in many rock-and-roll revival concerts and tours. In 1998 he was inducted into the Rock and Roll Hall of Fame.

BIBLIOGRAPHY

A. Shaw: *Honkers and Shouters: The Golden Years of Rhythm and Blues* (New York, 1978), 188
B. Dahl: "Lloyd Price: Mr. Personality," *Living Blues*, xxx/5 (Sept–Oct 1999), 10–21

BARRY KERNFELD/R

Price, (Mary Violet) Leontyne (*b* Laurel, MS, 10 Feb 1927). Soprano. While training as a music teacher, she sang with her college glee club at Central State University in Wilberforce, Ohio. In 1949 she won a scholarship to the Juilliard School where she sang Alice Ford (*Falstaff*) and met her teacher and mentor Page Kimball. In 1952 Virgil Thomson chose her for a Broadway revival of his opera *Four Saints in Three Acts*; thereafter she was immediately engaged as Bess in a new production of Gershwin's opera at the Ziegfeld Theatre (1953) and on a two-year world tour. The role of Porgy was taken by Price's then husband, WILLIAM WARFIELD. A concert career (including first performances of works by Barber and Sauguet) was interrupted by a highly successful NBC television appearance as Tosca (1955). She was the first African American opera singer to perform on television. This, and appearances at San Francisco in 1957 (as Madame Lidoine in *Dialogues des Carmélites* and as Aida), decided the course of her career. At her debuts at the Arena di Verona, Vienna, and Covent Garden (all 1958) and La Scala (1960), she had further triumphs as Aida. In 1960 she first appeared at the Salzburg Festival, as Donna Anna, returning there in 1962–3 as Leonora in *Il trovatore*; in the latter role she had made an acclaimed Metropolitan debut in 1961, which received a 45-minute ovation. Further roles there included Leonora (*La forza del destino*), Elvira (*Ernani*), Amelia (*Un ballo in maschera*), Butterfly, Minnie, Tosca, Pamina, and Fiordiligi. A notable appearance among many in New York was as Cleopatra in Barber's *Antony and Cleopatra*, commissioned for the opening of the new Metropolitan (1966); in 1975 she played Puccini's Manon there, and she made her farewell appearance as Aida in 1985. Though her repertory embraced Poppaea, Handel's Cleopatra, Tatyana, and Mozart and Puccini roles, it was principally in Verdi that she achieved fame as one of the world's foremost sopranos. Her voice was a true *lirico-spinto*, able to fill Verdi's long phrases with clean, full, dusky tone. Musically she was a subtle interpreter full of confidence, though her acting did not always evince dramatic involvement. Many recordings, of Mozart, Puccini and, especially, Verdi operas, faithfully document her career. She is the first opera singer to be awarded the Presidential Medal of Freedom (1964). Among her other significant awards are a Kennedy Center Honor (1980), a National Medal of Arts (1985), the Handel Medallion (1985), and a Grammy Lifetime Achievement Award (1989).

BIBLIOGRAPHY

A. Blyth: "Leontyne Price Talks to Alan Blyth," *Gramophone*, xlix (1971–2), 303 only
W. Sargeant: "Leontyne Price," *Divas* (New York, 1973), 135–67
J.B. Steane: *The Grand Tradition* (London, 1974/*R*), 407–13
R. Jacobson: "'Collard Greens and Caviar'," *ON*, l/1 (1985), 18–23, 28–31, 46–7

R. Story: *And So I Sing: African American Divas of Opera and Concert* (New York, 1993)

M. Loppert: "Price, Rysanek, Los Angeles," *Opera*, xlvii/11 (1996), 1277–84

ALAN BLYTH/MARTI NEWLAND

Price, (Noble) Ray (*b* Peach, TX, 12 Jan 1926). Country music singer-songwriter and guitarist. He was born in a small Texas community where his family farmed cotton and vegetables. Later they moved to Dallas. His mother eventually remarried, Price spending the school year in the city and summers working on the farm with his father. His opera-loving stepfather encouraged him to study classical voice which he did for six years during his early teens. While in college, he began to sing at Roy's House Café in Dallas. Price made his first record for Bullet at Jim Beck's Dallas studio in 1950 and appeared regularly on the *Big D Jamboree*. Troy Martin of Peer Southern was instrumental in Price being signed to Columbia Records by Don Law in March 1951. That fall he met Hank Williams who became a good friend and invited Price to make his *Grand Ole Opry* debut. After Williams's death on New Year's Day, 1953, Price continued working with Hank's band, the Drifting Cowboys. The next year Price decided to develop his own sound and recruited a band he named the Cherokee Cowboys. His insistence on its members wearing matching tailored outfits reflected his mother's own career in fashion. In 1956 "Crazy Arms" became his first no.1 hit. "My shoes keep walking back to you" (1957) and "City Lights" (1958) followed in the top position. Price's innovative 4/4 shuffle beat with strong bass, pedal steel, and single-string fiddle lead redefined the honky-tonk sound, giving country music a renewed life that helped sustain it through the invasion of rock and roll. Price's Cherokee Cowboys was a training ground for many musicians, including future stars Roger Miller, Willie Nelson, and Johnny Paycheck and noted instrumentalists Buddy Emmons, Tommy Jackson, and Pete Wade. In the first half of the 1960s, Price moved toward a smoother sound and several lush recordings in this style, including "For the Good Times" (1970), "I won't mention it again" (1971), and "You're the best thing that ever happened to me" (1973), all reached no.1 on *Billboard*'s country singles chart. His long association with Columbia, which brought him more than 62 hit records, ended in 1974. He has recorded with a series of different labels in the almost four decades since and continues to tour at the age of 87. Price was inducted into the Country Music Hall of Fame in 1996 and was honored by the museum's exhibition, "For the Good Times: The Ray Price Story," in 2006.

BIBLIOGRAPHY

B. Malone: "A Shower of Country Stars: Country Music since World War II," *Stars of Country Music*, ed. B.C. Malone and J. McCulloh (Urbana, IL, 1975), 397–445

M. McCall: "Don't Let the Stars Get in Your Eyes: Ray Price's Singular, Six-Decade Journey Forsakes Shine for Substance," *Journal of Country Music*, xxv/2 (2007), 30–43

CHARLES K. WOLFE/LINDA J. DANIEL

Pride, Charley (Frank) (*b* Sledge, MS, 18 March 1938). Country music singer. Born in the Mississippi Delta, a region long associated with the blues, Pride spent his boyhood listening to country music, particularly the *Grand Ole Opry*. He considered singing a hobby since he focused on a professional baseball career. After Army service in 1956–7, he played semipro baseball while working at a zinc smelter in Helena, Montana. An African American artist, he began singing country in area clubs and in 1962 met singers Red Sovine and Red Foley, who were in town for a concert. After hearing Pride sing, both suggested he go to Nashville. When an attempt to try out for the New York Mets failed in 1963, he visited Nashville. He elicited interest, but two years passed before he was summoned to record audition material revealing his rich, twangy baritone. Jack Clement, who produced these recordings, took them to Chet Atkins, who ran RCA's Nashville operations. With civil rights violence raging across America, Atkins got approval to sign Pride but released his earliest singles under the name "Country Charley Pride" without publicity photos. When two singles, including "Just Between You and Me" (1966), reached the country top ten, RCA issued Pride's first LP *Pride* (1966) with a cover photo. Pride's recordings appealed strongly to traditionalist fans disillusioned by the smoother "countrypolitan" music gaining popularity. Their enthusiasm for Pride's records and his warm reception at concerts eclipsed any concerns over race. Pride maintained a solid string of number-one singles including "Is anybody goin' to San Antone" (1970) and his biggest, the Grammy-winning "Kiss an angel good morning" (1971). Pride won numerous awards and, in 2000, became the first African American inducted into the Country Music Hall of Fame.

BIBLIOGRAPHY

C. Pride with J Henderson: *Pride: The Charley Pride Story* (New York, 1994)

RICH KIENZLE

Prima, Louis (*b* New Orleans, LA, 7 Dec 1910; *d* New Orleans, LA, 24 Aug 1978). Trumpeter, bandleader, singer, and composer. The son of Sicilian immigrants, Prima began his musical studies on the violin and later changed to trumpet. He cited early influences such as New Orleans musicians King Oliver and Louis Armstrong. As a teenager he played local theater gigs and joined Red Nichols and the Five Pennies before moving to New York and forming Prima's New Orleans Gang. His engagements at the Famous Door were popular, and as a composer he wrote a number of instrumentals and songs, including "Sing, Sing, Sing" (1936), which became forever associated with Benny Goodman and the swing era. In the 1940s he performed with his big band and released the popular novelty song "Angelina" (1944). In 1949 Prima met singer Keely Smith and in 1953 she became his fourth wife. Together with New Orleans saxophonist Sam Butera and the Witnesses, they performed as a Las Vegas act and also recorded for Capitol Records. In later years he graced the stage of the Sands Casino. Prima was noted for his raspy bass vocals, comical antics, and both lyrics and running commentary about Italian culture. His scat singing can also be heard in Disney's *The Jungle Book* (1967) for which he supplied the voice of King Louie. His stage presence and good looks were appreciated by Hollywood, and he starred in a handful of films, such as *You Can't Have Everything* (1937), and shorts throughout the 1930s and 40s.

BIBLIOGRAPHY
G. Boulard: *Louis Prima* (Urbana, IL, 2002)
T. Clavin: *That Old Black Magic: Louis Prima, Keely Smith, and the Golden Age of Las Vegas* (Chicago, 2010)

MONICA F. AMBALAL

Primavera String Quartet. String quartet. It was formed in New York in 1975 and, until it disbanded in the spring of 1983, it attracted much attention as one of the few all-women chamber music ensembles performing in the United States. The original members were first violinist Martha Caplin, second violinist Kathryn Caswell, the violist Diann Jezurski, and the cellist Melissa Meell (Deborah Berlin replaced Caswell in 1977; later second violinists were Mitsuru Tsubota and Catherine Metz). The ensemble won the Naumburg Award in 1977; their subsequent concert at Alice Tully Hall in April 1978 included the world premiere of Chihara's string quartet, written especially for the group. Perhaps due to frequent personnel changes, the Primavera String Quartet seldom achieved an extremely high level of ensemble refinement, but its interpretations were characteristically intelligent and sensitive.

JAMES WIERZBICKI

Primrose, George H. [Delaney, George H.] (*b* London, ON, 12 Nov 1852; *d* San Diego, CA, 23 July 1919). Minstrel. Of Irish descent, Primrose debuted with McFarland's Minstrels *c*1867 in Detroit as "Master Georgie," the infant clog dancer. While working with Skiff and Gaylord's in 1871 he met William H. West. Their ensuing song-and-dance partnership resulted in Barlow, Wilson, Primrose, and West's Minstrels (1877–82); Thatcher, Primrose, and West's Minstrels (1882–9); and Primrose and West's Minstrels (1889–98). Primrose subsequently teamed with Lew Dockstader (1898–1903), then ran Primrose's Minstrels and played vaudeville.

Both white and black dancers recognized Primrose as the leading exponent of the soft shoe. His grace, elegance, and compact, lithe body contributed to a seemingly effortless style; dancer Harland Dixon later compared him to Fred Astaire. Primrose was also a noted character actor and singer. Over the course of his 50-year career he inspired performers from James Bland to Bill Robinson, both of whom idolized him. Following Sam Hague's example in London, Primrose and West's lavish shows featured whiteface performers dressed in evening attire, prompting Lew Dockstader to grouse that they were refining all the fun out of minstrelsy. Even in blackface Primrose "talked white," according to Dixon. He performed his vaudeville act of the 1900s in whiteface, with supporting male dancers in blackface.

A shrewd businessman, Primrose managed his companies frugally and invested wisely in real estate, allowing him a relatively comfortable existence when many minstrels were struggling economically. He performed until shortly before his death; afterward his third wife managed his minstrel company and performed as interlocutor.

BIBLIOGRAPHY
E.L. Rice: *Monarchs of Minstrelsy, from "Daddy" Rice to Date* (New York, 1911)
M. Stearns and J. Stearns: *Jazz Dance: The Story of American Vernacular Dance* (New York, 1968)
R. Toll: *Blacking Up: The Minstrel Show in Nineteenth-Century America* (New York, 1974)

SANDRA JEAN GRAHAM

Primrose, William (*b* Glasgow, Scotland, 23 Aug 1904; *d* Provo, UT, 1 May 1982). Scottish viola player. He studied the violin in Glasgow with Camillo Ritter, then at the GSM in London and in Belgium under EUGÈNE YSAŸE (1925–7), who advised him to change to the viola. He toured as a soloist and in the London String Quartet (1930–35). Arturo Toscanini chose him as principal viola in the NBC SO (1937–42). Primrose appeared as a soloist with orchestras in Europe and the United States, becoming the foremost viola virtuoso. In 1939 he formed the Primrose Quartet. In 1944 he commissioned Béla Bartók to write a viola concerto and in 1949 gave the first performance of the work, which was completed by Tibor Serly after Bartók's death. Other composers who wrote for him were Benjamin Britten, Darius Milhaud, George Rochberg, Edmund Rubbra, and P.R. Fricker. He formed the Festival Quartet (1954–62) from the faculty of the Aspen Music School. In 1962 the University of Southern California, Los Angeles, invited Jascha Heifetz, Gregor Piatigorsky, and Primrose to teach their respective instruments and chamber music. The three also made recordings together.

In 1963 Primrose suffered a heart attack and from that year onwards devoted most of his time to teaching, first at Indiana University (1965–72) and later at the Tokyo National University of Fine Arts and Music (1972). In Japan he was also associated with Tōhō Gakuen School in Tokyo and Shin'ichi Suzuki's institute in Matsumoto. He gave master classes in the United States and Europe, judged many international music competitions, then taught at Brigham Young University from 1979 until his death. He wrote *Technique is Memory* (London, 1960) and also edited works from the viola repertory and made numerous arrangements for viola. His memoirs, *Walk on the North Side*, were published in 1978 (Provo, UT). He was made a CBE in 1953 and received an honorary doctorate from Eastern Michigan University.

Generally Primrose played on a viola of moderate size, producing a tone of rare sweetness and beauty. His first viola was an Amati of 1600, but he also played on a viola by Andrea Guarneri (1697) and two Stradivari instruments, the "Gibson" (1734) and the "MacDonald" (1700).

BIBLIOGRAPHY
D. Dalton: *Playing the Viola: Conversations with William Primrose* (Oxford, 1988)
D. Dalton: "The First Star of the Viola," *The Strad*, cv (1994), 148–55
T. Potter: "William Primrose on the Record," *The Strad*, cv (1994), 157–9

WATSON FORBES/R

Prince [Nelson, Prince Rogers] (*b* Minneapolis, MN, 7 June 1958). Popular recording artist, songwriter, and performer. Known for his prolific output and multi-instrumental proficiency, he released 19 albums of his own music on Warner Bros. before going independent in the late 1990s, and maintains a "vault" of unreleased material. A musician of African American heritage, he has explored and fused diverse musical genres, creating a multiplicity of musical style and personal image that some have interpreted as a postmodern deconstruction of identity and genre. His music has several distinct stylistic periods, but in each he has demanded creative freedom, utilized the latest advances in music technology, and explored themes of racial, religious, sexual, and gender identity.

Born and raised in Minneapolis, Prince taught himself piano, guitar, bass, and drums, and in high school led a band which performed in the competitive music scene of the city's predominantly African American Northside neighborhood. At age 19 he signed a contract with Warner Bros. that allowed him to produce his own recordings.

Prince's first two albums show the strong influence of soul and disco music, but also include rock-influenced electric-guitar and acoustic singer-songwriter numbers, and feature synthesizers instead of the horn sections common in R&B music of the period. On his third and fourth albums Prince established a distinctive stylistic fusion: in songs like "Dirty Mind" and "Controversy," Prince blended new wave's robotic synthesizer timbres with funk's polyrhythmic dance grooves and driving rock guitar. Influential rock critics heralded Prince's blend of "black" genres like disco, soul, and funk with "white" genres of rock, new wave, and punk, and dubbed it the Minneapolis sound. Prince also crossed boundaries of sexual and religious propriety with his taboo song lyrics and risqué performances. His musical blend reached an early peak on the album *1999*, which explored themes of technological dystopia and Armageddon, and which demonstrated his growing crossover popularity with two top-ten singles on Billboard's Hot-100 chart.

Released on 25 June 1984 as the soundtrack to his first feature film, *Purple Rain* is Prince's best-known album, achieving the RIAA's platinum certification (for a million units sold) by late August 1984, and surpassing 11 times multi-platinum status by July 1994. The movie blends live performances by Prince and his band of that time, the Revolution, into a seemingly autobiographical story, presenting Prince's character as a misunderstood musical genius. Heavily promoted by MTV, *Purple Rain* put Prince's Minneapolis sound into the mainstream, and the album spent 24 weeks at the top of the Billboard 200 album chart. Among its four top-ten singles are "When Doves Cry," a dance hit whose barren synthesizer-and-drum-machine texture and harmony vocals are highlighted by Prince's omission of bass guitar, and "Purple Rain," a slow rock-guitar anthem which earned Prince an Academy Award for Best Original Song Score.

After *Purple Rain*, Prince moved away from his Minneapolis sound, adding a horn section to his band and experimenting with different styles. *Around the World in a Day* and *Parade* include psychedelic rock, world music, cabaret music, and symphonic orchestrations, and yielded two top-ten hits, the psychedelic "Raspberry Beret" and "Kiss," whose sparse arrangement resembled "When Doves Cry." Released in 1987, *Sign o' the Times* was critically praised for its topical lyrics and stylistic breadth, which encompassed the austere synthesizer-and-drum-machine electronica of its title song, horn-heavy funk and soul, guitar-based rockers, and psychedelic experiments. Later that year construction was completed on Prince's Minnesota recording-studio complex, Paisley Park. His first project there was *Lovesexy*, a funk concept-album with a message about divinity and sexuality. Prince then recorded the soundtrack to Tim Burton's film *Batman* (1989) which generated a no.1 hit with the dance-rock fusion "Batdance." In 1990 he released his final Warner Bros. movie, *Graffiti Bridge*; filmed at Paisley Park and directed by Prince, the movie was not a critical success; its soundtrack produced one top-ten hit, "Thieves in the Temple."

In the 1990s Prince formed a new backing band, the New Power Generation, and incorporated hip hop into his music, a change that some critics interpreted as an attempt to recapture his vanguard position as an R&B artist. *Diamonds and Pearls* hit no.1 on Billboard's R&B album chart and no.3 on the mainstream chart; one of its hit singles was "Gett Off," a rap-rock hybrid that mixed hip-hop techniques such as rapping and sampling with the conventional R&B/rock instrumentation of live drums and instruments.

Prince, 1986. (Ron Wolfson/Landov)

During this period Prince began to have conflicts with Warner Bros. In 1993 he began performing with the word "slave" written on his face and changed his name to an un-pronounceable symbol; he fulfilled the terms of his contract by quickly releasing several albums, scoring one hit with the R&B ballad "The Most Beautiful Girl in the World." In 1986 he celebrated his freedom from Warner Bros. with the R&B- and hip-hop-inspired triple-album *Emancipation*, and a collection of songs from his vault, *Crystal Ball*. Seeking new ways to control his music's distribution, Prince released more than 40 songs through his online music-club and distributed albums through one-time arrangements with various labels.

Prince began the new millennium by focusing on funk and jazz, touring with a pedigreed R&B horn section that included James Brown's former saxophonist Maceo Parker. Released in 2001, *The Rainbow Children* is a jazz-fusion concept album exploring the Jehovah's Witness faith, and Prince followed it with the instrumental smooth-jazz album *N.E.W.S.* His next recording, *Musicology*, featured a title track that is a paean to 1960s R&B and was supported by a tour in 2004; it reached the top ten of Billboard's pop and R&B album charts. Prince was inducted into the Rock and Roll Hall of Fame that same year.

Since 2005 Prince's albums have included guitar rock, electronic dance music, contemporary R&B, old-school funk, and even his Minneapolis sound. Each has been distributed through a different label, newspaper, or retailer. In 2007 Prince was the featured performer at the Superbowl XLI halftime show and set an attendance record while performing over 21 consecutive nights at London's O2 arena. From 2010 to 2012, Prince toured sporadically, taking his Welcome 2 America tour to the United States, Canada, Europe, and Australia.

RECORDINGS
(selective list)

For You (1978); *Prince* (1979); *Dirty Mind* (1980); *Controversy* (1981); *1999* (1982); *Purple Rain* (1984); *Around the World in a Day* (1985); *Parade* (1986); *Sign o' the Times* (1987); *Lovesexy* (1988); *Batman* (1989); *Graffiti Bridge* (1990); *Diamonds and Pearls* (1991); [Symbol] (1992); *The Hits/The B-Sides* (1993); *Come* (1994); *Black Album* (1994); *The Gold Experience* (1995); *Chaos and Disorder* (1996); *Emancipation* (1996); *Crystal Ball* (1998); *Rave Un2 The Joy Fantastic* (1999); *The Rainbow Children* (2001); *One Nite Alone…Live!* (2002); *N.E.W.S.* (2003); *Musicology* (2004); *3121* (2006); *Planet Earth* (2007); *LotusFlow3r/MPLSound/Elixir* (2009); *20Ten* (2010)

BIBLIOGRAPHY

T. Carr: "Prince: a One-Man Band and a Whole Chorus, Too," *Minneapolis Tribune* (29 April 1978)
B. Adler. "Will the Little Girls Understand?" *Rolling Stone* (19 Feb 1981)
R. Palmer: "Is Prince Leading Music to a True Biracism?" *New York Times* (2 Dec 1981)
K. Tucker: "Love and Lust in Minneapolis: Prince, *Dirty Mind*," *Rolling Stone* (19 Feb 1981) [review]
J. Bream: *Prince: Inside the Purple Reign* (New York, 1984)
K. Loder: "Prince Reigns," *Rolling Stone* (30 Aug 1984)
N. Karlen: "Prince Talks," *Rolling Stone* (26 April 1985)
N.J. Holland: "Purple Passion: Images of Female Desire in 'When Doves Cry,'" *Cultural Critique* (1988), fall, 89–98
B. Hoskyns: *Prince: Imp of the Perverse* (London, 1988)
D. Hill: *Prince: a Pop Life* (New York, 1989)
J. Duffy: *Prince: the First Illustrated Biography* (New York, 1992)
S. Hawkins: "Prince: Harmonic Analysis of 'Anna Stesia,'" *Popular Music*, xi/3 (1992), 325–35
A. Leeds: disc notes, *Prince: the Hits/The B-Sides*, (1993)
R. Walser: "Prince as Queer Poststructuralist," *Popular Music and Society*, xviii/2 (1994), 79–89
J. Walsh: "The Artist Speaks," *St. Paul Pioneer Press* (17 Nov 1996); (18 Nov 1996)
A. Danielsen: "His Name was Prince: a Study of Diamonds and Pearls," *Popular Music*, xvi/3 (1997), 275–91
R. Doerschuk: "The Sound of Emancipation," *Musician Magazine* (1997), April, 28–30, 32, 34, 36, 75, 88–9
P. Nilsen: *Dance Music Sex Romance: Prince, the First Decade* (London, 1999, 2/2004)
S. Hawkins: "Subversive Musical Pleasures in 'The Artist (Again) Known as Prince,'" *Settling the Pop Score* (Burlington, VT, 2002), 160–95
A. Hahn: *Possessed: the Rise and Fall of Prince* (New York, 2003)
M. Matos: *Sign o' the Times* (New York, 2004)
P. Nilsen: *The Vault: the Definitive Guide to the Musical World of Prince* (Linghem, Sweden, 2004)
G.M. Woodworth: *"Just Another One of God's Gifts": Prince, African-American Masculinity, and the Sonic Legacy of the Eighties* (diss., UCLA, 2008)

GRIFFIN M. WOODWORTH

Prince, Faith (*b* Augusta, GA, 5 Aug 1957). Singer and actor. A University of Cincinnati College Conservatory of Music graduate, Faith Prince is a musical theater, film, and television actress of particularly fine comedic ability. She worked in New York musical reviews and in the campy movie *The Last Dragon* (1985) before making her Broadway debut in *Jerome Robbins' Broadway* (1989), for which she received a Tony Award nomination. She played Lorraine Bixby in the short-lived *Nick & Nora* (1991). Her performance as Miss Adelaide in the revival of *Guys and Dolls* (1992) earned her Drama Desk and Tony awards. She replaced Donna Murphy as Anna Leonowens in *The King and I* (opened 1996) revival and starred in two other revivals, as Belle in *Little Me* (1998) and as Ella Peterson in *Bells Are Ringing* (2001). After she created the starring role of Aggie in *A Catered Affair* (2008), she replaced Ursula in *The Little Mermaid* (opened 2008). She received both Tony and Drama Desk Award nominations for both *Bells Are Ringing* and *A Catered Affair*.

Prince's red hair, wide eyes and high cheekbones give her a distinctive appearance, well suited to madcap comedy roles. Her performances are marked by sweet charm and a sly sense of humor. Her strong character belt voice is accurate and attractive, if lacking in a nuanced color palette. While distinguishing herself in dramatic roles and in subtler styles of comedy, Prince's ability to bring believability, humanity, and likeability to an over-the-top character like Adelaide is memorable.

BIBLIOGRAPHY

R. Pogrebin: "The Party's Hardly Over for Faith Prince," *The New York Times* (1 May 2001), E1
T.S. Hischak: "Faith Prince," *The Oxford Companion to the American Musical: Theatre, Film and Television* (Oxford, 2008), 596–7

SHARON O'CONNELL CAMPBELL

Prince, George A. (*b* Boston, MA, 17 Feb 1818; *d* Buffalo, NY, 3 March 1890). Reed organ manufacturer. The son of a sea captain, he worked as a young man in a Boston music store owned by a relative. When the family moved to Buffalo in 1833 he opened a music store there. In 1846 (some sources say 1840) he began making melodeons in a room over the store, and soon took out several patents on improvements. In 1849 he is said to have employed 150 workers, and in 1851 he built a factory in Buffalo, where he was one of the first to engage in large-scale reed organ production. He was a major manufacturer of reed organs during the 1850s and 60s, although eventually outstripped by competitors in this rapidly expanding market, including Jeremiah Carhart and Emmons Hamlin, who had apprenticed with Prince. Hamlin, who had developed improved reed voicing techniques while with Prince, left in 1854 to become a partner of Henry Mason in the MASON & HAMLIN firm of Boston. During the 1850s Prince's melodeons were usually small parlor instruments, often with only one set of reeds, in attractive furniture-wood cases, but during the 1860s the firm began to cater to the demand for larger instruments, by the 1870s advertising a "New Organ Melodeon" for church use, having two manuals, four sets of reeds, and one and a half octaves of pedals. Competition in this area from larger factories proved too great, however, and in 1879 Prince retired. His business was taken over in 1880 by his brother, Samuel N. Prince, with Charles E. Bacon under the name of Prince & Bacon, but this enterprise was short-lived.

See also MELODEON, REED ORGAN.

BIBLIOGRAPHY

R.F. Gellerman: *The American Reed Organ* (Vestal, NY, 1973)
R.F. Gellerman: *Gellerman's International Reed Organ Atlas* (Lanham, MD, 2/1998)

BARBARA OWEN

Prince, Hal [Harold] **(Smith)** (*b* New York, NY, 30 Jan 1928). Producer and director. After graduating from the University of Pennsylvania, Prince worked for famed director George Abbott, running errands and, after a military stint, serving as stage manager for *Wonderful Town* (1953). In 1954 he began to produce shows with Robert E. Griffith (1907–61). Their first two efforts, both with scores by Adler and Ross and directed by Abbott, *The Pajama Game* (1954) and *Damn Yankees* (1955), each won a Tony Award for Best Musical. Prince and Griffith then took over Bernstein and Sondheim's innovative *West Side Story* (1957), which producer Cheryl Crawford had just left. They provided director Jerome Robbins with more rehearsal time, allowing him to suffuse the show with dance. Prince and Griffith then produced Bock and Harnick's Pulitzer Prize–winning *Fiorello!* (1959). In addition to Abbott, Robbins became one of Prince's greatest influences. Prince and Robbins next collaborated on *Fiddler on the Roof* (1964) with Bock and Harnick, investing a thoroughly ethnic plot with universal appeal.

Prince began his Broadway directing career in the early 1960s. His first success was *She Loves Me* (1963), and in 1966 he staged Kander and Ebb's *Cabaret*, a successful concept musical with a dark plot. Prince worked with Kander and Ebb on *Zorba* (1968), and between

1970 and 1981 renewed a striking partnership with Stephen Sondheim (whose *A Funny Thing Happened on the Way to the Forum* he produced in 1962) to direct a series of innovative shows: *Company, Follies, A Little Night Music, Pacific Overtures, Sweeney Todd,* and *Merrily We Roll Along*. Prince provided these productions with memorable, original concepts and stagings, and continued to nudge the musical theater into new emotional arenas. His carnival-like staging helped make a revival of Bernstein's *Candide* a major hit in 1974. Prince then directed two megamusicals: Rice and Lloyd Webber's *Evita* (1979), an exploration of media manipulation, and Hart and Lloyd Webber's *The Phantom of the Opera* (1986), a lavish evocation of 19th-century aesthetics. Prince's staging of Kander and Ebb's *Kiss of the Spider Woman* (1993) contrasted a political prison with escapist fantasies along with a frank treatment of homosexuality, and his revival of *Show Boat* (1994) included more emphasis on the plot's darker aspects than audiences had previously considered. Prince helped conceive *Parade* (1998), a musical about a Jew lynched in Georgia in 1913. Jason Robert Brown wrote a fine score, but the show was not commercially successful. Prince has won 21 Tony Awards for producing and directing, including three special awards.

WORKS
(selective list)

Producer: The Pajama Game (1954); Damn Yankees (1955); New Girl in Town (1957); West Side Story (1957); Fiorello! (1959); Tenderloin (1960); A Funny Thing Happened on the Way to the Forum (1962); Fiddler on the Roof (1964); Flora, The Red Menace (1965); Side by Side by Sondheim (1977)

Producer and Director: She Loves Me (1963); Cabaret (1966); Zorba (1968); Company (1970); Follies (1971); A Little Night Music (1973); Candide (1974); Pacific Overtures (1976); Merrily We Roll Along (1981)

Director: Baker Street (1965); On the Twentieth Century (1978); Sweeney Todd (1979); Evita (1979); The Phantom of the Opera (1988); Kiss of the Spider Woman (1993); Show Boat (1994); Parade (1998, also co-conceived); Lovemusik (2007)

BIBLIOGRAPHY

H. Prince: *Contradictions* (New York, 1974)
F. Hirsch: *Harold Prince and the American Musical Theatre* (Cambridge, 1989)
C. Ilson: *Harold Prince: From "The Pajama Game" to "Phantom of the Opera"* (Ann Arbor, MI, 1989; rev. as *Harold Prince: From "The Pajama Game" to "The Phantom of the Opera" and Beyond*, New York, 2/1992)
C. Zadan: *Sondheim & Co.* (New York, 2/1989)

ROBERT HOWIE/PAUL R. LAIRD

Prince Paul [Huston, Paul] (*b* Amityville, NY, 2 April 1967). DJ and producer. He began his music career as DJ and member of the group Stetsasonic and gained further prominence as a producer for De La Soul's first three albums, which are known for their liberal use of sampling. In addition to releasing two solo albums in the 1990s, Prince Paul joined the RZA, Frukwan, and Too Poetic to form the group Gravediggaz. He has also collaborated with producer Dan the Automator—forming the group Handsome Boy Modeling School—and with a number of rappers including Del tha Funkee Homosapien and Mike D (of the Beastie Boys). He is credited as one of the first producers to put skits (of comedy and other dialogue) on hip-hop albums, most notably De La Soul's debut *3 Feet High and Rising* (1989). As on his early productions, Prince Paul continues to use eclectic source material and collaborate with a diverse range of artists.

RECORDINGS
(selective list)
Psychoanalysis (What is it?) (Wordsound, 1996); *A Prince Among Thieves* (Tommy Boy, 1999); *Politics of the Business* (Razor & Tie/Antidote, 2003); *Itstrumental* (Female Fun, 2005)

BIBLIOGRAPHY
J. Wood: "Native Tongues: a Family Affair," *The Vibe History of Hip Hop*, ed. A. Light (New York, 1999), 187–99

JUSTIN A. WILLIAMS

Princeton University. Private university in Princeton, New Jersey, the fourth oldest university in the United States (chartered as the College of New Jersey in 1746). Although informal music-making was a part of campus activity as early as the 1760s, music entered the undergraduate curriculum only in 1934 with the appointment of Roy Dickinson Welch to the faculty. Student response to Welch's two initial courses was so strong that the number increased to seven only three years later. By 1937, 10% of all undergraduates were registering for at least one music course, and a BA degree in music was instituted. The MFA degree in music was announced in 1940, and the first PhD was awarded in 1950. In addition to his work in building Princeton's first music curriculum, Welch is remembered for attracting outstanding musical minds to Princeton's faculty including Roger Sessions, Milton Babbitt, Edward Cone, and Oliver Strunk.

Currently, study in applied music, while encouraged, does not carry academic credit, although a Certificate in Musical Performance requiring a combination of course work and solo/ensemble study can be earned. Doctoral programs in composition and musicology/ethnomusicology are highly respected, while the Firestone Library's music collection is a major repository for researchers.

BIBLIOGRAPHY
J.M. Knapp: "Department of Music," *A Princeton Companion*, ed. A. Leitch (Princeton, NJ, 1978)

NINA DAVIS-MILLIS/DAVID G. TOVEY

Prine, John (*b* Maywood, IL, 10 Oct 1946). Americana, folk, and country singer and songwriter. His first album, *John Prine* (1971), included the enduring "Sam Stone," about the plight of Vietnam veterans, and "Hello in There," which dealt with the insensitive treatment of elderly people. The recording brought him critical acclaim and an enthusiastic cult following but little mainstream success, a pattern that has continued since. Starting with 1975's *Common Sense*, he has explored country, rock, and rockabilly as platforms for his prolific compositions and often surprising covers. Prine's lyrics mix the topical with the surreal, often portraying ordinary people attempting to deal with extraordinary times in absurd, humorous, or painfully sad ways. His songs have been recorded by performers as diverse as Bonnie Raitt, Johnny

Cash, Norah Jones, Jim & Jesse, and Bette Midler. A 2010 album featured popular young artists such as the Avett Brothers covering Prine compositions.

Prine has continued to tour, compose, and record, owning his own successful recording label (Oh Boy!) for nearly 30 years. He has enjoyed the support of a solid core of fans. Following his bestselling album, the Grammy-winning *The Missing Years* in 1991, his studio releases have often featured collaborations with artists as diverse as Mac Wiseman and Iris Dement. He has also released several live albums and the studio project *Souvenirs* that offer new recordings of his classic titles. He survived cancer on his neck in 1998, returning to singing the next year with a raspier, yet gentler, more relaxed voice.

BIBLIOGRAPHY
C. Fanning: "John Prine's Lyrics," *AM*, v/1 (1987), 48–73
J. Kruth: "John Prine: One of the Good Guys" *Sing Out!*, xlix/4 (2006), 54–62
P.B. Helsel: "John Prine's Images of God and Male Melancholia: Terror, Forgiveness, and the Persistence of Desire," *Journal of Religion and Health*, xlvi/3 (2007), 359–68

KEN TUCKER/ART MENIUS

Printing and publishing. This article focuses on the history of music publishing in the United States, although the technology of printing is necessarily a part of the picture. The publishers cited in this text are given in the form most frequently encountered on title pages of editions, though minor modifications have been made in the interest of clarity (e.g., in company names "&" is used for "and" throughout, and, because of the many changes of title, such abbreviations as "Co." and "Inc." are omitted). For a full discussion of printing techniques, see Stanley Boorman and others, "Printing and Publishing of Music," *Grove 7*.

1. Early sacred music publishing. 2. Sheet music to 1865. 3. Commercial activity, 1865–1945. 4. Developments in publishing, 1945–85. 5. Printing and publishing in the digital age.

1. EARLY SACRED MUSIC PUBLISHING. Music printing in the New World dates from the 1540s, when several plainchant books were issued in Mexico by immigrant printers from Spain, but the earliest musical publication from the English colonies dates from a century later. The earliest surviving book printed in the English-speaking New World was a psalter, the Bay Psalm Book, issued in 1640 by Stephen Day at Cambridge in the Massachusetts Bay Colony. Containing no musical notation, it names the tunes to which the texts were to be sung, and the many editions that appeared during the next few decades showed a strong English influence in both content and method of production. The book was produced by letterpress, a process that involved fixing type or block cuts on a flat bed and inking them so as to transfer the text to the paper. Musical notation appeared for the first time only in the ninth edition ("printed by B. Green and J. Allen for Michael Perry" in Boston, 1698), and the crude woodcuts used to produce the eight-page tune supplement were reused in several of the later editions as well.

Freehand music engraving was introduced during the period when the New England reform movement of congregational singing flourished. It involved the incision of a text into a flat plate (at first usually of copper, but later of pewter); the plate was then inked and wiped clean so that the ink remaining in the incisions was transferred to the paper during pressing. The process was used in two celebrated instruction books published in Boston in 1721, one by John Tufts entitled *A Very Plain and Easy Introduction to the Singing of Psalm Tunes* (the first extant edition is the third, 1723, "printed from copper-plates, neatly engraven…for Samuel Gerrish"), and the other by Thomas Walter entitled *Grounds and Rules of Musick*, printed by James Franklin, also for the bookseller Gerrish.

Freehand engraving continued to be used in the early Yankee tunebooks, which bear the names of America's prominent copperplate engravers: Thomas Johnston, who engraved his own booklet of rules for singing (1755) as well as several editions of Walter's *The Grounds and Rules of Musick* around 1760; Henry Dawkins (James Lyon's *Urania*, 1761); Paul Revere (Josiah Flagg's *A Collection of the Best and Most Approved Tunes*, 1764, and *The New-England Psalm-singer* by William Billings, 1770); John Ward Gilman, who engraved several books around 1770, including American editions of works by the English psalmodist William Tans'ur; and Amos Doolittle, who prepared most of Daniel Read's compilations.

Movable type was introduced in the English colonies by Christopher Saur in Germantown, Pennsylvania; his sacred collection *Kern alter und neuer…geistreicher Lieder* (1752) was the first of several German religious books with music issued from his press in subsequent decades. Although Saur is thought to have cast the type himself, his matrices came from Europe, probably Frankfurt am Main. The music typeface used in William Dawson's *The Youth's Entertaining Amusement* (Philadelphia, 1754) appears to be unique; Wolfe (1980) identified the printer as Anton Armbrüster, who also issued a collection of *Tunes in Three Parts* in 1763. The last of the early American music typefaces (which was acquired from the Dutch firm of Johannes Enschedé) is seen in two books printed for the Reformed Protestant Dutch Church in New York, Francis Hopkinson's translation of *The Psalms of David* (1767) and *A Collection of the Psalm and Hymn Tunes* (1774).

Movable type began to be used more frequently in the 1780s, when the fonts were first imported from the Caslon foundry in London. This also marks the rise of specialty publishing (exemplified by a broadside songsheet printed by William Norman in Boston, 1783) and of religious music publishing. In 1785 Isaiah Thomas in Worcester and William M'Culloch in Philadelphia also imported fonts, and the adoption of this practice eventually led to the decline of freehand engraving, as well as to the establishment of a formal repertory of religious music and the tunebook as a distinct physical object. Set in movable type, such tunebooks were oblong in format and bound in heavy boards; a theoretical introduction generally preceded the music. The several hundred different tunebooks that appeared around the turn of the century were printed in the Caslon typeface, in the special music type without staff lines developed by Andrew Law for his solfège system, or in a new and tidier face (which also had a special solfège version) introduced soon after 1800 by the Binney & Ronaldson foundry in Philadelphia. Centered at first in the cities of the East Coast, interest in religious music publishing eventually spread to the West and South and resulted in the publication of collections of sacred music (especially hymns) by Lowell Mason and his contemporaries, as well as the shape-note tunebooks (*see* SHAPE-NOTE HYMNODY).

2. SHEET MUSIC TO 1865. As early as 1768 John Mein and John Fleming prepared a broadside engraving of *The New and Favourite Liberty Song*, the plates for which were used in *Bickerstaff's Boston Almanack* for 1769. In 1786 Chauncey Langdon's *The Select Songster* was engraved in New Haven by Amos Doolittle, and during the course of the next few years a group of prominent Philadelphians—Reinagle (composer), Aitken (engraver), Thomas Dobson (pressman), Henry Rice (bookseller), and Hopkinson (composer and patron)—assembled their talents to produce several major anthologies: vocal and instrumental collections by Reinagle (notably a set of keyboard variations thought to be the first solely secular musical publication in the United States), Hopkinson's famous *Seven Songs* (1788), and a Roman Catholic service book. The introduction of music engraving punches in America can probably be traced to these books. Each instance of a particular sign was identical, having been produced from the same punch; with freehand engraving, by contrast, each sign was drawn separately and therefore differed, albeit minutely, from all others of its kind.

Sheet-music publishing was firmly established in America by the mid-1790s. In 1793 J.C. Moller and Henri Capron established a music store in Philadelphia and published four issues of *Moller and Capron's Monthly Numbers*, a periodical collection of vocal and instrumental music (their business was taken over by George Willig the following year). Benjamin Carr settled in Philadelphia in 1793 and soon became established as a publisher; that year J.H. Smith and James Harrison founded their companies in New York. In 1794 Carr's father Joseph emigrated from London and opened a shop in Baltimore, and Frederick Rausch established another in New York. Peter Albrecht von Hagen started his own firm in Boston in the late 1790s. These firms were located in major urban centers and had close ties with the theatrical companies that were being founded at the time. Many of the publishers themselves had been theater musicians, and their catalogs consisted largely of theater songs. At the turn of the century two more major publishers were established, Gottlieb Graupner in Boston and George E. Blake in Philadelphia. While Philadelphia maintained its leadership through the shops of Willig and Blake, New York grew in importance through the work of smaller firms, including those of John Paff, Joseph Willson, the Geib family, and William Dubois.

Three interrelated events date from the late 1820s. The new printing method of lithography, involving a flat printing surface marked, dampened, and then inked so as to leave ink on only the marked areas for transfer to the paper, was first used in the United States by Henry Stone in Washington, DC, around 1822, but was taken up more extensively in New York five years later by Edward S. Mesier, Anthony Fleetword, and G. Melkham Bourne. The introduction of lithography coincided with the rise of blackface minstrelsy, and notable early examples of the process can be found in editions of *Jim Crow* and other works in this repertory (*see* Minstrelsy). These events may be seen in another context, as a reflection of the rise of "Jacksonian democracy," with its emphasis on the new values of the western frontier rather than the more traditional values cultivated in the eastern cities. Clearly, early music lithographs, with their imperfectly drawn musical figures but better prospects for music illustration, interested a different public from the one that purchased engraved music editions, which had become largely devoted to the fashionable repertories of Italian opera and guitar songs. Lithographic sheet music virtually disappeared in the 1830s, perhaps because the engraved editions looked so much less amateurish. The process re-emerged, however, in the 1840s with the development of chromolithography for cover illustrations; notable among the specialty shops using this technique, by which several colors could be printed, were John H. Bufford, W.S. and J.B. Pendleton, and B.W. Thayer in Boston; Peter S. Duval and Thomas Sinclair in Philadelphia; and Nathaniel Currier (famous through his later partnership with J. Merritt Ives), George Endicott, and Napoleon Sarony of Sarony, Major & Knapp in New York.

The publishers John Cole and the younger George Willig were particularly active in Baltimore around 1830. The 1840s saw the emergence of Charles Keith and George P. Reed in Boston; James G. Osbourn, Augustus Fiot, Leopold Meignen, and Lee & Walker in Philadelphia; and Frederick Benteen in Baltimore. It was during this decade that the family of William Cumming Peters became active, at first in Baltimore, and later in Pittsburgh, Cincinnati, and Louisville. Music publishing in San Francisco flourished for the first time during the Gold Rush years, the firm of Sherman & Hyde being particularly important. In the 1850s several new firms were established on the East Coast, notably S. T. Gordon in New York and Miller & Beacham in Baltimore, but more significant was the continuing activity in the West, involving such major firms as Balmer & Weber in St. Louis, Root & Cady in Chicago, and Silas Brainard in Cleveland. Confederate firms included A.E. Blackmar (in Vicksburg, MS; Augusta, GA; and New Orleans, LA) and W.T. Mayo, Philip P. Werlein, and Louis Grunewald in New Orleans. Foremost among America's music publishers by the middle of the century were the various partnerships of John Firth, William Hall, and William A. Pond in New York (who were responsible for publishing much of the music of Stephen Foster), and Oliver Ditson in Boston.

3. Commercial activity, 1865–1945. The period from the end of the Civil War to the end of World War II saw a vast expansion in publishing activity and an increase in specialization. An unprecedented amount of music for domestic use was published in what has been described as the "age of parlor music." The consolidation of over 50 firms under the control of Oliver Ditson during the second half of the 19th century was an event of crucial importance. Other significant firms publishing serious music emerged, many of them founded by German immigrants. The largest was probably G. Schirmer in New York (formally established in 1861 but active earlier), which began to publish the extensive Schirmer Library of Musical Classics in 1892 and achieved great success with its highly regarded catalog of art songs. Other firms established by German immigrants included Carl Fischer, founded in New York in 1872, specializing at first in band music, then in choral and orchestral works; Arthur P. Schmidt in Boston, founded in 1876, noted for its sponsorship of American composers, among them MacDowell and the Second New England School; and the smaller firm of J. Fischer in Dayton, founded in 1864 and specializing in Roman Catholic choral music. Theodore Presser, founded in 1883 in Lynchburg, Virginia, but soon moved to Philadelphia, enhanced its catalog by publishing what came to be the major music journal of the time, *The Etude*.

For the best editions of art music, however, purchasers in the United States (as elsewhere) looked mostly to Germany. Among those who attempted to promote American-born composers in the first part of the 20th century were Arthur Farwell, active from 1901 to 1912 at the Wa-Wan Press in Newton Centre, Massachusetts, and specializing in music derived from American Indian traditions; the members of the Society for the publication of American music, founded in 1919; and Henry Cowell, whose *New Music* series (1927–58) was substantially underwritten by Charles Ives.

Popular-music publishing emerged as a specialty in its own right after the Civil War as publishers began to look for "hit tunes." By the end of the century, the center for this kind of music publishing was midtown Manhattan, an area that came to be known as Tin pan alley. Among the major popular-music firms were Belwin-Mills, Leo Feist, Charles Foley, Sam Fox, T.B. Harms, Edward B. Marks, J.J. Robbins, Shapiro & Bernstein, and M. Witmark. Chicago also enjoyed bustling activity in this area, its practitioners including Sol Bloom, later a prominent member of the US Congress, and Will Rossiter. Detroit was known for its musical-comedy firms (among them Henry Whittemore, Clark J. Whitney, and Jerome H. Remick). Even Sedalia, Missouri, could claim John Stark, who issued the early rags of Scott Joplin. As Hollywood became the home of the film industry, Los Angeles developed a music publishing community of its own, one that in later years, however, degenerated into the center for "song shark" practices, whereby dealers with questionable reputations charged exorbitant fees to print and copyright a song and ostensibly to promote it into a lucrative hit.

Other sources of popular music were the Sunday newspapers that featured special music supplements printed in color (if on poor-quality paper). The Bromo Seltzer Company issued music with covers advertising its product, and countless local music shops offered printing, publishing, and retail services to local composers anxious to establish a reputation. Only as the recording industry began to flourish in the 1920s did the great age of popular-music publishing show the first signs of decline and redirection.

Other kinds of music publisher emerged to accommodate the particular needs of various types of performance. Educational firms provided materials for public-school use, continuing a tradition that had roots in the pedagogically oriented collections published by Lowell Mason. The "basic series" (i.e., sets of graded materials for use at the elementary school level) proved to be particularly valuable for general textbook publishers such as the American Book Company, Allyn & Bacon, Follett, Ginn, and Silver Burdett, as well as for such music firms as C.C. Birchard, Neil A. Kjos, and E.C. Schirmer. Band music continued to be issued nationally by Carl Fischer and another general music firm, John Church; it was also provided by such specialist publishers as E.F. Ellis in Washington, DC, J.W. Pepper in Philadelphia, Vandersloot in Williamsport, Pennsylvania, and C.L. Barnhouse in Oskaloosa, Iowa. Choral music was a specialty of E.C. Schirmer in Boston and H.W. Gray in New York, though amateur choirs requiring a simpler repertory turned to E.S. Lorenz in Dayton, Ohio. Hymnals were produced mostly under official denominational auspices or by individual evangelists, for instance Homer Rodeheaver of Winona Lake, Indiana, while topical songbooks were issued by or for innumerable political, ethnic, social, fraternal, and occupational groups. An important publisher of opera librettos was Fred J. Rullman, who was associated with the Metropolitan Opera in New York.

Common concerns of music publishers came to be addressed through special organizations, beginning with the BOARD OF MUSIC TRADE, founded in 1855 but moribund by the end of the century. In the 20th century, a growing concern for performance rights led to the establishment of the American Society of Composers, Authors and Publishers (ASCAP) in 1914 and Broadcast Music, Inc. (BMI) in 1940 (*see also* PERFORMING RIGHTS SOCIETIES). Music publishers now generally affiliate themselves with either THE MUSIC PUBLISHERS ASSOCIATION OF THE UNITED STATES founded in 1895 and serving chiefly the publishers of serious music, or the NATIONAL MUSIC PUBLISHERS' ASSOCIATION, founded in 1917 as the Music Publishers' Protective Association and serving mostly the publishers of popular music.

4. DEVELOPMENTS IN PUBLISHING, 1945–85. After a quarter-century of continued expansion, from about 1945 to about 1970, the industry went through an unsettling time of economic uncertainty and volatility. The arrival in the United States of experienced music publishers escaping the Holocaust had proved highly beneficial in serving the increasingly sophisticated tastes of performers and listeners during the 1950s, yet, in the 1960s, many of the stable giants of music publishing found themselves, for better or worse, absorbed into the great financial conglomerates. G. Schirmer and Associated Music Publishers, for instance, became subsidiaries of Macmillan, Inc. Although new firms continued to appear, many of them were small, serving only specialty audiences. Popular-music firms, which in more recent times have found a home in Nashville, have in many instances became extremely successful. Experimentation characterized methods of production (as reflected in the passing use of "black-line" prints and of the ozalid process, which involves special photocopying techniques applied to manuscript copies made on special papers); distribution, especially of music published for a limited audience, exemplified by the activities of the AMERICAN COMPOSERS ALLIANCE; and music rental. There has also been, on the other hand, a disturbing decline in local music retailing, with outlets being closed or forced to provide a more limited range of services to their customers. The inconvenience has perhaps been offset by the rise of national retailing activities and by the expanded services of public and academic music libraries.

Two overriding changes in music publishing since World War II—the burgeoning impact of the sound recording as a musical document and the demands made on publishers as a result of the Copyright Act of 1976 to collect and distribute royalties—served to direct the music publisher's attention increasingly toward legal and proprietary activities and away from printing, and often distribution as well. Photo-lithography (the copying of a page of music with a camera for reproduction by the lithographic process) came to be the dominant printing process, whether (as in the 1950s) for reprinting prewar editions of the standard repertory for use in performance, or (in the 1960s) for reprinting scholarly editions for use in the new and expanding libraries, or (in the 1980s) to replace music engraving through, for example, computerized layout of musical texts. Meanwhile, the rise of the quick photocopying machine severely diminished the sale of copies for music publishers, forcing increases in price and causing publishers to look even more to performance rights for their income.

5. PRINTING AND PUBLISHING IN THE DIGITAL AGE. With the rise of computing, the digital age, and the Internet, the publishing of music has changed dramatically. Music publishers have faced similar challenges, from attracting consumers to competing with other media, that have beset their counterparts in book publishing. Sheet music has become less and less popular, and many of the largest publishing companies have been sold to larger conglomerates focusing more on performance rights. Other companies, such as ALFRED MUSIC PUBLISHING, have chosen to focus on publishing instructional music rather than popular or classical titles. Recorded music is now typically packaged together, initially as records and tapes, subsequently on compact discs, CD-ROMs, or in digitized form.

The impact of the Internet and the development of new music software on publishing has been revolutionary. Countless websites offer depositories of vast quantities of musical material—including historical archives, personal websites, song databases, digitized audio, and much more—often circumventing traditional publishers entirely. The development and continual refinement of computer software—most notably the programs Finale and Sibelius—have enabled individuals to compose or transcribe music, and self-publish it in digital or printed form, without the editorial intervention of a traditional music publisher. The ease of distribution has also encouraged composers to make their own music readily available to musicians, often for no charge.

Both individuals and larger music publishers have come to use the Internet to distribute printed music, which is purchased, downloaded, and printed by the consumer at home. Internet sites have quickly become the primary distributors of sheet music, typically offering PDF versions of otherwise printed material. Some sites offer free downloads; others display individual titles that can be purchased separately; still others work on a membership model, requiring a monthly fee for unlimited downloads. Niche markets have enabled many small publishing companies to flourish on the Internet: for example, <http://www.jwpepper.com> offers music for church choirs, bands, and orchestras, while <http://www.sheetmusicdirect.com> focuses on popular music. Because digitized distribution allows for greater flexibility, some advanced Internet distributors offer consumers various options to manipulate their music purchases—including immediate transposition to a new key or a ready-to-go MIDI interface. With the continual development of new technologies, such as note recognition software, music printing and publishing in the United States will no doubt experience more change in the future.

BIBLIOGRAPHY
Grove7 ("Printing and publishing of music"; S. Boorman and others)

W.A. Fisher: *One Hundred and Fifty Years of Music Publishing in the United States* (Boston, 1933/*R*)

H. Dichter and E. Shapiro: *Early American Sheet Music: its Lure and its Lore* (New York, 1941, repr., 1970, as *Handbook of Early American Sheet Music*)

V.L. Redway: *Music Directory of Early New York City: a File of Musicians, Music Publishers and Music Instrument-Makers Listed in New York Directories from 1786 to 1835, together with the Most Important Music Publishers from 1836 through 1875* (New York, 1941)

W.T. Upton: "Early American Publications in the Field of Music," *Music and Libraries*, ed. R.S. Hill (Washington, DC, 1943), 60

J.H. Stone: "The Merchant and the Muse: Commercial Influences on American Popular Music before the Civil War," *Business History Review*, xxx (1956), 1

P.H. Lang, ed.: *One Hundred Years of Music in America* (New York, 1961) [incl. R.F. French: "The Dilemma of the Music Publishing Industry," 171]

D.J. Epstein: *Music Publishing in Chicago before 1871: the Firm of Root & Cady, 1858–1871* (Detroit, 1969)

G.T. Tanselle: *Guide to the Study of United States Imprints* (Cambridge, MA, 1971) [see also Krummel, 1972]

E.C. Krohn: *Music Publishing in the Middle Western States before the Civil War* (Detroit, 1972)

D.W. Krummel: "American Music Bibliography: Four Titles in Three Acts," *Yearbook for Inter-American Musical Research*, viii (1972), 137–46 [analysis of and addenda to Tanselle, 1971]

J.L. Fleming: *James D. Vaughan, Music Publisher, Lawrenceburg, Tennessee, 1912–1964* (diss., Union Theological Seminary, New York, 1972)

D.J. Epstein: "Introduction," *Complete Catalogue of Sheet Music and Musical Works*, ed. Board of Trade (New York, 1973) [original catalog, 1870]

D.W. Krummel: "Counting Every Star: or, Historical Statistics on Music Publishing in the United States," *Yearbook for Inter-American Musical Research*, x (1974), 175

C. Pavlakis: "Music Publishers," *The American Music Handbook* (New York, 1974), 625

D.P. McKay and R. Crawford: *William Billings of Boston* (Princeton, NJ, 1975)

K. Kroeger: "Isaiah Thomas as a Music Publisher," *Proceedings of the American Antiquarian Society*, lxxxvi (1976), 321

P. Dranov: *Inside the Music Publishing Industry* (White Plains, NY, 1980)

L. Feist: *An Introduction to Popular Music Publishing in America* (New York, 1980)

J. Taubman: *In Tune with the Music Business* (New York, 1980)

R.J. Wolfe: *Early American Music Engraving and Printing* (Urbana, IL, 1980)

C. Sachs, ed.: *An Introduction to Music Publishing* (New York, 1981)

"Small Music Presses," *Notes*, xxxviii/4 (1982) [complete issue, incl. articles by S. Smith, J. McKelvey, A. Seay]

R. Crawford and D.W. Krummel: "Early American Music Printing and Publishing," *Printing and Society in Early America*, ed. W.L. Joyce and others (Worcester, MA, 1983), 186–227

M.K. Duggan: "A Provisional Directory of Music Publishers, Music Printers, and Sheet-music Cover Artists in San Francisco, 1850–1906," *Kemble Occasional*, no.30 (1983), 1

"Music Publishing in America," *American Music*, i/4 (1983) [whole issue, incl. articles by P.R. Osterhout, R.D. Wetzel, D.P. Walker, R.H. Mead, and L.S. Levy]

R. Sanjek: *From Print to Plastic: Publishing and Promoting America's Popular Music (1900–1980)*, ISAMm, xx (Brooklyn, NY, 1984)

A.P. Britton, I. Lowens, and R. Crawford: *American Sacred Music Imprints, 1698–1810: a Bibliography* (Worcester, MA, 1990)

N. Tawa: "The Publishers of Popular Songs," *The Way to Tin Pin Alley: American Popular Song, 1866–1910* (New York, 1990), 37–53

P.A. Munstedt: "Kansas City music publishing: the first fifty years," *American Music*, ix/4 (1991), 353–83

R. Sanjek: *Pennies From Heaven: the American Popular Music Business in the Twentieth Century* (Cambridge, MA, 1996)

E.D. Bomberger: "Edward MacDowell, Arthur P. Schmidt, and the Shakespeare overtures of Joachim Raff: a case study in nineteenth-century music publishing," *Notes*, liv (1997), 11–26

R. Garofalo: "From music publishing to MP3: Music and industry in the twentieth century," *American Music*, xvii/3 (1999), 318–53

D. Goldmark: "Creating Desire on Tin Pan Alley," *MQ*, xc (2007), 197–229

D.W. KRUMMEL/R (1–4), JONAS WESTOVER (5)

Prinz, Le Roy (*b* St Joseph, MO, 14 July 1895; *d* Wadsworth, CA, 15 Sept 1983). Dance director of musical films. His father operated the Prinz School of Social Dance for Young Ladies and Gentlemen, where he and his brother Eddie were trained. As a teenager, he left home, went to New York, and learned to tap dance before going abroad to join the French Foreign Legion. In World War I, he distinguished himself as a combat pilot in Eddie Rickenbacker's squadron, surviving numerous crashes. Back in the States after the war, he became involved in theatrical productions, but wanderlust took him to Mexico City, where he opened a social dance school, and then to Havana, where he got into a row that put him in prison for some months. In the mid-1920s he was back in Europe, staging dance numbers for the Folies-Bergère in Paris and for Viennese impresario Max Reinhardt. Eventually landing back in New York

City, Prinz supervised the musical numbers for several Broadway shows before going to Hollywood in 1929. Arriving there just as sound came to the movies, he quickly found work on the new musical films. He assisted in staging the dances for *Innocents of Paris* (1929) and then was hired as dance director of *Madame Satan* (1930) by Cecil B. DeMille. He remained at MGM for some years and then worked at other studios, creating dances for more than sixty musical films in the course of his career. Among them are *Show Boat* (1936), *Yankee Doodle Dandy* (1942), *Shine On Harvest Moon* (1944), *Night and Day* (1946), *Look for the Silver Lining* (1947), *Lullaby of Broadway* (1951), and *South Pacific* (1958).

BIBLIOGRAPHY
T. Sennett: *Hollywood Musicals* (New York, 1981)
J. Kobal: *Gotta Sing, Gotta Dance: a History of Movie Musicals* (New York, rev. 1983)
L. Billman: *Film Choreographers and Dance Directors* (Jefferson, NC, 1997)

CLAUDE CONYERS

Prison music. A term that refers to both music made by inmates and media representations of music in prisons. Although almost any genre outside the walls has found its way into prison, overrepresentation of certain groups—especially African Americans and men—has influenced the types of music brought to and cultivated in prison. Furthermore, institutional policies have both limited and directed musical activity. Inmates have created and adapted music for a multitude of uses of their own, be it to temporarily escape, form communities, communicate, or contemplate the carceral experience. These uses have also affected the types of music and lyrical themes found in prison. Outside the walls, movies, television, and popular music have often developed narratives or characters, drawing upon and perpetuating stereotypes of prisoners and music making.

Early American prisons instituted solitary confinement and enforced silence. That silence—at least in the literature—broke after the Civil War. Documentation of music in prisons in newspapers, trade journals, folksong collections, and scholarly works reveals unconnected musical activities sequestered in countless institutions. The mention of music in prisons, however, confirms that American prisoners have been prolific. Music-making in prisons has fallen into three general categories: religious music, work songs, and music programs.

1. Religious music. 2. Southern prison work songs. 3. Music programs. 4. Prison music in popular culture.

1. RELIGIOUS MUSIC. Often, the only musical opportunities open to inmates have been church choirs and bands. Over the years, many institutional attempts at moral rehabilitation and inmate management have relied upon religious programming. Documentation of church choirs in prisons dates back to the Civil War. Christian groups have often partnered outside churches for both organizational support and funding. Some spiritual themes have had great resonance to those confined.

For example, many inmates who have sung within the African American gospel tradition use Christian notions of transcendence and redemption to signify real-world hopes of release and exoneration.

2. SOUTHERN PRISON WORK SONGS. Prison work songs developed from plantation work songs shortly after the end of slavery. During Reconstruction, a convict lease system emerged in the South. Convicts were privately leased from the state or used by the states themselves for agricultural work and infrastructure construction. These convict workers sang as they worked on prison farms and in chain gangs, fitting new expressions of protest to older song practices. Song styles were suited to different types of work: for instance, rhythmically timed ax and hammer songs in call-and-response form for coordinated labor or rhythmically free flat-weeding or harvesting songs for individual labor. Lyrics to songs were improvisatory, often concealing criticism of the singers' custodians for fear of retribution. Beginning in the 1930s folklorists such as John and Alan Lomax, Lawrence Gellert, John W. Work, and Harry Oster documented these songs, noting that performance of the older songs had persisted in prisons but disappeared outside. Bruce Jackson documented the last traces of these songs in Texas prisons in the 1960s. He noted that prison reform, radios, racial integration, and the changing demographics of inmates were eroding the prison work song tradition.

3. MUSIC PROGRAMS. Music has long been a part of prison programming, serving as a tool of rehabilitation and as an instrument of control linked to a system of privileges and punishment. The earliest documentation of music programming can be traced to the period following the Civil War, a time when an emphasis on solitude, silence, and work gave way to prison overcrowding, corruption, and chaos. Programs have included choruses, orchestral groups, and popular music bands. One of the most developed programs of the early years was created by Willem van de Wall, who designed and directed music therapy programs in New York and Pennsylvania prisons, hospitals, and asylums. He wrote about the benefits of music programs in institutions for much of the first half of the 20th century. Subsequently, jazz, songwriting, classical music, rap, and experimental music programs have been part of rehabilitation, therapy, recreation, and education programming. Occasionally, programs have been inmate-initiated efforts that emerge from recreational time dedicated to music. For instance, the composer Henry Cowell led a large music program while incarcerated at San Quentin in the late 1930s, and Charles Neville informally developed a jazz scene at the Louisiana State Penitentiary in the early 1970s. Given the lack of centralization of state prisons, tenuous budget appropriations, and the fact that many music directors in prisons are volunteers, these programs have mostly been restricted to local and often fleeting initiatives.

The largest prison arts program developed in the California state prison system from 1977 to 2003. The

Arts in Corrections program coordinated numerous fine arts programs, operating autonomously from the California Department of Corrections and Rehabilitation. Artist facilitators led inmates through recording projects, yard shows, musical theater productions, experimental sound sculpture, classical guitar lutherie, and music instruction in a variety of styles. Although proven to reduce recidivism and behavioral problems, the program was a victim to budget cuts and a lack of public support.

4. PRISON MUSIC IN POPULAR CULTURE. To much of the outside world, inmates have been rendered invisible while popular media have been drawn to representing the prison. In some cases current and former inmates have negotiated media attention and the prison bureaucracy. Some have expedited their release by generating public sympathy or endearing themselves to prison officials. This list includes Lead Belly in the 1930s, Reable Childs who sang in the Goree Girls in the 1940s, and Johnny Bragg in the 1950s. Most of these musicians hoped to avoid media attention after release, given the stigma of being an ex-con. Others, such as Lyfe Jennings, have leveraged the experience to help define a career after incarceration. The rapper C-Murder has managed to maintain a prolific career during his life sentence in Louisiana. Johnny Cash, who served only a short sentence in jail, managed to garner renewed attention through a series of recorded prison performances and prison-themed songs. Music has sometimes played a part in television shows and movies about prison. Seminal prison films such as *The Big House* (1930), *Cool Hand Luke* (1967), and *The Shawshank Redemption* (1994) have used diegetic music to develop narrative. For the most part, music has stood for human expression and protest under the harsh regiments of prison life.

BIBLIOGRAPHY

W. van de Wall: *Music in Correctional Institutions* (Albany, NY, 1923)

A. Lomax: "'Sinful Songs' of the Southern Negro," *MQ*, xx (1934), 177–87

B. Jackson: *Wake up Dead Man: Afro-American Worksongs from Texas Prisons* (Cambridge, MA, 1972, rev. 2/1999 as *Wake up Dead Man: Hard Labor and Southern Blues*)

H.B. Franklin: "Songs of an Imprisoned People," *MELUS*, vi/1 (1979), 6–22

M. Hicks: "The Imprisonment of Henry Cowell," *JAMS*, xliv/1 (1991), 92–119

M. Streissguth: *Johnny Cash at Folsom Prison: the Making of a Masterpiece* (Cambridge, MA, 2004)

M. Cohen: "Choral Singing and Prison Inmates: Influences of Performing in a Prison Choir," *Journal of Correctional Education*, lx/1 (2009), 52–65

L.G Brewster: "The California Arts-in-Corrections Music Program: a Qualitative Study," *International Journal of Community Music*, iii/1 (2010), 33–46

B. Harbert: *Doing Time: the Work of Music in Louisiana Prisons* (diss., UCLA, 2010)

R. Lee: "Music Education in Prisons: a Historical Overview," *International Journal of Community Music*, iii/1 (2010), 7–17

BENJAMIN J. HARBERT

Pro Arte Quartet. Belgian, and subsequently American, string quartet. It was founded in 1911–2 by students at the Brussels Conservatory. The leader, Alphonse Onnou (*b* Dolhain-Limbourg, 29 Dec 1893; *d* Madison, WI, 20 Nov 1940), was a pupil of Alexandre Cornelis. The other members were Laurent Halleux, a pupil of César Thomson; Germain Prévost, a pupil of Léon von Hout; and Fernand Auguste Lemaire, a pupil of Edouard Jacobs. The quartet made its debut in Brussels in 1913 and soon became known as an exponent of modern music. In 1918 Fernand Quinet became the cellist, but in 1921 he was replaced by Robert Maas. That year, with the aid of Paul Collaer and Arthur Prévost, the Pro Arte Concerts began, in which performances were given of new works by, among others, Bartók, Casella, Honegger, Martinů, Milhaud, and Rieti. The quartet performed with great success at the 1923 ISCM Festival in Salzburg, and the same year played new works commissioned by Elizabeth Sprague Coolidge at a concert in Rome. After touring Europe the quartet visited England for the first time in 1925, and the following year played at the inauguration of the Hall of Music in the Library of Congress, Washington, DC. This was followed by the first of several tours of the United States, and a tour of Canada. Subsequent visits to England included annual series of a week's performances in Cambridge (1932–8). In 1932 the quartet was granted the title Quatuor de la Cour de Belgique, in recognition of its services to Belgian music. Onnou, Halleux, and Prévost moved to the United States in 1939. Maas was trapped in Belgium, where he played in the Artis Quartet (with Alfred Dubois, Arthur Grumiaux, and Robert Courte). Onnou died in 1940, but the quartet continued until 1947 as quartet-in-residence at Wisconsin University, led first by Antonio Brosa and from 1944 by Rudolf Kolisch. Since then the title Pro Arte Quartet has been taken by the faculty quartet of the University of Wisconsin–Madison. The Pro Arte Quartet's most recent members include cellist Parry Karp, violinist Suzanne Beia, violinist David Perry, and violinist Sally Chisholm. The group celebrated its 100th anniversary in the 2011–2 season, making it the oldest continually active string quartet in the world.

At first the original Pro Arte Quartet was less consistently successful with the classical repertory than with modern works, to which it brought exceptional polish and ease; but in time it came to be equally highly regarded in Mozart, Haydn, and Schubert. Its style was without either the intensity of the Busch Quartet or the rich warmth of the Léner, but concentrated on finesse, lucidity of texture, and rhythmic buoyancy. Among its recordings were many of Haydn's quartets, several of which had not previously been recorded, as well as works by Mozart, Schubert, and Brahms, and the quartets of Franck, Fauré, Debussy, and Ravel. The current group continues to perform the standard classical repertoire, but also maintains its tradition of promoting new music. More recently, it has recorded all of Ernest Bloch's chamber music, the fourth and fifth quartets of Andrew Imbrie, and Tamar Diesendruck's first and second quartets. It commissioned Ralph Shapey's ninth quartet and premiered Walter Mays' Quartet in G Minor. In addition, it was awarded the Koussevitsky Foundation grants for new works by Brian Fennelly and Tamar Diesendruck.

BIBLIOGRAPHY
T. Potter: "Matchless Beauty of Arte," *The Strad*, cvii (1996), 790–95
ROBERT PHILIP/TULLY POTTER/MEGAN E. HILL

Process music. A term applied to one of the compositional practices generally referred to as MINIMALISM; it is associated particularly with the work of STEVE REICH.

Producer, record. A person who plans and oversees the execution of recording projects. Producers' specific roles vary considerably, depending on musical idiom, historical era, and an individual's qualifications. A useful breakdown of types is offered by Atlantic Records producer Jerry Wexler: "documentarian," "servant of the project," and "artist." While Wexler addressed his analysis to the roles of pop producers, the general concept applies to other idioms as well. The documentarian seeks to capture musical events with as little apparent intrusion as possible. The servant of the project takes a more active role, suggesting repertory, pairing performers, and offering aesthetic opinions on performances, arrangements, tempo, balance, and so forth. The producer as artist describes a person whose creative vision and stylistic inclinations exert a decisive influence on the project, an ultimate authority not unlike a film director. However a producer approaches the role, he or she is responsible for overseeing and judging the work of performers and recording engineers, for managing a project's budget and schedule, and for serving as a record company's agent on a given project.

Historically, producers were part of record companies' artist and repertoire (A&R) operation, charged with finding talent, matching performers with suitable repertory, and supervising recording sessions, which often meant performing the tasks of recording engineer as well. Among the first of such figures was Fred Gaisberg, an American who traveled through Europe recording such performers as Enrico Caruso, Adelina Patti, and Fyodor Chaliapin for the British Gramophone Company. He also recorded on location in India, Japan, and Russia, using his acoustic disc recorder to capture snapshots of the music he found. In the United States, itinerant recordists such as RALPH S. PEER and JOHN LOMAX III traveled in the American South recording blues, folk, and country musicians. All of these producers focused on capturing faithful representations of existing acoustic music traditions.

As the record industry matured and technologies evolved, record making became more complex, concerned not simply with capturing existing traditions but with the development of a new studio culture. Electrical recording, for example, which emerged in 1925, placed an amplifier between sound sources and the recording machine, introducing a mediating element with the potential to dramatically alter the acoustic musical sound. After 1945, tape recording presented new possibilities for editing and overdubbing. Moreover, the studio itself, as a performance venue, offered possibilities for instrumental combinations and textural balances unlike any in the natural sound world. As music and machinery became increasingly entwined, some producers (for example, JOHN HAMMOND) strove to keep the electronic process as transparent as possible. They aimed to create the impression of music "originat[ing] in the room instead of in the headphones," as a *Popular Mechanics* piece phrased it. Others, however, worked with recording engineers to shape acoustic parameters and musical arrangements according less to the laws of natural acoustics than to a desired aesthetic aim. For those so inclined, studio recording offered the possibility of crafting unique musical artifacts without real world counterpart. Such producers as MITCH MILLER and LES PAUL were at the forefront of a wave of postwar pop producers who made records as one-off electronic concoctions.

Producers working in idioms seeming to favor a documentarian approach—classical and jazz, for example—nevertheless shaped sonic images that became de facto textual elements augmenting the listener's overall musical impression. The jazz producer Alfred Lion, for example, was widely credited, along with his regular engineer, Rudy Van Gelder, with crafting a signature sound for his Blue Note records. Classical producer Wilma Cozart Fine, along with her husband and engineer Robert Fine, fashioned a distinctive sound for their Mercury recordings (often with a single microphone). A *New York Times* review of their 1950 recording of the Chicago Symphony's performance of Mussorgsky's *Pictures at an Exhibition* described the record as a "living presence," a term the company adopted for its classical music series. And the Columbia producer, Andrew Kazdin, both in his work with Glenn Gould and in his orchestral recordings, used close-up microphone techniques to create sharp sonic images reflecting not the acoustic space of the music's performative moment but an imaginary space crafted specifically for the record listener.

Postwar pop music, relatively unconstrained by traditional convention or aesthetic ideology and with the singular goal of commercial success, led the way in developing record production as a musical rhetoric. Claiming the market presence that had belonged previously to sheet music, records now became pop music's central currency, both commercially and creatively. With the sanction of the marketplace, many producers moved decisively in the direction of artifice, making records whose chief aim was a distinctive, novel sound. Recording studios became provinces of creative experiment and discovery. Often, ad hoc instrumental groupings were assembled for a single session or even a single song. (Miller was particularly fond of this approach.) Performers became increasingly aware that their recorded persona was something distinct from their live one. Indeed, as SAM PHILLIPS, owner of the Memphis Recording Service, put it, through the recording process a performer might discover a "possibly unknown talent." Most important, a notion developed that songs and records were of a piece—that is, the sonic rendering completed the song. Production, then, moved from a craft of sonic rendering to an integral component of compositional practice.

The 1960s saw a proliferation of records conceived in studios and at the time impossible to recreate in live performance. THE BEATLES and their producer George Martin led the way with such albums as *Revolver* and *Sgt Pepper's Lonely Heart Club Band*. On both records, Martin was not only the supervisor and organizer but also chief arranger. Commonly known as the "fifth Beatle," Martin presented an example of a producer as musical collaborator. On the other hand, the Beatles themselves became increasingly involved in aspects of the production process. Although such artist participation was not unprecedented, it was rare in previous pop eras. In the 60s, however, many recording artists became involved in producing or coproducing their records. Notable examples include Jimi Hendrix's *Electric Ladyland*, Sly and the Family Stone's *Stand!*, and the Grateful Dead's *American Beauty*.

In the final analysis, record producers serve as central figures charged with advancing a sometimes ineffable process in whatever way necessary. DANIEL LANOIS calls this "maximizing the room," getting the best from the people, the machines, and the acoustic space. Jim Dickinson puts it in terms of the musical "spirit" suffusing the enterprise. The producer's role is "to foster that spirit and to cause it to flourish—to capture it at its peak." The nature of the job changes continually, requiring a constant sensitivity to the life of the project, bearing in mind that the most effective production role may at times involve simply staying out of the way. As Mitchell Froom has explained, "If you can't make the decision to leave a good thing alone, you've no business being a producer."

See also RECORDED SOUND; RECORDING ENGINEER.

BIBLIOGRAPHY

T. Fox: *In the Groove: the People Behind the Music* (New York, 1986)

E. Olsen with P. Verna and C. Wolff: *The Encyclopedia of Record Producers* (New York, 1999)

H. Massey: *Behind the Glass: Top Record Producers Tell How They Craft the Hits* (San Francisco, 2000)

A. Zak: *The Poetics of Rock: Cutting Tracks, Making Records* (Berkeley, CA, 2001)

E. Eisenberg: *The Recording Angel: Music, Records and Culture from Aristotle to Zappa* (New Haven, CT, 2005)

V. Moorefield: *The Producer as Composer: Shaping the Sounds of Popular Music* (Cambridge, MA, 2005)

ALBIN ZAK

Production music. It typically comprises recorded music of a broad range of styles and genres, which is produced and owned by production music libraries and licensed for use in commercial media, such as theme music or background music in film, television, radio, and other media.

Music for productions has existed since the silent film era, early on supplied in the form of cue sheets and anthologies used by pianists, small orchestras, and other ensembles to be performed in real time with a film. Over time, recorded media has replaced printed materials as the main way to distribute music. Many large production music companies have compiled extensive sound and audio libraries for commercial distribution, including Boosey & Hawkes, Sony BMG, and many others. Since these libraries generally own the rights to the music, they license it directly to a client without the need to gain permission from composers or writers.

Revenue from production music is created through several models. The first is a licensing fee with the production music library, paid in advance for authorization to synchronize music from a particular library to a piece of film or video. A second practice is through performance royalties, generated when music is publicly performed. These fees are collected by PERFORMING RIGHTS SOCIETIES established to monitor usage and administer royalties on behalf of its member composers, artists, and publishers. Most countries have their own performance rights organizations, such as ASCAP, BMI, or other organizations such as the Production Music Association. Another method of revenue combines the comprehensive licensing of music already contained in the catalog of a production music library along with original music, created by a contracted composer to meet the artistic demands of a specific project. In this situation, the composer of the newly created music typically retains the rights to the music for a negotiated period of time; eventually the music is subsumed into the catalog of the music production company, at which time the library can license the new music as its property and recover its original production costs. Finally, the royalty free model offers for an upfront fee a way to purchase or license a compact disc of music (or to download the same music), which can then be used as many times as needed without any further payments or fees by the original purchaser. If the music is broadcast in any fashion, however, the broadcaster is responsible for performance royalties, hence the somewhat misleading nature of the practice.

TIMOTHY M. CRAIN

Professor Longhair [Byrd, Henry Roeland; Byrd, Roy; Fess] (*b* Bogalusa, LA, 19 Dec 1918; *d* New Orleans, LA, 30 Jan 1980). Rhythm-and-blues pianist and singer. He grew up in New Orleans, where he lived most of his life. He was a street tap dancer in his youth, and in his teens mastered the rough-hewn blues piano style played in the brothels and nightclubs of New Orleans. Among his influences were Isidore "Tuts" Washington, Robert Bertrand, and Sullivan Rock. He was drafted into the army in World War II, but returned to New Orleans in the mid-1940s and became a prominent figure in that city's rapidly evolving rhythm-and-blues scene. In 1949 he made his first recordings, playing the piano, singing, and whistling on recordings such as "Mardi Gras in New Orleans," accompanied by a small combo. "Bald Head" (1950) was his first and only national rhythm-and-blues hit.

Longhair's energetic piano playing, characterized by a rolling boogie-woogie bass, rumba rhythms, and good-humored syncopation, inspired New Orleans rock-and-roll musicians of the 1950s and 60s. As a performer and piano teacher, he helped shape the music of Fats Domino, Huey "Piano" Smith, Ernie-K-Doe, Allen Toussaint, James Booker, Mac ("Dr. John") Rebennack, and countless others; expressing a debt that many acknowledged, Toussaint dubbed him the "Bach of Rock."

In the late 1970s Longhair was discovered by rock critics and audiences, enabling him to tour again, appear at major jazz festivals, and record several fine albums. His songs "Tipitina" and "Mardi Gras in New Orleans" are frequently performed during Mardi Gras celebrations. He was inducted into both the Blues Hall of Fame and the Rock and Roll Hall of Fame.

BIBLIOGRAPHY

J. Broven: *Walking to New Orleans: the Story of New Orleans Rhythm and Blues* (Bexhill-on-Sea, England, 1974)

R. Palmer: "Professor Longhair: Deep South Piano and the Barrelhouse Blues," *Bluesland: Portraits of Twelve Major American Blues Masters*, eds. P. Welding and T. Byron (New York, 1991), 158–75

C.L. Keyes: "Funkin' with Bach: the impact of Professor Longhair on Rock 'n' Roll," *The Funk Era and Beyond: New Perspectives on Black Popular Culture*, ed. T. Bolden (New York, 2008), 213–26

LANGDON WINNER/R

Proffitt, Frank (*b* Laurel Bloomery, TN, 1913; *d* Reese, NC, 24 Nov 1965). Banjo maker and singer. He learned to make banjos and dulcimers from his father, and as an instrument maker became most famous for his banjos, which were typical of those made in the mountains of northwestern North Carolina where he lived. A fine traditional singer (who was also a tobacco farmer and part-time carpenter), he was important in the folk music revival of the late 1950s and early 1960s. He was the source of the song "Tom Dooley." The song collector and performer Frank Warner recorded this song from Proffitt in 1939, reshaped it over years of performing it himself, and taught his version to Alan Lomax, who published it in 1947 in *Folksong USA*, giving credit only to Warner. "Tom Dooley" became a commercial hit when the Kingston Trio recorded this version in 1957, giving credit to no one. This recording was largely responsible for initiating the urban folk music boom. Through Warner's efforts, Proffitt finally became known as the source of the song, which created a demand both for his appearance at folk festivals and for his handmade banjos. These are made out of native hardwoods, and are characterized by a long, fretless neck, a small body with a wide wooden rim into which is set a small skin head, and a wooden back with a small soundhole. Although this style has been taken to be the authentic mountain folk banjo, it is only one of the many varieties of homemade mountain banjos. Proffitt made recordings for Folk Legacy Records and Folkways Records.

BIBLIOGRAPHY

F. Warner: "Frank Proffitt," *Sing Out!*, xiii/4 (1963), 6–9

C.P. Heaton: "The 5-String Banjo in North Carolina," *Southern Folklore Quarterly*, xxxv (1971), 62–82

Appalachian Journal, i/3 (1973) [entire issue]

J. Warner: "Frank Proffitt: From Watauga County to Pinewoods Camp Warner," *Country Dance and Song*, xv (March 1985), 1–9

ROBERT B. WINANS/R

Progressive country music. Coined in 1972, the term initially described a new radio format of Austin, Texas, radio station KOKE-FM. Intended to challenge the strict country playlists promoted by the Country Music Association, the format freely blended current country hits, classic honky tonk and western swing recordings, the country-rock music of The Band, the Byrds, the Flying Burrito Brothers, and Gram Parsons, and the folk-rock of Jerry Jeff Walker and Michael (Martin) Murphey.

Also called "redneck rock" and "the Hill Country Sound," the term was soon applied not only to the radio format (which was also adopted in San Antonio, Houston, and Dallas) but also to the work of musicians performing in and around Austin. Progressive country musicians often exhibited a reverence for Texas history and folklife, as heard in such songs as Guy Clark's "Texas Cookin'" and "Desperados Waiting for a Train" and in the stylistic variety heard in the recorded work of Doug Sahm. Thriving in the live music scene that developed around such Austin clubs as the Armadillo World Headquarters and the Soap Creek Saloon, progressive country musicians worked to recreate a live aesthetic in their recordings, often recording few takes, hiring local musicians to participate in sessions, and eschewing the "sweetening" practices found in contemporary country music created in Nashville.

Although progressive country music was popular among young people in Texas, distribution to audiences beyond the Lone Star State proved challenging and ultimately led to the demise of the scene between 1978 and 1980. Hoping to discover a nationally viable act, executives at record labels such as MCA and Atlantic Records invested in Austin's music industry but earned minimal return. On the other hand, AUSTIN CITY LIMITS, a television series filmed in the University of Texas at Austin's Department of Radio-Television-Film and distributed via the Public Broadcasting Service, began broadcasting live performances of local artists in 1974 and, in 2010, celebrated its 35th season.

BIBLIOGRAPHY

B. Shank: *Dissonant Identities: the Rock 'n' Roll Scene in Austin, Texas* (Middletown, CT, 1994)

J. Reid: *The Improbable Rise of Redneck Rock* (Austin, TX, 1974/R2004)

T. Stimeling: *Cosmic Cowboys and New Hicks: the Countercultural Sounds of Austin's Progressive Country Music Scene* (New York and Oxford, 2011)

TRAVIS D. STIMELING

Progressive jazz. A stylistic offshoot of the white big band tradition that emerged on the West Coast toward the end of swing era. Coined by bandleader STAN KENTON in 1947 to underscore the alternative efforts of a younger generation of modernist bandleaders such as Woody Herman, Boyd Raeburn, Earl Spencer, and Kenton himself, the term denoted an approach or repertoire somehow removed from the jazz mainstream as perpetuated by earlier pop icons Benny Goodman, Glenn Miller, and Tommy Dorsey, among others. Broadly defined, progressive jazz featured expanded orchestration, bold harmonies, and occasional metric play—though the label is perhaps more accurately viewed as a shrewd promotional device than a bona fide stylistic subgenre. Often touted as an original strain indebted neither to swing nor bebop—Kenton, for instance, once characterized the music during this period of his career as "free swing"—the progressivity of this music in fact deliberately blended swing with elements of bop as well as European concert music.

Alongside the artistic thrust of bebop, progressive jazz groups contributed to an erosion of the longstanding commercial model in which live jazz primarily presented functional dance band music. This transformation initiated an important shift toward the modern concert setting that jazz audiences now take for granted. Inevitably, the most extreme progressive jazz arrangements reflected developments in 20th-century art music, occasionally adopting quasi-serialist techniques. Some jazz leaders and arrangers even pursued formal training under renowned classical composers—Dave Brubeck and Pete Rugolo, for example, both studied with Darius Milhaud.

BIBLIOGRAPHY

A. Jackson, "Boyd Raeburn," *Jazz Monthly*, xii/11 (1966), 5
A. Morgan, "The Progressives," *Jazz on Record*, ed. A. McCarthy (London, 1968), 361
S. DeVeaux: "The Emergence of the Jazz Concert, 1935–1945," *AM*, vii/1 (1989), 6–29
R.P. Jones: "'Free Swing' and the Emergent Neophonic: Forging Progressive Jazz with Stan Kenton in the 1947 Dance Hall," *Jazz Research Journal*, ii/1 (2008), 29–54

RYAN PATRICK JONES

Progressive rock. The term arose in the late 1960s as part of rock's redefinition in opposition to pop. "Progressive" was applied to artists who broke popular music conventions, for example, by making song forms and instrumental passages longer and more complicated, merging rock with other genres, or linking album tracks together through a common theme. Initially, progressive rock was broadly inclusive, describing older British Invasion groups who made concept albums (the Beatles, the Moody Blues), blues-based jam bands who improvised open-endedly (Cream, Ten Years After), psychedelic groups who experimented with timbre (Pink Floyd, the Jimi Hendrix Experience), "art rock" bands who merged rock with classical music (King Crimson, Genesis), and "Rock in Opposition" groups who joined rock with radical politics and avant-garde composition techniques (Henry Cow, Univers Zero). In the United States, progressive rock also drew from jazz and southern styles such as bluegrass and country, and sometimes overlapped with jazz-rock fusion (the Dixie Dregs, Kansas, Chicago). The genre in all these forms comprised exclusively male artists, and arose at a time when middle-class musicians, fans, and critics were redefining rock from their own cultural perspective.

Through the 1970s British art rock was the most cited form of progressive rock, very popular in the UK and North America owing to its highly theatrical and spectacular performing practices, well-suited to large arena concerts. This complemented the genre's fixation on concept albums and themes drawn from high literature, science fiction, and fantasy, which lent themselves to dramatic live treatment. Music critics turned on the genre in the mid-1970s, branding its lengthy songs, solos, and middlebrow lyrics pretentious and dull. Punk rock and new wave was touted as a negation of progressive rock's aesthetics, and many "prog" groups broke up or changed to a simpler, more conventional

rock style around 1978. During the early 1980s, however, Marillion, Pink Floyd, and American stadium rock bands like Styx found that tastes for concept albums and flashy musicianship remained strong among American rock audiences.

The genre was revitalized in the 1990s and 2000s by merging with heavy metal. Prog-metal first arose from mid-1970s experiments by King Crimson and Rush, and following metal's resurgence in the 1980s, American bands like Dream Theater, Fates Warning, and Queensrÿche revived prog features such as lengthy, episodic songs, changing time signatures, frequent key and tempo changes, and virtuosic solos. Neo-prog bands from the UK (Ozric Tentacles, Porcupine Tree) and the United States (Spock's Beard, Tiles) continue to serve a niche audience for the genre, which remains overwhelmingly male.

Progressive rock represents a neo-romantic strain in popular culture, elevating virtuosity, authenticity, anticommercial rhetoric, and romantic notions of "art" as key aesthetic considerations. Stylistically, progressive rock's odd meters, extended forms, elaborate and exacting musicianship, and conceptually dense lyrics lead it to overlap with other styles, including jazz-rock fusion (Mahavishnu Orchestra), extreme metal (Metallica, Opeth, Meshuggah), post-rock (Godspeed! You Black Emperor), and math rock (Don Caballero). Some artists, like Frank Zappa, fulfill the stylistic criteria of progressive rock though both the artist and his fans generally shun the term.

BIBLIOGRAPHY

E. Macan: *Rocking the Classics: English Progressive Rock and the Counterculture* (New York, 1997)
P. Stump: *The Music's All That Matters: a History of Progressive Rock* (London, 1997)
B. Martin: *Listening to the Future: the Time of Progressive Rock, 1968–1978* (Chicago, 1998)
K. Holm-Hudson, ed.: *Progressive Rock Reconsidered* (New York, 2002)
C. Anderton: "A Many-Headed Beast: Progressive Rock as European Meta-Genre," *Popular Music*, xxix/3 (2010), 417–35

CHRIS McDONALD

Pro-Musica Society. Society founded in New York in 1920 as the Franco-American Musical Society by the French pianist E. Robert Schmitz, who also directed its activities. It was one of several bodies formed in the 1920s to promote new and unfamiliar music, and it aimed, in particular, to internationalize music through greater exchange between France and the United States. After a few years the aims of the society broadened and its name was changed to Pro-Musica, Inc.; chapters were established in the West and Midwest, as well as in Canada, Europe, and East Asia. It was Schmitz's talents as a concert pianist, educator, and entrepreneur that made Pro-Musica a thriving organization for 12 years. He established more than 40 chapters in major cities and sought support from socially and financially prominent patrons for the advisory boards in each city. Schmitz's European education, reputation, and contacts abroad made possible the first American appearances of some of the most prominent composers of the century, including Ravel, Bartók, and Ottorino Respighi;

these three (independently) gave lecture recitals in 30 chapters in the United States and Canada in 1928. Divisions of the society came to be seen as a part of the established musical life in those cities, offering concerts by local performers along with more widely recognized guest composers. Early on in the life of the society, American composers were sent to the Paris chapter, and the tenor Roland Hayes sang in Moscow and Leningrad under the society's auspices. Among the many other artists and composers to appear under Pro-Musica sponsorship were Hindemith, Schoenberg, Arthur Honegger, Milhaud, Albert Roussel, Alexandre Tansman, Prokofiev, Alfredo Casella, Arthur Bliss, Germaine Tailleferre, Florent Schmitt, Kodály, Stravinsky, Webern, Alexander Tcherepnin, and Ernst Toch. From 1923 the society sponsored a series of International Referendum Concerts with programs suggested by its international advisory board. Several important premieres were given, such as two of Ives's *Three Quarter-tone Pieces* in 1925. The society published the *Pro-Musica Quarterly*, edited by Germaine Schmitz (Robert Schmitz's wife) under the pseudonym Ely Jade.

BIBLIOGRAPHY
V. Perlis: *Two Men for Modern Music*, ISAMm, ix (Brooklyn, NY, 1978)

VIVAN PERLIS/MEGAN E. HILL

Protestant Episcopal Church in the USA. *See* EPISCOPAL CHURCH.

Protest song. There is little agreement on what constitutes a protest song. Just as folksinger Pete Seeger defined folk songs as what folks sing, one might say that if folks think a song protests something, it is a protest song. Many protest songs are of unknown authorship, passed on by oral tradition, and altered to fit new times and contemporary problems.

Although protest songs did not become part of American mass culture until the activist 1960s, they have always been a part of American musical culture. Since most protest songs are topical, made for a particular time and place, they tend to date quickly and fade in significance. An abolitionist song such as "Get off the track" (1844) by the Hutchinson Family successfully addressed contemporary issues but it sprang from a now distant social context. To resonate with later musical generations, protest songs must reflect universal concerns or commonly shared problems. As these features are rare, there exists no canon of American protest song.

Topical protest songs held obvious charm for poorly educated and pragmatic American pioneers. They told simple stories and expressed simple emotions. Since the colonial era Americans have sung about wars, criminals, and economic misery. There have also been complaint songs: women generally protesting about the infidelity of husbands; men typically complaining about shrewish wives. Most early examples addressed general issues without pinpointing clear social goals. For instance, African American spirituals, such as "My God is a rock" and "O Freedom," contained subtle antislavery protests and issued broader calls for freedom.

American protest songs became distinctively modern in 1905, with the IWW (The Industrial Workers of the World), which used protest songs to help organize workers. The chief IWW songwriter, Joe Hill, arranged to have many of his protest songs printed in the *Little Red Songbook* (1909), which was handed to every new union member. Hill's song "There is power in the Union" remains a classic example.

The IWW was demolished by its opposition to World War I and both unionism and protest songs became rather irrelevant during the prosperous 1920s; however, both unionism and protest songs came back strong in the 1930s during the Great Depression. New unions such as the United Mine Workers sang on the picket lines during strikes. Songwriters penned songs about tough times. The leading writer of such songs was WOODY GUTHRIE, the Oklahoma-born folk icon who roamed the country writing songs about hard times and America's promise. He represents the most important bridge between the protest songs of Joe Hill and the folk-protest movement of the 1960s. Some of his early songs were made popular by 60s performers, including Bob Dylan, Joan Baez, and Guthrie's protégé, Pete Seeger.

Patriotism tempered unionism and protest during World War II, and intense patriotism carried over into the Cold War era. Suddenly the fear of a strong, aggressive Soviet Union and rumors of communist subversion within the United States made expressions of protest seem potentially un-American. In an era that saw musicians blacklisted, Guthrie and Seeger were among those suspected of communist ties. In response, they were instrumental in establishing People's Songs, a group that used song, performance, and direct action to criticize both hard cold war approaches to the Soviets and also Southern segregation. Although People's Songs failed to change America through song, it did produce ballads that became models for 1960s protest songs by younger artists. Additionally, a new generation of young folksingers brought up during the unpopular 1950s Korean War became adult performers during the even more unpopular 1960s Vietnam War. They venerated Guthrie and openly supported Seeger, when he and likeminded singers were banned from prime-time TV shows.

The key difference between the younger and older performers who delivered protest songs in the 1960s was personal involvement. For the older singers such as Seeger, songs were weapons to be used in a battle they had already joined. Younger singers, such as Bob Dylan, typically wrote songs as commentary on contemporary events covered by the mass media. With few exceptions, such as The Weavers and Joan Baez, the new generation castigated social evils, but did not personally act to cure them. The largest number of 1960s protest songs centered on civil rights and the Vietnam War. Other singers, including Phil Ochs and Tom Paxton, protested the arms race and America's military industrial complex. Protest songs eventually enabled The Kingston Trio, The Brothers Four, and Peter, Paul and Mary to hit the top ten charts in the later 1960s. These groups performed conventional pop tunes alongside protest songs, often composed with vague or obscure lyrics. By protesting anything, they sometimes ended up protesting nothing. Suddenly protest songs were part of the mainstream, pitched as entertainment. The more critical protest songs by singers such as Ochs, Paxton, and Seeger proved too divisive for radio and could only be heard on record or in concert.

Protest songs in the United States are generally identified as left wing, but even extremist right wing groups such as The Ku Klux Klan and The American Nazi Party wrote protest songs of their own in the 1920s. In the 1960s conservative protest songs, usually sung by country musicians, received radio play since they could be interpreted as patriotic. One such example was Merle Haggard's hit song, "Okie from Muskogee" (1969), which protested the actions of hippie college student protestors. Since the 1960s songs have appeared across the spectrum—including folk, rock, funk, soul, rap, and other genres—to lodge musical protests against social and political developments, ranging from US domestic policy to the wars in Afghanistan and Iraq. Clearly protest songs, both from the right and left, will continue to function in any era of social activism.

See also FOLK MUSIC; FOLK REVIVAL, THE.

BIBLIOGRAPHY

O. Brand: *The Ballad Mongers* (New York, 1962)

G.M. Smith: *Labor Martyr Joe Hill* (New York, 1969)

R.S. Denisoff: *Great Day Coming: Folk Music and the American Left* (Urbana, IL, 1971)

J. Rodnitzky: *Minstrels of the Dawn: the Folk Protest Singer as a Cultural Hero* (Chicago, 1976)

J. Klein: *Woody Guthrie: a Life* (New York, 1980)

A. Winkler: *"To Everything There is a Season": Pete Seeger and the Power of Song* (New York, 2009)

JERRY RODNITZKY

Proulx, Richard (*b* St. Paul, MN, 3 April 1937; *d* Chicago, IL, 18 Feb 2010). Composer, conductor, music editor, and organist. Proulx published more than 300 works, including liturgical music, sacred and secular choral works, two operas, film music, instrumental works, and organ music. He attended MacPhail College and the University of Minnesota, with further music studies at the American Boychoir School in Princeton, New Jersey, Saint John's Abbey in Collegeville, Minnesota, and the Royal School of Church Music in England. He also studied choral conducting with ROBERT SHAW and ROGER WAGNER. Proulx served as a consultant for *Worship II* (Roman Catholic, 1975), *The Hymnal* (Episcopal, 1982), and the *United Methodist Hymnal* (1989), and contributed to *Hymns, Psalms, and Spiritual Songs* (Presbyterian, 1990), among other hymnals. He served as music director and organist at several churches, most notably the Cathedral of the Holy Name in Chicago (1980–94), where he oversaw the installation of two new organs (the Casavant II/19 [Quebec, 1981] and the Flentrop IV/71 [Holland, 1989]). The Cathedral Singers, which Proulx founded, recorded more than 25 CDs.

His compositional style was greatly influenced by Gregorian chant and by the music of Hindemith, Copland, Vierne, Duruflé, and Pärt. His best-known liturgical composition, *A Community Mass* (1971; revised 1977), has been used by several denominations and is adaptable to many different performance situations and resources. In 1994 Proulx received an honorary doctorate from General Theological Seminary in New York City as well as the BENE award from *Modern Liturgy Magazine* as "the most significant liturgical composer of the last 20 years." In 1995 the National Association of Pastoral Musicians named him the Pastoral Musician of the Year and in 2006 the American Guild of Organists presented Proulx with its Distinguished Composer Award.

WORKS
(selective list)

Mass of the Redeemer, 1973; Festival Eucharist, 1975; Canticles, vv, perc, 1976; 3 Preludes, org, 1976; The Pilgrim, op, 1980; Missa Emmanuel, 1991; Antiphony, 2 tpt, 1997; 6 Hymn Preludes, 1997; 12 Hymn Settings, 3 tpt, org, 1997; 3 Alleluia Interludes, org, 2003; 2 Spirituals, kbd, 2003; 8 Choral Introits for Feasts and Solemnities, 2004

KATHLEEN SEWRIGHT

Providence. Capital city of Rhode Island (pop. 175,255; metropolitan area: 627, 690; 2010 US Census). Italian explorer Giovanni da Verrazano (1485–1528) wrote in 1524 that as he heard the natives singing while he voyaged through Narragansett Bay he was reminded of the voices in his native Florence. Indigenous people in what is now Rhode Island mourned their dead and worshiped through music. Highly spiritual, southern New England tribes would often connect to the earth by striking it with ground beaters as they sang and danced.

Puritan leader Roger Williams (*c*1603–83) moved to Rhode Island from Massachusetts in 1636 and soon acquired land for a new village at the head of what was then called the Great Salt River. Williams named the new village Providence. His followers were generally educated middle-class workers from England's urban centers. Extraordinarily pious, a cappella psalm singing was important to their worship.

Colonists in Anglican churches were needful of instruments to accompany sacred singing. In 1734, around 20 years after the first organ was built in Boston, CHARLES THEODORE PACHELBEL (1690–1750), son of German composer Johann Pachelbel, came to Newport to install an English-made organ at Trinity Church, founded in 1698. Pachelbel served as the church's first organist for approximately a year. In 1770 First Congregational became the first Providence church to install an organ.

A concert of instrumental music was held in 1768 in the home of Providence shipowner Joshua Hacker, and a reading of John Gay's *Beggar's Opera* took place there a year later. *The Poor Soldier*, a ballad opera by William Shield, was performed in Providence in 1795.

Entrepreneurial singing masters became important throughout the colonies in the 18th century. William Billings (1746–1800) conducted a singing-school at Providence's Congregational Church in 1774, and Andrew Law (1749–1821) was an active singing master in Rhode Island, beginning as a student at Rhode Island College (later to become Brown University), from which he graduated in 1775. Both Billings and Law compiled their own hymn collections.

NEWPORT GARDNER (1746–1826), born Occramer Mary-coo in what is now Sierra Leone, was brought to Newport around 1760 where he was sold into slavery at 14. Educated in music by his master's wife Catherine Gardner, he also studied with Andrew Law. Newport Gardner composed music, taught private lessons, and held singing schools in Newport.

Singing master Stephen Wardwell, who attended Billings's Providence singing-school, was the father of Stephen S. Wardwell and the grandfather of Stephen P. Wardwell, both musicians and composers. Moses Noyes conducted a singing-school and served as organist at the First Congregational Church. Oliver Shaw (1779–1848), who had begun his career as a singing master in Massachusetts where he was Lowell Mason's first teacher, was active in Providence as an organist and composer after 1807. He founded the Psallonian Society, a large choral organization incorporated by the state legislature in 1815.

Music was introduced into Providence's public schools in 1844, apparently at the behest of Henry Barnard (1811–1900) who became state commissioner of schools a year earlier. Rhode Island singer and organist Eben Tourjée (1834–91) established Boston's New England Conservatory in 1867. A founder of Music Teachers National Association in 1876, he served as the organization's first president.

Band music gained prominence in the 19th century. The American Band of Providence was founded in 1837 with Joseph C. Green as leader. David Wallis Reeves (1838–1900), whom John Philip Sousa called "the father of American band music," was conductor from 1866 to 1900. The band continues an active performing schedule today.

When Sissieretta Jones (1868–1933), the African American soprano who grew up in Providence and spent much of her life there, was excluded from singing at major venues because of her race, she formed her own troupe and traveled around the world giving concerts of classical and semiclassical music. Her operatic voice drew large audiences and brought her critical acclaim.

Author, composer, singer, dancer, actor, producer, and director George M. Cohan (1878–1942), born in Providence, changed Broadway's style from sedate to up-to-date. Songs like "Give my regards to Broadway" and "The Yankee Doodle Boy" exemplified America's transition from vaudeville to musical comedy. Other Rhode Islanders who became famous singing on stage include Nelson Eddy (1901–67) and Eileen Farrell (1920–2002). Eddy had an early career as an opera and concert artist, but is best known for his work in films of operettas and musicals. Farrell sang at a number of opera houses, including the Metropolitan Opera, and was also successful as a popular recording and concert artist.

Jazz has had a strong presence in Rhode Island since the first half of the 20th century. Accordionist Angelo DiPippo (*b* 1934), guitarist/vocalist Frank D'Rone (*b* 1932), percussionist Nick Fatool (1915–2000), tenor saxophonist Paul Gonsalves (1920–74), cornetist Bobby Hackett (1915–76), tenor saxophonist Scott Hamilton (*b* 1954), trombonist/composer George Masso (*b* 1926), pianist Dave McKenna (1930–2008), percussionist Paul Motian (1931–2011), guitarist Frank Potenza (*b* 1950), and vocalist Carol Sloane (*b* 1937) have all added to this legacy. Popular pianist and bandleader Frankie Carle (1903–2001) and the singing group The Cowsills, a vocal/instrumental group, began their careers in Newport in 1965, and the Westerly-based band Roomful of Blues was founded in 1967. The Ocean State supports numerous informal venues for performances by rock, country, and folk artists.

Rhode Island's summer music festivals founded during the last half of the 20th century still thrive. The Newport Jazz Festival opened in 1954 and soon influenced the public's perception of jazz. First presented in 1959, the Newport Folk Festival showcases musicians from traditionalist and revivalist camps. George Wein (*b* 1925) founded the festivals, which are held at Ft. Adams State Park in Newport. Although both underwent interruptions during their early years, they were restructured and resumed on more solid foundations. The Newport Music Festival began in its current form in 1969, specializing in introducing young international artists and performances of little-known chamber works. Concerts are held in Newport's historic mansions built as vacation homes during America's industrial age. Mark Malkovich III (1931–2010) directed the festival from 1975 to 2008, when Mark Malkovich IV assumed leadership. The Kingston Chamber Music Festival at the University of Rhode Island has existed since 1989 and was founded by David Kim.

The 1900-seat Veterans Memorial Auditorium, opened in 1950, is home to the Rhode Island PO (Larry Rachleff, present conductor), Festival Ballet Providence, and the Providence Singers. The 3100-seat Providence Performing Arts Center, which opened in 1928 as Loew's Movie Palace, is a venue for touring Broadway shows, concerts, community events, and traveling acts. The Mary K. Hail (1870–1948) Music Mansion's performance hall can accommodate up to a hundred. Hail's will left her 1928 home, and a trust fund for its care, to be used for recitals, music club meetings, and other such happenings. The 31,000-square-foot Dunkin' Donuts Center, formerly Providence Civic Center, accommodates large musical performances.

Quartered at Naval Station Newport, Navy Band Northeast was established in 1974 and gives over 500 performances a year in military and community venues. It includes the following performing units: The Concert Band, Ceremonial Band, The Northeast Navy Showband, Rhode Island Sound, Top Brass Quintet, VIP Combo, and Forecast.

Rhode Island is home to several universities and colleges that offer performance venues and grant music degrees. An AB degree with three tracks: music theory/history/composition, ethnomusicology, and computer music/multimedia, is available at Brown University in Providence; Brown grants PhDs in two areas: ethnomusicology and computer music/multimedia. A BA, a BM with a concentration in performance or music education, a MME, and a MAT are offered at Rhode Island College in Providence. The University of Rhode Island in Kingston grants a BA with a choice of three options: music performance/history/theory, music history/literature, and jazz studies. The URI BM degree has separate concentrations in performance, music education, and composition. The MM degree at URI offers both music education and performance options. An Associate of Fine Arts degree in music is available at the Community College of Rhode Island's Warwick campus. Roger Williams University in Bristol awards a BA in music, and Salve Regina University in Newport grants both a BA and a BAS in music.

Among the many active Rhode Island community-based performing organizations are the Rhode Island Civic Chorale and Orchestra of Providence, Opera Providence, The Chorus of Westerly, North Kingstown Community Chorus, Jamestown Community Band, Warwick Symphony Orchestra, and the Lusitania Portuguese American Band of Cumberland. A number of Celtic and Irish bands perform regularly in Rhode Island. Cajun and Zydeco bands are popular, as are klezmer bands. The Rhode Island St. Andrews society encourages the performance of traditional Scottish music and dance.

Informal outdoor summer concerts are held in Cranston, Cumberland, Narragansett, North Kingstown, Providence, and Westerly. Occasional powwows and other festivals offer the opportunity to hear and see authentic performances of Native American music. Theatre-by-the-Sea in Matunuck is a thriving summer enterprise that produces a selection of musicals every summer.

Rhode Island's musical history is long and diverse, embracing many professional and amateur music makers. The state is rich in the variety of musical experiences it offers residents and visitors.

BIBLIOGRAPHY

AGrove

H.C. Thrasher: *250 Years of Music in Providence, Rhode Island, 1636–1886* (MS, 1937; Providence, 1942)

W.G. McLoughlin: *Rhode Island: A History* (New York, 1986)

M.L. Mark and C.L Gary, eds.: *A History of American Music Education* (Reston, VA, 2/1999)

C. Livingston and D.E. Smith, eds.: *Rhode Island's Musical Heritage: An Exploration* (Sterling Heights, MI, 2008)

CAROLYN LIVINGSTON

Pruett, James W(orrell) (*b* Mount Airy, NC, 23 Dec 1932). Music librarian and musicologist. He attended the University of North Carolina, Chapel Hill (BA 1955, MA 1957, PhD 1962), and from 1955, he served as reference assistant and then music librarian (1961–76) there. In 1963 he joined the faculty of the music department, becoming professor of music in 1974 and chair in 1976; in 1987 he became chief of the Music Division at the Library of Congress until his retirement in 1995.

As librarian at Chapel Hill, Pruett's greatest accomplishments were in collection development—he was instrumental in creating one of the most significant academic research collections in the country—and in mentoring students. At the Library of Congress he was responsible for major acquisitions, including the personal papers of Irving Berlin, Leonard Bernstein, and Artur Rubinstein. He expanded concert offerings to include jazz and established the Leonore S. Gershwin/Library of Congress Recording and Publishing Project. As a scholar Pruett has been engaged in a multiplicity of topics including Moravian music, the work of Filippo Vitale, and the *Laborde chansonnier*. He has also published works in the areas of music bibliography and research methods.

Pruett has been active in the American Musicological Society and the Music Library Association (president, 1973–75). He was editor of *Notes* from 1974 to 1977. In 2007 the UNC Department of Music established the James W. Pruett Summer Research Fellowships for Music at the Library of Congress in his honor.

WRITINGS

with L. Rigsby: *A Selective Music Bibliography from the Period 1663–1763* (Raleigh, NC, 1962)

ed.: *Studies in Musicology: Essays in Memory of Glen Haydon* (Chapel Hill, NC, 1969)

with T.P. Slavens: *Research Guide to Musicology* (Chicago, 1985)

"Scholar-Librarian? Librarian-Scholar?" *Music Librarianship in America*, ed. Michael Ochs (Cambridge, MA, 1991), 65–69

BIBLIOGRAPHY

P.R. Laird and C.H. Russell: *Res Musicae: Essays in Honor of James W. Pruett* (Warren, MI, 2001)

PHILIP VANDERMEER

Pruslin, Stephen (Lawrence) (*b* Brooklyn, NY, 16 April 1940). Pianist, librettist, writer, and broadcaster. He studied music at Brandeis University (1958–61) and Princeton University (1961–3), teaching at Princeton until 1964. At the same time, he studied piano with Luise Vosgerchian and EDWARD STEUERMANN, the pianist whom Arnold Schoenberg contracted to give the premieres of many of his works, including *Pierrot lunaire*. In 1964, under the auspices of a Hertz Memorial Scholarship from the University of California, he went to Europe and settled in London, where he has remained. He is touted as a leading interpreter of contemporary keyboard music and has maintained an international career as a pianist, making his recital debut at the Purcell Room in London in 1970. His commanding performances of Elliott Carter's *Night Fantasies* and Sir Peter Maxwell Davies's Piano Sonata, written for him in 1981, established precedents for future performers. His renditions of late Beethoven piano sonatas and keyboard works by J.S. Bach and John Bull, performed on the piano, have also garnered international recording awards. Pruslin has composed or arranged music for film and theater, including Ken Russell's *The Devils* and *The Boy Friend*, Derek Jarman's *The Tempest*, and Peter Ustinov's *Beethoven's Tenth*.

In 1967 Pruslin began to gain firsthand access to the music of Davies as one of the founding members of the Pierrot Players, subsequently reconstituted as the Fires of London, both of whose names he coined. The ensemble, active for 20 years, offered definitive performances and recordings of Davies's music-theater works that were modeled on, and played alongside, *Pierrot lunaire*. The desire to perform the piece in English necessitated Pruslin's translation of *Pierrot*, which is remarkable for his crafting of supple, sonically flowing phrases through intricate alliteration and vowel configurations.

Pruslin has made other significant literary contributions, as a scholar and a creative writer. His edited volume *Peter Maxwell Davies: Studies from Two Decades* (London, 1979) was the first scholarly collection devoted to the composer. Pruslin's libretto for Harrison Birtwistle's *Punch and Judy* (1966–7) is one of the most celebrated of the postwar era, winning high praise from W.H. Auden, who called it "one of the most outstanding and original opera librettos of the century" (Pruslin, 2007). His second libretto, for Martin Butler's *Craig's Progress* (1993–4), exhibits calculated stylistic pluralism, the premise on which the opera was conceived. The BBC frequently engages him as a commentator and lecturer for television and radio programs.

SUSAN FEDER/JESSICA PAYETTE

Pryor, Arthur (Willard) (*b* St Joseph, MO, 22 Sept 1870; *d* West Long Branch, NJ, 18 June 1942). Trombonist, conductor, and composer. He began to study piano and cornet with his father at the age of six, changing to valve trombone when he was 11. By the age of 15 he was playing slide trombone in his father's band. He joined the Liberati Band in 1888, where he became known as "the boy wonder trombonist from Missouri." He served as conductor of the Stanley Opera Company from 1890 to 1892, when he was offered a position as trombone soloist with the Sousa Band. His solos, in a popular idiom that incorporated trombone glissandos or "smears," complemented Herbert L. Clarke's sophisticated cornet solos, and by 1900 Pryor was a star attraction of the band, second only to Sousa himself. He was also assistant conductor of the band from 1895 to 1902. Pryor left Sousa in 1903 to form his own band, which gave its first concert in New York on 15 November. It made six nationwide tours (1903–9), but thereafter its engagements were limited to Asbury Park, New Jersey (over 20 summers); Willow Park Grove, New Jersey (10 summers); and Royal Palm Park, Miami (10 winters); it also made recordings. Pryor retired in 1933, but his band continued to reassemble occasionally to give concerts.

Pryor was one of the greatest trombone virtuosos in the band tradition, and during his career played about 10,000 solos, earning the title "the Paganini of the trombone." He was also an eminent bandmaster and was a charter member of ASCAP (1914) and of the American Bandmasters Association (1929). He conducted what may have been the first commercial recording made by an American band, and directed the Sousa Band in many of its recordings, even after he had left the group; his own band made some 1000 recordings before 1930.

Pryor wrote over 300 compositions, including three operettas (apparently lost), *Jingaboo, On the Eve of her Wedding Day*, and *Uncle Tom's Cabin*. Most of his works are for band, including marches (e.g., *Will Rogers March*), rags (*Razzazza Mazzazza*), waltzes (*The Love Kiss Waltz*), and novelties (*The Whistler and his Dog*); he also wrote piano pieces and songs. Much of his

music was designed to display his own virtuosity. He limited himself to four forms of predictable format—theme and variations, "valse caprice," "valse de concert," and polka caprice—resulting in a certain similarity of style and repetition of musical ideas. These works were written at a time when the trombone had little solo repertory of consequence; they are technically demanding, and are still widely played. Among the most popular are *Blue Bells of Scotland, Love's Enchantment, The Patriot*, and *Thoughts of Love*. His music is principally published by Carl Fischer.

BIBLIOGRAPHY

DAB (P.E. Bierley)

C.H. Larkin: "Memories of Arthur Pryor and his Band," *School Musician*, xiv (1943), no.6, 8 only; no.7, 14 only

N.H. Quayle: "Arthur Pryor: Some Reminiscences," *MJ*, xii/3 (1954), 37 only

H.W. Schwartz: *Bands of America* (Garden City, NY, 1957/*R*), 198–200, 237–42

G. Bridges: *Pioneers in Brass* (Detroit, 1965), CD-ROM (Coupeville, WA, 2000)

J.R. Smart: disc notes, *The Sousa and Pryor Bands*, New World 282 (1976)

S. Wolfinbarger: "The Solo Trombone Music of Arthur Pryor," *International Trombone Association Journal*, xi/1 (1983), no.1, 3 only; no.2, 27 only; no.3, 20 only

D.E. Frizane: *Arthur Pryor (1870–1942): American Trombonist, Bandmaster, Composer* (diss., U. of Kansas, 1984)

L.J. Luper: *Arthur Pryor: His Trombone, His Band, His Music* (n.p., 1987)

W.H. Rehrig: *The Heritage Encyclopedia of Band Music* (Westerville, OH, 1991, suppl. 1996); CD-ROM (Oskaloosa, IA, 2005) [includes extensive list of works]

M. Meckna: *Twentieth-Century Brass Soloists* (Westport, CT, 1994)

L.D. Geiger: "Paganini of the Trombone," *Boombah Herald*, xxv/1 (1997), 21–31 [includes list of works]

JAMES M. BURK/RAOUL F. CAMUS

Psalmody. A general term for music sung in Protestant churches in England and America from the 17th to the early 19th centuries. The term was first associated with the chanting of psalms (following traditional practices of the Roman Catholic Church) and later with the singing of metrical psalms, but after these had been gradually replaced by hymns, the term was retained to cover all kinds of sacred music sung during the period.

1. Early psalm books, congregations, and singing-schools. 2. The rise of choirs, musical societies, and elaborate psalmody. 3. Musical style. 4. Reform.

1. EARLY PSALM BOOKS, CONGREGATIONS, AND SINGING-SCHOOLS. The singing of psalms in meter has a long history in the English Protestant church dating from the Reformation (*c*1530). When the Pilgrims landed at Plymouth in 1620 they carried with them Henry Ainsworth's *Book of Psalmes: Englished Both in Prose and Metre* (Amsterdam, 1612), which included 39 unharmonized tunes. The tunes in Ainsworth's psalter, many of them traceable to French and Dutch folk sources, were generally rather long (eight lines is typical) and often enlivened by syncopation. The Puritans who founded the Massachusetts Bay Colony in 1629 sang from Thomas Sternhold and John Hopkins's *The Whole Booke of Psalmes, Collected into Englishe Meter* (London, 1562),

later called the Old Version. Thomas Ravenscroft's *Whole Booke of Psalmes* (London, 1621), containing four-part settings of the British psalm-tune repertory for recreational use, also circulated in America during the 17th and 18th centuries. Ravenscroft's harmonizations, set mostly in block chords, still contained elements of the contrapuntal tradition. The earliest American psalmody was thus rooted in a European tradition of considerable musical power.

To these English publications 17th-century New Englanders added one of their own that attests to the importance they attached to psalmody. The first full-length book printed in the English-speaking colonies was a metrical psalter, *The Whole Booke of Psalmes* (Cambridge, MA, 1640, 3/1651; published thereafter as *The Psalms, Hymns, and Spiritual Songs of the Old and New Testament*), known as the Bay Psalm Book. The clergymen who assembled it sought fidelity to the original scriptures. They also discarded some of the more complex textual meters of Ainsworth and Sternhold and Hopkins. The ninth edition of the Bay Psalm Book (1698) was the first printed with music, and it marked the beginning of American tunebook publication. The 13 pieces, printed in the back of the book as a supplement, without texts, were the first musical works published in the British colonies.

All 150 psalms were sung to a few dozen tunes, based on the poetic meter of the text. The most common text meters were common meter, long meter, double common meter, and short meter. The meters are defined by the number of syllables per line. Common meter has four lines of eight and six syllables (8 : 6 : 8 : 6), long meter has four lines of eight syllables (8 : 8 : 8 : 8), and short meter has four lines of six and eight syllables (6 : 6 : 8 : 6). Double meters refer to the setting of two stanzas of poetry (*see* PSALMS, METRICAL).

Other psalters of note include Nahum Tate and Nicholas Brady's *New Version of the Psalms of David* published in 1696 (known as the New Version), along with a *Supplement to the New Version of Psalms* in 1700. Both became an important source of texts for psalmodists throughout the 18th century. In the first two decades of the 18th century Isaac Watts, an English Independent, published three collections of sacred texts that became popular later in the century, especially among more liberal Congregationalist churches (and American composers). The first was the *Horae lyricae* (1706), followed by *Hymns and Spiritual Songs* (1707), and *Psalms of David* (1719). All of these were first published in London.

For most New Englanders during the first century of British settlement, psalm singing was partly or entirely an oral practice. Calvinist theology, mistrustful of musical elaboration, encouraged congregations to make their own music, without instrumental accompaniment or professional leadership, and according to the wishes and skills of a majority of the congregation's members. As time passed, moreover, contact with Old World musical traditions lessened, the level of the settlers' musical skill declined, and the ability to read music grew rarer. Furthermore, literacy was by no means universal,

and not all worshipers could afford psalm books. Each of these factors helped to introduce oral elements into the practice of psalmody. By the 18th century most New England congregations sang their psalms at a slow, irregular tempo, with much sliding and ornamental embellishment, usually under the leadership of a clerk or precentor who may or may not have been an accomplished singer. The technique of lining out, in which the leader intoned or read the text line by line and the congregation sang back the lines in alternation with the leader, was widespread. Its appeal was at least partly practical, as a proponent in the 1780s explained: "It is impossible for all to get books; and if all had books, they could not be benefitted by them, some being old and dim-sighted, others young and not versed enough in reading to keep pace while singing." During the next century, this quasi-improvisatory practice came to be called the OLD WAY OF SINGING, or the usual way. (It may be noted, incidentally, that the encroachment of oral practice into what had first been a written tradition was paralleled in the parishes of the Church of England, where music making was also entrusted to congregations who sang without organs to lead them.)

Early in the 18th century New England clergymen, among them Cotton Mather and Thomas Symmes, began to express dissatisfaction with the way congregations sang. Some had come to believe that however satisfying to participants the old way might be, it was not contributing to a proper atmosphere in worship. From 1720 polemical tracts began to appear in Boston deploring the state of psalmody and recommending improvements. The agency for reform was the SINGING-SCHOOL, a series of instructional sessions led by an accomplished musician. A singing master typically advertised for classes lasting several months during the winter. The teacher would find an available space, such as a tavern or home, and meet two or three evenings per week. Singing-school students were typically teenagers of both sexes, who clearly enjoyed them as social as well as educational events. Scholars in the school would learn the rudiments of psalm singing: the basic elements of vocal technique, pronunciation, and the ability to read music from notation. Many schools ended with a concert, "singing exhibition," or a singing lecture or sermon. Here the students could demonstrate what they had learned. Then, when they returned to sing in their congregations, their mode of singing (i.e., "singing by rule") would presumably be followed by others, and the congregation would abandon the old way in favor of what was known as regular singing.

That was the theory. In fact, the process did not work out quite so neatly, for the reformers encountered strong resistance. Many colonial Protestants did not share the belief that the old way was a corruption of correct psalmody. Sanctioned by use, and gratifying in the relaxed freedom it allowed the singer, it was set aside only reluctantly and continued in many congregations, throughout the century and later, as an indigenous folk tradition that grew from a written practice.

Nevertheless, singing-schools are documented regularly in New England during the 1720s and flourished there and elsewhere through the rest of the 18th century and into the next. They began a process of disseminating musical learning which during the course of the century had a powerful effect on psalmody. One of the first results was the publication of tunebooks: collections of psalm tunes, usually including an instructional preface, designed for use in the singing-schools. The first compilers of these works were Congregational ministers: John Tufts, whose *A Very Plain and Easy Introduction to the Singing of Psalm Tunes* went through 11 editions between 1721 and 1744; and Thomas Walter, whose *Grounds and Rules of Musick* (1721) was still in print nearly half a century later as part of Daniel Bayley's *A New and Complete Introduction to the Grounds and Rules of Musick* (Newburyport, MA, 5/1768). A sizable majority of the sacred tunebooks published later in the century—and by the end of 1810 some 350 such works had been published in British North America—were designed for singing-school use. As well as stimulating the publication of tunebooks and, eventually, the composition of music to fill them, the singing-school served a second important function. It provided institutional support, however fragile, for musical professionalism. For most of the 18th century, and in some places well into the 19th, the only way a native American was likely to earn even a part of his living in music was as a singing master, a teacher of singing-schools. A third effect of the singing-school was that, by teaching Americans to sing with greater attention to vocal production and choral blend, and introducing them to musical notation, it inspired a wish for a more elaborate kind of music making than congregational singing could provide. In this impulse lies the beginning of the New England church choir, an institution that began to take shape shortly after the mid-18th century.

2. THE RISE OF CHOIRS, MUSICAL SOCIETIES, AND ELABORATE PSALMODY. As long as tunebooks were geared to the needs of beginning singing-school and congregational singing, there was no reason for them to contain more than a limited repertory. Before 1760 more than 30 separate publications containing sacred music appeared in the American colonies, including various editions of the Bay Psalm Book and the many issues of Tufts's and Walter's collections. Together these made available a repertory of no more than about 85 different tunes, almost all of British origin, which typically moved in uniform note values and were harmonized in block chords.

Urania (Philadelphia, 1761), compiled by James Lyon, is the earliest sign of the increase in the size and stylistic range of the printed repertory of psalmody in the 1760s. With its 198 pages and 96 works, it dwarfed all earlier American musical publications, and its inclusion of elaborate, modern British music (more than a dozen anthems and set-pieces, and several hymn tunes, as well as a selection of psalm tunes), most of it never before published in America, made it a landmark in American psalmody. Two publications by Josiah Flagg, *A Collection of the Best Psalm Tunes* (Boston, 1764) and

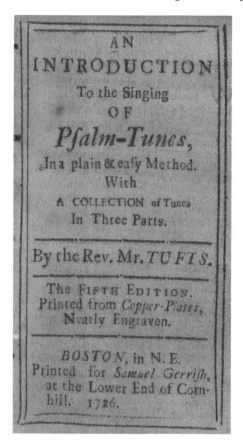

Title page of John Tuft's An Introduction to the Singing of Psalm-tunes, *1726. (Courtesy American Antiquarian Society)*

Sixteen Anthems (Boston, 1766), further established the American tunebook as a forum for the publication of new music. Finally, the American editions of William Tans'ur's *Royal Melody Complete* (Boston, 1767, with many later editions) and Aaron Williams's *Universal Psalmodist* (Newburyport, MA, 1769, published by Daniel Bayley with Tans'ur's work as *The American Harmony*) were another step towards broadening the stylistic framework of American psalmody. Between 1760 and 1770 the printed repertory burgeoned beyond oral command.

The tunebooks of the 1760s, both in number and in content, signal a new energy in American sacred music-making. Whereas in the two preceding decades only 12 tunebooks had been printed, roughly twice that many were published between 1760 and 1769. Moreover, more than 300 new compositions were added to the published repertory. Among them were many pieces incorporating texture changes, melismas, and—especially in fuging-tunes—brief contrapuntal sections. This new, more elaborate style was being developed around the mid-1700s by the psalmodists working in English parish churches. Tunebooks by Tans'ur, William Knapp, John Arnold, and other provincial English psalmodists circulated in America during the 1750s and 1760s; moreover, music by these men began to appear in tunebooks printed in the British colonies during the 1760s. The presence of so much new elaborate music in this decade signifies that a new branch of psalmody had been established, one in which singers were more accomplished and some degree of musical literacy was required.

The origins of the 18th-century New England Protestant church choir appear to lie in two impulses: a desire to improve and regularize congregational singing, and the singers' wish to perform. The former appears to have originated with the clergy, or church leaders, or perhaps the wishes of the congregation as a whole; the latter originated with the singers themselves. Although no systematic study of the 18th-century New England choir has been undertaken, evidence suggests that more often than not it was the singers' insistence that led to the formation of a choir. No Congregational church choirs are known to have existed before 1750, but a number were formed during the 1750s and 1760s, and by the 1780s and 1790s choirs were common.

Typically, choir members were singing-school alumni. When a school was held in a town, the more accomplished scholars sometimes expressed a wish after it was over to continue singing as a group. In many towns "the singers" petitioned to sit together during public worship, a request that was not always granted. That arrangement might be recommended, however, as in Boston's First Church (1758), because "skilful Singers, sitting together in some convenient place, would greatly tend to rectify our singing on the Lord's Day, and would render that part of Divine Worship more agreeable." It also gave the choir a chance to perform its own special music, including elaborate pieces of the kind that began to appear in American tunebooks of the 1760s—surely not by coincidence precisely the time when church choirs were beginning to spring up in New England.

Singing-schools and church choirs lie behind the sharp increase in the printed repertory in the 1760s, which testifies that the ability to read music was no longer a rare skill. Although the growth of repertory was slowed down by the Revolutionary War (1775–81), it continued during the rest of the century. By 1800 more than 1000 different compositions had been printed in American tunebooks. (By 1811 the figure had reached 7500.) When that figure is compared with the few tunes used by colonial Christians earlier in the century (85 tunes available in American tunebooks by 1760; 400 tunes printed before 1770), it is clear that the tradition was transformed by the appearance of new institutions and the impact of musical literacy, and that the 1760s were a crucial time in that transformation.

From 1770 the contributions of native composers increased. Much of the music in American tunebooks was still taken from British sources, but more music was composed by Americans who over the next several decades formed what some historians have called the First New England School of composers (*see* NEW ENGLAND COMPOSERS, SCHOOLS OF). Most of these men were Anglo-Celtic by lineage and Protestant (probably Congregational) by religion, born and brought up in the towns and villages of Massachusetts and Connecticut. Many were married and had children. Most were not full-time musicians but tradesmen who practiced music in their spare time. Few had training beyond what they had picked up in singing-schools and from British treatises. Few were tutored in orthodox European musical grammar. Nevertheless, they composed and published, and saw their music eagerly taken up by their countrymen. As a group they embodied the quality of self-reliance that Americans often associate with the beginnings of their history as a nation.

The most prominent of them and the first American composer of real consequence was William Billings, whose *New-England Psalm-singer* (Boston, 1770) represents another landmark. Published at a time when only a dozen or so American tunes had appeared in print, Billings's work, made up entirely of his own compositions, increased the figure tenfold. Moreover, the patriotic overtones of his prefatory remarks and of some of the texts he wrote and set, such as "Chester," were unprecedented. His unabashed confession of his own inexperience and unwillingness to follow established compositional rules provided musical Americans with a bold example of a native composer.

Billings's example was not ignored. By the end of 1782 compositions by at least 19 different Americans had appeared in print. The sudden increase can be traced to two Connecticut collections, *Select Harmony* (Cheshire, 1779) by Andrew Law and *The Chorister's Companion* (New Haven, 1782) by Simeon Jocelyn and Amos Doolittle. Like Lyon, Flagg, and Bayley before them, Law and Jocelyn were primarily compilers rather than composers. Many of the tunes introduced into print in their books soon became American favorites. The two works also provided a new model for American tunebooks. Earlier collections had generally been either assortments of British music, or entirely original, such as Billings's publications. *Select Harmony* and *The Chorister's Companion* were eclectic compilations in which both British tunes, many of them established favorites, and newly composed American tunes appeared. It is noteworthy that later tunebooks that went through many editions displayed a similar combination of European and American music, among them *The Worcester Collection* (Worcester, MA, 1786, 8/1803), Andrew Adgate's *Philadelphia Harmony* (Philadelphia, 1789, 9/1807), and *Village Harmony* (Exeter, NH, 1795, 17/1821). *The Worcester Collection* was the first tunebook printed by Isaiah Thomas from moveable type. Thomas was the leading publisher in early America and increasingly publishers followed his example of printing tunebooks from musical type rather than engraved plates.

The years between the end of the Revolutionary War and the beginning of the War of 1812 brought conspicuously increased activity in all areas of psalmody. Tunebook production grew from some 60 issues in the 1780s and more than 100 in the 1790s to more than 220 by the beginning of the 1800s. The first federal copyright law was passed in 1790, which stopped the unregulated reprinting of popular tunes without the composer's knowledge or permission. New Englanders traveled southward and westward, teaching singing-schools and establishing their books in New York State, Pennsylvania, Maryland, and the Carolinas, and making their regional music into a national music. Younger composers and compilers appeared—not only from Massachusetts and Connecticut but also from New Hampshire, Vermont, and Maine—setting their printed works before the singing public. (A reliable estimate is that by 1810 nearly 250 US natives or residents had published sacred music.)

While institutions like singing-schools and church choirs continued to flourish, more and more singers were forming musical societies—groups devoted to sacred music-making but existing independently of any structure of formal worship. Evidence of the existence of American musical societies can be found as early as the 1760s; but it was in the postwar period that the impulse to form such groups as the Stoughton Musical Society (MA, 1786; still in existence in the early 2010s), the Uranian Musical Society (NY, 1793–8), the Hampshire Musical Society (Hampshire Co., MA, c1800–02), and the Handel Society at Dartmouth College (Hanover, NH, c1810) really took hold. Like that of the church choir, the existence of musical societies demonstrates the desire of Americans to sing the most challenging and artistic music available to them and to perform at a high level of proficiency.

3. MUSICAL STYLE. Written for worship, recreational, and didactic use—for singing-schools, congregations, choirs, and musical societies—the choral music of 18th-century Americans answered specific needs and is best understood as a community practice. American psalmodists usually composed for four-part chorus, with the melody in the tenor voice. Set in open score, the music seldom calls for instrumental accompaniment, although from around 1800 "gallery orchestras" of treble instruments (flute, violin, clarinet) with bass support (most often cello or "church bass," but sometimes bassoon) often accompanied the singers by doubling voice parts. Since most American composers of the time lacked keyboard skills or knowledge of 18th-century European harmonic practice, their music often lacks harmonic direction and gives the impression of crudeness. That quality can be a strength, as in Daniel Read's fuging-tune "Sherburne," where instead of following the expected path to a cadence on the tonic, the first phrase discovers its destination as the submediant (ex.1). Such tonal freedom, and the sacred texts they set, could inspire the New Englanders to bold and memorable melodies. Timothy Swan's "China," celebrated in Harriet Beecher Stowe's novel *The Minister's Wooing* (1859; chap.38) as "one of those wild, pleading tunes, dear to the heart of New England" and long admired by both singers and scholars, skillfully balances leaps and stepwise motion, creating the effect of a good singer's spontaneous embellishment of a slow-moving triple-time dirge (ex.2).

Ex.1 Daniel Read: "Sherburne" (1785), bars 1–3

Ex.2 Timothy Swan: "China" (1801)

Most American tunes of the time set only one stanza of metrical text. Plain tunes—settings in block-chord texture in which the phrase structure reflects the textual meter exactly—are in the majority. Sometimes, however, the composer transcends the meter by repeating or extending certain words, resulting in a tune with extension. Fuging-tunes make particular demands on the composer's ability to compose imitative counterpoint (*see* FUGING-TUNE). Set-pieces—through-composed settings of metrical texts—and anthems constitute only a small proportion of the repertory composed by Americans (*see* SET-PIECE and ANTHEM). Limited compositional training is most apt to show up as a defect rather than an asset in these larger-scale works; many suffer for lack of tonal variety.

Billings's comments on composition emphasize the importance he attached to the independence of voice parts. "The grand difficulty in composition," he wrote in *The Continental Harmony* (Boston, 1794), "is to preserve the air through each part separately, and yet cause them to harmonize with each other at the same time" (p.31). His own custom was to compose the tenor part, the "air," or melody, first and then add the bass, treble (soprano), and counter (alto) parts in turn. Such an approach helps to explain how the New Englanders arrived at the kind of harmony found, for example, in the first part of Lewis Edson's fuging-tune "Lenox" (ex.3). Each phrase begins and ends with a consonance; but within each, a harmonic collision or unexpected chord occurs: an $f/f'\#$ clash, generated contrapuntally (bar 2, beat 4); a submediant chord where the bass movement seems to promise tonic (bar 4, beat 3); a second-inversion dominant and submediant, both in the same measure (bar 7, beats 2 and 4); and a free-floating 7th (bar 9, beat 2).

Once thought by some to be a unique New World practice, American psalmody can now be seen to have been modeled upon British prototypes, and several styles of English Protestant psalmody influential in America can be distinguished. Perhaps the clearest way of differentiating between them is to notice how each approaches the declamation of the text. A brief survey using well known American pieces as examples will illustrate this.

The basic style of Anglo-American psalmody, known as the common tune style, gives each syllable of text

Ex.3 Lewis Edson: "Lenox" (1782), bars 1–10

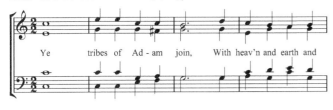

Ye tribes of Ad-am join, With heav'n and earth and

seas, And of-fer notes di-vine, To

your cre-a-tor's praise.

the same weight by moving in equal note values in slow duple time. English psalmody was given over almost exclusively to this kind of tune (e.g., "Old Hundredth" and "St. Anne") until the beginning of the 18th century; and Billings's plain tune "Lebanon," which is only lightly decorated, shows that as late as 1770 a compositional approach more than two centuries old could still serve a New World psalmodist (ex.4). Early in the 18th century two variations on the common tune style appeared in England, both animating its stolid tread. One retained duple meter but enlivened it with dactyls. Read's plain tune "Windham" (1785) shows an especially skillful use of dactylic motion; its first three phrases hammer home the text's grim message through a series of dactyls broken only in the fourth phrase (ex.5). The other approach introduced

Ex.4 William Billings: "Lebanon" (1770, in the revised version of 1778), bars 1–7, with text quoted from *The Village Harmony* (1796)

Death with his war-rant in__ his hand Comes

rush-ing on a-main,

iambic declamation in triple meter, assigning longer notes to accented syllables and opening the door to melodic embellishment. Billings's plain tune "Brookfield," by far the most widely circulated American triple-time sacred piece of its era, avoids any hint of the limping gait that such tunes sometimes assumed. It does so chiefly by a varying motion from phrase to phrase (ex.6).

Ex.5 Daniel Read: "Windham" (1785)

Broad is the road that leads to death,

And thou-sands walk to-geth-er there,

But wis-dom shows a nar-row path,

With here and there a trav-el-ler.

Ex.6 William Billings: "Brookfield" (1770), quoted from *The Worcester Collection* (1786)

'Twas on that dark, that__ dole-ful night, When

pow'rs__ of earth__ and hell__ a-rose, A-

gainst__ the Son__ of God's__ de-light, And

friends__ be-tray'd__ him to_____ his foes.

Each of the three styles noted so far arose within Anglican parish psalmody, the first at its beginning, the second apparently during the second decade of the 18th century, and the third perhaps slightly earlier. A fourth style, introduced by and associated with a dissenting sect that began within the Church of England but soon broke away, appeared around 1740; this so-called Methodist style of hymnody is described by Temperley (B1979) as "popular and strongly secular in style." Its hallmarks include a brisker tempo (usually notated as 4/4, 2/4, or 3/4 instead of the traditional 2/2 or 3/2); a three-voice texture; trochaic declamation, often with weak phrase-endings; melodic ornamentation, sometimes written as grace notes; and repetition of either text or music or both. "Middletown," a plain tune by Amos Bull first published in 1778, was one of the most widely accepted American attempts to seize the modern, cosmopolitan spirit of the Methodists' emphasis on catchy melodies (ex.7).

Ex.7 Amos Bull: "Middletown" (1778), bars 1–8

One other approach to declamation introduced by the mid-18th century English psalmodists had an especially strong impact on New England composers; it might be called declamatory duple style: the basic half-note beat is enlivened by bursts of quarter-notes, often sung on repeated pitches and tending to appear towards the end of a piece. The clearest and by far the most famous example of the declamatory duple style is the fuging-tune, a piece of strophic music containing at least one section involving contrapuntal vocal entries with overlapping text. Appearing in England before 1750, the fuging-tune first circulated in the colonies in English tunebooks. Beginning with Lyon's *Urania*, English fuging-tunes were also printed in American collections. By the 1780s rural American psalmodists had taken up the form and made it their own. Choral singers embraced it with enthusiasm, both because each voice part had its own chance to strike in with the subject and because the piling up of declamatory entries generated a momentum that inspired spirited performances. Edson's "Lenox," the most widely printed American fuging-tune of its time, demonstrates the appeal of the declamatory duple style especially well.

Beginning with four short, distinct phrases, separated by definite pauses, it then unleashes a fuge section that, with 26 consecutive quarter-note articulations, proceeds like a relentless rhythmic engine (ex.8).

Ex.8 Lewis Edson: "Lenox" (1782), bars 10–18

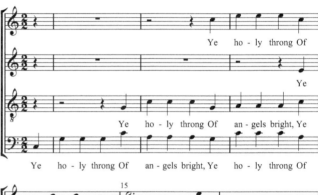

The fuging-tune, although a form in which the declamatory duple style flourished conspicuously, is by no means the only form in which it appeared. Oliver Holden's tune "Coronation," a popular American tune with extension, is a fine example of a declamatory duple piece (ex.9). And nowhere was it used to more dramatic effect than in Billings's *Anthem for Easter*, where the triumph of the Resurrection is dramatized in a burst of choral recitative with the force of a lightning bolt (ex.10).

With all of these styles of declamation at hand, American psalmodists of the period were equipped to set the available repertory of texts—chiefly, metrical psalms and hymns, and especially those versified by Isaac Watts—either in a single style or by mixing them, as Swan skillfully did in his fuging-tune "Bristol" (ex.11).

A stylistic gamut, with those American composers who were in close contact with cosmopolitan urban music-making at one end and those without such

Ex.9 Oliver Holden: "Coronation" (1793), bars 1–9

Ex.10 William Billings: *Anthem for Easter* (1787), bars 77–84

Ex.11 Timothy Swan: "Bristol" (1785), bars 1–15

contact at the other, revealed sharp differences in melodic–harmonic practice. Men such as Holden, Samuel Holyoke, and Jacob Kimball all knew, and perhaps studied with, the learned immigrant organist and composer Hans Gram. Their music tends to favor full triads and to move according to the formulae of 18th-century textbook harmony. Moreover, Holyoke, Timothy Olmstead, and Samuel Babcock, among others, explored the elaborately ornamented melodic style of Methodist music, an idiom seldom essayed successfully by Americans of their generation. If the melodic–harmonic idiom of these men closely resembles that favored in the cities, it diverges strongly from that of Edson, Oliver Brownson, Justin Morgan, Stephen Jenks, and Abraham Wood, at the other end of the gamut. These men were self-taught, spending their lives mostly in New England villages and the countryside, unexposed to more cosmopolitan musical learn-

ing. The folklike melody, harmonic exploration, and fondness for dissonant clashes that can be found in their music show that they worked more by trial and error than by precept. Beyond consistently setting textual accents to music, placing consonances on most strong beats, and giving each vocal part some melodic independence, they were bound by few conventions, which created differences in style. These differences make it awkward to consider them as a group. Somewhere closer to the center of the gamut might be placed the music of Billings, Read, and Swan, whose work is less polished and more clearly provincial in melody and harmony than that of the first group, but all of whom were more strongly affected than the second group by precepts derived from Europe. Each of these men produced enough music over a long enough period to have arrived at a distinctive melodic–harmonic style of their own. Of the three, Billings was perhaps the least pungent in his harmony and the most given to writing melodies with sweep and aggressive momentum, which he often did by sequentially repeating small units of text and music. The potent resource of Read's harmony and the craftsmanship of his melodies helped to make him especially skilled at plain tunes and short fuging-tunes, in which he wrote some of the most tersely concentrated music of his time. Swan was blessed with an exceptionally free imagination, capable of strikingly expressive responses to images in the text and unexpected melodic and harmonic twists. The widely varied melodic–harmonic idiom of these three and their contemporaries suggests that, when future studies of the sacred style of the First New England School of composers are undertaken, stylistic diversity is likely to be a chief topic.

4. REFORM. From the 1760s American psalmody had evolved without comparison to any stylistic standard or ideal. Towards the end of the century American collections frequently contained, printed side by side, tunes in the common style almost as old as Protestantism itself, recent pieces by Yankee psalmodists, and the often florid Methodist tunes from mid-18th century Britain—many of them drawn from Thomas Butts's *Harmonia sacra* (London, c1760) and Martin Madan's *Lock Hospital Collection* (London, 1769)—which in style resembled the Italianate solo songs favored in drawing rooms and theaters. Andrew Law, apparently the first to see any incongruity in this kind of musical mixture, attacked native composers in the preface of his *Musical Primer* (Cheshire, CT, 1793). His attack, and similar comments by others, expressed dissatisfaction with the absence of a standard in American psalmody. It signaled that a process of musical reform was under way that later set up a standard of musical style modeled on that of late 18th-century British psalmody.

Reform assumed a variety of guises. Some American composers began in the 1790s to follow British or European models more closely. Samuel Holyoke and Oliver Holden joined with Gram to produce *The Massachusetts Compiler* (Boston, 1795), a reform landmark which introduced an assortment of European or Europeanized compositions with a lengthy digest from prominent European "thoroughbass" manuals and instructional treatises. European music occupied an increasingly large proportion of the repertory in tunebooks published after the turn of the century, especially after 1805. The American tunes that did survive were often purged of at least some of their supposed crudities, as in William Cooper's *Beauties of Church Music* (Boston, 1804). Denunciations of the native idiom became increasingly frequent, and fuging-tunes came in for special attack—for example, by John Hubbard in his *Essay on Music* (Boston, 1808)—for their obfuscation of the text. Interestingly, however, the height of fuging-tune publication was the period from 1800 to 1809.

Some reformers sought to encourage the cultivation of increasingly elaborate music by European masters; others, viewing psalmody as a liturgical practice in which solemnity and decorum should outweigh all other qualities, advocated a return to the ancient common tunes in use before the Revolutionary War. The former impulse led to the establishment of more musical societies; the latter led to a rejection of musical elaboration and eventually to the formulation of a kind of latter-day common tune devotional style by Thomas Hastings, Lowell Mason, and their followers. However divergent these two approaches may have been, they shared a rejection of the First New England School of composers and of the American styles they developed.

The success of the reform movement in the cities of the Atlantic seaboard and New England marked the end, by 1820, of the indigenous New England compositional style as a creative force. It did not, however, end the circulation of its repertory. New England tunes survived in collections published in upstate New York, western Pennsylvania, Ohio, and the Shenandoah Valley of Virginia, as well as in the shape-note collections published farther south (*see* SHAPE-NOTE HYMNODY). In these outlying areas, and especially in the South, new traditions of provincial polyphonic hymnody were taking root, and New England psalmodists provided many of the pieces published in shape-note tunebooks. Meanwhile, in New England, beginning with *The Stoughton Collection* (Boston, 1829), favorite pieces from the earlier New England repertory were regularly reprinted in tunebooks whose avowed purpose was to keep the older repertory alive. Tunebooks such as *The Billings and Holden Collection* (Boston, 1836), *Ancient Harmony Revived* (Boston, 1847; five more editions), *Father Kemp's Old Folks' Concert Tunes* (Boston, 1860; three more editions), and *The Stoughton Musical Society's Centennial Collection* (Boston, 1878) carried works by Billings, Read, Holden, Swan, and their compatriots in something like their original form, giving pleasure both to those who had grown up with native psalmody and to others who could see value in the long-discredited music of their forefathers.

WORKS
EDITIONS
R. Crawford: *The Core Repertory of Early American Psalmody* (Madison, WI, 1984)

K. Kroeger: *Music of the New American Nation: Sacred Music from 1780 to 1820*, i, ii, iii, xv (New York, 1995–99)

K. Kroeger: *Early American Anthems*, i, ii (Madison, WI, 2000)

BIBLIOGRAPHY
CATALOGS
A. Britton, I. Lowens, and R. Crawford: *American Sacred Music Imprints 1698–1810: a Bibliography* (Worcester, MA, 1990)

K. Kroeger: *American Fuging-tunes 1770–1820: a Descriptive Catalog* (Westport, CT, 1994)

N. Temperley: *The Hymn Tune Index: a Census of English-language Hymn Tunes in Printed Sources from 1535 to 1820*, i–iv (New York, 1998)

K. Kroeger and M. Kroeger: *An Index to Anglo-American Psalmody in Modern Critical Editions*, RRAM, xl (Madison, WI, 2000)

N. Temperley: "The Hymn Tune Index," <http://hymntune.library.uiuc.edu/> (2012)

STUDIES AND OTHER RESOURCES
G. Hood: *A History of Music in New England* (Boston, 1846/R)

N. Gould: *Church Music in America* (Boston, 1853)

F. Metcalf: *American Writers and Compilers of Sacred Music* (New York, 1925/R)

A. Britton: *Theoretical Introductions in American Tune-books to 1800* (diss., U. of Michigan, 1949)

I. Lowens: *Music and Musicians in Early America* (New York, 1964)

R.T. Daniel: *The Anthem in New England before 1800* (Evanston, IL, 1966/R)

R.G. Appel: *The Music of the Bay Psalm Book, 9th Edition (1698)*, ISAMm, v (Brooklyn, NY, 1975)

K. Kroeger: *The Worcester Collection of Sacred Harmony and Sacred Music in America, 1786–1803* (diss., Brown U., 1976)

N. Temperley: *The Music of the English Parish Church* (Cambridge, England, 1979)

L. Inserra and H.W. Hitchcock: *The Music of Henry Ainsworth's Psalter* (Brooklyn, NY, 1981)

K. Kroeger: "Introduction," *The Complete Works of William Billings*, i (Charlottesville, VA, 1981), 13–28

N. Temperley: "The Old Way of Singing: its Origins and Development," *JAMS*, xxxiv/3 (1981), 511–44

R. Crawford and D.W. Krummel: "Early American Music Printing and Publishing," *Printing and Society in Early America*, ed. W. Joyce and others (Worcester, MA, 1983), 186, 215

N. Cooke: "Itinerant Yankee Singing Masters in the Eighteenth Century," *Itinerancy in New England and New York*, ed. P. Benes (Boston, 1986), 16–36

P. Osterhout: "Note Reading and Regular Singing in Eighteenth-century New England," *American Music*, iv/2 (1986), 125–44

K. Kroeger: "William Billings's 'Anthem for Easter': the Persistence of an Early American 'Hit,'" *Proceedings of the American Antiquarian Society*, xcvii (1987), 105–28

K. Kroeger: "William Tans'ur's Influence on William Billings," *Inter-American Music Review*, xi (1991), 1–12

S. Bullock: "'I Sing the Mason's Glory': Freemasonry and Musical Life in Early New England," *New England Music: the Public Sphere, 1600–1900*, ed. P. Benes (Boston, 1998), 80–91

J. Weiss: *The Relationship between the "Great Awakening" and the Transition from Psalmody to Hymnody in the New England Colonies* (diss., Ball State U., 1988)

A. Britton: "The How and Why of Teaching Singing Schools in Eighteenth Century America," *Bulletin of the Council for Research in Music Education*, xcix (1989), 23–41

N. Cooke: *American Psalmodists in Contact and Collaboration, 1770–1820* (diss., U. of Michigan, 1990)

R. Crawford: "'Ancient Music' and the Europeanizing of American Psalmody, 1800–1810," *A Celebration of American Music: Words and Music in Honor of H. Wiley Hitchcock*, ed. R. Crawford, R.A. Lott, and C.J. Oja (Ann Arbor, MI, 1990), 225–55

R. Crawford: "William Billings (1746–1800) and American Psalmody: a Study of Musical Dissemination," *The American Musical Landscape* (Berkeley, CA, 1993), 111–50

L. Davenport: *Divine Song on the Northeast Frontier: Maine's Sacred Tunebooks, 1800–1830* (Lanham, MD, 1996)

Quarterly Journal of Music Teaching and Learning, vii (1996) [William Billings issue]

M. Fawcett-Yeske: *The Fuging Tune in America, 1770–1820: an Analytical Study* (diss., U. of Colorado Boulder, 1997)

A.C. Buechner: "Thomas Walter and the Society for Promoting Regular Singing in the Worship of God: Boston, 1720–1723," *New England Music: the Public Sphere, 1600–1900*, ed. P. Benes (Boston, 1998), 48–60

D.C.L. Jones: "Early American Psalmody and the Core Repertory: a Perspective," *Vistas of American Music: Essays and Compositions in Honor of William K. Kearns*, ed. S. Porter and J. Graziano (Warren, MI, 1999), 39–62

A.C. Buechner: *Yankee Singing Schools and the Golden Age of Choral Music in New England, 1760–1800* (Boston, 2003)

F. Selch: *Instrumental Accompaniments for Yankee Hymn Tunes: an Investigation of the Evidence* (diss., New York U., 2003)

J. Ogasapian: *Church Music in America, 1620–2000* (Macon, GA, 2007)

L.J. Sampsel: *Samuel Babcock (1760–1813): Archetypal Psalmodist of the First New England School of Composers* (diss., U. of Pittsburgh, 2009)

RICHARD CRAWFORD/LAURIE J. SAMPSEL

Psalms, metrical. Paraphrases of the biblical psalms in verse, often designed for singing to tunes of a simple, popular type (which subsequently became known as hymn tunes). In the early years of the Protestant settlements of North America metrical psalm singing was often the only form of organized music. It occupied a most important place in the cultural life of the people and was invested with the strong feelings of a strug-

gling community far from home. The Puritans, in particular, treated the psalms and their tunes with veneration and sang them in everyday situations as well as at church on Sundays. The tradition naturally followed similar patterns to those of the parent countries in Europe. By the time a more assertively American school of psalmody had arisen in the late 18th century, metrical psalms were rapidly giving way to hymns in many churches. (A number of metrical psalms are included in Crawford, 1984.)

1. History of psalm singing. (i) Episcopal churches. (ii) Pilgrims. (iii) Dutch Reformed Church. (iv) Puritans. (v) Presbyterian churches. (vi) German Reformed Church. 2. Psalm books. (i) Function and character. (ii) The Bay Psalm Book.

1. HISTORY OF PSALM SINGING.

(i) Episcopal churches. The psalms of Calvin's French psalter were sung in America as early as 1564, during the Huguenot expeditions to Florida and South Carolina, just as Sir Francis Drake's men sang psalms, to the delight of the Indians, while camping on the coast of California in 1579. However, the first Protestant church to establish itself permanently on the American continent was from the Church of England: at Jamestown, Virginia, a church was built in 1607, the year that the colony was founded. Commercial enterprise rather than religious fervor was dominant in the minds of the early Virginian colonists. They were content to continue the traditions of the Anglican church, which was established there by law, as it was later in Maryland, North and South Carolina, and Georgia. Anglican churches were organized by the early 18th century in the northern colonies.

The bibles and prayer books imported from England had the usual metrical psalms bound in the back—*The Whole Booke of Psalmes, Collected into Englishe Meter* by Thomas Sternhold and John Hopkins (1562) and, later, *A New Version of the Psalms of David, Fitted to the Tunes Used in Churches* (1696) by Nahum Tate and Nicholas Brady. The singing was very much as it was in English parish churches. In the larger town churches organs were gradually acquired: at King's Chapel, Boston, in 1714; at Trinity Church, Newport, Rhode Island, in 1733; at Trinity Church, New York, in 1737; at five Virginia churches between 1737 and 1767; at two Connecticut churches by 1756; at all three Anglican churches in Philadelphia in the years 1762–6. In smaller churches parish clerks led the people in unaccompanied singing. Tate and Brady's *New Version of the Psalms*, which was first published in America in New York in 1710, was widely used by the mid-18th century. In some country churches, societies of singers were organized, first in Maryland during Thomas Bray's visitation of 1700.

After the Revolution authority over the congregations passed to the Protestant Episcopal Church, and for the first time, in 1789, a selection of psalms and hymns for use in the churches was laid down by authority and annexed to the Book of Common Prayer. It consisted of the entire *New Version* of Tate and Brady, with 27 hymns. A revised selection was made in 1833, still including a large number of Tate and Brady's psalms, and continued in use until 1866. Thus the Episcopal Church was one of the last to sing metrical psalms as a regular part of its services.

The tunes sung with these psalms were at first the same as those used in England, as can be seen from a tune supplement bound in with a Boston edition of Tate and Brady in 1720; they were also the same as those used by the Puritan churches. A later tune supplement to Tate and Brady was engraved and probably compiled by Thomas Johnston, who was also one of the first American organ builders; Daniel Bayley's collections indicate a more florid taste. On the whole, however, Episcopal churches were musically more conservative than Congregational ones, avoiding the excesses of fuging-tunes and elaborate "set-pieces." A most influential Anglican musician was Francis Hopkinson. His *Collection of Psalm Tunes…for the Use of the United Churches of Christ Church and St. Peter's Church in Philadelphia* (Philadelphia, 1763) contains some fairly ornate tunes, including some of Hopkinson's own, but they are in the *galant* taste of the time, resembling the music of town rather than country churches in England. The prevalence of organs and the stronger links with the mother country tended to keep Anglican church music closer to the European art music of the time. The same tendency is shown in the tunes of *The Book of Common Prayer…Proposed to the Use of the Protestant Episcopal Church* (Philadelphia, 1786) and in *Jacob Eckhard's Choirmaster's Book of 1809*, used at St. Michael, Charleston, South Carolina, together with a special *Selection of Psalms and Hymns* prepared by the rectors of the two principal Charleston churches in 1792 (ex.1).

See also EPISCOPAL CHURCH.

(ii) Pilgrims. The band of about 100 English Pilgrims who founded the colony at Plymouth, Massachusetts, in 1620 were members of a group of Separatists who had gone into exile at Leiden, Holland, in 1609. They had rejected the worship of the Church of England, and so instead of using Sternhold and Hopkins's psalms they adopted the version of Henry Ainsworth, pastor of a neighboring Separatist community at Amsterdam. Ainsworth was one of the most cultivated biblical scholars of his day, and in *The Book of Psalmes: Englished both in Prose and Metre* (Amsterdam, 1612) he offered not only a complete new prose translation of the psalms accompanied by a pithy commentary but also a new metrical version and an excellent selection of tunes. In his variety of meters and choice of tunes, Ainsworth was as much influenced by the Franco-Dutch psalter as by Sternhold and Hopkins:

> Tunes for the Psalms I find none set of God; so that each people is to use the most grave, decent and comfortable manner of singing that they know…The singing-notes, therefore, I have most taken from our former Englished Psalms, when they will fit the measure of the verse. And for the other long verses I have also taken (for the most part) the gravest and easiest tunes of the French and Dutch Psalms.

Details of Ainsworth's tunes and their origins are provided by Pratt and Frost. The tunes, like the rest of the book, are learned rather than popular and not all easy to sing. However, Edward Winslow recalled that there were "many of our congregation very expert in music" at Leiden; some of these must have been on the momentous voyage of the *Mayflower*, for Ainsworth's *Psalmes* were used for many years in the Plymouth colony, in the total absence of instrumental or professional aid. Later generations lost their predecessors' skill. In 1681 Plymouth church decided to institute

Ex.1 Peter Valton: "St. Peters," in *Jacob Eckhard's Choirmaster's Book of 1809*, where it is allocated to "Psalm 46," i.e., Psalm cl (*New Version*), verse 1 of which is underlaid here

lining out, and in 1691, on the amalgamation of the Plymouth colony with the much larger and more successful settlement to the north, the church formally recognized the "difficulties" of many of the Ainsworth tunes and allowed the substitution of easier ones used with the Bay Psalm Book. So Ainsworth's book was never to be widely popular in America, although it was used at Ipswich and Salem, both outside the Plymouth colony, until 1667. It was reprinted several times, but never in America.

(iii) Dutch Reformed Church. Dutch settlers first landed in what is now New York in 1613, but the first church was not organized until 1628, when the Dutch and French Protestant settlers combined; the two parts of the congregation knew identical tunes and sang them in their own languages. The Dutch psalter, prescribed by the Synod of Dort in 1618, was used with strict invariance for a full 100 years after the English conquest of the colony in 1664. An organ was erected in the New York church in 1727. The first English psalm book for the Dutch Reformed Church was *The Psalms of David...for the Use of the Reformed Dutch Church of the City of New York* (New York, 1767). Francis Hopkinson was the translator, and his job was the singular one of adapting the psalm versions of Tate and Brady to fit the tunes of varying meters in the old Dutch psalter. The music still remained unaltered.

The new book did not long satisfy the English-speaking congregations; many of the tunes in peculiar meters were unfamiliar through long disuse, and there was a demand to relax the strict confinement to psalms and to introduce some of the hymns popular in other American churches. The central Synod continued to maintain a strict control over the worship of individual congregations, but after the Revolution it authorized a new book (1789) that included 135 hymns selected by Dr. John Livingston. The psalms in this book were selected largely from Tate and Brady's and Watts's versions, with only a few of Hopkinson's remaining; and the great majority were in common, short, or long meter. No music was provided and no tunes suggested. Later editions increased the proportion of hymns until, in *Hymns of the Church* (New York, 1869), the remaining metrical psalms were mixed in with hymns.

Despite these updating procedures, congregational singing remained at a low ebb. In the parochial school system sponsored by the church, the leader of the church psalmody was also the schoolmaster; but he did not generally use his position to teach the schoolchildren how to sing. As a result congregations were generally unable to take part in the psalm singing. Until the mid-19th century the schoolmaster and the organist often performed the music alone.

See also REFORMED CHURCH IN AMERICA.

(iv) Puritans. The Massachusetts Bay colony was founded in 1629 by puritan members of the Church of England, who had at first no idea of seceding from the church, although they rejected its ritual. They brought with them Sternhold and Hopkins's psalms, and we may suppose that they sang them mainly to the handful of four-line tunes then in common use. They were not of a temper to concern themselves with artistic improvements in the singing. But they were unhappy with Sternhold and Hopkins because "their variations of the sense, and alterations of the sacred text too frequently, may justly minister matter of offence." Accordingly, a group of 30 divines assembled to prepare a still more literal translation, "that as wee doe injoye other, soe (if it were the Lord's will) we might injoye this ordinance also in its native purity." They published, in 1640, *The Whole Booke of Psalmes* (see §2(ii) below).

The Bay Psalm Book, or New England Psalm Book, as this collection came to be known, was at once adopted by almost every church in the colony. By means of lining out, which was in use in 1647 and perhaps earlier, the people could easily be taught to fit the new words to the old tunes. The compilers referred at the end of the book to 48 tunes to which the psalms might be sung, including 39 common-meter tunes "as they are collected, out of our chief musicians, by Tho. Ravenscroft." But it is highly unlikely that more than a handful of these were used in church. Copies of Ravenscroft's and Alison's harmonized settings are known to have been in the possession of early New England settlers, but as in the old country they would have been used domestically.

The Bay Psalm Book was used for more than a century and spread to other American colonies and even to many dissenting churches in Britain. There is no doubt that the new psalms continued to be sung to the old tunes. When for the first time a musical supplement appeared, with the ninth edition of 1698, the 13 tunes in it were all standard ones from English sources; they were set for tenor and bass, with fasola letters below the staves, suggesting that the basses were sung, not played, though they are angularly instrumental in character (ex.2). In later editions the tunes were printed without basses.

As in English country churches, the speed of singing had slowed to a drawl by this date. A type of melismatic heterophony, known to would-be reformers as the old way or common way, prevailed in Congregational churches everywhere until about 1720 (*see* OLD WAY OF SINGING). The long absence of professional musicians led to an almost primitive practice that many deplored. Something of the chaos that often prevailed may be gathered from entries in Samuel Sewall's *Diary*, describing services at the South Meeting House, Boston:

1705, Dec. 28. Mr. Willard...spoke to me to set the Tune, I intended Windsor and fell into High-Dutch, and then essaying to set another Tune went into a key much too high. So I pray'd Mr. White to set it, which he did well, Litchf[ield] Tune

1718, Feb. 2. In the Morning I set York Tune, and in the 2d going over, the Gallery carried irresistibly to St. David's which discouraged me very much.

But the people liked this way of singing and in some churches persisted with it despite efforts at reform. In the strongly individualistic, Congregational tradition of New England, every church was at liberty to govern its own practice.

Ex.2 "Low Dutch Tune," from the Bay Psalm Book (9/1698)

Psalm xxiii, as sung to the above tune (v.1)

The Lord to me a shepherd is,
Want therefore shall not I:
He in the folds of tender grass
Doth make me down to lie.

Reform got under way in 1720, with the appearance of the Reverend Thomas Symmes's anonymous pamphlet *The Reasonableness of Regular Singing, or Singing by Note.* In the following year John Tufts and Thomas Walter published two important singing methods. Each carried an appendix of psalm tunes, and Tufts introduced a new musical notation based on fasola letters. Walter's appendix presented the tunes in three-part harmony. (For discussion of the new era of American singing that resulted from these publications and from the formation of singing-schools, *see* PSALMODY.) It is sufficient to point out here that the teaching of singing from notes naturally generated church choirs, which tended, as in Anglican churches, to take the singing out of the hands of the people—if the people would let them. The attention that was thus focused on singing led in turn to a desire for better literary and musical materials to sing. The Bay Psalm Book soon gave way in popularity to more elegant if less literal translations—Tate and Brady's *New Version* and, particularly among Congregationalists, Isaac Watts's *Psalms of David Imitated in the Language of the New Testament* (first

American publication, Philadelphia, 1729). More conservative congregations stuck to the old book (revised in 1758), but the supplements attached to later editions show that the traditional psalms, as well as the newer ones, were sung to increasingly elaborate tunes.

Two tunes of this time appear to be the first printed compositions of American origin: "Southwel New Tune" (ex.3) from Walter (1721), and "100 Psalm New" from Tufts (1723). Some of the earliest tunes containing florid melismas ("Northampton," "Isle of Wight," "24 Psalm") were drawn from English sources. But in the mid-18th century two tune supplements from New England, engraved and possibly compiled by James Turner and Thomas Johnston respectively, include some ornate tunes probably of American origin. One of them in the Johnston supplement (1755), called "Psalm 136 Tune," comes near to being a fuging-tune, although for tenor and bass only (ex.4). In the latter part of the century, especially after the Revolution, there was a burgeoning of elaborate psalmody in which the Congregational churches (descendants of the old Puritan bodies) were often in the vanguard. It was perhaps partly for the

Ex.3 Thomas Walter: "Southwel New Tune" (1721) [originally on three staves]

Ex.4 "136 Psalm Tune," from Thomas Johnston's tune supplement to Nahum Tate and Nicholas Brady's *New Version* (1755), here underlaid with the first verse of Psalm cxxxvi

purpose of countering this trend that organs were gradually introduced in Congregational churches towards the end of the 18th century. The first was at Providence, Rhode Island, in 1770; in 1798 Bentley had heard of only four Congregational churches with organs in America, three in Boston and one in Newburyport.

Under the influence of the Great Awakening and subsequent evangelical movements, metrical psalms tended to be replaced by hymns, and by 1830 formed a small proportion of the verses in most Congregational hymnbooks (*see* HYMNODY).

See also UNITED CHURCH OF CHRIST.

(v) Presbyterian churches. The Presbyterians also claimed descent from the Puritans, but retained a more authoritarian and centralized form of church government by synod. From 1668, and especially in the 18th century, both in what is now the United States and in Canada, a constant influx of Scots and Scots-Irish produced a distinctive brand of Presbyterianism—one that was strongly resistant to liberal trends. *The Psalms of*

David in Meeter in the Scottish version of 1650 was to Presbyterian minds almost a part of the Bible with which it was usually bound. The success of the Scots in colonizing the frontier outposts of the American and Canadian interiors left them often remote from acculturating influences, and they continued to use the old way of singing long after it had been forgotten elsewhere. The 12 common tunes were lined out by a precentor and sung by the people in the old way, which survived well into the 20th century in remote places. In urban centers such as Boston, Philadelphia, and New York, there were schisms in the 18th century: "new side" synods welcomed the influence of the evangelical movement; "old side" synods preferred to continue in the old traditions. The psalm singing was, indeed, often the central issue in the fierce disputes that raged in Presbyterian circles at this date. James Lyon's *Urania* (Philadelphia, 1761) was subscribed to by a number of prominent Presbyterian clergymen; it must have represented the avant-garde of Presbyterian singing. In 1774 John Adams, accustomed to the elaborate choir singing of New England, reported that the Old Presbyterian Society of New York was still "in the *old way*, as we call it—all the drawling, quavering, discord in the world." A revision of Watts's *Psalms* in a conservative direction, restoring those portions that Watts had deliberately omitted, was prepared by Joel Barlow in 1785, and the synods of Philadelphia and New York left individual parishes to decide whether to use it or to continue to sing the old psalms in the old way. The *Directory for the Worship of God* (1788) at last substituted "singing psalms or hymns" for the 1644 Westminster directory's "singing of psalms," paving the way for the authorization of Watts's hymns in 1802. In town churches the sterner kind of Presbyterianism faded gradually; organs were purchased, choirs took over the psalms and hymns. Congregational singing survived only in the wild country places.

See also PRESBYTERIAN CHURCH.

(vi) German Reformed Church. Of the various sects that flourished among the German communities in Pennsylvania during the 18th century, only the Reformed Church, with its Calvinist ancestry, sang metrical psalms. The first settlements were founded by Dutch Reformed ministers early in the century. They used the Marburg Collection of psalms in Lobwasser's version, and in 1753 this book was reprinted by Christopher Sauer at Germantown, Pennsylvania, as *Neu-vermehrt und vollständiges Gesang-Buch*, with all the traditional tunes. But the knowledge of the old chorale melodies was disappearing among the people; lining out had to be introduced, and by the end of the century it often happened that the minister and the organist were the only audible singers. At a synod held in Reading in 1794, it was resolved "that a new hymn-book be prepared, of which the Psalms shall be taken from Lobwasser and Spreng's improved version, and the Palatine hymn-book shall form the basis of the hymns." This, the first officially authorized book, was published in 1797. The psalm tunes had been greatly reduced in number, by the omission of little-used tunes. Between 1800 and 1850 there was a gradual change to the English language in many churches, and the first English collection, *Psalms and Hymns for the Use of the German Reformed Church in the United States of America*, appeared in 1830: all 150 psalms were still included, but they were largely in Watts's version and drew on Anglo-American sources for their tunes. A newly compiled German book appeared in 1842, and another, *Deutsches Gesangbuch* (edited by Philip Schaff), in 1861. By this time such metrical psalms as survived were embedded in a large collection of hymns, arranged by the church year. Tunes were no longer printed with the words; suggestions for tunes showed, however, an interest in reviving the traditional German chorale melodies.

2. PSALM BOOKS.

(i) Function and character. Of the psalm books printed in America only those for the Dutch and German Reformed churches contained tunes printed with the psalms. In the Dutch version the tune was reprinted

over each verse of the psalm; in the German the first verse was underlaid and the rest printed beneath. These formats were modeled on European books that had been used with a tradition of accompanied singing. When an organ could not be obtained the congregation was at a loss and the knowledge of the tunes quickly faded. With the introduction of English psalms and hymns the older type of underlaid psalm book disappeared.

The great majority of psalm books in the English American tradition had no music at all (perhaps 80% of the surviving editions up to 1800). Before the era of the singing-schools, there were so few tunes that they were known from memory, having been sung unaccompanied for generations. After choirs were well established, they generally sang from their own books containing special selections of psalm and hymn tunes and through-composed set-pieces and anthems. Most of the tune supplements date from the intermediate period (*c*1720–75).

In the early days, when psalms were lined out, the congregation did not really need books at all in church. They knew the tunes, and they took the words from the parish clerk, elder, or minister. No doubt the Bay Psalm Book was designed, as much as anything, for domestic singing and private reading, as the title of the third edition suggests (see §ii below). In the same way the early tune supplements were for the benefit of devout singers at home rather than for the church; bass parts were soon found unnecessary. With the singing-school movement came the possibility of learning new music in parts, and for this Walter and Tufts prepared their in-

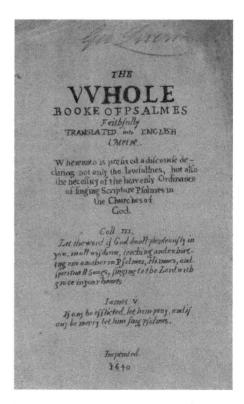

The Bay Psalm Book, 1640. (Library of Congress, Rare Book and Special Collections Division)

structional books. When the music was sung in church it was convenient for the singers to have it in the psalm book. The tune appendix of Tufts was itself used as a supplement for editions of psalm books; others had supplements of similar scope, usually (from 1737 onwards) in three parts. Tune supplements were only loosely attached to psalm books. The same supplement was used for different psalm books and vice versa, while most psalm books had no tunes at all. Evidently it was up to the purchaser to order whatever tunes he liked. Very probably the books with tunes were used by the members of the "choir"—those who had rehearsed them in the singing-school or psalmody society. The tunes attached to the 1774 Tate and Brady are entitled *A New Collection of Psalm Tunes Adapted to Congregational Worship*, which might seem to indicate an effort to prevent choirs from monopolizing the singing. But all the tunes in it are in four-part harmony, many are elaborate, and some are of the fully fuging variety. It seems that in some churches tunes of this sort were actually sung by congregations at large. With the disappearance of tune supplements and the flowering of psalmody books after the Revolution, choirs took over an increasing share of the music, singing anthems and set-pieces in which nobody could take part without rehearsal. After evangelical hymn singing made its way into churches congregations could once more take their full part (*see* HYMNODY). However, psalm books (without tunes) continued to appear until after the middle of the 19th century.

(ii) The Bay Psalm Book. The Bay Psalm Book (1640) was the first English book ever printed in America: 1700 copies were run off on a small press belonging to Harvard College. The compilers, like Barton and Rous in England, eliminated some of the more unusual meters found in Sternhold and Hopkins, thus allowing all 150 psalms to be sung to the few tunes that were at the command of congregations. The collection was thoroughly revised for the third edition (1651), chiefly by Henry Dunster and Richard Lyon. They polished the versification somewhat and added alternative translations. They further reduced unusual meters, so that 125 (instead of 112) out of 150 psalms were now in common meter; and they added 36 other "scripture-songs," still maintaining the Calvinistic principle that only inspired words were suitable for singing in worship. The new title was *The Psalms Hymns and Spiritual Songs of the Old and New Testament Faithfully Translated into English Metre for the Use, Edification, and Comfort of the Saints in Publick and Private, especially in New England.* This proved to be the definitive edition. It was reprinted under this title, with scarcely any alterations in the verbal text, for more than a century.

When for the first time a tune supplement, printed from woodblocks, was bound in with the ninth edition (1698), its 13 tunes and their basses were drawn from the 1679 edition of John Playford's *Breefe Introduction to the Skill of Musick*, although the preface and the idea of using fasola letters probably came from the 1672 edition of the same book. Lowens conjectured that the

TABLE 1: Contents of the tune supplement of the ninth edition of the Bay Psalm Book (1698)

Frost no.	Tune name	Meter	Key	Psalm
121	Oxford	CM	g	iv
25	Lichfield	CM	g	lxix
19	Low Dutch	CM	G	xxiii
205	York	CM	F	lxxiii
129	Windsor	CM	g	cxvi
154*a*	Cambridge Short	SM	g	lxx
234	St. David's	CM	F	xcv
209	Martyrs	CM	g	xxxix
333*a*	Hackney	CM	d	lxi
132	Psalm cxix Second Meeter	DCM	e	cxix
114	Psalm c First Meeter	LM	G	c
125	Psalm cxv [sic] First Meeter	8:8:8:8:8:8: 8:8:8:8:8:8	G	(cxiii)
174	Psalm cxlviii First Meeter	6:6:6:6:4:4: 4:4	C	cxlviii

CM – common meter; SM – short meter; LM – long meter; DCM – double common meter

supplement was printed in England as part of a lost London edition of the Bay Psalm Book, but it does not resemble other English music printing of the time. The tunes are as set out in Table 1. It is a curious fact that the allocation of "Lichfield" to Psalm lxix, like the rest, is copied from Playford, where it is actually a misprint for xcvi (through printing 69 for 96): the first verse of Psalm xcvi is printed under the tune in Playford. In New England, however, the tune (as a result of this misprint) came to be associated with Psalm lxix, the first verse of which is printed with it in editions from 1705 to 1730. Other misprints closely follow Playford, proving the provenance of the tunes beyond doubt.

For the 1705 edition the music was completely reset in a different style, without basses or fasola letters but with the first verse of the allocated psalm underlaid. Many of the tunes are transposed up a tone ("Martyrs" down a 3rd), a somewhat pointless maneuver for unaccompanied singing. The reason appears to have been that the 1705 tunes were copied from the 1694 or 1697 edition of Playford, where the same transpositions had been made to bring the tunes into line with Playford's *Whole Book of Psalms* (1677). The 13 tunes were reduced to 11 by omitting "Hackney" and "Psalm 115." The printer evidently had little competence in music: there are no clefs, several misprints, and "Oxford" has a key signature of one flat despite transposition to A minor. These mistakes were not corrected until 1726. The next few editions were similar to that of 1705, with one other tune, "Ten Commandments" (Frost no.178), appearing in some editions and not others. The tune selection was a standard one in New England, for the 1720 Boston edition of Tate and Brady had the same 11 tunes in a different order. One British edition of the Bay Psalm Book (Glasgow, 1720) contains a similar selection, printed by James Duncan, printer to the city of Glasgow.

The 1737 edition carries an entirely different tune supplement of a much more ambitious kind, along the lines of Tufts's and Walter's books. It has 34 tunes in three-part harmony, with fasola letters underlaid. The selection of tunes owes far more to Tufts and Walter than to the previous supplements, reprinting some of their most "advanced" and ornate tunes and such novelties as "100 Psalm New."

Two copies of the 1744 edition are bound up with the Tufts supplement itself, printed from the plates of the 1738 edition. The 1758 edition has Turner's supplement, first printed with a psalm book of local use only, made by John Barnard, minister of a church in Marblehead, Massachusetts. This edition has also a revised text, by Thomas Prince. But the days of the Bay Psalm Book were numbered. A few more editions were still to come, without music, but between 1761 and 1780 the *New Version* and Watts's *Psalms* each appeared in more than ten times as many editions.

See also PRINTING AND PUBLISHING.

BIBLIOGRAPHY

The Whole Booke of Psalms Faithfully Translated into English Metre (Cambridge, MA, 1640/R) [the Bay Psalm Book]

J. Cotton: *Singing of Psalms a Gospel Ordinance* (London, 1647)

T. Symmes: *The Reasonableness of Regular Singing, or Singing by Note* (Boston, 1720)

J. Tufts: *An Introduction to the Singing of Psalm-tunes* (Boston, 3/1723)

Das neue und verbesserte Gesang-Buch (Philadelphia, 1797)

G. Hood: *A History of Music in New England* (Boston, 1846/R)

D.D. Demarest: *History and Characteristics of the Reformed Protestant Dutch Church* (New York, 1856, enlarged 4/1889 as *The Reformed Church in America*)

J.S. Curwen: *Studies in Worship Music* (London, 1880–85), 57

C.W. Baird: *History of the Huguenot Emigration to America*, i (New York, 1885), 65

J. Sabin: *Bibliotheca americana*, xvi (New York, 1886), 27

O. Seidensticker: *The First Century of German Printing in America, 1728–1830* (Philadelphia, 1893)

S.L. Thorndike: "The Psalmodies of Plymouth and Massachusetts Bay," *Colonial Society of Massachusetts Publications*, i (1895), 228–38

J.H. Dubbs: "History of the Reformed Church, German," *American Church History*, viii (1902), 213–423

O.G.T. Sonneck: *Francis Hopkinson, the First American Poet-composer (1737–1791) and James Lyon, Patriot, Preacher, Psalmodist (1735–1794)* (Washington, DC, 1905/R)

A.H. Messiter: *A History of the Choir and Music of Trinity Church, New York* (New York, 1906/R)

W. Bentley: *Diary*, ii: *1793–1802* (Salem, MA, 1907), 259

L.F. Benson: *The English Hymn* (New York, 1915/R)

W.S. Pratt: *The Music of the Pilgrims* (Boston, 1921/R)

M. van Doren, ed.: *Samuel Sewall: Diary* (New York, 1927)

W.S. Pratt: *The Music of the French Psalter of 1562* (New York, 1939)

H.C. Macdougall: *Early New England Psalmody: an Historical Appreciation, 1620–1820* (Brattleboro, VT, 1940/R)

W.W. Sweet: *Religion in Colonial America* (New York, 1942)

D. Wing: *A Short-title Catalogue of Books Printed in England, Scotland and Ireland . . . 1641–1700* (New York, 1945–51, 2/1972)

A.P. Britton: *Theoretical Introductions in American Tune-books to 1800* (diss., U. of Michigan, 1949)

H.B. Satcher: "Music of the Episcopal Church in Pennsylvania in the Eighteenth Century," *Historical Magazine of the Protestant Episcopal Church*, xviii (1949), 372–413

M. Frost: *English and Scottish Psalm and Hymn Tunes c1543–1677* (London, 1953)

G. Chase: *America's Music: from the Pilgrims to the Present* (New York, 1955, 2/1966/R)

L. Ellinwood, ed.: *The Charleston Hymnal of 1792* (Charleston, 1956)

T.W. Dean: *The Organ in Eighteenth Century English Colonial America* (diss., U. of Southern California, 1960)

I. Lowens: *Music and Musicians in Early America* (New York, 1964)

T.M. Finney: "The Third Edition of Tufts' *Introduction . . .*," *JRME*, xiv/3 (1966), 163–70

C.K. Shipton and J.E. Mooney: *National Index of American Imprints through 1800* (n.p., 1969)

D.K. Stigberg: *Congregational Psalmody in Eighteenth Century New England* (thesis, U. of Illinois, 1970)

G.W. Williams, ed.: *Jacob Eckhard's Choirmaster's Book of 1809* (Columbia, SC, 1971)

N. Temperley: "John Playford and the Metrical Psalms," *JAMS*, xxv/3 (1972), 331–78

R.G. Appel: *The Music of the Bay Psalm Book, 9th Edition (1698)*, ISAMm, v (Brooklyn, NY, 1975)

N. Temperley: *The Music of the English Parish Church* (Cambridge, UK, 1979)

R.M. Wilson and K.V. Keller: *Connecticut's Music in the Revolutionary Era* (Hartford, 1979)

L. Inserra and H.W. Hitchcock: *The Music of Henry Ainsworth's Psalter*, ISAMm, xv (Brooklyn, NY, 1981)

N. Temperley: "The Old Way of Singing: its Origins and Development," *JAMS*, xxxiv/3 (1981), 511–44

N. Temperley and C.G. Manns: *Fuging Tunes in the Eighteenth Century* (Detroit, 1983)

R. Crawford, ed.: *The Core Repertory of Early American Psalmody*, RRAM, xi–xii (Madison, WI, 1984)

K.L. Carroll: "Singing in the Spirit of Early Quakerism," *Quaker History*, no.73 (1984), 1–13

A.P. Britton, I. Lowens, and R. Crawford: *American Sacred Music Imprints, 1698–1810: a Bibliography* (Worcester, MA, 1990)

E.R. Brink: "Metrical Psalmody in North America: a Story of Survival and Revival," *The Hymn*, xliv/4 (1993), 20–24

E.C. Wolf: "The Convivial Side of Scottish Psalm Tunes," *American Music*, xiv/2 (1996), 141–60

R.A. Stackhouse: *The Language of the Psalms in Worship: American Revisions of Watts' Psalter* (Lanham, MD, 1997)

D.W. Krummel: "The Bay Psalm Book Tercentenary, 1698–1998," *Notes*, lv/2 (1998), 281–87

D.W. Music: "Edward Taylor and the Metrical Psalms," *The Hymn*, xlix/4 (1998), 18–20

N. Temperley, C.G. Manns, and J. Herl: *The Hymn Tune Index: a Census of English-language Hymn Tunes in Printed Sources from 1535 to 1820* (Oxford, 1998)

P.V. Bohlman, and O. Holzapfel, ed.: *Land without Nightingales: Music in the Making of German America* (Madison, WI, 2002)

S.A. Marini: *Sacred Song in America: Religion, Music, and Public Culture* (Urbana, IL, 2003)

N. Temperley: *Bound for America: Three British Composers* (Urbana, IL, 2003)

P.V. Bohlman, E. L. Blumhofer, and M.M. Chow: *Music in American Religious Experience* (New York, 2006)

J. Ogasapian: *Church Music in America* (Macon, GA, 2007)

N. Reed Knouse, ed.: *The Music of the Moravian Church in America* (Rochester, NY, 2008)

D.J. Grimminger: *Sacred Song and the Pennsylvania Dutch* (Rochester, NY, 2012)

G. Goodman: "The Tears I Shed at the Songs of Thy Church": Seventeenth-Century Musical Piety in the English Atlantic World," *Journal of the American Musicological Society*, lxv/3 (2012), 691–725

G. Goodman: "But They Differ from Us in Sound: Indian Psalmody and the Soundscape of Colonialism, 1651–75," *William and Mary Quarterly*, 3rd series, lxix/4 (2012), 795–824

NICHOLAS TEMPERLEY/R

Psychedelic rock [acid rock]. A subgenre of rock music that first emerged around 1965 in San Francisco and London. Independently, musicians in both cities responded in similar ways to cultural and social developments, emphasizing an alternative lifestyle to mainstream culture, consciousness expansion, love, and drug use. Originally, psychedelic rock (or acid rock) reflected the LSD experience, but it eventually came to represent a musical style less strongly associated with its initial connotations.

Early influences included the "acid tests" staged by Ken Kesey and his Merry Pranksters from 1965 to 1966 throughout the San Francisco Bay Area. These all-night happenings, fueled by LSD, featured a light show, electronic sound manipulation, and live music by local bands such as the GRATEFUL DEAD. These events offered a blueprint for concerts staged by the Dead and other bands such as the JEFFERSON AIRPLANE, Big Brother and the Holding Company, and the Quicksilver Messenger Service. Bands in London such as Pink Floyd and Soft Machine played frequently at the UFO Club, a center of London's growing underground counterculture.

Colorful and eccentric clothing, elaborate light shows that mimicked hallucinatory movements, and posters with distorted lettering and shapes were visual accompaniments to the music. At first an underground scene, by 1967 hit records such as Jefferson Airplane's "Somebody to Love" and Cream's "I feel free" inspired a wave of mainstream psychedelic pop, including Tommy James and the Shondells' "Crimson and Clover" and the First Edition's "Just Dropped In."

Stylistically speaking, psychedelic rock draws from 1960s R&B, rock, country, and folk music as well as on extended improvisation by such jazz artists as John Coltrane and noise experiments by avant-garde composers including Karlheinz Stockhausen. Particular attention was paid to expanding and altering conventions of form and timbre. The Grateful Dead's "Viola Lee Blues" is one of many simple songs that the band stretched out with extensive improvisation. Timbres became warped, distorted, and unfixed: Jimi Hendrix used fuzz and wah-wah pedals on "Purple Haze," Donovan integrated a sitar into "Sunshine Superman," the Beatles used tape loops and the sound of a guitar played backwards on "Tomorrow never knows," and Pink Floyd utilized organs with rotating speakers to create a swirling sound on "Astronomy Domine." Sensations or impressions of psychedelic drug experiences were also coded in lyrics and represented in sound, as in the accumulative form of the Jefferson Airplane's "White Rabbit," with its entreaty to "Feed your head."

In 1967, high-profile media coverage of events such as the Human Be-In and successful concert promotion by impresario Bill Graham framed San Francisco as the center of the psychedelic scene. However, local scenes existed in cities such as Los Angeles, New York, and Austin, Texas. Bands such as Os Mutantes and CAN testify to the international reach of psychedelic rock, which continues to influence indie artists such as Animal Collective and Tame Impala in the 21st century.

BIBLIOGRAPHY

G. Sculatti and S. Seay: *San Francisco Nights: the Psychedelic Music Trip, 1965–1968* (New York, 1985)

S. Whiteley: *The Space Between the Notes: Rock and the Counter-Culture* (London, 1992)

M. Hicks: *Sixties Rock: Garage, Psychedelic, and Other Satisfactions* (Chicago, 1999)

J. DeRogatis: *Turn on Your Mind: Four Decades of Great Psychedelic Rock* (Milwaukee, 2003)

M. Carroll: "'Loneliness Is Such a Drag': Existential Psychedelia and Jimi Hendrix's 'The Burning of the Midnight Lamp,'" *Musicology Australia*, xxxii/2 (2010), 161–83

JACOB A. COHEN

Ptaszyńska, Marta (*b* Warsaw, 29 July 1943). Polish composer and percussionist. After graduating from the music academies of Warsaw and Poznań she received a French government grant to study with NADIA BOULANGER (1969–70). In 1972 she settled in the United States when a grant from the Kosciuszko Foundation enabled her to study at the Cleveland Institute of Music (1972–4) with DONALD ERB, Cloyd Duff, and Richard Weiner. During her time there she gave many lectures on Polish music and made concert appearances throughout the United States with a wide repertory that included her own works. She has taught at Bennington College, Vermont (1974–7), the University of California (1977–81), Indiana University, Northwestern University, and the University of Cincinnati; in 1998 she was appointed professor at the University of Chicago, and in 2005 she was named the Helen B. and Frank L. Sulzberger Professor of Music in the Humanities. Her *Siderals* and *Classical Variations* won prizes in Percussive Arts Society competitions in 1974 and 1976, and in 1986 *La novella d'inverno* was placed second at the UNESCO International Rostrum of Composers in Paris. She was a recipient of the Polish Cross of Merit and the Alfred Jurzykowski Foundation Award (New York). Her music, which ranges widely from pointillism to cantabile writing, is colorful and often delicate, with a keen sense of architecture and occasional use of aleatory procedures. Percussion instruments feature prominently in her works of the 1970s, while music after 1978 is more lyrical with a predominance of melodic and harmonic textures. She later returned to opera with *Magic Doremik* (libretto by G. Rodari) and the phenomenally successful children's opera, *Mister Marimba* (libretto by A. Osiecka). She is often inspired by surrealist paintings.

WORKS
(selective list)

Stage: Oskar z Alwy [Oscar from Alva] (op, 6 scenes, Z. Kopalko, after Byron), S, Mez, T, Bar, B, chorus, orch, 1971; Soirée snobe chez la princesse (music-theater), 2 kbd, tape, mimes, light projection, 1979; Mister Marimba (children's op, A. Osiecka), 11vv, children's chorus, orch, 1993–5; Magic Doremik (children's op, G. Rodari), 8vv, chbr ens, 2006–7

Orch: Improvisations, 1968; Phantasy in Black and White, 1973; Spectri sonori, 1973; Crystallites, 1974; Perc Conc., 1974; Conductus: a Ceremonial for Winds, ww, 1982; La novella d'inverno, str, 1984; Mar Conc., 1985; Sax Conc., 1988; Ode to Praise all Famous Women, 1992; Fanfare for Peace, 1994; Conc. grosse, 2 vn, chbr orch, 1996

Chbr: 4 Preludes, vib, pf, 1965; Scherzo, xyl, pf, 1967; Passacaglia and Fugue, org, perc, 1968; Jeuparti, harp, vib, 1970; Madrigals (Canticum sonarum), wind qt, str qt, tpt, trbn, gong, 1971; Sonospheres III, fl, cl, trbn, vc, pf, perc, 1973; Siderals, 2 perc qnts, light projection, 1974; Mobile, perc, 1975; Classical Variations, timp, str qt, 1976; Dream Lands, Magic Spaces, vn, pf, 6 perc, 1978; Kwiaty Księżyca [Moon Flowers], vc, pf, 1986; Ajikan: Unfolding Light, fl, perc, 1990; Poetic Impressions, ww qnt, pf, 1991; 4 Portraits, str qt, 1994; Mancala, 2 vn, 1997; Scherzo di fantasia, euphonium, pf, 1997; Linear Constructions in Space, perc ens, 1998

Solo inst: Model przestrzenny [Space Model], perc, 1971–5; Arabesque, hp, 1972; Stress, tape, perc, 1972; 2 Poems, tuba, 1973–5; Touracou, hpd, 1974; Quodlibet, db, tape, 1976; 6 Bagatelles, hp, 1979; Graffito, mar, 1988; Hommage à I.J. Paderewski, pf, 1992; Spider Walk, perc, 1994; Olympian Rings, steel drum, 1998

Vocal: Epigrams (Gk. poems), chorus, fl, hp, pf, perc, 1977; Un grand sommeil noir (P. Verlaine), Mez, fl, hp, 1978; Sonety do Orfeusza [Sonnets to Orpheus] (R.M. Rilke), 1v, chbr orch, 1981; Listy polskie [Polish Letters] (cant., S. Wyspiański and others), S, Mez, Bar, chorus, chbr orch, 1988; Pieśni rozpaczy i samotności [Songs of Despair and Loneliness] (Rilke, P. Verlaine, W. Shakespeare, F. García Lorca, L.

Staff), Mez, pf, 1989; Holocaust Memorial Cantata (L.W. Hedley, Y. Menuhin), S, T, Bar, chorus, chbr orch, 1992; Cantiones jubilationis (M. Duffy), women's chorus, 1995; Distant Echoes (Hedley and others), Mez, str qt, 1995; Liquid Light (Duffy), Mez, pf, perc, 1995

Principal publishers: Marks, Presser, PWM

BIBLIOGRAPHY

T. Marek: "Composer's Workshop: Marta Ptaszyńska's *Siderals*," *Polish Music* (1975), no.2, 20–23

B. Murray: "The Influence of Polish Music on American Culture," *Polish Music* (1976), no.1, 6; no.2, 10–18

D. Szwarcman: "The Colorful World of Marta Ptaszyńska," *Polish Music* (1988), nos.2–3, 25ff

R. Zierolf: "Composers of Modern Europe, Australia and New Zealand," *Women and Music*, ed. K. Pendle (Bloomington, IN, 1991), 187–207, esp. 199–202

B. Smolenska-Zielinska: "Concerto for Marimba by Marta Ptaszyńska," *Percussive Notes*, xxix/4 (1991), 78–82

J.R. Briscoe, ed.: *Historical Anthology of Music by Women* (Bloomington, IN, 1997), 241–59

M.A. Harley: "Composing in Color: Marta Ptaszyńska's Liquid Light," *Frau Musica (nova): Komponieren heute/Composing Today*, ed. M. Homma and H.-W. Boresch (Sinzig, 2000) 307–29

MICHAEL MECKNA (with BARBARA ZWOLSKA-STĘSZEWESKA)

Public Enemy. Rap group. Among the most influential rap artists, Public Enemy is best known for lyrics addressing the socio-political realities of African American youth and music featuring sonically complex beats infused with sirens, spoken samples, and scratching.

The group first came together in 1982 as the mobile DJ crew Spectrum City. Initial members included rapper CHUCK D (Carlton Douglas Ridenhour; *b* Roosevelt, Long Island, NY, 1 Aug 1960), DJs Hank and Keith Shocklee, and WBAU radio program director Bill Stephney. In 1986, Stephney helped Ridenhour secure a recording deal with Def Jam records where the two envisioned a rap group that would be musically experimental and commercially successful. With the addition of Flavor Flav (William Drayton; *b* Roosevelt, Long Island, NY, 16 March 1959), DJ Terminator X (Norman Rogers, *b* 5 Nov 1966) and "Minister of Information" Professor Griff (Richard Griffin, *b* 1 Aug 1960), Public Enemy was born, releasing their debut album *Yo! Bum Rush the Show* in 1987.

The group garnered attention for its overtly political songs and unique, energetic stage show. Performances included Flavor Flav acting as an MC and "hype man" responsible for exciting the audience through his wild interjections and call-and-response. His fashion eccentricities, which include a large clock worn as a necklace, and stage persona allowed him to act as comic foil to Chuck D's more serious persona. Public Enemy's militancy was enhanced in live performances and music videos through the addition of bodyguards who acted as stage performers. Named "The Security of the First World," or S1W, these men donned military fatigues and performed choreography which combined military drill, martial arts, and "step show" dances.

Subsequent albums for the Def Jam label, particularly *It Takes a Nation of Millions to Hold Us Back* (1989) and *Fear of a Black Planet* (1990), increased the collaged atmosphere of musical frenzy created by Public Enemy's production team, THE BOMB SQUAD. Fragmented and rhyth-

mically volatile, the music evoked cities in chaos, while Chuck D's forceful raps conveyed an urgency in their apocalyptic imagery. Memorably describing rap as "black America's CNN," Chuck D became a focal point for anti-establishment hostility felt by young African Americans; yet the group's music appealed to rebels of all ethnic backgrounds. Controversy followed the group due, in part, to their public support of Nation of Islam leader Louis Farrakhan; they came under further scrutiny in 1989 when Professor Griff made anti-Semitic comments that eventually led to his dismissal from the group. That same year, their song "Fight the power" was used to striking effect in Spike Lee's film, *Do the Right Thing*.

Later albums, *Apocalypse 91…The Enemy Strikes Black* (1991) and *Muse Sick-N-Hour Mess Age* (1994), were powerful, but sounded less turbulent than their earlier and more influential work. Particularly notable, however, is their collaboration with heavy metal band Anthrax on the 1991 remake of their single "Bring the noise," which helped give rise to a rap-metal subgenre. By the mid-1990s the group had fallen from prominence, but they continued to record, while Chuck D assumed his role as a public intellectual through lectures and writing.

BIBLIOGRAPHY

R. Walser: "Rhythm, Rhyme, and Rhetoric in the Music of Public Enemy," *EthM*, xxxix (1995), 259–71

J. Chang: *Can't Stop Won't Stop: a History of the Hip Hop Generation* (New York, 2005)

S. Reynolds: *Bring the Noise: 20 Years of Writing about Hip Rock and Hip Hop* (London, 2007)

D. Myrie: *Don't Rhyme for the Sake of Riddlin': the Authorized Story of Public Enemy* (New York, 2008)

DAVID TOOP/MARGARET JACKSON

Pueblo, eastern. Native American tribes of New Mexico that live along the Rio Grande and its tributaries. The ancestors of the modern Pueblo peoples have lived in this region for thousands of years, long before the first Europeans colonized the area and gave the name *pueblo* (Sp.: village) to settlements of sedentary Indians. Members of the 16 eastern Pueblo groups, who now number more than 25,000, share many cultural and musical characteristics and are grouped by language family. The Keresan-speaking eastern Pueblos include Cochiti, San Felipe, Santa Ana, Santo Domingo, and Zia. Those belonging to the Kiowa-Tanoan language family are divided into three subgroups: TEWA (Nambe, Pojoaque, San Ildefonso, Ohkay Owingeh or San Juan, Santa Clara, and Tesuque), Tiwa (Isleta, PICURIS, TAOS, and Sandia), and Towa (Jemez). Eastern Pueblo peoples participate in all aspects of contemporary musical life, while also maintaining their historic repertories, which are taught and learned through oral tradition. The diverse genres include songs to accompany social dances, gambling games, healing rituals, work, lullabies, and personal songs, but Pueblo peoples perform most of their traditional music in the context of collective ceremonies.

The semiarid environment of the eastern Pueblos strongly influences their spiritual beliefs and practices. Traditional ceremonies, which remain vital to Pueblo life, focus on weather control (especially rain), fertility, hunting, and the change of seasons. Some ceremonies occur on specific dates, others are seasonal, and a few are enacted throughout the year. The five general categories of ceremonies include rituals associated with secret societies as well as kachina dances, which involve masked representations of spirit beings; maskless kachina ceremonies, which resemble kachina dances but do not involve masked performers; ceremonies conducted by warrior or hunter associations, including game animal dances; dances that are more oriented toward entertainment but that retain Pueblo stylistic characteristics; and ceremonies associated with Catholic feast days, which often blend Pueblo and Spanish New Mexican stylistic characteristics. Visitors are welcome at many traditional dances, as long as they adhere to Pueblo law, including prohibitions against photography and audio recording. However, kachina dances and rituals performed by secret societies are closed. During the colonial period, severe religious persecution by European clergy forced the eastern Pueblo peoples to perform these ceremonies privately; restricting access by outsiders has helped preserve Pueblo cultural identity and integrity.

Most ceremonial songs are performed by men; the number of singers ranges from 1 to 200. The singers may also be dancing, or they may constitute a separate, well-rehearsed chorus. Some ceremonies feature male dancers only, while others involve men and women. Depending on the genre and the context, the performance may involve one dancer or a group of any size up to several hundred dancers. Pueblo songs are monophonic and use pentatonic, hexatonic, and heptatonic scales. In some kinds of songs, melodic movement begins with a phrase centered on a base pitch; the second phrase leaps up a fifth and then gradually returns to the base pitch by means of an undulating descent. Most Pueblo songs emphasize duple meter, but certain genres feature brief changes to triple meter, which is sometimes referred to as a patterned pause. Pueblo singers employ a moderately relaxed and open method of vocal production in most ceremonial genres, although tension occurs in some song types. Singers use vocal pulsations and strongly accented tones in some songs and emphasize the lower part of their vocal ranges, except among the northern Tiwa, for whom higher-pitched melodies reflect musical influence from Plains tribes. Pueblo singers perform in blended unison, which expresses the Pueblo values of moderation and lack of individual display. Song texts combine vocables with poetic lyrics in a Pueblo language. For these peoples, songs possess power, and therefore must be used only in appropriate situations, unless they have been altered in terms of structure, text, or both.

Pueblo music employs some of the most complex forms in all of Native North America. Pueblo musical form and design reflect cultural concepts of cyclic time and directionality. These are expressed through large-scale patterns of repetition, which symbolize circularity, and four-part phrase divisions, which symbolize the cardinal directions. Kachina and maskless kachina songs employ sectional form (*AABBA*), in which each main section contains four subdivisions. For example, within the *A* section, the first part, called the *puchano*, involves a short rhythmic pattern with an essentially level melodic contour that identifies the genre. The second part, considered the beginning of the song, is relatively long and contains meaningful lyrics as well as an extended cadence. The third part, called the chorus, usually begins with a dramatic upward leap and includes *ta'a* or patterned pauses, which result from changing meters. The fourth phrase, called the ending part, features increased melodic and rhythmic animation and includes *ta'a*. Each part within each section repeats, so that a complete performance of one song may last 10 minutes or longer. Other genres of traditional music, such as animal dances, usually feature paired phrase structure (such as *AABBCC*); for each dance appearance there is an entrance song, a slow dance song, and a fast dance song.

Some ceremonies feature songs passed down orally from generation to generation, whereas others require the composition of new songs each year. New compositions must fit the proper mold for a specific song type. Any member of the group responsible for conducting a ceremony can present an original song to the group, but most are made by recognized composers. In addition, new songs may undergo a process of collective revision, so that the final product represents a group effort. New songs often contain phrases from earlier compositions or melodies borrowed from other cultures and transformed into Pueblo style.

Traditional Pueblo songs are accompanied by various percussion instruments, many of which carry symbolic significance, as evident in the way they are constructed, decorated, named, and handled. Drums include large double-headed barrel drums, hand-crafted from logs and animal skins, sometimes containing small, symbolically significant wooden objects. Ceremonial drums may be brightly painted and are played with a padded stick. Other instruments include hand-held container rattles made from gourds, suspension rattles made of turtle shells and deer hooves and tied to a dancer's knee, or metal bells. Notched rasps accompany some kinds of ceremonial songs. Flutes are less common in eastern Pueblo traditional repertories, although the Plains courting flute has long been popular at Taos Pueblo. The fiddle and the guitar, adopted from Spanish colonizers, accompany *Matachines* dances.

While eastern Pueblo singers and dancers have maintained traditional styles, they have also expanded their repertory to include innovative genres oriented toward tourists, to enlarge roles for women singers, and to engage in the global popular music industry. During the 1890s some Pueblos designed new kinds of dances, inspired by Plains Indian styles and genres, for tourist shows within and outside of the pueblo. These performances developed into elaborate theatrical productions known as "ceremonials," which were most popular from the 1920s through the early 1980s. Since the 1970s, women have become more prominent in eastern Pueblo musical life. The Tewa Women's Choir, for example, performs traditional and original songs during Catholic church services and at various social events, combining Pueblo drums and rattles with choral music accompanied by the organ. Lillian Ranier (Taos Pueblo) learned to play the courting flute, a traditionally male instrument, from her father and became a concert and recording artist. In the realm of Native American popular music, the singer-songwriter Robert Mirabal (Taos Pueblo) has made important contributions, taking the tradition of Pueblo theatrical productions to new heights through contemporary media.

RECORDINGS

Pueblo Indian Songs from San Juan (1969, Canyon); Cloud Dance Songs of San Juan Pueblo (1972, Indian House); Pueblo Songs of the Southwest (1972, Indian House); Turtle Dance Songs from San Juan Pueblo (1972, Indian House); Oku Shareh: Turtle Dance Songs of San Juan Pueblo (1979, New World); Music of New Mexico: Native American Traditions (1992, Smithsonian Folkways); Heartbeat: Voices of First Nations Women (1995, Smithsonian Folkways); Songs of my People: Peter Garcia and the Garcia Brothers (1995, Music of the World); Music from a Painted Cave: Robert Mirabal with Rare Tribal Mob (2001, Silver Wave)

BIBLIOGRAPHY

G. Herzog: "A Comparison of Pueblo and Pima Musical Styles," *Journal of American Folklore*, xlix (1936), 283–417
F. Densmore: *Music of Santo Domingo Pueblo, New Mexico* (Los Angeles, 1938)
G.P. Kurath: "Cochiti Choreographies and Songs," *Cochiti*, ed. C.H. Lange (Austin, TX, 1959/R1968), 539–56
A. Ortiz: *The Tewa World* (Chicago, 1969)
G.P. Kurath and A. Garcia: *Music and Dance of the Tewa Pueblos* (Santa Fe, NM, 1970)
D.L. Roberts: "The Ethnomusicology of the Eastern Pueblos," *New Perspectives on the Pueblos*, ed. A. Ortiz (Albuquerque, NM, 1972), 243–55
D.N. Brown: "Dance as Experience: the Deer Dance of Picuris Pueblo," *Southwestern Indian Ritual Drama*, ed. C.J. Frisbie (Albuquerque, NM, 1980), 71–92
M. La Vigna: "Okushare, Music for a Winter Ceremony: the Turtle Dance Songs of San Juan Pueblo," *Selected Reports in Ethnomusicology*, iii/2 (1980), 77–100
D.L. Roberts: "A Calendar of Eastern Pueblo Indian Ritual Dramas," *Southwestern Indian Ritual Drama*, ed. C. Frisbie (Albuquerque, NM, 1980), 103–24
N. Yeh: "The Pogonshare Ceremony of the Tewa: San Juan, New Mexico," *Selected Reports in Ethnomusicology*, iii/2 (1980), 101–45
P. Humphreys: "The Tradition of Song Renewal among the Pueblo Indians of North America," *American Indian Culture and Research Journal*, vi/1 (1982), 9–24
J.D. Sweet: *Dances of the Tewa Pueblo Indians: Expressions of New Life* (Santa Fe, NM, 1985, 2/2004)
B. Romero: *The Matachines Music and Dance in San Juan Pueblo and Alcalde, New Mexico* (diss., U. of California, Los Angeles, 1993)
H. Huang: "The 1992 Turtle Dance (Oekuu Shadeh) of San Juan Pueblo: Lessons with the Composer, Peter Garcia," *American Indian Culture and Research Journal*, xxi/4 (1997), 171–215

DON L. ROBERTS/VICTORIA LINDSAY LEVINE

Pueblo, western. Native Americans of the southwestern United States. Western Pueblo Indians include the Acoma and Laguna, who speak Keresan; the Hano; the Hopi; and the Zuni.

Puente, Tito [Ernesto Antonio] (*b* New York, NY, 20 April 1923; *d* New York, NY, 31 May 2000). Percussionist, bandleader, composer, and arranger. He began performing with Los Happy Boys and other local bands as a child prodigy, and as a teenager played with Noro Morales and Machito. Following wartime service in the US Navy (1942–5), he studied at the Juilliard School of Music (1945–7). In 1946 he joined Jose Curbelo's band alongside the upcoming vocalist Tito Rodríguez. The following year he left to form the Piccadilly Boys, later called the Tito Puente Orchestra, and which became a training ground for such musicians as Mongo Santamaría, Willie Bobo, Ray Barretto, and Johnny Pacheco. Along with fellow "Mambo Kings" Machito and Rodríguez, Puente performed regularly at New York's Palladium Ballroom. During the 1950s he also recorded a series of albums devoted to authentic Cuban percussion. In the 1960s he made important recordings with the Cuban female vocalists Celia Cruz and La Lupe, and his career continued to flourish through the next three decades. He also collaborated with such musicians as Woody Herman and the trombonist Buddy Morrow. He composed more than 400 songs, made more than 100 recordings, and gained four Grammy awards and eight Grammy nominations. Among his most famous tunes are "Oye como va" (later popularized by the Chicano rock star Carlos Santana), "Ran Kan Kan," "Picadillo," and "El rey del timbal."

In addition to his popularization of Cuban-based dance music, he was renowned as a Latin jazz performer, best known for his brilliance on the timbales and vibraphone, although also playing conga, piano, and saxophone. He also recorded jazz big band and bossa nova albums. He hosted his own television show in 1968, appeared in the 1992 film *The Mambo Kings*, and became a symbol of the New York Puerto Rican identity, marching prominently in Puerto Rican parades. Puente played and recorded with nearly every major jazz and Latin musician and won numerous awards including an honorary doctorate from Old Westbury College (1994) and a star on the Hollywood Walk of Fame.

BIBLIOGRAPHY

S. Loza: *Tito Puente and the Making of Latin Music* (Urbana, IL, 1999)
K.R. Gartner: *Analysis of the Stylistic Development of Selected Tito Puente Timbale Solos in the Mambo Style* (diss., U. of Northern Colorado, 2001)

LISE WAXER/R

Puerling, Gene [Eugene Thomas] (*b* Milwaukee, WI, 31 March 1929; *d* San Anselmo, CA, 25 March 2008). Singer and arranger. He was born into a musical family but was largely self-taught. By the time he graduated from South Division High School he had already formed three small vocal groups. In 1951, he moved to Los Angeles where he sang with several small ensembles. In 1953, he formed the Hi-Lo's with Clark Burroughs, Bob Strasen, and Bob Morse. As the group's arranger, he borrowed tunes not only from the repertory of pop songs of the day but also from old standards. With sensitivity to vocal counterpoint and a desire for the right amount of tension and release in harmonic progressions, he sought to bring new life to old tunes. His arranging style reflected his practice of listening regularly to the music of classical composers. By the time they disbanded in 1964, the Hi-Los had performed with an array of well-known film and TV personalities and had produced a large number of recordings in a variety of formats.

In 1967, Puerling formed The Singers Unlimited in Chicago with Bonnie Herman, Don Shelton, and Len Dresslar. With this group he experimented with a new recording technique using multi-track machines. In the 1970s, TSU recorded fifteen LP albums in the MPS Studio in Villingen, Germany. Their first a cappella album won the *Deutscher Schallplattenpreis* in 1971.

In 1977, the Hi-Los reunited in a performance at the Monterey Jazz Festival. The following year they produced an LP titled *Back Again*. Puerling won a Grammy in 1982 for his arrangement of "A nightingale sang in Berkeley Square." He sang with the Hi-Los in a farewell concert in 1996 and continued his work as a clinician and workshop leader until well into his seventies.

EDITIONS
The Gene Puerling Sound (New York, 1975)

BIBLIOGRAPHY
D. Gold: "The Best Vocal Group Ever," *Chicago Tribune Magazine* (22 Dec 2002)
J. Warner: *The Billboard Book of American Singing Groups: A History, 1940–1990* (New York, 1992), 224, 507–8

WARREN FIELDS

Puerto Rican music. *See* LATINO MUSIC.

Puerto Rico. Island in the Greater Antilles (pop. 3,725,789) associated with the United States since 1898, with commonwealth status from 1952. It is located north of the Caribbean Sea and east of the Dominican Republic, Haiti, and Cuba. Puerto Rico is the name the Spanish conquistadors gave the biggest of a series of smaller islands that make up the Puerto Rican archipelago of which Vieques, Culebra, and Mona are best known. The original name was *Borikén*, given by the aboriginal Ameridian inhabitants of the Antilles, the Taino Indians, which means La Tierra del Gran Señor (Land of the Great Lord). Puerto Rico means "rich port," a reference to the gold recovered by the colonial soldiers, led by Christopher Columbus, who first visited the island in 1493. Colonization by Spain began in 1508, and the seat of government was established in San Juan, now the island's largest city and the center of commercial and cultural life.

As a result of the Spanish-American War, US troops invaded Puerto Rico, and Spain ceded the island to the United States in 1898. Initially, it became a territory or colonial possession, under military rule; in 1952, as a result of national unrest and demands made by Puerto Rican political parties, the United States granted Puerto Rico Commonwealth status (Estado Libre Asociado), which has remained unaltered to the present. After more than a century of political, economic, and cultural relationships between the colony and the metropolitan power, there are as many Puerto Ricans living in US cities as in the archipelago. Immigrants brought their traditional musical practices, and they have shared, adapted, synthesized, and created new musical genres

or forms that have contributed to the musical development of the United States.

1. Pre-Columbian societies. 2. Early church music. 3. Bomba. 4. Seis. 5. Secular festivities and institutions. 6. Danza. 7. Plena. 8. Salsa. 9. Reggaeton. 10. Bolero. 11. Classical composition since the 1950s. 12. Musical institutions.

1. PRE-COLUMBIAN SOCIETIES. It has been estimated that the Taino Indians inhabited *Borikén* for more than 2000 years before the arrival of the first Europeans. Their origins have been traced back to the Arawaks, who inhabited South America and gradually moved up throughout the islands until they reached and settled in the Lesser and Major Antilles. They built a well organized and successful society based on communal principles living mostly off of agricultural production of *yuca* (cassava) and fishing. Their local leader was the *cacique* or *cacica* and in turn they were organized in different *cacicazgos* around the island. Their most important cultural and musical expression was the AREÍTO (written also *areyto* or *areito*), a combination of playing, singing, dancing, and mimicking that was grounded on strong religious and magical beliefs; it was directed by the *tequina*, the religious leader of the tribe. The *areíto* incorporated voices—solo and choral—and antiphonal singing, using melodies based on a pentatonic scale. Melodic instruments included bamboo or bone flutes (which were also pentatonic) and the *güamos* or conch-shell, which functioned as a type of horn. The most important percussion instrument was the *mayohuacán*, made of a whole log of wood with two languets in an H-shape; it was struck like a xylophone with two wooden sticks. The *güiro*, a gourd made of a local fruit, and the *maracas*, made of the Indian fig-tree, were also used for percussion; according to Spanish descriptions, they produced combinations of rhythmic patterns or polyrhythms. They also tied *sonajeros*, timbrels made of small conch-shells, to their arms and legs.

For the Taino, music was considered to have magical powers and was used to enact their myths. The *maracas* were thought to possess the power to communicate with their ancestors. The *mayohuacán* was associated with the land, the moon, the sky, the rain, and thunder as well as with fertility rites. The *güiro* was associated mainly with rites of death, fertility, and resurrection. The *güamos* were associated with fecundity, death, resurrection, and the wind. None of their music has survived, although some of their instruments remain in use today. By the 17th century the native population had been decimated by war, disease, slavery, and emigration.

2. EARLY CHURCH MUSIC. During the first three centuries of Puerto Rican history, musical life centered on the church and the military garrison. Early records are scarce because many ecclesiastical archives and other sources of information were destroyed in fires, hurricanes, sackings and sieges. Early in the 16th century an organist and a *chantre* were requested for the cathedral, whose construction had begun in 1511. At the end of the 16th century the cathedral, described as being as beautiful as any in England, possessed a fine organ. Capitulary

Acts of 1660 indicate that the permanent musical staff of the cathedral consisted of an organist and a *sochantre*, but in 1672 two new posts were created, *maestro de capilla* and cantor. From 1698 until 1756 there is no record of specific nominations to posts in cathedral music. However, from 1756, records show a succession of organists, *maestros de capilla* and other musicians attached to the church. These musicians, including both clerics and laymen, provided the first regular music instruction in Puerto Rico.

3. BOMBA. To replace the depleted native work force, the Spanish government imported African slaves. The music and dance as well as the drum known as BOMBA had its origins in the first contingents of African slaves imported to Puerto Rico. They were taken from all regions of the African continent, especially from the lands now constituting Nigeria, Dahomey, Sierra Leone, Congo, Senegal, and Ghana. In the beginning, slaves served as forced labor in the gold mines. When the gold rush was over, they were moved to the sugar cane plantations of the coastal areas. Over time, and especially up to the official abolition of slavery in 1873, various musical forms and dances were synthesized and transformed into what is known as *bailes de bomba* (*bomba* dances). In the four centuries of African slavery in Puerto Rico, the *bailes de bomba* represented the most important social and cultural event in the hard and oppresive daily life of the slaves. These dances were only permitted by slave owners on Saturdays and Sundays, the official free-days, and at the end of the sugar cane harvest; only on these occasions were slaves permitted to observe their traditional ceremonies, perform customary rituals, and celebrate. It has been documented that these gatherings were also used to plan rebellions.

The amount and type of *bomba* dances are found in different proportions around Puerto Rico. In the Northern part of the Island (mainly Loíza and Fajardo), which represents the highest concentration of Yoruba culture, these dances are limited to a few. But in the southern part of Puerto Rico (Ponce, Santa Isabel, Salinas, Gúayama, Arroyo, and Patillas) there exists a much wider variety: *Holandés, Leró, Candungué, Mariangola, Cucalambé, cuembé* or *guembé, curiquinque, guateque, mariandá* or *mariyandá, bambulé, canlindé* or *calindá, cunyá, grasimé, leró,* and *sicá.* Other cultural and religious musical forms that developed in this era include the *Rosario Francés* (French Rosary) and the *Mendé* songs. After the abolition of slavery, *bomba* dances became one popular response to the bourgeois Puerto Rican plantation owners; for instance, the attire worn by women dancers of the *bomba* both imitated and ridiculed the aristocratic plantation lady.

Bomba music and dance is characterized by two types of call and response: between the solo singers and chorus, and as a dialogue between the dancer and the solo drum (*requinto*). The instruments used to accompany these dances and songs were the *bomba* drums (also called *barriles* or barrels because they are made from dried codfish, or rum barrels, with a goatskin head); the *cuá*, or sticks that are played on the side of the drum, not on the skin; and the *maracas*. The formal structure is antiphonal: either a solo voice or a chorus responds to a solo singer. The music features pentatonic melodies, syncopated rhythms, and polyrhythms produced by the percussion instruments.

4. SEIS. While *bomba* music recalls the island's African heritage, the *seis* symbolizes the major musical expression of Puerto Rican peasants who labored as subsistence farmers and sharecroppers in the central mountainous area of the coffee and tobacco *haciendas* (see SEIS PUERTORRIQUEÑO). They are called *jíbaros*, who remained culturally attached to their Spanish colonial models, which were, coincidentally, associated with the poorest areas of Spain. The *seis* takes its name from a six-couple dance, and refers to a variety of music and dance forms. Although historians have not yet determined the specific Old World origins of the *seis*, there is consensus that this musical form came to Puerto Rico from Spain during the time of colonization and settlement in the late 17th century. As Spanish music bears the mark of eight centuries of Moorish rule, the influence of Arabic culture on Spanish expressive culture can be heard in Puerto Rican music. Spanish settlers adapted a rich variety of Spanish/Arabic music styles to their new environment, with the *seis* becoming the most important genre of the Puerto Rican peasantry; other peasant music practices in Puerto Rico include AGUINALDO and *baquiné.* A similar process of adaptation occurred with traditional stringed instruments, which served as the basis for the development of the *bordonúa* (bass), *tiple,* and *requinto.* The *cuatro,* a variant of these string instruments, remains unique to Puerto Rico, and is most integrally associated with peasant music and stands as a national musical symbol. The *cuatro,* together with the guitar and *güiro* (scraped gourd of indigenous origin), came to form the typical peasant music ensemble.

With the exception of the *seis chorreao,* instrumental dance accompaniment, and the improvised *cuatro* interludes, the typical peasant music ensemble is used to accompany the solo-voice of the *trovador*—the improvisatory singer/poet. The melodies are characterized by short, two-to-four bar phrases and use standard tonic, dominant, and subdominant harmonies. Melodies often reveal an Arabic influence through reminders of the Andalusian *canto jondo,* and the *trovador's* vocalization of *le-lo-lai,* in preparation for improvisation, is also Arabic in origin. Most *seis* verses use the *décima* poetic structure: ten lines of eight syllables each, following a strict rhyming structure. Not all *seises* in the *décima* structure are improvised; some are part of a peasant poetic repertoire, while others are stock phrases that appear in many different songs.

Most *seises* obtain their names by the way they are danced: *chorreao, bombeao, zapateao,* and so on. Others are named after their town of origin—*fajardeño, viequense, bayamonés, comerieño*—or after animals common to their everyday life, such as *matatoros* and *culebra.* Some are named after the way they are sung or for the musicians that composed or popularized them, including Andino, Mapeyé, and Villarán. Their lyrics celebrate the natural beauty of the mountainous central region, and often venerate Puerto Rican women as well as the island itself.

5. SECULAR FESTIVITIES AND INSTITUTIONS. Secular music before the 19th century was connected mainly with public celebrations. Among these were events of religious significance, but mounted at the expense of secular authority: Corpus Christi and the celebration of the patron saints of Spain, Spanish West Indies, and Puerto Rico. In addition, *fiestas reales* were organized on occasions connected with accessions of Spanish monarchs and with other significant events in the Spanish world. The accession of Fernando VI in 1746 was marked by processions, balls, *comedias*, and other festivities extending over a period of nine days, and similar events occurred in 1789 on Carlos IV's accession to the throne. During the 18th and 19th centuries, military musicians were important figures in the colony's musical life. Attached to Spanish units serving in the Antilles, these musicians also performed for balls and other civil celebrations and provided the nucleus of orchestras formed for opera and concerts. They were among the first teachers of wind instruments in Puerto Rico, and many remained after completion of their military service as teachers, performers, and founders of musical families.

Construction of the island's first permanent theater began in 1824; the building, originally named the San Juan Teatro Municipal and still in use today as the Teatro Tapia, was officially inaugurated in 1832. A philharmonic society was formed by a group of professionals and amateur musicians. Among the goals of this society (many of which were realized) were the establishment of a music academy, the organization of an orchestra, and the presentation of locally mounted operas and zarzuelas. One of Puerto Rico's first native composers was Felipe Gutiérrez Espinosa (1825–99). He wrote the first opera on a Puerto Rican subject, *Guarionex* (1856), as well as two other operas, a zarzuela, and a large quantity of religious music.

6. DANZA. The Puerto Rican DANZA developed during the mid-19th century and flourished among the aristocratic and bourgeois classes. Its origins can be traced to a series of similar music and dance forms common to the Caribbean basin, Cuba, Venezuela, and Colombia. It is a variation of the Spanish *contradanza*, which was also common in Cuba, and elements can be traced to the 16th-century French *bransles* and the 17th-century English reels and jigs. The *danza* is written in 2/4 or 6/8 and it employs a formal structure: Introduction, which is called the *paseo*; two sections called *merengues*, one in the tonic and the other in the dominant; a contrasting section in the minor mode called the *trio*, which often featues the obligato of a solo wind instrument; a repeat of the first *merengue*; and a short coda. The development of the Puerto Rican danza can be attributed to three renowned composers: Manuel G. Tavárez

(1843–83), who composed *danzas* for the solo piano, reminiscent of Romantic composers like Fryderyk Chopin; JUAN MOREL CAMPOS (1857–1896), who popularized the *danza* as a dance form; and JOSÉ I. QUINTÓN (1881–1925), who brought the *danza* back to the recital hall and into the academy. The best known *danza* is *La Borinqueña*, a folkloric melody of Peruvian origin; Francisco Ramírez Ortiz (1884–1900), from the town of San Germán, provided new romantic verses and called it *Bellísima Trigueña*. These lyrics were later changed by Lola Rodriguez Tió in *El Grito de Lares* (1868), the revolutionary content of which supported the popular national uprising against the Spanish colonial government, symbolizing the birth of the Puerto Rican nation. With the establishment of the Commonwealth government *(Estado Libre Asociado)* in 1952, the melody of *La Borinqueña* was arranged by Ramón Collado into the official anthem of Puerto Rico.

7. PLENA. *Plena*, while rooted in *bomba* and *seis* traditions, is a product of more than one hundred years of development. Its origins responded to the change from Spanish to US colonial rule, and the economic upheaval following the abolition of slavery and the movement of displaced workers throughout Puerto Rico and the Caribbean. Most of these workers sought economic opportunity in the growing urban centers of the region, including cities on the southern coast such as Ponce, which is considered to be the birthplace of the *plena*. Although *plena* has its musical and social roots in *bomba*—many of the early *pleneros* were also *bomba players*, including Joselino "Bum-Bum" Oppenheimer—*plena* also owes much to peasant music, including its own traces of Spanish Arabic influences, and to European-style salon music such as the Puerto Rican *danza*. During its early years, the *plena* was also strongly influenced by styles from the English-speaking Carribbean islands, such as Nevis, St. Kitts, St. Thomas, and Barbados, whose displaced freed slaves also traveled throughout the Caribbean in search for work. The music that resulted from this cultural contact represents the sound of an emerging Puerto Rican working class. *Plena*, which literarilly means "full," symbolizes the synthesis of musical traditions in the 20th century. *Plena* instruments traditionally consist of three or more *panderetas* (hand-held frame drums of different sizes and pitches that resemble tambourines without the cymbals), and sometimes accordion or harmonica, and a guitar. The *panderetas* rhythmically interact with the soloist, choral voices, and dancing couples. *Plena* is known as the sung newspaper because it reports and comments critically upon the history and everyday life of the Puerto Rican people. Some of the best-known *plenas*—including *Tintorera del Mar* (The Shark), *Cortaron a Elena* (They Cut Up Elena), *Mamita, llegó el Obispo* (Look, Sweetie, the Bishop's Arrived), and *Aló, Quién llama?* (Hello? Who's Calling?)—all make reference to topical events of the day in four-verse stances called *coplas*. After the soloist sings the first verse, the chorus responds with the same lines, exchanging verses with the soloist. The soloist improvises each new verse

until the song reaches the main section. At this point the *pandereta requinto* (highest-pitched solo drum) improvises, and a talented *plenero* responds to these syncopated rhythmic units and takes the song to its climax.

8. SALSA. Although Puerto Rico has been a colonial posession throughout its history, the semi-feudal nature of the Spanish Empire differed from the capitalist system of the United States. Shortly after the birth of recording in the late 19th century, US music executives flocked to the Caribbean islands and Latin America in search of traditional music—including the Cuban *son*, the Argentinian tango, and the Cuban mambo—that could be recorded, packaged, and sold. Puerto Rico's traditional music was no exception. *Plena* music of different types has been recorded since the 1920s by artists such as the singer Manuel Jiménez Canario, the Latin big band led by César Concepción, and Ramón "Mon" Rivera, the well known *plenero* from Mayagüez. Perhaps the best known group to record both *bomba* and *plena* was CORTIJO Y SU COMBO with lead singer ISMAEL RIVERA. All of these traditional musical genres, as well as the *Seis* and even the traditional 19th-century *danza*, were recorded with the intention of selling records to the migrant Puerto Rican, Caribbean, and Latin American population in the United States, especially in the city of New York.

These musical styles represent the historical and musical antecedents of what was later known as *salsa* music. Rather than a typical musical genre, *salsa* (literally, sauce) is basically a commercial label, a kind of musical mixture containing anything that has a Latin flavor. It has drawn on the traditional music of Puerto Rico and different genres from the Caribbean and Latin America. In its most profound sense, *salsa* represents the musical expression of migrant Puerto Rican populations within the United States, especially New York City. The originator of what years later became commercially known as *salsa* music and dance in New York City was Puerto Rican musician and composer EDDIE PALMIERI, who sought to represent the Caribbean and Latin American population in such a multinational and multi-ethnic city. Palmieri drew on instrumentation, music, and stylistic elements adopted from musics including the Cuban *son* and the Puerto Rican *plena*. Salsa subsequently incorporated other Latin musical elements, including the Latin big band format, which is used by one of the world's top salsa orchestras, El Gran Combo de Puerto Rico.

9. REGGAETON. Puerto Rican reggaeton is a musical form whose style can be traced to Jamaican reggae, a dance hall music rhythm (called "Dembow"), and hip hop. It is the principal musical genre created by Jamaican workers who immigrated to build the Panama Canal. During the 1970s, it developed as a combination of Jamaican reggae with Spanish lyrics (called *Reggae en Español*). In Puerto Rico, the music took shape first as an underground musical form, due to political repression of urban youth. In the 1990s, Puerto Rican musical rhythms were added and mixed with singing and

rapping, and the style evolved into how it is known today. The first exponent of the new genre in Puerto Rico was Vico C., and his music and lyrics soon gained acceptance in the United States. Reggaeton performers include the commercially successful Daddy Yankee and the significant artist René Pérez, known as Residente Calle 13.

10. BOLERO. The establishment of the Commonwealth in 1952 and subsequent economic and cultural reforms brought relief and recovery to Puerto Rico. Just as the romantic *bolero* (the origins of which are still debated between Mexico and Cuba) captured the attention of Latin American, Caribbean, and mostly Puerto Rican migrants in postwar America, in Puerto Rico the 1950s became a decade filled with this popular solo song and dance. The two most important Puerto Rican *bolero* composers were PEDRO FLORES (1894–1979) and RAFAEL HERNÁNDEZ (1892–1965). Together they composed hundreds of *güarachas, plenas,* and, mostly, Puerto Rican *boleros*. While Flores chose to use a popular lyrical style in some compositions (*Borracho no vale*) and sublime poetry in others (*Bajo un Palmar* or the *bolero Obsesión*), the more musically trained Hernández experimented with complicated harmonies to support his romantic and patriotic *boleros*. Perhaps the most beloved *boleros* by Hernández were *Capullito de Alelí, Campanitas de Cristal,* and *Silencio*. But *boleros* like *Lamento Borincano*, with its criticism of the harsh economic and social conditions of the Puerto Rican peasantry, and *Preciosa,* a direct attack on the tyranny of the US colonial domination over the people of Puerto Rico, offered social commentary with a nationalist flavor.

11. CLASSICAL COMPOSITION SINCE THE 1950S. During the 1950s a Puerto Rican nationalist school of composition developed featuring the composers HÉCTOR CAMPOS PARSI (1922–98), AMAURY VERAY (1922–95), and JACK DELANO (1914–97). Campos Parsi studied European classical music composition in France and the United States, Veray studied in Italy (the Conservatory of Music of Santa Cecilia in Rome), and the Ukrainian-born Delano lived many years on the island. The principles guiding this school involved the use of folkloric and national Puerto Rican melodies, harmonies, and rhythms with modern classical forms, genres, and compositional techniques. The best known of these pieces are Campos Parsi's *Cuarteto de Cuerdas* (1950) and *Divertimiento del Sur* (1953), Veray's ballet *Cuando las Mujeres* (1957) and *Villancico yaucano* (1953), and Delano's *Sonata para Viola* (1953). Since 1960, composers have taken a much more eclectic view, embracing styles and techniques ranging from post-Romantic to serial, aleatory, and mixed-media expression. Composers active in Puerto Rico in recent decades have also included LUIS ANTONIO RAMÍREZ (1923–95), IGNACIO MORALES NIEVA (1928–2005), RAFAEL APONTE LEDÉE (*b* 1938), LUIS MANUEL ÁLVAREZ (*b* 1939), FRANCIS SCHWARTZ (*b* 1940), ERNESTO CORDERO (*b* 1946), WILLIAM ORTIZ ALVARADO (*b* 1947), ROBERTO SIERRA (*b* 1953), and RAYMOND TORRES SANTOS (*b* 1958).

12. MUSICAL INSTITUTIONS. The traditional music of Puerto Rico is alive and well throughout the island, accompanying all types of secular, religious, and social activity. In most public and private schools, traditional music is played in music theory and performance classes. There is a long history of public funding and support for musical education. The government also sponsors the Puerto Rican Institute of Culture which holds annual festivals of national and international folk music, and the Casals Festival where international classical European and Puerto Rican concert music is performed by acclaimed musicians and singers. In 1946, the government of Puerto Rico passed the Escuelas Libres de Música (Free Schools of Music) Act in order to train the professional musicians that were needed to play in the new hotels in the capital city of San Juan. In 1960, the government also founded the Conservatory of Music of Puerto Rico, to train the musicians that could play in the Puerto Rico Symphony Orchestra founded in 1958, and the Casals Festival Orchestra. Members of the Puerto Rico Symphony Orchestra accompany the major opera and ballet national companies seasons as well as visiting acts.

The publicly funded University of Puerto Rico, Río Piedras campus, includes a Music Department which grants the BA in music. Interamerican University of Puerto Rico (IUPR), a private nonprofit university, offers bachelor's and master's degrees in music performance and music education in two of its 11 campuses. While the San German Music Deparment of IUPR focuses on music education, the Metropolitan campus, located in the capital city of San Juan, specializes in the study and performance of traditional popular music in general with emphasis on Puerto Rican music.

See also LATINO MUSIC: PUERTO RICAN MUSIC.

BIBLIOGRAPHY

F. Callejo: *Música y músicos puertorriqueños* (San Juan, 1915/*R*)
M.L. Muñoz: *La Música en Puerto Rico: Panorama Histórico-Cultural* (Sharon, CT, 1966)
F. López Cruz: *La Música Folklórica de Puerto Rico* (Sharon, CT, 1967)
J. McCoy: *The Bomba and Aguinaldo of Puerto Rico as they have evolved from indigenous African and European Cultures* (diss., Florida State U., 1968)
H. Vega Drouet: *Some Musical Forms of African Descendants in Puerto Rico: Bomba, Plena and Rosario Frances* (thesis, Hunter College, 1969)
H. Campos Parsi: "Música," *La Gran Enciclopedia de Puerto Rico*, vii (Madrid, 1972)
M. Rosado, ed.: *Ensayos sobre la Danza Puertorriqueña* (San Juan, 1977)
H. Vega Drouet: *Historical and Ethnological Survey on the Probable African Origins of the Puerto Rican Bomba* (diss., Wesleyan U., 1979)
C.M. Rondón: *El Libro de la Salsa: Crónica de la Música del Caribe Urbano* (Caracas, 1980)
L. Acosta: *Música y Descolonización* (Habana, 1982)
J. Pérez Rolón: *La Bomba y la Plena Puertorriqueñas: Sincretismo Racial o Transformación Histórica-Musical?* (New York, 1982)
J. Pérez Rolón: *A Study of the Conservatory of Music of Puerto Rico with Implications for Future Development* (diss., Columbia U., 1983)
F. Echevarría Alvarado: *La Plena: Origen, sentido y desarrollo en el folklore puertorriqueño* (Santurce, 1984)
D. Thompson and A.F. Thompson: *Music and Dance in Puerto Rico from the Age of Columbus to Modern Times: an Annotated Bibliography* (Metuchen, NJ, 1991)
L. Acosta: *Del Tambor al Sintetizador* (Havana, Cuba, 1993)
R. Glasser: *My Music is My Flag: Puerto Rican Musicians and Their New York Communities (1917–1940)* (Berkeley, CA, 1995)
C. Díaz Ayala: *La Marcha de los Jíbaros (1898–1997): Cien Años de Música Puertorriqueña por el Mundo* (San Juan, 1998)
J.S. Roberts: *The Latin Tinge* (New York, 1979, 2/1999)
J. Flores: *From Bomba to Hip-Hop-Puerto Rican Culture and Latino Identity* (New York, 2000)
R. Moris Garcia: *El Rap vs. La 357: Tres Padres, Cinco Trabajos, Siete Dias de la Semana: Historia del Rap y Reggaeton en Puerto Rico* (San Juan, 2004)

JORGE A. PÉREZ ROLÓN

Pulido, Bobby (*b* Edinburg, TX, 25 April 1971). Singer. From a small Texas border town, he came on the scene one year after the 1995 death of Selena, perhaps the biggest-selling Tejana artist of all time. Pulido employed a danceable style similar to Selena's cumbia norteña, featuring keyboards alongside the accordion and focusing on smooth and slick pop vocals, which earned him a northern Mexican fan base as well as in Texas. His first release, *Desvelado* (Can't Sleep), went platinum, and his third album, *Llegaste a mi vida* (You Came into my Life), took honors at the annual Tejano Music Awards in 1997. As a singer and entertainer Pulido follows in the footsteps of his father, Roberto Pulido, a pioneer of the *tejano* (also, *orquesta tejana*) sound in the 1960s. The senior Pulido updated the folksy *conjunto* (ensemble) style and appealed to a broader Mexican American audience (working-class and *jaitón,* or upwardly mobile), though rarely south of the border.

CATHY RAGLAND

Pulitzer Prize. *See* AWARDS.

Pullen, Don (Gabriel) (*b* Roanoke, VA, 25 Dec 1941; *d* New York, NY, 22 April 1995). Jazz pianist, organist, composer, and bandleader. His early training ranged from classical music to gospel and the blues. His modern piano style took shape in 1964 after he left his studies as a pre-med student at Johnson C. Smith University to study with the AACM pianist MUHAL RICHARD ABRAMS. Pullen then moved to New York, where he associated himself with the avant-garde jazz scene, recorded with the Giuseppe Logan Quartet (1964–5), and released a self-produced duo album with drummer Milford Graves (1966). Pullen financially supported himself by accompanying various gospel and R&B artists during the late 1960s and accepting a one-year position as Nina Simone's musical director; he also worked as an arranger for King Records (*c*1968–9). He became known for his performances and four recordings with the Charles Mingus orchestra (1973–5). Despite his work in other genres and his ability to play swing, stride piano, and boogie-woogie, he was quickly labeled an avant-gardist and found it difficult to find an American record label to record him; many of the albums on which he appeared as leader were released on European labels such as Horo, Black Saint, and Soul Note.

Pullen was a member of the Mingus Dynasty band after the bassist's death in 1979; this band spawned the George Adams/Don Pullen quartet, which lasted until 1988. His most popular album, *New Beginnings*, was also recorded in 1988. His last major project, the African-Brazilian Connection (1990–5), mixed jazz with world music polyrhythms, which included dance scores and Native American music. His other notable collaborations after the 1970s included working with saxophonists Hamiet Bluiett, Jane Bunnett, and David Murray and AACM percussionist Famoudou Don Moye.

Pullen is remembered as an inside-outside player, incorporating a free jazz approach within traditional melodies, forms, or styles. His sound has been characterized as jagged and asymmetrical; he also used alternative techniques such as playing the inside of the piano and playing the keys with the back of his hand to create tone clusters that fit with the rhythm and harmony.

BIBLIOGRAPHY

H. Mandel: "Don Pullen: Piano Inside and Out," *DB*, lii/6 (1985), 20–1, 63
K. Whitehead: "Don Pullen: Reconciling Opposites," *DB*, lvi/11 (1989), 26–8
Obituary, *Billboard*, cvii/18 (1995)

RYAN D. W. BRUCE

P'ungmul. Originally from Korea, *p'ungmul* (wind object) is a vibrant form of percussion band music and dance that features the *changgo* (hourglass drum), the *puk* (barrel drum), the *sogo* (hand drum), the *ching* (large gong), and the *kkwaenggwari* (small gong). A complete ensemble also includes a double-reed instrument called the *t'aep'yŏngso*, flag bearers, and character actors called *chapsaek*. Based in agricultural village life, this music is also referred to as *nongak* (farmer's music) and as such is recognized as Important Intangible Cultural Asset no.11 in South Korea. Led by the head kkwaenggwari player, a typical South Korean band ranges from thirty to fifty members, although similar bands in the United States or Canada are often smaller. A distinguishing feature of p'ungmul is the practice of playing the instruments while dancing in various formations. Although all of the members incorporate footwork and rhythmic up-and-down movements, some performers (usually the sogo players) specialize in acrobatic flip-turns and other dazzling moves. Colorful costumes consist of white shirts and pants, contrasting vests or jackets, and banners of red, blue, and yellow that hang over one shoulder and tie at the waist. Performers traditionally wear eye-catching headwear ranging from paper hats decorated with huge flowers to tight-fitting headpieces fitted with long ribbons that are twirled and flipped into a variety of spectacular patterns. According to native beliefs, *p'ungmul* creates cosmological harmony by emphasizing inclusive, circular movements in space that connect the three elements of the universe: heaven, earth, and humans.

P'ungmul became established in the United States and Canada primarily through the formation of Korean American college groups and community-based organizations in the mid-1980s. The first groups were formed in metropolitan areas such as New York, Chicago, and Los Angeles and were primarily concerned with Korean and Korean American identity and cultural politics. About 50 groups have formed in both countries since then. Over time, p'ungmul activity has been integrated into other programs such as university ensembles, Korean language schools, martial arts, church programs, and camps for Korean immigrant children and adoptees. Although a handful of individuals play for purposes of entertainment and train in the more virtuosic, staged style called *samulnori*, the vast majority of groups today are driven by the educational and social needs of immigrant and adoptee Koreans adjusting to life in the United States and Canada.

BIBLIOGRAPHY

N. Hesselink: "Kim Inu's 'P'ungmulgut and Communal Spirit': Edited and Translated with an Introduction and Commentary," *Asian Music*, xxxi/1 (1999), 1–34
S. Pak: *Negotiating Identities in a Performance Genre: the Case of P'ungmul and Samulnori in Contemporary Seoul* (diss., U. of Pittsburgh, 2000)
D.L. Kwon: "The Roots and Routes of *P'ungmul* in the United States," *Music and Culture* (Korean Society for World Music), v (2001), 39–65
N. Hesselink: *P'ungmul: South Korean Drumming and Dance* (Chicago, 2006)

DONNA LEE KWON

Punk. It emerged as a rock subgenre in the mid-1970s, in part as a reaction to the contemporary mainstream rock industry and its aesthetics.

While the artistic precedents and sentiments that grew into punk surfaced at about the same time in such cities as Detroit, Los Angeles, and London, punk first coalesced into a recognizable, though disparate, musical movement in mid-1970s New York. It defied simple definition but often had either a spare sound or an aggressive, raw approach that countered a 1970s rock aesthetic that celebrated highly polished performances and the larger-than-life virtuoso musician. Instead, punk's do-it-yourself (DIY) ethic celebrated simplicity and amateurish enthusiasm. Punkers viewed commercial rock as a complacent, cookie-cutter, business-oriented shadow of its former self, reflecting a broader insipidness endemic to society at the time. Although punk began as rebellion against the mainstream music industry, it eventually challenged the status quo across society. Punks strove to be self-invented people, molding self-aware images through every aspect of life—music, clothes, books, and lived habitats. As much as a musical style, punk was a sensibility, one defined by individual subjectivity and faith in DIY efforts, both of which grew out of deep boredom with contemporary popular culture. Punks believed that rock and roll should be by and for young people and should emphasize the here and now.

In part because New York punk remained largely undiscovered for a few years, it was characterized by great diversity and camaraderie. As long as one challenged the rock status quo, one should be accepted into the fold. Thus Patti Smith's guitar-backed poetry coexisted with Television's art-rock dueling guitars, the Ramones' soon-to-be-classic three-chord punk minimalism, and

Johnny, Joey, Marky, and Dee Dee Ramone of The Ramones, Detroit, 1978. (Dalle/Sue Rynski/Landov)

Blondie's power pop. This diversity prefigured the emergence of myriad subgenres by the late 1970s. Although categorizing these subgenres in any way is problematic, most punk bands could be placed into one of two categories: art rock or back-to-basics rock. The United States did not experience an "art-school punk" movement like that in Britain, but New York bands such as Talking Heads and Television presented an artier, more intellectual version of punk, while bands such as the Ramones and the Dictators offered hard-driving homages to 1950s rock and roll.

In 1974, the burgeoning New York scene found a physical home in the Bowery dive CBGB & OMFUG (an acronym, ironically, for Country, BlueGrass, Blues and Other Music for Uplifting Gourmandizers), the first of several key factors that resulted in a self-identified punk scene by 1976. The next important step was attaching a name to the phenomenon. At first the disparate music had no commonly accepted appellation, although some called it "street rock." Increasingly, however, the scene's participants began to refer to it as punk rock, drawing on Bomp! Records owner Greg Shaw's moniker for 1960s garage bands such as the Seeds. The January 1976 publication of *PUNK*, a fan magazine that mixed enthusiasm for local music with *MAD* magazine's comically bizarre perspective, solidified a connection between New York street rock and the name "punk." The final institutionalizing component came when several key bands released albums. In late 1975, Patti Smith put out *Horses*, garnering attention for the scene. In 1976,

Sire signed the Ramones and Talking Heads, Stiff (a British label) released a Television EP, and Blondie's first album came out on Private Stock.

The year 1976 also witnessed the blossoming of punk in Great Britain, where promoters and artists blended punk with England's pub rock tradition and infused it with new meanings. British punks politicized their music more overtly than their American peers in two ways. First, the scandalous actions of bands such as the Sex Pistols, though not entirely new to punk, were much more visible in Britain owing to the tabloid nature of its media as well as the publicity savvy of Pistols manager Malcolm McLaren. When the Pistols cursed live on the BBC, they flouted mainstream mores and garnered the attention McLaren craved. Second, the Clash's lyrical "social realism" directly challenged British policies about topics such as imperialism's lingering effects, the welfare state, the era's political right turn, and police harassment. Unlike the American version, which found fleeting success in only a few early—and relatively tame—bands such as Blondie and Talking Heads, English punk achieved numerous hits in the U.K. throughout the late 1970s.

By this time, would-be punks had come together in the seedier parts of Hollywood, California, to begin their own DIY music culture. Los Angeles quickly became the new American punk mecca, and as the number of participants skyrocketed, semi-autonomous scenes sprouted up all over the greater metropolitan area. The L.A. punk sprawl paralleled the growth of

Addiction performs at CBGB on its closing night, 31 August 2005. (UPI Photo/Ezio Petersen/Landov)

scenes of varying size in cities throughout North America and Europe. In addition, southern California gave birth to HARDCORE, a subgenre that by the early 1980s dominated the public face of punk. Simultaneously, the fan base became younger. In the mid-1970s they were usually in their twenties; by the early 1980s teens dominated the genre—both as performers and fans.

In the 1970s American punk rockers believed they could transform and revitalize a "diseased" industry that they believed no longer represented rebellion or youth. Despite the early success of a few bands, punks failed to revolutionize the music industry or popular tastes. Over time they therefore abandoned efforts at large-scale reform and contented themselves with fostering a permanent underground built on DIY fanzines, record labels, and touring circuits. This underground continues today, as demonstrated by the longevity of such labels as Alternative Tentacles (San Francisco, 1979) and Dischord (Washington, DC, 1980). Punk remained culturally marginalized through the early 1990s but laid the groundwork for INDIE ROCK, a musical movement that picked up punk's DIY torch. And when grunge rockers such as Nirvana emerged in the early 1990s, they acknowledged their punk roots and thereby introduced the genre to mainstream audiences. The annual Warped Tour (from 1995), a national music and extreme sports festival where dozens of small-time bands share stages with bigger acts such as Bad Religion and NOFX, testifies to both the higher profile punk has attained since the tour's founding and the ongoing commitment of many punks to the DIY ethos.

BIBLIOGRAPHY

L. McNeil and G. McCain: *Please Kill Me: the Uncensored Oral History of Punk* (New York, 1997)

M. Spitz and B. Mullen: *We Got the Neutron Bomb: the Untold Story of L.A. Punk* (New York, 2001)

M. Andersen and M. Jensen: *Dance of Days: Two Decades of Punk in the Nation's Capitol* (New York, 2/2009)

D. MacLeod: *Kids of the Black Hole: Punk Rock in Postsuburban California* (Norman, OK, 2010)

R. Moore: *Sells Like Teen Spirit: Music, Youth Culture, and Social Crisis* (New York, 2010)

M. MONTGOMERY WOLF

Punta. Popular Garifuna social-commentary dance-song genre. Punta is also the name of the duple-meter ostinato on which the genre is based. The Garifuna are a people of African, Arawak, and Carib descent and live along the Caribbean coast of Belize, Guatemala, Honduras, and Nicaragua and in US urban centers. They share a common origin, language, system of rituals, and repertoire of music and dance. Punta songs are composed by women and address topics such as relationships, family, and work. The ostinato is played on the *segunda* (bass drum) and is accompanied by improvised passages on the *primero* (tenor drum). It features a quarter note and an eighth note played in the center of the drumhead followed by two sixteenth notes played near the rim. *Shakkas* (calabash rattles) and conch-shell trumpets provide additional accompaniment. The punta rhythm is almost identical to that of *paranda*, the guitar-accompanied, social-commentary genre of Garifuna men. Puntas and parandas serve as the basis for *punta rock*, the dance-oriented music created by Pen Cayetano that has become the predominant form of musical expression among Garifuna youth. The dance reenacts the cock-and-hen mating ritual and is characterized by rapid movement of the buttocks.

BIBLIOGRAPHY

E. Whipple: *The Music of the Black Caribs of British Honduras* (thesis, U. of Texas, Austin, 1971)

S. Cayetano and F. Cayetano: *Garifuna History, Language, and Culture of Belize, Central America, and the Caribbean* (Belize, 1997)

O.N. Greene Jr.: "Ethnicity, Modernity, and Retention in the Garifuan Punta," *Black Music Research Journal* xxii/2 (2002), 189–216

O.N. Greene Jr.: "Garifuna Music in Belize," *The Concise Garland Encyclopedia of World Music*, ed. D. Puchowski (London, 2008)

OLIVER GREENE

Purvis, Richard (Irven) (*b* San Francisco, CA, 25 Aug 1913; *d* San Francisco, CA, 25 Dec 1994). Organist. After early studies in piano and organ, in 1934 he entered the Curtis Institute of Music in Philadelphia, where he studied organ with ALEXANDER MCCURDY and conducting with FRITZ REINER. Further studies were with Josef Lhévinne in New York, Sir Edward C. Bairstow in England, Marcel Dupré in France, and after his graduation from Curtis (1940) with CHARLES M. COURBOIN and Charles Heinroth. During World War II, while serving as a bandmaster with the 28th Infantry Division, he was captured and held as a prisoner of war for six months. After the war an appointment to St. Mark's Lutheran Church took him back to his native city, and in 1947 he was appointed to Grace Cathedral, where he helped to form a cathedral school for boys, thus continuing the all-male choir tradition. Purvis's long and distinguished career was marked by elegant service playing, conducting, and composition. After his retirement in 1971 he continued to perform and compose. His compositions include a concerto for organ and orchestra, a partita on *Christ ist erstanden*, *Four Prayers in Tone* for organ, and *The Ballad of Judas Iscariot* for choir and orchestra.

CHARLES KRIGBAUM

Purvis, William (*b* Pennsylvania, 1948). Horn player. He studied at Haverford College and made his debut as horn soloist with the Pittsburgh Symphony at age 18. In addition to being a member of the New York Woodwind Quintet, the Orpheus Chamber Orchestra, and the Orchestra of St. Luke's, he has appeared as a soloist and chamber musician at noted music festivals including Tanglewood, Norfolk, Schleswig-Holstein, and Hong Kong. Purvis has performed with the Chamber Music Society of Lincoln Center and with the Tokyo, Mendelssohn, Sibelius, Fine Arts, and Orion String Quartets. In 1996 he toured with the Chamber Orchestra of Europe, presenting performances of the complete set of Beethoven symphonies. He has recorded and given premiere performances of works by György Ligeti, Milton Babbitt, Elliott Carter, Peter Maxwell Davies, Karlheinz Stockhausen, Paul Lansky, Peter Lieberson, and Chad Northcott. In addition, he has received critical acclaim as a performer and conductor with SPECULUM MUSICAE. Purvis is an artist-in-residence at Stony Brook University and holds appointments at Columbia University, the Juilliard School, and the Hochschule für Musik in Karlsruhe, Germany.

HEIDI LUCAS

Puthli, Asha (*b* Bombay [Mumbai], India, *c*1947). Indian singer and actress. From an affluent family, Puthli attended college in Mumbai. After studying Indian classical music and dance and Western opera as a youth, she began singing jazz and pop with local bands at age 13 and made her first recording in 1968. She met author Ved Mehta, who wrote about her in *Portrait of India* (New York, 1970). She appeared in two films by Ismail Merchant and James Ivory, *The Guru* (1969) and *Savages* (1972). A dance scholarship from the Martha Graham Company brought her in that same year to New York, where Mehta introduced her to CBS executive John Hammond. In 1972 she recorded two critically acclaimed tracks for Ornette Coleman's *Science Fiction* album. She recorded two pop and two disco albums of her own for CBS (1973–6) and a disco album for the TK label in 1979. Although her disco and jazz recordings became popular with audiences in Europe and India, as disco faded Puthli recorded sporadically before retiring during the 1980s to raise her son. She made a rare appearance in 1987 singing jazz with the Henry Threadgill Sextet. In the 1990s, hip-hop and techno/electronica artists, including Jay-Z and the Notorious B.I.G., began sampling her disco recordings, reviving her career. She has subsequently collaborated with several producers and DJs in these genres, singing classical Indian music. She has recorded more than 15 albums and co-produced shows with the India Broadcasting Network.

BIBLIOGRAPHY
R. Palmer, "Pop Life," *New York Times,* 30 July 1976
"Those Talking Heads," *The Times of India,* 9 Sept 1994
J. Pareles: "A Singer Embracing Countless Cultures," *New York Times,* 12 Aug 2006

GAYLE MURCHISON

Putnam, Ashley (Elizabeth) (*b* New York, NY, 10 Aug 1952). Soprano. Encouraged by her musical family, she began by playing the flute and honing her skills at the Interlochen Center for the Arts. She studied as a flute major at the University of Michigan but changed paths to pursue a vocal career. She then became an apprentice at Santa Fe and was a winner of the Metropolitan Opera National Council Auditions in 1976. She made her debut in that year as Lucia at Norfolk, Virginia, where she later sang the title role in the American premiere of Thea Musgrave's *Mary, Queen of Scots* (1978). She sang Angel More (*The Mother of Us All*) and Gilda at Santa Fe, Donna Elvira and Ophelia (*Hamlet*) at San Diego, Zdenka at Houston, and Konstanze at Miami. At the New York City Opera (1978–83) her roles included Violetta, Elvira (*I puritani*), Giselda (*I Lombardi*), Adèle (*Le comte Ory*), Marie (*La fille du régiment*), and Gaetano Donizetti's Mary Stuart. She made her European debut in 1978 as Musetta at Glyndebourne, where she later sang Arabella (1984) and Vitellia (1991). Returning to Santa Fe she sang Strauss's Danae (1985), Fiordiligi (1988), and the Marschallin (1989), a role she also sang at Los Angeles (1994). In 1983 she sang Xiphares (*Mitridate*) at Schwetzingen and Aix-en-Provence. She made her Covent Garden debut in 1986 as Jenůfa and her Metropolitan debut in 1990 as Donna Elvira. The following year she also sang Fusako in the US premiere of Hans Werner Henze's *Das verratene Meer* in San Francisco. During the 1970s and 80s Putnam's flexible, silver-toned voice was well suited to the bel canto repertory. In the 1990s she began to take on heavier, more dramatic roles such as Donna Anna, Kát'a Kabanová, Ellen Orford, and Eva, which she first sang at Cleveland in 1995. Putnam teaches privately in New York, where she is based. She also is on the faculty of the Manhattan School of Music, teaches masterclasses throughout the country, and frequently serves as a judge for the Metropolitan auditions.

ELIZABETH FORBES/JONAS WESTOVER

Puyallup. Native American group of the northwest coast; *see* COAST SALISH.

Pychowski, Jan Nepomucene (*b* Nowry Hrady [Grazen], Bohemia, 8 April 1818; *d* Hoboken, NJ, 18 March 1900). Bohemian pianist, composer, and teacher active in the United States. After early studies at the Prague Conservatory and with Jan Tomaschek, Pychowski immigrated to the United States in 1850. He married an American woman and settled in Hoboken, New Jersey, in 1855, spending the rest of his life as a teacher and performer there. He was an excellent chamber musician; his nerves prevented him from pursuing a vigorous solo career, but his name appears often in accounts of New York musical life in the 1850s. He was widely respected as a teacher, counting among his students WILLIAM H. SHERWOOD and AMY FAY. He published several works for solo piano, including *Adagio et polka brillante*, op.21 (New York, 1853) and *Les Sentiments d'un Polonais*, op.6 (Hamburg, 1856). His chamber works include *Duetto dramatique p. Pfte e Clarinetto [o Viola di Braccio]*, op.4 (Hamburg, 1856) and *Grande Sonate p. Pfte et Violon*, op.8 (Hamburg, 1857).

BIBLIOGRAPHY

W.S.B. Mathews, ed.: *a Hundred Years of Music in America* (Chicago, 1889/*R*), 138

"Death of John Pychowski," *New York Times* (25 March 1900), 18

V.B. Lawrence: *Strong on Music: the New York Music Scene in the Days of George Templeton Strong*, 3 vols. (New York, 1988–99)

E. DOUGLAS BOMBERGER

Qi Shu Fang (*b* Shanghai, China, 1943). Peking opera performer of Chinese birth. Born to a family of actors, she began learning Peking Opera at the age of four. She later enrolled in the Shanghai Theater School, joining the new Shanghai Youth Peking Drama Troupe following graduation. When she was 18 years old, she was chosen by Chairman Mao's wife to perform the female lead role in one of the national "model operas" created by China's communist government. At the age of 22, she was among the artists deemed talented enough to be selected by the government to perform modern Beijing revolutionary operas during the Cultural Revolution, a period when classic and traditional works were banned. Working in those politically dangerous and unstable circumstances, Qi became well known throughout the country. When the sanctions on artistic production became less stringent in the late 1970s, she again began performing in productions of traditional works. She immigrated to the United States in 1987, settling in New York with her husband, performer Ding Mei Kui, and other Chinese opera actors and musicians and founding the Qi Shu Fang Peking Opera Company there the following year. She has performed throughout Asia, Europe, and North America. Well known and admired by lovers of Chinese opera in the United States, she has been awarded the title of National Treasure of China, and in 2001 she was awarded the National Heritage Fellowship by the National Endowment for the Arts.

MEGAN E. HILL

QRS. Manufacturer of piano rolls. The company was established in 1900 as an adjunct to the Melville Clark Piano Co. of Chicago. Clark's invention of the "marking piano" in 1912 made possible the cutting of rolls that accurately captured specific performances, although without expression. Involved at an early stage in the recording of ragtime, QRS soon also turned to jazz, especially after Max Kortlander joined its staff and it transferred its main recording activities to New York about 1920. Among the notable musicians who cut rolls for the company were James P. Johnson (1921–7) and Fats Waller (as "Thomas Waller," 1923–31); in 1926 some

11 million rolls were cut. The company also established a record label of the same name, on which it put out three series of discs from the early 1920s until 1930; the second of these was most notable, with recordings supervised by Arthur E. Satherley. The third series appeared in 1929, shortly after QRS merged with a film company, the DeVry Corporation.

By this time the market for piano rolls had severely declined, and in 1931 Kortlander bought the company. For many years its existence was frequently precarious, and its employees often worked only part-time. The "marking piano" was abandoned in favor of "arranged" rolls, many of which were made by the stride pianist J. Lawrence Cook, some under the pseudonym Sid Laney. Cook's output over five decades included a remarkable series of Waller-like arrangements, and transcriptions of Art Tatum and Erroll Garner. By the 1950s production had dropped to around 200,000 rolls per year, although thereafter interest revived with the advent of new spinet player pianos. Kortlander died in 1961, and the company was acquired by Ramsi P. Tick, who moved production to Buffalo in 1966. Though "arranged" rolls have remained the company's mainstay, new recordings on the restored "marking piano" have been made by artists including Earl Hines, George Shearing, Marian McPartland, Peter Nero, and Liberace.

In 1987 QRS was sold to Richard A. Dolan, who brought out a MIDI-based player system for installation in acoustic pianos. The meaning of the acronym is unknown; the only interpretation ever to appear in official company literature was the slogan "Quality, Real Service," used in the late 1910s and early 20s.

BIBLIOGRAPHY
M. Wyler and B. Kumm: "QRS Past and Present," *Storyville*, no.7 (1966), 19–27 [incl. discography]
B. Kumm: "Mr. Piano Roll: J. Lawrence Cook," *Storyville*, no.10 (1967), 14–16
R.M.W. Dixon and J. Godrich: *Recording the Blues* (London, 1970), 58
T. Magnusson: "The Piano Rolls by Thomas Waller and by 'Fats' Waller," *Matrix*, no.106 (1975), 3–8
B. Rust: *The American Record Label Book* (New Rochelle, NY, 1978), 259

M. Montgomery: "James P. Johnson Rollography," F.H. Trolle James, *P. Johnson: Father of the Stride Piano*, ed. D.M. Bakker (Alphen aan den Rijn, 1981), 25–30

L. Wright: "Q.R.S.," *Storyville*, no.114 (1984), 218–25

BOB BERKMAN

Quadrille. A group dance performed in a square by four couples that was fashionable in the 19th century. The term "quadrille" was first applied to equestrian ballets popular at large outdoor events in 18th-century Germany and Austria. Its European ancestor was the 18th-century French *contredanse française*, which was performed in a square formation by eight dancers. Eventually the *contredanse française* was exported to England where it was known as a cotillion and performed in the same square formation as its relative. In a cotillion, the "figure" of the dance was alternately performed with "changes," of which there were usually ten.

Because the order of the figures and changes of the cotillion could be a challenge to remember in the ballroom, a simplified version, eventually called quadrille, appeared with a set of five figures, performed without the changes found in the cotillion.

The early, standard quadrille consisted of five figures that were titled "Le Pantalon," "L'Été," "La Poule," "Le Pastourelle," and "Finale." Occasionally, an additional figure, "La Trénis" was added. The music was usually composed in duple meter, although "La Poule" was often found in 6/8. The quadrille's music consisted of eight- or 16-bar measures, which were repeated as needed for the figures. Tunes were often based on popular songs and opera and operetta themes. A brief pause would separate each set. During the early 19th century, the dancers were required to bow to each other and their corners during the first eight bars of each set. By the middle of the century, they simply waited for the eight bars to pass before starting the figures. Examples of some of the components that made up figures included: Forward and Backward, Going to the Right and Left, Crossing Over, Balance (also known as Set to Partners), Hands Around, English Chain (also know as Right and Left), Ladies' Chain, and Moulinet. Often, the components were described by their French names, for example, the English Chain was called *chaine anglaise*. An example of the figure "Le Pantalon," consisted of the following figures:

Bow to your partner and corner	8 bars
English Chain	8 bars
Balance	4 bars
Turn Partners	4 bars
Ladies' Chain	8 bars
Half Promenade	4 bars
Half English Chain	4 bars

After the bows, the entire figure was performed first by the head couples then repeated by the side couples. Many manuals and pamphlets were published to provide a repertory of sets of quadrilles. One of the most valuable of these treatises was by the English dancing master Thomas Wilson, *The Quadrille and Cotillion Panorama* (c1818). In this work, Wilson analyzed the figures and components of the quadrille and suggested hundreds of combinations.

Late 18th-century *contredanses* were performed with a series of step sequences, and this tradition continued into the early 19th century. The most frequent combination of steps performed in early 19th-century quadrilles consisted of three *chassés*, a *jeté*, and an *assemble*, used for figures such as the English Chain, Ladies' Chain, and Half Promenade. *Elements and Principles of the Art of Dancing* (Philadelphia, 1817) by J.H.G. (J.H. Gourdoux-Daux), described step sequences that also required *sissoné*, two varieties of *échappe*, *temps levé*, and *glissade*. Other writers added more, often technically challenging steps and step sequences.

After the 1830s many of the steps were simplified or dancers would simply walk through the figures. Before then quadrille figures were not called by a caller, which required the dancers to know all the figures by memory. By mid-century dance manuals not only included directions for numerous quadrilles, including the popular set of figures known as Lancers, but provided instructions for callers and appropriate music. Edward Ferrero's *The Art of Dancing, Historically Illustrated* (1859) and Lucien O. Carpenter's *J.W. Pepper's Universal Dancing Master: Prompter's Call Book and Violinist's Guide* (1882) are two examples of dance manuals published in the United States that present quadrille figures, music, and instructions for performance.

BIBLIOGRAPHY

[J.H. Gourdoux-Daux]: *Elements and Principles of the Art of Dancing* (Philadelphia, 1817)

T. Wilson: *The Quadrille and Cotillion Panorama* (London, c1818)

L. Carpenter: *J.W. Pepper's Universal Dancing Master: Prompter's Call Book and Violinist's Guide* (Philadelphia, 1882)

E. Ferrero: *The Art of Dancing, Historically Illustrated* (New York, 1959)

E. Aldrich: *From the Ballroom to Hell: Grace and Folly in Nineteenth-century Dance* (Evanston, 1991)

ELIZABETH ALDRICH

Quebradita. A partner dance and music style of the southwest United States and Mexico. Its name means "little break," referring to the quick backbends of the female partner or the breaking of a wild horse. The dance references cowboy life in its use of Western attire, hat tricks, and vigorous moves like *caballito* (little horse). Mexican *folklórico* dances contributed to quebradita-style *zapateo* footwork; other influences came from country line dance and hip hop. Quebradita music is based on a fast *cumbia* rhythm usually played by *bandas*, *technobandas*, or *conjuntos norteños*. The rhythm is particularly associated with such Jalisco-based technobandas as Banda Machos, Banda Maguey, and Banda El Mexicano. Quebradita is often performed together with *música ranchera* and *valses*, *polkas*, or *sones* of the banda repertoire.

The 1990s quebradita craze was attributable in part to anti-immigrant politics in California, which caused many Mexican American youth to practice the new dance as a symbol of pride in Mexican identity. Hundreds of dance clubs formed in the border area and beyond and were widely cited as an alternative to gang activity. The quebradita has also been credited with the rise of banda as a major presence in the US Latin music market, and it influenced the subsequent development of *pasito duranguense* dance in Chicago.

BIBLIOGRAPHY

H. Simonett: *Banda: Mexican Musical Life across Borders* (Middletown, CT, 2001)

S. Hutchinson: *From Quebradita to Duranguense: Dance in Mexican American Youth Culture* (Tucson, 2007)

H. Simonett: "Quest for the Local: Building Musical Ties between Mexico and the United States," *Postnational Musical Identities: Cultural Production, Distribution, and Consumption in a Globalized Scenario*, ed. I. Corona and A.L. Madrid (Lanham, MD, 2008), 12–37

SYDNEY HUTCHINSON

Queen Ida [Guillory, Ida Lewis] (*b* Lake Charles, LA, 15 Jan 1929). Accordionist and zydeco composer and performer. She grew up among farmers, helping plant the annual rice crop. Music was one of the major forms of recreation for the Cajun community, and she was raised hearing French songs and zydeco dance music. In the mid-1970s, she moved to the San Francisco area and raised her family, driving a school bus for a living. Later in the decade, she returned to playing push-button accordion, which she had learned as a child, and soon became a well-known figure within the local transplanted Creole community, playing with her brother at the San Francisco Blues Festival in 1975 and at the Monterey Jazz Festival the following year. Her role as the queen at a Mardi Gras parade prompted her royal performance moniker. Her compilation album *Queen Ida and the Bon Temps Zydeco Band* (1982) won a Grammy award and launched her career in the United States. Women leaders of zydeco bands are quite rare, and she openly discussed the difficulties of holding such a position. Once her career blossomed, though, she remained successful on a global scale; throughout the 1980s and 90s, she regularly released recordings on the GNP Crescendo label and toured in Europe, Japan, Australia, and Africa. One of the key elements of her success was her family's involvement with the band, which included two of her brothers, her husband, and her children.

JONAS WESTOVER

Queen Latifah [Owens, Dana] (*b* Newark, NJ, 18 March 1970). Rapper, singer, and actress. She was the first solo female rapper to launch a commercially successful career. Latifah took her stage name from the Arabic word for "delicate," or "sensitive," after joining an all-female group, Ladies Fresh, in high school. Her recording career began during rap music's rapid expansion in the 1980s, continued during hip hop's mainstreaming in the 1990s, and eventually crossed over to feature films. As suggested by her royal stage name, Latifah has used commanding song lyrics and uplifting autobiographical writings to demand respect for herself and all other black women. For these reasons, she has been well received by black feminist scholars and critics who use her music as an example of anti-misogynistic, pro-woman, activist hip hop. These themes are evident in her 1989 duet "Ladies First" with protégé Monie Love. The Grammy-winning single "U.N.I.T.Y" from her third album, *Black Reign*, exemplifies the social critique in many of her songs by addressing violence toward black women. The size and strength of her voice and body helped her construct a powerful stage identity that blends conventionally feminine and masculine qualities: strong, yet nurturing, and politically conscious. Queen Latifah's shift from rap to acting speaks to her versatility, demonstrated by roles in more than 40 commercial films and television shows. Her deep vocal tone and powerful projection make her voice reminiscent of female blues artists of the 1920s. These traits enhanced her performance in the role of Matron Mama Morton in the film adaptation of the Broadway musical *Chicago*, for which she was nominated for the 2003 Academy Award for Best Supporting Actress. She was awarded the 2004 NAACP Image Award for her role in the film *Bringing Down the House* and a 2008 Golden Globe Award for her role in *Life Support*. In 2006 she became the first hip-hop artist to be given a star on the Hollywood Walk of Fame.

RECORDINGS

All Hail the Queen (1989, Tommy Boy); *Nature of a Sista* (1991, Tommy Boy); *Black Reign* (1993, Motown); *Order in the Court* (1998, Motown); *She's a Queen* (2002, Motown); *The Dana Owens Album* (2004, Motown); *Trav'lin Light* (2007, Verve); *Persona* (2009, Verve)

BIBLIOGRAPHY

T. Rose: *Black Noise: Rap Music and Black Culture in Contemporary America* (Middletown, CT, 1994)

G.D. Pough: *Check it While I Wreck it: Black Womanhood, Hip-Hop Culture, and the Public Sphere* (Boston, 2004)

ELIZABETH WHITTENBURG OZMENT

Queer music. *See* LESBIAN, GAY, BISEXUAL, TRANSGENDER, AND QUEER MUSIC.

Queler, Eve (*b* New York, NY, 1 Jan 1936). Conductor. She studied piano and conducting at Mannes College and, on a Martha Baird Rockefeller Fund grant, conducting with Joseph Rosenstock and accompaniment with PAUL ULANOWSKY and Paul Berl; her later teachers were Walter Susskind and LEONARD SLATKIN in St. Louis and Igor Markevich and HERBERT BLOMSTEDT in Europe. After working as music assistant to the New York City Opera and the Metropolitan Opera, she formed in 1968 the Opera Orchestra of New York (OONY), with herself as music director. Based from 1971 at Carnegie Hall, the OONY has since become America's leading exponent of forgotten opera, a forum for new singers, and a vehicle for Queler's talents as conductor, entrepreneur, and mentor. OONY has presented opera in concert only, and has offered more than 100 works. Many major singers, including June Anderson, Carlo Bergonzi, Montserrat Caballé, Placido Domingo, Jane Eaglen, Renée Fleming, and Renata Scotto, have appeared with her. Queler has also made a career as a guest conductor, appearing at the New York City Opera, the Kirov Mariinsky Opera, Australian Opera, the Hamburg Staatsoper, Prague National Theatre, Frankfurt Opera, Sydney Opera, and elsewhere. She has occasionally worked with symphony orchestras, and has appeared with the Philadelphia Orchestra, Montreal SO, Cleveland Orchestra, Edmonton Orchestra, and Honolulu SO. Queler has also written a number of journal articles and supervised critical editions of three of Gaetano Donizetti's operas. She has made studio recordings of *Jenůfa*, Richard Strauss's *Guntram*, and Arrigo Boito's *Nerone*. In 2002 Queler was named Chevalier de l'Ordre des Arts et des Lettres, in 2010 was recipient of the NEA Opera Honors award, and retired as OONY music director in late 2011.

ELIZABETH WOOD/CHARLES BARBER

Quezada (Borbón), Milly [Milagros del Rosario] (*b* Santo Domingo, Dominican Republic, 21 May 1952). Merengue singer born in the Dominican Republic. Quezada's family immigrated to New York (1965), where she attended high school and obtained a bachelor's degree in communications from the City College of New York (CCNY). In 1975 she and sister Jocelyn formed the merengue group Milly, Jocelyn y Los Vecinos, recording their first album the following year. As lead singers, the two women served as models for later female-led merengue orchestras while providing a vital connection to Dominican culture for others in their Washington Heights neighborhood. In 1982 Los Vecinos scored hits in the Dominican Republic, Colombia, and Panama. The group's international acceptance was a source of pride for diasporic Dominicans, and their incorporation of North American musical elements helped their merengue style gain popularity among non-Dominican Latinos.

In 1996, after recording two dozen albums, Los Vecinos broke up and Milly pursued a solo career. As a solo artist Milly won a Soberano (1998) at the Casandra Prizes, the Dominican Republic's highest arts award. That year her album *Vive* won a Latin Billboard Award for best female topical album, and in 2003 she won a Latin Grammy for best merengue album with *Pienso así*.

BIBLIOGRAPHY

P. Austerlitz: *Merengue: Dominican Music and Dominican Identity* (Philadelphia, 1997)

C. Batista Matos: *Historia y evolución del merengue* (Santo Domingo, 1999)

A. Gómez Sotolongo: *Los cien músicos del siglo* (Santo Domingo, 2000)

SYDNEY HUTCHINSON

Quickstep (i). *See* MARCH.

Quickstep (ii). An English ballroom dance that evolved from the fast FOXTROT of the ragtime era. In 1924 the Imperial Society of Teachers of Dancing, based in London, accepted the name "quickstep" to define a fast foxtrot done at 54 to 56 measures per minute. In 1927 an early version was performed as "the Quick Time Foxtrot and Charleston" at the Star Dance Championships. The couple who danced it, Frank Ford and Molly Spain, eliminated the characteristic Charleston knee actions, added some elements of the one-step, the shag, and the PEABODY, and presented a fast-paced, lighthearted dance that traveled quickly around the line of

dance. Today the quickstep is one of the five dances in the International Standard category of competitive BALLROOM DANCE. Its popularity with dancers in the United States, Canada, Australia, and continental Europe is rivaled only in the ballrooms of England, where its elegance, wit, and urbane style are valued as national characteristics.

Like the foxtrot, the quickstep is a smooth and glamorous dance that follows a 2/4 or 4/4 time signature. Over the years it has evolved into a dynamic dance of many patterns of traveling steps: running, skipping, gliding, sliding, hopping, and bouncing with flicking feet. While the basic figures are not exceptionally difficult, the tempo of the music makes proper execution a challenge. The quickstep is perhaps the most joyous of all ballroom dances, because its essential character seems to invite a carefree interpretation of its bright rhythm.

The quickstep is often danced to such standards as "Alexander's Ragtime Band," "Darktown Strutters' Ball," "Fidgety Feet," and "Don't sit under the apple tree." Among the recordings favored for dancing the quickstep are "I won't dance" by Ella Fitzgerald and Louis Armstrong, "I'm sitting on top of the world" by Bobby Darin, and "Those Lazy-Hazy-Crazy Days of Summer" by Nat King Cole. Best of all, however, is Louis Prima's 1936 hit "Sing, Sing, Sing," considered the ideal accompaniment for classic quickstep because of its strong, driving rhythm.

BIBLIOGRAPHY

A. Moore: *Ballroom Dancing, with 66 Diagrams and Photographs of the Quickstep, Waltz, Foxtrot, Tango, etc.* (London, 1936)

W. Fryer: *How to Dance: Slow Foxtrot, Waltz, Quickstep, Tango, Rumba, Samba, Square Dancing [and] the Jive* (London, 1953)

R.M. Stephenson and J. Iaccarino: *The Complete Book of Ballroom Dancing* (New York, 1980)

P. Bottomer: *Quickstep* (London, 1997)

A. Moore: *Ballroom Dancing, with 100 Diagrams and Photographs of the Quickstep, Waltz, Foxtrot, Tango, etc.* (New York, 10/2002)

CLAUDE CONYERS

Quilico, Louis (*b* Montreal, QC, 14 Jan 1925; *d* Toronto, ON, 15 July 2000). Canadian baritone. He studied with MARTIAL (JEAN-PAUL) SINGHER at the Conservatoire de Musique, Montreal, and Mannes College, New York, and with Teresa Pediconi and Riccardo Stracciari at the Accademia di S Cecilia, Rome. His principal teacher was the pianist Lina Pizzolongo (1925–91), whom he married in 1949. After winning several major Canadian competitions he made his professional debut with the Opera Guild of Montreal in 1954. In 1955 he won the Metropolitan Opera Auditions of the Air and the same year made his New York debut with the New York City Opera. He joined the Metropolitan Opera in 1973 and became one of its leading baritones. He performed such roles as Rigoletto (which became his calling card, played more than 500 times, the last in Ottawa in 1994), Giorgio Germont, Rodrigo (*Don Carlo*), Iago, Amonasro, Scarpia, Tonio, Golaud (*Pelléas et Mélisande*), and Falstaff at leading houses throughout the world, including Covent Garden, the Vienna Staatsoper, the Teatro Colón, the Rome Opera, the Bolshoi, San Francisco, and the Opéra de Montréal. He was also principal baritone of the Canadian Opera Company. Quilico sang in the premieres of Darius Milhaud's *Pacem in terris* (1963), a work he recorded, and *La mère coupable* (1966) and André Jolivet's *Le coeur de la matière* (1965); in 1991 he played the title role of Tony in Frank Loesser's *The Most Happy Fella* at the New York City Opera. His many recordings include operas ranging from Monteverdi to Verdi, Puccini, and Massenet. Quilico had a clear and ringing dramatic voice, particularly well suited to Verdi. He taught at the University of Toronto (1970–87) and at McGill University (1987–90) and gave masterclasses for young professional singers. He was awarded the Companion of the Order of Canada in 1974. In 1993 he married the Canadian pianist Christina Petrowska. After his retirement from the Metropolitan in 1998 Quilico continued to give concerts, appearing frequently with his wife. Upon his sudden death his widow set up the Christina and Louis Quilico Fund to help young singers, pianists, and composers for the voice. His son is the baritone Gino Quilico.

BIBLIOGRAPHY

C. Petrowska: *Mr. Rigoletto: in Conversation with Louis Quilico* (Toronto, 1996)

EZRA SCHABAS/R

Quinby. Family of brass instrument makers and inventors. Benjamin F(ranklin) Quinby (*b* Minot, ME, 3 July 1830; *d* Boston, MA, 9 July 1890) and his twin brother George W(ashington) Quinby (*b* Minot, ME, 3 July 1830; *d* Boston, MA, 13 Sept 1876) produced large quantities of brass instruments from 1861 to 1884 while associated with several instrument-making firms. Benjamin came to Boston as a machinist in 1853 and was followed by George in 1854. In 1861 they began a long association with the bandleader and instrument maker D.C. Hall, working first for a year with the firm Allen & Hall, then with Hall's own firm. In 1867 George W. Quinby and D.C. Hall formed the firm of Hall & Quinby. It was very successful, quickly becoming the largest brass instrument manufacturer in Boston. The business continued as Quinby Brothers in 1875, after Hall had withdrawn. Most of the instruments made by these firms were equipped with flat-windway Allen valves. In 1872 Benjamin F. Quinby patented a valve system for brass instruments featuring very simple construction and clear windways, but these "square or box valves" (as they were called) were not very successful. Quinby Brothers ceased making brass instruments in 1884 and began the manufacture of rotary machine shoe-brushes.

BIBLIOGRAPHY

Waterhouse-LangwillI

H.C. Quinby: *Genealogical History of the Quinby Family* (New York, 1915)

R.E. Eliason: "Early American Valves for Brass Instruments," *GSJ*, xxiii (1970), 86–96

R.E. Eliason: "D. C. Hall and the Quinby Brothers," *JAMIS*, xxxiii (2007), 84–91

ROBERT E. ELIASON

Quincy, George (Cochran) (*b* McAlester, OK, 8 Sept 1937). Composer, pianist, and conductor. While at the Juilliard School (BS 1961; MS 1962, piano) he worked as a rehearsal pianist for the Martha Graham Dance Company and subsequently served as a musical advisor to Graham for a number of years. He credits her with teaching him "how to be an artist." After graduating, he taught at Juilliard for five years while pursuing a concert career and composing incidental music and encores for off-Broadway theatrical productions. He went on to compose, orchestrate, and conduct music for theater, dance, opera, film, television, and the concert hall. Never having received formal instruction in music composition, Quincy credits his Choctaw heritage for his lyrical gifts and the training he received in Western art music for his analytical abilities. He reports that dreams are the source of many of his musical ideas, which he subsequently works out at the piano.

A member of the First Nations Composer Initiative, Quincy seeks to "develop the emotional and cultural fusion of classical music and Choctaw sounds" by combining Western compositional techniques with Choctaw traditions and instruments such as the water drum, rain stick, and native flute. These compositions include *Choctaw Nights*, which he recorded for Albany Records (2003) as a member of the New York Five, a chamber ensemble that has performed his music extensively. Another instrumental work, *Choctaw Diaries* (2008), evokes the composer's childhood recollections of the prairie landscape and sky: with orchestral strings, woodwinds, and percussion depicting the natural surroundings, the native flute, given a prominent role, evokes the Choctaw spirit world.

Quincy has received numerous awards from Meet the Composer and ASCAP (1997–2010), and his works have been performed at Alice Tully Hall, Carnegie Hall, and Town Hall and elsewhere in the United States, as well as in Europe. His opera *Young Woman Warrior who Came Home* (2011), based on a Navajo tale, was commissioned by the Arizona Opera for presentation in Indian reservations throughout that state. His chamber opera *Pocahontas at the Court of James I* (2006–7), on a libretto by his wife, Thayer Burch, was commissioned by the Queen's Chamber Band for the 400th anniversary of the founding of Jamestown, Virginia, and has been performed at the Smithsonian Institution and the National Museum of the American Indian, among other venues, and recorded on the Lyrichord Classical label.

S. TIMOTHY MALONEY

Quintana, Ismael (*b* Ponce, PR, 3 June 1937). Puerto Rican composer and singer. He is best known for his partnership as *sonero* with pianist EDDIE PALMIERI and his orchestra La Perfecta. Ten days after his birth, his mother took him to the South Bronx, where he grew up playing percussion instruments. Bandleader Angel Náter hired him as singer in 1959. At the request of Palmieri, he joined the newly formed La Perfecta in 1961, in a celebrated collaboration that lasted 12 years. Quintana then opted to pursue a solo career, preferably as a performer of *baladas* and slower boleros. As a *sonero*, Quintana is highly regarded for his fiery, ragged vocal style and his considerable improvisatory ability with the maracas and the claves. He wrote lyrics for most of the pieces he recorded with Palmieri, including "Vámonos pa'l monte," "Justicia," and "Puerto Rico." Other important compositions include his rumba-like "Tambó," his plena "Oí una voz," and his best-known salsa piece, "Mi debilidad." His lengthy catalog includes solo albums and collaborative recordings with Palmieri, the Fania All Stars, Cal Tjader, Tito Puente, and Jimmie Delgado.

EDGARDO DÍAZ DÍAZ

Quintero Rivera, Ángel G. (*b* Santurce, San Juan, PR, 29 Jan 1947). Sociologist. He received the doctorate in sociology from the London School of Economics and Political Science (1976). His research interests include historical sociology of the Hispanic Caribbean, focusing on popular culture, music, and festive activities. He is the author of *Music, Social Classes, and the National Question of Puerto Rico* (1989), and *Salsa, sabor y control! Sociología de la música tropical* (1998), for which he received the Casa de las Americas Prize in 1998 and the Latin American Studies Association Iberoamerican Prize in 2000. His 2009 book *Cuerpo y cultura: las músicas "mulatas" y la subversión del baile* was awarded the Frantz Fanon Book Award from the Association of Philosophy of the Caribbean the same year. He has also collaborated with Ana María García on the documentary *Cocolos y Rockeros* (1992). He is currently professor and director of the Social Science Research Center at the University of Puerto Rico. He has served as visiting professor at many universities and lectured worldwide. He is a founding member of the Centro de Estudios de la Realidad Puertorriqueña. In 2009 he was awarded the distinction of Humanist of the Year from the Puerto Rican Foundation of the Humanities.

MARYSOL QUEVEDO

Quintiliani, Barbara (*b* Quincy, MA, 24 Sept 1976). Soprano. She graduated from the New England Conservatory of Music, then took apprenticeships in the Young Artists programs of the Houston Grand Opera and the Washington National Opera. She has won a number of national and international vocal competitions; she was a National Grand Prize Winner in 1999 of the Metropolitan Opera National Council Auditions, and in 2006 became the first American woman in more than 25 years to win First Prize in the International Singing Contest Francisco Viñas. She made her United States operatic debut in 2002 with the Washington National Opera as Elettra in *Idomeneo* and reprised that role in 2006 for her international debut with the Gran Teatre del Liceu in Barcelona. Since then, Quintiliani has most often sung roles in operas by Giuseppe Verdi and Gaetano Donizetti, embracing the role of the title character of *Maria Padilla*, which she first sang at the 2009 Wexford Festival, as her special vocal vehicle. Also active as a concert artist and recitalist, she has performed Ludwig van Beethoven's Symphony no.9 with the National Symphony Orchestra and Samuel Barber's *Knoxville: Summer of 1915* with the Buffalo Philharmonic and has recorded Charles Griffes's *Three Poems*

of Fiona McLeod for the Naxos label. Her dramatic soprano voice has a large range of vocal colors, secure coloratura, and seemingly inexhaustible breath support.

KATHLEEN SEWRIGHT

Quintón, José I(gnacio) (*b* Caguas, PR, 1 Feb 1881; *d* Coamo, PR, 19 Dec 1925). Puerto Rican composer and pianist. He received lessons in harmony, counterpoint, composition, and piano from his father, who was a graduate of the Paris Conservatoire and a church organist. He was also influenced by the Spanish pianist Ernesto del Castillo and the Puerto Rican composer Angel Mislán but was to some extent self-educated. From the age of 12 until his death he lived in Coamo; he became a teacher of instrumental music at the Coamo Municipal Academy of Music and also organized several musical groups as well as the municipal band. As a composer Quintón appropriated Classical forms and a Romantic idiom while searching constantly for sonorities that he called "music of the future" (as a pianist he was one of the first to perform the music of Debussy, Ravel, and Schoenberg in Puerto Rico). He took a historic step in elevating the *danza* to the level of concert music. His several chamber works, including the String Quartet in D (1913), are Brahmsian in style.

WORKS
(selective list)

Edition: *Obras completas*, ed. J.I. Quintón (San Juan, PR, 1986)
Orch: Marcha triunfal, 1911; Conc. Ov., 1913
Chbr and solo inst: Str Qt, D, 1913; Pf Trio; several other ens works; pf works, incl. Variaciones sobre un tema de Hummel, 1913, Una página de mi vida, rhapsody, 1920, many danzas, waltzes; other character pieces
Vocal: Requiem, SATB, orch, 1903; 10 salve Reginas, SATB, orch

BIBLIOGRAPHY
F. Ferrer Callojo: *Música y músicos puertorriqueños* (San Juan, PR, 1915, 2/1971)
C. Dower: "Quintón Bridges Centuries," *Dateline Puerto Rico, U.S.A.*, iii/3 (1981), 38
R. Rivera Bermúdez: *Biografía de José Quintón* [MS in *NYp*]

GUSTAVO BATISTA

Quittmeyer, Susan (*b* Port Washington, NY, 27 Oct 1953). Mezzo-soprano. After studying voice at Illinois Wesleyan University and the Manhattan School of Music, she made her American opera debut in 1978 with the Opera Theatre in St. Louis as Chloe in Vicente Martín y Soler's *The Tree of Chastity*. In 1979 she sang Dorabella in *Così fan tutte* with the San Francisco Opera, the first of more than 20 different roles that she sang with that company through 1995. These included Rosette in *Manon* (1981), Cherubino in *Le Nozze di Figaro* (1982), the Composer in *Ariadne auf Naxos* (1983), Mistress Meg Page in *Falstaff* (1985), Marina in *Boris Godunov* (1992), and Nicklausse/the Muse in *Les Contes d'Hoffmann* (1987). She made her 1987 Metropolitan Opera debut in this last role; during her eight-year association with the Met, she sang Dorabella (1988), Idamante in *Idomeneo* (1989), Siebel in *Faust* (1990, 1991), Varvana in Leoš Janáček's *Kát'a Kabanová* (1991), and Cherubino (1991, 1994). From 1986 until 1994 she was also active in European opera houses. She made her debut as a concert soloist in 1981 in a San Francisco Symphony performance of Ludwig van Beethoven's Ninth Symphony under the baton of Leonard Slatkin, and she made her Carnegie Hall recital debut in 1985. She can be heard on a 1992 recording of *Falstaff* and a 1989 recording of *Das Rheingold*. In 1987 she married bass-baritone JAMES MORRIS. She retired from singing professionally around 2000.

BIBLIOGRAPHY

Baker 20th

KATHLEEN SEWRIGHT

Quivar, Florence (*b* Philadelphia, PA, 3 March 1944). Mezzo-soprano. Her highly acclaimed orchestral, opera, and solo performances encompass both the lyric and the dramatic repertoires. Her musicianship was nurtured at an early age by her mother, a piano and organ teacher, and Quivar gave her first public performance at age six. She entered college intending to major in education but quickly found a performance career irresistible. She graduated from the Philadelphia Music Academy and subsequently studied at the Juilliard School. With the instruction of MAUREEN (KATHLEEN STEWART) FORRESTER, Quivar mastered lieder and oratorio and shortly thereafter won the Boston Lyric Opera Competition and Marian Anderson Award, which launched her international career. Heralded for her rich timbre, she sang Marina (*Boris Godunov*) in her 1977 Metropolitan Opera debut. Her other notable roles include the title role in *Carmen*, Orpheus (*Orfeo ed Euridice*), Suzuki (*Madama Butterfly*), Isabella (*L'italiana in Algeri*), and Mother Marie (*Dialogues des Carmélites*), performed at the Royal Opera at Covent Garden, the Teatro Colon, the Deutsche Oper Berlin, and La Scala. Quivar sang with the New York Philharmonic, the Boston SO, and the Philadelphia Orchestra and performed in the premieres of Anthony Davis's *Amistad* as the Goddess of the Waters in 1999 and William Bolcom's song cycle *From the Diary of Sally Hemmings* in 2001. The 1976 recording of *Porgy and Bess* in which Quivar sang Serena won a Grammy award, and her 1990 album of spirituals with the Boys Choir of Harlem remains a hallmark recording. She serves on the voice faculty at Frost School of Music at the University of Miami.

MARTI NEWLAND

Quotation. The incorporation of a segment of existing music into another piece, akin to quotation in speech or literature; also, a segment of existing music so incorporated in a later piece. The term usually refers to melodic quotation, although the whole texture may be incorporated and solely rhythmic quotation is possible. Quotation is distinct from other forms of BORROWING in that the borrowed material is presented exactly or nearly so, unlike an ALLUSION, but is not part of the main substance of the work, as it would be if used as a theme in variations or other forms, or if presented complete in a transcription or medley. Quotation plays a role in other forms of borrowing, such as COLLAGE or the use of a previous work as a model. Music scholarship has not always observed these distinctions, and the term "quotation" has been used to refer to a variety of borrowing practices.

Quotations are often prominent and brief, suggesting that the composer or improviser expects listeners familiar with the quoted piece to recognize it from a short excerpt. It is also possible for listeners to perceive a quotation where none was intended, based on a coincidental similarity between pieces. In most cases quoting existing music is an act that conveys meaning through the text or through associations carried by the quoted music and the implications aroused by the way the quoted material is presented or manipulated in the new work. Like a synecdoche in literature, the quotation can stand for the entire piece of music from which it is extracted and thus for its composer, its genre, its era or region of origin, the musical tradition from which it comes, a performance of the piece, or a particular performer. Quotation has also been used to create humor through surprise or incongruous juxtapositions and, in 20th-century music, to comment on the distance between the present and the past.

In the music of North America, early examples include the quotations of patriotic songs in battle pieces such as James Hewitt's *The Battle of Trenton* (1797), which represent the opposing armies through the music of their bands. In programmatic music quotation can represent a performance of the quoted piece, like the pianola playing "Hello! Ma Baby" in Charles Ives's evocation of the sounds of a summer evening in *Central Park in the Dark* (*c*1909). An exact quotation may also signal another, less obvious relationship between two works; in Ives's song *West London* (1921), the appearance in the piano postlude of the opening phrase of the hymn "There is a fountain filled with blood" makes overt the source from which almost the entire vocal line has been paraphrased. Composers after World War II have used quotation to suggest the gulf between present and past by juxtaposing current and past musical idioms; in "Dream Images (Love–Death Music)" from George Crumb's *Makrokosmos I* for amplified piano (1972), the middle section of Chopin's *Fantaisie-Impromptu* appears "as if emerging from silence" amid Crumb's own sweetly dissonant modern sounds, "like the gentle caress of a faintly remembered music."

Quotation is even more common in popular music than in the classical tradition. Tin Pan Alley songwriters in the late 19th and early 20th centuries often quoted well-known tunes near the end of the chorus, as in George M. Cohan's "The Story of the Wedding March" (1901, with Mendelssohn's wedding march), or used quotation to suggest a scene or activity, as in James Thornton's "Streets of Cairo" (1895), which evokes exotic dancing by borrowing the tune that accompanied the hoochie-coochie dance performed at the Chicago World's Fair in 1893; both of these tunes have become among those most often quoted, as a few notes suffice to set a scene or make a reference. Quotations can convey meanings remarkably quickly through the associations carried by the quoted material, and this is often exploited in music for films and television. Jazz improvisers such as Louis Armstrong and Charlie Parker often quoted popular tunes, classical music, or other jazz artists in their solos, with aims that varied from homage to inside jokes. In popular music quotation has often been used for humor or to convey meanings, as in Frank Zappa's frequent references to the theme of the television show "The Twilight Zone" and other familiar sounds he called "Archetypal American Musical Icons." Digital sampling and other such technologies have made it easier to excerpt and manipulate recordings, fostering new forms of quotation that reproduce the exact sound of an existing performance and thus can refer to a particular performer (*see* SAMPLING AND SEQUENCING, HIP-HOP). RAP musicians have often used such samples to convey meanings beyond those associated with a song itself, for example, presenting a snippet of James Brown to suggest links to SOUL MUSIC and Black Power politics of the 1960s, while avant-garde artists use sampling to deconstruct the music of well known performers, as in Negativland's farcical take on the U2 song "I still haven't found what I'm looking for."

BIBLIOGRAPHY

GMO ("Quotation"; J.P. Burkholder)

MGG2 ("Zitat"; G. Gruber)

C. Kühn: *Das Zitat in der Musik der Gegenwart: mit Ausblicken auf bildende Kunst und Literatur* (Hamburg, 1972)

M. Hicks: *The New Quotation: its Origins and Functions* (diss., U. of Illinois, 1984)

K. Gabbard: "The Quoter and his Culture," *Jazz in Mind: Essays on the History and Meanings of Jazz*, ed. R.T. Bruckner and S. Weiland (Detroit, 1991), 92–111

J.P. Burkholder: *All Made of Tunes: Charles Ives and the Uses of Musical Borrowing* (New Haven, 1995)

C. Smith: "Broadway the Hard Way: Techniques of Allusion in the Music of Frank Zappa," *College Music Symposium*, xxxv (1995), 35–60

D. Metzer: *Quotation and Cultural Meaning in Twentieth-century Music* (Cambridge, 2003)

For further bibliography *see* BORROWING.

J. PETER BURKHOLDER